May 31–June 4, 2015
Melbourne, Victoria, Australia

Association for Computing Machinery

Advancing Computing as a Science & Profession

SIGMOD'15

Proceedings of the 2015 ACM SIGMOD International Conference on Management of Data

Sponsored by:

ACM SIGMOD

Supported by:

Microsoft, Oracle, Facebook, Google, IBM, SAP, Tableau, Twitter, Intel, RMIT University, NEC, Morgan & Claypool, and Elsevier

Association for
Computing Machinery

Advancing Computing as a Science & Profession

The Association for Computing Machinery
2 Penn Plaza, Suite 701
New York, New York 10121-0701

ISBN: 978-1-4503-2758-9 (Digital)

ISBN: 978-1-4503-3864-6 (Print)

Additional copies may be ordered prepaid from:

ACM Order Department
PO Box 30777
New York, NY 10087-0777, USA

Phone: 1-800-342-6626 (USA and Canada)
+1-212-626-0500 (Global)
Fax: +1-212-944-1318
E-mail: acmhelp@acm.org
Hours of Operation: 8:30 am – 4:30 pm ET

Printed in the USA

Welcome Message from the SIGMOD Chairs

Welcome to SIGMOD 2015 – officially, the 2015 ACM SIGMOD International Conference on the Management of Data! This year's conference is being held in the beautiful cultural capital of Australia, Melbourne. During the Gold Rush period of the 19th Century, Melbourne was the richest city in the world, and as a result it is filled with many unique neighborhoods and distinctive buildings. In addition to wonderful neighborhoods to explore, the city has great museums and other cultural attractions, as well as a fine multi-cultural atmosphere. For those who would like to explore the outdoors, popular highlights are the Phillip Island Nature Park (90 minutes away), which features wild penguins who return in a parade each day at sunset, and the Great Ocean Road, one of the world's most scenic coastal drives, including the famous towering 12 Apostles.

SIGMOD 2015's exciting technical program reflects not only traditional topics, but the database community's role in broader data science and data analytics. The keynote from Laura Haas, "The Power Behind the Throne: Information Integration in the Age of Data-Driven Discovery" highlights the role of database and data integration techniques in the growing field of data science. Jignesh Patel's talk, "From Data to Insights @ Bare Metal Speed," explains how hardware and software need to be co-evolved to support the needs of scalable data analytics. Jennifer Widom, winner of the 2015 ACM-W Athena Lecturer Award for fundamental contributions to computer science, will give her award talk, "Three Favorite Results," on Tuesday. Christopher Ré will lead a panel on "Machine Learning and Databases: The Sound of Things to Come or a Cacophony of Hype?," with participants Divyakant Agrawal, Magdalena Balazinska, Michael Cafarella, Michael Jordan, Tim Kraska, and Raghu Ramakrishnan. Of course, there are also 106 research paper presentations, 4 tutorials, 30 demonstrations, and 18 industrial papers. Papers will be presented both as talks during the research sessions, and as part of plenary Poster Sessions.

SIGMOD 2015 is preceded by the PhD Workshop, as well as workshops on leading-edge topics like data analytics (DanaC), databases and the Web (WebDB), exploratory search (ExploreDB), managing and mining spatial data (GeoRich), and graph data (GRADES); the New Researcher Symposium will take place on Wednesday. The banquet will be held in a Melbourne landmark, the Town Hall.

We are grateful to the many researchers who have shaped the conference program. Specific thanks go to the keynotes chair, Renée Miller; the panel chairs, Michael Franklin and Tova Milo; the tutorial chair, Wenfei Fan; the industrial program chairs, Sihem Amer-Yahia and Christopher Olston, as well as the industrial program committee members; the demonstrations chairs, Vanessa Braganholo and Juliana Freire, as well as the demonstration program committee members; the workshops chairs, Anastasia Ailamaki and Yi Chen; the undergraduate research chairs, Anisoara Nica and Anastasios Kementsietsidis; and the New Researcher Symposium chairs, Julia Stoyanovich and Alexandria Meliou. We would also like to express our immense gratitude to the members of the SIGMOD 2015 program committee and especially the "Group Leaders" who helped oversee the review process: Alin Deutsch, Yanlei Diao, Jens Dittrich, Luna Dong, Hank Korth, Alexandros Labrinidis, Feifei Li, Dan Olteanu, Jignesh Patel, Sunita Sarawagi, Pierre Senellart, Wang-Chiew Tan, Jun Yang, and Xiaofang Zhou.

As in recent years, we had two submission deadlines for SIGMOD this year, one in August and one in November. The review process was journal-style, with multiple rounds of reviews coordinated by the Group Leaders. We accepted 34 of 137 papers from the first deadline and 72 of 278 from the second deadline. The total acceptance rate was about 25.5%, and we believe that the revision process has improved the quality of the technical program.

We thank the members of the SIGMOD 2015 organizing committee, as well as the SIGMOD Executive Committee, for their invaluable help and guidance throughout the process leading up to the conference. The team includes the finance chair Xiuzhen Jenny Zhang, the publicity and social media chairs Egemen Tanin and Jagan Sankaranarayanan, the sponsorship chairs Nick Koudas and Mohamed Mokbel, the local arrangements chair Yanchun Zhang, the registration chair Arkady Zaslavsky, the demonstration and workshop local arrangements chair Benjamin Rubinstein, the web/information chair Kai (Kevin) Zheng, the travel award committee chairs Alexandra Meliou and Eugene Wu, the programming contest chair Thomas Neumann, and the wonderful team of ICE Australia who supported the whole organization. We also extend our appreciation to the student volunteers – the success of this conference is impossible without their hard work and dedication. Finally, we benefited from a great deal of advice and help from Tamer Ozsu, as a former Program Chair, and K. Selçuk Candan, as both a liaison to the SIGMOD Executive and as a former SIGMOD General Chair. We are also grateful to the Microsoft Research Conference Management Toolkit (CMT) team for their extremely prompt and helpful support throughout the complex conference reviewing process.

We thank the many SIGMOD 2015 supporters, whose contributions helped to keep the conference registration fees manageable, particularly for student attendees. Sponsors include: Platinum Level – Microsoft and Oracle; Gold Level – Facebook, Google, IBM Research, SAP, Tableau, and Twitter; and Silver Level – Intel and RMIT University. NEC has also supported SIGMOD 2015. Finally, Microsoft, Google, the National Science Foundation and the SIGMOD Executive Committee have generously financially the SIGMOD 2015 student travel award program.

Welcome to Melbourne, and we hope you enjoy the conference!

Timos Sellis	**Susan Davidson & Zachary Ives**	**Huiping Cao & Xiang Lian**
General Chair	*Program Co-Chairs*	*Proceedings Co-Chairs*

Table of Contents

Research Session 5 – Keyword Search and Text

Research Session 6 – Graph Primitives

Research Session 7 – Data Mining

Research Session 8 – Uncertainty and Linking

Research Session 10 – Privacy

Research Session 11 – Streams

Session: Demo A

Tutorial 2

Research Session 12 – Spatial Data

Research Session 13 – Crowdsourcing

Session: Demo B

Research Session 14 – Indexing & Performance

Research Session 15 – Data Cleaning

Research Session 16 – Transactions

Industry Session 3 – Novel Systems

Session: Demo C

Research Session 17 – Hardware-Aware Query Processing

Research Session 18 – Graph Propagation, Influence, Mining

Research Session 21 – RDF and SPARQL

Research Session 22 – Time Series & Graph Processing

Industry Session 5 – Usability

Research Session 23 – Advanced Query Processing

Research Session 24 – New Models

SIGMOD 2015 Conference Organization

General Chair: Timos Sellis (RMIT University, Australia)

Program Chairs: Susan B. Davidson (University of Pennsylvania, USA)
Zack Ives (University of Pennsylvania, USA)

Proceedings Chairs: Huiping Cao (New Mexico State University, USA)
Xiang Lian (University of Texas - Pan American, USA)

Tutorial Chair: Wenfei Fan (University of Edinburgh, UK)

Keynotes Chair: Renée Miller (University of Toronto, Canada)

Panels Chairs: Michael Franklin (University of California, Berkeley, USA)
Tova Milo (Tel Aviv University, Israel)

Industrial Program Chairs: Sihem Amer-Yahia (CNRS, Grenoble, France)
Christopher Olston (Google, USA)

Demonstration Chairs: Vanessa Braganholo (Universidade Federal Fluminense, Brazil)
Juliana Freire (New York University, USA)

Workshops Chairs: Anastasia Ailamaki (Ecole Polytechnique Federale de Lausanne, Switzerland)
Yi Chen (New Jersey Institute of Technology, USA)

Undergraduate Research Chairs: Anisoara Nica (SAP)
Anastasios Kementsietsidis (Google)

New Researcher Symposium Chairs: Julia Stoyanovich (Drexel University, USA)
Alexandra Meliou (University of Massachusetts Amherst, USA)

Finance Chair: Xiuzhen Jenny Zhang (RMIT University, Australia)

Publicity and Social Media Chairs: Egemen Tanin (University of Melbourne, Australia)
Jagan Sankaranarayanan (NEC Labs America, USA)

Sponsorship Chairs: Nick Koudas (University of Toronto, Canada)
Mohamed Mokbel (University of Minnesota, USA)

Programming Contest Chair: Thomas Neumann (Technische Universität München, Germany)

Local Arrangements Chair: Yanchun Zhang (Victoria University, Australia)

Registration Chair: Arkady Zaslavsky (CSIRO, Australia)

Demonstration and Workshop Local Arrangements Chair: Benjamin Rubinstein (University of Melbourne, Australia)

Travel Award Selection Committee Chairs: Alexandra Meliou (University of Massachusetts Amherst, USA)
Eugene Wu (Massachusetts Institute of Technology, USA)

Web/Information Chair: Kai (Kevin) Zheng (The University of Queensland, Australia)

Program Committee Group Leaders: Alin Deutsch (University of California, San Diego, USA)
Yanlei Diao (University of Massachusetts, Amherst, USA)
Jens Dittrich (Saarland University, Germany)
Luna Dong (Google, USA)
Hank Korth (Lehigh University, USA)
Alex Labrinidis (University of Pittsburgh, USA)
Feifei Li (University of Utah, USA)
Dan Olteanu (University of Oxford, UK)
Jignesh Patel (University of Wisconsin, USA)
Sunita Sarawagi (Indian Institute of Technology, Bombay, India)
Pierre Senellart (Telecom ParisTech, France)
Wang-Chiew Tan (University of California, Santa Cruz, USA)
Jun Yang (Duke University, USA)
Xiaofang Zhou (University of Queensland, Australia)

Program Committee Members: Yanif Ahmad (Johns Hopkins University, USA)
Reza Akbarinia (INRIA Sophia Antipolis, France)
Magda Balazinska (University of Washington, USA)
Zhuowei Bao (Facebook, USA)
Pablo Barcelo (Universidad de Chile, Chile)
Srikanta Bedathur (Indraprastha Institute of Information Technology, Delhi, India)
Spyros Blanas (Ohio State University, USA)
Philip Bohannon (Facebook, USA)
Stephane Bressan (National University of Singapore, Singapore)
Michael Cafarella (University of Michigan, USA)
K. Selçuk Candan (Arizona State University, USA)
Badrish Chandramouli (Microsoft Research, USA)
Shimin Chen (Chinese Academy of Science, China)
Lei Chen (The Hong Kong University of Science & Technology, China)
James Cheng (The Chinese University of Hong Kong, China)
Alvin Cheung (Massachusetts Institute of Technology, USA)

Program Committee Members (continued):

Fei Chiang (McMaster University, Canada)
Rada Chirkova (North Carolina State University, USA)
John Cieslewicz (Google, USA)
Sarah Cohen-Boulakia (LRI Université Paris Sud, France)
Dario Colazzo (Université Paris-Dauphine, France)
Tyson Condie (University of California, Los Angeles, USA)
Bin Cui (Peking University, China)
Antonios Deligiannakis (Technical University of Crete, Greece)
Amol Deshpande (University of Maryland, USA)
Daniel Deutch (Tel Aviv University, Israel)
Eduard Dragut (Temple University, USA)
Alan Fekete (University of Sydney, Australia)
Avrilia Floratou (IBM Almaden, USA)
Tim Furche (University of Oxford, UK)
Minos Garofalakis (Technical University of Crete, Greece)
Wolfgang Gatterbauer (Carnegie Mellon University, USA)
Tingjian Ge (University of Massachusetts, Lowell, USA)
Boris Glavic (Illinois Institute of Technology, Chicago, USA)
TJ Green (LogicBlox, USA)
Torsten Grust (University of Tübingen, Germany)
Carmem Hara (Universidade Federal do Parana, Brazil)
Michael Hay (Colgate University, USA)
Melanie Herschel (University Paris-Sud 11, France)
Vagelis Hristidis (University of California, Irvine, USA)
Panos Ipeirotis (New York University, USA)
Chris Jermaine (Rice University, USA)
Alekh Jindal (Massachusetts Institute of Technology, USA)
Panagiotis Karras (Skoltech, Russia)
Gjergji Kasneci (Hasso-Plattner-Institute, Germany)
Tasos Kementsietsidis (IBM Research, USA)
Oliver Kennedy (University at Buffalo, USA)
Martin Kersten (Centrum Wiskunde & Informatica, Netherlands)
Daniel Kifer (Pennsylvania State University, USA)
George Kollios (Boston University, USA)
Tim Kraska (Brown University, USA)
Wolfgang Lehner (Technische Universität Dresden, Germany)
Chengkai Li (University of Texas, Arlington, USA)
Guoliang Li (Tsinghua University, China)
Lipyeow Lim (University of Hawaii at Manoa, USA)
Xuemin Lin (University of New South Wales, Australia)
Chengfei Liu (Swinburne University of Technology, Australia)
Jiaheng Lu (Renmin University of China, China)
Qiong Luo (The Hong Kong University of Science and Technology, China)
Ashwin Machanavajjhala (Duke University, USA)

Program Committee Members (continued):

Nikos Mamoulis (University of Hong Kong, China)
Silviu Maniu (University of Hong Kong, China)
Amelie Marian (RutgersUniversity, USA)
Davide Martinenghi (Politecnico di Milano, Italy)
Sharad Mehrotra (University of California, Irvine, USA)
Alexandra Meliou (University of Massachusetts, USA)
Xiaofeng Meng (Renmin University of China, China)
Ahmed Metwally (Google, USA)
Sebastian Michel (Saarland University, Germany)
Arnab Nandi (Ohio State University, USA)
Thomas Neumann (Technische Universität München, Germany)
Fatma Özcan (IBM research, USA)
Olga Papaemmanouil (Brandeis University, USA)
Stelios Paparizos (Microsoft Research, USA)
Aditya Parameswaran (University of Illinois at Urbana-Champaign, USA)
Srinivasan Parasarathy (Ohio State University, USA)
Andy Pavlo (Carnegie Mellon University, USA)
Rachel Pottinger (University of British Columbia, Canada)
Nicoleta Preda (University of Versailles, France)
Li Qian (Facebook)
Jorge Quiané-Ruiz (Qatar Computing Research Institute, Qatar)
Rajeev Rastogi (Amazon, USA)
Chris Ré (Stanford University, USA)
Juan Reutter (Pontificia Universidad Católica de Chile, Chile)
Sudeepa Roy (University of Washington, USA)
Senjuti B Roy (University of Washington Tacoma, USA)
Elke A Rundensteiner (Worcester Polytechnic Institute, USA)
Florin Rusu (University of California, Merced, USA)
Cyrus Shahabi (University of Southern California, USA)
Mohamed A Sharaf (University of Queensland, Australia)
Dennis Shasha (New York University, USA)
Michael Spear (Lehigh University, USA)
Julia Stoyanovich (Drexel University, USA)
Kian-Lee Tan (National University of Singapore, Singapore)
Nan Tang (Qatar Computing Research Institute, Qatar)
Yufei Tao (The Chinese University of Hong Kong, China)
Nesime Tatbul (Massachusetts Institute of Technology, USA)
Evimaria Terzi (Boston University, USA)
Martin Theobald (University of Antwerp, Belgium)
Dimitrios Theodoratos (New Jersey Institute of Technology, USA)
Dimitrios Tsoumakos (National Technical University of Athens, Greece)
Vasilis Vassalos (Athens University of Economics and Business, Greece)
Marcos Vaz Salles (University of Copenhagen - DIKU, Denmark)

Program Committee Members (continued):

Stratis Viglas (University of Edinburgh, UK)
Haixun Wang (Google Inc., USA)
Steven E Whang (Google Inc., USA)
Sai Wu (Zhejiang University, China)
Yinghui Wu (University of California, Santa Barbara, USA)
Melanie Y Wu (Indiana University, USA)
Kuixiao Xiao (Nanyang Technological University, Singapore)
Jianliang Xu (Hong Kong Baptist University, China)
Ke Yi (The Hong Kong University of Science & Technology, China)
Cong Yu (Google, USA)
Wenyuan Yu (Facebook, USA)
Jeffrey Xu Yu (The Chinese University of Hong Kong, China)
Carlo Zaniolo (University of California, Los Angeles, USA)
Demetris Zeinalipour (University Cyprus, Cyprus)
Rui Zhang (University Melbourne, Australia)
Baihua Zheng (Singapore Management University, Singapore)
Kai Zheng (The University of Queensland, Australia)

Tutorial Program Committee Members:

Philip Bohannon (Facebook, USA)
Floris Geerts (University of Antwerp, Belgium)
Felix Naumann (Hasso Plattner Institut, Germany)
Meral Ozsoyoglu (Case Western Reserve University, USA)
Tamer Özsu (University of Waterloo, Canada)
Jignesh Patel (University of Wisconsin, USA)
Divesh Srivastava (AT&T Labs, USA)
Haixun Wang (Google, USA)

Demonstration Program Committee Members:

Amr El Abbadi (University of California Santa Barbara, USA)
Serge Abiteboul (INRIA, France)
Medha Atre (University of Pennsylvania, USA)
Luciano Barbosa (IBM Research, Brazil)
Yi Chen (New Jersey Institute of Technology, USA)
Sara Cohen (The Hebrew University of Jerusalem, Israel)
Eli Cortez (Microsoft Research, USA)
Lois Delcambre (Portland State, USA)
Boris Glavic (IIT Chicago, USA)
Todd Green (LogicBlox, USA)
Carmem Hara (Universidade Federal do Paraná, Brazil)
Thomas Heinis (Imperial College, UK)
Stratos Idreos (Harvard, USA)
Dmitri V. Kalashnikov (University of California Irvine, USA)
Verena Kantere (University of Geneva, Switzerland)

Demonstration Program Committee Members (cont'd):

Yannis Katsis (University of California San Diego, USA)
David Koop (UMass-Dartmouth, USA)
Flip Korn (Google Research)
Georgia Koutrika (HP Labs, USA)
Chao Li (Google Inc., USA)
Ashwin Machanavajjhala (Duke University, USA)
Ioana Manolescu (INRIA, France)
Yannis Manolopoulos (Aristotle University of Thessaloniki, Greece)
Paolo Merialdo (Universita Roma Tre, Italy)
Mirella Moro (Universidade Federal de Minas Gerais, Brazil)
Mario Nascimento (University of Alberta, Canada)
Eduardo Ogasawara (CEFET/RJ, Brazil)
Daniel Oliveira (Universidade Federal Fluminense, Brazil)
Andy Pavlo (Carnegie Mellon University, USA)
Lucian Popa (IBM Research, USA)
Maya Ramanath (IIT Delhi, India)
Sudeepa Roy (University of Washington, USA)
Yasin N. Silva (Arizona State University, USA)
Emad Soroush (GraphLab Inc, USA)
Valéria Times (Universidade Federal de Pernambuco, Brazil)
Ricardo Torres (UNICAMP, Brazil)
Pinar Tozun (EPFL, Switzerland)
Huy Vo (New York University, USA)
Xiaochun Yang (Northeastern University, China)
Wenchao Zhou (Georgetown University, USA)

Industrial Program Committee Members:

Jose Blakeley (Microsoft)
Paul Brown (Paradigm 4)
Ed H. Chi (Google, USA)
Carlo Curino (Microsoft)
Shel Finkelstein (University of California Santa Cruz)
Stratos Idreos (Harvard University, USA)
Mohsen Jamali (WalmartLabs)
Grigoris Karvounarakis (LogicBlox, Greece)
Donald Kossmann (ETH Zurich)
Benjamin Reed (Facebook)
Jean-Michel Renders (Xerox Labs, France)
Philippe Rigaux (Internet Memory, France)
Mehul Shah (Amiato)
Eric Simon (SAP, France)
Theo Vassilakis (Metanautix)
Todd Walter (Teradata)
Ken Yocum (Illumina)

Additional reviewers

(In alphabetical order by Last Name):

Afsin Akdogan
Cem Aksoy
Peter Alvaro
Panayiotis Andreou
Vaibhav Arora
Joy Arulraj
Mohammad Asghari
Ramoza Ashan
Andreas Behrend
Souvik Bhattacherjee
Panagiotis Bouros
Matteo Brucato
Francesca Bugiotti
Damian Bursztyn
Lei Cao
Bogdan Cautis
Aniket Chakrabarty
Lijun Chang
Georgios Chatzimilioudis
Amit Chavan
Muhammad Aamir Cheema
Rui Chen
Yan Chen
Shiwen Cheng
Yu Cheng
Shumo Chu
Eleonora Ciceri
Andrew Crotty
Mahashweta Das
Ananya Dass
Dingxiong Deng
Dong Deng
Aggeliki Dimitriou
Katerina Doka
S.M. Faisal
Liyue Fan
Ioannis Flouris
David Fuhry
Alexander Galakatos
Yihan Gao
Theodore Georgiou
Nikos Giatrakos
Anastasios Gounaris
Eric Gribkoff
Sairam Gurajada
Samuel Haney
Sona Hasani
Naeemul Hassan
Xi He
Zhenying He
Haibo Hu
Huiqi Hu
Silu Huang
Weihuang Huang
Xin Huang
Yuzheng Huang
Zengfeng Huang
Sergey Ivanov
Srini Iyer
Ayush Jain
Nandish Jayaram
Lilong Jiang
Niranjan Kamat
Zoi Kaoudi
Konstantinos Karanasos
Ashwin Kayyoor
Udayan Khurana
Albert Kim
Georgios Kollias
Ios Kotsogiannis
Christos Laoudias
Chuan Lei
Jianxin Li
Jinfeng Li
Yafei Li
Yaguang Li
Xiang Lian
Xika Lin
Miguel Liroz Gistau
Yi Lu
Ying Lu
Gerasimos Marketos
Thomas Marshall
Julian McAuley
Rui Meng
Xianrui Meng
Umar Farooq Minhas
Prasenjit Mitra

Additional reviewers (continued):

Jayanta Mondal
Tobias Müller
Faisal Nawab
Apostolos Papadopoulos
Nikolaos Papailiou
Huy Pham
Yann Ponty
Olga Poppe
Mohiuddin Abdul Qader
Li Qian
Chengjie Qin
Lu Qin
Teng Qin
Abdul Quamar
Nisarg Raval
Medhabi Ray
Alexandra Roatis
Yiye Ruan
Shouq Sadah
Cetin Sahin
Zechao Sang
Carlo Sartiani
Rebeca Schroeder
Vivek Shah
Moloud Shahbazi
Anil Shanbhag
Yingxia Shao
Jieming Shi
Juwei Shi
Yanchen Shi
Lefteris Sidirourgos
Afroza Sultana
Youze Tang
Yu Tang
Hien To
Yongxin Tong
Tassos Venetis
Domagoj Vrgoc
Chi Wang
Jingjing Wang
Sibo Wang
Wei Wang
Xiang Wang
Xiaolan Wang
Xiaoyang Wang
Zhengkui Wang
Mingrui Wei
Zhewei Wei
Zeyi Wen
Matthew Wiley
Huanhuan Wu
Xiaoying Wu
Yingjun Wu
Qin Xiao
Jie Xu
Da Yan
Fan Yang
Shiyu Yang
Erfan Zamanian
Stamatis Zampetakis
Gensheng Zhang
Jun Zhang
Xiaofei Zhang
Yang Zhang
Ying Zhang
Rui Zhou
Haohan Zhu
Linhong Zhu
Honglei Zhuang
Zhongfang Zhuang
George Zois
Zainab Zolaktaf
Andreas Zuefle

SIGMOD 2015 Sponsor & Supporters

Sponsor: ACM SIGMOD

Platinum Supporters: Microsoft, ORACLE

Gold Supporters: facebook, Google, IBM, SAP, tableau SOFTWARE, Twitter

Silver Supporters: intel, RMIT UNIVERSITY

Other Supporters: NEC Laboratories America — Relentless passion for innovation

Platinum Publisher:

MORGAN & CLAYPOOL PUBLISHERS

Gold Publisher:

ELSEVIER

Graft: A Debugging Tool For Apache Giraph

Semih Salihoglu, Jaeho Shin, Vikesh Khanna, Ba Quan Truong, and Jennifer Widom
Department of Computer Science, Stanford University
Stanford, CA, USA
semih@cs.stanford.edu, jaeho@cs.stanford.edu, vikesh@cs.stanford.edu,
bqtruong@cs.stanford.edu, widom@cs.stanford.edu

ABSTRACT

We address the problem of debugging programs written for Pregel-like systems. After interviewing Giraph and GPS users, we developed *Graft*. Graft supports the debugging cycle that users typically go through: (1) Users describe programmatically the set of vertices they are interested in inspecting. During execution, Graft captures the context information of these vertices across supersteps. (2) Using Graft's GUI, users visualize how the values and messages of the captured vertices change from superstep to superstep,narrowing in suspicious vertices and supersteps. (3) Users replay the exact lines of the `vertex.compute()` function that executed for the suspicious vertices and supersteps, by copying code that Graft generates into their development environments' line-by-line debuggers. Graft also has features to construct end-to-end tests for Giraph programs. Graft is open-source and fully integrated into Apache Giraph's main code base.

1. INTRODUCTION

The *Pregel* distributed graph-processing engine [18] and its open source versions, such as *Apache Giraph* [7], *Apache Hama* [11], and *GPS* [25], are being adopted by a growing number of applications for processing large-scale graphs. For example, Facebook is using Apache Giraph in production for its Graph Search application [22] and its recommendation algorithms, and PayPal is using Giraph for fraud detection and user credit risk [28]. Like *MapReduce* [3] and *Hadoop* [10] for record-oriented data, Pregel-like systems offer transparent scalability, automatic fault-tolerance, and a simple programming interface based around implementing a small set of functions.

The computational framework introduced by Pregel is based on the *Bulk Synchronous Parallel (BSP)* computation model [29]. At the beginning of the computation, the vertices of the graph are distributed across *Worker* tasks running on different compute nodes. Computation is broken down into iterations called *supersteps*, and all workers synchronize at the end of each superstep. Algorithms are implemented in a vertex-centric fashion inside a `vertex.compute()` function, which gets called on each vertex exactly once in every superstep. Inside `vertex.compute()`, vertices receive messages from the previous superstep, update their local values, and send messages to other vertices. In Giraph [7] and GPS [25], an optional `master.compute()` function is executed by the `Master` task between supersteps.

SIGMOD'15, May 31–June 4, 2015, Melbourne, Victoria, Australia.

http://dx.doi.org/10.1145/2723372.2735353.

We have tackled the challenge of debugging programs written for Pregel-like systems. Despite being a core component of programmers' development cycles, very little work has been done on debugging in these systems. We interviewed several Giraph and GPS programmers (hereafter referred to as "users") and studied how they currently debug their `vertex.compute()` functions. We found that the following three steps were common across users: (1) Users add print statements to their code to capture information about a select set of potentially "buggy" vertices, e.g., vertices that are assigned incorrect values, send incorrect messages, or throw exceptions. The captured set of vertices is typically quite small, sometimes containing as little as a single vertex with its neighbors, because it is slow to log, and difficult to inspect the information of a large number of vertices. (2) Then, users inspect the captured vertex information and mentally "replay" their graph algorithms superstep by superstep, until they narrow in on the most suspicious vertices and supersteps. (3) Finally, they return to their code and try to identify the part of `vertex.compute()` that must have executed on the suspicious vertices and supersteps, hoping to find the bug.

Based on our observations, we designed and developed *Graft*, a new replay-style debugger that is tailored specifically for the needs of Giraph users. Existing replay debuggers, e.g. [2, 6], capture and replay all low-level system calls made by a distributed application, such as memory reads and writes to the network drivers, which are usually not relevant for diagnosing bugs inside `vertex.compute()` functions. They also do not provide any replay functionality specific to Pregel's vertex-centric graph computations. Graft's approach is motivated by the three manual steps we observed in users' current debugging cycles, which we call *capture*, *visualize*, and *reproduce*, respectively:

- **Capture**: Users describe programmatically which vertices they are interested in capturing (details in Section 3.1). Graft captures the entire context information for these vertices, across all supersteps or a user-defined selection of supersteps. It is expected that the selected set of vertices will be relatively small, and the rich API encourages applying selective criteria.
- **Visualize**: Graft includes a graph-specific and superstep-based visual interface for users to replay the algorithm's effects on the vertices whose contexts have been captured. Users can see how the values and messages of these vertices change from superstep to superstep, narrowing in on suspicious values, messages, or exceptions.
- **Reproduce**: The last step involves code inspection, for which we rely on the user's *integrated development environment* (IDE), such as Eclipse [4] or IntelliJ [12]. The context that Graft cap-

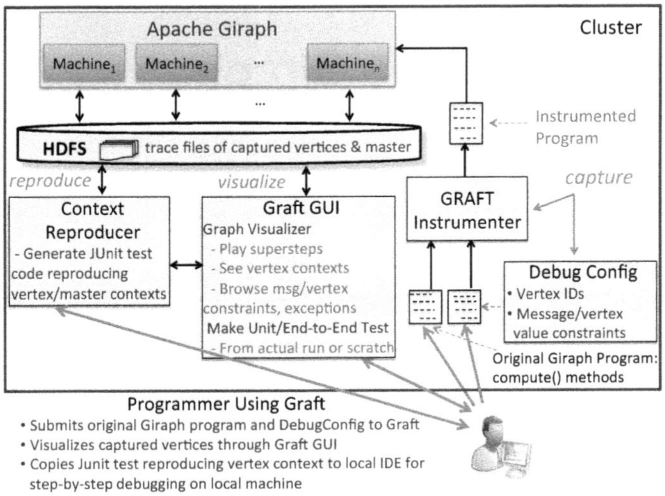

Figure 1: Graft architecture.

tures is sufficient to generate code that can reproduce exactly those lines of `vertex.compute()` that executed for a specific vertex and superstep. The user copies this code into the IDE and uses its line-by-line debugger. The code that Graft generates is a unit test file, which the user may wish to turn into a real unit test case for his `vertex.compute()` function.

Graft similarly helps users debug their `master.compute()` functions.

In our demo, we will show how Graft is used effectively under several different debugging scenarios (see Section 4), with low runtime overhead and small log files. Graft is fully implemented and integrated into Giraph's official code base [7].

2. BACKGROUND: GIRAPH API

The Giraph API consists of the four classes that were described in the original API of Pregel, and an optional `Master` class, which was introduced by GPS [25]. For the purposes of describing Graft, the important components are:

- **`vertex.compute()`**: Users subclass the `Vertex` class and code the vertex-centric logic of the computation by implementing the `vertex.compute()` function. Inside `vertex.compute()`, a vertex has access to five pieces of data: (1) the vertex ID; (2) its outgoing edges; (3) its incoming messages; (4) a set of `aggregators` (see below); and (5) *default global data* consisting of the current superstep number and the total number of vertices and edges in the graph. Each vertex also has an active/inactive flag; a vertex declares itself inactive by calling the `voteToHalt()` function in the API. The system terminates computation when all vertices become inactive or the `Master` class instructs the system to terminate. We note that in Giraph, the `vertex.compute()` function is not part of the `Vertex` class but a class called `Computation`. For simplicity of presentation, we will ignore this difference in class names.
- **`Aggregators`**: Global objects visible to all vertices; used for coordination, data sharing, and statistics aggregation. When multiple vertices update their local copy of an aggregator during a superstep, the system merges the updates at the end of the superstep using a user-specific merge function.
- **`master.compute()`**: Users can optionally subclass the `Master` class and implement the `master.compute()` function, which gets called at the beginning of each superstep. `master.compute()` can update the aggregators before they

```
public class RWDebugConfig {
  public int numRandomVerticesToCapture() { return 5; }
  public boolean captureNeighborsOfVertices () { return true ; }
  public boolean messageValueConstraint(Message msg, ID srcID,
    ID dstID, int superstep ) { return msg.value ≥ 0; }}
```

Figure 2: A `DebugConfig` file.

are broadcast to the vertices and also decide to terminate the computation. When algorithms are comprised of a sequence of different vertex-centric computations, the `master.compute()` function is typically used to coordinate phases.

3. THE GRAFT DEBUGGING TOOL

Figure 1 gives an overview of Graft's architecture. In the following subsections we explain the architecture and components in terms of the capture, visualize, and reproduce functionalities they implement.

3.1 Capture: The DebugConfig File and Graft Instrumenter

Users extend and implement a `DebugConfig` class to specify the vertices they are interested in capturing. Users can instruct Graft to capture all vertices in five categories: (1) vertices specified by their IDs, and optionally their neighbors; (2) a random set of a given number of vertices, and optionally their neighbors; (3) vertices that violate a specified constraint on vertex values; (4) vertices that send a message value that violates a specified constraint; and (5) vertices that raise exceptions. Alternatively, a user may specify that all active vertices should be captured. Users can also limit in which supersteps Graft captures vertices; by default Graft captures vertices in each superstep. For example, the `DebugConfig` shown in Figure 2 instructs Graft to capture 5 random vertices and their neighbors, and all vertices that send negative-valued messages, across all supersteps.

The Graft Instrumenter takes as input the user's `DebugConfig` file and `vertex.compute()` function. It uses Javassist [15] to wrap the `vertex.compute()` around a new instrumented one, which is the final program that is submitted to Giraph. When Giraph calls `compute()` on the instrumented code of a vertex v, the code calls the user's original `vertex.compute()` function, intercepting messages and value updates so it can check constraints. After the user's `vertex.compute()` function returns, the instrumented function checks whether v should be captured: (1) if v is in one of the five possible categories of `DebugConfig` (above); or (2) if the user instructed Graft to capture all active vertices. To capture v, the instrumented code logs the context of v, along with the messages that v sent, to a *trace file* in the Hadoop Distributed File System (HDFS)—the distributed file system that is used by Giraph [10]. The context of a `vertex.compute()` function consists of the five pieces of data that the Giraph API exposes to a vertex (recall Section 2). We note that there are some limitations to capturing only this small set of data, which we discuss in Section 7. We also note that the design of our debugger assumes that the captured set of vertices is relatively small, both for usability and performance. As a "safety net", we have built in an adjustable threshold, specifying a maximum number of captures, after which Graft stops capturing.

3.2 Visualize: Graft GUI

Users inspect the captured vertices through the Graft GUI in their browsers; screenshots are shown in Figures 3-5. Figures 3 and 4 are from a graph coloring algorithm, so the vertex values are color assignments. Figure 5 is from a connected components algorithm,

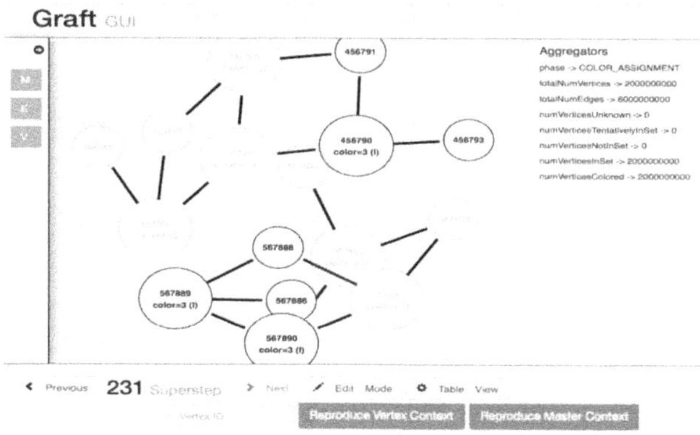

Figure 3: Node-link View.

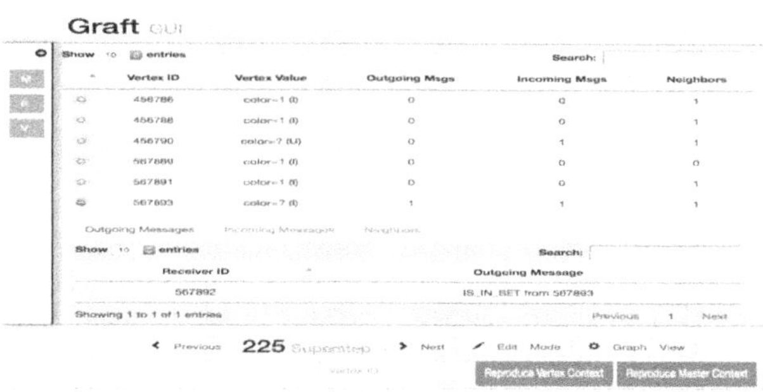

Figure 4: Tabular View.

where the values are vertex IDs. The GUI's Node-link View is for visualizing a small number of selected vertices and their graph structure. The Tabular View is for visualizing larger numbers of selected vertices. The Violations and Exceptions View is for inspecting those vertices that violate constraints or raise exceptions. We explain these views in detail, and explain the Reproduce Context buttons.

- **Node-link View (Figure 3)**: Shows the vertices that were captured by ID or by random selection as a node-link diagram. The IDs and values of vertices are displayed on the nodes, and edge values (if any) are displayed on the links. If a vertex is inactive in the displayed superstep, its color is dimmed. For example, in Figure 3 vertex 567890 is active in superstep 231, while vertex 567891 is inactive. If u is a neighbor of a captured vertex v but u is not captured, then u is shown as a small node and only u's ID is displayed. By clicking on a captured vertex, users can further see the incoming and outgoing messages of the vertex (omitted in the figure). In the upper-right corner, we see the aggregator values and default global data for the displayed superstep.

  Users can replay how vertex values, active/inactive states, incoming and outgoing messages, and aggregators change superstep by superstep by pressing the Next and Previous superstep buttons. On the left side, there are three boxes labeled as *M* for **m**essage value constraint, *V* for **v**ertex value constraint, and *E* for **e**xception. Green labels indicate that no violation or exception has occurred on any vertex during the superstep that is being displayed, and red labels indicate otherwise. When a label is red, users can click on the label and go to the Violations and Exceptions View to see the vertices that violated the constraint or raised an exception (see below).

- **Tabular View (Figure 4)**: If the user is debugging a large number of vertices, then the node-link diagram becomes difficult to use. The Graft GUI alternatively provides a tabular view of vertices, shown in Figure 4, where each row displays the summary of a captured vertex and can be expanded to see the entire context. This view also provides a simple search feature to find vertices by their IDs or their neighbors' IDs, their values, or messages they have sent and/or received. Similar to the Node-link View, the Tabular View allows stepping through vertex contexts superstep by superstep.

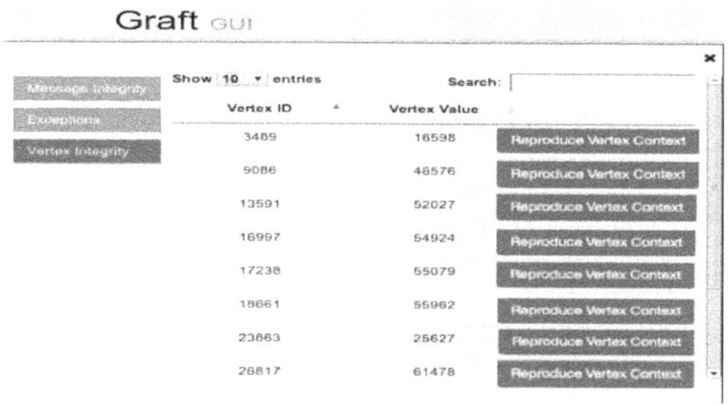

Figure 5: Violations and Exceptions View.

- **Violations and Exceptions View (Figure 5)**: Tabular view of vertices that have violated a vertex value or message constraint, or have raised an exception. Shows the constraint-violating vertex or message value, or the error message and stack trace of the exception.

- **Reproduce Context Buttons**: When the user wants to further investigate a vertex v, he clicks the "Reproduce Vertex Context" button that is available in all of the views. The GUI displays a piece of Java code the user can copy into his IDE to replay line-by-line which lines of `vertex.compute()` executed for the selected vertex. We will explain the details of this Java code in the next section.

3.3 Reproduce: Context Reproducer

When a user clicks on the Reproduce Vertex Context button for a vertex v in superstep i, Graft's Context Reproducer takes the trace file of v from superstep i and generates a JUnit test file [16], with the help of Apache Velocity's template-based code generation [30]. The generated code replicates the context of v through mock objects, then calls `v.compute()`. The user can copy this code into his IDE and use the IDE's line-by-line debugger to see exactly which lines of `v.compute()` executed in superstep i. Using Mockito [19], the mock objects emulate the behavior of the different objects that the `vertex.compute()` code depends on, such as v's data and ID, aggregators in superstep i, or the default global data exposed to v, thus replicating the context under which `v.compute()` executed in the cluster. (We will discuss a limitation of this approach in Section 7.) An example JUnit code snippet generated by Context Reproducer is shown in our longer online tech-report [24]. We believe the ability to replay the line-by-line execution of `vertex.compute()` for a specific vertex and superstep is a very powerful feature of Graft. It was also the most challenging component of Graft to implement.

Although JUnit is a standard testing framework to unit-test pieces of Java code, our primary use of JUnit is not to unit-test `vertex.compute()`, but to reproduce the context of `vertex.compute()` for a particular vertex in a particular superstep. However, users can edit the JUnit test code generated by Graft and turn it into a real unit test.

Name	Vertices	Edges	Description
web-BS	685K	7.6M (d), 12.3M (u)	A web graph from 2002
soc-Epinions	76K	500K (d), 780K (u)	Epinions.com "who trusts whom" network
bipartite-1M-3M	1M	6M (u)	A 3-regular bipartite graph

Table 1: Graph datasets for demonstration.

3.4 Other Features

Debugging Master.compute()

If the Giraph program submitted to Graft contains a `master.compute()` function, Graft automatically captures its context—just the aggregator values—in every superstep. By clicking on the "Reproduce Master Context" button in the GUI, users can generate a JUnit test file reproducing `master.compute()` execution in a particular superstep. In our experience, the most common bug inside `master.compute()` is setting the phase of the computation incorrectly (recall Section 2), which generally leads to infinite superstep executions or premature termination.

Small Graph Construction and End-To-End Tests

We discussed that the JUnit test files Graft produces can be retained as real unit tests. In addition to unit tests, which test `compute()` functions in a single superstep, users may wish to write "end-to-end" tests. In an end-to-end test, a user may construct a small graph, then execute the program locally from first superstep until termination, to verify that Giraph's final output is correct on the small graph. The Node-link View of the Graft GUI has an "offline" mode to help users construct small graphs for testing purposes. Users can add vertices and draw edges between vertices, and edit the values of the vertices and edges in an easy fashion. Users can also select premade graphs from a menu. After constructing a graph in the GUI, the user can obtain either a text file that contains the adjacency list representation of the graph and use it in an end-to-end test, or can obtain an end-to-end test code template, which contains code that constructs the graph programmatically.

4. DEBUGGING SCENARIOS

To illustrate Graft's debugging capabilities, our demo runs through three debugging scenarios that cover different features of Graft. Two of the scenarios demonstrate how Graft helps users debug their `vertex.compute()` functions, while the third demonstrates how Graft can also help users find problems in their input graphs. In each scenario, we run a Giraph algorithm on an eight-node cluster. To keep the demo interactive, we run each algorithm on one of the medium-scale directed (d) or undirected (u) input graphs from Table 1, so that each run takes only a few seconds.

4.1 Graph Coloring Scenario

Our first scenario is based on a report from an actual Graft user and illustrates the feature of capturing and inspecting a random set of vertices for debugging `vertex.compute()`. It is based on our Giraph implementation of a graph coloring algorithm from references [5, 26], which we call GC. Graph coloring is the problem of assigning a color to each vertex of an undirected graph so that no two adjacent vertices have the same color, using as few colors as possible. GC iteratively finds a maximal independent set (MIS) of vertices, i.e., a maximal set of vertices such that no pair of vertices are adjacent. The algorithm assigns the vertices in each MIS a new color, then removes them from the graph, until there are no vertices left in the graph.

Our implementation of GC contains a bug that incorrectly puts some adjacent vertices into the same MIS, so they are assigned the same color. In this scenario, a small sample of vertices is typically enough to see the bug. We run our implementation on the `bipartite-1M-3M` graph and use Graft to capture a random set of 10 vertices. We then go to the final superstep from the GUI to verify that the algorithm is correct, but we see that some vertices and their neighbors are assigned the same color, indicating a bug in our implementation. We then focus on two such vertices in the GUI, say 672 and 673, replay the computation superstep by superstep, and investigate how they end up with the same color. We notice at some point, say superstep 41, both vertices enter the MIS that the algorithm is constructing (indicated by a `type` field on their values). We generate a JUnit test case from the GUI replicating the lines of code that executed for vertex 672 in superstep 41. During line-by-line replay inside an IDE, we identify the buggy code that incorrectly puts vertex 672 into the MIS.

4.2 Random Walk Scenario

Our second scenario illustrates debugging using message value constraints. We use a random walk simulation algorithm from reference [25], which we call RW. Each vertex starts with an initial number of 100 walkers. In each superstep, each vertex declares a local counter for each of its neighbors, randomly increments one of the counters by one for each of its walkers, then sends the counters as messages to its neighbors.

To optimize the memory and network I/O, our implementation declares the counters and messages as 16-bit `short` primitive types. However, if a vertex u has a large number of walkers and the number of walkers from u to v exceeds Java's max `short` value of 32767, then u might send v a negative number of walkers. To detect this bug using Graft, we run RW on the `web-BS` graph with a simple message value constraint that messages are non-negative. After the run we see that the message value constraint icon is red in some supersteps, and in the Violations and Exceptions View we identify which vertices are sending negative messages. We generate a JUnit test case from a vertex v that has sent a negative message, and detect that the bug is due to overflowing of the `short` type counters.

4.3 Maximum-Weight Matching Scenario

Our third scenario illustrates that Graft can also be used to find errors in the input graph. We use an approximate maximum-weight matching algorithm from reference [23], which we call MWM. In this algorithm, the input is an undirected graph with edge weights. In each iteration of MWM, vertices select their maximum-weight neighbors. If u and v select each other, the edge (u, v) is added to M, and u and v (along with all edges incident to them) are removed from the graph. The iterations continue until there are no vertices left in the graph.

We run MWM on a weighted version of the `soc-Epinions` graph, which is encoded as undirected by having symmetric directed edges between every pair of adjacent vertices. However, a small fraction of the edges incorrectly have different weights on their symmetric edges. We run MWM on our erroneous `soc-Epinions` graph and see that it enters an infinite loop. We then run MWM with Graft and capture all active vertices after superstep 500, by which point the active graph is fairly small. We notice that some of the edge weights in the small remaining graph are asymmetric, which is the cause of the algorithm not converging.

Name	Vertices	Edges	Description
sk-2005	51M	1.9B (d), 3.5B (u)	Web graph of the .sk domain from 2005
twitter	42M	1.5B (d), 2.7B (u)	Twitter "who is followed by who" network
bipartite-2B-6B	2B	12B (u)	A 3-regular bipartite graph

Table 2: Graph datasets for performance experiments.

Name	Description
`DC-sp`	Captures 5 specified vertices
`DC-sp+nbr`	Captures 5 specified vertices and their neighbors
`DC-msg`	Specifies constraint that message values are non-negative
`DC-vv`	Specifies constraint that vertex values are non-negative.
`DC-full`	Captures 10 specified vertices and their neighbors, specifies message and vertex constraints, and checks for exceptions

Table 3: `DebugConfig` configurations.

5. PERFORMANCE

To evaluate the performance overhead of Graft, we ran the three algorithms from our scenarios with and without Graft, over large data sets. The graphs and the `DebugConfig` configurations we used are shown in Tables 2 and 3, respectively. We used a cluster of 36 machines, each with 50 GB of RAM, running Red Hat Linux OS and Giraph 1.0.0. We used the *3X* software tool to automate and manage our experiments [27]. Our 3X repository, which contains the exact configurations of our experiments and can be used to reproduce them, is available to download [9].

Figure 6 shows a sample of our experiments. In the figure, each cluster of bars corresponds to one algorithm and dataset as indicated on the x-axis. Individual bars of the cluster show the overhead of running the algorithm and dataset on a particular `DebugConfig` or without Graft ("no-debug" bars). The heights of the bars indicate the relative total run-time of a specific experiment against the no-debug configuration (normalized to 1.0 for each experiment). The number on each bar indicates the total number of vertex captures in the experiment. For example, the last bar of the RW-tw cluster indicates that the overhead of running `RW` on the `twitter` graph with the `DC-full` configuration was 26% compared to running without Graft, and Graft captured 24213 vertices during the experiment. We ran each experiment five times and report the average runtimes for each experiment. The variances across runs were small and are shown by the error bars.

Overall, Graft's overhead when capturing a set of 5 vertices randomly or by their IDs was less than 16% (`DC-sp`), and less than 17% when also capturing the neighbors of these vertices (`DC-sp+nbr`), across all of our experiments. The overhead was less than 20% when checking message and vertex value constraints (`DC-vv` and `DC-msg`). Finally, Graft's overhead when capturing a specified set of vertices and their neighbors, and also the vertices that violate a message and vertex value constraint was less than 29% (`DC-full`). The number of captures varied between 1 and 1,246,151.

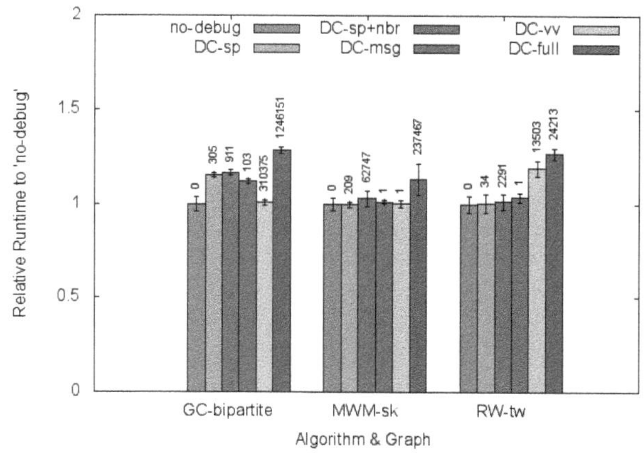

Figure 6: Graft's performance overhead.

6. RELATED WORK

We provide a very brief discussion of related work here; more extensive discussion and comparison against our approach is provided in our online technical report [24]. In brief, past work divides into three categories, none of which proposes and implements a debugger designed specifically for the needs of Pregel-like systems, or any other distributed graph-processing system.

- **Remote Debuggers of IDEs (e.g., [4, 12]):** Debugging must be attached to pieces of code running on a specific port of a specific machine—information that is usually unknown to Giraph users before launching their programs.
- **Replay Debuggers (e.g., [2, 6]):** These debuggers record low-level information such as OS calls, network messages, and memory accesses throughout the execution of a distributed application. Using this recorded information, users replay the execution of any group of processes offline to find bugs.
- **Debuggers of Dataflow Systems:** Distributed dataflow programs consist of a workflow of data operators, such as `map`, `filter`, `join`, and `groupBy`. IG [20] is a framework for building debugging tools for *Pig* [21], a dataflow system on top of *Hadoop* [10]. Daphne [14] is a set of debugging tools for DryadLINQ [31], a dataflow system on top of the Dryad [13] data-processing system. Arthur [1] is a new debugger for Spark [32] and Hadoop [10] programs. However, Pregel-like systems do not cast their graph computations as a workflow of operators that modify a set of input records, and these tools do not provide any useful visualizations for understanding graph algorithms.

7. LIMITATION AND FUTURE WORK

Because the APIs of Pregel-like systems are implemented in standard programming languages such as Java or C++, users can, in principle, write `compute()` functions that depend on "external" data beyond the five pieces of data that are exposed by the API. For example, programs can read external data from an HDFS file in Giraph, or vertices that are executed on the same Giraph worker thread can share information amongst themselves through static Java objects. If a user's `vertex.compute()` code has such external data dependencies, then the limited context information that Graft captures will not be enough to reproduce exactly what happened, which is a limitation of our approach. That said, we believe that such external data dependencies should be avoided in general, and every algorithm we have seen implemented in the code repositories of Pregel-like systems either had no external dependencies or could be implemented without such dependencies. There are ways, however, to capture external dependencies: we could, for example, employ techniques in some replay debuggers [2, 6] that capture enough context information to replay the entire execution of processes, which includes all function calls. For now, Graft is intended to be a very lightweight debugger, and employing techniques to capture and reproduce the complete data dependencies of `compute()` functions is beyond the scope of the initial system.

We outline three broad directions for future work.

- **More complex constraints:** During our interviews with Giraph users, several users expressed interest in more sophisticated vertex value and message constraints than what Graft currently offers. For example, in our GC algorithm, a user might wish to specify as a constraint that no two adjacent vertices should be assigned the same color. As another example, users might want to express message constraints that depend on the value of the destination vertex, which Graft does not currently allow—message constraints can only depend on the ID of the destination vertex. Extending `DebugConfig` and the Graft Instrumenter to specify and verify such constraints should not be overly difficult and could be a useful extension.
- **Debugging other vertex-centric systems:** With only minor modifications the Graft code could be used for other Pregel-like systems, such as Apache Hama [11] or GPS [25], which contain only minor API differences from Giraph. Some vertex-centric graph-processing systems, such as PowerGraph [8] and GraphChi [17], support both synchronous and asynchronous computations. We believe a Graft-like debugger could also be helpful in debugging synchronous programs written for these systems. However, asynchronous computations have no clear superstep by superstep divisions; it would be a challenging and interesting future direction to design intuitive GUIs to visualize asynchronous computations.
- **Extending Graft's unit-testing functionality:** During our interviews with Giraph users, we observed a prevalence of end-to-end tests, which verify the final output of their programs on small graphs, as opposed to unit tests, which verify the behavior of a vertex in a particular superstep and context. One reason is that it is much easier to construct a small input test graph, which is the input to an end-to-end test, than the entire context of a vertex in a particular superstep (mock vertex values, aggregators, global data, input messages, and neighbors of a vertex). However, our interviewees also recognized that at scale, `vertex.compute()` functions can be exposed to many contexts that are not tested during end-to-end tests on small graphs. We hope to extend the Graft GUI's offline mode to make it easy to generate unit tests that can test `vertex.compute()` functions under contexts that emerge at large scale.

8. ACKNOWLEDGEMENTS

We are grateful to Pavan Athivarapu, Avery Ching, Sergey Edunov, Nishant Gandhi, and Maja Kabilijo for numerous interviews, discussions, and valuable feedback. We also thank Andrej Krevl for his assistance with a variety of system issues.

9. REFERENCES

[1] A. Dave and M. Zaharia and I. Stoica. Arthur: Rich Post-Facto Debugging for Production Analytics Applications. Technical report, University of California, Berkeley, 2013.

[2] G. Altekar and I. Stoica. ODR: Output-deterministic Replay for Multicore Debugging. In *Proceedings of the ACM Symposium on Operating Systems Principles*, 2009.

[3] J. Dean and S. Ghemawat. MapReduce: Simplified data processing on large clusters. In *Proceedings of the Symposium on Operating System Design and Implementation*, 2004.

[4] Eclipse IDE. https://www.eclipse.org/.

[5] A. H. Gebremedhin and F. Manne. Scalable Parallel Graph Coloring Algorithms. *Concurrency - Practice and Experience*, 12(12), 2000.

[6] D. Geels, G. Altekar, S. Shenker, and I. Stoica. Replay Debugging for Distributed Applications. In *Proceedings of the USENIX Annual Technical Conference*, 2006.

[7] Apache Giraph. http://giraph.apache.org/.

[8] J. E. Gonzalez, Y. Low, H. Gu, D. Bickson, and C. Guestrin. PowerGraph: Distributed Graph-Parallel Computation on Natural Graphs. In *Proceedings of the Symposium on Operating Systems Design and Implementation*, 2012.

[9] 3X Repository of Graft Overhead Experiments. https://github.com/netj/graft-overhead-exp.

[10] Apache Hadoop. http://hadoop.apache.org/.

[11] Apache Hama. http://hama.apache.org/.

[12] IntelliJ IDE. https://www.jetbrains.com/idea/.

[13] M. Isard, M. Budiu, Y. Yu, A. Birrell, and D. Fetterly. Dryad: Distributed Data-parallel Programs from Sequential Building Blocks. *SIGOPS Operating Systems Review*, 41(3), Mar. 2007.

[14] V. Jagannath, Z. Yin, and M. Budiu. Monitoring and Debugging DryadLINQ Applications with Daphne. In *International Workshop on High-Level Parallel Programming Models and Supportive Environments*, 2011.

[15] Javassist Documentation. www.javassist.org.

[16] Junit Documentation. http://junit.org/.

[17] A. Kyrola, G. Blelloch, and C. Guestrin. GraphChi: Large-Scale Graph computation on Just a PC. In *Proceedings of the Symposium on Operating Systems Design and Implementation*, 2012.

[18] G. Malewicz, M. H. Austern, A. J. C. Bik, J. C. Dehnert, I. Horn, N. Leiser, and G. Czajkowski. Pregel: A System for Large-Scale Graph Processing. In *Proceedings of the ACM SIGMOD International Conference on Management of Data*, 2011.

[19] Mockito Home Page. https://code.google.com/p/mockito/.

[20] C. Olston and B. Reed. Inspector Gadget: A Framework for Custom Monitoring and Debugging of Distributed Dataflows. In *Proceedings of the ACM SIGMOD International Conference on Management of Data*, 2011.

[21] C. Olston, B. Reed, U. Srivastava, R. Kumar, and A. Tomkins. Pig Latin: A Not-So-Foreign Language for Data Processing. In *Proceedings of the ACM SIGMOD International Conference on Management of Data*, 2008.

[22] Facebook's Graph Search Puts Apache Giraph on the Map. http://www.pcworld.com/article/2046680/facebooks-graph-search-puts-apache-giraph-on-the-map.html.

[23] R. Preis. Linear Time 1/2-Approximation Algorithm for Maximum Weighted Matching in General Graphs. In *Proceedings of the Symposium On Theoretical Aspects of Computer Science*, 1998.

[24] S. Salihoglu and J. Shin and V. Khanna and B. Truong and J. Widom. Graft: A Debugging Tool For Apache Giraph. Technical Report, Stanford. http://ilpubs.stanford.edu:8090/1109/, 2014.

[25] S. Salihoglu and J. Widom. GPS: A Graph Processing System. In *Proceedings of the International Conference on Scientific and Statistical Database Management*, 2013.

[26] S. Salihoglu and J. Widom. Optimizing Graph Algorithms on Pregel-like Systems. In *Proceedings of the International Conference on Very Large Databases*, 2014.

[27] J. Shin, A. Paepcke, and J. Widom. 3X: A Data Management System for Computational Experiments. Technical Report, Stanford. http://ilpubs.stanford.edu:8090/1080/, 2013.

[28] J. Tang. Graph Mining with Apache Giraph. http://www.slideshare.net/Hadoop_Summit/tang-june26-205pmroom210cv2.

[29] L. G. Valiant. A Bridging Model for Parallel Computation. *Communications of the ACM*, 33(8), 1990.

[30] Velocity. http://velocity.apache.org/.

[31] Y. Yu, M. Isard, D. Fetterly, M. Budiu, U. Erlingsson, P. K. Gunda, and J. Currey. DryadLINQ: A System for General-purpose Distributed Data-parallel Computing Using a High-level Language. In *Proceedings of the USENIX Conference on Operating Systems Design and Implementation*, 2008.

[32] Zaharia, M. and Chowdhury, M. and Franklin, M. J. and Shenker, S. and Stoica, I. Spark: Cluster Computing with Working Sets. In *USENIX Conference on Hot Topics in Cloud Computing*, 2010.

Even Metadata is Getting Big: Annotation Summarization using InsightNotes *

Dongqing Xiao, Armir Bashllari, Tyler Menard, and Mohamed Eltabakh
Computer Science Department, Worcester Polytechnic Institute
Worcester, MA, US
dxiao@cs.wpi.edu, abashllari@cs.wpi.edu, tjmenard@cs.wpi.edu, meltabakh@cs.wpi.edu

ABSTRACT

In this paper, we demonstrate the *InsightNotes* system, a *summary-based annotation management engine over relational databases* [30]. InsightNotes addresses the unique challenges that arise in modern applications—especially scientific applications—that rely on rich and large-scale repositories of curation and annotation information. In these applications, the number and size of the raw annotations may grow beyond what end-users and scientists can comprehend and analyze. InsightNotes overcomes these limitations by integrating mining and summarization techniques with the annotation management engine in novel ways. The objective is to create concise and meaningful representations of the raw annotations, called *"annotation summaries"*, to be the basic unit of processing. The core functionalities of InsightNotes include: **(1) Extensibility**, where domain experts can define the summary types suitable for their application, **(2) Incremental Maintenance**, where the system efficiently maintains the annotation summaries under the continuous addition of new annotations, **(3) Summary-Aware Query Processing and Propagation**, where the execution engine and query operators are extended for manipulating and propagating the annotation summaries within the query pipeline under complex transformations, and **(4) Zoom-in Query Processing**, where end-users can interactively expand specific annotation summaries of interest and retrieve their detailed (raw) annotations. We will demonstrate the InsightNotes's features using a real-world annotated database from the ornithological domain (the science of studying birds). We will design an interactive demonstration that engage the audience in annotating the data, visualizing how annotations are summarized and propagated, and zooming-in when desired to retrieve more details.

1. INTRODUCTION

The virtue and merit of data curation and annotation is becoming increasingly important in modern applications. This is evident from scientific applications that collect and generate metadata information in the scale of orders-of-magnitudes larger than the base data, e.g., the number of annotations is around 30x, 120x, and 250x larger than the number of data records in DataBank biological database [2], Hydrologic Earth database [3, 29], and AKN ornithological database [4], respectively. Annotations may range from capturing scientists' observations about the data, attaching related articles or documents, exchanging auxiliary knowledge among users, to highlighting erroneous or conflicting values, and storing provenance and lineage information. Existing techniques in annotation management, e.g., [6, 10, 11, 15, 17, 20], have made it feasible to systematically capture such metadata annotations and efficiently integrate them into the data processing cycle. This includes propagating the related annotations along with queries' answers [6, 10, 11, 20, 28], querying the data based on their attached annotations [15, 20], annotation-based scientific workflows [5, 7, 25], and supporting semantic annotations such as provenance tracking [8, 9, 14, 27], and belief annotations [19].

Why Annotations are Not Data: Annotations are logically different from the base data since they are viewed as metadata information that should propagate automatically with the data. Since the data values may go though complex transformations during query processing, e.g., projection, join, grouping and aggregation, and duplicate elimination, the related annotations must also go though corresponding transformations by each query operator. If annotations are modeled as regular data, then the annotation management tasks are entirely delegated to end-users and higher-level applications starting from the storage and indexing of annotations and ending by explicitly encoding the propagation semantics within each of the users' queries (An example illustrating the complexity of annotation propagation is presented in Section 2.1). Evidently, this approach is not only error-prune, lacks optimizations, not feasible in some applications, but also render even simple queries very complex. That is why annotation management engines have been proposed to efficiently and transparently manage such complexities.

In this paper, we propose to demonstrate the *"InsightNotes"* system, *an advanced summary-based annotation management engine over relational databases* [22, 30]. InsightNotes overcomes a critical and common limitation to all existing techniques in annotation management, which is that they all manage and manipulate the raw annotations. As a result—under the current large repositories of annotations—a single output tuple may have 100s of raw annotations attached to it. For example, the L.H.S of Figure 1 illustrates a single data tuple having 100s of raw annotations attached to it. Hence, it is extremely hard for scientists to analyze the reported annotations and extract useful knowledge from them, e.g., finding out which ones carry provenance information vs. regular comments, which ones are obsolete or proven wrong, which ones are duplicates or have similar content, and which ones refute (or approve) the content of their tuples.

*This project is partially supported by NSF-CRI 1305258 grant.

SIGMOD'15, May 31–June 4, 2015, Melbourne, Victoria, Australia.

http://dx.doi.org/10.1145/2723372.2735355.

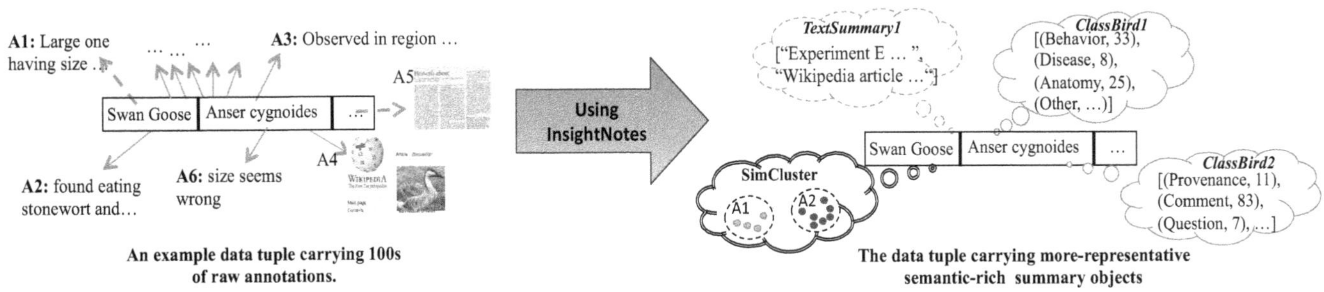

Figure 1: Example of Annotation Summaries in InsightNotes.

InsightNotes is fundamentally different from the existing techniques as it proposes a new annotation management model based on the new concept of *"annotation summaries"*. InsightNotes integrates data mining and summarization techniques with the annotation management engine. The objective is to create concise and meaningful representations of the raw annotations, i.e., the *annotation summaries*, to be the basic unit of processing and propagation. For example, the R.H.S of Figure 1 illustrates the same data tuple along with its attached summary objects using InsightNotes. The summary objects include, for example, Classifier-type objects, e.g., *ClassBird1* and *ClassBird2*, that classify the raw annotations into user-defined classes, Snippet-type objects, e.g., *TextSummary1*, that summarize the attached big articles and report snippets on each, and Cluster-type objects, e.g., *SimCluster*, that group similar annotations into groups and reports only one representative from each group. It is worth highlighting that these summary objects are created per data tuple, i.e., they summarize the annotations on a single tuple, and then they get attached back to this tuple as depicted in the figure.

In the demonstration, we will present the novel features and capabilities of the *InsightNotes* engine that enable the creation, manipulation, and propagation of the annotation summaries. These features include:

(1) Extensibility and Efficient Maintenance: InsightNotes is designed as an extensible engine where the database admins can define how to summarize the annotations in a way suitable for their applications, e.g., determining which classification techniques to use and what class labels to generate. The system only defines some properties and requirements that the integrated mining techniques should obey for efficient and incremental maintenance of the annotation summaries.

(2) Summary-Aware Query Processing: Unlike the raw annotations which are free-text objects, the annotation summaries have well-defined structures and properties. The challenge is how to extend the query engine to efficiently manipulate the annotation summaries at query time without retrieving the raw annotations. The semantics and algebra of each of the standard query operators, e.g., projection, join, grouping, and aggregation, have been extended to directly operate on the summary objects attached to each tuple. We also introduced new query operators specific for annotation summaries and integrated them into the query engine.

(3) Zoom-in Query Processing: After reporting the annotation summaries, end-users may get interested in retrieving the detailed (raw) annotations of specific summaries. For example, referring to the R.H.S of Figure 1, a scientist may be interested in retrieving the eight disease-related annotations attached to the given tuple, or in retrieving all annotations in the cluster represented by annotation *A2*. This feature is enabled in InsightNotes through an interactive *zoom-in* querying capability. We will demonstrate this feature coupled with smart caching techniques for efficient execution.

(4) InsightNotes Interface: Our team is developing an Excel-based GUI on top of the InsightNotes engine from which most of the proposed functionalities can be realized. We opt for an Excel-based tool since scientists are already familiar with Excel and its functionalities. The tool will enable, querying the data interactively, visualizing the reported annotation summaries, and optionally zooming-in to retrieve the detailed raw annotations.

2. InsightNotes OVERVIEW

In this section, we briefly highlight the core features of the InsightNotes system. The system has an extended data model, where each data tuple r carries its attribute values as well as the annotation summary objects that summarize the raw annotations on r (See Figure 1). InsightNotes supports three widely-used families (types) of data mining and summarization techniques, which are: (1) Text summarization techniques (Snippets), e.g., [24], for summarizing large-object annotations, e.g., big text values and large documents, and creating concise snippets from them, (2) Clustering techniques, e.g., [23], for clustering the annotations into distinct groups of similar content, and (3) Classification techniques, e.g., [12], for categorizing annotations according to user-defined classifiers. In the following, we highlight the query processing, extensibility, and scalability features of InsightNotes.

2.1 Summary-Aware Query Processing and Propagation

InsightNotes has an extended query engine for manipulating the annotation summaries attached to each data tuple under complex transformations, e.g., join, grouping, projection, and duplicate elimination. We proposed extended semantics for each query operator to compute the output annotation summaries from the input values without accessing the raw annotations. A key contribution of InsightNotes is that the summaries are manipulated in a pipelined fashion. As a result, summary-based processing can be plugged-in at any stage of the query plan, e.g., filtering, joining, or sorting the data tuples according to summary-based predicates. The following example demonstrates a Select-Project-Join (SPJ) query involving summary propagation in InsightNotes. The formal semantics of all query operators can be found in [30].

Example: *Assume an SQL query* `"Select r.a, r.b, s.z From R r, S s Where r.a = s.x And r.b = 2"` *over the two tuples r and s presented in Figure 2. Tuple r has four summary objects attached to it, while tuple s has only two attached summary objects. We proved in [30] in Theorems 1 and 2 that to guarantee identical summary propagation under different—but equivalent—query plans, InsightNotes needs to project out the un-needed annotations before any merge operation over the summary objects. Therefore, the projection operator in Step 1 in Figure 2 projects out attributes* r.c *and* r.d *and eliminates*

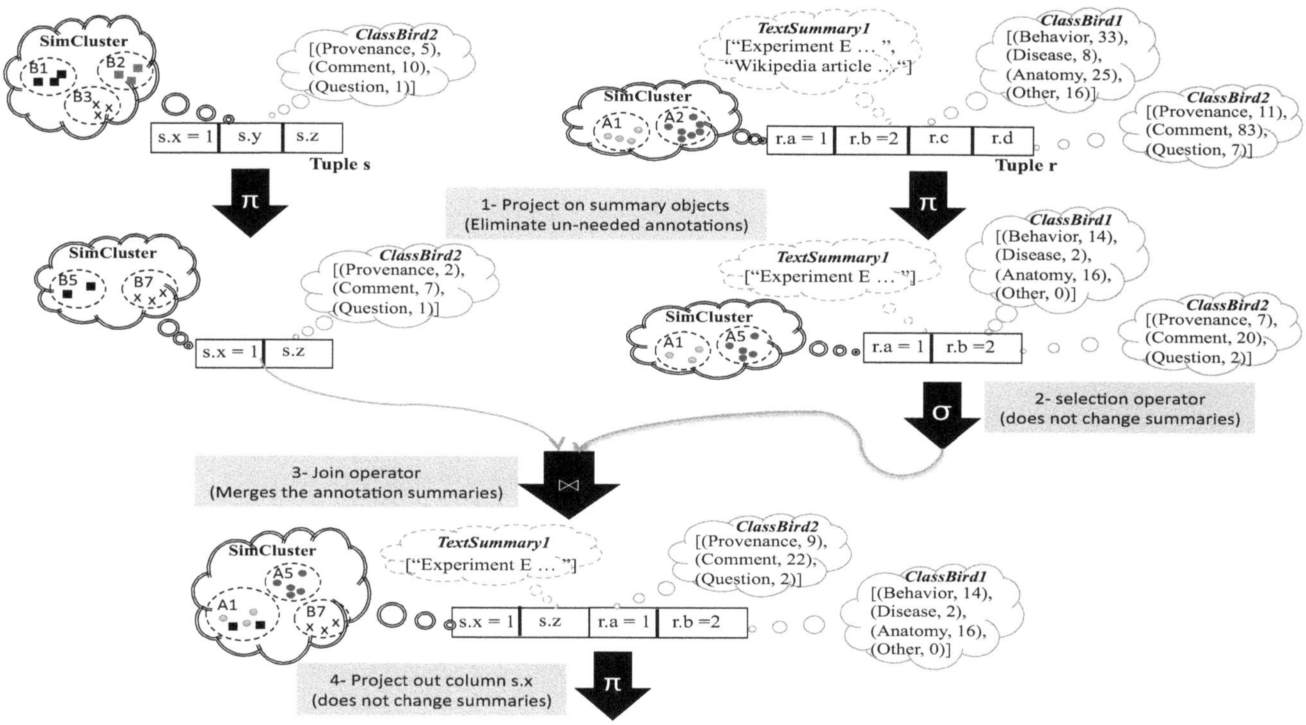

Figure 2: Example Query in InsightNotes.

the effect of their annotations from r's summary objects. For example, the `annotationCnt` *field in the classifier objects is decremented, the wikipedia article in the snippet object is deleted, and the cluster objects are modified, e.g., some annotations are dropped from each cluster, and hence the* `groupSize` *field is decremented. Moreover, if a cluster's representative is dropped, then another representative is elected (See A5 representative replacing the dropped A2 representative). The same operation takes place over tuple s, where the effect of all annotations attached to both s.x and s.y is removed from s's summary objects. The only difference is that s.x attribute will not be projected out because it is needed in the subsequent join operator.*

The next operator in the query plan is the selection operator over r (Step 2). Based on the query's predicate, r will pass the operator and all its summary objects will propagate without any change. Then, the produced tuples will join and their summary objects will be merged (Step 3). According to the merge procedure, r's summary objects `ClassBird1` *and* `TextSummary1` *will propagate without any change since they do have no counterpart objects over s. Whereas summary objects* `ClassBird2` *and* `SimCluster` *will be combined. This action takes into account the case where the same annotation may be attached to both tuples r and s, and hence the annotation's effect on the summary objects should not be double counted. For example, assuming that there are five common annotations on both r and s classified as* `Comment`, *then when the two objects are merged the sum of that classifier label will be 22 instead of 27 as illustrated in the figure. The merge of the cluster summary objects is slightly more complex. The main idea is that the overlapping groups from both sides, e.g., the groups represented by A1 and B5, will be combined together, whereas the non-overlapping groups, e.g., the groups represented by A5 and B7, will propagate separately as illustrated in the figure. Finally attribute s.x will be projected out before producing the output.*

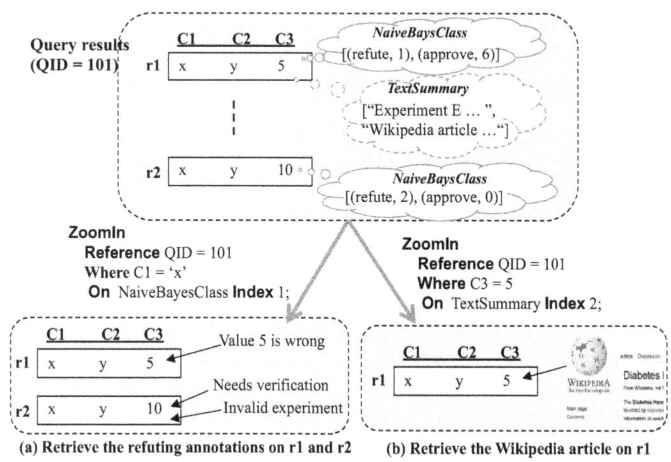

Figure 3: Zoom-In Query Processing.

2.2 Zoom-In Query Processing

After receiving the results of a query along with the attached annotation summaries, end-users may investigate the propagated summaries and get interested in zooming-in and retrieving more details about specific summaries (See Figure 3). The zoom-in capability in InsightNotes enables performing this operation interactively and efficiently. Users can reference queries that they have just executed (using unique QIDs assigned to the result), refine which tuples from the result they want to focus on (using predicates in the `ZoomIn` command), and then specify which summaries to retrieve their details. For example, in Figure 3(a), the `ZoomIn` command selects tuples r_1 and r_2, and retrieves the actual annotations refuting (disapproving) the content of these tuples (one annotation on r_1, and two annotations on r_2). The ZoomIn command specifies in the ON clause that the zoom-in operation is over the classifier summary object of type *NaiveBayesClass*, and the index of "1" indicates the 1st class label within the object, which is the *"refute"* label. Similarly, the second command, retrieves the complete Wikipedia article attached to r_1.

In addition to demonstrating the high-level feature, we will also demonstrate the underlying caching and materialization techniques behind the efficient execution of the zoom-in operation. For example, we proposed a materialization technique, which allows the queries' results to compete with each other over a limited disk-based cache—where they are temporarily kept to serve future zoom-in operations. Adding to (or evicting from) the cache is controlled by a new replacement policy, called *RCO* (stands for Recency, Complexity, and Overhead), that takes into account three factors for replacement, i.e., query complexity and cost, the results' size, and how frequently and recently the results have been referenced in a zoom-in operation. The demonstration will illustrate the effect of the cache on the zoom-in performance.

2.3 Extensibility & Scalable Maintenance

Different applications may maintain and manage annotations of different semantics, and hence they may target different types of summarization outputs. For example, in biological databases, it can be meaningful to classify the annotations attached to the gene tuples into the classes of {'FunctionPrediction', 'Provenance', 'Comment'}, while in ornithological databases it can be more meaningful to classify them into the classes of {'Behavior', 'Disease', 'Anatomy', 'Other'}. To achieve broader applicability, InsightNotes is designed as an extensible engine, where it only defines some properties and requirements that the integrated summarization techniques should obey, while the rest is customizable by domain experts and database admins.

Figure 4 illustrates the three-level summarization hierarchy of InsightNotes. The 1st level is the *Summary Types*, where the summarization types of *Cluster*, *Classifier*, and *Snippet* are integrated within the query engine and any instance of these types can be supported. The 2nd level is the *Summary Instances*, where domain experts and database admins can fully customize the desired instances, e.g., for a *Classifier* type, the instance defines the underlying algorithm to use, the output class labels, configuration parameters, and training datasets or classifier model. In this level, domain knowledge, e.g., ontologies for the available annotations, can be also integrated with the summarization technique. Finally, the created instances can be linked in a many-to-many relationship with users' relations. If an instance is linked to a given relation, say R, then the annotations on each of R's tuples will be summarizes by that instance. The summarization output creates the 3rd level of the hierarchy, which is the *Summary Objects*, and each tuple will carry these summary objects along with its data during the query execution.

Despite the extensibility and flexibility of InsightNotes, the system deploys various optimizations for efficient incremental maintenance of the annotation summaries. These optimizations enable the system to achieve scalability w.r.t both the number of raw annotations attached to the data and the number of summary instances defined on top of them. One example of these optimizations is controlled by the *Properties* field within the summary instance (See Figure 4). The Boolean *AnnotationInvariant* property indicates whether or not the summarization of a newly inserted annotation a over tuple t depends on t's current annotations. In contrast, the Boolean *DataInvariant* property indicates whether or not the summarization depends on t's content, i.e., the data values. If both

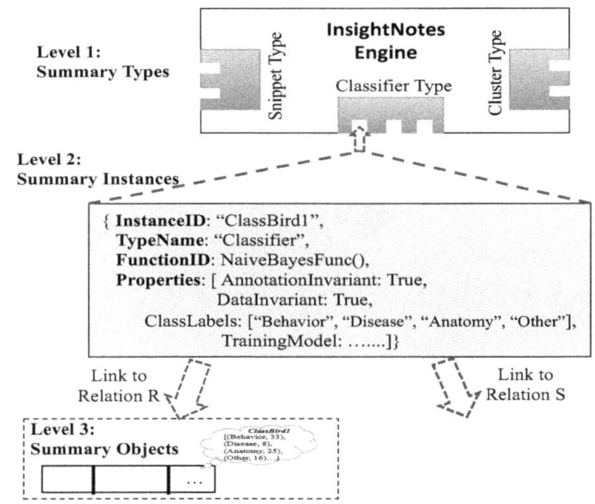

Figure 4: Extensibility and Summarization Hierarchy.

properties are True, then the summarization depends on neither of t's annotations nor t's content. Therefore, the system will summarize a only once even if it will attached to many data tuples.

3. DEMONSTRATION SCENARIOS

Interactive Demo using Ornithological Datasets: We plan to develop an interactive audience-engaged demonstration using real-world datasets obtained from the AKN system. In the AKN system, in addition to the base data, i.e., the birds' basic information such as scientific names, synonyms, geographic ranges, images, description, etc., there are more than 200,000 bird watchers and scientists who continuously provide observations and annotations on these birds. It is reported in [1] that, on average, bird watchers add 1.6 million annotations per month to the ebirds system, which is part of the AKN network. These annotations are free-text values that may describe anything related to the observed birds, e.g., color, body shape or weight, certain behavior or sound, eating habits, geographic location, or observed diseases. Therefore, in these databases the number of annotations can be more than two orders of magnitude larger than the number of data records. To encourage the audience's participation and engagement in annotating the data, we will select few widely-known birds to be the target dataset. The dataset set will be already annotated with various types of annotations and related documents, and then the audience can add to that.

InsightNotesGate & Demonstration Features: Our team is developing an Excel-based frontend tool, called *InsightNotesGate*, for visualizing the data and the queries' results as well as the annotation summaries (See Figure 5). We choose an Excel-based GUI because most scientists are already familiar with Excel-based tools and their functionalities. All of the new features and functionalities of the InsightNotes system will be performed through this GUI. The demonstration will involve:

(1) *Querying and Visualizing Summaries:* As illustrated in Figure 5, we developed a customized ribbon in InsightNotesGate that enables end-users to query their database either by entering an explicit SQL statement, or by filling-in fields in a Query-By-Example (QBE) section. The QBE mechanism is more user-friendly, but limited only to select-project queries. In contrast, the explicit SQL mechanism is more flexible as it allows for expressing more complex queries, e.g., join and aggregation. The audience can spec-

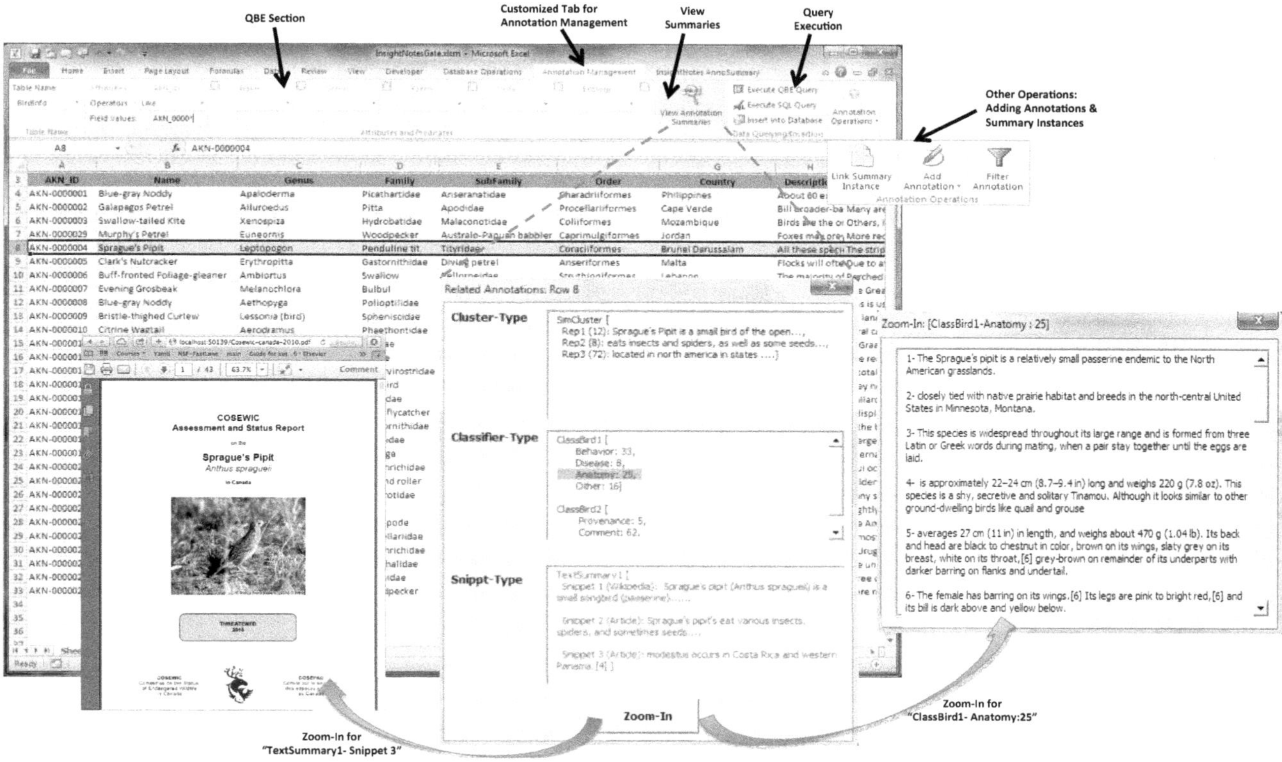

Figure 5: InsightNotesGate: InsightNotes Interactive Excel-Based GUI.

ify their query predicates in the QBE section, and then submit the query for execution. The resultset will be displayed in the excel sheet as depicted in the figure. By highlighting a specific data row, the attached annotation summaries can be visualized by clicking the button *"Visualize Annotation Summaries"*. The annotation summaries will be displayed in a separate window, and categorized into three sections, *Cluster-Type*, *Snippet-Type*, and *Classifier-Type*, as depicted in Figure 5. Recall that multiple summary instances of each type can be defined and linked to a single user's relation. For example, in the visualized scenario, there are two Classifier-Type, one Cluster-Type, and one Snippet-Type instances linked to the database table.

Audience will have the ability to examine the reported summaries, select specific objects, and then apply a zoom-in operation to retrieve the detailed raw annotations. For example, referring to Figure 5, by selecting the class label ("Anatomy : 25") within the *ClassBird1* summary object and clicking the *Zoom-In* button, the system will retrieve the detailed 25 raw annotations assigned to this label for display. Similarly, by selecting the 3rd snippet within the *TextSummary1* object and clicking the *Zoom-In* button, the system will retrieve the corresponding article for display.

(2) *Adding Annotations and Summary Instances:* The audience will be encouraged to add more annotations over the data. This feature is supported from InsightNotesGate by selecting specific table cell(s) or entire data row(s) from the displayed dataset, and then clicking the *"Add Annotation"* button (See Figure 5). A separate window will be opened allowing the insertion of free-text comment, or attaching auxiliary documents or files. The new annotation will be reflected to the database, update the existing summaries, and then the visualized resultset will be refreshed. To demonstrate the system's extensibility, the tool will also enable creating new links (or dropping existing links) between summary instances and users' relations, e.g., linking a new Classifier-type or Snippet-Type instances to the database table. As a result, the maintained and visualized summary objects will differ accordingly.

(3) *Under-the-Hood Execution:* In addition to the high-level features, an interesting experience for audience is to get exposed to the manipulation of annotation summaries within a query pipeline (e.g., similar to the illustration in Figure 2). Our plan is to design a query that involves some of the basic SQL operators, e.g., selection, join, projection, and duplicate elimination, and visualize its query tree. We then extend the InsightNotes's engine to allow the query operators to log and report their intermediate data, i.e., the data tuples along with their attached annotation summaries. This log information can be then visualized on the query tree.

4. RELATED WORK

The advances in data management and the increasing ability of applications to capture more metadata information have triggered the need for more feature-rich annotation management engines. On one hand, end-users and scientists are incapable of analyzing and extracting knowledge from the large number of reported annotations. On the other hand, the current annotation management techniques fall short in providing advanced processing over the annotations beyond just propagating them to end-users [6, 11, 15, 20, 21, 28]. The InsightNotes system has been proposed to bridge this gap by providing real insights on top of the raw annotations. Therefore, InsightNotes addresses several unique challenges that have not been addressed by existing techniques.

Scientific systems and workflow management techniques have also leveraged the concept of semantic and ontology-based annotations, e.g., [5, 7, 16, 25]. For example, the work in [25] uses the annotations drawn from a specific ontology to relate and measure the similarity among the scientific entities in the database. And hence, it uses the annotations as a similarity metric among the data entires. In contrast, the work in [5, 7] uses semantic annotations to either summarize complex workflows [5], or help in building and verifying workflows [7]. These systems are based on workflow- and process-centric annotations, e.g., annotations capturing the semantics of each function in a workflow, the structure of their input and output arguments, etc. In contrast, InsightNotes manages data-centric annotations that are independent from how the data is processed.

In the domains of e-commerce, social networks, and entertainment systems, e.g., [18], the annotations are usually referred to as *tags*. These systems deploy advanced mining and summarization techniques for extracting the best insight possible from the annotations to enhance users' experience. They use such extracted knowledge to take actions, e.g., providing recommendations and targeted advertisements [13, 26]. However, unlike relational DBs, the retrieval mechanisms in these systems are typically straightforward and do not involve complex processing or transformations, i.e., objects (products in Amazon or movies in Netflix) are usually queried as individual instances without going through a complex pipeline of query operators, e.g., projection, join, grouping, and aggregation operators. Therefore, no advanced query processing is required over the annotations summaries once created.

5. REFERENCES

[1] eBird Trail Tracker Puts Millions of Eyes on the Sky. `https://www.fws.gov/refuges/RefugeUpdate/MayJune_2011/ebirdtrailtracker.html`.

[2] Gene Ontology Consortium. `http://geneontology.org`.

[3] Hydrologic Information System CUAHSI-HIS. `(http://his.cuahsi.org`.

[4] The Avian Knowledge Network (AKN). `http://www.avianknowledge.net/`.

[5] P. Alper, K. Belhajjame, C. Goble, and P. Karagoz. Small Is Beautiful: Summarizing Scientific Workflows Using Semantic Annotations. In *IEEE BigData Congress*, pages 318–325, 2013.

[6] D. Bhagwat, L. Chiticariu, and W. Tan. An annotation management system for relational databases. In *VLDB*, pages 900–911, 2004.

[7] S. Bowers and B. LudŁscher. A Calculus for Propagating Semantic Annotations through Scientific Workflow Queries. In *In Query Languages and Query Processing (QLQP)*, 2006.

[8] P. Buneman, A. Chapman, and J. Cheney. Provenance management in curated databases. In *SIGMOD*, pages 539–550, 2006.

[9] P. Buneman, S. Khanna, and W. Tan. Why and where: A characterization of data provenance. *Lec. Notes in Comp. Sci.*, 1973:316–333, 2001.

[10] P. Buneman, E. V. Kostylev, and S. Vansummeren. Annotations are relative. In *Proceedings of the 16th International Conference on Database Theory*, ICDT '13, pages 177–188, 2013.

[11] L. Chiticariu, W.-C. Tan, and G. Vijayvargiya. DBNotes: a post-it system for relational databases based on provenance. In *SIGMOD*, pages 942–944, 2005.

[12] P. R. Christopher D. Manning and H. Schutze. Book Chapter: Text classification and Naive Bayes, in Introduction to Information Retrieval. In *Cambridge University Press*, pages 253–287, 2008.

[13] A. S. Das, M. Datar, A. Garg, and S. Rajaram. Google news personalization: scalable online collaborative filtering. In *Proceedings of the 16th international conference on World Wide Web (WWW)*, pages 271–280, 2007.

[14] S. B. Davidson and J. Freire. Provenance and scientific workflows: challenges and opportunities. In *SIGMOD*, pages 1345–1350, 2008.

[15] M. Eltabakh, W. Aref, A. Elmagarmid, and M. Ouzzani. Supporting annotations on relations. In *EDBT*, pages 379–390, 2009.

[16] M. Eltabakh, M. Ouzzani, and W. Aref. bdbms-database management system for biological data. In *CIDR*, pages 196–206, 2007.

[17] M. Y. Eltabakh, W. G. Aref, and A. K. Elmagarmid. A database server for next-generation scientific data management. In *ICDE Workshops*, pages 313–316, 2010.

[18] A. Gattani and et. al. Entity extraction, linking, classification, and tagging for social media: a wikipedia-based approach. *Proc. VLDB Endow.*, 6(11):1126–1137, 2013.

[19] W. Gatterbauer, M. Balazinska, N. Khoussainova, and D. Suciu. Believe it or not: adding belief annotations to databases. *Proc. VLDB Endow.*, 2(1):1–12, 2009.

[20] F. Geerts and et. al. Mondrian: Annotating and querying databases through colors and blocks. In *ICDE*, pages 82–93, 2006.

[21] F. Geerts and J. Van Den Bussche. Relational completeness of query languages for annotated databases. In *Proceedings of the 11th international conference on Database Programming Languages (DBPL)*, pages 127–137, 2007.

[22] K. Ibrahim, D. Xiao, and M. Y. Eltabakh. Elevating Annotation Summaries To First-Class Citizens In InsightNotes. In *EDBT Conference*, 2015.

[23] Y.-B. Liu, J.-R. Cai, J. Yin, and A. W. Fu. Clustering Text Data Streams. *Journal of Computer Science and Technology*, 23(1):112–128, 2008.

[24] A. Nenkova and K. McKeown. A Survey of Text Summarization Techniques. In *Book: Mining Text Data*, pages 43–76, 2012.

[25] G. Palma and et. al. Measuring Relatedness Between Scientific Entities in Annotation Datasets. In *International Conference on Bioinformatics, Computational Biology and Biomedical Informatics*, pages 367:367–367:376, 2013.

[26] A. Rae, B. Sigurbjörnsson, and R. van Zwol. Improving tag recommendation using social networks. In *Adaptivity, Personalization and Fusion of Heterogeneous Information*, RIAO, pages 92–99, 2010.

[27] Y. L. Simmhan, B. Plale, and D. Gannon. A survey of data provenance in e-science. *SIGMOD Record*, 34(3):31–36, 2005.

[28] W.-C. Tan. Containment of relational queries with annotation propagation. In *DBPL*, 2003.

[29] D. Tarboton, J. Horsburgh, and D. Maidment. CUAHSI Community Observations Data Model (ODM),Version 1.1, Design Specifications. In *Design Document*, 2008.

[30] D. Xiao and M. Y. Eltabakh. InsightNotes: Summary-Based Annotation Management in Relational Databases. In *SIGMOD Conference*, pages 661–672, 2014.

StoryPivot: Comparing and Contrasting Story Evolution

Anja Gruenheid, Donald Kossmann
Systems Group
Department of Computer Science
ETH Zurich
{agruen,donaldk}@inf.ethz.ch

Theodoros Rekatsinas
University of Maryland
thodrek@cs.umd.edu

Divesh Srivastava
AT&T Labs-Research
divesh@research.att.com

ABSTRACT

As the world evolves around us, so does the digital coverage of it. Events of diverse types, associated with different actors and various locations, are continuously captured by multiple information sources such as news articles, blogs, social media etc. day by day. In the digital world, these events are represented through *information snippets* that contain information on the involved entities, a description of the event, when the event occurred, etc. In our work, we observe that events (and their corresponding digital representations) are often inter-connected, i.e., they form *stories* which represent evolving relationships between events over time. Take as an example the plane crash in Ukraine in July 2014 which involved multiple entities such as "Ukraine", "Malaysia", and "Russia" and multiple events ranging from the actual crash to the incident investigation and the presentation of the investigator's findings. In this demonstration we present STORYPIVOT, a framework that helps its users to detect evolving stories in event datasets over time. To resolve stories, we differentiate between *story identification*, the problem of connecting events over time within a source, and *story alignment*, the problem of integrating stories across sources. The goal of this demonstration is to present an interactive exploration of both these problems and how events can be dynamically interpreted and put into context in real-world datasets.

1. INTRODUCTION

Lately there has been an increasing interest in monitoring news media, blogs, and social media from all over the world and extracting geo-referenced records that correspond to different real-world events and interactions between diverse groups of people, international organizations, countries etc. The extracted event records are commonly stored in repositories that get updated regularly whenever new extractions are obtained from a diverse collection of data sources. Example repositories of such extractions include GDELT [11] and EventRegistry [9] which are updated over fixed time intervals (e.g., daily). Extracted data is stored in a tuple format containing for example information about its origin, the type of the corresponding real-world event describing an activity linked with the event, the entities associated with the corresponding activity, a short description and a timestamp. An example of such a tuple is <New York Times, Accident, {Ukraine, Malaysian Airlines}, "Plane Crash", 07/17/2014>.

Extracted pieces of information over a fixed time-window represent only a snapshot of what is happening in the world. Real-world events are often connected over time forming *stories* that represent evolving relationships between different entities. Recovering the evolution and the dynamics of news stories across time is of tremendous value in different application domains, ranging from trend detection to economic analysis, and has been a focus of recent research literature [2, 10]. Nevertheless, the majority of proposed approaches for story detection focus on identifying current and thus often mentioned stories in streaming news. Thus, they do not provide means for tracking the evolution and dynamics of stories even though this type of story tracking has applications in different domains. For example analysts rely on temporal patterns of event occurrences to discover supporting evidence and validate their hypotheses. The most common paradigm to consider is political scientists who rely on historical data to forecast political crises [18, 8] and conflicts [20]. A different application domain that is increasingly popular is that of financial analytics based on political event extractions [7, 6].

Another limitation of currently employed systems is that they are oblivious to the presence of multiple data sources and their story reporting *perspectives*. Data sources have different perspectives on stories because they report the same story with varying content and with varying levels of timeliness [21]. Further, it has been recently shown that leveraging these individual source characteristics can lead to a significant accuracy improvement for difficult prediction tasks such as predicting civil unrest incidents [14]. Moreover, there has been an increasing interest in the database community to understand and exploit the characteristics of different data sources to either provide affordable analytics or to improve the quality of integrated data [4, 19, 15].

In this demonstration, we present STORYPIVOT, a novel story detection framework for detecting stories involving different entities over time. STORYPIVOT allows users to explore the evolution and dynamics of stories but also to understand the perspectives of different data sources when reporting these stories. To address the limitations mentioned above, we decompose the story detection problem into two subproblems (1) *story identification* and (2) *story alignment*. Story identification is the problem of finding those events that represent the same real-world story within a single source, and captures the individual story perspectives of each data source. Story alignment then integrates stories across multiple sources to enhance completeness and correctness. Due to the sheer number of available sources, one of the main challenges here is combining stories across

SIGMOD'15, May 31–June 4, 2015, Melbourne, Victoria, Australia.

http://dx.doi.org/10.1145/2723372.2735356.

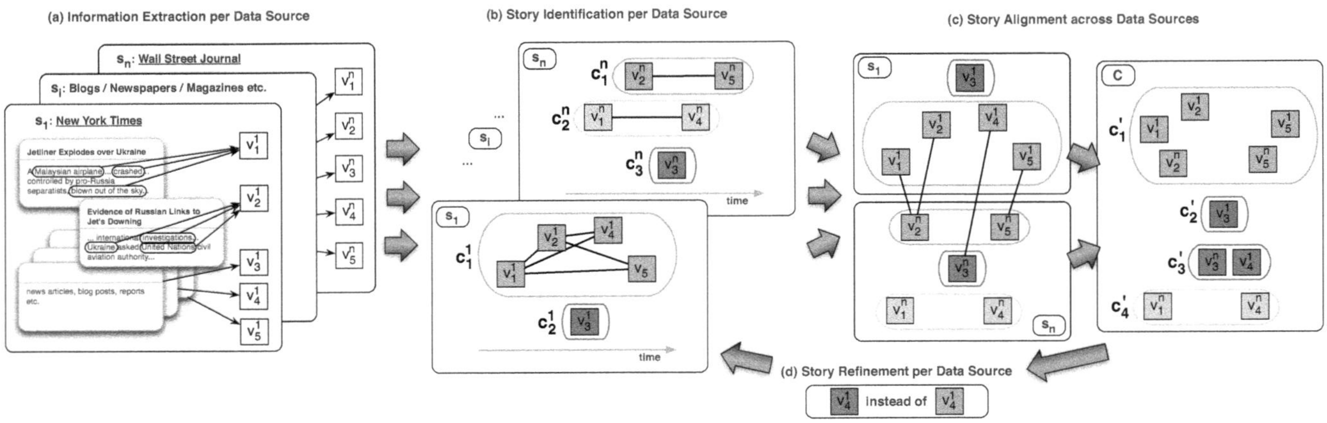

Figure 1: StoryPivot system overview.

data sources efficiently. In summary, we present the following features in our demonstration:

Interactive Framework. We provide an interactive interface for the users that allows them to examine the development of stories over time. It will provide visualization for both, story identification and story alignment, components of StoryPivot.

Large-Scale Experiments. To provide evidence of the scalability and efficiency of StoryPivot, we perform extensive experiments whose results are presented during the demo. Furthermore, the user can use the interactive visualizations to explore the results of these experiments as well.

The remainder of this demonstration description is structured as follows: First, we introduce the problem of story detection and a 2-phase mechanism to solve it in Section 2. It is applicable for a variety of use cases that we briefly describe in Section 3. Afterwards, we present the details on the technical demonstration in Section 4 and conclude this demonstration paper in Section 5.

2. STORY EVOLUTION

Identifying the evolution of stories requires detecting related events over multiple sources over time and combining them into a single cohesive story. In this section, we present an overview of StoryPivot which detects the evolution and dynamics of stories through processing event data. Furthermore, we present techniques on how to address story identification and story alignment efficiently.

2.1 Overview

An overview of StoryPivot is illustrated in Figure 1. Within the system, we use *information snippets* that are extracted from documents of varying data sources as elemental units of information. Let V be the set of all available information snippets. We make the following assumptions for the structure of these snippets: First, every snippet $v_i \in V$ is associated with a timestamp t_i which records when the event(s) in the snippet occurred in the real-world. Second, it is associated with a data source s_i. Data sources may correspond to newspapers such as the New York Times or the Wall Street Journal but can encompass all digital media that provide event-based information. Last, every snippet has a content that describes the characteristics of the snippet. This content may vary depending on the application scenario and the available extraction possibilities. For StoryPivot in its current state, we use a black box extraction mechanism as visualized in Figure 1(a). Specifically, our extraction pipeline works as follows: It first collects textual excerpts from documents found on EventRegistry [9], i.e., it extracts the documents and breaks their text down based on paragraphs, title, etc. These excerpts are then forwarded to Open Calais which is an open-source annotation tool [16]. This tool provides additional information if available, for example on entities or keywords associated with the excerpt. The original text analyzed for the excerpt as well as its corresponding annotations thus form the content of the snippet.

Once snippets have been correctly extracted, the problem of finding stories is to search V for all snippets $v_j \in V$ that form a story c_ℓ. Let C be the set of all stories that can be extracted from the snippets in V. To process information snippets, we adopt a two-phase strategy which first determines the stories $C_i \subseteq C$ that can be found in a single source s_i. To compute these stories, V is partitioned into subsets $V_i \subseteq V$ where subscript i corresponds to the data source s_i. These sets of information snippets are then processed independently of each other to identify the stories within s_i. A visualization of this phase is shown in Figure 1(b) per data source. For example, for every snippet v_i^1 found in data source s_1 and thus part of V_1, story identification proceeds as follows: It first determines the most likely story that v_i^1 can be matched to. If no such story exists, it generates a new story around this information snippet, otherwise it adds the snippet to its best matching story. After all snippets in V_1 have been evaluated, C_1 consists of $c_1^1, \ldots, c_m^1$ source-specific stories. The evolution of stories, and thus implicitly the relationship of snippets, depends on the evolution of the corresponding real-world events which have to be captured correctly. In that context, we observe that it is possible for stories to split into multiple substories or to merge into a bigger story. For example political and economic events were interwoven during the height of the Ukraine crisis while they started to separate after the situation had (temporarily) stabilized. In order to capture the evolution of stories, we incrementally construct stories [5] instead of using single pass story detection [1, 17].

Once story identification for all available sources has been completed, we align stories across data sources. The alignment step is crucial for story detection for two reasons. First, it allows users of StoryPivot to retrieve unbiased information, i.e., a complete view of all available information on a story from a variety of sources instead of a single perspective which is the case if data is retrieved from a single source. Second, it allows us to correct errors made during the story identification phase. In Figure 1, we show that v_4^1 has been wrongly assigned to story c_1^1. Story alignment helps to determine this mistake by correlating events across sources and finding irregularities in the matching process which are then corrected. We call this correction step story refinement (Figure 1(d)). More detailed descriptions of the story identification and story alignment phases are presented next. Finally, we point out that the proposed two-level approach allows us to handle changes to the set of available data sources efficiently. As new sources become available, we first identify the stories associated with them and then align them with existing stories extracted from previously available sources. This enables an efficient integration of new data sources into the established information flow.

2.2 Story Identification

To enable efficient information aggregation into a story, we propose an incremental solution for the problem of story identification. As explained previously, story identification is the task of finding those information snippets $v_j^i \in V_i$ that refer to the same story c_ℓ. Recall that an information snippet is described by its content, its data source, and its timestamp. The evolution of a story and the connectivity of snippets can thus be described by matching the content of different snippets along its temporal axis. If a snippet v_j^i is sufficiently similar to any other candidate snippets $v_k^i \in V_i$ they may be part of the same story. Analogously, if the content of v_j^i and v_k^i is sufficiently dissimilar, it is intuitive to assume that they belong to different stories.

For this framework, we explore two different matching techniques for two snippets v_j^i and v_k^i: The first mechanism follows a *complete* matching scheme, while the second one pursues a *temporal* scheme as illustrated in Figure 2. The complete mechanism serves as a baseline for our system as we observe that due to the evolving nature of stories, complete mechanisms overfit stories as they tend to add related snippets to the same story independently of the evolution of the story in between. In reality, story evolution means that characteristics of a story change over time. Consider the example shown in Figure 2. Imagine that snippet v_7^1 is compared with the existing story set C_1: Here, it is not useful to compare it against all events $v_1^1 \dots v_6^1$ associated with previously found stories (Figure 2a) because an event that happened a long time before v_7^1 can have completely different content, even if they both refer to the same entities. Take as an example the Ukraine crisis which started with civilian protests and evolved into a military conflict. Comparing snippets describing the fights around Donezk and protests on the Independence Square will not likely yield good results. In contrast, if we consider events closer to the fights such as the plane crash or the split of Crimea, there will be a higher overlap in entities and description between the single data snippets [12]. To leverage temporal information, we use a sliding window based technique for story identification. Instead of comparing v_7^1 to all other snippets, we thus reduce the window of comparison to all snippets $v_k^1 \in V_1$ for which the corresponding timestamp t_k^1 is in a range of $t_7^1 - \omega_1 \leq t_k^1 \leq t_7^1 + \omega_1$ (Figure 2b). Apart from providing a more realistic presentation of story evolution, sliding windows guarantee efficiency in information processing as the search space for related information snippets is reduced effectively.

2.3 Story Alignment

The story identification phase concludes with producing a set of stories C_i that contain all stories that have been identified for a data source s_i. These stories can then be used for cross-source story alignment, i.e., finding those stories in a data source s_i that contain the same semantic information as the stories in a different data source s_j. Imagine that there are two sources s_1, corresponding to the New York Times, and s_n, corresponding to the Wall Street Journal. Though both of these information sources provide details on events happening in the United States, they have different perspectives on topics expressed in their published documents. Here specifically, this difference is due to political orientation or different concepts for content presentation in the newspaper, amongst others. Story alignment helps to enrich the stories identified for each data source and enables providing end users with a more encompassing view of a story. This means that users are not only provided with source-specific and thus potentially biased information but have a structured way of exploring all perspectives of a story. These perspectives can be realized for stories that evolve over time but also for snippets capturing only one specific real-world event that can be correlated across data sources. In that sense, story alignment enhances the results found during the initial story identification phase.

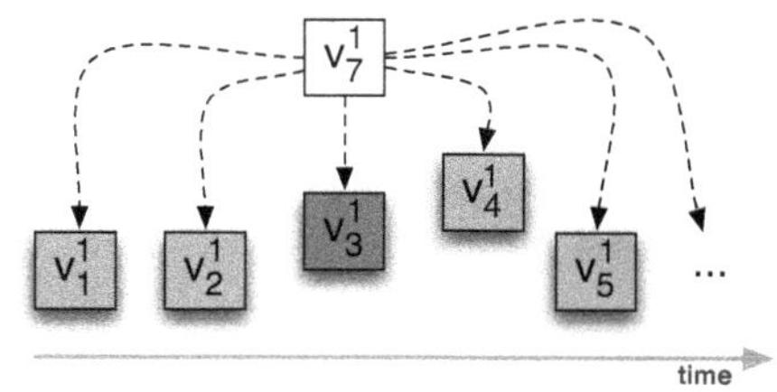

(a) Complete story identification.

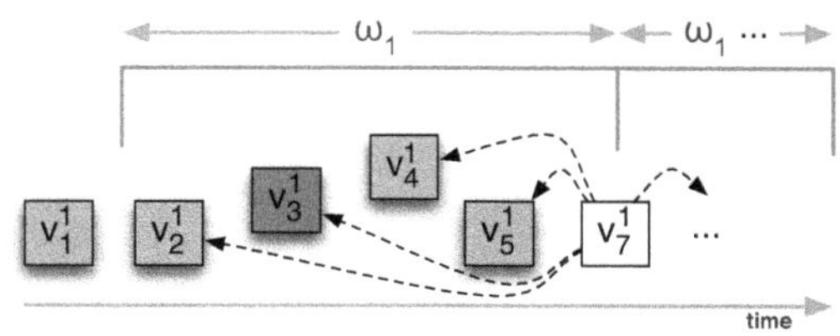

(b) Temporal story identification.

Figure 2: Story identification execution modes.

For story alignment, we observe that two stories are likely to refer to the same real-world story if their evolution is similar and their content is similar as well. It is highly unlikely that two stories c_1 and c_2 are similar if c_1 ends at time t_i and c_2 starts at t_j with $t_i \ll t_j$. We observe that in the alignment phase, we can partition information snippets into two categories considering their purpose for alignment: they can (a) help to align stories or (b) enrich stories. The first type is used for the actual alignment step as two snippets v_k^i and v_l^j from sources s_i and s_j provide aligning information if they contain similar entities, description, and are temporally (approximately) similar. If data snippets enrich a story instead, they provide additional information that is contained in data source s_i but not in s_j. Relevant examples include special reports, background information etc. that are produced by journalists working for one data source but not the other.

Once stories have been compared across sources, the last step of story alignment is to resolve conflicts between the results of story identification and story alignment. Consider the example shown in Figure 1. Here, story alignment reveals a mismatch in the story results of data sources s_1 and s_n: While v_1^1, v_2^1, v_4^1, and v_5^1 belong to the same story in s_1 (c_1^1), their related snippets are in different stories in s_n (c_1^n and c_3^n). After story alignment, the system contains for this example two integrated stories, c_1' and c_3'. Resolving conflicts between results of these two phases helps to refine the results of the story identification phase as the decisions made during story alignment can be propagated back into the story sets of data sources if desired. Nevertheless, even if a story cannot be aligned across different data sources, it is still going to be present in the result set after story alignment has been executed. That is, if stories appear only within a data source, they may still hold interest for a variety of users. Imagine for example ten data sources out of which nine focus on business data and one covers sports events. Users then may search for a specific sports club which will require STORYPIVOT to return both sports and business stories independently of how many data sources actually report each story.

2.4 Dynamic Interaction between Story Identification and Alignment

So far, we talked about batch processing a set of information snippets abstractly. If these snippets are extracted from online newspapers, blogs, etc., they are generated dynamically every time a news document is published online. Furthermore, there exist different types of data sources which do not necessarily publish their information in a temporally ordered manner. Local events for example usually get picked up faster by local newspapers and might be delayed in international media because of locality and interest in those events. To address these challenges, story identification and alignment need to be dynamically integrated and realized efficiently as to provide users with live information on ongoing stories. This integration needs to consider an efficient representation of stories to reduce the search space and thus provide near real-time integration and out-of-order integration of events into evolving stories. To achieve efficient integration of story identification and alignment, we propose to abstract from snippets and stories into one common format which we refer to as a *sketch* [13]. A sketch is a (smaller) unified representation of the snippet or story that allows for fast and efficient similarity comparisons between stories and snippets or amongst stories across different sources. Last, notice that data sources are not always known to end users. Hence any story detection system should allow the addition or removal of data sources. The goal of our work is to address all of these problems with temporal story evolution techniques that adhere to the principles and ideas mentioned in the previous sections.

3. USE CASES

STORYPIVOT has practical utility for a variety of users. In this section, we present two target groups of users of our system and describe specific scenarios in which they can employ STORYPIVOT to obtain information about stories that they are interested in. For both of these user types, we envision an interface where the users can explore stories and where our system supports different patterns of accessing information.

Expert Scientist. Given its two-phase construction of stories, our system can provide users with insights on a story from either within a source or aggregated across sources. This functionality is essential for example for political scientists or journalists who want to determine the evolution of conflicts or interactions: Examining data within a data source reveals source bias and explicitly contrasts the different points of view that arise around a specific story. The results from the story alignment phase then help to construct a complete view of a story and to put single pieces of information from different data sources into context.

Casual Reader. As a casual news reader, it is often difficult to obtain a clear picture of the reason for stories to evolve the way they do. For example, young news readers are often not fully aware of the historical developments and trends that influence politics. Also, readers might get interested in a story only after it has gained some traction in the media. Investigating the timeline of a story can help such users to get a comprehensive view of which events contribute to a story and to understand the implications certain events have on the development of this story.

In addition to these inherent features of our system, we can further extend it with interfaces to existing knowledge bases such as DBpedia [3]. Connecting STORYPIVOT to knowledge bases explicitly helps experts and casual users to obtain more information on the context of stories and to explore the data provided by our framework more extensively.

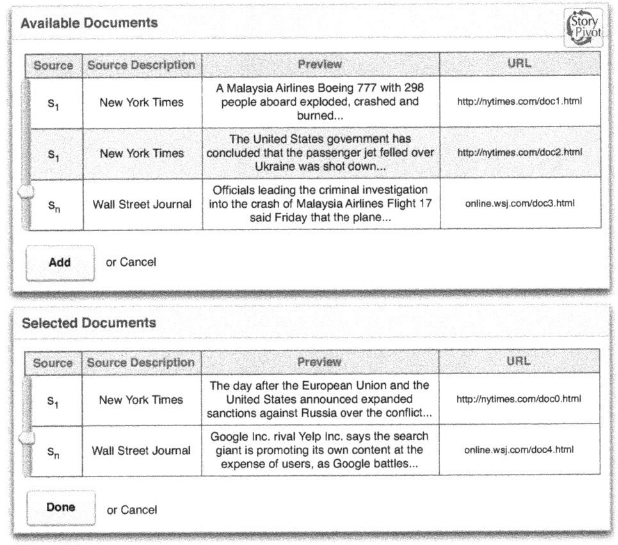

Figure 3: Document selection module.

4. DEMONSTRATION

In this section, we describe how we structure our demonstration and present the functionalities that will be available when interacting with the STORYPIVOT system.

4.1 Implementation

Our demonstration introduces STORYPIVOT, a system that efficiently processes event datasets to find semantically correlated events that form stories, i.e., that describe relationships between entities with evolving content. Users of STORYPIVOT can explore two different views on stories following the differentiation between story identification within a data source and alignment across data sources presented in Section 2. The backend processing of information extracted from documents is done as shown in Figure 1: First, we use an extraction mechanism that retrieves snippets of information which is followed by our implementation of the story identification and alignment steps. To realize story identification, we implemented the two different identification models shown in Figure 2, temporal story identification and complete story identification. For story alignment, we extend the techniques used in story identification to consider matching stories with each other instead of comparing a snippet to a story allowing for more tolerance in the temporal alignment of stories. The implemented methods can be combined on the fly by the user to test advantages and disadvantages as well as compare result quality for these varying techniques. The event data explored for this demonstration is taken from real-world online newspapers and blogs such as the New York Times and the Wall Street Journal as captured by existing event repositories such as GDELT [11] or EventRegistry [9].

4.2 Functionalities

For the demonstration, we will provide dynamic and static execution components. First, we will show how stories evolve on a small scale with a predefined example that the user can explore by adding and removing documents from the system. This will enable

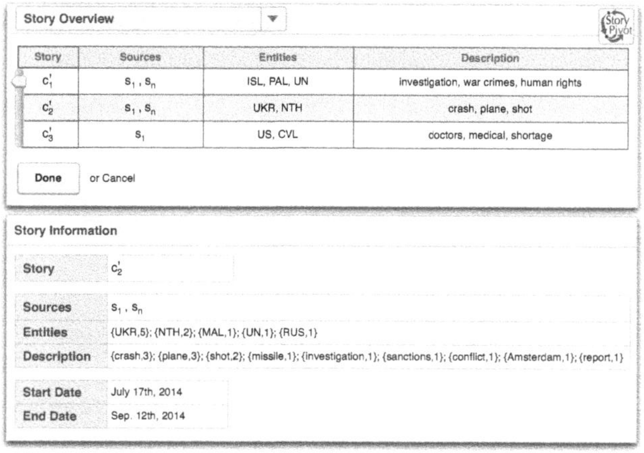

Figure 4: Story overview module.

users to understand how extracted information from a document changes the outcome of the story identification and alignment phases. Furthermore, this part of our demonstration serves to illustrate the applicability and output quality of our system. To understand the actual performance of STORYPIVOT and to be able to compare it against existing approaches, we will provide users with manually curated stories taken from well-known news providers. Furthermore, we also present examples of large scale story detection and examine the scalability and efficiency of STORYPIVOT when processing larger amounts of data. The purpose for this part of the demonstration is to show that real-time event integration can be achieved through efficient story identification and alignment mechanisms. Users will be able to explore the results of the larger integration run and can query STORYPIVOT to see the evolution of a story over time within and across sources. For simplicity, queries will consist of enquiries about specified real-world events or entities.

4.2.1 *Interactive Story Detection*

For this part of our demonstration, we will provide the user with an interface where a set of documents can be selected. Each of these documents is taken from real-world event data streams. An example for the document selection mechanism is shown in Figure 3. The data sources here are two well-known newspapers and documents correspond to news articles published on their corresponding websites. For this example specifically, the articles mainly focus on the downing of a plane in the Ukraine in July 2014. Once the user has selected a subset of these articles, an initial set of stories within the selected data sources is computed and then stories are aligned across data sources, as in Figure 4. After the computation has finished, the user will be able to explore the data in two different ways corresponding to the view (i) within and (ii) across data sources.

Stories per Source Module. The "Stories per Source" module, Figure 5, shows the computed stories within a source. Information snippets are sorted according to their story affiliation and can be browsed to understand why they are associated with the same or different stories. This module represents the story identification part of our work. Next to visualizing and explaining the correlation of snippets within a story, we also show the relationship of snippets across stories but within a data source. Take v_2^1 in Figure 5 as an example: We show that it is connected not only to v_1^1 and v_5^1 but also to v_4^1 which contains information on a call for investigation on some problems in the Israeli conflict around the same time as the jet's downing. As the entities for both snippets and the contents are similar, there exists such a connection intuitively though the events

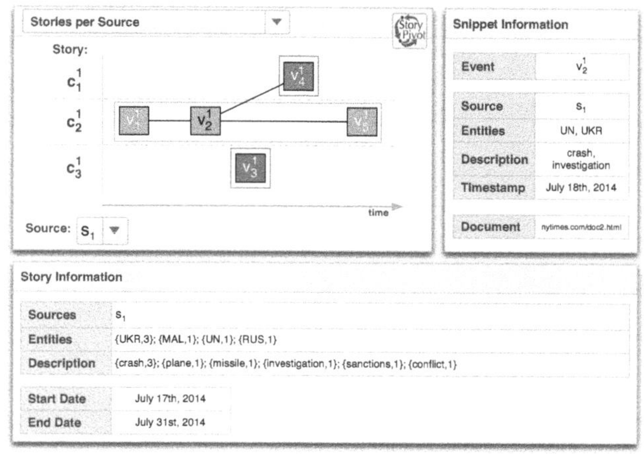

Figure 5: Stories per source module. Displays (subset of) stories for a selected source.

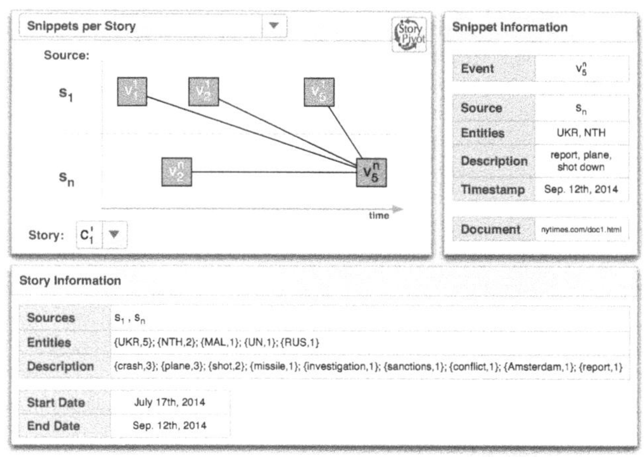

Figure 6: Snippets per story module. Displays (subset of) information snippets for a selected story.

can be separated through their context. Here, v_2^1 is similar to v_1^1 and v_5^1 which indicates that it is in fact part of a different story than v_4^1. In addition to providing this overview information per snippet, we allow users of STORYPIVOT to explore snippets within a data source in this module. Changing the selected snippet will automatically change the displayed content.

Snippets per Story Module. As the second exploration module, we provide a "Snippets per Story" module, as in Figure 6, which shows a user-selected story that has been aligned across data sources. Again, this module will help the user to understand why our algorithms make certain decisions through visualizing the story alignment phase. System users can select a story that they are interested in and again explore single information snippets within the story to determine their connectivity. In the example of Figure 6, the selected snippet, v_5^n, is well-connected within story c_1' which consists of information on the downing of the jet ranging from the initial news to results of the investigation.

Both Figure 5 and Figure 6 show snippet-centric views of story detection. We choose this form of visualization because it puts emphasis on the evolving nature of stories as a set of semantically connected pieces of information. To enable users to explore this evolution, additional documents can be added to the system after

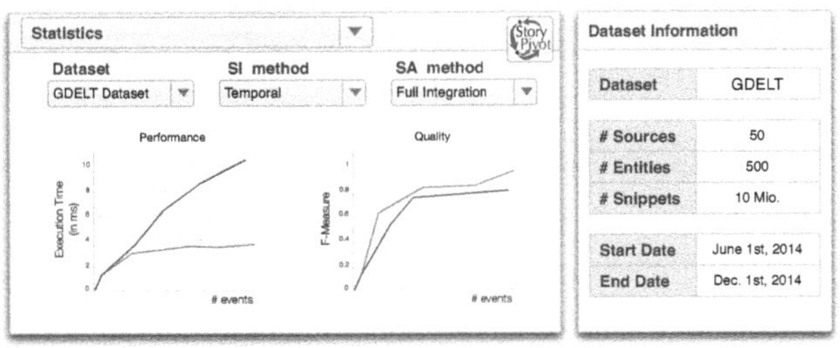

Figure 7: Statistics module. Displays information on experiments with larger datasets.

the initial import step. Furthermore, we allow users to remove documents from StoryPivot to explore how missing information affects the displayed stories.

4.2.2 Large Scale Story Detection

In this part of our demonstration, we want to show the effectiveness of our mechanisms for detecting story evolution on larger datasets. In contrast to the previously presented interactive components, we will not allow the user to add or remove single documents but present them with results from large-scale experiments run beforehand. Users are shown information and statistics on a set of extensive experiments through an overview module as visualized in Figure 7. Here, they can select all available datasets as well as different execution mechanisms that were run for these datasets. This will provide an intuition of which techniques are more advantageous than others in terms of data analysis but also performance over time.

Next to these static ways of exploring these datasets and the meta information on performance and quality, we also allow users to use the modules presented previously for an interactive exploration of these datasets. As a result, users develop an understanding of how stories evolve over time and how our system captures this evolution. It will not be possible to add or remove documents for this setup as the datasets will be fixed beforehand.

4.3 Take-away Points

With our work, we want to emphasize that story detection is an important and interesting problem that helps users to obtain information on real-world stories in a structured way. We use a two-step mechanism of story identification and story alignment for two reasons: First, it inherently guarantees that users can choose the granularity of stories presented to them. For example, they can decide to see a story from within a data source or as a (partial) integration across sources through our story alignment methods. With our interactive design, we want to show system users how these two mechanisms interact and help to build a better understanding of story evolution. Second, this two-step mechanism provides efficient implementation mechanisms and fast information processing because it makes effective use of incremental rather than complete computation of results. Remember that stories evolve over time which means that using and integrating all information snippets completely is more harmful than information processing in a time-aware manner. The stability and performance of our mechanisms are shown in large-scale experiments which help to obtain a better understanding of the efficiency of StoryPivot.

5. CONCLUSION

In this demonstration proposal, we have introduced a system called StoryPivot that constructs stories from information snippets that were extracted from news documents such as online blog entries, articles, reports, and others. We proposed to process this data in two steps through story identification and subsequently story alignment. Both of these can be interactively explored in our demonstration with a small predefined example which allows users to manipulate stories by adding and removing information at will. In the second part of our demonstration, we examine large scale datasets to show that the mechanisms devised for this system are stable over time in terms of performance and result quality. Furthermore, we allow users to explore the results of these large-scale experiments interactively to understand how StoryPivot forms stories.

6. REFERENCES

[1] J. Allan, R. Papka, and V. Lavrenko. On-line New Event Detection and Tracking. *SIGIR*, pages 37–45, 1998.
[2] A. Angel, N. Sarkas, N. Koudas, and D. Srivastava. Dense Subgraph Maintenance Under Streaming Edge Weight Updates for Real-time Story Identification. *PVLDB*, 5(6):574–585, 2012.
[3] S. Auer, C. Bizer, G. Kobilarov, J. Lehmann, R. Cyganiak, and Z. G. Ives. DBpedia: A Nucleus for a Web of Open Data. *ISWC*, pages 722–735, 2007.
[4] X. L. Dong, B. Saha, and D. Srivastava. Less is More: Selecting Sources Wisely for Integration. *PVLDB*, pages 37–48, 2013.
[5] A. Gruenheid, X. L. Dong, and D. Srivastava. Incremental Record Linkage. *PVLDB*, 7(9):697–708, 2014.
[6] J. I. Haidar. Sanctions and Trade Diversion: Exporter-Level Evidence from Iran. *ERF Annual Conference: Economic Development and Social Justice*, 2014.
[7] J. Hinz. The Ties that Bind: Geopolitical Motivations for Economic Integration. *Sixteenth Annual Conference of The European Trade Study Group ETSG*, 2014.
[8] Y. Keneshloo, J. Cadena, G. Korkmaz, and N. Ramakrishnan. Detecting and Forecasting Domestic Political Crises: A Graph-based Approach. *WebSci*, pages 192–196, 2014.
[9] G. Leban, B. Fortuna, J. Brank, and M. Grobelnik. Event Registry: Learning About World Events from News. *WWW Companion*, pages 107–110, 2014.
[10] P. Lee, L. V. S. Lakshmanan, and E. E. Milios. Incremental Cluster Evolution Tracking from Highly Dynamic Network Data. *ICDE*, pages 3–14, 2014.
[11] K. Leetaru and P. Schrodt. GDELT: Global Data on Events, Language, and Tone, 1979-2012. *Inter. Studies Association Annual Conf.*, 2013.
[12] P. Li, X. L. Dong, A. Maurino, and D. Srivastava. Linking Temporal Records. *PVLDB*, 4(11):956–967, 2011.
[13] S. Muthukrishnan. *Data Streams: Algorithms and Applications*. Now Publishers Inc, 2005.
[14] N. Ramakrishnan et al. 'Beating the News' with EMBERS: Forecasting Civil Unrest Using Open Source Indicators. *SIGKDD*, pages 1799–1808, 2014.
[15] T. Rekatsinas, X. L. Dong, L. Getoor, and D. Srivastava. Finding Quality in Quantity: The Challenge of Discovering Valuable Sources for Integration. *CIDR*, 2015.
[16] T. Reuters. Calais. *http://www.opencalais.com/*, 2008 – 2014.
[17] H. Sayyadi, M. Hurst, and A. Maykov. Event Detection and Tracking in Social Streams. *ICWSM*, 2009.
[18] S. Schutte and K. Donnay. Matched Wake Analysis: Finding Causal Relationships in Spatiotemporal Event Data. *Political Geography*, 41:1–10, 2014.
[19] P. Upadhyaya, M. Unutzer, M. Balazinska, D. Suciu, and H. Hacigumus. Affordable Analytics on Expensive Data. *Data4U*, page 19, 2014.
[20] M. D. Ward, N. W. Metternich, C. L. Dorff, M. Gallop, F. M. Hollenbach, A. Schultz, and S. Weschle. Learning from the Past and Stepping into the Future: Toward a New Generation of Conflict Prediction. *International Studies Review*, 15(4):473–490, 2013.
[21] N. Weller and K. McCubbins. Raining on the Parade: Some Cautions Regarding the GDELT Dataset. *Blog Post on Political Violance a Glance*, 2014.

The Flatter, the Better

Query Compilation Based on the Flattening Transformation

Alexander Ulrich Torsten Grust

Universität Tübingen
Tübingen, Germany

[alexander.ulrich, torsten.grust]@uni-tuebingen.de

ABSTRACT

We demonstrate the insides and outs of a query compiler based on the **flattening transformation**, a translation technique designed by the programming language community to derive efficient data-parallel implementations from iterative programs. Flattening admits the straightforward formulation of intricate query logic—including deeply nested loops over (possibly ordered) data or the construction of rich data structures. To demonstrate the level of expressiveness that can be achieved, we will bring a compiler frontend that accepts queries embedded into the Haskell programming language. Compilation via flattening takes places in a series of simple steps all of which will be made tangible by the demonstration. The final output is a program of lifted primitive operations which existing query engines can efficiently implement. We provide backends based on PostgreSQL and VectorWise to make this point—however, most set-oriented or data-parallel engines could benefit from a flattening-based query compiler.

Categories and Subject Descriptors: H.2.3 [**Database Management**]: Languages—*Query languages, Database (persistent) programming languages*

General Terms: Languages, Performance

Keywords: Nested data parallelism; flattening; list comprehensions

1. 20 YEARS OF FLATTENING

About 20 years ago, the **flattening transformation** has been devised to compile the NESL programming language into the data-parallel primitives of a vector machine [2]. Today, we demonstrate how flattening can be reinterpreted to compile expressive query languages into the bulk-oriented primitives of existing database engines. From NESL, we inherit (1) its ability to efficiently cope with iteration, even if nested deeply, (2) its support for nested and ordered data models, and (3) a functional and compositional semantics.

SIGMOD'15, May 31–June 4, 2015, Melbourne, Victoria, Australia.

ACM 978-1-4503-2758-9/15/05 ...$15.00.
http://dx.doi.org/10.1145/2723372.2735359.

In tandem with established query compilation techniques that we repeatedly draw on here, flattening enables a principled translation that proceeds in small digestible steps—a welcome advance over rather complex and monolithic approaches, including our own [7]. Flattening admits rich user-facing query languages and data models beyond those offered by recent related efforts (*query shredding* [4], for example, lacks support for ordered data, grouping, or aggregation). To make these points we express the examples in this paper in a comprehension-based language, *Database-Supported Haskell*[1], that is deeply embedded into Haskell [11]. The flattening idea is not tied to a particular frontend language, however. The core of flattening itself may be described by a compact set of transformation rules that trade nested iteration for a small library of—possibly lifted, see Section 3—query engine built-ins. Existing database backends can efficiently support these lifted built-ins. We will bring PostgreSQL [12] and Vectorwise [17] for demonstration, but it is a hypothesis of this work that a variety of database engines and data-parallel execution frameworks (*e.g.*, Stratosphere [1]) can be a driven by a flattening-based compiler.

The demonstration features a full-stack implementation of flattening, from the Haskell frontend to the database backend. All intermediary compilation artifacts are made tangible for the demo audience.

2. LOOPS, LISTS, AND LAYERS

Let us begin with a review of three sample queries, similar to those the demo audience will experience on site. The queries are formulated in Haskell, in a style that is idiomatic for programs that process lists. Flattening can compile query languages whose expressiveness and data model support comes close to those of general-purpose programming languages. We exploit this here to let the border between programs and queries vanish. (The details of this query embedding are orthogonal to flattening and have been described elsewhere [6].)

No knowledge of Haskell is required to grasp the present paper. The following should suffice: Principal query construct is the loop (or iteration), expressed in *list comprehension* syntax `[`e `|` x `<-` xs`,` p`]`, which iterates over the elements x of list xs. Expression e is evaluated for all x that pass predicate p (typically, x occurs free in e and p) to form the result list [3]. We write e :: a to denote that expression e has type a. Programs use e :: `Q`a to signal that they intend expression e to be evaluated by an un-

[1] `http://hackage.haskell.org/package/DSH`

trades

id	ts	day	price
ACME	1	10/20/2014	3.0
ACME	2	10/20/2014	4.0
ACME	3	10/20/2014	1.0
ACME	4	10/20/2014	7.0
⋮	⋮	⋮	⋮

Figure 1: Stock trading data. Rows have Haskell record type `Trade`. Fields of a row are accessed using selector functions: `price` x is `3.0` if x denotes the first row.

```
-- rolling minimum (mins [3,4,1,7] = [3,3,1,1])
mins :: Ord a => Q [a] -> Q [a]
mins xs =
  [ minimum [ y | (y,j) <- #xs, j <= i ] | (_,i) <- #xs ]

-- margin ≙ current value - minimum value up to now
margins :: (Ord a, Num a) => Q [a] -> Q [a]
margins xs = [ x - y | (x,y) <- zip xs (mins xs) ]

-- our profit is the maximum margin obtainable
profit :: (Ord a, Num a) => Q [a] -> Q a
profit xs = maximum (margins xs)

-- best profit obtainable for stock on given date
bestProfit :: Text -> Date -> Q [Trade] -> Q Double
bestProfit stock date trades =
  profit [ price t | t <- sortWith ts trades,
                     id t  == toQ stock,
                     day t == toQ date ]
```

Figure 2: Best profit obtainable if we buy, then sell stock. `bestProfit "ACME" "10/20/2014" trades` yields `6.0`.

derlying database system (*i.e.*, not by the regular Haskell runtime). Database tables are accessed like lists: for example, we use `trades :: Q [Trade]` to obtain the list of rows in table `trades` of Figure 1 in primary key order.

A list-based data model. With flattening, order is the default. Queries operate over lists (or: arrays, vectors) and use operations that preserve, depend on, or establish the order of list items.

Consider a trading application where a timestamp is used to record the price fluctuation of stocks over time (see column `ts` of table `trades` in Figure 1—this scenario is taken directly from [9]). What is the best possible profit if we buy and then sell `ACME` stocks on October 20? At timestamp t, our margin is `ACME`'s current price minus its minimum price at or before t. This margin is what we try to maximize. The list-based query of Figure 2 implements this strategy almost literally. Main function `bestProfit` sorts the trading data in timestamp order, filters the stock and day of interest, and then calls on auxiliary functions (`profit`, `margins`, and `mins`) to process the list of stock prices.

Note how function `mins` computes a rolling minimum (*e.g.*, `mins [3.0,4.0,1.0,7.0]` = `[3.0,3.0,1.0,1.0]`) and thus is of general utility (indeed `mins` will work for lists of any

```
1 SELECT MAX(margins.price - margins.min)
2 FROM (SELECT t.price, MIN(t.price)
3                          OVER (ORDER BY t.ts
4                                ROWS BETWEEN UNBOUNDED PRECEDING
5                                AND CURRENT ROW)
6       FROM   trades AS t
7       WHERE  t.id = 'ACME'
8       AND    t.day = '10/20/2014') AS margins(price,min);
```

Figure 3: SQL:1999 code generated for the `bestProfit` query.

customer

c_custkey	c_name	c_nationkey	c_phone	c_acctbal	c
c	Customer#01	n	30-555-···	5236.89	

lineitems

l_orderkey	l_partkey	l_extendedprice	l_discount	l
o	p	3712.08	0.05	

nation

n_nationkey	n_name	r
n	USA	

orders

o_orderkey	o_custkey	o_orderstatus	o_orderdate	c
o	c	P	10/20/14	

Figure 4: Relevant excerpt of the TPC-H schema with sample rows. Matching key symbols (c, n, o) indicate relationships.

```
-- average account balance of the customers cs
avgBalance :: Q [Customer] -> Q Double
avgBalance cs = avg [ c_acctbal c | c <- cs, c_acctbal c > 0.0 ]

-- the orders of customer c (possibly none)
ordersOf :: Q Customer -> Q [Order]
ordersOf c = [ o | o <- orders, o_custkey o == c_custkey c ]

-- high potentials among the customers cs
potentialCustomers :: Q [Customer] -> Q [Customer]
potentialCustomers cs =
  [ c | c <- cs, c_acctbal c > avgBalance cs, empty (ordersOf c) ]

-- country code (phone number prefix) for customer c
countryCodeOf :: Q Customer -> Q Text
countryCodeOf c = subString 2 (c_phone c)

-- does customer c live in any of the given countries?
livesIn :: Q Customer -> [Text] -> Q Bool
livesIn c countries = countryCodeOf c `elem` toQ countries

-- TPC-H query Q22
q22 :: [Text] -> Q [(Text, Integer, Double)]
q22 countries =
  sortWith (\(country, _, _) -> country)
    [ (country, length custs, sum (map c_acctbal custs)) |
      (country, custs) <- groupWith countryCodeOf pots ]
  where
    pots = potentialCustomers [ c | c <- customers,
                                    c `livesIn` countries ]
```

Figure 5: A Haskell formulation of TPC-H query *Q22*.

type `a` as long as its values may be ordered: `Ord a`). Auxiliary functions `mins` and `margins` themselves invoke the primitive operation `#` (to make item order explicit, `#[`x_1`,`…`,`x_n`]` = `[(`x_1`,1),`…`,(`x_n`,`n`)]`) and `zip` (to pair the items of lists, `zip [`x_1`,`…`,`x_n`] [`y_1`,`…`,`y_n`]` = `[(`x_1`,`y_1`),`…`,(`x_n`,`y_n`)]`).

Flattening plus subsequent code generation for PostgreSQL can translate this Haskell query into the SQL:1999 code of Figure 3. We argue that this generated SQL formulation is reasonable in that it closely resembles the hand-written solution to the best profit problem proposed in [9]. The semantics of timestamp ordering, in particular, do not infect the entire generated code but remain local to the ordered `MIN` window aggregate (lines 2 to 5).

Layered queries (primitive, generic, domain-specific). Dividing queries into cooperating, tiny (typically single-line) auxiliary functions can help to (1) formulate complex query logic and (2) identify reusable, generic query pieces. Once we adopt this style, well-known scenarios like the TPC-H database (see the excerpt in Figure 4) and its associated queries appear in a new light.

domain	`margins` `ordersOf` `revenue` ...
generic	`mins` `groupWith` `sortWith` `zip` `concat` `map` `elem` `reverse` `take`/`drop` `head` `!!`
primitive	`[·|·]` `#` aggregates (`sum`, `length`, `or`, ...) `++` `sort` `nub` `empty` simple expressions (`+`, `==`, ...)

Figure 6: Three layers of query abstractions. Operations in upper layers are definable in terms of those on lower layers.

```
SELECT substring(c.c_phone, 1, 2), COUNT(*), SUM(c.c_acctbal)
FROM customer AS c,
     (SELECT AVG(c1.c_acctbal)
      FROM customer AS c1
      WHERE substring(c1.c_phone, 1, 2) IN (VALUES ('44'),('49'))
        AND c1.c_acctbal > 0.0) AS avgBalance(c_acctbal)
WHERE substring(c.c_phone, 1, 2) IN (VALUES ('44','49')
      AND c.c_custkey NOT IN (SELECT o.o_custkey
                              FROM   orders AS o)
      AND c.c_acctbal > avgBalance.c_acctbal
GROUP BY substring(c.c_phone, 1, 2)
ORDER BY substring(c.c_phone, 1, 2);
```

Figure 7: PostgreSQL-executable code for q22 `["44","49"]`.

Given a list of countries, TPC-H query *Q22* [16] aims to identify potential customers: those whose accounts show an above-average balance but currently have not placed any order. Average account balance or current order placement are pervasive concepts in the TPC-H application domain which leads us to define designated functions (see **`avgBalance`** and **`ordersOf`** in Figure 5—**`ordersOf`**, in particular, embodies the *1:n* relationship between customers and orders). With these domain-specific functions in place, the core of the problem becomes a two-liner itself (lines 11 and 12). The residual query below line 15 filters, groups, and sorts customers (by phone country code) to prepare the answer format that *Q22* demands.

More generally, we obtain a multi-layered query language design (Figure 6) in which a small set of primitives are used to define generic, domain-agnostic query operations. The polymorphic types of the functions in this second layer (cf. the rolling minimum **`mins`**) hint at their reusability. Domain-specific functions in the top layer embody application-level concepts and can lead to very succinct query formulation ("one-liners").

It is particularly desirable to populate the top layers and keep the set of primitives as small as possible (in *AQuery* [9], for example, the equivalent of **`mins`** lives at the bottom layer). Flattening is fully compositional and makes the required unrestricted composition of query abstractions viable. Users are not bound to query templates of any form and are not penalized for the introduction or use of abstractions. Figure 7 shows the generated (monolithic) SQL code—the used abstractions have been compiled away.

Nested data: separation of contents and structure. Query languages whose data modeling capabilities are on par with programming languages are the exception rather than the rule [5]. With its roots in the programming language domain, flattening can compile queries that arbitrarily nest two principal type constructors—tuples `(·,·)` and lists `[·]`.

Nested data of this kind allows the construction of complex reports: function **`expectedRevenue`** (see Figure 8) pairs

```
-- is customer c a resident of nation?
hasNationality :: Q Customer -> Text -> Q Bool
hasNationality c nation =
  or [ n_name n == toQ nation && n_nationkey n == c_nationkey c |
       n <- nations ]

-- all orders of customer c with the given status (O, P, C)
ordersWithStatus :: Text -> Q Customer -> Q [Order]
ordersWithStatus status c =
  [ o | o <- ordersOf c, o_orderstatus o == toQ status ]

-- our revenue for order o
revenue :: Q Order -> Q Double
revenue o = sum [ l_extendedprice l * (1 - l_discount l) |
                  l <- lineitems, l_orderkey l == o_orderkey o ]

-- expected revenues (by customer, with details) in nation
expectedRevenue :: Text -> Q [(Text, [(Date, Double)])]
expectedRevenue nation =
  [ (c_name c, [ (o_orderdate o, revenue o) |
                 o <- ordersWithStatus "P" c ]) |
    c <- customers,
    c `hasNationality` nation ]
```

Figure 8: Expected revenue report (produces nested result).

each customer with the list of dates and expected revenues for her pending orders. True to layering, most of the query logic has been relocated into domain-specific functions to control complexity and promote reusability: while auxiliary function **`revenue`** embodies TPC-H's specific notion of order revenue, function **`ordersWithStatus`** builds on **`ordersOf`** (see above) to find all orders in condition **`status`** for customer **`c`**. The overall result type has shape `[(·,[(·,·)])]`.

Efficient support for such nested data structures poses a challenge for common database backend architectures with their rigid layout of data (*e.g.*, first normal form relational tables). Flattening follows a compilation scheme that separates data contents from any nesting structure. The separation and the subsequent re-imprinting of structure are essentially compile-time operations (Section 3). This scheme turns out to be a good fit for existing database backends which then can compute contents and structural aspects separately: the demo audience will understand how a query of list nesting depth d will yield d backend queries ($d = 2$ for the **`expectedRevenue`** example above).

3. 10 MINUTES OF FLATTENING

It is the prime purpose of this demonstration to provide a comprehensible and concise account of the role that flattening can play in query compilation. Following the *compilation by transformation* principle, the surface query syntax is lowered towards database-executable form in a series of steps, each of which yield human-readable and self-contained intermediate output. Here, we sketch the individual steps. The demo audience should be able to follow a complete walk-through in about 10 minutes. Figure 9 provides a road map.

① **Desugar and normalize.** As a preparatory step, the compiler removes domain-specific and generic query abstractions, replacing them with their primitive equivalents (cf. Figure 6). The bodies of user-defined functions like **`margins`** or **`revenue`** are unfolded at their call sites. (This implies that these functions must be non-recursive—primitives may embody recursive computation, however.) A polymorphic function in the generic layer is replaced by either

- its equivalent primitive comprehension form (refer to Figure 10) or

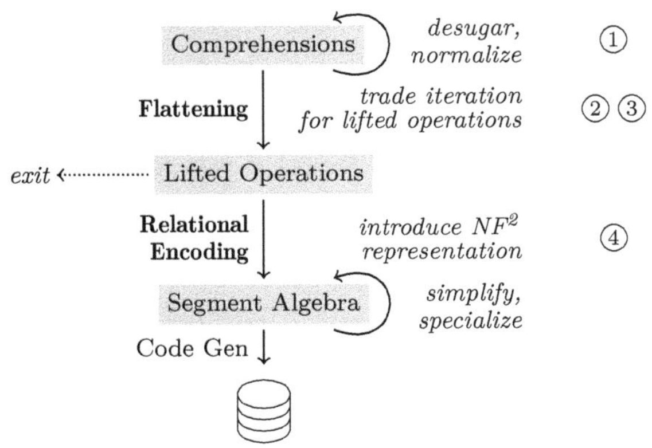

Figure 9: Compilation stages. Connect alternative backends at *exit* to receive the post-flattening input query.

generic	primitive
`groupWith f xs`	`[ (x,[ y | y <- xs, f y == x ]) | x <- nub (map f xs) ]`
`zip xs ys`	`[ (x,y) | (x,i) <- #xs, (y,j) <- #ys, i == j ]`
`concat xss`	`[ x | xs <- xss, x <- xs ]`
`take n xs`	`[ x | (x,i) <- #xs, i <= n ]`

Figure 10: Expressing generic query abstractions in terms of the primitive layer (excerpt).

- a special-purpose built-in primitive if that is provided by the underlying query engine (*e.g.*, `zip` may simply turn into the built-in `ZIP` if the engine features positional join support [10]).

After these replacements, the query of Figure 8 takes the form shown in Figure 11, for example.

Desugaring continues with normalizing rewrites that build on the extensive body of work on the unnesting and optimization of calculus-based or comprehension-style query languages [8, 15]: common comprehension patterns are traded for built-in operations which embody these patterns. Notably, this introduces list-based variants of joins, for example, `NESTJOIN` or `SEMIJOIN`.

② **Flattening: syntactic transformation.** All remaining comprehensions are in the normal form `[` e `|` x `<-` xs `]` (single generator, no predicates). Flattening, originally described by Blelloch [2] as well as Prins and Palmer [13], addresses the challenge of *nested data parallelism*: how to efficiently compile iterative programs of the given normal form if expression e itself contains iterative constructs. Typical for query-style programs, all examples in this paper manifest such nested iteration (up to depth 3, despite their simplicity).

Flattening revolves around the concept of *lifted functions* which consume and return—possibly in parallel—entire lists of items: the lifted variant of $F :: a \to b$ is $F^1 :: [a] \to [b]$. (In the following, we identify F and F^0.) This notion of lifting coincides with the bulk-oriented mode of processing in query engines which are tuned to efficiently apply operations to entire collections of data items (*e.g.*, tables of rows). Flattening is specified via few syntactic program transformation rules. The gist is the following rule that expresses the iterated application of F in terms of its lifted variant:

$$[\, F^n\, e \mid x \text{ <- } xs \,] \quad \mapsto \quad F^{n+1}\, [\, e \mid x \text{ <- } xs \,] \qquad (\uparrow)$$

```
[ (c.c_name,
   [ (o.o_orderdate,
      SUM [ l.l_extendedprice * (1.0 - l.l_discount) |
            l <- TABLE(lineitem),
            l.l_orderkey == o.o_orderkey ]) |
     o <- TABLE(orders),
     o.o_custkey == c.c_custkey,
     o.o_orderstatus == "P" ]) |
  c <- TABLE(customer),
  OR [ n.n_name == "USA" && c.c_nationkey == n.n_nationkey |
       n <- TABLE(nation) ]
]
```

Figure 11: The query of Figure 8 after domain-specific and generic abstractions have been unfolded. Comprehensions and primitives remain.

```
-- scan xs and identify spots (= True) where new maximum reached
climb :: Ord a => Q [a] -> Q [Bool]
climb xs = [ and [ y <= x | (y,j) <- #xs, j <= i ] | (x,i) <- #xs ]

-- does xs ascend monotonically?
monotonic :: Ord a => Q [a] -> Q Bool
monotonic xs = and (climb xs)
```

Figure 12: Function `climb xs`: identify where `xs` reaches new maxima (`climb [3,4,1,7] = [True,True,False,True]`).

Nested iteration yields liftings of order $n > 1$. For example, we obtain `[ [` $F\, y$ `|` y `<-` $G\, x$ `] |` x `<-` xs `]` $\mapsto F^2(G^1\, xs)$ through two applications of ($\uparrow$) and the identity `[` x `|` x `<-` xs `]` $\equiv xs$. Since $F :: a \to b$, consequently $F^2 :: [[a]] \to [[b]]$.

To provide a concise account of flattening, we trace the transformation of the one-liner `climb` function of Figure 12 (`climb`, quite similar to `mins` of Figure 2, and `monotonic` test whether the elements of a list grow monotonically). The transformation trace itself is found in Figure 13. After desugaring and normalization (step ①), the body of `climb` exhibits nested iteration:

```
[ ··· [ y <= x | (y,j) <- g ] | (x,g) <- ··· ]
```

The intermediate program after flattening (step ②) features the characteristic lifted built-ins (here: AND^1, $<=^2$, and pair projections like $.2^1$ or $.1^2$). Explicit iteration has been compiled away entirely.

③ **Flattening: reducing F^n to F^1.** Flattening becomes practicable with the insight that any lifted built-in F^n with $n \geqslant 2$

```
  [ and [ y <= x | (y,j) <- #xs, j <= i ] | (x,i) <- #xs ]

=     ① (desugar, normalize)

  [ AND [ y <= x | (y,j) <- g ] |
      ((x,i),g) <- NESTJOIN{Ⓛ.2 <= Ⓡ.2} #xs #xs ]

=     ② (flatten)

  let xg = NESTJOIN{Ⓛ.2 <= Ⓡ.2} #xs #xs
   in AND^1 (xg.2^1.1^2 <=^2 (DIST^1 xg.1^1.1^1 xg.2^1))

=     ③ (reduce F^n to F^1)

  let xg = NESTJOIN{Ⓛ.2 <= Ⓡ.2} #xs #xs
      y = IMPRINT_1 xg.2^1 (FORGET_1 xg.2^1).1^1
   in AND^1 (IMPRINT_1 y
       ((FORGET_1 y) <=^1 (FORGET_1 (DIST^1 xg.1^1.1^1 xg.2^1))))
```

Figure 13: Tracing the flattening of `climb` (Figure 12). Ⓛ/Ⓡ inside the predicate {···} of a built-in operation refer to its left/right input, .1/.2 access components of a pair.

lifted	F^n ($n \geqslant 2$, if F^1 is a built-in)
built-in	$\text{SEMIJOIN}^{0,1}$ $\text{NESTJOIN}^{0,1}$ $\text{RESTRICT}^{0,1}$ ... $\text{DIST}^{0,1}$ TABLE FORGET_n IMPRINT_n $\text{SORT}^{0,1}$ simple operators ($+^{0,1}$, $<=^{0,1}$, ...)

Figure 14: The underlying query engine is expected to provide the operations F^0 and F^1. Flattening reduces lifted operations F^n (with $n \geqslant 2$) to these built-ins.

can be reduced to its variant F^1. This reduction (1) temporarily *forgets* about the $n-1$ outer nesting layers of F^n's list argument xs, (2) applies F^1 to the—now presumed flat—argument, and then (3) *imprints* the outer list nesting layers on the result again:

$$\text{F}^n\ xs \quad \mapsto \quad \text{IMPRINT}_{n-1}\ xs\,(\text{F}^1\,(\text{FORGET}_{n-1}\ xs)) \qquad (\flat)$$

Query engines thus only need to implement the F^0 and F^1 variants. We have already said that F^1 fits well with the bulk-oriented execution model of these engines—this is obvious for simple operators like $\text{F} = +$ or $\text{F} = <=$ but extends to more complex built-ins like SEMIJOIN (our discussion of step ④ below touches on this). Figure 14 summarizes our expectations of which operations an underlying engine has to supply.

The efficiency of flattening–generated code hinges on the operations FORGET_n and IMPRINT_n to have *zero* run-time costs for any $n \geqslant 1$. Careful representations of nested data can provide this behavior (see below).

The end of step ③ marks the point where code generators for various query engines could be hooked up (cf. the *exit* in Figure 9). These engines will find opportunities for a bulk-oriented or data-parallel evaluation already made explicit through the lifting superscripts.

④ **Relational encoding.** Vanilla relational database systems are viable engines in the above sense. The zero run-time cost requirement for FORGET_n and IMPRINT_n suggest a data representation that *separates contents from structure*: given such a separation, $\text{FORGET}_n\ xs$ simply ignores the structure part of xs temporarily while $\text{IMPRINT}_n\ xs\ e$ applies (the already existing) structure of xs to e.

One relational representation of nested data that provides this separation is the trusted NF^2 model [14]. Lists of items are encoded in a ternary seg|pos|item contents table in which column pos keeps track of item order and column seg indicates the sub-list to which an item belongs. The order of these sub-lists is held in a *separate* seg|pos structure table referencing the contents table. A list nested to depth n will feature $n-1$ structure tables. Figure 15 visualizes how $\text{FORGET}_n/\text{IMPRINT}_n$ exploit this NF^2-style encoding of data: during the evaluation of the underlined subexpression of Figure 13, only $<=^1$ will incur run-time cost.

Relational engines already implement the operators F^0 (cf. Figure 14 again). For operators with atomic arguments and result ($\text{F} \in \{+, <=, \dots\}$), F^1 is readily obtained through projection (π, mapping). At least two options exist to obtain lifted variants of bulk-oriented, or algebraic, built-ins F:

(1) extend the engine to provide true data-parallel implementations of F^1—note that all F^1 are intrinsically "embarrassingly parallel"—or

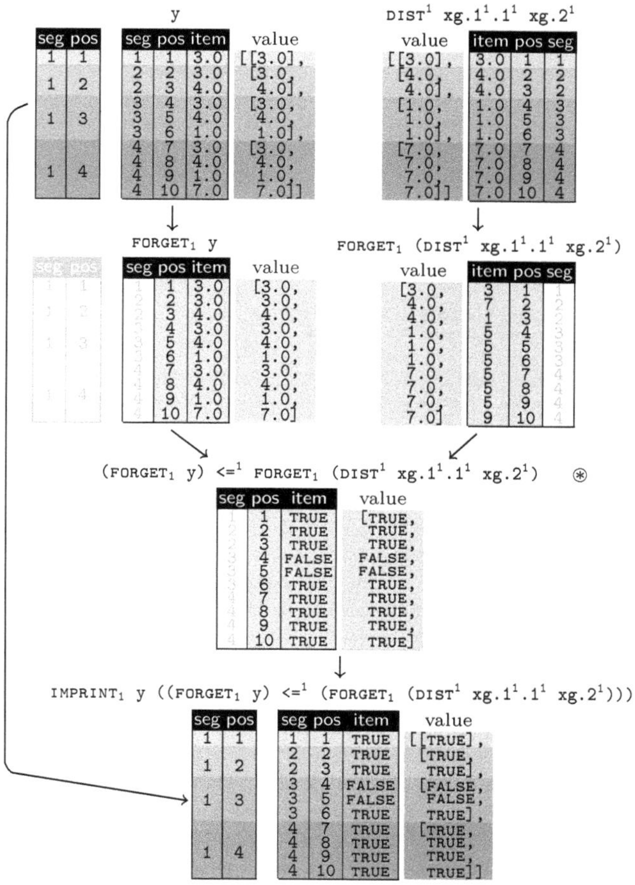

Figure 15: Evaluating the underlined expression in Figure 13. Operator $<=^1$ at ⊛ incurs the only run-time cost, FORGET_1 merely ignores (the grayed out) parts of the NF^2 encoding.

(2) parameterize the existing built-ins F to acknowledge list segmentation (column seg): $\text{SEMIJOIN}^1\{p\}$ then becomes $\ltimes\{$Ⓛ.seg = Ⓡ.seg $\wedge\, p\}$ and seg is prepended to the list of sort criteria in a SORT, for example.

The present work features a full implementation of option (2).

4. DEMONSTRATION SETUP

We will bring a demonstration setup that has been designed to facilitate both quick and deep impressions of flattening as a query compilation technique. A set of canned queries—similar to those discussed in this write-up— helps to provide an immediate overview of the flattening idea.

The demonstration does *not* run on rails, though: any canned query is editable, for example, to explore interesting edge cases in compilation. New ad hoc queries may be formulated. An interactive read-eval-print loop (REPL) promotes experimentation with queries, gives immediate feedback, and thus allows for quick "one-shot"demonstrations. Figure 16 shows the REPL (bottom of screenshot). Errors are signaled early: the system implements a static typing discipline that rejects programs for which no type assignment of the form $\text{Q}\,a$ can be found (these programs would not be database-executable).

The underlying relational backends, PostgreSQL and Vectorwise [17], will be preloaded with

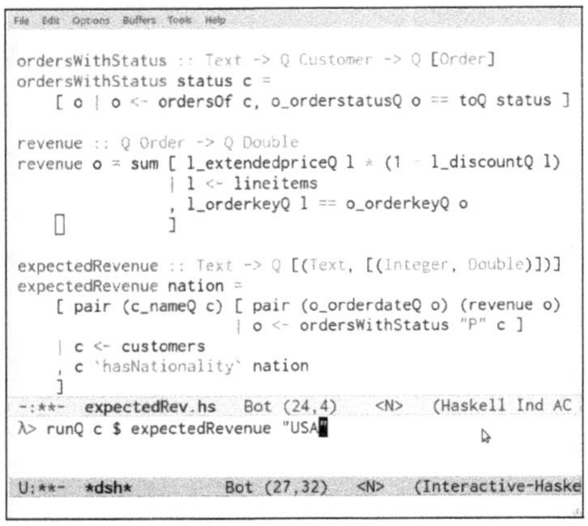

Figure 16: Haskell-embedded queries may be authored ad hoc and are evaluated in an interactive read-eval-print loop.

(1) toy data sets—that permit to explore query semantics since results may be checked item-by-item—as well as

(2) larger database instances so that the audience can assess backend performance once code has been generated.

We include familiar instances (*e.g.*, TPC-H) to ensure that attendees can easily follow the demonstration.

Going deeper. Along with the compiler implementation itself, the demonstration provides dedicated pretty-printers and visualizers for all intermediary program forms (screenshots in Figure 17). The inspection of the query after flattening (but before relational encoding) is of particular interest if new backends are to be connected. A peek at the code generated for the existing PostgreSQL and Vectorwise backends—SQL:1999 statements and algebraic plans, respectively—is provided as well. We hope to illustrate that a suitable encoding of segmented lists indeed (1) provides zero-cost implementations of $\texttt{FORGET}_n/\texttt{IMPRINT}_n$, and (2) leads to idiomatic relational queries that are not occupied with costly row order management.

5. REFERENCES

[1] A. Alexandrov et al. The Stratosphere Platform for Big Data Analytics. *VLDB Journal*, 2014.

[2] G. E. Blelloch and G. W. Sabot. Compiling Collection-Oriented Languages onto Massively Parallel Computers. *J. Parallel Distrib. Comput.*, 8(2), 1989.

[3] P. Buneman, L. Libkin, D. Suciu, V. Tannen, and L. Wong. Comprehension Syntax. *ACM SIGMOD Record*, 23(1), 1994.

[4] J. Cheney, S. Lindley, and P. Wadler. Query Shredding: Efficient Relational Evaluation of Queries Over Nested Multisets. In *Proc. SIGMOD*, 2014.

[5] G. Copeland and D. Maier. Making Smalltalk a Database System. In *Proc. SIGMOD*, 1984.

[6] G. Giorgidze, T. Grust, T. Schreiber, and J. Weijers. Haskell Boards the Ferry. In *Proc. IFL*, 2011.

[7] T. Grust, J. Rittinger, and T. Schreiber. Avalanche-Safe LINQ Compilation. In *Proc. VLDB*, 2010.

[8] T. Grust and M. H. Scholl. How to Comprehend Queries Functionally. *J. Intell. Inf. Syst.*, 12(2-3), 1999.

[9] A. Lerner and D. Shasha. AQuery: Query Language for Ordered Data, Optimization Techniques, and Experiments. In *Proc. VLDB*, 2003.

[10] S. Manegold, P. Boncz, N. Nes, and Martin Kersten. Cache-Conscious Radix-Decluster Projections. In *Proc. VLDB*, 2004.

[11] S. Marlow. *Haskell 2010: Language Report*, 2010. `haskell.org`.

[12] *The PostgreSQL Relational Database System*. `postgresql.org`.

[13] J. F. Prins and D. W. Palmer. Transforming High-Level Data-Parallel Programs into Vector Operations. In *Proc. PPOPP*, 1993.

[14] H.-J. Schek and M. H. Scholl. The Relational Model with Relation-Valued Attributes. *Information Systems*, 2(11), 1986.

[15] H. J. Steenhagen, R. A. de By, and H. M. Blanken. Translating OSQL Queries into Efficient Set Expressions. In *Proc. EDBT*, 1996.

[16] *TPC Benchmark H (Rev. 2.17.0)*, 2013. `tpc.org/tpch`.

[17] M. Zukowski, M. van de Wiel, and P. Boncz. Vectorwise: A Vectorized Analytical DBMS. In *Proc. ICDE*, 2012.

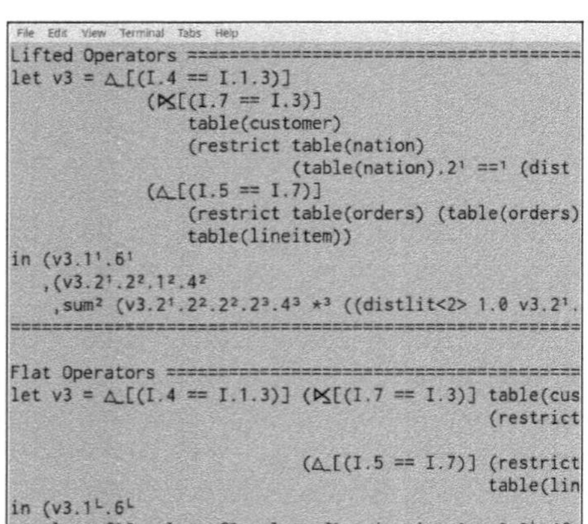

(a) Pretty-printed form after flattening and introduction of $\texttt{FORGET}_n/\texttt{IMPRINT}_n$ (compilation steps ② and ③).

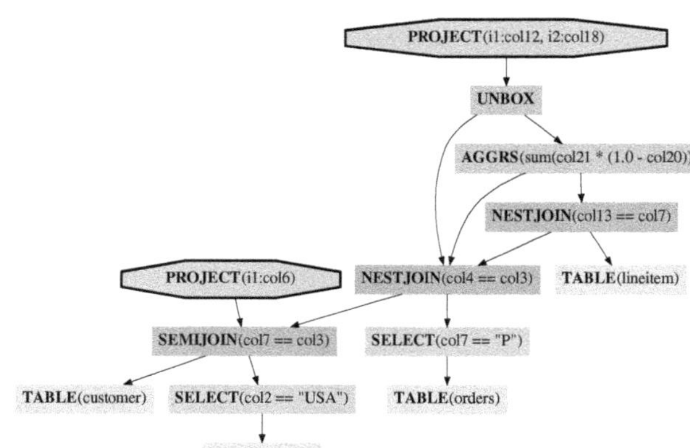

(b) Diagram of plan immediately before code generation. Two root nodes (⬭) represent a result of depth $d = 2$.

Figure 17: Compilation artifacts are tangible for the demonstration audience (here: program `expectedRevenue` of Figure 8).

D²WORM: A Management Infrastructure for Distributed Data-centric Workflows

Martin Jergler
Dept. for Computer Science,
Technische Universität
München, Germany.
jergler@in.tum.de

Mohammad Sadoghi
IBM T. J. Watson
Research Center,
Yorktown NY, USA.
msadoghi@us.ibm.com

Hans-Arno Jacobsen
Dept. for Computer Science,
Technische Universität
München, Germany.
jacobsen@in.tum.de

ABSTRACT

Unlike traditional activity-flow-based models, data-centric workflows primarily focus on the data to drive a business. This enables the unification of operational management, concurrent process analytics, compliance with process or associated data constraints, and adaptability to changing environments. In this demonstration, we present D²WORM, a Distributed Data-centric Workflow Management system. D²WORM allows users to (1) graphically model data-centric workflows in a declarative fashion based on the Guard-Stage-Milestone (GSM) meta-model, (2) automatically compile the modelled workflow into several fine-granular workflow units (WFUs), and (3) deploy these WFUs on distributed infrastructures. A WFU is a system component that manages a subset of the workflow's data model and, at the same time, represents part of the global control flow by evaluating conditions over the data. WFUs communicate with each other over a publish/subscribe messaging infrastructure that allows the architecture to scale from a single node to dozens of machines distributed over different data-centers. In addition, D²WORM is able to (4) concurrently execute multiple workflow instances and monitor their behavior in real-time.

Categories and Subject Descriptors

H.4 [**Information Systems Applications**]: General

Keywords

data-centric workflows, workflow distribution, publish/subscribe

1. INTRODUCTION

Data-centric workflows are becoming increasingly popular and receive growing attention from both industry [5, 16, 18, 20] and academia [4, 6, 7, 13, 14, 17]. Popular examples include Adaptive Case Management [20] and the emerging OMG CMMN standard [18], Business Artifacts [5, 16], scientific workflows [17], decentralized service orchestration [13], and even MapReduce-style processing [7].

SIGMOD'15, May 31–June 4, 2015, Melbourne, Victoria, Australia.

http://dx.doi.org/10.1145/2723372.2735362.

In recent decades, workflow technology in general has turned out to be essential for the efficient management of processes in business, governmental institutions, healthcare, science, and many other areas [10, 11, 20]. In general, a workflow represents a technical view on such business processes (BPs) by describing a set of computational or organizational tasks along with a well-defined execution order to achieve a higher-level objective. Although, a lot of research has been conducted to the present, today's requirements impose new challenges: Due to the increasing portion of knowledge-intense work, fast production cycles, and ever-changing business environments (e.g., legal constraints or policies), flexible and adaptable approaches are necessary [10, 11, 18, 20]. Furthermore, workflows often span across administrative and geographical boundaries (e.g., in multicorporate enterprises or B2B processes), or manage data that is inherently distributed [10]. Thus, decentralized coordination and distributed execution are inherent prerequisites for workflow management in practice [10, 15]. Workflows often structure processing as a graph of activities, in which nodes correspond to processing tasks and edges represent the flow between them. A prominent representative of these traditional activity-flow-based approaches is the Business Process Model and Notation (BPMN). Although explicit control flow is an intuitive way to describe workflows, it reveals several drawbacks. The static dependencies between the individual tasks make it hard to adapt the workflow. Also, with increasing numbers of tasks, the semantic correctness of the process is hard to ensure. Additional workflow goals that go beyond the operational management, like concurrent analytics, may even require their own solutions (e.g., data mining techniques for provenance). A mapping between separate approaches and different systems imposes massive inefficiencies and is cumbersome [11].

In data-centric workflows, however, the data fills the role that activity-flow plays in conventional models – hence, data becomes a first-class citizen [5, 11]. A data-centric workflow implicitly defines the order of task executions by using declarative rules to interpret the state of a global data model. This data model does not only represent application-level data but also status information about the workflow (e.g., which tasks are currently being executed). A particular system state is described by a snapshot of the underlying data. A specific task within the workflow lifecycle is triggered if the data has reached a certain state. The effects of task executions further evolve the data to a state that triggers the subsequent task. A trigger in this context is essentially a rule or a condition over the data model, and a particular result is linked with the invocation of the relevant task. This greatly facilitates flexibility as workflow adaptations can be achieved by changing the workflow's rule set, even dynamically at run-time.

Moreover, data-centric design also facilitates distributed management. In principle, there are two reasons for distributing workflows [8, 10, 15]. First, processes can reach scales that centralized systems simply cannot handle anymore; consider, for instance, the number of concurrent users and instances on sales platforms like Salesforce or Amazon [2]. Second, workflows are often defined over already existing data, which is either inherently distributed [10] (e.g., processes between subsidiaries in multicorporate enterprises) or must be physically spread across geographical areas due to legal constraints (e.g., the Data Protection Act in Great Britain [9]). Therefore, distributed workflow execution requires distributed management of (1) the underlying data and (2) the control flow that drives the process.

To address these challenges, we contribute by designing and developing D²WORM a holistic system for distributed data-centric workflow management. D²WORM allows the user to graphically model a workflow, transform this workflow into a set of interacting workflow units (WFUs), deploy WFUs on distributed infrastructures (e.g., a cloud [2], or a virtual cluster like in this demonstration), run sample instances of the workflow on that deployment, and monitor the execution. D²WORM is based on an industry-strength data-centric workflow meta-model, namely IBM Business Artifacts with Guard-Stage-Milestone (GSM) lifecycles [5]. Based on a formal mapping of GSM to Publish/Subscribe primitives [19], D²WORM transforms workflow models into fine-granular workflow units (WFUs). Each WFU manages a subset of the global data model and is responsible for a single or even multiple workflow rules. Workflow rules typically have the form: **if** *condition* **then** *action*, which means that if certain attributes in the data model have specific values (i.e., the condition is fulfilled), then the associated action is triggered (i.e., other attribute values are changed accordingly). As the workflow state is also represented as attributes of the data model, an attribute change might correspond, for instance, to the invocation of a new task. Such attribute changes, in turn, might also be relevant to other WFUs that want to evaluate a rule, which contains a condition including the updated attribute. Due to these characteristics, we believe that Publish/Subscribe (Pub/Sub) [12] provides a well-suited messaging infrastructure between WFUs.

Our novel Pub/Sub-based execution architecture decouples individual WFUs in a way that they do not have to know about each other. On one side, WFUs subscribe to attribute updates that are relevant for their rule evaluation, on the other side, WFUs simply publish the result of rule evaluation to the infrastructure. With this decoupling we enable a great potential for flexibility in terms of workflow deployment and execution. The load on workflow systems can vary significantly depending on the circumstances. For instance, a new service choreography might initially only attract a few users, so all WFUs could be deployed on a single node. As over time the number of users increases, certain WFUs can be migrated to other nodes and share the system load. In an extreme setting, each WFU would be deployed on its own node. For D²WORM, we use an agent-based deployment mechanism [15] where a manager publishes WFU descriptions and available agents subscribe to these. Agents that received such a description act as the respective WFU.

In summary, with D²WORM we demonstrate a holistic system architecture and implementation for integrated data-centric workflow management on distributed infrastructures. D²WORM supports the whole management lifecycle, including modeling, deployment, execution, and monitoring of workflows. In the remainder of this paper, we give a short overview about related approaches in Section 2 and elaborate on GSM in Section 3. The architecture of D²WORM and its components is then presented in Section 4 followed by our demonstration setup in Section 5.

2. RELATED WORK

In recent years, a plethora of approaches for execution of workflows has been proposed [1, 8, 13, 14, 15, 21]. However, these approaches are either not distributed [1, 14] or exclusively focus on activity-flow-based workflows [8, 15, 21]. Moreover, they are rather domain specific (e.g., scientific workflows [17]) or not flexible (e.g., no adaptability [13]).

The Amit situation manager specifies a language and a centralized execution mechanism in order to reduce complexity in active databases [1]. The situation concept extends composite events in its expressive power, flexibility, and usability; thus, baring some similarity with our notion of WFUs, which are partly realized by subscribing to update events. Amit, however, is a centralized system and focuses on rather isolated situations less complex workflows or interactions among situations. Another centralized object-aware framework that is trying to unify process and data is PHILharmonicFlows [14]. Here, workflows are modeled as micro processes, that represent the data and behavior of individual objects, and macro processes that represent the interactions among such objects.

Mentor was among the first approaches towards distributed execution of enterprise-wide workflows [21]. As in our approach, a workflow model is transformed into a representation that is appropriate for distributed execution, that captures all necessary synchronization information between different activities at the same time. The core difference is that Mentor relies on centralized state-chart models as opposed to a declarative, data-centric specification. Niños is a system for distributed execution of BPEL processes over a pure publish/subscribe substrate [8, 15]. Although resembling our approach in some respects (e.g., publish/subscribe-based messaging, agent-based deployment), Niños is a BPEL engine that only captures the control flow and neglects the underlying data. A distribution approach for BPEL processes that is based on stream processing units (SPUs) is presented in [3]. SPUs are abstraction for business functions and encapsulate their logic in the context of a business process. SPUs are similar to WFUs in our approach in a sense that they form the unit of distribution. However, they do not support data-centric workflows and build on stream processing primitives instead of publish/subscribe. A decentralized service orchestration architecture based on the Object Modeling System (OMS) is proposed in [13]. Data that is generated by a particular service is directly forwarded to the subsequent service without being passed through a centralized orchestration engine. Though focusing on the decentralization of data flow to enhance performance, the approach is not data-centric in a sense that the control flow is defined over data, which reduces its flexibility. Another system that focuses explicitly on scientific workflows is proposed in [17]. This approach is inspired by the work on relational algebra and enables automatic optimization by leveraging a parallel execution model. Workflows are represented as compositions of algebraic operations. The focus of the approach is on handling large collections of data (baring some similarity with MapReduce-style processing).

3. GSM WORKFLOW DECLARATIONS

We begin by giving the relevant background on data-centric workflow specifications and operational semantics by introduc-

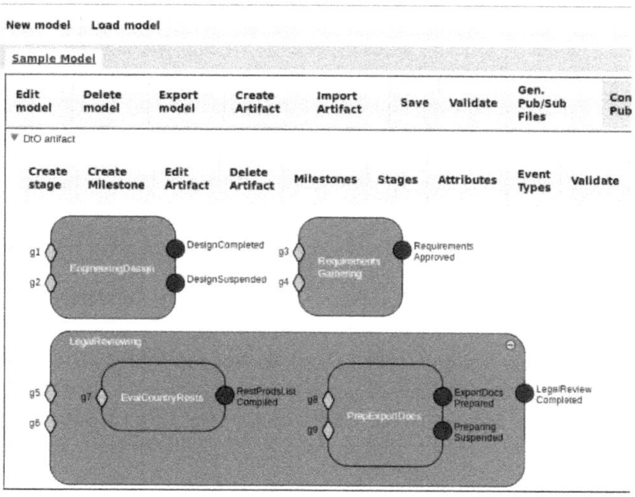

Figure 1: GSM model for "Design-To-Order" BP. Screenshot of D²WORM's web-based editor.

ing the Guard-Stage-Milestone (GSM) meta-model for business artifacts [5]. We elaborate on a sample process (cf. Figure 1) that we use as a running example throughout the paper to illustrate our system. This process will also serve as a use case during the system demonstration, where users can interactively control and monitor the workflow.

3.1 Business Use Case

The "Design-To-Order" BP that is depicted in Figure 1 was modeled with the web-based editor of D²WORM. It represents a typical design process that is structured into various phases [5]. Upon the reception of a new customer order, the associated requirements are approved. Once approved, the product designers can start with the actual design. Customers can change their requirements at any time, which results in a suspension of the design phase and requires a reapproval or requirements. Moreover, there is also a legal reviewing of the order that is comprised of two sub-phases. While the country restrictions of the destination country can be evaluated in parallel with the approval of requirements, the preparation of the export documents for the product requires a complete design. The latter one is, again, suspended and country restrictions have to be reevaluated if requirements change.

3.2 Model Elements & Execution Semantics

In GSM [5] a workflow like the BP depicted in Figure 1 is modeled as interactions of business-relevant entities (i.e., business artifacts). An artifact consists of a *lifecycle model* ($\mathcal{L}$) and an associated *information model* ($\mathcal{I}$) that captures all business relevant data (i.e., data attributes) and workflow-specific status information (i.e., status attributes). Interactions are specified in $\mathcal{L}$ and executed according to predefined operational semantics that evolve the artifact (i.e., $\mathcal{I}$).

GSM provides three fundamental elements to specify the behavior of a workflow. (1) *Milestones* are business-relevant objectives that can be achieved or invalidated. They are represented as circles in the graphical notation of GSM (cf. Figure 1). (2) *Stages* (i.e., rounded rectangles) that (hierarchically) cluster operational tasks and which are either *opened* or *closed*. During execution, multiple stages can be opened at a time, which naturally enables parallelism in task execution. The status attributes in $\mathcal{I}$ are Boolean attributes that capture which stages are currently opened or closed and which milestones are achieved or not. Stage opening is controlled by (3) *Guards* (i.e., diamonds), which are unlabeled in contrast to stages and milestones and internally specified using sentries. A sentry is a Boolean expression over a subset of status and data attributes. Besides stage opening, sentries are also used to express when milestones are achieved or invalidated, respectively.

For the execution of GSM workflows, operational semantics define the incorporation of *external events* into the current system snapshot, which corresponds to an instance of $\mathcal{I}$ (i.e., the impact on stage opening, status of milestones and data mutations). This reaction is encapsulated in a business step (B-Step), which is the smallest unit of business-relevant change in GSM. A B-Step is defined by a 5-tuple $(\Sigma, e, t, \Sigma', Gen)$, where Σ is the current system snapshot, e is an external event (e.g., a customer request to change the requirements) occurred at logical time t, Σ' is the updated system snapshot, and Gen is a set of generated events that is supposed to be published to the environment (e.g., a confirmation for the customer). More specifically, in each B-Step a set of workflow rules, which are derived from the model, are fired according to a specific order that is derived likewise. Each rule represents a micro-B-Step, which is an atomic data operation within a B-Step (e.g., the update of a particular milestone). Basically, there are six templates for such rules (i.e., for achieving/invalidating guards, for achieving/invalidating milestones and two rules for stage closing) [5].

3.3 Task Ordering & Invocation

The execution of GSM workflows is centered around B-Steps that specify the incorporation of external events by applying an ordered set of workflow rules to reveal the full impact of the respective event. Intuitively, these rules formally express what has been described rather informally in Sec. 3.1 (e.g., when exactly are stages opened or closed, when are milestones achieved or invalidated). Rules follow a common format and are expressed by a triple (π, α, γ). π describes a prerequisite on the state after the last B-Step, antecedent α represents state changes in the current B-Step (e.g., due to other rules), and γ is the effect on the system if π and α evaluate to true (i.e., the consequence). These rules are formulated as "Prerequisite-Antecedent-Consequence"-rules, or PAC-rules for short. For instance, the rule to capture the achieving of guard `g1`, which listens for a `NewOrder`-request to open the stage `RequirementsApproval` (`RA`), is

$$(\text{RA} = \text{false},\ \text{latestEvent} = \text{"NewOrder"},\ \text{RA} \leftarrow \text{true}),$$

which intuitively says that if the stage `RequirementsApproval` is currently closed and there is a new event of type `NewOrder` coming from the environment, then open this stage.

Another example is the invalidation of milestone `ExportDocsPrepared` (`edp`) (cf. Figure 1), which has three applicable rules. These rules only differ in their antecedents because they describe a separate, preceding system evolution within the B-Step due to different external events: Rule (1) captures a prior invalidation of milestone `DesignCompleted`. Rule (2) is based on an explicit external event of type `RedoExportDocs`. Rule (3) captures achieving milestone `DesignCompleted`. In combination with stage `LegalReviewing` being opened, this also requires to prepare export documents again and therefore to invalidate `edp`.

$$\begin{array}{lccc} 1: & (\text{edp} = \text{true}, & \text{DesignCompleted} \rightsquigarrow \text{false}, & \text{edp} \leftarrow \text{false}) \\ 2: & (\text{edp} = \text{true}, & \text{latestEvent} = \text{RedoExportDocs} & \text{edp} \leftarrow \text{false}) \\ & & \wedge\ \text{LR} = \text{true}, & \\ 3: & (\text{edp} = \text{true}, & \text{DesignCompleted} \rightsquigarrow \text{true} & \text{edp} \leftarrow \text{false}) \\ & & \wedge\ \text{LR} = \text{true}, & \end{array}$$

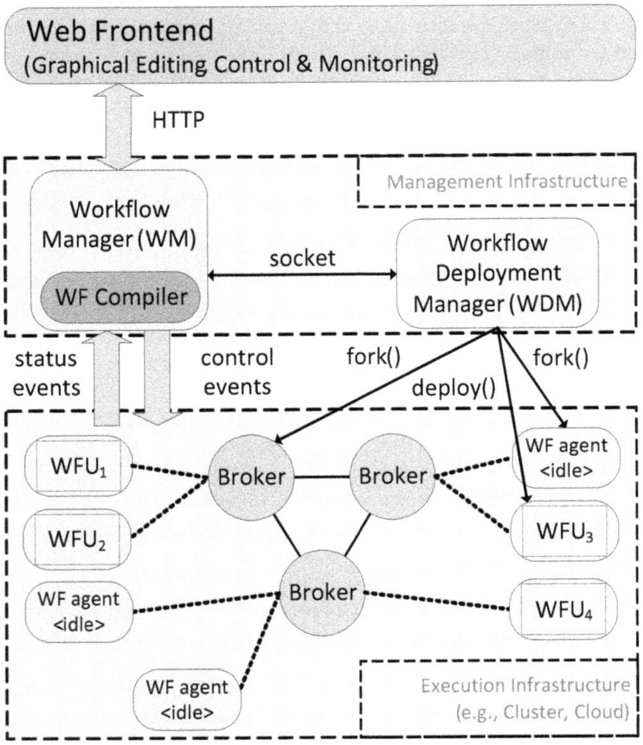

Figure 2: Overview of system architecture.

where, "=" checks the current state of an attribute and "$\rightsquigarrow$" indicates that the respective attribute value has been changed (toggled) within the current B-Step.

As prerequisite and consequent are equal for all three rules, they can be collapsed to a single PAC rule (π,$\mathcal{A}$,γ), where $\mathcal{A}$ is a disjunction over all antecedents of the original PAC rules. In D^2WORM, a WFU essentially describes a collapsed PAC rule.

WFUs express their interest in updates on attributes occurring in the prerequisite and antecedent of the rule and continuously interpret the data state according to the condition that is formed by the rule. Once data has reached a state that fulfills the condition, the corresponding rule fires. As a result, an event representing the consequent γ of the PAC rule is created and published to the system. On a global workflow level, this represents an update of $\mathcal{I}$ in the context of a particular B-Step.

4. DISTRIBUTED WORKFLOW MANAGEMENT & EXECUTION

We now present D^2WORM, our distributed data-centric workflow management system by giving an overview of the architecture and describing its individual components. We also describe the structure of WFU descriptions and explain the WFU interaction over our publish/subscribe middleware [12]. Furthermore, we outline the agent-based deployment process of WFUs, the publish/subscribe-based execution infrastructure and the monitoring system.

4.1 System Architecture

The architecture of D^2WORM is depicted in Figure 2. A core component of the system is the *Workflow Manager* (WM). It provides a web frontend and hosts a graphical workflow editor and the workflow compiler. The compiler translates workflow models into a set of WFUs. Besides managing the models, the WM also provides an interface to the *Workflow Deployment Manager* (WDM), and an event-based control interface to the execution infrastructure. The WDM takes the WFU descriptions resulting from the compilation and allocates them on a set of workflow agents in the execution infrastructure. These workflow agents are connected by a publish/subscribe broker network, which is also configured by the WDM, and execute the actual WFU logic.

4.2 Workflow Editor & Execution Monitor

The editor component of D^2WORM is implemented using the Google Web Toolkit (GWT) and is comprised of a server-side implementation to manage models and a web-based client application (cf. Figures 1). The editor enables the user to graphically model workflows according to the GSM specification [5]. Besides the graphical elements like guards, stages, and milestones, it also allows for the specification of external event types, service invocations, and sentry definitions. An automated validation routine guarantees that workflow models are always syntactically correct. We defined a XML schema definition for GSM that allows the generation of XML instance documents and equipped the editor with an export functionality.

As workflows can be directly compiled, deployed, and executed from the web frontend, D^2WORM also uses the graphical elements of the editor to monitor the execution (cf. Figure 5). For each workflow instance a new graphical instance of the workflow is generated and its progress is depicted by highlighting the currently active stages and the milestones that have already been achieved in green color. During the demonstration, the users can interact with a workflow instance over the WM control interface by issuing external events and track their impact on the workflow in real-time.

4.3 Compilation to Workflow Units

The workflow compiler of D^2WORM takes as input a GSM model that was generated with the editor component, and generates a set of WFU descriptions. A sample WFU description that corresponds to the opening of stage `RequirementsGathering` is depicted in Figure 3. WFUs are generated according to a formal mapping from GSM to publish/subscribe primitives [19]. This contains a direct mapping of workflow rules to WFUs and a set of additional generic WFUs that are necessary to maintain the GSM operational semantics in our distributed execution setting. Besides an encoding of the actual rule that needs to be evaluated (Rules), such descriptions also contain information about the attribute updates the WFU is interested in (Subscriptions), and the attributes the WFU can potentially update itself after evaluating the rule (Publications).

The encoding of Publications, Subscriptions, and Rules is based on conjunctions of predicates, which are expressed in a triple notation [12]. Here, a predicate consists of an `attribute_name`, an `operator`, and an associated `value`, meaning that the attribute with name `attribute_name` matches the predicate, if its value adheres to the specified `value` in combination with the order-relation imposed by the `operator`. For Subscriptions, this allows to specify the content of events, i.e., the attributes this WFU is interested in. Lines 2-4 in Figure 3, for instance, express the interest in an update of status attribute RequirementsGathering (if its value is false), and (&) an update of data attribute externalEvent having any String value.

In a similar way, the attribute updates that are possibly generated by the WFU are represented. In the example, there are

```
 1  Subscriptions={
      {[name,=,'RequirementsGathering'],[typ,=,'status'],[val,=,'false']}
    } & {
      {[name,=,'externalEvent'],[typ,=,'data'],[val,=,'@String']}
    }
 6
    Rules={
      {
        {
          [id,=,'R1'],[step,=,'latest'],[name,=,'RequirementsGathering'],
11        [typ,=,'status'],[val,=,'false']
        } & {
          [id,=,'R1'],[step,=,'current'],[name,=,'externalEvent'],
          [typ,=,'data'],[val,=,'Request:NewOrder']
        }
16    } || {
        {
          [id,=,'R2'],[step,=,'latest'],[name,=,'RequirementsGathering'],
          [typ,=,'status'],[val,=,'false']
        } & {
21        [id,=,'R2'],[step,=,'current'],[name,=,'externalEvent'],
          [typ,=,'data'],[val,=,'Request:CustomerChange']
        }
      }
    }
26
    Publications={
      {[id,=,'P1'],[name,=,'RequirementsGathering'],[typ,=,'toggling'],
        [val,=,'FALSEtoTRUE']
      } || {
31      [id,=,'P2'],[name,=,'RequirementsGathering'],[typ,=,'toggling'],
        [val,=,'TRUEtoTRUE']
      } || {
        [id,=,'P0'],[name,=,'Ach-RequirementsGathering'],[typ,=,'isVisited'],
        [val,=,'visited']
36    }
    }
```

Figure 3: WFU description for opening stage RequirementsGathering (cf. Figure 1).

three different publication templates for that account. Lines 26-27 in Figure 3, for instance, describe an attribute update for the toggling attribute RequirementsGathering, whereby its value toggles from `false` to `true`, i.e., the stage `RequirementsGathering` is opened.

Also the workflow rules can be expressed using the triple notation. Lines 7-23 in Figure 3 represent two different rules, R1 or (i.e., ||) R2 for the sample WFU. There are two rules because the original workflow rule also contained two separate antecedents (cf. Section 3.3). The reason for this is that two different external events (i.e., `NewOrder` and `CustomerChange`) are defined as opening guards for the stage. Both rules evaluate predicates for the latest and (i.e., &) the current B-Step.

Depending on the outcome of rule evaluation, which can be either `true`, if at least one rule was applicable, or `false`, if none was applicable, different publications are generated and sent. In the success case, the WFU will generate publications with id P1, in the other case publications with id P2. Independent of the evaluation outcome all publications with id P0 are generated and published by default. In the example there is one publication P0 that indicates that the rule has been processed already.

4.4 Execution Infrastructure

The execution infrastructure of D^{2}WORM is essentially comprised of a set of workflow agents (WF agents) that are connected to an overlay of publish/subscribe message brokers (cf. Figure 2). WF agents are software components that are able to execute the application logic of any WFU and implement the publish/subscribe interface to communicate with each other over the broker network. They are able to parse WFU descriptions (cf. Figure 3), subscribe to the desired attribute updates, instantiate the rule evaluation logic, and publish updates if required. In our setting the workflow manager is also connected with the broker overlay and, for demonstration purposes, acts as the external environment. On one side, the WM sends external events in the form of publications to interested WFUs. On the other side, it subscribe to events that notify milestone achievement and stage opening.

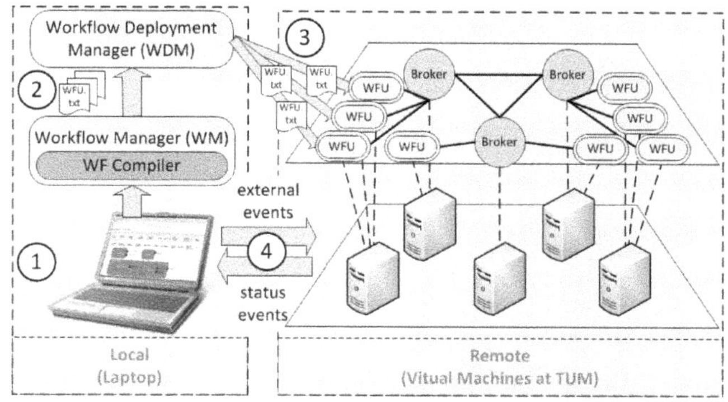

Figure 5: Setup for demonstration.

4.5 Infrastructure & Workflow Deployment

The deployment of a workflow on a distributed computing infrastructure, like a cloud or a cluster, is handled by the Workflow Deployment Manager (WDM). The deployment process itself is separated into two phases. First, the WDM spawns the broker and agent processes on the remote machines and establishes the overlay by connecting brokers and agents. Once the overlay is properly configured, in a second step, the WDM allocates the WFU descriptions on the WF agents. To bring descriptions to the right destination, we use the capabilities the publish/subscribe overlay already provides. WF agents subscribe to special control events including their own agent id. The WDM, in turn, generates such control publications with the id of the target agent and wraps the respective WFU description inside. WF agents receive these events, unwrap the description, and instantiate the WFU. The instantiation process of a WFU includes subscribing to the desired updates of other WFUs and announcing future publication of own attribute updates. As both interests must be matched in the broker network, the instantiation process of a single WFU also depends on the instantiation of other WFUs. To enable the WDM to determine when the overall instantiation process has succeeded, WFUs implement a mechanism to determine whether their subscriptions and announcements have been propagated through the whole overlay, and subsequently publish this state. Once the WDM receives acknowledgments from all WFUs, the WM is notified that the workflow has successfully deployed and the actual execution of the workflow can now begin.

5. LIVE DEMONSTRATION OF D^{2}WORM

The setup for our live demonstration of D^{2}WORM is depicted in Figure 5. The Workflow Manager, Workflow Compiler, and Workflow Deployment Manger are hosted on a physically present laptop (Intel Core i7-3520M 2.90 GHz, 8GB RAM, Ubuntu 14.04.1 LTS) and control the distributed workflow execution in the university infrastructure at TUM. The execution infrastructure is comprised of virtual machines (VMs) running in a clustered environment (2 vCPUs 2 GHz, 512 MB RAM, Ubuntu 12.04.5 LTS). VMs can be accessed over SSH from the laptop and can communicate with each other over arbitrary ports.

During the demonstration, users can basically experience the whole feature set of D^{2}WORM. We start with loading a sample process into the WM over the web frontend. In addition to the "Design-to-order" process described in the paper, we also

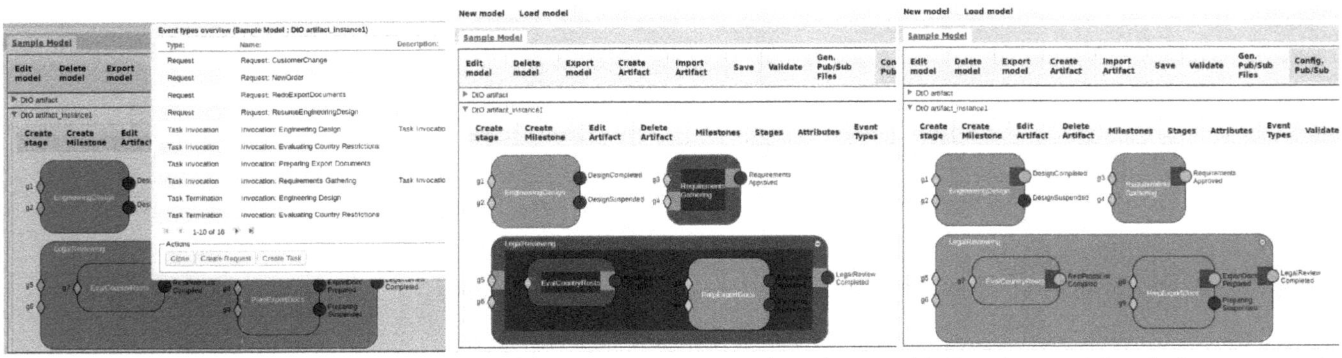

(a) Execution by issuing external events. (b) Some opened stages (green). (c) Complete workflow (milestones green)

Figure 4: D²WORM in action. Workflow emulation by issuing external events and real-time status monitoring.

provide a model for a claim management process. Users can then apply adaptations to these processes, e.g., add new stages, define a new milestones, validate their models, and export/import them (cf. Step 1 in Figure 5). Next, the workflow model is compiled into WFU descriptions right from the editor. WFUs are stored in text files and can be individually investigated for their contents (Step 2). For deployment (Step 3), we assume an existent and running virtual cluster environment with SSH access to all VMs. The WDM configures a static execution environment, e.g., three brokers and eight agents, and uniformly allocates the WFUs to agents. The progress of the deployment process can be monitored from the web interface. In addition, SSH connections to the VMs and inspection of log files are possible. After the workflow is successfully deployed, the process is executed and monitored (Step 4). Figure 5 shows some of the possible execution phases. Figure 4(a) shows how the user can select an external event type from the list of available events, instantiate it with additional data attributes, and fire it into the execution system. Figure 4(b) shows the impact of an external event of type `NewOrder` on the workflow execution. Stages that are opened in reaction to this event are highlighted in green. Similarly, Figure 4(c) shows a completed workflow, i.e., the sequence of external events has caused all milestones to be achieved. Again, these milestones are indicated in green color.

6. REFERENCES

[1] A. Adi and O. Etzion. Amit - The Situation Manager. *VLDB Journal '04*.

[2] Amazon. Amazon's Corporate IT Migrates Business Process Management to the Amazon Web Services Cloud. `https://media.amazonwebservices.com/AWS_Amazon_BPM_Migration.pdf`, 2011.

[3] S. Appel, S. Frischbier, T. Freudenreich, and A. Buchmann. Event Stream Processing Units in Business Processes. In *BPM'13*.

[4] D. Calvanese, G. De Giacomo, and M. Montali. Foundations of Data-aware Process Analysis: A Database Theory Perspective. In *PODS '13*.

[5] E. Damaggio, R. Hull, and R. Vaculín. On the equivalence of incremental and fixpoint semantics for business artifacts with Guard-Stage-Milestone lifecycles. *Information Systems*, 2013.

[6] M. Dumas. On the convergence of data and process engineering. In *ADBIS*, 2011.

[7] I. Elghandour and A. Aboulnaga. ReStore: Reusing Results of MapReduce Jobs. *In VLDB'12*.

[8] S. Ganesan, Y. Yoon, and H. Jacobsen. Niños Take Five: The Management Infrastructure for Distributed Event-Driven Workflows. In *DEBS'11*.

[9] Great Britain. Data Protection Act. 1998.

[10] C. Houy, P. Fettke, P. Loos, W. Aalst, and J. Krogstie. Business Process Management in the Large. *In BISE'11*.

[11] R. Hull and J. Su. NSF Workshop on Data-Centric Workflows (2009). `http://dcw2009.cs.ucsb.edu/report.pdf`.

[12] H.-A. Jacobsen, A. K. Y. Cheung, G. Li, B. Maniymaran, V. Muthusamy, and R. S. Kazemzadeh. The PADRES Publish/Subscribe System. In *Principles and Applications of Distributed Event-Based Systems*. IGI Global, 2010.

[13] B. Javadi, M. Tomko, and R. O. Sinnott. Decentralized Orchestration of Data-centric Workflows Using the Object Modeling System. In *CCGRID'12*.

[14] V. Künzle and M. Reichert. Philharmonicflows: Towards a framework for object-aware process management. *In Journal of Software Maintenance'11*.

[15] G. Li, V. Muthusamy, and H.-A. Jacobsen. A distributed service-oriented architecture for business process execution. *TWEB'10*.

[16] A. Nigam and N. S. Caswell. Business artifacts: An approach to operational specification. *IBM Syst. J.'03*.

[17] E. S. Ogasawara, J. Dias, V. Silva, F. S. Chirigati, D. de Oliveira, F. Porto, P. Valduriez, and M. Mattoso. Chiron: a parallel engine for algebraic scientific workflows. *Concurrency and Computation: Practice and Experience*, 2013.

[18] OMG. Case Management Model and Notation (CMMN). bmi/09-09-23.

[19] M. Sadoghi, M. Jergler, H.-A. Jacobsen, R. Vaculin, and R. Hull. Safe Distribution and Parallel Execution of Data-centric Workflows over the Publish/Subscribe Paradigm. Technical report, University of Toronto, 2012.

[20] K. D. Swenson. *Mastering the Unpredictable*. Meghan-Kiffer Press, 2010.

[21] D. Wodtke, J. Weißenfels, G. Weikum, and A. K. Dittrich. The Mentor Project: Steps Toward Enterprise-Wide Workflow Management. *ICDE '96*.

NL$_2$CM: A Natural Language Interface to Crowd Mining

Yael Amsterdamer, Anna Kukliansky and Tova Milo
Tel Aviv University, Tel Aviv, Israel
{yaelamst,annaitin,milo}@post.tau.ac.il

ABSTRACT

The joint processing of *general data*, which can refer to objective data such as geographical locations, with *individual data*, which is related to the habits and opinions of individuals, is required in many real-life scenarios. For this purpose, *crowd mining* platforms combine searching knowledge bases for general data, with mining the crowd for individual, unrecorded data. Existing such platforms require queries to be stated in a formal language. To bridge the gap between naïve users, who are not familiar with formal query languages, and crowd mining platforms, we develop NL$_2$CM, a prototype system which translates natural language (NL) questions into well-formed crowd mining queries.

The mix of general and individual information needs raises unique challenges. In particular, the different types of needs must be identified and translated into separate query parts. To account for these challenges, we develop new, dedicated modules and embed them within the modular and easily extensible architecture of NL$_2$CM. Some of the modules interact with the user during the translation process to resolve uncertainties and complete missing data. We demonstrate NL$_2$CM by translating questions of the audience, in different domains, into OASSIS-QL, a crowd mining query language which is based on SPARQL.

1. INTRODUCTION

A useful distinction between information needs in real-life tasks classifies such needs into two types: *general information* needs, which involve data not tied to a particular person, such as the locations of places or opening hours; and *individual knowledge* needs, which concerns individual people, e.g., their actions and opinions. The first type of data can often be fetched from standard databases or knowledge bases, whereas obtaining individual data about the members of a certain population often requires posing questions to (a sample of) the relevant people. As an example, based on a real question posted in a travel-related forum, consider a group of travelers who booked a hotel in Buffalo, NY. The group members may be interested in the answer to the question "What are the most interesting places near Forest Hotel, Buffalo, we should visit in the fall?" Answering this question requires processing mixed data: the sights in Buffalo and their proximity to Forest Hotel is a general data that can be found, e.g., in a geographical ontology such as LinkedGeoData;[1] the interestingness of places is an individual opinion; and which places one should visit in the fall is an individual recommendation. As another example, consider a dietician wishing to study the culinary preferences in some population, focusing on food dishes rich in fiber. While nutritional facts can be found in a (general) knowledge base, the eating habits of people are individual information.

The example tasks mentioned above could be performed using standard tools such as web search or forums. However, these tools have shortcomings in processing mixed general and individual knowledge: search engines are very efficient nowadays, but cannot ask people to provide individual data that is not already recorded in the search engine's repository, when such data is required; web forums allow fetching individual data from web users, but do not search relevant general data in knowledge bases; and both tools may incur post-processing efforts to the user, in manually analyzing their text-based output, filtering irrelevant results, aggregating answers and identifying consensus, etc. This calls for a *hybrid and automated approach*, which involved searching a general knowledge base, asking and analyzing the answers of people, and jointly processing the results.

Such an alternative approach is studied in our recent work about *crowd mining* [1, 2]. In [2], a novel query language was defined, OASSIS-QL, whose syntax splits individual information needs from general ones. This allows OASSIS-QL queries to be evaluated by an efficient, crowd-powered query engine, such that general query parts are evaluated against a knowledge base (ontology) and the individual parts are evaluated with the help of the crowd of web users.

While existing crowd mining tools such as OASSIS-QL are a major step towards processing mixed general and individual information needs, one cannot expect naïve users (like the travelers in our first example above) to write complex queries in a formal language. To overcome this, we introduce NL$_2$CM. This prototype system allows users to express their requests in natural language (NL), identifies and isolates specific general and individual information needs, and automatically translates these needs into well-formed queries. We exemplify the operation of this framework for OASSIS-QL, which is evaluated over RDF-modeled data. However, the

SIGMOD'15, May 31–June 4, 2015, Melbourne, Victoria, Australia.

http://dx.doi.org/10.1145/2723372.2735370.

[1]LinkedGeoData. `http://linkedgeodata.org/`

principles we develop and the modular architecture of NL$_2$CM, may cater for other crowd mining platforms that support query languages over, e.g., relational or XML data.

The problem of developing NL interfaces to query engines has been studied in previous work for queries over general, recorded relational/XML/RDF data (e.g., [5, 6, 7, 12]). However, the mix of individual and general information needs in the scenarios we consider add new challenges to the problem. For instance, individual and general information needs may be mixed in an intricate manner in an NL question. Until now, no existing tools could account for distinguishing the different types of needs, which is necessary for the translation process. Existing NL tools can identify only individual expressions of sentiments and opinions, but do not account, e.g., for individual habits. Moreover, naïve approaches, such as checking which parts of the query do not match to the knowledge base, cannot facilitate this task since most knowledge bases are incomplete.

Our solution to these challenges consists of (i) a modular architecture, reusing existing NL tools where possible; (ii) a newly-developed module for distinguishing individual information needs from general ones; and (iii) seamless integration of individual and general query parts into a well-formed query. The translation process can be outlined as follows. First, off-the-shelf NL tools are instrumented for parsing the free text and converting it into well-defined data structures, which represent the semantic roles of text parts. These structures then undergo decomposition into their general and individual parts by our new module, which employs means of declarative pattern matching and dedicated vocabularies. Each part is separately processed, and in particular, an existing *General Query Generator* is used to process the general query parts, whereas the individual parts are processed by new modules. The processed query parts are integrated to form the final output query. NL$_2$CM implements these ideas and further *interacts with the user* in order to deal with uncertainties and missing details (e.g., "Buffalo" is ambiguous) in the user request.

We next provide a brief overview of the demonstration of NL$_2$CM and of related work. Section 2 explains the design and the techniques used in the translation framework. The implementation details of these ideas, along with the interaction of the user with the system are explained in Section 3. An elaborate demonstration scenario is described in Section 4.

Demonstration Overview. We will demonstrate the operation of NL$_2$CM in three stages, to gradually introduce it to the audience members. First, we will demonstrate the translation of real-life NL requests collected from web forums into OASSIS-QL queries, and observe the correspondences between different query parts and parts of the original NL sentence. Second, we will invite the audience members to contribute questions on any topic that interests them. These NL requests will also be translated into OASSIS-QL, and we will execute some of the queries via the OASSIS query engine, to gain further intuition about the semantics of the generated queries and their results. Last, we will demonstrate the interaction of NL$_2$CM with the user in cases when either rephrasing the question or adding information is required. In parallel, we will gain an insight into the system operation through its administrator mode screen. See Section 4 for full details.

```
SELECT VARIABLES
WHERE
    {$x instanceOf Place.
     $x near       Forest_Hotel,_Buffalo,_NY}
SATISFYING
    {$x  hasLabel "interesting"}
    ORDER BY DESC(SUPPORT)
    LIMIT 5
   AND
    {[]  visit $x.
     []  in    Fall}
    WITH SUPPORT THRESHOLD = 0.1
```

Figure 1: Sample OASSIS-QL Query, $\mathcal{Q}$

Related Work. A recent line of work studies the use of crowdsourcing platforms for performing different data processing tasks with the help of the crowd (e.g., [3, 4, 9, 13, 14]). The idea of *ontology-based crowd mining* was originally introduced in [1], and extended to support the evaluation of user-specified declarative queries in [2], by the OASSIS system. NL$_2$CM forms an important enabling tool for crowd mining systems like OASSIS, since it makes them accessible to the public, and allows any user to formulate even complex queries in an intuitive manner. Previous work includes a line of NL interfaces to declarative systems, e.g., [5, 6, 7, 12], many of which employ interactive request refinement as is done in NL$_2$CM. In particular, FREyA [5] translates NL into SPAQRL, and interacts with the user to resolve unrecognized or ambiguous terms. We employ it for processing general information needs, as described in Section 3. However, to our knowledge, no prior work can account for NL requests concerning individual data.

2. TECHNICAL BACKGROUND

The process of automated query translation can be viewed as converting between two types of data representations, namely, the source and target languages. In our setting, we use NL parsing tools to generate a standard representation of the source NL text (see below). This representation allows processing the text to detect and isolate the general and individual query parts, and eventually convert them to the representation of the target query language.

Next, we review the design and techniques used in the NL$_2$CM translation framework. As explained in the Introduction, this framework is modular and can be adapted to support different query languages. To make the discussion concrete, we describe here the translation of NL to OASSIS-QL, which is also used in our demonstration scenario. We will mention throughout the section which parts of the solutions are specific to OASSIS-QL, and changes that can be made to support other languages. For background, we start by briefly explaining the syntax and semantics of OASSIS-QL, a full description of which can be found in [2]. Then, we describe the modular architecture of NL$_2$CM, and the interaction between the framework modules.

2.1 Query Language Overview

As mentioned in the Introduction, OASSIS-QL queries are evaluated against an ontology of general knowledge as well as the individual knowledge of the crowd. An RDF model is used to represent both types of knowledge, and thus, the syntax of OASSIS-QL is defined as an extension of SPARQL, the RDF query language, to crowd mining.

An OASSIS-QL query has three parts: (i) a SELECT clause, which defines the output of the query; (ii) a WHERE clause, which is evaluated against an ontology; and (iii) a `SATISFYING` clause, which defines the data patterns to be mined from the crowd. The returned output is composed of data patterns that capture the *relevant* and *significant* habits and opinions of the crowd. We briefly review below the `OASSIS-QL` syntax, using the example question "What are the most interesting places near Forest Hotel, Buffalo, we should visit in the fall?". Figure 1 displays the query $\mathcal{Q}$, which is the translation of this NL question into `OASSIS-QL`.

The `SELECT` clause (line 1) specifies that the output should be *significant variable bindings*, i.e., bindings to the query variables which yield significant data patterns. In this example, $\mathcal{Q}$ contains a single variable `$x`, and its bindings to places in Buffalo that match the query, e.g., the Delaware Park and Buffalo Zoo may be returned. The language also allows projecting the results over a subset of the variables.

The `WHERE` clause (lines 2-4) defines a SPARQL-like selection query on the ontology. It consists of triples of the form entity-relation-entity, which correspond to the RDF ontology triple structure. The ontology triples represent general knowledge *facts*, e.g., the triple {`Delaware_Park instanceOf Place`} signifies that Delaware Park is a name of a place. The triples in the query `WHERE` clause may further contain variables (e.g., `$x`), and are used to perform a selection over the ontology facts. This returns all variable bindings such that the resulting set of triples is contained in the ontology.

The `SATISFYING` clause (lines 5-12), to which we apply the previously found variable bindings, defines the data patterns (fact-sets) to be mined from the crowd. Each pattern appears in a separate subclause in curly brackets (lines 6 and 10-11). Consider, e.g., the fact-set {`[] visit $x. [] in Fall`}, where `[]` stands, intuitively, for "anything". Combined with the binding `$x` $\mapsto$ `Delaware_Park`, this fact-set corresponds to a habit of visiting Delaware Park in the fall. The system can then ask crowd members how frequently they engage in this habit, if at all. Intuitively, the *support* of a data pattern captures a habit frequency or a level of agreement to a statement, aggregated from the answers of several crowd members. In `OASSIS-QL`, one can select the patterns with the k-highest(lowest) support values, using `ORDER` and `LIMIT` (lines 7-8). Alternatively, one can set a minimal support threshold for the patterns (line 12). Note that neither the limit nor the support threshold values are specified in our example NL request. In this common scenario, the system can either use default values that are pre-configured at the system administrator level, or interact with the user to obtain them (See Section 4.1).

2.2 NL Parsing Modules

We now proceed to describe the modules of the translation framework. To parse the input user request, two standard NL tools are used: *POS (Part-Of-Speech) tagger* and *dependency graph parser*. A Part-of-Speech (POS) tagger assigns a linguistic category to every meaningful unit in a given text [8]. E.g., in the running example question, "Buffalo" is a *proper noun* and "interesting" is an *adjective*. A dependency graph parser produces a directed acyclic graph (typically, a tree), whose nodes correspond to meaningful units and its edges are labeled by semantic relationships between these units [8]. E.g., an edge labeled "subject" may connect a verb node with its grammatical subject.

The dependency graph along with the POS tags serve for higher-level data processing by the subsequent modules.

2.3 Individual Expression Detection

In order to distinguish the individual and general parts of the parsed NL request, we use an *Individual eXpression (IX) Detector*. This module identifies and extracts the individual parts from the dependency graph.

As mentioned in the Introduction, no existing tools can account for IX detection. Some previous work considers identifying expressions of sentiment or subjectivity in texts (e.g., [10]), but these expressions are only a subset of individual expressions. For instance, they do not capture individual habits such as where people visit, what they cook, etc. We thus develop a dedicated solution for IX detection, based on a general technique in NL processing, namely, pattern matching. This technique is simple and transparent (in comparison with, e.g., machine learning), and by defining the IX detection patterns in a declarative manner, allows a system administrator to easily manage, change or add the predefined set of patterns. By our analysis of user requests with individual parts, we have identified different IX patterns and classified them into the three following types.

- **Lexical individuality** stems from a term in the text. E.g., "interesting" conveys an individual opinion.
- **Participant individuality** stems from participants or agents in the text that are relative to the person addressed by the request. E.g., "you" in "Where do *you* visit in Buffalo?" is an individual participant.
- **Syntactic individuality** stems from the sentence syntax. For example, in "Obama *should* visit Buffalo", the verb auxiliary "should" denotes the speaker's opinion.

Every IX detection pattern of the above types matches a *connected subgraph* within the dependency graph (which corresponds to a set of semantically related text units). We define IX detection patterns in a SPARQL-like syntax, in terms of the POS tags; the dependency graph edges; and dedicated vocabularies. For lack of space, we will not explain here the detection pattern syntax but give an intuition about it via an example: the following simple pattern detects IXs with a verb that has an individual subject, a particular case of an individual participant.

```
$x subject $y
filter(POS($x) = "verb" && $y in V_participant)
```

Intuitively, the query above selects a verb (`$x`) which is connected by a `subject`-labeled edge to its subject (`$y`). The `filter` statement enforces that `$x` is a grammatical verb by its POS tag, and that `$y` is in the vocabulary `V_participant`, dedicated to individual participants.

More generally, individuality in NL can be very complex, and almost every expression can appear in a (non-)individual context. Thus, the IX detection patterns and vocabularies should be designed to capture expressions which appear in individual contexts with *high probability*.

2.4 General Query Generator

The different query parts should now be converted into the basic building blocks of the query. As mentioned in the Introduction, since the problem of translating NL to queries over general data has been studied in previous work (e.g., [5, 6, 7, 12]), it is preferable to reuse an existing tool for this task. Thus, we embed in the translation framework an off-the-shelf General Query Generator for processing the general parts of the query, i.e., the parts of the dependency graph which were not identified as IXs. In the particular case of translation to OASSIS-QL, the syntax of the general query parts is based on SPARQL, and thus a SPARQL Query Generator such as [5] can be used. From the Generator's output, we can extract the SPARQL triples that will form the WHERE part of the target OASSIS-QL query. The crux in reusing an existing Query Generator lies in having it translate *only the general request parts* rather than the full request. The way to resolve this issue may depend on the choice of Query Generator. The particular solution used in our implementation is described in Section 3.

2.5 Individual Query Parts Creation

While the general parts of the query are translated by a General Query Generator, translating the IXs is done by a new module. Unlike the Query Generator, this module cannot rely on aligning the request parts to the ontology, since these parts do not correspond to an ontology. Instead, a mapping is defined from certain grammatical patterns within the IXs into query parts, according to the syntax of the query language. In the case of OASSIS-QL they are mapped to query triples. For example, consider the IX "places we should visit", which corresponds to a subgraph where "we" and "places" are, respectively, the subject and object of "visit". A mapping would then generate the triple {[] visit $x}, where $x corresponds to "places"; and [] corresponds to "we", meaning that this individual participant is projected out, which is necessary for aggregating the answers of different crowd members about the same habit.[2]

2.6 Query Composition

The last module of the architecture combines the generated individual query parts with the general query parts, created by the Query Generator. In the case of OASSIS-QL, forming the query mainly means creating the subclauses of the SATISFYING clause, aligning the variables of the WHERE and SATISFYING clause, and creating the SELECT clause. Intuitively, the subclause creation phase ensures that every subclause defines a data pattern to be mined from the crowd that corresponds to a single event or property. For example, the visit of Buffalo, in our running example, is described as occurring in the fall and thus their corresponding triples are put in the same subclause (lines 10-11 in Figure 1). For each subclause, either a support threshold or a top/bottom-k support selection is defined. The alignment of variables is done such that every reference to a particular term in the original sentence is represented by an occurrence of the same variable. By default, the generated SELECT clause is simple and does not project out any variables (as in Figure 1), which means that the query returns bindings to all the variables. In Section 4.1 we discuss interacting with the user to determine which variables should be projected out.

3. IMPLEMENTATION DETAILS

To complete the picture, we now provide the details of the implementation of NL_2CM. The main system modules are depicted top-down in Figure 2 according to the formerly described architecture. In this Figure, the modules and data repositories painted black are new.

[2]"should" does not appear in the query, since it is implied by the fact the SATISFYING clause handles individual data.

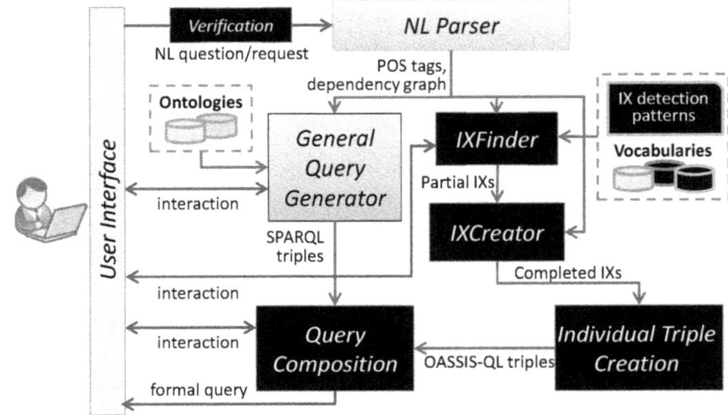

Figure 2: System Architecture

NL_2CM is implemented in Java 7, and its graphical user interface is web-based, and written in PHP 5.3 using jQuery 1.x. Users can write their questions/requests as free text in a text field (see Figure 3). The text then undergoes a basic verification process, which checks for certain types of questions/requests that are not supported by the system. In our case, one common example is *descriptive questions* such as "How to...?" "Why...?" "For what purpose...?", whose answer semantics is not supported by OASSIS-QL. In the case that NL_2CM detects an unsupported question, it displays an adequate warning to the user along with a link to an explanation and tips how to rephrase the question.

The questions that pass the verification step are sent to the NL parsing modules. In NL_2CM, we use the Stanford Parser [8] to obtain both the dependency graph representation and POS tags of the input request, that are passed on the subsequent modules (See Section 2.2).

Our newly developed IX Detector is split in Figure 2 into two components: the *IXFinder* uses vocabularies and a set of predefined patterns in order to find IXs within the dependency graph, as described in Section 2.3. We use a dedicated vocabulary for each type of IX pattern: for *lexical* individuality, we use the Opinion Lexicon [3], which contains expressions of sentiment or subjectivity. For the other types we use vocabularies of our own making (hence, some of the vocabularies in Figure 2 are painted black). The second module, the *IXCreator*, is responsible for completing the subgraphs representing the IXs. For example, if some verb is found to have an individual subject, this component further retrieves other parts belonging to the same semantic unit, e.g., the verb's objects.

The Query Generator is responsible for translating the general query parts into SPARQL triples. For that, NL_2CM employs the FREyA system [5] as a black-box module. Since FREyA only accepts full sentences as an input, NL_2CM feeds it with the dependency graph and POS tags of the original user request, *including the IXs*. Some of the IXs may be wrongly matched by FREyA to the ontology and translated into general query triples. To overcome this problem, the Query Composition module later deletes generated SPARQL triples that correspond to detected IXs.

The Individual Triple Creation module receives the IXs, and converts them, in this case, into OASSIS-QL triples, as described in Section 2.5. These triples are then composed

[3]http://www.cs.uic.edu/ liub/FBS/sentiment-analysis.html

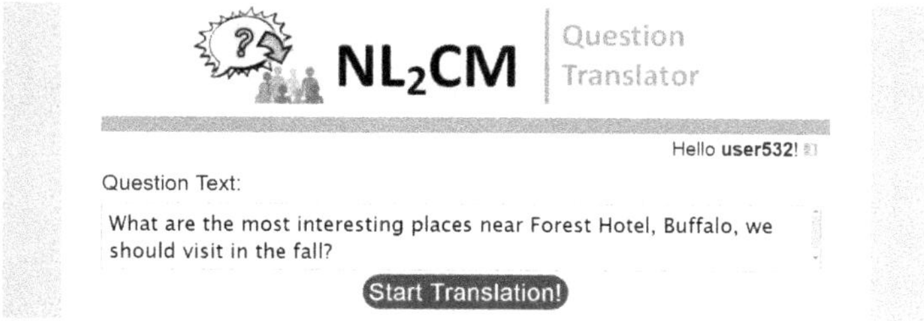

Figure 3: Enter NL question (UI screenshot)

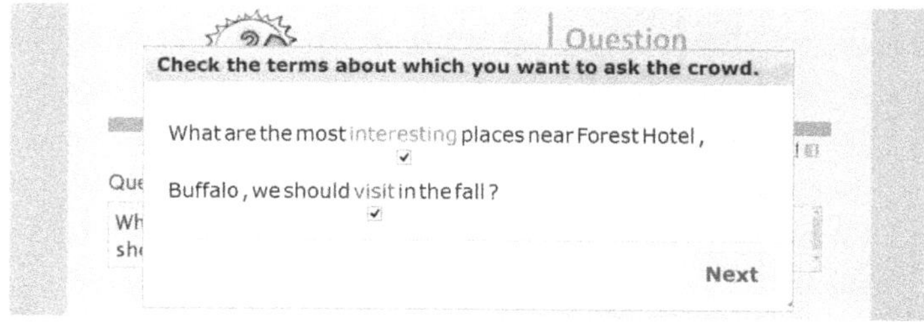

Figure 4: Verify the IXs (UI screenshot)

with the generated SPARQL triples into a well-formed query by the Query Creation module, as described in Section 2.6.

The UI of NL$_2$CM allows manually editing the output query (Figure 6). For convenience, the design of NL$_2$CM allows connecting it directly to OASSIS, the OASSIS-QL evaluation platform. This further enables the user to submit the query via the NL$_2$CM UI to be executed with the crowd, track the progress of the evaluation process through OASSIS's UI, etc.

4. DEMONSTRATION

The usage of NL$_2$CM includes optional interaction with the users. Next, we describe this interaction, and then give the full details about the interactive demonstration scenario.

4.1 User Interaction

Our user studies show that the quality of our developed translation is high for real user questions even without interacting with the user. Yet, user interaction may still be useful (i) for manually adjusting certain query parameters instead of using default values; and (ii) in cases of input questions that are ambiguous or vague. Thus, as depicted in Figure 2, some of the translation framework modules may interact with the user via the UI of NL$_2$CM. The optional points of interaction are exemplified in Figures 3-6, for the running example question. To minimize the user effort, the system may be configured to always skip certain interaction points, or skip them when there is no uncertainty.

Figure 4 depicts the first possible point of interaction with the user in NL$_2$CM, by the IX Detection module. An IX detection pattern can be marked as "uncertain", in which case the IX Detector asks the user to verify IXs detected by this pattern. For that, the uncertain individual parts are highlighted (each by a different color), and the user can check the parts about which the crowd should be asked. (For the sake of the example, in Figure 4 we have marked all the IX detection patterns as uncertain.)

The General Query Generator may also interact with the user to align ambiguous NL terms with the ontology concepts. This kind of interaction is already employed by FREyA, and we have thus plugged it into the UI of NL$_2$CM. For example, FREyA can ask the user whether "Buffalo" refers to Buffalo, NY, USA, to Buffalo, IL, USA, or to other entities in the ontology that are named Buffalo. The response of the user is recorded and serves to improve the ranking of optional entities in subsequent user interactions with the system [5].

Next, the Query Composition module may interact with the user to complete missing details that are required for composing the query. As noted in Section 2.1, user questions rarely contain explicit values which can be used in the LIMIT or THRESHOLD expressions of an OASSIS-QL query.[4] In other cases, the system may either use default values or ask the user to specify the missing values. In Figure 5, the user is asked to specify the value of k for the top-k query over interesting places, which sets the value of the LIMIT expression in the query $\mathcal{Q}$ in Figure 1, line 8. The user is also asked to select the minimal frequency of the "visit in the fall" event, which is translated to a threshold between 0 and 1, and can be plugged into the THRESHOLD expression in line 12 of $\mathcal{Q}$.

Last, by default, the SELECT clause does not project out any variables. In the running example question this makes sense, since the only variable in $\mathcal{Q}$ corresponds to "places", and the relevant places are indeed the answer to the original question. However, consider the variation "What are the most interesting places ... we should visit *with a tour guide*?". The user may or may not want to get, along with each place, the name of the tour guide that recommends it. Moreover, if we replace "a tour guide" with "locals", the user is probably not interested in specific names of locals with whom to visit Buffalo. Thus, the system can ask the users for which terms, out of the terms that correspond to query variables, they want to receive instances (variable bindings). After this last interaction with the user, the final query is composed and displayed (Figure 6).

4.2 Full Demonstration Scenario

To introduce NL$_2$CM to the conference participants, we will demonstrate its translation of NL questions to OASSIS-QL, its interaction with the users, and the execution of the resulting queries by the OASSIS engine. The demonstration will be split into three parts: (i) translating real-life NL questions collected from web forums; (ii) translating NL questions from the audience members; and (iii) observing the feedback of the system about questions that could not be directly translated. We will use three monitors, for the NL$_2$CM interactive UI, for the OASSIS crowd UI, and for the NL$_2$CM administrator mode, which will provide the audience a peek "under the hood" of the system. The system will use the publicly available general data ontologies LinkedGeoData and DBPedia.[5]

For the first step of the demonstration, we have collected a set of example questions that were originally posted on the question-and answer platforms Yahoo! Answers [11]. These questions concern various topics, including travel ("Which hotel in Vegas has the best thrill ride?"), shopping ("What type of digital camera should I buy?"), health ("Is chocolate milk good for kids?"), and others. We will ask the audience

[4]Note, however, that similar values are likely to be required by other query languages.

[5]http://dbpedia.org/About

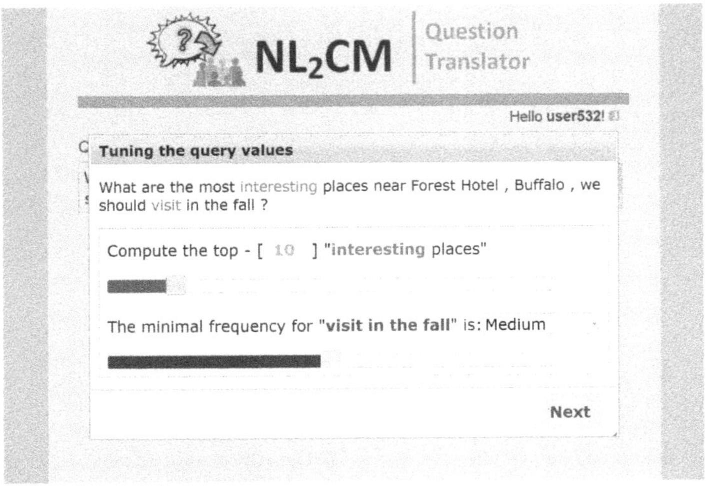

Figure 5: Select the LIMIT value (UI screenshot)

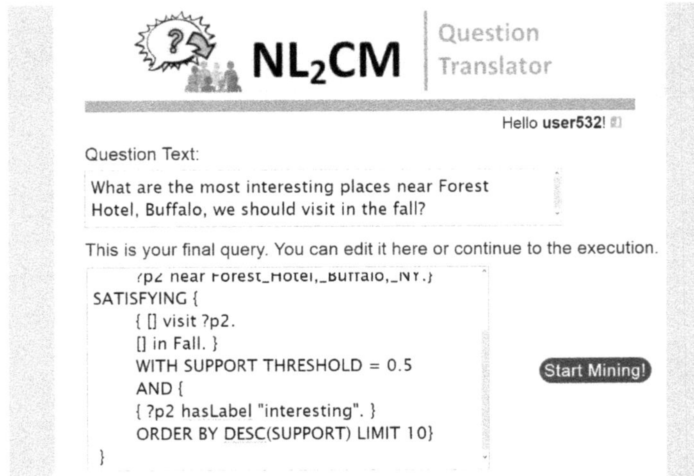

Figure 6: Final query (UI screenshot)

to choose a topic of interest, and then feed a sample question about this topic to NL$_2$CM. Then, we will demonstrate the translation process and inspect the generated query; this will give us a better understanding of the query structure and the mapping performed by system. To gain further intuition about the query semantics, we will instruct the system to feed some of the generated queries into OASSIS and, via the second monitor, view the tasks that are generated to the crowd by the query engine.

In the second step, we will invite volunteers to write questions of their own and feed them to the system. If a question does not pass the verification step, the system will point out to the user where the difficulty occurred, as well as provide tips on how to rephrase the question, where possible. Otherwise, our volunteer users will be able to interact with the system, verify the detected IX or provide additional information that is necessary for composing the query (as shown for the running example question in Figures 3-6), and will finally observe the resulting OASSIS-QL queries.

To complete the picture, in the case that all the questions in the previous stage passed the verification, we will give a few examples for real-life questions from Yahoo! Answers that do not pass the verification. We will explain what is the reason that certain types of question are not supported, and show the tips NL$_2$CM provides for rephrasing them. For instance, "How should I store coffee?" is a descriptive question which is not supported, but the similar question "*At what container* should I store coffee?" is supported (and for this example, may capture the original user's intention just as well).

While the volunteer users interact with NL$_2$CM, we will also turn the attention of the audience to the administrator mode monitor, which will display the intermediate outputs passed between the NL$_2$CM modules. We will be able to observe the structure and content of these outputs, and gain additional intuition about the operation of the system.

Acknowledgements. This work has been partially funded by the European Research Council under the FP7, ERC grant MoDaS, agreement 291071 and by the Israel Ministry of Science.

5. REFERENCES

[1] A. Amarilli, Y. Amsterdamer, and T. Milo. On the complexity of mining itemsets from the crowd using taxonomies. In *ICDT*, 2014.

[2] Y. Amsterdamer, S. B. Davidson, T. Milo, S. Novgorodov, and A. Somech. OASSIS: query driven crowd mining. In *SIGMOD*, 2014.

[3] A. Bozzon, M. Brambilla, S. Ceri, and A. Mauri. Reactive crowdsourcing. In *WWW*, 2013.

[4] V. Crescenzi, P. Merialdo, and D. Qiu. A framework for learning web wrappers from the crowd. In *WWW*, 2013.

[5] D. Damljanovic, M. Agatonovic, H. Cunningham, and K. Bontcheva. Improving habitability of NL interfaces for querying ontologies with feedback and clarification dialogues. *J. Web Sem.*, 19, 2013.

[6] F. Li and H. V. Jagadish. Constructing an interactive natural language interface for relational databases. *PVLDB*, 8(1), 2014.

[7] Y. Li, H. Yang, and H. V. Jagadish. NaLIX: A generic natural language search environment for XML data. *ACM Trans. DB Syst.*, 32(4), 2007.

[8] M. D. Marneffe, B. Maccartney, and C. D. Manning. Generating typed dependency parses from phrase structure parses. In *LREC*, 2006.

[9] A. D. Sarma, A. Parameswaran, H. Garcia-Molina, and A. Halevy. Crowd-powered find algorithms. In *ICDE*, 2014.

[10] Stanford Sentiment Analysis tool. http://nlp.stanford.edu/sentiment.

[11] Yahoo! webscope dataset ydata-yanswers-all-questions-v1_0. http://research.yahoo.com/Academic_Relations.

[12] M. Yahya, K. Berberich, S. Elbassuoni, M. Ramanath, V. Tresp, and G. Weikum. Deep answers for naturally asked questions on the web of data. In *WWW*, 2012.

[13] C. Zhang, Z. Zhao, L. Chen, H. V. Jagadish, and C. Cao. CrowdMatcher: crowd-assisted schema matching. In *SIGMOD*, 2014.

[14] L. Zhang, D. V. Kalashnikov, and S. Mehrotra. Context-assisted face clustering framework with human-in-the-loop. *IJMIR*, 3(2), 2014.

Optimistic Recovery for Iterative Dataflows in Action

Sergey Dudoladov[1], Chen Xu[1], Sebastian Schelter[1], Asterios Katsifodimos[1], Stephan Ewen[2], Kostas Tzoumas[2], Volker Markl[1]
[1]Technische Universität Berlin
firstname.lastname@tu-berlin.de
[2]Data Artisans GmbH
firstname@data-artisans.com

ABSTRACT

Over the past years, parallel dataflow systems have been employed for advanced analytics in the field of data mining where many algorithms are iterative.

These systems typically provide fault tolerance by periodically checkpointing the algorithm's state and, in case of failure, restoring a consistent state from a checkpoint.

In prior work, we presented an optimistic recovery mechanism that in certain cases eliminates the need to checkpoint the intermediate state of an iterative algorithm. In case of failure, our mechanism uses a *compensation function* to transit the algorithm to a consistent state, from which the execution can continue and successfully converge. Since this recovery mechanism does not checkpoint any state, it achieves optimal failure-free performance while guaranteeing fault tolerance.

In this paper, we demonstrate our recovery mechanism with the Apache Flink data processing engine. During our demonstration, attendees will be able to run graph algorithms and trigger failures to observe the algorithms recovering with compensation functions instead of checkpoints.

Categories and Subject Descriptors

H.2.4 [**Database Management**]: Parallel databases

Keywords

Iterative Algorithms; Fault-Tolerance; Optimistic Recovery

1. INTRODUCTION

In recent years, the growing demand for large-scale data analysis has led to the development of new data-parallel computing platforms like MapReduce [6], SCOPE [5], Apache Flink [1] and Apache Spark [15]. Such platforms on a day-to-day basis execute a variety of data mining tasks ranging from simple grep-style log analysis to complex machine learning algorithms.

[1]Apache Flink originated from the Stratosphere research project [1]. See `https://flink.apache.org`

SIGMOD'15, May 31–June 4, 2015, Melbourne, Victoria, Australia.

http://dx.doi.org/10.1145/2723372.2735372.

An important primitive present in many machine learning algorithms is *iteration* (or recursion). Iteration repeats a certain computation until a termination condition is met. The need for efficient execution of iterative algorithms spawned the development of specialized systems [10, 11] as well as integration of iterations into existing dataflow systems [3, 8].

Iterative dataflow computations are often deployed in large clusters of commodity machines, where failures are common. This makes a dataflow system's ability to deal with failures important. The usual approach to fault tolerance is to periodically checkpoint the algorithm state to stable storage. Upon failure, the system restores the state from a checkpoint and continues the algorithm's execution. This method is often referred to as *rollback recovery* [7].

This pessimistic approach works well if failures happen regularly. However, real-world use cases indicate that many computations do not run for such a long time or on so many nodes that failures become commonplace [17]. In the case of less frequent failures checkpoints may unnecessarily increase the latency of a computation [16]. Since one still needs to protect against failures, other approaches to recovery may be worth investigating.

In prior work [14], we exploited the convergence properties of certain classes of iterative algorithms to provide an optimistic recovery mechanism. Instead of restoring the lost state from a checkpoint, our mechanism restores the lost state through a *compensation function*. This user-supplied function generates a consistent algorithm state, and the algorithm then resumes execution converging to a correct result as if no failures had occurred.

In this paper, we demonstrate this recovery technique using Apache Flink as a testbed. To exemplify how iterative computations can recover without checkpoints, we employ the Connected Components and PageRank algorithms: Schelter et al. [14] have previously shown them to converge after recovery with compensation functions. We implement a graphical user interface (GUI) with which conference attendees will be able to choose Flink tasks to fail during the algorithms' execution. The failures lead to the partial loss of intermediate results; attendees can observe how compensation functions restore the lost state and how the algorithms converge afterwards.

2. BACKGROUND

Section 2.1 introduces the Apache Flink data processing engine and describes its support for efficient execution of iterative algorithms. Section 2.2 discusses the optimistic recovery of iterative computations with compensation functions.

2.1 Apache Flink

Because of the suboptimal performance when executing complex dataflows and iterative computations [2], the MapReduce computational model has been extended by newly emerging dataflow systems [1, 2, 3, 15, 12]. These systems typically represent a program as a directed acyclic graph (DAG). In such a graph, vertices represent individual tasks running user-defined functions (UDFs) and edges represent data exchanges among vertices. The systems explicitly provide mechanisms for efficient execution of iterative computations in a distributed manner [8, 3, 15, 12].

We build upon Apache Flink, which extends the MapReduce paradigm with several higher-order functions such as *Join* (for applying a UDF to the result of an equi-join between two datasets) or *Cross* (for applying a UDF to the cross product of two datasets). A user expresses a data analysis program in terms of these functions and UDFs using the high-level language API. Flink then compiles the program into a DAG of operators, optimizes it and runs in a cluster. Flink allows the user to mark a part of the DAG as iterative. The system then repeatedly executes that part of the DAG by forwarding the output of its last operator to its first operator. The execution finishes when either a predefined number of iterations has been run or a user-supplied termination criterion is met [8].

Flink provides two ways to execute iterative parts of a DAG: bulk iterations and delta iterations. *Bulk iterations* always recompute intermediate result of an iteration as a whole. However, in many cases parts of the intermediate state converge at different speeds, e.g. in single-source shortest path computations in large graphs. In such cases, the system would waste resources by always recomputing the whole intermediate state, including the parts that do not change anymore. To alleviate this issue, Flink offers *delta iterations*. This mode models an iterative computation with two datasets: the *solution set* holds the current intermediate result, while the *working set* holds updates to the solution set. During a delta iteration the system consumes the working set, selectively updates elements of the solution set, and computes the next working set from the updates. The delta iteration terminates once the working set becomes empty.

2.2 Optimistic Recovery

To execute algorithms on massive datasets in a distributed manner, algorithms' intermediate results must be partitioned among machines. Failures cause the loss of a subset of these partitions; to continue execution, the system has to restore the lost data first. Rollback recovery is a popular method to ensure fault tolerance [7]. The idea is to periodically checkpoint the algorithm state to stable storage. Upon failure, the system halts execution, restores a consistent state from a previously written checkpoint and resumes execution. This approach has the drawback that it always incurs overhead to the execution, even in failure-free cases. An alternative is lineage-based recovery [15], which retains lineage, i.e. information about how a partition was derived. After a failure, lineage allows the system to recompute the lost partitions only. Unfortunately, lineage-based recovery does not perform well for many iterative computations, because a partition of the current iteration may depend on all partitions of the previous iteration (e.g. when a reducer is run during an iteration). In such cases after a failure the iteration has to be restarted from scratch to re-compute lost partitions.

In previous work [14], we proposed to exploit the robust nature of a large class of fixpoint algorithms for an optimistic recovery mechanism. These algorithms can converge to the correct solutions from many intermediate states, not only from the one checkpointed before the failure. We introduce a user-defined *compensation function* which a system uses to re-initialize lost partitions. This function restores a consistent state from which an algorithm can converge. For example, if the algorithm computes a probability distribution, the compensation function has to ensure that probabilities in all partitions sum up to one.

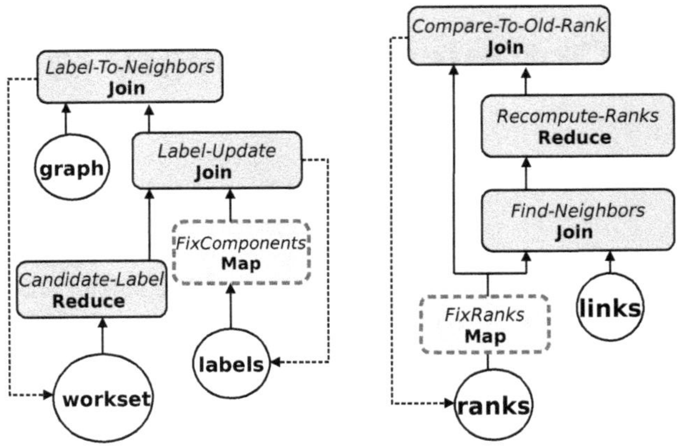

(a) Connected Components. (b) PageRank.

Figure 1: Dataflows with compensations.

Failure-free execution proceeds as if no fault tolerance is needed: the system neither checkpoints intermediate state nor it tracks the lineage. Therefore, this approach provides optimal failure-free performance. When a failure occurs, the system pauses the current iteration ignoring the failed tasks and re-assigns the lost computations to newly acquired nodes. After that, the system invokes the compensation function on all partitions to restore a consistent state and resumes the execution. Essentially, the compensation function brings the computation "back on track": the function and subsequent iterations correct errors introduced by the data loss.

To illustrate our approach, we describe how to optimistically recover two well-known fixpoint algorithms, namely Connected Components and PageRank, via a compensation function.

2.2.1 Recovering Connected Components

The Connected Components algorithm identifies connected components of an undirected graph, i.e. maximum cardinality sets of vertices that can reach each other. We use the diffusion-based algorithm that propagates the minimum label of each component through a graph [9]. Figure 1(a) shows the conceptual Flink dataflow for finding connected components[2] with delta iterations. Initially, we assign a unique label to each vertex (c.f. the 'labels' input which also serves as the solution set). The workset consists of all vertices that updated their labels during the previous iteration; it initially equals to the 'labels' input. The 'graph' dataset contains the edges of a graph. At every iteration,for every vertex we compute the minimum label of its neighbors from the workset via the 'candidate-label' reduce. Next, we compare the resulting candidate labels to the current labels from the solution set in the 'label-update' join. If the candidate label is smaller than the current label, we update the solution set and forward the new label to the 'label-to-neighbors' join. This join computes the workset for the next iteration, which consists of the updated labels and the neighboring vertices of a vertex that was updated. The algorithm converges when there are no more label updates. At convergence, all vertices in a connected component share the same label, namely the minimum of the initial labels of vertices in this component.

[2]Blue rectangles denote operators, white circles denote data sources and brown rectangles denote compensation functions. The dotted line around the functions signifies that they are invoked only after failures and are absent from the dataflow otherwise.

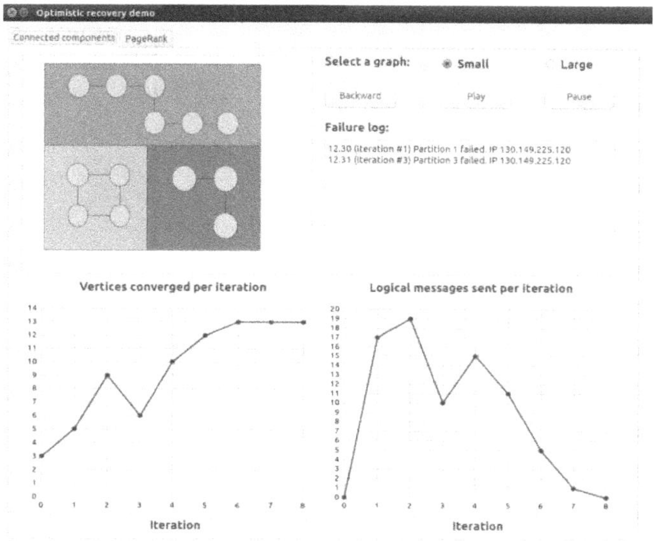

Figure 2: GUI for demonstrating optimistic recovery of the Connected Components algorithm.

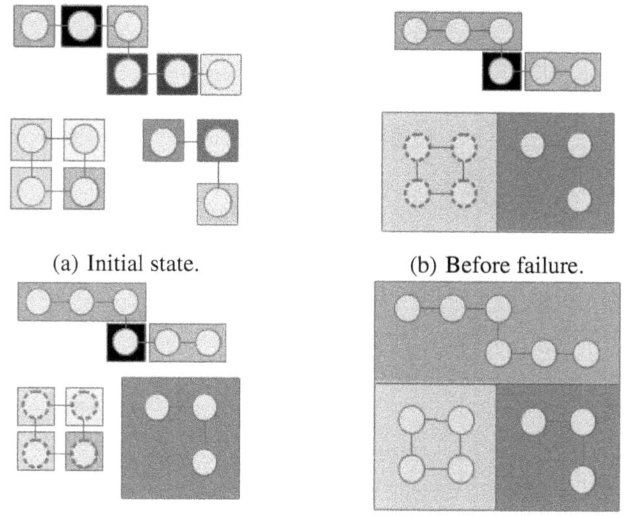

(a) Initial state. (b) Before failure. (c) After compensation. (d) Converged state.

Figure 3: Connected Components algorithm convergence.

Compensation function for Connected Components: Failures during the course of the algorithm destroy computed labels for a subset of vertices. Simply re-initializing lost vertices to their initial labels guarantees convergence to the correct solution [14]. The 'fix-components' map executes this compensation function in the dataflow illustrated in Figure 1(a).

2.2.2 *Recovering PageRank*

PageRank is a well-known algorithm for ranking the vertices of a large network by importance with respect to its link structure [13]. The algorithm works by computing the steady-state probabilities of a random walk on the network. Figure 1(b) illustrates the dataflow for modeling PageRank with a Flink bulk iteration. The input consists of the initial vertices' ranks (c.f. the 'ranks' dataset) and the edges with transition probabilities (c.f. the 'links' dataset). During a PageRank iteration, every vertex propagates a fraction of its rank to its neighbors via the 'find-neighbors' join. Next, we re-compute the rank of each vertex from the contributions of its neighbors in the 'recompute-ranks' reduce. At the end of each iteration, we compare the old and new ranks of every vertex to check for convergence (c.f. the 'compare-to-old-rank' join).

Compensation function for PageRank: Losing partitions during the execution of PageRank means that we lose the current ranks of the vertices contained in the failed partitions. As long as all ranks sum up to one, the algorithm will converge to the correct solution [14]. Therefore, it is sufficient to uniformly redistribute the lost probability mass to the vertices in the failed partitions. The 'fix-ranks' map in Figure 1(b) takes care of this.

3. DEMONSTRATION

Section 3.1 introduces the demo infrastructure. Sections 3.2 and 3.3 describe the demonstration scenario and visualization of the failure-recovery process for the Connected Components and PageRank, respectively.

3.1 Setup

The demo setup comprises a laptop and a graphical user interface (GUI). Figures 2 and 4 depict the user interface. By switching the tabs at the top of the interface, users can choose PageRank, if they want to watch the recovery of bulk iterations, or Connected Components, if they want to watch the recovery of delta iterations. Next, attendees pick the input to the chosen algorithm: either a small hand-crafted graph or a larger graph derived from real-world data. Running the demo on the small graph makes it easy to comprehend visually; we slow down the small graph demo so that demo visitors can easily trace each iteration. For the larger graph, we use a publicly available snapshot[3] of the Twitter's social network [4]. We only visualize the small hand-crafted graph in the GUI; for the larger graph, the attendees can track the demo progress only via plots of statistics of the algorithms' execution.

Once the parameters are set, the user presses the "play" button to run the demo. The system then executes the algorithm and visualizes results of each iteration. The "backward" button jumps to the previous iteration; the "pause" button stops the demo at the end of the current iteration. The progression of algorithms on the small graphs is visualized: after an iteration finishes, the interface depicts connected components or page ranks as given by the intermediate results calculated at this iteration.

Conference attendees will be able to choose which partitions to fail and in which iterations via our GUI. The demo tracks such failures and applies the relevant compensation function to restore the lost partitions.

3.2 Connected Components

Figure 2 illustrates the GUI for demonstrating the recovery of Connected Components. Attendees will observe the following demo behavior on the small graph: a distinct color highlights the area enclosing each connected component. Initially, the area around every vertex has a distinct color, as every vertex starts out in its own component (Figure 3(a)). When an iteration finishes, the vertices that changed labels in this iteration are redrawn with a new enclosing color. The new color indicates that the vertices form a new intermediate component. The color comes from the

[3] http://twitter.mpi-sws.org/data-icwsm2010.html

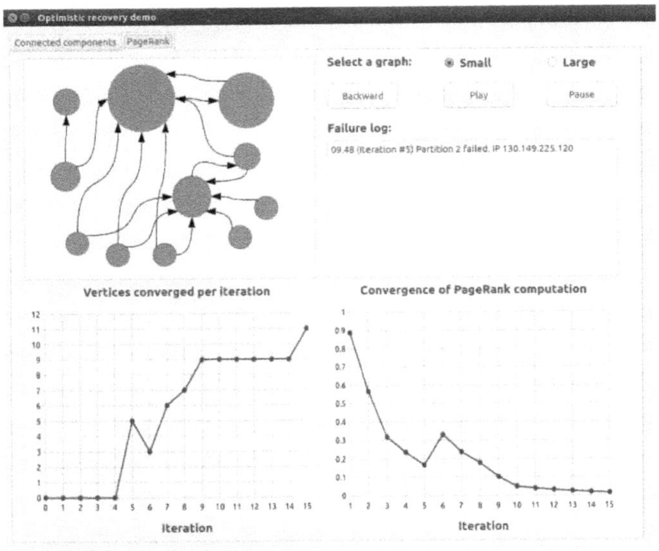

Figure 4: GUI for demonstrating optimistic recovery of the PageRank algorithm.

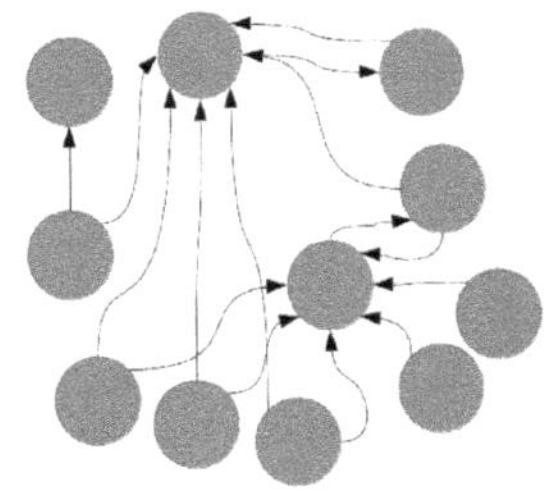

(a) Initial state.

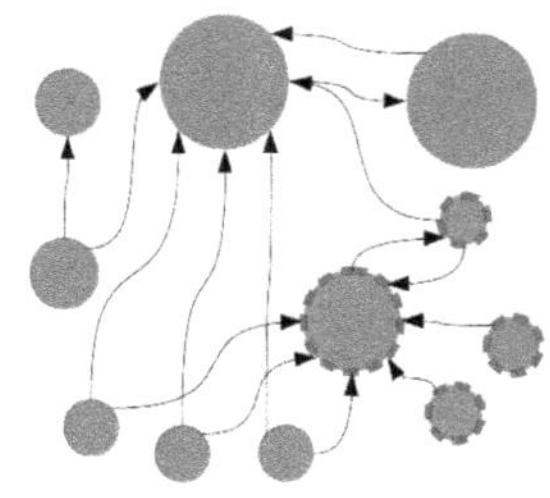

(b) Before failure.

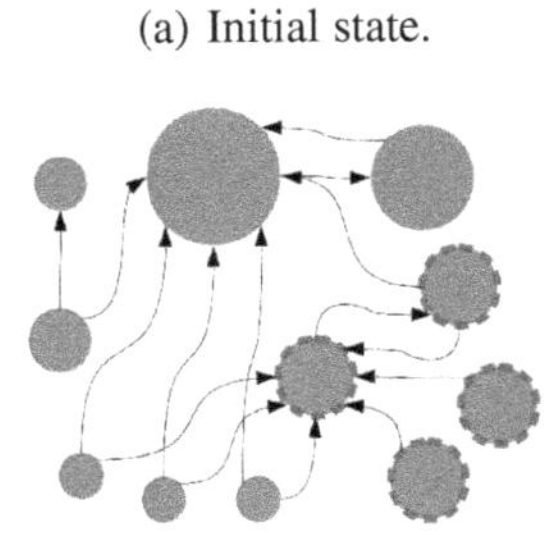

(c) After compensation.

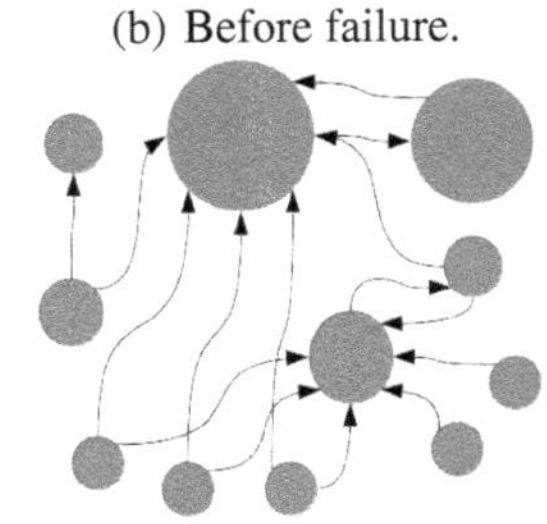

(d) Converged state.

Figure 5: PageRank algorithm convergence.

vertex from which the (updated) vertices accepted their new minimum labels. During the execution, areas of the same color grow as the algorithm discovers larger and larger parts of the connected components. The number of colors decreases; by that attendees can track the convergence of the algorithm. In case of a failure, our GUI highlights the lost vertices (Figure 3(b)), and the compensation function restores them to their initial state (Figure 3(c)). In the end, the algorithm converges and the number of distinct colors equals the number of connected components: the same color encloses all vertices in the same component (Figure 3(d)).

The demo GUI in Figure 2 shows (i) the number of vertices converged to their final connected components [4] at each iteration and (ii) the number of messages (candidate labels send to neighbors) per iteration. The GUI bottom left corner contains the first plot: note the plummet at the third iteration corresponding to the detected failure. Attendees can expect to see similar plummets each time a failure causes a loss of a partition with already converged vertices. The plot at the bottom right corner illustrates the messages sent per iteration. The increased amount of messages at iterations 2 and 4 corresponds to the effort to recover from failures in previous iterations. The system processes more messages compared with a failure-free case, because the vertices restored to their initial labels by the compensation function (as well as their neighbors) have to propagate their labels again.

3.3 PageRank

Figure 4 illustrates the GUI for visualizing the recovery of PageRank. We make the size of a vertex represent the magnitude of its PageRank value: the higher the rank, the larger the vertex. PageRank starts from a uniform rank distribution: all the vertices are of the same size in the beginning (Figure 5(a)). At the end of each iteration, we rescale each vertex proportionally to its recomputed rank. Thus, attendees can watch the convergence of the algorithm: vertices grow and shrink and over time reach their final size, meaning that they converged to their true rank. In the case of a failure, we lose the ranks of the vertices contained in the failing partition. The GUI highlights those vertices (Figure 5(b)), and the compensation function restores their ranks by uniformly distributing the lost probability mass over them (Figure 5(c)). In the end, the vertices converge to their true ranks, irrespective of the compensation (Figure 5(d)).

Analogously to Connected Components, our GUI from Figure 4 plots several statistics collected during the execution: (i) the number of vertices converged to their true PageRank at each iteration and (ii) the convergence behavior of PageRank. The bottom left corner of the GUI shows the first plot. A loss of partitions with converged vertices corresponds to the plummet in the plot in the iteration 6 after the failure in the iteration 5. The second plot (bottom right corner) shows the L1-norm of the difference between the current estimate of the PageRank vector and the estimate from the previous iteration. Over the course of the algorithm, the difference between the estimates at each pair of consecutive iterations becomes smaller and smaller because of the convergence. Hence the downward trend in the plot. Failures appear as spikes in the plot (iteration 6), because the ranks computed during a failure-free iteration are to be closer to the estimates obtained in the previous iteration than the rescaled ranks compensated after failures. Hence, we can expect to observe an increase in the difference after an iteration with failures.

[4]We precompute the true values for presentation reasons.

4. ACKNOWLEDGMENTS

The authors would like to acknowledge the invaluable help of Mingliang Qi in developing the GUI of this demonstration. This work has been supported through grants by the German Science Foundation (DFG) as FOR 1306 Stratosphere, by the German Ministry for Education and Research as Berlin Big Data Center BBDC (funding mark 01IS14013A) and by the EIT ICT Labs as EUROPA 2014 EITs Cloud-Based Data project (activity code 12115).

5. REFERENCES

[1] A. Alexandrov, R. Bergmann, S. Ewen, J. C. Freytag, F. Hueske, A. Heise, O. Kao, M. Leich, U. Leser, V. Markl, F. Naumann, M. Peters, A. Rheinländer, M. J. Sax, S. Schelter, M. Höger, K. Tzoumas, and D. Warneke. The Stratosphere platform for big data analytics. *The VLDB Journal'14*, pp. 939–964.

[2] S. Babu and H. Herodotou. Massively Parallel Databases and MapReduce Systems. *Foundations and Trends in Databases'12*, 5(1):1–104.

[3] Y. Bu, B. Howe, M. Balazinska, and M. D. Ernst. HaLoop: Efficient Iterative Data Processing on Large Clusters. *VLDB'10*, pp. 285–296.

[4] M. Cha, H. Haddadi, and K. P. Gummadi. Measuring User Influence in Twitter: The Million Follower Fallacy. *ICWSM'10*, pp. 10–17.

[5] R. Chaiken, B. Jenkins, P. Larson, B. Ramsey, D. Shakib, S. Weaver, and J. Zhou. SCOPE: Easy and Efficient Parallel Processing of Massive Data Sets. *PVLDB'08*, pp. 1265–1276.

[6] J. Dean and S. Ghemawat. MapReduce: Simplified Data Processing on Large Clusters. *Communications of the ACM* '08, 51(1):107–113.

[7] E. N. M. Elnozahy, L. Alvisi, Y.-M. Wang, and D. B. Johnson. A Survey of Rollback-Recovery Protocols in Message-Passing Systems. *ACM Computing Survey'02*, 34(3):375–408.

[8] S. Ewen, K. Tzoumas, M. Kaufmann, and V. Markl. Spinning Fast Iterative Data Flows. *PVLDB'12*, 5(11):1268–1279.

[9] U. Kang, C. E. Tsourakakis, and C. Faloutsos. PEGASUS: A Peta-Scale Graph Mining System Implementation and Observations. *ICDM'09*, pp. 229–238.

[10] Y. Low, D. Bickson, J. Gonzalez, C. Guestrin, A. Kyrola, and J. M. Hellerstein. Distributed GraphLab: A framework for machine learning and data mining in the cloud. *VLDB'12*, pp. 716–727.

[11] G. Malewicz, M. H. Austern, A. J. Bik, J. C. Dehnert, I. Horn, N. Leiser, and G. Czajkowski. Pregel: a system for large-scale graph processing. *SIGMOD'10*, pp. 135–146.

[12] D. G. Murray, F. Mcsherry, R. Isaacs, M. Isard, P. Barham, and S. Valley. Naiad: A Timely Dataflow System. *SOSP '13*, pp. 439–455, 2013.

[13] L. Page, S. Brin, R. Motwani, and T. Winograd. The PageRank Citation Ranking: Bringing Order to the Web. *Stanford Infolab'98*, pp. 1–17.

[14] S. Schelter, S. Ewen, K. Tzoumas, and V. Markl. "All Roads Lead to Rome:" Optimistic Recovery for Distributed Iterative Data Processing. *CIKM'13*, pp. 1919–1928.

[15] M. Zaharia, M. Chowdhury, M. J. Franklin, S. Shenker, and I. Stoica. Spark: Cluster Computing with Working Sets. *HotCloud'10*, pp. 1–7.

[16] P. Upadhyaya, Y. Kwon, and M. Balazinska. A Latency and Fault-Tolerance Optimizer for Online Parallel Query Plans. *Proceedings of the 2011 International Conference on Management of Data - SIGMOD '11*.

[17] Y. Chen, S. Alspaugh, and R. Katz. Interactive Analytical Processing in Big Data Systems: A Cross-industry Study of MapReduce Workloads. *Proceedings of the 2012 VLDB Endowment*, pp. 1802–1813.

A Secure Search Engine for the Personal Cloud

Saliha Lallali [1,2] Nicolas Anciaux [1,2] Iulian Sandu Popa [1,2] Philippe Pucheral [1,2]

[1]INRIA Rocquencourt
78153 Le Chenay Cedex, France
FisrtName.LastName@inria.fr

[2]Université de Versailles Saint-Quentin en Yvelines
78035 Versailles Cedex, France
FirstName.LastName@uvsq.fr

ABSTRACT

The emerging Personal Could paradigm holds the promise of a Privacy-by-Design storage and computing platform where personal data remain under the individual's control while being shared by valuable applications. However, leaving the data management control to user's hands pushes the security issues to the user's platform. This demonstration presents a Secure Personal Cloud Platform relying on a query and access control engine embedded in a tamper resistant hardware device connected to the user's platform. The main difficulty lies in the design of an inverted document index and its related search and update algorithms capable of tackling the strong hardware constraints of these devices. We have implemented our engine on a real tamper resistant hardware device and present its capacity to regulate the access to a personal dataspace. The objective of this demonstration is to show (1) that secure hardware is a key enabler of the Personal Cloud paradigm and (2) that new embedded indexing and querying techniques can tackle the hardware constraints of tamper-resistant devices and provide scalable solutions for the Personal Cloud.

Categories and Subject Descriptors

E.2 [**Data Storage Representations**]: Composite structures; H.3.3 [**Information Search and Retrieval**]: Search process; H.3.1 [**Content Analysis and Indexing**]: Dictionaries, Indexing methods.

Keywords

Embedded Search Engine, Access Control, Personal Cloud.

1. INTRODUCTION

We are witnessing an exponential increase in the acquisition of personal data by administrations and companies, and by the individuals themselves e.g., through quantified-self devices [1, 10]. In fine, all this data ends up in servers where it remains organized in *silos*, each under the control of their data collector. However, the pressure increases to link data between different silos thereby increasing business opportunities. Hence the strategy of major internet companies that search to horizontally control multiple data silos (domains of interest, leisure, geolocation, health, etc.). However, the PRISM affair[1] has made clear that centralizing and processing all one's data in a single server (or multiple servers controlled by a single actor) introduces a major threat on privacy. Moreover, this introduces a monopolistic situation impeding the free development of many valuable applications by others.

To face this situation, the World Economic Forum formulates the need for *a data platform that allows individuals to manage under their control the collection, usage and sharing of their data*[2]. This is precisely what the Personal Cloud paradigm aims to provide. Because it gives a tangible source of trust, the *home cloud* is the most emblematic form of Personal Cloud. It can be thought of as a dedicated box connected to the user's internet gateway, equipped with storage, computing and communication facilities [17], running a personal server and acquiring personal data from multiple sources [3, 22]. This personal server is in charge of organizing the personal dataspace in a document database style to ease its management, to allow crossing data from multiple "local silos" and to protect it against loss, theft and abusive use. Many projects and startups currently investigate this direction, e.g., OpenPDS[3], CozyCloud[4], Younity[5], Lima[6], OwnCloud[7], Tonido[8].

Leaving the data management control into the user's hands pushes the security issues to the user's computing platform as well. Documents can still be stored encrypted in Cloud servers but these servers never get access to the cryptographic keys and their role shrinks to guaranteeing the availability and resiliency of encrypted data. Hence, encryption/decryption, metadata management (e.g., indexing and search) and access control management is under the responsibility of the Personal server. This charge is paramount considering that all silos of personal data are now grouped in the user's hands.

This demonstration precisely tackles this challenge. The proposed solution combines a traditional home cloud data system organizing the document dataspace and a secure hardware-based co-server managing the encryption/decryption of documents and enforcing the access control rules. Our objective is to demonstrate that (1) such combination of software and tamper-resistant hardware can provide the individuals with the tangible source of trust required for a wide Personal Cloud adoption and (2) new search engine techniques embedded in tamper-resistant hardware can be devised to manage large-scale personal dataspaces with surprisingly good performance.

2. ARCHITECTURE AND SCENARIOS

Let us consider the Secure Personal Cloud Platform of Alice as pictured in Figure 1. The main component is a home cloud data

[1] See e.g. the Wikipedia page on PRISM surveillance program

[2] The World Economic Forum. Rethinking Personal Data: Strengthening Trust. May 2012.

[3] OpenPDS: http://openpds.media.mit.edu/

[4] CozyCloud: https://www.cozycloud.cc

[5] Younity: http://getyounity.com/

[6] Lima : https://meetlima.com/

[7] OwnCloud : https://owncloud.org/

[8] Tonido : http://www.tonido.com/

SIGMOD'15, May 31–June 4, 2015, Melbourne, Victoria, Australia.
Copyright 2015 ACM 978-1-4503-2758-9/15/05...$15.00
http://dx.doi.org/10.1145/2723372.2735376

system gathering personal data from multiple sources (employer, banks, hospitals, commercial web sites, etc) and devices (smart meters, quantified-self devices, smartphones, cameras, etc.). The Personal Cloud can be implemented by any type of computing platform with storage facilities such as a set-up box or a plug computer. This data system is associated to a secure co-server which can be hosted by any type of tamper-resistant devices flourishing today, e.g., Mobile Security Card[9] (produced by Giesecke & Devrient), Personal Portable Security Device[10] (produced by Gemalto and Lexar), Multimedia SIM card or Secure Portable Token [4, 18]. Whatever its commercial name and form factor, a tamper-resistant device, called *secure token* hereafter, embeds a secure microcontroller (e.g., a smart card chip) connected to a large NAND Flash memory (e.g., a SD card) and can communicate with a host through a USB, Bluetooth or Ethernet port.

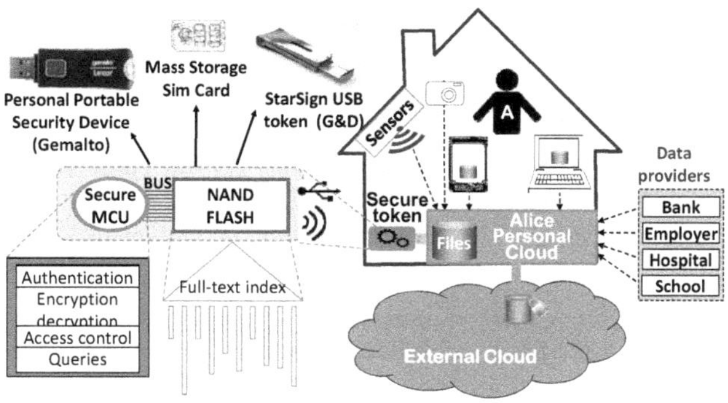

Figure 1. Secure Personal Cloud platform.

The documents entering Alice's dataspace can be any form of files (pictures, text files, pdf files, mails, data streams produced by sensors, etc). To help Alice query this diversity of documents, we consider the use of a simple keyword search engine, in the spirit of Google desktop or Spotlight. Terms are extracted from the file content and from metadata describing it (e.g., name, type, date, creator, tags set by the user herself). Since keywords seem the most convenient way to query Alice's dataspace, it make sense to let her express access control rules with a similar paradigm, that is through logical expressions on terms associated to documents. Hence, a query issued by a user or an application can be any form of term search expression, with a ranking function (e.g., *tf-idf* [23]) identifying the top-k most relevant documents (see Section 3). Only the documents granted to the user/application must appear in the query result (e.g., a query issued by the *mailer* application can only see documents tagged with the terms *email* or *contact*).

The question is how to make this architecture secure? To answer information retrieval queries, search engines usually rely on an inverted index containing all relevant terms extracted from the content and metadata of all the documents in the collection. This inverted index is thus as sensitive as the document collection itself and must be protected accordingly. However, Alice (as most of the typical users) is not a world-class security expert. Therefore, her home computing platform cannot reasonably be considered trusted. The unique source of security is provided by the secure token connected to her home platform (see Figure 1). This means that the inverted index and the query and access control engine must be embedded in the secure token to avoid any data disclosure at query execution time, except the final result. The high level of security (and hence trust) of this architecture is rooted in the combination of hardware and software security and data decentralization, which we detail in Section 5.3.

Designing such embedded query and access control engine is however very challenging due to a combination of severe and conflicting hardware constraints from the secure tokens. To the best of our knowledge, no state of the art work can meet document insertion performance and query scalability at the same time in this context (see Section 3). Moreover none of them support file deletions and updates, nor consider access control, which are mandatory in the Personal Cloud context.

3. TECHNICAL CHALLENGES

Search Engine Requirements. We consider that the search engine of interest in our context has a similar functionality as a Google desktop for secure tokens. Hence, we use the terminology introduced in the Information Retrieval literature for full-text search. Then, a document refers to any form of data files, terms refers to any form of data/metadata elements, term frequencies refer to data/metadata element weights and a query is equivalent to a full-text search. Full-text search has been widely studied by the information retrieval community since decades (see [23] for a recent survey). The core problem is, given a collection of documents and a user query expressed as a set of terms $\{t_i\}$, to retrieve the k most relevant documents that the querier is granted access to. In the wide majority of works, the *tf-idf* score is used to rank the query results: $tf\text{-}idf\,(d) = \sum_{t \in Q} \log(f_{d,t} + 1) \cdot \log(N/F_t)$, where $f_{d,t}$ is the frequency of term t in document d, N is the total number of indexed documents, and F_t is the number of documents that contain t. This formula is given for illustrative purpose, the weight between $f_{d,t}$ and N/F_t varying depending on the proposals. Classically, full-text search queries are evaluated efficiently using a B-tree-like inverted index storing for each term t the number F_t and the list of $(d, f_{d,t})$ pairs.

In our context, the same index will be used to rank the documents pertaining to the query result and to filter out those which do not match the access control rule. For example, Bob can search in Alice's dataspace for the k most relevant files containing (or tagged with) terms 'vacation', '2014', 'France' but will see only those which have been tagged by Alice with the term 'friends'.

Secure Tokens' Hardware Constraints. As mentioned earlier, the inverted index and the query and access control engine must be embedded in the secure token to enforce the security of the Personal Cloud. Whatever their form factor and usage, secure tokens share strong commonalities in terms of data management. Indeed, a large NAND Flash storage is used to persistently store data, metadata and indexes, and a microcontroller (MCU) executes the embedded code, both being connected by a bus. Hence, the architecture inherits hardware constraints from both the MCU and the Flash memory. Note that the tamper-resistance of the MCU provides a high level of protection against physical and side-channel attacks, and in particular for the data residing in RAM since the RAM memory is located inside the MCU. Also, all the persistently stored data in the NAND Flash is cryptographically protected.

[9] http://www.gi-de.com/en/products_and_solutions/products/strong_authentication/Mobile-Security-Card-31488.jsp

[10] "Smart Guardian" http://cardps.com/product/gemalto-smart-guardian or "Smart Enterprise Guardian" http://cardps.com/product/gemalto-smart-enterprise-guardian

The MCU usually has a low power CPU, a tiny RAM (few KB), and a few MB of persistent memory (ROM, NOR or EEPROM) used to store the embedded code and secrets (e.g., cryptographic keys). The NAND Flash component (either raw NAND Flash chip or SD/micro-SD card) also exhibits strong limitations [7, 9]. In NAND Flash, the minimum unit for a read and a write operation is the page (usually 512 Bytes, also called a sector). Pages must be erased before being rewritten but the erase operation must be performed at a block granularity (e.g., 256 pages). Erases are then costly and a block wears out after about 10^4 repeated write/erase cycles. In addition, the pages have to be written sequentially in a block. Therefore, NAND Flash badly supports random writes.

State-of-the-Art solutions. Tiny RAM and NAND Flash persistent storage introduce conflicting constraints. Indeed, the index maintenance generates costly random writes in Flash which can be alleviated only at the expense of an extensive use of RAM. This leads to split state of the art on embedded search engines in two families. The *insert-optimized family* (e.g., [15, 16, 19, 21]) reaches insertion scalability thanks to a small indexed structure buffered in RAM (e.g., a small hash table) and sequentially flushed in Flash, thereby precluding costly random writes in Flash. This good insertion behavior is however obtained to the detriment of query scalability, the performance of searches being roughly linear with the index size in Flash (e.g., linear scan of very large hash buckets). Conversely, the *query-optimized family* (e.g., [2, 8, 12, 20]) reaches query scalability by adapting traditional indexing structures (e.g., B^+-Tree) to Flash storage, to the detriment of insertion scalability. The key idea in these approaches is to buffer the updates in log structures to amortize the Flash write cost in the same index nodes and to index this log in RAM to keep acceptable query performance. Hence, the number of random writes in Flash (linked to the log commit frequency) is roughly inversely proportional to the RAM capacity.

In conclusion, the existing solutions are scalable either for queries or insertions when considered in our context (please refer to [5] for an extensive evaluation of the representative full-text search methods). In addition, we are not aware of state of the art works addressing the crucial problems of random document deletions and of access control management in the context of an embedded search engine.

In the light of this discussion, the problem we address can be formulated as designing an embedded full-text search engine that meets three properties, namely:

(1) *Bounded RAM*: to consume a small and bounded amount of RAM to comply with the widest population of secure tokens (thereby precluding any solution where this consumption depends on the size of the document set).

(2) *Full scalability:* be scalable for queries and updates (insertion, deletion of documents) without distinction to comply with the widest usages.

(3) *Security:* to enforce access control rules and defeat tampering actions.

4. DESIGN OF THE SOLUTION

To tackle the challenge above, we proposed in [5] a novel indexing method that relies on the following design principles.

P1. Write-Once Partitioning: *Split the inverted index structure I in successive partitions such that a partition is flushed only once in Flash and is never updated.*

By precluding random writes in Flash, Write-Once Partitioning aims at satisfying update scalability. Considering the Bounded RAM property, the consequence of this principle is to parse documents and maintain I in a streaming way. Conceptually, each partition can be seen as the result of indexing a window of the document input flow, the size of which is limited by a predefined RAM_Bound. Therefore, I is split in an infinite sequence of partitions $<I_0, I_1,\ldots, I_p>$, each partition I_i having the same internal structure as I. When the size of the current I_i partition stored in RAM reaches RAM_Bound, I_i is flushed in Flash and a new partition I_{i+1} is initialized in RAM for the next window.

A second consequence of this design principle is that document deletions have to be processed similar to document insertions since the partitions cannot be modified once they are written. This means adding compensating information in each partition that will be considered by the query process to produce correct results.

P2. Linear Pipelining: *Compute each query Q with respect to the Bounded RAM property in such a way that the execution cost of Q over* $<I_0, I_1,\ldots, I_p>$ *is in the same order of magnitude as the execution cost of Q over I.*

Linear Pipelining aims at satisfying query scalability under the Bounded RAM agreement. A unique structure I (e.g., a traditional B^+-Tree) is assumed to satisfy query scalability by nature and is considered as providing a lower bound in terms of query execution time. Hence, the objective of Linear pipelining is to keep the performance gap between Q over $<I_0, I_1,\ldots, I_p>$ and Q over I, both small and predictable. Computing Q as a set-oriented composition of a set of Q_i over I_i, (with i=0,...p) would unavoidably violate the Bounded RAM property as p increases, since it will require to store all Q_i's intermediate results in RAM. Hence the necessity to organize the processing in pipeline such that the RAM consumption remains independent of p, and therefore of the number of indexed documents. Also, the term *linear* pipelining conveys the idea that the query processing must preclude any iteration (i.e., repeated accesses) over the same data structure to reach the expected level of performance. This disqualifies brute-force pipeline solutions where the *tf-idf* scores of documents are computed one after the other, at the price of reading the same inverted lists as many times as the number of documents they contain.

However, Linear Pipelining alone cannot prevent the performance gap between Q over $<I_0, I_1,\ldots, I_p>$ and Q over I to increase with the increase of p as (*i*) multiple searches in several small indexes are more costly than a single search in a large index and (*ii*) the inverted lists in $<I_0, I_1,\ldots, I_p>$ are likely to occupy only fractions of Flash pages, multiplying the number of Flash I/Os to access the same amount of data. A third design principle is then required.

P3. Background Linear Merging: *To limit the total number of partitions, periodically merge partitions in a way compliant with the Bounded RAM agreement and without hurting update scalability.*

The objective of partition merging is therefore to obtain a lower number of larger partitions to avoid the drawbacks mentioned above. Partition merging must meet three requirements. First the merge must be performed in pipeline to match the Bounded RAM property. Second, since its cost can be significant (i.e., proportional to the total size of the merged partitions), the merge must be processed in background to avoid locking the index structure for unbounded periods of time. Since multi-threading is not supported by the targeted platforms, background processing can simply be understood as the capacity to interrupt and recover the merging process at any time. Third, update scalability requires that the total cost of a merge run be always smaller than the time to fill out the next bunch of partitions to be merged.

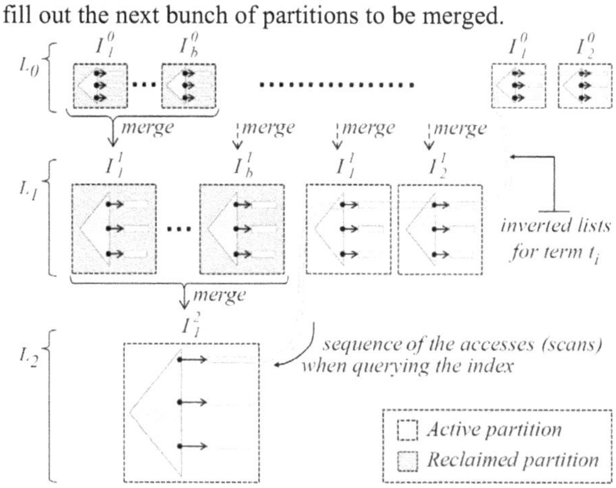

Figure 2. SSF index structure.

Taken together, principles P1 to P3 reconcile the Bounded RAM and Full scalability properties. These principles lead to the inverted index structure named SSF (Scalable and Sequential Flash index) pictured in Figure 2. This figure shows the incremental merging of partitions producing larger and larger indexes while generating only sequential writes in Flash. At each point of time, only the white partitions are active, the grey partitions being reclaimed by the merging process. For a same term *t*, the inverted list of $(d, f_{d,t})$ pairs traverses several partitions (from L_0 to L_2 in the figure), I^0_2 containing the most recent inserted documents and I^2_1 the oldest ones.

At query time, one buffer is allocated in RAM to sequentially scan the inverted list of each term involved in the query. Traditionally, a RAM variable is also allocated to each document *d* to compute its *tf-idf* score. This however hurts the bounded RAM property, the size of the document set being likely to be much larger than the available RAM. Conversely, we allocate a RAM variable only to the *k* documents having currently the best scores and compute the *tf-idf* scores in pure pipeline. Document ids reflecting the insertion ordering, the inverted lists are naturally sorted. Hence, the *tf-idf* computation sums up to a simple linear pipeline merging process of the inverted lists for all terms $t \in Q$ in each partition. The management of document deletions and updates and the fact that large documents can cross several partitions makes this process trickier. We refer the interested reader to [5] for a detailed presentation of the algorithms and performance evaluation.

The enforcement of access control rules is integrated seamlessly in the query computation. Access control rules are boolean expressions over terms present in or associated to the documents (e.g., authorize Bob to access all documents containing a given keyword or set of keywords or tags, as defined by tag-based access control models [6, 13, 14]). At query execution time, the inverted lists of terms involved in the access control rules are merged in pipeline with the inverted lists for all terms $t \in Q$. Then, a document enters in the set of the current *k* best documents if (1) its own *tf-idf* score is better than the worst of the *k* current best scores and (2) it satisfies the access control rule expression over its terms/tags.

5. DEMONSTRATION

In this section, we present our prototype platform and describe the demonstration scenario covering the security and the performance of the proposed solution for the Personal Cloud paradigm.

5.1 Demonstration platform

The Hardware Platform. The demonstration platform is an instance of the architecture presented in Figure 1. A PC plays the role of the home cloud data system organizing the document dataspace. In addition, the secure co-server manages the encryption/decryption of documents, indexes them, processes the queries and enforces the defined access control rules. The secure co-server runs on a tamper-resistant token produced by the ZED company and has an architecture representative for secure tokens (see Figure 3). Our secure token has the following characteristics: the MCU is equipped with a 32 bit RISC CPU clocked at 120 MHz, a crypto-coprocessor implementing AES and SHA in hardware, 128 KB of static RAM and 1 MB of NOR Flash. The MCU is connected to a smartcard chip hosting the cryptographic material and to a µSD card reader where the inverted index resides. The documents themselves are stored encrypted on the PC (i.e., the home cloud data system).

The secure token can communicate with the outside word either though the USB or the Bluetooth protocol. It is also equipped with a fingerprint reader providing a strong physical authentication of the queriers. The fingerprint reader can be used to identify the owner of the token that can either connect to her own token with all privileges or connect to another user's remote token with restricted privileges, which are regulated by access control rules established by the owner of the remote token.

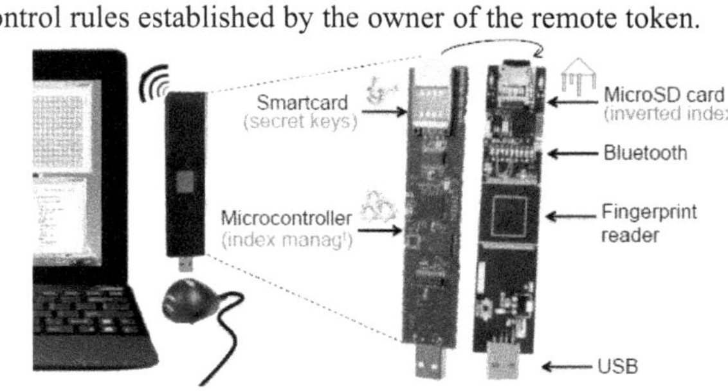

Figure 3. Secure token

The Graphical User Interface (GUI). The demonstration interface reflects the external APIs of our secure search engine enabling the insertion and deletion of sets of terms extracted from sets of documents, the keyword search and the definition of access control rules for the different subjects (see Figure 4, left part). When a given subject (e.g., an application, the data owner or a remote user) opens a session with the secure token, it first chooses an inverted index corresponding to a particular datasets. Then, it can add (or select) a set of files to (from) a (virtual) directory, to be inserted into (or deleted from) the index. Terms are extracted from these files and are completed with the appropriate tags before being inserted in the index embedded in the secure token. After insertion, the files appear encrypted on the host. The encryption key is automatically generated by the token from the document identifier and the secret key stored in the SIM smartcard and is unique for each file. Then, the encryption can be either performed by the host or by the token.

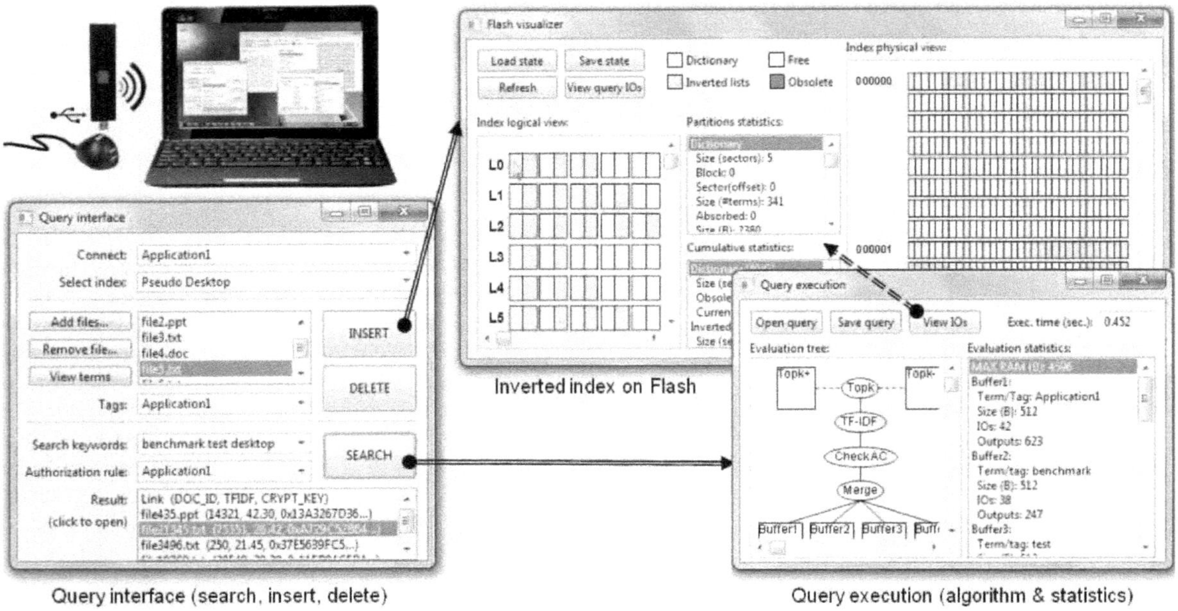

Figure 4. Demonstration graphical interface

The connected subject is able to issue keyword search queries to retrieve the relevant files. The relevant documents are ranked according to the *tf-idf* score and the top-*k* results are returned to the user. A link provides access to each result file, which can be decrypted on demand. The search queries conform to the access control rules. However, in the demonstration interface, a rule can be dynamically edited to show the effect on the result and the efficiency of the system whatever the access rule.

To demonstrate the behavior of the index, the interface also plots (see Figure 4, right upper part) the logical view of the index partitions and their corresponding physical view of the blocks/sectors in the Flash memory. Many useful statistics that describe the current state of each index partition, as well as the cumulative values maintained since the index creation, are also provided. For each insertion, deletion and search query, a synopsis of the underlying evaluation algorithm is also pictured (see Figure 4, right lower part) along with detailed statistics of their respective RAM consumption and IO patterns.

5.2 Demonstration scenario

The first part of the demonstration presents the motivation of the approach and shows the benefits of our search engine in terms of security and privacy protection in the context of the Personal Cloud. We use two representative collections of personal documents with their predefined query sets: a Pseudo-desktop Collection [11] composed of 27000 documents (emails, photos, pdf, docs, and ppts) and a large collection of emails (available at https://www.cs.cmu.edu/~enron/) containing more than 500 thousand emails to show the scalability of our platform. Representative applications (e.g., email) and users (data owner or remote users) are predefined with their respective access control rules (i.e., the files have been tagged accordingly). The attendees will be able to connect to the Personal Cloud as subjects granted with different access control rules, and will issue queries (insert, delete and search) to evaluate the usability and performance of the proposed technology. The enforcement of the access control rules will be illustrated with well prepared queries. Finally, the attendees may enroll their fingerprint on the token, insert a few files in the Personal Cloud tagged with their own keywords. We will then show that the files inserted by an attendee remain hidden to the other enrolled subjects.

The second part of the demonstration will focus on the search engine performance, scalability and compliance with the low RAM constraint. To demonstrate the scalability of the solution, we will use the large email data set. New files will be added or removed by the attendees and search queries will be executed on the indexed data set containing more than 500 thousand files. For each insertion, deletion and search query, the underlying execution plan is plotted with detailed statistics of memory consumption, IO costs and NAND Flash usage. The graphical user interface also shows the logical index structure and its physical representation in Flash memory. The IO pattern of each search query will be also visualized in the graphical interface, to better explain the scalability and efficiency of the search engine.

5.3 Demonstration results

Security. The primary expected result of this demonstration is to convince the audience that building a secure personal cloud platform where the evaluation of the access control rules is enforced by a secure token is within reach. The trustworthiness in the platform is rooted in two things. First, compared to a solution centralizing the personal data of millions of people in a single proprietary Cloud, the intrinsic decentralization of the Personal cloud decreases the incentive for attacks. Second, the use of secure hardware at the user's side strongly increases the difficulty and cost of an attack. Indeed, (1) the secure token provides a closed execution environment (no code can be installed and executed by the MCU but the original code and cryptographically signed versions of its upgrades), (2) the attacker must be in physical possession of the token to attack it, (3) tamper-resistance provides state of the art guarantees against physical and side-channel attacks, (4) the data at rest (stored in the NAND Flash) are cryptographically protected, (5) strong authentication is mandatory to unlock the personal server and no DBA or any other third party interfere in the loop. Hence, the ratio cost/benefit of an attack, which provides an accurate measure of the security level of a system, is greatly improved.

Bounded RAM. The second result is to demonstrate that a full-fledged search engine integrating access control can manage hundreds of thousands of documents while consuming kilobytes of RAM. The RAM consumption is indeed bounded by the number of terms involved in the query and in the access control rules and remains independent of the size of the document set. This results from the ability to execute any query in a pure pipeline way even in the case where the document set is subject to updates (modifications and deletions of documents).

Full scalability. The third result is to show that improving query execution time is not always synonym of insertion/update degradation and vice-versa. This results from a sequential partitioned indexing structure providing linear performance for queries and insertions for a limited number of documents combined with a background reorganization process reaching logarithmic performance while the document set increases in size. The demonstration shows that the storage penalty incurred by this strategy is rather acceptable.

6. CONCLUSION

The emerging Personal Could paradigm holds the promise of a Privacy-by-Design storage and computing platform where personal data remains under the individual's control while being shared by valuable applications. However, this paradigm puts in the user's hand the responsibility of protecting all these data against multiple threats. While many personal cloud platforms are flourishing, riding the wave of repeated scandals blemishing the typical centralized management of personal data, none of them provide a tangible source of trust to the individuals. We hope that the platform demonstrated here contributes to the wider adoption of the Personal Could paradigm and emphasizes the interest of studying new database techniques embedded in secure hardware for the database community.

7. ACKNOWLEDGMENTS

This work is partially funded by project ANR-11-INSE-0005 KISS. Special thanks are due to Benjamin André from Cozy Cloud for fruitful discussions on the Personal Cloud paradigm.

8. REFERENCES

[1] Aggarwal, C. C., Ashish, N., and Sheth, A. The internet of things: A survey from the data-centric perspective. In Managing and mining sensor data, 2013.

[2] Agrawal, D., Ganesan, D., Sitaraman, R., Diao, Y. and Singh, S. Lazy-adaptive tree: An optimized index structure for flash devices. In *VLDB*, 2(1), 2009.

[3] Anciaux, N., Bonnet, P., Bouganim, L., Nguyen, B., Sandu Popa, I., and P. Pucheral. Trusted cells: A sea change for personal data services. In *CIDR*, 2013.

[4] Anciaux, N., Bouganim, L., Pucheral, P., Guo, Y., Folgoc, L. L., Yin, S. 2014. Milo-db: a personal, secure and portable database machine. In *Distributed and Parallel Databases*.

[5] Anciaux, N., Lallali, S., Sandu-Popa, I., Pucheral, P. A Scalable Search Engine for Mass Storage Smart Objects. *Technical report*, accessible at: http://www.prism.uvsq.fr/~isap/files/RT.pdf.

[6] Yeung, C., A., Kagal, L., Gibbin, N., Shadbolt, N. Providing Access Control to Online Photo Albums Based on Tags and Linked Data. AAAI Spring Symposium on Social Semantic Web: Where Web 2.0 Meets Web 3.0, 2009.

[7] Bjorling, M., Bonnet, P., Bouganim, L., and Jonsson, B. T. 2010. Uflip: Understanding the energy consumption of flash devices. In *IEEE Data Eng. Bull.*, 33(4).

[8] Debnath, B., Sengupta, S., and Li, J. Skimpystash: Ram space skimpy key-value store on flash-based storage. In *SIGMOD*, 2011.

[9] Diao, Y., Ganesan, D., Mathur, G., and Shenoy, P. J. Rethinking data management for storage-centric sensor networks. In *CIDR*, 2007.

[10] Huang, Y.-M., Lai, Y.-X. Distributed energy management system within residential sensor-based heterogeneous network structure. In *Wireless Sensor Networks and Ecological Monitoring*, 3, 2013.

[11] Kim, J. Y. and Croft, W. B. Retrieval Experiments using Pseudo-Desktop Collections. In *CIKM*, 2009.

[12] Li, Y., He, B., Yang, R. J., Luo, Q., and Yi, K. Tree Indexing on Solid State Drives. *VLDB*, 3(1-2), 2010

[13] Mazurek, M., L. A. Tag-Based, Logical Access-Control Framework for Personal File Sharing. 2014. PhD thesis.

[14] Klemperer, P., Liang, Y., Mazurek, M., Sleeper, M., Ur, B., Bauer, L., Cranor, F., L., Gupta, N., and Reiter, M. Tag, you can see it!: using tags for access control in photo sharing. In *SIGCHI*, 2012.

[15] Tan, C. C., Sheng, B., Wang, H., and Li, Q. Microsearch: When search engines meet small devices. *Pervasive Computing*, 2008.

[16] Tan, C. C., Sheng, B., Wang, H., Li, Q. 2010. Microsearch: A search engine for embedded devices used in pervasive computing. *ACM Trans. Embed. Comput. Syst.*, 9(4).

[17] To, Q.-C., Nguyen, B., and Pucheral, P. Privacy-Preserving Query Execution using a Decentralized Architecture and Tamper Resistant Hardware. In *EDBT*, 2014.

[18] Tsiftes, N. and Dunkels, A. A database in every sensor. In *ACM SenSys*, 2011.

[19] Wang, H., Tan, C. C., Li, Q. 2010. Snoogle: A search engine for pervasive environments. *IEEE Transactions on Parallel and Distributed Systems*, 21(8).

[20] Wu, C.-H., Kuo, T.-W., and Chang, L.-P. 2007. An efficient b-tree layer implementation for flash-memory storage systems. *ACM Trans. Embed. Comput. Syst.*, 6(3).

[21] Yan, T., Ganesan, D., and Manmatha, R. Distributed image search in camera sensor networks. In *ACM SenSys*, 2008.

[22] Yap, K.-K., Srinivasan, V., Motani, M. Max. 2008. Wide area human-centric search of the physical world. In *ACM Transactions on Sensor Networks*, 4(4).

[23] Zobel, J. and Moffat, A. 2006. Inverted files for text search engines. In *ACM Comput. Surv.*, 38(2).

IReS: Intelligent, Multi-Engine Resource Scheduler for Big Data Analytics Workflows

Katerina Doka
Computing Systems Lab
National Technical University of Athens, Greece
katerina@cslab.ece.ntua.gr

Nikolaos Papailiou
Computing Systems Lab
National Technical University of Athens, Greece
npapa@cslab.ece.ntua.gr

Dimitrios Tsoumakos
Department of Informatics
Ionian University
Corfu, Greece
dtsouma@ionio.gr

Christos Mantas
Computing Systems Lab
National Technical University of Athens, Greece
cmantas@cslab.ece.ntua.gr

Nectarios Koziris
Computing Systems Lab
National Technical University of Athens, Greece
nkoziris@cslab.ece.ntua.gr

ABSTRACT

Big data analytics tools are steadily gaining ground at becoming indispensable to businesses worldwide. The complexity of the tasks they execute is ever increasing due to the surge in data and task heterogeneity. Current analytics platforms, while successful in harnessing multiple aspects of this "data deluge", bind their efficacy to a single data and compute model and often depend on proprietary systems. However, no single execution engine is suitable for all types of computation and no single data store is suitable for all types of data. To this end, we demonstrate *IReS*, the *Intelligent Resource Scheduler* for complex analytics workflows executed over multi-engine environments. Our system models the cost and performance of the required tasks over the available platforms. *IReS* is then able to match distinct workflow parts to the execution and/or storage engine among the available ones in order to optimize with respect to a user-defined policy. During the demo, the attendees will be able to execute workflows that match real use cases and parametrize the input datasets and optimization policy. The underlying platform supports multiple compute and data engines, allowing the user to choose any subset of them. Through the inspection of the produced plan, its execution and the collection and presentation of numerous cost and performance metrics, the audience will experience first-hand how *IReS* takes advantage of heterogeneous runtimes and data stores and effectively models operator cost and performance for actual and diverse workflows.

Categories and Subject Descriptors

H.4.m [**Information Systems Applications**]: Miscellaneous

SIGMOD'15, May 31–June 4, 2015, Melbourne, Victoria, Australia.
Copyright © 2015 ACM 978-1-4503-2758-9/15/05 ...$15.00.
http://dx.doi.org/10.1145/2723372.2735377.

Keywords

Multi-Engine Optimization, Cost Modelling, Profiling, Big Data, Analytics Workflows

1. INTRODUCTION

Big data analytics have become a necessity for the majority of industries [17], taking the lead in risk assessment, business process effectiveness, market analysis, etc. [23, 16]. Enabling engineers, analytics experts and scientists alike to tap the potential of vast amounts of business-critical data has grown increasingly important. Such data analysis demands a high degree of parallelism in both storage and computation: Modern datacenters host huge volumes of data, stored over large numbers of nodes with multiple storage devices and process them using thousands or millions of cores.

The demand for near-real-time, data-driven analytics has given rise to diverse execution engines and data stores that target specific data and computation types (e.g., [1, 4, 2, 13, 3, 10]). Many of these systems are now offered as a service by IaaS providers, enabling a very wide deployment range. There also exist approaches in the literature that manage to optimize their performance (e.g., [20, 22]) by automatically tuning a number of configuration parameters. Yet, these schemes assume strictly single-engine environments (mainly the Hadoop ecosystem), thus considering specific data formats and query/analytics task types.

However, modern workflows have become increasingly long and complex [19]. Specifically, workflows may include multiple data types (e.g., relational, key-value, graph, etc.) generated from different resources. What is more, they are executed under varying constraints and policies (e.g., optimize performance or cost, require different fault-tolerance degrees, etc.). Finally, workflow operators can be greatly diverse, from simple Select-Project-Join (SPJ) and data movement to complex NLP-, graph- or custom business-related operations. There currently exists no single platform that can optimize for this complexity [27].

Sensing this trend, cloud software companies now offer software distributions in pre-cooked VM images or as a service. These distributions incorporate different processing frameworks, data stores and libraries to alleviate the burden of multiple installations and configurations (e.g., [5, 9,

8, 12]). Yet, such multi-engine environments lack a *meta-scheduler* that could automatically match tasks to the right engine(s) according to multiple criteria, deploy and run them without manual intervention. A recent attempt along this line [25, 26] focuses more on lower-level database operators, emphasizing on their automatic translation from/to specific engines via an XML-based language. Yet, this is a proprietary tool with limited applicability and extension possibilities for the community.

To address multi-engine analytics workflow optimization we present the *Intelligent Multi-Engine Resource Scheduler (IReS)*, an integrated, open source platform for managing, executing and monitoring complex analytics workflows[1]. Its goal is to provide adaptive, cost-based and customizable resource management of the diverse execution and storage engines available. IReS incorporates a modelling framework that constantly evaluates the cost, quality and performance of data and computational resources in order to decide on the most advantageous store, indexing and execution pattern.

To that direction, our system handles existing open-source execution models (e.g., Map-Reduce, Bulk Synchronous Parallel) as well as state-of-the-art centralized and distributed storage engines (RDBMSs, NoSQL, distributed file-systems, etc.) in order to have a broad applicability and increased performance gains. IReS is able to optimize workflows consisting of tasks that range from simple group-by, aggregation or complex joins between different data sources to machine-learning tasks and queries on graph data in combination with relational data. In the current implementation, the system bases its operation on the following elements:

- A profiling and modelling engine that benchmarks operator performance and cost for different engine configurations. Outputs are collected via budget-constraint executed benchmarks. The learned models are stored and utilized for the planning phase of the workflow.
- A JSON-based metadata framework that describes operators in abstract and instantiated forms, enabling search and matching of operators that perform a similar task in the planning phase.
- A decision-making and enforcing process that chooses among different equivalent workflow execution plans (i.e., on different engines, resulting in equivalent output) based on cost and performance models and schedules the execution.

The resulting optimization is orthogonal to (and in fact enhanced by) any optimization effort within a single engine. Unlike [25, 26], IReS is a fully open-source platform that targets both low (e.g., join, sort, etc.) as well as high level (e.g., machine learning, graph processing) operators, treating them as black boxes. The generic profiling/modelling method it relies upon allows for easy addition of new operators and engines.

Our demonstration of the IReS system will showcase its ability to i)model operator performance according to different engines and their resources and ii)adaptively decide on which operator version to run based on the optimization policy and the available engines. The demonstration platform will integrate Hadoop [1], Hama [2], Spark [4] and PostgreSQL [11] with HDFS [7], HBase [3] and Elasticsearch [6] and operate upon real-life and synthetic workflows chosen to include diverse datasets and computation types. The participants will have a rich interaction with IReS, controlling policy and input aspects, while being able to evaluate the advantages of multi-engine optimization by inspecting generated plans and output.

[1]IReS is a central component of the *ASAP (Adaptive, highly Scalable Analytics Platform)* EU-funded project. ASAP envisions a unified, open-source execution framework for scalable data analytics. `http://www.asap-fp7.eu/`

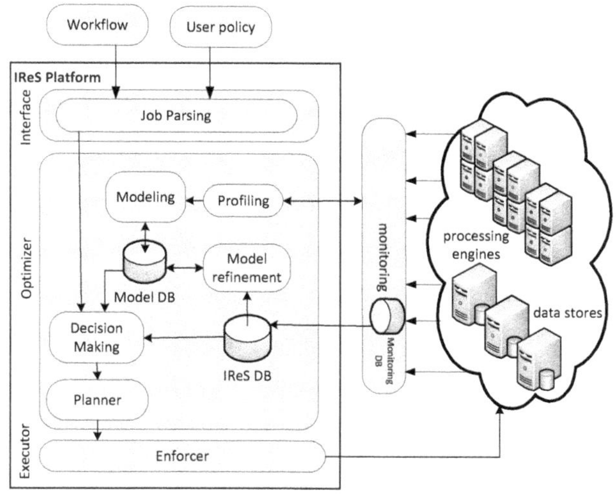

Figure 1: Architecture of the IReS platform

2. ARCHITECTURE

IReS focuses on highly efficient and user-customizable execution of analytics tasks (or workflows). This is made possible through the transparent modeling, monitoring and scheduling that involves different execution engines and storage technologies. Consequently, our system is able to execute all types of analytics workflows by adaptively choosing to execute each sub-part of the workflow to a (possibly different) deployed engine. The IReS platform assigns sub-tasks to the most advantageous technology(-ies) available and ensures resource and dataflow scheduling in order to enhance performance: If a single engine is used, enhancement will be achieved through optimized resource allocation and elasticity modeling (e.g., execute on more VMs, or on smaller cluster with larger main memory, etc.); if multiple ones are required, enhancements will relate both to single-engine optimization and to workflow management that decides what is the best execution plan and data-flow (e.g., execute sub-task 1 first, intermediate results should be stored on a NoSQL engine and then sub tasks 2 and 3 run in parallel and write final results to HDFS files).

The central notion behind the IReS platform is to create detailed models of the costs and performance characteristics of various analytics operations over multiple execution engines. These models are then used to match the user optimization policy with the available execution engines.

The architecture of the IReS platform is depicted in Figure 1. IReS comprises of three layers, the *interface*, the *optimizer* and the *executor* layer.

The *interface layer* is responsible for communicating with the application UI in order to receive the input that is necessary for its operations. It consists of the *job parser* module, which identifies execution artifacts such as operators, data, their dependencies and accompanying metadata. Moreover,

```
{"joinOp": {
  "constraints": {
    "input1": {
      "data_info": {
        "attributes": ["attr1", "attr2"]}},
    "input2": {
      "data_info": {
        "attributes": ["attr1", "attr2"]}},
    "output1": {
      "data_info": {
        "attributes": ["attr1", "attr2"]}},
    "op_specification": {
      "algorithm": {
        "join": {
          "join_condition":
            "input1.attr1=input2.attr1"}}}}}}
```

Figure 2: Metadata description of the abstract join operator

it validates the user-defined policy. All this information must be robustly identified, structured in a dependency graph and stored.

The *optimizer layer* is responsible for optimizing the execution of an analytics workflow with respect to the policy provided by the user. The core component of the optimizer is the *Decision Making* module, which determines the optimal execution plan in real-time. This entails deciding on where each subtask is to be run, under what amount of resources provisioned, the plan for moving data to/from their current locations and between runtimes (if more than one is chosen) and defining the output destinations. Such a decision must rely on the characteristics of the analytics task in hand and the models of all possible engines. These models are produced by the *Modeling* module and stored in a database called *Model DB*. The initial model of an engine results from profiling and benchmarking operations in an offline manner, through the *Profiling* module. This module directly interacts with the pool of physical resources and the monitoring layer in-between. While the workflow is being executed, the initial models are refined in an online manner by the *Model refinement* module, using monitoring information of the actual run. Such monitoring information is kept in the IReS DB and is utilized by the decision making module as well, to enable real-time, dynamic adjustments of the execution plan based on the most up-to-date knowledge.

The *executor layer* is the layer that enforces the optimal plan over the physical infrastructure. It includes methods and tools that translate high level "start runtime under x amount of resources", "move data from site Y to Z" type of commands to a workflow of primitives as understood by the specific runtimes and storage engines. Moreover, it is responsible for ensuring fault tolerance and robustness through real-time monitoring.

In the following, we describe in more detail the role, functionality and internals of the most important modules of the platform.

Job Parsing Module: This module takes as input the user-defined workflow, formulated in a dependency graph format and expressed in a way that allows for various levels of abstraction using a metadata framework. Moreover, the module takes as input the user optimization parameters, which could translate to performance, cost, availability, etc.

The main challenge of defining a workflow description metadata framework is the fact that it requires to be abstract at the user level. The user should be able to describe the data and operators that comprise her workflow in a way as abstract as she desires. The IReS planner and workflow scheduler need to remove that abstraction, find all the alternative ways of materializing the workflow and select the most beneficial, according to the user-defined policy.

Our proposed metadata framework describes *data* and *operators*. Data and operators can be either *abstract* or *materialized*. Abstract are the operators and datasets that are described partially or in a high level by the user when composing her workflow whereas materialized are the actual operator implementations and existing datasets, either provided by the user or residing in a repository.

Both data and operators need to be accompanied by a set of metadata, i.e., properties that describe them and can be used to match (a) abstract operators to materialized ones and (b) data to operators. Such properties include input data types and parameters of operators, location of data objects or operator invocation scripts, data schemata, implementation details, engines, etc. The metadata defined for each object have a generic tree format (JSON). To avoid restricting the user and allow for extensibility, the first levels of the metadata tree are predefined, while users can add their ad-hoc subtrees to define their custom data or operators. Moreover, some fields (mostly the ones related to the operator and data requirements) are *compulsory* while the rest (e.g., known cost models, statistics, etc.) are *optional*. Materialized data and operators need to have all their compulsory fields filled in with information. Abstract data and operators do not adhere to this rule. Apart from having empty fields, they can also support regular expressions (e.g., the * symbol under a field means that the abstract object matches materialized ones with any value of that field).

Let us take a `join` operator on a single attribute as an example. In its abstract form, the `joinOP` operator (see Figure 2) needs only define two input parameters, the condition under which they are joined and an output parameter. Each of the input parameters and the output are abstract `data_info` objects with two attributes: "attr1" represents the field of the join predicate while "attr2" represents the second available field in each `data_info` object. The `op_specification` field of this operator specifies its operation, a single join algorithm, and defines the join condition (in this case an inner join). In short, the abstract join operator defines a format that any join operator implementing the specific functionality needs to follow.

The materialized operators include, on top of that, all information required in order to perform the operation on an execution engine. In `join_1` (see Figure 3.a), the operator executes the join over Hadoop; it thus includes Hadoop-specific information about the input, output and the engine. The inputs and output in this case have specific attribute types and an engine specification (under `engine`) containing the location of the data and information about their structure. The operator itself also has an engine specification (`engine_specification`) indicating its execution location. The example in Figure 3.b describes `join_2`, which joins an HBase and a relational table and outputs the result to HDFS. It runs as a local Java process.

To discover the actual implementations that comply with the description of an abstract operator provided by the user, we employ a tree matching algorithm to make sure that all metadata constraints are met, i.e., all compulsory fields are consistent. This is performed by the decision making mod-

```
{"join_1": {
   "constraints": {
     "input1": {
       "data_info": {
         "attributes": [
           {"attr1": {"type": "ByteWritable"}},
           {"attr2": {"type": "List<ByteWritable>"}}]},
       "engine": {
         "DB.NoSQL.Hbase": {
           "key:": "attr1",
           "value": "attr2",
           "location": "127.0.0.1"}}},
     "input2": {...},
     "output1": {...},
   "op_specification": {...},
   "engine_specification": {
     "Distributed.MapReduce": {
       "location": "83.212.118.9"}}},
  "optimization": {
   "cost_model": {
     "exec_time": "10*(input1.size+input2.size)"}}}}
```

(a)

```
{"join_2": {
  "constraints": {
    "input1": {
      "data_info": {
        "attributes": [
          {"attr1": {"type": "Varchar(15)"}},
          {"attr2": {"type": "Varchar(15)"}}]},
      "engine": {
        "DB.Relational.PostgreSQL": {
          "key:": "attr1",
          "value": "attr2",
          "location": "83.212.118.9" }}},
    "input2": {...},
    "output1": {...},
    "op_specification": {...},
    "engine_specification": {
      "Centralized.Java": {"location": "localhost"}}},
  "optimization": {
    "cost_model": {
      "profile":
        ["execution_time", "required_ram"]}}}}
```

(b)

Figure 3: Metadata descriptions of the two materialized join operators

ule, described subsequently. In our example, both `join_1` and `join_2` match `joinOP` and are thus considered when constructing the optimized execution plan.

Apart from the compulsory fields, which are necessary for the matching of abstract to materialized operators, the metadata descriptions of the materialized joins both contain the optional `optimization` field, which holds additional information that assists in the optimization of the workflow. In the case of `join_1`, a cost function is provided by the developer of the operator while for `join_2` the platform is instructed to create one by profiling over specific metrics (execution time and required RAM in our case).

Modelling Module: This module is responsible for constructing models on a per operator–engine combination basis. The relevant literature review [18, 28, 24] has revealed that models already exist for a very limited number of operators and engines and some of them entail knowledge of the code to be executed. Contrarily, we treat materialized operators as "black boxes", assuming no prior knowledge of their internals, and model them using profiling in an offline mode, as well as machine learning over actual runs.

Profiling Module: The profiling module functions in an operator-agnostic way, having no prior knowledge other than the profiler input parameters. These parameters fall into three categories:

- Data specific parameters: These parameters describe the data to be used for the operator profiling, e.g., the type of data and its size.
- Operator specific parameters: These parameters relate to the algorithm of the operator, e.g., the number of output clusters in k-means.
- Resource specific parameters: These parameters define the resources to be tweaked during profiling, e.g., cluster size, storage size, main memory, etc.

The output of each run is the profiled operator's performance and cost (e.g., completion time and I/O operations, average memory and CPU consumption, etc) under each combination of the input parameter values for specific user-defined optimization metrics, such as cost in $ or I/O, latency, throughput, etc. Both the input parameters as well as the output metrics are given by the user/developer.

The aim of the profiling module is to create a surrogate estimation model [21], including neural networks, SVM, interpolation and curve fitting techniques, for each operator running over a specific engine. To that end, we need to sample the operator function by running automated experiments for various values of each of the input parameters and measure the outputs. To create the most accurate surrogate within a budget of experiments, adaptive sampling techniques are adopted to select the combinations of values to be used as input of each run.

Decision Making Module: This module performs the intelligent exploration of all the available execution plans and the discovery of the optimal execution plan according to the user-defined optimization objectives. Initially, it transforms the abstract workflow representation, described as a DAG graph, into a materialized workflow DAG graph that contains all the alternative paths of materialized operators that match the abstract workflow. To do so, for each abstract operator, it searches the library of available materialized operators to find all matches. Our decision module is using an efficient tree matching algorithm to avoid unnecessary comparisons and follow the hierarchical structure of the tree-based metadata constrains. When all operator matches are discovered, the decision making module intelligently consults the input and output specifications of the materialized operators and adds the required move/transform operators. Those operators are needed in order to connect operators of different engines and input/output configurations and generate the final materialized workflow DAG graph.

To find the optimal execution plan, our decision module uses a dynamic programming planner that explores the materialized workflow DAG in order to find the plan that best matches the user optimization policy. To estimate operator performance metrics, our planner consults the profiler module that holds surrogate estimator models for each one of the materialized operators. In our current implementation, our planner can be configured to optimize one metric or a function of multiple performance metrics that the user is interested in. We are currently investigating methods for optimizing multiple dimensions of performance metrics, like finding Pareto frontier execution plans.

In the course of the workflow execution, the real-time monitoring information is fed back to the decision making module in order to take into account current running conditions and adapt accordingly. Moreover, our planner considers more than a single final plan to ensure that alternatives will exist in case of failures or other unpredictable circumstances without having to run the whole decision making process from scratch. These alternatives include the top-k (instead of the best) plans according to the user's optimization preferences or a sample of the multi-dimensional space covering different environments.

Enforcer Module: The enforcer module undertakes the execution of the ensuing plan. First, the enforcer needs to validate the plan by checking the availability of resources and data, the load of the engines, etc. After ensuring that everything is correct, it enforces the plan actions by translating the plan steps to standard, low-level API calls. Such actions might entail code and/or data shipment if necessary. In case of faults and failures occurring on-the-fly, an alternative plan will substitute the current.

3. DEMONSTRATION DESCRIPTION

Our system is controlled by a comprehensive web-based GUI that attendees will utilize. The basic interaction dimensions include input parametrization, operator model visualization, execution plan inspection and execution output evaluation. The GUI controls a cloud-based deployment of several runtime engines and data stores over 16 virtual machines of an Openstack cluster hosted in our lab.

Workflows and Datasets: The users will have the opportunity to test the IReS platform either using one of four predefined workflows or assembling their own, using operators from the ASAP operator library. A diverse set of operations of varying complexity and execution parameters is covered including basic SQL queries (selections, projections, joins), ML algorithms (classification and clustering) as well as NLP methods (named entity recognition).

Three of the predefined workflows represent real use cases driven by business needs. These cover complex data manipulations in the areas of business analytics on telecommunication data and web data analytics, provided by a large telecommunications company and a well-known web archiving organization respectively. The input datasets for these workflows consist of anonymized telecommunication traces and web content data (WARC files). Subsets of those datasets can be used for each of the available workflows. A short description for each workflow follows:

Web analytics - Clustering: The workflow starts by selecting a subset of the initial web content indexed by Elasticsearch. Feature-extraction (e.g., tf-idf) is performed on these documents; the outputs are clustered using k-means clustering (chosen among weka, mahout and MLlib running centrally or over Hadoop or Spark respectively).

Web analytics - Named Entity Recognition: A subset of the dataset (obtained via a query over Elasticsearch as before) undergoes named entity extraction. The results are joined with the YAGO external ontology database [15] to find possible matches and output them.

Telco analytics - Peak Detection: The workflow involves processing of anonymized CDR data (residing in an RDBMS) via clustering along time and space in order to detect peaks in load, according to a set of criteria. The results of this phase enrich a database (relational or graph DB)

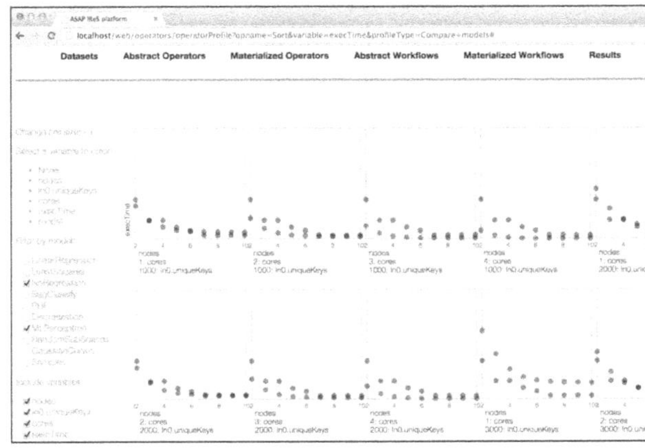

Figure 4: IReS web application GUI - Materialized Operator models

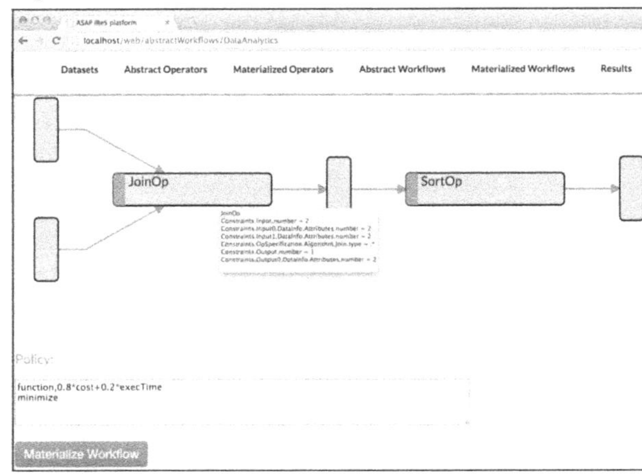

Figure 5: IReS web application GUI - Abstract Workflow

that contains peaks detected in previous runs. The dataset of peaks is used to discover clusters of calls that occur with or without regularity.

Synthetic workflow: A sample workflow that showcases a simple join operation between two datasets residing in different stores, namely PostgreSQL and HBase, followed by a sorting operation. For this workflow, we use synthetic data produced by the popular TPC-H [14] benchmark generator.

User defined workflow: The users will have the opportunity to construct custom workflows by utilizing the current library of operators and datasets.

Interface: Through the platform's front-end, users are able to inspect available operators and datasets, construct the workflow they want to execute or choose one of the pre-defined ones, specify the input parameters, review the proposed execution plan and monitor its progress and output. Our proposed interface consists of 6 sections, namely: *Datasets*, *Abstract Operators*, *Materialized Operators*, *Abstract Workflow*, *Materialized Workflow* and *Results*.

In the *Datasets* tab, the user can browse through the available datasets and view their metadata. In the *Abstract Operator* tab, the user can chose an existing abstract operator and customize it by changing its accompanying metadata. Among others, the user can specify the engine(s) on which an operator will be run or the storage where the data will be saved. The engines supported by IReS include JVM,

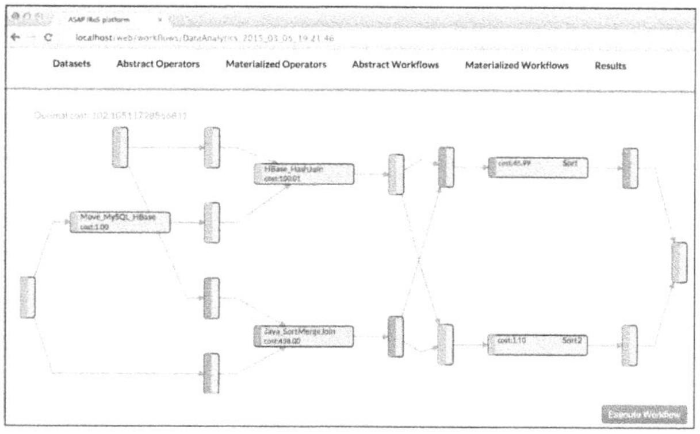

Figure 6: IReS web application GUI - Materialized Workflow tab

Hadoop MapReduce [1], Spark [4], Hama [2] for processing and HDFS [7], HBase [3], Elasticsearch [6], PostgreSQL [11] and local file system for storage.

The *Materialized Operator* tab visualizes the materialized operator models that have been created offline and are stored in the Model DB. The user can plot the modelled metrics (e.g., execution time) versus various parameters (e.g., number of nodes, dataset size, etc.) for a plethora of machine learning models (Figure 4).

The *Abstract Workflow* tab gives the user the opportunity to view the predefined workflows and choose one of them or create one of her own by combining abstract operators and datasets. Either way, the workflow is visualized in its abstract form as a graph, consisting of operator and data nodes (Figure 5). Moreover, the user can specify the policy for which the platform will optimize the execution plan. The supported choices include minimizing cost, execution time or a function of them.

After selecting the abstract workflow and its input parameters, the user is able to move forward to the *Materialized Workflow* tab (Figure 6). A preview of the materialized plan is presented here and the user can inspect the platform's choices for each of the operators and the intermediate results, along with an estimation of the execution cost and performance. At this stage, the user should be able to validate the strategy that will be followed in order to optimize for the chosen attributes. It is also possible to go back and change the input parameters if the user wants to override some of the system's decisions.

The *Results* section offers a live preview of the execution so far. For each finished workflow stage, a summary of its execution aspects is presented, including execution time, resources allocated to each operator, resources actually used, operator throughput and I/O and network costs (if applicable). The cost of each operation as calculated by its cost model is also shown. For the execution steps that have not yet been concluded, an approximation for the anticipated performance and cost measures is presented, if possible via previous knowledge of the operator.

4. ACKNOWLEDGEMENTS

This work has been supported by the European Commission in terms of the ASAP FP7 ICT Project under grant agreement no 619706. Nikolaos Papailiou has received funding from IKY fellowships of excellence for postgraduate studies in Greece - SIEMENS program.

5. REFERENCES

[1] Apache Hadoop. `http://hadoop.apache.org/`.
[2] Apache Hama. `https://hama.apache.org/`.
[3] Apache HBase. `http://hbase.apache.org/`.
[4] Apache Spark. `https://spark.apache.org/`.
[5] Cloudera Distribution CDH 5.2.0. `http://www.cloudera.com/content/cloudera/en/downloads/cdh/cdh-5-2-0.html`.
[6] elasticsearch. `http://www.elasticsearch.org/overview/elasticsearch/`.
[7] Hadoop Distributed File System. http://hadoop.apache.org/docs/r1.2.1/hdfs_design.html.
[8] heroku add-ons. `https://addons.heroku.com/`.
[9] Hortonworks Sandbox 2.1. `http://hortonworks.com/products/hortonworks-sandbox/`.
[10] monetdb. `https://www.monetdb.org/`.
[11] Postgresql. http://www.postgresql.org/.
[12] Running Databases on AWS. `http://aws.amazon.com/running_databases/`.
[13] Stratosphere Project. `http://stratosphere.eu/`.
[14] TPC-H benchmark. *http://www.tcp.org/hspec.html*.
[15] YAGO2s: A High-Quality Knowledge Base. `http://www.mpi-inf.mpg.de/departments/databases-and-information-systems/research/yago-naga/yago/`.
[16] The Power of Combining Big Data Analytics with Business Process Workflow. CGI Whitepaper, 2013.
[17] 84% Of Enterprises See Big Data Analytics Changing Their Industries' Competitive Landscapes In The Next Year . Forbes Magazine, 2014.
[18] S. Babu. Towards automatic optimization of mapreduce programs. In *ACM symposium on Cloud computing*, 2010.
[19] M. Ferguson. Architecting a big data platform for analytics. *A Whitepaper Prepared for IBM*, 2012.
[20] H. Herodotou et al. Starfish: A Self-tuning System for Big Data Analytics. In *CIDR*, 2011.
[21] Y. Jin. Surrogate-assisted evolutionary computation: Recent advances and future challenges. *Swarm and Evolutionary Computation*, 2011.
[22] H. Lim, H. Herodotou, and S. Babu. Stubby: A Transformation-based Optimizer for Mapreduce Workflows. *VLDB*, 2012.
[23] A. Pariyani, U. G. Oktem, and D. L. Grubbe. Process risk assessment uses big data, 06-03-2013. http://bit.ly/1vDlTVk.
[24] B. Sharma, T. Wood, and C. R. Das. Hybridmr: A hierarchical mapreduce scheduler for hybrid data centers. In *ICDCS*. IEEE, 2013.
[25] A. Simitsis, K. Wilkinson, U. Dayal, and M. Hsu. HFMS: Managing the Lifecycle and Complexity of Hybrid Analytic Data Flows. In *ICDE*. IEEE, 2013.
[26] A. Simitsis, K. Wilkinson, and P. Jovanovic. xPAD: A Platform for Analytic Data Flows. In *SIGMOD 2013*.
[27] D. Tsoumakos and C. Mantas. The Case for Multi-Engine Data Analytics. In *Euro-Par 2013: Parallel Processing Workshops*. Springer, 2014.
[28] Z. Zhang, L. Cherkasova, A. Verma, and B. T. Loo. Automated profiling and resource management of pig programs for meeting service level objectives. In *Conference on Autonomic computing*. ACM, 2012.

Just can't get enough - Synthesizing Big Data

Tilmann Rabl
Middleware Systems
Research Group
University of Toronto
Canada
tilmann.rabl@utoronto.ca

Manuel Danisch,
Michael Frank,
Sebastian Schindler
bankmark UG
Passau, Germany
{first.last}@bankmark.de

Hans-Arno Jacobsen
Middleware Systems
Research Group
University of Toronto
Canada
jacobsen@eecg.toronto.edu

ABSTRACT

With the rapidly decreasing prices for storage and storage systems ever larger data sets become economical. While only few years ago only successful transactions would be recorded in sales systems, today every user interaction will be stored for ever deeper analysis and richer user modeling. This has led to the development of big data systems, which offer high scalability and novel forms of analysis. Due to the rapid development and ever increasing variety of the big data landscape, there is a pressing need for tools for testing and benchmarking.

Vendors have little options to showcase the performance of their systems but to use trivial data sets like TeraSort or WordCount. Since customers' real data is typically subject to privacy regulations and rarely can be utilized, simplistic proof-of-concepts have to be used, leaving both, customers and vendors, unclear of the target use-case performance. As a solution, we present an automatic approach to data synthetization from existing data sources. Our system enables a fully automatic generation of large amounts of complex, realistic, synthetic data.

1. INTRODUCTION

Data generation is a tedious part of the daily routine of researchers testing new algorithms, database administrators testing new configurations, and performance engineers testing new optimizations. Typically, the data is generated using scripting solutions, which are written and rewritten for each individual use case. While this is manageable for simple and small data sets, databases are ever increasing in size and complexity. Database testing typically is done on simple scenarios, however, customers demand ever more realistic benchmarks that match their use cases [21]. Modern enterprise systems comprise hundreds to thousands of tables, which frequently have more than fifty columns. System vendors that can show the performance of their systems in a most realistic setup have an advantage over vendors that present generic, simple benchmarks.

To this end, multiple generic data generators have been developed, that enable a fast description of data models and correlations [10, 9, 1, 4]. Although all of these systems feature more efficient and more realistic generation of data none has reached wide adoption in the industry. While building custom data generators for each use case is highly inefficient, generic tools are either too limited in their features or their learning curve is too steep to be accepted by developers. This has led to a dilemma, where it is often infeasible for customers to find the best solution for their use case since they can only give metadata but not real data to vendors and vendors are not able to cover the complex schemas and dependencies in their proof of concept systems.

What is needed is a simple solution, that is able to automatically generate realistic data based only on meta information of the original data. Because of ever increasing data sizes and the prevalent increase of cores, processors, and physical machines in deployed systems, the solution has to be performant and scalable. The data has to be rich in features even in single values, since big data systems do not stop processing at the value level. With these requirements in mind, we have developed DBSynth, a fully automatic data generation solution that can reproduce realistic data sets based on schema information and sampling. Unlike any other generic data generator, it can extract features on the value level and generate new relevant values.

DBSynth is an extension to the Parallel Data Generation Framework (PDGF), a generic data generator suite [17]. PDGF is the basis for the data generator of the new industry standard ETL benchmark TPC-DI, which was released by the Transaction Processing Performance Council (TPC) in January 2014 [16] and was also used to implement the data generator for BigBench, the first end-to-end proposal for a big data analytics [7].

Our main contributions are the following, we demonstrate DBSynth, which is the answer to one of the fundamental challenges in the big data space today - finding the best system for a given use case. DBSynth is the first tool, which can generate complete data models from large complex databases on a variety of systems, sample data sets and automatically create relevant dictionaries and Markov models. Furthermore, we demonstrate PDGF, a highly advanced generic data generator, which can use models created by DBSynth to create big, realistic, synthetic data. PDGF is faster and more efficient than any other generic generator and can be run with perfect speedup in multi-core and multi-node environments. PDGF can write data in various formats (e.g., CSV, JSON, XML, and SQL) to files, database systems, streaming systems, and modern big data storage systems (e.g., HDFS).

The remainder of this paper is structured as follows. We describe PDGF briefly in Section 2 and then show the core functionality of DBSynth in Section 3. After an evaluation in Section 4, we explain our demonstration in Section 5. In Section 6, we give an overview of related work, before concluding in Section 7.

SIGMOD'15, May 31–June 4, 2015, Melbourne, Victoria, Australia.

ACM 978-1-4503-2758-9/15/05 ...$15.00.
http://dx.doi.org/10.1145/2723372.2735378.

2. PDGF

The Parallel Data Generation Framework (PDGF) is a versatile, generic data generator [17]. PDGF has a novel computation-based generation strategy that enables a completely parallel generation of data. PDGF's generation strategy is based on the exploitation of determinism in pseudo random number generators (PRNG). Random number sequences generated using PRNGs are repeatable, which means that the exact same sequence can be generated over and over again. PDGF uses xorshift random number generators, which behave like hash functions. Repeatable, parallel data generation is possible using an elaborate seeding strategy (depicted in Figure 1). In the example, starting with a project seed one seed per table is generated. This seed is used to create one seed per column, which again is used to generate one seed per abstract time unit and finally per field. The field seed is used to generate the random number sequence for the value generation. The values are generated using *field value generators*. These can be simple generators, like number generators, generators based on dictionaries, or reference generators, but also *meta generators*, which can concatenate results from other generators or execute different generators based on certain conditions [18]. The concept of meta generators enables a functional definition of complex values and dependencies using simple building blocks. Although the seeding hierarchy and meta generator stacking seems expensive, most of the seeds can be cached and the cost for generating single values is very low. We will show an analysis of the exact costs in Section 4.

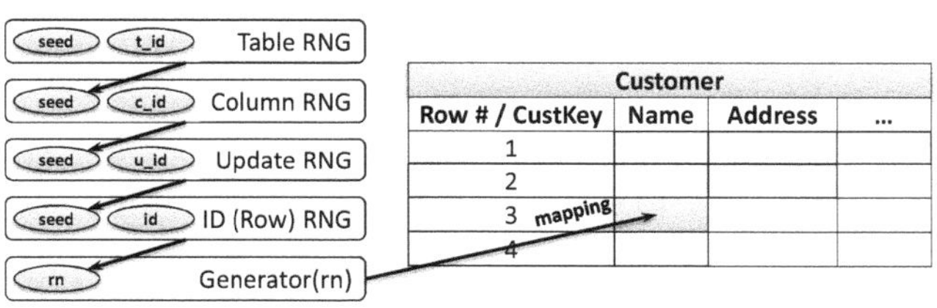

Figure 1: PDGF's seeding strategy

PDGF's architecture is shown in Figure 2. The user specifies two XML configuration files, one for the data model and one for the formatting instructions. These will be explained in more detail in Section 3. Additionally, all previously specified properties of a model and format (e.g., scale factors, table sizes, probabilities) can be changed in the command line interface. The controller then initializes the system. The meta scheduler manages multi-node scheduling, while the scheduler assigns work packages to the workers. A work package is a set of rows of a table that need to be generated. The workers then initialize the correct generators using the seeding system and the update black box. Whenever a work package is generated, it is sent to the output system, where it can be formatted and sorted.

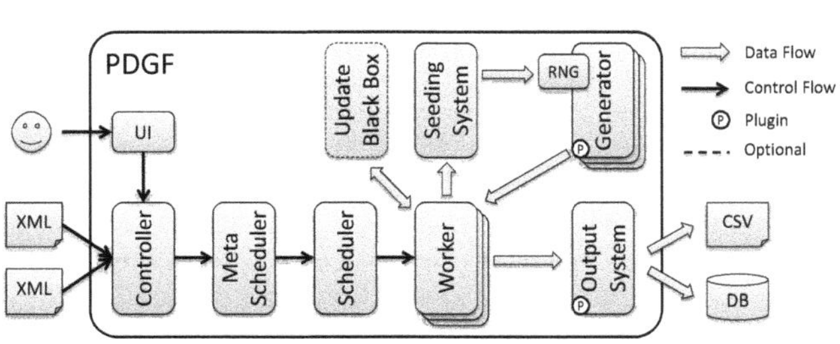

Figure 2: PDGF's architecture

PDGF has been successfully used to implement a variety of benchmarks, e.g., TPC-H [17], the Star Schema Benchmark [19], TPC-DI [6], and BigBench [7].

3. DBSYNTH

DBSynth is an extension to PDGF that automates the configuration and enables the extraction of data model information from an existing database. DBSynth's abstract architecture and mode of operation can be seen in Figure 3. In DBSynth, the user specifies projects, which integrate workflows, such as data generation, data extraction, etc. The figure shows the complete automatic workflow, from model extraction to data generation. Not all steps are necessary for a given project.

DBSynth connects to a source database via JDBC, using the model creation tool, schema information and a configurable level of additional information of the data model are extracted. Possible information includes min/max constraints, histograms, NULL probabilities, as well as statistic information collected by the database system such as histograms. DBSynth also features a rule based system that searches for key words in the schema information and adds predefined generation rules to the data model. For example, numeric columns with name *key* or *id* will be generated with an *ID generator*.

If sampling the database is permissible, the data extraction tool builds histograms and dictionaries of text-valued data and stores the according probabilities for values. Users can specify the amount of data sampled and the sampling strategy. In future versions, we will include a dynamic sampling, which adapts the sample size and sampling strategy according to the base data. If the text data contains multiple words, DBSynth uses a Markov chain generator, which analyzes the word combination frequencies and probabilities. These are stored and linked to the data model.

Using the generated data model, PDGF can generate the data. The model is translated into a SQL schema, which is loaded into the target database using JDBC. The data can be loaded into the target database either using SQL statements generated by PDGF or a bulk load option, if featured by the target database.

Listing 1 presents an excerpt of the automatically generated configuration for a TPC-H data set [15]. The excerpt shows the general structure of the PDGF schema configuration. It contains the project's seed, changing the seed will modify every value of the generated data set, the random number generator, PdgfDefaultRandom is a custom built, very fast xorshift PRNG, property definitions, which can also be changed from the command line, and the schema information itself. A default property is the scaling factor *SF*, which is used to determine the size of the data set. DBSynth will generate a size property for each table and assign it the product of the scale factor and the original table size. This way other scaling dependencies can be easily specified in a centralized point in the model. Furthermore, all boundaries for numerical values and dates are stored in properties.

The schema model is specified in form of table entries. Each table specifies its size, which DBSynth sets to be linear with the scale factor as shown in the example. However, any formula can be used to calculate the size. Then the columns of the table are specified in form of field entries. The first field is "l_orderkey", the name and size are extracted from the database's schema information. The fact that it is a key is deduced from the column name, this is the reason why DBSynth chooses an ID generator for this column. The next field is "l_partkey", which is a reference to the table "partsupp". This is specified in the schema, which is why DBSynth chooses a DefaultReferenceGenerator, which will generate consistent references to this table. The final field that is shown is "l_comment",

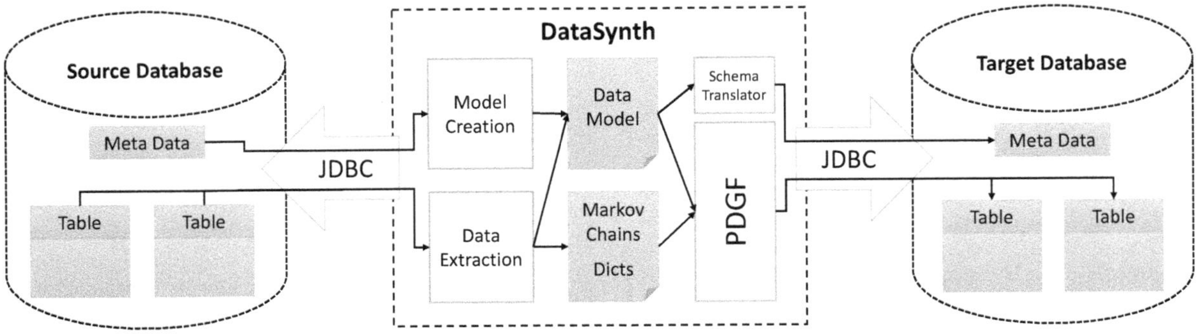

Figure 3: Abstract architecture and data flow in DBSynth

a text field containing free text. DBSynth chooses the Markov-Generator for this field, thus it will sample the original database to build the Markov model. For a TPC-H data set the comment field model contains 1500 words and 95 starting states, which can easily be fit in memory. The choice of the generator type used for a field is based first on referential integrity constraints, i.e., a reference will always be generated by a reference generator independent of its type. Then the data type determines if a number generator, e.g., Long, Integer, Double, or a date generator, or a text generator is used, DBSynth and PDGF support all SQL 92 datatypes. If the database is not sampled, the column name is parsed to determine whether a matching high level generator construct exists, e.g., names, addresses, comment. In case nothing is found a random string is generated. The Markov generator builds dictionaries for single word text fields and Markov chains for free text, the parameters for the Markov model are adjusted based on the original data. If the original data cannot be sampled or analyzed, DBSynth falls back to random values based on the database statistics as well as predefined generators for URLs, addresses, etc.

4. EVALUATION

We evaluated the performance of PDGF and DBSynth on a 24 node, dual socket, dual core cluster and on a single node with two sockets and eight cores per socket. Where possible, generated data was written to */dev/null* to ensure the throughput was not I/O bound. In the experiments, we used either the BigBench data set or our custom implementation of the TPC-H data set.

In the first experiment, we evaluate the performance of PDGF by generating a BigBench data set of scale factor 5000, which results in a total data size of 4392 GB on the 24 node cluster. The results of this experiment can be seen in Figure 4. As is shown in the figure, PDGF has linear throughput scaling in the number of nodes.

In the second experiment, we benchmark the scale out performance of PDGF by increasing the number of workers and thus threads used for the data generation. This experiment is conducted on the single node. The results can be seen in Figure 5. PDGF's throughput increases linearly with the number of cores (16) and further increases with the number of hardware threads (32), but not as significantly as for the number of cores. An interesting observation is that scheduling exactly the same number of workers as the number of system cores or threads is not optimal due to the additional internal scheduling and I/O threads.

In Figure 6, a comparison of the data generator DBGen and PDGF is shown. As can be seen, both tools achieve a similar performance. In parallel mode, it is not possible to write to /dev/null using DBGen, which is why in this experiment the throughput of both, DBGen and PDGF, was disk-bound. We also show PDGF's CPU-bound performance, which is 33% higher than its disk-bound performance. DBGen's parallelization is non-transparent. This means that for each parallel stream a new instance is started, which writes its own files. As a result, DBGen's parallel output will be split in as many files as instances were started, whereas PDGF writes sorted output into a single file. PDGF also supports the same parallel generation strategy as DBGen does, which is starting multiple instances and generating a distinct range of the data set with each instance. With this approach it is possible to scale out the generation to shared nothing systems with linear speedups [17]. When comparing the single process performance, i.e., starting only a single DBGen instance and running PDGF with a single worker, DBGen achieves 48 MB/s and PDGF 30 MB/s. Thus, PDGF is has the

```
<?xml version="1.0" encoding="UTF-8"?>
<schema name="tpch">
 <seed>12456789</seed>
 <rng name="PdgfDefaultRandom"></rng>
 <property name="SF" type="double">1</property>
 <property name="lineitem_size" type="double">6000000 *
      ${SF}</property>

 <table name="lineitem">
  <size>${lineitem_size}</size>

  <field name="l_orderkey" size="19" type="BIGINT"
       primary="true">
   <gen_IdGenerator>
   </gen_IdGenerator>
  </field>

  <field name="l_partkey" size="19" type="BIGINT"
       primary="false">
   <gen_DefaultReferenceGenerator>
    <reference table="partsupp"
        field="ps_partkey"></reference>
   </gen_DefaultReferenceGenerator>
  </field>
  [..]
  <field name="l_comment" size="44" type="VARCHAR"
       primary="false">
   <gen_NullGenerator> probability=".0000d"
    <gen_MarkovChainGenerator>
     <min>1</min>
     <max>10</max>
     <file>markov\l_comment_markovSamples.bin</file>
    </gen_MarkovChainGenerator>
   </gen_NullGenerator>
  </field>
 </table>
 [..]
```

Listing 1: Excerpt of the schema definition for TPC-H

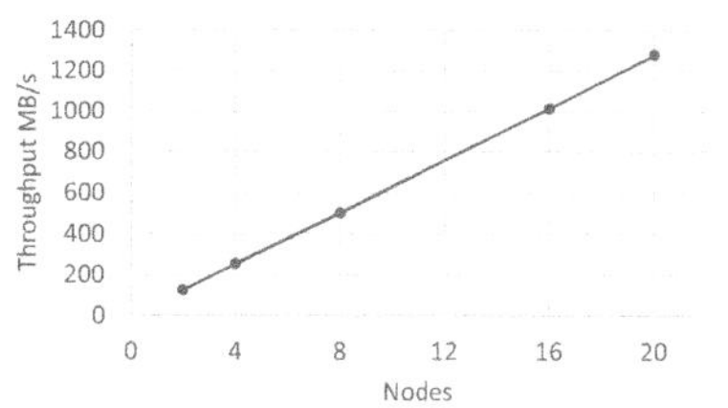

Figure 4: PDGF BigBench scale-out performance

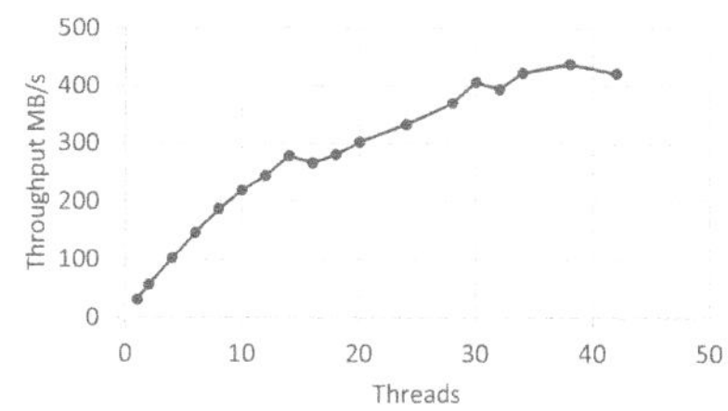

Figure 5: PDGF TPC-H scale-up performance

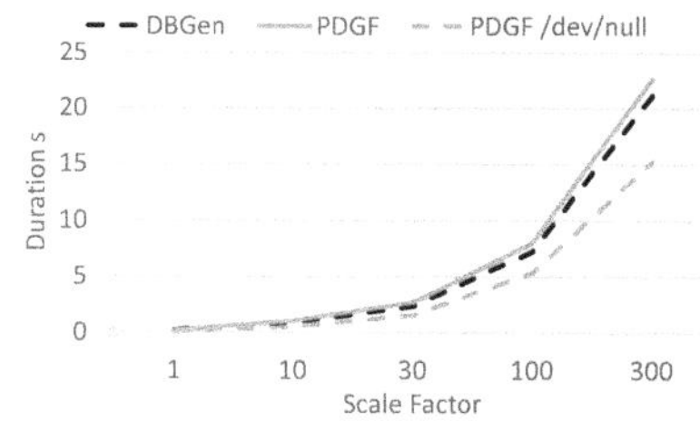

Figure 6: DBGen vs PDGF performance

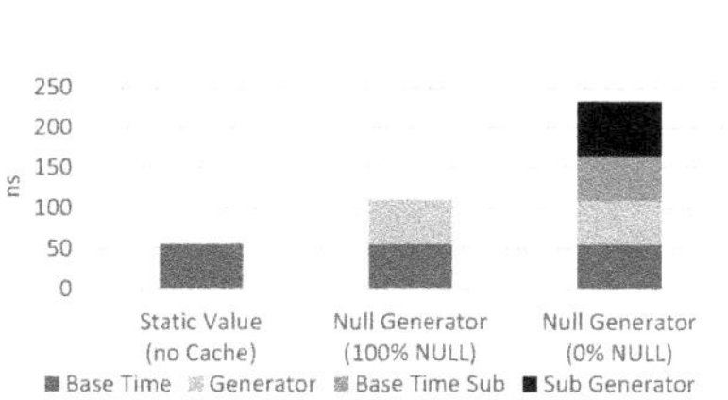

Figure 7: Generation latency

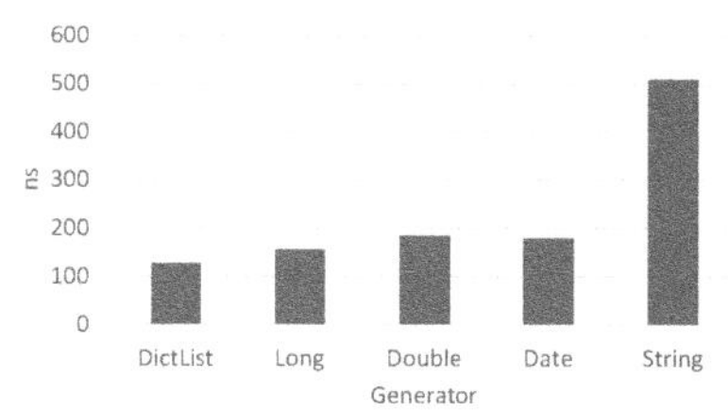

Figure 8: Basic generator latency

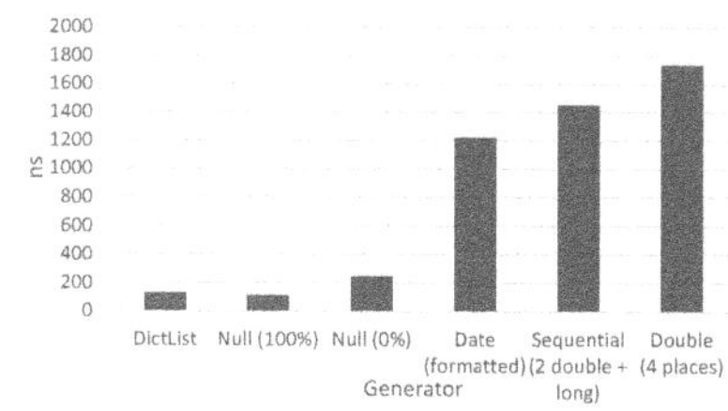

Figure 9: Complex generator latency

same order of performance as DBGen, although being completely generic and adaptable.

We conducted further experiments to determine the sources of latencies for the individual value generation. The experiments were done in a single threaded setup, to get the per value overhead. These results show the pure computational requirements and do not discuss latencies added by the I/O subsystem. In Figure 7, the latency of independent value generation is broken down into its subparts. For a static value, i.e., a column contains only one unique value that is never changed, the pure system overhead can be seen. It is in the order of 50 Nanoseconds (ns). If a NULL value generator is wrapped around a static value that is NULL with 100% probability, the overhead of the NULL generator is added to the generation of the (static) NULL value, this is again in the order of 50 ns. The definition of the NULL value generator can be seen in Listing 1. Finally, if the NULL probability is 0% the inner static value generator has to be executed in all cases, this adds the base time for the subgenerator and the actual value generation, both of which are again ca 50 ns. Thus the total duration for each value is in the order of 200 ns. In Figure 8, it can be seen that this is a good ballpark number for simple values that are not formatted. Picking values from dictionaries, computing random numbers, and generating random strings are all in the range of 100 ns - 500 ns. String formatting is the most expensive operation in data generation in Java, this can seen in Figure 9. Formatting a date value (e.g., "11/30/2014") increases the generation cost to 1200 ns, which is similar to generating a value that consists of a formula that references 2 double values and concatenates it with a long. Although the formatting is expensive, its cost is fixed since PDGF does lazy formatting, which means even very complex values will only be formatted once. This analysis shows that using subgenerators incurs nearly negligible cost (ca. 100 ns) and it also shows that computing values rather than rereading them is much more efficient. While generating complex values might cost up to 2000 ns, doing a single random read will cost ca. 10 ms on disk, which means the computational approach is 5000 times faster than an approach that reads previously generated data to solve dependencies. Furthermore, the computational approach enables a completely parallel generation of data, which is not possible using reading based approach without replicating data or extensive network communication.

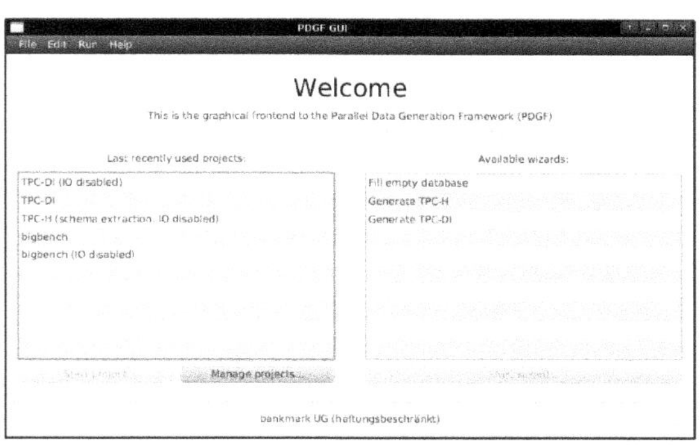

Figure 10: Standard screen of DBSynth

In our final experiment, we tested the performance of the DBSynth metadata extraction. Using a TPC-H database with scale factor 1 loaded in a PostgreSQL DBMS, it takes 600 ms to get the schema information, 1.3 s to get the table sizes, 600 ms to get NULL probabilities, 10 seconds to get all min and max constraints, and between 800 ms (0.001% samples) and 200 s (100% samples) to retrieve data for the Markov chains. These results indicate an interactive response time for data model generation. Using PDGF's preview generation, which shows samples of the generated data instantaneously, data models can be built and improved very fast.

5. DEMONSTRATION

To show the ease of use of DBSynth, we will demonstrate typical work flows for data generation. We will start by generating industry standard data sets such as TPC-H. The data will be generated using PDGF, but this configuration is compliant to the TPC-H data set [15] and was developed in cooperation with the TPC-H subcommittee. This is a default project in DBSynth. The according selection screen can be seen in Figure 10. We will generate a 10 GB TPC-H data set. We will show how the data can be altered

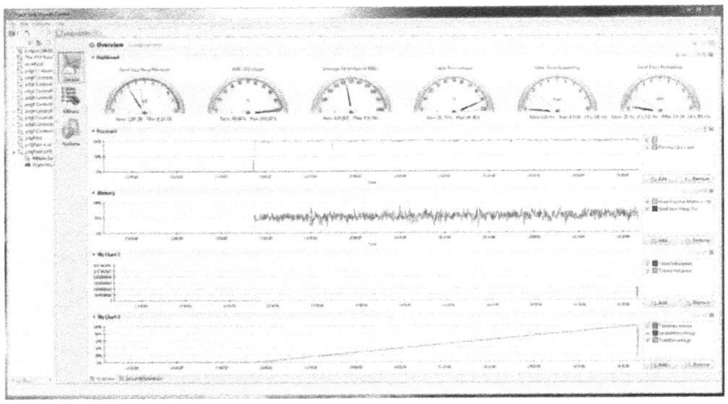

Figure 11: Mission Control interface for PDGF

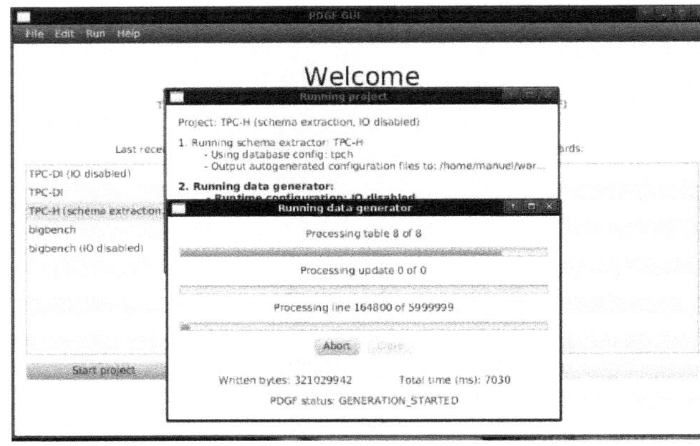

Figure 12: Data generation screen of DBSynth

by changing the output format. To this end, the data will be written in CVS and XML format. The generation progress and system utilization will be monitored using Java Mission Control[1]. PDGF uses the Java Management Extensions internally for inter process communication and using these interfaces, the progress of single tables and the complete data set as well as general performance parameters can be visualized. This can be seen in Figure 11.

After the data generation, we will demonstrate the configuration generation. To show a real use case, we will use the publicly available parts of the IMDb database[2]. The data set is hosted in a MySQL database, which was loaded using the imdbpy2sql.py script, which is part of the IMDbPY package[3]. We will first use a basic schema extraction, where only the schema information is retrieved from the database and no tables are accessed. The generated XML file will be explained, which contains the model for the data generation. Then we will do a second more elaborate schema extraction, where min/max constraints, NULL values, and data samples for Markov chains will be read from the database. We will compare the newly extracted model with the first one and then generate the data. The according screen can be seen in Figure 12. We will show excerpts of the generated data in comparison to the original data and verify the quality by running SQL queries on the original data and the generated data and compare the results. To this end, the generated data will be loaded to a database system.

Finally, we will explain how the model can be changed or adapted. We will change the automatically generated configuration by adding additional columns to the model and refining correlations that could not automatically be detected. This will be done using an automatically generated version of the TPC-H configuration. We will then show the differences between the original TPC-H configuration and the newly generated configuration and compare the generated data sets.

6. RELATED WORK

There is a rich body of work on data generation for database benchmarking and testing. In the following, we will first give an overview of related work on data generation in general and then show other approaches for synthesizing existing data sets.

Even though there are many generic data generation tools, most data generators either produce very simple data or are non-reusable hard coded programs or collections of scripts. Examples for simple data generation are the data generator used by all variations of the sorting benchmark (e.g., TeraSort[4]) and the Yahoo Cloud Serving Benchmark data generator [5]. Examples for hard coded generators are all TPC data generators, with the notable exceptions of TPC-DS [14] and TPC-DI [16]. While simple data is helpful for testing basic functionality it does not represent real world use cases. However, hard coded data generators cannot easily be adapted for changing requirements and for different systems. In many cases real data can be used, but due to the impossiblity of scaling, privacy constraints and cost of storage and transportation it is not feasible for benchmarking.

An important characteristic for benchmarking data is repeatablity. Basis for repeatable parallel data generation is the work by Gray et al. on synthetic data generation [8]. This work describes how to generate non uniform data in parallel on shared nothing systems. These techniques along with parallel pseudo random number generators for the basis of our Parallel Data Generation Framework.

Modern generic data generators can be divided into three subsets according to their reference and correlation generation: (1) no reference generation; (2) reference tracking; and (3) reference computation. Many data generators do not generate references or correlations explicitly, but rely on users providing correct statistic distributions to generate correlating values. Generators that track references either compute all references at the same time that the original value is generated, or they track the original value when a references is generated. The former approach is frequently done using graph models [10, 11] or declarative description [2, 24] which can lead to realistic data, however, typically is very slow and hard to parallelize. Tracking references is done by rereading the previously generated data. This approach was for example presented by Bruno et al. [4], this approach is very flexible but also very slow and does not scale well. A faster approach is generating all related data at the same time. Generic suites that use this approach include MUDD [22] and PSDG [9]. The fastest way of generating correct references in most cases is recomputing them. This approach was first implemented in PDGF. A very similar data generator, Myriad, was built at the Technical University of Berlin [1]. It shares the same generation strategy with PDGF, however, does does not include many of the features of PDGF, such as update generation and text generation.

As part of the BigDataBench suite of test cases for big data systems, an early version of PDGF is used to generate structured data [13]. The suite comprises additional generators for graphs

[1]http://www.oracle.com/technetwork/java/javaseproducts/mission-control/java-mission-control-1998576.html

[2]http://www.imdb.com/interfaces

[3]https://github.com/alberanid/imdbpy

[4]`https://hadoop.apache.org/docs/current/api/org/apache/hadoop/examples/terasort/package-summary.html`

and a similar text generator as the current version of PDGF features. Unlike PDGF's text generator, the different generators are not connected and, therefore, cannot generate heterogeneous data sets with references in between different data sets, e.g., references from structured data into text.

Although synthetic data is usually better suited for benchmarking purposes, synthetic data should reflect characteristics of real data. Therefore, typically real data sets are analyzed for modeling data sets for benchmarking. Although this step is typically manual, it can be automated. Like DBSynth other tools use the metadata stored in database systems to get information about the distribution and structure of the data. RSGen reads metadata and schema information of existing data sets and generates similar data sets by using histograms of the original data [20]. Although similar to DBSynth, the approach is limited to numerical data. Another tool that is able to scale existing data sets is UpSizeR [23]. It builds a graph of the original schema information and correlation information and generates data accordingly. However, the individual, non-key values are deemed application specific and thus have to be specified by the user. DBSynth uses sampling of the data set to generate dictionaries and Markov chains for non-key, non-numerical values. Furthermore, DBSynth uses its built in dictionaries to increase the value domain in scale out scenarios. Myriad also comes with configuration generation tool Oligos, which can analyze the schema and statistical information of a DB2 database [1]. However, it cannot not sample a database and also has no tools to analyze and synthesize values.

A line of work that is orthogonal to our work is test data generation for queries. QAGen analyzes queries to generate data that produces desired results and intermediate results to cover all required test cases [3]. A similar tool is MyBenchmark [12]. Analyzing queries to ensure desired results is currently not a feature of our tool, but will be included in future versions. Given the deterministic approach of data generation, our tool will then also be able to directly execute the query without ever generating the data, which can be used to verify results for correctness.

Although many of the features of DBSynth are covered to some extent by other projects, none of these does include synthetic value generation. Values are always treated as atomic units. This is problematic for big data sets, where values frequently are texts that have to be further analyzed using machine learning techniques. To generate data sets, which satisfy requirements of big data use cases, DBSynth includes Markov chain generators and dictionaries that can generate realistic, synthetic values based on sampled data.

7. CONCLUSION

We demonstrate DBSynth, an extension to the Parallel Data Generation Framework, which enables a fully automatic configuration of the data generator based on existing databases. DBSynth can build realistic data models from a deployed database extracting schema information, sampling, and analyzing the database. It uses heuristics for data type determination and builds dictionaries and Markov models for data generation. The generated models and configuration can be directly used by PDGF to generate data for a target database. A simple, intuitive graphical user interface ties all parts together and features wizards to guide users through every step of the process. In our demonstration, we showcase the ease of use, the high performance, and the flexibility of the system.

In future work, we will extend DBSynth to automate the complete benchmarking process. To this end, we will generate the queries consistently using PDGF and build additional driver and analysis modules. Furthermore, we will include query analysis to generate data sets with predefined (intermediate) results and generate verification results for queries for given data models.

8. REFERENCES

[1] A. Alexandrov, K. Tzoumas, and V. Markl. Myriad: Scalable and Expressive Data Generation. In *VLDB*, 2012.

[2] A. Arasu, R. Kaushik, and J. Li. Data Generation Using Declarative Constraints. In *SIGMOD*, 2011.

[3] C. Binnig, D. Kossmann, E. Lo, and M. T. Özsu. QAGen: Generating Query-aware Test Databases. In *SIGMOD*, 2007.

[4] N. Bruno and S. Chaudhuri. Flexible Database Generators. In *VLDB*, pages 1097–1107, 2005.

[5] B. F. Cooper, A. Silberstein, E. Tam, R. Ramakrishnan, and R. Sears. Benchmarking Cloud Serving Systems with YCSB. In *SoCC*, pages 143–154, 2010.

[6] M. Frank, M. Poess, and T. Rabl. Efficient Update Data Generation for DBMS Benchmark. In *ICPE*, 2012.

[7] A. Ghazal, T. Rabl, M. Hu, F. Raab, M. Poess, A. Crolotte, and H.-A. Jacobsen. BigBench: Towards an industry standard benchmark for big data analytics. In *SIGMOD*, 2013.

[8] J. Gray, P. Sundaresan, S. Englert, K. Baclawski, and P. J. Weinberger. Quickly Generating Billion-Record Synthetic Databases. In *SIGMOD*, pages 243–252, 1994.

[9] J. E. Hoag and C. W. Thompson. A Parallel General-Purpose Synthetic Data Generator. *SIGMOD Record*, 36(1):19–24, 2007.

[10] K. Houkjær, K. Torp, and R. Wind. Simple and Realistic Data Generation. In *VLDB*, pages 1243–1246, 2006.

[11] P. J. Lin, B. Samadi, A. Cipolone, D. R. Jeske, S. Cox, C. Rendón, D. Holt, and R. Xiao. Development of a Synthetic Data Set Generator for Building and Testing Information Discovery Systems. In *ITNG*, pages 707–712, Washington, DC, USA, 2006. IEEE Computer Society.

[12] E. Lo, N. Cheng, and W.-K. Hon. Generating Databases for Query Workloads. *PVLDB*, 3(1-2):848–859, 2010.

[13] Z. Ming, C. Luo, W. Gao, R. Han, Q. Yang, L. Wang, and J. Zhan. BDGS: A Scalable Big Data Generator Suite in Big Data Benchmarking. In *WBDB*, 2013.

[14] M. Poess and C. Floyd. New TPC Benchmarks for Decision Support and Web Commerce. *SIGMOD Record*, 29(4):64–71, 2000.

[15] M. Poess, T. Rabl, M. Frank, and M. Danisch. A PDGF Implementation for TPC-H. In *TPCTC*, 2011.

[16] M. Poess, T. Rabl, H.-A. Jacobsen, and B. Caufield. TPC-DI: The First Industry Benchmark for Data Integration. *PVLDB*, 13(7):1367–1378, 2014.

[17] T. Rabl, M. Frank, H. M. Sergieh, and H. Kosch. A Data Generator for Cloud-Scale Benchmarking. In *TPCTC*, pages 41–56, 2010.

[18] T. Rabl, M. Poess, M. Danisch, and H.-A. Jacobsen. Rapid Development of Data Generators Using Meta Generators in PDGF. In *DBTest*, 2013.

[19] T. Rabl, M. Poess, H.-A. Jacobsen, P. E. O'Neil, and E. O'Neil. Variations of the Star Schema Benchmark to Test Data Skew in Database Management Systems. In *ICPE*, 2013.

[20] E. Shen and L. Antova. Reversing Statistics for Scalable Test Databases Generation. In *DBTest*, 2013.

[21] V. Sikka. Does the World Need a New Benchmark? `http://www.saphana.com/community/blogs/blog/2013/09/16/does-the-world-need-a-new-benchmark`, 2013.

[22] J. M. Stephens and M. Poess. MUDD: a multi-dimensional data generator. In *WOSP*, pages 104–109, 2004.

[23] Y. Tay, B. T. Dai, D. T. Wang, E. Y. Sun, Y. Lin, and Y. Lin. UpSizeR: Synthetically Scaling an Empirical Relational Database. *Information Systems*, 38(8):1168–1183, 2013.

[24] E. Torlak. Scalable Test Data Generation from Multidimensional Models. In *FSE*, 2012.

Rack-Scale In-Memory Join Processing using RDMA

Claude Barthels, Simon Loesing, Gustavo Alonso, Donald Kossmann*
Systems Group
Department of Computer Science
ETH Zurich, Switzerland
{firstname.lastname}@inf.ethz.ch

ABSTRACT

Database systems running on a cluster of machines, i.e. rack-scale databases, are a common architecture for many large databases and data appliances. As the data movement across machines is often a significant bottleneck, these systems typically use a low-latency, high-throughput network such as InfiniBand. To achieve the necessary performance, parallel join algorithms must take advantage of the primitives provided by the network to speed up data transfer.

In this paper we focus on implementing parallel in-memory joins using Remote Direct Memory Access (RDMA), a communication mechanism to transfer data directly into the memory of a remote machine. The results of this paper are, to our knowledge, the first detailed analysis of parallel hash joins using RDMA. To capture their behavior independently of the network characteristics, we develop an analytical model and test our implementation on two different types of networks. The experimental results show that the model is accurate and the resulting distributed join exhibits good performance.

1. INTRODUCTION

The ability to efficiently process complex queries over large datasets is a basic requirement in real-time analytics. Given the increase of data volume, a platform of choice for data processing are rack-scale clusters composed of several multi-core machines connected by a high-throughput, low-latency network such as InfiniBand [17]. The adoption of rack-scale architectures has been further accelerated through the introduction of several data appliances such as Oracle Exadata [26], IBM Netezza [18] and SAP HANA [29], which follow a similar architecture.

In these systems, efficient inter-machine data movement is critical, forcing join algorithms to be aware of machine boundaries and to employ communication patterns suited for the underlying network technology. A natural question to ask is how join algorithms can be optimized to operate in such environments, how well they can scale with the number of machines, and which bottlenecks arise when scaling out in these architectures. However, little work is available on adapting join algorithms to make efficient use of modern high-speed networks.

Several low-latency networks provide Remote Direct Memory Access (RDMA) as a light-weight communication mechanism to transfer data. RDMA is essential for high performance applications because the data is immediately written or read by the network card, thus eliminating the need to copy the data across intermediate buffers inside the operating system (kernel bypass). This, in turn, reduces the overall CPU costs of large data transfers. However, these performance advantages can only be leveraged through thoughtful design of the distributed algorithm, in particular through careful management of the RDMA-enabled buffers used for sending and receiving data and through interleaving computation and network communication [11].

In this paper we analyze the behaviour of a radix hash join using RDMA. Building upon recent work on main-memory multi-core join algorithms [19, 2, 6, 4], we analyze how a hash join needs to be adapted in order to run on a rack-scale database cluster. In the description of the algorithm we place special emphasis on the registration, de-registration and management of RDMA-enabled buffers as these are critical components. To generalize our findings, we develop a theoretical model allowing us to predict the performance of the algorithms based on the system configuration and input data size. Last but not least, we evaluate our prototype implementation on two database clusters: a ten node cluster composed of multi-core machines connected by a Quad Data Rate (QDR) InfiniBand network and a four node cluster connected by a Fourteen Data Rate (FDR) InfiniBand network. The experimental results validate the accuracy of the analytical model and provide insights on the importance of interleaving computation and communication, the role of the network protocol, the effects of skew, and of different relation and tuple sizes.

To the best of our knowledge, this is the first detailed description, analytical model, and experimental evaluation of a state-of-the-art distributed join operator using RDMA.

The paper is structured as follows: Sections 2 and 3 present related work and discuss the necessary background on the radix hash join and InfiniBand networks. Section 4 describes the RDMA-based hash join. Section 5 provides a detailed analytical model. In Section 6 we evaluate the proposed algorithm experimentally. We discuss our findings in Section 7 and present our conclusions in Section 8.

*The author is currently on leave at Microsoft Research

SIGMOD'15, May 31–June 4, 2015, Melbourne, Victoria, Australia.

http://dx.doi.org/10.1145/2723372.2750547.

2. RELATED WORK

2.1 Parallel and Distributed Joins

In the Gamma database machine [7, 8] tuples are routed to processing nodes using hash-based split tables. Identical split tables are applied to both input relations, thus sending matching tuples to the same processing node. This method reduces a join of two large relations to a set of separate joins which can be executed in parallel.

Schneider et al. [30] compared hash and sort-merge joins on the Gamma database machine. They conclude that with a sufficient amount of main-memory, hash-based join algorithms have superior performance to sort-merge joins.

Most modern hash join algorithms build upon the idea of the Grace hash join [20], where both input relations are first scanned and partitioned according to the join attribute before a hash table is created for each partition of the inner relation and probed with the tuples from the corresponding partition of the outer relation.

The findings of Shatdal et al. [31] and Manegold et al. [23] showed that a Grace hash join which partitions the data such that the resulting hash tables fit into the processor cache can deliver higher performance because it reduces the number of cache misses while probing the hash tables. To avoid excessive Translation Lookaside Buffer (TLB) misses during the partitioning phase caused by random memory access to a large number of partitions, Manegold et al. [23] proposed a partitioning strategy based on radix-clustering. When the amount of partitions exceeds the number of TLB entries or cache lines, the partitioning is performed in multiple passes.

2.2 Join Algorithms on Modern Hardware

Kim et al. [19] have compared hash and sort-merge joins to determine which type of algorithm is better suited to run on modern multi-core machines. In addition to their experiments, the authors also developed a model in order to predict the performance of the algorithms on future hardware. Although modern hardware currently favours hash join algorithms, they estimated that future hardware with wider single instruction over multiple data (SIMD) instructions would significantly speed up sort-merge joins.

Blanas et al. [6] reexamined several hash join variants, namely the no partitioning join, the shared partitioning join, the independent partitioning join and the radix join. The authors argue that the no partitioning join, which skips the partitioning stage, can still outperform other algorithms because modern machines are very good in hiding latencies caused by cache and TLB misses. Their results indicate that the additional cost of partitioning can be higher than the benefit of having a reduced number of cache and TLB misses, thus favouring the no partitioning join.

Albutiu et al. [2] looked at parallel sort-merge join algorithms. The authors report that their implementation of the massively parallel sort-merge (MPSM) join is significantly faster than hash joins, even without SIMD instructions.

Balkesen et al. [4] implemented efficient versions of two hash join algorithms – the no partitioning join and the radix join – in order to compare their implementations with the ones from [6]. They show that a carefully tuned hardware-conscious radix join algorithm outperforms a no partitioning join. Furthermore, the authors argue that the number of hardware-dependent parameters is low enough, such that hardware-conscious join algorithms are as portable as their hardware-oblivious counterparts. In [3], the authors further show that the radix hash join is still superior to sort-merge approaches for current SIMD/AVX sizes.

Lang et al. [21] show the importance of NUMA-awareness for hash join algorithms on multi-cores. Their implementation of a NUMA-aware join claims an improvement over [4] by a factor of more than two.

2.3 Distributed Join Algorithms

Goncalves et al. [16, 15] and Frey et al. [12, 13] have developed a join algorithm, called cyclo-join, suited for ring network topology networks. In the setup phase of the cyclo-join, both relations are fragmented and distributed over all n machines. During the execution, data belonging to one relation is kept stationary while the second relation are passed on from one machine to the next. Similar to our approach, the idea is that the data is too large to fit in one machine, but can fit in the distributed memory of the machines connected on the ring [11]. The cyclo-join uses RDMA as a transport mechanism. The cyclo-join differs from our work in that the cyclo-join is an experimental system that explores how to use the network as a form of storage. The hot set data is kept rotating in the ring and several mechanism are proposed to identify which data should be put on the storage ring [16]. In DaCyDB the authors use RDMA to connect several instances of MonetDB in a ring architecture [15].

Polychroniou at al. [27] propose three variants of a distributed join algorithm which minimize the communication costs. The authors tested their implementation of the proposed join algorithms on a Gigabit Ethernet network. They show that the 3-phase and 4-phase track join algorithms can significantly reduce the overall network traffic.

Rödiger et al. [28] propose locality-sensitive data shuffling, a set of techniques, including optimal assignment of partitions, network communication scheduling, adaptive radix partitioning, and selective broadcast indented to reduce the amount of communication of distributed operators.

Recent work around distributed joins [1, 25] in map-reduce environments focuses on carefully mapping the join operator to the relevant data in order to minimizing network traffic.

These contributions show that the network is the main bottleneck for join processing.

3. BACKGROUND

3.1 Radix Hash Join

The radix hash join proposed by Manegold et al. [23] is a hardware-conscious main-memory hash join. The algorithm operates in two stages. First, both input relations R and S are divided into disjoint partitions according to the join attributes. The goal of the partitioning stage is to ensure that the resulting partitions fit into the private cache of CPU cores. Second, a hash table is built over each partition of the inner relation and is probed using the data of the corresponding partition of the outer relation. Having partitions and hash tables which fit into the processor cache has a major impact on performance compared to accessing large hash tables, which results in a higher cache miss rate [31].

The partitioning algorithm of the radix hash join determines the position of a tuple based on the key's b lower bits, thus creating 2^b partitions in total. The creation of the partitions is performed in p passes (multi-pass partitioning), each pass $i \in \{1 \ldots p\}$ operating on a different non-overlapping

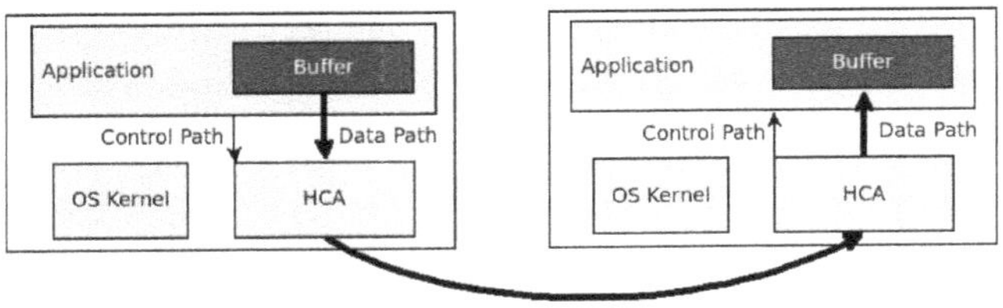

Figure 1: Example of an RDMA transfer from one machine to another. Control and data path are separated. The operating system is completely bypassed.

subset b_i of the b bits such that the number of simultaneously created partitions 2^{b_i} does not exceed the number of TLB entries or cache lines. The multi-pass partitioning scheme employed by the radix hash join avoids excessive TLB misses and cache trashing, and therefore allows to generate a large number of partitions without compromising performance.

The radix join can be parallelized by dividing both input relations into non-overlapping parts and assigning the individual parts to different worker threads. Each thread partitions the data to which it was assigned and afterwards adds the result to a task queue. Finally, each task is consumed during the build-probe phase [4, 6].

3.2 RDMA and InfiniBand

3.2.1 *Benefits and Challenges of RDMA*

Remote Direct Memory Access (RDMA) is a mechanism allowing direct access and placement of data in the main-memory of a remote machine. RDMA is offered by InfiniBand [17] and other recent hardware implementations, for example, RDMA over Ethernet (iWARP and RoCE).

For a memory region to be accessible by the network card, it needs to be registered. During the memory registration process, the memory is pinned to avoid those pages being swapped out while being accessed by the network card. A registered part of memory is referred to as a memory region (MR). As shown by Frey et al. [11], the memory region registration cost increase with the number of registered pages. To reduce the overall registration cost and to avoid pinning large parts of main-memory, efficient buffer management is crucial for high performance. An algorithm should reuse existing RDMA-enabled buffers as often as possible and avoid registering new memory regions on the fly.

Main-memory can directly be accessed by an InfiniBand Host Channel Adapter (HCA) or an RDMA-enabled network interface card (RNIC). This mechanism allows to bypass the network stack, avoids context switches and makes large data transfers more efficient as it eliminates the need to copy the data across intermediate buffers inside the operating system. A message which has not been copied into any temporary buffer during its transmission is called a zero-copy message (see Figure 1).

RDMA separates control and data path. Requests to read or write remote memory are added to a queue and executed asynchronously by the network card. The data transfer therefore does not involve any CPU operation, meaning that the processor remains available for processing while a network operation is taking place. In order to prevent processor cores from becoming idle, an algorithm needs to be able to interleave computation and communication.

Dragojevic et al. [9] have developed FaRM, a distributed computing platform that makes use of RDMA. FaRM combines the memory of multiple machines into one shared address space. In their evaluation on a 40 Gbit/s RoCE network, the authors show that accessing remote memory is slower than local memory accesses, even when using RDMA. This is an important observation as it highlights the importance of hiding the network latency by interleaving computation and communication when using RDMA.

3.2.2 *Programming Abstractions*

RDMA provides one-sided and two-sided operations. When using one-sided read and write operations (memory semantics), data is directly written into or read from a specified RDMA-enabled buffer without any interaction from the remote host. Two-sided calls on the other hand implement send/receive message-passing operations (channel semantics). The receiver registers memory regions into which incoming messages will be written and will receive a notification when a write has occurred. No significant performance difference between one-sided and two-sided operations has been observed in previous work [10].

Multiple message-passing systems, like MPICH2 [22] have been implemented over InfiniBand. Furthermore, InfiniBand also provides upper-layer protocol support such as IP-over-InfiniBand (IPoIB), which provides a transparent interface to any IP-based application.

4. ALGORITHMIC DETAILS

In this section we present a distributed variant of the radix hash join. In a distributed system with many multi-core and multi-processor machines, the ability to generate a sufficiently large number of partitions without being limited by the TLB or cache capacity is important in order to be able to assign partitions to every available core and preventing cores from becoming idle. Because there is no data dependency between the individual partitions, these can be processed with a high degree of parallelism. The radix hash join with its multi-pass partitioning strategy prevents excessive TLB and cache misses while partitioning the data into a large number of partitions, thus making it a good candidate to be transformed into a distributed algorithm. Furthermore, the authors of [4, 3] clearly show that a carefully tuned radix hash join is superior to other join algorithms on multi-core machines.

For the distributed variant of the radix hash join, we propose a couple of modifications to the partitioning, build and probe phases of existing parallel hash join solutions.

4.1 Histogram Computation Phase

As a first step, all threads compute a histogram over the input data. By assigning the threads to sections of the input relations of equal size, we can ensure an even load distribution among the worker threads.

Next, all the threads within the same machine exchange their histograms and combine them into one machine-level histogram providing an overview of the data residing on a particular machine. Computing the machine-level histograms is identical to the histogram computation of the join algorithm described in [4].

The machine-level histograms are then exchanged over the network. They can either be sent to a predesignated coordinator or distributed among all the nodes. The machine-level histograms are in turn combined into a global histogram providing a global overview of the partition sizes and the

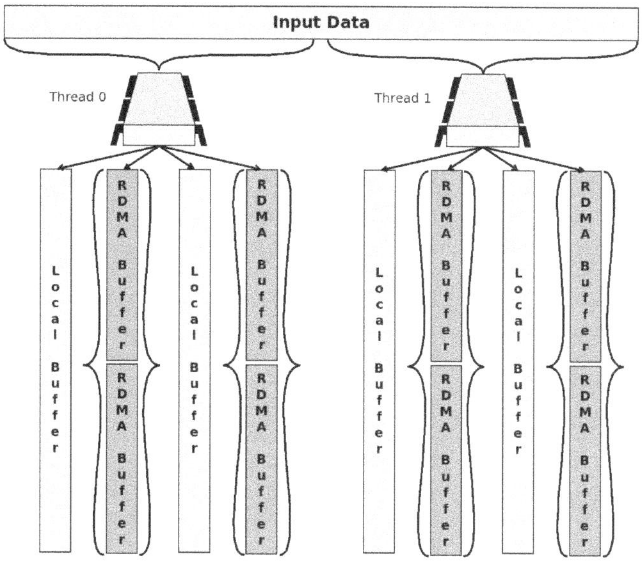

Figure 2: Two threads partitioning the input data into a set of local and RDMA-enabled buffers.

necessary size of the buffers which need to be allocated to store the data received over the network.

From the machine-level and global histograms the join algorithm can compute a machine-partition assignment for every node in the cluster. This assignment can be dynamic or static. The algorithm computing the machine-partition assignment is independent of the rest of the join algorithm. For the experiments we implemented a static round-robin assignment and, for skewed workloads, a dynamic algorithm which first sorts the partitions based on their element count and then assigns them evenly over all machines.

4.2 Partitioning Phase

The purpose of the partitioning phase of the radix hash join is to ensure that the partitions and hash tables fit into the processor cache. For the distributed radix join, we additionally want to ensure maximum resource utilization, in particular we need to be able to assign at least one partition to each processor core. Therefore, the number of partitions needs to be at least equal to the total number of CPU cores in order to prevent cores from becoming idle.

In the multi-pass partitioning phase of the algorithm we distinguish between two different types of partitioning passes: (i) a network partitioning pass which interleaves the computation of the partitions with the network transfer and (ii) local partitioning passes which partition the data locally in order to ensure that the partitions fit into the processor cache. The latter does not involve any network transfer.

4.2.1 Network Partitioning Pass

To efficiently use the asynchronous nature of RDMA, the data needs be transmitted over the network in parallel with the computation. When designing the algorithm, we need to avoid having a separate network transmission phase during which the processor cores are idle. To achieve these goals, we introduce the concept of a network-partitioning pass in which the data is partitioned and distributed in parallel.

Crucial for high performance processing is the management of the partitioning buffers, in particular the ability to reuse existing RDMA-enabled buffers. For each partition which will be processed locally, a thread receives a local buffer for writing the output. Based on the histogram computation, the required size of the local buffers can be determined such that local buffers do not overflow. Remote partitions need to be transmitted over the network. For processing remote partitions, a thread receives multiple fixed-sized RDMA-enabled buffers. Data belonging to a remote partition is partitioned directly into these buffers. When a remote buffer is full, it will be transmitted over the network to the target machine. In order to be able to continue processing while a network operation is taking place, at least two RDMA-enabled buffers are assigned to each thread for a given partition. The buffers assigned to one partition can be used in turn and reused once the preceding network operation completes. To hide the buffer registration costs, the RDMA-enabled buffers are drawn from a pool containing preallocated and preregistered buffers. All buffers, both local buffers and RDMA-enabled buffers, are private to each thread, such that no synchronization is required while partitioning the input relations (see Figure 2).

4.2.2 Receiving Incoming Data

Depending on the available amount of main memory on the receiving machine, we can chose between one-sided and two-sided operations. If the amount of main memory is large enough to hold all the data, one-sided operations can be used. In such a setup, the receiver needs to allocate one large RDMA-enabled buffer for each partition and each remote machine. The necessary size of these buffers is known from the histogram phase. No interaction from the receiving machine is required during the partitioning as the incoming data is directly written into the destination buffers by the network card. On the other hand, if only a small amount of memory is at our disposal, we want to avoid that large parts of main-memory are registered for RDMA transfer. Otherwise pages cannot be swapped out, which would significantly impact the performance of other applications and concurrent queries. In such a case, we use two-sided RDMA operations and only register a predefined number of small RDMA-enabled buffers in order to receive incoming data. In addition to these receive buffers, we allocate larger non-RDMA buffers for each partition into which the data from the receive buffers will be copied. The receive buffers can be reused once the copy operation terminated successfully.

At the end of the network partitioning pass, the partitions are assembled for further processing by combining the buffers containing the local data with the buffers holding the data received over the network.

4.2.3 Local Partitioning Passes

The goal of the partitioning phase is to speed up the build-probe phase by creating cache-sized partitions. To ensure that the partitions fit into the processor cache, subsequent partitioning passes not involving network operations might be required depending on the data size.

4.3 Build & Probe Phases

In the build-probe phase a hash table is built over the data of each partition of the inner relation. Data from the corresponding partition of the outer relation is used to probe the hash table. Because there is no data dependency between two partitions, they can be processed in parallel.

The result containing the matching tuples can either be output to a local buffer or written to RDMA-enabled buffers,

Symbol	Description
$\|R\|$ $\|S\|$	Size of the inner/outer relation [MB]
N_{M}	Number of machines
$N_{\mathrm{C/M}}$	Number of cores per machine
$ps_{\mathrm{Part.}}$	Partitioning speed of a thread [MB/s]
net_{max}	Network bandwidth per host [MB/s]
hb_{Thread}	Hash table build speed of a thread [MB/s]
hp_{Thread}	Hash table probe speed of a thread [MB/s]

Table 1: List of basic symbols.

depending on the location where the result will be further processed. Similar to the partitioning phase, we transmit an RDMA-enabled buffer over the network once it is full. To be able to continue processing, each thread receives multiple output buffer for transmitting data. The buffers can be reused when the proceeding network operation completed.

When operating on a skewed data set, the computation of the build-probe phase of a partition can be shared among multiple threads. If the partition of the outer relation contains more tuples than a predefined threshold, it is split into distinct ranges. Multiple threads can then be used to probe the hash table, each operating on its range of the outer relation. No synchronization between the threads is needed as the accesses to the common hash table are read-only. Skew on the inner relation can cause that the hash tables do not fit into the processor cache. This can be compensated by splitting the large hash table into a set of smaller hash tables. In this case the tuples of the outer relation need to be used to probe multiple tables, however, this probing can also be executed in parallel.

5. ANALYTICAL MODEL

In this section, we present a model describing the individual phases of the distributed hash join algorithm. In addition we want to find (i) an optimal number of processor cores per machine as well as (ii) an optimal number of machines for a given input size.

Table 1 provides an overview of the symbols used in the analytical model.

5.1 Partitioning Phase

The partitioning phase is composed of multiple partitioning passes which can be of two types: (i) network partitioning passes involving the partitioning and transfer of the data over the network and (ii) subsequent local partitioning passes which ensure that the partitions fit into the processor caches but do not involving any network operations.

In this model, we assume that every thread runs on the same identical processor core and that each individual thread can read a tuple from the input, determine its partition and write the tuple to the corresponding buffer at a rate $ps_{\mathrm{Part.}}$.

5.1.1 Network Partitioning Pass

The partitioning speed ps_{Thread} at which a thread can partition its input data is composed of two parts: (i) the speed at which tuples are written to the respective buffers $ps_{\mathrm{Part.}}$ and (ii) the speed at which tuples belonging to remote partitions can be transmitted over the network ps_{Network}.

The total network speed net_{Max} is shared equally among all partitioning threads on the same machine. When using two-sided RDMA calls, one thread is responsible for processing incoming partitions and has the full incoming bandwidth at its disposal, while the remaining $N_{\mathrm{C/M}} - 1$ partitioning threads share the outgoing network bandwidth.

$$ps_{\mathrm{Network}} = \frac{net_{\mathrm{Max}}}{N_{\mathrm{C/M}} - 1} \tag{1}$$

Assuming uniform distribution of the data over all N_{M} machines, we can estimate that $(|R|+|S|) \cdot \frac{1}{N_{\mathrm{M}}}$ tuples belong to local partitions, the rest is send to remote machines.

At this point, the system can either be limited by the partitioning speed of the threads (CPU-bound) or by the available network bandwidth on each host (network-bound). A system is network-bound if the tuples belonging to remote partitions are output at a faster rate than the network is able to transmit.

$$\frac{N_{\mathrm{M}} - 1}{N_{\mathrm{M}}} \cdot ps_{\mathrm{Part.}} > ps_{\mathrm{Network}} \tag{2}$$

In systems which are CPU-bound, the overall processing rate is fully determined by the partitioning speed of each thread $ps_{\mathrm{Part.}}$. The entire system is composed of N_{M} machines, each of which contains $N_{\mathrm{C/M}}$ processor cores. Equation 3 gives us the global partitioning speed of the network partitioning pass ps_1 for CPU-bound systems.

$$ps_1 = N_{\mathrm{M}} \cdot \left(N_{\mathrm{C/M}} - 1\right) \cdot ps_{\mathrm{Part.}} \tag{3}$$

On the other hand, if the system is network-bound, meaning the partitioning speed exceeds the maximum network processing speed, threads have to wait for network operations to complete before they are able to reuse RDMA-enabled buffers. The observed partitioning speed of each thread is a combination of $ps_{\mathrm{Part.}}$ and ps_{Network}.

$$\begin{aligned} ps_{\mathrm{Thread}} &= \frac{1}{\frac{\frac{1}{N_{\mathrm{M}}}}{ps_{\mathrm{Part.}}} + \frac{\frac{N_{\mathrm{M}}-1}{N_{\mathrm{M}}}}{ps_{\mathrm{Network}}}} \\ &= \frac{N_{\mathrm{M}} \cdot ps_{\mathrm{Part.}} \cdot ps_{\mathrm{Network}}}{(N_{\mathrm{M}} - 1) \cdot ps_{\mathrm{Part.}} + ps_{\mathrm{Network}}} \end{aligned} \tag{4}$$

From Equations 1 and 4 we can determine the overall partitioning speed of network-bound systems.

$$\begin{aligned} ps_1 &= N_{\mathrm{M}} \cdot \left(N_{\mathrm{C/M}} - 1\right) \cdot ps_{\mathrm{Thread}} \\ &= \frac{{N_{\mathrm{M}}}^2 \cdot (N_{\mathrm{C/M}} - 1) \cdot ps_{\mathrm{Part.}} \cdot net_{\mathrm{Max}}}{(N_{\mathrm{C/M}} - 1) \cdot (N_{\mathrm{M}} - 1) \cdot ps_{\mathrm{Part.}} + net_{\mathrm{Max}}} \end{aligned} \tag{5}$$

5.1.2 Local Partitioning Passes

Local partitioning passes do not involve any network transfer and all threads in the system partition the data at their maximum partitioning rate $ps_{\mathrm{Part.}}$. Therefore, the global processing speed of this phase (ps_2) increases with the total number of available CPU cores.

$$ps_2 = N_{\mathrm{M}} \cdot N_{\mathrm{C/M}} \cdot ps_{\mathrm{Part.}} \tag{6}$$

5.1.3 Combining Partitioning Passes

The partitioning phase is composed of p passes, one of them involving the transfer of the data over the network, the other $p-1$ passes operate on local data only. We can derive an expression for the time required to partition both input relations of size $|R|$ and $|S|$.

$$t_{\mathrm{partitioning}} = (|R| + |S|) \cdot \left(\frac{1}{ps_1} + \frac{(p-1)}{ps_2}\right) \tag{7}$$

5.2 Build & Probe Phases

In the build phase, each thread is creating a cache-sized hash table over the inner relation of size $|R|$ at an average build speed hb_{Thread}. Building hash tables over the partitions can be done in parallel as there is no data dependency between partitions.

$$hb = N_{\text{M}} \cdot N_{\text{C/M}} \cdot hb_{\text{Thread}} \tag{8}$$

$$t_{\text{build}} = \frac{|R|}{hb} \tag{9}$$

During the probe phase, tuples from the outer relation of size $|S|$ are used to probe the hash tables at a rate hp_{Thread}. Partitions can be processed in parallel during the probe phase. The global speed at which hash tables can be probed increases with the number of available cores.

$$hp = N_{\text{M}} \cdot N_{\text{C/M}} \cdot hp_{\text{Thread}} \tag{10}$$

$$t_{\text{probe}} = \frac{|S|}{hp} \tag{11}$$

5.3 Optimal Number of Cores and Machines

Maximum utilization of the available resources is achieved in the network partitioning phase if the processing speed at which each thread can partition the data is equal to the maximum thread partitioning speed (maximum CPU utilization) and the data belonging to remote partitions is transmitted over the network at the maximum network transmission speed per host (maximum network utilization).

$$\begin{aligned} \frac{N_{\text{M}}-1}{N_{\text{M}}} \cdot ps_{\text{Part.}} &= \frac{net_{\text{Max}}}{N_{\text{C/M}}-1} \\ \Leftrightarrow \left(N_{\text{C/M}}-1\right) &= \frac{N_{\text{M}}}{N_{\text{M}}-1} \cdot \frac{net_{\text{Max}}}{ps_{\text{Part.}}} \end{aligned} \tag{12}$$

From the above we can determine that the optimal number of processor cores is such that it can exactly saturate the available network bandwidth. The optimal number of cores should therefore be equal to the ratio of the network bandwidth and the partitioning rate of a thread.

In the network partitioning pass, data is partitioned into N_{P1} partitions. Within a machine each of the $N_{\text{C/M}} - 1$ partitioning threads has N_{P1} partitioning buffers. These buffers can either be local buffers or RDMA-enabled buffers. RDMA-enabled buffers are of a fixed predetermined size $S_{\text{RDMA-Buffer}}$. If the smaller inner relation R is spread across too many machines, these RDMA-enabled buffers will no longer be fully filled before being transmitted over the network, thus resulting in an inefficient usage of the network.

$$\begin{aligned} &\frac{|R|}{N_{\text{M}} \cdot N_{\text{P1}} \cdot \left(N_{\text{C/M}}-1\right) \cdot S_{\text{RDMA-Buffer}}} \geq 1 \\ \Leftrightarrow\ &N_{\text{M}} \leq \frac{|R|}{N_{\text{P1}} \cdot \left(N_{\text{C/M}}-1\right) \cdot S_{\text{RDMA-Buffer}}} \end{aligned} \tag{13}$$

Equation 13 determines an upper-bound of the number of machines given a specific workload (size of the inner relation) and system configuration (size of the RDMA-buffers). Scaling above this number will lead to loss of bandwidth in the network partitioning pass.

In addition, we need to ensure that every core is assigned to at least one partition for further processing. Therefore the total number of processor cores should not exceed N_{P1}.

$$N_{\text{C/M}} \cdot N_{\text{M}} \leq N_{\text{P1}} \tag{14}$$

6. EXPERIMENTAL EVALUATION

6.1 Experimental Setup

We evaluated our implementation of the distributed join on a cluster of ten machines connected by an QDR InfiniBand network as well as a four-machine cluster featuring an FDR InfiniBand network.

The goal of this evaluation is to understand how to use RDMA in the context of distributed rack-scale databases, rather than to compare the performance of a distributed join to that of a single-machine algorithm. Because of a lower overhead in terms of coordination and communication, a single-machine algorithm is expected to always be faster. In this paper, we use the algorithm of [4] as it makes the results comparable to a public baseline.

Like [21], we noticed that the algorithm in [4] did not run beyond certain amounts of data. We have extended the algorithm such that it can process large data sizes. In order to have a more realistic baseline, we have also modified the algorithm in [4] to make it more NUMA-aware. In particular we created multiple task queues, one for each NUMA region. If a buffer is located in region i, it is added to the i-th queue. A thread first checks the task queue belonging to the local NUMA-region and only when there is no local work to be done, will it check other queues. Furthermore, we have implemented both the first and second partition passes with SIMD/AVX vector instructions. With these modifications, the single-machine algorithm of [4] reaches a throughput of 700 million join argument tuples-per-second, similar to that of [21] (see Figure 5a).

In addition, we implemented a network component using TCP/IP and evaluated our algorithm using IPoIB, which gives a bandwidth slightly larger to a 10Gbit Ethernet network. To better compare both versions, we evaluated the RDMA implementation which uses channel semantics.

Our C++ implementation of a distributed join is partially based on the source code made available by [4][1] and [6][2].

Details on the hardware can be found in Table 2.

6.1.1 Workloads

In order to compare our results to the results of [4] and [6], we have selected a workload composed of narrow tuples, each consisting of a join key and a record id (e.g., <key, rid>). The tuples are 16 byte wide. In the data loading phase the input data is distributed evenly across all available machines. The Rids are range-partitioned at load time and each machine is assigned a particular range of Rids.

Similar to [4] and [6], we focus on highly distinct value joins. For each tuple in the inner relation, there is at least one matching tuple in the outer relation. The ratio of the inner and outer relation sizes which are used throughout the experiments are either 1:1, 1:2, 1:4, 1:8 or 1:16. To analyze the impact of data skew, we generated two skewed datasets, with different values of the Zipf distribution: a low skew

[1] http://www.systems.ethz.ch/projects/paralleljoins
[2] http://pages.cs.wisc.edu/~jignesh/

	FDR Cluster	QDR Cluster	Multi-Core Server
CPUs	Intel Xeon E5-4650 v2 2.40 GHz	Intel Xeon E5-2609 2.40 GHz	Intel Xeon E5-4650 v2 2.40 GHz
Cores/Threads	40/80	8/8	40/80
Memory	512 GB	128 GB	512 GB
Cache Sizes	64 KB 256 KB 25 MB	64 KB 256 KB 10 MB	64 KB 256 KB 25 MB
InfiniBand	Mellanox FDR HCA	Mellanox QDR HCA	-

Table 2: Hardware used in our evaluation.

dataset with a value of 1.05 and high skew with a skew factor of 1.20. To gain insights on the behaviour of the join not only for column stores but for row stores as well, we also use a workload with a variable payload. These tuples can either be 16, 32 or 64 bytes wide.

6.2 Size of RDMA Buffers

As explained in Section 4, the primary communication abstraction is the sending and receiving of RDMA-enabled buffers. Therefore, a natural question to ask is how much buffer space should be allocated and which impact the buffer size has on the network throughput.

InfiniBand networks can either be bound by the maximum package rate which can be processed by the HCA or by the available network bandwidth. Figure 3 shows the observed bandwidth on both the QDR and FDR network between two machines for message sizes ranging from 2B to 512KB. One can observe that both systems can reach and maintain full bandwidth for buffers larger than 8KB.

Unless otherwise stated, the size of the RDMA-enabled buffers is fixed to 64KB for the rest of the experiments.

6.3 Joins on Rack-Scale Systems

One of the first questions to ask is how the hash join algorithm behaves on the different hardware configurations described in Table 2. In order to be able to compare the distributed join with the implementation from [4], we selected a high-end multi-processor server containing four sockets using eight out of the ten CPU cores on each socket and compared it against four nodes from the FDR and QDR cluster. On each of the cluster machines we used eight cores. Thus, the total number of processor cores for each of the hardware configurations is 32 physical cores.

Inside the high-end server the CPUs are connected via QuickPath (QPI). Each processor is attached to two neighbours. Using the STREAM benchmark [24], we measured the bandwidth with which one core can write to a remote NUMA region. The total bandwidth offered by QPI is not fully available to a single core. On different hardware configurations, we measured different values for the per-core write bandwidth, even within the same processor family. In this paper, we show the results for the configuration which offered us the highest inter-socket bandwidth, which peaked at 8.4 GB/s. The distributed system is composed of individual machines connected to each other via a single InfiniBand switch. The measured bandwidth on the QDR network is around 3.4 GB/s. The FDR network offers a higher bandwidth with a peak performance close to 6.0 GB/s. The architecture of both systems is illustrated in Figure 4.

In the first experiment we used three different workloads consisting of 1024 million, 2048 million and 4096 million tuples per relation. The results are shown in Figure 5a. The centralized algorithm outperforms the distributed version for all data sizes. This is expected because the algorithm has a lower coordination overhead and the bandwidth between cores is significantly higher than the inter-machine bandwidth. For large data sizes, the distribution overhead is amortized. The execution time 2048 million and 4096 million tuples per relation shows an increase less than 30%.

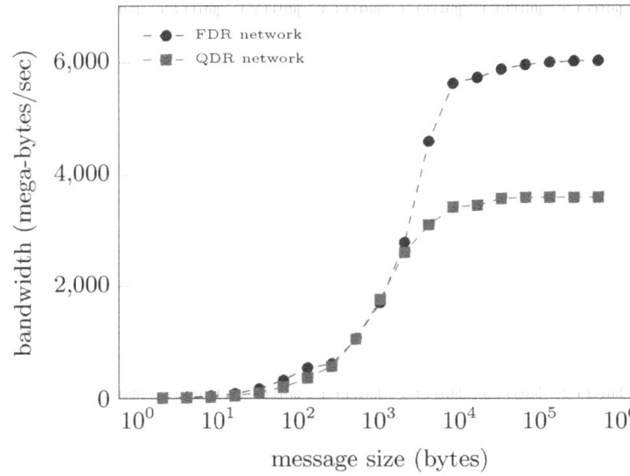

Figure 3: Point-to-point bandwidth for different message sizes on the QDR and FDR networks.

In Figure 5b we compare the TCP/IP version and two RDMA-based implementations. The first RDMA-based variant does not interleave computation and communication. After issuing an RDMA request, a thread waits for the network transfer to finish before it continues processing. Hence, partitioning and network communication are never interleaved. The second RDMA-based version is the algorithm described in Section 4. It tries to hide the network latency by interleaving computation and communication.

We can observe that the differences in execution time is caused only by differences in the network partitioning pass. The TCP/IP versions takes long to complete this phase. The reasons for this performance difference are three-fold: (i) although FDR InfiniBand provides 6.0 GB/s of network bandwidth, we cannot reach this throughput using IPoIB. We measured the IPoIB bandwidth to be only 1.8 GB/s, slightly higher than the bandwidth provided by 10Gb Ethernet; (ii) when using TCP/IP, a context switch into the kernel is required which causes additional overhead; and (iii) the message needs to be copied across intermediate buffers during the network transfer.

We can also see a small difference between the execution time of the interleaved and non-interleaved RDMA implementations. Although both can benefit from the increased bandwidth, the version which interleaves computation and communication hides parts of the network latency leading to a reduced execution time of the network partitioning pass.

From the second experiment we can conclude that we cannot rely on the upper-layer protocol support of the network in order to achieve the full performance. Instead we have to use the RDMA primitives. Furthermore, interleaving computation and communication also brings down the execution time of the network partitioning pass by an additional 35%. We expect that this benefit is more pronounced as more data needs to be transmitted over the network.

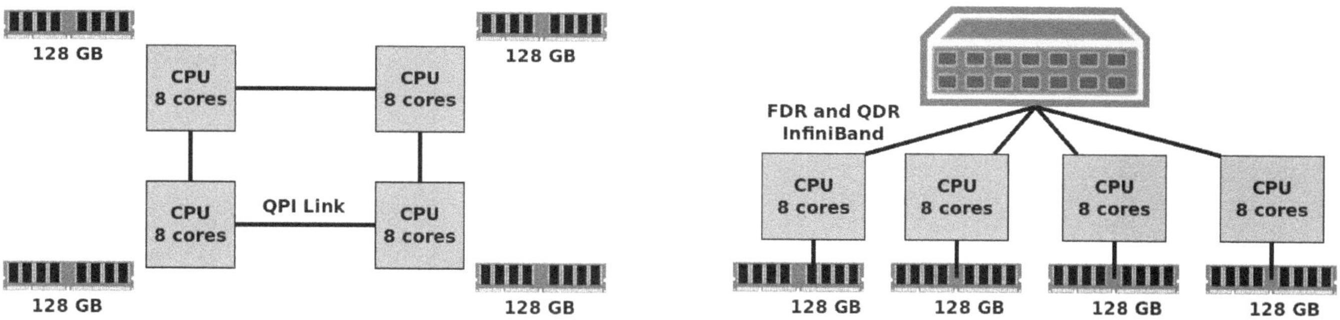

Figure 4: Comparison of the single-machine and distributed setup: The multi-processor machine has 4 CPUs connected by a QPI link. The distributed setup is composed of 4 distinct machines. The machines are connected by a QDR and FDR InfiniBand network.

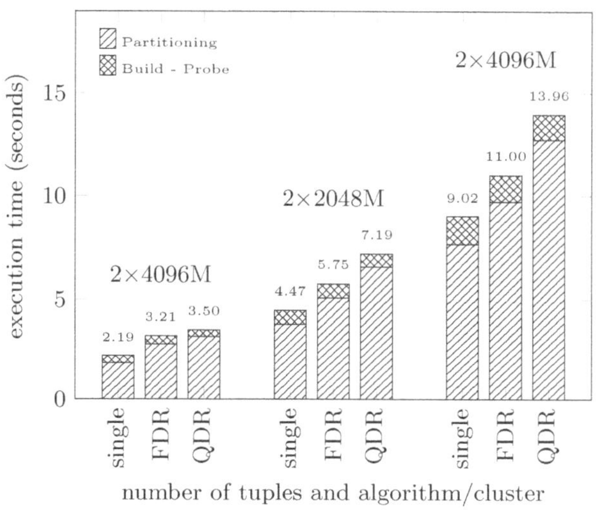

(a) Comparison of the execution time on the high-end server and the distributed setup with 4 machines on the QDR and FDR network. The total number of CPU cores for all three experiments is 32 cores.

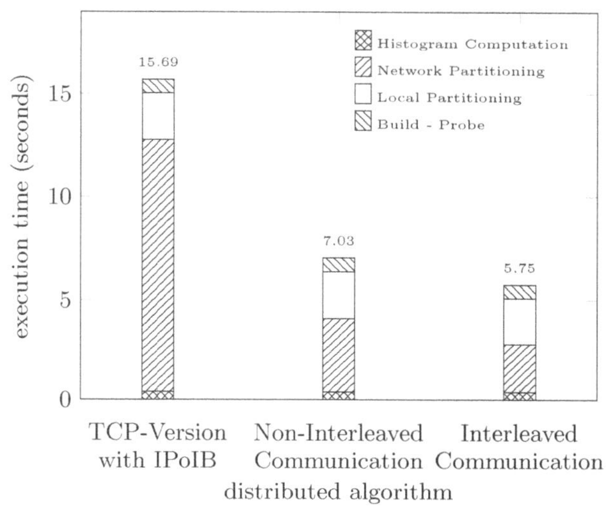

(b) Execution time of a join of 2×2048 million tuples for three variants of the distributed radix hash join. All experiments run on 4 machines with 32 CPU cores in total (FDR cluster). The TCP/IP-based version runs over IPoIB.

Figure 5: Baseline experiments. The distributed radix hash join is compared against a single-machine algorithm running on a high-end server and a TCP/IP-based implementation.

6.4 Horizontal Scale-Out Behaviour

6.4.1 Large-to-Large Table Joins

To study the impact of the input relation sizes on the performance of the distributed join, we varied the input relation sizes and the number of machines. In large-to-large table joins, both input relations are of the same size and each element of the inner relation is matched with exactly one element of the outer relation. In this experiment, we use relations ranging from 1024 million to 4096 million tuples per relation, and we increase the number of machines from two to ten machines. The experiment was conducted on the QDR cluster.

Due to the available memory, the largest workload containing 2×4096 million tuples (≈ 128 GB) cannot be executed on two machines.

Figure 6a presents the average execution time for each of the three workloads using different numbers of machines. We can observe that the execution time doubles when doubling the amount of input data. The relative difference in execution time between the first two workloads is on average a factor of 1.98. The difference between the second and third workload is a factor of 1.92.

The experiment shows that the execution time for a large-to-large join increases linearly with the size of both input relations: doubling the relation sizes results in a doubling of the total execution time of the join algorithm.

The execution time for all three workloads goes down as we increase the number of machines. However, we can also observe a sub-linear speed-up when comparing the configuration with two and ten nodes. The optimal speed-up in such a setup should lead to a five times improvement in the execution time, which cannot be observed in this experiment. The reason for this sub-linear scale-out behavior on the QDR cluster will be studied in greater detail in Section 6.4.3 and Section 6.6.

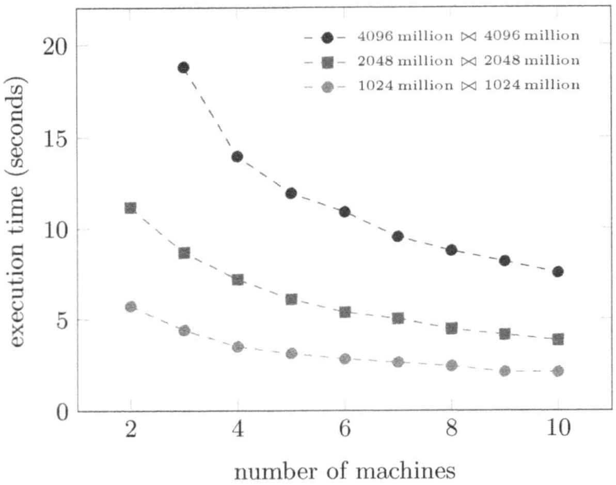

(a) Execution time of the distributed hash join for different large-to-large joins using a variable number of machines. The experiment was conducted on the QDR cluster.

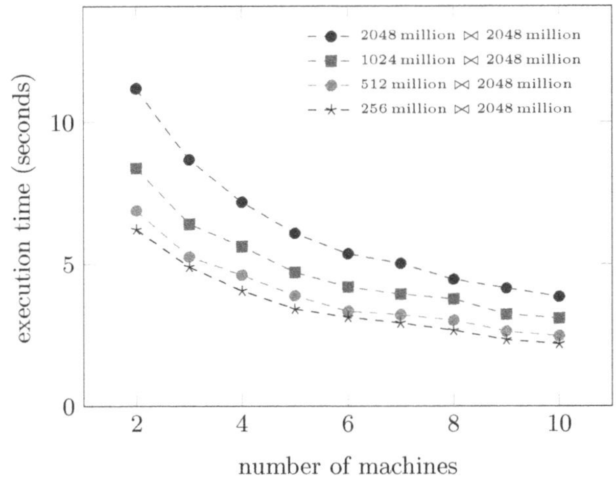

(b) Execution time of the distributed hash join for small-to-large joins with different relative relation sizes. The experiment was conducted on the QDR cluster.

Figure 6: Execution time for large-to-large and small-to-large table joins.

6.4.2 *Small-to-Large Table Joins*

To explore the impact of the relative sizes of the inner and outer relations, we measured the performance of the distributed join using an outer relation of fixed size, composed of 2048 million tuples, and a variable number of tuples for the inner relation ranging from 2048 million tuples (1-to-1 workload) to 256 million tuples (1-to-8 workload). All measurements were taken on the QDR cluster.

From Figure 6b we can see that the execution time of the join decreases when reducing the size of the inner relation. The execution time of the radix hash join is dominated by the time to partition the data. These partitioning costs decrease linearly with the size of both input relations. Therefore, when keeping the size of the outer relation fixed at 2048 million tuples and decreasing the number of tuples in the inner relation, we can see a reduction in the execution time by almost half when comparing the 1-to-1 workload to the 1-to-8 workload.

6.4.3 *Execution Time Break Down*

In the previous experiments we see a sub-linear reduction in the execution when increasing the number of machines. To understand the cause of this behaviour, we take a closer look at the 2048 million ⋈ 2048 million tuple join on the QDR cluster.

Figure 7a visualizes the execution time of the different phases of the join and illustrates the effects of scale-out in more detail. The partitioning phase is composed of two passes, each creating 2^{10} partitions. The resulting 2^{20} partitions are $\sim$ 32KB in size and fit into the processor caches.

During the first partitioning pass the data is distributed over the network. This phase is completed once all the data has been send out and acknowledged by the receiving hosts. When increasing the number of machines from two to ten machines we expect – in an ideal scenario – a speed-up factor of 5. However, when examining the execution time of the individual phases (Figure 7a), one can observe a near-linear speed-up for the second partitioning pass (speed-up by 4.73) and for the build/probe phase (speed-up by 5.00). The speed-up of the first partitioning pass on the other hand is limited because the network transmission speed of 3.4 GB/s is significantly lower than the partitioning speed of a multi-core machine. As a consequence, the network presents a major performance bottleneck and limits the speed-up.

With an increasing number of machines, a larger percentage of the input data needs to be transmitted over the network, which puts additional pressure on the network component and does not allow us to fully leverage the performance gains of the increased parallelism. Furthermore, adding machines to the network is likely to increase overall network congestion during the network partitioning pass if communication is not scheduled carefully. The overall speed-up when scaling from two to ten machines is 2.91.

6.4.4 *Scale-Out with Increasing Workload*

In order to deal with ever increasing workload sizes, a common approach is to add more resources to an existing system to maintain a constant execution time despite the increase in data volumes.

In the experiment, we vary the workload size from 2×1024 million ($\approx$ 60 GB) to 2×5120 million ($\approx$ 300 GB) tuples. For each increase in the data size by 512 million tuples per relation, we add another machine to the system.

Figure 7b shows the execution time of each phase. One can observe that the algorithm maintains a constant performance for the second partitioning pass as well as the build-probe phase. On the other hand, we see a significant increase in the execution time of the network partitioning pass as we add more machines.

When increasing the input sizes along with the number of machines, the amount of data which needs to be processed per machine remains identical. Thus all local partitioning passes and the build-probe phase show constant performance. However, increasing the number of machines, leads to a higher percentage of the data that needs to be exchanged over the network. Because the QDR network bandwidth is significantly lower than the combined partitioning speed of all threads, the network will become a significant performance bottleneck, thus leading to a notable increase in the execution time of the network partitioning phase.

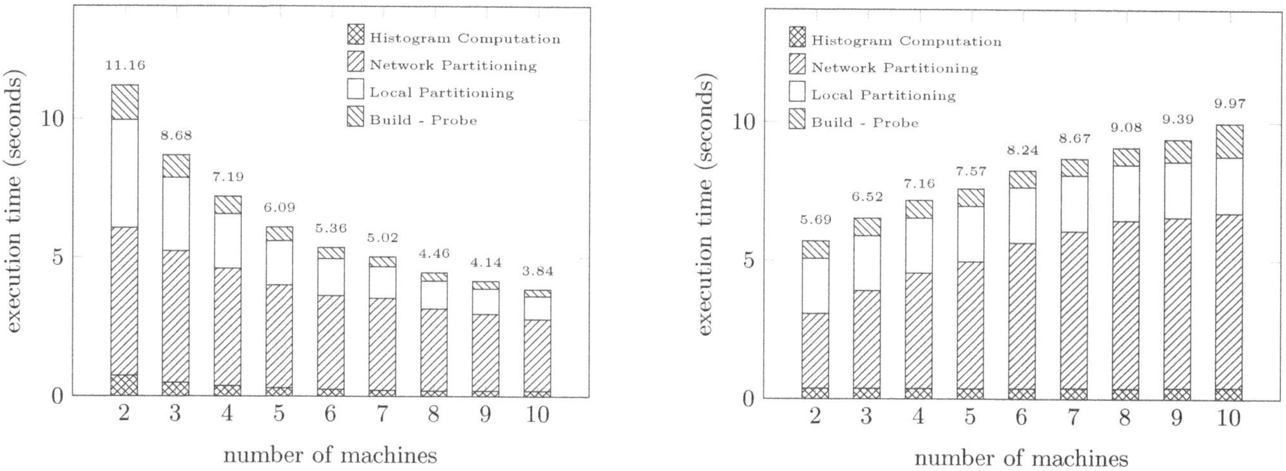

(a) Execution time of each phase of the distributed hash join for a workload of 2048 million ⋈ 2048 million tuples on a variable number of machines. The experiment was conducted on the QDR cluster.

(b) Execution time of each phase of the distributed hash join for an increasing number of tuples and machines. The relation size increases by 2×512 million tuples for each machine that is added. The experiment was conducted on the QDR cluster.

Figure 7: Scale-out behaviour for constant and increasing relation sizes.

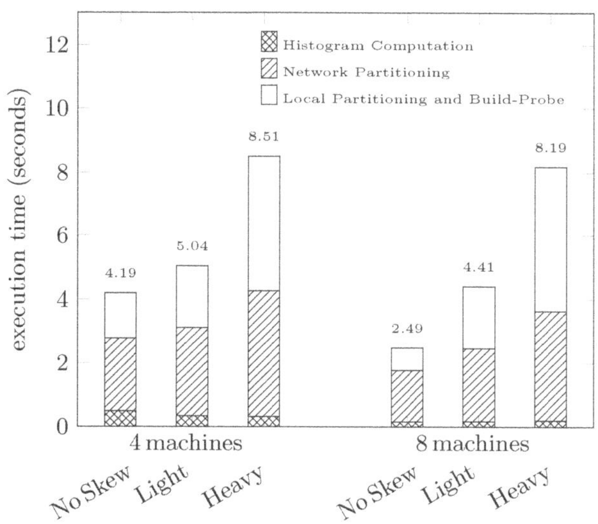

Figure 8: Effect of data skew for two skew factors and hardware configurations on the QDR cluster.

6.5 Impact of Data Skew

In this section, we study the effects of data skew. Similar to the authors of [6] we populate the foreign key column of the outer relation with two data sets. The first one with a low data skew which follows a Zipf distribution law with a skew factor of 1.05 and a highly skewed data set with a factor of 1.2. The relation sizes are 128 million tuples for the inner relation and 2048 million tuples for the outer relation.

In order to ensure that two skewed partitions are not assigned to the same machine, we use a dynamic partition-machine assignment. In this dynamic assignment the partitions are first sorted in decreasing order according to their element count before being distributed in a round-robin manner, thus preventing that the largest partitions are assigned to the same machine. In the build-probe phase, partitions are split according to the description in Section 4.3 when they contain more than twice the average number of tuples.

In Figure 8 we see an increase in the execution time for both workloads and configurations. We notice an increase in execution time for the network partitioning pass and local processing part, i.e. local partitioning and build-probe phase. The network phase is dominated by the time it takes to send all the data to the machine responsible for processing the largest partition. Similarly, the execution time of the local processing part is also dominated by that same machine. This effect is more pronounced for higher skew factors.

This result highlights the need to share tasks between machines. Although heavily skewed partitions can be split and distributed among threads in order to allow for a higher degree of parallel processing, the current implementation only allows work sharing among threads within the same machine and not across multiple machines, thus not fully exploiting the parallelism of the entire system. Nevertheless, we are confident that this issue can be addressed by extending the algorithm to allow work sharing between machines.

6.6 Comparing Joins on QDR and FDR

The experiments on the QDR cluster showed limited scalability of the network partitioning pass because of the limit network bandwidth. To address this issue we deployed the algorithm on a second cluster composed of four machines connected by an FDR InfiniBand network, offering close to twice the available network bandwidth.

For a 2048 million ⋈ 2048 million tuple join conducted on two, three and four machines on the FDR cluster, we can observe identical execution times for the phases not involving any network operation, i.e. the local partitioning pass as well as the build-probe phase. The increase in performance compared to the QDR cluster is due to the shorter network partitioning pass which benefits from the extra bandwidth.

The available network bandwidth of 6.0 GB/s cannot be over-saturated by the seven partitioning threads when running on two and three machines. In this configuration, the system is fully CPU-bound. The partitioning threads reach the maximum network bandwidth on four nodes, in which case $^3/_4$ of the data will be exchanged over the network.

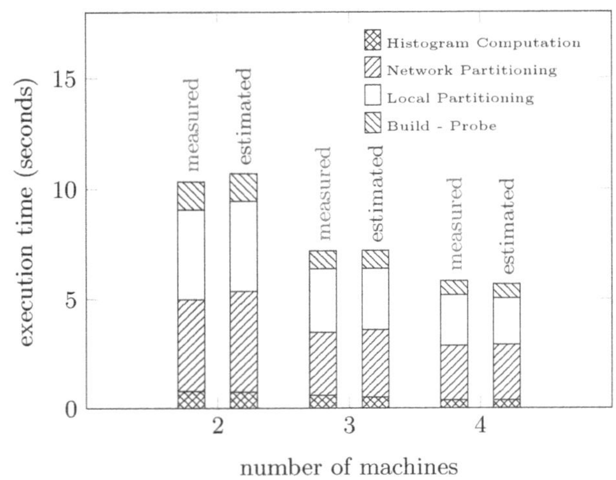

(a) Measured and estimated execution times on the FDR cluster for up to 4 machines.

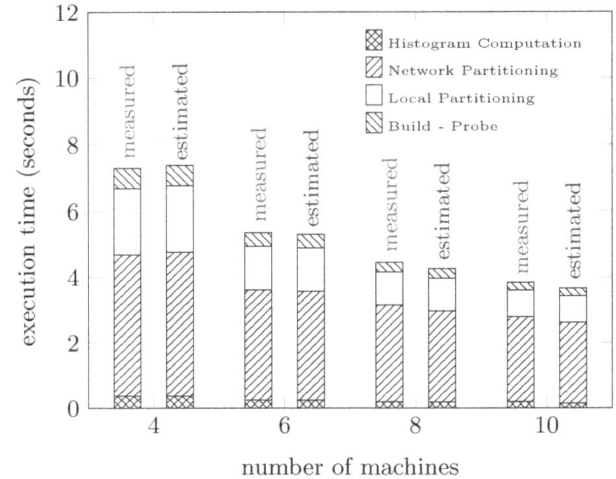

(b) Measured and estimated execution times on the QDR cluster for 4, 6, 8 and 10 machines.

Figure 9: Model verification for a 2048M ⋈ 2048M join on the FDR and QDR cluster.

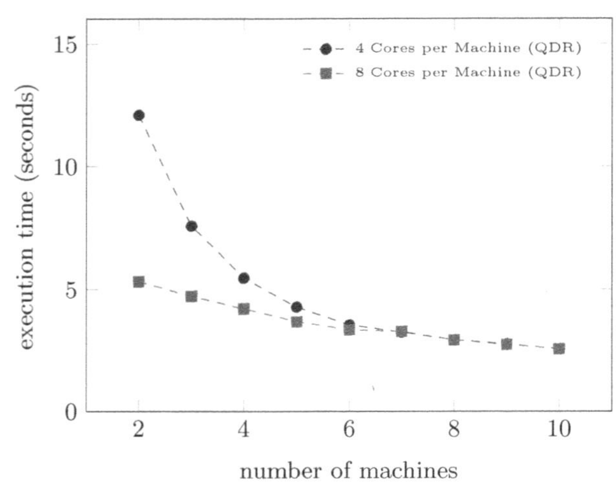

(a) Execution time of the network partitioning phase with 4 and 8 threads per machine on the QDR cluster.

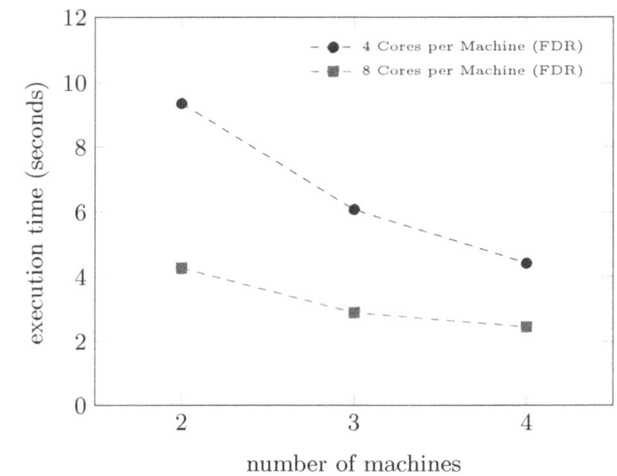

(b) Execution time of the network partitioning phase with 4 and 8 threads per machine on the FDR cluster.

Figure 10: Execution time of the network partitioning pass for a 2048 million ⋈ 2048 million join on both clusters for 4 and 8 threads.

The speed-up factor from two to four nodes of the network partitioning pass alone is 1.7 on the FDR cluster compared to only 1.3 on the QDR cluster.

From this experiment we can conclude that the network partitioning phase can scale to a large number of machines, provided that a sufficient amount of inter-machine bandwidth is available.

6.7 Impact of Wide Tuples

In previous experiments we focused on narrow tuples composed of 8-byte keys with and 8-byte record id in order to evaluate the performance of the join for column-store systems. To get additional insides into the behavior of the join for row-stores, we use tuples with variable payload size.

To keep the overall data size constant, we use relations composed of 2048 million 16-byte tuples, 1024 million 32-byte tuples and 512 million 64-byte tuples. We observed that the execution time of the join, as well as the execution time of each phase, is identical for all three workloads.

This results highlights that data movement is the primary performance factor of distributed join processing. The execution time is determined by the data size, independent whether the workload is composed of a large number of small tuples or a small number of large tuples.

6.8 Model Verification

In this section we validate the accuracy of the analytical model described in Section 5 by comparing its predictions to the experimental results gathered on both clusters.

The measured network throughput is 6.0 GB/s on the FDR network, respectively 3.4 GB/s on the QDR network. In addition, we observed a small performance degradation when increasing the number of machines on the QDR cluster. This decrease is due to the fact that adding machines increases the overall network congestion. On each machine we use eight cores. Each thread is able to reach a local partitioning speed of 955 MB/s.

$$ps_{\text{FDR}}(N_M) = \frac{6000}{8-1} \quad [\text{MB/s}]$$

$$ps_{\text{QDR}}(N_M) = \frac{3400-(N_M-1)*110}{8-1} \quad [\text{MB/s}] \tag{15}$$

$$ps_{\text{Part.}} = 955 \quad [\text{MB/s}]$$

Using Equation 2 we know that the join is CPU bound on the FDR network for two and three machines and is close to being network-bound on four machines. Thus, for two and three machines we can assume that all threads partition the data at their full capacity $ps_{\text{Part.}}$ (CPU-bound). In all the other cases the join is network-bound. Using Equation 4 we can compute the partitioning speed of a thread for the network partitioning pass. The second local partitioning pass is always executed at the local partitioning rate $ps_{\text{Part.}}$.

Figure 9a shows the predicted and measured performance of a 2×2048 million tuple join on the FDR cluster, while Figure 9b compares the model to the results gathered on the QDR machines. One can clearly see that the predictions closely match the experimental results, varying on average by only 0.17 seconds.

6.8.1 *Finding an Optimal Number of Threads*

The analytical model allows us to find the optimal number of threads for a given hardware specification. Given Equation 12, we know that in order to achieve maximum utilization of the network and processing resources, the number of partitioning threads should be such that it can saturate the network without being fully network-bound.

Given the network speed and partitioning rate from Equation 15, we can determine the required number of processor cores for each of the two networks, which is four cores per machine on the QDR and seven cores per machine on the FDR cluster. To verify this result, we conducted two runs of experiments: the first run was performed with four and the second run with eight threads.

In Figure 10a we compare the execution times of the network partitioning pass on the QDR cluster. When increasing the number of machines, the percentage of data which needs to be exchanged over the network increases. We can observe that from five machines onwards, three partitioning threads are sufficient to fully saturate the QDR network. Adding additional cores (i.e. eight threads) will not speed up the execution as threads need to wait for network operations to complete before being able to reuse the RDMA-buffers.

Figure 10b shows the same experiment on the FDR cluster. Given that four threads are not able to fully saturate the available network bandwidth, increasing the number of cores will speed up the network partitioning pass.

7. DISCUSSION

In this paper we have developed a distributed version of the parallel radix hash join using RDMA. However, the ideas described in this work, i.e. RDMA buffer pooling, reuse of RDMA buffers, and interleaving computation and communication are general techniques which can be used to create distributed versions of many database operators like sort-merge joins or aggregation.

In this work we treated the join operation as part of an operator pipeline in which the result of the join is materialized at a later point in the query execution. We are aware that distributed result materialization involves moving large amounts of data over the network and will therefore be an expensive operation. We leave studying the combination of join computation and result materialization to future work.

Our experimental evaluation focuses on running one join operator at a time. Scheduling concurrent database operators in a distributed setup remains an open research area. However, we are confident that recent work on query plan deployment for multi-core systems [14] can also be applied to rack-scale databases.

The experiments clearly show that distributed joins are at a similar level of performance than parallel join algorithms. In fact, our results indicate that modern multi-core hardware should be treated more and more as a distributed system as it has been suggested for operating systems [5].

Although it is not the goal of this paper to compare distributed to centralized algorithms, our findings suggest that the answer to the question whether join performance can be improved by scaling up or scaling out is dependent on the bandwidth provided by the NUMA interconnect and the network. For instance, faster CPU interconnects and a higher number of cores per processor favor vertical scale-up, whereas a higher inter-machine bandwidth would favor horizontal scale-out. In the experimental evaluation we could show that our implementation of a distributed join exhibits good performance, despite the network being a major bottleneck. Current technical road-maps project that InfiniBand will be able to offer a bandwidth of 25 GB/s (HDR) by 2017 [17], which suggests that the network bottleneck will be reduced, which would increase the performance of the proposed algorithm.

8. CONCLUSIONS

In this paper we presented a distributed hash join algorithm which makes use of RDMA as a light-weight communication mechanism. We described how RDMA-enabled buffers can be used to partition and distribute the data efficiently. We were able to show that that the scalability of the distributed join algorithm is highly dependent on the right combination of processing power and network bandwidth. Although the algorithm in its current form is susceptible to data skew, we believe that this can be addressed by introducing inter-machine workload sharing.

In addition to the prototype implementation, we presented an analytical model of the algorithm and were able to show that it can be used to predict the performance of the algorithm with very high accuracy. We performed an experimental evaluation of the algorithm on multiple hardware platforms using two different low-latency networks.

To the best of our knowledge this is the first paper to combine a detailed analysis, analytical model, and experimental evaluation of a distributed join using RDMA.

9. ACKNOWLEDGMENTS

The authors would like to thank the anonymous reviewers for their valuable comments and suggestions. This work has been funded in part by a grant from Oracle Labs. The authors would like to thank Oracle Labs, in particular Cagri Balkesen, Vikas Aggarwal and Michael Duller.

10. REFERENCES

[1] F. N. Afrati and J. D. Ullman. Optimizing Joins in a Map-Reduce Environment. In *EDBT'10*, pages 99–110, 2010.

[2] M. Albutiu, A. Kemper, and T. Neumann. Massively Parallel Sort-Merge Joins in Main Memory Multi-Core Database Systems. *PVLDB*, 5(10):1064–1075, 2012.

[3] C. Balkesen, G. Alonso, J. Teubner, and M. T. Özsu. Multi-Core, Main-Memory Joins: Sort vs. Hash Revisited. *PVLDB*, 7(1):85–96, 2013.

[4] C. Balkesen, J. Teubner, G. Alonso, and M. T. Özsu. Main-Memory Hash Joins on Multi-Core CPUs: Tuning to the Underlying Hardware. In *ICDE'13*, pages 362–373, 2013.

[5] A. Baumann, P. Barham, P. Dagand, T. L. Harris, R. Isaacs, S. Peter, T. Roscoe, A. Schüpbach, and A. Singhania. The Multikernel: A new OS Architecture for Scalable Multicore Systems. In *SOSP'09*, pages 29–44, 2009.

[6] S. Blanas, Y. Li, and J. M. Patel. Design and Evaluation of Main Memory Hash Join Algorithms for Multi-Core CPUs. In *SIGMOD'11*, pages 37–48, 2011.

[7] D. J. DeWitt, R. H. Gerber, G. Graefe, M. L. Heytens, K. B. Kumar, and M. Muralikrishna. GAMMA - A High Performance Dataflow Database Machine. In *VLDB'86*, pages 228–237, 1986.

[8] D. J. DeWitt, S. Ghandeharizadeh, D. A. Schneider, A. Bricker, H. Hsiao, and R. Rasmussen. The Gamma Database Machine Project. *IEEE Trans. Knowl. Data Eng.*, 2(1):44–62, 1990.

[9] A. Dragojevic, D. Narayanan, M. Castro, and O. Hodson. FaRM: Fast Remote Memory. In *NSDI'14*, pages 401–414, 2014.

[10] P. W. Frey. *Zero-copy network communication*. PhD thesis, ETH Zurich, 2010.

[11] P. W. Frey and G. Alonso. Minimizing the Hidden Cost of RDMA. In *ICDCS'09*, pages 553–560, 2009.

[12] P. W. Frey, R. Goncalves, M. L. Kersten, and J. Teubner. Spinning Relations: High-Speed Networks for Distributed Join Processing. In *DaMoN'09*, pages 27–33, 2009.

[13] P. W. Frey, R. Goncalves, M. L. Kersten, and J. Teubner. A Spinning Join That Does Not Get Dizzy. In *ICDCS'10*, pages 283–292, 2010.

[14] J. Giceva, G. Alonso, T. Roscoe, and T. Harris. Deployment of Query Plans on Multicores. *PVLDB*, 8(3):233–244, 2014.

[15] R. Goncalves. *The Data Cyclotron - Juggling Data and Queries for a Data Warehouse Audience*. PhD thesis, CWI, 2013.

[16] R. Goncalves and M. L. Kersten. The Data Cyclotron query processing scheme. In *EDBT'10*, pages 75–86, 2010.

[17] InfiniBand Trade Association. InfiniBand Architecture Specification. http://www.infinibandta.org/. Nov. 2014.

[18] International Business Machines Corporation. IBM Netezza. http://www.netezza.com/. Nov. 2014.

[19] C. Kim, E. Sedlar, J. Chhugani, T. Kaldewey, A. D. Nguyen, A. D. Blas, V. W. Lee, N. Satish, and P. Dubey. Sort vs. Hash Revisited: Fast Join Implementation on Modern Multi-Core CPUs. *PVLDB*, 2(2):1378–1389, 2009.

[20] M. Kitsuregawa, H. Tanaka, and T. Moto-Oka. Application of Hash to Data Base Machine and Its Architecture. *New Generation Comput.*, 1(1):63–74, 1983.

[21] H. Lang, V. Leis, M. Albutiu, T. Neumann, and A. Kemper. Massively Parallel NUMA-Aware Hash Joins. In *IMDM'13*, pages 3–14, 2013.

[22] J. Liu, W. Jiang, P. Wyckoff, D. K. Panda, D. Ashton, D. Buntinas, W. D. Gropp, and B. R. Toonen. Design and implementation of MPICH2 over infiniband with RDMA support. In *IPDPS'04*, 2004.

[23] S. Manegold, P. A. Boncz, and M. L. Kersten. Optimizing Main-Memory Join on Modern Hardware. *IEEE Trans. Knowl. Data Eng.*, 14(4):709–730, 2002.

[24] J. D. McCalpin. Memory Bandwidth and Machine Balance in Current High Performance Computers. *IEEE Technical Committee on Computer Architecture Newsletter*, pages 19–25, 1995.

[25] A. Okcan and M. Riedewald. Processing Theta-Joins using MapReduce. In *SIGMOD'11*, pages 949–960, 2011.

[26] Oracle Corporation. Oracle Exadata. http://www.oracle.com/us/products/database/exadata-database-machine/. Nov. 2014.

[27] O. Polychroniou, R. Sen, and K. A. Ross. Track Join: Distributed Joins with Minimal Network Traffic. In *SIGMOD'14*, pages 1483–1494, 2014.

[28] W. Rödiger, T. Mühlbauer, P. Unterbrunner, A. Reiser, A. Kemper, and T. Neumann. Locality-Sensitive Operators for Parallel Main-Memory Database Clusters. In *ICDE'14*, pages 592–603, 2014.

[29] SAP AG. SAP HANA. http://www.saphana.com/. Nov. 2014.

[30] D. A. Schneider and D. J. DeWitt. A Performance Evaluation of Four Parallel Join Algorithms in a Shared-Nothing Multiprocessor Environment. In *SIGMOD'89*, pages 110–121, 1989.

[31] A. Shatdal, C. Kant, and J. F. Naughton. Cache Conscious Algorithms for Relational Query Processing. In *VLDB'94*, pages 510–521, 1994.

Self-Tuning, GPU-Accelerated Kernel Density Models for Multidimensional Selectivity Estimation

Max Heimel
Technische Universität Berlin
max.heimel@tu-berlin.de

Martin Kiefer
Technische Universität Berlin
kiefer@campus.tu-berlin.de

Volker Markl
Technische Universität Berlin
volker.markl@tu-berlin.de

ABSTRACT

Quickly and accurately estimating the selectivity of multidimensional predicates is a vital part of a modern relational query optimizer. The state-of-the art in this field are multidimensional histograms, which offer good estimation quality but are complex to construct and hard to maintain. Kernel Density Estimation (KDE) is an interesting alternative that does not suffer from these problems. However, existing KDE-based selectivity estimators can hardly compete with the estimation quality of state-of-the art methods.

In this paper, we substantially expand the state-of-the-art in KDE-based selectivity estimation by improving along three dimensions: First, we demonstrate how to numerically optimize a KDE model, leading to substantially improved estimates. Second, we develop methods to continuously adapt the estimator to changes in both the database and the query workload. Finally, we show how to drastically improve the performance by pushing computations onto a GPU.

We provide an implementation of our estimator and experimentally evaluate it on a variety of datasets and workloads, demonstrating that it efficiently scales up to very large model sizes, adapts itself to database changes, and typically outperforms the estimation quality of both existing Kernel Density Estimators as well as state-of-the-art multidimensional histograms.

1. INTRODUCTION

Estimating the cardinality of intermediate result sets is an integral part of the query optimization pipeline in a modern database: The optimizer uses these estimates to make assumptions about the costs of candidate plans [21]. Since the estimation quality directly impacts plan quality [35], incorrect estimates can cause unexpectedly bad query performance [10, 29]. An important subproblem of cardinality estimation is to compute the selectivity of multidimensional range queries over real-valued attributes [14]. Multiple authors have suggested special estimators for this case – usually variants of multidimensional histograms [7, 14, 34].

SIGMOD'15, May 31–June 4, 2015, Melbourne, Victoria, Australia.

ACM 978-1-4503-2758-9/15/05 ...$15.00.
http://dx.doi.org/10.1145/2723372.2749438.

While multidimensional histograms generate very good estimates, they also have shortcomings that have prevented major commercial adoption. In particular, they are often complex to construct, and hard – or even impossible – to maintain under updates. An alternative class of estimators are *Kernel Density Estimators* (KDEs), which compute selectivities from a random data sample by averaging local probability distributions – the kernels – that are centered on the sampled items. A KDE model is very simple: Essentially it just consists of a data sample, making model construction and maintenance extremely easy. Since it also has statistical advantages [1], multiple authors suggested using KDE to estimate range selectivities [4, 14].

However, existing KDE-based selectivity estimators are still immature and can hardly compete with state-of-the-art multidimensional histograms. There are three major reasons for this: First, they are expensive to evaluate, given that computing an estimate requires to scan the complete sample. Second, their estimation quality is often suboptimal since they do not adjust the *bandwidth* parameter, which has a strong impact on estimation quality [1, 4, 14]. Finally, to the best of our knowledge, the question of how to maintain a KDE-based selectivity estimator under database changes has not been covered by the literature so far.

In a prior publication, we already discussed how to tackle the first problem by offloading computations to a graphics card [16]: KDE can be efficiently parallelized, and the required computations are well-suited to be accelerated by a GPU. In this paper, we substantially extend upon their work and approach the other two problems: Selecting the optimal bandwidth parameters and maintaining the model under database updates and workload changes. In particular, we make the following contributions:

1. We demonstrate how to drastically improve the estimation quality of a KDE-based selectivity estimator by solving an optimization problem over query feedback to pick the optimal bandwidth. We also show how to automatically adjust the bandwidth to workload changes via online learning.
2. We introduce a method to efficiently maintain the underlying data sample under database updates by tracking the impact of individual sample points on estimation quality and selectively replacing "bad" points.
3. We provide a GPU-accelerated implementation[1] of our estimator integrated into Postgres and evaluate it on a variety of synthetic and real-world datasets.

[1] The source code is available at: `goo.gl/aQSQNd` .

The remainder of this paper is structured as follows: In the next section, we discuss related work and introduce required concepts. The subsequent two sections provide a theoretical overview of our self-tuning, optimal KDE-based selectivity estimator, with Section 3 introducing the idea of numerically optimizing the bandwidth, and Section 4 providing details on how to automatically adjust the model. In Section 5, we give an overview of our implementation and discuss details of the GPU-acceleration. Finally, Section 6 presents the experimental evaluation, Section 7 summarizes our findings, and Section 8 concludes the paper by discussing possible directions for future work.

2. BACKGROUND & RELATED WORK

2.1 Problem Description

Given a relation R with attributes $(A_1, \ldots, A_d)$, and an arbitrary query region $\Omega \subseteq D_1 \times \ldots \times D_d$ – where D_i denotes the domain of attribute A_i –, selectivity estimators aim to estimate the fraction $|\sigma_{\vec{x}\in\Omega}(R)|/|R|$ of tuples from R that fall within Ω. In this paper, we discuss the subproblem where Ω is a hyper-rectangle, i.e., it is the Cartesian product of intervals within the d attribute domains: $\Omega = (l_1, u_1) \times \ldots \times (l_d, u_d)$. Furthermore, we assume that all attributes are real-valued, meaning that $\Omega \subseteq \mathbb{R}^d$. Note that – contrary to the authors of [14] –, we do not make any further assumptions about the attribute domains. In particular, we do not assume that the data in R is chosen from a known region, such as the unit cube.

2.2 Multidimensional Selectivity Estimators

The easiest way to estimate the selectivity of a multidimensional range query is to assume that attributes are independent of each other. In this case, a d-dimensional estimate can be computed by multiplying d one-dimensional estimates, e.g. obtained from histograms. However, since real datasets are almost always correlated, this *attribute-value independence assumption* often leads to significant estimation errors in real-world cases. These errors can cause incorrect decisions by the query optimizer, which in turn result in bad query performance [10].

Improving the quality of multidimensional selectivity estimates is a classical database research problem, and authors have actively investigated and suggested methods for over 15 years. Most suggested methods rely on multidimensional histograms, which partition the data space into buckets and track the number of tuples within those [32]. Prominent representatives include *MHIST* [34], *Genhist* [14], *STHoles* [7], and ISOMER [38]. Other discussed methods include wavelets [30], discrete cosinus transformations [26], kernel methods [4] and sampling [25, 28].

For a much more detailed overview, we refer the reader to the following two surveys: In [20], the authors give an historic overview over the development of histograms and other estimator techniques. In [14], the authors provide an experimental comparison of the selectivity estimation quality of kernel methods, wavelets, sampling techniques, and multidimensional histograms on real-valued attributes.

2.3 Kernel Density Estimation

One approach for multidimensional selectivity estimation are multivariate *Kernel Density Estimators*. Kernel Density Estimation is a well-known and appreciated tool from statistics that has been around since the late 1950s [1]. It is a data-driven technique to estimate a probability distribution from a data sample [1]. Figure 1 visualizes the method for a two dimensional dataset: Given a data sample (Figure 1(b)), local probability distributions – known as *kernels* – are centered around the sample points (Figure 1(c)). The estimate is then computed by averaging these local contributions (Figure 1(d)). Essentially, this amounts to sampled points contributing *probability mass* to their immediate neighborhood, which is why KDE assigns high probability to regions that lie in the vicinity of sampled data points. Kernel Methods are generally accepted to be among the most accurate estimators in statistics literature [1], and – compared to alternative methods – they offer several advantages:

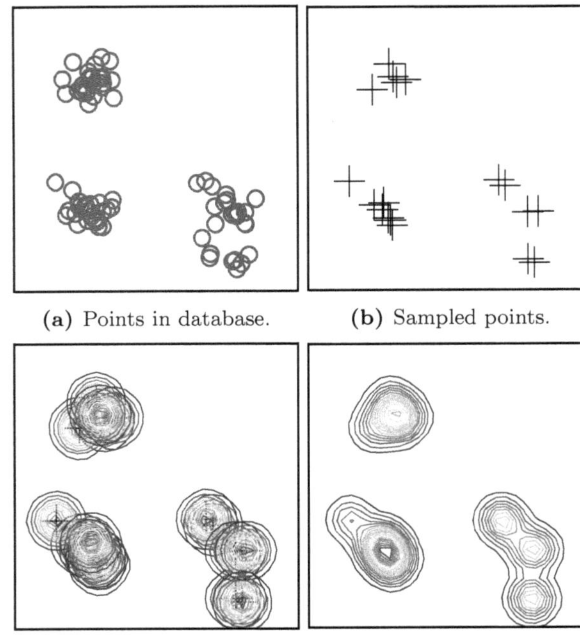

(a) Points in database. (b) Sampled points. (c) Kernels. (d) Estimated distribution.

Figure 1: A Kernel Density Estimator approximates the underlying distribution of a given dataset (a) by picking a random sample of data points (b), centering local probability distributions (kernels) around the sampled points (c), and averaging those local distributions (d).

- KDE has been shown to converge faster to the underlying distribution than histograms do [1]. Furthermore, compared to methods that "naïvely" evaluate the query on a sample [25, 28], KDE has been shown to consistently offer superior estimation quality [14].

- KDE models are easy to construct and to use: After the sample is collected, they are ready to be used. In particular, they do not require any additional model assumptions, like splitting or bucketization rules.

- Since a KDE model is inherently a data sample, the estimator implicitly follows any data distribution without having to explicitly model the domain space. This makes KDE very robust against effects from correlated or degenerate data.

- Compared to histograms, maintaining KDE-based selectivity estimators under database updates is comparably easy: KDE models consist primarily of a data sample, which is why maintaining them is identical to the well-understood sample maintenance problem [13].

Despite these advantages, the amount of database research literature published on KDE-based selectivity estimation is surprisingly scarce. The first paper that suggested KDE to predict selectivities – albeit only for the single-dimensional case – was published in 1999 by Blohsfeld et. al. [4]. They experimentally demonstrated that KDE is generally preferable over a purely sample-based estimator, matches the estimation quality of equi-width histograms and can drastically outperform them in case of sufficiently smooth data. In 2005, Gunopulos et. al. generalized KDE-based selectivity estimation for the multidimensional case and compared it against Genhist, their variant of a multidimensional histogram [14]. They demonstrated that KDE offers comparable estimation quality to histograms in the multidimensional case and also highlighted the comparably cheap construction costs. While those are the only publications that primarily discuss aspects of KDE-based selectivity estimation, there are publications that suggest further use-cases for KDE, including approximate range query processing [15], estimating stream cardinalities [18], online outlier detection [39], and predicting the results of skyline queries [46].

2.4 GPU-assisted Selectivity Estimation

A major disadvantage of KDE is its performance impact: For each estimate, the whole data sample has to be scanned, which can be quite expensive. Since database systems need to trade off between the time spent on query optimization and execution, the improved estimation quality offered by KDE is often simply not worth the additional cost.

In a prior publication, we suggested a possible approach to solve this problem by using a graphics card as a *statistical co-processor* that computes selectivity estimates [16]. Modern graphics cards bundle high-bandwidth memory with a massively parallel processor, making them an interesting platform to accelerate data-intensive operations. In particular, they are well-suited to accelerate the types of computations encountered in Kernel Density Estimation[2], and we could observe roughly a ten-fold speedup compared to a CPU implementation when running KDE on an off-the-shelf graphics card.

Besides being faster, pushing selectivity estimation to a graphics card also has further advantages: First, it allows the database to perform other tasks while selectivities are computed. Second, it enables us to use much larger model sizes within the same time budget. Since the quality of an estimator is directly proportional to its model size [1], this directly results in better estimates. Interestingly, since better estimates usually improve plan quality [21], running selectivity estimation on a graphics card is one of the only applications of GPUs in database systems that can also accelerate traditional disk-based systems [16].

[2]Note that increased transfer across the PCI Express bus – which is typically the bottleneck of any GPU-accelerated application – is of little concern: The sample is kept on the graphics card at all times, meaning that the only required transfers are the query bounds and the computed estimate.

3. OPTIMAL KDE MODELS

In this section, we introduce how to build optimal KDE-based selectivity estimators by adjusting model parameters over query feedback.

3.1 The Formal View

Formally, based on a sample $\mathcal{S} = \left\{\vec{t}^{(1)}, \ldots, \vec{t}^{(s)}\right\}$ of size s from a d-dimensional dataset, multivariate KDE defines an estimator $\hat{p}_H(\vec{x}) : \mathbb{R}^d \to \mathbb{R}$ that assigns a probability density to each point $\vec{x} \in \mathbb{R}^d$. The estimator is defined as:

$$\hat{p}_H(\vec{x}) = \frac{1}{s \cdot |H|} \sum_{i=1}^{s} K\left(H^{-1}\left[\vec{t}^{(i)} - \vec{x}\right]\right) \tag{1}$$

In this equation, $K : \mathbb{R}^d \to \mathbb{R}$ denotes the *kernel function*, which defines the shape of the local probability distributions. The matrix $H \in \mathbb{R}^{d \times d}$ is the *bandwidth matrix*, which controls the spread of the local probability distributions.

3.1.1 KDE-based Range Selectivity Estimation

The probability density $\hat{p}_H(\vec{x})$ from equation (1) can be interpreted as the likelihood of finding a tuple at point $\vec{x}$. In order to approximate the selectivity $\hat{p}_H(\Omega)$ for a query region Ω, we have to integrate (1) over the region:

$$\begin{aligned}\hat{p}_H(\Omega) &= \int_\Omega \hat{p}(\vec{x})\, d\vec{x} \\ &= \frac{1}{s}\sum_{i=1}^{s} \underbrace{\int_\Omega \frac{K\left(H^{-1}\left[\vec{t}^{(i)} - \vec{x}\right]\right)}{|H|} d\vec{x}}_{=\hat{p}_H^{(i)}(\Omega)}\end{aligned} \tag{2}$$

In this equation, $\hat{p}_H^{(i)}(\Omega)$ denotes the *individual probability mass contribution* of the i-th sample point to region Ω. Equation (13) – derived in Appendix Section B – provides the closed-form expression. The selectivity estimate is then simply the average contribution across all sample points.

3.1.2 The Kernel Function

The *kernel function* $K : \mathbb{R}^d \to \mathbb{R}$ in equation (1) defines the shape of the local probability distributions – any function that defines a symmetric probability distribution is a valid choice. Since the shape of the kernel function barely impacts estimation quality [1], K is often chosen based on certain desired properties. In our case, we require that the Kernel is continuously differentiable: Possible choices include the *Gaussian* – a standard normal distribution –, or the *Epanechnikov*, a truncated second-order polynomial.

3.1.3 The Bandwidth

Selecting a good *bandwidth matrix* $H \in \mathbb{R}^{d \times d}$ is much more important than choosing the kernel function [1, 23]. The bandwidth controls the spread of the local distributions, i.e., the larger its magnitude is, the further will sample points distribute probability mass into their neighborhood. Figure 2 illustrates the effect of choosing different bandwidth parameters for the estimator from Figure 1: If the bandwidth is chosen too small (Figure 2(a)), the estimator isn't smooth enough, resulting in a very spiky distribution that overfits the sample. On the other hand, if the bandwidth is chosen too large (Figure 2(b)), the estimator is smoothed too strongly, losing much of the local information and underfitting the distribution.

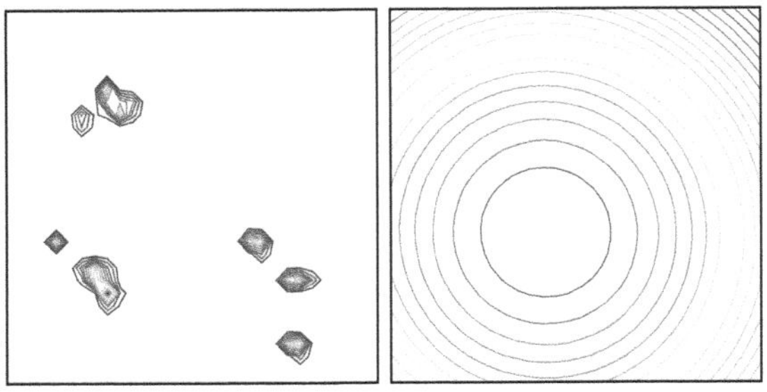

(a) Bandwidth too small. (b) Bandwidth too large.

Figure 2: Choosing the bandwidth has a crucial impact on estimation quality. If the bandwidth is too small (a), the estimator overfits the sample. If it is too large (b), all local information is lost.

A typical simplification – which we also adopt in this paper – is to assume that the bandwidth matrix H is diagonal, i.e. $H = diag(h_1, \ldots, h_d)$, where h_i is a scalar that controls the spread of the local distributions along the i-th attribute. While this simplification can have an impact on estimation quality [44], it vastly simplifies operations and allows us to derive closed-form expressions that do not exist for full bandwidth matrices [1].

3.2 The Bandwidth Selection Problem

Selecting the optimal – or even just a "good enough" – bandwidth is a challenging problem that has been under heavy investigation by the statistics community [1, 23]. The primary goal behind this *bandwidth selection problem* is to select H in a way that minimizes the "distance" between the Kernel Density Estimator $\hat{p}_H(\vec{x})$ and the true distribution $p(\vec{x})$. Most methods aim to minimize the *mean integrated square error* $\mathbb{E}\left[\int_{\vec{x}} (p(\vec{x}) - \hat{p}_H(\vec{x}))^2 \, d\vec{x}\right]$, which is just the expected L_2 loss between distributions p and $\hat{p}_H$.

What makes this problem challenging is that the true distribution is generally assumed to be unknown [1]. Bandwidth selectors solve this problem by selecting H based on an approximation of the true distribution. The most straightforward approach is to replace $p(\vec{x})$ by the Normal distribution $\mathcal{N}(\mu, \Sigma)$ with the observed mean μ and covariance matrix Σ of the data sample. In this case, the optimal (diagonal) bandwidth matrix has a closed-form form expression that can be computed via *Scott's rule* [1]:

$$\hat{h}_i^{scott} = s^{-\frac{1}{d+4}} \cdot \sigma_i \tag{3}$$

In this formula, s denotes the sample size, d the dimensionality, and σ_i the standard deviation of the i-th attribute in the sample. However, since real-world data is seldom normal, Scott's rule often leads to overly smoothed estimators that underfit the true distribution and can produce arbitrarily large estimation errors [14, 23].

More sophisticated selection methods follow the same general principle, but apply better methods to approximate $p(\vec{x})$. In particular, the two most prominent classes of bandwidth selectors are *Cross-Validation* methods, which use leave-one-out cross-validation based on the data sample to approximate $p(\vec{x})$ [5, 37], and *Plug-In* methods, which iteratively refine a pilot distribution for $p(\vec{x})$ that was plugged into the bandwidth optimization [45]. While these methods produce drastically better bandwidth estimates than Scott's rule, they are also expensive to compute, making their usage hard to justify in time-critical settings.

The bandwidth selection problem for KDE-based methods has also been covered in the database literature. However, while all KDE-related publications acknowledge the problem, most simply rely on Scott's rule due to its simplicity [14, 15, 16, 18, 39]. In fact, there are only three papers that discuss alternatives: In [4], Blohfeld et. al. demonstrate that a Plug-In method can drastically improve the selectivity estimation performance of a one-dimensional KDE model. Instead of relying on an existing method, Zhang et. al. introduce a Newton-based optimization method in [46] that directly minimizes the skyline cardinality estimation error based on a sampled test set from the database. While their method is conceptually similar to the one introduced in this paper, it only discusses the case of a single bandwidth parameter that is used for all dimensions. Finally, in [2], Andrzejewski et. al. demonstrate how to reduce the performance impact of a Cross-Validation bandwidth selector by using GPU-acceleration.

3.3 Bandwidth Selection in a Database

Most bandwidth selection methods have one thing in common: They are built on the assumption that the true distribution $p(\vec{x})$ is unknown. In the case of a selectivity estimator, we can relax this assumption since we have a clear and measurable objective: Our estimator is used to approximate the dataset that is stored in the database. Accordingly, we should pick the bandwidth in a way that minimizes the estimation error between our model and the database.

Exploiting this observation, we can re-formulate the bandwidth selection problem for a KDE-based selectivity estimator into the following constrained optimization problem:

$$H^* = \underset{H}{\operatorname{argmin}} \, \mathbb{E}\left[\mathcal{L}\left(\hat{p}_H(\Omega), \frac{|\sigma_{\vec{x}\in\Omega}(R)|}{|R|}\right)\right] \quad \text{s.t. } \forall i : h_i > 0 \tag{4}$$

In this formula, $|R|$ denotes the cardinality of relation R and $|\sigma_{\vec{x}\in\Omega}(R)|$ denotes the number of tuples from R that fall into the region Ω. Summarizing the optimization problem, we want to pick the (positive) bandwidth that minimizes the expected value of a given loss function $\mathcal{L} : \mathbb{R}^2 \to \mathbb{R}$ over the range queries on relation R. The actual choice of loss function is arbitrary, typical choices are quadratic (L2), absolute (L1), or relative. Appendix Section C.1 provides a list of commonly used error metrics and explains how to apply them to this method.

In order to solve optimization problem (4), we need to compute the expected estimation error across all possible range queries on R. Since this is obviously infeasible to compute, we will instead solve a tractable approximation. In particular, we can approximate the expected error by averaging the estimation error over a small set of representative range queries. This method yields an asymptotically correct approximation and can be efficiently computed. In other words, given a training set of range queries $Q = \{\Omega_1, \ldots, \Omega_q\}$, we obtain the optimal bandwidth by solving the following modified optimization problem:

$$H^* = \underset{H}{\operatorname{argmin}} \frac{1}{q} \sum_{i=1}^{q} \mathcal{L}\left(\hat{p}_H(\Omega_i), \frac{|\sigma_{\vec{x}\in\Omega_i}(R)|}{|R|}\right) \tag{5}$$
$$\text{s.t. } \forall i: h_i > 0$$

We derive the closed-form expression for the gradient $\nabla_H \mathcal{L}$ of the error function with respect to the bandwidth in Appendix Section C. Based on this, we can compute the optimal bandwidth by simply plugging the estimation error and its gradient into any off-the-shelf optimization algorithm for bound constrained problems.

There are two issues to consider: First, the problem is non-convex, meaning it can have multiple local minima. It is therefore important to use a global optimization algorithm when solving the problem. However, it should be noted that we found that the actual number of minima is very low, typically only one or two. Second, finding the optimal bandwidth requires a viable set of representative range queries. One possibility is to use a random workload, which would result in the model being optimized under the assumption that every region is equally likely to be queried. However, in real-world scenarios this is rarely the case, as there are usually regions that the users query more frequently. Accordingly, the model optimization should prioritize estimation quality in these regions, which can be achieved by collecting a set of user queries and solving problem (5) for them.

3.4 An Optimal KDE Selectivity Estimator

Summarizing our approach, we can construct an optimal KDE-based selectivity estimator for a given relation R by the following three steps:

1. Collect a set of representative queries on relation R, e.g. by keeping the last q user queries in a ring buffer. Increasing q leads to a more robust optimization, but at the same time makes the process more expensive. We found that a good choice for q is on the order of a few hundred queries.

2. Collect a random sample of size s from the target relation and initialize the bandwidth using Scott's rule from equation (3). Increasing the sample size improves the estimation quality, but also makes it more expensive to compute. Therefore, s should be chosen as large as possible, while still guaranteeing that the time to estimate a selectivity stays within a given time budget.

3. Pick the optimal bandwidth H^* by plugging optimization problem (5) into your favorite gradient-based numerical solver for bound constrained optimization problems. The required closed-form expression for the gradient $\nabla_H \mathcal{L}$ is given in Appendix Section C.2. In our experiments, we made good experiences with first running a coarse global optimization algorithm (e.g. MLSLS [24]) to get us into the right neighborhood, followed by a local optimization algorithm (e.g. L-BFGS-B [8] or MMA [40]) to refine the bandwidth.

4. SELF-TUNING KDE MODELS

The method outlined in the previous section describes how to build an optimal KDE-based selectivity estimator. However, if either the database or the workload characteristics change, we have to rebuild the estimator to remain optimal. Obviously, this is not ideal, as periodic rebuilding could incur significant performance overhead. Ideally, the estimator should adjust itself to compensate for any occurring changes. In this section, we present two complementary methods to build such a self-tuning KDE model.

Listing 1: Adaptively adjusting the bandwidth.

$\vec{g}^{(0)} = [0, \ldots, 0]^T$ *//Gradient accumulator.*
$\vec{m} = [0, \ldots, 0]^T$ *//Running average magnitude.*
$\vec{\lambda} = [1, \ldots, 1]^T$ *//Initial learning rates.*
$i = 0;\ t = 0$
foreach query Ω:
  Compute $\hat{p}_H(\Omega)$ according to (2).
  Run query Ω.
  Collect $|\sigma_{\vec{x}\in\Omega}(R)|$ from query feedback.
  $\vec{g}^{(t)} = \vec{g}^{(t)} + \nabla_H \mathcal{L}\left(\hat{p}_H(\Omega), |\sigma_{\vec{x}\in\Omega}(R)|/|R|\right)$
  $i = i + 1$
  if $(i \bmod N == 0)$:
    $\vec{g}^{(t)} = \vec{g}^{(t)}/N$
    foreach dimension d:
      $m_d = \alpha \cdot m_d + (1-\alpha) \cdot \left(g_d^{(t)}\right)^2$
      if $(g_d^{(t)} \cdot g_d^{(t-1)} > 0)$ $\lambda_d = min(\lambda_d \cdot \lambda_{inc}, \lambda_{max})$
      if $(g_d^{(t)} \cdot g_d^{(t-1)} < 0)$ $\lambda_d = max(\lambda_d \cdot \lambda_{dec}, \lambda_{min})$
      $h_d = \max\left(0.5 \cdot h_d, h_d - \lambda_d/\sqrt{m_d} \cdot g_d^{(t)}\right)$
    $t = t + 1;\ \vec{g}^{(t)} = [0, \ldots, 0]^T$

4.1 Adaptive Bandwidth Maintenance

Changes in the query workload and to the database can lead to a gradual change in the optimal bandwidth configuration. In order to counter these changes, we propose to continuously update the bandwidth by incrementally solving optimization problem (5) via a variant of *stochastic gradient descent* (SGD). The principle idea is simple: Instead of optimizing the bandwidth based on a set of pre-collected user queries, we directly update the bandwidth after each incoming query by subtracting the gradient $\nabla_H \mathcal{L}$ of our error function. This leads to a reactive optimization procedure that automatically adjusts itself to changes.

There are some issues to consider: First, SGD is susceptible to outliers since extreme gradients from single observations can lead to strong bandwidth fluctuations between queries. We mitigate this problem by using a *mini-batch* approach, where we average the gradients from a small number of queries before updating the model. Second, the convergence behavior of SGD is controlled by the *learning rate*, which determines how strongly each observation changes the model. This rate should tend towards zero for static workloads to accelerate convergence, but increase again when the workload changes for quick and reactive model updates. In our estimator we use *RMSprop* [42], which is the mini-batch variant of the earlier *Rprop* [36], to achieve this behavior. RMSprop changes the learning rate based on the direction of previous gradients: If the directions of the last gradients agree, the rate is increased, otherwise it is decreased. Before updating the model, RMSprop also scales the gradients by the average magnitude of recent gradients to achieve better convergence behavior. RMSprop is a simple and cheap learning algorithm that we found to work well in our experiments. Finally, we need to ensure that the positivity constraint from optimization problem (5) is never violated. SGD is an unconstrained optimization algorithm, meaning we have to manually guarantee positivity. We do this by artificially restricting model updates towards zero to at most half the current bandwidth's value.

Listing 1 gives a detailed overview of this adaptive bandwidth learning algorithm: When a new query arrives, we compute the selectivity estimate (line 6), pass the estimate to the database, and let the query run (line 7). After the query finished, we receive query feedback, compute the error gradient according to Appendix Section C.2, and add it to the current mini-batch (line 9). If the mini-batch is full, we average the accumulated gradient (line 12) and use it to update the running average of gradient magnitudes (line 14). We then perform the RMSprop learning rate update for each dimension (lines 15 and 16), and update the individual bandwidth parameters by subtracting the scaled gradients (line 17), enforcing the positivity constraint as discussed.

There are a few important parameters in this algorithm: The mini-batch size N controls how many gradients are averaged per mini-batch. We found that a value around 10 works well. The smoothing rate α limits the influence of historic gradients on the gradient scaling. In our implementation, this is set to 0.9. Parameters λ_{min} and λ_{max} are the smallest and largest allowed learning rates. They are set to 10^{-6} and 50 respectively, which are the suggested values from [42]. The final two parameters are λ_{inc} and λ_{dec}, which are the multiplicative factors by which the learning rate is in-/decreased. These are also set to their suggested values from [42], which are 1.2 and 0.5 respectively.

4.2 Karma-based Sample Maintenance

The second major source of estimation errors are updates to the database: These updates invalidate our data sample, forcing us to apply corrective measures to keep it representative. In our case, this is an especially challenging problem, since the sample resides on the graphics card, while database updates occur on the host. Keeping sample and database in sync via traditional sample maintenance algorithms [12, 33] would require us to continuously transfer information to the graphics card. Depending on the workload, these additional transfers could easily clog the limited bandwidth of the PCI Express bus, resulting in severe performance penalties. We therefore had to develop a novel sample maintenance algorithm that avoids data transfers where possible.

The first scenario we consider are insert-only workloads. In this case, we utilize the well-known *reservoir sampling algorithm* [43]. Reservoir sampling adds newly inserted data to the sample with probability $|S|/|R|$, replacing a random point in the process. It is optimal with regard to transfers, as all decisions are made independently by the host and only points that will end up in the sample are transferred to the graphics card.

Things get more complicated for workloads that also contain deletions or updates, as reservoir sampling is insufficient in this case. In our estimator, we use an approximate, but transfer-efficient, maintenance algorithm. Our method piggybacks on the query feedback information that is sent to the graphics card for the adaptive bandwidth optimization. It uses this information to identify and selectively replace points that consistently hurt our estimation quality. In order to derive the approach, let us recall equation (2): The selectivity estimate $\hat{p}_H(\Omega)$ is computed by averaging the individual contributions $\hat{p}_H^{(i)}(\Omega)$ from all points in the sample. We can now remove the i-th point's contribution from the estimate:

$$\hat{p}_H^{-(i)}(\Omega) = \frac{\hat{p}_H(\Omega) \cdot s - \hat{p}_H^{(i)}(\Omega)}{s-1} \quad (6)$$

This *adjusted estimate* $\hat{p}_H^{-(i)}(\Omega)$ tells us how the estimator would have performed if the i-th point had been absent. Our key assumption is, that if a point significantly improves estimation quality by its absence, it is likely outdated and should be replaced. In order to track this, we introduce the *Karma score*, which we define as the estimation error change a given point causes for a given query Ω:

$$K^{(i)}(\Omega) = \left[\mathcal{L}\left(p(\Omega), \hat{p}_H^{-(i)}(\Omega)\right) - \mathcal{L}\left(p(\Omega), \hat{p}_H(\Omega)\right)\right] \quad (7)$$

Large positive Karma values correspond to sample points that significantly improved the estimation quality in query region Ω, while negative values are associated with points that had a negative impact. By aggregating the Karma over multiple queries, we obtain a solid indicator to tell us which points consistently helped and which hurt us. Accordingly, we define the i-th point's *cumulative Karma* as follows:

$$K_{t+1}^{(i)} = \min\left(K_t^{(i)} + K^{(i)}(\Omega), K_{\max}\right) \quad (8)$$

Based on this equation, the estimator updates the cumulative Karma for all points after each query. If a point's Karma falls below a given threshold, it is marked as outdated and is replaced by a newly sampled point from the database. It should be noted that – strictly speaking –, this approach is not a true maintenance algorithm, as changes in the database are not applied instantaneously to the sample. Instead they propagate over time as the Karma of deleted points decays. We play two tricks to reduce this sample convergence time. First, we limit the maximum cumulative Karma that a point can collect through the saturation constant $K_{\max}$ in equation (8)[3]. Second, we use a shortcut to quickly identify and replace sample points that fall into an empty query region. Details of this shortcut are explained in Appendix Section E.

5. GPU-ACCELERATED KDE MODELS

In a prior publication, we introduced the idea of tapping into the massive raw computational power of modern consumer graphics cards to enable more advanced methods for selectivity estimation [16]. KDE models are especially well-suited for GPU-acceleration: All major operations – including estimation, model optimization, and sample maintenance – can be expressed as summations over individual probability contributions from sampled points. Computing these is an embarrassingly parallel problem that can be efficiently accelerated by a GPU (or any other massively parallel processor for that matter).

Figure 3 illustrates the general implementation overview of our self-tuning estimator, the required operations, and the relations between them. Our implementation is integrated into Postgres 9.3.1 and uses OpenCL to achieve portable performance across a multitude of devices, including modern GPUs and multi-core CPUs [17]. In the following sections, we discuss the single components in more detail. However, for lack of space, we will not provide a highly detailed rundown of our implementations. Instead, we convey the general ideas, and refer to the provided source code for further details. We also assume that the reader is familiar with the kernel-based programming model that is typically used for GPU programming.

[3]We found that a good value for $K_{\max}$ is four.

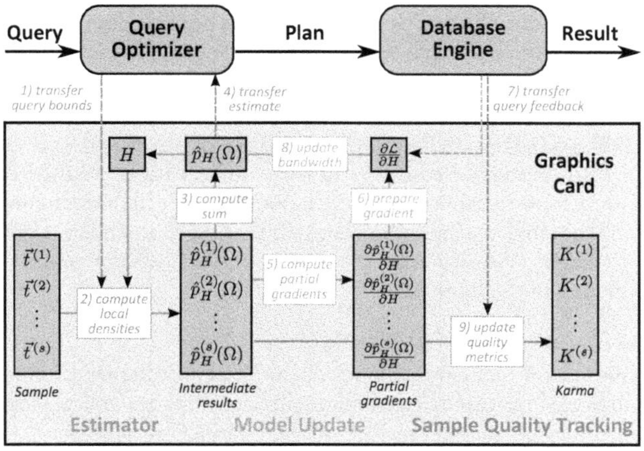

Figure 3: Computing the selectivity on a graphics card.

5.1 Data Representation

The most memory-intensive part of our estimator is the sample buffer, which is used to keep the sampled data points on the graphics card. We represent the sample in row-major format, using floating point numbers to store attribute values. While a columnar data layout would likely be preferable from a performance perspective [6, 17], the row-major format allows us to efficiently update points in the sample using only a single PCI Express transfer.

In order to reduce the performance impact of the row-major format, we use templated kernel code and runtime code generation: When an estimator is initialized for a table, we compile specific kernels for it, passing both the configured floating point precision and the table's dimensionality as compile-time constants to the OpenCL runtime compiler. This helps the runtime compiler to apply device-specific code optimizations like loop-unrolling or data access reordering.

5.2 Initializing the Estimator

Model construction is triggered by Postgres' ANALYZE command. When called, we utilize Postgres' internal routines to collect a random sample of the requested size. We copy this sample row-by-row into a host buffer, transforming data types where necessary. This buffer is then copied over to a pre-allocated sample buffer on the graphics card. Note that this is the only major data transfer that is required by the estimator! Besides preparing the data sample, we also initialize the estimator bandwidth via Scott's rule from equation (3). The most expensive part of this formula is to compute the standard deviation within the dimensions: We efficiently compute this on the graphics card by summing up the single dimensions' values and their squares in a parallel binary reduction scheme [19], and then using the identity: $\sigma^2 = {}^1\!/\!{}_n \sum_j x_i^2 - \left({}^1\!/\!{}_n \sum_i x_i\right)^2$.

5.3 Optimizing the Bandwidth

In order to optimize the bandwidth based on a query workload as described in Section 3.4, we first transfer the query bounds and the observed selectivities of the workload to the graphics card. The actual optimization of problem (5) then happens in two steps: We first run a global optimization step via MLSL [24] to (hopefully) get us near the global minimum, followed by a local optimization via L-BFGS-B [8] to refine the bandwidth. Note that we did not implement these optimization algorithms ourselves. Instead, we plug the optimization problem into off-the-shelf implementations from the optimization library NLopt [22]: During every internal iteration, NLopt calls one of our functions to compute the estimation error and the gradient for the current bandwidth. Internally, this function copies the current bandwidth to the graphics card and then lets each thread compute the partial gradient and estimation error for a single user query according to equation (17). Afterwards, the partial gradients are summed up using a parallel binary reduction scheme and shipped back to he host, where the final gradient is returned to NLopt, which uses it to update the bandwidth according to the selected optimization algorithm. After a few iterations, NLopt will converge to the optimal bandwidth, which we then transfer to the graphics card.

5.4 Computing Estimates

The actual estimator is mostly implemented as outlined in [16]: First, we transfer the query bounds Ω to the device (1). Based on these bounds, and the current bandwidth H, the graphics card computes the local densities in parallel, with each thread using equation (13) to compute the individual contribution $\hat{p}_H^{(i)}(\Omega)$ of a single sample item (2). The local contributions are written to a temporary buffer, which is afterwards aggregated via a parallel binary reduction scheme (3). The resulting estimate $\hat{p}_H(\Omega)$ is transferred back to the host (4), where it is passed on to the query optimizer. The only major difference to our previous implementation is that we do not discard the temporary buffer that stores the individual contributions until after the query returns from the database, as we need them for the sample maintenance.

5.5 Model Updates

The adaptive bandwidth optimization method outlined in Section 4.1, requires us to compute the gradient of the current estimation error after each query, which is quite expensive to do. Luckily, we can hide these costs behind the query runtime. As derived in Appendix Section C, the gradient is the product of two factors: The first one is the partial derivative of the estimator with respect to the bandwidth, as given by equation (15). This part is expensive to compute, but is independent of the actual estimation error, meaning we can compute it on the graphics card while the database is busy running the query. The computation itself is parallelized over the sample items, with each thread using equation (16) to compute the partial gradient contribution for one sample point (5). Afterwards, all partial contributions are aggregated using a parallel binary reduction scheme (6). The second factor is the partial derivative of the estimation error, which is a simple scalar that is computed from the estimated and the true selectivity. After we receive the true selectivity (7), the host computes this factor according to equation (14) and ships it to the graphics card. There it is multiplied with the pre-computed model-dependent factor, and accumulated on the current mini-batch. Once a full mini-batch is collected, we update the bandwidth (8) as described in Listing 1.

Another implementation aspect we did not cover so far are logarithmic bandwidth updates. In our experiments, we found that updating the logarithm of the bandwidth often leads to improved estimates and a more stable optimization behaviour. In fact, we observed improvements over the non-logarithmic case in 68% of all experiments. Appendix Section D provides further details about this method.

5.6 Sample Maintenance

The final major component is the sample maintenance algorithm, which consists of two components: Reservoir Sampling is used to deal with insertions and Karma-based Sample Maintenance to deal with updates.

Our implementation of Reservoir Sampling follows the algorithm specification from [43]: Whenever a new tuple is inserted into relation R, the sample maintenance routine gets notified by the database engine. The host then decides whether the new tuple should be inserted into the sample as explained in [43]. If the tuple should be inserted, a PCI Express transfer is scheduled to copy it to a random position in the sample, overwriting the point that is stored there.

Karma-based Sample Maintenance tracks the cumulative Karma as described in Section 4.2 based on the (retained) individual contributions $\hat{p}_H^{(i)}(\Omega)$, the estimated, and the true selectivity. This computation happens in a single pass over the sample, with each thread evaluating equation (6) for one point. Afterwards, the same thread updates the point's cumulative Karma according to equation (8) (9). If this update results in a point's Karma falling below a threshold – or if the true selectivity is zero, and condition (20) holds –, the point is deemed outdated and will be replaced. The actual replacement happens in a two-step procedure: First, a bitmap is generated in parallel that indicates which tuples must be replaced. This bitmap is transferred back to the host, which samples the requested number of tuples from the database and schedules transfers to copy them to the positions indicated in the bitmap.

6. EVALUATION

In this section, we present the experimental evaluation of our proposed estimator. The experiments were designed to cover the following four areas: 1) Estimation quality on static datasets, 2) Estimation behavior with increasing model size, 3) Performance impact of our method & advantage of GPU-acceleration, and 4) Estimation quality on changing datasets.

6.1 Experimental Setup

We will now describe the datasets, workloads, and estimators that were used for the experiments.

6.1.1 Compared Estimators

We compared the following five estimators:

KDE heuristic: The "naïve" variant of a Kernel Density Estimator, using Scott's rule (c.f. equation (3)) to compute the bandwidth. This is our baseline to compare against existing KDE estimators.

KDE SCV: A Kernel Density Estimator using the bandwidth chosen by a state-of-the-art bandwidth selection method. In particular, we use the bandwidth selector *Hscv.diag* from the R package *ks*[4], which is based on the Smoothed Cross Validation approach from [11].

STHoles: STHoles [7] is a self-tuning, multidimensional histogram that continuously refines its model based on query feedback. We use STHoles as a proxy to compare our estimator against the quality of state-of-the-art multidimensional histograms.

KDE batch: The optimal KDE estimator, as described in Section 3. In this configuration, we optimize the bandwidth during model construction based on an initial training set of user queries.

KDE adaptive: The adaptive variant of our estimator, as described in Section 4. In this configuration, we initialize the model according to Scott's rule, and then continuously adjust the bandwidth based on query feedback. We also use the Karma-based sample maintenance techniques.

6.1.2 Evaluated Datasets

We based our experiments on a variety of synthetic and real-world[5] datasets from multiple domains to get a solid and unbiased understanding of the estimation quality:

Bike: Hourly aggregated usage statistics for the Washington DC bike sharing system. The dataset consists of 17,379 data points with 16 continuous attributes.

Forest: Geological survey of forest cover types in the US. The dataset consists of 581,012 points with 54 attributes, of which we use a projection on the 10 continuous ones.

Power: Time series describing the electric power consumption in a single household with one-minute resolution. The dataset consists of 2,075,259 data points with 9 attributes containing continuous and discrete values.

Protein: Physiochemical properties of the tertiary structure of proteins. The dataset contains 45,730 points with 9 continuous attributes.

Synthetic: Synthetic dataset from [14], consisting of one million points. It is generated by randomly placing hyper-rectangular clusters with a uniform interior distribution, and then adding uniformly distributed noise.

For all datasets, we generated versions with three and eight dimensions. These were created by projecting the full dataset onto a random subset of the available attributes.

6.1.3 Query Workloads

We generated our workloads according to the method outlined in [7]: Each workload is specified by a distribution for the query centers and a target measure that the queries have to meet. Based on this approach, we defined the following four workloads, which cover a variety of usage scenarios:

DT: Queries with a target selectivity of 1% whose centers are following the data distribution. This workload corresponds to a set of well-defined user queries that return roughly the same number of tuples.

DV: Queries with a target volume of 1% of the data space whose centers are following the data distribution. This workload corresponds to a set of explorative user queries having a wide spectrum of different selectivities.

UT: Queries with a target selectivity of 1%, whose centers are randomly distributed across the data space. This workload corresponds to a random workload with queries having highly diverse query volumes.

UV: Queries with a target volume of 1% of the data space, whose centers are randomly distributed across the data space. This workload corresponds to a random workload with mostly empty queries.

[4]`http://cran.r-project.org/web/packages/ks`

[5]Obtained from the UCI Machine Learning repository [3].

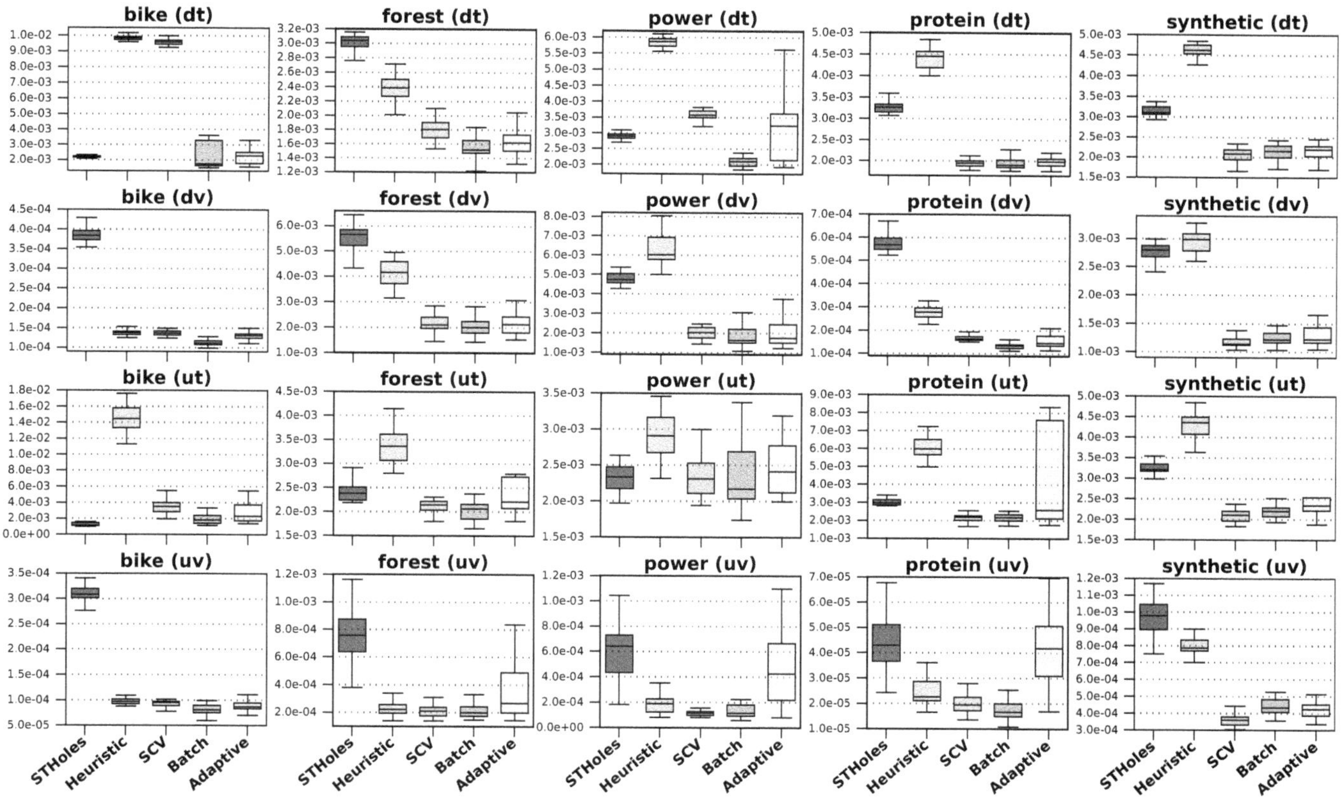

Figure 4: Estimation quality on static datasets (3D). The y-axis shows the absolute selectivity estimation error.

6.2 Estimation Quality on Static Data

In the first series of experiments, we compared the estimation quality on static datasets with fixed workloads. The primary goal of these experiments was to answer the following three questions:

1. Does selecting the bandwidth by solving optimization problem (5) from Section 3 actually improve the estimation quality of a KDE-based selectivity estimator, especially when compared to using Scott's rule, or alternative bandwidth selection methods?
2. How does the adaptive bandwidth optimization from Section 4 compare against the batch method?
3. How does the estimation quality of the batch-optimized and the adaptive estimator compare against state-of-the art multidimensional histograms?

We ran these experiments using the following protocol: We randomly selected 100 training and 300 test queries from the selected workload. Then, we initialized the estimators, and – if applicable – optimized their model parameters based on the training queries. Finally, we measured the average absolute selectivity estimation error on the test set. This process was repeated 25 times to measure how strongly the estimation quality fluctuates. During each run, all estimators were given the exact same set of queries to avoid measuring workload-dependent changes. Furthermore, all KDE-based estimators were built using the same random sample. Finally, in order to make the comparisons fair, we restricted all estimators to use the same amount of memory. In particular, we allowed $d{\cdot}4\,\text{kB}$, where d is the dimensionality of the dataset.

	STHoles	Heuristic	SCV	Batch	Adaptive	All
STHoles	-	*52.5*	*19.4*	*14.4*	*24.5*	*8.4*
Heuristic	*46.0*	-	*5.7*	*6.7*	*12.1*	*0.7*
SCV	*79.0*	*94.3*	-	*37.0*	*46.3*	*26.3*
Batch	*84.1*	*90.8*	*63.0*	-	*64.5*	*43.2*
Adaptive	*71.3*	*81.8*	*53.5*	*35.5*	-	*21.4*

Table 1: Comparing the estimation quality of the different estimators: Cells list the percentage of experiments in which the row's estimator performed better than the one on top.

The results of these experiments are shown in Figure 4 for the three-, and in Figure 5 for the eight-dimensional datasets. Each plot shows the result for a single workload and dataset, using boxplots to illustrate how estimation errors were distributed over the 25 repetitions. Furthermore, Table 1 lists the percentage of experiments in which a given estimator performed better than a given other one.

Let us discuss the results: First, the plots clearly show that our methods indeed substantially improve the estimation quality of KDE. In fact, *Batch* performed better than *Heuristic* in over 90% of all experiments! It should also be noted that *Batch* even outperformed *SCV* in a majority of cases (> 60%). While this seems counter-intuitive at first, it is expected: *SCV* picks the bandwidth by minimizing the Cross Validation error on the sample. *Batch* has two advantages: It directly minimizes the selectivity estimation error, and – through the user workload – takes additional information about the data distribution into account, allowing it to better tune the bandwidth.

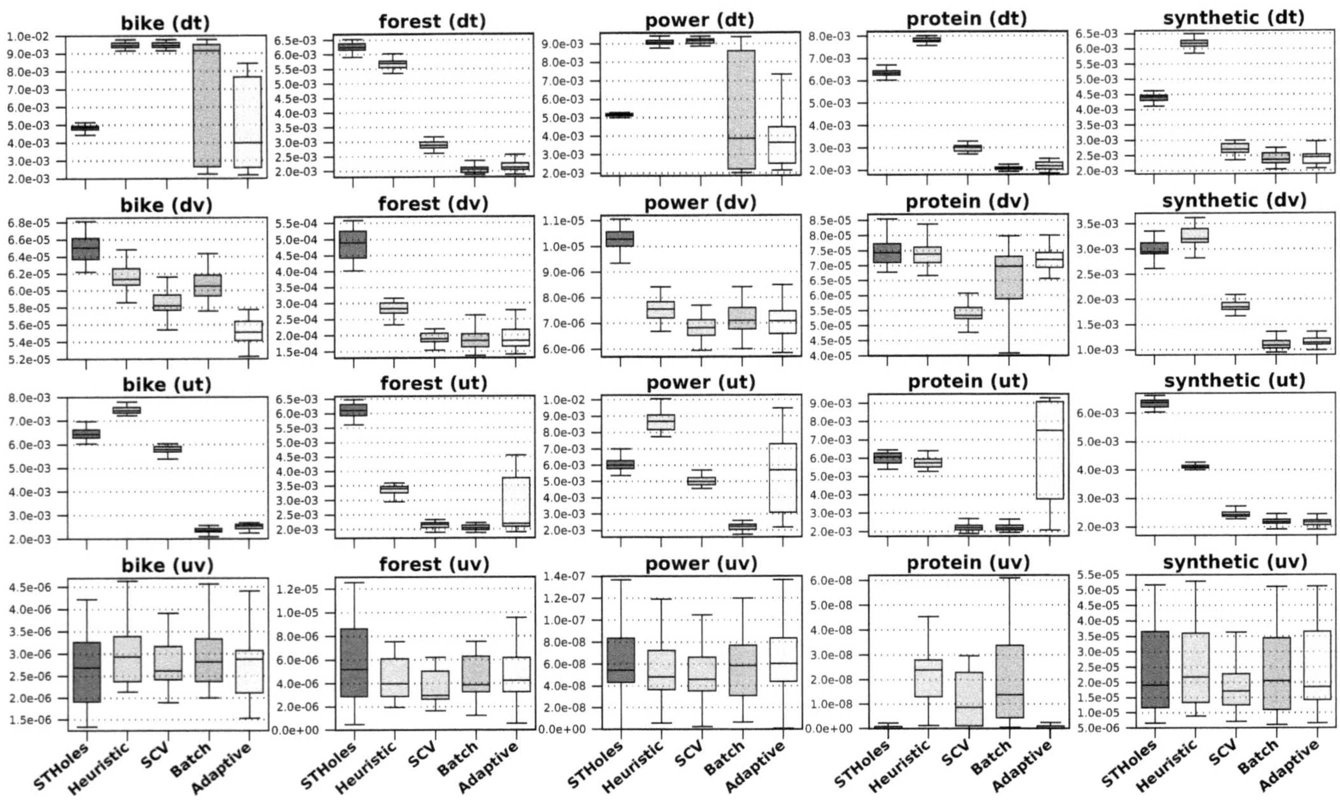

Figure 5: Estimation quality on static datasets (8D). The y-axis shows the absolute selectivity estimation error.

Second, while *Adaptive* does not fully match the estimation quality of *Batch*, it still performs admirably, clearly outperforming *Heuristic* and matching the quality of *SCV*. However, there are several cases in which *Adaptive* leads to a much higher variance than *Batch* or *SCV*. There are two primary reasons for this behavior: First, the stochastic nature of online learning leads to a higher variance in the produced bandwidth estimates. Second, in contrast to *Batch*, *Adaptive* does not use global optimization, meaning it can get stuck in local minima more easily. Still, *Adaptive* generally offers competitive performance, while not requiring us to collect user queries or run an expensive optimization routine.

Finally, let's compare with *STHoles*. In general, both *Batch* and *Adaptive* are clearly superior, with *Batch* producing better estimates in 84% and *Adaptive* in 71% of all experiments. However, *STHoles* still has the advantage of producing more stable estimates: Since bandwidth optimization is a non-convex problem, there is some chance of the estimator getting stuck in a local minima, leading to a large variance – as can be seen in Bike(8D) DT and Power(8D) DT. Nevertheless, we could demonstrate that our bandwidth selection methods clearly improve the estimation quality of a state-of-the-art KDE-based selectivity estimator, and push them into a range where KDE actually becomes a reasonable alternative to multidimensional histograms.

6.3 Quality Impact of Model Size

In this experiment, we investigated how the estimators' quality scales when increasing the model size. Note that we focused on *Heuristic*, *Batch* & *Adaptive* – a discussion of *STHoles'* scaling behavior can be found in [7].

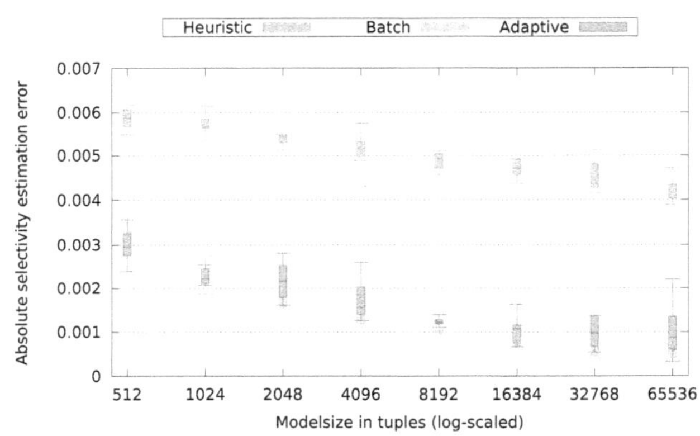

Figure 6: Estimation quality with growing model size.

The experiment was set up like the previous section, using the 8D Forest dataset and the DT workload. Estimators were built based on 100 randomly selected queries, the estimation quality – the absolute selectivity estimation error – was measured based on another 100 queries. Each experiment was repeated ten times, the results are illustrated in Figure 6, note the logarithmically scaled x-axis. The plots clearly show that, for all models, using larger samples leads directly to improved estimates: By increasing the sample size from 1024 to 32768, we could decrease the estimation error to roughly one third. In general, the error decreases exponentially with a negative exponent with increasing sample size. Furthermore, the experiment again demonstrates the impact of bandwidth optimization, as the optimized estimators are roughly twice as accurate as *Heuristic*.

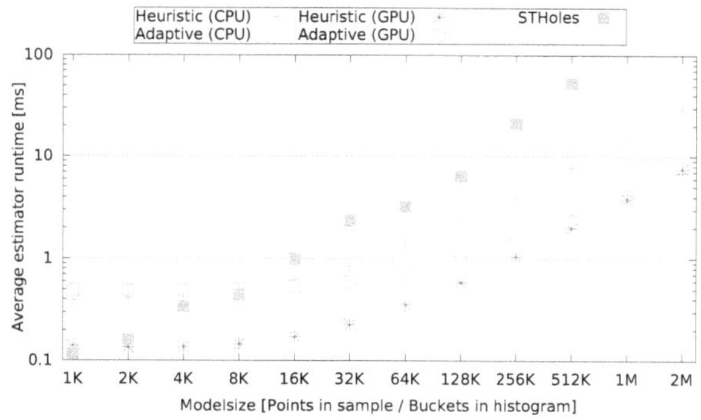

Figure 7: Estimator runtime with growing model size.

6.4 Performance & GPU-Acceleration

In the next experiment, we measured the estimator runtime overhead with growing model sizes, answering the following questions:

1. How does the runtime of our estimators scale with increasing model size?
2. What is the runtime impact of the adaptive bandwidth optimization method?
3. How much does GPU-acceleration help?
4. How does the runtime of our methods compare to state-of-the-art multidimensional histograms?

In this experiment, we measured the total estimation overhead for 100 random UV queries on a synthetic 8D table with three million rows. We compared the performance of *Heuristic*, *Adaptive* & *STHoles* – *Batch* was left out as it is as fast as *Heuristic*. For *Heuristic* and *Adaptive*, we measured both the CPU and the GPU variant. Measuring the runtime of STHoles was somewhat tricky, as it incrementally builds a histogram by adding buckets (or "holes") based on query feedback until a limit is reached. Therefore, the estimation speed of STHoles gradually decreases over time until the histogram is full. This is different from KDE, whose runtime overhead is constant and only depends on the model size. In order to compensate for this, we report the runtime overhead for the full STHoles model, which was constructed over a large-enough training workload. Furthermore, we only measured estimation time, excluding the time that STHoles spends on maintaining the histogram.

The experiment was run on custom server with a Quad-Core Intel Xeon E5620 @ 2.4GHz and 32GB of DDR3-1066 RAM, running Scientific Linux 6.4. It is equipped with a middle-class NVIDIA GTX-460 graphics card having 2GB of DDR4 memory. The GPU is controlled by NVIDIA's 340.32 driver, we used Intel's OpenCL SDK 2014 to run the estimators on the CPU. Figure 7 illustrates the results, note that both axes are scaled logarithmically.

First, let us take a look at how estimation overhead scales with increasing model sizes. On both CPU & GPU, *Heuristic* and *Adaptive* show a flat curve until the model size reaches $\approx 16-32K$ points. Afterwards, the estimator scales linearly with the model size, as expected. The flat start is likely caused by the OpenCL runtime, which introduces latency penalties for each scheduled data transfer and kernel execution. Only for larger models is this latency shadowed by the actual computation. Second, let us discuss the runtime difference between *Adaptive* and *Heuristic*. Interestingly, this difference is constant and does not seem to depend on the model size. This behavior demonstrates nicely that efficiently hide the additional computations required by *Adaptive*: They run concurrently while Postgres executes the query, making the only measurable performance impact of *Adaptive* the latency penalties incurred by the additional kernel calls and data transfers.

Let us now discuss the performance impact of using a graphics card: Looking at the plot, we can see that GPU-acceleration gives us a speed-up of around a factor of four, both for *Heuristic* and for *Adaptive*. In particular, the GPU can estimate a selectivity with *Adaptive* on a model of $128K$ elements in under $1ms$. The CPU is slightly slower, but still delivers impressive performance, being able to estimate selectivities based on models of $\approx 32K$ elements in $1ms$. This is a nice indication of the portable performance of OpenCL, and demonstrates that our estimator is also very efficient when being run without a graphics card. This impressive scaling behaviour has some interesting consequences: In the first series of experiments, we restricted our samples to $32kB$ of memory. Judging from the performance measurements, we could easily increase this size to at least $2MB$ without seeing any major performance impact. Looking at the previous section, increasing the sample by a factor of 64 would cut our estimation error by at least a factor of three. This demonstrates one of the strongest advantages of KDE: Since they can be efficiently parallelized, KDE models scale much better, and can benefit much stronger from modern hardware than multidimensional histograms or comparable methods could.

Finally, let us compare *STHoles* and *KDE*. The plot shows that *STHoles* is generally faster than KDE for small models – due to the OpenCL overhead –, but gets much slower when the model size is increased. In fact, for large models, STHoles is around a factor of $7-10$ slower than KDE on the GPU, and around a factor of 3 than KDE on the CPU. Note however that this comparison is only indicative and should be taken with a grain of salt: First, we only measured the estimation component of *STHoles*, excluding the time spent on model maintenance. This is actually highly significant, given that *STHoles'* maintenance time can quickly add up to several seconds on larger models. Second, even though we implement all performance improvements outlined in [7], *STHoles* only uses a sequential implementation, meaning it has somewhat sub-optimal performance-

6.5 Estimation Quality on Changing Data

In the final experiment, we wanted to demonstrate the self-tuning aspects of *Adaptive*, in particular the Karma-based sample maintenance from Section 4.2. For this experiment, we used a synthetic workload, combining insertions, deletions, and selections. The workload starts by loading 4500 tuples, evenly distributed among three random clusters. Afterwards the workload features ten cycles of slowly creating a new cluster by gradually inserting 1500 tuples into it, followed by deleting all tuples belonging to one of the old clusters. These dataset changes are interleaved with a DT query workload that queries older clusters less frequently than newer ones. This scenario mirrors an evolving database where new data is queried more frequently, and older data is periodically moved into an archive. We ran this workload ten times each on *STHoles*, *Heuristic*, and *Adaptive*, measuring the progression of the absolute estimation error. As in the first series of experiments, we restricted the estimators to $d{\cdot}4\,\mathrm{kB}$ of memory.

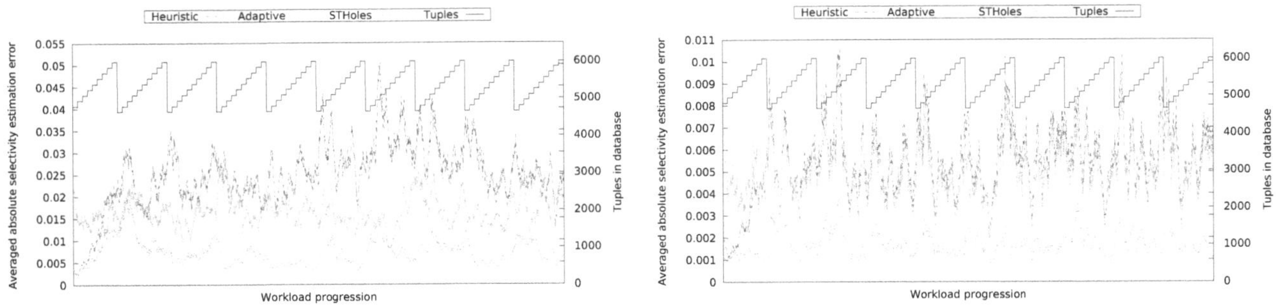

(a) 5D (b) 8D

Figure 8: Estimation quality on changing datasets.

Figure 8 illustrates the results of this experiment, with Figure 8a containing the 5D, and Figure 8b the 8D case. The black lines on top illustrate the progression of the number of tuples in the database. The observed behaviors are as expected: *Heuristic* is unable to keep up with the ongoing database changes. *STHoles* is somewhat in the middle: Due to its self-tuning nature, it does a better job of adjusting to the changes, but cannot compete with *Adaptive*.

7. CONCLUSION

In this paper, we proposed a modern multidimensional selectivity estimator based on Kernel Density Estimation (KDE). KDE is a statistical to estimate probability densities from a data sample that has several advantages over histograms. However, existing KDE-based selectivity estimators were a) suboptimal, because they did not adjust the important bandwidth parameter, b) non-adaptive, because they did not use sample maintenance routines, and c) expensive to evaluate. These shortcomings prevented KDE-based selectivity estimators from becoming a reasonable alternative to multidimensional histograms.

We tackled these challenges and significantly advanced the state-of-the-art in KDE-based selectivity estimation. First, we demonstrated how to numerically optimize the bandwidth based on query feedback to improve estimation quality. Then, we presented two orthogonal methods enabling self-tuning models based on query feedback: A learning algorithm to continuously adjust the bandwidth, and a transfer-efficient sample maintenance algorithm to identify and replace outdated sample points. Finally, we explained how these methods can be efficiently accelerated by graphics cards and multi-core CPUs, and provided a working prototype of the estimator integrated into Postgres. We validated our estimator in an extensive evaluation, demonstrating that its estimation quality outperforms state-of-the-art multidimensional histograms, that it is efficient to evaluate, can automatically adjust itself to database updates, and can be scaled up to very large model sizes without showing a significant performance impact.

8. FUTURE WORK

In order to conclude the paper, we now present and discuss selected topics that we believe to be interesting directions for future work in the field of KDE-based selectivity estimation.

Join Selectivity Estimation. An important subproblem in selectivity estimation research is how to estimate selectivities over joined tables. Extending KDE-based models for this case is very interesting. If the predicate is known beforehand – for instance in case of PK-FK joins –, it can be done by building the estimator based on a sample collected directly from the join result, e.g. by using the sampling algorithms presented in [9]. Estimating arbitrary theta joins is more complex: Since KDE defines a continuous estimator, we should in theory be able to express join selectivities by a joint integral over the two estimators. However, it remains to be seen whether such a formulation is a viable approach, and whether it can be computed efficiently.

Support for Discrete and String Data. KDE works best on continuous data that has strong neighborhood properties, i.e. where the presence of data increases the likelihood of finding other data. However, in real-world databases, we also have to deal with non-continuous data. Extending KDE-based selectivity estimators for discrete and string data is therefore very important. While we did not demonstrate this behavior in the evaluation, our estimator already handles discrete attributes to a certain degree: The bandwidth optimization will observe that it does not profit from increasing the bandwidth for discrete attributes and therefore set it to a very small value. Effectively, this means that the estimator automatically degrades to counting matching tuples on discrete attributes. However, this support is fairly limited, and further investigation is required. One starting point is statistics literature, where this topic was already studied in the context of KDE over mixed continuous and discrete variables [27].

Variable Kernel Density Models. Variable – or adaptive – KDE models are an extension of KDE using distinct bandwidth parameters for each sample point that can be individually modified [41]. These models have shown very promising results in density estimation for very high-dimensional spaces. In theory, our bandwidth optimization approach should be portable to variable KDE models as well, and it would be interesting to investigate how this additional complexity affects estimation quality and runtime overhead.

Integrating with a GPU-accelerated DBMS. Another interesting direction is integrating our estimator with a GPU-accelerated database system [6]. In this case, the estimator would have to compete with the query processor for resources on the GPU. This requires methods for resource sharing that can trade-off estimation quality with resource impact. In particular, using techniques such as *device fission*, modern graphics cards can be virtually partitioned into several sub-devices that can run code concurrently. This technique could allow a GPU-accelerated database system to allocate a given fraction of the graphics card – say 10% – for selectivity estimation without affecting query performance. It would also be interesting to investigate how to accelerate KDE estimation across multiple graphics cards.

9. REFERENCES

[1] *Multivariate Density Estimation - Theory, Practice and Visualization.* John Wiley & Sons, Inc., 1992.

[2] W. Andrzejewski, A. Gramacki, and J. Gramacki. Graphics processing units in acceleration of bandwidth selection for kernel density estimation. *Int. J. Appl. Math. Comput. Sci*, 23(4):869–885, 2013.

[3] K. Bache and M. Lichman. UCI machine learning repository, 2013.

[4] B. Blohsfeld, D. Korus, and B. Seeger. A comparison of selectivity estimators for range queries on metric attributes. *SIGMOD Record*, 28(2):239–250, 1999.

[5] A. W. Bowman. An alternative method of cross-validation for the smoothing of density estimates. *Biometrika*, 71(2):353–360, 1984.

[6] S. Breß, M. Heimel, N. Siegmund, L. Bellatreche, and G. Saake. Gpu-accelerated database systems: Survey and open challenges. In *Transactions on Large-Scale Data-and Knowledge-Centered Systems XV*, pages 1–35. Springer, 2014.

[7] N. Bruno, S. Chaudhuri, and L. Gravano. Stholes: a multidimensional workload-aware histogram. *SIGMOD Record*, 30(2):211–222, 2001.

[8] R. H. Byrd, P. Lu, J. Nocedal, and C. Zhu. A limited memory algorithm for bound constrained optimization. *SIAM Journal on Scientific Computing*, 16(5):1190–1208, 1995.

[9] S. Chaudhuri, R. Motwani, and V. Narasayya. On random sampling over joins. *SIGMOD Record*, 28(2):263–274, 1999.

[10] S. Christodoulakis. Implications of certain assumptions in database performance evauation. *ACM Transactions on Database Systems (TODS)*, 9(2):163–186, 1984.

[11] T. Duong and M. L. Hazelton. Cross-validation bandwidth matrices for multivariate kernel density estimation. *Scandinavian Journal of Statistics*, 32(3):485–506, 2005.

[12] R. Gemulla, W. Lehner, and P. J. Haas. Maintaining bounded-size sample synopses of evolving datasets. *The VLDB Journal*, 17(2):173–201, 2008.

[13] P. B. Gibbons, Y. Matias, and V. Poosala. Maintaining a random sample of a relation in a database in the presence of updates to the relation, Jan. 4 2000. US Patent 6,012,064.

[14] D. Gunopulos, G. Kollios, J. Tsotras, and C. Domeniconi. Selectivity estimators for multidimensional range queries over real attributes. *The VLDB Journal*, 14(2):137–154, 2005.

[15] D. Gunopulos, G. Kollios, V. J. Tsotras, and C. Domeniconi. Approximating multi-dimensional aggregate range queries over real attributes. *ACM SIGMOD Record*, 29(2):463–474, 2000.

[16] M. Heimel and V. Markl. A first step towards gpu-assisted query optimization. In *International Workshop on Accelerating Data Management Systems using Modern Processor and Storage Architectures (ADMS), Istanbul, Turkey*, pages 33–44, 2012.

[17] M. Heimel, M. Saecker, H. Pirk, S. Manegold, and V. Markl. Hardware-oblivious parallelism for in-memory column-stores. *Proceedings of the VLDB Endowment*, 6(9):709–720, 2013.

[18] C. Heinz and B. Seeger. Cluster kernels: Resource-aware kernel density estimators over streaming data. *Knowledge and Data Engineering, IEEE Transactions on*, 20(7):880–893, 2008.

[19] D. Horn. Stream reduction operations for gpgpu applications. *Gpu gems*, 2:573–589, 2005.

[20] Y. Ioannidis. The history of histograms (abridged). In *Proceedings of the 29th VLDB conference*, pages 19–30. VLDB Endowment, 2003.

[21] Y. E. Ioannidis and S. Christodoulakis. On the propagation of errors in the size of join results. *SIGMOD Record*, 20(2):268–277, 1991.

[22] S. G. Johnson. The NLopt nonlinear-optimization package. `http://ab-initio.mit.edu/nlopt`.

[23] M. C. Jones, J. S. Marron, and S. J. Sheather. A brief survey of bandwidth selection for density estimation. *Journal of the American Statistical Association*, 91(433):401–407, 1996.

[24] A. R. Kan and G. Timmer. Stochastic global optimization methods part ii: Multi level methods. *Mathematical Programming*, 39(1):57–78, 1987.

[25] P.-A. Larson, W. Lehner, J. Zhou, and P. Zabback. Cardinality estimation using sample views with quality assurance. In *Proceedings of the 2007 ACM SIGMOD Conference*, pages 175–186. ACM, 2007.

[26] J.-H. Lee, D.-H. Kim, and C.-W. Chung. Multi-dimensional selectivity estimation using compressed histogram information. *SIGMOD Record*, 28(2):205–214, 1999.

[27] Q. Li and J. Racine. Nonparametric estimation of distributions with categorical and continuous data. *journal of multivariate analysis*, 86(2):266–292, 2003.

[28] R. J. Lipton, J. F. Naughton, and D. A. Schneider. *Practical selectivity estimation through adaptive sampling*, volume 19. ACM, 1990.

[29] V. Markl, P. J. Haas, M. Kutsch, N. Megiddo, U. Srivastava, and T. M. Tran. Consistent selectivity estimation via maximum entropy. *The VLDB journal*, 16(1):55–76, 2007.

[30] Y. Matias, J. S. Vitter, and M. Wang. Wavelet-based histograms for selectivity estimation. *SIGMOD Record*, 27(2):448–459, 1998.

[31] G. Moerkotte, T. Neumann, and G. Steidl. Preventing bad plans by bounding the impact of cardinality estimation errors. *Proceedings of the VLDB Endowment*, 2(1):982–993, 2009.

[32] M. Muralikrishna and D. J. DeWitt. Equi-depth multidimensional histograms. *SIGMOD Record*, 17(3):28–36, 1988.

[33] F. Olken and D. Rotem. Maintenance of materialized views of sampling queries. In *Data Engineering, 1992. Proceedings. Eighth International Conference on*, pages 632–641. IEEE, 1992.

[34] V. Poosala and Y. E. Ioannidis. Selectivity estimation without the attribute value independence assumption. In *Proceedings of the 23rd VLDB conference*, pages 486–495. VLDB Endowment, 1997.

[35] N. Reddy and J. R. Haritsa. Analyzing plan diagrams of database query optimizers. In *Proceedings of the 31st VLDB conference*, pages 1228–1239. VLDB Endowment, 2005.

[36] M. Riedmiller and H. Braun. A direct adaptive method for faster backpropagation learning: The rprop algorithm. In *Neural Networks, 1993., IEEE International Conference on*, pages 586–591. IEEE, 1993.
[37] S. R. Sain, K. A. Baggerly, and D. W. Scott. Cross-validation of multivariate densities. *Journal of the American Statistical Association*, 89(427):807–817, 1994.
[38] U. Srivastava, P. J. Haas, V. Markl, M. Kutsch, and T. M. Tran. Isomer: Consistent histogram construction using query feedback. In *Data Engineering, 2006. ICDE'06. Proceedings of the 22nd International Conference on*, pages 39–39. IEEE, 2006.
[39] S. Subramaniam, T. Palpanas, D. Papadopoulos, V. Kalogeraki, and D. Gunopulos. Online outlier detection in sensor data using non-parametric models. In *Proceedings of the 32nd VLDB conference*, pages 187–198. VLDB Endowment, 2006.
[40] K. Svanberg. A class of globally convergent optimization methods based on conservative convex separable approximations. *SIAM journal on optimization*, 12(2):555–573, 2002.
[41] G. R. Terrell and D. W. Scott. Variable kernel density estimation. *The Annals of Statistics*, pages 1236–1265, 1992.
[42] T. Tieleman and G. Hinton. Lecture 6.5-rmsprop: Divide the gradient by a running average of its recent magnitude. *COURSERA: Neural Networks for Machine Learning*, 4, 2012.
[43] J. S. Vitter. Random sampling with a reservoir. *ACM Transactions on Mathematical Software (TOMS)*, 11(1):37–57, 1985.
[44] M. Wand and M. Jones. Comparison of smoothing parameterizations in bivariate kernel density estimation. *Journal of the American Statistical Association*, 88(422):520–528, 1993.
[45] M. Wand and M. Jones. Multivariate plug-in bandwidth selection. *Computational Statistics*, 9(2):97–116, 1994.
[46] Z. Zhang, Y. Yang, R. Cai, D. Papadias, and A. Tung. Kernel-based skyline cardinality estimation. In *Proceedings of the 2009 ACM SIGMOD Conference*, pages 509–522. ACM, 2009.

APPENDIX

A. PRELIMINARIES

In the following, we provide an overview of the math behind various interesting aspects of KDE-based selectivity estimator. In particular, we will derive the closed-form expression that is used to compute a KDE range estimate based on a data sample, derive the gradient of the estimation error with regard to the bandwidth, explain how to perform logarithmic bandwidth updates, and introduce a shortcut to quickly identify which sample points fall into a given query region. We demonstrate these topics for a Gaussian Kernel, which has the following form:

$$K(\vec{x}) = (2\pi)^{-\frac{d}{2}} \exp -\frac{1}{2}\vec{x}^T\vec{x} \tag{9}$$

Note that we use the Gaussian Kernel primarily to simplify the following derivations. In principle, our methods can be applied to any differentiable kernel function. Another interesting choice is for instance the *Epanechnikov Kernel*, which is a truncated second-degree polynomial. Compared to the Gaussian, the Epanechnikov Kernel is much cheaper to compute. However, its limited support make the derivation more cumbersome.

B. KDE FOR RECTANGULAR REGIONS

Equation (2) defines how to compute the KDE-based selectivity estimate $\hat{p}_H(\Omega)$ for a given query region Ω. In order to evaluate this equation, we need to derive a closed-form expression for the individual probability mass contribution $\hat{p}_H^{(i)}(\Omega)$ from a given sample point $\vec{t}^{(i)}$:

$$\hat{p}_H^{(i)}(\Omega) = \int_\Omega \frac{1}{|H|} K\left(H^{-1}\left[\vec{t}^{(i)} - \vec{x}\right]\right) d\vec{x} \tag{10}$$

In general, the integral in this term doesn't have a closed form solution for arbitrary regions [1]. However, since we assume that Ω is rectangular, i.e. $\Omega = (l_1, u_1) \times \ldots \times (l_d, u_d)$, we can integrate by each dimension individually:

$$p_H^{(i)}(\Omega) = \int_{l_1}^{u_1} \ldots \int_{l_d}^{u_d} \frac{K\left(H^{-1}\left[\vec{t}^{(i)} - \vec{x}\right]\right)}{|H|} dx_d \ldots dx_1 \tag{11}$$

We can now simplify (11) via the following observations:

1. The assumption of a diagonal bandwidth matrix $H = \operatorname{diag}(h_1, \ldots, h_d)$ allows us to simplify the computation of the determinant $|H|$ to: $\prod_{i=1}^d h_i$. We can also express the product $H^{-1}\left[\vec{t}^{(i)} - \vec{x}\right]$ in terms of single dimensions: $\left[\frac{1}{h_1}\left(x_1 - t_1^{(i)}\right), \ldots, \frac{1}{h_d}\left(x_d - t_d^{(i)}\right)\right]^T$.
2. The multivariate Gaussian Kernel is a product kernel [1], meaning it can be expressed as a product of single-dimensional kernels: $K(\vec{x}) = \prod_{i=1}^d K(x_i)$. In particular, this allows us to evaluate the d-dimensional integral in (11) as a product of d one-dimensional integrals.

Plugging the definition of the Gaussian Kernel from (9) into (11) and applying the discussed simplifications, we arrive at:

$$p_H^{(i)}(\Omega) = \prod_{j=1}^{d} \int_{l_j}^{u_j} \underbrace{\frac{(2\pi)^{-\frac{1}{2}}}{h_j} \exp\left(-\frac{\left(x_j - t_j^{(i)}\right)^2}{2 \cdot h_j^2}\right)}_{=\mathcal{N}_{t_j^{(i)}, h_j^2}(x_j)} dx_j \tag{12}$$

In equation (12), $\mathcal{N}_{\mu,\sigma^2} : \mathbb{R} \rightarrow \mathbb{R}$ denotes the *probability density function* of the one-dimensional normal distribution with variance σ^2 and mean μ. We can now get rid of the integral by plugging the *cumulative distribution function* of the normal distribution into equation (12):

$$\begin{aligned} p_H^{(i)}(\Omega) &= \prod_{j=1}^{d} \frac{1}{2}\left[\operatorname{erf}\left(\frac{u_j - t_j^{(i)}}{\sqrt{2} \cdot h_j}\right) - \operatorname{erf}\left(\frac{l_j - t_j^{(i)}}{\sqrt{2} \cdot h_j}\right)\right] \\ &= \frac{1}{2^d}\prod_{j=1}^{d} \left[\operatorname{erf}\left(\frac{u_j - t_j^{(i)}}{\sqrt{2} \cdot h_j}\right) - \operatorname{erf}\left(\frac{l_j - t_j^{(i)}}{\sqrt{2} \cdot h_j}\right)\right] \end{aligned} \tag{13}$$

Where $\operatorname{erf} : \mathbb{R} \rightarrow \mathbb{R}$ denotes the *error function*, which is defined as $\operatorname{erf}(x) = \frac{2}{\sqrt{\pi}} \int_0^x e^{-\tau^2} d\tau$.

C. GRADIENT OF THE LOSS FUNCTION

In order to numerically solve optimization problem (5) with a gradient-based solver, we need to derive the gradient $\nabla_H \mathcal{L} = \left[\frac{\partial \mathcal{L}}{\partial h_1}, \ldots, \frac{\partial \mathcal{L}}{\partial h_d}\right]^T$ of the chosen loss function $\mathcal{L}$ with respect to the bandwidth H. Looking at the partial derivative with respect to h_i and applying the chain rule, we arrive at:

$$\frac{\partial \mathcal{L}}{\partial h_i} = \frac{\partial \mathcal{L}}{\partial \hat{p}_H(\Omega)} \cdot \frac{\partial \hat{p}_H(\Omega)}{\partial h_i} \tag{14}$$

According to this equation, we can compute each element of the gradient as the product of two partial derivatives. The first derivative is independent of the estimator and encodes information about the chosen loss function $\mathcal{L}$. The second derivative encodes how the estimator reacts when we change the bandwidth of the i-th attribute. We will now take a closer look at both factors individually.

C.1 Partial Derivative of the Loss Function

Let us first take a look at the partial derivative $\frac{\partial \mathcal{L}}{\partial \hat{p}_H(\Omega)}$ of the loss function. This partial derivative encodes information about the chosen loss function. In particular, it specifies how the selected error function behaves when the estimated selectivity changes. By changing this factor, we can modify which error metric the model optimization will minimize, allowing us to fine-tune the bandwidth of our KDE-based estimator with regard to any differentiable error metric. The following list gives loss functions and closed-form partial derivatives for several important metrics:

- Quadratic (L2) Error:

$$\mathcal{L}_{\text{Quadratic}} = \left(\hat{p}_H(\Omega) - p(\Omega)\right)^2$$
$$\frac{\partial \mathcal{L}_{\text{Quadratic}}}{\partial \hat{p}_H(\Omega)} = 2 \cdot \left(\hat{p}_H(\Omega) - p(\Omega)\right)$$

- Absolute (L1) Error:

$$\mathcal{L}_{\text{Absolute}} = \left|\hat{p}_H(\Omega) - p(\Omega)\right|$$
$$\frac{\partial \mathcal{L}_{\text{Absolute}}}{\partial \hat{p}_H(\Omega)} = \begin{cases} -1 & \hat{p}_H(\Omega) < p(\Omega) \\ 0 & \hat{p}_H(\Omega) = p(\Omega) \\ 1 & \hat{p}_H(\Omega) > p(\Omega) \end{cases}$$

- Relative Error[6]:

$$\mathcal{L}_{\text{Relative}} = \frac{\left|\hat{p}_H(\Omega) - p(\Omega)\right|}{\lambda + p(\Omega)}$$
$$\frac{\partial \mathcal{L}_{\text{Relative}}}{\partial \hat{p}_H(\Omega)} = \frac{1}{\lambda + p(\Omega)} \cdot \begin{cases} -1 & \hat{p}_H(\Omega) < p(\Omega) \\ 0 & \hat{p}_H(\Omega) = p(\Omega) \\ 1 & \hat{p}_H(\Omega) > p(\Omega) \end{cases}$$

- Squared Relative Error[5]:

$$\mathcal{L}_{\text{Relative}^2} = \left(\frac{\hat{p}_H(\Omega) - p(\Omega)}{\lambda + p(\Omega)}\right)^2$$
$$\frac{\partial \mathcal{L}_{\text{Relative}^2}}{\partial \hat{p}_H(\Omega)} = 2 \cdot \frac{\hat{p}_H(\Omega) - p(\Omega)}{\lambda + p(\Omega)}$$

- Squared Q-Error[5] [31]:

$$\mathcal{L}_{\text{Q}^2} = \left[\log\left(\lambda + \hat{p}_H(\Omega)\right) - \log\left(\lambda + p(\Omega)\right)\right]^2$$
$$\frac{\partial \mathcal{L}_{\text{Q}^2}}{\partial \hat{p}_H(\Omega)} = 2 \cdot \frac{\log\left(\lambda + \hat{p}_H(\Omega)\right) - \log\left(\lambda + p(\Omega)\right)}{\lambda + \hat{p}_H(\Omega)}$$

C.2 Partial Derivative of the Estimator

The second partial derivative from equation (14) encodes the model-specific part of the gradient. In particular, it specifies how strongly the estimators' selectivity estimate changes when we modify the bandwidth of the i-th attribute. We derive the closed-form expression for this factor by applying the sum and the constant factor derivation rule to the definition of the estimator from equations (2) and (13):

$$\frac{\partial \hat{p}_H(\Omega)}{\partial h_i} = \frac{1}{2^d \cdot s} \sum_{j=1}^{s} \frac{\partial}{\partial h_i} \prod_{k=1}^{d} \left[\operatorname{erf}\left(\frac{u_k - t_k^{(j)}}{\sqrt{2} \cdot h_k}\right) - \operatorname{erf}\left(\frac{l_k - t_k^{(j)}}{\sqrt{2} \cdot h_k}\right)\right] \tag{15}$$

We now apply the product rule to further simply the equation:

$$\frac{\partial \hat{p}_H(\Omega)}{\partial h_i} = \frac{1}{2^d \cdot s} \sum_{j=1}^{s} \frac{\partial}{\partial h_i}\left[\operatorname{erf}\left(\frac{u_i - t_i^{(j)}}{\sqrt{2} \cdot h_i}\right) - \operatorname{erf}\left(\frac{l_i - t_i^{(j)}}{\sqrt{2} \cdot h_i}\right)\right] \prod_{k \neq i} \left[\operatorname{erf}\left(\frac{u_k - t_k^{(j)}}{\sqrt{2} \cdot h_k}\right) - \operatorname{erf}\left(\frac{l_k - t_k^{(j)}}{\sqrt{2} \cdot h_k}\right)\right] \tag{16}$$

Applying the chain rule and observing that $\frac{d}{dx} \operatorname{erf}\left(\frac{c}{x}\right) = -\frac{2 \cdot c}{\sqrt{\pi} \cdot x^2} \cdot \exp\left(-\left(\frac{c}{x}\right)^2\right)$, we arrive at the closed-form formula to compute the partial derivative of the estimator with regard to the bandwidth of the i-th attribute:

$$\frac{\partial \hat{p}_H(\Omega)}{\partial h_i} = \frac{\sqrt{2}}{\sqrt{\pi} \cdot h_i^2 \cdot 2^d \cdot s} \cdot \sum_{j=1}^{s} \left[\left(l_i - t_i^{(j)}\right) \cdot \exp\left(-\frac{\left(l_i - t_i^{(j)}\right)^2}{2 \cdot h_i^2}\right) - \left(u_i - t_i^{(j)}\right) \cdot \exp\left(-\frac{\left(u_i - t_i^{(j)}\right)^2}{2 \cdot h_i^2}\right)\right] \prod_{k \neq i} \left[\operatorname{erf}\left(\frac{u_k - t_k^{(j)}}{\sqrt{2} \cdot h_k}\right) - \operatorname{erf}\left(\frac{l_k - t_k^{(j)}}{\sqrt{2} \cdot h_k}\right)\right] \tag{17}$$

D. LOGARITHMIC MODEL UPDATES

As mentioned in Section 5.5, we found in our experiments that we can improve stability and quality of the adaptive bandwidth optimization routine by scaling the gradient to update the logarithm of the bandwidth. In order to perform these logarithmic updates, we need to slightly modify the gradient from Section C. In particular, if we define

[6] λ is a small positive smoothing constant to prevent divisions by zero.

$h_i^* = \ln h_i$, we need to compute the modified partial gradient $\partial\mathcal{L}/\partial h_i^*$ to update the model. We can easily derive this gradient by applying the chain rule and a few simple transformations:

$$\begin{aligned}\frac{\partial\mathcal{L}}{\partial h_i^*} &= \frac{\partial\mathcal{L}}{\partial h_i}\cdot\frac{\partial h_i}{\partial h_i^*} = \frac{\partial\mathcal{L}}{\partial h_i}\cdot\frac{\partial \exp h_i^*}{\partial h_i^*}\\ &= \frac{\partial\mathcal{L}}{\partial h_i}\cdot \exp h_i^* = \frac{\partial\mathcal{L}}{\partial h_i}\cdot h_i \qquad (18)\end{aligned}$$

In other words, we can directly optimize the logarithmic bandwidth by scaling each dimension of the gradient by the (non-logarithmic) value of the bandwidth. Besides scaling the gradient, we need to make another small change to the adaptive learning algorithm outlined in Listing 1: We have to remove the positivity safeguard from line 17, since it would prevent negative logarithmic bandwidths, and thus bandwidth values smaller than one.

E. IDENTIFYING POINTS IN A REGION

As discussed in Section 4.2, our estimator identifies outdated sample points by tracking their *Karma score*, i.e. their net contribution to the estimation quality. While this approach is very efficient with regard to the required data transfers, it also results in the sample lagging behind the database, as updates only propagate over time. One shortcut to reduce this convergence time is to exploit when the system receives a query over a region $\Omega_0 = (l_1, u_1) \times \ldots \times (l_d, u_d)$ for which the database does not contain any tuples. Obviously, all sample points falling into Ω_0 are outdated and can be instantly replaced by newly sampled points, vastly accelerating sample convergence in this region. In order to do this efficiently, we need to quickly identify which points from the sample are falling into a given region, for instance by scanning the sample.

Another option, that does not require a full scan of the sample, is to examine the individual probability contributions $p_H^{(i)}(\Omega_0)$. The basic idea is simple: A point from within the query region will typically produce a higher probability contribution than a point from outside of it. If we can bound the maximum probability that a point from outside of Ω_0 can contribute, any point with a higher contribution must necessarily be from within Ω_0. While this approach will not identify all points from within Ω_0, we can piggyback the computations while updating the Karma Scores, making it very cheap to run.

Since the Gaussian Kernel is unimodal and symmetric, the theoretically maximum probability contribution from points outside of the query region is 0.5. However, this bound is only tight if the bandwidth is very small compared to the query region. In order to get a general tight bound, we first need to derive the largest possible probability contribution from points *within* Ω_0. Obviously, the point $\vec{t}_{(0)} = \left(\frac{l_1+u_1}{2}, \ldots \frac{l_d+u_d}{2}\right)$, which is directly at the center of Ω_0, will produce this contribution. Inserting $\vec{t}_{(0)}$ into equation (13), we arrive at:

$$p_H^{\max}(\Omega_0) = \prod_{j=1}^{d} \operatorname{erf}\left(\frac{u_j - l_j}{2\cdot\sqrt{2}\cdot h_j}\right) \qquad (19)$$

Based on this, we can easily derive the maximum probability contribution from a point outside of Ω_0 by moving $\vec{t}_{(0)}$ along one of the dimensions until we hit the boundary. For example, if we move along dimension j, we arrive at $\vec{t}_{(j)} = \left(\frac{l_1+u_1}{2}, \ldots, l_j, \ldots, \frac{l_d+u_d}{2}\right)$. This ensures that the probability contributions from all but one dimensions remain at maximum, while the contribution from the j-th dimension is the largest possible for a point just outside of Ω_0. Now, since the estimator uses different bandwidth parameters for each dimension, we will receive different contributions for $\vec{t}_{(1)}$ to $\vec{t}_{(d)}$. Out of those d contributions, the largest one is the bound we are looking for.

Summarizing the approach, we can guarantee that point $\vec{t}^{(i)}$ is contained within query region Ω if the following condition holds:

$$p_H^{(i)}(\Omega) \geq \frac{p_H^{\max}(\Omega)}{2}\cdot\max_{j=1}^{d}\frac{\operatorname{erf}\left(\frac{u_j-l_j}{\sqrt{2}\cdot h_j}\right)}{\operatorname{erf}\left(\frac{u_j-l_j}{2\cdot\sqrt{2}\cdot h_j}\right)} \qquad (20)$$

Acknowledgments

This work was partially funded by the German Federal Ministry of Education and Research (BMBF) under funding code 01IS12056. Furthermore, we thank the anonymous reviewers for their helpful comments in preparing the paper's final version.

Rethinking SIMD Vectorization for In-Memory Databases

Orestis Polychroniou*
Columbia University
orestis@cs.columbia.edu

Arun Raghavan
Oracle Labs
arun.raghavan@oracle.com

Kenneth A. Ross†
Columbia University
kar@cs.columbia.edu

ABSTRACT

Analytical databases are continuously adapting to the underlying hardware in order to saturate all sources of parallelism. At the same time, hardware evolves in multiple directions to explore different trade-offs. The MIC architecture, one such example, strays from the mainstream CPU design by packing a larger number of simpler cores per chip, relying on SIMD instructions to fill the performance gap. Databases have been attempting to utilize the SIMD capabilities of CPUs. However, mainstream CPUs have only recently adopted wider SIMD registers and more advanced instructions, since they do not rely primarily on SIMD for efficiency. In this paper, we present novel vectorized designs and implementations of database operators, based on advanced SIMD operations, such as gathers and scatters. We study selections, hash tables, and partitioning; and combine them to build sorting and joins. Our evaluation on the MIC-based Xeon Phi co-processor as well as the latest mainstream CPUs shows that our vectorization designs are up to an order of magnitude faster than the state-of-the-art scalar and vector approaches. Also, we highlight the impact of efficient vectorization on the algorithmic design of in-memory database operators, as well as the architectural design and power efficiency of hardware, by making simple cores comparably fast to complex cores. This work is applicable to CPUs and co-processors with advanced SIMD capabilities, using either many simple cores or fewer complex cores.

1. INTRODUCTION

Real time analytics are the steering wheels of big data driven business intelligence. Database customer needs have extended beyond OLTP with high ACID transaction throughput, to interactive OLAP query execution across the entire database. As a consequence, vendors offer fast OLAP solutions, either by rebuilding a new DBMS for OLAP [28, 37], or by improving within the existing OLTP-focused DBMS.

*Work partly done when first author was at the Oracle Labs.

†Supported by NSF grant IIS-1422488 and an Oracle gift.

SIGMOD'15, May 31–June 4, 2015, Melbourne, Victoria, Australia.

http://dx.doi.org/10.1145/2723372.2747645.

The advent of large main-memory capacity is one of the reasons that blink-of-an-eye analytical query execution has become possible. Query optimization used to measure blocks fetched from disk as the primary unit of query cost. Today, the entire database can often remain main-memory resident and the need for efficient in-memory algorithms is apparent.

The prevalent shift in database design for the new era are column stores [19, 28, 37]. They allow for higher data compression in order to reduce the data footprint, minimize the number of columns accessed per tuple, and use column oriented execution coupled with late materialization [9] to eliminate unnecessary accesses to RAM resident columns.

Hardware provides performance through three sources of parallelism: *thread parallelism*, *instruction level parallelism*, and *data parallelism*. Analytical databases have evolved to take advantage of all sources of parallelism. Thread parallelism is achieved, for individual operators, by splitting the input equally among threads [3, 4, 5, 8, 14, 31, 40], and in the case of queries that combine multiple operators, by using the pipeline breaking points of the query plan to split the materialized data in chunks that are distributed to threads dynamically [18, 28]. Instruction level parallelism is achieved by applying the same operation to a block of tuples [6] and by compiling into tight machine code [16, 22]. Data parallelism is achieved by implementing each operator to use SIMD instructions effectively [7, 15, 26, 30, 39, 41].

The different sources of parallelism were developed as a means to deliver more performance within the same power budget available per chip. Mainstream CPUs have evolved on all sources of parallelism, featuring massively superscalar pipelines, out-of-order execution of tens of instructions, and advanced SIMD capabilities, all replicated on multiple cores per CPU chip. For example, the latest Intel Haswell architecture issues up to 8 micro-operations per cycle with 192 reorder buffer entries for out-of-order execution, 256-bit SIMD instructions, two levels of private caches per core and a large shared cache, and scales up to 18 cores per chip.

Concurrently with the evolution of mainstream CPUs, a new approach on processor design has surfaced. The design, named the many-integrated-cores (MIC) architecture, uses cores with a smaller area (transistors) and power footprint by removing the massively superscalar pipeline, out-of-order execution, and the large L3 cache. Each core is based on a Pentium 1 processor with a simple in-order pipeline, but is augmented with large SIMD registers, advanced SIMD instructions, and simultaneous multithreading to hide load and instruction latency. Since each core has a smaller area and power footprint, more cores can be packed in the chip.

The MIC design was originally intended as a GPU [33], but now targets high performance computing applications. Using a high FLOPS machine to execute compute-intensive algorithms with superlinear complexity is self-evident. Executing analytical queries in memory, however, consists of data-intensive linear algorithms that mostly "move" rather than "process" data. Previous work to add SIMD in databases has optimized sequential access operators such as index [41] or linear scans [39], built multi-way trees with nodes that match the SIMD register layout [15, 26], and optimized specific operators, such as sorting [7, 11, 26], by using *ad-hoc* vectorization techniques, useful only for a specific problem.

In this paper, we present good design principles for SIMD vectorization of main-memory database operators, without modifying the logic or the data layout of the baseline scalar algorithm. The baseline algorithm is defined here as the most straightforward scalar implementation. Formally, assume an algorithm that solves a problem with optimal complexity, its simplest scalar implementation, and a vectorized implementation. We say that the algorithm can be *fully vectorized*, if the vector implementation executes $O(f(n)/W)$ vector instructions instead of $O(f(n))$ scalar instructions where W is the vector length, excluding random memory accesses that are by definition not data-parallel. We define fundamental vector operations that are frequently reused in the vectorizations and are implemented using advanced SIMD instructions, such as non-contiguous loads (*gathers*) and stores (*scatters*). The fundamental operations that are not directly supported by specific instructions can be implemented using simpler instructions at a performance penalty.

We implement vectorized operators in the context of main-memory databases: selection scans, hash tables, and partitioning, which are combined to build more advanced operators: sorting and joins. These operators cover a large portion of the time needed to execute analytical queries in main memory. For selection scans, we show branchless tuple selection and in-cache buffering. For hash tables, we study both building and probing across using multiple hashing schemes. For partitioning, we describe histogram generation, including all partitioning function types: radix, hash, and range. We also describe data shuffling, including inputs larger than the cache. All of the above are combined to build radixsort and multiple hash join variants that highlight the impact of vectorization on determining the best algorithmic design.

We compare our vectorized implementations of in-memory database operators against the respective state-of-the-art scalar and vector techniques, by evaluating on the Intel Xeon Phi co-processor and on the latest mainstream CPUs. Xeon Phi is currently the only available hardware based on the MIC architecture and is also the only generally available hardware that supports *gathers* and *scatters*, while the latest mainstream CPUs (Intel Haswell) support gathers.

We use the sorting and join operator to compare a Xeon Phi 7120P co-processor (61 P54C cores at 1.238 GHz, 300 Watts TDP) against four high-end Sandy Bridge CPUs (4×8 Sandy Bridge cores at 2.2 GHz, 4 × 130 Watts TDP), and found that they have similar performance, but on a different power budget, since Xeon Phi spends almost half the energy.

The next generation of Xeon Phi will also be available as a standalone CPU,[1] even if the current generation is only available as a co-processor, and will support more advanced SIMD instructions (AVX 3), also supported by the next generation of mainstream CPUs.[2] Our work does not focus on evaluating Xeon Phi as a co-processing accelerator, such as GPUs, that would also be bound by the PCI-e bandwidth, but as an alternative CPU design that is suitable and more power efficient for executing analytical database workloads.

We summarize our contributions:

- We introduce design principles for efficient vectorization of in-memory database operators and define fundamental vector operations that are frequently reused.
- We design and implement vectorized selection scans, hash tables, and partitioning, that are combined to design and build sorting and multiple join variants.
- We compare our implementations against state-of-the-art scalar and vectorized techniques. We achieve up to an order of magnitude speedups by evaluating on Xeon Phi as well as on the latest mainstream CPUs.
- We show the impact of vectorization on the algorithmic design of in-memory operators, as well as the architectural design and power efficiency of hardware, by making simple cores comparably fast to complex cores.

The rest of the paper is organized as follows. Section 2 presents related work. Sections 4, 5, 6, and 7 discuss the vectorization of selection scans, hash tables, Bloom filters, and partitioning. Sections 8 and 9 discuss algorithmic designs for sorting and hash join. We present our experimental evaluation in Section 10, we discuss how SIMD vectorization relates to GPUs in Section 11, and conclude in Section 12. Implementation details are provided in the Appendix.

2. RELATED WORK

Previous work that added SIMD instructions in database operators is briefly summarized. Zhou et al. used SIMD for linear scans, index scans, and nested loop joins [41]. Ross proposed probing multiple keys per bucket for cuckoo hashing [30]. Willhalm et al. optimized decompression of bit packed data [39]. Inoue et al. proposed data-parallel combsort and merging [11]. Chhugani et al. optimized bitonic merging for mergesort [7]. Kim et al. designed multi-way trees tailored to the SIMD layout [15]. Polychroniou et al. discussed trade-offs for updating heavy hitter aggregates [25], fast range partitioning via a range function index [26], and Bloom filter probing using gathers [27]. Schlegel et al. described scalable frequent itemset mining on Xeon Phi [32].

Database operators have been extensively optimized for modern processors. Manegold et al. introduced hash joins with cache-conscious partitioning [19], which Kim et al. extended to multi-core CPUs and compared against SIMD sort-merge joins [14]. Cieslewicz et al. and Ye et al. studied contention-free aggregation [8, 40]. Blanas et al. and Balkesen et al. evaluated hardware-tuned hash joins [3, 5]. Albutiu et al. introduced NUMA-aware joins and Balkesen et al. evaluated join variants on multiple CPUs [1, 4]. Satish et al. and Wassenberg et al. introduced buffered partitioning for radixsort [31, 38]. Polychroniou et al. introduced in-place and range partitioning for sorting variants [26]. Jha et al. optimized hash joins on Xeon Phi, but used SIMD partially only to compute hash functions and load hash buckets [12].

[1] newsroom.intel.com/community/intel_newsroom/blog/2014/06/23/intel-re-architects-the-fundamental-building-block-for-high-performance-computing

[2] software.intel.com/blogs/2013/avx-512-instructions

Compilers partially transform scalar to SIMD code based on loop unrolling [17] and control flow predication [34]. Our designs are far more complicated and not strictly equivalent. Database operators can be compiled directly [22], thus manual vectorization is also desirable to maximize performance.

GPUs have also been used in databases for generic queries [2] and to accelerate operators, such as indexes [15], sorting [31], joins [13, 24], and selections [36]. SIMT GPU threads are organized in *warps* that execute the same scalar instruction per cycle by predicating all control flow. In SIMD code, control flow is converted to data flow in software. We discuss the similarities between SIMD and SIMT code and to what extent our work is applicable to SIMT GPUs in Section 11.

3. FUNDAMENTAL OPERATIONS

In this section we define the fundamental vector operations that we will need to implement vectorized database operators. The first two operations, termed *selective load* and *selective store*, are spatially contiguous memory accesses that load or store values using a *subset* of vector lanes. The last two operations are spatially non-contiguous memory loads and stores, termed *gathers* and *scatters* respectively.

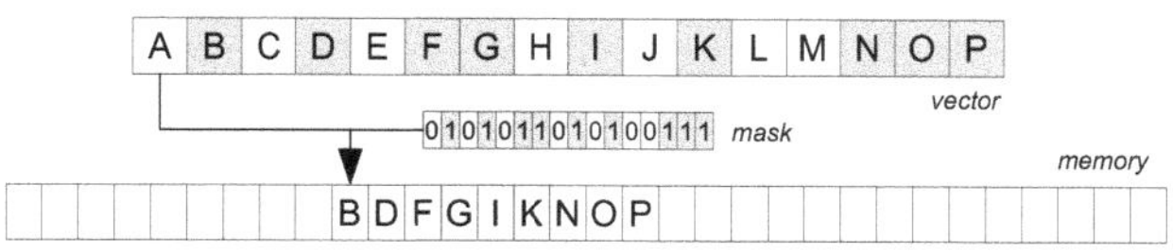

Figure 1: Selective store operation

Selective stores write a specific subset of the vector lanes to a memory location contiguously. The subset of vector lanes to be written is decided using a vector or scalar register as the mask, which must not be limited to a constant.

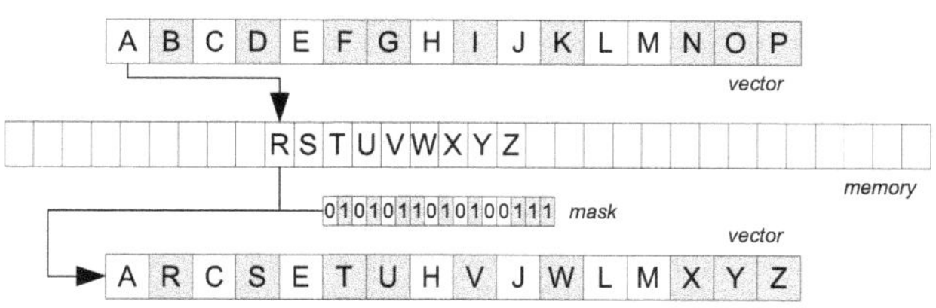

Figure 2: Selective load operation

Selective loads are the symmetric operation that involves loading from a memory location contiguously to a subset of vector lanes based on a mask. The lanes that are inactive in the mask retain their previous values in the vector.

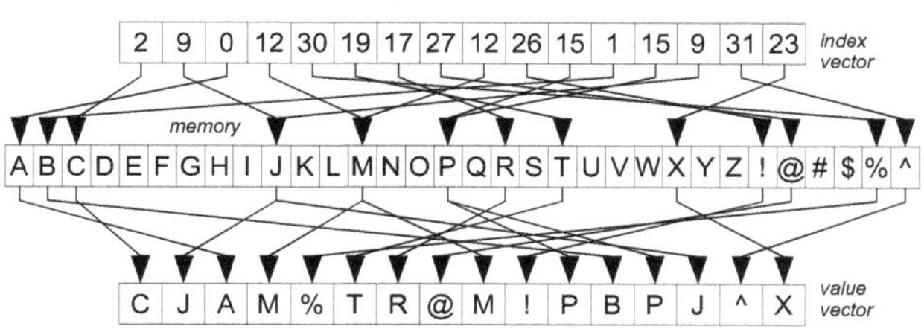

Figure 3: Gather operation

Gather operations load values from non-contiguous locations. The inputs are a vector of indexes and an array pointer. The output is a vector with the values of the respective array cells. By adding a mask as an input operand, we define the selective gather that operates on a subset of lanes. The inactive mask lanes retain their previous contents.

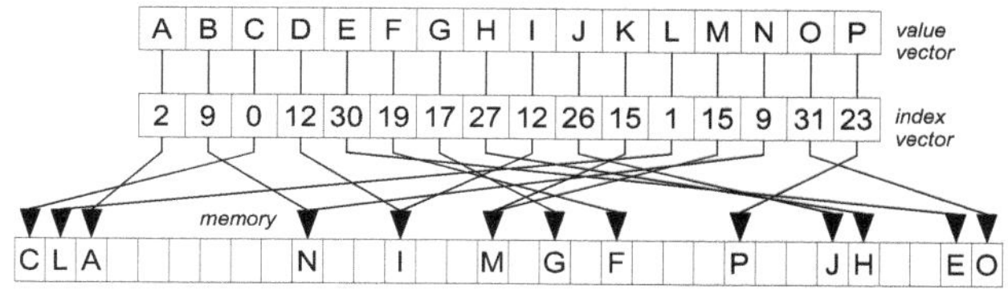

Figure 4: Scatter operation

Scatter operations execute stores to multiple locations. The input is a vector of indexes, an array pointer, and a vector of values. If multiple vector lanes point to the same location, we assume that the rightmost value will be written. By adding a mask as an input we can store lanes selectively.

Gathers and scatters are not really executed in parallel because the (L1) cache allows one or two distinct accesses per cycle. Executing W cache accesses per cycle is an impractical hardware design. Thus, random memory accesses have to be excluded from the $O(f(n)/W)$ vectorization rule.

Gathers are supported on the latest mainstream CPUs (Haswell) but scatters are not. Older mainstream CPUs (e.g., Sandy Bridge) support neither. Emulating gathers is possible at a performance penalty, which is small if done carefully. We discuss more hardware details in Appendix B.

Selective loads and stores are also not supported on the latest mainstream CPUs, but can be emulated using vector permutations. The lane selection mask is extracted as a bitmask and is used as an array index to load a permutation mask from a pre-generated table. The data vector is then permuted in a way that splits the active lanes of the mask to the one side of the register and the inactive lanes to the other side. In case of a selective store we can store the vector (unaligned) and in case of a selective load, we load a new vector (unaligned) and blend the two vectors to replace the inactive lanes. This technique was first used in vectorized Bloom filters [27] on CPUs, without defining the operations. We describe the Xeon Phi instructions in Appendix C.

4. SELECTION SCANS

Selection scans have re-emerged for main-memory query execution and are replacing traditional unclustered indexes in modern OLAP DBMSs [28]. Advanced optimizations include lightweight bit compression [39] to reduce the RAM bandwidth, generation of statistics to skip data regions [28], and scanning of bitmaps-zonemaps to skip cache lines [35].

Linear selective scan performance has been associated with branch mispredictions, if the operator is implemented as shown in Algorithm 1. Previous work has shown that converting control flow to data flow can affect performance, making different approaches optimal per selectivity rate [29]. Branches can be eliminated as shown in Algorithm 2 to avoid misprediction penalties, at the expense of accessing all payload columns and eagerly evaluating all selective predicates.

Algorithm 1 Selection Scan (Scalar - Branching)

$j \leftarrow 0$ ▷ *output index*
for $i \leftarrow 0$ **to** $|T_{keys\_in}| - 1$ **do**
  $k \leftarrow T_{keys\_in}[i]$ ▷ *access key columns*
  if $(k \geq k_{lower})$ && $(k \leq k_{upper})$ **then** ▷ *short circuit and*
    $T_{payloads\_out}[j] \leftarrow T_{payloads\_in}[i]$ ▷ *copy all columns*
    $T_{keys\_out}[j] \leftarrow k$
    $j \leftarrow j + 1$
  end if
end for

Algorithm 2 Selection Scan (Scalar - Branchless)

```
j ← 0                                          ▷ output index
for i ← 0 to |T_keys_in| − 1 do
    k ← T_keys_in[i]                           ▷ copy all columns
    T_payloads_out[j] ← T_payloads_in[i]
    T_keys_out[j] ← k
    m ←(k ≥ k_lower ? 1 : 0) & (k ≤ k_upper ? 1 : 0)
    j ← j + m       ▷ if-then-else expressions use conditional ...
end for        ▷ ... flags to update the index without branching
```

Vectorized selection scans use selective stores to store the lanes that satisfy the selection predicates. We use SIMD instructions to evaluate the predicates resulting in a bitmask of the qualifying lanes. Partially vectorized selection extracts one bit at a time from the bitmask and accesses the corresponding tuple. Instead, we use the bitmask to selectively store the qualifying tuples to the output vector at once.

When the selection has a very low selectivity, it is desirable to avoid accessing the payload columns due to the performance drop caused by the memory bandwidth. Furthermore, when the branch is speculatively executed, we issue needless loads to payloads. To avoid reducing the bandwidth, we use a small cache resident buffer that stores indexes of qualifiers rather than the actual values. When the buffer is full, we reload the indexes from the buffer, gather the actual values from the columns, and flush them to the output. This variant is shown in Algorithm 3. Appendix A describes the notation used in the algorithmic descriptions.

When we materialize data on RAM without intent to reuse them soon, we use streaming stores. Mainstream CPUs provide non-temporal stores that bypass the higher cache levels and increase the RAM bandwidth for storing data. Xeon Phi does not support scalar streaming stores, but provides an instruction to overwrite a cache line with data from a vector without first loading it. This technique requires the vector length to be equal to the cache line and eliminates the need for write-combining buffers used in mainstream CPUs. All operators that write the output to memory sequentially, use buffering, which we omit in the algorithmic descriptions.

Algorithm 3 Selection Scan (Vector)

```
i, j, l ← 0                      ▷ input, output, and buffer indexes
r⃗ ← {0, 1, 2, 3, ..., W − 1}             ▷ input indexes in vector
for i ← 0 to |T_keys_in| − 1 step W do      ▷ # of vector lanes
    k⃗ ← T_keys_in[i]                  ▷ load vectors of key columns
    m ← (k⃗ ≥ k_lower) & (k⃗ ≤ k_upper)       ▷ predicates to mask
    if m ≠ false then                          ▷ optional branch
        B[l] ←_m r⃗                       ▷ selectively store indexes
        l ← l + |m|                          ▷ update buffer index
        if l > |B| − W then                         ▷ flush buffer
            for b ← 0 to |B| − W step W do
                p⃗ ← B[b]                      ▷ load input indexes
                k⃗ ← T_keys_in[p⃗]              ▷ dereference values
                v⃗ ← T_payloads_in[p⃗]
                T_keys_out[b + j] ← k⃗      ▷ flush to output with ...
                T_payloads_out[b + j] ← v⃗     ▷ ... streaming stores
            end for
            p⃗ ← B[|B| − W]                     ▷ move overflow ...
            B[0] ← p⃗                          ▷ ... indexes to start
            j ← j + |B| − W                   ▷ update output index
            l ← l − |B| + W                   ▷ update buffer index
        end if
    end if
    r⃗ ← r⃗ + W                                ▷ update index vector
end for                       ▷ flush last items after the loop
```

5. HASH TABLES

Hash tables are used in database systems to execute joins and aggregations since they allow constant time key lookups. In hash join, one relation is used to build the hash table and the other relation probes the hash table to find matches. In group-by aggregation they are used either to map tuples to unique group ids or to insert and update partial aggregates.

Using SIMD instructions in hash tables has been proposed as a way to build bucketized hash tables. Rather than comparing against a single key, we place multiple keys per bucket and compare them to the probing key using SIMD vector comparisons. We term the approach of comparing a single input (probing) key with multiple hash table keys, *horizontal vectorization*. Some hash table variants such as bucketized cuckoo hashing [30] can support much higher load factors. Loading a single 32-bit word is as fast as loading an entire vector, thus, the cost of bucketized probing diminishes to extracting the correct payload, which requires $\log W$ steps.

Horizontal vectorization, if we expect to search fewer than W buckets on average per probing key, is wasteful. For example, a 50% full hash table with one match per key needs to access ≈ 1.5 buckets on average to find the match using linear probing. In such a case, comparing one input key against multiple table keys cannot yield high improvement and takes no advantage of the increasing SIMD register size.

In this paper, we propose a generic form of hash table vectorization termed *vertical vectorization* that can be applied to any hash table variant without altering the hash table layout. The fundamental principle is to process a different input key per vector lane. All vector lanes process different keys from the input and access different hash table locations.

The hash table variants we discuss are linear probing (Section 5.1), double hashing (Section 5.2), and cuckoo hashing (Section 5.3). For the hash function, we use multiplicative hashing, which requires two multiplications, or for 2^n buckets, one multiplication and a shift. Multiplication costs very few cycles in mainstream CPUs and is supported in SIMD.

5.1 Linear Probing

Linear probing is an open addressing scheme that, to either insert an entry or terminate the search, traverses the table linearly until an empty bucket is found. The hash table stores keys and payloads but no pointers. The scalar code for probing the hash table is shown in Algorithm 4.

Algorithm 4 Linear Probing - Probe (Scalar)

```
j ← 0                                          ▷ output index
for i ← 0 to |S_keys| − 1 do          ▷ outer (probing) relation
    k ← S_keys[i]
    v ← S_payloads[i]
    h ← (k · f) × ↑ |T|    ▷ "× ↑": multiply & keep upper half
    while T_keys[h] ≠ k_empty do           ▷ until empty bucket
        if k = T_keys[h] then
            RS_R_payloads[j] ← T_payloads[h]     ▷ inner payloads
            RS_S_payloads[j] ← v                 ▷ outer payloads
            RS_keys[j] ← k                           ▷ join keys
            j ← j + 1
        end if
        h ← h + 1                                  ▷ next bucket
        if h = |T| then                    ▷ reset if last bucket
            h ← 0
        end if
    end while
end for
```

Algorithm 5 Linear Probing - Probe (Vector)

```
i, j ← 0                          ▷ input & output indexes (scalar register)
o⃗ ← 0                            ▷ linear probing offsets (vector register)
m ← true                          ▷ boolean vector register
while i + W ≤ |S_keys_in| do      ▷ W: # of vector lanes
    k⃗ ←_m S_keys[i]               ▷ selectively load input tuples
    v⃗ ←_m S_payloads[i]
    i ← i + |m|
    h⃗ ← (k⃗ · f) × ↑ |T|           ▷ multiplicative hashing
    h⃗ ← h⃗ + o⃗                    ▷ add offsets & fix overflows
    h⃗ ← (h⃗ < |T|) ? h⃗ : (h⃗ − |T|)  ▷ "m ? x⃗ : y⃗": vector blend
    k⃗_T ← T_keys[h⃗]               ▷ gather buckets
    v⃗_T ← T_payloads[h⃗]
    m ← k⃗_T = k⃗
    RS_keys[j] ←_m k⃗              ▷ selectively store matching tuples
    RS_S_payloads[j] ←_m v⃗
    RS_R_payloads[j] ←_m v⃗_T
    j ← j + |m|
    m ← k⃗_T = k_empty             ▷ discard finished tuples
    o⃗ ← m ? 0 : (o⃗ + 1)           ▷ increment or reset offsets
end while
```

The vectorized implementation of probing a hash table using a linear probing scheme is shown in Algorithm 5. Our vectorization principle is to process a different key per SIMD lane using gathers to access the hash table. Assuming W vector lanes, we process W different input keys on each loop. Instead of using a nested loop to find all matches for the W keys before loading the next W keys, we reuse vector lanes as soon as we know there are no more matches in the table, by selectively loading new keys from the input to replace finished keys. Thus, each key executes the same number of loops as in scalar code. Every time a match is found, we use selective stores to write to the output the vector lanes that have matches. In order to support each key having executed an arbitrary number of loops already, we keep a vector of offsets that maintain how far each key has searched in the table. When a key is overwritten, the offset is reset to zero.

A simpler approach is to process W keys at a time and use a nested loop to find all matches. However, the inner loop would be executed as many times as the maximum number of buckets accessed by any one of the W keys, underutilizing the SIMD lanes, because the average number of accessed buckets of W keys can be significantly smaller than the maximum. By reusing vector lanes dynamically, we are reading the probing input "out-of-order". Thus, the probing algorithm is no longer *stable*, i.e., the order of the output does not always match the previous order of the probing input.

Building a linear probing table is similar. We need to reach an empty bucket to insert a new tuple. The scalar code is shown in Algorithm 6 and the vector code in Algorithm 7.

Algorithm 6 Linear Probing - Build (Scalar)

```
for i ← 0 to |R_keys| − 1 do      ▷ inner (building) relation
    k ← R_keys[i]
    h ← (k · f) × ↑ |T|           ▷ multiplicative hashing
    while T_keys[h] ≠ k_empty do  ▷ until empty bucket
        h ← h + 1                 ▷ next bucket
        if h = |T| then
            h ← 0                 ▷ reset if last
        end if
    end while
    T_keys[h] ← k                 ▷ set empty bucket
    T_payloads[h] ← R_payloads[i]
end for
```

Algorithm 7 Linear Probing - Build (Vector)

```
l⃗ ← {1, 2, 3, ..., W}     ▷ any vector with unique values per lane
i, j ← 0 , m ← true       ▷ input & output index & bitmask
o⃗ ← 0                    ▷ linear probing offset
while i + W ≤ |R_keys| do
    k⃗ ←_m R_keys[i]               ▷ selectively load input tuples
    v⃗ ←_m R_payloads[i]
    i ← i + |m|
    h⃗ ← o⃗ + (k⃗ · f) × ↑ |T|       ▷ multiplicative hashing
    h⃗ ← (h⃗ < |T|) ? h⃗ : (h⃗ − |T|)  ▷ fix overflows
    k⃗_T ← T_keys[h⃗]               ▷ gather buckets
    m ← k⃗_T = k_empty             ▷ find empty buckets
    T[h⃗] ←_m l⃗                    ▷ detect conflicts
    l⃗_back ←_m T_keys[h⃗]
    m ← m & (l⃗ = l⃗_back)
    T_keys[h⃗] ←_m k⃗               ▷ scatter to buckets ...
    T_payloads[h⃗] ←_m v⃗           ▷ ... if not conflicting
    o⃗ ← m ? 0 : (o⃗ + 1)           ▷ increment or reset offsets
end while
```

The basics of vectorized probe and build of linear probing hash tables are the same. We process different input keys per SIMD lane and on top of gathers, we now also use scatters to store the keys non-contiguously. We access the input "out-of-order" to reuse lanes as soon as keys are inserted. To insert tuples, we first gather to check if the buckets are empty and then scatter the tuples only if the bucket is empty. The tuples that accessed a non-empty bucket increment an offset vector in order to search the next bucket in the next loop.

In order to ensure that multiple tuples will not try to fill the same empty bucket, we add a conflict detection step before scattering the tuples. Two lanes are conflicting if they point to the same location. However, we do not need to identify both lanes but rather the leftmost one that would get its value overwritten by the rightmost during the scatter. To identify these lanes, we scatter arbitrary values using a vector with unique values per lane (e.g., [1,2,3,...,W]). Then, we gather using the same index vector. If the scattered matches the gather value, the lane can scatter safely. The conflicting lanes search the next bucket in the next loop.

Future SIMD instruction sets include special instructions that can support this functionality (`vpconflictd` in AVX 3), thus saving the need for the extra scatter and gather to detect conflicts. Nevertheless, these instructions are not supported on mainstream CPUs or the Xeon Phi as of yet.

If the input keys are unique (e.g., join on a candidate key), we can scatter the keys to the table and gather them back to find the conflicting lanes instead of a constant vector with unique values per lane. Thus, we save one scatter operation.

The algorithmic descriptions show the keys and values of the hash table on separate arrays. In practice, the hash table uses an interleaved key-value layout. To halve the number of cache accesses, we pack multiple gathers into fewer wider gathers. For example, when using 32-bit keys and 32-bit payloads, the two consecutive 16-way 32-bit gathers of the above code can be replaced with two 8-way 64-bit gathers and a few shuffle operations to split keys and payloads. The same applies to scatters (see Appendix E for details).

For both probing and building, selective loads and stores assume there are enough items in the input to saturate the vector register. To process the last items in the input, we switch to scalar code. The last items are bounded in number by $2 \cdot W$, which is negligible compared to the total number of input tuples. Thus, the overall throughput is unaffected.

5.2 Double Hashing

Duplicate keys in hash tables can be handled by storing the payloads in a separate table, or by repeating the keys. The first approach works well when most matching keys are repeated. The second approach works well with mostly unique keys, but suffers from clustering duplicate keys in the same region, if linear probing is used. Double hashing uses a second hash function to distribute collisions so that the number of accessed buckets is close to the number of true matches. Thus, we can use the second approach for both cases. Comparing multiple hash table layouts based on the number of repeats is out of the scope of this paper.

Algorithm 8 Double Hashing Function

$\vec{f}_L \leftarrow m \;?\; f_1 : f_2$ ▷ *pick multiplicative hash factor*
$\vec{f}_H \leftarrow m \;?\; |T| : (|T|-1)$ ▷ *the collision bucket ...*
$\vec{h} \leftarrow m \;?\; 0 : (\vec{h}+1)$ ▷ *... is never repeated*
$\vec{h} \leftarrow \vec{h} + ((\vec{k} \times \downarrow \vec{f}_L) \times \uparrow \vec{f}_H)$ ▷ *multiplicative hashing*
$\vec{h} \leftarrow (\vec{h} < |T|) \;?\; \vec{h} : (\vec{h} - |T|)$ ▷ *fix overflows (no modulo)*

Algorithm 8 shows the double hashing scheme that we propose. Here, m is the subset of vector lanes that have probed at least one bucket. If the primary hash function h_1 is in $[0, |T|)$, the collision hash function h_2 is in $[1, |T|)$, and $|T|$ is prime, then $h = h_1 + N \cdot h_2$ modulo $|T|$ (double hashing) *never* repeats the same bucket for $N < |T|$ collisions. To avoid the expensive modulos, we use $h - |T|$ when $h \geq |T|$.

5.3 Cuckoo Hashing

Cuckoo hashing [23] is another hashing scheme that uses multiple hash functions. and is the only hash table scheme that has been vectorized in previous work [30], as a means to allow multiple keys per bucket (horizontal vectorization). Here, we study cuckoo hashing to compare our (vertical vectorization) approach against previous work [30, 42]. We also show that complicated control flow logic, such as cuckoo table building, can be transformed to data flow vector logic.

The scalar code for cuckoo table probing, which we omit due to space requirements, can be written in two ways. In the simple way, we check the second bucket only if the first bucket does not match. The alternative way is to always access both buckets and blend their results using bitwise operations [42]. The latter approach eliminates branching at the expense of always accessing both buckets. Still, it has been shown to be faster than other variants on CPUs [42].

Algorithm 9 Cuckoo Hashing - Probing

$j \leftarrow 0$
for $i \leftarrow 0$ **to** $|S| - 1$ **step** W **do**
  $\vec{k} \leftarrow S_{keys}[i]$ ▷ *load input tuples*
  $\vec{v} \leftarrow S_{payloads}[i]$
  $\vec{h}_1 \leftarrow (\vec{k} \cdot f_1) \times \uparrow |T|$ ▷ *1st hash function*
  $\vec{h}_2 \leftarrow (\vec{k} \cdot f_2) \times \uparrow |T|$ ▷ *2nd hash function*
  $\vec{k}_T \leftarrow T_{keys}[\vec{h}_1]$ ▷ *gather 1st function bucket*
  $\vec{v}_T \leftarrow T_{payloads}[\vec{h}_1]$
  $m \leftarrow \vec{k} \neq \vec{k}_T$
  $\vec{k}_T \leftarrow_m T_{keys}[\vec{h}_2]$ ▷ *gather 2nd function bucket ...*
  $\vec{v}_T \leftarrow_m T_{payloads}[\vec{h}_2]$ ▷ *... if 1st is not matching*
  $m \leftarrow \vec{k} = \vec{k}_T$
  $RS_{keys}[j] \leftarrow_m \vec{k}$ ▷ *selectively store matches*
  $RS_{S\_payloads}[j] \leftarrow_m \vec{v}$
  $RS_{R\_payloads}[j] \leftarrow_m \vec{v}_T$
  $j \leftarrow j + |m|$
end for

Vectorized cuckoo table probing is shown in Algorithm 9. No inner loop is required since we have only two choices. We load W keys with an aligned vector load and gather the first bucket per key. For the keys that do not match, we gather the second bucket. Cuckoo tables do not directly support key repeats. Probing is stable by reading the input "in-order", but accesses remote buckets when out of the cache.

Building a cuckoo hashing table is more complicated. If both bucket choices are not empty, we create space by displacing the tuple of one bucket to its alternate location. This process may be repeated until an empty bucket is reached.

Algorithm 10 Cuckoo Hashing - Building

$i, j \leftarrow 0$, $m \leftarrow$ true
while $i + W \leq |R|$ **do**
  $\vec{k} \leftarrow_m R_{keys\_in}[i]$ ▷ *selectively load new ...*
  $\vec{v} \leftarrow_m R_{payloads\_in}[i]$ ▷ *... tuples from the input*
  $i \leftarrow i + |m|$
  $\vec{h}_1 \leftarrow (\vec{k} \cdot f_1) \times \uparrow |B|$ ▷ *1st hash function*
  $\vec{h}_2 \leftarrow (\vec{k} \cdot f_2) \times \uparrow |B|$ ▷ *2nd hash function*
  $\vec{h} \leftarrow \vec{h}_1 + \vec{h}_2 - \vec{h}$ ▷ *use other function if old*
  $\vec{h} \leftarrow m \;?\; \vec{h}_1 : \vec{h}$ ▷ *use 1st function if new*
  $\vec{k}_T \leftarrow T_{keys}[\vec{h}]$ ▷ *gather buckets for ...*
  $\vec{v}_T \leftarrow T_{payloads}[\vec{h}]$ ▷ *... new & old tuples*
  $m \leftarrow m \;\&\; (\vec{k}_T \neq k_{empty})$ ▷ *use 2nd function if new ...*
  $\vec{h} \leftarrow m \;?\; \vec{h}_2 : \vec{h}$ ▷ *... & 1st is non-matching*
  $\vec{k}_T \leftarrow_m T_{keys}[\vec{h}]$ ▷ *selectively (re)gather ...*
  $\vec{v}_T \leftarrow_m T_{payloads}[\vec{h}]$ ▷ *... for new using 2nd*
  $T_{keys}[\vec{h}] \leftarrow \vec{k}$ ▷ *scatter all tuples ...*
  $T_{payloads}[\vec{h}] \leftarrow \vec{v}$ ▷ *... to store or swap*
  $\vec{k}_{back} \leftarrow T_{keys}[\vec{h}]$ ▷ *gather (unique) keys ...*
  $m \leftarrow \vec{k} \neq \vec{k}_{back}$ ▷ *... to detect conflicts*
  $\vec{k} \leftarrow m \;?\; \vec{k}_T : \vec{k}$ ▷ *conflicting tuples are ...*
  $\vec{v} \leftarrow m \;?\; \vec{v}_T : \vec{v}$ ▷ *... kept to be (re)inserted*
  $m \leftarrow \vec{k} = k_{empty}$ ▷ *inserted tuples are replaced*
end while

Vectorized cuckoo table building, shown in Algorithm 10, reuses vector lanes to load new tuples from the input. The remaining lanes are either previously conflicting or displaced tuples. The newly loaded tuples gather buckets using one or both hash functions to find an empty bucket. The tuples that were carried from the previous loop use the alternative hash function compared to the previous loop. We scatter the tuples to the hash table and gather back the keys to detect conflicts. The lanes with newly displaced tuples, which were gathered earlier in this loop, and the conflicting lanes are passed through to the next loop. The other lanes are reused.

6. BLOOM FILTERS

Bloom filters are an essential data structure for applying selective conditions across tables before joining them, a *semi join*. A tuple qualifies from the Bloom filter, if k specific bits are set in the filter, based on k hash functions. Aborting a tuple as soon as one bit-test fails is essential to achieve high performance, because most tuples fail after a few bit tests.

Vectorized Bloom filter probing was recently shown to get a significant performance boost over scalar code on the latest mainstream CPUs, especially when the Bloom filter is cache resident [27]. The design and implementation follows the principle of processing different input keys per lane and is one of our influences for this paper. However, no fundamental vector opeations were explicitly defined. Here, we evaluate the vectorized Bloom filter design [27] on Xeon Phi.

7. PARTITIONING

Partitioning is a ubiquitous operation for modern hardware query execution as a way to split large inputs into cache-conscious non-overlapping sub-problems. For example, join and aggregation operators can use hash partitioning to split the input into small partitions that are distributed among threads and now fit in the cache [3, 4, 5, 14, 19, 26]. We study all types of partitioning: radix, hash, and range.

7.1 Radix & Hash Histogram

Prior to moving any data, in order to partition into contiguous segments, we use a histogram to set the boundaries. To compute the histogram, we increment a count based on the partition function of each key. By using multiplicative hashing, hash partitioning becomes equally fast to radix.

Algorithm 11 Radix Partitioning - Histogram

$\vec{o} \leftarrow \{0, 1, 2, 3, ..., W-1\}$
$H_{partial}[P \times W] \leftarrow 0$ ▷ *initialize replicated histograms*
for $i \leftarrow 0$ **to** $|T_{keys\_in}| - 1$ **step** W **do**
  $\vec{k} \leftarrow T_{keys\_in}[i]$
  $\vec{h} \leftarrow (\vec{k} << b_L) >> b_R$ ▷ *radix function*
  $\vec{h} \leftarrow \vec{o} + (\vec{h} \cdot W)$ ▷ *index for multiple histograms*
  $\vec{c} \leftarrow H_{partial}[\vec{h}]$ ▷ *increment W counts*
  $H_{partial}[\vec{h}] \leftarrow \vec{c} + 1$
end for
for $i \leftarrow 0$ **to** $P - 1$ **do**
  $\vec{c} \leftarrow H_{partial}[i \cdot W]$ ▷ *load W counts of partition*
  $H[i] \leftarrow$ sum_across($\vec{c}$) ▷ *reduce into single result*
end for

Vectorized histogram generation, shown in Algorithm 11, uses gathers and scatters to increment counts. However, if multiple lanes scatter to the same histogram count, the count will still be incremented by 1 and all items (over)written to the same location. To avoid conflicts, we replicate the histogram to isolate each lane. Thus, lane j increments $H'[i \cdot W + j]$ instead of $H[i]$. In the end, the W histograms are reduced into one. If the histograms do not fit in the fastest cache, we use 1-byte counts and flush on overflow.

7.2 Range Histogram

Radix and hash partitioning functions are significantly faster than range partitioning functions. In range function, we execute a binary search over a sorted array of splitters. Although the array is cache resident, the number of accesses is logarithmic and all accesses are dependent on each other, thus the cache hit latency in the critical path is exposed [26]. Branch elimination only marginally improves performance.

Binary search can be vectorized using gather instructions to load the splitters from the sorted array, as shown in Algorithm 12, by processing W keys in parallel. The search path is computed by blending low and high pointers. We can assume without loss of generality that $P = 2^n$, since we can always patch the splitter array with maximum values.

Algorithm 12 Range Partitioning Function

$\vec{l} \leftarrow 0$, $\vec{h} \leftarrow P$ ▷ *$\vec{l}$ is also the output vector*
for $i \leftarrow 0$ **to** $\log P - 1$ **do**
  $\vec{a} \leftarrow (\vec{l} + \vec{h}) >> 1$ ▷ *compute middle*
  $\vec{d} \leftarrow D[\vec{a} - 1]$ ▷ *gather splitters*
  $m \leftarrow \vec{k} > \vec{d}$ ▷ *compare with splitters*
  $\vec{l} \leftarrow m\ ?\ \vec{a} : \vec{l}$ ▷ *select upper half*
  $\vec{h} \leftarrow m\ ?\ \vec{h} : \vec{a}$ ▷ *select lower half*
end for

Recently, a range index was proposed where each node has multiple splitters that are compared against one input key using SIMD comparisons [26]. Each node is at least as wide as a vector and scalar code is used for index arithmetic and to access the nodes (without gathers), relying on the superscalar pipeline to hide the cost of scalar instructions. The SIMD index can be seen as horizontal vectorization for binary search and is evaluated on simple and complex cores.

7.3 Shuffling

The data shuffling phase of partitioning involves the actual movement of tuples. To generate the output partitions in contiguous space, we maintain an array of partition offsets, initialized by the prefix sum of the histogram. The offset array is updated for every tuple transferred to the output.

Vectorized shuffling uses gathers and scatters to increment the offset array and scatters the tuples to the output. However, if multiple vector lanes have tuples that belong to the same partition, the offset would be incremented by one and these tuples would be (over)written to the same location.

We compute a vector of conflict offsets, by using gathers and scatters to detect conflicts iteratively, as shown in Algorithm 13. First, we scatter unique values per lane to an array with P entries. Then, we gather using the same indexes and compare against the scattered vector to find conflicts. We increment the conflicting lanes and repeat the process for these lanes only until no lanes conflict. Even if W iterations are executed, the total number of accesses to distinct memory locations is always W, i.e., if a_i is the number of accesses to distinct memory locations in iteration i, then $\sum a_i = W$.

Algorithm 13 Conflict Serialization Function ($\vec{h}$, A)

$\vec{l} \leftarrow \{W-1, W-2, W-3, ..., 0\}$ ▷ *reversing mask*
$\vec{h} \leftarrow$ permute($\vec{h}, \vec{l}$) ▷ *reverse hashes*
$\vec{c} \leftarrow 0$, $m \leftarrow$ true ▷ *serialization offsets & conflict mask*
repeat
  $A[\vec{h}] \leftarrow_m \vec{l}$ ▷ *detect conflicts*
  $\vec{l}_{back} \leftarrow_m A[\vec{h}]$
  $m \leftarrow m\ \&\ (\vec{l} \neq \vec{l}_{back})$ ▷ *update conflicting lanes*
  $\vec{c} \leftarrow m\ ?\ (\vec{c} + 1) : \vec{c}$ ▷ *increment offsets ...*
until $m =$ false ▷ *... for conflicting lanes*
return permute($\vec{c}, \vec{l}$) ▷ *reverse to original order*

Since the rightmost lane is written during conflicts, tuples of the same partition in the same vector are written in reverse order. Also, per group of k conflicting lanes, the rightmost lane will incorrectly increment the offset by 1, not by k. By reversing the index vector during serialization, we update the offsets correctly and also maintain the input order. *Stable* partitioning is essential for algorithms such as LSB radixsort. Vectorized shuffling is shown in Algorithm 14.

Algorithm 14 Radix Partitioning - Shuffling

$O \leftarrow$ prefix_sum(H) ▷ *partition offsets from histogram*
for $i \leftarrow 0$ **to** $|T_{keys\_in}| - 1$ **step** W **do**
  $\vec{k} \leftarrow T_{keys\_in}[i]$ ▷ *load input tuples*
  $\vec{v} \leftarrow T_{payloads\_in}[i]$
  $\vec{h} \leftarrow (\vec{k} << b_L) >> b_R$ ▷ *radix function*
  $\vec{o} \leftarrow O[\vec{h}]$ ▷ *gather partition offsets*
  $\vec{c} \leftarrow$ serialize_conflicts($\vec{h}, O$) ▷ *serialize conflicts*
  $\vec{o} \leftarrow \vec{o} + \vec{c}$ ▷ *add serialization offsets*
  $O[\vec{h}] \leftarrow \vec{o} + 1$ ▷ *scatter incremented offsets*
  $T_{keys\_out}[\vec{o}] \leftarrow \vec{k}$ ▷ *scatter tuples*
  $T_{payloads\_out}[\vec{o}] \leftarrow \vec{v}$
end for

7.4 Buffered Shuffling

Shuffling, as described so far, is fast if the input is cache resident, but falls into certain performance pitfalls when larger than the cache. First, it suffers from TLB thrashing when the partitioning fanout exceeds the TLB capacity [20]. Second, it generates many cache conflicts [31] and in the worst case, may be bound by the size of the cache associativity set. Third, using normal stores, we trigger cache loads to execute the stores and reduce the bandwidth due to loading cache lines that will only be overwritten [38].

The vectorized implementation of simple non-buffered shuffling improves performance, but suffers from the same performance pitfalls as the scalar version. In general, vectorization improves performance compared to its scalar counterpart, but does not overcome algorithmic inefficiencies.

To solve these problems, recent work proposed keeping the data in buffers and flushing them in groups [31]. If the buffers are small and packed together, they will not cause TLB or cache misses. Thus, with W buffer slots per partition, we reduce cache and TLB misses to $1/W$. If the buffers are flushed with non-temporal stores, we facilitate hardware write combining and avoid polluting the cache with output data [38]. The fanout is bounded by the cache capacity to keep the buffer cache resident. The scalar code for buffered shuffling is thoroughly described in previous work [4, 26].

The improvement of vectorized buffered shuffling shown in Algorithm 15 over vectorized unbuffered shuffling shown in Algorithm 14, is scattering the tuples to the cache resident buffer rather than directly to the output. For each vector of tuples, once the tuples are scattered, we iterate over the partitions that the current W input tuples belong to, and flush to the output when all available buffer slots are filled.

Algorithm 15 Radix Partitioning - Buffered Shuffling

$O \leftarrow \text{prefix\_sum}(H)$ ▷ *partition offsets from histogram*
for $i \leftarrow 0$ **to** $|T_{keys\_in}| - 1$ **step** W **do**
  $\vec{k} \leftarrow T_{keys\_in}[i]$ ▷ *load input tuples*
  $\vec{v} \leftarrow T_{payloads\_in}[i]$
  $\vec{h} \leftarrow (\vec{k} << b_L) >> b_R$ ▷ *radix function*
  $\vec{o} \leftarrow O[\vec{h}]$ ▷ *gather partition offsets*
  $\vec{c} \leftarrow \text{serialize\_conflicts}(\vec{h}, O)$ ▷ *serialize conflicts*
  $\vec{o} \leftarrow \vec{o} + \vec{c}$ ▷ *add serialization offsets*
  $O[\vec{h}] \leftarrow \vec{o} + 1$ ▷ *scatter incremented offsets*
  $\vec{o}_B \leftarrow \vec{o} \,\&\, (W - 1)$ ▷ *buffer offsets in partition*
  $m \leftarrow \vec{o}_B < W$ ▷ *find non-overflowing lanes*
  $m' \leftarrow !m$
  $\vec{o}_B \leftarrow \vec{o}_B + (\vec{h} \cdot W)$ ▷ *buffer offsets across partitions*
  $B_{keys}[\vec{o}_B] \leftarrow_m \vec{k}$ ▷ *scatter tuples to buffer ...*
  $B_{payloads}[\vec{o}_B] \leftarrow_m \vec{v}$ ▷ *... for non-overflowing lanes*
  $m \leftarrow \vec{o}_B = (W - 1)$ ▷ *find lanes to be flushed*
  if $m \neq$ false **then**
    $H[0] \leftarrow_m \vec{h}$ ▷ *pack partitions to be flushed*
    for $j \leftarrow 0$ **to** $|m| - 1$ **do**
      $h \leftarrow H[j]$
      $o \leftarrow (O[h] \,\&\, -W) - W$ ▷ *output location*
      $\vec{k}_B \leftarrow B_{keys}[h \cdot W]$ ▷ *load tuples from buffer*
      $\vec{v}_B \leftarrow B_{payloads}[h \cdot W]$
      $T_{keys\_out}[o] \leftarrow \vec{k}_B$ ▷ *flush tuples to output ...*
      $T_{payloads\_out}[o] \leftarrow \vec{v}_B$ ▷ *... using streaming stores*
    end for
    $B_{keys}[\vec{o}_B - W] \leftarrow_{m'} \vec{k}$ ▷ *scatter tuples to buffer ...*
    $B_{payloads}[\vec{o}_B - W] \leftarrow_{m'} \vec{v}$ ▷ *... for overflowing lanes*
  end if
end for ▷ *cleanup the buffers after the loop*

Since multiple tuples can be written to the buffer for the same partition on each loop, we identify which vector lanes will not cause overflow and scatter them selectively before flushing the buffers that are full. After the buffers are flushed, we scatter the remaining tuples to the buffer.

We identify which vector lanes point to partitions that have filled their buffers using the output index. Given that tuples in multiple vector lanes can belong to the same partition, we identify the lanes that wrote to the last partition slot and ensure that we will not flush the same data twice in the same loop. Flushing occurs "horizontally" one partition at a time, after selectively storing the partitions in the stack.

Flushing data from the buffers to the output is done by streaming stores to avoid polluting the cache with output data [38]. Note that we are streaming to multiple outputs, thus, single output buffering (Section 4) does not apply.

Hash partitioning is used to split the data into groups with non-overlapping keys and has no need to be stable. Instead of conflict serialization, we detect and process conflicting lanes during the next loop. Performance is slightly increased because very few conflicts normally occur per loop if $P > W$.

As in hash tables, if the tuples are keys and rids stored on separate arrays, we do fewer and wider scatters by interleaving the two columns before storing to the buffers.

To partition multiple columns of payloads, we can either shuffle all the columns together as a unified tuple or shuffle one column at a time. Shuffling unified tuples should optimally compile specific code for each query at run time. Otherwise, we can process one column at a time using precompiled type-specialized code. In the latter approach, which we use here, during histogram generation, we store partition destinations alongside the conflict serialization offsets in a temporary array. Thus, we avoid reloading the wider keys as well as redoing conflict serialization for each column. The temporary array must be $\log P + \log W$ bits wide per entry.

8. SORTING

Sorting is used in databases as a subproblem for join and aggregation. Sorting is also used for declustering, index building, compression, and duplicate elimination. Recent work showed that large-scale sorting is synonymous to partitioning. Radixsort and comparison sorting based on range partitioning have comparable performance, by maximizing the fanout to minimize the number of partition passes [26].

Here, we implement least-significant-bit (LSB) radixsort, which is the fastest method for 32-bit keys [26]. We do not evaluate larger keys as Xeon Phi only supports 32-bit integer arithmetic in vector code. Parallel LSB radixsort splits the input equally among threads and uses the prefix sum of the histograms from all threads to interleave the partition outputs. Histogram generation and shuffling operate shared-nothing maximizing thread parallelism. By using vectorized buffered partitioning, we also maximize data parallelism.

9. HASH JOIN

Joins are one of the most frequent operators in analytical queries that can be expensive enough to dominate query execution time. Recent work has focused on comparing main-memory equi-joins, namely sort-merge join and hash join. The former is dominated by sorting [4, 14]. In the baseline hash join, the inner relation is built into a hash table and the outer relation probes the hash table to find matches.

Partitioning can be applied to hash join forming multiple variants with different strengths and weaknesses. Here, we design three hash join variants using different degrees of partitioning that also allow for different degrees of vectorization. Because the inputs are much larger than the cache, we use buffered shuffling during partitioning (Section 7.4).

In the first variant termed *no partition*, we do not use partitioning. The building procedure builds a shared hash table across multiple threads using atomic operations. The threads are synchronized using a barrier. The read-only probing procedure then proceeds without atomics. On the other hand, building the hash table cannot be fully vectorized because atomic operations are not supported in SIMD.

In the second variant termed *min partition*, we use partitioning to eliminate the use of atomics by not building a shared hash table. We partition the inner (building) relation into T parts, T being the number of threads, and build T hash tables without sharing across threads. During probing, we pick both which hash table and which bucket to search. All parts of the algorithm can be fully vectorized, after we slightly modify the code to probe across the T hash tables.

In the third variant termed *max partition*, we partition both relations until the inner relation parts are small enough to fit in a cache-resident hash table. In our implementation, the original partitioning phase splits both relations across T threads and each part is further partitioned by a single thread in one or more passes. The resulting partitions are used to build and probe hash tables in the cache, typically the L1. All parts of the algorithm can be fully vectorized.

10. EXPERIMENTAL EVALUATION

We use three platforms throughout our evaluation. The first is a Xeon Phi co-processor based on the MIC design, the second has one Haswell CPU, and the third has four high-end Sandy Bridge CPUs. Details are shown in Table 1.

We use the Haswell CPU to compare our vectorized implementations against scalar and state-of-the-art vectorized implementations, because Haswell has 256-bit SIMD registers and supports gathers, being the closest to the 512-bit SIMD registers of Xeon Phi. However, because one CPU cannot match the scale of Xeon Phi, we use four Sandy Bridge CPUs with comparable processing power and memory bandwidth to measure aggregate performance and power efficiency.

Platform	1 CoPU	1 CPU	4 CPUs
Market Name	Xeon Phi	Xeon	Xeon
Market Model	7120P	E3-1275v3	E5-4620
Clock Frequency	1.238 GHz	3.5 GHz	2.2 GHz
Cores × SMT	61 × 4	4 × 2	(4 × 8) × 2
Core Architecture	P54C	Haswell	Sandy Bridge
Issue Width	2-way	8-way	6-way
Reorder Buffer	N/A	192-entry	168-entry
L1 Size / Core	32+32 KB	32+32 KB	32+32 KB
L2 Size / Core	512 KB	256 KB	256 KB
L3 Size (Total)	0	8 MB	4 × 16 MB
Memory Capacity	16 GB	32 GB	512 GB
Load Bandwidth	212 GB/s	21.8 GB/s	122 GB/s
Copy Bandwidth	80 GB/s	9.3 GB/s	38 GB/s
SIMD Width	512-bit	256-bit	128-bit
Gather & Scatter	Yes & Yes	Yes & No	No & No
Power (TDP)	300 W	84 W	4 × 130 W

Table 1: Experimental platforms

To compile for Xeon Phi, we use ICC 15 with the `-mmic` and the `-no-vec` flag to avoid automatic vectorization. To compile for mainstream CPUs, we use either ICC 15 or GCC 4.9, the fastest per case. In all cases we use `-O3` optimization. For the Haswell CPU we use `-mavx2` (AVX 2) and for the Sandy Bridge CPUs we use `-mavx` (SSE 4 with VEX). Xeon Phi runs Linux 2.6 as an embedded OS, the Haswell machine has Linux 3.13 and the Sandy Bridge machine has Linux 3.2.

Unless specified otherwise, we use all hardware threads, including SMT, to minimize load and instruction latencies. All data are synthetically generated in memory and follow the uniform distribution. Uniform data are used in the most common analytical DBMS benchmarks, such as TPC-H, and are not particularly favorable to any specific operation. In fact, previous work has shown that joins, partitioning, and sorting are faster under skew [5, 26]. Nevertheless, optimizing for skew efficiency is out of the scope of this paper.

10.1 Selection Scans

Figure 5 shows the performance of selection scans on Xeon Phi and Haswell. The input table consists of 32-bit keys and 32-bit payloads and the selective condition on the key column is $k_{min} \leq k \leq k_{max}$, as shown in Section 4, where k_{min} and k_{max} are query constants. We vary the selectivity and measure the throughput of six selection scan versions, two scalar with and without branching [29], and four vectorized using two orthogonal design choices. First, we either select the qualifying tuples by extracting one bit at a time from the bitmask, or use vector selective stores. Second, we either access both keys and payloads during predicate evaluation and buffer the qualifiers, or we load the key column only and buffer the indexes of qualifiers, which are used to dereference the actual key and payload values during buffer flushing.

On Xeon Phi, scalar code is almost an order of magnitude slower than vector code, whereas on Haswell, vector code is about twice faster. Low selectivities are faster because RAM loading is faster than copying, and more payload column accesses are skipped. Branch elimination [29] improves performance on Haswell, but decreases performance on Xeon Phi due to slow `set` instructions. On Haswell, all vector versions are almost identical by saturating the bandwidth, while the branchless scalar code catches up on 10% selectivity. On Xeon Phi, avoiding payload column accesses dominates low selectivities, while using selective stores instead of extracting one tuple at a time dominates high selectivities. On the simple cores of Xeon Phi, vectorization is essential to saturate the bandwidth. On the complex cores of mainstream CPUs, vectorization remains useful for low selectivities.

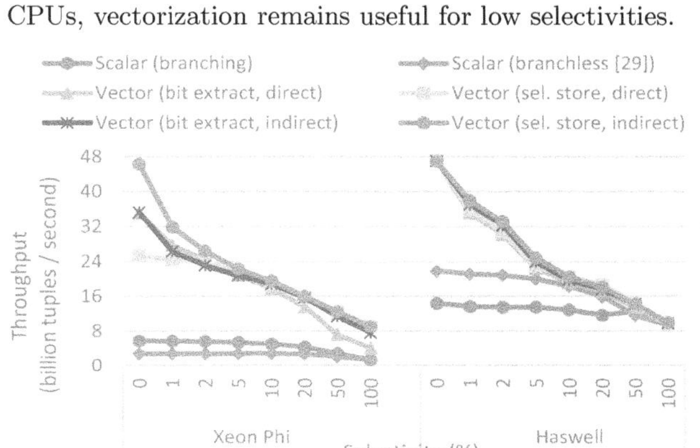

Figure 5: Selection scan (32-bit key & payload)

10.2 Hash Tables

In this section we evaluate hash table vectorization. The first set of experiments measures the probing throughput and compares against state-of-the-art scalar and vectorized approaches, on both Xeon Phi and Haswell. The second set evaluates iterative building and probing of shared-nothing hash tables on Xeon Phi only since Haswell has no scatters.

Figure 6 shows linear probing (LP) and double hashing (DH). The input is a 32-bit column with 10^9 keys, the output is a 32-bit column with the payloads of matches, almost all keys match, and the hash table is half full. The horizontal vector code uses bucketized hash table where each input key is compared against multiple table keys [30]. In our approach, vertical vector code, we compare multiple input keys against one hash table key each using gathers. We are up to 6X faster than everything else on Xeon Phi, and gain a smaller speedup for cache resident hash tables on Haswell.

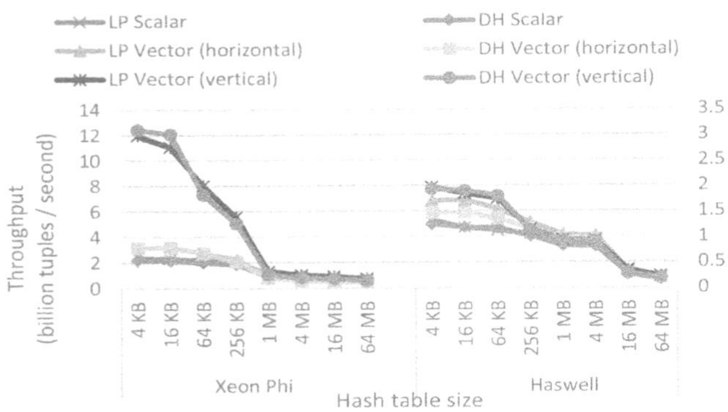

Figure 6: Probe linear probing & double hashing tables (shared, 32-bit key → 32-bit probed payload)

Figure 7 shows the probing throughput of cuckoo hashing, with the same setting as Figure 6. The scalar versions are either branching or branchless [42], and the vector versions are either horizontal (bucketized) [30] or vertical, where we evaluate two vertical techniques, loading both buckets and blending them, or loading the second bucket selectively. The branchless scalar version [42] is slower than branching scalar code on both Xeon Phi and Haswell. Also, branching scalar code is faster than branchless on Haswell using ICC, while GCC produces very slow branching code. Vertically vectorized code is 5X faster on Xeon Phi and 1.7X on Haswell.

Bucketized hash table probing is faster by using 128-bit SIMD (SSE 4) to probe 4 key, rather than use 256-bit SIMD (AVX 2) to probe 8 keys, due to faster in-register broadcasts.

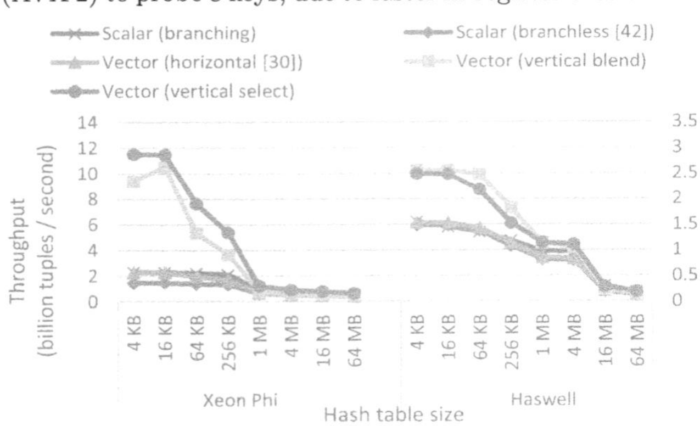

Figure 7: Probe cuckoo hashing table (2 functions, shared, 32-bit key → 32-bit probed payload)

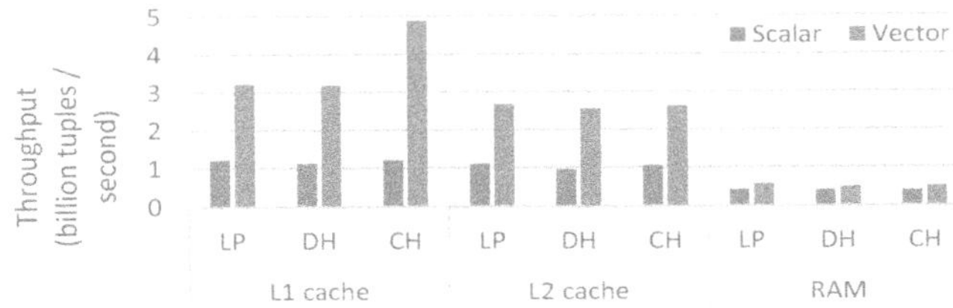

Figure 8: Build & probe linear probing, double hashing, & cuckoo hashing on Xeon Phi (1:1 build–probe, shared-nothing, 2X 32-bit key & payload)

Figure 8 interleaves building and probing of shared-nothing tables, as done in the last phase of partitioned hash join, using Xeon Phi. The build to probe ratio is 1:1, all keys match, and we vary the hash table size. The hash tables are $\approx$ 4 KB in L1, 64 KB in L2, and 1 MB out of cache. Both inputs have 32-bit keys and payloads, the output has the matching keys and the two payloads, the load factor is 50%, and we saturate Phi's memory. Throughput is defined as $(|R| + |S|)/t$. The speedup is 2.6–4X when the hash table resides in L1, 2.4–2.7X in L2, and 1.2–1.4X out of the cache.

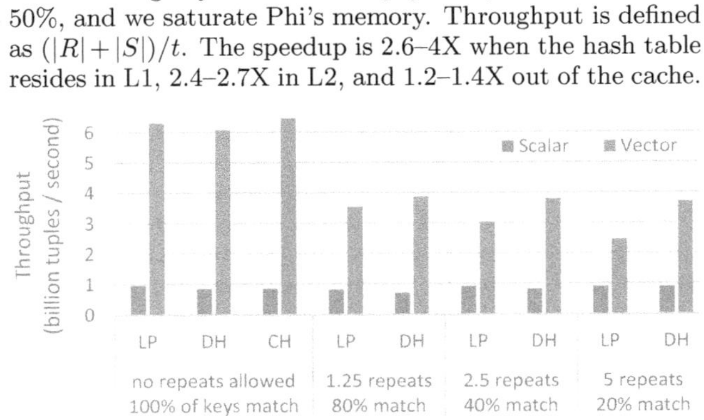

Figure 9: Build & probe linear probing, double hashing, & cuckoo hashing on Xeon Phi (1:10 build–probe, L1, shared-nothing, 2X 32-bit key & payload)

In Figure 9, we modify the experiment of Figure 8 by varying the number of key repeats with the same output size. All tables are in L1 and the build to probe ratio is 1:10. The other settings are as in Figure 8. With no key repeats, the speedup is 6.6–7.7X, higher than Figure 8, since building is more expensive than probing and also detects conflicts. Here, building alone gets a speedup of 2.5–2.7X. With 5 key repeats, the speedup is 4.1X for DH and 2.7X for LP. Thus, DH is more resilient to key repeats than LP.

10.3 Bloom Filters

In Figure 10, we measure Bloom filter probing throughput using the design of [27] with selective loads and stores for Xeon Phi. We disable loop unrolling and add buffering. The speedup is 3.6–7.8X on Xeon Phi and 1.3–3.1X on Haswell

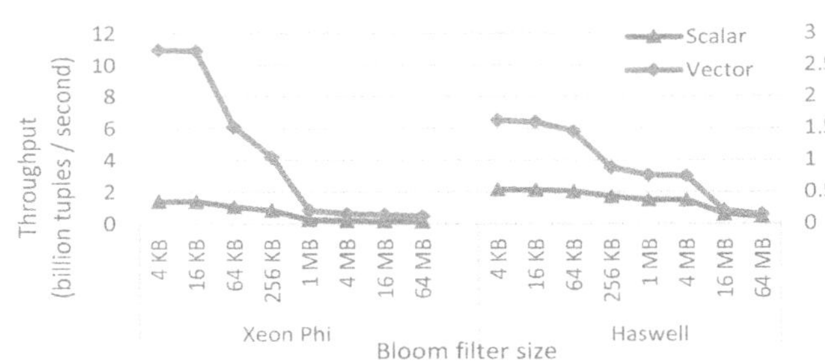

Figure 10: Bloom filter probing (5 functions, shared, 10 bits / item, 5% selectivity, 32-bit key & payload)

10.4 Partitioning

Figure 11 shows radix and hash histogram generation on Xeon Phi. On mainstream CPUs, the memory load bandwidth is saturated [26]. Scalar code is dominated by the partition function. By replicating each count W times, we get a 2.55X speedup over scalar radix. A slowdown occurs when we exceed the L1, but we can increase P by compressing to 8-bit counts. Conflict serialization does not replicate but is slower, especially if $P \leq W$. If P is too large, both count replication and conflict serialization are too expensive.

Figure 11: Radix & hash histogram on Xeon Phi

Figure 12 shows the performance of computing the range partition function. The binary search vectorization speedup is 7–15X on Xeon Phi and 2.4–2.8X on Haswell. SIMD range indexes [26] are even faster on Haswell but are slower on Xeon Phi, where the pipeline is saturated by scalar instructions. Each node has W keys and the root stays in registers.

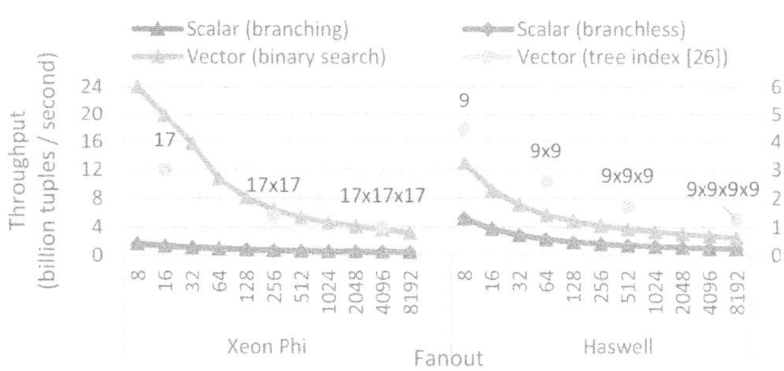

Figure 12: Range function on Xeon Phi (32-bit key)

Figure 13 measures shuffling on Xeon Phi using inputs larger than the cache. On mainstream CPUs, shuffling cannot be fully vectorized without scatters, but saturates the memory copy bandwidth at higher fanout [4, 26]. On Xeon Phi, among the unbuffered versions, vectorization achieves up to 1.95X speedup. Among the scalar versions, buffering achieves up to 1.8X speedup. Among the buffered versions, vectorization achieves up to 2.85X speedup, using up to 60% of the bandwidth. The optimal fanout, maximizing throughput × bits, is 5–8 radix bits per pass. Unstable hash partitioning, shown here, is up to 17% faster than stable radix.

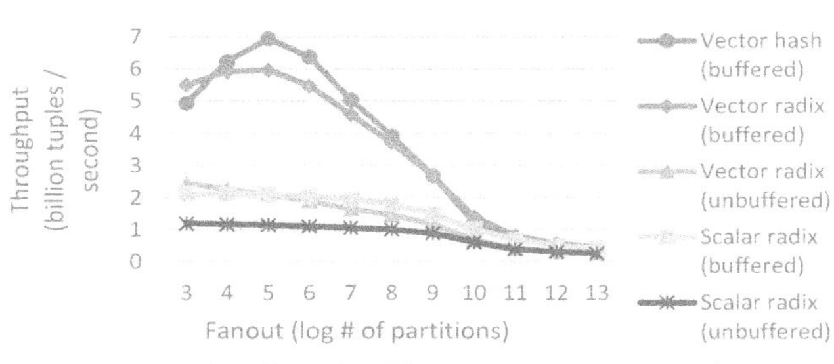

Figure 13: Radix shuffling on Xeon Phi (shared-nothing, out-of-cache, 32-bit key & payload)

10.5 Sorting & Hash Join

We now evaluate sorting and hash joins in three stages: first, we measure performance on Xeon Phi and highlight the impact of vectorization on algorithmic designs; second, we compare against 4 high-end CPUs to highlight the impact on power efficiency; and third, we study the cost of a generic implementation and materialization of multiple columns.

10.5.1 Vectorization Speedup & Algorithmic Designs

Figure 14 shows the performance of LSB radixsort on Xeon Phi. The vectorization speedup is 2.2X over state-of-the-art scalar code and time scales with size. In mainstream CPUs, we are already almost saturated, since each partitioning pass runs close to the bandwidth [31, 26, 38].

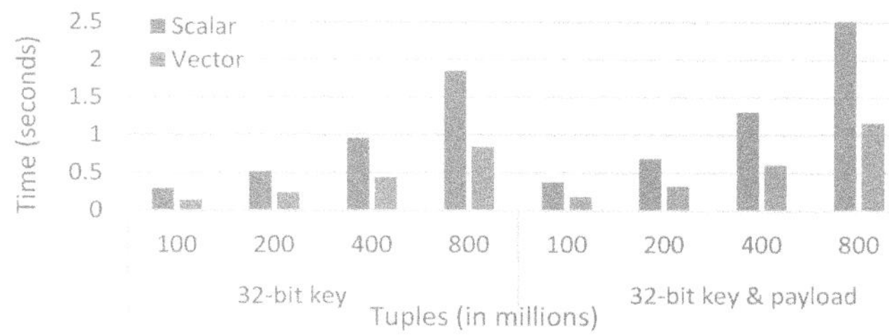

Figure 14: Radixsort on Xeon Phi (LSB)

Figure 15 shows the performance of the three hash join variants as described in Section 9, on Xeon Phi. We assume a foreign key join but our implementation is generic. The "no-partition" and the "min-partition" methods get small 1.05X and 1.25X speedups, while the fully partitioned gets a 3.3X speedup and becomes the fastest overall by a 2.25X gap, which is too large to justify hardware-oblivious joins [12]. Hash join is faster than sort-merge join [4, 14], since we sort $4 \cdot 10^8$ in 0.6 seconds and join $2 \times 2 \cdot 10^8$ tuples in 0.54 seconds.

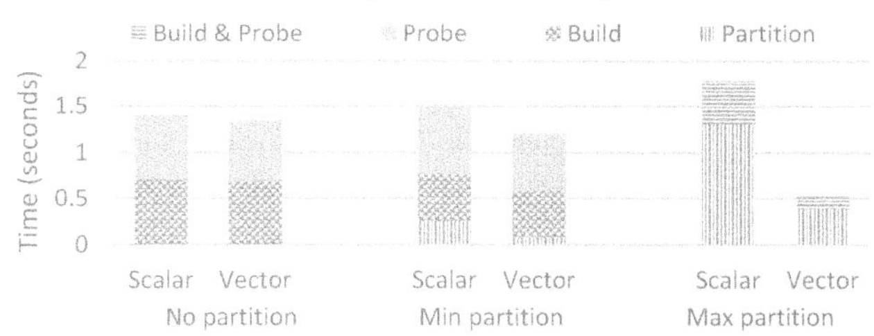

Figure 15: Multiple hash join variants on Xeon Phi ($2 \cdot 10^8 \bowtie 2 \cdot 10^8$ 32-bit key & payload)

Figure 16 shows the thread scalability of radixsort and partitioned hash join on Xeon Phi. The speedup is almost linear, even when using 2-way and 4-way SMT due to hiding load and instruction latencies. On Xeon Phi, using 4-way SMT is essential to hide the 4-cycle vector instruction latencies. On mainstream CPUs, LSB radixsort is again saturated, gaining only marginal speedup from 2-way SMT [26].

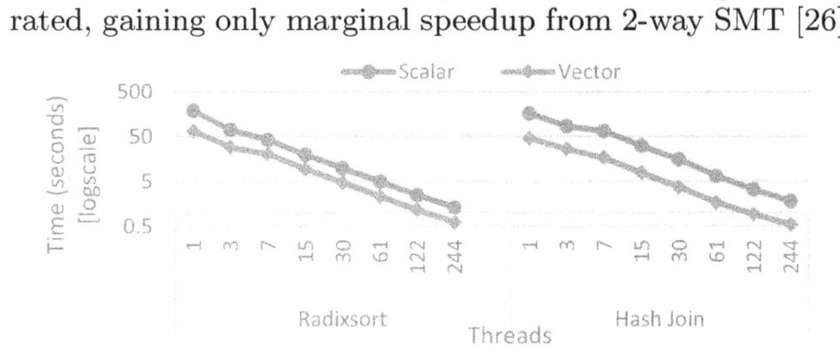

Figure 16: Radixsort & hash join scalability ($4 \cdot 10^8$ & $2 \cdot 10^8 \bowtie 2 \cdot 10^8$ 32-bit key & payload, log/log scale)

10.5.2 Aggregate Performance & Power Efficiency

We now compare Xeon Phi to 4 Sandy Bridge (SB) CPUs in order to get comparable performance, using radixsort and hash join. On the SB CPUs, we implemented partitioned hash join and use the source code of [26] for LSB radixsort.

Partitioning passes on the SB CPUs are memory bound, thus cannot benefit from full vectorization. Both radixsort and hash join on SB are NUMA aware and transfer the data at most once across CPUs [26]. To join the partitions in cache, we use horizontal linear probing, shown in Figure 6.

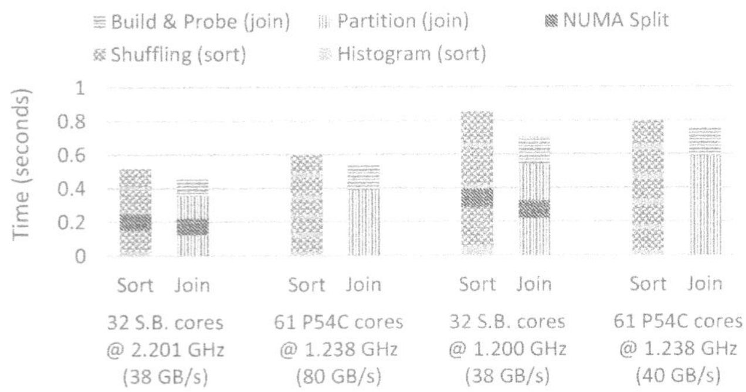

Figure 17: Radixsort & hash join on Xeon Phi 7120P versus 4 Xeon E5 4620 CPUs (sort $4 \cdot 10^8$ tuples, join $2 \cdot 10^8 \bowtie 2 \cdot 10^8$ tuples, 32-bit key & payload per table)

As shown in Figure 17, radixsort and hash join are both $\approx$ 14% slower on the Phi compared to the 4 SB CPUs. If we assume the operating power of both platforms to be equally proportional to TDP, both radixsort and hash join are $\approx$ 1.5X more power efficient on the Phi. We also include results after equalizing the two platforms. We set the frequency of the SB CPUs to 1.2 GHz and halve the bandwidth of the Phi to 40 GB/s for copying, which is done by adjusting the code to access twice as many bytes as are processed. Phi is then 7% faster for radixsort and 8% slower for hash join.

As shown in previous work [4, 14], hash joins outperform sort-merge joins. Here, we join $2 \times 2 \cdot 10^8$ tuples faster than sorting $4 \cdot 10^8$ tuples alone, also materializing the join output.

10.5.3 Multiple Columns, Types & Materialization

Vector code cannot handle multiple types as easily as scalar code. So far we used 32-bit columns, which suffices for sorting orders and join indexes of 32-bit keys. Also, type-generic materialization methods, such as radix-decluster [21], can only do a single pass that is bounded by the cache capacity. Type-generic buffered shuffling can solve both problems.

Figure 18 measures radixsort with 32-bit keys by varying the number and width of payload columns. Per pass, we generate the histogram once and shuffle one column at a time. Shuffling 8-bit or 16-bit columns costs as much as 32-bit columns since we are compute-bound. Also, Xeon Phi upcasts 8-bit and 16-bit operations to 32-bit vector lanes. This approach scales well with wider columns, as we sort 8-byte tuples in 0.36 seconds and 36-byte tuples in 1 second.

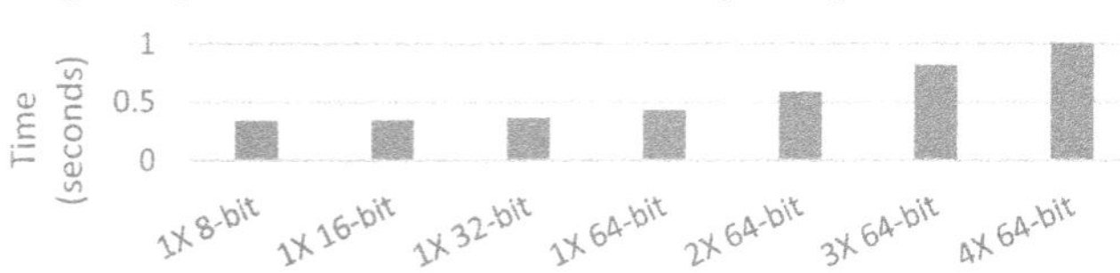

Figure 18: Radixsort with varying payloads on Xeon Phi ($2 \cdot 10^8$ tuples, 32-bit key)

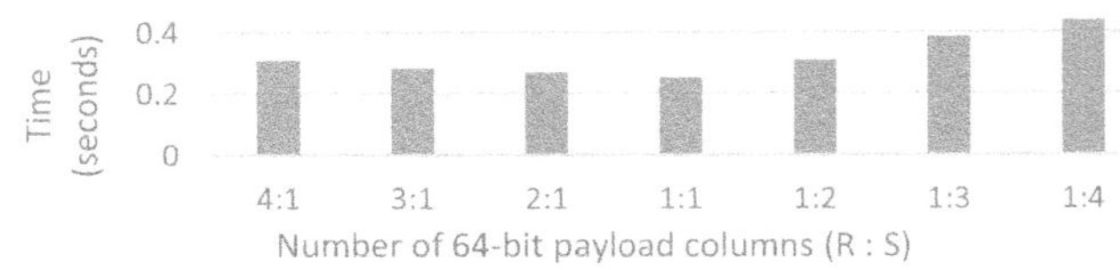

Figure 19: Hash join with varying payload columns on Xeon Phi ($10^7 \bowtie 10^8$ tuples, 32-bit keys)

Figure 19 shows partitioned hash join with 32-bit keys and multiple 64-bit payload columns. Out of the cache, we shuffle one column at a time as in Figure 18. In the cache, we store rids in hash tables and then dereference the columns.

A different materialization strategy would be, after joining keys and rids, to cluster to the order of the side with shorter payloads, and then re-partition to the order of the other side. Thus, instead of using radix-decluster [21] that is done in a single pass, we partition the shorter payloads in one or more passes to remain cache-conscious. Neverthless, finding the fastest strategy per case is out of the scope of this paper.

11. SIMD CPUS & SIMT GPUS

The SIMT model in GPUs exhibits some similarity to SIMD in CPUs. SIMT GPUs run scalar code, but "tie" all threads in a *warp* to execute the same instruction per cycle. For instance, gathers and scatters are written as scalar loads and stores to non-contiguous locations. Horizontal SIMD instructions can be supported via special shuffle instructions that operate across the warp. Thus, CPU threads are analogous to GPU warps and GPU threads are analogous to SIMD lanes. However, while conditional control flow is eliminated in SIMD code "manually", SIMT transforms control flow to data flow automatically, by executing all paths and nullifying instructions from paths that are not taken per thread.

One-to-one conversion from SIMD to SIMT code is of limited use for in-memory database operators, due to the vastly different memory hierarchy dynamics. The speedup from SIMD vectorization is maximized for cache-conscious processing, which is achieved by partitioning. On the other hand, GPUs are fast even without partitioning [13, 24], due to good memory latency hiding. Sequential operators, such as selection scans, have already been studied in detail [36].

A comparison of GPUs and Xeon Phi is out of the scope of this paper. We view Xeon Phi as a potential CPU design and study the impact of vectorization on making it more suitable for analytical databases. Thus, we do not transfer data through the PCI-e bus of Xeon Phi in our evaluation.

12. CONCLUSION

We presented generic SIMD vectorized implementations for analytical databases executing in-memory. We defined fundamental vector operations and presented good vectorization principles. We implemented selection scans, hash tables, and partitioning using entirely vector code, and then combined them to build sorting and join operators. Our implementations were evaluated against scalar and state-of-the-art vector code on the latest mainstream CPUs, as well as the Xeon Phi co-processor that is based on many simple cores with large SIMD vectors. In the context of in-memory database operators, we highlighted the impact of vectorization on algorithmic designs, as well as the architectural designs and power efficiency, by making the simple cores comparable to complex cores. Our work is applicable to all SIMD processors, using either simple or complex cores.

13. REFERENCES

[1] M.-C. Albutiu et al. Massively parallel sort-merge joins in main memory multi-core database systems. *PVLDB*, 5(10):1064–1075, June 2012.
[2] P. Bakkum et al. Accelerating SQL database operations on a GPU with CUDA. In *GPGPU*, pages 94–103, 2010.
[3] C. Balkesen et al. Main-memory hash joins on multi-core CPUs: Tuning to the underlying hardware. In *ICDE*, pages 362–373, 2013.
[4] C. Balkesen et al. Multicore, main-memory joins: Sort vs. hash revisited. *PVLDB*, 7(1):85–96, Sept. 2013.
[5] S. Blanas et al. Design and evaluation of main memory hash join algorithms for multi-core CPUs. In *SIGMOD*, pages 37–48, 2011.
[6] P. Boncz et al. MonetDB/X100: Hyper-pipelining query execution. In *CIDR*, 2005.
[7] J. Chhugani et al. Efficient implementation of sorting on multi-core SIMD CPU architecture. In *VLDB*, pages 1313–1324, 2008.
[8] J. Cieslewicz et al. Automatic contention detection and amelioration for data-intensive operations. In *SIGMOD*, pages 483–494, 2010.
[9] D. J. DeWitt et al. Materialization strategies in a column-oriented DBMS. In *ICDE*, pages 466–475, 2007.
[10] J. Hofmann et al. Comparing the performance of different x86 SIMD instruction sets for a medical imaging application on modern multi- and manycore chips. *CoRR*, arXiv:1401.7494, 2014.
[11] H. Inoue et al. AA-sort: A new parallel sorting algorithm for multi-core SIMD processors. In *PACT*, pages 189–198, 2007.
[12] S. Jha et al. Improving main memory hash joins on Intel Xeon Phi processors: An experimental approach. *PVLDB*, 8(6):642–653, Feb. 2015.
[13] T. Kaldewey et al. GPU join processing revisited. In *DaMoN*, 2012.
[14] C. Kim et al. Sort vs. hash revisited: fast join implementation on modern multicore CPUs. In *VLDB*, pages 1378–1389, 2009.
[15] C. Kim et al. Fast: fast architecture sensitive tree search on modern CPUs and GPUs. In *SIGMOD*, pages 339–350, 2010.
[16] K. Krikellas et al. Generating code for holistic query evaluation. In *ICDE*, pages 613–624, 2010.
[17] S. Larsen et al. Exploiting superword level parallelism with multimedia instruction sets. In *PLDI*, pages 145–156, 2000.
[18] V. Leis et al. Morsel-driven parallelism: A NUMA-aware query evaluation framework for the many-core age. In *SIGMOD*, pages 743–754, 2014.
[19] S. Manegold et al. Optimizing database architecture for the new bottleneck: Memory access. *J. VLDB*, 9(3):231–246, Dec. 2000.
[20] S. Manegold et al. What happens during a join? dissecting CPU and memory optimization effects. In *VLDB*, pages 339–350, 2000.
[21] S. Manegold et al. Cache-conscious radix-decluster projections. In *VLDB*, pages 684–695, 2004.
[22] T. Neumann. Efficiently compiling efficient query plans for modern hardware. *PVLDB*, 4(9):539–550, June 2011.
[23] R. Pagh et al. Cuckoo hashing. *J. Algorithms*, 51(2):122–144, May 2004.
[24] H. Pirk et al. Accelerating foreign-key joins using asymmetric memory channels. In *ADMS*, 2011.
[25] O. Polychroniou et al. High throughput heavy hitter aggregation for modern SIMD processors. In *DaMoN*, 2013.
[26] O. Polychroniou et al. A comprehensive study of main-memory partitioning and its application to large-scale comparison- and radix-sort. In *SIGMOD*, pages 755–766, 2014.
[27] O. Polychroniou et al. Vectorized Bloom filters for advanced SIMD processors. In *DaMoN*, 2014.
[28] V. Raman et al. DB2 with BLU acceleration: So much more than just a column store. *PVLDB*, 6(11):1080–1091, Aug. 2013.
[29] K. A. Ross. Selection conditions in main memory. *ACM Trans. Database Systems*, 29(1):132–161, Mar. 2004.
[30] K. A. Ross. Efficient hash probes on modern processors. In *ICDE*, pages 1297–1301, 2007.
[31] N. Satish et al. Fast sort on CPUs and GPUs: a case for bandwidth oblivious SIMD sort. In *SIGMOD*, pages 351–362, 2010.
[32] B. Schlegel et al. Scalable frequent itemset mining on many-core processors. In *DaMoN*, 2013.
[33] L. Seiler et al. Larrabee: A many-core x86 architecture for visual computing. *ACM Trans. Graphics*, 27(3), Aug. 2008.
[34] J. Shin. Introducing control flow into vectorized code. In *PACT*, pages 280–291, 2007.
[35] L. Sidirourgos et al. Column imprints: A secondary index structure. In *SIGMOD*, pages 893–904, 2013.
[36] E. A. Sitaridi et al. Optimizing select conditions on GPUs. In *DaMoN*, 2013.
[37] M. Stonebraker et al. C-store: A column-oriented DBMS. In *VLDB*, pages 553–564, 2005.
[38] J. Wassenberg et al. Engineering a multi core radix sort. In *EuroPar*, pages 160–169, 2011.
[39] T. Willhalm et al. SIMD-scan: ultra fast in-memory table scan using on-chip vector processing units. *PVLDB*, 2(1):385–394, Aug. 2009.
[40] Y. Ye et al. Scalable aggregation on multicore processors. In *DaMoN*, 2011.
[41] J. Zhou et al. Implementing database operations using SIMD instructions. In *SIGMOD*, pages 145–156, 2002.
[42] M. Zukowski et al. Architecture-conscious hashing. In *DaMoN*, 2006.

APPENDIX

A. NOTATION

We now explain the notation of the vectorized algorithmic descriptions. Boolean vector operations result in boolean vector bitmasks that are shown as scalar variables. For example, $m \leftarrow \vec{x} < \vec{y}$ results in the bitmask m. Assignments such as $m \leftarrow$ true, set the W bits of m. Vectors as array indexes denote a gather or a scatter. For example, $\vec{x} \leftarrow A[y]$ is a vector load, while $\vec{x} \leftarrow A[\vec{y}]$ is a gather. Selective loads and stores as well as selective gathers and scatters use a bitmask as a subscript in the assignment. For example, $\vec{x} \leftarrow_m A[y]$ is a selective load, while $\vec{x} \leftarrow_m A[\vec{y}]$ is a selective gather. $|m|$ is the bit population count of m and $|T|$ is the size of array T. If-then-else statements, such as $\vec{x} \leftarrow m\ ?\ \vec{y} : \vec{z}$, use vector blending. Finally, scalar values in vector expressions use vectors generated before the main loop. For example, $\vec{x} \leftarrow \vec{x} + k$ and $m \leftarrow \vec{x} > k$ use a vector with k in all lanes.

B. GATHER & SCATTER

In the latest mainstream CPUs (AVX 2), gathers and scatters are executed in one instruction. On Xeon Phi, each instruction call accesses one cache line and is called repeatedly until all W lanes are processed. If N distinct cache lines are accessed, the instructions are issued N times with $N \leq W$.

An implementation for 16-way gather on Xeon Phi is shown below. The `rax` scalar register holds the array pointer. The 512-bit `zmm0` vector holds the indexes and `zmm1` vector holds the loaded values. `k1` is a 16-bit boolean vector set by `kxnor`. Each call to `vpgatherdd` finds the leftmost set bit in `k1`, extracts the index from `zmm0`, identifies other lanes pointing to the same cache line, loads the values in `zmm1`, and resets the bits in `k1`. The `jknzd` branches back if `k1` has more set bits.

```
       kxnor        %k1, %k1
loop:  vpgatherdd   (%rax, %zmm0, 4), %zmm1 {%k1}
       jknzd        loop, %k1
```

Scatters are symmetric to gathers. If multiple lanes of the index vector have the same value, the value in the rightmost lane is written but all respective bits in k1 are reset. We can detect multiple references to the same cache line by checking if multiple bits of k1 were reset, but we cannot distinguish between conflicts and distinct writes in the same cache line.

Non-selective gathers and scatters initially have all bits in k1 set. Selective gathers and scatters, use k1 and zmm1 as both inputs and outputs to load a subset of lanes determined by k1. The rest lanes in zmm1 not set in k1 are unaffected.

The latency and throughput of each gather or scatter operation is determined by the number of cache lines accessed. Assuming all cache lines are L1 resident, the operation is faster if assembled in fewer cache lines. For the same cache lines, accessing fewer items reduces the total latency [10].

In Haswell gathers, k1 is a vector. The asymmetry between Xeon Phi and Haswell on how gather instructions work, is possibly due to the fact that out-of-order CPUs can overlap a single high-latency branchless gather with other instructions more effectively. Haswell gathers have been shown to perform almost identically in L1 and L2. Also, loading W items from distinct cache lines in L1 or L2 has been shown to be almost as fast as loading the same item W times [10].

On Xeon Phi, mixing gather and scatter instructions in the same loop reduces performance. Thus, executing gather and scatter operations in a loop of gather and scatter instructions offers no performance benefit. Ideally, we would like to combine the spatial locality aware gathers and scatters of Xeon Phi with the single instruction of Haswell, also implementing the logic to iterate over $W' \leq W$ distinct cache lines inside the execution unit without branching.

Gathers and scatters can be emulated, if not supported. We did a careful implementation of gathers using other vector instructions and used it in linear probing and double hashing tables. We found that we lose up to 13% probing performance compared to the hardware gathers (Figure 6), which reduces as the table size increases. When the loads are not cache resident, there is no noticeable difference, which is expected since gathers and scatters go through the same memory access path as loads and stores to a single location.

C. SELECTIVE LOAD & STORE

Selective loads and stores must be able to access unaligned memory. Thus, a load can span across two cache lines. Xeon Phi provides two instructions for these two cache lines. In Haswell, we use unaligned vector accesses and permutations, which are shown in the code examples of Appendix D and E.

```
void _mm512_mask_packstore_epi32(int32_t *p, // pointer
                                  __mmask16 m, // mask
                                  __m512i v) // vector
{ _mm512_mask_packstorelo_epi32(&p[0], m, v):
  _mm512_mask_packstorehi_epi32(&p[16], m, v); }
```

The selective load of 16 32-bit data for Xeon Phi is shown above. The symmetric selective store is shown below. The functions with prefix _mm are intrinsics available online.[3]

```
__m512i _mm512_mask_loadunpack_epi32(__m512i v,
                                      __mmask16 m,
                                 const int32_t *p)
{ v = _mm512_mask_loadunpacklo_epi32(v, m, &p[0]):
  v = _mm512_mask_loadunpackhi_epi32(v, m, &p[16]);
  return v; }
```

[3]software.intel.com/sites/landingpage/IntrinsicsGuide/

D. SELECTION SCANS

The code for selection scans assuming 32-bit keys and payloads in Xeon Phi is shown below. We use the version that was described in Section 4 that stores input pointers of qualifiers in a cache resident buffer and then gather the data from the input. The selective condition is $k_{lower} \leq k \leq k_{upper}$. The buffer must be small enough to be L1 resident. The streaming store instruction (_mm512_storenrngo_ps) mechanism is to not read back the cache line that is overwritten. The input and output here must be aligned in cache lines.

```
for (i = j = k = 0;  i < tuples;  i += 16) {
  /* load key column and evaluate predicates */
  key = _mm512_load_epi32(&keys[i]);
  m = _mm512_cmpge_epi32_mask(key, mask_lower);
  m = _mm512_mask_cmple_epi32_mask(k, key, mask_upper);
  if (!_mm512_kortestz(m, m)) {    // jkzd
    /* selectively store qualifying tuple indexes */
    _mm512_mask_packstore_epi32(&rids_buf[k], m, rid);
    k += _mm_countbits_64(_mm512_mask2int(m)); }
    if (k > buf_size - 16) {
      /* flush the buffer */
      for (b = 0;  b != buf_size - 16;  b += 16) {
        ptr = _mm512_load_epi32(&rids_buf[b]);
        /* dereference column values and stream */
        key_f = _mm512_i32gather_ps(ptr, keys, 4);
        pay_f = _mm512_i32gather_ps(ptr, pays, 4);
        _mm512_storenrngo_ps(&keys_out[b + j], key_f);
        _mm512_storenrngo_ps(&pays_out[b + j], pay_f);}
      /* move extra items to the start of the buffer */
      ptr = _mm512_load_epi32(&rids_buf[b]);
      _mm512_store_epi32(&rids_buf[0], ptr);
      j += buf_size - 16;
      k -= buf_size - 16; } }
  rid = _mm512_add_epi32(rid, mask_16); }
```

We now show the same code in Haswell using AVX 2 intrinsics. The selective store is replaced by a 2-way partition that loads the permutation mask from a lookup array [27].

```
for (i = j = k = 0;  i < tuples;  i += 8) {
  /* load key columns and evaluate predicates */
  key = _mm256_load_si256((__m256i*) &keys[i]);
  cmp_lo = _mm256_cmpgt_epi32(mask_lower, key);
  cmp_hi = _mm256_cmpgt_epi32(key, mask_upper);
  cmp = _mm256_or_si256(cmp_lo, cmp_hi);
  cmp = _mm256_xor_si256(cmp, mask_minus_1);
  if (!_mm256_testz_si256(cmp, cmp)) {
    /* load permutation mask for selective store */
    m = _mm256_movemask_ps(_mm256_castsi256_ps(cmp));
    perm_comp = _mm_loadl_epi64(&perm[m]);
    perm = _mm256_cvtepi8_epi32(perm_comp);
    /* permute and store the input pointers */
    cmp = _mm256_permutevar8x32_epi32(cmp, perm);
    ptr = _mm256_permutevar8x32_epi32(rid, perm);
    _mm256_maskstore_epi32(&rids_buf[k], cmp, ptr);
    k += _mm_popcnt_u64(m);
    if (k > buf_size - 8) {
      /* flush the buffer */
      for (b = 0;  b != buf_size - 8;  b += 8) {
        /* dereference column values and store */
        ptr = _mm256_load_si256(&rids_buf[j]);
        key = _mm256_i32gather_epi32(keys, ptr, 4);
        pay = _mm256_i32gather_epi32(pays, ptr, 4);
        _mm256_stream_si256(&keys_out[b + j], key);
        _mm256_stream_si256(&pays_out[b + j], pay); }
      /* move extra items to the start of the buffer */
      ptr = _mm256_load_si256(&rids_buf[b]);
      _mm256_store_si256(&rids_buf[0], ptr);
      j += buf_size - 8;
      k -= buf_size - 8; } }
  rid = _mm256_add_epi32(rid, mask_8); }
```

E. HASH TABLES

The code for probing a hash table using linear probing for Xeon Phi is shown below. The probing input has 32-bit keys and payloads and the table stores 32-bit keys and payloads. The output includes keys and the two payload columns.

```
m = _mm512_kxnor(m, m);                  // set mask
off = _mm512_xor_epi32(off, off);  // reset vector
for (i = j = 0;  i + 16 <= S_tuples;) {
  /* replace invalid keys & payloads */
  key=_mm512_mask_loadunpack_epi32(key, m, &S_keys[i]);
  pay=_mm512_mask_loadunpack_epi32(pay, m, &S_pays[i]);
  i += _mm_countbits_64(_mm512_mask2int(m));
  /* hash keys and add linear probing offset */
  hash = _mm512_mullo_epi32(key, mask_factor);
  hash = _mm512_mulhi_epu32(hash, mask_buckets);
  hash = _mm512_add_epi32(hash, off);
  /* gather key-payload pairs (buckets) */
  lo = _mm512_i32logather_epi64(hash, table, 8);
  hash =_mm512_permute4f128_epi32(hash, _MM_PERM_BADC);
  hi = _mm512_i32logather_epi64(hash, table, 8);
  /* unpack keys and payloads from pairs */
  _MM512_UNPACK_EPI32(lo, hi, table_key, table_pay);
  /* selectively store matches to output (or buffer) */
  m = _mm512_cmpeq_epi32_mask(key, table_key);
  _mm512_mask_packstore_epi32(&keys_out[j], m, key);
  _mm512_mask_packstore_epi32(&S_pays_out[j], m, pay);
  _mm512_mask_packstore_epi32(&R_pays_out[j], m,
  /* update output index */   table_pay);
  j += _mm_countbits_64(_mm512_mask2int(m));
  /* search empty buckets using special key value */
  m = _mm512_cmpeq_epi32_mask(table_key, mask_empty):
  /* increment or reset linear probing offsets */
  off = _mm512_add_epi32(off, mask_1);
  off = _mm512_mask_xor_epi32(off, m, off, off); }
```

The code for building linear probing hash tables with 32-bit keys and payloads for Xeon Phi is shown below. The implementation of double hashing is very similar with the difference being in the way the hash index is computed.

```
m = _mm512_kxnor(m, m);                  // set mask
off = _mm512_xor_epi32(off, off);  // reset vector
for (i = 0;  i + 16 <= R_tuples;) {
  /* replace invalid keys & payloads */
  key=_mm512_mask_loadunpack_epi32(key, m, &R_keys[i]);
  pay=_mm512_mask_loadunpack_epi32(pay, m, &R_rids[i]);
  i += _mm_countbits_64(_mm512_mask2int(m));
  /* hash keys and add linear probing offsets */
  hash = _mm512_mullo_epi32(key, mask_factor);
  hash = _mm512_mulhi_epu32(hash, mask_buckets);
  hash = _mm512_add_epi32(hash, off);
  /* gather keys from buckets */
  tab = _mm512_i32gather_epi32(hash, table, 8);
  /* check if buckets are empty */
  m = _mm512_cmpeq_epi32_mask(tab, mask_empty);
  /* scatter unique values per vector lane */
  _mm512_mask_i32scatter_epi32(table, m, hash,
  /* gather back values */      mask_unique, 8);
  tab = _mm512_mask_i32gather_epi32(tab, m, hash,
  /* detect non-conflicting */      table, 8);
  m=_mm512_mask_cmpeq_epi32_mask(m, tab, mask_unique);
  /* packs keys and payloads in pairs */
  _MM512_PACK_EPI32(key, pay, lo, hi);
  /* scatter key-payload pairs 1-8 */
  _mm512_mask_i32loscatter_epi32(table, m, hash,
  /* scatter key-payload pairs 9-16 */  lo, 8);
  hash =_mm512_permute4f128_epi32(hash, _MM_PERM_BADC);
  mt = _mm512_kmerge2l1h(m, m);
  _mm512_mask_i32loscatter_epi32(table, mt, hash,
  /* increment or reset offsets */      hi, 8);
  off = _mm512_add_epi32(off, mask_1);
  off = _mm512_mask_xor_epi32(off, m, off, off); }
```

The constants used in the procedures are the multiplicative hashing factor (**mask_factor**), the number of hash table buckets (**mask_buckets**), a special key for empty buckets (**mask_empty**), and constant numbers. The tuples are stored in the table using an interleaved layout, thus, we access the hash table buckets using 64-bit gathers. The code used to unpack the 32-bit keys and payloads from registers with 64-bit pairs (**_MM512_UNPACK_EPI32**) as well as the code for the inverse packing (**_MM512_PACK_EPI32**), are omitted.

Conflict detection, used here for hash table building, is the most common problem in vectorization with scatters. The future AVX 3 ISA provides specialized instructions (e.g., **_mm512_conflict_epi32**) that compare all pairs of vector lanes i, j for $i < j$ and generate a bitmask per lane of vector lanes to the left with the same value. The zero lanes are non-conflicting and thus we avoid using gathers and scatters.

Hash table probing may or may not reuse the output directly. In such a case, we must use the same buffering technique we used for selection scans. The difference from the code shown is that selective stores are used to write the data to the buffer, which is then flushed with streaming stores.

We now show the same hash table probing code for Haswell, using both selective loads and stores through permutation.

```
inv = _mm256_cmpeq_epi32(inv, inv);    // set mask
off = _mm256_xor_si256(off, off);      // reset vector
for (i = j = 0;  i + 8 <= S_tuples;) {
  /* load new items and skip reloads */
  new_key = _mm256_maskload_epi32(&S_keys[i], inv);
  new_pay = _mm256_maskload_epi32(&S_vals[i], inv);
  key = _mm256_andnot_si256(inv, key);
  pay = _mm256_andnot_si256(inv, pay);
  key = _mm256_or_si256(key, new_key);
  pay = _mm256_or_si256(pay, new_pay);
  /* compute the hash function and add offsets */
  hash = _mm256_mullo_epi32(key, mask_factor);
  off = _mm256_add_epi32(off, mask_1);
  off = _mm256_andnot_si256(inv, off);
  hash = _mm256_mulhi_epu32(hash, mask_buckets);
  hash = _mm256_add_epi32(hash, off);
  /* gather data from table and unpack */
  lo = _mm256_i32gather_epi64(table_64, hash, 8);
  hash = _mm256_permute4x64_epi64(hash, 14);
  hi = _mm256_i32gather_epi64(table_64, hash, 8);
  _MM256_UNPACK_EPI32(lo, hi, table_key, table_val);
  /* check who qualifies and who is invalid */
  inv = _mm256_cmpeq_epi32(table_key, mask_empty);
  out = _mm256_cmpeq_epi32(table_key, key);
  /* load permutation masks */
  m_out = _mm256_movemask_ps(_mm256_castsi256_ps(out));
  m_inv = _mm256_movemask_ps(_mm256_castsi256_ps(inv));
  perm_out_comp = _mm_loadl_epi64(&perm[m_out]);
  perm_inv_comp = _mm_loadl_epi64(&perm[m_inv ^ 255]);
  perm_out = _mm256_cvtepi8_epi32(perm_out_comp);
  perm_inv = _mm256_cvtepi8_epi32(perm_inv_comp);
  /* permute matching items */
  out    = _mm256_permutevar8x32_epi32(out, perm_out);
  RS_key = _mm256_permutevar8x32_epi32(key, perm_out);
  S_pay  = _mm256_permutevar8x32_epi32(pay, perm_out);
  R_pay  = _mm256_permutevar8x32_epi32(table_val,
  /* store matching items */             perm_out);
  _mm256_maskstore_epi32(  &keys_out[j], out, RS_key);
  _mm256_maskstore_epi32(&S_pays_out[j], out, S_pay);
  _mm256_maskstore_epi32(&R_pays_out[j], out, R_pay);
  j += _mm_popcnt_u64(m_out);
  /* permute invalid items */
  inv = _mm256_permutevar8x32_epi32(inv, perm_inv);
  key = _mm256_permutevar8x32_epi32(key, perm_inv);
  off = _mm256_permutevar8x32_epi32(off, perm_inv);
  i += _mm_popcnt_u64(m_inv); }
```

F. PARTITIONING

We show the code for radix histogram generation using 32-bit keys for Xeon Phi below. For the radix function, we use two shifts (`mask_shift_left`, `mask_shift_right`). To compute the replicated histogram index, we multiply by the vector lanes (`mask_16`) and add the lane offset (`mask_lane`).

```
for (i = 0;  i < tuples;  i += 16) {
  /* load keys and compute the radix */
  key = _mm512_load_epi32(&keys[i]);
  part = _mm512_sllv_epi32(key, mask_shift_left);
  part = _mm512_srlv_epi32(part, mask_shift_right);
  /* compute locations in the replicated histograms */
  part = _mm512_fmadd_epi32(part, mask_16, mask_lanes);
  /* increment the partial histograms */
  count = _mm512_i32gather_epi32(part, hists, 4);
  count = _mm512_add_epi32(count, mask_1);
  _mm512_i32scatter_epi32(hists, part, count, 4); }
/* merge partial histograms */
for (p = 0;  p != partitions;  ++p) {
  count = _mm512_load_epi32(&hists[p << 4]);
  hist[p] = _mm512_reduce_add_epi32(count); }
```

To compress the partial histograms in cache, we use 8-bit counts and add code to handle overflows. The assembly of Xeon Phi allows us to specify modifiers to gather and scatter instructions, that load or store 8-bit and 16-bit memory locations. The operations are executed on 16 32-bit lanes.

We also show vectorized binary search of 32-bit keys for Xeon Phi, which is used to compute range functions. We can patch the array so that $P = 2^n$. Haswell code is identical.

```
  hi = mask_partitions;            // broadcast P
  lo = _mm512_xor_epi32(lo, lo);  // the output vector
  for (i = 0;  i != log_partitions;  ++i) {
    /* gather middle splitter */
    mid = _mm512_add_epi32(lo, hi);
    mid = _mm512_srli_epi32(mid, 1);
    del = _mm512_i32gather_epi32(mid, &splitters[-1],
    /* compare and update pointers */ 4);
    m = _mm512_cmpgt_epi32(key, del);
    lo = _mm512_mask_blend_epi32(m, lo, mid);
    hi = _mm512_mask_blend_epi32(m, mid, hi); }
```

The code for conflict serialization using gathers and scatters is shown below. The constant permutation mask used to reverse the lanes of a vector (`mask_reverse`), also used to detect conflicts since due to having distinct values per lane. Using the conflict detection instruction provided by AVX 3, we can also implement conflict serialization. Given that AVX 3 does not provide vectorized bit count, we run a loop that clears one bit at a time per lane using `x & (x - 1)` and increments the non-zero lanes in the resulting offset vector.

```
__m512i _mm512_serialize_conflicts(__m512i part,
  /* reverse order of indexes */   int32_t *array) {
  part = _mm512_permutevar_epi32(part, mask_reverse);
  __m512i back, res = _mm512_xor_epi32(res, res);
  __mmask16 m = _mm512_kxnor(m, m);
  do {
    /* scatter unique values per lane */
    _mm512_mask_i32scatter_epi32(array, m, part,
    /* gather back values */      mask_reverse);
    back = _mm512_mask_i32gather_epi32(back, m, part,
    /* detect conflicting lanes */     array, 4);
    m = _mm512_mask_cmpneq_epi32_mask(m, back,
    /* increment offsets */            mask_reverse);
    res = _mm512_mask_add_epi32(res, m, res, mask_1);
  } while (!_mm512_kortestz(m, m));
  /* reverse result back to original order */
  return _mm512_permutevar_epi32(res, mask_reverse); }
```

The code for stable buffered shuffling for radix partitioning using 32-bit keys and payloads for Xeon Phi is shown below. Both the input and the output are assumed to be aligned on cache line boundaries. After the loop, we clean the buffer by flushing remaining tuples. If multiple threads are used, the buffer cleanup occurs after synchronizing, to fix the first cache line of each partition that may be corrupted.

When partitioning columns of multiple widths, assuming we partition one column at a time, the number of buffered items per partition varies. We implement 8-bit, 16-bit, 32-bit, and 64-bit shuffling by storing 64, 32, 16, and 8 items in the buffer per partition respectively. When we partition 64-bit columns, because 16 64-bit values can span across two cache lines, we scatter the tuples to the buffers in three phases instead of two, as overflows can occur twice per loop.

```
for (i = 0;  i < tuples;  i += 16) {
  /* load keys and payloads */
  key = _mm512_load_epi32(&keys[i]);
  pay = _mm512_load_epi32(&pays[i]);
  /* compute partition function (radix) */
  part = _mm512_sllv_epi32(key, mask_shift_left);
  part = _mm512_srlv_epi32(part, mask_shift_right);
  /* load current partition offsets */
  off = _mm512_i32gather_epi32(part, offsets, 4);
  /* detect conflicts (pollutes offsets array) */
  ser_off = _mm512_serialize_conflicts(part, offsets);
  /* scatter updated offsets (fixes offsets array) */
  off_back = _mm512_add_epi32(off_back, mask_1);
  off_back = _mm512_add_epi32(off, ser_off);
  _mm512_i32scatter_epi32(offsets, part, off_back, 4);
  _MM512_PACK_EPI32(key, pay, lo, hi);
  /* compute partition offsets in buffers */
  off = _mm512_and_epi32(off, mask_15);
  off = _mm512_add_epi32(off, ser_off);
  off_lo = _mm512_fmadd_epi32(part, mask_16, off);
  off_hi = _mm512_permute4f128_epi32(off_lo,
  /* find non-overflowing lanes */   _MM_PERM_BCDC);
  m = _mm512_cmpgt_epi32_mask(mask_15, off);
  mt = _mm512_knot(m);
  /* scatter pairs 1-8 to buffers (non-overflowing) */
  _mm512_mask_i32loscatter_epi64(buffers, m, off_lo,
  /* scatter pairs 9-16 to buffers ... */  lo, 8);
  m = _mm512_kmerge2l1h(m, m);
  _mm512_mask_i32loscatter_epi64(buffers, m, off_hi,
  /* find lanes with partitions to flush */  hi, 8);
  m = _mm512_cmpeq_epi32_mask(off, mask_15);
  if (!_mm512_kortestz(m, m)) {
    /* pack partitions that need to be flushed */
    _mm512_mask_packstorelo_epi32(flush_part, m, part);
    /* count how many partitions to flush */
    j = 0, k = _mm_countbits_64(_mm512_mask2int(m));
    do {
      p = flush_part[j];                // which partition
      o = (offsets[p] & -16) - 16;  // output location
      /* load key-payload pairs from the buffer */
      lo_f = _mm512_load_ps(&buffers[(p << 4) + 0]);
      hi_f = _mm512_load_ps(&buffers[(p << 4) + 8]);
      /* unpack pairs into keys and payloads */
      _MM512_UNPACK_PS(lo_f, hi_f, key_f, pay_f);
      /* flush to output using streaming stores */
      _mm512_storenrngo_ps(&keys_out[o], key_f);
      _mm512_storenrngo_ps(&pays_out[o], pay_f);
    } while (++j != k);
    if (!_mm512_kortestz(mt, mt)) {
      /* scatter pairs 1-8 to buffers (overflowing) */
      _mm512_mask_i32loscatter_epi64(&buffers[-16], mt,
      /* scatter pairs 9-16 ... */  off_lo, lo, 8);
      mt = _mm512_kmerge2l1h(mt, mt);
      _mm512_mask_i32loscatter_epi64(&buffers[-16], mt,
/* flush buffers after the loop */  off_hi, hi, 8);}}}
```

A Padded Encoding Scheme to Accelerate Scans by Leveraging Skew

Yinan Li Craig Chasseur Jignesh M. Patel

University of Wisconsin–Madison
{yinan, chasseur, jignesh}@cs.wisc.edu

ABSTRACT

In-memory data analytic systems that use vertical bit-parallel scan methods generally use encoding techniques. We observe that in such environments, there is an opportunity to turn skew in *both* the data and predicate distributions (usually a problem for query processing) into a benefit that can be leveraged to encode the column values. This paper proposes a *padded encoding* scheme to address this opportunity. The proposed scheme creates encodings that map common attribute values to codes that can easily be distinguished from other codes by only examining a few bits in the full code. Consequently, scans on columns stored using the padded encoding scheme can safely prune the computation without examining all the bits in the code, thereby reducing the memory bandwidth and CPU cycles that are consumed when evaluating scan queries. Our padded encoding method results in a fixed-length encoding, as fixed-length encodings are easier to manage. However, the proposed padded encoding may produce longer (fixed-length) codes than those produced by popular order-preserving encoding methods, such as dictionary-based encoding. This additional space overhead has the potential to negate the gains from early pruning of the scan computation. However, as we demonstrate empirically, the additional space overhead is generally small, and the padded encoding scheme provides significant performance improvements.

Categories and Subject Descriptors

H.2.4 [**Information Systems**]: Database Management—*systems*

Keywords

Encoding; Skew; Scan; Bit-parallel; Analytics

1. INTRODUCTION

There has been a recent flurry of interest in efficient scan methods for main memory analytic data processing systems (e.g. [7, 17, 25, 33, 40, 41, 46]). The key motivation for this interest is the frequent use of scans in these systems. There is also a recent trend towards building scan-based data processing engines, (e.g. [2, 13, 26, 28, 33, 38]). Such systems leverage the simplicity of scan operations to improve the effectiveness and predictability of the system, both in terms of query performance and scalability, when running in a distributed environment or on many-core machines.

To achieve maximum efficiency for the scan operation, data is often stored in compressed form using dictionary encoding or other fixed-length encoding schemes, e.g. null suppression and prefix suppression. Such schemes compress columns (attributes) and convert the native column (attribute) value to a code. The data for a column is represented using these codes, and these codes only use as many bits as are needed for the fixed-length encoding. The small code size presents opportunities to optimize the scan by performing predicate evaluation on multiple codes in parallel. However, existing encoding schemes do not exploit skew in the data distribution.

In this paper, we propose an encoding scheme called *padded encoding* to leverage skew to enhance scan performance. Similar to the well-known Huffman encoding [16], padded encoding assigns smaller code lengths to frequent values. However, in contrast to the Huffman encoding, padded encoding preserves the order of codes to match the order of the native column domain values, thereby allowing for predicate evaluation on the (compressed) codes directly for higher performance. Our encoding method pads these variable-length codes to a fixed-length code block, producing a fixed-length encoding scheme. Such fixed-length encoding are desirable, as they make storage management and query processing easier.

Scans on columns stored using our padded encoding scheme can *safely prune* the computation early without examining all the bits in each code when the code is stored in a vertical bit-packed representation. Such representations – e.g. [25, 29, 34] – store each bit position in a column separately (think of these as column-stores but at the bit level). Safe *early pruning* in such methods reduces the memory bandwidth and CPU cycles that are consumed when evaluate scan queries, thus improving performance. Our padded encoding scheme can enhance this early pruning effect.

We note that our proposed padded encoding may produce longer codes than those produced by simpler popular methods such as dictionary-based encoding. However, the average number of bits that we need to access when evaluating a scan predicate is actually reduced when there is skew in the data and/or predicate literals, resulting in improved scan performance. A subtle but crucial point to note is that the encoding that we propose takes into account *both* the distribution of the column values and the distribution of the values that are used in query predicates to improve the scan performance. Accounting for only one of these aspects potentially misses opportunities for holistic optimization.

With the design of the padded encoding scheme in place, we next develop a cost function to capture the effects of both data and predicate skew for improved scan performance. We present an algorithm that can construct an optimal padded encoding in $O(n^3)$ time, where n is the number of distinct codes/values in an encoding.

SIGMOD'15, May 31–June 4, 2015, Melbourne, Victoria, Australia.

http://dx.doi.org/10.1145/2723372.2737787.

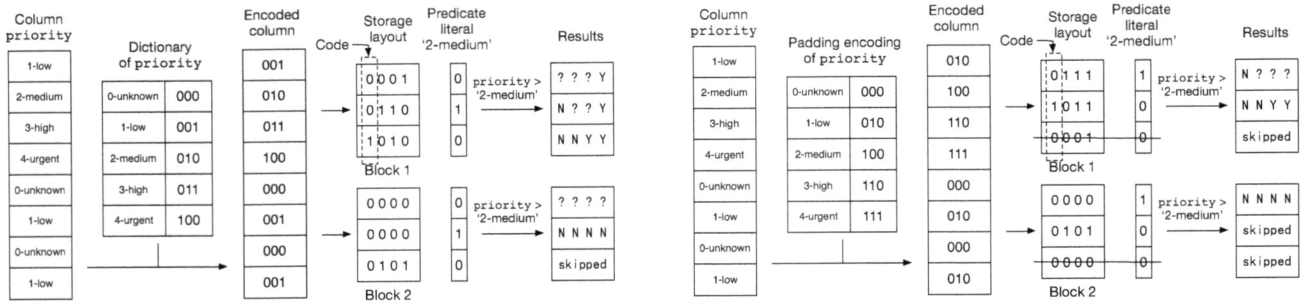

(a) Fixed-length encoding E_0 (b) Padded encoding E_2 (with base encoding E_1 from Figure 3)

Figure 1: Workflow of evaluating the predicate "`priority` > 2-medium" on the column `priority` with the example values.

However, this algorithm may be prohibitively expensive in practice when applied to a large domain of values. The next key contribution of this paper is to propose a more practical padded encoding algorithm that uses heuristics to provide a near-optimal solution while significantly reducing the algorithmic time complexity.

We have conducted an evaluation of the padded encoding using both micro-benchmarks and queries from the TPC-H benchmark. Our evaluation shows that the use of the padded encoding method improves scan performance by up to 3.8X for a highly skewed distribution. The additional overhead associated with the longer codes produced by the padded encoding is generally small, even in the worst-case where the padded encoding is constructed based on an incorrect distribution. We also evaluate our methods on the scan component of TPC-H queries, and show that the scan component can be accelerated as much as 3.4X. An astute reader may have noticed that the TPC-H dataset has no skew in the distribution of the column values, so any gains (even for scans) may seem surprising. We note that TPC-H dataset is in fact not an ideal test dataset for our method for precisely this reason, but our methods still improve the scan performance for some queries in the benchmark as these queries have predicate literal skew – i.e. certain constants in predicates appear more frequently, and our methods can leverage that skew. When the data also has skew, there is a synergistic effect and the relative advantage of our method increases, and the results with synthetic datasets show this effect. Conversely, if *both* the data and the predicate literals are uniformly distributed, our methods do not improve scan performance, and we acknowledge this fact.

This paper makes four contributions. First, to the best of our knowledge, this is the first work to draw insight from the observation that skew in the distribution of the constants in query predicates can be leveraged for improved scan performance. Second, we design a padded encoding scheme that leverages data and predicate literal skew to improve scan performance. Third, we map the padded encoding problem to existing work, and then design a new practical (heuristic) algorithm to compute a padded encoding. Finally, we empirically demonstrate the effectiveness of our method.

The remainder of this paper is organized as follows: Section 2 contains some preliminaries. Section 3 describes data and predicate literal skew. Section 4 describes the new padded encoding scheme, and Section 5 presents the algorithms to construct such encodings. Section 6 contains our experimental results. Related work is covered in Section 7, and Section 8 contains our concluding remarks.

2. BACKGROUND

2.1 Encoding techniques for database systems

Encoding techniques have been extensively used in main memory analytical data processing settings in both the research community (e.g. [1,4,5,10,20,25,26,35]), and in industry (e.g. [11,22,23, 32,41]). An encoding scheme compresses columns, or attributes, using a fixed-length order-preserving scheme, and converts a native column value to a *code*. In this paper, we use the term "code" to refer to an encoded column value. The data for a column is represented using these codes, and these codes only use as many bits as are needed for the fixed-length encoding. Note that the size of a code can be an arbitrary number of bits, and the code need not be aligned to the boundaries of a byte or a processor word.

In these compression methods, all value types, including numeric and string types, are encoded as an unsigned integer code, resulting in a discrete domain for column values. For example, an order-preserving dictionary can map strings to unsigned integers [5,20]. Floating point numbers can be converted using a scale scheme that multiples by a certain factor [10,36]. These compression methods maintain an order-preserving one-to-one mapping between the column values and the codes. As a result, column scans can often be directly evaluated on the codes. Codes may need to be recomputed if the underlying values change (i.e. new values are inserted/updated), but in many analytic settings the data is read-mostly. Nevertheless, methods to re-encode the database efficiently may be needed, and it is an interesting direction for future work.

2.2 Vertical bit-packing

This paper focuses on data stored in columnar vertical bit-packing format, such as [25,29,34], as these have been shown to be very efficient (see [25]). In this paper, we call these methods *vertical bit-packing*, as they use a bit-level columnar data organization; i.e., the highest-order bits of all column codes are arranged sequentially, followed by the second highest-order bit, and so on.

The example shown in Figure 1(a) illustrates how a scan operation work on a vertical bit-packed column. Here, the column `priority` is encoded using an order-preserving dictionary, converting the native column values to 3-bit codes. With vertical bit-packing, the eight codes in the column are broken into two fixed-length blocks. In each block, we store the most significant bits of the four codes in the first processor word (this example assumes 4-bit processor words), followed by the second most significant bits, and finally the least significant bits. Thus, the vertical dashed box in the figure represents the code for the first column value.

A scan operation on a vertical bit-packed column leverages a key insight that within each processor clock cycle there is "abundant parallelism" as the processor's ALU operates on multiple bits in parallel. To find the tuples with a priority value higher than "2-medium", we evaluate the predicate on each block independently. For each block, a vertical bit-packing scan algorithm compares each pair of bits at the same bit position of the column code and a code that is obtained by encoding the predicate literal using the same dictionary, starting from the most significant bits to the least significant bits. In addition, the scan performs this bitwise comparison operation on a vector of codes in parallel. Consider Block 1 in Figure 1(a). By comparing the first bit of the predicate constant code (0) with the first bits of the four codes (0001), we notice that only the 4th code is guaranteed to be greater than the constant at this point (we use the symbol "?" to denote an unknown result in the figure). Next, we expand the comparison to the second bit between the constant and the column codes. Now, we also know that the 1st code is less than the constant because their first two bits (00) are less than the first two bits of the constant (01). Finally, by looking at the least significant bits, we obtain the comparison results for all the four column codes. The predicate evaluation is converted to a bitwise logical computation on processor words that are fully filled with bits from different column codes.

In many cases, we can further improve the efficiency of a vertical bit-packed scan operation by safely pruning the computation without looking at all the bits in the column. The intuition behind this *early pruning* technique is as follows. Consider Block 2 in Figure 1(a). By comparing the leading two bits of the predicate literal code with the leading two bits of the four column codes in this block, we know that all the four codes (and hence the underlying column values) are less than "2-medium", and do not match the predicate. At this point, all the codes have a *definite* answer with respect to this predicate, and we can terminate the computation on this block. Organizing the column codes at the bit level allows us to skip over less significant bit positions once a predicate has been conclusively evaluated for all the codes in a block.

In general, each block contains a fixed number of codes, denoted as b. The block size b equals to the number of bits in a processor word ($b = 64$ for modern processor ALU words and 128 or 256 bits for SIMD vectors). The probability of early pruning increases at successively larger bit position numbers (counting from the most significant bit at position 0). More specifically, let $f(i)$ denote the early pruning probability at bit position i. According to the definition, $f(i)$ equals to the probability that the b column codes are all different from the predicate literal in the most significant i bits. Assume that a column code and the predicate literal have the same value at a certain bit position with a probability of 1/2 (which is true when the column values and the predicate literals are uniformly distributed, and the column values span the entire range of values that can be encoded by b bits.). Then, we have:

$$f(i) = (1 - (\frac{1}{2})^i)^b. \quad (1)$$

When $b = 64$, the early pruning probability at the bit position 12, $f(12)$, is above 99%, which indicates that in many cases we can *safely* terminate the scan after looking at the first 12 bits.

In this paper, we focus on designing encodings that go beyond simple dictionary encoding to further enhance scan performance by exploring two opportunities: 1) assigning short codes to frequent predicate literals such that scans only need to access the prefixes of column value codes to compute a definite result for the predicate; 2) assigning short codes to frequent column values such that we relax the assumption that column codes and predicate literal codes have the same value at a bit position with a probability value of 1/2 as discussed above, and make the early pruning occur at an earlier bit position. We will continue the example in Section 4 to show the basic idea behind the proposed encoding (Figure 1(b)).

3. WORKLOAD ANALYSIS

Data skew is a well-known phenomenon that has been extensively studied in the context of database systems. The term "data skew" loosely refers to several related but distinct types of skew. The key focus of this paper is on two types of data skew: column value skew and predicate literal skew. Both column values and predicate literals need to be converted to codes using the encoding algorithms that are proposed in this paper.

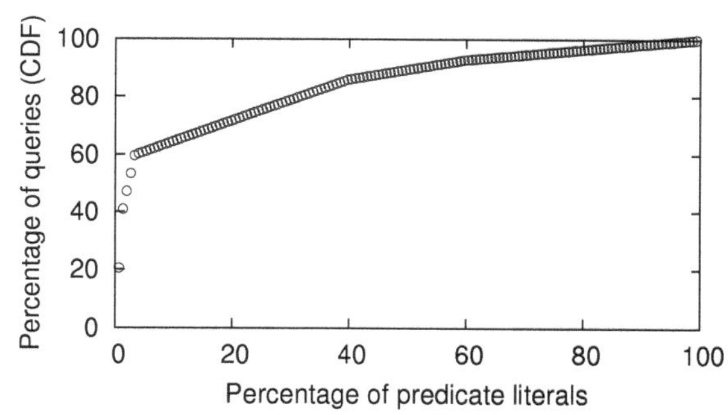

Figure 2: The distribution of predicate literals for the column `l_shipdate` in the TPC-H benchmark.

Column Value Skew (CVS). Column value skew, or attribute value skew, is the best-known type of data skew. It broadly denotes a non-uniform distribution of column (attribute) values in databases. Column value skew is a property of the real-world data, and is also called *intrinsic skew* in the literature [39]. In order to compute a column value distribution, we simply count the number of occurrences of each distinct column values in a certain column.

Predicate Literal Skew (PLS). Predicate literal skew denotes an uneven distribution in the literals that appear in query predicates, which generally tend to choose certain values more frequently than others. Like column value skew, predicate literal skew derives from real-world data, independent of the storage or query processing algorithms. In order to calculate the distribution of predicate literals, for each predicate in the form of $R.a \circ A$, where the operator $\circ \in \{<, >, =, \neq, \leq, \geq\}$, we increment the weight of the literal A; for each range predicate in the form of $R.a$ `between` A_0 `and` A_1, we update the weights of both A_0 and A_1 (a BETWEEN predicate is equivalent to a conjunction of two inequalities); for each IN predicate $R.a$ `in` $A_0, A_1, \cdots, A_n$, we increment the weights of all literals in the list, i.e. $A_0 \sim A_n$ (an IN predicate is equivalent to a disjunction of several equality predicates). We note that the distribution of predicate literals is independent of the operations that the predicate literal is involved in (e.g $<, >, =,$ `BETWEEN`, `IN`).

Predicate literal skew is related to but distinct from predicate skew, also known as filter skew [3, 36]. Predicate skew refers to a non-uniform distribution of the range of values that a predicate matches, whereas predicate literal skew refers to uneven distribution of the start and end values of the range, without regard to values between those bounds. For instance, the predicates "$R.a$ between A_0 and A_1" and "$R.a$ between A_0 and A_2" are two distinct predicates, but they share a common predicate literal A_0. Thus, the distribution on the predicate literals A_0, A_1, and A_2 is more skewed than the distribution on the predicates denoted by their range $[A_0, A_1]$ and $[A_0, A_2]$. In general, predicate literal skew has a higher degree of skew than predicate skew on a given database workload.

As a concrete example of predicate literal skew, consider the column `l_shipdate` in the TPC-H benchmark [37], which records the shipping dates of items. For each predicate literal on this column, e.g. the literal "1998-12-01" in the predicate "`l_shipdate` < 1998-12-01", we calculate its weight, i.e. how many instances of this literal occur in a predicate in one of the 22 TPC-H queries. Figure 2 plots the cumulative percentage of TPC-H queries that use a certain number of predicate literals from all those that appear in the benchmark. It is clear that the distribution of predicate literals on the column `l_shipdate` is highly skewed. (See [36] for other examples of skews in distribution of predicates.)

We note that the distribution of column values and the distribution of predicate literals can be unrelated. For example, one can imagine that shipping-date columns in a database may have frequent column values for dates that are close to holiday seasons, such as Thanksgiving and Christmas seasons, as there are likely more purchases made during these periods. In contrast, the frequent predicate literals that are used to query this attribute often include the first and the last day of each year, each quarter, each month, etc. These dates are frequently selected as predicate literals to run analysis queries on an annual, quarterly, and monthly basis.

The encoding algorithms proposed in this paper focus on scenarios with both skewed column values and skewed predicate literals.

4. PADDED ENCODING

There are two broad categories for data encoding schemes: *fixed-length encoding*, where each code consists of the same number of bits, and *variable-length encoding*, where the codes consist of a variable number of bits. Figure 3 shows a fixed-length encoding E_0 and a variable-length encoding E_1 constructed for the example column `priority`. While a variable-length encoding can leverage data skew to speed up scans by assigning smaller codes to frequent values, it is inefficient to locate and decode a code in an encoded column, and it is problematic to perform predicate evaluation on a set of codes in parallel (as we discussed in Section 2.2). Fixed-length encoding, on the other hand, misses the opportunity to leverage skew in the distribution of the column codes or the predicate literals to enhance scan performance for frequent values. Therefore, in this section, we propose a new encoding scheme, called *padded encoding*, to capture the best of both worlds.

Terminology. In this paper, we use the word *code* to refer to a finite sequence of bits (binary digits). An *encoding* is a mapping that associates a code c_i with each column value a_i in a database column. A code c is said to be in an encoding E if there exists one value which could be converted to c using E. We use $l(c)$ to denote the length of a code c in terms of the number of bits. In addition, we use $l(E)$ to denote the maximum length of all codes in an encoding E. We say that we *encode* a value a to mean that we convert the value a to a code, and *decode* a code c to mean that we convert the code c to its corresponding (native) value.

Values	Fixed-length encoding E_0	Variable-length encoding E_1	Padded encoding E_2
0-unknown	000	00	000
1-low	001	01	010
2-medium	010	10	100
3-high	011	110	110
4-urgent	100	111	111

Figure 3: Example encodings E_0, E_1, and E_2 constructed for the example column `priority`.

4.1 Basic idea behind padded encoding

The basic idea behind the padded encoding method is to pad the codes produced by a variable-length encoding scheme into a fixed-length code block, making all codes in the padded encoding identical in code length. Formally, given a variable-length encoding E', we construct a padded encoding E on E' as follows: for each code c' in E', we add a sequence of $l(E') - l(c')$ zeros at the end of the binary representation of the code c', producing a new code c, i.e. $c = c' \underbrace{00\cdots00}_{l(E')-l(c')}$; then, c is the code associated with the value of c' in the padded encoding E. We use the term *base encoding* to mean the variable-length encoding that the padded encoding is constructed upon. We define the *effective length* of a code c, denoted as $l^*(c)$, in a padded encoding E as the length of the corresponding code c' in the base encoding E', i.e. $l^*(c) = l(c')$.

Example: *Figure 3 shows the padded encoding E_2 that is constructed on the variable-length encoding E_1 for the example column values. Thus, E_1 is the base encoding of E_2. To produce E_2, zeros are appended to the codes 00, 01 and 10 associated with the values "0-unknown", "1-low", and "2-medium", respectively. Thus, all codes in E_2 have a 3-bit representation.*

The padded encoding method provides an opportunity for performing efficient predicate evaluation on an encoded column. On one hand, as all codes in a padded encoding have an identical code length, it is nearly as efficient as a fixed-length encoding to locate a code or perform predicate evaluation on an encoded column in parallel. On the other hand, it leverages the variable-length codes embedded in the padded encoded codes to speed up the predicate evaluation on frequent values (we will discuss two key properties that are required to achieve this goal in the section below). In short, the padded encoding has the potential to capture the best of both worlds in terms of scan performance on an encoded column.

4.2 Key properties

Two key properties are required of a base encoding in order to leverage padded encodings for efficient predicate evaluation on skewed column codes, or with skewed predicate literals:

- *Order-preserving property*. An encoding E has the order-preserving property if the numerical binary order of the codes (comparing bits lexicographically first-to-last) in E corresponds to the order of the associated values in E.
- *Prefix property*. A base encoding E' has the prefix property if no code in E' is a prefix of any other code in E'.

The order-preserving property of the base encoding enables predicate evaluation directly on the code domain when performing a scan. Lemma 4.1 shows that the order-preserving property is retained when constructing a padded encoding on a base encoding. The proof for this lemma appears in Appendix A.

LEMMA 4.1. *A padded encoding has the order-preserving property if its base encoding has the order-preserving property.*

To perform a scan on an order-preserving padded encoded column, it is usually unnecessary to convert all codes in the column to the native column values and compare them with the predicate literal. Instead, since the order-preserving property guarantees that the order of codes is identical to the order of native column values, we can encode the predicate literal and compare all codes with the code of the predicate literal directly without decoding. For example, say that we wished to find all tuples whose priority is higher than "2-medium" using the order-preserving example padded encoding E_2 in Figure 3. To accomplish this task, we simply convert the predicate literal to a code "100" using E_2, and then scan the column to find all tuples whose code is greater than "100".

The base (variable-length) encoding should also have the prefix property to speed up scans with frequent predicate constants. The lemma below shows the basic principle behind this observation.

LEMMA 4.2. *The answer to a comparison between two codes c_1 and c_2 in a padded encoding E can be obtained by comparing up to $\min(l^*(c_1), l^*(c_2))$ leading bits so long as E's base encoding has the prefix property.*

PROOF. Let $P_l(c)$ denote the prefix of a code c of length l bits. We use c_1' and c_2' to denote the corresponding codes of c_1 and c_2 in the base encoding of E, respectively. According to the definitions, we have $c_1' = P_{l^*(c_1)}(c_1)$ and $c_2' = P_{l^*(c_2)}(c_2)$. Without loss of generality, we assume $l^*(c_1) < l^*(c_2)$. If we have $P_{l^*(c_1)}(c_1) = P_{l^*(c_1)}(c_2)$, then c_2 must be identical to c_1, because there does not exist another code in the base encoding of E whose prefix is the same as $c_1' = P_{l^*(c_1)}(c_1)$, according to the prefix property of the base encoding. If $P_{l^*(c_1)}(c_1) < P_{l^*(c_1)}(c_2)$, we have $c_1 < P_{l^*(c_1)}(c_1) + 1 \leq P_{l^*(c_1)}(c_2) \leq c_2$, which implies $c_1 < c_2$. Similarly, if $P_{l^*(c_1)}(c_1) > P_{l^*(c_1)}(c_2)$, we have $c_2 < P_{l^*(c_1)}(c_2) + 1 \leq P_{l^*(c_1)}(c_1) \leq c_1$, which implies $c_1 > c_2$. In summary, the comparison result between $P_{l^*(c_1)}(c_1)$ and $P_{l^*(c_1)}(c_2)$ implies the comparison result between c_1 and c_2. Thus, we can compare the prefixes of length $l^*(c_1) = \min(l^*(c_1), l^*(c_2))$ to obtain the comparison result between c_1 and c_2. This completes the proof. □

Using Lemma 4.1 and Lemma 4.2, we can devise an efficient scan method for skewed column values and skewed predicate literals using padded encoding.

With predicate literal skew it is only necessary to access enough leading bits of the codes, i.e. the effective length of the literal code, until we get a definite result on the predicate. Given a vertical bit-packed column where all bit positions are stored separately (see Section 2.2), this method could enhance the scan performance by reducing both the number of instructions and the memory bandwidth that is needed to compute the scan operation.

Example: *Figure 1(b) shows the process of evaluating the example predicate on a column encoded with the padded encoding E_2. The effective length of the code associated with the predicate literal "2-medium" is two. Thus, we only need to access the leading two bits of each code to obtain the comparison results. Let us first focus on Block 1 in Figure 1(b). Even though the 2nd code has the same value as the predicate literal code in the leading two bits, we can still safely terminate the comparison at this bit position, as the 2nd code is guaranteed to be equal to the predicate literal code according to Lemma 4.2. Consequently, the scan with E_2 has the potential to achieve a 1.5X speedup over the scan with E_0 that accesses all three bits of all codes in Block 1 (shown in Figure 1(a)).*

For column value skew, we could quickly get definite results when comparing a set of column codes to a literal code, increasing the probability that the comparison between the whole set of column codes in a block and the literal code safely terminates at an early bit position. To achieve this goal, we assign short codes for frequent column values, which in turn increases the likelihood that codes have distinct bit values in the leading bits.

Example: *Reconsider Block 2 in Figure 1. Recall that with the encoding E_0, the column values "0-unknown" and "1-low" have the same bit value as the predicate literal "2-medium" at the 1st bit position (as shown in Figure 1(a)). The early pruning then occurs at the 2nd bit position. In contrast, the padded encoding E_2 assigns codes with short effective lengths to the frequent values "0-unknown", "1-low", and "2-medium" (as shown in Figure 1(b)), which generally increases the likelihood that the codes have different values in the leading bits. In the case of Block 2, the column codes (000, 010) and the predicate literal code (100) have a distinct bit value at the most significant bit position. Thus, we can prune the predicate evaluation on Block 2 earlier at the first bit position. As compared to E_0, E_2 has the potential to be 2X faster when evaluating the scan on Block 2.*

4.3 Additional Discussion

We discuss several additional optimizations for padded encodings in Appendix C. More specifically, we present a method to support scans that compare two distinct columns in Appendix C.1. Then, we discuss why and how we construct a padded encoding for clustered columns in Appendix C.2. In Appendix C.3, we describe a method that transforms a predicate to a semantically identical predicate, but with a more frequent predicate literal. Finally, we discuss how we preserve data locality in Appendix C.4.

5. ENCODING ALGORITHMS

In this section, we present a series of encoding algorithms to construct optimal and near-optimal variable-length encodings. Then, a padded encoding can be constructed by appropriately padding these variable-length encodings.

5.1 Problem definition

Encoding algorithms for data skew take as input a sequence of n values, $a_0, a_1, \cdots, a_{n-1}$, that have been sorted in a domain-specific order, e.g. an alphabetical order for string values. We define the distribution of predicate literals as a sequence of weights, $p_0, p_1, \cdots, p_{n-1}$, where p_i represents the frequency that the value a_i is selected as a predicate literal in queries. Similarly, we define the distribution of column values as a sequence of weights, $q_0, q_1, \cdots, q_{n-1}$, where q_i represents the frequency that the value a_i occurs in a column. The sum of all column value weights and predicate literal weights equals 1, i.e. $p_0 + p_1 + \cdots + p_{n-1} = 1$, and $q_0 + q_1 + \cdots + q_{n-1} = 1$.

The encoding problem is to find a variable-length encoding E with minimum value for the *cost of encoding* $C(E)$ amongst all variable-length encodings that have both the order-preserving property and the prefix property. The cost of encoding $C(E)$ is derived in more detail below in Section 5.2.

Symbol	Definition
n	The number of distinct values in the column
b	The number of codes in a block
a_i	The i-th value
c_i	The code of a_i
$l(c_i)$	The code length of c_i
p_i (q_i)	The predicate literal (column value) frequency of a_i
u_i (v_i)	The i-th internal (leaf) node in the binary tree
$w_p(u)$ ($w_q(u)$)	The predicate literal (column value) weight of a subtree rooted at an internal node u

Table 1: Summary of notations.

5.2 Cost model

In this section, we present a framework to capture data and predicate skews, and then use that framework to produce a mathematical model to create an optimal encoding. Given a variable-length encoding E, we quantify the cost of encoding $C(E)$ in terms of the expected cost of running a scan operation with this encoding. We validate this cost function in Appendix F. The notations used in this section are summarized in Table 1.

In the interest of simplicity of presentation, we use a binary tree representation to show a variable-length encoding. Each leaf node of the binary tree corresponds to a value in the encoding whose binary code defines a path from the root of the binary tree to the corresponding leaf node. In this path traversal, choosing the left branch at the level i corresponds to setting the i-th bit in the code to 0, and choosing the right branch maps to a bit value of 1. Figure 4 shows the binary tree representation of the example variable-length encoding E_1 from Figure 3.

The values associated with the leaf nodes are sorted in the domain specific order of the values, ensuring the encoding's order-preserving property. Let v_i denote the $(i + 1)$-th leaf node in the

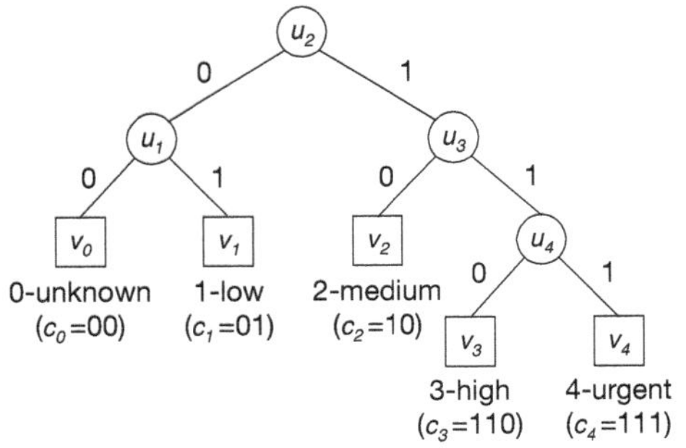

Figure 4: The binary tree representation of the example variable-length encoding E_1 from Figure 3.

binary tree. Thus, the leaf node v_i corresponds to the value a_i with the predicate literal weight p_i and the column code weight q_i. Also, we use $u_1 \sim u_{n-1}$ to denote the $n-1$ internal nodes. Here, u_i is the i-th internal node in symmetric order (i.e. in-order). We also use $w_p(u)$ to denote the predicate literal weight of a subtree rooted at an internal node u, i.e. the sum of the predicate literal weights p_i of all leaf nodes in this subtree. Similarly, $w_q(u)$ denotes the column code weight of a subtree rooted at the internal node u.

With the binary tree representation, the cost of encoding $C(E)$ can be calculated as the sum of the cost for each internal node, denoted as $C(u_i)$, as shown in Formula 2. Formula 3 shows the cost function for each internal node $C(u_i)$. Collectively, Formula 2 and 3 provide the cost function that is needed by the encoding algorithms. The unit of cost in these formula is the cost of accessing and comparing at one bit position.

$$C(E) = \sum_{i=1}^{n-1} C(u_i). \tag{2}$$

$$C(u_i) = (1 - (1 - w_q(u_i))^b) \cdot w_p(u_i). \tag{3}$$

Note that the cost of each internal node $C(u_i)$ only relies on the predicate literal weights and the column value weights of nodes that are in the subtree rooted at the internal node u_i, as $w_p(u_i)$ (or $w_q(u_i)$) represents the sum of the predicate literal (or the column value) weights of all leaf nodes in the subtree under u_i. This key property implies that we can design more efficient recursive encoding algorithms compared to an algorithm that exhaustively searches over all possible encodings.

Example: *Consider computational cost of the encoding E_1 shown in Figure 4. Assume that the column value weight of a value is the frequency that the value occurs in the example column shown in Figure 1. Thus we have $q_0 = 2/8$, $q_1 = 3/8$, $q_2 = q_3 = q_4 = 1/8$. We also suppose that the only value that can be used as a predicate literal is "2-medium", thus we have $p_2 = 1.0$, $p_0 = p_1 = p_3 = p_4 = 0.0$. Suppose that the block size b is 4 in this example. Then, we can calculate the cost associated with the internal node u_3 using Formula 3 as: $C(u_3) = (1-(1-(1/8+1/8+1/8))^4)\cdot 1 = 0.847$. Similarly, the cost of the root node is $C(u_2) = (1-(1-1)^4)\cdot 1 = 1$. The costs of other internal nodes are all zeros. Finally, we obtain the cost of the encoding E_1 as: $C(E_1) = C(u_2)+C(u_3) = 1.847$. In this case, E_1 actually has the minimum cost amongst all encodings that have both the prefix and the order-preserving properties.*

In the remainder of this section, we illustrate how we derive the cost function shown in Formula 2 and 3. The cost of the encoding $C(E)$ is the weighted sum of the cost of each literal code c_k, denoted as $C(c_k)$, over all possible literal codes in E, i.e. $c_0 \sim c_n$. Note that if a predicate literal is not present in the encoding, then it cannot be converted to a code. In this case, we transform it to a value in the encoding, without changing the semantic meaning of the predicates, using the method presented in Appendix C.3. Thus, we can express $C(E)$ in terms of the number of values (i.e. n as defined in the beginning of Section 5.1) as follows:

$$C(E) = \sum_{k=0}^{n-1} C(c_k) \cdot p_k \tag{4}$$

Next, we analyze the cost of a literal code c_k, $C(c_k)$, in terms of the cost of a scan operation on a block containing b codes, i.e. the cost of comparing a vector of b column codes to the literal code c_k. According to Lemma 4.2, the number of bits that must be accessed in order to obtain a definite answer for a comparison of a column code with the literal code c_k, is bounded by the length of the literal code: $l(c_k)$. Thus, even in the worst-case, we can always complete the comparison between the entire block and the literal code c_k by comparing each bit of the literal code c_k. In certain cases, the comparison terminates before accessing all the $l(c_k)$ bits due to early pruning (see Section 2.2). We use $f(i)$ to denote the early pruning probability at the i-th bit position, i.e. the probability that we can terminate the computation at the i-th bit position (note, $f(0) = 0$ as the early pruning cannot occur before the first bit position). Let us assume that the cost of accessing a bit position is 1. Then, the cost associated with the i-th bit position can be represented by the probability that early pruning does not occur in its immediately previous bit position, i.e. $1 - f(i-1)$. Thus, the total cost for the predicate literal c_k is the sum of the costs at each bit position of c_k, i.e.:

$$C(c_k) = \sum_{i=1}^{l(c_k)} (1 - f(i-1)). \tag{5}$$

Next, we derive the early pruning probability $f(i)$, i.e. the probability that the b column codes in a block are all different from the predicate literal c_k in the most significant i bits, by using the binary tree representation of the encoding. With the binary tree representation, the literal code c_k corresponds to a path from the root to the leaf node v_k. Let $U_i(c_k)$ denote the node at level i on the path associated with c_k (thus, the edge between nodes $U_{i-1}(c_k)$ and $U_i(c_k)$ corresponds to the i-th bit of c_k). The codes that share the common prefix of length i with the literal code c_k are exactly those in the subtree rooted at $U_i(c_k)$. Consequently, the probability that a code is identical to the literal code c_k in the leading i bits is the probability that the column code is in the subtree rooted at $U_i(c_k)$, i.e. the column value weight of the subtree $w_q(U_i(c_k))$. Hence, the early pruning probability on a block of b column codes is:

$$f(i) = (1 - w_q(U_i(c_k)))^b \tag{6}$$

By substituting Equation 5 and Equation 6 into Equation 4, the cost of the encoding E can be rewritten as:

$$C(E) = \sum_{k=0}^{n-1} (\sum_{i=0}^{l(c_k)-1} 1 - (1 - w_q(U_i(c_k)))^b) \cdot p_k \tag{7}$$

Now, we reformulate formula 7 so that the cost of the encoding E is the sum of the cost on each internal node u_i, denoted as $C(u_i)$, of the binary tree associated with E. For a given literal code c_k, Formula 7 essentially adds the cost $(1-(1-w_q(U_i(c_k)))^b)\cdot p_k$ to each internal node $U_i(c_k)$ that we encounter in the path corresponding to c_k (note that the leaf nodes, which can be represented by $U_{l(c_k)}(c_k)$ in a path for c_k, are not involved in Equation 7). Thus, the cost associated with each internal node $C(u_i)$ is the sum of the cost associated with u_i in $C(c_k)$ for all possible literal codes c_k that are in the subtree rooted at u_i, as shown in Formula 3. Finally, we complete our derivation by rewriting Equation 7 as the sum of cost of all the internal nodes, obtaining Formula 2.

5.3 Optimal algorithm

We first present the optimal algorithm to find the minimum cost binary tree. The binary tree with the minimum cost, $C(E)$, is called an *optimal tree*. A key observation for an optimal tree is stated in the Lemma below. (The proof for this lemma is in Appendix A.)

LEMMA 5.1. *All subtrees of an optimal tree are optimal.*

According to the lemma above, the problem at hand exhibits an optimal substructure: that is, the solution to the entire problem relies on solutions to subproblems. Naturally then, we can use a dynamic programing-based solution for this problem. Let us define a function $C(i,j)$ as the minimum cost of a binary tree built on a sequence of leaf nodes starting from the i-th leaf node v_i to the j-th leaf node v_j, where $(0 \leq i \leq j < n)$. In addition, we use $W_p(i,j)$ to denote the predicate literal weight of a subtree built on $v_i \sim v_j$, i.e. $W_p(i,j) = \sum_{k=i}^{j} p_k$. Similarly, let $W_q(i,j)$ denote the column code weight of a subtree built on $v_i \sim v_j$, i.e. $W_q(i,j) = \sum_{k=i}^{j} q_k$.

We can define $C(i,j)$ recursively as follows. If $i = j$, the problem is trivial; the tree consists of just one node with the cost equal to 0. To compute $C(i,j)$ when $i < j$, we take advantage of the optimal substructure shown in Lemma 5.1. We enumerate the value of k between i and j, splitting the tree between the $(k-1)$-th and k-th leaf nodes. Then $C(i,j)$ equals the minimum cost to compute the left subtree and the right subtree, plus the cost associated with the root node. Note that according to Equation 3, the cost of the root node is independent of the structure of the tree, and can be calculated as: $(1-(1-W_q(i,j))^b) \cdot W_p(i,j)$. Thus, we have

$$C(i,j) = \begin{cases} 0 & \text{, if } i = j \\ \min\limits_{i<k\leq j} (C(i,k-1) + C(k,j)) + & \\ \qquad (1-(1-W_q(i,j))^b) \cdot W_p(i,j) & \text{, if } i < j. \end{cases}$$

Algorithm 1 shows the pseudocode for an iterative implementation of this dynamic-programming solution (we omit the pseudocode for constructing the optimal tree). This solution requires a running time of $O(n^3)$ to find the optimal tree, because there are $O(n^2)$ cells in the matrix of $C(i,j)$, and it takes $O(n)$ instructions to compute each cell. The algorithm requires $O(n^2)$ space to the store the $C(i,j)$ matrix.

Algorithm 1 Computing the optimal encoding

Input: The predicate literal weights $p_0, p_1, \cdots, p_{n-1}$
The column code weights $q_0, q_1, \cdots, q_{n-1}$
Output: The minimum cost of the tree
$W_p(i,j) := \sum_{k=i}^{j} p_k$, for $0 \leq i \leq j < n$
$W_q(i,j) := \sum_{k=i}^{j} q_k$, for $0 \leq i \leq j < n$
$C_q(i,i) := 0$, for $0 \leq i < n$
for $d := 2 \dots n$ **do**
  for $i := 0 \dots n-d$ **do**
    $j := i + d - 1$
    $C(i,j) := \infty$
    for $k := i+1 \dots j$ **do**
      if $C(i,k-1) + C(k,j) < C(i,j)$ **then**
        $C(i,j) := C(i,k-1) + C(k,j)$
    $C(i,j) := C(i,j) + (1-(1-W_q(i,j))^b) \cdot W_p(i,j)$
return $C(0, n-1)$;

5.4 Near-optimal algorithm: AMPE

Since the optimal algorithm has an $O(n^3)$ time complexity, it is impractical for large values of n. In this section, we present a heuristic-based approach that provides a faster, but near-optimal solution. We call the algorithm AMPE for **A**pproximate **M**ethod to compute **P**added **E**ncoding. The AMPE algorithm uses two primary heuristics, namely the monotonicity heuristic and the early pruning heuristic, and the code size reduction technique (presented in Appendix E). We describe the two heuristics next.

5.4.1 *Monotonicity heuristic*

The first heuristic is from Knuth's solution to the problem of the optimal binary search tree [18, 19]. Knuth observed that there is a *monotonicity property* in the optimal binary search tree problem: that is, the root of the optimal tree constructed on a sequence of continuous leaf nodes $v_i \sim v_j$, where $(0 \leq i \leq j < n)$, is never on the left of the root of the optimal tree constructed on the leaf nodes $v_i \sim v_{j-1}$. Formally, let $R(i,j)$ denote the root position for the subtree for the leaf nodes $v_i \sim v_j$. Let r denote the node that is the root of this subtree. Then, the $R(i,j)$ value is computed as the index of the leaf node that is the leftmost leaf node in the right subtree of the node r. For example, in the encoding tree shown in Figure 4, $R(0,4) = 2$ and $R(2,4) = 3$. The monotonicity property states that $R(i,j-1) \leq R(i,j)$. We can also obtain $R(i,j) \leq R(i+1,j)$ according to the symmetric property.

The encoding problem does not have a monotonicity property, as it uses a different cost function from the optimal binary search tree problem (see Appendix D for a counterexample). Nevertheless, we observe that it is fairly rare that the root position of the optimal tree breaks the monotonicity property. Thus, we use the monotonicity property as a heuristic to quickly find a near-optimal solution.

The monotonicity heuristic suggests an improved algorithm. When computing the minimum value of $C(i,j)$, it is not necessary to enumerate all values in the entire range $(i \leq k < j)$ to find the root position of the optimal tree, but we can focus on the limited range between $R(i,j-1)$ and $R(i+1,j)$. We show the pseudocode for the modified dynamic programming approach with the monotonicity heuristic in Appendix B. With the monotonicity heuristic, the running time of the algorithm is reduced to $O(n^2)$ [18].

5.4.2 *Early pruning heuristic*

This second heuristic is based on an observation of the early pruning technique (see Section 2.2). When comparing a block of b column codes to a literal code starting from the most significant bit, the probability for early pruning increases as the bit position number increases. At a certain position, the early pruning probability becomes very close to 100%, which indicates that in many cases we can safely terminate the scan after looking at a limited number of leading bits. In other words, the effects of both the predicate literal weights and the column code weights decline as we go down the binary tree from the root to the bottom levels, leading to a relatively balanced tree structure near the bottom of the binary tree. It is also the case that the leaf nodes that are close to the root in an optimal tree are usually associated with the most frequent values.

With this early pruning heuristic, we now present a preprocessing algorithm. Given a sequence of n values, we first find up to $2k$ values, called *frequent values*, which includes values with the top k predicate literal weights or with the top k column code weights. The other values remaining in the sequence are then split into a set of segments by the frequent values. For each segment, we construct a balanced binary tree. The root of each balanced binary tree is treated as a "virtual" value with the predicate literal (column code) weight equal to be the sum of the predicate literal (column code) weights of all the values in this subtree. A follow-up encoding algorithm is then performed on up to $2k$ frequent values and the up to $2k + 1$ "virtual" values.

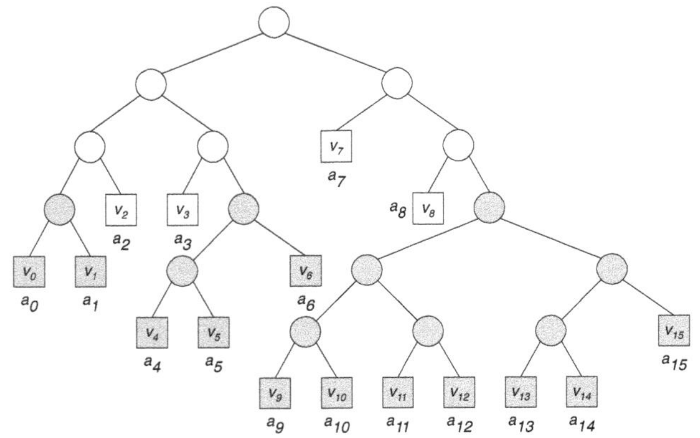

Figure 5: The tree constructed with the early pruning heuristic.

Figure 5 shows an example binary tree constructed on 16 values using the early pruning heuristic. In this example, we construct the binary tree with the 4 most frequent values (a_2, a_3, a_7, and a_8) ($k = 4$). Other values are split into three segments ($a_0 \sim a_1$, $a_4 \sim a_6$, and $a_9 \sim a_{15}$). For each segment, we build a balanced binary tree (marked grey in the figure), forming the subtrees with 2, 3, and 7 leaf nodes, respectively. Thus, a follow-up encoding algorithm needs to process only 7 nodes (4 frequent nodes plus the 3 roots of these balanced subtrees), instead of all the 16 nodes.

We select the value of k according to the bit position number where early pruning occurs with a fairly high probability. We denoted this bit position as e. Then, there are up to 2^e leaf nodes in the top part of the optimal tree that has a relatively unbalanced structure. Hence, we set $k = 2^e$. For example, when the block size $b = 64$, $e \approx 12$, then we set $k = 2^{12} = 4196$.

This algorithm takes $O(n \log k)$ time to find the frequent values, and then $O(n)$ time to construct balanced binary subtrees. Together with the monotonicity heuristic, the follow-up encoding algorithm requires a running time of $O(k^2)$, as there are up to $2k$ frequent values and up to $2k + 1$ "virtual" values after the preprocessing algorithm. Thus, the time complexity of the near-optimal algorithm is $O(n \log k + k^2)$. The algorithm's space complexity is $O(n + k^2)$. With this near-optimal encoding algorithm, it now becomes practical to tackle the encoding problem for large values of n.

6. EVALUATION

Our experimental server has dual 2.0 GHz Intel Xeon E5-2620 6-core processors, and 32GB of 1600 MHz DDR3 main memory. The server runs 64-bit Linux 2.6.32. All experiments are run in an in-memory setting as the database fits entirely in memory.

We have implemented the encoding techniques proposed in this paper in C++. We used an implementation of the BitWeaving/V [25] technique, as the vertical bit-packing method to store and scan the encoded columns. We compiled the code using g++ 4.4.7 with optimization flags (-O3 -march=native).

6.1 Micro-benchmark evaluation

For the first experiment, we create a table `R` with a single column `a`. The column `R.a` contains one billion values. (We have also experimented with different cardinalities for this table, and found that the results are similar to the case with one billion values; thus, we omit these additional results in the interest of space.) The column values are integer numbers in the range of $[0, 2^d)$, where d is a parameter to adjust the domain size. By default, the parameter d is set to 12, but we evaluate the impact of this parameter (see Section 6.1.3). The performance of an encoding is evaluated by the time it takes to execute a scan query on the column with a simple predicate `R.a < A`. The value of `A` is selected based on the distribution of the predicate literals. The performance for other predicates is similar to that with the less than (<) predicate, and is omitted in interest of space.

In the evaluation below, we generate three set of workloads with: a) only skewed predicate literals, called *UD-SP* (Uniform-Data-Skewed-Predicates), b) only skewed column values, called *SD-UP* (Skewed-Data-Uniform-Predicates), and c) with both skewed predicate literals and skewed column values, called *SD-SP* (Skewed-Data-Skewed-Predicates). The skewed column values/predicate literals follow a Zipfian distribution, with the skew factor varying from 1.0 to 2.0. For SD-SP, the distribution of column values are different from the distribution of predicate literals.

We construct padded encodings on the three sets of workloads. The encodings are constructed on all integer values in the domain, no matter whether or not a value appears in the column. For the workload UD-SP (or SD-UP), we set equal values for the column value (or predicate literal) weights, i.e. $q_0 = q_1 = \cdots = q_{n-1} = \frac{1}{n}$, (or $p_0 = p_1 = \cdots = p_{n-1} = \frac{1}{n}$). We use the AMPE algorithm (see Section 5.4) to construct the padded encodings.

To serve as a yardstick, we also include the performance on an uniformly distributed workload, called *UD-UP* (Uniform-Data-Uniform-Predicates). To encode this workload, we use a simple null suppression encoding that removes leading zeros and converts the column values in the range $[0, 2^d)$ to d-bit codes. This simple encoding does not exploit the skewed distribution of column values and predicate literals.

Each experiment was run 10 times with different datasets that are produced by our Zipfian data generator. For each run, we generate 100 queries based on the predicate literal distribution. We report the average execution time for the 10×100 queries.

6.1.1 Varying skew factor

In this evaluation below, we evaluate the scan performance (the focus of this paper) with the padded encoding on the three sets of workloads (UD-SP, SD-UP, and SD-SP).

Figure 6(a) shows the scan performance with padded encoding when varying the skew factor of the Zipfian distribution. We also mark a horizontal line in the figure to indicate the scan performance of the simple encoding on UD-UP. As can be seen in the figure, not surprisingly, the scan execution time reduces as the skew increases on all the three workloads. On UD-SP, the padded encoding improves scan performance by up to 3.6X over the simple encoding. On SD-UP, the padded encoding is relatively less effective than that on UD-SP, achieving an up to 65% speedup over the simple encoding. The reason for this behavior is because the scan performance is determined by: 1) the effective code lengths of all column codes in a block, and 2) the effective code length of the only predicate literal code. Thus, a short code may enhance the scan performance if it is used as a predicate literal, but might not necessarily improve the scan performance if it is contained in a block as a column code.

As can be seen in Figure 6(a), the padded encoding results in the best scan performance on SD-SP, achieving up to 4.0X speedup over the simple encoding. We see that the performance improvement on SD-SP is mainly due to predicate literal skew, rather than column value skew, as the SD-SP curve is much closer to the UD-SP curve. The small gap between the SD-SP and the UD-SP curves is due to the fact that the encoding on SD-SP is also optimized for column value skew, in addition to predicate literal skew.

To better understand the effects of the padded encoding on the three workloads, we plot the range of *effective code length*, i.e. the code length without the padded zeros, on UD-SP, SD-UP, and SD-SP in Figure 6(b), 6(c), and 6(d), respectively. In these figures,

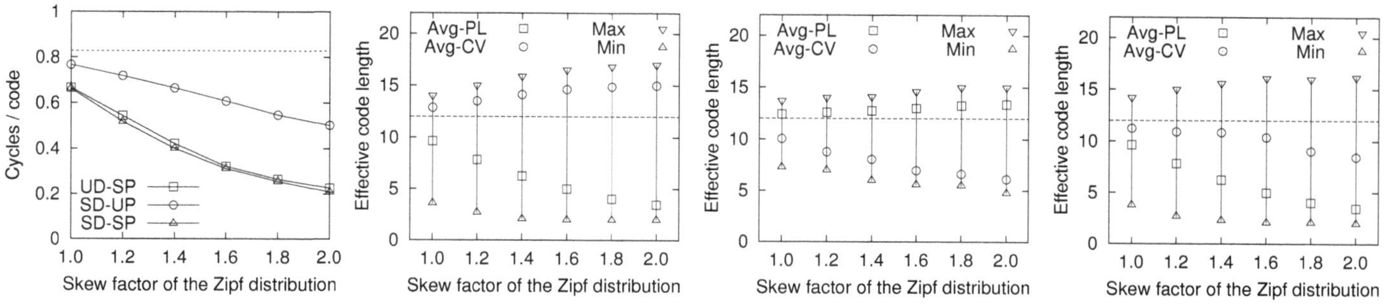

(a) Execution time (b) Effective code length on UD-SP (c) Effective code length on SD-UP (d) Effective code length on SD-SP

Figure 6: Execution time and effective code length of the padded encoding scheme when varying the Zipfian skew factor.

the bar at each skew factor value represents the range of effective code length of the padded encoding (thus, the low-end and high-end of the bar represent the minimum and maximum effective code length). We also plot two points in each bar corresponding to the weighted average effective code length based on the predicate literal weights (with the tag "Avg-PL"), and column value weights (with the tag "Avg-CV"), respectively. Essentially, the "Avg-PL" point represents the average effective code length of the values that are used in predicates, whereas the "Avg-CV" point shows the average effective code length of the codes in the column. In these figures, we also draw a horizontal line at 12 to represent the code length of the simple encoding scheme.

As can be seen from Figure 6(b) $\sim$ 6(d), the maximum code length of the encodings on the UD-SP, the SD-UP, and the SD-SP datasets are 17.0, 15.0, and 16.2, respectively. All these padded encodings amplify the size of codes, as compared to the code length 12 of the simple encoding. In spite of this, the average effective code length generally decreases as the skew increases. On the UD-SP dataset, the average effective code length with the predicate literal weights (Avg-PL) drops quickly. However, since the encoding on the UD-SP dataset only optimizes for predicate literal skew, the weighted average effective code length with the column value weights (Avg-CV) increases as the maximum effective code length increases. Similarly, the encoding on the SD-UP dataset only reduces the average effective code length with the column value weights. On the SD-SP dataset, nevertheless, the encoding makes a trade-off between the predicate literal skew and column value skew, and therefore reduces the average effective code length with the column value weights and the predicate literal weights. We also see that the encoding on the SD-SP dataset reduces the code length by around 1 bit while improving the scan performance relative to that on the UD-SP dataset.

The space that is needed to store an encoded column is proportional to the code length of the encoding, i.e. the maximum effective code length of the padded encoding (the "Max" points in Figure 6 (b-d)), or the code length of the simple encoding (the dashed lines in Figure 6 (b-d)). Thus, as can be seen in Figure 6 (b-d), the column encoded with the padded encoding is up to 42%, 25%, or 35% larger than that with the simple encoding on the UD-SP, the SD-UP, and the SD-SP datasets, respectively.

6.1.2 Varying locality

Next, we evaluate the effects of the locality of frequent values on the scan performance with padded encoding. Consider the shipping date example that we discussed previously in Section 3. The frequent values are the dates that are close to holiday seasons. Thus, the frequent values tend to be located closer to each other sequentially. We call this phenomenon the *locality of frequent values*. In this experiment, in order to study the effect of the locality, we restrict the top 1% frequent values in the range $[0, 2^{12} \cdot \alpha)$, where α is a locality factor and is varied from 1% to 100%. For example, when $\alpha = 10\%$, the top 1% frequent values are within a small key range from 0 to $2^{12} \times 10\%$.

Figure 7 plots the execution time of the scans on the UD-SP and the SD-UP datasets, and with the locality factor set to 1%, 10%, and 100%. On the SD-UP dataset, the scan speed is further improved by up to 30% when there exists strong locality of frequent values. In this case, most column codes in a block tend to have similar prefixes. As a result, it is more likely that the early pruning occurs at an earlier bit position, which in turn enhances the scan performance. Also, when values exhibit strong locality, the encoding algorithm can often construct a more effective binary tree as frequent values are closer to each other. In contrast, the encoding on the UD-SP dataset only achieves marginal additional speedups with locality of frequent values. The effect of locality of frequent values on the SD-SP dataset is similar to that on the UD-SP dataset, and is omitted in the interest of space.

6.1.3 Varying domain sizes

Next, we evaluate the performance when varying the domain size from $[0, 2^4)$ to $[0, 2^{28})$. Note that the code size of an encoding is determined by the size of the domain that the encoding is constructed on. For example, the code size of the simple encoding is varied from 4 to 28 for the domains evaluated in this experiment.

Figure 8 compares the scan speeds with the simple encoding and the padded encoding with varying domain sizes. When the domain size is 2^4, scans on the UD-SP and the SD-SP datasets are only 50% faster than those on the UD-UP and the SD-UP datasets. As the domain size increases to 2^8, the execution time of the scan on the UD-UP dataset quickly rises, while those on the UD-SP and the SD-SP datasets change very little. When the domain size exceeds 2^{12}, the execution time of scans on the four workloads no longer increases, as at this point the early pruning occurs in nearly all cases. In summary, the performance improvement of the padded encoding scheme over the simple encoding scheme increases when the domain size is smaller than 2^{12}, and does not change once the domain size exceeds 2^{12}. Note that the execution time of scans on the UD-SP and the SD-SP datasets remains nearly constant across all domain sizes.

6.1.4 Robustness evaluation

In this experiment, we evaluate the robustness of the padded encoding scheme, i.e. the performance of padded encoding if the distribution that the encoding is constructed on does not match the real distribution. Note that the distribution of column values changes slowly as new values are inserted into the column, especially when

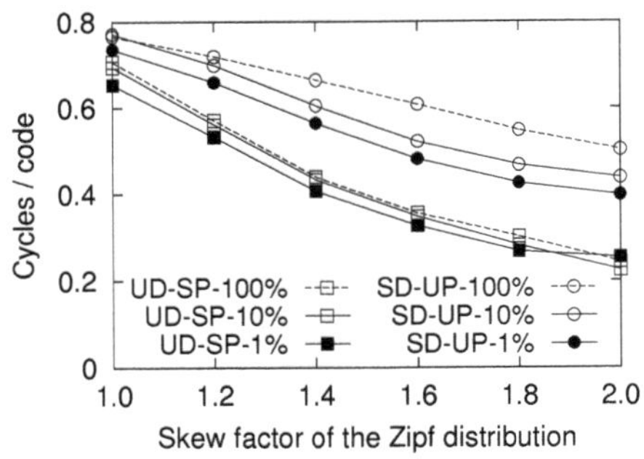

Figure 7: Execution time of scans varying the locality of frequent values.

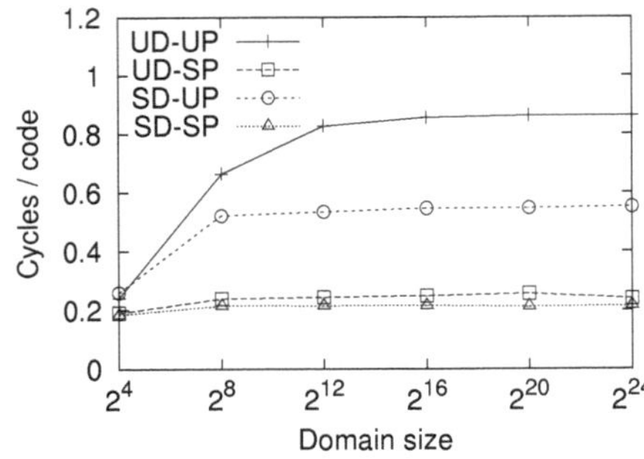

Figure 8: Execution time of scans varying the domain sizes.

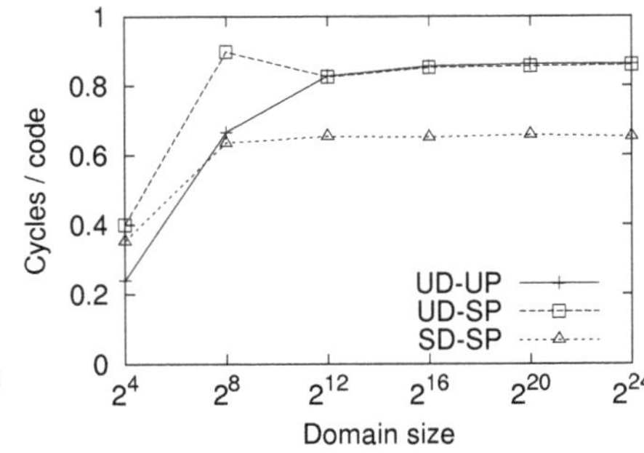

Figure 9: Robustness evaluation.

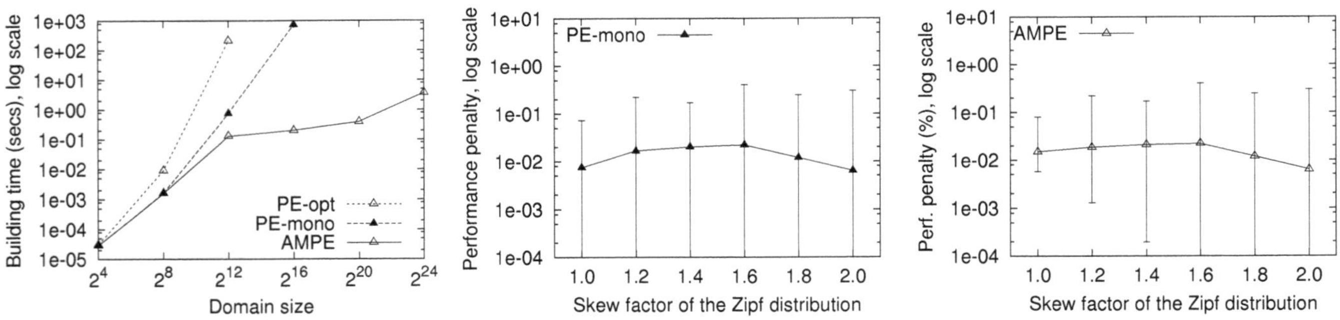

(a) Building time (b) Performance penalty of PE-mono (c) Performance penalty of AMPE

Figure 10: Comparisons between the optimal and near-optimal encoding algorithms on the SD-SP dataset.

the number of new values is a small fraction of the original dataset. As a result, the old distribution is often still fairly accurate. Thus, we focus on the scenario where the distribution of predicate literals changes, i.e. we construct padded encodings on the UD-SP and the SD-SP datasets based on a Zipfian distribution with the scale factor set to 2.0, but generated queries with uniformly distributed predicate literals (thus, SD-SP and UD-SP temporarily become SD-UP and UD-UP, respectively).

Figure 9 plots the execution time of scans with the encodings that are constructed on an incorrect distribution of predicate literals. We include the performance of the simple encoding on UD-UP as a yardstick of performance. The results on SD-UP are omitted here, as its performance is irrelevant to the distribution of predicate literals. When the domain size is smaller than 2^{12}, the incorrect distribution imposes an up to 66% performance penalty (relative to UD-UP) on the UD-SP and the SD-SP datasets. This is because the padded encodings often have wider codes than the simple encoding. If the distribution of predicate literals is incorrect, then the scan does not benefit from the small codes associated with the frequent values in the padded encoding, but suffers from the increased code size of the entire encoding. However, when the domain size exceeds 2^{12}, there is no performance penalty on the UD-SP and the SD-SP datasets, because nearly all comparisons safely terminate around bit position 12 due to early pruning, even for the codes whose length is extended by the padded encodings.

From the results shown in Figure 9, we see that the scan on the SD-SP dataset is still 25% faster than the scan on the UD-UP dataset, even though the encoding is constructed on an incorrect distribution on predicate literals. This performance improvement results from the effect of column value skew. In this case, the encoding on the SD-SP dataset has a similar effect to the padded encoding on the SD-UP dataset. Although the padded encoding with both predicate literal skew and column value skew is only slightly faster than that with predicate literal skew (see Figure 6(a)), it is more resilient to changes in the distribution of predicate literals.

6.1.5 Optimal vs. near-optimal encodings

Finally, we compare the optimal and near-optimal encoding algorithms in terms of the encoding building time and the scan performance. The tag "PE-opt" and "PE-mono" refer to the optimal encoding algorithm (c.f. Section 5.3), and the near-optimal algorithm with the monotonicity heuristic (c.f. Section 5.4.1), whereas "AMPE" refers to the near-optimal algorithm with both monotonicity and early pruning heuristics (c.f. Section 5.4).

Figure 10(a) plots the building time of the optimal and near-optimal encoding algorithms when varying the domain size. Not surprisingly, the building time of PE-opt and PE-mono quickly increases as the domain size increases, due to their high time complexity. The AMPE method is much faster than both PE-opt and PE-mono, taking less than four seconds to construct a padded encoding with $2^{24} = 16$ million values. Thus AMPE enables practical applications of our proposed padded encoding scheme.

Figure 10(b) and 10(c) show the average performance penalty of the two near-optimal encodings, PE-mono and AMPE, over the optimal encoding PE-opt, respectively. The error bars represent the minimum and maximum performance penalty in 100 runs for each experiment. The performance penalty is shown as a percentage of the increase in the execution time of scans. Since the measured execution time of scans is not sufficiently accurate to reflect the performance penalty, we measured the performance penalty based on the cost function we developed in Section 5.2. As can be seen from the figure, the average performance penalty of PE-mono is between 0.1% and 0.0001%. AMPE adds extra penalty when the skew factor is low, and has similar penalty with PE-mono when the skew factor increases. The maximum performance penalty for both near-optimal algorithms across all skew factors is less than 1%.

6.2 TPC-H evaluation

In the evaluation below, we use the TPC-H benchmark [37] to evaluate the encoding methods. These experiments were run against a TPC-H dataset at scale factor 10. The total size of the database is approximately 10GB.

Although the TPC-H data generator assumes a uniform distribution for data in the database, some of the predicate constants in the TPC-H queries are not uniformly distributed, e.g. the first of January of each year is frequently used on predicates. As a result, we produced padded encodings for the TPC-H benchmark based on the distribution of predicate literals, as per the TPC-H specification. To capture the uniform data distribution aspect of the benchmark dataset, we simply set the column value weights to $1/n$.

Encoding names	Columns	Code sizes
skew_date	o_orderdate, l_shipdate, l_commitdate, l_receiptdate	17 (12)
skew_partname	p_name	24 (21)
skew_container	p_container	8 (6)
skew_size	p_size	7 (6)
skew_shipinstruction	l_shipinstruction	2 (2)
skew_shipmode	l_shipmode	4 (3)
skew_delta_date	l_commitdate - l_receiptdate, l_shipdate - l_commitdate	9 (8)

Table 2: Padded encodings used in the TPC-H benchmark. The numbers in parentheses are the code sizes with the simple encoding. With the padded encodings, codes in these columns need 0 – 5 extra bits to represent the column values, as compared to using the simple encoding.

Table 2 summarizes the padded encodings that we constructed for the TPC-H dataset. For each encoding, we calculated the distribution of predicate literals across the 22 TPC-H queries. The columns in the same domain use identical padded encoding, thus codes in these columns can be compared directly without additional decoding operations. For example, the "skew_date" encoding shown in Table 2 is used to encode all `DATE` columns. The predicate literal distribution for this padded encoding is calculated by merging the distribution of predicate literals on each `DATE` column. In addition, using the method presented in Appendix C.1, we created two "delta columns." on the expressions `l_commitdate - l_receiptdate` and `l_shipdate - l_commitdate`, as well as the associated padded encodings on these "delta columns". As a baseline method, we use a simple encoding method to encode column values. More specifically, we use null suppression encoding for integer and date columns, and the simple dictionary encoding for string columns. The encoding and loading time for the simple encoding scheme is around 90 minutes. With the AMPE algorithm, this time increases by only 2 minutes to construct the padded encodings. This time includes 5 seconds to construct all the encodings that are listed in Table 2. Thus, the extra time in loading the data with the padded encoding scheme is small.

To mitigate the performance overhead associated with fetching codes from padded encoded columns in projection and aggregation operations, we use the padded encoded column as a secondary index only for evaluating scans. In this method, the columns involved in projections or aggregations are fetched from the associated base column representations for these attributes. With this method, 0.9GB of extra space is needed to store all the padded encoding column indices listed in Table 2, increasing the size of the underlying database by 10%. We discuss the alternative method, i.e. using padded encoded columns as base column representations, at the end of this section.

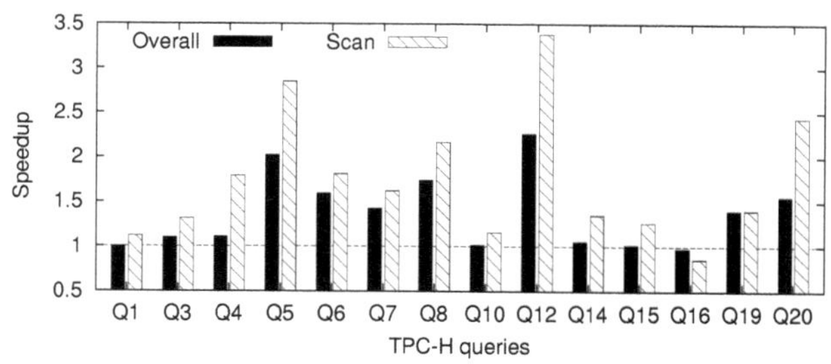

Figure 11: Speedup of the padded encoding over the simple encoding with the TPC-H queries.

In the evaluation below, we focus on 14 of the 22 TPC-H queries (Q1, Q3 - Q8, Q10, Q12, Q14 - Q16, Q19-Q20), as the other 8 queries in the TPC-H benchmark do not involve the columns listed in Table 2. (In other words, the padded encodings have neither a positive nor a negative effect on the performance of these remaining 8 queries.) Following previous work [25, 36], we materialize the join component in these queries, and then ran scan operations on the pre-joined materialized tables so as to stress the scan performance (the focus of this study). All the 14 queries that we focus on, except for Q19, contain a predicate clause that is a conjunction of one to five predicates. Q19 has a more complex predicate clause, which includes a disjunction of three predicate clauses, each of which is a conjunction of six predicates, some of which are performed on the padded encoded columns. These queries contain a variety of predicates, including $<$, $>$, $=$, $<>$, `BETWEEN`, and `IN`. Some queries also involve predicates that perform comparisons between two columns. For most queries, there are complex aggregation operations following the scan operations.

Figure 11 plots the speedup of the padded encoding over the simple encoding with the 14 queries in the TPC-H benchmark. (The corresponding graph showing the raw execution time is in Appendix G.) The total execution time of a query includes the time for the scan phase, and the time on other operations, e.g. aggregations and grouping. As the encoding methods have an immediate effect on scans but an insignificant effect on other operations, we show the speedup for scans and other operations in this figure separately.

For scan operations, the speedup of the padded encoding scheme over the simple encoding scheme ranges from 0.9X to 3.4X, with a geometric mean (GM) of 1.6X. The speedup that the padded encodings achieve depends on many query characteristics, including the number of predicates that involve the padded encoded columns, and the frequency of the predicate constants used in these queries. Q12, for instance, contains five scan predicates, four of which are performed on padded encoded columns or padded encoded delta columns. The two predicates on the column `l_shipdate` always choose the most frequent literals, i.e. the first of January of each year, as the predicate constants to filter the table. Consequently, the computation comparing the column codes and the predicate literals can be safely pruned by only looking at the first 3-4 of the 17 bits. In addition, the use of padded encoded delta columns speeds up the evaluation of the two predicates that compare two date columns. Consequently, the padded encoding scheme achieves a 3.4X speedup over the simple encoding on Q12. In contrast, Q1 randomly selects a day between 30 and 60 days prior to a certain day as the literal for the predicate on the column `l_shipdate`. As those dates are rarely chosen by other queries, the padded encodings achieve only 1.1X speedup over the simple encoding for Q1. Also notice that Q16 shows a 10% degradation in the scan performance, as the predicate literals in this query are randomly selected from all possible values in the column `p_size`.

Taking other operations into consideration, the speedup of the padded encodings over the simple encoding ranges from 0.98X to 2.3X, with a GM of 1.3X. The speedup reduces significantly for many queries, e.g. Q3, Q4, Q10, Q14, and Q15, as the scan phase contributes a smaller portion to the total execution time for these queries. More specifically, the scan times for Q3, Q4, Q10, Q14, and Q15 account for 37%, 22%, 12%, 21%, and 8% of the total execution time, respectively.

We also evaluated the performance on these queries when the base columns shown in Table 2 are stored using padded encoding. With this method, the execution time of the scan phase is generally the same as that when using the padded encoded columns as indices. However, the performance of some aggregation operations that need to access these (padded encoded) columns slows down. For instance, Q7 uses the column `l_shipdate` as a part of the grouping key. With the padded encoding scheme, the size of the codes that are associated with the column `l_shipdate` grows from 12 bits to 17 bits, which increases the time it takes to fetch these column values for the aggregation operation. As a result, the positive effect of padded encoding on the scan operation (62% faster) is offset by the negative effect on the aggregation operations (36% slower), resulting in a reduced net improvement (20%) in the total running time for Q7. Similarly, the performance degradation on Q16 increases from 2% to 25% when using the padded encoded column as the base column representation. The performance for other queries remains largely unchanged from that presented above.

7. RELATED WORK

Encoding techniques in database systems. Encoding techniques have been extensively used for main memory analytical databases in both the research community [1, 4, 5, 10, 20, 25, 26, 35], and in the industry, e.g. SAP HANA [11, 41], IBM DB2 BLU [23, 32], Vertica [22]. Most systems listed here use the simple encoding techniques, e.g. dictionary encoding and null suppression encoding, and do not take the distribution of data into consideration.

IBM Blink [33] and its commercial successor IBM DB2 BLU [32] employ an encoding technique called frequency compression or frequency partitioning to exploit column value skew. Based on the frequency of data, a column is split into multiple partitions, each of which uses an independent fixed-length encoding. Thus, the partitions containing frequent column values use shorter codes. Similar to padded encoding, this technique can be viewed as a hybrid between the fixed-length encoding and variable-length encoding. Unlike frequency compression/partitioning, our work is based on a distinct storage format (vertical bit-packing storage), and exploits skew in the distribution of predicate literals in addition to the distribution of column values. Furthermore our methods can be used in addition to their methods to encode each partition (with padding).

Recently, there has been increasing interest in using encoding techniques to speed up query execution, instead of reducing data space usage, i.e. compression. With the use of encoding techniques, the reduced code size introduces an opportunity to operate on multiple small codes in parallel. Many efficient scan methods have been proposed recently (e.g. [7, 17, 25, 33, 40, 41, 46]) to exploit the parallelism available for small codes. A recent work also studied joins over encoded data [23]. We leverage these methods in our work, and note that our work is complementary to this body of work, as we use these methods to scan the encoded columns.

Skew handling in database systems. Data skew is a well-known phenomenon that has been extensively studied in nearly all aspects of data processing systems, e.g. query processing [8, 24, 31, 42, 44, 45], indexing [9, 43], query optimization [27, 39], partitioning [30], data skipping [3, 36], and MapReduce processing [6, 21]. The focus of this work is on exploiting skew in data distribution to construct efficient skew-aware encodings. Unlike most previous work that attempted to reduce the performance degradation caused by data skew, we leverage data skew to speed up query performance.

Optimum binary search tree. Several algorithms have been devised to compute an optimum Binary Search Tree (BST) [12, 14, 15, 18]; this is, to find a binary search tree with the minimum expected search cost with given frequencies. A key application for this problem is alphabetic encoding [14]: by assigning 0 to the left branch in the binary tree and 1 for a right branch, we obtain an alphabetic encoding which has the minimum expected code length amongst all variable-length encodings that have both the prefix property and the order-preserving property.

Our padded encoding is inspired by alphabetic encoding, as both encodings require the order-preserving property and the prefix property. However, in contrast to alphabetic encoding, the padded encoding needs a more complicated cost function (as shown in Section 5.2). Thus, existing algorithms for the alphabetic encoding (and optimum BST) problem can not be used to solve the padded encoding problem.

The first solution to the optimum BST problem was given by Gilbert and Moore [14]. This solution is based on the dynamic-programming technique and has a time complexity of $O(n^3)$. We adapted this algorithm to the padded encoding problem and obtained the optimal algorithm (see Section 5.3). Knuth improved this solution and reduced the time complexity to $O(n^2)$ with the use of the monotonicity property [18]. This property is not guaranteed to hold for the padded encoding problem, and is used as the first heuristic in our near-optimal solution. Hu and Tucker [15] found a solution in $O(n \log n)$ steps. This solution was further simplified as the Garsia-Wachs algorithm [12]. However, these solutions cannot be adapted to the padded encoding problem directly.

8. CONCLUSIONS AND FUTURE WORK

Scans are a crucial primitive in real-time analytic data processing systems, and in this paper we propose a scheme called padded encoding that leverages skew in the data and predicate literals to improve the performance of scans. To construct a padded encoding, an algorithm (called AMPE) was proposed to efficiently build a near-optimal encoding while reducing the overhead associated with the code size. We have empirically demonstrated the effectiveness of the padded encoding scheme to speed up scan performance. There are a number of directions for future work, including developing methods to automatically pick an encoding scheme based on the workload, exploring the use of padded encoding when replicating data for high availability, and extending the use of padded encoding for operations other than scans.

Acknowledgments

We would like to thank the reviewers of this paper for their insightful feedback on an earlier draft of this paper. This work was supported in part by the National Science Foundation under grants IIS-0963993, IIS-1110948, and IIS-1250886, the Anthony Klug NCR Fellowship, and a gift donation from Google.

9. REFERENCES

[1] D. J. Abadi, S. Madden, and M. Ferreira. Integrating compression and execution in column-oriented database systems. In *SIGMOD Conference*, pages 671–682, 2006.

[2] L. Abraham, J. Allen, O. Barykin, V. R. Borkar, B. Chopra, C. Gerea, D. Merl, J. Metzler, D. Reiss, S. Subramanian, J. L. Wiener, and O. Zed. Scuba: Diving into data at facebook. *PVLDB*, 6(11):1057–1067, 2013.

[3] K. Alexiou, D. Kossmann, and P. Larson. Adaptive range filters for cold data: Avoiding trips to siberia. *PVLDB*, 6(14):1714–1725, 2013.

[4] T. Apaydin, G. Canahuate, H. Ferhatosmanoglu, and A. S. Tosun. Approximate encoding for direct access and query processing over compressed bitmaps. In *VLDB Conference*, pages 846–857, 2006.

[5] C. Binnig, S. Hildenbrand, and F. Färber. Dictionary-based order-preserving string compression for main memory column stores. In *SIGMOD Conference*, pages 283–296, 2009.

[6] S. Blanas, J. M. Patel, V. Ercegovac, J. Rao, E. J. Shekita, and Y. Tian. A comparison of join algorithms for log processing in mapreduce. In *SIGMOD Conference*, pages 975–986, 2010.

[7] Z. Chen, J. Gehrke, and F. Korn. Query optimization in compressed database systems. In *SIGMOD Conference*, pages 271–282, 2001.

[8] D. J. DeWitt, J. F. Naughton, D. A. Schneider, and S. Seshadri. Practical skew handling in parallel joins. In *VLDB Conference*, pages 27–40, 1992.

[9] C. Faloutsos and H. V. Jagadish. On b-tree indices for skewed distributions. In *VLDB Conference*, pages 363–374, 1992.

[10] W. Fang, B. He, and Q. Luo. Database compression on graphics processors. *PVLDB*, 3(1):670–680, 2010.

[11] F. Färber, N. May, W. Lehner, P. Große, I. Müller, H. Rauhe, and J. Dees. The SAP HANA database – an architecture overview. *IEEE Data Eng. Bull.*, 35(1):28–33, 2012.

[12] A. M. Garsia and M. L. Wachs. A new algorithm for minimum cost binary trees. *SIAM J. Comput.*, 6(4):622–642, 1977.

[13] G. Giannikis, P. Unterbrunner, J. Meyer, G. Alonso, D. Fauser, and D. Kossmann. Crescando. In *SIGMOD Conference*, pages 1227–1230, 2010.

[14] E. N. Gilbert and E. F. Moore. Variable-length binary encodings. *Bell System Technical Journal*, 38(4):933–967, 1959.

[15] T. C. Hu and A. C. Tucker. Optimal computer search trees and variable-length alphabetical codes. *SIAM Journal on Applied Mathematics*, 21(4):514–532, 1971.

[16] D. A. Huffman et al. A method for the construction of minimum redundancy codes. *Proc. IRE*, 40(9):1098–1101, 1952.

[17] R. Johnson, V. Raman, R. Sidle, and G. Swart. Row-wise parallel predicate evaluation. *PVLDB*, 1(1):622–634, 2008.

[18] D. E. Knuth. Optimum binary search trees. *Acta Inf.*, 1:14–25, 1971.

[19] D. E. Knuth. *The Art of Computer Programming, Volume III: Sorting and Searching, 2nd Edition*. Addison-Wesley, 1998.

[20] J. Krüger, C. Kim, M. Grund, N. Satish, D. Schwalb, J. Chhugani, H. Plattner, P. Dubey, and A. Zeier. Fast updates on read-optimized databases using multi-core CPUs. *PVLDB*, 5(1):61–72, 2011.

[21] Y. Kwon, M. Balazinska, B. Howe, and J. A. Rolia. Skewtune: mitigating skew in mapreduce applications. In *SIGMOD Conference*, pages 25–36, 2012.

[22] A. Lamb, M. Fuller, R. Varadarajan, N. Tran, B. Vandier, L. Doshi, and C. Bear. The vertica analytic database: C-store 7 years later. *PVLDB*, 5(12):1790–1801, 2012.

[23] J.-G. Lee, G. K. Attaluri, R. Barber, N. Chainani, O. Draese, F. Ho, S. Idreos, M.-S. Kim, S. Lightstone, G. M. Lohman, K. Morfonios, K. Murthy, I. Pandis, L. Qiao, V. Raman, V. K. Samy, R. Sidle, K. Stolze, and L. Zhang. Joins on encoded and partitioned data. *PVLDB*, 7(13):1355–1366, 2014.

[24] W. Li, D. Gao, and R. T. Snodgrass. Skew handling techniques in sort-merge join. In *SIGMOD Conference*, pages 169–180, 2002.

[25] Y. Li and J. M. Patel. BitWeaving: fast scans for main memory data processing. In *SIGMOD Conference*, pages 289–300, 2013.

[26] Y. Li and J. M. Patel. WideTable: An accelerator for analytical data processing. *PVLDB*, 7(10):907–918, 2014.

[27] C. A. Lynch. Selectivity estimation and query optimization in large databases with highly skewed distribution of column values. In *VLDB Conference*, pages 240–251, 1988.

[28] S. Melnik, A. Gubarev, J. J. Long, G. Romer, S. Shivakumar, M. Tolton, and T. Vassilakis. Dremel: Interactive analysis of web-scale datasets. *PVLDB*, 3(1):330–339, 2010.

[29] P. E. O'Neil and D. Quass. Improved query performance with variant indexes. In *SIGMOD Conference*, pages 38–49, 1997.

[30] A. Pavlo, C. Curino, and S. B. Zdonik. Skew-aware automatic database partitioning in shared-nothing, parallel OLTP systems. In *SIGMOD Conference*, pages 61–72, 2012.

[31] O. Polychroniou and K. A. Ross. High throughput heavy hitter aggregation for modern SIMD processors. In *DaMoN Workshop*, page 6, 2013.

[32] V. Raman, G. K. Attaluri, R. Barber, N. Chainani, D. Kalmuk, V. KulandaiSamy, J. Leenstra, S. Lightstone, S. Liu, G. M. Lohman, T. Malkemus, R. Müller, I. Pandis, B. Schiefer, D. Sharpe, R. Sidle, A. J. Storm, and L. Zhang. DB2 with BLU acceleration: So much more than just a column store. *PVLDB*, 6(11):1080–1091, 2013.

[33] V. Raman, G. Swart, L. Qiao, F. Reiss, V. Dialani, D. Kossmann, I. Narang, and R. Sidle. Constant-time query processing. In *ICDE Conference*, pages 60–69, 2008.

[34] D. Rinfret, P. E. O'Neil, and E. J. O'Neil. Bit-sliced index arithmetic. In *SIGMOD Conference*, pages 47–57, 2001.

[35] B. Schlegel, R. Gemulla, and W. Lehner. Fast integer compression using SIMD instructions. In *DaMoN Workshop*, pages 34–40, 2010.

[36] L. Sun, M. J. Franklin, S. Krishnan, and R. S. Xin. Fine-grained partitioning for aggressive data skipping. In *SIGMOD Conference*, pages 1115–1126, 2014.

[37] Transaction Processing Performance Council. *TPC Benchmark H. Revision 2.17.0*. April 2014.

[38] P. Unterbrunner, G. Giannikis, G. Alonso, D. Fauser, and D. Kossmann. Predictable performance for unpredictable workloads. *PVLDB*, 2(1):706–717, 2009.

[39] C. B. Walton, A. G. Dale, and R. M. Jenevein. A taxonomy and performance model of data skew effects in parallel joins. In *VLDB Conference*, pages 537–548, 1991.

[40] T. Willhalm, I. Oukid, I. Müller, and F. Faerber. Vectorizing database column scans with complex predicates. In *ADMS Workshop*, pages 1–12, 2013.

[41] T. Willhalm, N. Popovici, Y. Boshmaf, H. Plattner, A. Zeier, and J. Schaffner. SIMD-scan: Ultra fast in-memory table scan using on-chip vector processing units. *PVLDB*, 2(1):385–394, 2009.

[42] J. L. Wolf, D. M. Dias, P. S. Yu, and J. Turek. An effective algorithm for parallelizing hash joins in the presence of data skew. In *ICDE Conference*, pages 200–209, 1991.

[43] K. Wu and P. S. Yu. Range-based bitmap indexing for high cardinality attributes with skew. In *COMPSAC Conference*, pages 61–67, 1998.

[44] Y. Xu and P. Kostamaa. Efficient outer join data skew handling in parallel DBMS. *PVLDB*, 2(2):1390–1396, 2009.

[45] Y. Xu, P. Kostamaa, X. Zhou, and L. Chen. Handling data skew in parallel joins in shared-nothing systems. In *SIGMOD Conference*, pages 1043–1052, 2008.

[46] J. Zhou and K. A. Ross. Implementing database operations using SIMD instructions. In *SIGMOD Conference*, pages 145–156, 2002.

APPENDIX

A. PROOFS

LEMMA 4.1. *A padded encoding has the order-preserving property if its base encoding has the order-preserving property.*

PROOF. We use a_1 and a_2 to denote two values. Let c_1 and c_2 denote the codes of a_1 and a_2 in the padded encoding, and c_1' and c_2' to denote their corresponding codes in the base encoding. If the base encoding has the order-preserving property, then we have $c_1' > c_2' \Leftrightarrow a_1 > a_2$. It is clear that adding zeros to the end of codes does not change the numerical binary order of c_1' and c_2', i.e. $c_1 > c_2 \Leftrightarrow c_1' > c_2'$. Thus, we obtain $c_1 > c_2 \Leftrightarrow a_1 > a_2$; that is, the padded encoding also has the order-preserving property. □

LEMMA 5.1. *All subtrees of an optimal tree are optimal.*

PROOF. Suppose, to the contrary, that there exists a subtree T' in an optimal tree T that is not optimal. Then, there exists another subtree T'' that is built on all leaf nodes of T' and has a lower cost than T', i.e. $C(T'') < C(T')$. According to Equation 2, the cost associated with the tree T is the sum of the cost associated with T' and the cost associated with all other internal nodes that are not in T'. According to Equation 3, the cost associated with an internal node is only related to the predicate literal weights and the column code weights of codes that belongs to the subtree rooted at the node. Then, we can reduce the cost associated with T', without changing the cost of all other nodes in T, by substituting the subtree T' with T'', which results in reducing the cost associated with the tree T. This contradicts the supposition that T is optimal. Thus, Lemma 5.1 follows by contradiction. □

B. ADDITIONAL PSEUDOCODE

Algorithm 2 shows the pseudocode for the modified dynamic programming approach with the monotonicity heuristic (see Section 5.4.1). The modified lines are marked with the symbol ◁.

With the monotonicity heuristic, the running time of the algorithm is reduced to $O(n^2)$ [18]. The cost of the inner loop (Line 6-13) in Algorithm 2 is given by: $\sum_{0 \le i \le n-d, j=i+d-1}(R(i+1,j) - R(i,j-1)+1) = R(n-d+1,n) - R(n-d,n-1) + R(n-d,n-1) - R(n-d-1,n-2) + \cdots - R(0,d-1) + n-d+1 = R(n-d+1,n) - R(0,d-1) + n - d + 1 < 2n$. Then, as the outer loop takes on $n-1$ values, the algorithm requires a running time of $O(n^2)$.

Algorithm 2 Computing the near-optimal tree for the general case

Input: The predicate literal weights $p_0, p_1, \cdots, p_{n-1}$
The column code weights $q_0, q_1, \cdots, q_{n-1}$
Output: The minimum cost of the tree
1: $W_p(i,j) := \sum_{k=i}^{j} p_k$, for $0 \le i \le j < n$
2: $W_q(i,j) := \sum_{k=i}^{j} q_k$, for $0 \le i \le j < n$
3: $C_q(i,i) := 0$, for $0 \le i < n$
4: $R(i,i) := i$, for $0 \le i < n$ ◁
5: **for** $d := 2 \ldots n$ **do**
6: **for** $i := 0 \ldots n-d$ **do**
7: $j := i+d-1$
8: $C(i,j) := \infty$
9: **for** $k := R(i,j-1) \ldots R(i+1,j)$ **do** ◁
10: **if** $C(i,k-1) + C(k,j) < C(i,j)$ **then**
11: $C(i,j) := C(i,k-1) + C(k,j)$
12: $R(i,j) := k$ ◁
13: $C(i,j) := C(i,j) + (1-(1-W_q(i,j))^b)) \cdot W_p(i,j)$
14: **return** $C(0,n-1)$;

C. OPTIMIZATIONS FOR THE PADDED ENCODING SCHEME

In this section, we discuss several techniques that further improve the padded encoding scheme in terms of performance and its applicability.

C.1 Handling comparisons between columns

So far the main focus of the type of predicates is a comparison between a column and a predicate literal. There is another common type of predicate that compares two distinct columns, which can be represented canonically as $R.a1 - R.a2 \circ A$, where the operator $\circ \in \{<, >, =, \neq, \le, \ge\}$, and A is a predicate literal. For example, we might want to find the sale records whose shipping date is within one week of the order date by using the predicate `shipdate ≤ orderdate + 7`. However, scans with this type of predicate do not directly benefit from the encoding techniques proposed in this paper so far.

To handle predicates that compares two columns $R.a1$ and $R.a2$, we propose adding a *delta column*, which is a materialized column representing the expression $R.a1 - R.a2$. Thus, predicates that compare these two columns, i.e. $R.a1 - R.a2 \circ A$, now becomes a "regular" predicate that compares a delta column to a predicate literal, i.e. $delta(R.a1, R.a2) \circ A$. An encoding can now be constructed on the delta column based on the column value weights and predicate literal weights of the values appearing in the delta column, making it feasible to leverage our padded encoding technique to speed up scans with this type of predicate.

Considering the above example again, assume that the predicate literal 7 is a frequent predicate literal on the delta column that is built on `shipmate - orderdate`. Then, the scan with the example predicate runs at a higher speed as we can assign a short code to the value 7 in the encoding constructed for the delta column.

In practice, we only construct delta columns for comparisons that actually show up frequently in the query workload. These delta columns consume extra space, and present a space vs. time tradeoff for speeding up scan operations on these columns.

C.2 Encoding for clustered columns

The assumption that an encoding is constructed on a single column can be relaxed. Thus, we can produce an encoding for a cluster of columns that share the same domain, and have a similar distribution for their column values. To construct an encoding for a set of columns, the predicate literal weights and the column value weights have to be computed across all columns that share the encoding. Then, we encode the values in these columns using the constructed encoding. As all codes in these columns are produced by using the same encoding, it is efficient to compare the column values from two different columns.

For instance, we can directly compare the codes for the columns `shipdate` and `orderdate` without decoding, if the two columns use the same encoding. The shared encoding also reduces the space consumption that is used to store multiple individual dictionaries.

C.3 Transforming predicates

A predicate on a scan operation can often be transformed into a semantically identical predicate but with a distinct predicate literal. This is because the domain of an encoded column is discrete, consisting of the values in the encoding. Thus, we can replace the literal in a predicate with its immediate previous or next value in the domain and correspondingly change the comparator. For example, a predicate `shipdate <= '2014-10-31'` can be rewritten as `shipdate < '2014-11-01'` without changing the semantic meaning of the predicate.

There are three primary reasons to consider transforming predicates. The first reason is that we could switch to a more frequent predicate literal by transforming the predicate. In the example above, it is worthwhile to transform the predicate to `shipdate < '2014-11-01'` if the predicate literal weight for the date "2014-11-01" is higher than that of "2014-10-31", leading to a scan with a shorter predicate literal code.

Second, the predicate transformation may produce a predicate literal distribution with a higher degree of skew, which often results in a more efficient encoding. For example, if we transform the predicate literal "2014-10-31" in all queries of a database to the literal "2014-11-01", then the predicate literal weight of the date "2014-10-31" is shifted to that of the date "2014-11-01". Thus,

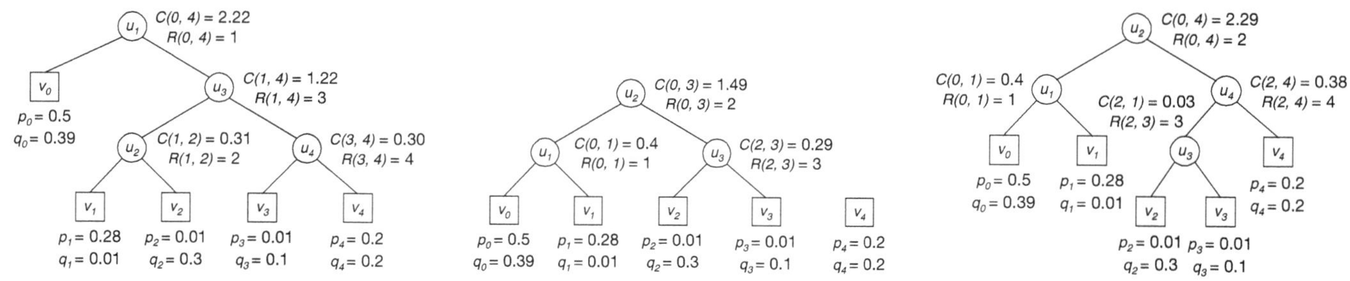

(a) Optimal tree on $v_0 \sim v_4$ (b) Optimal subtree on $v_0 \sim v_3$ (c) Near-optimal tree on $v_0 \sim v_4$

Figure 12: The counterexample encoding tree for the monotonicity heuristic.

we now have a more skewed distribution for the predicate literals, which improves the efficiency of the padded encoding scheme.

Finally, we have to transform the predicate if the predicate literal is not in the encoding. For instance, if the date column does not contain the date value "2014-10-31," but a query is issued with the predicate `shipdate < '2014-10-31'`, then there is no assigned code for the date "2014-10-31" in the encoding. In this case, we have to convert the predicate literal with the immediate previous or next value in the encoding. Note that the decision between choosing the immediate previous value or next value can be made based on the weights of these two values.

C.4 Preserving data locality

Although the padded encoding method may increase the code lengths and may allow the scan operation to skip over some bit positions, the storage layout of the BitWeaving(/V) method naturally preserves the data locality for the padded encoding. With the BitWeaving storage layout, a column of codes is broken down into fixed-length segments. The codes in a segment are then transposed into the vertical bit-packing representation, and are further divided into fixed sized bit groups. This storage layout is designed to improve the data locality and fully utilize the memory bandwidth. In the interest of space, we omit a detailed discussion of this aspect in this paper, and refer interested readers to the original paper [25].

D. COUNTEREXAMPLE FOR THE MONOTONICITY HEURISTIC

Figure 12 shows a counterexample for the monotonicity heuristic. There are five values in the encoding, with the predicate literal weights $p_0 = 0.5$, $p_1 = 0.28$, $p_2 = 0.01$, $p_3 = 0.01$, $p_4 = 0.2$, and with the column value weights $q_0 = 0.5$, $q_1 = 0.28$, $q_2 = 0.01$, $q_3 = 0.01$, $q_4 = 0.2$. Figure 12(a) illustrates the optimal encoding tree on the five leaf nodes $v_0 \sim v_4$. However, this optimal encoding tree cannot be obtained by using the monotonicity heuristic. To illustrate the reason, Figure 12(b) shows the optimal subtree on the leaf nodes $v_0 \sim v_3$. The left subtree and the right subtree is split on the leaf node v_2, i.e. $R(0,3) = 2$. Thus, according to the monotonicity heuristic, $R(0,4)$ should be equal to or greater than $R(0,3)$. Nevertheless, the left subtree of the root and the right subtree in the optimal encoding tree (Figure 12(a)) are split at the leaf node v_1, i.e. $R(0,4) = 1 < R(0,3)$. As a result, with the monotonicity heuristic, we fail to find the optimal encoding tree. Figure 12(c) show the near-optimal encoding tree constructed with the monotonicity heuristic, whose cost (2.29) is slightly higher than that of the optimal encoding tree (2.22).

E. REDUCING THE CODE SIZE

Our padded encoding method results in a fixed-length encoding, as fixed-length encodings are easier to manage for storage and query processing. However, the padded encoding method may produce longer (fixed-length) codes than those produced by popular order-preserving encoding methods, such as dictionary-based encoding. This additional space overhead has the potential to negate the performance gains of the padded encoding as: a) it increases the space that is needed to store the encoded column(s); b) it could hinder the scan performance if the distribution of the column values or the predicate literals changes; and c) it increases the execution time to fetch a code from the encoded column(s). In this section, we present a method to reduce the maximum code length of a padded encoding.

Algorithm. The basic idea behind this algorithm follows the early-pruning heuristic (see Section 5.4.2): the effects of both the predicate literal weights and the column code weights decline as we go down the binary tree from the root to the bottom levels, leading to a relatively balanced tree structure at the bottom of the binary tree. In the remainder of this section, we use the binary tree representation of the encoding. Thus, given a binary encoding tree, we replace the subtree that contains the deepest leaf node of the encoding tree with a balanced binary tree, reducing the maximum level of the encoding tree.

Algorithm 3 Reducing the maximum level of an encoding tree

Input: The binary encoding tree T
The level l
Output: A binary encoding tree T'
1: $T' := T$
2: $l_{max} := 0$
3: **for all** internal node u at level l of T **do**
4: $n :=$ the number of nodes in the subtree rooted at u
5: $l_{max} := \max(l_{max}, \lceil \log_2 n \rceil + l)$
6: **for all** internal node u at level l of T **do**
7: $l_u :=$ the maximum level of nodes in the subtree rooted at u
8: **if** $l_u > l_{max}$ **then**
9: Replace the subtree rooted at u in T' by a balanced tree
10: **return** T'

Algorithm 3 shows the pseudocode for the algorithm that reduces the maximum level of a binary encoding tree, starting from an input level l. In the first loop (Line 3 to Line 5), we compute the maximum level (l_{max}) of the encoding tree if we replace the subtree rooted at each internal node at the level l by a balanced binary subtree. Then, in the second loop (Line 6 to Line 9), we perform the substitution process. However, if the maximum level in a subtree is lower than l_{max}, replacing this subtree cannot reduce the maximum level of the encoding tree, but could degrade the performance of scans with this encoding. As a result, we only substitute a subtree if the maximum level of the subtree exceeds l_{max}. We note that all nodes above the level l remain unchanged using this

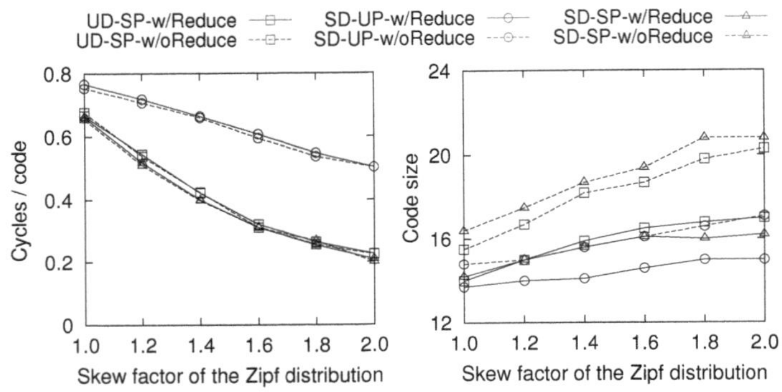

(a) Execution time (b) Code size

Figure 13: Performance comparison between the padded encodings with and without reducing the code length.

algorithm. This solution requires a running time of $O(n)$, because we need to access and reconstruct all subtrees below the level l in the worst-case.

Evaluation. Next, we empirically evaluate the behavior of this algorithm with varying code sizes. Figure 13(a) plots the execution time of scans with the padded encoding before and after the code size reduction on the three set of workloads (UD-SP, SD-UP, and SD-SP) that we used in Section 6. We set the level l to 8 in this experiment, and vary this value in the next experiment. We see that the performance degradation with the code size reduction is generally small, across all skew factors. The maximum performance penalty we measured is 3%. Figure 13(b) shows the code length of the padded encoding before and after reducing the code length. Each experiment was run 10 times. Without the code size reduction, the average code size of the padded encodings are up to 20.3, 17.1, and 20.8 on the UD-SP, the SD-UP, and the SD-SP datasets, respectively. The additional code length over the simple encoding (with the code length of 12) is reduced by around 40% on the UD-SP and the SD-UP datasets, and around 50% on the SD-SP dataset. In summary, we empirically demonstrate that the algorithm effectively reduces the code size of the padded encodings, while preserving the scan performance.

Figure 14 plots the scan performance and code size when varying the parameter l in the algorithm. When $l = 0$, we substitute the entire encoding tree with a balanced binary tree, reducing the padded encoding to a simple encoding with a code size of 12. As the parameter l increases, the scan performance improves while the

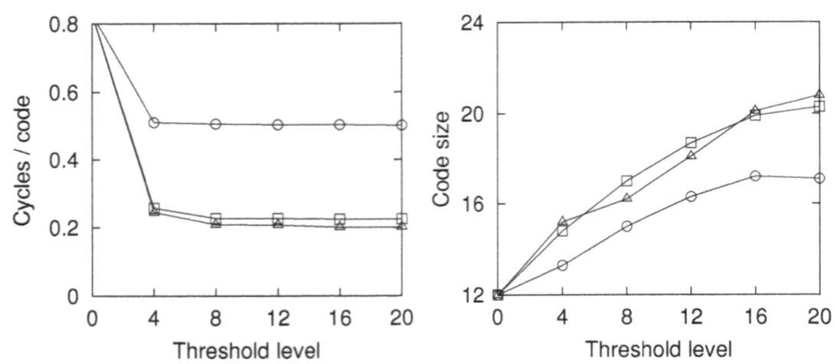

(a) Execution time (b) Code size

Figure 14: Scan performance and the code size when varying the level parameter l.

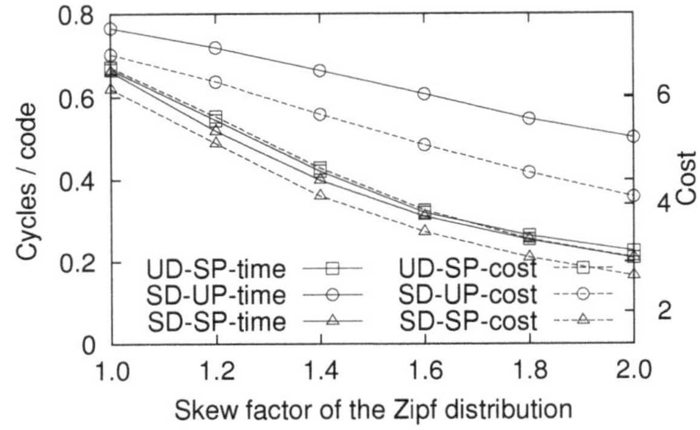

Figure 15: Comparison between the execution time and the theoretical cost of a scan operation with the padded encodings.

overhead associated with the extra code length increases. We observe that choosing $l = 8$ is a reasonable trade-off between the scan performance and code size, as at this point the scan performance is nearly the same as that before reducing the code size, while the code size is smaller.

F. VALIDATING THE COST FUNCTION

Figure 15 compares the measured time and the theoretical cost of scan operations with the padding encodings on the UD-SP, the SD-UP, and the SD-SP datasets. The solid curves represent the measured execution time, whereas the dashed curves show the theoretical cost according to the cost model (present in Section 5.2). With the UD-SP dataset, the theoretical cost matches the measured time across all the skew factors. With the SD-UP and the SD-SP datasets, the lines associated with the measured time have a similar trend to that associated with the theoretical cost, but are generally below the the cost curves. The reason for this behavior is because the implementation of the early pruning mechanism imposes an extra performance overhead that is not accounted for in the theoretical model. Improving the implementation of the early pruning mechanism is an interesting direction for future work.

G. ADDITIONAL TPC-H RESULTS

Figure 16 shows the execution time of the 14 queries in the TPC-H benchmark. The left bar for each query in the figure represents the execution time of the scans and other operations with the simple encoding scheme, while the right bar shows the execution time with the padded encoding scheme.

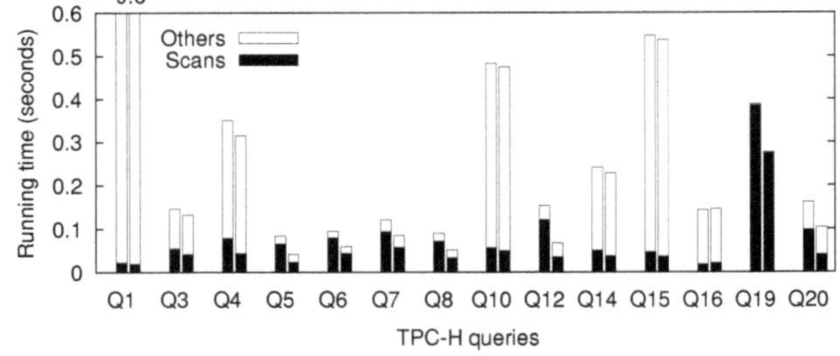

Figure 16: Performance comparison between the simple encoding scheme (the left bars) and the padded encoding scheme (the right bars) with the TPC-H queries.

GetReal: Towards Realistic Selection of Influence Maximization Strategies in Competitive Networks

Hui Li
School of Cyber Engineering
Xidian University, China
hli@xidian.edu.cn

Sourav S Bhowmick
School of Computer Engineering
Nanyang Technological University, Singapore
assourav@ntu.edu.sg

Jiangtao Cui
School of Cyber Engineering
Xidian University, China
cuijt@xidian.edu.cn

Yunjun Gao
College of Computer Science
Zhejiang University, China
gaoyj@cs.zju.edu.cn

Jianfeng Ma
School of Cyber Engineering
Xidian University, China
jfma@mail.xidian.edu.cn

ABSTRACT

State-of-the-art classical *influence maximization* (IM) techniques are "competition-unaware" as they assume that a group (company) finds seeds (users) in a network independent of other groups who are also simultaneously interested in finding such seeds in the same network. However, in reality several groups often compete for the same market (*e.g., Samsung*, *HTC*, and *Apple* for the smart phone market) and hence may attempt to select seeds in the same network. This has led to increasing body of research in devising IM techniques for *competitive* networks. Despite the considerable progress made by these efforts toward finding seeds in a more realistic settings, unfortunately, they still make several unrealistic assumptions (*e.g.,* a new company being aware of a rival's strategy, *alternate* seed selection, etc.) making their deployment impractical in real-world networks. In this paper, we propose a novel framework based on game theory to provide a more realistic solution to the IM problem in competitive networks by jettisoning these unrealistic assumptions. Specifically, we seek to find the "best" IM *strategy* (an algorithm or a mixture of algorithms) a group should adopt in the presence of rivals so that it can maximize its influence. As each group adopts some strategy, we model the problem as a game with each group as competitors and the expected influences under the strategies as payoffs. We propose a novel algorithm called GetReal to find each group's best solution by leveraging the competition between different groups. Specifically, it seeks to find whether there exist a *Nash Equilibrium* (NE) in a game, which guarantees that there exist an "optimal" strategy for each group. Our experimental study on real-world networks demonstrates the superiority of our solution in a more realistic environment.

SIGMOD'15, May 31–June 4, 2015, Melbourne, Victoria, Australia.

http://dx.doi.org/10.1145/2723372.2723710.

Categories and Subject Descriptors

F.2.2 [**Analysis of Algorithms and Problem Complexity**]: Non-numerical Algorithms and Problems

Keywords

Influence Maximization; competitive network; game theory; nash equilibrium; pure and mixed strategies

1. INTRODUCTION

Given a social network as well as an *influence propagation* (or *cascade*) model, the problem of *influence maximization* (IM) is to find a set of initial users of size k (referred to as *seeds*) so that they eventually influence the largest number of individuals (referred to as *influence spread*) in the network [18]. Kempe et al. [18] proved that this problem is NP-hard and presented a greedy approximate algorithm and guarantee that the influence spread is within $(1 - 1/e)$ of the optimal influence spread. Since then a long stream of greedy and heuristic-based techniques [8, 12, 13, 19–21] have been proposed to improve efficiency and scalability of the IM problem.

Despite the significant progress made by state-of-the-art IM approaches, they inevitably suffer from a key drawback primarily due to the unrealistic assumption of the social network to be *non-competitive* in nature. Specifically, these techniques are effective for a network where only *one* company (*i.e.,* group)[1] is maximizing the influence of a product irrespective of the absence or presence of other competitors. Unfortunately, this scenario rarely occurs in the real world as competition for market between rivals is ubiquitous. Given a market of a particular product category (*e.g.,* mobile phone market), there exist several rival groups (*e.g., Apple*, *Samsung*, *HTC*) attempting to maximize their influences[2]. A common concern of these groups is the scenario where their rivals may take precedence in the market.

[1]In the sequel, we shall use the terms "company" and "group" interchangeably.

[2]In this paper, we do not consider a market which is heavily monopolized by a certain group where users have no other choice but to buy their product(s). For such monopoly market the most important problem is not IM but price setting.

As a result, competitive new products from rival companies are often promoted during the same period[3]. For example, *HTC* and *Samsung* promoted *HTC One* and *Samsung Galaxy S4*, respectively, almost simultaneously. Consequently, these companies also desire to maximize the influence of their products in the market at the same time. Unfortunately, the aforementioned IM techniques generate unsatisfactory results when deployed over such *competitive* networks (detailed in Section 6). Several groups in the competition may adopt the same or similar IM algorithms, leading to poor estimations of influence spreads.

1.1 Motivating Example

Consider the social network in Figure 1(a). In order to maximize the influence of a new mobile phone model, assume that *Samsung* adopts a state-of-the-art IM algorithm to select two users ($k = 2$) whom it wishes to provide free samples of the phone. Suppose *Samsung* decided to choose *Ada* and *Bob* as candidate seeds based on the output of the algorithm. These users eventually influence nine persons in the network. Now consider Figure 1(b). Assume that *Samsung* has a rival in the mobile phone market, namely *HTC*. Similar to *Samsung*, *HTC* also wants to maximize the influence of their new mobile phone which is released almost simultaneously. Thus, *HTC* may also adopt a state-of-the-art IM algorithm to select the candidate seeds. It is indeed possible for *HTC* to select the same candidate seeds as *Samsung* (*Ada* and *Bob*) based on the output of the chosen IM algorithm. However, in reality, *Ada* or *Bob* may adopt *only one* mobile phone model (which they prefer) to recommend to their friends. For instance, *Ada* may adopt *Samsung* whereas *Bob* may adopt *HTC*. Note that users who are influenced by both *Ada* and *Bob* (persons in brown color in Figure 1(b)), will rarely buy both phones. Instead, they may need to make a choice between these two phones. Consequently, in reality *both companies may not eventually influence a large number of users as expected*, especially when both of them adopt IM algorithms that recommend similar candidate seeds. Clearly, this will lead to inferior influence spread quality.

Now consider the case where we assume that *Samsung* and *HTC* adopt different IM algorithms. In this case, it is possible to have lesser degree of overlap between the candidate seed sets. However, existing IM techniques still estimate the seed set of one group *disregarding* the impact of the influence spread of the other group. *In this paper, we propose a novel framework to study the* IM *problem under competitive networks where more than one competing groups want to maximize their influence.*

1.2 IM Research in Competitive Networks

Due to the aforementioned limitations, there have been increasing research efforts to address the IM problem in competitive networks [1–3, 5, 15, 29, 31] (detailed in Section 2). Although these efforts assume the existence of competing groups in a network, they suffer from two key limitations that may impede their adoption in real-world settings. First, they assume that a company A, who has already selected the seeds, is unaware of the existence of their new competitor B (*e.g., Samsung* is unaware of *HTC*). However, this is highly unlikely in reality as a company is typically aware of their potential rivals. Note that due to this unrealistic assumption, a company A may fail to adapt their IM *strategy* to one that is suitable for a competitive network (in the presence of the rival B) in order to maximize influence. In this paper, an IM *strategy* refers to an IM algorithm or a mixture of IM algorithms that a group adopts to maximize their influence. Second, they assume that the new company B is aware of its rival A's strategy and selected seeds (target users) to whom free samples of a product have been provided. Clearly, this is highly unlikely to happen as majority of these companies who are promoting their products in social networks (*e.g., Twitter*) do not own these networks to track rivals' strategies or seeds.

[3]For simplicity, we assume that the companies promote their own products without seeking any aid from a third-party for promotion.

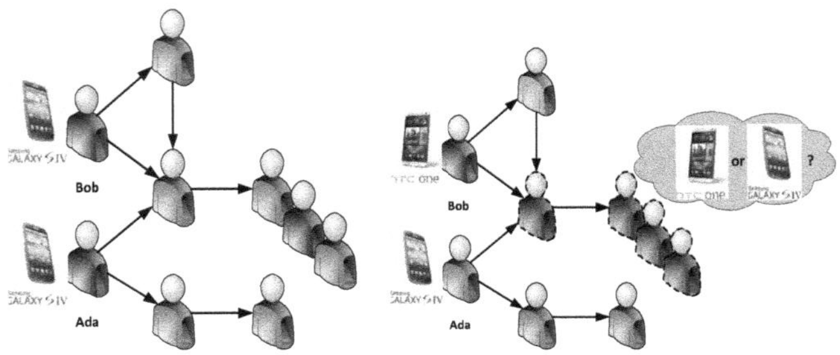

(a) Non-competitive (b) Competitive

Figure 1: [Best viewed in color] Influence propagation in different networks.

More recently, game theory is leveraged to investigate the IM problem in competitive networks [10, 11, 26, 32]. Specifically, the efforts in [10, 26] assume that each individual is able to alternate their choices at arbitrary time step, which deviates from traditional settings of the IM problem. In real applications, especially in viral marketing, whenever a user buys a product she is viewed as being influenced. Consequently, as the user is already influenced by a product, it is highly unlikely that she is going to be influenced by any other products. In [11] and [32], the authors investigate the IM problem between non-cooperative companies who select the seeds *alternately*. However, the assumption of "alternate seed selection" is unrealistic in may real-world applications as it is extremely difficult for companies to select targets alternatively (like playing chess).

1.3 Overview

In this paper, we take an important step towards reconsidering the IM problem in a competitive network under *more* realistic settings. Specifically, we jettison the aforementioned assumptions (*e.g.,* a new company being aware of a rival's strategy, competing companies may select seeds alternatively) made by state-of-the-art IM techniques. Instead, we make the following more realistic assumptions to address the IM problem in competitive networks.

- Firstly, given r different groups $\Psi = \{p_1, \dots, p_r\}$ who are maximizing their influences in a competitive network G, each group p_i may *independently* select k seeds under some strategy (algorithm). Note that different groups may or may not select seeds simultaneously.
- Secondly, we assume that each group p_i is aware of the existence of their rivals $p_1, \dots, p_{i-1}, p_{i+1}, \dots, p_r$ but is unaware of the IM strategies adopted by them.
- Thirdly, as motivated in Section 1.1, we assume that during influence propagation once a node in G is influ-

enced by some group p_i, it cannot be affected by any other groups.

Based on the above assumptions, we seek to find the "best" IM strategy (strategy for brevity) for each group in Ψ either by maximizing its influence or by minimizing its rivals', or both. Specifically, we provide an answer to the following question: *which existing* IM *strategy a company should adopt in the presence of rivals so that it can maximize its influence?*

Towards this goal, we model the IM problem in a competitive network as a game with each group as competitors and the expected influences under the strategies as payoffs. Consequently, we reformulate the IM task in such networks as the *optimal* IM *strategy selection* problem in a game (detailed in Section 3). By leveraging game theory, we first show that *pure* and *mixed* strategies may achieve *Nash Equilibrium* (NE) [16] (*i.e.*, a state in which none of the groups in the competition can influence more users by changing their strategies) and then discuss how to select the "best" IM strategy by finding the existence of NE (Section 4). To realize this solution, in Section 5 we propose a novel algorithm called GETREAL[4] (**G**am**E** **T**heory-based **RE**alistic M**A**ximization of Inf**L**uence) that seeks to find whether there exist a NE and returns both *pure* and *mixed* strategies for NE in a competitive network with r players and z strategies. Note that finding the existence of NE is particularly important as it guarantees that there exist an "optimal" strategy (strategy that exhibits the most expected influence in comparison with other strategies for all scenarios) for each group despite it being oblivious to their competitors' seeds. We experimentally demonstrate that GETREAL enables us to obtain superior quality influence spread in a competitive network compared to state-of-the-art IM techniques. We also show that this is primarily due to the fact that it can find the best strategy for a group in a competitive network attempting to maximize its influence against its rivals. In summary, we make the following contributions in this paper.

- We reformulate the IM problem in a competitive network where several companies are competing to influence the users over the same product almost simultaneously under more realistic settings compared to the state-of-the-art.
- We conduct a series of game theoretic analysis over the combinations of IM strategies by different companies in the competition. Based on our analysis, we propose a novel and generic algorithm called GETREAL to generate optimal solutions for these companies by finding the *Nash Equilibrium* (NE) under different conditions. Note that our solution ensures that GETREAL is not tightly coupled to any specific influence propagation model. This enhances its generality as well as portability as it can be easily realized over several popular models such as the *independent cascade* (IC) model and the *linear threshold* (LT) model.
- By applying GETREAL to real-world datasets under more realistic assumptions, we show its effectiveness and superiority over state-of-the-art methods.

[4] The name is inspired by an award-winning television programme in Singapore called *Get Real!* (pronounced as "get real") that takes a "fresh and hard look" at real-world issues related to life and living in Singapore. Similarly, in this paper we take a fresh and hard look at the real-world assumptions made by state-of-the-art IM techniques.

Table 1: Key notations used in this paper.

Symbol	*Definition*
$G(V,E)$	A social network graph
n	number of vertices in G
m	number of edges in G
$\Psi = \{p_1, \dots, p_r\}$	r different groups competing for influence
$\Phi = \{\phi_1, \dots, \phi_z\}$	z different IM algorithms each group may choose from
ϕ_j^i	p_i adopts ϕ_j
S_i	the initial seeds selected by p_i
A_i^j	the nodes eventually activated by p_i in j-th round, thus A_i^0 is the initial seeds that are eventually activated by p_i
$\sigma(\cdot)$	expected number of influenced node
$\sigma^0(\cdot)$	expected number of influenced node in singleton form, without competition
$\sigma_i(\phi_{t1}, \dots, \phi_{tr})$	the expected influence of p_i with $p_1, \dots, p_r$ adopting strategies $\phi_{t1}, \dots, \phi_{tr}$, respectively
$\Sigma(\Psi^r, \Phi^r)$	expected influence in competitive network with groups Ψ, each of which can choose a strategy from Φ
R	number of rounds of simulation
$E_{\phi_{t1} \dots \phi_{tr}}(\sigma(\cdot))$	expected $\sigma(\cdot)$ when p_i adopts ϕ_{ti}, $\forall i = 1, \dots, r$

The rest of this paper is organized as follows. We review related work in Section 2. In Section 3, we formally define a more realistic setting of the IM problem in competitive networks. We propose a game theory-driven method to solve the problem of selecting best IM strategies for groups in a competitive network in Section 4. In Section 5, we present the GETREAL algorithm to identify the "best" IM strategies involving r groups and z strategies. We present the experimental results in Section 6. Finally, the last section concludes this paper. The key notations used in this paper are given in Table 1.

2. RELATED WORK

2.1 IM in Non-competitive Networks

Kempe et al. [18] proved that the IM problem is NP-hard. Hence, they proposed an approximate greedy algorithm based on the fact that if a greedy maximization algorithm of a *submodular* function f returns the result A_{greedy}, then the following holds $f(A_{greedy}) \geq (1 - 1/e) \max_{|A| \leq k} f(A)$ [24]. That is, a greedy algorithm can give near optimal solution to the problem of maximization of a submodular function. Since then a large body of greedy [8,12,18,20–22] and heuristic-based [6–9,13,17,19] IM techniques are reported in the literature to improve efficiency, scalability, and influence spread quality. However, as discussed in Section 1, these techniques are suitable for maximizing influence in a non-competitive network. In reality, competition is ubiquitous. Consequently, if all competitors in a particular product market adopt the aforementioned approaches to influence the most number of users, then the initial seeds determined by these approaches may be shared by many competitors. Given that a user may eventually be influenced by a single competitor's product among many alternative options, existing IM approaches naturally fail to influence the expected number of users in a competitive network.

2.2 IM in Competitive Networks

Carnes et al. [5] and Bharathi et al. [1] are among the first to investigate the IM problem in competitive networks.

They proved that maximizing the influence of a competing group with the prior knowledge of rival side's initial seeds is NP-hard and submodular. Thus, they proposed a pair of hill-climbing algorithms to maximize the influence with prior knowledge of rival side's choice. Borodin et al. [2] studied similar problem under the LT model and further extended the solution to general threshold model [18]. The efforts in [3,15,31] investigate the problem of limiting the spread of a given campaign, which shares similarity with the IM problem in competitive networks. More recently, [29] proposed to solve the same problem with a minimal number of seeds selected by a latter group, who is maximizing its influence, given that another group have already influenced a number of users. However, as remarked in Section 1, these approaches suffer from several limitations stemming primarily from unrealistic assumptions. This limits their deployment in competitive networks.

Clark and Poovendran [10] and Pathak et al. [26] assumed that each individual is able to alternate their choice at arbitrary time step in a competitive influence maximization environment. However, in viral marketing, whenever a user buys a product she is viewed as being influenced. Consequently, once a user is influenced, she may not be influenced by other products subsequently. Recently, Fazeli et al. [11] and Tzoumas et al. [32] have investigated the IM problem between non-cooperative companies who select seeds alternately using game theory. They assume that a pair of companies select the seeds alternately in sequence, until both companies have selected k seeds. Unfortunately, in the real world it is highly unlikely that a competitor of a company is aware (or informed) every time the latter selects a seed. Furthermore, these techniques attempt to maximize the overall influence of both companies by leveraging a third party association. However, such scenario may not happen frequently in practice as many companies tend to maximize their own influence while minimizing their competitors'. They typically adopt their own strategies without knowing their competitors'. In contrast, GETREAL assumes that each individual company is unaware of the choices of their competitors.

Goyal and Kearns [14] jettisoned the aforementioned unrealistic assumptions and similar to our proposed technique assume that each group is unaware of their competitors' choices. However, this approach has the following drawbacks. Firstly, for the initial seeds which are simultaneously selected by both groups, namely p_1 and p_2, they assume that each node is infected by p_1 and p_2 with a probability proportional to the number of initial *adopters* of p_1 and p_2. However, this strategy may run into a dilemma as the number of initial adopters of p_1 and p_2 cannot be determined in reality *before* all the initial seeds for each group p_1 and p_2 are identified. In contrast, in our work a seed is activated by both groups with equal chance. Secondly, they defined a novel cascade model where the probability of a node to be activated is proportional to the fraction of active nodes in its neighborhood. However, in popular cascade models for the IM problem (*e.g.,* IC, WC) the probability of a node to be activated is affected by the exponential of the number of activated neighbors. Hence, the aforementioned technique has a limited applicability whereas, as we shall see later, our method can be applied to any cascade models. Thirdly, according to their model, the neighbors of a node v attempt to activate v at the same time. Hence, if v is not infected by its neighbors, it cannot be considered as a candidate seed. However, in IC, WC and LT models, if a node v is not affected by some neighbor, it is indeed possible to be affected by other neighbors at some step later.

Additionally, the work in [11,14,32] theoretically analyzed the existence of NE and the expected payoffs of competitors within the game without proposing any method to search for the NE. Furthermore, no simulation or experimental study has been undertaken on real-world networks to validate the approaches. In contrast, we not only analyze the existence of NE but also propose an algorithm that searches for NE given the *group space* and *strategy space*. Furthermore, we demonstrate its effectiveness with simulation on several real-world networks.

In [27], Prakash et al. theoretically showed winner takes all in the context of *epidemic propagation problem*, where a node i can be infected by a particular virus with probability β and cured with probability δ. Then when $\beta/\delta \geq \tau = \lambda_{1,A}$ (*i.e.*, the largest eigenvalue of adjacency matrix A) the epidemic survives, otherwise it dies out. IM problem is completely different as it only assumes that a node can transmit from inactive to active mode but not vice versa. Hence, influence cannot die out as long as it activates some nodes. Furthermore, the authors argued that even if two viruses both satisfy the *epidemic threshold* τ, one will dominate over the other. This is because a node can transmit from "infected by virus v_1" to "cured" and then to "infected by virus v_2". Such scenario does not happen in the IM problem setting.

3. PROBLEM DESCRIPTION

In this section, we formally define the problem of IM *strategy selection* in competitive networks. We begin by formally defining the notion of IM *strategy*. To facilitate our discussion, we focus on the *Independent Cascade* (IC) and *Weighted Cascade* (WC) models as these are the most popular cascade models [7, 8, 18–20]. However, our proposed technique is orthogonal to any specific cascade model as it provides a general solution to the proposed problem.

3.1 IM Strategy

We model a social network as directed graph $G = (V, E)$, where nodes in V represent individuals in the network and edges in E represent relationships between them. In contrast to classical IM techniques, influence diffusion in a competitive network does not happen in a "singleton" form. Instead, multiple pieces of influence diffuse simultaneously from competitive groups in the network. Each competing group aims to maximize their own influence considering the fact that some nodes may not be influenced if they have already been influenced by another group. Moreover, each group may adopt different IM *strategies*. Formally, an IM *strategy* is defined as follows.

DEFINITION 1. *Given a network $G(V, E)$ and a cascade model C, a* ***strategy*** *is an algorithm or a mixture of algorithms that a group adopts to maximize their influence subject to a budget k. All algorithms (*e.g., *Hill-climb algorithms, Heuristic algorithms, etc.) that a group may adopt form a strategy space and is denoted by $\Phi = \{\phi_1, \ldots, \phi_z\}$. If a single algorithm is adopted, it is called a* ***pure strategy****. Otherwise, we refer to it as a* ***mixed strategy****. We denote a mixed strategy as $\phi^* = \{\rho_1\phi_1, \ldots, \rho_z\phi_z\}$ where $\sum_{i=1}^{z} \rho_i = 1$. That is, ϕ^* is a mixture of Φ, namely, each player selecting seeds using ϕ_i with a probability ρ_i.* ∎

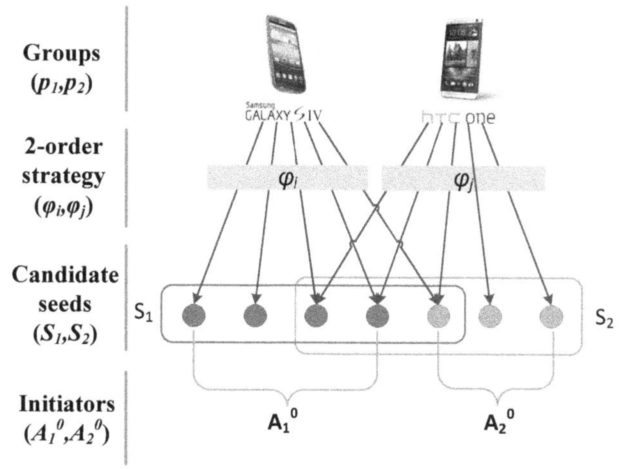

Figure 2: The seeds in a competitive network ($r = 2, z = 2$).

3.2 IM Strategy Selection Problem

Clearly, IM algorithms for non-competitive networks are unsuitable to provide superior solution to the IM problem in competitive networks. On the other hand, existing IM algorithms for competitive networks make several unrealistic assumptions. Hence, we revisit the IM problem in competitive networks under relatively more realistic settings and cast it to the problem of *optimal* selection of IM strategies in a competitive network. In the sequel, we refer to this reformulation of the IM problem in competitive networks as *influence maximization with competition* (IMC), which is formally defined below.

DEFINITION 2. *Let $\Psi = \{p_1, p_2, \ldots, p_r\}$ be the set of groups, each of which is maximizing their influence in a network $G(V, E)$. Let $\Phi = \{\phi_1, \ldots, \phi_z\}$ be a set of IM strategies that $p_i \in \Psi$ can choose from. Assume that each $v \in V$ can be activated by at most one $p_i \in \Psi$ and p_i is unaware of the strategies and seeds of other groups in Ψ. Given a specific cascade model C and a budget number k, the* ***influence maximization with competition (IMC) problem*** *is to choose $\phi_j \in \Phi$ for each $p_i \in \Psi$ that finds a seed set S_i in G where $|S_i| = k$ such that the expected number of nodes that are influenced by S_i, $\sigma(S_i)$, is the largest. That is,*

$$S_i = \underset{S'_i \subseteq V, |S'_i| = k}{\arg\max} \ \sigma(S'_i).$$

∎

Remark. It is worth noting that the goal of the above problem is not to propose yet another new IM technique that leverages local adoption dynamics and competition during the diffusion process to generate superior influence spreads. Instead, it *selects the best existing* IM *strategy from Φ for each competing group in Ψ in a competitive network*[5]. Since there are already an array of IM algorithms for non-competitive networks, in this paper we explore how a group can leverage them by choosing the "best" algorithm(s) (strategy) from this existing collection to maximize influence in a competitive network.

[5]Similar to [14], we assume groups have the same budget k. Our technique can be easily extended to arbitrary budgets for different groups.

Recall that a common concern of each group in the competition is that their rivals may take precedence in the market. As a result, competitive new products from rival companies are often promoted at similar times. To this end, in our model each group in a competitive network simultaneously selects the seed set and triggers off the diffusion process. Consider the simplest case where there is only one group. Then the selected seed nodes are eventually initiated by the group, which we refer to as *initiators* of the group. That is, the initiators and seeds are the same in a non-competitive IM problem. However, this may not be the case when there are multiple groups. In this case, each group may select their own seed set, which may overlap with one another. Without loss of generality, let S_i be the seeds selected by p_i and A_i^0 be the set of initiators of p_i. As depicted in Figure 2, S_1 and S_2 represent the seeds selected by p_1 and p_2, respectively. Observe that some of the seeds are selected by both p_1 and p_2. However, in reality they can only act as seeds of only one group (p_1 or p_2). Hence we can consider the nodes that eventually act as seeds of p_1 as *initiators* (denoted as A_1^0). Obviously, A_1^0 comprises of two parts: the nodes in $S_1 \setminus S_2$, which definitely act as seeds of p_1; the nodes in $S_1 \cap S_2$, which act as seeds of p_1 with *certain probabilities.*

Let $\mathcal{S} = \{S_1, S_2, \ldots S_r\}$ be the seed sets of $\Psi = \{p_1, p_2, \ldots, p_r\}$ in $G(V, E)$. A node selected by p_i can also be selected as a seed by other groups. Hence, we can use a bitmap $B = \{0, 1\}^r$ to denote whether a seed of p_i is also selected by other groups. Specifically, if a seed of p_i is also a seed of p_j, we set $b_j = 1$. Hence, all seeds of p_i can be matched to 2^{r-1} different bitmaps where $b_i = 1$. These seeds can be classified into two groups according to their bitmaps. The first group of seeds corresponds to the sequence $B = b_1 \ldots b_r$ where $b_i = 1, b_j \neq 1$ for $\forall j \neq i$. Note that these seeds are selected by p_i exclusively and definitely belong to the initiators of p_i, A_i^0. The second group of seeds corresponds to the sequences $B = b_1 \ldots b_r$ where $b_i = 1$ and $\exists j1, \ldots, js \neq i$ such that $b_{jh} = 1$ for $h = 1, \ldots, s$ (*i.e.*, these seeds are selected by not only p_i but also some other groups $p_{j1}, \ldots, p_{js}$). These seeds will be eventually initiating the influence propagation of only one group with equal probability $\frac{1}{s+1}$. Obviously, there are $2^{r-1} - 1$ bitmaps belonging to the second group. Seeds corresponding to each of these $2^{r-1} - 1$ bitmaps form a fuzzy set Q, for each seed $v \in Q$, it belongs to A_i^0 with probability $\frac{1}{|\{j|b_j^v = 1\}|}$ where b_j^v is j-th bit in v's bitmap $B^v = b_1^v b_2^v \ldots b_{i-1}^v 1 b_{i+1}^v \ldots b_r^v$.

Therefore, based on the pigeonhole principle, the expected size of A_i^0 should be less than or equal to k.

The example depicted in Figure 2 illustrates the relationship between A_i^0 and S_i. Let p_1 (*e.g., Samsung*) adopts a strategy ϕ_i which returns the seeds S_1; p_2 (*e.g., HTC*) adopts a strategy ϕ_j which returns the seeds S_2 ($|S_1| = |S_2| = k = 5$). Observe that there are three nodes in $S_1 \cap S_2$, which are eventually influenced by one group, either p_1 or p_2. Let us assume that two out of these three nodes in $S_1 \cap S_2$ are eventually influenced by p_1. Hence, these two nodes along with the other two nodes $v \in S_1 \setminus S_2$ are the initiators of p_1, denoted as A_1^0.

Extension of Cascade Models. We now extend the IC and WC models to competitive networks describing how multiple influences diffuse simultaneously in a given network. Note that according to the IC model, if there are t neighbors of v that are in A^i, then $v \in A^{i+1}$ with probability

		p_2	
		ϕ_1	ϕ_2
p_1	ϕ_1	$(\lambda g, \lambda g)$	$(\alpha g, \beta h)$
	ϕ_2	$(\beta h, \alpha g)$	$(\gamma h, \gamma h)$

Table 2: Expected influence under $\Psi \times \Phi$.

$1-(1-p)^t$. Hence, IC model in competitive networks can be defined as follows.

Let A_j^i be the set of nodes that are influenced by p_j in the i-th round and $|A_j^0| \leq k$. If there are t_j neighbors of v that are in A_j^i, then $v \in A_j^{i+1}$ with probability:

$$\frac{t_j}{\sum_{j=1}^r t_j}(1-(1-p)^{\sum_{j=1}^r t_j}).$$

Similarly, in the WC model for competitive networks, v belongs to A_j^{i+1} with the following probability:

$$\frac{t_j}{\sum_{j=1}^r t_j}(1-(1-1/v.degree)^{\sum_{j=1}^r t_j}).$$

In the following section, we propose a game theoretic strategy to investigate the solutions for groups maximizing their influences in a competitive network under these two models.

4. FINDING BEST STRATEGIES

As discussed in the preceding section, the goal of IMC problem is to select the best IM strategy from Φ for each competing group in Ψ in a competitive network such that the influence of each group is maximized under a specified cascade model. To this end, in this section we propose a novel method using game theory to find the best solution for groups that are competing for influence scope with a set of rivals. We first describe the strategies that each group may adopt. As remarked earlier, each strategy is correlated to seed selection according to a specific IM algorithm or even a mixture of algorithms. With each group adopting some strategy, a game can be formed with each group as competitors and the expected influence under the strategies as payoffs. Hence, we can seek NE within the game, from which the best strategy for each group is obtained.

To simplify our discussion, we assume the competitive network involves two groups and two strategies. That is, $r=2$ (*i.e.*, $\Psi=\{p_1,p_2\}$) and $z=2$ (*i.e.*, $\Phi=\{\phi_1,\phi_2\}$) (*e.g.*, Figure 2). It is worth noting that although it is widely acknowledged that game between 2 or 3 competitive players is prevalent in many real markets (*e.g., Samsung* vs. *Apple* in smartphone; *AMD* vs. *Intel* in desktop CPUs; *Verizon, Sprint* and *AT&T* in US mobile service market) [25], the solution proposed in this paper is not limited to this setting. Particularly, it is applicable to more complex competitive networks with more than two groups and two strategies.

Let g and h be the expected influence using strategies ϕ_1 and ϕ_2, respectively. Clearly, in a competitive network with $\Psi=\{p_1,p_2\}$, the expected influence of p_1 and p_2 both adopting the same strategy ϕ_1 (*resp.*, ϕ_2) should be equal to each other. Let us denote it as λg (*resp.*, γh). In the case where p_1 adopts ϕ_1 and p_2 adopts ϕ_2, the expected influence of p_1 and p_2 can be represented as αg and βh, respectively. Similarly, in the symmetric case where p_1 adopts ϕ_2 while p_2 adopts ϕ_1, the expected influence of p_1 and p_2 are βh and αg, respectively. Thus, we have the matrix in Table 2 showing the expected influences under all combinations in $\Psi \times \Phi$.

Definition 3. *Let Ψ and Φ be the group space and strategy space, respectively. Then a* ***r-order strategy*** *can be denoted as Φ^r, and an instance of r-order strategy $\Phi_j^r = (\phi_{j1},\ldots,\phi_{jr}) \in \Phi^r$ refers to the case where p_i adopts ϕ_{ji} for $i=1,\ldots,r$, respectively.* ∎

Definition 4. *Let Ψ and Φ be the group space and strategy space, respectively. The* ***expected influence over all groups for a r-order strategy*** *Φ^r is defined as $\Sigma:\Phi^r \mapsto \mathbb{R}^r$. Let $\sigma_i(\Phi_j^r)$ be the expected influence of a r-order strategy Φ_j^r. Then the expected influence over all r-order strategies is given as follows:*

$$\begin{aligned}\Sigma(\Phi^r) &= ((\sigma_1(\phi_1,\ldots,\phi_1),\ldots,\sigma_r(\phi_1,\ldots,\phi_1)),\\ &\quad (\sigma_1(\phi_1,\ldots,\phi_1),\ldots,\sigma_{r-1}(\phi_1,\ldots,\phi_1),\\ &\quad \sigma_r(\phi_1,\ldots,\phi_1,\phi_2)),\\ &\quad \vdots\\ &\quad (\sigma_1(\phi_{z-1},\phi_z,\ldots,\phi_z),\sigma_2(\phi_{z-1},\phi_z,\ldots,\phi_z),\\ &\quad \ldots,\sigma_r(\phi_{z-1},\phi_z,\ldots,\phi_z)),\\ &\quad (\sigma_1(\phi_z,\ldots,\phi_z),\ldots,\sigma_r(\phi_z,\ldots,\phi_z))).\end{aligned}$$

Obviously, the number of element $|\Sigma(\Phi)| = z^r$, each of which is a vector in $\mathbb{R}^r$ space. ∎

Table 2 shows the expected influences of 2-order strategies in a competitive network with $r=2, z=2$. By transferring the expected influence for 2-order strategies into such a table, the IMC problem can be reformulated as a Nash Equilibrium (NE) existence problem in the field of game theory. For the sake of completeness, we first briefly introduce the notion of Nash Equilibrium.

Nash Equilibrium (NE). In game theory, the Nash Equilibrium is a solution concept of a non-cooperative game involving two or more players, in which each player is assumed to know the equilibrium strategies of the other players, and no player has anything to gain by changing only his own strategy unilaterally [16, 23]. If each player has chosen a strategy and no player can benefit by changing strategies while the other players keep theirs unchanged, then the current set of strategy choices and the corresponding payoffs constitute a NE. Stated simply, p_1 and p_2 are in NE if p_1 is making the best decision she can, taking into account p_2's decision, and p_2 is making the best decision he can, taking into account p_1's decision. Likewise, a group of players are in NE if each one is making the best decision that he or she can, taking into account the decisions of the others. In the following, we discuss the solution to the NE from the parameters in Table 2. In particular, in contrast to [11,14,32], we present a generalized technique, which is applicable to *any* existing cascade model, for finding the existence of NE.

4.1 The Values of γ, λ, α and β

Solving the NE within the expected influence of r-order strategies shown in Table 2 requires detailed comparison over the adjacent entries in the table. We now discuss the entries in the expected influence of r-order strategy table. Through the discussion, we are able to show how the expected influence of strategies affect the existence of NE. In the next section, we shall propose an algorithm for solving the problem in more general case.

THEOREM 1. *Let g, h be the expected influence for strategies ϕ_1, ϕ_2 with seeds set size k, respectively, in a network without competition. The expectation for the expected influence of 2-order strategy when both groups adopt the same strategy in a competitive network (*i.e., *$(\sigma_1(\phi_1,\phi_1), \sigma_2(\phi_1,\phi_1))$ and $(\sigma_1(\phi_2,\phi_2), \sigma_2(\phi_2,\phi_2)))$ can be represented as $(\lambda g, \lambda g)$ and $(\gamma h, \gamma h)$, respectively. Moreover, the following holds $\lambda \in [\frac{1}{2}, 1-\frac{\epsilon_1}{2g}]$ and $\gamma \in [\frac{1}{2}, 1-\frac{\epsilon_2}{2h}]$ where $\epsilon_i = E_{\phi_i}(\sigma(S_1 \cap S_2))$.*[6]

PROOF. Let $\sigma^0(S)$ be the expected number of influenced nodes with initial seeds set S in a network without competition. As S is generated from a randomized algorithm ϕ_i, we use $E_{\phi_i}(\sigma^0(S))$ to denote the expected $\sigma^0(S)$ that is computed over ϕ_i. Then $E_{\phi_1}(\sigma^0(S)) = g$ when we adopt ϕ_1 strategy. Hence, $E_{\phi_1}(\sigma^0(S_1)) = E_{\phi_1}(\sigma^0(S_2)) = g$.

On one hand, as $\sigma^0(\cdot)$ is monotonically increasing [18], the following holds: $g = E_{\phi_1}(\sigma^0(S_1)) \leq E_{\phi_1}(\sigma^0(S_1 \cup S_2))$. Also, $S_1 \cup S_2 = A_1^0 \cup A_2^0$ and $A_1^0 \cap A_2^0 = \emptyset$. Thus,

$$E_{\phi_1}(\sigma^0(S_1 \cup S_2)) = E_{\phi_1}(\sigma(S_1 \cup S_2)) = E_{\phi_1}(\sigma(A_1^0 \cup A_2^0)).$$

As there is no overlap between A_1^∞ and A_2^∞, then the following holds:

$$\begin{aligned} E_{\phi_1}(\sigma(A_1^0 \cup A_2^0)) &= E_{\phi_1}(|A_1^\infty|) + E_{\phi_1}(|A_2^\infty|) \\ &= \lambda g + \lambda g = 2\lambda g. \end{aligned}$$

Thus, $g \leq 2\lambda g$ which indicates $\lambda \geq \frac{1}{2}$.

Similarly, $h \leq 2\gamma h$ under strategy ϕ_2. Thus, $\gamma \geq \frac{1}{2}$.

On the other hand, as $\sigma^0(\cdot)$ is submodular [18][7], the following holds under strategy ϕ_1:

$$\begin{aligned} \sigma^0(S_1 \cup S_2) - \sigma^0(S_1) &= \sigma^0(S_1 \cup (S_2 \setminus S_1)) - \sigma^0(S_1) \\ &\leq \sigma^0((S_1 \cap S_2) \cup (S_2 \setminus S_1)) \\ &\quad -\sigma^0(S_1 \cap S_2). \end{aligned}$$

In fact, $E_{\phi_1}(\sigma^0(S_1 \cup S_2)) = E(|A_1^\infty|) + E(|A_2^\infty|) = 2\lambda g$ and

$$\begin{aligned} E_{\phi_1}(\sigma^0((S_1 \cap S_2) \cup (S_2 \setminus S_1))) &= E_{\phi_1}(\sigma^0(S_2)) \\ &= E_{\phi_1}(\sigma^0(S_1)) = g. \end{aligned}$$

If we represent $E_{\phi_1}(\sigma^0(S_1 \cap S_2))$ as ϵ_1, then $2\lambda g - g \leq g - \epsilon_1$ which indicates $\lambda \leq 1 - \frac{\epsilon_1}{2g}$.

Similarly, $2\gamma h - h \leq h - \epsilon$. Hence, $\gamma \leq 1 - \frac{\epsilon_2}{2h}$ where $\epsilon_2 = E_{\phi_2}(\sigma^0(S_1 \cap S_2))$. □

COROLLARY 1. *Let g, h be the expected influences for strategies ϕ_1, ϕ_2, respectively, in a network without competition. The expectation for the expected influence of 2-order strategy where both groups adopt different strategies in a competitive network (*i.e., *$(\sigma_1(\phi_1,\phi_2)$, $\sigma_2(\phi_1,\phi_2))$ and $(\sigma_1(\phi_2,\phi_1)$, $\sigma_2(\phi_2,\phi_1)))$ can be represented as $(\alpha g, \beta h)$ and $(\beta h, \alpha g)$, respectively. Moreover, the following holds $\alpha + \beta \in [1, 1 + \frac{g-\epsilon}{h}]$ where*

$$\epsilon = E_{\phi_1\phi_2}(\sigma(S_1 \cap S_2)) = E_{\phi_2\phi_1}(\sigma(S_1 \cap S_2)).$$

PROOF. Similar to the proof for Theorem 1, the following holds:

$$g + h - \epsilon \geq \alpha g + \beta h \geq g.$$

On the other hand, according to the result in [8], $g \geq h$. Thus,

$$(\alpha + \beta)h \leq \alpha g + \beta h \leq (\alpha + \beta)g.$$

Combining both sets of inequalities together, we can generate the following inequalities:

$$\begin{cases} (\alpha+\beta)h \leq g + h - \epsilon \\ (\alpha+\beta)g \geq g \end{cases}$$

Hence,

$$\begin{cases} \alpha + \beta \leq 1 + \dfrac{g-\epsilon}{h} \\ \alpha + \beta \geq 1 \end{cases}$$

□

In fact, the values of γ, λ, α and β are affected by the degree of overlap between the seeds generated from different algorithms, which is eventually decided by the topological characteristics of the network and the adopted influence cascade model. For instance, if a network always generates the same initial seeds according to a specific algorithm, the values of λ and γ are $\frac{1}{2}$. Otherwise, if a network generates different initial seeds according to the same algorithm, the values of λ and γ are close to the upper bound. Note that α and β are also affected by the topological characteristics of networks in the same way. Experimental results in Section 6 shall justify our conclusion.

4.2 Pure Strategy Nash Equilibrium

Next we show in detail the NE that can be found from the expected influence table of 2-order strategy. We begin by formally defining NE in the context of the IMC problem.

DEFINITION 5. *A r-order strategy $\Phi_j^r = (\phi_{t1}, \ldots, \phi_{tr})$ is an **equilibrium** for p_s if $\forall \phi'_{ts} \in \Phi$ and $\phi'_{ts} \neq \phi_{ts}$, the following holds: $\sigma_s(\phi_{t1}, \ldots, \phi_{t(s-1)}, \phi_{ts}, \phi_{t(s+1)}, \ldots, \phi_{tr}) \geq \sigma_s(\phi_{t1}, \ldots, \phi_{t(s-1)}, \phi'_{ts}, \phi_{t(s+1)}, \ldots, \phi_{tr})$. If a r-order strategy Φ_j^r is an equilibrium for all groups $p_i \in \Psi$, then it is a **Nash Equilibrium**[8].* ▮

Let (ϕ_i, ϕ_j) be the 2-order strategy where p_1 adopts ϕ_i while p_2 adopts ϕ_j. We iteratively examine each 2-order strategies in Table 2. If a 2-order strategy dominates the others with respect to the expected influence for both groups p_1 and p_2, it is a *pure strategy* NE.

If $\lambda g \geq \beta h$ and $\alpha g \geq \gamma h$, the 2-order strategy (ϕ_1, ϕ_1) is the NE. It can be explained as follows. In case p_2 adopts ϕ_1, ϕ_1 is superior to ϕ_2 for p_1 as the following holds

$$\sigma_1(\phi_1, \phi_1) = \lambda g \geq \beta h = \sigma_1(\phi_2, \phi_1).$$

In the other case when p_2 adopts ϕ_2, ϕ_1 is also superior to ϕ_2 for p_1, as

$$\sigma_1(\phi_1, \phi_2) = \lambda g \geq \beta h = \sigma_1(\phi_2, \phi_2).$$

Thus, no matter whichever strategy p_2 adopts, p_1 has to adopt ϕ_1. Similarly, it is easy to see that p_2 has to adopt ϕ_1 in both cases (*i.e.*, p_1 adopts ϕ_1 or ϕ_2).

[6]Note that as all greedy IM algorithms are in fact based on sampling method, the seeds selected by the same algorithm may not be exactly the same.

[7]Note that $\sigma^0(S)$ is the expected number of influenced nodes with initial seeds set S in a network without competition and therefore satisfies submodularity. Hence, we do not need to know whether $\sigma(S)$, the competitive version, is submodular or not.

[8]We only consider dominant strategy nash equilibrium. The strategy of every player (*i.e.*, p_1, p_2, ...) in this equilibrium always dominates other strategies no matter how other players choose their strategies. This is consistent with our problem settings where companies are unaware of each other's strategy and aim to maximize their own benefits while not dominated by any other groups.

Similarly, If $\lambda g \leq \beta h$ and $\alpha g \leq \gamma h$, the 2-order strategy (ϕ_2, ϕ_2) is the NE. Particularly, Nash [23] has proved that in a symmetric game where the players are commutative with each other, if there is a NE, it exists when all the players adopt the same strategy (*i.e.*, (ϕ_1, ϕ_1) or (ϕ_2, ϕ_2))[9].

4.3 Mixed Strategy Nash Equilibrium

Observe that when none of the 2-order strategy dominates all the other ones, there does not exist a NE based on pure strategy. However, there exists another type of solution, namely *mixed strategy*, where players choose a probability distribution over possible strategies. Nash [23] has proved for a game with finite set of actions (*i.e.*, strategies), at least one mixed strategy NE must exist in such a game.

DEFINITION 6. *A r-order **mixed strategy** is a r-order strategy $\Phi^r_j = (\phi^*_1, \ldots, \phi^*_r)$ where ϕ^*_i is a probabilistic strategy that p_i adopts $\phi_1, \ldots, \phi_z$ with probability $\rho_{i1}, \ldots, \rho_{iz}$ ($\sum_{j=1}^{z} \rho_{ij} = 1$), respectively.* ∎

Hence, in a network with $r = 2, z = 2$, the expectation for p_1 adopting ϕ_1 can be given as follows.

$$E[\rho\sigma_1(\phi_1, \phi_1) + (1 - \rho)\sigma_1(\phi_1, \phi_2)] = \rho\lambda g + (1 - \rho)\alpha g. \quad (1)$$

On the other hand, the expectation for p_1 adopting ϕ_2 is given as:

$$E[\rho\sigma_1(\phi_2, \phi_1) + (1 - \rho)\sigma_1(\phi_2, \phi_2)] = \rho\beta h + (1 - \rho)\gamma h. \quad (2)$$

Nash [23] proved that the mixed strategy exists when both equations equal to each other. Specifically, all the players in a symmetric game where the players are commutative with each other, will *adopt the same mixed strategy*: $\phi^*_1 = \cdots = \phi^*_r$. Hence, let $\rho\lambda g + (1 - \rho)\alpha g = \rho\beta h + (1 - \rho)\gamma h$. Then a mixed strategy NE can be found when the following holds.

$$\rho = \frac{\gamma h - \alpha g}{\gamma h - \alpha g + \lambda g - \beta h} \quad (3)$$

That is, in a problem where pure strategy NE does not exist, the best solution for each group (*i.e.*, p_1, p_2) is to adopt a mixed strategy by adopting ϕ_1, ϕ_2 with the following probabilities, respectively.

$$\frac{\gamma h - \alpha g}{\gamma h - \alpha g + \lambda g - \beta h} \quad (4)$$

$$\frac{\lambda g - \beta h}{\gamma h - \alpha g + \lambda g - \beta h} \quad (5)$$

Next, we propose a framework to solve the IMC problem by exploiting NE in the expected influence for r-order strategy.

5. THE GETREAL ALGORITHM

In the preceding section, we have formally defined r-order strategy as well as the corresponding expected influence (Definitions 3 and 4). Using the r-order strategy, we reformulate the IMC problem as a NE existence problem. By investigating the simplest case, namely the existence of pure NE in IMC problem with $r = 2, z = 2$ (Theorem 1 and Corollary 1), we describe a method to find the pure NE in general IMC problem with $r \geq 2, z \geq 2$ in Section 4.2. In case there is no pure strategy, we additionally show how to find the mixed NE in general IMC problem with $r \geq 2, z \geq 2$ in Section 4.3. Hence we now have all the machinery in place to present the GETREAL algorithm.

Algorithm 1: The GETREAL Algorithm.

Input: network $G(V, E)$, group space $\Psi = \{p_1, \ldots, p_r\}$, seeds sets $S_1, \ldots, S_z$ generated by strategies $\phi_1, \ldots, \phi_z$, respectively; the expected influence function $\sigma_i(S_{t1}, \ldots, S_{tr})$ under a given influence cascade model.

Output: the best strategy $\phi^* = \{\rho_1\phi_1, \ldots, \rho_z\phi_z\}$ for each group, where $\sum_{i=1}^{z} \rho_i = 1$.

begin
  foreach $\psi = (\phi_{t1}, \ldots, \phi_{tr}) \in \psi(\Phi^r)$ **do**
    foreach $p_i \in \Psi$ **do**
      compute $\sigma_i(\psi) = \sigma_i(S_{t1}, \ldots, S_{tr})$;
  foreach $\phi_i \in \Phi$ **do**
    if $\forall p_s \in \Psi$ *and* $\phi^s_j \neq \phi_i$, $\sigma_s(\phi_i, \ldots, \phi_i) \geq \sigma_s(\phi^1_i, \ldots, \phi^{s-1}_i, \phi^s_j, \phi^{s+1}_i, \ldots, \phi^r_i)$ **then**
      return $\phi^* = \{\phi_i\}$ /* the pure strategy */;
  Solve the equation set
  $\sum_{\vec{\ell} \in L} \vec{\rho} \odot \vec{\ell}\sigma_1(\phi_1, \phi_{-1}(\vec{\ell})) = \sum_{\vec{\ell} \in L} \vec{\rho} \odot \vec{\ell}\sigma_1(\phi_2, \phi_{-1}(\vec{\ell}))$;
  $= \cdots = \sum_{\vec{\ell} \in L} \vec{\rho} \odot \vec{\ell}\sigma_1(\phi_z, \phi_{-1}(\vec{\ell}))$;
  return $\phi^* = \{\rho_1\phi_1, \ldots, \rho_z\phi_z\}$ where $(\rho_1, \ldots, \rho_z) = \vec{\rho}$
  /* the mixed strategy */;

The main idea of the algorithm is as follows. Given a competitive network $G(V, E)$ with group space $\Psi = \{p_1, \ldots, p_r\}$ and strategy space $\Phi = \{\phi_1, \ldots, \phi_z\}$, let $f : \Psi \mapsto \Phi$ be a function that maps every element of Ψ to an element in Φ. Hence, each function f corresponds to a specific case in the game where each group adopts a specific strategy. We compute the expected influence of each group under each function. If there exist any strategy which exhibits the most expected influence under all functions, it is output as a pure strategy that is correlated to a pure NE. Otherwise, we need to find the mixed strategy by searching for mixed NE solution as follows. Let $\sigma_i(\phi_j, \phi_{-i})$ be the expected influence of p_i while p_i adopts ϕ_j and other groups adopt a combination over all the strategies, namely ϕ_{-i}. Clearly, ϕ_{-i} contains z^{r-1} cases. For instance, ϕ_{-1} contains the cases $(\phi^1_2, \ldots, \phi^1_r), (\phi^1_2, \ldots, \phi^1_{r-1}, \phi^2_r), \ldots, (\phi^z_2, \ldots, \phi^z_r)$. That is, the number of remaining $r-1$ users adopting an arbitrary strategy ϕ_i follows a distribution $L = (\ell_1, \ldots, \ell_z)$ subject to $\sum_{i=1}^{z} \ell_i = r - 1$, where ℓ_i indicates the number of players adopting ϕ_i. Let $\phi_{-i}(L)$ denote the case where players other than ψ_i adopt strategies according to the distribution L. Hence, ϕ_{-1} contains all the possible distributions of L which contains z^{r-1} cases. Generally, given that ϕ_{-1} follows a distribution $L = (\ell_1, \ldots, \ell_z)$ and for each player ϕ_i occurs with probability ρ_i, then L occurs with a probability $\prod_{i=1}^{r} \rho_i^{\ell_i}$. Formally, we denote $\prod_{i=1}^{r} \rho_i^{\ell_i}$ as $\vec{\rho} \odot \vec{\ell}$ where $\vec{\rho} = (\rho_1, \ldots, \rho_r)$ and $\vec{\ell} = (\ell_1, \ldots, \ell_r)$. We now present the GETREAL algorithm to find the best solution.

Algorithm 1 outlines the GETREAL algorithm. Firstly, for each instance of r-order strategy in Φ^r, the algorithm com-

[9]We do not consider the asymmetric nash equilibrium, where an equilibrium is formed by groups adopting different pure strategy. In this case, there is at least one group dominated by the others in any nash equilibrium, and thus that group will reject the nash. In our algorithm, we tackle this using a randomized mixed strategy NE.

Table 3: Description of real-world networks.

Network	*No. of nodes*	*No. of edges*
Phy	37,154	231,584
Hep	15,233	58,891
Wiki-talk	2,394,385	5,021,410

putes the expected influence for each group $p_i \in \Psi$ using $\sigma(\Phi^r)$ (Lines 2-4). Obviously, there are z^r instances in r-order strategy set Φ^r. For each instance, the algorithm computes the expected influence for r different groups. Next, it tests whether there exist any pure strategy NE as described in Definition 5 (Lines 5-7). Note that we have also shown in Section 4.3, if there is a NE in a symmetric game where the players are commutative with each other, it exist when all players adopt the same strategy. Hence, we examine only z instances in the r-order strategy space, namely, $(\phi_i, \dots, \phi_i)$ for all $i = 1, \dots, z$ (Lines 5). For each of these instances, namely $(\phi_i, \dots, \phi_i)$, the algorithm checks whether there is an increase in the expected influence of p_s for all $s = 1, \dots, r$ when p_s changes its strategy (Lines 6). If there is any increase, the r-order strategy $(\phi_i, \dots, \phi_i)$ is rejected and we turn on to $(\phi_{i+1}, \dots, \phi_{i+1})$. Otherwise, the pure strategy NE happens when each group adopts ϕ_i (Lines 7). Recall that we only aim to find symmetric pure strategy where NE happens when all groups adopt the same strategy. We do not consider the asymmetric NE where an equilibrium is formed by groups adopting different pure strategy. For this case, the best strategy is to adopt a randomized mixed strategy NE which is guaranteed to exist in finite action games [23]. Specifically, it exists when all the z expectations of the payoff (*i.e.*, expected influence) for p_s adopting each strategy equal to each other. Thus, GETREAL finds the solution (*i.e.*, $\rho_1, \dots, \rho_z$) towards the equation set with z equations (Lines 8-10) based on our discussion in Section 4.3. Note that it has been proven that finding the mixed equilibrium in a game with r players (*i.e.*, groups) and z actions (*i.e.*, strategies) is NP-complete [28]. Hence, it works effectively in games where $z, r \leq 3$, which represents many real-world scenarios [25]. Observe that GETREAL can easily be extended (by replacing Lines 8-10 with a state-of-the-art *approximate* approach in game theory [4, 28]) to handle more complex networks (*i.e.*, $z, r \geq 4$) by solving NE in complex games[10].

6. PERFORMANCE STUDY

GETREAL is implemented in C++. We ran all experiments on 3.2GHz Quad-Core Intel i5 machines with 8GB RAM, running Windows 7. Note that there is no existing IM algorithm for competitive networks which we can compare with GETREAL. This is because, in addition to the unrealistic assumptions, the efforts in [11, 14, 32] do not provide solutions for finding NE as they focus on theoretical study of the existence of NE.

6.1 Experimental Setup

Table 3 summarizes the three real-world social network graphs used in our experiments. *Phy* and *Hep* are two academic collaboration networks[11] which are also used in several prior studies such as [7, 8, 13, 18, 20]. The *Wiki-talk*[12] is a large network containing millions of nodes representing all the users and discussions in Wikipedia from its inception to January 2008. Nodes in the network represent Wikipedia users and edges represent talk page editing relationship.

Recall that the goal of this work is to choose an optimal existing IM strategy for each group so that each group can maximize influence. Hence, we report the following experiments under different cascade models. Recall from Section 4, 2-player game is the most classic game in many real applications [25]. Hence, we focus our experimental study on 2-order strategies. Note that the qualitative results on 3-order strategies are similar and we do not report them here due to space constraints (requires 27 graphs for a single dataset).

- Firstly, we show the optimal 2-order strategy that is selected by our framework and compare it with the other two 2-order strategies under each model (IC and WC). Hence, there are six different 2-order strategies as listed below.
- Secondly, we show the impact of our realistic assumptions on the IM problem by comparing GETREAL with some of the state-of-the-art algorithms designed for non-competitive networks.
- Thirdly, for the case when pure NE does not exist, we show the 2-order mixed strategy found by our framework and compare it with other 2-order strategies as well as the random strategy.

We denote the strategies involved in these experiments as follows:

- "DDIC-MGIC": 2-order strategy (*DegreeDiscountIC*, *MixGreedyIC* [8]).
- "MGIC-MGIC": 2-order strategy (*MixGreedyIC*, *MixGreedyIC*).
- "DDIC-DDIC": 2-order strategy (*DegreeDiscountIC*, *DegreeDiscountIC*).
- "SDWC-MGWC": 2-order strategy (*SingleDiscount*, *MixGreedyWC* [8]).
- "MGWC-MGWC": 2-order strategy (*MixGreedyWC*, *MixGreedyWC*).
- "SDWC-SDWC": 2-order strategy (*SingleDiscount*, *SingleDiscount*).
- "S-MGIC": running *MixGreedyIC* in non-competitive network.
- "S-MGWC": running *MixGreedyWC* in non-competitive network.
- "*Mixed Str.*": 2-order strategy ($\phi^* = \rho\phi_1, (1-\rho)\phi_2$) with both p_1 and p_2 adopt ϕ_1, ϕ_2 with probability $\rho, 1-\rho$, respectively.
- "*Random*": both p_1 and p_2 adopt ϕ_1, ϕ_2 randomly.

Observe that we chose the popular IM techniques in [8] as representative strategies. However, our strategy space is not limited to these selected algorithms. Particularly, GETREAL is orthogonal to any specific choice of IM techniques. Other IM techniques such as [7, 19] can be chosen as well.

[10]Pure NE can be found in polynomial time and is not the main challenge in such complex game.

[11]Hep and Phy are downloaded from `http://research.microsoft.com/enus/people/weic/graphdata.zip`.

[12]Downloaded from `http://snap.stanford.edu/data/wiki-Talk.html`.

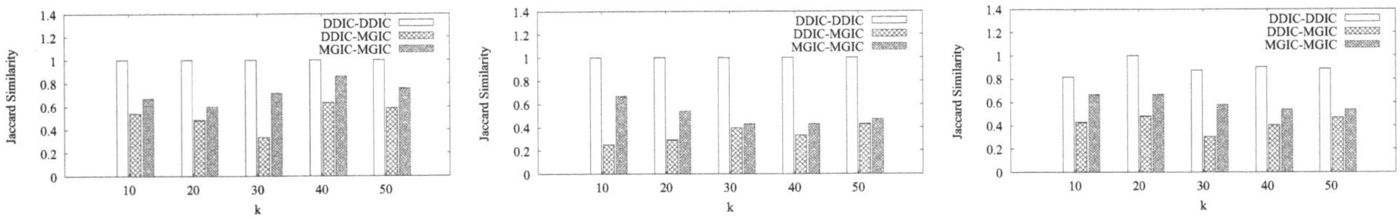

(a) *Hep* (b) *Phy* (c) *Wiki*

Figure 3: Overlap between S_1 and S_2 (IC model).

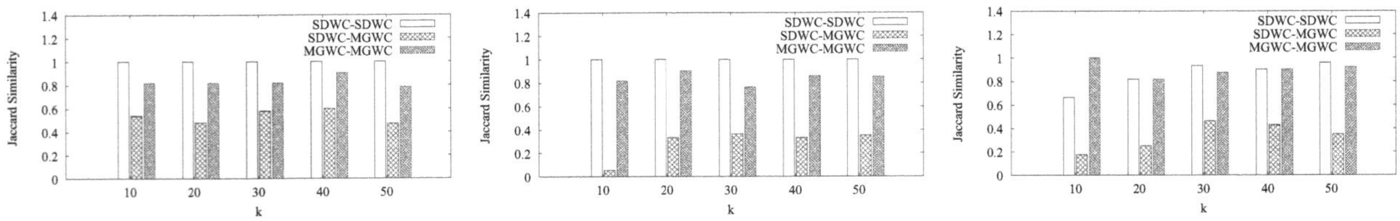

(a) *Hep* (b) *Phy* (c) *Wiki*

Figure 4: Overlap between S_1 and S_2 (WC model).

6.2 Experimental Results

Similarity Between the Selected Seeds Sets. We ran a series of 2-order strategies with $\phi_1 =$ *MixGreedy* (IC) and $\phi_2 =$ *DegreeDiscount* (IC). Before comparing the influence spread, we compare the selected seeds in the three different 2-order strategies, namely, "DDIC-MGIC", "MGIC-MGIC" and "DDIC-DDIC". We compute the jaccard similarity between S_1 and S_2 under each 2-order strategy, which is computed as follows:

$$Sim(S_1, S_2) = \frac{|S_1 \cap S_2|}{|S_1 \cup S_2|}.$$

Note that it can also be computed as follows.

$$Sim(S_1, S_2) = \frac{2k - (|A_1^0| + |A_2^0|)}{|A_1^0| + |A_2^0|}.$$

Figure 3 plots $Sim(S_1, S_2)$ by varying $k = 10, \ldots, 50$ for the three datasets. Obviously, the 2-order strategies "DDIC-DDIC" and "MGIC-MGIC" exhibit higher similarity than the strategy "MGIC-DDIC". Specifically, the seeds selected by the same IM algorithms have larger overlap and is consistent with our discussion in Section 1. We also evaluated the jaccard similarities when $\phi_1 =$ *MixGreedy* (WC) and $\phi_2 =$ *SingleDiscount*. The results are reported in Figures 3(b), 3(c), and 4. All these cases show similar behavior as Figure 3(a).

The Pure Strategy Solutions. The aim of this set of experiments is to find the best pure strategy a group should choose, given all the possible pure strategies their competitors may choose from. Based on the seeds selected by different algorithms under three r-order strategies under IC model, we compute the expected influence for groups p_1 and p_2. Based on Algorithm 1, we find the pure strategy NE solution towards *Hep* dataset as "MGIC-MGIC". That is, the best solution for p_1 to maximize their influence is to choose *MixGreedy* (IC model) to select the seeds, no matter which strategy p_2 adopts (*MixGreedy* or *DegreeDiscount*). In fact, p_2 will also select *MixGreedy* (IC) for the same reason as p_1. Figures 5(a) and 5(b) justify our conclusion. In both figures we plot the expected influence of p_1 by fixing the strategy of p_2. The curve "MGIC" (*resp.*, "DDIC") means p_1 adopts *MixGreedy* (*resp.*, *DegreeDiscount*). In Figure 5(a) we fix p_2 to adopt "MGIC" and vary the approaches for p_1. Clearly, "MGIC" dominates "DDIC". That is, p_1 should adopt "MGIC" when p_2 adopts "MGIC". In Figure 5(b) we fix p_2 to adopt "DDIC" and vary the approaches for p_1. Again "MGIC" dominates "DDIC". That is, p_1 should adopt "MGIC" when p_2 adopts "DDIC". Thus, p_1 should adopt "MGIC" no matter whichever strategy p_2 adopts ("MGIC" or "DDIC"). Similarly, p_2 should also select "MGIC" as p_2 and p_1 is symmetric. Likewise, we can also find pure strategy NE in the other four scenarios, namely, *Phy* and *Wiki* datasets under both IC and WC models. These are reported in Figures 6 and 7, respectively.

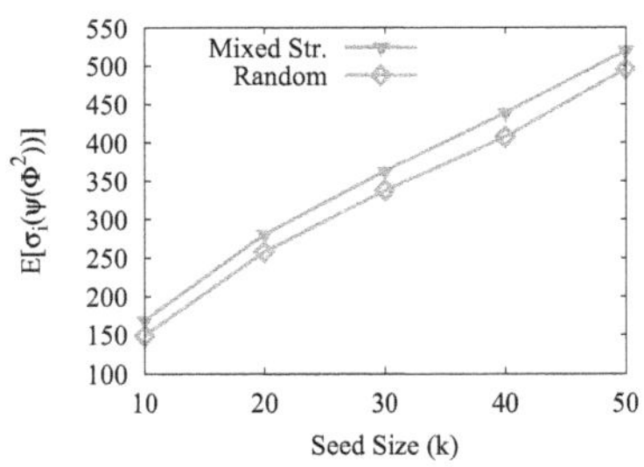

Figure 8: Comparison between mixed ($\rho = 0.582$) and random strategies (*Hep* under WC model).

The Mixed Strategy Solutions. In all the datasets and cascade scenarios discussed above, there exist one case where we cannot find a pure strategy solution: *Hep* under WC model (Figures 5(c) and 5(d)). Hence, we search for mixed strategy (Lines 8-10 in Algorithm 1). Executing GETREAL on this scenario computes the value of ρ as 0.582. That is, the mixed strategy for p_1 (*resp.*, p_2) is to adopt *MixGreedy* and *SingleDiscount* with probabilities 0.582 and 0.418, respectively.

In order to test the performance of mixed strategy NE, we simulate the influence propagation for $R = 50$ rounds by choosing each 2-order strategy pair according to ρ. Specifically, "MGWC-SDWC" and "SDWC-MGWC" are adopted with probability $0.582 \times 0.418 = 0.243$, respectively. "MGWC-MGWC" and "SDWC-SDWC" are adopted with probabilities $0.582^2 = 0.339$ and $0.418^2 = 0.175$, respectively. The his-

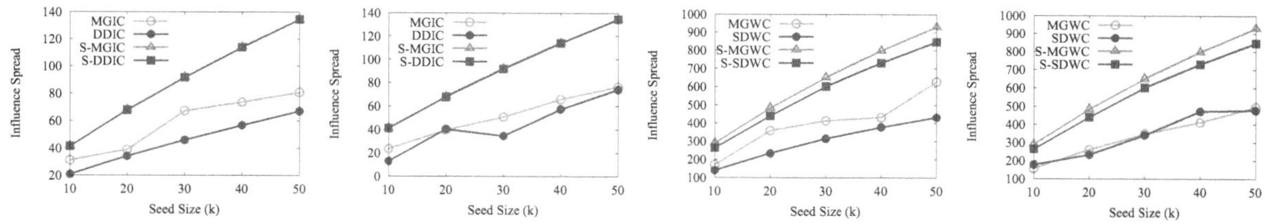

(a) p_2 adopts "MGIC" (IC) (b) p_2 adopts "DDIC" (IC) (c) p_2 adopts "MGWC"(WC) (d) p_2 adopts "SDWC" (WC)

Figure 5: [Best viewed in color] Influence spread in competitive network ($z = 2, r = 2$, *Hep* dataset).

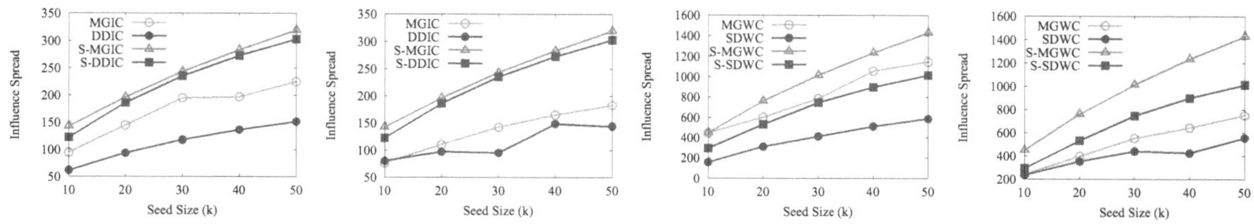

(a) p_2 adopts "MGIC" (IC) (b) p_2 adopts "DDIC" (IC) (c) p_2 adopts "MGWC"(WC) (d) p_2 adopts "SDWC" (WC)

Figure 6: [Best viewed in color] Influence spread in a competitive network ($z = 2, r = 2$, *Phy* dataset).

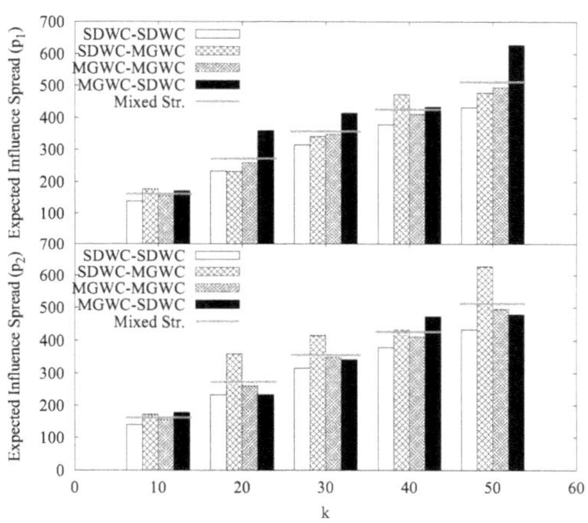

Figure 9: Average influence under different 2-order strategies (*Hep* under WC model).

Table 4: Response Times.

network	Hep		Phy		Wiki-talk	
model	IC	WC	IC	WC	IC	WC
($r = z = 2$)	0.022s	0.034s	0.024s	0.024s	0.023s	0.03s
($r = z = 3$)	0.043s	0.083s	0.044s	0.092s	0.098s	0.44s

tograms in Figure 9 show the average influence spread of different 2-order pure strategies for p_1 and p_2. The horizontal lines in the figure represent the average number of eventually influenced nodes under 2-order mixed strategy with $\rho = 0.582$ over all 50 rounds for each group. Obviously, there does not exist a histogram, namely 2-order strategy, which dominates others for both p_1 and p_2. Thus, there does not exist a pure strategy NE. In this case, p_1 or p_2 has no idea which strategy they should adopt. Hence, we propose to use mixed strategy, the performance of which is shown by the horizontal lines. The optimal mixed strategy with $\rho = 0.582$ outperforms the influence spread of "MGWC-MGWC" and "SDWC-SDWC" by 20% and 9%, respectively. On the other hand, the area under each horizontal line is larger than the area covered by all the histograms for each k. In other words, the expectation of the mixed strategy at $\rho = 0.582$ is superior to the strategy which randomly select a 2-order strategy with equal probability 0.25. This result is shown in Figure 8. For both p_1 and p_2, mixed strategy is better than random selection by 7%. Observe that the degree of improvement over random selection depends on the difference between the expected influence of pure strategy, as the expected influence under mixed strategy is bounded by the minimum and maximum of that under a particular pure strategy within the strategy space. In the above case, the difference between the expected influences of p_1 adopting MGWC and SDWC is small. Hence, the expected influence of mixed strategy of p_1 is limited. In fact, regardless of the existence of pure strategy NE, randomly selecting seeds over strategy space is not the optimal solution.

Response times. Table 4 reports the response time of finding NE (Lines 5-11 in Algorithm 1) when there are 2 (resp. 3) players and 2 (resp. 3) strategies. Observe that, given the expected influence of different strategies for each group, it is able to return the NE less in than a second.

Values of $\gamma, \lambda, \alpha, \beta$. Finally, we evaluate the values of $\gamma, \lambda, \alpha, \beta$. For both IC and WC models, we compute the values from the results generated under three 2-order strategies. Figures 10(a)-(b) plot the values for different $k = 10, \ldots, 50$ in *Hep*. In both figures, λ and γ are within the range [0.5,0.59], which supports Theorem 1. Moreover, both λ and γ are close to 0.5, which indicates that the summation over the influence of p_1 and p_2 is close to that of the influence in regular form without competition. In other words, it can be interpreted as follows. By adopting the same strategy (*i.e.*, *MixGreedy* or *DegreeDiscount*), p_1 and p_2 select almost the same seeds (*i.e.*, $|\frac{|S^1 \cap S^2|}{|S^1 \cup S^2|} - 1| < \epsilon$). As p_1 and p_2 are symmetric in the competition, the expectation over the seeds initially activated by them is the same (*i.e.*, $E(|A_1^0|) = E(|A_2^0|)$). The summation over them equals to the total number of seeds activated, which in this case is close to k. Hence, both of $E(|A_1^0|)$ and $E(|A_2^0|)$ are close to $k/2$. In both figures, $(\alpha+\beta)$

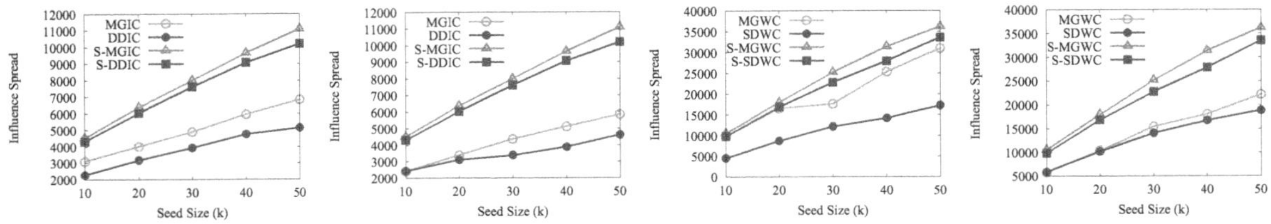

(a) p_2 adopts "MGIC" (IC) (b) p_2 adopts "DDIC" (IC) (c) p_2 adopts "MGWC"(WC) (d) p_2 adopts "SDWC" (WC)

Figure 7: [Best viewed in color] Influence spread in a competitive network ($z = 2, r = 2$, *Wiki* dataset).

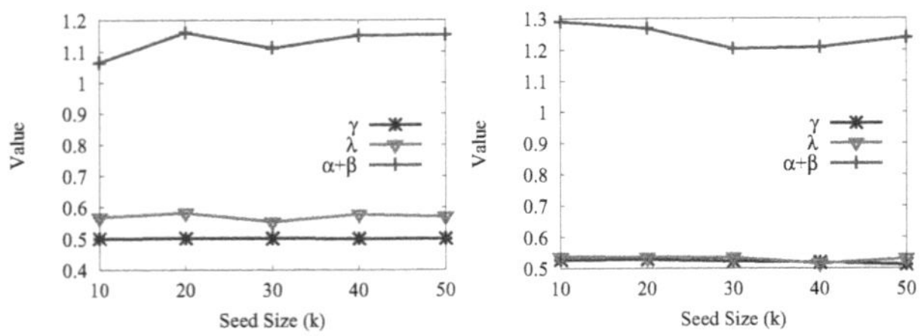

(a) IC model (*Hep*) (b) WC model (*Hep*)

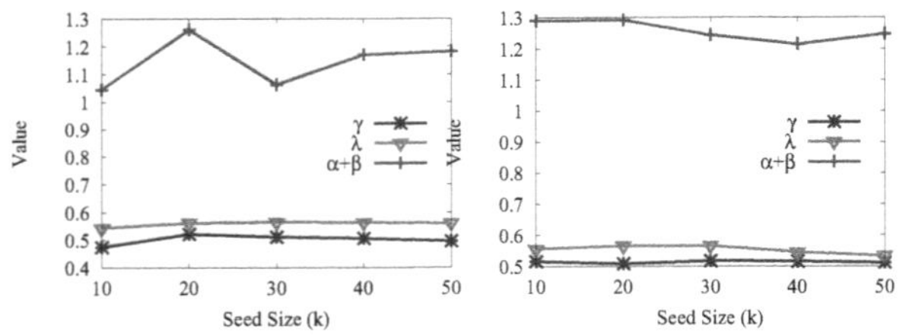

(c) IC model (*Phy*) (d) WC model (*Phy*)

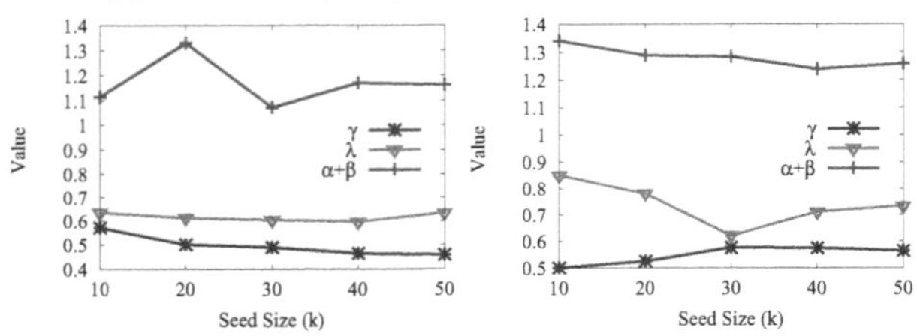

(e) IC model (*Wiki*) (f) WC model (*Wiki*)

Figure 10: [Best viewed in color] Values of $\gamma, \lambda, \alpha, \beta$.

values are within the range [1.08,1.16] (*resp.,* [1.2,1.29]) under IC model (*resp.,* WC model), which justifies our discussion in Corollary 1.

Observe that the values of γ, λ, α, and β do not vary significantly. However, they are different in the two models. For instance, λ ranges from 0.56 to 0.59 in the IC model. However, it is between 0.51 and 0.52 in the WC model. This phenomenon indicates that γ, λ, α, and β are unaffected by k. Instead they are influenced by the cascade models and network topology. This is consistent with our discussion in Section 4.1. The values of γ, λ, α, and β for *Wiki* and *Phy* under these two models are reported in Figures 10(c)-(f) and also show similar characteristics as above.

7. CONCLUSIONS & FUTURE WORK

State-of-the-art IM techniques for non-competitive networks can seldom be deployed in real-world applications as they ignore competitions between rival companies to maximize influence of a product. That is, they are not suitable for the case where multiple groups are maximizing their influence simultaneously in a network. Our work reported here contributes towards the goal of enhancing usefulness of IM techniques by designing a pragmatic IM solution that is competition-aware and is grounded on several realistic assumptions. In particular, we study the setting where each group is aware of the existence of their rivals but is unaware of the strategies adopted by their rivals. We propose a framework that finds the best solution for each group, who are maximizing their influences, based on game theory. To this end, we propose a novel algorithm called GETREAL that seeks to find whether there exists a Nash Equilibrium (NE) (*i.e.,* whether there exists an optimal strategy that will exhibit the most influence spread in comparison with other strategies for all scenarios). Specifically, it can find either pure strategy NE or mixed strategy NE in a network with competition. Experimental results demonstrate that it can find the optimal strategy for each group no matter which strategy their rivals adopt.

Despite considering more realistic assumptions compared to the state-of-the-art techniques for the IM problem, complex social behaviors of users and groups in a competitive network may engender some special scenarios where some of these assumptions may not hold. For instance, a user may buy a product of a company p_1 and then change her mind to buy another product from a rival p_2. In this case, the assumption that once a user is influenced by some group, it cannot be affected by any other groups, does not hold. Furthermore, under certain scenarios the game may become a *biased* one. For example, two groups p_1 and p_2 may collude with each other secretly to compete with p_3. In this case, p_1 and p_2 not only know each other's strategy, but also can design a *cooperative* strategy to minimize the influence of p_3. Therefore, p_1 and p_2 can be viewed as a special company which selects $2k$ seeds in the game. It may also happen that p_1 and p_2 may explicitly form an alliance (*e.g.,* buying either product leads to customer services from both companies). In this case the influence probability for p_1 and p_2 may increase. Hence, as part of future work, we plan to investigate such *biased competition* where groups exhibit different cascade models and explore efficient methods to solve the IMC problem in a more complex competitive networks.

Acknowledgment

Hui Li, Sourav S Bhowmick, Jiangtao Cui and Jianfeng Ma are supported by National Nature Science Foundation of China (No. 61202179, 61173089, 61472298 and U1135002), National High Technology Research and Development Program (863 Program) (No. 2015AA011704), SRF for ROCS, SEM and the Fundamental Research Funds for the Central Universities.

8. REFERENCES

[1] S. Bharathi, D. Kempe, and M. Salek. Competitive influence maximization in social networks. In *WINE*, 2007.

[2] A. Borodin, Y. Filmus, and J. Oren. Threshold models for competitive influence in social networks. In *WINE*, 2010.

[3] C. Budak, D. Agrawal, and A. El Abbadi. Limiting the spread of misinformation in social networks. In *ACM WWW*, 2011.

[4] I. Caragiannis, A. Fanelli, N. Gravin, and A. Skopalik. Approximate pure nash equilibria in weighted congestion games: existence, efficient computation, and structure. In *ACM ICEC*, 2012.

[5] T. Carnes, C. Nagarajan, S. M. Wild, and A. van Zuylen. Maximizing influence in a competitive social network: a follower's perspective. In *ACM ICEC*, 2007.

[6] W. Chen, A. Collins, R. Cummings, T. Ke, Z. Liu, D. Rincón, X. Sun, Y. Wang, W. Wei, and Y. Yuan Influence maximization in social networks when negative opinions may emerge and propagate. In *SDM*, 2011.

[7] W. Chen, C. Wang, and Y. Wang. Scalable influence maximization for prevalent viral marketing in large-scale social networks. In *KDD*, 2010.

[8] W. Chen, Y. Wang, and S. Yang. Efficient influence maximization in social networks. In *KDD*, 2009.

[9] W. Chen, Y. Yuan, and L. Zhang. Scalable influence maximization in social networks under the linear threshold model. In *ICDM*, 2010.

[10] A. Clark and R. Poovendran. Maximizing influence in competitive environments: a game-theoretic approach. In *GameSec*, 2011.

[11] A. Fazeli and A. Jadbabaie. Game theoretic analysis of a strategic model of competitive contagion and product adoption in social networks. In *CDC*, 2012.

[12] A. Goyal, F. Bonchi, and L. V. S. Lakshmanan. A data-based approach to social influence maximization. *PVLDB*, 2011.

[13] A. Goyal, W. Lu, and L. V. S. Lakshmanan. Simpath: An efficient algorithm for influence maximization under the linear threshold model. In *ICDM*, 2011.

[14] S. Goyal and M. Kearns. Competitive contagion in networks. In *STOC*, 2012.

[15] X. He, G. Song, W. Chen, and Q. Jiang. Influence blocking maximization in social networks under the competitive linear threshold model. In *SDM*, 2012.

[16] O. M. J and A. Rubinstein. A course in game theory. 1994.

[17] K. Jung, W. Heo, and W. Chen. IRIE: Scalable and Robust Influence Maximization in Social Networks. In *ICDM*, 2012.

[18] D. Kempe, J. M. Kleinberg, and É. Tardos. Maximizing the spread of influence through a social network. In *KDD*, 2003.

[19] J. Kim, S. Kim, and H. Yu. Scalable and parallelizable processing of influence maximization for large-scale social networks. In *ICDE*, 2013.

[20] J. Leskovec, A. Krause, C. Guestrin, C. Faloutsos, J. M. VanBriesen, and N. S. Glance. Cost-effective outbreak detection in networks. In *KDD*, 2007.

[21] H. Li, S. S. Bhowmick, and A. Sun. Cinema: conformity-aware greedy algorithm for influence maximization in online social networks. In *EDBT*, 2013.

[22] H. Ma, H. Yang, M. R. Lyu and I. King. Mining social networks using heat diffusion processes for marketing candidates selection. In *CIKM*, 2008.

[23] J. Nash. Non-cooperative games. *The Annals of Mathematics*, 54(2):286–295, Sept. 1951.

[24] G. L. Nemhauser, L. A. Wolsey, and M. L. Fisher. An analysis of approximations for maximizing submodular set functions. *Math. Programming*, 14(3):265–294, 1978.

[25] J. von Neumann and O. Morgenstern. Theory of Games and Economic Behavior. *Princeton University Press*, 2007.

[26] N. Pathak, A. Banerjee, and J. Srivastava. A generalized linear threshold model for multiple cascades. In *ICDM*, 2010.

[27] B. A. Prakash, A. Beutel, R. Rosenfeld, and C. Faloutsos. Winner takes all: competing viruses or ideas on fair-play networks. In *WWW*, 2012.

[28] G. R. Schoenebeck, and S. Vadhan. The computational complexity of nash equilibria in concisely represented games. *ACM Trans. Comput. Theory*, 4(2):4:1–4:50, May 2012.

[29] S. Shirazipourazad, B. Bogard, H. Vachhani, A. Sen, and P. Horn. Influence propagation in adversarial setting: how to defeat competition with least amount of investment. In *CIKM*, 2012.

[30] Y. Tang, X. Xiao, and Y. Shi. Influence Maximization: Near-Optimal Time Complexity Meets Practical Efficiency. *In SIGMOD*, 2014,

[31] J. Tsai, T. H. Nguyen, and M. Tambe. Security games for controlling contagion. In *AAAI*. 2012.

[32] V. Tzoumas, C. Amanatidis, and E. Markakis. A game-theoretic analysis of a competitive diffusion process over social networks. In *WINE*, 2012.

Influence Maximization in Near-Linear Time: A Martingale Approach

Youze Tang Yanchen Shi Xiaokui Xiao
School of Computer Engineering
Nanyang Technological University
Singapore
tangyouze@gmail.com shiy0017@e.ntu.edu.sg xkxiao@ntu.edu.sg

ABSTRACT

Given a social network G and a positive integer k, the *influence maximization* problem asks for k nodes (in G) whose adoptions of a certain idea or product can trigger the largest expected number of follow-up adoptions by the remaining nodes. This problem has been extensively studied in the literature, and the state-of-the-art technique runs in $O((k+\ell)(n+m)\log n/\varepsilon^2)$ expected time and returns a $(1-1/e-\varepsilon)$-approximate solution with at least $1-1/n^\ell$ probability.

This paper presents an influence maximization algorithm that provides the same worst-case guarantees as the state of the art, but offers significantly improved empirical efficiency. The core of our algorithm is a set of estimation techniques based on *martingales*, a classic statistical tool. Those techniques not only provide accurate results with small computation overheads, but also enable our algorithm to support a larger class of information diffusion models than existing methods do. We experimentally evaluate our algorithm against the states of the art under several popular diffusion models, using real social networks with up to 1.4 billion edges. Our experimental results show that the proposed algorithm consistently outperforms the states of the art in terms of computation efficiency, and is often orders of magnitude faster.

Categories and Subject Descriptors

H.2.8 [**Database Applications**]: Data mining

Keywords

Influence maximization; sampling

1. INTRODUCTION

Given a social network G and a positive integer k, the *influence maximization* problem asks for k nodes (in G) whose adoptions of a certain idea or product can trigger the largest expected number of follow-up adoptions by the remaining nodes. This problem originates from *viral marketing* [14, 31], where a company provides free samples of a product to a set of *influential* individuals in a social network, aiming to create a cascade of product adoptions via the word-of-mouth effect. Kempe et al. [25] formulate influence maximization as a combinatorial optimization problem, and show that it is NP-hard; as a solution, they propose a greedy approach that yields $(1-1/e-\varepsilon)$-approximations under several formal models of information diffusion. Since then, a plethora of techniques [4–9,15,18,19,24–27,29,32,33,37] have been proposed for efficient influence maximization in large social networks.

Most existing techniques, however, either trade approximation guarantees for practical efficiency, or vice versa. In particular, methods [5,8,20,25,29] that provide $(1-1/e-\varepsilon)$-approximation solutions often require days to process small social networks with several thousands of nodes and edges; on the other hand, techniques that offer empirical efficiency rely on heuristics, due to which they are unable to offer any worst-case performance guarantee. The only exception is two recent techniques called *TIM* and *TIM*$^+$ [33]: both techniques run in $O((k+\ell)(n+m)\log n/\varepsilon^2)$ expected time and return $(1-1/e-\varepsilon)$-approximations with at least $1-1/n^\ell$ probability, where n and m are the numbers of nodes and edges, respectively, in the social network; furthermore, their empirical performance is shown to be comparable to the state-of-the-art heuristic solutions.

Although *TIM* and *TIM*$^+$ offer strong theoretical guarantees and good practical efficiency, they still leave much room for improvement in terms of their computational costs. Specifically, *TIM* consists of two phases, namely, *parameter estimation* and *node selection*. The node selection phase samples a number θ of node sets from the social network G, and then utilizes them to derive a size-k node set with a large expected influence. The value of θ is crucial: to ensure a $(1-1/e-\varepsilon)$-approximate solution, it is shown that θ should be at least λ/OPT [33], where OPT is the maximum expected influence of any size-k node set, and λ is a function of k, ℓ, n, and ε. To derive an appropriate θ, the parameter estimation phase of *TIM* first computes a lower bound of OPT, and then sets θ as λ over the lower bound. This approach, albeit intuitive, has two deficiencies. First, the lower bound derived by *TIM* is rather conservative and can be n/k times smaller than OPT in the worst case. As a consequence, θ could be excessively large, resulting in unnecessary overheads in the node selection phase. Second, the computation of the lower bound itself is costly – as we show in Section 6, the time required for deriving the lower bound can be more than 3 times longer than that required for node selection.

TIM$^+$ improves upon *TIM* by adding an intermediate step (between parameter estimation and node selection) that heuristically refines θ into a tighter lower bound of OPT, which leads to higher efficiency. However, in the worst case, even the improved lower bound may still be as small as $\frac{k}{n}OPT$. Furthermore, adding the in-

SIGMOD'15, May 31 - June 04, 2015, Melbourne, VIC, Australia.

ACM 978-1-4503-2758-9/15/05 ...$15.00.
http://dx.doi.org/10.1145/2723372.2723734.

termediate step does not address the significant overheads incurred by the node selection phase.

Contributions. The paper presents *IMM*[1], an influence maximization algorithm that overcomes the deficiencies of *TIM* and TIM^+, while retaining their superior approximation guarantee and expected time complexity. The core of *IMM* is a set of estimation techniques based on *martingales* [38], a classic statistical tool. With those techniques, *IMM* adopts the two-phase paradigm of *TIM*, but incorporates a drastically different parameter estimation phase, which is able to derive a lower bound of OPT that is asymptotically tight. Specifically, the lower bound obtained by *IMM* is no less than $OPT \cdot (1 - 1/e)/(1 + \varepsilon')^2$ with a high probability, where ε' is a tunable parameter. In addition, the computation of the lower bound is optimized, so that it incurs a considerably smaller overhead than in the case of *TIM* and TIM^+. Furthermore, the node selection phase of *IMM* is significantly improved with a martingale approach, which helps eliminate a large amount of unnecessary computation that is otherwise unavoidable. With the above optimizations, *IMM* significantly outperforms *TIM* and TIM^+ in terms of practical performance. In particular, we experimentally evaluate *IMM* against *TIM* and TIM^+ on a variety of social networks with up to 1.4 billion edges, and our results show that *IMM*'s running time is up to two orders of magnitude smaller than that of *TIM* and TIM^+. Moreover, when we set $\varepsilon = 0.5$ and $\ell = 1$, *IMM* even yields higher efficiency than the state-of-the-art heuristic solutions, while still offering empirically accurate results.

In addition, we show that *IMM* can be extended to support any diffusion model for which a certain sampling procedure is well-defined. As an application, we present a variant of *IMM* for the *continuous-time independent cascade (CTIC)* model [6, 16, 30], which is widely adopted in the machine learning literature [15, 17, 18] but not supported by *TIM*. We compare our approach with the most advanced method under the CTIC model, and demonstrate that *IMM* is vastly superior in both asymptotic and practical performance.

In summary, our contributions are as follows:

1. We propose *IMM*, an influence maximization algorithm runs in $O((k+\ell)(n+m)\log n/\varepsilon^2)$ expected time and returns a $(1-1/e-\varepsilon)$-approximation with at least $1-1/n^\ell$ probability under the triggering model [25], a general diffusion model adopted by most existing work. (Section 3)
2. We investigate the conditions under which *IMM* can be extended to a larger class of diffusion models, while still retaining the $(1-1/e-\varepsilon)$-approximation ratio. As an application, we present an extended version of *IMM* that supports the CTIC model [16]. (Section 4)
3. We experimentally evaluate *IMM* with the largest social networks ever tested in the literature, and show that it is orders of magnitude faster than the state-of-the-art methods for several popular diffusion models. (Section 6)

2. PRELIMINARIES

This section formally defines the influence maximization problem, and presents an overview of *TIM* [33] to facilitate the discussions of our solution in subsequent sections.

2.1 Problem Definition

Let G be a social network with a set V of n nodes and a set E of m directed edges. For any two nodes $u, v \in V$, if $\langle u, v \rangle$ is an edge in E, we say that v is an outgoing neighbor of u, and u is an incoming neighbor of v. We consider a time-stamped diffusion process on G as follows:

1. At the first timestamp, we *activate* a set S of nodes, and set the remaining nodes *inactive*.
2. When a node u is first activated at a certain timestamp, it samples a set of its outgoing neighbors according to a certain probability distribution, and activates them at the next timestamp. After that, u cannot activate any other nodes.
3. Once a node becomes activated, it remains activated in all subsequent timestamps.

Let $I(S)$ be the number of activated nodes in G when the above process converges, i.e., when no more nodes can be activated. We refer to S as the *seed set*, and $I(S)$ as the *influence* of S. Note that $I(S)$ is a random variable that depends on the probability distributions from which each node samples out-neighbors to activate. We refer to the collection of those probability distributions as the *diffusion model* that underlies the diffusion process.

Problem Statement. Given G, a diffusion model M, and a positive integer k, the influence maximization problem asks for a size-k node set S_k with the maximum expected influence $\mathbb{E}[I(S_k)]$.

2.2 Diffusion Models

Unless specified otherwise, we focus on the *triggering model* [25] , which is a classic and general diffusion model adopted by most existing work on influence maximization. To explain the triggering model, we first introduce one of its special cases referred to as the *independent cascade (IC)* [25] model, for ease of exposition. The IC model originates from the marketing literature [22, 23], and it assumes that each edge $e \in E$ is associated with a probability $p(e) \in [0, 1]$. For any node u and any of its outgoing neighbors v, if u is first activated at timestamp i, then it has $p(\langle u, v \rangle)$ probability to activate v at timestamp $i + 1$. In other words, whether or not u can activate v is independent of the history of diffusion before u is activated, and hence, the order of node activations does not affect the diffusion results. For such a model, the diffusion process from a seed set S has an equivalent formulation as follows [25]:

1. We flip a coin for each edge e in G and remove it with $1 - p(e)$ probability. Let g be the resulting social network.
2. We activate the nodes in S, as well as any nodes in g that can be reached[2] from S.

Kempe et al. [25] show that the above formulation is essential in establishing the hardness and constant approximations for influence maximization under the IC model.

The triggering model is a generalization of the IC model, and it has a formulation similar to the one mentioned above. Specifically, it assumes that each node v in G is associated with a distribution $\mathcal{T}(v)$ over subsets of v's incoming neighbors. We refer to $\mathcal{T}(v)$ as the *triggering distribution* of v, and refer to a sample from $\mathcal{T}(v)$ as a *triggering set* of v. For any seed set S, a diffusion process from S under the triggering model is formulated as follows:

1. For each node v, we sample a triggering set of v from $\mathcal{T}(v)$, and remove any incoming edge of v that starts from a node not in the triggering set. Let g be the resulting social network.
2. We activate the nodes in S, as well as any nodes in g that can be reached from S.

[1] Influence **M**aximization via **M**artingales

[2] We say that a node v in g can be reached from S, if there exists a directed path in g that starts from a node in S and ends at v.

For convenience, we use $\mathcal{G}$ to denote the distribution of g induced by the randomness in sampling from each node's triggering distribution.

As with many existing solutions under the triggering model (e.g., [4–6,8,15,18–20,25,26,29,32,33]), our influence maximization algorithms require taking samples from various nodes' triggering distributions, as a means to evaluate the expected influence of various node sets. The cost of this sampling process varies with the specific type of triggering model considered. For example, under the IC model, sampling from the triggering distribution $\mathcal{T}(v)$ of a node v requires flipping a coin for each of v's incoming edges, which takes time linear to the number x of incoming edges that v has. As another example, under the *linear threshold (LT)* model [25] (which is another special case of the triggering model), a sample from $\mathcal{T}(v)$ has p_i ($i \in [1, x]$) probability to be a unit set containing the i-th incoming neighbor of v, and has $1 - \sum_{i=1}^{x} p_i$ probability to be an empty set. Such a sample can be derived in $O(x)$ time as follows. We first generate a random number μ from a uniform distribution on $[0, 1]$. If $\mu > \sum_{i=1}^{x} p_i$, we return $\emptyset$; otherwise, we identify the smallest j ($j \in [1, x]$) such that $\sum_{i=1}^{j} p_j > \mu$, and return the j-th incoming neighbor of v. Note that the complexity of this sampling process can even be reduced to $O(1)$, if we allow $O(x)$-time preprocessing on $\mathcal{T}(v)$ [12, 35].

In general, with some pre-computation, the sampling methods in [12, 35] allow us to sample a random number from an arbitrary discrete distribution in $O(1)$ time. Given such methods, we can sample from an arbitrary triggering distribution $\mathcal{T}(v)$ in $O(x)$ time, by first spending $O(1)$ time to choose a triggering set based on $\mathcal{T}(v)$, and then returning the chosen triggering set in $O(x)$ time. (Recall that each triggering set contains at most x elements.)

In the remainder of the paper, we assume that the input graph G is properly preprocessed so that sampling from $\mathcal{T}(v)$ requires $O(x)$ time for any $v \in G$. Note that this assumption does not unfairly favor our algorithms, since all influence maximization methods considered in this paper (e.g., *TIM* and *TIM*$^+$) rely on efficient methods to sample from triggering distributions. In addition, the same assumption is implicitly adopted in previous work [33]. Furthermore, for the IC and LT models (i.e., the two diffusion models considered in most existing work), the assumption holds even without preprocessing G, as we previously analyzed.

2.3 Revisiting *TIM* and *TIM*$^+$

As mentioned in Section 1, both *TIM* and *TIM*$^+$ [33] have a parameter estimation phase and a node selection phase, the latter of which samples numerous node sets from the social network G to derive a solution for influence maximization. The type of node sets sampled by *TIM* and *TIM*$^+$ is referred to as *random RR sets*, defined as follows:

DEFINITION 1 (REVERSE REACHABLE SET). *Let v be a node in V. A* reverse reachable (RR) set *for v is generated by first sampling a graph g from $\mathcal{G}$, and then taking the set of nodes in g that can reach v. A* random RR set *is an RR set for a node selected uniformly at random from V.*

Intuitively, if a node u appears in an RR set of another node v, then a diffusion process from a seed set containing u should have a certain probability to activate v. This connection between RR sets and node activations is formalized in the following lemma.

LEMMA 1 ([5]). *For any seed set S and any node v, the probability that a diffusion process from S can activate v equals the probability that S overlaps an RR set for v.* □

Based on Lemma 1, the node selection phase of *TIM* (resp. *TIM*$^+$) adopts the following approach for influence maximization:

1. Generate a sizable set $\mathcal{R}$ of *independent* random RR sets.
2. Consider the *maximum coverage* problem [34] of selecting k nodes to *cover*[3] the maximum number of RR sets in $\mathcal{R}$. Apply the standard greedy algorithm to obtain a $(1 - 1/e)$-approximate solution S_k^* to the problem.
3. Return S_k^* as the answer for influence maximization.

To understand why the above approach works, observe that for any seed set S, the fraction of RR sets in $\mathcal{R}$ covered by S is an unbiased estimator of $\mathbb{E}[I(S)]$ (this is due to Lemma 1). Therefore, a seed set S_k^* that covers a large number of RR sets in $\mathcal{R}$ is likely to have a large expected influence, which makes S_k^* a good solution to the influence maximization problem.

To ensure that S_k^* provides a $(1 - 1/e - \varepsilon)$-approximation with at least $1 - 1/n^\ell$ probability, it is shown [33] that the number of RR sets in $\mathcal{R}$ should be at least λ/OPT, where OPT is the maximum expected influence of any size-k node set in G, and λ is a function of k, ℓ, n, and ε. Since OPT is unknown in advance, *TIM* sets $|\mathcal{R}| = \lambda/KPT$, where KPT is a lower bound of OPT that is derived by the parameter estimation phase of *TIM*. As mentioned in Section 1, however, KPT can be considerably smaller than OPT (which leads to an excessive number of RR sets in $\mathcal{R}$), and its derivation often incurs significant computational costs. To alleviate this issue, *TIM*$^+$ incorporates a heuristic approach to refine KPT. In particular, it selects a certain size-k node set S_k, and then estimates S_k's expected influence $\mathbb{E}[I(S_k)]$. After that, *TIM*$^+$ uses the larger one between KPT and $\mathbb{E}[I(S_k)]$ as an improved lower bound of OPT. Although this heuristic approach tends to yield a tighter lower bound of OPT, it does not reduce the significant overhead in deriving KPT. Furthermore, in the worst case when $KPT \geq \mathbb{E}[I(S_k)]$, the heuristic approach would fail to offer any improvement over *TIM*.

3. PROPOSED SOLUTION

This section presents *IMM*, an influence maximization technique that borrows ideas from *TIM* and *TIM*$^+$ [33] but adopts a novel algorithm design to reduce computational costs. At a high level, *IMM* consists of two phases as follows:

1. **Sampling.** This phase iteratively generates random RR sets and puts them into a set $\mathcal{R}$, until a certain stopping condition is met.
2. **Node Selection.** This phase applies the standard greedy algorithm for maximum coverage [34] to derive a size-k node set S_k^* that covers a large number of RR sets in $\mathcal{R}$. It then returns S_k^* as the final result.

The node selection phase of *IMM* is similar to that of *TIM* and *TIM*$^+$; however, *TIM* and *TIM*$^+$ requires all random RR sets in $\mathcal{R}$ to be independent, which is not the case in *IMM*. In particular, the random RR sets generated by *IMM* are dependent because, in the sampling phase of *IMM*, whether the $(i+1)$-th RR set is generated relies on whether the first i RR sets satisfy the stopping condition. Allowing such dependencies among RR sets makes *IMM*'s theoretical guarantees more difficult to analyze, but it is crucial for *IMM*'s efficiency as it enables *IMM* to eliminate a considerable amount of redundant computation that is unavoidable in *TIM* and *TIM*$^+$ (see Section 3.4). Meanwhile, the sampling phase of *IMM* considerably differs from the parameter estimation phase of *TIM* and *TIM*$^+$, in that it employs a more advanced statistical method to decide the number θ of RR sets required. This method not only provides more

[3]We say that a node set S covers an RR set R if $S \cap R \neq \emptyset$.

Notation	Description
$G=(V,E)$	a social network G with a node set V and an edge set E
n, m	the numbers of nodes and edges in G, respectively
k	the size of the seed set for influence maximization
$\mathcal{T}(v)$	the triggering distribution of a node $v \in V$
$\mathcal{G}$	the distribution of social networks induced by the triggering distribution of each node (see Section 2.1)
$I(S)$	the influence of a node set S in a diffusion process on G
$\mathbb{E}(\cdot)$	the expectation of a random variable
$\mathcal{R}$	the set of RR sets generated by *IMM*'s sampling phase
θ	the number of RR sets in $\mathcal{R}$
$F_{\mathcal{R}}(S)$	the fraction of RR sets in $\mathcal{R}$ that are covered by a node set S
OPT	the maximum expected influence of any size-k node set S

Table 1: Frequently used notations.

accurate choice of θ, but also leads to a significantly smaller cost of parameter estimation than in the case of *TIM* and *TIM*$^+$.

In the following, we first introduce the concept of *martingales* [10], which is crucial in our analysis of the dependent RR sets in $\mathcal{R}$. After that, we discuss the condition under which the node selection phase of *IMM* returns a good solution, and then we clarify the details of the sampling phase. For ease of reference, Table 1 lists the notations that we frequently use. Unless specified otherwise, all logarithms in this paper are to the base e.

3.1 A Martingale View of RR Sets

Let $R_1, R_2, \ldots, R_\theta$ be the sequence of random RR sets generated in the sampling phase of *IMM*. Let S be any set of nodes in G, and x_i ($i \in [1,\theta]$) be a random variable that equals 0 if $S \cap R_i = \emptyset$, and 1 otherwise. By Lemma 1 and the linearity of expectation,

$$\mathbb{E}[I(S)] = \frac{n}{\theta} \cdot \mathbb{E}\left[\sum_{i=1}^{\theta} x_i\right]. \qquad (1)$$

Accordingly, the node selection phase of *IMM* uses $\frac{n}{\theta} \cdot \sum_{i=1}^{\theta} x_i$ as an estimator of $\mathbb{E}[I(S)]$. To ensure that this estimation is accurate, it is essential that $\sum_{i=1}^{\theta} x_i$ should not deviate significantly from its expectation. A classic tool to prove such concentration results is the Chernoff bounds [10], but it requires all x_i to be independent, which contradicts the dependencies among x_i caused by the stopping condition in *IMM*'s sampling phase. We circumvent this issue with an analysis based on *martingales* [10], defined as follows:

DEFINITION 2 (MARTINGALE). *A sequence of random variables $Y_1, Y_2, Y_3, \ldots$ is a* martingale, *if and only if* $\mathbb{E}[|Y_i|] < +\infty$ *and* $\mathbb{E}[Y_i \mid Y_1, Y_2, \ldots, Y_{i-1}] = Y_{i-1}$ *for any i.* □

To establish the connections between x_i ($i \in [1,\theta]$) and martingales, we first introduce two properties of *IMM*'s sampling phase. First, each R_i ($i \in [1,\theta]$) is generated for a node v selected uniformly at random, and it contains nodes that can reach v on a graph g sampled from $\mathcal{G}$. Second, the choices of v and g are independent of $R_1, R_2, \ldots, R_{i-1}$ (although the decision to generate R_i depends on $R_1, R_2, \ldots, R_{i-1}$). Due to these properties, for any $i \in [1,\theta]$,

$$\mathbb{E}[x_i \mid x_1, x_2, \ldots, x_{i-1}] = \mathbb{E}[x_i] = \mathbb{E}[I(S)]/n.$$

Let $p = \mathbb{E}[I(S)]/n$ and $M_i = \sum_{j=1}^{i}(x_j - p)$. Then, we have $\mathbb{E}[M_i] = 0$, and

$$\mathbb{E}[M_i \mid M_1, M_2, \ldots, M_{i-1}] = M_{i-1}.$$

Algorithm 1: NodeSelection ($\mathcal{R}$, k)

```
Initialize a node set S*_k = ∅.;
for i = 1 to k do
    Identify the vertex v that maximizes F_R(S*_k ∪ v) − F_R(S*_k);
    Insert v into S*_k;
return S*_k;
```

Therefore, by Definition 2, $M_1, M_2, \ldots, M_\theta$ is a martingale.

The following lemma from [10] shows two concentration results for martingales that have similar flavor to the Chernoff bounds.

LEMMA 2 ([10]). *Let $Y_1, Y_2, Y_3, \ldots$ be a martingale, such that $|Y_1| \le a$, $|Y_j - Y_{j-1}| \le a$ for any $j \in [1,i]$, and*

$$Var[Y_1] + \sum_{j=2}^{i} Var[Y_j \mid Y_1, Y_2, \ldots, Y_{j-1}] \le b,$$

where $Var[\cdot]$ denotes the variance of a random variable. Then, for any $\lambda > 0$,

$$\Pr\left[Y_i - \mathbb{E}[Y_i] \ge \gamma\right] \le \exp\left(-\frac{\gamma^2}{\frac{2}{3}a\gamma + 2b}\right). \qquad \square$$

Consider the martingale $M_1, M_2, \ldots, M_\theta$. We have $|M_1| \le 1$ and $|M_j - M_{j-1}| \le 1$ for any $j \in [2,\theta]$. By the properties of R_i ($i \in [1,\theta]$), we also have

$$\begin{aligned} Var[M_1] + \textstyle\sum_{j=2}^{\theta} Var[M_j \mid M_1, M_2, \ldots, M_{j-1}] \\ = \textstyle\sum_{j=1}^{\theta} Var[M_j] = \theta p \cdot (1-p). \end{aligned}$$

Then, by Lemma 2 and $M_\theta = \sum_{i=1}^{\theta}(x_i - p)$, we have the following corollary.

COROLLARY 1. *For any $\varepsilon > 0$,*

$$\Pr\left[\sum_{i=1}^{\theta} x_i - \theta p \ge \varepsilon \cdot \theta p\right] \le \exp\left(-\frac{\varepsilon^2}{2 + \frac{2}{3}\varepsilon} \cdot \theta p\right). \quad \square$$

In addition, by applying Lemma 2 on the martingale $-M_1, -M_2, \ldots, -M_\theta$, we have the following result.

COROLLARY 2. *For any $\varepsilon > 0$,*

$$\Pr\left[\sum_{i=1}^{\theta} x_i - \theta p \le -\varepsilon \cdot \theta p\right] \le \exp\left(-\frac{\varepsilon^2}{2} \cdot \theta p\right). \quad \square$$

In Section 3.2, we will utilize the above corollaries to establish the approximation guarantees of *IMM*.

3.2 Node Selection Phase

Let $\mathcal{R} = \{R_1, R_2, \ldots, R_\theta\}$ be the set of random RR sets generated by the sampling phase of *IMM*, and $F_{\mathcal{R}}(S)$ be the fraction of RR sets in $\mathcal{R}$ that are covered by a node set S. Algorithm 1 shows the pseudo-code of the node selection phase of *IMM*, which takes as input $\mathcal{R}$ and a positive integer k, and returns a size-k node set S_k^*. The algorithm corresponds to the standard greedy approach for the maximum coverage problem [34], which guarantees that $F_{\mathcal{R}}(S_k^*)$ is at least $(1 - 1/e)$ times the fraction of RR sets covered by any size-k node set. In what follows, we show that when the number θ of RR sets in $\mathcal{R}$ is sufficiently large, S_k^* ensures a $(1 - 1/e - \varepsilon)$-approximation to the influence maximization problem with a high probability.

Consider the size-k node set S_k° with the maximum expected influence. Let $OPT = \mathbb{E}[I(S_k^\circ)]$. By Equation 1, $n \cdot F_{\mathcal{R}}(S_k^\circ)$ is an unbiased estimator of OPT. Then, by Corollary 2, $F_{\mathcal{R}}(S_k^\circ)$ should be close to OPT when θ is sizable, as shown in the following lemma.

LEMMA 3. *Let $\delta_1 \in (0,1)$, $\varepsilon_1 > 0$, and*

$$\theta_1 = \frac{2n \cdot \log(1/\delta_1)}{OPT \cdot \varepsilon_1^2}. \tag{2}$$

If $\theta \geq \theta_1$, then $n \cdot F_{\mathcal{R}}(S_k^\circ) \geq (1-\varepsilon_1) \cdot OPT$ holds with at least $1-\delta_1$ probability. □

Suppose that $n \cdot F_{\mathcal{R}}(S_k^\circ) \geq (1-\varepsilon_1) \cdot OPT$ holds. By the properties of the greedy approach,

$$\begin{aligned} n \cdot F_{\mathcal{R}}(S_k^*) &\geq (1-1/e) \cdot n \cdot F_{\mathcal{R}}(S_k^\circ) \\ &\geq (1-1/e) \cdot (1-\varepsilon_1) \cdot OPT. \end{aligned} \tag{3}$$

Intuitively, Equation 3 indicates that the expected influence of S_k^* is likely to be large, since $n \cdot F_{\mathcal{R}}(S_k^*)$ is an indicator of $\mathbb{E}[I(S_k^*)]$. We formalize this intuition in the following lemma:

LEMMA 4. *Let $\delta_2 \in (0,1)$, $\varepsilon_1 < \varepsilon$, and*

$$\theta_2 = \frac{(2-2/e) \cdot n \cdot \log\left(\binom{n}{k}/\delta_2\right)}{OPT \cdot (\varepsilon - (1-1/e) \cdot \varepsilon_1)^2}. \tag{4}$$

If Equation 3 holds and $\theta \geq \theta_2$, then with at least $1-\delta_2$ probability, $\mathbb{E}[I(S_k^*)] \geq (1-1/e-\varepsilon) \cdot OPT$. □

Lemmas 3 and 4 lead to the following theorem.

THEOREM 1. *Given any $\varepsilon_1 \leq \varepsilon$ and any $\delta_1, \delta_2 \in (0,1)$ with $\delta_1 + \delta_2 \leq 1/n^\ell$, setting $\theta \geq \max\{\theta_1, \theta_2\}$ ensures that the node selection phase of IMM returns a $(1-1/e-\varepsilon)$-approximate solution with at least $1-1/n^\ell$ probability.* □

Parametrization. Assume that OPT is known. Then, by Theorem 1, we can obtain a $(1-1/e-\varepsilon)$-approximation from *IMM* with at least $1-1/n^\ell$ probability as follows: We first choose ε_1, δ_1, and δ_2 according to the conditions stated in Theorem 1; after that, we calculate θ_1 and θ_2 based on Equations 2 and 4, respectively, and compute $\theta = \max\{\theta_1, \theta_2\}$; finally, we ensure that $\mathcal{R}$ contains at least θ RR sets. A natural question is, how should we select ε_1, δ_1, and δ_2 to minimize θ? Getting an exact answer to this question is difficult, due to the complex relationships among ε_1, δ_1, δ_2, and θ. However, there exists a relatively simple method to derive a near-minimum θ, as explained in the following.

First, we set $\delta_1 = \delta_2 = 1/(2n^\ell)$. Under this setting, θ is minimized when $\theta_1 = \theta_2$. In turn, $\theta_1 = \theta_2$ holds if and only if $\varepsilon_1 = \varepsilon \cdot \frac{\alpha}{(1-1/e)\cdot\alpha+\beta}$, where

$$\begin{aligned} \alpha &= \sqrt{\ell \log n + \log 2}, \text{ and} \\ \beta &= \sqrt{(1-1/e) \cdot \left(\log \binom{n}{k} + \ell \log n + \log 2\right)}. \end{aligned} \tag{5}$$

In that case,

$$\theta = \frac{2n \cdot ((1-1/e)\cdot\alpha+\beta)^2}{OPT \cdot \varepsilon^2}.$$

Denote the above θ as θ^*. The following lemma shows that θ^* is near-optimal with respect to Theorem 1:

LEMMA 5. *Given ε, ℓ, let θ° be the smallest possible θ under the conditions stated in Theorem 1. We have*

$$\theta^\circ \leq \theta^* \leq \theta^\circ \cdot \frac{\ell \log n + \log 2}{\ell \log n}. \quad \square$$

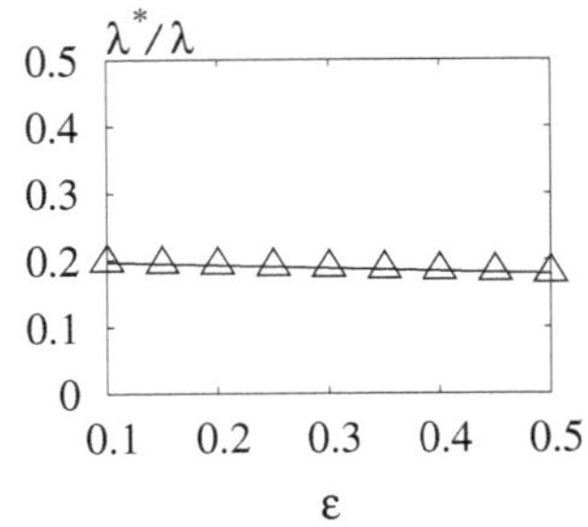

Figure 1: λ^*/λ **vs.** ε.

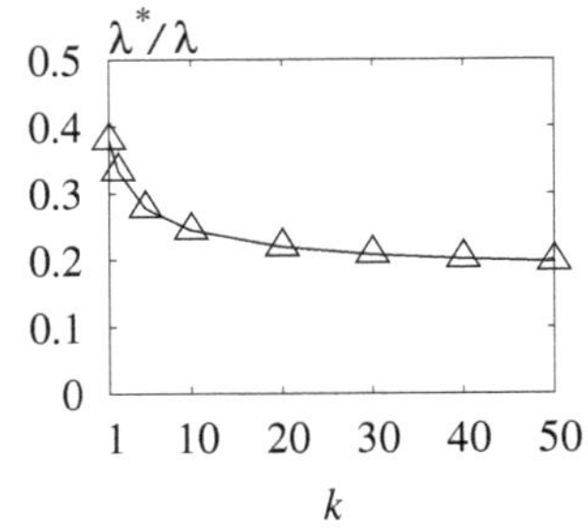

Figure 2: λ^*/λ **vs.** k.

In summary, the node selection phase of *IMM* returns a $(1-1/e-\varepsilon)$-approximation with at least $1-1/n^\ell$ probability, if we ensure that the number θ of RR sets in $\mathcal{R}$ is at least λ^*/OPT, where

$$\lambda^* = 2n \cdot \left((1-1/e)\cdot\alpha+\beta\right)^2 \cdot \varepsilon^{-2}. \tag{6}$$

Nevertheless, ensuring $\theta \geq \lambda^*/OPT$ is non-trivial, since OPT is unknown in advance. In Section 3.3, we address this issue by setting $\theta = \lambda^*/LB$, where LB is a lower bound of OPT that is almost tight.

Finally, we have the following result regarding the time complexity of Algorithm 1.

COROLLARY 3. *Algorithm 1 runs in $O\left(\sum_{R\in\mathcal{R}} |R|\right)$ time.* □

The above corollary follows from the fact that Algorithm 1 corresponds to the standard greedy approach for maximum coverage, which runs in time linear to the total size of its input [34].

Comparison with the Node Selection Phase of *TIM* and *TIM*$^+$. Previous work [33] utilizes Algorithm 1 as part of the node selection phase of *TIM* and *TIM*$^+$, and establishes two conditions for Algorithm 1 to return a $(1-1/e-\varepsilon)$-approximation with at least $1-1/n^\ell$ probability. First, all random RR sets in $\mathcal{R}$ should be independent. Second, $\theta \geq \lambda/OPT$, where

$$\lambda = (8+2\varepsilon)n \cdot \left(\ell \log n + \log \binom{n}{k} + \log 2\right) \cdot \varepsilon^{-2}. \tag{7}$$

In comparison, our results are more general in that we allow dependencies among the RR sets in $\mathcal{R}$. Furthermore, our analysis leads to a θ that is near-optimal with respect to Theorem 1, whereas the θ given in [33] roughly corresponds to a suboptimal case in Theorem 1 with $\delta_1 = 1/\left(n^\ell \cdot \binom{n}{k}\right)$, $\delta_2 = 1-\delta_1$, and $\varepsilon_1 = \varepsilon/2$.

To illustrate the differences between our results and those in [33], Figure 1 compares λ^* (in Equation 6) and λ (in Equation 7) under a realistic setting where $n = 10^6$, $\ell = 1$, $k = 50$, and ε varies from 0.1 to 0.5. Observe that $\lambda^* \leq 0.2\lambda$ in all cases. Figure 2 shows λ^*/λ as a function of k, with $\varepsilon = 0.1$, $n = 10^6$, and $\ell = 1$. Again, λ^* is considerably smaller than λ, regardless of the value of k.

3.3 Sampling Phase

Recall that *IMM*'s node selection phase requires as input a set $\mathcal{R}$ of random RR sets with $|\mathcal{R}| \geq \lambda^*/OPT$, where λ^* is as defined in Equation 6. As OPT is not known a priori, we aim to identify a lower bound LB of OPT and then set $|\mathcal{R}| = \lambda^*/LB \geq \lambda^*/OPT$. Ideally, LB should be as close to OPT as possible, so as to minimize the computational cost of generating $\mathcal{R}$. However, it is challenging to derive such an LB, given the NP-hardness of the influence maximization problem.

To address the above challenge, our idea is to design a statistical test $B(x)$, such that if $OPT < x$, then $B(x) = false$ with a high probability. With such a test, we can easily identify a lower bound of OPT by running $B(x)$ on $O(\log n)$ values of x, e.g., $x =$

Algorithm 2: Sampling (G, k, ε, ℓ)

1 Initialize a set $\mathcal{R} = \emptyset$ and an integer $LB = 1$;
2 Let $\varepsilon' = \sqrt{2} \cdot \varepsilon$;
3 **for** $i = 1$ *to* $\log_2 n - 1$ **do**
4   Let $x = n/2^i$;
5   Let $\theta_i = \lambda'/x$, where λ' is as defined in Equation 9;
6   **while** $|\mathcal{R}| \leq \theta_i$ **do**
7   Select a node v from G uniformly at random;
8   Generate an RR set for v, and insert it into $\mathcal{R}$;
9   Let S_i = NodeSelection($\mathcal{R}$);
10   **if** $n \cdot F_{\mathcal{R}}(S_i) \geq (1 + \varepsilon') \cdot x$ **then**
11         $LB = n \cdot F_{\mathcal{R}}(S_i)/(1 + \varepsilon')$;
12   **break**;
13 Let $\theta = \lambda^*/LB$, where λ^* is as defined in Equation 6;
14 **while** $|\mathcal{R}| \leq \theta$ **do**
15   Select a node v from G uniformly at random;
16   Generate an RR set for v, and insert it into $\mathcal{R}$;
17 **return** $\mathcal{R}$

$n/2, n/4, n/8, \ldots, 2$. (Note that $OPT \in [1, n]$.) Interestingly, the algorithm used in *IMM*'s node selection phase provides a means to implement $B(x)$, as shown in the following lemma:

LEMMA 6. *Let $x \in [1, n]$ and $\varepsilon', \delta_3 \in (0, 1)$. Suppose that we invoke Algorithm 1 on a set $\mathcal{R}$ containing θ random RR sets, with*

$$\theta \geq \frac{(2 + \frac{2}{3}\varepsilon') \cdot \left(\log \binom{n}{k} + \log(1/\delta_3)\right)}{\varepsilon'^2} \cdot \frac{n}{x}. \quad (8)$$

Let S_k^* be the output of Algorithm 1. Then, if $OPT < x$, we have $n \cdot F_{\mathcal{R}}(S_k^*) < (1 + \varepsilon') \cdot x$ with at least $1 - \delta_3$ probability. □

The rationale of Lemma 6 is as follows. First, if OPT is large, then Algorithm 1 is likely to return a node set S_k^* that covers a large portion of RR sets in $\mathcal{R}$, i.e., $F_{\mathcal{R}}(S_k^*)$ should be large. Conversely, if we observe that $F_{\mathcal{R}}(S_k^*)$ is small, then OPT is also likely to be small (modulo the sampling error in $\mathcal{R}$). Therefore, we can use $F_{\mathcal{R}}(S_k^*)$ as an indicator of the magnitude of OPT.

Based on Lemma 6, Algorithm 2 presents the pseudo-code of the sampling phase of *IMM*. Given G, k, ε, and ℓ, the algorithm first initializes a set $\mathcal{R} = \emptyset$, and an integer $LB = 1$ (Line 1). After that, it sets a parameter $\varepsilon' = \sqrt{2} \cdot \varepsilon$, and enters a for loop with at most $\log_2 n - 1$ iterations (Lines 3 - 12). (We will explain our choice of ε' shortly.)

In the i-th iteration, the algorithm computes $x = n/2^i$, and then derives $\theta_i = \lambda'/x$, where

$$\lambda' = \frac{(2 + \frac{2}{3}\varepsilon') \cdot \left(\log \binom{n}{k} + \ell \cdot \log n + \log \log_2 n\right) \cdot n}{\varepsilon'^2}. \quad (9)$$

It can be verified that θ_i equals the smallest θ that satisfies Equation 8 when $\delta_3 = n^\ell \cdot \log_2 n$. As a next step, the algorithm inserts random RR sets into $\mathcal{R}$ until $|\mathcal{R}| = \theta_i$ (Lines 6-8), after which it invokes Algorithm 1 on $\mathcal{R}$ to obtain a size-k node set S_i. By Lemma 6, if

$$n \cdot F_{\mathcal{R}}(S_i) \geq (1 + \varepsilon') \cdot x, \quad (10)$$

then $OPT \geq x$ should hold with at least $1 - 1/(n^\ell \cdot \log_2 n)$ probability. In other words, once Equation 10 holds, we can terminate the for loop and identify x as a lower bound of OPT. This explains Line 10-12 in Algorithm 2, except that the algorithm uses $LB = n \cdot F_{\mathcal{R}}(S_i)/(1 + \varepsilon')$ as a lower bound of OPT, instead of setting $LB = x$. (Notice that the former is a tighter lower bound, due to Equation 10.) Our choice of LB is justified by the following lemma.

LEMMA 7. *Let x, ε', δ_3, $\mathcal{R}$, and S_k^* be as defined in Lemma 6. If $OPT \geq x$, then we have $OPT \geq n \cdot F_{\mathcal{R}}(S_k^*)/(1 + \varepsilon')$ with at least $1 - \delta_3$ probability.* □

The above discussions assume that Equation 10 holds in a ceratin iteration of the for loop in Algorithm 2. On the other hand, if Equation 10 does not hold in any of the $\log_2 n - 1$ iterations, then the algorithm sets $LB = 1$. In either case, once LB is determined, the algorithm computes $\theta = \lambda^*/LB$, where λ^* is as defined in Equation 6, and then it adds more random RR sets into $\mathcal{R}$ until $|\mathcal{R}| = \theta$ (Lines 13-16). Finally, it terminates by returning $\mathcal{R}$.

Theoretical Analysis. Let $j = \left\lceil \log_2 \frac{n}{OPT} \right\rceil$. By Lemma 6 and the union bound, Algorithm 2 has at most $(j - 1)/(n^\ell \cdot \log_2 n)$ probability to terminate its for loop before the j-th iteration. Then, by Lemma 7 and the union bound, Algorithm 2 sets $LB \leq OPT$ with at least $1 - n^\ell$ probability. Therefore, we have the following result.

THEOREM 2. *With at least $1 - n^\ell$ probability, Algorithm 2 returns a set $\mathcal{R}$ of RR sets with $|\mathcal{R}| \geq \lambda^*/OPT$, where λ^* is as defined in Equation 6.* □

In addition, we can show that LB is close to OPT with a high probability. Towards this end, we prove that Algorithm 2 is likely to stop its for loop soon after the j-th iteration, as shown in the following lemma.

LEMMA 8. *Let x, ε', δ_3, $\mathcal{R}$, and S_k^* be as defined in Lemma 6. Let $c \geq 1$. If $OPT \geq c \cdot \frac{(1+\varepsilon')^2}{1-1/e} \cdot x$, then $n \cdot F_{\mathcal{R}}(S_k^*) < (1 + \varepsilon') \cdot x$ holds with at most $(\delta_3)^c$ probability.* □

Based on Lemma 8, we have the following result regarding LB.

LEMMA 9. *Let $\mathcal{R}$ be the output of Algorithm 2, and LB be as in Line 13 of Algorithm 2. We have $LB \geq \frac{1-1/e}{(1+\varepsilon')^2} \cdot OPT$ with at least $1 - 1/n^\ell$ probability. In addition, when $1/n^\ell \leq 1/2$,*

$$\mathbb{E}[|\mathcal{R}|] \leq \frac{3 \max\{\lambda^*, \lambda'\} \cdot (1 + \varepsilon')^2}{(1 - 1/e) \cdot OPT},$$

where λ' is as defined in Equation 9. □

In Section 3.4, we will utilize Lemma 9 to analyze the total running time of *IMM* and compare it with that of *TIM* and *TIM*$^+$ [33].

Parametrization. It remains to explain why we set $\varepsilon' = \sqrt{2} \cdot \varepsilon$ in Algorithm 2. As shown in Lemma 9, the expected number of RR sets generated by Algorithm 2 is bounded by a quantity proportional to $\max\{\lambda^*, \lambda'\} \cdot (1 + \varepsilon')^2$. Ideally, we should choose an ε' that minimizes $\max\{\lambda^*, \lambda'\} \cdot (1 + \varepsilon')^2$, but it is difficult given the complex expressions of λ^* and λ'. As an alternative, we roughly approximate $\max\{\lambda^*, \lambda'\} \cdot (1 + \varepsilon')^2$ with a simple function of ε' and ε, and then derive $\varepsilon' = \sqrt{2} \cdot \varepsilon$ as a minimizer of the function. Our experiments show that this choice of ε' leads to reasonably good performance of *IMM*.

3.4 Putting It Together

In summary, *IMM* first invokes Algorithm 2 to generate a set $\mathcal{R}$ of RR sets, and then feeds $\mathcal{R}$ to Algorithm 1 to obtain a size-k node set S_k^* as the final output. By Theorems 1 and 2 as well as the union bound, *IMM* returns a $(1 - 1/e - \varepsilon)$-approximate solution to influence maximization with at least $1 - 2/n^\ell$ probability. The success probability of *IMM* can be easily improved to $1 - 1/n^\ell$, by increasing ℓ by a factor of $1 + \log 2/\log n$. Algorithm 3 shows the pseudo-code of a version of *IMM* with the improved success probability.

Algorithm 3: IMM $(G, k, \varepsilon, \ell)$

1 $\ell = \ell \cdot (1 + \log 2 / \log n)$;
2 $\mathcal{R}$ = Sampling (G, k, ε, ℓ);
3 S_k^* = NodeSelection ($\mathcal{R}, k$);
4 **return** S_k^*

In what follows, we discuss the time complexity of *IMM*. We focus on the sampling phase of *IMM* (i.e., Algorithm 2), since the time complexity of the node estimation phase (i.e., Algorithm 1) has been established in Corollary 3. Observe that the major computational cost of Algorithm 2 is incurred by the construction of RR sets. On the other hand, the time required in generating a random RR set R is $O(w(R))$, where $w(R)$ denotes the number of edges in G that point to the nodes in R. Specifically, the generation of R requires (i) sampling an edge set from the triggering distribution of each node in R and (ii) traversing all edges in the edge sets sampled. The former requires $O(w(R))$ time, since a sample from a node v's triggering distribution incurs a linear cost to the number of incoming edges of v. Meanwhile, the latter takes $O(w(R))$ time, since the sampled edge sets contain $O(w(R))$ time in total.

Let EPT be the expected value of $w(R)$. We have the following result from [33].

LEMMA 10 ([33]). $n \cdot EPT \leq m \cdot OPT$. □

Now consider the set $\mathcal{R}$ of RR sets generated by Algorithm 2. By Lemma 9,

$$\mathbb{E}[|\mathcal{R}|] \leq \frac{3\max\{\lambda^*, \lambda'\} \cdot (1+\varepsilon')^2}{(1-1/e)\cdot OPT} = O\left((k+\ell)n\log n \cdot \varepsilon^{-2}/OPT\right). \quad (11)$$

If $|\mathcal{R}|$ is independent of $w(R)$ for each $R \in \mathcal{R}$, then by Lemma 10 and Equation 11, the expected total time to generate $\mathcal{R}$ is

$$\mathbb{E}\Big[\sum_{R\in\mathcal{R}} w(R)\Big] = \mathbb{E}\big[|\mathcal{R}|\big] \cdot EPT = O\left((k+\ell)(n+m)\log n/\varepsilon^2\right). \quad (12)$$

However, $|\mathcal{R}|$ is correlated with the RR sets in $\mathcal{R}$, because $|\mathcal{R}|$ depends on when Algorithm 2 terminates its for loop, which in turn is decided by the RR sets in $\mathcal{R}$. But interestingly, we can prove that Equation 12 still holds, by utilizing the *optional stopping theorem* [38] for martingales. For our discussion, we introduce a simplified version of the theorem[4] as follows.

THEOREM 3 ([38]). *Let $Y_1, Y_2, Y_3, \ldots$ be a martingale, and τ be a random variable such that the event $\tau = i$ is independent of any Y_j with $j > i$. If $Pr[\tau < +\infty] = 1$, then*

$$\mathbb{E}[Y_\tau] = \mathbb{E}[Y_1]. \quad (13)$$

An intuitive way to understand Theorem 3 is as follows. Suppose that we retrieve $Y_1, Y_2, \ldots$ one by one, and we have a certain algorithm that examines the Y_i that we obtain and decides when we should stop the retrieval process. (That is, the algorithm determines the value of τ.) Then, as long as the algorithm always terminates in finite time, the expectation of the last retrieved Y_i is equal to $\mathbb{E}[Y_1]$.

Based on Theorem 3, we prove Equation 12 as follows. First, let R_i be the i-th RR set generated by Algorithm 2, and $Z_i = \sum_{j=1}^{i}\big(w(R_i) - EPT\big)$. It can be verified that $Z_1, Z_2, \ldots$ is a martingale. Let τ be a random variable that denotes the total number of RR sets generated by Algorithm 3. Observe that $\tau < +\infty$ always holds. Thus, by Theorem 3, $\mathbb{E}[Z_\tau] = \mathbb{E}[Z_1]$. Notice that

$$\mathbb{E}[Z_1] = \mathbb{E}\big[w(R_1) - EPT\big] = 0, \text{ and}$$

$$\begin{aligned}\mathbb{E}[Z_\tau] &= \mathbb{E}\left[\textstyle\sum_{j=1}^{\tau}\big(w(R_i) - EPT\big)\right] \\ &= \mathbb{E}\left[\textstyle\sum_{j=1}^{\tau} w(R_i)\right] - \mathbb{E}[\tau]\cdot EPT \\ &= \mathbb{E}\left[\textstyle\sum_{R\in\mathcal{R}} w(R)\right] - \mathbb{E}\big[|\mathcal{R}|\big]\cdot EPT.\end{aligned}$$

Therefore, Equation 12 holds.

With the above discussions, we can prove that the expected running time of *IMM* equals the right hand side of Equation 12. This leads to the following theorem.

THEOREM 4. *Algorithm 3 returns a $(1-1/e-\varepsilon)$-approximate solution with at least $1 - 1/n^\ell$ probability, and runs in $O\left((k+\ell)(n+m)\log n/\varepsilon^2\right)$ expected time.* □

Comparison with *TIM* and *TIM*$^+$. *IMM*, *TIM*, and *TIM*$^+$ have the same approximation guarantee and expected time complexity, but *IMM* provides much higher efficiency in practice since it requires generating a much smaller number of RR sets. Specifically, the number of RR sets constructed in *IMM* is $O((k+\ell)n\log n \cdot \varepsilon^{-2}/OPT)$, whereas *TIM* requires $O((k+\ell)n\log n \cdot \varepsilon^{-2}/KPT)$ RR sets, where KPT is the expected influence of a node set obtained by sampling k nodes with replacement from G, with the sampling probability of each node being proportional to its in-degree [33]. It can be verified that $KPT < OPT$ always holds, and $KPT/OPT = O(k/n)$ in the worst case. Therefore, *TIM* incurs a much larger overhead than *IMM*. Meanwhile, although *TIM*$^+$ improves upon *TIM* in terms of efficiency, its parameter estimation phase is identical to that of *TIM*, due to which it also requires producing a large number of RR sets to estimate KPT. As a consequence, *TIM*$^+$'s practical performance is much inferior to that of *IMM*, as we show in Section 6.

In addition, there exists another crucial difference between *IMM* and *TIM* (resp. *TIM*$^+$). In *IMM*, all RR sets generated in the sampling phase are re-used in the node selection phase. In contrast, *TIM*'s node selection phase is unable to recycle any RR sets produced in the parameter estimation phase, due to which it has to re-generate a large number of RR sets from scratch for influence maximization. The reason is that the node selection phase of *TIM* demands that all RR sets used should be independent, whereas the RR sets produced in *TIM*'s parameter estimation phase are correlated. This results in a considerable amount of redundant computation, which degrades *TIM*'s efficiency. *TIM*$^+$ suffers from the same issue since its node selection and parameter estimation phases are the same as those of *TIM*. Meanwhile, *IMM* circumvents this issue because its node selection phase accommodates dependencies among RR sets, which in turn is due to the martingale approach adopted in *IMM*.

4. EXTENSIONS

This section extends *IMM* beyond the triggering model, and demonstrates an application of *IMM* to the continuous-time model [16], a diffusion model not supported by *TIM* and *TIM*$^+$ [33].

4.1 Generalization of *IMM*

Our discussions in the previous sections have assumed the triggering model. However, observe that the algorithms used by *IMM* (i.e., Algorithms 1, 2, and 3) do not rely on anything specific to the triggering model, except that they require a method to generate

[4] In its original form, the optional stopping theorem states three sufficient conditions for Equation 13. For simplicity, we include only one condition in Theorem 3, but it suffices for our purpose.

random RR sets. To extend *IMM* to other diffusion models, we first generalize the definition of RR sets in a model-independent manner as follows.

DEFINITION 3 (REVERSE INFLUENCE SET). *Let v be a node in V. A* reverse influence (RI) set *for v is a node set $R \subseteq V$, such that for any node set $S \subseteq V$, the probability that $R \cap S \neq \emptyset$ equals the probability that S as a seed set can activate v in a diffusion process. A* random RI set *is an RI set for a node selected uniformly at random from V.* □

Notice that RR sets are a special case of RI sets under the triggering model, due to Lemma 1.

Let $\mathcal{R}$ be a set of RI sets under a certain diffusion model $\mathcal{M}$. Then, by Definition 3 and the linearity of expectation, we have

$$\mathbb{E}[I(S)] = n \cdot \mathbb{E}[F_{\mathcal{R}}(S)], \tag{14}$$

where $I(S)$ denotes the influence of S under $\mathcal{M}$, and $F_{\mathcal{R}}(S)$ denotes the fraction of RI sets in $\mathcal{R}$ that overlaps S. Given Equation 14 and the concentration results in Corollaries 1 and 2, it can be verified that all theoretical analysis in Section 3.2 holds under $\mathcal{M}$, if the input to Algorithm 1 is a set $\mathcal{R}$ of random RI sets generated under $\mathcal{M}$. It then follows that all results in Section 3.3 are still valid, even if we modify Algorithm 2 so that it generates random RI sets under $\mathcal{M}$ instead of random RR sets. As a consequence, Algorithm 3 is guaranteed to return a $(1-1/e-\varepsilon)$-approximation under $\mathcal{M}$, with at least $1 - 1/n^{\ell}$ probability.

On the other hand, the time complexity of *IMM* under $\mathcal{M}$ may differ from that stated in Theorem 4, since Theorem 4 assumes $n \cdot EPT \leq m \cdot OPT$ (see Lemma 10), which does not necessarily hold under $\mathcal{M}$. Nonetheless, if we re-define EPT as the expected cost to generate a random RI set under $\mathcal{M}$, then it follows from Theorem 3 that *IMM* has an expected time complexity of $O\left(\frac{EPT}{OPT} \cdot (k+\ell)(n+m)\log n/\varepsilon^2\right)$.

In summary, *IMM* can be extended to any diffusion model $\mathcal{M}$ for which random RI sets can be generated efficiently. In addition, it provides the following theoretical guarantees under $\mathcal{M}$.

THEOREM 5. *Under a diffusion model where a random RI set takes $O(EPT)$ expected time to generate, Algorithm 3 returns a $(1-1/e-\varepsilon)$-approximation with at least $1-1/n^{\ell}$ probability, and runs in $O\left(\frac{EPT}{OPT} \cdot (k+\ell)(n+m)\log n/\varepsilon^2\right)$ expected time.* □

Remark. The above extension of *IMM* requires a procedure for generating random RI sets under the diffusion model $\mathcal{M}$. However, such a procedure may not exist. For example, consider a diffusion model $\mathcal{M}$ under which the expected influence of a node set S is not a submodular function of S. Then, it can be verified that it is impossible to generate RI sets under $\mathcal{M}$ that satisfy the condition stated in Definition 3. We leave as future work to characterize the diffusion models under which random RI sets can be produced.

4.2 Application to Continuous-Time Models

The *continuous-time independent cascade (CTIC) model* [6, 16, 30] assumes that each directed edge e in the social network G is associated with a *length distribution* $\mathcal{L}(e)$. Given a seed set S and a threshold t, a diffusion process under the CTIC model first samples a length $l(e)$ for each edge e, and then activates any node that can be reached from a node in S via a path with a length no more than t. The rationale behind this model is that $w(e)$ represents the time required to transmit information from the starting point of e to its ending point, and accordingly, the diffusion process from S with a threshold t captures the effect of information cascade within a certain time frame. Such a model is useful in practice since, in viral marketing, a marketer is often concerned about the effectiveness of a marketing campaign within a given time (e.g., one month from the start of the campaign) [15].

In what follows, we demonstrate that our generalization of *IMM* in Section 4.1 can be applied to handle the CTIC model. Towards that end, we first present an efficient algorithm to construct an RI set $R(v)$ for any given node v. Conceptually, the algorithm works in three steps. First, it decides the length of each edge e in G by taking a sample from $\mathcal{L}(e)$. Let g be the resulting weighted graph. Then, the algorithm invokes the Dijkstra's algorithm [13] on g to identify the shortest distance from each node to v. Finally, it returns the set $R(v)$ of all nodes whose distance to v is no more than t (i.e., the threshold parameter in the CTIC model).

For practical efficiency, we implement the above algorithm as follows. We invoke the Dijkstra's algorithm to traverse G with v as the starting point, following only the incoming edge of each node. Each time we encounter an edge e whose length has not been decided, we sample its length from $\mathcal{L}(e)$. By the properties of the Dijkstra's algorithm [13], it would maintain a priority queue Q during the traverse of G, and it removes a node u from Q only if the shortest path from u to v is determined. Accordingly, we monitor each node u' removed from Q by the algorithm, and we terminate the algorithm whenever the shortest path from u' to v is longer than t. After that, we return the set $R(v)$ of all nodes that have been removed from Q, except u'. We refer to this algorithm as *RI-Gen*.

It can be verified that the running time of *RI-Gen* is $O(n^* \log n^* + m^*)$, where n^* and m^* are the numbers of nodes and edges inspected by *RI-Gen* during the traversal of G. Although $n^* = n$ and $m^* = m$ in the worst case, we will show that when v is selected from G uniformly at random, the expected time complexity of *RI-Gen* can be much smaller than $O(n \log n + m)$. Before that, we first establish the correctness of *RI-Gen*.

LEMMA 11. *Suppose that we feed a node v as input to RI-Gen, and obtain a node set $R(v)$ as the output. Then, for any node set S, the probability that S overlaps $R(v)$ equals the probability that S as a seed set can activate v in a diffusion process under the CTIC model.* □

Based on Lemma 11, we have the following result related to *RI-Gen*'s running time.

LEMMA 12. *Let OPT^* be the largest expected influence of any size-1 node set in G under the CTIC model. Suppose that we choose a node v from G uniformly at random, and feed v as input to RI-Gen. Let m^* be the number of edges inspected by RI-Gen. Then,*

$$n \cdot \mathbb{E}[m^*] \leq m \cdot OPT^*.$$ □

Given Lemma 12, it can be derived that the expected time complexity of *RI-Gen* is $O\left(\frac{n \log n}{m} OPT\right)$. Meanwhile, Lemma 11 shows that we can extend *IMM* to tackle the CTIC model, by adopting *RI-Gen* to generate random RI sets. Then, by Theorem 5, we have the following result.

THEOREM 6. *Under the CTIC model, Algorithm 3 returns a $(1-1/e-\varepsilon)$-approximation with at least $1-1/n^{\ell}$ probability, and runs in $O\left((k+\ell)(n+m)\log^2 n/\varepsilon^2\right)$ expected time.* □

Comparison with *ConTinEst* [15]. *ConTinEst* is the state-of-the-art solution for influence maximization under the CTIC model. It first generates c weighted versions of G, denoted as $g_1, g_2, \ldots, g_c$, such that in each g_i ($i \in [1, c]$), the length of each edge e is sampled from $\mathcal{L}(e)$ independently. After that, it constructs a *sketch* [11] on each g_i, and utilizes the sketches for influence maximization. Du et al. [15] provide an analysis of *ConTinEst*'s accuracy guarantee, but do not formally discuss its time complexity. In the following, we analyze the time complexity of *ConTinEst* based on the theoretical results from [15], and compare it with *IMM*.

First, the sketch on each g_i ($i \in [1, c]$) is parameterized with a positive integer d, and it takes $O(dn \log^2 n + dm \log n)$ time to construct [11]. Second, by Theorems 1 and 2 in [15], *ConTinEst* returns a $(1 - 1/e - \varepsilon)$-approximate solution with at least $1 - 1/n^\ell$ probability, if

$$c \geq \frac{\Lambda \cdot 4k^3(\ell + 1)(\log n + \log 2)}{\varepsilon^2 \cdot OPT^2}, \text{ where} \quad (15)$$

$$\Lambda = \max_{S \subseteq V, |S| \leq k} \left(\tfrac{2}{d-2}\mathbb{E}[I(S)]^2 + \tfrac{d-1}{d-2}Var[I(S)] + \tfrac{4\varepsilon \cdot r(S)}{3k} OPT \right),$$

and $r(S)$ denotes the maximum number of nodes that S can activate under the CTIC model. We observe that Λ is unknown in advance, and hence, it is unclear how a user can select an appropriate c to ensure a $(1 - 1/e - \varepsilon)$-approximation. However, this issue is not addressed in [15]. For our discussion, we use a loose lower bound of Λ to derive an optimistic estimation of *ConTinEst*'s time complexity, and then compare it with that of *IMM*. (Note that this is to the advantage of *ConTinEst*.)

Let S_k° be the size-k node set with the largest expected influence under the CTIC model. Then, $E[I(S_k^\circ)] = OPT$ and $r(S_k^\circ) \geq OPT$. Therefore,

$$\begin{aligned} \Lambda &\geq \left(\tfrac{2}{d-2}\mathbb{E}[I(S_k^\circ)]^2 + \tfrac{4\varepsilon \cdot r(S_k^\circ)}{3k} OPT \right) \\ &\geq \left(\tfrac{2}{d-2} + \tfrac{4\varepsilon}{3k} \right) OPT^2 \end{aligned}$$

By setting $\Lambda = \left(\frac{2}{d-2} + \frac{4\varepsilon}{3k} \right) OPT^2$ in Equation 15, we have

$$c \geq \left(\tfrac{8}{d-2} + \tfrac{16\varepsilon}{3k} \right) \cdot k^3(\ell + 1)(\log n + \log 2)/\varepsilon^2. \quad (16)$$

Given that *ConTinEst* needs to construct a sketch on each g_i ($i \in [1, c]$), and that each sketch takes $O(dn \log^2 n + dm \log n)$ time to generate, the time complexity of *ConTinEst* is at least

$$O\left(k^3(\ell + 1)(n \log n + m) \log^2 n/\varepsilon^2\right).$$

Observe that this time complexity is larger than that of *IMM* (see Theorem 6) by a factor of more than k^2. In Section 6, we will demonstrate that the empirical efficiency of *ConTinEst* is also inferior to that of *IMM*.

5. RELATED WORK

Kempe et al. [25] presents the first algorithmic study on influence maximization. They show that the problem is NP-hard in general, but can be approximated with a factor of $1 - 1/e - \varepsilon$ under the triggering model using a polynomial-time greedy algorithm. The key of Kempe et al.'s algorithm is a monte-carlo approach for estimating the expected influence of any node set S. In particular, it simulates the diffusion process from S for a large number r of times, and then takes the average influence of S in the r simulations as an estimation of $\mathbb{E}[I(S)]$. With this monte-carlo approach, Kempe et al.'s algorithm greedily selects the node in G that leads to the largest increment of estimated influence (with respect to the nodes that are already selected), until k nodes are chosen.

Kempe et al.'s algorithm is simple and effective, but it incurs a high time complexity of $O(knmr)$, which restricts its application to very small graphs. This motivates numerous techniques [4–9, 15–19, 24–27, 29, 32, 33, 37] that improve upon Kempe et al.'s algorithm in terms of efficiency. Among them, the methods in [8, 20, 29] follow Kempe et al.'s greedy framework and retain its approximation ratio under the triggering model, while providing higher empirical efficiency by using branch-and-bound approaches to omit node sets whose expected influence are small. Those techniques, however, still entail $O(kmnr)$ computation time, due to which cannot scale to large graphs with millions of nodes. In contrast, techniques in [7–9, 19, 24, 27, 37] offer much better scalability by exploiting heuristics in node selection, but none of them retains the $(1 - 1/e - \varepsilon)$-approximation ratio achieved by Kempe et al.'s approach.

Very recently, Borg et al. [5] make a theoretical breakthrough on influence maximization by presenting a near-linear time algorithm under the independent cascade (IC) model (which is a special case of the triggering model). In particular, Borg et al.'s algorithm runs in $O(k\ell^2(m + n) \log^2 n/\varepsilon^3)$ time, and returns a $(1 - 1/e - \varepsilon)$-approximate solution with at least $1 - 1/n^\ell$ probability. As pointed out in [33], however, Borg et al.'s algorithm incurs significant overheads in practice, due to the ε^{-3} term and the large hidden constant factor in its time complexity. Tang et al. [33] address this deficiency and propose an improved algorithm (i.e., *TIM*) that runs in $O((k + \ell)(m + n) \log n/\varepsilon^2)$ while providing the same approximation guarantee with Borg et al.'s approach. In addition, Tang et al. show that *TIM* can be extended to support the triggering model, and it offers much higher empirical efficiency than any existing method that returns a $(1 - 1/e - \varepsilon)$-approximation under the same model. Nevertheless, as we explain in Section 3.4, *TIM* is inferior to *IMM* in that it incurs unnecessary computational costs.

In addition, Du et al. [15] present a $(1 - 1/e - \varepsilon)$-approximation algorithm (i.e., *ConTinEst*) for influence maximization under the CTIC model. The algorithm adopts a greedy framework similar to that of Kempe et al.'s approach [25], but it applies an advanced sketch method [11] to estimate the expected influence of all relevant node sets in a batch manner, which considerably reduces computation overheads. Nevertheless, as we discuss on Section 4.2, *ConTinEst*'s approximation guarantees rely on parameters that are unknown in advance, and its time complexity is at least a factor of k^2 larger than that of *IMM*.

Table 2: Datasets.

Name	n	m	Type	Corresponding Site
NetHEPT	15.2K	31.4K	undirected	arxiv.org
Pokec	1.6M	30.6M	directed	pokec.azet.sk
LiveJournal	4.8M	69.0M	directed	www.livejournal.com
Orkut	3.1M	117.2M	undirected	www.orkut.com
Twitter	41.7M	1.5G	directed	twitter.com

6. EXPERIMENTS

This section experimentally evaluates *IMM* against the states of the art, on a linux machine with an Intel Xeon 2.4GHz CPU and 64GB memory.

6.1 Experimental Settings

Datasets. We use five real social networks in our experiments, as shown in Table 2. Among them, *Pokec*, *LiveJournal*, *Orkut*, and *Twitter* are the largest datasets ever used in the literature of influence maximization. All datasets are publicly available: *Pokec*, *LiveJournal*, and *Orkut* can be obtained from [1], while *NetHEPT* and *Twitter* can be obtained from [2] and [3], respectively.

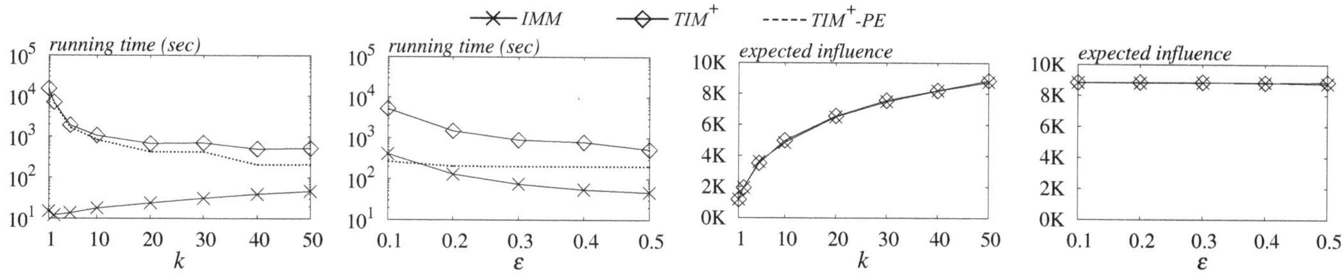

(a) Running time vs. k ($\varepsilon = 0.5$) (b) Running time vs. ε ($k = 50$) (c) Expected influence vs. k ($\varepsilon = 0.5$) (d) Expected influence vs. ε ($k = 50$)

Figure 3: Running time and expected influence on *Twitter* under the IC model ($l = 1$ for *IMM* and *TIM*$^+$).

Diffusion Models. We consider three well-adopted diffusion models in our experiments, namely, the *independent cascade (IC)* model [25] (see Section 2.2), the *linear threshold (LT)* model [25], and the *continuous time independent cascade (CTIC)* model [6, 16, 30] (see Section 4.2). For the IC model, we set the propagation probability $p(e)$ of each edge e to $1/i$, where i denotes the number of edges that share the same ending point with e. This setting is adopted in previous work [7, 19, 24, 36]. For the CTIC model, we set the length distribution of each edge e to be a *Weibull distribution* [28], with the following pdf:

$$f(x) = \tfrac{a}{b} \cdot (\tfrac{x}{b})^{a-1} \cdot e^{-(x/b)^a},$$

where a and b are sampled from $[0, 10]$ uniformly at random for each edge e. In addition, the threshold parameter t of the CTIC model is varied from 1 to 10 in our experiments. These settings follow from the experiments in [15] for evaluating *ConTinEst* [15].

Recall from Section 2.2 that the LT model is a special case of the triggering model where each sample from a node v's triggering distribution $\mathcal{T}(v)$ is a unit set containing only one incoming neighbor of v. Following previous work [6], we construct $\mathcal{T}(v)$ as follows. First, for each of v's incoming neighbors u, we assign to u a number selected from $[0, 1]$ uniformly at random. Then, we normalize the numbers assigned to all incoming neighbors, so that they sum up to one. Finally, we set the normalized number of each incoming neighbor as the probability that it is sampled from $\mathcal{T}(v)$.

Algorithms. We compare *IMM* with five algorithms, namely, *TIM* [33], *TIM*$^+$ [33], *IRIE* [24], *SIMPATH* [21], and *ConTinEst* [15]. In particular, *TIM* and *TIM*$^+$ are the state-of-the-art techniques that return $(1 - 1/e - \varepsilon)$-approximations under the triggering model, while *ConTinEst* is a method the yields the same approximation result under the CTIC model. On the other hand, *IRIE* and *SIMPATH* are the most advanced heuristic solutions under the IC and LT models, respectively. We implement *IMM* with C++, and we adopt the C++ implementations of the other algorithms made available by their inventors.

Parameter Settings. For *IMM*, *TIM*, *TIM*$^+$, we set $\varepsilon = 0.5$, $\ell = 1$, and $k = 50$ by default. For *IRIE* and *SIMPATH*, we set their internal parameters as recommended in [24] and [21], respectively. In each of our experiments, we run each method 5 times and report the average measurements. In addition, to compare the quality of the seed sets returned by each method, we estimate the expected influence of any seed set S by taking its average influence in 10000 simulations of the diffusion process.

6.2 Results under the IC Model

In our first set of experiments, we compare four methods that support the IC models, namely, *IMM*, *TIM*, *TIM*$^+$, and *IRIE*. Figure 3a shows the computational costs of *IMM* and *TIM*$^+$ on *Twitter* (i.e., our largest dataset), with k varying from 1 to 50. We omit *TIM* and *IRIE*, since the former incurs prohibitive cost on *Twitter*, while the latter requires more than 64G memory to process the data. Observe that *IMM* consistently outperforms *TIM*$^+$ in terms of running time, and is faster than *TIM*$^+$ by three orders of magnitude when $k = 1$. The reason that *TIM*$^+$ is inferior to *IMM* is two-fold. First, as we point out in Section 3, the node selection phase of *TIM*$^+$ requires generating a large number of RR sets, due to the facts that (i) it cannot reuse RR sets produced in the parameter estimation phase, and (ii) it makes sub-optimal choices when setting its internal parameters. Second, the parameter estimation phase of *TIM*$^+$ (denoted as *TIM*$^+$*-PE*) incurs significant overheads when k is small. The rationale is that, when k decreases, the optimal expected influence OPT also tends to decrease, in which case it is more challenging to derive a reasonable lower bound of OPT. To illustrate *TIM*$^+$*-PE*'s computational overhead, we plot it in Figure 3 along with *IMM* and *TIM*$^+$. Observe that *TIM*$^+$*-PE* runs even slower than *IMM*. Furthermore, when k = 1, *TIM*$^+$*-PE* accounts for 97% of *TIM*'s computation time. In contrast, *IMM* does not suffer from this issue, since it adopts a more effective statistical test in its sampling phase.

Figure 3b illustrates the running time of *IMM* and *TIM*$^+$ on *Twitter* as a function of ε. Regardless of the value of ε, the processing cost of *IMM* is lower than that of *TIM*$^+$ by an order of magnitude. The computation time of both *IMM* and *TIM* decreases with ε, since a larger ε leads to a less stringent theoretical guarantee, which is easier to achieve. The overhead of *TIM*$^+$*-PE* is insensitive to ε, which is consistent with the fact that its time complexity is independent of ε. Figure 3c (resp. Figure 3d) shows the expected influence of *IMM* and *TIM*$^+$ when k (resp. ε) varies. In all cases, *IMM* and *TIM*$^+$ yield similar results.

Figure 4 plots the running time of *IMM*, *TIM*, *TIM*$^+$, and *IRIE* against k for the four smaller datasets. Again, *IMM* consistently outperforms *TIM*$^+$, especially when k is small. Furthermore, the parameter estimation phase of *TIM*$^+$ (i.e., *TIM*$^+$*-PE*) alone incurs a higher cost than *IMM* in most cases. On the other hand, *TIM*$^+$ is more efficient *TIM*, due to the heuristic optimization that it adopts to reduce computational overhead of its node selection phase (see Section 2.3). *IRIE* outperforms *IMM* on *NetHEPT* when $k \leq 5$, but is inferior to *IMM* in all other cases. In particular, the running time of *IRIE* is around two orders of magnitude larger than that of *IMM* on *Pokec*, *LiveJournal*, and *Orkut*, when $k \geq 20$.

Figure 5 shows the expected influence of each method on the four smaller datasets. *IMM*, *TIM*, and *TIM*$^+$ produce comparable results in all scenarios. Meanwhile, on *LiveJournal*, the quality of seed sets returned by *IRIE* are noticeably worse than those returned by *IMM*, *TIM*, and *TIM*$^+$. The reason is that *IMM*, *TIM*, and *TIM*$^+$ all provide asymptotic guarantees in terms of the accuracy of their solutions, whereas *IRIE* is a heuristic method that does not offer any worst-case assurance.

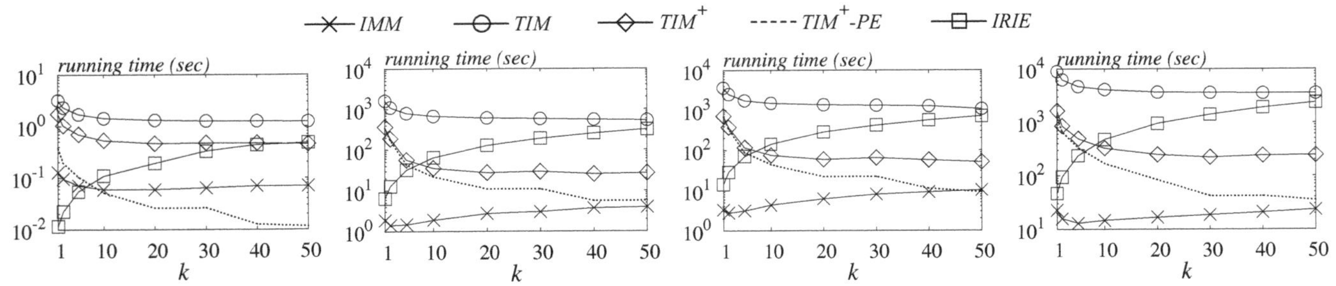

(a) *NetHEPT* (b) *Pokec* (c) *LiveJournal* (d) *Orkut*

Figure 4: Running time vs. k under the IC model ($\varepsilon = 0.5$ and $\ell = 1$ for *IMM*, *TIM*, and *TIM*$^+$).

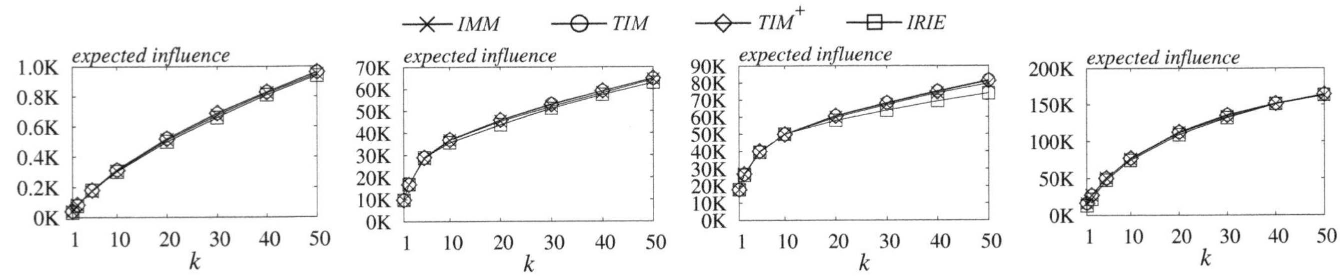

(a) *NetHEPT* (b) *Pokec* (c) *LiveJournal* (d) *Orkut*

Figure 5: Expected influence vs. k under the IC model ($\varepsilon = 0.5$ and $\ell = 1$ for *IMM*, *TIM*, and *TIM*$^+$).

Remark. We have also evaluated the effect of ε on the performance of *IMM*, *TIM*, and *TIM*$^+$ on the four smaller datasets. We vary ε from 0.1 to 0.5, and find that *IMM* consistently surpasses both *TIM* and *TIM*$^+$ in terms of efficiency, while achieving similar expected influence. We omit the results due to the space constraint.

6.3 Results under the LT model

Our second set of experiments compares four methods that support the LT model, i.e., *IMM*, *TIM*, *TIM*$^+$, and *SIMPATH*. Figure 6 shows the running time and expected influence of *IMM* and *TIM*$^+$ on *Twitter*, omitting *TIM* and *SIMPATH* since they entail prohibitive costs on the dataset. As with the case under the IC model, *IMM* considerably outperforms *TIM*$^+$ in all cases, and is even more efficient than the parameter estimation phase of *TIM*$^+$ (denoted as *TIM*$^+$*-PE*). At the same time, there is no noticeable difference between the quality of the results returned by *IMM* and *TIM*$^+$.

Figure 7 (resp. Figure 8) illustrates the computational overheads (resp. expected influence) of all methods on the four smaller datasets. The relative performance of *IMM*, *TIM*, and *TIM*$^+$ is qualitatively similar to that in Figures 4 and 5, with *IMM* surpassing *TIM* and *TIM*$^+$ in terms of efficiency. On the other hand, *SIMPATH* incurs a much larger overheads than all other methods, and its result accuracy on on *Pokec* and *LiveJournal* is considerably lower than that of *IMM*, *TIM*, and *TIM*$^+$.

6.4 Results under the CTIC Model

Our last set of experiments compares *IMM* with *ConTinEst* under the CTIC model. We first consider the case when both *IMM* and *ConTinEst* return $(1 - 1/e - \varepsilon)$-approximate solutions with $\varepsilon \leq 0.5$. Towards this end, we tune *ConTinEst*'s parameters c and d as follows. First, we set $d = 5$, following the experiments in [15]. Then, we let c be the smallest value that satisfies Equation 15. Note that this setting is to the advantage of *ConTinEst* because, as we analyze in Section 4.2, *ConTinEst* may require a much larger c to ensure $(1 - 1/e - \varepsilon)$-approximations.

Figure 9a illustrates the computation time of *IMM* and *ConTinEst* on *NetHEPT*, when $\varepsilon = 0.5$, $t = 10$, and k varies from 1 to 5. (Recall that t is the threshold parameter in the CTIC model.) We use only *NetHEPT* in this experiment, since *ConTinEst* incurs prohibitive overheads on the larger datasets. Observe that the running time of *ConTinEst* increases significantly with k. The reason is that, when the approximation ratio of *ConTinEst* if fixed, its computational cost is roughly proportional to k^3, as we analyze in Section 6.4. In contrast, *IMM* scales much better with k, and it is three orders of magnitude faster than *ConTinEst* when $k = 5$.

Figure 9b shows the overheads of *IMM* and *ConTinEst* when $\varepsilon = 0.5$, $k = 3$, and t varies from 1 to 10. The running time of *IMM* increases with t. To explain, recall that under the CTIC model, *IMM* generates each RI set by invoking the Dijkstra's algorithm on a weighted version of G to identify nodes that are within t distance to a given node v. When t increases, there exists a larger number of nodes in G that are within t distance to v, and hence, the construction of RI sets incurs a larger overhead. This renders *IMM* less efficient. In contrast, the computational cost of *ConTinEst* is insensitive to t. That said, even when $t = 10$, *IMM* is still more than 250 times faster than *ConTinEst*. Finally, Figure 9c plots the processing costs of *IMM* and *ConTinEst* when $k = 3$, $t = 10$, and ε varies from 0.1 to 0.5. The costs of *IMM* and *ConTinEst* both decrease with the increase of ε, but *IMM* is significantly more efficient than *ConTinEst* in all cases.

7. CONCLUSION

This paper presents *IMM*, an influence maximization algorithm runs in $O((k + \ell)(n + m)\log n/\varepsilon^2)$ expected time and returns a $(1 - 1/e - \varepsilon)$-approximation with at least $1 - 1/n^\ell$ probability under the triggering model. *IMM* has the same approximation guarantee and time complexity as the state of the art, but achieves higher empirical efficiency with a novel algorithm design based on martingales. In addition, *IMM* can be extended to a large class of diffusion models beyond the triggering model, while still retaining

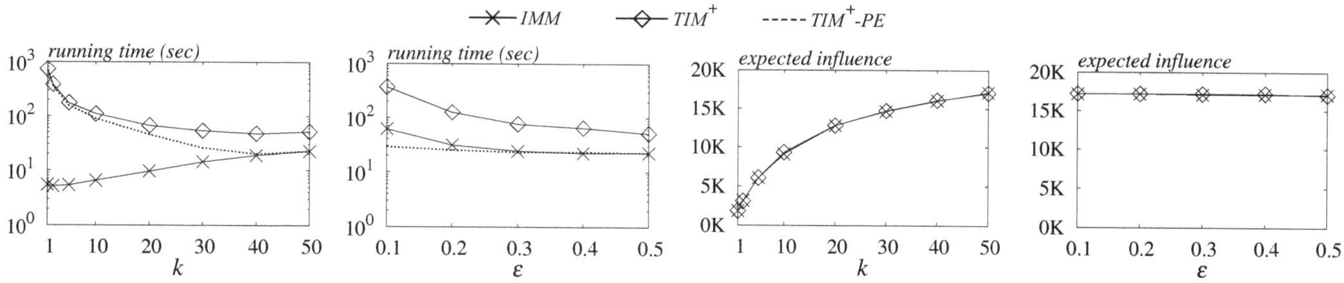

(a) Running time vs. k ($\varepsilon = 0.5$) (b) Running time vs. ε ($k = 50$) (c) Expected influence vs. k ($\varepsilon = 0.5$) (d) Expected influence vs. ε ($k = 50$)

Figure 6: Running time and expected influence on *Twitter* under the LT model ($l = 1$ for *IMM* and *TIM*$^+$).

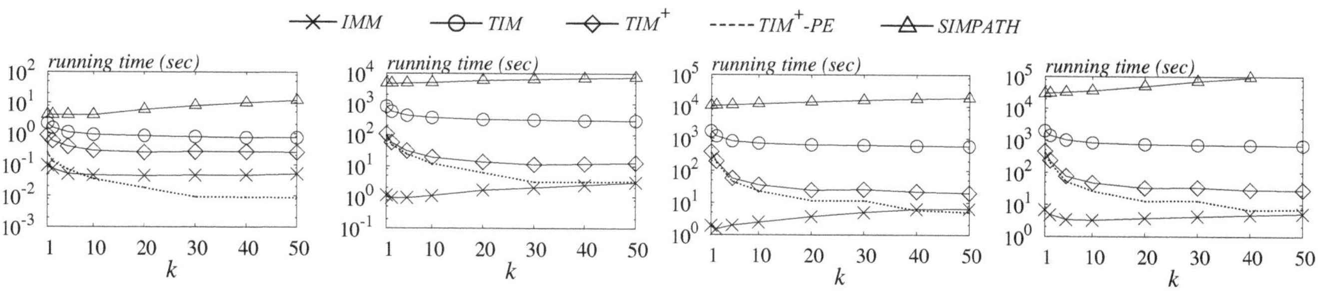

(a) *NetHEPT* (b) *Pokec* (c) *LiveJournal* (d) *Orkut*

Figure 7: Running time vs. k under the LT model ($\varepsilon = 0.5$ and $\ell = 1$ for *IMM*, *TIM*, and *TIM*$^+$).

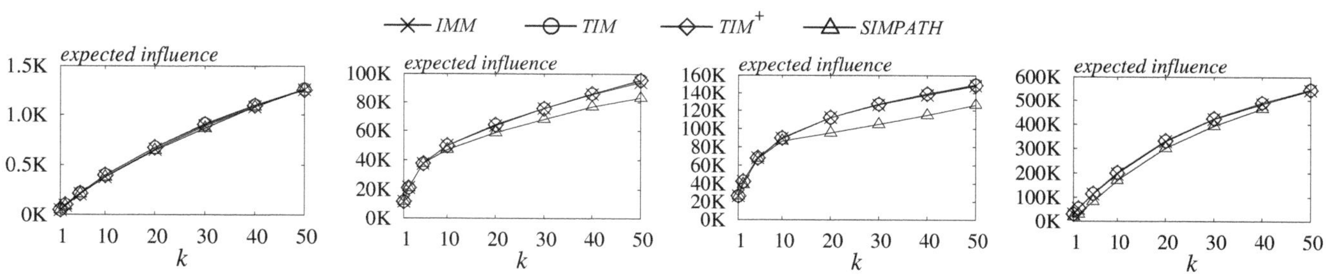

(a) *NetHEPT* (b) *Pokec* (c) *LiveJournal* (d) *Orkut*

Figure 8: Expected influence vs. k under the LT model ($\varepsilon = 0.5$ and $\ell = 1$ for *IMM*, *TIM*, and *TIM*$^+$).

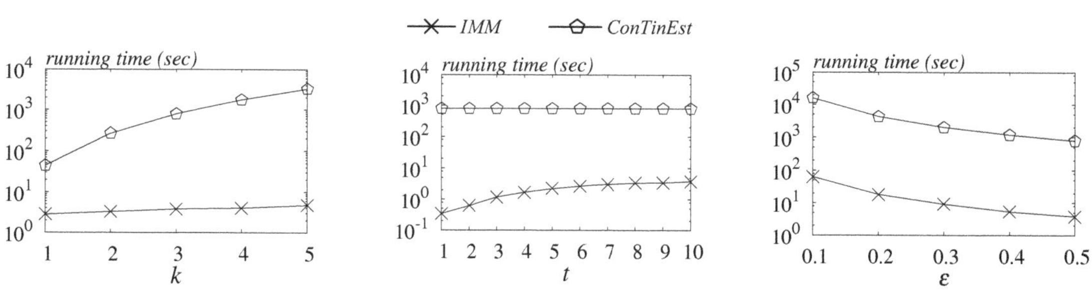

(a) Vary k ($t = 10$ and $\varepsilon = 0.5$). (b) Vary t ($k = 3$ and $\varepsilon = 0.5$). (c) Vary ε ($k = 3$ and $t = 10$).

Figure 9: Running time of *IMM* and *ConTinEst* under the CTIC model.

the $(1 - 1/e - \varepsilon)$-approximation ratio. We experimentally evaluate *IMM* against the state-of-the-art methods under the IC, LT, triggering, and CTIC models, using real social networks with up to 1.4 billion edges. Our experimental results show that *IMM* consistently outperforms the states of the art in terms of computation efficiency, and is often orders of magnitude faster. For future work, we plan to investigate a precise characterization of the diffusion models for which our extension of *IMM* (in Section 4.2) is applicable.

8. ACKNOWLEDGMENTS

This work was supported by AcRF Tier 2 Grant ARC19/14 from the Ministry of Education, Singapore, an SUG Grant from the Nanyang Technological University, and a gift from the Microsoft Research Asia. The authors would like to thank the anonymous reviewers for their constructive and insightful comments.

9. REFERENCES

[1] https://snap.stanford.edu/data/.

[2] http://research.microsoft.com/en-us/people/weic/graphdata.zip.

[3] http://an.kaist.ac.kr/traces/WWW2010.html.

[4] S. Bharathi, D. Kempe, and M. Salek. Competitive influence maximization in social networks. In *WINE*, pages 306–311, 2007.

[5] C. Borgs, M. Brautbar, J. Chayes, and B. Lucier. Maximizing social influence in nearly optimal time. In *SODA*, pages 946–957, 2014.

[6] W. Chen, W. Lu, and N. Zhang. Time-critical influence maximization in social networks with time-delayed diffusion process. In *AAAI*, 2012.

[7] W. Chen, C. Wang, and Y. Wang. Scalable influence maximization for prevalent viral marketing in large-scale social networks. In *KDD*, pages 1029–1038, 2010.

[8] W. Chen, Y. Wang, and S. Yang. Efficient influence maximization in social networks. In *KDD*, pages 199–208, 2009.

[9] W. Chen, Y. Yuan, and L. Zhang. Scalable influence maximization in social networks under the linear threshold model. In *ICDM*, pages 88–97, 2010.

[10] F. R. K. Chung and L. Lu. Concentration inequalities and martingale inequalities: A survey. *Internet Mathematics*, 3(1):79–127, 2006.

[11] E. Cohen. Size-estimation framework with applications to transitive closure and reachability. *J. Comput. Syst. Sci.*, 55(3):441–453, 1997.

[12] L. Devroye. *Non-Uniform Random Variate Generation*. Springer-Verlag, New York, NY, USA, 1986.

[13] E. W. Dijkstra. A note on two problems in connection with graphs. *Numerical Mathematics*, 1:269–271, 1959.

[14] P. Domingos and M. Richardson. Mining the network value of customers. In *KDD*, pages 57–66, 2001.

[15] N. Du, L. Song, M. Gomez-Rodriguez, and H. Zha. Scalable influence estimation in continuous-time diffusion networks. In *NIPS*, pages 3147–3155, 2013.

[16] M. Gomez-Rodriguez, D. Balduzzi, and B. Schölkopf. Uncovering the temporal dynamics of diffusion networks. In *ICML*, pages 561–568, 2011.

[17] M. Gomez-Rodriguez, J. Leskovec, and B. Schölkopf. Modeling information propagation with survival theory. In *ICML*, pages 666–674, 2013.

[18] M. Gomez-Rodriguez and B. Schölkopf. Influence maximization in continuous time diffusion networks. In *ICML*, 2012.

[19] A. Goyal, F. Bonchi, and L. V. S. Lakshmanan. A data-based approach to social influence maximization. *PVLDB*, 5(1):73–84, 2011.

[20] A. Goyal, W. Lu, and L. V. S. Lakshmanan. Celf++: optimizing the greedy algorithm for influence maximization in social networks. In *WWW*, pages 47–48, 2011.

[21] A. Goyal, W. Lu, and L. V. S. Lakshmanan. Simpath: An efficient algorithm for influence maximization under the linear threshold model. In *ICDM*, pages 211–220, 2011.

[22] E. M. J. Goldenberg, B. Libai. Talk of the network: A complex systems look at the underlying process of word-of-mouth. *Marketing Letters*, 12(3):211–223, 2001.

[23] E. M. J. Goldenberg, B. Libai. Using complex systems analysis to advance marketing theory development. *American Journal of Sociology*, 9:1, 2001.

[24] K. Jung, W. Heo, and W. Chen. Irie: Scalable and robust influence maximization in social networks. In *ICDM*, pages 918–923, 2012.

[25] D. Kempe, J. M. Kleinberg, and É. Tardos. Maximizing the spread of influence through a social network. In *KDD*, pages 137–146, 2003.

[26] D. Kempe, J. M. Kleinberg, and É. Tardos. Influential nodes in a diffusion model for social networks. In *ICALP*, pages 1127–1138, 2005.

[27] J. Kim, S.-K. Kim, and H. Yu. Scalable and parallelizable processing of influence maximization for large-scale social networks. In *ICDE*, pages 266–277, 2013.

[28] J. F. Lawless. *Statistical Models and Methods for Lifetime Data*. Wiley-Interscience, 2002.

[29] J. Leskovec, A. Krause, C. Guestrin, C. Faloutsos, J. VanBriesen, and N. Glance. Cost-effective outbreak detection in networks. In *KDD*, pages 420–429, 2007.

[30] B. Liu, G. Cong, D. Xu, and Y. Zeng. Time constrained influence maximization in social networks. In *ICDM*, pages 439–448, 2012.

[31] M. Richardson and P. Domingos. Mining knowledge-sharing sites for viral marketing. In *KDD*, pages 61–70, 2002.

[32] L. Seeman and Y. Singer. Adaptive seeding in social networks. In *FOCS*, pages 459–468, 2013.

[33] Y. Tang, X. Xiao, and Y. Shi. Influence maximization: near-optimal time complexity meets practical efficiency. In *SIGMOD*, pages 75–86, 2014.

[34] V. V. Vazirani. *Approximation Algorithms*. Springer, 2002.

[35] M. D. Vose. A linear algorithm for generating random numbers with a given distribution. *IEEE Trans. Software Eng.*, 17(9):972–975, 1991.

[36] C. Wang, W. Chen, and Y. Wang. Scalable influence maximization for independent cascade model in large-scale social networks. *Data Min. Knowl. Discov.*, 25(3):545–576, 2012.

[37] Y. Wang, G. Cong, G. Song, and K. Xie. Community-based greedy algorithm for mining top-k influential nodes in mobile social networks. In *KDD*, pages 1039–1048, 2010.

[38] D. Williams. *Probability with Martingales*. Cambridge University Press, 1991.

APPENDIX

Proof of Lemma 3. Define a random variable x_i for each $R_i \in \mathcal{R}$, such that $x_i = 1$ if $S_k^\circ \cap R_i \neq \emptyset$, and $x_i = 0$ otherwise. Then, $F_{\mathcal{R}}(S_k^\circ) = \sum_{i=1}^{\theta} x_i/\theta$. Let $p = \mathbb{E}\left[F_{\mathcal{R}}(S_k^\circ)\right]$. By Lemma 1,

$$p = \mathbb{E}\left[F_{\mathcal{R}}(S_k^\circ)\right] = \mathbb{E}\left[I(S_k^\circ)\right]/n = OPT/n.$$

By Corollary 2,

$$\begin{aligned}
&\Pr\left[n \cdot F_{\mathcal{R}}(S_k^\circ) \leq (1-\varepsilon_1)\cdot OPT\right] \\
&= \Pr\left[n \cdot F_{\mathcal{R}}(S_k^\circ) \leq (1-\varepsilon_1)\cdot np\right] \\
&= \Pr\left[\theta \cdot F_{\mathcal{R}}(S_k^\circ) \leq (1-\varepsilon_1)\cdot \theta p\right] \\
&= \Pr\left[\textstyle\sum_{i=1}^{\theta} x_i - \theta p \leq -\varepsilon_1 \cdot \theta p\right] \\
&\leq \exp\left(-\varepsilon_1^2 \cdot p\theta/2\right) \leq \exp\left(-\varepsilon_1^2 \cdot p\theta_1/2\right) \\
&= \delta_1.
\end{aligned}$$

Thus, the lemma is proved. □

Proof of Lemma 4. Let S_k be an arbitrary size-k node set. We say that S_k is *bad*, if $\mathbb{E}[I(S_k)] < (1-1/e-\varepsilon)\cdot OPT$. To prove the lemma, we will show that each bad size-k node set has at most $\delta_2/\binom{n}{k}$ probability to be returned by the node selection phase of *IMM*. This suffices to establish the lemma because (i) there exist only $\binom{n}{k}$ bad size-k node sets, and (ii) if each of them has at most $\delta_2/\binom{n}{k}$ probability to be returned, then by the union bound, there is at least $1-\delta_2$ probability that none of them is output by the node selection phase.

Consider any bad size-k node set S_k. Define a random variable x_i for each $R_i \in \mathcal{R}$, such that $x_i = 1$ if $S_k \cap R_i \neq \emptyset$, and $x_i = 0$ otherwise. We have $F_{\mathcal{R}}(S_k) = \sum_{i=1}^{\theta} x_i/\theta$. Let $p = \mathbb{E}[F_{\mathcal{R}}(S_k)] = \mathbb{E}[I(S_k)]/n$ and $\varepsilon_2 = \varepsilon - (1-1/e)\cdot\varepsilon_1$. We have

$$\begin{aligned}&\Pr\left[n\cdot F_{\mathcal{R}}(S_k) - \mathbb{E}[I(S_k)] \geq \varepsilon_2\cdot OPT\right]\\ =\ &\Pr\left[\theta\cdot F_{\mathcal{R}}(S_k) - \theta p \geq \tfrac{\varepsilon_2\cdot OPT}{np}\cdot\theta p\right]\end{aligned} \qquad (17)$$

Let $\zeta = \frac{\varepsilon_2\cdot OPT}{np}$. By Corollary 1 and $p < ((1-1/e-\varepsilon)\cdot OPT)/n$,

r.h.s of Eqn. 17

$$\begin{aligned}&\leq \exp\left(-\frac{\zeta^2}{2+\frac{2}{3}\zeta}\cdot\theta p\right)\\ &= \exp\left(-\frac{\varepsilon_2^2\cdot OPT^2}{2n^2p+\frac{2}{3}\varepsilon_2 n\cdot OPT}\cdot\theta\right)\\ &< \exp\left(-\frac{\varepsilon_2^2\cdot OPT^2}{2n(1-1/e-\varepsilon)\cdot OPT+\frac{2}{3}\varepsilon_2 n\cdot OPT}\cdot\theta\right)\\ &< \exp\left(-\frac{(\varepsilon-(1-1/e)\varepsilon_1)^2\cdot OPT}{(2-2/e)\cdot n}\cdot\theta\right)\\ &\leq \exp\left(-\frac{(\varepsilon-(1-1/e)\varepsilon_1)^2\cdot OPT}{(2-2/e)\cdot n}\cdot\theta_2\right)\\ &\leq \delta_2/\tbinom{n}{k}.\end{aligned}$$

Therefore, the lemma holds. □

Proof of Theorem 1. By Lemma 4, $\mathbb{E}[I(S_k^*)] \geq (1-1/e-\varepsilon)\cdot OPT$ holds with at least $1-\delta_2$ probability under the condition that Equation 3 holds. And by Lemma 3, Equation 3 holds with at least $1-\delta_1$ probability. By the union bound, $\mathbb{E}[I(S_k^*)] \geq (1-1/e-\varepsilon)\cdot OPT$ holds with at least $1-\delta_1-\delta_2 \geq 1/n^{\ell}$ probability. Thus, the theorem is proved. □

Proof of Lemma 5. We rewrite θ_1 (resp. θ_2) as a function f_1 (resp. f_2) as follows:

$$\begin{aligned}f_1(\varepsilon_1,\delta_1) &= \frac{2n\cdot\log(1/\delta_1)}{OPT\cdot\varepsilon_1^2}, \text{ and}\\ f_2(\varepsilon_1,\delta_2) &= \frac{(2-2/e)\cdot n\cdot\log\left(\binom{n}{k}/\delta_2\right)}{OPT\cdot(\varepsilon-(1-1/e)\cdot\varepsilon_1)^2}.\end{aligned}$$

Observe that f_1 monotonically decreases with the increase of ε_1 or δ_1, and f_2 monotonically increases with ε_1 but monotonically decreases with the increase of δ_2. Assume that θ^o is obtained when $\varepsilon_1 = \varepsilon_1^o$, $\delta_1 = \delta_1^o$, and $\delta_2 = \delta_2^o$. Since θ^o is the smallest possible θ, the following equations hold:

$$\begin{aligned}f_1(\varepsilon_1^o,\delta_1^o) &= f_2(\varepsilon_1^o,\delta_2^o) = \theta^o, \quad\text{and}\\ \delta_1^o+\delta_2^o &= 1/n^{\ell}.\end{aligned}$$

Meanwhile, we have $\theta^* = f_1(\varepsilon_1^*, 1/(2n^{\ell})) = f_2(\varepsilon_1^*, 1/(2n^{\ell}))$, where $\varepsilon_1^* = \varepsilon\cdot\frac{\alpha}{(1-1/e)\cdot\alpha+\beta}$. Since $\theta^o \leq \theta$, we have

$$f_1(\varepsilon_1^o,\delta_1^o) \leq f_1\left(\varepsilon_1^*, 1/(2n^{\ell})\right) \qquad (18)$$

The remaining part of our proof consists of three steps. First, we prove that $f_1(\varepsilon_1', 1/n^{\ell}) < f_1(\varepsilon_1^o,\delta_1^o)$, where ε_1' is the positive real root of the equation $f_1(\varepsilon_1', 1/n^{\ell}) = f_2(\varepsilon_1', 1/n^{\ell})$. For this purpose, we consider two cases based on whether $\varepsilon_1^o \leq \varepsilon_1'$. When $\varepsilon_1^o \leq \varepsilon_1'$, it can be verified that $f_1(\varepsilon_1', 1/n^{\ell}) < f_1(\varepsilon_1^o,\delta_1^o)$ given $\delta_1^o < 1/n^{\ell}$. Meanwhile, if $\varepsilon_1^o > \varepsilon_1'$, we have

$$f_1(\varepsilon_1', 1/n^{\ell}) = f_2(\varepsilon_1', 1/n^{\ell}) < f_2(\varepsilon_1^o,\delta_2^o) = f_1(\varepsilon_1^o,\delta_1^o). \quad (19)$$

Second, we show that $M \leq \frac{\ell\log n+\log 2}{\ell\log n}\cdot f_1(\varepsilon_1', 1/n^{\ell})$, where $M = \max\left\{f_1(\varepsilon_1', 1/(2n^{\ell})), f_2(\varepsilon_1', 1/(2n^{\ell}))\right\}$. We have

$$\begin{aligned}\frac{f_1(\varepsilon_1', 1/(2n^{\ell}))}{f_1(\varepsilon_1', 1/n^{\ell})} &= \frac{\ell\log n+\log 2}{\ell\log n}, \text{ and}\\ \frac{f_2(\varepsilon_1', 1/(2n^{\ell}))}{f_1(\varepsilon_1', 1/n^{\ell})} &= \frac{f_2(\varepsilon_1', 1/(2n^{\ell}))}{f_2(\varepsilon_2', 1/n^{\ell})}\\ &= \frac{\ell\log n+\log\binom{n}{k}+\log 2}{\ell\log n+\log\binom{n}{k}}\\ &< \frac{\ell\log n+\log 2}{\ell\log n}.\end{aligned}$$

It then follows that

$$M \leq \frac{\ell\log n+\log 2}{\ell\log n}\cdot f_1(\varepsilon_1', 1/n^{\ell}). \qquad (20)$$

Finally, we prove that $f_1(\varepsilon_1^*, 1/(2n^{\ell})) \leq M$. We consider two cases based on whether $\varepsilon_1^* \geq \varepsilon_1'$. When $\varepsilon_1^* \geq \varepsilon_1'$, we have

$$f_1(\varepsilon_1^*, 1/(2n^{\ell})) \leq f_1(\varepsilon_1', 1/(2n^{\ell})) \leq M.$$

Meanwhile, if $\varepsilon_1^* < \varepsilon_1'$, we have

$$f_1(\varepsilon_1^*, 1/(2n^{\ell})) = f_2(\varepsilon_1^*, 1/(2n^{\ell})) \leq f_2(\varepsilon_1', 1/(2n^{\ell})) \leq M.$$

Therefore, the following equation holds

$$f_1(\varepsilon_1^*, 1/(2n^{\ell})) \leq M. \qquad (21)$$

Combining Equations 18, 19, 20 and 21, we have

$$f_1(\varepsilon_1^o,\delta_1^o) \leq f_1(\varepsilon_1^*, 1/(2n^{\ell})) < \frac{\ell\log n+\log 2}{\ell\log n}\cdot f_1(\varepsilon_1^o,\delta_1^o).$$

Thus, the lemma is proved. □

Proof of Lemma 6. Let S_k be an arbitrary size-k node set and $p = \mathbb{E}[F_{\mathcal{R}}(S_k)]$. Define a random variable x_i for each $R_i \in \mathcal{R}$ such that $x_i = 1$ if $S_k \cap R_i \neq \emptyset$, and $x_i = 0$ otherwise. Then, we have $F_{\mathcal{R}}(S_k) = \sum_{i=1}^{\theta} x_i/\theta$ and

$$p = \mathbb{E}[F_{\mathcal{R}}(S_k)] = \mathbb{E}[I(S_k)]/n \leq OPT/n < x/n. \quad (22)$$

let $\zeta = \frac{(1+\varepsilon')\cdot x}{np} - 1$. By Equation 22, we have $\zeta > \varepsilon'\cdot x/(np) > \varepsilon'$. Then, by Corollary 1,

$$\begin{aligned}&\Pr[n\cdot F_{\mathcal{R}}(S_k) \geq (1+\varepsilon')\cdot x]\\ =\ &\Pr\left[\theta\cdot F_{\mathcal{R}}(S_k) - \theta p \geq \left(\frac{(1+\varepsilon')\cdot x}{np} - 1\right)\cdot\theta p\right]\\ \leq\ &\exp\left(-\frac{\zeta^2}{2+2\zeta/3}\cdot\theta p\right)\\ <\ &\exp\left(-\frac{\varepsilon'\cdot x/(np)}{2/\zeta+2/3}\cdot\frac{(2+\frac{2}{3}\varepsilon')\cdot\log(\binom{n}{k}/\delta_3)}{\varepsilon'^2}\cdot\frac{np}{x}\right)\\ <\ &\exp\left(-\frac{1}{2/\varepsilon'+2/3}\cdot\frac{(2+\frac{2}{3}\varepsilon')\cdot\log(\binom{n}{k}/\delta_3)}{\varepsilon'}\right)\\ =\ &\delta_3/\tbinom{n}{k}.\end{aligned}$$

By the union bound, we can have $n \cdot F_{\mathcal{R}}(S_k^*) < (1+\varepsilon') \cdot x$ with at least $1 - \delta_3$ probability. Thus, the lemma is proved. □

Proof of Lemma 7. Let S_k be an arbitrary size-k node set. We say that S_k is *bad*, if $OPT < n \cdot \mathbb{E}[F_{\mathcal{R}}(S_k)]/(1+\varepsilon')$. To prove the lemma, we will show that each bad size-k node set has at most $\delta_3/\binom{n}{k}$ probability to be returned by Algorithm 1. This suffices to establish the lemma because (i) there exist only $\binom{n}{k}$ bad size-k node sets, and (ii) if each of them has at most $\delta_3/\binom{n}{k}$ probability to be returned, then by the union bound, there is at least $1 - \delta_3$ probability that none of them is output by the node selection phase.

Consider any bad size-k node set S_k. Define a random variable x_i for each $R_i \in \mathcal{R}$, such that $x_i = 1$ if $S_k \cap R_i \neq \emptyset$, and $x_i = 0$ otherwise. We have $F_{\mathcal{R}}(S_k) = \sum_{i=1}^{\theta} x_i/\theta$. Let $p = \mathbb{E}[F_{\mathcal{R}}(S_k)] = \mathbb{E}[I(S_k)]/n$. We have

$$\begin{aligned} &\Pr\left[OPT < n \cdot F_{\mathcal{R}}(S_k)/(1+\varepsilon')\right] \\ \leq\ & \Pr\left[\theta \cdot F_{\mathcal{R}}(S_k) - \theta p \geq \tfrac{\varepsilon' \cdot OPT}{np} \cdot \theta p\right] \end{aligned} \tag{23}$$

Let $\zeta = \frac{\varepsilon' \cdot OPT}{np}$. By Corollary 1 and $OPT \geq x$,

r.h.s of Eqn. 23

$$\begin{aligned} &\leq \exp\left(-\frac{\zeta^2}{2+\frac{2}{3}\zeta} \cdot \theta p\right) \\ &= \exp\left(-\frac{\varepsilon'^2 \cdot OPT^2}{2n^2 p + \frac{2}{3}\varepsilon' n \cdot OPT} \cdot \theta\right) \\ &< \exp\left(-\frac{\varepsilon'^2 \cdot OPT}{2n + \frac{2}{3}\varepsilon' n} \cdot \frac{2+\frac{2}{3}\varepsilon'}{\varepsilon'^2} \cdot \frac{n}{x} \cdot \log(\tbinom{n}{k}/\delta_3)\right) \\ &< \exp\left(-(OPT/x) \cdot \log(\tbinom{n}{k}/\delta_3)\right) \\ &\leq \delta_3/\tbinom{n}{k}. \end{aligned}$$

Therefore, the lemma holds. □

Proof of Theorem 2. Let $j = \lceil \log_2 \frac{n}{OPT} \rceil$. By Lemma 6 and the union bound, Algorithm 2 has at most $(j-1)/(n^\ell \cdot \log_2 n)$ probability to terminate its for loop before the j-th iteration. Then, by Lemma 7 and the union bound, Algorithm 2 sets $LB \leq OPT$ with at least $1 - n^\ell$ probability. Therefore, the theorem holds. □

Proof of Lemma 8. Let S_k^+ be the size-k node set that maximizes $F_{\mathcal{R}}(S_k^+)$. By the properties of the greedy algorithm for maximum coverage, we have

$$F_{\mathcal{R}}(S_k^*) \geq (1-1/e) \cdot F_{\mathcal{R}}(S_k^+) \geq (1-1/e) \cdot F_{\mathcal{R}}(S_k^\circ).$$

Let $p = \mathbb{E}[F_{\mathcal{R}}(S_k^\circ)]$. We have $p = OPT/n$. Since $OPT \geq c \cdot \frac{(1+\varepsilon')^2}{1-1/e} \cdot x$,

$$\begin{aligned} &\Pr[n \cdot F_{\mathcal{R}}(S_k^*) \leq (1+\varepsilon') \cdot x] \\ \leq\ & \Pr[n(1-1/e) \cdot F_{\mathcal{R}}(S_k^\circ) \leq (1+\varepsilon') \cdot x] \\ \leq\ & \Pr[n \cdot F_{\mathcal{R}}(S_k^\circ) \leq OPT/(1+\varepsilon')] \\ \leq\ & \Pr[\theta_i \cdot F_{\mathcal{R}}(S_k^\circ) - \theta_i p \leq -\varepsilon' \cdot \theta_i p/(1+\varepsilon')] \end{aligned} \tag{24}$$

Let $\zeta = \varepsilon'/(1+\varepsilon')$. By Corollary 2,

$$\begin{aligned} \text{r.h.s of Eqn. 24} &\leq \exp\left(-\frac{\zeta^2}{2} \cdot \theta_i p\right) \\ &= \exp\left(-\frac{\varepsilon'^2}{2 \cdot (1+\varepsilon')^2} \cdot \frac{2+2\varepsilon'/3}{\varepsilon'^2} \cdot \frac{np}{x} \cdot \log(\tbinom{n}{k}/\delta_3)\right) \\ &= \exp\left(-\frac{1+\varepsilon'/3}{(1+\varepsilon')^2} \cdot \frac{OPT}{x} \cdot \log(\tbinom{n}{k}/\delta_3)\right) \\ &\leq \exp\left(-\frac{1+\varepsilon'/3}{(1+\varepsilon')^2} \cdot \frac{(1+\varepsilon')^2}{1-1/e} \cdot \log(\tbinom{n}{k}/\delta_3) \cdot c\right) \\ &< (\delta_3/\tbinom{n}{k})^c \end{aligned}$$

By the union bound, for all possible size-k node set S_k^* we have $n \cdot F_{\mathcal{R}}(S_k^*) \leq (1+\varepsilon') \cdot x$ holds with at most $(\delta_3)^c$ probability. Thus, the lemma is proved. □

Proof of Lemma 9. Assume that $OPT \geq \frac{(1+\varepsilon')^2}{1-1/e} \cdot x$ first holds in the j-th iteration. Let $z \geq j$, and $c = 2^{z-j}$. Then, in the z-th iteration, we have $OPT \geq c \cdot \frac{(1+\varepsilon')^2}{1-1/e} \cdot \frac{n}{2^z}$. Let I_z be the event that *IMM* executes the z-th iteration of its for loop. By Lemma 8,

$$P[I_z] \leq 1/(n^\ell \cdot \log_2 n)^c \leq 1/(n^\ell \cdot \log_2 n)$$

Taking into account all iterations from the j-th one to the $(\log_2 n - 1)$-th one, we have

$$\textstyle\sum_{z \geq j} P[I_z] \leq 1/n^\ell$$

Thus, Algorithm 2 terminates before the j-th iteration with at least $1 - 1/n^\ell$ probability. In that case, we have $OPT \leq \frac{(1+\varepsilon')^2}{1-1/e} \cdot x$, which leads to

$$LB = n \cdot F_{\mathcal{R}}(S_i)/(1+\varepsilon') \geq x \geq \frac{1-1/e}{(1+\varepsilon')^2} \cdot OPT.$$

Meanwhile, the expected total number of RR sets generated in the first $j-1$ iterations is at most

$$\begin{aligned} &\max\left\{\frac{\lambda^*}{LB}, \frac{\lambda'}{n/2^{j-1}}\right\} \cdot \left(1 - \textstyle\sum_{z \geq j} P[I_z]\right) \\ \leq\ & \frac{2\max\{\lambda^*, \lambda'\} \cdot (1+\varepsilon')^2}{(1-1/e) \cdot OPT} \cdot (1 - 1/n^\ell) \\ <\ & \frac{2\max\{\lambda^*, \lambda'\} \cdot (1+\varepsilon')^2}{(1-1/e) \cdot OPT}. \end{aligned} \tag{25}$$

In addition, when $1/n^\ell \leq 1/2$, the expected total number of RR sets from the j-th to the $(\log_2 n - 1)$-th iteration is at most

$$\begin{aligned} &\sum_{z \geq j} \max\left\{\frac{\lambda^*}{LB}, \frac{\lambda'}{n/2^z}\right\} \cdot P[I_z] \\ =\ & \textstyle\sum_{z \geq j} \frac{\max\{\lambda^*, \lambda'\}}{n/2^z} \cdot P[I_z] \\ \leq\ & \frac{1}{\log_2 n} \cdot \textstyle\sum_{z \geq j} \frac{\max\{\lambda^*, \lambda'\}}{(n^\ell)^c \cdot n/2^z} \\ \leq\ & \frac{\max\{\lambda^*, \lambda'\}}{n \cdot \log_2 n} \cdot \textstyle\sum_{z \geq j} 2^{-2^{z-j}+z} \\ <\ & \frac{\max\{\lambda^*, \lambda'\}}{n \cdot \log_2 n} \cdot \log_2 n \\ \leq\ & \frac{\max\{\lambda^*, \lambda'\} \cdot (1+\varepsilon')^2}{(1-1/e) \cdot OPT}. \end{aligned} \tag{26}$$

Combining Equations 25 and 26, we have

$$\mathbb{E}[|\mathcal{R}|] \leq \frac{3\max\{\lambda^*, \lambda'\} \cdot (1+\varepsilon')^2}{(1-1/e) \cdot OPT},$$

which proves the lemma. □

Proof of Theorem 4. By combining Theorems 1 and 2, we obtain that Algorithm 3 returns a $(1 - 1/e - \varepsilon)$-approximate solution with at least $1 - 1/n^\ell$. In the following, we focus on *IMM*'s time complexity. Observe that the computation cost of *IMM* mainly consists of two parts, namely, the cost of generating the set $\mathcal{R}$ of random RR sets, and the cost of invoking Algorithm 1. As discussed in Section 3.4, the expected total cost of constructing $\mathcal{R}$ is $O\left((k+\ell)(n+m)\log n/\varepsilon^2\right)$. Therefore, it suffices to prove that the total cost incurred by Algorithm 1 is no more than $O\left((k+\ell)(n+m)\log n/\varepsilon^2\right)$.

Observe that *IMM* invokes Algorithm 1 at most $\log_2 n$ times, i.e., once in each iteration of the for loop in Algorithm 2, and once for the node selection phase. Let R_i be the version of $\mathcal{R}$ in the i-th iteration of Algorithm 2. By Corollary 3, when given $\mathcal{R}_i$ as input, Algorithm 1 runs in $O(\sum_{R\in\mathcal{R}_i}|R|)$ time. Notice that $|\mathcal{R}_i|$ doubles after each iteration, i.e., $|\mathcal{R}_1|, |\mathcal{R}_2|, \ldots$ is a geometric sequence with a common ratio 2. Combining this with Theorem 3, it can be verified that the expected total cost incurred by invoking Algorithm 1 in Algorithm 2 is $O(\mathbb{E}[\sum_{R\in\mathcal{R}}|R|])$. On the other hand, the node selection phase executes Algorithm 1 once on the $\mathcal{R}$ generated by Algorithm 2, which takes $O(\sum_{R\in\mathcal{R}}|R|)$ time. In summary, the expected total cost incurred by Algorithm 1 is $O(\mathbb{E}[\sum_{R\in\mathcal{R}}|R|])$.

Note that $|R| \le w(R)$ for any $R \in \mathcal{R}$. Then, by Equation 12,

$$\begin{aligned} O(\mathbb{E}[\textstyle\sum_{R\in\mathcal{R}}|R|]) &\le O(\mathbb{E}[\textstyle\sum_{R\in\mathcal{R}} w(R)]) \\ &= O\left((k+\ell)(n+m)\log n/\varepsilon^2\right), \end{aligned}$$

which proves the theorem. □

Proof of Theorem 5. The approximation guarantees of *IMM* under $\mathcal{M}$ follow from the discussions in Section 4.1. In the following, we focus on *IMM*'s time complexity. Similar to the case of the triggering models, the computation cost of *IMM* under $\mathcal{M}$ also mainly consists of two parts, namely, the cost of generating the set $\mathcal{R}$ of random RI sets, and the cost of invoking Algorithm 1.

Let $w(R)$ be a random variable that denote the cost of generating a specific RI set R under $\mathcal{M}$. Using a derivation similar to the proof of Equation 12 in Section 3.4, we can prove that

$$\begin{aligned} \mathbb{E}\left[\textstyle\sum_{R\in\mathcal{R}} w(R)\right] &= \mathbb{E}[|\mathcal{R}|]\cdot EPT \\ &= O\left(\tfrac{EPT}{OPT}(k+\ell)(n+m)\log n/\varepsilon^2\right). \end{aligned}$$

In other words, the expected total cost of generating $\mathcal{R}$ is $O\left(\frac{EPT}{OPT}(k+\ell)(n+m)\log n/\varepsilon^2\right)$. To prove the theorem, it suffices to show that the expected total cost incurred by Algorithm 1 is also no more than $O\left(\frac{EPT}{OPT}(k+\ell)(n+m)\log n/\varepsilon^2\right)$.

Following from the analysis in the proof of Theorem 4, the expected total cost incurred by Algorithm 1 is $O(\mathbb{E}[\sum_{R\in\mathcal{R}}|R|])$. Note that $|R| \le w(R)$ for any $R \in \mathcal{R}$. Therefore, we have

$$\begin{aligned} O(\mathbb{E}[\textstyle\sum_{R\in\mathcal{R}}|R|]) &\le O(\mathbb{E}[\textstyle\sum_{R\in\mathcal{R}} w(R)]) \\ &= O\left(\tfrac{EPT}{OPT}(k+\ell)(n+m)\log n/\varepsilon^2\right), \end{aligned}$$

which completes the proof. □

Proof of Lemma 11. First, we show that if $R(v)$ is constructed by the conceptual algorithm in Section 4.2, then the lemma holds. Let p_1 be the probability that S overlaps $R(v)$, and p_2 be the probability that S as a seed set can activate v in the diffusion process under the CTIC model. Observe that the conceptual algorithm first constructs g and then identifies nodes within t distance to v. Hence, p_1 equals the probability that g contains a directed path that starts from a node in S, ends at v, and has a length no more than t. In addition, p_2 equals the probability that v is reachable from S within t distance. Thus, we have $p_1 = p_2$.

Second, we prove that our implementation of the conceptual algorithm does not alter its output. In our implementation, we only sample the length of an edge at the first time that we encounter it. For any edge inspected in the algorithm, the effect of sampling its length on the fly is the same as sampling its length at the very beginning of the algorithm. Therefore, the node set $R(v)$ returned by our implementation is identical to the output of the conceptual algorithm. Thus, the lemma is proved. □

Proof of Lemma 12. Let R be the RI set generated from v by *RI-Gen*, and $w(R)$ be the number of edges in G that point to the nodes in R. $\mathbb{E}[m^*] \le \mathbb{E}[w(R)]$ holds because every edge inspected by *RI-Gen* must point to a node in R. Define a probability distribution $\mathcal{V}'$ over all nodes, such that each node has the probability mass that proportional to its in-degree in G. Let v' be a random sample from $\mathcal{V}'$, and p_R be the probability that an edge selected uniformly at random from G would point to a node in R. By the definition of $w(R)$ and p_R, we have

$$m\cdot\mathbb{E}[p_R] = \mathbb{E}[p_R\cdot m] = \mathbb{E}[w(R)].$$

Define a function $f(v', R)$ for each v' sampled from $\mathcal{V}'$, such that $f(v', R) = 1$ if $v' \in R$, and $f(v', R) = 0$ otherwise. Regarding v' as a random variable and R as a fixed set, we have

$$p_R = \textstyle\sum_{v'} \Pr[v']\cdot f(v', R).$$

Next, we fix v' and consider R as a random variable. Define $p_{v'}$ to be the probability that R overlaps $\{v'\}$. We have

$$p_{v'} = \textstyle\sum_R Pr[R]\cdot f(v', R).$$

By Lemma 11, we have $p_{v'}$ equals the probability that $\{v'\}$ as a seed set can activate v. Thus, we have

$$n\cdot\mathbb{E}[p'_v] = \mathbb{E}[I(\{v'\})].$$

Since OPT^* is the largest expected influence of any size-1 node set, $\mathbb{E}[I(\{v'\})] \le OPT^*$ holds. Combining all equations above, we have

$$\begin{aligned} n\cdot\mathbb{E}[m^*] &\le n\cdot\mathbb{E}[w(R)] \\ &= n\cdot m\cdot\mathbb{E}[p_R] \\ &= n\cdot m\cdot\textstyle\sum_R \Pr[R]\cdot p_R \\ &= n\cdot m\cdot\textstyle\sum_R \left(\Pr[R]\cdot\sum_{v'}\Pr[v']\cdot f(v', R)\right) \\ &= n\cdot m\cdot\textstyle\sum_{v'} \left(\Pr[v']\cdot\sum_R\Pr[R]\cdot f(v', R)\right) \\ &= n\cdot m\cdot\textstyle\sum_{v'} \Pr[v']\cdot p_{v'} \\ &= n\cdot m\cdot\mathbb{E}[p_{v'}] \\ &= m\cdot\mathbb{E}[I(\{v'\})] \\ &\le m\cdot OPT^*. \end{aligned}$$

Thus, the lemma is proved. □

Proof of Theorem 6. Let n^* and m^* be the number of nodes and edges inspected by *RI-Gen* respectively. Recall that *RI-Gen* runs in $O(n^*\log n^* + m^*)$ time. We have $n^*\log n^* + m^* = O(m^*\log n)$. By Lemma 12, we have

$$\mathbb{E}[m^*\log n] \le \frac{m}{n}\cdot OPT^*\log n.$$

Observe that OPT^* is no more than the largest expected influence of a size-k node set, i.e., $OPT^* \le OPT$ for any $k \ge 1$. Then, by Theorem 5, Algorithm 3 returns a $(1-1/e-\varepsilon)$-approximation with at least $1-1/n^\ell$ probability under the CTIC model, and runs in $O\left((k+\ell)(n+m)\log^2 n/\varepsilon^2\right)$ expected time. Thus, the theorem is proved. □

Community Level Diffusion Extraction

Zhiting Hu[1,3], Junjie Yao[2], Bin Cui[1], Eric P. Xing[3]
[1]Key Lab of High Confidence Software Technologies (MOE), School of EECS, Peking University
[2]East China Normal University
[3]Language Technologies Institute, Carnegie Mellon University
{zhitingh,epxing}@cs.cmu.edu, junjiey@gmail.com, bin.cui@pku.edu.cn

ABSTRACT

How does online content propagate on social networks? Billions of users generate, consume, and spread tons of information every day. This unprecedented scale of dynamics becomes invaluable to reflect our zeitgeist. However, most present diffusion extraction works have only touched individual user level and cannot obtain comprehensive clues.

This paper introduces a new approach, i.e., COmmunity Level Diffusion (COLD), to uncover and explore temporal diffusion. We model topics and communities in a unified latent framework, and extract inter-community influence dynamics. With a well-designed multi-component model structure and a parallel inference implementation on GraphLab, the COLD method is expressive while remaining efficient.

The extracted community level patterns enable diffusion exploration from a new perspective. We leverage the compact yet robust representations to develop new prediction and analysis applications. Extensive experiments on large social datasets show significant improvement in prediction accuracy. We can also find communities play very different roles in diffusion processes depending on their interest. Our method guarantees high scalability with increasing data size.

Primary Classification:

H.4.0 [**Information Systems**]: General

Keywords:

Information Diffusion, Community Detection, Graph Model

1. INTRODUCTION

A longstanding question in communication media research is Lasswell's 5W maxim: "Who says What to Whom in What channel with What effect?" [15, 33]. In the prevalent online social networks, such as Twitter, Facebook and Weibo, billions of users share messages and interact with others. User activities exhibit rich temporal dynamics. Understanding these dynamics can reveal unique insight into our society. As a first and critical step, what popular topics do users talk and how do they spread the topics?

SIGMOD'15, May 31–June 4, 2015, Melbourne, Victoria, Australia.

http://dx.doi.org/10.1145/2723372.2723737.

Recently, there have been extensive studies in this direction [11, 7, 13, 27]. On one hand, most information diffusion extraction works focus on individual-level interactions and structural topologies [19, 27, 22], where the influence between individual users and the bridging nodes (structural hole) spanning network structures are used to model the diffusion process. On the other hand, temporal modeling methods are developed to capture aggregated temporal trends of online content [24, 16].

These variety of diffusion extraction methods have enjoyed impressive success but still have large drawbacks. First, the structural methods largely ignore topical differences and cannot capture the rich diversity of information patterns. Moreover, the highly volatile user behaviors usually render it difficult to accurately uncover diffusion patterns for *individual level* approaches. Finally, the aggregation methods fail to reveal detailed dissemination processes.

Can we unify these different lines, and obtain a rich spectrum of online temporal diffusion? This paper offers a new perspective. We propose to extract *community level* diffusion, i.e., modeling diffusion patterns of topics across different communities. Community is a collection of users with more intense interactions amongst its members than the rest of the global network [17]. It provides the basis for user engagement in social networks. Meanwhile, the "Strength of Weak Ties" theory[1] [9] has suggested a critical role of inter-community interactions in online diffusion. In this work, we extract communities' temporal dynamics as well as influence between communities, and provide a coarse-grained diffusion representation. The compact community level extraction captures the backbone of information spreading, improves temporal modeling, and finally better predicts and analyzes the diffusion.

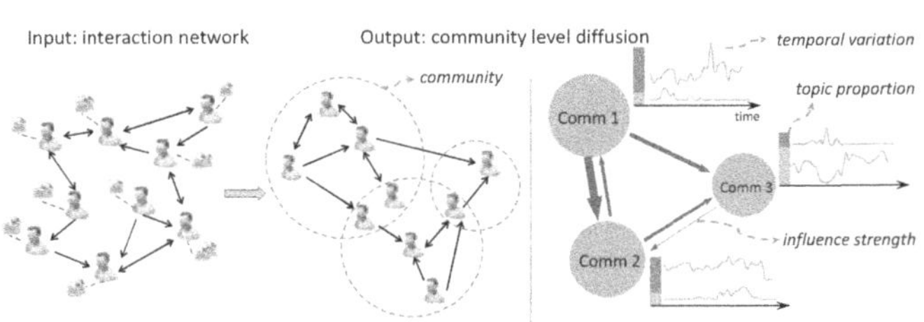

Figure 1: Overview of Community Level Diffusion.

Figure 1 shows an overview of the community level diffusion problem. The input is an interaction network among users, along with user-generated content over time. Our goal

[1]Weak social ties are responsible for the majority of the information spreading through human networks.

is to uncover the information dynamics across communities, including the communities' varying interest in different topics (topic proportion),

Community level diffusion extraction is challenging. Communities and topics are both hidden. Pipeline approaches to extract these two factors in sequence fail to capture their interdependence. Though in recent years an array of techniques [39, 21, 12] have been developed for jointly leveraging these two critical factors, they all fall short of suitably modeling the correlation between them. Besides the task of simultaneously extracting community and topics, we are even required to include vibrant temporal factors.

To tackle the difficulties, this paper develops a latent model, COLD (COmmunity Level Diffusion), to extract communities, topics, and community level topic dynamics in a unified way. We model community and topic as latent variables, and set up a generative process for observed network, text, and time to accurately characterize the topic diffusion at community level. An efficient sampling-based inference algorithm and its parallel implementation are designed.

Based on the extraction, we design an effective diffusion prediction method. Extensive experiments on large datasets show our approach greatly improves the prediction accuracy. We further use COLD to investigate rich social dynamics from the new community level perspective, and reveal meaningful diffusion patterns, such as the interest shift of communities and the time lag of topic spreading. Finally, we demonstrate how the new representation and improved prediction can lead to novel real-world applications such as influential community identification for viral marketing.

Our latent model brings up several innovations. We model users in overlapping communities with various affiliation degrees to capture users' personalities. Each community is associated with a mixture of topics, indicating its diverse interest with varying levels. This improves over previous one-to-one topical community limitations. We also associate each topic with community-specific temporal distributions, which is able to distinguish different dynamic processes within different communities.

To summarize, we make the following contributions:

1. **Novel Perspective**. We identify the problem of community level diffusion. It brings up new insights into the information dissemination process. To the best of our knowledge, such a new angle has not been studied before.
2. **Comprehensive Model**. We propose a latent model to uncover the hidden topics and communities as well as capture the community-specific temporal diffusion. It exhibits improved capacity to model information dynamics.
3. **Scalable Inference**. We decouple the model into several components, based on which an efficient inference algorithm is developed. We further set up a scalable parallel implementation.
4. **Inspiring Prediction & Exploration**. An effective diffusion prediction approach is developed which leverages community level patterns and shows significant superiority. We also study the real-world applications of COLD in viral marketing.

The rest of this paper is organized as follows: §2 reviews related literature. §3 formulates the problem and introduces the model. §4 describes the inference method and parallel implementation. §5 illustrates the model analysis and develops a new prediction approach. §6 evaluates the solution. And finally, we conclude this work in §7.

2. RELATED WORK

Information Diffusion. Online information diffusion has received increasing interests over the recent years [11]. One fundamental problem is to estimate the influence strength (or diffusion probabilities) between users [19, 27]. However, the large volume of existing works have only focused on individual level, i.e., extracting user-to-user influence directly from the volatile individual behaviors. This can be limited and fragile to noises. In contrast, our approach proposes to model diffusion at community level, a new granularity that provides compact yet robust representations.

The extracted influence strength can be used in downstream applications such as future propagation prediction [31, 8] and influential spreader identification [29, 7, 13], and eventually promote viral marketing and social network management. We develop an effective prediction method based on the new community level patterns and improve the previous work significantly.

Temporal Modeling. Another line of research captures temporal trends of content [35, 24, 32]. Topics Over Time (TOT) [32] is a latent generative model over the text and time stamps of documents. These works only reveal the aggregated topical trends, while ignoring the diversity of different users' temporal behaviors. By comparison, our work distinguishes temporal dynamic patterns across different communities, and provides a more thorough and versatile view.

Community Detection. Communities are natural groups formed by users with close connections and similar interest [17]. A mixed membership stochastic block model is introduced in [1] where each user has a probability distribution over communities. A growing number of recent works [26, 36] incorporate both the network structure and content to improve community detection performance, e.g., Link-PLSA-LDA [25], RTM [3], and PMTLM [39]. In these models, content and links are both generated by the same latent variables. Thus communities are limited to have one-to-one correspondence with topics. Our model decomposes these two factors, which opens up an array of meaningful and desired extraction such as community interest over varying topics and popularity variation of topics across different communities.

3. COMMUNITY LEVEL DIFFUSION EXTRACTION METHOD

The central task is to extract community level diffusion patterns from social records (§3, §4), and utilize them to promote novel diffusion prediction and analysis (§5).

In this section, we first formulate the diffusion modeling problem from the new community level perspective. We then propose COLD (COmmunity Level Diffusion), a comprehensive latent variable model, to address the problem.

3.1 Problem Formulation

The notations used in this paper are listed in Table 1.

Definition 1. **(Interaction Network)**. Consider a social network $\mathcal{G} = (\mathcal{U}, \mathcal{E})$. $\mathcal{U}$ is a set of U users. The link set $\mathcal{E}$ denotes interactions between users and can be derived from various types of user interactions such as following, retweeting and commenting. A directed link $(i, i') \in \mathcal{E}$ represents there exists communication from user i to i', e.g., i' once retweeted i.

Symbol	Description
U, T, C, K	number of users, time slices, communities, and topics
D_i, E_i	number of posts by user i, and links from user i
d_{ij}	the jth post by user i
t_{ij}	the time stamp of post d_{ij}
w_{ijl}	the lth word in post d_{ij}
c_{ij}	community associated with post d_{ij}
z_{ij}	topic associated with post d_{ij}
$e_{ii'}$	indicator of the existence of link (i, i')
$s_{ii'}, s'_{ii'}$	communities associated with user i and i' in link (i, i')
$\boldsymbol{\pi}_i$	multinomial distribution over communities specific to user i
$\boldsymbol{\theta}_c$	multinomial distribution over topics specific to community c
$\boldsymbol{\phi}_k$	multinomial distribution over words specific to topic k
$\boldsymbol{\psi}_{kc}$	multinomial distribution over time specific to topic k and community c
$\eta_{cc'}$	general influence strength (diffusion probability) from community c to c'
$\zeta_{kcc'}$	influence strength on topic k from community c to c'
λ_0, λ_1	Beta priors on $\boldsymbol{\eta}$

Table 1: Notations Used in This Paper.

Each user $i \in \mathcal{U}$ is associated with a set of D_i posts, denoted as $\mathcal{D}_i$, where each post d_{ij} contains a bag of words from a given vocabulary, along with a posting time stamp t_{ij}. We use $\mathcal{E}_i$ to denote the set of links from i to other users, and define $E_i = |\mathcal{E}_i|$.

Community is a collection of users with more intense interactions amongst its members than the rest of the global network. It can be characterized not only by interaction link structures, but also the content (i.e. posts) generated by its members. While existing works on community modeling generally assume one community corresponds to one interest/topic, we associate each community with a topic distribution representing its different topical interests and give the following new definition.

Definition 2. **(Community)**. A community $c \in \{1, \ldots, C\}$ has two components: a multinomial distribution over topics $\boldsymbol{\theta}_c$, where each component θ_{ck} represents the probability that a post from the community is related with the corresponding topic k; and a probability vector $\boldsymbol{\eta}_c$ where each component $\eta_{cc'}$ is the mean of a Bernoulli distribution representing the diffusion probability from a user in community c to a user in community c'.

In social networks, users usually bear multiple roles and are influenced by different community contexts [34]. We therefore employ the *mixed-membership* approach: each user i is associated with a multinomial distribution over communities $\boldsymbol{\pi}_i$, where π_{ic} indicates her affiliation degree to community c.

Definition 3. **(Topic)**. A topic $k \in \{1, \ldots, K\}$ is a multinomial distribution over the vocabulary, denoted as $\boldsymbol{\phi}_k$.

A topic has changing popularity over time. We represent it as a temporal distribution. Besides, a topic can exhibit very different temporal dynamics within different communities, which leads to the following definition:

Definition 4. **(Community-level Temporal Variation)**. At community level, a temporal topic k is associated with a set of C multinomial distributions $\boldsymbol{\psi}_k = \{\boldsymbol{\psi}_{k1}, \boldsymbol{\psi}_{k2}, \ldots, \boldsymbol{\psi}_{kC}\}$, each of which represents the changing popularity of topic k within the corresponding community, i.e., a multinomial distribution over time slices.

Different communities are expected to play different roles in topic dissemination process. This can be modeled by influence strength between communities:

Definition 5. **(Community-level Influence Strength)**. For each topic k, the community-level influence strength is represented as the diffusion probabilities between any two communities c and c', denoted as $\zeta_{kcc'}$.

Note that we aim to model *topic-sensitive* influence between communities. The topics and communities are both latent factors to be extracted, and we are also required to uncover their correlations over time, i.e., community-level temporal variations and influence strength on topics.

The perspective of community level diffusion is quite different from prior works which study diffusion at individual level and largely ignore the effects of community structure. The new granularity provides a compact yet accurate representation, but also brings about unique complexity in modeling and computing. Next we develop our new model by describing its general structure as well as three properly decoupled components.

3.2 Model Structure

COLD is a generative model jointly over text, time and network. It uncovers latent communities and topics, and infers community-level dynamics in a unified way.

Although some of its building blocks are inspired by recent successful attempts, including the Mixed Membership Stochastic Blockmodel (MMSB) [1] over networks, and Topics over Time (TOT) [32] over text and time, COLD significantly goes beyond those on more comprehensive input features and powerful modeling ability. Compared to previous joint text and link models, COLD better fits the social network setting by accurate community interest recovering and refined user post treatment.

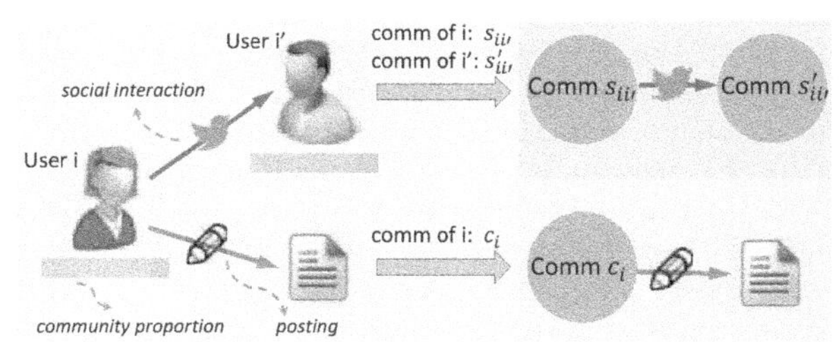

Figure 2: An illustration Showing the User Behaviors Explained by Community-specific Context. The color of each component corresponds to that of Figure 3.

COLD aims to model two basic types of user behaviors, i.e., posting (which generates text) and social interaction (which forms links), together. Figure 2 illustrates the user behavior modeling. Specifically, each user may assume different community memberships when taking these behaviors, and each behavior is further explained by *community-specific context*. That is, for the behavior of posting, the words and time stamp of the post are assumed to be generated by community-specific mixture of topics (i.e. $\boldsymbol{\theta}_c$); while for the behavior of social interaction, the link is governed by the community-specific interaction strengths with other communities (i.e. $\boldsymbol{\eta}_c$).

Figure 3 shows the graphical structure of COLD. By jointly considering the two types of user behaviors with properly separated generative process, COLD naturally combines content and network data while still keeping the model tractable. Both community interest over topics and topic dynamics within communities can be inferred from the timestamped posts specific to particular communities.

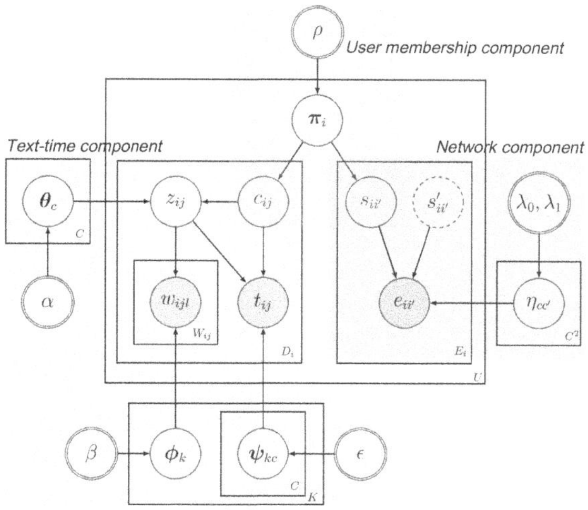

Figure 3: Graphical Model Representation of COLD. The latent variable $s'_{ii'}$ is represented as dashed circle since it is drawn from $\boldsymbol{\pi}_{i'}$ which is not shown in the graphical model.

3.3 Individual Components

Figure 3 shows three components together form COLD: the *text-time component* uncovers the semantic topics, and captures topic temporal variations; the *network component* accounts for the link structure; and the *user membership component* models user membership to communities, which also serves to seamlessly unify the other two components.

User membership component. Users in social network usually have multiple community memberships. We associated each user i with a community probability vector $\boldsymbol{\pi}_i$. Each post $d_{ij} \in \mathcal{D}_i$ is assigned to a community c_{ij}, denoting the community membership of user i when she writes the post. In addition, each link $e_{ii'} \in \mathcal{E}_i$ is associated with two communities $s_{ii'}$ and $s'_{ii'}$, one for each of the two users i and i' respectively, denoting their community memberships when user i builds relationship with i'.

The community membership vector $\boldsymbol{\pi}$ captures the personality of individual user, which can be utilized for predicting message propagation between users (§5).

Text-time component. Each post $d_{ij} \in \mathcal{D}_i$ contains a bag of words $\{w_{ij1}, \ldots, w_{ij|d_{ij}|}\}$ where $|d_{ij}|$ denotes the length of the post. In traditional topic models such as latent Dirichlet allocation (LDA) [2], a document is associated with a mixture of topics and each word has a topic label. This is reasonable for long documents such as academic papers. However, on social media like micro-blog, a post is usually short, and thus is most likely to be about a single topic [5]. We therefore associate with d_{ij} a single latent topic variable z_{ij} drawn from $\boldsymbol{\theta}_{c_{ij}}$ to indicate its topic. The words are then sampled from the corresponding word distribution $\boldsymbol{\phi}_{z_{ij}}$.

To model the temporal information of posts, we first discretize the time by dividing the entire time span of all users' posts into T time slices, then use a multinomial distribution $\boldsymbol{\psi}_{kc}$ over time slices to model the temporal variation specific to each topic k and each community c. Thus, a post d_{ij} is generated at the time t_{ij} drawn from $\boldsymbol{\psi}_{z_{ij}c_{ij}}$. Moreover, compared to Topics over Time (TOT) [32] which uses a Beta distribution to model time variations and only allows a unimodal distribution over time for each topic, our use of multinomial distribution can capture multimodal variations. It is more flexible and expressive in capturing real-life topics which usually rise and fall for many times.

Network component. We use pairwise community Bernoulli distributions $\boldsymbol{\eta}$ to model the presence and absence of links between pairs of users. For each link (i, i'), a boolean indicator $e_{ii'}$ is drawn from $\eta_{s_{ii'}s'_{ii'}}$ which represents the relationship strength between community $s_{ii'}$ and $s'_{ii'}$.

Social network is typically sparse, thus we only model positive links: the variables $s_{ii'}, s'_{ii'}$ exist if and only if $(i, i') \in \mathcal{E}_i$. As in [12], the negative links $(i, i') \notin \mathcal{E}_i$ are implicitly modeled in a Bayesian fashion: we use a Beta(λ_0, λ_1) prior on each $\eta_{cc'}$, and set $\lambda_0 = \kappa \cdot \ln(n_{neg}/C^2)$ and $\lambda_1 = 0.1$, where $n_{neg} = U(U-1) - \sum_i |\mathcal{E}_i|$ is the number of negative links and κ is a tunable weight. In this way, we reduce large amount of computation and achieve linear complexity on network modeling, as explained later in §4.2.

3.4 Generative Process

The generative process is summarized in Alg 1. Consider a user i who posts and interacts with others. When she publishes a post d_{ij}, she first selects the community membership c_{ij} by her community distribution $\boldsymbol{\pi}_i$, then selects a topic by the community's topic distribution $\boldsymbol{\theta}_{c_{ij}}$. With the chosen topic, words are generated from the topic's word distribution, and time stamp from the temporal distribution of that community and topic. On the other hand, when she interacts another user i', a community is sampled for each of them by their own community distributions, and the link is formed by community-community influence strength.

Algorithm 1 Generative Process for COLD

1. For each topic $k = 1, 2, \ldots, K$,
   (a) Sample the distribution over words, $\boldsymbol{\phi}_k|\beta \sim \text{Dir}(\beta)$.
   (b) For each community $c = 1, 2, \ldots, C$,
      i. Sample the distribution over time stamps, $\boldsymbol{\psi}_{kc}|\epsilon \sim \text{Dir}(\epsilon)$.
2. For each community $c = 1, 2, \ldots, C$,
   (a) Sample the distribution over topics, $\boldsymbol{\theta}_c|\alpha \sim \text{Dir}(\alpha)$.
   (b) For each community $c' = 1, 2, \ldots, C$,
      i. Sample community-community link probability, $\eta_{cc'}|\lambda_0, \lambda_1 \sim \text{Beta}(\lambda_0, \lambda_1)$.
3. For each user $i = 1, 2, \ldots, U$
   (a) Sample the distribution over communities, $\boldsymbol{\pi}_i|\rho \sim \text{Dir}(\rho)$.
   (b) For each post $j = 1, 2, \ldots,$
      i. Sample community indicator, $c_{ij}|\boldsymbol{\pi}_i \sim \text{Mul}(\boldsymbol{\pi}_i)$.
      ii. Sample topic indicator, $z_{ij}|\boldsymbol{\theta}_{c_{ij}} \sim \text{Mul}(\boldsymbol{\theta}_{c_{ij}})$.
      iii. For each word $l = 1, 2, \ldots,$
         A. Sample word, $w_{ijl}|\boldsymbol{\phi}_{z_{ij}} \sim \text{Mul}(\boldsymbol{\phi}_{z_{ij}})$.
      iv. Sample time stamp, $t_{ij}|\boldsymbol{\psi}_{z_{ij}c_{ij}} \sim \text{Mul}(\boldsymbol{\psi}_{z_{ij}c_{ij}})$.
   (c) For each link $(i, i') \in \mathcal{E}_i$,
      i. Sample community indicator, $s_{ii'}|\boldsymbol{\pi}_i \sim \text{Mul}(\boldsymbol{\pi}_i)$.
      ii. Sample community indicator,$s'_{ii'}|\boldsymbol{\pi}_{i'} \sim \text{Mul}(\boldsymbol{\pi}_{i'})$.
      iii. Sample link, $e_{ii'}|\boldsymbol{\eta}_{s_{ii'}s'_{ii'}} \sim \text{Ber}(\boldsymbol{\eta}_{s_{ii'}s'_{ii'}})$.

3.5 Discussion

COLD is designed to reveal the rich spectrum of online temporal diffusion across communities. Such a highly expressive model had not been explored due to its inherent complexity in modeling and computing. Here we discuss the modeling choices for handling the complexity.

Previous works on text and link modeling [39, 12, 3, 25] have assumed one-to-one correspondence between communities and topics. Such modeling is limited since the rich correlation between communities and topics are ignored. We decouple these two factors, which not only improves both community and topic extraction (§6), but also opens up an array of meaningful and desired extraction. For instance, we can explore communities' varying topical interest by associating each community with a mixture of topics; we are also enabled to distinguish topic's temporal variation across communities, which, compared to previous aggregation methods [24, 32], leads to new insights in user attention shift (§5.3).

However, the decomposition also leads to $C \cdot C \cdot K$ parameters in the *topic-sensitive* community-level diffusion ($\zeta_{kcc'}$), which can be prohibitive for inference. We therefore employ a *two-stage* approach by first inferring the general inter-community influence $\eta_{cc'}$ and the community interest θ_{ck}, then deriving $\zeta_{kcc'}$ as combination of these intermediate parameters (§5.1). The formulation effectively reduces the complexity to $C \cdot (C+K)$, and still exhibits strong predictive power in diffusion prediction (§5.2).

It is also worth noting that previous text-link methods are typically proposed for the document citation network, which, in the social network setting, requires to view each user's post collection as a huge document. A latent topic is then selected for each word of the "document". In contrast, COLD models individual posts separately, which helps to preserve the correlation among words in each post—we can associate a single topic to each post as a whole. This has not only overcome the heavy noise in social network-style text, but also decreased the inference complexity.

Finally, as discussed above, the carefully-designed Bayesian prior avoids explicit modeling of the negative links. Hence the computation for network modeling is drastically reduced given that social networks are typically very sparse.

4. INFERENCE & IMPLEMENTATION

This section develops an efficient inference method for COLD. We first present the basic inference algorithm using a sampling method. It scales linearly w.r.t. the data size, which is still intolerant for growing large social data. To ensure its scalability, we further design a parallel implementation based on GraphLab.

4.1 Approximate Inference

Exact inference for COLD model is difficult due to the intractable normalizing constant of the posterior distribution (see the appendix for more details), we therefore exploit collapsed Gibbs sampling [10] for approximate inference. As a widely used *Markov chain Monte Carlo* (MCMC) algorithm, Gibbs Sampling iteratively samples latent variables (i.e. $\{\boldsymbol{c}, \boldsymbol{s}, \boldsymbol{z}\}$ in COLD) from a Markov chain, whose stationary distribution is the posterior. The samples can therefore be used to estimate the distributions of interest (i.e. $\{\boldsymbol{\pi}, \boldsymbol{\theta}, \boldsymbol{\eta}, \boldsymbol{\phi}, \boldsymbol{\psi}\}$).

At each iteration of our Gibbs sampler, for each post d_{ij} by user i, we sample both the corresponding community indicator c_{ij} and the topic indicator z_{ij}; for each link (i, i'), we sample the corresponding community indicators $s_{ii'}$ and $s'_{ii'}$. Here we directly give the sampling formulas, and provide the detailed derivation in the appendix (Appx A).

Sampling community indicator c_{ij} for post d_{ij} according to,

$$P(c_{ij} = c | z_{ij} = k, t_{ij} = t, \boldsymbol{c}_{-ij}, \boldsymbol{s}, \boldsymbol{z}_{-ij}, \boldsymbol{t}_{-ij}, .) \propto \frac{n_i^{(c)} + \rho}{n_i^{(\cdot)} + C\rho} \cdot \frac{n_c^{(k)} + \alpha}{n_c^{(\cdot)} + K\alpha} \cdot \frac{n_{ck}^{(t)} + \epsilon}{n_{ck}^{(\cdot)} + T\epsilon}, \quad (1)$$

where $n_i^{(c)}$ denotes the number of posts and links of user i assigned to community c; $n_c^{(k)}$ is the number of posts assigned to community c and generated by topic k; $n_{ck}^{(t)}$ denotes the number of times that time stamp t is generated by community c and topic k. Marginal counts are represented with dots; e.g., $n_{ck}^{(\cdot)}$ denotes the total number of time stamps generated by community c and topic k. All the counters are calculated with the post d_{ij} excluded.

Sampling community indicators $s_{ii'}$ and $s'_{ii'}$ for link (i, i'). Recall that we only model $s_{ii'}$ and $s'_{ii'}$ for positive links $e_{ii'} = 1$:

$$P(s_{ii'} = c, s'_{ii'} = c' | e_{ii'} = 1, \boldsymbol{s}_{-ii'}, \boldsymbol{c}, \boldsymbol{e}, .) \propto \frac{n_i^{(c)} + \rho}{n_i^{(\cdot)} + C\rho} \cdot \frac{n_{i'}^{(c')} + \rho}{n_{i'}^{(\cdot)} + C\rho} \cdot \frac{n_{cc'} + \lambda_1}{n_{cc'} + \lambda_0 + \lambda_1}, \quad (2)$$

where $n_{cc'}$ is the number of positive links, with (i, i') excluded, whose communities indicators are $\{c, c'\}$.

Sampling topic indicator z_{ij} for post d_{ij} according to:

$$P(z_{ij} = k | c_{ij} = c, t_{ij} = t, \boldsymbol{c}_{-ij}, \boldsymbol{z}_{-ij}, \boldsymbol{w}, \boldsymbol{t}_{-ij}, .) \propto \frac{n_c^{(k)} + \alpha}{n_c^{(\cdot)} + K\alpha} \cdot \frac{n_{ck}^{(t)} + \epsilon}{n_{ck}^{(\cdot)} + T\epsilon} \cdot \frac{\prod_{v=1}^{V} \prod_{q=0}^{n_{ij}^{(v)}-1} (n_k^{(v)} + q + \beta)}{\prod_{q=0}^{n_{ij}^{(\cdot)}-1} (n_k^{(\cdot)} + q + V\beta)}, \quad (3)$$

where $n_{ij}^{(v)}$ is the number of times word v occurs in the post d_{ij}; $n_k^{(v)}$ denotes the number of times word v is assigned to topic k. Note that $n_k^{(v)}$ and $n_k^{(\cdot)}$ are calculated with the post d_{ij} excluded.

After a sufficient number of sampling iterations as described above, we obtain a set of samples. The unknown distributions can then be computed by integrating across the samples [10].

4.2 Time Complexity

We now analyze the time complexity of our inference algorithm. It is shown that the devised algorithm scales linearly in terms of the size of data, i.e., the number of words and positive links.

In each iteration, the communities of user posts are first sampled. Since all the counters (e.g. $n_i^{(c)}$) involved in Eq.(1) can be cached and updated in constant time for each c_{ij} being sampled, Eq.(1) can be calculated in constant time. Thus, sampling all $\boldsymbol{c}$ takes linear time w.r.t. the number of posts. Next, we sample community indicators $\boldsymbol{s}$ using Eq.(2). Since we have implicitly modeled negative links in Bayesian prior (i.e., the Beta prior for $\eta_{cc'}$), we only need to sample $s_{ii'}$ and $s'_{ii'}$ for positive links $e_{ii'} = 1$. Hence the complexity is reduced from quadratic (w.r.t. the number of users) to linear (w.r.t. the number of links). It significantly saves computation cost due to the sparseness of networks. Finally, sampling all $\boldsymbol{z}$ by Eq.(3) is linear in the number of words.

Though linear computational complexity might not seem prohibitive, it limits the applicability of the model for growing data. We further give a parallel implementation of the inference algorithm to scale up our model to large social dataset.

4.3 Parallel Implementation

We implement a parallel COLD inference algorithm on the distributed GraphLab system [23]. GraphLab is a vertex-centric programming framework, expressing computational dependencies with a distributed graph. It has demonstrated superior performance over popular parallel systems, e.g., MapReduce and Spark, for many machine learning algorithms.

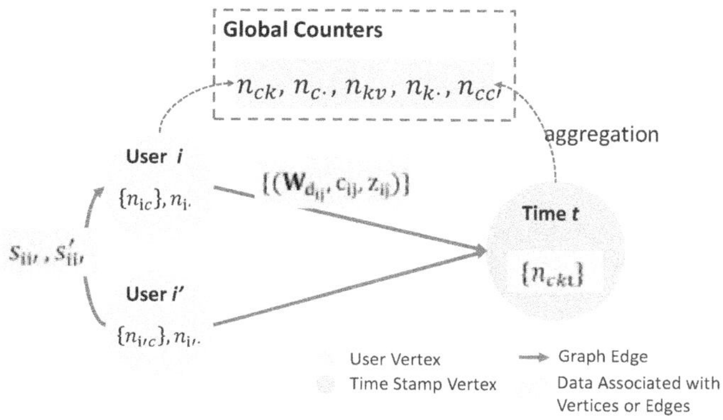

Figure 4: Abstraction of the Distributed Gibbs Sampler.

GraphLab implements the *gather-apply-scatter (GAS)* model which abstracts the program into three phases. In the *gather* phase, each vertex aggregates data from its neighborhood, and uses the result to update its own associated data in the *apply* phase. In the *scatter* phase, each vertex triggers neighboring vertex or modifies adjacent edge data.

The parallelization of our collapsed Gibbs Sampler is achieved by drawing new assignments in Eqs.(1–3) simultaneously. We first define the graph abstraction of our algorithm as shown in Figure 4. Specifically, we construct a bipartite graph connecting each user with each time stamp. An edge between a user i and a time stamp t contains the words of posts generated by user i at time t, as well as the community and topic indicators for the posts. We then incorporate the network data by connecting corresponding user vertices, where each edge contains the community indicators of two users.

The counters in Eqs.(1–3) are either maintained globally or in vertices. Global counters are aggregated from the vertices periodically, while counters in vertices are updated during the gather and apply phases. The program samples new assignments in the scatter phase. Alg 2 shows the GAS procedures of COLD Gibbs Sampler. We monitor the convergence of the algorithm by periodically computing the likelihood of training data [10].

The designed graph abstraction and GAS decomposition ensure most of the state maintenance to be processed locally, while global counters are generally only related to latent spaces which are low-dimensional. This maximizes the parallelism of the algorithm. Meanwhile, the data, as well as computation tasks, is partitioned into fine granularity and evenly distributed to each vertex and edge (Figure 4). Such an abstraction can promote better load balance among cluster nodes in the distributed setting.

Finally, as we avoid directly modeling the absence of links, a tremendous amount of communication is saved. Equipped with all the above features, our inference implementation leads to satisfying efficiency and scalability on large real data, as shown latter in our empirical study.

Algorithm 2 Vertex Program (GAS) of COLD Gibbs Sampler

Gather (v, e)
if $v.type = user$ **then**
  if $e.type = user\_time\_edge$ **then**
    return counts of each comm acc. to $e.\{c_{ij}\}$
  else if $e.type = user\_user\_edge$ **then**
    return counts of each comm acc. to $e.s_{ii'}$ or $e.s'_{ii'}$
  end if
else if $v.type = time$ **then**
  return counts of each comm-topic pair acc. to $e.\{z_{ij}, c_{ij}\}$
end if

Apply (v, $gather\_result$)
if $v.type = user$ **then**
  update $v.n_{ic}$ by $gather\_result$
else if $v.type = time$ **then**
  update $v.n_{ckt}$ by $gather\_result$
end if

Scatter (v, e)
if $e.type = user\_time\_edge$ **then**
  for all doc j in e **do**
    sample $e.c_{ij}$ by Eq.(1) and $e.z_{ij}$ by Eq.(3)
  end for
else if $e.type = user\_user\_edge$ **then**
  sample $e.s_{ii'}$ and $e.s'_{ii'}$ by Eq.(2)
end if

5. DIFFUSION PREDICTION & ANALYSIS

Modeling information diffusion at community level can provide insights into social dynamics at a brand new granularity. This section first illustrates the compact diffusion patterns extracted by COLD, based on which novel prediction methods and diffusion analysis are designed.

5.1 Community Level Diffusion

Here we demonstrate how our approach can be utilized to reveal topic dynamics and diffusion across communities.

In COLD, $\eta_{cc'}$ models the *general* influence strength of a community c on another community c', while θ_{ck} and $\theta_{c'k}$ captures the interest levels on topic k of community c and community c', respectively. As discussed in § 3.5, we can combine these intermediate factors to infer the *topic-specific* influence strength of c on c':

$$\zeta_{kcc'} = \theta_{ck}\theta_{c'k}\eta_{cc'}. \tag{4}$$

An example excerpted from our empirical study is shown in Figure 5, which demonstrates the extracted community level diffusion. The word cloud of topic *Movie The Journey to the West* and its diffusion path across different communities are included. Each community is represented as a *"pie chart"*-style node showing its top-5 interested topics (acc.

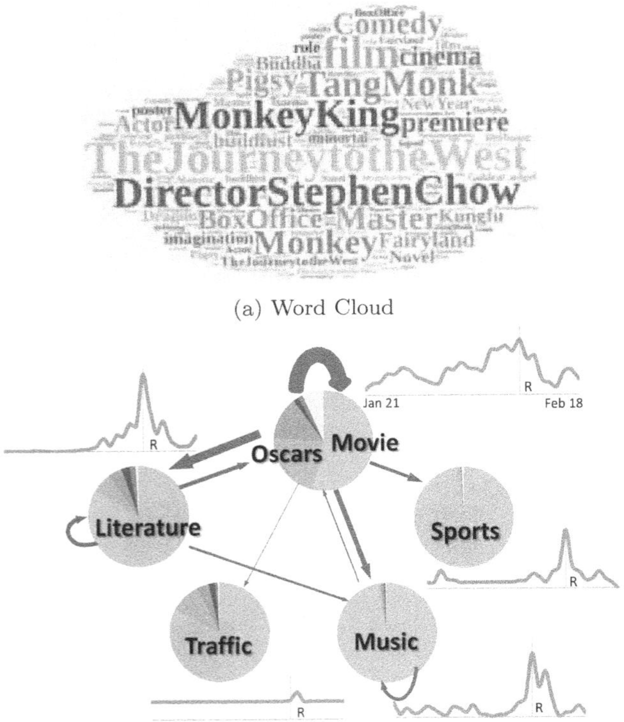

(a) Word Cloud

(b) Diffusion Path

Figure 5: Community-level Diffusion of Topic *Movie The Journey to the West*—a record-breaking box-office hit in China. We refer to the topic as *Journey West* for short.

to $\boldsymbol{\theta}$), with the dominant ones manually labeled by concise names. The time line near each community node shows the temporal variation (i.e. $\boldsymbol{\psi}$) of the topic specifically inside that community. The spike (time stamp R) of each line coincides with the release date of the movie. Interestingly, the spikes in communities *Literature*, *Sports* and *Music* are huge. In contrast, though community *Movie-Oscars* exhibited increasing activities at that time, the degree is not remarkable. We investigate the seemingly unintuitive phenomenon in §5.3.

The thickness of edges represents the influence strength between communities at this topic (i.e. $\boldsymbol{\zeta}$). We can clearly see that the community most interested in *Movie* and *Oscar* is the most influential one on topic *Journey West*. We formally discuss in §6.6 how COLD can be applied to identify most influential communities which is critical in viral marketing. The community *Traffic* is not active on the topic. By investigating the data we found this is because the majority of its members are traffic police official accounts.

The community level diffusion not only reveals compact yet meaningful overview of the topic diffusion process, but also forms the bases for the accurate diffusion prediction and in-depth analyses of social media dynamics, as shown next.

5.2 Prediction Method

A common task of diffusion analysis is to predict whether a message will propagate from one individual to another [11]. Taken retweeting as the example, given the content $\mathbf{w}_d$ of a message d, its publisher i, and another user i' (e.g. a follower of i), the objective is to estimate the probability that i' will retweet d from i.

Motivated by the above COLD model and the identified diffusion patterns, we develop our diffusion prediction method. Unlike traditional diffusion prediction methods which attempts to extract user-to-user diffusion probability directly from individual's interaction history, our solution conducts a two-step strategy: we first get the community-level diffusion probability as described in Eq.(4), and then combine personality of individuals through user-specific community memberships.

Our solution takes advantage of the community members' collective behavior patterns which are stable and predictable over time. User-specific community memberships can also be accurately captured based on both text and network features. In contrast, traditional methods can be ineffective due to the volatility of individual's actions and the sparsity of individual's records. We present the details of our method as follows.

Given a user-user-post triple (i, i', d), we estimate the probability that the post d will be spread from user i to user i'. Based on the topic modeling component in COLD, we first infer the underlying topics of the post through its text and its publisher's interest:

$$\begin{aligned} P(k|d,i) &\propto P(\mathbf{w}_d|k)P(k|i) \\ &\propto \prod_l \phi_{kw_{dl}} \cdot \sum_{c\in\mathbf{TopComm}(i)} \pi_{ic}\theta_{ck}, \end{aligned} \quad (5)$$

where $P(k|i)$ is the topical preferences of user i; $\mathbf{TopComm}(i)$ is the set of top communities of user i according to $\boldsymbol{\pi}_i$. Prior study has shown that a user on social media is typically active in a small number of communities [34], indicating that just the top few (e.g. 5 to 10) communities are sufficient enough to characterize the user's interest. We thus fix the size of **TopComm** as a small constant value (i.e. 5 in our setting).

Next, for one topic k, the influence of user i on user i' at topic k can be inferred by combining user community memberships and community-level influence strengths:

$$P(i,i'|k) = \sum_{\substack{c\,\in\,\mathbf{TopComm}(i)\\ c'\,\in\,\mathbf{TopComm}(i')}} \pi_{ic}\pi_{i'c'}\zeta_{kcc'}. \quad (6)$$

By combining Eq.(5) and (6), we obtain the final user-to-user diffusion probability of post d from user i to i':

$$P(i,i',d) = \sum_k P(k|d,i)P(i,i'|k). \quad (7)$$

Though seeming costly by combining several components together, we can actually get the result efficiently by offline filtering. In practice, we pre-collect the top communities of each user and then get her topic preferences. These are processed offline. In online determining of diffusion for user pairs, we simply collect the intermediate representation and calculate the final value, which only requires a weighted linear combination (Eq.(7)). The online computation complexity is $O(K|\mathbf{w}_d|)$, making the prediction very efficient, as further validated in Section 6.4.

Unlike most traditional diffusion prediction methods, the proposed approach also accounts for the semantics of spreading messages by comprehensive topic modeling as shown above, and is able to distinguish different diffusion processes across topics. The advantage and improved performance of COLD's prediction method will be illustrated in the experimental study.

5.3 Diffusion Patterns

Here we reveal several interesting and useful characters of diffusion based on the extracted community-level representations. We focus on the rich interplay between user interest and temporal dynamics.

Correlation between Community Interest and Topic Fluctuation. Users' concern usually changes over time, which is reflected by the popularity trends of topics. Here we study the connection between topics' temporal trends (i.e. ψ) and communities' topical focus (i.e. θ). Specifically, how do topics with varying interest levels fluctuate within communities? What is the difference between the variation patterns of topics with high weights and those with low?

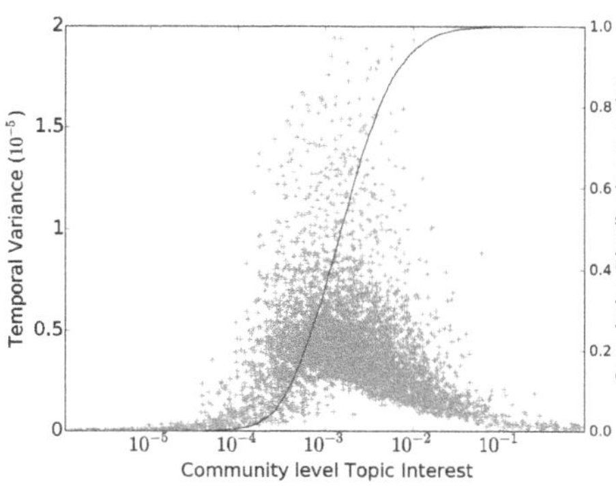

Figure 6: Topic Fluctuation and Community Interest. (X-axis is log scale.)

We use the *variance* of topic's community-specific temporal distribution ψ_{kc} to measure the fluctuation intensity of topic popularity. The scatter diagram in Figure 6 displays its relation with community's topic preference degree θ_{ck}. We also include the cumulative distribution function for the distribution of all communities' interest strengths. Topic popularity tends to fluctuate heavily throughout the time period within those communities with moderate interest in that topic. It generally exhibits higher variance when the topic has a proportion between 0.01% and 1% in community's interest distribution. In contrast, the popularity usually keeps steady in other communities which exhibit extremely low and high preference.

We can conclude that temporal topics are usually more dynamic in medium-interested communities. Members' attention on these topics tends to rise and fall intensely over time; in contrast, their engagement in communities' dominant topics is more stable.

Popularity lag between different communities. The influence strengths between communities have revealed the diffusion paths of topics. We then try to determine the time lag of topic propagating across communities. Specifically, how much time does it take for a topic diffusing from its initiators to others?

Figure 5, along with the above study, shows that different communities have varying temporal popularity on a specific topic. We can generally classify two categories of communities, i.e., communities with high preference for the topic and those with medium interest. Take the topic *Oscars2013* for example, the *Movie* and *Literature* communities (Figure 5) have the highest preference and others' are lower. We recognize the top 10 communities with largest probability on this topic as the highly-interested ones, yielding a set of communities whose average probability on the topic is 4.1%. Medium-interested communities are the remaining communities except those with extremely low probability (threshold is set to 0.01%), which have an average probability 0.37%. Due to the scale of social data, these thresholds are not low.

We then plot the *median topic dynamic curve* [16] for these two categories of communities. Specifically, for each community category, we align all of its community-specific temporal distributions of *Oscars2013* so that the peak popularity is equal to 1; we then at each time stamp plot the median probability over these aligned curves. Figure 7 shows the two categories' peak-time curves for topic *Oscars2013*.

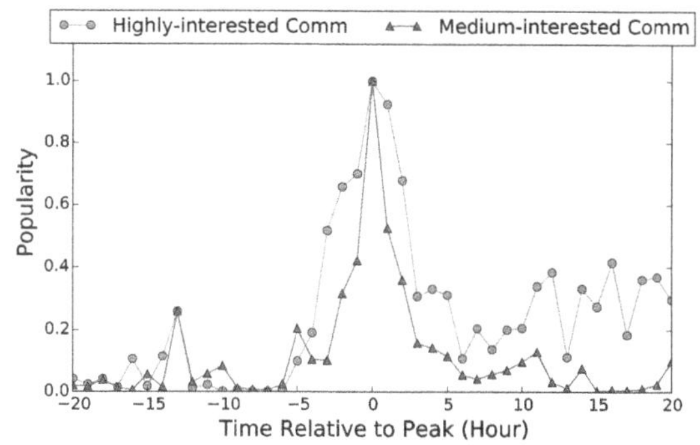

Figure 7: Time Lag between Highly and Medium-interested Communities on Topic *Oscars2013*.

We find that the topic popularity in the highly-interested communities rises earlier than the medium-interested communities. Moreover, the popularity in highly-interested communities lasts longer. It has a durable popularity. Investigating this time lag phenomenon on other topics, we also find similar results. Due to the space limit, we omit them.

The diffusion path and time lag confirm the usefulness of community level diffusion analysis and can be valuable in a variety of applications such as viral marketing, which we study in §6.6.

6. EMPIRICAL DEMONSTRATION

We conduct extensive experiments on large real datasets to evaluate the extraction and prediction performance of the proposed approach. The empirical study is divided into multiple stages. We first quantitatively evaluate the model's capability to extract topics and communities. We then test the diffusion prediction of the proposed approach, where the temporal modeling accuracy and the diffusion prediction performance are reported. Besides, efficiency and scalability of our model are validated by measuring the running time of model training, parallel extension, and online prediction. We also systematically study the sensitivity of model parameters. At last, we demonstrate novel real-world applications supported by our method.

All experiments are conducted on a cluster of Linux machines, each with eight 2.4GHz CPU cores and 48G memory. Data is stored in a RAID5 SAS storage server.

6.1 Setup

Datasets. Two real-world datasets are crawled from Sina Weibo[2], one of the most popular micro-blog platforms. We uniformly at random sample temporal messages from its streaming API. The messages are distributed nearly evenly

[2]http://weibo.com

in a three-month period from Dec 2012 through Feb 2013. Both datasets choose hour as the basic time interval.

Dataset 1. After removing stop words and low active users (with fewer than 20 posts), we create a dataset consisting of about 53K users, 11M posts and 91M words. The vocabulary size of these messages is 89K. Interaction network is derived from retweeting interactions between users, i.e., a link from user i to i' exists if i' once retweeted i's post. 2.7M links are observed.

Dataset 2. To evaluate the scalability of our approach, we also generate a larger dataset obtained in a similar manner as the first dataset. It consists of about 0.52M users, 10M links, 14M posts and 112M words.

Baselines. We compare the proposed COLD approach with several latest competitors. As there exists no prior approach capable of modeling communities and topic dynamics at the same time, we carefully select appropriate state-of-the-art methods to cover different aspects of diffusion modeling methods.

Table 2 lists the characters of these methods. Be aware that though some methods can be tuned to be used in several tasks, they are inadequate or uncompetitive compared with others; thus we omit them in this paper.

	features			tasks			
	text	social	time	topic ext	comm detec	temp modl	diff pred
PMTLM [39]	•	•		•	•		
MMSB [1]		•			•		
EUTB [37]	•	•	•	•		•	
Pipeline	•	•	•	•	•	•	
WTM [31]	•	•					•
TI [20]	•	•		•			•
COLD	•	•	•	•	•	•	•

Table 2: Feature and Task Comparison of Different Methods

Methods (1-2) models text and network features. Methods (3-5) aim at modeling temporal dynamics by integrating text and temporal features. At last, we include two diffusion prediction methods, which are used to compare the performance of direct individual diffusion modeling against community level modeling.

1. **Poisson Mixed-Topic Link Model (PMTLM).** PMTLM [39] defines a generative process for both text and links between users. Text generation follows the LDA [2] model, and links are modeled as a Poisson distribution. In PMTLM, links and text are generated by the same latent factor, which means one community is bounded to one topic (the latent factor is treated as community when generating links, and topic when generating text).

2. **Mixed Membership Stochastic Block model (MMSB)** [1] uses pairwise Bernoulli distributions to model links, and infers a distribution over communities for each user.

3. **Enhanced User-Temporal Model with Burst-weighted Smoothing (EUTB)** [37] assumes a topic is generated either by a user or a time stamp. It models the topic distributions for both users and time stamps. With network regularization and burst-weighted smoothing, EUTB performs best in time stamp prediction task among a set of competitors.

4. **COLD without Link (COLD-NoLink).** As a subpart of COLD without network component, COLD-NoLink can be used to test the contributions of network features.

5. **Pipelined Approach of Community-level Temporal Dynamics (Pipeline).** We first use MMSB model to assign each user to two most probable communities. Then we extract topic variation in particular communities by running TOT [32] on the posts generated by their members. This approach does not include interdependence between network and content.

6. **Whom to Mention (WTM)** [31] proposes a ranking method aimed at finding top users who would retweet a post and make contribution to its further diffusion. Features including user interest match, content-dependent user relationship and user influence are adopted.

7. **Topic-level Influence (TI)** [20] is a probabilistic generative model capturing influence between users at different topics. Both direct and indirect user influences are considered when predicting whether a user will retweet a friend's post.

6.2 Latent Factor Extraction

We report the model's capacity in extracting latent factors, showing its accurate modeling ability in both topic and community identification.

Topic Extraction. For an intuitive understanding of the extracted topics, we present four example word clouds in Figure 8. Meaningful subjects can be observed.

Figure 8: Word Clouds of Extracted Topics.

We next quantitatively evaluate COLD's topic extraction capacity by *perplexity* [2]. As a widely used metric in text modeling, perplexity measures how well a probability model predicts a sample. It can be interpreted as being proportional to the distance (formally, the cross-entropy) between the word distribution learned by the model and the actual distribution in test set [4]. Thus lower scores are better, indicating the model distribution is closer to the actual one. For a test set of M posts,

$$perplexity(\mathrm{D}_{test}) = \exp\left\{ - \frac{\sum_{d=1}^{M} \log p(\mathbf{w}_d)}{\sum_{d=1}^{M} N_d} \right\},$$

where N_d is the length of the test post d, and $p(\mathbf{w}_d)$ is the probability of the words in the post; for COLD, it is computed as:

$$p(\mathbf{w}_d) = \sum_c \pi_{ic} \sum_k \theta_{ck} \prod_l \phi_{k w_{dl}},$$

where i is the post author.

We use a 5-fold cross validation testing, i.e., at each time interval, 80% of the posts as the train set, while the remaining 20% posts and all links as test set. Figure 9 shows the perplexity values under varying number of topics. It reveals that COLD ($K = 100$, $C = 100$) has the lowest perplexity, indicating best topic discovery performance among all the competitors. Perplexity scores for EUTB and COLD are close, and both significantly outperform PMTLM. PMTLM's topics are tangled with communities in the same latent factor, weakening their fitness in modeling text.

In contrast, COLD comprehensively models communities and topics while explaining text well. Compared to EUTB, COLD not only models the dynamic content, but further captures social influence between users by incorporating network features. Therefore, the proposed method delievers improved advantages in topic extraction.

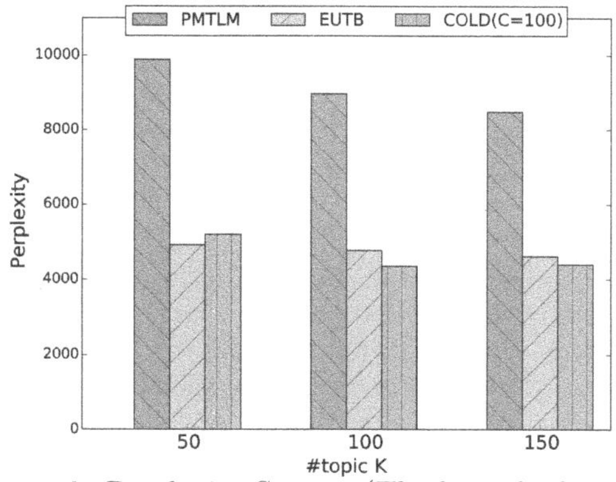

Figure 9: Perplexity Scores. (The less, the better.)

Community Detection. We then continue to evaluate the quality of the extracted communities. An example of the mixed-membership communities is visualized in Figure 16. We can see most users are clustered at the pentagon's corners and sides/diagonal lines, indicating that most of them have primary communities for engagement.

For quantitative evaluation, since no ground truth is available on Weibo network (which is the most common situation on social networks), we use link prediction, a widely-used quantitative measurement in the mixed-membership community setting without community labels [28].

Link prediction [18] is defined to estimate the probability of a link between two users. The probability of a link from user i to i' is measured by:

$$P_{i \to i'} = \sum_{s} \sum_{s'} \pi_{is} \pi_{i's'} \eta_{ss'}.$$

Since there is no pre-defined threshold for link existence, we turn to *area under the receiver operating characteristic curve* (AUC)[3] as the prediction accuracy. Given a rank of all non-observed links, the AUC value can be interpreted as the probability that a randomly chosen true positive link is ranked above a randomly chosen true negative link. In 5-fold cross validation, each time we use 20% of the positive links and randomly select 1% of the negative links to evaluate AUC; models are trained on the remaining links and all posts.

Figure 10 shows the AUC values for the three models. COLD ($K = 100$, $C = 100$) outperforms all other methods. Moreover, PMTLM and COLD are significantly more accurate than MMSB, showing that incorporating content feature benefits network structure modeling. COLD is also slightly better than PMTLM, with the comprehensive modeling ability.

[3]http://en.wikipedia.org/wiki/Roc_curve

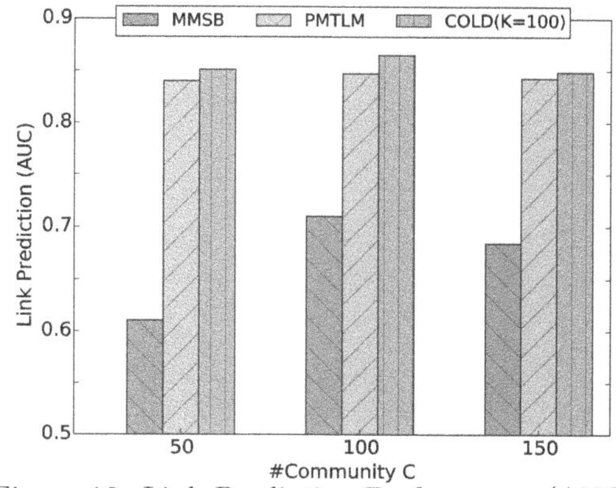

Figure 10: Link Prediction Performance (AUC).

The above two latent extraction experiments show the proposed COLD is versatile enough to simultaneously capture the critical characters in temporal diffusion. Though PMTLM performs almost as well as COLD in network modeling, the low topic extraction quality hinders its ability in modeling communities and topics at the same time. It reveals that, a single latent variable is not expressive enough to capture the diverse structures underlying the rich heterogeneous text and network context. COLD decouples these two critical factors and suitably models their correlations, ensuring both flexibility and accuracy.

6.3 Diffusion Prediction

Here we demonstrate the significant superiority of COLD over existing methods in terms of diffusion modeling and prediction.

Temporal Modeling. Time stamp prediction [32] is to estimate the occurring time stamp of a previously unseen document. Given the words in a post d and its author user i, we choose its time stamp as the candidate giving maximum likelihood:

$$\hat{t}_d = \arg\max_t \sum_c \pi_{ic} \sum_k \theta_{ck} \psi_{kct} \prod_l \phi_{k w_{dl}}.$$

Here 5-fold cross validation is used. The best results are obtained by setting $K = 100$ for the four models, and $C = 100$ for COLD and COLD-NoLink. Figure 11 shows the prediction accuracy for different models as a function of tolerance range, i.e., the maximum allowed difference between the real and predicted time stamps. COLD performs best among all competitors. COLD-NoLink outperforms EUTB, showing that the superiority of our approach derives not only from the the integration of network feature, but also from the fine-grained representation by distinguishing temporal topic dynamics across different communities.

It is notable that Pipeline, despite taking into account community specific topic dynamics, has poor performance. The reason is that it exploits network and content information separately, and ignores the interdependence between them. This experiment further justifies the advantage of the unified way which COLD uses to model dynamic social data.

Diffusion Prediction. The prediction task is to estimate whether a post d by a user i will be retweeted by another user i'. We use the averaged AUC values [6]. Specifically, given a tuple $\mathcal{RT}_{id} = (i, d, \mathcal{U}_{id}, \overline{\mathcal{U}}_{id})$, where $\mathcal{U}_{id}$ is the set of i's followers who retweeted d from i while $\overline{\mathcal{U}}_{id}$ is the rest of i's followers who ignored d, its AUC is computed by treating

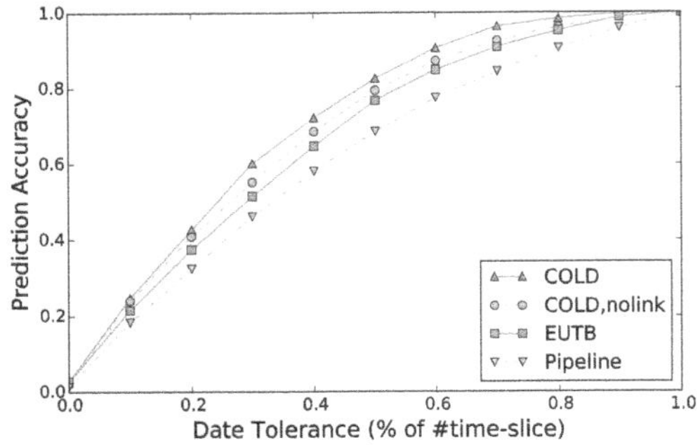

Figure 11: Time Stamp Prediction Accuracy.

the set $\{(i, i', d) | i' \in \mathcal{U}_{id}\}$ as positive examples and the set $\{(i, i', d) | i' \in \overline{\mathcal{U}}_{id}\}$ as negative examples. We then average the AUC values for all the tuples in test set. Here 5-fold cross validation is used by randomly holding out 20% tuples (with non-empty $\mathcal{U}_{id}$ and $\overline{\mathcal{U}}_{id}$) from the dataset as the test set each time.

Figure 12 gives the averaged AUC values for the three competitors. COLD ($K = 100$, $C = 100$) outperforms all other methods. Both TI and WTM attempt to model diffusion probability directly based on individual records, which can be prohibited by the volatility of individual behaviors as well as the sparsity of individual data. In contrast, COLD adopts a new paradigm by taking the advantage of the stability and predictability of collective behaviors of community members; user-specific characters are captured by user distribution over communities which can be accurately modeled by leveraging both text and network features.

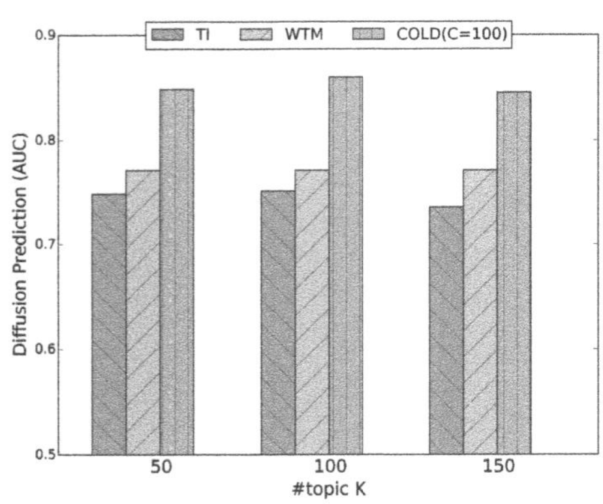

Figure 12: Diffusion Prediction Performance (AUC).

6.4 Efficiency

Parallel Scaling. We deploy our inference algorithm on the distributed GraphLab system to tackle the challenge of large data size. We study its scalability on the larger dataset with 0.52M users, 10M links and 14M posts. Training time is reported under different machine and data settings in Figure 13.

Figure 13(a) shows that the required time increases linearly as the data size grows. This confirms that by implicitly modeling negative links in Bayesian prior, our proposed collapsed Gibbs Sampler scales linearly with the size of dataset, as analyzed in §4.2.

The results in Figure 13(b) demonstrate satisfying efficiency of our distributed implementation on GraphLab. The running time decreases significantly with growing size of distributed GraphLab nodes. We reduce the training time for 10M links and 14M posts from hundred hours to just a few. This clearly shows the advantage of parallel processing. The model structure of COLD is loosely coupled enough to guarantee the parallel processing, showing advantage in growing social data size.

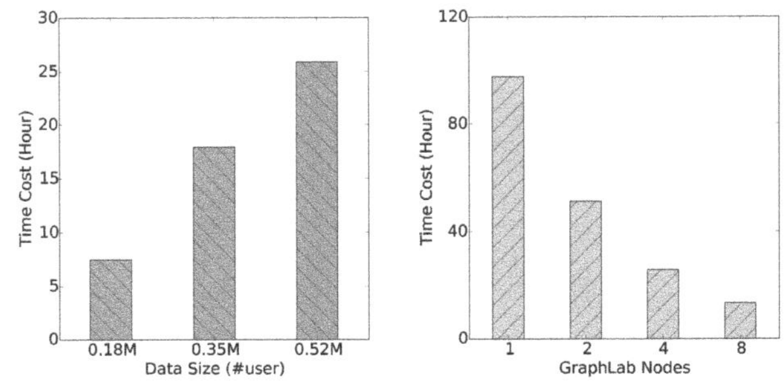

(a) Three Subsets, 4 Nodes. (b) Whole Dataset, # nodes.
Figure 13: Training Time of COLD on Parallel GraphLab.

Training time. Figure 14 shows the running time of different methods on the whole dataset. Note that while COLD jointly models text, network and time information, the baselines generally only account for a limited portion of the data. Though the basic implementation of COLD is costly, the parallel implementation guarantees the efficiency very well. It is feasible in actual deployment.

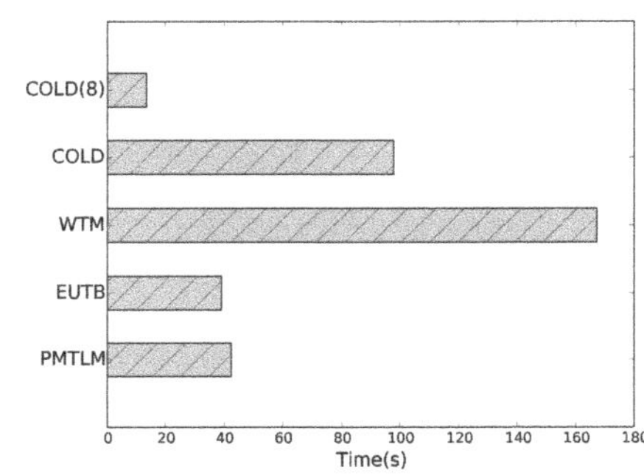

Figure 14: Training Time (C=K=100). "COLD (8)" is the distributed implementation on 8 nodes.

Prediction Time. Figure 15 presents the online diffusion prediction time of different methods after model training.

Our proposed method has lowest cost. In contrast, the baseline methods, i.e., TI and WTM are usually costly. This can be attributed to their lack of compact representation of user's profile. Specifically, TI's prediction is based on the influence of a user's multi-hop friends which can be a large set and require much processing time. For WTM, due to the absence of topic modeling, computing content-dependent features can be costly. Different from these methods, our proposed approach is able to characterize user's profile by extracted communities' representations, which can be efficiently computed by only a few operations.

6.5 Parameter Sensitivity

Though seeming complex, hyper-parameters for Bayesian priors, as discussed later, generally have negligible impact. COLD model is largely affected by two parameters, i.e., community number C and topic number K. We test the sensitivity in different tasks. The empirical results show that K primarily impacts topic modeling, while C has an effect

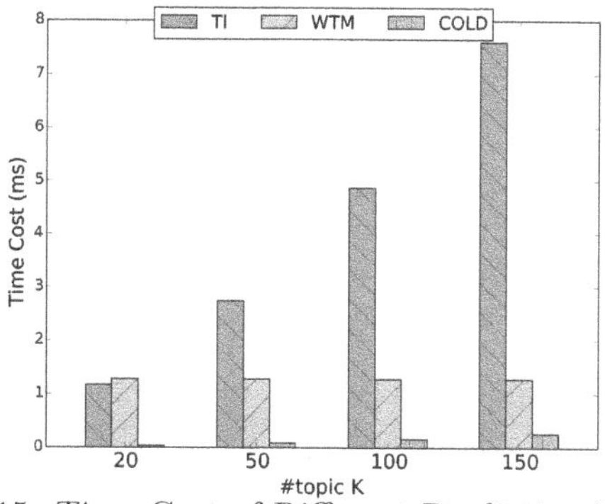

Figure 15: Time Cost of Different Prediction Methods.

mainly on community extraction. They together exert influence on diffusion prediction accuracy. The performance is stable under a broad range of parameter settings, indicating little tuning is required in actual deployment. Due to the space limitations, we defer the experimental results of parameter effects to the appendix (Appx B).

It is worth pointing out that Dirichlet hyper-parameters have low impact on model performance, and can be set as fixed values following the common strategy [5, 38] (i.e., $\rho = 50/C, \alpha = 50/K, \beta = \epsilon = 0.01$), while λ_0 and λ_1 are set as described in §3 for modeling negative links. Empirical studies also show our model is insensitive to these hyperparameters, which we omit due to space limitations.

6.6 Application of COLD

The improved diffusion prediction and the compact community level representation can not only help in traditional diffusion analysis, but also open up various novel applications at community scale. Here we demonstrate a concrete application to show how COLD can be applied to identify influential users and communities, which can be crucial in viral marketing and social network management [11].

Mining the influential nodes on social network has been studied extensively. Most existing works [29, 13, 8] usually assume pre-defined influence strength between users and focus on the information cascade simulation. Hence COLD is complementary, and can be directly applied, to these works by providing accurate influence strength estimation.

Moreover, COLD also enables us to go beyond the traditional user level and study the most *influential communities*. Selecting communities as the initial target has been increasingly employed due to its economy (e.g. by creating fanpages on Facebook) [30, 7] and effectiveness (e.g. by word-of-month among closely-connected members) [14]. Therefore, influential community identification enjoys practical values.

Analogous to measuring user's influence degree [19], we compute the influence degree of each community by setting the single community as the seedset and applying the well-known Independent Cascade [8] model on the extracted community level diffusion graph (e.g. Figure 5). Figure 16 shows the 4 most influential communities on topic *Sports*, as well as the aggregated other communities, by the 5 corners of a pentagon. Every user i is displayed as a point whose position is determined by her community membership π_i, i.e., a π_i-weighted convex combination of the 5 pentagon corners. For better understanding of the result, we also compute the influence degree of users, which is reflected by the size of the points in the figure. The characteristics of communities can then be obtained by analyzing their influential members. We can see that most of the influential users are from

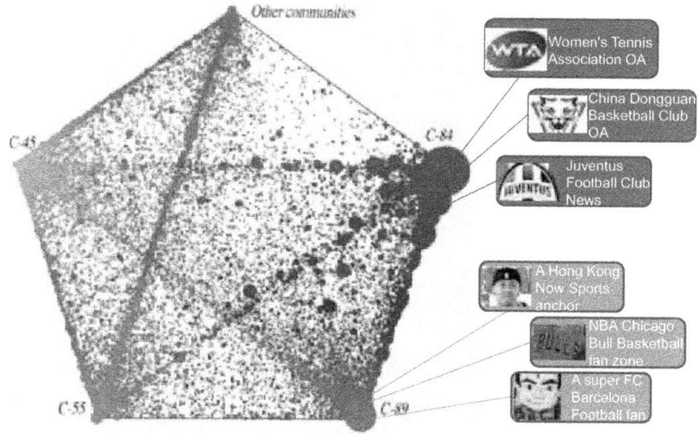

Figure 16: The Most Influential Communities on Topic *Sports*. Points at the pentagon's corners represent single-membership users, while points on the sides and diagonal lines represent users with mixed-membership in 2 communities. Only the top 20k influential users are shown (thus the points around "other communities" are few). Top-3 influential members of community 84 and 89 are labeled, where "OA" stands for "Official Account". Best viewed in color.

community 84 (blue) and 89 (green), which are the top-2 influential communities. Figure 16 further labels the top-3 users of each community. Interestingly, the top members of C-84 are usually the official accounts of sports organizations, while those of C-89 are personal or unofficial ones, indicating distinct interaction patterns of these two influential types.

7. CONCLUSION

This paper addressed the problem of community-level diffusion analysis. We presented COLD (COmmunity Level Diffusion), a generative latent model jointly over network, text and time, to simultaneously uncover the hidden topics, communities, and inter-community influence.

With the well-designed model structure and parallel inference, COLD is effective and scalable. Based on the extracted community level representations, we developed an effective diffusion prediction approach. We also applied the model on real large datasets and performed temporal diffusion analysis. Meaningful patterns were discovered. COLD can be further used in influential community identification to promote viral marketing.

The community level diffusion analysis is a novel angle, and opens up several promising future directions. For example, the mechanism behind the coarse-grained diffusion and user engagement are beneficial for better temporal analysis and user targeting. More efficient and compact summarization techniques are also vital for dynamic and noisy data scenarios. We would like to extend current extraction method for advanced prediction and diffusion problems.

Acknowledgement: The research is supported by the National Natural Science Foundation of China under Grant No. 61272155, 61272340 and 61232006, and 973 program under No. 2014CB340405. This work is also supported by NSF IIS1218282.

8. REFERENCES

[1] E. M. Airoldi, D. M. Blei, S. E. Fienberg, and E. P. Xing. Mixed membership stochastic blockmodels. *JMLR*, 9:1981–2014, 2008.

[2] D. M. Blei, A. Y. Ng, and M. I. Jordan. Latent dirichlet allocation. *JMLR*, 3:993–1022, 2003.

[3] J. Chang and D. M. Blei. Relational topic models for document networks. In *Proc. of AISTATS*, pages 81–88, 2009.

[4] C. Chemudugunta, A. Holloway, P. Smyth, and M. Steyvers. *Modeling documents by combining semantic concepts with unsupervised statistical learning*. Springer, 2008.

[5] Q. Diao, J. Jiang, F. Zhu, and E.-P. Lim. Finding bursty topics from microblogs. In *Proc. of ACL*, pages 536–544, 2012.

[6] L. Dietz, S. Bickel, and T. Scheffer. Unsupervised prediction of citation influences. In *Proceedings of the 24th international conference on Machine learning*, pages 233–240. ACM, 2007.

[7] M. Eftekhar, Y. Ganjali, and N. Koudas. Information cascade at group scale. In *Proc. of KDD*, pages 401–409. ACM, 2013.

[8] J. Goldenberg, B. Libai, and E. Muller. Talk of the network: A complex systems look at the underlying process of word-of-mouth. *Marketing letters*, 12(3):211–223, 2001.

[9] M. Granovetter. The strength of weak ties: A network theory revisited. *Sociological theory*, 1(1):201–233, 1983.

[10] T. L. Griffiths and M. Steyvers. Finding scientific topics. *PNAS*, 101(Suppl 1):5228–5235, 2004.

[11] A. Guille, H. Hacid, C. Favre, and D. A. Zighed. Information diffusion in online social networks: A survey. *ACM SIGMOD Record*, 42(1):17–28, 2013.

[12] Q. Ho, R. Yan, R. Raina, and E. P. Xing. Understanding the interaction between interests, conversations and friendships in facebook. *CoRR*, abs/1211.0028, 2012.

[13] D. Kempe, J. Kleinberg, and É. Tardos. Maximizing the spread of influence through a social network. In *Proc. of KDD*, pages 137–146, 2003.

[14] R. V. Kozinets, K. De Valck, A. C. Wojnicki, and S. J. Wilner. Networked narratives: understanding word-of-mouth marketing in online communities. *Journal of marketing*, 74(2):71–89, 2010.

[15] H. D. Lasswell. The structure and function of communication in society. *The communication of ideas*, 37, 1948.

[16] J. Leskovec, L. Backstrom, and J. Kleinberg. Meme-tracking and the dynamics of the news cycle. In *Proc. of KDD*, pages 497–506, 2009.

[17] J. Leskovec, K. J. Lang, and M. Mahoney. Empirical comparison of algorithms for network community detection. In *Proc. of WWW*, pages 631–640, 2010.

[18] D. Liben-Nowell and J. Kleinberg. The link prediction problem for social networks. In *Proc. of CIKM*, pages 556–559, 2003.

[19] S. Lin, F. Wang, Q. Hu, and P. S. Yu. Extracting social events for learning better information diffusion models. In *Proc. of KDD*, pages 365–373, 2013.

[20] L. Liu, J. Tang, J. Han, M. Jiang, and S. Yang. Mining topic-level influence in heterogeneous networks. In *Proc. of CIKM*, pages 199–208, 2010.

[21] Y. Liu, A. Niculescu-Mizil, and W. Gryc. Topic-link lda: joint models of topic and author community. In *Proc. of ICML*, pages 665–672, 2009.

[22] T. Lou and J. Tang. Mining structural hole spanners through information diffusion in social networks. In *Proc. of WWW*, pages 825–836, 2013.

[23] Y. Low, D. Bickson, J. Gonzalez, C. Guestrin, A. Kyrola, and J. M. Hellerstein. Distributed graphlab: a framework for machine learning and data mining in the cloud. *PVLDB*, 5(8):716–727, 2012.

[24] Y. Matsubara, Y. Sakurai, B. A. Prakash, L. Li, and C. Faloutsos. Rise and fall patterns of information diffusion: model and implications. In *Proc. of KDD*, pages 6–14, 2012.

[25] R. M. Nallapati, A. Ahmed, E. P. Xing, and W. W. Cohen. Joint latent topic models for text and citations. In *Proc. of KDD*, pages 542–550, 2008.

[26] Y. Ruan, D. Fuhry, and S. Parthasarathy. Efficient community detection in large networks using content and links. In *Proc. of WWW*, pages 1089–1098, 2013.

[27] J. Tang, J. Sun, C. Wang, and Z. Yang. Social influence analysis in large-scale networks. In *Proc. of KDD*, pages 807–816. ACM, 2009.

[28] L. Tang and H. Liu. Community detection and mining in social media. *Synthesis Lectures on Data Mining and Knowledge Discovery*, 2(1):1–137, 2010.

[29] Y. Tang, X. Xiao, and Y. Shi. Influence maximization: Near-optimal time complexity meets practical efficiency. In *Proc. of SIGMOD*, pages 75–86, 2014.

[30] C. Treadaway and M. Smith. *Facebook marketing: An hour a day*. John Wiley & Sons, 2012.

[31] B. Wang, C. Wang, J. Bu, C. Chen, W. V. Zhang, D. Cai, and X. He. Whom to mention: expand the diffusion of tweets by@ recommendation on micro-blogging systems. In *Proc. of WWW*, pages 1331–1340, 2013.

[32] X. Wang and A. McCallum. Topics over time: a non-markov continuous-time model of topical trends. In *Proc. of KDD*, pages 424–433, 2006.

[33] S. Wu, J. M. Hofman, W. A. Mason, and D. J. Watts. Who says what to whom on twitter. In *Proc. of WWW*, pages 705–714, 2011.

[34] J. Xie, S. Kelley, and B. K. Szymanski. Overlapping community detection in networks: The state-of-the-art and comparative study. *ACM Comput. Surv.*, 45(4):43:1–43:35, Aug 2013.

[35] J. Yang and J. Leskovec. Patterns of temporal variation in online media. In *Proc. of WSDM*, pages 177–186, 2011.

[36] T. Yang, R. Jin, Y. Chi, and S. Zhu. Combining link and content for community detection: a discriminative approach. In *Proc. of KDD*, pages 927–936, 2009.

[37] H. Yin, B. Cui, H. Lu, Y. Huang, and J. Yao. A unified model for stable and temporal topic detection from social media data. In *Proc. of ICDE*, 2013.

[38] H. Yin, Y. Sun, B. Cui, Z. Hu, and L. Chen. Lcars: a location-content-aware recommender system. In *Proc. of KDD*, pages 221–229, 2013.

[39] Y. Zhu, X. Yan, L. Getoor, and C. Moore. Scalable text and link analysis with mixed-topic link models. In *Proc. of KDD*, pages 473–481, 2013.

APPENDIX

A. INFERENCE VIA COLLAPSED GIBBS SAMPLING

Here we describe the inference algorithm for COLD based on collapsed Gibbs Sampling.

Given an interaction network $\mathcal{G} = (\mathcal{U}, \mathcal{E})$ with a set of posts $\mathcal{D}$, and the pre-defined hyperparameters $\rho, \alpha, \beta, \epsilon$ and $\boldsymbol{\lambda}$, COLD specifies the following full posterior distribution:

$$\begin{aligned}
&P(\boldsymbol{\pi}, \boldsymbol{\theta}, \boldsymbol{\eta}, \boldsymbol{\phi}, \boldsymbol{\psi}, \boldsymbol{c}, \boldsymbol{s}, \boldsymbol{z} | \mathcal{U}, \mathcal{E}, \mathcal{D}, \rho, \alpha, \beta, \epsilon, \boldsymbol{\lambda}) \propto \\
&\Big(P(\boldsymbol{\pi}|\rho) P(\boldsymbol{\theta}|\alpha) P(\boldsymbol{\eta}|\boldsymbol{\lambda}) P(\boldsymbol{\phi}|\beta) P(\boldsymbol{\psi}|\epsilon) P(\boldsymbol{c}, \boldsymbol{s}|\boldsymbol{\pi}) P(\boldsymbol{z}|\boldsymbol{\theta}, \boldsymbol{c}) \\
&P(\boldsymbol{w}_{\mathcal{D}}|\boldsymbol{\phi}, \boldsymbol{z}) P(\boldsymbol{t}_{\mathcal{D}}|\boldsymbol{\psi}, \boldsymbol{c}, \boldsymbol{z}) P(\boldsymbol{e}_{\mathcal{E}}|\boldsymbol{\eta}, \boldsymbol{s}) \Big),
\end{aligned} \tag{8}$$

where $\boldsymbol{w}_{\mathcal{D}}$ is the words in the post set; $\boldsymbol{t}_{\mathcal{D}}$ is the time stamps of the posts; $\boldsymbol{e}_{\mathcal{E}}$ is the set of positive links; the constant of proportionality is the marginal likelihood of the observed data.

The task of posterior inference for COLD is to determine the probability distribution of the hidden variables given the observed words, time stamps and network. However, exact inference is intractable due to the difficulty of calculating the normalizing constant in the above posterior distribution.

We use collapsed Gibbs Sampling, a well-established Markov chain Monte Carlo (MCMC) technique for approximate inference. In collapsed Gibbs Sampling, the multinomial distributions $\boldsymbol{\Phi} = \{\boldsymbol{\pi}, \boldsymbol{\theta}, \boldsymbol{\eta}, \boldsymbol{\phi}, \boldsymbol{\psi}\}$ are first marginalized (collapsed), a Markov chain over the latent indicators $\{\boldsymbol{c}, \boldsymbol{s}, \boldsymbol{z}\}$ is then constructed, whose stationary distribution is the posterior. We obtain samples of latent variables from the Markov chain. Point estimates for the collapsed distributions $\boldsymbol{\Phi}$ can then be computed given the samples, and predictive distributions are computed by averaging over multiple samples.

Sampling Procedure. Gibbs Sampler repeatedly samples each latent variable conditioned on the current states of other hidden variables and observations; a configuration of latent states of the system is then obtained. Next we provide the derivation of the sampling formulas (Eqs.(1–3)).

By marginalizing out $\boldsymbol{\Phi}$ in Eq.(8), we obtain:

$$\begin{aligned}
&P(\boldsymbol{c}, \boldsymbol{s}, \boldsymbol{z}|.) \\
&\propto P(\boldsymbol{c}, \boldsymbol{s}|\rho) P(\boldsymbol{z}|\boldsymbol{c}, \alpha) P(\boldsymbol{w}|\boldsymbol{z}, \beta) P(\boldsymbol{t}|\boldsymbol{c}, \boldsymbol{z}, \epsilon) P(\boldsymbol{e}|\boldsymbol{s}, \boldsymbol{\lambda}) \\
&= \int P(\boldsymbol{\pi}|\rho) P(\boldsymbol{c}, \boldsymbol{s}|\boldsymbol{\pi}) d\boldsymbol{\pi} \int P(\boldsymbol{\theta}|\alpha) P(\boldsymbol{z}|\boldsymbol{\theta}, \boldsymbol{c}) d\boldsymbol{\theta} \\
&\cdot \int P(\boldsymbol{\phi}|\beta) P(\boldsymbol{w}|\boldsymbol{\phi}, \boldsymbol{z}) d\boldsymbol{\phi} \int P(\boldsymbol{\psi}|\epsilon) P(\boldsymbol{t}|\boldsymbol{\psi}, \boldsymbol{c}, \boldsymbol{z}) d\boldsymbol{\psi} \\
&\cdot \int P(\boldsymbol{\eta}|\boldsymbol{\lambda}) P(\boldsymbol{e}|\boldsymbol{\eta}, \boldsymbol{s}) d\boldsymbol{\eta}.
\end{aligned} \tag{9}$$

The conditional of c_{ij} can be computed by dividing the joint distribution of all variables by the joint of all variables except c_{ij} (denoted as $\boldsymbol{c}_{-ij}$):

$$\begin{aligned}
&P(c_{ij} = c|\boldsymbol{c}_{-ij}, \boldsymbol{s}, \boldsymbol{z}, \boldsymbol{t}, .) \\
&= \frac{P(\boldsymbol{c}, \boldsymbol{s}, \boldsymbol{z}|.)}{P(\boldsymbol{c}_{-ij}, \boldsymbol{s}, \boldsymbol{z}|.)} \\
&= \frac{P(\boldsymbol{c}, \boldsymbol{s}|\rho)}{P(\boldsymbol{c}_{-ij}, \boldsymbol{s}|\rho)} \cdot \frac{P(\boldsymbol{z}|\boldsymbol{c}, \alpha)}{P(\boldsymbol{z}|\boldsymbol{c}_{-ij}, \alpha)} \cdot \frac{P(\boldsymbol{t}|\boldsymbol{c}, \boldsymbol{z}, \epsilon)}{P(\boldsymbol{t}|\boldsymbol{c}_{-ij}, \boldsymbol{z}, \epsilon)}.
\end{aligned} \tag{10}$$

We now derive the first fraction of Eq.(10), i.e.,

$$\frac{P(\boldsymbol{c}, \boldsymbol{s}|\rho)}{P(\boldsymbol{c}_{-ij}, \boldsymbol{s}|\rho)} = \frac{\int P(\boldsymbol{\pi}|\rho) P(\boldsymbol{c}, \boldsymbol{s}|\boldsymbol{\pi}) d\boldsymbol{\pi}}{\int P(\boldsymbol{\pi}|\rho) P(\boldsymbol{c}_{-ij}, \boldsymbol{s}|\boldsymbol{\pi}) d\boldsymbol{\pi}}. \tag{11}$$

As we assume each c is generated from a multinomial distribution $\boldsymbol{\pi}$, and the hyper-parameter for conjugate Dirichlet prior is ρ, we have:

$$\begin{aligned}
&\int P(\boldsymbol{\pi}|\rho) P(\boldsymbol{c}, \boldsymbol{s}|\boldsymbol{\pi}) d\boldsymbol{\pi} \\
&= \int \prod_i \frac{\Gamma(C\rho)}{\prod_c \Gamma(\rho)} \prod_c \pi_{ic}^{\rho-1} \cdot \prod_i \prod_c \pi_{ic}^{n_i^{(c)}} d\boldsymbol{\pi} \\
&= \prod_i \frac{\Gamma(C\rho)}{\prod_c \Gamma(\rho)} \cdot \frac{\prod_c \Gamma(n_i^{(c)} + \rho)}{\Gamma(n_i^{(\cdot)} + C\rho)}.
\end{aligned}$$

Combining the above equation with Eq.(11) leads to:

$$\begin{aligned}
\frac{P(\boldsymbol{c}, \boldsymbol{s}|\rho)}{P(\boldsymbol{c}_{-ij}, \boldsymbol{s}|\rho)} &= \frac{\Gamma(n_i^{(c_{ij})} + \rho)\Gamma(n_{i,-ij}^{(\cdot)} + C\rho)}{\Gamma(n_{i,-ij}^{(c_{ij})} + \rho)\Gamma(n_i^{(\cdot)} + C\rho)} \\
&= \frac{n_{i,-ij}^{(c)} + \rho}{n_{i,-ij}^{(\cdot)} + C\rho},
\end{aligned} \tag{12}$$

where the count with subscript $-ij$ denotes a quantity with the current instance (i.e. post d_{ij}) excluded. Here we use the identity $\Gamma(x+1) = x\Gamma(x)$. The second and third fractions of Eq.(10) can be derived analogously. The Dirichlet-Multinomial conjugates ensure the tractability of the integrals. Specifically, the second fraction can be written as:

$$\frac{P(\boldsymbol{z}|\boldsymbol{c}, \alpha)}{P(\boldsymbol{z}|\boldsymbol{c}_{-ij}, \alpha)} = \frac{n_{c,-ij}^{(k)} + \alpha}{n_{c,-ij}^{(\cdot)} + K\alpha}, \tag{13}$$

while the third fraction as:

$$\frac{P(\boldsymbol{t}|\boldsymbol{c}, \boldsymbol{z}, \epsilon)}{P(\boldsymbol{t}|\boldsymbol{c}_{-ij}, \boldsymbol{z}, \epsilon)} = \frac{n_{ck,-ij}^{(t)} + \epsilon}{n_{ck,-ij}^{(\cdot)} + T\epsilon}. \tag{14}$$

Finally, by combining Eqs.(12-14) we obtain the sampling formula as in Eq.(1). Note that we omit the subscripts $-ij$ in Eq.(1) for clarity. Eq.(2) and Eq.(3) are derived in a similar manner.

Distribution Estimation. After a sufficient number of sampling iterations, we obtain a set of samples. For any single sample, we can estimate the unknown distributions as follows:

$$\hat{\pi}_{ic} = \frac{n_i^{(c)} + \rho}{n_i^{(\cdot)} + C\rho},$$

$$\hat{\theta}_{ck} = \frac{n_c^{(k)} + \alpha}{n_c^{(\cdot)} + K\alpha},$$

$$\hat{\eta}_{cc'} = \frac{n_{cc'} + \lambda_1}{n_{cc'} + \lambda_0 + \lambda_1},$$

while $\boldsymbol{\phi}$ and $\boldsymbol{\psi}$ can be estimated similarly. The final predictive distributions are obtained by integrating across all the samples.

B. RESULTS ON PARAMETER SENSITIVITY

***K* on Topic Extraction.** Figure 17 shows the topic perplexity values under different parameter settings. Given a fixed C, the perplexity decreases with the increasing number of topics, and levels off after K is larger than 100. On the other hand, under any fixed K, the result remains stable as C varies, indicating that the number of communities is less important than the number of topics for text modeling. In COLD, text is generated by mixture of topics, hence the number of topics directly impacts the capacity of modeling text. In contrast, although there exists correlations between content and network, the influence of communities on text modeling is indirect.

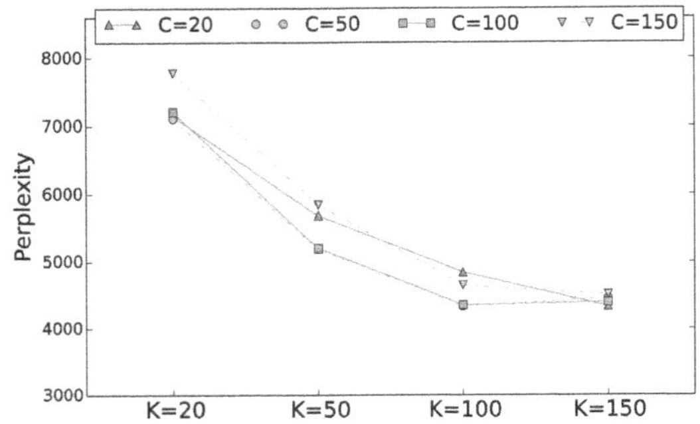

Figure 17: #Community C and #Topic K Impacts on Topic Extraction.

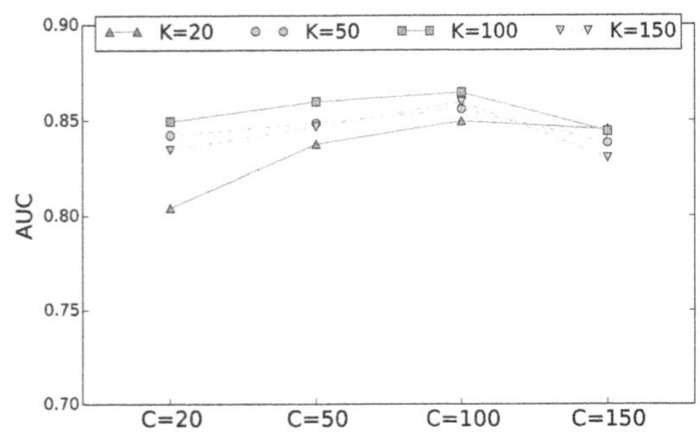

Figure 18: #Community C and #Topic K Impacts on Link Prediction.

***C* on Community Extraction.** Figure 18 shows the impacts of C and K w.r.t. the quality of COLD in community modeling. The AUC value at first increases as C increases, and there is an intermediate value of C (i.e. 100) at which COLD performs best. After that the AUC value decreases as C continues to increase. In contrast, the result fluctuates slightly without a clear pattern as K varies. The result is expected as links are directly generated by mixture of communities. The effect of topic number is not significant.

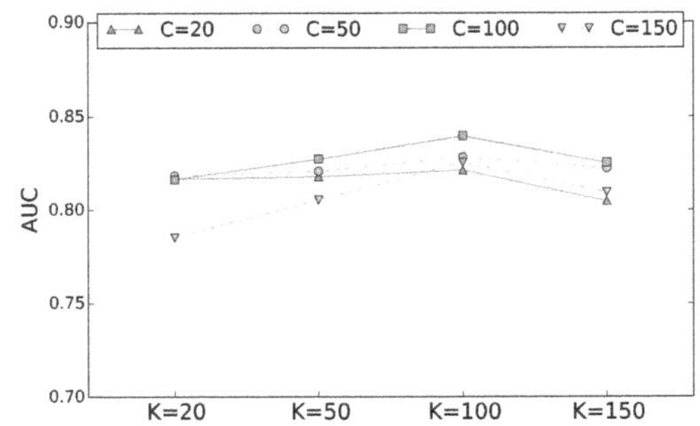

Figure 19: #Community C and #Topic K Impacts on Diffusion Prediction.

Joint Impacts on Diffusion Prediction. Figure 19 shows the diffusion prediction performance under different parameter settings. We find that the prediction AUC values are affected by both C and K, e.g., the performance gets better when K and C increases from 20 to 100, respectively. The joint effect indicates that communities and topics are both critical factors in modeling diffusion process. Besides, the clear trends w.r.t. K and C provide a useful guidance for model selection, e.g., a wide range of K values (from 20 to 100 for this data) would provide good performance.

BEAR: Block Elimination Approach for Random Walk with Restart on Large Graphs

Kijung Shin
Seoul National University
koreaskj@snu.ac.kr

Jinhong Jung
KAIST
montecast@kaist.ac.kr

Lee Sael
The State University of New York (SUNY) Korea
sael@sunykorea.ac.kr

U Kang
KAIST
ukang@cs.kaist.ac.kr

ABSTRACT

Given a large graph, how can we calculate the relevance between nodes fast and accurately? Random walk with restart (RWR) provides a good measure for this purpose and has been applied to diverse data mining applications including ranking, community detection, link prediction, and anomaly detection. Since calculating RWR from scratch takes long, various preprocessing methods, most of which are related to inverting adjacency matrices, have been proposed to speed up the calculation. However, these methods do not scale to large graphs because they usually produce large and dense matrices which do not fit into memory.

In this paper, we propose BEAR, a fast, scalable, and accurate method for computing RWR on large graphs. BEAR comprises the preprocessing step and the query step. In the preprocessing step, BEAR reorders the adjacency matrix of a given graph so that it contains a large and easy-to-invert submatrix, and precomputes several matrices including the Schur complement of the submatrix. In the query step, BEAR computes the RWR scores for a given query node quickly using a block elimination approach with the matrices computed in the preprocessing step. Through extensive experiments, we show that BEAR significantly outperforms other state-of-the-art methods in terms of preprocessing and query speed, space efficiency, and accuracy.

Categories and Subject Descriptors

H.2.8 [**Database Management**]: Database Applications—*Data Mining*

General Terms

Design, Experimentation, Algorithms

Keywords

Proximity; relevance score; random walk with restart

SIGMOD'15, May 31–June 4, 2015, Melbourne, Victoria, Australia.

http://dx.doi.org/10.1145/2723372.2723716.

1. INTRODUCTION

Measuring the relevance (proximity) between nodes in a graph becomes the base for various data mining tasks [3, 6, 19, 21, 29, 39, 41, 40, 43, 46] and has received much interest from the database research community [5, 13, 16, 44]. Among many methods [1, 22, 31, 34] to compute the relevance, random walk with restart (RWR) [34] has been popular due to its ability to account for the global network structure [21] and the multi-faceted relationship between nodes [40]. RWR has been used in many data mining applications including ranking [42], community detection [3, 19, 43, 46], link prediction [6], and anomaly detection [39].

However, existing methods for computing RWR are unsatisfactory in terms of speed, accuracy, functionality, or scalability. The iterative method, which naturally follows from the definition of RWR is not fast: it requires repeated matrix-vector multiplications whose computational cost is not acceptable in real world applications where RWR scores for different query nodes need to be computed. Several approximate methods [3, 18, 39, 42] have also been proposed; however, their accuracies or speed-ups are unsatisfactory. Although top-k methods [16, 44] improve efficiency by focusing on finding the k most relevant nodes and ignoring irrelevant ones, finding top-k is insufficient for many data mining applications [3, 6, 18, 21, 39, 41, 43, 46] which require the relevance scores of all nodes or the least relevant nodes. Existing preprocessing methods [16, 17], which achieve better performance by preprocessing the given graph, are not scalable due to their high memory requirements.

In this paper, we propose BEAR, a fast, scalable, and accurate method for computing RWR on large graphs. BEAR comprises two steps: the preprocessing step and the query step. In the preprocessing step, BEAR reorders the adjacency matrix of a given graph so that it contains a large and easy-to-invert submatrix, and precomputes several matrices including the Schur complement [10] of the submatrix. In the query step, BEAR computes the RWR scores for a given query node quickly using a block elimination approach with the matrices computed in the preprocessing step. BEAR has two versions: an exact method BEAR-EXACT and an approximate method BEAR-APPROX. The former provides accuracy assurance; the latter gives faster query speed and requires less space by allowing small accuracy loss.

Through extensive experiments with various real-world datasets, we demonstrate the superiority of BEAR over

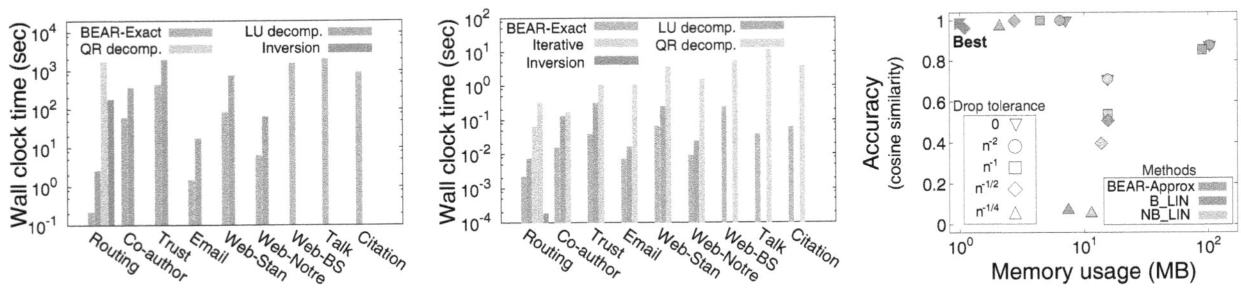

(a) Preprocessing time of exact methods

(b) Query time of exact methods

(c) Space for preprocessed data vs. Accuracy in approximate methods

Figure 1: Performance of BEAR. (a) and (b) compare exact methods, while (c) compares approximate methods. In (a) and (b), bars are omitted if and only if the corresponding experiments run out of memory. (a) In the preprocessing phase, BEAR-EXACT is the fastest and the most scalable among all preprocessing methods. (b) BEAR-EXACT is the fastest in the query phase except for the smallest Routing dataset. Due to its up to 300× faster query speed, BEAR-EXACT outperforms the iterative method, despite the preprocessing cost, when RWR scores for different query nodes are required. (c) BEAR-APPROX achieves both space efficiency and accuracy. Details of these experiments are explained in Section 4.

other state-of-the-art methods as seen in Figure 1. We also discuss how our method can be applied to other random-walk-based measures such as personalized PageRank [33], effective importance [9], and RWR with normalized graph Laplacian [42]. The main characteristics of our method are the followings:

- **Fast.** BEAR-EXACT is faster up to 8× in the query phase and up to 12× in the preprocessing phase than other exact methods (Figures 1(a) and 1(b)); BEAR-APPROX achieves a better time/accuracy trade-off in the query phase than other approximate methods (Figure 8(a)).
- **Space-efficient.** Compared with their respective competitors, BEAR-EXACT requires up to 22× less memory space (Figure 5), and BEAR-APPROX provides a better space/accuracy trade-off (Figure 1(c)).
- **Accurate.** BEAR-EXACT guarantees exactness (Theorem 1); BEAR-APPROX enjoys a better trade-off between accuracy, time, and space than other approximate methods (Figure 8).
- **Versatile.** BEAR can be applied to diverse RWR variants, including personalized PageRank, effective importance, and RWR with normalized graph Laplacian (Section 3.4).

The binary code of our method and several datasets are available at `http://kdmlab.org/bear`. The rest of the paper is organized as follows. Section 2 presents preliminaries on RWR. Our proposed BEAR is described in Section 3 followed by experimental results in Section 4. After providing a review on related work in Section 5, we make conclusion in Section 6.

2. PRELIMINARIES

In this section, we describe the preliminaries on random walk with restart and its algorithms. Table 1 lists the symbols used in this paper. We denote matrices by boldface capitals, e.g., $\mathbf{A}$, and vectors by boldface lowercases, e.g., $\mathbf{q}$.

2.1 Random Walk with Restart

Random walk with restart (RWR) [42] measures each node's relevance w.r.t. a given seed node s in a given graph. It assumes a random surfer who occasionally gets bored with following the edges in the graph and restarts at node s. The surfer starts at node s, and at each current node, either restarts at node s (with probability c) or moves to a neighboring node along an edge (with probability $1-c$). The probability that each edge is chosen is proportional to its weight in the adjacency matrix. $\tilde{\mathbf{A}}$ denotes the row-normalized adjacency matrix, whose (u, v)th entry is the probability that a surfer at node u chooses the edge to node v among all edges from node u. The stationary probability of being at each node corresponds to its RWR score w.r.t. node s, and is denoted by $\mathbf{r}$, whose uth entry corresponds to node u's RWR score. The vector $\mathbf{r}$ satisfies the following equation:

$$\mathbf{r} = (1-c)\tilde{\mathbf{A}}^{\mathbf{T}}\mathbf{r} + c\mathbf{q} \tag{1}$$

where $\mathbf{q}$ is the starting vector with the index of the seed node s is set to 1 and others to 0. It can be obtained by solving the following linear equation:

$$(\mathbf{I} - (1-c)\tilde{\mathbf{A}}^{\mathbf{T}})\mathbf{r} = c\mathbf{q}$$
$$\Leftrightarrow \mathbf{Hr} = c\mathbf{q}. \tag{2}$$

Table 1: Table of symbols.

Symbol	Definition
G	input graph
n	number of nodes in G
m	number of edges in G
n_1	number of spokes in G
n_2	number of hubs in G
n_{1i}	number of nodes in the ith diagonal block of $\mathbf{H_{11}}$
b	number of diagonal blocks in $\mathbf{H_{11}}$
s	seed node (=query node)
c	restart probability
ξ	drop tolerance
$\tilde{\mathbf{A}}$	$(n \times n)$ row-normalized adjacency matrix of G
$\mathbf{H}$	$(n \times n)$ $\mathbf{H} = \mathbf{I} - (1-c)\tilde{\mathbf{A}}^{\mathbf{T}}$
$\mathbf{H_{ij}}$	$(n_i \times n_j)$ (i, j)th partition of $\mathbf{H}$
$\mathbf{S}$	$(n_2 \times n_2)$ Schur complement of $\mathbf{H_{11}}$
$\mathbf{L_1}, \mathbf{U_1}$	$(n_1 \times n_1)$ LU-decomposed matrices of $\mathbf{H_{11}}$
$\mathbf{L_2}, \mathbf{U_2}$	$(n_2 \times n_2)$ LU-decomposed matrices of $\mathbf{S}$
$\mathbf{q}$	$(n \times 1)$ starting vector
$\mathbf{q_i}$	$(n_i \times 1)$ ith partition of $\mathbf{q}$
$\mathbf{r}$	$(n \times 1)$ relevance vector
$\mathbf{r_i}$	$(n_i \times 1)$ ith partition of $\mathbf{r}$
T	number of SlashBurn iterations
k	number of hubs removed at a time in SlashBurn
t	rank in B_LIN and NB_LIN
ϵ	threshold to stop iteration in iterative methods
ϵ_b	threshold to expand nodes in RPPR and BRPPR

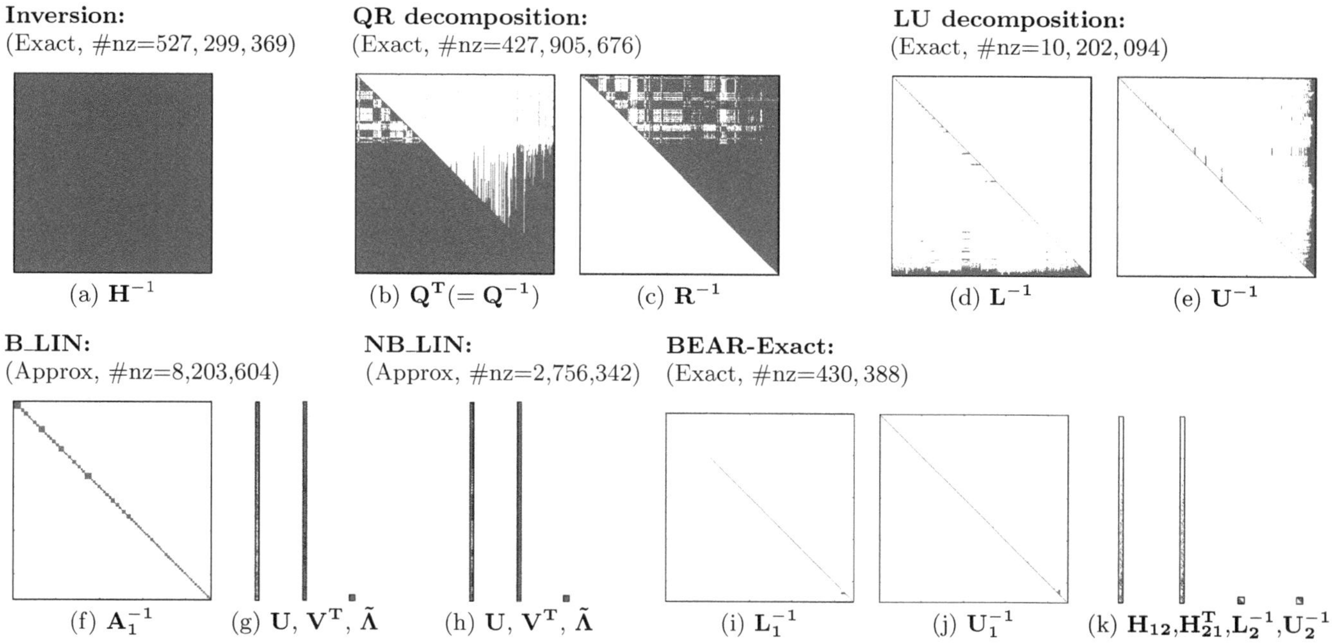

Figure 2: Sparsity patterns of the matrices resulted from different preprocessing methods on the Routing dataset (see Section 4.1 for the details of the dataset). Exact: exact method, Approx: approximate method, #nz: number of non-zero elements in the precomputed matrices. For B_LIN and NB_LIN, rank t is set to 500 and drop tolerance ξ is set to 0. Precomputed matrices are loaded into memory to speed up the query phase; for the reason, the number of non-zero entries in them determines the memory usage of each method and thus its scalability. Our exact method BEAR-EXACT produces the smallest number of non-zero entries than all other methods including the approximate methods (1200× than Inversion and 6× than the second best method). Our approximate method BEAR-APPROX further decreases the number of non-zero entries, depending on drop tolerance ξ.

Personalized PageRank. Personalized PageRank (PPR) [33] is an extension of RWR. PPR calculates the relevance of nodes according to the preference of each user, and is widely used for personalized search. A random surfer in PPR either jumps to a random node according to the probability distribution (user preference distribution) given by $\mathbf{q}$ (with probability c) or moves to a neighboring node (with probability $1-c$). PPR can be viewed as a generalized version of RWR with multiple seed nodes. Equations (1) and (2) can be directly applied to PPR with the modified $\mathbf{q}$.

2.2 Algorithms for RWR

We review two basic methods for RWR computation and four recent methods for addressing the limitations of the basic methods. We also point out a need for improvement which we will address in the following section. Since most applications require RWR scores for different seed nodes, whether at once or on demand, we separate the preprocessing phase, which occurs once, from the query phase, which occurs for each seed node.

Iterative method. The iterative method repeats updating $\mathbf{r}$ until convergence ($|\mathbf{r}^{(i)} - \mathbf{r}^{(i-1)}| < \epsilon$) by the following update rule:

$$\mathbf{r}^{(i)} \leftarrow (1-c)\tilde{\mathbf{A}}^{\mathbf{T}}\mathbf{r}^{(i-1)} + c\mathbf{q} \qquad (3)$$

where the superscript i denotes the iteration number. If $0 < c < 1$, $\mathbf{r}^{(i)}$ is guaranteed to converge to a unique solution [27]. This method does not require preprocessing (one-time cost) but has expensive query cost which incurs a repeated matrix-vector multiplication. Thus, it is inefficient when RWR scores for many query nodes are required.

RPPR / BRPPR. Gleich et al. [18] propose restricted personalized PageRank (RPPR), which speeds up the iterative method by accessing only a part of a graph. This algorithm uses Equation 3 only for a subgraph and the nodes contained in it. The subgraph is initialized to a given seed node and grows as iteration proceeds. A node contained in the subgraph is on the boundary if its outgoing edges (in the original graph) are not contained in the subgraph, and the outgoing edges and outgoing neighbors of the node are added to the subgraph if the RWR score of the node (in the current iteration) is greater than a threshold ϵ_b. The algorithm repeats iterations until RWR scores converge. The RWR scores of nodes outside the subgraph are set to zero. Boundary-restricted personalized PageRank (BRPPR) [18] is a variant of the RPPR. It expands nodes on the boundary in decreasing order of their RWR scores (in the current iteration) until the sum of the RWR scores of nodes on the boundary becomes less than a threshold ϵ_b. Although these methods reduce the query cost of the iterative method significantly, they do not guarantee exactness.

Inversion. An algebraic method directly calculates $\mathbf{r}$ from Equation (2) as follows:

$$\mathbf{r} = c(\mathbf{I} - (1-c)\tilde{\mathbf{A}}^{\mathbf{T}})^{-1}\mathbf{q} = c\mathbf{H}^{-1}\mathbf{q}. \qquad (4)$$

The matrix $\mathbf{H}$ is known to be invertible when $0 < c < 1$ [27]. Once $\mathbf{H}^{-1}$ is computed in the preprocessing phase, $\mathbf{r}$ can be obtained efficiently in the query phase. However, this is again impractical for large graphs because calculating $\mathbf{H}^{-1}$ is computationally expensive and $\mathbf{H}^{-1}$ is usually too dense to fit into memory as seen in Figure 2(a).

QR decomposition. To avoid the problem regarding $\mathbf{H}^{-1}$, Fujiwara et al. [17] decompose $\mathbf{H}$ using QR decomposition, and then use $\mathbf{Q}^{\mathbf{T}}(=\mathbf{Q}^{-1})$ and $\mathbf{R}^{-1}$ instead of $\mathbf{H}^{-1}$ as follows:

$$\mathbf{r} = c\mathbf{H}^{-1}\mathbf{q} = c\mathbf{R}^{-1}(\mathbf{Q}^{\mathbf{T}}\mathbf{q})$$

where $\mathbf{H} = \mathbf{QR}$. They also propose a reordering rule for $\mathbf{H}$ which makes $\mathbf{Q^T}$ and $\mathbf{R}^{-1}$ sparser. However, on the most datasets used in our experiments, QR decomposition results in dense matrices as shown in Figures 2(b) and 2(c); thus, its scalability is limited. This fact agrees with the claim made by Boyd et al. [10] that it is difficult to exploit sparsity in QR decomposition.

LU decomposition. To replace $\mathbf{H}^{-1}$, Fujiwara et al. [16] also exploit LU decomposition using the following rule:

$$\mathbf{r} = c\mathbf{H}^{-1}\mathbf{q} = c\mathbf{U}^{-1}(\mathbf{L}^{-1}\mathbf{q})$$

where $\mathbf{H} = \mathbf{LU}$. Prior to the decomposition, $\mathbf{H}$ is reordered based on nodes' degrees and community structure. This makes matrices $\mathbf{L}^{-1}$ and $\mathbf{U}^{-1}$ sparser as seen in Figures 2(d) and 2(e). We incorporate their idea into our method to replace inverse terms, which will be explained in detail in Section 3.

B_LIN / NB_LIN. Tong et al. [42] partition a given graph and divide $\tilde{\mathbf{A}}^\mathbf{T}$ into $\mathbf{A_1}$ (inner-partition edges) and $\mathbf{A_2}$ (cross-partition edges). Then, they use a heuristic decomposition method with given rank t to approximate $\mathbf{A_2}$ with low-rank matrix $\mathbf{U\Sigma V}$ where $\mathbf{U}$, $\mathbf{\Sigma}$, and $\mathbf{V}$ are $n \times t$, $t \times t$, and $t \times n$ matrices, respectively. In the query phase, they apply Sherman-Morrison lemma [35] to efficiently calculate $\mathbf{r}$ as follows:

$$\begin{aligned}\mathbf{r} &= c(\mathbf{I} - (1-c)\tilde{\mathbf{A}}^\mathbf{T})^{-1}\mathbf{q} \\ &\approx c(\mathbf{I} - (1-c)\mathbf{A_1} - (1-c)\mathbf{U\Sigma V})^{-1}\mathbf{q} \\ &= c(\mathbf{A_1}^{-1}\mathbf{q} + (1-c)\mathbf{A_1}^{-1}\mathbf{U}\tilde{\mathbf{\Lambda}}\mathbf{V}\mathbf{A_1}^{-1}\mathbf{q})\end{aligned}$$

where $\tilde{\mathbf{\Lambda}} = (\mathbf{\Sigma}^{-1} - c\mathbf{V}\mathbf{A_1}^{-1}\mathbf{U})^{-1}$. To sparsify the precomputed matrices, near-zero entries whose absolute value is smaller than ξ are dropped. This method is called B_LIN, and its variant NB_LIN directly approximates $\tilde{\mathbf{A}}^\mathbf{T}$ without partitioning it. Both methods do not guarantee exactness.

As summarized in Figure 2, previous preprocessing methods require too much space for preprocessed data or do not guarantee accuracy. Our proposed BEAR, explained in the following section, achieves both space efficiency and accuracy as seen in Figures 2(i) through 2(k).

3. PROPOSED METHOD

In this section, we describe BEAR, our proposed method for fast, scalable, and accurate RWR computation. BEAR has two versions: BEAR-EXACT for exact RWR, and BEAR-APPROX for approximate RWR. BEAR-EXACT guarantees accuracy, while BEAR-APPROX improves speed and space efficiency by sacrificing little accuracy. A pictorial description of BEAR is provided in Figure 3. BEAR exploits the following ideas:

- The adjacency matrix of real-world graphs can be reordered so that it has a large but easy-to-invert submatrix, such as a block-diagonal matrix as shown in the upper left part of Figure 4(b).
- A linear equation like Equation (2) is easily solved by block elimination using Schur complement if the matrix contains a large and easy-to-invert submatrix such as a block-diagonal one.
- Compared with directly inverting an adjacency matrix, inverting its LU-decomposed matrices is more efficient in terms of time and space.

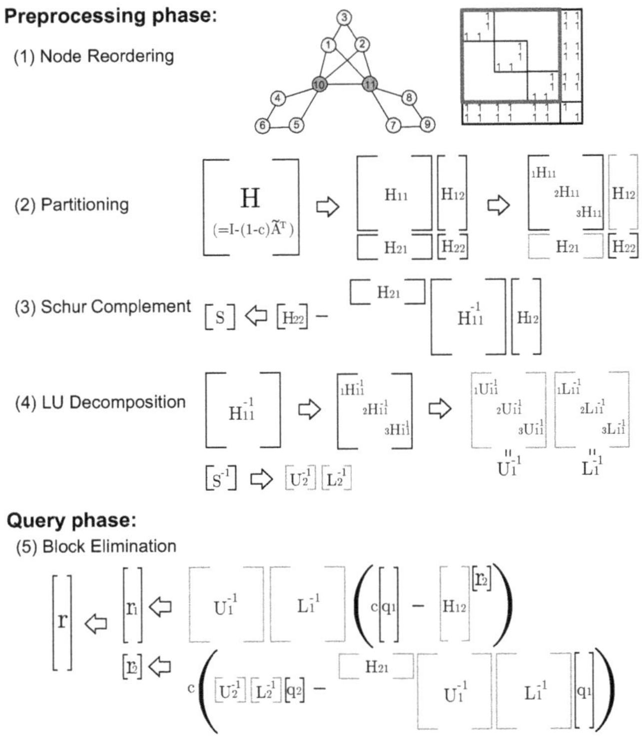

Figure 3: A pictorial description of BEAR. The output matrices of the preprocessing phase are red-bordered. (1) Reorder nodes so that the adjacency matrix has a large block-diagonal submatrix (the blue-bordered one). (2) Partition $\mathbf{H}$ into four blocks so that $\mathbf{H_{11}}$ corresponds to the submatrix. (3) Compute the Schur complement $\mathbf{S}$ of $\mathbf{H_{11}}$. (4) Since $\mathbf{S}^{-1}$ and the diagonal blocks of $\mathbf{H_{11}^{-1}}$ are likely to be dense, store the inverse of the LU decomposed matrices of $\mathbf{S}$ and $\mathbf{H_{11}}$ instead to save space. Notice that these can be computed efficiently in terms of time and space because $\mathbf{S}$ and the diagonal blocks of $\mathbf{H_{11}}$ are relatively small compared with $\mathbf{H}$. (5) Compute the RWR score vector $\mathbf{r}$ for a query vector $\mathbf{q}$ (the concatenation of $\mathbf{q_1}$ and $\mathbf{q_2}$) fast by utilizing the precomputed matrices.

Algorithms 1 and 2 represent the procedure of BEAR. Since RWR scores are requested for different seed nodes in real world applications, we separate the preprocessing phase (Algorithm 1), which is run once, from the query phase (Algorithm 2), which is run for each seed node. The exact method BEAR-EXACT and the approximate method BEAR-APPROX differ only at line 9 of Algorithm 1; the detail is in Section 3.1.4. To exploit their sparsity, all matrices considered are saved in a sparse matrix format, such as the compressed sparse column format [36], which stores only non-zero entries.

3.1 Preprocessing Phase

The overall preprocessing phase of BEAR is shown in Algorithm 1 and the details in the following subsections.

3.1.1 Node Reordering (lines 2 through 4)

In this part, we reorder $\mathbf{H}(= \mathbf{I} - (1-c)\tilde{\mathbf{A}}^\mathbf{T})$ and partition it. Our objective is to reorder $\mathbf{H}$ so that it has a large but easy-to-invert submatrix such as a block-diagonal one. Any node reordering method (e.g., spectral clustering [32], cross association [11], shingle [14], etc.) can be used for this purpose; in this paper, we use a method which improves on SlashBurn [23] since it is the state-of-the-art method in concentrating the nonzeros of adjacency matrices

Algorithm 1: Preprocessing phase in BEAR

Input: graph: G, restart probability: c, drop tolerance: ξ
Output: precomputed matrices: $\mathbf{L_1^{-1}}$, $\mathbf{U_1^{-1}}$, $\mathbf{L_2^{-1}}$, $\mathbf{U_2^{-1}}$, $\mathbf{H_{12}}$, and $\mathbf{H_{21}}$

1: compute $\tilde{\mathbf{A}}$, and $\mathbf{H} = \mathbf{I} - (1-c)\tilde{\mathbf{A}}^{\mathbf{T}}$
2: find hubs using SlashBurn [23], and divide spokes into disconnected components by removing the hubs
3: reorder nodes and $\mathbf{H}$ so that the disconnected components form a block-diagonal submatrix $\mathbf{H_{11}}$ where each block is ordered in the ascending order of degrees within the component
4: partition $\mathbf{H}$ into $\mathbf{H_{11}}, \mathbf{H_{12}}, \mathbf{H_{21}}, \mathbf{H_{22}}$
5: decompose $\mathbf{H_{11}}$ into $\mathbf{L_1}$ and $\mathbf{U_1}$ using LU decomposition and compute $\mathbf{L_1^{-1}}$ and $\mathbf{U_1^{-1}}$
6: compute the Schur complement of $\mathbf{H_{11}}$, $\mathbf{S} = \mathbf{H_{22}} - \mathbf{H_{21}}(\mathbf{U_1^{-1}}(\mathbf{L_1^{-1}}(\mathbf{H_{12}})))$
7: reorder the hubs in the ascending order of their degrees in $\mathbf{S}$ and reorder $\mathbf{S}$, $\mathbf{H_{21}}$ and $\mathbf{H_{12}}$ according to it
8: decompose $\mathbf{S}$ into $\mathbf{L_2}$ and $\mathbf{U_2}$ using LU decomposition and compute $\mathbf{L_2^{-1}}$ and $\mathbf{U_2^{-1}}$
9: (BEAR-APPROX only) drop entries whose absolute value is smaller than ξ in $\mathbf{L_1^{-1}}$, $\mathbf{U_1^{-1}}$, $\mathbf{L_2^{-1}}$, $\mathbf{U_2^{-1}}$, $\mathbf{H_{12}}$, and $\mathbf{H_{21}}$
10: **return** $\mathbf{L_1^{-1}}$, $\mathbf{U_1^{-1}}$, $\mathbf{L_2^{-1}}$, $\mathbf{U_2^{-1}}$, $\mathbf{H_{12}}$, and $\mathbf{H_{21}}$

Algorithm 2: Query phase in BEAR

Input: seed node: s, precomputed matrices: $\mathbf{L_1^{-1}}$, $\mathbf{U_1^{-1}}$, $\mathbf{L_2^{-1}}$, $\mathbf{U_2^{-1}}$, $\mathbf{H_{12}}$, and $\mathbf{H_{21}}$
Output: relevance scores: $\mathbf{r}$

1: create $\mathbf{q}$ whose sth entry is 1 and the others are 0
2: partition $\mathbf{q}$ into $\mathbf{q_1}$ and $\mathbf{q_2}$
3: compute $\mathbf{r_2} = c(\mathbf{U_2^{-1}}(\mathbf{L_2^{-1}}(\mathbf{q_2} - \mathbf{H_{21}}(\mathbf{U_1^{-1}}(\mathbf{L_1^{-1}}\mathbf{q_1})))))$
4: compute $\mathbf{r_1} = \mathbf{U_1^{-1}}(\mathbf{L_1^{-1}}(c\mathbf{q_1} - \mathbf{H_{12}}\mathbf{r_2}))$
5: create $\mathbf{r}$ by concatenating $\mathbf{r_1}$ and $\mathbf{r_2}$
6: **return** $\mathbf{r}$

of graphs (more details in Appendix A). We first run SlashBurn on a given graph, to decompose the graph into hubs (high-degree nodes), and spokes (low-degree nodes which get disconnected from the giant connected component if the hubs are removed). Within each connected component containing spokes, we reorder nodes in the ascending order of degrees within the component. As a result, we get an adjacency matrix whose upper-left area (e.g., $\mathbf{H_{11}}$ in Figure 4(a)) is a large and sparse block diagonal matrix which is easily inverted, while the lower-right area (e.g., $\mathbf{H_{22}}$ in Figure 4(a)) is a small but dense matrix. Let n_1 denote the number of spokes and n_2 denote the number of hubs. After the reordering, we partition the matrix $\mathbf{H}$ into four pieces: $\mathbf{H_{11}}$ ($n_1 \times n_1$ matrix), $\mathbf{H_{12}}$ ($n_1 \times n_2$ matrix), $\mathbf{H_{21}}$ ($n_2 \times n_1$ matrix), and $\mathbf{H_{22}}$ ($n_2 \times n_2$ matrix), which correspond to the adjacency matrix representation of edges between spokes, from spokes to hubs, from hubs to spokes, and between hubs, respectively.

3.1.2 Schur Complement (lines 5 through 6)

In this part, we compute the Schur complement of $\mathbf{H_{11}}$, whose inverse is required in the query phase.

DEFINITION 1 (SCHUR COMPLEMENT [10]). *Suppose a square matrix $\mathbf{A}$ is partitioned into $\mathbf{A_{11}}$, $\mathbf{A_{12}}$, $\mathbf{A_{21}}$, and $\mathbf{A_{22}}$, which are $p \times p$, $p \times q$, $q \times p$, and $q \times q$ matrices, resp., and $\mathbf{A_{11}}$ is invertible. The Schur complement $\mathbf{S}$ of the block $\mathbf{A_{11}}$ of the matrix $\mathbf{A}$ is defined by*

$$\mathbf{S} = \mathbf{A_{22}} - \mathbf{A_{21}}\mathbf{A_{11}^{-1}}\mathbf{A_{12}}.$$

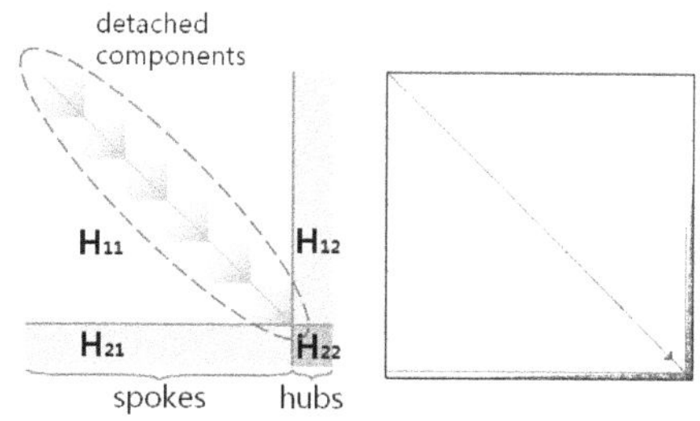

(a) Node reordering method (b) Result on the Routing datset

Figure 4: The node reordering method of BEAR and its result on the Routing dataset. BEAR reorders nodes so that edges between spokes form a large but sparse block-diagonal submatrix ($\mathbf{H_{11}}$). Diagonal blocks correspond to the connected components detached from the giant connected component when hubs are removed. Nodes in each block are sorted in the ascending order of their degrees within the component.

According to the definition, computing the Schur complement $\mathbf{S}$ ($n_2 \times n_2$ matrix) of $\mathbf{H_{11}}$ requires $\mathbf{H_{11}^{-1}}$. Instead of directly inverting $\mathbf{H_{11}}$, we LU decompose it into $\mathbf{L_1}$ and $\mathbf{U_1}$, then compute $\mathbf{L_1^{-1}}$ and $\mathbf{U_1^{-1}}$ instead (the reason will be explained in Section 3.1.3). Consequently, $\mathbf{S}$ is computed by the following rule:

$$\mathbf{S} = \mathbf{H_{22}} - \mathbf{H_{21}}(\mathbf{U_1^{-1}}(\mathbf{L_1^{-1}}\mathbf{H_{12}})). \quad (5)$$

3.1.3 LU Decomposition (lines 7 through 8)

The block elimination method, which will be explained in Section 3.2, requires $\mathbf{H_{11}^{-1}}$ and $\mathbf{S^{-1}}$ to solve Equation (2). Directly inverting $\mathbf{H_{11}}$ and $\mathbf{S}$, however, is inefficient since $\mathbf{S^{-1}}$ as well as each diagonal block of $\mathbf{H_{11}^{-1}}$ is likely to be dense. We avoid this problem by replacing $\mathbf{H_{11}^{-1}}$ with $\mathbf{U_1^{-1}}\mathbf{L_1^{-1}}$ as in Equation (5) and replacing $\mathbf{S^{-1}}$ with $\mathbf{U_2^{-1}}\mathbf{L_2^{-1}}$ where $\mathbf{L_2}$ and $\mathbf{U_2}$ denote the LU-decomposed matrices of $\mathbf{S}$. To compute $\mathbf{L_1^{-1}}$, $\mathbf{U_1^{-1}}$, $\mathbf{L_2^{-1}}$, and $\mathbf{U_2^{-1}}$ efficiently and make them sparser, we exploit the following observation [16] and lemma.

OBSERVATION 1. *Reordering nodes in the ascending order of their degrees speeds up the LU decomposition of an adjacency matrix and makes the inverse of the LU-decomposed matrices sparser.*

LEMMA 1. *Suppose $\mathbf{A}$ is a non-singular block-diagonal matrix that consists of diagonal blocks, $\mathbf{A_1}$ through $\mathbf{A_b}$. Let $\mathbf{L}$ and $\mathbf{U}$ denote the LU-decomposed matrices of $\mathbf{A}$, and let $\mathbf{L_i}$ and $\mathbf{U_i}$ denote those of $\mathbf{A_i}$ for all i ($1 \le i \le b$). Then, $\mathbf{L^{-1}}$ and $\mathbf{U^{-1}}$ are the block-diagonal matrices that consist of $\mathbf{L_1^{-1}}$ through $\mathbf{L_b^{-1}}$ and $\mathbf{U_1^{-1}}$ through $\mathbf{U_b^{-1}}$, respectively.*

PROOF. See Appendix B. □

These observation and lemma suggest for $\mathbf{H_{11}^{-1}}$ the reordering method we already used in Section 3.1.1. Since we computed $\mathbf{L_1^{-1}}$ and $\mathbf{U_1^{-1}}$ in Section 3.1.2, we only need to process $\mathbf{S}$. We first rearrange the hubs in the ascending order of their degrees within $\mathbf{S}$, which reorders $\mathbf{H_{12}}$, $\mathbf{H_{21}}$, and $\mathbf{H_{22}}$ as well as $\mathbf{S}$. Note that computing $\mathbf{S}$ after reordering the hubs, and reordering the hubs after computing $\mathbf{S}$ produce the same result. After decomposing $\mathbf{S}$ into $\mathbf{L_2}$ and $\mathbf{U_2}$, we compute $\mathbf{L_2^{-1}}$ and $\mathbf{U_2^{-1}}$.

3.1.4 Dropping Near-zero Entries (line 9, BEAR-Approx only)

The running time and the memory usage in the query phase of our method largely depend on the number of non-zero entries in $\mathbf{L_1^{-1}}$, $\mathbf{U_1^{-1}}$, $\mathbf{L_2^{-1}}$, $\mathbf{U_2^{-1}}$, $\mathbf{H_{12}}$, and $\mathbf{H_{21}}$. Thus, dropping near-zero entries in them saves time and memory space in the query phase although it sacrifices little accuracy of $\mathbf{r}$. BEAR-Approx drops entries whose absolute value is smaller than the drop tolerance ξ. The effects of different ξ values on accuracy, query time, and memory usage are empirically analyzed in Section 4. Note that, contrary to BEAR-Approx, BEAR-Exact guarantees the exactness of $\mathbf{r}$, which will be proved in Section 3.2, and still outperforms other exact methods in terms of time and space, which will be shown in Section 4.

3.2 Query Phase

In the query phase, BEAR computes the RWR score vector $\mathbf{r}$ w.r.t. a given seed node s by exploiting the results of the preprocessing phase. Algorithm 2 describes the overall procedure of the query phase.

The vector $\mathbf{q} = \begin{bmatrix}\mathbf{q_1}\\ \mathbf{q_2}\end{bmatrix}$ denotes the length-n starting vector whose entry at the index of the seed node s is 1 and otherwise 0. It is partitioned into the length-n_1 vector $\mathbf{q_1}$ and the length-n_2 vector $\mathbf{q_2}$. The exact RWR score vector $\mathbf{r}$ is computed by the following equation:

$$\mathbf{r} = \begin{bmatrix}\mathbf{r_1}\\ \mathbf{r_2}\end{bmatrix} = \begin{bmatrix}\mathbf{U_1^{-1}}(\mathbf{L_1^{-1}}(c\mathbf{q_1} - \mathbf{H_{12}}\mathbf{r_2}))\\ c(\mathbf{U_2^{-1}}(\mathbf{L_2^{-1}}(\mathbf{q_2} - \mathbf{H_{21}}(\mathbf{U_1^{-1}}(\mathbf{L_1^{-1}}\mathbf{q_1})))))\end{bmatrix}. \tag{6}$$

To prove the correctness of the above equation, we use the block elimination method.

Lemma 2 (Block elimination [10]). *Suppose a linear equation $\mathbf{Ax} = \mathbf{b}$ is partitioned as*

$$\begin{bmatrix}\mathbf{A_{11}} & \mathbf{A_{12}}\\ \mathbf{A_{21}} & \mathbf{A_{22}}\end{bmatrix}\begin{bmatrix}\mathbf{x_1}\\ \mathbf{x_2}\end{bmatrix} = \begin{bmatrix}\mathbf{b_1}\\ \mathbf{b_2}\end{bmatrix}$$

where $\mathbf{A_{11}}$ and $\mathbf{A_{22}}$ are square matrices. If the submatrix $\mathbf{A_{11}}$ is invertible, and $\mathbf{S}$ is the Schur complement of the submatrix $\mathbf{A_{11}}$ in $\mathbf{A}$,

$$\mathbf{x} = \begin{bmatrix}\mathbf{x_1}\\ \mathbf{x_2}\end{bmatrix} = \begin{bmatrix}\mathbf{A_{11}^{-1}}(\mathbf{b_1} - \mathbf{A_{12}}\mathbf{x_2})\\ \mathbf{S^{-1}}(\mathbf{b_2} - \mathbf{A_{21}}\mathbf{A_{11}^{-1}}\mathbf{b_1})\end{bmatrix}. \tag{7}$$

Theorem 1 (The correctness of BEAR-Exact). *The $\mathbf{r}$ in Equation (6) is equal to the $\mathbf{r}$ in Equation (2).*

Proof. *$\mathbf{H_{11}}$ is invertible because its transpose is a strictly diagonally dominant matrix for $0 < c < 1$ [8]. Thus, by Lemma 2, the following holds for Equation (2):*

$$\mathbf{r} = \begin{bmatrix}\mathbf{r_1}\\ \mathbf{r_2}\end{bmatrix} = \begin{bmatrix}\mathbf{H_{11}^{-1}}(c\mathbf{q_1} - \mathbf{H_{12}}\mathbf{r_2})\\ \mathbf{S^{-1}}(c\mathbf{q_2} - \mathbf{H_{21}}\mathbf{H_{11}^{-1}}(c\mathbf{q_1}))\end{bmatrix}.$$

Equation (6) only replaces $\mathbf{H_{11}^{-1}}$ with $\mathbf{U_1^{-1}}\mathbf{L_1^{-1}}$ and $\mathbf{S^{-1}}$ with $\mathbf{U_2^{-1}}\mathbf{L_2^{-1}}$ where $\mathbf{H_{11}} = \mathbf{L_1}\mathbf{U_1}$ and $\mathbf{S} = \mathbf{L_2}\mathbf{U_2}$. □

3.3 Complexity Analysis

In this section, we analyze the time and space complexity of BEAR. We assume that all the matrices considered are saved in a sparse format, such as the compressed sparse column format [36], which stores only non-zero entries, and that all the matrix operations exploit such sparsity by only considering non-zero entries. We also assume that the number of edges is greater than that of nodes (i.e., $m > n$) for simplicity. The maximum number of non-zero entries in each precomputed matrix is summarized in Table 2 where b denotes the number of diagonal blocks in $\mathbf{H_{11}}$, and n_{1i} denotes the number of nodes in the ith diagonal block. The maximum numbers of non-zero entries in $\mathbf{L_1^{-1}}$ and $\mathbf{U_1^{-1}}$ depend on the size of diagonal blocks because the LU-decomposed matrices and inverse of a block-diagonal matrix are also block-diagonal matrices with the same block sizes (see Lemma 1).

Table 2: Maximum number of non-zero entries in the precomputed matrices.

Matrix	Max nonzeros
$\mathbf{H_{12}}$ & $\mathbf{H_{21}}$	$O(\min(n_1 n_2, m))$
$\mathbf{L_1^{-1}}$ & $\mathbf{U_1^{-1}}$	$O(\sum_{i=1}^{b} n_{1i}^2)$
$\mathbf{L_2^{-1}}$ & $\mathbf{U_2^{-1}}$	$O(n_2^2)$

3.3.1 Time Complexity

The time complexity of each step of BEAR is summarized in Table 3. In this section, we provide proofs for nontrivial analysis results starting from the following lemma:

Lemma 3 (Sparse matrix multiplication). *Suppose $\mathbf{A}$ and $\mathbf{B}$ are $p \times q$ and $q \times r$ matrices, respectively, and $\mathbf{A}$ has $|\mathbf{A}|$ ($> p, q$) non-zero entries. Calculating $\mathbf{C} = \mathbf{AB}$ using sparse matrix multiplication takes $O(|\mathbf{A}|r)$.*

Proof. *Each non-zero entries in $\mathbf{A}$ is multiplied and then added up to r times.* □

Lemma 4. *It takes $O(\sum_{i=1}^{b} n_{1i}^3)$ to compute $\mathbf{L_1^{-1}}$ and $\mathbf{U_1^{-1}}$.*

Proof. *By Lemma 1, each block of $\mathbf{H_{11}}$ is processed separately. Since the LU decomposition of $p \times p$ matrix takes $O(p^3)$ [10], it takes $O(\sum_{i=1}^{b} n_{1i}^3)$ to LU decompose the diagonal blocks of $\mathbf{H_{11}}$. Since the inversion of $p \times p$ matrix takes $O(p^3)$ [10], it takes $O(\sum_{i=1}^{b} n_{1i}^3)$ to invert the decomposed blocks.* □

Lemma 5. *It takes $O(n_2 \sum_{i=1}^{b} n_{1i}^2 + \min(n_1 n_2^2, n_2 m))$ to compute $\mathbf{S} = \mathbf{H_{22}} - \mathbf{H_{21}}(\mathbf{U_1^{-1}}(\mathbf{L_1^{-1}}\mathbf{H_{12}}))$.*

Proof. *By Lemma 3 and Table 2, it takes $O(n_2 \sum_{i=1}^{b} n_{1i}^2)$ to compute $\mathbf{R_1} = \mathbf{L_1^{-1}}\mathbf{H_{12}}$, $O(n_2 \sum_{i=1}^{b} n_{1i}^2)$ to compute $\mathbf{R_2} = \mathbf{U_1^{-1}}\mathbf{R_1}$, $O(\min(n_1 n_2^2, n_2 m))$ to compute $\mathbf{R_3} = \mathbf{H_{21}}\mathbf{R_2}$, and $O(n_2^2)$ to compute $\mathbf{S} = \mathbf{H_{22}} - \mathbf{R_3}$.* □

Theorem 2. *Preprocessing phase in BEAR takes $O(T(m + n\log n) + \sum_{i=1}^{b} n_{1i}^3 + n_2 \sum_{i=1}^{b} n_{1i}^2 + n_2^3 + \min(n_2^2 n_1, n_2 m))$*

Proof. *See Lemma 4, Lemma 5, and Table 3.* □

Theorem 3. *Query phase in BEAR takes $O(\sum_{i=1}^{b} n_{1i}^2 + n_2^2 + \min(n_1 n_2, m))$*

Proof. *Apply Lemma 3 and the results in Table 2 to each steps in $\mathbf{r_2} = c(\mathbf{U_2^{-1}}(\mathbf{L_2^{-1}}(\mathbf{q_2} - \mathbf{H_{21}}(\mathbf{U_1^{-1}}(\mathbf{L_1^{-1}}\mathbf{q_1})))))$ and $\mathbf{r_1} = \mathbf{U_1^{-1}}(\mathbf{L_1^{-1}}(c\mathbf{q_1} - \mathbf{H_{12}}\mathbf{r_2}))$ as in Lemma 5.* □

In real-world graphs, $\sum_{i=1}^{b} n_{1i}^2$ in the above results can be replaced by m since the number of non-zero entries in $\mathbf{L_1^{-1}}$ and $\mathbf{U_1^{-1}}$ is closer to $O(m)$ than $O(\sum_{i=1}^{b} n_{1i}^2)$ as seen in Table 4.

Table 3: Time complexity of each step of BEAR.

Line	Task	Time complexity
		Preprocessing phase (Algorithm 1)
2	run SlashBurn	$O(T(m + n \log n))$ [23]
3	reorder $\mathbf{H}$	$O(m + n + \sum_{i=1}^{b} n_{1i} \log n_{1i})$
5	compute $\mathbf{L_1^{-1}}$ and $\mathbf{U_1^{-1}}$	$O(\sum_{i=1}^{b} n_{1i}^3)$
6	compute $\mathbf{S}$	$O(n_2 \sum_{i=1}^{b} n_{1i}^2 + \min(n_1 n_2^2, n_2 m))$
8	compute $\mathbf{L_2^{-1}}$ and $\mathbf{U_2^{-1}}$	$O(n_2^3)$
9	drop near-zero entries	$O(\sum_{i=1}^{b} n_{1i}^2 + n_2^2 + min(n_1 n_2, m))$
Total		$O(T(m + n \log n) + \sum_{i=1}^{b} n_{1i}^3 + n_2 \sum_{i=1}^{b} n_{1i}^2 + n_2^3 + \min(n_2^2 n_1, n_2 m))$
		Query phase (Algorithm 2)
3	compute $\mathbf{r_2}$	$O(\sum_{i=1}^{b} n_{1i}^2 + n_2^2 + \min(n_1 n_2, m))$
4	compute $\mathbf{r_1}$	$O(\sum_{i=1}^{b} n_{1i}^2 + \min(n_1 n_2, m))$
Total		$O(\sum_{i=1}^{b} n_{1i}^2 + n_2^2 + \min(n_1 n_2, m))$

3.3.2 *Space Complexity*

THEOREM 4. BEAR *requires* $O(\sum_{i=1}^{b} n_{1i}^2 + \min(n_1 n_2, m) + n_2^2)$ *memory space for precomputed matrices:* $\mathbf{H_{12}}$, $\mathbf{H_{21}}$, $\mathbf{L_1^{-1}}$, $\mathbf{U_1^{-1}}$, $\mathbf{L_2^{-1}}$, *and* $\mathbf{U_2^{-1}}$.

PROOF. *See Table 2.* □

For the same reason, as in the time complexity, $\sum_{i=1}^{b} n_{1i}^2$ in the above result can be replaced by m in real-world graphs.

Theorems 2, 3, and 4 imply that BEAR works efficiently when the given graph is divided into small pieces (small $\sum_{i=1}^{b} n_{1i}^2$ and $\sum_{i=1}^{b} n_{1i}^3$) by removing a small number of hubs (small n_2), which is true in many real world graphs [2, 23].

3.4 Application to RWR Variants

Our BEAR method is easily applicable to various RWR variants since BEAR does not assume any unique property of RWR contrary to other methods [16, 44]. In this section, we show how BEAR can be applied to three of such variants.

Personalized PageRank. As explained in Section 2.1, personalized PageRank (PPR) selects a restart node according to given probability distribution. PPR can be computed by replacing $\mathbf{q}$ in Algorithm 2 with the probability distribution.

Effective importance. Effective importance (EI) [9] is the degree-normalized version of RWR. It captures the local community structure and adjusts RWR's preference towards high-degree nodes. We can compute EI by dividing each entry of $\mathbf{r}$ in Algorithm 2 by the degree of the corresponding node.

RWR with normalized graph Laplacian. Instead of row-normalized adjacency matrix, Tong et al. [42] use the normalized graph Laplacian. It outputs symmetric relevance scores for undirected graphs, which are desirable for some applications. This score can be computed by replacing $\tilde{\mathbf{A}}$ in Algorithm 1 with $\mathbf{D^{-1/2}AD^{-1/2}}$ where $\mathbf{A}$ is an unnormalized adjacency matrix and $\mathbf{D}$ is a diagonal matrix whose (i, i)th entry is the degree of ith node.

4. EXPERIMENTS

To evaluate the effectiveness of our exact method BEAR-EXACT, we design and conduct experiments which answer the following questions:

- **Q1. Preprocessing cost (Section 4.2).** How much memory space do BEAR-EXACT and its competitors require for their precomputed results? How long does this preprocessing phase take?
- **Q2. Query cost (Section 4.3).** How quickly does BEAR-EXACT answer an RWR query compared with other methods?
- **Q3. Effects of network structure (Section 4.4).** How does network structure affect the preprocessing time, query time, and space requirements of BEAR-EXACT?

For our approximate method BEAR-APPROX, our experiments answer the following questions:

- **Q4. Effects of drop tolerance (Section 4.5).** How does drop tolerance ξ affect the accuracy, query time, and space requirements of BEAR-APPROX?
- **Q5. Comparison with approximate methods (Section 4.6).** Does BEAR-APPROX provide a better trade-off between accuracy, time, and space compared with its competitors?

4.1 Experimental Settings

Machine. All the experiments are conducted on a PC with a 4-core Intel i5-4570 3.2GHz CPU and 16GB memory.

Data. The graph data used in our experiments are summarized in Table 4. A brief description of each real-world dataset is presented in Appendix C. For synthetic graphs, we use R-MAT [12] with different p_{ul}, the probability of an edge falling into the upper-left partition. The probabilities for the other partitions are set to $(1 - p_{ul})/3$, respectively.

Implementation. We compare our methods with the iterative method, RPPR [18], BRPPR [18], inversion, LU decomposition [16], QR decomposition [17], B_LIN [42], and NB_LIN [42], all of which are explained in Section 2.2. Methods only applicable to undirected graphs [3] or top-k search [20, 44] are excluded. All the methods including BEAR-EXACT and BEAR-APPROX are implemented using MATLAB, which provides a state-of-the-art linear algebra package. In particular, our implementation of NB_LIN and that of RPPR optimize their open-sourced implementations[1,2] in terms of preprocessing speed and query speed, respectively. The binary code of our method and several datasets are available at `http://kdmlab.org/bear`.

[1]http://www.cs.cmu.edu/~htong/pdfs/FastRWR_20080319.tgz
[2]http://www.mathworks.co.kr/matlabcentral/fileexchange/11613-pagerank

Table 4: Summary of real-world and synthetic datasets. |**M**| denotes the number of non-zero entries in the matrix **M**. A brief description of each real-world dataset is presented in Appendix C.

dataset	n	m	n_2	$\sum_{i=1}^{b} n_{1i}^2$	$\lvert\mathbf{H}\rvert$	$\lvert\mathbf{H_{12}}\rvert + \lvert\mathbf{H_{21}}\rvert$	$\lvert\mathbf{L_1^{-1}}\rvert + \lvert\mathbf{U_1^{-1}}\rvert$	$\lvert\mathbf{L_2^{-1}}\rvert + \lvert\mathbf{U_2^{-1}}\rvert$
Routing	22, 963	48, 436	572	678, 097	119, 835	72, 168	86, 972	271, 248
Co-author	31, 163	120, 029	4, 464	1, 364, 443	271, 221	118, 012	202, 482	18, 526, 862
Trust	131, 828	841, 372	10, 087	3, 493, 773	972, 627	317, 874	318, 461	81, 039, 727
Email	265, 214	420, 045	1, 590	566, 435	684, 170	358, 458	554, 681	1, 149, 462
Web-Stan	281, 903	2, 312, 497	16, 017	420, 658, 754	2, 594, 400	1, 423, 993	26, 191, 040	55, 450, 105
Web-Notre	325, 729	1, 497, 134	12, 350	77, 441, 937	1, 795, 408	611, 408	5, 912, 673	12, 105, 579
Web-BS	685, 230	7, 600, 595	50, 005	717, 727, 201	8, 285, 825	4, 725, 657	25, 990, 336	547, 936, 698
Talk	2, 394, 385	5, 021, 410	19, 152	3, 272, 265	7, 415, 795	3, 996, 546	4, 841, 878	246, 235, 838
Citation	3, 774, 768	16, 518, 948	1, 143, 522	71, 206, 030	20, 293, 715	9, 738, 225	6, 709, 469	408, 178, 662
R-MAT (0.5)	99, 982	500, 000	17, 721	1, 513, 855	599, 982	184, 812	204, 585	260, 247, 890
R-MAT (0.6)	99, 956	500, 000	11, 088	1, 258, 518	599, 956	145, 281	205, 837	104, 153, 333
R-MAT (0.7)	99, 707	500, 000	7, 029	705, 042	599, 707	116, 382	202, 922	43, 250, 097
R-MAT (0.8)	99, 267	500, 000	4, 653	313, 848	599, 267	104, 415	199, 576	19, 300, 458
R-MAT (0.9)	98, 438	500, 000	3, 038	244, 204	598, 438	107, 770	196, 873	8, 633, 841

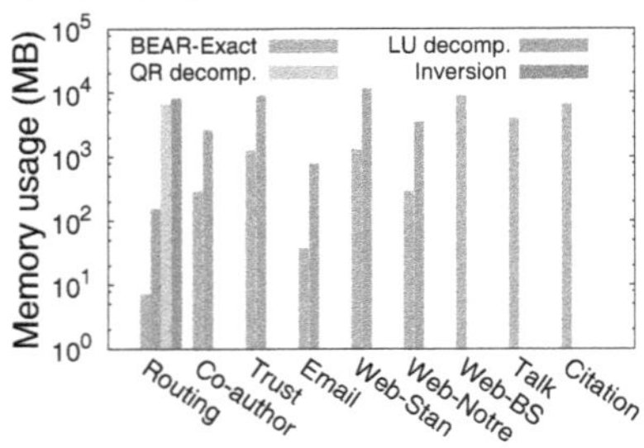

Figure 5: Space for preprocessed data. BEAR-EXACT requires the least amount of space for preprocessed data on all the datasets. Due to its space efficiency, only BEAR-EXACT successfully scales to the largest Citation dataset (with 3.8M nodes) without running out of memory.

Parameters. We set the restart probability c to 0.05 as in the previous work [42][3]. We set k of SlashBurn to $0.001n$ (see Appendix A for the meaning of k), which achieves a good trade-off between running time and reordering quality. The convergence threshold ϵ of the iterative method is set to 10^{-8}, which gives accurate results. For B_LIN and NB_LIN, we use the heuristic decomposition method proposed in their paper, which is much faster with little difference in accuracy compared with SVD in our experiments. The number of partitions in B_LIN, the rank in B_LIN and NB_LIN, and the convergence threshold of RPPR and BRPPR are tuned for each dataset, which are summarized in Table 5 in Appendix D.

4.2 Preprocessing Cost

We compare the preprocessing cost of BEAR-EXACT with that of other exact methods. Figures 1(a) and 5 present the preprocessing time and space requirements of the methods except the iterative method, which does not require preprocessing. Only BEAR-EXACT successfully preprocesses all the datasets, while others fail due to their high memory requirements.

Preprocessing time is measured in wall-clock time and includes time for SlashBurn (in BEAR-EXACT) and community detection (in LU decomposition). BEAR-EXACT requires the least amount of time, which is less than an hour, for all the datasets as seen in Figure 1(a). Especially, in the graphs with distinct hub-and-spoke structure, BEAR-EXACT is up to 12× faster than the second best one. This fast preprocessing of BEAR-EXACT implies that it is better at handling frequently changing graphs.

To compare space efficiency, we measure the amount of memory required for precomputed matrices of each method. The precomputed matrices are saved in the compressed sparse column format [36], which requires memory space proportional to the number of non-zero entries. As seen in Figure 5, BEAR-EXACT requires up to 22× less memory space than its competitors in all the datasets, which results in the superior scalability of BEAR-EXACT compared with the competitors.

4.3 Query Cost

We compare BEAR-EXACT with other exact methods in terms of query time, which means time taken to compute **r** for a given seed node. Although time taken for a single query is small compared with preprocessing time, reducing query time is important because many applications require RWR scores for different query nodes (e.g., all nodes) or require the real-time computation of RWR scores for a query node.

Figure 1(b) shows the result where y axis represents average query time for 1000 random seed nodes. Only BEAR-EXACT and the iterative method run successfully on all the graphs, while the others fail on large graphs due to their high space requirements. BEAR-EXACT outperforms its competitors in all the datasets except the smallest one, which is the only dataset that the inversion method can scale to. BEAR-EXACT is up to 8× faster than LU decomposition, the second best one, and in the Talk dataset, it is almost 300× faster than the iterative method, which is the only competitor. Although BEAR-EXACT requires a preprocessing step which is not needed by the iterative method, for real world applications where RWR scores for many query nodes are required, BEAR-EXACT outperforms the iterative method in terms of total running time.

Furthermore, BEAR-EXACT also provides the best performance in personalized PageRank, where the number of seeds is greater than one. See Figure 11 of Appendix E.1 for the query time of BEAR-EXACT with different number of seeds, and see Figure 10 of Appendix E.1 for the comparison of the query time of BEAR-EXACT with that of others in personalized PageRank.

4.4 Effects of Network Structure

The complexity analysis in Section 3.3 indicates that the performance of BEAR-EXACT depends on the structure of

[3]In this work, c denotes (1 - restart probability)

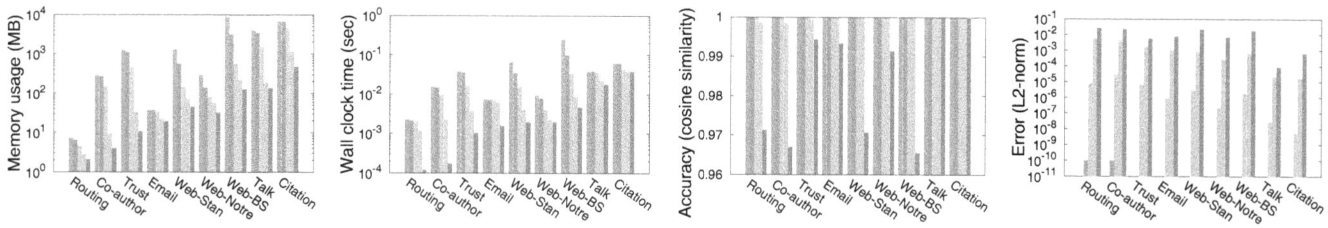

(a) Space for preprocesseed data

(b) Query time

(c) Accuracy (cosine similarity)

(d) Error (L2-norm of error)

0 (BEAR-Exact) n^{-2} n^{-1} $n^{-1/2}$ $n^{-1/4}$

Figure 6: Effects of drop tolerance on the performance of BEAR-APPROX. Drop tolerance changes from 0 to $n^{-1/4}$. As drop tolerance increases, space requirements and query time are significantly improved, while accuracy, measured by cosine similarity and L2-norm of error, remains high.

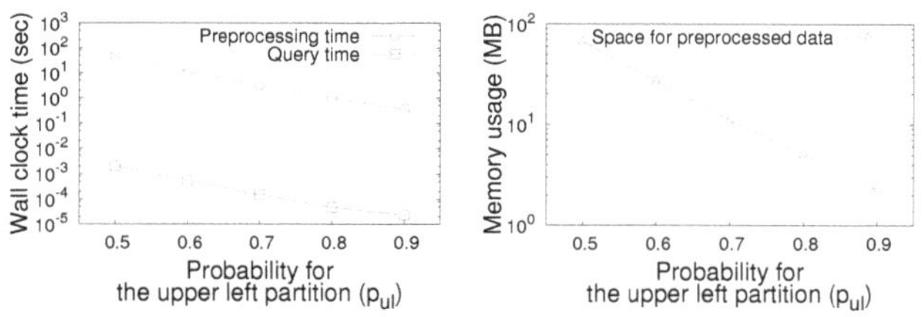

(a) Preprocessing time and Query time

(b) Space for preprocessed data

Figure 7: Effects of network structure. BEAR-EXACT becomes fast and space-efficient on a graph with distinct hub-and-spoke structure (a graph with high p_{ul}).

a given graph. Specifically, the analysis implies that BEAR-EXACT is fast and space-efficient on a graph with strong hub-and-spoke structure where the graph is divided into small pieces by removing a small number of hubs. In this experiment, we empirically support this claim using graphs with similar sizes but different structures.

Table 4 summarizes four synthetic graphs generated using R-MAT [12] with different p_{ul}, the probability of an edge falling into the upper-left partition. As p_{ul} increases, hub-and-spoke structure becomes stronger as seen from the number of hubs (n_2) and the size of partitions ($\sum_{i=1}^{b} n_{1i}^2$) of each graph. Figure 7 shows the performance of BEAR-EXACT on theses graphs. Preprocessing time, query time, and space required for preprocessed data decline rapidly with regard to p_{ul}, which is coherent with what the complexity analysis implies.

4.5 Effects of Drop Tolerance

As explained in Section 3.1.4, BEAR-APPROX improves the speed and space efficiency of BEAR-EXACT by dropping near-zero entries in the precomputed matrices although it loses the guarantee of accuracy. In this experiment, we measure the effects of different drop tolerance values on the query time, space requirements, and accuracy of BEAR-APPROX. We change the drop tolerance, ξ, from 0 to $n^{-1/4}$ and measure the accuracy using cosine similarity[4] and L2-norm of error[5] between $\mathbf{r}$ computed by BEAR-EXACT and $\hat{\mathbf{r}}$ computed by BEAR-APPROX with the given drop tolerance.

Figure 6 summarizes the results. We observe that both the space required for preprocessed data and the query time of BEAR-APPROX significantly decrease compared with those of BEAR-EXACT, while the accuracy remains high. When ξ is set to n^{-1}, BEAR-APPROX requires up to 16× less space and 7× less query time than BEAR-EXACT, while cosine similarity remains higher than 0.999 and L2-norm remains less than 10^{-4}. Similarly, when ξ is set to $n^{-1/4}$, BEAR-APPROX requires up to 117× less space and 90× less query time than BEAR-EXACT, while cosine similarity remains higher than 0.96 and L2-norm remains less than 0.03.

[4]$(\mathbf{r}\cdot\hat{\mathbf{r}})/(||\mathbf{r}||\,||\hat{\mathbf{r}}||)$, ranging from -1 (dissimilar) to 1 (similar)
[5]$||\hat{\mathbf{r}}-\mathbf{r}||$, ranging from 0 (no error) to $||\hat{\mathbf{r}}||+||\mathbf{r}||$ (max error bound)

4.6 Comparison with Approximate Methods

We conduct performance comparison among BEAR-APPROX and other state-of-the-art approximate methods. Dropping near-zero entries of precomputed matrices is commonly applied to BEAR-APPROX, B_LIN, and NB_LIN, and provides a trade-off between accuracy, query time, and storage cost. We analyze this trade-off by changing drop tolerance from 0 to $n^{-1/4}$. Likewise, we analyze the trade-off between accuracy and time provided by RPPR and BRPPR by changing the threshold to expand nodes, θ_b, from 10^{-4} to 0.5. RPPR and BRPPR do not require space for preprocessed data. Accuracy is measured using cosine similarity[4] and L2-norm of error[5] as in Section 4.5.

Figure 8 summarizes the result on two datasets. In Figure 8(a), the points corresponding to BEAR-APPROX lie in the upper-left zone, indicating that it provides a better trade-off between accuracy and time. BEAR-APPROX with $\xi = n^{-1/4}$ achieves 254× speedup in query time compared with other methods with the similar accuracy. It also preserves accuracy (> 0.97), while other methods with similar query time produce almost meaningless results.

BEAR-APPROX also provides the best trade-off between accuracy and space requirements among preprocessing methods as seen in Figure 8(b). BEAR-APPROX with $\xi = n^{-1/4}$ saves 50× on storage compared with B_LIN with $\xi = 0$ while providing higher accuracy (> 0.97). NB_LIN with $\xi = 0$ requires 7× more space compared with BEAR-APPROX with $\xi = n^{-1/4}$ despite its lower accuracy (< 0.71).

Experiments using L2-norm (Figures 8(c) and 8(d)) show similar tendencies. BEAR-APPROX lies in the lower-left zone, which indicates that it provides the best trade-off. The results on other datasets are given in Figure 13 of Appendix E.3. The preprocessing times of the approximate methods are also compared in Figure 12 of Appendix E.2.

5. RELATED WORK

In this section, we review related work, which can be categorized into four parts: (1) relevance measures and applica-

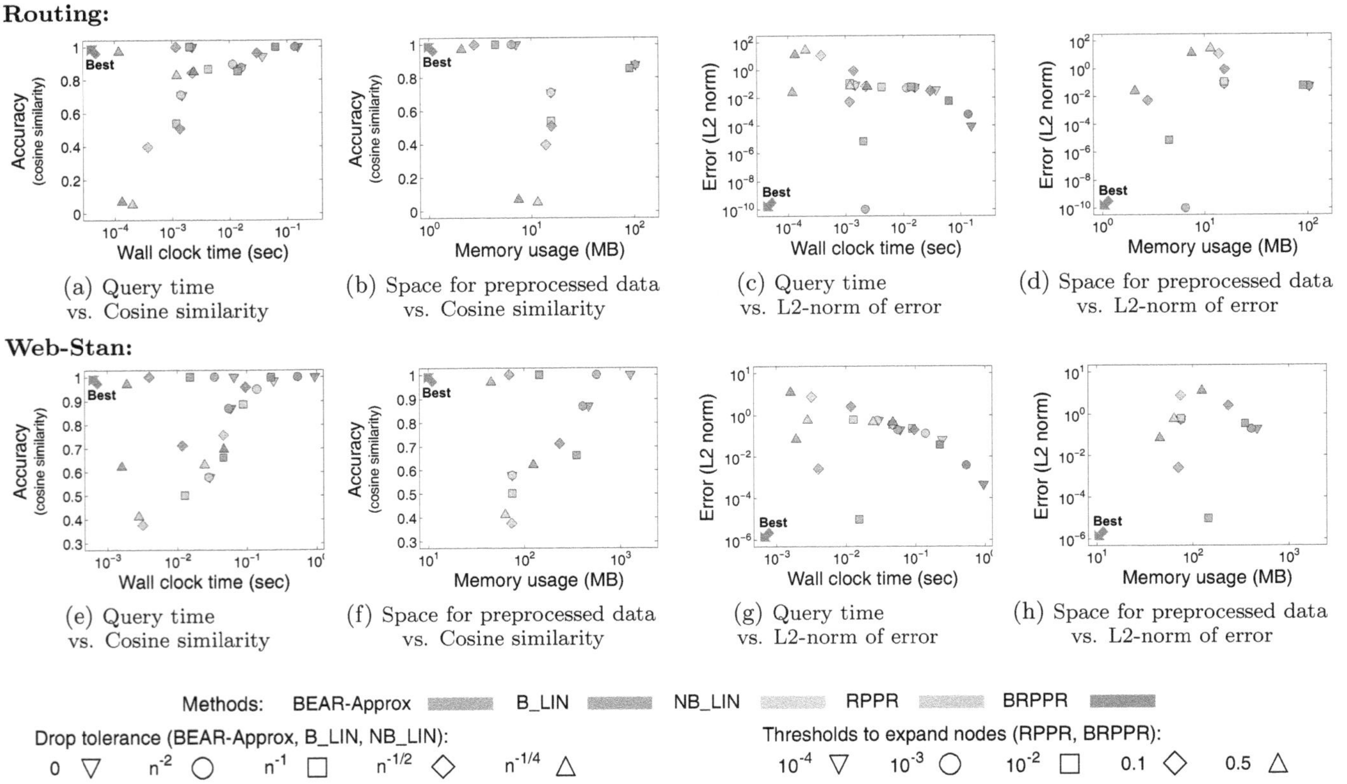

(a) Query time vs. Cosine similarity
(b) Space for preprocessed data vs. Cosine similarity
(c) Query time vs. L2-norm of error
(d) Space for preprocessed data vs. L2-norm of error
(e) Query time vs. Cosine similarity
(f) Space for preprocessed data vs. Cosine similarity
(g) Query time vs. L2-norm of error
(h) Space for preprocessed data vs. L2-norm of error

Figure 8: Trade-off between time, space, and accuracy provided by approximate methods. The above four subfigures show the results on the Routing dataset, and the below ones show the results on the Web-Stan dataset. The colors distinguish the methods, and the shapes distinguish the drop tolerance (for BEAR-APPROX, B_LIN, and NB_LIN) or the threshold to expand nodes (for RPPR and BRPPR). RPPR and BRPPR do not appear in the subfigures in the second and fourth columns because they do not require space for preprocessed data. In the left four subfigures, upper-left region indicates better performance, while in the right ones, lower-left region indicates better performance. Notice that BEAR-APPROX provides 1) the best trade-off between accuracy and query speed, and 2) the best trade-off between accuracy and space requirements, among preprocessing methods.

tions, (2) approximate methods for RWR, (3) top-k search for RWR, and (4) preprocessing methods for RWR.

Relevance measures and applications. There are various relevance (proximity) measures based on random walk, e.g., penalized hitting probability (PHP) [45], effective importance (EI) [9], discounted hitting time (DHT) [38], truncated hitting time (THT) [37], random walk with restart (RWR) [34], effective conductance (EC) [15], ObjectRank [7], SimRank [22], and personalized PageRank (PPR) [33]. Among these measures, RWR has received much interests and has been applied to many applications including community detection [3, 19, 43, 46], ranking [42], link prediction [6], graph matching [41, 25], knowledge discovery [26], anomaly detection [39], content based image retrieval [21], and cross modal correlation discovery [34]. Andersen et al. [3] proposed a local community detection algorithm which utilizes RWR to find a cut with small conductance near a seed node. This algorithm was used to explore the properties of communities in large graphs since it is fast and returns tight communities [28]. Considerable improvements of the algorithm have been made regarding seed finding [19, 43] and inner connectivity [46]. Backstrom et al. [6] proposed a link prediction algorithm called supervised random walk, which is a variant of RWR. In the algorithm, transition probabilities are determined as a function of the attributes of nodes and edges, and the function is adjusted through supervised learning. Tong et al. [41] proposed G-Ray, which finds best-effort subgraph matches for a given query graph in a large and attributed graph. They formulated a goodness function using RWR to estimate the proximity between a node and a subgraph. Kasneci et al. [26] exploited RWR as a measure of node-based informativeness to extract an informative subgraph for given query nodes. Sun et al. [39] utilized RWR for neighborhood formulation and abnormal node detection in bipartite graphs. He et al. [21] employed RWR to rank retrieved images in their manifold ranking algorithm. Pan et al. [34] proposed a method adopting RWR to compute the correlations between a query image node and caption nodes.

Approximate methods for RWR. The iterative method, which comes from the definition of RWR, is not fast enough in real world applications where RWR scores for different query nodes need to be computed. To overcome this obstacle, approximate approaches have been proposed. Sun et al. [39] observed that the relevance scores for a seed node are highly skewed, and many real-world graphs have a block-wise structure. Based on these observations, they performed random walks only on the partition containing the seed node and assigned the proximities of zero to the other nodes outside the partition. Instead of using a precomputed partition, Gleich et al. [18] proposed methods which adaptively determine the part of a graph used for RWR computation in the query phase as explained in Section 2.2. Andersen et al. [3] also proposed an approximate method based on local information. This method, however, is only applicable to undirected graphs. Tong et al. [42] proposed approximate approaches called B_LIN and NB_LIN. They achieved higher accuracy than previous methods by applying a low-rank approximation to cross-partition edges instead of ignoring them. However, our proposed BEAR-APPROX outperforms them by providing a better trade-off between accuracy, time, and space.

Top-k search for RWR. Several recent works focus on finding the k most relevant nodes of a seed node instead of calculating the RWR scores of every node. Gupta et al. [20] proposed the basic push algorithm (BPA), which finds top-k nodes for personalized PageRank (PPR) in an efficient way. BPA precomputes relevance score vectors w.r.t. hub nodes and uses them to obtain the upper bounds of PPR scores. Fujiwara et al. [16] proposed K-dash, which computes the RWR scores of top-k nodes exactly. It computes the RWR scores efficiently by exploiting precomputed sparse matrices and pruning unnecessary computations while searching for the top-k nodes. Wu et al. [44] showed that many random walk based measures have the no-local-minimum (or no-local-maximum) property, which means that each node except for a given query node has at least one neighboring node having lower (or higher) proximity. Based on this property, they developed a unified local search method called Fast Local Search (FLoS), which exactly finds top-k relevant nodes in terms of measures satisfying the no-local-optimum property. Furthermore, Wu et al. showed that FLoS can be applied to RWR, which does not have the no-local-optimum property, by utilizing its relationship with other measures. However, top-k RWR computation is insufficient for many data mining applications [3, 6, 19, 21, 39, 41, 43, 46]; on the other hand, BEAR computes the RWR scores of all nodes.

Preprocessing methods for RWR. As seen from Section 2.2, the computational cost of RWR can be significantly reduced by precomputing $\mathbf{H}^{-1}$. However, matrix inversion does not scale up. That is, for a large graph, it often results in a dense matrix that cannot fit to memory. For this reason, alternative methods have been proposed. NB_LIN, proposed by Tong et al. [41], decomposes the adjacency matrix using low-rank approximation in the preprocessing phase and approximates $\mathbf{H}^{-1}$ from these decomposed matrices in the query phase using Sherman-Morrison Lemma [35]. Its variant B_LIN uses this technique only for cross-partition edges. These methods require less space but do not guarantee accuracy. Fujiwara et al. inverted the results of LU decomposition [16] or QR decomposition [17] of $\mathbf{H}$ after carefully reordering nodes. Their methods produce sparser matrices that can be used in place of $\mathbf{H}^{-1}$ in the query phase but still have limited scalability. Contrary to the earlier methods, our proposed BEAR-EXACT offers both accuracy and space efficiency.

In addition to the approaches described above, distributed computing is another promising approach. Andersen et al. [4] proposed a distributed platform to solve linear systems including RWR. In order to reduce communication cost, they partitioned a graph into overlapping clusters and assigned each cluster to a distinct processor.

6. CONCLUSION

In this paper, we propose BEAR, a novel algorithm for fast, scalable, and accurate random walk with restart computation on large graphs. BEAR preprocesses the given graph by reordering and partitioning the adjacency matrix and uses block elimination to compute RWR from the preprocessed results. We discuss the two versions of BEAR: BEAR-EXACT and BEAR-APPROX. The former guarantees accuracy, while the latter is faster and more space-efficient with little loss of accuracy. We experimentally show that the preprocessing phase of the exact method BEAR-EXACT takes up to 12× less time and requires up to 22× less memory space than that of other preprocessing methods guaranteeing accuracy, which makes BEAR-EXACT enjoy the superior scalability. BEAR-EXACT also outperforms the competitors in the query phase: it is up to 8× faster than other preprocessing methods, and in large graphs where other preprocessing methods run out of memory, is almost 300× faster than its only competitor, the iterative method. The approximate method BEAR-APPROX consistently provides a better trade-off between accuracy, time, and storage cost compared with other approximate methods. Future research directions include extending BEAR to support frequently changing graphs [24].

Acknowledgment

This work was supported by the IT R&D program of MSIP/IITP [10044970, Development of Core Technology for Human-like Self-taught Learning based on Symbolic Approach], and Basic Science Research Program through the NRF of Korea funded by the MSIP [2013005259].

7. REFERENCES

[1] L. A. Adamic and E. Adar. Friends and neighbors on the web. *Social Networks*, 25(3):211–230, 2003.

[2] R. Albert, H. Jeong, and A.-L. Barabasi. Error and attack tolerance of complex networks. *Nature*, 406(6794):378–382, 2000.

[3] R. Andersen, F. Chung, and K. Lang. Local graph partitioning using pagerank vectors. In *FOCS*, pages 475–486, 2006.

[4] R. Andersen, D. F. Gleich, and V. Mirrokni. Overlapping clusters for distributed computation. In *WSDM*, pages 273–282, 2012.

[5] I. Antonellis, H. G. Molina, and C. C. Chang. Simrank++: Query rewriting through link analysis of the click graph. *PVLDB*, 1(1):408–421, 2008.

[6] L. Backstrom and J. Leskovec. Supervised random walks: Predicting and recommending links in social networks. In *WSDM*, pages 635–644, 2011.

[7] A. Balmin, V. Hristidis, and Y. Papakonstantinou. Objectrank: Authority-based keyword search in databases. In *VLDB*, pages 564–575, 2004.

[8] S. Banerjee and A. Roy. *Linear Algebra and Matrix Analysis for Statistics*. CRC Press, 2014.

[9] P. Bogdanov and A. Singh. Accurate and scalable nearest neighbors in large networks based on effective importance. In *CIKM*, pages 1009–1018, 2013.

[10] S. Boyd and L. Vandenberghe. *Convex Optimization*. Cambridge University Press, 2009.

[11] D. Chakrabarti, S. Papadimitriou, D. S. Modha, and C. Faloutsos. Fully automatic cross-associations. In *KDD*, pages 79–88, 2004.

[12] D. Chakrabarti, Y. Zhan, and C. Faloutsos. R-mat: A recursive model for graph mining. In *SDM*, volume 4, pages 442–446, 2004.

[13] S. Chakrabarti, A. Pathak, and M. Gupta. Index design and query processing for graph conductance search. *PVLDB*, 20(3):445–470, 2011.

[14] F. Chierichetti, R. Kumar, S. Lattanzi, M. Mitzenmacher, A. Panconesi, and P. Raghavan. On compressing social networks. In *KDD*, pages 219–228, 2009.

[15] P. G. Doyle and J. L. Snell. Random walks and electric networks. *AMC*, 10:12, 1984.

[16] Y. Fujiwara, M. Nakatsuji, M. Onizuka, and M. Kitsuregawa. Fast and exact top-k search for random walk with restart. *PVLDB*, 5(5):442–453, 2012.

[17] Y. Fujiwara, M. Nakatsuji, T. Yamamuro, H. Shiokawa, and M. Onizuka. Efficient personalized pagerank with accuracy assurance. In *KDD*, pages 15–23, 2012.

[18] D. Gleich and M. Polito. Approximating personalized pagerank with minimal use of web graph data. *Internet Mathematics*, 3(3):257–294, 2006.

[19] D. F. Gleich and C. Seshadhri. Vertex neighborhoods, low conductance cuts, and good seeds for local community methods. In *KDD*, pages 597–605, 2012.

[20] M. Gupta, A. Pathak, and S. Chakrabarti. Fast algorithms for topk personalized pagerank queries. In *WWW*, pages 1225–1226, 2008.

[21] J. He, M. Li, H.-J. Zhang, H. Tong, and C. Zhang. Manifold-ranking based image retrieval. In *ACM Multimedia*, pages 9–16, 2004.

[22] G. Jeh and J. Widom. Simrank: a measure of structural-context similarity. In *KDD*, pages 538–543, 2002.

[23] U. Kang and C. Faloutsos. Beyond 'caveman communities': Hubs and spokes for graph compression and mining. In *ICDM*, pages 300–309, 2011.

[24] U. Kang and C. Faloutsos. Big graph mining: algorithms and discoveries. *SIGKDD Explorations*, 14(2):29–36, 2012.

[25] U. Kang, H. Tong, and J. Sun. Fast random walk graph kernel. 2012.

[26] G. Kasneci, S. Elbassuoni, and G. Weikum. Ming: mining informative entity relationship subgraphs. In *CIKM*, pages 1653–1656, 2009.

[27] A. N. Langville and C. D. Meyer. *Google's PageRank and Beyond: The Science of Search Engine Rankings.* Princeton University Press, 2011.

[28] J. Leskovec, K. J. Lang, A. Dasgupta, and M. W. Mahoney. Community structure in large networks: Natural cluster sizes and the absence of large well-defined clusters. *Internet Mathematics*, 6(1):29–123, 2009.

[29] D. Liben-Nowell and J. Kleinberg. The link-prediction problem for social networks. *J. Amer. Soc. Inf. Sci. and Tech*, 58(7):1019–1031, 2007.

[30] Y. Lim, U. Kang, and C. Faloutsos. Slashburn: Graph compression and mining beyond caveman communities. *IEEE Trans. Knowl. Data Eng.*, 26(12):3077–3089, 2014.

[31] Z. Lin, M. R. Lyu, and I. King. Matchsim: a novel neighbor-based similarity measure with maximum neighborhood matching. In *CIKM*, pages 1613–1616, 2009.

[32] A. Y. Ng, M. I. Jordan, and Y. Weiss. On spectral clustering: Analysis and an algorithm. *NIPS*, 2:849–856, 2002.

[33] L. Page, S. Brin, R. Motwani, and T. Winograd. The pagerank citation ranking: Bringing order to the web. *Technical report, Stanford University*, 1999.

[34] J.-Y. Pan, H.-J. Yang, C. Faloutsos, and P. Duygulu. Automatic multimedia cross-modal correlation discovery. In *KDD*, pages 653–658, 2004.

[35] W. W. Piegorsch and G. Casella. Inverting a sum of matrices. *SIAM Review*, 32(3):470–470, 1990.

[36] W. H. Press. *Numerical recipes 3rd edition: The art of scientific computing.* Cambridge university press, 2007.

[37] P. Sarkar and A. W. Moore. A tractable approach to finding closest truncated-commute-time neighbors in large graphs. In *UAI*, pages 335–343, 2007.

[38] P. Sarkar and A. W. Moore. Fast nearest-neighbor search in disk-resident graphs. In *KDD*, pages 513–522, 2010.

[39] J. Sun, H. Qu, D. Chakrabarti, and C. Faloutsos. Neighborhood formation and anomaly detection in bipartite graphs. In *ICDM*, pages 418–425, 2005.

[40] H. Tong and C. Faloutsos. Center-piece subgraphs: problem definition and fast solutions. In *KDD*, pages 404–413, 2006.

[41] H. Tong, C. Faloutsos, B. Gallagher, and T. Eliassi-Rad. Fast best-effort pattern matching in large attributed graphs. In *KDD*, pages 737–746, 2007.

[42] H. Tong, C. Faloutsos, and J.-Y. Pan. Random walk with restart: fast solutions and applications. *KAIS*, 14(3):327–346, 2008.

[43] J. J. Whang, D. F. Gleich, and I. S. Dhillon. Overlapping community detection using seed set expansion. In *CIKM*, pages 2099–2108, 2013.

[44] Y. Wu, R. Jin, and X. Zhang. Fast and unified local search for random walk based k-nearest-neighbor query in large graphs. In *SIGMOD*, pages 1139–1150, 2014.

[45] C. Zhang, L. Shou, K. Chen, G. Chen, and Y. Bei. Evaluating geo-social influence in location-based social networks. In *CIKM*, pages 1442–1451, 2012.

[46] Z. A. Zhu, S. Lattanzi, and V. Mirrokni. A local algorithm for finding well-connected clusters. In *ICML*, pages 396–404, 2013.

APPENDIX

A. DETAILS OF SLASHBURN

SlashBurn [23, 30] is a node reordering method for a graph so that the nonzeros of the resulting adjacency matrix are concentrated. For the purpose, SlashBurn first removes k hub nodes (high-degree nodes) from the graph so that the graph is divided into the giant connected component (GCC) and the remaining disconnected components. Then, SlashBurn reorders nodes such that the hub nodes get the highest node ids, the nodes in the disconnected components get the lowest node ids, and the nodes in the GCC get the ids in the middle. The above procedure repeats on the GCC until the size of GCC becomes smaller than k. When SlashBurn finishes, the adjacency matrix of the graph contains a large

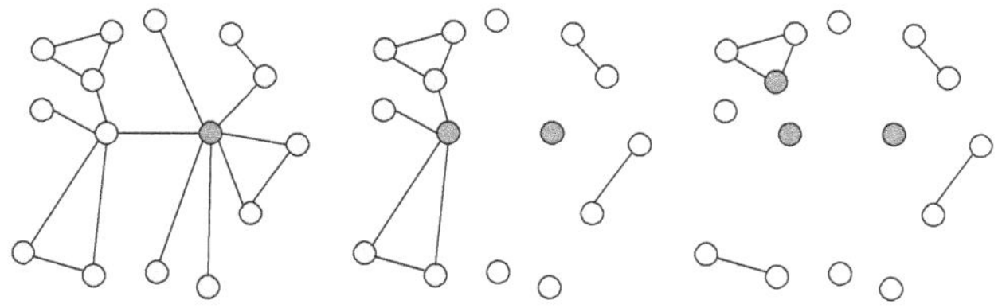

(a) Step 1 (b) Step 2 (c) Step 3

Figure 9: Hub selection in SlashBurn when $k = 1$. Hub nodes are colored red, nodes in the giant connected component are colored yellow, and nodes in disconnected components are colored white.

and sparse block diagonal matrix in the upper left area, as shown in Figure 4(b). Figure 9 illustrates this process when $k = 1$.

B. THE PROOF OF LEMMA 1

PROOF. Let $\mathbf{L}'$ and $\mathbf{U}'$ be the block-diagonal matrices that consist of $\mathbf{L}_1$ through $\mathbf{L}_\mathbf{b}$ and $\mathbf{U}_1$ through $\mathbf{U}_\mathbf{b}$, respectively. Then, $\mathbf{L} = \mathbf{L}'$ and $\mathbf{U} = \mathbf{U}'$ because: (1) $\mathbf{L}'$ is a unit lower triangular matrix; (2) $\mathbf{U}'$ is an upper triangular matrix; (3) $\mathbf{L}'\mathbf{U}'$ is the block-diagonal matrix that consists of $\mathbf{L}_1\mathbf{U}_1$ through $\mathbf{L}_\mathbf{b}\mathbf{U}_\mathbf{b}$ which is equal to $\mathbf{A}$; and (4) $\mathbf{L}'$ and $\mathbf{U}'$ satisfying (1)$\sim$(3) are the unique LU decomposition of $\mathbf{A}$ [8]. The multiplication of $\mathbf{L}$ and $\mathbf{L}^{-1}$ defined in Lemma 1 results in the block-diagonal matrix that consist of $\mathbf{L}_1\mathbf{L}_1^{-1}$ through $\mathbf{L}_\mathbf{b}\mathbf{L}_\mathbf{b}^{-1}$ which is an identical matrix. Likewise, the multiplication of $\mathbf{U}$ and $\mathbf{U}^{-1}$ defined in Lemma 1 results in an identical matrix. □

C. EXPERIMENTAL DATASETS

Below, we provide a short description of the real-world datasets used in Section 4.

- **Routing**[6]. The structure of the Internet at the level of autonomous systems. This data was reconstructed from BGP tables collected by the University of Oregon Route Views Project[7].
- **Co-author**[8]. The co-authorship network of scientists who posted preprints on the Condensed Matter E-Print Archive[9]. This data include all preprints posted between Jan. 1, 1995 and June. 30, 2003.
- **Trust**[10]. A who-trust-whom online social network taken from Epinions.com[11], a general consumer review site. Members of the site decide whether to trust each other, and this affects which reviews are shown to them.
- **Email**[12]. An email network taken from a large European research institution. This data include all incoming and outgoing emails of the research institution from October 2003 to May 2005.
- **Web-Notre**[13]. The hyperlink network of web pages from University of Notre Dame in 1999.
- **Web-Stan**[14]. The hyperlink network of web pages from Stanford University in 2002.
- **Web-BS**[15]. The hyperlink network of web pages from University of California, Berkeley and Stanford University in 2002.
- **Talk**[16]. A who-talks to-whom network taken from Wikipedia[17], a free encyclopedia written collaboratively by volunteers around the world. This data include all the users and discussion (talk) from the inception of Wikipedia to January 2008.
- **Citation**[18]. The citation network of utility patents granted in U.S. between 1975 and 1999.

D. PARAMETER SETTINGS FOR B_LIN, NB_LIN, RPPR, AND BRPPR

Table 5: Parameter values of B_LIN, NB_LIN, RPPR, and BRPPR used for each dataset. $\#p$ denotes the number of partitions, t denotes the rank, and ϵ denotes the convergence threshold.

dataset	B_LIN		NB_LIN	RPPR	BRPPR
	$\#p$	t	t	ϵ	ϵ
Routing	200	200	100	10^{-4}	10^{-4}
Co-author	200	500	1,000	10^{-4}	10^{-4}
Trust	100	200	1,000	10^{-4}	10^{-5}
Email	1,000	100	200	10^{-3}	10^{-5}
Web-Stan	1,000	100	100	10^{-3}	10^{-4}
Web-Notre	500	100	200	10^{-4}	10^{-5}
Web-BS	2,000	100	100	10^{-3}	10^{-5}
Talk	-	-	200	10^{-3}	10^{-6}
Citation	-	-	100	10^{-4}	10^{-5}

For each dataset, we determine the number of partitions ($\#p$) and the rank (t) of B_LIN among $\{100, 200, 500, 1000, 2000\}$ and $\{100, 200, 500, 1000\}$, resp., so that their pair provides the best trade-off between query time, space for preprocessed data, and accuracy. Likewise, the rank (t) of NB_LIN is determined among $\{100, 200, 500, 1000\}$, and the convergence threshold (ϵ) of RPPR and BRPPR is determined among $\{10^{-7}, 10^{-6}, 10^{-5}, 10^{-4}, 10^{-3}, 10^{-2}\}$. The parameter values used for each dataset are summarized in Table 5. B_LIN runs out of memory on the Talk dataset and the Citation dataset regardless of parameter values used.

E. ADDITIONAL EXPERIMENTS

E.1 Query Time in Personalized PageRank

We measure the query time of exact methods when the number of seeds is greater than one, which corresponds to personalized PageRank. We change the number of seeds (non-zero entries in $\mathbf{q}$) from 1 to 1000. As seen in Figure 10, BEAR-EXACT is the fastest method regardless of the number of seeds in all the datasets except the smallest Routing dataset The query time of the inverse method increases rapidly as the number of seeds increases. It increases by 210× on the Routing dataset, while the query time of BEAR-EXACT increases by 3×. Figure 11 summarizes the effect of the number of seeds on the query time of

[6]http://www-personal.umich.edu/~mejn/netdata/as-22july06.zip
[7]http://www.routeviews.org/
[8]http://www-personal.umich.edu/~mejn/netdata/cond-mat-2003.zip
[9]http://arxiv.org/archive/cond-mat
[10]http://snap.stanford.edu/data/soc-sign-epinions.html
[11]http://www.epinions.com/
[12]http://snap.stanford.edu/data/email-EuAll.html
[13]http://snap.stanford.edu/data/web-NotreDame.html
[14]http://snap.stanford.edu/data/web-Stanford.html
[15]http://snap.stanford.edu/data/web-BerkStan.html
[16]http://snap.stanford.edu/data/wiki-Talk.html
[17]http://www.wikipedia.org/
[18]http://snap.stanford.edu/data/cit-Patents.html

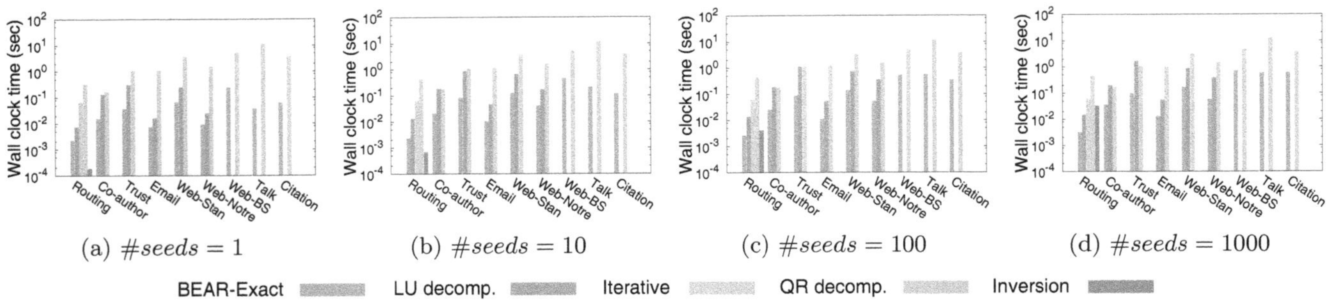

Figure 10: Query time of exact methods with different number of seeds. If a method cannot scale to a dataset, the corresponding bar is omitted in the graphs. BEAR-EXACT is the fastest method regardless of the number of seeds in all the datasets except the smallest Routing dataset.

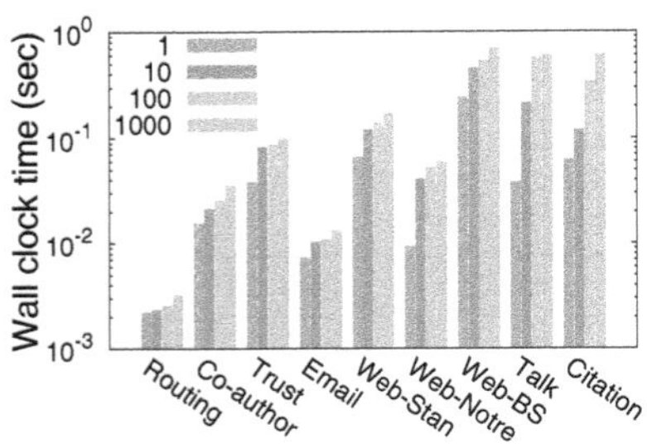

Figure 11: Effect of the number of seeds on the query time of BEAR-EXACT. Query time increases as the number of seeds increases, but the rate of increase slows down.

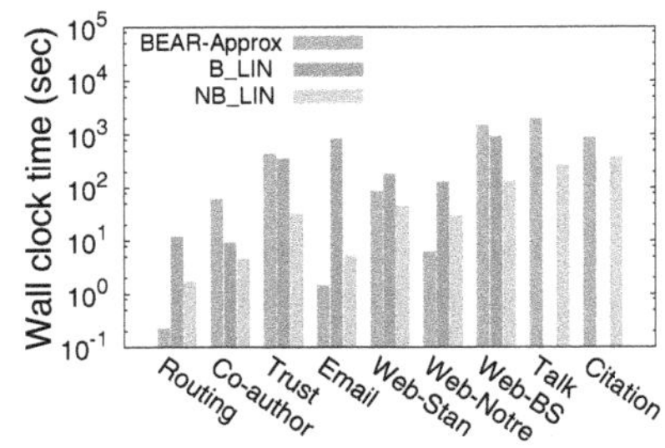

Figure 12: Preprocessing time of approximate methods. The relative performances among the methods depend on the characteristics of data.

BEAR-EXACT. In most datasets, the effect of the number of seeds diminishes as the number of seeds increases. The query time increases by up to 16× depending on the number of seeds.

E.2 Preprocessing Time of Approximate Methods

Figure 12 presents the preprocessing time of approximate methods. Preprocessing time is measured in wall-clock time and includes time for SlashBurn (in BEAR-APPROX) and community detection (in B_LIN). B_LIN cannot scale to the Talk dataset and the Citation dataset because it runs out of memory while inverting the block diagonal matrices. The relative performances among the methods depend on the structure of graphs, as summarized in Table 4. BEAR-APPROX tends to be faster than the competitors on graphs with a small number of hubs (such as the Routing and Email datasets) and slower on those with a large number of hubs (such as the Web-BS and Citation datasets).

E.3 Comparison with Approximate Methods

Figure 13 shows the result of the experiments described in Section 4.6 on other datasets. In most of the datasets, BEAR-APPROX gives the best trade-off between accuracy and time. It also provides the best trade-off between accuracy and storage among all preprocessing methods.

Co-author:

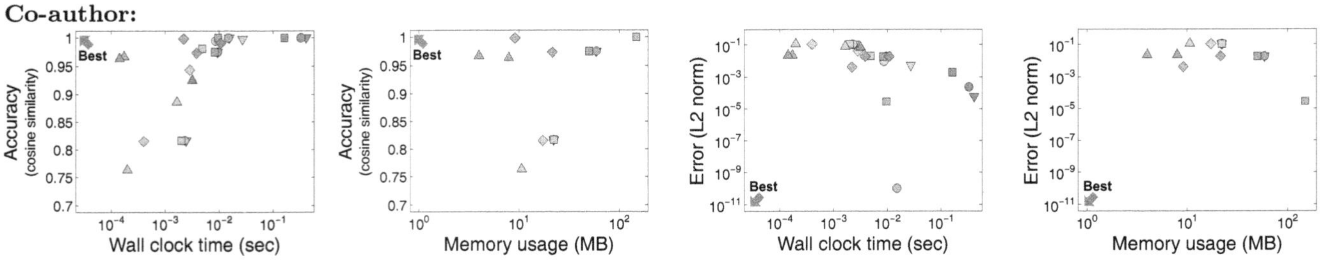

Trust:

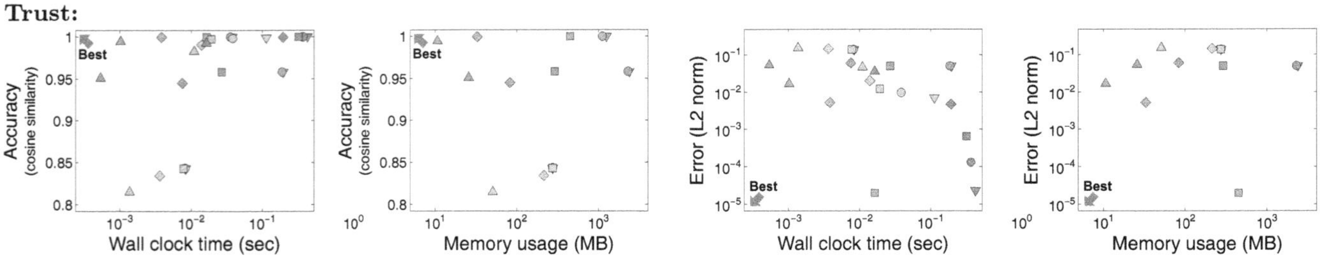

(continues on the next page)

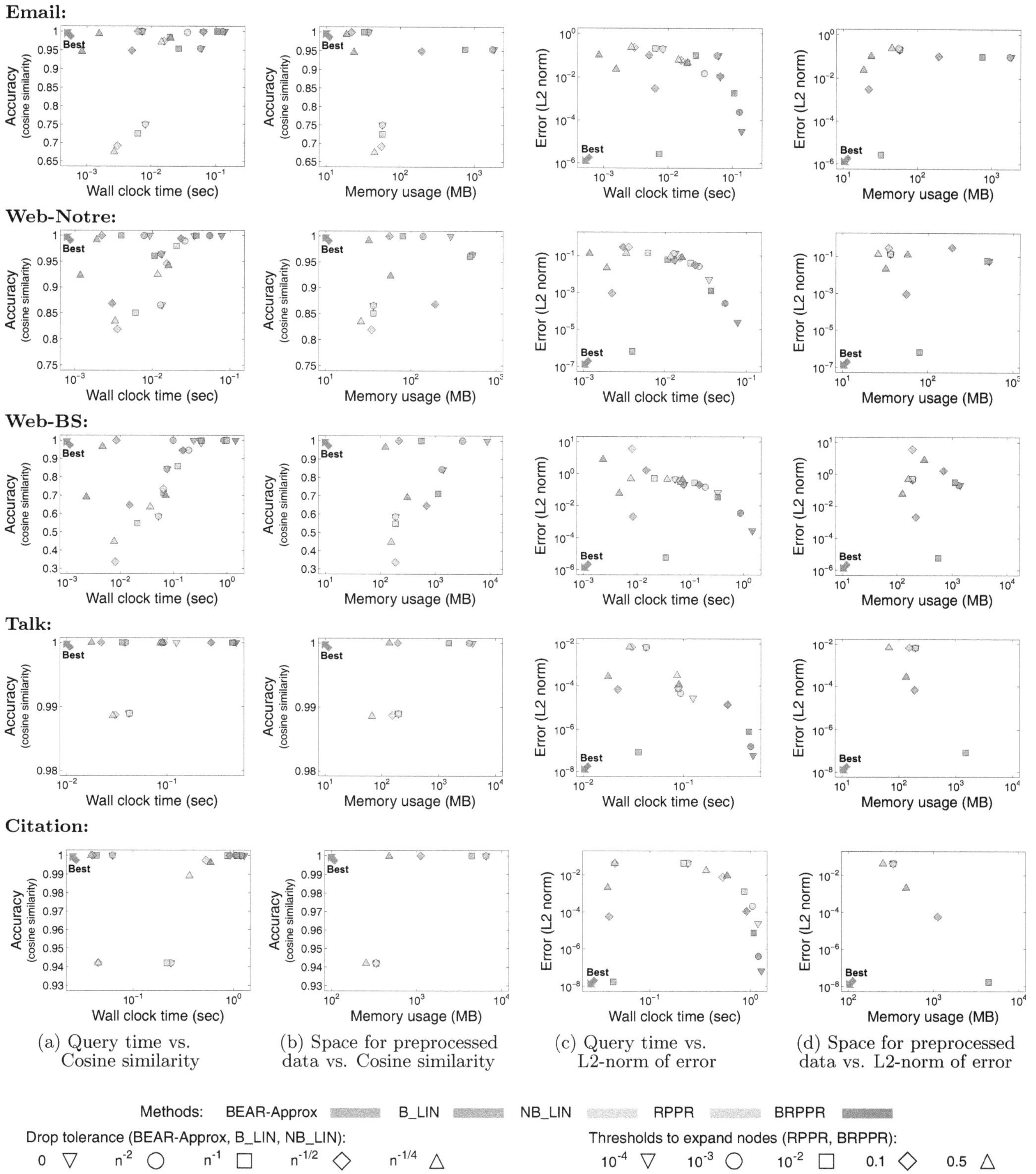

(a) Query time vs. Cosine similarity

(b) Space for preprocessed data vs. Cosine similarity

(c) Query time vs. L2-norm of error

(d) Space for preprocessed data vs. L2-norm of error

Figure 13: Trade-off between time, space, and accuracy provided by approximate methods. The subfigures in each row show the results on the corresponding dataset. The colors distinguish the methods, and the shapes distinguish the drop tolerance (for BEAR-APPROX, B_LIN, and NB_LIN) or the threshold to expand nodes (for RPPR and BRPPR). RPPR and BRPPR do not appear in the subfigures in the second and fourth columns because they do not require space for preprocessed data. In the subfigures in the left two columns, upper-left region indicates better performance, while in the subfigures in the right two columns, lower-left region indicates better performance. BEAR-APPROX is located more closely to those regions than the competitors in most of the datasets.

The Minimum Wiener Connector Problem

Natali Ruchansky
Computer Science Dept.
Boston University, USA
natalir@bu.edu

Francesco Bonchi David García-Soriano
Francesco Gullo Nicolas Kourtellis
Yahoo Labs, Barcelona
{bonchi,davidgs,gullo,kourtell}@yahoo-inc.com

ABSTRACT

The Wiener index of a graph is the sum of all pairwise shortest-path distances between its vertices. In this paper we study the novel problem of finding a *minimum Wiener connector*: given a connected graph $G = (V, E)$ and a set $Q \subseteq V$ of query vertices, find a subgraph of G that connects all query vertices and has minimum Wiener index.

We show that MIN WIENER CONNECTOR admits a polynomial-time (albeit impractical) exact algorithm for the special case where the number of query vertices is bounded. We show that in general the problem is **NP**-hard, and has no PTAS unless $\mathbf{P} = \mathbf{NP}$. Our main contribution is a constant-factor approximation algorithm running in time $\widetilde{O}(|Q||E|)$.

A thorough experimentation on a large variety of real-world graphs confirms that our method returns smaller and denser solutions than other methods, and does so by adding to the query set Q a small number of "important" vertices (i.e., vertices with high *centrality*).

1. INTRODUCTION

Suppose we have identified a set of subjects in a terrorist network suspected of organizing an attack. Which other subjects, likely to be involved, should we keep under control? Similarly, given a set of patients infected with a viral disease, which other people should we monitor? Given a set of proteins of interest, which other proteins participate in pathways with them?

Each of these questions can be modeled as a graph-query problem: given a graph $G = (V, E)$ and a set of query vertices $Q \subseteq V$, find a subgraph H of G which *"explains"* the connections existing among the nodes in Q, that is to say that H must be connected and contain all query vertices in Q. We call this query-dependent subgraph a *connector*.

While there exist many methods for query-dependent subgraph extraction (discussed later in Section 1.1), the bulk of this literature aims at finding a "community" around the set of query vertices Q: the implicit assumption is that the vertices in Q belong to the same community, and a good solution will contain other vertices belonging to the same community of Q. When such an assumption is satisfied, these methods return reasonable subgraphs. But when the query vertices belong to different modules of the input graph, these methods tend to return too large a subgraph, often so large as to be meaningless and unusable in real applications.

The goal of this paper is different, as we do not aim at reconstructing a community. Instead we seek a *small* connector: a connected subgraph of the input graph which contains Q and a small set of *important additional vertices*. These additional vertices could explain the relation among the vertices in Q, or could participate in some function by acting as important links among the vertices in Q. We achieve this by defining a new, *parameter-free* problem where, although the size of the solution connector is left unconstrained, the objective function itself takes care of keeping it small.

Specifically, given a graph $G = (V, E)$ and a set of query vertices $Q \subseteq V$, our problem asks for the connector H^* minimizing the sum of shortest-path distances among all pairs of vertices (i.e., the *Wiener index* [57]) in the solution H^*:

$$H^* = \underset{G[S]:S \subseteq V}{\arg\min} \sum_{\{u,v\} \in S} d_{G[S]}(u, v)$$

where $G[S]$ denotes the subgraph induced by a set of nodes S, and $d_{G[S]}(u, v)$ denotes the shortest-path distance between nodes u and v in $G[S]$. We call H^* the *minimum Wiener connector* for query Q.

This is a very natural problem to study: shortest paths define fundamental structural properties of graphs, playing a role in all the basic mechanisms of networks such as their evolution [39] and the formation of communities [26]. The fraction of shortest paths that a vertex takes part in is called its *betweenness centrality* [8], and is a well established measure of the importance of a vertex, i.e., the extent to which an actor has control over information flow. As our experiments in Section 6 show, a consequence of our definition of minimum Wiener connector is that our solutions tend to include vertices which hold an important position in the network, i.e., vertices with high betweenness centrality.

Consider social and biological networks with their modular structure [26] (i.e., the existence of communities of vertices densely connected inside, and sparsely connected with the outside). When the query vertices Q belong to the same community, the additional nodes added to Q to form the minimum Wiener connector will tend to belong to the same community. In particular, these will typically be vertices with higher "centrality" than those in Q: these are likely to be influential vertices playing leadership roles in the community. These might be good users for spreading information, or to target for a *viral marketing* campaign [34].

SIGMOD'15, May 31–June 4, 2015, Melbourne, Victoria, Australia.
Copyright © 2015 ACM 978-1-4503-2758-9/15/05 ...$15.00.
http://dx.doi.org/10.1145/2723372.2749449.

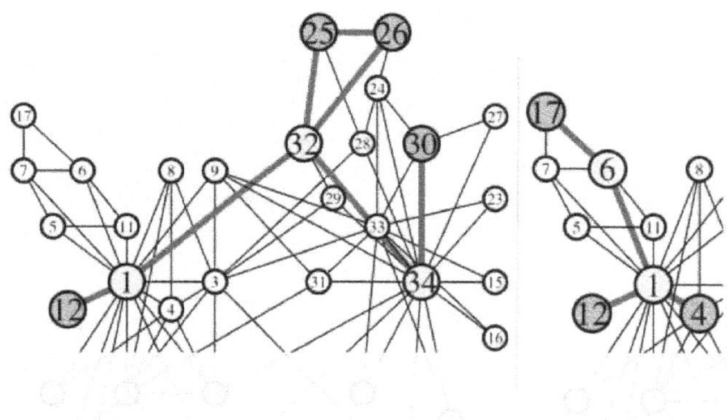

Figure 1: Example of two minimum Wiener connectors on the Zachary's "karate club" social network: on the left the query vertices Q (in dark gray) belong to different communities, on the right they belong to the same community.

Instead, when the query vertices in Q belong to different communities, the additional vertices added to Q to form the minimum Wiener connector will contain vertices adjacent to edges that "bridge" the different communities. These also have strategic importance: information has to go over these bridges to propagate from a community to others, thus the vertices incident to bridges enjoy a strategically favorable position because they can block information, or access it before other individuals in their community. These vertices are said to span a *"structural hole"* [9]: they are the best candidates to target for blocking the spread of rumors or viral diseases in a social network, or the spread of malware in a network of computers. In a protein-protein interaction network these vertices can represent proteins that play a key role in linking modules and whose removal can have different phenotypic effects.

As an example, consider the classic Zachary's "karate club" toy social network [60] with known community structure: a dispute between the club president (vertex 34) and the instructor (vertex 1) led to the club splitting into two. In Figure 1 we show two different minimum Wiener connectors: the one on the left has the query nodes Q (in dark gray) belonging to the two different communities, while in the example on the right, all the query vertices belong to the same community. As discussed above, we can observe that when the query vertices span over different communities, the minimum Wiener connector will include vertices incident to bridging edges. This is the case in our example in Figure 1 (left): given $Q = \{12, 25, 26, 30\}$ the solution subgraph H^* adds to Q the vertices 1 and 34 (the leaders of the two communities) and the vertex 32, which is one of the few vertices connecting 1 and 34 (which do not have a direct connection) and thus practically bridging the two communities. By contrast, in the example on the right, the query vertices $Q = \{4, 12, 17\}$ belong to the same community, and as expected the solution remains inside the community: in this case we just add two vertices, one of which is the community leader (vertex 1), which holds a very central position.

1.1 Related work

At a high level our problem can be described as the problem of finding an interesting connected subgraph of G containing a set of query vertices Q. Several problems of this type have been studied under different names, depending on the objective function adopted: local community detection, seed set expansion, connectivity subgraphs, just to mention a few. As discussed above, most of the existing approaches aim at finding a community around the seeds in Q: these methods end up producing very large solutions, especially when the query vertices are not in the same community. Our goal instead is to produce a small connector by adding a few central vertices. Another important distinction is that many researchers have considered only the cases where $|Q| = 1$ [3, 14, 15, 31] or $|Q| = 2$ [19]. Finally, our method is *parameter-free*, while several existing methods have many parameters which make a direct comparison complicated. In the following we provide a brief overview of this body of literature, highlighting the distinctions w.r.t. our proposal.

Random-walk methods. Many authors have adopted random-walk-based approaches to the problem of finding vertices related to a seed of vertices: this is the basic idea of Personalized PageRank [33, 29]. Spielman and Teng propose methods that start with a seed and sort all other vertices by their degree-normalized PageRank with respect to the seed [49]. Andersen and Lang [2] and Andersen et al. [1] build on these methods to formulate an algorithm for detecting overlapping communities in networks. In a recent work, Kloumann and Kleinberg [37] provide a systematic evaluation of different methods for *seed set expansion* on graphs with known community structure. They assume that the seed set Q is made of vertices belonging to the same community C: under this assumption they measure precision and recall in reconstructing C. Their main findings are that (*i*) PageRank-based methods outperform other methods, (*ii*) few iterations (two or three) of the PageRank update rule are sufficient for convergence, and (*iii*) standard PageRank is to be preferred over degree-normalized PageRank [2, 1].

Closer to our goals, Faloutsos et al. [19] address the problem of finding a subgraph that connects two query vertices ($|Q| = 2$) and contains at most b other vertices, optimizing a measure of proximity based on *electrical-current flows*. Tong and Faloutsos [53] extend the work of [19] to deal with query sets of any size, but again having a budget b of additional vertices. They introduce the concept of *Center-piece Subgraph*, the computation of which is based on the Hadamard (i.e., component-wise) product of a set of vectors, where each vector is obtained by doing a random walk with restart from a query vertex. The efficiency and scalability of the method is severely limited by the processing time of random walks with restart. Koren et al. [38] redefine proximity using the notion of *cycle-free effective conductance* and propose a branch and bound algorithm.

All the approaches described above require several parameters: common to all is the size of the required solution, plus all the usual parameters of PageRank methods, e.g., the jumpback probability, or the number of iterations. We recall that instead our problem definition and algorithms are completely parameter-free.

Other methods. Asur and Parthasarathy [3] introduce the concept of *viewpoint neighborhood analysis* in order to identify neighbors of interest to a particular source in a dynamically evolving network. The authors also show a connection of their measure with heat diffusion. However, the method of Asur and Parthasarathy has several parameters, such as the budget, the stopping threshold, and minimum number of viewpoint neighborhoods for a vertex.

More recently, Sozio and Gionis [48] provide a parameter-free combinatorial optimization formulation. Their problem asks to find a connected subgraph containing Q and maximizing the minimum degree. Sozio and Gionis show that the problem is solvable in polynomial time and propose an efficient algorithm. However, their algorithm tends to return extremely large solutions (it should be noted that for the same query Q many different optimal solutions of different sizes exist). To circumnavigate this drawback they also study a constrained version of their problem, with an upper bound on the size of the output community. In this case the problem becomes **NP**-hard. The authors propose a heuristic where the quality of the solution produced (i.e., its minimum degree) can be arbitrarily far away from the optimal value of a solution to the unconstrained problem.

Cui et al. [15] propose a local-search method to improve the efficiency of the algorithm by Sozio and Gionis [48]; however, their method does not solve the issue of the size of the solutions produced. Moreover, their method works only for the special case $|Q| = 1$.

Steiner Tree and MAD Spanning Trees. Given a graph and a set of terminal vertices, the *Steiner tree* problem asks to find a minimum-cost tree that connects all terminals. This is an extremely well-studied problem: a plethora of methods to solve/approximate it and many variants of the problem have been defined [22]. We will explain in detail (Section 2) how our MIN WIENER CONNECTOR problem differs from the Steiner tree problem.

Another related problem is *Minimum Average Distance* (MAD) *Spanning Trees*: given a graph G, find a spanning tree of G that minimizes the average shortest-path distance among all pairs of vertices [30]. This problem is related to Wiener index as a MAD Spanning Tree is a spanning tree that minimizes the Wiener index. However, this problem still remains different from our MIN WIENER CONNECTOR as the latter asks for subgraphs containing a given set of query vertices rather than asking to span the whole input graph. In a sense, our problem is to MAD Spanning Trees as Steiner Tree is to Minimum Spanning Tree.

Wiener index. The notion of *Wiener index* is rooted in chemistry, where in 1947 Harry Wiener introduced it to characterize the topology of chemical compounds [57]. In general, the Wiener index captures how well connected a set of vertices are, thus bearing resemblance to centrality measures and finding application in several fields, such as communication theory, facility location, and cryptography [18]. A recent work also considers the Wiener index in the context of event detection in activity networks [46]. Existing literature on Wiener index focuses on computing it efficiently [42], finding a tree that minimizes/maximizes it among all trees with a prescribed degree sequence [56, 61, 11], characterizing the trees which minimize [21] or maximize [21, 50] the Wiener index among all trees of a given size and maximum degree, or solving the inverse Wiener index problem [20].

To the best of our knowledge, the problem of finding a minimum-Wiener-index subgraph containing a given set of query vertices has never been studied before.

In our experiments in Section 6 we will compare our method with prior contributions which allow $|Q| > 2$: following the findings of [37] we will use a standard PageRank (with no normalization) personalized over the query vertices Q (PPR for short), the so-called *Center-piece Subgraph* [53] (CPS for short) which is closer in spirit to our goal of finding a connector and not a community, the so-called *Cocktail Party Problem* [48] (CTP) which is parameter free, and the classic Steiner Tree (ST for short).

1.2 Contributions and roadmap

In this paper we initiate the study of the MIN WIENER CONNECTOR problem, a novel *parameter-free* graph query problem, whose objective function favors small connected subgraphs, obtained by adding few *central* vertices to the query vertices. Beyond this main contribution, we provide a series of theoretical and empirical results:

- We show that, when the number of query vertices is small, MIN WIENER CONNECTOR can be solved exactly in polynomial time (§3). However, in the general case our problem is **NP**-hard and it has no PTAS unless $\mathbf{P} = \mathbf{NP}$ (§2): note that, while the inapproximability result says that the problem cannot be approximated within *every* constant, it leaves open the possibility of approximating it within *some* constant.
- In fact, our central result is an efficient constant-factor approximation algorithm for MIN WIENER CONNECTOR (§4), which runs in $\widetilde{O}(|Q||E|)$ time.
- We devise integer-programming formulations of our problem (§5). We use them to compare our solutions for small graphs with those found using state-of-the art solvers, and show empirically that our solutions are indeed close to optimal (§6.2).
- We empirically confirm that existing methods for query-dependent community extraction tend to produce large solutions, which become even larger when the query set Q is made of vertices belonging to different communities (§6.4). Our method instead produces solution subgraphs which are smaller in size, denser, and which include more central nodes (§6.3), regardless of whether the query vertices belong to the same community or not.
- We show interesting case-studies in biological and social networks, confirming that our method returns small solutions that include important vertices (§7).

2. PROBLEM STATEMENT

Preliminaries. We consider simple, connected, undirected, unweighted graphs. We denote the vertex set (resp., edge set) of a graph G by $V(G)$ (resp., $E(G)$).

Given a graph G and $S \subseteq V(G)$, we denote by $G[S]$ the subgraph of G induced by S: $G[S] = (S, E|S)$, where $E|S = \{(u,v) \in E \mid u \in S, v \in S\}$. For any connected graph H and $u, v \in V(H)$, let $d_H(u,v)$ denote the shortest-path distance between u and v in H. Clearly, if H is a subgraph of G, it holds that $d_G(u,v) \le d_H(u,v)$.

The *Wiener index* $\mathbf{W}(H)$ of a (sub)graph H is the sum of pairwise distances between vertices in H [57]:

$$\mathbf{W}(H) = \sum_{\{u,v\} \subseteq V(H)} d_H(u,v), \tag{1}$$

where the sum is taken over unordered pairs.

For ease of notation, we identify any $S \subseteq V(G)$ with its induced subgraph $G[S]$. Thus, we use the shorthand $d_S(u,v)$ (resp., $\mathbf{W}(S)$) to denote $d_{G[S]}(u,v)$ (resp., $\mathbf{W}(G[S])$.

The input to our problem is a connected graph G and a set $Q \subseteq V(G)$ of *query vertices* (or *terminals*). A *connector* for Q in G is a connected subgraph of G containing Q.

Problem definition. In this work we aim at finding subgraphs of the input graph that connect a given set of query vertices while minimizing the Wiener index.

PROBLEM 1 (MIN WIENER CONNECTOR). *Given a graph $G = (V, E)$ and a query set $Q \subseteq V$, find a connector H^* for Q in G with the smallest Wiener index.*

Clearly we may restrict the search to *vertex sets* and their corresponding induced subgraphs.

Note that $\mathbf{W}(H)$ may be written as the product of $\binom{|V(H)|}{2}$ and the average distance between pairs of distinct vertices of H. Therefore, Problem 1 encourages solutions that attain a proper tradeoff between having small pairwise distances *and* using few vertices. In fact, while adding vertices may decrease distances, it also increases the number of terms to be summed up in Eq (1).

Hardness results. We next prove that the problem is **NP**-hard, hence unlikely to admit efficient exact solutions. In fact we show a stronger result, namely that it does not admit a polynomial-time approximation scheme: unless $\mathbf{P} = \mathbf{NP}$, one cannot obtain a polynomial-time c-factor approximation algorithm for every $c > 1$. This inapproximability result says that the problem cannot be approximated within *every* constant, but leaves open the possibility of approximating it to *some* constant; in fact we will show this possible.

Our proof makes use of the following inapproximability result for VERTEX COVER IN BOUNDED DEGREE GRAPHS:

THEOREM 1 (DINUR AND SAFRA [17]). *There exist constants $d \in \mathbb{N}$, $\alpha \in \mathbb{R}^+$ with the following property: given a degree-d graph G and an integer $k \in \mathbb{N}$, it is **NP**-hard to distinguish instances where the minimum vertex cover of G has size larger than $k(1+\alpha)$ from instances where the minimum vertex cover of G has size at most k.*

THEOREM 2. *There is some constant $\varepsilon \in \mathbb{R}^+$ such that Problem 1 is **NP**-hard to approximate within a $1+\varepsilon$ factor.*

PROOF. We present a gap-preserving reduction from VERTEX COVER IN BOUNDED DEGREE GRAPHS to MIN WIENER CONNECTOR. Let α and d be as in Theorem 1. Let $\langle G, k\rangle$ be an instance of the decision version of VERTEX COVER IN BOUNDED DEGREE GRAPHS, where the degree of G is at most d. We need to show that there is some constant $\varepsilon > 0$ such that, given $\langle G, k\rangle$, we can construct in polynomial time an instance $\langle G', Q\rangle$ of MIN WIENER CONNECTOR and a bound $B \in \mathbb{N}$ with the following properties:

(a) if G has a vertex cover of size at most k, then $\langle G', Q\rangle$ has a connector with Wiener index at most B;

(b) if every vertex cover of G has size larger than $k(1+\alpha)$, then every connector of $\langle G', Q\rangle$ has Wiener index larger than $B(1+\varepsilon)$.

Let G have n vertices and m edges. We may assume that $m \geq k \geq \frac{m}{d}$, for otherwise the vertex cover instance can be answered trivially. Furthermore, for any fixed constant c we may assume that $k > c \cdot d$ (if not, we can solve the vertex cover instance in polynomial time.)

Our graph G' is built as follows. Let the vertex set of G' be composed of:

- a distinguished "root" node r;
- n vertices $v_1, \ldots, v_n$ corresponding to vertices of G;
- m vertices $e_1, \ldots, e_m$ corresponding to edges of G.

Put an edge between r and every vertex in $\{v_1, \ldots, v_n\}$, and connect v_i to e_j if and only if v_i is an endpoint of e_j in G. Note that to every v_i correspond at most d such e_j's, and the degree of each e_j is exactly two. Finally, let $Q = \{e_1, \ldots, e_m\} \cup \{r\}$ be the set of query vertices.

Observe that any solution to the original VERTEX COVER instance gives rise to a feasible solution to MIN WIENER CONNECTOR that contains Q and a subset $\mathcal{X} \subseteq \{v_1, \ldots, v_s\}$; conversely, any solution to MIN WIENER CONNECTOR is of the form $Q \cup \mathcal{X}$, where $\mathcal{X} \subseteq \{v_1, \ldots, v_s\}$ is a vertex subset whose corresponding vertices in G cover all the edges of G.

We claim that, if $|\mathcal{X}| = t$ and $Q \cup \mathcal{X}$ forms a connected subgraph, then the Wiener index of the induced subgraph of G' containing Q and $\mathcal{X}$ is at most $u(t) = t^2 + 3mt + 2m^2$ and at least $l(t) = u(t) - O(md)$. Indeed, the contribution to the Wiener index from r to the t chosen vertices is exactly t, and its contribution to the m edges is exactly $2m$. The sum of induced distances among the t chosen vertices is precisely $\binom{t}{2} \cdot 2 = t^2 - t$. The contribution of the t chosen vertices to $e_1, \ldots, e_n$ is $t(3m - O(d))$, because the distance from v_i to e_j is exactly 3 except in the case that e_j has an edge to v_i (meaning that e_j was an endpoint of v_i in the original graph G, and there are at most d such edges for any v_i). Similarly, the contribution from $e_1, \ldots, e_m$ to themselves is $\frac{1}{2}m(4m - O(d)) = 2m^2 - O(md)$. The total is $t^2 + 2m^2 + 3tm - O(md)$.

If we pick $B = u(k)$, we know that condition (a) is satisfied. Regarding condition (b), a straightforward computation shows that $u(k) \leq 6d^2k^2$ and $u(k(1+\alpha)) \geq u(k) + 5\alpha k^2$, hence using the fact that $m \leq kd$ we get

$$\frac{l((1+\alpha)k) - u(k)}{u(k)} \geq \frac{5\alpha k^2 - O(md)}{6d^2k^2} \geq \frac{5\alpha}{6d^2} - \frac{O(1)}{k}.$$

For some large enough $k_0 = \Theta(d^2/\alpha)$, let $\varepsilon = \frac{5\alpha}{6d^2} - \frac{O(1)}{k_0}$; the above shows that $\varepsilon > 0$ and

$$\frac{l((1+\alpha)k) - u(k)}{u(k)} > \varepsilon,$$

so condition (b) holds as well, completing the proof. $\square$

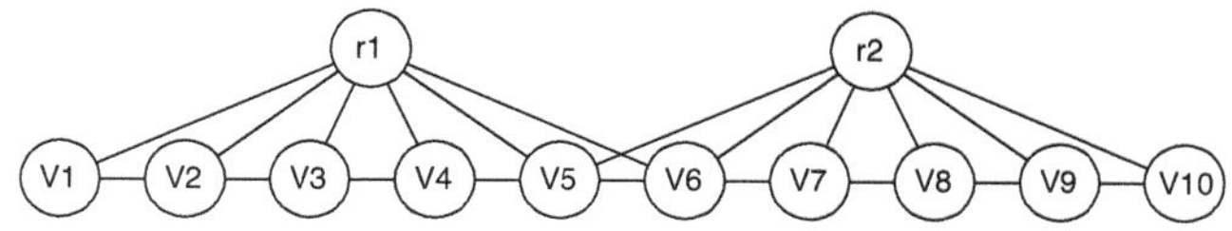

Figure 2: Example showing that a solution to STEINER TREE may exhibit a large Wiener index. Note that similar situations arise also in real-world instances (see §6.4).

Min Wiener Connector vs. Steiner tree. At first glance, Problem 1 may resemble the well-known STEINER TREE problem (see, e.g, [22]): given a graph G and a set Q of terminal vertices of G, find a minimum-sized connector for Q. (The size is measured as the total cost of edges used, which for unweighted graphs is one less than the number of vertices used.) Such an optimal subgraph must be a tree.

Although related (see Section 4), the two problems are different. In fact, a solution for STEINER TREE may be arbitrarily bad for MIN WIENER CONNECTOR. To see this, take a look at the graph in Figure 2. Let $Q = \{v_1, \ldots, v_{10}\}$ be the set of query/terminal vertices. The unique optimal solution to the STEINER TREE problem is obviously Q itself, which has Wiener index $\mathbf{W}(Q) = 165$. However, adding either vertex r_1 or r_2 would lower the index to $\mathbf{W}(Q \cup \{r_1\}) = \mathbf{W}(Q \cup \{r_2\}) = 151$, and the optimal solution to our MIN WIENER CONNECTOR problem is given by $Q \cup \{r_1, r_2\}$, which has Wiener index 142. Also note that no tree is an optimal solution to this example, showing that the addition of extra edges may help decrease the cost.

In general, the fact that the STEINER TREE problem seeks connectors with as few edges/vertices as possible hinders the minimization of pairwise distances. We can generalize the example in Figure 2 to a line of length h and a root r connected to all of them. The optimal STEINER TREE solution exhibits a Wiener index of $\Omega(h^3)$, determined by the $\Omega(h^2)$ pairs of vertices and an average distance of $\Omega(h)$; on the other hand, a solution to MIN WIENER CONNECTOR can include r so as to achieve constant average distance, lowering the Wiener index to $O(h^2)$.

3. AN EXACT ALGORITHM

Here we address the question of how to solve the MIN WIENER CONNECTOR problem exactly. If the input graph has n vertices, a straightforward solution would be to try all 2^n vertex subsets and compute their Wiener index; this gives a running time of $2^n \operatorname{poly}(n)$. On the other hand, there are some polynomial-time solvable special cases. As an example, for unweighted graphs (like the ones studied in this work), when $|Q| = 2$, any shortest path between the two terminals yields an optimal solution. As many problems like satisfiability, coloring, etc., turn from easy to **NP**-hard as the "size" parameter switches from 2 to 3, it is natural to wonder if the same happens here. Interestingly, the answer is negative: the problem admits an exact algorithm that runs in polynomial time for any *fixed* bound on the maximum size of the query set. The result is of limited practical interest, but gives insight into the nature of the problem.

THEOREM 3. *The* MIN WIENER CONNECTOR *problem can be solved in polynomial time when $|Q| = O(1)$.*
That is, there is a function $f : \mathbb{N} \to \mathbb{N}$ such that the MIN WIENER CONNECTOR *problem can be solved in time $n^{f(|Q|)}$.*

The proof is in Appendix A.1. The intuition is that an optimal solution has $f(|Q|) = \operatorname{poly}(|Q|)$ "pivotal" vertices that are useful in connecting several query vertices together or are query vertices themselves. Any other vertices in the solution are simply "pass-through" vertices needed to connect pairs of pivotal vertices via shortest paths; they could be replaced by vertices in another arbitrary shortest path between the required pivotal vertices. Thus, if we try all possible sets of pivotal vertices and connection patterns among them, and then find shortest paths in G to actually connect them, we are guaranteed to find an optimal solution.

4. AN APPROXIMATION ALGORITHM

As we cannot hope for efficient exact solutions to MIN WIENER CONNECTOR, in this section we design an efficient algorithm with provable approximation guarantees. Specifically, we achieve a constant-factor approximation in roughly the same time it takes to compute shortest-path distances from the terminals to every other vertex in the graph.

Proof outline. We need to introduce a series of relaxations of MIN WIENER CONNECTOR to arrive at a problem for which it is easier to derive an approximation algorithm. First we show that we can approximate the cost of any solution in terms of the number of vertices in it and the single-source shortest-path distances to a suitably chosen root vertex $r \in V(G)$. Then we introduce a further relaxation where distances are measured according to the original graph; using the techniques developed by [35] to find light approximate shortest path trees, we show how to make use of a solution to this relaxation. Then we apply a linearization technique to show that if we knew a certain parameter λ controlling the ratio between the size of the optimal solution and the sum of distances to r in the optimal solution, we could reduce our problem to NODE-WEIGHTED STEINER TREE. It turns out that our particular instances of the latter problem admit an $O(1)$-approximation (unlike the general case). Finally, we explain how to search quickly for the correct values of r and λ; as an optimization, we also prove that we can further restrict the search of candidates for r. Finally, we combine these arguments to prove the correctness and efficiency of our algorithm.

Step 1: from Min Wiener Connector to Min-A Connector. First we need the following lemma, whose proof may be found in Appendix A.2.

LEMMA 1. *For any graph H,*

$$\min_{r \in V(H)} \sum_{v \in V(H)} d_H(v,r) \le \frac{2\,W(H)}{|V(H)|} \le 2 \min_{r \in V(H)} \sum_{v \in V(H)} d_H(v,r).$$

Lemma 1 justifies the introduction of the following problem. Given a subgraph H of G and $r \in V(H)$, let

$$\begin{aligned} \mathbf{A}(H,r) &= |V(H)| \cdot \sum_{u \in V(H)} d_H(u,r) \\ \mathbf{A}(H) &= \min_{r \in V(H)} \mathbf{A}(V(H),r). \end{aligned}$$

PROBLEM 2 (MIN-A CONNECTOR). *Given a graph G and a query set $Q \subseteq V(G)$, find a connector H for Q in G minimizing $\mathbf{A}(H)$.*

Note that standard Steiner tree problems do *not* minimize $\mathbf{A}(H)$, but the number (or total cost) of the edges in H.

COROLLARY 1. *Any α-approximate solution to Problem 2 is a 2α-approximate solution to* MIN WIENER CONNECTOR.

Step 2: from Min-A Connector to Min Weak-A Rooted Connector via distance adjustments. One approach to solve Problem 1 is to "guess" the correct vertex r and then find a connector H for Q that minimizes $\mathbf{A}(H,r)$. However, the objective function depends on the induced distances of the unknown solution. In order to simplify our task, we now introduce a "weak" relaxation of the above problem where shortest-path distances are measured in the input graph G instead.

Given a subgraph H of G and a vertex $r \in V(H)$, define

$$\widetilde{\mathbf{A}}(H,r) = |V(H)| \cdot \sum_{u \in V(H)} d_G(u,r) \qquad (2)$$

PROBLEM 3 (MIN WEAK-A ROOTED CONNECTOR). *Given graph G, root $r \in V(G)$ and query set $Q \subseteq V(G)$, find a Steiner tree T for Q in G minimizing $\widetilde{\mathbf{A}}(T)$.*

Here we insist that the solution be a tree (unlike in Problem 2, where we allowed non-tree solutions, even though an optimal solution may easily seen to be a tree as well). The reason will become apparent shortly.

We are now faced with an additional complication, namely that a good solution to MIN WEAK-A ROOTED CONNECTOR may not give a good solution to MIN-A CONNECTOR. Hence the need to perform a post-processing step on every candidate solution to ensure that distances in the modified solution resembles distances in G as closely as possible.

LEMMA 2. *Let T be a subtree of G and $r \in V(T)$. There is another subtree T' of G with the following properties:*

(a) $V(T') \supseteq V(T)$;

(b) $|V(T')| \leq (1+\sqrt{2})|V(T)|$;

(c) for all $v \in V(T')$, $d_{T'}(r,v) \leq (1+\sqrt{2})\, d_G(r,v)$.

(d) $\sum_{v \in V(T')} d_G(r,v) \leq \sqrt{2} \sum_{v \in V(T)} d_G(r,v)$.

Furthermore, given T, a BFS tree from r in G, and $d_G(r,v)$ for all $v \in V(G)$, it is possible to construct T' in time $O(|V(T)|)$.

This follows from a slight modification of an algorithm by Khuller et al for balancing spanning trees and shortest-path trees [35, Lemma 3.2]; although they state it for *minimum* spanning trees and shortest path trees with the same vertex set, a careful examination of their proof establishes Lemma 2 as well. For completeness, we reproduce the proof in Appendix A.3.

COROLLARY 2. *Any α-approximation to Problem 3 can be used to obtain a $(4+3\sqrt{2})\alpha$-approximation to Problem 2.*

PROOF. We can try all possible choices of r. For each of them, let T be an α-approximation to Problem 3. Then we can find a tree T' as in Lemma 2. Since $V(T) \subseteq V(T')$, T' is also a connector for Q and satisfies

$$\begin{aligned}\widetilde{\mathbf{A}}(T',r) &= |V(T')| \sum_{v \in V(T')} d_G(r,v) \\ &\leq (1+\sqrt{2})\,|V(T)| \sum_{v \in V(T')} d_G(r,v) \\ &\leq (1+\sqrt{2})\,\sqrt{2}\,|V(T)| \sum_{v \in V(T)} d_G(r,v) \\ &= (2+\sqrt{2})\,\widetilde{\mathbf{A}}(T,r),\end{aligned}$$

and $\mathbf{A}(T',r) \leq (1+\sqrt{2})\widetilde{\mathbf{A}}(T',r) \leq (4+3\sqrt{2})\widetilde{\mathbf{A}}(T,r)$. □

Step 3: from Min Weak-A Rooted Connector to Min-B Rooted Steiner Tree. We further relax Problem 3 so as to employ a modified objective function where the product between the number of vertices in H and the sum of original distances to the chosen root r is replaced with a linear combination of the two. The rationale here is to make the overall objective function linear and, as such, more amenable to standard approximation techniques.

Given (a subgraph induced by) a subset of vertices $H \subseteq V(G)$, a root vertex $r \in V(H)$, and a parameter $\lambda \in \mathbb{R}^+$, the modified objective we consider is:

$$\mathbf{B}(H,r,\lambda) = \lambda\, |H| + \frac{\sum_{u \in V(H)} d_G(r,u)}{\lambda}. \tag{3}$$

PROBLEM 4 (MIN-B ROOTED STEINER TREE). *Given a graph G, a query set $Q \subseteq V(G)$, a root vertex $r \in V$, and a parameter $\lambda \in \mathbb{R}^+$, find a Steiner tree for $Q \cup \{r\}$ in G minimizing $\mathbf{B}(H,r,\lambda)$.*

We next show that, by choosing λ in the proper way, any approximate solution to Problem 4 yields an approximate solution to Problem 3 too. The right choice of λ is given by the following lemma, proved in Appendix A.4.

LEMMA 3. *For any graph G with $|V(G)| \geq 2$, query set $Q \subseteq V(G)$ and $r \in V(G)$, there is $\lambda \in [1/\sqrt{2}, \sqrt{|V(G)|}]$ such that for any $\alpha \in \mathbb{R}^+$, every α-approximate solution to Problem 4 is also an α^2-approximate solution to Problem 3.*

Step 4: approximating Min-B Rooted Steiner Tree. Our next step aims to find approximate solutions to Problem 4. To this end, we note that Problem 4 can be cast as a NODE-WEIGHTED STEINER TREE problem, where the cost of a node u is equal to $\lambda + d_G(r,u)/\lambda$. However, no approximation factor better than $\Omega(\log |Q|)$ is possible in general for NODE-WEIGHTED STEINER TREE, unless every problem in **NP** can be solved in quasipolynomial time [36]. Nevertheless, we show that our particular problem admits a constant-factor approximation, by shifting the cost from vertices to edges and reducing it to a classical STEINER TREE problem. The reason is that in our instance the cost of two adjacent vertices from the root r cannot differ by more than 1, thus the overall solution cost is nearly preserved despite the cost shift. We formalize this intuition next.

LEMMA 4. *Given a graph $G=(V,E)$, a query set $Q \subseteq V$, a root vertex $r \in V$, and a parameter $\lambda \in \mathbb{R}^+$, let $G_{r,\lambda}$ be a weighted graph with vertex set V, edge set E, and weight on each edge (u,v) equal to $w(u,v) = \lambda + \frac{\max\{d_G(r,u), d_G(r,v)\}}{\lambda}$. Then any Steiner tree T for $Q \cup \{r\}$ satisfies the following:*

$$\mathbf{B}(T,r,\lambda) - \lambda \;\leq \sum_{(u,v) \in E(T)} w(u,v) \;\leq\; 2\,(\mathbf{B}(T,r,\lambda) - \lambda).$$

PROOF. Observe that the cost $w(u,v)$ of each edge $(u,v) \in E(T)$ lies in the range $[\lambda + d_G(r,u)/\lambda, \lambda + (d_G(r,u)+1)/\lambda]$, as u and v are adjacent in T. Notice that in every edge (u,v) of T, either u is the parent of v or v is the parent of u. Hence, writing $A = V(T) \setminus \{r\}$, we can bound

$$\underbrace{\sum_{u \in A}\left(\lambda + \frac{d_G(r,u)}{\lambda}\right)}_{\mathbf{B}(T,r,\lambda)-\lambda} \leq \sum_{(u,v) \in E(T)} w(u,v) \leq \sum_{u \in A}\left(\lambda + \frac{d_G(r,u)+1}{\lambda}\right),$$

The result follows by noticing that the right-hand side is at most

$$\mathbf{B}(T,r,\lambda) - \lambda + \frac{|V(T)|-1}{\lambda} \;\leq\; 2\,(\mathbf{B}(T,r,\lambda) - \lambda).$$

□

Lemma 4 entails a reduction from Problem 4 to the well-studied STEINER TREE tree problem. The best known algorithm for the latter is the 1.39-factor approximation algorithm of Byrka et al. [10]. However, it is based on solving a linear program, in contrast to quicker combinatorial algorithms that achieve a factor-2 approximation. The fastest among the latter is due to Mehlhorn [41].

COROLLARY 3. *A 4-approximation to Problem 4 can be computed in time $O(|E|+|V|\log|V|)$, provided that shortest-path distances from Q in G have been precomputed.*

PROOF. We can construct the graph of Lemma 4 in time $O(|V|+|E|)$, and use the 2-approximation algorithm of [41] for Steiner tree, which runs in time $O(|E|+|V|\log|V|)$. By Lemma 4, the result is a 4-approximation for Problem 4. □

Step 5: choosing r and λ. At this point, we know that, with the right choice of λ (which depends on the problem instance), we can get a constant-factor approximate solution to Problem 3. For any given graph G and query set $Q \subseteq V(G)$, the algorithm would run as follows:

- For every vertex $r \in V$ do:
  - Compute $d_G(r, u)$ from r to every other vertex u;
  - Guess λ matching the value stated in Lemma 3;
  - Construct the weighted graph $G_{r,\lambda}$ of Lemma 4;
  - Find an α-approximate solution S_r^* to the STEINER TREE problem on graph $G_{r,\lambda}$ and terminals $Q \cup \{r\}$;
- Take the S_r^* that minimizes $\mathbf{B}(S_r^*, r, \lambda)$.

However, we still need to explain how to guess λ. Since there are only poly($|V(G)|$) many possible values for λ^2, we could try all of them in polynomial time. A faster way is to fix some $\beta > 0$ and then try all powers of $(1+\beta)$ in the interval $[\sqrt{1/2}, \sqrt{|V|}]$, of which there are only $O(\log |V|/\beta)$ many; this will guarantee that one of the candidate values of λ tried will be off by a factor of at most $1+\beta$. It is not hard to generalize Lemma 3 to show that using a $1+\beta$ approximation for the true value of λ results in the loss of another multiplicative $(1+\beta)^2$ factor in the overall approximation.

Step 6: restricting the number of root vertices. Finally, we show that trying all possible root vertices $r \in V$ is overkill if we are willing to settle for a somewhat larger approximation factor. The next result shows that we can restrict our search to elements of the query set (notice that an optimal solution to Problem 2 is a tree with leaves in Q).

LEMMA 5. *Let T be a tree, $r \in V(T)$, and let x^* be a leaf of T closest to r. Then $\sum_{u \in V(T)} d_T(x^*, u) \leq 3 \sum_{u \in V(T)} d_T(r, u)$, hence $\mathbf{A}(T, x^*) \leq 3 \cdot \mathbf{A}(T, r)$.*

PROOF. For any vertex $x \in V(T)$, let $d(x) = \sum_{u \in V(T)} d_T(u, x)$. It suffices to show that $d(x^*) - d(r) \leq 2d(r)$. To this end, partition $V(T)$ into levels according to the distance to r: $L_i = \{u \in V(T) \mid d_T(r, u) = i\}$. Let $\ell = d_T(r, x^*)$ and for $t \in \mathbb{N}$ write $L_{\leq t} = \bigcup_{j \leq t} L_j$, $L_{>t} = \bigcup_{j>t} L_j$. On the one hand,

$$d(x^*) - d(r) = \sum_{u \in V(T)} (d_T(u, x^*) - d_T(u, r)) \quad (4)$$

$$\leq \sum_{u \in V(T)} |d_T(u, x^*) - d_T(u, r)| \leq (|L_{\leq \ell}| + |L_{>\ell}|)\, \ell.$$

On the other hand, observe that by our choice of x^*, it is guaranteed that $|L_0| \leq |L_1| \leq \ldots \leq |L_\ell|$, as every vertex at level $i < \ell$ has at least one child (and they are distinct as H is acyclic). This implies that we can partition $L_{\leq \ell}$ into a collection of pairs $\{a, b\}$ where $a \neq b$ and $d_T(r, a) + d_T(r, b) \geq \ell$, possibly along with a singleton element from $L_{\geq \ell/2}$. Therefore, the average distance from the elements of $L_{\leq \ell}$ to r is at least $\ell/2$. Furthermore, every element of $L_{>\ell}$ is at distance $> \ell$ from r by definition. Hence

$$d(r) \geq |L_{\leq \ell}| \frac{\ell}{2} + |L_{>\ell}|(\ell + 1). \quad (5)$$

Combining Equations (4) and (5) yields the result. □

Putting it all together. The pseudocode for our approach is shown as Algorithm 1. The following theorem summarizes the results about solution quality and running time.

Algorithm 1 WienerSteiner

Input: A graph $G = (V, E)$; a set of query vertices $Q \subseteq V$.
Output: A set of vertices $Q \subseteq H^* \subseteq V$.

1: For all $q \in Q$ and for all $u \in V$, compute $d_G(q, u)$
2: $\mathcal{H} = \emptyset$ ▷ set of candidate solutions
3: $\beta \leftarrow$ any constant > 0 ▷ e.g., $\beta = 1$
4: **for** $t = 1, \ldots, \lceil \log_{1+\beta} |V| \rceil$ **do**
5: $\quad \lambda \leftarrow (1+\beta)^t$ ▷ guess the right balance
6: $\quad$ **for** $r \in Q$ **do** ▷ guess a "root" vertex
$\quad\quad$ ▷ Compute $G_{r,\lambda} = (V, E, w)$ (Lemma 4)
7: $\quad\quad$ **for** $(u, v) \in E$ **do**
8: $\quad\quad\quad w(u, v) \leftarrow \lambda + \frac{\max\{d_G(r,u), d_G(r,v)\}}{\lambda}$
9: $\quad\quad$ **end for**
10: $\quad\quad T \leftarrow$ APPROXSTEINERTREE$(G_{r,\lambda}, Q)$
11: $\quad\quad H \leftarrow$ ADJUSTDISTANCES(T) ▷ see Lemma 2
12: $\quad\quad \mathcal{H} \leftarrow \mathcal{H} \cup \{(H, r)\}$
13: $\quad$ **end for**
14: **end for**
15: $H^* \leftarrow \arg\min_{(H,r) \in \mathcal{H}} \mathbf{A}(H, r)$ ▷ see Remark 1

THEOREM 4. *There is a constant-factor approximation algorithm for the* MIN WIENER CONNECTOR *problem running in $O\left(|Q|\ (|E| \log |V| + |V| \log^2 |V|)\right)$.*

PROOF. First we prove correctness. Let H denote an optimal solution to MIN WIENER CONNECTOR. By Lemma 1, $\mathbf{A}(H) \leq 2 \cdot \mathbf{W}(H)$, so there is $r \in V(H)$ with $\mathbf{A}(H, r) \leq 2 \cdot W(H)$. By Lemma 5, there exists $q \in Q$ with $\mathbf{A}(H, q) \leq 3 \cdot \mathbf{A}(H, r) \leq 6 \cdot \mathbf{W}(H)$; henceforth we take q to be the "root" vertex in our problems. Let K denote an optimal solution to Problem 3 with root q; clearly $\widetilde{\mathbf{A}}(K, q) \leq \widetilde{\mathbf{A}}(H, q) \leq \mathbf{A}(H, q)$. Let $\lambda \in \mathbb{R}^+$ be as in Lemma 3, and let $L \subseteq V(G)$ be an optimal solution to Problem 4. Then for any connector X, the conclusion of Lemma 3 says that if $\mathbf{B}(X, q, \lambda) \leq \alpha \mathbf{B}(L, q, \lambda)$, then $\widetilde{\mathbf{A}}(X, q) \leq \alpha^2 \widetilde{\mathbf{A}}(K, q)$.

The main loop is guaranteed to try at some point this choice of q and also a $(1+\beta)$-approximation λ' for λ. It is readily seen that, for any Y, $\mathbf{B}(Y, q, \lambda') \leq (1+\beta)\mathbf{B}(Y, q, \lambda)$. By Corollary 3, we can find an 4-factor approximation to Problem 4 with q and λ'; in particular we find X, q and λ' with $\mathbf{B}(X, q, \lambda') \leq 4\mathbf{B}(L, q, \lambda') \leq 4(1+\beta)\mathbf{B}(L, q, \lambda)$. Therefore $\widetilde{\mathbf{A}}(X, q) \leq 16(1+\beta)^2 \widetilde{\mathbf{A}}(K, q) \leq 96(1+\beta)^2 \mathbf{W}(H)$.

By Corollary 2, line 11 obtains a graph X' with

$$\mathbf{A}(X', q) \leq (4 + 3\sqrt{2})\widetilde{\mathbf{A}}(X, q) \leq 96(1+\beta)^2(4 + 3\sqrt{2})W(H).$$

Therefore, another application of Lemma 1 tells us that

$$\mathbf{W}(X') \leq \mathbf{A}(X', r) \leq 792(1+\beta)^2 \mathbf{W}(H) = O(\mathbf{W}(H)),$$

as we wished to prove.

As for the running time, computing the initial shortest-path distances (Line 1) takes $O(|Q|\ (|V| + |E|))$ time, while the main loop in Lines 3–14 is repeated $O(|Q| \log |V|)$ times. Lines 6–10 compute the weighted graph $G_{r,\lambda}$ and find an approximated Steiner tree, thereby solving Problem 4. By Corollary 3, they run in time $O(|E| + |V| \log |V|)$. Line 11 adjusts large distances and run in linear time (Lemma 2). Finally, computing $\mathbf{A}(H, r)$ in Line 15 can be done in linear time for each element of $\mathcal{H}$ (of which there are $O(Q \log |V|)$). In summary, the overall runtime of Algorithm 1 is $O\left(|Q|\ (|E| \log |V| + |V| \log^2 |V|)\right)$. □

REMARK 1. *The last line of Algorithm 1 is intended to return the best solution found. It may be replaced with $H^* \leftarrow \arg\min_{H | (H,r) \in \mathcal{H}} \mathbf{W}(H)$, which can only lead to better* *solutions. The trouble is that computing $\mathbf{W}(H)$ exactly may be very costly for large H; this poses no difficulty in practice as the sets found are typically small. However, for the worst-case analysis of the running time bounds, it is important to use $\mathbf{A}(H,r)$ as a proxy for the actual Wiener index $\mathbf{W}(H)$.*

5. LOWER BOUNDS

In this section we design methods to prove *lower bounds* on the optimal Wiener index. The idea is to have a way to somehow compare the Wiener index of the solution outputted by our method with the optimum. As the optimal solution is unknown, we compare against a lower bound on its cost. While this is pessimistic approach, proving that our solutions are close to the lower bound allows us to state with certainty that they are close to optimal as well.

To compute the desired lower bound, we show an integer-programming formulation of the MIN WIENER CONNECTOR problem. Let S denote the vertices in a feasible solution, i.e., a connector of Q in G. We set a variable y_u to 1 for each $u \in S$ (in particular $y_u = 1$ for all $u \in Q$), and another variable p_{st} for each pair $s,t \in V(G)\times V(G)$. In the intended solution, $p_{st} = 1$ iff $y_s = y_t = 1$; we model this by the linear constraint $p_{st} \geq y_s + y_t - 1$. Notice that the connectivity requirement is equivalent to being able to route an unit of flow from s to t whenever $p_{st} = 1$. We add two variables f^{st}_{uv} and f^{st}_{vu} for each edge $\{u,v\}$ in G and each pair $s,t \in V$; f^{st}_{uv} which will be set to one when a fixed shortest path from s to t traverses edges u to v in that direction. For each s,t and $v \in V \setminus \{s,t\}$, the flow constraints indicate that the net flow through v is zero: $\sum_{u\in N(v)}[f^{st}_{uv} - f^{st}_{vu}] = 0$, where $N(v)$ are the neighbours of v in G. Also, the net flow through s must be $-p_{st}$ and for t must be p_{st}. Since $d_S(s,t) = \sum_{u,v} f^{st}_{uv}$ and the latter sum vanishes when $p_{st} = 0$, $\mathbf{W}(S) = \frac{1}{2}\sum^{s,t}_{u,v} f^{st}_{uv}$. The complete program is shown next.

$$
\begin{array}{lrcll}
\min & \multicolumn{4}{l}{\frac{1}{2}\sum_{u,v,s,t} f^{st}_{uv}} \\
\text{s.t.} & \sum_{u\in N(v)} [f^{st}_{uv} - f^{st}_{vu}] & = & \begin{cases} -p_{st} & \text{if } v = s \\ p_{st} & \text{if } v = t \\ 0 & \text{otherwise} \end{cases} & \forall s,t,v \in V \\
& f^{st}_{uv} & \leq & y_u & \forall \{u,v\} \in E \\
& p_{st} & \geq & y_s + y_t - 1 & \forall s,t \in V \\
& y_u & = & 1 & \forall u \in Q \\
& f^{st}_{uv}, p_{st} & \geq & 0 & \\
& y_u & \in & \{0,1\} &
\end{array} \tag{6}
$$

THEOREM 5. *Program* (6) *models the* MIN WIENER CONNECTOR *problem.*

The proof is reported in Appendix A.5.

Program (6) uses more than $2|E||V|^2$ variables and more than $|V|^3$ constraints, which can be problematic for large graphs. A way to reduce the size of the program is to ask for minimization of the pairwise sum of distances in the original graph: this is a safe relaxation as our solutions typically respect the original distances. Applying this relaxation, the objective function becomes a linear function of $p_{s,t}$, thus eliminating the need for separate flow variables for each s,t pair and leading to a program significantly smaller in size.

Let y_u and p_{st} be as before. The Wiener index of any solution is at least $\sum_{u,v} d_G(u,v)\cdot p_{uv}$. To express the condition that the variables with $y_u = 1$ form a connected subgraph, we add two variables x_{uv} and x_{vu} for each edge (u,v) of G. Pick an arbitrary $q \in Q$ and any directed spanning tree T_q of S rooted at q; the intended solution will have $x_{uv} = 1$ if and only if v is the parent of u in T_q. One constraint is that $x_{uv} + x_{vu} \leq y_u$: edge (u,v) can be used only in one direction, and in order to use it from u to v, we must choose u as well. Also, for any $u \neq q$, $\sum_{u\in N(v)} x_{uv} = y_v$ (any chosen vertex must have exactly one parent in T_q). Finally, we need to make sure that the edges with $x_{uv} + x_{vu} = 1$ form an undirected tree. A tree with k vertices has $k-1$ edges and no cycles; hence we enforce the constraint $\sum_{u,v}[x_{uv}+x_{vu}] = \sum y_u - 1$ and, in order to avoid cycles, we add constraints saying that the sum of $x_{uv} + x_{vu}$ for all edges (u,v) in every cycle C of G is at most $|C| - 1$.

$$
\begin{array}{lrcll}
\min & \multicolumn{4}{l}{\frac{1}{2}\sum_{s,t} d_G(s,t)\cdot p_{st}} \\
\text{s.t.} & \sum_{u\in N(v)} x_{uv} & = & y_u & \forall v \in V\setminus\{q\} \\
& \sum_{\{u,v\}\in E} [x_{uv} + x_{vu}] & = & \sum_u y_u - 1 & \\
& \sum_i [x_{z_i,z_{i+1}} + x_{z_{i+1},z_i}] & \leq & t - 1 & \forall \text{cycle } z_0,\dots,z_t = z_0 \\
& x_{uv} + x_{vu} & \leq & y_u & \forall \{u,v\} \in E \\
& p_{st} & \geq & y_s + y_t - 1 & \forall s,t \in V \\
& y_u & = & 1 & \forall u \in Q \\
& x_{uv}, p_{st} & \geq & 0 & \\
& y_u & \in & \{0,1\} &
\end{array} \tag{7}
$$

We reduced the number of variables to a more manageable $O(V^2)$, in exchange for exponentially many constraints (one per cycle in G). This is not a serious issue because the program above has a *separation oracle* [27], and commercial solvers support the addition of *lazy constraints* [28].

6. EXPERIMENTS

In this section we report the results of our empirical analysis. Here we anticipate the main findings:

- Our approximation algorithm produces solutions which are close to optimal (§6.2).
- When compared to other concepts of query-dependent subgraphs extraction such as personalized PageRank [37] (PPR), *Center-piece Subgraph* [53] (CPS), or the *Cocktail Party Subgraph* [48] (CTP), the minimum Wiener connector is several orders of magnitude smaller in size, it is much denser, and it includes vertices with higher centrality (§6.3).
- When the query set Q includes vertices belonging to different communities, PPR, CPS, and CTP return solutions that are 5 to 10 times larger than the case where the whole of Q belongs to the same community. The minimum Wiener connector is only slightly larger (§6.4).
- Steiner tree produces solutions that are much closer to the minimum Wiener connector than the other methods. However, in addition to having smaller Wiener index (§6.5), the Steiner-tree solutions are nearly always less dense, and include vertices with lower centrality. Also, interestingly, the size of our solutions is comparable to the size of Steiner-tree solutions, despite the fact that Steiner tree explicitly optimizes for solution size.

Table 1: Summary of graphs used. δ: density, ad: average degree, cc: clustering coefficient, ed: effective diameter. Datasets with ground truth communities (*). Classical Steiner Tree benchmarks with given query workload (#).

Dataset	$\|V\|$	$\|E\|$	δ	ad	cc	ed
football	115	613	9.4e-2	21.3	0.40	3.9
jazz	198	2742	1.4e-1	55.4	0.62	3.8
celegans	453	2025	2.0e-2	17.9	0.65	4.0
email	1133	5452	8.5e-3	9.62	0.22	8
yeast	2224	6609	2.6e-3	5.94	0.14	11
oregon	10670	22002	3.8e-4	4.12	0.30	4.4
astro	18772	198110	1.1e-3	22.0	0.63	5
dblp*	317080	1049866	2.1e-5	6.62	0.63	8.2
youtube*	1134890	2987624	4.6e-6	5.27	0.08	6.5
wiki	2394385	5021410	1.8e-6	4.19	0.22	3.9
livejournal	3997962	34681189	4.3e-6	17.3	0.28	6.5
twitter	11316811	85331846	1.3e-6	15.1	0.09	5.9
dbpedia	18268992	172183984	1.0e-6	18.9	0.17	5.0
puc#	64-4096	448-24574	-	-	-	-
vienna#	1991-8755	3176-14449	-	-	-	-

6.1 Experimental set up

Algorithms. We compare our algorithm WS-Q with several alternative methods described next. Following the literature on random walks with restart [54, 24, 59], CPS is initialized with a restart parameter c=0.85, number of iterations m=100, and a convergence error threshold $\xi=10^{-7}$. To allow CPS to converge to the best possible solution, no budget constraint is given a priori: we greedily add to the solution the highest-score vertex, until we connect the vertices in Q. For the personalized PageRank method, PPR, we use the same settings as CPS, as well as the same way of selecting which and how many vertices to add to the solution.

For CTP [48] we found that the parameter-free version typically returns too large solutions (often with a size comparable to the original graph). In order to limit the size of the solutions returned while keeping it parameter-free, we first execute a BFS from each query vertex until all other vertices in Q are connected, among all these subgraphs we pick the smallest one, and run over it the greedy algorithm of [48]. For Steiner tree (ST) we use the approximation algorithm by Mehlhorn [41], which is the same that WS-Q uses internally to solve the Steiner tree instances it generates (§4). All algorithms are implemented in C++.

Datasets and query workloads. We use real-world publicly-available graphs of various types and sizes, spanning different domains: communication over emails and wiki pages, citation and co-authorship networks, road networks, social networks, and web graphs (Table 1).

Small datasets are used for assessing approximation quality (§6.2) of our algorithm WS-Qw.r.t. the best provable bounds obtained by solving the integer program in §5.

Medium-large datasets are used for characterizing the solutions produced by the various algorithms described above, in terms of size, density, and centrality (§6.3).

In all these datasets, the query workloads are made of random query-sets Q, with controlled size and average distance of the query vertices. Datasets marked with (*) contain ground-truth community structure [58]: these are used to create different workloads with query vertices in Q belonging to the same community or to different communities (§6.4). As we delve deeper in the comparison between MIN WIENER CONNECTOR and Steiner tree (§6.5), we use benchmarks with predefined query workloads which are used for assessing Steiner tree algorithms.[1] These are marked with (#) in Table 1: benchmark puc contains 25 problems on small graphs with $|Q| \in [8, 2048]$, while benchmark vienna contains 85 problems with $|Q| \in [50, \approx 5k]$.

For scalability assessment (§6.6) we use the larger graphs in Table 1, plus synthetic graphs generated according to the Erdős-Rényi and Power-Law models.[2]

Table 2: Comparison of the Wiener index of WS-Q's solution with the lower (G_L) and upper (G_U) bounds found by Gurobi solver for different datasets and query set sizes. The cost of the optimal solution is guaranteed to be in $[G_L, G_U]$. †Numbers based on the best lower bound the solver could prove *before it ran out of memory*; they give an *upper bound* on the error that is likely to be an overestimate.

Dataset	|Q|	WS-Q	G_U	G_L	Error interval
football	3	40	40	40	0
	5	172	172	164	[0, 4.9%]
	10	656	598	538	[9.6%, 22%]
	20	2352	2018	1546†	[16.5%, 52.2%†]
jazz	3	16	16	16	0
	5	44	44	44	0
	10	276	276	260	[0, 6.2%]
	20	1014	964	936	[5.1%, 8.4%]
celegans	3	36	36	36	0
	5	106	106	106	0
	10	330	330	326	[0, 1.3%]
	20	1204	1196	1192	[0.66%, 1.1%]
email	3	58	58	58	0
	5	250	250	240	[0, 4.2%]
	10	1352	1208	1033†	[11.9%, 30.9%†]
	20	5490	5490	4032†	[0, 36.2%†]

6.2 Approximation quality

Table 2 reports the Wiener index of the solution produced by WS-Q, and how it compares with the best provable bounds obtained with the integer-programming formulation reported in Program (7) (§5) and the state-of-the-art Gurobi solver [28]. This comparison was carried out on small graphs as otherwise the number of variables would be too large to even formulate the integer program. We initialize the solver with our solution so that the solver's upper bound can never be worse by construction. A match in the solver's upper and lower bounds indicates an optimal solution was found. When they do not coincide, either there is a gap between the best solution and the lower bound from Program (7), or the solver ran out of memory during the optimization phase (in which case we report the best lower bound found so far).

We also report an error interval obtained by comparing our solution with the solver's best upper and lower bounds. Observe that, for small query sets (three to five vertices), WS-Q produces solutions that are optimal or very close to it (with error in the interval [0, 5%]). The worst discrepancy between our and the solver's best solution is 16.5% (football with $|Q| = 20$); and here all we can prove is that our solution is at most 52.2% from optimal. However, note in this case there is also a significant gap between the solver's own lower and upper bounds, thus 52.2% is likely to be an overestimate. It should also be noted that this query set size is approximately 1/5 the size of the whole vertex set V.

[1] `http://steinlib.zib.de/`

[2] `http://snap.stanford.edu/snap/index.html`

Table 3: Main characteristics of the solution H returned by different algorithms on 6 datasets, with $|Q| = 10$ and average distance of 4 among the vertices in Q. Each experiment is run 5 times and we report averages of size of the solution $|V[H]|$, density of the solutions $\delta(H) = |E[H]|/\binom{|V[H]|}{2}$, average betweenness centrality $bc(H)$ of vertices in H, and Wiener index $\mathbf{W}(H)$.

	email	yeast	oregon	astro	dblp	youtube	
$\lvert V[H]\rvert$	671	819	9028	12758	11804	17865	CTP
	155	188	4556	1735	7349	5615	CPS
	137	100	1846	598	842	684	PPR
	26	**24**	26	26	25	19	ST
	24	**24**	**23**	**23**	**23**	**17**	WS-Q
$\delta(H)$	0.016	0.016	0.01	<0.01	<0.01	0.01	CTP
	0.047	0.028	0.02	0.019	0.01	<0.01	CPS
	0.029	0.039	0.02	0.07	0.01	0.02	PPR
	0.080	0.088	0.090	0.09	0.08	0.1	ST
	0.093	**0.091**	**0.106**	**0.13**	**0.11**	**0.13**	WS-Q
$bc(H)$	<0.01	<0.01	<0.01	<0.01	<0.01	<0.01	CTP
	0.03	0.02	<0.01	<0.01	<0.01	<0.01	CPS
	0.03	<0.01	<0.01	0.02	0.01	<0.01	PPR
	0.09	0.07	0.10	0.11	0.10	0.13	ST
	0.11	**0.11**	**0.12**	**0.14**	**0.12**	**0.18**	WS-Q
$\mathbf{W}(H)$	$\approx 750k$	$\approx 2M$	$\approx 137M$	$\approx 292M$	$\approx 400M$	$\approx 1.5G$	CTP
	54 598	69 296	$\approx 50M$	$\approx 8.3M$	$\approx 12.6M$	$\approx 561M$	CPS
	52 222	15 838	$\approx 7.5M$	40 079	$\approx 1.2M$	$\approx 1.3M$	PPR
	1 200	1 259	1 164	1 318	3 371	1 324	ST
	968	**931**	**923**	**1 007**	**2 043**	**956**	WS-Q

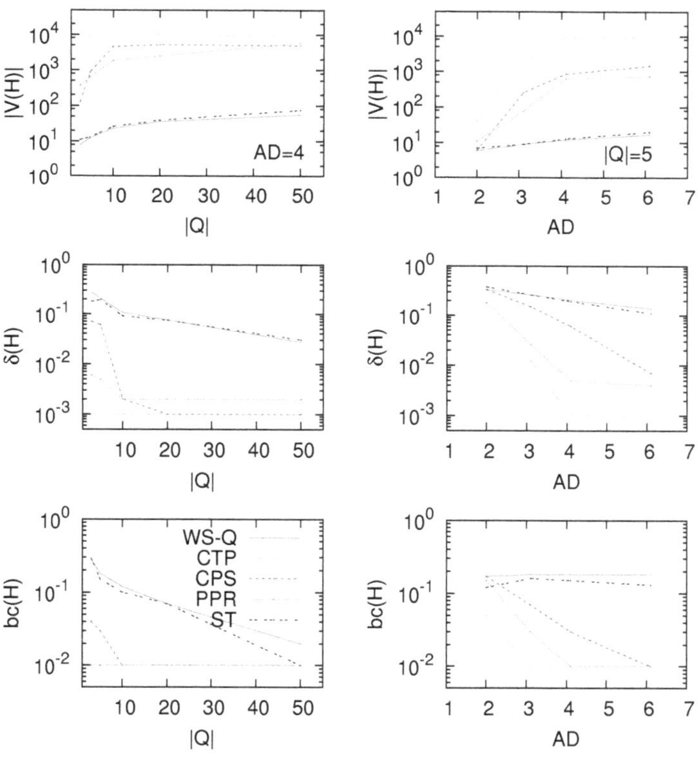

Figure 3: Left column: fixed average distance $AD = 4$ among query vertices, varying $|Q|$. Right column: fixed query set size $|Q| = 5$, varying average distance among query vertices. We report $|V(H)|$, $\delta(H)$, and $bc(H)$ on oregon.

6.3 Solution characterization

Table 3 and Figure 3 report a characterization of the solutions produced by the various algorithms in terms of number of vertices in the solution ($|V(H)|$), density of the solution ($\delta(H)$) and betweenness centrality of the vertices in the solution ($bc(H)$). Table 3 reports results for various graphs with a fixed size of Q, and a fixed average distance among the vertices in Q, while Figure 3 shows the same statistics for a single dataset (oregon) with varying size of Q and average distance of the query vertices. Results confirm that WS-Q produces solutions which are always smaller, denser and contain vertices with higher betweenness centrality than the other methods. The difference is striking with all the methods, with Steiner tree being much closer to the type of solutions produced by WS-Q. As expected, since the other methods do not try to optimize it, WS-Q produces solutions with a Wiener index that is orders of magnitude smaller. Moreover, the solutions WS-Q provides have much smaller index the Steiner-tree solutions. A deeper comparison between WS-Q and ST is reported in Section 6.5.

Table 4: Average solution size for query workloads based on ground-truth communities: dc = query vertices in different communities, sc = query vertices in the same community, and dc/sc = the ratio of the previous two columns.

	dblp-dc	dblp-sc	dblp:dc/sc	youtube-dc	youtube-sc	youtube:dc/sc	
$\lvert V[H]\rvert$	1.4e5	2.8e4	**5.03**	8e5	2.3e5	**3.5**	CTP
	4.1e4	3.69e3	**11.3**	3.6e5	5.0e4	**7.4**	CPS
	3.4e4	3.5e3	**8.6**	3.9e5	4.1e4	**9.2**	PPR
	40	29	**1.43**	20	16	**1.3**	ST
	36	26	**1.38**	18	14	**1.3**	WS-Q

6.4 Ground-truth communities workload

Next, we compare the behavior of the various methods when the query set Q belongs to a community or to multiple communities. To this end, we use graphs with ground-truth community structure (dblp and youtube) and produce two query workloads for each graph: one with query vertices belonging the *same community* (denoted sc) and one with query vertices coming from *different communities* (denoted dc). Each workload contains 40 queries, 10 for each size $|Q| \in \{3, 5, 10, 20\}$. For sc workloads, we pick the community at random, but avoiding small communities (of size smaller than 100 vertices).

The results are reported in Table 4. We observe that when Q belongs to multiple communities, random-walk-based methods (PPR and CPS) produce solutions which are from 7 to 11 times larger than when Q belongs to only one community. While the ratio is less striking for CTP (3 to 5 times larger), the solutions produced are already extremely large in both workloads.

The results confirm that these methods are conceived to reconstruct a community around a given seed set of vertices Q, implicitly assumed to belong to the same community; thus, they tend to return significantly larger results when this does not hold. By contrast, WS-Q and ST do not rely on such assumptions, and the difference in average solution size between the two workloads is much smaller.

6.5 Comparison on Steiner tree benchmarks

We have shown that the types of solutions produced by community-oriented methods have very different characteristics from those by the minimum Wiener connector and the Steiner tree. We next delve deeper in the comparison between the minimum Wiener connector and the Steiner tree, using Steiner-tree benchmarks with predefined query workloads, and focusing on the two objective functions of the two problems: the size of the solution (Steiner) and the sum of the pairwise shortest-path distances (Wiener).

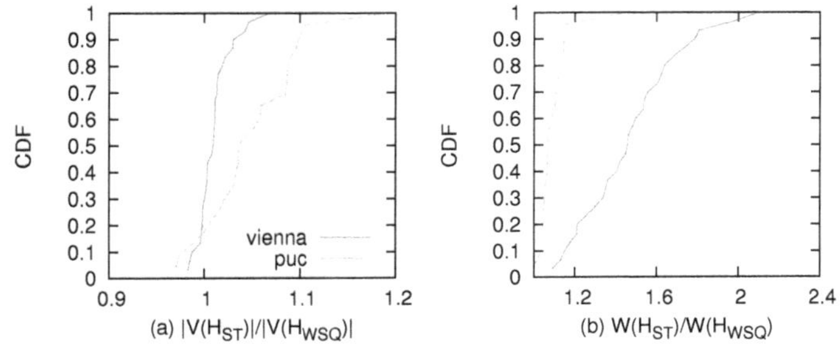

Figure 4: CDFs of the ratio of (a) solution size and (b) Wiener index on benchmarks vienna and puc.

Figure 4 reports the cumulative distribution functions (CDFs) of the ratio of solution size (left) and Wiener index (right) between ST and WS-Q, on the two benchmarks puc and vienna. As expected, WS-Q produces solutions which have a much smaller sum of the pairwise shortest-path distances. Also interesting to observe is the fact that our algorithm WS-Q often outperforms the well-established Steiner-tree approximation-algorithm by Mehlhorn [41] with respect to the size of the solution, which is the objective function of the Steiner tree (recall that the MIN WIENER CONNECTOR objective function implicitly favors small solutions).

Interestingly, we also observe that many problem instances on the vienna benchmark are real-world instances of the situation depicted earlier in Figure 2 – that is to say WS-Q produces a slightly larger solution in number of vertices, yet with a significantly smaller Wiener index.

6.6 Scalability

We now focus on WS-Q's runtime performance and scalability with an increasing graph or query set size. We use Erdős-Rényi (ER) and Power-Law (PL) models to generate synthetic graphs with varying size, while keeping constant other graph properties. We also use the larger real-world graphs in Table 1. Results are reported in Figure 5. First, we note that the performance of the algorithm is not significantly affected by the type of graph (random or power-law). Second, runtime has an almost linear relationship with the query set size, as well as the input graph size. However, as expected by Theorem 4, runtime is most impacted by the graph size rather than the query-set size.

Parallelization. Examining Algorithm 1 we notice that we can easily speed-up our method via parallelization (e.g., via a Map-Reduce execution), assuming the graph G fits in memory. In fact, by launching $|Q|$ threads in parallel (Map), we can achieve a linear speedup of $|Q|$. Each thread examines one root $r \in Q$ and computes shortest-path distances in G from r to construct and solve the Steiner tree instances for different choices of the parameter λ. Then, all possible solutions can be collected (Reduce), and the best one chosen. To this end, each thread needs to evaluate its candidate solutions. Since these are typically small in practice, the thread can compute the induced shortest-path distances from all vertices in its solutions and compute their Wiener indices exactly. In the (unlikely) scenario that a solution is large, we can instead approximate the Wiener index (see Remark 1). This preserves the approximation guarantee while providing an overall speedup of $|Q|$. If G is too large to fit in memory, it becomes necessary to employ techniques for parallel and/or approximate shortest-distance computations [52, 4, 40, 45], but these are beyond the scope of this work.

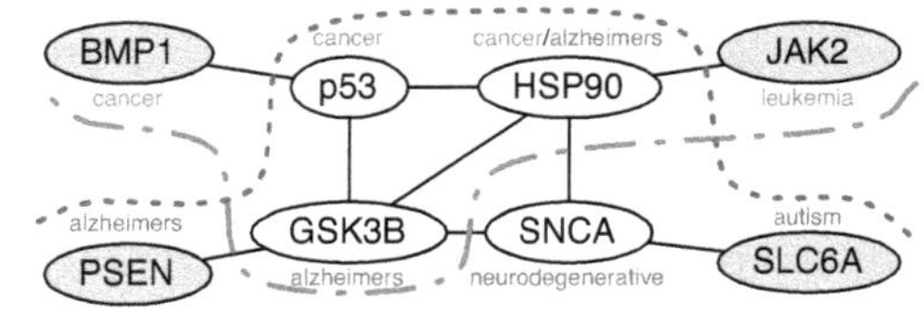

Figure 6: A minimum Wiener connector extracted from a PPI network and links genes associated with cancer and Alzheimer's disease.

7. CASE STUDIES

Protein-Protein-Interaction network. Network analysis has established itself as a central component of computational and systems biology. Barabasi et al [5] drew attention to the great potential of *"network medicine"* in the study of diseases. This work highlighted the utility of identifying not only vertices with high betweenness centrality, but also those that act as links between diseases. Finding such vertices may lead to the discovery of new protein-disease associations and a deeper understanding of the relationships between diseases [13, 12, 47, 7].

The minimum Wiener connector fits well in this setting, as it aims at finding few central vertices that connect a given set of query vertices. As a proof of concept we use a human Protein-Protein-Interaction (PPI) network collected from BioGrid[3] with 15 312 vertices. To demonstrate the utility of WS-Q we require a ground truth about the relationship, so we select query proteins that have been the subject of previous biological study. In Figure 6 we report the minimum Wiener connector for a query set shown in grey, and the solution connector-vertices in white. For each query node we analyze the disease-association of its next-hop in the connector, and find that it is indicative of the studied association of the query node. For example, we observe that the next-hop of *BMP1* is *p53* which is widely regarded as central in cancer; we then verify in the literature that in fact *BMP1* has also been linked to cancer [55, 51]. Similar literature-verified examples are:

- *PSEN* is related to the other query nodes through *GSK3B* – uncovering its role in Alzheimer's disease.
- *JAK2* is connected through *HSP90* which has been studied for its potential therapeutic role in JAK-related diseases [6, 23].
- *SLC6A4* is suspected to play a role in Alzheimer disease, and is connected to *SNCA*, a known factor in Alzheimer's.

Further, the high connectivity of the inner nodes insinuates a close relationship between Cancer and Alzheimer's (e.g., as seen by the interaction between *p53* and *GSK3B*), which has in fact been a topic of interest and study [44, 32, 25].

This sample query is exemplary of the quality and potential of finding the minimum Wiener connector. Identifying not only high betweenness and important nodes, but also those that act as links, gives potential for new directions of investigation for protein-disease and disease-disease relationships. The connector also provides a concise summary of the relationships that is amenable to visualization.

Social network. The next case study is based on a graph created over Twitter users taking part in the ACM SIGKDD 2014 conference. The graph contains 1 141 Twitter users whose tweets over the three-day period contained the hash-

[3] `http://thebiogrid.org/`

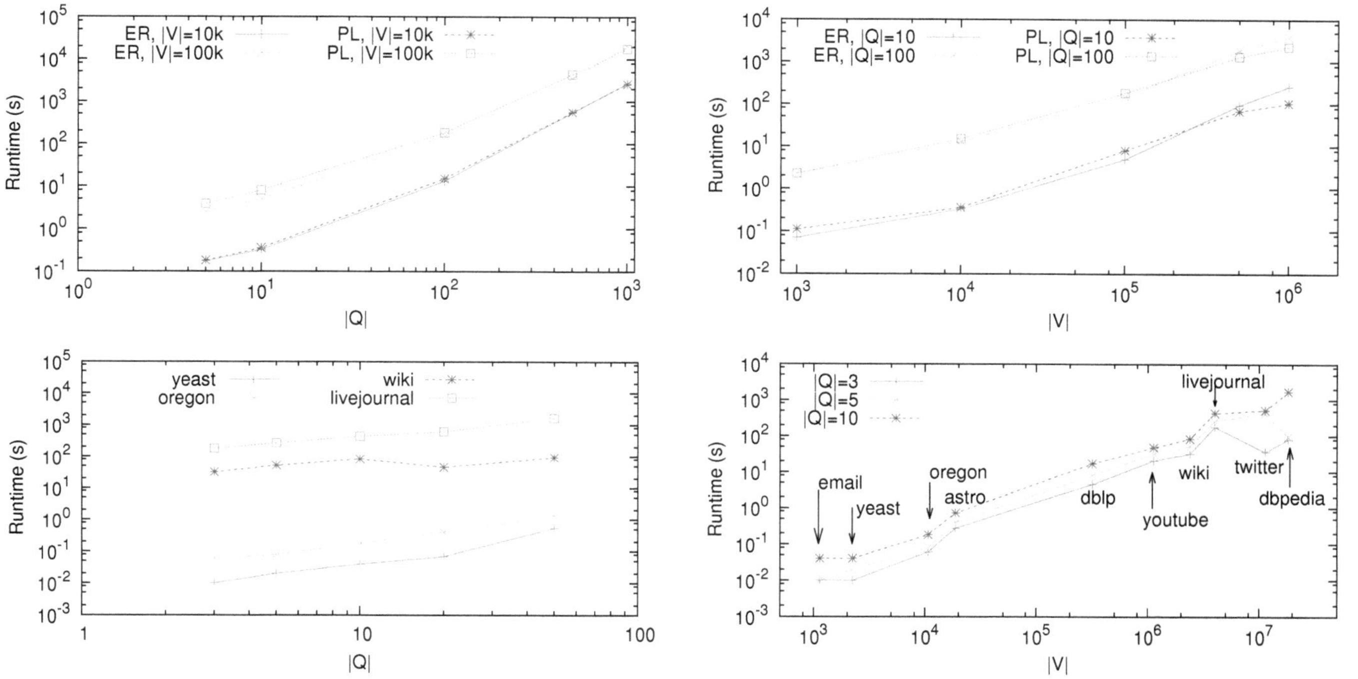

Figure 5: Computational runtime of WS-Q on different synthetic Power-Law (PL) and Erdős-Rényi (ER) graphs (first row) and real-world graphs (second row), with varying query set size and fixed graph size (left column), and varying graph size and fixed query set size (right column).

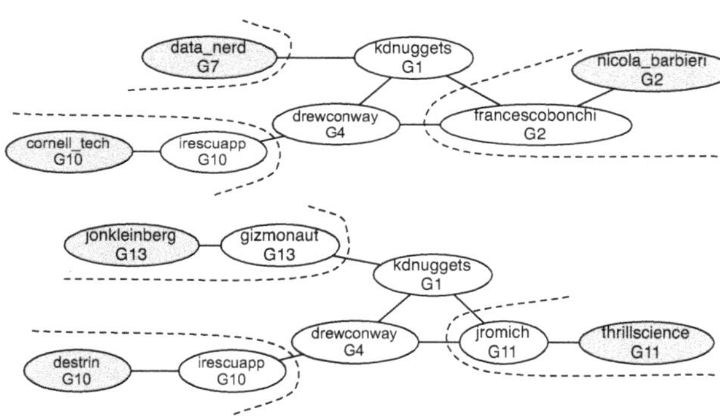

Figure 7: Two minimum Wiener connectors extracted from the Twitter #*kdd*2014 graph.

tag #*kdd*2014, or who replied to or were mentioned in these tweets. There is an edge between two users for each reply or mention. The Clauset-Newman-Moore algorithm was used to cluster the graph into 10 communities.[4]

Figure 7 reports two minimum Wiener connectors extracted with query sets Q (shown in gray) consisting of vertices belonging to different communities. The vertices chosen to be combined with Q to produce the solution subgraph H are, in both cases, users that exhibit some influence or leadership. In particular, we observe that in both examples, H contains the users *kdnuggets* and *drewconway*, each of which have a very large set of Twitter followers ($23.1k$ and $10k$ respectively), and turn out to be the top mentioned and replied-to users in the whole #*kdd*2014 dataset. Table 5 contains more detailed information. In particular it shows that the other intermediate vertices included in the minimum Wiener connectors also exhibit high levels of activity and are among the top-10 mentioned or replied-to users in their respective communities.

[4] https://nodexlgraphgallery.org/Pages/Graph.aspx?graphID=26533

Table 5: Statistics on Tweeters in #*kdd*2014 graph.

UserId	Followers	Notes
kdnuggets	23.1k	Top-1 mentioned in entire graph & G1
		Top-1 betweenness in entire graph
		Top-3 word in entire graph & G1
		Top-6 mentioned in G2-G8
		Top-10 word in G4
		Top-2 replied-to in G8
drewconway	10.7k	Top-7 mentioned in entire graph & G1, G4
		Top-4 replied-to in entire graph & G2, G3
		Top-6 word in G4
gizmonaut	304	Top-9 tweeter in G10
irescuapp	204	Top-7 mentioned in G10
jromich	165	Top-7 replied-to in G1
francescobonchi	619	Top-7 mentioned in G2

8. CONCLUSIONS

In this paper we introduced the MIN WIENER CONNECTOR problem: given a graph and a set of query vertices, find a subgraph that connects the query vertices while minimizing the sum of pairwise shortest-path distances within that subgraph. In such simple and elegant formulation, the objective function favors small solutions built by adding important (central) vertices to connect the given query vertices. Thanks to these features, the minimum Wiener connector lends itself naturally to applications in biological and social network analysis.

We showed that the problem is **NP**-hard, cannot admit any PTAS, and has an exact (yet impractical) algorithm that runs in polynomial time for the special case where the size of the query set is constant. Also, as a major contribution, we provided a constant-factor approximation algorithm that runs in time proportional (up to logarithmic factors) to the size of the input graph and the number of query vertices.

9. REFERENCES

[1] R. Andersen, F. R. K. Chung, and K. J. Lang. Local graph partitioning using PageRank vectors. In *FOCS 2006*.

[2] R. Andersen and K. J. Lang. Communities from seed sets. In *WWW 2006*.

[3] S. Asur and S. Parthasarathy. A viewpoint-based approach for interaction graph analysis. In *KDD 2009*.

[4] D. Bader and K. Madduri. Parallel algorithms for evaluating centrality indices in real-world networks. In *Int. Conf. on Parallel Processing*, pages 539–550, 2006.

[5] A.-L. Barabási, N. Gulbahce, and J. Loscalzo. Network medicine: a network-based approach to human disease. *Nature Reviews Genetics*, 12(1):56–68, 2011.

[6] J. Bareng, I. Jilani, M. Gorre, H. Kantarjian, F. J. Giles, A. Hannah, and M. Albitar. A potential role for HSP90 inhibitors in the treatment of JAK2 mutant-positive diseases as demonstrated using quantitative flow cytometry. *Leukemia & lymphoma*, 48(11):2189–2195, 2007.

[7] A. Baryshnikova, M. Costanzo, C. L. Myers, B. Andrews, and C. Boone. Genetic interaction networks: toward an understanding of heritability. *Annual review of genomics and human genetics*, 14:111–133, 2013.

[8] A. Bavelas. A mathematical model of group structure. *Human Organizations*, 7:16–30, 1948.

[9] R. Burt. *Structural Holes: The Social Structure of Competition.* Harvard University Press, 1992.

[10] J. Byrka, F. Grandoni, T. Rothvoss, and L. Sanità. Steiner tree approximation via iterative randomized rounding. *J. ACM*, 60(1):6:1–6:33, Feb. 2013.

[11] E. Çela, N. S. Schmuck, S. Wimer, and G. J. Woeginger. The Wiener maximum quadratic assignment problem. *Discret. Optim.*, 8(3):411–416, 2011.

[12] S. Chandrasekaran and D. Bonchev. A network view on Parkinson's disease. *Computational and structural biotechnology journal*, 7(8):1–18, 2013.

[13] X. Chang, T. Xu, Y. Li, and K. Wang. Dynamic modular architecture of protein-protein interaction networks beyond the dichotomy of 'date' and 'party' hubs. *Scientific reports*, 3, 2013.

[14] W. Cui, Y. Xiao, H. Wang, Y. Lu, and W. Wang. Online search of overlapping communities. In *SIGMOD*, pages 277–288, 2013.

[15] W. Cui, Y. Xiao, H. Wang, and W. Wang. Local search of communities in large graphs. In *SIGMOD*, pages 991–1002, 2014.

[16] M. Dietzfelbinger, A. R. Karlin, K. Mehlhorn, F. Meyer auf der Heide, H. Rohnert, and R. E. Tarjan. Dynamic perfect hashing: Upper and lower bounds. *SIAM J. Comput.*, 23(4):738–761, 1994.

[17] I. Dinur and S. Safra. On the hardness of approximating minimum vertex cover. *Annals of Mathematics*, 162(1):439–485, 2005.

[18] A. Dobrynin, R. Entringer, and I. Gutman. Wiener index of trees: Theory and applications. *Acta Applicandae Mathematica*, 66(3):211–249, 2001.

[19] C. Faloutsos, K. S. McCurley, and A. Tomkins. Fast discovery of connection subgraphs. In *KDD*, 2004.

[20] J. Fink, B. Lužar, and R. Škrekovski. Some remarks on inverse Wiener index problem. *Discrete Appl. Math.*, 160:1851–1858, 2012.

[21] M. Fischermann, A. Hoffmann, D. Rautenbach, L. Székely, and L. Volkmann. Wiener index versus maximum degree in trees. *Discrete Appl. Math.*, 122(1–3):127–137, 2002.

[22] D. S. R. Frank K. Hwang and P. Winter, editors. *The Steiner Tree Problem.* Annals of Discrete Mathematics. Elsevier, 1992.

[23] J. S. Fridman and N. J. Sarlis. The interplay between inhibition of JAK2 and HSP90. *JAK-STAT*, 1(2):77–79, 2012.

[24] Y. Fujiwara, M. Nakatsuji, M. Onizuka, and M. Kitsuregawa. Fast and exact top-k search for random walk with restart. *Proc. VLDB Endow.*, 5(5):442–453, 2012.

[25] C. Gao, C. Hölscher, Y. Liu, and L. Li. Gsk3: a key target for the development of novel treatments for type 2 diabetes mellitus and Alzheimer disease. *Reviews in the Neurosciences*, 23(1):1–11, 2012.

[26] M. Girvan and M. E. J. Newman. Community structure in social and biological networks. *National Academy of Sciences of USA*, 99(12):7821–7826, June 2002.

[27] M. Grötschel, L. Lovász, and A. Schrijver. The ellipsoid method and its consequences in combinatorial optimization. *Combinatorica*, 1(2):169–197, 1981.

[28] Gurobi Optimization, Inc. Gurobi optimizer reference manual, 2015.

[29] T. H. Haveliwala. Topic-sensitive pagerank. In *WWW 2002*.

[30] T. C. Hu. Optimum communication spanning trees. *SIAM J. Comput.*, 3(3):188–195, 1974.

[31] X. Huang, H. Cheng, L. Qin, W. Tian, and J. X. Yu. Querying k-truss community in large and dynamic graphs. In *SIGMOD*, pages 1311–1322, 2014.

[32] K. M. Jacobs, S. R. Bhave, D. J. Ferraro, J. J. Jaboin, D. E. Hallahan, and D. Thotala. GSK-3: A bifunctional role in cell death pathways. *International journal of cell biology*, 2012, 2012.

[33] G. Jeh and J. Widom. Scaling personalized web search. In *WWW 2003*.

[34] D. Kempe, J. M. Kleinberg, and É. Tardos. Maximizing the spread of influence through a social network. In *KDD*, 2003.

[35] S. Khuller, B. Raghavachari, and N. E. Young. Balancing minimum spanning trees and shortest-path trees. *Algorithmica*, 14(4):305–321, 1995.

[36] P. Klein and R. Ravi. A nearly best-possible approximation algorithm for node-weighted Steiner trees. *Journal of Algorithms*, 19(1):104–115, July 1995.

[37] I. M. Kloumann and J. M. Kleinberg. Community membership identification from small seed sets. In *KDD 2014*.

[38] Y. Koren, S. C. North, and C. Volinsky. Measuring and extracting proximity graphs in networks. *TKDD*, 1(3), 2007.

[39] G. Kossinets and D. J. Watts. Empirical analysis of an evolving social network. *Science*, 311(5757):88–90, 2006.

[40] N. Kourtellis, T. Alahakoon, R. Simha, A. Iamnitchi, and R. Tripathi. Identifying high betweenness centrality nodes in large social networks. *Social Network Analysis and Mining*, 3:899–914, 2013.
[41] K. Mehlhorn. A faster approximation algorithm for the Steiner problem in graphs. *Inf. Proc. Letters*, 27(3):125–128, 1988.
[42] B. Mohar and T. Pisanski. How to compute the Wiener index of a graph. *J. Mathematical Chemistry*, 2(3):267–277, 1988.
[43] R. Pagh and F. F. Rodler. Cuckoo hashing. *J. Algorithms*, 51(2):122–144, 2004.
[44] C. J. Proctor and D. A. Gray. GSK3 and p53-is there a link in Alzheimer's disease? 2010.
[45] M. Riondato and E. M. Kornaropoulos. Fast Approximation of Betweenness Centrality Through Sampling. In *WSDM*, 2014.
[46] P. Rozenshtein, A. Anagnostopoulos, A. Gionis, and N. Tatti. Event detection in activity networks. In *KDD*, pages 1176–1185, 2014.
[47] J. A. Santiago and J. A. Potashkin. A network approach to clinical intervention in neurodegenerative diseases. *Trends in Molecular Medicine*, 20(12):694 – 703, 2014.
[48] M. Sozio and A. Gionis. The community-search problem and how to plan a successful cocktail party. In *KDD*, pages 939–948, 2010.
[49] D. A. Spielman and S. Teng. Nearly-linear time algorithms for graph partitioning, graph sparsification, and solving linear systems. In *STOC 2004*.
[50] D. Stefanovic. Maximizing Wiener index of graphs with fixed maximum degree. *MATCH Commun. Math. Comput. Chem.*, 60:71–83, 2008.
[51] J. P. Thawani, A. C. Wang, K. D. Than, C.-Y. Lin, F. La Marca, and P. Park. Bone morphogenetic proteins and cancer: review of the literature. *Neurosurgery*, 66(2):233–246, 2010.
[52] M. Thorup and U. Zwick. Approximate distance oracles. *J. ACM*, 52(1):1–24, 2005.
[53] H. Tong and C. Faloutsos. Center-piece subgraphs: problem definition and fast solutions. In *KDD*, pages 404–413, 2006.
[54] H. Tong, C. Faloutsos, and J.-Y. Pan. Fast random walk with restart and its applications. In *ICDM*, pages 613–622, 2006.
[55] B. Vogelstein, S. Sur, and C. Prives. p53: the most frequently altered gene in human cancers. *Nature Education*, 3(9):6, 2010.
[56] H. Wang. The extremal values of the Wiener index of a tree with given degree sequence. *Discrete Appl. Math.*, 156(14):2647–2654, 2008.
[57] H. Wiener. Structural determination of paraffin boiling points. *J. Am. Chem. Soc*, 69(1):17–20, 1947.
[58] J. Yang and J. Leskovec. Defining and evaluating network communities based on ground-truth. *Knowl. Inf. Syst.*, 42(1):181–213, 2015.
[59] A. W. Yu, N. Mamoulis, and H. Su. Reverse top-k search using random walk with restart. *Proc. VLDB Endow.*, 7(5):401–412, 2014.
[60] W. Zachary. An information flow model for conflict and fission in small groups. *J. Anthropol. Res.*, 33(4):452–473, 1977.
[61] X.-D. Zhang and Q.-Y. Xiang. The Wiener index of trees with given degree sequences. *MATCH Commun. Math. Comput. Chem.*, 60:623–644, 2008.

APPENDIX

A. REMAINING PROOFS

A.1 Proof of Theorem 3 (Section 3)

Recall that a *homomorphism* between two graphs H and H' is a mapping $\phi : V(H) \to V(H')$ such that $(u, v) \in E(H)$ implies $(\phi(u), \phi(v)) \in E(H')$.

LEMMA 6. *Let $\phi : H \to H$ be a surjective graph homomorphism. Then $\mathbf{W}(H') \leq \mathbf{W}(H)$.*

PROOF. The existence of a homomorphism implies that for every path p in H, there is a corresponding path in H' (which may not be simple even if p is). Therefore $d_{H'}(\phi(u), \phi(v)) \leq d_H(u, v)$, and

$$\begin{aligned}\mathbf{W}(H) &= \sum_{u,v \in V(H)} d_H(u, v) \\ &\geq \sum_{u,v \in V(H)} d_{H'}(\phi(u), \phi(v)) \\ &\geq \sum_{u',v' \in \phi(V(H))} d_{H'}(u', v') \\ &= \sum_{u',v' \in V(H')} d_{H'}(u', v').\end{aligned}$$

The second inequality uses the fact that every pair u', v' from the image of $V(H)$ under ϕ is counted at least once as $d_{H'}(\phi(u), \phi(v))$ for some $u, v \in V(H)$. The last equality is by the surjectivity of ϕ. □

LEMMA 7. *Let G be a graph, H be a connected subgraph of G, $Q \subseteq V(H)$ and let*

$$A = Q \cup \{v \in V(H) \mid \deg_H(v) > 2\}.$$

We call A the set of pivotal vertices *of H with respect to Q.*
Call a path p between two vertices of A basic *if the internal vertices of p are outside A; say that an unordered pair of vertices $u, v \in A$ is* neighbouring *if $u, v \in V(H)$ and there is a basic path from u to v. Suppose we construct a graph H' by including the vertices and edges of an arbitrary shortest path in G between each pair of neighbouring elements of A. Then $Q \subseteq V(H')$ and either $\mathbf{W}(H') = \mathbf{W}(H)$, or H is not a minimum Wiener connector for Q.*

PROOF. It suffices to show that if H is a minimum Wiener connector for Q, then we can construct a surjective homomorphism ϕ from H to H' whose restriction to A is the identity. Indeed, then clearly $Q \subseteq A \subseteq V(H')$, and Lemma 6 would imply $\mathbf{W}(H') \leq \mathbf{W}(H)$.

For each neighbouring pair $(u, v) \in A \times A$, there is a unique basic path $p = p_0 \dots p_t$ in H between $u = p_0$ and $v = p_t$ (otherwise removing some path yields a smaller connector). The graph H' contains a path $q_0, \dots, q_{t'}$ in G (where $t' \leq t$); define $\phi(p_i) = q_{\min(i,t')}$ for $i \in \{0, \dots, t'\}$. The map ϕ is well-defined because the internal vertices of all these paths in H are distinct, as their degree is 2. By construction, ϕ is surjective on $V(H')$ and $\phi(u) = u$ for all $u \in A$. Moreover, the image of every edge in the unique basic path between a pair of neighbouring vertices is an edge of H'. Since any edge of H must belong to some basic path (or else we could remove one of its endpoints while reducing the Wiener index of H), it follows that ϕ is a homomorphism, as claimed. □

LEMMA 8. *Let H be a connected graph and let $\mathcal{P} = (\{s_i, t_i\})_{i\in[m]}$ denote a sequence of m unordered pairs of distinct vertices of H. Write $T = \bigcup_{i\in[m]}\{s_i, t_i\}$ and call a sequence $p_1, \dots, p_m$ of paths in H valid if for all $i \in [m]$, p_i is a shortest path between s_i and t_i. There is a valid sequence $p_1, \dots, p_m$ of paths in H such that in the subgraph $H' = \bigcup_{i\in[m]} p_i$ of H there are at most $m(m-1)$ vertices with degree different from two, and $\mathbf{W}(H') \le \mathbf{W}(H)$.*

PROOF. Since H is connected, there is some valid sequence of paths; what we need to show is that there is one with the degree property. We argue by induction on m. When $m = 1$, all the internal vertices of any shortest pair between s_1 and t_1 have degree two, so we are done. Suppose the theorem holds for $m-1$ vertex pairs; let $p_1, \dots, p_{m-1}$ be the paths in the conclusion of the lemma, and take an arbitrary shortest path p_m from s_m to t_m. We claim that we can replace the path p_m with another path p'_m such that, for each p_i with $i < m$, at most two vertices have a different successor or predecessor in the two paths p'_m and p_i. This is easy to see because if p_m meets p_j, leaves it and intersects it for a second time, we can replace the part of p_m between the two intersections by a subpath of p_j.

Consequently, when we add the edges in path p'_m to the subgraph $\bigcup_{i\in[m-1]} p_i$, for any $i < m$ we increase the degree of at most two vertices that belong to p_i. Therefore the total number of vertices of degree larger than two is at most $(m-1)(m-2) + 2(m-1) = m(m-1)$, as desired.

Finally, note that the above path-replacement procedure cannot increase the Wiener index as H' is a subgraph of H that maintains shortest-path distances. □

LEMMA 9. *Let $k = |Q|$. For any graph G, there is an optimal solution to* MIN WIENER CONNECTOR *where at most k^4 vertices have degree in H larger than two.*

Note that such H is not necessarily an induced subgraph.

PROOF. Let H be an optimal solution. Consider a sequence $\mathcal{P}$ containing all $m = \binom{k}{2}$ pairs of distinct query nodes. By Lemma 8, there is a sequence $p_1, \dots, p_m$ of shortest paths in H (one for each pair of query nodes) such that in the graph H' formed by the union of all these paths, there are most $m(m-1)$ vertices with degree different from two. Clearly H' is a connector for Q (since it contains paths linking each pair of query nodes). Since $\mathbf{W}(H') \le \mathbf{W}(H)$ and H is optimal, it follows that $\mathbf{W}(H') = \mathbf{W}(H)$. Also, there cannot be any non-query vertices of degree 1, otherwise we could remove them from H' and still obtain a connector of Q with smaller Wiener index. So the total number of vertices of degree larger than 2 in H' is at most $k + m(m-1) \le k^4$. □

Proof of Theorem 3. Let $k = |Q|$. We can loop over all possible $\binom{n}{k^4}$ vertex subsets of size k^4; by Lemma 9 one of them will be the set X of vertices of degree 2 in the optimal solution H^*. Then $X \cup Q$ is the set of pivotal vertices of H^* with respect to Q; we can construct in polynomial time a graph H' as in Lemma 7, and we will have $\mathbf{W}(H') \le \mathbf{W}(H^*)$, hence $\mathbf{W}(H^*) = W(H')$.

Overall, the algorithm runs in time $n^{\mathrm{poly}(k)}$. □

A.2 Proof of Lemma 1 (Section 4)

Let $r^* = \operatorname{argmin}_r \sum_v d_H(v, r)$. Observe that

$$|V(H)| \cdot \sum_v d_H(v, r^*) = \sum_w \Big(\sum_v d_H(v, r^*)\Big) \le \sum_w \Big(\sum_v d_H(v, w)\Big) = 2\,\mathbf{W}(H),$$

$$\text{and } 2\,\mathbf{W}(H) \le \sum_w \Big(\sum_v [d_H(v, r^*) + d_H(r^*, w)]\Big) = \sum_{v,w} d_H(v, r^*) + \sum_{v,w} d_H(r^*, w) = 2\sum_{v,w} d_H(v, r^*) = 2\,|V(H)| \cdot \sum_v d_H(v, r^*),$$

where we used the choice of r^* in the first inequality and the triangle inequality for d_H in the second inequality. □

A.3 Proof of Lemma 2 (Section 4)

Let T_S be the shortest-path tree from r to the elements of T, determined by an array of distances $d_S[]$ and an array of parent links $p_S[]$. Consider the algorithm below, which traverses T and performs a series of edge relaxations that add additional vertices from T_S in order to decrease distances to the root r. The important invariant maintained is that the edges $\{(p[v], v)\} \mid d[v] \ne \infty\}$ form a subtree of $T \cup T_S$, with $d[v]$ an upper bound on the distance between the root and v in the tree.

Algorithm 2 AdjustDistances

Input: A graph $G = (V, E)$; a subtree T; a root node $v \in V(T)$; and a BFS tree from r with parent array $p_S[]$ and distance array $d_S[]$.
Output: A tree.

Construct hash tables $d[], p[]$, with default values $p[v] =$ **nil** and $d[v] = \infty$ for all $v \in V(G)$.
$d[r] \leftarrow 0$.
dfs(r).
return the tree $T' = \{(v, p[v]) \mid v \in V(G) \wedge p[v] \ne$ **nil**$\}$.

Algorithm 3 dfs

Input: A vertex u.
if $d[u] > (1 + \sqrt{2})d_S[u]$ **then**
  AddPath(u)
end if
for each child v of u in T **do**
  relax(u, v)
  dfs(v)
  relax(v, u)
end for

Algorithm 4 AddPath

Input: A vertex u.
$v \leftarrow u$
while $d[v] > d_S[v]$ **do**
  relax($p_S[v], v$)
  $v \leftarrow p[v]$
end while

We need to show that AdjustDistances runs in time $O(|V(T)|)$ and returns a tree T' satisfying the following:

(a) $V(T') \supseteq V(T)$;

Algorithm 5 Relax

```
Input: two adjacent vertices u, v.
if d[v] > d[u] + 1 then
    d[v] ← d[u] + 1
    p[v] ← u
end if
```

(b) $|V(T')| \leq (1+\sqrt{2})|V(T)|$;

(c) for all $v \in V(T')$, $d_{T'}(r,v) \leq (1+\sqrt{2})\, d_G(r,v)$.

(d) $\sum_{v\in V(T')} d_G(r,v) \leq \sqrt{2}\sum_{v\in V(T)} d_G(r,v)$.

Property a) holds because every time we insert a new vertex u in the tree (that is, $p[u]$ becomes $\neq$ nil), it is never removed again; and the call dfs(r) visits all vertices of T. Property c) holds because $d[u] = d_S[u]$ for all $u \in V(T') \setminus V(T)$, and whenever $d[u] > (1+\sqrt{2})d_S[u]$ for some $u \in V(T)$, we add a path to achieve $d[u] = d_S[u]$.

Next we analyze the running time. For $d[]$ and $p[]$ we use a resizable hash table with constant expected amortized update/lookup time [16, 43]. When an element v is not in the table, we insert $p[v] \leftarrow$ **nil** and $d[v] \leftarrow \infty$. This way lines 1-2 of AdjustDistances take time $O(1)$. We also keep track of which elements $v \in V(G)$ have been assigned values in the table, so line 4 takes time $O(|V(T')|)$ rather than $O(|V(G)|)$. The running time of dfs(r) (excluding line 1, which is run $O(|V(T)|)$ times) is proportional to the number of calls to relax made by AddPath and the recursive calls to dfs. The number of relaxations is $O(|V(T')|)$ because every edge of T or T_S is relaxed at most twice by dfs and at most once by AddPath. Therefore the running time of dfs(r) is $O(|V(T')|)$, which is also $O(|V(T)|)$ assuming property b).

Now we show property b). As the algorithm executes, define a potential function Φ to be the distance estimate of the current vertex (for ease of notation we omit the dependence of Φ on the current time). When a shortest path of length $\ell = d_S[u]$ to the current vertex u is added by AddPath(u), $\phi = d[u] > \alpha\ell$, where $\alpha = 1+\sqrt{2}$. Adding the path lowers $d[u]$ to ℓ, decreasing ϕ by at least $(\alpha-1)\ell$. Hence the total length of the added paths is bounded by the sum of the decrements to ϕ during the course of the algorithm, divided by $\alpha - 1$. Since ϕ is initially 0 and always nonnegative, the sum of the decreases is at most the sum of the increments. The potential Φ increases only when the current vertex changes from some vertex u to a vertex v after the edge (u,v) was relaxed, which ensures that $d[v] \leq d[u]+1$ and that Φ increases by at most 1. Since each edge is traversed twice, the total of the increases to Φ during the course of the algorithm is bounded by twice the number of edges in T. This establishes that the total length of the added paths is bounded by $2/(\alpha-1) = \sqrt{2}$ times the total number of edges of T. Thus, $|V(T')| \leq (1+\sqrt{2})|V(T)|$, showing b).

Only property d) remains to be shown. Define analogously a potential Ψ to be $\binom{d[v]+1}{2}$ when the current vertex is $v \in V(T)$. Adding a shortest path of length ℓ when $d[v] > (1+\sqrt{2})\ell$ lowers Ψ by at least $\ell^2(1+\sqrt{2})$. The vertices added increase the sum of distances from r by at most $\binom{\ell-1}{2} \leq \ell^2/2$. Hence the total increase in sum of distances is bounded by the sum of the decrements to Ψ, divided by $2(1+\sqrt{2})$. The sum of the deceases is at most the sum of the increases. The potential Ψ increases by at most $d_G(v)$ when relaxing an edge (u,v). Since each edge is traversed twice, the total of the increases to Ψ is bounded by $\frac{2}{2(1+\sqrt{2})}\sum_{v\in V(T)} d_G(v)$. Hence $\sum_{v\in V(T')\setminus V(T)} d_G(v) \leq \frac{1}{1+\sqrt{2}}\sum_{v\in V(T)} d_G(v)$, which implies c). $\square$

A.4 Proof of Lemma 3 (Section 4)

We need the following lemma.

LEMMA 10. *Let $x_0, y_0 \in \mathbb{R}^+$ and $\lambda = \sqrt{\frac{y_0}{x_0}}$. Then, for all $x, y \in \mathbb{R}^+$ it holds that*

$$\frac{xy}{x_0y_0} \leq \left(\frac{x\lambda + \frac{y}{\lambda}}{x_0\lambda + \frac{y_0}{\lambda}}\right)^2.$$

PROOF. Our choice of λ implies that $4x_0y_0 = \left(x_0\lambda + \frac{y_0}{\lambda}\right)^2$. Recall that, by the AM–GM inequality, $\sqrt{ab} \leq \frac{a+b}{2} \Rightarrow 4ab \leq (a+b)^2$ for all $a, b \in \mathbb{R}^+$. Hence

$$\frac{xy}{x_0y_0} = \frac{4xy}{4x_0y_0} = \frac{4\,(x\lambda)\left(\frac{y}{\lambda}\right)}{\left(x_0\lambda + \frac{y_0}{\lambda}\right)^2} \leq \left(\frac{x\lambda + \frac{y}{\lambda}}{x_0\lambda + \frac{y_0}{\lambda}}\right)^2. \quad \square$$

Now we are ready to show Lemma 3. Let A^* denote the optimal solution to Problem 3 and set $\lambda = \sqrt{\frac{\sum_{u\in A^*} d_G(r,u)}{|A^*|}}$. It is easy to see that $\lambda \in [1/\sqrt{2}, \sqrt{|V(G)|}]$ as all distances $d_G(r,u)$ but one (i.e., $d_G(r,u)$ which is equal to 0) are in the range $[1, |V(G)|]$ and $|A^*| \geq 2$. Let B^* (resp., B) denote the optimal solution (resp., an α-approximate solution) to Problem 4. By our choice of λ, Lemma 10 implies that

$$\begin{aligned}\frac{\widetilde{\mathbf{A}}(B,r)}{\widetilde{\mathbf{A}}(A^*,r)} &= \frac{|B|\sum_{u\in B} d_G(r,u)}{|A^*|\sum_{u\in A^*} d_G(r,u)} \\ &\leq \left(\frac{|B|\lambda + \frac{1}{\lambda}\sum_{u\in B} d_G(r,u)}{|A^*|\lambda + \frac{1}{\lambda}\sum_{u\in A^*} d_G(r,u)}\right)^2 \\ &= \left(\frac{\mathbf{B}(B,r)}{\mathbf{B}(A^*,r)}\right)^2 \leq \left(\frac{\mathbf{B}(B,r)}{\mathbf{B}(B^*,r)}\right)^2,\end{aligned}$$

where the last inequality follows from $\mathbf{B}(A^*,r) \geq \mathbf{B}(B^*,r)$ (due to the optimality of B^* for Problem 4). To complete the proof, note that $\frac{\mathbf{B}(B,r)}{\mathbf{B}(B^*,r)} \leq \alpha$ holds by hypothesis. $\square$

A.5 Proof of Theorem 5 (Section 5)

We have to show that an optimal solution to (6) gives an optimal solution to our problem, and viceversa.

It is clear that any solution $S \subseteq V(G)$ to MIN WIENER CONNECTOR yields a feasible solution to (6): set $y_u = 1$ and $p_{uv} = 1$ iff $u, v \in S$, and for each $s, t \in S$, pick a shortest path $z_0 = s, z_1, \ldots, z_t = t$ from s to t in S and set $f^{st}_{z_i, z_{i+1}} = 1$; set all other variables to 0. This satisfies all constraints and the objective function coincides with $\mathbf{W}(S)$.

Conversely, consider an optimal solution to (6) and let $S = \{u \in V \mid y_u = 1\}$; note that $S \supseteq Q$. We show that the objective function is at least $\mathbf{W}(G[S])$. For any $s, t \in S$, $p_{st} \geq y_s + y_t - 1 \geq 1$. The constraints now imply that we can route $p_{st} \geq 1$ units of flow from s to t, where the capacity of directed edge (u,v) is at most y_u. Note that once y_u and p_{st} have been fixed, all remaining constraints involve only flow variables and constants, and only flow variables with the same pair s, t. Therefore, the only way to minimize the objective function is to find, for each s, t, a min-cost flow of value p_{st} (where the cost and capacity of every edge is one), i.e., a shortest-path from s to t in S. Thus there is such a path p, and the sum of f^{st}_{uv} for the directed edges (u,v) of p is at least $d_S(s,t)$. As this holds for all s, t, the result follows. $\square$

From Group Recommendations to Group Formation

Senjuti Basu Roy[†], Laks V. S. Lakshmanan [⋄], Rui Liu[†].
[†] University of Washington Tacoma, [⋄] University of British Columbia
{senjutib,ruiliu}@uw.edu,laks@cs.ubc.ca

ABSTRACT

There has been significant recent interest in the area of group recommendations, where, given groups of users of a recommender system, one wants to recommend top-k items to a group that maximize the satisfaction of the group members, according to a chosen semantics of group satisfaction. Examples semantics of satisfaction of a recommended itemset to a group include the so-called *least misery* (LM) and *aggregate voting* (AV). We consider the complementary problem of *how to form groups* such that the users in the formed groups are most satisfied with the suggested top-k recommendations. We assume that the recommendations will be generated according to one of the two group recommendation semantics – LM or AV. Rather than assuming groups are given, or rely on ad hoc group formation dynamics, our framework allows a *strategic* approach for forming groups of users in order to maximize satisfaction. We show that the problem is NP-hard to solve optimally under both semantics. Furthermore, we develop two efficient algorithms for group formation under LM and show that they achieve *bounded absolute error*. We develop efficient heuristic algorithms for group formation under AV. We validate our results and demonstrate the scalability and effectiveness of our group formation algorithms on two large real data sets.

1. INTRODUCTION

There is a proliferation of *group recommender systems* that cope with the challenge of addressing recommendations for groups of users. YuTV [31] is a TV program recommender for groups of viewers, LET'S BROWSE [21] recommends web pages to a group of two or more people who are browsing the web together, and FlyTrap [9] recommends music to be played in a public room. What all these recommender systems have in common is that they assume that the groups are *ad hoc*, are *formed organically and are provided as inputs*, and focus on designing the most appropriate *recommendation semantics* and effective algorithms. *In all these systems, all members of a group are recommended a common list of items to consume.* Indeed, designing semantics to recommend items to ad-hoc groups has been a subject of recent research [14, 23, 1, 27], and several algorithms have been developed for recommending items personalized to *given* groups of users [8, 1].

We, on the other hand, study the *flip problem* and address the question, *if group recommender systems follow one of these existing popular semantics, how best can we form groups to maximize user satisfaction.* In fact, we pose *this as an optimization problem to form groups in a principled manner, such that, after the groups are formed and the users inside the group are recommended an itemset to consume together, following the existing semantics and group recommendation algorithms, they are as satisfied as possible.* We describe several motivating applications next.

Applications: Travel planning for user groups is a popular group recommendation application [11], where several hundreds of travelers can register their individual preferences to visit certain points of interest (POIs) in a city. A group vacation planning agency typically supports only a few customized groups, say 25 different user groups. Given these groups, they accordingly design 25 different plans, where each plan consists of a list of $5-10$ different POIs tailored to each group. Consequently, the registered customers are to be partitioned to form 25 different groups. Each group will be recommended a plan of k items ($5 \leq k \leq 10$), based on a "standard" group recommendation semantics.

Other emerging applications, such as, recommending news [24], music [9], book, restaurants [22], and TV programs [31] to groups, make use of similar settings. The size of the user population, the number of groups, the length of the recommended item list, or the most appropriate group recommendation semantics may be application dependent and are best decided by the domain experts; for example, an online news agency may create hundreds of segments of their large reader-base (with several thousands of users) to serve the top-10 news, whereas a TV recommender system may only form a few groups to serve the most appropriate 3 programs to a family. What ties all these applications together is the applicability of the same underlying settings.

For all these scenarios, we study, *if group recommender systems follow a given semantics, how best can we can partition the user-base to form a pre-defined number of groups, such that the recommended top-k items to the groups maximize user satisfaction.* We exploit existing popular group recommendation semantics and do not propose a new one. Clearly, our problem is a *non-intrusive addition* to existing operational recommender systems and has clear practical impact in all these applications.

In fact, our *strategic* group formation is potentially of interest to all group recommender system applications, as long as they use certain recommendation semantics. Instead of ad-hoc group formation [31, 21, 9, 24, 8, 1], or grouping individuals based on similarity in preferences [22], or meta-data (e.g., socio-demographic factors [31, 21, 9]), we explicitly embed the underlying group recommendation semantics in the group formation phase, which may

SIGMOD'15, May 31–June 4, 2015, Melbourne, Victoria, Australia.

http://dx.doi.org/10.1145/2723372.2749448 .

dramatically improve user satisfaction. For example, two users with similar socio-demographic attributes may still have very distinct preferences for watching TV or listening to music; therefore, a meta-data based group formation strategy may place them in the same group, and thus a group recommendation semantics may end up recommending items to them that are not satisfactory to both. We attempt to bridge that gap and propose systematic investigation of the group formation problem. More concretely, our focus in this work is to formalize *how to form a set of user groups for a given population, such that, the aggregate satisfaction of all groups w.r.t. their recommended top-k item lists, generated according to existing popular group recommendation semantics using existing group recommendation algorithms, is maximized.*

Our work is also orthogonal to existing *market based strategies [6, 18, 20] on daily deals sites*, such as Groupon and LivingSocial. Most of these works focus on *recommending deals* (i.e., items or bundles of items) to users. They rely on incentivizing formation of groups via price discounting. The utility of such recommendation strategies is to *maximize revenue*, whereas, our group formation problem is purely designed to *maximize user satisfaction*. We elaborate on this interesting but orthogonal research direction further in the related work section.

Contributions: Our first contribution is in proposing a formalism to create groups in the context of an existing group recommender system, that naturally fits many emerging applications. In particular, we study the group formation problem under two popular group recommendation semantics, namely *least misery* (LM) and *aggregate voting* (AV) [14, 23, 1, 27, 31]. Given an item and a group, LM sets the preference rating of the item for the group to be the preference rating of the least happy member of that group for that item. On the other hand, AV sets the preference rating of the item for the group to be the aggregated (sum) preference rating of that item over the members of the group. In this paper, *given a user population of a recommender system, a set of items, and a number ℓ, we seek to partition the users into at most ℓ non-overlapping groups, such that when each group is recommended a top-k list of items under a group recommendation semantics (LM or AV), the aggregate (sum) satisfaction of the created groups is maximized.* Given a group, its satisfaction with a recommended top-k item list could be measured in many ways: by considering the group preference of the most preferred item, the least preferred item (i.e., k-th recommended item), or the sum of group preferences over all k items. These alternatives are discussed in Section 2.

Our second contribution is computational. We provide an in-depth analysis of the group formation problem and prove that finding an optimal set of groups is NP-hard under both group recommendation semantics, LM and AV. We propose two efficient approximation algorithms for group formation under LM with provable theoretical guarantees. In particular, our proposed algorithms `GRD-LM` have *absolute error* [16] guarantees. Additionally, we also describe efficient heuristic algorithms `GRD-AV` for forming groups under AV semantics and analyze the complexity of both algorithms. We also propose an integer programming based optimal solution for both LM and AV semantics (referred to Section A in appendix) which will not scale, but can be used as a reference with which to calibrate scalable algorithms w.r.t. the quality of the solution, on small data sets.

Finally, we conduct a detailed empirical evaluation by using two large scale real world data sets (Yahoo! Music and MovieLens) to demonstrate the effectiveness as well as the scalability of our proposed solutions. We also compare our proposed solutions with intuitive baseline algorithms both qualitatively and w.r.t. various performance metrics. Our experimental results indicate that our proposed algorithms successfully form groups with high satisfaction scores w.r.t. the top-k recommendations made to the groups. Additionally, we demonstrate that the proposed solutions are highly scalable and terminate within a couple of minutes in most cases. Furthermore, we conduct a user study involving users from Amazon Mechanical Turk. Our results demonstrate that our proposed formalism is indeed effective for forming multiple groups, with the individuals being highly satisfied w.r.t. the suggested top-k group recommendations. Based on our experimental analysis, our group formation algorithms consistently outperform the baseline algorithms both qualitatively and on various performance metrics.

In summary, we make the following contributions:

- We initiate the study of how to form groups in the context of recommender systems, considering popular group recommendation semantics. We formalize the task as an optimization problem, with the objective to form groups, such that the aggregated group satisfaction w.r.t. the suggested group recommendation is maximized (Section 2).
- We provide an in-depth analysis of the problem and prove that finding an optimal set of groups is NP-hard under both LM and AV semantics (Section 3). We present several simple and efficient algorithms for group formation (Sections 4 and 5). We show that our algorithms for LM semantics under both Min and Sum aggregation, achieve a bounded absolute error w.r.t. the optimal solutions (Section 4). We also work out a clean integer programming based formulation of the optimal solution under both LM and AV semantics (Appendix A).
- We conduct a comprehensive experimental study (Section 7) on Yahoo! Music and MovieLens data sets and show that our algorithms are effective in achieving high aggregate satisfaction scores for user groups compared to the optimum, lead to relatively balanced group sizes, high average group satisfaction, and scale very well w.r.t. number of users, items, items recommended, and number of groups allowed. Our user study results demonstrate the effectiveness of our proposed solutions.

Section 6 presents extensions of the proposed work. Section 8 presents related work. Finally, we conclude the paper in Section 9 and outline future research directions.

2. PRELIMINARIES & PROBLEM DEFINITION

In this section, we first discuss the preliminaries and describe our data model. We also present two running examples that are used throughout the paper. Finally, we formalize the group formation problem in sub-section 2.4.

2.1 Data Model

We assume an item-set $\mathcal{I} = \{i_1, i_2, \ldots, i_m\}$ containing m items and a user set $\mathcal{U} = \{u_1, u_2, \ldots, u_n\}$ with n users. A group g corresponds to a subset of users, i.e., $g \subseteq \mathcal{U}$. In this paper, we consider recommender systems with explicit feedback, which means users' feedback on items is in the form of an explicit rating $sc(u, i) \in \mathcal{R}$, where $\mathcal{R}$ is typically a discrete set of positive integers, e.g., $\mathcal{R} = \{1, ..., 5\}$, with r^{min} and r^{max} being the minimum and maximum possible ratings respective (e.g., r^{min} may be 0 and r^{max} may be 5). Without causing confusion, we also use $sc(u, i)$ to denote the rating of item i predicted for user u by the recommender system.[1] Thus, in general, $sc(u, i)$ denotes *user u's*

[1]Predicted ratings may be real numbers.

User-item Ratings	u_1	u_2	u_3	u_4	u_5	u_6
i_1	1	2	2	2	3	1
i_2	4	3	5	5	1	2
i_3	3	5	1	1	1	5

Table 1: User Item Preference Rating for Example 1

User-item Ratings	u_1	u_2	u_3	u_4	u_5	u_6
i_1	3	1	2	2	1	3
i_2	1	4	5	5	2	2
i_3	4	3	1	1	3	1

Table 2: User Item Preference Rating for Example 2

preference for item i, whether user provided or system predicted. We sometimes also refer to $sc(u, i)$ as the *relevance of an item for a user*. The recommended top-k item list for a group g is denoted $\mathcal{I}_g^k$, where $\mathcal{I}_g^k \subseteq \mathcal{I}$ and $|\mathcal{I}_g^k| = k$. Furthermore, we denote the k-th item score for group g as $sc(g, i^k)$, where i^k denotes the k-th item (i.e., the worst item) in the top-k item list $\mathcal{I}_g^k$ recommended to g. We note that $sc(g, i^k)$ is a quantity that is defined according to a chosen group satisfaction semantics such as LM or AV, as explained in the next subsection.

EXAMPLE 1. Imagine that the user set $\mathcal{U} = \{u_1, u_2, u_3, u_4, u_5, u_6\}$ contains 6 members and the itemset $\mathcal{I} = \{i_1, i_2, i_3\}$ has 3-items. The user's preference for the itemset is given (or predicted) as in Table 1. Imagine that the user set needs to be partitioned into at most 3 groups ($\ell \leq 3$). □

EXAMPLE 2. Imagine that the same user set and with the same itemset has now different ratings, as presented in Table 2. Let us assume that the user set needs to be partitioned into at most 2 groups ($\ell \leq 2$). □

2.2 Group Recommendation Semantics

A group recommendation semantics spells out a numeric measure of just how satisfied a group is with an item recommended to it. Two popular semantics of group recommendation that have been employed in the literature on group recommendations are: (i) aggregate voting and (ii) least misery. Given a group g and item i, the aggregated voting score of item i for the group is the sum of the preference ratings of item i for each member $u \in g$. On the other hand, the least misery score of item i for group g is the minimum preference rating of item i across all members of g.

DEFINITION 1 (LEAST MISERY SEMANTICS $\mathcal{F}_{LM}$). *[14, 23, 1, 27] The group satisfaction score of item i for group g is the least score of i across members of g, i.e.,* $sc(g, i) := min_{u \in g} sc(u, i)$.

DEFINITION 2 (AGGREGATED VOTING SEMANTICS $\mathcal{F}_{AV}$). *[14, 23, 1, 27] The group satisfaction score of item i for g is the aggregated score of i for all members of g, i.e.,* $sc(g, i) := \sum_{u \in g} sc(u, i)$.

2.3 Group Satisfaction Aggregation

Given a group g and a list of k recommended items $\mathcal{I}_g^k$, there are multiple ways of aggregating the scores of the k items in order to define the group g's satisfaction with the recommended list $\mathcal{I}_g^k$. Some of the natural alternatives are described below.

- Max-aggregation: Satisfaction of the group is measured as the score of the very top item in the list, i.e., $g^s(\mathcal{I}_g^k) := sc(g, i^1)$.
- Min-aggregation: Satisfaction of the group is measured as the score of the k-th item in the list, i.e., $g^s(\mathcal{I}_g^k) := sc(g, i^k)$.
- Sum-aggregation: Satisfaction of the group is measured as the sum of scores of all items in the list, i.e., satisfaction of group g is, $g^s(\mathcal{I}_g^k) := \Sigma_{i \in \mathcal{I}_g^k} sc(g, i)$. It is also possible to design a Weighted Sum aggregation function, where each of the k items is assigned a differential weight correlated with its position i. We present a brief discussion of this extension in Section 6.

Notice that when $k = 1$, Max, Min, and Sum-aggregation coincide.

2.4 Problem Definition

Recommendation Aware Group Formation (GF): Given items $\{i_1, i_2, \ldots i_m\}$ and users $\{u_1, u_2, \ldots u_n\}$, a group recommendation semantics LM or AV, two integers k and ℓ, create a set of at most ℓ non-overlapping groups, where each group g is associated with a top-k itemset $\mathcal{I}_g^k$ in accordance with semantics LM or AV, s.t.:

- The aggregated group satisfaction of the created groups is maximized; i.e., maximize $Obj = \sum_{j=1}^{\ell} g_j^s(\mathcal{I}_{g_j}^k)$.

3. COMPLEXITY ANALYSIS

In this section, we show that the recommendation-aware group formation (GF) problem is NP-hard. Our hardness reduction is from Exact Cover by 3-Sets (X3C), known to be NP-hard [12]. Since a direct reduction is involved, we first prove a helper lemma, which shows that a restricted version of Boolean Expected Component Sum (ECS[2]), called Perfect ECS (PECS for short), is NP-hard. We then reduce PECS to GF.

An instance of PECS consists of a collection V of m-dimensional boolean vectors, i.e., $V \subset \{0, 1\}^m$, and a number K. The question is whether there exists a disjoint partition of V into K subsets $V_1, \ldots, V_K$ such that $\sum_{i=1}^{K} max_{1 \leq j \leq m} (\sum_{\vec{v} \in V_i} \vec{v}[j]) = |V|$. We have:

LEMMA 1. *PECS is NP-complete.*

PROOF. The membership of PECS in NP is straightforward.

To prove hardness, we reduce a known NP-Complete problem, namely, Exact Cover by 3-sets (X3C) [12] to PECS.

X3C: An instance $\mathcal{I}$ of X3C consists of a ground set $\mathcal{X}$ with $3q$ elements and a collection $\mathcal{C} = \{S_1, \ldots, S_m\}$ of 3-element subsets of $\mathcal{X}$. The problem is to find if there exists a subset $\mathcal{C}' \subseteq \mathcal{C}$, such that $\mathcal{C}'$ is an exact cover of $\mathcal{X}$, i.e., each element of $\mathcal{X}$ occurs in exactly one subset in $\mathcal{C}'$.

Given an instance $\mathcal{I}$ of X3C, we create an instance $\mathcal{J}$ of PECS as follows. Transform each element $x_i \in \mathcal{X}$ into a boolean vector $\vec{v}_i \in \{0, 1\}^m$ by setting $\vec{v}_i[j] = 1$ if $x_i \in S_j$ and $\vec{v}_i[j] = 0$ otherwise. Thus, $V = \{\vec{v}_1, \ldots, \vec{v}_{3q}\}$, where vector $\vec{v}_i$ corresponds to ground element $x_i \in \mathcal{X}$. By construction, subset $S_j \in \mathcal{C}$ corresponds to dimension j of the vectors. Notice that at most three vectors have a 1 in any given dimension. Thus, instance $\mathcal{J}$ consists of the vectors V and the number $K := q$.

We claim that $\mathcal{I}$ is a YES-instance of X3C iff $\mathcal{J}$ is a YES-instance of PECS.

($\Rightarrow$): Suppose $\mathcal{C}' = \{S_{j_1}, \ldots, S_{j_q}\} \subseteq \mathcal{C}$ is an exact (disjoint) cover of $\mathcal{X}$. Then consider the partition $[V_1, \ldots, V_q]$ of V, where $\vec{v}_i \in V_k$ iff $x_i \in S_{j_k}$. Notice that each V_k consists of exactly three

[2]Expected Component Sum is also NP-hard [12].

vectors. Since $\mathcal{C}'$ is an exact cover of $\mathcal{X}$, each element $x \in \mathcal{X}$ appears in exactly one subset $S_k \in \mathcal{C}'$. Thus, $\max_{1 \le \ell \le m} \sum_{\vec{v} \in T_i} \vec{v}[\ell] = 3$ and hence $\sum_{k=1}^{q} (\max_{1 \le \ell \le m} \sum_{\vec{v} \in T_i} \vec{v}[\ell]) = 3q$, showing $\mathcal{J}$ is a YES-instance.

($\Leftarrow$): Let π be a partition of V such that $\sum_{T \in \pi} (\max_{1 \le \ell \le m} \sum_{\vec{v} \in V_i} \vec{v}[\ell]) = 3q$, witnessing the fact that $\mathcal{J}$ is a YES-instance. Observe that any block $T \in \pi$ with > 3 vectors in it cannot contribute more than 3 to the sum above. As well, any block $T \in \pi$ with < 3 vectors will surely contribute less than 3 to the sum above. Since the overall sum is $3q$, it follows that every block must have exactly three vectors in it. For a block $T \in \pi$, let $dim(T) = argmax\{\sum_{\vec{v} \in T} \vec{v}[j] \mid 1 \le j \le m\}$, i.e., $dim(T)$ is the dimension which maximizes the component sum. Then consider the collection $\mathcal{C}' = \{S_{dim(T)} \in \mathcal{C} \mid T \in \pi\}$. It is easy to verify that $|\mathcal{C}'| = q$ and that every element $x \in \mathcal{X}$ appears in exactly one set $S \in \mathcal{C}'$.

□

THEOREM 1. *The Group Formation Problem is NP-hard under both the least misery and aggregated voting semantics.*

PROOF. We prove hardness of the restricted version of GF, where $k = 1$ item is to be recommended to each group such that sum of satisfaction measures of each group is maximized, from which the theorem follows. We prove this hardness by reduction from PECS. Given an instance $\mathcal{I}$ of PECS, consisting of a set of boolean vectors $V \subset \{0, 1\}^m$ and an integer K, we create an instance $\mathcal{J}$ of GF as follows. Each vector $\vec{v} \in V$ corresponds to a user's preference over the m items, where preferences are binary. The decision version of GF asks whether there exists a disjoint partition of V into K groups $g_1, ..., g_K$ such that $\sum_{j=1}^{K} \max_{1 \le \ell \le m} (min_{\vec{v} \in g_j} \vec{v}[\ell]) \ge K$. We claim that this is true iff $\mathcal{I}$ is a YES-instance.

($\Rightarrow$): Suppose there are $g_1, ..., g_K$ such that $\sum_{j=1}^{K} \max_{1 \le \ell \le m} (min_{\vec{v} \in g_j} \vec{v}[\ell]) \ge K$. This sum can never be $> K$. If we replace the min by a sum in the objective function above, it is easy to see that the value will be exactly $|V|$, showing $\mathcal{I}$ is a YES-instance.

($\Leftarrow$): Suppose there is a disjoint partition of V into K subsets showing that $\mathcal{I}$ is a YES-instance. Again, replacing the innermost summation by a min in the objective function of PECS, will result in a value of K, showing $\mathcal{J}$ is a YES-instance.

Hardness under the aggregated voting semantics follows trivially from the construction above.

□

4. APPROXIMATION ALGORITHMS: LM

In this section, we investigate efficient algorithms for group formation based on LM. Notice that when $k = 1$, the Max, Min, and Sum aggregation (see Section 2.3) coincide. When $k > 1$, basing the LM score on the bottom item (i.e., the k-th item in the top-k list) corresponds to Min aggregation while basing it on the top item corresponds to Max aggregation, and the entire top-k set corresponds to Sum aggregation. Unless otherwise stated, we henceforth focus on Min and Sum aggregation.

We propose two greedy algorithms, where both of them have respective *absolute error guarantees*. Algorithm GRD-LM-MIN is designed for LM considering Min aggregation and Algorithm GRD-LM-SUM is for Sum aggregation.

For simplicity of exposition, we use our running example 1 and 2 from Section 2. We interleave our exposition of the algorithm with an illustration of how it works on these examples for $k = 1$ as well as $k = 2$ (i.e., top-1 or top-2 items are recommended).

4.1 Min Aggregation

Our proposed algorithm operates in a top-down fashion and gradually forms the groups. Intuitively, the algorithm consists of the following three high level steps.

Step 1 - forming a set of intermediate groups: It begins with the user set $\mathcal{U}$ and leverages a preference list ($\mathcal{L}$) of items for each user u, sorted in non-increasing order of item ratings. In our running example, for user u_2 in Example 1, $\mathcal{L}^{u_2} = \langle i_3, 5; i_2, 3; ; i_1, 2 \rangle$. After that, the algorithm creates a set of intermediate groups. Each group g *contains a set of users who have the same top-k item sequence*, as well as the *same preference rating for the bottom item* across all users in the group. E.g., the group $\{u_2, u_6\}$ shares the same top-1 item (i_3) and the same rating for it (5). Thus, for $k = 1$, this is a valid group. On the other hand, for $k = 2$, even though u_2 and u_6 share the same top-2 sequence of items ($i_3; i_2$), they have distinct ratings for the bottom item, namely 3 and 2, and so they cannot be in the same group for $k = 2$.

Assuming Min-aggregation, the interesting observation is that, for each group, it is a good strategy to form these groups on the common top-k item sequence, as long as the group members (users) match on the preference rating of the bottom item. This is because the objective function (LM score) is based on the ratings of the bottom (i.e., k-th) item among group members. On the other hand, a subtle point is that it is *not* a good strategy to consider just the bottom item only (even though the aggregation is on that item) instead of the entire top-k sequence. The reason is that the bottom item recommended to a group containing a user u may differ from u's personal bottom item. We next illustrate this with an example.

EXAMPLE 3. Consider a group consisting of two users u_1, u_2 whose individual ratings over items $i_1, ..., i_3$ are respectively $u_1 = (5, 4, 1)$ and $u_2 = (1, 4, 5)$. For $k = 2$, the second best (i.e., bottom) item for either user in isolation is i_2, and yet under LM semantics, it can be easily verified that the top-2 item list recommended to the group $\{u_1, u_2\}$ is $(i_2; i_*)$, where i_* could be any one of the remaining items. Notice that the bottom item recommended to the group is different from the indidual bottom preference of every group member, even though they all shared the same item i_2 as their bottom preference, with identical ratings (4). The reason this happened is because i_2 ended up having the ***highest*** LM score for this group, among *all items*. When i_2 is moved to the top position, no matter which other item is chosen as the top-2 (bottom) item for the group, its LM score is just 1 in this example. This shows that forming a group solely based on shared bottom item and score can lead to a group with a poor LM score, when $k > 1$. □

To generalize this observation, our algorithm needs to store the top-k common sequence as well as the rating of the item on which the group satisfaction (i.e., the LM score of that group) is aggregated. Next, we describe how one can execute this first step above efficiently.

For every user u, we create a sequence $\langle i_1^u, i_2^u, ..i_k^u : sc(u, i^k) \rangle$ comprising her top-k ranked items (in sequence) followed by the preference rating of the k-th (bottom) item, $sc(u, i^k)$. We use a hash map to hash each user u using $(\langle i_1^u, i_2^u, ..i_k^u : sc(u, i^k) \rangle)$ as the key and the user id u as the value. Then, we create a heap $\mathcal{H}$ to store the LM scores $sc(u, i^k)$ for various users.[3] This data structure enables us to efficiently retrieve the highest LM score, needed for Step 2 below. In our Example 1, when $k = 1$, we hash user u_2 with key $\langle i_3 : 5 \rangle$ and value u_2. We add the entry $sc(u, i^k)$ to the heap, i.e., $\mathcal{H}.insert(sc(u, i^k))$. Notice that, users with same keys get hashed together and the associated value gets

[3]It is sufficient to store the value once per intermediate group formed.

updated with their union after each such operation in the hash map. For example, $\{u_3, u_4\}$ gets hashed together, with key $\langle i_2 : 5\rangle$ and value $\{u_3, u_4\}$. Finally, we preserve the association between the hash keys and the corresponding LM scores in another data structure. This operation generates the set of intermediate groups, where users with same keys belong to the same group.

For our running example (Example 1), when $k = 1$, we form the following set of intermediate user groups: $\{u_2, u_6\}$ on item i_3, $\{u_3, u_4\}$ on item i_2, and two singleton groups for $\{u_1\}$ and $\{u_5\}$, since they do not share a common top-1 item. When $k = 2$, $\{u_3, u_4\}$ will be grouped together with key $\langle i_2, i_1 : 2\rangle$ and value $\{u_3, u_4\}$. $\{u_3, u_4\}, \{u_1\}, \{u_2\}, \{u_5\}, \{u_6\}$ are the groups that get created this way. Observe that the sets of intermediate groups generated for $k = 1$ and for $k = 2$ are different.

Step 2 - greedy selection of $\ell - 1$ groups: Recall that the group formation problem requires that we form at most ℓ groups of users. Observe that the objective function value *Obj* (see Section 2.4) is maximized when all ℓ groups are formed. Accordingly, in this step, the algorithm runs in $\ell - 1$ iterations. Continuing with Example 1, suppose $\ell = 3$, then this means that this step of the algorithm runs for 2 iterations. In iteration i, it retrieves the *maximum element* from the heap $\mathcal{H}$ (i.e., highest associated LM score), extracts the corresponding key and uses that to output the user group from the hash map. After that, it deletes that $\langle key, value\rangle$ entry from the hash map and deletes the corresponding LM score from the heap.

When $k = 1$, in Example 1, iteration 1 outputs the group $\{u_3, u_4\}$ with score 5 and iteration 2 outputs $\{u_2, u_6\}$ with score 5. When $k = 2$, for the same example instance, iteration 1 outputs the group $\{u_1\}$ with score 3 and iteration 2 outputs $\{u_2\}$ with score 3.

Step 3 - forming the ℓ-th group: Finally, the last group g_ℓ is formed by considering all the remaining users from the hash map and a top-k LM score is assigned to this group. For our running example (Example 1), when $k = 1$, this group is $\{u_1, u_5\}$ with LM score of 1. When $k = 2$, this last group is $\{u_3, u_4, u_5, u_6\}$ with LM score of 1. Our algorithm terminates after this iteration. When $k = 1$, the final set of groups are $\{u_3, u_4\}$, $\{u_2, u_6\}$, $\{u_1, u_5\}$ and the corresponding value *Obj* of the objective function is $5 + 5 + 1 = 11$. When $k = 2$, the final set of groups are $\{u_1\}$, $\{u_2\}$, $\{u_3, u_4, u_5, u_6\}$. The corresponding value of *Obj* is $3+3+1 = 7$. The pseudo-code of the algorithm is presented in Algorithm 1.

In general, the grouping formed by Algorithm GRD-LM-MIN is sub-optimal. For Example 1, we saw that the objective function value achieved by the grouping found by GRD-LM-MIN is 11. It may be verified that the optimal grouping for Example 1 is $\{u_1, u_3, u_4\}$, $\{u_2, u_6\}$, $\{u_5\}$ with an overall *Obj* value of $4 + 5 + 3 = 12$.

4.2 Sum Aggregation

The greedy algorithm for Sum aggregation, GRD-LM-SUM, exploits a similar framework, except that it primarily differs in *Step-1, i.e., in the intermediate groups formation step* of the previous algorithm. Notice that GRD-LM-MIN forms these intermediate groups by bundling those users who have the same top-k sequence, as well as the same preference rating for the k-th item. Obviously, this strategy falls short for GRD-LM-SUM, where, we are interested to aggregate satisfaction over the entire k-itemset. Therefore, GRD-LM-SUM forms these intermediate user groups by hashing users who have not only the *same top-k item sequence, but also the same score for each item.*

More concretely, for every user u, we create a sequence $\langle i_1^u : sc(u, i^1), i_2^u : sc(u, i^2), ..i_k^u : sc(u, i^k)\rangle$ comprising her top-k ranked items and scores. We use a hash map to hash each user u using $\langle i_1^u : sc(u, i^1), i_2^u : sc(u, i^2), ..i_k^u : sc(u, i^k)\rangle$ as the key and the user id u as the value. Then, in the heap $\mathcal{H}$, we store

Algorithm 1 Algorithm GRD-LM-MIN

Require: Preference lists $\mathcal{L}^u \forall u \in \mathcal{U}$, k, group recommendation semantics $\mathcal{F}_{LM}$, ℓ; hash map h and heap $\mathcal{H}$;

for every user u, generate top-k preference list $\mathcal{L}^{u^k}$ from $\mathcal{L}^u$;
for every user u, generate top-k item sequence and the k-th item score $sc(u, i^k)$, i.e., $\langle i_1^u, i_2^u, ..i_k^u : sc(u, i^k)\rangle$;
For every distinct $\langle i_1^u, i_2^u, ..i_k^u : sc(u, i^k)\rangle$, create $h.key = \langle i_1^u, i_2^u, ..i_k^u : sc(u, i^k)\rangle$, $h.value = \{u\}$, where each user u has same $sc(u, i^k)$;
Perform $\mathcal{H}.insert = sc(u, i^k)$, associated with every unique key;
$\mathcal{G} = \{$ values present in h$\}$;
$Obj = 0$;
$j = 0$;
while $(j < (\ell - 1))$ **do**
    Retrieve the maximum LM score SC from $\mathcal{H}(Maximum)$;
    Retrieve the sequence key $\mathcal{S}$ associated with SC;
    Retrieve the value for the given key, $g = h.key(\mathcal{S})$;
    $Obj = Obj + SC$;
    Remove $\mathcal{S}$ from h;
    Remove SC from $\mathcal{H}$;
    $j = j + 1$;
end while
Form group g_ℓ with all the remaining users in $\mathcal{U}$;
$g_\ell^s(\mathcal{I}_{g_\ell}^k) = \min_{\forall u \in g_\ell} sc(u, i^k)$;
$Obj = Obj + g_\ell^s(\mathcal{I}_{g_\ell}^k)$;
return $g_1, g_2, \ldots g_\ell$ groups and Obj;

the aggregated LM scores $sc(u, \sum_{j=1}^{k} i^j)$ for various users - i.e., we perform, $\mathcal{H}.insert(sc(u, \sum_{j=1}^{k} i^j))$. In our Example 1, when $k = 2$, this way, users u_3 and u_4 are hashed together with key $\langle i_2 : 5, i_1 : 2\rangle$ and value $\{u_3, u_4\}$. The other four users get hashed in 4 individual buckets, as their top-2 item rating sequences do not match. We insert a score of $5 + 2 = 7$ in the heap for users u_3 and u_4, and the respective sum scores of top-2 items for the other four users.

Steps 2 and 3 of GRD-LM-SUM are akin to that of GRD-LM-MIN, except for the obvious difference, that the group satisfaction score is now aggregated over all k-items. We omit the details for brevity. Using Example 1, this algorithm may form the following three groups at the end - $\{u_3, u_4\}$, $\{u_1, u_5, u_6\}$, $\{u_2\}$ with the total objective function value as $(5 + 2) + (1 + 1) + (5 + 3) = 17$. Appendix B gives an example where the grouping produced by GRD-LM-SUM is suboptimal.

4.3 Analysis

In this subsection, we analyze the performance of the greedy algorithms for LM, compared to optimal grouping. We also analyze the running time complexity of the algorithms.

Approximation Analysis: Our analysis focuses on the absolute error of the greedy algorithms, compared to their optimal solutions.

DEFINITION 3 (ABSOLUTE ERROR [16]). Let Π be a problem, I an instance of Π, $A(I)$ be the solution provided by algorithm A, $f(A(I))$ be the value of the objective function for that solution. Let $OPT(I)$ be the value of the objective function for an optimal solution on instance I. We say Algorithm A solves the problem with a guaranteed absolute error of η, provided for every instance I of Π, $|f(A(I)) - OPT(I)| <= \eta$. □

THEOREM 2. *Algorithm* GRD-LM-MIN *solves the group formation problem under LM semantics using min-aggregation with a guaranteed absolute error of at most r^{max}, where $r^{max} \in \mathcal{R}$ is the maximum value in the rating scale.*

PROOF. Let $g_1, g_2, \ldots g_\ell$ (resp., $g_1', g_2', \ldots g_\ell'$) be the set of groups formed by Algorithm GRD-LM-MIN (resp., the optimal algorithm).

Sort the groups w.r.t. the group's LM score and assume that the orders $g_1, ..., g_\ell$ and $g'_1, ..., g'_\ell$ are non-increasing in the group LM scores.

Recall that $\mathcal{I}_g^k$ denotes the top-k item list recommended to a group g under the group recommendation semantics under consideration, which, for this theorem, is LM. Similarly, $g^s(\mathcal{I}_g^k)$ denotes the LM score of group g w.r.t. the recommended top-k item list $\mathcal{I}_g^k$. Let $\texttt{OPT}(i) := \sum_{j=1}^{i} g_j'^s(\mathcal{I}_{g'_j}^k)$ and $\texttt{GRD}(i) := \sum_{j=1}^{i} g_j^s(\mathcal{I}_{g_j}^k)$, i.e., they are the partial sum of LM scores of the first i groups formed by the two algorithms. Clearly, $\texttt{OPT}(\ell)$ and $\texttt{GRD}(\ell)$ are the final objective function values achieved by both algorithms and $\texttt{OPT}(\ell) = \texttt{OPT}(\ell-1) + g_\ell'^s(\mathcal{I}_{g'_\ell}^k)$ and similarly, $\texttt{GRD}(\ell) = \texttt{GRD}(\ell-1) + g_\ell^s(\mathcal{I}_{g_\ell}^k)$. The overall proof hinges on the following points.

(1) The aggregated satisfaction score generated by the best $\ell - 1$ groups of GRD is always larger or equal to that of OPT, i.e., $\texttt{GRD}(\ell - 1) \geq \texttt{OPT}(\ell - 1)$. We prove this below with a simple domination argument.

First, notice that the LM score of g_1 cannot be less than that of g'_1. By construction, g_1 consists of a set of users who are indistinguishable w.r.t. their top-k list and bottom item score, which is what determines the LM score of a group; besides, g_1 has the highest such bottom score and hence highest possible LM score among all possible groups. Let $i < \ell$ be the smallest number such that the LM score of g_i is less than that of g'_i. Removal of any user from g_i leaves its LM score unchanged while adding a new user to g_i cannot possibly increase its LM score. This contradicts the assumption. We just showed for $1 \leq i < \ell$, g_i dominates g'_i. Thus, $\texttt{GRD}(\ell - 1) \geq \texttt{OPT}(\ell - 1)$.

(2) For the ℓ-th group, notice that $g_\ell^s(\mathcal{I}_{g_\ell}^k) \geq g'^s_\ell(\mathcal{I}_{g'_\ell}^k) - r^{max}$, since the maximum possible rating value is r^{max}.

The theorem follows from (1) and (2). □

THEOREM 3. *Algorithm* GRD-LM-SUM *solves the group formation problem under LM semantics using Sum aggregation with a guaranteed absolute error of at most* $k \times r^{max}$, *where* $r^{max} \in \mathcal{R}$ *is the maximum value in the rating scale.*

PROOF. (Sketch): We omit the details for brevity but note that this proof uses similar reasoning as above. Akin to GRD-LM-MIN, only the ℓ-th group of GRD-LM-SUM is subject to error compared to OPT, where each of the k-items can accrue at most r^{max} error. Therefore, the aggregated error over all k items, i.e., the absolute error of GRD-LM-SUM, is upper-bounded by $k \times r^{max}$. □

Running time complexity: We first describe the running time complexity of GRD-LM-MIN. *Line 2* of Algorithm GRD-LM-MIN takes $O(nk)$ time overall to produce top-k item list per user. *Line 3* takes $O(n)$ time to hash all users. Adding LM score to the heap also takes $O(n)$ time overall. The *while loop* runs for $(\ell - 1)$ iterations and in each iteration the highest LM score is obtained in constant time from the heap, and rebuilding the heap takes $O(\log n)$ time. Therefore, the entire *while loop* takes $O(\ell \log n)$ time. Forming the ℓ-th group (*lines 17-18*) can take at most $O(n \log k)$ time. Therefore, the overall complexity of the algorithm is $O(nk + n + \ell \log n)$ or simply $O(nk + \ell \log n)$. Similarly, it can be shown that the running time of GRD-LM-SUM is also $O(nk + \ell \log n)$.

5. ON APPROXIMATION ALGORITHMS : AV

Next, we describe algorithms to produce groups with high satisfaction scores under the semantics of aggregate voting (AV) considering both Min and Sum aggregation. Unlike least misery (LM), aggregate voting defines the satisfaction score of a group as the sum of the preference scores of the individual users in the group, for the recommended top-k itemset.

An insight for forming good groupings under the AV semantics is that users who share the same top-k sequence of items could be grouped together, irrespective of the underlying aggregation function (Min/Max/Sum). Notice that the grouping principle differs from that used by the greedy algorithms for LM, which look for not only common top-k item sequence but also a common rating for the bottom (k-th) item (GRD-LM-MIN) or for all k items (GRD-LM-SUM). To see why the above grouping principle is intuitive, notice that a group formed in this way preserves the personal top-k list associated with each group member. Secondly, the contribution of this group to the overall satisfaction score of the grouping is the sum of ratings of the bottom item (Min aggregation), or all k-items (Sum aggregation). Two users who have the same sequence of top-k item sequence therefore are best grouped together, irrespective of their individual item preference. Thus, grouping on item's score is not a useful operation for AV semantics.

We devise two algorithms GRD-AV-MIN (for Min aggregation) and GRD-AV-SUM (for Sum aggregation) that exploit the same algorithmic framework as that of greedy algorithms for LM.

Min Aggregation: GRD-AV-MIN also runs in a top-down manner (starting with a single group with all users and forming a set of intermediate groups from there) and consists of three primary steps. Computationally, it has only two major differences with GRD-LM-MIN, described next:

(1) Consider *Lines 2 and 3* of Algorithm 1 which hash every unique *top-k item sequence and the bottom item score* in the hash map. By contrast, as explained above, GRD-AV-MIN hashes *only the top-k item sequence and not the k-th item score.* Because of this, GRD-AV-MIN is likely to generate fewer unique hash keys (and hence fewer intermediate groups). This observation is corroborated by our experiments, in Section 7.1.

(2) The other difference is more obvious: the group satisfaction score is computed differently in GRD-AV-MIN compared to GRD-LM-MIN. What we store in heap $\mathcal{H}$ in *line 4* is the aggregated group satisfaction score $\sum_u sc(u, i^k)$, where each user u has the same top-k item sequence, and $sc(u, i^k)$ is their respective bottom item score.

The remaining operations of Algorithms GRD-AV-MIN and GRD-LM-MIN are essentially similar.

Consider Example 2 and assume the groups are to be formed using Min-aggregation function over top-2 ($k = 2$) recommended itemset under AV.

Step-1 of GRD-AV-MIN will only group $\{u_3, u_4\}$ together as they have the same top-2 item sequence, $h.key = \langle i_2, i_1 \rangle$ and $h.value = \{u_3, u_4\}$. The heap $\mathcal{H}$ will insert 4 as the corresponding AV score. The remaining four users will form singleton groups.

Step-2 of GRD-AV-MIN will have only one iteration (as $\ell - 1 = 1$). It will retrieve that element from the heap with the highest AV score on the top-2 item for item i_1, which is 4. Consequently, it will produce $\{u_3, u_4\}$ as the first group. The top-2 itemset for this group will be (i_2, i_1).

Step-3 of GRD-AV-MIN will form the second group by merging the remaining singleton groups into $\{u_1, u_2, u_5, u_6\}$. The AV score on the top-2 item is 9 considering item i_2. This group will be recommended the following top-2 itemset, (i_3, i_2). The algorithm terminates after that and achieves the objective function value 13.

Notice that, GRD-AV-MIN may produce sub-optimal answers as well. For Example 2, the optimal two user groups are instead $\{u_1, u_3, u_4\}$, $\{u_2, u_5, u_6\}$. Now, the first group has the same recommended item list as that of the first group of GRD-AV-MIN, however, the second group has $\{i_2, i_3\}$ as the recommended itemset. The overall objective function value is now 14, which is higher.

Sum Aggregation: Operationally, there is no difference between `GRD-AV-MIN` and `GRD-AV-SUM`, except for the obvious difference, that the latter aggregates the group satisfaction score over the entire k-itemset (not just on the k-th item). Using Example 2 again, Step-1 of `GRD-AV-SUM` will group $\{u_3, u_4\}$ together, as they have the same top-2 item sequence, $h.key = \langle i_2, i_1 \rangle$ and $h.value = \{u_3, u_4\}$, but will insert $(5+2)+(5+2) = 14$ as the corresponding AV score in the heap. Other than that, the rest of the users will form four singleton groups. `GRD-AV-SUM` will result in the same set of user groups as that of `GRD-AV-MIN` but the overall objective function value is $14 + 20 = 34$, as the second group $\{u_1, u_2, u_5, u_6\}$ will now have a satisfaction score of $(4+3+3+1)+(1+4+2+2) = 20$ based on the Sum-aggregation.

5.1 Analysis

Akin to Section 4.3, we present both qualitative and runtime analyses of the greedy algorithms for AV.

Qualitative Analysis: Unlike `GRD-LM` algorithms, greedy algorithms for AV do not come with any guarantees about the total satisfaction score of the grouping they provide. While at this time the approximability of optimal group formation under AV semantics is open, we *conjecture* that the problem is MAX-SNP-Hard [15] and cannot be approximated within a constant factor. We next give an example to bring out the subtleties of AV semantics. The point is that, *by grouping a user u with others such that the resulting top-k order is personally arguably worse for user u, can still produce a group with higher group satisfaction score, than if u had been grouped with users with the same top-k item list.*

EXAMPLE 4. Consider four users $u_1, ..., u_4$ and two items i_1, i_2. Let the ratings for the users, respectively be $u_1 = (5, 4)$, $u_2 = u_3 = (4, 5)$, and $u_4 = (3, 2)$. Let $k = 2$. Suppose we wish to form two groups. Considering Min aggregation, grouping based on common top-2 item list would produce the groups $\{u_1, u_4\}$ (satisfaction score $4+2 = 6$) and $\{u_2, u_3\}$ (satisfaction score $4+4 = 8$) for an overall satisfaction score of 14. However, suppose u_1 is grouped together with u_2, u_3 and u_4 is left alone. The top-2 list for the group $\{u_1, u_2, u_3\}$ becomes $(i_2; i_1)$, whereas i_1 is u_1's favorite. Yet, the satisfaction scores are $5 + 4 + 4 = 13$ for the first group and 2 for the second, for a total satisfaction score of 15. Even though u_1's top-2 order changed to something sub-optimal for u_1, the overall satisfaction has improved! This kind of behavior is impossible under LM semantics. This illustrates that it's tricky to reason about forming groups that even approximate the optimal satisfaction score for AV semantics. □

Running time complexity: Running time of the greedy algorithms of AV is similar to that of the LM algorithms, except that the group satisfaction score needs to iterate over all the users to compute the sum or iterate over all k items for the Sum-aggregation. Therefore, adding AV scores to the heap for `GRD-AV-MIN` and `GRD-AV-SUM` now take $O(nk)$ time. The *while loop* will overall take $O(\ell \log n)$ time. The last step will now take $O(nk)$ time. Therefore, both the algorithms accept same time complexity, i.e., $O(nk + \ell \log n)$.

6. DISCUSSION

In this section, we present some extensions to our proposed group formation framework. In particular, we describe how to extend Sum Aggregation to consider differential weights, as briefly discussed in Section 2.3. Intuitively, *Weighted Sum Aggregation* can assign different weights to the top-k items and not treat them equally. We next describe two natural alternatives.

Weights at the item list level: For any group, we can assign a weight to each of the top-k recommended items, where the weights could simply be inversely proportional to the position or its logarithm. This way, the top items will have higher weight than the lower ones. Then instead of Sum, we compute Weighted Sum LM or AV. This extension does not introduce any complications to our proposed algorithms, as we only need to consider the weights when the overall objective function value is calculated.

Weights at the user level: A more interesting scenario is to consider weighted aggregation at the user level. More specifically, how satisfied an individual user is with the recommended top-k items could be measured using IR techniques, such as, *NDCG* (Normalized Discounted Cumulative Gain) [5]. Using a graded relevance scale, NDCG computes the user satisfaction (i.e., gain) for an item, given its position in the result list. The gain is then aggregated from the top of the item list to the bottom and the gain of each item is discounted at lower ranks. After weighted satisfaction of each user is computed, any group recommendation semantics (such as, LM or AV) could be used to compute the group satisfaction. Our proposed solutions do not require any significant change even here, except for the fact that the user satisfaction will be computed in a weighted fashion that our objective function must account for. Notice that, except for the ℓ-th group in our greedy algorithm, all the users in the first $\ell - 1$ groups are fully satisfied, i.e., the recommended top-k lists exactly match their individual top-k lists. Only for users in the ℓ-th group, dissatisfaction may occur, which does not affect the theoretical guarantees.

7. EXPERIMENTAL EVALUATIONS

We evaluate our proposed algorithms w.r.t. their effectiveness and efficiency. We also conduct a small scale user study on Amazon Mechanical Turk (AMT) to evaluate effectiveness.

The development and experimentation environment uses Python on a 2.9 GHz Intel Core i7 with 8 GB of memory using OS X 10.9.5 OS. We use IBM CPLEX for solving the IP instances. All numbers are presented as the average of three runs.

Datasets: (1) Yahoo! Music: This dataset represents a snapshot of the Yahoo! Music community's preferences for various songs. Standard pre-processing for collaborative filtering and rating prediction was applied to prepare this data set. The data has been trimmed so that each user has rated at least 20 songs, and each song has been rated by at least 20 users. The data has been randomly partitioned so as to correspond to 10 equally sized sets of users, in order to enable cross-validation. We use a subset of this dataset in our experiments. The ratings values are on a scale from 1 to 5, 5 being the best. More information about this dataset can be found at Yahoo! Research Alliance Webscope program[4].

(2) MovieLens: We use the MovieLens 10M ratings dataset [5]. MovieLens is a collaborative rating dataset where users provide ratings ranging on a 1–5 scale. Table 3 contains the statistics of both these datasets. Additionally, Section 7.3 conducts a user study using *Flickr data*.

Algorithms Compared: In addition to the greedy algorithms (Sections 4 and 5), we also developed optimal algorithms for group formation, based on integer programming (IP) (Appendix A). In addition to these, we also implemented two baseline algorithms (`BaseLine-LM` and `BaseLine-AV`), described below, by adapting prior work [22]. All three aggregation functions (Min/Max/Sum) are considered.

[4]http://research.yahoo.com

[5]*http://movielens.umn.edu*

dataset name	# users	# items
Yahoo! Music	200,000	136736
MovieLens	71,567	10,681

Table 3: Dataset Descriptions

The baseline algorithms work as follows: For every user pair u, u', we measure the Kendall-Tau distance [25] between them based on their individual ranking of items, induced by the ratings they provide. This way, we obtain $dist(u, u')$ for each u, u'. Notice that it is not *sufficient to consider only top-k items to compute this ranked distance, because two users may have a very small overlap on their top-k itemset; therefore, we consider all the items to obtain* $dist(u, u')$. After that, we use *K-means clustering* [13] to form a set of ℓ user groups. Once these groups are formed, for each group, we compute the top-k item list and respective group satisfaction scores (using Min/Max/Sum aggregation) based on LM or AV semantics. We aggregate these scores over ℓ groups to produce the final objective function value. The maximum number of iterations in the clustering is set to 100 by default.

Experimental Analysis Setup: Wherever applicable, we compare the aforementioned algorithms both qualitatively and quantitatively. For evaluation of quality, we measure the *objective function value* (for AV or LM), as well as *average group satisfaction score on the top-k item lists across the groups,* $\frac{\sum_{x=1}^{\ell}\sum_{j=1}^{k}\overline{sc(g_x, i^j)}}{\ell}$, where $\overline{sc(g_x, i^j)}$ is the average j-th item for group g_x. We additionally present the distribution of group sizes to examine whether our solution can give rise to many degenerated groups (i.e., singleton groups). For scalability experiments, we primarily measure the clock time to produce the groups and their respective top-k item list. We typically vary number of users (n), number of items (m), number of groups (ℓ), and the number of recommended items (k). In user study, we evaluate the effectiveness of our group formation algorithms compared with the baselines.

Preview of Experimental Results: Our key findings are: (1) We find that our proposed group formation algorithms effectively maximize the objective function compared to the optimal algorithms, i.e., the average group satisfaction, for all three aggregation functions (Min/Max/Sum). (2) Our results indicate the practical usefulness of Min aggregation, where *the average aggregate group satisfactions over the entire top-k item lists* are presented. Even though Min aggregation only optimizes on the k-th item, our results demonstrate high aggregate user satisfaction over the entire list. (3) We observe that our solution produces groups that are quite balanced in size, i.e., the variation in size is small. This observation establishes that our greedy algorithms are also practically viable. (4) We observe that our proposed algorithms are scalable and form groups efficiently, even when the number of users, items, or groups is large. We also observe that we outperform the baseline algorithms quite consistently in all cases – both qualitatively and w.r.t. performance (efficiency, satisfaction scores). (5) Our user study results indicate that, with statistical significance, our optimization guided group formation algorithms produce user groups, in which, the users are more satisfied with the top-k recommendations than that of the baseline algorithms. This observation is consistent across the datasets. Sections 7.1, 7.2, and 7.3 present the quality, scalability, and the user study results, respectively.

For lack of space, we only present a subset of results. The results are representative and the omitted ones are similar.

7.1 Quality Experiments

The IP-based optimal algorithms do not complete in a reasonable time, beyond 200 users, 100 items, and 10 groups. Our default settings are as follows: number of users = 200, number of items = 100, number of groups = 10, $k = 5$ and Max-aggregation. We vary # users, # items, # groups, and k in the top-k list. We measure two quality metrics: (1) the objective function value, i.e., the total satisfaction score of a grouping under LM or AV semantics, (2) the average group satisfaction score over all the recommended top-k items, (3) present the distribution of group sizes for both LM and AV.

Interpretation of Results: We observe that the `GRD` algorithms outperform the corresponding baseline algorithms, over both of these datasets. With increasing number of users, the objective function value as well as the average group satisfaction on the recommended top-k itemset decrease for a given value of the number of groups ℓ, as larger number of users typically add more variance in user preference. On the other hand, with increasing number of groups, both of these values increase, as there is more room for similar users to be grouped together, thereby improving overall satisfaction. With increasing k, both of these values decrease again (except Sum aggregation).

7.1.1 *Measuring Objective Function*

For lack of space, we only present the results for Yahoo! Music dataset. Results on MovieLens are similar.

Number of users: We vary the number of users and use the default settings for the rest of the parameters. Figure 1(a) depicts the results. With increasing number of users, the objective function value decreases in general, because, more users typically introduce larger variation in the preference and smaller LM score. The results also clearly demonstrate that `GRD-LM-MAX` consistently outperforms `Baseline-LM-MAX` and achieves an objective function value comparable to `OPT-LM-MAX`.

Number of items: Figure 1(b) shows that with increasing number of items, the objective function value typically increases. This is also intuitive, because, the top items of each group are likely to improve leading to higher LM score. Also, `GRD-LM-MAX` consistently outperforms the `Baseline-LM-MAX`.

Number of groups: When number of groups is increased, the overall objective function value also increases. Notice that the objective function reaches its maximum possible value when number of groups equals the number of users. Therefore, with more groups, users get the flexibility to be with other users who are "similar" to them. Figure 1(c) presents these results. Similar to the above two cases, `GRD-LM-MAX` outperforms the baseline.

Top-k on Min and Sum aggregation: In this experiment, we vary k and produce the objective function value over the least preferred (i.e., bottom) item on the recommended top-k item list. For Min-aggregation, Figure 2(a) shows that with increasing k, the objective function value decreases across the algorithms. This is natural, because, group satisfaction based on the bottom element typically decreases with increasing value of k. Figure 2(b) shows the Sum aggregation , where the objective function value increases across the algorithms with increasing k, although the rate of increase is smaller for higher k. These results demonstrate that `GRD-LM` algorithms are highly effective, their respective objective function values are quite comparable with that of `OPT-LM`.

7.1.2 *Avg Group Satisfaction Over top-k List*

For lack of space, for this set of experiments, we only present the results on MovieLens dataset considering AV semantics. Here, we measure the average user satisfaction over *all* the recommended top-k items, i.e., $\frac{\sum_{x=1}^{\ell}\sum_{j=1}^{k}\overline{sc(g_x, i^j)}}{\ell}$, where $\overline{sc(g_x, i^j)}$ is the average AV score on the j-th item for group g_x using Min aggregation. While `GRD-AV-MIN` is not specifically optimized for this measure, our experimental results indicate that the formed groups have very high average satisfaction nevertheless.

Number of users: Figure 3(a) presents the results where we vary the number of users. Notice that for 10 user groups, the maximum possible satisfaction per group over the top-k item list could be as high as 25 when 5 items are recommended (and the ratings are in the scale of $1-5$). This is indeed true, because, $\sum_{j=1}^{5} \overline{sc(g, i^j)} \leq$ 25. Interestingly, GRD-AV-MIN consistently produces a score that is close to 25 and outperforms the baseline algorithm.

Number of items: When number of items is increased, the group satisfaction score is likely to increase, as the algorithms now have more options to recommend the top-k items from, for each group. Figure 3(b) presents these results. The average group satisfaction score of both algorithms improves slightly with more items and again GRD-AV-MIN consistently beats the baseline.

Number of groups: The results are shown in Figure 3(c). As expected, we observe that the aggregated group satisfaction over the top-k items improves with the increasing number of groups. As explained before, with increasing number of groups, the algorithms have more flexibility to form groups with users who are highly similar in their top-k item preferences.

Top-k on Min-aggregation: Finally, we vary top-k and compute the aggregated group satisfaction score over all top-k items (results in Figure 3(d)). With increasing k, the aggregation is done over more number of items, thus increasing the overall score. As shown in the figure, GRD-AV-MIN produces highly comparable results with that of OPT-AV-MIN and consistently outperforms the baseline algorithm Baseline-AV-MIN.

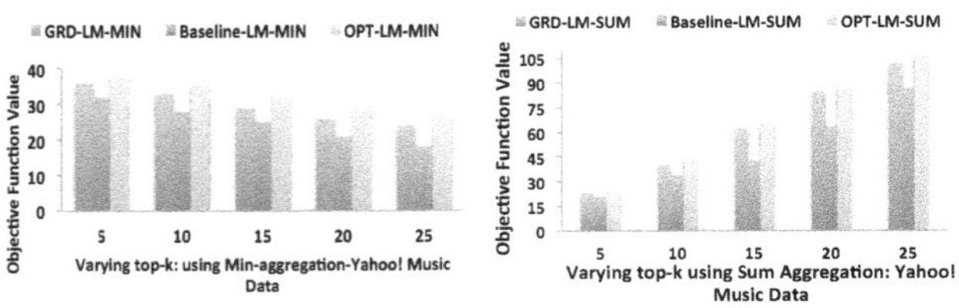

(a) (b)

Figure 2: We measure the objective function value by varying top-k for Min and Sum-aggregation using Yahoo! Music. The default parameters are # users = 200, # items = 100, # groups = 10, $k=5$.

7.1.3 *Distribution of Group Sizes*

We randomly select 200 users and 100 items with the objective to form $\ell = 10$ groups and recommend top-k ($k = 5$) items to each group using both datasets. In each sample of 200 users, we measure the number of users in each of these 10 groups. We repeat this experiment 3 times and present the average variation in group size using a 5-point summary : average minimum size, average 25% percentile (Q1), average median, average 75% percentile (Q3), average maximum size. This representation is akin to the box-plot summary [13]. The underlying algorithms are GRD-LM and GRD-AV considering both Max and Sum-aggregation. These results are summarized in Table 4. It is evident that the groups that are generated by our algorithms are balanced in general. Unsurprisingly, GRD-LM-MAX produces more uniform groups than GRD-LM-SUM, as the latter imposes stricter condition on grouping members (needs to match both top-k sequence and ratings). Interestingly, notice that the generated group sizes have smaller average variation under AV than under LM. This is expected, because GRD-AV only requires users to have the same top-k item sequence (irrespective of the specific ratings on the bottom item) to belong to the same group. Thus, AV tends to produce relatively larger groups and results in smaller variation in size across the generated groups.

Distribution of Average Group Size			
Semantics	Quantile	GRD-⋆-MAX	GRD-⋆-SUM
LM	Minimum	11.33	8.33
	Q1	15.75	11.5
	Median	18.5	13.66
	Q3	23.58	19.33
	Maximum	31.33	39.33
AV	Minimum	20.33	14.33
	Q1	22.4	19.35
	Median	25.4	22.5
	Q3	28.66	25.95
	Maximum	30.33	33.75

Table 4: Distribution of Average Group Size

7.2 Scalability Experiments

For brevity, we present the results for only the larger dataset, Yahoo! Music, and present a subset of results. As mentioned earlier, OPT-LM and OPT-AV do not terminate beyond 200 users, 100 items, and 10 groups, and are thus omitted. Our default settings here are as follows: number of users= $100,000$, number of items = $10,000$, number of groups =10, $k = 5$ and Min-aggregation. Again, we vary # users, # items, # groups, and k.

Interpretation of Results: The running time of GRD is primarily affected by the number of users (n), number of groups (ℓ), and k. Therefore, as it would be seen throughout the results, varying number of items does not impact the computational cost of either GRD-LM or GRD-AV. Between GRD-LM or GRD-AV, the latter takes more time, as it has to aggregate the satisfaction of all the users in a single group to produce the group satisfaction score. Running time of GRD-LM-MIN and GRD-LM-SUM are observed to be comparable, which corroborates our theoretical analysis. For the baseline algorithms (Baseline), running time increases with increasing number of users, and number of groups. Additionally, to produce the top-k recommendations once the groups are formed, the last step of these algorithms has to sift through the item-ratings of all users inside every group. Given a group obtained using clustering, the ranked item lists of users may not be aligned. Thus, to form the group's overall top-k list, one may have to consider arbitrarily many items in the individual ranked items lists of the group members. Therefore, the computation time of the baseline algorithms increases with increasing m or k. In case of our greedy algorithms, groups are formed by insisting that group members are aligned on the top-k item sequence. Thus, forming the overall top-k list for a group is straightforward in this case, for all groups but the ℓ-th group formed by the greedy algorithms. For the ℓ-th group, it sifts through the top-k items per user to generate score.

7.2.1 *Scalability Experiments : LM*

Number of users: We vary the number of users and measure the clock time of group formation and top-k recommendation time for GRD-LM-MIN and Baseline-LM-MIN. (For the record, the optimal algorithms do not complete even after one hour.) Figure 4(a) presents the results in minutes. As expected, GRD-LM-MIN increases linearly and always terminates within 2 minutes. These results also exhibit that the clustering based baseline algorithm is non-linear that our algorithm significantly outperforms.

Number of items: Next, we vary the number of items and measure the clock time. As can be seen from Figure 4(b), the running time of our proposed algorithm is less affected by varying number of items. This result is also consistent with our theoretical anal-

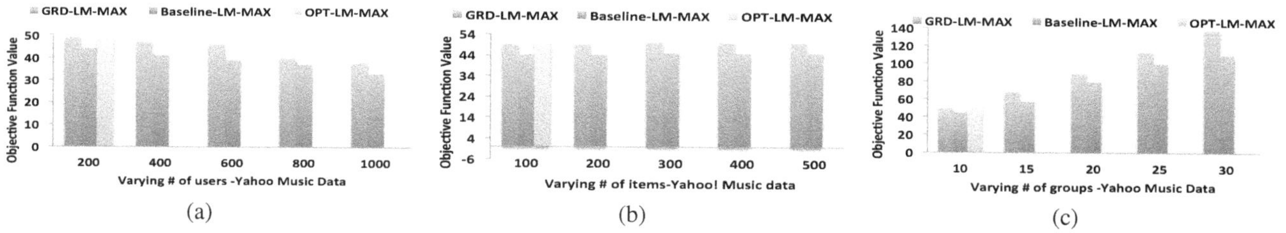

Figure 1: We measure the objective function value by varying # users, # items, # groups, respectively, one at a time. The default parameters are # users = 200, # items = 100, # groups = 10, $k = 5$ and Max-aggregation. The underlying dataset is Yahoo! Music.

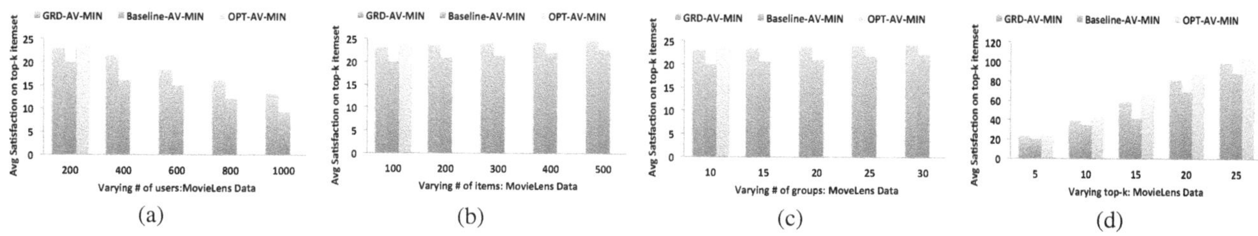

Figure 3: We measure the average group satisfaction score on the top-k item list $\frac{\sum_{x=1}^{\ell}\sum_{j=1}^{k}\overline{sc(g_x,i^j)}}{\ell}$ by varying # users, # items, # groups, and top-k, respectively, one at a time. The default parameters are # users = 200, # items = 100, # groups = 10, $k = 5$. The underlying dataset is MovieLens.

ysis. Recall from Section 4.3 that the running time of both the algorithms is $O(nk + \ell \log n)$, which is independent of the number of items m. Since GRD-LM-MIN leverages the sorted top-k list of items, more items do not necessarily lead to higher computational cost. On the contrary, the clustering based baseline has to produce the top-k itemset for each user group once the groups are formed. As explained earlier, this requires considerable work since top-k lists of cluster members may not be aligned. Figure 4(b) clearly demonstrates that Baseline-LM is rather sensitive to the increasing number of items. GRD-LM-MIN of course beats the baseline.

Number of groups: These results are presented in Figure 4(c). Both Baseline-LM-MIN and our algorithm take more time with increasing number of groups. This observation is also consistent with our theoretical analyses, as the running time of both these algorithms depends on the number of groups. GRD-LM-MIN scales linearly with the increasing number of groups and outperform its baseline counterpart quite consistently.

Top-k on Min and Sum aggregation: We vary top-k for both GRD-LM-MIN and Baseline-LM-MIN and present the running time in Figure 5(a). While GRD-LM-MIN consistently outperforms Baseline-LM-MIN, both these algorithms are not very sensitive to increasing k. The computation time of the first $\ell - 1$ groups are not so much affected by k and only determining the LM score and hence top-k list of the last group (i.e., ℓ-th group) is affected. The same observation holds for the baseline, as it incurs majority of its computations in forming the clusters that do not depend on k. Figure 5(b) presents the running time of both GRD-LM-SUM and Baseline-LM-SUM. GRD consistently outperforms Baseline, as expected, similar to Min aggregation.

7.2.2 Scalability Experiments : AV

Number of users: In this final set of scalability experiments, we again vary number of users and compute the running time of group formation algorithms under AV semantics. Figure 6(a) presents the results. These results are similar to those of LM, except that AV takes more time to compute than LM. Then, as expected, the running time of Baseline-AV is similar to that of Baseline-LM in Figure 4(a), as the clustering algorithm does not exploit the (AV) semantics in the group formation process. Our proposed greedy algorithm consistently outperforms the baseline algorithm.

Number of items: We vary the number of items and present the computation time in Figure 6(b). GRD-AV-MIN takes more time to terminate compared to that of GRD-LM-MIN (Figure 4(a)), this slight increase is due to the extra computation that GRD-AV-MIN has to perform to aggregate AV score for each group. On the other hand, GRD-AV-MIN is not sensitive to the increasing number of items, similarly to GRD-LM-MIN. The figure clearly illustrates that Baseline-AV-MIN takes more time, as the number of items is increased. As usual, GRD outperforms Baseline.

Number of groups: We vary number of groups and observe that both algorithms incur higher processing time with increased number of groups. Figure 6(c) presents these results. As expected, GRD-AV-MIN scales linearly with the increasing number of groups and consistently outperforms the baseline algorithm.

Top-k on Min and Sum aggregation: We vary k and measure the computation time in Figures 5(c) and Figure 5(d). With increased values of k, running time increases overall. However, GRD-AV-MIN takes significantly less time to terminate, compared to its baseline counterpart. Similar computation times are taken by Baseline-LM-MIN and Baseline-AV-MIN for the same values of k, as these baseline algorithms do not make use of the underlying group recommendation semantics during the group formation process. Sum aggregation results are presented in Figure 5(d) and the behavior is consistent, as before.

7.3 User Study

We use publicly available Flickr data to set up the user study in AMT for New York city. Given a Flickr log of a particular city, each row in that log corresponds to a user itinerary that is visited in a 12-hour window. From this log, we extract the most popular 10 POIs. The user study is designed in two phases overall, where Phase 1 is used to create three different sets of users – similar, dissimilar, and random. Phase 2 is used to assess the performance of the algorithms on each of these sets, under different semantics and aggregation functions.

Phase 1: Preference Collection and Group Formation: First, we set up a HIT (Human Intelligence Task) in AMT, where we ask

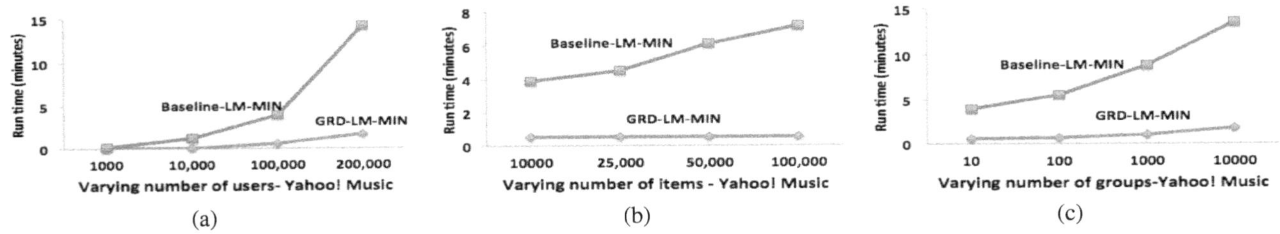

Figure 4: We present the average running time (measured in minutes) of the group formation algorithms under LM semantics with varying # users, # items, # groups respectively, one at a time. The default parameters are # users = $100,000$, # items = $10,000$, # groups = 10, $k = 5$, considering Min-aggregation. The underlying dataset is Yahoo! Music.

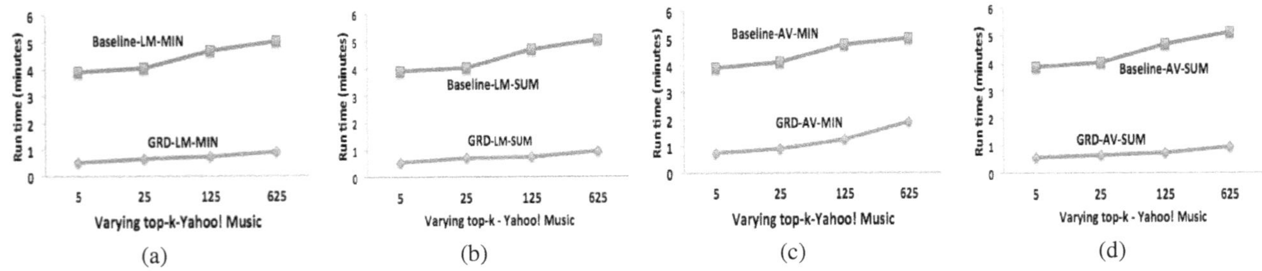

Figure 5: We present the average running time (measured in minutes) varying top-k, using Sum and Min aggregation for LM and AV. The default parameters are # users = $100,000$, # items = $10,000$, # groups = 10. The underlying dataset is Yahoo! Music.

each AMT user to rate one of these 10 POIs on a scale of $1-5$, higher rating implying greater preference. This data is collected from 50 workers. From this collected dataset, we create user samples. Sampling is conducted to select a seed user.

Similar user sample: We select a subset of 10 users who have provided very similar ranking on the 10 POIs. We compute normalized pair-wise similarity, considering each item in the top-10 ranked item lists for each user pair and aggregating that over all 10 items, as follows: $sim(u,u') = \sum_{j=1}^{10} \frac{sim(u,u',j)}{10}$

$$sim(u,u',j) \quad = \begin{cases} 1 - \frac{|sc(u,i^j) - sc(u',i^j)|}{5} & \text{if } i_j^u = i_j^{u'} \\ 0 & \text{otherwise} \end{cases}$$

Dissimilar user sample We select a different subset of 10 users who has the smallest aggregate pair-wise similarity.

Random user sample In our third sample, we select another subset of 10 users who are chosen randomly from the 50 users (workers).

For brevity, we only report results on LM semantics for these experiments and set the number of groups to be $\ell = 3$. We apply GRD-LM and Baseline-LM (both Sum and Min) to each sample and each algorithm produces three groups.

Step 2: Group Satisfaction Evaluation: In this phase, for each user sample (similar, dissimilar, and random), we set up 6 HITs in AMT (3 for Min and another 3 for Sum), where each HIT comprises the $(3+3)$ groups created by GRD-LM and Baseline-LM. In each HIT, we first show the individual user preference ratings for all 10 users in the sample, over all 10 items. We do not disclose the underlying group formation algorithm (but refer to them as Method-1 and Method-2) and produce the groups formed by GRD-LM and Baseline-LM. We note that our settings mimic the set-up of previous user studies in group recommendation research [14, 1, 26]. We also request the worker to regard herself as one of the individuals in the sample and ask her to rate the following questions (higher is better): (1) Her satisfaction with the formed groups by Method-1; (2) Her satisfaction with the formed groups by Method-2, (3) In an absolute sense, which method she prefers more. Each HIT is undertaken by 10 unique users, thereby involving 60 new users in this phase (30 for Min and another 30 for Sum). For each HIT, we average the ratings and present them in Figures 7(b) and 7(c). Standard error bars are added for statistical significance.

Additionally, we aggregate and compute the percentage of users who prefer GRD-LM versus Baseline-LM in Figure 7(a).

Interpretation of Results: We make the following key observations from the results presented in Figures 7(a), 7(b), 7(c). First and foremost, our proposed algorithm GRD-LM gives rise to higher satisfaction compared to the baseline, in all cases. In fact, this difference in satisfaction seems to be higher when the user population is dissimilar in its individual preferences. During our post-analysis, we see, indeed the clustering based baseline algorithm becomes ineffective, when the individual user preferences are dissimilar from each other. For the same reason, the difference in the average satisfaction of our greedy algorithm from the baseline algorithm is the highest for dissimilar users and smallest for similar users. A random user population consists of both similar and dissimilar users, hence the effectiveness falls in the middle. These results clearly demonstrate that our proposed solutions can effectively exploit existing group recommendation semantics and form groups that lead to high group satisfaction in practice.

8. RELATED WORK

While no prior work has addressed the problem of group formation in the context of recommender systems, we still discuss existing work that appears to be contextually most related.

Group Recommendation: Group recommendation has been designed for various domains such as news pages [24], tourism [11], music [9], book, restaurants [22], and TV programs [31].

There are two dominant strategies for group recommendations [8, 1]. The first approach creates a pseudo-user representing the group and then makes recommendations to that pseudo-user, while the second strategy computes a recommendation list for each group member and then combines them to produce a group's list. For the latter, a widely adopted approach is to apply an aggregation function to obtain a *consensus group preference* for a candidate

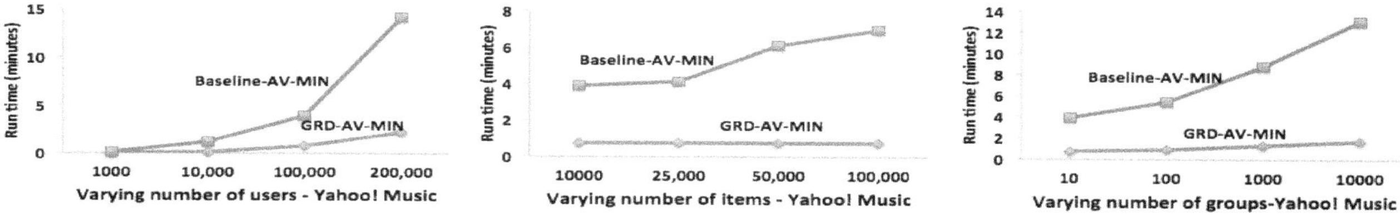

(a) (b) (c)

Figure 6: We present the average running time (measured in minutes) of the group formation algorithms under AV semantics with varying # users, # items, # groups respectively, one at a time. The default parameters are # users = $100,000$, # items = $10,000$, # groups = 10, $k = 5$, considering Min-aggregation. The underlying dataset is Yahoo! Music.

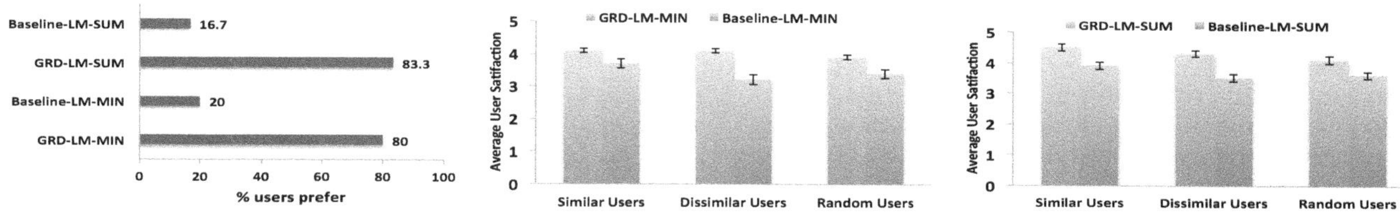

(a) (b) (c)

Figure 7: User Study Results: Figures 7(b) and 7(c) present the average user satisfaction score of `GRD-LM` and that of `Baseline-LM` for both Min and Sum aggregation with statistical significance analyses. Figure 7(a) indicates about 80% of the users prefers `GRD` over the `Baseline` algorithms.

item. Popular aggregation functions, such as, *least misery*, *aggregate voting* are popularly used in existing works [14, 1, 26]. [22] pre-clusters the users and the individual recommendations are generated for group members using that member's cluster. After that group aggregation function is applied.

In these works, groups are created beforehand, either by a random set of users with different interests, or by a number of users who explicitly choose to be part of a group.

Market-based Strategies: Existing research on market based strategies [6, 18, 20] studies problems on daily deals sites, such as Groupon and LivingSocial, that are orthogonal to our group formation problem. These works focus on *recommending deals* (i.e., items) to the users and groups For example, [18] proposes new algorithms for daily deals recommendation based on the explore-then-exploit strategy. [20] recommends the best deals to the users, among a set of candidate deals, to maximize revenues. Real-time bidding strategy for group-buying deals based on the online optimization of bid values is studied in [6]. This body of works essentially relies on price discounts to incentivize group formation around deals, with the objective of maximizing revenue. By contrast, we investigate *how to form groups to maximize user satisfaction* under existing group recommendations semantics. Our work is directly deployable as a non-intrusive addition to group recommender systems where explicit incentives may not be present.

Team Formation: Team formation problems [19, 7, 33, 3, 4] are often modeled using Integer Programming, or heuristic solutions using Simulated Annealing [7] or Genetic Algorithms [29] are designed. These problems are assignment problems.

In general, group formation is not a matching or generalized assignment problem [17, 10]. There are no resources to match the users to. We need to "match" users to one another. In that sense, it's closer in spirit to clustering [13]. However, as we demonstrate in the paper, a clustering algorithm which is agnostic to the group recommendation semantics (LM or AV) is likely to perform poorly for purposes of maximizing group satisfaction.

Community Detection: These problems [28] discover communities (a set of users) with common interests. Again, our groups have a more explicit connotation (in the sense of having clearly defined satisfaction scores) than communities. One can potentially generate a graph of users based on a suitable notion of distance or similarity between users in terms of tastes and find communities. Once again, this approach falls short, as it does not take group recommendation semantics into account.

Multi-way Partition: Minimization problems over multiway partition functions are studied in [32, 2], with graphs or hypergraphs as the underlying abstract model. They attempt to partition the nodes to optimize certain outcome (e.g., variants of k-cut problems). While these problems are NP-hard, efficient algorithms with provable approximation factors are known, when the objective function exhibit certain properties [32, 2]. If we are to use such a weighted graph, the weight on each edge is local to just two users and does not capture the essence of group recommendation semantics, which renders those solutions to our problem far from ideal.

9. CONCLUSION

We initiate *the study of forming groups in the context of group recommender systems.* We consider two popular group recommendation semantics (LM and AV) and formalize the problem of creating a set of non-overlapping groups over an underlying user population, such that the aggregate satisfaction of the formed groups, with their recommended top-k lists, is maximized. We prove that optimal group formation is computationally intractable under both group recommendation semantics. We present efficient greedy group formation algorithms and show that they achieve absolute error guarantees for LM. We present a comprehensive experimental analysis that demonstrates the effectiveness as well scalability of our proposed solutions. We also conduct a user study on Amazon Mechanical Turk that shows that users by far are more satisfied with the groups formed by our solutions than that of the baseline ones.

The approximability of group formation under AV semantics remains open although we conjecture that it may be hard to approximate. Identifying natural special cases that are tractable is an interesting open problem. Forming groups where the individual members are not treated equally, or groups that are possibly overlapping are also worthy of study. Finally, the problem we studied in this paper implicitly assumes that user interests are static. How to form groups where the group members' interests drift and start to diverge over time, remains to be an important problem.

APPENDIX

A. OPTIMAL ALGORITHMS

Despite the fact that the optimal group formation problem is computationally intractable, we describe optimal algorithms under both LM and AV semantics by formulating them as integer programming problems. We can make use of existing integer programming solvers (such as CPLEX) to solve these problems. Since IP is also NP-hard [30] and could be exponential in the worst case, the proposed solutions are not scalable. Nevertheless, the formulation is useful when the numbers of users and items are fairly small.

For both formulations the following Boolean decision variables are defined: u_{ig} captures whether user u_i is part of group g. To describe the top-k itemset of each group, an additional Boolean decision variable, y_{jg} checks, if item j is the k-th item for group g, whereas, w_{jg} is used to check if item j is *one of the top-*$(k-1)$ *items* for group g. The following formulation is provided assuming Min-aggregation for a general value of $k > 1$. To consider Max-aggregation formulation, we no longer need w_{jp} and one has to check if y_{jg} is indeed the top-1 item for the recommended itemset. Similarly, Sum aggregation could be performed by modifying the objective function to aggregate over all k-items.

A.1 IP Formulation for Least Misery

The objective function for LM aims to form ℓ groups such that their sum of scores is maximized. The first two constraints capture the fact that the score of an item j is to be computed by considering the minimum score of that item over all users. The third and fourth constraints are used to capture the top-$(k-1)$ items. The rest of the constraints simply state that the $k-$th item is a single item for every group, whereas, there should be a total of $k-1$ additional items whose score is higher than that of the k-th item. Finally, we assert that only ℓ groups are to be formed, whereas, a user can belong to only one of these groups (satisfying disjointness).

$$\text{Maximize } \Sigma_{g=1}^{\ell}\{y_{jp} \times sc(g,j)\} \tag{1}$$

s.t.

$$\left.\begin{aligned} sc(j,g) &= r \\ r &\leq \{\forall u_{ig}=1\}u_{ig} \times sc(u_i,j) \\ w_{ig} \times sc(g,i) &\geq y_{jg} \times sc(g,j) \times w_{ig} \\ (1-w_{jg}) \times sc(g,j) &\leq y_{jg} \times sc(g,j) \end{aligned}\right\}$$

$$\left.\begin{aligned} \Sigma_{j=1}^{m} y_{jg} &= 1 \\ \Sigma_{i=1}^{m} w_{ig} &= k-1 \\ \ell &\leq n \end{aligned}\right\}$$

$$\left.\begin{aligned} y_{jg} &= 1/0, \forall j = 1,2,\ldots,m \\ w_{jg} &= 1/0, \forall j = 1,2,\ldots,m \\ \Sigma_{g=1}^{\ell} u_{ig} &= 1, \forall i = 1,2,\ldots,n \\ u_{ig} &= 1/0, \forall i = 1,2,\ldots,n, \forall g = 1,2,\ldots,\ell \end{aligned}\right\}$$

When this IP is run on Example 1, considering $k = 1$, the following groups are produced: $\{u_1, u_3, u_4\}$, $\{u_2, u_6\}$, $\{u_5\}$ with an overall *Obj* value of $4 + 5 + 3 = 12$.

A.2 IP Formulation for Aggregate Voting

The formulation of optimal group formation under aggregate voting is similar to that of LM, except for the fact that the score of an item j for a group g is the summation of scores of j over all users in g.

$$\text{Maximize } \Sigma_{p=1}^{\ell}\{y_{jg} \times sc(g,j)\} \tag{2}$$

s.t.

$$\left.\begin{aligned} sc(g,j) &= \Sigma_{\{\forall u_{ig}=1\}} u_{ig} \times sc(u_i,j) \\ w_{ig} \times sc(g,i) &\geq y_{jg} \times sc(g,j) \times w_{ig} \\ (1-w_{jg}) \times sc(g,j) &\leq y_{jp} \times sc(g,j) \end{aligned}\right\}$$

$$\left.\begin{aligned} \Sigma_{j=1}^{m} y_{jg} &= 1 \\ \Sigma_{i=1}^{m} w_{ig} &= k-1 \\ \ell &\leq n \end{aligned}\right\}$$

$$\left.\begin{aligned} y_{jg} &= 1/0, \forall j = 1,2,\ldots,m \\ w_{jg} &= 1/0, \forall j = 1,2,\ldots,m \\ \Sigma_{g=1}^{\ell} u_{ig} &= 1, \forall i = 1,2,\ldots,n \\ u_{ig} &= 1/0, \forall i = 1,2,\ldots,n, \forall g = 1,2,\ldots,\ell \end{aligned}\right\}$$

When run on Example 2, the optimal grouping with two groups consists of the following groups: $\{u_1, u_3, u_4\}$, and $\{u_2, u_5, u_6\}$, with the overall objective function value of 14.

B. SUBOPTIMAL GROUP FORMATION BY GRD-LM-SUM

EXAMPLE 5. Consider the user set $\mathcal{U} = \{u_1, u_2, u_3, u_4, u_5, u_6\}$ and the itemset $\mathcal{I} = \{i_1, i_2, i_3\}$. The users' preferences for the itemset are given (or predicted) as in Table 5. Suppose the users need to be partitioned into at most 3 groups ($\ell \leq 3$), where each group has to be recommended $k = 2$ items. □

Using `GRD-LM-SUM`, this will form the following 3 groups at the end: $\{u_2\}$, $\{u_3, u_4\}$, $\{u_1, u_5, u_6\}$ with the overall objective function value as $(5+3)+(5+2)+(3+2) = 20$, whereas, the optimal grouping will give a different solutions to form 3 groups, $\{u_2, u_6\}$, $\{u_3, u_4\}$, $\{u_1, u_5\}$ with the overall objective function value of $(5+2)+(5+2)+(4+3) = 21$.

User-item Ratings	u_1	u_2	u_3	u_4	u_5	u_6
i_1	1	2	2	2	2	1
i_2	4	3	5	5	4	2
i_3	3	5	1	1	3	5

Table 5: User Item Preference Rating for Example 5

C. REFERENCES

[1] S. Amer-Yahia, S. B. Roy, A. Chawla, G. Das, and C. Yu. Group recommendation: Semantics and efficiency. *PVLDB*, 2(1):754–765, 2009.

[2] O. Amini, F. Mazoit, N. Nisse, and S. Thomassé. Submodular partition functions. *Discrete Mathematics*, 309(20):6000–6008, 2009.

[3] A. Anagnostopoulos, L. Becchetti, C. Castillo, A. Gionis, and S. Leonardi. Power in unity: forming teams in large-scale community systems. In *Proceedings of the 19th ACM international conference on Information and knowledge management*, pages 599–608. ACM, 2010.

[4] A. Anagnostopoulos, L. Becchetti, C. Castillo, A. Gionis, and S. Leonardi. Online team formation in social networks. In *Proceedings of the 21st international conference on World Wide Web*, pages 839–848. ACM, 2012.

[5] R. Baeza-Yates, B. Ribeiro-Neto, et al. *Modern information retrieval*, volume 463. ACM press New York, 1999.

[6] R. Balakrishnan and R. P. Bhatt. Real-time bid optimization for group-buying ads. In *Proceedings of the 21st ACM international conference on Information and knowledge management*, pages 1707–1711. ACM, 2012.

[7] A. Baykasoglu, T. Dereli, and S. Das. Project team selection using fuzzy optimization approach. *Cybernetics and Systems: An International Journal*, 38(2):155–185, 2007.

[8] S. Berkovsky and J. Freyne. Group-based recipe recommendations: analysis of data aggregation strategies. In *RecSys*, pages 111–118, 2010.

[9] A. Crossen, J. Budzik, and K. J. Hammond. Flytrap: intelligent group music recommendation. In *Proceedings of the 7th international conference on Intelligent user interfaces*, pages 184–185. ACM, 2002.

[10] L. Fleischer, M. X. Goemans, V. S. Mirrokni, and M. Sviridenko. Tight approximation algorithms for maximum general assignment problems. In *Proceedings of the seventeenth annual ACM-SIAM symposium on Discrete algorithm*, pages 611–620. ACM, 2006.

[11] I. Garcia, L. Sebastia, and E. Onaindia. On the design of individual and group recommender systems for tourism. *Expert Syst. Appl.*, 38(6):7683–7692, 2011.

[12] M. R. Garey and D. S. Johnson. *Computers and Intractability: A Guide to the Theory of NP-Completeness*. 1979.

[13] J. Han and M. Kamber. *Data Mining: Concepts and Techniques*. Morgan Kaufmann, 2000.

[14] A. Jameson and B. Smyth. Recommendation to groups. In *The adaptive web*, pages 596–627. Springer, 2007.

[15] V. Kann. Maximum bounded 3-dimensional matching is max snp-complete. *Information Processing Letters*, 37(1):27–35, 1991.

[16] V. Kann. *On the approximability of NP-complete optimization problems*. PhD thesis, Royal Institute of Technology Stockholm, 1992.

[17] S. O. Krumke and C. Thielen. The generalized assignment problem with minimum quantities. *European Journal of Operational Research*, 228(1):46–55, 2013.

[18] A. Lacerda, A. Veloso, and N. Ziviani. Exploratory and interactive daily deals recommendation. In *RecSys*, 2013.

[19] T. Lappas, K. Liu, and E. Terzi. Finding a team of experts in social networks. In *SIGKDD*, pages 467–476, 2009.

[20] T. Lappas and E. Terzi. Daily-deal selection for revenue maximization. In *21st ACM International Conference on Information and Knowledge Management, CIKM'12, Maui, HI, USA, October 29 - November 02, 2012*, pages 565–574, 2012.

[21] H. Lieberman, N. Van Dyke, and A. Vivacqua. Let's browse: a collaborative browsing agent. *Knowledge-Based Systems*, 12(8):427–431, 1999.

[22] E. Ntoutsi, K. Stefanidis, K. Nørvåg, and H.-P. Kriegel. Fast group recommendations by applying user clustering. In *ER*, pages 126–140, 2012.

[23] M. OâĂŹconnor, D. Cosley, J. A. Konstan, and J. Riedl. Polylens: a recommender system for groups of users. In *ECSCW 2001*, pages 199–218. Springer, 2001.

[24] S. Pizzutilo, B. De Carolis, G. Cozzolongo, and F. Ambruoso. Group modeling in a public space: Methods, techniques, experiences. In *Proceedings of the 5th WSEAS International Conference on Applied Informatics and Communications*, AIC'05, pages 175–180, Stevens Point, Wisconsin, USA, 2005. World Scientific and Engineering Academy and Society (WSEAS).

[25] C. Romesburg. *Cluster analysis for researchers*. Lulu. com, 2004.

[26] S. B. Roy, S. Thirumuruganathan, S. Amer-Yahia, G. Das, and C. Yu. Exploiting group recommendation functions for flexible preferences. In *ICDE Conference*, 2014.

[27] C. Senot, D. Kostadinov, M. Bouzid, J. Picault, A. Aghasaryan, and C. Bernier. Analysis of strategies for building group profiles. In *User Modeling, Adaptation, and Personalization*, pages 40–51. Springer, 2010.

[28] M. Sozio and A. Gionis. The community-search problem and how to plan a successful cocktail party. In *Proceedings of the 16th ACM SIGKDD international conference on Knowledge discovery and data mining*, pages 939–948. ACM, 2010.

[29] H. Wi, S. Oh, J. Mun, and M. Jung. A team formation model based on knowledge and collaboration. *Expert Systems with Applications*, 36(5):9121–9134, 2009.

[30] L. A. Wolsey. *Integer programming*, volume 42. Wiley New York, 1998.

[31] Z. Yu, X. Zhou, Y. Hao, and J. Gu. TV Program Recommendation for Multiple Viewers Based on user Profile Merging. *User Modeling and User-adapted Interaction*, 16:63–82, 2006.

[32] L. Zhao, H. Nagamochi, and T. Ibaraki. Greedy splitting algorithms for approximating multiway partition problems. *Mathematical Programming*, 102(1):167–183, 2005.

[33] A. Zzkarian and A. Kusiak. Forming teams: an analytical approach. *IIE transactions*, 31(1):85–97, 1999.

Real-Time Multi-Criteria Social Graph Partitioning: A Game Theoretic Approach

Nikos Armenatzoglou[1] Huy Pham[2] Vasilis Ntranos[2] Dimitris Papadias[1] Cyrus Shahabi[2]

Hong Kong University of Science and Technology
Clear Water Bay, Hong Kong
{nikos, dimitris}@cse.ust.hk

University of Southern California
Los Angeles, USA
{huyvpham, shahabi, ntranos}@usc.edu

Abstract

Graph partitioning has attracted considerable attention due to its high practicality for real-world applications. It is particularly relevant to social networks because it enables the grouping of users into communities for market analysis and advertising purposes. In this paper, we introduce RMGP, a type of real-time multi-criteria graph partitioning for social networks that groups the users based on their connectivity and their similarity to a set of input classes. We consider RMGP as an on-line task, which may be frequently performed for different query parameters (e.g., classes). In order to overcome the serious performance issues associated with the large social graphs found in practice, we develop solutions based on a game theoretic framework. Specifically, we consider each user as a player, whose goal is to find the class that optimizes his objective function. We propose algorithms based on best-response dynamics, analyze their properties, and show their efficiency and effectiveness on real datasets under centralized and decentralized scenarios.

Categories and Subject Descriptors

E.1 [**Data Structures**]: Graphs and Networks; G.2.2 [**Graph Theory**]: Graph Algorithms; H.2.4 [**Systems**]: Query processing

Keywords

social networks; graph partitioning; game theory

1. INTRODUCTION

In this paper, we introduce RMGP a novel framework for Real-time Multi-criteria Graph Partitioning. RMGP partitions a social network into a set of input classes, so that users in the same class are socially connected, and at the same time they have high similarity to the class' properties. Formally, let $G = (V, E, W)$ be a social graph, where V is the set of users, E is the set of edges (i.e., social connections), and W is the set of edge weights (denoting the strength of social connections). The edges may be directed (e.g., representing the *follow* relationship in Twitter), and the weights may be binary (i.e., indicating simply the presence or absence of a friendship). Let P be a set classes given at query time, and $c : V \times P \rightarrow \mathbb{R}^+$ a function that measures the cost of assigning a user to a class, i.e., $c(v, s_v)$ is the cost of assigning $v \in V$ to $s_v \in P$. Then, RMGP returns an assignment of each user v to a single class s_v that minimizes the following function:

$$RMGP(G, P, \alpha) = \alpha \cdot \sum_{v \in V} c(v, s_v) + (1 - \alpha) \cdot \sum_{\substack{e=(v,f) \in E \wedge \\ s_v \neq s_f}} w_e \quad (1)$$

The first sum in Equation 1 represents the *assignment cost*, while the second one corresponds to the *social cost*, i.e., the total weight of edges crossing classes. The *preference* parameter $\alpha \in (0, 1)$ adjusts the relative importance of the two factors (i.e., if $a > 0.5$, the partition process should aim more at minimizing the assignment cost at the expense of the social aspect). Each class becomes a partition, so that the weighted sum of assignment and social costs is minimized. Conversely, the similarities between users and their assigned classes, as well as the social connectivity inside classes are maximized.

EXAMPLE 1. *Location-Aware Graph Partitioning (LAGP). Assume that a geo-social network wishes to promote upcoming events to users based on proximity and social connectivity. Each event corresponds to a class, and the cost of assigning a user to a class is his/her current distance, or travel time, to the respective event.* RMGP *assigns each user to an event that minimizes (i) the distance/travel time between the user and the event, and (ii) the social connectivity between users assigned to different events. Consequently, a user is assigned to an event that is nearby and, at the same time, it is recommended to several of his friends.*

We illustrate LAGP through the example of Figure 1, with users $V = \{v_1, v_2, v_3, v_4, v_5, v_6\}$ and a set of three locations $P = \{p_1, p_2, p_3\}$ (each location corresponds to an event/class). The edge weights indicate the strength of social connections. The table in Figure 1 shows the Euclidean distance $||v_i, p_j||$ between each user $v_i \in V$ and location $p_j \in P$, which serves as the cost $c(v_i, p_j)$ (the larger the distance, the higher the cost of assigning v_i to class p_j). Assuming $\alpha = 0.5$, RMGP assigns v_1 to event p_3, v_2 and v_5 to event p_2, and v_3, v_4, v_6 to event p_1 (users have the same color as the event they are assigned to). Observe that user v_4 is assigned to p_1, and not to the closest location p_2, because his friends v_3 and v_6 are also assigned to p_1. The bold edges are the ones that contribute to the social cost, i.e., connecting friends in different events.

EXAMPLE 2. *Topic-Aware Graph Partitioning (TAGP). Consider that an on-line discussion forum wishes to place an advertisement for each user, in a manner that maximizes the "word of*

SIGMOD'15, May 31–June 4, 2015, Melbourne, Victoria, Australia.

http://dx.doi.org/10.1145/2723372.2749450.

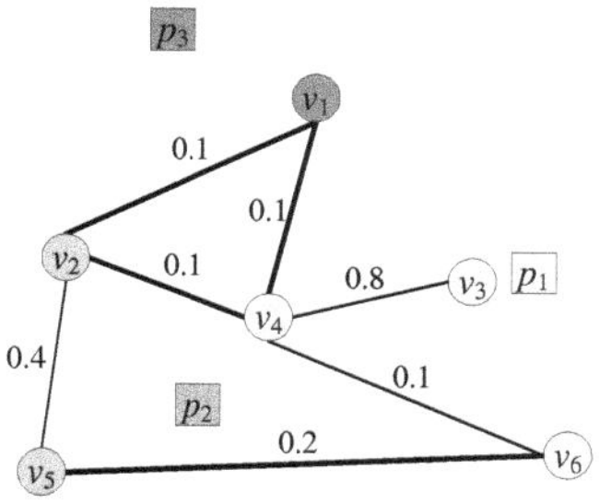

	$\|v_i, p_1\|$	$\|v_i, p_2\|$	$\|v_i, p_3\|$
v_1	0.48	0.6	0.27
v_2	0.8	0.34	0.44
v_3	0.1	0.54	0.67
v_4	0.47	0.2	0.54
v_5	0.94	0.3	0.8
v_6	0.34	0.67	0.99

Figure 1: Running Example

mouth" effect. In the corresponding RMGP *task, each potential advertisement constitutes a class. The assignment cost of a user is based on some (dis-)similarity measure (e.g., tf-idf) between his current discussions and the advertisement topic. The social connectivity between users is based on the number of common discussions in which they have participated. Thus, users are likely to be assigned advertisements that match their own interests, and those of their frequent discussion co-participants.*

In general, RMGP refers to the partition of a graph according to connectivity, and one or more additional criteria. Specifically, in addition to social connectivity, we have the travel cost in LAGP and the text similarity in TAGP. A combination of multiple criteria can also be supported. For example, if each user has a profile, the assignment cost could take into account both the distance of each user and his preference to an event (e.g., based on textual similarity between the profile and the event description). Note that the combination of different criteria is application-dependent, and orthogonal to RMGP; e.g., the assignment cost $c(v, s_v)$ of Equation 1 could be a linear combination (or any other scoring function) of the distance and the preference of user v to event s_v.

We consider RMGP as an on-line process because input parameters change frequently. Specifically, in LAGP, locations of users maybe updated through check-ins, while new events may appear frequently [1]. Therefore, RMGP recommendations should be efficiently generated in order to accommodate the fast-pace changes. Moreover, for some tasks only a subset of the network, determined at query time, may participate in RMGP. For instance, if a geo-social network wishes to advertise events at a certain area, only the users who recently checked-in that area, and the corresponding induced sub-graph, are relevant.

Another important issue in RMGP, and all tasks that partition a graph according to connectivity and additional criteria, is how to set the relative importance of the social aspect in the total cost. For instance, in LAGP the distance-based assignment cost can be in the order of thousands (of meters), whereas the edge weights may be in the range $[0, 1]$. In general, vast differences in the assignment and social costs render the value of the preference parameter α (and all types of relative weights) irrelevant. *Normalization* is crucial for adjusting the importance of the assignment and social costs as expressed by α, and eliminating the effects of factors such as the extent of the data space.

Graph partitioning has been studied extensively in social networks, where users are classified into groups or communities for advertising and analysis purposes. However, existing approaches focus on different versions of the problem, where the graph is partitioned based on connectivity and/or similarities between node attributes [33][29], but not between nodes and input classes. On the other hand, RMGP can be considered as an instance of Uniform Metric Labeling (UML) [13]. UML is a well-known NP-Hard problem that has only been studied theoretically in the context of approximation algorithms. Thus, all existing (approximate) solutions aim at small instances, and are not applicable to the large graphs commonly found in social networks. Moreover, they do not consider the real-time and decentralized nature of the problem, which is fundamental in our setting.

To effectively solve RMGP in real world social networks, we model the problem as a *game*, where each user corresponds to a player: his goal is to find the class that minimizes his assignment and social costs. As we show, the game reaches an equilibrium, i.e., a local minimum where no user has incentive to deviate. Modeling and solving RMGP as a game has several advantages. First, the game mimics the behavior of individual *real-world* users who aim at optimizing their own objectives, independently of those of the others. Consequently it yields recommendations (i.e., solutions) that are likely to be followed by the users. On the other hand, optimization methods that minimize the global cost, without considering the individual objectives, could lead to recommendations that are not followed by numerous users (e.g., in LAGP, users assigned to far events), rendering the solution meaningless. Moreover, the resulting algorithms are fast, allowing the real-time execution of queries, and facilitate distributed processing.

We first develop a baseline algorithm based on *best-response dynamics*, and analyze its properties. Our experimental evaluation shows that even the baseline algorithm is many orders of magnitude faster than state-of-the art UML methods and yields solutions that are very close to the optimal approximation. Then, we propose optimizations that enhance pruning of the search space by pre-computing a set of valid strategies per user and utilizing parallelism. Moreover, we apply our algorithms in decentralized scenarios (where the social graph is distributed at different servers), using an implementation that reduces the communication costs between processing units. Finally, we discuss and solve normalization issues that arise in RMGP due to the different values/measurements used for the assignment and social costs. Our contributions are summarized as follows:

- We introduce RMGP, and model the problem based on a game theoretic framework.
- We propose highly optimized algorithms that can efficiently solve RMGP tasks for large social networks in real-time.
- We apply our techniques to decentralized implementations of social networks.
- We show how to solve normalization issues in RMGP.
- We illustrate the effectiveness of our techniques through extensive experiments with real datasets under centralized and decentralized settings.

The rest of the paper is organized as follows. Section 2 overviews the related work and presents background on game theory. Section 3 proposes the baseline algorithm and analyzes its behavior. Section 4 describes multiple optimizations. Section 5 introduces a framework for applying RMGP in decentralized environments. Section 6 includes our experiments, and Section 7 concludes the paper with directions for future work.

2. RELATED WORK

Section 2.1 presents related work on graph partition algorithms and Section 2.2 provides background on game theory.

2.1 Graph Algorithms

Existing work on graph partitioning can be grouped into three main categories: i) attribute-based, ii) connectivity-based, and iii) attribute and connectivity-based. Attribute-based methods partition the graph based only on the similarity of node attributes, without considering the social connectivity [27]. Connectivity-based approaches partition the graph based only on connectivity, e.g., normalized cut [26], structural density [32], and modularity [24]. Partitioning can also be based on multiple objective functions on the graph's structural properties. For instance, [4] minimizes both the weight of edges that cross partitions, and the shortest path length connecting two nodes in different partitions.

Methods in the third category partition a graph based on both connectivity and attribute similarity [33]. For example, Van Gennip et al. [30] create groups of users in a geo-social graph so that users in the same group are nearby and socially connected. [33] defines a distance function between two nodes that combines their social connectivity and attribute similarity. A conventional clustering algorithm, such as K-Medoids [12], can then be adapted to partition the graph using the distance function. Even though the above techniques partition a graph using multiple objectives none of them can be used for RMGP. In particular, besides the social connectivity, we consider the similarity of each node to a set of input classes, instead of the similarity between two nodes based on their attribute values.

On the other hand, RMGP is closely related to the Uniform Metric Labeling (UML) problem. The input of UML is (i) an undirected edge-weighted graph $G = (V, E, W)$, (ii) a set L of k labels, (iii) a function $c(v, l)$ that denotes the cost of assigning label $l \in L$ to node $v \in V$, and (iv) a uniform function $d(l, l')$ that returns 1 if $l \neq l'$; 0 otherwise. UML assigns a label l to every node v (the assignment is denoted as v_l), such that the following objective function is minimized.

$$\sum_{v \in V} c(v, v_l) + \sum_{e=(u,v) \in E} w_e \cdot d(v_l, u_l) \tag{2}$$

Comparing the objective function of UML with Equation 1, it is easy to verify that they are equivalent. Specifically, the labels of UML correspond to classes in RMGP. Moreover, Equation 2 can incorporate the preference parameter α by simply modifying $c(v, v_l)$ and w_e.

UML can be formulated as an integer linear program (ILP), which is NP-hard. Existing solutions are based on linear programming (LP) relaxations [13] [7] and focus on providing theoretical approximation guarantees to bound the integrality gap between the optimal (ILP) and the rounded (LP) solutions that can be obtained in polynomial time. Even though both LP methods provide a 2-approximation algorithm for UML, their respective complexities, $O\left((|E| + k \cdot |V|)^{3.5}\right)$ and $O\left((k \cdot (|V| + k \cdot |E|)^{3.5})\right)$, are still prohibitive for practical applications. To avoid linear programming, Bracht et al. [5] propose a greedy approach that runs in $O(k \cdot |V|^{3.6})$, but guarantees a much looser approximation ratio $8 \log |V|$. Furthermore, the algorithm requires extensive graph transformations; i.e., for each class it generates a new graph that connects the class to all nodes.

Due to their high complexity, UML algorithms have only been experimentally evaluated on small graphs with up to a few hundreds of nodes. In this paper, we compare our techniques to the above approaches and show that our solutions can be computed several orders of magnitude faster and are very close to the theoretical 2-approximation obtained by LP. Moreover, previous UML algorithms do not take into consideration the real-time and decentralized nature of the problem, which is fundamental in our setting.

Several platforms, such as Giraph [3], Pregel [19], GraphLab [18] have been used for implementing graph partitioning algorithms. These approaches aim at offline tasks as they were designed for graph analytics. A recent paper [17] studies LAGP tasks assuming that events have minimum and maximum participation constraints that cannot be violated (i.e., events that cannot reach the minimum number of participants are canceled). Finally, Metis [11], a well-known graph partitioning tool, focuses on k-way graph partitioning, i.e., it creates k clusters that minimize the cut based on connectivity only. In our experimental evaluation, we design a benchmark solution based on Metis.

2.2 Game Theory

In *strategic games*, players compete with each other over the same resources in order to optimize their individual objective functions. Under this framework, a player chooses a *strategy* that minimizes his own cost without taking into account the effect of his choice on other players' objectives. Formally, a strategic game is a tuple $< V, \{S_v\}_{v \in V}, \{C_v : \times_{u \in V} S_u\}_{v \in V} \rightarrow \mathbb{R} >$, where S_v represents all the possible decisions that player v can take during the game to optimize his function C_v. The optimization of C_v depends on v's own strategy, as well as the strategies of the other players. Thus, the objective function of each player takes as input the *strategic space* $S = S_1 \times S_2 \times \cdots \times S_{|V|}$, which is the Cartesian product of the strategies of all players. A strategic game has a *pure Nash equilibrium* [23], if there exist a specific choice of strategies $s_v \in S_v$ such that the following condition is true for all $v \in V$:

$$C_v(s_1, ..., s_v, ..., s_{|V|}) \leq C_v(s_1, ..., s'_v, ..., s_{|V|}), \ \forall s'_v \in S_v$$

In other words, no player has incentive to deviate from his current strategy. Figure 2 illustrates a common framework for studying the dynamic process of decision-making in a strategic game. Initially, a random strategy is assigned to every player. Then, in an iterative manner, each player selects his best strategy in response to the current strategies of all the other players; v chooses $s^*_v = \arg\min_{s_v \in S_v} C_v(s_1, ..., s_v, ..., s_{|V|})$, i.e, the strategy that minimizes his own cost function. This decision is called the *best-response*, and the process *best-response dynamics* [8].

Input: Strategic game $< V, \{S_v\}_{v \in V}, \{C_v : \times_{u \in V} S_u\}_{v \in V} \rightarrow \mathbb{R} >$
Output: Nash equilibrium

```
Assign a random strategy to each player
Repeat
    For each player v ∈ V
        compute v's best strategy wrt the other players' strategies
        let v follow his best strategy
Until Nash equilibrium //no player has incentive to change his strategy
Return the strategy of each player
```

Figure 2: Best-Response Dynamics

Issues related to the framework of Figure 2 involve: (i) whether a Nash equilibrium exists, (ii) how fast it can be found (speed of convergence), (iii) how good is the resulting solution (quality). Three measures have been widely used to evaluate the quality of equilibria : (i) *social optimum* (OPT), (ii) *price of stability* (PoS), and (iii) *price of anarchy* (PoA). The social optimum is the solution that yields the optimal values to all the objective functions, so that their total cost (or utility) is minimum (or maximum). The PoS of a strategic game is the ratio between the best value among its equilibria and the social optimum i.e., PoS = best equilibrium / OPT. On the other hand, the PoA of a game is the ratio between the worst value among its equilibria and the social optimum i.e., PoA = worst equilibrium / OPT. Intuitively, PoS corresponds to the best solution, while PoA to the worst possible solution found.

Potential games constitute special class of strategic games, in which a single function $\Phi : \times_{v \in V} S_v \rightarrow \mathbb{R}$, called the *potential function*, can be used to express the objective functions of all the players [20]. Let $\overline{s_v}$ denote the set of strategies followed by all players except v, i.e., $\overline{s_v} = \{s_1, ..., s_{v-1}, s_{v+1}, ..., s_{|V|}\}$. A potential game is *exact*, if there exist a potential function Φ, such that for all s_i and all possible combinations of $\overline{s_i} \in \times_{j \in N \setminus \{i\}} S_j$, the following condition holds:

$$C_v(s_v, \overline{s_v}) - C_v(s'_v, \overline{s_v}) = \Phi(s_v, \overline{s_v}) - \Phi(s'_v, \overline{s_v})$$

For potential games, the best-response dynamics of Figure 2 always converge to a pure Nash equilibrium [20]. Therefore, we can use the local search algorithm of Figure 2 to obtain solutions for any combinatorial problem that falls in the above framework. In most cases the potential function Φ can be directly obtained by the objective function of the corresponding optimization problem and C_v can be defined accordingly. Since Φ represents the objective functions of all players, the set of Nash equilibria can be found by locating the local minima of Φ.

Game theory has been used for solving numerous well-known graph problems, e.g., minimum spanning tree and community detection [9][25][22]. To the best of our knowledge, there is no work that considers a game theoretic approach for the UML problem.

3. RMGP: GAME THEORETIC METHOD

In order to model RMGP as a game, we assume that each user is a player, whose goal is to join a class with low assignment cost that contains many of his closest friends. Initially, players are randomly assigned to classes, and then they start changing classes according to their best-responses until they reach a Nash equilibrium. In the rest of the section, we describe the algorithmic framework, and we analyze its properties.

3.1 Baseline Algorithm

The RMGP game is a tuple $< V, \{S_v\}_{v \in V}, \{C_v : \times_{u \in V} S_u \rightarrow \mathbb{R}\}_{v \in V} >$, where each user/player $v \in V$ has a set of strategies S_v and a cost function C_v. Let $s_v \in S_v$ be a specific strategy of player v, which represents the class that v is assigned to, and $c(v, s_v)$ be its cost. Given s_v and the strategies $\overline{s_v}$ of the other players, the total cost $C_v(s_v, \overline{s_v})$ of v is the weighted sum of (i) the *assignment cost* $c(v, s_v)$, and (ii) the *social cost*, i.e., half[1] of the total weight of edges that connect v with the subset of his friends in $adj(v)$, who are assigned to different classes. The goal of each player $v \in V$ is to find the class s_v that minimizes his own total cost as expressed by Equation 3. Similar to Equation 1, parameter α adjusts the relative importance of the assignment and social costs.

$$C_v(s_v, \overline{s_v}) = \alpha \cdot c(v, s_v) + (1 - \alpha) \cdot \sum_{\substack{f \in adj(v) \wedge \\ s_f \neq s_v}} \frac{1}{2} w_{(v,f)} \quad (3)$$

It is important to note that the RMGP objective function in Equation 1 is equal to the sum of all individual user costs, i.e., $RMGP(G, P, \alpha) = \sum_{v \in V} C_v(s_v, \overline{s_v})$. This decomposition of the RMGP objective into a sum of individual (per user) costs functions provides a natural motivation for modeling RMGP as a game, since users' own goals are considered for reaching a global solution. Consequently, recommendations generated by the RMGP game are likely to be followed by the users.

[1] The social cost of assigning two users v, f in different classes is evenly divided between v and f, i.e., for an edge $(v, f) \in E$, only $\frac{1}{2} w_{(v,f)}$ is attributed to the cost C_v.

Figure 3 depicts the baseline algorithm $RMGP_b$, which applies the framework of Figure 2 to RMGP. Initially, $RMGP_b$ assigns every player to a random class and computes the maximum social cost $maxSC_v$, assuming that all friends of v are assigned to a different class. Then, it starts the best-response procedure (Lines 4-14). Each iteration of the repeat-loop corresponds to a *round*. A round computes, for each player v, the cost of assigning v to every class. Initially the cost of a class is set as the assignment cost plus $maxSC_v$ (Lines 8-9). Then, for each strategy s_f followed by a friend f of v, the social cost of s_f is reduced according to the weight of the edge (v, f) (Lines 9-10). Lines 11-13 assign v to the strategy with the minimum cost. The algorithm terminates when there is no class change for any user during a round. The output is the final class s_v assigned to each player v.

Input: Social Graph $G = (V, E, W)$, Classes P
Output: Nash equilibrium

1. **For** each player $v \in V$
2. assign $v \in V$ to a random class/strategy
3. $maxSC_v = (1 - \alpha) \cdot \sum_{f \in adj(v)} \frac{1}{2} \cdot w_{(v,f)}$
4. **Repeat**
5. **For** each player $v \in V$
6. $minCost = \infty$
7. **For** each class $p \in P$
8. $cost_v[p] = \alpha \cdot c(v, p) + maxSC_v$
9. **For** each friend f of v
10. $cost_v[s_f] = cost_v[s_f] - (1 - \alpha) \cdot \frac{1}{2} \cdot w_{(v,f)}$
11. **For** each class $p \in P$
12. **If** $cost_v[p] < minCost$
13. $minCost = cost_v[p]$, $s_v = p$
14. **Until** Nash equilibrium
15. **Return** players' strategies

Figure 3: $RMGP_b$ Algorithm

Table 1 shows all the execution steps of $RMGP_b$ for our running example with $\alpha = 0.5$. Initially (first row), we randomly assign each player to a location/class $p \in P$, e.g., players v_1 and v_4 to location p_1. The value of the cost function for each player is shown inside the parenthesis next to his id (e.g., $C_{v_1} = 0.265$). Next, we iterate over the players, starting with v_1. The first column contains the cost for each of the three classes, and the best response is underlined (e.g., the best-response of v_1 is p_3 with cost 0.185). The pair of gray cells per row indicates strategy deviations; the cell with a bold value represents the new class. For instance, v_1, following his best response, switches from p_1 to p_3. A round terminates when all players have been examined. At the first round v_1, v_3 and v_6 change strategies. During the second round, there are no strategy deviations (i.e., there are no gray cells). Thus, $RMGP_b$ has reached an equilibrium and it terminates, returning the final assignments (v_3, v_4, v_6 to p_1, v_2, v_5 to p_2, and v_1 to p_3).

The performance of $RMGP_b$ can be improved by some simple heuristics. Specifically, in Line 2, instead of a random initialization, we can assign each player to the class that yields the minimum assignment cost (e.g., the closest event). Moreover, instead of selecting players at random in each round (Line 5), we can consider them in decreasing order of their degrees. The intuition behind this choice is that strategy changes of highly connected users (community leaders) will propagate fast to the other players, decreasing the number of rounds. We examine the effects of these heuristics in the experimental evaluation.

Steps		p_1	p_2	p_3
Initialization		$v_1(0.265), v_4(0.485)$	$v_2(0.22), v_5(0.15), v_6(0.36)$	$v_3(0.535)$
Round 1	$v_1(0.265, 0.325, \underline{0.185})$	$v_4(0.485)$	$v_2(0.22), v_5(0.15), v_6(0.36)$	$\mathbf{v_1(0.185)}, v_3(0.535)$
	$v_2(0.525, \underline{0.22}, 0.345)$	$v_4(0.485)$	$\mathbf{v_2(0.22)}, v_5(0.15), v_6(0.36)$	$v_1(0.185), v_3(0.535)$
	$v_3(\underline{0.05}, 0.47, 0.535)$	$\mathbf{v_3(0.05)}, v_4(0.485)$	$v_2(0.22), v_5(0.15), v_6(0.36)$	$v_1(0.185)$
	$v_4(\underline{0.31}, 0.325, 0.52)$	$v_3(0.05), \mathbf{v_4(0.31)}$	$v_2(0.22), v_5(0.15), v_6(0.36)$	$v_1(0.185)$
	$v_5(0.62, \underline{0.15}, 0.55)$	$v_3(0.05), v_4(0.31)$	$v_2(0.22), \mathbf{v_5(0.15)}, v_6(0.36)$	$v_1(0.185)$
	$v_6(\underline{0.22}, 0.36, 0.0.57)$	$v_3(0.05), v_4(0.31), \mathbf{v_6(0.22)}$	$v_2(0.22), v_5(0.15)$	$v_1(0.185)$
Round 2	$v_1(0.265, 0.325, \underline{0.185})$	$v_3(0.05), v_4(0.31), v_6(0.22)$	$v_2(0.22), v_5(0.15)$	$\mathbf{v_1(0.185)}$
	$v_2(0.525, \underline{0.22}, 0.345)$	$v_3(0.05), v_4(0.31), v_6(0.22)$	$\mathbf{v_2(0.22)}, v_5(0.15)$	$v_1(0.185)$
	$v_3(\underline{0.05}, 0.47, 0.535)$	$\mathbf{v_3(0.05)}, v_4(0.31), v_6(0.22)$	$v_2(0.22), v_5(0.15)$	$v_1(0.185)$
	$v_4(\underline{0.285}, 0.35, 0.52)$	$v_3(0.05), \mathbf{v_4(0.285)}, v_6(0.22)$	$v_2(0.22), v_5(0.15)$	$v_1(0.185)$
	$v_5(0.57, \underline{0.2}, 0.55)$	$v_3(0.05), v_4(0.285), v_6(0.22)$	$v_2(0.22), \mathbf{v_5(0.2)}$	$v_1(0.185)$
	$v_6(\underline{0.22}, 0.36, 0.57)$	$v_3(0.05), v_4(0.285), \mathbf{v_6(0.22)}$	$v_2(0.22), v_5(0.2)$	$v_1(0.185)$

Table 1: $RMGP_b$ **Example**

$RMGP_b$ can perform graph partitioning by combining connectivity with arbitrary criteria. For instance, in LAGP (running example), the assignment cost $c(v, s_v)$ in Line 8 could take into account both the distance of each user and his preference to an event (e.g., based on textual similarity between the profile and the event description). Moreover, it can easily handle cases where only a subset of the graph participates in the game (e.g., only users in a certain geographic area) by adding appropriate conditions in Lines 5 and/or 9. Finally, if multiple executions are required (e.g., in a scenario sending location-based advertisements every hour), the solution of the last execution can be used as the seed of the next one, in order to minimize the number of rounds.

3.2 Analysis

We first analyze the running time of $RMGP_b$ and then investigate the quality of its solutions. Let $k = |P|$ be the number of input classes, and $|V|$, $|E|$ be the node and edge cardinality respectively.

LEMMA 1. *The complexity of each round is* $\Theta(k \cdot |V| + |E|)$.

PROOF. The best response of a user v requires initializing the costs for k strategies (Lines 7-8), each involving constant time. Lines 10-11 reduce the cost of classes that contain the d_v friends of v, where d_v is the degree of v. Finally, Lines 11-13 find, among the k classes, the one incurring the minimum cost for v. Summarizing, the total cost for a single user is $2 \cdot k + d_v$. Repeating the same process for all users yields: $\sum_{v \in V}(2 \cdot k + d_v) = 2 \cdot k \cdot |V| + \sum_{v \in V} d_v = 2 \cdot k \cdot |V| + 2 \cdot |E| = \Theta(k \cdot |V| + |E|)$. □

In order to obtain the number of rounds, we first show that RMGP is an exact potential game (see Section 2.2). Specifically, the players' best responses according to their own objective function (Equation 3) reduce the value of the potential function $\Phi(S)$ given below. Note that $\Phi(S)$ is *not* the same as the RMGP objective function given in Equation 1 (due to the $\frac{1}{2}$ factor in the social cost) and it will only be used in the following as a tool for our analysis.

$$\Phi(S) = \alpha \cdot \sum_{v \in V} c(v, s_v) + (1 - \alpha) \cdot \sum_{e=(v,f) \in E \wedge s_v \neq s_f} \frac{1}{2} w_e \quad (4)$$

THEOREM 1. RMGP *constitutes an exact potential game.*

PROOF. Recall from Section 2.2, that it suffices to show that for every player v, who changes his strategy from the current one s_v to the best-response s'_v, and for all possible combinations of the other players' strategies $\overline{s_v}$ it holds that: $C_v(s_v, \overline{s_v}) - C_v(s'_v, \overline{s_v}) = \Phi(s_v, \overline{s_v}) - \Phi(s'_v, \overline{s_v})$. Indeed, we have $\Phi(s_v, \overline{s_v}) - \Phi(s'_v, \overline{s_v}) = \alpha \cdot (c(v, s_v) - c(v, s'_v)) + (1 - \alpha) \cdot (\sum_{f \in adj(v) \wedge s_v \neq s_f} \frac{1}{2} w_{(v,f)} - \sum_{f \in adj(v) \wedge s'_v \neq s_f} \frac{1}{2} w_{(v,f)}) =$
$\alpha \cdot c(v, s_v) + (1 - \alpha) \cdot \sum_{f \in adj(v) \wedge s_v \neq s_f} \frac{1}{2} w_{(v,f)} - (\alpha \cdot c(v, s'_v) + (1 - \alpha) \cdot \sum_{f \in adj(v) \wedge s'_v \neq s_f} \frac{1}{2} w_{(v,f)}) =$
$C_v(s_v, \overline{s_v}) - C_v(s'_v, \overline{s_v})$ □

Since RMGP is an exact potential game, and the set of strategic configurations S is finite, players need to change their strategies a finite number of times before a Nash equilibrium is reached. In order to provide an upper bound for the number of rounds required for convergence of $RMGP_b$, we consider a scaled version of the problem where the objective function takes integer values. More specifically, we assume an equivalent game with potential function $\Phi_{\mathbb{Z}}(S) = d \cdot \Phi(S)$, where d is a positive multiplicative factor chosen such that $\Phi_{\mathbb{Z}}(S) \in \mathbb{Z}, \forall S$. Notice that d is a constant that depends on the choice of $c(v, s_v)$, w_e and α, and does not scale with the size of the problem. Moreover, this scaling only serves the purpose of proving the following theorems and the actual execution of the algorithm can be performed on decimal values.

Let $C^* \triangleq d \cdot \sum_{v \in V} \max_{p \in P} c(v, p)$, and $W^* \triangleq \frac{d}{2} \cdot \sum_{e \in E} w_e$. Intuitively, C^* corresponds to the (scaled) maximum assignment cost, assuming that each user is assigned to his "worst" strategy. Similarly, W^* is the (scaled) maximum social cost of any solution, assuming that all edges cross classes. The following lemma describes an upper bound on the number of rounds required until $RMGP_b$ converges to a Nash equilibrium. The main idea behind the proof of the lemma is that in each round $\Phi_{\mathbb{Z}}(S)$ will decrease by at least 1 and hence the total number of rounds cannot be more that the difference between its maximum and the minimum values.

LEMMA 2. *The number of rounds required until* $RMGP_b$ *converges to an equilibrium is upper bounded by* $\max\{C^*, W^*\}$.

PROOF. We can easily see that the scaled version of $RMGP_b$ with potential function $\Phi_{\mathbb{Z}}(S) = d \cdot \Phi(S) = \alpha \cdot \sum_{v \in V} c'(v, s_v) + (1 - \alpha) \cdot \sum_{e=(v,f) \in E \wedge s_v \neq s_f} w'_e$, where $c'(v, s_v) = d \cdot c(v, s_v)$ and $w'_e = d \cdot w_e / 2$, will converge to an equilibrium in the same number of rounds as $RMGP_b$. The cost reduction in $\Phi_{\mathbb{Z}}$ after each strategy change of a player is at least 1, i.e., $\Phi_{\mathbb{Z}}(s_v, \overline{s_v}) - \Phi_{\mathbb{Z}}(s'_v, \overline{s_v}) \geq 1$ for all players $v \in V$ and all possible strategies S. This is because i) a player deviates only if his cost decreases according to his best response, ii) the improvement is at least 1 as $\Phi_{\mathbb{Z}}$ takes integer values, and iii) the improvement of a user's cost is the same as the improvement of the global potential function due to the property of exact potential game. Consequently, the total number of rounds is at most the maximum possible value of $\Phi_{\mathbb{Z}}$, denoted as Φ_{max}, minus the minimum possible value, denoted as Φ_{min}. In the worst case, $\Phi_{min} = 0$ and $\Phi_{max} \leq \alpha \cdot C^* + (1 - \alpha) \cdot W^* \leq \max\{C^*, W^*\}$. Therefore, the number of rounds to reach an equilibrium is upper-bounded by $\max\{C^*, W^*\}$, as stated by the lemma. □

Next, we continue our discussion with some theoretical results on the quality of the solutions of $RMGP_b$.

THEOREM 2. *In $RMGP_b$, the price of stability (PoS) is bounded by 2, and the price of anarchy (PoA) is bounded by* $PoA \leq 1 + \frac{(1-\alpha)}{\alpha} \frac{deg_{avg} \cdot w_{avg}}{2 \cdot c^*_{avg}}$, *where deg_{avg} is the average degree, $w_{avg} = \frac{1}{|E|} \sum_{e \in E} w_e$ is the average edge weight and $c^*_{avg} = \frac{1}{|V|} \sum_{v \in V} \min_{s_v \in P} c(v, s_v)$ is the average minimum per user cost.*

PROOF. Let $\mathcal{C}(S)$ denote the summation of all players' costs, $\mathcal{C}(S) \triangleq \sum_{v \in V} C_v(s_v, \overline{s_v})$, and recall that $\mathcal{C}(S)$ is equal to the RMGP objective function of given in Equation 1. From the definition of the potential function $\Phi(S)$ (Equation 4) we can directly see that for any strategic configuration S, we have that

$$\frac{1}{2}\mathcal{C}(S) \leq \Phi(S) \leq \mathcal{C}(S). \tag{5}$$

Let S^* be the globally optimal set of strategies that minimize $\mathcal{C}(S)$, and let $OPT = \mathcal{C}(S^*)$. Further, let S^{**} be the set of strategies that yields the minimum of the potential function $\Phi(S)$, i.e., the best Nash equilibrium. From the bound in (5) and since $\mathcal{C}(S^*) \leq \mathcal{C}(S), \forall S$ and $\Phi(S^{**}) \leq \Phi(S), \forall S$, we have: $\mathcal{C}(S^{**}) \leq 2\Phi(S^{**}) \leq 2\Phi(S^*) \leq 2\mathcal{C}(S^*) = 2 \cdot OPT$, and hence the PoS is bounded by 2 as stated by the Theorem.

Now, let $S^{\#}$ be the strategic configuration of any Nash equilibrium (e.g., the one obtained by $RMGP_b$). Since $S^{\#}$ is a Nash equilibrium, all the user cost functions are locally minimized and hence we have that $C_v(s_v^{\#}, \overline{s_v}^{\#}) \leq C_v(s'_v, \overline{s_v}^{\#})$, for all $v \in V$ and all $s'_v \in P$. Choosing s'_v to be the strategy with the smallest assignment cost for user v (i.e., $s'_v = \arg\min_{s_v \in P} c(v, s_v)$) we obtain $\mathcal{C}(S^{\#}) = \sum_{v \in V} C_v(s_v^{\#}, \overline{s_v}^{\#}) \leq \sum_{v \in V} C_v(s_v', \overline{s_v}^{\#}) =$

$$\begin{aligned}
&= \alpha \sum_{v \in V} \min_{s_v \in P} c(v, s_v) + (1-\alpha) \sum_{v \in V} \sum_{\substack{f \in adj(v) \wedge \\ s'_v \neq s_f^{\#}}} \frac{1}{2} w_{(f,v)} \\
&\leq \alpha \sum_{v \in V} \min_{s_v \in P} c(v, s_v) + (1-\alpha) \sum_{v \in V} \sum_{f \in adj(v)} \frac{1}{2} w_{(f,v)} \\
&= \alpha \sum_{v \in V} \min_{s_v \in P} c(v, s_v) + (1-\alpha) \sum_{e \in E} w_e \\
&= \alpha |V| c^*_{avg} + (1-\alpha)|E| w_{avg}
\end{aligned} \tag{6}$$

Since $\mathcal{C}(S^*) \geq \alpha \cdot |V| \cdot c^*_{avg}$, we have that $PoA = \mathcal{C}(S^{\#})/\mathcal{C}(S^*) \leq 1 + \frac{1-\alpha}{\alpha} \cdot \frac{|E| \cdot w_{avg}}{|V| \cdot c^*_{avg}}$, and since $|E| = |V| \cdot deg_{avg}/2$ we obtain the required bound. ☐

3.3 Normalization Issues

In several applications, the assignment and social costs may not be comparable. For instance, in LAGP the assignment cost per user is defined on distance and can be in the order of thousands (of meters), whereas edge weights may be in the range $[0, 1]$. On the other hand, for TAGP the assignment cost is based on similarity and is usually in the range $[0, 1]$, while the social cost (e.g., based on the number of common discussions threads) may be in the order of thousands. Even for the same type of task, costs may exhibit huge fluctuations depending on the problem characteristics; e.g., distances in LAGP may be defined in a unit space (i.e., a square with extent 1 per axis), or may be given in meters, miles etc.

In such cases, the direct application of RMGP algorithms, or any partition method that combines social with other criteria, may be meaningless; if distances are very large compared to edge weights, most users are likely to be assigned to the closest event independently of their friends because the total cost is dominated by the assignment cost (i.e., distances to events). On the other hand, for high edge weights (compared to distances), users are likely to be grouped based only on their social connections, independently of their distance to events. To avoid the effect of the specific problem characteristics and measurements, we introduce the *normalized version* RMGP^{N} of multi-criteria graph partitioning.

The aim of RMGP^{N} is to regularize the assignment and social costs so that they are comparable: when $\alpha = 0.5$ the two sums of Equation 1 should have similar values; other values of α should indeed reflect the input preferences (e.g., $\alpha = 0.9$ should mean that the assignment cost is about 9 times more important that the social aspect). As a first step, recall that the objective function of conventional RMGP (Equation 1) can be written in terms of the per user costs (Equation 3) as $RMGP(G, P, \alpha) = \sum_{v \in V} C_v(s_v, \overline{s_v})$. If AC_v (and SC_v) denote the *average* assignment (and social) cost per user, $RMGP(G, P, \alpha)$ can be rewritten as

$$RMGP(G, P, \alpha) = \alpha \cdot |V| \cdot AC_v + (1-\alpha) \cdot \frac{1}{2} \cdot |V| \cdot SC_v$$

In RMGP^{N} for $\alpha = 0.5$, the average assignment and social costs must be equal; i.e., it should hold that:

$$|V| \cdot AC_v = \frac{1}{2} \cdot |V| \cdot SC_v \Rightarrow AC_v = \frac{1}{2} \cdot SC_v$$

To achieve this, the costs should be normalized, by re-adjusting the assignment cost or the edge weights. In the following we focus on the normalization of assignment cost. Let the *normalization constant* be $c_N = \frac{SC_v}{2 \cdot AC_v}$; then, RMGP^{N} aims at minimizing the function of Equation 7:

$$RMGP^N(G, P, \alpha) = c_N \cdot \alpha \cdot \sum_{v \in V} c(v, s_v) + (1-a) \cdot \sum_{\substack{e=(v,f) \in E \wedge \\ s_v \neq s_f}} w_e \tag{7}$$

The value of c_N depends on the problem characteristics. We focus on LAGP before discussing other applications. Let $||v_i, p_j||$ be the distance between user $v_i \in V$ and event $p_j \in P$. Equation 7 essentially normalizes this distance to $c_N \cdot ||v_i, p_j||$; if $c_N > 1$, the data space is expanded, whereas if $c_N < 1$ the data space contracts. However, we cannot compute the exact value of c_N because it requires AC_v and SC_v, which can only be obtained after solving the problem. Instead, we approximate c_N using estimations of AC_v and SC_v based on two heuristic approaches.

The *optimistic* approach considers that among the k events, every user is assigned to the closest one. Therefore, $AC_v = dist_{min}$, where $dist_{min}$ is the average minimum distance between every user and any event, and it can be derived by cost models [28], or it can be computed at an initialization phase. Regarding SC_v, let deg_{avg} be the average node degree and w_{avg} be the average edge weight, both of which are query-independent and available apriori. We assume that among the deg_{avg} friends of a user, only a fraction $\frac{1}{\sqrt{k}}$ is assigned to different events, so that $SC_v = \frac{deg_{avg} \cdot w_{avg}}{\sqrt{k}}$ (e.g., if there are 16 events, 1/4 of the friends of a user are expected to be in other classes). Thus, the estimation for the normalization constant is $C_{Nopt} = \frac{deg_{avg} \cdot w_{avg}}{2 \cdot dist_{min} \cdot \sqrt{k}}$.

The *pessimistic* approach considers that each user is assigned to the event with the median distance, i.e., $AC_v = dist_{med}$, where $dist_{med}$ is the average median distance between every user and event. For the estimation of SC_v, we assume that users are uniformly assigned to k events, so that there are $\frac{deg_{avg} \cdot (k-1)}{k}$ edges connecting a user with friends at different events. Accordingly, $SC_v = \frac{deg_{avg} \cdot (k-1) \cdot w_{avg}}{k}$ and $C_{Npes} = \frac{deg_{avg} \cdot (k-1) \cdot w_{avg}}{2 \cdot dist_{med} \cdot k}$. C_{Npes} may be larger or smaller than C_{Nopt} depending on the values of the above parameters.

According to either the optimistic or the pessimistic approach, the *normalization constant* c_N, involves graph-dependent parameters deg_{avg}, w_{avg}, and application-dependent parameters $dist_{min}$, $dist_{med}$. In other applications, the values of $dist_{min}$, $dist_{med}$ should be computed accordingly. For instance, in TAGP, a pessimistic approach would set $dist_{med}$ as the average median dissimilarity between every user and advertisement. In case of multiple criteria (e.g., both distance and text dissimilarity), the values of $dist_{min}$, $dist_{med}$ should take into account all criteria. In general, the computation of application-dependent parameters is orthogonal to the normalization framework. Since normalization only involves multiplication of the assignment cost by c_N, RMGP^{N} preserves all the properties of RMGP presented in this section. It can also easily accommodate the optimizations of the next section. Moreover, our experimental evaluation confirms that normalization is indeed necessary in order to obtain meaningful results.

4. OPTIMIZATIONS

In this section we present optimizations that improve the performance of the baseline algorithm without compromising the convergence guarantee. Section 4.1 describes the elimination of strategies that can never be followed, regardless of the decisions of other players. Section 4.2 investigates how independent strategies can be utilized to achieve parallelism. Section 4.3 enhances efficiency at the expense of space by exploring a global table of strategies. The proposed optimizations are orthogonal and can be applied in any combination.

4.1 Pruning by Strategy Elimination

$RMGP_b$ computes the cost functions of all players for each strategy in every round. However, there are strategies that cannot be assigned to some users. For example, in LAGP, a user with a small number of friends will be assigned to an event in his vicinity. Consequently, we can reduce the strategic space, i.e., prune the events that are far from the user, and avoid redundant computations.

Let $s_{v,min}$ be the strategy with the minimum assignment cost for player v, and W_v be half the sum of the edge weights incident to v, i.e., $s_{v,min} = \arg\min_{s_v \in S_v} c(v, s_v)$ and $W_v = \sum_{f \in adj(v)} \frac{1}{2} \cdot w_{v,f}$, respectively. In the worst case (i.e., assuming that none of his friends follows $s_{v,min}$), the total cost of assigning v to $s_{v,min}$ is:

$$\alpha \cdot c(v, s_{v,min}) + (1 - \alpha) \cdot W_v$$

The *reduced strategic space* of v, denoted as S_v^r, contains only the possible strategies that v may follow. A strategy $p \in S_v^r$ if and only if the lowest possible total cost of assigning p to v does not exceed $\alpha \cdot c(v, s_{v,min}) + (1 - \alpha) \cdot W_v$. The lowest cost for p is achieved when all friends of v follow p, i.e., $\alpha \cdot c(v,p) + (1-\alpha) \cdot 0 = \alpha \cdot c(v,p)$. Consequently, p belongs to S_v^r if:

$$\alpha \cdot c(v,p) \leq \alpha \cdot c(v, s_{v,min}) + (1 - \alpha) \cdot W_v$$

The *valid region* VR_v of player v is a bound such that no strategy with assignment cost higher than VR_v can be assigned to v:

$$VR_v = \frac{\alpha \cdot c(v, s_{v,min}) + (1 - \alpha) \cdot W_v}{\alpha}$$

Equivalently, the reduced strategic space S_v^r of v contains only those strategies, whose assignment cost does not exceed VR_v. In the running example of Figure 1, if $\alpha = 0.5$, then $VR_{v_1} = 0.37$. $S_{v_1}^r$ contains only p_3, since $c(v_1, p_1) = 0.48$, $c(v_1, p_2) = 0.6$, and $c(v_1, p_3) = 0.27$. Therefore, we can directly remove v_1 from the game, and directly assign v_1 to p_3. Similarly, we can eliminate v_6 and prune p_1 from $S_{v_2}^r$.

We refer to the version of the algorithm that includes strategy elimination as $RMGP_{se}$. In a initialization step, $RMGP_{se}$ computes the valid regions for all users and eliminates the strategies that can never be followed. If during this process, it discovers a user v that can only be assigned to a single strategy (i.e., the one with the minimum assignment cost), it directly assigns v and removes him from the game. Since $RMGP_{se}$ never prunes best responses, it has the same convergence guarantees as $RMGP_b$.

4.2 Parallelism with Independent Strategies

In each round, $RMGP_b$ computes the best response of all users sequentially, in a round-robin fashion. This is a fundamental requirement in best response dynamics: if multiple players change strategies simultaneously their decisions may be based on "outdated" information and there is the chance that the overall potential function increases. However, in our setting, if two users are *not socially connected*, the strategic deviations of one will not affect the best-response of the other; i.e., these two users can select their best responses *simultaneously*. Based on this observation, we can partition the users in N_g groups such that no two users in the same group share an edge. In the running example of Figure 1 we could have three (or more groups), e.g., $\mathcal{G}_1 = \{v_1, v_5\}$, $\mathcal{G}_2 = \{v_2, v_3, v_6\}$, and $\mathcal{G}_3 = \{v_4\}$. The best responses of the users in the same group (e.g., v_2, v_3 and v_6) are computed in parallel, either by the same machine through multi-threading, or by different machines.

We refer to this game as $RMGP_{is}$. As shown in Figure 4, $RMGP_{is}$ examines each group in a round-robin manner. Since there are implementation limits on the number of threads that can be created, the algorithm takes as input a parameter T that defines the maximum threads that can run simultaneously. For each group $\mathcal{G}_i$, $RMGP_{is}$ creates T sets of users, each consisting of at most $\lceil |\mathcal{G}_i|/T \rceil$ users (Lines 3-6). The threads are executed in parallel, computing the best response of the users in the corresponding group sequentially (Line 7). $RMGP_{is}$ waits for all threads to finish in order to continue to the next group (Line 8). The algorithm terminates when none of the users in any group changes strategy.

Input: Social Graph $G = (V, E, W)$, Classes P, Colored Groups $\mathcal{G}_i$, Number of threads T
Output: Nash equilibrium

1. assign each player $v \in V$ to a class/strategy
2. **Repeat**
3.   **For** $i \in [1, N_g]$
4.   users per thread $upt = \lceil |\mathcal{G}_i|/T \rceil$
5.   **For** each $t \in [1, T]$
6. $\mathcal{U}_t$ = choose at most upt users from $\mathcal{G}_i$
7.   start thread: compute best responses of users in $\mathcal{G}_i^t$
8. $\mathcal{G}_i = \mathcal{G}_i \setminus \mathcal{U}_t$
9.   wait for all threads to finish
10. **Until** Nash equilibrium
11. **Return** players' strategies

Figure 4: $RMGP_{is}$ Algorithm

Groups can be computed by a graph coloring algorithm. In particular, graph coloring assigns colors to nodes such that no two incident nodes share the same color. The problem of coloring a graph using the minimum number of colors is NP-Hard. However, there are polynomial greedy approaches (e.g., $O(|V|^2)$, [31]) that use at most $d_{max} + 1$ colors, where d_{max} is the maximum degree. We apply such an algorithm off-line to create groups of nodes with the same color.

4.3 Scheduling with Global Table

Depending on the strategy deviations, numerous redundant computations can be avoided with proper book-keeping. In particular, for a class/strategy p and a user v, if the set of v's friends, who followed p does not change, then the cost of assigning v to p remains the same. Even if some of v's friends have switched strategies, it is possible that v is not affected, and the costly examination of his strategies can be avoided. Based on these observations we propose the $RMGP_{gt}$ optimization.

$RMGP_{gt}$ randomly assigns each player v to a strategy and computes his cost for each strategy. This information is stored in a $|V| \cdot k$ array (k is the class cardinality), referred to as the *global table*, which is kept updated in the following manner. A Boolean variable h_v indicates whether user v is happy, i.e., if his current strategy has the minimum total cost among the strategies. The method only examines those players for which h_v is $false$. In more detail, assume that the algorithm considers player v, where s_v is his current strategy, and s'_v is his best-response. First, v updates his strategy from s_v to s'_v, and sets $h_v = true$. Then, he informs his friends so that they will update their costs for the corresponding strategies. Specifically, for each friend f of v, the cost of s_v increases by $(1-\alpha) \cdot \frac{1}{2} \cdot w_{(v,f)}$ due to the class change of v; on the other hand, the cost of s'_v decreases by $(1-\alpha) \cdot \frac{1}{2} \cdot w_{(v,u)}$. If, after the changes, the current strategy of f is the one with the lowest cost, h_f is set to $true$. The algorithm terminates when all players are happy.

Figure 5 depicts the pseudocode of $RMGP_{gt}$. Initially, $RMGP_{gt}$ computes the global table GT and sets v as happy or unhappy accordingly (Lines 3-6). Then, it processes the game described above until reaching a Nash equilibrium. $RMGP_{gt}$ performs the same number of rounds as $RMGP_b$, assuming that both use the same initial assignments. However, $RMGP_{gt}$ is faster since it only schedules unhappy users that will switch strategies, as opposed to all players in $RMGP_b$. Therefore, the cost of each round in $RMGP_{gt}$ is lower than that of $RMGP_b$, and it gradually decreases. The trade-off is that $RMGP_{gt}$ needs to maintain in main memory, for each user v, the cost of every strategy. The space requirement can be reduced if, during the construction of the global table, we apply the optimization of Section 4.1 to eliminate strategies that can never be followed. Finally, $RMGP_{gt}$ follows the definitions of $RMGP_b$ for cost and potential functions; therefore, convergence is guaranteed and the PoS and PoA remain the same.

Input: Social Graph $G = (V, E, W)$, Classes P
Output: Nash equilibrium

1. initialize array GT of size $|V| \times k$
2. assign each player $v \in V$ to a class/strategy
3. **For** each player $v \in V$
4.   **For** each class/strategy $p \in P$
5. $GT[v][p] = C_v(p, \overline{s_v})$
6.   **If** $s_v = \arg\min_{p \in P} GT[v][p]$ then $h_v = true$; $false$ otherwise
7. **Repeat**
8.   **For** each player $v \in F$
9.   **If** $h_v = false$
10. $s'_v = \arg\min_{p \in P} GT[v][p]$, $h_v = true$
11.   **For** each friend $f \in adj(v)$
12. $GT[f][s'_v] = GT[f][s'_v] - (1-\alpha) \cdot \frac{1}{2} \cdot w_{(v,f)}$
13. $GT[f][s_v] = GT[f][s_v] + (1-\alpha) \cdot \frac{1}{2} \cdot w_{(v,f)}$
14.   **If** $s_f = \arg\min_{p \in P} GT[f][p]$
15. $h_f = true$; $false$ otherwise
16. **Until** Nash equilibrium
17. **Return** players' strategies

Figure 5: $RMGP_{gt}$ Algorithm

5. DECENTRALIZED GAME

Commercial social networks usually distribute the social graph across multiple servers in order to improve content delivery and accommodate the geographically diverse nature of data generation and demand. Computation in decentralized storage systems is usually performed through a distributed data access interface (API) between the application and the corresponding servers. One such example is Facebook's TAO [6]. Following a similar approach, one could perform RMGP on a distributed social graph by fetching the data over the network through the API to a master processing unit and executing the algorithm locally. We refer to this approach as fetch-and-execute (FaE). However, for large problem instances, transferring the data to a server can be a major bottleneck in performance. Moreover, a single server may not be able to store the entire graph due to memory limitations.

To avoid these shortcomings, we propose a framework for performing RMGP in a decentralized manner. Our framework assumes that the graph is distributed over several *slave nodes* that have processing capabilities. The partitioning scheme used for assigning the data to the slaves is orthogonal to our problem. A *master node* M acts as a game coordinator that manages the data exchange between the slave nodes. We call this framework DG, for decentralized game. DG requires that the social graph has been colored using a distributed graph coloring technique such as [14]. Although we assume that the slaves can only communicate through M, DG can be easily extended to handle direct data exchange between slaves.

We describe DG through an LAGP scenario, e.g., we wish to assign users, who are currently checked-in within the bounds of a specific geographical area to k events. Figure 6 depicts the processing method and communication steps between M and the slave nodes. First, M sends an initialization command to all slave nodes, which contains the query (i.e., events, α, area of interest) along with a strategy initialization method, e.g., random or closest event. Then, each slave: i) determines the users who are stored locally and will participate in the game, i.e., are within the area of interest, ii) initializes players' strategies based on the method decided by M, and iii) sends the strategic vector of the local users, referred to as the local strategic vector LSV, along with the distinct colors of the players to M. M integrates the union of all LSVs into a global strategic vector GSV, and sends it to the slaves that will participate to the game (slaves that do not contain users within the area of interest are excluded). Once a slave node receives GSV, it i) stores it locally, ii) performs additional initialization tasks, e.g., computes the global table if processing is based on $RMGP_{gt}$, and iii) sends an acknowledgment to M, denoting that it is ready to start the game.

After M has received an acknowledgment from *all* slaves, it starts the execution of the game. Each iteration of the repeat loop (Lines 14-25) corresponds to a round of the game. In every round, M sends to the slave nodes a command to compute the best response of all users with a specific color. Upon receiving the command, each slave computes the best responses and sends back to M only the strategy changes. Next, M updates GSV and redistributes the changes. When a slave node receives such a message, it updates the local GSV and the global table if required, and sends an acknowledgment to M. The round finishes when all colors are processed. The algorithm terminates if M receives no strategic updates in a round.

Compared to FaE, DG improves the overall performance in two ways. First, it lessens the communication overhead by allowing slave nodes to locally process their data and exchange only strategy changes through the network. This is an important feature since

```
M sends q and initialization parameters to the all slave nodes
Each slave node
    determines the local players
    initializes the strategies of the local players
    sends the strategies and the distinct colors of the local players' to M
let D denote all slave nodes that participate to the game
let CL be the set containing the distinct colors of players
M computes GSV
M distributes GSV to all slave nodes in D
Each slave node in D
    stores GSV locally
    performs additional initialization tasks (if required)
    sends ACK to M
Repeat
    For each color c ∈ CL
        M sends "compute c" command to all slave nodes in D
        Each slave node in D
            computes the best responses of the users in group c
            sends the strategic changes to M
        M updates GSV
        M distributes the changes to the slave nodes in D
        Each slave node in D
            updates its local strategic vector and players' scores
            sends ACK to M
Until no strategic changes
```

Figure 6: Decentralized Game

data transfers may significantly burden the performance of decentralized systems. Second, DG reduces the query response time by enabling slaves to work in parallel.

6. EXPERIMENTS

We evaluate the proposed approaches assuming a LAGP task, where the users of a geo-social network are assigned to events based on proximity and social aspects (i.e., the running example). The graph and the locations of users are stored in two main-memory hash tables where the user IDs are used as keys. In the social hash table, for each user there is an adjacency list of pairs (friend id, edge weight). The location hash table maintains the coordinates of the last check-in of each user. All algorithms were implemented in C++, under Linux Ubuntu and executed on an Intel Xeon E5-2660 2.20GHz with 16GB RAM.

We use two real datasets: Gowalla and Foursquare. Gowalla [2] consists of i) 12,748 users in the Dallas and Austin metropolitan area, ii) their check-ins over a weekend in February 2009, and iii) 48,419 edges/friendships among them. 128 different social events that took place during the same weekend in Dallas and Austin, were obtained from Eventbrite [2]. Foursquare [16], collected in September 2013, consists of 2,153,471 users and their check-ins, 27,098,490 friendships, and 1,143,092 events/venues. In both datasets, all edge weights equal to 1. For experiments, where we need to reduce the size of the social graph, we use the Forest Fire sampling technique [15]. For decreasing the event cardinality, we randomly select the required number of events.

Section 6.1 compares the performance of $RMGP_b$ with algorithms for related problems. Section 6.2 investigates the effect of normalization on the quality of the solutions. Section 6.3 evaluates the optimizations of the baseline approach in a centralized setting. Section 6.4 studies RMGP in a decentralized setting.

6.1 Comparison with Other Approaches

Since as discussed in Section 2 existing graph partitioning methods focus on different problems, in order to evaluate the proposed techniques we use the following benchmarks. (i) The Metis-Hungarian approach (MH), which initially computes the minimum unbalanced k-way social cut using METIS, and then it assigns every partition (i.e., group of users) to an event using the Hungarian method [21], so that each partition is assigned to a different event and the total assignment cost is minimized. (ii) The linear programming UML algorithm (UML_{lp}) [13], which guarantees an approximation ratio 2. (iii) The faster greedy UML approach (UML_{gr}) [5], which guarantees a looser approximation ratio $8 \log |V|$.

We compare the above techniques with the *unoptimized* $RMGP_b$ in terms of efficiency and solution quality. $RMGP_b$ applies random initial assignment and random order for considering users in each round. Since UML methods aim at small datasets, we reduce the size of Gowalla through Forest Fire. Moreover, we pre-compute the costs (distances) of the assignments because they are required by UML_{lp} and UML_{gr} as input. In order to solve UML_{lp}, we use CVX [10].

Figure 7(a) assesses the execution time (in ms) as a function of the number k of events, for $|V| = 200$. $RMGP_b$ is more than 3 orders of magnitude faster than UML_{gr} and UML_{lp} because both UML algorithms have high complexity and require graph transformations at execution time. MH is slightly slower than $RMGP_b$. Figure 7(b) shows the solution quality (i.e., total assignment cost according to Equation 1) versus k. UML_{lp} yields the lowest cost because in the worst case it generates a 2-approximation of the optimal solution. Actually, in most settings, the linear relaxation gave integral solutions, which means that the output of UML_{lp} is optimal (this is not expected for larger graph instances). The assignments of $RMGP_b$ have higher cost, but still comparable to UML_{lp}. However, the solutions of UML_{gr} and MH are significantly worse; UML_{gr} is bounded by a higher (worse) approximation ratio $8 \log |V|$, while MH minimizes the social cost (i.e., k-way cut) but yields high assignment costs. To better demonstrate the difference, for $k = 7$, given a user, the average number of his/her friends recommended to the same event is 14.2 and 13.7 for $RMGP_b$ and MH, respectively. Similarly, the average distance between each user and the recommended event is 9.4km in $RMGP_b$ and 13.6km in MH.

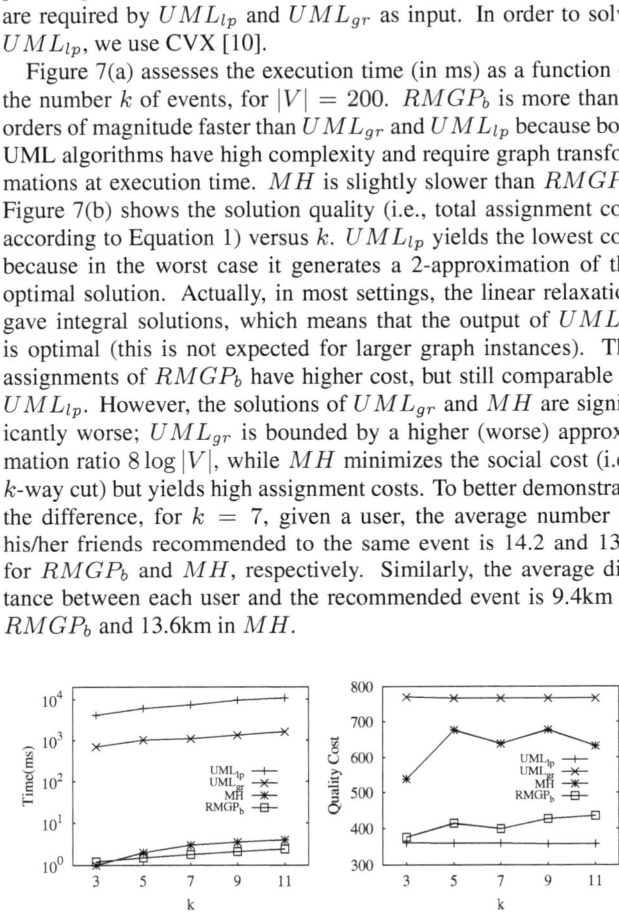

(a) Time vs. k (b) Quality vs. k

Figure 7: $RMGP_b$, MH, UML_{lp} and UML_{gr} vs. k

Figure 8 plots the running time and quality cost versus the node cardinality $|V|$, for $k = 7$. Similar to the previous experiment, $RMGP_b$ is the most efficient algorithm while the quality of its solutions remains close to UML_{lp} (which in most cases is optimal). Note that the quality cost grows with the size of the graph, because there are more users to assign. We restrict the maximum number of nodes to 300, because otherwise UML_{lp} and UML_{gr} would be too slow. In the remaining experiments, we focus on game theoretic algorithms using the complete real datasets. We exclude UML_{lp} and UML_{gr} because they are inefficient for large graphs, and MH since it generates solutions of low quality.

[2]http://www.eventbrite.com

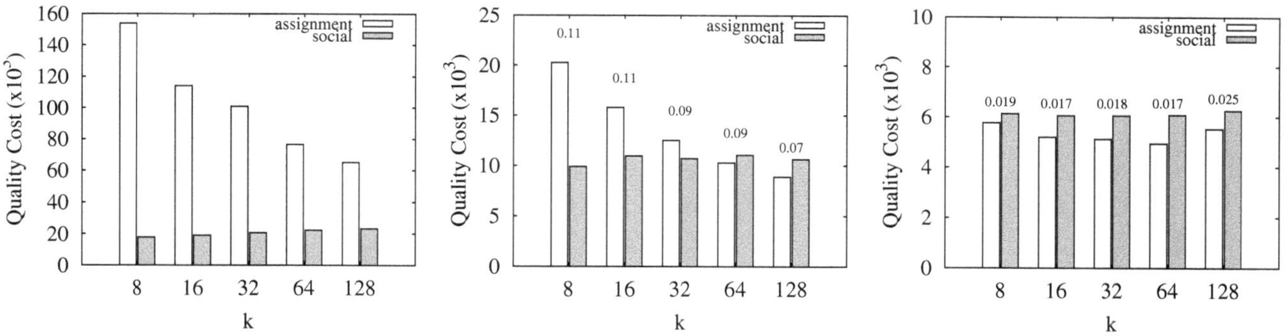

(a) No normalization (b) Optimistic normalization (c) Pessimistic normalization

Figure 9: Effect of Normalization, Cost vs. *k* ($\alpha = 0.5$)

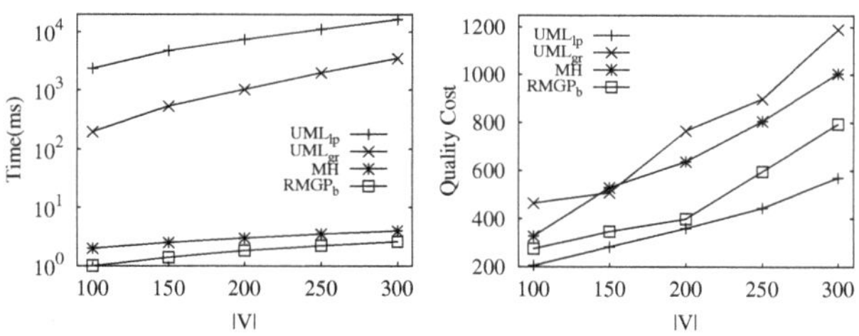

(a) Time vs. $|V|$ (b) Quality vs. $|V|$

Figure 8: $RMGP_b$, MH, UML_{lp} and UML_{gr} vs. $|V|$

6.2 Effect of Normalization

To demonstrate the effect of normalization, we use Gowalla. Figure 9(a) shows the assignment and social costs as a function of the number of events k for the original (non-normalized) RMGP. Figures 9(b) and 9(c) illustrate the corresponding diagrams for RMGP^{N} according to the optimistic and pessimistic normalization, respectively. In all cases, the preference parameter α is set to 0.5 so that the assignment and social costs are considered equally important. The solutions are obtained by $RMGP_b$, where initially all users are assigned to the closest event.

According to Figure 9(a), the assignment dominates the social cost for all values of k before the normalization. This happens because the average distance between a user and an event is above 100 (kms) for all values of k, whereas the edge weights are equal to 1 and the average node degree is 7.6. Consequently, even if all friends of a user are assigned to different events, the social cost is likely to be a small fraction of the assignment cost, and most users stay at the closest event. For instance, if $k = 8$, only 1434 users are re-assigned to a new event, while 11314 remain at their initial assignment; the social gain of moving to a further event attended by friends cannot compensate for the increase in the distance.

On the other hand, the normalized versions of the problem exhibit a much more balanced behavior, especially with the pessimistic approach, for which the assignment and social costs are similar for all values of k (recall that α is set to 0.5). For $k = 8$, in the optimistic (pessimistic) approach 3459 (6583) users are re-assigned to events that reduce their social cost. The numbers on top of the columns for RMGP^{N} show the values of the normalization constant c_N used for the specific value of k (see Section 3.3). Finally, note that the overall costs in the three diagrams are not directly comparable since they are based on different formulae (Equation 1 for RMGP and Equation 7 for RMGP^{N}), or different approximations of c_N (for the two versions of RMGP^{N}). Moreover, they correspond to different solutions.

Since the solutions of the non-normalized version of RMGP are futile, in all the following experiments we assume RMGP^{N} normalized according to the pessimistic approach.

6.3 Centralized RMGP

We examine the behavior of $RMGP_b$ assuming a single server, which maintains the Gowalla dataset and performs query processing. Recall that $RMGP_b$ initializes users to random events, and each round considers users in a random order. We slightly modify the baseline to create two versions: i) $RMGP_{b+i}$ that initializes users to their closest event, and ii) $RMGP_{b+i+o}$, which in addition considers users in decreasing order of their degree.

Figure 10(a) illustrates the CPU time of the three variants as a function of the number k of events, for $\alpha = 0.5$. $RMGP_{b+i}$ improves significantly the performance of $RMGP_b$, whereas the additional effect of $RMGP_{b+i+o}$ is evident only for $k = 128$. Figure 10(b) shows the quality of the final solutions produced by the algorithms, for the same settings. For each value of k, the first column corresponds to the cost of $RMGP_b$, the second to the cost $RMGP_{b+i}$, and the third to the cost $RMGP_{b+i+o}$. The white part of a column indicates its assignment (i.e., distance) cost, whereas the gray part is the social component. Observe that the two components have comparable costs because $\alpha = 0.5$ and the problem is normalized. Usually $RMGP_{b+i}$ and $RMGP_{b+i+o}$ reach the same solution since they start with the same initialization, and their differences in terms of quality are negligible. On the other hand, the solutions produced by $RMGP_b$ are inferior in all settings.

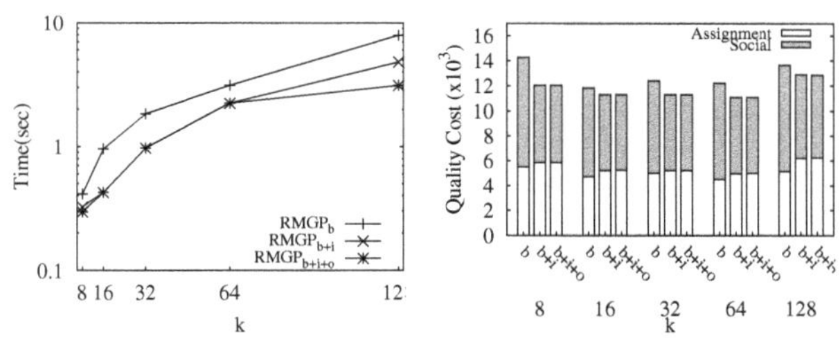

(a) Time vs. k (b) Quality vs. k

Figure 10: Behavior of $RMGP_b$ ($\alpha = 0.5$)

Figure 11(a) studies the effect of α on the running time, for $k = 32$. Similar to Figure 10(a), $RMGP_{b+i}$ and $RMGP_{b+i+o}$ have almost identical performance, and they are both better than $RMGP_b$. The value of α does not have a significant impact, and in all cases the heuristic versions require between 5 and 8 rounds to terminate, whereas the original algorithm needs between 9 and 11 rounds. Figure 11(b) measures the effect of α on the quality of

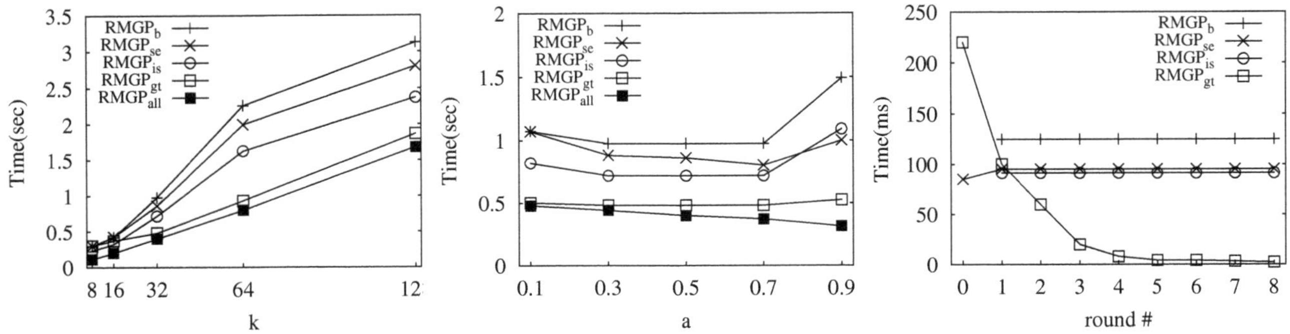

(a) Time vs. k ($\alpha = 0.5$) (b) Time vs. α ($k = 32$) (c) Time vs. round

Figure 12: Effect of Optimizations

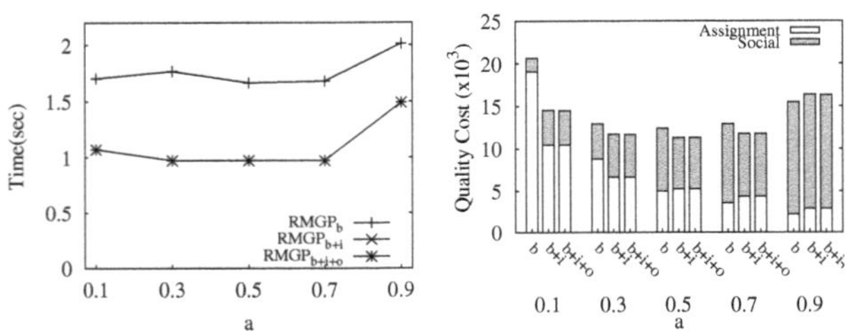

(a) Time vs. α (b) Quality vs. α

Figure 11: Behavior of $RMGP_b$ ($k = 32$)

solutions. Small values of α indicate low importance of the assignment cost, and the algorithms aim at minimizing mainly the social cost. This explains the small contribution of the gray (i.e., social) component in the leftmost columns of the diagram. As α increases, the assignment cost becomes more important; for $\alpha = 0.9$, the social component dominates the total cost because the algorithms tend to assign users to their closest events. Similar to Figure 10(b), $RMGP_{b+i}$ and $RMGP_{b+i+o}$ yield, in general, better solutions than $RMGP_b$. Since $RMGP_{b+i+o}$ has the best overall performance, we use it as the baseline algorithm for subsequent experiments.

Next we evaluate the optimizations of Section 4, namely $RMGP_{se}$, $RMGP_{is}$, $RMGP_{gt}$. Recall that i) $RMGP_{se}$ prunes events that cannot be assigned to a user (independently of the friend assignments) during an initialization round, ii) $RMGP_{is}$ exploits parallelization through independent strategies, and iii) $RMGP_{gt}$ utilizes a global table to only examine users who deviate (i.e., are re-assigned to a different event). $RMGP_{all}$ applies all three optimizations. Since the algorithms start with the same initial assignments (users are assigned to the closest events initially), they reach similar solutions. Thus, in the following, we exclude experiments on the quality of the solutions and only focus on efficiency.

Figure 12(a) measures the running time as a function of the number of events k, for $\alpha = 0.5$. The time of all approaches increases with k because the number of possible assignments per user grows linearly. $RMGP_{gt}$ achieves the best gains among individual optimizations because it only schedules unhappy users that will switch strategies. Therefore, the cost of each round in $RMGP_{gt}$ is lower than that of the other optimizations, and it gradually decreases (see also Figure 12(c)).

Figure 12(b) examines the effect of α on the running time, for $k = 32$. As α increases the spatial component starts dominating the total cost and users tend to be assigned to the closest events. Accordingly, the pruning power of $RMGP_{se}$ increases since the valid regions shrink (eliminating more users), and for $\alpha = 0.9$ it outperforms $RMGP_{is}$. $RMGP_{all}$ has the best performance in all cases as it incorporates all optimizations.

Figure 12(c) shows the running time per individual round for a random query with $k = 32$ and $\alpha = 0.5$. All algorithms terminate after 8 rounds. Round 0 constitutes the initialization step, which involves the cost of sorting the users in decreasing order of their degree and assigning them to their closest event (i.e., the two basic heuristics). In addition, for $RMGP_{se}$ it includes the computation of valid regions, and for $RMGP_{gt}$ it includes the generation of the global table. Thus, Round 0 is more expensive for these methods. Subsequent rounds have fixed cost for $RMGP_b$, $RMGP_{se}$ and $RMGP_{is}$ because they incur exactly the same computations. The savings of $RMGP_{se}$ and $RMGP_{is}$ with respect to $RMGP_b$ are due to strategy elimination and parallelism respectively. On the other hand, in the case of $RMGP_{gt}$ the running time per round gradually decreases because the the number of users who are re-assigned drops as the algorithm approaches convergence.

6.4 Decentralized RMGP

In this section we evaluate DG, the framework presented in Section 5, versus FaE, which involves fetching the data to a server and executing the query locally. We use three identical servers (Intel Xeon E5-2660 2.20GHz with 16GB RAM) that communicate using an 100Mbps Ethernet connection. The Foursquare dataset is distributed to two of the servers. In DG, the third server acts as the master node, while in FaE it receives the entire dataset and performs all computations. Both DG and FaE employ $RMGP_{all}$ as the underlying algorithm since it has been shown to be the most efficient in the previous experiments.

Figure 13 depicts the execution time (in sec) versus k, for $\alpha = 0.5$. The columns represent the cost of FaE, which is split into transfer (gray) and execution (white) time. The first factor corresponds to the time required for the processing server to receive the social graph from the other servers, and is query-independent. For values of k up to 128 it dominates the total cost of FaE. DG avoids this cost and can start the game earlier. On the other hand, the execution time of FaE is comparable to DG, although the latter involves communication with the slaves during the game, while FAE executes $RMGP_{all}$ locally. This can be explained by the high cost of initialization (Round 0). For instance, if $k = 1024$ more than 2.2 billion computations of euclidean distances among users and events are required. In DG, slaves perform, in parallel, initializations for users in their partition, compensating for the additional data transfers during the rounds. For both FaE and DG the execution time increases linearly with k, mainly due to the cost of the initialization step. Observe that the running time (up to 5 minutes for the largest instance) is small compared to the size of the problem (2,153,471 users, 27,098,490 edges, up to 1,024 events), especially considering that we only use two slaves. Recall that UML methods require comparable times for graphs of a few hundred nodes.

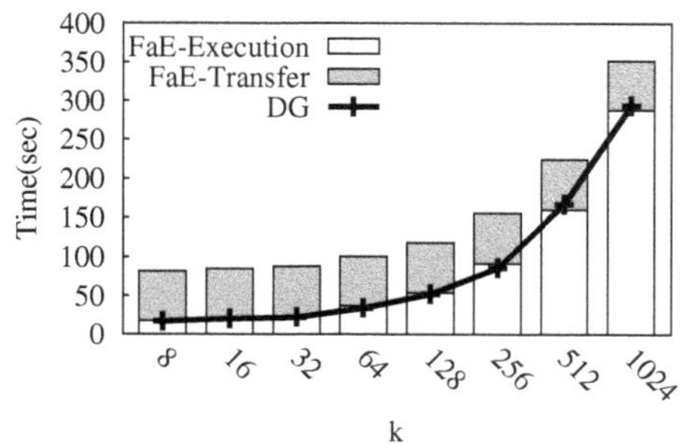

Figure 13: Decentralized Game: time versus k

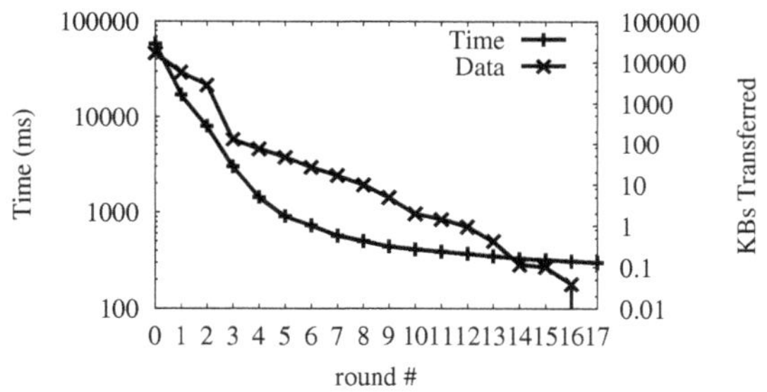

Figure 14: Decentralized Game: bytes transferred per round

Figure 14 plots the processing time (left axis) and data transferred (right axis) per round by DG for a random query with $k = 256$. The game terminates in 17 rounds. Round 0 incurs 58 seconds due to the initialization. The processing time of subsequent rounds gradually decreases because fewer users change strategies; this results in reduced data transfers and update operations at the master and slave nodes. Note that even the last round consumes some time because of the network communication (e.g., command and acknowledgment messages). The maximum amount of data (16MBs) is transferred at Round 0 because each slave obtains an up-to-date version of the entire strategic vector. Subsequent rounds only communicate strategy changes, and the amount of data transferred diminishes in accordance with the processing time.

7. CONCLUSION

This paper studies a type of multi-criteria graph partitioning, which assigns users of a social network to a set of input classes so that their assignment and social costs are minimized. To achieve efficiency, we model the problem as a game, develop a best-response algorithm, and propose several optimizations to enhance its performance. We implement our methods in both centralized and decentralized settings, where the social graph is distributed at different servers. In addition, we apply normalization to resolve issues that arise due to large differences in the assignment and social costs. Finally, we demonstrate the effectiveness of the proposed techniques with extensive experiments on real datasets. Given that our methods significantly outperform existing UML algorithms, they could be used to provide solutions to UML problems in real-time, even for large graphs.

Acknowledgments

Nikos Armenatzoglou and Dimitris Papadias were supported by GRF grant 16207914 from Hong Kong RGC. Huy Pham and Cyrus Shahabi were supported by NSF grants IIS-1115153, IIS-1320149, and CNS-1461963.

8. REFERENCES

[1] Socialbakers: check-in statistics. http://www.socialbakers.com/blog/167-interesting-facebook-places-numbers.

[2] Stanford large network dataset collection,. https://snap.stanford.edu.

[3] Apache Giraph. http://http://giraph.apache.org/, 2014.

[4] C. Ababei, N. Selvakkumaran, K. Bazargan, and G. Karypis. Multi-objective circuit partitioning for cutsize and path-based delay minimization. In *ICCAD*, 2002.

[5] E. C. Bracht, L. A. Meira, and F. K. Miyazawa. A greedy approximation algorithm for the uniform metric labeling problem analyzed by a primal-dual technique. *Journal of Experimental Algorithmics (JEA)*, 10:2–11, 2005.

[6] N. Bronson, Z. Amsden, G. Cabrera, P. Chakka, P. Dimov, H. Ding, J. Ferris, A. Giardullo, S. Kulkarni, H. C. Li, et al. Tao: Facebook's distributed data store for the social graph. In *USENIX*, 2013.

[7] C. Chekuri, S. Khanna, J. S. Naor, and L. Zosin. Approximation algorithms for the metric labeling problem via a new linear programming formulation. In *SODA*, 2001.

[8] D. Fudenberg and T. Jean. *Game Theory*. MIT Press, Cambridge, 1991.

[9] D. Granot and G. Huberman. Minimum cost spanning tree games. *Mathematical Programming*, 21(1):1–18, 1981.

[10] M. Grant and S. Boyd. Graph implementations for nonsmooth convex programs. Lecture Notes in Control and Information Sciences. 2008.

[11] G. Karypis and V. Kumar. METIS: Unstructured Graph Partitioning and Sparse Matrix Ordering System. www.cs.umn.edu/karypis/metis, 1995.

[12] L. Kaufman and P. Rousseeuw. Clustering by means of medoids. *Statistical Data Analysis based on the L1 Norm*, pages 405 – 416, 1987.

[13] J. Kleinberg and E. Tardos. Approximation algorithms for classification problems with pairwise relationships: Metric labeling and markov random fields. *Journal of the ACM (JACM)*, 49(5):616–639, 2002.

[14] F. Kuhn and R. Wattenhofer. On the complexity of distributed graph coloring. In *ACM PODC*, 2006.

[15] J. Leskovec and C. Faloutsos. Sampling from large graphs. In *KDD*, 2006.

[16] J. J. Levandoski, M. Sarwat, A. Eldawy, and M. F. Mokbel. Lars: A location-aware recommender system. In *ICDE*, 2012.

[17] K. Li, W. Lu, S. Bhagat, L. V. Lakshmanan, and C. Yu. On social event organization. In *SIGKDD*, 2014.

[18] Y. Low, D. Bickson, J. Gonzalez, C. Guestrin, A. Kyrola, and J. M. Hellerstein. Distributed graphlab: a framework for machine learning and data mining in the cloud. *PVLDB*, 5(8):716–727, 2012.

[19] G. Malewicz, M. H. Austern, A. J. Bik, J. C. Dehnert, I. Horn, N. Leiser, and G. Czajkowski. Pregel: a system for large-scale graph processing. In *SIGMOD*, 2010.

[20] D. Monderer and L. S. Shapley. Potential games. *Games and economic behavior*, 14(1):124–143, 1996.

[21] J. Munkres. Algorithms for the assignment and transportation problems. *Journal of the Society for Industrial & Applied Mathematics*, 5(1):32–38, 1957.

[22] R. Narayanam and Y. Narahari. A game theory inspired, decentralized, local information based algorithm for community detection in social graphs. In *ICPR*, 2012.

[23] J. F. Nash. Equilibrium points in n-person games. *Proceedings of the national academy of sciences*, 36(1):48–49, 1950.

[24] M. E. Newman and M. Girvan. Finding and evaluating community structure in networks. *Physical review E*, 69(2):026113, 2004.

[25] N. Nisan. *Algorithmic game theory*. Cambridge University Press, 2007.

[26] J. Shi and J. Malik. Normalized cuts and image segmentation. *TPAMI*, 22(8):888–905, 2000.

[27] J. Sun, C. Faloutsos, S. Papadimitriou, and P. S. Yu. Graphscope: parameter-free mining of large time-evolving graphs. In *KDD*, 2007.

[28] Y. Tao, J. Zhang, D. Papadias, and N. Mamoulis. An efficient cost model for optimization of nearest neighbor search in low and medium dimensional spaces. *TKDE*, 16(10):1169–1184, 2004.

[29] Y. Tian, R. A. Hankins, and J. M. Patel. Efficient aggregation for graph summarization. In *SIGMOD*, 2008.

[30] Y. van Gennip, B. Hunter, R. Ahn, P. Elliott, K. Luh, M. Halvorson, S. Reid, M. Valasik, J. Wo, G. E. Tita, et al. Community detection using spectral clustering on sparse geosocial data. *SIAM Journal on Applied Mathematics*, 73(1):67–83, 2013.

[31] D. J. Welsh and M. B. Powell. An upper bound for the chromatic number of a graph and its application to timetabling problems. *The Computer Journal*, 10(1):85–86, 1967.

[32] X. Xu, N. Yuruk, Z. Feng, and T. A. Schweiger. Scan: a structural clustering algorithm for networks. In *KDD*, 2007.

[33] Y. Zhou, H. Cheng, and J. X. Yu. Graph clustering based on structural/attribute similarities. *PVLDB*, 2(1):718–729, 2009.

Utility-Aware Social Event-Participant Planning

Jieying She[†], Yongxin Tong[‡], Lei Chen[†]
[†]Department of Computer Science and Engineering, The Hong Kong University of Science and Technology, Hong Kong SAR, PR China
[‡]SKLSDE Lab, School of Computer Science and Engineering, Beihang University, PR China
[†]{jshe, leichen}@cse.ust.hk [‡]yxtong@buaa.edu.cn

ABSTRACT

Online event-based social network (EBSN) platforms are becoming popular these days. An important task of managing EBSNs is to arrange proper social events to interested users. Existing approaches usually assume that each user only attends one event or ignore location information. The overall utility of such strategy is limited in real world: 1) each user may attend multiple events; 2) attending multiple events will incur spatio-temporal conflicts and travel expenses. Thus, a more intelligent EBSN platform that provides personalized event planning for each participant is desired. In this paper, we first formally define the problem of *Utility-aware Social Event-participant Planning* (USEP), which is proven to be NP-hard. To solve the USEP problem, we first devise a greedy-based heuristic algorithm, which performs fast under certain circumstances but has no approximation guarantee. We then present a two-step approximation framework, which not only guarantees a $\frac{1}{2}$-approximation ratio but also includes a series of optimization techniques to improve its space/time efficiency. Finally, we verify the efficiency and effectiveness of the proposed methods through extensive experiments on real and synthetic datasets.

Categories and Subject Descriptors

H.2.8 [**Database Management**]: Database Applications

Keywords

Event-based social network; Event planning

1. INTRODUCTION

A new type of social media, event-based social network (EBSN)[21], is becoming popular recently. In EBSNs, *online* users organize and register for *offline* social activities. For example, Plancast[1] provides a platform for users to organize, attend and share social events, and Meetup[2] allows users to create groups and organize events for other users to join. Such EBSNs facilitate social event organization and ease the recruitment of activity participants.

However, existing EBSNs only provide an information sharing platform[21] without strategic event organization and personalized event planning. Recently, the problem of global event organization strategy in EBSNs has been brought to attention. [19] proposes the Social Event Organization (SEO) problem to assign events to users, which maximizes the overall satisfaction of users towards the arranged events and also the social affinity among the users participating the same event. However, this work only considers a simple case of assigning one single event to each participant and thus naturally ignores both spatio-temporal conflicts of different events and multiple events planning for each participant. [26] also studies a global event organization strategy, but does not take travel expenditure into consideration. Imagine the following scenario. Being a sports enthusiast and a music fan, Alice attends various sports activities and concerts published on Meetup on weekends. However, Alice encounters a dilemma on Friday night since Meetup recommends her three interesting but conflicting activities on Saturday: a running club activity from 9:00 a.m. to 11:00 a.m., a tennis match from 10:00 a.m. to 1:30 p.m., and a jazz music party from 2:00 p.m. to 3:00 p.m. In addition to time conflicts, location information is another concern since Alice needs a half hour by taxi or two hours by bus from the tennis gymnasium to the party venue. Although Alice is interested in all the three events, she has to face trade-offs according to spatio-temporal conflicts of events and her budget of travel expenditure in terms of time, money, etc. Clearly, the approaches in [19][26] cannot handle the aforementioned scenario since the constraints of spatio-temporal conflicts, multiple events allocation for each participant or travel expenditure are ignored.

As discussed above, many users often face the dilemma of choosing events to attend properly from a long and probably conflicting recommendation list on EBSN platforms. On the other hand, existing EBSNs focus on pushing recommendation to all potential participants for each event, in which case the capacities of events are out of consideration, and the satisfaction for both event organizers and participants is not optimized. Therefore, it is appealing to have a new event-participant planning strategy that satisfies spatio-temporal conflict and travel expenditure constraints, and optimizes the planning benefits on a global scale as well.

In this paper, we propose a new global event planning problem considering both spatio-temporal conflict and travel

[1]http://plancast.com
[2]http://www.meetup.com

SIGMOD'15, May 31–June 4, 2015, Melbourne, Victoria, Australia.

http://dx.doi.org/10.1145/2723372.2749446.

Table 1: Utility between Events and Users and Time of Events

	u_1 (59)	u_2 (29)	u_3 (51)	u_4 (9)	u_5 (33)	Time
$v_1(1)$	0.2	0.6	0.7	0.3	0.6	1-4p.m.
$v_2(3)$	0.5	0.1	0.3	0.9	0.5	3-6p.m.
$v_3(4)$	0.6	0.2	0.9	0.4	0.5	1-2p.m.
$v_4(2)$	0.4	0.7	0.2	0.5	0.1	6-7p.m.

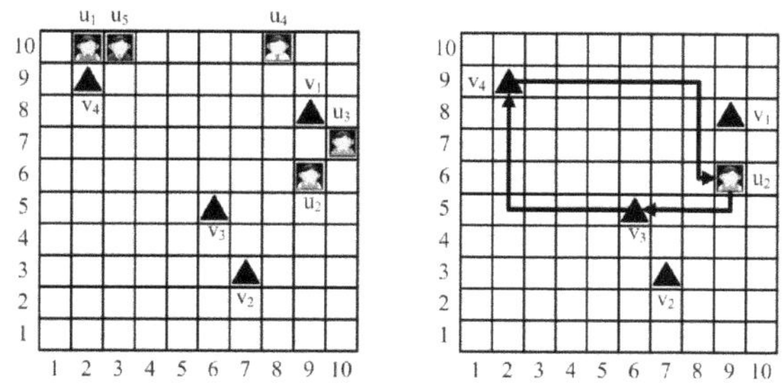

(a) (b)

Figure 1: Example 1.

expenditure constraints to maximize the overall satisfaction of event participants. Specifically, given a set of events and a set of users, each event is associated with a location and a capacity, which is the maximum number of attendees allowable, and each user is also associated with a location, which is her/his initial location from which s/he travels to the first attended event and also the final location to which s/he returns from the last attended event. Each event is additionally associated with a time period. Note that users can only attend events that are non-overlapping in time. Each user is additionally associated with a travel budget, which is the maximum travel expenditure the user would like to spend in order to attend the arranged events. There is also a travel cost between each pair of events/users. Users may have different preferences towards the events, each of which is measured as a non-negative "utility value". The satisfaction of a user is defined as a linear combination of the sum of utility values over her/his attended events. Our task is to find an event-participant planning to maximize the overall satisfaction of users, such that the capacity, spatio-temporal conflict and travel budget constraints are satisfied. Similar to [19][26], we also adopt the sum of satisfaction over all users as the overall utility of the planning.

EXAMPLE 1. *Suppose we have four events($v_1 - v_4$) and five users($u_1 - u_5$) in an EBSN. Table 1 shows the utility values between each event-user pair, and also the time intervals of the events. The capacities of the events and the budgets of the users are shown in brackets, e.g. v_1 has capacity 1, and u_4 has budget 9. Figure 1a shows the locations of users and events, and we use Manhattan distance to calculate the cost among them. Existing methods do not consider conflicts and budgets and thus cannot yield a feasible planning. Figure 1b shows a feasible schedule of u_2.*

Notice that for event planning, many other constraints can be taken into consideration, for example, considering friends who may want to attend the same event, reliability of event organizers, etc. We choose to consider spatio-temporal conflict and travel cost as constraints when optimizing users' interests in this planning problem of EBSNs with the following reasons. First, spatio-temporal conflicts among events are prevalent in real-life EBSNs, which have to be taken into consideration to make a feasible planning for users. Second, travel cost is the fundamental constraint in a planning problem. [6] indicates that venue constraints (e.g. locations), time constraints (e.g. time budget and transit time between venues) and users' preferences are the three main factors that must be taken into consideration in a planning problem. Also, travel cost, in terms of time or money, is the major constraint considered in many existing planning problems [24][8][4].

Table 2: Summary of Symbol Notations

Notation	Description
$V = \{v_1, \cdots, v_{\|V\|}\}$	Set of events
$U = \{u_1, \cdots, u_{\|U\|}\}$	Set of users
c_v	Capacity of v
t_1^v	Start time of v
t_2^v	End time of v
b_u	Travel budget of u
$cost(v_i, v_j)$	Travel cost from v_i to v_j
$cost(u, v)$ $(cost(v, u))$	Travel cost from $u(v)$ to $v(u)$
$\mu(v, u)$	Utility value between v and u
S_u	Schedule of u
$A = \cup_u \{S_u\}$	A planning for all users
$\Omega(A)$ $(\Omega(S_u))$	Total utility score of A (S_u)
cr	Conflict ratio of the set of events
f_b	Budget factor of the set of users

The contributions of our work are summarized as follows.

- To the best of our knowledge, this is the first work to formulate the *Utility-aware Social Event-participant Planning (USEP) problem*, which conducts strategic multiple-event planning for every user and considers the constraints of spatio-temporal conflicts and travel cost. We prove that this problem is NP-hard.
- We develop a greedy-based heuristic algorithm, which is efficient but has no approximation guarantee, to address the USEP problem.
- We present a two-step framework, which not only provides a $\frac{1}{2}$-approximation ratio but also includes a series of optimization techniques to improve its space and time efficiency.
- We verify the effectiveness and efficiency of the proposed methods through extensive experiments on real and synthetic datasets.

The rest of the paper is organized as follows. In Section 2, we formally formulate the USEP problem and prove its NP-hardness. Section 3 presents a greedy-based heuristic algorithm. Section 4 proposes a two-step framework and its optimization techniques. Section 5 gives an empirical study and Section 6 reviews the related work. Section 7 concludes the paper.

2. PROBLEM STATEMENT

Let V be a set of events. For each $v \in V$, it is associated with a capacity c_v, a location l_v, and a time interval $[t_1^v, t_2^v]$ that describes the starting and ending time of the event. Notice that c_v is any integer in $\mathbb{Z}_+$. For events that may not have capacity constraints, such as firework shows, we can simply set c_v to an extremely large integer. U is a set of users. For each $u \in U$, it is associated with a location l_u that is the initial and also the final location of the user, and a travel budget b_u. We take b_u as an input parameter, following the assumptions of other planning problems [6][24][8][4]. We denote $S_u = \{v_1^u, v_2^u, ..., v_{|S_u|}^u\}$ as the schedule of arranged events in increasing time order for user u. We call two events in a schedule *neighboring* if one will be attended right after the other one finishes. The schedule is feasible if and only if there is no time conflict among the arranged events. And we define the feasibility of a schedule formally as follows.

DEFINITION 1 (FEASIBLE SCHEDULE). *A schedule is feasible if and only if* $t_2^{v_i^u} \leq t_1^{v_{i+1}^u}, \forall 1 \leq i \leq |S_u| - 1$.

Each user u has a utility value for each event v, denoted as $\mu(v, u) \in [0, 1]$. Notice that this value can be discovered by existing data mining techniques [36]. However, calculation of the value is not our focus in this work. There is a travel cost (e.g. time, money) between each pair of events v_i, v_j. Without loss of generality, for any two events, suppose their time order is $t_1^{v_i} \leq t_1^{v_j}$. If v_i and v_j do not conflict in time and users can attend v_j on time after attending v_i, the travel cost $cost(v_i, v_j)$ is a bounded non-negative integer. Otherwise, $cost(v_i, v_j) = +\infty$. There is also travel cost, $cost(u, v)$ and $cost(v, u)$, between a user and an event, which is the travel cost from l_u to l_v and also that from l_v returning to l_u. The cost between any event-event(event-user) pair satisfies the triangle inequality.

We finally define our Utility-aware Social Event-participant Planning (USEP) problem as follows.

DEFINITION 2 (USEP PROBLEM). *Given a set of events V and a set of users U and their associated attributes, find a planning $A = \cup_u \{S_u\}$ for the users to maximize the total utility score $\Omega(A)$ of the planning A such that the following constraints are satisfied:*

1. *Capacity constraint of events: no event is arranged to users more than its capacity, i.e.* $\sum_u \mathbf{1}_{S_u}(v) \leq c_v, \forall v$, *where* $\mathbf{1}_{S_u}(v)$ *is the indicator function.*
2. *Budget constraint of users: no user needs to spend more than her/his budget to complete the schedule, i.e.* $cost(u, v_1^u) + \sum_{i=2}^{|S_u|} cost(v_{i-1}^u, v_i^u) + cost(v_{|S_u|}^u, u) \leq b_u, \forall u$
3. *Feasibility constraint: each user is arranged a feasible schedule.*
4. *Utility constraint: no user is arranged events that s/he is not interested in at all, i.e.* $\mu(v, u) > 0, \forall v \in S_u, \forall u$.

where the total utility score $\Omega(A)$ is defined as follows:

$$\Omega(A) = \sum_u \sum_{v \in S_u} \mu(v, u) \tag{1}$$

Note that $\Omega(A)$ is the overall utility of the planning towards both event organizers and users.

Remark1. Another setting of the USEP problem is that instead of arranging events from the entire set V for a user, each user u can provide a set $V_u \subseteq V$, only events in which will be arranged to u. That is, $S_u \subseteq V_u$. This variation of the USEP problem can be reduced to the original USEP problem by letting $\mu(v, u) = 0, \forall v \in V \setminus V_u$.

Remark2. Another variance of travel cost is that there is a participation fee fee_v for an event v. This variance can be reduced to the original USEP problem by taking $cost$ as cost of money and letting $cost'(u, v) = cost(u, v) + fee_v$ and $cost'(v_i, v_j) = cost(v_i, v_j) + fee_{v_j}$, where $cost'(u, v)$ ($cost'(v_i, v_j)$) is the new travel cost in this variance of USEP, and $cost(u, v)$ ($cost(v_i, v_j)$) is the original travel cost in the original USEP problem.

The notations of symbols are summarized in Table 2. And we have the following theorem that states the hardness of USEP, the proof of which is in the Appendix.

THEOREM 1. *The USEP problem is NP-hard.*

3. GREEDY-BASED ALGORITHM

In this section, we present a greedy-based heuristic algorithm, RatioGreedy for the USEP problem. To make a planning that has a high total utility score, we need to consider both the utility value and the travel cost induced by each event-user pair. On one hand, an event-user pair with larger utility value will result in a higher total utility score if the pair is included in the planning. On the other hand, a pair with lower induced travel cost will possibly allow more pairs to be added to the schedule of the user if the pair is included in the planning. Thus, the RatioGreedy algorithm is to consider the utility-cost ratio of each unarranged event-user pair and add the pair with the largest ratio value into the planning if it satisfies all the constraints.

Specifically, the utility-cost ratio for each event-user pair that is not yet in A is defined as follows.

$$ratio(v, u) = \frac{\mu(v, u)}{inc\_cost(v, u)} \tag{2}$$

$$inc\_cost(v, u) = \begin{cases} cost(u, v) + cost(v, u) & S_u = \emptyset \\ cost(u, v) + cost(v, v_1^u) - cost(u, v_1^u) & t_2^v \leq t_1^{v_1^u} \\ cost(v_i^u, v) + cost(v, v_{i+1}^u) - cost(v_i^u, v_{i+1}^u) & t_2^{v_i^u} \leq t_1^v, t_2^v \leq t_1^{v_{i+1}^u}, 1 \leq i < |S_u| \\ cost(v_{|S_u|}^u, v) + cost(v, u) - cost(v_{|S_u|}^u, u) & t_2^{v_{|S_u|}^u} \leq t_1^v \\ \infty & otherwise \end{cases} \tag{3}$$

In Equation (2), $inc\_cost(v, u)$ is the additional travel cost that will be induced if the v is added to the current schedule S_u of u. Equation (3) defines $inc\_cost(v, u)$ formally. Specifically, when S_u is empty, the additional cost is that of traveling to v and returning to u if v is arranged for u. When S_u is non-empty, the additional cost depends on the time order of S_u if v is arranged for u, which is determined by the time interval of v and also those of the events that are already in S_u. If v will the first event to be attended when it is added to the current schedule, the additional cost is that of traveling from u to v and then to v_1^u subtracting the cost traveling from u to v_1^u (since u will no longer travel to v_1^u directly if v is added to the schedule), where v_1^u is the first event to be attended in the current schedule. If v will be attended after v_i^u and before v_{i+1}^u, where v_i^u and v_{i+1}^u are some neighboring events in S_u, the additional cost is that of traveling from v_i^u to v and then to v_{i+1}^u subtracting the cost from v_i^u to v_{i+1}^u (since u will no longer travel from v_i^u to v_{i+1}^u directly if v is added to the schedule). Similarly, if v will be the last event to be attended, the additional cost is that of traveling from $v_{|S_u|}^u$ to v and then retuning to u subtracting the cost from $v_{|S_u|}^u$ to u (since u will not long return to her/his initial location after attending $v_{|S_u|}^u$ if v is added to the schedule), where $v_{|S_u|}^u$ is the last event to be attended in the current schedule.

The detailed algorithm is as follows. Initially, the planning A is empty, i.e. $S_u = \emptyset, \forall u \in U$. We maintain a heap H for storage of unarranged event-user pairs. At each iteration, we extract a pair (v, u) with the largest ratio value from H and add it to A if possible. Initially, for each $v_i \in V$, we find a $u_{v_i} \in U$ such that $ratio(v_i, u_{v_i}) \geq ratio(v_i, u')$ for all u'

Algorithm 1: RatioGreedy

input : $V, U, \{c_v\}, \{\mu(v,u)\}, \{t_1^v, t_2^v\}, \{b_u\}, \{cost\}$
output: A feasible planning A

1 $S_u \leftarrow \emptyset, \forall u$;
2 $H \leftarrow \emptyset$;
3 **foreach** v **do**
4 $\quad u_v \leftarrow \arg\max_{u|S_u=\{v\} \text{ is valid}} ratio(v,u)$;
5 $\quad$ Push (v, u_v) into H if $u_v\exists$;
6 **foreach** u **do**
7 $\quad v_u \leftarrow \arg\max_{v|S_u=\{v\} \text{ is valid}} ratio(v,u)$;
8 $\quad$ Push (v_u, u) into H if $v_u\exists$ and $(v_u, u) \notin H$;
9 **while** $H \neq \emptyset$ **do**
10 $\quad$ Pop (v,u) with the largest $ratio(v,u)$ from H;
11 $\quad$ Add v into S_u if $\{v\} \cup S_u$ is valid;
12 $\quad$ **if** *v is not full of capacity* **then**
13 $\quad\quad u_v \leftarrow \arg\max_{u'|S_{u'}=\{v\}\cup S_{u'} \text{ is valid and } v\notin S_{u'}} ratio(v,u')$;
14 $\quad\quad$ Push (v, u_v) into H if $u_v\exists$ and $(v, u_v) \notin H$;
15 $\quad$ **foreach** *original* $(v_k, u) \in H$ **do**
16 $\quad\quad$ Remove (v_k, u) from H if $inc\_cost(v_k, u)$ changes, continue otherwise;
17 $\quad\quad u_{v_k} \leftarrow \arg\max_{u'|S_{u'}=\{v_k\}\cup S_{u'} \text{ is valid and } v_k\notin S_{u'}} ratio(v_k,u')$;
18 $\quad\quad$ Push (v_k, u_{v_k}) into H if $u_{v_k}\exists$ and $(v_k, u_{v_k}) \notin H$;
19 $\quad v_u \leftarrow \arg\max_{v'|S_u=\{v'\}\cup S_u \text{ is valid and } v'\notin S_u} ratio(v',u)$;
20 $\quad$ Push (v_u, u) into H if $v_u\exists$ and $(v_u, u) \notin H$;
21 $A \leftarrow \cup_u\{S_u\}$;
22 **return** A

whose schedule $\{v_i\}$ satisfies all the constraints. If there are multiple u_{v_i}'s whose ratio values are the same, we pick the one with the least *inc_cost*. We also find a v_{u_j} for each $u_j \in U$ in a similar way. Each pair $(v_i, u_{v_i})((v_{u_j}, u_j))$ is pushed into H. If for some i and j, $v_i = v_{u_j}$ and $u_{v_i} = u_j$, only one pair will be in H. Whenever a pair (v,u) is popped from H, we update H as follows. If v is not yet full of capacity, we find the next u_v such that $ratio(v,u_v) \geq ratio(v,u')$ for all u' such that v is not yet in $S_{u'}$ and the schedule $\{v\} \cup S_{u'}$ satisfies all the constraints. Again, if there are multiple u's whose ratio values are the same, we pick the one with the least *inc_cost*. For u, we also find its corresponding v_u in a similar way. The new found pair(s) will be pushed into H. If there are some other pairs (v_k, u) in H that are incident to u, since the schedule of u may have been updated and thus $inc\_cost(v_k, u)$ may have changed, we need to find a possibly new u_{v_k} for each v_k to ensure that for v_k, the pair (v_k, u_{v_k}) that has the largest ratio value and satisfies all the constraints is in H. Therefore, we update the u_{v_k} for each v_k and also update H accordingly. The whole procedure terminates when no more feasible pair can be pushed into H and H is empty.

The procedure of the RatioGreedy algorithm is illustrated in Algorithm 1. In lines 2-8, we initialize H by finding a valid event-user pair with the largest ratio value for each event(user). In lines 9-20, we repetitively pop the pair (v,u) with the largest ratio value from H, add the pair to the planning if possible and update H. In lines 12-14 and lines 19-20, we find a new valid event-user pair with the largest ratio value for v and u respectively. In lines 15-18, we update the elements in H that contain u in case that the *inc_cost*'s and thus the ratio values for such elements have changed. The iteration terminates when H is empty.

Table 3: Example 2

	u_1	u_2	u_3	u_4	u_5
v_1	0.011(18)	0.15(4)	0.175(4)	0.05(6)	0.0375(16)

	States of H
After Initialization	(v_4,u_1) : 0.2(2), (v_1,u_3) : 0.175(4), (v_1,u_2) : 0.15(4), (v_3,u_3) : 0.075(12), (v_1,u_4) : 0.05(6), (v_1,u_5) : 0.0375(16), (v_2,u_5) : 0.023(22)
After 1st Iteration	(v_1,u_3) : 0.175(4), (v_1,u_2) : 0.15(4), (v_3,u_3) : 0.075(12), (v_1,u_4) : 0.05(6), (v_1,u_5) : 0.0375(16), (v_3,u_1) : 0.0375(16), (v_4,u_2) : 0.035(20), (v_2,u_5) : 0.023(22)

EXAMPLE 2 (RATIOGREEDY). *Back to our running example in Example 1. Initially, H is empty. In the second row of Table 3, we present the ratio values between v_1 and different users and also the inc_cost (in brackets). As pair (v_1, u_3) is valid and has the largest ratio value, we push (v_1, u_3) into H. We continue the initialization step, and present the state of H after initialization in Table 3, where we present the ratio value of each event-user pair in H and also its inc_cost (in bracket). Then during the 1st iteration, the pair v_4, u_1 is popped from H as it has the largest ratio value 0.2. Then we add v_4 to S_{u_1}, and update H, the state of which is presented in Table 3. The procedure continues until H is empty, and we have the following planning $S_{u_1} = \{v_3, v_4\}, S_{u_2} = \{v_3, v_4\}, S_{u_3} = \{v_1\}$ and $S_{u_5} = \{v_3, v_2\}$, which has total utility score* 3.6.

Complexity analysis. In RatioGreedy, initializing H takes $O(|V||U|)$ time as we scan through each event-user pair. Then during each iteration, it takes $O(|S_u|)$ time to check the validity of the popped pair and $O((|V|+|U|)|S_u|)$ time to push new pairs into H. Also, as there are at most $|V|$ event-user pairs in H that are incident to u, it takes at most $O(|V||U||S_u|)$ additional time to update the elements in H. Since there are at most $|V||U|$ event-user pairs, the number of iterations is $O(|V||U|)$. Thus, the overall time complexity of RatioGreedy is $O(|V||U|(|V|+|U|+|V||U|)|S_u|)$ in the worst case. The major space consumption of RatioGreedy comes from H and S_u. Thus, the space complexity of RatioGreedy is $O(|V||U|)$.

4. A TWO-STEP APPROXIMATION FRAMEWORK

In this section, due to the NP-hardness of the USEP problem, we present a two-step approximate solution framework. Based on the framework, we present a *Decomposed Dynamic Programming (DeDP)* approximation algorithm with approximation ratio $\frac{1}{2}$. To improve the space and time efficiency and also the effectiveness of the DeDP algorithm, we further present techniques that optimize the DeDP algorithm. Finally, we present a DeGreedy algorithm following the two-step approximation solution framework, which is faster than the DeDP algorithm but returns a planning with lower total utility score.

4.1 Preliminary

We first introduce some background of the framework. Specifically, our framework is based on the decomposition idea of Local Ratio Theorem[3][7], which is stated as follows.

THEOREM 2 (LOCAL RATIO[3]). *Let* $\max f(x) = w \cdot x$ *be the objective function, where* $w \in \mathbb{R}^n$ *is a weight vector, and* $x \in \mathbb{R}^n$ *is a solution vector satisfying a set of constraints* C*. Let* $w = w_1 + w_2$*, and* $x \in \mathbb{R}^n$ *be an* r*-approximate solution w.r.t.* $w_1 \in \mathbb{R}^n$ *and* $w_2 \in \mathbb{R}^n$*, then* x *is also an* r*-approximate solution w.r.t.* w*.*

Theorem 2 indicates that we can decompose the weight function and thus the USEP problem into a set of simpler problems and aggregate the solutions of the simpler problems to obtain a final solution for the USEP problem. Details of the algorithm are presented in the following.

4.2 DeDP Algorithm

In the DeDP algorithm, the main idea is to first decompose the USEP problem into $|U|$ problems following [3][7], where in each of the $|U|$ problems we design a dynamic programming algorithm to find a feasible schedule for a user u that can maximize the total utility score of the schedule. In the second step, we combine the solutions of each user and resolve the case where certain constraints are violated.

4.2.1 First Step

In the first step, we decompose the original USEP problem into $|U|$ problems. First, we sort the events in V in non-descending order of t_2^v, and denote the i-th element in the sorted list as v_i. That is, $t_2^{v_j} \leq t_2^{v_i}, \forall j < i$. Second, we construct a set of *pseudo-events* with cardinality c_{v_i} for each v_i. Specifically, for each $v_i \in V$ with capacity c_{v_i}, we construct a set of pseudo-events $\{v_{i,k}\}$ where $1 \leq k \leq c_{v_i}$, and each $v_{i,k}$ is identical to v_i except that $c_{v_{i,k}} = 1, \forall 1 \leq k \leq c_{v_i}$. Notice that if $c_{v_i} > |U|$, we simply change c_{v_i} to $|U|$. Thus, $c_{v_i} \leq |U|, \forall v_i$. When arranging events for users, instead of arranging v_i to users directly, we arrange one of the pseudo-events $\{v_{i,k}\}$ to a user. Each $v_{i,k}$ is associated with a utility value $\mu(v_{i,k}, u)$ w.r.t. each user u, where $\mu(v_{i,k}, u) = \mu(v_i, u), \forall 1 \leq k \leq c_{v_i}$ initially. The values of $\mu(v_{i,k}, u)$ will be decomposed as we solve the problem, details of which will be presented shortly. Finally, after constructing the pseudo-event sets, we decompose the USEP problem into $|U|$ problems and iteratively solve each decomposed problem. In the r-th decomposed problem, we find a schedule for user u_r with a dynamic programming algorithm, and update the values of $\mu(v_{i,k}, u)$ accordingly.

More specifically, in the r-th iteration, where $1 \leq r \leq |U|$, we find a schedule for user u_r. For easy illustration, we denote $\mu^r(v_{i,k}, u)$ as the value of $\mu(v_{i,k}, u)$ when we start to process the r-th user, which is updated after the last $((r-1)$-th) iteration. Particularly, $\mu^1(v_{i,k}, u) = \mu(v_{i,k}, u)$ initially. Then for each event v_i, we first find from its pseudo-event set $\{v_{i,k}\}$ the element that has the largest updated utility value w.r.t. u_r, i.e. $\max_k \mu^r(v_{i,k}, u_r)$, denoted as $\hat{v}_i$ (ties are broken arbitrarily). Let $V_r = \{\hat{v}_i | \mu^r(\hat{v}_i, u_r) > 0\}$. Thus, any $\hat{v}_i$ with non-positive utility value is excluded from V_r. We next find a schedule for user u_r from V_r with a dynamic programming algorithm.

LEMMA 1. *For any* v_i *such that* $cost(u, v_i) + cost(v_i, u) > b_u$*, it cannot be included in any valid schedule of* u*.*

Lemma 1, the proof of which is in the Appendix, indicates that we can remove events with $cost(u_r, \hat{v}_i) + cost(\hat{v}_i, u_r) > b_{u_r}$ from V_r as they cannot be in the schedule of u_r. Denote V'_r as the resulted set of events. Then in the dynamic programming algorithm, we scan through each pseudo-event $\hat{v}_i \in V'_r$, and find the best utility score we can obtain with $\hat{v}_i$ being the last event to attend in the schedule. Let $S_{u_r}^{i,T} = \{v^{u_r,i,T}\}$ (simplified as $S^{i,T} = \{v^{i,T}\}$) denote the schedule for u_r with $\hat{v}_i$ being the last event to attend and T being the total travel cost of completing the schedule at $\hat{v}_i$, i.e. $T = cost(u_r, v_1^{i,T}) + \sum_{j=2}^{|S^{i,T}|} cost(v_{j-1}^{i,T}, v_j^{i,T})$ and $v_{|S^{i,T}|}^{i,T}$ is $\hat{v}_i$. Let $\Omega(i,T)$ be the largest utility score of $S^{i,T}$. And we have the following equation to compute $\Omega(i,T)$.

$$\Omega(i,T) = \begin{cases} \mu^r(\hat{v}_i, u_r) & T = cost(u_r, \hat{v}_i) \\ \max_{1 \leq l \leq l_i} & \\ \{\Omega(l, T - cost(\hat{v}_l, \hat{v}_i)) & T \geq cost(\hat{v}_l, \hat{v}_i) \text{ and} \\ +\mu^r(\hat{v}_i, u_r)\} & T + cost(\hat{v}_i, u_r) \leq b_{u_r} \\ 0 & otherwise \end{cases} \quad (4)$$

In Equation (4), l_i is the largest index l such that $t_2^{v_l} \leq t_1^{v_i}$. Recall that $t_2^{v_j} \leq t_2^{v_i}, \forall j < i$. Therefore, $\forall l > l_i$, we have $t_2^{v_l} > t_1^{v_i}$ and thus $\hat{v}_i$ cannot be attended if $\hat{v}_l$ is in the schedule of u_r. By computing $\Omega(i,T)$, we can then find a schedule $\hat{S}_{u_r}$ that corresponds to the largest $\Omega(i,T)(\forall i, 0 \leq T \leq b_{u_r})$ value for u_r.

After finding schedule $\hat{S}_{u_r}$, we finally update the values of μ^r as follows. If the schedule $\hat{S}_{u_r}$ contains pseudo-event $\hat{v}_i$ (recall that $\hat{v}_i$ is one of $\{v_{i,k}\}$), $\mu^{r+1}(\hat{v}_i, u_j)$ is updated as $\mu^r(\hat{v}_i, u_j) - \mu^r(\hat{v}_i, u_r)$ for all $j > r$. In addition, $\mu^{r+1}(v_{i,k}, u_r) = 0, \forall i, k$. The other μ^{r+1} values are the same as their corresponding μ^r. The intuition is to ensure that when $\hat{v}_i$ is arranged to u_r, $\hat{v}_i$ will be rearranged to $u_j (j > r)$ only if $\mu^j(\hat{v}_i, u_j) > 0$ and thus $\mu(v_i, u_j) > \mu(v_i, u_r)$ initially. Then in our second step, $\hat{v}_i$ will be removed from $\hat{S}_{u_r}$ in such case to ensure that $\hat{v}_i$ is only arranged to one single user. Details of this step will be described shortly. After updating the values of $\mu^r(v_{i,k}, u)$, we proceed to the next iteration to find a schedule for user u_{r+1} until $r = |U|$.

The procedure of finding individual schedule for each user is presented in Algorithm 2. In line 1, we construct V'_r according to Lemma 1. In lines 2-9, we compute $\Omega(i,T)$ according to Equation (4). In lines 10-11, we find the schedule with the largest $\Omega(i,T)$ value as $\hat{S}_{u_r}$.

4.2.2 Second Step

In the second step, we resolve the case where $v_{i,k}$ is arranged to multiple users, which violates the capacity constraint of $v_{i,k}$ and thus also that of v_i, since every $v_{i,k}$ must be arranged in this case. Specifically, we scan through u_r in the order of $r = |U|, |U|-1, ..., 1$. For $r = |U|$, $S_{u_r} = \hat{S}_{u_r}$. And for each $r < |U|$, any $v_{i,k}$ that is already in $\cup_{j>r} S_{u_j}$ is removed from $\hat{S}_{u_r}$, which results in S_{u_r} as the final schedule for u_r. After this step, we obtain a planning where each $v_{i,k}$ is arranged to only one user and thus the capacity constraint of v_i is satisfied. The other three constraints (i.e. budget constraint, feasibility constraint and utility constraint), which are ensured to be satisfied in the first step, are not affected by the removal of events from a schedule. Therefore, the resulted planning of the DeDP algorithm is feasible.

Algorithm 2: DPSingle

input : $V_r, u_r, \mu^r, \{t_1^v, t_2^v\}, b_{u_r}, \{cost\}$
output: A feasible schedule $\hat{S}_{u_r}$
$V_r' \leftarrow \{v \in V_r | cost(u_r, v) + cost(v, u_r) \leq b_{u_r}\}$;
for $i \leftarrow 1$ **to** $|V_r'|$ **do**
  $\Omega(i, cost(u_r, \hat{v}_i)) \leftarrow \mu^r(\hat{v}_i, u_r)$;
  $path(i, cost(u_r, \hat{v}_i) \leftarrow 0$;
  for $l \leftarrow 1$ **to** l_i **do**
    foreach T *s.t.* $\Omega(l, T) > 0$ **do**
      if $T + cost(\hat{v}_l, \hat{v}_i) + cost(\hat{v}_i, u_r) \leq b_{u_r}$ *and* $\Omega(l, T) + \mu^r(\hat{v}_i, u_r) > \Omega(i, T + cost(\hat{v}_l, \hat{v}_i))$ **then**
        Update $\Omega(i, T + cost(\hat{v}_l, \hat{v}_i))$;
        $path(i, T + cost(\hat{v}_l, \hat{v}_i)) \leftarrow l$;
Find the largest $\Omega(i, T)$;
Construct $\hat{S}_{u_r}$ according to $path(i, T)$;
return $\hat{S}_{u_r}$

Algorithm 3: DeDP

input : $V, U, \{c_v\}, \{\mu(v, u)\}, \{t_1^v, t_2^v\}, \{b_u\}, \{cost\}$
output: A feasible planning A
1 $\forall v_i$ s.t. $c_{v_i} > |U| : c_{v_i} \leftarrow |U|$;
2 $\mu^1(v_{i,k}, u_j) \leftarrow \mu(v_i, u_j), \forall 1 \leq i \leq |V|, 1 \leq k \leq c_{v_i}, 1 \leq j \leq |U|$;
3 **for** $r \leftarrow 1$ **to** $|U|$ **do**
4   $V_r \leftarrow \{\hat{v}_i | \mu^r(\hat{v}_i, u_r) > 0\}$;
5   $\hat{S}_{u_r} \leftarrow$ `DPSingle` $(V_r, u_r, \mu^r, \{t_1^v, t_2^v\}, b_{u_r}, \{cost\})$;
6   Update μ^r;
7 **for** $r \leftarrow |U|$ **downto** 1 **do**
8   $S_{u_r} \leftarrow \{v_i | \text{the corresponding } \hat{v}_i \in \hat{S}_{u_r} \setminus (\cup_{j>r} \hat{S}_{u_j})\}$;
9 $A \leftarrow \cup_u \{S_u\}$;
10 **return** A

4.2.3 Summary

The main procedure of the DeDP algorithm is summarized in Algorithm 3. In line 1, we temporally let $c_{v_i} \leq |U|, \forall v_i \in V$. In line 2, we initialize μ^1. In lines 3-6, which is the first step of DeDP, we decompose the USEP problem into $|U|$ problems by finding a schedule for each u_r. In line 4, we construct the set V_r using the selected pseudo-events. We find the schedule for u_r using Algorithm 2 and update μ^r in lines 5-6. In lines 7-9, which is the second step of DeDP, we resolve the case where $v_{i,k}$ is contained in multiple schedules.

EXAMPLE 3. *Back to our running example in Example 1. Note that in this example, the sorted list of V is v_3, v_1, v_2, v_4, and we still use the original subscript of v's instead of referring to v_3 as v_1, v_1 as v_2 etc. as we do in the algorithm. In the first iteration, the values of μ^1 are identical to those of μ. We present the selected pseudo-events and their corresponding μ^1 values (in bracket) in the second row of Table 4. We then construct V_1', which is presented in Table 5, and find a schedule for u_1 using dynamic programming, events of which are shown in bold font in Table 5. Then the values of μ^2 are updated. We show the selected pseudo-events and their updated μ^2 values (in bracket) in the third row of Table 4. After updating μ^2, we then proceed to find a schedule for u_2. After the first step, the initial planning is shown in bold font in Table 5. Then after the second step, we have the final planning: $S_{u_1} = \{v_3, v_2\}, S_{u_2} = \{v_1, v_4\}, S_{u_3} = \{v_3, v_2\}, S_{u_5} = \{v_3, v_2\}$. The total utility score is 4.6.*

Table 4: Updated μ^r of Example 3

	$\hat{v}_1$	$\hat{v}_2$	$\hat{v}_3$	$\hat{v}_4$
u_1	$v_{1,1}(0.2)$	$v_{2,1}(0.5)$	$v_{3,1}(0.6)$	$v_{4,1}(0.4)$
u_2	$v_{1,1}(0.6)$	$v_{2,2}(0.1)$	$v_{3,2}(0.2)$	$v_{4,1}(0.7)$
u_3	$v_{1,1}(0.1)$	$v_{2,2}(0.3)$	$v_{3,2}(0.9)$	$v_{4,2}(0.2)$
u_4	$v_{1,1}(-0.3)$	$v_{2,3}(0.9)$	$v_{3,3}(0.4)$	$v_{4,2}(0.5)$
u_5	$v_{1,1}(0)$	$v_{2,3}(0.5)$	$v_{3,3}(0.5)$	$v_{4,2}(0.1)$

Table 5: Results of First Step of Example 3

User	V_r'
u_1	$\mathbf{v_{3,1}}$, $v_{1,1}$, $\mathbf{v_{2,1}}$, $v_{4,1}$
u_2	$v_{3,2}$, $\mathbf{v_{1,1}}$, $v_{2,2}$, $\mathbf{v_{4,1}}$
u_3	$\mathbf{v_{3,2}}$, $v_{1,1}$, $\mathbf{v_{2,2}}$, $v_{4,2}$
u_4	$\emptyset$
u_5	$\mathbf{v_{3,3}}$, $\mathbf{v_{2,3}}$, $v_{4,2}$

Complexity analysis. In the first step of DeDP, the number of iterations is $|U|$. Then in each of the decomposed $|U|$ problems, it takes $O(|V| \max_v\{c_v\})$ time to construct V_r and $O(|V|^2 \max_u\{b_u\})$ time to compute each $\Omega(i, CT)$ value in the worst case. Constructing $\hat{S}_{u_r}$ takes $O(|V|)$ time. Updating μ^r takes $O(|V||U|)$time. Therefore, the first step of DeDP takes $O(|U|(|V|^2 \max_u\{b_u\} + |V||U|))$ time. The second step of DeDP takes $O(|V||U|)$ time to obtain the final schedules. Thus, the overall time complexity of DeDP is $O(|U|(|V|^2 \max_u\{b_u\} + |V||U|))$.

The major space consumption of DeDP comes from storing values of μ^r, which takes $O(|V||U| \max_v\{c_v\})$ space. Computing $\Omega(i, CT)$ takes $O(|V| \max_u\{b_u\})$ space, and storing schedules of users takes $O(|V||U|)$ space. Thus, the overall space complexity of DeDP is $O(|V||U| \max_v\{c_v\} + |V| \max_u\{b_u\})$.

Approximation ratio. We next present the approximation ratio of DeDP with the following theorem, the proof of which is in the Appendix.

THEOREM 3. *DeDP has approximation ratio of $\frac{1}{2}$, i.e. $\Omega(A) \geq \frac{1}{2}\Omega(A^\star)$, where A is the planning returned by DeDP, and $A^\star$ is the optimal planning.*

4.3 Optimizing DeDP Algorithm

Note that though the DeDP algorithm returns a planning with guaranteed approximation ratio of $\frac{1}{2}$, it has the following issues. First, notice that storing values of μ^r requires $O(|V||U| \max_v\{c_v\})$ space, which is infeasible especially when $|U|$ and c_v are large. Also, updating values of μ^r takes time, which reduces the efficiency of DeDP. Second, since some events may be removed from some users' schedules, it is possible that the removed events may be added to some schedules to improve the resulted planning. In this subsection, we address these two issues and propose two enhanced algorithms, DeDPO and DeDPO+RG, which still have guaranteed approximation ratio of $\frac{1}{2}$.

4.3.1 Optimizing Space and Speed

We first optimize the space consumption of DeDP by reducing the space of μ^r, which is the major space consumption of DeDP. Reducing μ^r can also speed up DeDP. We call this improved algorithm DeDPO. We first present the following lemma, the proof of which is in the Appendix.

Algorithm 4: DeDPO

input : $V, U, \{c_v\}, \{\mu(v,u)\}, \{t_1^v, t_2^v\}, \{b_u\}, \{cost\}$
output: A feasible planning A

1 $\forall v_i$ s.t. $c_{v_i} > |U| : c_{v_i} \leftarrow |U|$;
2 $select(v_i, k) \leftarrow 0, \forall 1 \leq i \leq |V|, 1 \leq k \leq c_{v_i}$;
3 **for** $r \leftarrow 1$ **to** $|U|$ **do**
4   **for** $i \leftarrow 1$ **to** $|V|$ **do**
5     $k' \leftarrow \arg\max_k(\{\mu(v_i, u_r) | select(v_i, k) = 0\} \cup \{\mu(v_i, u_r) - \mu(v_i, select(v_i, k)) | select(v_i, k) > 0\})$;
6     $\hat{v}_i \leftarrow v_{i,k'}$;
7     $\mu'(\hat{v}_i) \leftarrow \mu(v_i, u_r)$ if $select(v_i, k') = 0$ or $\mu(v_i, u_r) - \mu(v_i, select(v_i, k'))$ otherwise;
8   $V_r \leftarrow \{\hat{v}_i | \mu'(\hat{v}_i) > 0\}$;
9   $\hat{S}_{u_r} \leftarrow$ `DPSingle` $(V_r, u_r, \mu', \{t_1^v, t_2^v\}, b_{u_r}, \{cost\})$;
10   Update *select*;
11 $S_{u_r} \leftarrow \emptyset, \forall 1 \leq r \leq |U|$;
12 **for** $i \leftarrow 1$ **to** $|V|$ **do**
13   **for** $k \leftarrow 1$ **to** c_{v_i} **do**
14     $S_{select(v_i,k)} \leftarrow S_{select(v_i,k)} \cup \{v_i\}$ if $select(v_i, k) > 0$;
15 $A \leftarrow \cup_u \{S_u\}$;
16 **return** A

LEMMA 2. *For a pseudo-event $v_{i,k}$, let $u_{r_1}, u_{r_2}, ..., u_{r_n}$ be the list of users who have $v_{i,k}$ in their schedules $\hat{S}_{u_{r_j}}$, where $1 \leq r_1 < ... < r_j < ... < r_n \leq |U|$. It holds that $\forall l$ s.t. $1 \leq l \leq r$,*

$$\mu^l(v_{i,k}, u_r) = \begin{cases} \mu(v_i, u_r) & 1 \leq l \leq r_1 \\ \mu(v_i, u_r) - \mu(v_i, u_{r_{j_l}}) & r_{j_l} < l \leq r_{j_l+1}, j_l \geq 1 \end{cases} \quad (5)$$

Notice that the values of $\mu^r(v_{i,k}, u_r)$ are used only when DeDP is performing the r-th iteration in the first step. Lemma 2 states that instead of keeping tracking of and updating $\mu^r(v_{i,k}, u_r)$ during the whole procedure of the first step of DeDP, we only need to know *who is the last user to have $v_{i,k}$ in her/his schedule $\hat{S}$* when DeDP starts to process the r-th user in the first step, which has similar consideration as [7]. Therefore, we can remove storage of μ^r values by defining a new $|V| \times c_v$ array $select(v_i, k)$, where $select(v_i, k)$ keeps tracking of the last user to have $v_{i,k}$ in her/his $\hat{S}$ before execution of the r-th iteration of the first step. That is, $select(v_i, k) = \max\{j | 1 \leq j < r, v_{i,k} \in \hat{S}_{u_j}\}$.

The procedure of the improved algorithm DeDPO is illustrated in Algorithm 4. In line 2, we initialize $select(v_i, k)$. In lines 4-7, we find the pseudo-event with the largest utility value for each v_i as we do in DeDP, and calculate the updated μ values, which are stored in a temperate array μ'. Note that $\mu'(\hat{v}_i)$ is equivalent to $\mu^r(\hat{v}_i, u_r)$ in DeDP. We construct V_r in line 8 and find an optimal schedule for u_r based on μ' in line 9. In line 10, we update the values of $select(v_i, k)$ with u_r if $v_{i,k}$ is included in $\hat{S}_{u_r}$. In lines 11-14, we construct the planning by arranging v_i to the last user who has $v_{i,k}$ in $\hat{S}$, which is already recorded in $select(v_i, k)$. Thus, step 2 of DeDPO is equivalent to step 2 of DeDP.

Complexity analysis. DeDPO improves the time efficiency of DeDP by saving $O(|V||U|)$ time to update the values of μ^r in each iteration. Therefore, the first step of DeDPO takes $O(|U|(|V|^2 \max_u\{b_u\} + |V| \max_v\{c_v\}))$ time. The second step of DeDP takes $O(|V| \max_v\{c_v\})$ time to obtain the final schedules. Thus, the overall time complexity of DeDPO is $O(|U|(|V|^2 \max_u\{b_u\} + |V| \max_v\{c_v\}))$, which reduces that of DeDP by $O(|U||V|(|U| - \max_v\{c_v\}))$.

DeDPO improves the space consumption of DeDP by saving $O(|V||U| \max_v\{c_v\})$ space to store values of μ^r while introduces $O(|V| \max_v\{c_v\})$ extra space to store values of *select*. Therefore, the overall space complexity of DeDPO is $O(|V| \max_v\{c_v\} + |V| \max_u\{b_u\} + |V||U|)$, which reduces that of DeDP by one order of magnitude.

4.3.2 Optimizing Utility

Notice that in second step of DeDPO (DeDP), some of the events may not be full in terms of capacity, i.e. some of the $select(v_i, k)$ may be 0 for some v_i. Also. some arranged events in $\hat{S}$ of some users may be removed in the second step, and thus such users may still have enough budget to attend some more events. Therefore, our second optimization for DeDPO (DeDP) is to improve the total utility score of the planning by adding events whose capacity are not yet full to schedules of users whose budgets are not yet exceeded.

Specifically, after running the DeDPO(DeDP) algorithm, we obtain an initial planning A. We construct a set of events $V' = \{v | v \text{ is not full of capacity}\}$, including all the events that are not yet full of capacity w.r.t. A. We next run RatioGreedy algorithm with input V' and U to add more arranged pairs into A if possible. Note that when running RatioGreedy (Algorithm 1), in lines 1-8, the *inc_cost* of each event-user pair should be calculated by taking the existing schedules of A into consideration. We call this algorithm DeDPO+RG. Note that the planning A' returned by DeDPO+RG is still a $\frac{1}{2}$-approximate solution.

4.4 DeGreedy Algorithm

Note that the DeDP algorithm, even the DeDPO algorithm, could be time-consuming since in each decomposed problem of the first step, it takes $O(|V|^2 \max_u\{b_u\})$ time to find an optimal schedule for the user using the dynamic programming algorithm. Thus, in this subsection, we introduce the DeGreedy algorithm, where instead of using the dynamic programming algorithm to solve each decomposed problem, we use a ratio-based greedy algorithm to find a suboptimal schedule for each user in a faster way.

More specifically, the framework of DeGreedy is the same as that of DeDPO, as we use the techniques of DeDPO to improve the space and time efficiency of DeGreedy. The only difference is that we find a schedule for user u_r in the r-th iteration of the first step in a greedy way. We then only describe the details of the greedy algorithm to find a schedule for u_r. Initially, $\hat{S}_{u_r}$ is empty. We then iteratively add a valid event v with the largest ratio score, which is defined in Equation (2), into $\hat{S}_{u_r}$. The validity of v is that adding v into $\hat{S}_{u_r}$ does not violate the travel budget and schedule feasibility constraints of u_r. Note that the utility constraint is ensured to be satisfied when we construct V_r. We maintain a heap H to keep tracking of feasible event candidates and pop the one with the largest ratio score from H and add it to $\hat{S}_{u_r}$ during each iteration.

The details of maintaining H are as follows. Initially, H is empty. We then scan through each pseudo-event in V_r', which is constructed as in Algorithm 2, and push the one with the largest ratio score into H. Each time an pseudo-event $\hat{v}_i$ is popped from H and added to $\hat{S}_{u_r}$, we update H as follows. Let p_i be the index of the precedent of $\hat{v}_i$ in $\hat{S}_{u_r}$, and s_i be index of the successor of $\hat{v}_i$ in $\hat{S}_{u_r}$ if

Algorithm 5: GreedySingle

input : $V_r, u_r, \mu^r, \{t_1^v, t_2^v\}, b_{u_r}, \{cost\}$
output: A feasible schedule $\hat{S}_{u_r}$
1 $V_r' \leftarrow \{v \in V_r | cost(u_r, v) + cost(v, u_r) \leq b_{u_r}\}$;
2 $v \leftarrow \arg\max_{v \in V_r'} ratio(v, u_r)$;
3 Push v into H;
4 $\hat{S}_{u_r} \leftarrow \emptyset$;
5 **while** $H \neq \emptyset$ **do**
6 Pop $\hat{v}_i$ with the largest $ratio(\hat{v}_i, u_r)$ from H;
7 Add $\hat{v}_i$ into $\hat{S}_{u_r}$;
8 **if** *$\hat{v}_i$ is the first in $\hat{S}_{u_r}$* **then**
9 $v' \leftarrow \arg\max_{\text{valid } v \in \{\hat{v}_1, \cdots, \hat{v}_{i-1}\} \cap V_r'} ratio(v, u_r)$;
10 **else**
11 $v' \leftarrow \arg\max_{\text{valid } v \in \{\hat{v}_{p_i+1}, \cdots, \hat{v}_{i-1}\} \cap V_r'} ratio(v, u_r)$;
12 Add v' into H if $v' \exists$;
13 **if** *$\hat{v}_i$ is the last in $\hat{S}_{u_r}$* **then**
14 $v' \leftarrow \arg\max_{\text{valid } v \in \{\hat{v}_{i+1}, \cdots, \hat{v}_{|V|}\} \cap V_r'} ratio(v, u_r)$;
15 **else**
16 $v' \leftarrow \arg\max_{\text{valid } v \in \{\hat{v}_{i+1}, \cdots, \hat{v}_{s_i-1}\} \cap V_r'} ratio(v, u_r)$;
17 Add v' into H if $v' \exists$;
18 **return** $\hat{S}_{u_r}$

they exist. That is, u_r attends $\hat{v}_{p_i}$, $\hat{v}_i$ and $\hat{v}_{s_i}$ respectively in order w.r.t. $\hat{S}_{u_r}$. We then scan through each pseudo-event in $\{\hat{v}_{p_i+1}, \hat{v}_{p_i+2}, \cdots, \hat{v}_{i-1}\}$ ($\{\hat{v}_1, \hat{v}_2, \cdots, \hat{v}_{i-1}\}$ if $\hat{v}_i$ is the first event in $\hat{S}_{u_r}$), and push the one that is valid and has the largest ratio score into H. Similarly, we scan through each pseudo-event in $\{\hat{v}_{i+1}, \hat{v}_{i+2}, \cdots, \hat{v}_{s_i-1}\}$ ($\{\hat{v}_{i+1}, \hat{v}_{i+2}, \cdots, \hat{v}_{|V|}\}$ if $\hat{v}_i$ is the last event in $\hat{S}_{u_r}$), and push the one that is valid and has the largest ratio score into H. The following lemma states that the way we maintain H ensures that we pop a valid event with the largest ratio score among all the other valid event candidates from H each time, the proof of which is in the Appendix.

LEMMA 3. *Let v be the latest event popped from H. It holds that $ratio(v, u_r) = \max_{valid\ v' \in V_r' \setminus \hat{S}_{u_r}} ratio(v', u_r)$.*

The main procedure of DeGreedy is the same as that of Algorithm 4, except that in line 9 of Algorithm 4, we call procedure *GreedySingle* instead to find the schedule $\hat{S}_{u_r}$. The procedure of *GreedySingle* is illustrated in Algorithm 5. In line 1, we construct V_r' as we do in DeDPO. In lines 2-3, we find a valid event with the largest ratio value and push it into H. In lines 5-17, we keep popping events from H and updating $\hat{S}_{u_r}$ and H until H is empty.

EXAMPLE 4. *Back to our running example in Example 1. DeGreedy returns the following planning after the first step: $\hat{S}_{u_1} = \{v_{3,1}, v_{4,1}\}, \hat{S}_{u_2} = \{v_{1,1}, v_{4,2}\}, \hat{S}_{u_3} = \{v_{3,2}, v_{2,1}\}, \hat{S}_{u_5} = \{v_{3,3}, v_{2,2}\}$. After the second step, the final planning is as follows: $S_{u_1} = \{v_3, v_4\}, S_{u_2} = \{v_1, v_4\}, S_{u_3} = \{v_3, v_2\}, S_{u_5} = \{v_3, v_2\}$. The total utility score is 4.5.*

Notice that similar to DeDPO+RG, we can also run the RatioGreedy algorithm after the second step of the DeGreedy algorithm to improve the total utility score if possible. We call this improved algorithm DeGreedy+RG.

Table 6: Real Datasets

City	$\|V\|$	$\|U\|$	Mean of c_v	cr
Vancouver	225	2012	50	0.25
Auckland	37	569		
Singapore	87	1500		

Table 7: Synthetic Datasets

Factor	Setting
$\|V\|$	20, 50, **100**, 200, 500
$\|U\|$	100, 200, 500, 1000, **5000**
$\mu(v, u)$	**Uniform**, Normal(0.5, 0.25), Power: 0.5, 4
Mean of c_v	10, 20, **50**, 100, 200
Distributions of c_v	**Uniform**, Normal
f_b	0.5, 1, **2**, 5, 10
Distributions of b_u	**Uniform**, Normal
cr	0, **0.25**, 0.5, 0.75, 1
Scalability	$\|U\|$ = 10K, 20K, 30K, 40K, 50K, 100K

Complexity analysis. The difference between DeDPO and DeGreedy is GreedySingle. In GreedySingle, it takes $O(|V|)$ time to update H each time, and the number of iterations is at most $|V|$. Therefore, the overall complexity of DeGreedy is $O(|U|(|V|^2 + |V| \max_v\{c_v\}))$, and the space complexity is $O(|V| \max_v\{c_v\} + |V||U|)$.

5. EXPERIMENTAL STUDY

5.1 Experiment Setup

Parameters. We first define a *conflict ratio cr* to reflect the conflicting degree of events. Specifically, conflict ratio is the percentage of pairs of events that are spatio-temporally conflicting with each other. The time and cost values are generated based on the conflict ratio.

We next use a *budget factor* f_b to control the budget of user b_u. Specifically, given f_b, which is universal for all users, for each user u, the value of b_u is generated uniformly in $[2\min_v cost(u, v), 2\min_v cost(u, v) + mid \times f_b \times 2]$, where $mid = \frac{1}{2}(\max_{v,v'} cost(v, v') + \min_{v,v'} cost(v, v'))$.

Datasets. We use the Meetup dataset from [21] as real dataset. In the dataset, each user is associated with a set of tags and a location. Each event in the dataset is also associated with a location, and we use the tags of the group who creates the event as the tags of the event itself since the events themselves do not have tags. We use the similarity of the tags between an event and a user as their utility scores[36]. Since it is unlikely for a user living in a city to attend a meet-up event held in another city, we focus on the event/users pairs located in the same city. We select three popular cities, Vancouver, Auckland and Singapore, and extract events and users located within the area around each city. We use the Manhatan distance between a user and an event or that between two events as their travel cost in our experiments. We generate capacities of events following Uniform distribution, and generate the time and budgets with varying parameters described previously. TABLE 6 presents the statistics and configuration. We also use synthetic dataset for evaluation. We generate the utility values following Uniform, Normal and Power distributions respectively. The statistics and configuration of synthetic data are illustrated in TABLE 7, where we mark our default settings in bold font.

Notice that spatio-temporal conflicts, capacities and travel budgets are also generated syntactically for real datasets. The reason is that though such information is often contained or can be inferred from the description of events on Meetup, it is not contained in the dataset of [21].

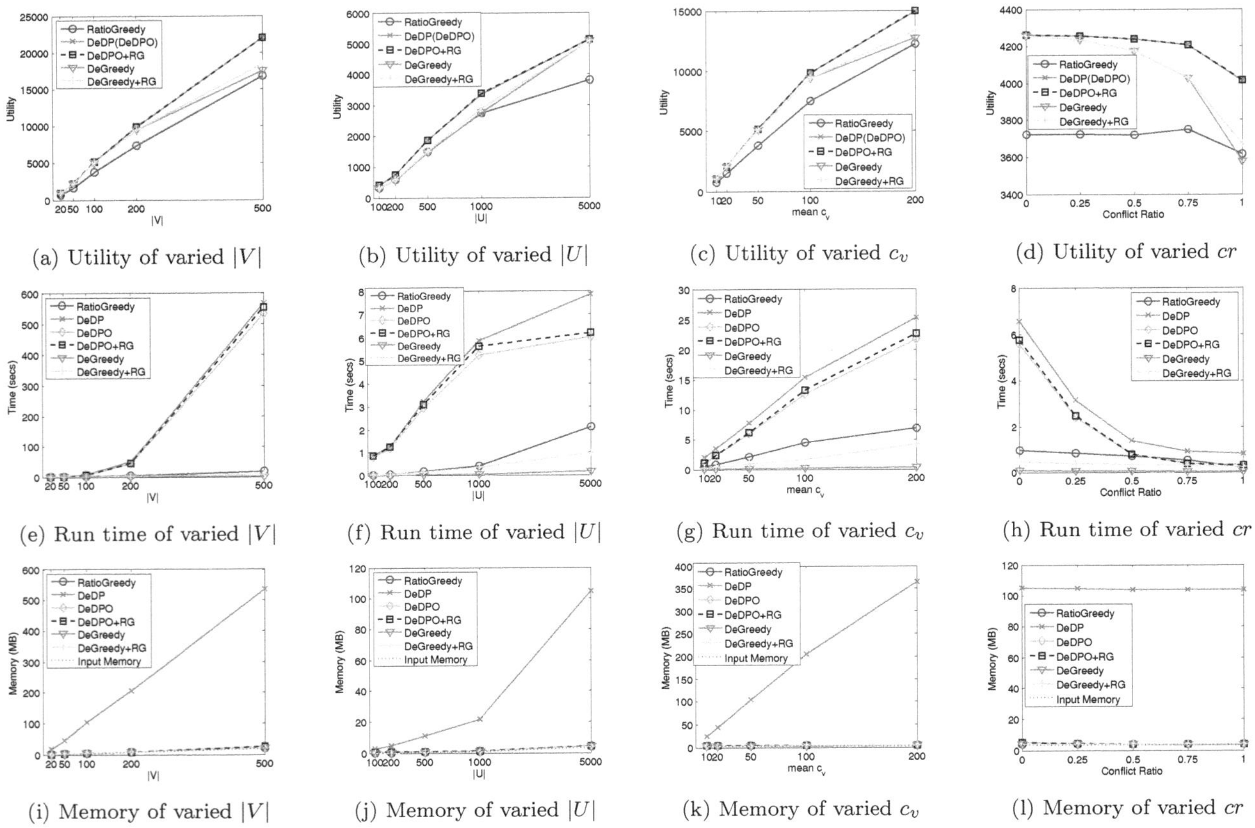

(a) Utility of varied $|V|$ (b) Utility of varied $|U|$ (c) Utility of varied c_v (d) Utility of varied cr

(e) Run time of varied $|V|$ (f) Run time of varied $|U|$ (g) Run time of varied c_v (h) Run time of varied cr

(i) Memory of varied $|V|$ (j) Memory of varied $|U|$ (k) Memory of varied c_v (l) Memory of varied cr

Figure 2: Results on varied $|V|$, $|U|$, mean of c_v, and conflict ratio.

We evaluate RatioGreedy, DeDP, DeDPO, DeDPO+RG, DeGreedy, and DeGreedy+RG in terms of total utility score, running time and memory cost, and study the effect of different parameters on the performance of the algorithms. The algorithms are implemented in C++, and the experiments were performed on a Windows 7 machine with Intel i7-2600 3.40GHZ 8-core CPU and 8GB memory.

5.2 Experiment Results

Effect of cardinality of V. We first study the effect of $|V|$. The first column of Figure 2 presents the results when $|V|$ varies from 20 to 500. In terms of total utility scores, we can first observe that DeDP-based algorithms, i.e. DeDP(DeDPO) and DeDPO+RG, perform the best, while the heuristic-based RatioGreedy algorithm achieves the lowest utility scores. Note that the difference between two total utility scores can be considered as at least how many more interesting events are suggested to users. For example, the difference of 4500 and 5000 when $|V| = 100$ indicates that in the planning with utility score of 5000, at least 500 more interesting events are suggested to users compared to the one with total utility score of 4500. Second, DeGreedy+RG enhances DeGreedy to a certain degree, while DeDPO+RG does not enhance DeDPO significantly. The reason is that DeGreedy returns a worse planning than DeDPO does, and thus there could be more available event-user pairs in the planning returned by DeGreedy, which increases the possibility that the enhanced algorithm can add some more event-user pairs to the original planning. Third, we can observe that the utility scores increase as $|V|$ increases, which is natural as there are more events available for users when $|V|$ increases. As for running time, we can observe that DeDP-based algorithms run slower than other algorithms do, especially when $|V|$ is as large as 500. We can also see that DeDPO is slightly faster than DeDP as expected. Finally, in terms of memory consumption, we can observe that all the algorithms perform well except DeDP, which is highly memory-consuming. The results reflect that our techniques that optimize DeDP are very effective. Overall, DeDPO-based algorithms are the best in terms of utility score, while DeGreedy-based algorithms have a better trade-off between total utility score and running time.

Effect of cardinality of U. We next study the effect of varying $|U|$, the results of which are presented in the second column of Figure 2. $|U|$ is varied from 100 to 5K. For utility score, we can again observe that DeDP-based algorithms perform the best, while RatioGreedy performs the worst. However, DeGreedy-based algorithms are almost as good as DeDP-based algorithms when $|U|$ is as large as 5000. The reason is that when $|U|$ is 5000, the number of events w.r.t. users is relatively small, and thus the optimality of DeDP-based algorithms in finding a schedule for each user becomes less significant. As for running time, we can observe that DeGreedy is the fastest, while DeDP is again the slowest among the six. Also, we can see that DeDPO is again more time-efficient than DeDP. Finally, for memory consumption, we can observe once again that DeDP, without optimization, performs much worse than the other algorithms. Overall, DeDPO-based algorithms still return the best planning, while DeGreedy-based algorithms again show better trade-off between optimality and running time.

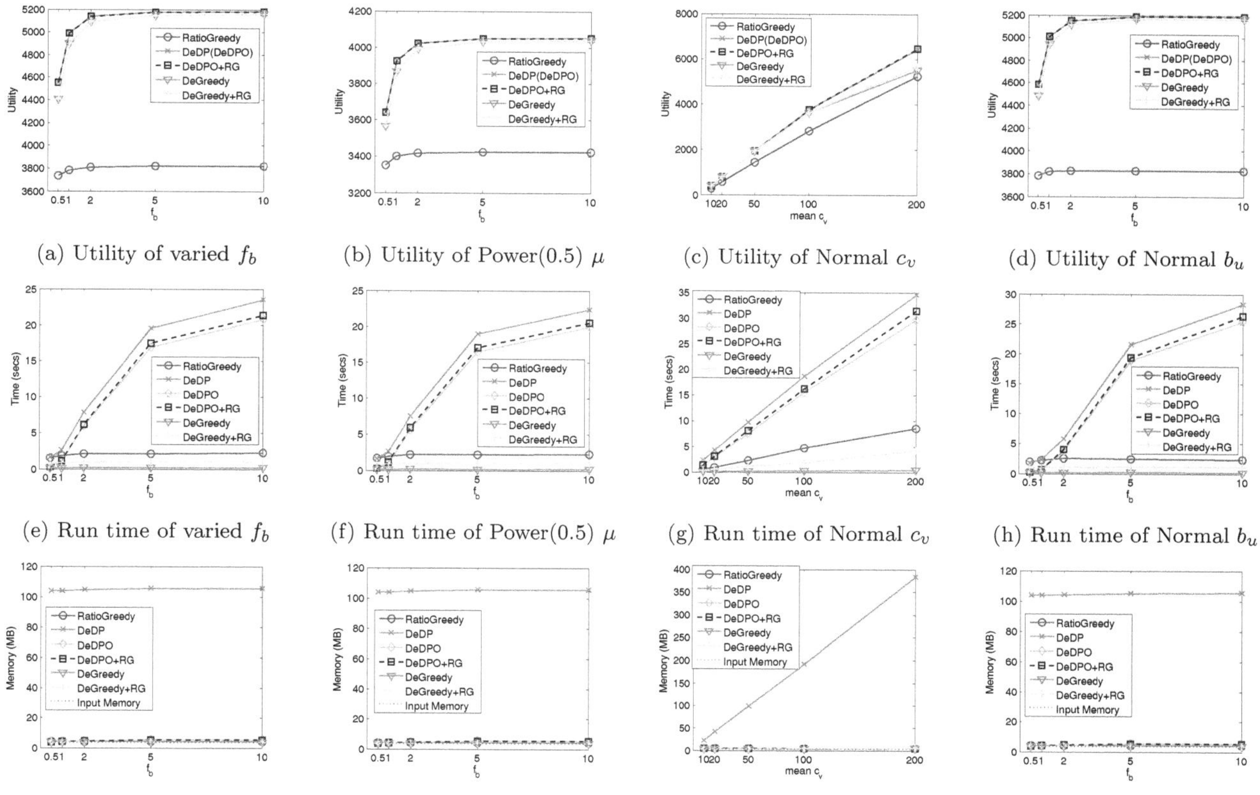

(a) Utility of varied f_b (b) Utility of Power(0.5) μ (c) Utility of Normal c_v (d) Utility of Normal b_u

(e) Run time of varied f_b (f) Run time of Power(0.5) μ (g) Run time of Normal c_v (h) Run time of Normal b_u

(i) Memory of varied f_b (j) Memory of Power(0.5) μ (k) Memory of Normal c_v (l) Memory of Normal b_u

Figure 3: Results on varied f_b and distributions.

Effect of capacity. We next study the effect of varying the mean of c_v, the results of which are presented in the third column of Figure 2. We vary the mean of c_v from 10 to 200. For utility score, we can first observe that the utility scores increase as the mean of c_v increases, which is reasonable as more event-pairs can be added to the planning when the capacity of events increases. Second, DeDP-based algorithms again achieve the best utility results, while RatioGreedy is still the worst. We can finally observe that DeDPO+RG improves the utility results of DeDP(DeDPO) slightly, while DeGreedy+RG improves the utility results of DeGreedy more significantly. For running time, the running time of all algorithms increases as the mean of c_v increases, which makes sense as each event can be arranged for more users. Second, we can again obesve that DeGreedy is the fastest, while DeDP is the least time-efficient. Finally, as for memory consumption, DeDP without optimization is still the most memory-consuming algorithm.

Effect of conflict ratio. We then study the effect of varying conflict ratio cr, the results of which are presented in the last column of Figure 2. We vary the conflict ratio from 0.0 to 1.0. For utility score, our first observation is that the utility scores decrease as the conflict ratio increases. The reason is that when more pairs of events are conflicting with each other, the availability of events is decreased when the algorithms find schedules for users. As we can see from Figure 2d, the utility scores are quite low when $cr = 1$, in which case each user can attend at most one event as all events are conflicting with each other. Finally, we can observe that DeDP-based algorithms perform significantly better than the other algorithms when the conflict ratio increases. The reason is that DeDP-based algorithms always return optimal schedules for each user in each decomposed problem, while DeGreedy-based algorithms may return much worst schedules in each decomposed problem when the conflict ratio increases since the greedy strategy of DeGreedy does not consider conflicting degree of events. As for running time, the first interesting observation is that the running time of all the algorithms, especially that of DeDPO-based algorithms and DeGreedy-based algorithms, decreases as cr increases. The major reason is that when more events are conflicting with each other, the number of iterations for both DeDPO-based algorithms and DeGreedy-based algorithms will decrease. As we can see from Figure 2h, DeDPO-based algorithms are nearly as fast as DeGreedy-based algorithms when cr is 0.5 or above, in which cases the time efficiency advantage of the greedy strategy adopted by DeGreedy-based algorithms becomes less significant. Finally, for memory consumption, DeDP is once again the worst among all the algorithms. Overall, DeDPO-based algorithms demonstrate their advantages in utility results when conflict ratio increases, and they can be as fast as DeGreedy-based algorithms when conflict ratio increases.

Effect of budget factor. We next study the effect of varying budget factor f_b, the results of which are presented in the first column of Figure 3. We vary f_b from 0.5 to 10. For utility, we can first observe that the utility scores increase as f_b increases, which makes sense as users can attend more events as f_b increases and thus b_u increases. However, when $f_b \geq 2$, the utility scores increase much slower as f_b increases. The reason is that though budgets of users increase, the number of events available to users is limited.

Thus, when f_b is large, all events may have been full of capacity and thus no more events can be added to users' schedules though users' budgets are sufficient. As for running time and memory consumption results, we can observe again that DeGreedy-based algorithms are the most time-efficient and DeDP is the most memory-consuming.

Effect of distribution. We then study the effect of varying distributions of μ, c_v and b_u respectively. In the second column of Figure 3, we present the results when values of μ are generated following a power distribution with parameter 0.5. We plot against different f_b values, and the other parameters are set to default. We can observe that the trending patterns of utility scores, running time and memory consumption are similar to those in the first column of Figure 3, where values of μ are generated uniformly. We also generate values of μ following normal distribution with mean 0.5 and std 0.25 and a power distribution with parameter 4, whose results are similar and we omit them for brevity.

In the third column of Figure 3, we present the results when values of c_v are generated following a normal distribution, whose mean is varied from 10 to 200 and the std is the mean value multiplied by 0.25. The trending patterns of utility scores, running time and memory consumption are also similar to those in the third column of Figure 2, where the values of c_v are generated uniformly.

Finally, in the last column of Figure 3, we present the results when values of b_u are generated following a normal distribution, whose mean is $2\min_v cost(u,v) + mid * f_b$ and standard deviation is the mean value multiplied by 0.25, where $mid = \frac{1}{2}(\max_{v,v'} cost(v,v') + \min_{v,v'} cost(v,v'))$. We vary f_b from 0.5 to 10. Again, we can observe that the trending patterns of utility scores, running time and memory consumption are similar to those in the first column of Figure 3, where the values of b_u are generated uniformly.

Scalability. We next test the scalability of the algorithms. Since DeDP is memory-consuming and thus not scalable as our previous results show, we only test the scalability of RatioGreedy, DeDPO, DeDPO+RG, DeGreedy and DeGreedy+RG. The results are presented in the first three columns of Figure 4, where we set $|V|$ to 100, 200 and 500 respectively and vary $|U|$. The mean of c_v is set to 200, and the other parameters are set to default. For utility, we can see that DeDPO-based algorithms still perform the best, while RatioGreedy is the worst. For running time, we can observe that RatioGreedy is not very scalable as its running time increases quickly as the scale of data increases. We can also see that DeGreedy-based algorithms are highly-efficient even when the scale of data is large. Particularly, DeGreedy is much more efficient than the other algorithms when $|U|$ is as large as 100K. In our special test case where $|V| = 500$, $|U| = 200K$ and the mean of c_v is 500, DeGreedy returns a planning with total utility score of 229,234 in around 13 minutes while DeDPO returns one with totally utility score of 230,585 in more than 1.4 hours. It indicates that DeGreedy has better a trade-off between optimality and running time. As for DeDPO-based algorithms, though they are slower than the DeGreedy-based algorithms, their running time increases slowly as the scale of data increases. Finally, for memory consumption, all the algorithms consume only very little memory in addition to the memory taken up by input data. Thus, all algorithms are scalable in space. Overall, DeDPO-based algorithms return the best planning among all the algorithms and are scalable. DeGreedy-based algorithms return worse planning but are more scalable, and are preferable on extremely large datasets, e.g. cities with millions of citizens, given their high efficiency.

Real datasets. We finally study results on real datasets. In the last column of Figure 4, we present the results on the Singapore dataset. We vary values of f_b, and set the other parameters to default. We can observe that the trending patterns are similar to those in the first column of Figure 3, where synthetic data is used. The results on the other two real datasets are similar, and we omit them for brevity.

Summary. We finally summarize our findings.

- DeDPO improves the space and time efficiency of DeDP significantly, and is much more scalable than DeDP.
- DeDP(DeDPO)-based algorithms always achieve the largest total utility score among all the algorithms. DeGreedy-based algorithms are the most time-efficient, though achieve slightly worse total utility score than DeDP(DeDPO)-based algorithms do.
- Both DeDPO-based algorithms and DeGreedy-based algorithms are scalable in space and time.

6. RELATED WORK

In this section, we review the related work from three categories, mining and managing event-based social networks, location and event recommendation in social networks and bipartite graph matching.

Mining and managing event-based social networks. With the prevalence of various kinds of EBSN platforms, [21] is the first work on formulating and analysing the properties of EBSNs. Recently, some other problems in EBSN are studied. A set of studies, such as [36][10][13], utilize learning-based models to train data of EBSNs and then recommend events to related users. However, they focus on recommendation rather than optimizing a global planning.

[11] studies the problem of discovering influential event organizers based on the influence maximization problem[14] and team formation problem[17][2], which only considers interests of event organizers. Our work differs from them in that we study the maximum utility event-participant planning problem.

In particular, a closely related research, *Social Event Organization (SEO)* problem [19], has been proposed recently. This problem aims to maximize the overall satisfaction of users towards the arranged events and the social affinity among the users participating the same event. In SEO, each event is associated with a lower bound and an upper bound on the number of attendees, and every pair of users attending the same event contributes to the social affinity score. Due to the pair-wise social affinity score, the SEO problem is NP-hard to approximate and thus only heuristics are proposed. More importantly, the SEO problem substantially differs from ours since this work only considers a simple case of assigning one single event to each participant and thus naturally ignores both the spatio-temporal conflicts of events and also multiple-event planning for each user.

Another related work [26] also studies a global event assignment strategy, but does not consider travel expenditure. [29] studies another objective function, max-min, regarding the event arrangement problem, but still does not consider travel cost between events.

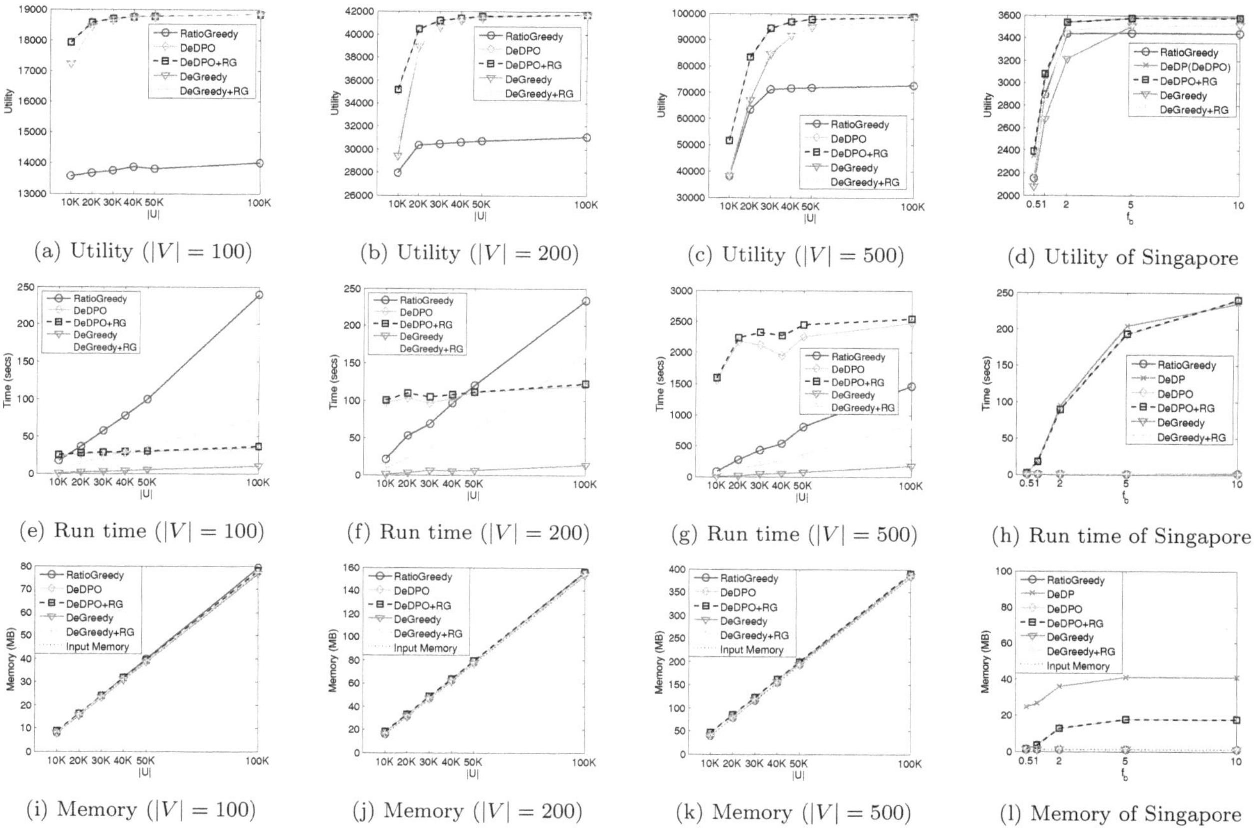

(a) Utility ($|V| = 100$) (b) Utility ($|V| = 200$) (c) Utility ($|V| = 500$) (d) Utility of Singapore

(e) Run time ($|V| = 100$) (f) Run time ($|V| = 200$) (g) Run time ($|V| = 500$) (h) Run time of Singapore

(i) Memory ($|V| = 100$) (j) Memory ($|V| = 200$) (k) Memory ($|V| = 500$) (l) Memory of Singapore

Figure 4: Results on scalability test and real dataset.

Location recommendation in social networks. Due to the recent popularity of location-based social networks (LBSNs), this topic is quite hot [25][18][21][34][20][9][28][35][22][15][15][1]. However, they focus on mining single user's interests in certain venues and make user-oriented recommendation. Also, they do not consider spatio-temporal conflicts, capacity of events or travel budget of users. Our problem is different from theirs since we satisfy the interests of most users with a systematic planning while consider spatio-temporal conflicts and travel cost.

In addition, location-based travel route recommendation[16][6][24][8][4] tries to recommends some landmarks to tourists, where travel expenditure is considered. However, these works focus on making recommendation to one single user and do not consider conflicts, and we differ from them in that we make a global planning for users. Thus, their solutions cannot be applied to our problem.

Bipartite graph matching. The maximum weighted bipartite matching [32][5] is quite related to our problem. However, the bipartite matching problem does not take spatio-temporal conflicts or travel cost between nodes or capacity of nodes into consideration. Recent works [33][31][30][27][23] study the problem of spatial matching, which integrates spatial information and capacities of nodes into the weighted bipartite matching problem. However, they still do not consider spatio-temporal conflicts or travel cost of nodes. Notice the original maximum weighted bipartite matching can be solved in polynomial time. However, our problem is different since our problem is NP-hard due to the conflicts and travel cost between nodes.

7. CONCLUSION

In this paper, we propose a novel social event-participant planning problem called *utility-aware social event-participant planning* (USEP). We first analyze our differences with other problems in EBSNs and prove the NP hardness of our problem. In order to solve this problem, we first devise a greedy-based heuristic solution, called RatioGreedy, which performs fast in certain circumstances but has no approximation guarantee. To obtain better approximation quality, a two-step approximation framework is presented. Based on this framework, we first propose the DeDP algorithm which has a $\frac{1}{2}$-approximation ratio but consumes more space for large datasets. In order to improve the time/space efficiency of the DeDP algorithm, we further devise the DeDPO algorithm using a series of optimized techniques. Furthermore, to address the challenge of massive data, we also design the DeGreedy algorithm following the two-step approximation framework, which runs faster than the DeDP algorithm but returns a planning with a lower total utility score. We conduct extensive experiments that verify the efficiency, effectiveness and scalability of the proposed approaches.

Acknowledgements: We are grateful to anonymous reviewers for their constructive comments on this work. This work is supported in part by the Hong Kong RGC Project N_HKUST637/13, National Grand Fundamental Research 973 Program of China under Grant 2014CB340303, NSFC Grant No. 61328202/61300031, Microsoft Research Asia Gift Grant, Google Faculty Award 2013 and Microsoft Research Asia Fellowship 2012.

8. REFERENCES

[1] S. Amer-Yahia, S. B. Roy, A. Chawlat, G. Das, and C. Yu. Group recommendation: Semantics and efficiency. In *VLDB'09*.

[2] A. Anagnostopoulos, L. Becchetti, C. Castillo, A. Gionis, and S. Leonardi. Online team formation in social networks. In *WWW'12*.

[3] R. Bar-Yehuda, K. Bendel, A. Freund, and D. Rawitz. Local ratio: A unified framework for approximation algorithms. in memoriam: Shimon even 1935-2004. *ACM Computing Surveys (CSUR)*, 2004.

[4] I. Brilhante, J. A. Macedo, F. M. Nardini, R. Perego, and C. Renso. Where shall we go today?: Planning touristic tours with tripbuilder. In *CIKM'13*.

[5] R. E. Burkard, M. Dell'Amico, and S. Martello. *Assignment Problems, Revised Reprint*. 2009.

[6] C. Chen, D. Zhang, B. Guo, X. Ma, G. Pan, and Z. Wu. Tripplanner: Personalized trip planning leveraging heterogeneous crowdsourced digital footprints. *IEEE Transactions on Intelligent Transportation Systems (T-ITS)*, 2014.

[7] R. Cohen, L. Katzir, and D. Raz. An efficient approximation for the generalized assignment problem. *Information Processing Letters*, 2006.

[8] M. De Choudhury, M. Feldman, S. Amer-Yahia, N. Golbandi, R. Lempel, and C. Yu. Automatic construction of travel itineraries using social breadcrumbs. In *HT'10*.

[9] T. De Pessemier, J. Minnaert, K. Vanhecke, S. Dooms, and L. Martens. Social recommendations for events. In *CEUR Workshop'13*.

[10] R. Du, Z. Yu, T. Mei, Z. Wang, Z. Wang, and B. Guo. Predicting activity attendance in event-based social networks: Content, context and social influence. In *UbiComp '14*.

[11] K. Feng, G. Cong, S. S. Bhowmick, and S. Ma. In search of influential event organizers in online social networks. In *SIGMOD'14*.

[12] M. R. Garey and D. S. Johnson. *Computers and intractability: A guide to the theory of NP-completeness*. 1979.

[13] S. Karanikolaou, I. Boutsis, and V. Kalogeraki. Understanding event attendance through analysis of human crowd behavior in social networks. In *DEBS'14*.

[14] D. Kempe, J. Kleinberg, and É. Tardos. Maximizing the spread of influence through a social network. In *KDD'03*.

[15] H. Khrouf and R. Troncy. Hybrid event recommendation using linked data and user diversity. In *RecSys'13*.

[16] T. Kurashima, T. Iwata, G. Irie, and K. Fujimura. Travel route recommendation using geotags in photo sharing sites. In *CIKM'10*.

[17] T. Lappas, K. Liu, and E. Terzi. Finding a team of experts in social networks. In *KDD'09*.

[18] J. J. Levandoski, M. Sarwat, A. Eldawy, and M. F. Mokbel. Lars: A location-aware recommender system. In *ICDE'12*.

[19] K. Li, W. Lu, S. Bhagat, L. V. S. Lakshmanan, and C. Yu. On social event organization. In *KDD'14*.

[20] G. Liao, Y. Zhao, S. Xie, and P. S. Yu. An effective latent networks fusion based model for event recommendation in offline ephemeral social networks. In *CIKM'13*.

[21] X. Liu, Q. He, Y. Tian, W.-C. Lee, J. McPherson, and J. Han. Event-based social networks: linking the online and offline social worlds. In *KDD'12*.

[22] X. Liu, Y. Tian, M. Ye, and W.-C. Lee. Exploring personal impact for group recommendation. In *CIKM'12*.

[23] C. Long, R. C.-W. Wong, P. S. Yu, and M. Jiang. On optimal worst-case matching. In *SIGMOD'13*.

[24] E. H.-C. Lu, C.-Y. Chen, and V. S. Tseng. Personalized trip recommendation with multiple constraints by mining user check-in behaviors. In *GIS'12*.

[25] E. Minkov, B. Charrow, J. Ledlie, S. Teller, and T. Jaakkola. Collaborative future event recommendation. In *CIKM'10*.

[26] J. She, Y. Tong, L. Chen, and C. C. Cao. Conflict-aware event-participant arrangement. In *ICDE'15*.

[27] Y. Sun, J. Huang, Y. Chen, R. Zhang, and X. Du. Location selection for utility maximization with capacity constraints. In *CIKM'12*.

[28] Y.-C. Sun and C. C. Chen. A novel social event recommendation method based on social and collaborative friendships. In *SocInfo'13*.

[29] Y. Tong, R. Meng, and J. She. On bottleneck-aware arrangement for event-based social networks. In *ICDE Workshop SSEPM'15*.

[30] L. H. U, K. Mouratidis, M. L. Yiu, and N. Mamoulis. Optimal matching between spatial datasets under capacity constraints. *ACM Transactions on Database Systems (TODS)*, 2010.

[31] L. H. U, M. L. Yiu, K. Mouratidis, and N. Mamoulis. Capacity constrained assignment in spatial databases. In *SIGMOD'08*.

[32] D. B. West. *Introduction to graph theory*. 2001.

[33] R. C.-W. Wong, Y. Tao, A. W.-C. Fu, and X. Xiao. On efficient spatial matching. In *VLDB'07*.

[34] H. Yin, Y. Sun, B. Cui, Z. Hu, and L. Chen. Lcars: A location-content-aware recommender system. In *KDD'13*.

[35] Q. Yuan, G. Cong, and C.-Y. Lin. Com: a generative model for group recommendation. In *KDD'14*.

[36] W. Zhang, J. Wang, and W. Feng. Combining latent factor model with location features for event-based group recommendation. In *KDD'13*.

APPENDIX

Proof of Theorem 1:

PROOF. In order to complete the proof, we reduce the knapsack problem, which is a well-known NP-complete problem [12], to the USEP problem. The following is an instance of the knapsack problem. Given n items $\{x_1, x_2, ..., x_n\}$, each with value $a_i > 0$ and weight $w_i > 0$, the maximum weight W that a bag can carry, decide if there is a collection of items $C = \{x_{s_1}, x_{s_2}, ..., x_{s_m}\}$ (without loss of generality $s_i < s_j, \forall 1 \leq i < j \leq m$) such that $\sum_{i=1}^{m} a_{s_i} = K$ and $\sum_{i=1}^{m} w_{s_i} \leq W$.

We then construct an instance of the USEP problem from the instance of the knapsack problem accordingly:

(1) Let $|U| = 1$, $U = \{u\}$, and $b_u = W$.

(2) Each item of the knapsack instance corresponds to an event. Let $\mu(v_i, u) = \frac{a_i}{\max a_i}, \forall 1 \leq i \leq n$, and $c_{v_i} = 1, \forall 1 \leq i \leq n$.

(3) Assign any value to $\{t_1^{v_i}, t_2^{v_i}\}$ subject to $t_1^{v_i} < t_2^{v_i}, \forall 1 \leq i \leq n$ and $t_2^{v_i} < t_1^{v_{i+1}}, \forall 1 \leq i < n$.

(4) The travel cost between u and an event v_i is constructed as: $cost(u, v_i) = cost(v_i, u) = \frac{w_i}{2}, \forall 1 \leq i \leq n$.

(5) The travel cost between two events is constructed as:

$$cost(v_i, v_j) = \begin{cases} \frac{w_i + w_j}{2} & 1 \leq i < j \leq n \\ +\infty & \text{otherwise} \end{cases}$$

We want to decide if there is a feasible schedule S_u for u such that $\sum_{v_i \in S_u} \mu(v_i, u) = \frac{K}{\max a_i}$ and it satisfies all the constraints.

We can see that if the collection C exists, then the schedule $S_u = \{v_{s_1}, v_{s_2}, ..., v_{s_m}\}$ is feasible, and it satisfies that $\sum_{v_i \in S_u} \mu(v_i, u) = \frac{K}{\max a_i}$ and that $cost(u, v_{s_1}) + cost(v_{s_m}, u) + \sum_{i=2}^{m} cost(v_{s_i - 1}, v_{s_i}) = \sum_{i=1}^{m} w_{s_i} \leq W$. On the other hand, if the schedule $S_u = \{v_{s_1}, v_{s_2}, ..., v_{s_m}\}$ exists, then there exists a collection $C = \{x_{s_1}, x_{s_2}, ..., x_{s_m}\}$ satisfying that $\sum_{i=1}^{m} a_{s_i} = K$ and that $\sum_{i=1}^{m} w_{s_i} \leq W$. This completes the proof. □

Proof of Lemma 1:

PROOF. If $|S_u| = 1$ and $S_u = \{v_i\}$, it is clear that S_u violates the budget constraint of u. If $|S_u| > 1$ and $v_i \in S_u$, due to the triangle inequality property of *cost*, it is clear that $cost(u, v_1^u) + \sum_{j=2}^{|S_u|} cost(v_{j-1}^u, v_j^u) + cost(v_{|S_u|}^u, u) \geq cost(u, v_i) + cost(v_i, u) > b_u$. Thus, S_u is infeasible. □

Proof of Theorem 3:

PROOF. Let $A_r = \cup_{j \geq r}\{S_{u_j}\} \subseteq A$ be the solution w.r.t. μ^r, i.e. $\Omega(A_r) = \sum_{j \geq r} \sum_{v_{i,k} \in S_{u_j}} \mu^r(v_{i,k}, u_j)$. Notice that according to the way we update μ^r, $\mu^{r+1}(v_{i,k}, u_r) = 0, \forall 1 \leq i \leq |V|, 1 \leq k \leq c_{v_i}$. Since $\mu^{r+1}(v_{i,k}, u_j) = \mu^r(v_{i,k}, u_j)$, $\forall 1 \leq i \leq |V|, 1 \leq k \leq c_{v_i}, j < r$, it is easy to see that $\mu^{r+1}(v_{i,k}, u_j) = 0, \forall 1 \leq i \leq |V|, 1 \leq k \leq c_{v_i}, j \leq r$. Thus, when calculating the total utility score of a solution w.r.t. μ^r, we do not need to sum over users in $\{u_j | j < r\}$.

We then prove by induction and start from the last user, i.e. $r = |U|$. When $r = |U|$, since the dynamic programming algorithm returns an optimal schedule for $u_{|U|}$, $A_{|U|} = \{S_{u_{|U|}}\}$ is an optimal solution w.r.t. $\mu^{|U|}(\hat{v}., u_{|U|})$. Since $\mu^{|U|}(\hat{v}_i, u_{|U|}) \geq \mu^{|U|}(v_{i,k}, u_{|U|}), \forall 1 \leq i \leq |V|, 1 \leq k \leq c_{v_i}$, $\Omega(A_{|U|}) = \Omega(A^{\star}_{|U|}) \geq \frac{1}{2}\Omega(A^{\star}_{|U|})$, where $A^{\star}_{|U|}$ is the optimal solution w.r.t. $\mu^{|U|}$.

Suppose A_{r+1} is a $\frac{1}{2}$-approximate solution w.r.t. μ^{r+1}. We next prove that A_r is also a $\frac{1}{2}$-approximate solution w.r.t. μ^r. Recall that $\mu^{r+1}(v_{i,k}, u_r) = 0, \forall 1 \leq i \leq |V|, 1 \leq k \leq c_{v_i}$. Thus, the schedule of u_r does not affect the total utility score of the solution w.r.t. μ^{r+1}. Since $A_{r+1} \subseteq A_r$ and A_{r+1} is a $\frac{1}{2}$-approximate solution w.r.t. μ^{r+1}, clearly A_r is also a $\frac{1}{2}$-approximate solution w.r.t. μ^{r+1}.

We then define μ_o^r as follows.

$$\mu_o^r(v_{i,k}, u_j) = \begin{cases} \mu^r(v_{i,k}, u_r) & (j = r) \text{ or } (j > r \text{ and } v_{i,k} \in \hat{S}_{u_r}) \\ 0 & \textit{otherwise} \end{cases} \tag{6}$$

Consider an arbitrary feasible planning $A' = \cup_j\{S'_{u_j}\}$ w.r.t. μ_o^r, and we have

$$\begin{aligned} \Omega_o(A') &= \sum_j \sum_{v_{i,k} \in S'_{u_j}} \mu_o^r(v_{i,k}, u_j) \\ &= \sum_{j \geq r} \sum_{v_{i,k} \in S'_{u_j}} \mu_o^r(v_{i,k}, u_j) \\ &= \sum_{v_{i,k} \in S'_{u_r}} \mu^r(v_{i,k}, u_r) \\ &+ \sum_{j > r} \sum_{v_{i,k} \in \hat{S}_{u_r} \cap S'_{u_j}} \mu^r(v_{i,k}, u_r) \end{aligned} \tag{7}$$

Notice that in the planing A', each $v_{i,k}$ can be included in at most one of $S'_{u_j}, \forall j > r$. Therefore, we have

$$\sum_{j > r} \sum_{v_{i,k} \in \hat{S}_{u_r} \cap S'_{u_j}} \mu^r(v_{i,k}, u_r) \leq \sum_{v_{i,k} \in \hat{S}_{u_r}} \mu^r(v_{i,k}, u_r) \tag{8}$$

Note that the schedule $\hat{S}_{u_r}$ returned by the dynamic programming algorithm for u_r is an optimal solution w.r.t. $\mu^r(\hat{v}., u_r)$ and that $\mu^r(\hat{v}_i, u_r) \geq \mu^r(v_{i,k}, u_r), \forall 1 \leq i \leq |V|, 1 \leq k \leq c_{v_i}$. Therefore, we have

$$\sum_{v_{i,k} \in S'_{u_r}} \mu^r(v_{i,k}, u_r) \leq \sum_{v_{i,k} \in \hat{S}_{u_r}} \mu^r(v_{i,k}, u_r) \tag{9}$$

Combining Equations (8) and (9), we have

$$\Omega_o(A') \leq 2 \sum_{v_{i,k} \in \hat{S}_{u_r}} \mu^r(v_{i,k}, u_r) = 2\Omega_o(\hat{S}_{u_r}) \tag{10}$$

Notice that regarding A_r, for each $v_{i,k} \in \hat{S}_{u_r}$, it is either in S_{u_r} or in $\cup_{j > r} S_{u_j}$, and appears only once in A_r. For the other $v_{i,k}$'s that are not in $\hat{S}_{u_r}$, they cannot be in S_{u_r} and do not affect $\Omega_o(A_r)$ according Equation (6). Therefore, we have $\Omega_o(A_r) = \Omega_o(\hat{S}_{u_r}) \geq \frac{1}{2}\Omega_o(A')$. Thus, A_r is a $\frac{1}{2}$-approximate solution w.r.t. μ_o^r. Notice that $\mu^r(\cdot,\cdot) = \mu^{r+1}(\cdot,\cdot) + \mu_o^r(\cdot,\cdot)$. Based on Theorem 2, A_r is thus a $\frac{1}{2}$-approximate solution w.r.t. μ^r.

By induction, $A = \cup_j\{S_{u_j}\}$ is a $\frac{1}{2}$-approximate solution w.r.t. $\mu^1 = \mu$, which completes the proof. □

Proof of Lemma 2:

PROOF. Clearly, for $1 \leq l \leq r_1, l \leq r$, it holds that $\mu^l(v_{i,k}, u_r) = \mu(v_i, u_r)$ since $v_{i,k}$ is not included in any of

$\hat{S}_{u_j}, 1 \leq j < r_1$ and thus $\mu^l(v_{i,k}, u_r)$ does not change in the first $r_1 - 1$ iterations according to the way we update μ^r.

We prove the remaining of the claim by induction. For $r_1 < l \leq r_2, l \leq r$, we have

$$\begin{aligned}
\mu^l(v_{i,k}, u_r) &= \mu^{l-1}(v_{i,k}, u_r) \\
&= \cdots \\
&= \mu^{r_1+1}(v_{i,k}, u_r) \\
&= \mu^{r_1}(v_{i,k}, u_r) - \mu^{r_1}(v_{i,k}, u_{r_1}) \\
&= \mu(v_i, u_r) - \mu(v_i, u_{r_1})
\end{aligned} \tag{11}$$

Suppose $\mu^l(v_{i,k}, u_r) = \mu(v_i, u_r) - \mu(v_i, u_{r_{j_l}})$ holds for $j_l = j - 1$, i.e. $r_{j-1} < l \leq r_j, l \leq r$, we next prove that the equation also holds for $r_j < l \leq r_{j+1}, l \leq r$. For $r_j < l \leq r_{j+1}, l \leq r$, we have

$$\begin{aligned}
\mu^l(v_{i,k}, u_r) &= \mu^{l-1}(v_{i,k}, u_r) \\
&= \cdots \\
&= \mu^{r_j+1}(v_{i,k}, u_r) \\
&= \mu^{r_j}(v_{i,k}, u_r) - \mu^{r_j}(v_{i,k}, u_{r_j}) \\
&= (\mu(v_i, u_r) - \mu(v_i, u_{r_{j-1}})) \\
&\quad - (\mu(v_i, u_{r_j}) - \mu(v_i, u_{r_{j-1}})) \\
&= \mu(v_i, u_r) - \mu(v_i, u_{r_j})
\end{aligned} \tag{12}$$

which completes the proof. □

Proof of Lemma 3:

PROOF. We prove by induction. Before the 1st iteration, it is clear that we have pushed a valid event with the largest ratio value into H during in the initialization step. Suppose before the i-th iteration, the valid event with the largest ratio value must be in H. We next prove that after updating H in the i-th iteration, all valid event candidates with the possibly largest ratio value must be in H.

Denote $\hat{v}_i$ as the event popped from H in the i-th iteration. First, if $\hat{v}_i$ is the only event in $\hat{S}_{u_r}$, the way we update H ensures that we scan through the remaining $V_r' \setminus \{\hat{v}_i\}$ events to push the next valid event candidates with the largest ratio values into H. Second, if $\hat{v}_i$ is the first but not the only event in $\hat{S}_{u_r}$, recall that $\hat{v}_{s_i}$ is the successor of $\hat{v}_i$ in $\hat{S}_{u_r}$. Notice that only the *inc_cost* values of the events in $\{\hat{v}_1, \hat{v}_2, \cdots, \hat{v}_{i-1}\}$ and $\{\hat{v}_{i+1}, \hat{v}_{i+2}, \cdots, \hat{v}_{s_i-1}\}$ will be changed when $\hat{v}_i$ is added into $\hat{S}_{u_r}$, and these events are not yet in H. Also, the way we update H ensures that the valid event candidates in $\{\hat{v}_1, \cdots, \hat{v}_{i-1}\}$ and $\{\hat{v}_{i+1}, \cdots, \hat{v}_{s_i-1}\}$ with the largest ratio values will be scanned. For the other events whose *inc_cost* values do not change, they have been scanned through in previous iterations. Therefore by induction, the next valid event candidate with the largest ratio value must be in H. Similarly, if $\hat{v}_i$ is the last but not the only event in $\hat{S}_{u_r}$, the way we update H ensures that we scan through all events whose *inc_cost* are changed and the next valid event with the largest ratio value must be in H. Finally, if $\hat{v}_i$ has a precedent $\hat{v}_{p_i}$ and a successor $\hat{v}_{s_i}$ in $\hat{S}_{u_r}$, we also scan through all events whose *inc_cost* are changed. Therefore, in all cases, the next valid event with the largest ratio value must be in H after we update H in the i-th iteration if it exists, which completes the proof. □

Online Video Recommendation in Sharing Community

Xiangmin Zhou
School of Computer Science and Info Tech.
RMIT University, Australia
xiangmin.zhou@rmit.edu.au

Lei Chen
Department of Computer Science and Engineering,
Hong Kong University of Science and Technology,
Hong Kong, China
leichen@cs.ust.hk

Yanchun Zhang
Centre for Applied Informatics,
Victoria University, Australia
School of Computer Science,
Fudan University, China
yanchun.zhang@vu.edu.au

Longbing Cao
Advanced Analytics Institute
University of Technology, Sydney, Australia
longbing.cao@uts.edu.au

Guangyan Huang
School of Information Technology
Deakin University, Australia
guangyan.huang@deakin.edu.au

Chen Wang
CSIRO, Sydney Australia
chen.wang@csiro.au

ABSTRACT

The creation of sharing communities has resulted in the astonishing increasing of digital videos, and their wide applications in the domains such as entertainment, online news broadcasting etc. The improvement of these applications relies on effective solutions for social user access to video data. This fact has driven the recent research interest in social recommendation in shared communities. Although certain effort has been put into video recommendation in shared communities, the contextual information on social users has not been well exploited for effective recommendation. In this paper, we propose an approach based on the content and social information of videos for the recommendation in sharing communities. Specifically, we first exploit a robust video cuboid signature together with the Earth Mover's Distance to capture the content relevance of videos. Then, we propose to identify the social relevance of clips using the set of users belonging to a video. We fuse the content relevance and social relevance to identify the relevant videos for recommendation. Following that, we propose a novel scheme called sub-community-based approximation together with a hash-based optimization for improving the efficiency of our solution. Finally, we propose an algorithm for efficiently maintaining the social updates in dynamic shared communities. The extensive experiments are conducted to prove the high effectiveness and efficiency of our proposed video recommendation approach.

Categories and Subject Descriptors

H.3.3 [**Information Storage and Retrieval**]: Information Search and Retrieval

Keywords

Online Video Recommendation; Social Relevance

SIGMOD'15, May 31–June 4, 2015, Melbourne, Victoria, Australia

http://dx.doi.org/10.1145/2723372.2749444.

1. INTRODUCTION

The popularity of online video shared communities has created an opportunity to share media information at an unprecedented scale. Users access to these communities, operate and comment on videos for various purposes such as entertainment, online news broadcasting and advertisement. In sharing communities, the behavior of people is highly affected by the recommendations from the system. According to a white paper released in February 2012 by Unruly Media, viewers enjoy online videos they discover from a recommendation more than ones they discover through browsing, which reports 65% of viewers who watched a recommended video enjoyed it, representing a 14% increase from 57% who enjoyed a video found through browsing [3]. Therefore, an appropriate recommendation is a promising way of increasing the viewing rate to specific media data, enhancing the effect of online news broadcasting and advertisement. Although many existing video sharing communities, such as Youtube, Netflix, MySpace and Google Video, have provided recommendation services, the recommendations on relevant videos are produced based on social texts. The content and social connections have not been fully exploited in the video recommendation so far.

In this paper, we focus on the problem of online video recommendation in a shared community like Youtube, where unregistered users can get accesses to social videos. Traditional recommendation systems generate the recommendations by matching the recommended items and the user input profiles, and deliver them to the appropriate users. However, in sharing communities, it is very common that unregistered users access to the social videos, where these users' profiles are unavailable. Some users are just beginners for a certain sharing community, and have no user history. Especially, in recent years, some unregistered new users may disable their cookies or use public machines when they get access to videos in sharing communities for the purpose of privacy protection [20]. The recent statistics data show that 19.1% users use the private browsing mode [2]. Therefore, for such cases, traditional recommendation is not workable any more. Unlike traditional recommendation using users' registered information, our video recommendation takes a user clicked video as the input, and returns a list of recommended videos that are relevant to the user's current view. Technically, our video recommendation is highly related to the video search in multimedia database field. From this point of view, techniques for video search can be extended for video recommendation task. But different from the video search which returns the matched clips in content of a video, our video recommendation system returns the relevant videos that include both the matched clips and those relevant but unmatched ones. Thus, directly using video identification methods will lose some relevant videos that are unmatched to the query. Fortunately, although many users may access the video content anonymously as the *subjects* receiving recommendation from the system, many other registered users comment on videos using their real identities, which provides important *social data source* in sharing communities. Exploiting the social information that named users provided is very promising for recommending videos to anonymous social users. Though Yang etc proposed to recommend online videos based on video content and relevance feedback [33], they have not considered the social information of videos in sharing communities.

Motivated by the limitation of traditional video search and recommendation systems, we propose a multiple feature-based video recommendation in sharing communities using the content and social connections. We first exploit a compact video signature over video segments to capture the spatial and temporal content information. The similarity between two signatures is measured to identify the matched videos that are similar in content with the query. Then we capture the social information of each video by extracting the social users who comment on it. The social information of a video reflects the users who are interested in it. The social similarity between two videos is identified by the Jacard similarity between their user sets. The final video recommendation is performed by a late fusion of the content and social features. Our contributions in this paper are summarized as follows.

1. We propose a new framework which exploits multiple content and social features of videos for video recommendation in sharing communities. While the content feature identifies the matched videos, the social connection captures the relevant unmatched clips.
2. We propose a new complementary video matching based on content and social fusion. The new approach well embeds the rich social information into video content, thus appropriate to the application of social video recommendation.
3. We propose a novel sub-community-based approximation relevance scheme (SAR) and a hash-based optimization for improving the efficiency of our framework. With the SAR, a robust user dictionary is constructed by extracting several sub-communities, and each user is mapped to its sub-community number. Accordingly the social context of each video is converted into a vector. The optimization strategy greatly improves the efficiency of social context vectorization.
4. Last but not the least, we propose a novel algorithm which well maintains the social updates in dynamic sharing social communities. We conduct extensive experiments on hundreds hours of real video data to verify the effectiveness and efficiency performance of the proposed solution.

The rest of the paper is organized as follows: Section 2 reviews the related research on social video recommendation. Section 3 describes the framework of the proposed social video recommendation system. We present our proposed Multiple Feature-based video recommendation approach together with our SAR and hash-based schemes over our relevance identification modal, and social updates maintenance algorithm in section 4. The high effectiveness and efficiency of our approach is evaluated in section 5. Finally, we conclude the whole work in section 6.

2. RELATED WORK

In this section, we review the existing research on two problems closely related to our work, including the video recommendation and near duplicate video detection.

2.1 Video Recommendation

Approaches have been proposed for video recommendation. In [29], Setten et al. use prediction strategies for personalized TV recommendation. In [8], Christakou et al. apply content-based and collaborative filtering to predict personalized movie recommendations. In [4], Baluja et al. presented a personalized approach which generates recommendations based on the analysis of the user-video graph for videos from Youtube. In [19], Luo et al. developed a personalized news video recommendation system, which first detects reliable news topics based on the multimodal information, and then integrates the topic network based on contextual relationship with the users' profiles considered for interactive navigation and exploration of news videos. In [17], a news recommendation was proposed by considering the item characteristics including the news content, access patterns, named entities, popularity and recency. Li et al model the news articles based on the contexts of users and articles [16]. Sedhain et al recommend content in Facebook by a social affinity filtering [22]. In [11], authors introduced a news video recommender system that exploits semantic augmentation of news stories, and represents dynamic user profile by capturing users' evolving information. In [9], the video recommendation system for Youtube was discussed. The system produces personalized recommendations based on users' activity on the site. All these approaches focus on the personalized recommendations, which recommend videos matching to users' profiles or interests, while not the item itself. In [39], a content-based framework VideoTopc was proposed for movie recommendation. VideoTopic exploits both visual features and textual features of videos to construct a topic model, which represents the video content and links to its user interests. The video recommendation problem is transformed into finding the videos that have minimal topic distribution difference with user interests. This topic model-based approach naturally links video content and user interests. However, the user interests need to be learnt from the topics of users' browsing history. In [34], a hybrid recommendation approach has been proposed for video recommendation over social networks by considering the user relationship strength and the interest degree of video. For a given user, the recommendation score of a video candidate is decided by the interest degree of the video by the user's friends, and the relationship strengths between the user and his friends. However, this approach requires the information of users who receive recommendations. Practically, most users access to video sharing communities anonymously, where users' profiles are not available for the system. This poses a challenge for personalized recommendations.

To handle the cases where users' profiles are absent, Yang et al. proposed to perform online video recommendation by exploiting textual, visual and audio information [33]. The relevance values from all modalities are fused to improve the results of recommendations by attention fusion function and relevance feedback. However, for the video recommendation in a shared social community, the feasibility of this approach has been challenged due to two reasons. First, it does not consider the social connection among users, which is an important characteristic of videos in sharing communities. Thus, the social relevance of videos can not be identified. Second, the existing work [33] focused on designing a multimodal relevance identification method, while the efficiency issue has not been addressed. In this work, we fully exploit the social connections attached to videos, and propose a set of query optimization techniques including the SAR scheme and chained hash-based optimization to overcome the disadvantages of the existing work.

2.2 Near Duplicate Video Detection

Video representation and similarity measure are two basic tasks in near duplicate video detection. Generally, based on the video representation, existing video detection approaches can be put into three categories, global feature-based [6, 13, 12, 24], local feature-based [15, 31, 36, 27], and signature-based [14, 40, 32, 35, 23].

Global feature-based approaches extracted visual features such as color histograms to represent frames, and construct compact representations over these visual features. Typical examples on global feature-based approaches include Video Signature (Visig) [6], Video Triplet (ViTri) [24], bounded coordinate system (BCS) [13] and video distance trajectory (VDT) [12]. In [6], Cheung et al. represent each video as a set of frame samples called Video Signature(ViSig), and perform video matching based on the percentage of similar frames shared by two sequences, which is further estimated by computing the percentage of similar ViSig frame pairs. In [24], Shen et al. estimate the distance between videos by comparing their video clusters and estimating the number of video frames shared by them. In [13], Huang et al. summarize each video as a single representation called bounded coordinate system (BCS) that captures the correlation of it. The video matching is performed by integrating the global difference between two frame sets, the content changing trends and ranges. In [12], Huang et al. describe a video as a series of video distance trajectories, and perform video matching using a weighted edit distance. However, due to the limitation of global visual features, these approaches suffer from severe information loss, leading to low effectiveness of video detection.

Local feature-based approaches extract visual features from a set of local interest points captured in each frame, and improve the efficiency of detection by effective search mechanisms or constructing compact representations over local descriptors. Recent examples on this line include local interest trajectory [15], Hierarchical detection [31], and multiple feature hashing [27]. In [15], Law-To et al. construct trajectories over local interest points of adjacent frames, and use a voting function based on the signal description, the contextual information and the combination of relevant labels for video matching. In [31], Wu et al. proposed a video matching that extracts a number of local descriptors from each keyframe, and compares two videos by calculating the matched local descriptor pairs shared by their keyframes. The search efficiency is improved by using a global feature based filtering before the local descriptor based matching. In [27], Song et al. proposed a multiple feature hashing based on both global and local features for near duplicate video detection. The comparison between two videos is performed over hash codes by approximating the common bits along all dimensions shared by them. In [36], Zhou et al. construct a tensor series over the local descriptors of each video, and perform Hamming based tensor series matching for near duplicate video identification. Using local descriptors, more discriminative information can be captured. However, these approaches either suffer from high computation cost [15, 31], the sensitivity of local descriptors over streams [36], or highly depend on the selected video training dataset [27], thus not robust in sequence detection.

Signature-based approaches extracted compact signatures from video frames or video segments to leverage the effectiveness and efficiency of detection. Typical signature-based approaches include color shift signature [40], cut signature [40], centroid signature [40], ordinal signature [14], sketch representation [32], STF-CE and STR-LBP signatures [23], video cuboid signature [35]. In [40], various types of compact signatures, such as cut length, color shift and centroid signatures, are used for video matching. Here, cut length signature is extracted by detecting the cuts in a video and counting the number of frames between two adjacent cuts. Color shift signature is obtained by detecting the color difference between neighboring frames. Centroid signature describes the shift of the lightest and darkest areas between neighboring frames. In [14], Kim et al. partition each keyframe into a number of small equal size blocks that are represented as ordinal signatures based on the average intensity values of these blocks. The comparison between two videos is performed by calculating the normalized distance of their ordinal signatures. In [32], Yan et al. proposed a frame partition based sketch representation and a set based measure for video matching over streams. In [23], Shang et al. proposed two compact signatures, STF-CE and STR-LBP, which use ordinal relations of keyframe blocks for video matching. While some signatures suffer from severe information loss [40], others are sensitive to the spatial editing of frames [14, 32, 23]. In [35], Zhou et al. proposed a video cuboid signature that captures the spatial and temporal information change of a video segment. The similarity between two video cuboid signatures is decided by the EMD distance between them, and the final video matching is performed by a set based measure with the similarity between each matched signature pair embedded. Video cuobid signatures capture the discriminative local information of videos, and the EMD-based signature set measure well handles the spatial and temporal editing of videos, thus more robust for video detection. Therefore, we will apply the video cuboid signature model and fuse the social information of videos for clip recommendation in sharing communities. The notation used in this paper is listed in Table 1 for easy reference.

Table 1: Notation

Notation	Meaning
Q, V	A video
q_f	The visual feature of a video
q_s	The social connection of a video
Sim	A social video relevance function
S	A list of videos
S_1, S_2	A signature series
D_V	A set of user ids
id_{Vi}	id of a user commenting v.
k	The number of sub-communities
K	The number of top score videos
w	The lightest edge weight
ω	The weight of the social relevance
s	A string
h_i	An intermediate hash value
$e,$	An edge between two users
$\{e_i\}$	An edge set
G_I	A UIG graph
U_i, U_j	Social users
n	Number of returned videos
N	Number of retrieved videos with rating score bigger than 4
γ	The rank of a returned video
$\mathcal{Q}$	The number of queries
$\mathcal{H}$	A chained hash table

3. FRAMEWORK OF OUR SOLUTION

This section describes the framework of our proposed approach for social video recommendation. In our social video recommendation, the input of our system is a user selected video document in a sharing community, which is represented as a pair $Q = (q_f, q_s)$, where q_f denotes its visual feature described as a signature series and q_s is its social connection described as a set ids of users commenting it. Given a social video Q selected by a user, a social video relevance function Sim, the task of video recommendation returns a list of videos S with the best relevance to Q, i.e., for any $V_1 \in S$ and $V_2 \notin S$, $Sim(Q, V_1) \geq Sim(Q, V_2)$ holds. The proposed system framework exploiting multiple features for social video recommendation is shown in Figure 1.

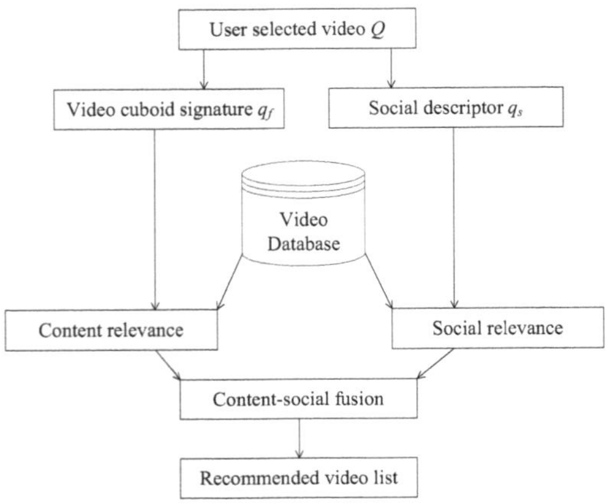

Figure 1: Framework of our social recommendation

Our social video recommendation system consists of three important parts. First, each video is represented using a compact signature to perform the content based relevance identification. Then, the social context of each video is described with a set of social users for social relevance identification. After that, the social relevance and content relevance are fused for the final video recommendation in a sharing community. Finally, based on our multi-feature relevance model, we further design a sub-community-based approximation relevance scheme, and a chained hashing scheme to improve the efficiency of our online video content-social based similarity recommendation.

4. MULTIPLE FEATURE-BASED RECOMMENDATION

Social videos are compositions of video sequences and social contexts, each delivers important information on the relevance of a selected clip. Therefore, multiple feature-based relevance is described by the combination of the relevance from all the features. We will detail the content and social relevance in this section.

4.1 Content Relevance

We aim to find the content relevance between a user selected clip and a video in a shared community. Because of the high complexity and huge amount of video data in sharing communities, the task of efficient content relevance identification has been challenging. To overcome the difficulties of this task, we need to find a number of video segments, and describe them compactly. Then, the similarity between two videos is decided based on the representations of their segments. We use the existing techniques, and focus on how to select a suitable approach for our purpose.

We identify content relevance of user selected clips based on video segments. Given a video, we exploit the state-of-the-art shot detection technique proposed in [18] to detect a number of cuts. A series of segments are then obtained by extracting the subsequences between adjacent cuts. These segments can be further represented for video matching using a good representation model. A typical representation is to describe each segment as its keyframe that is described by its global visual features [13, 38], local interest points [31, 37], or compact signatures [14, 40, 32, 35, 12, 36]. However, local interest points based approaches incur high computation cost, while using global visual features, such as color histograms, is neither discriminative enough nor robust to photometric variation and encoding methods. Signature based methods overcome the weakness of local feature-based and global feature-based methods, thus more applicable to content relevance identification.

Conventional video signatures include the ordinal signature, color shift signature, cut signature, local intensity shift signature and video cuboid signature etc. Among them, the ordinal signature is not robust to the frame editing in videos, while the global transformation of videos is well handled by it. The color shift signature is robust to different video transformation and frame editing operations, but not discriminative enough. Though the local intensity shift signature takes the advantages of both ordinal signature and color shift signature, it can not handle the content shift within frames. Video cuboid signature is a more advanced signature comparing with other signature representation models. It captures the spatial and temporal information of videos, and is robust to the content shift with the support of earth mover's distance over signatures. Considering the advantages of video cuboid signatures, we apply it to this work for the content relevance identification in social video recommendation. A video cuboid signature is constructed over a number of temporally consecutive keyframes, and consists of video cuboids that constitute spatially and temporally adjacent pixels. Given a video $q-gram$ consisting of q keyframes, its video cuboids are generated by first dividing each keyframe into a fixed number of equal-size blocks, and then merging the spatially adjacent similar blocks in a reference keyframe. Based on the variable-size blocks in the reference frame, video cuboids are produced by grouping the temporally adjacent blocks, and each is described as a pair (v, μ), where v is the average intensity change between temporally adjacent blocks and μ denotes its weight indicating the block size. To simplify the video cuboid signature, we use bigrams and each v is a single value.

The similarity between video cuboid signatures is measured by the EMD that permits the comparison between two signatures consisting of different numbers of video cuboids. The EMD of two signatures measures the minimal amount of work necessary to transform one signature into another. Formally, the EMD between two video cuboid signatures can be computed as follows [35].

Definition 1. Given two video cuboid signatures $C_1 = \{(v_{1i}, \mu_{1i})\}$ and $C_2 = \{(v_{2j}, \mu_{2j})\}$, $\forall 1 \leq i \leq |C_1| : \mu_{1i} > 0$ and $\forall 1 \leq j \leq |C_2| : \mu_{2j} > 0$ of normalized total mass $\sum_{i=1}^{|C_1|} \mu_{1i} = \sum_{j=1}^{|C_2|} \mu_{2j} = 1$, and c_{ij} the cost to transform a video cuboid unit $v_{1i} \in C_1$ to $v_{2j} \in C_2$, The EMD between them is defined as a minimization over all possible flows $F = [f_{ij}]$ under positivity constraints CPos, source constraints CSource and target constraints CTarget:

$$EMD_c(C_1, C_2) = \min_F \{\sum_{i=1}^{|C_1|} \sum_{j=1}^{|C_2|} c_{ij} f_{ij} | Constraints\} \quad (1)$$

with $Constraints = CPos \wedge CSource \wedge CTarget$:

$$\begin{aligned} &CPos : \forall 1 \leq i \leq |C_1|, 1 \leq j \leq |C_2| : f_{ij} \geq 0 \\ &CSource : \forall 1 \leq i \leq |C_1| : \Sigma_{j=1}^{|C_2|} f_{ij} = \mu_{1i} \\ &CTarget : \forall 1 \leq j \leq |C_2| : \Sigma_{i=1}^{|C_1|} f_{ij} = \mu_{2j} \end{aligned} \quad (2)$$

where c_{ij} defines how much dissimilarity one unit of flow from video cuboid v_{1i} to v_{2j} induces, f_{ij} is the fraction of flow units between v_{1i} to v_{2j} that minimizes the total dissimilarity, $CPos$ rules out negative flow, $CSource$ ensures that the total flow from cluster (v_{1i}, μ_{1i}) of C_1 is equal to (v_{2j}, μ_{2j}) and $CTarget$ restricts the total flow to (v_{2j}, μ_{2j}) of C_2. The similarity between C_1 and C_2 is derived from the EMD between them, and is computed by [35].

$$SimC(C_1, C_2) = \frac{1}{1 + EMD_c(C_1, C_2)} \quad (3)$$

Given two signature series, S_1 and S_2, the similarity between them is computed by an extended Jaccard similarity which incorporates the similarity between matched video cuboid signatures.

$$\kappa J(S_1, S_2) = \frac{\sum_{C_i \in S_1, C_j \in S_2} SimC(C_i, C_j)}{|S_1 \cup S_2|} \quad (4)$$

Video cuboid representation model has several advantages when processing short video segments. It captures the spatial and temporal information of a video segment locally by the intensity change of frame blocks over time. Moreover, since the intensity changes over time are invariant to global video transformations and the EMD based measure is robust to frame editing, video cuboid signature model is effective for processing our video segments with various transformation and editing operations. Different from global visual features that totally ignore the local information of frames, video cuboid signatures are extracted from keyframe blocks locally, thus more differentiable. Meanwhile, unlike local interest points that consider local information at a finer level, video cuboid signatures capture the local information of video segments at a coarser level, thus more robust to the feature variations over streams. Therefore, we select video cuboid signature together with its EMD based signature measure for video segment matching. Applying video cuboid signature model on the video segments, we can transform each video into a signature sequence for matching. To improve the efficiency of video signature sequence matching, we also apply the locality sensitive hashing based optimization strategy used in [35] and exploit LSB-index structure which is a B^+-tree-based hash index proposed in [28] for Z-order values of hash keys, to reduce the number of EMD-based signature measures.

4.2 Social Relevance

In this section, we first propose our social modeling together with the optimization schemes including the SAR and chained hashing schemes, for improving the social relevance identification cost. We then discuss the maintenance of sub-communities under social updates in dynamic environment.

4.2.1 Social Modeling

Using video cuboid signature model, the content similarity between videos can be captured to find the matched ones in content, identifying their content relevance. However, video recommendation applications concerns not only the content relevance of clips. There are still some videos which are relevant to the user selected clip, but unmatched to it in content, thus not searchable using content relevance. This has raised new challenge for effective social video recommendation. Fortunately, the interaction of social users on video data in shared communities provides rich social information that can be exploited to identify the relevant but unmatched clips from the aspect of social relevance.

Intuitively, when registered social users review some videos in shared communities, they tend to comment on those interesting ones to them. Meanwhile, a user is usually interested in certain types of media data. While users commenting to a single video have common interests to some extent, two videos commented by a group of common users are usually relevant to each other from some aspects. Thus, exploiting the social interaction of users on videos is a promising way of solving the social relevance problem in video sharing communities. We describe the social user interaction on a video as a social descriptor. Given a video V, its social descriptor is constructed by obtaining a set including its owner user and those users commenting it. The social descriptor of the video V is represented as a set of user ids, i.e. $D_V = \{id_{Vi}\}$, where id_{Vi} is the id of a user commenting V. We identify the social relevance between two videos based on the Jaccard similarity coefficient. Suppose that D_V and D_Q are the social descriptors of videos V and Q respectively, their social relevance is computed by the common users shared by their descriptors, which is defined as:

$$sJ = \frac{|D_V \cap D_Q|}{|D_V \cup D_Q|} \quad (5)$$

The social relevance reflects the number of common users interested in two compared videos. Practically, in video sharing communities, the number of comments to a single video is usually very large, especially for some popular videos. When using sJ measure for social relevance calculation, we encounter two challenges. First, the computation complexity of the measure is quadratic to the number of elements in two compared social descriptors. Second, the number of elements for comparison to the compared videos is usually very large, usually several hundreds to tens thousands, thus the computation cost for social relevance identification becomes prohibitively expensive. Next, we will estimate the sJ calculation by proposing two schemes, the SAR and chained hashing index, for fast social relevance identification, and discuss on how we handle social updates in dynamic environment.

4.2.2 Complexity Reduction

As discussed previously, in real applications, it is vital to reduce the complexity of social relevance identification for online video recommendation. We propose a scheme called sub-community-based approximation relevance (SAR) to reduce the computation complexity and the number of elements for comparison. The basic idea of SAR is to transform the user comparison in sJ calculation into the comparison over a sub-community level. SAR approximates the social relevance computation by three major steps: *sub-community extraction*, *social descriptor vectorization*, and *social relevance approximation*. The social users are first grouped into a small number of sub-communities based on their interests on videos in the whole collection. Then the social descriptor of each video is converted into a vector of user histogram over a small number of sub-communities. Finally the sJ between two descriptors is approximated based on the difference of their user histograms.

Sub-Community Extraction We propose a graph partition approach to discover a number of sub-communities related to the social users of the video collection. A user interest graph (UIG) is first constructed over all users of a video collection. It consists of a set of nodes that represent the social users of a video collection and are linked by a number of weighted edges. The weight of an edge linking two users denotes the number of common interested videos shared by them. Given a collection of 8 videos, $V_1, ..., V_8$, and 5 users, $u_1, ..., u_5$, suppose that we have their interest relationship as follows: $(u_1, < V_1, V_3, V_8 >)$, $(u_2, < V_3, V_8 >)$, $(u_3, < V_2, V_4, V_5 >)$, $(u_4, < V_1, V_4, V_5 >)$, $(u_5, < V_4, V_5, V_6, V_7 >)$, Figure 2 shows the UIG of the users of this collection.

Once the user interest graph is constructed over a set of social users, we can discover a number of sub-communities by graph partition. There are several existing algorithms, such as balanced min-cut and spectral clustering [30], for clustering graph nodes. The spectral clustering is a more advanced algorithm comparing with balanced min-cut clustering. However, the spectral clustering does not perform very well, because of the information loss in dimen-

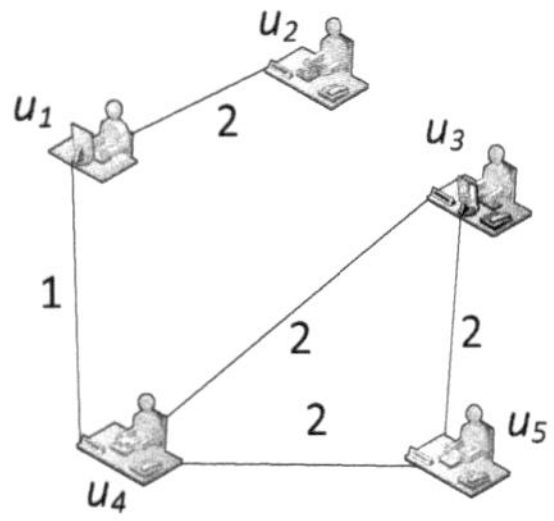

Figure 2: An example of user interest graph

Procedure SubgraphExtraction.
input: G_I - UIG graph k - Number of sub-communities
output: $S_{\mathcal{G}}$ - Set of sub-communities
1. Extract components disconnected with each other, put them in $S_{\mathcal{G}}$.
2. Let $p(G_I)$ be the number of connected components in G_I
3. **while** $p(G_I) < k$
4. $e \leftarrow$FindLightestEdge($S_{\mathcal{G}}$)
5. remove e from $S_{\mathcal{G}}$
6. Let U_i and U_j be two users connecting e
7. **if** U_i and U_j are disconnected
8. $p(G_I) \leftarrow p(G_I) + 1$
9. Put all connected components of G_I into $S_{\mathcal{G}}$
10. return $S_{\mathcal{G}}$

Figure 3: Extracting subgraphs.

sionality reduction over very large number of social users. We propose a new approach for sub-community extraction. Figure 3 shows the detailed algorithm for extracting k sub-communities from UIG. Given a UIG graph, and the number of sub-communities k, our algorithm performs in two steps. In the first step, we extract the originally separated components, each corresponds to a sub-community, and put these sub-communities from the original UIG graph into the sub-community set (line 1). In the second step, we recursively remove the edges with lowest weights from the user interest graph until k disconnected subgraphs are obtained (lines 2-9). As the distribution of user connections varies in the user interest graph, we permit the sub-communities to be of different sizes, so the users in a sub-community can be highly similar and high effectiveness can be achieved in recommendation. The set containing k subgraphs is finally returned after the extraction process stops (line 10). Each subgraph is a connected component in the whole user interest graph, and corresponds to a sub-community over the whole user space. We set the subgraph number k as a parameter for evaluation, which balances the sub-community size given a social dataset and fixes the dimensionality in social descriptor vectorization.

We evaluate the superiority of our algorithm over the best practice, the spectral clustering, using a standard metric called *Silhouette Coefficient*, where a bigger value indicates a better overall clustering result [10]. We randomly select 2000 video samples from our whole dataset, and cluster their users using our subgraph extraction approach and spectral clustering algorithm. We measure the average *Silhouette Coefficient* of the partition results produced by our approach and that produced by spectral clustering. The average *Silhouette Coefficient* of our results is 0.498, while that of spectral clustering is only 0.242. This has proved that our algorithm produces better clustering results.

Social Descriptor Vectorization After extracting k sub-communities by graph partition, we map the whole user space into a k-dimensional sub-community space. Users in different sub-communities are stored in a dictionary for later social descriptor vectorization. Using a k-dimensional dictionary, a social descriptor of n users $< u_1, ..., u_n >$ can be converted into a k-dimensional vector $< d_1, ..., d_k >$ by simply counting the number of users in each sub-community.

Social Relevance Approximation The social relevance can be approximated by comparing the social descriptor vectors of different videos. Given two videos Q and V, suppose that their social descriptor vectors are $< d_{Q1}, ...d_{Qk} >$ and $< d_{V1}, ..., d_{Vk} >$ respectively, the social relevance between them can be approximated as follows.

$$\tilde{sJ} = \frac{\sum_{i=1}^{k} \min(d_{Qi}, d_{Vi})}{\sum_{i=1}^{k} \max(d_{Qi}, d_{Vi})} \tag{6}$$

Using social relevance approximation, the computation complexity of social relevance identification is linear.

4.2.3 Social Relevance Optimization

We use hash table to organize the sub-communities for improving the mapping from a social user to its sub-community, thus further improve the efficiency of social relevance identification. To effectively index the social users in the sub-communities using hash, we need to create a hash structure and a class of hash functions that map each hash key into a hash code. We use chained hash tables to organize the social users because of its simplicity and flexibility on the element number in them. For hashing function selection, since the class of *shift-add-xor* string hashing functions satisfy four important properties including uniformity, universality, applicability and efficiency, and has been proved to be appropriate for practical applications [21], we use it for mapping social users to hash codes. Let $s = c_1, ...c_m$ be a string of m characters, v a seed and h_i an intermediate hash value after examination of i characters. The components in the class of *shift-add-xor* are defined as:

$$\begin{array}{rl} init(v) = v & (a) \\ step(i, h, c) = h \bigoplus (\mathcal{L}_L(h) + \mathcal{R}_R(h) + c) & (b) \\ final(h, v) = h \| T & (c) \end{array} \tag{7}$$

Here, $\mathcal{L}_L(h)$ denotes the left-shift of value h by L bits, $\mathcal{R}_R(h)$ is the right-shift of value h by L bits. Given a social user name, its hash code is computed by first generating an initial hash code using the equation 7 (a), then recursively computing the intermediate hash code over its first i characters using the equation 7 (b), and finally yielding the modulo value of the hash code over its m characters. For a given video collection, the social users can be organized as a chained hash table containing a list of hash buckets. Each element of the hash table is a triad formed as $< key, cno, nextptr >$, where key denotes the social user name, cno refers to the sub-community id of the key, and $nextptr$ is the pointer to the next element having the same hash code. Given a user in a collection, we first generate its hash code, by which its hash bucket is located. The triad of the user is then inserted at the head of this appropriate bucket. A chained hash table is formed by inserting the triads of all the social users in the data collection. Figure 4 shows a chained hash table of our social data collection.

Given a user selected social video, we first capture all the users interested in it. For each social user, we map it to a sub-community id by first mapping it to a hash bucket, and then comparing its user name with all users in this bucket. Using our chained hashing index structure, the mapping from a social user name to its sub-community id is quickly performed.

We estimate the time complexity for social descriptor vectorization based on approximation with the support of our hash structure. The time cost for the vectorization of a social descriptor is decided by the number of its social users, and the number of string comparison for users with hash collisions. Given a social descriptor containing n social users, suppose the average number of collisions for each social user is η, the cost of each string comparison is a constant β. Then the time complexity for vectorization is $n * \eta * \beta$. We ana-

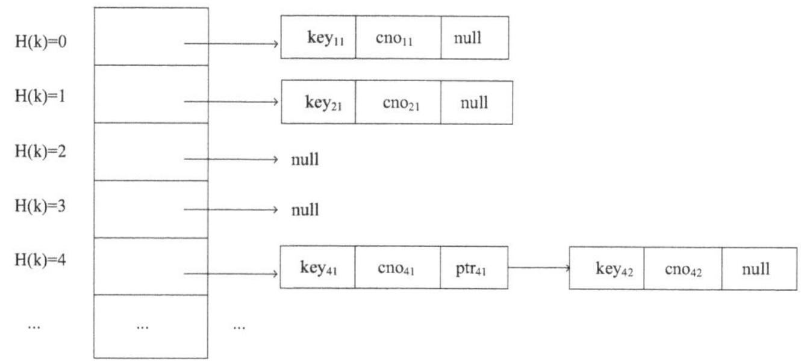

Figure 4: The chained hash table structure

lyze the space complexity of our optimization strategies. The space complexity for our social descriptor vectorization and optimization is determined by the size of video database and the number of social users in the database. Suppose that the database size is C_d, and the number of social users in database is C_u, let k be the number of sub-communities, then the space required to store the hash-tree and social descriptor vectors would be $O(C_d * k + C_u)$.

4.2.4 Social Updates Maintenance

This section discuss how to deal with the dynamic issues in video sharing communities. Practically, sharing communities are highly dynamic and social connections change frequently. Considering our social relevance model, the social connections between users are often updated as well. On the one hand, when new comments come, new user connections are built. On the other hand, as the interests of people may change over time, users in a sub-community may not comment the same types of videos any more after a time period. Accordingly, existing user connections may become invalid. We are concerned about how sub-communities are updated to reflect the most recent user connections, how the chained hash table is updated according to the sub-community changes, and how the social descriptor of a video is updated.

We maintain the sub-communities periodically by checking the status of each sub-community and its interactions with other sub-communities. Figure 5 shows the algorithm details for handling the social updates. Given a set of new social connections in the recent time period, our algorithm performs the maintenance mainly in three steps: (1) find recently formed bigger new sub-communities by checking if strong connections have been formed in the new time period, and union the multiple sub-communities if necessary (lines 1-13); (2) find sub-communities which can be split into multiple new sub-communities (lines 14-18); (3) update the index structure (lines 9, 19) and user descriptor vectors (lines 10, 20). We search the hash index, and find the biggest edge weight connecting two sub-communities and that belonging to each single sub-community respectively. Let the lightest edge of the connection in original sub-communities be w. If an edge between two sub-communities is bigger than w, we merge these two sub-communities, and update the chained hash table by replacing the ids of the two original sub-communities with a single new id. For a single sub-community, if the biggest edge between its users over the new social connection set is smaller than w, this sub-community will be further divided into two subgraphs. Once the sub-communities change, the social descriptors of interested videos are updated over the updated dimensions accordingly. As such, the sub-communities are well maintained to better reflect the recent social updates.

4.2.5 Social Update Cost Analysis

We estimate the cost of social update in our proposed algorithm. Let $E = \{e_i\}$ be a set of new connections. Denote the cardinality of the connection set as $|E|$. Suppose that we have the sub-community set undergoing union operation $\{g_{ui}\}$ and the size of its sub-community $|g_{ui}|$, the number of videos to g_{ui} denoted as $\mathcal{N}_{ui}$, the sub-community set undergoing split operation $\{g_{si}\}$ and the size of its sub-community $|g_{si}|$, the number of videos to g_{si} denoted as $\mathcal{N}_{si}$. The social update cost T_{mc} can be estimated as:

$$|E|*c_h + \sum_{i=1}^{|\{g_{ui}\}|} (|g_{ui}|*t_1 + \mathcal{N}_{ui}*t_2) + \sum_{i=1}^{|\{g_{si}\}|} (|g_{si}|*(t_1+t_3) + \mathcal{N}_{si}*t_2) \quad (8)$$

where c_h, t_1, t_2, t_3 are constant, which denote the cost used for the mapping from a social user name to its sub-community id, the index update on a sub-community element, the user descriptor update on a dimension, and the element checking in sub-community partition, respectively. Clearly, the cost of social updates maintenance is linear to the cardinality of the new connection set, those of the sub-communities with union and split operations, and the number of videos involved in social updates. In addition, as we adopt incremental updating strategy in our algorithm, the maintenance operation is only performed over the sub-communities involved in update operations and their corresponding videos, which are much smaller comparing with the whole video data collection. Therefore, the cost of social updates can be well controlled.

Procedure SocialUpdatesMaintenance.
input: $\{e_i\}$ - A set of connections in recent time period
$S_{\mathcal{G}}$ - Set of sub-communities
w - The lightest edge weight in the sub-communities
output: k updated sub-communities
1. Let U_i and U_j be two users connected by e_i
2. for each $e_i \in \{e_i\}$,
3. $SearchIndex(\{e_i\})$
4. $id_i \leftarrow MapUser2subCommunity(U_i)$
5. $id_j \leftarrow MapUser2subCommunity(U_j)$
6. if the weight of e_i is bigger than w
7. if id_i is not equal to id_j /*not in the same sub-community*/
8. $UnionSubCommunities(id_i, id_j, e_i)$
9. $UpdateIndex(id_i, id_j)$
10. $UpdateUserDescriptor(id_i, id_j)$
11. $SetStatusofSubCommunityAsSplit(id_i)$
12. else if id_i is equal to id_j /* in the same sub-community*/
13. $SetStatusofSubCommunityAsSplit(id_i)$
14. while $|S_{\mathcal{G}}| < k$
15. For all sub-commpunities with Split status
16. $id_i \leftarrow Getsub-communitywithLightestEdge$
17. $Splitsub-community(id_i)$
18. $S_{\mathcal{G}} \leftarrow PutNewsubCommunities(id_i)$
19. $UpdateIndex(id_i)$
20. $UpdateUserDescriptor(id_i, id_j)$
21. return $S_{\mathcal{G}}$

Figure 5: Maintaining social updates.

4.3 Content-Social Fusion

Once we define the content relevance and social relevance of videos, we can fuse them using a good integration function to perform effective recommendation in video sharing communities. Borrowing the idea of search fusion in [26], the relevance fusion can be simply performed by taking the average of the content relevance and social relevance, or retaining the higher relevance score between them. However, while the former approach ignores the importance difference of them in recommendation, the later one completely ignores one of them in relevance identification. As the content relevance and social relevance may contribute to the final recommendation to different extent, we need to find out the best parameter that leads to effective video recommendation.

In this work, we care about the video ranking based on their final relevance in recommendation, while the absolute relevance score of each video is ignored. Given two videos V and Q, let S_V and S_Q be their video cuboid signature series, and D_V and D_Q be their social descriptors, the overall relevance between them is defined as:

$$FJ(V,Q) = (1-\omega)\kappa J(S_V, S_Q) + \omega sJ(D_V, D_Q) \quad (9)$$

where ω is the parameter adjusting the weight of the content relevance and that of social relevance in the final relevance function. FJ fuses the content and social relevance, and takes the difference of their contributions in recommendation. We will discuss the selection of an optimal ω in the experimental study.

4.4 KNN Search

With FJ relevance function, we can identify the top score videos from a given data set, which considers both the video content and social information. To quickly identify the social relevance, we use k inverted files, each of which stores a sub-community id and a list of its corresponding videos $\{v_i\}$. For content relevance, we combine the locality sensitive hashing based technique in [35] and the LSB-index that is a B^+-tree structure in [28], to identify the nearest video cuboids of each signature in a query video. We use the existing index structure for content relevance, and extend it for multiple video cuobids and embed social relevance in KNN search. Specifically, we embed EMD-metric into L_1-norm space like [35], and use LSB-index to index Z-order values of points obtained by hash conversion as in [28]. Meanwhile, we record the video id of each data entry together with its video cuboid signature in our application. Similar to [28], we perform KNN search by continuously finding the next longest common prefix with the query. Unlike the KNN search which processes a single point query in [28], we handle a set of signatures in a query video at the same time to obtain their overall content similarity. Figure 6 shows the detailed algorithm for computing K top score videos.

Given a query video Q, our algorithm performs KNN search by three important steps. (1) Find a list video candidates based on social relevance by vectorizing query social descriptor, obtaining the video candidates related to the query social descriptor and ranking these video candidates (lines 1-3); (2) Obtain a set of video candidates based on the content relevance by searching the next longest common prefix with all query signatures (lines 5-6); (3) Refine the video candidates by first obtaining the most relevant candidate set, and then calculating the overall relevance between the query and each candidate based on FJ function (lines 7-9). The KNN_list is updated if the relevance score of the current candidate is bigger than that of its top K relevant video (line 10). The algorithm recursively performs the operations in steps (2) and (3), until all K top score videos are found (lines 4-11). The final search results are returned to the users (line 12).

Procedure K**TopScoreVideoSearch**.
input: $\mathcal{H}$ - A chained hash table I-Inverted file
$\mathcal{LSB}$ - An LSB-tree $Q :< Q_f, Q_s >$-A query video
K - Number of top score videos
output: KNN_list - A list of K top score videos
1. $\{d_{Qi}\} \leftarrow$ SocialDescriptorVectorization($\mathcal{H}, Q_s$)
2. $\{V_i\} \leftarrow$ GetSocialRelevanceCandidates($I, \{d_{Qi}\}$)
3. $\{V_{ri}\} \leftarrow$ RankRelevanceCandidates($\{V_i\}$)
4. **Repeat** /*SearchLSB($\mathcal{LSB}, Q_f$)*/
5. for each $Q_{fi} \in Q_f$, pick the leaf entry, e_{fi}, from $\mathcal{LSB}$ having the next longest common prefix with Q_{fi}
6. $\{V_{fi}\} \leftarrow$ GetVideoCandidates($\{e_{fi}\}$)
7. $V_n \leftarrow$ GetNextMostRelevantVideo($\{V_{ri}\}$)
8. for each $V_i \in \{v_{fi}\} \bigcup \{V_n\}$
9. ComputeFJ
10. UpdateKNN_list
11. **Until** K top score videos are found
12. return KNN_list

Figure 6: Computing K top score videos.

Table 2: 5 queries collected from Youtube

Query id	Query description
q_1	youtube
q_2	mariah carey
q_3	miley cyrus
q_4	american idol
q_5	wwe

5. EXPERIMENTAL EVALUATION

We demonstrate the high effectiveness and efficiency of our proposed content-social based approach for video recommendation in sharing communities.

5.1 Experimental Setup

We conduct the experiments on a 200-hour video collection that is collected by crawling Youtube website based on the recent popular queries [1]. We selected 5 most popular youtube queries listed in Table 2 to retrieve the top favorite videos of each query from Youtube. Following [31], we only kept the short clips with time duration no more than 10 minutes. For each video, we kept its context information including its owner user and the users who comment it as well. Following [33], for each query, we select the top two videos as the source videos and get 10 in total for recommendation.

We conducted a subjective user study. 10 evaluators majored in computer science, including eight graduate students and two undergraduate students, participated in the user study. Each individual is given the recommended videos returned by the three approaches in a random order. After viewing these videos, they were asked to give a rating score from 1 to 5 indicating whether the recommended videos are relevant to current source video. Here, higher score indicates more relevance.

5.2 Evaluation Methodology

We evaluate our proposed social video recommendation approach in terms of effectiveness and efficiency. First, we evaluate the effect of different content distance selection, the effect of two parameters, the relevance weighting ω and the number of sub-communities k, to obtain their optimal values. Then the effectiveness and efficiency of our recommendation approach are evaluated using the optimal parameter settings. For each source video, we use the following four schemes to recommend different video lists, and compare our two proposed alternatives,SR and CSF, and two existing video recommendation approaches, AFFRF and CR.

- AFFRF: Using text, visual, aural and relevance feedback for recommendation [33].
- CR: Using content relevance for recommendation [35].
- SR: Using social relevance for recommendation.
- CSF: Using content-social fusion for recommendation.

To evaluate the effectiveness of our recommendation approach, we use three metrics in [33], the average rating score (AR), average accuracy (AC) and mean average precision (MAP) of top 5, 10, and 20 recommended videos, as the measurements. Here, AC is defined as the proportions of videos with the rating bigger than 4 to all recommended videos. The mean average precision is a standard TRECVID metric, which is computed by the mean of non-interpolated average precisions (AP) of all queries [25]. Let n be

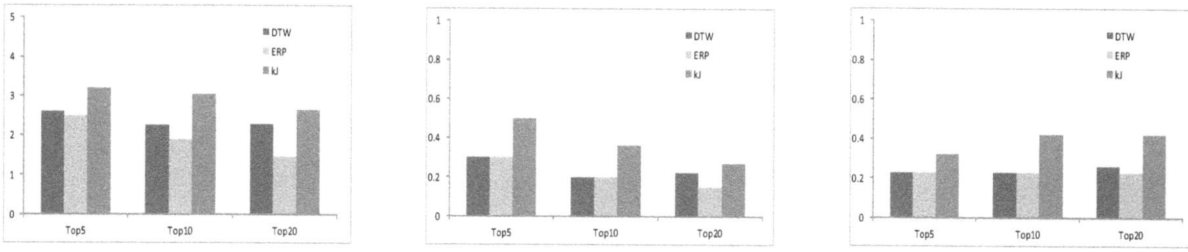

(a) AR (b) AC (c) MAP

Figure 7: Effect of content relevance measures

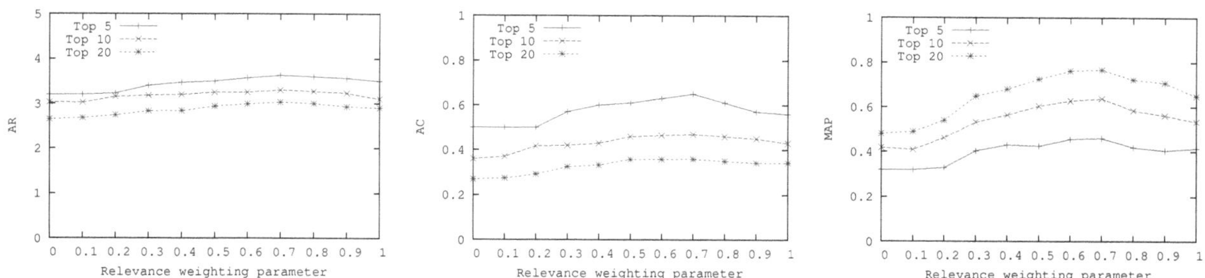

(a) AR (b) AC (c) MAP

Figure 8: Effect of ω

the number of retrieved videos, r_i the rating score of the ith returned video, N the number of retrieved videos with rating score bigger than 4. The formal equations for computing these three metrics are as below.

$$AR = \frac{\sum_{i=0}^{n} r_i}{n} \quad (a) \qquad AC = \frac{N}{n} \quad (b) \tag{10}$$

$$AP = \sum_{\gamma=1}^{n} (P(\gamma) * rel(\gamma)) \tag{11}$$

$$MAP = \frac{\sum AP_{\vec{q}=1}^{\mathcal{Q}} AP(\vec{q})}{\mathcal{Q}} \tag{12}$$

Here,γ is the rank, $rel()$is a binary function on the relevance of a given rank, $P()$ is the precision of the system at a given cut-off rank, $\mathcal{Q}$ is the number of queries.

We evaluate the efficiency of our approach over 200-hour real videos from Youtube in terms of time costs during the recommendation. We compare our SAR scheme, CSF-SAR, and our optimization using SAR and chained hashing, CSF-SAR-H, with the original content-social-based and the content-based recommendations. All the experiments were performed on Window 7 platform with Intel(R) Core(TM) i5-4570S CPU (2.9GHz)and 8GB RAM.

5.3 Effectiveness Evaluation

We first compare three existing content similarity measures for content relevance to select an optimal one as a base of our multi-feature based recommendation. Then we evaluate the effect of parameters by conducting content-social-based video recommendation. After that, we compare our proposed approach with the state-of-art video recommendation approaches by performing the video recommendation over the collected Youtube video dataset. Finally, we prove the scalability of our approach to social updates.

5.3.1 Effect of content relevance measures

We conduct experiments to test the effectiveness of the system using three typical content similarity measures including (1) ERP [5]; (2) DTW [7]; and (3) κJ [35], for selecting an optimal content relevance measure in our content-social fusion modal. Figures 7 (a)-(c) show the effectiveness comparison of three similarity measures in terms of average rating score, average accuracy and mean average precision respectively.

As we can see, κJ obtains the best effectiveness among three content similarity measures. This is because κJ performs measure in a more flexible manner comparing with ERP and DTW, thus better captures content relevance. For one thing, ERP and DTW perform video similarity measure by considering the temporal order of the whole sequence, similar videos may not be identified because of temporal sequence editing. For another, κJ considers only the temporal order in each video segment, which captures the temporal information of videos. At the same time, as an EMD-based measure, κJ allows the space shift of videos and does not care about the order between different segments, thus the video sequence and frame editing operations can be well handled. Based on the results, we select κJ as an optimal content relevance measure, which is the base of our multi-feature fusion model.

5.3.2 Effect of ω

We evaluate the effect of the relevance weighting parameter, ω, on the average rating score, average accuracy and mean average precision using 10 source videos. We vary the value of ω from 0 to 1. For each ω, we recommend top 5, top 10 and top 20 respectively. Figures 8 (a)-(c) show the ω changes on average rating score, average accuracy and mean average precision of our system.

As we can see, with the increasing of ω, the average rating score, average accuracy and mean average precision of our recommendation increase gradually from 0 to 0.7 to different extent, and reach to their peak values. With the further increasing of ω after 0.7, the effectiveness of our recommendation system drops under all three metrics. This is caused by two reasons. On the one hand, when ω is set to a value between 0 to 0.7, a bigger ω ensures that more information on social user connection is captured, which enhances the effectiveness of our system accordingly. On the other hand, after the peak point 0.7, content information of videos re-

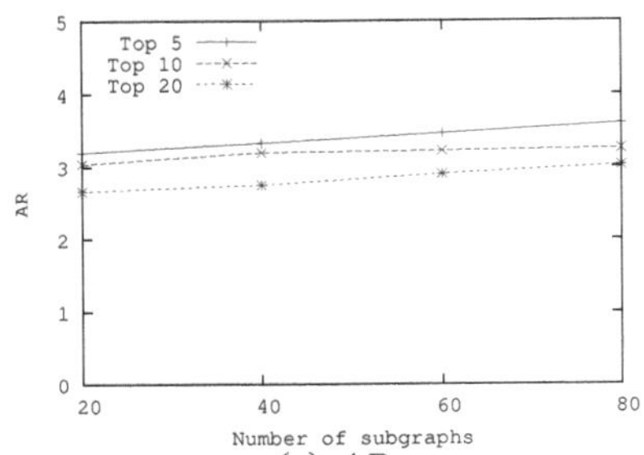

(a) AR

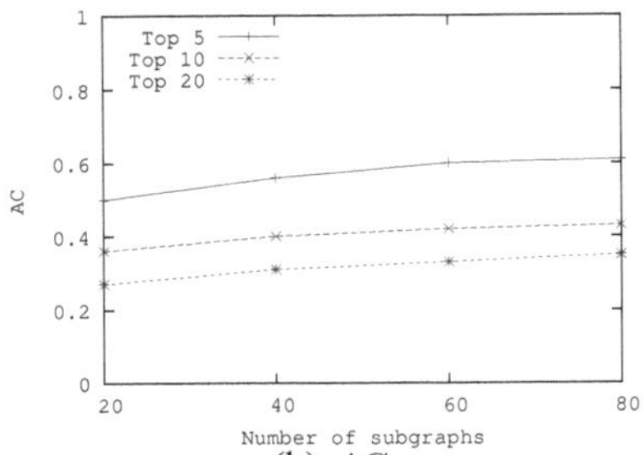

(b) AC

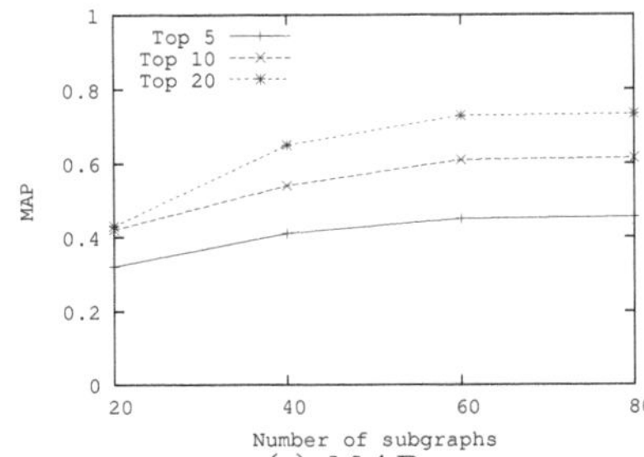

(c) MAP

Figure 9: Effect of k

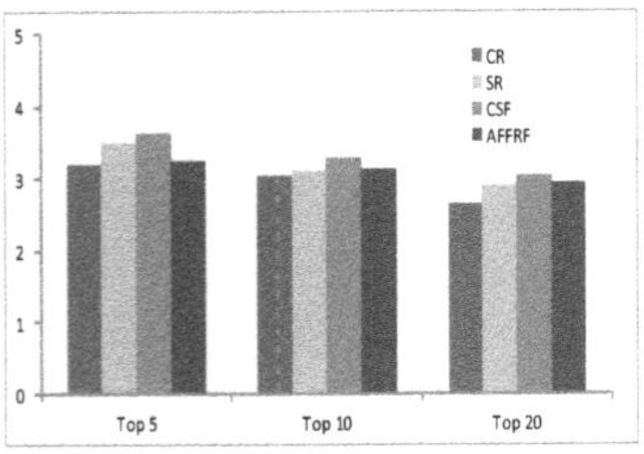

(a) AR

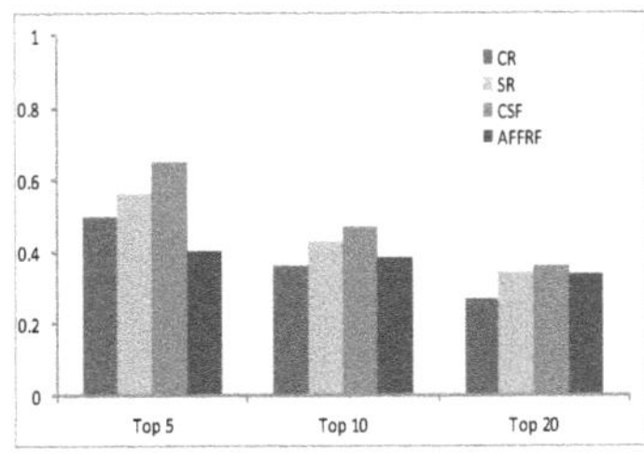

(b) AC

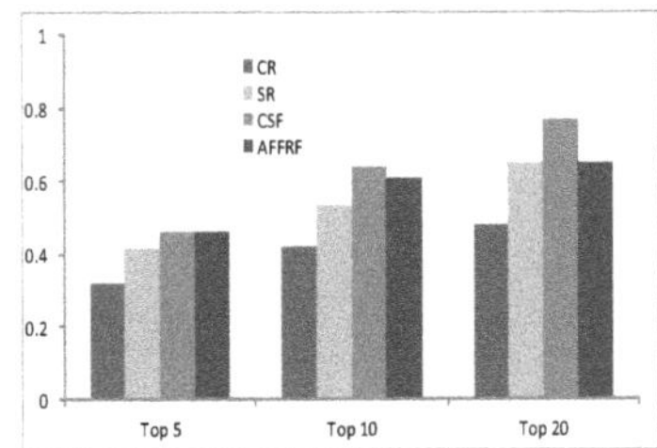

(c) MAP

Figure 10: Effectiveness comparison

duces because of the increase of social information. As a group of social users may be interested in videos on multiple unrelated topics, some videos with relevant content are replaced by those irrelevant ones with common social connections. Consequently, an ω bigger than 0.7 weakens the determinativeness of content relevance. Therefore we set ω to 0.7 as its default value to obtain an optimal effectiveness of the recommendation.

5.3.3 *Effect of* k

We evaluate the effect of the subgraph number in our SAR scheme, k, on the effectiveness of the system by applying our content-social recommendation. In this test, the k is varied from 20 to 80, and the optimal ω is applied.

Figures 9 (a)-(c) show the performance change trends of the average rating score, average and mean average precision of our approach. Clearly, with the increasing of the sub-community number in our SAR scheme, the effectiveness of our approach has been improved with the change of k from 20 to 60. The effectiveness on three metrics keeps steady when k is further increased from 60 to 80. This is mainly caused by the information loss of our SAR approximation scheme. When we transform the social user set matching in social relevance computation into the linear compact vector matching, we describe a group of interactive social users as their common community id, which is a user representation over a coarser level. A smaller k value produces coarser social user presentations, leading to more serious social information loss. With the increasing of k value from 20 to 60, the social information loss decreases, thus better effectiveness can be obtained at a bigger k value point. When k is changed from 60 to 80, most removed social connections are redundancy, which does not affect the effectiveness of our approach. Thus, considering a good balance of effectiveness and efficiency, the default value of k in our test is set to 60.

5.3.4 *Comparing Different Recommendations*

We conduct experiments to evaluate the effectiveness of four video recommendation approaches, including two proposed alternatives, SR and CSF, and the existing competitors for video detection and recommendation, CR and AFFRF. For our CSF, we set the parameters, ω and k, to their optimal values. Figures 10 (a)-(c) show the comparison of four approaches in terms of the average rating score, average accuracy, and mean average precision.

As we can see, our content-social based recommendation (CSF) achieves a better performance on all three metrics comparing with the other alternative, the social relevance (SR). This is because the CSF approach exploit the information from both the robust visual content and social user connections, which finds more relevant and rejects more irrelevant videos than other alternatives do in recommendation process. Comparing with two existing recommendation approaches, the content relevance (CR) and the multimodal with relevance feedback, our content-social based recommendation obtains much higher effectiveness because of the fully exploiting of social interaction information and robust video content in our approach. Although AFFRF uses multiple features in their recommendation, our content-social based recommendation still performs better in terms of effectiveness metrics. This is because of two factors. For one thing, videos are user uploaded data in Youtube, and a large portion of them have been edited or undergone different variations. The global video features like color histogram, and aural or text features are not fully reliable, which directly degrades the effectiveness of recommendation. For another thing, the social connections between users are not considered, thus some relevant videos with irrelevant content can not be identified. The high effectiveness of our content-social based recommendation has proved its superiority over other competitors.

5.3.5 *Effect of Social Updates*

We test the effect of social updates on effectiveness of the video recommendation. We divide the whole social collections into two parts: (1) a test set containing connections in recent 4 months; and (2) a source set containing connections appearing in a year before the 4 months. We measure the effectiveness of our recommendation system under social update operations by fixing our source set

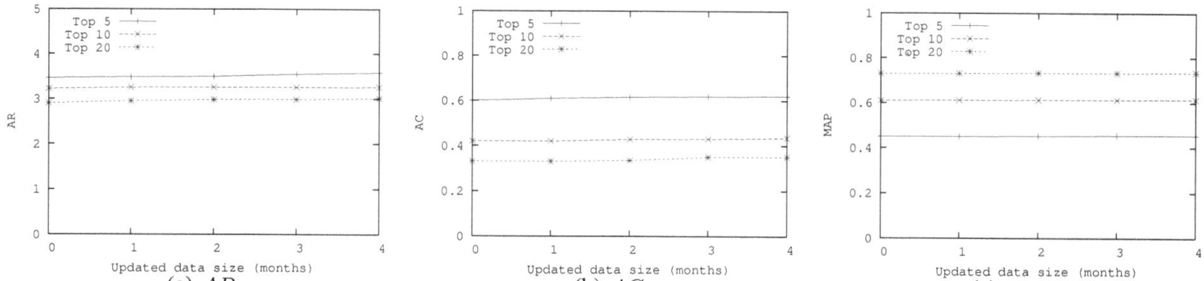

(a) AR (b) AC (c) MAP

Figure 11: Effect of social updates

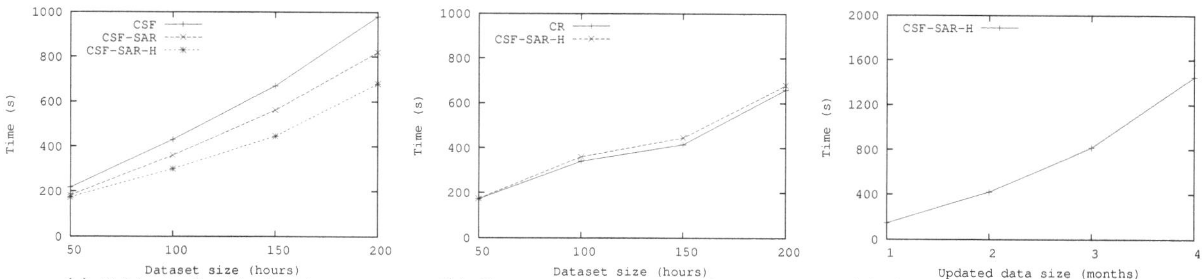

(a) $Effect\ of\ optimization$ (b) $Comparing\ recommendations$ (c) $Cost\ of\ updates\ maintenance$

Figure 12: Efficiency evaluation

and varying the test sets from 1 month to 4 months updates. Figures 11 (a)-(c) show the performance changes with respect to the size of social updates. As we can observe, with more social updates, the effectiveness of our approach remains steady. This has demonstrated the good scalability of our approach over high dynamic social environment.

5.4 Efficiency Evaluation

We evaluate the efficiency of our recommendation approach by first testing the effect of our sub-community-based approximation relevance scheme SAR and the SAR with chained hashing scheme SAR-H, then comparing our approach with the existing content-based recommendation (CR) [35], and finally testing the cost of social updates. Since there is no any strategy proposed for improving the efficiency of AFFRF-based recommendation [33], we omit the efficiency comparison with this approach.

5.4.1 Effect of Social Relevance Optimization

We evaluate the effect of our SAR scheme and chained hashing scheme by varying the video dataset size from 50 to 200 hours, and reporting the average time cost of video recommendation using different optimization approach: (1)CSF; (2) CSF-SAR; and (3) CSF-SAR-H, for each dataset size. Figure 12 (a) shows the time cost change trends of three different approaches.

As we can see, CSF-SAR-H performs best, followed by CSF-SAR. The original content-social based recommendation incurs highest time cost. With SAR, the recommendation cost has been reduced significantly comparing with the original content-social based recommendation. This is caused by two factor. For one thing, SAR scheme transforms the original string set to a video into a single vector, which greatly compresses the video representation. For another thing, while the original sJ computation suffers from the high computation complexity, which is exponential to the user set sizes of videos, the time complexity of social information matching under SAR scheme is linear. CSF-SAR-H further reduces the mapping cost of SAR scheme by exploiting a chained hash structure.

5.4.2 Comparing Different Recommendations

We compare our content-social based video recommendation with the state-of-the-art technique in terms of the overall time cost. We test the time cost of the recommendation over 50 to 200 hours video datasets. Figure 12 (b) compares our CSF-SAR-H approach with the content based video recommendation (CR) in terms of the time cost used for recommendation.

As we can see, our CSF-SAR-H performs as good as CR in terms of efficiency, although huge amount of social information is embedded in the process of recommendation to improve the effectiveness. This is because CSF-SAR-H adopts SAR scheme and chained hash structure, which greatly reduces the time cost of the social relevance computation and the mapping from social user sets to sub-community id vectors. Comparing with the content relevance computation in CR, the time cost of social relevance computation can be neglected. Thus, our CSF-SAR-H achieves competitive efficiency performance, while the effectiveness is improved greatly as demonstrated in Section 5.3.4. Consequently, our approach greatly improves the overall performance of the social video recommendation system.

5.4.3 Efficiency of Social Updates

We test the cost of social updates using different sizes of updates. We use the social connections to our 200 hours video dataset collected based on the five most popular queries. We divide the whole social collections into two parts: (1) a test set containing connections in recent 4 months (Sept.2014-Dec.2014); and (2) a source set containing connections appearing in a year before the recent 4 months. We fix our source set, and vary the test sets from 1 month to 4 months updates. The time costs of social updates over different time periods are reported in figure 12 (c).

As shown in the results, the time cost is only hundreds of seconds for maintaining social updates within 3 months, and about 1500s for 4 months. The results show that we can maintain the social updates efficiently as we adopt incremental maintenance strategy and hash scheme.

6. CONCLUSIONS

In this paper, we study the problem of video recommendation in sharing communities. First, we propose a novel multiple feature-based model for video relevance identification in social recommendation. Then, we propose a sub-community-based approximation relevance scheme for improving the social relevance computation. Finally, we propose to optimize the efficiency of our social video recommendation by designing a chained hash structure, and performing hash-based mapping from user sets to sub-community id vectors. In addition, the maintenance of sub-communities and our chained hash structure has been discussed for the dynamic environment with social updates. We have conducted extensive experiments to evaluate the effectiveness and efficiency of our proposed recommendation approach. The experimental results have proved that our proposed approach outperforms the existing methods in terms of the efficacy.

7. ACKNOWLEDGMENTS

The research presented in this paper has been supported via ARC projects DP140100841 and DP130102691, NSFC project 61332013, the Hong Kong SRFDP&RGC ERG Joint Research Scheme M-HKUST602/12, National Grand Fundamental Research 973 Program of China under Grant 2014CB340303 , Microsoft Research Asia Gift Grant and Google Faculty Award 2013.

8. REFERENCES

[1] https://spreadsheets.google.com/spreadsheet/pub?key =0am4ow7xs15awchn6z3hka0o4rzzzmktjskcwsfpnrgc& gid=1.

[2] https://www.elie.net/blog/privacy/19-of-users-use-their-browser-private-mode.

[3] http://www.marketingcharts.com/direct/online-viewers-prefer-socially-recommended-videos-21011.

[4] S. Baluja, R. Seth, D. Sivakumar, Y. Jing, J. Yagnik, S. Kumar, D. Ravichandran, and M. Aly. Video suggestion and discovery for youtube: taking random walks through the view graph. In *WWW*, pages 895–904, 2008.

[5] L. Chen and R. Ng. On the marriage of edit distance and L_p norms. In *VLDB*, pages 792–803, 2004.

[6] S.-C. S. Cheung and A. Zakhor. Efficient video similarity measurement with video signature. *IEEE Trans. Circuits Syst. Video Techn.*, 13(1):59–74, 2003.

[7] C.-Y. Chiu, C.-H. Li, H.-A. Wang, C.-S. Chen, and L.-F. Chien. A time warping based approach for video copy detection. In *ICPR*, pages 228–231, 2006.

[8] C. Christakou and A. Stafylopatis. A hybrid movie recommender system based on neural networks. In *ISDA*, pages 500–505, 2005.

[9] J. Davidson, B. Liebald, J. Liu, P. Nandy, T. Van Vleet, U. Gargi, S. Gupta, Y. He, M. Lambert, B. Livingston, and D. Sampath. The youtube video recommendation system. In *RecSys*, pages 293–296, 2010.

[10] J. Han. *Data Mining: Concepts and Techniques*. Morgan Kaufmann Publishers Inc., San Francisco, CA, USA, 2005.

[11] F. Hopfgartner. Adaptive interactive news video recommendation: An example system. In *SEMAIS*, pages 21–25, 2011.

[12] Z. Huang, H. T. Shen, J. Shao, B. Cui, and X. Zhou. Practical online near-duplicate subsequence detection for continuous video streams. *IEEE Trans. on Multimedia*, 12(5):386–398, 2010.

[13] Z. Huang, H. T. Shen, J. Shao, X. Zhou, and B. Cui. Bounded coordinate system indexing for real-time video clip search. *ACM Trans. Inf. Syst.*, 27(3):17:1–17:33, 2009.

[14] C. Kim and B. Vasudev. Spatiotemporal sequence matching for efficient video copy detection. *IEEE Trans. Circuits Syst. Video Techn.*, 15(1):127–132, 2005.

[15] J. Law-To, O. Buisson, V. Gouet-Brunet, and N. Boujemaa. Robust voting algorithm based on labels of behavior for video copy detection. In *ACM Multimedia*, pages 835–844, 2006.

[16] L. Li, W. Chu, J. Langford, and R. E. Schapire. A contextual-bandit approach to personalized news article recommendation. In *WWW*, pages 661–670, 2010.

[17] L. Li, D. Wang, T. Li, D. Knox, and B. Padmanabhan. SCENE: a scalable two-stage personalized news recommendation system. In *SIGIR*, pages 125–134, 2011.

[18] Z. Liu, E. Zavesky, D. Gibbon, B. Shahraray, and P. Haffner. At&t research at trecvid 2007. In *TRECVID*, 2007.

[19] H. Luo, J. Fan, and D. A. Keim. Personalized news video recommendation. In *ACM Multimedia*, pages 1001–1002, 2008.

[20] J. Mayer and J. Mitchell. Third-party web tracking: Policy and technology. In *Security and Privacy (SP), 2012 IEEE Symposium on*, pages 413–427, 2012.

[21] M. V. Ramakrishna and J. Zobel. Performance in practice of string hashing functions. In *DASFAA*, pages 215–224, 1997.

[22] S. Sedhain, S. Sanner, L. Xie, R. Kidd, K. Tran, and P. Christen. Social affinity filtering: recommendation through fine-grained analysis of user interactions and activities. In *Conference on Online Social Networks*, pages 51–62, 2013.

[23] L. Shang, L. Yang, F. Wang, K.-P. Chan, and X.-S. Hua. Real-time large scale near-duplicate web video retrieval. In *ACM Multimedia*, pages 531–540, 2010.

[24] H. T. Shen, B. C. Ooi, and X. Zhou. Towards effective indexing for very large video sequence database. In *SIGMOD*, pages 730–741, 2005.

[25] A. F. Smeaton, P. Over, and W. Kraaij. Evaluation campaigns and trecvid. In *MIR*, 2006.

[26] J. R. Smith, A. Jaimes, C.-Y. Lin, M. R. Naphade, A. Natsev, and B. L. Tseng. Interactive search fusion methods for video database retrieval. In *ICIP (1)*, pages 741–744, 2003.

[27] J. Song, Y. Yang, Z. Huang, H. T. Shen, and R. Hong. Multiple feature hashing for real-time large scale near-duplicate video retrieval. In *ACM Multimedia*, pages 423–432, 2011.

[28] Y. Tao, K. Yi, C. Sheng, and P. Kalnis. Quality and efficiency in high dimensional nearest neighbor search. In *SIGMOD*, pages 563–576, 2009.

[29] M. van Setten, M. Veenstra, A. Nijholt, and B. van Dijk. Prediction strategies in a tv recommender system - method and experiments. In *ICWI*, pages 203–210, 2003.

[30] U. von Luxburg. A tutorial on spectral clustering. *Statistics and Computing*, 17(4):395–416, 2007.

[31] X. Wu, A. G. Hauptmann, and C.-W. Ngo. Practical elimination of near-duplicates from web video search. In *ACM Multimedia*, pages 218–227, 2007.

[32] Y. Yan, B. C. Ooi, and A. Zhou. Continuous content-based copy detection over streaming videos. In *ICDE*, pages 853–862, 2008.

[33] B. Yang, T. Mei, X.-S. Hua, L. Yang, S.-Q. Yang, and M. Li. Online video recommendation based on multimodal fusion and relevance feedback. In *CIVR*, pages 73–80, 2007.

[34] X. Zhao, J. Yuan, R. Hong, M. Wang, Z. Li, and T.-S. Chua. On video recommendation over social network. In *Advances in Multimedia Modeling*, volume 7131 of *Lecture Notes in Computer Science*, pages 149–160. Springer Berlin Heidelberg, 2012.

[35] X. Zhou and L. Chen. Monitoring near duplicates over video streams. In *ACM Multimedia*, pages 521–530, 2010.

[36] X. Zhou, L. Chen, and X. Zhou. Structure tensor series-based matching for near-duplicate video retrieval. In *ACM Multimedia*, pages 1057–1060, 2011.

[37] X. Zhou, X. Zhou, L. Chen, A. Bouguettaya, N. Xiao, and J. A. Taylor. An efficient near-duplicate video shot detection method using shot-based interest points. *IEEE Trans. on Multimedia*, 11(5):879–891, 2009.

[38] X. Zhou, X. Zhou, L. Chen, Y. Shu, A. Bouguettaya, and J. A. Taylor. Adaptive subspace symbolization for content-based video detection. *IEEE Trans. Knowl. Data Eng.*, 22(10):1372–1387, 2010.

[39] Q. Zhu, M.-L. Shyu, and H. Wang. Videotopic: Content-based video recommendation using a topic model. In *ISM*, pages 219–222, 2013.

[40] J. Zobel and T. C. Hoad. Detection of video sequences using compact signatures. *ACM Trans. Inf. Syst.*, 24(1):1–50, 2006.

Large-scale Predictive Analytics in Vertica: Fast Data Transfer, Distributed Model Creation, and In-database Prediction

Shreya Prasad Arash Fard Vishrut Gupta Jorge Martinez
Jeff LeFevre Vincent Xu Meichun Hsu Indrajit Roy+

HP Vertica, +HP Labs

{shreya.prasad,afard,vishrut.gupta,jms}@hp.com
{jeff.lefevre,vincent.xu,meichun.hsu,indrajitr}@hp.com

ABSTRACT

A typical predictive analytics workflow will pre-process data in a database, transfer the resulting data to an external statistical tool such as R, create machine learning models in R, and then apply the model on newly arriving data. Today, this workflow is slow and cumbersome. Extracting data from databases, using ODBC connectors, can take hours on multi-gigabyte datasets. Building models on single-threaded R does not scale. Finally, it is nearly impossible to use R or other common tools, to apply models on terabytes of newly arriving data.

We solve all the above challenges by integrating HP Vertica with Distributed R, a distributed framework for R. This paper presents the design of a high performance data transfer mechanism, new data-structures in Distributed R to maintain data locality with database table segments, and extensions to Vertica for saving and deploying R models. Our experiments show that data transfers from Vertica are 6× faster than using ODBC connections. Even complex predictive analysis on 100s of gigabytes of database tables can complete in minutes, and is as fast as in-memory systems like Spark running directly on a distributed file system.

Categories and Subject Descriptors

H.2 [**Database Management**]: Systems; H.3.4 [**Information Storage and Retrieval**]: Systems and software—*distributed systems*

General Terms

Design, Performance

Keywords

HP Vertica; R; Machine Learning; In-database

SIGMOD'15, May 31–June 4, 2015, Melbourne, Victoria, Australia.

ACM 978-1-4503-2758-9/15/05 ...$15.00
http://dx.doi.org/10.1145/2723372.2742789.

1. INTRODUCTION

Data scientists rely on advanced statistical tools, such as R and MATLAB, for exploratory analysis: modeling historical data using different algorithms and then applying these models on new data. Since operational data is generally stored in databases, data scientists extract data from databases, import it in their statistical tool, and then use their tool for both creating and deploying models. This workflow is slow and cumbersome. Extracting data using ODBC connectors can take hours, and statistical tools are typically single process, in-memory systems that cannot handle 100s of gigabytes of data.

HP Vertica, Teradata, IBM Netezza, Pivotal Greenplum and others currently implement a handful of data mining algorithms inside the database [22, 14, 2]. Yet, data scientists continue to prefer their external statistical tools because of ease-of-use, the rigor of the algorithm implementations in these tools (for regulatory compliance), and availability of thousands of functions (such as 6000 packages in R). Given the popularity of statistical tools, vendors of these tools have enhanced their systems for parallel processing, which means the number of scalable algorithms will continue to grow in these systems [4, 9, 26]. Additionally, when in-database implementation of an algorithm is unavailable, data scientists are anyway forced to extract data from a database. Hence, in addition to extending in-database capabilities, there is a need to improve the performance of workflows that use both database and statistical tools. In this paper, we describe how HP Vertica integrates with R to solve the challenges of customers who use both database and statistical tools.

Using statistical tools, such as R, with a database is challenging for multiple reasons. First, there is high overhead in transferring data from the database and converting to R's format. Second, even if machine learning models are created in R, it is ill-suited for applying the model on large amounts of data in a timely manner. Third, when database and R instances run on the same node, resource contention can degrade performance.

1.1 Challenges

To understand the challenge in data transfer, consider the case when 50GB to 150GB of table data has to be transferred from a database to R. Figure 1 compares two cases (1) when data is transferred from Vertica to a single R instance and (2) when extensions to R, such as Distributed

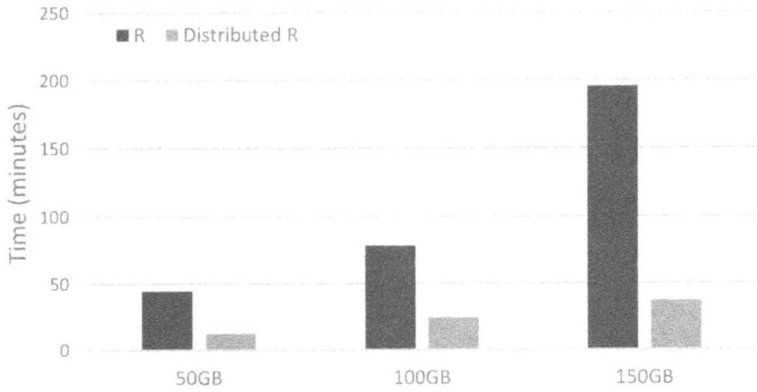

Figure 1: Extracting data from a database is slow. R and Distributed R use ODBC connections in this setup. Lower is better.

R [3], are used to extract data in parallel from a database. We use a 5-node database installation, where both R and Distributed R make connections via ODBC. Using a single R instance (a common scenario with customers), loading even 50 GB takes close to an hour. Parallel analytics engines, such as Distributed R (prior name Presto [26]) or ScaleR [9] may improve performance by starting multiple ODBC connections to the database. Even this approach has limitations. Multiple simultaneous SQL queries can overwhelm the database. For example, an installation of Distributed R on five 24-core servers will simultaneously start 120 ODBC connections, stressing the database. Additionally, ODBC connections destroy data locality when data is moved from the database to concurrent R instances. Figure 1 shows what happens if we launch Distributed R with 120 instances where each R instance concurrently requests $1/120^{th}$ of the table rows in the database. Even with all of this parallelism, loading 150 GB of data can still take close to 40 minutes. Ironically, many machine learning analyses, such as regression, can complete in a few minutes even at these data sizes (Section 7). Using these current approaches means that data scientists may spend more time waiting for data to load than to perform analysis.

Regarding the second challenge, extensions to R provide parallel algorithms that speed up model creation. However, models are typically created by training on a subset of data, while deployment of models can occur on terabytes of new data, and may have real-time constraints. Consider the case of media buying platforms (such as RocketFuel [7]), which bid on digital media advertisement in real time. These platforms may create offline regression models on user characteristics (such as websites visited and demographics), and then use these models to bid, in real-time, on advertisement slots auctioned by Google, Facebook, and other online services. While R is a good fit for offline model creation, it is ill-suited for real-time model deployment–transferring data from a database is slow, and so is managing newly arriving terabytes of data in R.

Finally, brokering shared resources between the database and R is challenging. Machine learning computations are generally compute as well as memory intensive. As an example, a single R instance can easily use 100% of a CPU core during computations, and have a large memory footprint. Running R computations on the same nodes as the database can lead to resource starvation and poor performance for both R jobs and database queries.

1.2 Contributions

This paper describes how HP Vertica solves the above challenges by integrating the Vertica database with Distributed R, HP's open source enhancement to single-threaded R. The integrated product leverages the strengths of both Vertica and R to provide the following features:

- Fast, parallel data transfer between Vertica and R
- Creation of distributed machine learning models in R using database tables
- In-database model deployment and prediction

For fast, parallel data data transfer, our key idea is to reduce the number of simultaneous database queries issued to fetch data, and still allow parallel transfer from Vertica to Distributed R. Only the master node in Distributed R needs to issue a SQL query and initiate data transfer. The new transfer mechanism works irrespective of whether R instances are on the same or different nodes as the database. Our methods enable users to choose between different policies to indicate their preference for maintaining data locality versus ensuring evenly partitioned data in Distributed R.

For model creation, data scientists can leverage high performance parallel algorithms in Distributed R to create models. We have added new data-structures to Distributed R so that parallel algorithms work on data loaded from the database.

For model deployment, we have extended Vertica to save R models and apply them on tables. Since models can sometimes be very large, and inappropriate for storing in table format, we serialize R objects and store them in Vertica's internal distributed file system. Models in Vertica can be accessed by the query engine to run distributed prediction functions. We use Hadoop YARN to broker shared resources when Vertica and Distributed R are installed on the same machines.

Our evaluation shows dramatic increase in performance of workflows that use R on database data. For instance, data transfer is now about 6× faster than using a traditional ODBC connector. As an example, 400GB of data can be loaded into Distributed R in less than 10 minutes. Additionally, in-database prediction takes only a few minutes on billions of rows. We also compare against Spark, an in-memory platform, which is 100× faster than MapReduce for iterative algorithms [28]. Spark loads data directly from Hadoop file system (HDFS) and is expected to be faster than executing machine learning via external tools (such as R) on database tables. Our results show that with Vertica integration, Distributed R executes machine learning algorithms as fast as Spark even when data resides in a database. These results are encouraging because, unlike the low overhead of loading data directly from HDFS, interfacing with a database is slower because the database first loads data from the local filesystem, deserializes and decompresses data, converts it to a standard format and then hands it to Distributed R for parsing and converting into R objects.

2. OVERVIEW

Vertica is a disk-based, columnar store with MPP architecture [23]. Distributed R, on the other hand, extends R

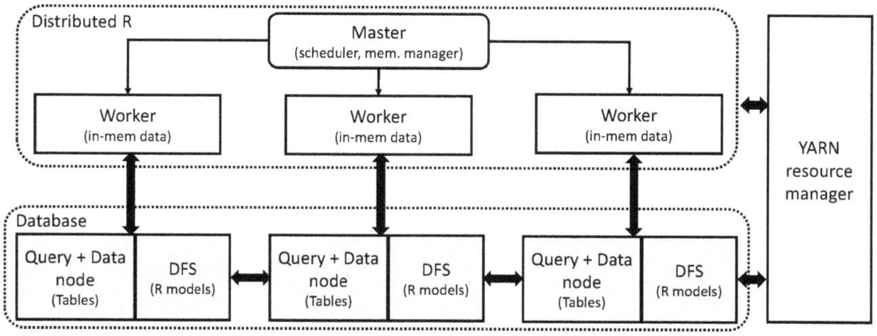

Figure 2: Architectural diagram of Vertica and Distributed R integration

with distributed, in-memory data structures (such as arrays and lists) to execute parallel machine learning algorithms [26]. Distributed R currently handles only data that fits in the aggregate memory of the cluster. For larger datasets, the operating system may invoke virtual memory swapping and substantially increase overheads. In this work we have integrated Vertica with Distributed R by adding functionality to both systems. The new techniques support fast data transfers, maintain data locality, and include the ability to deploy R models inside the database.

Figure 2 shows the architecture of the integrated product. Both Vertica and Distributed R run on commodity Linux nodes. For good performance, we recommend well-provisioned network such as nodes with 10Gb ethernet connection. Distributed R can be installed on either the same nodes as the Vertica database or on remote nodes. We use Hadoop YARN, a resource manager, to broker shared resources between Vertica and Distributed R. YARN uses Linux containers for isolation between processes, and can enforce memory and CPU usage restrictions. YARN ensures that Vertica queries and Distributed R jobs do not adversely interfere with each other.

To begin an R session, users connect to the Distributed R master node shown in Figure 2. During the workflow, data is transferred from Vertica's on-disk tables to Distributed R's in-memory data structures. The data transfer occurs in parallel. For high performance, data is read from local disks, adhering to the table segmentation scheme of Vertica. Once data is loaded in Distributed R, users can manipulate it using R functions and also apply distributed machine learning algorithms. After creating machine learning models, users can store them in the database for later use. If the model has a reference to data spread across Distributed R nodes, then the data is first fetched from Distributed R workers to the master, embedded into an R model object, and then transferred from the Distributed R master to the Vertica node. Within the Vertica node, R models are stored in an internal distributed file system (DFS) and hence accessible to the database query engine including user-defined functions.

The seamless integration between Vertica and Distributed R ensures that users can leverage the strengths of both systems. In a typical enterprise scenario, customers use standard ETL processes to first load data into Vertica. During a predictive analytics workflow, pre-processing steps such as feature extraction can be accomplished inside Vertica itself using SQL operators, sometimes in conjunction with user-defined functions. After pre-processing, machine learning

```
#Start Distributed R session
1 : library(distributedR)
2 : library(HPdregression)
3 : distributedR_start()
4 : ...

#Load features
5 : data<-db2darray(''mytable'',
          list(''def''), list(''A'',''B''))

#Run distributed regression and cross validation
6 : model<-hpdglm(data$Y, data$X,
            family=binomial(link=logit))
7 : cv.hpdglm(data$Y, data$X, model)
8 : print(coef(model))

#Deploy model to database
9 : deploy.model(model, 'rModel')

#Run in-db predictions
10: q<-''SELECT glmPredict(A,B
          using PARAMETERS model='rModel')
          OVER (PARTITION BEST) from mytable2''
11: res<-sqlQuery(conn,q)
```

Figure 3: Regression analysis. Illustrates data transfer, distributed model creation, and model deployment.

models can be created in Distributed R. For instance, Figure 3 shows an example R code which uses Vertica and Distributed R to perform distributed regression analysis. In lines 1-3, the user starts Distributed R from an R console. In line 5, the `db2darray` function selects features from a Vertica table and loads it in a distributed array in R. In line 6, `hpdglm` executes distributed logistic regression R. The user can then inspect the regression model, such as the coefficients using `coeff`, and include other types of analysis in R (line 8). Using `deploy.model` in line 9, the regression model is serialized and stored in Vertica. Finally, the user can run predictions inside the database using SQL commands, which can be invoked at the Vertica SQL prompt or through R (line 10-11).

3. VERTICA FAST TRANSFER

We have implemented a new data transfer mechanism, called Vertica Fast Transfer (VFT), that solves two challenges. First, it overcomes the problem that hundreds of simultaneous ODBC connections from Distributed R can

```
select ExportToDistributedR(col1, col2, col3,
        USING PARAMETERS DR_workers =
        'worker1:port|worker2:port',
        partitionSize=100000,
        policy = 'uniform')
      over(PARTITION BEST) from Samples;
```

Figure 4: SQL query issued internally to initiate data transfer

overwhelm the database and make transfers slow. Second, it provides the ability to optimize data transfer for different partitioning policies such as those preserving locality or balancing load. To understand the second challenge, consider the case of multiple R instances connecting to a database. As each instance loads data from the database table, data locality is destroyed. For example, the first R instance will request the first N rows of a table (e.g., 1 to 1 million rows), the second instance will request the next N rows (e.g., 1 million to 2 million rows), and so on. However, the first million rows may be spread across the database nodes (depending upon the segmentation scheme). Extracting these rows from multiple nodes and transferring it to each R instance hurts data locality and increases transfer overheads.

Vertica Fast Transfer has two components. On the database side, once a data request arrives from Distributed R, Vertica starts parallel data streams to Distributed R nodes. Vertica user-defined functions handle these streams and also determine the data partitioning scheme. On the Distributed R side, data streams are stored in-memory, optionally combined, and then converted into R objects. All of these steps are hidden from the user by a single line of R function, i.e., `db2darray` on line 5 of Figure 3.

3.1 Extracting tables

Initially data resides as tables in Vertica and is stored as *segments* on the database nodes. After transfer to Distributed R, the data becomes part of distributed datastructures (such as arrays). To depict that the data distribution may be different in Distributed R compared to the original database table, we call chunks of data local to Distributed R nodes as *partitions*. As an example, a 5-node Distributed R cluster may load a database table as an R array with 5 partitions. The union of these partitions correspond to the complete data in the table.

To initiate data loading, the Distributed R master node issues a single SQL query to Vertica. At the same time, Distributed R workers start listening for network connections from Vertica processes. The SQL query invokes a Vertica user-defined function, `ExportToDistributedR` to start data transfer. The query also relays meta-data information that is used in subsequent steps to perform the parallel data transfer. Figure 4 shows the three key arguments that are included in the `ExportToDistributedR` function. First, network information such as the hostname and ports of the Distributed R workers, is passed. This information tells Vertica which R instances to connect to. Second, approximate sizes of partitions that R instances expect, is provided. Partition sizes are calculated by dividing the the number of rows in the Vertica table by the total number of R instances waiting to receive the data. This calculation is performed by the Distributed R code that invokes the data transfer. Partition sizes are used as hints by Vertica to determine how much

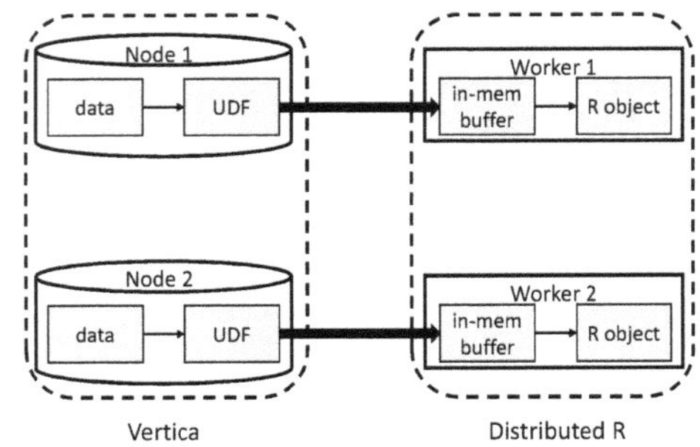

Figure 5: Locality preserving data transfer policy

data should be buffered before transferring to R instances. Third, the transfer policy argument determines how data should be spread across R instances.

Once all data transfer related information is received, Vertica spawns multiple instances of user-defined functions (UDFs) to extract data from its columnar storage. UDFs on each database node read a unique segment of the table stored on that node. The partitioning policy determines how the database table should be split for each UDF instance to operate. Generally, the `PARTITION BY` clause on a particular table column is used. However, in many cases there is no natural column to partition the table, and the only requirement is to transfer table contents to Distributed R without ordering constraints. In such cases, Vertica's `PARTITION BEST` scheme is appropriate as it processes data that is local to each Vertica node and sends it to the corresponding R instance. Using this scheme, we avoid the costly data movement of simultaneous ODBC connections that fetch ordered sequence of rows from a table. Vertica's `PARTITION BEST` takes into account resource availability, such as CPU and memory usage, to determine the optimal number of UDF instances to spawn. The UDFs use in-memory buffers to stage table contents before pushing them to R instances.

3.2 Data distribution policies

Vertica can currently transfer data to Distributed R using one of the two policies– *locality preserving* and *uniform distribution*. As shown in Figure 5 and 6, these policies provide users control over how data is distributed. Figure 5 illustrates the locality preserving policy. This policy adheres to the data segmentation on Vertica, i.e., there is one-to-one mapping of data transfer between Vertica nodes and Distributed R workers. In this policy, all UDF instances executing on Vertica node 1 will send data to Distributed R worker 1 and so on. This approach is used when Vertica and Distributed R have the same number of nodes. In the common case, where Vertica and Distributed R are installed on the same nodes, there is additional advantage as network overhead is minimized.

While data locality is important, it can sometimes lead to load imbalance and hence poor performance of machine learning algorithms in Distributed R. For example, if tables in Vertica have skewed segmentation, once loaded in Distributed R, some R instances will hold more data than others. During the execution of distributed machine learning algorithms, this data skew can lead to straggler tasks, and hence poor performance [20]. Figure 6 illustrates the uniform distribution policy, which addresses the issue of data

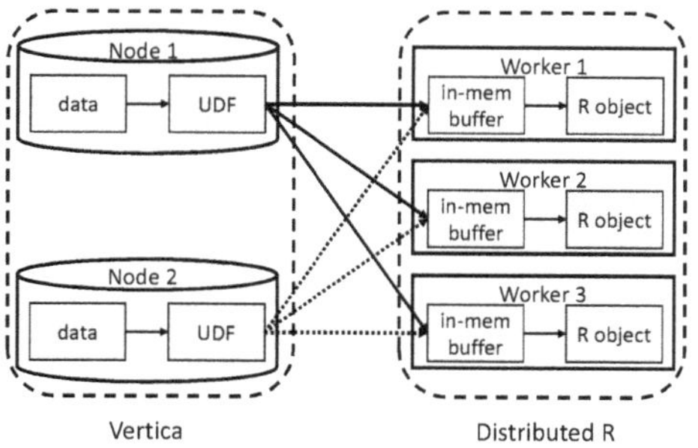

Figure 6: Uniform distribution data transfer policy

skew. The key idea is to sprinkle data across Distributed R workers such that data distribution is largely uniform, i.e., each R instance will contain the same amount of data. In this policy, each UDF instance connects and transfers data equally to Distributed R workers in a round-robin fashion until all local table data has been processed. This policy can be employed irrespective of the relative number of Distributed R and Vertica nodes.

3.3 Receiving data in R

As each Distributed R node receives data from Vertica, it stores them as in-memory data files (typically in /dev/shm). For parallelism, each Distributed R node uses a threadpool to accept data streams from multiple Vertica UDF instances. The conversion of incoming data into distributed data-structures happens in two steps. First, an empty distributed data-structure (such as a distributed array) is creates in R. This empty data-structure will have a symbol table in the Distributed R master node, which points to empty partitions on worker nodes. Once R instances on the workers receive enough rows from Vertica, the in-memory files are converted into R objects and assembled into partitions. Thus, the empty pointers in the distributed data-structure start pointing to the now filled partitions. At the end of this stage, data from Vertica is available for use by Distributed R algorithms.

4. NEW DATA STRUCTURES ADDED TO DISTRIBUTED R

Distributed R enhances R's data structures such as arrays, data-frames, and lists to store data in-memory across nodes. Data in Distributed R is partitioned by rows, columns, or blocks (sub-matrices). Using these data-structures, R programmers can manipulate remote data and express distributed algorithms. For example, to add two distributed arrays, programmers write a R function that takes corresponding partitions of the two arrays and adds them. In this section, we describe novel additions to Distributed R for integrating with Vertica. To simplify the discussion we focus on distributed arrays. We first discuss the existing state of distributed arrays and then describe the enhancements.

In current distributed arrays, all partitions, except for the last one, are of the same size. The last partition may be slightly smaller if the total number of rows in the data is not divisible by the number of partitions. Figure 7 shows an example where the input table has 2 columns and 6

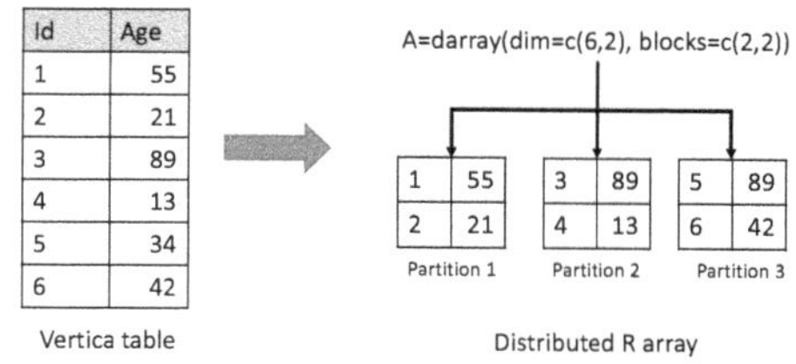

Figure 7: Distributed arrays originally supported only equal sized partitions

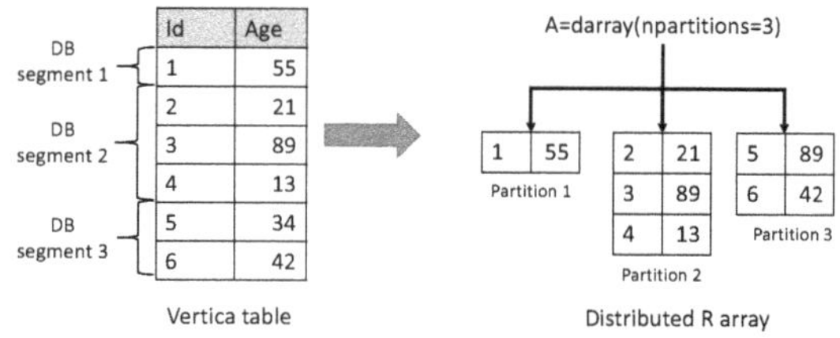

Figure 8: New data-structures now handle arrays with different partition sizes

rows (ignoring the names of the columns). The programmer can declare an array using `A = darray(dim=c(6,2), blocks=c(2,2))` and load the input data into Distributed R. This array definition creates a distributed array of size 6×2, where each partition is a 2×2 sub-array. Therefore, the array has equal sized partitions.

Forcing partitions to be the same size has multiple advantages. First, R programmers can treat distributed arrays just like normal R arrays. For example, the syntax of declaring distributed arrays (`darray(dim=,blocks=)`) is same as R arrays, except that `blocks` represents the partition size. Second, in many distributed algorithms different arrays may need to be co-partitioned, i.e., partitioned in the same manner for parallel processing to occur. As an example, to add distributed arrays, the arrays should be partitioned in the same manner (such as by rows) and be of the same size. It is fairly simple to use `blocks` to declare arrays that have the same partition size. Finally, knowledge of array dimension and partition sizes during declaration simplifies how Distributed R allocates and manages its memory space.

To integrate with Vertica, we need to handle arrays with different partition sizes. In fact, partition sizes are not known at the time distributed arrays are declared. Instead, partition sizes become available once data has been transferred from Vertica to Distributed R. The reason for the different partition sizes is that the Vertica table segments present on each node depend on the segmentation scheme and may contain different numbers of elements. Therefore, when using the *locality preserving* data transfer policy, partitions of the distributed array correspond to table segments and will be of uneven size. Figure 8 shows an example where an input table is initially stored in a 3-node Vertica database. In this case the first row of the table is in database node one, the next three rows are in the second node, and the remaining in the last node. If we want to maintain data locality while loading data in Distributed R, we need distributed data-structures that can store different sized partitions in R.

Functionality	Description
`darray(npartitions=)`	Create a distributed array with specified number of partitions
`dframe(npartitions=)`	Create a distributed data-frame with specified number of partitions
`dlist(npartitions=)`	Create a distributed list with specified number of partitions
`partitionsize(A,i)`	Return size of ith partition or of all partitions if i is missing.
`clone(A,nrow=,ncol=)`	Return another object with the same structure, such as number partitions, as input A .

Table 1: New language constructs in Distributed R

To handle different sized partitions, we have added new data-structures in Distributed R. Table 1 lists the new data-structures and helper functions in Distributed R. Users can declare distributed arrays without providing any size information (**darray(npartitions=)**). After declaration, meta-data related to **darray** is created on the Distribute R master node, but no memory is reserved on the workers to store data contents. Users can call R functions to either generate data for each partition or load data from Vertica. Even though each partition can be of different size, Distributed R checks for conformity between adjacent partitions. For example, if data is row partitioned, each partition may have variable number of rows, but the same number of columns. These checks ensure that arrays constitute well-formed matrices.

Figure 8 illustrates an example of array partitions when data has been loaded from Vertica to Distributed R. The Distributed R array has three partitions, each of which is of a different size. The first array partition contains only one row which is the data present in the first segment of the database. The second and third array partitions contain three and two rows respectively, which correspond to the remaining two database segments.

We have implemented multiple machine learning algorithms in Distributed R that use these new data-structures. In many of these algorithms, intermediate steps require arrays which have the same partitioning scheme as other arrays. Since arrays can have hundreds of different sized partitions, we provide high level functions such as **clone** to copy the structure of an existing array.

Figure 9 illustrates how a table from Vertica is loaded into a distributed array **X**, in order to run algorithms. The first step, **X<-db2darray(..)**, loads data from the table *Samples* to the array **X**. The array **X** has two partitions but each with different number of rows. Next, a user may run the **Y<-clone(..)** command to create a vector **Y**. **Y** has the same number of partitions as **X**, same number of rows, one column, and the partitions are co-located with those of array **X**. In the figure, the Distributed R memory manager is located on the master node. The memory manager tracks the location and meta-data of each partition.

5. IN-DATABASE MODEL DEPLOYMENT AND PREDICTION

After creating machine learning models in Distributed R, data scientists typically use the model for predictions. We have added new features in Vertica to store and apply ma-

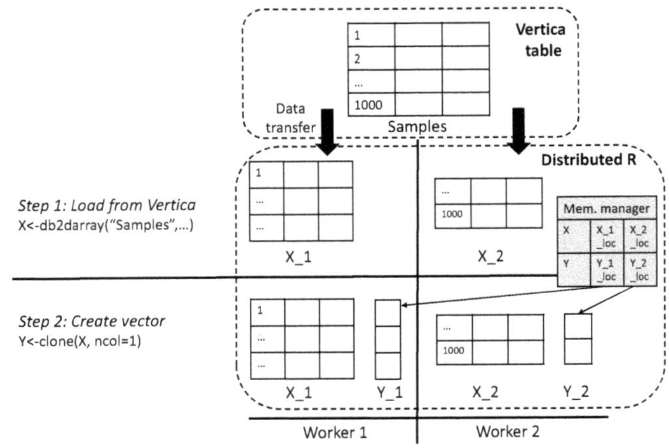

Figure 9: Distributed arrays with different partition sizes

```
=> select * from R_Models;

model  | owner | type        | size | description
-------------------------------------------------
model1 | X     | kmeans      | 100  | clustering
model2 | Y     | regression  |  20  | forecasting
```

Figure 10: Vertica R models table

chine learning models in the database. Saving models in Vertica eliminates the need to move data to an external analytical tool to perform predictions. Therefore, models can be applied on terabytes of data as well as on newly arriving data which is streamed into the database.

Once a model has been created in Distributed R, users can deploy them in the database using the **deploy.model** function. Users simply pass the R model as well as a name with which the model can be referred to (e.g., Figure 3 line 9). Internally, models are first serialized and then transferred to the database using a Vertica user-defined function (UDF). Since models can be large (sometimes gigabytes), we don't store them as part of a regular table. Instead, models are stored as binary blobs in Vertica's distributed file system (DFS). The Vertica DFS was primarily created for storing unstructured data that are accessible by the query engine. The DFS can replicate files across nodes to ensure that they are available at all nodes. While models are stored in the DFS, meta-data related to the models are stored in a database table called **R_Models**. Figure 10 shows an example of what the model table may contain. Models can be assigned security permissions to grant access or modification rights to database users. Models stored in the DFS provide the same fault-tolerance guarantees as Vertica tables.

Users can explore models and apply them on tables by providing R functions that perform predictions. Prediction functions are algorithm specific because both the data contained in the model, and how it should be used depends upon the machine learning algorithm. As an example, a K-means clustering model may contain information about centers while a regression model may contain only coefficients. Applying a K-means model on new data involves calculating distance from the centers while for linear regres-

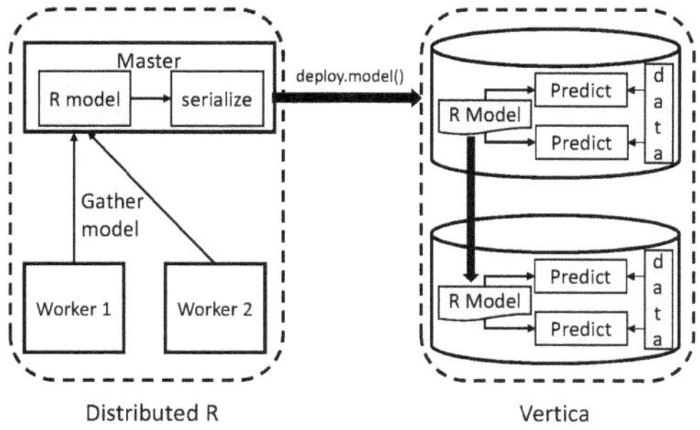

Figure 11: Model deployment and prediction

sion coefficients have to be multiplied with values in a row. We have added prediction functions in Vertica for common machine learning models such as clustering, regression, and randomforest. Users have the flexibility to create their own prediction functions for custom models and register them with Vertica.

Figure 11 illustrates the complete workflow of how models are created in Distributed R and then deployed in Vertica for predictions. If the content of a machine learning model is distributed across Distributed R workers, the master first gathers the model from R workers, and then sends them to one of the Vertica nodes. The Vertica DFS internally replicates the model, and makes it available to different nodes for prediction functions. When prediction functions are invoked, Vertica starts user-defined functions that first retrieve the models from DFS, deserialize and load them in R, and call the prediction function on the input data. The Vertica query planner starts many parallel instances of user-defined functions. The amount of parallelism is dependent on resources available and how the input table is partitioned. When the table is well partitioned among the nodes of the Vertica cluster, a near linear speedup can be achieved through parallel prediction.

6. RESOURCE MANAGEMENT

Distributed R and Vertica can be deployed on the same node or on separate nodes. There are advantages and disadvantages to both setup options. Using just a single set of nodes means that in many cases network overhead is minimized and transferring data from Vertica to Distributed R is fast. Node consolidation also leads to better resource utilization so that the database and R processes can share resources when needed. The disadvantage of such an approach is that resource isolation is a thorny issue. Under heavy usage, both SQL queries and machine learning processes will see performance degradation, especially when resources are insufficient. Deploying Vertica and Distributed R on separate nodes can be considered a case of static resource allocation. It ensures that machine learning analysis does not affect production SQL queries. However, if machine learning analysis is infrequent or SQL queries occur in bursts, node resources remain idle and underutilized.

We use Hadoop's YARN resource manager for allocating and isolating resources. YARN uses a two level scheduler, supports different allocation policies such as capacity and fairness, and is cognizant of data locality. To use YARN, each framework requires an application manager which makes requests to YARN for resources. Instead of

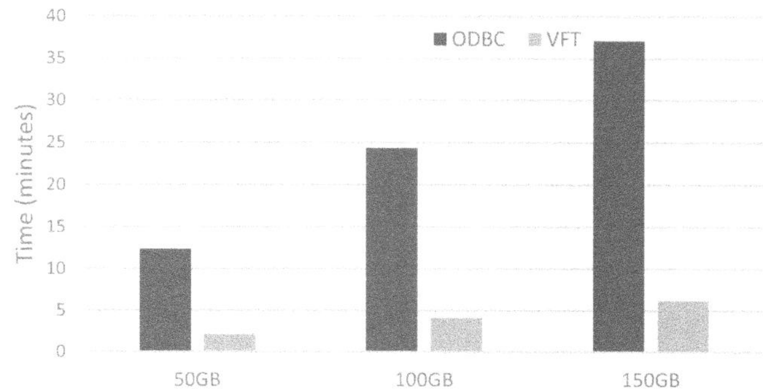

Figure 12: ODBC vs. Vertica Fast Transfer in a 5-node cluster. Lower is better.

creating a new resource manager, we leverage YARN because it is a natural choice for multi-engine software stacks.

Since releasing resources and tearing down a database is costly, Vertica requests resources from YARN for long term use. Distributed R, on the other hand, requests resources from YARN whenever a user starts a session. When starting a Distributed R session, users can specify resources such as the number of cores or amount of memory to be used in that session. These user specified resources are requested from YARN, with a preference for data locality with Vertica. When scheduled on the same nodes, Vertica and Distributed R processes are isolated using Linux `cgroups` [6]. These enforcement mechanisms ensure that each process is restricted to the allocated amount of CPU and memory usage.

7. PERFORMANCE BENEFITS

By integrating Vertica and Distributed R, we address two major customer complaints– extracting data from databases is slow and R cannot be used for analysis on really large data. In this section we empirically evaluate the benefits of our integration.

Setup. Our experiments use a cluster of 24 HP SL390 servers running CentOS 6.4. Each server has 24 hyper-threaded 2.67 GHz cores (Intel Xeon X5650), 196 GB of RAM, 120 GB SSD, and are connected with full bisection bandwidth on a 10Gbps network. We use Vertica 7.1 and Distributed R 1.0.0. For the comparison study with Spark, we use Spark 1.1.0 running on HDFS. HDFS is set to the default 3-way data replication. Spark machine learning algorithms are from the MLlib package which uses optimized linear algebra libraries.

7.1 Vertica Fast Transfer

The aim of our new Vertica Fast Transfer (VFT) mechanism is to ensure that data can be loaded in an external analytics engine in a matter of minutes. Figure 12 compares the performance of loading data in Distributed R using parallel ODBC connections versus VFT. In this experiment, we use a 5-node Vertica cluster, with Distributed R installed on a separate 5-node cluster. For VFT we use the locality-preserving policy. Distributed R starts 24 R instances on each node, and each R instance connects using an ODBC connection or uses the VFT mechanism. We vary the Vertica table size from 50 GB to 150 GB data (approximately 1 billion to 3 billion rows). The results show that VFT can load datasets as large as 150 GB in less than 6 minutes, com-

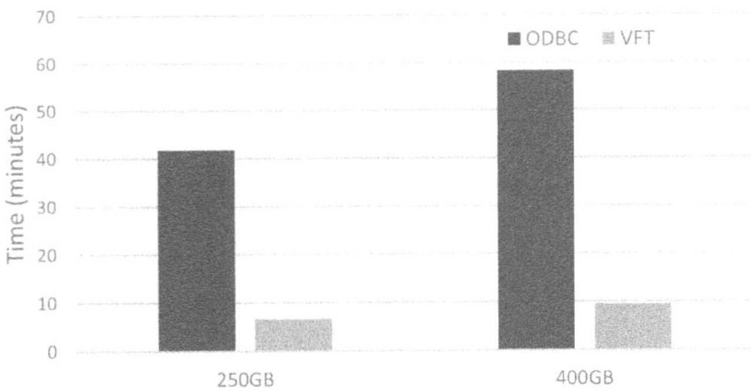

Figure 13: ODBC vs. Vertica Fast Transfer in a 12-node cluster. Lower is better.

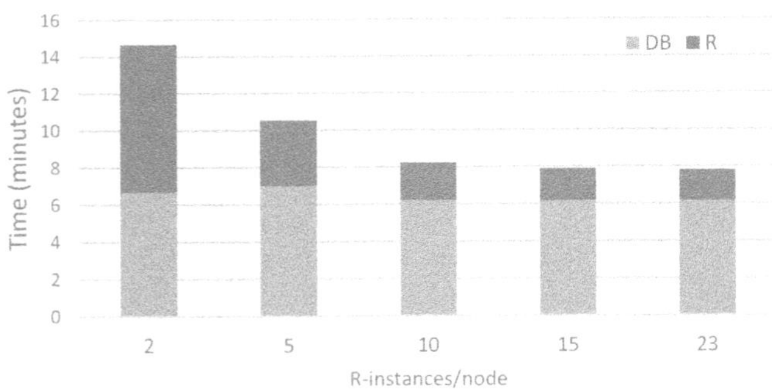

Figure 14: Time breakdown in Vertica Fast Transfer. 12-node cluster setup with 400 GB data.

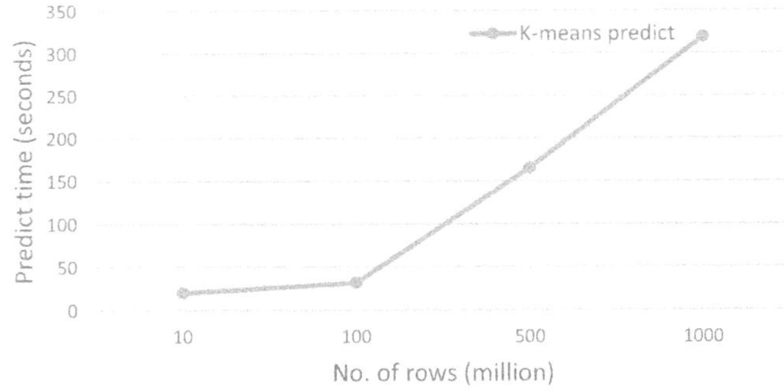

Figure 15: Scalability of in-database K-means prediction.

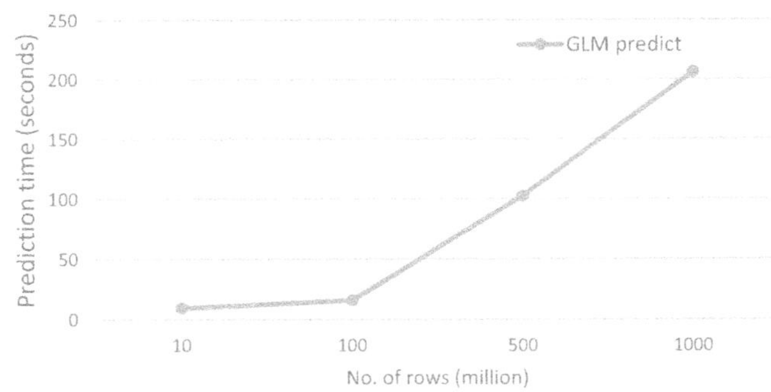

Figure 16: Scalability of in-database linear regression prediction.

pared to about 40 minutes in the case of ODBC connectors. We noticed that running Distributed R and Vertica on the same servers has similar performance, which means that the network is not a bottleneck. Instead, disk, database, and R execution are the bottlenecks.

Figure 13 shows similar results on a 12-node cluster and with up to 400 GB size tables. For the ODBC case, Distributed R will spawn 288 (12*24) connections to the database. Unfortunately, even with these many parallel connections and a large database cluster, it takes almost an hour to load 400 GB of data. With VFT, the load time is less than 10 minutes. Figure 14 shows a breakdown of the time spent in VFT, as we increase the number of R instances on each server. The *DB* part includes time taken by Vertica to read 400 GB data from disk, serialize, and send it across the network. The R part includes the time taken by Distributed R instances to receive data, buffer it, and finally convert to an R object. The results show that when there are only a couple of R instances per server, almost half of the transfer time is spent in buffering data and converting into R objects. Time taken by the database is constant and independent of the parallelism in Distributed R. The reason is that the database, irrespective of Distributed R, uses the same amount of parallelism and resources as specified by its query planner. As we increase the number of R instances (more parallelism in Distributed R), the time to create R objects decreases.

7.2 Scalable model deployment in Vertica

Once machine learning models are created, they can be stored in the database for later use. Customers can, therefore, use Vertica itself for predictions. To measure the performance of in-database prediction, we use a 5-node Vertica cluster, and populate tables with six columns and up to a billion rows. We test the performance of prediction on two machine learning models, K-means and linear regression.

Figure 15 shows the time taken to apply the K-means model on Vertica tables. A K-means model contains the final centers into which the training data was clustered. By applying the predict function (`KmeansPredict`), each point in the table is mapped to its nearest cluster center. For each row in the table, `KmeansPredict` calculates the euclidean distance of the point to the centers. The prediction function runs in parallel inside Vertica and, as shown in Figure 15, takes less than 20 seconds to execute on 10 million rows. As we increase the table size to a billion rows, the prediction time increases to 318 seconds. The execution time shows close to linear scaling because both the dataset and execution time grows by approximately 100×.

Figure 16 shows a similar behavior for linear regression. The linear regression model consists of coefficients that define a line best fitting the training data. The Vertica predict function (`GlmPredict`) applies these coefficients on the input table and outputs the response value. As shown in Figure 16, Vertica takes less than 10 seconds to run prediction on a 10 million row table. Even on a 1 billion row table, it takes only 206 seconds to complete prediction. Similar to K-means pre-

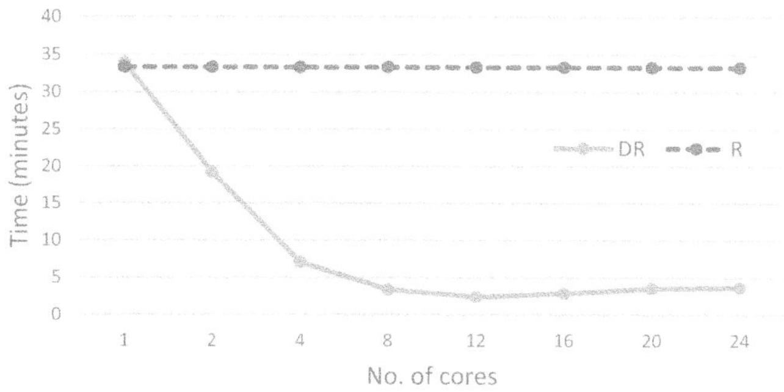

Figure 17: Distributed R vs. R: K-means clustering on a single node. Lower is better.

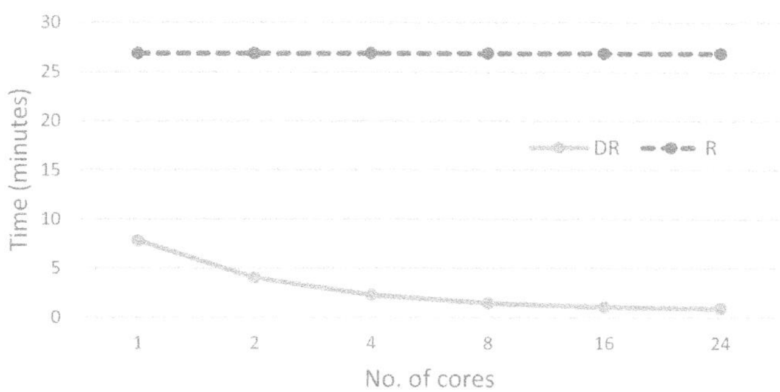

Figure 18: Distributed R vs. R: Linear regression on a single node. Lower is better.

diction, the linear regression prediction function shows near linear scalability as the dataset size is increased.

7.3 Comparison with R and Spark

Vertica's integration with Distributed R not only helps users overcome the limitations of R, but also allows them to efficiently analyze their data stored in the database. We use experiments to show how our solution compares against the state-of-the-art.

7.3.1 Advantages over R

R, due to its single-threaded nature, has limitations regarding both the dataset size and performance. HP Vertica Distributed R solves many of these limitations by scaling R to multi-core and multi-node settings. We have open sourced different clustering, classification, and graph algorithms in Distributed R, and made them available on GitHub [3]. This section provides evidence of the performance and scalability benefits of Distributed R. Here, we use K-means and linear regression as example machine learning applications. We exclude the time taken to load data from Vertica because single-threaded R, using one ODBC connection, takes a long time to load from a database (as shown earlier in Figure 1).

K-means clustering assigns points to one of K groups based on their similarity. In each iteration, points are first mapped to their closest centers and then new centers are calculated by averaging the groups. In this experiment, we set the number of centers, i.e., K, to 1000 and use a synthetic dataset with 1 million points, each with 100 features, to compare the performance of R and Distributed R on a sin-

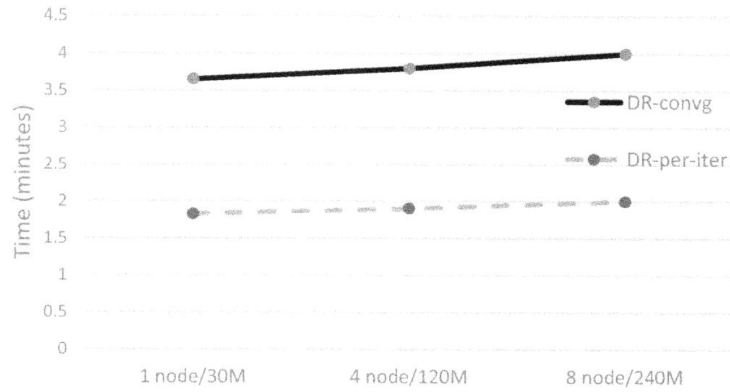

Figure 19: Scalability of linear regression in Distributed R. Both per-iteration and convergence time are shown. Lower is better.

gle node as we vary the number of cores from 1–24. Figure 17 plots the time taken per iteration for both R and Distributed R . Figure 17 shows that R takes approximately 35 minutes to complete an iteration of K-means, even as the number of cores is increased. In contrast, on a single node Distributed R can reduce the per-iteration time to less than 4 minutes by using 12 or more cores. The performance plateaus beyond 12 cores because the node has only 12 physical cores and the K-means algorithm is compute bound. Overall, Distributed R shows 9× speedup over stock R by using 12 cores.

We also compare against R using regression analysis, which is widely used by financial firms for forecasting, such as predicting sales based on customer characteristics. Figure 18 compares the performance of regression on a dataset with 100 million rows and 7 columns. On this dataset, R takes more than 25 minutes to converge to the result. In comparison, Distributed R takes less than 10 minutes even with a single core. The reason for this difference is because R uses matrix decomposition to implement regression, while Distributed R uses the Newton-Raphson technique [27]. Even though the final answer is the same, these techniques result in different running time. Irrespective of the implementation technique, Distributed R shows good single-core performance as well as scalability with the number of cores. As the number of cores is increased from 1 to 24, the execution time of Distributed R drops from about 8 minutes to less than a minute, representing a 9× speedup.

Scaling on multiple nodes. While R is restricted to a single node and single core, Distributed R can scale horizontally and utilize multiple nodes to analyze multi-gigagbyte datasets. Figure 19 shows how distributed linear regression scales on upto 8 nodes. For the experiments, we synthetically generated datasets by creating vectors around coefficients that we expect to fit the data. This methodology ensures that we can check for accuracy of the answers by Distributed R. We use 100 features per dataset, and the number of rows are 30M, 120M, and 240M for 1, 4, and 8 nodes respectively, representing a proportional data increase per node. Figure 19 shows that Distributed R completes each Newton-Raphson iteration in less than 2 minutes, and converges in just 4 minutes (2 iterations).

7.3.2 Comparison with Spark on HDFS

Due to the prevalent belief that loading data into a database and then exporting data out of a database is slow,

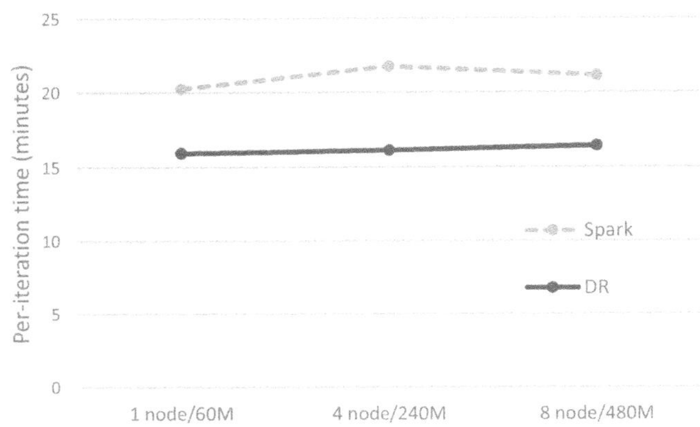

Figure 20: Distributed R vs. Spark: K-means algorithm. Lower is better.

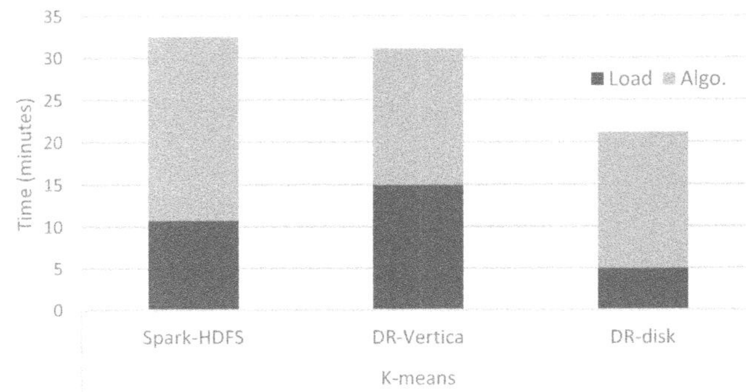

Figure 21: End-to-end comparison between Vertica-Distributed R and Spark. We use a 4-node cluster setup. Lower is better.

Hadoop, especially the HDFS filesystem, has become a common choice for storing raw data. On this data, analysts may use MapReduce, Spark, and other programming paradigms for different kinds of analysis. While MapReduce and systems built on top of it are known to be slow, Spark provides a fast, in-memory computation layer, and is an order of magnitude faster.

In this section we show that Vertica with Distributed R can be as fast as Spark running on top of HDFS. These numbers are encouraging because loading data directly from a distributed file system is expected to be much faster than reading data out of a database and running analytics in an external tool. This is because the database has to read data from the local filesystem, deserialize and decompress data, convert it into a standard format (such as csv), and may even need to serialize again if the client is using a network connection. The external tool, such as R, will then parse the incoming data and convert it into objects. In comparison, Spark which is tightly integrated with HDFS, reads the data directly from the local HDFS node and optionally deserializes the data before converting into its own data-structures.

We run K-means on multi-gigabyte datasets and compare the end-to-end application performance between Vertica and Spark. We use three setups: 1 node cluster, 4 node cluster, and 8 node cluster running Distributed R on Vertica and Spark on HDFS.

K-means. We use three synthetic datasets, with 60M, 240M, and 480M rows. Each dataset has 100 features, and we set the number of centers (K) to 1000. These datasets correspond to approximately 45GB, 180GB, and 360GB on-disk data.

Figure 20 compares the performance of Spark and Distributed R. We exclude the load time to first measure the scalability of each system. As we increase the number of nodes from 1 to 4 and finally 8, we proportionally increase the number of rows in the dataset from 60M to 240M, and then to 480M. Therefore, in an ideal distributed system the per-iteration execution time should remain constant. In the figure, `Spark` and `DR` denote the same implementation of the K-means algorithm, and hence an apples-to-apples comparison.

Figure 20 shows that Distributed R takes approximately 16 minutes to complete each iteration at 8 nodes while Spark requires 21 minutes or more. Both Distributed R and Spark scale well as the number of servers and the dataset size is increased. Overall, Distributed R and Spark have similar performance, with Distributed R faster about 20%.

End-to-end experiments. While the previous experiment shows that machine learning algorithms available in Distributed R are slightly faster than Spark, the results exclude one important aspect–time to load data. Our final experiment compares end-to-end performance, i.e, application time plus the time taken to load data from Vertica compared to Spark loading data from HDFS.

We run K-means in the 4-node setup. The datasets are the same as in the previous experiment, 240M rows and 100 features. For K-means, Distributed R takes 15 minutes to load the data from Vertica and 16 minutes per-iteration. Spark, on the other hand, needs 11 minutes to load the data from HDFS and 21 minutes per-iteration. Overall, this means that Spark and Distributed R take almost the same time to run K-means end-to-end. We also measure the case when data resides as files in the local ext4 filesystem of each node, and Distributed R loads data directly from these files. `DR-disk` in the figure shows that it takes just 5 minutes to load all the data from files in ext4, about 2× faster than Spark on HDFS and 3× faster than loading via Vertica. These numbers indicate the higher overheads involved in extracting data from distributed filesystems and databases.

Summary. Our comparison with Spark shows that interfacing an external tool, such as R, with a database is not necessarily slow. With proper integration, R applications can read data from a database at comparable speeds to systems like Spark that are tightly integrated with HDFS, and read directly from the distributed file system.

8. RELATED WORK

There are many systems that provide the ability to perform machine learning analysis. We briefly survey the relevant systems below.

Machine learning infrastructure. Matlab [5], SAS [11], R [8], and others are traditional statistical tools used by data scientists for different types of analysis including machine learning and graph processing. Each of these tools has a wide user base, sometimes in the order of millions of customers. R, given it's open source nature, has become increasingly popular and has more than 6000 packages available. All of these tools are generally single-threaded and known to have limitations on large datasets. Therefore, the common usage model is to install these tools on laptops and desktops, and perform analysis on sampled data to avoid hitting the data size limitations. Several recent efforts have extended these tools for parallel processing on a single machine(parallel Matlab [4], ScaleR [9]), distributed computing (Distributed R [26]), and even integration with Hadoop (SAS on Hadoop [12], RHadoop [10]).

The last few years has seen a surge in distributed computing infrastructure for machine learning and graph processing. Google's MapReduce pushed the scale of distributed computing to thousands of commodity, but unreliable, servers [18]. A prominent use of the MapReduce infrastructure is for graph analysis, such as calculating PageRank of the Web graph [15]. The Hadoop ecosystem, an open source version of MapReduce, added many machine learning and graph analysis algorithms under the Mahout library [1]. However, the MapReduce paradigm is inefficient for machine learning algorithms, since they are iterative in nature. There have been efforts to improve performance of iterative algorithms by using techniques such as caching (HaLoop [16], Twister [19]). Another line of research has abandoned the MapReduce interface completely for specialization, such as a vertex centric programming for graph processing (Pregel [24], GraphLab [20]). Spark generalizes the programming paradigm of MapReduce by supporting LINQ like API which include aggregation and filter functions [28]. Spark improves over the performance of other systems by using main memory for computations, avoiding disk accesses, but still guaranteeing fault-tolerance. Spark's machine learning and SQL interface are an order of magnitude faster than similar systems on Hadoop.

Many of the techniques in this paper, such as extracting data from databases, are independent of the choice of the external analytics tool. For example, one could use the mechanisms in this paper to integrate Vertica with Spark instead of Distributed R. The integration of Vertica and Distributed R ensures that customers can continue to use the popular tool R along with industrial strength SQL by Vertica, and get competitive performance.

Databases and machine learning. Database vendors use three main approaches to support machine learning analysis (1) provide ways to extract data from database to R like tools, (2) support R within the database, and (3) implement distributed algorithms in the database. We contrast these approaches below.

ODBC based connectors are commonly used to extract data from databases. As mentioned in this paper, ODBC connections are slow and do not meet the performance requirements on large data. Solutions such as Teradata Parallel Transporter (TPT) FastExport supports parallel data transfer from Teradata to a client [13]. It uses multiple sessions to extract partitioned table data, and is similar to using multiple ODBC connections. Unlike mechanisms expressed in this paper, TPT does not transfer data to the memory of remote analytics engines, nor does it support different transfer policies such as partitioning data for load balance or data locality. RICE shows how to bridge SAP HANA with single-threaded R [21]. The key idea is to use shared memory on the node to convert database tables to R data-frames with low overhead. The data format conversion techniques in RICE are complementary to Vertica's fast transfer mechanism. As an example, Distributed R uses shared memory to not only stage data arriving from Vertica but also to share data across multiple R processes. However, unlike RICE, Vertica also focuses on reducing the overhead of transferring data in parallel to multiple R instances, and supports different data distribution policies.

Many prominent database vendors such as Oracle, Vertica, and others embed R in the database. This approach provides the ability to call R with user defined functions (UDF). Unfortunately, such an approach is limited by the single threaded implementation of the algorithm in the UDF. As an example, a customer can call single threaded R K-means by funneling a table through a single R UDF, but they cannot create a distributed K-means function by simple invoking multiple K-means UDFs. Ricardo is an example system that combines R and Hadoop [17]. Ricardo performs coarse grained decomposition by delegating large scale aggregation queries to Hadoop and small-scale statistical analysis to single-threaded R. Vertica has similar goals of delegating pre-processing and model deployment to the database, but provides new mechanisms for integrating with a distributed system such as Distributed R.

Finally, MADlib exemplifies the approach of expressing distributed, in-database, machine learning algorithms via user-defined functions, and SQL statements [22]. SciDB goes a step further by providing support for arrays in the database instead of retrofitting them on relational tables [25]. MADlib like approaches can leverage the SQL query optimizer and reduce data movement overhead. However, to contribute algorithms one needs to follow the programming paradigm proposed by MADlib. Vertica's integration with Distributed R is an orthogonal approach. It leverages the strengths of both relational databases and R. Our approach uses the database for model deployment, but does not rule out implementing distributed algorithms inside the database (such as pattern mining in Vertica [2]). However, by integrating Vertica with Distributed R, Vertica customers get the familiarity and power of R. Additionally, since most data scientists use R like tools to implement their analysis, one expects R based package contributions to grow rapidly, and these new algorithms will become automatically available to Vertica customers.

9. CONCLUSIONS

By integrating Vertica with Distributed R, we have not only expanded the functionality of Vertica but also solved multiple performance issues that customers face when using R with a database. This paper shows how customers can now use Vertica's industrial strength SQL engine for preprocessing data, deploying machine learning models, and applying predictions on database tables. Our new data transfer mechanism and parallel algorithms in Distributed R improve the end-to-end execution time of workflows by an order of magnitude compared to using R on a database.

10. ACKNOWLEDGMENTS

We are thankful to Sunil Venkayala, Dan Huang, Hua Zhang, Elena Chan, and Kyungyong Lee for their contributions to the HP Distributed R product. We are grateful to the reviewers, especially our shepherd Mehul Shah, for their valuable feedback and help in improving this paper.

11. REFERENCES

[1] Apache Mahout. http://mahout.apache.org.

[2] Comparing pattern mining on a billion records with HP Vertica and Hadoop. http://www.vertica.com/2013/04/08/comparing-pattern-mining-on-a-billion-records-with-hp-vertica-and-hadoop/.

[3] HP Vertica Distributed R. https://www.vertica.com/distributedR.

[4] MATLAB–parallel computing toolbox. http://www.mathworks.com/products/parallel-computing/.

[5] MATLAB–the language of technical computing. http://www.mathworks.com/products/matlab.

[6] Process containers. http://lwn.net/Articles/236038/.

[7] Programmatic media buying. http://rocketfuel.com/.

[8] The R project for statistical computing. http://www.r-project.org.

[9] Revolution R enterprise scaler. http://www.revolutionanalytics.com/revolution-r-enterprise-scaler.

[10] RHadoop and MapR. https://www.mapr.com/resources/rhadoop-and-mapr.

[11] SAS analytics. http://www.sas.com.

[12] SAS in-memory statistics for Hadoop. http://www.sas.com/en_us/software/sas-hadoop/in-memory-hadoop.html.

[13] Teradata parallel transporter. http://www.teradata.com/tools-and-utilities/parallel-transporter/.

[14] Teradata Warehouse Miner. http://www.teradata.com/products-and-services/teradata-warehouse-miner/.

[15] S. Brin and L. Page. The anatomy of a large-scale hypertextual Web search engine. In *WWW7*, 1998.

[16] Y. Bu, B. Howe, M. Balazinska, and M. D. Ernst. HaLoop: Efficient iterative data processing on large clusters. *PVLDB*, 3(1–2), 2010.

[17] S. Das, Y. Sismanis, K. S. Beyer, R. Gemulla, P. J. Haas, and J. McPherson. Ricardo: Integrating R and Hadoop. In *SIGMOD*, 2010.

[18] J. Dean and S. Ghemawat. MapReduce: Simplified data processing on large clusters. *Commun. ACM*, 51(1), 2008.

[19] J. Ekanayake, H. Li, B. Zhang, T. Gunarathne, S.-H. Bae, J. Qiu, and G. Fox. Twister: A runtime for iterative MapReduce. In *HPDC*, 2010.

[20] J. E. Gonzalez, Y. Low, H. Gu, D. Bickson, and C. Guestrin. PowerGraph: Distributed graph-parallel computation on natural graphs. In *OSDI*, 2012.

[21] P. Große, W. Lehner, T. Weichert, F. Färber, and W.-S. Li. Bridging two worlds with RICE integrating R into the SAP in-memory computing engine. *PVLDB*, 4(12), 2011.

[22] J. M. Hellerstein, C. Ré, F. Schoppmann, D. Z. Wang, E. Fratkin, A. Gorajek, K. S. Ng, C. Welton, X. Feng, K. Li, and A. Kumar. The MADlib analytics library: Or MAD skills, the SQL. *PVLDB*, 5(12), 2012.

[23] A. Lamb, M. Fuller, R. Varadarajan, N. Tran, B. Vandiver, L. Doshi, and C. Bear. The Vertica analytic database: C-store 7 years later. *PVLDB*, 5(12), 2012.

[24] G. Malewicz, M. H. Austern, A. J. Bik, J. C. Dehnert, I. Horn, N. Leiser, and G. Czajkowski. Pregel: A system for large-scale graph processing. In *SIGMOD*, 2010.

[25] E. Soroush, M. Balazinska, and D. Wang. ArrayStore: A storage manager for complex parallel array processing. In *SIGMOD*, 2011.

[26] S. Venkataraman, E. Bodzsar, I. Roy, A. AuYoung, and R. S. Schreiber. Presto: Distributed machine learning and graph processing with sparse matrices. In *EuroSys*, 2013.

[27] T. J. Ypma. Historical development of the Newton-Raphson method. *SIAM Rev.*, 37(4), 1995.

[28] M. Zaharia, M. Chowdhury, T. Das, A. Dave, J. Ma, M. McCauley, M. J. Franklin, S. Shenker, and I. Stoica. Resilient distributed datasets: a fault-tolerant abstraction for in-memory cluster computing. In *NSDI*, 2012.

Oracle Workload Intelligence

Quoc Trung Tran* Konstantinos Morfonios
Oracle USA
{quoc.trung.tran, konstantinos.morfonios}@oracle.com

Neoklis Polyzotis*
Google, Inc
npolyzotis@google.com

ABSTRACT

Analyzing and understanding the characteristics of the incoming workload is crucial in unraveling trends and tuning the performance of a database system. In this work, we present Oracle Workload Intelligence (WI), a tool for workload modeling and mining, as our attempt to infer the processes that generate a given workload. WI consists of two main functionalities. First, WI derives a model that captures the main characteristics of the workload without overfitting, which makes it likely to generalize well to unseen instances of the workload. Such a model provides insights into the most frequent code paths in the application that drives the workload, and also enables optimizations inside the database system that target sequences of query statements. Second, WI can compare the models of different snapshots of the workload to detect whether the workload has changed. Such changes might indicate new trends, regressions, problems, or even security issues. We demonstrate the effectiveness of WI with an experimental study on synthetic workloads and customer-provided application benchmarks.

Categories and Subject Descriptors

H.2.m [**Database Management**]: Miscellaneous

General Terms

Management; Performance; Verification; Measurement.

Keywords

Workload Intelligence; Workload Modeling; Significant Pattern.

1. INTRODUCTION

Analyzing and understanding the characteristics of the incoming workload plays an important role in unraveling trends and optimizing the performance of database systems. One example is identifying a small representative subset that captures the characteristics of a larger workload [8]. Another example is summarizing features of the statement distribution in the workload [20]. Each of these methods illuminates a particular aspect of the workload and a database administrator (DBA) is likely to utilize several methods in tandem in order to gain information on the application logic that generates the workload and thus tune the system accordingly.

*Work done while authors were affiliated with UC Santa Cruz

SIGMOD'15, May 31–June 4, 2015, Melbourne, Victoria, Australia.

ACM 978-1-4503-2758-9/15/05 ...$15.00.
http://dx.doi.org/10.1145/2723372.2742791.

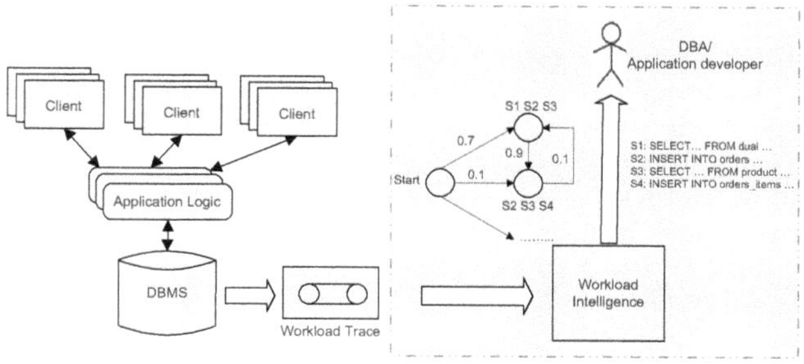

Figure 1: Oracle Workload Intelligence.

This paper introduces an additional tool that the DBA can use to mine knowledge about the incoming workload. Specifically, we introduce the Workload Intelligence (WI) tool that infers information about the application logic that generates the workload. The input to WI is a sequence of statements executed by the database management system (DBMS), which in turn can be obtained from a workload capture service (e.g., from Oracle Database Replay [11]) or from the query logs that contain time order information. After analyzing this input, WI outputs a Markov model that essentially describes how the application logic generates sequences of statements. In turn, this model can be used to predict which statement patterns are likely to be observed in a running system or to compare different instances of the workload.

WI was developed as a supplement to Oracle Database Replay, a popular tool that enhances database manageability. In brief, Oracle Database Replay allows DBAs to record a real workload running in the database server of their production system, and subsequently replay the recorded workload in the database server of a test system in a realistic fashion. Oracle Database Replay captures a large amount of information in the recorded workload (also referred to as *workload trace*) such as SQL text and identifiers, bind values, timing data, and identifiers of objects that have been accessed. Given that the information captured in the recorded workload is so rich, WI was initiated to mine knowledge out of the workload trace.

Applications. WI can be useful for DBAs and application developers in many different contexts:

Understanding application logic. In many scenarios the DBAs may not be fully informed about the application logic that drives the database workload. As an example, Figure 1 shows a typical database application following the three-tier architecture. In this setup, one or more applications maintain pools of connections to a database server and submit queries through these connections. Depending on which code path of the application is executed during a task, a series of queries is executed inside the DBMS. In the common case, the DBA does not have access to the source code of the applications and sees them as black boxes. Hence, the DBA does not have immediate access to the aforementioned code paths. As another example, the DBAs for database-as-a-service (DaaS) offerings (e.g., Oracle Cloud, Microsoft Azure [6], or Salesforce.com) also have little knowledge about the application logic that drives the workload. The models computed by WI can provide insights into the driving logic. More specifically, by using WI, the DBA can obtain a useful model for the workload trace, from which they can identify patterns of queries corresponding to application code paths and gain a better insight of what is running in the database they are responsible for. In Figure 1, the output of WI includes the Markov model for the input workload trace and a pattern consisting of four SQL statements. The output in Figure 1 provides the DBAs with information about the process that generates the workload, i.e., the pattern corresponds to a code path that places an order for some customers. (More details are provided in the experimental section.) Besides, the information provided by WI can also help application designers verify that the application logic works as intended.

Hints for optimization. WI provides statistics about entire patterns in the workload rather than individual statements; hence, it can enhance existing reports that are useful in optimizing the performance of the DBMS by enriching them with context information that is currently missing. Moreover, if the WI model reveals that a specific sequence is frequent, then the optimizer, a DBA, or an application developer may be able to optimize the corresponding code path accordingly. Note that the frequency of executed code paths could be measured explicitly by instrumenting the source code. However, such instrumentation may be cumbersome or impossible, if some application components are black boxes.

Comparing workload models. WI may be also useful for comparing different workload models of the same application that may differ in various ways, such as, in terms of time, location, or release version. The results of such a comparison may be used to deduce the profile of application users, or detect changes that can be attributed to errors, regressions, or security issues. For example, two models may represent workloads of the same application recorded in the U.S.A in July and December, respectively. The comparison of these models may indicate that customers browse more in one case and purchase more in the other. Such information may help a merchant in determining an advertising strategy. In another example, a significant decrease in the frequency of purchases in December might indicate an unexpected condition, for instance, some server that is not responding, or some script that is hitting an error.

Generating artificial workloads. A model derived by WI can be used to generate artificial workloads that are close to the actual workload but may have random mutations/omissions. Such artificial workloads can be tuned to be larger or smaller than the original workload. Experimenting with artificial workloads of different scale-up factors can be useful for capacity planning, stress testing, or other applications.

Challenges. We had to address several technical challenges in implementing WI. First, there is the general issue of balancing between overfitting and generalization for the derived model: we want a model that describes the captured workload well and at the same time is likely to describe well unseen instances of the workload. Second, due to connection pooling in the DBMS (which is a very common feature), the statements coming from a single code path may be logged through different connections and hence may be separated in the query logs, i.e., they will not be adjacent in the log. Moreover, the statements of one code path may be interleaved with statements of other code paths. Hence, one key question is whether it is even feasible to recover a model of the workload given these "discontinuities" in the logs. Our work shows that simple assumptions go a long way in overcoming this obstacle and yield good results in practice.

Our contributions. The contributions of our work are as follows:

- (Section 3) We introduce a methodology to build a model for the sequence of statements in a given workload. To guide the search for a good model, we follow the Minimum Description Length (MDL) principle. Essentially, MDL chooses the model that is sufficiently complex to describe the workload but is also likely to generalize to other instances of the workload.
- (Section 4) Using the Markov-based model as the foundation, we introduce WI as a tool for workload analysis. WI works both offline, building a model for a given sequence of statements, and online, continuously maintaining a model of the workload based on a sliding window of the most recent statements. Such a model can be used for mining significant patterns of statements, or for comparison against a reference model in order to detect significant changes or anomalies.
- (Section 5) We evaluate WI experimentally using both synthetic workloads and customer-provided application benchmarks. The results demonstrate that WI can recover meaningful information about application code paths, and is efficient enough to perform continuous workload analysis with low overhead.

Given the availability of workload recording, our work shows that it is feasible to obtain a meaningful model for a database workload without any knowledge of the driving application logic. In turn, such a model can be used as the basis for several interesting optimizations inside the DBMS, and also as a tool for workload monitoring. These features make WI an important tool in the arsenal of DBAs, particularly in the context of DaaS platforms where the DBA has little knowledge about the applications driving the database workload.

The offline feature of WI (i.e., building a model for a given statement sequence) has been implemented in Oracle Database 12c.

2. PRELIMINARIES

In this section, we provide some basic definitions (Section 2.1) and then discuss the techniques that we utilize to build WI. In particular, Section 2.2 reviews the Markov Chain model which we will use to model the workload. Section 2.3 reviews the MDL principle, which we will use to select a good Markov model for the given workload. Finally, Section 2.4 reviews the Kolmogorov-Smirnov (KS) test, which we will use to compare different models for an evolving workload. For ease of reference, Table 1 summarizes the key symbols that we introduce in this section.

2.1 Basic Definitions

The input to our tool is a sequence of statements **T** that represent the workload executed at the DBMS. The collection of **T** is rather straightforward in modern systems, as most commercial database vendors provide profiling tools that enable logging of SQL activity on the server over a period of time (e.g., [8, 11]). In practice, a system may generate several such sequences corresponding to different DBMS connections, but we assume that there is a single

Symbol	Explanation
$\mathbf{T}$	The sequence of statements gathered from the database logs.
n	Length of sequence $\mathbf{T}$.
$\mathbf{T}[i]$	Statement at position i (i.e., in $\mathbf{T}$), $1 \leq i \leq n$.
S	Alphabet of $\lvert S\rvert$ statements. This is basically the set of possible statements.
$\mathbf{p}$	Sequence of $\lvert\mathbf{p}\rvert$ statements from S. This is the pattern.
$\mathbf{p}[j]$	Statement at position j, $1 \leq j \leq \lvert\mathbf{p}\rvert$.
$embed(\mathbf{p}, \mathbf{T})$	The set of embeddings of $\mathbf{p}$ in $\mathbf{T}$.
τ	A threshold to determine if a transition probability $Prob(a\lvert b)$ is significant.
h	The maximum order of all Markov models that are considered.
θ	A threshold to determine if a sequence of statements from $\mathbf{T}$ is significant.

Table 1: Notation.

sequence $\mathbf{T}$ for the time being in order to simplify our presentation. We extend our techniques to the general case in Section 3.

The input statements may have been processed to substitute constants with bind variables, thus turning each statement in a form of "template". This templatization can help hide details of the application logic that are not important for the discovery of patterns. For instance, consider an e-commerce application and specifically the code path that handles the addition of an item in the user's shopping cart. This code path may issue several SQL queries, each having the user id and the item id as constants. By substituting the specific constants with variables, it becomes possible to equate statements that come from different users and different items and thus to surface the underlying code path. In our work, we assume a complete templatization method that substitutes all constants with abstract bind variables. Templatization reduces the number of distinct statements and thus increases the chances of discovering frequent patterns and reduces the running time of WI.

We stress that such a templatization step is solely a way to preprocess the input of WI in order to facilitate the computation of a workload model, i.e., it does not affect the core ideas of our techniques. Of course, the choice of the templatization strategy will affect the final model. Our experimental results suggest that the simple method that we mentioned earlier (complete substitution of constants with variables) yields good results in practice. Applying more involved methods is an interesting direction for future work and we discuss some ideas in Appendix A.

We use S to denote the set of possible statements and S^k to denote the set of possible sequences that contain k statements from S. We note that $\mathbf{T}$ is a member of S^n, i.e., a sequence of n statements.

A pattern $\mathbf{p}$ is a member of $S^{\lvert\mathbf{p}\rvert}$ and essentially represents the sequence of statements in a code path. Let e be a contiguous subinterval of $[1,n]$. We say that e is an *embedding* of $\mathbf{p}$ in $\mathbf{T}$ if $\mathbf{T}[e[i]] = \mathbf{p}[i]$ for all $1 \leq i \leq \lvert\mathbf{p}\rvert$. In a slight abuse of notation, we will use e to also denote the subsequence of $\mathbf{T}$. Given a pattern $\mathbf{p}$, we use $embed(\mathbf{p}, \mathbf{T})$ to denote the set of all possible embeddings of $\mathbf{p}$ in $\mathbf{T}$.

EXAMPLE 1. *Consider a sequence of statements $\mathbf{T} = ababc$. In our notation, the length of the sequence is $n = 5$. The set of statements is $S = \{a,b,c\}$. The set of patterns of length 2 of $\mathbf{T}$ is $S^2 = \{ab, ba, bc\}$. Consider the pattern $p = ab$. We observe that $e_1 = [1,2]$ is an embedding of p in $\mathbf{T}$, since $T[e_1[1]] = p[1] = a$ and $T[e_1[2]] = p[2] = b$. Similarly, $e_2 = [3,4]$ is another embedding of p in $\mathbf{T}$.* □

One aspect of our formulation is that a pattern (i.e., statements in a code path) can be embedded in the workload as a contiguous subsequence without gaps. Our driving assumption is that the possibility that two code paths are randomly interleaved is really small and hence such cases will be harmless noise within large sequences. This is a conscious design choice that was driven by two assumptions. First, there is a separate log that traces the sequence of incoming statements for every different DBMS connection. Second, the applications running on top of the DBMS employ connection affinity to execute DBMS statements in the same code path. So, even in the presence of connection pooling, we expect that an application will not decide to switch connections in the middle of a given task. Our experience shows that these assumptions are realistic. Note that the two assumptions imply that statements that are coming from the same code path are likely to appear together in a logged sequence and not to be interleaved accross multiple logs or spread in different areas of the same log. Extending our model to consider gaps would allow us to lift these assumptions, but we believe that the complexity of dealing with gaps outweighs any potential benefits in computing a better workload model. Moreover, there are cases where an approach that considers gaps may lead to a worse workload model. Consider the following example, which is modeled after a real-world application that we examined with WI:

```
execute query a;
if (condition) then
    execute query b;
end if
execute query c;
```

Depending on the condition, some executions of the previous code would generate the sequence *abc*, whereas some other executions would generate *ac*. By considering gaps of length 1, an algorithm might decide to omit *b* and report a single pattern *ac* to represent both code paths. Such a result would be clearly misleading.

2.2 Markov Chain Model

Markov models are widely used to represent statistical regularities in data [15]. Basically, we can think of the workload $\mathbf{T}$ as a sequence $X_1, X_2, \cdots, X_n$ of random variables taking values from the set of statements S. The sequence of random variables are said to form a kth-order Markov chain model if

$$Prob(X_i|X_1 \ldots X_{i-1}) = Prob(X_i|X_{i-k}, \ldots, X_{i-2}, X_{i-1})$$

for all values of i. Formally, a Markov Chain is uniquely defined by the following information:

1. The order k.
2. The associated probabilities $Prob(s_{k+1}|s_1 \ldots s_k)$ for each statement s_{k+1} and sequence $s_1 \ldots s_k$.

We view the values of X_i as *states* and $Prob(s_{k+1}|s_1 \ldots s_k)$ as the probability that the model will transition to state s_{k+1} given that the k previous states were $s_1, s_2, \ldots, s_k$ respectively. We use $\theta(k)$ to denote an assignment of these probabilities for a specific k, and $M^{\theta(k)}$ to denote the corresponding model. We use $\mathscr{M}^k$ for the set of all possible models for some fixed k.

We want to limit our search to models relevant to the given workload. Specifically, the probability terms $Prob(s_{k+1}|s_1 \ldots s_k)$ should reflect the characteristics of $\mathbf{T}$, e.g., if a specific pattern *abc* is frequently occurring in $\mathbf{T}$, then we would like to have a high probability for $Prob(c|ab)$. As it turns out, there is a standard method to compute these conditional probabilities as follows:

$$Prob(s_{k+1}|s_1 \ldots s_k) = \frac{|embed(s_1 \ldots s_k s_{k+1}, \mathbf{T})|}{|embed(s_1 \ldots s_k, \mathbf{T})|}$$

The previous expression yields the *maximum-likelihood (ML) estimator* of $Prob(s_{k+1}|s_1 \ldots s_k)$. We henceforth assume that the probabilities in $\theta(k)$ are computed under the ML estimator assumption. Obviously, specifying $\theta(k)$ is equivalent to describing the counts $|embed(\mathbf{p},\mathbf{T})|$ for all $\mathbf{p} \in S^{k+1}$. Note that this information is sufficient for deriving $|embed(\mathbf{p}',\mathbf{T})|$ for all $\mathbf{p}' \in S^k$ by performing a simple marginalization. In particular, $|embed(\mathbf{p}',\mathbf{T})|$ is the summation of all $|embed(\mathbf{p},\mathbf{T})|$'s where $\mathbf{p}'$ is a prefix of length k of $\mathbf{p}$.

We can now define the high-level problem solved by WI: Given an input sequence $\mathbf{T}$ that we will treat as training data, we wish to compute k and a Markov model $M^{\theta(k)} \in \mathscr{M}^k$ such that $M^{\theta(k)}$ is a "good" abstraction for the process that generated $\mathbf{T}$. Intuitively, goodness means that frequent patterns should have a high probability of occurring according to $M^{\theta(k)}$, but also that $M^{\theta(k)}$ should not overfit the input $\mathbf{T}$. To illustrate this point, consider the $(n-1)$-th order chain that sets $prob(\mathbf{T}[n]|\mathbf{T}[1]\ldots\mathbf{T}[n-1]) = 1$ and all other probability terms to zero. This model captures perfectly the training data in $\mathbf{T}$ but offers little insight in terms of the application that generated the workload. Going for the simplest possible model may not be a good choice either. Specifically, the 0-th order Markov Chain records only the probability terms $Prob(s_i)$ for each statement and essentially assumes independence of state transitions. This is a simple model that avoids overfitting, but is also (most likely) a poor representation of the application that generated the workload, since it ignores the dependencies between statements. As we discuss below, a good model must strike a balance between its complexity (which is indicative of overfitting) and its accuracy in describing the training data.

2.3 Minimum Description Length Principle

The MDL Principle is a well-known solution for the problem of selecting a model out of several candidates [12]. The intuition is to select the model that is both a good representative of the training data and has good generalization power (i.e., it avoids overfitting).

MDL is based on the following insight. Let D be data generated by the process that M is meant to model. (In our case, D represents a sequence of statements.) Then, MDL can be viewed as a method to generate a binary encoding of D, by first transcoding M and then transcoding an optimal (i.e., the shortest) representation of D according to M. For the case of Markov Models, we would first transcode M by encoding its order and the associated probabilities in a binary string, and then transcode D as a sequence of binary strings that represent D in terms of the states in M. As it turns out, the optimal choice for these binary strings (in terms of the length of the transcoding) corresponds to the log likelihood of observing D given M, i.e., if $Prob(D|M)$ is high then this transcoding will have a small length. Note that the specific choice of these binary strings is not important for the application of MDL. What matters again is that the length of encoding D given M is proportional to $-logProb(D|M)$.

Looking at the total number of bits as the cost to transcribe D, we will write $cost(M,D) = cost(M) + cost(D|M)$. The MDL principle argues that, all else being equal, the best model minimizes this cost, i.e., M is compact ($cost(M)$ is small) and yet M is a good representative of the data ($cost(D|M)$ is small, which means that the $Prob(D|M)$ is high). This is another manifestation of Occam's Razor, the guiding principle that a good model should strike a balance between complexity and accuracy in capturing the training data.

Back to our previous example with the two extreme Markov models ($k = 0$ and $k = n-1$), we see that the MDL principle penalizes both choices but in different ways: $k = 0$ has a high $cost(D|M)$ due to the poor representative power of the model, whereas $k = n-1$ has a high $cost(M)$ due to the complexity of the model.

2.4 Kolmogorov-Smirnov Test

The KS test is one of the most useful and general methods for comparing two samples when we cannot make any assumptions about the distribution of data [7]. It is a good fit for our purpose to compare workload models, since the workloads can be arbitrary and do not follow any known distributions such as Gaussian or exponential. Basically, the KS test determines whether two workload models differ significantly with a confidence level. In the following, we review how to perform the KS test [7].

Consider two samples (e.g., two periods of a workload): a first sample $Y_1, \cdots, Y_p$ of size p and a second sample $Z_1, \cdots, Z_q$ of size q. In our context, each Y_i (resp. Z_j) is a pattern in the workload. The KS test is based on the empirical cumulative distribution function (c.d.f), which is an estimate (from the data) of the true cumulative distribution function of the population.

The cdf of a random variable X is a function, F, given by

$$F(x) = Prob(X \leq x).$$

Here, the domain of X and x is the set $\{Y_1, \cdots, Y_p\} \cup \{Z_1, \cdots, Z_q\}$. Note that we need a total order among Y_i's and Z_j's to compute $F(x)$. In our case, we choose the lexicographical order of patterns. At a high level, the cdf tells us how much probability has been accumulated up to a certain point.

The emperical cdf is defined as

$$\hat{F}(x) = (\text{fraction of observations} \leq x).$$

The KS statistic looks at the maximum absolute difference between the empirical cdf of sample 1 and the empirical cdf of sample 2:

$$D_{p,q} = max_x|\hat{F_1}(x) - \hat{F_2}(x)|$$

The computed value $D_{p,q}$ is used to validate the following hypothesis: both samples come from a population with the same distribution. We reject the above hypothesis at a significance level (or confidence level) α if $D_{p,q} > D_{p,q,\alpha}$ where $D_{p,q,\alpha}$ is computed as:

$$D_{p,q,\alpha} = c(\alpha) \times \sqrt{\frac{p+q}{p \times q}}$$

where $c(\alpha)$ is pre-computed in the Kolmogorov-Smirnov Table [7].

3. APPLYING MDL FOR WORKLOAD MODELING

In this section, we describe the application of the MDL principle (see Section 2.3) to our problem of modeling the input sequence $\mathbf{T}$ with a Markov model. We structure the presentation in two parts. We first describe the straightforward application of MDL to our problem in order to illustrate the key concepts of the methodology. However, we also show that this approach is not likely to work well in practice, and hence we subsequently present a refined methodology which is the one implemented by WI.

3.1 MDL Principle with Full Models

Let $x \in S^n$ be the message we need to transmit. We assume that x is generated by the same process that generates $\mathbf{T}$, and for the time being that $x = \mathbf{T}$. (As explained below, it is actually desirable to set $x \neq \mathbf{T}$.) The metric $cost(x, M^{\theta(k)})$ gives us the minimum number of bits needed to transmit x using the model $M^{\theta(k)}$.

$$cost(x, M^{\theta(k)}) = (\text{number of bits to transmit } M^{\theta(k)}) - \log Prob(x|M^{\theta(k)})$$

The second component comes out of the MDL methodology and represents the optimal code to transmit x once the receiver knows the model $M^{\theta(k)}$. We note that this component is equivalent to $cost(D|M)$ as discussed in Section 2.3. For the first component, we need to transmit the following information:

1. The integer k. This requires $2\log k+1$ bits, following the uniform code for integers [12]. For $k=0$, we need one bit to encode k. For the sake of simplicity, in this corner case, we substitute $\log 0$ with 0.
2. The counts $|embed(\mathbf{p},\mathbf{T})|$ for $\mathbf{p}\in S^{k+1}$. Each count requires $\log n$ bits, and there are $|S|^{k+1}$ such counts. We can assume that the counts are transmitted in lexicographical order of the corresponding sequences, so the receiver knows how to decode them.

Putting everything together, the description-length metric (DL) is a cost computed as:

$$cost(x,M^{\theta(k)}) = 2\log k+1+|S|^{k+1}\log n-\log Prob(x|M^{\theta(k)})$$

EXAMPLE 2. *Let us consider a sequence of statements* $\mathbf{T}=ababc$. *We discuss how to compute the MDL-based metric of a model of order* $k=1$ *that describes* $\mathbf{T}$. *We have* $S=\{a,b,c\}$, *the length of* $\mathbf{T}$ *is* $n=5$, *and* $x=\mathbf{T}$. *In addition,*

$$Prob(\mathbf{T}|M^{\theta(1)}) = Prob(a)\times Prob(b|a)\times Prob(a|b)\times Prob(b|a)\times Prob(c|b)$$

To compute $Prob(\mathbf{T}|M^{\theta(1)})$, *we apply the maximum-likelihood principle and obtain the following:*

- $Prob(a)=\frac{1}{|S|}=\frac{1}{3}$,
- $Prob(b|a)=\frac{|embed(ab,\mathbf{T})|}{|embed(a,\mathbf{T})|}=\frac{2}{2}=1$
- $Prob(a|b)=\frac{|embed(ba,\mathbf{T})|}{|embed(b,\mathbf{T})|}=\frac{1}{2}$
- $Prob(c|b)=\frac{|embed(bc,\mathbf{T})|}{|embed(b,\mathbf{T})|}=\frac{1}{2}$

By replacing the values of these terms, we obtain the following result $cost(\mathbf{T},M^{\theta(1)})=2\log 1+1+3^2\log 5-\log\frac{1}{12}$. □

We can make some interesting observations about the metric.

- The DL can be computed on a sequence x that is different than $\mathbf{T}$. This is more principled, as we do not measure the goodness of the model on the training data.
- Only the last term depends on the actual model. The remaining terms do not depend on $\theta(k)$ and are the same for all models in $\mathscr{M}^k$.
- Assume that we compute the DL for two models $M_1\in\mathscr{M}^k$ and $M_2\in\mathscr{M}^{k+l}$. The following equivalence is straightforward:

$$cost(x,M_2)<cost(x,M_1)\Leftrightarrow$$
$$\log\frac{Prob(x|M_2)}{Prob(x|M_1)}>2\log\frac{k+l}{k}+|S|^{k+1}(|S|^l-1)\log n$$

The inequality shows clearly that a model of higher order will require a huge increase in probability in order to have a smaller DL metric.

It is instructive to examine the last property for the simple case where $k=0$ and $l=1$, i.e., M_1 employs complete independence and M_2 has a memory buffer of size one. In this case, the inequality is reduced as follows:

$$\log\frac{Prob(x|M_2)}{Prob(x|M_1)}>|S|(|S|-1)\log n$$

For $n>1$, the inequality implies that $Prob(x|M_2)$ has to be at least $2^{|S|(|S|-1)}$ times higher than $Prob(x|M_1)$ in order for M_2 to be more attractive under the MDL. Even for $|S|=2$, this implies a ratio of 4. For more realistic sizes of S, e.g., more than a hundred symbols in S, M_2 is much less likely to be better than M_1 according to the MDL principle.

3.2 MDL Principle with Pruned Models

One of the inherent shortcomings of the previous approach is that the complexity of any model in $\mathscr{M}^k$ is very high, even if only few of the probability terms are significant. One solution is to switch to a class of "pruned" models, where the assumption is that only a subset of the transition probabilities are significant and hence described precisely, and the remaining probabilities are approximated using a uniform distribution.

We illustrate this idea with an example. Suppose that $k=2$ and $S=\{a,b,c\}$. In total, $\theta(k)$ will comprise $|S|^{k+1}=3^3$ conditional probabilities. Suppose that only two probabilities, say $Prob(a|bc)$ and $Prob(c|ab)$, exceed some predefined threshold τ and are thus deemed significant. We can assume that all remaining probabilities are uniformly distributed as follows:

- The terms $Prob(b|bc)$ and $Prob(c|bc)$ are both equal to $(1-Prob(a|bc))/2$. Here, $1-Prob(a|bc)$ is the remaining total probability for the non-significant transitions out of state bc.
- Similarly, the terms $Prob(a|ab)$ and $Prob(b|ab)$ are equal to $(1-Prob(c|ab))/2$.
- Consider state ac. Since there are no significant transitions out of it, we assume that $Prob(a|ac)=Prob(b|ac)=Prob(c|ac)=1/3$. A similar reasoning is applied to all other states.

A Markov model that is defined using these rules is termed a pruned model. We will use $\mathscr{P}^k$ to denote the class of pruned models of order k.

Clearly, a model $M\in\mathscr{P}^k$ can be described much more succinctly. In the previous example, it suffices to define the two significant probability terms instead of the twenty seven terms of the conventional model. More generally, suppose that M contains m significant terms. To transmit the model, we need to transmit the following information:

1. The order k. This takes again $2\log k+1$ bits.
2. The number of significant terms m. This takes $2\log m+1$ bits.
3. The m terms. For each term $Prob(s|s_1\ldots s_k)$, we transmit the sequence $s_1\ldots s_k s$ and the two counts that define the maximum-likelihood estimate [1]. This requires a total of $(k+1)\log|S|+2logn$ per term.

Putting it all together, the DL of a pruned model M is a cost computed as follows:

$$\begin{aligned}cost(x,M^{\theta(k)}) &= 2\log k+1+2\log m+1\\ &\quad +m((k+1)\log|S|+2\log n)\\ &\quad -\log Prob(x|M^{\theta(k)})\end{aligned}$$

We notice that the model description length grows with $m\times k\times\log|S|$ instead of $|S|^k$. In general, we expect $m<|S|^k$, since only few transitions are expected to be significant. Going back to the previous example with models M_1 and M_2, it now becomes possible to select M_2 without requiring a huge value for the ra-

[1]In this case we cannot use simply the count of the sequence containing s, since the receiver has incomplete knowledge of the sequence counts. Note that the counts corresponding to non-significant transitions are not transferred.

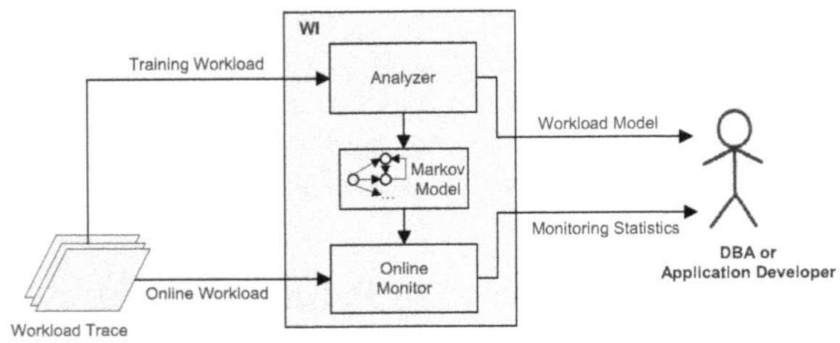

Figure 2: The functionality of WI.

tio $Prob(x|M_2)/Prob(x|M_1)$. The selection among the two actually depends (in part) on the number of significant terms in each case.

What is a good threshold τ for determining significance? A simplistic approach is to set $\tau = 1/|S|$, so that the uniform distribution yields no significant terms. A more robust approach is to use statistical significance tests that can isolate the frequencies that deviate from uniformity, although such tests may be inefficient. Our implementation follows the former one for efficiency reasons and we have found that this approach returns good results in practice.

3.3 Extensions to Multiple Trace Files

Up to this point, we have assumed that all the executed statements are logged in a single sequence $\mathbf{T}$. In practice, a DBMS may log such statements in several files, which correspond to the open physical connections between the application and the DBMS. (This is the case for Oracle Database Replay, for example.) Our techniques extend to such cases with minimal modifications.

Specifically, assume that the input now comprises a collection of ℓ sequences of statements $\mathbf{T}_1, \cdots, \mathbf{T}_\ell$, which are all generated by the same application logic. We wish again to compute a model $M^{\theta(k)}$ that captures the generation of these statements. Using MDL, we define $cost(D,M)$ as the cost to encode the *aggregate* training data (i.e., all sequences) using M. We use a simple scheme that first encodes ℓ (the total number of sequences) followed by an encoding of each sequence. Then, the cost of the model can be computed as:

$$cost(\mathbf{T}, M^{\theta(k)}) = c + \sum_{i=1}^{\ell} cost(\mathbf{T}_i, M^{\theta(k)}),$$

where $cost(\mathbf{T}_i, M^{\theta(k)})$ is computed as described previously, and c is the number of bits to encode ℓ, which is constant across all models.

Note that we do not consider embeddings that straddle different sequences, i.e., $embed(s_1 \dots s_k, \mathbf{T}) = \bigcup_{i=1}^{\ell} embed(s_1 \dots s_k, \mathbf{T}_i)$. This design choice is driven by the same considerations that we described in Section 2, when we discussed the handling of gaps: since code paths are assumed to generate short subsequences, connection affinity is likely to use the same physical connection for a code path, and hence the corresponding subsequence must be logged in the same sequence $\mathbf{T}_i$. This expectation is verified by the results we observed in practice. In fact, the one case where we observed code paths to straddle sequences was an artifact of the application logic, which explicitly switched physical connections for load balancing. The generated model was able to capture this logic, indicating frequent subsequences that corresponded to the split points. Such knowledge can be informative to a DBA who wishes to understand the querying behavior of the application, and in this case, it was also useful to an application developer, who was able to verify that the application logic worked as expected.

4. WI: IMPLEMENTATION & FEATURES

Figure 2 describes the functionality of WI, which comprises two main modules: the **analyzer**, which derives a workload model and predicts which statement patterns are likely to be observed in a running system, and the **online monitor**, which continuously analyzes the workload in order to recompute its current model and detect changes in its trends by comparing the current model with previous ones that represent different phases of the evolving workload.

Algorithm 1: $MODEL(\mathbf{T}, h)$

1 let TR be the trie to be built
2 **for** $i = 1$ *to* n **do**
3 | insert $\mathbf{T}[i]\mathbf{T}[i+1] \cdots \mathbf{T}[i+\min\{h, n-i\}]$ into TR
4 **for** $\ell = 0$ *to* h **do**
5 | **foreach** *node* n_p *of* TR *at level* ℓ **do**
6 | | **foreach** *node* n_c *of* TR *that is a child of* n_p **do**
7 | | | $seq \leftarrow$ the conceptual key of n_p
8 | | | $x \leftarrow$ the label of the edge between n_p and n_c
9 | | | $seq' \leftarrow seq \,||\, x$
10 | | | $Prob(x|seq) \leftarrow \frac{|embed(seq', \mathbf{T})|}{|embed(seq, \mathbf{T})|} = \frac{val(n_c)}{val(n_p)}$
11 | Compute $cost(\mathbf{T}, M^{\theta(\ell)})$ based on all significant $Prob(x|seq)$ computed in this loop
12 $cost(\mathbf{T}, \ell_{min}) \leftarrow \min_{\ell \in [0,h]} \{cost(\mathbf{T}, M^{\theta(\ell)})\}$
13 **return** $M^{\theta(\ell_{min})}$

4.1 Analyzer

The user invokes this module to analyze a training workload.

Computing workload models. Our approach is outlined in Algorithm 1. The algorithm takes as inputs: (1) a training workload $\mathbf{T}$, and (2) the maximum order of all models to be considered h, which is a control knob for our algorithm. We expect the value of h to be small in practice. Having a very large h will make it more difficult for the DBA to understand the patterns. The output of the analyzer is a Markov model that minimizes the DL metric.

Recall from Section 3 that specifying the assignment of transition probabilities (i.e., $\theta(k)$) is equivalent to describing the counts $|embed(\mathbf{p}, \mathbf{T})|$ for every $\mathbf{p} \in S^{k+1}$. For this purpose, WI builds a trie to encode these counts (line 3). A trie, or prefix tree, is an ordered tree data structure [9]. It has $h+1$ levels of nodes. The root node is at level 0, whereas the last level of leaf nodes is at level h. All the children of a node in the trie are ordered based on the labels of the edges from the node to each child. In our case, an edge label is a symbol in S. The key of a node is obtained by concatenating the labels of all the edges in the path from the root to this node. For space efficiency, WI does not physically store such keys. It only associates each node n with a value, denoted as $val(n)$, which represents the value of $|embed(\mathbf{p}, \mathbf{T})|$, where the pattern $\mathbf{p}$ corresponds to the key of the node. We note that if the trie cannot fit into the main memory, we can resort to the use of a disk-based version of the trie, such as the B-trie, which has been proven to store and retrieve variable-length strings efficiently on disk [4].

EXAMPLE 3. *Consider a sequence* $\mathbf{T} = ababababadac$ *and assume that* $h = 1$. *Figure 3 shows the trie that* WI *builds to encode all the counts of patterns of length at most* $h+1 = 2$ *in* $\mathbf{T}$. *The trie consists of* 10 *nodes, which we denote as* n_i *for* $i \in [0,9]$.

We now explain the components associated to each node. For instance, node n_5 *has the key "ab", which is the concatenation of edges in the path from the root node* n_0 *to this node:* $n_0 \xrightarrow{a} n_1 \xrightarrow{b} n_5$. *We associate node* n_5 *with the value* $val(n_5) = 3$ *indicating the event that the pattern "ab" appears three times in* $\mathbf{T}$.

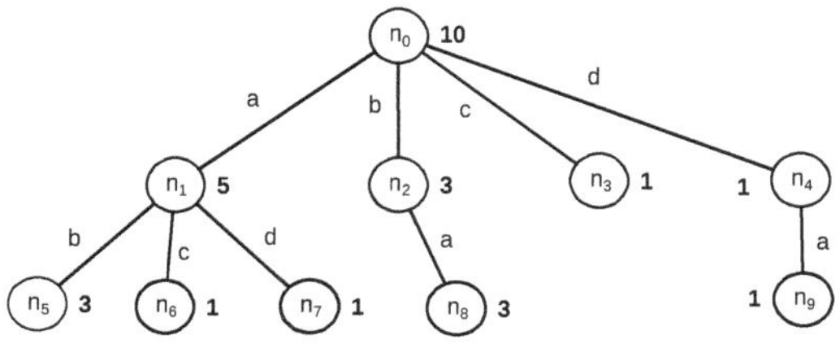

Figure 3: An example of a trie built by WI to derive patterns from the workload $\mathbf{T} = abababadac$.

Algorithm 2: $PATTERN(\mathbf{T}, \ell)$

```
let R be the set of all significant patterns to be found
sig ← T[1]...T[ℓ]
i ← ℓ+1
while i ≤ n − ℓ do
    if Prob(T[i] |T[i−ℓ]...T[i−1]) ≥ θ then
        sig ← sig || T[i]
        i ← i+1
    else
        R ← R ∪ {sig}
        sig ← T[i]...T[i+ℓ−1]
        i ← i+ℓ
return R
```

To build the trie, WI *performs one scan over* $\mathbf{T}$*: it first inserts the subsequence* $T[1]T[2] = ab$ *into the trie, then inserts the next subsequence* $T[2]T[3] = ba$*, then the next subsequence* $T[3]T[4] = ab$*, and so on. Node* n_0 *is at level 0; nodes* $n_i, i \in [1,4]$ *are at level 1; and nodes* $n_i, i \in [5,9]$ *are at level 2.* □

After the trie has been built, WI visits all nodes of level ℓ to compute the DL metric of the model of order ℓ (lines 7- 11). Under the MDL principle with a pruned model (Section 3.2), a term $Prob(x|seq)$ is deemed significant, if and only if its value is no smaller than some predefined threshold τ (we set $\tau = 1/|S|$.) We assume that all remaining probabilities are uniformly distributed. We omit the mathematical formulas to compute such "insignificant" terms, but instead, we provide an example to illustrate the idea.

EXAMPLE 4. *We reconsider Example 3 and assume that* $\tau = 1/4$*. To compute the DL metric for a model of order* 1*,* WI *first visits node* n_1 *and its child nodes* n_5 *-* n_7*. The term* $Prob(b|a) = val(n_5)/val(n_1) = 3/5$ *is deemed significant since it is greater than* $1/4$*. Other transition probabilities from state "a" (i.e.,* $Prob(a|a)$*,* $Prob(c|a)$*,* $Prob(d|a)$*) are insignificant, since their values are less than* τ*. Thus, we assume they are uniformly distributed and estimate their values as* $(1 - Prob(b|a))/3 = 2/15$*.* □

Mining significant patterns. Based on the derived Markov model, WI can predict which statement patterns are likely to be observed in a running system using a heuristic solution. The high level idea is based on the following intuition: if a transition probability $Prob(s|c_1 \ldots c_k)$ is high (e.g., no smaller than 0.7), then the pattern $c_1 \ldots c_k s$ is likely to be observed in a running system. We consider such a pattern *significant*. We assume that there is a user-defined threshold $\theta \in [0,1]$ to determine significant patterns. The implementation of this feature is rather straightforward. We outline the details in Algorithm 2. The input ℓ of Algorithm 2 is the order of the good model computed by Algorithm 1.

Algorithm 3: $LOOP(p)$

```
let R denote a set of different representations of p
for ℓ = 1 to |p|/2 do
    let r_ℓ denote a representation of p where all loops in r_ℓ
    have length ℓ
    r_ℓ ← an empty string
    i ← 1
    while i ≤ |p| do
        j ← i+ℓ
        while j ≤ |p| − ℓ + 1 do
            if p[i]...p[i+ℓ−1] = p[j]...p[j+ℓ−1] then
                j ← j+ℓ
            else
                break
        if j > i+ℓ /* We have found a loop    */
        then
            r_ℓ ← r_ℓ || (p[i]...p[i+ℓ−1])+
            i ← j
        else
            r_ℓ ← r_ℓ || p[i]
            i ← i+1
    R ← R ∪ {r_ℓ}
let r_min be one of r ∈ R such that r_min has the minimum length
return r_min
```

EXAMPLE 5. *We discuss how* WI *derives significant patterns from the sequence of statements given in Example 3, assuming that* $\theta = 0.7$ *and* $\ell = 1$*. First,* WI *initializes* $sig = \mathbf{T}[1] = a$*. For the next symbol* $\mathbf{T}[2] = b$*, since* $Prob(\mathbf{T}[2]|\mathbf{T}[1]) = Prob(b|a) = 3/5 < \theta$*,* WI *reports* $sig = a$ *as significant pattern and resets* $sig = b$*. For the next symbol* $\mathbf{T}[3] = a$*, since* $Prob(\mathbf{T}[3]|\mathbf{T}[2]) = Prob(a|b) = 1 > \theta$*,* WI *updates* $sig = ab$*. Similarly, for the next symbol, since* $Prob(\mathbf{T}[4]|\mathbf{T}[3]) = Prob(b|a) = 3/5 < \theta$*,* WI *reports* $sig = ba$ *as a significant pattern.* WI *continues the process and finally derives* $\{a, ba, d, c\}$ *as the set of significant patterns.* □

Detecting loops in patterns. WI performs a simple additional post-processing step to detect loops in each derived significant pattern. For instance, given a pattern $p = abcbc$, we observe that the subsequence "*bc*" appears more than once in p. Thus, WI represents p in a more compact form as $p' = a(bc)^+$. Here, we use $(bc)^+$ to indicate that there is a loop on the subsequence "*bc*" in the pattern. Note that it is also possible to record the number of times that each subsequence appears in the significant pattern. However, WI chooses to report the loops with the goal to represent repeating user actions or loops in the code paths of a real application. For instance, let us assume that a code path executes a statement a followed by a loop that executes statements b and c. Then, the patterns "*abcbc*" and "*abcbcbc*" generated from this code path should be considered as the same. In contrast, if we had recorded the number of times that each subsequence appears in the pattern, then "*abcbc*" and "*abcbcbc*" would be identified as different patterns. The outline of our approach is given in Algorithm 3.

4.2 Online Monitor

WI maintains a model that is continuously recomputed based on the latest sequences in the workload. More concretely, WI maintains a sliding window over the current workload (the length of the window is a parameter decided by the user), and then derives the model M_{slide} using the sliding window as the training workload.

Each new sequence of statements in the running workload causes an update of the window and a recomputation of M_{slide}.

Once computed, the up-to-date model M_{slide} is compared against the current model M_{curr}. WI outputs a level of confidence, between 0% and 100%, on the similarity of the two models. This output, which is essentially a time series since M_{slide} is being continuously updated, can inform the user about the change in the trend of the running workload.

Assume we need to compare two Markov models M_1 and M_2 that are built for two sequences $\mathbf{T}_1$ and $\mathbf{T}_2$, respectively. (M_1 corresponds to M_{curr} and M_2 corresponds to M_{slide}.)

Models of the same order. We first consider the case when the two models have the same order k. Recall from the previous section that specifying the parameters of a Markov model is equivalent to describing the counts $|embed(\mathbf{p},\mathbf{T})|$ for all $\mathbf{p} \in S^{k+1}$. Intuitively, if the distributions of all patterns of length $k+1$ of $\mathbf{T}_1$ and $\mathbf{T}_2$ are very different, then the two models are likely very different. Based on this observation, WI collects a sample of all patterns of length $(k+1)$ from each workload, and then applies the KS test [7] on the two samples to compute the similarity of the two models. The KS test has the advantage of making no assumption about the distribution of data, which is a good fit for our case. The output of the KS test (and thus the online monitor module) is a value $x \in [0,1]$ stating that the two models are similar with a level of $100 \times x\%$ confidence.

EXAMPLE 6. *Consider a workload* $\mathbf{T} = ababababadac$*, and assume that* WI *needs to derive two models* M_1 *(corresponding to* M_{curr}*) and* M_2 *(corresponding to* M_{slide}*) for the corresponding two subsequences* $\mathbf{T}_1 = abababad$ *and* $\mathbf{T}_2 = ababadac$ *of* $\mathbf{T}$*. The two models have the same order* $k = 1$.

From $\mathbf{T}_1$*,* WI *derives a collection of all patterns of length* $k+1 = 2$ *as* $C_1 = [ab,ba,ab,ba,ab,ba,ad]$*. Similarly, from* $\mathbf{T}_2$*,* WI *derives a collection of patterns of length* $k+1 = 2$ *as* $C_2 = [ab,ba,ab,ba,ad,da,ac]$*. The similarity between* $\mathbf{T}_1$ *and* $\mathbf{T}_2$ *is computed based on the KS test on the two samples* C_1 *and* C_2*, which results in the value 70%. Thus, we can conclude that* $\mathbf{T}_1$ *is similar to* $\mathbf{T}_2$*, which matches our intuition.* □

Models of different orders. We now consider two Markov models $M_1^{\theta(k_1)}$ and $M_2^{\theta(k_2)}$ that have different orders and assume that $k_1 > k_2$. In this case, describing the counts $|embed(\mathbf{p},\mathbf{T}_2)|$ for all $\mathbf{p} \in S^{k_1+1}$ of $\mathbf{T}_2$ is sufficient to specify the parameters of the Markov model of order k_2 for $\mathbf{T}_2$. The reason is that we can easily compute $|embed(\mathbf{p},\mathbf{T}_2)|$ for all $\mathbf{p} \in S^{k_2+1}$ from the counts of $|embed(\mathbf{p}',\mathbf{T}_2)|$ with $\mathbf{p}' \in S^{k_1+1}$. Specifically, $|embed(\mathbf{p},\mathbf{T}_2)|$ is the summation over all $|embed(\mathbf{p}',\mathbf{T}_2)|$, where $\mathbf{p}$ is a prefix of $\mathbf{p}'$. Note that $\mathbf{p}$ is of length k_2+1 and $\mathbf{p}'$ is of length k_1+1 and $k_2 < k_1$. Therefore, WI collects all patterns of length (k_1+1) from the two workloads, and then applies the same KS test as described for the case of models of a same order, to compute the similarity of the two workloads.

EXAMPLE 7. *Consider a workload* $\mathbf{T} = ababababadabcdef$*, and assume that* WI *needs to derive the models* M_1 *(corresponding to* M_{curr}*) and* M_2 *(corresponding to* M_{slide}*) for the following two subsequences* $\mathbf{T}_1 = abababad$ *and* $\mathbf{T}_2 = adabcdef$ *of* $\mathbf{T}$*. In this case, the model* M_1 *for* $\mathbf{T}_1$ *has the order* $k_1 = 1$*, whereas the model* M_2 *for* $\mathbf{T}_2$ *has the order* $k_2 = 0$.

From $\mathbf{T}_1$*,* WI *derives a collection of all patterns of length* $k_1 + 1 = 2$ *as* $C_1 = [ab,ba,ab,ba,ab,ba,ad]$*. Similarly, from* $\mathbf{T}_2$*,* WI *derives a collection of patterns of length* $k_1 + 1 = 2$ *as* $C_2 = [ad,da,ab,bc,cd,de,ef]$*. The similarity of* $\mathbf{T}_1$ *and* $\mathbf{T}_2$ *is computed based on the KS test on the two samples* C_1 *and* C_2*, which results in the value 9%. We can conclude that* $\mathbf{T}_1$ *is very different from* $\mathbf{T}_2$*, which matches our intuition.* □

Optimization. WI reuses the computations calculated during the previous window to derive the model for the current window. In more detail, WI updates the trie with the sequences that are removed/added into the current window, and then traverses the trie, as described in the previous section, to derive the model. This optimization is much more beneficial than the naive approach of building the trie for the sequence in the current window from scratch. The reason is that the current window should typically share a large portion of patterns with the previous window.

5. EXPERIMENTAL RESULTS

This section presents the results of the experimental study that we conducted to evaluate the effectiveness and the efficiency of WI. In what follows, we first discuss the experimental methodology and then present our findings, based on the results of our experiments.

5.1 Methodology

In our experiments, we have used a prototype implementation of WI written in Java. The prototype implements both main features described in this paper (Analyzer and Online Monitor), whereas the currently released version of WI in Oracle 12c implements only the first one (the Analyzer). So, we have used the prototype in all the experiments for consistency reasons. Note that the results for the feature that is implemented both in the prototype and as part of our released product are similar. We have conducted our experiments on a machine running 64-bit Ubuntu OS with four-core Intel(R) Core(TM) i7 Q820 @1.73GHz CPU and 4GB RAM.

Workloads. We have used four in-house benchmark (*IB*) workloads captured using Oracle Database Replay [11]:

- **tpcc**: TPC-C benchmark [3] is a benchmark widely referenced in the database literature. It portrays a wholesale supplier with a number of geographically distributed sales districts and associated warehouses.
- **swingbench**: Swingbench [1] is a benchmark designed to stress test a database server. It simulates the workload coming from concurrent customers that place orders.
- **siebel**: Siebel is a workload that has been generated by running Oracle Siebel CRM application [2].
- **billing**: Billing is a workload generated by a customer-provided application benchmark. It performs resource usage monitoring and calculates the cost of provided services.

As described in Section 2, WI first transforms each statement by substituting constants (e.g., appearing in predicates) by abstract variables before analyzing the workloads. Table 2 shows the characteristics of these workloads in terms of: (1) the length of the workload, which is the total number of statements in the workload, (2) the number of distinct statements in the workload, and (3) the number of trace files. Note that the number of trace files is exactly the same as the number of open physical connections to the DBMS when the workload was recorded.

In addition to these IB workloads, we have used synthetic workloads generated by specific Markov Models. For such workloads, we have more information about the logic of the process that generates them, and thus better insights into the results of WI. In our data generator, we have varied the following parameters: the number of distinct statements $|S|$, the original order k_{org} of the model, the length of the workload n, and a core transition threshold $\alpha \in [0,1]$.

Workload	Length	# Statements	# Trace files
tpcc	445783	78	100
billing	1693111	6	101
swingbench	17775484	24	399
siebel	743184	277	122

Table 2: Characteristics of the *IB* workloads.

Parameter	Values
The original order (k_{org})	1, 2, **3**, 4, 5
Number of distinct statements (S)	20, **40**, 60, 80
The length (n)	$\mathbf{6}\times 10^6$, 8×10^6, 10×10^6, 12×10^6
The core transition threshold (α)	0.6, **0.7**, 0.8, 0.9

Table 3: Parameters to generate synthetic workloads (default values in bold).

We have used the parameter α as follows. For each "base" sequence $s_1 \dots s_k$ with $s_1 \in S, \cdots, s_k \in S$, we have randomly selected a symbol $s \in S$ and set the following transition probabilities:

$$Prob(s|s_1 \dots s_k) = \alpha$$
$$Prob(c|s_1 \dots s_k) = \frac{1-\alpha}{|S|-1}, \ \forall c \in S - \{s\}$$

If α is large (e.g., $\alpha > 0.5$), the pattern $s_1 \dots s_k s$ appears more frequently than other patterns that have the same prefix (i.e., $s_1 \cdots s_k c$) in the generated workload.

Control knobs. WI has two control knobs: the knob h that limits the order of all Markov models being considered, and the threshold θ to mine significant patterns. We have set the default values of h and θ to be 6 and 0.7, respectively. We also report the results with other value settings of these knobs in later sections.

5.2 The Analyzer

IB workloads. We begin with experiments that evaluate the effectiveness of WI on deriving Markov models for the *IB* workloads.

Table 4 reports the order of the Markov models derived by WI for the *IB* workloads and the number of significant patterns discovered, for different values of the knob θ. Intuitively, the higher the value of θ is, the smaller the number of significant patterns WI derives. The number of significant patterns found by WI is much smaller than the number of patterns that we would have discovered if the appearence of statements was completely random. As a concrete example, according to Table 2, in our siebel workload, there are 277 distinct statements. Also, in Table 4, we see that the chosen order for the Markov model that describes this workload is 1. An order of 1 indicates that we expect to find rather short patterns of statements that on average are of length 2. The number of possible pairs of statements is $277 \times 277 = 76,729$. This gives us the maximum number of pairs that we would have discovered if the appearence of statements was completely random. Instead, in our experiments (Table 4), we found a number of 325, 297, and 216

Workload	Order	# significant patterns		
		$\theta = 0.6$	$\theta = 0.7$	$\theta = 0.8$
tpcc	1	49	49	49
billing	2	10	8	2
swingbench	5	230	148	146
siebel	1	325	297	216

Table 4: Order of the Markov models for the *IB* workloads and number of significant patterns.

Workload	Running time	Space
tpcc	0.8sec	2.8MB
billing	0.4sec	3.7KB
swingbench	3.4sec	8.9KB
siebel	1.0sec	3.8MB

Table 5: Running time and space usage of WI for *IB* workloads.

significant patterns respectively, for various values of parameter θ. These numbers are significantly smaller than the calculated maximum. WI also reports the top patterns that have been identified in the given workload ordered by different useful metadata, including the DB time (i.e., the time that a pattern has consumed in the database server), the number of executions, and the pattern lengths. Figure 4 shows an example of such a report on swingbench.

In terms of efficiency, Table 5 reports the running time and space usage of WI while processing each *IB* workload. Clearly, WI takes only a few seconds to analyze each *IB* workload, and consumes a small amount of main memory.

Examples of significant patterns. We have presented the significant patterns discovered by WI to some expert users of the IB benchmarks or applications and they have verified that the discovered patterns reflect real patterns of statements that are executed in the respective workloads. Table 6 shows two examples of such frequent patterns automatically identified by WI in the swingbench workload. We have chosen the particular workload in our example, because it comes from an open source benchmark and we can therefore show the SQL text of queries that are executed in the database as part of it.

Pattern 1 corresponds to a codepath that places an order. We note that pattern 1 is exactly the first pattern (i.e., the pattern with ID 2) shown in Figure 4. It consists of five distinct statements (S1-S5). First, it creates a new order identifier (S1). Then, it inserts the order information in table ORDERS (S2), it retrieves some information about the product that is ordered (S3-S4), and finally it inserts the items that correspond to this order into table ORDER_ITEMS. The subsequence S3, S4, S5 forms a loop in pattern 1, indicating that it appears more than once in the pattern. This reflects the fact that the given order may include one or more items.

Similarly, pattern 2 corresponds to a codepath that creates a new customer and then signs the customer in into the system. The pattern consists of four statements (S6-S9). First, it creates a new customer identifier (S6) and inserts some customer's information into table CUSTOMERS (S7). Subsequently, it records that the particular customer has logged in (S8) and retrieves some information related to the customer (S9). Also, the subsequence S8, S9 forms a loop in pattern 2. The pattern reflects a registration of a new customer, followed by multiple (one or more) logins.

It is clear from this example that WI's output has a high correlation with the code paths inside the application logic. A user can gain insight about what the application is doing by observing the aforementioned patterns, among others. Note that we are associating the patterns with more useful metadata as described above (e.g., the number of executions and the time that a pattern has consumed in the database server). Furthermore, an analysis of the patterns may reveal potential optimizations. In our example, for instance, the result set of statement S3 is part of the result set of S4. Hence, a potential optimization in this case would be combining the two statements in one.

Note that the length of the two patterns is five and four respectively, but both of them contain loops, which means that some of the statements they contain are executed one or more times in a row. This matches the order of the Markov Chain identified by WI,

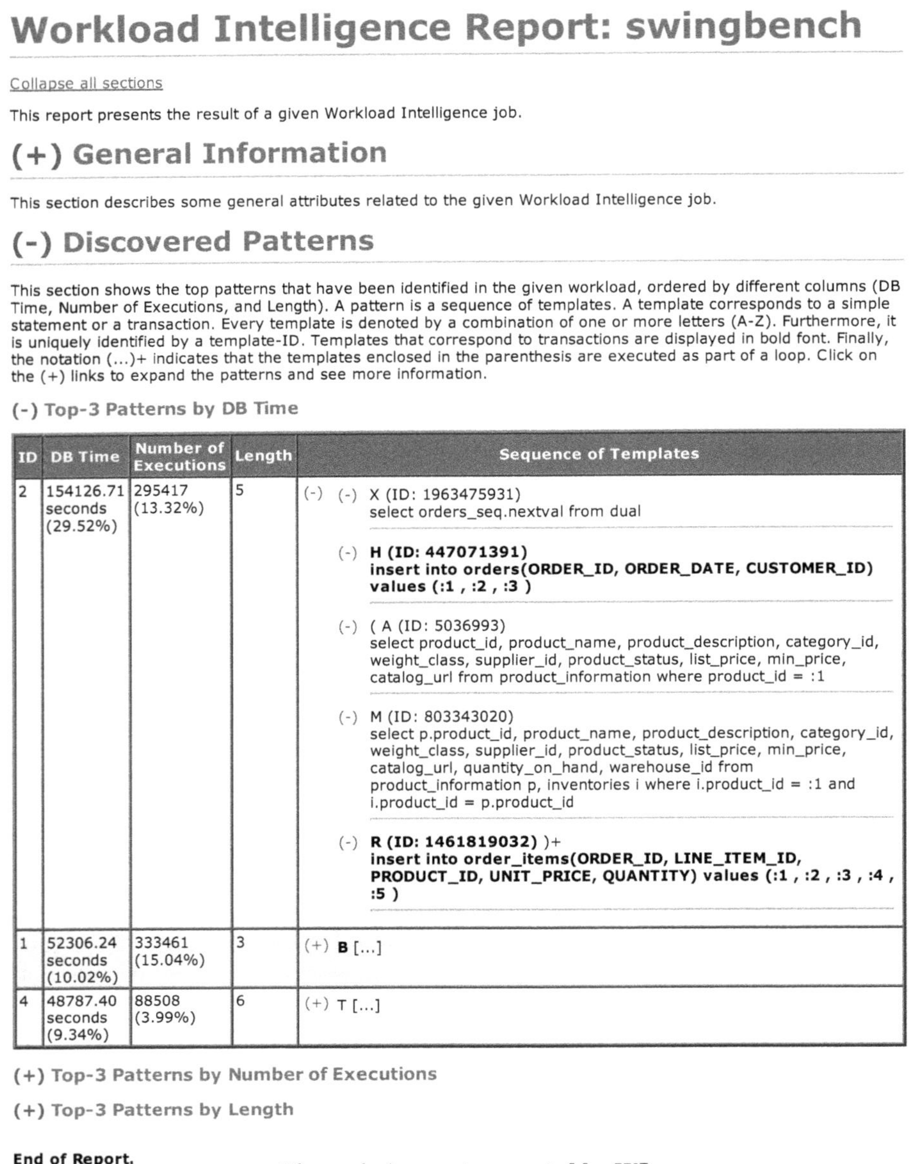

Workload Intelligence Report: swingbench

Collapse all sections

This report presents the result of a given Workload Intelligence job.

(+) General Information

This section describes some general attributes related to the given Workload Intelligence job.

(-) Discovered Patterns

This section shows the top patterns that have been identified in the given workload, ordered by different columns (DB Time, Number of Executions, and Length). A pattern is a sequence of templates. A template corresponds to a simple statement or a transaction. Every template is denoted by a combination of one or more letters (A-Z). Furthermore, it is uniquely identified by a template-ID. Templates that correspond to transactions are displayed in bold font. Finally, the notation (...)+ indicates that the templates enclosed in the parenthesis are executed as part of a loop. Click on the (+) links to expand the patterns and see more information.

(-) Top-3 Patterns by DB Time

ID	DB Time	Number of Executions	Length	Sequence of Templates
2	154126.71 seconds (29.52%)	295417 (13.32%)	5	(-) (-) X (ID: 1963475931) select orders_seq.nextval from dual (-) **H (ID: 447071391) insert into orders(ORDER_ID, ORDER_DATE, CUSTOMER_ID) values (:1 , :2 , :3)** (-) (A (ID: 5036993) select product_id, product_name, product_description, category_id, weight_class, supplier_id, product_status, list_price, min_price, catalog_url from product_information where product_id = :1 (-) M (ID: 803343020) select p.product_id, product_name, product_description, category_id, weight_class, supplier_id, product_status, list_price, min_price, catalog_url, quantity_on_hand, warehouse_id from product_information p, inventories i where i.product_id = :1 and i.product_id = p.product_id (-) **R (ID: 1461819032)**)+ **insert into order_items(ORDER_ID, LINE_ITEM_ID, PRODUCT_ID, UNIT_PRICE, QUANTITY) values (:1 , :2 , :3 , :4 , :5)**
1	52306.24 seconds (10.02%)	333461 (15.04%)	3	(+) **B** [...]
4	48787.40 seconds (9.34%)	88508 (3.99%)	6	(+) T [...]

(+) Top-3 Patterns by Number of Executions

(+) Top-3 Patterns by Length

End of Report.

Figure 4: A report generated by WI.

which reflects the fact that a typical pattern of this workload has a length of at least six statements.

Synthetic workloads. We now study the effectiveness of WI in analyzing synthetic workloads generated by varying the four parameters: $|S|$, α, k_{org}, and n. For this task, we compare the order of the model derived by WI against the original order of the model that was used to generate the corresponding workload.

First, we vary $|S|$ and α. (The original k_{org} and the length of the file are set according to their default values: $k_{org} = 3$ and $n = 6 \times 10^6$.) WI is able to discover the model that is used to generate the corresponding workload in all cases. This capability is enabled due to the usage of the DL metric to evaluate the goodness of each computed Markov model.

To gain insights into the above result, we study the details of the DL metrics of all models considered by WI. Figure 5 shows the details of the models built for the synthetic workload generated by setting $\alpha = 0.6$ and $|S| = 40$, as an example. Recall that the DL metric of a model, $cost(D,M)$, is the sum of the cost to encode the model, $cost(M)$, and the cost to encode the workload using the model, $cost(D|M)$. Some general trends that we observed follow:

- The cost to encode a higher-order model is much higher than that of a lower-order model. For instance, in Figure 5, $cost(M^{\theta(4)})$ is six times greater than $cost(M^{\theta(3)})$. The reason is that the value of $M^{\theta(k)}$ grows with $mk \log|S|$, where k and $\log|S|$ are small in this case, and m is the number of significant transition probabilities. The value of m is 400K in $M^{\theta(4)}$, which is much larger than the corresponding value 64K for $M^{\theta(3)}$. Essentially, the number of significant terms (i.e., transition probabilities) in $M^{\theta(3)}$ matches the number of significant terms that is used when generating the data set. There are two reasons for this. First, the data set follows a Markov model of order 3. Second, recall from Section 3.2 that a probability $Prob(c|s_1s_2s_3)$ is deemed significant if it is greater than a predefined threshold τ, which is set to be $1/|S| = 0.025$ in our case. Because of the way we generate the synthetic workload, for each base sequence $s_1s_2s_3$, with $s_i \in S$ and $i \in [1,3]$, there is

Statement	SQL
S1	**SELECT** orders_seq.nextval **FROM** dual
S2	**INSERT** into orders(ORDER_ID, ORDER_DATE, CUSTOMER_ID) values (:1 , :2 , :3)
S3	**SELECT** product_id, product_name, product_description, category_id, weight_class, supplier_id, product_status, list_price, min_price, catalog_url **FROM** product_information **WHERE** product_id = :1
S4	**SELECT** p.product_id, product_name, product_description, category_id, weight_class, supplier_id, product_status, list_price, min_price, catalog_url, quantity_on_hand, warehouse_id **FROM** product_information p, inventories i where i.product_id = :1 and i.product_id = p.product_id
S5	**INSERT** into order_items(ORDER_ID, LINE_ITEM_ID, PRODUCT_ID, UNIT_PRICE, QUANTITY) values (:1 , :2 , :3 , :4 , :5)
Pattern 1	S1 S2 (S3 S4 S5)+
S6	**SELECT** customer_seq.nextval **FROM** dual
S7	**INSERT** into customers (customer_id, cust_first_name, cust_last_name, nls_language, nls_territory, credit_limit, cust_email, account_mgr_id) values (:1 , :2 , :3 , :4 , :5 , :6 ,:7 , :8)
S8	**INSERT** into logon values(:1 ,:2)
S9	**SELECT** customer_id, cust_first_name, cust_last_name, nls_language, nls_territory, credit_limit, cust_email, account_mgr_id **FROM** customers **WHERE** customer_id = :1
Pattern 2	S6 S7 (S8 S9)+

Table 6: Examples of significant patterns discovered by WI for the swingbench workload.

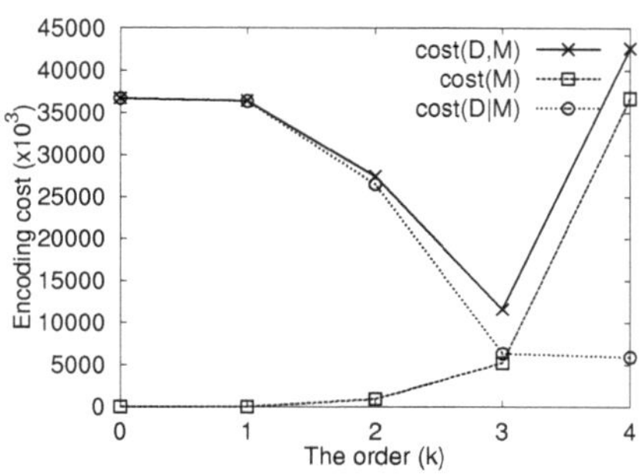

Figure 5: Details of the DL metrics on synthetic workloads.

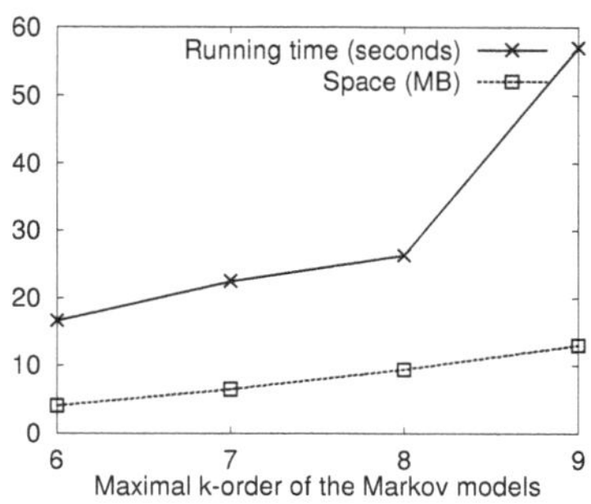

Figure 6: Running time and space.

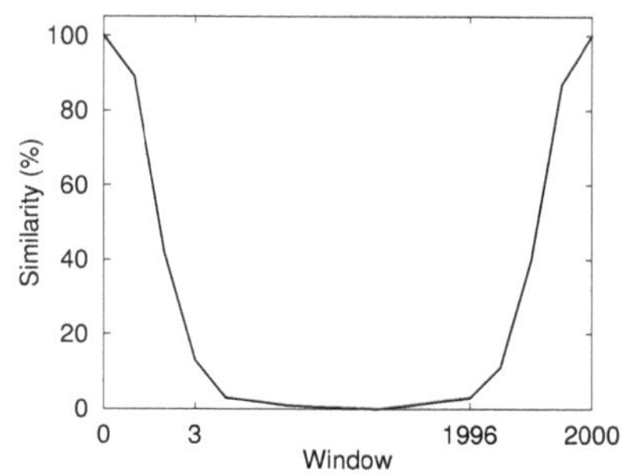

Figure 7: Online monitor.

exactly *one symbol* $s \in S$ such that $Prob(s|s_1s_2s_3) = 0.6 > \tau = 0.025$. As a result, $Prob(s|s_1s_2s_3)$ is deemed significant in our model, whereas $Prob(c|s_1s_2s_3)$ is not significant for every $c \neq s$. Therefore, the number of significant terms in $M^{\theta(3)}$ is $|S|^3 = 40^3$.

- The cost to represent the workload using a higher-order model is smaller than that of a lower-order model. For example, in Figure 5, $cost(D|M^{\theta(2)})$ is double the value of $cost(D|M^{\theta(3)})$. As another example, $cost(D|M^{\theta(3)})$ is larger than $cost(D|M^{\theta(4)})$, although the difference is negligible. Again, this result matches our intuition, since the higher the order of the model, the more details the model can capture about the workload. Also, the data set follows a Markov model of order 3; thus, the difference between $cost(D|M^{\theta(3)})$ and $cost(D|M^{\theta(k)})$ is small for all $k > 3$.

Overall, the model of order 3 has the minimal DL value, and thus WI chooses the particular model to represent the workload. Note that, in Figure 5, we do not show the details of DL values for models of orders greater than 4, since these values are in the order of 10^8 and are much larger than other values shown in the figure.

We have also studied the effectiveness of WI when varying the length n and the original order k_{org}. The results show that these parameters do not affect the result of WI. We omit the details here.

In terms of efficiency, Figure 6 shows the average running time and the memory consumption of WI for the synthetic workload considered above (i.e., $S = 40$, $\alpha = 0.6$, $k_{org} = 3$ and $n = 6$M), as we vary the knob on the maximal order of all Markov models (h). As is expected, the higher the value of h, the more space and the more running time that WI needs to derive the model. Based on our experience and our experimental results, we suggest setting the value of h to a relatively low value as a best practice. Larger values not only require more computational resources, but may also lead to longer patterns that may be more difficult for a DBA to interpret. Overall, our experiments indicate that WI typically runs very efficiently and consumes a small amount of memory.

5.3 Online Monitor

We next study the online monitoring functionality of WI by using a new workload *WI-dyn*, generated by mixing together appropriate portions from workloads billing and swingbench. Specifically, workload *WI-dyn* goes through three phases: the first phase is a sample of statements from workload swingbench, the next phase transitions to statements from workload billing, and the last phase has the same distribution as the first phase.

We assume that, initially, the system is using a model that represents the first phase of workload *WI-dyn*. WI continuously computes the optimal Markov model for a workload that consists of a sliding window. The sliding window comprises the last 2M statements from the workload and is updated every 2K statements. Note that WI does not record the full text of each statement. A fingerprint value suffices; hence, the memory required to store the sliding window is actually modest. WI computes a new model every time the window is updated and then compares it to the initial model.

Figure 7 shows the monitoring statistics produced by WI for workload *WI-dyn*. The output shows that the similarity between the two models (current and initial) decreases after the first five updates of the sliding window, when the workload shifts to the second phase of *WI-dyn*. However, when the workload shifts back to the original distribution, the output shows a high similarity. At the end of phase three, the similarity is 100% as the distribution completely comes back to the distribution of the workload in the beginning of phase one. Interestingly, WI requires only a few seconds to update the model for a new sequence of symbols of the workload.

6. RELATED WORK

The work related to WI can be broadly classified into two areas.

Mining significant subsequences. Our work relates to the problem of identifying frequent and statistically relevant subsequences in a sequence (e.g., [5, 13]), since we also find significant patterns that are likely to be observed in a running system. Methods proposed in this area find subsequences that are not necessarily contiguous. In contrast, WI builds a different model for the workload, for which frequent subsequences with gaps are not a good fit. As mentioned in Section 1, the workload model can be used to infer information about the application logic that generates the workload. As a result, WI can be useful in various applications such as query optimization, comparing workloads and generating artificial workloads.

There is another line of research on *frequent sequence mining (FSM)* (e.g., [14, 19]) that also relates to our work. Given a collection of input sequences of items (e.g., a set of text documents), the goal of FSM is to find all subsequences (e.g., word sequences) that appear in sufficiently many input sequences. In WI, we are interested not only in the patterns that are likely to be observed in a running system, but also in building a richer model of the workload. Such a rich model aims at inferring information about the application logic that generates the workload. FSM techniques do not provide such functionality; they are therefore not sufficient for WI.

Another work [17] addresses the problem of identifying contiguous significant patterns from a sequence, based on the count of the characters in each subsequence, without taking into account the order in which these characters appear. By doing so, the methods described in the corresponding paper [17] cannot infer the application logic that drives the workload, which is our main goal in WI.

Workload analysis for optimizing database systems. Previous workload studies focus on describing the statistical summaries of run-time behavior [8, 20], predicting the buffer hit ratio [10], and improving caching performance [18]. These studies employ rather simple approaches, since they do not take into account a model of the application that generates the workload. In WI, we overcome this drawback by combining the MDL logic with Markov chain models that, as shown in this paper, provide a rich representation of a given workload.

Modeling workloads with Markov models has also been introduced in a previous work, Houdini [16], in the context of shared-nothing parallel databases. Given the current state of a transaction (e.g., which query has just been executed), Houdini relies on the Markov model to predict which actions the transaction would perform next. This information is then used to guide database optimization, e.g., executing the transaction at the node with the partition of data that it will access the most. Both WI and Houdini share the idea of using Markov models to model database workloads. However, WI differs from Houdini in the following two aspects. First, the Markov models built in Houdini are first order (i.e., Houdini only considers transitions from one statement to another one), whereas the models that WI considers can be of a higher order, chosen by employing the MDL logic. As discussed in Section 2, WI needs to find a good model that strikes a balance between its complexity and its accuracy in describing the data. Houdini's first-order Markov model cannot guarantee the same property and can potentially build a poor representation of the application that generated the workload. Second, WI utilizes the Markov model for other applications as well, such as comparing workloads or generating artificial workloads. Houdini does not support such applications.

7. CONCLUSION

In this paper, we presented WI, an effective tool for workload modeling and mining. Part of WI has been implemented in Oracle Database 12c. The goal of WI is to build a Markov model for a given sequence of statements in a workload. Such a model can be used in several applications, including (a) prediction of statement patterns that are likely to be observed in a running system, (b) gathering statistics and metadata related to the aforementioned patterns that can yield a better insight of what is running in the database server and enable optimizations that target sequences of statements, (c) generation of artificial workloads with similar characteristics as the original one, and (d) comparison of different instances of a given workload. We demonstrated the effectiveness of WI with an experimental performance study on synthetic workloads and customer-provided application benchmarks.

8. REFERENCES

[1] http://www.dominicgiles.com/swingbench.html.

[2] http://www.oracle.com/us/products/applications/siebel.

[3] http://www.tpc.org/tpcc/.

[4] N. Askitis and J. Zobel. B-tries for disk-based string management. *The VLDB Journal*, 18(1), 2009.

[5] M. J. Atallah and W. Szpankowski. Detection of significant sets of episodes in event sequences. In *ICDM*, 2004.

[6] P. Bernstein, I. Cseri, N. Dani, N. Ellis, A. Kalhan, G. Kakivaya, D. Lomet, R. Manne, L. Novik, and T. Talius. Adapting Microsoft SQL server for cloud computing. In *ICDE*, 2011.

[7] C. M. Bishop. *Pattern Recognition and Machine Learning (Information Science and Statistics)*. 2006.

[8] S. Chaudhuri, P. Ganesan, and V. Narasayya. Primitives for workload summarization and implications for sql. In *VLDB*, 2003.

[9] J. Clément, P. Flajolet, and B. Vallée. Dynamical sources in information theory: A general analysis of trie structures. *Algorithmica*, 29(1), 2001.

[10] A. Dan, P. S. Yu, and J. Y. Chung. Characterization of database access pattern for analytic prediction of buffer hit probability. *The VLDB Journal*, 4(1), 1995.

[11] L. Galanis, S. Buranawatanachoke, R. Colle, B. Dageville, K. Dias, J. Klein, S. Papadomanolakis, L. L. Tan, V. Venkataramani, Y. Wang, and G. Wood. Oracle database replay. In *SIGMOD Conference*, 2008.

[12] P. Grunwald. A tutorial introduction to the minimum description length principle. In *Advances in Minimum Description Length: Theory and Applications*, 2005.

[13] H. Mannila, H. Toivonen, and A. Inkeri Verkamo. Discovery of frequent episodes in event sequences. *Data Min. Knowl. Discov.*, 1(3), 1997.

[14] I. Miliaraki, K. Berberich, R. Gemulla, and S. Zoupanos. Mind the gap: large-scale frequent sequence mining. In *SIGMOD Conference*, 2013.

[15] J. R. Norris. *Markov chains*. Cambridge series in statistical and probabilistic mathematics. Cambridge University Press, 1998.

[16] A. Pavlo, E. P. C. Jones, and S. Zdonik. On predictive modeling for optimizing transaction execution in parallel oltp systems. *Proc. VLDB Endow.*, 5(2), 2011.

[17] M. Sachan and A. Bhattacharya. Mining statistically significant substrings using the chi-square statistic. *PVLDB*, 5(10), 2012.

[18] C. Sapia. Promise: Predicting query behavior to enable predictive caching strategies for olap systems. In *DaWaK*, 2000.

[19] R. Srikant and R. Agrawal. Mining sequential patterns: Generalizations and performance improvements. In *EDBT*, 1996.

[20] P. S. Yu, M.-S. Chen, H.-U. Heiss, and S. Lee. On workload characterization of relational database environments. *IEEE Trans. Softw. Eng.*, 18(4), 1992.

APPENDIX

A. EXTENSIONS

In this section, we present some ideas related to the issue of identifying an appropriate templatization method for WI.

Recall from Section 2.1 that before building the model of a given workload, WI preprocesses the input statements by executing a templatization algorithm that assigns each one of them into an appropriate template. The rationale is that we want to group together into the same template statements that perform a similar task. By doing so, we reduce the number of symbols in our alphabet S. Intuitively, a good templatization algorithm should increase the chances of discovering meaningful patterns.

There is a wide spectrum of choices for the templatization algorithm. Here, we present a few examples of options that such an algorithm could use in order to group different statements together into the same template:

- Statements whose SQL text matches after removing literal values, extra whitespaces, new line characters, comments, and variable names.
- Statements that access the same objects.
- Statements that contain the same joins.
- Statements of the same type. For example, a templatization algorithm could use one template to represent all selects, another one for all inserts, and different ones for updates, and deletes.
- Equivalent statements. For example, a sophisticated templatization algorithm could be immune to permutations of table names, column names, and predicates. Furthermore, it could ignore table aliases, or even rewrite queries that contain views as new queries against the base tables.

The templatization algorithm in WI currently implements only the first option from the previous list to avoid costly transformations by keeping templatization simple, while preserving the nice characteristics we mentioned above. We believe that our choice is good enough for the typical cases we consider, since WI has been designed mainly for workloads generated by applications running on top of a database server, rather than workloads containing ad hoc SQL text. In the future, we plan to extend our algorithm to use more sophisticated transformations and rules, and determine which rules to apply on-the-fly.

Purity: Building Fast, Highly-Available Enterprise Flash Storage from Commodity Components

John Colgrove, John D. Davis, John Hayes, Ethan L. Miller, Cary Sandvig,
Russell Sears*, Ari Tamches, Neil Vachharajani, and Feng Wang
Pure Storage
Mountain View, CA, USA
coz,johnd,jhayes,elm,cary,sears,ari,neil,fwang@purestorage.com

ABSTRACT

Although flash storage has largely replaced hard disks in consumer class devices, enterprise workloads pose unique challenges that have slowed adoption of flash in "performance tier" storage appliances. In this paper, we describe Purity, the foundation of Pure Storage's Flash Arrays, the first all-flash enterprise storage system to support compression, deduplication, and high-availability.

Purity borrows techniques from modern database and key-value storage architectures, and introduces novel storage primitives that have wide applicability to data management systems. For instance, all writes in Purity are monotonic, and deletions are handled using an atomic predicate-based tuple *elision* primitive.

Purity's redundancy mechanisms are optimized for SSD failure modes and performance characteristics, allowing for fast recovery from component failures and lower space overhead than the best hard disk systems. We built deduplication and data compression schemes atop these primitives.

Flash changes storage capacity/performance tradeoffs: unlike disk-based systems, flash deployments are rarely performance bound. A single Purity appliance can provide over 7 GiB/s of throughput on 32 KiB random I/Os, even through multiple device failures, and while providing asynchronous off-site replication. Typical installations have 99.9% latencies under 1 ms, and production arrays average 5.4× data reduction and 99.999% availability.

Purity takes advantage of storage performance increasing more rapidly than computational performance to build a simpler (with respect to engineering, installation, and management) scale-up storage appliance that supports hundreds of terabytes of highly-available, high-performance storage. The resulting performance and capacity supports many customer deployments of multiple applications, including scale-out and parallel systems, such as MongoDB and Oracle RAC, on a single Purity appliance.

*Corresponding author

SIGMOD'15, May 31–June 4, 2015, Melbourne, Victoria, Australia.

ACM 978-1-4503-2758-9/15/05 ...$15.00.
http://dx.doi.org/10.1145/2723372.2742798

Categories and Subject Descriptors

D.4.2 [**Storage Management**]: Storage hierarchies; Secondary storage

Keywords

Storage Area Networks; Enterprise Flash Storage; Deduplication; Log structured storage; High availability; Scale up architectures

1. INTRODUCTION

Most "performance tier" applications—those that favor I/O rate over capacity—store their data in virtual block devices that are exposed over the network by enterprise storage arrays. Historically, such systems used hard disks, so random reads and writes were expensive, but raw storage capacity was cheap. As a result, large-scale storage resorted to scale-out architectures to achieve reasonable performance.

Flash reverses this capacity/performance tradeoff and, as flash storage capacity becomes cheaper, it has begun to displace disk for performance tier applications. However, enterprise users demand resiliency, high availability, and scalability in addition to performance, and want it all at no higher cost per gigabyte than they pay for high-performance disk. In this paper, we present Purity, a system that uses commodity solid state disks (*SSDs*) and servers to meet these requirements.

Enterprise storage users frequently make clones, snapshots, and off-site copies of volumes to provide data resiliency. To make these operations more efficient and less disruptive, we store data in *mediums*—coarse-grained mappings that we expose as virtual containers. This allows us to virtualize all storage resources, making many of the system features that conserve capacity easier to implement, at the expense of additional random reads.

We leverage flash's ability to perform fast random reads and sequential writes by compressing data and storing a single instance of duplicate blocks written to different logical addresses. Using these and other techniques, we significantly reduce the amount of flash capacity needed for a given workload. This provides us cost parity with disk capacity at significantly higher levels of availability and performance than disk.

Although they continue to improve, SSDs pay a large penalty for random writes [55], so Purity uses log-structured indexes and data layouts to ensure that data is written in large sequential chunks. We stripe the data written by these structures across many drives, and use Reed-Solomon encoding for redundancy, allowing Purity to tolerate the loss of two SSDs without losing availability. In fact, we encourage potential customers to pull drives and unplug controllers as they evaluate Purity and competitive products.

Flash products for higher performance environments focus on direct-attached storage instead of redundant deployments. This causes them to become unavailable during machine failures, and prevents deduplication and load balancing across multiple tenants. In contrast, Purity allows quick failover from one controller to a live spare by having the spare "follow" the primary system, at significantly lower costs.

On average, these data reduction and fault tolerance techniques provide real-world applications with 5.4× more effective storage than the physical storage in the system, excluding gains from "thin provisioning," which would count unused space as application data. On average, our customers provision approximately 12× more virtual space than physical storage. We publish these numbers continuously[1] as averages across customer installations that are constantly monitored by our operations team.

This paper makes the following contributions: In Section 2 we examine the implications of flash storage on disk-based enterprise and scale-out storage architectures. Section 3 presents a set of design principles, motivated by these hardware trends and recent research results, upon which Purity is based. Next, in Section 4 we discuss Purity's implementation in more detail, showing that aggressive data reduction can be integrated with solid state storage while maintaining high performance. Finally, Section 5 discusses lessons learned from real-world deployments of Purity, and the implications of flash storage on application and database infrastructure.

2. BACKGROUND

Storage software designs are closely coupled to the performance and reliability characteristics of the underlying storage devices. As solid state disks replace hard disks, they are forcing a rewrite of legacy storage systems. Purity is one such redesign, aimed at efficiently using commodity flash drives to provide enterprise-quality block storage.

This section provides an overview of solid state disk (SSD) technology, and then describes the approaches that existed when we began development of Purity. We describe the impact of affordable SSDs on enterprise storage, and then argue that the vast majority of performance-oriented disk-based key-value applications are now better served by scale-up storage architectures.

2.1 Solid State Disks

SSDs are much faster and more reliable than mechanical disks, but they have performance quirks that prevent unmodified legacy storage systems from using them optimally. Purity and other SSD-optimized storage systems make up much of the difference by acting as a translation layer for existing applications.

An SSD consists of a set of flash chips that store data persistently and an ASIC with a purpose-built processor, error correction and redundancy hardware (Figure 1). This is driven by firmware that is at least as complicated as the operating system storage stack. The ASIC and firmware

[1] `http://www.purestorage.com/`

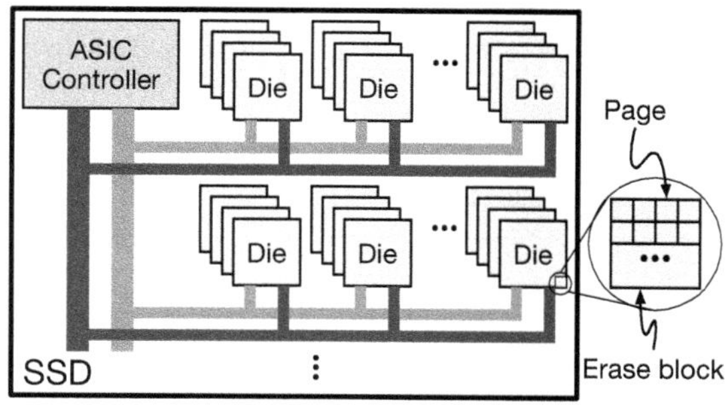

Figure 1: Architecture of an SSD.

combination is usually called a flash translation layer (FTL). Each flash chip contains a set of independent dies that can run in parallel; typical SSDs do not reach peak throughput with read queue depths less than 32.

Each die is broken into erase blocks of 2–16 MiB, which are, in turn, broken into pages of 512–4096 bytes. Pages are the minimum read/write unit. However, a page must be erased at some point before being written, and an entire erase block is erased in a single operation.

Because SSDs cannot efficiently overwrite data in place, the FTL must maintain mappings between logical sector addresses and physical locations. This process is complex and undocumented, and varies across vendors, models, and even firmware revisions, leading to performance quirks. Worse, while an SSD is erasing a block, it cannot read data from physically-related blocks, leading to read latency spikes. Purity goes to great lengths to expose simple append-only write workloads to the SSDs, and to avoid creating situations that expose these performance issues, as described in Section 4.4. We also carefully validate firmware revisions to ensure that this approach leads to deterministic, reliable behavior in practice.

Modern SSDs can store from 1–4 bits per cell. Storing more bits per cell increases data density, but decreases *endurance*—the number of times a given cell may be erased and still reliably store data. SLC SSDs, which store 1 bit per cell, are rated to support about 100,000 program/erase (P/E) cycles. Multi-level cell (MLC) SSDs store 2 bits per cell, and typically support 3000–5000 P/E cycles, while newer technologies such as TLC and QLC store 3 bits and 4 bits per cell, respectively, further increasing density at the expense of fewer P/E cycles. Purity systems currently store data in consumer-grade MLC SSDs. Because of the way Purity uses flash, P/E ratings significantly underestimate real-world endurance. Section 5.1 discusses the discrepancy and describes the flash failure modes we have encountered.

2.2 Disk-based enterprise storage

Enterprise applications can require tens of thousands of random I/O operations per second (IOPS), but a typical performance hard disk provides only a few hundred IOPS. To work around this mismatch, enterprise computing environments incorporate block storage appliances that aggregate large numbers of disks behind a small number of controllers, making them accessible to applications such as scale-up databases, virtual machines, and file servers via standard protocols such as iSCSI and FibreChannel. For example, EMC's midrange VNX-7500 supports 1,000 spinning disks in its largest configuration, while EMCs VMAX

Table 1: Comparison of Purity and a disk array.

Metric	Purity	Disk	Improvement
Peak IOPS @ 32 KB	200K	65K	3.08×
Latency	1ms	5ms	5×
Usable Capacity	40 TB	25 TB	1.6×
Rack Units (RUs)	8	28	3.5×
Installation	4 hours	40 hours	10×
Power	1240 W	3500 W	2.82×
Annual Power Cost	$13,034	$36,792	2.82×
$/GB	**$5**	**$18**	**3.6×**
IOPS/RU	**25,000**	**2321**	**10.7×**
IOPS/W	**161**	**18.6**	**8.6×**
IOPS/$	**1**	**0.144**	**6.9×**

arrays leverage custom silicon to scale to even larger configurations.

Enterprise arrays typically consist of a large number of RAID-protected disks, a battery-backed RAM to accelerate commit of data and logs to "stable" storage, and a large data cache for the hottest data. Database engines and operating systems assume disk is slow, and thus cache their working sets in client (host) DRAM, allowing the total amount of cache to scale linearly with the number of clients and avoiding network latencies for cache hits.

Although they do not provide high-availability and other important enterprise features, consumer-oriented SSDs deliver 100–1000× more IOPS than enterprise spinning disks, suggesting that drastically simpler deployments should be able to match the throughput of these thousand-disk arrays.

This intuition is borne out in Table 1, which compares the published specifications for the VNX and a Purity array [46]. The numbers are from a description of our reference architecture for Oracle databases, which includes benchmark results and explains how to deploy Oracle RAC atop a Purity array.

Although the Purity array outperforms the disk array across all our metrics, the difference in cost/performance is striking: Purity cuts the cost of an I/O by about an order of magnitude while decreasing the cost of usable capacity. This has changed the way users manage storage: IOPS cost less than careful performance provisioning, so most customers simply throw hardware at the problem rather than spending their time manually configuring the disk array to ensure that important applications are not starved for IOPS.

2.3 High-performance scale-out storage

Enterprise storage only scales up to a certain point. As companies attempted to leverage it for Internet workloads, they discovered that the largest available systems were unable to service consumer-facing web sites [11].

Unlike most enterprise applications, these services did not require strong isolation or consistency, so homegrown scale-out storage systems with relaxed consistency models were sufficient. As with enterprise storage, these systems targeted spinning disk. Given the advantages of solid state storage, it is natural to ask if they are still necessary or cost-effective.

In this section, we compare high-performance scale-out disk storage with a large Purity array that targets data center storage consolidation. The FA-450 provides clients with 200,000 32 KiB peak IOPS, and can be configured with up to 70 TB of physical (250 TB effective) storage. We pessimistically assume object sizes of 32 KiB, which is larger than typical key-value store records.

Conveniently, the YCSB benchmarking study provides us with directly comparable numbers for a wide range of key value stores [16]. They all achieve approximately 1600 ops/s per machine in the best case, which is less than 1% the throughput of a FA-450.

Where sufficient information is available, we repeat this calculation in Table 2 by looking at published numbers from real-world disk-based scale-out deployments, and, again, estimate that one Purity array can replace hundreds of disk-based machines. We use disk-based key-value store hardware requirements and scalability bottlenecks from the literature, focusing on 2010–2014, when SSD storage deployments began to become practical.

We believe our estimated 100–250:1 consolidation ratios apply to a wide-range of disk-based storage solutions, and our customers have reported similar ratios (Section 5.4).

Recall that application designers were forced to move to key-value storage systems because their applications were too demanding to be stored in a scale-up system. However, the cost of managing a large scale-out cluster is significant, pushing these applications to consolidate onto a small number of monolithic clusters.

The deployments in the table are meant to serve dozens to thousands of applications. The vast majority of such applications require only a small fraction of a scale-up flash storage system. This eliminates the need for extremely large consolidated storage infrastructure, and allows applications to migrate to simpler scale-up solutions that provide strong application-level consistency.

The logistical improvements associated with 100:1 consolidations are significant. It takes approximately four hours to unpack a Purity array, physically install it and finish provisioning volumes. We help customers run on-site evaluations of our products on their own workloads before making a purchase. This is simply not practical for custom-built scale-out storage clusters.

The transition from disk to flash is driving aggressive storage consolidation. Even the largest scale-out applications from just a few years ago are now better served by a few scale-up machines than by large-scale clusters. In turn, this is improving application semantics, reducing costs, and enabling new classes of applications.

3. DESIGN PRINCIPLES

The previous section describes the approaches taken by existing systems and the storage trends that led us to break from those designs. Purity was designed around several core principles that are based upon the use of SSDs rather than disks for the underlying storage. These design principles are used throughout Purity's implementation.

To recap, Purity exposes virtual block devices over local networks. Systems such as databases and virtual machine infrastructure use these block devices to store data. These applications run in highly-available environments, and standard protocols such as iSCSI allow them to coordinate access to a given block device amongst multiple machines.

Simple applications run in primary-secondary mode. One machine obtains an exclusive lease on the block device. If the primary fails, the secondary obtains the lease and continues operation. Higher-level issues (such as client session management) are handled by the applications deployed atop Purity.

Table 2: Key-value store deployment sizes and estimated Purity FA-450 consolidation ratios. Purity arrays improve data center storage densities by orders of magnitude, and can service multiple scale-out applications.

Service	Scale	Year	Scope	Apps	Nodes	≈FA-450's	$\frac{Nodes}{FA-450}$	$\frac{Apps}{FA-450}$
PNUTS [15,16]	1.6M op/s (design target)	2010	Data center	-	1000	8	120	-
Spanner [18]	1-10 PB (design target)	2010	Data center	300	10^3-10^4	4-40	250	7.5-75
S3 [31]	1.5M op/s (peak)	2013	Global	-	-	6*	-	-
DynamoDB [32]	2.6M op/s (mean)	2014	Region	-	-	13	-	-

*S3 mixes large and small objects; our estimate ignores large objects.

In systems such as parallel databases, multiple machines simultaneously access the same block devices. The clients manage issues such as cache coherence, often by leveraging block-level leases on the underlying storage.

In addition to carefully managing faults, Purity generates and manages large amounts of metadata. Despite the relative simplicity of block-oriented storage, users demand high-level volume management features such as snapshotting, off-site replication and security. Furthermore, Purity relies on compression and deduplication to provide storage capacities at costs comparable to hard disks. Purity stores the resulting metadata in log structured relational structures.

For these reasons, Purity includes from-scratch implementations of locking and indexing primitives that should be familiar to database implementors. Indeed, Purity incorporates a wide range of recent advances in database implementation techniques.

3.1 Perform extra reads to conserve space

Flash capacity is more expensive than disk, requiring that we reduce the total amount of storage actually required as much as possible. Our system implements both compression and deduplication on the fly, cutting storage requirements by a factor of 3–10× or more, depending on the workload, while still providing very high performance. Purity's deduplication and error correction coding techniques incur additional random reads, but our use of SSDs makes the cost acceptable [54]. Purity employs compression judiciously, reducing the amount of data transferred between storage and RAM [34]. Update-in-place systems must align compressed data to fixed boundaries to allow future updates. In contrast, like other log-structured systems, Purity is able to pack data tightly, leading to simpler, more efficient compression techniques [12, 50, 53, 56].

3.2 Leverage logical monotonicity

Purity represents all persistent data as immutable facts (tuples). Deletions are represented as immutable retractions of facts, e.g., "X is no longer true." Facts incorporate sequence numbers, allowing us to represent arbitrary insertion and deletion schedules. This makes it easier to reason about complex parallel schedules and failure scenarios.

Over time, machines have become increasingly parallel, and SSDs have drastically lowered the price of I/O operations. However, the cost of synchronization primitives has remained relatively flat. In order to leverage the computational power and storage bandwidth of modern systems, we need to be extremely careful to avoid unnecessary synchronization across CPU sockets and cores. Similarly, Purity arrays contain multiple storage devices and caches. For performance, we process updates in parallel whenever possible.

Since insertions and deletions simply insert immutable facts into Purity relations, they are idempotent and commutative. This allows us to use relaxed synchronization and ordering primitives without sacrificing correctness. It also enables a novel approach to deletion we call *elision*. Elision allows us to atomically delete all tuples that match a predicate, and is discussed in more detail in Section 4.10.

Unlike standard key-value stores, Purity stores retractions in a separate table from normal facts, and readers are allowed to run in a relaxed consistency mode that simply ignores retractions, allowing them to observe tuples that no longer exist. Similarly, confused or lagging writers may safely reorder inserts and deletes to no ill-effect.

Our approach to insertions and deletions is similar to the programming methodology espoused by the CALM theorem [3], which states that eventually consistent programs are exactly those that can be built by monotone logic. Logically monotone programs are those in which facts that become true never become false. Sequence numbers violate this property because the current sequence number changes over time, so they act as a controlled source of non-monotonicity.

Purity uses this to implement semantics stronger than eventual consistency, such as total ordering of writes to each sector, atomic snapshots and crash consistency. Similarly, we can implement linearizable updates by having write requests wait until their corresponding sequence number has propagated throughout the system. See the CRON principle for a more theoretical grounding of this approach [4].

As far as we know, Purity is the first data management system to uniformly apply these principles across every layer of the stack. Indeed, Purity was implemented as the CALM conjecture and CRON principle were published. As we describe Purity's implementation in Section 4, we present practical applications of these ideas in more detail.

3.3 Carefully manage writes

Although SSDs provide higher raw write bandwidth than hard disks, SSD writes come with hidden costs. They wear out the underlying flash, and, despite good average performance, flash translation layers behave erratically when exposed to random writes [43]. In theory, FTL behavior should improve, but a few issues prevent this in practice.

First, consumer use cases drive FTL designs. We have characterized and validated SSDs from a range of vendors over the last five years. Enterprise performance frequently regresses, even as consumer benchmarking scores improve.

More fundamentally, our x86 controller has a global view of the workload and much more computational power than the SSD FTL, allowing it to apply optimizations and make global decisions that the drives are incapable of.

Purity manages writes in a few different ways. As discussed above, Purity uses log-structured layouts and data reduction techniques to translate application-level random writes into compressed sequential writes. This simplifies the job of the FTL, though we still need to verify that each SSD revision we ship behaves predictably when confronted with sequential writes. Also, we schedule reads to avoid SSDs that are performing writes, reducing read latency variance.

Materialized aggregates are a significant source of writes in Purity. Queries such as *"How many references are there to this block?"* are common. Instead of keeping precise answers in flash, we keep approximations and then fix them up by issuing additional reads at runtime.

3.4 Virtualize resources

Purity provides an update-in-place abstraction atop log-structured storage primitives. This level of indirection enables optimizations such as compression and deduplication, and it also breaks the direct correspondence between application disk blocks and physical disk blocks. This allows us to choose data layouts that directly support features such as volume cloning and snapshots. When implemented carefully, using these abstractions to virtualize volumes adds negligible runtime overhead. We use mediums to implement such functionality.

4. IMPLEMENTATION

Based on the hardware trends and design principles outlined in the previous sections, we implemented a scale-up storage appliance capable of servicing all but the largest workloads. A scale-up appliance based on commodity servers combined with consumer-grade SSDs provided the right balance of cost, performance, reliability, and capacity. Our challenge was to implement Purity in an environment that could easily become CPU-bound, not I/O bound, as legacy disk-based systems are.

Significant software development is required to use performant, low-cost consumer SSDs in Purity. For example, we use several data reduction techniques to increase the effective system capacity and we trade SSD throughput performance for consistently low I/O latency. Likewise, the hardware platform provides multiple paths to storage to enable software to maintain 24/7 availability, even during systems upgrades and hardware failures. Finally, fully virtualizing and abstracting the storage resources enables low-overhead features such as snapshots and image cloning, which also dovetails well with our deduplication features.

This section starts at the lowest levels of Purity's design, and describes how we progressively layer higher levels of the stack upon the foundation we have already described. Purity borrows concepts heavily from the literature; we cite existing work when possible, and focus on novel aspects here.

4.1 Flash Array hardware

Pure Flash Arrays consist entirely of commodity hardware (Figure 2). Each array contains two controllers, which are standard dual-socket x86 machines. Like most commodity servers, these machines include standard redundancy features, such as dual power supplies. Purity provides access to virtual block devices in *active-active* mode, which means that clients treat network ports on the two servers interchangeably, allowing clients to transparently redirect traffic in the event of a controller failure.

However, only one Purity controller serves traffic at a time. The other forwards requests to the primary via internal InfiniBand connections. The InfiniBand links are the throughput bottleneck in our current arrays. As a side effect, Purity latencies improve slightly when the secondary fails. This is preferable to degrading application performance during failures, which risks losing availability.

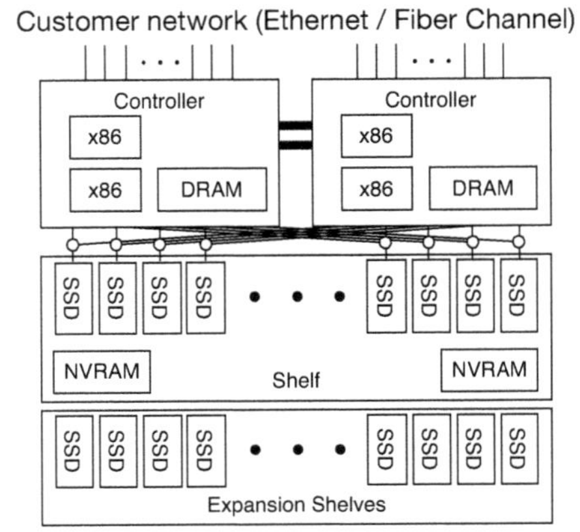

Figure 2: Flash Array consists of commodity components. At failure, interposers transfer control of the SSDs to the secondary. The controllers are stateless.

Flash Array appliances connect to customer networks via multiple links. Currently, our largest model provides 7 GB/s of storage bandwidth via up to 12 × 16 Gb/s fiber channel links, 12 × 10 Gb/s Ethernet iSCSI links, or various combinations of the two technologies. All Flash Arrays include network replication ports.

The controllers connect to *shelves* that contain between 11 and 24 MLC drives. We use consumer grade SATA SSDs with SAS interposers. The interposers connect each drive to both controllers. When one of the controllers fails, the remaining controller immediately gains access to the SSDs.

In addition to the SSDs, shelves contain NVRAM devices for logging frequently updated structures. The NVRAM is part of the shelf so that the controllers themselves are stateless and easily replaced.

When Purity launched, NVRAM was not widely available. Instead, we use an extremely high-performance SLC flash part that provides us with bounded latency, and many more P/E cycles than the rest of the flash in the system. Below, we use the word "NVRAM" to refer to this device, since its performance characteristics are closer to NVRAM than to commonly deployed flash.

4.2 Physical storage layout

Purity stores data in *segments* (Figure 3) each of which is striped across multiple SSDs, using a high-performance software implementation of Reed-Solomon [45] to ensure that no data is lost even if two SSDs fail. In addition, Purity can leverage the parity pages *within* each SSD; flash translation layers can quickly recover a single corrupted page without the need to read data from the other drives in the segment.

A segment is composed of one *allocation unit* (AU) from each of the drives across which it is striped; the specific drives may be different for each segment and are chosen when the segment is written. Allocation units, which are 8 MB in current systems, are the minimum allocation granularity for an SSD; future AUs could be different sizes. Within a segment, each SSD is written atomically in *write units*, which are currently 1 MB. A horizontal stripe of write units across the segment, called a *segio*, accumulates compressed

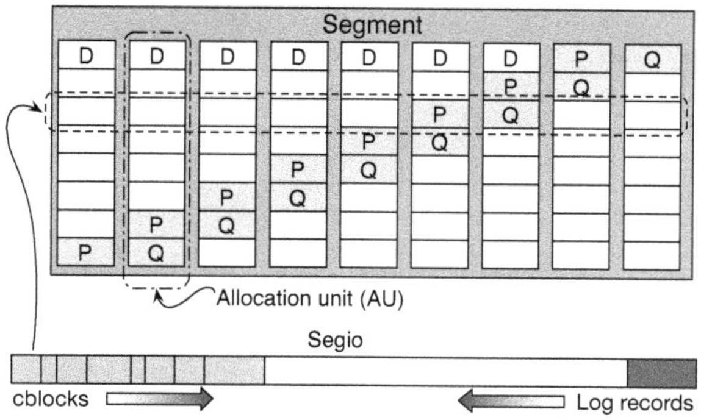

Figure 3: Data layout in Purity. Segios are parity protected and striped across devices. Data accumulates from the front of the segio, and log records (tuples) are written from the back. When the segio is full, it is flushed to the SSDs.

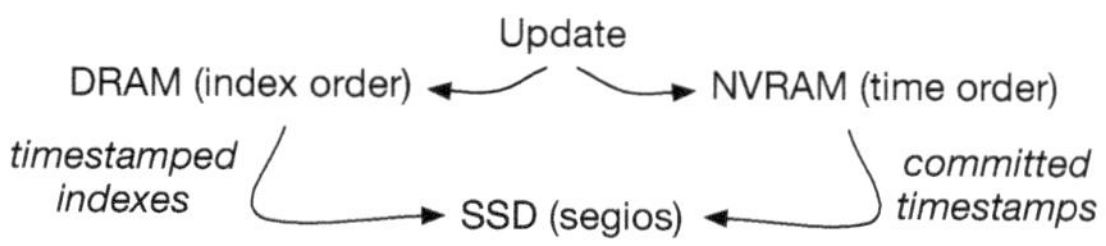

Figure 4: Monotonic write-ahead logging implementation. The segio layer joins the commit stream with a stream of time-bounded indexes, and then trims the DRAM and NVRAM (not shown).

user data from the front, and accumulates log records from the back (Figure 3). When the two sections meet, the segio is completed and marked for flush to SSD. However, Purity is very flexible; a segio may only contain user data or log records, as well.

Writing log entries is less expensive than re-writing entire data sections. However, it still involves writing multiple megabytes of data, and is too high-latency to be useful for committing application writes. Instead, we commit writes to NVRAM, and then write them back to segios (Figure 4). The commit path implementation is monotonic; commits are expressed in terms of immutable facts that flow through the system. We describe the benefits of this below, in the discussion of recovery and pyramids.

In the remainder of the paper, we ignore the existence of segios, and refer to them as segments instead. Segios are an optimization that allows us to flush data to SSDs in smaller chunks, so distinguishing between segios and segments would complicate our discussion considerably, to little benefit.

4.3 Recovery

At recovery, we scan segment headers. This allows us to discover facts that were persisted shortly before crash, since segment headers contain information about the sequence numbers they encode. Segments are self-describing, and early versions of Purity simply checked each header in the system at boot.

Segments are fairly large, and random SSD reads are inexpensive, so this approach worked reasonably well. However, it is linear in the size of the Purity array's storage. Although this scan was never the dominant cost of a cold boot, controller failover performs a segment scan, and its performance is critical. During failover, the Purity array

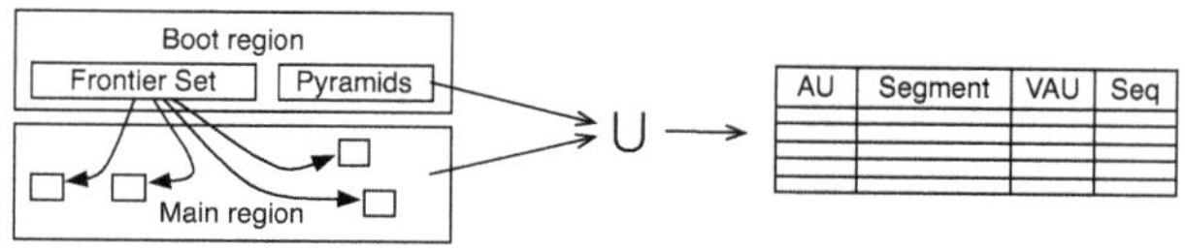

Figure 5: Purity always writes large sequential chunks, and therefore scatters log records amongst user data. Instead of scanning all AUs for log records, we maintain a *frontier set*—the list of AUs that we plan to use soon. Purity stores all its data as immutable facts, so recovery consists of computing set unions over the discovered tuples.

cannot respond to I/O requests, and typical clients time out after 30 seconds. Therefore, to avoid application failures during controller failure, we have to guarantee that recovery will complete in under 30 seconds.

It is tempting to synchronously ship the log to the secondary during normal operation. However, doing so would cause the system to become unresponsive if the secondary failed. Instead, the primary controller asynchronously warms the cache of the secondary, reducing the total amount of I/O required for failover. With this optimization, the scan takes 12 seconds on recent hardware; combined with other, less expensive, aspects of recovery, this brought previous versions of Purity dangerously close to the 30 second timeout.

Purity divides storage into two regions. The *main region* contains application data, medium tables, deduplication information, and the other metadata Purity maintains during forward operation. The *boot region* is a tiny percentage of the total storage, and contains the locations of the relations and allocator state for the main region.

Instead of scanning all segment headers to find log records at failover, we store a *frontier set* in Purity's boot region (Figure 5). This stores the set of free AUs that are ready to be reused. We constrain the allocator to allocate AUs from the currently persisted frontier set, allowing us to limit log record scans to segments in the frontier set. As an optimization, we also store *speculative* and *transition* sets that contain approximations of future frontier sets. These usually contain adequate approximations of future frontier sets, allowing us to rewrite the frontier set less frequently.

An early prototype took this idea one step further, and stored portions of the frontier set in log records. Ultimately, this was untenable: trimming segments could break the chain of log records, forcing us to block space reclamation on log updates. This was complicated and deadlock prone, so we abandoned chained frontier sets, and instead use the scheme in Figure 5.

In practice, frontier set writes consist of well under 1% of writes, and reduce startup scan times from 12 s to 0.1 s on our current arrays. This further reduces the impact of controller failover on applications, and keeps us well below the 30 second hard limit.

Scanning NVRAM and the log records provides us with a set of facts that might be missing from the persistent copies of Purity's indexes. We leverage logical monotonicity, and simply insert these facts into the indexes in question. Since all tuples in Purity are immutable facts, inserting stale or duplicate records is harmless.

Recovery must be robust against corrupted pages and missing drives. Since log records are stored in segments, they are automatically protected by Purity's ECC scheme.

4.4 I/O scheduling

Purity aims to service all application requests with less than a 1 ms tail latency. To this end, we implemented Purity in event-driven C++, with a single thread pinned to each core. Event handlers run with affinity to NUMA groups to avoid cache synchronization traffic. We carefully instrument and bound the latencies of each request handler in the system, preventing one application or background request from monopolizing an x86 core. Whenever feasible, the event handlers are lock-free, further reducing the chances that requests will lead to CPU stalls and impact the latency of unrelated requests.

Before shipping SSDs to customers, we carefully qualify both the physical hardware, and also the firmware revisions that are allowed into our appliances. This allows us to avoid drives with unpredictable request latencies.

As is common practice with other large-scale storage systems [19], we measure the latency of each request and use Reed-Solomon to reconstruct requested data whenever a request takes longer than our 95th percentile latency.

Despite all of these efforts, the SSDs still cause stalls, and, as of Purity release 4.0, slow SSD requests are the leading cause of high latency application requests.

Since we cannot avoid using SSDs and FTLs with unpredictable latencies, we have to work around the underlying hardware. The vast majority of slow SSD reads happen while the SSD is in the process of servicing segment write requests. Therefore, we try to avoid writing to more than two SSDs per ECC group at the same time, and treat SSDs that are in the process of writing data as though they have failed.

Instead of reading from the busy SSDs, we rebuild the data using parity data. Purity uses 7 + 2 Reed-Solomon encoding, with each segment written across a (potentially different) set of the 11 drives in a write group. In the worst case, we service $\frac{2}{11}$ of reads in this way, each of which requires reading 7 drives, increasing costs by $7 \times \frac{2}{11} \approx 1.3\times$ for write-heavy workloads.

With these optimizations, Purity provides an order of magnitude lower tail latencies than the best disk or hybrid disk-flash appliances, more than compensating for the throughput penalties.

4.5 Mediums

The vast majority of data stored in Purity is compressed block data from applications. Unlike metadata, this data is stored without regard for locality or careful ordering by key. Garbage collection strategies for unordered storage are well-understood, and are significantly less expensive than approaches for ordered indexes [48, 52, 58].

Purity exports a volume-based interface to users: blocks are addressed by $\langle$*volume*, *offset*$\rangle$. Internally, however, Purity maintains a single mapping structure for *all* user data, regardless of the volume on which it is stored. Rather than associate data with a particular volume, Purity logically stores user data in containers called *mediums*; each user-visible data block is thus accessed using a $\langle$*medium*, *offset*$\rangle$ key.

The medium table (Figure 6) is used to identify all possible keys that might be used to find the value for a given $\langle$*volume*, *offset*$\rangle$ lookup. Figure 6 shows examples of snapshots (14 is a snapshot of 12, 20 is a snapshot of 18, and 22 is a snapshot of 21) and clones (15 and 18 are clones of part of 12). In medium 22, it also shows that the table facilitates shortcuts: since blocks 500–999 haven't been written since the snapshot was taken of 12, medium 22 can refer *directly* to 12, allowing for fewer lookups. Purity uses additional flags to optimize lookup and reduce the number of references that need to be made to the table, including flags that indicate when no blocks have been written to a range and flags that terminate recursion.

Source		Target		
Medium	Start:End	Medium	Offset	Status
12	0:3999	none		RO
14	0:3999	12	0	RW
15	0:999	12	2000	RW
18	0:999	12	2000	RO
20	0:999	18	0	RO
21	0:999	20	0	RO
22	0:499	21	0	RW
22	500:999	12	2500	RW
22	1000:1999	none		RW

Figure 6: Information maintained for each medium.

4.6 Cblocks

Existing storage protocols dictate a minimum block size of 512 B, which we use as the minimum unit of deduplication and compression in Purity. Mediums store blocks of application data in a compressed format called a *cblock*. Each medium contains a set of cblocks that act as a patch to be applied to the underlying medium. Although mediums could be stacked arbitrarily, Purity's garbage collector rewrites trees of mediums in a flattened form so that application reads never have to access more than three cblocks.

Most applications perform I/O operations much larger than 512 B: across our customer installations, I/O requests are $\approx$ 55 KiB on average. Most flash and hard disk arrays force administrators to set a single optimal block size per volume. Such systems attempt to align application pages with RAID stripe geometries. This does not work well in practice, since most systems perform I/Os of multiple sizes. For example, customer telemetry data tells us that Oracle aggressively prefetches pages, leading to a minimum effective I/O size well above the configured database page size. Also, it chooses different transfer sizes for log and data accesses, forcing customers using other arrays to configure multiple virtual block devices with different RAID geometries for each database instance.

We went to great lengths to avoid exposing tuning knobs to customers. Purity is often used to consolidate multiple workloads, making it extremely difficult to manually tune. Also, Purity's simplicity of installation and administration is an important selling point to most customers.

Instead of having administrators guess optimal block sizes, Purity infers optimal transfer sizes by observing I/O requests. The vast majority of read requests access data using the same alignment and block size as the write request that created the data in question. Although Purity cblocks can represent as little as 512 B of data, they are sized to match application writes, up to 32 KiB. This improves compression ratios and also access times. Since the data is likely to be retrieved with the same granularity as the write, small read requests generally retrieve a single cblock.

4.7 Deduplication

Purity tracks deduplication blocks at 512 B granularity, but only records the hash value of every eighth block written, using hashes no larger than 64 bits. While only 1/8 of all hashes are recorded, *all* hashes are looked up. If a block's hash value matches one already stored, Purity performs a byte-level check to confirm that the block is a duplicate, allowing us to use shorter hashes with a collision rate of 10^{-6} or worse, since collisions only cost a data block comparison and do *not* affect correctness. We then use the duplicate block as an "anchor" to find other, nearby duplicates. This approach detects most duplicate sequences of at least 8 blocks (4 KiB), regardless of alignment, and is a reasonable tradeoff between occasionally missing duplicates and maintaining a small index of block hash values. For duplicates, Purity records a mapping from the new logical address to the $\langle$*segment*, *offset*$\rangle$ of the existing data.

Purity performs inline deduplication, allowing it to detect duplicates before writing the duplicate value somewhere on SSDs. We use a number of heuristics to improve inline deduplication performance. For instance, inline deduplication only checks for duplicates of recently written data and frequently deduplicated data; in practice, inline deduplication finds most duplicates. Later, as garbage collection scans SSDs in the background, it performs a more expensive deduplication pass, and deduplicates the blocks we did not have time to process earlier. Garbage collection also attempts to segregate deduplicated blocks into their own segments, since blocks with multiple references are less likely to become completely unreferenced due to overwrites.

4.8 Log structured indexes

Purity stores its metadata in relations that are indexed by zero or more log-structured merge trees called *pyramids*. Pyramids are tightly coupled to our NVRAM and segment persistence schemes.

Insertions are handled by *persist* operations that assign a sequence number to a batch of tuples and insert them into NVRAM. Each of these batches is also cached in DRAM, where it is sorted and indexed in key order.

The segment (segio) writer (Figure 4) subscribes to two event streams. One contains a list of sequence numbers that have been persisted to NVRAM; the other contains *patches*, index-ordered data that is annotated with sequence numbers. The segment writer enforces write-ahead logging by ensuring that indexes are not written to segments until after the corresponding sequence numbers are persisted to NVRAM.

Patches are analogous to *levels* or *components* in other LSM-Tree implementations, and describe differences between the previous version of the pyramid and the new one. We track key ranges and sequence numbers for each patch. *Merge* operations combine patches with contiguous sequence numbers, and *flatten* operations replace old patches with the newly merged ones.

The implementation of merge and flatten are idempotent, allowing everything below the top level of the pyramid to be implemented in a lock-free fashion. Furthermore, merge and flatten operations are always safe, ensuring that index maintenance is deadlock free, and simplifying recovery from failures during in-progress merge operations. LSM-Tree merge strategies are covered in detail elsewhere [10, 35, 39, 41, 44, 47, 51]; we refer readers to those discussions for more information about LSM-Tree algorithms and implementations.

In addition to the medium table and elide tables described below, important Purity tables include the segment table, deduplication tables, and link tables that manage relationships between segments for garbage collection.

4.9 Metadata layout

Purity stores metadata in tables that are compressed using formats similar to those used in column stores [1, 33, 50]. Each page has a "dictionary" header used to compress or decompress the tuples in the page. The dictionary has an entry for each tuple field that contains *bases* $b_0, \ldots, b_{B-1}$ and a width W for the offset from the base encoded in each tuple. A tuple value $v = b_x + o$ is then encoded as $\langle x, o \rangle$, where b is a $\lceil \lg B \rceil$-bit integer and o is a W-bit integer. Note that W can be 0, as can $\lceil \lg B \rceil$. This encoding is a highly efficient variant of run length encoding, allowing us to include extra fields that aren't needed: as long as their value is the same for every tuple, the extra fields take up no space. Another advantage is that the system can scan a page for a particular value without decompressing the tuples, all of which are the same length in bits. Instead, we treat the page as a bit stream and look for a particular bit pattern based on the compressed representation at the appropriate offset from the start of each tuple.

As a special case, Purity also implements extremely efficient range encoding schemes. These are used to bound the size of the elide tables.

4.10 Elision

Most LSM-Trees implement delete by inserting *tombstone* records into the tree. Tombstone records contain the key of the record to be deleted. Upon encountering a tombstone, LSM-Trees lookups ignore any older tuples with the same key. When tombstones reach the oldest level of the tree they can be discarded.

Purity takes a different approach. Each table has a set of *elide rules* associated with it, which refer to a set of *elision tables*, and explain the table's deletion policy. Typical tables have a single elision table, which is indexed by an auto increment key or sequence number. Tuples in this table represent deletion predicates, and Purity treats all tuples that match the predicate as though they have been deleted. Unlike tombstones, elide records do not need to be keyed in the same way as the table.

Mediums are the motivating example for elision: to drop all of the pages in a given medium, we simply insert a single record into the appropriate elide table. Traditional techniques, such as hierarchical locking [26] would obtain medium-level locks. We wish to avoid such synchronization primitives in Purity, since the data in question is accessed using lock-free operations. Also, inserting an elide record is much less expensive than deleting one cblock at a time.

As with all other tuples in Purity, elide records are immutable facts. Elide operations are idempotent and do not need to be protected by a locking protocol. Requests read the base data as normal. In circumstances in which they must return failure if the records have been deleted, they query the elide table for predicates that match the records they are about to return, and filter their results accordingly. Such readers simply read immutable data, and do not need to acquire locks or synchronize with other threads.

Purity's garbage collector understands elide records, and consults elide tables as part of the merge process. Tuples that have been deleted are immediately dropped. This allows space to be reclaimed more quickly than tombstone-based approaches, which must wait for the tombstone to propagate to the level that stores the data to be deleted. Timely space reclamation is important, because it allows us to immediately begin reclaiming segments after snapshots and other large structures have been dropped. This reduces the risk of deadlock due to running out of space inside the garbage collector.

However, it leaves us with a new problem: We must make sure that elide records do not accumulate over time, permanently leaking space. Rather than introduce another deletion mechanism, we encode elide records as ranges, and merge contiguous ranges. In the worst case, this forces us to store one range for every elide tuple. Since we use dense, monotonically increasing numbers as the keys for elide tables, the ranges collapse rapidly, preventing the elide tables from growing without bound. Moreover, the number of elide ranges can be no larger than the number of *valid* tuples, which itself is limited by the amount of physical or logical storage in the system, depending on the table. Since we never reuse sequence numbers, there is never a need to remove an elide record to allow new records to be written.

5. CUSTOMER DEPLOYMENTS

In Section 2, we contrasted Purity's design goals with those of state-of-the-art performance disk systems. Here, we talk about real-world deployments of Purity, and compare to currently deployed solutions.

Although an alpha version of Purity began shipping in 2010, it began to hit critical mass in 2013 and 2014. At that point, Purity had mature support for the most important enterprise storage features.

5.1 Reliability

We sell service plans that include continuous health and telemetry monitoring of customer arrays, as well as installation services for failed components. In areas with sufficient customer density, our operations team offers customers a four hour hardware replacement SLA.

When an array phones home with a hardware failure, we dispatch a technician to pick up the necessary replacement equipment from a local warehouse, arrive at the customer site, and install the part.

Telemetry data provides us with detailed insights into customer workloads, including I/O request rates, request sizes, volume sizes, and deduplication ratios. We do not expose tuning knobs to customers. Instead, if a Purity array's performance begins to degrade, we perform a root cause analysis (remotely, or on site), and contact the customer before taking action to mitigate the problem. Along with Purity's architecture, this proactive approach to array maintenance has led to 99.999% availability across our customers' production arrays.

For example, a bug in our garbage collection routines was causing suboptimal deduplication performance at a few of our customer sites. We detected the issue, patched and validated a new version of Purity, and then contacted the impacted customers so they could install the patch at a time that minimized the risk of disruption to their production applications.

SSDs are much more reliable than we anticipated. At this point, Purity arrays have replaced hundreds of EMC VMAX installations. Across all Purity installations, only two SSDs have failed. Of course, this number will increase over time, but the chances that a Purity array will encounter a failed drive are extremely low. Instead, components such as fans and DIMMs account for the lion's share of hardware replacement calls.

Unlike hard disks, which fail catastrophically, SSDs simply begin losing pages as they age. Even this is rare, as most enterprise workloads are read heavy, and typical customers never approach the P/E ratings of the consumer MLC drives we sell. We are confident enough in this statement to offer free SSD replacements to customers that actually manage to wear out SSDs in arrays covered by support contracts.

In the process of validating Purity, we built an array out of worn-out flash. We first used synthetic data to overwrite drives until they reached their rated number of P/E cycles. Next, we formatted the drives using Purity, and ran stress tests against the resulting system. We did not encounter any application-level hardware errors in this test.

In addition to all of the error correction techniques that Purity employs, it periodically scrubs the underlying storage to proactively detect data loss. Worn-out flash leaks charge faster than new flash, and P/E ratings are calculated under the assumption that the SSD will be powered off for a year. Periodically scrubbing and rewriting data ensures that the worn-out flash is rewritten more frequently than the P/E calculations assumed, allowing our arrays to run well past rated wear out. In practice, we do not let customer arrays reach such a state, and instead, proactively replace the few worn SSDs we encounter in production.

5.2 Database deployments

Our customers routinely deploy databases atop our arrays, and we have published detailed descriptions of reference installations of popular options, including Oracle, SQL Server and MongoDB. At the high end, customers deploy parallel, shared-disk database solutions such as Oracle RAC against one of our arrays. However, it is much more common for customers to deploy dozens or even hundreds of independent database instances on top of each Purity array.

Instead of recapping details about these installations, we discuss the implications of all-flash arrays on well-known database performance models.

5.2.1 Transaction rollback rates

Stateless clients scale linearly with request latencies and parallelism. Typical Purity latencies are $\frac{1}{10}$ those of disk based solutions, reducing the number of concurrent requests customer compute boxes must track. Similarly, Purity provides much higher throughput than disk-based systems, allowing more requests to be processed per unit time. Taken together, these effects can significantly reduce memory usage on modern database application servers. However, such servers run stateless applications, and are typically compute bound.

Contrast the case of stateless servers with database transactions, which must roll back in the face of conflicts. As latencies increase, so too does transaction concurrency and runtime, increasing the probability of transaction rollbacks. It is well known that these effects lead to non-linear increases in rollback rates [25].

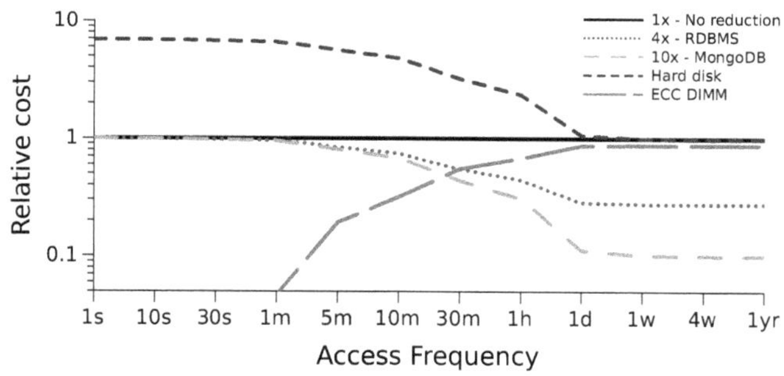

Figure 7: The relative cost of storing data in Purity arrays, disk arrays and main memory. Data reduction significantly changes the tradeoffs between disk, flash and RAM.

A number of mitigating techniques exist, including running transactions at lower consistency levels, rewriting applications from scratch without transactions, and purchasing extremely expensive database licenses.

We frequently encounter customers facing this dilemma, and offer an alternative solution: Purity decreases request latencies by an order of magnitude, potentially reducing rollback rates by more than 10×. In practice, this allows customers to avoid upgrading to more complicated database infrastructure, or even to migrate from proprietary solutions to simpler open source systems such as Postgres and MySQL.

Interestingly, these effects cause customers to underestimate Purity's potential throughput improvements. For instance, given a production database running at 60% CPU time and 40% I/O wait time, one would not expect more than a doubling of throughput due to storage improvements. In contrast, replacing disk-based storage with Purity often leads to speedups closer to 10× in such scenarios.

5.2.2 The five minute rule

The database literature is well-poised to answer another common customer concern: *Given the rapid changes to storage hardware, what should we purchase?*

The "five minute rule" provides a rule of thumb for provisioning storage systems [24]. Traditionally, data accessed more often than once every five minutes belonged in RAM, and colder data belonged on disk.

The cost of storing data can be divided into the price of the capacity the data occupies, and the price of the device time it takes to transfer the data to storage. Small, fast devices, like RAM are a good fit for hot data, and large, slow devices are better for cold data.

Using Table 1, and information from customer deployments, we computed relative costs for Purity and hard-disk arrays: Typical Purity deduplication ratios are 3–8× for relational databases and 10× for document stores such as MongoDB. I/Os are 55 KiB on average. We assume a price of $1000 for 64 GiB of ECC LR-DIMM RAM.

Based on the results in Figure 7, we present the following rules of thumb:

1. Performance disk is dead.
2. Without data reduction, store everything you can afford to lose in RAM (or non-redundant direct attached disks).
3. With data reduction, never cache data that is accessed less frequently than every half hour. It is cheaper to store it in fault tolerant storage than RAM.
4. Important data follows a ten-minute rule: For data colder than that, the cost of the second cached copy is comparable to the cost of accessing the storage.

With Purity, it makes sense to move warm data from RAM to persistent storage, reducing the amount of RAM necessary to support a given set of compute nodes. This has second-order benefits. High-density, low profile DIMMs are roughly 50% more expensive than physically larger models. Reducing memory capacities can allow customers to purchase less expensive processors with fewer memory channels, and to fit more machines into a given number of rack units. These effects increase the incremental cost of storing data in RAM in ways we ignored in our computation.

5.3 Virtualization environments

Virtualization is another common use case for Purity, and can be divided into two classes of workloads: server and desktop virtualization. Server virtualization allows companies to reduce the number of physical machines required to service their backend infrastructure, and has side benefits, such as facilitating hardware upgrades and centralizing backup and other storage management tasks.

Customers often run hundreds or thousands of virtual machines atop a single Purity array. Many are database servers, while others run database applications, mail servers, file servers and other such services. Typical deduplication ratios for these systems are 5–10×.

Scale-out database applications are commonplace, and typically run atop stateless clones of the same operating system image. Purity can efficiently clone such instances. Alternatively, as updates are rolled out to the cloned images, Purity aggressively deduplicates data modified by the updates. Effects such as these sometimes lead to much higher deduplication rates.

We see similar effects with virtual desktop deployments that manage thousands of similar virtual machine images, which are in turn used to power cash registers, terminals, and standardized software environments. Depending on the exact use case, it is possible to achieve deduplication ratios in excess of 20× with such workloads.

5.4 Cloud service providers

Section 2.3 estimates storage requirements of large scale-out storage installations, and concludes that Purity arrays and scale-out performance storage clusters have comparable capabilities at drastically different price points. Indeed, we have begun selling Purity arrays to cloud service providers.

Our customers report data center footprint reductions on the order of 40% when moving from spinning disk to Purity, with the majority of the remaining footprint allocated to compute nodes. Client-visible request latencies improve dramatically, as does throughput. In a representative deployment, virtual machine provisioning times went from nine minutes to forty five seconds (12× faster), and the customer plans to back 500 relational database instances with a single FA-420 array.

Based on customer experiences and proof of concept installations, we have found that an eight-rack-unit Purity appliance provides service providers with similar capabilities as 160 rack units of white-box OpenStack storage nodes. This is similar to the footprint reductions reported by our customers, as well as the estimates we presented in Section 2.3.

Cloud service providers resell fractions of Purity arrays to customers that ultimately provision their own resources. Purity includes automation tooling that is appropriate for this task, and has been certified to work well with the major infrastructure stacks in use at cloud service providers. As with our other use cases, customer-facing simplicity and usability are major differentiators here. Providers resell Purity storage to a large number of customers. To the extent that the array automates performance tuning and provisioning, providers can focus manpower on other tasks.

Similarly, data reduction leads directly to improvements in the providers' cost per gigabyte, allowing our customers to charge rates comparable to their competitors' non-redundant cache storage rates.

In such environments, Purity's tail latencies and 99.999% availability have become key differentiators for cloud service providers. These benefits translate directly to improved application-level availability and performance, and cloud service providers are able to charge a premium for this.

6. RELATED WORK

Purity builds upon an extremely large body of related work, including LSM-Trees and other sorted [2,10,13,39,40, 44,51], and unordered indexes [5,37,43].

Gupta, *et al.* use flash for content-addressable storage in a way that improves locality [30]. We do this for our index. While interesting, memory optimized indexes such as SILT have write amplifications that are too high for our purposes [41]. Debnath has published a number of other interesting small-memory flash structures [21–23]. Salus is another flash optimized persistent block store [57].

There are a large number of scale out distributed systems; we mention a few that target high performance workloads and modern storage hardware here. FAWN takes the opposite approach as Purity, and uses extremely inexpensive servers to build scale out flash storage [6]. Similarly, RAMcloud targets main-memory scale-out storage [49]. Like Purity, its implementation makes heavy use of logs and sequence numbers. Strata is another system in this category [17].

A number of key-value workload studies provided us with insight into scale-out storage performance [7,16].

Our use of sequence numbers for consistency is reminiscent of the approach taken in Corfu, which implements a large, high-throughput distributed flash log [8]. Tango [9] layers persistent data structures atop this simple primitive.

We were informed by insights from a wide range of studies of flash hardware limitations. Flash performance is known to degrade in the face of random writes [29,43]. Purity already uses horizontal and vertical erasure coding [38]; over time, we expect flash densities to increase at the expense of error rates, and adaptive techniques that handle variable error rates will probably be necessary [27,28].

Chen, *et al.* found that coalescing writes extends flash lifetime [14]. We do so in our compression, deduplication and garbage collection algorithms, and use SLC SSDs (our "NVRAM") to absorb low latency writes that we cannot coalesce. Deferred writes have been applied elsewhere [20].

Deduplication studies show that, depending on workloads, whole-file deduplication performs well [42]. However, we target virtual machine deployments which are known to provide opportunities for deduplication [36], and therefore perform block-level deduplication. It is well known that database workloads compress well [34], and we use techniques from the column store compression literature [1,33].

7. CONCLUSION

We have presented Purity, the first all-flash enterprise storage system to support compression, deduplication and high-availability. Hardware trends are disrupting existing storage system architectures, and enabling rapid consolidation of existing storage infrastructure as well as new classes of applications.

Purity leverages these trends, and a wide body of work from the literature to provide applications with order of magnitude performance and density improvements at comparable or lower cost per gigabyte than existing systems.

8. ACKNOWLEDGMENTS

Purity is the work of the entire Pure Storage team. Our conversations with Chas. Dye about customer deployments were invaluable, as were Costa Sapuntzakis's descriptions of Purity. Thanks to Marco Sanvido for the description and motivation for frontier sets, which were developed by Marco Sanvido, Rich Hankins, Nidhi Doshi and Huihui Cheng. We thank our shepherd, Carlo Curino, and Christopher Douglas for their feedback on earlier drafts of this work.

9. REFERENCES

[1] D. Abadi, S. Madden, and M. Ferreira. Integrating compression and execution in column-oriented database systems. In *Proc. SIGMOD Conf.*, pages 671–682, 2006.

[2] D. Agrawal, D. Ganesan, R. Sitaraman, Y. Diao, and S. Singh. Lazy-adaptive tree: An optimized index structure for flash devices. In *Proc. 35th VLDB Conf.*, Aug. 2009.

[3] P. Alvaro, N. Conway, J. Hellerstein, and W. R. Marczak. Consistency analysis in Bloom: a CALM and collected approach. In *Proc. CIDR*, pages 249–260, 2011.

[4] T. J. Ameloot and J. Van den Bussche. Positive Dedalus programs tolerate non-causality. *Journal of Computer and System Sciences*, 80(7):1191–1213, 2014.

[5] A. Anand, C. Muthukrishnan, S. Kappes, A. Akella, and S. Nath. Cheap and large CAMs for high performance data-intensive networked systems. In *Proc. 7th NSDI Symp.*, 2010.

[6] D. G. Andersen, J. Franklin, M. Kaminsky, A. Phanishayee, L. Tan, and V. Vasudevan. FAWN: A fast array of wimpy nodes. In *Proc. 22nd SOSP Conf.*, pages 1–14, Oct. 2009.

[7] B. Atikoglu, Y. Xu, E. Frachtenberg, S. Jiang, and M. Paleczny. Workload analysis of a large-scale key-value store. In *Proc. 2012 SIGMETRICS*, pages 53–64, 2012.

[8] M. Balakrishnan, D. Malkhi, V. Prabhakaran, T. Wobber, M. Wei, and J. D. Davis. CORFU: A shared log design for flash clusters. In *Proc. 9th NSDI Symp.*, Apr. 2012.

[9] M. Balakrishnan, D. Malkhi, T. Wobber, M. Wu, V. Prabhakaran, M. Wei, J. D. Davis, S. Rao, T. Zou, and A. Zuck. Tango: Distributed data structures over a shared log. In *Proc. 24th SOSP Conf.*, pages 325–340, Nov. 2013.

[10] M. A. Bender, M. Farach-Colton, J. T. Fineman, Y. R. Fogel, B. C. Kuszmaul, and J. Nelson. Cache-oblivious streaming B-trees. In *Proc. 19th Symp. on Parallel Algorithms and Architectures*, pages 81–92, 2007.

[11] E. A. Brewer. Lessons from giant-scale services. *IEEE Internet Computing*, 5(4):46–55, Aug. 2001.

[12] M. Burrows, C. Jerian, B. Lampson, and T. Mann. On-line data compression in a log-structured file system. In *Proc. 5th ASPLOS*, pages 2–9, Oct. 1992.

[13] F. Chang, J. Dean, S. Ghemawat, W. C. Hsieh, D. A. Wallach, M. Burrows, T. Chandra, A. Fikes, and R. E. Gruber. Bigtable: A distributed storage system for structured data. In *Proc. 7th OSDI Symp.*, Nov. 2006.

[14] F. Chen, T. Luo, and X. Zhang. CAFTL: A content-aware flash translation layer enhancing the lifespan of flash memory based solid state drives. In *Proc. 9th FAST Conf.*, Feb. 2011.

[15] B. F. Cooper, R. Ramakrishnan, U. Srivastava, A. Silberstein, P. Bohannon, H.-A. Jacobsen, N. Puz, D. Weaver, and R. Yerneni. PNUTS: Yahoo!'s hosted data serving platform. In *Proc. 34th VLDB Conf.*, Aug. 2008.

[16] B. F. Cooper, A. Silberstein, E. Tam, R. Ramakrishnan, and R. Sears. Benchmarking cloud serving systems with ycsb. In *Proc. 1st ACM Symp. on Cloud Computing*, 2010.

[17] B. Cully, J. Wires, D. Meyer, K. Jamieson, K. Fraser, T. Deegan, D. Stodden, G. Lefebvre, D. Ferstay, and A. Warfield. Strata: High-performance scalable storage on virtualized non-volatile memory. In *Proc. 12th FAST Conf.*, Feb. 2014.

[18] J. Dean. Designs, lessons and advice from building large distributed systems. Keynote from LADIS, 2009.

[19] J. Dean and L. A. Barroso. The tail at scale. *Communications of the ACM*, 56(2):74–80, 2013.

[20] B. Debnath, M. F. Mokbel, D. J. Lilja, and D. Du. Deferred updates for flash-based storage. In *Proc. 26th IEEE Conf. on Mass Storage Systems and Technologies*, 2010.

[21] B. Debnath, S. Sengupta, and J. Li. ChunkStash: Speeding up inline storage deduplication using flash memory. In *Proc. 2010 USENIX Annual Technical Conference*, June 2010.

[22] B. Debnath, S. Sengupta, and J. Li. FlashStore: High throughput persistent key-value store. In *Proc. 36th VLDB Conf.*, Sept. 2010.

[23] B. Debnath, S. Sengupta, and J. Li. SkimpyStash: RAM space skimpy key-value store on flash-based storage. In *Proc. SIGMOD Conf.*, 2011.

[24] J. Gray and G. Graefe. The five-minute rule ten years later, and other computer storage rules of thumb. *ACM Sigmod Record*, 26(4):63–68, 1997.

[25] J. Gray, P. Helland, P. O'Neil, and D. Shasha. The dangers of replication and a solution. In *Proc. SIGMOD Conf.*, pages 173–182, June 1996.

[26] J. N. Gray, R. A. Lorie, G. R. Putzolu, and I. L. Traiger. Granularity of locks and degrees of consistency in a shared data base. In *Proc. IFIP Working Conf. on Modelling in Data Base Management Systems*, pages 365–394, 1976.

[27] K. M. Greenan, D. D. Long, E. L. Miller, T. J. E. Schwarz, S.J., and A. Wildani. Building flexible, fault-tolerant flash-based storage systems. In *Proc. 5th Workshop on Hot Topics in System Dependability*, June 2009.

[28] L. M. Grupp, J. D. Davis, and S. Swanson. The bleak future of NAND flash memory. In *Proc. 10th FAST Conf.*, Feb. 2012.

[29] L. M. Grupp, J. D. Davis, and S. Swanson. The harey tortoise: Managing heterogeneous write performance in SSDs. In *Proc. 2013 USENIX Annual Technical Conference*, June 2013.

[30] A. Gupta, R. Pisolkar, B. Urgaonkar, and A. Sivasubramaniam. Leveraging value locality in optimizing NAND flash-based SSDs. In *Proc. 9th FAST Conf.*, Feb. 2011.

[31] J. Hamilton. Why scale matters and why the cloud is different. AWS re:Invent, 2013.

[32] J. Hamilton. AWS innovation at scale. AWS re:Invent, 2014.

[33] A. L. Holloway, V. Raman, G. Swart, and D. J. DeWitt. How to barter bits for chronons: compression and bandwidth trade offs for database scans. In *Proc. SIGMOD Conf.*, pages 389–400, 2007.

[34] B. R. Iyer and D. Wilhite. Data compression support in databases. In *Proc. 20th VLDB Conf.*, pages 695–704, 1994.

[35] C. Jermaine, E. Omiecinski, and W. G. Yee. The partitioned exponential file for database storage management. *Proc. VLDB Endowment*, 16:417–437, 2007.

[36] K. Jin and E. L. Miller. The effectiveness of deduplication on virtual machine disk images. In *Proc. SYSTOR 2009*, May 2009.

[37] W. K. Josephson, L. A. Bongo, K. Li, and D. Flynn. DFS: A file system for virtualized flash storage. *ACM Trans. on Storage*, 6(3), Sept. 2010.

[38] Y. Kang and E. L. Miller. Adding aggressive error correction to a high-performance compressing flash file system. In *Proc. 9th ACM & IEEE Conf. on Embedded Software (EMSOFT '09)*, Oct. 2009.

[39] LevelDB: A fast and lightweight key/value database library by Google. https://code.google.com/p/leveldb/.

[40] Y. Li, B. He, Q. Luo, and K. Yi. Tree indexing on flash disks. In *Proc. 25th Int'l Conf. on Data Engineering*, 2009.

[41] H. Lim, B. Fan, D. G. Andersen, and M. Kaminsky. SILT: a memory-efficient, high-performance key-value store. In *Proc. 23rd SOSP Conf.*, Oct. 2011.

[42] D. T. Meyer and W. J. Bolosky. A study of practical deduplication. In *Proc. 9th FAST Conf.*, Feb. 2011.

[43] C. Min, K. Kim, H. Cho, S.-W. Lee, and Y. I. Eom. SFS: Random write considered harmful in solid state drives. In *Proc. 10th FAST Conf.*, Feb. 2012.

[44] P. O'Neil, E. Cheng, D. Gawlick, and E. O'Neil. The log-structured merge-tree (LSM-tree). *Acta Informatica*, 33:351–385, 1996.

[45] J. S. Plank, K. M. Greenan, and E. L. Miller. Screaming fast Galois field arithmetic using Intel SIMD instructions. In *Proc. 11th FAST Conf.*, Feb. 2013.

[46] Pure Storage reference architecture for Oracle databases, 2014.

[47] RocksDB: A fork of LevelDB by Facebook. https://github.com/facebook/rocksdb/.

[48] M. Rosenblum and J. K. Ousterhout. The design and implementation of a log-structured file system. *ACM Trans. on Computer Systems*, 10(1):26–52, Feb. 1992.

[49] S. M. Rumble, A. Kejriwal, and J. Ousterhout. Log-structured memory for DRAM-based storage. In *Proc. 12th FAST Conf.*, Feb. 2014.

[50] R. Sears, M. Callaghan, and E. Brewer. Rose: Compressed, log-structured replication. In *Proc. 34th VLDB Conf.*, pages 526–537, Aug. 2008.

[51] R. Sears and R. Ramakrishnan. bLSM: A general purpose log structured merge tree. In *Proc. SIGMOD Conf.*, pages 217–228, May 2012.

[52] D. J. Sheehy and D. Smith. Bitcask. a log-structured hash table for fast key value data. Technical report, Technical report, Basho Technologies, 04 2010, 2010.

[53] V. Sikka, F. Färber, W. Lehner, S. K. Cha, T. Peh, and C. Bornhövd. Efficient transaction processing in SAP HANA database: the end of a column store myth. In *Proc. SIGMOD Conf.*, pages 731–742, 2012.

[54] K. Srinivasan, T. Bisson, G. Goodson, and K. Voruganti. iDedup: Latency-aware, inline data deduplication for primary storage. In *Proc. 10th FAST Conf.*, Feb. 2012.

[55] R. Stoica, M. Athanassoulis, R. Johnson, and A. Ailamaki. Evaluating and repairing write performance on flash devices. In *DaMoN*, pages 9–14, June 2009.

[56] M. Stonebraker, D. J. Abadi, A. Batkin, X. Chen, M. Cherniack, M. Ferreira, E. Lau, A. Lin, S. Madden, E. O'Neil, P. O'Neil, A. Rasin, N. Tran, and S. Zdonik. C-store: a column-oriented DBMS. In *Proc. 31st VLDB Conf.*, pages 553–564, 2005.

[57] Y. Wang, M. Kapritsos, Z. Ren, P. Mahajan, J. Kirubanandam, L. Alvisi, and M. Dahlin. Robustness in the Salus scalable block store. In *Proc. 10th NSDI Symp.*, pages 357–370, 2013.

[58] H. Yadava. *The Berkeley DB Book*. Apress, 2014.

On Improving User Response Times in Tableau

Pawel Terlecki
Tableau Software
pterlecki@tableau.com

Fei Xu
Tableau Software
fxu@tableau.com

Marianne Shaw
Tableau Software
mshaw@tableau.com

Valeri Kim
Tableau Software
vkim@tableau.com

Richard Wesley
Tableau Software
hawkfish@tableau.com

ABSTRACT

The rapid increase in data volumes and complexity of applied analytical tasks poses a big challenge for visualization solutions. It is important to keep the experience highly interactive, so that users stay engaged and can perform insightful data exploration.

Query processing usually dominates the cost of visualization generation. Therefore, in order to achieve acceptable response times, one needs to utilize backend capabilities to the fullest and apply techniques, such as caching or prefetching. In this paper we discuss key data processing components in Tableau: the query processor, query caches, Tableau Data Engine [1, 2] and Data Server. Furthermore, we cover recent performance improvements related to the number and quality of remote queries, broader reuse of cached data, and application of inter and intra query parallelism.

1. INTRODUCTION

Data visualization and big data processing have become key elements of modern analytic platforms. Lower hardware prices allow customers to purchase powerful computational clusters, collect high volumes of detailed data and perform sophisticated ad hoc analysis. Moreover, there is a growing demand for standardized solutions in related areas, such as: data federation, exploration of semi-structured and graph data sets, and data preparation or knowledge discovery. The increasing popularity of visual analytics is driving development in these fields and provides the research community with new data processing and usability challenges.

In the past years, Tableau has become a leader in providing easy-to-use data visualization tools. It currently connects to over 40 different data sources, from simple file-based sources, through SQL/MDX databases or web data sources, to Hadoop clusters. In a common intuitive interface, it allows for rich analysis of different areas of data, including filtering, custom calculations – potentially at different levels of detail, window and statistical functions and many others.

Tableau aims to provide a fast interactive environment for data exploration. A key challenge, both today and as we continue to add more sophisticated data analysis, is maintaining high responsiveness of the interface. To achieve that across all the supported data sources, one often needs to apply dedicated optimization techniques to alleviate efficiency and capability shortcomings of various architectures.

During data exploration, each user interaction with the application generates an adhoc query workload. This workload is difficult to predict and requires powerful analytic databases, e.g. column stores, to process requests with low latencies. Additionally, we leverage caching and query optimization techniques to provide high levels of interactivity.

Sharing the results of data exploration via Tableau Server in the intranet or Tableau Online, in the cloud, presents a different set of workload challenges. Users can combine visualizations created during data exploration into dashboards and publish them to Server. A dashboard consists of multiple visualizations; they are often linked by actions, such as filtering of one view based on selection in another.

The query workload generated by published dashboards is easier to predict than the adhoc workload generated during exploratory analysis. This is because queries are generated by interacting with schema components already defined in the dashboard. Moreover, caching is more efficient as it can be applied across multiple users accessing the same dashboards.

Although with different emphasis, providing a highly interactive experience in both aforementioned scenarios depends upon the efficient retrieval of new data from external sources and maximal utilization of previously obtained results. In this paper, we present recent performance improvements focused on increasing product interactivity, including:

- Query batch preparation and concurrent query execution to improve dashboard generation;
- Persisted and distributed intelligent cache to improve response times across users and their interactions;
- Parallel plans and fast scanning of RLE encoded columns in Tableau Data Engine;
- Managing data models and extracts in Data Server along with temporary table support.

The text is organized accordingly. Section 2 covers the general background. In Sect. 3 we describe how dashboards are generated focusing on query processing and caching. Section 4 gives an overview of the Tableau Data Engine and its recent performance features. In Sect. 5 we look at connection and data model management in the Data Server. Section 6 covers related work. Future plans are given in Sect. 7 and the paper is concluded in Sect. 8.

SIGMOD'15, May 31–June 4, 2015, Melbourne, Victoria, Australia.

http://dx.doi.org/10.1145/2723372.2742799

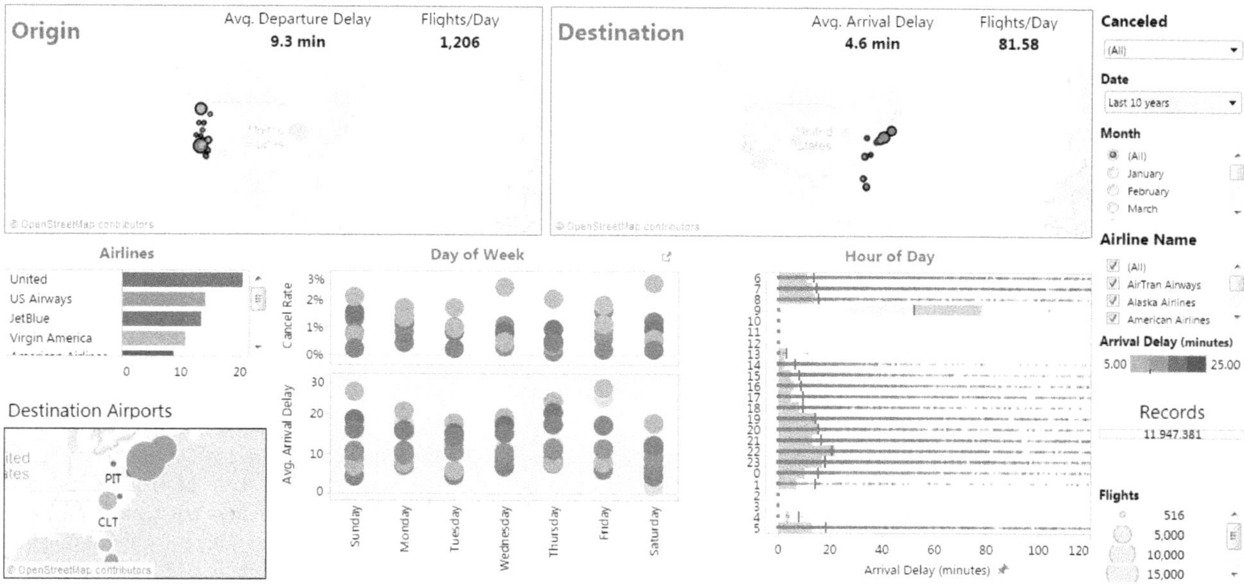

Figure 1: Sample dashboard for the FAA Flights On-Time dataset

2. BACKGROUND

Tableau is an application for rapid interrogation of structured data. The application has a simple, intuitive drag-and-drop interface that generates queries against a wide spectrum of data sources. The application has a large number of built-in chart types. Users are offered a rich environment for analyzing their data, including defining new calculations, forecasting, filtering, and combining data from heterogeneous data sources [47].

User actions that add and remove items in a worksheet are represented with VizQL [40], a set of specialized algebraic operations. This representation is used to automatically generate queries against a specified data source. Queries are issued and the results are interpreted to produce the requested visualization. As the user interacts with elements of the visualization, additional queries may be issued to the underlying database.

The Tableau Data Engine (TDE) is a proprietary column store database that can be used to allow users to extract data from an existing database or text file. When a TDE extract is incorporated into a user's workbook, a user can continue to interrogate their data when a network connection to the database is not available. Additionally, the extract reduces the query load on the backing database. Users can easily switch from an extract back to a live connection, and extracts can be refreshed when appropriate.

Tableau Server allows users to easily share their visualizations with others. Users publish data sources or visualizations to Server and specify sharing permissions for them. These visualizations can be viewed and interacted with via another Tableau application, or simply through a Web browser. If visualizations are published with accompanying TDE extracts, a schedule can be created to automatically refresh the extracts, ensuring the data is always current.

3. QUERY PROCESSING FOR DASHBOARDS

Dashboards are a vital element of many data visualization platforms. Each covers a certain area of data and allows users to view it from different angles. Quality of experience depends on the degree of interactivity, a factor that distinguishes dashboards from old-fashioned static reports.

A dashboard is a collection of zones organized according to a certain layout. Different zone types include various charts, maps, filters, calculated text, images etc. One defines the behavior of individual zones first and then specifies dependencies between them. Complicated scenarios might involve tens or even hundreds of zones.

Let us consider a simple example of a dashboard (Fig. 1) defined for the popular FAA Flights On-time dataset [43]. It covers all the flights in the US in the past decade. The two upper maps show the number of flight origins and destination by state and, at the same time, allow specifying origins and destinations for the slave charts at the bottom. Each chart is annotated with average delays and flights per day. The bottom charts cover airlines operating the flights, destination airports, breakdown of cancellations and delays by weekdays, and distribution of arrival delays broken down by hours of a day. The right-hand side has filtering, total count of visible records and static legends.

Rendering a dashboard requires retrieving necessary data and post-processing it for visualization. Due to dependencies between zones, the entire process might take several iterations in which obtained responses are used to specify subsequent requests; the process is discussed in detail in Sect. 3.3.

Most zones require data from one or more data sources in order to be rendered. The requests are specified internally by queries with expressiveness matching the capabilities of the data sources. These internal queries eventually get turned into textual queries in appropriate dialects and sent to the corresponding data sources.

In the next section we discuss efficient data retrieval and generation of high-quality remote queries as both vastly contribute to the latency of dashboard interactions.

3.1 Single Query Processing

The internal queries formulated by components in Tableau closely follow the concepts of the application. In general, the queries express aggregate-select-project scenarios, with potential subqueries for computed columns of different levels of detail and more sophisticated filters, such as top-n.

A query gets executed against a certain view on the data of a single data source. Users can specify views as single tables (e.g. denormalized SQL relations, OData sources, and text files), multi-table joins (often star or snowflake schemas), parameterized custom SQL queries, stored procedures or cubes.

Before a query can be sent to a relevant backend, it undergoes a compilation process consisting of structural simplification and implementation. First, a query is translated into a tree of elementary operations to facilitate subsequent transformations. Numerous optimizations are applied to the tree, including join culling, predicate simplification and externalization of large enumerations with temporary secondary structures. The query compiler incorporates information about cardinalities, domains, and overall capabilities of the data source, such as support for subqueries, temporary table creation and indexing, or insertion over selection.

A simplified query is subsequently translated into a textual representation that matches the dialect of the underlying data source. While most supported data sources speak a variant of SQL or MDX, each has their own exceptions to the standard and non-compliances. Moreover, out of the wide spectrum of scalar and aggregate functions available in the system, the native implementations might vary a lot due to type promotion and casting, function efficiency or even feasibility. As a result, some operations may need to be locally applied in the post-processing stage.

Tableau communicates with remote data sources by means of connections. Most often a connection maps to a database server connection maintained over a network stack. In some cases it might be entirely handled on the side of the application, e.g. parsing of text or Excel files. Communication with the drivers is encapsulated in external processes to isolate failures in the third-party software and potentially greedy resource allocation from the rest of the system. Retrieved results are streamed back in a tabular format.

3.2 Query Caching

Generating visualizations is expensive, therefore, Tableau utilizes several levels of caching. In this section we focus on the product's use of query-related caches, as data retrieval is the most time-consuming stage of the entire process. Other examples include caching entire visualizations, image and map tiles, etc.

As a user interacts with a dashboard, it is likely that identical or similar visualizations will be requested at each refresh of the view. In a multi-user scenario, it is even more common to get identical or similar requests, since different users are working with the same shared dashboards. An extreme example of this is seen in Tableau Public, which allows for publishing visualizations and data, and referencing them in personal articles or blogs. The user-generated traffic is saturated by initial load requests, as many viewers just read content with the initial state of a dashboard and make further interactions rarely.

Tableau incorporates two levels of query caching: intelligent and literal. The intelligent cache maps the internal query structure to a key that is associated with the query results [48]. When a new query is to be executed, a cache key is generated and the intelligent cache is searched for a match. When looking for matches, we attempt to prove that results of the stored query subsume the requested data [19, 20]. While currently we accept the first match, in the future release, we plan to choose the entry that requires the least post-processing. Also, even though the matching logic is designed to be fast, we are planning to maintain an index over the cache to minimize the lookup time.

The applicability of the intelligent cache is limited by proving capabilities and efficiency, e.g. analyzing implications of predicates, potentially large or formulated in different equivalent ways, and by post-processing capabilities. The latter includes roll-up, filtering, calculation projection, and column restriction. It is worth noting that certain operations cannot be performed locally, in particular, if they involve native function calls or collation conflicts.

The intelligent cache can be treated as a database view-matching component. It keeps the application highly responsive as long as covering data is available and can be post-processed. The additional post-processing usually does not require much time as we retrieve data in small, pre-filtered and pre-aggregated volumes. For many queries, the number of tuples returned is of smaller size than the number of un-aggregated, unfiltered rows in the database. Local post-processing occurs on this relatively small set of aggregated data. The query processor might choose to adjust queries before sending, in order to make the results more useful for future reuse.

The literal query cache contains low-level queries that are not directly related to visualization generation; it is keyed on the query text. It is used to match internal queries that end up having the same textual representation but where a match could not be proven upfront without performing complete query compilation. Predicate simplification based on domains or join culling are some examples of this scenario.

Cache entries in both the literal and intelligent cache are purged based upon a combination of entry age, usage, and the expense of re-evaluating the query. Entries are also purged when a connection to a data source is closed or refreshed.

Let us revisit the sample dashboard in Fig. 1 in the context of caching. Note that the queries for the domains of filters on the right need to be sent only once. Further interactions might change the selection but not the domains. Furthermore, data for other charts got cached with all the filtering values selected. If a user deselects some of the values on the right, the intelligent cache will be able to filter out the necessary rows for the results for other charts, as long as the filtering columns are included.

In Tableau Desktop query caches get persisted to enable fast response times across different sessions with the application. Tableau Server does not persist the caches but it utilizes a distributed layer based on REDIS [41] or Cassandra [42] depending on the configuration. This allows sharing data across nodes in the cluster and keeping data warm regardless of which node handles particular requests. For efficiency, recent entries are also stored in memory on the nodes processing particular queries. In general, we cache all the query results unless computation time is comparable with a cache lookup time or the results are excessively large

3.3 Query Batch Processing

From a user's perspective, the ultimate goal is to immediately load an entire dashboard or refresh it after a given interaction. Therefore, the data retrieval task is not formulated with respect to individual queries but in terms of minimizing the latency of processing all of them.

Due to dependencies between zones, rendering of a dashboard might require several iterations to complete. Consider the dashboard in Fig. 2, which shows the Flights/Day for a Market, Carrier, and Airline Name for the FAA Flights data from Figure 1. The Carrier zone is filtered to the top 5 carriers, based upon number of flights, that have more than 1,400 Flights/Day. The dashboard has two interactive filter actions defined: (1) selecting a field in the Market zone will filter the results in the Carrier and Airline Name zones, and (2) selecting a carrier in the Carrier zone will filter the Airline Name zone. In Figure 2, the user has already selected a Market (LAX-SFO) and a Carrier (AA).

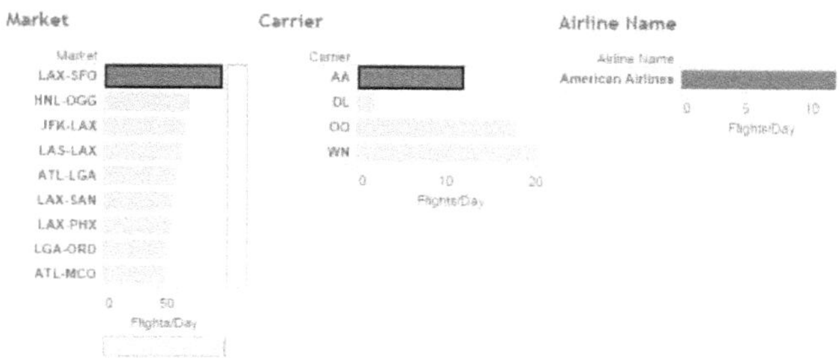

Figure 2: A dashboard with three zones, linked by two interactive filter actions. Selecting items in either the Market or Carrier zones filters the viz results.

If the user selects HNL-OGG in Market, the interactive filter actions will cause the Airline Name and Carrier zones to be updated with a filter on HNL-OGG. One side-effect of these updated results is that the previous user-selection (AA) in the Carrier zone is eliminated, as AA is not a carrier for the HNL-OGG market. Subsequently, the interactive filter action will cause a query without a filter on Carrier to be generated to update the Airline Name zone.

Zones that participate in an iteration generate queries that together comprise a query batch of this iteration. As the iteration and, thus, the corresponding batches are processed independently, here we examine the optimization of a single query batch.

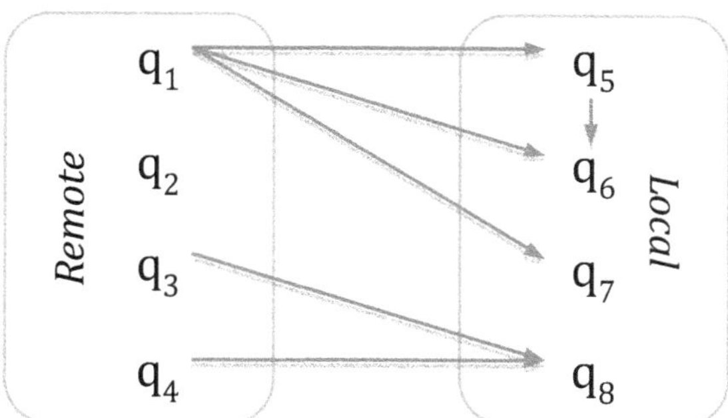

Figure 3: Sample cache hit opportunities graph with partition of queries into local and remote

Consider a query batch B=[q_1, .. , q_n] and assume that the target data sources are all idle and have all the resources available. In addition, to express cache hit opportunities, consider a directed graph G with the queries as nodes and edges pointing from q_i to q_j iff the result of q_j can be computed from the results of q_i (Fig. 3). The latter is determined by the matching logic of the intelligent query cache.

One way of executing these queries is to send them one by one in a certain order, and each time wait for the query to complete. This way each query has all the resources for itself and its processing time is the shortest. Note that the query execution order matters and topological orders in G are most beneficial, as the queries with incoming edges will be answered from the cache. This strategy roughly corresponds to processing zones serially.

Serial execution of queries minimizes their individual processing times but does not utilize available resources to the fullest. Therefore, executing queries concurrently might reduce the overall rendering time of a dashboard. In order to maximize cache usage we process the batch in two phases. First, we analyze it and partition the nodes of G into two sets. One set contains queries that need to be sent to the remote back-ends; they correspond to the source nodes, i.e. the nodes without incoming edges. The second set contains queries that are cache hits that can be processed locally. In the second phase, remote queries are submitted for execution concurrently and the local ones are processed as soon as any of their predecessors in G finishes.

3.4 Query fusion

Grouping queries in batches creates an opportunity to utilize multi-query optimization techniques. One basic optimization we apply across queries before executing a query batch is combining groups of queries defined over the same relation and potentially different with respect to their top-level projection lists. Strictly speaking, we replace a group of queries of the form [$\pi_{P1}(R)$, .. , $\pi_{Pn}(R)$] with a single query $\pi_P(R)$, where R is the common relation, P_1, .., P_n are respective projection lists and $P = \cup_{i=1,..,n} P_i$. We refer to this transformation as *query fusion*.

One obvious advantage of this approach is a reduction of the number of queries in a batch and, thus, the overall overhead of dispatching queries in corresponding data sources and necessary communication. Since it is quite common for different zones of a dashboard to share the same filters but request different columns, the reduction might be substantial.

More importantly processing of a fused query is often much more efficient than processing of the individual queries that were fused, as the underlying relation needs to be computed only once. Although it is possible that a physical layout of the data can lead to a performance regression, this optimization brings significant gains in our visualization benchmarks.

3.5 Concurrent Execution of Queries

In order to process dashboards in parallel, Tableau needs to concurrently execute queries against external data sources. Since the capabilities, stability and efficiency of the many supported back-ends often vary dramatically, the communication and execution layers need to be universal. This section explains the design choices and their consequences for different data source architectures.

As noted in Sect. 3.1, Tableau uses the abstraction of a connection to communicate with external data sources. There are basically two strategies to submit queries concurrently: by using a single or multiple connections. The first route is rarely supported by databases and usually comes with functional or performance limitations. SQL Server with MARS enabled is one example here. On the contrary, maintaining separate connections to allow for concurrent access from independent clients belongs to a basic repertoire of most database servers. Their responsibility is to govern resources appropriately across the corresponding workloads and make sure none gets starved.

Tableau manages a certain number of active connections to each data source to implement concurrent execution of remote queries. The process of opening a connection, retrieving configuration information and metadata are costly, therefore, connections are pooled and kept around even if idle.

In addition, connection pooling plays an important role in preserving and reusing temporary structures stored in remote sessions. For example, temporary tables created for large filters or multi-dimensional sets during query processing are likely to be useful while formulating queries within the same query batch or within batches originating from interactions with the same dashboard. An age-wise eviction policy is used in case of local memory pressure or to release remote resources unused for longer periods of time.

Queries submitted by different components of the system are multiplexed across connections regardless of their remote state. That means that popular temporary structures will be duplicated in several connections. While this adds a certain overhead to the backend, it also makes the connections potentially more useful for subsequent queries. Some architectures allow to alleviate this overhead and share a single remote session across multiple connections, however, this comes at a price of more complicated locking on the server side to resolve concurrent changes across the participating connections.

While Tableau generates a highly parallel workload, the overall efficiency of the system depends on the processing ability of the back-ends. The latter is determined by several aspects of the database architecture and the underlying hardware. First of all, the sooner a database server receives a workload the better it can schedule execution of the participating queries. Generally, databases do not perform cross-query optimization with respect to query plans. This would require substantial pre-processing and affect short-running queries. Nonetheless, certain optimizations might be applied in lower layers. One example is the shared scans feature [45] present in several systems, including SQL Server. It allows the storage layer to pipe pages of a single table scan to multiple concurrently handled execution plans.

Resource allocation on the remote side plays a pivotal role in handling a concurrent workload efficiently. While some queries are already being executed, an arrival of a new query might cause the previously assigned resources to be reclaimed. Furthermore, even though clients might be sending a high number of concurrent queries, the database is likely to throttle them based on available resources or a hard-coded threshold. One might need to tune the system to appropriately manage resources of the entire cluster or their allocation across connections. Also, it is worth noting that some systems impose limitations on the overall number of connections or the number of concurrently executed queries.

Moreover, the way a database allocates CPU in the single query execution substantially affects performance. Many architectures use a single thread per query. That means that a serial execution of a query batch would leave a tremendous amount of processing power idle. On the contrary, massively parallel clusters or non-clusters solutions that support parallel plans, such as SQL Server, the TDE (see 3.2) and many others, will attempt to allocate many machines/CPUs to reduce the individual latencies. This makes the resource allocation harder, as it needs to take into account overheads of parallelism, data migration, etc. Also, scalability limitations, such as restricting query execution or its certain stages, e.g. aggregation, to a single node, allow for higher performance of a more concurrent workload.

Our experiments show that using multiple connections to handle concurrent workloads boosts performance, often dramatically, across the architectures supported by Tableau. Obviously, the positive effect is observable if idle resources are available and can be utilized. Note that some resources can be shared easily, such as CPU, and some not, such as memory. In addition, any bottleneck in the system can slow down the entire pipeline. For example, in certain databases, session-local DDL operations for temporary structures take a high-level lock. We have also observed higher contention on disc controllers to affect the overall performance.

4. Tableau Data Engine

The Tableau Data Engine (TDE) is a read-only column store implemented by Tableau. It has been described in [1] and [2]. Most features described in the above papers have been shipped before Tableau 9.0, except for the new performance improvements covered in Sect. 4.2 and 4.3. The TDE is used both in the client environment with Tableau Desktop and in the server environment with Tableau Server. This section first gives an overview of the TDE, and then discusses these improvements.

4.1 TDE Overview

The TDE is designed to support the Extract scenario: extracting a fraction of or the entire dataset from the lively connected data source for offline analysis. Popular use cases include reducing the workload to a live database, getting better performance for analysis, making a snapshot and without worrying about data change, working on an airplane, etc. This scenario imposes a few requirements that are not fully satisfied by existing open-source and commercial systems: support fast execution of complex analytical queries, column level collated strings, 32-bit hardware with limited resource, single database file, and small installation footprint. The single database file is an important convenience feature for users to move, share, and publish the data. The TDE is also used in the Tableau Server environment, where it is deployed as a cluster of nodes through either shared-nothing or shared-everything architecture. The TDE's design is largely influenced by the extensive research work around MonetDB [3]. And it has a few advantages over existing systems:

1. The TDE supports all popular platforms, such as Windows, Mac and Linux. It also supports both 32bit and 64 bit systems.
2. As an analytical engine, the TDE supports column level collated strings.
3. The TDE models column decompression using regular logical operators. Special logical operators are also introduced to utilize the compression to speed up the query execution. This provides a uniform view for all the operations in the TDE.
4. The TDE has a very small installation package. It is easy to download and install.
5. The TDE is able to run as a client application on cheap hardware and limited resource. It can also be deployed as a shared-nothing or shared-everything cluster in the server environment.
6. The TDE is specially tuned for interactive analysis of complicated analytical queries. Features such as fact table culling directly address this kind of a workload

7. The TDE is able to compact a database into a single file.

This section gives an overview of the TDE. We focus on the following aspects of its architecture:

- the storage layer
- the compiler and optimizer
- the execution engine.

We also discuss how TDE is deployed in both the client and server environment.

4.1.1 Storage Layer

Like most database systems, the TDE has a three-layer namespace for logical objects in a database: schema, table and column. It has a simple on-disk storage layout, which makes packing the entire database into a single file easy. The three-layer namespace matches on-disk storage layout: each database is a top-level directory that contains schemas. Each schema is the next level directory that contains tables. Each table is a directory that contains columns. Each column is a set of related files. The metadata is stored in the reserved SYS schema. This directory is packaged into a single file once created.

The TDE implements column-level compression. Each column stores uncompressed fixed-width data, or compressed fixed length or variable-length data. The TDE uses a dictionary-based compression. When data is compressed, the fixed tokens are stored in the original column. Each compressed column also owns an associated dictionary for the original fixed length (array compression) or variable length (heap compression) values. The TDE also employs lightweight compression storage format, such as run-length or delta encodings, for storing fixed-width data. This form of compression is called *encoding* in the TDE. The dictionary-compression is visible to the outside of the storage layer while encoding is a storage format that is typically invisible outside this layer.

Unlike most analytical databases, the TDE supports column-level collated strings. This is important for keeping behavior in the live and Extract scenario in Tableau consistent, as most live databases do support column-level collated strings.

4.1.2 Compiler and Optimizer

The TDE uses a logical tree style language called Tableau Query Language (TQL). It supports logical operators present in most databases, such as TableScan, Select, Project, Join, Aggregate, Order, and TopN. It has a classic query compiler that accepts a TQL query as text and translates it into some logical operator tree structure. The compiler does parsing, syntax checking, binding and semantic analysis. In addition, the compiler also performs classic rewrites of the tree, for example, expressing SELECT DISTINCT as a GROUP BY query. It also rewrites the tree to model the decompression as a normal join and introduces special logical operators to speed up query execution by utilizing the compression. This will be further discussed in Sect. 3.3.

The TDE optimizer is a rule-based optimizer. It derives properties, such as column dependencies, equivalence sets, uniqueness, sorting properties and utilizes them to perform a series of optimizations, such as filter and project push-down/pull-up, removal of unnecessary joins, removal of unnecessary orderings, common sub-expression elimination etc. The TDE optimizer is specially optimized for interactive analysis of complicated analytical queries. For example, removal of the fact table from a join is critical for performance of domain queries, frequently sent by Tableau.

4.1.3 Execution Engine

The TDE execution engine is based on the Volcano execution framework. It has implementations for a set of operators such as filter, join, etc. Each query is compiled into an execution tree by the compiler and optimizer. The query tree is executed by iterating over all the rows of the root of the tree. Operators are of two types: streaming, and stop-and-go. The first type of operators can immediately generate output rows while consuming input rows. The second type of operator needs to consume the entire input before generating any output.

4.1.4 TDE Deployment in the Client and Server Environments

The TDE is a part of any Tableau Desktop deployment and gets executed as a separate process in its process tree. When the TDE is used in the server environment, it is deployed either as a shared-nothing architecture or shared-everything architecture. Each node in the cluster is a separate TDE program. In the shared-everything architecture, storage is shared across all the nodes. A load balancer dispatches queries to different nodes in the TDE cluster.

In both cases Tableau, treats the TDE like any other supported database. It pre-processes query batches, compiles queries in TQL and executes them against the engine.

4.2 Parallel Query Execution

The TDE is able to run different queries in parallel on a single host. For a single query, however, the first version of the TDE did not use multiple parallel threads. In Tableau 8.1, we introduced a limited implementation that targeted expensive calculations in filters and projections. In the current release, we redesigned the parallel execution in the TDE to use parallel scans, which provides a much greater degree of parallelism. This section discusses the implementation of parallel execution.

4.2.1 Parallel Execution Runtime Operators

Like most database systems, the TDE execution engine uses the Exchange operator [4] to handle the parallel part of the query plan. The TDE has an implementation of the Exchange operator that is able to take N inputs and produce M outputs. It has a capability to repartition the data and can preserve the order of the input if needed.

Besides the Exchange operator, the TDE implements parallelism by means of additional operators: SharedTable and FractionTable. SharedTable is used to share access to a table across multiple threads and handles synchronization. FractionTable enables the TDE to read the table in parallel, since each fraction can be read by a separate thread.

4.2.2 Parallel Plan Generation Algorithm

Like VectorWise [9], the TDE optimizer takes a serial plan, and transforms it into a parallel plan by determining the degree of parallelism, and inserting Exchange operators [4] into the tree. In Tableau 9.0, we limited the usage of the Exchange operator to only support N inputs and one output. This means that the parallel plans we consider do not support repartitioning. The only data partitioning happens in TableScan. We also do not utilize the order preserving capability in the Exchange operator. In the coming releases, we will explore how repartitioning and order-preservation can benefit the performance of Tableau's workloads.

For brevity, we first describe the parallel plan generation for the case of a query without any joins. The algorithm to parallelize such a serial query follows the bottom-up scheme:

1. Leaf nodes are TableScan operators. At the TableScan operator the optimizer looks at the metadata, and makes a decision to partition the table into N fractions, where N is at least one.
2. If the parent is a flow operator such as Select or Project, the parent inherits the degree of parallelism from the child.
3. If the parent is a stop-and-go operator, such as Aggregate, Order or TopN, the optimizer inserts an Exchange operator between the child and the parent.
4. If the root has a degree of parallelism that is larger than one, the optimizer inserts an Exchange operator to close the parallelism.

Figure 3 shows some parallel plan examples generated by the algorithm.

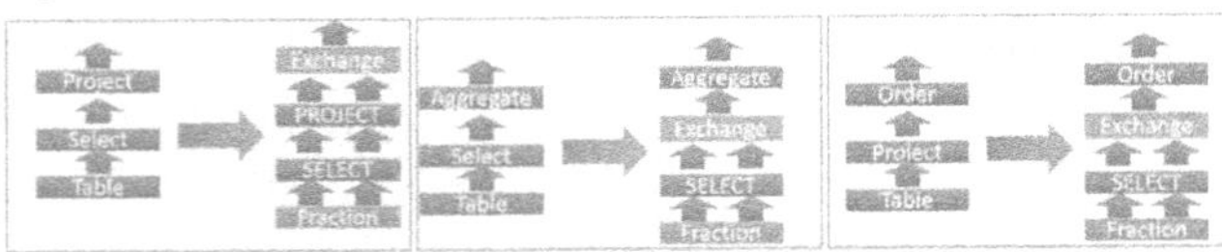

Figure 3: Parallel Plan Examples

We notice that because the Exchange operator has only one output, once the optimizer decides to put an Exchange operator to close the parallelism, the entire tree above the Exchange operator runs in serial. This is a limitation that we plan to explore and alleviate in the next release.

Determining the degree of parallelism in TableScan relies on metadata, such as data volume stored in a table. The TDE also has a cost profile for different supported elementary functions. The cost constants are obtained by empirical measuring. Certain operations, such as string manipulations, are much more expensive than others, even though the engine employs vectorization in expression evaluation. The cost profile is used to determine how expensive an expression could be. This further affects the decision of the parallelization.

Since joins in Tableau are usually between the fact table and multiple dimension tables, the TDE uses a left-deep tree to represent the joins, where the leftmost leaf table is the fact table. The TDE's execution engine processes the join by building a hash table for the right-side input, and probing the left-side input for matches.

Extending the parallel plan generation algorithms to handle join is straightforward and can be described as follows:

1. The left sub-tree of the join participates in the main parallelism
2. The right sub-tree forms a separate and independent parallel unit, and the resulting table is shared between threads.
3. A single hash table is built from the shared table and then shared for every left-hand block to probe.

Figure 4 shows a parallel plan example with join.

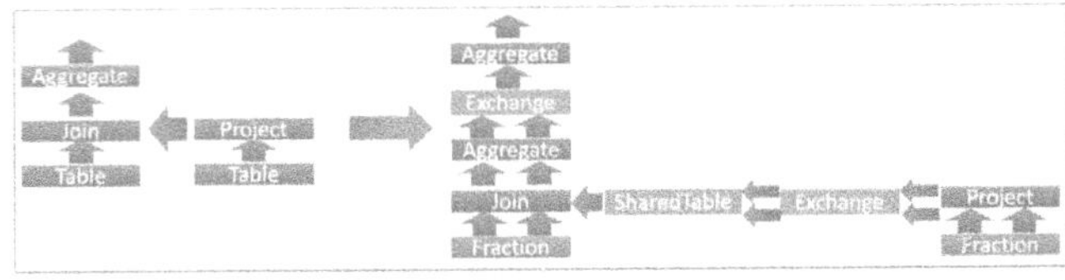

Figure 4: Parallel Plan with Join

4.2.3 Optimizing Aggregations in the Parallel Plan

Aggregations are very common in TQL queries. The simple parallel plan generation algorithm puts an Exchange operator to close a parallelized block and then applies the aggregation function serially on top of the output of the Exchange operator.

This approach can be improved by using local/global aggregation. The basic idea is simple: we apply the aggregate on each partition in parallel, let the Exchange operator to merge those partially aggregated results, and again apply the aggregate on top of the output of the Exchange operator. The local/global aggregation approach reduces the total size of data that goes into the Exchange operator. The same approach can also be applied to the TopN operator. Figure 5 shows how the parallel plan looks like when local/global aggregation is applied.

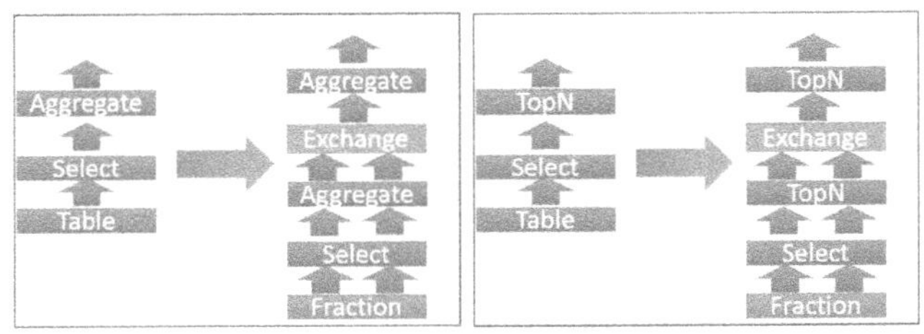

Figure 5: Parallel Plan with Local/Global Aggregation

Even if we apply local/global aggregation to the query tree, aggregation is still a serialization point. We can do even better by removing the Exchange operator and the global aggregation completely from the tree and keep the plan in parallel. This requires a more careful partitioning of the data. If we can guarantee that all the records of each unique group appear in one and exactly one partition, the global aggregation is redundant. In the remaining part of this section, we explore how to make this possible.

Typically, database systems use three types of partitioning: hash partitioning, range partitioning, and random partitioning. Random partitioning means that there is no constraint on which record goes to which partition. The system just sends records to partitions in an arbitrary fashion. The TDE is able to perform random partitioning for any table. Most tables are sorted according to one or more columns, and for those tables, the TDE is also able to perform range partitioning on the major sort. Performing range partitioning sometimes is important because interesting orders [13] on columns involved in the partitioning may be helpful in optimizing the query.

In this section, we discuss the conditions when the global aggregate and the associated Exchange operator can be removed, under the constraint that the TDE is either able to perform a random partitioning, or a range partitioning on a sorted table. A sufficient condition for removing the global aggregation is: if there exists a subset of GROUP BY columns such that a permutation of these columns is a prefix of the sorted column list, a range partition is able to be delivered for removing the global aggregation and the associated Exchange operator. We briefly prove this through the following lemmas:

Lemma 1: A sorted table on an ordered set of columns $\{c_1, .., c_n\}$ *can be range partitioned on a prefix of the ordered set.*

Proof. If a table is sorted on an ordered set, it is also sorted on any prefix of the ordered set. Therefore, we are able to range partition on any prefix. ■

Lemma 2: If a table is range partitioned on a subset of group by columns, the partition guarantees that each unique group appears in one and only one of the partitions.

Proof. If a table is range partitioned on a subset of group by columns, the partition guarantees each unique group with respect to the subset appears in one and only one of these partitions. Since any group according to the full column set is a subset of some group according to the subset, all the records of such a group must be in one and only one of the partitions. ■

Lemma 3: If some permutation of a subset of the group by columns is a prefix of a sorted table's ordered column set, there exists at least one range partitioning scheme that allows aggregates to be computed in parallel.

Proof. Lemma 1 says that we can range partition on a prefix of the ordered set. Lemma 2 says that range partitioning on a subset of group by columns enables parallel execution for aggregates. By combining the two lemmas, Lemma 3 is proved. ■

The TDE today implements range partitioning by allowing the Aggregate operator to push down the partitioning requirements. TableScan can then utilize this information along with the metadata that indicates whether the table is sorted on one or more columns, to make a decision whether a range partitioning is appropriate. Multiple layers of Aggregates may accumulate more than one partition requirements along the tree from the root to the leaf. Inferring the relationship and finding a best partition is an interesting topic. In Tableau 9.0, we did not explore this problem space. Instead, the TableScan only gets the partition requirements from the nearest Aggregate operator.

Data skew and low cardinality are other concerns related to range partitioning. Namely, if the data is skewed or if the partition key has very low cardinality (e.g. partitioning on gender), range partitioning may be slower than the local/global aggregation approach. Therefore, range partitioning in the TDE is applied conservatively today.

4.2.4 Interaction between Parallelization and Other Query Optimizations

The TDE query optimizer performs a series of optimizations. Some of them are affected by the introduction of parallelism to the plans. For example, the optimizer derives sorting properties that are used in certain rewrites. One of the usages is to determine whether a streaming implementation can be used for an aggregate function. Strictly speaking, if the data is grouped according to the group by columns, streaming aggregates can be applied. The TDE only tracks sorting properties but sorting is a sufficient (but not a necessary) condition to satisfy the grouping requirements.

The Exchange operator disturbs the sorting properties. Choosing between a streaming aggregate while the query is running in serial, and the parallel plan while we need to use a normal aggregate (currently based on hashing only in the TDE) is a cost-based decision. One can also consider variations of the parallel plans with resorting or order-preserving Exchange but both strategies performed badly on our testing workloads. In general, parallelization introduces more alternatives into the search space and the current rule-based query optimizer does not explore all the additional ones.

4.3 Leverage Encoding for Query Execution

The TDE optimizer is able to utilize the encoding information to speed up query execution. Such techniques have been discussed in [2]. The implementation has now become part of the Tableau 9.0 release. This section gives a quick overview of one specific technique and is largely a summary of Sect. 5.2 from [2].

For a run length encoded column, the optimizer can generate an IndexTable, which consists of three columns: *value*, *count* and *start*. The IndexTable can then be joined back to the main table on a range predicate:

Index.start <= Main.rank < Index.start + Index.count.

While this join by itself is not interesting, combining with the operator pushdown allows the optimizer to push a filter condition on the run length encoded column to the IndexTable. As a result, it produces a much smaller output that normally only contains a few rows. This join then significantly reduces the output of the TableScan. Furthermore, since this is a special join, we implement the join that translates the range specifications directly into disk accesses. This approach allows us to express range skipping simply as a join in the query plan. Parallel execution is implemented by distributing the result from the IndexTable across multiple threads. These threads then scan different ranges of the same input table.

Given the parallel plan introduced in Tableau 9.0, the specific approach described above does not always make the query execution faster. Although it reduces the total amount of data to be read from the disk, it may also reduce the degree of parallelism. Furthermore, this approach can introduce data skew among different threads in the parallel execution. We are looking into how to better choose the best plan among different alternatives. We are also looking for different ways to utilize the encoding for faster query execution.

4.4 Shadow Extract for Text and Excel Files

Tableau is able to connect to a wide range of data sources, including text and Microsoft Excel files. Both text and Excel files are highly popular file formats for storing data.

In the past Tableau used Microsoft Jet/Ace drivers to query text and Excel files. This approach had a number of drawbacks, such as lack of portability to other operating systems and a 4GB parsing limit. Furthermore, running analytical queries over these data sources was inherently slow because the system had to parse the file for every query.

Shadow extracts have been introduced to speed up the query execution and overcome the Jet limitations. When a text or excel file is connected, Tableau extracts the data from the file, and stores them in temporary tables in the TDE. Subsequently, all queries are executed by the TDE instead of parsing the entire file each time. This greatly improves the query execution time, however, we need to pay a one-time cost of creating the temporary database. Last but not least, the system can persist extracts in workbooks to avoid recreating temporary tables at every load.

In order to effectively extract data from text and Excel files, and overcome the Jet/Ace limitations, Tableau uses an in-house parser for parsing text files and LibXL [6] for parsing Excel files. These parsers are both more efficient, do not have the 4GB limitation, and are cross-platform. The text parser accepts a schema file as additional input if one is available. Otherwise, it attempts to discover the metadata by performing type and column name inference.

5. Improving Interactivity of Tableau Server

Tableau Server enables users to share their visualizations in an organization. Tableau 9.0 has improved the interactivity of Tableau Server significantly. In this section, we first discuss the limitations of using Tableau Server for sharing. We then present the Data Server component, which was introduced to address these problems. The rest of this section discusses the performance improvements in Tableau Server for interactivity.

5.1 Sharing Visualizations in Tableau Server

Tableau users share their data visualizations by publishing them to Tableau Server as collections of visualizations, called workbooks. Users interact with these published visualizations via a Web browser. The visualizations may rely on either live connections to data sources or data extracts. Extracts can be automatically refreshed by Server to prevent stale data.

Except for their connections to live data sources, Tableau workbooks are self-contained. Customized calculations and fields are defined within the workbook. TDE extracts are contained in the workbook.

Bundling all data source definitions and extracts within a workbook makes sharing a workbook simple, but prevents other workbooks from sharing the contained calculations and extracts. Users wishing to use the same calculations and fields defined in a published workbook must manually copy the definitions into their own workbooks. If a calculation needs to be modified, all workbooks containing the calculation must also be updated.

Similarly, TDE extracts must be generated and included in each workbook that references it. If hundreds of workbooks all use the same large extract, considerable disk resources are consumed by redundant data. Refreshing the workbooks' extracts daily to prevent stale data incurs a significant and redundant load on the underlying database.

5.2 Tableau Data Server Overview

The Tableau Data Server is a part Tableau Server that reduces the overhead of sharing calculations and extracts across workbooks. Data Server also allows filters to be applied to a published data source to restrict individual users' access to the data. For example, an individual salesperson may only be able to see customers in their region, while their manager can see customers in all regions.

Users publish data sources that can be leveraged, without duplication, by multiple workbooks to Data Server. By publishing a data source to Data Server, a complex calculation in a data source can be defined once and used everywhere. Categorical bins and multi-dimensional sets of thousands of constants can be manually defined once. Modifications to a published data source affect all visualizations that refer to it.

TDE extracts can be published with a data source. Instead of 100 workbooks with distinct copies of the same extract, a single extract is created. Refreshing a single extract daily -- rather than all copies of it – significantly reduces the query load on the underlying database.

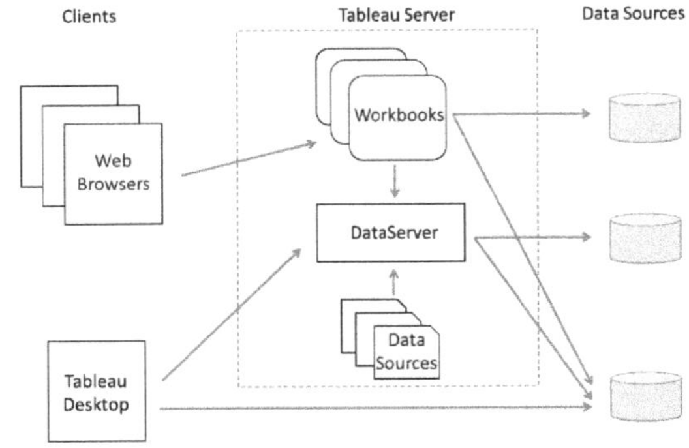

Figure 6: Data Server in the Tableau eco-system

Figure 6 depicts Data Server in the larger Tableau eco-system. Clients can directly connect to databases or connect to data sources published to Data Server, which acts as a proxy between clients and the underlying database.

When a client connects to a published data source, it receives metadata (e.g. schema) about the published data source from Data Server. The client populates its data window with this information. As the user drags fields on to the visualization, queries are dispatched from the client to Data Server.

Data Server parses the query into an internal representation, optimizes it and generates the query for the specific underlying database. Databases have different capabilities and the query optimization and generation process takes these capabilities into account. The generated query is evaluated against the underlying database and the retrieved results are returned to the client for display.

5.3 Improving Interactivity of Published Data Sources

Data Server as any other proxy adds on a certain overhead. However, other than imposing data permissions, there is conceptually no reason why proxied interactions with underlying data sources would be different from the ones against equivalent direct connections.

In the past, in certain cases the queries from Data Server could be less optimal. This is because Data Server was using a separate optimization pipeline from the one in Tableau Desktop (Sect. 3.1). In Tableau 9.0, these pipelines got unified, which allows both applications to take advantage of the same rich optimizations. Another shortcoming was related to managing a remote state. Namely, when a client directly connects to a database, Tableau creates temporary data structures on the database to improve interactivity. For example, a filter on a large cardinality database field may be stored as a temporary table on the database. Instead of issuing a query with a very long and complicated filter to the database, the temporary table is used in the query.

We have introduced temporary tables to the Data Server to improve the user experience for published data sources. The temporary data structures provide two different performance improvements: (1) reduced network traffic between the client and the Data Server if a temporary data structure is used repeatedly in subsequent queries, and (2) improved query execution times on the database.

When a client connects to a published data source on Data Server, the Data Server establishes a connection to the underlying database and determines if it supports the creation of temporary tables. This information is conveyed back to the client with the data source metadata.

As fields are dragged to the visualization, the client issues a series of requests to Data Server to create and populate a temporary table, causing the Data Server to construct an in-memory temporary table. Subsequent queries from the client to the Data Server may reference this temporary table. On the Data Server, the temporary table's definition is incorporated during query optimization, compilation, and evaluation. In some cases, the query may be evaluated without interacting with the underlying database.

If the generated query must be evaluated by the underlying database, the Data Server will create a temporary table on the database. The generated query is modified to use the temporary table on the database and executed. If the Data Server fails to create a temporary table on the database, the query is rewritten to produce a query that can be evaluated without it.

5.4 State Management

Temporary table state is maintained in two different places in Data Server: in memory and on the underlying database. In both cases, this state is maintained while the client connection to Data Server remains active; it is reclaimed when the connection is closed or expired due to inactivity.

To alleviate the in-memory cost of temporary tables, temporary table definitions are shared across client connections. These definitions are updated as clients create and drop temporary tables. The definitions are removed when all references to them are removed.

If desired, in-memory temporary tables on Data Server can be disabled. While network traffic between the client and Data Server will increase, users will still benefit from improved query execution times on the underlying database.

6. RELATED WORK

The TDE is a column store for analytical queries. C-store [7] is a column store that has been commercialized as Vertica. MonetDB [3, 8] from CWI is another column store that has wide impact. Vectorwise [9] is the commercialized MonetDB/X100 [3] project that has an Ingres front-end and many additional improvements. Also, SAP Hana [11] is a column store that supports both OLTP and analytical queries.

A parallel database has a long history of research and commercial development since early 1990s. It is beyond the scope of this section to give an overview of this area, for details see [10]. The TDE's execution model is based on the Volcano system [4]. In particular, it uses the Exchange operator to perform parallel execution. Vectorwise's parallel optimizer [12] provides some good data structure to track the requests from the parents to the children and the delivery from the children to the parents. The TDE's parallelizer has largely borrowed the notations from Vectorwise's optimizer. Property derivation has a long history. System R [13] pioneered this technique by tracking the ordering information for intermediate query results. Partition property derivation was first discussed in [5].

Eliminating redundant operations, such as joins has been widely studied [14, 15, 16, 17, 18]. In particular, elimination of redundant joins in [14, 15] is based on the concept of tableaux and is only able to treat a sub-class of relational algebras. [16] enhanced the tableaux approach by using so-called tagged selection tableaux. Removing redundant joins in queries involving views has been studied in [17]. The approach uses functional dependencies and source level transformations of SQL to remove redundant joins. Join culling is widely applied in Tableau and the TDE to improve query execution latency for better interactive experience.

Query matching plays an important role in Tableau's caching infrastructure. It has been widely studied in the database literature, mostly in the context of database views. Giving an overview of the research for database views is beyond the scope of this section. A good survey is provided in [13]. Query containment and query equivalence are two important concepts in the research literature. They enable comparison between different queries. The theory of query containment and equivalence has been widely studied [18, 21, 22, 23, 24, 25]. GMAP [26, 27] pioneered the view matching approach in the database system. In [28], the authors provide a similar algorithm for view matching. A transformation rule based approach for view matching in the SQL Server's optimizer is discussed in [29]. This approach introduces the filter-tree index to dramatically speed up the matching process.

Multiple query processing has been widely studied in the database literature, mostly in the context of multiple query optimization [30, 31, 32, 33, 34, 35]. Much of the work [30, 31, 34] has focused on finding common subexpressions and materializing the results temporarily for sharing among these queries. Researchers also studied multiple query processing beyond the common subexpression detection. For example, Tan and Lu [36, 37] investigated how to schedule query fragments to better share the data in memory and across multiprocessors. Pipelining the data between processes to share the same data is studied in [38]. Furthermore, scheduling the queries carefully using a middleware to improve sharing between queries has been studied in [39].

7. FUTURE PLANS

Tableau constantly adds new data sources and types of analysis, which often requires implementation of dedicated performance features. In particular, we are planning to add end-to-end support for federated and semi-structured data sources, where appropriate optimization techniques, efficient extraction and management in Data Server play important roles.

Regarding the query processing pipeline we plan to apply more multi-query processing techniques to take advantage of sophisticated commonalities between queries in a batch. That fits well with incorporating more classic optimizations to improve our plans and generated remote queries. Furthermore, in order to alleviate frequently substantial local post-processing, we are going to explore multi-level caching similar to [44].

Substantial sizes of federated datasets and rapidly growing popularity of our SaaS platform put more pressure on the Tableau Data Engine to process larger extracts. Therefore, we are considering using data partitioning in a distributed architecture.

Last but not least, both data exploration and dashboard generation could become more responsive if requested data has been accurately predicted and prefetched. Materialization of secondary structures and prediction approaches such as DICE [46], are good examples in this field.

8. SUMMARY

In this paper we have discussed several performance improvements that contribute to high interactivity of visual data analysis. They are available in the new release of the product, Tableau 9.0.

Most of all, in dashboard generation, we have suggested query batch processing with an initial batch optimization phase, query fusion and concurrent query submission. Using two levels of query caches, intelligent and literal, that can be persisted on the client or distributed in the server environment, further magnifies the responsiveness. Furthermore, performance of the TDE has been improved thanks to addition of parallel plans and index scans for RLE-encoded columns. Last but not least, temporary table support has been added to Tableau Data Server to improve performance of published data sources.

9. REFERENCES

[1] Richard Wesley, Matthew Eldridge, and Pawel T. Terlecki. 2011. An analytic data engine for visualization in tableau. In *Proceedings of the 2011 ACM SIGMOD International Conference on Management of data* (SIGMOD '11). ACM, New York, NY, USA, 1185-1194. DOI= http://doi.acm.org/10.1145/1989323.1989449

[2] Richard Michael Grantham Wesley and Pawel Terlecki. 2014. Leveraging compression in the tableau data engine. In *Proceedings of the 2014 ACM SIGMOD international conference on Management of data* (SIGMOD '14). ACM, New York, NY, USA, 563-573. DOI=http://doi.acm.org/10.1145/2588555.2595639

[3] Boncz, P., Zukowski, M., and Nes, N. MonetDB/X100: Hyper-Pipelining Query Execution. In *International Conference on Innovative Data Systems Research (CIDR)*, Jan. 2005, 225-237.

[4] G. Graefe, "Volcano: An extensible and parallel query evaluation system," IEEE Transactions on Knowledge and Data Engineering, 120-135, 1994.

[5] J. Zhou, P. Larson, and R. Chaiken. Incorporating partitioning and parallel plans into the SCOPE optimizer. In ICDE, 2010.

[6] LibXL http://www.libxl.com/

[7] Abadi, D. J., Madden, S. R., and Hachem, N. 2008. Column-stores vs. row-stores: how different are they really? In *Proceedings of the 2008 ACM SIGMOD international Conference on Management of Data* (Vancouver, Canada, June 09 - 12, 2008). SIGMOD '08. ACM, New York, NY, 967-980.

[8] Boncz, P. *Monet: A Next-Generation DBMS Kernel For Query-Intensive Applications*. Doctoral Thesis, Universiteit van Amsterdam, Amsterdam, The Netherlands, May 2002.

[9] Zukowski, Marcin, and Peter A. Boncz. "Vectorwise: Beyond column stores."*IEEE Data Engineering Bulletin* 35.1 (2012): 21-27.

[10] Shivnath Babu and Herodotos Herodotou (2013), "Massively Parallel Databases and MapReduce Systems", Foundations and Trends® in Databases: Vol. 5: No. 1, pp 1-104. http://dx.doi.org/10.1561/1900000036

[11] Franz Färber, Norman May, Wolfgang Lehner, Philipp Große, Ingo Müller, Hannes Rauhe, and Jonathan Dees. The SAP HANA Database – An Architecture Overview. IEEE Data Engineering Bulletin, 35(1):28–33, 2012.

[12] Anikiej K. Multi-core Parallelization of Vectorized Queries [dissertation]. University of Warsaw and VU University of Amsterdam, 2010.

[13] P. G. Selinger, M. M. Astrahan, D. D. Chamberlin, R. A. Lorie, and T. G. Price. Access path selection in a relational database management system. In Proceedings of SIGMOD Conference, 1979.

[14] M. Majster-Cederbaum. Elimination of redundant operations in relational queries with general selection operators. Computing, 34(4):303-323, 1984.

[15] A. V. Aho, C. Beeri, and J. D. Ullman. The theory of joins in relational databases. ACM Trans. on Database Systems, 4(3): 297-314, 1979.

[16] A. V. Aho, Y. Sagiv, and J. D. Ullman. Efficient optimization of a class of relational expression. ACM Trans. on Database Systems, 4(4):435-454, 1979.

[17] Nikolaus Ott, Klaus Horländer, Removing redundant join operations in queries involving views, Information Systems, Volume 10, Issue 3, 1985, Pages 279-288

[18] Y. Sagiv and M. Yannakakis. Equivalences among relational expressions with the union and difference operator. Journal of the ACM, 27(4):633-655, 1980.

[19] Halevy, Alon Y. "Answering queries using views: A survey." The VLDB Journal 10.4 (2001): 270-294.

[20] Sara Cohen, Werner Nutt, and Yehoshua Sagiv. 2003. Containment of Aggregate Queries. In *Proceedings of the 9th International Conference on Database Theory* (ICDT '03), Diego Calvanese, Maurizio Lenzerini, and Rajeev Motwani (Eds.). Springer-Verlag, London, UK, UK, 111-125.

[21] Chandra A.K., Merlin P.M. Optimal implementation of conjunctive queries in relational databases. In: Proc. Ninth AnnualACMSymposium on Theory of Computing.pp 77–90, 1977

[22] Zhang X., Ozsoyoglu M.Z. On efficient reasoning with implication constraints. In: Proc. of DOOD. pp 236–252, 1993

[23] Chaudhuri S., Vardi M. Optimizing real conjunctive queries. In: Proc. of PODS. pp 59–70, Washington D.C., USA, 1993

[24] Chaudhuri S., Vardi M. On the complexity of equivalence between recursive and nonrecursive datalog programs. In: Proc. of PODS. pp 55–66, Minneapolis, Minn., USA, 1994

[25] Kolaitis P., Martin D., Thakur M. On the complexity of the containment problem for conjunctive queries with built-in predicates. In: Proc. of PODS. pp 197–204, Seattle,Wash., USA, 1998

[26] Tsatalos O.G., Solomon M.H., Ioannidis Y.E. The GMAP: a versatile tool for physical data independence. In: Proc. of VLDB. pp 367–378, Santiago, Chile, 1994

[27] Tsatalos O.G., Solomon M.H., Ioannidis Y.E. The GMAP: a versatile tool for physical data independence. VLDB J. (2):101–118, 1996

[28] Chaudhuri, S., Krishnamurthy, R., Potamianos, S., & Shim, K. (1995, March). Optimizing queries with materialized views. In 2013 IEEE 29th International Conference on Data Engineering (ICDE) (pp. 190-190). IEEE Computer Society.

[29] Goldstein J., Larson P.A. Optimizing queries using materialized views: a practical, scalable solution. In: Proc. of SIGMOD. pp 331–342, 2001

[30] JarkeM. Common subexpression isolation in multiple query optimization. Query Processing in Database Systems, KimW, Reiner DS, Batory DS (eds.). Springer: Berlin, 1985

[31] Park J, Segev A. Using common subexpressions to optimize multiple queries. Proceedings of the 4th International Conference on Data Engineering. IEEE Computer Society: Washington, DC, 1988; 311–319.

[32] Sellis T. Multiple query optimization. ACM Transactions on Database Systems 1988; 13(1):23–52.

[33] Cosar A, Lim E, Srivastava J. Multiple query optimization with depth-first branch-and-bound and dynamic query ordering. CIKM 93, Proceedings of the Second International Conference on Information and Knowledge Management. ACM, 1993; 433–438.

[34] Chen F, Dunham M. Common subexpression processing in multiple-query processing. IEEE Transactions on Knowledge and Data Engineering 1988; 10(3):493–499.

[35] Roy P et al. Efficient and extensible algorithms for multi query optimization. Proceedings of the 2000 ACM SIGMOD International Conference on Management of Data. ACM Press: New York, 2000; 249–260.

[36] Tan K, Lu H. Workload scheduling for multiple query processing. Information Processing Letters 1995; 55(5):251–257.

[37] Tan K, Lu H. Scheduling multiple queries in symmetric multiprocessors. Information Sciences 1996; 95(1/2):125–153.

[38] Dalvi N et al. Pipelining in multi-query optimization. J. Comput. Syst. Sci. 2003; 66(4):728–762.

[39] O'Gorman, Kevin, Amr El Abbadi, and Divyakant Agrawal. "Multiple query optimization in middleware using query teamwork." Software: Practice and Experience 35.4 (2005): 361-391.

[40] Stolte, C., Tang, D., and Hanrahan, P. 2008. Polaris: a system for query, analysis, and visualization of multidimensional databases. *Commun. ACM* 51, 11 (Nov. 2008), 75-84.

[41] http://redis.io/

[42] Lakshman, Avinash, and Prashant Malik. "Cassandra: a decentralized structured storage system." ACM SIGOPS Operating Systems Review 44.2 (2010): 35-40.

[43] https://www.faa.gov/data_research/

[44] Milena G. Ivanova, Martin L. Kersten, Niels J. Nes, and Romulo A.P. Gonçalves. 2009. An architecture for recycling intermediates in a column-store. In Proceedings of the 2009 ACM SIGMOD International Conference on Management of data (SIGMOD '09), Carsten Binnig and Benoit Dageville (Eds.). ACM, New York, NY, USA, 309-320

[45] Parag Agrawal , Daniel Kifer , Christopher Olston, Scheduling shared scans of large data files, Proceedings of the VLDB Endowment, v.1 n.1, August 2008

[46] Prasanth Jayachandran, Karthik Tunga, Niranjan Kamat, Arnab Nandi. Combining User Interaction, Speculative Query Execution and Sampling in the DICE System. PVLDB 7(13): 1697-1700 (2014)

[47] Kristi Morton, Ross Bunker, Jock Mackinlay, Robert Morton, and Chris Stolte. 2012. Dynamic workload driven data integration in tableau. In Proceedings of the 2012 ACM SIGMOD International Conference on Management of Data (SIGMOD '12). ACM, New York, NY, USA, 807-816. http://doi.acm.org/10.1145/2213836.2213961

[48] Shaul Dar , Michael J. Franklin , Björn Þór Jónsson , Divesh Srivastava , Michael Tan. Semantic Data Caching and Replacement, *Proceedings of the 22th International Conference on Very Large Data Bases*, p.330-341, September 03-06, 1996

Data Management in Non-Volatile Memory

Stratis D. Viglas
School of Informatics
University of Edinburgh, UK
sviglas@inf.ed.ac.uk

ABSTRACT

Non-volatile memory promises to bridge the gap between main memory and secondary storage by offering a universal storage device. Its performance profile is unique in that its latency is close to main memory and it is byte addressable, but it exhibits asymmetric I/O in that writes are more expensive than reads. These properties imply that it cannot act as a drop-in replacement for either main-memory or disk. Therefore, we must revisit the salient aspects of data management in light of this new technology. In what follows we present the current work in the area with a view towards identifying the open problems and exposing the research opportunities. In particular, we address issues like: (*a*) incorporating non-volatile memory into the data management stack, (*b*) supporting transactions and ensuring persistence and recovery, and (*c*) query processing.

Categories and Subject Descriptors

H.2.4 [**Database Management**]: Systems; D.4.2 [**Storage Management**]: Secondary storage

Keywords

Non-volatile memory; Persistence; Performance; Recovery; Query processing

1. INTRODUCTION

Non-volatile memory (NVM), also referred to as persistent memory, is a new type of storage medium that aims to bring forth, for the first time, a universal storage device. That is, a device that bridges the gap between volatile main memory and non-volatile, block-based secondary storage. Its performance characteristics are such that it is close to main memory (DRAM) in terms of access latency—albeit slower—but much faster than flash memory and magnetic disks (see also Figure 1 for a comparison). The key properties of non-volatile memory, apart from its performance and persistence, are byte-addressability and write-read cost asymmetry. Byte-addressability means that NVM is not a block-storage device and it is certainly feasible, depending on how vendors choose to expose it to the system, for it to be accessible through memory load/store operations. Likewise, we can perform byte-level I/O as opposed to block-level I/O without having to amortize the I/O cost by increasing the block size. At the same time, NVM exhibits some of the pathologies of flash memory: writes are more expensive than reads both in terms of response time (*i.e.*, they simply need longer to be completed) and in terms of how they affect the lifetime of the medium. Note, however, that the physical mechanisms used in contemporary NVM designs are not the same as those in flash memory [2, 22]—see also Section 2.1. As such, NVM requires new techniques for masking this asymmetry from the users.

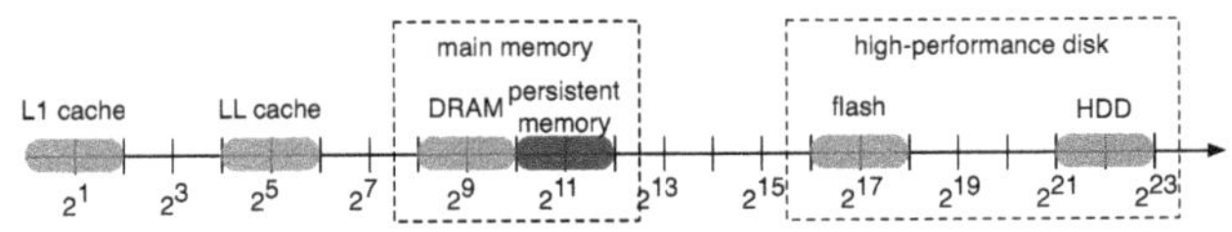

Figure 1: Typical access latency in processor cycles on a 4GHz processor (figure adapted from [33])

Given the above, the question is how do we expose NVM to developers and users? Treating persistent memory as persistent storage means that we will be downplaying its performance merits and using algorithms and techniques that have been designed for a different medium. Treating persistent memory as volatile memory means that we will need to rethink our data structures in light of the new available capacity and assume that everything can be memory-resident. In both alternatives, by treating persistent memory as yet another persistent storage device or yet another additional volatile memory device, we are effectively reusing a prior abstraction that has been originally built for different performance characteristics. In doing that, we are missing an opportunity to bring out the best of each abstraction and drop all the bloat that it may be carrying with it.

Objectives In this work, our aims are: (*a*) to present this new type of storage technology in more detail and focus on what makes it different and why it requires a study of its own; (*b*) to give insight into how this technology can be seamlessly integrated into the data management stack; (*c*) to give an overview of the recent work in the area and explain the key techniques in more detail; (*d*) to identify both the immediate research opportunities and the longer-term fundamental problems that require attention; and (*e*) to jump-start researchers and practitioners in the area.

SIGMOD'15, May 31–June 4, 2015, Melbourne, Victoria, Australia.

http://dx.doi.org/10.1145/2723372.2731082.

2. BACKGROUND

NVM is a class of memory, rather than a specific type of storage medium. There are many competing implementations that are classified as NVM even though they do not necessarily share the same underlying technology. We will first present an overview of the different technologies that have been proposed in the literature and have picked up significant traction to be considered as the forerunners when NVM becomes mainstream. After addressing the technological side of NVM we will look at how it can be introduced into the system stack, *i.e.*, we will present ways that existing systems can immediately start using NVM as a drop-in replacement for either DRAM or for secondary storage. We will next turn our attention to the use-cases that are most relevant to data management. We will start with the most basic guarantee that NVM provides: persistence. Persistence is guaranteed by the medium, but only at the level of ensuring that data is not lost if power is lost. There are various aspects that need to be addressed when higher-level workflows like database systems are taken into account. Immediately following persistence is recovery. Not only do we want to ensure long-term access to the data, we also need to have sufficient mechanisms in place to allow us to recover portions of the database in the event of a power failure. This is a departure from the typical database architecture where all processing takes place in a DRAM-backed bufferpool and I/O is performed in blocks. The runtime must now guarantee the recoverability of each individual byte change, as NVM is byte-addressable. A repercussion of different persistent and recovery mechanisms is that we need to develop new mechanisms for transactional support as well. Finally, we will address query processing. We will discuss how the fundamentals of query processing need to be revisited in the context of NVM. In the last part of the presentation we will focus on the open challenges in the area with an eye towards identifying future research directions. A more detailed discussion of the various topics follows.

2.1 The inner workings

NVM is an umbrella term that encompasses both read-only memories and persistent random-access memories. The most widely used underlying technology used in NVMs is the floating-gate transistor, which acts as a single memory cell. It works by having the device controller apply device-specific operating voltages to the gate to trap or release electrical charge. The recorded value can then be read by sensing the charge (no charge equals 0, charge equals 1). This technology forms the basis of various implementations like the (Electrical) Erasable Programmable Read Only-Memory (EEPROM), or the most widely used flash memory. In flash memory, multiple cells are blocked and are not individually set. Operations take place at the granularity of an entire block, which is erased and reprogrammed (also referred to as the the erase-before-write property of flash memory). Floating-gate transistors can only go through a limited number of erase/program cycles, thus reducing the lifetime of the device. Limited endurance and block-level I/O, combined with the physical property of setting voltage taking longer than sensing, result in writing to flash memory being much slower than reading. The key difference between flash memory and the wider class of NVMs is the method by which information is stored and sensed: rather than storing and sensing charge, NVM technologies alter some physical property of the medium thereby changing its electrical resistance, which they then sense to read back the information.

Phase-Change Memory, or PCM, is the most widely known NVM technology. Information is recorded using a mechanism similar to that of optical media. A heating element heats the silicone of each memory cell, either changing it to an amorphous state, or crystallizing it. The two different states, or phases, have different electrical resistance, thus recording one bit. An electrical current is applied to measure the electrical resistance and sense the state of each cell. There are various other phases in between an amorphous and a completely crystallized state. Thus, a single cell can record more than one bit of information. The main merit of PCM is its high density. Its main disadvantage is that it is not a purely electrical device as it requires a heating element for programming and thus it is more power-hungry and dissipates more heat during operation. Additionally, there is considerable voltage drift due to the resistance of the amorphous state increasing over time according to a power law. So, as times goes by, it becomes increasingly difficult for the device to store multiple bits in a single cell, thus losing capacity. Therefore, even though the technology is capable of high density in the offset, this capability is lost over time.

Resistive Random Access Memory, or ReRAM, works in a similar way to PCM. The main difference is that instead of affecting the crystallization of the medium, a heating element physically opens a conduction path on the material for the current to pass. That physical path can be closed on demand. The existence (or not) of the physical path affects the electrical resistance of the material, which can thus be used to record information. As electrical current passing through the material, in addition to sensing the electrical resistance, is used to read the stored information.

Magnetoresistive Random Access Memory, or MRAM, employs the magnetic properties of the medium in addition to its electrical ones. The memory cells are magnetic storage elements formed by two magnetic plates separated by a thin insulating layer, each capable of holding a magnetic field. One of the plates is a permanent magnet, whereas the other plate's field can be set at will. The two fields generate a magnetic tunnel, whose electrical resistance changes depending on the orientation of the two fields. The electrical resistance can be measured if current is supplied to the two plates. The polarity of the fields of the plates results in two levels of resistance that can record one bit of information.

All these technologies support byte-addressable fine-grained control of the medium and alleviate some of the performance problems associated with the large-scale erase-to-program operations of flash memory. However, setting the physical properties takes as long a time and requires a heating element (for PCM and ReRAM) or polarization of the medium (for MRAM); in all cases, energy consumption is greater. Thus, the problem has only been alleviated and writes still hurt performance more than reads, whether the performance metric is response time, energy consumption, or device lifetime. All vendors aim to produce NVM at high densities, and thus capacities, but at a much lower energy consumption point, thereby making NVM cost-effective.

2.2 Integrating NVM into the stack

NVM presents a new level in the memory hierarchy so a salient decision is how to best integrate it with the rest of the system stack. There are two main options: the first option is to treat NVM as secondary storage and use file I/O operations to access it. If that is the case, we need to optimize the I/O substrate of the system for persistent memory, as opposed to optimizing the memory subsystem for persistence. The second option is to treat NVM as byte-addressable DRAM with persistence guarantees through persistent memory regions. We then need to extend the system to support NVM through either: (*a*) changes to the memory controller so that it can guarantee persistence through its firmware; or (*b*) extending the system's instruction set architecture to expose persistent memory to the developer through specialized memory load/store operations; or (*c*) exposing a higher-level API to the operating system and then relying on software to guarantee persistence and to decide on data placement. These alternatives can be refined further into four main designs that have been used in practice.

RAM disk The first approach is to employ a memory-mounted filesystem over NVM. RAM disks are lightweight filesystems that bypass disk-related overheads. They do not incur disk I/O, though they support persistence. RAM disks bypass the filesystem cache with writes and reads being synchronous to the portion of main memory allocated to the RAM disk. Therefore, RAM disks bridge the mismatch between block devices and byte-addressable NVM by employing filesystem practices to manage NVM.

Byte-addressable filesystem The second option is to use a filesystem optimized for persistent memory such as PMFS [13] or BPFS [9]. These are typically implemented as kernel extensions and thus reduce the overhead of system calls and employ low-level fine-grained persistence primitives to implement file-level access through CPU load/store instructions, thereby minimizing overhead.

Heap-based approaches The third option is to substitute the runtime's memory allocator (*e.g.*, `malloc()`) with one that uses the non-volatile memory for allocations, as opposed to the system's heap (see, *e.g.*, [8, 40] for two approaches). This affects the memory allocator, but not the way by which data structures allocate memory. In applying this approach we use main memory data structures implemented for volatile memory. Thus, we may be using patterns that are not optimized for NVM. Consider, for instance, a dynamic array like a C++ `vector`. C++ `vectors` have an initial capacity; when that capacity is reached they allocate a memory chunk twice as big as their current capacity; copy the elements over; and release the memory they had previously occupied. The doubling of allocated memory and, more importantly, the copying of elements over are far from ideal for NVM as they incur a large number of writes.

Optimized blocked memory Finally, we can use a combination of the previous options. We can keep the interface of a heap-based allocator, but change the implementation of our data structures so they use lightweight logging approaches to record changes to NVM and export a byte addressable interface to the user. Such an approach has been proven to decouple the persistence guarantees from the implementation of data structures and the memory allocator and incurs a minimal overhead [39].

2.3 Persistence

Persistent regions have been proposed to support persistent virtual memory and user-accessible heaps [17, 34, 44]. These attempts either provide persistence guarantees for heap-allocated data, or employ a mapping to block-level I/O devices and file abstractions to implement persistence. Recoverability relies on staging persistence and logging through combining volatile main memory and persistent disk storage. In [25], the authors use battery-backed DRAM for persisting the file cache [5]. They also invoke disk-based I/O and uses a coarse-grained region approach to log undo information.

Two recent proposals [8, 40] provide implementations of heaps for persistent memory to user applications. Such support can act as a drop-in replacement for `malloc()` and enables the developers to seamlessly integrate persistent memory regions into their applications. Moreover, heaps in NVM can be used as building blocks for programmers to create and manage their own recovery protocols. Fang *et al.* [14] propose an NVM-based log manager for DBMSs, which relies on a client-server design and uses epoch barriers to guarantee persistence. Giles *et al.* [15] address embedded transaction management in user code. They introduce custom hardware to force parts of the log to NVM before committing, while keeping user updates in a dedicated buffer before persisting the log. Other recent work [16] explicitly addresses redo logging without in-place updates. Similarly, [47] embeds transaction management in user code by assuming the existence of a non-volatile cache that is used as a drop-in replacement for a log. Finally, [3] studies the update semantics of NVM data in lock-based code (as opposed to transactional code) and the mechanisms used for logging and recovery in NVM.

2.4 Recovery

Prior to NVM, researchers proposed battery-backed DRAM and buffer manager extensions to support recoverability [28]. For instance, [10] uses battery-backed DRAM with an ARIES-like protocol, and assumes page-level I/O for data and log updates. DBMSs optimized for volatile memory [11, 19] can be used as starting points for integrating persistent memory, even though they are sometimes subject to the inefficiencies of a block-based design towards durability.

Pelley *et al.* [32] address the problem of supporting durability for OLTP workloads executed over NVM. They first show that NVM can act as a drop-in replacement for disk drives and gives almost instantaneous recovery in the event of failure. However, this comes at the price of a reduction in throughput during transactional processing. They identify the barrier latency in NVM as one of the main culprits for this discrepancy, and introduce distributed logging and group commits for mitigating the impact of suboptimal barrier implementations. Similarly, [41] examines more closely the impact of NVM and non-uniform memory access on multicore and multi-socket architectures. The authors argue that distributed logging is not elected but enforced by the environment and propose passive group commit as an implementation mechanism for distributed logging. Passive group commit exhibits a minimal overhead and enables distributed commit to scale well in logging-intensive workloads. Along the same lines, Oukid *et al.* [30] proposed a framework by which NVM is combined with DRAM for recovery. The insight is that updates should happen in-place on NVM but in small batches to better take advantage of the performance profile of NVM. Doing so results in almost instantaneous restart in the event of failure.

Logging and recovery for NVM is also addressed in [4] where the authors present REWIND: a user-mode library approach to managing transactional updates directly from user code written in an imperative general-purpose language.

REWIND starts from write-ahead logging and adapts it for NVM. It relies on a custom persistent in-memory data structure for the log that supports recoverable operations on itself. The scheme also employs a combination of batching in the memory layout of the log data, non-temporal updates, persistent memory fences, and lightweight logging to optimize performance. The authors show that such an optimized logging scheme can be orders of magnitude faster than disk-based approaches ported to persistent memory, or than data-structure-specific recoverability extensions.

Other work has considered more general data management tasks. For instance, [35] compares both DBMSs and file systems to custom alternatives; while [18] quantifies the overhead of several DBMS functionalities. There has also been recent interest in extending file systems for NVM. For example, [31] presents an extended transactional and recoverable I/O interface for multiple, non-consecutive blocks.

2.5 Query processing

There has been a large body of work dealing with query processing but in the context of flash memory. Research has focused on flash-specific bufferpool management schemes [20, 21, 29, 45], query evaluation techniques [12, 27, 36], or indexing [23, 24, 38, 42, 43, 46]. Though this host of work addresses the write-read asymmetry of the medium, it does not cater for byte addressability. The differences in block- *vs.* byte-level access suggest that considerable effort will be necessary to port these approaches to persistent memory.

Chen *et al.* [6] explored how database algorithms need to be changed in the presence of phase-change memory. The authors argued for a radical reimplementation of algorithms by eliminating data copying and using pointers to data in order to reduce memory stores. This resulted in substantial benefits both in terms of performance and in terms of lifetime and power consumption of the device.

A strand of work tackles algorithms for query processing, when these algorithms work over data stored in NVM. For example, [37] describes the necessary optimizations if sorting is to be applied over data in PCM. The authors propose and evaluate mechanisms for using a small DRAM buffer ahead of PCM to optimize performance. Similarly, [39] introduces write-limited algorithms for fundamental query processing operations. These are families of algorithms for sorting and join processing that trade expensive writes for cheaper reads with the goal of achieving the same performance as traditional query processing algorithms, but at a fraction of the write cost. Write-limited algorithms are accompanied by a runtime that dynamically tracks reads and writes and decides whether intermediate results should be materialized, or deferred and regenerated on demand from their primary sources. Further, different ways of incorporating NVM into the stack are also explored, along the lines of Section 2.2. The choice of algorithm in addition to the choice of how to best access NVM from query processing code is a complicated problem that requires a carefully crafted cost model and runtime, if informed decisions are to be made.

Data structures have also been tackled in the context of NVM. In [7], the authors present three schemes to optimize B^+-trees for phase-change memory: keeping node entries unsorted, allowing underflow in nodes, or allowing overflow chains. All three methods aim to optimize write performance. The authors show that the three proposed schemes can reduce the response time and improve device lifetime and energy consumption. Similarly, [38] proposes the introduction of controlled imbalance in the B^+-tree to cope with asymmetric I/O. The observation is that if we know the write-to-read cost ratio of the device we can afford to introduce imbalance as that will manifest as extra reads, which are cheaper than writes. Once the savings from those extra reads are spent, we can rebalance the tree. The unbalanced B^+-tree exhibited performance improvements over the traditional B^+-tree in a variety of settings.

Finally, query optimization has been addressed in [1]. The authors argue that even though the optimization algorithm is robust, its cost models are suboptimal when dealing with asymmetric storage. The reason is that the big differentiating factor in performance so far has been random *vs.* sequential I/O. In asymmetric media, however, it is the number of write *vs.* the number of read operations that should be used as the basis for cost functions. The authors implement an asymmetry-aware cost model for PostgreSQL and show how it can lead to more efficient execution plans. In addition, they propose mechanisms by which the system can automatically tune the cost model to the host hardware. It would be interesting to extend and refine this work to account for the byte addressability of NVM. This can be further improved with main memory execution models that take the CPU's cache hierarchy into account [26].

3. OUTLOOK

Non-volatile memory has the potential to become a universal storage device that bridges the gap between main memory and secondary storage. Even though non-volatile memory is a general term encompassing a multitude of technologies, regardless of the specific type of technology the performance profile of non-volatile memory is unique. Non-volatile memory is asymmetric with writes being more expensive than reads, and it is also byte-addressable. The combination of these factors requires that all aspects of data management are revisited: from transactional processing, to persistence and recovery, to query processing. A related, but salient question, apart from the actual use of non-volatile memory for data management, is how to best integrate non-volatile memory in the data management stack at the system level. There has been some preliminary work on non-volatile memory, but the area is certainly fresh with plenty of opportunities for original and high-impact work.

4. REFERENCES

[1] D. Bausch, I. Petrov, and A. Buchmann. Making cost-based query optimization asymmetry-aware. In *DaMoN*, 2012.

[2] P. Bonnet, L. Bouganim, I. Koltsidas, and S. D. Viglas. System co-design and data managment for flash devices. *PVLDB*, 4, 2011.

[3] D. Chakrabarti and H.-J. Boehm. Durability semantics for lock-based multithreaded programs. In *HOTPAR*, June 2013.

[4] A. Chatzistergiou, M. Cintra, and S. D. Viglas. Rewind: Recovery write-ahead system for in-memory non-volatile data-structures. *PVLDB*, 8, 2015.

[5] P. M. Chen, W. T. Ng, S. Chandra, C. Aycock, G. Rajamani, and D. Lowell. The Rio file cache: Surviving operating system crashes. In *ASPLOS*, 1996.

[6] S. Chen, P. B. Gibbons, and S. Nath. Rethinking database algorithms for phase change memory. In *CIDR*, 2011.

[7] P. Chi, W.-C. Lee, and Y. Xie. Making b+-tree efficient in pcm-based main memory. In *ISLPED*, 2014.

[8] J. Coburn, A. M. Caulfield, A. Akel, L. M. Grupp, R. K. Gupta, R. Jhala, and S. Swanson. NV-heaps: Making persistent objects fast and safe with next-generation, non-volatile memories. In *ASPLOS*, 2011.

[9] J. Condit, E. B. Nightingale, C. Frost, E. Ipek, D. Burger, B. Lee, , and D. Coetzee. Better I/O through byte-addressable, persistent memory. In *SOSP*, 2009.

[10] G. Copeland, T. Keller, R. Krishnamurthy, and M. Smith. The case for safe RAM. In *VLDB*, 1989.

[11] C. Diaconu, C. Freedman, E. Ismert, P.-A. Larson, P. Mittal, R. Stonecipher, N. Verma, and M. Zwilling. Hekaton: SQL server's memory-optimized OLTP engine. In *SIGMOD*, 2013.

[12] J. Do and J. M. Patel. Join processing for flash SSDs: remembering past lessons. In *DaMoN*, 2009.

[13] S. R. Dulloor, S. Kumar, A. Keshavamurthy, P. Lantz, D. Reddy, R. Sankaran, and J. Jackson. System software for persistent memory. In *EuroSys*, 2014.

[14] R. Fang, H.-I. Hsiao, C. Mohan, and Y. Wang. High performance database logging using storage class memory. In *ICDE*, 2011.

[15] E. Giles, K. Doshi, and P. Varman. Bridging the programming gap between persistent and volatile memory using WrAP. In *CF*, 2013.

[16] E. Giles, K. Doshi, and P. Varman. Software support for atomicity and persistence in non-volatile memory. In *MEAOW*, October 2013.

[17] J. Guerra, L. Marmol, D. Campello, C. Crespo, R. Rangaswami, and J. Wei. Software persistent memory. In *ATC*, 2012.

[18] S. Harizopoulos, D. J. Abadi, S. Madden, and M. Stonebraker. OLTP through the looking glass, and what we found there. In *SIGMOD*, 2008.

[19] R. Kallman, H. Kimura, J. Natkins, A. Pavlo, A. Rasin, S. Zdonik, E. P. C. Jones, S. Madden, M. Stonebraker, Y. Zhang, J. Hugg, and D. J. Abadi. H-Store: a high-performance, distributed main memory transaction processing system. *PVLDB*, 1(2), 2008.

[20] H. Kim and S. Ahn. BPLRU: a buffer management scheme for improving random writes in flash storage. In *FAST*, 2008.

[21] I. Koltsidas and S. D. Viglas. Flashing up the storage layer. *Proc. VLDB Endow.*, 1(1), 2008.

[22] I. Koltsidas and S. D. Viglas. Data management over flash memory. In *SIGMOD*, 2011.

[23] X. Li *et al.* A new dynamic hash index for flash-based storage. In *WAIM*, 2008.

[24] Y. Li *et al.* Tree indexing on flash disks. In *ICDE*, 2009.

[25] D. E. Lowell and P. M. Chen. Free transactions with Rio vista. In *SOSP*, 1997.

[26] S. Manegold, P. A. Boncz, and M. L. Kersten. Generic Database Cost Models for Hierarchical Memory Systems. In *VLDB*, 2002.

[27] D. Myers. On the use of NAND flash memory in high-performance relational databases. MSc Thesis, MIT, 2007.

[28] W. T. Ng and P. M. Chen. Integrating reliable memory in databases. In *VLDB*, 1997.

[29] Y. Ou *et al.* CFDC: a flash-aware replacement policy for database buffer management. In *DAMON*, 2009.

[30] I. Oukid, D. Booss, W. Lehner, P. Bumbulis, and T. Willhalm. Sofort: A hybrid scm-dram storage engine for fast data recovery. In *DaMoN*, 2014.

[31] X. Ouyang, D. Nellans, R. Wipfel, D. Flynn, and D. K. Panda. Beyond block I/O: Rethinking traditional storage primitives. In *HPCA*, 2011.

[32] S. Pelley, T. F. Wenisch, B. T. Gold, and B. Bridge. Storage management in the NVRAM era. *PVLDB*, 7(2), 2014.

[33] M. K. Qureshi, S. Gurumurthi, and B. Rajendran. *Phase Change Memory: from devices to systems.* Morgan & Claypool, 2012.

[34] M. Satyanarayanan, H. H. Mashburn, P. Kumar, D. C. Steere, and J. J. Kistler. Lightweight recoverable virtual memory. In *SOSP*, 1993.

[35] R. Sears and E. Brewer. Stasis: Flexible transactional storage. In *OSDI*, 2006.

[36] D. Tsirogiannis, S. Harizopoulos, M. A. Shah, J. L. Wiener, and G. Graefe. Query processing techniques for solid state drives. In *SIGMOD*, 2009.

[37] M. Vamsikrishna, Z. Su, and K.-L. Tan. A write efficient pcm-aware sort. In *DEXA*, 2012.

[38] S. D. Viglas. Adapting the B+-tree for asymmetric I/O. In *ADBIS*, 2012.

[39] S. D. Viglas. Write-limited sorts and joins for persistent memory. *PVLDB*, 7(5), 2014.

[40] H. Volos, A. J. Tack, and M. M. Swift. Mnemosyne: Lightweight persistent memory. In *ASPLOS*, 2011.

[41] T. Wang and R. Johnson. Scalable logging through emerging non-volatile memory. *PVLDB*, 7(10), 2014.

[42] C.-H. Wu, L.-P. Chang, and T.-W. Kuo. An efficient R-tree implementation over flash-memory storage systems. In *GIS*, 2003.

[43] C.-H. Wu, T.-W. Kuo, and L. P. Chang. An Efficient B-tree Layer Implementation for Flash-Memory Storage Systems. *Trans. on Embedded Computing Sys.*, 6(3), 2007.

[44] M. Wu and W. Zwaenepoel. eNVy: A non-volatile, main memory storage system. In *ASPLOS*, 1994.

[45] S. yeong Park, D. Jung, J. uk Kang, J. soo Kim, J. Lee, S. yeong Park, D. Jung, J. uk Kang, J. soo Kim, and J. Lee. CFLRU: a replacement algorithm for flash memory. In *CASES*, 2006.

[46] D. Zeinalipour-Yazti, S. Lin, V. Kalogeraki, Dimitrios, and W. A. Najjar. Microhash: an efficient index structure for flash-based sensor devices. In *FAST*, 2005.

[47] J. Zhao, S. Li, D. H. Yoon, Y. Xie, and N. P. Jouppi. Kiln: Closing the performance gap between systems with and without persistence support. In *MICRO*, 2013.

TEGRA: Table Extraction by Global Record Alignment

Xu Chu[1*], Yeye He[2], Kaushik Chakrabarti[2], Kris Ganjam[2]

[1]University of Waterloo, Waterloo, Canada
[2]Microsoft Research, Redmond, USA

[1]x4chu@uwaterloo.ca
[2]{yeyehe, kaushik, krisgan}@microsoft.com

ABSTRACT

It is well known today that pages on the Web contain a large number of content-rich relational tables. Such tables have been systematically extracted in a number of efforts to empower important applications such as table search and schema discovery. However, a significant fraction of relational tables are *not* embedded in the standard HTML table tags, and are thus difficult to extract. In particular, a large number of relational tables are known to be in a "list" form, which contains a list of clearly separated rows that are not separated into columns.

In this work, we address the important problem of automatically extracting multi-column relational tables from such lists. Our key intuition lies in the simple observation that in correctly-extracted tables, values in the same column are *coherent*, both at a syntactic and at a semantic level. Using a background corpus of over 100 million tables crawled from the Web, we quantify semantic coherence based on a statistical measure of value co-occurrence in the same column from the corpus. We then model table extraction as a principled optimization problem – we allocate tokens in each row sequentially to a fixed number of columns, such that the sum of coherence across all pairs of values in the same column is maximized. Borrowing ideas from $A^\star$ search and metric distance, we develop an efficient 2-approximation algorithm. We conduct large-scale table extraction experiments using both real Web data and proprietary enterprise spreadsheet data. Our approach considerably outperforms the state-of-the-art approaches in terms of quality, achieving over 90% F-measure across many cases.

1. INTRODUCTION

Relational tables on the Web have long been established as a rich source of structured data. Early studies suggest that the number of meaningful relational tables on the Web is well over a hundred million [10, 26], and is thus considered to be by far the largest relational data repository [10]. The sheer number of tables has spawned many interesting applications including table search [1, 2], table integration [9, 27], and knowledge discovery [26] among many others.

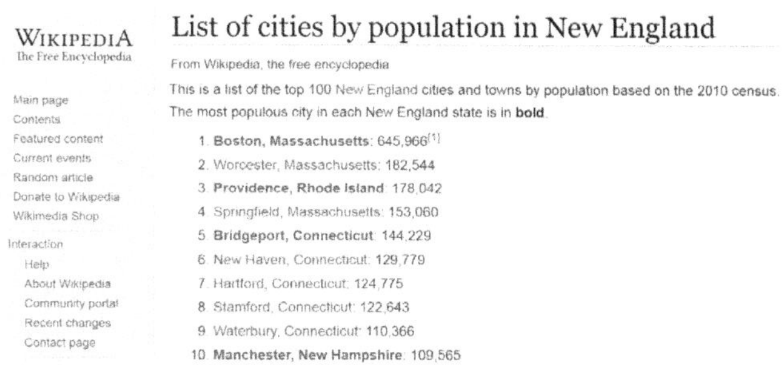

Figure 1: An example relational table in HTML list

All these useful applications hinge on the successful extraction of high-quality relational tables. While many relational tables on the Web are embedded in *HTML table* tags, and are thus easy to extract (since both row boundaries and column boundaries are clearly marked), a significant fraction of tables do *not* use HTML table tags. In particular, a large number of relational tables are in *HTML list* tags, which provide a set of clearly separated rows, but do not segment the rows into columns. Figure 1 shows one such example list containing a relational table with city name, state name, and population of cities in New England.

It is estimated in [16] that the number of useful relational tables that can be extracted from HTML lists is at least tens of millions (a number consistent with our analysis to be discussed later). Tables in lists thus represent a significant source of relational tables. Extracting such tables brings obvious benefits for downstream applications. For example, a table search system [1, 2] powered by an enhanced table corpus extracted from lists is more likely to return relevant tables (e.g., the table in Figure 1 can be returned for a query "top New England city population").

The pioneering work from Google, named `ListExtract` [16], is the only work that specifically targets the problem of extracting tables from lists on the Web. The authors rightfully point out the challenges therein – column delimiters in lists are implicit, which can be any special characters. Delimiters can also vary from one list to another, or even within the same list. In Figure 1, for example, a comma (",") and a semi-colon (":") are used as column delimiters, yet the second comma (",") is not a delimiter. In addition, white-spaces (" ") is often used as delimiters, as in the additional example in Figure 2 (which should parse into a three-column table shown in Figure 3). In Figure 1, however, white-spaces should not be used as delimiters. The bottom line is that any special characters or punctuation can be used as column de-

*Work done at Microsoft Research.

SIGMOD'15, May 31–June 4, 2015, Melbourne, Victoria, Australia.

http://dx.doi.org/10.1145/2723372.2723725.

l_1	Los Angeles California United States
l_2	Toronto Canada
l_3	New York City New York USA

Figure 2: An example input list L

t_1	Los Angeles	California	United States
t_2	Toronto		Canada
t_3	New York City	New York	USA

Figure 3: An extracted output table T

limiters, which greatly complicates the extraction problem. [1]

Previous approaches. The authors in [16] were the first to recognize the value of extracting tables from We lists, and proposed an approach called `ListExtract`. To date, [16] is the only published approach specifically addressing the problem of extracting tables from general Web lists fully automatically (other related methods will be reviewed in Section 6).

At a high level, the `ListExtract` approach works in three steps: (1) It utilizes various signals, such as a language model, to greedily identify token subsequences in each line that are likely to be individual cells (e.g., "New York" and "USA"), so that each line is independently split into multiple cells. (2) It counts the number of segmented cells in each line and use the majority vote to guess the correct number of columns, k, in the output table. Records that are not split into k columns in the previous step are re-split to produce exactly k columns. (3) Adjustments are made for values that appear inconsistent to produce the final output. A more detailed discussion of `ListExtract` can be found in Appendix A.

We observe that `ListExtract` makes *local* splitting decisions in each line *independently* early in the process, regardless of segmentations in other lines. Once such local decisions are made, it becomes difficult to recover from these decisions that are in fact suboptimal globally. For example, in l_3 of Figure 2, the language model may be very confident that "New York" is more likely to be a cell entry than "New York City" because of the popularity of the name. However, once "New York" is greedily split into a cell, it becomes very difficult to segment subsequent tokens starting with "City" (e.g., "City", "City New", or "City New York") to align them well with values from other rows in the same column. Such local greedy decisions negatively affect the quality of the extraction.

Highlights of our approach. In light of these issues, in this work we propose a principled approach called Table Extraction by Global Record Alignment (TEGRA), which models table extraction as a global optimization problem. We observe that in a correctly extracted table, cell values in the same column should be coherent, either semantically (e.g., "Los Angeles" and "Toronto" are coherent because they are in the same domain and co-occur in the same column frequently), or syntactically (e.g., values should have similar token length, etc.). Using a Web table corpus with over 100 million tables, we quantify semantic coherence by statistical value co-occurrence in the same column (e.g., "Los Angeles" and "Toronto" co-occur much more frequently than mere coincidence in the corpus, thus their coherence is strong). Using the notion of coherence, we formulate table extraction as an optimization problem – we sequentially allocate tokens to a fixed number of columns, so that the sum of coherence score across all pairs of values in the same column can be maximized.

[1]The work in [16] provides additional HTML lists that are excellent motivating examples.

While this is a natural formulation that captures the "goodness" of a well-formatted table, the formal problem is intractable in general. We design a mechanism to decompose the objective function into more tractable components while guaranteeing 2-approximation. We further develop an efficient algorithm utilizing ideas from A* search that can prune away unpromising segmentations without affecting quality.

TEGRA has a number of salient features. First, by using coherence as the objective function in our formulation, we perform *global* optimization, where splitting decisions in different lines are optimized *holistically* to ensure the best alignment.

Second, our coherence score takes advantage of a large table corpus with over 100 million tables. By using a data-driven approach to measure the compatibility of two values in the same column ("Los Angeles" and "Toronto"), it easily generalizes to a wide variety of domains, which works well for both public Web data as well as proprietary enterprise data, as will be shown in our experiments. In comparison, previous research on unsupervised record segmentation [3, 14,28] mostly relies on a specific reference table or knowledge base that need to match the target table of interest, and as we will show, cannot handle general tables on the Web.

Third, in order to scale to millions of lists on the Web and extract tables automatically, our approach is designed to be fully unsupervised, for user input can be too expensive at this scale. Note that in our problem, we need to extract content with heterogeneous schemas from *every* lists. This is in contrast to techniques such as wrapper induction [4, 12, 17], that utilize training examples to extract targeted relations with a specific schema.

Finally, although the intended application is offline relation table extraction (the *offline unsupervised variant*), our approach is general and capable of handling an interactive online scenario for ad-hoc table extraction (the *online supervised variant*), where a certain amount of user feedback is given in the form of segmentations for a few example rows to further improve the quality of tables extracted.

Contributions. We make the following contributions.

- We model table extraction as a principled optimization problem that captures the conceptual goodness of a table. We show experimentally that this objective function strongly correlates with the quality of extracted tables.
- We develop an efficient 2-approximation algorithm utilizing ideas from $A^\star$ search and a mechanism to decompose the objective function.
- We demonstrate that our approach can also be adapted to handle user supervision in the same framework.
- We conduct extensive experiments using real datasets from both the public Web and a proprietary enterprise. TEGRA achieves high accuracy and outperforms the state-of-the-art in all scenarios we evaluated.

2. PROBLEM STATEMENT

In this section, we formally define the problem of *table extraction from lists.* We start by defining what table segmentation or table extraction is[2].

2.1 Definition of Segmentation

Let tok be a tokenization function that splits an unsegmented line l into a sequence of tokens $tok(l)$, based on a set of user defined delimiters (e.g., white spaces, commas, etc.). We use $l[w]$ to index the wth token, and use $l[i \dots j], i \leq j$,

[2]We use both table segmentation and extraction interchangeably when the context is clear.

to represent a consecutive subsequence of tokens starting at $l[i]$ and ending at $l[j]$. We define a *segmentation* t of line l as follows.

Definition 1. *An m-column segmentation t of line l is defined as $t = (l[i_1 \dots j_1], \dots, l[i_m \dots j_m])$, where $i_1 = 1, j_m = |l|$, and $i_{k+1} = j_k + 1, \forall 1 \leq k \leq m-1$. Denote by $s_m(l)$ the domain of all possible m-column segmentations of l.*

The notion of segmentation is quite natural – it is a set of m subsequences of tokens that collectively covers all tokens in l. We intentionally make a distinction by denoting an unsegmented line as l and a segmented tuple/record[3] as t.

Example 1. *Consider an unsegmented line l_1 in our running example in Figure 2. Using white spaces as delimiters, l_1 can be split into a sequence of tokens as follows.*

l_1:	Los	Angeles	California	United	States

A possible segmentation of l_1 is $t = (l[1 \dots 2], l[3 \dots 3], l[4 \dots 5])$

t:	Los Angeles	California	United States

Finally, a table segmentation for a list of lines L is simply the union of segmentations of all lines in L.

2.2 The Goodness of Segmentation

There are many ways to segment a line, and exponentially more to segment a list into a table. Among all these options, we need a criteria to measure the goodness of a segmented table in order to guide the algorithm to pick the best segmentation. Intuitively, when a human looks at a table, if values in the same column are not *coherent*, then he would judge the segmentation as "bad". For example, if a person's name "John Smith" and a city name "New York City" are in the same column, the segmentation would be judged as "bad" because **semantically** these values are not in the same conceptual domain. Similarly, if a numerical value "159.3" and a city name "New York City" are aligned in the same column, or if a long string value "New York City New York" and a short string "Toronto" are aligned in the same column, then the alignment is also likely to be bad, because we expect values in the same column of a correctly-segmented table to be **syntactically** similar (e.g., similar number of tokens, similar value types, etc.).

Mimicking this human intuition, we say a segmented table is good if it is overall coherent. For technical reasons, in this work we use the notion of *distance*, which is the reverse of coherence – that is, pairs of cell values with *high* coherence (similarity) have *low* distance (dis-similarity), and vice versa. With this, we can equivalently say that a segmented table is good if its overall distance is low.

2.3 Quantify Goodness: Distance Functions

In order to quantify the overall distance of a table, we first define the distance between two cell values. Given two string values s_1 and s_2, we use $d(s_1, s_2)$ to denote the *distance* (in-coherence) score of s_1 and s_2. As motivated above, $d(s_1, s_2)$ should be a combination of *syntactic distance*, $d_{syn}(s_1, s_2)$, and *semantic distance*, $d_{sem}(s_1, s_2)$. Namely,

$$d(s_1, s_2) = \alpha\ d_{syn}(s_1, s_2) + (1 - \alpha)\ d_{sem}(s_1, s_2) \quad (1)$$

where α controls the relative importance of the two components. By default, we set α to be 0.5.

In this work, we focus on distance $d(s_1, s_2)$ that satisfies the natural properties used in metric distance, namely, non-negativity, symmetry, and triangular inequality.

- Non-negativity: $d(s_1, s_2) \geq 0$
- Symmetry: $d(s_1, s_2) = d(s_2, s_1)$
- Triangle inequality: $d(s_1, s_2) + d(s_1, s_3) \geq d(s_2, s_3)$

[3]Tuple and record are used interchangeably for a segmented row in the paper.

2.3.1 Semantic Distance

As discussed above, semantic distance $d_{sem}(s_1, s_2)$ should capture the likelihood that s_1 and s_2 are in the same semantic domain (e.g., "New York City" and "Toronto"). While specialized Knowledge Bases (KBs) capture some of these semantic information, they are of limited domain coverage and/or entity coverage (let alone name variations, etc.). Since our goal is to extract tables from millions of general lists on the Web regardless of domain, KBs are unsuitable as a universal way to define distance because it cannot possibly cover all entities that can be found on the Web (we will explore this in our experiments).

We propose a data-driven way to define semantic distance that generalizes to all values. Specifically, using a table corpus of over 100 million tables crawled from the Web, we measure the statistical co-occurrence of s_1 and s_2 in the same column. This embodies our intuition that values in the same semantic domain ("New York City" and "Toronto") should co-occur frequently in the same column.

In particular, let $C(s_1)$ and $C(s_2)$ be the set of Web table columns that s_1 and s_2 occur in, respectively. If $C(s_1) \cap C(s_2)$ is large relative to $C(s_1)$ and $C(s_2)$, then s_1 and s_2 are likely to be semantically coherent (low semantic distance).

In this work, we use a probabilistic measure called *point-wise mutual information* [11], PMI(s_1, s_2), defined as follows. Let N be the total number of columns. Then $p(s_1) = \frac{|C(s_1)|}{N}$, $p(s_2) = \frac{|C(s_2)|}{N}$, are the probabilities of seeing s_1, s_2 respectively, and $p(s_1, s_2) = \frac{|C(s_1) \cap C(s_2)|}{N}$ is the probability of seeing (s_1, s_2) together in the same column. PMI is defined as:

$$\text{PMI}(s_1, s_2) = \log \frac{p(s_1, s_2)}{p(s_1)p(s_2)}$$

Example 2. *Let s_1 = Canada, and s_2 = Republic of Korea. Suppose $N = 100M$ (there are a total of 100M columns), $|C(s_1)| = 1000$, $|C(s_2)| = 500$, and $|C(s_1) \cap C(s_2)| = 300$ (individually, the two strings occur 1000 and 500 times respectively; together they co-occur 300 times). It can be calculated that PMI$(s_1, s_2) = 4.77 > 0$, strongly indicating that they are semantically related (even though syntactically s_1 and s_2 are very different, by the number of tokens, etc.)*

Note that PMI actually measures coherence instead of distance. We apply the following normalization and transformation to ensure that the resulting semantic distance satisfies triangle inequality[4].

$$d_{sem}(s_1, s_2) = 0.75 - 0.25\text{NPMI}(s_1, s_2)$$

where NPMI $\in [-1, 1]$ is the normalized PMI, defined as:

$$\text{NPMI}(s_1, s_2) = \frac{\text{PMI}(s_1, s_2)}{-\log p(s_1, s_2)}$$

Discussions. In principle other metric distances such as Jaccard distance, Angular distance (the metric version of Cosine similarity) can also be used to define $d_{sem}(s_1, s_2)$. We choose NPMI because it is a symmetric measure that is robust to asymmetric sets. Appendix H gives more discussion on this, as well as our experience of using Jaccard (which also produces decent results).

2.3.2 Syntactic Distance

The main motivation of using syntactic distance is that not all strings are semantically meaningful. For example, if

[4]This is by virtue of the fact that $d_{sem} \in [0.5, 1]$ after transformation of NPMI. When other metric distances are used in place of NPMI the triangle inequality is naturally respected.

s_1 = SKU-926434 and s_2 = SKU-09393. There is unlikely sufficient statistical co-occurrence to justify that they are semantically coherent.

At a high level, we define syntactic distance $d_{syn}(s_1, s_2)$ as:

$$d_{syn}(s_1, s_2) = \frac{d_{len}(s_1, s_2) + d_{char}(s_1, s_2) + d_{type}(s_1, s_2)}{3}$$

where d_{len} represents the difference in the number of tokens, d_{char} the difference at the character level, and d_{type} the difference based on certain predefined types (e.g., numeric values, email address, date and time, etc) as determined by regular expressions. The exact definition of these functions can be found in Appendix I.

Note that the use of syntactic features for segmentations has been extensively studied [3,8,16]. Our syntactic distance function uses well-known ideas from existing literature, and we do not claim to make new contributions in this respect.

2.4 An Optimization-based Formulation

Using distance functions, we can formally quantify the goodness of an extracted table as follows.

The objective function. Given a list $L = \{l_1, l_2, \ldots, l_n\}$ containing n unsegmented lines, the table we extract $T = \{t_1, t_2, \ldots, t_n\}$ should be such that each record t_i is a segmentation of l_i, and furthermore every record has the same number of columns m.

Let $t[k]$ be the k-th column of record t. Given a segmented table T with m columns, we can define our objective function, termed *sum of pairs (SP) distance*, as the sum of distance of every pair of cell values, $t_i[k]$ and $t_j[k]$, in the same column. Namely,

$$SP_m(T) = \sum_{1 \leq k \leq m} \sum_{1 \leq i < j \leq n} d(t_i[k], t_j[k]) \quad (2)$$

Since the summations are commutative, we can rewrite as

$$SP_m(T) = \sum_{1 \leq i < j \leq n} \sum_{1 \leq k \leq m} d(t_i[k], t_j[k]) \quad (3)$$

Let $d(t_i, t_j)$ be the distance between two records, defined as

$$d(t_i, t_j) = \sum_{1 \leq k \leq m} d(t_i[k], t_j[k]) \quad (4)$$

We can simplify Equation (3) to have

$$SP_m(T) = \sum_{1 \leq i < j \leq n} d(t_i, t_j) \quad (5)$$

Example 3. *We revisit our running example in Figure 3. By Equation (4), the distance $d(t_1, t_2)$ between t_1 and t_2 is calculated as:*

$$d(t_1, t_2) = d(\textit{Los Angeles, Toronto}) + d(\textit{California, null}) + d(\textit{United States, Canada})$$

$SP_3(T)$ can then be written as the sum of all pairs distance, where $d(t_1, t_3)$ and $d(t_2, t_3)$ are defined similarly.

$$SP_3(T) = d(t_1, t_2) + d(t_1, t_3) + d(t_2, t_3)$$

The use of all pair distance as the objective is natural – it captures the idea that a table is coherent if all pairs of values in the same column are coherent. We note that sum of pairs is also used in clustering [5], bioinformatics [22], and facility location problems [19], among other things.

Problem statement. Suppose we know the number of columns that lists need to be segmented into, we can define the problem ***Table Segmentation Given Column Number*** as follows.

Definition 2. ***Table segmentation given column number.*** *Given a list $L = \{l_1, l_2, \ldots, l_n\}$ and the desired number of columns m. The problem here is to find a table segmentation $T = \{t_1, t_2, \ldots, t_n\}$ that minimizes the sum of pair distance $SP_m(T)$ over all possible table segmentations.*

In the unsupervised setting where the number of columns m is not given, we can test all possible m's up to some upper limit (e.g., the maximum number of tokens in all lines), and pick the m that produces the best SP score *per column.*

Definition 3. ***Unsupervised table segmentation.*** *Given a list $L = \{l_1, l_2, \ldots, l_n\}$, the problem of unsupervised segmentation is to find a segmentation $T = \{t_1, t_2, \ldots, t_n\}$ that minimizes the per column objective score $\frac{SP_m(T)}{m}$ over all possible table segmentations and m.*

Note that we use the *per column* SP score as the objective function in the unsupervised setting, because we need to normalize the aggregate SP score for a fair comparison between segmentations with different number of columns m.

Example 4. *When the number of columns m is 2, the table T' in Figure 4 achieves the best $SP_2(T')$ for list L in Figure 2. Note that values in the first column of T' have high semantic distance values, because their co-occurrence in Web tables corpus are almost non-existent. This is an artifact of the $m = 2$ column constraint. If we specify $m = 3$, we will have the table T in Figure 3, where semantic distances are very low. In this case, $\frac{SP_3(T')}{3}$ will be lower than $\frac{SP_2(T)}{2}$, indicating that 3-column is the right segmentation of L.*

t_1	Los Angeles California	United States
t_2	Toronto	Canada
t_3	New York City New York	USA

Figure 4: Table T' with minimal $SP_2(T')$

Notice that for ***unsupervised table segmentation***, since we can try all numbers of columns m up to $|l_{max}|$, where $|l_{max}|$ can be the maximum number of tokens in any line, or some reasonable upper limit of columns we expect to see in a table (e.g., 20), for the rest of the paper we will only discuss ***table segmentation given column number*** for unsupervised table segmentation and treat m as a given input.

3. THE TEGRA ALGORITHM

While the SP objective function naturally captures the desirable property of a good table, we show that the general problem of unsupervised table segmentation is NP-hard using a reduction from multiple sequence alignment.

Theorem 1. *The decision version of unsupervised table segmentation is NP-hard.*

A proof of Theorem 1 can be found in Appendix B.

In light of the hardness, we propose the TEGRA algorithm that solves the segmentation problem with an approximation guarantee. In particular, in Section 3.1, we design a mechanism to decompose the objective function into more tractable components with quality guarantees. In Section 3.2, we further optimize the segmentation algorithm using ideas reminiscent of A* search. These together produce an efficient table segmentation algorithm.

3.1 A Conceptual Approximation Algorithm

In the following, we define the notion of *anchor* and *anchor distance* to decompose the SP distance.

Definition 4. *Let record $t_i \in T$ be an anchor record, the anchor distance of t_i, denoted as $AD_m(t_i, T)$, is the sum of distances between t_i, and all other records in T.*

$$AD_m(t_i, T) = \sum_{t_j \in T, j \neq i} d(t_i, t_j) \quad (6)$$

Using the definition of anchor distance and symmetry of distance d, SP distance is decomposed as the half of the sum of the anchor distance for all anchors. Namely,

$$\begin{aligned} SP_m(T) &= \sum_{1 \le i < j \le n} d(t_i, t_j) \\ &= \frac{1}{2} \sum_{1 \le i \le n} AD_m(t_i, T) \end{aligned} \quad (7)$$

We will omit subscript m in $SP_m(T), AD_m(t_i, T)$ when the context is clear.

Example 5. *Consider the example table T in Figure 3. For each anchor record we have*

$$AD_3(t_1, T) = d(t_1, t_2) + d(t_1, t_3)$$
$$AD_3(t_2, T) = d(t_2, t_1) + d(t_2, t_3)$$
$$AD_3(t_3, T) = d(t_3, t_1) + d(t_3, t_2)$$

Given that $SP_3(T) = d(t_1, t_2) + d(t_1, t_3) + d(t_2, t_3)$,
we have $SP_3(T) = \frac{1}{2}(AD_3(t_1, T) + AD_3(t_2, T) + AD_3(t_3, T))$.

Intuitively, transforming SP to AD is to make the problem more tractable. SP considers n^2 pairs of interaction between record pairs in T, where a change of segmentation in one record has complex implications. In comparison, when computing AD, once the segmentation of anchor t_i is fixed, the best (minimal) $AD(t_i, T)$ over all possible T can be found by segmenting all other lines *independently* against t_i.

Formally, let $s(l_i)$ [5] be a segmentation function that maps a line l_i to all possible segmentations. Similarly $s(L)$ maps a list L to all possible tables. Given a segmented t_i, the best segmentation for each line l_j against t_i, denoted by t_j^{i*}, is the one that achieves the minimal distance with t_i.

$$t_j^{i*} = \arg\min_{t_j \in s(l_j)} d(t_i, t_j) \quad (8)$$

Notice that t_i and the segmentations of all other lines t_j^{i*} together induce a table, denoted as $R(t_i)$.

$$R(t_i) = \{t_j^{i*} | 1 \le j \le n, j \ne i\} \cup t_i \quad (9)$$

where $R(t_i)$ is the *table induction function* for anchor t_i.

By the definition of the anchor distance AD, we know $R(t_i)$ minimizes $AD(t_i, R(t_i))$ over all possible tables.

$$R(t_i) = \arg\min_{T \in s(L)} AD(t_i, T) \quad (10)$$

Equation (10) follows from the fact that in the definition of $AD(t_i, T)$ (Equation (6)), only distance scores between anchor t_i and other records count, distance between other records, $d(t_j, t_k), j \ne i \wedge k \ne i$, do not contribute to AD. Thus, each line can be independently optimized in Equation (8), yet the union of all lines in Equation (9) still minimizes AD anchored on t_i (Equation (10)).

Notice that finding table segmentations $R(t_i)$ through AD minimization is more tractable, because only one pair (t_i, l_j) needs to be considered at a time, as opposed to considering n lines simultaneously in SP optimization.

Interestingly, we show that the table segmentation found by minimizing $AD(t_i, R(t_i))$ over all possible anchor t_i is not bad compared to the global optimal $SP(T)$.

Define t_i^* to be the segmentation of l_i that minimizes $AD(t_i^*, R(t_i^*))$ over all possible $t_i \in s(l_i)$:

$$t_i^* = \arg\min_{t_i \in s(l_i)} AD(t_i, R(t_i)) \quad (11)$$

[5]The segmentation function $s()$ is defined with subscript m in Definition 1 but also used without subscript when context is clear.

Let c be the index that minimizes $AD(t_i^*, R(t_i^*))$ over all choices of i:

$$(t_c^*, R(t_c^*)) = \arg\min_{1 \le i \le n} AD(t_i^*, R(t_i^*)) \quad (12)$$

Let $T^* = \arg\min_{T \in s(L)} SP(T)$ be the global optimal segmentation with minimum $SP(T)$. In the following theorem, we can show that the SP distance, $SP(R(t_c^*))$, of the segmentation $R(t_c^*)$ induced by picking the best t_c^*, is not far away from the global optimal $SP(T^*)$.

Theorem 2. *Let $R(t_c^*)$ be the table segmentation with minimum AD distance over all possible choices of anchors as defined in Equation (12). Let T^* be the global optimal segmentation with the minimum $SP(T^*)$. If d satisfies triangle inequality, then $SP(R(t_c^*)) \le 2SP(T^*)$*

The idea here to bound $SP(R(t_c^*))$ using $SP(T^*)$ is to utilize triangle inequality, the fact that $R(t_c^*)$ minimizes AD over all possible anchor segmentation, and the relationship between AD and SP outlined in Equation (7). A proof of this theorem can be found in Appendix C. Using this result, we develop `TEGRA-naive` in Algorithm 1 that has 2-approximation.

Algorithm 1: `TEGRA-naive`

Input: List $L = \{l_1, l_2, \ldots, l_n\}$, number of columns m
Output: Segmented table $T = \{t_1, t_2, \ldots, t_n\}$

1 **for** *each* $l_i \in L$ **do**
2   **for** *each* $t_i \in s(l_i)$ **do**
3         $AD(t_i, R(t_i)) = 0$
4   **for** *each* $l_j \in L, j \ne i$ **do**
5             $t_j^{i*} = \arg\min_{t_j \in s(l_j)} d(t_i, t_j)$
6             $AD(t_i, R(t_i)) += d(t_i, t_j^{i*})$
7     $t_i^* = \arg\min_{t_i \in s(l_i)} AD(t_i, R(t_i))$
8 $c = \arg\min_{1 \le i \le n} AD(t_i^*, R(t_i^*))$
9 **Return** $R(t_c^*)$

`TEGRA-naive` works as follows. It first picks each line $l_i \in L$ as an anchor. Then for each anchor segmentation $t_i \in s(l_i)$, it segments every other line l_j to t_j^{i*} so that it minimizes distance $d(t_i, t_j^{i*})$ over all possible $s(l_j)$ (Line 5). The anchor segmentation t_i^* that has the minimum AD distance is picked (Line 7). This induces a table segmentation $R(t_i^*)$ using a table induction function $R()$ that unions all line segmentations in Equation (8), (9). We return as result the table $R(t_c^*)$ induced by anchor t_c^* that has minimum AD distance over all anchor lines.

Example 6. *Consider list L in Figure 2:*
For line l_1, `TEGRA-naive` tries all possible segmentations t_1. For every t_1 such as the one in Figure 3, it will find the best t_2^{1*} out of all possible t_2 for l_2 such that $d(t_1, t_2^{1*})$ is minimal and the best t_3^{1*} out of all possible t_3's such that $d(t_1, t_3^{1*})$ is minimal. It will remember the t_1^* that results in the minimal $AD(t_1^*, T_1^*) = d(t_1^*, t_2^{1*}) + d(t_1^*, t_2^{1*})$, where $T_1^* = \{t_1^*, t_2^{1*}, t_3^{1*}\}$.
Similarly, T_2^* is derived for l_2, and T_3^* for l_3.
`TEGRA-naive` returns one of T_1^*, T_2^*, T_3^* whose $AD(t_i^*, T_i^*)$ is minimal among all $1 \le i \le 3$.

While the naive version of the algorithm is logically clear, each of the two steps at Line 2 and Line 5 requires enumerating all possible segmentations $t \in s(l)$ for a line l, which is prohibitively expensive with a large number of columns. In the next section, we will explain how these two key components can be optimized. We also note that even in this naive algorithm, when assuming the number of desired columns is no more than a fixed constant (e.g., it is shown that over 95% Web tables have less than 10 columns [10]), the complexity of `TEGRA-naive` is already a polynomial of the input.

3.2 Optimization Strategies

As discussed above, there are two places in `TEGRA-naive` that require exhaustive enumeration of possible segmentations of a line l. In order to optimize this, we need to address two problems efficiently: (1) **Pruning Anchor Segmentation (PAS)**: How to prune away unpromising segmentations so that the t_i^* that minimizes $AD(t_i^*, R(t_i^*))$ can be found efficiently without looking at all possible segmentations (Line 2 and Line 7 of Algorithm 1). (2) **Segment a Line Given a Record (SLGR)**: Given a segmented t_i, how to segment another line l_j such that $d(t_i, t_j)$ is minimized (Line 5 of Algorithm 1). For technical reasons, we will discuss SLGR first and then PAS in the following.

3.2.1 *Segment a Line Given a Record (SLGR)*

We are given an unsegmented line l_j, and a segmented record t_i. The goal is to find $t_j^{i*} \in s(l_j)$ that minimizes $d(t_i, t_j^{i*})$. Recall that the distance of two records $d(t_i, t_j)$ is defined as the sum of distance of all m pairs of cells in the same column, $\sum_{1 \leq k \leq m} d(t_i[k], t_j[k])$.

We define a *partial alignment cost function* $M_{l_j,t_i}[p, w]$, that calculates the cost of aligning the first p columns of t_i, using the first w tokens of l_j.

Definition 5. *The partial alignment cost function, denoted as $M_{l_j,t_i}[p, w]$, with $0 \leq p \leq m$ and $0 \leq w \leq |l_j|$, is defined as follows.*

$$M_{l_j,t_i}[p, w] = \min_{t' \in s_p(l_j[1 \ldots w])} \sum_{1 \leq k \leq p} d(t'[k], t_i[k]) \tag{13}$$

Recall that $l_j[1 \ldots w]$ represents the consecutive subsequence of l_j that ends at the w-th token, and $s_p(l_j[1 \ldots w])$ is the segmentation function that enumerates all possible p-column segmentations of $l_j[1 \ldots w]$.

When the context is clear we omit the subscript l_j, t_i in $M_{l_j,t_i}[p, w]$. Notice that by definition, the final segmentation corresponding to $M[m, |l_j|]$ is exactly the desired segmentation t_j^{i*}, which minimizes $d(t_i, t_j^{i*})$.

There is an *optimal sub-structure* [13] in $M[p, w]$, namely

$$M[p, w] = \min \begin{cases} M[p-1, x] + d(l_j[x+1 \ldots w], t_i[p]) \\ \qquad\qquad\qquad\qquad \forall 0 \leq x < w \\ M[p-1, w] + d(\text{null}, t_i[p]) \end{cases} \tag{14}$$

$M[p, w]$ is calculated based on where the first $p-1$ columns end. If the first $p-1$ columns end at a token $x < w$, then the pth column is $l_j[x+1 \ldots w]$. Thus $M[p, w]$ equals $M[p-1, x]$ plus the distance of aligning $l_j[x+1 \ldots w]$ with $t_i[p]$. If the first $p-1$ columns end at token w, then the pth column is null. Thus $M[p, w]$ equals $M[p-1, w]$ plus aligning null with $t_i[p]$. $M[p, w]$ takes the minimum of all those choices. This is clearly amenable to dynamic programming. The actual algorithm can be found in Appendix D.

Example 7. *Revisiting our running example, suppose t_1 in Figure 3 has been segmented. Given l_2 in Figure 2, in SLGR, we need to find the min-cost segmentation t_2^{1*} of l_2 so that $d(t_1, t_2^{1*})$ is minimized.*

Figure 5 shows a sample matrix $M[p, w]$. The final segmentation t_2^{1*} is also t_2 in Figure 3.

In the $M[p, w]$ matrix in Figure 5, $M[0, 1], M[0, 2]$ is initialized to be ∞ because the 0th column (a hypothetic column) cannot consume any tokens. Suppose $d(null, *) = 0.9$. We have $M[1, 0], M[2, 0], M[3, 0]$ populated as $0.9, 1.8, 2.7$ respectively because of this.

Using Equation (14), it can be calculated that $M[1, 1] = d(l_2[1], t_1[1]) = d(Toronto, Los\ Angeles) = 0.3$. Similarly,

$$M[2, 1] = \min \begin{cases} M[1, 0] + d(Toronto, t_1[2]) = 0.9 + 0.5 = 1.4 \\ M[1, 1] + d(null, t_1[2]) = 0.3 + 0.9 = 1.2 \end{cases}$$

Thus $M[2, 1]$ has an arrow from $M[1, 1]$. The final result t_2^{1*} is constructed by back tracing the computation from $M[3, 2]$ via arrows. For instance, $t_2^{1*}[3]$ is "Canada" because $M[3, 2]$ comes from $M[2, 1]$, meaning the second token "Canada" is used in the third column.

p \ w	0	1 (Toronto)	2 (Canada)
0	0	∞	∞
1	0.9	0.3	0.8
2	1.8	1.2	1.1
3	2.7	2.1	1.5

Figure 5: Matrix $M[p, w]$ for aligning l_2 with t_1.

3.2.2 *Pruning Anchor Segmentations (PAS)*

In this section, we develop techniques to prune away unpromising anchor segmentations in $s(l_i)$ while still finding $t_i^* = \arg\min_{t_i \in s(l_i)} AD(t_i, R(t_i))$ correctly (Line 2 to Line 7 in Algorithm 1).

Example 8. *The following segmentation t_1', for instance, is a bad choice for segmenting l_1 in Figure 2.*

t_1'	*Los*	*Angeles California United*	*States*

This is because there is no subsequence of tokens in any other line of Figure 2, that can possibly have a low distance score with $t_1'[1]$ ("Los"). The same is true for the second column $t_1'[2]$ and third column $t_1'[3]$.

Conceptually, we need a way to systematically avoid such segmentations. In the following, we will first show that the space of possible segmentations $s(l_i)$ can be naturally encoded in a graph. We will then show that finding the best segmentation translates to finding a path on the graph with minimum cost, which motivates us to use ideas from A* for efficient pruning of segmentations.

Anchor Segmentation Graph. Efficient pruning of segmentations requires us to first represent the space of segmentations $s(l_i)$. We define a search graph G_i for l_i that can compactly encode all segmentations as follows. Nodes in the graph are labeled as $l_i[p, w]$ (abbreviated to $[p, w]$ when context is clear), for all $1 \leq p \leq m-1$, and $0 \leq w \leq |l_i|$. There is a special start node $[0, 0]$ and a target node $[m, |l_i|]$. There is an edge going from $[p_j, w_j]$ to $[p_k, w_k]$, if $p_k = p_j + 1$ and $w_j \leq w_k$.

Notice that in this graph, a path from the start node to the end node represents a segmentation of l_i. In fact the union of all paths in the graph G_i captures all possible segmentations $s(l_i)$. This gives us a natural and compact representation of the search space.

More formally, a *complete path* from the start node to target node specifies a complete segmentation t_i for a line l_i. A *partial prefix path* is a path from the start node to $[p, w]$, specifying only the partial segmentations of the first p columns using the first w tokens. Similarly, a *partial suffix*

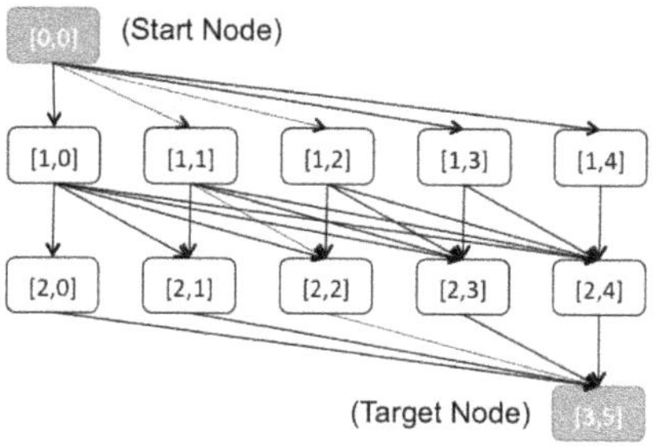

Figure 6: Search space G_1 for segmenting l_1

path is a path from $[p, w]$ to the target node, specifying only the partial segmentations of the last $m - p$ columns using remaining tokens starting at position $w + 1$.

Example 9. *Figure 6 shows the search graph for segmenting l_1 into three columns. The start node is $[0, 0]$. The is target node $[3, 5]$, because l_1 has five tokens and we need to segment into three columns.*

The complete path $Z : [0, 0] \to [1, 2] \to [2, 3] \to [3, 5]$ fully specifies one possible segmentation: the first column is "Los Angeles" (using 2 token for 1 column), the second column "California" (3 token for 2 columns), and the third column "United States" (5 tokens for 3 columns).

The partial prefix path $X : [0, 0] \to [1, 2]$ corresponds to a partial segmentation, where the first column is "Los Angeles", and the last two columns are yet to be segmented using the remaining three tokens "California United States".

Similarly the partial suffix path $Y : [2, 3] \to [3, 5]$ corresponds to a partial segmentation with only the third column specified as "United States".

Having created G_i, we need to assign cost/lengths to graph paths, to represent the current distance cost of the (partial) segmentation.

Definition 6. *Path length in G_i is defined as follows.*

- ***Length of a complete path** Z. Let t_i^Z be the segmentation specified by path Z. The length of the path $L(Z)$ is:*

$$L(Z) = \sum_{\substack{1 \le j \le n \\ j \neq i}} M_{l_j, t_i^Z}[m, |l_j|]$$

Where M_{l_j, t_i} is the alignment cost function defined in Definition 5. Note that here all m columns and $|l_j|$ tokens have been aligned.

- ***Length of a partial prefix path** X **to node** $[p, w]$. Let t_i^X be the partial segmentation specified by X. The length of the path $L(X)$ is defined as:*

$$L(X) = \sum_{\substack{1 \le j \le n \\ j \neq i}} \min_{0 \le k \le |l_j|} M_{l_j, t_i^X}[p, k]$$

- ***Length of a partial suffix path** Y **from node** $[p, w]$. Let t_i^Y be the partial segmentation specified by Y. The length of the path $L(Y)$ is defined as:*

$$L(Y) = \sum_{\substack{1 \le j \le n \\ j \neq i}} \min_{\forall 0 \le k \le |l_j|} N_{l_j, t_i^Y}[p, k]$$

where $N_{l_j, t_i^Y}[p, w]$ is defined similar to M only backwards: it represents the minimal sum of distance between the last $m - p$ columns of t_i, and the last $m - p$ columns starting at the $(w + 1)$-th token of l_j. Matrix N can be calculated similar to M using Algorithm 3.

Note that the length of a complete path Z is the sum of distances between t_i^Z and all other lines, which is exactly our anchor distance $AD(t_i^Z, R(t_i^Z))$.

t_1^X		Los Angeles	California United States
t_2^X		Toronto	Canada
t_3^X		New York	City New York USA

Figure 7: Calculating the length of partial prefix path X. The gray cells are unsegmented.

When calculating the length of a partial prefix path X, since the remaining $m - p$ columns of t_i are not fully segmented yet, we do not know the best way to segment the first p columns in l_j to align with t_i. Therefore, we test all possible ending tokens for the first p columns in l_j to align with $t_i[1 \dots p]$. The length of a partial suffix path $L(Y)$ is defined similar to $L(X)$ except that the backward DP matrix N is used.

Our definition of path lengths is not additive and thus different from traditional graph paths. Namely, for some partial prefix path X ending at $[p, w]$, partial suffix path Y starting from $[p, w]$, and complete path $Z = X \cup Y$, we have $L(X) + L(Y) \neq L(Z)$. However, we show that our paths are *super-additive*, which is a nice property.

Lemma 1. *The paths of search graph G_i defined above are super-additive. That is, for any partial prefix path X ending at $[p, w]$, partial suffix path Y starting from $[p, w]$, and complete path $Z = X \cup Y$, we have $L(X) + L(Y) \le L(Z)$.*

Intuitively, $L(X) + L(Y) \le L(Z)$ is true because the definition of partial paths allows other lines l_j to use a flexible number of tokens to align with p columns from t_i, thus giving partial paths more freedom in minimizing their lengths, making the sum of lengths of two partial paths smaller than the length of the full path. A proof of Lemma 1 can be found in Appendix F. Super-additivity allows us to estimate (underestimate) $L(Z)$ by estimating $L(X), L(Y)$ separately.

Example 10. *For a partial prefix path $X : [0, 0] \to [1, 2]$ in G_1, the corresponding partial segmentation $t_1^X[1]$ is shown in Figure 7. Figure 7 also shows the partial segmentations of other lines $t_2^X[1], t_3^X[1]$, that have the minimal distance with $t_1^X[1]$ respectively. Notice that although in the final result "New York City" in t_3 should align with "Los Angeles" from t_1, here "New York" is aligned with "Los Angeles" when calculating $L(X)$ because it has a smaller distance with "Los Angeles" than "New York City".*

Pruning anchor segmentations (PAS) using A^* Search. Now that we have defined graph G_i to encode all segmentations of l_i, finding the minimum AD cost segmentation naturally translates to finding the shortest path, where ideas from A* search [23] are directly applicable.

In A* search, there is a concept called heuristic/future function h [23] , which gives an estimate of the cost of the path from an intermediate node to the target node (note that in spite of the name heuristic, it always finds the correct min-cost path). It can be shown that if h never overestimates the true cost of reaching the target, then A* can be used to safely prune away unpromising paths. We refer readers to Appendix E for a more detailed overview of A*.

Given the defined lengths of paths, it is important to design an appropriate h function that closely approximates but always underestimates the future cost. Specifically, the h function takes as input a node $[p, w]$, and returns an underestimate of the min-cost path from $[p, w]$ to the target.

Notice that while the past cost of a partial prefix path X at $[p, w]$ can be calculated following Definition 6, the future cost starting from $[p, w]$ cannot be calculated in the same way, because the future path Y is not known at this point yet. The idea then is to segment the remaining $m - p$ columns in l_i while allowing other lines to align with these $m-p$ columns fully flexibly to produce a safe underestimate.

In order to achieve this, for any candidate column c in l_i that is $c = l_i[a \ldots b]$, define a *free distance* of c as follows.

Definition 7. *The free distance of c and l_j, denoted as $freeD(c, l_j)$, is*

$$freeD(c, l_j) = \min_{1 \le a_j \le b_j \le |l_j|} d(l_i[a \ldots b], l_j[a_j \ldots b_j])$$

The free distance of c, denoted as $freeD(c)$, is simply the summation of $freeD(c, l_j)$ for all $l_j, j \ne i$.

$$freeD(c) = \sum_{\substack{1 \le j \le n \\ j \ne i}} freeD(c, l_j)$$

Intuitively, the free distance of c and l_j is the minimum distance between c and any subsequence in l_j regardless of other alignments (hence the name free).

Example 11. *In Figure 7, suppose we are calculating $freeD$("California") in t_1^X. Candidate column "Canada" in l_2, "New York" in l_3 have the smallest distance with "California" respectively. Notice that although in final table, "null" in l_2 is aligned with "California", in $freeD$ calculation "Canada" is used for "California" because they have a smaller distance.*

Our h function uses free distance to (under-)estimate future costs. In particular, Let $r = l_i[w+1 \ldots |l_i|]$ be remaining tokens at $[p, w]$ for conciseness. Using $freeD$, we can define a heuristic function $h(p, w)$ as follows.

$$h(p, w) = \min_{t' \in s_{m-p}(r)} \sum_{1 \le k \le m-p} freeD(t'[k]) \qquad (15)$$

The heuristic function $h(p, w)$ is the minimal sum of free distances of all $(m-p)$-column segmentation of r. Notice that Equation (15) is similar to Equation (13). Thus they share a similar optimal sub-structure as in Equation (14). A similar DP can thus be used to compute $h(p, w)$.

We empirically observe that the heuristic function designed here is effective in pruning away unlikely paths and achieves significant efficiency improvements as demonstrated in the experiments.

Lemma 2. *$h(p, w)$ is admissible [23], i.e., it underestimates the length of any path from $[p, w]$ to target node. Furthermore, $h(p, w)$ is monotonic [23], i.e., $L(X) + h(p, w) \le L(X') + h(p+1, w')$ where X is a path from starting node to node $[p, w]$, and X' is a path extending X with an additional node $[p+1, w']$.*

The actual algorithm for calculating $h(p, w)$ and a proof of Lemma 2 can be found in Appendix G.

Algorithm 2 describes the $A^\star$ search procedure for finding T_i^* with the minimal $AD(t_i^*, T_i^*)$. It keeps a closed set of nodes, representing a set of visited node whose shortest path from start node has already been found, and a set of open nodes, representing a set of node to be visited ordered according to a node's f function. Each node $[p, w]$ in G_i stores the following information: (1) the current path X from start node to $[p, w]$ that has the minimal length, denoted as $[p, w].X$; (2) the length $L(X)$ of the current path X, i.e., the g function in $A^\star$ search; (3) the underestimated distance between the current node to the destination node, i.e., h function in $A^\star$ search; and (4) the f function in $A^\star$ search, which is equal to $g+h$. At each step of Algorithm 2, the node with the lowest f is removed from the set of open nodes, and the f, g, X of its neighbors are updated accordingly (Lines 8-12). The loop terminates when the target node is removed from open nodes (Line 5).

Algorithm 2: `Minimizing Anchor Distance`

Input: List L, Number of columns m, anchor line l_i
Output: $t_i^*, R(t_i^*)$, such that $AD_m(t_i^*, R(t_i^*))$ is minimized

```
1  Initialize the openset, add start node [0,0] to it
2  Initialize the closedset, initially empty
3  while openset ≠ ∅ do
4      [p,w] ← the node with the lowest f score
5      break if [p,w] is the target node, construct t_i*
6      remove [p,w] from openset, add [p,w] to closedset
7      for neighbor nodes [p+1,w'] of [p,w] do
8          continue if [p+1,w'] is in the closedset
9          X' ← [p,w].X ∪ [p+1,w']
10         if [p+1,w'] ∉ openset or L(X') < g(p+1,w') then
11             update X, g, f of [p+1,w']
12             add [p+1,w'] to openset if it is not in there
13 construct R(t_i*) by aligning every l_j with t_i*
14 Return t_i* and R(t_i*)
```

Theorem 3. *Algorithm 2 terminates with a table T_i that has the minimal $AD(t_i^*, R(t_i^*))$.*

The correctness of Algorithm 2 follows directly from the proof of the correctness of $A^\star$ search [23] and the fact that our h function is admissible and monotonic as shown in Lemma 2.

We note that an improved algorithm `TEGRA` thus replaces Lines 2- 7 in `TEGRA-naive` with Algorithm 2.

4. THE SUPERVISED VARIANT

While we set out to design algorithms that can extract tables fully automatically, we note that our approach applies directly in the scenario where user supervision is provided.

In an online ad-hoc table extraction scenario (such as in spreadsheets), users may be willing to provide example segmentations for a few lines. Suppose in addition to the unsegmented lines $L = \{l_i | i \in [n]\}$, we have a set of user provided segmentation examples, denoted as $E = \{l_i | i \in [k]\}$, for some $k < n$.

In such cases, we can modify the objective function to have $SP'_m(T) = \sum_{1 \le i < j \le n} w_{ij} d(t_i, t_j)$, where w_{ij} reflects the relative importance of examples. This way, $SP'_m(T)$ can then assign more weights to record pairs involving user examples because they are generally more reliable.

Definition 8. ***Supervised table segmentation.*** *Given $L = \{l_i | i \in [n]\}$ and user segmented examples $E = \{l_i | i \in [k]\}$ for some $k < n$. Our goal is to produce $T = \{t_i | i \in [n]\}$ with m columns, such that $SP_m(T)$ is minimized.*

We present one way to assign w_{ij} given k user examples:

$$w_{ij} = \begin{cases} \frac{n}{k} & \text{if } t_i \in E \text{ or } t_j \in E \\ 1.0, & \text{otherwise} \end{cases}$$

These w_{ij} ensures that the user-provided examples are more important, i.e., $w_{ij} \ge 1$ if t_i or t_j is user provided. Furthermore, the importance of user examples $\frac{n}{k}$ are adjusted based on the total number of lines and number of user examples, so that the impact of user examples is neither overwhelming nor underwhelming.

The TEGRA approach applies directly in this supervised problem variant, which is also shown to outperform alternative approaches in our experiments.

5. EXPERIMENTS

We conduct extensive experiments to understand the performance of different algorithms.

Data set	avg # of rows	avg # of cols	avg % of numeric cells
Web	14.2	6.2	43.1%
Wiki	11.8	5.0	42.1%
Enterprise	15.0	4.5	56.8%

Table 1: Some characteristics of three data sets. Numbers are averaged over 10,000 tables.

5.1 Experimental Setup

5.1.1 Algorithms compared

• `ListExtract` [16]. This work addresses the exact same problem as ours. As discussed in Appendix A, `ListExtract` makes local splitting decisions first, and then tries to make adjustment to the local decisions. It is the most relevant work directly comparable to TEGRA.

• `Judie` [14]. `Judie` represents a large class of record segmentation techniques [3,14,28] that rely on the existence of a reference table / knowledge base (KB) in the matching domain of the input list (e.g., a recipe knowledge base [14]). While it has been shown to work well when the matching KB in that narrow domain is provided, it is unclear how this class of approaches perform when segmenting general lists on the Web using general purpose KBs. We compare with a recent work `Judie` that is shown to outperform other techniques, including the unsupervised CRF `U-CRF` [28]. We use the popular Freebase [6] as the general purpose KB.

• `TEGRA`. This is our method discussed in Section 3.

5.1.2 Data preparation

We crawl two table corpora for our experiments.

First, we crawl over 100 million tables from the document index of a commercial search engine, henceforth referred to as `Web-All`. These tables are classified as high-quality relational content (e.g., not HTML tables for formatting, etc.). This corpus covers diverse relational content in almost all possible domains available on the public Web.

We also crawl over 500,000 tables from Excel spreadsheets in the Intra-net of a large IT company. This is referred to as `Enterprise-All`.

5.1.3 Benchmark table sets

In order to evaluate quality of tables extracted, for each unsegmented list we need a ground truth table that is the correct segmentation of the list. Manual labeling cannot scale to a test set large enough to draw any reliable conclusion, due to the high cost of labeling (authors in [16] for instance manually labeled segmentations for 20 lists). In order to perform large scale experiments for a reliable quality comparison, yet without actually labeling data, we automatically construct test datasets similar to [16]. We randomly sample existing tables, and then we concatenate cells in the same row into a line using white-spaces as delimiters. For instance, the table in Figure 3 crawled from the Web is concatenated into a list in Figure 2 and used as input. The original table can then be used as the ground truth to evaluate segmentation quality.

We prepare three datasets of different characteristics as our benchmark sets, namely `Web`, `Wiki` and `Enterprise`, each with 10,000 tables. The `Web` dataset is randomly sampled from `Web-All`, which contains relational tables crawled from the Web. The `Wiki` dataset is also sampled from `Web-All` but restricted to the *wikipedia.org* domain, which are generally of high quality compared to the `Web` dataset. The `Enterprise` benchmark set is sampled from `Enterprise-All` that contains spreadsheets crawled from an enterprise. Table 1 reports some characteristics of these three data sets.

As an additional sanity check to validate the large scale evaluation using automatic methods above, we also manually sample 20 real Web lists spanning across domains such as airports, movies, cartoons, presidents, and sports. We manually segment these lists into tables as ground truth. Note that these lists use many different delimiters such as comma, semicolon, dash, and tab. This dataset is henceforth referred to as `Lists`.

5.1.4 The background table corpus

Given that our semantic coherence requires co-occurrence computation like PMI from a background table corpus to determine semantic distance (Section 2.3.1), we use `Web-All` and `Enterprise-All` for this purpose.

The `Web-All` corpus covers diverse relational content in almost all possible domains available on the public Web. We construct the background corpus `Background-Web` as `Background-Web` = `Web-All` \ (`Web` ∪ `Wiki`).

Note that we intentionally exclude benchmark sets from the background corpus, to ensure that the quality numbers genuinely reflect algorithms' capability of segmenting tables not seen before. This is similar to the classical training set / testing set separation used in Machine Learning.

Given the excellent coverage of `Background-Web`, and the fact that it is of public nature such that anyone with sufficient resources could crawl this corpus, we use this as the default background corpus across our experiments.

In addition, we create a background corpus `Background-Enterprise` = `Enterprise-All` \ `Enterprise`. Since the benchmark set `Enterprise` is obtained from the same source as `Background-Enterprise`, `Background-Enterprise` provides additional co-occurrence information specific to the `Enterprise` test set (e.g., organization names, customer names, etc.). Thus, we report quality of extracting `Enterprise` using `Background-Enterprise` in addition to `Background-Web`.

5.1.5 Evaluation metric

Direct comparisons between an output table T_a and the ground truth table T_g can be tricky, since there may be multiple, equally correct ways of segmenting lists into tables, and T_a and T_g may have different number of columns. For instance, suppose Table 2 is the ground truth table T_g we crawled, and Table 3 is the output T_a of an algorithm. Although first-name/last-name are separated into two columns in ground truth T_g, they are concatenated in T_a. Similarly month/date columns are segmented in T_a but not T_g.

Table 2: T_g

Jenny	Scott	Jan 12
John	Smith	Nov 20

Table 3: T_a

Jenny Scott	Jan	12
John Smith	Nov	20

Intuitively, both segmentations are reasonable in this particular case, since we could easily find tables on the Web that segment first-name/last-name and month/date in two columns, as well as tables that concatenate them. Even human labelers may disagree on the right segmentation.

Our observation is that segmenting one column into multiple ones, or conversely concatenating multiple consecutive columns into one still provides some utility. For instance, regardless of whether first-name/last-name are concatenated or not, the extracted table still provides useful information. However, traditional set-based precision/recall evaluation does not take this into account.

We are not the first to recognize this problem. It has been shown [15,18] that in certain matching and alignment problems, traditional precision/recall is not suitable, and generalized P/R evaluations has been proposed [15,18]. In the following we describe the metric that we use, which is similar in spirit to [18].

Define a *column mapping* M as a mapping from one column in T_g to multiple consecutive columns in T_a, or one column in T_a to multiple consecutive columns in T_g. Denote by $M(T)$ the column(s) of T that participates in M. Also let $l(M(T))$ be the values of columns $M(T)$ in line l.

Define $|M|$ as the total number of correctly aligned row values between columns $M(T_a)$ and $M(T_g)$, namely $|M| = |\{i : l_i(M(T_a)) = l_i(M(T_g)), i \in [n]\}|$.

A *mapping set* $\mathcal{M} = \{M_i : i \in [k]\}$ is a set of column mappings M_i such that no two different mappings touch overlapping columns in T_g and T_a. In other words, $\forall i \neq j$, $M_i(T_a) \cap M_j(T_a) = \emptyset$ and $M_i(T_g) \cap M_j(T_g) = \emptyset$.

Let $|\mathcal{M}| = \sum_{i \in [k]} |M_i|$, which is the number of correctly aligned values, and $|\mathcal{M}_{best}| = \max_{\mathcal{M}} |\mathcal{M}|$ be the best possible set of mappings.

We define the precision (P), recall (R), and f-measure (F) as follows:

$$P = \frac{|\mathcal{M}_{best}|}{|T_a|} \quad R = \frac{|\mathcal{M}_{best}|}{|T_g|} \quad F = \frac{2PR}{P+R}$$

where $|T|$ denotes the total number of cells in T.

As a concrete example, for T_g and T_a in Table 2 and 3, $\mathcal{M}_{best}$ has two column mappings: M_1 that maps the first two columns in T_g to the first column in T_a, where $|M_1| = 2$ (mappings in both rows are correct); and M_2 that maps the third column in T_g to the last two columns in T_a, where $|M_2| = 2$. $|\mathcal{M}_{best}| = |M_1| + |M_2| = 4$. $P = \frac{4}{6} = 0.67$ and $R = \frac{4}{6} = 0.67$. Note that using this metric, we only get partial credits when we over-segment or under-segment in a consistent manner. Observe that in this case where the produced a table T_a that is clearly useful, the our P/R values are only 0.67.

5.2 Overall table quality comparison

Unsupervised. Table 4 shows the the overall quality comparison when extracting tables from lists without any user input. It is clear from the table that TEGRA significantly outperforms both `ListExtract` and `Judie` across all benchmark sets. Notice that the difference in F-measures between TEGRA and `ListExtract` (the second-best method) is quite significant – the results are 0.9 vs 0.76, 0.9 vs 0.73 and 0.87 vs 0.79 for the three automatically generated test sets respectively, and 0.91 vs 0.7 for the manually label test set. This validates our belief that a principled formulation that performs global optimization is superior to `ListExtract` that uses local decisions that can be sub-optimal.

We observe that while the recall numbers of `ListExtract` come relatively close to TEGRA, its precision numbers lag much behind (0.89 vs 0.69, 0.89 vs 0.65, 0.88 vs 0.75, and 0.89 vs 0.63 respectively). We believe this is because of the way `ListExtract` works. Recall that it greedily extract the most confident cells from each row independently, which tends to lead to over-segmentation, because shorter token subsequences are naturally more popular in a language model and other sources (e.g., "New York" is a popular name and is likely to be extracted first despite the token "City" that comes after "New York"). Since it is more aggressive in splitting, its precision numbers suffer the most.

The `Judie` approach does not perform as well as others. This is not entirely surprising – the algorithm relies on a domain-specific reference table / knowledge base (KB) to perform segmentation correctly through essentially KB lookups. In the case of general lists on the web, even a general-purpose KB like Freebase [6] does not have nearly enough entities to cover values that can possibly occur in wide range of tables on the Web, not to mention various naming variations (e.g., a KB may have the entry "United Kingdom" but not "UK" or "Britain") and ambiguity of names (e.g., "United" may refer to airline or country). Thus, the class of techniques represented by `Judie` is not suitable for general table extraction from lists on the Web.

		TEGRA	ListExtract	Judie
Web	P	**0.89**	0.69	0.37
	R	**0.94**	0.88	0.45
	F	**0.90**	0.76	0.40
Wiki	P	**0.89**	0.65	0.44
	R	**0.94**	0.85	0.50
	F	**0.90**	0.73	0.46
Enterprise	P	**0.88**	0.75	0.43
	R	**0.89**	0.87	0.49
	F	**0.87**	0.79	0.45
Lists	P	**0.89**	0.63	0.60
	R	**0.94**	0.82	0.64
	F	**0.91**	0.70	0.62

Table 4: Quality Comparison (unsupervised)

		TEGRA	ListExtract	Judie
Web	$P/R/F$	**0.97**	0.70	0.39
Wikipedia	$P/R/F$	**0.96**	0.71	0.50
Enterprise	$P/R/F$	**0.94**	0.81	0.49
Lists	$P/R/F$	**0.95**	0.71	0.61

Table 5: Quality Comparison (supervised)

Supervised. We show an overall quality comparison when user feedback is given (i.e., the supervised setting) in Table 5. We emulate the user input by randomly selecting two records from the ground truth table as input.

It is worth noting that while user feedback gives a quality boost to all three algorithms, TEGRA benefits the most. This demonstrates the usefulness of the proposed framework – using the same technique and a little user feedback, the quality of TEGRA can be greatly improved. We report additional experiments in the supervised setting in Appendix K due to space limit.

SP Distance Analysis. In order to analyze the correlation between our objective function and the "goodness" of tables extracted, we sort extracted tables based on their objective scores normalized on a per tuple-pair basis, and bucketize the tables into five bins. We plot the score bucket percentile on the x-axis and F-measure on the y-axis in Figure 8(a). The overall trend is that as the normalized objective score increases, table quality as measured by F-measure decreases across all three datasets. This validates the usefulness of our formulation and scoring – by minimizing SP distance we are indeed producing high quality tables.

5.3 Sensitivity to different tables

In this section we vary input tables to understand the performance of the three algorithms in response to tables of different characteristics. We skip the results on `Wiki` dataset since the results are similar to `Web`.

First, we observe that tables with more number of tokens per cell are generally more difficult to segment (because algorithms are more likely to make mistakes in picking wrong splitting positions). In contrast tables with fewer number of tokens per cell are easier, which are often tables dominated by 1-token numerical columns that are easy to seg-

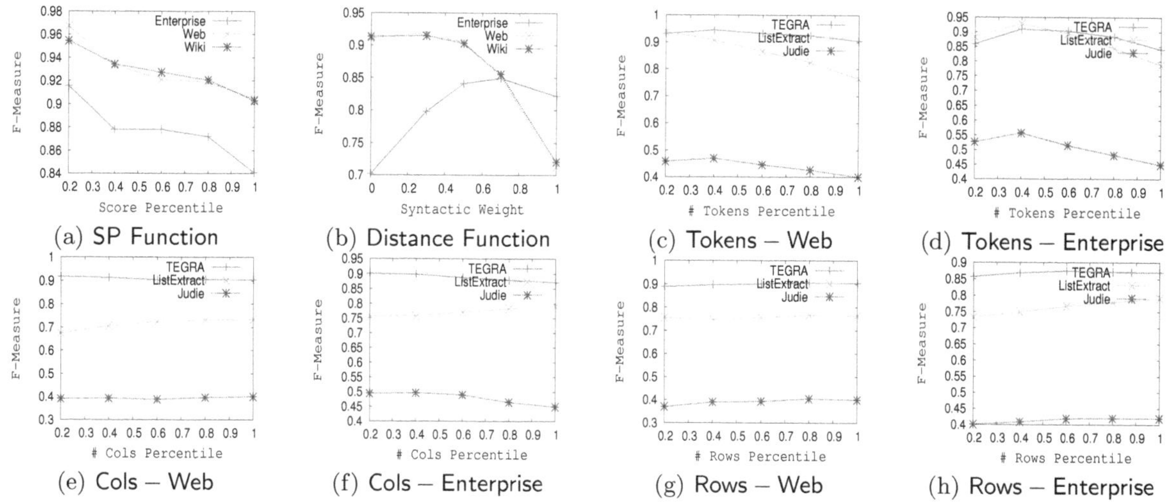

Figure 8: Experiments in the unsupervised setting

ment. Using this observation, we sort tables based on their average number of tokens per cell, which is a proxy measure of segmentation "difficulty". We again bucketize tables into 5 buckets, and plot the corresponding F-measure in Figures 8(c) and 8(d).

When the average number of tokens per cell is low, the F-measure of `ListExtract` and `TEGRA` are very close, since a large fraction of these tables are actually dominated by 1-token numerical columns, which are not difficult to segment. As the average number of tokens per cell increases, segmentation becomes non-trivial, and the F-measure drops quite significantly for `ListExtract`. Note that even in the hard-to-segment cases, `TEGRA` performs surprisingly well – in fact, its quality numbers stay almost the same across all five table buckets. The fact that `TEGRA` can segment difficult (and more meaningful) tables almost as well as trivial 1-column numerical tables underlines the robustness of TEGRA.

Second, we vary tables by the number of columns. We observe in Figures 8(e) and 8(f) that as the number of columns increases, quality results only drop slightly. This is somewhat surprising and contrary to our initial belief that tables with more columns are more difficult to segment. An analysis reveals that tables with more columns are actually mixed, with both tables that are genuinely difficult to segment, and tables with mostly 1-token numerical columns that are trivial to segment. Since our test sets are uniformly sampled from the corpus, in aggregate the results are not sensitive to the number of columns.

Finally, we bucketize tables by the number of rows. We observe in Figures 8(g) and 8(h), as the number of rows increases, quality results of all three algorithms stay relatively the same. This is mostly expected – the number of rows does not correlate much with the hardness of segmentation.

5.4 Sensitivity to distance scoring

In this section, we vary the relative importance of syntactic distance and semantic distance, namely α in Equation (1), with the goal of understanding the importance of score components in different settings. In Figure 8(b), we vary the weight of the syntactic component α used in the distance function in Equation (1).

For `Web` and `Wiki`, starting with only semantic distance ($\alpha = 0$) the quality of `Web` and `Wiki` is already fairly good. As we increase the importance of syntactic distance the quality results improves slightly. When we move to the rightmost point with only syntactic distance ($\alpha = 1$), quality numbers suffer. This shows the importance of semantic distance for `Web` and `Wiki`, where syntactic features like the number of tokens is not sufficient to capture semantic coherence between values like "New York City" and "Toronto".

On the other hand, on the `Enterprise` data set, the quality results using only semantic distance ($\alpha = 0$) are not very good. As we increase the importance of syntactic distance quality numbers improve significantly. However when we reach the extreme with only syntactic distance ($\alpha = 1$) the performance falls again. This shows that syntactic distance is perhaps more important in the `Enterprise` data set, because a significant fraction of data is proprietary (e.g., customer names, internal ID codes, etc.) that cannot be found in `background-Web` crawled from the public domain. When semantic distance is not as indicative, syntactic distance naturally becomes more important.

Across all three benchmark sets `Web`, `Wiki` and `Enterprise`, both syntactic distance and semantic distance are shown to be important – using some combination of syntactic distance and semantic distance gives the best performance. This demonstrates the usefulness of both scoring components. Empirically we find $\alpha = 0.5$ to be a good setting (equal weights between semantic and syntactic distance), which is used as default in our experiments.

5.5 Impact of matching background corpus

In Table 6, we evaluate the effect of using different background corpora, namely, `background-Enterprise`, `background-Web` and `background-Combined` (which combines the previous two). It is quite clear that in all these cases, using the matching background corpus (e.g., `background-Enterprise` for test set `Enterprise`) or the combined corpus (`background-Combined`) provides the best performance.

On the other hand, when using *mismatched* corpus, e.g., `background-Enterprise` for `Web`, the performance drops significantly. We believe that `background-Enterprise` does not really cover the diverse data found on the Web, thus cannot provide meaningful semantic distance. Surprisingly, using `background-Web` on `Enterprise` performs reasonably well, perhaps because `background-Web` is already diverse enough to cover certain aspect of `Enterprise` (e.g., geography data, product data, etc.). This is encouraging, because it show that the general purpose approach of using the public `background-Web` can actually provide reasonable performance on proprietary `Enterprise` data, which underscores the general applicability of our approach.

5.6 Efficiency study

Figures 9(a) and Figure 9(b) show the scalability of different approaches when varying the number of columns and number of rows, respectively. It is not really surprising that the `TEGRA` line (second from the top) takes considerably more

Test-Dataset \	Background	TEGRA	ListExtract	Judie
Web	B-Web	**0.90**	**0.76**	0.40
	B-Enterprise	0.68	0.73	0.40
	B-Combined	**0.90**	**0.76**	0.40
Wiki	B-Web	**0.90**	**0.73**	0.46
	B-Enterprise	0.70	0.71	0.46
	B-Combined	**0.90**	**0.73**	0.46
Enterprise	B-Web	0.84	0.78	0.45
	B-Enterprise	**0.87**	**0.80**	0.45
	B-Combined	**0.87**	0.79	0.45

Table 6: F-Measure using different background corpus (unsupervised)

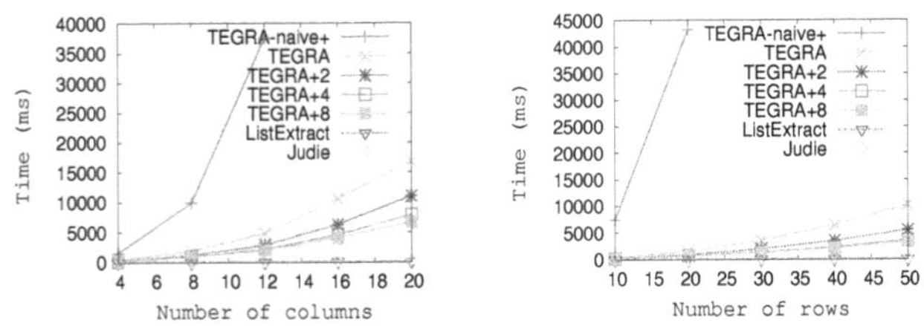

(a) Varying # columns (b) Varying # rows

Figure 9: Scalability Analysis

time than ListExtract and Judie, since both use greedy procedures that lack formal quality guarantees. Given the significant quality improvement TEGRA provides, and the fact that our main targeted application is to extract tables from Web lists offline, we believe that the cost in execution time can be justified (we scale out the extraction process using a production Map Reduce system).

In comparison to TEGRA, TEGRA-naive+ line here uses the dynamic programming in SLGR, but no A* optimization is performed. TEGRA-naive+ actually takes over 40 seconds to segment a table with 20 rows, and over a few minutes when the number of rows increases (off the chart in Figure 9(b)). The significant improvement of TEGRA over TEGRA-naive+ shows the effectiveness of our A* optimization in Section 3.

We note that previous studies [16] as well as our own show that the majority (over 95%) of Web tables have less than 10 columns, in which case the unoptimized TEGRA can already finish within 4 seconds on average as shown in Figures 9(a). Furthermore, since the anchor-distance calculations are trivial to parallelize on a per row basis, we also experiment using multi-threading to see its impact on latency (denoted as TEGRA+n, where n is the number of threads used). We note that with modest multi-threading, e.g. TEGRA+4, we can reduce segmentation time for a 10-column table to around 1 second, which may already be acceptable for certain online applications like interactive table segmentation.

5.7 Estimate useful lists on the Web

As an empirical analysis of the number of useful relational tables in lists, we extract a sample of 770K Web HTML lists embedded in $\langle ul \rangle \langle /ul \rangle$ HTML tags from a small fraction of the Web crawl. We filter away lists with too many or two few rows, and those with very long rows, which leaves us with around 40K lists. We run our segmentation algorithms on these lists. The number of resulting tables that have a good empirical per-tuple quality score (based on Figure 8(a)) is around 2K. Given that the sampled Web chunk is about 0.006% of the whole index, we estimate that there are over 30 million lists on the Web with good relational content, which is in line with what is reported in [16].

6. RELATED WORK

The pioneering work in [16] is the only work that automatically extracts tables from general Web lists to our knowledge, and is reviewed in Appendix A. Because it greedily makes local splitting decisions for each line independently early in the process without giving consideration to global alignment, it can get stuck with sub-optimal local decisions.

There are several approaches, e.g., Judie [14], CRAM [3], U-CRF [28], that segment text into records utilizing a knowledge base (KB) or a reference table in the *matching* domain of the target content. Our experience shows that for these approaches to work well, a large fraction of values to be segmented must be covered in the matching KB. In the case of Web-scale table extraction where finding a matching KB for each target list is infeasible, using general KB like Freebase [6] does not work well (Section 5). We believe the reason lies in the fact that data on the Web are so diverse that even a general KB cannot provide sufficient coverage for the variety of values that can possibly occur in tables. In contrast, TEGRA obviates the need for specific KBs by taking advantage of statistical co-occurrence using a large table corpus that provides exhaustive content coverage.

Graphical models like CRF have been demonstrated to be useful for table segmentation, especially in supervised settings [21]. A recent approach, U-CRF [28], adapts CRF for the unsupervised setting and can be used without training examples. It is conceptually similar to Judie [14] in that it also requires matching KBs to be provided. Since it is shown in [14] that Judie outperforms U-CRF for unsupervised record parsing, we only compare with Judie in this paper. HMM has also been adapted for record segmentation in [8,25]. However, [8] uses training examples, and [25] requires explicit target schema, which make them unsuitable for extraction of tables from Web lists.

Our problem is also related to information extraction, and more specifically wrapper induction for structured Web data extraction [4,12,17]. However, all these approaches above are supervised in nature, requiring some examples to be given, which cannot scale to the general problem of extracting tables from millions of lists on the Web. Example driven extraction using program synthesis techniques (e.g., [20]) is another related line of work.

Sequence alignment in bioinformatics [22] addresses the problem of aligning biological sequences to identify similar regions, where similarity is predefined for pairs of symbols. The all-pairs objective function we use is reminiscent of the sum-of-pairs in the multiple sequence alignment (MSA) literature [22]. However, because symbols are always the unit of alignment in MSA, when pairs of sequences (a, b) and (a, c) are aligned, it is trivial to align the three sequences (a, b, c) together. In contrast, in table alignment this property does not hold, because token sequences become the unit of alignment and additivity of tokens no longer holds, which makes table alignment more difficult.

7. CONCLUSIONS AND FUTURE WORK

Motivated by the need to extract relational tables from HTML lists, we propose a principled formulation for the problem of table extraction. We design efficient algorithms with 2-approximation guarantees, which produce tables of superior quality compared to the state-of-the-art. Our approach also shows great promise in the supervised setting when user examples are provided, which is an interesting area that warrants further investigations.

8. REFERENCES

[1] Google Web Tables. http://research.google.com/tables.

[2] Microsoft Excel Power Query. http://office.microsoft.com/powerbi.

[3] E. Agichtein and V. Ganti. mining reference tables for automatic text segmentation. In *KDD*, 2004.

[4] E. Agichtein and L. Gravano. Snowball: extracting relations from large plain-text collections. In *DL*, 2000.

[5] Y. Bartal, M. Charikar, and D. Raz. Approximating min-sum clustering in metric spaces. In *STOC*, 2001.

[6] K. Bollacker, C. Evans, P. Paritosh, T. Sturge, and J. Taylor. Freebase: a collaboratively created graph database for structuring human knowledge. In *SIGMOD*, 2008.

[7] P. Bonizzoni and G. D. Vedova. The complexity of multiple sequence alignment with sp-score that is a metric. In *Theoretical Computer Science*, 2001.

[8] V. R. Borkar, K. Deshmukh, and S. Sarawagi. Automatic segmentation of text into structured records. In *SIGMOD*, 2001.

[9] M. J. Cafarella, A. Y. Halevy, and N. Khoussainova. Data integration for the relational web. In *VLDB*, 2009.

[10] M. J. Cafarella, E. Wu, A. Halevy, Y. Zhang, and D. Z. Wang. Webtables: Exploring the power of tables on the web. In *VLDB*, 2008.

[11] K. W. Church and P. Hanks. Word association norms, mutual information, and lexicography. In *Computational Linguistics*, 1990.

[12] W. W. Cohen, M. Hurst, and L. S. Jensen. A flexible learning system for wrapping tables and lists in html documents. In *WWW*, 2002.

[13] T. Cormen, C. Leiserson, R. Rivest, and C. Stein. *Introduction to Algorithms*. 2001.

[14] E. Cortez, D. Oliveira, A. S. da Silva, E. S. de Moura, and A. H. F. Laender. Joint unsupervised structure discovery and information extraction. In *SIGMOD*, 2011.

[15] H. Do, S. Melnik, and E. Rahm. Comparison of schema matching evaluations. In *Workshop on Web Databases*, 2002.

[16] H. Elmeleegy, J. Madhavan, and A. Y. Halevy. Harvesting relational tables from lists on the web. *PVLDB*, 2009.

[17] D. W. Embley, Y. Jiang, and Y.-K. Ng. Record-boundary discovery in web documents. In *SIGMOD*, 2009.

[18] J. Euzenat. Semantic precision and recall for ontology alignment evaluation. IJCAI'07, 2007.

[19] R. L. Francis, T. J. Lowe, and H. D. Ratliff. Distance constraints for tree network multifacility location problems. In *Operations Research*, 1978.

[20] S. Gulwani, W. R. Harris, and R. Singh. Spreadsheet data manipulation using examples. In *CACM*, 2012.

[21] R. Gupta and S. Sarawagi. Answering table augmentation queries from unstructured lists on the web. In *PVLDB*, 2009.

[22] D. Gusfield. Efficient methods for multiple sequence alignment with guaranteed error bounds. *Bulletin of Mathematical Biology*, 1993.

[23] P. E. Hart, N. J. Nilsson, and B. Raphael. A formal basis for the heuristic determination of minimum cost paths. *SIGART Bull.*, 1972.

[24] W. Just. Computational complexity of multiple sequence alignment with sp-score. In *Journal of Computational Biology*, 2001.

[25] A. Machanavajjhala, A. S. Iyer, P. Bohannon, and S. Merugu. Collective extraction from heterogeneous web lists. In *WSDM*, 2011.

[26] M. Yakout, K. Ganjam, K. Chakrabarti, and S. Chaudhuri. Infogather: entity augmentation and attribute discovery by holistic matching with web tables. In *SIGMOD*, 2012.

[27] M. Zhang and K. Chakrabarti. Infogather+: Semantic matching and annotation of numeric and time-varying attributes in web tables. In *SIGMOD*, 2013.

[28] C. Zhao, J. Mahmud, and I. Ramakrishnan. Exploiting structured reference data for unsupervised text segmentation with conditional random fields. In *SDM*, 2008.

APPENDIX

A. ALGORITHM OVERVIEW IN [16]

Given an input list $L = \{l_1, l_2, \ldots, l_n\}$, `ListExtract` in [16] extracts a table $T = \{t_1, t_2, \ldots, t_n\}$ in three phases: an *independent splitting* phase, an *alignment* phase, and an *refinement* phase.

In the first phase, each line l_i is independently split into a multi-column record t_i based on *Field Quality Score* $FQ(f)$. $FQ(f)$ has three components: type support, language model support, and table corpus support.

In the alignment phase, since each line might be split into different number of columns in the previous step, the algorithm use the most common columns number m to re-split all lines. Records with number of columns less than m are expanded by inserting empty columns using a dynamic programming procedure to maximize consistency among cells in the same column. A *Field-to-Filed Consistency Score*, $F2FC(f_1, f_2)$, is used to measure the consistency of two fields f_1, f_2 being the same column. Records with number of columns more than m are merged and re-split into a record using the same algorithm in the independent splitting phase given m as a constraint.

In refinement phase, `ListExtract` tried to rectify some local decisions made before by identifying sequences of fields (termed streaks) in a record that are deemed to be incorrect. A field is deemed to be incorrect if its score with other fields in the same column is less than a predefined threshold. Each streak is then merged together and re-split.

B. PROOF OF THEOREM 1

We obtain the hardness result by a reduction from multiple sequence alignment (MSA) [24]. Recall that given a set $S = \{s_i | 1 \leq i \leq k\}$ of k strings over an alphabet Σ, a multiple alignment of is a $k \times l$ matrix A where row i contains string s_i interleaved by spaces. The score for a multiple alignment is the sum of all pairs of rows in the alignment, where the cost of a pair of rows is in turn the sum of all aligned symbol pairs. The penalty costs of all symbol pairs $P : (\Sigma, \Sigma) \rightarrow \mathbb{R}$ are pre-defined. The decision version of MSA is to determine if there exists a multiple alignment with cost no more than some given constant C.

For any instance of MSA, we construct an Unsupervised Table Segmentation(UTS) as follows. We create k unsegmented lines $L = \{s_i | 1 \leq i \leq k\}$ exactly using S, and define the cost function in UTS for each pair of token subsequences as:

$$d(l_i[a_i \ldots b_i], l_j[a_j \ldots b_j]) = \begin{cases} P(l_i[a_i \ldots b_i], l_j[a_j \ldots b_j]), \\ \qquad\qquad \text{if } a_i = b_i \wedge a_j = b_j \\ \infty, \text{ if } a_i \neq b_i \vee a_j \neq b_j \end{cases}$$

That is, if $l_i[a_i \ldots b_i]$ and $l_j[a_j \ldots b_j]$ are single symbols, then we use exactly P from MSA, otherwise we force it to ∞.

We show that if there exists a solution to MSA, i.e., a multiple alignment with cost at most C, then there is a solution to UTS with cost at most C. Suppose the multiple alignment solution A has l number of columns. It can be shown that $l \leq \sum_{1 \leq i \leq k} |s_i|$. In the corresponding UTS, if we try all number of columns $m \leq \sum_{1 \leq i \leq k} |s_i|$, then when using l number of columns, the best UTS will have a cost at most C. This is because the alignment A is a feasible segmentation of L in UTS with exactly the same cost. Thus the solution to UTS must have a cost at most C.

We then show it in the other direction – if there exists a solution to UTS, i.e., a table segmentation with cost at most C, then there is a solution to MSA with cost at most C. Since there is a table segmentation with cost at most C, then all columns in the segmentations must be single-symbol or null (otherwise the cost is ∞ by construction). Thus this table segmentation is also a valid multiple alignment, meaning the solution to MSA must have a cost at most C.

Since MSA is shown to be NP-hard [24], this completes our hardness proof. Note that MSA is shown to be NP-hard even with metric distance [7]. It follows that UTS is also NP-hard even with metric distance.

C. PROOF OF THEOREM 2

Let $T_c^* = R(t_c^*)$ be the table returned by Algorithm 1 that has the minimal $AD(t_c^*, T_c^*)$, and $T^\star$ be the table with the minimal SP distance. Then we have

$$\begin{aligned} SP_m(T_c^*) &= \frac{1}{2} \sum_{1 \le i \le n} \sum_{\substack{1 \le j \le n \\ j \ne i}} d(t_i, t_j) \\ &\le \frac{1}{2} \sum_{1 \le i \le n} \sum_{\substack{1 \le j \le n \\ j \ne i}} \left(d(t_i, t_c^*) + d(t_c^*, t_j) \right) \quad (16) \\ &= (n-1) \sum_{\substack{1 \le i \le n \\ i \ne c}} d(t_c^*, t_i) \\ &\le (n-1) AD(t_c^*, T_c^*) \quad (17) \end{aligned}$$

Note that Equation (16) holds by triangle inequality.

Overall, Equation (17) shows that $SP_m(T_c^*)$ can be bounded by $AD(t_c^*, T_c^*)$ from above. We further show that $SP_m(T^\star)$ can be bounded by $AD(t_c^*, T_c^*)$ from below.

$$\begin{aligned} SP_m(T^\star) &= \frac{1}{2} \sum_{1 \le i \le n} AD(t_i, T^\star) \quad \text{(By definition of AD)} \\ &\ge \frac{1}{2} \sum_{1 \le i \le n} AD(t_i, T_i^*) \quad (18) \\ &\ge \frac{n}{2} AD(t_c^*, T_c^*) \quad \text{(By definition of } t_c^*, T_c^*) \quad (19) \end{aligned}$$

Note that Equation (18) is true because T_i^* is defined to be the table that minimizes anchor distance of t_i among all possible tables segmentations, which include $T^\star$.

Dividing (17) by (19), we have:

$$\frac{SP_m(T_c^*)}{SP_m(T^\star)} \le \frac{2(n-1)nAD(t_c^*, T_c^*)}{nAD(t_c^*, T_c^*)} = 2 - \frac{2}{n} < 2$$

D. ALGORITHM FOR SLGR

Algorithm 3 describes a dynamic programming procedure to calculate $M[p, w]$ and the optimal segmentation t_j^{i*}. Lines 1-5 initialize $M[p, w]$ and address boundary cases. Line 8 uses the optimal substructure for calculating $M[p, w]$. The complexity of the procedure is $O(m|l_j|^2)$, where the size of the M matrix is $O(m|l_j|)$, and the calculation of each cell requires $O(|l_j|)$ comparisons.

E. $A^\star$ SEARCH OVERVIEW.

$A^\star$, an informed search algorithm, is designed to find a least-cost path from a start node to an end node quickly. It keeps a priority queue of alternate paths sorted by their underestimated cost to the end node. It traverses the graph by following a path that has least expected cost.

Algorithm 3: Segment a Line Given Record (SLGR)

Input: A record t_i and a line l_j
Output: Segmentation t_j^{i*} of l_j that minimizes $d(t_i, t_j^{i*})$

1 $M[0, 0] \leftarrow 0$
2 **for** *each* $w \in 1 \ldots |l_j|$ **do**
3 $\quad M[0, w] \leftarrow \infty$
4 **for** *each* $p \in 1 \ldots m$ **do**
5 $\quad M[p, 0] \leftarrow M[p-1, 0] + d(null, t_i[k])$
6 **for** *each* $p = 1 \ldots m$ **do**
7 $\quad$ **for** *each* $w = 1 \ldots |l_j|$ **do**
8
$$M[p, w] = \min \begin{cases} M[p-1, x] + d(l_j[x+1 \ldots w], t_i[p]) \\ \qquad \forall 0 \le x < w \\ M[p-1, w] + d(\text{null}, t_i[p]) \end{cases}$$
9 $t_j^{i*} \leftarrow$ construct segmentation by back tracing $M[m, |l_j|]$
10 **Return** t_i

For every node x in the search graph, $A^\star$ keeps a cost function $f(x)$ to determine the order in which $A^\star$ visits the nodes in the graph. $f(x)$ consists of two components: $g(x)$ and $h(x)$. $g(x)$ is the currently known least cost from start node to x. $h(x)$ is an estimated cost from x to the end node. $h(x)$ must be *admissible*, i.e., $h(x)$ must underestimate the actual cost from x to the end node. $h(x)$ being admissible guarantees the the path $A^\star$ finds is the least cost path when terminated. $h(x)$ is said to be *monotonic* if it satisfies $L(X) + h(x) \le L(Y) + h(y)$, where X is any path from start node to x, and Y is the path extending X with an additional node y. If $h(x)$ is monotonic, any node only needs to be processed once, making the search more efficient.

F. PROOF OF LEMMA 1

Let t_i^Z be the segmentation corresponding to Z, t_i^X be the partial segmentation corresponding to X, and t_i^Y be the partial segmentation corresponding to Y, we have $t_i^Z[k] = t_i^X[k], \forall 1 \le k \le p$ and $t_i^Z[k] = t_i^Y[k], \forall p < k \le m$. Let t_j^Z be the record aligning l_j with t_i^Z, t_j^X be the record aligning l_j with t_i^X, and t_j^Y be the record aligning l_j with t_i^Y. we have (20):

$$\begin{aligned} L(Z) &= \sum_{\substack{1 \le j \le n \\ j \ne i}} \sum_{1 \le k \le m} d(t_i^Z[k], t_j^Z[k]) \\ &= \sum_{\substack{1 \le j \le n \\ j \ne i}} \sum_{1 \le k \le p} d(t_i^Z[k], t_j^Z[k]) + \sum_{\substack{1 \le j \le n \\ j \ne i}} \sum_{p < k \le m} d(t_i^Z[k], t_j^Z[k]) \\ L(X) &= \sum_{\substack{1 \le j \le n \\ j \ne i}} \sum_{1 \le k \le p} d(t_i^X[k], t_j^X[k]) \\ L(Y) &= \sum_{\substack{1 \le j \le n \\ j \ne i}} \sum_{p < k \le m} d(t_i^Y[k], t_j^Y[k]) \quad (20) \end{aligned}$$

$$L(X) \le \sum_{\substack{1 \le j \le n \\ j \ne i}} \sum_{1 \le k \le p} d(t_i^Z[k], t_j^Z[k]) \quad (21)$$

$$L(Y) \le \sum_{\substack{1 \le j \le n \\ j \ne i}} \sum_{p < k \le m} d(t_i^Z[k], t_j^Z[k]) \quad (22)$$

(21) holds because $t_i^Z[k] = t_i^X[k], \forall 1 \le k \le p$ and t_j^X is the

record that achieves the minimal distance with t_i^X according to the definition of $L(X)$, which is certainly smaller or equal to any other record's (including t_j^Z) distance with first p columns of t_i. (22) holds for similar reasons.

Combining (20) (21) (22), we have $L(X) + L(Y) \leq L(Z)$.

G. HEURISTIC FUNCTION

Algorithm 4 describes the procedure for calculating h function for every node $[p, w]$ in G_i. Lines 1-8 initialize $freeD(c_1)$ for every candidate column c_1 in l_i. Lines 9-13 initialize and take care of corner cases of $h_{l_i}(p, w)$. Lines 14-16 use a dynamic programming procedure to initialize all entries of $h_{l_i}(p, w)$ similar to the one used in Algorithm 3.

Algorithm 4: `Calculate` h `Function`

Input: List L, number of columns m, anchor line l_i
Output: $h_i(p, w)$ for $1 \leq p \leq m$ and $1 \leq w \leq |l_i|$

1 **for** *candidate column* $c_1 \in l_i$ **do**
2 $\quad freeD(c_1) \leftarrow 0$
3 $\quad$ **for** *Line* $l_j \in L$ *and* $l_j \neq l_i$ **do**
4 $\quad\quad freeD(c_1, l_j) \leftarrow$ Double.Max
5 $\quad\quad$ **for** *candidate column* $c_2 \in l_j$ **do**
6 $\quad\quad\quad$ **if** $d(c_1, c_2) < freeD(c_1, l_j)$ **then**
7 $\quad\quad\quad\quad freeD(c_1, l_j) \leftarrow d(c_1, c_2)$
8 $\quad\quad freeD(c_1) \leftarrow freeD(c_1) + freeD(c_1, l_j)$
9 $h_{l_i}(m, |l_i|) \leftarrow 0$
10 **for** $w = |l_i| - 1 \rightarrow 1$ **do**
11 $\quad h_{l_i}(m, w) \leftarrow \infty$
12 **for** $p = m - 1 \rightarrow 1$ **do**
13 $\quad h_{l_i}(p, |l_i|) \leftarrow h_{l_i}(p + 1, |l_i|) + freeD(\text{null})$
14 **for** $p = m \rightarrow 1$ **do**
15 $\quad$ **for** $w = |l_i| \rightarrow 1$ **do**
16
$$h_{l_i}(p, w) = \min \begin{cases} h_{l_i}(p + 1, x) + freeD(l_i[w + 1 \ldots x]) \\ \qquad\qquad \forall w < x \leq |l_i| \\ h_{l_i}(p + 1, w) + freeD(\text{null}) \end{cases}$$
17 **Return** $h_i(p, w)$

Proof of Lemma 2. h function is admissible by definition since for every candidate column s_1 in l_i, it finds the best candidate column in every other line to align with s_1.

According to Line 16 in Algorithm 4, we have:

$$h(p, w) \leq h(p + 1, w') + freeD(l_i[w + 1 \ldots w']) \quad (23)$$

Let t_i^X be the segmentation corresponding to X and $t_i^{X'}$ be the segmentation corresponding to X'. We have $t_i^X[k] = t_i^{X'}[k], \forall 1 \leq k \leq p$. For every other line l_j, let t_j^X be the record of aligning l_j with t_i^X and $t_j^{X'}$ be the record of aligning l_j with $t_i^{X'}$. We have the following:

$$L(X) = \sum_{\substack{1 \leq j \leq n \\ j \neq i}} \sum_{1 \leq k \leq p} d(t_i^X[k], t_j^X[k])$$

$$L(X') = \sum_{\substack{1 \leq j \leq n \\ j \neq i}} \sum_{1 \leq k \leq p+1} d(t_i^{X'}[k], t_j^{X'}[k])$$

$$= \sum_{\substack{1 \leq j \leq n \\ j \neq i}} \sum_{1 \leq k \leq p} d(t_i^{X'}[k], t_j^{X'}[k]) + \sum_{\substack{1 \leq j \leq n \\ j \neq i}} d(t_i^{X'}[p + 1], t_j^{X'}[p + 1]) \quad (24)$$

Similar to the argument in Proof F, we have 25.

$$L(X) \leq \sum_{\substack{1 \leq j \leq n \\ j \neq i}} \sum_{1 \leq k \leq p} d(t_i^{X'}[k], t_j^{X'}[k]) \quad (25)$$

Because $l_i[w+1 \ldots w'] = t_i^{X'}[p+1]$, we have (26) for every line l_j from the definition of $freeD$.

$$freeD(l_i[w + 1 \ldots w'], l_j) \leq d(t_i^{X'}[p + 1], t_j^{X'}[p + 1]) \quad (26)$$

Summing up (26) for every $j \neq i$, we have:

$$freeD(l_i[w + 1 \ldots w']) \leq \sum_{\substack{1 \leq j \leq n \\ j \neq i}} d(t_i^{X'}[p + 1], t_j^{X'}[p + 1]) \quad (27)$$

Combining Equations (23) (24) (25) (27), we have:

$$L(X) + h(p, w) \leq L(X') + h(p + 1, w')$$

H. JACCARD DISTANCE

Since Jaccard distance also reflects the strength of co-occurrence between s_1, s_2, we also used Jaccard for semantic distance. Recall that $JaccardDist(s_1, s_2) = 1 - \frac{|C(s_1) \cap C(s_2)|}{|C(s_1) \cup C(s_2)|}$.

While using Jaccard distance also achieves reasonable quality, its performance is not as good as using NPMI. We suspect that the reason lies in the fact that Jaccard cannot handle asymmetric sets well. In particular, suppose s_1 is very popular (e.g. "USA") but s_2 is not (e.g., "Congo"). When using Jaccard, just because s_1 is so popular, even if s_2 always co-occurs with s_1 the Jaccard similarity is low and Jaccard distance is high. In comparison, NPMI is information theoretic and handles asymmetry better – even if s_2 is not popular, as long as s_1 and s_2 always co-occur their NPMI will never be negative. Thus NPMI is more robust to asymmetric sets and is a better measure to use in our setting.

I. DETAILS OF SYNTACTIC DISTANCE

At a high level, our syntactic distance $d_{syn}(s_1, s_2)$ is

$$d_{syn}(s_1, s_2) = \frac{d_{len}(s_1, s_2) + d_{char}(s_1, s_2) + d_{type}(s_1, s_2)}{3}$$

We use three main components to capture syntactic distance. First, length difference is defined as $d_{len}(s_1, s_2) = \frac{||s_1| - |s_2||}{\max(|s_1|, |s_2|)}$, where $|s_1|$ denotes the number of tokens in s_1. One can prove that d_{len} satisfies triangular inequality. Second, character distance $d_{char}(s_1, s_2)$ looks at s_1 and s_2 in character level, and determines if they have same number of digits, capital letters, punctuation marks, symbols, and letters. $d_{char}(s_1, s_2)$ equals to the number of types of characters s_1 and s_2 have the same number, divided by the total types of characters, which is 5. Third, type distance indicates $d_{type}(s_1, s_2)$ whether s_1 and s_2 belong to the same predefined type, e.g., numerical value, phone number, email address, all of which determined by predefined regular expressions. Define $d_{type}(s_1, s_2)$ to be 0 when they s_1 and s_2 have the same type, and 1 otherwise. It can be shown that $d_{syn}(s_1, s_2)$ satisfies triangle inequality.

Note that when calculating the distance between a string s and a null string, i.e., $d(\text{null}, s)$, we treat null as an empty string for calculating the syntactic distance $d_{syn}(\text{null}, s)$, i.e., we use $d_{syn}(\text{""}, s)$ for $d_{syn}(\text{null}, s)$; we give 1.0 for the semantic distance $d_{sem}(\text{null}, s)$ since empty string does not carry any meaningful semantics.

Also note that our design $d(s_1, s_2)$ did not include the likelihood of s_1 or s_2 being a cell in a table, called single value distance, which also seems to be a valid component of $d(s_1, s_2)$. Appendix J provides an explanation about this.

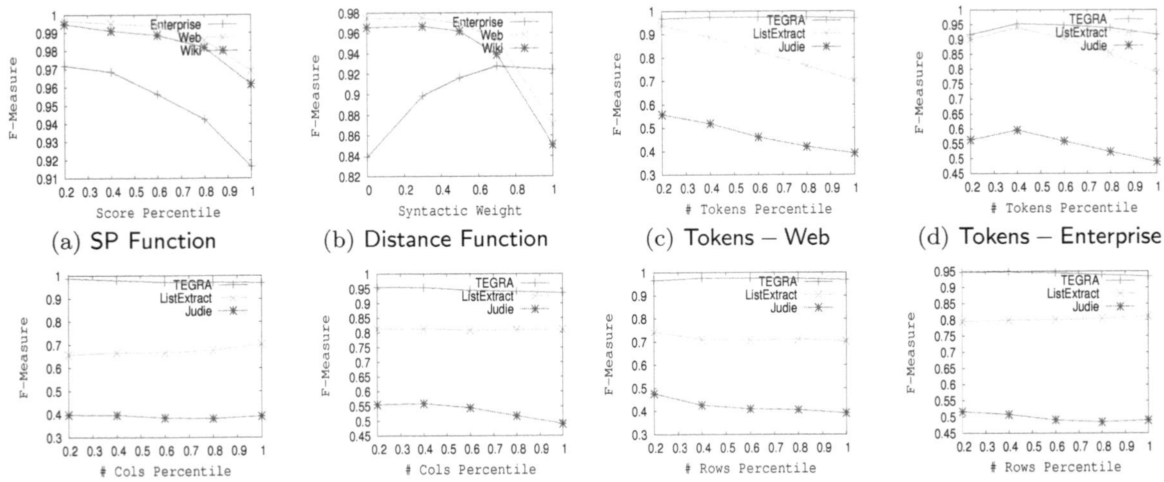

(a) SP Function (b) Distance Function (c) Tokens – Web (d) Tokens – Enterprise (e) Cols – Web (f) Cols – Enterprise (g) Rows – Web (h) Rows – Enterprise

Figure H.1: Experiments in supervised setting

Lastly, our syntactic distance do not work well for lists with very long texts (e.g., paragraphs). In practice, very long lists are unlikely to have good relational tables, so we simply discard lists whose lengths exceed certain limit. Images and other HTML constructs are sometimes embedded in lists. These however can be easily identified by HTML tags and are removed from the input lists by an upstream table/list extraction job.

J. SINGLE VALUE DISTANCE

$d(s_1, s_2)$ reflects the likelihood of s_1, s_2 being in the same column of a table, which include $d_{syn}(s_1, s_2)$ and $d_{sem}(s_1, s_2)$. $d(s_1, s_2)$ could also include two additional components: the likelihood of s_1 being a cell in a table $d(s_1)$ and the likelihood of s_2 being a cell in a table $d(s_2)$. $d(s_1)$ could include the language model of s_1, the frequency of s_1 in a column of the web tables corpus, etc. We chose not to include $d(s_1)$ and $d(s_2)$ in our design of $d(s_1, s_2)$ for several reasons: (1) we found that the $d(s_1)$ and $d(s_2)$ is already partially expressed by $d(s_1, s_2)$. For instance, if s_1 occurs infrequently in the web tables corpus, so will the occurrence of s_1, s_2; (2) it is quite difficult to tune the relative weights of four components, $d_{syn}(s_1, s_2)$, $d_{sem}(s_1, s_2)$, $d(s_1)$, and $d(s_2)$; and (3) we found in experiments that bad relative weight assignment of the four components will greatly degrade the tables quality. Furthermore, the best quality of resulted tables after fine turning the relative weights is not so much better than our current much simpler distance function design.

K. MORE EXPERIMENTS

We also experiment with the supervised scenario where users need to segment an ad-hoc list into tables, and example row segmentations can be provided. By default we use two example segmentations as input.

Table 7 varies the background corpus, where we have similar observations as Table 6 in the unsupervised setting.

Figure H.1 reports the same set of experiments as ones in Figure 8, but this time with supervision. We observe similar trends in the supervised setting.

Figure K.1 analyzes how quality improves as more user feedback is provided. The leftmost point ($x = -1$) corresponds to the unsupervised scenario where lists are segmented fully automatically. In the next set of points ($x = 0$), the correct number of columns are given as input. As we move to the right with $x > 0$ number of fully segmented rows as input, quality numbers further improve. We observe that

Test-Dataset	Background	TEGRA	ListExtract	Judie
Web	B-Web	**0.97**	**0.70**	0.39
	B-Enterprise	0.79	0.67	0.39
	B-Combined	**0.97**	**0.70**	0.39
Wiki	B-Web	**0.96**	**0.71**	0.50
	B-Enterprise	0.79	0.69	0.50
	B-Combined	**0.96**	**0.71**	0.50
Enterprise	B-Web	0.92	0.79	0.49
	B-Enterprise	0.92	**0.83**	0.49
	B-Combined	**0.94**	0.81	0.49

Table 7: F-Measure using different background corpus (supervised)

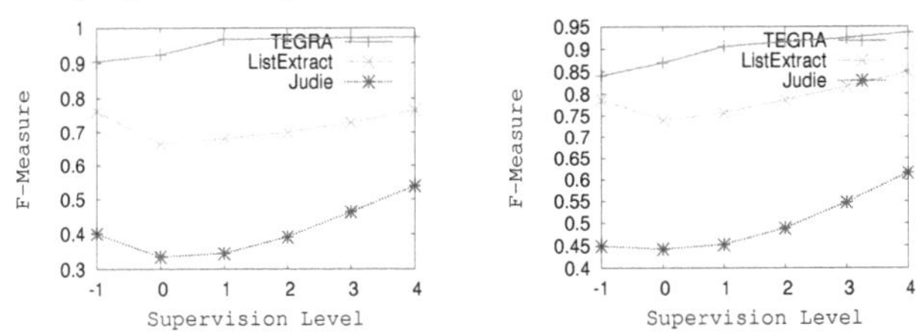

(a) Web (b) Enterprise

Figure K.1: Varying supervision level

TEGRA gets a significant boost with only 1 example row, and the incremental gain of have more example segmentations quickly diminishes. This shows that in the supervised setting TEGRA can achieve very high quality with very limited feedback. It is somewhat surprising that for ListExtract, knowing the number of columns ($x = 0$) actually hurts its quality. We suspect that the reason lies in the fact that ListExtract splits lines using a language model, which favors shorter token sequences (e.g., "New York" over "New York City"). As such, it tends to be too aggressive and over-segment. When the number of columns are constrained, however, the local splitting decisions cannot be reconciled by using more number of columns, thus destroying the structure of the extracted table and negatively affecting performance.

Mining Quality Phrases from Massive Text Corpora

Jialu Liu[†*] Jingbo Shang[†*] Chi Wang[‡] Xiang Ren[†] Jiawei Han[†]
[†]Department of Computer Science, University of Illinois at Urbana-Champaign, Urbana, IL, USA
[‡]Microsoft Research, Redmond, WA, USA
[†]{jliu64, shang7, xren7, hanj}@illinois.edu [‡]chiw@microsoft.com

ABSTRACT

Text data are ubiquitous and play an essential role in big data applications. However, text data are mostly unstructured. Transforming unstructured text into structured units (*e.g.*, semantically meaningful phrases) will substantially reduce semantic ambiguity and enhance the power and efficiency at manipulating such data using database technology. Thus mining quality phrases is a critical research problem in the field of databases. In this paper, we propose a new framework that extracts quality phrases from text corpora integrated with phrasal segmentation. The framework requires only limited training but the quality of phrases so generated is close to human judgment. Moreover, the method is scalable: both computation time and required space grow linearly as corpus size increases. Our experiments on large text corpora demonstrate the quality and efficiency of the new method.

1. INTRODUCTION

Mining quality phrases refers to automatically extracting salient phrases from a given corpus. It is a fundamental task for text analytics of various domains, such as science, news, social media and enterprise documents. In these large, dynamic collections of documents, analysts are often interested in variable-length phrases, including scientific concepts, events, organizations, products, slogans and so on. Efficient extraction of quality phrases enable a large body of applications to transform from word granularity to phrase granularity. Examples of such applications include topic tracking [21], OLAP on multi-dimensional text collections [40], and document categorization. For keyword search, the extracted phrases facilitate selective indexing, query suggestion and other tasks. Also, extraction of phrases is critical towards information extraction because many concepts, entities and relations are manifested in phrases.

Though the study of this task originates from the natural language processing (NLP) community, the challenge has been recognized of applying NLP tools in the emerging big data that deviate from rigorous language rules. Query logs, social media messages, and textual transaction records are just a few examples. Therefore, researchers have sought more general data-driven approaches, primarily based on the frequent pattern mining principle [2, 34]. The early work focuses on efficiently retrieving recurring word sequences, but many such sequences do not form meaningful phrases. More recent work filters or ranks them according to frequency-based statistics. However, the raw frequency from the data tends to produce misleading quality assessment, and the outcome is unsatisfactory, as the following example demonstrates.

Example 1 (Raw Frequency-based Phrase Mining). Consider a set of scientific publications and the raw frequency counts of two phrases 'relational database system' and 'support vector machine' and their subsequences in the *frequency* column of Table 1. The numbers are hypothetical but manifest several key observations: (i) the frequency generally decreases with the phrase length; (ii) both good and bad phrases can possess high frequency (*e.g.*, 'support vector' and 'vector machine'); and (iii) the frequency of one sequence (*e.g.*, 'relational database system') and its subsequences can have a similar scale of another sequence (*e.g.*, 'support vector machine') and its counterparts. ■

Obviously, a method that ranks the word sequences solely according to the frequency will output many false phrases such as 'vector machine'. In order to address this problem, different heuristics have been proposed based on comparison of a sequence's frequency and its sub-(or super-)sequences, assuming that a good phrase should have high enough (normalized) frequency compared with its sub-sequences and/or super-sequences [29, 12]. However, such heuristics can hardly differentiate the quality of, *e.g.*, 'support vector' and 'vector machine' because their frequency are so close. Finally, even if the heuristics can indeed draw a line between 'support vector' and 'vector machine' by discriminating their frequency (between 160 and 150), the same separation could fail for another case like 'relational database' and 'database system'.

Using the frequency in Table 1, all heuristics will produce identical predictions for 'relational database' and 'vector machine', guaranteeing one of them wrong. This example suggests the intrinsic limitations of using raw frequency counts, especially in judging whether a sequence is too long (longer than a minimum semantic unit), too short (broken and not informative), or right in length. It is a critical bottleneck for all frequency-based quality assessment.

In this work, we address this bottleneck, proposing to rectify the decisive raw frequency that hinders discovering the true quality of a phrase. The goal of the *rectification* is

*Equal Contribution

SIGMOD'15, May 31–June 4, 2015, Melbourne, Victoria, Australia.

http://dx.doi.org/10.1145/2723372.2751523. .

Table 1: A hypothetical example of word sequence raw frequency

sequence	frequency	phrase?	rectified	sequence	frequency	phrase?	rectified
relational database system	100	yes	70	support vector machine	100	yes	80
relational database	150	yes	40	support vector	160	yes	50
database system	160	yes	35	vector machine	150	no	6
relational	500	N/A	20	support	500	N/A	150
database	1000	N/A	200	vector	1000	N/A	200
system	10000	N/A	1000	machine	1000	N/A	150

to estimate how many times each word sequence should be interpreted in whole as a phrase in its occurrence context. The following example illustrates this idea.

Example 2 (Rectification). Consider the following occurrences of the 6 multi-word sequences listed in Table 1.

1. A ⌈relational database system⌋ for images...
2. ⌈Database system⌋ empowers everyone in your organization...
3. More formally, a ⌈support vector machine⌋ constructs a hyperplane...
4. The ⌈support vector⌋ method is a new general method of ⌈function estimation⌋...
5. A standard ⌈feature vector⌋ ⌈machine learning⌋ setup is used to describe...
6. ⌈Relevance vector machine⌋ has an identical ⌈functional form⌋ to the ⌈support vector machine⌋...
7. The basic goal for ⌈object-oriented relational database⌋ is to ⌈bridge the gap⌋ between... ■

The first 4 instances should provide positive counts to these sequences, while the last three instances should not provide positive counts to 'vector machine' or 'relational database' because they should not be interpreted as a whole phrase (instead, sequences like 'feature vector' and 'relevance vector machine' can). Suppose one can correctly count true occurrences of the sequences, and collect rectified frequency as shown in the *rectified* column of Table 1. The rectified frequency now clearly distinguishes 'vector machine' from the other phrases, since 'vector machine' rarely occurs as a whole phrase.

The success of this approach relies on reasonably accurate rectification. Simple arithmetics of the raw frequency, such as subtracting one sequence's count with its quality super sequence, are prone to error. First, which super sequences are quality phrases is a question itself. Second, it is context-dependent to decide whether a sequence should be deemed a whole phrase. For example, the fifth instance in Example 2 prefers 'feature vector' and 'machine learning' over 'vector machine', even though neither 'feature vector machine' nor 'vector machine learning' is a quality phrase. The context information is lost when we only collect the frequency counts.

In order to recover the true frequency with best effort, we ought to examine the context of every occurrence of each word sequence and decide whether to count it as a phrase. The examination for one occurrence may involve enumeration of alternative possibilities, such as extending the sequence or breaking the sequence, and comparison among them. The test for word sequence occurrences could be expensive, losing the advantage in efficiency of the frequent pattern mining approaches.

Facing the challenge of accuracy and efficiency, we propose a segmentation approach named *phrasal segmentation*, and integrate it with the phrase quality assessment in a unified framework with linear complexity (w.r.t the corpus size). First, the segmentation assigns every word occurrence to only one phrase. In the first instance of Example 2, 'relational database system' are bundled as a single phrase. Therefore, it automatically avoids double counting 'relational database' and 'database system' within this instance. Similarly, the segmentation of the fifth instance contributes to the count of 'feature vector' and 'machine learning' instead of 'feature', 'vector machine' and 'learning'. This strategy condenses the individual tests for each word sequence and reduces the overall complexity while ensures correctness. Second, though there are an exponential number of possible partitions of the documents, we are concerned with those relevant to the phrase extraction task only. Therefore, we can integrate the segmentation with the phrase quality assessment, such that (i) only frequent phrases with reasonable quality are taken into consideration when enumerating partitions; and (ii) the phrase quality guides the segmentation, and the segmentation rectifies the phrase quality estimation. Such an integrated framework benefits from mutual enhancement, and achieves both high quality and high efficiency. Finally, both the phrase quality and the segmentation results are useful from an application point of view. The segmentation results are especially desirable for tasks like document indexing, categorization or retrieval.

The main contributions lie in the following aspects:

- Realizing the limitation of raw frequency-based phrase mining, we propose a segmentation-integrated framework to rectify the raw frequency. To the best of our knowledge, it is the first work to integrate phrase extraction and phrasal segmentation and mutually benefit each other.
- The proposed method is scalable: both computation time and required space grow linearly as corpus size increases. It is easy to parallelize as well.
- Experimental results demonstrate that our method is efficient, generic, and highly accurate. Case studies indicate that the proposed method significantly improves applications like *interesting phrase mining* [5, 17, 28] and *relevant word/phrase search* [27].

2. RELATED WORK

2.1 Quality Phrase Mining

Automatic extraction of quality phrases (*i.e.*, multiword semantic units) from massive, dynamically growing corpora gains increasing attention due to its value in text analytics of various domains. As the origin, the NLP community has conducted extensive studies [38, 16, 30, 41, 4]. With predefined POS rules, one can generate noun phrases from each document[1]. However, such rule-based methods usually suffer

[1] http://www.nltk.org/howto/chunk.html

in domain adaptation. Supervised noun phrase chunking techniques [31, 39, 10] leverage annotated documents to automatically learn rules based on POS-tagged corpus. These supervised methods may utilize more sophisticated NLP features such as dependency parser to further enhance the precision [20, 25]. The various kinds of linguistic processing, domain-dependent language rules, and expensive human labeling make it challenging to apply to emerging big corpora.

Another kind of approaches explore frequency statistics in document collections [13, 32, 29, 12, 15]. Most of them leverage a variety of statistical measures derived from a corpus to estimate phrase quality. Therefore, they do not rely on linguistic feature generation, domain-specific rules or large training sets, and can process massive corpora efficiently. In [29], several indicators, including frequency and comparison to super/sub-sequences, were proposed to extract n-grams that are not only popular but also concise as concepts. Deane [13] proposed a heuristic metric over frequency distribution based on Zipfian ranks, to measure lexical association for phrase candidates.

Different from aforementioned methods, this work considers integrating phrasal segmentation with phrase quality estimation to further rectify the inaccurate phrase quality initially estimated, based on local occurrence context. Meanwhile, our phrase quality estimation explores statistical features using rectified phrase frequencies, which provides a principled way to refine the phrase quality assessment.

Our work is also related to *keyphrase extraction* in terms of deriving a variety of statistical measures for finding quality phrases [26, 19, 24]. However, keyphrase extraction focuses on deriving from each single document most prominent phrases, instead of from the entire corpus. In [5, 17, 28], interesting phrases can be queried efficiently for ad-hoc subsets of a corpus, while the phrases are based on simple frequent pattern mining methods.

2.2 Word Sequence Segmentation

In our solution, phrasal segmentation is integrated with phrase quality assessment, as a critical component for rectifying phrase frequency. Formally, phrasal segmentation aims to partition a sequence into disjoint subsequences each mapping to a semantic unit, *i.e.*, word or phrase. In terms of identifying semantic units, existing work includes query segmentation [36, 23], phrase chunking [37, 7, 14], and Chinese word segmentation [35, 9], following either supervised setting on labeled data, or unsupervised setting on large corpus. In [36], Tan and Pang proposed a generative model in unsupervised setting which adopted n-gram frequency from a large corpus and used expectation maximization for computing segment scores. Li *et al.* [23] leveraged query click-through data based on a bigram language model and further refined retrieval model with query segmentation.

The phrasal segmentation step in our proposed framework incorporates the estimated phrase quality as guidance on partition of sequences, which does not rely on external sources such as Wikipedia and click-through data and achieves good efficiency. It mainly serves the purpose of rectifying phrase frequencies.

3. PRELIMINARIES

This paper deals with quality phrase extraction from a large collection of documents. The input documents can be any textual word sequences with arbitrary lengths, such as articles, titles, queries, tags, memos, messages and records. A phrase is a sequence of words that appear contiguously in the text, and serves as a whole (non-composible) semantic unit in certain context of the given documents. Its raw frequency is the total count of its occurrences. There is no universally accepted definition of *phrase quality*. However, it is useful to quantify phrase quality based on certain criteria. We use a value between 0 and 1 to indicate the quality of each phrase, and specify four requirements of a good phrase, which conform with previous work.

- **Popularity:** Since many phrases are invented and adopted by people, it could change over time or occasions whether a sequence of words should be regarded as a non-composible semantic unit. When relational database was first introduced in 1970 [11], 'data base' was a simple composition of two words, and then with its gained popularity people even invented a new word 'database', clearly as a whole semantic unit. 'vector machine' is not a meaningful phrase in machine learning community, but it is a phrase in hardware design. Quality phrases should occur with sufficient frequency in a given document collection.
- **Concordance:** Concordance refers to the collocation of tokens in such frequency that is significantly higher than what is expected due to chance. A commonly-used example of a phraseological-concordance is the two candidate phrases 'strong tea' and 'powerful tea' [18]. One would assume that the two phrases appear in similar frequency, yet in the English language, the phrase 'strong tea' is considered more proper and appears in much higher frequency. Because a concordant phrase's frequency deviates from what is expected, we consider them belonging to a whole semantic unit.
- **Informativeness:** A phrase is informative if it is indicative of a specific topic. 'This paper' is a popular and concordant phrase, but not informative in research publication corpus.
- **Completeness:** Long frequent phrases and their subsets may both satisfy the above criteria. A complete phrase should be interpreted as a whole semantic unit in certain context. In the previous discussion of Example 2, the sequence 'vector machine' does not appear as a complete phrase. Note that a phrase and its subphrase can both be valid in appropriate context. For example, 'relational database system', 'relational database' and 'database system' can all be valid in certain context.

Efficiently and accurately extracting quality phrases is the main goal of this study. For generality, we allow users to provide a few examples of quality phrases and inferior ones. The estimated quality should therefore align with these labeled examples. Previous work has overlooked some of the requirements and made assumptions against them. For example, most work assumes a phrase candidate should either be included as a phrase, or excluded entirely, without analyzing the context it appears. Parameswaran *et al.* [29] assumed that if a phrase candidate with length n is a good phrase, its length $n-1$ prefix and suffix cannot be a good phrase simultaneously. We do not make such assumptions. Instead, we take a context-dependent analysis approach – phrasal segmentation.

A *phrasal segmentation* defines a partition of a sequence into subsequences, such that every subsequence corresponds to either a single word or a phrase. Example 2 shows instances of such partitions, where all phrases with high quality are marked by brackets $\lceil \rfloor$. The phrasal segmentation is distinct from word, sentence or topic segmentation tasks in natural language processing. It is also different from the syntactic or semantic parsing which relies on grammar to decompose the sentences with rich structures like parse trees. Phrasal segmentation provides the necessary granularity we need to extract quality phrases. The total count of times for a phrase to appear in the segmented corpus is called *rectified frequency*.

It is beneficial to acknowledge that a sequence's segmentation may not be unique, due to two reasons. First, as we mentioned above, a word sequence may be regarded as a phrase or not, depending on the adoption customs. Some phrases, like 'bridge the gap' in the last instance of Example 2, are subject to a user's requirement. Therefore, we seek for segmentation that accommodates the phrase quality, which is learned from user-provided examples. Second, a sequence could be ambiguous and have different interpretations. Nevertheless, in most cases, it does not require perfect segmentation, no matter if such a segmentation exists, to extract quality phrases. In a large document collection, the popularly adopted phrases appear many times in a variety of context. Even with a few mistakes or debatable partitions, a reasonably high quality segmentation (*e.g.*, yielding no partition like 'support $\lceil$vector machine$\rfloor$') would retain sufficient support (*i.e.*, rectified frequency) for these quality phrases, albeit not for false phrases with high raw frequency.

With the above discussions, we have formalizations:

Definition 1 (Phrase Quality). Phrase quality is defined to be the possibility of a multi-word sequence being a coherent semantic unit, according to the above four criteria. Given a phrase v, its phrase quality is:

$$Q(v) = p(\lceil v \rfloor | v) \in [0, 1]$$

where $\lceil v \rfloor$ refers to the event that the words in v compose a phrase. For a single word w, we define $Q(w) = 1$. For phrases, Q is to be learned from data. ■

For example, a good quality estimator is able to return Q(relational database system) ≈ 1 and Q(vector machine) ≈ 0.

Definition 2 (Phrasal Segmentation). Given a word sequence $C = w_1 w_2 \dots w_n$ of length n, a segmentation $S = s_1 s_2 \dots s_m$ for C is induced by a boundary index sequence $B = \{b_1, b_2, \dots, b_{m+1}\}$ satisfying $1 = b_1 < b_2 < \dots < b_{m+1} = n+1$, where a segment $s_t = w_{b_t} w_{b_t+1} \dots w_{b_t+|s_t|-1}$. Here $|s_t|$ refers to the number of words in segment s_t. Since $b_t + |s_t| = b_{t+1}$, for clearness we use $w_{[b_t, b_{t+1})}$ to denote word sequence $w_{b_t} w_{b_t+1} \cdots w_{b_t+|s_t|-1}$. ■

Example 3 . Continuing our previous Example 2 and specifically for the first instance, the word sequence and marked segmentation are

C = a relational database system for images

S = / a / relational database system / for / images /

with a boundary index sequence $B = \{1, 2, 5, 6, 7\}$ indicating the location of segmentation symbol /. ■

Based on these definitions, the main input of quality phrase mining task is a corpus with a small set L of labeled quality phrases and $\bar{L}$ of inferior ones. The corpus can be represented by a giant word sequence $\mathcal{C} = C_1 \dots C_D$, where C_d is the word sequence of document $d, d = 1 \dots D$. Each document can be further partitioned into smaller pieces based on different properties of the corpus, such as sentences according to punctuation. The output is a ranked list of phrases with decreasing quality, together with a segmented corpus.

4. QUALITY PHRASE MINING

We first present the full procedure of phrase mining. Then we introduce each of them in following subsections.

1. Generate frequent phrase candidates according to popularity requirement (Sec. 4.1).
2. Estimate phrase quality based on features about concordance and informativeness requirements (Sec. 4.2).
3. Estimate rectified frequency via phrasal segmentation (Sec. 4.3).
4. Add segmentation-based features derived from rectified frequency into the feature set of phrase quality classifier (Sec. 4.4). Repeat step 2 and 3.
5. Filter phrases with low rectified frequencies to satisfy the completeness requirement as post-processing step.

An complexity analysis for this framework is given at Sec 4.5 to show that both of its computation time and required space grow linearly as the corpus size increases.

4.1 Frequent Phrase Detection

Algorithm 1: Frequent Phrase Detection

Input: Corpus $\mathcal{C}$, minimum support threshold τ.
Output: Raw frequency dictionary f of frequent phrases and words.

$f \leftarrow$ an empty dictionary
index $\leftarrow$ an empty dictionary
for $i \leftarrow 1$ **to** $|\mathcal{C}|$ **do**
    index$[\mathcal{C}[i]] \leftarrow$ *index*$[\mathcal{C}[i]] \cup i$
while *index is not empty* **do**
    index' $\leftarrow$ an empty dictionary
    for $u \in$ *index.keys* **do**
        if $|$*index*$[u]| \geq \tau$ **then**
            $f[u] \leftarrow |$*index*$[u]|$
            for $j \in$ *index*$[u]$ **do**
                $u' \leftarrow u \oplus \mathcal{C}[j+1]$
                index'$[u'] \leftarrow$ *index'*$[u'] \cup \{j+1\}$
    index $\leftarrow$ *index'*
return f

The task of detecting frequent phrases can be defined as collecting aggregate counts for all phrases in a corpus that satisfy a certain minimum support threshold τ, accordding to the popularity requirement. In practice, one can also set a maximum phrase length ω to restrict the phrase length. Even if no explicit restriction is added, ω is typically a small constant. For efficiently mining these frequent phrases, we draw upon two properties:

1. Downward Closure property: If a phrase is not frequent, then any its super-phrase is guaranteed to be not frequent. Therefore, those longer phrases will be filtered and never expanded.
2. Prefix property: If a phrase is frequent, any its prefix units should be frequent too. In this way, all the frequent phrases can be generated by expanding their prefixes.

The algorithm for detecting frequent phrases is given in Alg. 1. We use $\mathcal{C}[\cdot]$ to index a word in the corpus string and $|\mathcal{C}|$ to denote the corpus size. The $\oplus$ operator is for concatecating two words or phrases. Alg. 1 returns a key-value dictionary f. Its keys are vocabulary $\mathcal{U}$ containing all frequent phrases $\mathcal{P}$, and words $\mathcal{U} \setminus \mathcal{P}$. Its values are their raw frequency.

4.2 Phrase Quality Estimation

Estimating phrase quality from only a few training labels is challenging since a huge number of phrase candidates might be generated from the first step and they are messy. Instead of using one or two statistical measures [16, 30, 15], we choose to compute multiple features for each candidate in $\mathcal{P}$. A classifier is trained on these features to predict quality Q for all unlabeled phrases. For phrases not in $\mathcal{P}$, their quality is simply 0.

We divide the features into two categories according to concordance and informativeness requirements in the following two subsections. Only representative features are introduced for clearness. We then discuss about the classifier in Sec. 4.2.3.

4.2.1 *Concordance Features*

This set of features is designed to measure concordance among sub-units of a phrase. To make phrases with different lengths comparable, we partition each phrase candidate into two disjoint parts in all possible ways and derive effective features measuring their concordance.

Suppose for each word or phrase $u \in \mathcal{U}$, we have its raw frequency $f[u]$. Its probability $p(u)$ is defined as:

$$p(u) = \frac{f[u]}{\sum_{u' \in \mathcal{U}} f[u']}$$

Given a phrase $v \in \mathcal{P}$, we split it into two most-likely sub-units $\langle u_l, u_r \rangle$ such that *pointwise mutual information* is minimized. Pointwise mutual information quantifies the discrepancy between the probability of their true collocation and the presumed collocation under independence assumption. Mathematically,

$$\langle u_l, u_r \rangle = \arg \min_{u_l \oplus u_r = v} \log \frac{p(v)}{p(u_l)p(u_r)}$$

With $\langle u_l, u_r \rangle$, we directly use the pointwise mutual information as one of the concordance features.

$$PMI(u_l, u_r) = \log \frac{p(v)}{p(u_l)p(u_r)}$$

Another feature is also from information theory, called pointwise Kullback-Leibler divergence:

$$PKL(v \| \langle u_l, u_r \rangle) = p(v) \log \frac{p(v)}{p(u_l)p(u_r)}$$

The additional $p(v)$ is multiplied with pointwise mutual information, leading to less bias towards rare-occurred phrases.

Both features are positively correlated with concordance.

4.2.2 *Informativeness Features*

Some candidates are unlikely to be informative because they are functional or stopwords. We incorporate the following stopword-based features into the classification process:

- Whether stopwords are located at the beginning or the end of the phrase candidate;

which requires a dictionary of stopwords. Phrases that begin or end with stopwords, such as 'I am', are often functional rather than informative.

A more generic feature is to measure the informativeness based on corpus statistics:

- Average inverse document frequency (IDF) computed over words;

where IDF for a word w is computed as

$$\text{IDF}(w) = \log \frac{|\mathcal{C}|}{|\{d \in [D] : w \in \mathcal{C}_d\}|}$$

It is a traditional information retrieval measure of how much information a word provides in order to retrieve a small subset of documents from a corpus. In general, quality phrases are expected to have not too small average IDF.

In addition to word-based features, punctuation is frequently used in text to aid interpretations of specific concept or idea. This information is helpful for our task. Specifically, we adopt the following feature:

- Punctuation: probabilities of a phrase in quotes, brackets or capitalized;

higher probability usually indicates more likely a phrase is informative.

Besides these features, many other signals like knowledge-base entities and part-of-speech tagging can be plugged into the feature set. They are less generic quality estimators and require more training or external resources. It is easy to incorporate these features in our framework when they are available.

4.2.3 *Classifier*

Our framework can work with arbitrary classifiers that can be effectively trained with small labeled data and output a probabilistic score between 0 and 1. For instance, we can adopt random forest [8] which is efficient to train with a small number of labels. The ratio of positive predictions among all decision trees can be interpreted as a phrase's quality estimation. In experiments we will see that 200–300 labels are enough to train a satisfactory classifier.

Just as we have mentioned, both quality phrases and inferior ones are required as labels for training. To further reduce the labeling effort, some machine learning ideas like PU-learning [22] can be applied to automatically retrieve negative labels. Active learning [33] is another popular mechanism to substantially reduce the number of labels required via iterative training. Moreover, it is possible to train a transferable model on one document collection and adapt it to the target corpus. We plan to explore these directions in future work.

Finally, it's noteworthy that in order to extract features efficiently we have designed an adapted Aho-Corasick Automaton to rapidly locate occurrences of phrases in the corpus. Please refer to the appendix for details about this part.

4.3 Phrasal Segmentation

The discussion in Example 1 points out the limitations of using only raw frequency counts. Instead, we ought to examine the context of every word sequence's occurrence and decide whether to count it as a phrase, as introduced in Example 2. The segmentation directly addresses the completeness requirement, and indirectly helps with the concordance requirement via rectified frequency. Here we propose an efficient phrasal segmentation method to compute rectified frequency of each phrase. We will see that combined with aforementioned phrase quality estimation, bad phrases with high raw frequency get removed as their rectified frequencies approach zero.

Furthermore, rectified phrase frequencies can be fed back to generate additional features and improve the phrase quality estimation. This will be discussed in the next subsection.

We now propose the phrasal segmentation model integrated with the aforementioned phrase quality Q. Given a word sequence C, and a segmentation $S = s_1 \dots s_m$ induced by boundary index sequence $B = \{b_1, \dots, b_{m+1}\}$, where $s_t = w_{[b_t, b_{t+1})}$, the joint probability is factorized as:

$$p(S, C) = \prod_{t=1}^{m} p\left(b_{t+1}, \lceil w_{[b_t, b_{t+1})} \rfloor \middle| b_t\right) \quad (1)$$

where $p(b_{t+1}, \lceil w_{[b_t,b_{t+1})} \rfloor | b_t)$ is the probability of observing a word sequence $w_{[b_t,b_{t+1})}$ as the t-th quality segment. As segments of a word sequence usually have weak dependence on each other, we assume they are generated one by one for the sake of both efficiency and simplicity.

We now describe the generative model for each segment. Given the start index b_t of a segment s_t, we first generate the end index b_{t+1}, according to a prior distribution $p(|s_t| = b_{t+1} - b_t)$ over phrase lengths. Then we generate the word sequence $w_{[b_t,b_{t+1})}$ according to a multinomial distribution over all segments of length $(b_{t+1} - b_t)$. Finally, we generate an indicator whether $w_{[b_t,b_{t+1})}$ forms a quality segment according to its quality $p(\lceil w_{[b_t,b_{t+1}} \rfloor | w_{[b_t,b_{t+1})}) = Q(w_{[b_t,b_{t+1})})$. We formulate its probabilistic factorization as follows:

$$p(b_{t+1}, \lceil w_{[b_t,b_{t+1})} \rfloor | b_t) = p(b_{t+1}|b_t) p(\lceil w_{[b_t,b_{t+1})} \rfloor | b_t, b_{t+1})$$
$$= p\Big(b_{t+1} - b_t\Big) p\Big(w_{[b_t,b_{t+1})} \Big| |s_t| = b_{t+1} - b_t\Big) Q(w_{[b_t,b_{t+1})})$$

The length prior $p(|s_t| = b_{t+1} - b_t)$ is explicitly modeled to counter the bias to longer segments as they result in fewer segments. The particular form of $p(|s_t|)$ we pick is:

$$p(|s_t|) \propto \alpha^{1-|s_t|} \quad (2)$$

Here $\alpha \in R^+$ is a factor called *segment length penalty.* If $\alpha < 1$, phrases with longer length have larger value of $p(|s_t|)$. If $\alpha > 1$, the mass of $p(|s_t|)$ moves towards shorter phrases. Smaller α favors longer phrases and results in fewer segments. Tuning its value turns out to be a trade-off between precision and recall for recognizing quality phrases. At the end of this subsection we will discuss how to estimate its value by reusing labels in Sec. 4.2. It is worth mentioning that such segment length penalty is also discussed by Li *et al.* [23]. Our formulation differs from theirs by posing a weaker penalty on long phrases.

We denote $p(w_{[b_t,b_{t+1})} \Big| |s_t|)$ with $\theta_{w_{[b_t,b_{t+1})}}$ for convenience. For a given corpus $\mathcal{C}$ with D documents, we need to estimate $\theta_u = p(u \Big| |u|)$ for each frequent word and phrase $u \in \mathcal{U}$, and infer segmentation S. We employ the maximum a posteriori principle and maximize the joint probability of the corpus:

$$\sum_{d=1}^{D} \log p(S_d, C_d) = \sum_{d=1}^{D} \sum_{t=1}^{m_d} \log p\left(b_{t+1}^{(d)}, \lceil w_{[b_t,b_{t+1}}^{(d)} \rfloor \middle| b_t^{(d)}\right) \quad (3)$$

Algorithm 2: Dynamic Programming (DP)

Input: Word sequence $C = w_1 w_2 \dots w_n$, phrase quality Q, normalized frequency θ, segment length penalty α.
Output: Optimal segmentation S.
$h_0 \leftarrow 1,\ h_i \leftarrow 0\ (0 < i \le n)$
denote ω as the maximum phrase length
for $i = 1$ *to* n **do**
  for $\delta = 1$ *to* ω **do**
    if $h_i \cdot p(b_{t+1} = b_t + \delta, \lceil w_{[i+1,i+\delta+1)} \rfloor \Big| b_t) > h_{i+\delta}$ **then**
      $h_{i+\delta} \leftarrow h_i \cdot p(b_{t+1} = b_t + \delta, \lceil w_{[i+1,i+\delta+1)} \rfloor \Big| b_t)$
      $g_{i+\delta} \leftarrow i$
$i \leftarrow n$
$m \leftarrow 0$
while $i > 0$ **do**
  $m \leftarrow m + 1$
  $s_m \leftarrow w_{g_i+1} w_{g_i+2} \dots w_i$
  $i \leftarrow g_i$
return $S \leftarrow s_m s_{m-1} \dots s_1$

Algorithm 3: Viterbi Training (VT)

Input: Corpus $\mathcal{C}$, phrase quality Q, length penalty α.
Output: θ.
initialize θ with normalized raw frequencies in the corpus
while *not converge* **do**
  $\theta'_u \leftarrow 0,\ \forall\ u \in \mathcal{U}$
  for $d = 1$ *to* D **do**
    $S_d \leftarrow DP(C_d, Q, \theta, \alpha)$ via Alg. 2
    assume $S_d = s_1^{(d)} \cdots s_m^{(d)}$
    for $t = 1$ *to* m **do**
      $u \leftarrow w_{[b_t,b_{t+1})}^{(d)}$
      $\theta'_u \leftarrow \theta'_u + 1$
  normalize θ' w.r.t. different length as in Eq. (4)
  $\theta \leftarrow \theta'$
return θ

To find the best segmentation to maximize Eq. (3), one can use efficient dynamic programming (DP) if θ is known. The algorithm is shown in Alg. 2.

To learn θ, we employ an optimization strategy called Viterbi Training (VT) or Hard-EM in the literature [3]. Generally speaking, VT is an efficient and iterative way of parameter learning for probabilistic models with hidden variables. In our case, given corpus $\mathcal{C}$, it searches for a segmentation that maximizes $p(\mathcal{S}, \mathcal{C}|Q, \theta, \alpha)$ followed by coordinate ascent on parameters θ. Such a procedure is iterated until a stationary point has been reached. The corresponding algorithm is given in Alg. 3.

The hard E-step is performed by DP with θ fixed, and the M-step is based on the segmentation obtained from DP. Once the segmentation S is fixed, the closed-form solution of θ_u can be derived as:

$$\theta_u = \frac{\sum_{d=1}^{D} \sum_{t=1}^{m_d} \mathbb{1}_{s_t^{(d)} = u}}{\sum_{d=1}^{D} \sum_{t=1}^{m_d} \mathbb{1}_{|s_t^{(d)}| = |u|}} \quad (4)$$

where $\mathbb{1}$ denotes the identity indicator. We can see that θ_u is the rectified frequency of u normalized by the total

Table 2: Effects of segmentation feedback on phrase quality estimation

phrase	quality before feedback	quality after feedback	problem fixed by feedback
np hard in the strong sense	0.78	0.93	slight underestimate
np hard in the strong	0.70	0.23	overestimate
false positives and false negatives	0.90	0.97	N/A
positives and false negatives	0.87	0.29	overestimate
data base management system	0.60	0.82	underestimate
data stream management system	0.26	0.64	underestimate

Algorithm 4: Penalty Learning

```
Input: Corpus C, labeled quality phrases L, phrase
quality Q, non-segmented ratio r_0.
Output: Desired segment length penalty α.
up ← 200, low ← 0
while not converge do
    α ← (up + low)/2
    θ ← VT(C, Q, α) via Alg. 3
    r ← r_0 × |L|
    for i = 1 to |L| do
        S ← DP(L_i, Q, θ, α) via Alg. 2
        if |S| = 1 then
            r ← r − 1
    if r ≥ 0 then
        up ← α
    else
        low ← α
return (up + low)/2
```

frequencies of the segments with length $|u|$. For this reason, we name θ *normalized rectified frequency*.

Note that Soft-EM (*i.e.*, Bawm-Welch algorithm [6]) can also be applied to find a maximum likelihood estimator of θ. Nevertheless, VT is more suitable in our case because:

1. VT uses DP for the segmentation step, which is significantly faster than Bawm-Welch using forward-backward algorithm for the E-step;
2. Majority of the phrases get removed as their θ approaches 0 during iterations, which further speeds up our algorithm.

It has also been reported in [3] that VT converges faster and results in sparser and simpler models for Hidden Markov Model-like tasks. Meanwhile, VT is capable of correctly recovering most of the parameters.

Previously in Eq. (2) we have defined the formula of segment length penalty. There is a hyper-parameter α that needs to be determined outside the VT iterations. An overestimate α will segment quality phrases into shorter parts, while an underestimate of α tends to keep low-quality phrases. Thus an appropriate α reflects the user's trade-off between precision and recall. To judge what α value is reasonable, we propose to reuse the labeled phrases used in the phrase quality estimation. Specifically, we try to search for the maximum value of α such that VT does not segment positive phrases. A parameter r_0 named *non-segmented ratio* controls the trade-off mentioned above. It is the expected ratio of phrases in L not partitioned by dynamic programming. The detailed searching process is described in Alg. 4 where we initially set upper and lower bounds of α and then perform a binary search. In Alg. 4, $|S|$ denotes the number of segments in S and $|L|$ refers to the number of positive labels.

4.4 Feedback as Segmentation Features

Rectified frequencies can help refine the feature generation process in Sec. 4.2 and improve the quality assessment. The motivation behind this feedback idea is explained with the examples shown in Table 2. 'Quality before feedback' listed in the table is computed based on phrase quality estimation introduced in Sec. 4.2. For example, the quality of 'np hard in the strong' is significantly overestimated according to the raw frequency. Once we correctly segment the documents, its frequency will be largely reduced, and we can use it to guide the quality estimator. For another example, The quality of phrases like 'data stream management system' were originally underestimated due to its relatively lower frequency and smaller concordance feature values. Suppose after the segmentation, this phrase is not broken into smaller units in most cases. Then we can feed that information back to the quality estimator and boost the score.

Based on this intuition, we design two new features named *segmentation features* and plug them into the feature set introduced in Sec. 4.2. Given a phrase $v \in \mathcal{P}$, these two segmentation features are defined as:

$$\log \frac{p(S,v)|_{|S|=1}}{\max_{|S|>1} p(S,v)}$$

$$p(S,v)|_{|S|=1} \log \frac{p(S,v)|_{|S|=1}}{\max_{|S|>1} p(S,v)}$$

where $p(S,v)$ is computed by Eq. (1). Instead of splitting a phrase into two parts like the concordance features, we now find the best segmentation with dynamic programming introduced in the phrasal segmentation, which better models the concordance criterion. In addition, normalized rectified frequencies are used to compute these new features. This addresses the context-dependent completeness requirements. As a result, misclassified phrase candidates in the above example can get mostly corrected after retraining the classifier, as shown in Table 2.

A better phrase quality estimator can guide a better segmentation as well. In this way, the loop between the quality estimation and phrasal segmentation is closed and such an integrated framework is expected to leverage mutual enhancement and address all the four phrase quality requirements organically.

Note that we do not need to run quality estimation and phrasal segmentation for many iterations. In our experiments, the benefits brought by rectified frequency can penetrate after the first iteration, leaving performance curves over the next several iterations similar. It will be shown in the appendix.

4.5 Complexity Analysis

Frequent Phrases Detection: Since the operation of Hash table is $\mathcal{O}(1)$, both the time and space complexities are

$\mathcal{O}(\omega|\mathcal{C}|)$. ω is a small constant indicating the maximum phrase length, so this step is linear to the size of corpus $|\mathcal{C}|$.

Feature Extraction: When extracting features, the most challenging problem is how to efficiently locate these phrase candidates in the original corpus, because the original texts are crucial for finding the punctuation and capitalization information. Instead of using some dictionaries to store all the occurrences, we take the advantage of the Aho-Corasick Automaton algorithm and tailor it to find all the occurrences of phrase candidates (some prefix issues are addressed by the adapted version in the appendix). The time complexity is $\mathcal{O}(|\mathcal{C}|+|\mathcal{P}|)$ and space complexity $\mathcal{O}(|\mathcal{P}|)$, where $|\mathcal{P}|$ refers to the total number of frequent phrase candidates. As the length of each candidate is limited by a constant ω, $\mathcal{O}(|\mathcal{P}|) = \mathcal{O}(|\mathcal{C}|)$, so the complexity is $\mathcal{O}(|\mathcal{C}|)$ in both time and space.

Phrase Quality Estimation: As we only labeled a very small set of phrase candidates, as long as the number and depth of decision trees in the random forest are some constant, the training time for the classifier is very small compared to other parts. For the prediction stage, it is proportional to the size of phrase candidates and the dimensions of features. Therefore, it could be $\mathcal{O}(|\mathcal{C}|)$ in both time and space, although the actual magnitude might be smaller.

Viterbi Training: It is easy to observe that Alg. 2 is $\mathcal{O}(n\omega)$, which is linear to the number of words. ω is treated as a constant, and thus the VT process is also $\mathcal{O}(|\mathcal{C}|)$ considering Alg. 3 ususally finishes in a few iterations.

Penalty Learning: Suppose we only require a constant ϵ to check the convergence of the binary search. Then after $log_2 \frac{200}{\epsilon}$ rounds, the algorithm converges. So the number of loops could be treated as a constant. Because VT takes $\mathcal{O}(|\mathcal{C}|)$ time, Penalty learning also takes $\mathcal{O}(|\mathcal{C}|)$ time.

Summary. Because the time and space complexities of all components in our framework are $O(|\mathcal{C}|)$, our proposed framework has a linear time and space complexities and is thus very efficient. Furthermore, the most time consuming parts, including penalty learning and VT, could be easily parallelized because of the nature of independence between documents and sentences.

5. EXPERIMENTAL STUDY

In this section, experiments demonstrate the effectiveness and efficiency of the proposed methods in mining quality phrases and generating accurate segmentation. More complete experiments regarding parameter selection and case studies are reported in the appendix. We begin with the description of datasets.

5.1 Datasets

Two real-world data sets were used in the experiments and detailed statistics are summarized in Table 3.

- The **Academia** dataset[2] is a collection of major computer science journals and proceedings. We use both titles and abstracts in our experiments.
- The **Yelp** dataset[3] provides reviews of 250 businesses. Each individual review is considered as a document.

[2] http://arnetminer.org/citation

[3] https://www.yelp.com/academic_dataset

Table 3: Statistics about datasets

dataset	#docs	#words	#labels
Academia	2.77M	91.6M	300
Yelp	4.75M	145.1M	300

5.2 Compared Methods

To demonstrate the effectiveness of the proposed approach, we compared the following phrase extraction methods.

- **TF-IDF** ranks phrases by the product of their raw frequencies and inverse document frequencies;
- **C-Value** proposes a ranking measure based on frequencies of a phrase used as parts of their super-phrases following a top-down scheme;
- **ConExtr** approaches phrase extraction as a market-baskets problem based on an assumption about relationship between n-gram and prefix/suffix $(n-1)$-gram;
- **KEA**[4] is a supervised keyphrase extraction method for long documents. To apply this method in our setting, we consider the whole corpus as a single document;
- **TopMine**[5] is a topical phrase extraction method. We use its phrase mining module for comparison;
- **ClassPhrase** ranks phrases based on their estimated qualities (removing step 3–5 from our framework);
- **SegPhrase** combines ClassPhrase with phrasal segmentation to filter overestimated phrases based on normalized rectified frequency (removing step 4 from our framework);
- **SegPhrase+** is similar to SegPhrase but adds segmentation features to refine quality estimation. It contains the full procedures presented in Sec. 4.

The first two methods utilize NLP chunking to obtain phrase candidates. We use the JATE[6] implementation of the first two methods, *i.e.*, TF-IDF and C-Value. Both of them rely on OpenNLP[7] as the linguistic processor to detect phrase candidates in the corpus. The rest methods are all based on frequent n-grams and the runtime is dramatically reduced. The last three methods are variations of our proposed method.

It is also worth mentioning that JATE contains several more implemented methods including Weirdness [1]. They are not reported here due to their unsatisfactory performance compared to the baselines listed above.

5.3 Experimental Setting

We set minimum phrase support τ as 30 and maximum phrase length ω as 6, which are two parameters required by all methods. Other parameters required by baselines were set according to the open source tools or the original papers.

For our proposed methods, training labels for phrases were collected by sampling representative phrase candidates from groups of phrases pre-clustered on the normalized feature space by k-means. We labeled research areas, tasks, algorithms and other scientific terms in the Academia dataset as quality phrases. Some examples are 'divide and conquer', 'np complete' and 'relational database'. For the Yelp dataset, restaurants, dishes, cities and other related concepts are

[4] https://code.google.com/p/kea-algorithm

[5] http://web.engr.illinois.edu/~elkishk2/

[6] https://code.google.com/p/jatetoolkit

[7] http://opennlp.apache.org

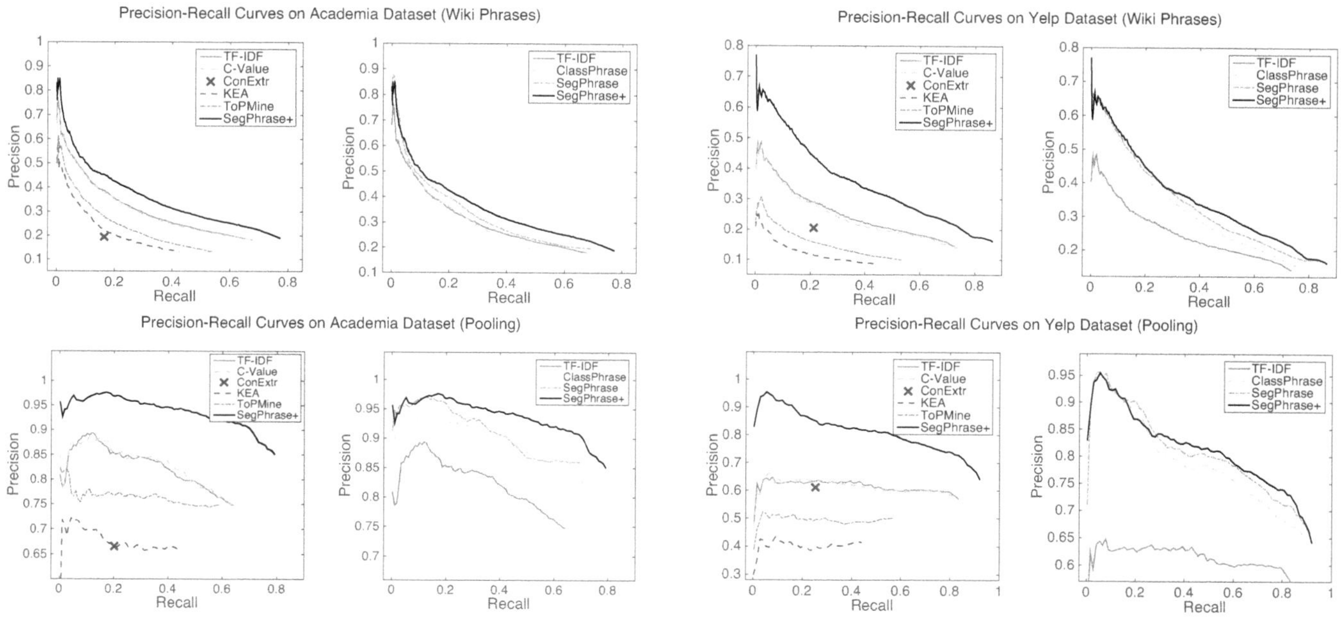

Figure 1: Precision-recall in 4 groups of experiments: (Academia, Yelp) × (Wiki phrase, pooling). Within each group, two figures are shown on par: the left compares SegPhrase+ with existing methods, and the right compares among the 3 proposed methods in this paper together with TF-IDF baseline

labeled to be positive. In contrast, phrases like 'under certain assumptions', 'many restaurants' and 'last night' were labeled as negative. We down-sample low quality phrases because they are dominant over quality phrases. The number of training labels in our experiments are reported in Table 3. To automatically learn the value of segment length penalty, we set the non-segmented ratio r_0 in Alg. 4 as 1.0 for Academia dataset and 0.95 for Yelp dataset. The selection of this parameter will be discussed in detail later in this section.

To make outputs returned by different methods comparable, we converted all the phrase candidates to lower case and merged plural with singular phrases. The phrase lists generated by these methods have different size, and the tail of the lists are low quality. For the simplicity of comparison, we discarded low-ranked phrases based on the minimum size among all phrase lists except ConExtr. ConExtr returns all phrases without ranking. Thus we did not remove its phrases. The remaining size of each list is still reasonably large (> 40,000).

5.4 Evaluation

The goal of our experiments is to study how well our methods perform in terms of "precision" and "recall" and compare with baselines. Precision is defined as the number of quality phrases divided by the number of phrase candidates. Recall is defined as the number of quality phrases divided by the total number of quality phrases.

Wiki Phrases: The first set of experiments were conducted by using Wikipedia phrases as ground truth labels. Wiki phrases refer to popular mentions of entities by crawling intra-Wiki citations within Wiki content. To compute precision, only the Wiki phrases are considered to be positive. For recall, we combine Wiki phrases returned by different methods altogether and view them as all quality phrases. Precision and recall are biased in this case because positive labels are restricted to Wiki phrases. However, we still expect to obtain meaningful insights regarding the performance difference between the proposed and baselines.

Pooling: Besides Wiki phrases, we rely on human evaluators to judge whether the rest of the candidates are good. We randomly sampled k Wiki-uncovered phrases from the returned candidates of each method mentioned at Sec. 5.2. These sampled phrases formed a pool and each of them was then evaluated by 3 reviewers independently. The reviewers could use a popular search engine for the candidates (thus helping reviewers judge the quality of phrases that they were not familiar with). We took the majority of the opinions and used these results to evaluate the methods on how precise the returned quality phrases are. Throughout the experiments we set $k = 500$.

5.5 Results

Precision-recall curves of different methods evaluated by both Wiki phrases and pooling phrases are shown in Fig. 1. The trends on both datasets are similar.

Among the existing work, the chunking-based methods, such as TF-IDF and C-Value, have the best performance; ConExtr reduces to a dot in the figure since its output does not provide the ranking information. Our proposed method, SegPhrase+, outperforms them significantly. More specifically, SegPhrase+ can achieve a higher recall while its precision is maintained at a satisfactory level. That is, many more quality phrases can be found by SegPhrase+ than baselines. Under a given recall, precision of our method is higher in most of the time.

For variant methods within our framework, it is surprising that ClassPhrase could perform competitively to the chunking-based methods like TF-IDF. Note that the latter requires large amounts of pre-training for good phrase chunking. However, ClassPhrase's precision at the tail is slightly worse than TF-IDF on Academia dataset evaluated by Wiki phrases. We also observe a significant difference between

SegPhrase and ClassPhrase, indicating phrasal segmentation plays a crucial role to address the completeness requirement. In fact, SegPhrase already beats ClassPhrase and baselines. Moreover, SegPhrase+ improves the performance of SegPhrase, because of the use of phrasal segmentation results as additional features.

An interesting observation is that the advantage of our method is more significant on the pooling evaluations. The phrases in the pool are not covered by Wiki, indicating that Wikipedia is not a complete source of quality phrases. However, our proposed methods, including SegPhrase+, SegPhrase, and ClassPhrase, can mine out most of them (more than 80%) and keep a very high level of precision, especially on the Academia dataset. Therefore, the evaluation results on the pooling phrases suggest that our methods not only detect the well-known Wiki phrases, but also work properly for the long tail phrases which might occur not so frequently.

From the result on Yelp dataset evaluated by pooling phrases, we notice that SegPhrase+ is a little weaker than SegPhrase at the head. As we know, SegPhrase+ has tried to utilize phrasal segmentation results from SegPhrase to refine the phrase quality estimator. However, segmentation features do not add new information for bigrams. If there are not many quality phrases with more than two words, SegPhrase+ might not have significant improvement and even can perform slightly worse due to the overfitting problem by reusing the same set of labeled phrases. This overfitting problem has been verified in the appendix regarding the iterative SegPhrase+ experiments. In fact, on Academia dataset, the ratios of quality phrases with more than 2 words are 24% among all Wiki phrases and 17% among pooling phrases. In contrast, these statistics go down to to 13% and 10% on Yelp dataset, which verifies our conjecture and explains why SegPhrase+ has slightly lower precision than SegPhrase at the head.

5.6 Model Selection

The goal of model selection is to study how well our methods perform in terms of "precision" and "recall" on various candidate models with different parameters. We specifically want to study two potentially interesting questions:

- How many labels do we need to achieve good results of phrase quality estimation?
- How to choose non-segmented ratio r_0 for deciding segment length penalty?

Experiments for other parameters are provided in the appendix due to the space limit.

5.6.1 Number of Labels

To evaluate the impact of training data size on the phrase quality estimation, we focus on studying the classification performance of ClassPhrase. Table 4 shows the results evaluated among phrases with positive predictions (*i.e.*, $\{v \in \mathcal{P} : Q_v \geq 0.5\}$). With different numbers of labels, we report the precision, recall and F1 score judged by human evaluators (Pooling). The number of correctly predicted Wiki phrases is also provided together with the total number of positive phrases predicted by the classifier. From these results, we observe that the performance of the classifier becomes better as the number of labels increases. Specifically, on both datasets, the recall rises up as the number of labels increases, while the precision goes down. The reason is the down-sampling of low quality phrases in the training data. Overall, the F1 score is monotonically increasing, which indicates that more labels may result in better performance. 300 labels are enough to train a satisfactory classifier.

Table 4: Impact of training data size on ClassPhrase (Top: Academia, Bottom: Yelp)

#labels	prec.	recall	f1	#wiki phr.	#total
50	0.881	0.372	0.523	6,179	24,603
100	0.859	0.430	0.573	6,834	30,234
200	0.856	0.558	0.676	8,196	40,355
300	0.760	0.811	0.785	11,535	95,070

#labels	prec.	recall	f1	#wiki phr.	#total
50	0.948	0.491	0.647	6,985	79,091
100	0.948	0.540	0.688	6,692	57,018
200	0.948	0.554	0.700	6,786	53,613
300	0.944	0.559	0.702	6,777	53,442

5.6.2 Non-segmented Ratio

The non-segmented ratio r_0 is designed for learning segment length penalty, which further controls the precision and recall phrasal segmentation. Empirically, under higher r_0, the segmentation process will favor longer phrases, and vice versa. We show experimental results in Table 5 for models with different values of r_0. The evaluation measures are similar to the previous setting but they are computed based on the results of SegPhrase. One can observe that the precision increases with lower r_0, while the recall decreases. It is because phrases are more likely to be segmented into words by lower r_0. High r_0 is generally preferred because we should preserve most positive phrases in training data. We select $r_0 = 1.00$ and 0.95 for Academia and Yelp datasets respectively, because quality phrases are shorter in Yelp dataset than in Academia dataset.

Table 5: Impact of non-segmented ratio r_0 on SegPhrase (Top: Academia, Bottom: Yelp)

r_0	prec.	recall	f1	#wiki phr.	#total
1.00	0.816	0.756	0.785	10,607	57,668
0.95	0.909	0.625	0.741	9,226	43,554
0.90	0.949	0.457	0.617	7,262	30,550
0.85	0.948	0.422	0.584	7,107	29,826
0.80	0.944	0.364	0.525	6,208	25,374

r_0	prec.	recall	f1	#wiki phr.	#total
1.00	0.606	0.948	0.739	7,155	48,684
0.95	0.631	0.921	0.749	6,916	42,933
0.90	0.673	0.846	0.749	6,467	34,632
0.85	0.714	0.766	0.739	5,947	28,462
0.80	0.725	0.728	0.727	5,729	26,245

5.7 Computational Complexity Study

The following execution time experiments were all conducted on a machine with 20 cores of Intel(R) Xeon(R) CPU E5-2680 v2 @ 2.80GHz. Our framework is mainly implemented in C++ while a small part of preprocessing is in Python. As shown in Fig. 3, the linear curves of total runtime of SegPhrase+ on different proportions of data verifies our linear time complexity analyzed in Sec. 4.5.

dataset	file size	#words	time
Academia	613MB	91.6M	0.595h
Yelp	750MB	145.1M	0.917h

Besides, the pies in Fig. 4 show the ratios of different components of our framework. One can observe that Feature Extraction and Phrasal Segmentation occupy most of the runtime. Fortunately, almost all components of our frameworks can be parallelized, such as Feature Extraction, Phrasal Segmentation and Quality Estimation, which are the most expensive parts of execution time. It is because sentences can be proceeded one by one without any impact on each other. Therefore, our methods could be very efficient for massive corpus using parallel and distributed techniques. Here we do not compare the runtime with other baselines because they are implemented by different programming languages and some of them further rely on various third-party packages. Among existing implementations, our method is empirically one of the fastest.

5.8 Feature Contribution

We conducted experiments to show the contributions of different features in the classifier of SegPhrase+ in Fig. 2. Feature contributions are determined by aggregating mean squared errors for nodes in decision trees of the random forest classifier. Generally speaking, we can observe that the contributions of features in different aspects vary for two datasets. As the Yelp dataset is noisier and less formal compared to the Academia dataset, the stopword and IDF features are more important in Yelp, whereas the concordance and segmentation features are more important in Academia. Also, due to the subjectivity in Yelp review data, its punctuation feature is less significant. Fig. 2 indicates that supervision is necessary for phrase quality assessment. Meanwhile, it suggests our proposed criteria for judging phrase quality is reasonable since each feature can be a strong signal of the final phrase quality in certain datasets.

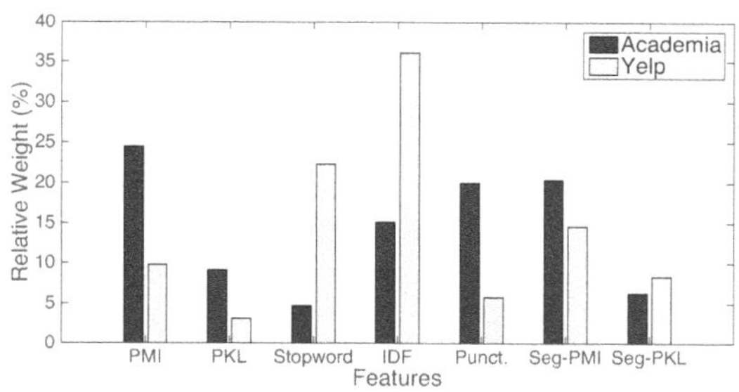

Figure 2: Contributions of features for phrase quality estimation of SegPhrase+

5.9 Case Study

Previous experiments are focused on evaluating phrase quality quantitatively. In this subsection, we show two case studies based on applications taking segmented corpora as input. Recall that the segmented corpus is the other output of the proposed phrase mining framework. In the appendix, we provide a fraction of the ranked phrase list produced by our framework.

5.9.1 *Interesting Phrase Mining*

The first application is to mine interesting phrases in a subset of given corpus. Interesting phrases are defined to be phrases frequent in the subset $\mathcal{C}'$ but relatively infrequent in the overall corpus $\mathcal{C}$ [5, 17, 28]. Given a phrase v, its interestingness is measured by $freq(v, \mathcal{C}') \cdot purity(v, \mathcal{C}', \mathcal{C}) = freq(v, \mathcal{C}')^2 / freq(v, \mathcal{C})$, which considers both phrase frequency and purity in the subset.

We list a fraction of interesting phrases in Table 6 mined from papers published in SIGMOD and SIGKDD conferences. Each series of proceedings form a subset of the whole Academia corpus. Two segmentation methods are compared. The first one relies on dynamic programming using phrase quality estimated by SegPhrase+. The other is based on the phrase chunking method adopted in JATE, which is further used to detect phrase candidates for TF-IDF and C-Value methods. To be fair, we only show phrases extracted by SegPhrase+, TF-IDF and C-Value methods in the table. Because TF-IDF and C-Value perform similarly and they both rely on the chunking method, we merge their phrases and report mining results in one column named 'Chunking'. Phrases in SegPhrase+ but missing in the chunking results are highlighted in purple (red vice versa). One can observe that the interesting phrases mined by SegPhrase+ based on the segmentation result are more meaningful and the improvement is significant. Relatively speaking, phrases mined from the chunking method are of inferior quality. Therefore, many of them are not covered by SegPhrase+. For more experimental results regarding this application, readers can refer to the appendix.

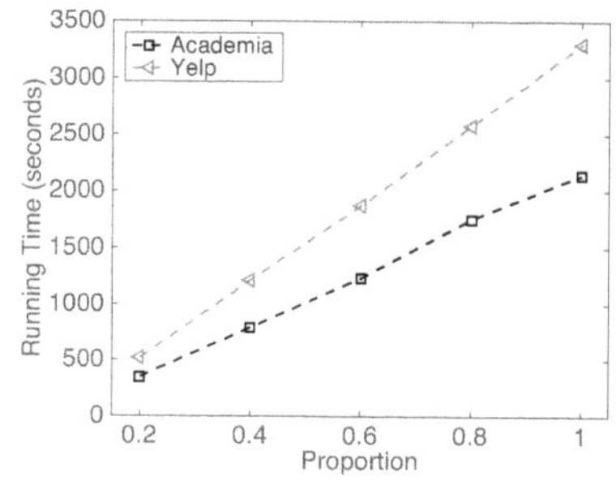

Figure 3: Runtime on different proportions of data

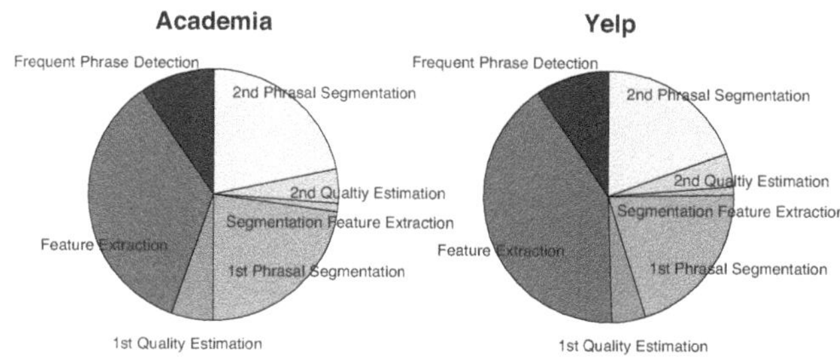

Figure 4: Runtime of different modules in our framework on Academia and Yelp dataset

5.9.2 *Word/Phrase Similarity Search*

With a segmented corpus, one could train a model to learn *distributed vector representations* of words and phrases [27]. Using this technique, words and phrases are mapped into a vector space such that semantically similar words and phrases have similar vector representations. It helps other text mining algorithms to achieve better performance by grouping similar units. The quality of the learned vector representation is closely related to the quality of the input segmented corpus. Accurate segmentation results in good vector representation and this performance gain is usually evaluated by comparing similarity scores between word/phrase pairs. To be specific, one could compute top-k similar words or phrases given a query and compare the ranked lists. We use this to verify the utility of both quality phrase mining and quality segmentation.

Table 6: Interesting phrases mined from papers published in SIGMOD and SIGKDD conferences

Conference	SIGMOD		SIGKDD	
Method	SegPhrase+	Chunking	SegPhrase+	Chunking
1	data base	data base	data mining	data mining
2	database system	database system	data set	association rule
3	relational database	query processing	association rule	knowledge discovery
4	query optimization	query optimization	knowledge discovery	frequent itemset
5	query processing	relational database	time series	decision tree
...	...	...	...	...
51	sql server	database technology	association rule mining	search space
52	relational data	database server	rule set	domain knowledge
53	data structure	large volume	concept drift	important problem
54	join query	performance study	knowledge acquisition	concurrency control
55	web service	web service	gene expression data	conceptual graph
...	...	...	...	...
201	high dimensional data	efficient implementation	web content	optimal solution
202	location based service	sensor network	frequent subgraph	semantic relationship
203	xml schema	large collection	intrusion detection	effective way
204	two phase locking	important issue	categorical attribute	space complexity
205	deep web	frequent itemset	user preference	small set
...	...	...	...	...

Table 7: Top-5 similar words or phrases for representative queries (Top: Academia, Bottom: Yelp)

Query	data mining		olap	
Method	SegPhrase+	Chunking	SegPhrase+	Chunking
1	knowledge discovery	driven methodologies	data warehouse	warehouses
2	text mining	text mining	online analytical processing	clustcube
3	web mining	financial investment	data cube	rolap
4	machine learning	knowledge discovery	olap queries	online analytical processing
5	data mining techniques	building knowledge	multidimensional databases	analytical processing

Query	blu-ray		noodle		valet parking	
Method	SegPhrase+	Chunking	SegPhrase+	Chunking	SegPhrase+	Chunking
1	dvd	new microwave	ramen	noodle soup	valet	huge lot
2	vhs	lifetime warranty	noodle soup	asian noodle	self-parking	private lot
3	cd	recliner	rice noodle	beef noodle	valet service	self-parking
4	new release	battery	egg noodle	stir fry	free valet parking	valet
5	sony	new battery	pasta	fish ball	covered parking	front lot

We show the results in Table 7 from SegPhrase+ and the chunking method mentioned in the previous interesting phrase mining application. Queries were chosen to be capable of showing the difference between the two methods for both Academia and Yelp datasets. Distributed representations were learned through an existing tool [27] and ranking scores were computed based on cosine similarity. Additional comparisons are provided in the appendix.

From the table, one can easily tell that the rank list from SegPhrase+ carries more sense than that from phrase chunking. One of the possible reasons is that chunking method only detects noun phrases in the corpus, providing less accurate information of phrase occurrences than SegPhrase+ to the vector representation learning algorithm.

6. CONCLUSIONS

In this paper, we introduced a novel framework for extracting quality phrases from text corpora. The framework is data-driven and requires only limited training to achieve outstanding performance. The key idea is to rectify the raw frequency of phrases which misleads quality estimation. We develop a segmentation-integrated approach for this purpose, which significantly boosts the final quality of extracted phrases. It is the first work to explore the mutual benefit of phrase extraction and phrasal segmentation. By intergrating them, this work addresses a fundamental limitation of phrase mining and empowers widespread applications. Meanwhile, the method is scalable: both computation time and required space grow linearly as corpus size increases.

A number of open problems need to be solved to allow further development of the proposed phrase mining framework. One direction is to investigate reducing the number of training labels. The current framework requires the model to be trained by 300 labeled phrases. It would be preferable if a transferable model can be pretrained on general document collection and adapt itself to the target corpus. An alternative is to use a domain-independent phrase collection as the training source. Overlapped phrases are first identified and then used to serve as the positive labels. Another direction is to replace Viterbi Training by other parameter estimation approaches to further improve the phrasal segmentation. For instance, one can find top-k best segmentations instead of one for each text snippet. This is less deterministic than the current design but consumes more computational power. Finally, it is now possible to reconsider many text data management problems with this technique. For example, text can be represented by bag of phrases instead of words. The best way to exploit this representation is open for exploration.

7. ACKNOWLEDGEMENTS

Research was sponsored in part by the U.S. Army Research Lab. under Cooperative Agreement No. W911NF-09-2-0053 (NSCTA), the Army Research Office under Cooperative Agreement No. W911NF-13-1-0193, National Science Foundation IIS-1017362, IIS-1320617, and IIS-1354329, HDTRA1-10-1-0120, trans-NIH Big Data to Knowledge (BD2K) initiative grant 1U54GM114838 awarded by NIGMS, and MIAS, a DHS-IDS Center for Multimodal Information Access and Synthesis at UIUC.

References

[1] K. Ahmad, L. Gillam, and L. Tostevin. University of surrey participation in trec8: Weirdness indexing for logical document extrapolation and retrieval (wilder). In *The Eighth Text REtrieval Conference (TREC-8)*, Gaithersburg, Maryland.

[2] H. Ahonen. Knowledge discovery in documents by extracting frequent word sequences. *Library Trends*, 48(1), 1999.

[3] A. Allahverdyan and A. Galstyan. Comparative analysis of viterbi training and maximum likelihood estimation for hmms. In *NIPS*, pages 1674–1682, 2011.

[4] T. Baldwin and S. N. Kim. Multiword expressions. *Handbook of Natural Language Processing, second edition. Morgan and Claypool*, 2010.

[5] S. Bedathur, K. Berberich, J. Dittrich, N. Mamoulis, and G. Weikum. Interesting-phrase mining for ad-hoc text analytics. *VLDB*, 3(1-2):1348–1357, 2010.

[6] C. M. Bishop. *Pattern recognition and machine learning*, volume 1. springer New York, 2006.

[7] G. Blackwood, A. De Gispert, and W. Byrne. Phrasal segmentation models for statistical machine translation. In *COLING*, 2008.

[8] L. Breiman. Random forests. *Machine learning*, 45(1):5–32, 2001.

[9] P.-C. Chang, M. Galley, and C. D. Manning. Optimizing chinese word segmentation for machine translation performance. In *ACL Workshop on Statistical Machine Translation*, 2008.

[10] K.-h. Chen and H.-H. Chen. Extracting noun phrases from large-scale texts: A hybrid approach and its automatic evaluation. In *ACL*, 1994.

[11] E. F. Codd. A Relational Model for Large Shared Data Banks. *Communications of The ACM*, 13:377–387, 1970.

[12] M. Danilevsky, C. Wang, N. Desai, X. Ren, J. Guo, and J. Han. Automatic construction and ranking of topical keyphrases on collections of short documents. In *SDM*, 2014.

[13] P. Deane. A nonparametric method for extraction of candidate phrasal terms. In *ACL*, 2005.

[14] H. Echizen-ya and K. Araki. Automatic evaluation method for machine translation using noun-phrase chunking. In *ACL*, 2010.

[15] A. El-Kishky, Y. Song, C. Wang, C. R. Voss, and J. Han. Scalable topical phrase mining from text corpora. *VLDB*, 8(3), Aug. 2015.

[16] K. Frantzi, S. Ananiadou, and H. Mima. Automatic recognition of multi-word terms:. the c-value/nc-value method. *JODL*, 3(2):115–130, 2000.

[17] C. Gao and S. Michel. Top-k interesting phrase mining in ad-hoc collections using sequence pattern indexing. In *EDBT*, 2012.

[18] M. A. Halliday. Lexis as a linguistic level. *In memory of JR Firth*, pages 148–162, 1966.

[19] K. S. Hasan and V. Ng. Conundrums in unsupervised keyphrase extraction: making sense of the state-of-the-art. In *COLING*, 2010.

[20] T. Koo, X. Carreras, and M. Collins. Simple semi-supervised dependency parsing. *ACL-HLT*, 2008.

[21] J. Leskovec, L. Backstrom, and J. Kleinberg. Meme-tracking and the dynamics of the news cycle. In *KDD*, KDD '09, pages 497–506, 2009.

[22] X. Li and B. Liu. Learning to classify texts using positive and unlabeled data. In *IJCAI*, volume 3, pages 587–592, 2003.

[23] Y. Li, B.-J. P. Hsu, C. Zhai, and K. Wang. Unsupervised query segmentation using clickthrough for information retrieval. In *SIGIR*, 2011.

[24] Z. Liu, X. Chen, Y. Zheng, and M. Sun. Automatic keyphrase extraction by bridging vocabulary gap. In *Proceedings of the Fifteenth Conference on Computational Natural Language Learning*, pages 135–144. Association for Computational Linguistics, 2011.

[25] R. McDonald, F. Pereira, K. Ribarov, and J. Hajič. Non-projective dependency parsing using spanning tree algorithms. In *EMNLP*, 2005.

[26] R. Mihalcea and P. Tarau. Textrank: Bringing order into texts. In *ACL*, 2004.

[27] T. Mikolov, I. Sutskever, K. Chen, G. S. Corrado, and J. Dean. Distributed representations of words and phrases and their compositionality. In *NIPS*, pages 3111–3119, 2013.

[28] D. P, A. Dey, and D. Majumdar. Fast mining of interesting phrases from subsets of text corpora. In *EDBT*, 2014.

[29] A. Parameswaran, H. Garcia-Molina, and A. Rajaraman. Towards the web of concepts: Extracting concepts from large datasets. *Proceedings of the Very Large Data Bases Conference (VLDB)*, 3((1-2)), September 2010.

[30] Y. Park, R. J. Byrd, and B. K. Boguraev. Automatic glossary extraction: beyond terminology identification. In *COLING*, 2002.

[31] V. Punyakanok and D. Roth. The use of classifiers in sequential inference. In *NIPS*, 2001.

[32] C. Ramisch, A. Villavicencio, and C. Boitet. Multiword expressions in the wild? the mwetoolkit comes in handy. In *COLING*, pages 57–60, 2010.

[33] B. Settles. *Active Learning*. Synthesis Lectures on Artificial Intelligence and Machine Learning. Morgan & Claypool Publishers, 2012.

[34] A. Simitsis, A. Baid, Y. Sismanis, and B. Reinwald. Multidimensional content exploration. *Proc. VLDB Endow.*, 1(1):660–671, Aug. 2008.

[35] R. Sproat, W. Gale, C. Shih, and N. Chang. A stochastic finite-state word-segmentation algorithm for chinese. *Computational linguistics*, 22(3):377–404, 1996.

[36] B. Tan and F. Peng. Unsupervised query segmentation using generative language models and wikipedia. In *WWW*, 2008.

[37] E. F. Tjong Kim Sang and S. Buchholz. Introduction to the conll-2000 shared task: Chunking. In *CONLL*, 2000.

[38] I. H. Witten, G. W. Paynter, E. Frank, C. Gutwin, and C. G. Nevill-Manning. Kea: Practical automatic keyphrase extraction. In *Proceedings of the fourth ACM conference on Digital libraries*, pages 254–255. ACM, 1999.

[39] E. Xun, C. Huang, and M. Zhou. A unified statistical model for the identification of english basenp. In *ACL*, 2000.

[40] D. Zhang, C. Zhai, and J. Han. Topic Cube: Topic Modeling for OLAP on Multidimensional Text Databases. In *SDM*, pages 1123–1134, 2009.

[41] Z. Zhang, J. Iria, C. A. Brewster, and F. Ciravegna. A comparative evaluation of term recognition algorithms. *LREC*, 2008.

8. APPENDIX

8.1 Adapted Aho-Corasick Automaton

The Aho-Corasick Automaton is similar to the data structure Trie, which could utilize the common prefix to save the memory usage and also make the process more efficient. It also computes the field "failed" referring to the node which could continue the matching process. In this paper, we adopt standard Aho-Corasick Automaton definition and construction process. Algorithm 5 introduced a "while" loop to fix the

Algorithm 5: Locating using Aho-Corasick Automaton

Input: The Aho-Corasick Automaton root, the corpus string $\mathcal{C}$.
Output: All occurrences of phrases in the automaton $\mathcal{O}$.
$\mathcal{O} \leftarrow \emptyset$
$u \leftarrow$ root
for $i \leftarrow 1$ **to** $|\mathcal{C}|$ **do**
  while $u \neq$ *root and* $\mathcal{C}[i]$ *not in* u.*next* **do**
    $u \leftarrow u$.failed
  if $\mathcal{C}[i]$ *in* u.*next* **then**
    $u \leftarrow u$.next[$\mathcal{C}$[i]]
  $p \leftarrow u$
  while $p \neq$ *root and p.isEnd* **do**
    $\mathcal{O} \leftarrow \mathcal{O} \cup$ [i - p.depth + 1, i]
    $p \leftarrow p$.failed
return $\mathcal{O}$

Table 8: Runtime of locating phrase candidates

	Academia	Yelp
Aho-Corasick Automaton	154.25s	198.39s
Unordered Map (Hash Table)	192.71s	366.67s

issues brought by prefix (*i.e.*, there might be some phrase candidates which are the prefix of the others), which is slightly different from the traditional matching process and could help us find all occurrences of the phrase candidates in the corpus in a linear time.

An alternative way is to adopt the hash table. However, one should carefully choose the hash function for hash tale and the theoretical time complexity of hash table is not exactly linear. For the comparison, we implemented a hash table approach using the unordered map in C++, while the Aho-Corasick Automaton was coded in C++ too. The results can be found in Table 8 We can see that Aho-Corasick Automaton is slightly better because of its exact linear complexity and less memory overhead.

8.2 Convergence Study of Viterbi Training

Our time complexity analysis in Sec. 4.5 assumes Viterbi Training in Alg. 3 converges in few iterations. Here we verify this through empirical studies. From Table 9, VT converges extremely fast on both datasets. This owes to the good initialization based on raw frequency as well as the particular property of Viterbi Training discussed in Sec. 4.3.

8.3 Iterations of SegPhrase+

SegPhrase+ involves only one iteration of re-estimating phrase quality using normalized rectified frequency from phrasal segmentation. Here we show the performance of SegPhrase+ with more iterations in Fig. 5 based on human-labeled phrases. For comparison, we also report performance of ClassPhrase+ which is similar with ClassPhrase but contains segmentation feature generated by results of phrasal segmentation from the last iteration.

We can see that the benefits brought by rectified frequency can be fully digested within the first iteration, leaving F1 scores over the next several iterations close. One can also

Table 9: Objective function values of Viterbi Training for SegPhrase and SegPhrase+

Dataset	Academia		Yelp	
Method	SegPhrase	SegPhrase+	SegPhrase	SegPhrase+
Iter.1	-6.39453E+08	-6.33064E+08	-9.33899E+08	-9.27055E+08
Iter.2	-6.23699E+08	-6.17419E+08	-9.12082E+08	-9.06041E+08
Iter.3	-6.23383E+08	-6.17214E+08	-9.11835E+08	-9.05946E+08
Iter.4	-6.23354E+08	-6.17196E+08	-9.11819E+08	-9.05940E+08
Iter.5	-6.23351E+08	-6.17195E+08	-9.11818E+08	-9.05940E+08

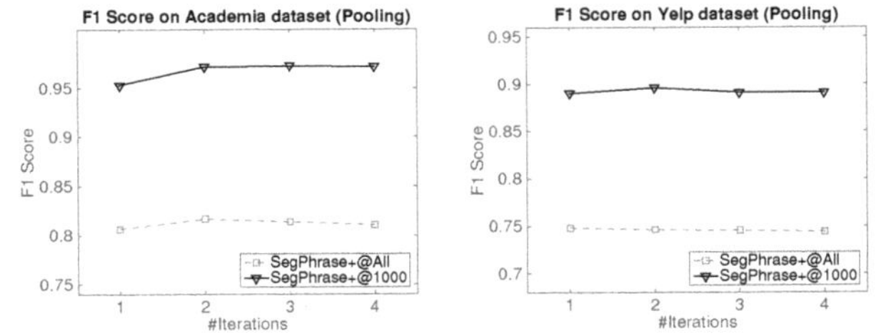

Figure 5: Performance variations of SegPhrase+ and ClassPhrase+ with increasing iterations

observe a slight performance decline over the next two iterations especially for the top-1000 phrases. Recall that we are reusing training labels for each iteration. Then this decline can be well explained by overfitting because segmentation features added by later iterations become less meaningful. Meanwhile, more meaningless features will undermine the classification power of random forest. Based on this, we can conclude that there is no need to do the phrase quality re-estimation multiple times.

8.4 Experiments on Larger Datasets

Since both Yelp and Academia dataset are relatively small in file size, we additionally tested our framework's running time on a larger data set composed of all Wikipedia articles as well as its performance considering all Wiki phrases to be ground truth. The statistics of Wikipedia dataset is shown in the following table and one can verify the linearality of computational complexity compared with previous experiments on Academia and Yelp reported in Table 10. The column *#wiki* shows the number of correctly predicted Wiki phrases of SegPhrase+. The precision-recall curves are reported in Fig. 6. Similar patterns can be observed compared to Fig. 1 that SegPhrase+ beats the other two proposed baselines and integration of phrasal segmentation with phrase mining boosts performance a lot.

Table 10: Statistics of experiments on Wiki dataset

file size	#words	time	#wiki phr.	# total
20.23GB	3.26G	28.08h	718,840	1,390,632

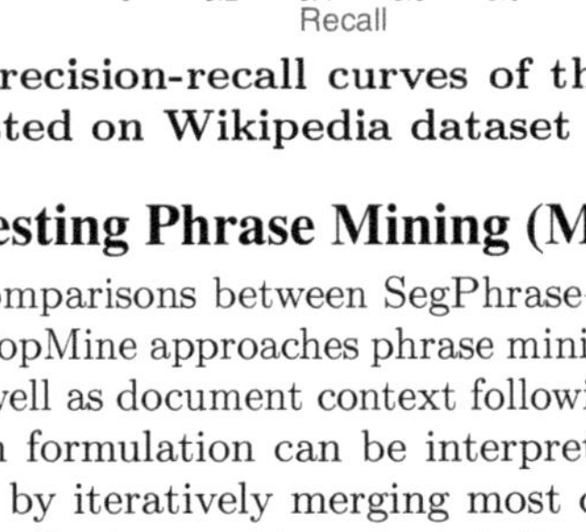

Figure 6: Precision-recall curves of the 3 proposed methods tested on Wikipedia dataset

8.5 Interesting Phrase Mining (More)

We show comparisons between SegPhrase+ and TopMine in Table 11. TopMine approaches phrase mining based on raw frequency as well as document context following a bottom-up fashion. Such formulation can be interpreted as a greedy segmentation by iteratively merging most correlated units in a sentence. Such a greedy segmentation is not optimal compared to our segmentation framework using dynamic programming. Moreover, TopMine removes stopwords before greedy segmentation. This loses important information

Table 11: **Interesting phrases mined from SIGMOD and SIGKDD conferences (SegPhrase+ v.s. TopMine)**

Conference	SIGMOD		SIGKDD	
Method	SegPhrase+	TopMine	SegPhrase+	TopMine
1	data base	data base	data mining	data mining
2	database system	query optimization	data set	data set
3	relational database	database system	association rule	knowledge discovery
...	...	...	...	...
51	sql server	aggregation function	association rule mining	data item
52	relational data	query answering	rule set	user profile
53	data structure	query rewriting	concept drift	user preference
54	join query	data access	knowledge acquisition	rule discovery
55	web service	hash join	gene expression data	sequential pattern
...	...	...	...	...
201	high dimensional data	logical and physical	active learning	
202	location based service	transitive closure	frequent subgraph	algorithm is efficient
203	xml schema	performance study	intrusion detection	approach is proposed
204	two phase locking	disk access	categorical attribute	data cube
205	deep web	object oriented	user preference	distance metric
...	...	...	...	...

Table 12: **Interesting phrases mined from SIGMOD and SIGKDD conferences (SegPhrase+ v.s. SegPhrase)**

Conference	SIGMOD		SIGKDD	
Method	SegPhrase+	SegPhrase	SegPhrase+	SegPhrase
1	data base	data base	data mining	data mining
2	database system	database system	data set	data set
3	relational database	query processing	association rule	association rule
...	...	...	...	...
51	sql server	subsequence matching	association rule mining	association rule mining
52	relational data	sql server	rule set	rule set
53	data structure	relational data	concept drift	concept drift
54	join query	data structure	knowledge acquisition	knowledge acquisition
55	web service	web service	gene expression data	gene expression data
...	...	...	...	...
201	high dimensional data	query containment	web content	web search engine
202	location based service	buffer management	frequent subgraph	better than
203	xml schema	garbage collection	intrusion detection	previously proposed
204	two phase locking	moving object	categorical attribute	application domain
205	deep web	on demand	user preference	wide range
...	...	...	...	...

because stopwords can be naturally serving as boundaries between meaningful phrases. From the table we can exactly tell that interesting phrases mined from our segmented corpus are better.

Comparisons between SegPhrase+ and SegPhrase are in Table 12. The results are basically similar but we can notice that phrases generated based on SegPhrase+'s segmentation are better in quality than SegPhrase's.

8.6 Relevant Word/Phrase Mining (More)

We show comparisons between SegPhrase+ and TopMine in Table 13, SegPhrase+ and SegPhrase in Table 14. From these two tables one can tell that SegPhrase+ beats TopMine while behaves similar to SegPhrase. This is reasonable because we are only listing the most similar words/phrases. As SegPhrase+ and SegPhrase are sharing the same phrasal segmentation module, the differences among top-ranked phrases will not be significant.

8.7 Case Study of Quality Phrases

We show some phrases from ranking lists generated by ClassPhrase, SegPhrase and SegPhrase+ in Table 15. In general, phrase quality drops with number goes up. ClassPhrase always performs the worst among the three methods. SegPhrase+ is slightly better than SegPhrase, which is noticeable for phrases ranked after 20,000. It's worth mentioning that the minimum sizes of phrase lists are 50,577 and 42,989 for two datasets respectively.

8.8 Error Analysis

We analyze of errors of SegPhrase+ from the aspects of false positive and false negative.

- False positive (reflected in precision): Through our studies, phrases with poor quality are mistakenly predicted as good ones due to the fixed collocation among words. For example, 'experiments are conducted' gets 0.88 quality score and 'at the network layer' gets 0.77. Such cases become more frequent when the phrases are close to the bottom of the ranking list.
- False negative (reflected in recall): Quality phrases are underestimated because their frequencies in the corpus is significantly lower than those of their sub-components. For example, 'topic model's score is 0.44, compared to 'topic modeling' which gets 0.72. As 'topic' and 'model' are both very frequent in the corpus, it is more difficult for 'topic model' to be predicted as quality phrase.

Based on the above error analysis, there are three inspired directions to improve the model. The first is to modify the quality estimator by incorporating syntactic features obtained from a pre-trained POS tagger. The second is to improve the viterbi training module in phrasal segmentation. One alternative is to find top-k segmentations instead of the best one given a text snippet. This is less deterministic in performing segmentation than the current design but consumes more computational power. Meanwhile, segment length penalty can be designed in a more sophisticated way by dynamically changing its value based on the local context instead of setting a global value. However, this will inevitably require more labels or predefined rules. The third aspect is to do normalization on words in the corpus such as stemming. This may merge 'topic modeling' and 'topic model' and make their predictions consistent.

Table 13: Top-5 similar words/phrases for queries from Academia/Yelp datasets (SegPhrase+ v.s. TopMine)

Query	data mining		olap	
Method	SegPhrase+	TopMine	SegPhrase+	TopMine
1	knowledge discovery	knowledge discovery	data warehouse	olap system
2	text mining	integrating data mining	online analytical processing	online analytical processing olap
3	web mining	data mining tools	data cube	olap queries
4	machine learning	mining	olap queries	data cube
5	data mining techniques	data mining dm	multidimensional databases	queries in olap

Query	blu-ray		noodle		valet parking	
Method	SegPhrase+	TopMine	SegPhrase+	TopMine	SegPhrase+	TopMine
1	dvd	movie	ramen	noodles the noodles	valet	valet
2	vhs	recordable	noodle soup	noodles weren	self-parking	valet service
3	cd	adobe's	rice noodle	noodle dish	valet service	parking and valet
4	new release	itunes	egg noodle	rice noodles	free valet parking	free valet
5	sony	bootable	pasta	noodle texture	covered parking	valet your car

Table 14: Top-5 similar words/phrases for queries from Academia/Yelp datasets (SegPhrase+ v.s. SegPhrase)

Query	data mining		olap	
Method	SegPhrase+	SegPhrase	SegPhrase+	SegPhrase
1	knowledge discovery	knowledge discovery	data warehouse	data warehouse
2	text mining	text mining	online analytical processing	online analytical processing
3	web mining	machine learning	data cube	data cube
4	machine learning	data mining techniques	olap queries	multidimensional database
5	data mining techniques	mining	multidimensional databases	olap operations

Query	blu-ray		noodle		valet parking	
Method	SegPhrase+	TopMine	SegPhrase+	TopMine	SegPhrase+	TopMine
1	dvd	dvd	ramen	noodle soup	valet	valet
2	vhs	new release	noodle soup	egg noodle	self-parking	valet service
3	cd	on netflix	rice noodle	ramen	valet service	self parking
4	new release	vhs	egg noodle	rice noodles	free valet parking	complimentary valet
5	sony	cd	pasta	noodle and	covered parking	parking

Table 15: Sampled quality phrases from Academia and Yelp datasets

Method	ClassPhrase	SegPhrase	SegPhrase+
1	virtual reality	virtual reality	self organization
2	variable bit rate	variable bit rate	polynomial time approx. scheme
3	shortest path	shortest path	least squares
...	...	...	...
501	finite state	frequency offset estimation	health care
502	air traffic	collaborative filtering	gene expression
503	long term	ultra wide band	finite state transducers
...	...	...	...
10001	search terms	test plan	airline crew scheduling
10002	high dimensional space	automatic text	integer programming
10003	delay variation	adaptive bandwidth	web log data
...	...	...	...
20001	test coverage	implementation costs	experience sampling
20002	adaptive sliding mode control	error bounded	virtual execution environments
20003	random graph models	free market	nonlinear time delay systems
...	...	...	...
50001	svm method	harmony search algorithm	asymptotic theory
50002	interface adaptation	integer variables	physical mapping
50003	diagnostic fault simulation	nonlinear oscillators	distinct patterns
...	...	...	...

Method	ClassPhrase	SegPhrase	SegPhrase+
1	taco bell	taco bell	tour guide
2	wet republic	wet republic	yellow tail
3	pizzeria bianco	pizzeria bianco	vanilla bean
...	...	...	...
501	panoramic view	art museum	rm seafood
502	pretzel bun	ice cream parlor	pecan pie
503	spa pedicure	pho kim long	master bedroom
...	...	...	...
10001	seated promptly	carrot soup	gary danko
10002	leisurely stroll	veggie soup	benny benassi
10003	flavored water	pork burrito	big eaters
...	...	...	...
20001	buttery toast	late night specials	cilantro hummus
20002	quick breakfast	older women	lv convention center
20003	slightly higher	worth noting	iced vanilla
...	...	...	...
40001	friday morning	conveniently placed	coupled with
40002	start feeling	cant remember	way too high
40003	immediately start	stereo system	almost guaranteed
...	...	...	...

Mining Subjective Properties on the Web

Immanuel Trummer*
EPFL
Lausanne, Switzerland
immanuel.trummer@epfl.ch

Alon Halevy
Google, Inc.
Mountain View, USA
halevy@google.com

Hongrae Lee
Google, Inc.
Mountain View, USA
hrlee@google.com

Sunita Sarawagi
Google, Inc. and IIT Bombay
Mountain View, USA/Mumbai, India
sarawagi@google.com

Rahul Gupta
Google, Inc.
Mountain View, USA
grahul@google.com

ABSTRACT

Even with the recent developments in Web search of answering queries from structured data, search engines are still limited to queries with an objective answer, such as EUROPEAN CAPITALS or WOODY ALLEN MOVIES. However, many queries are subjective, such as SAFE CITIES, or CUTE ANIMALS. The underlying knowledge bases of search engines do not contain answers to these queries because they do not have a ground truth. We describe the SURVEYOR system that mines the dominant opinion held by authors of Web content about whether a subjective property applies to a given entity. The evidence on which SURVEYOR relies is statements extracted from Web text that either support the property or claim its negation. The key challenge that SURVEYOR faces is that simply counting the number of positive and negative statements does not suffice, because there are multiple hidden biases with which content tends to be authored on the Web. SURVEYOR employs a probabilistic model of how content is authored on the Web. As one example, this model accounts for correlations between the subjective property and the frequency with which it is mentioned on the Web. The parameters of the model are specialized to each property and entity type.

SURVEYOR was able to process a large Web snapshot within a few hours, resulting in opinions for over 4 billion entity-property combinations. We selected a subset of 500 entity-property combinations and compared our results to the dominant opinion of a large number of Amazon Mechanical Turk (AMT) workers. The predictions of SURVEYOR match the results from AMT in 77% of all cases (and 87% for test cases where inter-worker agreement is high), significantly outperforming competing approaches.

*This work was done while the author was at Google, Inc.

SIGMOD'15, May 31–June 4, 2015, Melbourne, Victoria, Australia.
ACM 978-1-4503-2758-9/15/05.
http://dx.doi.org/10.1145/2723372.2750548.

Categories and Subject Descriptors

H.4 [**Information Systems Applications**]: Miscellaneous

Keywords

Text mining; subjective properties; user behavior model

1. INTRODUCTION

In recent years, Web search engines have invested heavily in answering queries with structured data. For example, queries such as WOODY ALLEN MOVIES or AMERICAN PRESIDENTS will yield a display of the appropriate entities. These queries are enabled by large knowledge bases about important entities and properties of these entities. Albeit vast, these knowledge bases are restricted to objective properties of the entities. Hence, queries with subjective properties such as BIG CITIES, SAFE CITIES, or CUTE ANIMALS would not trigger search results from structured data. Considering that queries about subjective properties are very common in the query stream, this implies lost opportunities for offering rich information.

We describe the SURVEYOR system whose goal is to mine from the Web the dominant opinion about whether a particular property applies to entities of a particular type. Given a property, typically expressed as an adjective (e.g., CUTE), a type (e.g., ANIMALS) and a set of entities of that type from the knowledge base, SURVEYOR decides whether the majority of users associate the property with the entity. The purpose is to build a knowledge base of subjective properties and entities. To the best of our knowledge, we are the first to study this problem.

The state-of-the-art approach to building SURVEYOR would be to use an information extraction or natural-language processing method to simply *count* the number of occurrences on the Web in which the property is attributed to the entity and the number of times in which a negative assertion about the property applying to the entity is found. We would then decide if a property applies to an entity based on a count-based estimator such as the majority vote. Such an approach would be appropriate if we had a sufficiently large and unbiased sample of statements about each entity. In practice, this assumption does not hold for the following reasons.

First, the statement sample might be biased because users with one specific opinion are more likely to express themselves than the others. For example, users who experience a certain city as being NOT SAFE might be more likely to point that out than other users who experience the same city as SAFE. Therefore, finding more statements claiming that a certain city is NOT SAFE does not necessarily mean that this is the majority opinion. Second, there are many entities and properties for which only very few statements can be found on the Web. This does not mean that we cannot infer the dominant opinion for them. Consider, for example, the property-type combination BIG CITY. Big cities are mentioned more frequently than small cities. A city about which we find no mentions is likely NOT BIG. Furthermore, such correlations are specific to a particular property-type combination.

To overcome all these challenges, we need a model that captures biases and correlations in how users create content on the Web, and therefore enables us to make inferences that go beyond majority voting on assertions. To that end, a critical component underlying SURVEYOR is a probabilistic model of how assertions about properties of entities are generated in Web content. The parameters of the model are instantiated differently for each combination of entity type and property. We use an iterative expectation-maximization approach [9] to infer optimal parameter values automatically for each type and property. Our method is therefore completely unsupervised, enabling us to scale to large numbers of types and properties. Figure 1 illustrates the flow of SURVEYOR.

The contributions of this paper are the following:

1. We introduce the problem of mining subjective properties of entites from the Web, complementing the current capabilities of search engines to answer queries from structured data. We describe the specific challenges that this problem poses, based on an analysis of several use cases.

2. We describe the architecture and implementation of the SURVEYOR system which parses Web snapshots to extract statements involving entities from the knowledge base and subjective properties. SURVEYOR analyzes sets of statements gathered about specific entity-property pairs to derive the probability that the property applies to the entity according to the dominant opinion.

3. We present a probabilistic model of how authors generate content on the Web. Our model is a parametric Bayesian network whose variables capture hidden author biases. We derive an efficient training and inference algorithm whose time complexity is linear in the number of entities and independent of the number of mentions. Thus our probabilistic model is applicable to Web-scale data.

4. We describe our experience of applying SURVEYOR to a Web snapshot of 40 TB, leading to extractions concerning 7 million property-type combinations and resulting in probabilities for over 4 billion entity-property pairs with a processing time of few hours on a large cluster. We evaluate the precision of SURVEYOR by comparing its output to opinions collected from a large number of Amazon Mechanical Turk workers; SURVEYOR outperforms baselines by more than 20 $\sim$ 30% in precision.

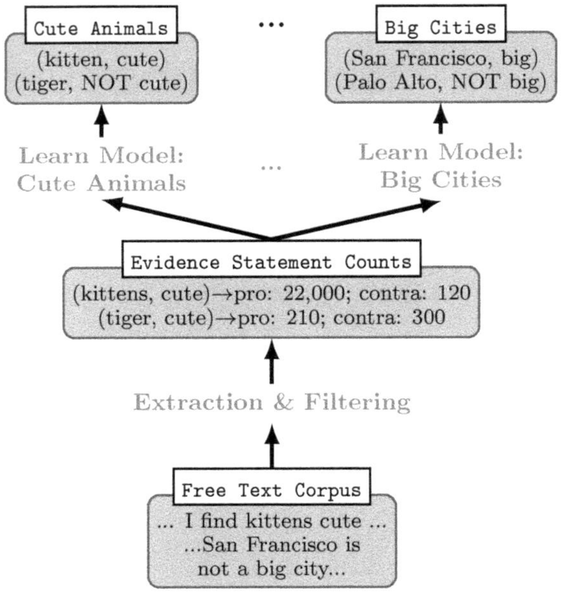

Figure 1: Surveyor begins by extracting positive and negative statements about entity-property pairs and counting the number of each. It then learns and applies a type and property specific probabilistic model to decide whether the counts entail a dominant opinion w.r.t. the property and the entity.

The remainder of this paper is organized as follows. In Section 2 we give a formal problem statement and analyze a representative use case leading to several insights that motivate specific design decisions later. We present the architecture of our system in Section 3. In Section 4 we describe the natural language processing methods by which we detect positive and negative statements. In Section 5 we describe our probabilistic model of user behaviour that is based on the observations from Section 2. We derive equations to calculate optimal parameter values for that model in Section 6. In Section 7 we describe the properties of the full data set generated by our system, and experimentally evaluate our system against baseline approaches. In Section 8 we discuss related work in more detail.

2. PROBLEM STATEMENT

We begin by introducing our terminology and defining the addressed problem. Then, we present an empirical analysis of an example scenario that uncovered many of the challenges we faced and motivated the proposed solution.

Definitions

A *subjective property* in our scenario is an adjective, optionally associated with preceding adverbs. Example properties include CUTE, DENSELY POPULATED, or VERY SMALL. We focus on properties that are subjective, meaning that there is no objective ground truth about whether they apply to certain entities. While different users might disagree on whether subjective properties apply to certain entities, we assume that there is a *dominant opinion* for many entity-property combinations, meaning that a significant part of the user base agrees on whether the property applies to the entity. When being asked whether the property CUTE applies

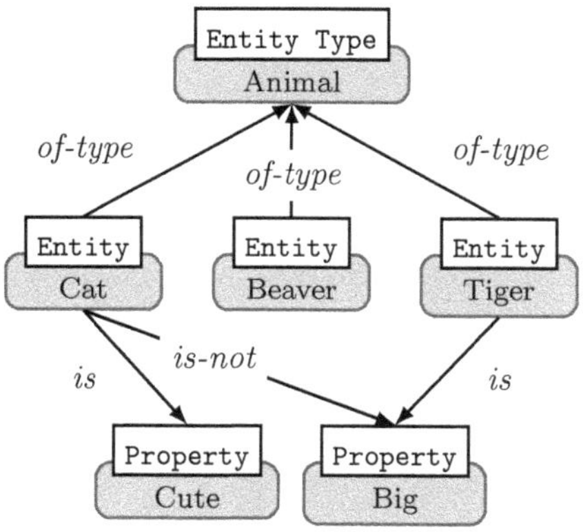

Figure 2: Graphical depiction of problem setting for entity type ANIMAL: typed entities can be connected to subjective properties with positive (is) or negative (is-not) polarity.

to PUPPY or whether BIG applies to LOS ANGELES, without being given any specific context, a majority of users would intuitively answer with YES. In such cases we have a *positive* dominant opinion while otherwise we have a *negative* dominant opinion.

We assume that a *knowledge base* is available which stores entities with their associated entity type (e.g., entity TIGER of type ANIMAL), as well as additional (objective) information on those entities. *Subjective queries* use subjective properties to characterize entities. This requires us to find out which subjective properties the average user associates with which entities in the knowledge base. Upon receipt of a subjective query, the search engine can exploit high-confidence entity-property associations and offer links to supporting content on the Web as query result.

This leads to the *subjective property mining* problem which is defined as follows: Given a document corpus W, an entity e, and a subjective property p, determine the polarity of the dominant opinion on the entity-property pair (e, p) among the authors of W, i.e., whether the majority of authors would intuitively associate the property with the entity. Given a document corpus W and a threshold ρ, Surveyor solves the *all pairs* version of the subjective property mining problem that determines dominant opinions for all pairs (e, p) where entities of the same type co-occur with the property p in at least ρ statements in W. See Figure 2 for a graphical depiction of our problem setting.

The region a user comes from can influence the probability that (s)he associates certain entities with certain properties. For example, Chinese users might have different ideas than American users about what constitutes a BIG CITY. SURVEYOR can produce region-specific results if the input is restricted to Web sites with specific domain extensions. In general, we can specialize the output of SURVEYOR for any user group by restricting the input to documents that have been authored by that group.

Empirical Analysis

We considered a test scenario where we had to decide for 461 Californian cities whether the property BIG applies (additional test scenarios are shown in Appendix A). We collect evidence for a specific city X by issuing Google queries for positive statements of the form "X IS A BIG CITY" and

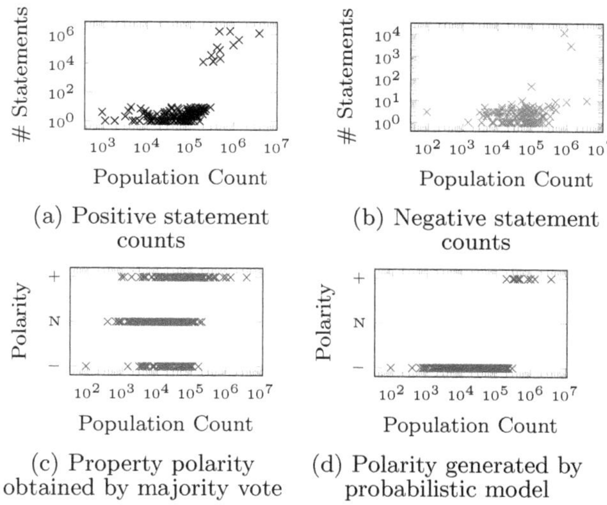

(a) Positive statement counts

(b) Negative statement counts

(c) Property polarity obtained by majority vote

(d) Polarity generated by probabilistic model

Figure 3: We interpret the statement counts (Figures 3(a)/3(b)) using majority vote (Figure 3(c)) and a probabilistic user model (Figure 3(d)).

queries for negative statements of the form "X IS NOT A BIG CITY". Note that in our actual system we used a more sophisticated Natural Language Processing (NLP) approach to extract the statements, which recognizes a much broader class of patterns.

We checked the names of all cities that received at least 100 hits in total for ambiguity and discarded 11 out of 23 of those cities since the top search result did not return the city that the population count refers to. We conclude that disambiguation is crucial in our scenario; our extraction mechanism that we present in Section 4 uses annotated Web documents as input that have been pre-processed by an entity tagger using state-of-the-art means for disambiguation.

Unlike our final evaluation of SURVEYOR with Mechanical Turk, in this exploration we use the population of the city as a proxy for its size. We chose this example because population correlates with the property BIG, but in general, the property will not necessarily be correlated to knowledge in the knowledge base. Figures 3(a) and 3(b) show the number of positive and negative statements for all cities that passed the ambiguity test, ordered by population count. There are many cities for which we find a non-negligible number of positive and negative statements at the same time. This means that a significant fraction of users disagrees with the dominant opinion. Therefore, we must take into account *subjectivity* and must aggregate contradictory results.

The first approach that comes to mind for aggregating contradictory results is to take the majority vote. Under the assumption that we find sufficiently large and unbiased sets of statements about each entity, the majority vote is representative for the dominant opinion. Figure 3(c) shows the result of the majority vote: for each city, we compare the number of positive statements with the number of negative statements and mark it as BIG (polarity=+) if the number of positive statements is higher; we mark it as NOT BIG (polarity=−) if the number of negative statements is higher. We mark polarity=N if both counters are equal. The figure shows that we find more negative than positive statements for some cities. Such cities should probably be marked as

NOT BIG which underscores the need to use NLP technology that can distinguish positive from negative assertions, and excludes the use of purely occurrence-based approaches that have been used by prior work in product tagging [2, 4, 5].

Despite the fact that we distinguish negative and positive statements, the result quality in Figure 3(c) seems rather low. Many cities are marked as big despite a relatively low population count. Looking for an explanation, we find that the total number of negative statements (see Figure 3(b)) is much lower than the number of positive statements (see Figure 3(a)). We have no reason to suspect that our sample contains mainly big cities (the opposite is probably true given the population counts). This indicates that counters of positive and negative statements can follow different probability distributions, i.e. we might have a *polarity bias.*

In addition to the lack of a correlation between property polarity and population counts, the results in Figure 3(c) are poor for another reason: for many cities, we cannot decide whether they are big or not because we could not extract positive or negative statements about them. At first glance, this problem seems hard to solve. Looking again at Figures 3(a) and 3(b), we realize however that the total number of positive and negative statements is correlated with the population count. Big cities tend to be mentioned more often on the Web than small cities. If we are able to automatically detect such correlations, we can infer that a city that is never mentioned on the Web is not big with high probability. Note that the lack of mentions for an entity is rather meaningless when working with a small collection of documents. But when considering the entire Web, finding no occurrences of an entity means that billions of content-generating users made the decision not to mention the entity; at sufficiently large scale, the lack of any evidence can be evidence as well. We conclude that taking into account *occurrence bias*, the correlation between property polarity and occurrence frequency, can be helpful.

Our hypothesis is that it is possible to account all types of bias by using a probabilistic user behavior model. Figure 3(d) shows the result of applying an early version of the probabilistic model presented in Section 5 to interpret the statement counts from Figures 3(a) and 3(b). The result quality is markedly better than in Figure 3(c): we obtain a decision for each city and polarity is strongly correlated with population count.

As we have seen, users are more likely to write about cities if they associate the property BIG with them. This implies that users are *less* likely to mention cities if they associate the property SMALL with them, as big and small are antonyms. This means that the occurrence bias for those two properties is different. In general, we observed that all types of bias mentioned before may differ across properties but also across entity types. We conclude that polarity bias and occurrence bias do *not generalize* and must be inferred separately for different property-type combinations.

The method that we present in the following sections is based on all those observations.

3. SYSTEM OVERVIEW

Algorithm 1 provides a high-level description of SURVEYOR. The input is a collection of annotated Web documents W, from which we extract evidence, a knowledge base KB containing entities with their types, and a threshold parameter ρ whose semantics we discuss later. The output of Algorithm 1 is a set of tuples assigning entity-property combinations to a polarity representing the dominant opinion.

Algorithm 1 Surveyor algorithm

// W: Web snapshot; KB: Knowledge base
// ρ: occurrence threshold
function SURVEYOR(W, KB, ρ)
    Iterate over documents in W to extract evidence
    for $\langle type, property \rangle$: at least ρ extractions **do**
        Learn model parameters
        for $entity \in KB$: entity is of *type* **do**
            Calculate $prb = \Pr(\text{property applies})$
            Add $\langle entity, property, + \rangle$ to *result* if $prb > \frac{1}{2}$
            Add $\langle entity, property, - \rangle$ to *result* if $prb < \frac{1}{2}$
        end for
    end for
    return *result*
end function

Extracting Evidence. We extract positive and negative evidence from a text corpus containing a snapshot of the Web. The corpus text was preprocessed using NLP tools and contains annotations mapping text mentions of entities to our knowledge base which is an extension of Freebase. We consider each mention of a knowledge base entity and analyze the surrounding free text. We use several patterns to detect evidence statements and to extract the properties that they connect to the entity and the polarity of the association. Section 4 provides more details on the extraction phase.

Next, we group evidence by the entity-property pair it refers to. For each pair, we compute two counters: the total number of positive statements and the total number of negative statements. Those counters are the input for the next step of the algorithm.

Evidence Interpretation. We interpret the collected evidence to calculate the probability that a specific property applies to a given entity. The knowledge base associates each entity with an entity type (the knowledge base may actually associate multiple types with an entity but we use only the most notable type). We group evidence by entity type, and aggregate for each property-type combination the total number of extracted statements. We only compute probabilities for property-type combinations for which the number of extracted statements is sufficiently high.

We consider each property-type combination separately. For each combination, we first use the collected evidence to instantiate a probabilistic model of how authors decide to issue positive or negative statements. Section 5 describes the model and justifies the underlying assumptions. The model is parameterized and we show in Section 6 how to learn optimal parameter values in an iterative approach. The instantiated model can be used to determine for a given entity the probability that the dominant opinion on it is positive, based on the collected evidence. We calculate probabilities for all entities in the knowledge base that belong to the current entity type. In paritcular, this includes entities for which no evidence was extracted at all. For some property-type pairs, SURVEYOR may draw conclusions for these unmentioned entities as well.

We currently assume a positive dominant opinion if the probability is greater than 0.5, and a negative dominant

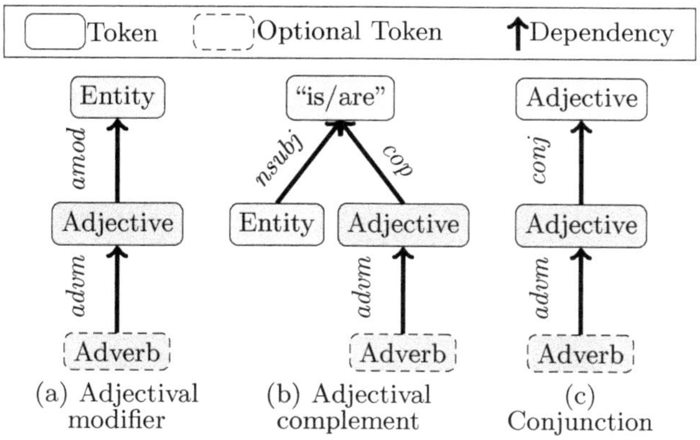

Figure 4: Evidence extraction patterns as Stanford typed dependency trees: property tokens are red.

Table 1: Example extractions

Statement	Pattern	Entity	Property
Snakes are dangerous animals	Adjectival modifier	snake	dangerous
Chicago is very big	Adjectival complement	Chicago	very big
Soccer is a fast and exciting sport	Conjunction	soccer	exciting

opinion if it is less than 0.5. We can chose a different threshold if we want to trade precision for recall.

4. EXTRACTING EVIDENCE

In this section we describe some of the details of evidence extraction in SURVEYOR. In particular, we describe our extraction patterns, how we limit the extraction to intrinsic evidence, and how we determine the polarity of evidence.

An evidence statement connects an entity to a property; a positive statement claims that the property applies to the entity, a negative statement claims the opposite. We recall that in our setting, a property is an adjective, optionally associated with adverbs (e.g., DENSELY POPULATED, VERY BIG). The input for evidence extraction is an annotated Web snapshot that was preprocessed using NLP tools similar to the Stanford parser[1] and by an entity extractor that identifies mentions of knowledge base entities using disambiguation techniques. The annotations contain the resulting dependency tree representation of sentences and the links to knowledge base entities. We consider sentences in our text corpus that mention at least one entity from the knowledge base and analyze their dependency parse trees.

We manually devised several patterns against which we match the sentences in the corpus. Figure 4 shows a simplified representation of those patterns. We obtain the properties associated with an entity by matching the corresponding pattern with the dependency tree. The tokens that together form the property are colored in red in Figure 4. Table 1 shows an example statement for each of the three patterns and the corresponding extractions. In the first example, note that ANIMALS is coreferential with SNAKES, i.e. those are two mentions of the same entity. Property DANGEROUS is adjectival modifier of the second mention. Also note that the third statement contains two patterns: using the adjectival modifier pattern we can also extract property FAST for entity SOCCER.

Our patterns do not explicitly target subjective properties (e.g., we might extract objective properties such as AMERICAN for a city), but most extracted properties turn out to be subjective in practice. The patterns depicted in Figure 4 are relatively restrictive. We tried several variations of those patterns (see Appendix B), allowing for instance an extended set of verbs for the top node of the adjectival complement pattern depicted in Figure 4(b), but came to the conclusion that the patterns in Figure 4 offer the best tradeoff between precision and recall for our application. In general, our design of the extraction and filtering mechanisms prioritizes precision over recall since we apply SURVEYOR to large input document collections where recall is less critical.

Once an evidence statement is extracted, we apply several heuristics to filter out non-intrinsic evidence statements. An example of a non-intrinsic statement is NEW YORK IS BAD FOR PARKING because it only refers to a specific aspect of the city (in contrast to the statement NEW YORK IS BAD). While it would be possible to use expressions such as BAD FOR PARKING as properties, we assume that the number of statements found for such complex properties would be too low to allow reliable inference. In order to recognize non-intrinsic statements that refer only to a specific aspect of an entity, we search for sub-trees in the dependency tree that could represent constrictions. We search for sub-trees that have a specific position in the dependency tree relative to the detected pattern (e.g., additional sub-trees of the top level node in Figure 4(b)) and contain nodes with specific labels (e.g., labels indicating prepositions). If such a sub-tree is found, we assume that the statement is non-intrinsic. While this filtering mechanism can be rather conservative at times, we found it to improve precision significantly.

As another example, compare the statements SOUTHERN FRANCE IS WARM and GREECE IS A SOUTHERN COUNTRY. Both statements use the adjective SOUTHERN as adjectival modifier for an entity of type COUNTRY. They differ in that the first statement uses the adjective to refer to a specific part of a country (France) while the second statement claims that SOUTHERN is an intrinsic property of an entire country (Greece). To filter out non-intrinsic statements that refer to a part of an entity (instead of distinguishing the entity from other entities of the same type), we require sentences in which the adjectival modifier pattern was detected to be coreferential. Note that this test distinguishes the two example statements given above.

Next, we determine the polarity of the statement by exploiting annotations in the dependency tree that indicate negations: for example, the sentence I DON'T THINK THAT SNAKES ARE NEVER DANGEROUS contains two negations (the negations DON'T and NEVER). Figure 5 shows the dependency tree representation of that sentence (negations are marked in red). Note that this sentence is recognized as evidence since a sub-tree (SNAKES ARE DANGEROUS) matches the adjectival complement pattern from Figure 4.

We decide the polarity by following the path in the dependency tree from the property token to the root: starting

[1]http://nlp.stanford.edu/software/stanford-dependencies.shtml

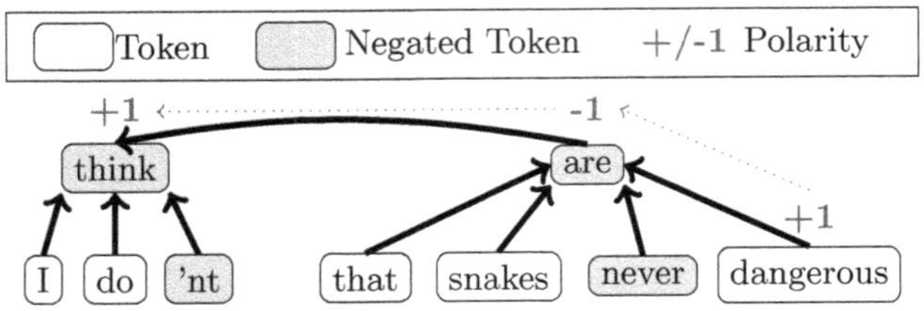

Figure 5: We detect the polarity of the example statement by counting the negated tokens on the path from property (dangerous) to tree root (think).

with a polarity of +1, we change the sign every time we encounter a negated token on that path (a negated token has a negation as child element). If the number of negated tokens is odd, then the polarity of the statement is negative, and otherwise it is positive. Note that this method recognizes even double negations which are rare but do sometimes appear for the properties we consider.

We considered taking into account antonym relationships between adjectives when identifying negations, e.g., interpreting the statement PALO ALTO IS SMALL as negation of PALO ALTO IS BIG. We decided against it for two reasons: First, even if two adjectives are registered as antonyms (e.g., within a database such as WordNet), they usually do not represent the exact opposite of each other. Users who consider a city as NOT BIG do not necessarily consider it SMALL. Second, we consider adverb-adjective combinations for which it is often impossible to find any antonyms at all.

5. MODELING USER BEHAVIOR

As we described in Section 2, the simple approach to estimating the probability of the dominant opinion based on majority vote counting does not work very well because it fails to model the different types of bias that underlie authoring on the Web. To address this fundamental challenge, SURVEYOR employs a probabilistic model that explicitly accounts for behavior of authors on the Web and takes into consideration the different types of biases. This section describes the model, beginning with an overview. Section 6 describes how we learn the model parameters for specific property-type combinations.

5.1 Model Overview

We assume in the following that one specific property-type combination is considered. The output of the extraction stage, described in Section 4, is an evidence tuple $\langle C_i^+, C_i^- \rangle$ for each entity; the evidence consists of the total count of positive statements, C_i^+, and the total count of negative statements, C_i^-, gathered during extraction about the entity and the current property.

Our probabilistic model assumes that each evidence tuple was drawn from one of two possible probability distributions: in the first distribution, we assume that the dominant opinion applies the property to the entity, whereas in the second, the dominant opinion does not. If we know how to express those two probability distributions then we can calculate for each evidence tuple the probability with which it was drawn from one distribution or the other; this is at the same time the probability that the entity to which the evidence tuple refers, does or does not have the current property.

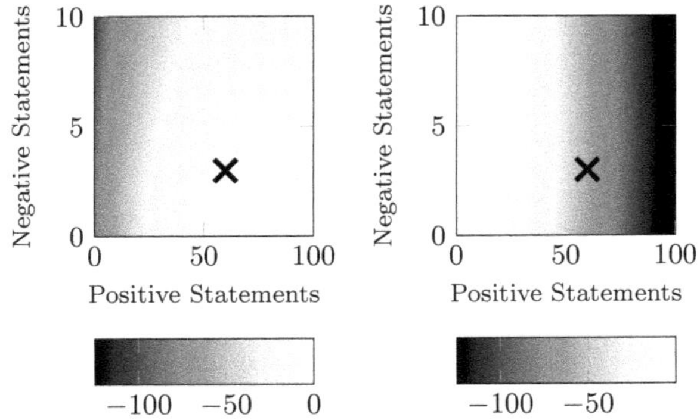

(a) Log-probability for entities with positive dominant opinion

(b) Log-probability for entities with negative dominant opinion

Figure 6: Each property-type combination is associated with two probability distributions over the statement counters: the dominant opinion on the entity for which we receive the counts ⟨60, 3⟩, marked by X, is more likely to be positive.

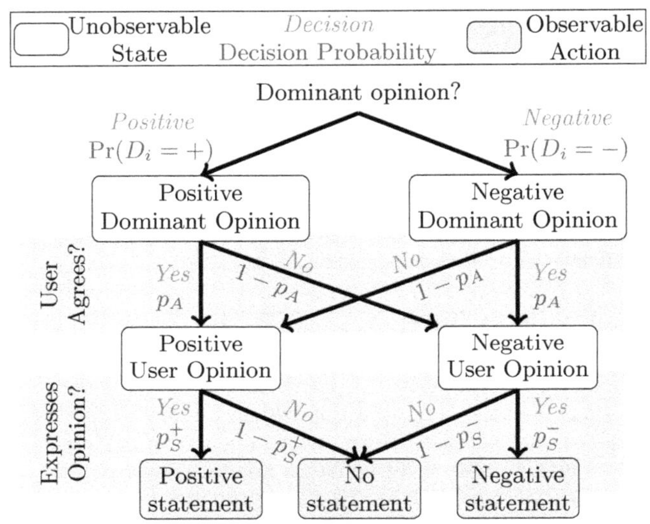

Figure 7: Probabilistic user behavior model: users agree with the dominant opinion on specific entity-property pairs with probability p_A; they state their opinion with probability p_S^+ if it is positive and probability p_S^- if it is negative.

EXAMPLE 1. *Figure 6 illustrates the scenario described above: we have two two-dimensional probability distributions that assign tuples of positive and negative statement counts to probabilities, lighter colors represent higher probabilities in the figure. Assume we receive the evidence tuple ⟨60, 3⟩ for an entity (this point is marked by the black X in Figure 6). As the distribution for entities with positive dominant opinion (depicted in Figure 6(a)) assigns a higher probability to that tuple than the distribution for entities with negative dominant opinion (depicted in Figure 6(b)), the current property is more likely to apply to that entity than not.*

Statements are issued by users who have a certain opinion about an entity and decide to express that opinion on the

Web. In order to model the probability to receive a certain number of positive or negative statements, we must model the probability that a single user decides to issue a positive or negative statement.

Figure 7 is a graphical depiction of our user model. We denote the dominant opinion for entity i of the given type by D_i. The top node, the dominant opinion about an entity-property pair, is what we are trying to compute. However, the only observable variables are the green rectangles at the bottom, namely, the actual statements (positive and negative) that we can extract from the text corpus. The probabilistic model contains internal variables that model how actual statements on the Web are created relative to a given dominant opinion.

First, the dominant opinion could be either positive or negative, which is represented by the two rectangles below the dominant opinion. We denote the probability for a positive dominant opinion by $\Pr(D_i = +)$ and the probability for a negative dominant opinion by $\Pr(D_i = -)$. Those probabilities are initially unknown but the model enables us to calculate them.

Second, given the polarity of the dominant opinion, an author of a web page may or may not agree with it. This connects to our observation from Section 2 that subjectivity plays an important role in our scenario. We will denote by p_A the probability that an author agrees with the dominant opinion, and therefore the transition from the second layer of Figure 7 to the third layer is done with probabilities p_A and $1 - p_A$, depending on the direction.

Finally, we model the probability that an author will actually write a statement about whether the property applies to the entity. We have observed various types of bias in Section 2, leading us to believe that the probability for writing a statement may depend on the user opinion. We therefore introduce two separate parameters, p_S^+ and p_S^-, representing the probability that a user mentions an entity with which (s)he associates the current property (p_S^+) and the probability that a user mentions an entity with which (s)he does not associate the current property (p_S^-).

We note that the model is parameterized per each property-type combination, as opposed to, for instance, all types-property, or all types-all properties pairs. This choice is based on our observation (in Section 2) that the right settings for the parameters vary across entity types for a fixed property but also across properties for a fixed type. Our experiences when collecting ground truth data for our experimental evaluation, described in Section 7.3, further support this design decision.

5.2 Model Details

The process described in the previous subsection can be expressed as a Bayesian network as illustrated in Figure 8. We use random variables D_i, C_i^+ and C_i^- to model the dominant opinion on the i-th entity, the number of positive statements and the number of negative statements collected for the i-th entity. We conceptually introduce two variables, O_{iw} and S_{iw}, for the Web document with index $w \in \{1, \ldots n\}$. Variable O_{iw} represents the opinion of the corresponding author about whether the current property applies to the i-th entity; this opinion may be positive or negative (represented by $O_{iw} = +$ and $O_{iw} = -$ respectively), it is consistent with the dominant opinion (i.e., $O_{iw} = D_i$) with probability p_A and inconsistent with probability $1 - p_A$.

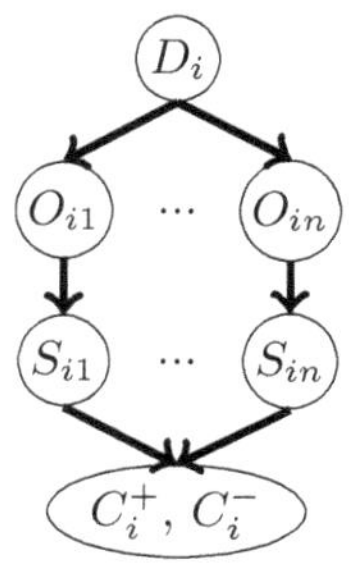

$\Pr(O_{iw}|D_i)$

O_{iw} \ D_i	+	−
+	p_A	$1 - p_A$
−	$1 - p_A$	p_A

$\Pr(S_{iw}|O_{iw})$

S_{iw} \ O_{iw}	+	−
+	p_S^+	0
N	$1 - p_S^+$	$1 - p_S^-$
−	0	p_S^-

Figure 8: Probabilistic model as Bayesian network with conditional probabilities

Variable S_{iw} captures whether the author of document w decided to make a positive or negative or no statement about whether the current property applies to entity i; those three cases are represented by $S_{iw} = +$, $S_{iw} = -$, or $S_{iw} = N$ respectively. The probability of making a statement is p_S^+ if $O_{iw} = +$ and p_S^- if $O_{iw} = -$. The counter variable C_i^+ counts the number of documents w such that $S_{iw} = +$ and variable C_i^- counts the number of documents such that $S_{iw} = -$. Note that the values for the parameters p_A, p_S^+, and p_S^- are fixed for each property-type combination. We illustrate those definitions by an example.

EXAMPLE 2. *Assume we want to find out which* ANIMALS *are considered* CUTE. *Let* KITTEN, DOG, SPIDER *be the list of entities (animals) that we consider. Then D_i for $1 \leq i \leq 3$ represents the dominant opinion about whether the i-th animal in that list is* CUTE, *counter C_i^+ represents the number of times the i-th animal was mentioned as being* CUTE *on the Web, and C_i^- is the number of times the animal was mentioned as being* NOT CUTE. *If $O_{1w} = +$ and $S_{1w} = N$, for some Web site w, then the author of that site considers* KITTENS *as* CUTE *but did not decide to express that opinion.*

Assume that there is generally a high agreement between users whether specific animals are cute or not. Then we expect to obtain a relatively high agreement parameter p_A for this property-type combination from the parameter learning algorithm presented in Section 6. Users are more likely to state the fact that they find a specific animal CUTE *than the fact that they consider an animal* NOT CUTE *and this is why we expect to obtain statement probabilities such that $p_S^+ \gg p_S^-$. Note that it might be the inverse for other property-type combinations: for instance, users might have a bias towards rather expressing their opinion if they consider a city* NOT SAFE *than if they consider it* SAFE. *Therefore, we expect to infer parameter values such that $p_S^- \gg p_S^+$ for property-type combination* SAFE CITIES.

Our goal now is to estimate the distribution over the variable D_i given the observed counts, i.e., $\Pr(D_i|C_i^+, C_i^-)$. We elaborate on how to compute $\Pr(D_i|C_i^+, C_i^-)$ with respect to the Bayesian network in Figure 8. First note that $\Pr(D_i|C_i^+, C_i^-) \propto \Pr(C_i^+, C_i^-|D_i) \Pr(D_i)$. Since we wish to be agnostic about the prior probability of D_i we set $\Pr(D_i = +) = \Pr(D_i = -) = 0.5$. Since the counts C_i^+, C_i^- are deterministic functions of S_{iw}, we first solve for $\Pr(S_{iw}|D_i)$.

From the Bayesian network, we obtain

$$(S_{iw}|D_i) = \sum_{O_{iw} \in \{+,-\}} \Pr(S_{iw}|O_{iw}) \Pr(O_{iw}|D_i).$$

By substituting, $D_i = +$ or $-$ and $S_{iw} = +$ or $-$, we get four possibilities as follows:

$$\Pr(S_{iw} = +|D_i = +) = p_A \cdot p_S^+$$
$$\Pr(S_{iw} = -|D_i = +) = (1 - p_A) \cdot p_S^-$$
$$\Pr(S_{iw} = +|D_i = -) = (1 - p_A) \cdot p_S^+$$
$$\Pr(S_{iw} = -|D_i = -) = p_A \cdot p_S^-$$

The variables C_i^+, C_i^- are obtained by summing up n variables S_{iw} each of which can be $+,-$, or neutral. We assume that the variables S_{iw} are independent for different w since the chances that two randomly selected documents on the Web are authored by the same person are negligible. This implies that (C_i^+, C_i^-) follows a Multinomial distribution where $\Pr(C_i^+ = a, C_i^- = b|D_i = +) =$

$$\frac{n!}{a!b!(n-a-b)!}(p_+^+)^a(p_+^-)^b(1 - p_+^+ - p_+^-)^{n-a-b}$$

where p_+^+ and p_+^- denote $\Pr(S_{iw} = +|D_i = +)$, and $\Pr(S_{iw} = -|D_i = +)$ respectively (i.e. the subscript is the dominant opinion and the superscript is the user opinion).

We can approximate this multinomial distribution as a product of two Poisson distributions since n is expected to be very large compared to both (C_i^+, C_i^-) [14, 18] since for any entity and property, the number of Web sites on which they appear together is very small compared to the total number of Web sites. Thus, we can rewrite the above expression as $\Pr(C_i^+ = a, C_i^- = b|D_i = +) = \Pr(C_i^+ = a|D_i = +)\Pr(C_i^- = b|D_i = +) =$

$$\text{Pois}(a; \lambda_+^+ = np_+^+)\text{Pois}(b; \lambda_+^- = np_+^-)$$

We derive a similar expression for the case where $D_i = -$.

In summary, we obtain four different Poisson distributions that can be described using the three parameters p_A, p_S^+, and p_S^-: the two counter distributions for positive and negative statements for entities to which the current property applies according to the dominant opinion, and the two corresponding distributions for entities to which the property does not apply. Each of the four distributions is described by one of four Poisson parameters $\lambda_{\sigma 1}^{\sigma 2}$ with $\sigma_1, \sigma_2 \in \{+,-\}$ where the subscript σ_1 refers to the dominant opinion and the superscript σ_2 to the statement polarity such that $(C_i^{\sigma 2}|D_i = \sigma 1) \sim \text{Pois}(\lambda_{\sigma 1}^{\sigma 2})$. The following equations express the Poisson parameters in terms of the three model parameters:

$$\lambda_+^+ = n \cdot p_A \cdot p_S^+ \qquad \lambda_+^- = n \cdot (1 - p_A) \cdot p_S^-$$
$$\lambda_-^- = n \cdot p_A \cdot p_S^- \qquad \lambda_-^+ = n \cdot (1 - p_A) \cdot p_S^+$$

EXAMPLE 3. *Assume we choose $p_A = 0.9$, $np_S^+ = 100$, and $np_S^- = 5$. The agreement parameter is relatively high and p_S^+ significantly higher than p_S^-; those are the characteristics of Example 2. We obtain $\lambda_+^+ = 90$, $\lambda_+^- = 0.5$, $\lambda_-^- = 4.5$, and $\lambda_-^+ = 10$. The corresponding distributions over the evidence tuples are the ones shown in Figure 6.*

Algorithm 2 Learning model parameters

```
// E: All evidence about one property-type pair
// X: number of iterations
function EM(E, X)
    Guess initial parameter vector θ_0
    for k ← 1 to X do
        Calculate opinion probabilities Pr(D|E, θ_{k-1})
        Calculate θ_k using opinion probabilities
    end for
    return θ_X
end function
```

6. CALCULATING PARAMETER VALUES

The probabilistic model introduced in the last section contains at the same time unknown parameters (p_A, p_S^+, and p_S^-) and unobservable random variables (the dominant opinion D_i on each entity). Knowing all parameter values would allow to infer the dominant opinion on each entity from the counts of positive and negative statements. Knowing the dominant opinion on each entity would allow to calculate optimal parameter values from the statement counts. We know however neither parameter values nor the dominant opinion and adopt therefore an iterative expectation-maximization (EM) approach [9].

Algorithm 2 shows a high-level overview of the expectation-maximization approach, applied to our scenario. The function represented in Algorithm 2 uses the evidence E that was collected about one specific property-type combination as input, i.e. $E = \{\langle c_i^+, c_i^- \rangle | i = 1..m\}$ is the count of positive and negative statements concerning the current property for all entities of the current type. The output is a three-dimensional vector θ_X containing near-optimal values for the three model parameters. The algorithm is iterative and executes X times the following two steps. First, it uses the estimates for the parameter values derived in the last iteration (or a vector of default values for the first iteration) to calculate probabilities for the dominant opinion about each entity. Second, it uses the opinion probabilities to calculate the most likely values for the parameters. We provide details on the second step in this section; the last section sketched how opinion probabilities can be calculated. Note that Algorithm 2 is executed separately for each property-type pair.

The EM approach is an extension of the Maximum- Likelihood (ML) method [9]. The goal of the ML method is to maximize a likelihood function $L(\Theta)$ in the parameter values Θ. The likelihood function represents the probability of obtaining given observations when assuming specific parameter values. The EM approach introduces a likelihood function that depends not only on the parameters but also on the unobservable random variables. In our scenario, this likelihood function $L(d, \Theta) := \Pr(E, D = d|\Theta)$ depends on the parameters $\Theta = \langle p_A, p_S^+, p_S^- \rangle$ but also on the values $d = \langle d_1, \ldots, d_m \rangle$ for the vector $D = \langle D_1, \ldots, D_m \rangle$ of unobservable dominant opinions. Algorithm 2 calculates a probability distribution over D in the first step of each iteration. Following the EM approach, we use that distribution in the second step to calculate function $Q_k(\Theta)$, representing the expected value of the logarithm of the likelihood function in the k-th iteration:

$$Q_k(\Theta) = \sum_{d \in \{+,-\}^m} \Pr(D = d|\theta_{k-1}, E) \log L(d, \Theta) \qquad (1)$$

We choose the new parameter estimate by maximizing Q_k:

$$\theta_k = \arg\max_{\theta}(Q_k(\theta)).$$

Note that the formula for Q_k contains the variable Θ, in which we maximize, as well as the constant vector θ_{k-1} that was calculated in the last iteration. In the following, we outline how Q_k can be expressed and maximized. Evaluating (1) directly is inefficient since the sum has an exponential number of terms in the number of entities. By summarizing the corresponding terms, we obtain a formula for Q_k with a linear number of terms in the number of entities:

$$\sum_{i=1}^{m} \sum_{d_i \in \{+,-\}} \left[\log(\Pr(D_i = d_i, E_i|\theta)) \Pr(D_i = d_i|\theta_{k-1}, E_i)\right]$$

We use $r_i^+ := \Pr(D_i = +|\theta_{k-1}, E_i)$ to denote the probability that the dominant opinion on the i-th entity is positive. Maximizing Q_k is equivalent to maximizing Q'_k which is obtained by neglecting constant factors in Q_k and yields:

$$Q'_k(\Theta) = \sum_i [r_i^+(c_i^+ \log(\lambda_+^+) - \lambda_+^+ + c_i^- \log(\lambda_+^-) - \lambda_+^-) + (1 - r_i^+)(c_i^+ \log(\lambda_-^+) - \lambda_-^+ + c_i^- \log(\lambda_-^-) - \lambda_-^-)]$$

Details of the transformation from Q_k to Q'_k are given in Appendix C. We can find the maximum of Q'_k by setting the partial derivatives $\partial Q'_k/\partial p_A$, $\partial Q'_k/\partial p_S^+$, and $\partial Q'_k/\partial p_S^-$ to zero. In our implementation, we speed up computations by trying a fixed set of values for p_A and maximizing Q'_k in p_S^+ and p_S^- for each value of p_A by setting the partial derivatives for p_S^+ and p_S^- to zero. We introduce several short notations to be able to conveniently express the formulas for p_S^+ and p_S^- that maximize Q'_k for fixed value of p_A. By $g_{\sigma 1}^{\sigma 2}$ with $\sigma_1, \sigma_2 \in \{+, -\}$, we denote the estimated number of statements with polarity σ_2 for entities with property polarity σ_1 according to the dominant opinion (e.g., g_+^- is the estimated number of negative statements about positive entities). By g_+ we denote the estimated number of entities with positive dominant opinion and by g_- the number of entities with negative dominant opinion:

$$g_+^+ = \sum_i (c_i^+ r_i^+) \qquad g_+^- = \sum_i (c_i^- r_i^+)$$

$$g_-^+ = \sum_i (c_i^+ (1 - r_i^+)) \qquad g_-^- = \sum_i (c_i^- (1 - r_i^+))$$

$$g_+ = \sum_i r_i^+ \qquad g_- = \sum_i (1 - r_i^+)$$

Now we can finally express the formulas for np_S^+ and np_S^- (we prefer working with np_S^+ and np_S^- over working with p_S^+ and p_S^- in our implementation to minimize rounding errors) that maximize Q'_k and Q_k for fixed values of p_A:

$$np_S^+ = (g_+^+ + g_-^+)/(g_- + p_A g_+ - p_A g_-)$$

$$np_S^- = (g_+^- + g_-^-)/(g_+ + p_A g_- - p_A g_+)$$

We derived expressions for the parameters values that can be evaluated in $O(m)$, i.e. in linear time in the number of entities. This allows SURVEYOR to scale to large entity sets as demonstrated in the next Section.

7. EXPERIMENTAL EVALUATION

We used SURVEYOR to solve the all common pairs version of the subjective property mining problem. Our input corpus was a snapshot of the entire Web. Section 7.1 quantifies input and output data set sizes as well as processing times for the different processing steps. Section 7.2 presents statistics concerning the number of extracted statements for different entities, properties, and types. We selected a limited set of entity-property combinations as sample to evaluate the precision of SURVEYOR in comparison to simpler approaches. Evaluating precision requires us to establish some kind of ground truth to compare against. Our ground truth is the dominant opinion among Web users about whether certain subjective properties apply to certain entities; we can approximate that dominant opinion by asking a sufficient number of *Amazon Mechanical Turk* (AMT) workers. Section 7.3 describes the test samples and how we approximate the dominant opinion on them using AMT. Section 7.4 compares SURVEYOR with alternative approaches against AMT. We summarize and discuss all results in Section 7.5.

7.1 Mining Subjective Properties on Web Scale

The data processing pipeline was executed on up to 5000 nodes. We used an annotated Web snapshot of 40 TB as input. Extracting evidence statements from that snapshot took around one hour. We thereby extracted over 922 million evidence statements concerning over 60 million entity-property combinations. Our knowledge base is an extension of Freebase; extracting the relevant information from the knowledge base (entities with their most notable types) took around 20 minutes. Combining information obtained from the knowledge base with evidence extracted from the Web snapshot and grouping entities by type took around one hour. The grouping of 60 million entity-property pairs by type, yielded 7 million distinct property-type pairs. We filtered this set down to 380,000 by removing the property-type pairs with fewer than 100 evidence sentences. On each property-type pair we ran the EM algorithm of Section 6 to get dominant opinions for 4 billion entity-property pairs subsumed by the 380,000 type-property pairs. The total time for this step was only 10 minutes. We attribute the efficiency of the EM step to the closed-form expressions we derived for each of the E and M steps.

7.2 Extraction Statistics

Figure 9 shows statistics concerning the number of extracted statements for entities, properties, and types. Figure 9(a) shows percentiles for the number of statements extracted about specific knowledge base entities: the 20th percentile shows for instance the number of statements such that for 20% of all knowledge base entities at most that many statements were extracted per entity. All percentiles up to the 95th percentile are close to zero. This means that most entities are rarely mentioned while few popular entities are the subject of most extracted statements.

Figure 9(b) shows the distribution of extracted statements over different property-type combinations. The distribution is skewed, meaning that a big part of all extracted statements concerns a few popular property-type combinations.

As discussed before, we only consider property-type combinations for which at least 100 statements are extracted. Figure 9(c) shows the distribution of considered properties over the entity types. The distribution is skewed again,

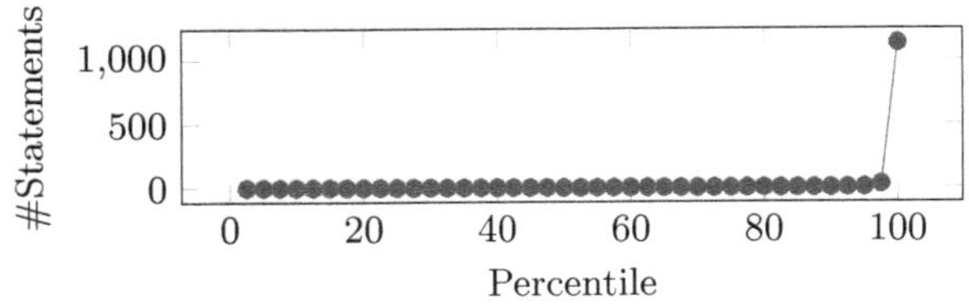

(a) Number of statements extracted about specific knowledge base entities

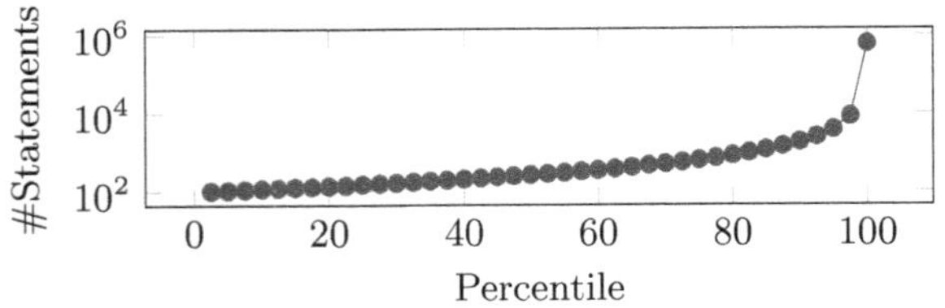

(b) Number of statements extracted about specific property-type combinations

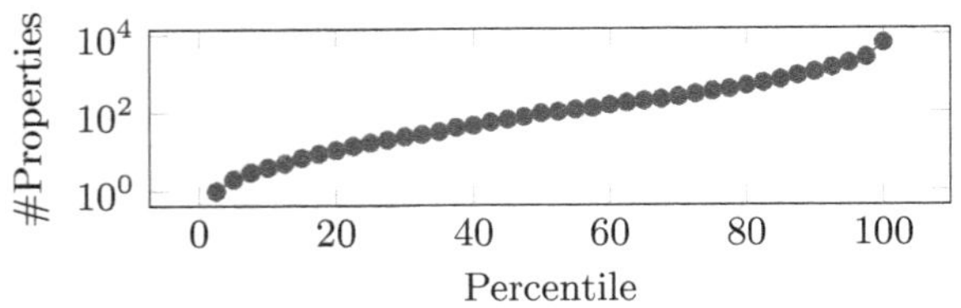

(c) Number of properties for which more than 100 statements are extracted for specific types

Figure 9: Extraction statistics: a big part of all extracted statements refers to a small set of popular entities and popular property-type combinations; few types are associated with many properties.

meaning that many properties are considered for few types while few properties are considered for most types.

7.3 Test Cases

We evaluate the accuracy of our system against a test dataset containing dominant opinions gathered from AMT workers. Our test dataset comprised 500 entity-property pairs: we selected five entity types and for each type 20 entities and five subjective properties as summarized in Table 2. We selected diverse types and properties that are common in the query stream. We safeguard against undesirable bias that this selection might introduce by reporting on a second series of evaluations over randomly selected entity-property pairs in Appendix D.

Since the goal of SURVEYOR is to find the dominant opinion, we tapped the crowd to collect ground truth data. We approximate the dominant opinion by asking AMT workers: we asked 20 workers about each of the 500 entity-property combinations such that we collected in total 10,000 opinions. We payed a fixed amount of 10 cents for providing an opinion on all entities of the same type for one specific property such that the total cost was 50 US dollars.

Figure 10 shows the results that we obtained from AMT for the property-type combination CUTE ANIMALS: for each animal, we report the number of AMT workers that would associate the property CUTE with it (out of 20 workers in total). Even if CUTE is a subjective property, we see that there is often a strong agreement between workers about

Table 2: Evaluated property-type combinations

Entity Type	Properties
Animals	dangerous, cute, big, friendly, deadly
Celebrities	cool, crazy, pretty, quiet, young
Cities	big, calm, cheap, hectic, multicultural
Professions	dangerous, exciting, rare, solid, vital
Sports	addictive, boring, dangerous, fast, popular

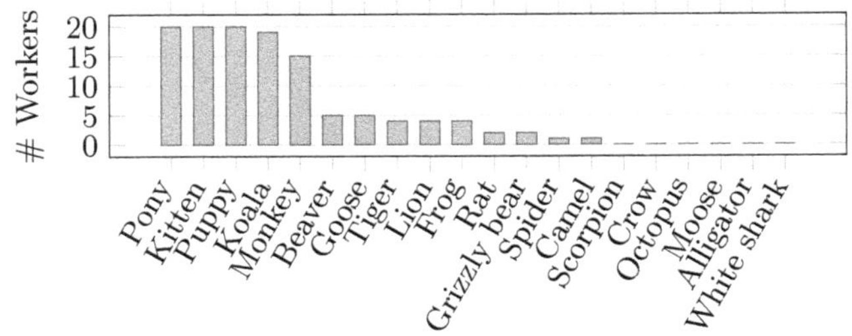

Figure 10: Test case example: how many out of 20 AMT workers call the animal "cute"?

whether specific animals are considered cute or not. In Figure 11 we show the distribution of the worker agreement values over all 500 test cases. We calculated worker agreement as the number of AMT workers that share the same opinion. We observe that there is indeed a dominant opinion that is worth searching for. Averaged over all 500 test cases, we had a worker agreement of 17 out of 20 with almost 180 cases enjoying perfect agreement. Only for 4% of the cases we got ties. We removed these cases from our test set.

While overall agreement was high, we noticed differences across different types and properties. Worker agreement was for instance higher when deciding which ANIMALS are DANGEROUS (average agreement: 18) than when deciding which SPORTS are DANGEROUS (average agreement: 16). Also, people agree more on which SPORTS are DANGEROUS than on which SPORTS are BORING (average agreement: 15). This means that the agreement parameter p_A should be chosen differently for each of the three combinations DANGEROUS ANIMALS, DANGEROUS SPORTS, and BORING SPORTS. This justifies our design decision of treating different property-type combinations separately.

7.4 Experimental Results

We evaluate SURVEYOR on the test cases presented in Section 7.3 by comparing its output to the opinions we collected from AMT. For a given test case, SURVEYOR will either assign positive polarity, negative polarity, or not generate any output (if we calculate a probability of 0.5 for the dominant opinion being positive). We consider the test case unsolved in the latter case. We use three measures to evaluate: coverage, precision, and F1. *Coverage* is the ratio of solved test cases to test cases. *Precision* is the ratio of correctly solved test cases to solved test cases. *F1* score is the harmonic mean of precision and coverage.

SURVEYOR uses a sophisticated probabilistic model to infer the dominant opinion given the counts of positive and negative statements. We compare this approach against two simpler methods: majority vote and scaled majority vote. *Majority Vote* (MV) decides that a property applies to an entity if the number of positive statements exceeds the number of negative statements and decides that the property does not apply if the number of negative statements exceeds the number of positive statements. No decision is possible if the two statement counters are equal. *Scaled Majority Vote* (SMV) is similar but scales the number of negative statements by the average ratio of positive to negative statements. As we will show this provides a gross adjustment of the inherent bias against negative statements.

As we discuss in Section 8, we are aware of no existing work on associating subjective properties to entities that can work on a Web scale without any supervision. The closest related work is the WebChild knowledge base [22] that associates entities with adjectives. The goal of WebChild is to associate an entity with all applicable adjectives like shape, color, and taste. WebChild does not explicitly model subjectivity and does not include negations of adjectives. Therefore, these comparisons are not entirely fair. In our comparison, we treat the absence of a property for an entity in WebChild as a negative assertion. Therefore, the only reason for loss of coverage for WebChild is that an entity is not contained in the knowledge base.

We first compare these four methods on aggregate performance over all 500 test cases and later present the results against varying levels of agreement among AMT workers. Table 5 shows that SURVEYOR is significantly better than the other methods according to all criteria. MV has low coverage indicative of the many cases with equal number of positive and negative statements which is often zero. SMV is able to improve on test cases where the number of negative statements is non-zero, explaining the slightly increased coverage. The coverage of WebChild is similar to the baseline's. The coverage of SURVEYOR is nearly doubled in comparison to the baselines because SURVEYOR employs a type and property specific model that allows inference even for entities that are not mentioned on the Web. SURVEYOR also performs significantly better in terms of precision. MV has the worst precision since it does not account for polarity bias. SMV has better precision but is still limited by the fact that it assumes universal polarity bias, meaning that its scaling factor is not type and property dependent. The precision of WebChild is significantly higher than for the two baselines. WebChild is however targeted at commonsense properties and not at subjective properties, so it does not explicitly detect negations; for certain property-type combinations (e.g., CUTE ANIMALS) we observed a high number of false positives from WebChild and suspect a connection. SURVEYOR suffers from none of those limitations; it detects negations and its model adapts to the type and property specific polarity bias.

We next compare the different approaches against varying levels of agreement among AMT workers. It seems more important that our system takes the right decisions for entity-property combinations where worker agreement is high. Figure 11 shows how many entity-property combinations satisfy different thresholds on the worker agreement. We observe that there is significant variation in the level of agreement; we have perfect agreement on 180 cases and less than 75% agreement on 100 cases. Figure 12 shows how precision and coverage vary with varying worker agreement. We see that

Table 3: Comparison of different methods for interpreting statement counters

Approach	Coverage	Precision	F1
Majority Vote	0.483	0.29	0.36
Scaled Majority Vote	0.486	0.37	0.42
WebChild	0.477	0.54	0.51
Surveyor	0.966	0.77	0.84

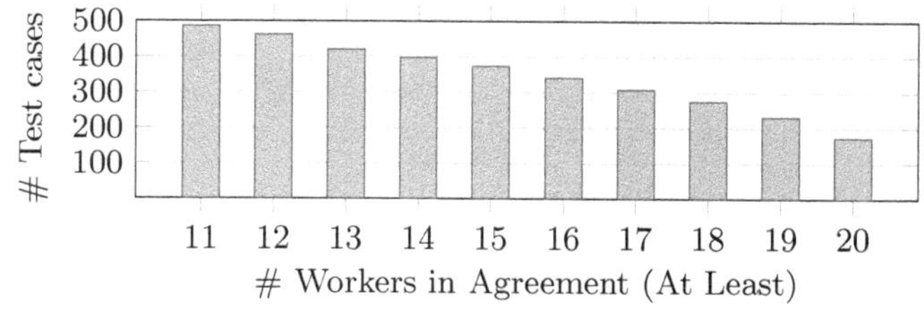

Figure 11: Number of test cases with AMT worker agreement above threshold

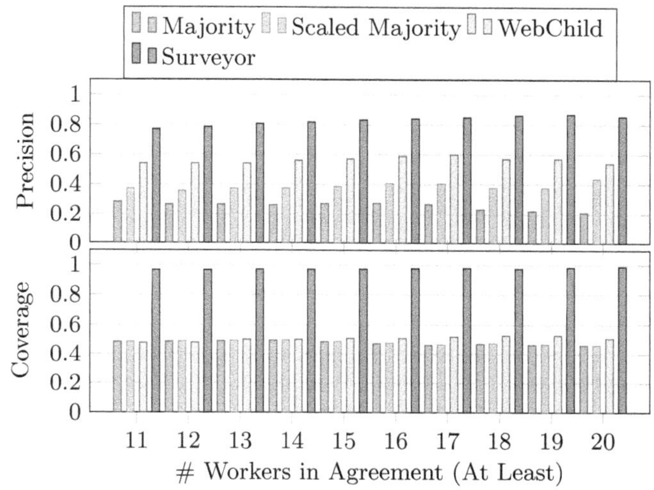

Figure 12: Precision and coverage for test cases with agreement above threshold

the precision of SURVEYOR increases with the worker agreement. It increases from 77% when considering all test cases to 87% when at most one worker disagreed. Figure 11 shows that almost half of all test cases fall into this category. MV cannot benefit from growing worker agreement while the precision of SMV increases from 37% to 44%. The effect is inconclusive for WebChild. Altogether, SURVEYOR performs better for test cases with high worker agreement which are at the same time the test cases that matter most.

We also experimented with randomly selected entities and properties which leads to similar precision values for all approaches while the coverage gap between SURVEYOR and the baselines increases. Details are given in Appendix D.

7.5 Discussion

The results show that our problem scope is reasonable: even if we consider subjective properties, the average agreement of 17 out of 20 for our test cases shows that a dominant opinion exists for many entity-property combinations. SURVEYOR outperforms competing approaches significantly in terms of precision and coverage. We believe that this is mainly due to the following properties of our approach. First, we distinguish between affirmative and negative statements which is important for controversial properties. Second, we do not treat different entities independently from each other but treat all entities of the same type together for each property. This increases coverage since it sometimes allows inferences for entities that are rarely mentioned (this is the case for most entities as shown in Section 7.2). Also, it improves precision since it allows to take type and property specific bias influencing the number of positive and negative statements into account.

8. RELATED WORK

We discuss the most closely related work in this section while we discuss additional publications in Appendix E.

Our work belongs to a broad family of approaches that parse free text to gain information about entities [2, 3, 4, 5, 22]. WebChild [22] associates nouns with adjectives over fine-grained relations such as has-shape or has-taste. The focus is on finding commonsense associations (e.g., carrot has-color orange) that are expected to be noncontroversial (e.g., we do not expect statements claiming that carrots are not orange). Therefore, WebChild does not search for statements claiming that a property does not apply to an entity and has no mechanisms to aggregate conflicting opinions. We compare our system against WebChild in Section 7. Chakrabarti et al. [4] and Cheng et al. [5] associate properties (*tags* in their terminology) with entities if the co-occurrence frequency (i.e., the number of documents in which property and entity appear close to each other) is statistically significant. Chakrabarti et al. [3] and Agrawal et al. [2] associate URLs with entities and rank entities based on the number of associated URLs that a search engine returns when querying for product features. The focus of these papers is less controversial properties like product features. They do not distinguish positive from negative statements, and do not deal with bias in mentions. As shown in Section 7, both of these are essential for subjective properties.

Sophisticated probabilistic models have been developed in the context of *Information Extraction* [8] to consolidate conflicting fact extractions (e.g., [6, 7, 20]). Those models are unsuitable for the scenario that we consider because their purpose is to explain the behavior of extraction algorithms in order to calculate a confidence from the number of consistent extractions. The purpose of our model is to explain the behavior of users in order to infer the majority opinion from the potentially non-representative set of statements that we collect. This is why our model integrates parameters modeling subjectivity and bias between positive and negative statements. This is what enables us to make inference even from the fact that we do not harvest any statements about specific entities. The models that are used in information extraction do not model subjectivity (assuming that inconsistent extractions are always due to mistakes of the extraction algorithm) and all inference is based on the fact that information was extracted (but not on the fact that no information was extracted).

The OpenEval system [19] is similar to our system in that it tries to connect entities to predicates. It differs however from our system since it uses supervised learning and would require us to specify by hand positive and negative samples for each property-type combination; this approach does not scale to large numbers of types and properties. Also, OpenEval uses Google queries to collect statements and is not able to mine a large number of opinions for a given entity-property combination as it only examines the first few result sites for each query. OpenEval is designed for scenarios in which the ground truth can be collected from a few reliable sources and it is not necessary to mine many conflicting opinions in order to obtain a reliable estimate of the majority opinion.

Opinion Mining and Sentiment Analysis [24, 23, 15] techniques extract and aggregate sentiments from text snippets; the goal is to detect expressions of positive or negative sentiments. One of the main challenges in this field is how to associate text snippets with sentiments, which are often expressed in subtle ways. Corresponding approaches classify text snippets on n-grams that are known to be associated with positive or negative sentiments. Such n-grams with associated polarity can be manually entered [21], learned from labeled reviews [16, 15], obtained from synonym and antonym relationships in WordNet[2], or seeded from a manually created list [11]. Our terminology is similar to the one used in sentiment analysis but the semantic differs: positive and negative statements in our case are not associated with positive or negative sentiments. In our scenario, statements connect entities to properties and the entities and properties are explicitly mentioned; there is no need to interpret subtle nuances. Unlike most approaches in sentiment analysis, our method does not require any labeled training samples nor dictionaries; instead, we rely on a fixed set of extraction patterns that are specific to our scenario. Opinion mining and sentiment analysis systems might include a final aggregation stage but this simply involves counting the number of sentences (or reviews) in which positive or negative sentiments are expressed [11, 13, 25] or calculating a rating average [15]. In contrast, our focus is on a intelligent aggregation step that adjusts for user bias and thus goes beyond counting and averaging.

9. CONCLUSION AND OUTLOOK

Users often use subjective properties to restrict the scope of their Web queries. If search engine providers want to be able to respond to such queries with structured information then they must learn how to associate entities with subjective properties. SURVEYOR represents our first step into this direction. Our experimental results justify our problem scope as well as our overall approach.

In future work, we plan to use SURVEYOR to connect subjective properties to objective properties. We could for instance try to find a lower bound on the population count of a city starting from which an average user would call that city BIG. Inferring and exploiting such relationships should allow to improve precision and coverage for the subset of subjective properties for which such correlations can be found.

10. ACKNOWLEDGEMENTS

We thank Niket Tandon for his support during the comparison of SURVEYOR against the WebChild system.

[2]http://wordnet.princeton.edu

11. REFERENCES

[1] Special issue: nonresponse bias in household surveys. *Public Opinion Quarterly*, 70(5), 2006.

[2] S. Agrawal and K. Chakrabarti. Query portals: dynamically generating portals for entity-oriented web queries. *SIGMOD*, pages 1171–1174, 2010.

[3] K. Chakrabarti. Ranking objects by exploiting relationships: computing top-k over aggregation. *SIGMOD*, pages 371–382, 2006.

[4] K. Chakrabarti and S. Chaudhuri. Entitytagger: automatically tagging entities with descriptive phrases. *WWW*, pages 3–4, 2011.

[5] T. Cheng, K. Chakrabarti, S. Chaudhuri, V. Narasayya, and M. Syamala. Data services for e-tailers leveraging web search engine assets. In *ICDE*, pages 1153–1164, 2013.

[6] A. Culotta and A. McCallum. Confidence estimation for information extraction. *HLT-NAACL*, pages 109–112, 2004.

[7] D. Downey, O. Etzioni, and S. Soderland. A probabilistic model of redundancy in information extraction. In *IJCAI*, pages 1034–1041, 2005.

[8] O. Etzioni, M. Banko, S. Soderland, and D. S. Weld. Open information extraction from the web. *Communications of the ACM*, 51(12):68–74, 2008.

[9] R. Fisher. On an absolute criterion for fitting frequency curves. *Messenger of Mathematics*, 41:155–160, 1912.

[10] C. Giuliano. Fine-grained classification of named entities exploiting latent semantic kernels. In *CoNLL*, pages 201–209, 2009.

[11] M. Hu and B. Liu. Mining and summarizing customer reviews. *KDD*, pages 168–177, 2004.

[12] X. Ling and D. Weld. Fine-grained entity recognition. In *AAAI*, pages 94–100, 2012.

[13] B. Liu, M. Hu, and J. Cheng. Opinion observer: analyzing and comparing opinions on the web. In *WWW*, pages 342–351, 2005.

[14] D. McDonald. On the poisson approximation of the multinomial distribution. *Canadian Journal of Statistics*, 8(1):115–118, 1980.

[15] S. Moghaddam and M. Ester. Opinion digger. In *CIKM*, pages 18–25, 2010.

[16] B. Pang, L. Lee, and S. Vaithyanathan. Thumbs up? Sentiment classification using machine learning techniques. In *Empirical methods in natural language processing*, pages 79–86, 2002.

[17] A. Popescu, B. Nguyen, and O. Etzioni. OPINE: Extracting product features and opinions from reviews. In *HLT/EMNLP on interactive demonstrations*, pages 32–33, 2005.

[18] B. Roos. On the rate of multivariate Poisson convergence. *Journal of Multivariate Analysis*, 69(1):120–134, 1999.

[19] M. Samadi and M. Blum. OpenEval : Web information query evaluation. In *AAAI*, pages 1163–1169, 2013.

[20] M. Skounakis and M. Craven. Evidence combination in biomedical natural-language processing. *BIOKDD*, pages 2–9, 2003.

[21] M. Taboada, J. Brooke, and M. Tofiloski. Lexicon-based methods for sentiment analysis. *Computational linguistics*, 37(2):267–307, 2011.

[22] N. Tandon, G. de Melo, F. Suchanek, and G. Weikum. WebChild: harvesting and organizing commonsense knowledge from the Web. In *WSDM*, pages 523–532, 2014.

[23] M. Tsytsarau, S. Amer-Yahia, and T. Palpanas. Efficient sentiment correlation for large-scale demographics. *SIGMOD*, pages 253–264, 2013.

[24] M. Tsytsarau and T. Palpanas. Survey on mining subjective data on the web. *KDD*, 24(3):478–514, 2011.

[25] L. Zhuang, F. Jing, and X.-Y. Zhu. Movie review mining and summarization. In *CIKM*, pages 43–50, 2006.

APPENDIX

A. EXTENDED EMPIRICAL STUDY

We describe the results for additional property-type combinations that we tried during our empirical study. In addition to the property-type combination BIG CITY, we tried the combinations WEALTHY COUNTRY, BIG LAKE, and HIGH MOUNTAIN. The experimental setup is the same as in Section 2: for each subjective property, we determine a numerical property that it should correlate with. Whether a country is considered wealthy should correlate with its GDP per capita. Whether a lake is considered big or not should correlate with its area and whether a mountain is considered high should correlate with its height.

For each of the three property-type combinations, we identified an HTML table on the Web that contains entities of the corresponding type and specifies the required numerical property for them. We selected a table containing countries with their GDP per capita as estimated by the IMF for 2013, a table containing lakes in Switzerland with their associated area in square kilometers, and a table containing mountains on the British Islands with their relative height in meters. We issued Google queries for all entities in the corresponding tables as described in Section 2, thereby counting affirmative and negative statements on the Web. Then we use the majority vote and the probabilistic model to estimate for each entity the polarity from its statement counts.

Figure 13 compares the polarity results in terms of how well they correlate with the numerical properties that we specified before. For all three scenarios, the correlation is significantly better for the probabilistic model. In addition, the probabilistic model is even able to classify entities for which no statements were collected. The latter problem concerns in particular the scenarios with lakes and mountains. Those scenarios are representative for the bigger part of property-type combinations that SURVEYOR considers; as our knowledge base is large, it contains many entities for which no statements can be collected on the Web (see statistics in Section 7.2). The SURVEYOR system can cope with sparseness since it considers sets of entities of the same type together; the majority vote approach considers each entity separately and cannot deal well with sparseness. Note that we use a qualitative evaluation approach here, while we use a quantitative approach to compare the probabilistic model against majority vote and other baselines in the experimental section.

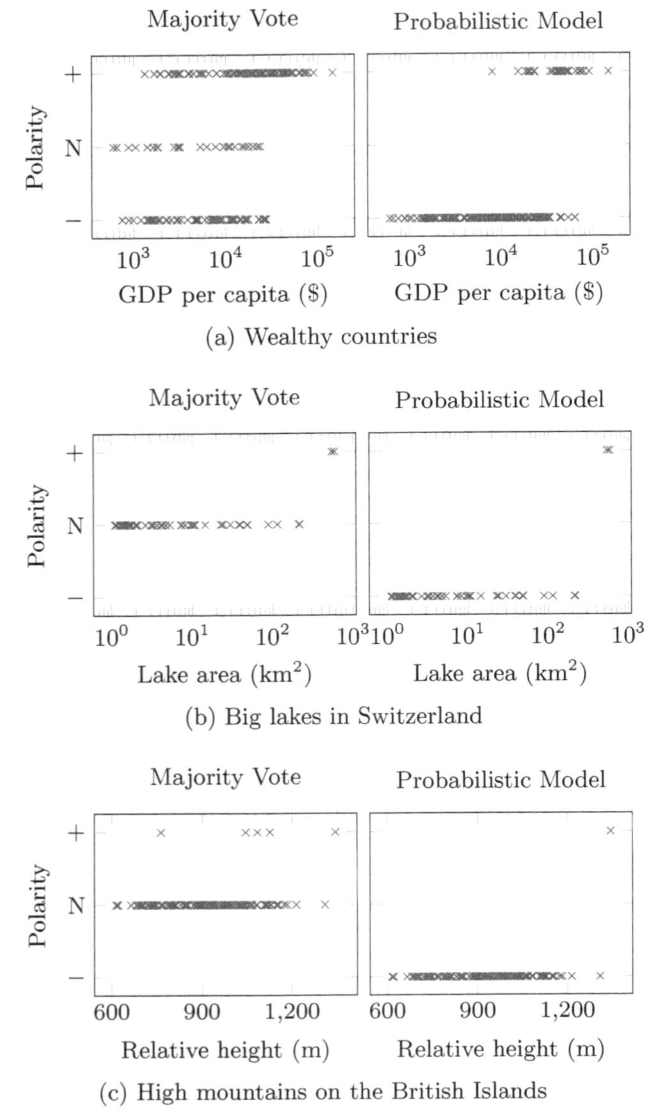

(a) Wealthy countries

(b) Big lakes in Switzerland

(c) High mountains on the British Islands

Figure 13: Result comparisons of majority vote (left side) and probabilistic model (right side).

B. EVOLUTION OF PATTERNS

We provide details on the different extraction patterns that we tried out before opting for the version that is presented in Section 4. Table 4 shows the different versions that we developed and tried out consecutively. The modifiers column describes the types of connections between adjectives and nouns that we considered for extraction; amod abbreviates adjectival modifier and captures cases such as "the cute cat" while acomp abbreviates accompanying modifier and captures cases such as "the cat is cute". The verbs column describes the verbs we considered for connecting adjectives to nouns; the class of copula verbs comprises all verbs that are commonly used to connect the subject of a sentence to a predicate. The other alternative is to be more restrictive and to consider only the verb "to be". The checks column indicates whether we filter out non-intrinsic statements. The statements column describes how many statements were extracted by the corresponding version.

Table 4: Comparison of different pattern versions

Vers.	Modifiers	Verbs	Check	Statements
1	amod	copula	no	1321194344
2	amod+acomp	copula	no	1779253966
3	acomp	to be	yes	98574972
4	amod+acomp	to be	yes	922299774

Our first version did not filter out non-intrinsic statements and used only the adjectival modifier pattern. After adding the accompanying modifier pattern for the second version, the number of extracted statements increased by over 30%. While the number of extractions was satisfactory, the quality of the extracted statements was not sufficient as we verified by studying example extractions. Our goal for the third version was to improve extraction quality; we therefore added the intrinsicness tests that are described in Section 4 and restricted ourselves to the accompanying modifier pattern and the verb "to be". This increased extraction quality indeed but at the same time decreased the number of extractions by more than one order of magnitude. For the final version, we used the adjectival modifier and accompanying modifier patterns together again but left the intrinsicness checks in place. The quality of the extractions now seemed significantly better than in the first versions while the number of extracted statements was still relatively close to the maximum. We used the fourth version for the experiments as it seemed to offer the best trade-off between precision and recall.

We also report extraction times for the different versions of the extraction patterns. Using version 1, extraction took around 2 hours and 40 minutes on a cluster with 1000 nodes. We increased the cluster size for executing version 2; extraction took around 50 minutes on a cluster with 5000 nodes. Version 3 took around 48 minutes with 5000 nodes. For our final version, extraction time was around one hour. Note that run time was not our primary criterion for selecting between extraction patterns.

C. ANALYSIS DETAILS

We provide more details on the analysis that we sketched in Section 6, leading to our formulas for calculating optimal parameter values. More precisely, we show how we obtain function $Q'_k(\Theta)$ which becomes maximal for the same parameter values as $Q_k(\Theta)$. The formula for Q_k is:

$$\sum_{i=1}^{m} \sum_{d_i \in \{+,-\}} \left[\log(\Pr(D_i = d_i, E_i|\theta)) \Pr(D_i = d_i|\theta_{k-1}, E_i) \right]$$

The factor $\Pr(D_i = d_i|\theta_{k-1}, E_i)$ is a constant in iteration k and we focus on transformations of the factor $\log(\Pr(D_i = d_i, E_i|\theta))$ in the following. The following transformations use the formula of conditional probabilities and basic properties of the logarithm function:

$$\begin{aligned} &\log(\Pr(D_i = d_i, E_i|\theta)) \\ =& \log(\Pr(D_i = d_i|\theta) \cdot \Pr(E_i|D_i = d_i, \theta)) \\ =& \log(\Pr(D_i = d_i|\theta)) + \log(\Pr(E_i|D_i = d_i, \theta)) \end{aligned}$$

The term $\log(\Pr(D_i = d_i|\theta))$ does not directly depend on the parameters since we do not consider the evidence E_i yet (the parameters concern only the connection between the probability for the dominant opinion and the collected evidence). We can therefore neglect the term when maximizing Q_k as it has no influence on the position of the maximum. We focus on the term $\log(\Pr(E_i|D_i = d_i, \theta))$ in the following and only consider the special case $D_i = d_i = +$ (while the analysis for the opposite case is analogue). The following transformations exploit the definition of the evidence $E_i = (C_i^+ = c_i^+ \wedge C_i^- = c_i^-)$ (i.e., the evidence consists of receiving a specific number c_i^+ of positive and a specific number c_i^- of negative statements), the assumed independence between the counts of positive and negative statements, the assumption that the number of evidence statements is distributed according to the Poisson distribution, and basic properties of the logarithm function:

$$\begin{aligned}
&\log(\Pr(E_i|D_i = +, \theta)) \\
=&\log(\Pr(C_i^+ = c_i^+|D_i = +, \theta) \cdot \Pr(C_i^- = c_i^-|D_i = +, \theta)) \\
=&\log(\text{Pois}(c_i^+; \lambda_+^+) \cdot \text{Pois}(c_i^-; \lambda_+^-)) \\
=&\log(\text{Pois}(c_i^+; \lambda_+^+)) + \log(\text{Pois}(c_i^-; \lambda_+^-))
\end{aligned}$$

We focus on the term $\log(\text{Pois}(c_i^+; \lambda_+^+))$ in the following while the analysis of the term $\log(\text{Pois}(c_i^-; \lambda_+^-))$ is analogue. We use the definition of the Poisson distribution and the logarithm rules:

$$\begin{aligned}
&\log(\text{Pois}(c_i^+; \lambda_+^+)) \\
=&\log(\frac{(\lambda_+^+)^{c_i^+} e^{-\lambda_+^+}}{c_i^+!}) \\
=&\log((\lambda_+^+)^{c_i^+} e^{-\lambda_+^+}) - \log(c_i^+!)
\end{aligned}$$

The term $\log(c_i^+!)$ does not depend on θ and we can neglect it when maximizing Q_k in θ. We transform the remaining term $\log((\lambda_+^+)^{c_i^+} e^{-\lambda_+^+})$ using our definition of the Poisson parameter λ_+^+:

$$\begin{aligned}
&\log((\lambda_+^+)^{c_i^+} e^{-\lambda_+^+}) \\
=&c_i^+ \cdot \log(\lambda_+^+) - \lambda_+^+ \\
=&c_i^+ \cdot \log(np_A p_S^+) - np_A p_S^+
\end{aligned}$$

We can apply analogue transformations to all terms in Q_k to obtain the formula for Q'_k that was specified in Section 6.

D. ADDITIONAL EXPERIMENTS

For the experiments in Section 7, we selected entity types and properties that frequently appear in queries. This reflects our main application scenario of interpreting queries. In this section, we provide additional results for types and properties that are sampled randomly from our large result set. We sampled 803 property-type combinations and for each combination we randomly sampled seven entities. This results in a total of over 5500 randomly sampled test cases.

We use those test cases to compare the performance of the same four approaches that we already evaluated in the experimental section. We used all test cases to evaluate coverage for the four approaches, as coverage can be calculated automatically: for scaled and naive majority vote we just verify whether the scaled or raw number of affirmative and negative statements are equal, for WebChild we check whether the entity that the test case refers to is included in the knowledge base.

Table 5: Comparison for random sample of property-type combinations

Approach	Coverage	Precision	F1
Majority Vote	0.0766	0.333	0.125
Scaled Majority Vote	0.0773	0.417	0.130
WebChild	0.173	0.615	0.270
Surveyor	0.999	0.784	0.879

Precision cannot be checked automatically but requires ground truth data to compare the output of the four approaches against. We therefore selected 80 property-type combinations and generated ground truth data for one randomly sampled entity per combination. We excluded six clearly offensive combinations such as "obnoxious ethnicity". In contrast to Section 7, we did not use AMT to generate the ground truth data. The reason is the following: our knowledge base is very large and when selecting random entities, we obtain in most cases entities that are very specific and not known to the general public. Our random sample of test cases includes for instance the Latin name of a disease ("Hiatal hernia"), a Portuguese artist named "Maria Lusitano", and the car model "Ford Cougar". Deciding for instance whether hiatal hernia should be counted as a MAJOR DISEASE required us to execute an Internet search and to read through corresponding material. We therefore do not expect to obtain meaningful results from AMT as this platform is rather targeted at simple and quickly executable tasks. The types and properties that we selected in Section 7 (e.g., animals) are more appropriate for an evaluation using AMT since those entities should be known to the general public.

Note that the aforementioned entities might still be useful to answer specific queries (e.g., a query asking for major diseases with specific properties that is issued by a person with a medical background).

Table 5 shows the results: our system is the only one which can slightly improve its F1 score comparing with the results in Section 7. For the three other approaches, the drop in F1 score is significant. In particular, there is a drop in coverage since the randomly sampled entities are less frequently mentioned on the Web, while the values for precision are comparable to the ones in Section 7. While the results in Table 5 are very favorable for our system, we still believe that the results reported in Section 7 are more relevant since they refer to entities that we expect to be more common in queries than the ones we randomly sampled. Our goal was however to show that our selection of test cases did not penalize the baseline approaches.

E. ADDITIONAL RELATED WORK

We pick one popular probabilistic model from *Information Extraction*, the one proposed by Downey et al. [7], as example to show why such models are ill-suited for our task. The model by Downey et al. models each extractor by a probabilistic "urn", fact extractions (e.g., the fact that New York is a city) are modeled as draws from the urns. The model calculates a confidence that specific facts are correct, based on the number of times the corresponding fact was extracted and the total number of draws. This model is not suitable for our scenario for several reasons. First, it cannot infer anything for the common case that no extractions were made for specific entity-property pairs; our model can give meaning to that case since it connects the likelihood that users express their opinion to their opinion. Second, the model by Downey et al. does not explicitly take into account mutual exclusion constraints between extracted facts. To map our scenario onto their model, we need to conceptually introduce for each property one extractor for positive statements and one extractor for negative statements. Then the latter model might for a given city calculate a probability for that city being big according to the dominant opinion and a probability for that city being not big such that those two probabilities do not sum up to one. The model that we introduce in this paper takes such exclusions into account.

Entity Classification [10, 12] is a sub-field of information extraction; the goal is to infer the type of entities mentioned in free text, using the surrounding text for the classification. Such techniques are a prerequisite for our approach since we group entities according to their type in order to learn type-specific content generation patterns. At the same time, the problem solved by SURVEYOR can be seen as a form of entity classification as well since for each property we classify entities into those to which the property applies and those where it does not apply. Our scenario poses however specific challenges since we consider properties that are controversially discussed; our prior discussion contrasting the probabilistic models used in information extraction from our model applies as well.

Feature Mining is often used as pre-processing step for opinion mining [11, 17, 15]; Hu and Liu [11] mine for instance product features (e.g., "picture quality" as feature of "camera") before extracting ratings for those features in a second step (we already discussed approaches for extracting ratings in the previous paragraph). Features are associated with entity types while subjective properties are associated with entities (e.g., the feature "picture quality" applies to all cameras, independently of whether they have good or bad picture quality, while the property "cute" only applies to a subset of animals but not to all of them). So the problem model of feature mining does not map to the problem model of subjective property mining. Also, features are usually frequent nouns [15] while subjective properties are usually adjectives and adverbs and associating properties with entities based on occurrence frequency alone creates problems since it neglects negation.

In *Classical Surveys*, participants are explicitly asked for their opinion. The bias introduced by the fact that some participants refuse to participate in a survey is known as non-response bias [1]. This case is considered rather rare and research usually focuses on bounding the effect of this bias or trying to avoid it by appropriate survey design. Our scenario differs from a traditional survey since we do not solicit participation but rather collect opinions that users decided to post themselves. This makes the "non-response" bias an important fact in our case since we have no control over the selection of participants. On the other side, our survey is simplistic comparing with traditional surveys, as we only have two options for each entity-property combination. This gives us the possibility to sometimes even infer something from the fact that we find "no participants".

Microblog Entity Linking with Social Temporal Context

Wen Hua [§†], Kai Zheng [§‡], Xiaofang Zhou [§‡]
[§] School of Information Technology and Electrical Engineering, The University of Queensland, Brisbane, Australia
[†] School of Information, Renmin University of China, Beijing, China
[‡] School of Computer Science and Technology, Soochow University, Suzhou, Jiangsu, China
w.hua@uq.edu.au {kevinz, zxf}@itee.uq.edu.au

ABSTRACT

Nowadays microblogging sites, such as Twitter and Chinese Sina Weibo, have established themselves as an invaluable information source, which provides a huge collection of manually-generated tweets with broad range of topics from daily life to breaking news. Entity linking is indispensable for understanding and maintaining such information, which in turn facilitates many real-world applications such as tweet clustering and classification, personalized microblog search, and so forth. However, tweets are short, informal and error-prone, rendering traditional approaches for entity linking in documents largely inapplicable. Recent work addresses this problem by utilising information from other tweets and linking entities in a batch manner. Nevertheless, the high computational complexity makes this approach infeasible for real-time applications given the high arrival rate of tweets. In this paper, we propose an efficient solution to link entities in tweets by analyzing their social and temporal context. Our proposed framework takes into consideration three features, namely entity popularity, entity recency, and user interest information embedded in social interactions to assist the entity linking task. Effective indexing structures along with incremental algorithms have also been developed to reduce the computation and maintenance costs of our approach. Experimental results based on real tweet datasets verify the effectiveness and efficiency of our proposals.

Categories and Subject Descriptors

H.3.3 [**Information Systems**]: Information Storage and Retrieval—*Information Search and Retrieval*

General Terms

Algorithms; Experimentation

Keywords

Microblog entity linking; Social temporal context; Entity popularity; Entity recency; User interest

SIGMOD'15, May 31–June 4, 2015, Melbourne, Victoria, Australia.

http://dx.doi.org/10.1145/2723372.2751522.

1. INTRODUCTION

Twitter[1], an online social networking and microblogging service, has attracted worldwide attention since its birth in March 2006. With more than 500 million registered users in 2012, it received over 340 million tweets per day[2] about topics ranging from daily life to breaking news. This huge collection of tweets make Twitter an invaluable information source, as well as a platform to maintain social interactions. Obviously, a better understanding of the content published on Twitter can benifit many real-world applications such as tweet clustering and classification, personalized microblog search, and so forth.

Consider microblog search as a motivation example throughout the paper. One of the most important issues faced by microblog search is **entity ambiguity**. Teevan et al. [1], based on analysis on large-scale query logs, observed that users search Twitter mostly to find information about breaking news or people of interest (e.g., celebrities), both of which involve named entities. Meanwhile, according to the statistics of a randomly sampled and manually annotated tweet corpus used in [2], about 45.08% of tweets have at least one named entity mention. In short, queries and tweets are full of named entities that, however, are usually ambiguous in practice, i.e., the same entity mention can correspond to multiple real-world entities. Therefore identifying the exact references for named entities can bring tremendous benefit to improving the accuracy and user experience of microblog search. Consider the example shown in Fig. 1, wherein the leftmost part are entity mentions occurring in tweets (e.g., "Jordan"), in the middle are named entities in a knowledgebase (e.g., *Jordan (country)*, *Air Jordan*, *Michael Jordan (basketball)*, and *Michael Jordan (machine learning expert)*), and each user u_i posts multiple tweets d_j at time t_j. Given a query with some entity mentions (e.g., "Jordan"), if we can successfully link them to the right entities (e.g., *Michael Jordan (basketball)*), the corresponding tweets (e.g., d_5, d_{13} and d_{15}) can be retrieved as the personalized search result. As we will show shortly, the performance of existing entity linking methodologies still needs to be improved, which is the focus of this work.

Next we will first review the state-of-the-art development in entity linking problem with a brief summary of differences between our proposal and existing approaches, and then bring out the challenges and our contributions.

1.1 Literature of Entity Linking

Entity linking is a task of automatically linking entity mentions to real-world entities stored in large-scale machine-understandable knowledgebases (e.g., Wikipedia[3]). Recently, significant progresses

[1] https://twitter.com/
[2] http://en.wikipedia.org/wiki/Twitter
[3] http://www.wikipedia.org/

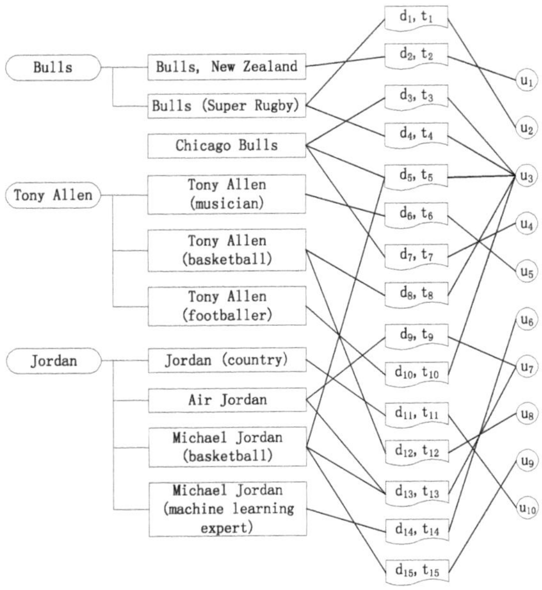

Figure 1: Entity linking for personalized microblog search.

have been achieved in linking named entities detected from Web documents with knowledgebases [3, 4, 5, 6, 7, 8, 9]. Many of them [3, 4] measure mention-entity correspondence by context similarity, i.e., similarity between text around the entity mention and the document describing the entity in a knowledgebase. However, tweets in microblogging sites are usually too short to have sufficient information to calculate context similarity accurately, which leads to unsatisfactory performance. Other approaches [5, 6, 7, 8, 9] assume that entities mentioned in a single document are likely to be topically coherent, and can collectively link mentions in a document by considering the interdependence between corresponding entities. Nevertheless, in the microblogging environment, there are usually too few available mentions to derive a joint and interdependent entity assignment due to the word limitation per tweet.

Recently, increasing attention has been paid to entity linking in short texts like tweets [10, 11, 12, 2, 13]. Regardless of their improvements over methods that link entities in a single tweet by considering topical coherence [14], these approaches are still not flawless. First, most of them [11, 12, 2] utilise information obtained from other tweets, and disambiguate entity mentions in these tweets collectively. They leverage the feature that Twitter users are content generators and hence their interest, which is helpful for entity linking, might be scattered in messages they broadcast. However, the topics of users' tweets vary significantly, making it difficult to detect user interest from such a diverse stream of tweets. Moreover, a large amount of Twitter users are information seekers (rather than content generators) who rarely tweet [15], which also increases the difficulty of learning their interest. Second, some work [13] enriches contextual information of tweets with knowledge from external sources such as Web documents. While such a strategy is feasible in an offline setting, it cannot handle the online tasks such as microblog search where thousands of tweets per second are to be processed in real time. Last but not least, none of them considers the popularity and recency of entities, which are important for capturing the dynamic nature of microblogging environment. In other words, their approaches always link *Michael Jordan* in queries or tweets issued by a user interested in computer science to *Michael Jordan (machine learning expert)*. This is obviously unreasonable, since *Michael Jordan (basketball)* is so popular and well-known that even machine learning experts sometimes talk about him. Furthermore, users' interest can be influenced by recent events and change over time. For example, *Michael Jordan (basketball)* is more likely to be mentioned during NBA seasons while *Michael Jordan (machine learning expert)* is probably a better candidate entity when ICML (International Conference on Machine Learning) is being held.

Our proposed method differs from existing approaches mainly in the following aspects.

- Instead of estimating user interest from her broadcasting history that is widely adopted in existing content-based methods, we resort to social interactions between users, namely the followee-follower relationship. This avoids the difficulty and inaccuracy of modeling user interest from limited amount of tweets with diverse topics.
- We propose a novel feature, entity recency, to model the evolving user interest influenced by recent events in the real world, which is important to capture the dynamic nature of microblogging sites.
- Different from existing collective entity linking methods, our framework links entities independently without considering any intra-tweet or inter-tweet relationships. This makes our approach much more efficient and suitable for online applications with real-time requirement.

1.2 Challenges and Contributions

In this paper, we propose to disambiguate entity mentions derived from microblog queries or tweets by leveraging several contextual information, namely user interest, entity popularity, and entity recency. In order to maintain the accuracy and efficiency of our framework, we need to overcome several challenges as elaborated in below.

Challenge 1. The first challenge is concerned with *measuring user interest by social interactions*. After offline entity linking using state-of-the-art approaches [2], entities in the knowledgebase are linked to tweets along with their timestamps and authorship. In other words, each entity is complemented with a community, namely a collection of users mentioning that entity. For example in Fig. 1, the communities associated with *Michael Jordan (basketball)* and *Michael Jordan (machine learning expert)* are $\{u_3, u_7, u_9\}$ and $\{u_6\}$ respectively. Therefore, measuring a user's interest in a candidate entity is equivalent to measuring her interest in the corresponding community. A straightforward method to estimate a user's interest in a community is to check her reachability with every user in that community through her social network. However, this approach has several drawbacks. First, conventional reachability test only considers connectivity between users. The *small-world* theory indicates that users in Twitter can reach each other within 4.12 hops in average [16], implying that just "reachable" does not mean "interested". Second, it is unreasonable to treat users in a community equally, since different people have different influences to a community, and a user's interest in influential people contributes more to her interest in that community. Third, reachability test between random users is time consuming in large-scale followee-follower network. Fourth, it is very expensive to aggregate reachability between the target user and every other user in a community, given that communities associated with popular entities are extremely large.

Contribution. To tackle the first challenge, we propose a novel concept of weighted reachability to model a user's personal interest in others. Instead of merely checking whether a path exists between two users, we also consider the number of paths in-between as well as the length of each path. We design indexing structures along with incremental algorithms to reduce the time cost for weighted reachability evaluation over the entire followee-follower network. Moreover, effective ways to estimate user influence in a community and incorporate it into measuring a user's interest in that community are also proposed.

Challenge 2. The second challenge is related to *gathering entity recency from tweets*. Entity recency is modeled by a burst of tweets talking about that entity during recent time period. In other words, entity recency represents an entity's recent popularity, so it is infeasible to pre-calculate and store entity recency offline. Another issue concerning entity recency estimation is that recency could be reinforced between related entities. For example, there might not be any tweets about *Michael Jordan (machine learning expert)* at the beginning of *ICML*. However, the possibility that users search for or tweet about *Michael Jordan (machine learning expert)* in the near future cannot be ignored. It is quite challenging to develop an efficient algorithm to evaluate entity recency on-the-fly while taking their mutual reinforcement into consideration. We capture this phenomenon with recency propagation, through which any change in some entity's recency can affect many other related ones.

Contribution. To cope with above challenge, we measure topical relatedness between entities based on their hyperlinks in the knowledgebase, with the rational that highly related entities should propagate recency to each other in a larger extent. To overcome the efficiency issue, we detect clusters of entities with strong connection, and ignore recency propagation between less relevant ones to avoid expensive recency diffusion. A PageRank-style algorithm has been proposed to conduct recency propagation, which can incorporate both recency gathered from underlying tweets and that reinforced by other highly related entities.

The rest of this paper is organized as follows: in Sec. 2, we briefly summarize development in the literature of graph reachability which is quite related with our work; then we define the problem of entity linking formally in Sec. 3, along with a brief introduction of notations adopted in this work; our approaches and experiments are described in Sec. 4 and Sec. 5 respectively, followed by a conclusion and discussion of future work in Sec. 6. The appendix includes a more detailed review of existing work on named entity recognition, two theorem proofs, dataset descriptions and two additional sets of experiments. At the end we also put a discussion about the issues of handling new entities/meanings and our thoughts of preliminary solution.

2. RELATED WORK

Reachability (Shortest Path Distance) Queries. One of the most important research topics related to our work is the reachability (shortest path distance) between two nodes over a network. Existing approaches to reachability checking trade-off between query efficiency and indexing cost, and thus can be classified into three categories: online search, transitive closure, and 2-hop labeling.

To determine reachability between two nodes u and v, the online search approach traverses from u to v using breadth- or depth-first search over the network G. This incurs $O(|E|)$ cost of query processing time, where $|E|$ is the number of edges contained in G. Lots of efforts [17, 18, 19] have been devoted to pruning the search space of BFS or DFS by pre-computing certain auxiliary information on G. For example, GRAIL [19] assigns each node in G with an interval such that u cannot reach v if u's interval does not fully contain v's interval. Given a reachability query from u to v, the algorithm starts DFS from the source node u and avoids visiting nodes whose interval does not cover that of the terminal node v, since they can never reach v. In spite of these pruning strategies, the online search approach still takes much more time than methods in the other two categories, making it inapplicable to real-time applications where query efficiency is a major concern.

The transitive closure approach [20, 21, 22, 23, 24, 25, 26], on the contrary, answers reachability queries within constant time. For each node u in G, it pre-calculates and maintains on disk a collection of all nodes that u can reach, namely a *transitive closure*. In this way, the algorithm determines reachability from u to v simply by checking whether (u, v) exists in the transitive closure matrix of the network. Obviously, the transitive closure approach is quite efficient, but it results in significant pre-computation and high storage consumption, and hence cannot easily scale to large networks. However, such an approach is still useful in situations where query efficiency is much more critical than storage consumption, as long as efficient algorithms can be proposed to reduce pre-computation.

To the best of our knowledge, 2-hop labeling approach [27, 28, 29, 30, 31, 32, 33, 34] is the most widely-adopted indexing scheme for reachability queries on large networks. It targets on designing indexes to reduce the space consumption of transitive closure and at the same time answer reachability queries efficiently. Typically, a *2-hop cover* of a network $G = (V, E)$ consists of two label sets $\{L_{in}(v)\}_{v \in V}$ and $\{L_{out}(v)\}_{v \in V}$, where $L_{in}(v)$ (resp. $L_{out}(v)$) represents the collection of nodes that can reach v (resp. nodes reachable from v). For any two nodes u and v, u can reach v if and only if $L_{out}(u) \cap L_{in}(v) \neq \emptyset$. Therefore, a reachability query can be answered within linear time by checking the intersection of the source node's out-label set and the terminal node's in-label set. Obviously, the 2-hop labeling approach also provides satisfying query efficiency, and thus can be regarded as a wonderful alternative for the transitive closure method when storage is limited.

3. PROBLEM STATEMENT

In this section, we briefly introduce some basic concepts and notations employed in the remaining of the paper, as well as a formal definition of entity linking. After that, we present an overview of our framework to entity linking. Table 1 summarizes major notations used in the paper.

Table 1: Summary of notations.

Notation	Definition
m	entity mention
e	entity
$\mathbb{E}_m$	candidate entity set of mention m
d	tweet with timestamp $d.t$ and author $d.u$
$\mathbb{D}_e$	tweets linked to entity e
$\mathbb{U}_e$	community associated with entity e
$Inf(u, \mathbb{U}_e)$	user u's influence in community associated with entity e
$R(u, v)$	weighted reachability between users u and v
$S_{in}(u, e)$	user u's interest in entity e
$S_p(e)$	popularity score of entity e
$S_r(e)$	recency score of entity e

3.1 Preliminary and Problem Definition

Definition 1 (Entity). *An entity e corresponds to a real-world object which exists in itself.*

Definition 2 (Mention). *A mention m is a sequence of words extracted from text and referring to some entities.*

Mentions are ambiguous while entities are unique, meaning that there exists many-to-many correspondence between mentions and entities. Specifically, A mention can refer to multiple entities. In Fig. 1, "Jordan" is a mention of *Jordan (country)*, *Air Jordan*, *Michael Jordan (basketball)*, and *Michael Jordan (machine learning expert)* as well. Meanwhile, an entity might have multiple mentions corresponding to it. For example, both "NYC" and "The Big Apple" can refer to the entity *New York City*. To resolve such a many-to-many correspondence between mentions and entities, entity linking is required.

DEFINITION 3 (**ENTITY LINKING**). *Entity linking is the task of determining the most probable entity e^* for a mention m.*

A typical strategy adopted by existing work on entity linking [3][4][5][6][7][8][9][10][11][12][2][13] includes two steps:

1. Candidate Generation. Given a mention m, a candidate entity set $\mathbb{E}_m$ is generated where each $e_i \in \mathbb{E}_m$ is a possible entity that m might refer to. In Fig. 1, the candidate entity set of "Jordan" is $\mathbb{E}_{Jordan}$ ={*Jordan (country), Air Jordan, Michael Jordan (basketball), Michael Jordan (machine learning expert)*};

2. Scoring and Ranking. For each entity in the candidate entity set $e_i \in \mathbb{E}_m$, a score $S(e_i)$ is calculated based on features which are application-dependent sometimes. After that, the most probable entity e^* is determined directly according to the ranking of scores.

Our focus in this work is how to calculate scores of entities in the candidate entity set, in order to achieve a reasonable ranking of candidate entities. we will briefly describe our approach to candidate generation in the next subsection. One thing to note is that a knowledgebase is required to enable machines to generate candidate entities automatically.

DEFINITION 4 (KNOWLEDGEBASE). *A knowledgebase $\mathbb{K}$ is a collection of mentions and entities along with mappings between them.*

DEFINITION 5 (COMPLEMENTED KNOWLEDGEBASE). *A complemented knowledgebase $\mathbb{K}'$ is a knowledgebase where each entity is associated with a list of tweets mentioning that entity along with their timestamps and authors, as illustrated in Fig. 1.*

We have discussed in Section 1.1 that the most important features for entity linking in Web documents are contextual similarity and topical coherence. Wikipedia, which is also the knowledgebase adopted in our work, is sufficient to provide these statistical information. However, queries and tweets are naturally short and informal, making both contextual similarity and topical coherence inapplicable. One of the most notable contributions of our work is that we propose new and effective features, namely user interest by social interactions, entity popularity and entity recency, which we believe are better options for entity linking in queries and tweets. In order to calculate these features, the original Wikipedia requires to be complemented with additional knowledge. Specifically, we pre-process a collection of tweets using current state-of-the-art approach to entity linking [2], and complement each entity in Wikipedia with a list of tweets mentioning that entity along with their timestamps and authors. We denote the collection of tweets linked to entity e as $\mathbb{D}_e$. Fig. 1 illustrates part of the complemented knowledgebase, where tweets associated with entities e_1 = *Michael Jordan (basketball)* and e_2 = *Michael Jordan (machine learning expert)* are $\mathbb{D}_{e_1} = \{d_5, d_{13}, d_{15}\}$ and $\mathbb{D}_{e_2} = \{d_{14}\}$ respectively. In the rest of this paper, we will use *Knowledgebase* and *Complemented Knowledgebase* interchangeably whenever context is clear.

We also mentioned in Section 1.2 that social interaction between users (i.e., followee-follower relationship) is a better choice to learn user interest, compared with tweet history. Although topics of users' broadcastings range from daily activities to breaking news and it is relatively difficult to detect user interest from such a diverse stream of tweets, users subscribe to others largely based on what they care. Therefore, a user's interest in an entity can be modeled as her interest in following users talking about that entity.

DEFINITION 6 (COMMUNITY). *A community $\mathbb{U}_e$ is a collection of users tweeting about a specific entity e, namely $\mathbb{U}_e = \{d.u | d \in \mathbb{D}_e\}$ where $d \in \mathbb{D}_e$ represents that tweet d is linked to entity e in our complemented knowledgebase.*

In Fig. 1, the communities associated with entities e_1 = *Michael Jordan (basketball)* and e_2 = *Michael Jordan (machine learning expert)* are $\mathbb{U}_{e_1} = \{u_3, u_7, u_9\}$ and $\mathbb{U}_{e_2} = \{u_6\}$ respectively.

3.2 Framework Overview

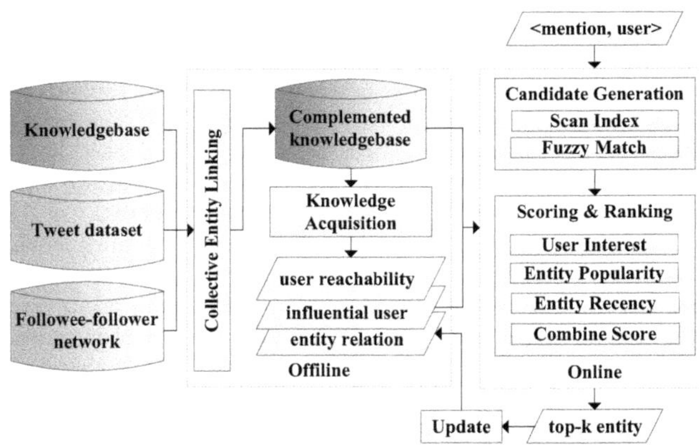

Figure 2: Framework overview.

Fig. 2 illustrates the framework of our prototype system for entity linking, which consists of two parts: offline knowledge acquisition and online inference. The workflow of our system is as below:

3.2.1 Offline Knowledge Acquisition

This module complements the original knowledgebase (Wikipedia) by pre-processing a set of tweets using current state-of-the-art approach to entity linking [2], and associating each entity in the knowledgebase with a list of tweets mentioning that entity along with their timestamps and authors, as demonstrated in Fig. 1. After that, it harvests essential knowledge which will be used during online inference.

Collective entity linking. [2] conducts entity linking in a batch manner. It assumes that each microblog user has an underlying interest distribution over named entities. Therefore, the intra-tweet entity relatedness and the inter-tweet user interest information can be integrated into a unified graph-based framework for collective entity linking. Specifically, given a set of entity mentions derived from all tweets posted by a user, it first constructs a graph between candidate entities where edge weights are calculated using the Wikipedia Link-based Measure (WLM) described in [35]. Then it estimates an initial interest score for each entity by considering its popularity, context similarity, as well as topical coherence, and employs a PageRank-like algorithm to propagate user interest from one entity to another. Finally, entities with the largest interest scores are regarded as the entity linking results.

Knowledge acquisition. We collect three types of knowledge during this process, namely weighted reachability between users, collections of most influential users broadcasting about each entity, and topical relatedness between entities. In this work, we determine a user's interest in an entity e by considering her interest in following the community broadcasting about e, namely $\mathbb{U}_e$. This requires a reachability checking between the target user and users in $\mathbb{U}_e$. In order to improve efficiency, we identify a set of most influential users for each community and check reachability only with these users. We describe the details of reachability checking and influential user detection in Sec. 4.1. Entity recency, which is aggregated from associated tweets, is also important for entity linking. We observe that recency can be propagated among related entities. Therefore, we pre-calculate topical relatedness between entities to facilitate recency propagation, as described in Sec. 4.2.

3.2.2 *Online Inference*

Given an entity mention along with its author, this module first generates a collection of candidate entities. Then for each candidate, it calculates a score which is a combination of user interest, entity popularity, and entity recency. Finally, it outputs a list of top-k entities according to the estimated scores. One thing to note is that our framework for entity linking can be easily designed to support personalized microblog search. Specifically, if the input entity mention comes from a keyword query, our system will collect tweets linked to the top-k entities from the complemented knowledgebase and regard them as answers to that query; but if the entity mention is derived from a tweet, our system will interactively consult users for the correctness of the top-k entities, and link the tweet as well as its timestamp and author to each of the correct entities in the knowledgebase, and update existing knowledge such as user influences in the corresponding communities.

Candidate generation. Since this is not the focus of our work, we simply adopt approaches proposed in previous work [9, 36]. In particular, given an entity mention m, we generate a set of candidate entities $\mathbb{E}_m$ which might by referred to by m. To ensure flexibility, our knowledgebase contains various surface forms of named entities, such as name variations, nicknames, abbreviations, and so forth, which are derived from Wikepedia's *entity pages*, *redirect pages*, *disambiguation pages* and *hyperlinks in Wikipedia articles* (details described in [9]). For example in Fig. 1, if the entity mention m matches knowledgebase entry "Jordan", its candidate entity set will be $\mathbb{E}_m$ ={*Jordan (country)*, *Air Jordan*, *Michael Jordan (basketball)*, *Michael Jordan (machine learning expert)*}. As we know, queries and tweets are full of misspellings. Therefore, we build a segment-based index on knowledgebase entries and adopt fuzzy matching to obtain candidate entities based on *edit distance* similarity (details described in [36]).

Scoring and ranking. The score of each candidate entity in $\mathbb{E}_m$ is a combination of user interest, entity popularity and entity recency, namely:

$$S(e) = \alpha \cdot S_{in}(u, e) + \beta \cdot S_p(e) + \gamma \cdot S_r(e) \tag{1}$$

In Eq. 1, $\alpha + \beta + \gamma = 1$ are parameters indicating the importance of each feature for entity linking, which can be manually set based on experience or learned from labeled data. $S_{in}(u, e)$ measures user u's interest in entity e, and is calculated through reachability checking between u and the most influential users in e's community $\mathbb{U}_e$. We describe the details in Sec. 4.1. $S_r(e)$ is the recency score of entity e, which will be discussed in Sec. 4.2. $S_p(e)$ is the popularity score of entity e, and is calculated as follows:

$$S_p(e) = \frac{count(e)}{\sum_{e_i \in \mathbb{E}_m} count(e_i)} \tag{2}$$

where *count*(e) is the number of tweets linked to entity e in the knowledgebase, and $\mathbb{E}_m$ is the candidate entity set of mention m.

4. METHODOLOGY

In this section, we describe some technical details in our framework for entity linking, including estimation of user interest by social interactions, as well as calculation and propagation of entity recency.

4.1 User Interest by Social Interactions

Traditional approaches to modeling user interest in microblogging sites are basically content-based, by assuming that users' interest might be scattered in their broadcastings. However, the topics of users' tweets usually range from daily activities to breaking news, making it difficult to detect user interest from such a diverse message stream. Furthermore, a large amount of microblogging users are information seekers who tweet rarely, which also enhances the difficulty to estimate their interest.

Fortunately, besides being content generators, microblogging users are also social network members, and they subscribe to others largely based on what they care. Therefore, we resort to social interactions between users (i.e., the followee-follower relationship) in this work, to avoid the difficulty and inaccuracy of modeling users' interest from their postings. In particular, we model a user's interest in an entity as her interest in following the community (i.e., the collection of users) broadcasting about that entity.

4.1.1 *Weighted Reachability Checking*

A straightforward way to measure a user's interest in a community is to calculate the number of users she subscribes to in that community, or in other words the proportion of overlapping between the community and her friend circle (i.e., followees). However, this naive method ignores users' interest in people several hops away. Such an indirect interest is also the motivation of friend recommendation in microblogging sites. Therefore, a better approach is to consider average reachability from the target user to people in the community through the directed followee-follower network.

$$S_{in}(u, e) = S_{in}(u, \mathbb{U}_e) = \frac{\sum_{v \in \mathbb{U}_e} R(u, v)}{|\mathbb{U}_e|} \tag{3}$$

In Eq. 3, $S_{in}(u, e)$ denotes user u's interest in entity e, which is transformed into u's interest in the community associated with entity e in our knowledgebase, namely $S_{in}(u, \mathbb{U}_e)$. And $R(u, v)$ denotes reachability from user u to user v.

However, Conventional reachability only considers connectedness between two nodes over a network, which is different from interestedness. The *small-world* theory guarantees that users in Twitter can be reachable within 4.12 steps in average ([16]), but it is obviously impossible for normal users to be interested in every other user. In order to achieve a meaningful measurement of users' interest in subscribing to other users, **reachability should be weighted**. We propose following heuristics:

- The shorter the distance from users u to v in the followee-follower network, the higher the probability of u following v;
- The larger the number of u's followees who participate in a shortest path from u to v, the higher the probability of u following v.

The second heuristic formulates strength of connection between users in the followee-follower network. Take 2-hop relationship as an example. If most of u's followees subscribe to v, then u is probably interested in following v. Based on these heuristics, we define weighted reachability from u to v as follows:

$$R(u, v) = \frac{1}{d_{uv}} \cdot \frac{|F_{uv}|}{|F_u|} \tag{4}$$

In Eq. 4, F_u denotes the collection of users that u subscribes to (i.e., u's followees), and F_{uv} represents u's followees participating in at least one shortest path from u to v. Formally, $F_{uv} = \{t | t \in F_u \wedge t \in u \leadsto^* v\}$, where $u \leadsto^* v$ is the set of shortest paths from u to v whose length (i.e., number of edges in-between) is denoted as d_{uv}.

Extended Transitive Closure Framework

Since query efficiency is a major concern when conducting entity linking for personalized microblog search, we first assume access to unlimited storage resource and extend the transitive closure approach [20, 21, 22, 23, 24, 25, 26] for weighted reachability checking. Our focus here is to design algorithms to reduce time cost for offline pre-computation.

Obviously, a traverse over the entire followee-follower network is required to calculate weighted reachability between each pair of users. This is extremely time-consuming and thus unacceptable, even if reachability is calculated offline. In this work, we design an **incremental algorithm** to improve efficiency of reachability checking, as illustrated in Algo. 1.

Algorithm 1 Incremental algorithm for extended transitive closure

```
Input:
    G = (V, E) /*followee-follower network*/
    H /*maximum number of hops*/
Output:
    R /*weighted reachability matrix*/
 1: Initialize each element of R_{|V|·|V|} as 0
 2: for each e = (u, v) ∈ E do
 3:     R(u, v) = 1
 4: end for
 5: for len=2:H do
 6:     for each u ∈ V do
 7:         T = {t|R(u, t) = 1} /*followees of u*/
 8:         for each t ∈ T do
 9:             V_t = {v|R(t, v) ≠ 0} /*reachable from t in len − 1 hops*/
10:         end for
11:         V = ⟨v, n_v⟩ /*n_v is the number of V_t containing v*/
12:         for each v ∈ V do
13:             if R(u, v) = 0 then
14:                 R(u, v) = (1/len) · (n_v/|T|) /*no shorter path from u to v, then update
                    weighted reachability*/
15:             end if
16:         end for
17:     end for
18: end for
```

Our incremental algorithm works by increasing the number of hops (i.e., the length of shortest path) one at a time. Given the followee-follower network $G = (V, E)$, we construct a matrix $R_{|V|\cdot|V|}$ to maintain weighted reachability between each pair of users. We traverse the network once and set reachability between connected users as 1 (lines 2-4). For each user u, her followees can be easily obtained by searching for elements in the reachability matrix $R(u, *)$ whose value is 1 (line 7). The key technique in this incremental algorithm lies in how to determine whether a followee of u (say t) participates in a shortest path from u to v, by leveraging existing knowledge about reachability.

THEOREM 1. *There exists a len-hop shortest path from u to v which passes through u' followee t only if the shortest path distance from t to v is len − 1 hops.*

According to Theorem 1, we can determine whether to insert t into u's followee set participating in the *len*-hop shortest path from u to v simply by checking whether t can reach v within $len - 1$ hops (or whether $R(t, v) \neq 0$ after the $(len - 1)$-th iteration). We collect such followees, and update the weighted reachability matrix using Eq. 4 (lines 8-16).

Compared with the naive method which traverses the followee-follower network for reachability checking between each pair of users, our incremental algorithm directly or indirectly scans the network only H (i.e., maximum number of hops) times. More formally, the naive method needs to calculate pairwise weighted reachability for $O(|V|^2)$ times, where $|V|$ is the number of users in the followee-follower network. For each reachability checking, it uses a breadth-first search which traverses $O(|E|) = O(|V|^2)$ users. Altogether, the time complexity of the naive method is $O(|V|^4)$. Our incremental algorithm, on the other hand, can leverage existing information about reachability and thus achieves $O(H \cdot |V|^2)$ time complexity. According to a previous study on Twitter's network structure, users can be connected within 4.12 steps in average [16]. In other words, H is guaranteed to be a small value.

Extended 2-Hop Cover Framework

The transitive closure approach requires $O(|V|^2)$ space consumption, making it inapplicable when storage resource is limited. Recent work mostly targets on designing indexes to reduce the space consumption of transitive closure and at the same time answer reachability queries efficiently. We believe the 2-hop labeling approach [27, 28, 29, 30, 31, 32, 33, 34] is the most efficient and widely-used indexing method for reachability queries on large graphs. Therefore, we also consider extending the 2-hop cover framework in this work, to support weighted reachability queries when storage is limited.

Typically, a *2-hop cover* of a graph $G = (V, E)$ consists of two label sets $\{L_{in}(v)\}_{v \in V}$ and $\{L_{out}(v)\}_{v \in V}$, where $L_{in}(v)$ (resp. $L_{out}(v)$) represents the collection of nodes that can reach v (resp. nodes that can be reached from v). Given a reachability query $Query(s, t, L_{in}, L_{out})$ from node s to node t, the algorithm first retrieves the out-label set of s and the in-label set of t, and then calculates the intersection of these two label sets:

$$Intersect(s, t) = (L_{out}(s) \cup \{s\}) \cap (L_{in}(t) \cup \{t\})$$

If the intersection set $Intersect(s, t)$ is empty, then the algorithm returns $FALSE$ to reachability query $Query(s, t, L_{in}, L_{out})$; otherwise, t is regarded to be reachable from s.

In Eq. 4, we define weighted reachability from node u to node v in terms of the shortest path distance between u and v, as well as the number of u's followees who participate in at least one shortest path. Therefore, an extension of the original 2-hop cover is required to incorporate these information and support weighted reachability queries. In particular, we define two label sets for each node $v \in V$:

$$L_{in}(v) = \{(s, d_{sv})\}$$

$$L_{out}(v) = \{(t, d_{vt}, F_{vt})\}$$

where s in $L_{in}(v)$ (resp. t in $L_{out}(v)$) is a node that can reach v (resp. a node reachable from v), and d_{sv} (resp. d_{vt}) is the shortest path distance from s to v (resp. from v to t). F_{vt} in $L_{out}(v)$ is a collection of v's followees participating in the shortest path from v to t, namely $F_{vt} = \{u | u \in F_v \wedge u \in v \leadsto^* t\}$.

In order to calculate weighted reachability from users s to t (i.e., $R(s, t)$), we issue a weighted reachability query $Query(s, t, L_{in}, L_{out})$

to retrieve information required in Eq. 4 (i.e., d_{st} and F_{st}):

$$(d_{st}, F_{st}) = Query(s, t, L_{in}, L_{out})$$
$$= \begin{cases} d_{st} = \min\{d_{sv} + d_{vt} | (v, d_{sv}, F_{sv}) \in L_{out}(s) \wedge (v, d_{vt}) \in L_{in}(t)\} \\ F_{st} = \bigcup_{d_{sv}+d_{vt}=d_{st}} F_{sv} \end{cases} \quad (5)$$

Here, d_{st} is the shortest path distance from nodes s to t, and $d_{st} = \infty$ when s cannot reach t within H (i.e., predefined maximum number of hops) steps. F_{st} is the collection of followees that participate in the shortest path from s to t.

THEOREM 2. *If the shortest path from s to v passes through s's followee f, and v lies in the shortest path from s to t, then f participates in the shortest path from s to t.*

According to Theorem 2, we calculate F_{st} in Eq. 5 by aggregating F_{sv} where v lies in the shortest path from s to t. For example, assume that $L_{out}(s) = \{(v_1, 2, \{f_1, f_2, f_3\}), (v_2, 3, \{f_2, f_4\})\}$ and $L_{in}(t) = \{(v_1, 2), (v_2, 1)\}$, then the shortest path distance from s to t is obviously $d_{st} = 4$ and s's followees participating in its shortest path to t is $F_{st} = \{f_1, f_2, f_3, f_4\}$.

Algorithm 2 Index construction for extended 2-hop labeling

Input:
$G = (V, E)$ /*followee-follower network*/
H /*maximum number of hops*/
Output:
$L_{in}^{|V|}$ and $L_{out}^{|V|}$ /*2-hop labels of G*/
1: Sort V by their degrees in descending order
2: **for** k=1:|V| **do**
3: $\forall v \in V$, $L_{in}^{k}(v) = L_{in}^{k-1}(v)$ and $L_{out}^{k}(v) = L_{out}^{k-1}(v)$
4: /*Conduct backward BFS to find all nodes that can reach v_k, and update L_{out}^{k}'s distances and followee sets when necessary*/
5: Q = an empty queue; Enqueue $\langle v_k, 0\rangle$ onto Q
6: **while** Q is not empty **do**
7: Dequeue $\langle u, len\rangle$ from Q
8: $len = len + 1$
9: **for all** $s \in N_{in}(u)$ **do**
10: $(d_{sv_k}, F_{sv_k}) = Query(s, v_k, L_{in}^{k-1}, L_{out}^{k-1})$
11: **if** $len < d_{sv_k}$ **then**
12: /*If distance is shortened, then update L_{out}^{k} and add the current node onto the queue*/
13: **if** $v_k \in L_{out}^{k}(s)$ **then**
14: Remove $(v_k, d_{sv_k}, F_{sv_k})$ from $L_{out}^{k}(s)$
15: **end if**
16: $L_{out}^{k}(s) = L_{out}^{k}(s) \cup \{(v_k, len, \{u\})\}$
17: **if** $len < H \wedge s \notin Q$ **then**
18: Enqueue $\langle s, len\rangle$ onto Q
19: **end if**
20: **else if** $len = d_{sv_k} \wedge u \notin F_{sv_k}$ **then**
21: /*If a new shortest path is found, then update followee set*/
22: **if** $v_k \in L_{out}^{k}(s)$ **then**
23: $L_{out}^{k}(s).F_{sv_k} = L_{out}^{k}(s).F_{sv_k} \cup \{u\}$
24: **else**
25: $L_{out}^{k}(s) = L_{out}^{k}(s) \cup \{(v_k, len, \{u\})\}$
26: **end if**
27: **end if**
28: **end for**
29: **end while**
30: Conduct forward BFS to find all nodes that v_k can reach, and update L_{in}^{k} only when distance is shortened
31: **end for**

Our offline indexing algorithm for the extended 2-hop labeling framework is depicted in Algo. 2. Inspired by the Pruned Landmark Labeling (PLL, [32, 33]) approach, we sort nodes in $G = (V, E)$ by their degrees in descending order (line 1), and construct 2-hop labels L_{in}^{k} (resp. L_{out}^{k}) from L_{in}^{k-1} (resp. L_{out}^{k-1}) using information obtained by pruned forward (resp. backward) BFS from the node v_k (lines 2-31). Specifically, suppose that we are handling a node t with distance *len* during the forward BFS from v_k. We issue a weighted reachability query from v_k to t, namely $(d_{v_k t}, F_{v_k t}) = Query(v_k, t, L_{in}^{k-1}, L_{out}^{k-1})$. If $len < d_{v_k t}$ (i.e., we find a shorter path from v_k to t), then we add (v_k, len) to $L_{in}^{k}(t)$ (i.e., $L_{in}^{k}(t) = L_{in}^{k}(t) \cup (v_k, len)$) and insert t into a queue for further BFS. One thing to note is that the index updating strategy for L_{out} is slightly different. Since $L_{out}^{k}(s)$ records both the shortest path distance from s to v_k and the collection of s's followees participating in the shortest path, special attention is required to maintain the followee set when updating $L_{out}^{k}(s)$ (lines 5-29). Assume that we are visiting a node s with distance *len* during the backward BFS from node v_k, and the shortest path distance (resp. followee set) obtained by a weighted reachability query from s to v_k is d_{sv_k} (resp F_{sv_k}). We consider two situations here which trigger updates of $L_{out}^{k}(s)$: 1) $len < d_{sv_k}$ (lines 11-19). Like before, a shorter path from s to v_k (i.e., $s \rightarrow u \rightsquigarrow v_k$) is detected in this situation. We add $(v_k, len, \{u\})$ to $L_{out}^{k}(s)$ where u is the followee of s in the *len*-hop path from s to v_k, and insert s into a queue for further BFS. Since we traverse nodes using a backward BFS, s's followees u can be directly recorded during this process. 2) $len = d_{sv_k}$ (lines 20-27). A new *len*-hop shortest path from s to v_k (i.e., $s \rightarrow u \rightsquigarrow v_k$) is detected in this situation. We need to check whether the information that s's followee u participates in a shortest-path from s to v_k has been encoded in existing 2-hop labels. If not, we insert u into the followee set, namely $L_{out}^{k}(s).F_{sv_k} = L_{out}^{k}(s).F_{sv_k} \cup \{u\}$. Since the shortest path distance from s to v_k stays unchanged, which means the distances from s's ancestors to v_k passing through s must also be the same, we do not need to add s into the queue for further BFS.

We evaluate the performance of the extended transitive closure framework and the extended 2-hop cover framework for weighted reachability queries in Sec. 5, in terms of query efficiency, space consumption, as well as pre-computation time.

4.1.2 Detecting influential users

As depicted in Eq. 3, measuring a user u's interest in an entity e requires reachability checking between u and other users in the community associated with e. Although these information can be obtained directly from the pre-computed weighted reachability matrix, aggregating such a great amount of reachability during online inference is still a waste of time. Moreover, it is obviously inappropriate to treat every user as equal. Different people have different influences in a community, and a user's interest in influential people has more contribution to her interest in the community. To improve both the accuracy and the efficiency of user interest estimation, we propose to detect a collection of most influential users for each community and consider reachability only with those influential users.

Intuitively, a user is influential in a community associated with an entity if:

- She posts a large proportion of tweets linked to that entity;
- She is discriminative among candidate entities.

The second intuition guarantees that the influential user of an entity has a *distinct* interest in broadcasting about that entity, and such an interest *remains stable* over time. For example, a machine learning expert might also has a major interest in basketball, and will talk about both *Michael Jordan (basketball)* and *Michael Jordan (machine learning expert)* in her tweets. Hence, estimating target user u's interest in following such a user makes little contribution to discriminating candidate entities of the mention "Jordan". On the contrary, NBA's official account in Twitter (i.e., @NBAOfficial) hardly broadcasts about *Jordan (country)*, *Air Jordan*, or *Michael Jordan (machine learning expert)*, making u's subscription to @NBAOfficial an important hint of her interest in basketball. In this case, mentions of "Jordan" in u's queries and tweets should probably be linked to *Michael Jordan (basketball)*.

Tfidf-Based Approach

One possible approach to identify influential users in a community considering the aforementioned intuitions is to adopt the tf-idf weighing strategy. Given the candidate entity set $\mathbb{E}_m$ of mention m, we can obtain documents and community associated with each candidate entity e from our complemented knowledgebase, namely $\mathbb{D}_e$ and $\mathbb{U}_e$ respectively. We use the following formula to measure the influence of a user u in community $\mathbb{U}_e$:

$$Inf(u, \mathbb{U}_e) = \frac{|\mathbb{D}_e^u|}{|\mathbb{D}_e|} \cdot \log \frac{|\mathbb{E}_m|}{|\mathbb{E}_m^u|} \quad (6)$$

In Equation 6, $\mathbb{D}_e^u = \{d|d \in \mathbb{D}_e \wedge d.u = u\}$ denotes the collection of tweets linked to entity e which are posted by user u. Hence, $\frac{|\mathbb{D}_e^u|}{|\mathbb{D}_e|}$ indicates u's enthusiasm in broadcasting about entity e. On the other hand, $\log \frac{|\mathbb{E}_m|}{|\mathbb{E}_m^u|}$ reflects u's ability to differentiate candidate entities (namely whether u's interest is unique or diversified among all candidate entities), where $\mathbb{E}_m^u = \{e_i|e_i \in \mathbb{E}_m \wedge \exists d \in \mathbb{D}_{e_i}, d.u = u\}$ denotes the set of candidate entities that user u has mentioned at least once in her tweets.

Entropy-Based Approach

In practice, it is possible that an influential user in a community (say @NBAOfficial) occasionally tweets about candidate entities of other communities (say *Air Jordan*). Such an incident posting should not cause huge impact on her influence in the original community. In this sense, the tfidf-based approach is inappropriate, since it penalizes a user's influence as long as she has broadcastings in many communities. A better approach is to consider the probability distribution of a user's tweets among candidate entities.

Entropy can be regarded as a quantitative description of the shape of a probability distribution, which maximizes when the distribution is uniform. Obviously, a user is discriminative among candidate entities if and only if the probability distribution of her tweets among these entities is biased, which in turn means a small entropy value. Therefore, we propose an entropy-based approach to estimate user influence in a community:

$$Inf(u, \mathbb{U}_e) = \frac{|\mathbb{D}_e^u|}{|\mathbb{D}_e|} \cdot \frac{1}{entropy(u, \mathbb{E}_m)} \quad (7)$$

As before, $\frac{|\mathbb{D}_e^u|}{|\mathbb{D}_e|}$ in Eq. 7 reflects user u's contribution of tweets to the community associated with entity e. $entropy(u, \mathbb{E}_m)$ measures u's ability to differentiate candidate entities, which is calculated as below:

$$entropy(u, \mathbb{E}_m) = -\sum_{e_i \in \mathbb{E}_m} p(u, e_i) \log p(u, e_i)$$

$$p(u, e_i) = \frac{|\mathbb{D}_{e_i}^u|}{\sum_{e_k \in \mathbb{E}_m} |\mathbb{D}_{e_k}^u|}$$

Here, $p(u, e_i)$ is the probability of user u mentioning entity e_i in her tweets, as compared with other entities in the candidate entity set $\mathbb{E}_m$. And $\mathbb{D}_{e_i}^u = \{d|d \in \mathbb{D}_{e_i} \wedge d.u = u\}$ is the collection of tweets written by user u about entity e_i.

We will evaluate the effectiveness of both tfidf-based and entropy-based approaches to user influence estimation in Sec. 5. Given influence scores of users in a community $\mathbb{U}_e$, the collection of most influential users in that community can be identified by a simple ranking:

$$\mathbb{U}_e^* = \arg\max_u Inf(u, \mathbb{U}_e)$$

After that, we can estimate a user's interest in entity e by her interest in following those influential users, which is in turn estimated through weighted reachability checking. Formally,

$$S_{in}(u, e) = S_{in}(u, \mathbb{U}_e^*) = \frac{\sum_{v \in \mathbb{U}_e^*} R(u, v)}{|\mathbb{U}_e^*|} \quad (8)$$

where $\mathbb{U}_e^*$ is the set of influential users associated with entity e, and $R(u, v)$ is the weighted reachability from users u to v.

4.2 Entity Recency

As discussed in Sec. 1, recency is important to entity linking especially when it is conducted to support personalized microblog search. Entity recency can be obtained indirectly by gathering temporal information of tweets talking about that entity. However, linking a single newly-generated tweet to an entity does not necessarily mean a refresh of entity recency. Instead, entity recency can be identified only when a burst of tweets about that entity occurs within short time. In this work, we adopt a simple but effective approach to measure entity recency - **sliding window**.

Given a time window τ, we define *recent tweets* of entity e as those linked to e and published within τ till the current time. If the number of recent tweets exceeds a predefined threshold θ_1, we believe that there has been a burst of attention on entity e, which implies the freshness of e. Since entity recency is proposed as a feature to support entity linking, namely estimating the probability of mapping an entity mention to a specific entity in the candidate entity set, we normalize recency of entity e over all candidate entities:

$$S_r(e) = \begin{cases} \frac{|\mathbb{D}_e^\tau|}{\sum_{e_i \in \mathbb{E}_m} |\mathbb{D}_{e_i}^\tau|} & |\mathbb{D}_e^\tau| \geq \theta_1 \\ 0 & \text{otherwise} \end{cases} \quad (9)$$

In Eq. 9, $\mathbb{D}_e^\tau = \{d|d \in \mathbb{D}_e \wedge d.t \geq now - \tau\}$ denotes recent tweets of entity e concerning time window τ.

Besides a burst of tweets mentioning entity e, recency of e can also be indirectly signified by that of related entities. For example, the recency of *Chicago Bulls* and *NBA* (National Basketball Association) enhances that of *Michael Jordan (basketball)*. Similarly, increasing amount of tweets about *ICML* (International Conference on Machine Learning) implies more attention on machine learning experts like Michael Jordan *(machine learning expert)*. Therefore, we propose a **recency propagation model** to incorporate mutual reinforcement of recency between related entities.

We adopt the Wikipedia Link-based Measure (WLM) described in [4] to calculate topical relatedness between entities. WLM assumes that two Wikipedia articles are topically related if the number of Wikipedia articles linked to both of them is large. Formally, given two entities e_i and e_j, we define topical relatedness between them as follows:

$$Rel(e_i, e_j) = 1 - \frac{\log(\max(|A_{e_i}|, |A_{e_j}|)) - \log(|A_{e_i} \cap A_{e_j}|)}{\log(|A|) - \log(\min(|A_{e_i}|, |A_{e_j}|))} \quad (10)$$

where A is the entire set of Wikipedia articles, and A_e is the set of Wikipedia articles that link to Wikipedia article describing entity e. Obviously, the more topically related e_i and e_j are, the larger $Rel(e_i, e_j)$ will be.

Fig. 3 illustrates an example of the recency propagation network whose nodes are entities in our knowledgebase. We propose several heuristics on constructing the network:

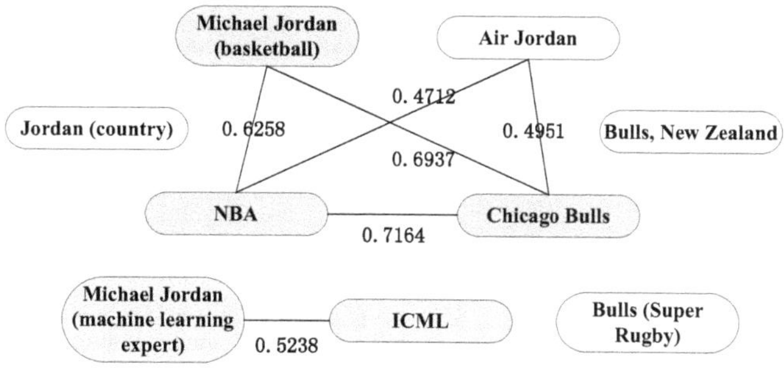

Figure 3: Example of recency propagation network.

- Since recency is used to find the best mention-entity mapping, it should not be propagated between candidate entities of the same entity mention;
- If two entities are more interdependent or topically related with each other, recency should be propagated between them in a larger extent;
- Only highly related entities can reinforce recency of each other. This avoids extensive recency diffusion to slightly related entities.

The first heuristic indicates that candidate entities of the same mention, such as *Jordan (country)*, *Air Jordan*, *Michael Jordan (basketball)*, and *Michael Jordan (machine learning expert)*, should not be connected in the recency propagation network; The second heuristic implies that edge weight should be defined as the topical relatedness between corresponding entities; And according to the third heuristic, we remove edges whose weights are smaller than a predefined threshold θ_2 from the entity relatedness network, and conduct a *Graph-Cut* to find clusters of strongly connected entities. We add edges between entities in such clusters into the recency propagation network.

Given the recency propagation network $G = (V, E)$, our propagation algorithm runs as follows: First, we initialize recency of entities in our knowledgebase based on their recent tweets, namely Eq. 9. This results in an initial recency vector denoted as $\vec{S_r}^0$. Then we reinforce recency between entities iteratively using a PageRank-like algorithm. Edges in the recency propagation network constitute a path to propagate recency from one entity to another. We normalize edge weights as below, to formulate the probability of recency reinforcing:

$$P(e_i, e_j) = \frac{w(e_i, e_j)}{\sum_{(e_i, e_k) \in E} w(e_i, e_k)}$$

Here, $w(e_i, e_j)$ is the edge weight (i.e., topical relatedness) between entities e_i and e_j. Given the initial recency vector $\vec{S_r}^0$ and the recency propagation matrix P, we can get the final recency vector using the following iterative process:

$$\vec{S_r}^i = \lambda \cdot \vec{S_r}^0 + (1 - \lambda) \cdot P \cdot \vec{S_r}^{i-1} \quad (11)$$

In Eq. 11, λ is a parameter to trade-off between recency gathered from underlying tweets and that reinforced by other entities.

5. EXPERIMENT

We conducted extensive experiments to evaluate the effectiveness and efficiency of our framework for entity linking in microblogging services. All the algorithms were implemented in C#, and all the experiments were conducted on a server with 2.90GHz Intel Xeon E5-2690 CPU and 192GB memory.

5.1 Experimental Setting

5.1.1 *Wikipedia dataset*

We downloaded the July 2014 version of English Wikipedia, which was used to construct our original knowledgebase defined in Sec. 3. The Wikipedia dump contains 6.3 million redirect pages, 0.2 million disambiguation pages, and 19.2 million entity pages. 380 million hyperlinks are established between entity pages, and from anchor texts associated with these hyperlinks we extracted 3.8 million nicknames of entities. Altogether, we obtained 29.3 million mentions (e.g., "Bulls", "Tony Allen", and "Jordan" in Fig. 1) and 19.2 million entities (e.g., *Chicago Bulls*, *Tony Allen (basketball)*, and *Michael Jordan (basketball)* in Fig. 1) together with mappings between them. We pre-calculated topical relatedness between entities using Wikipedia Link-base Measure (WLM, Eq. 10), which will be used in our recency propagation model, as well as the estimation of topical coherence considered in current state-of-the-art approaches to entity linking [14, 2]. We also harvested the popularity and the context of each entity from Wikipedia, to calculate intra-tweet features adopted in [14] and [2].

5.1.2 *Twitter dataset*

To guarantee that our knowledgebase has integrated as many entities mentioned in tweets as possible, the tweets we collect for experiments should be generated before the timestamp of Wikipedia dump. In particular, we used Twitter's API to download a collection of 29.3 million tweets which were published by 5 million users between September 2012 and February 2013. After conducting Named Entity Recognition (NER) using current start-of-the-art approaches to NER in tweets [37, 38], we observed that 12 million tweets in our dataset (40.96%) contain at least one named entity mention. This is slightly smaller that the 45.08% percentage found in previous work [2].

We conducted a collective entity linking [2] on part of the tweet dataset to complement our knowledgebase. Since [2] assumes that a user's interest is scattered amongst her broadcastings, it requires that the target user should have sufficient amount of historical tweets to infer her interest. Therefore, we extracted a set of active users with more than θ postings during this period, and used their tweets for the collective entity linking. We ranged θ from 10 to 90 incremented by 20, and obtained five tweet datasets: $\mathbb{D}10$, $\mathbb{D}30$, $\mathbb{D}50$, $\mathbb{D}70$, and $\mathbb{D}90$. In this work, we claim that one of the most notable superiorities of our framework is its ability to maintain accuracy of entity linking for information seekers who tweet rarely. To verify this, we randomly sampled 200 inactive users (with less than 10 broadcastings) and used their tweets for testing: $\mathbb{D}test$. Table 2 summarizes the statistics of these tweet datasets.

Table 2: Statistics of tweet datasets.

$\mathbb{D}10$		$\mathbb{D}30$		$\mathbb{D}50$	
#user	#tweet	#user	#tweet	#user	#tweet
311,835	6.76M	46,476	2.69M	16,015	1.56M
$\mathbb{D}70$		$\mathbb{D}90$		$\mathbb{D}test$	
#user	#tweet	#user	#tweet	#user	#tweet
7698	1.01M	4422	0.82M	200	649

5.1.3 *Evaluation Method*

We compared our approach to entity linking in tweets with two state-of-the-art methods, in terms of both accuracy and efficiency.

[14] conducts entity linking on-the-fly (i.e., tweet by tweet), by considering intra-tweet features such as entity popularity in Wikipedia, context similarity between mentions and entities, topical coherence within tweets, and so forth. [2] combines intra-tweet features with inter-tweet interest distributions, and thus achieves entity linking in a batch manner. We invited three colleagues to help with the labeling, by providing them with the entity linking results of each tweet along with its author, as well as some recent tweets containing the same entity mentions. Annotators were required to examine the friend network of the target user, her historical broadcastings and the recent tweets, to make their decisions. The final labels were based on majority voting. Table 3 lists default values of parameters used in this work.

Table 3: Default values of parameters.

importance of user interest, entity recency, and popularity		
α	β	γ
0.6	0.3	0.1
# recent tweet within time window		highly-related
τ	θ_1	θ_2
3 days	10	0.6

5.2 Experimental Results

5.2.1 *Effectiveness*

Fig. 4 (a) illustrates the accuracy of entity linking achieved by on-the-fly approach [14], collective approach [2], and our prototype system respectively. We present the percentage of correctly linked mentions, and that of tweets whose mentions are all correctly linked. As expected, the accuracy of mentions is always larger than that of tweets. We observe that the collective entity linking method performs better than the on-the-fly counterpart, since it considers users' interest distribution among their tweets, and combines inter-tweet features with traditional intra-tweet features to conduct entity linking. However, such an improvement is not as significant as that discovered in [2]. This is mainly because the collective method requires large amount of tweets to estimate a user's interest distribution. Whereas we focus on entity linking for information seekers with limited tweets in this work. Specifically, users in our test dataset only have 3.25 tweets in average, making the improvement of collective method insignificant. Our approach, on the other hand, achieves better performance by inferring user interest based on social interactions, and combining such interest with entity recency and entity popularity to detect the best linking.

An important prerequisite to our entity linking approach is the quality of the complemented knowledgebase. Therefore, we compared the accuracies of entity linking when complementing Wikipedia with different sizes of datasets. Fig. 4 (b) shows the result. We can see that with increasing amount of tweets appended to the original knowledgebase, the accuracy of entity linking improves gradually. This is consistent with our expectation. Nevertheless, we still observe a slight degradation of performance from $\mathbb{D}70$ to $\mathbb{D}50$, which is caused by mistakenly linked tweets when conducting collective entity linking on users with limited number of tweets. This is actually a trade-off between quality and coverage of the knowledgebase.

In our propotype system, we combine user interest, entity recency, and entity popularity to conduct entity linking. In Eq. 1, α, β, and γ reflect their relative contributions to the overall scoring. Table 4 illustrates the accuracies achieved by considering these features separately and all together. We can see that user interest is the most important feature to support personalized entity linking.

Table 4: Effectiveness of user interest, entity recency, and entity popularity for entity linking.

	$\alpha = 1$	$\beta = 1$	$\gamma = 1$	all features
tweet	0.6281	0.6000	0.5906	0.6375
mention	0.7190	0.6860	0.6777	0.7273

And the performance of user interest estimation using social interactions is better than that obtained using content-based approaches (i.e., 0.686 mention accuracy and 0.6 tweet accuracy achieved by collective method in Fig. 4 (a)), especially for information seekers. Entity recency performs better than entity popularity, since recency is a time-dependent feature which measures an entity' recent popularity. By combining all these features, our framework achieves the highest accuracy.

In this work, we propose new approaches to estimate user interest and entity recency respectively. We evaluated their effectiveness in our experiments. We measure a user's interest in an entity by examining her interest in following the community (i.e., set of users) tweeting about that entity, which is in turn formulated as the average weighted reachability between the target user and the most influential users in the community. We propose two methods to calculate user influence: tfidf-based and entropy-based. Fig. 4 (c) demonstrates their performance reflected by the accuracy of entity linking. We can see that the entropy-based approach performances better than the tfidf counterpart, since it allows for the case that an influential user in a community (e.g., @NBAOfficial) occasionally tweets about entities in other communities (e.g., *Air Jordan*). We propose a recency propagation model to estimate entity recency. Fig. 4 (d) shows the necessity and performance of recency reinforcing. As we have discussed before, the recency of *NBA* will increase that of *Michael Jordan (basketball)*. And similarly the recency of *ICML* might also indicates a burst of tweets about *Michael Jordan (machine learning expert)*. Therefore, the accuracy of entity linking which incorporates propagated recency outperforms that without recency reinforcement in Fig. 4 (d).

5.2.2 *Efficiency*

Entity linking is usually regarded as an online task, or an underlying step of many other text processing algorithms such as clustering and classification. This requires that it should be conducted within short time. Fig. 5 (a) illustrates the time requirement of our framework for entity linking, compared with current state-of-the-art methods. We present the average time required to link a single mention and a whole tweet respectively. As expected, existing on-the-fly approach is the most efficient, since it only considers intra-tweet features which can be calculated easily. The collective method incorporates inter-tweet features. It propagates user interest among entities extracted from all the tweets of a specific user, which is obviously time-consuming when the user has a large amount of tweets. However, since we focus on entity linking for information seekers in our experiments, the collective method only needs to handle a few mentions each time. In our test dataset, each user has 3.25 tweets and each tweet has 1.36 mentions in average, making the collective method to be extremely fast. Our approach, on the contrary, employs a PageRank-like algorithm to model recency reinforcement between related entities. Since a popular entity (e.g., *Michael Jordan (basketball)*) usually has a large number of related entities (e.g., *NBA*, *Chicago Bulls*, *Kobe Bryant*, etc.), the efficiency of our framework is incomparable with existing on-the-fly method. Nevertheless, our approach can still link entities of a tweet within 0.5 milliseconds by constraining recency propagation only between highly related entities, which we believe is

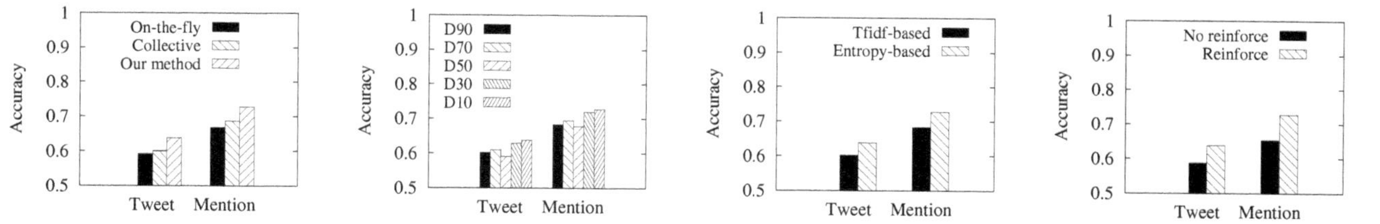

(a) effectiveness of our framework compared with state-of-the-art methods. (b) effectiveness of different tweet datasets used for knowledgebase complementation. (c) effectiveness of tfidf-based and entropy-based approach for user influence estimation. (d) necessity and performance of recency propagation model.

Figure 4: Results of effectiveness evaluation.

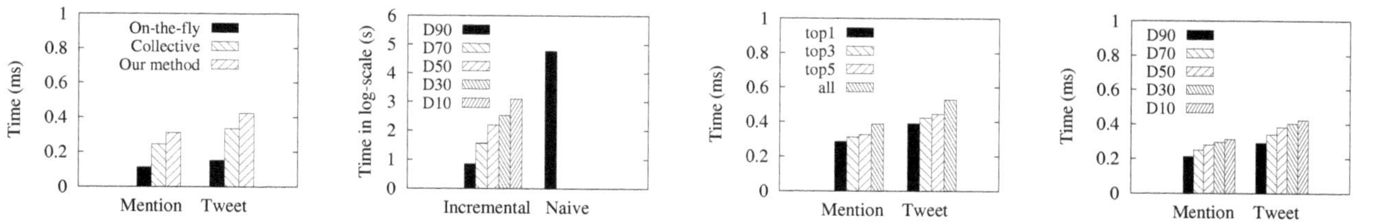

(a) efficiency of our framework compared with state-of-the-art methods. (b) efficiency of the naive and incremental algorithms to calculate reachability transitive closure. (c) efficiency improved by considering the most influential users. (d) efficiency of our framework when knowledgebase expands.

Figure 5: Results of efficiency evaluation.

sufficiently fast for most real-world applications. For example, Twitter's data showed that 200 million users send over 400 million tweets daily as of September 2013[4], which means 5000 postings are generated every second. Given that 40% of tweets contain at least one named entity mention, the entity linking framework needs to handle each tweet within 0.5 milliseconds. In this sense, our approaches are feasible for entity linking in real-time. Besides, our framework can be easily parallelized, since it conducts entity linking independently (i.e., tweet by tweet or even mention by mention) and requires no information from any other tweet. This can further improve the efficiency and applicability of our methods for online entity linking.

In this work, we measure a user's interest in an entity by calculating weighted reachability between the target user and users in the community associated with that entity. Since efficiency is the major concern in order to support online entity linking, we assume access to unlimited storage consumption, and extend the transitive closure framework for weighted reachability query. Naive approach to offline transitive closure construction needs to traverse the entire followee-follower network to calculate reachability for each pair of users, and thus is inefficient. We propose an incremental algorithm to improve the efficiency. Fig. 5 (b) shows the pre-computation time for transitive closure in log-scale. We omit results of index construction that cannot be finished within one day. From Fig. 5 (b) we can see that our incremental algorithm is extremely faster than the naive method. In particular, it takes less than 20 minutes to calculate all the pairwise weighted reachability in our largest dataset.

We also extend the 2-hop cover framework to support weighted reachability queries in case of limited storage resource, considering its ability to reduce space consumption of the transitive closure and at the same time answer reachability queries efficiently. We evaluated the performance of the extended transitive closure framework and the extended 2-hop cover framework on our datasets, in terms of query efficiency, index size, as well as pre-computation time. In addition to the filtered datasets adopted in previous experiments (i.e., $\mathbb{D}10$, $\mathbb{D}30$, $\mathbb{D}50$, $\mathbb{D}70$ and $\mathbb{D}90$), we also evaluated our approaches on the whole crawled dataset (i.e., $\mathbb{D}$ with 5 million users), as well as a public Twitter social network dataset[5] consisting of 11.3 million users. In order to evaluate query efficiency, we randomly sampled 1000 source nodes and another 1000 terminal nodes from each dataset, and generated 1,000,000 weighted reachability queries. We calculated the average query time to measure the efficiency of our approaches. Table 5 illustrates the statistics of these datasets and the performance of our indexing strategies for weighted reachability queries. As for the extended transitive closure framework, we only present the index construction time after applying our incremental algorithm. Results for index construction that cannot be finished within one day or that occupies excessive memory resource are ignored. We can see that the transitive closure approach answers reachability queries much faster than the 2-hop cover counterpart, at the cost of higher storage consumption and longer index construction time. On the other hand, the 2-hop cover framework, besides reducing index sizes dramatically, can still answer reachability queries efficiently, which makes it a wonderful alternative to handle large graphs (e.g., $\mathbb{D}$ and Twitter in Table 5) when storage resource is limited. Note that the index sizes, indexing time, and query efficiency of our approaches are slightly worse than those achieved in previous work on reachability queries. But this is mainly due to the fact that extra operations are required to maintain the followee sets in-between the shortest paths from nodes s to t, in order to calculate weighted reachability.

Although reachability can be retrieved directly after offline pre-calculation, estimating a user's average reachability with a community is still time-consuming, since the communities associated with popular entities are usually very large. Therefore, we propose to detect a collection of most influential users in a community, and check reachability only with those influential users. Fig. 5 (c) illustrates

[4]http://en.wikipedia.org/wiki/Twitter#Growth

[5]http://www.datatang.com/data/44253/

Table 5: Performance of the extended transitive closure framework and the extended 2-hop cover framework.

	#node	#edge	avg degree	max degree	indexing time		index size		query time	
					transitive closure	2-hop	transitive closure	2-hop	transitive closure	2-hop
$\mathbb{D}$90	4.6K	52.3K	22.6	0.7K	7s	2s	67MB	11MB	0.1μs	0.3μs
$\mathbb{D}$70	7.9K	123.07K	31.1	1.1K	36s	16s	154MB	31MB	0.1μs	0.4μs
$\mathbb{D}$50	16.2K	343.1K	42.3	1.9K	156s	86s	655MB	102MB	0.2μs	1.2μs
$\mathbb{D}$30	46.7K	899.1K	38.5	3.5K	328s	239s	1.8GB	271MB	0.1μs	0.8μs
$\mathbb{D}$10	312.1K	5.8M	34.3	6.8K	1217s	471s	8.7GB	1.4GB	0.2μs	1.5μs
$\mathbb{D}$	5.0M	71.4M	28.61	412.76K	-	1893s	-	16GB	-	4.7μs
Twitter	11.3M	85.3M	15.1	564.8K	-	3417s	-	38GB	-	4.2μs

the variation of time requirement when we increase the number of users to check reachability with. We observe an insignificant difference in Fig. 5 (c). This is mainly because that the tweet dataset we used for knowledgebase complementation in our experiments is quite small compared with the whole tweet dataset in Twitter. Hence, even the communities associated with popular entities contain only a small number of users. However, we can still find a trend of increasement of time when calculating reachability with more users.

At last, we examined the scalability of our framework for entity linking. From Fig. 5 (d), we can see that the time requirement of our system remains stable when we complement our knowledgebase with increasingly larger tweet dataset. The most time-consuming modules in our framework are reachability checking with community and the recency propagation model. However, after restricting reachability checking only with influential users and recency propagation only between highly related entities, both modules are insensitive to the number of tweets complemented to the original knowledgebase.

6. CONCLUSION

In this paper, we propose an on-the-fly approach to entity linking in tweets, which takes into consideration a combination of user interest, entity recency, and entity popularity. Unlike existing content-based methods, we measure user interest by social interactions, considering the difficulty and inaccuracy in inferring user interest from a diverse stream of tweets with highly diversified topics. We formulate a user's interest in an entity as her interest in subscribing to the community tweeting about that entity, which is calculated by weighted reachability between the target user and the most influential users in the community. We propose two approaches for user influence estimation within a community, namely tfidf-based approach and entropy-based approach. Effective indexing structures along with incremental algorithms are developed to reduce the time requirement for calculating weighted reachability. We adopt a simple but effective method - sliding window - to estimate an entity's initial recency, and propose a page-rank style recency propagation model to incorporate recency reinforced by other highly related entities. Empirical studies have demonstrated the superior effectiveness of our approach compared with state-of-the-art methods and the efficiency feasibility for online applications with real-time requirement.

Currently, we evaluate our approaches by providing annotators with top-k entities for each mention, and asking them to examine the correctness of the entity linking result, which is labour-intensive, time consuming and sometimes subjective. A better approach is to build an interface for our methods on Twitter, and invite tweet authors themselves to conduct the evaluation. We are currently working on this development. Furthermore, our framework for entity linking can be easily extended to support personalized microblog search. However, in order to build a robust search engine, the entire followee-follower network as well as an extremely huge collection of tweets are required. We are seeking for cooperations with companies and other research teams to achieve this goal.

Acknowledgement

This work was partially supported by the Australian Research Council (ARC) (under Grant DP140103171) and National Natural Science Foundation of China (NSFC) (under Grant 61472263).

7. REFERENCES

[1] J. Teevan, D. Ramage, and M. R. Morris. #twittersearch: A comparison of microblog search and web search. In *WSDM*, pages 35–44, 2011.

[2] W. Shen, J. Wang, P. Luo, and M. Wang. Linking named entities in tweets with knowledge base via user interest modeling. In *KDD*, pages 68–76, 2013.

[3] R. Mihalcea and A. Csomai. Wikify!: Linking documents to encyclopedic knowledge. In *CIKM*, pages 233–242, 2007.

[4] D. Milne and I. H. Witten. Learning to link with wikipedia. In *CIKM*, pages 509–518, 2008.

[5] X. Han and J. Zhao. Named entity disambiguation by leveraging wikipedia semantic knowledge. In *CIKM*, pages 215–224, 2009.

[6] X. Han and J. Zhao. Structural semantic relatedness: A knowledge-based method to named entity disambiguation. In *ACL*, pages 50–59, 2010.

[7] S. Kulkarni, A. Singh, G. Ramakrishnan, and S. Chakrabarti. Collective annotation of wikipedia entities in web text. In *KDD*, pages 457–466, 2009.

[8] X. Han, L. Sun, and J. Zhao. Collective entity linking in web text: A graph-based method. In *SIGIR*, pages 765–774, 2011.

[9] W. Shen, J. Wang, P. Luo, and M. Wang. Linden: Linking named entities with knowledge base via semantic knowledge. In *WWW*, pages 449–458, 2012.

[10] E. Meij, W. Weerkamp, and M. de Rijke. Adding semantics to microblog posts. In *WSDM*, pages 563–572, 2012.

[11] A. Davis, A. Veloso, A. S. da Silva, W. Meira Jr., and A. H. F. Laender. Named entity disambiguation in streaming data. In *ACL*, pages 815–824, 2012.

[12] X. Liu, Y. Li, H. Wu, M. Zhou, F. Wei, and Y. Lu. Entity linking for tweets. In *ACL*, pages 1304–1311, 2013.

[13] Y. Li, C. Wang, F. Han, J. Han, D. Roth, and X. Yan. Mining evidences for named entity disambiguation. In *KDD*, pages 1070–1078, 2013.

[14] P. Ferragina and U. Scaiella. Tagme: On-the-fly annotation of short text fragments (by wikipedia entities). In *CIKM*, pages 1625–1628, 2010.

[15] A. Java, X. Song, T. Finin, and B. Tseng. Why we twitter: Understanding microblogging usage and communities. In *WebKDD/SNA-KDD*, pages 56–65, 2007.

[16] H. Kwak, C. Lee, H. Park, and S. Moon. What is twitter, a social network or a news media? In *WWW*, pages 591–600, 2010.

[17] L. Chen, A. Gupta, and M. E. Kurul. Stack-based algorithms for pattern matching on dags. In *VLDB*, pages 493–504, 2005.

[18] S. Tribl and U. Leser. Fast and practical indexing and querying of very large graphs. In *SIGMOD*, pages 845–856, 2007.

[19] H. Yildirim, V. Chaoji, and M. J. Zaki. Grail: Scalable reachability index for large graphs. *PVLDB*, 3(1-2):276–284, 2010.
[20] R. Agrawal, A. Borgida, and H. V. Jagadish. Efficient management of transitive relationships in large data and knowledge bases. In *SIGMOD*, pages 253–262, 1989.
[21] H. Wang, H. He, J. Yang, P. S. Yu, and J. X. Yu. Dual labeling: Answering graph reachability queries in constant time. In *ICDE*, pages 75–75, 2006.
[22] Y. Chen and Y. Chen. An efficient algorithm for answering graph reachability queries. In *ICDE*, pages 893–902, 2008.
[23] R. Jin, Y. Xiang, N. Ruan, and H. Wang. Efficiently answering reachability queries on very large directed graphs. In *SIGMOD*, pages 595–608, 2008.
[24] S. J. van Schaik and O. de Moor. A memory efficient reachability data structure through bit vector compression. In *SIGMOD*, pages 913–924, 2011.
[25] Y. Chen and Y. Chen. Decomposing dags into spanning trees: A new way to compress transitive closures. In *ICDE*, pages 1007–1018, 2011.
[26] S. Seufert, A. Anand, S. Bedathur, and G. Weikum. Ferrari: Flexible and efficient reachability range assignment for graph indexing. In *ICDE*, pages 1009–1020, 2013.
[27] J. Cheng, J. X. Yu, X. Lin, H. Wang, and P. S. Yu. Fast computing reachability labelings for large graphs with high compression rate. In *EDBT*, pages 193–204, 2008.
[28] R. Jin, Y. Xiang, N. Ruan, and D. Fuhry. 3hop: A high-compression indexing scheme for reachability query. In *SIGMOD*, pages 813–826, 2009.
[29] J. Cai and C. K. Poon. Path-hop: Efficiently indexing large graphs for reachability queries. In *CIKM*, pages 119–128, 2010.
[30] J. Cheng, Z. Shang, H. Cheng, H. Wang, and J. X. Yu. K-reach: Who is in your small world. *PVLDB*, 5(11):1292–1303, 2012.
[31] J. Cheng, S. Huang, H. Wu, and A. W. Fu. Tf-label: A topological-folding labeling scheme for reachability querying in a large graph. In *SIGMOD*, pages 193–204, 2013.
[32] Y. Yano, T. Akiba, Y. Iwata, and Y. Yoshida. Fast and scalable reachability queries on graphs by pruned labeling with landmarks and paths. In *CIKM*, pages 1601–1606, 2013.
[33] T. Akiba, Y. Iwata, and Y. Yoshida. Fast exact shortest-path distance queries on large networks by pruned landmark labeling. In *SIGMOD*, pages 349–360, 2013.
[34] R. Jin and G. Wang. Simple, fast, and scalable reachability oracle. *PVLDB*, 6(14):1978–1989, 2013.
[35] I. Witten and D. Milne. An effective, low-cost measure of semantic relatedness obtained from wikipedia links. In *AAAI*, pages 25–30, 2008.
[36] G. Li, J. Hu, J. Feng, and K. Tan. Effective location identification from microblogs. In *ICDE*, pages 880–891, 2014.
[37] C. Li, J. Weng, Q. He, Y. Yao, A. Datta, A. Sun, and B. Lee. Twiner: Named entity recognition in targeted twitter stream. In *SIGIR*, pages 721–730, 2012.
[38] D. M. de Oliveira, A. H. F. Laender, A. Veloso, and A. S. da Silva. Fs-ner: A lightweight filter-stream approach to named entity recognition on twitter data. In *WWW*, pages 597–604, 2013.
[39] K. Takeuchi and N. Collier. Use of support vector machines in extended named entity recognition. In *CONLL*, pages 1–7, 2002.
[40] H. Isozaki and H. Kazawa. Efficient support vector classifiers for named entity recognition. In *COLING*, pages 1–7, 2002.
[41] H. L. Chieu and H. T. Ng. Named entity recognition: A maximum entropy approach using global information. In *COLING*, pages 1–7, 2002.
[42] O. Bender, F. J. Och, and H. Ney. Maximum entropy models for named entity recognition. In *CONLL*, pages 148–151, 2003.
[43] J. R. Curran and S. Clark. Language independent ner using a maximum entropy tagger. In *CONLL*, pages 164–167, 2003.
[44] G. Zhou and J. Su. Named entity recognition using an hmm-based chunk tagger. In *ACL*, pages 473–480, 2002.
[45] A. McCallum and W. Li. Early results for named entity recognition with conditional random fields, feature induction and web-enhanced lexicons. In *CONLL*, pages 188–191, 2003.
[46] A. Ritter, S. Clark, Mausam, and O. Etzioni. Named entity recognition in tweets: An experimental study. In *EMNLP*, pages 1524–1534, 2011.
[47] X. Liu, S. Zhang, F. Wei, and M. Zhou. Recognizing named entities in tweets. In *HLT*, pages 359–367, 2011.
[48] X. Liu, M. Zhou, F. Wei, Z. Fu, and X. Zhou. Joint inference of named entity recognition and normalization for tweets. In *ACL*, pages 526–535, 2012.

APPENDIX

A. ADDITIONAL RELATED WORK

Named Entity Recognition (NER). One of the prerequisites to entity linking is Named Entity Recognition, namely detecting named entities from texts written in natural languages. Existing approaches to NER can be classified into two categories: linguistic-based and knowledge-based.

Linguistic-based approaches are the current dominant techniques for addressing the NER problem. Most of them formulate NER as a *sequential labeling* task, and apply various machine learning algorithms, including Support Vector Machine (SVM) [39, 40], Maximum Entropy Model (ME) [41, 42, 43], Hidden Markov Model (HMM) [44], and Conditional Random Field (CRF) [45], to determine the NE labels of tokens collectively. The features they employ are basically linguistic-based such as capitalization, digitalization, punctuation, part-of-speech tags, and so forth. Despite the already satisfying performance that linguistic-based approaches to NER have achieved on news articles and Web documents, they cannot be applied directly to short texts like tweets. This is partially due to the fact that tweets are informal and error-prone, making traditional linguistic features (e.g., capitalization) inapplicable. Recently, much work [46, 47, 48] has been devoted to designing linguistic features to capture tweets' unique characteristics and training tweet-specific models to extract named entities. For example, Ritter et. al [46] explore features including retweets, @usernames, hashtags, URLs, and Brown clustering results to train tweet-specific POS tagger (T-POS) and shallow parsing (T-CHUNK), whose results are then regarded as features to train a CRF model for named entity recognition (T-NER). Liu et. al [47] leverage cross-tweet information by using a KNN-based classifier to conduct word-level pre-labeling, and then feed those information into a CRF model to conduct finer-grained NER. However, due to their supervised nature, these approaches require a vast amount of labeled data which is usually expensive to come by.

Knowledge-based approaches [37, 38] to NER are unsupervised, making them more feasible for handling texts in a streaming manner. A knowledgebase (also called gazetteer, lexicon, or dictionary) is required in such methods, and named entity recognition is conducted by simply checking for existence or frequency of a phrase in the knowledgebase. For example, the widely-used Longest-Cover method searches for longest terms contained in the knowledgebase while scanning a text. Like many recent attempts to entity linking in short texts [14, 2], we also adopt the knowledge-based approach as a pre-step to extract entity mentions, considering its simplicity and real-time nature. Note that most knowledge-based approaches implicitly require candidate phrases to exactly match at least one element in the knowledgebase, but some flexibility can be added by allowing for word stemming or fuzzy matching.

B. METHODOLOGY

In this section, we prove the theorems proposed in this work to verify the correctness of our algorithms.

B.1 Proof of Theorem 1.

Theorem 1 claims that there exists a *len*-hop shortest path from u to v which passes through u' followee t only if the shortest path distance from t to v is $len-1$ hops. We restate this theorem formally as below:

THEOREM 3. $\forall t \in F_u, d_{uv} = len \wedge t \in u \rightsquigarrow^* v \Rightarrow d_{tv} = len - 1$, *or simply* $\forall t \in F_u, t \in u \rightsquigarrow^* v \Rightarrow d_{tv} = d_{uv} - 1$.

where F_u denotes the collection of u's followees, and d_{uv} the shortest path distance from u to v. $t \in u \rightsquigarrow^* v$ means that u's followee t participates in a *len*-hop path from u to v.

PROOF. Assume by contradiction that $d_{tv} \neq len-1$, which means either t cannot reach v or the shortest path distance from v to t is longer or shorter than $len - 1$ hops. 1) If v is not reachable from t (i.e., $t \not\rightsquigarrow v$), then u cannot reach v through its followee t (i.e., $t \notin u \rightsquigarrow v$); 2) If the shortest path distance from t to v is longer than $len - 1$ hops (i.e., $d_{tv} > len - 1$), then the distance of path $u \rightarrow t \rightsquigarrow v$ is larger than *len*, implying that t cannot participate in a *len*-hop shortest path from u to v (i.e., $t \notin u \rightsquigarrow^* v$); 3) If the shortest path distance from t to v is shorter than $len - 1$ hops (i.e., $d_{tv} < len - 1$), then the distance of path $u \rightarrow t \rightsquigarrow v$ is smaller than *len*, which means a shorter path from u to v has been detected (i.e., $d_{uv} < len$). □

COROLLARY 1. $\forall t, d_{uv} = Len \wedge d_{ut} = len \wedge t \in u \rightsquigarrow^* v \Rightarrow d_{tv} = Len - len$, *or simply* $\forall t, t \in u \rightsquigarrow^* v \Rightarrow d_{tv} = d_{uv} - d_{ut}$.

where d_{uv} is the shortest path distance from u to v, and $t \in u \rightsquigarrow^* v$ means that t participates in the shortest path from u to v. Corollary 1 can be proved similarly as in the above theorem.

B.2 Proof of Theorem 2.

Theorem 2 claims that if the shortest path from s to v passes through s's followee f, and v lies in the shortest path from s to t, then f participates in the shortest path from s to t. We restate this theorem formally as below:

THEOREM 4. $\forall f \in F_s, f \in s \rightsquigarrow^* v \wedge v \in s \rightsquigarrow^* t \Rightarrow f \in s \rightsquigarrow^* t$

where F_s denotes the collection of s's followees, and $f \in s \rightsquigarrow^* t$ means that f participates in the shortest path from s to t.

PROOF. Assume the shortest path distance from s to t is $d_{st} = Len$. Since s subscribes to f, it suffices to prove that there exists a $(Len - 1)$-hop path from f to t. From $f \in s \rightsquigarrow^* v$ and $v \in s \rightsquigarrow^* t$, we can obtain that f can reach v which in turn reaches t. In other words, we have successfully detected a path from f to t, namely $f \rightsquigarrow v \rightsquigarrow t$. Now we only need to show that the distance of path $f \rightsquigarrow v \rightsquigarrow t$ is $Len-1$ hops. Assume the shortest path distance from s to v is $d_{sv} = len$. According to Corollary 1, $d_{fv} = d_{sv} - 1 = len - 1$ and $d_{vt} = d_{st} - d_{sv} = Len - len$. Hence, there exists a path $f \rightsquigarrow v \rightsquigarrow t$ whose distance is $d_{fv} + d_{vt} = Len - 1$. This completes our proof. □

C. ADDITIONAL EXPERIMENTS

C.1 Generalizability of our system

Different microblogging sites. We used Twitter dataset in our experiments considering the wide-spread adoption and the availability of large-scale tweet dataset for empirical study in this community. However, our approaches can apply to solve entity linking problem on any microblogging social network (e.g., Facebook, Google+, Pinterest, Chinese Sina Weibo, etc), since we do not exploit any features that are unique to Twitter.

To verify this, we collected 23.3 million tweets published between January 2012 and October 2012 as well as the followee-follower network using Chinese Sina Weibo's API. We downloaded the July 2014 version of Chinese Wikipedia from which 5.1 million mentions and 3.5 million entities were extracted to construct our knowledgebase. We conducted a collective entity linking [2] on part of the Sina Weibo dataset published by active users to complement the original knowledgebase, and used postings of inactive users for testing. The experimental results are consistent with those found in Twitter. Due to limitation of paper length, we only present the comparison of our framework and existing state-of-the-art approaches to entity linking in terms of both accuracy and efficiency, as illustrated in Fig. 6 (a) and (b) respectively. From Fig. 6 (a) we can see that our approaches still outperform existing On-the-fly method [14] and Collective method [2] when applied to Chinese Sina Weibo, although the improvement is slightly smaller than that achieved in Twitter (3.7% mention accuracy improvement and 2.6% tweet accuracy improvement in Sina Weibo vs. 6% mention accuracy improvement and 4.5% tweet accuracy improvement in Twitter - Fig. 4 (a)). Postings in Sina Weibo usually contain more entities (2.3 entities per tweet in our Sina Weibo dataset) than Twitter, making it much more reliable to consider topical coherence for entity disambiguation, which in turn leads to better performance of the On-the-fly method in Sina Weibo compared with Twitter. Fig. 6 (b) demonstrates that our framework can link entities of a tweet in Sina Weibo within 0.5 milliseconds in average. This is also sufficiently fast for most real-world applications. For example, Sina Weibo reported that about 100 million messages were posted each day in the year 2012[6], which requires an entity linking framework to handle each tweet within 2 milliseconds. In this sense, our approaches are also feasible for real-time entity linking in Chinese Sina Weibo.

Varying tweet length. We do not theoretically restrict the number of entities per posting in our framework, though we believe there should not be too many entity mentions in each tweet in a microblogging site like Twitter. We conduct an experiment in the paper to study the differences between our framework and existing state-of-the-art approaches with varying tweet lengths. We divide our test dataset into 4 parts according to tweet length (i.e., number of entity mentions per tweet) and then apply these methods to each part. As illustrated in Fig. 6 (c), the accuracy of our framework for entity linking remains quite stable when tweet length ranges from 1 to 4. This is mainly due to the fact that we handle each entity mention separately without considering their interdependence. We notice that the superiority of our method over other content-based counterparts is even more considerable when the target tweet contains only 1 entity mention. In this case, topical coherence adopted in [14] is no longer applicable, making the entity linking results unsatisfactory. [2] can improve the situation a little bit by estimating users' interest from their historical postings and linking all the entities mentioned by a single user collectively. However, such an improvement is insignificant for information seekers with few tweeting histories. Although Fig. 6 (c) shows an accuracy improvement of [14] and [2] when tweet length increases, our framework is still in a very competitive position since most microblogging sites (e.g., Twitter, Chinese Sina Weibo, etc.) impose a words limitation on their content, which in turn limit the number of entities per posting.

Different entity categories. It is also important to see how our framework performs on different categories of entities, in order to verify its generalizability. We asked annotators to manually classify the entities mentioned in our test dataset into 5 categories - Person

[6]https://en.wikipedia.org/wiki/Sina_Weibo

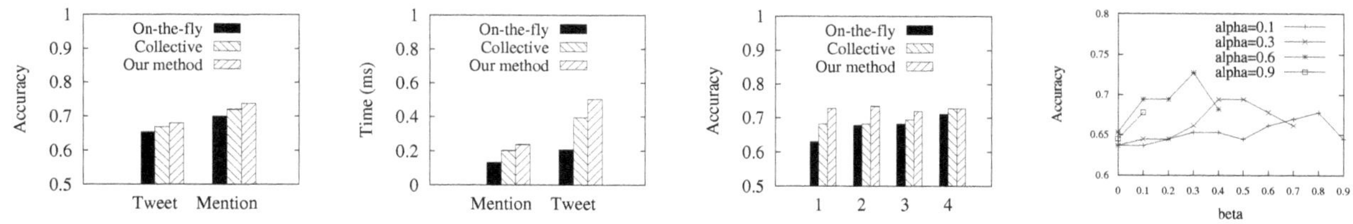

(a) effectiveness of our framework compared with state-of-the-art methods on Sina Weibo. (b) efficiency of our framework compared with state-of-the-art methods on Sina Weibo. (c) effectiveness of our framework when tweet length varies. (d) sensitivity of our framework to parameters.

Figure 6: Additional experimental results.

(71.35%), Location (8.38%), Company (2.6%), Product (2.27%), and Movie&Music (15.4%), and evaluate the accuracy of entity linking respectively. We find Location category gets the best accuracy (74.32%) and Movie&Music category has the worst (71.32%), which demonstrates that the performances of our framework on these five categories are similar and also irrelevant to the number of entities in each category. This is an expected result, since we do not employ any features specific to a particular category of entities.

C.2 Sensitivity of our system to parameters

In this work, we combine user interest, entity recency, and entity popularity to derive an overall ranking of candidate entities for a target entity mention. We adopt a linear combination of these three features in the current model, and use α, β and γ to reflect the relative contributions of these features to the final scoring of candidate entities. From Table 4 we can see that the performance of user interest estimation using social interactions is better than that obtained using traditional content-based approaches, and that entity recency performs better than entity popularity, since recency is a time-dependent feature which measures an entity's recent popularity. By combining all these features, our framework achieves the highest accuracy. In order to get a better insight of the sensitivity of our framework to the values of α, β and γ, we conduct an experiment by setting α to 0.1, 0.3, 0.6, and 0.9 respectively and measuring the performance of our system with various combinations of β and γ. Fig. 6 (d) shows that our method is indeed sensitive to the settings of these parameters. For each value of α, the best performance can be achieved only when neither β nor γ are equal to 0, verifying the importance of both entity recency and entity popularity for entity linking. Furthermore, the peak value of accuracy is always obtained on the right side of Fig. 6 (d) (i.e., when β is larger than γ), which indicates the superior of entity recency over entity popularity. This is consistent with the result in Table 4. In practice, these three parameters can be manually defined or automatically learned using existing machine learning methods. We choose to set them manually due to lack of large-scale training dataset. Section 5.1 reports the best combination of α, β and γ according to the experimental results.

D. DISCUSSION

It is important to think about the impact of vocabulary on linking quality, considering the dynamic feature of microblogging sites. Usually the knowledgebase should periodically check if new entities or new meanings for old entities appear in the Web and update its entity database accordingly. If new entities/meanings do appear but have not been reflected in knowledgebase, these entity mentions cannot be detected from tweets or be linked to the new meanings, since the nature of entity linking problem is to recognize and link an entity mention to the most appropriate entity meaning that already existed in the knowledgebase. The knowledgebase can be updated manually (e.g., Wikipedia) or automatically (e.g., Probase). There have been a lot of interesting discussions on the update policy for knowledgebase, which is out of the scope of this work. However, there are indeed two issues we need to consider, as detailed below.

First, we should avoid the false-positive error before the knowledgebase is updated. More specifically, an entity mention should not be linked to any of the existing entity meanings if the target user is found to have no interest in existing meanings of the entity. Since our framework adopts a linear combination of user interest, entity recency and entity popularity, any candidate entity meaning the target user is not interested in will receive an overall score no greater than $\beta + \gamma$. Therefore, we can set a threshold at $\beta + \gamma$ and only output top-k entities whose score exceeds the threshold. In this way, we avoid the false-positive error even before knowledgebase has been updated properly. Moreover, when the entity linking result is empty, it is most probable that the target entity mention should be linked to a new meaning which does not exist in the current knowledgebase. In this case, we can interactively ask the user to add a new entity meaning. By this means our framework can also help updating the knowledgebase in proactive manner.

Second, we should avoid the true-negative error after the knowledgebase is updated. This means the new entity meanings should be able to be linked to after knowledgebase updates. Since we complement the original knowledgebase using historical broadcastings, the newly-generated tweets containing mentions to new entity meanings have not been complemented to the knowledgebase. Therefore, a system warm-up is required, which can also been done through the aforementioned interactive process. In particular, when no entity linking result can be derived or the target user finds the top-k entity meanings unsatisfactory, we provide her with the new meaning and allow her to decide whether it is the desired one.

Graph-Aware, Workload-Adaptive SPARQL Query Caching

Nikolaos Papailiou* Dimitrios Tsoumakos† Panagiotis Karras◇ Nectarios Koziris*

*National Technical University of Athens, Greece
{npapa, nkoziris}@cslab.ece.ntua.gr

†Ionian University, Greece
dtsouma@ionio.gr

◇Skoltech, Russia
karras@skoltech.ru

ABSTRACT

The pace at which data is described, queried and exchanged using the RDF specification has been ever increasing with the proliferation of Semantic Web. Minimizing SPARQL query response times has been an open issue for the plethora of RDF stores, yet SPARQL result caching techniques have not been extensively utilized. In this work we present a novel system that addresses graph-based, workload-adaptive indexing of large RDF graphs by caching SPARQL query results. At the heart of the system lies a SPARQL query canonical labelling algorithm that is used to uniquely index and reference SPARQL query graphs as well as their isomorphic forms. We integrate our canonical labelling algorithm with a dynamic programming planner in order to generate the optimal join execution plan, examining the utilization of both primitive triple indexes and cached query results. By monitoring cache requests, our system is able to identify and cache SPARQL queries that, even if not explicitly issued, greatly reduce the average response time of a workload. The proposed cache is modular in design, allowing integration with different RDF stores. Incorporating it to an open-source, distributed RDF engine that handles large scale RDF datasets, we prove that workload-adaptive caching can reduce average response times by up to two orders of magnitude and offer interactive response times for complex workloads and huge RDF datasets.

1. INTRODUCTION

The RDF standard [6] together with the SPARQL[8] query language have been acknowledged as the de facto technologies to represent and query resources in the Semantic Web era. The schema-free nature of RDF data allows the formation of a common data framework that facilitates the integration of data originating from different application, enterprise, and community boundaries. This property has led to an unprecedented increase in the rate at which RDF data is created, stored and queried, even outside the purely academic realm (e.g., [9, 2]) and consequently to the development of many RDF stores [37, 29, 40, 11, 30, 12] that target RDF indexing and high SPARQL querying performance.

SIGMOD'15, May 31–June 4, 2015, Melbourne, Victoria, Australia.

http://dx.doi.org/10.1145/2723372.2723714.

However, the move from the schema-dependent SQL data to the schema-free RDF data has introduced new indexing and querying challenges and made a lot of the well-known relational database optimizations unusable. In fact, RDF databases assume limited knowledge of the data structure mainly in the form of RDFS triples [5]. However, RDFS information is not as rich and obligatory as the SQL schema; it can be incomplete and change rapidly along with the dataset. Therefore, most RDF databases are targeting the indexing of individual RDF edges resulting in query executions with much more joins than processing the same dataset in a schema-aware relational database. In contrast, RDF databases that use RDFS information to store and group RDF data [34, 35], fail to effectively adapt to schema changes and to non-conforming, to the schema, data. In general, RDF databases have not yet effectively benefited from the classic schema-aware optimizations used in SQL databases:

- Grouping data that are accessed together using tables.
- Indexing according to filtering and join operations.
- View materialization of frequently queried data patterns.

We argue that all those optimizations can be employed by an RDF database, without any prior knowledge of both the data schema and the workload, by actively monitoring query requests and adapting to the workload.

Result caching is a methodology that has been successfully employed over different applications and computing areas to boost performance and provide scalability. Given the complexity and very high execution latencies [29, 30] of several SPARQL query patterns, caching of frequent RDF subgraphs has the potential of boosting performance by even orders of magnitude. While indexing of graph patterns is extensively used in state of the art graph databases [41, 38], RDF stores have not yet taken advantage of these techniques. What is more, these schemes focus on *static* indexing of important graph patterns, namely they index subgraphs based solely on the underlying dataset, without any regard for the workload. However, the diversity of the applied SPARQL workloads together with the requirement for high performance for all the different workloads calls for dynamic, workload-driven indexing solutions (e.g., [18]).

In this work we argue for a *workload-adaptive* RDF caching engine that manages to dynamically index frequent workload subgraphs in real time, and utilize them to decrease response times. The major contributions of this paper are:

- A SPARQL query *canonical labelling* algorithm that is able to generate canonical string labels, identical among all

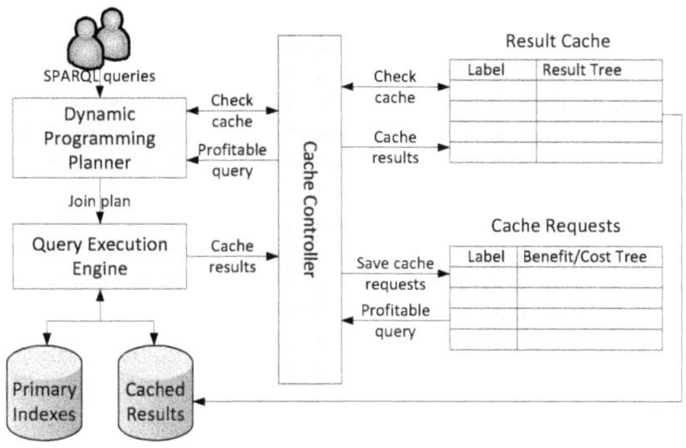

Figure 1: System architecture

isomorphic forms of a SPARQL query. We use these labels to identify and request query graphs to or from the cache. Most importantly, this scheme enables unique identification of all common subgraphs inside any SPARQL workload.

• We integrate our SPARQL query *canonical labelling* algorithm with a state-of-the-art *Dynamic Programming Planner* [28] by issuing cache requests for all query subgraphs using their canonical label. The resulting optimal execution plan may thus involve, in part or in whole, cached query subgraphs. In addition, we not only examine the utilization of exact cached subgraphs, but also larger, more general graphs that can be used to provide the input of a query subgraph.

• A *Cache Controller* process complements the caching framework. The controller monitors all cache requests issued by the workload queries, enabling it to detect cross-query *profitable* subgraphs and trigger their execution and caching.

Our caching framework is modularly designed to be able to support different RDF processing engines and their respective indexing and cost models. It specifically targets disk-based caching of RDF graphs for read-only workloads. Persistent storage can support immense volumes of cached results, that can be also indexed according to the engine's indexing capabilities. We integrate our prototype implementation with H_2RDF+ [30], a state of the art distributed query execution engine that utilizes multiple RDF indexes along with efficient distributed merge and sort-merge joins. Utilizing HBase and HDFS as the cache storage backends, our system is able to handle arbitrarily large RDF graphs. Extensive evaluation results using diverse workloads show that our caching framework is able to effectively detect, cache and utilize SPARQL query results to offer interactive, millisecond-range average response times for several workloads, reducing them up to two orders of magnitude.

2. SOLUTION OVERVIEW

The goal of this work is to provide an efficient, *workload-based* caching system that can adapt cache contents according to the query requests, trying to minimize response times for any SPARQL workload.

As depicted in Figure 1, query resolution starts from the *Dynamic Programming Planner* (Section 4) that identifies the optimal execution plan. We adapt a state-of-the-art dynamic programming planner [27], in order to efficiently discover and utilize all possibly usable cached query patterns that relate to the query in hand. To achieve robust tagging of query graphs in the face of multiple *isomorphs*, we employ a novel *canonical SPARQL query labelling* algorithm (Section 3) that allow us to uniquely index and refer to SPARQL query patterns. Meta-data about cached results are stored in-memory, indexed using their canonical labels, in the *Result Cache* table. To compute the optimal cost for each SPARQL query, our planner iterates over all its subgraphs issuing cache checks using their canonical label. The benefit of utilizing cached results is evaluated by our planner using the execution engine's cost model, resulting in query execution plans that can contain operators over both RDF primary indexes (e.g., *spo* tables) and cached results.

To enhance the cache hit ratio as well as decrease query response times, we not only examine exact query subgraphs but also search for more general cached results that can provide input for a query subgraph by executing a filtering operation over one or several of its variables. Our *Cache Controller* module (see Section 5) is responsible for accessing the *Result Cache*, as well as for recording all cache requests using the *Cache Requests* table. During query execution, all intermediate and final results are considered for caching according to the specified result caching strategy. The *Cache Controller* is responsible for monitoring cache requests and maintaining detailed benefit estimations for possibly usable query patterns as well as for their materialization cost. Utilizing this information, we trigger the execution and caching of *profitable* queries (frequently requested but not cached queries) in order to boost the cache utilization. The resulting architecture is pictorially described in Figure 1.

3. SPARQL QUERY CANONICAL LABELLING

In this section we address the problem of efficiently indexing SPARQL query results. Indexing graph patterns is a challenging task because it requires to tackle the graph isomorphism problem [19], a fundamental problem in graph theory. This problem arises when the same query pattern appears in different queries with small deviations such as pattern reordering, variable renaming etc. For example the following SPARQL queries are isomorphic.

`?p ub:worksFor "MIT" .`	`?v1 ub:name ?v2 .`
`?p ub:name ?name .`	`?v1 ub:emailAddress ?v3 .`
`?p ub:emailAddress ?email .`	`?v1 ub:worksFor "MIT"`

All "isomorphs" of the same SPARQL graph must be identified and linked to the same cache entry for a graph caching scheme to work. To address this issue, we extend a solution for graph canonical labelling and introduce the concept of SPARQL graph canonical labelling.

DEFINITION 1. *A graph labelling algorithm C takes as input a graph G and produces a unique label L=C(G). C is a canonical graph labelling algorithm if and only if for every graph H which is isomorphic to G we have C(G)=C(H). We call L a canonical label of G. Additionally, L introduces a canonical total ordering between the vertices of G.*

The canonical labelling problem shares the same computational complexity with the graph isomorphism problem and belongs to the GI complexity class. GI is one of the few open complexity classes that is not known to be either polynomial-time solvable, or NP-complete[19, 15]. To date, there exists a lot of heuristic evidence that GI is not NP-complete and there are many efficient open-source implementations for both graph isomorphism and canonical labelling algorithms [4, 1, 7] that are able to handle really large graphs. One of the first and most powerful canonical labelling algorithms is McKay's *nauty* algorithm [24] that introduced an innovative use of automorphisms to prune the isomorphism search space. In this paper we select to use *Bliss* [1] for computing graph canonical labels. *Bliss* extends *nauty* by introducing some extra heuristics that boost its performance on difficult graphs. Furthermore, it offers a very efficient C++ library that can compute canonical labels for graphs with thousands of vertices in milliseconds making it ideal to handle even the most complex SPARQL query graphs. The most descriptive format that *Bliss* and most of the above algorithms work with is the directed vertex-colored graph.

DEFINITION 2. *A directed vertex-colored graph is a graph* $G=(V,E,c)$*, where* $V=\{1,2,...,n\}$ *is a vertex set,* $E \subseteq V \times V$ *is a set of directed edges, and* $c: V \to N$ *is a function that associates to each vertex a non-negative integer(color).*

In order to use the existing canonical labelling algorithms, we need to transform SPARQL queries to directed vertex-colored graphs without losing any information that can introduce false positives or false negatives, i.e., non-isomorphic SPARQL queries having the same label or isomorphic queries having different labels. Our first task is to transform SPARQL queries to directed vertex-and-edge-colored graphs.

DEFINITION 3. *A directed vertex-and-edge-colored graph is a graph* $G=(V,E,c_v,c_e)$*, where* $V=\{1,2,...,n\}$ *is a finite set of vertices,* $E \subseteq V \times V$ *is a set of directed edges,* $c_v: V \to N$ *and* $c_e: E \to N$ *are color functions for vertices and edges.*

As a running example, let us assume that we need to get a canonical label for the following SPARQL query:

```
?prof ub:teacherOf ?gcourse .  (1)
?prof ub:teacherOf ?ugcourse .  (2)
?ugcourse rdf:type ub:UndergraduateCourse .  (3)
?gcourse rdf:type ub:GraduateCourse .  (4)
```

Initially, we transform the query to a graph where each triple query is represented by a vertex and triple queries that share a common variable are linked with an edge. This graph is depicted on the left of Figure 2, where the vertex IDs correspond to the triple query labels presented above. In the next stage, we remove all information related to the variable names. To do so, for each triple query we create a label that consists of three IDs, one for each position inside the triple. Bound nodes are translated to integer IDs using a String to ID dictionary while variables are translated to zero. For the current example, let us assume that the String-ID dictionary contains: {teacherOf→15, type→3, UndergraduateCourse→52, GraduateCourse→35}. The label of the first triple query would be, for example, "0_15_0". We handle *OPTIONAL* triple query patterns by appending a special character '|' at the beginning of their label. We also direct and color the edges according to the type of join that they represent. All possible types are {SS, SP, SO, PS, PP, PO, OS, OP, OO}. As we will see later in this section, the number of edge colors affects the labelling performance so we need to reduce it as much as possible. To do so, we introduce a position ordering (S<P<O) and only add edges whose source position is lower than or equal to their destination position. We only require the following 6 edge types {SS, SP, SO, PP, PO, OO}. In the second graph of Figure 2, we can see both the vertex and edge labels for our query.

In the final step, we translate the vertex and edge labels to non-negative integers(colors). We just sort the vertex labels and use as color the position of the label in the sorted set. For edge labels we use the following translation {SS→1, SP→2, SO→3, PP→4, PO→5, OO→6}. The final graph is a directed vertex-and-edge-colored graph and can be seen in the first graph of Figure 3. We note here that we do not use

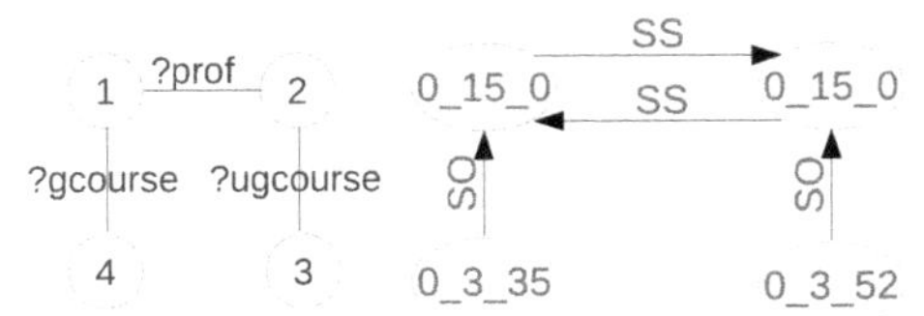

Figure 2: SPARQL query transformation

grouping, ordering, filtering and projection information for labelling SPARQL queries. Queries that are isomorphic but differ for example in result ordering will get the same label but they will be handled as different versions of the same result by our dynamic planner described in Section 4.

The above transformation removes all information relevant to variable naming while managing to maintain all structural information of the query using the directed join edges. To prove this, we note that isomorphic queries that contain different variable names would generate the same labelled graph because variable names do not affect the labels. Respectively, we can generate an isomorphic SPARQL query from the transformed graph by assigning variable names. We initially give unique names to all variables, labelled as 0. We then iterate over all edges, equating their source and destination variable names using the edge label information. This process generates an isomorphic query proving that our transformation maintains all structural query information.

In [25], McKay presents a practical way to transform directed edge-colored graphs to simple directed graphs without changing their automorphism group. We use this technique to transform directed vertex-and-edge-colored graphs to directed vertex-colored graphs. More specifically, if there are v vertex colors and all available edge colors are integers in $\{1, 2, \ldots, 2^d - 1\}$, we construct a graph with d layers, each of which contains n vertices, where n is the number of vertices of the initial graph. We require only 6 edge colors, one for each possible type of triple pattern join, and thus d equals to 3 leading to a new graph that contains $3n$ vertices. We vertically connect the vertices of the different layers (each corresponding to one vertex of the original graph) using paths. The vertex colors of the first layer remain the same as in the original graph and they get propagated to higher layers by adding v to the corresponding color of the lower layer. For each edge of the original graph the binary expansion of its color number tells us which layers should contain the horizontal edge. For example, an edge with color 3, whose binary expansion is 011, will be placed both in the first and the second layer of the new graph. The transformation for the above example is depicted in the second graph of Figure 3, where the vertex IDs represent the assigned colors.

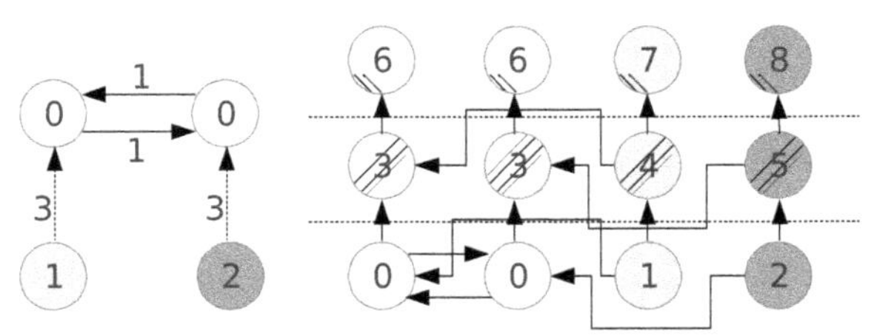

Figure 3: Transformation to directed vertex-colored graph

At this point we can use *Bliss* to produce a canonical label for the above graph. The canonization process returns a canonical order of the graph's vertices. As stated in [25], the order by which a canonical labelling of the new graph labels the vertices of the first layer can be taken to be a canonical labelling order of the original graph. Thus, after executing *Bliss* we can get a canonical ordering for our initial query. For our example the canonical ordering is {1,2,4,3}, where the ids are the SPARQL triple query ids used in the initial graph. Using this ordering, we generate the string canonical label of the SPARQL query graph. We iterate through the triple queries using this canonical ordering and, for each triple query we append its signature at the end of the label string. While iterating, we also generate the canonical ordering of the variables, i.e. variable ?prof is the first variable that we find and thus it gets the canonical ID ?1. In our example, the canonical variable mapping is {?prof→?1, ?gcourse→?2, ?ugcourse→?3} and the generated string label is ?1_15_?2&?1_15_?3&?2_3_35&?3_3_52. Our algorithm produces the exact same string label for any isomorphic SPARQL query and thus is a canonical labelling algorithm for SPARQL query graphs. This label is used as key in both our Result Cache and Cache Requests tables and provides a robust and efficient way to store and retrieve information about SPARQL query graphs.

4. QUERY PLANNING

Finding the optimal join plan for complex queries has always been a major research challenge in optimizing database systems. In addition, our system needs to effectively discover which of the maintained cached results can be used to provide input for a query's subgraph. Both these tasks have exponential complexity to the size of the query because they need to at least check all its subgraphs. While there exist several greedy, heuristic approaches for SPARQL query planning [36, 30], they cannot be easily integrated with a cached result discovery algorithm that finds *all* relevant cached results. In contrast, dynamic programming query planning approaches [27, 29] explore all subgraphs of a query and thus can be easily modified to achieve both optimal query planning and cached result discovery.

One of the oldest and most efficient dynamic programming algorithms for join planning is *DPsize* [13] that is widely used in commercial databases like IBM's DB2. *DPsize* limits the search space to left-deep trees and generates plans in increasing order of size. A more recent approach, *DPccp* [27] and its variant *DPhyp* [28] are considered to be the most efficient, state-of-the-art dynamic programming algorithms for query optimization. They reduce the search space by examining all connected subgraphs of the query in a bottom-up fashion. In addition, *DPccp* is successfully utilized to generate optimal SPARQL join plans in RDF-3X [29]. In this paper, we extend the *DPccp* algorithm and add support for cached result discovery for all query subgraphs.

4.1 Cached result discovery

In this section, we describe how our dynamic programming planner discovers all cached results that can enhance the execution of the query in hand. Detailed descriptions and pseudocodes of the proposed algorithms can be found in Appendix C. The main idea is that while the planner examines all the connected subgraphs of the query, it generates for each one a canonical label and issues a cache check. The benefit of all discovered cached results is examined by the cost model during the planner's execution. The above approach locates all cached results that exactly match a subgraph of the query and evaluates their usability for the generation of the optimal query plan. However, it cannot discover results that can provide input for a subgraph by executing a filtering operation over one or several of their variables. Lets examine the following query:

```
?prof ub:worksFor "MIT" .  ?prof ub:emailAddress ?email .
?prof ub:name "Mike" .
```

Using exact matching, our planner would only issue the cache requests that contain all the bound literals and URIs of the initial query, depicted in Figure 4.

?prof ub:worksFor "MIT" . ?prof ub:name "Mike" .	?prof ub:worksFor "MIT" . ?prof ub:emailAddress ?email .
?prof ub:emailAddress ?email . ?prof ub:name "Mike" .	?prof ub:worksFor "MIT" . ?prof ub:emailAddress ?email . ?prof ub:name "Mike" .

Figure 4: Exact cache requests

However, we notice that the following indexed cached result, while not examined, could also be beneficial for answering the query, transforming it to a simple index lookup:

```
{ ?prof ub:worksFor ?univ .  ?prof ub:emailAddress ?email
?prof ub:name ?name } index by ?univ ?name
```

To address this scenario, we need to also examine more general graphs as well as their indexing properties that can help reduce the filtering operation overhead. For example and in the above case, caching the general result without any indexing might be useless, if for instance its size was significantly larger than the size of the filtered results, as we should read all its data in order to find the relevant ones. In addition, the usability of a cached result also depends on the join operation that must be applied on it. For example, if we need to join this result with another triple pattern according to variable `?prof`, we would like to have it sorted in order to perform a merge join operation and not a more complex and inefficient hash or sort-merge join operation. Furthermore, we need to take into account the case of cached results or queries that contain more complex filters on variables, projection and group-by clauses. To achieve all these goals, we need to find an efficient way to examine which of the cached results can provide input for a query subgraph, due to filtering, projection and grouping properties, and search them to find the one that incurs the least cost.

To tackle this problem, we first abstract our query graph. We remove all bound query nodes that reside in the subject or object position of a triple query and replace them with variables along with the respective equality filters. In the above example, the query would be transformed to:

```
{ ?prof ub:worksFor ?univ .  ?prof ub:emailAddress ?email
?prof ub:name ?name } filter(?univ="MIT", ?name="Mike")
```

We use this abstract query graph in our dynamic programming planner and thus check all its subgraphs issuing cache requests. Each cache request is issued having as key the canonical label of the abstract query subgraph and is accompanied by the filter, projection and group-by clauses of the query as well as by a request for a join variable. As mentioned in Section 3, filters, projections and groupings are not used to generate the canonical label and thus queries with the same abstract structure will be grouped together using their label. The use of canonical labels as cache keys reduces the results that we need to examine for every query subgraph but we still need an efficient way to select the best result from the list of all existing results that share the same abstract structure. Each cache record, related to an abstract query label, maintains all cached results that share this label

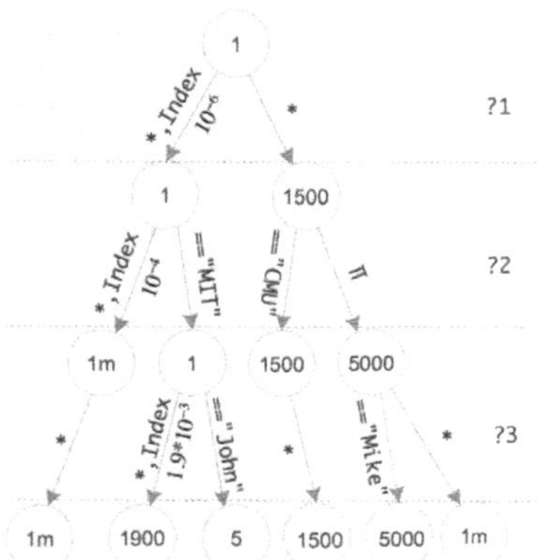

Figure 5: Cached Result Tree

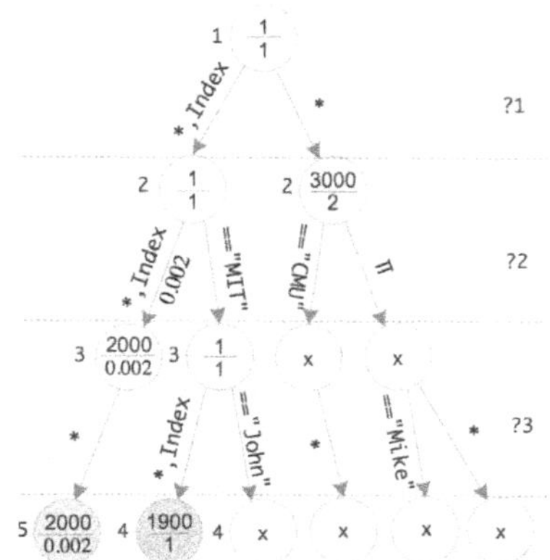

Figure 6: Search Result Tree

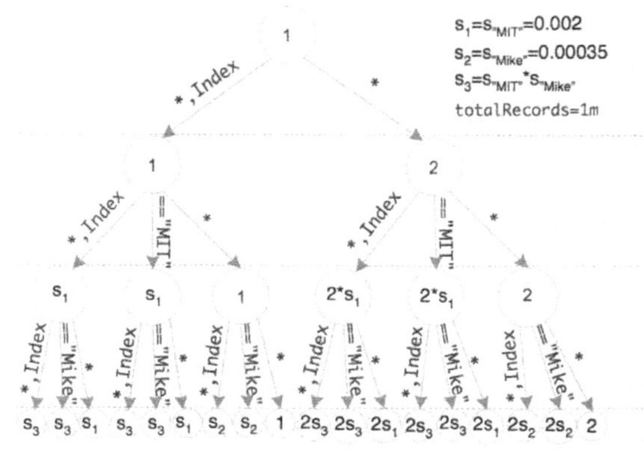

Figure 7: Benefit Estimation Tree

using a tree structure. This structure can be used to efficiently search for the best result with respect to the request's auxiliary information(filters, projections, groupings). Figure 5 depicts this structure for the following abstract query:

```
{ ?prof ub:worksFor ?univ .  ?prof ub:name ?name }
```

For this example, we assume that our cache contains several cached results with the same abstract query pattern. As discussed in Section 3, the canonical labelling of the abstract query provides a canonical ordering of its variables. Let's assume that the canonical ordering for our current example is {?prof→?1, ?univ→?2, ?name→?3}. Each level of the tree encodes the information related to the respective variable. Each leaf of the tree represents a cached result and therefore the path that connects it with the root node encodes all its auxiliary information. For example, an edge with label *"*, Index"* means that the result contains no filter on this variable and provides an index for it. An edge labeled *=="MIT"* appearing at the second level of the tree denotes that the result contains the filter *?2="MIT"*. A "Π" edge denotes that the respective variable is projected out in the result. If the query contains a group-by clause it is encoded as a last level edge in the cached result tree. To check the usability of cached results for a cache request we can traverse the tree from the root node and find the results that can be utilised to answer it by following only the edges that provide more generic results than the query request.

Apart from checking the usability of cached results for a cache request, we also need to be able to evaluate their cost and find the result that best matches each cache request. As cost of a cached result we refer to the amount of records that need to be accessed for using it. To estimate this cost in the presence of several indexed variables and query filters, we need to extend our tree structure with selectivity estimations and result sizes. The procedure of inserting a cached result in the result tree can be seen in Algorithm 2. The *treeInsert* method recursively adds a new leaf node, representing the current result, along with its size in number of records. The *minResults* value of each tree node, visible inside each node of Figure 5, represents an estimation of the smallest cost that can be achieved by the results of its respective subtree. Having guarantees for the smallest cost of a subtree, we can perform the search for a cache request using efficient A* search and prune entire subtrees that do not contain relevant results. To create the minimum cost estimations, each leaf node contains the actual result size; we propagate this value to the parent nodes by keeping each time the minimum value among all children. In the case of indexed edges, we apply the selectivity estimations before we propagate the value from the child to the parent node. If a request contains a filter on a variable that is indexed, we need to reduce the cost of the result by the expected selectivity of the filtering operation on the index. Edges that contain no indexes do not change the cost of the result because we would need to access all their data to perform the filtering operation.

Our cache implementation does not depend on the specific way that an RDF execution engine handles selectivity estimations. To create the cached result tree we only require the maximum selectivity that can be achieved by doing a filtering operation on a certain index. For each indexed edge of a cached result we generate a selectivity value $s = minRecords/totalRecords$, depicted along the indexed edges of Figure 5. In our running example, an index on the general result(1 million records), on variable `?2 (?univ)` has a minimum amount of 100 records and thus its maximum selectivity is $s = 100/1m = 10^{-4}$. To handle the estimation of multiple filtering operations on different variables we follow the independency assumption i.e. the selectivity of two filtering operations with selectivities s_1 and s_2 is $s = s_1 \cdot s_2$. This property allows us to follow paths of filtering operations on the cached result tree and maintain a total estimation by just multiplying the individual selectivities while crossing indexed edges. The *treeInsert* method (Algorithm 2) starts by adding the respective leaf along with its amount of records. We then move from the leaf to the root node and update the minimum values of the parent nodes. When crossing an indexed edge we apply the maximum selectivity by multiplying it with the child's number of records. We also set a minimum value of 1 for the costs of nodes. The complexity of the add operation is linear to the amount of variables contained in the abstract query pattern.

Figure 6 depicts the execution of the *searchTree* method (Algorithm 1) when searching for the cache request:

```
{ ?prof ub:worksFor ?univ .  ?prof ub:name ?name
} filter(?univ="MIT"), joinVar(?prof)
```

As mentioned before, we use the minimum cost estimations of the tree nodes in order to perform an A* search and prune subtrees with large costs. The search procedure starts from the root node and checks all nodes in a best first search according to cost estimations. In Figure 6, each node contains two numbers; its estimated cost (upper number) and its selectivity(lower number). Only edges that can be used for answering the request are followed. For example, the edge with label *?3="John"* will not be followed because it is more restrictive than the request. Furthermore, when crossing indexed edges that match with a filtering operation of the request we need to apply their selectivity. For example, when crossing the edge *(?2: "*,Indexed")* we need to apply the selectivity of the filter *?2="MIT"*. To do so, we consult the selectivity estimator of the abstract result for the respective variable. We use the abstract result to estimate selectivities because a tree edge can belong to several results with different sizes and we want to have an estimation for the maximum selectivity. In this case the selectivity of *?2="MIT"* is 0.002 because it is expected to return 2000 records and the abstract result contains 1 million records. To estimate the selectivity of several consecutive filtering operations we maintain a selectivity estimation for each open node and propagate it to children nodes by multiplying it when crossing indexed edges with filter operations. Additionally, when crossing join variable edges we multiply the selectivity by 2 if the edge is not indexed due to the fact that the overhead of performing a hash or sort-merge join algorithm instead of a merge join can be approximated by the time to read the input data twice [29]. The minimum cost estimation for each node (upper value) is computed by multiplying its selectivity with the *minResults* estimation depicted in Figure 5.

Our cost estimations can deviate from the actual costs due to the use of the abstract result selectivity estimator and our assumption of independency for filtering operations. Therefore, we perform a top-k search for results and then further examine the cost of each result, inside *DPccp*, using the detailed cost model of the execution engine. In Figure 6, we perform a top-2 search depicting on the side of each node the step in which it was opened. Nodes marked with an $\times$ were not opened; grey coloured nodes depict the results. We observe that we only required 5 steps to find the top-2 cached results and our search managed to prune a large part of the search tree due to auxiliary info mismatches and minimum cost estimations.

5. CACHE CONTROLLER

In this section, we describe the functionality of our Cache Controller module. Its main challenges are the generation and caching of *profitable* query patterns and the cache replacement strategy. As *profitable* query patterns we define queries that, even if not exactly issued by users or executed as intermediate results, could benefit the execution of the workload if cached. For example, consider a workload of queries having the same abstract query structure but random bound selective IDs. Caching only the intermediate results of those queries would not offer a great benefit to the workload because it would achieve cache hits only for queries that share the exact same selective IDs. In contrast, caching the abstract query pattern indexed according to the variable that contains the selective IDs would introduce benefits for all queries, in this special type of workload, transforming them to index scans. Apart from identifying abstract results and their indexing, our cache controller can intelligently identify cross-query frequent subgraphs and index them according to: 1) Their most common filtering variables and 2) their most common join variables.

5.1 Generation of profitable cached results

As discussed in the previous section, our dynamic programming planner issues cache requests for all subgraphs of the abstract query. In addition, these cache requests are issued while optimizing the query plan and can thus be recorded along with estimations about their effect to the execution time of the respective query. Maintaining such a detailed log of cache requests provides valuable information about which query patterns can provide the most benefit to the workload. The exact benefit computation of all cached requests $Q_i = (V_i, E_i)$ to the execution of a query $Q = (V, E)$ would require the execution of *DPccp* for each one of them. To avoid this, we use the following function, that multiplies the query's cost by the fraction of triple patterns covered by the subgraph, to compute a benefit estimation.

$$B(Q_i|Q) = \frac{|V_i|}{|V|} \cdot cost(Q) \tag{1}$$

This benefit estimation requires the optimal cost of the query Q and can be computed at the end of our planning process. Therefore, during the planning process our planner records all non satisfied cache requests (Q_i) and at the end compiles a list of requests along with their respective benefit and sends it to the Cache Controller for further processing. This means that the complexity cost of attributing benefits to possibly usable query patterns does not affect the execution and planning time of queries because it is done in an offline manner by the separate thread of the Cache Controller module. The Controller maintains a Cache Requests structure containing request benefits indexed by their abstract canonical label. Each record holds a tree structure encoding benefit estimations for requests sharing the same label. Figure 7 depicts this benefit estimation tree, generated by the *addBenefit* method (Algorithm 3), for the following cache request (Q_i) with benefit $B = 3sec$:

```
{ ?prof ub:worksFor ?univ .  ?prof ub:name ?name }
filter(?univ="MIT", ?name="Mike"), joinVar(?prof)
```

Each leaf of the tree represents a query pattern that can possibly benefit the cache request. To attribute benefits to all possibly usable results at each level of the tree we at least follow the *"*, Index"* and the *"*"* edges. If the respective variable contains a filter, we also add an edge containing it. Furthermore, if the record of the Cache Requests table already contained benefits for results with filters that can be used for the current request, they are also followed. For example, if a previous query had a regular expression filter $?name$ = "$M*$" we would also attribute benefits to its subtree. The values inside the nodes represent the selectivity estimations for the respective pattern. To generate these estimations we only require a selectivity estimator of the abstract result and the total amount of records of the abstract result. We again use the independency property to estimate the selectivities for multiple filters on different variables. Therefore, we just need to propagate the selectivity estimation from the parent to the child node by multiplying with the selectivity of the respective edge. The benefit for each usable result, leaf node, is:

$$b = B - s \cdot R/thr \tag{2}$$

where B is the total benefit of the request, s is the selectivity of the result, R is the number of records of the abstract query, and thr is the engine's read throughput (e.g. 100k records/sec). The second part of the equation represents the cost to read the result. In Figure 7, the benefit for a result with selectivity s_3 is $b_3 = 3sec - s_3 * 1m/100k \simeq 3sec$. We also ignore benefits that are less than 0, for example the non indexed abstract result, rightmost leaf, has selectivity 2 and benefit $b = 3sec - 2 * 1m/100k = -17sec$. When the benefits of all patterns are estimated, the Cache Controller sums the previously existing benefit values with the new ones and stores the tree inside the record of the Cache Results table. The Controller, running our planner, estimates the execution cost of the most prominent requests and maintains an ordered list of (request, benefit/cost) pairs (Algorithm 5) used by the *profitableQueryGeneration* method to trigger the caching of the most *profitable* queries.

The query pattern tree grows exponentially to the number of variables in an abstract query and there are various computed and maintained benefits for results that will never be the most profitable. However, this exponential complexity does not affect our query response times because it is done independently of the query execution. To alleviate the problem of maintaining all the benefit estimations, we have an offline process (Algorithm 5) that runs in configurable time-frames (e.g. every 10sec or every 10 queries) and maintains only the top-k leaf nodes of the Cache Requests table. Furthermore, to avoid promoting only queries with large costs, we normalize the benefit estimation of a query pattern using its execution cost. Thus, in the previous example, if we had queries that mostly targeted "MIT", both the indexed version of the abstract result and the version that contains only records for "MIT" would gather the same benefit but eventually the more specific result would be cached due to its lower cost of execution.

In addition, queries issue cache requests adding benefit to all their subgraphs. When one query pattern gets selected for caching the corresponding benefit should be removed from all other patterns that were requested by the same queries as they were *satisfied*. Not reducing benefits for *satisfied* queries can lead to: 1) executing all subgraphs of a frequent query pattern, 2) difficulties in identifying new profitable cache requests due to obsolete benefit estimations of *satisfied* requests. To alleviate this problem, we maintain for each query pattern in the Cache Requests table a list of query IDs that attributed to its benefit. This list is used to reduce the benefit of cache requests after the execution of a *profitable* query. We reduce the benefit of each request by the fraction of its query IDs that belonged to the *profitable*'s query ID list. In our example above, if we decided to execute the abstract query indexed according to variable $?univ$, all query profits would go to zero because the *profitable* query gathered benefit from all workload queries. Thus, no more queries would be executed by the Controller. To avoid maintaining obsolete benefit estimations for cache requests, we additionally decrease their benefit with time.

5.2 Cache replacement strategy

In this paper, we target disk based cached results keeping only their meta-data in main memory. Thus, the amount of the maintained cached results is only limited by the available disk space. However, the user can set limits on the disk space capacity dedicated for storing cached results. When a new cached result cannot be stored without exceeding those limits we need to remove some of the existing cached results. To be able to intelligently select which result should be evicted from the cache, the Controller also maintains a benefit estimation for each cached result. This benefit estimation is updated using the method *addResultBenefit* (Algorithm 4) and differs from the one described in the previous section. After the execution of a query that used a cached result, the Controller executes the planner one more time, restricting the use of this cached result. This gives us the cost of the query without utilizing the respective cached result. The controller adds the difference between this cost and the actual cost to the result's benefit value. Benefits, also, decrease with time in order to avoid maintaining obsolete results. We prioritize cache evictions using Algorithm 6 that utilizes this benefit estimation. New results can only evict cached results that have less benefit. In addition, if the cache size constraints are violated, our controller will not execute new *profitable* queries unless their benefit is larger than the lowest cached result benefit. To evict multiple results, due to its size, a new result must have benefit greater than the sum of benefits of all evicted results.

6. RELATED WORK

In this section, we present related research on SPARQL result caching techniques as well as on RDF databases, discussing the effect of our caching framework on them.

6.1 SPARQL result caching

Here, we present some of the most relevant research approaches on SPARQL query result caching. While this is a challenging problem, few relevant approaches to address it exist. A first attempt to introduce SPARQL caching was made in [23], where a meta-data relational database is responsible for storing information about cached query results. However, this approach cannot tackle the isomorphism problem introduced when the same SPARQL graph pattern is requested from different queries with small deviations such as pattern reordering, variable renaming, etc.

A more sophisticated approach was presented in [39], where the cache keys consisted of normalized Algebra Expression Trees (AETs) that correspond to cached join plans. However, a cached AET is only used in join plans that exactly contain it as a subtree. This is also not a general subgraph caching framework and leads to inferior cache utilization.

In [22], the authors introduce a similarity-based matching algorithm that can detect cached queries that resemble the query in hand. Yet, this greedy technique cannot find all candidate subgraph matches for a SPARQL query. They also propose some heuristics used to augment the workload queries and prefetch SPARQL query results, which resembles our *profitable* query execution. Their approach is again based on heuristic techniques that can not examine the benefit of all possibly usable results as well as their indexing. To sum up, current caching frameworks fail to effectively locate all subgraph matches and subsequently use them to produce optimal query plans for SPARQL queries.

Apart from SPARQL result caching there are other relevant techniques that try to tackle parts of the problem that we address in this paper. Many of the state-of-the-art approaches in graph database indexing propose the use of frequent pattern indexing [41, 38]. Frequent and discriminative subgraphs are discovered and indexed during the import phase of the dataset and can be then utilized to efficiently answer queries that contain them. In addition, large amount of research has been done in the area of multi-query optimization [33] and view selection [26] for relational databases. Approaches for multi-query optimization have also been proposed for SPARQL query processing [21]. All these techniques depend either on knowledge of the workload queries or on expensive import procedures that find frequent patterns in the dataset. In contrast, our approach assumes no a-priori knowledge on both the dataset and the workload and targets the adaptive indexing and caching of frequent query patterns by actively monitoring the workload queries.

6.2 RDF datastores

One of the first and most widely used ideas for indexing and querying RDF data was presented in Hexastore [37]. According to it, the materialization of all six *permutations* of subject-predicate-object values is required in order to retrieve any triple pattern at minimal cost and extensively use efficient merge joins. A similar indexing approach is followed in RDF-3X [29] which maintains all Hexastore indices as well as additional indices that collect statistical information amounting to a total of 15 indices. RDF-3X also uses the *DPccp* algorithm in order to find the optimal join execution plan and thus our caching framework can be easily integrated and offer the respective performance gains.

BitMat [11] is an alternative approach for storing RDF triples via a 3-dimensional bit matrix. Each matrix element is a bit denoting the presence or absence of the corresponding triple. This 3-d bit matrix is flattened to multiple 2-d matrices used for query execution. BitMat uses a greedy technique to chose the sequence of matrix operations that need to be performed for the execution of a SPARQL query.

To tackle the big-data challenge, research has recently moved onward to distributed RDF data management systems. A first attempt to utilize MapReduce and HBase was made in H_2RDF [31] which materializes three RDF triple indexes using HBase tables. H_2RDF performs joins using the MapReduce framework, employing a greedy planner that decides on the sequence of joins as well as their type of execution ranging from centralized to distributed joins.

An alternative proposal is presented by Huang et al. [17]; this method starts out by partitioning the RDF graph into distinct subgraphs, each stored in a single node running a local RDF-3X instance. Moreover, in a replication scheme, each node keeps information on the graph contents within n *hops* from the contents it owns. This provision allows for unobstructed parallel processing of SPARQL queries satisfying an n *hop guarantee*. In case this guarantee is not satisfied, Hadoop is invoked for distributed join processing.

Lastly, Trinity-RDF [40] is a distributed, memory-based graph engine for RDF data. It stores RDF triples as graph edges using distributed memory hashmaps. Utilizing graph exploration techniques it avoids join execution overheads and takes advantage of the quick random access provided by the memory resident data. Trinity-RDF depends on a DP planner to find the best graph exploration execution plan.

To sum up, all the aforementioned systems utilize different RDF indexing and query execution techniques. They also rely on a range of techniques for query optimization, from dynamic programming planners to greedy heuristic planners. However, none of the above systems effectively utilizes cached results or adaptive indexing techniques. We argue that our caching framework can be integrated with and benefit these systems transparently because:

- The *DPccp* algorithm is generic and can handle the query optimization for all those systems.
- Cost models for the different operators of the various systems can be plugged into the *DPccp* algorithm and used to devise the optimal query execution plan for each engine.
- Our labelling algorithm is based on the SPARQL standard and thus is applicable to all systems.
- Our caching implementation only depends on query metadata and thus query results can be stored and reused using the system's native storage format.

7. EXPERIMENTS

In this section, we present a thorough performance evaluation of our generic RDF caching framework. We choose to integrate our caching framework on top of the open source[1], distributed H_2RDF+ database [30, 32] that combines the Hadoop and HBase to index and query RDF data. H_2RDF+ generates HBase indexes for all permutations of RDF elements, namely *spo, pso, pos, ops, osp* and *sop* [37], along with aggregated statistic indexes that can provide a detailed join cost model. In addition, H_2RDF+ is highly scalable, utilizing MapReduce to perform distributed Merge and Sort-Merge joins. Joins can be executed using either single-machine or distributed jobs according to the join cost resulting in small response times for selective queries. H_2RDF+ utilizes aggressive byte-level compression and result grouping in order to reduce its result space consumption. As we focus on disk-based result caching, aggressive compression is a major plus and boosts the caching efficiency by allowing more results to be maintained.

Our caching framework is independent to the query execution engine and thus only small changes are required for H_2RDF+, as well as for other RDF stores, to support it. Our cache depends on indexing cached results for: 1) filtering operations, 2) boosting performance for join execution. Most RDF databases, including H_2RDF+, utilize order preserving indexes that can be used to efficiently perform both operations. H_2RDF+'s indexed results can be used in both Merge and Sort-Merge joins in the same way as H_2RDF+'s primary triple indexes [30]. Non-indexed results have no ordering properties and are stored in plain HDFS files.

7.1 SPARQL query canonical labelling

In this section we test the performance of our SPARQL query canonical labelling algorithm. Its performance is tightly coupled with *Bliss*'s, with an added transformation overhead introduced when translating SPARQL queries into directed, vertex-colored graphs. To evaluate the efficiency of our algorithm, we measure the time required to canonically label a set of different SPARQL query graphs consisting of paths, stars, cycles and path-stars. Path-stars are graphs that contain a star subgraph and each of the branches of the star consists of a path of two triple patterns.

First, we generate SPARQL query graphs using only one type of triple pattern query, e.g., `?v1 ub:takesCourse ?v2`. This means that all vertexes of the transformed graph, depicted in Figure 2, will have the same label. *Bliss* and *nauty* use vertex color and graph structure information to break the graph symmetry and prune the isomorphism search space when searching for a canonical label. Consequently, for SPARQL queries that contain only one type of triple pattern, our canonical labelling algorithm can benefit only from the graph structure. The response times required to label queries with variable number of triple patterns (of a *single* type) are depicted in the first graph of Figure 8. Path and cycle queries require almost stable labelling time, close to 0.2 ms, due to their small number of isomorphs. In contrast, star queries require a labelling time exponential in the number of triple patterns. Our labelling transformation

[1]http://h2rdf.googlecode.com

generates graphs with edges corresponding to join variables and thus it transforms star SPARQL queries to cliques because all triple patterns are joined according to the central variable of the star. Path-stars are a combination of a star and multiple paths and thus their complexity is higher than that of a simple path with the same size but lower than the complexity of the respective star graphs.

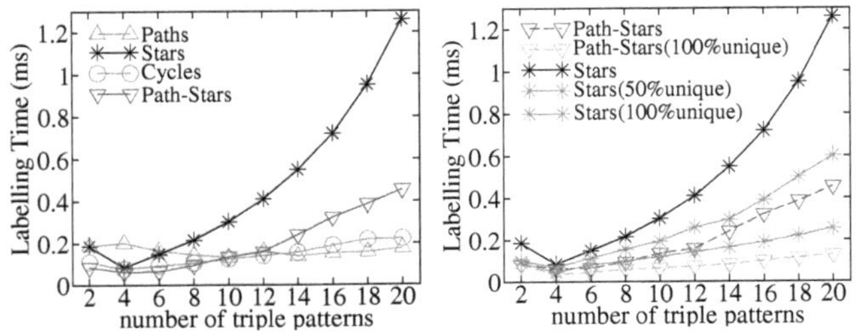

Figure 8: SPARQL query canonical labelling evaluation against queries of variable complexity and size

The second graph of Figure 8 depicts the effect of having different types of triple patterns in the queries. Different triple patterns give our canonical labelling algorithm more information to prune the isomorphism search space. We measure the time needed to label star and path-star queries with variable number of nodes while ranging the percentage of unique triple patterns. For stars we examine queries with 0%, 50% and 100% of the query's patterns being unique while the rest of the patterns are duplicates. We notice that the required labelling time decreases when queries contain more unique patterns that help our algorithm break the graph symmetry. This performance gain is also visible in path-star queries. Finally, this gain is exponential especially in the case of star queries leading to almost linear labelling complexity for both star and path-star queries with 100% unique triple queries. In general, our algorithm is able to label most real-life SPARQL queries in less than 1 ms.

7.2 Dynamic Programming Planner

In this section, we evaluate our dynamic programming planner that integrates *DPccp* [27] with our canonical labelling algorithm. The first graph of Figure 9 depicts the time required for our planner to generate canonical labels for all the query subgraphs, check for existing usable cached results and compute the optimal join plan for several types of SPARQL query graphs. We use a set of query graphs consisting of paths, cycles, stars, path-stars and grids and vary the number of their triple queries. *DPccp* utilizes the edge-graph representation of SPARQL queries, depicted in the left graph of Figure 2. When processing star queries *DPccp* faces an exponential complexity to the amount of triple queries. This is expected because star SPARQL queries are transformed to cliques in the edge-graph and thus contain exponential amount of connected subgraphs that need to be enumerated. However, we can generate optimal plans for star queries with up to 10 triple queries in milliseconds. In contrast, for path and cycle queries that do not contain as many subgraphs, the planner exhibits great performance and is able to process queries with up to 20 relations in less than 30ms. Path-star and grid query graphs, due to their more complex graph structure, present higher complexity than paths and cycles resulting in millisecond response times for queries with up to 14 triple queries.

Another major parameter that affects the complexity of

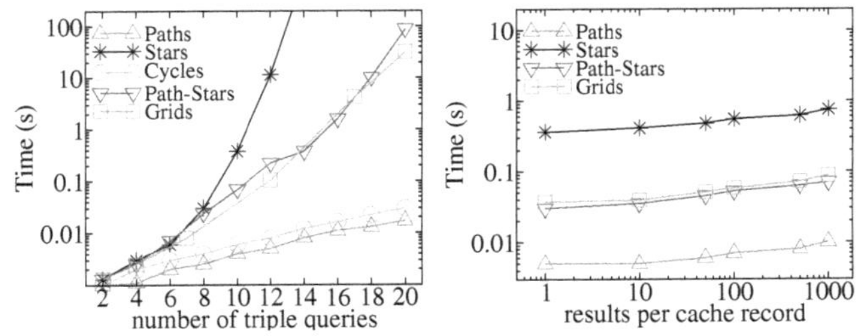

Figure 9: Query planning performance

our planner is the tree search for cached results inside a cache record. This procedure mainly depends on the amount of results that are stored inside a cache record. As explained in Section 4.1, we perform a top-k, A* search to find the best results inside each cache record. From our experimentation, we have discovered that a top-3 search inside each cache record is sufficient to discover the best cached results in all our query examples and therefore we utilize a top-3 search in all the experiments of this section. The second graph of Figure 9, depicts the effect of the amount of cached results to the planners execution time. To test the impact of the amount of cached results to the execution of our planner, we select a set of query graphs all consisting of 10 triple queries and range the number of cached results per cache record, utilized by the results, by randomly generating and loading 1 to 1000 cached results. We assume that 1000 results per unique abstract query subgraph suffice to evaluate our planner's performance even for the most challenging caching scenario. From the experimental results, we note that the performance of our planner scales logarithmically to the amount of cached results for all query patterns. This means that our A* search manages to effectively prune large parts of the cached result trees due to their filtering constraints and our minimum cost estimations. The time needed for our planner to evaluate the same query in the presence of 1 and 1000 cached results per cache record only increases by a factor of 2 for all query patterns. To sum up, our dynamic programming planner is able to both effectively locate cached results and generate the optimal join plan in less than a second for most realistic SPARQL queries; this includes all benchmark queries used in the following sections.

7.3 Cache efficiency

In this section we evaluate the ability of our cache to effectively generate *profitable* results in order to decrease query response times for several diverse SPARQL workloads.

7.3.1 Cluster configuration and Datasets

Our evaluation cluster consists of 10 worker nodes plus a single machine in the role of the Hadoop and HBase master. Each of our workers features a 2 Quad-Core E5405 Intel Xeon®CPUs at 2.00GHz, 8 GB of RAM and a 500GB disk, while the master has similar CPU and disk and 4 GB of RAM. Each worker is set to concurrently run 5 mappers and 5 reducers, each consuming 512MB of RAM. In our experiments, we used Hadoop v1.1.2 and HBase v0.94.5.

We utilize the LUBM dataset generator[14] that creates RDF datasets with academic domain information, enabling a variable number of triples by controlling the number of *university* entities. LUBM is widely used to compare the performance and scalability of triple stores due its ability to create arbitrarily large datasets. We use two datasets in our experiments: LUBM10k (10k universities, 1.38 billion triples and a total of 250GB of data) and LUBM20k (20k universities, 2.8 billion triples and 500GB of data).

7.3.2 SPARQL query workloads

To evaluate caching performance, we use the suite of LUBM read-only benchmark queries [3]. Our caching framework as well as the integrated execution engine (H_2RDF+) offer limited OWL functionality. Thus, we do not consider queries that require complex OWL reasoning in the current evaluation. To better present the advantages of our system we generate 4 representative query workloads:

Selective query workload (W1): This workload consists of queries that contain selective triple patterns, such as `?student ub:takesCourse` <`Course1`>. These selective patterns can be efficiently used to reduce the size of data processed because they can be directly retrieved using the maintained hexastore triple indexes. H_2RDF+ executes selective queries in a centralized manner resulting to great response times. The LUBM queries for this workload can be found in Appendix A. Our workload issues queries sequentially choosing each time randomly one of the above queries. To make this a more challenging workload, we also randomly alter the bound nodes of each query. For example, LQ1 will be issued each time containing a different graduate course. We can easily generate random IDs because all LUBM URIs follow the format <http://www.Department1.University8.edu /GraduateCourse5>, thus making it easy to generate random department, university and course IDs. The same is true for all IDs present in the aforementioned queries.

Non selective query workload (W2): This workload consists of queries that do not contain any selective triple pattern and require to retrieve and join large relations using distributed joins. Queries in this category have both small and large result sizes because their selectivity is based on graph pattern selectivity and not basic triple-pattern selectivity. Representative LUBM queries from this workload can be found in Appendix A. For example, LQ2 is quite selective because it retrieves the graduate students that are members of the *same* university that they graduated from. While all graduate students have graduated from a university and are members of another university only few of them satisfy the triangle pattern and thus the selectivity of the query is based on the selectivity of this triangular relation. LQ15 produces a large output because it generates information for all universities professors and courses. To make this workload more challenging, we randomly alter the `type` of the triple queries. For example, in LQ9 we randomly generate its first 3 triple queries by alternating between Professor, FullProfessor, AssistantProfessor, AssociateProfessor and Lecturer. In general, there are not many subclasses we can select from and thus the executed workload consists of 19 distinct SPARQL queries.

Subgraph pattern query workload (W3): Another strong point of our caching algorithm is the ability to detect cross-query frequent subgraphs and use them to effectively reduce the workload's response time. To highlight this scenario, we generate a workload of queries that all contain the triangular query patten:

```
?x ub:memberOf ?z .  ?z ub:subOrganizationOf ?y .
?x ub:undergraduateDegreeFrom ?y .
```

Each query in this workload consists of this subgraph along with a set of other triple patterns that are different across the set of queries. Two of the workload queries contain only non selective triple queries like: `?x ub:name ?n, ?x ub:email ?em`, etc. We also add two queries that contain selective patterns like: `?x ub:memberOf` <`Department0.University0.edu`> and `?z ub:subOrganizationOf` <`University0`> with random selective IDs. The last query of this workload is the LQ2 which also contains the triangular subgraph along with randomly selected type triple patterns.

General query workload (W4): This workload contains all the queries of the previous workloads. It consists of 14 different SPARQL query types containing both selective and non selective queries. It also contains inter-query subgraph dependencies as discussed above.

7.3.3 Workload caching

In this section we test the caching performance of our system for the aforementioned workloads utilizing the LUBM10k dataset. For each workload, we examine the impact of our cache implementation to the average query response time and highlight the strong and weak points of our system. Figure 10 presents the average query response times for our four query workloads. To highlight the distinct contributions of our system we depict the average response time for: 1) the baseline H_2RDF+ system, 2) our caching implementation with exact cache checks labelled "Exact" and 3) our fully functional system with abstract query cache checks labelled "Abstract". In all cases, we use unlimited cache size by default. We average query response times using a window of 10 queries in order to avoid large randomness in the figures and achieve quick responsiveness to the cache changes. Finally, our Cache Controller is configured to check the Cache Requests table and generate *profitable* queries every 10 sec.

W1: The first graph of Figure 10 illustrates the behaviour of the average query response time for the selective workload. Initially, we note that our baseline H_2RDF+ system has a stable average performance that ranges between 1 and 2.5 seconds. This is expected due to the use of centralized joins that take advantage of HBase indexes. By including the caching mechanism, average response times are gradually decreased to 500ms within 400 sec. Our abstract query cache check technique is especially useful in this workload. Due to the fact that the workload contains random selective IDs, it is true that no exact subgraph of the issued queries could be efficiently used to improve the execution of the consequent queries. This is the reason that the "exact" version behaves in the same way as H_2RDF+. In contrast, when using abstract cache checks our system can effectively discover, execute and index *profitable* SPARQL queries. For example, the controller will cache the following query (Q_c)

```
{ ?x ub:worksFor ?y .  ?x ub:name ?n .
?x ub:emailAddress ?em .  ?x ub:telephone ?t .
?x rdf:type ub:Professor .} index by ?y
```

that can convert the execution of LQ4 from a complex join that takes nearly 2sec, to a simple HBase index access that requires, on average, only several milliseconds. The same holds for all W1 queries, resulting in an average response time of 0.5sec (an average 75% reduction in the mean response time). The response time thus gradually decreases during workload execution as more queries get effectively cached. The 400 sec, required for the response time to reach its lowest point, correspond to the distributed execution and indexing of 6 complex SPARQL queries (like Q_c); yet, their execution does not introduce large overheads to the que-

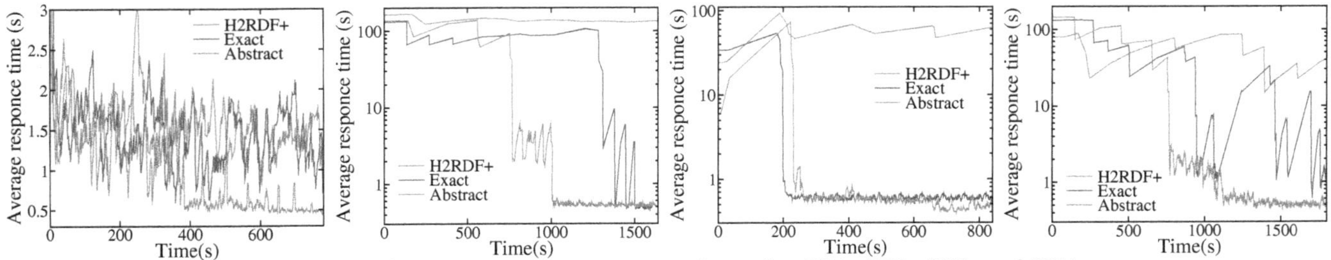

Figure 10: Average query response times for W1, W2, W3 and W4

ries of the workload that run at the same time. Finally, we note that while H$_2$RDF+'s basic indexes occupy 62GB of disk space, our system requires only an additional 1.3GB of disk space to cache the corresponding results and decrease the average response time for this workload. Although the workload queries are selective, the generated cached results are quite large because they contain information for all their selective nodes. The small size of cached results is mainly attributed to H$_2$RDF+'s aggressive compression scheme.

W2: The average response times for the compared systems are presented in the second graph of Figure 10. This workload is a lot more execution-intensive than the previous one, leading to an average response time of nearly 130 sec for the plain H$_2$RDF+ approach. However, our fully functional caching system is able to achieve interactive, millisecond-range response times for this workload in less than 1000 seconds (over two orders of magnitude reduction in the mean response time). Again, our caching system takes advantage of the abstract cache requests technique in order to capture the changes in the type fields of the queries and generate the most profitable cached results. It only requires the execution and indexing of 3 results to offer interactive response times for this workload. For example, the profitable cached result that corresponds to LQ9 is:

```
{?y ub:teacherOf ?z .  ?x ub:advisor ?y .
?x ub:takesCourse ?z .  ?x rdf:type ?t1 .
?y rdf:type ?t2 .  ?z rdf:type ?t3} index by ?t1 ?t2 ?t3
```

The time required to execute these 3 queries is actually around 400 sec. The additional time required to minimize the average response times is introduced by: 1) the fact that the result discovery process will not be very effective until enough entries are gathered in the Cache Requests table, 2)the concurrent distributed execution of workload queries affects the execution time of profitable queries. We notice that the "exact" version of our algorithm can also reduce the average response time for this workload but it needs nearly 1500 sec to do so. As mentioned before, when we do not utilize abstract cache requests we can only benefit from exact subgraph cache matches. However, this workload actually contains only 19 distinct queries and therefore we only need to execute each query once and then all queries will be directly found in the result cache. Despite being execution intensive only one of those queries, LQ15, has large output that requires 5.8GB of disk space. LQ2 and LQ9 are in fact very selective and require not more than 3MB of disk space.

W3: The third graph of Figure 10 depicts the average response times achieved for the subgraph pattern based workload. We can observe that both versions of our caching algorithm are presenting similar average response time behaviours. This is due to the fact that the common triangular query pattern, despite its complexity, is quite selective, with less than 3000 results. Both our algorithms can detect this inter-query dependency and in fact this is the first *profitable* query that is cached in both cases. The selectivity of this pattern is quite large, leading to really efficient, interactive execution times after only 240 sec. After caching the triangular subgraph, our fully functional version will also continue with caching indexed results for all the selective queries of the workload. This procedure leads to another small gain in performance, which can be seen after 600 sec. At this point the results could be directly retrieved using an HBase scan rather than executing a small join, showing over two orders of magnitude reduction in workload's mean response time. The disk size occupied by our cached results in this workload is only 50KB.

W4: The caching efficiency for this workload is depicted in the last graph of Figure 10. We observe that this is a quite challenging workload for our baseline H$_2$RDF+ engine as it presents an average response time of around 60 sec.

Regarding our caching implementation that only uses exact subgraph matching, we note that it is able to reduce the average response time by an order of magnitude resulting in average response times that oscillate around 3 seconds after 2000 seconds. Our "exact" version is able to cache: 1) the non selective results due to their small distinct number, 2) the frequent subgraph queries by caching their common subgraph. Nevertheless, this caching framework is not able to further reduce the execution time of small selective queries.

Using abstract cache requests we manage to reduce the average response time by two orders of magnitude for this challenging workload, resulting in interactive response times that stabilize close to 500 msec. As mentioned in Section 5.1, our Cache Controller prioritizes the execution of *profitable* queries according to their expected benefit and thus the queries that correspond to the costly, non selective SPARQL queries will be issued first. The large benefits of caching costly queries are obtained early, leading to one order of magnitude better response times after the first 700 sec. After caching large queries, our Cache Controller gradually improves the execution efficiency for the rest of the queries, requiring less than 1300 sec to execute and cache all the relevant, profitable SPARQL queries and drop response times to their lowest values. Due to the aggressive compression of H$_2$RDF+, the disk space occupied by all the cached results is only 7.5GB, leading us to assume that we can easily scale and handle even more complex datasets and workloads.

7.4 Caching techniques comparisson

To present a more detailed comparison of all different caching techniques for RDF data we use the *Detailed Cost Saving Ratio (DCSR)* metric presented in [20].

$$DCSR = \frac{\sum_i s_i}{\sum_i c_i} \tag{3}$$

where c_i is the execution cost for query q_i without utilising the cache and s_i is the savings provided by using the cache:

$$s_i = \begin{cases} 0, & \text{if } q_i \text{ does not use the cache} \\ c_i, & \text{if there is an exact match for } q_i \\ c_i - cf_i, & \text{if } q_i \text{ uses the cache and has cost } cf_i \end{cases} \quad (4)$$

DCSR captures the different levels of effectiveness of the materialized results against the workload queries and can be used to accurately compare different caching techniques.

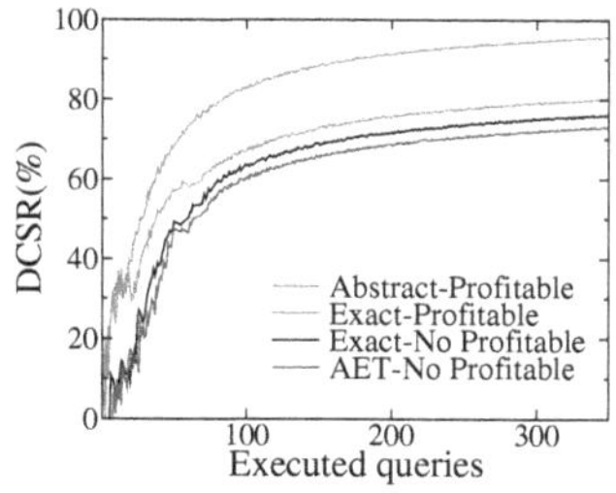

Figure 11: Effectiveness of caching techniques

The $DCSR(\%)$ measurements, for our generic workload **W4**, for four different RDF caching techniques are presented in Figure 11. To compare our system to the related RDF caching techniques we choose as baseline the AET-based caching [39] which caches normalized join execution trees and is the most efficient among the related work systems. We also compare the effectiveness of our techniques for: 1) utilizing more general results using the abstract cache requests, 2) generating *profitable* results using our benefit estimations. Figure 11, shows that our fully functional cache implementation can achieve the best cost saving ratio stabilising to 96% after 350 queries. We also note that the cache efficiency is reduced by nearly 15% when removing our abstract request functionality and another 4% when removing the discovery of *profitable* results. Lastly, our system outperforms the AET based caching by nearly 24% due to its ability to utilize all possibly usable cached results. The cost savings achieved by the AET based technique are limited to the caching of non-selective queries that do not vary much across the workload. The efficiency difference compared to our cache would increase for workloads with more variable query types and filtering values.

7.5 Dataset Size and Caching Policy effects

The left part of Figure 12 depicts the efficiency of our cache for W4, utilizing LUBM10k and LUBM20k. The major differences between the two are:

- The average response time in the beginning of the execution is larger for LUBM20k. When increasing the dataset size, the response time for non-selective queries increases respectively while the performance of selective queries remains almost stable. This is why the baseline average response time increases but remains less than double.
- The time needed for our caching framework to give millisecond-range average response times increases. While for LUBM10k our framework requires 1300 sec, 2000 sec are required for fully caching the general workload for LUBM20k. This is due to the fact that most of the *profitable* queries are non-selective, thus their execution time increases along with the dataset size.

To evaluate the effectiveness of the described caching policy heuristics described in Section 5, we execute W4 three times: 1) with unlimited cache and without using our benefit estimation to discover *profitable* queries, 2) with unlimited cache and using the proposed benefit estimation, 3) with benefit estimation and 2GB cache size. The experimental results are presented on the right part of Figure 12. For the

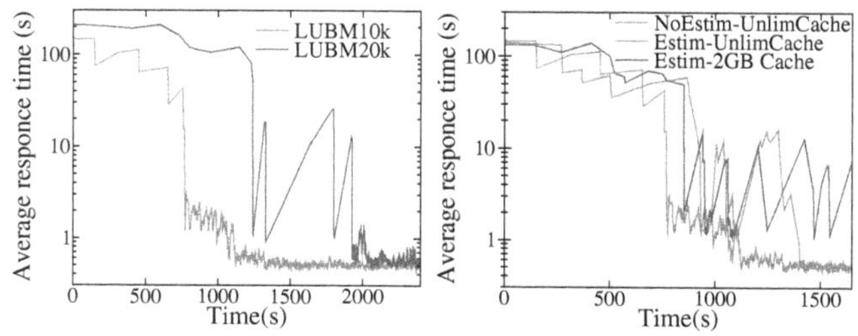

Figure 12: Cache performance for different dataset, caching policies and cache size

no estimation policy, instead of maintaining benefit estimations we just maintain a counter for each cache request, incremented by 1 each time the query graph is requested. We observe that both policies can eventually minimize the average response time of the workload but the proposed simple benefit-based approach manages to smoothly decrease the response times by caching the *profitable* queries in the most suitable order. In contrast, the policy that uses no benefit estimations cannot effectively order the caching of *profitable* results, leading to large deviations in the average response time due to the fact that costly queries happen to get cached later than selective queries.

When limiting the cache size, we note that the large output of LQ15 cannot be cached, while all the rest cached results fit inside our cache, requiring nearly 1.7GB of disk space. LQ15 requires 182 sec to be executed by H_2RDF+. While all other queries present interactive response times after 800 sec, the execution of LQ15 triggers the oscillations of the average response time.

8. CONCLUSIONS

In this paper we presented a novel SPARQL caching framework that is able to effectively cache and utilize query results. We introduced a SPARQL canonical labelling algorithm that manages to generate canonical labels for most real life SPARQL queries in less than a millisecond. Furthermore, we extended the *DPccp* dynamic programming planner by adding support for subgraph cache checks and generation of optimal query plans that consider the utilization of cached query subgraphs. We introduced a Cache Controller module that is able to discover and cache *profitable* SPARQL queries to reduce the response times for several workloads. Our caching framework was integrated on top of a state-of-the-art distributed RDF datastore, reducing its average response time by up to two orders of magnitude and offering interactive response times for complex workloads and huge RDF datasets.

9. ACKNOWLEDGMENTS

Nikolaos Papailiou has received funding from IKY fellowships of excellence for postgraduate studies in Greece - SIEMENS program. This work has received funding from the European Union, Seventh Framework Programme (FP7/ 2007-2013) under grant agreement no 619706.

10. REFERENCES

[1] Bliss. http://www.tcs.tkk.fi/Software/bliss/index.html.
[2] data.gov.uk. http://data.gov.uk/.
[3] LUBM queries. http://swat.cse.lehigh.edu/projects/lubm.
[4] Nauty and Traces. http://pallini.di.uniroma1.it/.
[5] RDFS. http://www.w3.org/TR/rdf-schema/.
[6] Resource Description Framework (RDF). http://www.w3.org/RDF/.

[7] Saucy. http://vlsicad.eecs.umich.edu/BK/SAUCY/.
[8] SPARQL. http://www.w3.org/TR/rdf-sparql-query/.
[9] Sports Refresh: Dynamic Semantic Publishing. http://www.bbc.co.uk/blogs/bbcinternet/2012/04/sports_dynamic_semantic.html.
[10] V. Arvind and J. Köbler. Graph isomorphism is low for zpp (np) and other lowness results. In *STACS 2000*. Springer, 2000.
[11] M. Atre, J. Srinivasan, and J. Hendler. BitMat: A Main-memory Bit Matrix of RDF Triples for Conjunctive Triple Pattern Queries. In *ISWC*, 2008.
[12] V. Bonstrom, A. Hinze, and H. Schweppe. Storing rdf as a graph. In *Web Congress, 2003*.
[13] P. Gassner, G. M. Lohman, K. B. Schiefer, and Y. Wang. Query optimization in the IBM DB2 family. *IEEE Data Eng. Bull.*, 16(4), 1993.
[14] Y. Guo, Z. Pan, and J. Heflin. LUBM: A Benchmark for OWL Knowledge Base Systems. *Web Semantics: Science, Services and Agents on the World Wide Web*, 3(2), 2005.
[15] S. G. Hartke and A. Radcliffe. Mckay's canonical graph labeling algorithm. *Communicating mathematics*, 479, 2009.
[16] J. Hoffart, F. M. Suchanek, K. Berberich, E. Lewis-Kelham, G. de Melo, and G. Weikum. YAGO2: Exploring and Querying World Knowledge in Time, Space, Context, and Many Languages. WWW, 2011.
[17] J. Huang, D. J. Abadi, and K. Ren. Scalable SPARQL Querying of Large RDF Graphs. *PVLDB*, 4(11), 2011.
[18] S. Idreos, I. Alagiannis, R. Johnson, and A. Ailamaki. Here are my Data Files. Here are my Queries. Where are my Results? In *CIDR*, 2011.
[19] J. Köbler, U. Schöning, and J. Torán. *The graph isomorphism problem: its structural complexity*. 1994.
[20] Y. Kotidis and N. Roussopoulos. Dynamat: a dynamic view management system for data warehouses. In *ACM SIGMOD Record*, 1999.
[21] W. Le, A. Kementsietsidis, S. Duan, and F. Li. Scalable multi-query optimization for sparql. In *ICDE*. IEEE, 2012.
[22] J. Lorey and F. Naumann. Caching and prefetching strategies for sparql queries. In *ESWC*. 2013.
[23] M. Martin, J. Unbehauen, and S. Auer. Improving the performance of semantic web applications with SPARQL query caching. In *The Semantic Web: Research and Applications*. 2010.
[24] B. D. McKay. *Practical Graph Isomorphism*. Department of Computer Science, Vanderbilt University, 1981.
[25] B. D. McKay and A. Piperno. Nauty and Traces User's Guide.
[26] H. Mistry, P. Roy, S. Sudarshan, and K. Ramamritham. Materialized view selection and maintenance using multi-query optimization. In *ACM SIGMOD Record*, 2001.
[27] G. Moerkotte and T. Neumann. Analysis of two existing and one new dynamic programming algorithm for the generation of optimal bushy join trees without cross products. In *VLDB*, 2006.
[28] G. Moerkotte and T. Neumann. Dynamic programming strikes back. In *SIGMOD*. ACM, 2008.
[29] T. Neumann and G. Weikum. The RDF-3X Engine for Scalable Management of RDF Data. *VLDBJ*, 19(1), 2010.
[30] N. Papailiou, I. Konstantinou, D. Tsoumakos, P. Karras, and N. Koziris. H2RDF+: High-performance Distributed Joins over Large-scale RDF Graphs. In *IEEE Big Data*, 2013.
[31] N. Papailiou, I. Konstantinou, D. Tsoumakos, and N. Koziris. *H_2RDF*: Adaptive Query Processing on RDF Data in the Cloud. In *WWW*, 2012.
[32] N. Papailiou, D. Tsoumakos, I. Konstantinou, P. Karras, and N. Koziris. H2RDF+: An Efficient Data Management System for Big RDF Graphs. ACM SIGMOD, 2014.
[33] P. Roy, S. Seshadri, S. Sudarshan, and S. Bhobe. Efficient and extensible algorithms for multi query optimization. *ACM SIGMOD Record*, 2000.
[34] H. Stuckenschmidt, R. Vdovjak, G.-J. Houben, and J. Broekstra. Index structures and algorithms for querying distributed rdf repositories. In *WWW*, 2004.
[35] T. Tran and G. Ladwig. Structure index for rdf data. In *SemData*, 2010.
[36] P. Tsialiamanis, L. Sidirourgos, I. Fundulaki, V. Christophides, and P. Boncz. Heuristics-based query optimisation for SPARQL. In *ICDT*. ACM, 2012.
[37] C. Weiss, P. Karras, and A. Bernstein. Hexastore: Sextuple Indexing for Semantic Web Data Management. *PVLDB*, 1(1), 2008.
[38] X. Yan, P. S. Yu, and J. Han. Graph indexing: a frequent structure-based approach. In *SIGMOD*, 2004.
[39] M. Yang and G. Wu. Caching intermediate result of sparql queries. In *WWW 2011*.
[40] K. Zeng, J. Yang, H. Wang, B. Shao, and Z. Wang. A Distributed Graph Engine for Web Scale RDF Data. *PVLDB*, 6(4), 2013.
[41] P. Zhao, J. X. Yu, and P. S. Yu. Graph indexing: tree+ delta<= graph. In *VLDB*, 2007.

APPENDIX

A. WORKLOAD QUERIES

For completeness, we include the LUBM SPARQL queries described in Section 7.3.2.

A.1 Selective query workload (W1):

LQ1: ?x rdf:type ub:GraduateStudent .
?x ub:takesCourse <GraduateCourse0>
LQ3: ?x rdf:type ub:Publication .
?x ub:publicationAuthor <AssistantProfessor0>
LQ4: ?x ub:worksFor <Department0.University0.edu> .
?x ub:name ?n . ?x ub:emailAddress ?em .
?x ub:telephone ?t . ?x rdf:type ub:Professor
LQ5: ?x rdf:type ub:GraduateStudent .
?x ub:memberOf <Department0.University0.edu>
LQ7: ?x rdf:type ub:Student . ?y rdf:type ub:Course .
?x ub:takesCourse ?y .
<AssociateProfessor0> ub:teacherOf ?y
LQ8: ?x rdf:type ub:Student . ?y rdf:type ub:Department .
?x ub:memberOf ?y . ?x ub:emailAddress ?em .
?y ub:subOrganizationOf <University0> .

A.2 Non selective query workload (W2):

LQ2: ?z rdf:type ub:Department .
?x ub:memberOf ?z . ?x rdf:type ub:GraduateStudent .
?z ub:subOrganizationOf ?y . ?y rdf:type ub:University .
?x ub:undergraduateDegreeFrom ?y .
LQ9: ?x rdf:type ub:Student . ?y rdf:type ub:Professor .
?z rdf:type ub:Course . ?x ub:advisor ?y .
?y ub:teacherOf ?z . ?x ub:takesCourse ?z .
LQ15: ?p rdf:type ?tp . ?p ub:worksFor ?d .
?s ub:takesCourse ?c . ?p ub:teacherOf ?c

B. EXTENDED EXPERIMENTS

In order to test our system with real-life RDF data and SPARQL queries that contain more edges and selective nodes, we utilize the Yago2 dataset [16]. This dataset consists of real data gathered from various resources such as Wikipedia, WordNet, GeoNames, etc., and contains more than 120 million triples. It is smaller than the various LUBM datasets we used in our experimental section but introduces more complex query and data structures. To test our system, we generate a workload consisting of SPARQL queries, also used in [29], containing up to 10 triple patterns:

YQ1: ?gn <hasGivenName> ?p. ?fn <hasFamilyName> ?p. ?p <type> "scientist?. ?p <wasBornIn> ?city. ?p <hasAcademicAdvisor> ?a. ?a <wasBornIn> ?city2. ?city <isLocatedIn> "Switzerland". ?city2 <isLocatedIn> "Germany".

YQ2: ?a <type> "actor". ?a <livesIn> ?city . ?a <actedIn> ?m1 . ?a <directed> ?m2 . ?city <isLocatedIn> ?s. ?s <isLocatedIn> "United States". ?m1 <type> "movie" . ?m1 <isLocatedIn> "Germany". ?m2 <type> "movie" . ?m2 <isLocatedIn> "Canada".

YQ3: ?p1 <hasGivenName> ?n1 . ?p1 <wasBornIn> "Berlin". ?p1 <isMarriedTo> ?p2. ?p2 <hasGivenName> ?n2 . ?p2 <wasBornIn> "London".

In order to make this workload more challenging, our workload generator utilizes random city and country names. This workload resembles the selective W1 used in Section

7.3.2. All the above queries have complex query graph structures with several triple patterns but their selectivity is small and thus the average execution time of the workload without caching is in the range of 2.5 seconds.

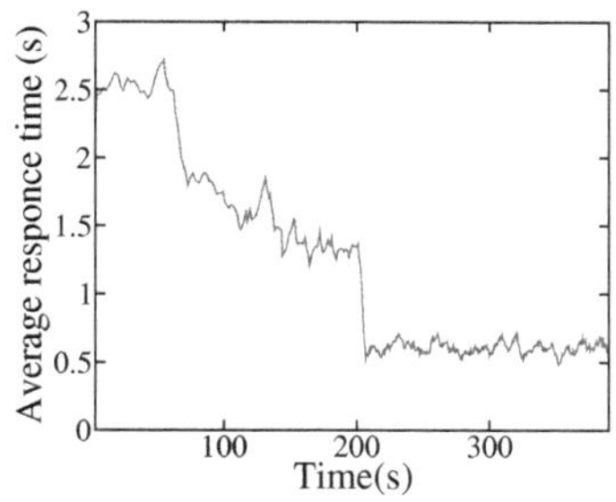

Figure 13: Yago2 query workload

As depicted in Figure 13, our caching framework can gradually reduce the average query execution time for this workload after nearly 200 seconds. This time is required to execute and index the 3 abstract queries that contain information for all possible selective IDs. In fact, query structure complexity (number of triple patterns, graph structure) mainly affects the planning time of the query, as was tested in Section 7.2, while the execution complexity of the query mainly depends on the underlying data and join algorithms. Therefore, the major conclusion of this experiment is that our system has the same effects on workloads with complex query structures. Its overhead depends on the planning overhead, which is in the range of milliseconds, while the join execution complexity occupies the major part of the query time, especially in the case of large non-selective queries. As depicted in this experiment, even for small selective queries the query structure complexity introduces negligible overheads to the average query response times.

C. ALGORITHMS

In this section, we formally describe our proposed algorithms using pseudocodes. We start with the *checkCache* method described in Algorithm 1. This algorithm is used inside the *DPccp* planner to find usable cached results for every connected subgraph (csg) of the abstract query graph. The abstraction procedure, as mentioned in Section 4.1, removes all the bound subject and object nodes and introduces the respective filters that are contained in the auxiliary query info (*aux*). This auxiliary query info also contains the filtering, projection, grouping and result ordering information of the initial query. Furthermore, the *checkCache* method also searches for the k most relevant results in the ResultCache. The major steps of this algorithm are the canonical labelling and the top-k tree search on top of the respective result tree. An important part of the *searchTree* method is the selectivity estimation of a cached result edge according to the auxiliary query info, described using function *selectivity*(*edge*, *aux*). This function computes: 1) the usability of cached results for the query in hand, 2) the selectivity of the usable cached results using the abstract query estimator (line 42) of Section 4.1.

Another important algorithm of our caching framework is the *cacheResult* Algorithm 2 that inserts the meta-data of a result in our cache structure. Again, the algorithm consists of two major steps, the canonical labelling and the tree insertion to the respective result tree. The *treeInsert* method, as mentioned in Section 4.1, is responsible for creating the respective tree node along with the parent nodes that do not already exist. It also updates the *minResults* value of each node that takes part in the insertion procedure by propagating the result size from the leaf node to the root node, applying selectivity estimations when crossing indexed edges.

Our next algorithm is the *addBenefit* Algorithm 3 that attributes the benefit for a specific query subgraph using

Algorithm 1 CHECKCACHE

```
1: function checkCache(V, E, aux, k)
2:     //V, E : vertices and edges of the abstract query subgraph
3:     //aux : auxiliary query info(filters, projections, etc)
4:     //k : search for the top-k results
5:     label ← canonicalLabel(V, E)
6:     resultTree ← ResultCache.get(label)
7:     //resultTree : the result tree for a certain canonical label
8:     return searchTree(resultTree, aux, k)
9: function searchTree(resultTree, aux, k)
10:    results ← {}
11:    //openNodes : priority queue with pairs (node, cost)
12:    openNodes ← {(resultTree.root, 1)}
13:    while openNodes ≠ {} do
14:        //get the open node with the minimum cost
15:        n ← openNodes.removeHead()
16:        if (results.size = k)and(n.cost ≥ results.maxCost) then
17:            //We have found k results and all open nodes
18:            //have greater cost than the current results
19:            return results
20:        processNode(n, openNodes, results, aux, k)
21:    return results
22: function processNode(n, openNodes, results, aux, k)
23:    for (edge, child) ∈ n.children() do
24:        if (s = selectivity(edge, aux)) > 0 then
25:            child.selectivity ← s * n.selectivity
26:            child.cost ← child.minResults * child.selectivity
27:            if child.isLeaf() then
28:                //maintain the k best results
29:                if results.size < k then
30:                    results.add(child)
31:                else if results.maxCost > child.cost then
32:                    results.removeMaxAndAdd(child)
33:            else
34:                openNodes.add({child, child.cost})
35: function selectivity(edge, aux)
36:    //compute edge selectivity for aux info
37:    selectivity ← 1
38:    for a ∈ aux.get(edge.variable) do
39:        //check edge usability
40:        if edge.subsumes(a) then
41:            if a.isFilter() then
42:                if edge.isIndexed then
43:                    //filter selectivity estimation
44:                    //using the abstract result estimator
45:                    selectivity ← selectivity * filterSelectivity(a)
46:            else if a.isJoinVariable() then
47:                if edge.isNotIndexed() then
48:                    selectivity ← selectivity * 2
49:        else
50:            selectivity ← 0
51:    return selectivity
```

its canonical label. This algorithm, introduced in Section 5.1, follows all possibly usable results in the benefit tree (at least 3 for each tree level, see lines 20-22) and attributes the respective benefit, computed using its selectivity estimation and Equation 2. It also prunes sub-trees with benefit ≤ 0 and adds the query ID to the list of the query IDs that contributed to the benefit of a cache request.

Algorithm 4 describes the complete processing of a SPARQL query. It starts with the abstraction of the query graph updating its *aux* info. It then calls the extended *DPccp* planner that issues cache requests and records their benefit using Equation 1. The optimal query plan is executed and then the CacheController thread handles the caching of produced intermediate results, the request and result benefit attribution (lines 8-10). The *cacheResults* method tries to cache all computed results consulting our caching policy. The *addRequestBenefits* updates benefits for all recorded cache requests using Algorithm 3. Lastly, the *addResultBenefit* method updates the benefit of all utilized cached results. It computes their contribution to the query execution by checking the optimal execution time computed by the *DPccp* without the use of the respective cached result.

Our caching policy, described in Section 5.2, is depicted in Algorithm 6. The *evictions* function, called if the cache constraints are violated, tries to find a set of results that cover the new result size and have cumulative benefit that is lower than the benefit of the new result. Furthermore, the *decreaseBenefits* function is presented that handles the update of benefits after the execution of a profitable result mentioned in the end of Section 5.1.

Lastly, Algorithm 5 presents our periodic processes. The *updateBenefits* method is responsible for decreasing the benefit estimations for both cached results and requests through time. To do so it uses a configurable decrease factor $0 < a < 1$. It also maintains the ordered lists of results and requests used in our other algorithms. In the case of cache requests, we remove requests that are not in the top-k most profitable ones and also compute their execution cost. The *profitableQueryGeneration* method iterates over all cache requests in decreasing order of benefit/cost and, consulting our caching policy, selects the most profitable request for execution. It proactively checks the caching policy using an estimation of the query size, in order to avoid executing requests that cannot be cached due to their size and benefit constraints.

Algorithm 2 CACHERESULT

```
function cacheResult(V, E, aux, size)
    //V, E : vertices and edges of the abstract query graph
    //aux : auxiliary query info(filters, projections, etc)
    //size : the size of the result in records
    label ← canonicalLabel(V, E)
    resultTree ← ResultCache.get(label)
    treeInsert(resultTree.root, aux, size)
function treeInsert(node, aux, size)
    if node.isLeaf() then
        node.minResults = size
    else
        aInfo ← aux.get(node.variable)
        if ((edge, child) = node.getEdge(aInfo)) = null) then
            //Edge does not exist, create new
            (edge, child) = newEdge(aInfo)
        treeInsert(child, aux, size)
        if aInfo.isIndexed() then
            //compute the maximum selectivity of the index
            maxSel ← maxSelectivity(edge)
            results = child.minResults * maxSel
        else
            results = child.minResults
        if results < node.minResults then
            if results ≤ 1 then
                results ← 1
            node.minResults = results
```

D. COMPLEXITY

In this section, we formally examine the time and space complexities of our proposed algorithms. Our first algorithm is the canonical labelling algorithm proposed in Section 3. The complexity of this algorithm is directly associated with the complexity of the *Bliss* algorithm that attempts to solve the graph isomorphism (GI) problem. GI is known to have time complexity at most $O(2^{\sqrt{n \log n}})$ for graphs with n vertices [10]. However, this is not a representative bound for *Bliss* because its complexity mainly depends on the amount of automorphisms present in the graph structure rather than on the number of its vertices. Indeed, there are graph examples that result in exponential labelling times but for general graphs *Bliss* presents sub-exponential complexity. Our extended SPARQL query labelling algorithm introduces a polynomial time, $O(n)$, transformation of the input query which is negligible compared to the worst-case exponential time complexity of *Bliss*. The major overhead of our scheme is the fact that it transforms the n vertices of the query graph to $3n$ vertices and thus introduces a polynomial increase to the input size. However, this overhead does not substantially affect the worst-case complexity of *Bliss*.

Our second algorithm is the top-k, A* search, (searchTree in Algorithm 1) performed in order to search results that share the same canonical label. The irregularity of the A* search does not allow us to set a useful upper bound for this algorithm. Of course, an upper bound for the algorithm is the maximum size of the tree stored inside each cache record but this bound does not take into account the intelligent pruning of the search space performed. In the worst case, the tree search will have complexity O(r), where r is the maximum amount of cached results that share the same graph structure and thus the same canonical label. We note here that r is also bound by the cache size constraints and we can therefore expect that it will not grow limitless.

Our checkCache Algorithm 1, generates a canonical label and then performs a tree search in the respective result tree. As mentioned before, the canonical labelling time will, in the worst case, dominate the checkCache mechanism due to its

Algorithm 3 ADDBENEFIT

```
function addBenefit(label, aux, benefit, qID)
    //label : the canonical label of the abstract query graph
    //aux : auxiliary query info(filters, projections, etc)
    //benefit : the estimated benefit for the query
    //qID : the query ID
    benefitTree ← CacheRequests.get(label)
    treeAddBenefit(benefitTree.root, aux, benefit, 1, qID)
function treeAddBenefit(node, aux, benefit, s, qID)
    //s : parent node selectivity
    if node.isLeaf() then
        b = benefit − s * R/thr //Equation 2
        if b > 0 then
            node.benefit = node.benefit + b
            node.queryIDs.add(qID)
    else
        aInfo ← aux.get(node.variable)
        newEdgeIfNotExists("*")
        newEdgeIfNotExists("*, Index")
        newEdgeIfNotExists(aInfo)
        for (edge, child) ∈ node.children() do
            //check usability, selectivity of existing edges
            selectivity ← s * selectivity(edge, aInfo)
            //prune subtrees with benefit ≤ 0
            if (benefit − selectivity * R/thr) > 0 then
                treeAddBenefit(child, aux, benefit, selectivity)
```

Algorithm 4 EXECUTEQUERY

```
function executeQuery(query)
    (q, aux) ← abstractQuery(query)
    //q: abstract query, aux: auxiliary query info
    cacheRequests ← {}
    plan ← DPccp(q, aux, cacheRequests)
    results ← execute(plan) //RDF engine
    //handled offline by the CacheController thread
    CacheController.cacheResults(results)
    CacheController.addRequestBenefits(cacheRequests, qID)
    CacheController.addResultBenefit(q, plan)
function cacheResults(results)
    //cache computed results
    for result ∈ results do
        //get the respective benefit from the cache requests
        request ← CacheRequests.get(result)
        result.benefit ← request.benefit
        result.queryIDs ← request.queryIDs
        cache(result, result.benefit)
function addRequestBenefits(cacheRequests, qID)
    for (req, benefit) ∈ cacheRequests do
        addBenefit(req.label, req.aux, benefit, qID)
function addResultBenefit(q, plan)
    //update the benefit of utilized cached results
    for result ∈ plan.usedCachedResults do
        newPlan ← DPccpWithoutResult(q, result)
        result.benefit+ = (newPlan.cost − plan.cost)
```

Algorithm 5 CACHE CONTROLLER PERIODIC PROCESS

```
// methods that run in configurable time or query intervals
function updateBenefits
    //OrderedResults : benefit ordered list of cached results
    for result ∈ ResultCache do
        //decrease benefit with time using paramater 0 < a < 1
        result.benefit = result.benefit * a
        OrderedResults.insert(result)
    //OrderedRequests : benefit ordered list with max size
    for request ∈ CacheRequests do
        //decrease benefit with time
        request.benefit = request.benefit * a
        OrderedRequests.insert(request)
    //remove cache requests that are not in OrderedRequests
    removeFromCacheRequests(OrderedRequests)
    for request ∈ OrderedRequests do
        //estimate cost for best requests using DPccp
        request.benefit = request.benefit/estimateCost()
function profitableQueryGeneration
    //iterate in decreasing order of benefit/cost
    for req ∈ OrderedRequests do
        //proactively check cache replacement
        evict ← evictions(estimateSize(req), req.benefit)
        if evict.satisfied then
            result ← executeQuery(req)
            return
```

Algorithm 6 CACHINGPOLICY

```
function cache(result, benefit)
    evict ← evictions(result.size, benefit))
    if evict.satisfied then
        removeCachedResults(evict)
        cacheResult(result.V, result.E, result.aux, result.size)
        decreaseBenefits(result.queryIDs)
        return
function evictions(size, benefit)
    //cache replacement policy
    evict ← {}
    if availableCacheSize ≥ size then
        evict.satisfied = true
        return evict
    //iterate cached results in decreasing benefit order
    for result ∈ OrderedResults do
        if result.benefit ≤ benefit then
            evict.add(result)
            if evict.totalSize ≥ size then
                break
    if evict.totalSize ≥ size then
        evict.satisfied = true
    else
        evict.satisfied = false
    return evict
function decreaseBenefits(queryIDs)
    for request ∈ CacheRequests do
        oldSize ← request.queryIDs.size
        //remove common query IDs
        request.queryIDs = request.queryIDs \ queryIDs
        newSize ← request.queryIDs.size
        request.benefit = request.benefit * newSize/oldSize
```

exponential time complexity and due to the fact that the tree search has bounded worst-case performance. However, as shown in our experimental evaluation, our checkCache mechanism is practical and presents acceptable time complexity for general graphs.

We now examine the time complexity of our dynamic programming query planner that integrates the *DPccp* algorithm with our checkCache algorithm. *DPccp* bases its enumeration procedure on finding all csg-cmp-pairs in the query graph [28]. Csg-cmp-pairs are pairs containing a connected subgraph(csg) of the query graph and one of its connected complement subgraphs(cmp).

DEFINITION 4. *(csg-cmp-pair). Let G=(V,E) be a query graph and S1, S2 two subsets of V such that* $S1 \subseteq V$ *and* $S2 \subseteq (V \setminus S1)$ *are a connected subgraph and a connected complement respectively. If there further exists an edge (u, v)∈E such that u⊆S1 and v⊆S2, we call (S1, S2) a csg-cmp-pair.*

For each unique csg, connected subgraph of the query graph, we call the checkCache algorithm in order to search for usable cached results. Therefore, if s is the amount of connected query subgraphs and m is the amount of csg-cmp-pairs, the complexity of our planner is $O(s \cdot c + m)$ where c is the complexity of the checkCache mechanism. The complexity of the original *DPccp* is $O(m)$. In the worst case m is exponentially larger than s because for each csg we need to enumerate all the respective cmp subgraphs. In fact, for the worst case of clique graphs $s = O(2^n)$ and $m = O(3^n)$ [27]. Therefore, the worst-case complexity of our extended dynamic programming planner is $O(2^n \cdot 2^{\sqrt{n \log n}} + 3^n)$ which does not largely deviate from the original complexity of the *DPccp* algorithm. However, as depicted in our experiments and in the extensive complexity evaluations of both *DPccp* [27] and *Bliss* [1], the above worst-case complexity does not arise for general graphs and the algorithms are practical for all tested query graphs.

We now discuss the complexity of our offline operations handled by the CacheController module. By offline we mean that they are not part of the critical path of executing a SPARQL query. Initially, we study the complexity of the cacheResult method presented in Algorithm 2. This operation consists of a canonical labelling step and one execution of the treeInsert method. The complexity of the treeInsert method is linear in the amount of variables in the query graph and thus is linear, $O(n)$, in the input graph size. The treeInsert method has also linear space complexity because it only inserts one node in the result tree along with its respective parent nodes that do not already exist. Therefore, the complexity of the cacheResult method is dominated by the worst-case complexity of our canonical labelling.

The *addRequestBenefits* method, presented in Algorithm 4, is responsible for attributing benefits to all possibly usable query patterns for all the cache requests issued during the planning of a query. The number of cache requests for a query graph is bound by the number of its connected subgraphs(csg) s. For every csg the addBenefit method is called (Algorithm 3). The worst-case time and space complexity of the addBenefit method is $O(d^v)$ where d is the maximum degree of the tree nodes (at least 3) and v is the number of variables in the query. In total, the worst-case complexity of the *cacheRequests* method is $O(s \cdot d^v)$. This worst-case complexity is tamed by: (i) the offline pruning of the benefit trees that maintains the top-k most profitable tree nodes for all query labels and (ii) the ability of the addBenefit method to prune entire subtrees with benefit ≤ 0.

The *profitableQueryGeneration* method, presented in Algorithm 5, iterates, in a benefit order, over the benefit estimations checking the caching policy in order to select the query that is going to be executed and cached. Our caching policy check has linear complexity, $O(res)$, in the amount of cached results res because, in the worst case, it needs to check the removal of all cached queries. Therefore, its worst-case complexity is $O(req \cdot res)$ where req is the number of maintained request benefit estimations. As stated above, this number is regulated by our offline request pruning process in order not to grow exponcentially. The res parameter is also regulated by the cache size constraints.

Our *updateBenefits* method, presented in Algorithm 5, has complexity $O(res \cdot \log res + req \cdot creq + req \cdot \log req + req \cdot dp)$. It sorts res cached results, it maintains and sorts req of the $creq$ accumulated requests. It also executes req times the *DPccp* algorithm, with complexity dp as presented above. The main memory space complexity of our caching framework is $O(res + req + creq)$ which is regulated using the configurable res and req values. The $creq$ value is regulated by the execution frequency of the *updateBenefits* method.

Left Bit Right: For SPARQL Join Queries with OPTIONAL Patterns (Left-outer-joins)

Medha Atre*
Pune, India
medha.atre@gmail.com

ABSTRACT

SPARQL basic graph pattern (BGP) (a.k.a. SQL inner-join) query optimization is a well researched area. However, optimization of OPTIONAL pattern queries (a.k.a. SQL left-outer-joins) poses additional challenges, due to the restrictions on the *reordering* of left-outer-joins. The occurrence of such queries tends to be as high as 50% of the total queries (e.g., DBPedia query logs).

In this paper, we present *Left Bit Right* (LBR), a technique for *well-designed* nested BGP and OPTIONAL pattern queries. Through LBR, we propose a novel method to represent such queries using a graph of *supernodes*, which is used to aggressively prune the RDF triples, with the help of compressed indexes. We also propose novel optimization strategies – first of a kind, to the best of our knowledge – that combine together the characteristics of *acyclicity* of queries, *minimality*, and *nullification*, *best-match* operators. In this paper, we focus on OPTIONAL patterns without UNIONs or FILTERs, but we also show how UNIONs and FILTERs can be handled with our technique using a *query rewrite*. Our evaluation on RDF graphs of up to and over one billion triples, on a commodity laptop with 8 GB memory, shows that LBR can process *well-designed* low-selectivity complex queries up to 11 times faster compared to the state-of-the-art RDF column-stores as Virtuoso and MonetDB, and for highly selective queries, LBR is at par with them.

Categories and Subject Descriptors

H.2.4 [**Systems**]: Query Processing

Keywords

Query optimization; SPARQL OPTIONAL patterns; Left-outer-joins; Semi-joins; Compressed bitvectors.

*Initial part of this work was completed when the author was at Rensselaer Polytechnic Institute and University of Pennsylvania.

SIGMOD'15, May 31–June 4, 2015, Melbourne, VIC, Australia.

http://dx.doi.org/10.1145/2723372.2746483.

1. INTRODUCTION

Resource Description Framework (RDF) [8] is a widely accepted standard for representing *semantically linked* data on the web, and SPARQL [9] is a standard query language for it. RDF data is a directed edge-labeled multi-graph, where each unique edge (S P O) is called a *triple* – P is the label on the edge from the node S to node O.

SPARQL query language, like SQL, provides various syntactic constructs to form *structured* queries for RDF graphs. Two types of queries of our interest are *Basic Graph Pattern* (BGP) and *OPTIONAL* pattern (OPT) queries. Any SPARQL BGP query can be methodically translated into an equivalent SQL inner-join query [20], and an OPT pattern query can be methodically translated into an SQL left-outer-join query [19]. Like SQL, the SPARQL grammar allows nested OPT queries, i.e., a query composed of an intermix of BGPs and OPT patterns. Since SPARQL BGP queries are same as SQL inner-joins (denoted by symbol $\bowtie$) and OPT queries are same as SQL left-outer-joins (denoted by $⟕$), we will use these terms, acronyms, and symbols interchangeably in the rest of the text. BGP and OPT queries tend to be performance intensive, especially for very large RDF data. An extensive amount of research has gone in the optimization of SQL inner-join queries. The database and semantic web communities have taken these optimizations further along with the novel ideas of indexing and BGP query processing over RDF data [15, 28, 29, 33, 42, 44, 45].

Why OPT queries? RDF is a semi-structured data, and adherence of RDF "instance data" to its Ontology specification (a.k.a. schema), and in turn its completeness, is not always enforced especially for the data published on the web (e.g., DBPedia [2]), and that which is compiled from many diverse sources of RDF graphs (e.g., Linked Open Data[1]). This makes OPT queries a crucial tool for the end users. For example, consider an RDF network describing movie and TV sitcom/soap actors. Not all the actors may have their contact info, such as email and telephone numbers listed. Then an OPT query (**Q1**) as given below fetches **all** the *actors* with their respective *name* and *address*. Along with that, it gets *email* and *tele* numbers of those who have them listed, and for the rest it marks *email* and *tele* values by *NULL*s.

```
SELECT ?actor ?name ?addr ?email ?tele WHERE {
    ?actor :name ?name .
    ?actor :address ?addr .
    OPTIONAL {
      ?actor :email ?email .
      ?actor :telephone ?tele .}}
```

[1] http://linkeddata.org/

Query logs of SPARQL endpoints on the web indeed concur with this intuition, e.g., DBPedia query logs show as high as 50% occurrence of OPT queries [27, 35], with as many as eight OPT patterns in a query. These statistics make OPT queries a non-negligible component of SPARQL "join" query optimization. Now consider a modified version (**Q2**) of the previous query:

```
SELECT ?friend ?sitcom WHERE {
  :Jerry :hasFriend ?friend .
  OPTIONAL {
    ?friend :actedIn ?sitcom .
    ?sitcom :location :NewYorkCity .}}
```

This query asks for all friends of *:Jerry* that have acted in a sitcom located in the *:NewYorkCity*. In this query, let (*:Jerry :hasFriend ?friend*) be tp_1, (*?friend :actedIn ?sitcom*) tp_2, and (*?sitcom :location :NewYorkCity*) tp_3. Then the query can be expressed as $(Query = tp_1 ⟕ (tp_2 \bowtie tp_3))$, where tp_1 forms a BGP (say P_1) with only one triple pattern, and $(tp_3 \bowtie tp_4)$ forms another BGP (say P_2).

BGP queries ($\bowtie$) are *associative* and *commutative*, i.e., a change in the order of triple patterns and joins between them does not change the final results. But for a nested OPT query, ⟕ operator is not associative and commutative, e.g., in the case of **Q2** above, left-outer-join between tp_1 and tp_2 cannot be performed before the inner-join $P_2 = (tp_2 \bowtie tp_3)$. This limits the number of query plans an optimizer can consider.

Let us assume that this actor network has thousands of actors, and many of them have acted in sitcoms located in the *:NewYorkCity*. But *:Jerry* has just two friends, *:Larry* and *:Julia*, and among them only *:Julia* has acted in *:Seinfeld*, which has *:NewYorkCity* as the location. So the final results of this query are just two with the respective values of *?friend* and *?sitcom* set as {(*:Larry, NULL*), (*:Julia, :Seinfeld*)}. However, the inner-join $P_2 = tp_2 \bowtie tp_3$ has to be evaluated before the left-outer-join $P_1 ⟕ P_2$, due to the restrictions on the reorderability of left-outer-joins. Since there are several actors who have acted in the sitcoms located in *:NewYorkCity*, these two triple patterns have a *low selectivity*[2], which increases the evaluation time and cost of their inner-join. To overcome such a limitation, for conventional databases, Rao et al [38, 39], and Galindo-Legaria, Rosenthal [26] have proposed ways of reordering nested inner and left-outer joins using additional operators as *nullification* and *best-match* [39] (*Generalized Outerjoin* in [26]).

On this background, we propose *Left Bit Right* (LBR), and make the following main contributions.

- We propose a novel way to represent a nested BGP-OPT query with a graph of *supernodes* (Section 2).
- We extend the previously known properties of *acyclicity* of queries, *minimality* of triples, and *nullification, best-match* operations, to propose novel optimization strategies – first of a kind, to the best of our knowledge – for acyclic and cyclic *well-designed* OPT queries (Sections 3.2, 3.3, 5). We mainly focus on the "join" component of SPARQL, i.e., OPT patterns without UNIONs, FILTERs, or Cartesian products. Nevertheless, in Section 5.2 we show how these constructs can be handled using our technique.
- Finally, we show LBR's performance using a commodity laptop of 8 GB memory over three popular RDF datasets, UniProt [10], LUBM [4], and DBPedia [2], with up to and over a billion triples, in comparison with the state-of-the-art RDF column-stores like Virtuoso v7.1.0 and MonetDB v11.17.21. Through our evaluation on queries with varying degrees of selectivity, complexity, and running times, we show that for complex, low selectivity "*well-designed*" queries, LBR is up to 11 times faster than Virtuoso and MonetDB, and for highly selective queries, it is at par with them (Section 6).

[2]Selectivity of a triple pattern is high if it has fewer number of triples associated with it and vice versa.

2. QUERY GRAPH OF SUPERNODES

An OPT query with an intermix of Basic Graph Patterns (BGPs $\bowtie$) and OPT patterns (⟕) establishes restrictions on the order of join processing, e.g., **Q1**, **Q2** in Section 1. In this section we introduce a novel idea of constructing a *graph of supernodes* (GoSN) to capture the nesting of OPT patterns in a query. GoSN makes an important part of our query processing techniques discussed in Sections 3 and 5.

2.1 GoSN Construction

Supernodes: In a SPARQL OPT pattern of the form $(P_1 ⟕ P_2)$, P_1 may in turn have nested BGPs and OPT patterns inside it, e.g., $P_1 = (P_3 ⟕ P_4)$. P_2 may have nested BGPs and OPT patterns inside it too, or either of P_1 and P_2 can be OPT-free. Generalizing it, if a pattern P_i does not have any OPT pattern nested inside it, we call P_i to be an *OPT-free Basic Graph Pattern*. From a given nested OPT query, first we extract all such OPT-free BGPs, and construct a *supernode* (SN_i) for each P_i. The triple patterns (TPs) in P_i are *encapsulated* in SN_i.

Next, we serialize a nested OPT query using its OPT-free BGPs, $\bowtie$ (inner-join), ⟕ (left-outer-join) operators, and proper parentheses. E.g., we serialize **Q2** in Section 1 as $(P_1 ⟕ P_2)$, where P_1 and P_2 are OPT-free BGPs, SN_1 of P_1 encapsulates just tp_1, and SN_2 of P_2 encapsulates tp_2 and tp_3 (see Figure 2.1a).

Unidirectional edges: From the serialized query, we consider each OPT pattern of type $P_m ⟕ P_n$. P_m or P_n may have nested OPT-free BGPs inside them. Using the serialized-parenthesized form of the query, we identify the *leftmost* OPT-free BGPs nested inside P_m and P_n each. E.g., if $P_m = ((P_a ⟕ P_b) \bowtie (P_c ⟕ P_d))$, and $P_n = (P_e ⟕ P_f)$, P_a and P_e are the *leftmost* OPT-free BGPs in P_m and P_n respectively, and SN_a and SN_e are their respective supernodes. We add a directed edge $SN_a \rightarrow SN_e$. If either P_m or P_n does not nest any OPT-free BGPs inside it, we treat the very pattern as the *leftmost* for adding a directed edge. With this procedure, we can treat OPT patterns in a query in any order. But for all practical purposes, we start from the *innermost* OPT patterns, and recursively go on considering the outer OPT patterns using the parentheses in the serialized query. E.g., if a serialized query is $((P_a ⟕ P_b) \bowtie (P_c ⟕ P_d)) ⟕ (P_e ⟕ P_f)$, with $P_a ... P_f$ as OPT-free BGPs, we add directed edges as follows: (1) $SN_a \rightarrow SN_b$, (2) $SN_c \rightarrow SN_d$, (3) $SN_e \rightarrow SN_f$, (4) $SN_a \rightarrow SN_e$.

Bidirectional edges: Next we consider each inner-join of type $P_x \bowtie P_y$ in a serialized query. If P_x or P_y has nested OPT-free BGPs inside, we add a bidirectional edge between the supernodes of *leftmost* OPT-free BGPs. E.g., if $P_x = (P_a ⟕ P_b)$, and $P_y = (P_c ⟕ P_d)$, we add a bidirectional edge $SN_a \leftrightarrow SN_c$. If P_x or P_y does not nest any OPT-free BGPs inside it, we consider the very pattern to be the *leftmost* for adding a bidirectional edge. We add bidirectional edges starting from the *innermost* inner-joins ($\bowtie$)

using the parentheses in the serialized query, and recursively go on considering the outer ones, until no more bidirectional edges can be added. Considering the same example given under unidirectional edges, we add a bidirectional edge between $SN_a \leftrightarrow SN_c$. The *graph of supernodes* (GoSN) for this example is shown in Figure 2.1b.

Thus we completely capture the nesting of BGPs and OPT patterns in a query using this GoSN, and establish an order among the supernodes, which is described in Section 2.2.

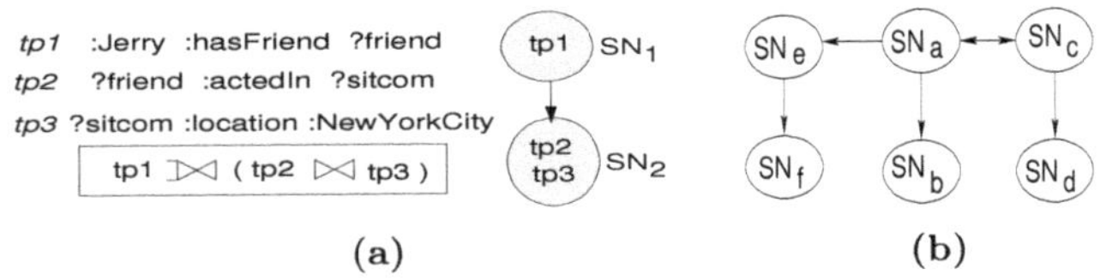

Figure 2.1: GoSN for – (a) Q2 in Section 1, (b) $((\mathbf{P_a} ⟕ \mathbf{P_b}) \bowtie (\mathbf{P_c} ⟕ \mathbf{P_d})) ⟕ (\mathbf{P_e} ⟕ \mathbf{P_f})$

2.2 Nomenclature

In this section, we highlight the nomenclature that we use in the context of GoSN, OPT patterns, and RDF graphs.

Master-Slave: In an OPT pattern $P_c ⟕ P_d$, we call pattern P_c to be a *master* of P_d, and P_d a *slave* of P_c. This master-slave relationship is *transitive*, i.e., if a supernode SN_f is reachable from another supernode SN_c by following *at least* one unidirectional edge in GoSN, then SN_c is called a master of SN_f (see Figure 2.1b).

Peers: We call two supernodes to be peers if they are connected to each other through a bidirectional edge, or they can be reached from each other by following *only* bidirectional edges in GoSN, e.g., SN_a and SN_c in Figure 2.1b.

Absolute masters: Supernodes that are *not* reachable from any other supernode through a path involving *at least one* unidirectional edge are called the *absolute masters*, e.g., SN_a and SN_c in Figure 2.1b are absolute masters.

These master-slave, peer, and absolute master nomenclatures and relationships apply to any triple patterns enclosed within the respective supernodes too.

Well-designed patterns: As per the definition given by Pérez et al [34], a *well-designed* OPT query is – for every subpattern of type $P' = P_k ⟕ P_l$ in the query, if a join variable "?j" in P_l appears outside P', then "?j" also appears in P_k. A query that violates this condition is said to be *non-well-designed*. In this paper, we have focused on well-designed queries, because they occur most commonly for RDF graphs, and remain unaffected by the difference between SPARQL and SQL algebra over treatment of NULLs. Nevertheless, we discuss *non-well-designed* queries in Appendices B and C for the completeness of the text.

NULLs and blank nodes: Unlike relational tables, RDF graphs do not have NULLs. Note that NULLs represent *non-existence* of entities, whereas "blank nodes" in an RDF graph have "blank node identifiers" to represent entities without distinct URIs[3], and in SPARQL queries, they are treated similar to the entities that have URIs. An OPT query may generate NULLs, and joins over NULLs happen only in *non-well-designed* patterns. SPARQL and SQL algebra handles joins over NULLs differently, and Appendix C elaborates on this issue. Well-designed patterns, however, remain unaffected by this – which are the focus of this paper.

[3] www.w3.org/TR/REC-rdf-syntax/#section-Syntax-blank-nodes

3. OPTIMIZATION STRATEGIES

In Figure 3.1 we point out that LBR can process all the nested BGP-OPT queries, but not all of them can avoid *nullification* and *best-match*, and we mainly focus on the *well-designed* queries in this paper. Our technique can be applied to *non-well-designed* queries too, but we have not focused on them due to lack of evidence of such queries in practice, disparity between pure SPARQL and SPARQL-over-SQL engines for joins over NULLs (refer to Appendices B and C), and space limitations.

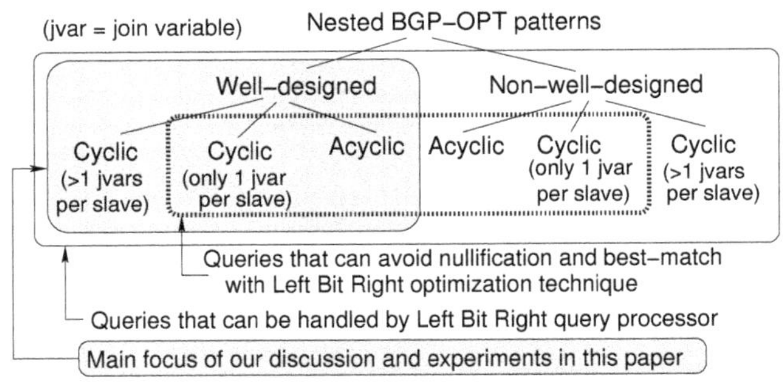

Figure 3.1: Classification of OPT queries

In Section 3.1, briefly ignoring GoSN, we describe the conceptual foundation of our technique by combining the properties of *nullification*, *best-match*, *acyclicity* of queries, and *minimality* of triples. Then in Section 3.2 we present our optimization strategies to "prune" the triples for *acyclic* well-designed patterns using GoSN, and in Section 3.3 we discuss pruning for *cyclic* well-designed patterns. For the discussion in Sections 3.1, 3.2, 3.3 we do not take into consideration the underlying indexes on RDF graphs, because the optimization strategies are agnostic to them. Then in Section 4 we describe our indexes, and in Section 5 we show how to prune the triples using our indexes, and generate the final query results using *multi-way-pipelined* join for both, acyclic as well as cyclic well-designed queries.

3.1 Preliminaries

Typically, for a pairwise join processing plan, if nested inner and left-outer joins are reordered, *nullification* and *best-match* (a.k.a. *minimum-union*) operations are required. We explain them here with a brief example for the completeness of the text, and refer the reader to [24, 39] for the details.

Nullification, Best-match: Consider the same query given in Figure 2.1a, along with the sample data associated with it in Figure 3.2. *:NewYorkCity* has been the location for a lot of American sitcoms, and a lot of actors have acted in them (they are not shown in the sample data for conciseness). But, among all such actors, *:Jerry* has only two friends, *:Julia* and *:Larry*. Hence, tp_1 is more *selective* than tp_2 and tp_3. A left-outer-join reordering algorithm as proposed in [26, 39] will typically reorder these joins as $(tp_1 ⟕ tp_2) ⟕ tp_3$. Due to this reordering, all four sitcoms that *:Julia* has acted in show up as bindings of *?sitcom* (see Res1 in Fig. 3.2), although only *:Seinfeld* was located in the *:NewYorkCity*. To fix this, *nullification* operator is used, which ensures that variable bindings across the reordered joins are consistent with the original join order in the query (see Res2 in Figure 3.2).

We can see that the *nullification* operation caused results that are *subsumed* within other results. A result r_1

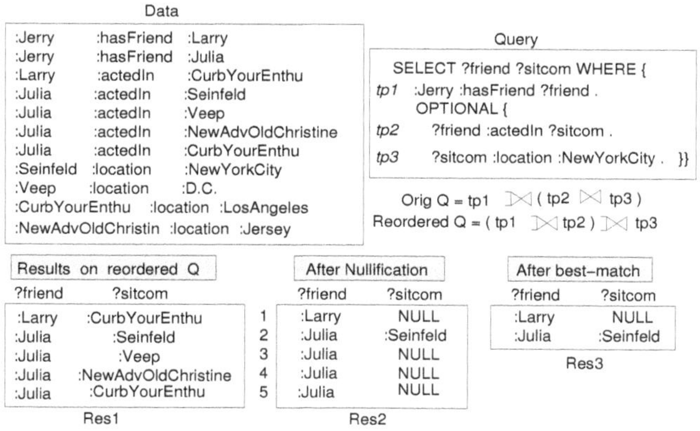

Figure 3.2: Nullification and best-match example

is said to be subsumed within another result r_2 ($r_1 \sqsubset r_2$), if for every non-null variable binding in r_1, r_2 has the same binding, and r_2 has more non-null variable bindings than r_1. Thus results 3–5 in Res2 are subsumed within result 2. The *best-match* operator removes all the subsumed results (see Res3). Final results of the query are given as *best-match(nullification((*tp_1 ⟕ tp_2*)* ⟕ tp_3*))*.

Semi-join ($\ltimes$) is a well-known concept in databases, with which triples associated with a triple pattern (TP) can be removed due to restrictions on the variable bindings coming from another TP, without actually performing a join between the two. $tp_2 \ltimes_{?j} tp_1 = \{t \mid t \in tp_2, t.?j \in (\pi_{?j}(tp_1) \cap \pi_{?j}(tp_2))\}$. Here t is a triple matching tp_2, and $t.?j$ is a variable binding (value) of variable $?j$ in t. After this semi-join, tp_2 is left with only triples whose $?j$ bindings are also in tp_1, and all other triples are removed. Now let triple patterns, $tp_1, tp_2, ...tp_n$ all share join variable *?j*. Then we define a **clustered-semi-join** over them as follows.

Definition 3.1. *A clustered-semi-join(?j,* $\{tp_1, tp_2, ..., tp_n\}$*) is performed as follows: Let* $\mathcal{J} = \{\pi_{?j}(tp_1) \cap ... \cap \pi_{?j}(tp_n)\}$. *For each triple pattern* $tp_i, 1 \le i \le n$, $tp_i = \{t \mid t \in tp_i, t.?j \in \mathcal{J}\}$.

This definition shows that a clustered-semi-join is nothing but many semi-joins performed together for TPs that share a join variable.

Example-1: Now let us evaluate the query in Figure 3.2 using semi-joins and clustered-semi-joins. We do a semi-join $tp_2 \ltimes_{?friend} tp_1$, because tp_1 does a left-outer-join with tp_2 over *?friend*. That keeps only *:Larry* and *:Julia* bindings of *?friend* in tp_2, and removes any other bindings, and in turn triples generating those bindings from tp_2 (they are not shown in the figure for conciseness). Followed by it, we do a *clustered-semi-join(?sitcom,* $\{tp_2, tp_3\}$*)*. That removes *:CurbYourEnthu*, *:Veep*, and *:NewAdvOldChristine* bindings of *?sitcom*, and the respective triples from tp_2. Notice that this clustered-semi-join also removes the *:Larry* binding of *?friend* from tp_2 as a *ripple effect* of the removal of *:CurbYourEnthu* binding of *?sitcom*. In the end, tp_1 and tp_3 has the same set of triples, but tp_2 now has only one triple *(:Julia :actedIn :Seinfeld)*. Now if we evaluate the original join (tp_1 ⟕ ($tp_2 \bowtie tp_3$)) or a reordered one (tp_1 ⟕ tp_2) ⟕ tp_3 on these *reduced* set of triples, *we do not need nullification to ensure consistent bindings of ?sitcom, and there are no subsumed results*, because each TP has a *minimal* set of triples. **Minimality** of triples is defined as follows.

Let $\mathcal{R}$ be the final results of a query Q, and tp be a TP in Q. Let $tp.s$, $tp.p$, $tp.o$ be the respective subject, predicate, and object positions in tp. Let Q be such that it SELECTs *all* the variables as well as fixed positions in *all* the TPs in Q. E.g., for the query in Figure 3.2, *"SELECT :Jerry :hasFriend ?friend :actedIn ?sitcom :location :NewYorkCity WHERE..."* selects *everything* in the query, and the final results will be {*(:Jerry, :hasFriend, :Larry, :actedIn, NULL, :location, :NewYorkCity), (:Jerry, :hasFriend, :Julia, :actedIn, :Seinfeld, :location, :NewYorkCity)*}. Note that this assumption of SELECTion is just for the ease of definition of minimality, and not a required condition. Let Δ_{tp} be the triples associated with a tp after a semi-join or clustered-semi-join. Then minimality of Δ_{tp} is defined as follows.

Definition 3.2. *Let* $\mathcal{R}_{tp} = (non\text{-}NULL)\pi_{tp.s,tp.p,tp.o}(\mathcal{R})$, *i.e.,* $\mathcal{R}_{tp}$ *is a projection of the respective distinct bindings of* $tp.s, tp.p, tp.o$ *from* $\mathcal{R}$ *without any NULLs. Then* Δ_{tp} *is said to be minimal, if* $\Delta_{tp} = \mathcal{R}_{tp}$ *(*Δ_{tp} *and* R_{tp} *can be empty as well). In short, in a BGP-OPT query, the set of triples associated with a triple pattern is minimal, if every triple creates one or more variable bindings in the final results. There does not exist any triple which may get eliminated as a result of an inner or left-outer-join.*

Next we see why minimality of triples is important in the context of an OPT pattern query.

Lemma 3.1. *If every triple pattern in an OPT pattern has a minimal set of triples associated with it, nullification and best-match operations are not required if an original query* tp_1 ⟕ ($tp_2 \bowtie tp_3$) *is reordered as* (tp_1 ⟕ tp_2) ⟕ tp_3. □

The proof of Lemma 3.1 is given in Appendix A.1.

Example-1 and Lemma 3.1 together interest us to find if the set of triples associated with each TP in an OPT pattern can be reduced to minimal through semi-joins and clustered-semi-joins alone, because then nullification and best-match can be avoided even if the joins are reordered.

Acyclicity: Bernstein et al [16, 17] and Ullman [43] have proved previously that if a "graph of tables" (GoT) of an inner-join query is a "tree" (i.e., it is acyclic), a bottom-up followed by a top-down pass with semi-joins at each table in this tree, reduces the set of tuples in each table to a minimal. In the context of a SPARQL query, GoT is a graph of TPs, where each TP is treated as a unique table, and two TPs are connected with an undirected edge if they share a join variable. Any redundant cycles in GoT are removed as suggested in [16, 17][4]. We use and extend the acyclicity property of GoT for our optimization strategies. For this, we construct a "graph of join-variables" (GoJ) as follows. Each unique join variable (jvar) in a query is a node (jvar-node). There is an undirected edge between two jvar-nodes, if they appear together in a TP. Figure 3.3 shows GoT and GoJ for the query given in Figure 3.2. For clarity and simplicity, we treat both GoT and GoJ separate from GoSN.

Lemma 3.2. *For a join query, if the GoT is acyclic, then the GoJ is acyclic too.* □

Acyclicity of GoJ follows from its construction. We have given the proof of Lemma 3.2 in Appendix A.2. From Lemma 3.2, we also observe the following property.

[4]Redundant cycles may occur if multiple TPs join over same variable.

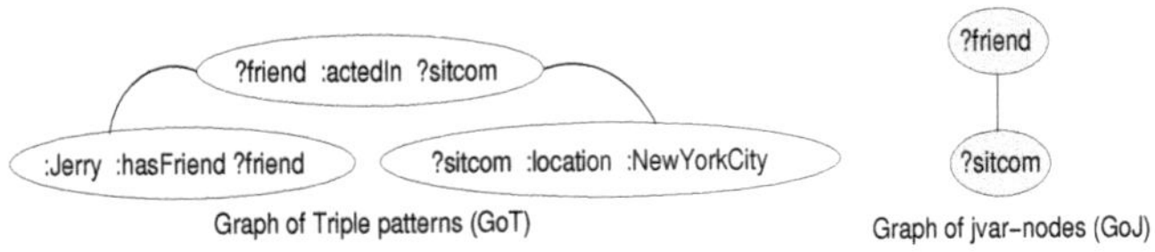

Figure 3.3: GoT and GoJ

PROPERTY 3.1. *For a BGP query without OPT patterns (inner-joins only), if the GoJ is acyclic (is a tree), a bottom-up followed by a top-down pass on the GoJ with "clustered-semi-joins" performed at each jvar-node, reduces the set of triples associated with each TP in the query to a minimal.*

Note: We use the query and GoSN in Figure 2.1a, its respective data in Figure 3.2, and GoJ in Figure 3.3 together as a running example in the rest of the text in this paper without mentioning it explicitly every time.

3.2 Acyclic well-designed OPT patterns

In Section 3.1, through Example-1 and Lemma 3.1, we showed that if each TP in an OPT query has minimal triples, nullification and best-match are not required. We showed how minimality of triples can be achieved for an acyclic OPT-free BGP through Lemma 3.2 and Property 3.1. *But can we combine all these observations to use the acyclicity of GoJ of a nested OPT query using its graph of supernodes (GoSN)?* We explore it next.

Let the GoJ of a nested OPT pattern without Cartesian products be acyclic, i.e., the GoJ is *connected* and is a *tree*. Cyclic GoJ and Cartesian products are discussed separately in Sections 3.3 and 5.2 respectively. We choose the *least selective* jvar node that appears in an *absolute master* supernode, and fix it as the root of the GoJ tree. Jvar-nodes can be ranked for selectivity as follows: A jvar-node $?j_1$ is considered more selective than $?j_2$, if the most selective TP having $?j_1$ has fewer triples than the most selective TP having $?j_2$, and so on.

With the root fixed as given before, this GoJ tree has all the jvars in absolute masters towards the *top* of the tree (root and internal nodes), and jvars in the slaves towards the *bottom*. This observation follows from the facts that there are no Cartesian products, GoJ is a tree, and we chose the *root* from an absolute master. We can traverse this tree bottom-up with semi-joins and clustered-semi-joins performed at each jvar-node $?j$ as follows:

- We perform a clustered-semi-join among the TPs that contain $?j$, and which appear either in the same supernode, or their supernodes are *peers* of each other.
- We perform a semi-join between pairs of TPs that are in a *master-slave* relationship.

We can do a top-down pass following the same rules. E.g., we choose *?friend* as the root of GoJ tree in our example, because it appears in absolute master SN_1. In the bottom-up pass, we perform a clustered-semi-join over *?sitcom* among the peers tp_2 and tp_3, no semi-join for *?sitcom*, because there are no *master-slave* TPs with *?sitcom*. We perform a semi-join $tp_2 \ltimes_{?friend} tp_1$, no clustered-semi-join for *?friend* because there are no peer TPs with *?friend*. Next, in the top-down pass, we process *?friend* first followed by *?sitcom*. This process leaves each TP with a *minimal* set of triples.

But does this give us an optimal order of processing jvars? No, because a bottom-up pass on the GoJ tree is same as processing OPT patterns per the order imposed in the original query – recall that all the jvars in slaves appear towards the *bottom* of the tree, and all the jvars in masters towards the *top* of the tree. So this hardly fetches us any benefits of the selectivity of the master TPs. *We want to find an optimal order of processing jvars, which exploits the selectivity of the masters to aggressively prune the triples.*

For that we use **get_jvar_order** (Alg. 3.1). From the GoJ tree of an OPT pattern, we consider an *induced subtree* consisting only of jvars that appear in the absolute master supernodes (ln 4). Since there are no Cartesian products, this induced subtree is connected. We choose a jvar with the *least selectivity* as the root of this induced subtree, do a bottom-up pass on it, and store the order in $order_{bu}$ (ln 5–7). Choosing a jvar with least selectivity as the *root* ensures that it is processed *last*.

Algorithm 3.1: get_jvar_order

```
input : GoSN, GoJ
output: order_bu, order_td
1  if GoJ is cyclic then
2  |   order_greedy = greedy-jvar-order(GoSN, GoJ);
3  |   return order_greedy, order_greedy
4  J_m = jvars in absolute master supernodes;
5  root = ?j ∈ J_m with least selectivity;
6  T_m = get-tree(J_m, root);
7  order_bu = bottom-up(T_m);
8  SN_ss = order remaining slaves with masters first;
9  for each slave supernode SN_i in SN_ss do
10 |   J_s = jvars in SN_i;
11 |   root = ?j ∈ masters(SN_i);
12 |   T_s = get-tree(J_s, root);
13 |   order_bu = order_bu.append(bottom-up(T_s));
14 order_td = top-down(T_m);
15 for each slave supernode SN_i in SN_ss do
16 |   J_s = jvars in SN_i;
17 |   root = ?j ∈ masters(SN_i);
18 |   T_s = get-tree(J_s, root);
19 |   order_td = order_td.append(top-down(T_s));
20 return order_bu, order_td;
```

Algorithm 3.2: prune_triples

```
input: order_bu, order_td, GoSN
1  for each ?j in order_bu do
2  |   for each tp_i do
3  |   |   for each tp_j do
4  |   |   |   if slave-of(tp_j, tp_i) then
5  |   |   |   |   semi-join (?j, tp_j, tp_i);      // tp_j ⋉_?j tp_i
6  |   for each SN_i with ?j do
7  |   |   S_tp = {tp | ?j ∈ tp, tp ∈ (SN_i ∪ peers-of(SN_i))};
8  |   |   clustered-semi-join(?j, S_tp);
9  for each ?j in order_td do
10 |   for each tp_i do
11 |   |   for each tp_j do
12 |   |   |   if slave-of(tp_j, tp_i) then
13 |   |   |   |   semi-join (?j, tp_j, tp_i);      // tp_j ⋉_?j tp_i
14 |   for each SN_i with ?j do
15 |   |   S_tp = {tp | ?j ∈ tp, tp ∈ (SN_i ∪ peers-of(SN_i))};
16 |   |   clustered-semi-join(?j, S_tp);
```

We order the remaining supernodes as – masters before their respective slaves, and among any two peer supernodes, a supernode with a more selective triple pattern is ordered first. This order is SN_{ss} (ln 8). Note that such an ordering of supernodes favours *selective masters* to be processed before their non-selective peers and slaves, thus benefiting the pruning process. For each supernode SN_i in SN_{ss}, we consider an induced subtree of GoJ consisting only of jvars in SN_i, and choose a *root* jvar such that it also appears in a master of SN_i (ln 11). Note that since GoJ is a *connected tree*, a slave supernode shares *at least* one jvar with a master. We make a bottom-up pass on this induced subtree of SN_i, and append it to $order_{bu}$ (ln 9–13). For a top-down pass, we reverse the above procedure. Starting with the induced subtree of absolute masters, we do a top-down pass, and store it in $order_{td}$ (ln 14). Using the same order of supernodes, SN_{ss}, for an induced subtree of each SN_i in SN_{ss}, we do a top-down pass, and append it to $order_{td}$ (ln 15–19).

With $order_{bu}$ and $order_{td}$ of jvar-nodes, we prune the triples associated with TPs in a query using **prune_triples** (Alg. 3.2). For each jvar *?j* in $order_{bu}$, first we do a **semi-join** between TPs that are in a master-slave relationship (ln 2–5). Then we do a **clustered-semi-join** among TPs having *?j*, and which appear in the same supernode, or are peers of each other (ln 6–8). Recall that the master-slave or peer relationship among TPs is determined by GoSN. We repeat the same process, but now by following $order_{td}$ of jvars (ln 9–16). Notice that in this process, **semi-joins** transfer the restrictions on variable bindings from master TPs to the slaves *without* actually performing left-outer-joins, and **clustered-semi-joins** transfer restrictions on variable bindings among all the peers without actually doing inner-joins. Through $order_{bu}$, $order_{td}$ of pruning we ensure that jvars in masters always get pruned before those in slaves.

Example-2: Recalling our running example, which has an acyclic GoJ, we get $order_{bu}$ = [(*?friend*), (*?sitcom*, *?friend*)], and $order_{td}$ = [(*?friend*), (*?friend*, *?sitcom*)] from **get_jvar_order**, and with these we use **prune_triples** to do **semi-joins** and **clustered-semi-joins** among the TPs in the master-slave and peer relationships respectively.

LEMMA 3.3. *For a well-designed OPT query with an acyclic GoJ, Algorithm 3.1 followed by Algorithm 3.2 leaves a minimal set of triples for each triple pattern.* □

The proof of Lemma 3.3 is given in Appendix A.3.

3.3 Cyclic well-designed OPT patterns

For OPT-free BGPs, i.e., pure inner-joins, with cyclic GoJ, minimality of triples cannot be guaranteed using clustered-semi-joins [16, 17, 43]. This result carries over immediately to cyclic OPT patterns too. For a cyclic OPT pattern, minimality of triples cannot be guaranteed, so we simply return $order_{greedy}$ from **get_jvar_order** (ln 3), which is a *greedy* order of jvars, i.e., all the jvars are ranked in the descending order of their selectivity. Recall from Section 3.2, that the relative selectivity between two jvars can be determined from the selectivity of the TPs which have those jvars. In **prune_triples**, we use $order_{greedy}$ in place of $order_{bu}$ and $order_{td}$, and follow the rest of the procedure as is. Since minimality of triples in each TP is not guaranteed, we need to use the *nullification* and *best-match* operations in a re-ordered query to ensure consistent variable bindings, and to remove any subsumed results.

This observation in general holds for all cyclic OPT queries, but we identify a *subclass* of cyclic OPT queries that can *avoid* nullification and best-match by just using $order_{greedy}$ in place of $order_{bu}$ and $order_{td}$ in **prune_triples** – *in such cyclic OPT queries, each slave supernode has only one jvar in it* (slaves can have one or more non-join variables).

LEMMA 3.4. *For a well-designed OPT query with a cyclic GoJ, if each slave supernode has only one jvar in it, nullification and best-match can be avoided by using Algorithm 3.1 followed by Algorithm 3.2.* □

We have given the proof in Appendix A.4.

From Alg. 3.1 and 3.2, it may seem that **prune_triples** is a "heavy-weight" procedure, than simply doing pairwise joins between the TPs. But as shown by our evaluation in Section 6, our pruning procedure is in fact quite "light-weight", especially for low-selectivity complex OPT patterns (please note the T_{prune} values compared to T_{total} in the query times, and "#initial triples" and "#triples aft pruning" columns in Tables 6.2, 6.3, 6.4). We achieve this through the usage of compressed bitvector indexes on RDF graphs, and procedures that directly work on these compressed indexes without decompressing them. These are described in Section 4. Together they give a competitive query performance.

4. INDEXING THE RDF GRAPH

In the recent few years, there have been a lot of advances in the efficient storage and indexing of RDF graphs, with many research systems, e.g., RDF-3X [33], TripleBit [45], BitMat [15], as well as large scale open-source and commercial engines, e.g., Virtuoso [12], MonetDB [7, 42]. Among these options, we have chosen BitMats as the base index structure for implementing our technique. Our reasons of choice are given after we give a brief overview of BitMat, our enhancements in it, and the **fold, unfold** operations for the completeness of the text.

If V_s, V_p, and V_o are the sets of unique subject, predicate, and object values in an RDF dataset, then a 3D bitcube of RDF data has $V_s \times V_p \times V_o$ dimensions. Each cell in this bitcube represents a unique RDF triple formed by the coordinate values (S P O). If this (S P O) triple is present in the given RDF dataset, that bit is set to 1 in the bitcube. To facilitate joins on S-O dimensions, same S and O values are mapped to the same coordinates of the respective dimensions[5]. Due to space constraints, the exact details of this procedure are given in Appendix D for reader's convenience. They are borrowed from the details given in Section 3 of [15]. The 3D bitcube of the data given in Figure 3.2 is shown in Figure 4.1.

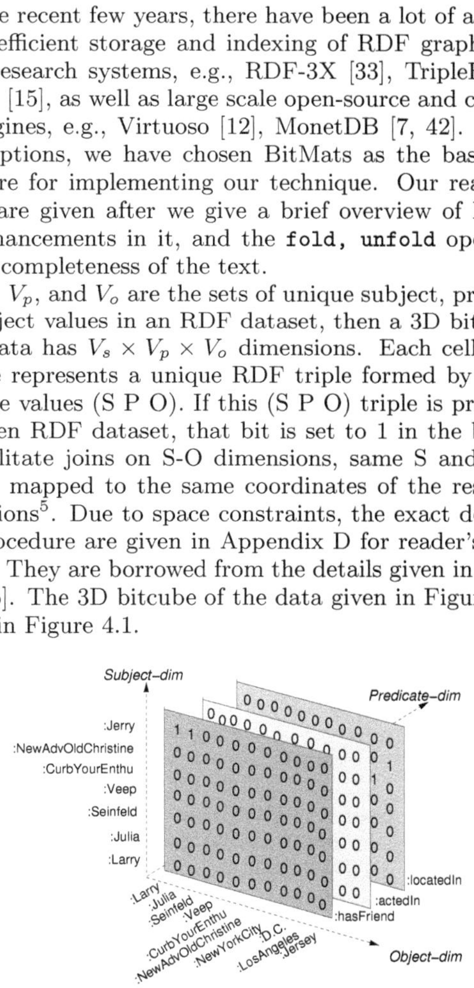

Figure 4.1: 3D Bitcube of RDF data in Figure 3.2

This bitcube is conceptually sliced along each dimension, and the 2D BitMats are created. In general, four types of 2D BitMats are created: (1) S-O and O-S BitMats by slicing the

[5]For the scope of this paper, we do not consider joins on S-P or O-P dimensions.

P-dimension (O-S BitMats are nothing but *transpose* of the respective S-O BitMats), (2) P-O BitMats by slicing the S-dimension, and (3) P-S BitMats by slicing the O-dimension. Altogether we store $2 * |V_p| + |V_s| + |V_o|$ BitMats for any RDF data. Figure 4.1 shows 2D S-O BitMats that we can get by slicing the predicate dimension (others are not shown for conciseness). Intuitively, a 2D S-O or O-S BitMat of predicate *:hasFriend* represents all the triples matching a triple pattern of kind (*?a :hasFriend ?b*), a 2D P-S BitMat of O-value *:Seinfeld* represents all triples matching triple pattern (*?c ?d :Seinfeld*), and so on.

Each row of these BitMats is compressed using run-length-encoding. A bit-row like "1110011110" is represented as "[1] 3 2 4 1", and "0010010000" is represented as "[0] 2 1 2 1 4". Notably, in the second case, the bit-row has only two set bits, but it has to use five integers in the compressed representation. So we use a *hybrid* representation in our implementation that works as follows – if the number of set bits in a bit-row are less than the number of integers used to represent it, then we simply store the set bit positions. So "0010010000" will be compressed as "3 6" (3 and 6 being the positions of the set bits). This hybrid compression fetches us as much as 40% reduction in the index space compared to using only run-length-encoding as done in [1].

Fold operation is represented as '**`fold(BitMat, RetainDimension) returns bitArray`**'. It takes a 2D BitMat and *folds* it by retaining the *RetainDimension*. More succinctly, a fold operation is nothing but *projection* of distinct values of the particular BitMat dimension, by doing a bitwise OR on the other dimension. It can be represented as:

$$\texttt{fold}(\texttt{BM}_{\texttt{tp}}, \texttt{dim}_{?\texttt{j}}) \equiv \pi_{?j}(BM_{tp})$$

BM_{tp} is a 2D BitMat holding the triples matching *tp*, and $dim_{?j}$ is the dimension of BitMat that represents variable $?j$ in *tp*. E.g., for a triple pattern (*?friend :actedIn ?sitcom*), if we consider the O-S BitMat of predicate *:actedIn*, *?friend* values are in the "column" dimension, and *?sitcom* values are in the "row" dimension of the BitMat.

Unfold is represented as '**`unfold(BitMat, MaskBitArray, RetainDimension)`**'. For every bit set to 0 in the *MaskBitArray*, *unfold* clears all the bits corresponding to that position of the *RetainDimension* of the BitMat. *Unfold* can be simply represented as:

$$\texttt{unfold}(\texttt{BM}_{\texttt{tp}}, \beta_{?j}, \texttt{dim}_{?\texttt{j}}) \equiv \{t \mid t \in BM_{tp}, t.?j \in \beta_{?j}\}$$

t is a triple in BM_{tp} that matches *tp*. $\beta_{?j}$ is the *MaskBitArray* containing bindings of $?j$ to be retained. $dim_{?j}$ is the dimension of BM_{tp} that represents $?j$, and $t.?j$ is a binding of $?j$ in triple t. In short, `unfold` keeps only those triples whose respective bindings of $?j$ are set to 1 in $\beta_{?j}$, and removes all other.

Reasons for choice of BitMats: RDF stores that achieve high compression ratio using variable length or *delta* encoding, have to decode/decompress the *variable length* IDs, and get them in 4-byte integers for performing joins. This ends up being an overhead for queries that have to access a large amount of data. In BitMats, IDs and in turn triples are represented by *bits* compressed with 4-byte run-lengths, which are manipulated through the `fold-unfold` procedures without decompressing them. Hence we have chosen BitMats as the base index structure in our implementation.

5. QUERY PROCESSING

Up to this point, we saw how to construct a GoSN to capture the nesting of OPT patterns in a query in Section 2.1. In Sections 3.2 and 3.3, we presented our optimization strategies to "prune" the triples associated with TPs in acyclic and cyclic well-designed queries, without considering the underlying index structure for RDF data. Then in Section 4, we described BitMat – our index structure.

Now, in this section, we "connect the dots", i.e., we present how triples associated with TPs in a query are pruned using BitMats, how **`semi-join`** and **`clustered-semi-join`** in **`prune_triples`** (Alg 3.2) are achieved through BitMats and **`fold-unfold`** by consulting GoSN, and finally how output results are generated using a *multi-way pipelined join* for any *acyclic or cyclic well-designed* query. We put all these concepts together in Algorithm 5.1.

Algorithm 5.1: Query processing

input : Original BGP-OPT query
output: Final results

1 GoSN = `get-graph-supernodes(`*Orig BGP-OPT query*`)`;
2 GoJ = `get-graph-jvars(`*Orig BGP-OPT query*`)`;
3 **for** *each* tp_i *in GoSN* **do**
4 | $\{tp_i \Rightarrow BM_{tp_i}\}$ = `init()`;
5 **bool** *NB-reqd* = `decide-best-match-reqd(`*GoSN, GoJ*`)`; `// Alg 3.1`
6 $(order_{bu}, order_{td})$ = `get_jvar_order(`*GoSN, GoJ*`)`
7 `prune_triples(`$order_{bu}$, $order_{td}$, *GoSN*`)`; `// Alg 3.2`
8 sorted-tps = sort TPs in master-slave hierarchy; `// Final result generation - Alg 5.4`
9 *allres* = `multi-way-join(`*vmap, sorted-tps, visited, NB-reqd*`)`;
10 **if** *NB-reqd* **then**
11 | *finalres* = `best-match(`*allres*`)`;
12 **else**
13 | *finalres* = *allres*;
14 **return** *finalres*;

Algorithm 5.2: `semi-join`

input: $?j$, tp_j, tp_i

1 $\beta_{?j}$ = `fold(`BM_{tp_i}, $dim_{?j}$`)` AND `fold(`BM_{tp_j}, $dim_{?j}$`)`;
2 `unfold(`BM_{tp_j}, $\beta_{?j}$, $dim_{?j}$`)`;

Algorithm 5.3: `clustered-semi-join`

input: $?j$, $\{tp_1, ..., tp_k\}$

1 $\beta_{?j}$ = bitarray with all bits set to 1;
2 **for** *each* tp_i *in* $\{tp_1, ..., tp_k\}$ **do**
3 | $\beta_{?j} = \beta_{?j}$ AND `fold(`BM_{tp_i}, $dim_{?j}$`)`;
4 **for** *each* tp_i *in* $\{tp_1, ..., tp_k\}$ **do**
5 | `unfold(`BM_{tp_i}, $\beta_{?j}$, $dim_{?j}$`)`

In Algorithm 5.1, we first construct the GoSN and GoJ (ln 1-2). Then with `init`, we load a BitMat for each TP in the query that contains the triples matching that TP (ln 4). Recall from Section 4, that we have, in all, four types of BitMats. We choose an appropriate BitMat for each TP as follows. If the TP in the query is of type (?var :fx1 :fx2), i.e., with two fixed positions, we load only one row corresponding to :fx1 from the P-S BitMat for :fx2. Similarly for a TP of type (:fx1 :fx2 ?var), we load only one row corresponding to :fx2 from the P-O BitMat for :fx1. E.g., for (*?sitcom :location :NewYorkCity*) we load only one row corresponding to *:location* from the P-S BitMat of *:NewYorkCity*. If the TP is of type (?var1 :fx1 ?var2), we load either the S-O or O-S BitMat of :fx1. If ?var1 is a join variable and ?var2 is not, we load the S-O BitMat and vice versa. If both,

?var1 and ?var2, are join variables, then we check which of ?var1 and ?var2 appears in $order_{bu}$ before the other. If ?var1 comes before ?var2, we load the S-O BitMat and vice versa. Recalling Example-2 from Section 3.2, for (*?friend :actedIn ?sitcom*) we load the S-O BitMat of *:actedIn* because *?friend* comes before *?sitcom* in $order_{bu}$.

While loading the BitMats with `init`, we do active pruning using the TPs that may have been initialized previously. E.g., if we first load BitMat BM_{tp_1} containing triples matching (*:Jerry :hasFriend ?friend*), then while loading BM_{tp_2}, we use the bindings of *?friend* in BM_{tp_1} to actively prune the triples in BM_{tp_2} while loading it. Then while loading BM_{tp_3}, we use the bindings of *?sitcom* in BM_{tp_2} to actively prune the triples in BM_{tp_3}. We check whether two TPs are joining with each other over an inner or left-outer join using GoSN with the *master-slave* or *peer* relationship, and then decide whether to use other BitMat's variable bindings.

Next we decide if nullification and best-match are required – they are required for a cyclic query where slaves have more than one jvars (ln 5). Then using `get_jvar_order` (ln 6) we get an optimal order of jvars for the bottom-up and top-down passes on GoJ. Recall that for a *cyclic* GoJ, `get_jvar_order` simply returns ($order_{greedy}$, $order_{greedy}$). Next, we prune the triples in BitMats using `prune_triples` (ln 7 in Alg 5.1). This procedure has already been explained in Section 3.2, hence we refer the reader to it. Two important operations in `prune_triples` are `semi-join` and `clustered-semi-join` – to remove the triples from the BitMats. These operations make use of the `fold` and `unfold` primitives. We have shown how `fold` and `unfold` are used in `semi-join` and `clustered-semi-join` with Algorithms 5.2 and 5.3 respectively.

Recall from `prune_triples` (Alg 3.2) that we do a `semi-join` (Alg 5.2) between two TPs, if they are in a master-slave relationship over a shared a jvar. The slave TP takes the restrictions on the variable bindings from the master. In `fold` we project out the bindings of $?j$ from tp_i and tp_j in the form of bitarrays. Through a bitwise AND we take an intersection of these bindings and store the intersection result in $\beta_{?j}$. Then we use $\beta_{?j}$ as the *MaskBitArray* in `unfold` to remove any triples whose respective bindings for $?j$ were dropped as a result of the intersection. `Clustered-semi-join` (Alg 5.3) is same as `semi-join`, except that we transfer the restrictions on the variable bindings across all the TPs that share a join variable and are *peers* of each other. Recall Example-2 from Section 3.2, which shows how `semi-join` and `clustered-semi-join` are used.

If an OPT query is *acyclic*, after `prune_triples`, each TP BitMat has a *minimal* set of triples (Lemma 3.3). In case of a *cyclic* OPT query, `prune_triples` only reduces the triples in the BitMats, but they may not be minimal. Note that using `prune_triples`, we prune the triples in BitMats, but we need to actually "join" them to produce the final results. For that we use `multi-way-join` (ln 9 in Alg 5.1). This procedure is described separately in Section 5.1. After `multi-way-join`, we use `best-match` to remove any subsumed results only if the query is cyclic and its slaves have more than one jvars (ln 11) – recall Lemmas 3.3 and 3.4. In `best-match`, we externally sort all the results generated by `multi-way-join`, and then remove the subsumed results with a single pass over them.

In the `init` and `prune_triples` processes, we do a "simple optimization" – if at any point, a TP in an absolute master supernode has zero triples, we take that as a hint of an empty result, and abandon any further query processing.

Currently Algorithm 5.1 is a main-memory process, i.e., all the TP BitMats are kept in memory during the query processing, and there is no disk spooling. This may pose some limitations on the total size of BitMats in a query. But as seen in our evaluation, LBR could handle low-selectivity queries with up to 13 TPs on a dataset with more than a billion triples on a machine with 8 GB memory, exhibiting the scalability of our technique. Presently LBR does not handle TPs with all variable positions (*?a ?b ?c*), and supporting them is currently under development.

5.1 Multi-way Pipelined Join

Before calling `multi-way-join`, we first sort all the TPs in the query as follows. Considering the TPs in absolute master supernodes, we sort them in an ascending order of the number of triples left in each TP's BitMat. Then we sort remaining TPs in the descending order of master-slave hierarchy and selectivity. That is, among two supernodes connected as $SN_1 \rightarrow SN_2$, TPs in SN_1 and any *peers* of SN_1 are sorted before those in SN_2. Among the peer TPs, they are sorted in the ascending order of the number of triples left in their BitMats (ln 8 in Alg 5.1). This order is `stps`. In `multi-way-join` we use at most $\sum_{tp_i \in Q} vars(tp_i)$ additional memory buffer, where $vars(tp_i)$ are the variables in every tp_i in the query Q. This is `vmap` in Alg 5.4. Thus we use negligible additional memory in `multi-way-join`.

At the beginning, `multi-way-join` gets an empty `vmap` for storing the variable bindings, `stps`, an empty `visited` list, and a flag `nulreqd` indicating if nullification is required (depending on the cyclicity of the query). In `multi-way-join`, we go over each triple in BM_{tp_1} of the first TP in `stps`, generate bindings for the variables in tp_1, and store them in `vmap`. We add tp_1 to the `visited` list, and call `multi-way-join` recursively for the rest of the TPs (ln 6–11). Note that in each recursive call, `multi-way-join` gets a partially populated `vmap` and a `visited` list that tells which TP's variable bindings are already stored in `vmap`. Then we check if any variables in a non-visited tp_i are already mapped in `vmap` (ln 16–18). Recall that since the query does not have Cartesian products, we always find *at least* one tp_i, which has one or more of its variables mapped in `vmap`. Also notice that `stps` order ensures that a master TP's variable bindings are stored in `vmap` before its slaves. If there exist one or more triples t in BM_{tp_i} consistent with the variable bindings in `vmap`, then for each such t we generate bindings for all the variables in tp_i, store them in `vmap`, and proceed with the recursive call to `multi-way-join` for the rest of the TPs (ln 20–25). Notice that, this way we *pipeline* all the BitMats, and do not do pairwise joins or use any other intermediate storage like hash-tables.

If we do not find any triple in BM_{tp_i} consistent with the existing variable bindings in `vmap`, then – (1) if tp_i is an absolute master, we *rollback* from this point, because an absolute master TP cannot have NULL bindings (ln 28), else (2) we map all the variables in tp_i to NULLs, and proceed with the recursive call to `multi-way-join` (ln 29–32). When all the TPs in the query are in the `visited` list, we check if we require `nullification` to ensure consistent variable bindings in `vmap` across all the slave TPs, and `output` one result (ln 1–4). We continue this recursive procedure till triples in BM_{tp_1} are exhausted (ln 6–11).

Algorithm 5.4: `multi-way-join`

input : vmap, stps, visited, nulreqd
output: all the results of the query

1 **if** *visited.size == stps.size* **then**
2   **if** *nulreqd* **then**
3   `nullification` (vmap);
4   `output` (vmap);   `// generate a single result`
5   **return**;
6 **if** *visited is empty* **then**
7   tp_1 = first TP from stps;
8   visited.add(tp_1);
9   **for** *each triple* $t \in BM_{tp_1}$ **do**
10   generate bindings for vars(tp_1) from t, store in vmap;
11   `multi-way-join`(*vmap, stps, visited, nulreqd*);
12 **else**
13   **for** *each* tp_i *in stps* **do**
14   **if** $tp_i \in$ *visited* **then**
15   **continue**;
16   get bindings for vars(tp_i) from vmap;
17   **if** *no bindings found* **then**
18   **continue**;
19   *atleast-one-triple* = **false**;
20   **for** *each triple* $t \in BM_{tp_i}$ *with same bindings* **do**
21   *atleast-one-triple* = **true**;
22   store vars(tp_i) bindings from t in vmap;
23   visited.add(tp_i);
24   `multi-way-join`(*vmap, stps, visited, nulreqd*);
25   visited.remove(tp_i);
26   **if** *(atleast-one-triple* == **false**) **then**
27   **if** tp_i *is an absolute master* **then**
28   **return**;
            `// This means` tp_i `is a slave`
29   set all vars(tp_i) to NULL in vmap;
30   visited.add(tp_i);
31   `multi-way-join`(*vmap, stps, visited, nulreqd*);
32   visited.remove(tp_i);

Intuitively, `multi-way-join` is reminiscent of a relational join plan with reordered left-outer-joins – that is, in `stps` we sort selective masters before their non-selective peers and slaves, and masters generate variable bindings before slaves in `vmap`. *But note that we pipeline all the joins together, and we can skip nullification and best-match for acyclic queries and cyclic queries with only one jvar per slave, because of our optimization techniques,* `get_jvar_order` (Alg 3.1), `prune_triples` (Alg 3.2), and Lemmas 3.3 and 3.4.

Recall Example-2 from Section 3.2. After `prune_triples`, tp_1 has two triples, and tp_2, tp_3 have one triple each in their BitMats. We sort the TPs as `stps` = [tp_1, tp_2, tp_3]. In `multi-way-join`, we first generate a binding of $tp_1.?friend$ and store it in `vmap`. In the recursive calls, we locate triples with the same *?friend* binding in BM_{tp_2}. For each such triple, we generate $tp_2.?friend$, $tp_2.?sitcom$ bindings in `vmap`, and proceed to tp_3. In a recursive call, if we do not find any triple with the same variable bindings in tp_2 or tp_3, we set variables in that TP to null in `vmap`. Since this is an acyclic query, we do not need `nullification`. While `output`ting a result, we pick variable bindings generated by masters over their slaves for common variables in `vmap`, e.g., we pick binding of *?friend* from $tp_1.?friend$ over $tp_2.?friend$.

5.2 Discussion

For our experiments, we assume that *all* the variables in a query – join as well as non-join – are SELECTed for projection, because analysis of DBPedia query logs shows that over 95% of the queries SELECT all the variables [35]. As per W3C specifications, SPARQL algebra follows "bag semantics" [9], so SELECTion (projection) of particular variables from a query can be readily supported in LBR by just intercepting the `output(vmap)` statement at line-4 in `multi-way-join`, which will output only mappings of the SELECTed variables from `vmap`.

For the scope of this paper, we have focused on the "join" component of SPARQL, i.e., BGP-OPT patterns without UNIONs, FILTERs, or Cartesian products. But for the completeness of the text, here we discuss how our technique can be extended to handle them.

UNION: For this discussion, we assume *well-designed* UNIONs (UWD), which are – for every subpattern $P' = (P_1 \cup P_2)$ in a query, if a variable $?j$ in P' appears outside P', then it appears in both P_1 and P_2. UWDs tend to have high occurrence (e.g., 99.97% as shown in [35]). Also UWDs remain unaffected by the difference between SPARQL and SQL over the treatment of NULLs [36], and following equivalences hold on them [34] – (1) $(P_1 \cup P_2) ⟕ P_3 \equiv (P_1 ⟕ P_3) \cup (P_2 ⟕ P_3)$, (2) $(P_1 \cup P_2) \bowtie P_3 \equiv (P_1 \bowtie P_3) \cup (P_2 \bowtie P_3)$. Additionally we also rewrite - (3) $P_1 ⟕ (P_2 \cup P_3)$ as $(P_1 ⟕ P_2) \cup (P_1 ⟕ P_3)$, and remove any spurious results in the end[6]. Using these rules, we rewrite a *well-designed* BGP-OPT-UNION query in the *UNION normal form* (UNF) [34], i.e., a query of the form $P_1 \cup P_2 \cup \, .. \, \cup P_n$ where each sub-pattern P_i $(1 \leq i \leq n)$ is UNION-free. We evaluate each UNION-free P_i using the same LBR technique, remove any spurious results if rule (3) of rewrite is used, and *add* the results from all the P_is. Note that we can *add* the output of all the P_is without a conventional *set-union*, because SPARQL UNION follows "bag semantics" [9, 41].

FILTER: For this discussion, we assume *safe* FILTERs [34, 36], i.e., for $P_x\mathcal{F}(R)$, where R is a filter to be applied on P_x, all the variables in R appear in P_x, $vars(R) \subseteq vars(P_x)$. *Unsafe* filters can alter the semantics of OPT patterns (ref [34]). In addition to the previous rewrite rules introduced under UNION, for a *well-designed* BGP-OPT-UNION query with *safe* filters, following equivalences hold [34, 41] – (4) $(P_1 ⟕ P_2)\mathcal{F}(R) \equiv (P_1\mathcal{F}(R)) ⟕ P_2$, (5) $(P_1 \cup P_2)\mathcal{F}(R) \equiv (P_1\mathcal{F}(R)) \cup (P_2\mathcal{F}(R))$. Using these five rewrite rules, we *push in* filters, *push out* unions, and bring the query in the UNF, i.e., $P_1 \cup P_2 \cup ... \cup P_n$ where each sub-pattern P_i $(1 \leq i \leq n)$ is union-free.

Now we can evaluate each P_i using an augmented LBR technique as follows. We apply filters either by intercepting `init` (ln 4) and `prune_triples` (ln 7) in Alg 5.1, or we apply them using a new *filter-and-nullification* (`FaN`) routine, in place of `nullification` (ln 3 in `multi-way-join`). The decision depends on the type of filters, e.g., if a filter has variables from two or more TPs, then we apply it in `FaN` when variable bindings from all the TPs are generated in `vmap`. Through `FaN`, we apply filters as well as do nullification for a cyclic P_i. We apply `best-match` in the end if `FaN` nullifies *at least* one variable binding in `vmap` or P_i is cyclic. We remove any spurious results introduced due to rule (3) of UNION rewrite, and obtain the final results by adding the results from each P_i in the UNF – please recall our note about SPARQL "bag semantics" under UNION. We can use some "cheap" filter optimizations before rewriting a query, e.g., a filter $P_1\mathcal{F}(?m = ?n)$ can be eliminated by replacing

[6]Spurious results may get introduced if either P_2 or P_3 is empty, or P_2 or P_3 does not have any matching variable bindings to that of P_1.

every ?n by ?m in all the TPs in P_1. Extending LBR technique for OPT patterns with UNIONs and FILTERs is a part of our ongoing work.

Cartesian products ($\times$): If a query is in the *Cartesian normal form*, i.e., $P_1 \times P_2 \times .. \times P_n$ where each sub-pattern P_i ($1 \leq i \leq n$) is $\times$-free, then we can evaluate each $\times$-free P_i using the same LBR technique presented in this paper, and generate the final results by taking a cross product of the results from each P_i sub-pattern. However, a query with an arbitrary nesting of ⟕ and $\times$ poses challenges, because ⟕ is *not distributive* over $\times$. A naïve way of handling such a query can be – use the technique presented in this paper only for the sub-patterns that are $\times$-free, and then resort to the standard relational technique of performing pairwise joins or $\times$-products to get the final results. As a part of the future work, we plan to extend LBR's technique to handle such nested OPT-Cartesian queries using an *augmented* GoSN construction and modified `multi-way-join` (Alg 5.4). Note that queries with Cartesian products are rare for RDF data. Previously published SPARQL queries in the literature do not have Cartesian products [15, 28, 32, 33, 35, 45, 46].

6. EVALUATION

We developed *Left Bit Right* (LBR) query processing technique with C/C++ language, compiled with g++ v4.8.2, -O3 -m64 flags, on a 64 bit Linux 3.13.0-34-generic SMP kernel (Ubuntu 14.04 LTS distribution). For running the experiments, we used a Lenovo T540p laptop with Intel Core i3-4000M 2.40GHz CPU, 8 GB memory, 12 GB swap space, and 1 TB Western Digital 5400RPM SATA hard disk.

6.1 Setup for Experiments

RDF Stores: To evaluate the competitive performance of LBR's techniques, we used two columnstores Virtuoso v.7.1.0 [12] and MonetDB v11.17.21 [7], which are popular for RDF data storage. LBR's core query processing algorithm works with the integer IDs assigned to the subjects, predicates, objects. Hence we loaded RDF triples with integer valued subjects, predicates, objects in Virtuoso and MonetDB's native columnstore, and translated all the OPT pattern queries to their equivalent SQL counterpart. We setup all the required indexes, configuration, and "vectorized query execution" in Virtuoso as outlined in [13, 23]. For MonetDB, we created separate predicate tables with triples of only that predicate, ordered on S-O columns as outlined in [42], and also created an O-S index on each of these tables. However, due to a large number of predicates in the DBPedia dataset (see Table 6.1), MonetDB failed to create a separate table for each predicate. Hence we loaded the entire DBPedia data in one 3-column table, and created four indexes PSO, POS, SPO, OPS on that table – same as what LBR and Virtuoso use. Thus we ensured that both Virtuoso and MonetDB have an optimized setup. Current published sources of RDF-3X [33] and TripleBit [45] cannot process OPT queries. GH-RDF3X[7], a third party system built using sources of RDF-3X for OPT pattern support, could not correctly process many OPT queries.

Datasets and Queries: We used three popular RDF datasets, (1) Lehigh University Benchmark (LUBM) – a synthetically generated dataset over 10,000 universities using their data generator program, (2) UniProt [10] – a real life protein network, and (3) DBPedia (English) 2014 [2] – a real life RDF dataset created from Wikipedia. The characteristics of these datasets are given in Table 6.1.

Datasets	#triples	# S	# P	# O
LUBM	1,335,081,176	217,206,845	18	161,413,042
UniProt	845,074,885	147,524,984	95	128,321,926
DBPedia	565,523,796	29,747,387	57,453	153,561,757

Table 6.1: Dataset characteristics

For a competitive evaluation of the three systems, we used a mix of *well-designed* OPT queries with varying degrees of selectivity, complexity, and running times. The LUBM data generator is popular for scalability analysis [15, 28, 44, 45]. However, its queries do not cover OPT patterns well. Therefore, to get a good coverage, we used UniProt queries from [5, 11], and LUBM queries from [6, 15], and introduced OPTIONAL patterns in them by studying the Ontology and graph structure. Similarly, we used DBPedia queries from [32] by removing union and filter clauses wherever necessary, because the main focus of our paper is on the nested BGP-OPT queries. Note that our approach is similar to that of other research systems, which focus on specific SPARQL components [15, 28, 33, 45, 46]. The current RDF benchmarks suffer from limitations as highlighted in [21]. Consequently, several systems use generated queries for specific SPARQL constructs. We evaluated all three systems over the same OPT queries, and they are given in Appendix E.

Evaluation Metrics: We used the following metrics for evaluation: (1) Time required for the `init` process in Alg 5.1 (T_{init}), i.e., the time to load the BitMats associated with all the triple patterns in a query. (2) Time required for `prune_triples` (Alg 3.2) (T_{prune}). (3) Total query execution time (warm cache) for each system averaged over 5 runs, i.e., end-to-end *clock-time* (T_{total}, T_{Virt}, T_{Monet} for LBR, Virtuoso, and MonetDB respectively). We ran each query 6 times by discarding the first runtime to warm up the caches. Also, for reporting this time fairly, we redirected output results of all the three systems to `/dev/null`, to eliminate any overhead of I/O latency in writing the results to the disk. Thus this reported time is the core query processing time spent by each system. T_{total} of LBR is $T_{init} + T_{prune} + T_{multiway}$. $T_{multiway}$ (Alg 5.4) is not explicitly shown in the evaluation for conciseness, as it can be computed by simply subtracting $T_{init} + T_{prune}$ from T_{total}. (4) Initial number of triples – the sum of triples matching each triple pattern in the query before the `init` and `prune_triples` procedures. (5) Sum of triples left in all the BitMats after `prune_triples`. (6) Number of final results. (7) Number of results, which have one or more NULL valued bindings, i.e., their result rows do not have all the variables bound due to the left-outer-joins in the query. These latter four metrics help us highlight the selectivity properties of the queries. (8) Whether `nullification` and `best-match` operations were required for LBR (see Section 5). Query processing times over all the three datasets are given in Tables 6.2, 6.3, and 6.4.

Note that the LBR system does not run in "server mode" as Virtuoso and MonetDB do, and it does not use any sophisticated cache management techniques of its own. It may only benefit from the underlying operating system kernel's file-system cache management.

[7] `https://github.com/gh-rdf3x/gh-rdf3x`

	T_{init} (*LBR*)	T_{prune} (*LBR*)	T_{total} (*LBR*)	T_{Virt}	T_{Monet}	#initial triples	#triples aft pruning	#total results	#results with nulls	best-match reqd?
Q1	5.88	3.95	**32.69**	104.67	>30min	649,375,261	61,662,975	10,448,905	336,455	No
Q2	22.63	7.33	**122.75**	197.84	>30min	758,743,140	157,571,451	226,641	8449	No
Q3	7.55	6.21	**140.02**	436.91	>30min	631,261,274	77,041,410	32,828,280	0	No
Q4	0.38	0.86	1.29	**0.015**	1466.14	352,340,574	1,701,020	11	6	Yes
Q5	0.36	0.85	1.26	**0.018**	1506.9	352,340,566	1,700,979	10	3	Yes
Q6	0.57	0.54	1.22	**0.03**	42.71	438,912,504	1,700,913	7	0	No

Table 6.2: Query proc. times (in seconds, warm cache, best times boldfaced) – LUBM 1.33 billion triples

	T_{init} (*LBR*)	T_{prune} (*LBR*)	T_{total} (*LBR*)	T_{Virt}	T_{Monet}	#initial triples	#triples aft pruning	#total results	#results with nulls	best-match reqd?
Q1	2.53	1.4	**8.2**	13.1	10.8	546,188,591	13,889,249	917,773	130,161	No
Q2	1.6	0	**1.6**	16.68	1.79	162,444,409	0	0	0	No
Q3	0.89	0.73	**3.25**	7.94	6.57	38,089,712	11,196,191	1,009,371	1,001,134	No
Q4	0.83	0.04	**3.61**	39.7	23.71	16,757,285	6,079,367	6,079,367	6,079,367	No
Q5	0.78	0.47	1.44	**0.49**	1.88	49,696,660	16,258,093	5625	5625	No
Q6	1.22	0.73	2.8	**1.55**	1.81	42,463,971	14,503,826	98,842	73,672	No
Q7	2.38	0.48	4.04	3.37	**2.92**	34,666,636	18,833,950	272,822	1	No

Table 6.3: Query proc. times (in seconds, warm cache, best times boldfaced) – UniProt 845 million triples

	T_{init} (*LBR*)	T_{prune} (*LBR*)	T_{total} (*LBR*)	T_{Virt}	T_{Monet}	#initial triples	#triples aft pruning	#total results	#results with nulls	best-match reqd?
Q1	1.19	0.19	**3.36**	6.65	>10min	22,460,545	3,165,560	515,003	446,204	No
Q2	0.025	0	0.025	**0.011**	>10min	2,231,035	0	0	0	No
Q3	0.036	0	0.036	**0.017**	>10min	15,799,901	0	0	0	No
Q4	0.63	0.15	0.81	**0.15**	>10min	13,493,622	501,240	4919	4917	No
Q5	0.37	0.04	0.44	**0.023**	0.68	8,624,878	94,336	5330	22	No
Q6	0.4	0.06	0.48	**0.02**	0.83	50,439,668	48	36	36	No

Table 6.4: Query proc. times (in seconds, warm cache, best times boldfaced) – DBPedia 565 million triples

6.2 Analysis of the Evaluation

From Tables 6.2, 6.3, and 6.4, we can see that for queries with low selectivity, LBR's technique clearly excels over Virtuoso and MonetDB.

Queries Q1–Q3 of LUBM need to access more than 50% of the data (see "#initial triples" column for the respective queries). These queries have a large number of triple patterns, have multiple OPT patterns, and generate a large number of results. Notably, these three queries have cyclic graphs of join-variables (GoJ), but only one join variable in each slave supernode. So LBR does not need to use nullification and best-match operations (see Section 3.2 and Lemma 3.4). For these three queries LBR gives several fold better performance than Virtuoso and MonetDB.

Queries Q4–Q6 of LUBM are short running, simpler queries with one OPT pattern. A closer look at these queries shows us that they have one or two highly selective triple patterns, with fixed values in predicate and object positions, and joins on S-S positions. This helps Virtuoso by way of fast merge-joins. Notice the column "#triples aft pruning", which shows that these queries actually deal with a very small fraction of the entire data - about a million triples out of more than a billion triple dataset, and they produce very small number of results. Notably, for these queries, while Virtuoso performs much better, MonetDB suffers a lot. We conjecture that for such queries with highly selective *master* triple patterns, Virtuoso probably uses the idea of basic reordering of the inner and left-outer joins. Virtuoso's "explain" tool revealed that it uses a combination of hash and bloom filters to join the selective master with a non-selective slave. Q4 and Q5 have a cycle in their respective GoJ, and since they also have more than one jvars in their slave supernodes, LBR uses nullification and best-match operations to remove any subsumed results (ref Section 3.3).

Among UniProt queries, for Q1–Q4, LBR performs much better. These queries have multiple nestings of BGP-OPT patterns, and do not have highly selective triple patterns in them. Notably, for Q4 a `semi-join` between master and slave removes all the bindings in the slave. Virtuoso however could not exploit this situation (as it did for LUBM Q4–Q6), because this master TP is not very selective and has only predicate position fixed. LBR's pruning method with semi-joins shows a benefit here. For Q2, LBR's `init` procedure with active pruning detects empty results of the query much earlier, and abandons further query processing (recall our "simple optimization" from Section 5). Whereas, Virtuoso and MonetDB detect empty results much later in their query processing. All seven UniProt queries are *acyclic*.

Similar to our previous observations, in case of DBPedia queries, for a query like Q1, which needs to handle larger amount of data, and produces more results, LBR comes out as a clear winner. Q2–Q6 access a much smaller fraction of the data, and generate a small set of results. In case of Q2–Q3, LBR's initialization with active pruning detects an empty set of results early on and abandons further query processing. MonetDB suffers badly for Q1–Q4. We conjecture that this is because it was unable to create 57,453 distinct predicate tables. We successfully created four types of indexes on MonetDB's DBPedia table, but its documentation revealed to us that MonetDB does not always honor user created indexes; it relies on its own policies of indexing and managing the data. All six DBPedia queries are acyclic.

In general, observe that for low selectivity queries, Q1–Q3 (LUBM), Q1–Q4 (UniProt), and Q1 (DBPedia), LBR prunes a significant portion of the initial triples (see columns "#initial triples" and "#triples aft pruning"), in a relatively small amount of time (T_{prune} is a very small portion of T_{total}). We believe that our novel technique of jvar-tree traversal (see Section 3.2) along with the compressed index structure and *fold-unfold* operations (see Section 5) make the pruning procedure efficient. Also please notice that LBR processes long running queries *several* seconds or minutes faster than Virtuoso and MonetDB ($T_{Virt} - T_{total}$). Virtuoso does better for short running queries, but the difference ($T_{total} - T_{Virt}$) is just about *a second*. We feel that for such queries, in the future, LBR can probably use a more sophisticated cache management technique by running in server mode. We trust that for long running queries, the essence of LBR's optimization technique gets highlighted.

To summarize, our evaluation shows that LBR works much better than the contemporary columnstores for queries with lower selectivity and higher complexity, e.g., queries Q1–Q3 (LUBM), Q1-Q4 (UniProt), and Q1 (DBPedia). The geometric mean of the presented queries for each dataset was as follows – for UniProt, 3.05 sec (LBR), 5.61 sec (Virtuoso), 4.35 (MonetDB), for LUBM, 10.18 sec (LBR) and 2.04 sec (Virtuoso), and for DBPedia 0.28 sec (LBR) and 0.07 sec (Virtuoso). The geometric mean of Virtuoso is lower than LBR for LUBM and DBPedia due to short running queries like Q4–Q6 (LUBM) and Q2–Q6 (DBPedia). We did not compute the geometric mean of MonetDB on LUBM and DBPedia as it took very long time for some of the queries.

Index Sizes: The on disk size of LBR indexes, i.e., $2|V_p| + |V_s| + |V_o|$ BitMats, with our enhancements of "hybrid compression" technique is 20 GB, 32 GB, and 41 GB for DBPedia, UniProt, and LUBM datasets respectively. But note that we do not need to load all these indexes in memory. For any given query, we just load the BitMats associated with the triple patterns in the query, which are typically a smaller fraction of the total indexes. We ran our experiments on a machine with 8 GB memory, which could fit the BitMats associated with the triple patterns in the queries. For Virtuoso, the on-disk size of the stored data and indexes was 5.5 GB, 9.5 GB, and 11 GB for DBPedia, UniProt, and LUBM datasets respectively, and for MonetDB it was 32 GB, 23 GB, 35 GB for DBPedia, UniProt, and LUBM respectively.

7. RELATED WORK

While the SPARQL OPT-free basic graph pattern (BGP) queries and their optimization have enjoyed quite bit of attention from the research community in the past few years, the discussion about OPTIONAL pattern queries has mostly remained theoretical. Previous work, such as [14, 22, 34, 41], has extensively analyzed the semantics of well-designed OPT patterns, as they have high occurrence [27, 35], bear desirable properties for the complexity analysis of the evaluation, and remain unaffected by the disparity between SPARQL and SQL algebra about joins over NULLs. Our query graph of supernodes (GoSN) is reminiscent of well-designed pattern trees (WDPT) [30, 31], but WDPTs are undirected and unordered, whereas GoSN is directed, and establishes an order among the patterns (*master-slave*, *peers*), which is an integral part of our optimization technique. While the work on WDPTs focuses on the analysis of containment and equivalence of well-designed patterns and identifying the tractable components of their evaluation, we use GoSN to focus on the practical aspects of OPT pattern evaluation.

From the practical aspects of the optimization of SQL left-outer-joins, most prominently, Galindo-Legaria, Rosenthal [24, 25, 26] and Rao et al [38, 39] have proposed ways of achieving it through reordering inner and left-outer joins. Rao et al have proposed *nullification* and *best-match* operators to handle inconsistent variable bindings and subsumed results respectively (see Section 3.1). In their technique, nullification and best-match are required for each reordered query, as the minimality of tuples is not guaranteed (see Lemma 3.1). They do not use methods like semi-joins to prune the candidate tuples. Bernstein et al and Ullman [16, 17, 43] have proved the properties of *minimality* for *acyclic inner-joins* only. Through LBR, we have taken a step forward by extending these semi-join properties in the context of SPARQL OPT patterns, by analyzing the graph of jvar-nodes (GoJ), and finding ways to avoid overheads like *nullification* and *best-match* operations.

For inner-join optimization, RDF engines like TriAD [28], RDF-3X [33], gStore [46] take the approaches like graph summarization, sideways-information-passing etc for an early pruning of triples. Systems like TripleBit [45] use a variable length bitwise encoding of RDF triples, and a query plan generation that favors queries with "star" joins, i.e., many triple patterns joining over a single variable. RDF engines built on top of commercial databases such as DB2RDF [18] propose creation of *entity-oriented* flexible schemas and better data-flow techniques through the query plan to improve the performance of "star" join queries. Along with this, there are distributed RDF processing engines such as H-RDF-3X [29] and SHARD [40]. While many of these engines mainly focus on efficient indexing of RDF graphs, BGP queries, and exploiting "star" patterns in the queries, we have focused on the OPT patterns that may have multiple S-O joins, which cannot exploit the benefits of "star" query optimizers.

Our indexes and pruning procedure resemble the BitMat system [15]. However, BitMat only handles BGP queries. Their query graph cannot capture the structural aspects of a nested BGP-OPT query, and their query processing does not honor any left-outer-joins. Additionally, while using their index structure as a base in our system, we have enhanced it further to reduce as much as 40% of the index size compared to their original method [1].

8. CONCLUSION

In this paper, we proposed *Left Bit Right* (LBR), for optimizing SPARQL OPTIONAL pattern queries. We proposed a novel concept of a query graph of *supernodes* to capture the structure of a nested OPT query. We proposed optimization strategies – first of a kind, to the best of our knowledge – that extend the previously known properties of acyclicity, minimality, nullification, and best-match. We presented LBR's evaluation in comparison with the two mainstream RDF columnstores, Virtuoso and MonetDB, and showed that LBR's technique works much better for low-selectivity OPT queries with multiple OPT patterns, and for highly selective simpler queries, it gives at par performance with the other systems. In the future, we plan to extend our query processor to handle other SPARQL constructs such as unions, filters, and we intend to investigate methods for better cache management especially for short running queries.

Acknowledgements

We are grateful to Dr. Sujatha Das Gollapalli and Dr. Sudeepa Roy for their valuable inputs, and the three anonymous reviewers for their detailed feedback, which significantly helped us in improving the presentation of our paper.

9. REFERENCES

[1] BitMat sources. http://sourceforge.net/projects/bitmatrdf/.

[2] DBPedia Datasets 2014. http://wiki.dbpedia.org/Downloads2014.

[3] Jena TDB. http://jena.apache.org/documentation/tdb/index.html.

[4] Lehigh University Benchmark. http://swat.cse.lehigh.edu/projects/lubm/.

[5] LifeScience SPARQL queries. http://www.w3.org/wiki/LifeSciencesQueries/SPARQL.

[6] LUBM Queries. http://swat.cse.lehigh.edu/projects/lubm/queries-sparql.txt.

[7] MonetDB. http://www.monetdb.org/.

[8] RDF 1.1 N-triples. http://www.w3.org/TR/n-triples/.

[9] SPARQL 1.1 Query Language. http://www.w3.org/TR/2013/REC-sparql11-query-20130321/.

[10] UniProt Protein Network. http://www.uniprot.org/.

[11] UniProt SPARQL queries. http://beta.sparql.uniprot.org/.

[12] Virtuoso Opensource Edition. http://virtuoso.openlinksw.com/dataspace/doc/dav/wiki/Main/.

[13] Virtuoso RDF Performance Tuning. http://virtuoso.openlinksw.com/dataspace/doc/dav/wiki/Main/VirtRDFPerformanceTuning.

[14] M. Arenas and J. Pérez. Querying semantic web data with SPARQL. In *PODS*, 2011.

[15] M. Atre, V. Chaoji, M. J. Zaki, and J. A. Hendler. Matrix "Bit"loaded: A Scalable Lightweight Join Query Processor for RDF Data. In *WWW*, 2010.

[16] P. A. Bernstein and D. W. Chiu. Using semi-joins to solve relational queries. *Journal of the ACM*, 28(1), 1981.

[17] P. A. Bernstein and N. Goodman. Power of natural semijoins. *SIAM Journal of Computing*, 10(4), 1981.

[18] M. A. Bornea, J. Dolby, A. Kementsietsidis, K. Srinivas, P. Dantressangle, O. Udrea, and B. Bhattacharjee. Building an Efficient RDF Store over a Relational Database. In *SIGMOD*, 2013.

[19] A. Chebotko, S. Lu, and F. Fotouhi. Semantics preserving SPARQL-to-SQL translation. *Data Knowledge Eng.*, 68(10), 2009.

[20] R. Cyganiak. A Relational Algebra for SPARQL. *Technical Report, HP Laboratories Bristol*, (HPL-2005-170), 2005.

[21] S. Duan, A. Kementsietsidis, K. Srinivas, and O. Udrea. Apples and Oranges: A Comparison of RDF Benchmarks and Real RDF Datasets. In *SIGMOD*, 2011.

[22] Egor V. Kostylev and Bernardo Cuenca Grau. On the Semantics of SPARQL Queries with Optional Matching under Entailment Regimes. In *ISWC*, 2014.

[23] O. Erling. Virtuoso, a Hybrid RDBMS/Graph Column Store. http://sites.computer.org/debull/A12mar/vicol.pdf.

[24] C. A. Galindo-Legaria. Outerjoins As Disjunctions. In *SIGMOD*, 1994.

[25] C. A. Galindo-Legaria and A. Rosenthal. How to Extend a Conventional Optimizer to Handle One- and Two-Sided Outerjoin. In *ICDE*, 1992.

[26] C. A. Galindo-Legaria and A. Rosenthal. Outerjoin Simplification and Reordering for Query Optimization. *ACM Trans. on Database Systems*, 22(1), 1997.

[27] M. A. Gallego, J. D. Fenández, M. A. Martínez-Prieto, and P. de la Fuente. An Empirical Study of Real-World SPARQL Queries. In *Usage Analysis and the Web of Data at WWW*, 2011.

[28] S. Gurajada, S. Seufert, I. Miliaraki, and M. Theobald. TriAD: A Distributed Shared-nothing RDF Engine Based on Asynchronous Message Passing. In *SIGMOD*, 2014.

[29] J. Huang, D. J. Abadi, and K. Ren. Scalable SPARQL querying of large RDF graphs. *PVLDB*, 2011.

[30] A. Letelier, J. Pérez, R. Pichler, and S. Skritek. Static Analysis and Optimization of Semantic Web Queries. In *PODS*, 2012.

[31] A. Letelier, J. Pérez, R. Pichler, and S. Skritek. Static Analysis and Optimization of Semantic Web Queries. *ACM Trans. on Database Systems*, 38(4), 2013.

[32] M. Morsey, J. Lehmann, S. Auer, and A. N. Ngomo. DBpedia SPARQL Benchmark – Performance Assessment with Real Queries on Real Data. In *ISWC*, 2011.

[33] T. Neumann and G. Weikum. Scalable join processing on very large RDF graphs. In *SIGMOD*, 2009.

[34] J. Pérez, M. Arenas, and C. Gutierrez. Semantics and complexity of SPARQL. *ACM Trans. on Database Systems*, 34(3), 2009.

[35] F. Picalausa and S. Vansummeren. What are real SPARQL queries like? In *SWIM workshop at SIGMOD*, 2011.

[36] A. Polleres. From SPARQL to Rules (and back). In *WWW*, 2007.

[37] R. Ramakrishnan and J. Gehrke. *Database Management Systems*. third edition, 2003.

[38] J. Rao, B. G. Lindsay, G. M. Lohman, H. Pirahesh, and D. E. Simmen. Using EELs, a Practical Approach to Outerjoin and Antijoin Reordering. In *ICDE*, 2001.

[39] J. Rao, H. Pirahesh, and C. Zuzarte. Canonical Abstraction for Outerjoin Optimization. In *SIGMOD*, 2004.

[40] K. Rohloff and R. E. Schantz. Clause-iteration with MapReduce to Scalably Query Datagraphs in the SHARD Graph-store. In *DIDC*, 2011.

[41] M. Schmidt, M. Meier, and G. Lausen. Foundations of SPARQL Query Optimization. In *ICDT*, 2010.

[42] L. Sidirourgos et al. Column-store support for RDF data management: not all swans are white. In *PVLDB*, 2008.

[43] J. D. Ullman. *Principles of Database and Knowledge-Base Systems, Volume II.* Computer Science Press, 1989.

[44] C. Weiss, P. Karras, and A. Bernstein. Hexastore: Sextuple Indexing for Semantic Web Data Management. In *PVLDB*, 2008.

[45] P. Yuan, P. Liu, B. Wu, H. Jin, W. Zhang, and L. Liu. TripleBit: A Fast and Compact System for Large Scale RDF Data. In *PVLDB*, 2013.

[46] L. Zou, J. Mo, L. Chen, M. T. Özsu, and D. Zhao. gStore: Answering SPARQL Queries via Subgraph Matching. In *PVLDB*, 2011.

APPENDIX

A. PROOFS

A.1 Lemma 3.1

PROOF. Let nullification be required with a minimal set of triples in each TP in a query. This means that there are one or more variable bindings and triples that will be removed as a result of an inner or left-outer-join that caused NULL values for the respective variable bindings. This is a contradiction to our assumption of minimality.

Let us assume that there are subsumed results with a minimal set of triples, and best-match is required to remove them. Let result r_2 be subsumed by r_1 ($r_2 \sqsubset r_1$), and $non\text{-}null(r_1)$ and $non\text{-}null(r_2)$ be the non-NULL variable bindings in r_1 and r_2 respectively. Let $S_1 = non\text{-}null(r_1) \setminus non\text{-}null(r_2)$ and $S_2 = non\text{-}null(r_1) \cap non\text{-}null(r_2)$. Per the definition of subsumption, $non\text{-}null(r_2) \subset non\text{-}null(r_1)$. This means that S_1 are the variable bindings contributed by a "slave" TP, which is why they could be set to NULL in r_2 (see the definition of master-slave in Section 2.2). This also means that S_2 variable bindings had corresponding bindings of variables in S_1 in r_1 but not in r_2, implying that those S_1 bindings and the respective triples were *removed* in the process of joins. This is a contradiction to our assumption of minimality of triples. □

A.2 Lemma 3.2

PROOF. Consider a query with three join variables, ?a, ?b, ?c, that form a three-cycle in GoJ. Let us assume that the respective GoT of the query is acyclic. An edge between ?a and ?b indicates that there exists a triple pattern tp_1, which has both ?a and ?b in it. Similarly there must be a tp_2 with join variables ?b and ?c, and tp_3 with join variables ?a and ?c. Now, tp_1 and tp_2 join on ?b, tp_1 and tp_3 join on ?a, and tp_2 and tp_3 join on ?c. This indicates a cycle among the TPs which is a contradiction. The same analysis can be extended to a join-variable cycle of more than three length.

Now consider a GoJ with no cycles, i.e., it is a tree. Consider that there exists a cycle involving TPs $tp_1...tp_n$ in GoT, such that each tp_i and tp_{i+1}, $1 \leq i < n$, join over join variable $?j_i$, and tp_1 and tp_n join over $?j_n$. This means that jvar-node graph has an edge between every pair of jvar-nodes $?j_i$ and j_{i+1}, $1 \leq i < n$, and there is an edge between $?j_n$ and $?j_1$. This indicates a cycle in the jvar-node graph, which is a contradiction. □

A.3 Lemma 3.3

PROOF. Let an OPT pattern be $P_k ⟕ P_l$ with P_k and P_l as OPT-free BGPs. Let us temporarily ignore the left-outer-join between P_k and P_l, and consider the two BGPs independently. P_k and P_l both have an acyclic connected GoJ. This observation follows from the fact that GoJ of P_k and P_l together is acyclic, and there are no Cartesian products in the query. Doing a bottom-up followed by top-down pass on the induced subtrees of P_k and P_l *independently*, with only *clustered-semi-joins* for each jvar, ensures that TPs in P_k and P_l are left with a minimal set of triples. This follows from Property 3.1 and is proved in [16]. Now consider $P_k ⟕ P_l$. Let $\mathcal{J} = jvars(P_k) \cap jvars(P_l)$, and $\mathcal{J} \neq \phi$ because GoJ of $P_k ⟕ P_l$ is connected. In Algorithm 3.1, line 11 chooses one of the jvars in $\mathcal{J}$ to be the root of P_l's induced subtree. Considering only jvars in $\mathcal{J}$ and acyclicity, this means that P_l has an induced subtree where jvar-nodes shared with its masters ($\mathcal{J}$) appear as the *ancestors* of the jvars that appear only in P_l, but not in P_k.

A bottom-up pass over jvar subtrees of P_k and P_l (ln 1–8 in Alg 3.2), transfers the restrictions on the variable bindings across respective TPs in P_k and P_l. Note that `semi-join` transfers the restrictions on variable bindings from P_k to P_l, and `clustered-semi-join` transfers the restrictions on bindings among peers. Recall that we build $order_{td}$ such that induced subtree of P_k is traversed before P_l's (ln 14–19 in Alg 3.1). A top-down pass on the jvar subtree of P_k (ln 9–16 in Alg 3.2) leaves a *minimal* set of triples in the TPs in P_k. Hence a top-down pass on the jvar subtree of P_l after P_k's, leaves a minimal set of triples in the TPs in P_l as a *ripple effect*.

This analysis can be inductively applied for any nesting of BGP and OPT patterns, as long as their GoJ is acyclic and connected. Hence with the procedures in Algorithms 3.1 and 3.2, we can get a minimal set of triples in each TP in a nested acyclic BGP-OPT query. □

A.4 Lemma 3.4

PROOF. We need to use *nullification* and *best-match* if a slave supernode has more than one jvars, because removal of bindings of one jvar may change the bindings of another due to the *ripple effect* through GoJ. Let us consider an OPT pattern of kind $tp_1 ⟕_{?j} (tp_2 \bowtie_{?j} tp_3)$. Let $P_1 = (tp_1)$ and $P_2 = (tp_2 \bowtie_{?j} tp_3)$. P_2 has only one jvar $?j$, that it shares with the master P_1. In `prune_triples` (Alg 3.2), we transfer the restrictions on bindings of $?j$ from tp_1 to tp_2 and tp_3 through a `semi-join`. Through a `clustered-semi-join` we ensure that restrictions on bindings of $?j$ are transferred among tp_2 and tp_3. So even if the original OPT pattern is reordered as $(tp_1 ⟕ tp_2) ⟕ tp_3$, there will not be any subsumed results. This is because, after a `clustered-semi-join`, tp_3 does not have any bindings of $?j$ that do not appear in tp_2 and vice versa.

An alternate way to look at it is: Consider a cyclic OPT pattern where slaves have more than one jvars. Then if a final result r_4 of the query is subsumed by r_3 ($r_4 \sqsubset r_3$), $non\text{-}null(r_3) \setminus non\text{-}null(r_4)$ have at least one jvar that appears *only* in the slaves of the query, i.e., $non\text{-}null(r_3) \setminus non\text{-}null(r_4)$ variables do not appear in *absolute masters* – that is why they could be set to NULLs. Let $S_1 = non\text{-}null(r_3) \setminus non\text{-}null(r_4)$, $S_2 = non\text{-}null(r_3) \cap non\text{-}null(r_4)$. Note that *not all* S_1 can be non-jvars from slaves, because it would mean that while variables in S_2 had the respective bindings for those in S_1 in r_3, they did not find any bindings for S_1 in r_4. As per our `prune_triples` procedure (Alg. 3.2), we only prune the bindings of jvars; bindings of non-jvars get removed as a *side effect* of the pruning of jvar bindings. So if S_1 has all non-jvars, this will be a contradiction. Hence, S_1 would have at least one join variable that *appears only in a slave*, for subsumed result r_4. But for a cyclic OPT pattern (without Cartesian products) with each slave having only one jvar, each jvar appears in an *absolute master* too. This in turn means that none of the jvars in the query can be set to NULL. S_1 does not have any jvars that appear only in slaves, which means that subsumed results cannot be generated.

Thus we do not need *nullification* and *best-match*, for a cyclic OPT pattern query, where each slave has only one jvar. □

B. NON-WELL-DESIGNED PATTERNS

As defined by Pérez et al in [34], a SPARQL nested BGP-OPT pattern query P is said to be *well-designed* (WD) if for every subpattern $P' = (P_i ⟕ P_j)$ of P, if a join variable $?j$ occurs in P_j and outside P', then $?j$ occurs in P_i as well. An OPT pattern that violates this condition is called a non-well-designed (NWD) pattern.

Before we discuss the evaluation of NWD patterns, it is important to take into consideration how NULLs are treated in left-outer-joins or inner-joins. There is a disparity between the SPARQL and SQL algebra over this, which mainly creates a problem for NWD queries. The same NWD query evaluated over a pure SPARQL engine, e.g., Jena, gives counter-intuitive results than a SPARQL-over-SQL engine, e.g. Virtuoso, when there are joins over NULLs. This issue is discussed in detail with an example in Appendix C. However, using the same assumption of "null-intolerant" (or null-rejecting) joins in SQL as done in the previous literature by Rao et al and Galindo-Legaria, Rosenthal [39, 26], we give a way of simplifying NWD patterns. In a "null-intolerant" join evaluation, NULL values are not matched with anything including other NULL values. E.g., in a left-outer-join $P_a ⟕_{?j} P_b$, if $?j$ has NULL values in P_b *before the join*, they get eliminated during the left-outer-join evaluation. NULLs are only introduced as a result of a left-outer-join for missing values in the right hand side pattern.

For any OPT query (WD or NWD), we first serialize it using OPT-free BGPs, join operators $\bowtie$, $⟕$, and proper parentheses; then build a graph of supernodes (GoSN) as described in Section 2.1. If the given query is NWD, we identify all OPT-free BGPs that *violate* the WD condition, and the corresponding OPT-free BGPs with which they do a violation. E.g., if the query is $P_x \bowtie (P_y ⟕ P_z)$, where P_z has a join variable $?j$ that appears in P_x but not in P_y, then we say, *"P_z violates WD condition with P_x, and (P_z, P_x) is a violation pair"*. We identify all such violation pairs in the query, and their corresponding violation supernode pairs in the GoSN. For this example (SN_z, SN_x) will be the violation pair of supernodes. Temporarily ignoring the directionality of edges in GoSN, we identify the undirected path between each such supernode violation pair. Note that according to GoSN's construction, there is a unique undirected path between any pair of supernodes. Next, considering the original directionality of edges on this path, we convert any unidirectional edges into bidirectional edges.

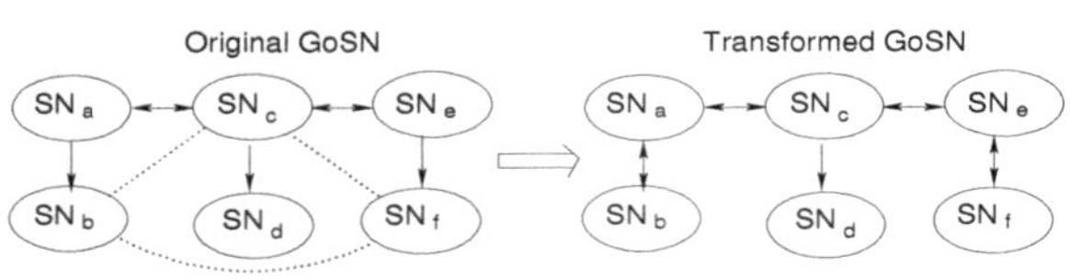

Figure B.1: NWD query GoSN transformation

Conversion of unidirectional edges into bidirectional edges is continued this way until all the violation pairs in GoSN are treated. Note that this is a monotonic process, and always converges – we always convert unidirectional edges into bidirectional edges, and never the other way round. This effectively means we convert one or more left-outer-joins in the original query into inner-joins (recall that a unidirectional edge represents a left-outer-join, and a bidirectional edge represents inner-join). E.g., consider a serialized query $(P_a ⟕ P_b) \bowtie ((P_c ⟕ P_d) \bowtie (P_e ⟕ P_f))$, where P_b violates WD condition over variable $?j_1$ with P_c, and P_f also violates WD condition over the same variable $?j_1$ with P_c. In turn, P_b and P_f too violate WD condition with each other over $?j_1$. In Figure B.1, we show the original GoSN and the transformed GoSN for this query. The dotted lines in the original GoSN indicate the pairs of respective supernodes that are in violation of the WD condition.

After this transformation process, we use the same query processing techniques given in Algorithms 3.1, 3.2, and 5.1 on this GoSN with null-intolerant join assumption.

C. TREATMENT OF NULLS

Unlike relational tables, RDF instance data does not contain NULLs[8]. Hence the issue of treatment of NULLs predominantly arises in case of non-well-designed OPT queries. This is because of the difference between the semantics of left-outer-joins between the SPARQL specifications [9] and SQL algebra. Borrowing the definitions from Pérez et al in [34], if we have a pattern $P_i ⟕ P_j$ with Ω_i and Ω_j as the set of *mappings* (variable bindings) of P_i and P_j respectively, then a SPARQL OPT pattern is defined as:

$$\Omega_i ⟕ \Omega_j = (\Omega_i \bowtie \Omega_j) \cup (\Omega_i \setminus \Omega_j)$$

This definition allows $P_i ⟕ P_j$ to have results which may have different *arity*. For example, considering the query in Figure 3.2, per above definition, the results will be {(:Larry), (:Julia, :Seinfeld)}. Note that the first result has arity 1, whereas the second one has arity 2.

This causes a problem if we do an inner-join of these results (mappings) with another pattern over *?sitcom* (as may happen in case of a non-well-designed query). Per SPARQL semantics of inner-join ($\bowtie$), two mappings are considered *join-compatible*, if they match on the variables that are *bound* in the respective mappings. For any unbound variables, the mappings are still considered compatible. E.g., if we join the above mappings with {(:Friends)} over the *?sitcom* variable, the result will be counter-intuitive – {(:Larry, :Friends)}. Note that mapping (:Julia, :Seinfeld) got removed, but (:Larry) was preserved, because it does not have an explicit NULL value for *?sitcom.*

In relational databases, evaluation of joins over NULL values has had different interpretations in different contexts (see [34, 38] for a discussion). However, for all practical purposes, most mainstream relational database systems assume a "null-intolerant" join evaluation. Also relational algebra assumes that the two sets of mappings (tuples) that are unioned, are *union compatible*, i.e., they have the same arity and same attributes [37]. Due to these differences in the join and union semantics of SQL and SPARQL, RDF stores that are built on top of relational databases, e.g., Virtuoso, give different results for a non-well-designed query, compared to a native SPARQL processing engine, when joining over NULLs.

We observed that pure SPARQL processing engines, such as ARQ/Jena [3], follow the join semantics which allow union of mappings with different arity, and a *null-tolerant* join, whereas relational RDF stores such as Virtuoso or MonetDB follow the SQL semantics of union-compatibility and null-intolerant joins.

[8]The difference between NULLs and "blank nodes" is elaborated in Section 2.2.

D. CONCEPTUAL BITCUBE

Borrowing the description of conceptual bitcube construction from [15], here we elaborate on the process of mapping the unique S, P, O values in the RDF data to the each bitcube dimension. As described in Section 4, the dimensions of the 3D bitcube of an RDF dataset are $V_s \times V_p \times V_o$. The unique values of S, P, O in the original RDF data are first mapped to integer IDs, which in turn are mapped to the respective bitcube dimensions. Let $V_{so} = V_s \cap V_o$. Set V_{so} is mapped to a sequence of integers 1 to $|V_{so}|$. Set $V_s - V_{so}$ is mapped to a sequence of integers $|V_{so}| + 1$ to $|V_s|$. Set $V_o - V_{so}$ is mapped to a sequence of integers $|V_{so}| + 1$ to $|V_o|$, and set V_p is mapped to a sequence of integers 1 to $|V_p|$. The common S-O identifier assignment (V_{so}) is for the sake of S-O joins.

The 2D BitMats are created by slicing this bitcube along each dimension, and they are compressed using our "hybrid compression" scheme as described in Section 4. Other meta-information such as, the number of triples, and condensed representation of all the non-empty rows and columns in each BitMat, is also stored along with them. This information helps us in quickly determining the number of triples in each BitMat and its selectivity without counting each triple in it, while processing the queries.

E. QUERIES

E.1 LUBM Queries

PREFIX ub: <http://www.lehigh.edu/~zhp2/2004/0401/univ-bench-.owl#>

Q1: SELECT * WHERE {{ ?st ub:teachingAssistantOf ?course . **OPTIONAL** { ?st ub:takesCourse ?course2 . ?pub1 ub:publicationAuthor ?st . }} { ?prof ub:teacherOf ?course . ?st ub:advisor ?prof . **OPTIONAL** { ?prof ub:researchInterest ?resint . ?pub2 ub:publicationAuthor ?prof . }}}
Q2: SELECT * WHERE {{ ?pub rdf:type :Publication . ?pub ub:publicationAuthor ?st . ?pub ub:publicationAuthor ?prof . **OPTIONAL** { ?st ub:emailAddress ?ste . ?st ub:telephone ?sttel . }}{?st ub:undergraduateDegreeFrom ?univ . ?dept ub:subOrganizationOf ?univ . **OPTIONAL** { ?head ub:headOf ?dept . ?others ub:worksFor ?dept . }}{ ?st ub:memberOf ?dept . ?prof ub:worksFor ?dept . **OPTIONAL** {?prof ub:doctoralDegreeFrom ?univ1 . ?prof ub:researchInterest ?resint1 . }}}
Q3: SELECT * WHERE { { ?pub ub:publicationAuthor ?st . ?pub ub:publicationAuthor ?prof . ?st rdf:type :GraduateStudent . **OPTIONAL**{ ?st ub:undergraduateDegreeFrom ?univ1 . ?st ub:telephone ?sttel . }} { ?st ub:advisor ?prof . **OPTIONAL** { ?prof ub:doctoralDegreeFrom ?univ . ?prof ub:researchInterest ?resint . }}{ ?st ub:memberOf ?dept . ?prof ub:worksFor ?dept . ?prof a ub:FullProfessor . **OPTIONAL** { ?head ub:headOf ?dept . ?others ub:worksFor ?dept . }}}
Q4: SELECT * WHERE { ?x ub:worksFor <http://www.Department9.University9999.edu> . ?x a ub:FullProfessor . **OPTIONAL** { ?y ub:advisor ?x . ?x ub:teacherOf ?z . ?y ub:takesCourse ?z . }
Q5: SELECT * WHERE {{ ?x ub:worksFor <http://www.Department0.University12.edu> . ?x a ub:FullProfessor . **OPTIONAL** { ?y ub:advisor ?x . ?x ub:teacherOf ?z . ?y ub:takesCourse ?z . } }
Q6: SELECT * WHERE { ?x ub:worksFor <http://www.Department0.University12.edu> . ?x a ub:FullProfessor> . **OPTIONAL** { ?x ub:emailAddress ?y1 . ?x ub:telephone ?y2 . ?x ub:name ?y3 . } }

E.2 UniProt queries

PREFIX uni: <http://purl.uniprot.org/core/>
PREFIX schema: <http://www.w3.org/2000/01/rdf-schema#>

Q1: SELECT * WHERE { { ?protein rdf:type uni:Protein . ?protein uni:recommendedName ?rn . **OPTIONAL** { ?rn uni:fullName ?name . ?rn rdf:type ?rntype . } } { ?protein uni:encodedBy ?gene . **OPTIONAL** { ?gene uni:name ?gn . ?gene rdf:type ?gtype . } } { ?protein uni:sequence ?seq . ?seq a ?stype . } }
Q2: SELECT * WHERE { { ?a rdf:subject ?b . ?a uni:encodedBy ?vo . **OPTIONAL** { ?a schema:seeAlso ?x } } { ?b a :Protein . ?b uni:sequence ?z . **OPTIONAL** { ?b uni:replaces ?c . } } { ?z a uni:Simple_Sequence . **OPTIONAL** { ?z uni:version ?v . } } }
Q3: SELECT * WHERE { { ?protein rdf:type uni:Protein . ?protein uni:organism <http://purl.uniprot.org/taxonomy/9606> . **OPTIONAL** { ?protein uni:encodedBy ?gene . ?gene uni:name ?gname . } } { ?protein uni:annotation ?an . **OPTIONAL** { ?an rdf:type uni:Disease_Annotation . ?an schema:comment ?text . } } }
Q4: SELECT * WHERE { ?s uni:encodedBy ?seq . **OPTIONAL** { ?seq uni:context ?m . ?m schema:label ?b . } }
Q5: SELECT * WHERE { { ?a uni:replaces ?b . **OPTIONAL** { ?a uni:encodedBy ?gene . ?gene uni:name ?name . ?gene rdf:type uni:Gene . } } { ?b rdf:type uni:Protein . ?b uni:modified "2008-01-15" . **OPTIONAL** { ?b uni:sequence ?seq . ?seq uni:memberOf ?m . } } }
Q6: SELECT * WHERE { { ?protein a uni:Protein . ?protein uni:organism <http://purl.uniprot.org/taxonomy/9606> . **OPTIONAL** { ?protein uni:annotation ?an . ?an a uni:Natural_Variant_Annotation . ?an schema:comment ?text . } } { ?protein uni:sequence ?seq . ?seq rdf:value ?val . } }
Q7: SELECT * WHERE { ?protein a uni:Protein . ?protein uni:annotation ?an . ?an a uni:Transmembrane_Annotation . **OPTIONAL** { ?an uni:range ?range . ?range uni:begin ?begin . ?range uni:end ?end . } }

E.3 DBPedia queries

PREFIX dbpedia: <http://dbpedia.org/resource/>
PREFIX dbpowl: <http://dbpedia.org/ontology/>
PREFIX dbpprop: <http://dbpedia.org/property/>
PREFIX dbpyago: <http://dbpedia.org/class/yago/>
PREFIX dbpcat: <http://dbpedia.org/resource/Category/>
PREFIX rdf: <http://www.w3.org/1999/02/22-rdf-syntax-ns#>
PREFIX rdfs: <http://www.w3.org/2000/01/rdf-schema#>
PREFIX foaf: <http://xmlns.com/foaf/0.1/>
PREFIX geo: <http://www.w3.org/2003/01/geo/wgs84_pos#>
PREFIX owl: <http://www.w3.org/2002/07/owl#>
PREFIX xsd: <http://www.w3.org/2001/XMLSchema#>
PREFIX skos: <http://www.w3.org/2004/02/skos/core#>
PREFIX georss: <http://www.georss.org/georss/>

Q1: SELECT * WHERE { { ?v6 a dbpowl:PopulatedPlace . ?v6 dbpowl:abstract ?v1 . ?v6 rdfs:label ?v2 . ?v6 geo:lat ?v3 . ?v6 geo:long ?v4 . **OPTIONAL** { ?v6 foaf:depiction ?v8 . } } **OPTIONAL** { ?v6 foaf:homepage ?v10 . } **OPTIONAL** { ?v6 dbpowl:populationTotal ?v12 . } **OPTIONAL** { ?v6 dbpowl:thumbnail ?v14 . } }
Q2: SELECT * WHERE { ?v3 foaf:page ?v0 . ?v3 a dbpowl:SoccerPlayer . ?v3 dbpprop:position ?v6 . ?v3 dbpprop:clubs ?v8 . ?v8 dbpowl:capacity ?v1 . ?v3 dbpowl:birthPlace ?v5 . **OPTIONAL** { ?v3 dbpowl:number ?v9 . } }
Q3: SELECT * WHERE { ?v5 dbpowl:thumbnail ?v4 . ?v5 rdf:type dbpowl:Person . ?v5 rdfs:label ?v . ?v5 foaf:page ?v8 . **OPTIONAL** { ?v5 foaf:homepage ?v10 . } }
Q4: SELECT * WHERE { { ?v2 a dbpowl:Settlement . ?v2 rdfs:label ?v . ?v6 a dbpowl:Airport . ?v6 dbpowl:city ?v2 . ?v6 dbpprop:iata ?v5 . **OPTIONAL** { ?v6 foaf:homepage ?v7 . } } **OPTIONAL** { ?v6 dbpprop:nativename ?v8 . } }
Q5: SELECT * WHERE { ?v4 skos:subject ?v . ?v4 foaf:name ?v6 . **OPTIONAL** { ?v4 rdfs:comment ?v8 . } }
Q6: SELECT * WHERE { ?v0 rdfs:comment ?v1 . ?v0 foaf:page ?v . **OPTIONAL** { ?v0 skos:subject ?v6 . } **OPTIONAL** { ?v0 dbpprop:industry ?v5 . } **OPTIONAL** { ?v0 dbpprop:location ?v2 . } **OPTIONAL** { ?v0 dbpprop:locationCountry ?v3 . } **OPTIONAL** { ?v0 dbpprop:locationCity ?v9 . ?a dbpprop:manufacturer ?v0 . } **OPTIONAL** { ?v0 dbpprop:products ?v11 . ?b dbpprop:model ?v0 . } **OPTIONAL** { ?v0 georss:point ?v10 . } **OPTIONAL** { ?v0 rdf:type ?v7 . } }

How to Build Templates for RDF Question/Answering —An Uncertain Graph Similarity Join Approach

Weiguo Zheng
Peking University
Beijing, China
zhengweiguo@pku.edu.cn

Lei Zou
Peking University
Beijing, China
zoulei@pku.edu.cn

Xiang Lian
University of Texas - Pan American
Texas, USA
lianx@utpa.edu

Jeffrey Xu Yu
The Chinese Univ. of Hong Kong
Hong Kong, China
yu@se.cuhk.edu.hk

Shaoxu Song
Tsinghua University
Beijing, China
sxsong@tsinghua.edu.cn

Dongyan Zhao
Peking University
Beijing, China
zhaody@pku.edu.cn

ABSTRACT

A challenging task in the natural language question answering (Q/A for short) over RDF knowledge graph is how to bridge the gap between unstructured natural language questions (NLQ) and graph-structured RDF data (G). One of the effective tools is the "template", which is often used in many existing RDF Q/A systems. However, few of them study how to generate templates automatically. To the best of our knowledge, we are the first to propose a join approach for template generation. Given a workload D of SPARQL queries and a set N of natural language questions, the goal is to find some pairs $\langle q, n \rangle$, for $q \in D \wedge n \in N$, where SPARQL query q is the best match for natural language question n. These pairs provide promising hints for automatic template generation. Due to the ambiguity of the natural languages, we model the problem above as an uncertain graph join task. We propose several structural and probability pruning techniques to speed up joining. Extensive experiments over real RDF Q/A benchmark datasets confirm both the effectiveness and efficiency of our approach.

Categories and Subject Descriptors

H.2.8 [**Database Management**]: Database Applications—*RDF, Graph Database, Question Answering*

1. INTRODUCTION

Recently, knowledge graphs have attracted lots of attentions in both academia and industry. As Resource Description Framework (RDF) is de facto standard of a knowledge graph, we focus on RDF repository in this paper. A key issue is how to access knowledge graphs and quickly obtain the desired information. Although SPARQL is a structural query language over RDF graphs, it is impractical for non-professional users to query RDF graphs using SPARQL, because of the complexity of the SPARQL syntax and RDF schema. We illustrate a SPARQL query example over DBpedia as follows.

```
SELECT ?person WHERE {
?person rdf:type Artist.
?person graduatedFrom Harvard_University.}
```

1.1 Motivation

To hide the complexity of SPARQL syntax, RDF question/answering (Q/A) systems provide an easy-to-use interface for users, which has attracted extensive attention in both NLP (natural language processing) [19, 23, 20] and DB (database) communities [24, 33]. A challenging task is how to translate natural language questions (NLQ) into structural queries, such as SPARQL, over a large knowledge graph G. One of the effective tools is the "template", which is used in many existing RDF Q/A systems [19, 20].

A typical system is EVI (http://www.evi.com/, formally TrueKnowledge), which logged over one million users within four months of launch in January 2012. EVI was acquired by Amazon in October 2012, and is now part of the Amazon group of companies. EVI aims to directly answer questions posed in plain English text over knowledge base. It employs a template-based approach to answer natural language questions, where a template describes how to turn a class of natural language questions into correct structural queries. However, EVI has to manually define the translation templates [19].

It is clear that the quality of templates determines the answer quality. The challenge is how to generate a large number of high quality templates automatically. Few previous works study this issue but all have to manually define the templates [19, 20]. Obviously, it is expensive to manually define these templates, especially for open-domain Q/A systems over large-scale RDF knowledge graphs. In this paper, we study how to generate templates automatically.

Figure 1 presents the framework for RDF Q/A using templates. It consists of two tasks: *how to generate templates* and *how to use these templates in RDF Q/A*.

To address the first issue (the focus of this paper), we propose a query workload-based approach for automatic template generation. Specifically, the inputs for the template generation task are two query workloads, as shown in Fig-

SIGMOD'15, May 31–June 4, 2015, Melbourne, Victoria, Australia.

http://dx.doi.org/10.1145/2723372.2747648.

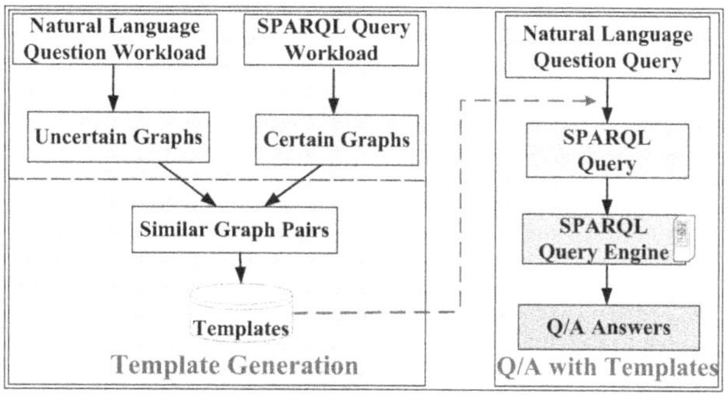

Figure 1: Framework for Template-based RDF Q/A

ure 1. One is a set D of SPARQL queries on the RDF repository (such as DBpedia workload[1]). The other one is a set N of natural language questions, which can be collected from some community-driven question-and-answer (Q&A) sites (such as Yahoo Answers) or search engine query workload (such as WebQuestions[2]). The whole process is done in three steps as follows.

Step 1. Uncertain Graph Generation. According to the method in [33], natural language questions can be interpreted into semantic query graphs. Due to the ambiguity of the interpretation, we model the semantic query graph as an uncertain graph, i.e, each vertex/edge has multiple possible labels with different probabilities. Here, labels are uncertain due to semantic ambiguity. For example, let us consider the question "which actor from USA is married to Michael Jordan born in a city of NY" in Figure 2. There are three persons named "Michael Jordan" in the DBpedia RDF graph, i.e., an NBA star, a professor, and an actor, each of which is associated with a probability. "NY" also has two possible mappings, i.e., state and city. Therefore, we can obtain an uncertain graph containing nodes with multiple labels, each associated with a probability.

Step 2. Finding Similar Graph Pairs. The goal is to find some pairs $\langle q, g\rangle$, for $q \in D \wedge g \in U$, where D corresponds to the SPARQL queries and U are the uncertain graphs derived from natural language questions.[3] Here, we utilize graph edit distance, which is widely used to measure graph similarity, to compute the similarity between q and g.

Step 3. Generating Templates with Similar Graph Pairs. Given a returned pair $\langle q, g\rangle$, based on the mapping between q and g (the mapping is found when computing graph edit distance at Step 2), we can build the templates.

In order to generate templates, the key problem is how to find the similar graph pairs efficiently (i.e. Step 2). This is the focus of this paper. We propose a novel approach, i.e., Similarity Join over uncertain graphs, denoted as *SimJ* (formally defined in Def. 7). Specifically, we propose a series of effective bounds to improve the performance.

Given the templates generated, a natural language question is translated into a SPARQL query using the templates generated in the first task. Then, the SPARQL query is searched over the knowledge graphs. The existing systems, such as Jena [2], RDF-3x [15], Virtuoso[4] and gStore [34], can be utilized to complete the search.

[1]aksw.org/Projects/DBPSB.html

[2]A natural language question log, the website is www-nlp.stanford.edu/software/sempre/

[3]We focus on the basic graph patterns of OPT-free SPARQL queries and do not handle other questions.

[4]http://virtuoso.openlinksw.com/

1.2 Challenges and Our Contributions

Challenge 1: *Effectiveness*. Since the templates are built based on the returned graph pairs, we need to guarantee that the returned pairs $\langle q, n\rangle$ are similar to each other. In our method, we represent the natural language question n as an uncertain graph g, due to the ambiguity of natural language phrases. To tackle this challenge, we propose a notion, called the *similarity probability*, $SimP_{\tau}(q, g)$, to measure the probability that (uncertain) graph g and q are similar under graph edit distance constraints, which will be formally defined in Def. 6. Our experiments on DBpedia SPARQL query workload and WebQuestions natural language question workload generate more than 8,000 templates with precision 86.54%. More experimental results on other real datasets are reported in Section 7.

Challenge 2: *Efficiency*. Another critical issue is related to efficient *SimJ* processing. To our best knowledge, no prior works studied this *SimJ* problem in the context of uncertain graphs. One straightforward method to solve the *SimJ* problem is to employ the *possible world* semantics [18, 3] to uncertain graphs, where each *possible world* is a materialized instance of uncertain graphs. However, since there are an exponential number of possible worlds, it is rather inefficient to materialize all possible worlds and perform graph similarity join on them. Therefore, efficient computations of *SimJ* answers are challenging and non-trivial.

There are several existing lower bounds for graph edit distances in the literature, such as *c-star* in [29], *k-Adjacent Tree* in [21], *paths* in [31], and *Pars* in [30]. However, these bounds are based on the deterministic vertex/edge labels. If we utilize them in uncertain graphs, there are two extreme solutions. One is to enumerate all possible worlds of an uncertain graph and compute lower bounds for each possible world. The other one is to ignore all vertex/edge labels and only consider structures of graphs. Obviously, the former is not efficient due to an exponential number of possible worlds; while the latter's pruning power is low. It is not straightforward to revise the existing lower bounds to provide both efficient and effective pruning in uncertain graphs.

We derive a novel edit distance lower bound (called CSS-based lower bound) that utilizes the relationship between graph edit distance (GED) and *common structural subgraph* (CSS) in the uncertain graph context. An advantage of CSS-based bound is that there is a uniform CSS-based lower bound between q and all possible worlds of uncertain graph g (see Theorem 3). In other words, we do not have to enumerate all possible worlds of g. Our lower bound considers structure and uncertainty together instead of using them separately. Compared with existing lower bounds, our bound is tighter, and can thus achieve higher pruning power.

Applying the relationship between GED and CSS, we also design an upper bound for similarity probability between q and g. Section 5 discusses more details about that.

To summarize, we make the following contributions.

- We propose a graph similarity join (SimJ) approach to generate SPARQL query templates for RDF Q/A automatically. Due to the inherent ambiguity of the natural language phrases, we study SimJ in the context of uncertain graphs.

- None of existing lower bounds of GED can be applied in SimJ over uncertain graphs. We propose a novel lower bound that is independent on the possible worlds of a uncertain graph, which is based on the relationship between GED and common structural subgraphs.

- We devise an upper bound for similarity probability between q and g to prune unpromising candidates.
- To optimize query performance, we further propose a cost-based technique. That is, dividing uncertain graphs into fine-grained groups so as to attain higher pruning power.
- We conduct extensive experiments over real (including QALD-3 benchmark) datasets to confirm the effectiveness and efficiency of our proposed approach. The precisions on QALD-3 and WebQuestions datasets achieve 97.67% and 86.54%, respectively.

2. OVERVIEW AND RUNNING EXAMPLE

2.1 Template Generation

As mentioned in Section 1, there are three steps to build templates. We illustrate the detailed steps.

Step 1: Uncertain Graph Generation. There are two phases, i.e., generating semantic query graphs and assigning uncertain labels, in order to generate uncertain graphs for natural language questions (NLQ).

Generating semantic query graphs. Consider each question n in the NLQ workload. n is translated into a *semantic query graph* (Def. 1) using the approach in [33]. A semantic query graph is a collection of *semantic relations*. A semantic relation is a triple $\langle rel, arg1, arg2\rangle$, where rel is a relation phrase, $arg1$ and $arg2$ are the two argument phrases.

Definition 1. **(Semantic Query Graph** [33]**).** A semantic query graph is denoted as Q^S, in which each vertex v_i is associated with an argument and each edge $\overline{v_i v_j}$ is associated with a relation phrase, $1 \le i, j \le |V(Q^S)|$.

Let us consider a natural language question "Which actor from USA is married to Michael Jordan born in city of NY ?" in Figure 2. We can extract four semantic relations from the question, i.e., ⟨"from", "which actor", "USA"⟩, ⟨"be married to", "which actor", "Michael Jordan" ⟩, ⟨"born in", "Michael Jordan", "city"⟩, ⟨"located in", "city", "NY"⟩, each of which is represented as an edge in the semantic query graph Q^S. Two edges share one common vertex if the corresponding relations share one common argument in Q^S.

Assigning Uncertain Vertex Labels. The uncertain labels of Q^S is from the ambiguity of natural language phrases. Each vertex in Q^S is an argument arg, which is a natural language phrase, such as "Michael Jordan" and "NY". Applying entity linking techniques [4], an argument arg (i.e., a vertex) in Q^S may be linked to multiple entities associated with different existence confidences. We use the corresponding type of entities to denote the vertex label. For example, "Michael Jordan" in Q^S may correspond to three different persons, i.e., an NBA player, a professor and an actor. Therefore, we replace "Michael Jordan" in Q^S (i.e., vertex v_2) with three possible classes, i.e., ⟨NBA_plaryer⟩, ⟨Professor⟩ and ⟨Actor⟩, each of which is associated with an existence confidence. Many entity linking algorithms can provide the confidence probability, such as [4]. Furthermore, all variable vertices are assigned the same label (a wildcard label), i.e., all the labels starting with "?" can match any vertex label.

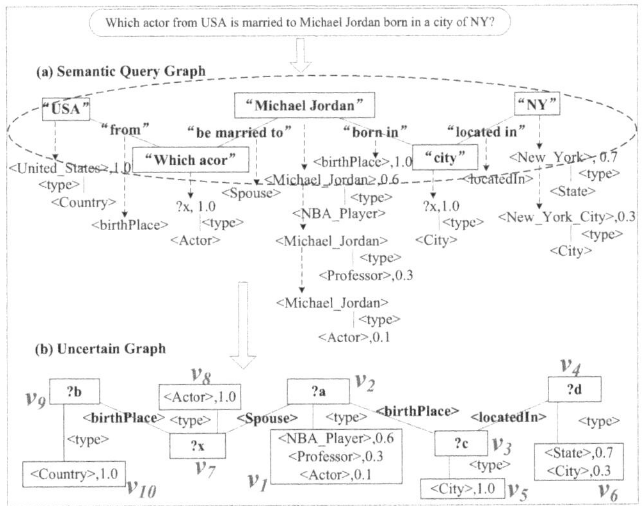

Figure 2: Uncertain graph generation

Assigning Uncertain Edge Labels. Similarly, one relation rel in Q^S may correspond to multiple predicates [33]. Zou et al. proposed a graph mining-based relation paraphrasing algorithm [33]. Thus, an edge in Q^S may also have multiple labels, each of which is a predicate associated with a confidence probability.

Step 2: Finding Similar Graph Pairs. Let U denote all uncertain graphs that are generated from natural language question (NLQ) workload in the first step. It is straightforward to represent each SPARQL query (in the SPARQL workload) as a certain graph q, all of which are collected to form a certain graph dataset D. As shown in Figure 3, our goal of this step is to find similar graph pairs $\langle q, g\rangle$, where $q \in D$ and $g \in U$ are similar to each other with high probability in the uncertain model.

We use minimum graph edit distance (GED for short), a widely used error-tolerant measure, to evaluate the graph similarity. Finding similar graph pairs by joining D with U is challenging, since computing GED is an NP-hard problem [29] and an uncertain graph $g \in U$ has an exponential number of possible worlds. The existing lower bounds of GED cannot be used directly unless that we materialize all possible worlds or ignore all vertex/edge labels of g, as these lower bounds are designed for certain graphs. To improve the performance, a careful-designed lower bound for a certain graph q (derived from a SPARQL query) and an uncertain graph g (derived from a natural language question) is desirable.

In this paper, we propose a common structural subgraph (CSS for short)-based lower bound, which avoids enumerating possible worlds of g and also considering the vertex/edge labels. The technical details are given in Sections 3 to 6. In the running example, we find two similar graph pairs $\langle g_1, q_2\rangle$ and $\langle g_2, q_1\rangle$. Note that the similar graph pair does not necessarily mean that the two queries (such as g_1 and q_2) ask for the same question, but they potentially generate a good template (see the next step) based on the matching between g_1 and q_2 under the graph edit distance constraint.

Step 3: Generating Templates with Similar Graph Pairs. Assume that we have obtained the similar graph pairs (such as $\langle g_1, q_2\rangle$ and $\langle g_2, q_1\rangle$), the next step is to build the templates automatically. We illustrate the detailed process using the running example. Consider the graph pair

$\langle g_2, q_1 \rangle$ in Figure 3, where g_2 corresponds to the second question "Which politician graduated from CIT?".

Figure 4(b) gives the uncertain graph g_2 that is generated based on the semantic query graph as shown in Figure 4(a). In computing graph edit distance, we obtain the mapping between the uncertain graph g_2 and SPARQL query q_1. The dashed lines in Figure 4(b) and (c) illustrate the mappings between g_2 and q_1, such as $\langle politician \leftrightarrow Artist \rangle$, $\langle CIT \leftrightarrow Harvard\_University \rangle$. It also shows the mappings between phrases in natural language questions and the entities/classes in SPARQL queries. We replace these specific entities/classes as slots and also keep the mappings, which lead to some templates, as shown in Figure 4(d).

2.2 Q/A with Templates

Given a new natural language question n, if a template t can match the question n, we translate n into a SPARQL query using the template. Then, any SPARQL query engine can be used to answer the SPARQL query. There are two main steps: *finding a template matching the question, slot filling*, and *entity linking*.

Finding a template matching the question and slot filling. Given a natural language question, we first find which natural language template can match the question. Then, based on the match, we can find the mapping between the phrases (in natural language question) and the slots (in templates). Here we propose a syntactic dependency tree based alignment for the slot filling task.

Syntactic dependency tree based alignment. First, by using the NLP (Natural Language Processing) parsers, e.g., Stanford Parser [13], the natural language question and the natural language part of templates are parsed into syntactic dependency trees, respectively. Many tree edit distance (TED)-based approaches have been proposed to find the alignment between two dependency trees in NLP literature, such as [6, 9, 26]. Based on these existing methods, we try to find a template's dependency tree that best aligns with the dependency tree of the natural language question sentence (i.e., the minimum tree edit distance). Once the alignment is found, it is straightforward to fill the slot with the corresponding phrases in the natural language question sentences. We give an example to illustrate the whole process.

Example 1. *Given a natural language question "Which physicist graduated from CMU?" and a natural language part of a query template "Which ⟨__⟩ graduated from ⟨__⟩?", they are parsed into two syntactic dependency trees as shown in Figure 5. By aligning these two syntactic dependency trees, we can fill the slots according to the mapping.*

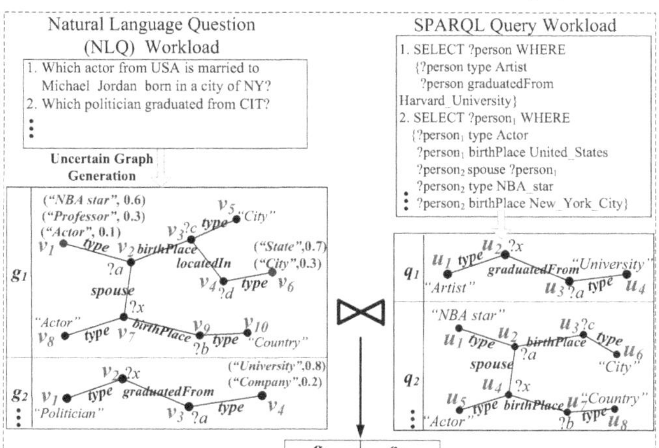

Figure 3: Finding Similar Graph Pairs

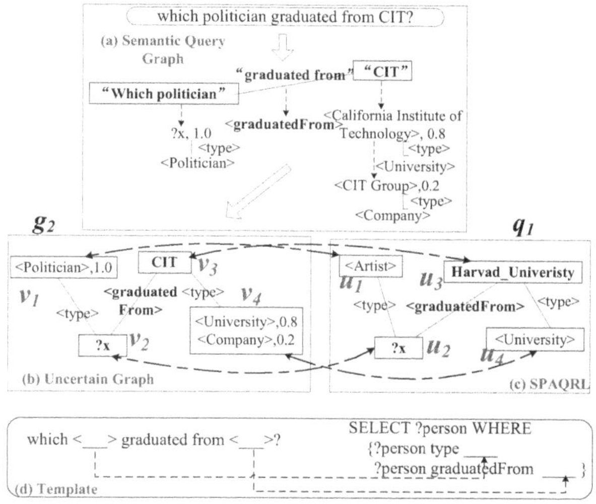

Figure 4: Template Generation.

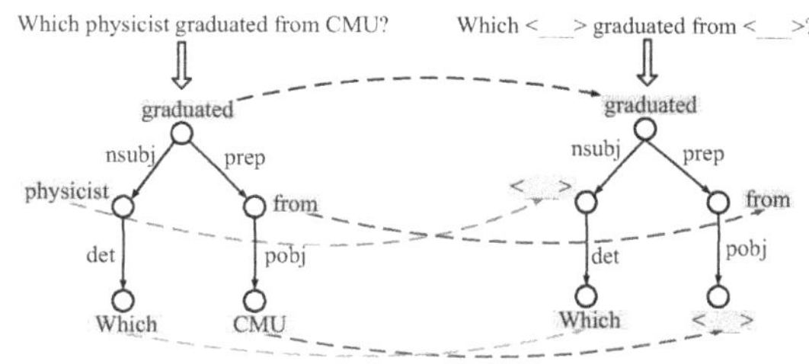

Figure 5: Syntactic dependency graph alignment

Entity Linking. Obtaining the mapping between entities and slots, we need to find the entities (in the underlying knowledge graph) that correspond to phrases filled at the slot. Actually, this is a classical entity linking problem, which has been extensively studied [4, 16, 32]. When it is done, we have obtained a complete SPARQL statement.

3. FINDING SIMILAR GRAPH PAIRS

We have outlined the whole process of our solution. As mentioned earlier, a challenging task is Step 2 of the template generation, i.e., how to find similar graph pairs from an uncertain graph set U (derived from the NLQ workload) and a certain graph set D (derived from the SPARQL query workload). We model this task as a graph similarity join problem. From this section, we focus on finding similar graph problem. In this section, we first give some preliminary knowledge in Section 3.1 and then formalize finding similar graph pair problem (denoted as SimJ) in Section 3.2 and discuss the steps of computing SimJ problem in Section 3.3. Table 1 lists the major notations in this paper.

Table 1: Notations and Descriptions

Notation	Description
D	certain graphs corresponding to SPARQL queries
U	uncertain graphs derived from language questions
q	a (certain) query graph, $q \in D$
g	an uncertain graph, $g \in U$
$pw(g)$ or g^c	possible world of uncertain graph g
$Pr\{pw(g)\}$	the appearance probability of $pw(g)$
τ	user-specified threshold of GED
α	user-specified threshold of similarity probability
$ged(\cdot,\cdot)$	the GED between two (un)certain graphs
$SimP_\tau(q,g)$	the similarity probability between q and g

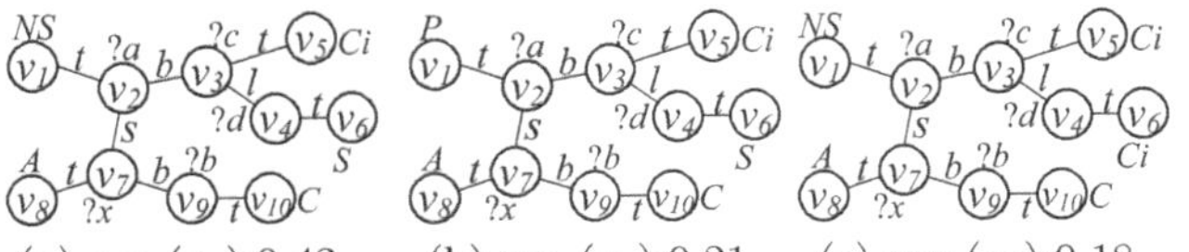

(a) $pw_1(g_1)$:0.42 (b) $pw_2(g_1)$:0.21 (c) $pw_3(g_1)$:0.18

Figure 6: Possible worlds of the uncertain graph g_1

3.1 Preliminary

In order to handle the uncertainty in the semantic query graph Q^S, we resort to the classical uncertain model—possible world [3]—in uncertain graphs (Section 3.1.1). We use a popular graph similarity measure—minimum graph edit distance (GED)—to evaluate the graph similarity (Section 3.1.2).

3.1.1 Uncertain Graph Model

Definition 2. (**Uncertain Graph Model**) An uncertain graph g is defined as a five-tuple $g = \{V(g), E(g), F_L(g), \Sigma_V(g), \Sigma_E(g)\}$, where $V(g)$ is a set of vertices, $E(g)$ is a set of edges, $F_L(g)$ is a mapping function: $V(g) \times V(g) \to E(g)$, that maps from vertices to edges, $\Sigma_V(g)$ is an uncertain vertex label set which contains possible labels, $l(v)$, of vertex $v \in V(g)$ with *existence probability* $l(v).p \in (0, 1]$, and $\Sigma_E(g)$ is an edge label set.

Def. 2 provides an uncertain graph model. Each vertex v in uncertain graphs is assigned with one or multiple *mutually exclusive* labels $l(v)$, each with an existence probability $l(v).p$, where $\sum_{\forall l(v)} l(v).p \leq 1$. In this work, we use the existing entity linking technique [4] to assign the probability $l(v).p$. In fact, a certain graph, g^c, is a special case of the uncertain graph g, where each vertex v has only one deterministic label $l(v)$ with existence probability $l(v).p = 1$. Note that for ease of presentation, we do not discuss the edge label uncertainty in finding similar graph pair (i.e., SimJ) problem, although it is straightforward to handle the general case. For example, we can introduce fictitious vertices to represent (uncertain) edges and assigning uncertain labels of edges to these new vertices.

In order to model the uncertain graph, we consider the well-defined *possible world* semantics [3] as follows.

Definition 3. (**Possible Worlds of an Uncertain Graph**) Let $PW(g)$ denote a set of all possible worlds in uncertain graph g. A possible world, $pw(g) \in PW(g)$, of an uncertain graph g is a deterministic graph instance, materialized from g, in which each vertex v is assigned with a certain label $l(v)$. Each possible world $pw(g)$ has an appearance probability $Pr\{pw(g)\} = \prod_{\forall v \in pw(g)} l(v).p$.

In Def. 3, each possible world is a materialized instance of uncertain graph g, which corresponds to one label assignment in vertices of g. Thus, the probability that a possible world appears in the real world is given by multiplying existence probabilities of vertex labels.

Example 2. *Due to the space limit, Figure 6 only shows an example of 3 possible worlds for uncertain graph g_1 in Figure 3. For simplicity, we use the acronym of each original label to denote this label, e.g., "NBA star"(NS), "State"(S), "type"(t). The existence probability of possible world $pw_1(g_1)$, $Pr\{pw_1(g_1)\}$, can be given by multiplying existence probabilities of vertex labels in $pw_1(g_1)$, that is, $Pr\{pw_1(g_1)\} = \prod_{i=1}^{10} l(v_i).p = 0.6 \times 1 \times 1 \times 1 \times 1 \times 0.7 \times 1 \times 1 \times 1 \times 1 = 0.42$.*

To keep our notations simple, we will use $pw(g)$ and g^c interchangeably to denote either a possible world of uncertain graph g or a certain graph, when there is no ambiguity.

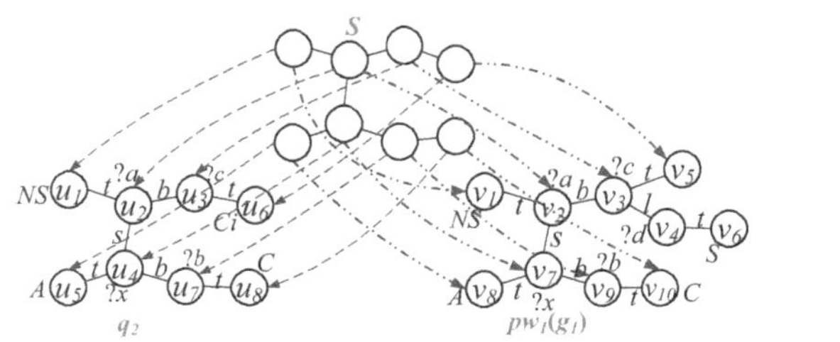

Figure 7: The CSS of q_2 and $pw_1(g_1)$

3.1.2 Graph Edit Distance

We use *minimum graph edit distance* [31], a widely used error-tolerant measure, to compute graph similarity.

Graph Edit Distance Between Certain Graphs. There are six *primitive edit operations* [29] on a certain graph g^c:

- insert/delete an isolated vertex with label;
- insert/delete an edge between two vertices; and
- substitute a (or an) vertex/edge label.

Given two certain graphs g_1^c and g_2^c, there exist many sequences of primitive edit operations to transform g_1^c to g_2^c. However, among them, the sequence with the shortest length is called the *minimum graph edit distance* (GED for short) [8] (i.e., dissimilarity) between two graphs. Computing GED between two certain graphs is NP-hard [29]. In the literature, previous works usually focus on its efficient computation [17, 31]. The most widely used approach is based on the A^* algorithm incorporating some heuristics [17].

3.1.3 Graph Edit Distance VS. Common Structural Subgraph

In this section, we presentation the relationship between graph edit distance and common structural subgraph (CSS) [1], which is used to design our bounds.

Definition 4. (Structurally Subgraph Isomorphism [1]). Given two certain graphs g_1^c and g_2^c, g_1^c is structurally subgraph isomorphic to g_2^c if and only if there exists a bijection $f : V(g_1^c) \to V(g_2^c)$, *s.t.*, 1) $\forall\ v \in V(g_1^c), f(v) \in V(g_2^c)$; 2) $\forall v_1, v_2 \in V(g_1^c)$, $\overrightarrow{v_1 v_2} \in E(g_1^c) \Leftrightarrow \overrightarrow{f(v_1) f(v_2)} \in E(g_2^c)$.

Note that, "structurally subgraph isomorphism" in Def. 4 does not consider the constraint of vertex/edge labels.

Definition 5. (Common Structural Subgraph [1], CSS) Given two certain graphs q and g^c, a graph s is a *common structural subgraph* (CSS) of q and g^c, if s is *structurally subgraph isomorphic* to both q and g^c, respectively.

For example, the graph s is a CSS of graph q_2 and the possible world $pw_1(g_1)$ in Figure 7. In this paper, we assume that the cost of each primitive edit operation is 1.

Lemma 1. *(Graph Edit Distance VS. CSS [1]) Given two certain graphs, q and g^c, s is a CSS of q and g^c. The following equation about $ged(q, g^c)$ holds.*

$$
\begin{aligned}
&ged(q, g^c) \\
&= \min_{\forall s}\{(|V(q)| + |E(q)|) - (|V(s)| + |E(s)|) && \text{(Part 1)} \\
&\quad + (|V(g^c)| + |E(g^c)|) - (|V(s)| + |E(s)|) && \text{(Part 2)} \\
&\quad + (|V_s| + |E_s|)\} && \text{(Part 3)} \\
&= |V(q)| + |E(q)| + |V(g^c)| + |E(g^c)| - F(q, g^c) && (1)
\end{aligned}
$$

where V_s and E_s are subsets of vertices and edges in CSS s, respectively, whose labels need to be substituted, and we have

$$F(q, g^c) = \max_{\forall s}\{2 \cdot (|V(s)| + |E(s)|) - (|V_s| + |E_s|)\}. \quad (2)$$

Lemma 1 provides a formula of calculating GED through CSS. The intuition is as follows. Part 1 in Eq. (1) is the cost of deleting those vertices/edges in q that do not belong to CSS s. Part 2 in Eq. (1) is the cost of inserting those vertices/edges in g^c that do not belong to CSS s. Part 3 in Eq. (1) is the cost of substituting some vertex/edge labels in CSS s. Since we may have multiple CSSs between q and g^c, the graph edit distance $ged(q, g^c)$ corresponds to a CSS that minimizes Eq. (1). According to Lemma 1, in order to compute the lower bound of $ged(q, g^c)$, we need to find the upper bound of $F(q, g^c)$ in Eq. (2).

Remarks. The work in [1] only presents the relationship between GED and CSS. As one of our technical contributions, we are the first to utilize the relationship to derive a novel lower bound so as to reduce the search space. Furthermore, we also extend the bound to handle uncertain graphs.

3.2 Finding Similar Graph Pairs: SimJ

As mentioned earlier, we obtain two graph datasets before the template generation. One is an uncertain graph dataset U derived from natural language questions, while the other one is a certain graph dataset D that collects all SPARQL query graphs in the workload. To provide promising hints for generating templates, we aim to find similar graph pairs $\langle q, g\rangle$, where $q \in D$ and $g \in U$. Since each graph $g \in U$ is uncertain, we need to consider the graph similarity measure in the uncertain graph model. Therefore, we propose a GED-based *similarity probability* as follows.

Definition 6. (Similarity Probability) Given a deterministic graph q, an uncertain graph g, and a graph edit distance threshold τ, we define the similarity probability, $SimP_\tau(q, g)$, between q and g as:

$$SimP_\tau(q,g) = \sum_{pw(g) \in PW(g)} Pr\{pw(g) | ged(q, pw(g)) \leq \tau\} \quad (3)$$

Formally, finding similar graph pairs by joining a deterministic graphs D and a set of uncertain graphs U (SimJ for short) is formulated as follows:

Definition 7. (Finding Similar Graph Pairs) Given a set of deterministic graphs D (derived from the SPARQL query workload), a set of uncertain graphs U (derived from natural language question workload), a graph edit distance threshold τ, and a similarity probability threshold $\alpha \in (0, 1]$, a *SimJ* query returns the graph pairs $\langle q, g\rangle$ ($q \in D$ and $g \in U$) with $SimP_\tau(q, g) \geq \alpha$, where the similarity probability $SimP_\tau(q, g)$ is given by Eq. (3).

Intuitively, in Def. 7, the *SimJ* query retrieves those graph pairs $\langle q, g\rangle$ such that g is within τ graph edit distance from q with high confidence.

Example 3. *We consider two graphs q_2 and g_1 in Figure 3. Let the GED threshold be $\tau = 4$. We add up the appearance probabilities of the possible worlds ($pw_1(g_1)$ and $pw_2(g_3)$) whose graph edit distances to q_1 are not larger than τ, that is, $SimP_\tau(q_2, g_1) = 0.42 + 0.18 = 0.6$.*

A straightforward solution to the *SimJ* problem is: performing a nested loop join algorithm over graph sets U and D. The graph pairs whose similarity probabilities are no less than the threshold are returned as final results.

Clearly, it is an inefficient solution since uncertain graphs may have an exponential number of possible worlds. Furthermore, it involves the time-consuming computation of GED. Therefore, we need to design effective and efficient approaches, which is challenging and non-trivial.

3.3 Framework for Finding Similar Graph Pairs

We propose a filtering-and-refinement framework for processing the *SimJ* problem efficiently.

Pruning Phase. We first prune the search space to avoid the expensive computation of $SimP_\tau(q, g)$ by two techniques.

1) *Structural Pruning*: Utilizing the CSS, we design a tighter lower bound for GED between graphs q and g (Section 4). If the lower bound is larger than the GED threshold τ, the graph pair $\langle q, g\rangle$ can be filtered out.

2) *Probabilistic Pruning*: We also deduce an upper bound for the similarity probability $SimP_\tau(q, g)$ (Section 5). We can prune the candidate graph pair whose upper bound is less than the similarity probability threshold α.

Refinement Phase. For those remaining uncertain graph candidates that cannot be pruned, we compute their exact similarity probabilities, and return actual *SimJ* answers.

4. COMMON STRUCTURAL SUBGRAPH-BASED PRUNING

We present a structural pruning strategy, namely CSS (Common Structural Subgraph)-based pruning. It prunes graph pairs that are definitely not similar to each other.

Pruning Heuristics. The function $SimP_\tau(q, g)$ (as given in Eq. (3)) sums up probabilities of all possible worlds, $pw(g)$, that satisfy $ged(q, pw(g)) \leq \tau$. Therefore, based on this definition, if the inequality above does not hold for any possible world $pw(g)$, then we have $SimP_\tau(q, g) = 0$, and the graph pair $\langle q, g\rangle$ can be safely pruned (since $0 \not\geq \alpha$).

Since there are an exponential number of possible worlds for uncertain graphs, it is not efficient to enumerate all possible worlds. Moreover, for each possible world $pw(g)$, the calculation of $ged(q, pw(g))$ in Eq. (3) is also very costly. Therefore, the basic idea of our solution is as follows. Given a deterministic graph q and an uncertain graph g, we propose a uniform lower bound for GED between q and each possible world of g. If the lower bound is larger than τ, it means that the GED between q and each possible world of g is larger than τ. Hence, $\langle q, g\rangle$ can be pruned safely.

Since our lower bound is based on the relationship between GED and common structural subgraph (see Section 3.1.3), the lower bound is called CSS-based lower bound. In the sequel, we first introduce CSS-based lower bound for certain graph and then extend it to the uncertain model.

4.1 Lower Bound for Certain Graph

Recall that Lemma 1 illustrates the relationship between GED and CSS. To obtain a lower bound of $ged(q, g^c)$, we can, instead, compute an upper bound, $ub\_F(q, g^c)$, of function $F(q, g^c)$ (as given in Eq. (2) of Lemma 1). Specifically, we use $\lambda_V(q, g^c)$ and $\lambda_E(q, g^c)$ to denote the common vertex/edge labels between q and g^c, i.e., $\lambda_V(q, g^c) = |\Sigma_V(q) \cap \Sigma_V(g^c)|$ and $\lambda_E(q, g^c) = |\Sigma_E(q) \cap \Sigma_E(g^c)|$, where $|\Sigma_V(\cdot)|$ and $|\Sigma_E(\cdot)|$ are the numbers of vertex or edge labels, respectively, in graphs. Due to the property of $\lambda_V(q, g^c)$ and $\lambda_E(q, g^c)$, we have the following inequalities about vertex/edge labels:

$$2 \cdot |V(s)| - |V_s| \leq |V(s)| + \lambda_V(q, g^c) \quad (4)$$

$$2 \cdot |E(s)| - |E_s| \leq |E(s)| + \lambda_E(q, g^c) \quad (5)$$

Intuitively, during the transformation from graph q to g^c, the number of vertex/edge labels that are not substituted is upper bounded by that of common vertex/edge labels between graphs q and g^c.

By substituting Eqs. (4) and (5) into Eq. (2), we can obtain the following inequality about function $F(\cdot,\cdot)$:

$$F(q,g^c) \le |V(s)| + \lambda_V(q,g^c) + |E(s)| + \lambda_E(q,g^c). \quad (6)$$

Thus, given two graphs q and g^c, in order to obtain an upper bound of $F(q,g^c)$, we need to derive the upper bound of $(|V(s)|+|E(s)|)$ for any CSS s, since $\lambda_V(q,g^c)$ and $\lambda_E(q,g^c)$ are constants (when q and g^c are given).

Lemma 2. *Given two certain graphs q and g^c, the maximum value of $(|V(s)|+|E(s)|)$ in Inequality (6) is achieved if and only if $|V(s)| = \min\{|V(q)|, |V(g^c)|\}$, where s is a CSS between q and g^c.*

PROOF. (proof by contradiction) According to the definition of CSS, we know $|V(s)| \le \min\{|V(q)|, |V(g^c)|\}$. Assume that $(|V(s)|+|E(s)|)$ is largest when $|V(s)| < \min\{|V(q)|, |V(g^c)|\}$. It means that $(V(q) - V(s)) \ne \phi$ and $(V(g^c) - V(s)) \ne \phi$. Therefore, we can arbitrarily introduce two vertices in $(V(q) - V(s))$ and $(V(g^c) - V(s))$, respectively, into the current CSS s to form another CSS s'. It means that we can obtain another CSS s' between q and g^c, where $|V(s')| + |E(s')| > |V(s)| + |E(s)|$. Obviously, it is contradicted to the assumption that $|V(s)| + |E(s)|$ is maximum. Therefore, Lemma 2 holds. □

Without loss of generality, we assume that $|V(q)| \le |V(g^c)|$. The above Lemma tells us that $(|V(s)| + |E(s)|)$ is maximum if and only if $|V(s)| = |V(q)|$, i.e, the CSS s covers all vertices in graph q. For simplicity of notations, let $|V(s)| = |V(q)| = m$ and $|V(g^c)| = n$ and $m \le n$. In order to estimate the upper bound of $(|V(s)|+|E(s)|)$, we should estimate the upper bound of $|E(s)|$ where $|V(s)| = |V(q)| = m$. We propose the following method. Readers can skip to Lemma 4 and Theorem 1 directly if they are not interested in the detailed derivation process.

Since s is a CSS between q and g^c, there must exist a subgraph q' in q, where q' is structurally graph isomorphic to s. Analogously, we can also find a subgraph $g^{c\prime}$ in g^c, where $g^{c\prime}$ is also structurally graph isomorphic to s. Since $|V(s)| = m$, thus both q' and $g^{c\prime}$ have m vertices, respectively. Assume that the m vertices in q' are u_1, ..., u_m and the m vertices in $g^{c\prime}$ are v_1, ..., v_m. It is easy to know q' is structurally graph isomorphic to $g^{c\prime}$. We assume that the graph isomorphism is defined under an injective function f from $\{u_1, ..., u_m\}$ to $\{v_1, ..., v_m\}$. A naive upper bound for $|E(s)|$ is $|E(s)| \le |E(q)|$. Obviously, this naive bound is not tight. Thus, we need to tighten the bound.

We need to delete some edges in q to form CSS s. To estimate the upper bound for $E(s)$, we need to delete as few edges as possible from q to form s. We utilize the degree differences between q and s to count how many edges that should be deleted. Let $d(u_1, q)$ denote the u_1's degree in graph q. $d(u_1, s)$ is the u_1's degree in CSS s. Deleting one edge in q affects two vertex degrees. Therefore, we need to delete $[\frac{d(u_1,q)-d(u_1,s)}{2}]$ edges to degrade $d(u_1, q)$ to $d(u_1, s)$. In a word, we have the following equation.

$$DelEdge = |E(q)| - |E(s)| = \sum_{i=1}^{i=m} \frac{d(u_i,q) - d(u_i,s)}{2}$$

where $DelEdge$ denotes the number of edges that should be deleted from q.

Now, in order to estimate the lower bound for $DelEdge$, we define an operator $\ominus$ as follows.

Definition 8. Given two integers a and b, a binary operator, denoted by $\ominus$, is defined as

$$a \ominus b = \begin{cases} a - b, & \text{if} \quad a > b, \\ 0, & \text{otherwise.} \end{cases} \quad (7)$$

Let $f(u_i)$ denote the mapping vertex in graph g^c under the injective function f. It is straightforward to know $d(u_i, s) \le d(f(u_i), g^c)$. Therefore, we have the following inequality.

$$DelEdge = |E(q)| - |E(s)| = \sum_{i=1}^{i=m} \frac{d(u_i,q)-d(u_i,s)}{2}$$
$$\ge \sum_{i=1}^{i=m} \frac{d(u_i,q) \ominus d(f(u_i),g^c)}{2} \quad (8)$$

According to Eq. (8), we need to estimate the lower bound of $\sum_{i=1}^{i=m} \frac{d(u_i,q)\ominus d(f(u_i),g^c)}{2}$. Fortunately, Lemma 3 holds.

Without loss of generality, assuming $m \le n$, we define the *degree distance*, $dif(q, g^c)$, of q and g^c as follows.

Definition 9. (Degree Distance) Given two certain graphs q and g^c with sorted degree sets in non-increasing order, i.e., $d(u_1, q) \ge ... \ge d(u_m, q)$ and $d(v_1, g^c) \ge ... \ge d(v_n, g^c)$. The degree distance between q and g^c, denoted by $dif(q, g^c)$, is:

$$dif(q,g^c) = \sum_{i=1}^{m} (d(u_i,q) \ominus d(v_i,g^c)) \quad (9)$$

Lemma 3. *Let us consider two certain graphs q and g^c with m and n vertices, $m \le n$. For any injective function f from m vertices $\{u_1, ..., u_m\}$ in q to n vertices $\{v_1, ..., v_n\}$ in g^c, the following inequality holds.*

$$\sum_{i=1}^{i=m} \frac{d(u_i,q) \ominus d(f(u_i),g^c)}{2} \ge \frac{dif(q,g^c)}{2} \quad (10)$$

PROOF. The proof can be achieved by induction. For details, please refer to Appendix A. □

Lemma 4. *Let us consider two certain graphs q and g^c with m and n vertices, $m \le n$. s is a CSS between q and g^c and $|V(s)| = |V(q)|$. The upper bound of $|E(s)|$ is as follows.*

$$|E(s)| \le |E(q)| - \frac{dif(q,g^c)}{2} \quad (11)$$

where $dif(q, g^c)$ is defined in Def. 9.

PROOF. According to Eqs. (8), (9) and (10), we have:

$$DelEdge = |E(q)| - |E(s)| \ge \frac{dif(q,g^c)}{2}$$

Finally, we derive the upper bound for $E(s)$. □

THEOREM 1. (CSS-Based Lower Bound of Graph Edit Distance for Certain Graphs) *Let us consider two certain graphs q and g^c. Without loss of generality, assume that $|V(q)| \le |V(g^c)|$. The lower bound for graph edit distance between q and g^c is:*

$$ged(q,g^c) \ge lb\_ged_{CSS}(q,g^c)$$
$$= |V(g^c)| + |E(g^c)| - \lambda_E(q,g^c) + \frac{dif(q,g^c)}{2} - \lambda_V(q,g^c) \quad (12)$$

where $dif(q, g^c)$ is defined in Eq. (9).

PROOF. According to Lemma 2 and Eqs. (6) and (11),

$$F(q,g^c) \le |V(s)| + \lambda_V(q,g^c) + |E(s)| + \lambda_E(q,g^c)$$
$$\le |V(q)| + \lambda_V(q,g^c) + |E(q)| - \frac{dif(q,g^c)}{2} + \lambda_E(q,g^c),$$

Thus, based on Eq. (1) we obtain the following inequality $ged(q, g^c) \ge |V(g^c)| + |E(g^c)| - \lambda_E(q, g^c) + \frac{dif(q,g^c)}{2} - \lambda_V(q, g^c)$. □

Pruning Effect Analysis of CSS-Based Lower Bound. Our CSS-based bound falls into the first category, namely, "global filter". Please refer to our discussion about global filters in the related work section (Section 8). More importantly, our CSS-based lower bound is proven to be tighter than the two existing ones in [29] and [31]. Note that, we only need to compare our lower bound with the label-multiset-based lower bound in [31], denoted as $lb\_ged_{LM}(q, g^c)$, since [31] has proven that $lb\_ged_{LM}(q, g^c)$ is tighter than the vertex/edge number-based lower bound in [29].

THEOREM 2. *Given two certain graphs q and g^c, it holds that*

$$lb\_ged_{CSS}(q, g^c) \geq lb\_ged_{LM}(q, g^c),$$

where $lb\_ged_{LM}(q, g^c) = \max\{|V(q)|, |V(g^c)|\} - \lambda_V(q, g^c) + \max\{|E(q)|, |E(g^c)|\} - \lambda_E(q, g^c)$.

PROOF. For details, please refer to Appendix B. □

4.2 Lower Bound for Uncertain Graphs

In this section, we discuss how to compute a lower bound for GED between graph q and uncertain graph g. Let us recall $lb\_ged_{CSS}(q, g^c)$ in Theorem 1. If we utilize Eq. (12) to compute the bound for uncertain graph g, all elements in Eq. (12) are constants except for $\lambda_V(q, g^c)$. Therefore, the only remaining issue is to compute an upper bound of $\lambda_V(q, g^c)$ for all possible worlds g^c of uncertain graph g.

Definition 10. (Vertex Label Bipartite Graph) Given a certain graph q and an uncertain graph g, we can construct a vertex label bipartite graph $G_b = (V(g), V(q))$. There is an edge between $v_i (\in V(g))$ and $u_j (\in V(q))$ iff $l(u_j) \in l(v_i)$.

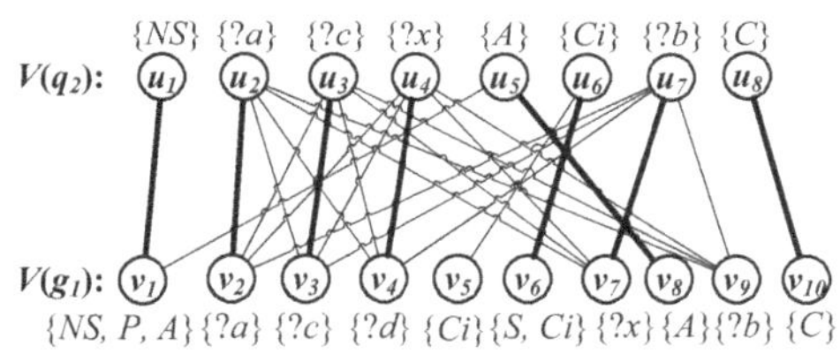

Figure 8: Vertex label bipartite graph of g_1 and q_2

Figure 8 shows an example of a vertex label bipartite graph of q_2 and g_1. Since $\lambda_V(q, g) \leq \max_{g^c \in PW(g)} \{\lambda_V(q, g^c)\}$, we need to estimate the maximum value for $\lambda_V(q, g^c)$ in all possible worlds g^c of uncertain graph g. We can reduce the problem of estimating the maximum value for $\lambda_V(q, g^c)$ to the maximum matching problem. A maximum matching is exactly to identify the largest set of non-adjacent matching edges, which can be solved by a classic algorithm, e.g., *Hungarian algorithm* [10].

The upper bound for $\lambda_V(q, g)$ equals to the number of matching edges in the maximum matching. According to the above analysis, we have the following theorem.

THEOREM 3. *(CSS-Based Lower Bound of Graph Edit Distance for Uncertain Graphs) Let us consider a certain graph q and an uncertain graph g. The CSS-based lower bound, $lb\_ged_{CSS}(q, g)$, of graph edit distance $ged(q, g)$ is given by:*

$$\begin{aligned} ged(q, g) &\geq lb\_ged_{CSS}(q, g) \\ &= |V| + |E| - \lambda_E(q, g) + \frac{dif(q, g)}{2} - \lambda_V(q, g), \end{aligned} \tag{13}$$

where $|V| = \max\{|V(g)|, |V(q)|\}$, $|E|$ is the number of edges in graph q or g with more vertices, $\lambda_E(q, g) = |\sum_E(q) \cap \sum_E(g)|$, $dif(q, g)$ is defined in Eq. (9) and $\lambda_V(q, g)$ is the size of the maximal matching in vertex label bipartite graph.

5. PROBABILISTIC PRUNING

The basic idea of probabilistic pruning is: utilizing the similarity probability threshold to filter out false alarms. Specifically, the intuition is to prune those graph pairs $\langle q, g \rangle$ with low similarity probabilities (i.e., $SimP_\tau(q, g) < \alpha$).

By replacing graph edit distance $ged(q, pw(g))$ (given in Eq. (3)) with the CSS-based lower bound $lb\_ged_{CSS}(q, pw(g))$ (Theorem 3), we obtain an upper bound of $SimP_\tau(q, g)$ under possible world semantics. That is, we have:

$$SimP_\tau(q, g) \leq \sum_{pw(g) \in PW(g)} Pr\{pw(g) | lb\_ged_{CSS}(q, pw(g)) \leq \tau\}. \tag{14}$$

Let $C(q, g)$ be $|V| + |E| - \lambda_E(q, g) + \frac{dif(q, g)}{2}$, which is a constant (given q and g). By substituting $C(q, g)$ into Eq. (14), we can rewrite Eq. (14) as:

$$\begin{aligned} SimP_\tau(q, g) &\leq \sum_{pw(g) \in PW(g)} Pr\{pw(g) | \lambda_V(q, pw(g)) \geq C(q, g) - \tau\} \\ &= Pr\{\lambda_V(q, g) \geq C(q, g) - \tau\}. \end{aligned} \tag{15}$$

The Rewriting of Probability Upper Bound. Next, the only remaining issue is how to compute the upper bound of $SimP_\tau(q, g)$ in Inequality (15). Intuitively, $\lambda_V(q, g)$ in Inequality (15) is the number of common vertex label pairs between graphs q and g. In other words, we can define a mapping from $V(g)$ to $V(q)$, and count the number of matching vertex labels.

Without loss of generality, we assume that graph g has m vertices, which correspond to m variables $x_1, x_2, \ldots$, and x_m, respectively. Each variable x_i has the value domain $\{0, 1\}$. If a vertex $v_i \in V(g)$ has a matching with $u_j \in V(q)$ such that $l(v_i) = l(u_j)$, then variable x_i (w.r.t. vertex v_i) is set to 1, otherwise x_i is set to 0. As a result, we can prove that the RHS of Inequality (15) is equivalent to: $Pr\{\sum_{i=1}^m x_i \geq C(q, g) - \tau\}$. Specifically, we have the following lemma.

Lemma 5. *Given a deterministic graph q and an uncertain graph g, it holds that: $SimP_\tau(q, g) \leq Pr\{\sum_{i=1}^m x_i \geq C(q, g) - \tau\}$.*

Note that, in a matching each vertex in q can be only matched with one vertex in g at most. It indicates that variables x_i take different values in different possible worlds $pw(g)$, and sometimes they might be correlated with each other. Thus, we will further relax this probability upper bound in Lemma 5, by using independent variables directly.

To reduce the computation cost w.r.t. correlated variable x_i, we introduce new variable y_i for each vertex $v_i \in V(g)$ to further relax the probability upper bound in Lemma 5. Specifically, similar to variables x_i, we also assume that $y_i = 1$, if $l(v_i) = l(u_j)$. The difference is that each vertex u_j can be used more than one time (i.e., matching with more than one vertices in $V(g)$). In this case, we know that it always holds that $y_i \geq x_i$. Thus, we obtain the following lemma.

Lemma 6. *Given a graph q and an uncertain graph g, it holds that: $Pr\{\sum_{i=1}^m x_i \geq C(q, g) - \tau\} \leq Pr\{\sum_{i=1}^m y_i \geq C(q, g) - \tau\}$.*

Furthermore, our newly defined m variables $y_1, y_2, \ldots$, and y_m are independent. Therefore, we denote $(y_1 + y_2 + \ldots + y_m)$ as a single random variable Y. By applying the Markov's inequality [5], we derive an upper bound as follows:

THEOREM 4. *(Probabilistic Upper Bound for Similarity Probability) Let us consider a deterministic graph q and an uncertain graph g. The upper bound for $SimP_\tau(q,g)$ is given as follows.*

$$SimP_\tau(q,g) \le ub\_SimP_\tau(q,g) = \frac{E(Y)}{C(q,g)-\tau} \quad (16)$$

where $E(Y) = \sum_{i=1}^{m} E(y_i)$ *and* $E(y_i) = \Sigma_{l_j \in l(v_i)} Pr(l_j | l_j \cap \Sigma_V(q) \neq \emptyset)$ *and* $C(q,g) = |V| + |E| - \lambda_E(q,g) + \frac{dif(q,g)}{2}$, *and* $|V|$, $|E|$, $\lambda_E(q,g)$ *and* $dif(q,g)$ *are defined in Theorem 3.*

PROOF. According to Lemmas 5 and 6, we have $SimP_\tau(q,g) \le Pr\{\sum_{i=1}^{m} y_i \ge C(q,g) - \tau\}$. Let us denote $(y_1 + y_2 + \ldots + y_m)$ as a single random variable Y. Thus, $SimP_\tau(q,g) \le Pr\{Y \ge C(q,g) - \tau\}$. Based on the Markov's inequality [5], we obtain $SimP_\tau(q,g) \le \frac{E(Y)}{C(q,g)-\tau}$. □

Example 4. *Assume that $\tau = 4$ and $\alpha = 0.6$. Considering the deterministic graph q_1 and uncertain graph g_1 in Figure 3, $E(Y) = \sum_{i=1}^{10} E(y_i) = 5$. According to Eq. (16), we have $ub\_SimP_\tau(q_1, g_1) = 5/13 \approx 0.38 < 0.6$. Thus, we prune the graph pair $\langle q_1, g_1 \rangle$ safely.*

We also consider correlations among variables x_i directly and derive tight upper bounds by the law of total probability [5]. Due to space limit, we have to put it in our future work.

6. SIMJ QUERY PROCESSING

We first present how to conduct *SimJ* processing. Then, we propose a cost-based query optimization technique, which divides possible worlds of uncertain graphs into fine-grained groups and thus attains higher pruning power.

6.1 SimJ Procedure

Algorithm 1 (please refer to Appendix D) presents the procedure of our *SimJ* processing approach. For each pair of graphs, we will first compute the lower bound $lb\_ged_{CSS}(q,g)$ of GED via Theorem 3 (line 3). If $lb\_ged_{CSS}(q,g)$ is larger than τ, the graph pair $\langle q,g \rangle$ can be pruned safely; otherwise, we compute the upper bound of the similarity probability by Theorem 4 (line 5). If the probability upper bound is smaller than α, then we can safely filter out the graph pair $\langle q,g \rangle$; otherwise, we need to conduct the verification (lines 6-15). Regarding the computation of GED between two certain graphs for the refinement (as given in Eq. (3)), any existing method, such as [17], can be adopted.

We give the time complexity of Algorithm 1. For more details please refer to Appendix D.

6.2 Cost-Based Query Optimization

In order to improve the pruning power, we propose to divide all possible worlds of an uncertain graph g into disjoint possible world groups (denoted as PWG_i). Each PWG_i contains fewer possible worlds. Thus, we can obtain tighter lower/upper bounds of the graph edit distance and similarity probability. Algorithm 2 (in Appendix E) gives the details.

Specifically, the uncertain graph g is divided into k possible world groups $PWG_1, \ldots, PWG_k$. Each lower bound $lb\_ged_{CSS}(q, PWG_i)$ is computed according to Theorem 3. The groups satisfying the inequality $lb\_ged_{CSS}(q, PWG_i) > \tau$ can be pruned. Then, we can sum up upper bounds, $ub\_SimP_\tau(q, PWG_i)$, of similarity probabilities for the remaining groups, which can be used for probabilistic pruning.

Partitioning Strategy. Given an uncertain graph g, we can partition g into different possible world groups, which may lead to different bounds for the pruning. Hence, a challenging problem arises, that is, how to partition possible worlds of g so that we can gain a tighter lower bound.

Process of Partitioning Possible Worlds. Our partitioning strategy starts with one group, and then recursively selects one group to split into two groups, until the number of groups reaches a predefined threshold. Here, we will select a group with the smallest lower bounds of graph edit distance and/or the one with the largest upper bound of similarity probability. Intuitively, such a group incurs low pruning power, and thus needs to be further partitioned to improve the pruning power.

Dividing a Possible World Group into Two Groups. Next, we discuss how to partition a possible world group, PWG_i, into two groups by splitting uncertain labels of a selected vertex, which is based on the two observations below. First, according to Theorem 3, it is intuitive that the less uncertainties g contains, the tighter the lower bound $lb\_ged_{CSS}(q,g)$ is. Second, as mentioned in Section 5, if the number of possible labels that a vertex contains is small and $P(x_i = 1 | L(v_i) = l)$ is small, the probability $P(x_i = 1)$ is small.

From observations above, we have the following two principles to select a vertex (in PWG_i) to split uncertain labels, and divide PWG_i into two groups.

- Select a vertex with high (total) existence probabilities of uncertain labels in PWG_i to split;
- Select a vertex with more possible labels to split.

We only need to sum up $ub\_SimP_\tau(q, PWG_i)$ for groups whose GED lower bounds are no larger than τ, and minimize the summation to obtain tighter similarity probability upper bounds.

Cost Model for Evaluating the Partitioning. We present a cost model to evaluate our grouping results:
$\arg\min\{ub\_SimP_\tau(q, PWG_i) | lb\_ged_{CSS}(q, PWG_i) \le \tau\}$.

With the heuristics/principles above, we can obtain different partitioning strategies, which are evaluated by our cost model. We select one partitioning strategy that minimizes the proposed metric (provided by our cost model).

7. EXPERIMENTAL RESULTS

7.1 Experiment Setting

7.1.1 Datasets

Real Dataset 1. QALD-3[5]: A benchmark delivered in the third evaluation campaigns on question answering over linked data. It contains 200 natural language questions, each of which has the corresponding SPARQL query.

Real Dataset 2. WebQuestions+DBpedia SPARQL: WebQuestions[6] is an open dataset created by Berant et al. It contains 5,810 natural language questions, denoted by *WebQ*. DBpedia SPARQL[7] is a set of SPARQL query logs which are actually posed queries against the DBpedia knowledge base. We randomly select 73,000 SPARQL queries from the whole dataset and create the deterministic graphs.

For natural language questions, we generate its corresponding uncertain graphs, denoted by U, utilizing the method

[5]http://greententacle.techfak.uni-bielefeld.de/~cunger/qald/index.php?x=home&q=3
[6]http://www-nlp.stanford.edu/software/sempre/
[7]http://aksw.org/Projects/DBPSB.html

Table 2: Statistics of Data sets

Dataset	$\|U\|$	avg.$\|V\|$	avg.$\|E\|$	avg.$\|L_V\|$	$\|D\|$
QALD3	200	5.73	4.51	4.50	200
WebQ	5,810	6.15	5.14	4.39	73,057
ER	100,000	64.86	157.07	9.39	100,000
SF	100,000	63.35	88.61	13.52	100,000
MM	23,250	5.35	4.92	4.21	2,500

introduced in Section 2.1. Regarding the SPARQL queries, we build their deterministic graphs, denoted by D.

Real Dataset 3. MM Workloads[8]**:** It contains both NLQ workloads and SPARQL query workloads, which are based on a closed domain, i.e., music and movies.

Furthermore, in order to evaluate efficiency of our SimJ algorithm, we construct two synthetic datasets as follows.

Synthetic Datasets. ER and **SF:** For the ER model, we randomly connect M pairs of vertices as edges in the graph; for the SF model, we use a graph generator *gengraph win*[9] to generate graphs whose vertex degrees, d, satisfy the power law distribution. We generate two sets of deterministic graphs for ER and SF, respectively. Table 2 lists statistics of all datasets used in the experiments.

7.1.2 *Evaluation Measures*

Metrics. We adopt several metrics for the evaluation: (1) Correct Answers ($|C|$), the number of the returned correct graph pairs[10]; (2) *Precision* (p), as $p = \frac{|C|}{|R|}$, where R is the set of returned answers for all questions; (3) *Response Time*, the time cost of filtering out false alarms and refining; (4) *Candidate Ratio*, the number of candidate graph pairs (after pruning) divided by $|U| \times |D|$. (5) Matching Proportion ϕ, which is defined as follows:

$$\phi = \frac{|\text{words covered by template P}|}{|\text{words in the whole question NLQ}|}$$

Correct answers: Consider a returned pair $\langle q, n \rangle$, where q is a SPARQL query and n is a natural language question. For natural language question n, we manually issue the corresponding SPARQL query q'. If q matches q' except for entity phrases, we regard that the returned pair is correct; otherwise, it is wrong. 10 students helped evaluate the results returned by our algorithm.

Setup. All experiments are conducted on a Windows 7 PC with a 2.9GHz Pentium IV CPU and 4GB main memory. All programs were implemented in C++.

7.2 Effectiveness Evaluation

Effect of GED threshold τ. To guarantee the quality of answers, the GED theshold τ is varied from 0 to 2. The similarity probability threshold α is fixed to be 0.9. When $\tau = 0$, the precisions over QALD-3 query log and WebQ are both 100%. It means that all the graph pairs delivered are correct, i.e., the corresponding natural language question and the SPARQL query has the same query intention. However, the number of answers is limited, i.e., 3 and 55, respectively. When $\tau = 1$, the correct answers are more enough with only a small sacrifice of the precisions.

In summary, as shown in Table 3, the precision becomes low with the growth of τ. But the number of correct answers grows with the increasing of τ. That is because smaller τ restricts the difference between two graphs. If τ becomes larger, some noises may be introduced, that is, some unrevelent graph pairs will be returned.

[8]a dataset acquired from a search engine company

[9]http://fabien.viger.free.fr/liafa/generation/

[10]Since it is hard to compute the recall, we utilize $|C|$ to measure the coverage of our method.

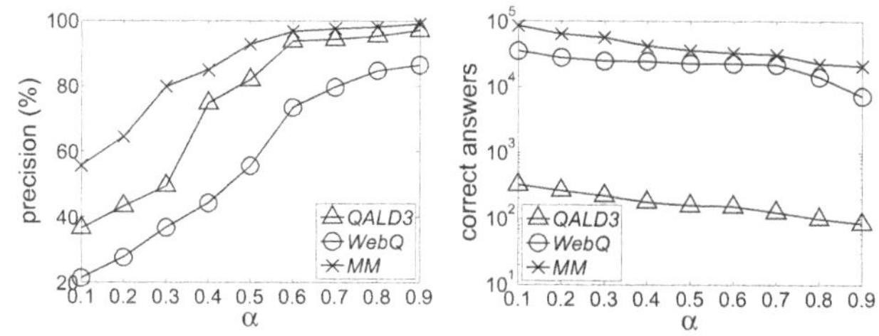

(a) Precision *vs.* α (b) Correct answers *vs.* α

Figure 9: Effect of similarity probability threshold α

Table 3: Effect of GED threshold τ

	QALD-3 Query Log			WebQ		
τ	$\|R\|$	precision	time(s)	$\|R\|$	precision	time(s)
0	3	100%	1.453	55	100%	76.851
1	86	97.67%	1.862	8,351	86.54%	100.316
2	2,421	52.33%	2.113	179,227	37.69%	652.947

Effect of Similarity Probability Threshold α. We fix the GED threshold τ to be 1, and vary the similarity probability threshold α from 0.1 to 0.9. Figure 9 shows the effect of α on $|C|$ and precision over real datasets. The precision grows with the increasing of α. It is reasonable that high probability threshold filters out the low-quality graph pairs. For example, when α is 0.7, the precision achieves 80%. Meanwhile, the number of correct answers decreases when α is larger as depicted in Figure 9(b).

The precision on MM dataset is better than that on QALD-3 and WeQ datasets. It is because that MM dataset is based on a knowledge graph of specific type (music and movies), which indicates that both natural language questions and SPARQL queries focus on similar topics.

Case Study. We provide a case study over the experiment "QALD-3 + DBpedia" (using QALD-3 questions and DBpedia queries) in Figure 10. *SimJ* identifies meaningful results of high quality. As an example, for the question "Give me all movies directed by Francis Ford Coppola", we find the SPARQL "SELECT ?film where $\{\langle ?film\ type\ Film \rangle\ \langle ?film\ director\ Joel\_Schumache \}$". Note that, the returned graph pairs do not necessarily ask the same question. The key is that we can build templates based on these graph pairs. Using the method discussed in step 3 of Section 2.1, we can obtain the templates. The corresponding templates are shown in Figure 16 (please refer to Appendix F). We also provide the analysis of the results in Appendix F.1.

To evaluate the quality of the generated templates, we use the questions of QALD to test the effectiveness. We translate the questions into SPARQL queries utilizing these generated templates, and then search these SPARQL queries over DBpedia. The precision and recall of our method are both 0.65 and outperform the competitors significantly. We include the details in Appendix F.2.

What is the ruling party in Lisbon?	SELECT ?uri WHERE { Germany type Country. Germany leaderParty ?uri. }
Give me all movies directed by Francis Ford Coppola	SELECT ?film WHERE { ?film type Film. ?film director Joel_Schumache. }
Which software has been developed by organizations founded in California?	SELECT ?product WHERE { ?company type Organisation. ?company foundationPlace Bangalore. ?product developer ?company. ?product type Software. }

Figure 10: Case study over DBpedia+QALD-3

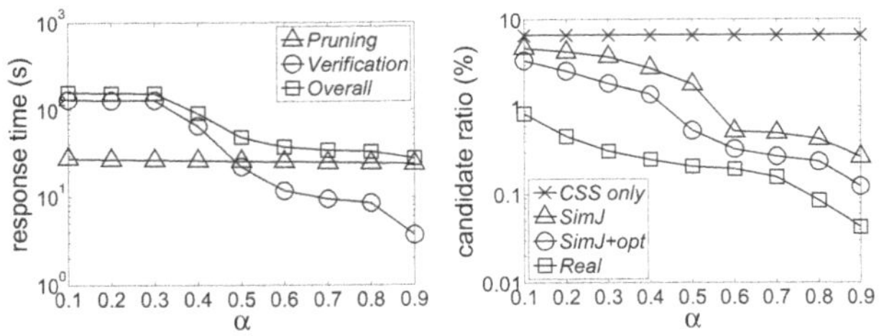

(a) Response time *vs.* α (b) Candidate ratio *vs.* α

Figure 11: Effect of threshold α (WebQ)

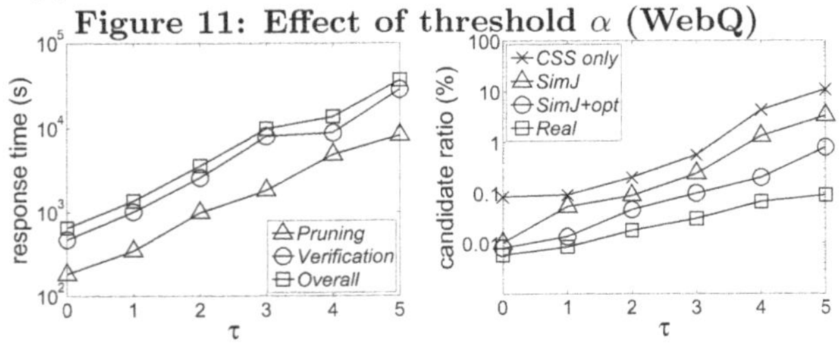

(a) Response time *vs.* τ (b) Candidate ratio *vs.* τ

Figure 12: Effect of GED Threshold τ (ER)

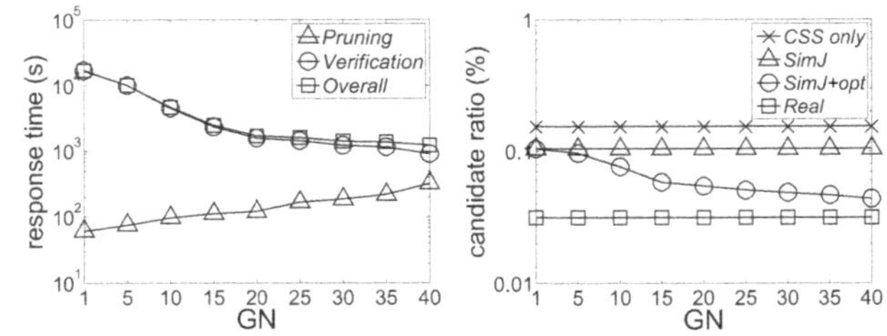

(a) Response time *vs.* GN (b) Candidate ratio *vs.* GN

Figure 13: Effect of group number GN (SF)

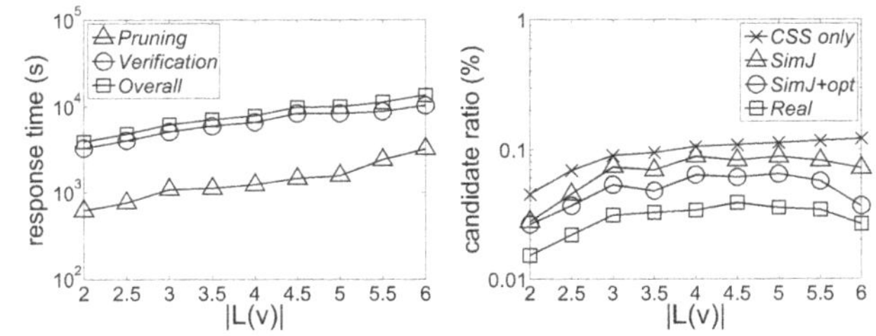

(a) Response time *vs.* $|L(v)|$ (b)Candidateratio *vs.* $|L(v)|$

Figure 14: Effect of $|L(v)|$ (ER)

7.3 Efficiency Evaluation

In order to evaluate the efficiency of our method, we test three *SimJ* answering techniques: the "CSS only" approach applies the CSS-based pruning method (without using the probabilistic pruning); the "*SimJ*" approach uses CSS-based and probabilistic pruning methods; the "*SimJ*+opt" approach employs the cost-based optimization by dividing possible worlds into groups to enhance the pruning power.

Effect of Similarity Probability Threshold α. We study the effect of α over the performance by varying similarity probability thresholds α from 0.1 to 0.9. As presented in Figure 11(a), the threshold has little impact on the pruning time. When α is larger, the candidates will become less. Therefore the overall time consumed decreases. As depicted in Figure 11(b), employing the optimization technique, the pruning power of the "*SimJ+opt*" is higher than "*SimJ*". Note that, the similarity threshold has no impact on the pruning ability of "CSS only".

Effect of Graph Edit Distance Threshold τ. Next, we vary GED thresholds τ from 0 to 5. Figure 12(a) shows the response time including pruning time and verification time. The overall response time grows with the increasing of τ, since large τ will result in more returned answers, as demonstrated in Figure 12(b). Notice that "*SimJ*" adopts the probability pruning in addition to the CSS-based pruning. Therefore, "*SimJ*" incurs fewer candidates, which can greatly reduce the refinement cost. Furthermore, the "*SimJ*+opt" approach considers the pruning with multiple possible world groups (rather than 1 group in "*SimJ*"), so that we can obtain tighter probability upper bound and thus enhance the pruning power. Thus, "*SimJ*+opt" has fewer candidates than "*SimJ*". When τ becomes larger, the improvement degrades slightly since larger τ decreases the upper bound of similarity probability as shown in Eq. 16.

7.4 Scalability Evaluation

Effect of Group Number GN. Here, we study the effect of group number, GN, which is varied from 1 to 40 stepped by 5. As shown in Figure 13(a), the time consumed by "*SimJ+opt*" grows with the increasing of GN. Clearly, the more groups we generate, the more filtering time we may need in the join processing. Meanwhile, the uncertain information in each group will be less, which is beneficial to filtering out more false alarms as confirmed in Figure 13(b). As expected, the group number has no impact on "*SimJ*" and "CSS only" approaches.

Effect of the Number of Possible Labels $|L(v)|$. For a specific data set, we average the number of possible labels, and vary this number from 2 to 6. Figs. 14(a) and 14(b) report the response time and pruning power, respectively. The response time increases as $|L(v)|$ increases, because "*SimJ*" invokes computing the upper bound of the maximum matching in a bipartite graph. Moreover, the more uncertain labels g contains, the larger the bipartite graph may be. Thus, more time will be consumed. The pruning ability decreases when $|L(v)|$ becomes larger as shown in Figure 14(b). Note that, the pruning powers of "*SimJ*" and "*SimJ+opt*" become higher when $|L(v)|$ is larger than 5. The reason is that although there are more uncertain labels incident to each vertex, the existence probability of each uncertain label is smaller, which favors the computation of the similarity probability upper bound.

Comparisons With Existing Works. To confirm the performance of our CSS-based method, we compare it with existing algorithms that are devised for deterministic graphs. As discussed in Theorem 2, our CSS-based lower bound has been proven to be tighter than the two existing global filters. Regarding these outstanding algorithms proposed recently, i.e., path [31], SEGOS [22], and Pars [30], in order to handle uncertain graphs, they must enumerate all possible worlds or ignore vertex labels. It is impractical for the first case due to the exponential number of possible worlds. Thus, we implement these methods by only considering the graph structure to handle uncertain graphs. Figs. 15(a) and 15(b) show the filtering time and candidate ratio *vs.* GED threshold τ, respectively, for the comparison.

Clearly, the computation of the CSS approach is the most efficient, and it outperforms its competitors greatly in terms of filtering time. More importantly, as shown in Figure 15(b) our proposed GED lower bound, $lb\_ged_{CSS}(q, g)$, has the highest pruning power compared to other competitors.

8. RELATED WORK

8.1 Question/Answering (Q/A) over RDF

RDF Q/A systems have attracted extensive attentions in both NLP (natural language processing) [19, 23, 20] and DB (database) communities [24, 33].

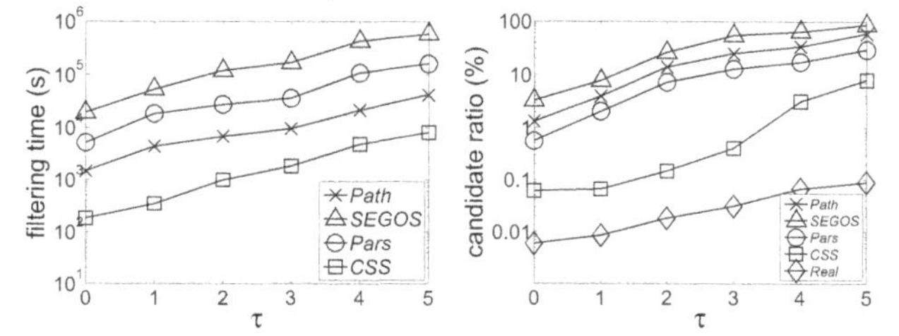

(a) Filtering time *vs.* τ (b) Candidate ratio *vs.* τ

Figure 15: Comparison with Existing Works (AIDS)

To solve the problem of RDF Q/A, templates are widely used [19, 20]. In the well-known True Knowledge Q/A system, a natural language question is turned into a structural query using some manually defined templates [19]. The templates used in this system are manually defined in the offline phase. It is expensive to pre-define all the templates especially for the open-domain RDF knowledge graphs. The authors in [20] propose a template-based method to answer the aggregate-like questions. They parese the questions to SPARQL templates, and instantiate the templates by entity/predicate mapping [20]. To the best of our knowledge, none of existing work study how to generate templates automatically for RDF Q/A. We are the first to propose a join-based approach for building templates automatically.

There are also some work that do not utilize templates, such as DEANNA [23] and gAnswer [33]. DEANNA [23] builds a disambiguation graph and reduces disambiguation as an integer linear programming problem. gAnswer translates a natural language question into a semantic query graph Q^S and tries to find the top-k matches over RDF graph with the highest confidence probabilities. Fader et al. [7] introduce a machine learning approach to answer factual questions. However, they only focus on single-relation queries. Yao et al. [25] associates question features with answer patterns described by Freebase to answer natural language questions.

Note that, although we adopt the method in gAnswer to generate the semantic query graph Q^S for each natural language question, we address the different issue. In this paper, we study how to build high-quality templates for RDF Q/A. These templates can be used in the template-based RDF Q/A systems.

8.2 Graph Edit Distance

Recently, edit distance-based graph similarity search has been well studied in certain graphs. Since it is an NP-hard problem to compute GED, lots of lower bounds have been proposed to speed up computation. They are categorized into *global filters*, *n-gram filters*, and *partition-based filters*.

1. global filter. There are two existing global filters. The first one is to compute the differences of vertex number and edge number as the lower bound [29]. The second one is the difference of vertex labels and edge labels [31].

2. n-gram filter. The basic idea is to represent a graph as a set of small-size substructures (called n-grams), such as *c-star* in [29], *k-Adjacent Tree* in [21] and *paths* in [31]. The intuition lies in that the two graphs must share lots of common n-grams if they are similar to each other (i.e., their graph edit distances are less than a threshold).

Although experiment results in existing work [29, 21, 31] show that n-gram filters are better than the two global filters in some real graph datasets, their superiorities over global filters cannot be proven theoretically. Furthermore, it is easy to find some cases that the global filters can beat these n-gram methods. However, we can prove that our filter can beat the two existing global filters from a theoretical perspective (See Theorem 2).

3. Partition-based filter. Pars [30] proposes a partition-based method. It main idea is to decompose data graphs into non-overlapping partitions, and compute the lower bound according to the number of mismatchings of these partitions.

Note that, all of these filters are proposed for certain graphs. It is not easy to extend them to uncertain scenarios. One of the technical contributions in this work is to propose a tight lower bound for GED in uncertain graphs.

The most widely used method computes exact graph edit distance based on A^* algorithm incorporating heuristics [17]. It explores the space of all possible vertex mappings between two graphs to find the optimal mapping. Zhao et al. [31] improve A^* with two heuristics. Specifically, exploiting minimum edit filtering and local label filtering to give a heuristic estimate of the distance from the current state to the goal. Note that our work focuses on the filtering phase, which are independent of the verification algorithms.

8.3 Uncertain Graph Management

Managing and mining uncertain graphs have attracted extensive attentions due to noises and inaccuracies. For example, Zou et al. study the problem of frequent subgraph mining on uncertain graphs under probabilistic semantics [35]. Kollios et al. use expected edit distance , which is extended from edit distance based graph clustering, to probabilistic graphs [14]. There are two existing work [27, 28] investigate subgraph search over uncertain graphs. However, their uncertain graph models do not measure the uncertainty of labels as does in our uncertain graph model (Def. 2). Beyond that, the work [27] proposes the similarity model based on maximum common subgraph, not the edit distance that is studied in this paper. There are some previous works [11, 12] that study probabilistic XML data. In contrast, we focus on general uncertain graph data in this paper (instead of tree structure).

9. CONCLUSIONS

To build templates for RDF Q/A, we propose a novel approach, i.e., performing graph similarity join over large uncertain graphs under the constraint of graph edit distance. Following the filtering-and-verification paradigm, we propose Common Structural Subgraph (CSS)-based pruning and probabilistic pruning to filter out as many false alarms as possible. In order to improve the pruning ability, we divide each uncertain graph to a number of groups based on a cost model. Extensive experiments over real and synthetic datasets have confirmed the effectiveness and efficiency of our solution.

Acknowledgments. This work was supported by 863 project (2015AA015402), NSFC funding (61370055,61202008, 61272344), the RGC of Hong Kong SAR (No. CUHK 418512) and UTPA Start Up Fund (No. 21ENCS018 - ENCS Enhancements). Authors are also grateful to anonymous reviewers for their constructive comments. This work was partially done (i.e., the uncertain technique part) when the first author was as a visiting student in UTPA. Lei Zou is the corresponding author of this work.

APPENDIX

A. REFERENCES

[1] L. Brun, B. Gaüzère, and S. Fourey. Relationships between graph edit distance and maximal common structural subgraph. In *SSPR/SPR*, pages 42–50, 2012.

[2] J. J. Carroll, I. Dickinson, C. Dollin, D. Reynolds, A. Seaborne, and K. Wilkinson. Jena: implementing the semantic web recommendations. In *WWW*, pages 74–83, 2004.

[3] N. N. Dalvi and D. Suciu. Efficient query evaluation on probabilistic databases. *VLDB J.*, 16(4), 2007.

[4] M. Dredze, P. McNamee, D. Rao, A. Gerber, and T. Finin. Entity disambiguation for knowledge base population. In *COLING*, pages 277–285, 2010.

[5] R. Durrett. *Probability: Theory and Examples.* Cambridge University Press, 2010.

[6] J. Eisner. Learning non-isomorphic tree mappings for machine translation. In *ACL*, pages 205–208, 2003.

[7] A. Fader, L. S. Zettlemoyer, and O. Etzioni. Paraphrase-driven learning for open question answering. In *ACL*, pages 1608–1618, 2013.

[8] X. Gao, B. Xiao, D. Tao, and X. Li. A survey of graph edit distance. *Pattern Anal. Appl.*, 13(1):113–129, 2010.

[9] M. Heilman and N. A. Smith. Tree edit models for recognizing textual entailments, paraphrases, and answers to questions. In *NAACL*, pages 1011–1019, 2010.

[10] H.W.Kuhn. The hungarian method for the assignment problem. In *Naval Research Logistics*, pages 83–97, 1955.

[11] B. Kimelfeld, Y. Kosharovsky, and Y. Sagiv. Query efficiency in probabilistic xml models. In *SIGMOD*, pages 701–714, 2008.

[12] B. Kimelfeld and P. Senellart. Probabilistic xml: Models and complexity. In *Advances in Probabilistic Databases for Uncertain Information Management*, pages 39–66. 2013.

[13] D. Klein and C. D. Manning. Accurate unlexicalized parsing. In *ACL*, pages 423–430, 2003.

[14] G. Kollios, M. Potamias, and E. Terzi. Clustering large probabilistic graphs. *IEEE Trans. Knowl. Data Eng.*, 25(2):325–336, 2013.

[15] T. Neumann and G. Weikum. RDF-3X: a risc-style engine for RDF. *PVLDB*, 1(1):647–659, 2008.

[16] D. Rao, P. McNamee, and M. Dredze. Entity linking: Finding extracted entities in a knowledge base. In *A book chapter in Multi-source, Multi-lingual Information Extraction and Summarization*, 2011.

[17] K. Riesen, S. Fankhauser, and H. Bunke. Speeding up graph edit distance computation with a bipartite heuristic. In *MLG*, 2007.

[18] D. Suciu and N. N. Dalvi. Foundations of probabilistic answers to queries. In *SIGMOD Conference*, 2005.

[19] W. Tunstall-Pedoe. True knowledge: Open-domain question answering using structured knowledge and inference. *AI Magazine*, 31(3):80–92, 2010.

[20] C. Unger, L. Bühmann, J. Lehmann, A.-C. N. Ngomo, D. Gerber, and P. Cimiano. Template-based question answering over rdf data. In *WWW*, pages 639–648, 2012.

[21] G. Wang, B. Wang, X. Yang, and G. Yu. Efficiently indexing large sparse graphs for similarity search. *TKDE*, 24(3):440–451, 2012.

[22] X. Wang, X. Ding, A. K. H. Tung, S. Ying, and H. Jin. An efficient graph indexing method. In *ICDE*, pages 210–221, 2012.

[23] M. Yahya, K. Berberich, S. Elbassuoni, M. Ramanath, V. Tresp, and G. Weikum. Natural language questions for the web of data. In *EMNLP-CoNLL*, pages 379–390, 2012.

[24] M. Yahya, K. Berberich, S. Elbassuoni, and G. Weikum. Robust question answering over the web of linked data. In *CIKM*, pages 1107–1116, 2013.

[25] X. Yao and B. V. Durme. Information extraction over structured data: Question answering with freebase. In *ACL*, pages 956–966, 2014.

[26] X. Yao, B. V. Durme, C. Callison-Burch, and P. Clark. Answer extraction as sequence tagging with tree edit distance. In *NAACL*, pages 858–867, 2013.

[27] Y. Yuan, G. Wang, L. Chen, and H. Wang. Efficient subgraph similarity search on large probabilistic graph databases. *PVLDB*, 5(9):800–811, 2012.

[28] Y. Yuan, G. Wang, H. Wang, and L. Chen. Efficient subgraph search over large uncertain graphs. *PVLDB*, 4(11):876–886, 2011.

[29] Z. Zeng, A. K. H. Tung, J. Wang, J. Feng, and L. Zhou. Comparing stars: On approximating graph edit distance. *PVLDB*, 2(1):25–36, 2009.

[30] X. Zhao, C. Xiao, X. Lin, Q. Liu, and W. Zhang. A partition-based approach to structure similarity search. *PVLDB*, 7(3):169–180, 2013.

[31] X. Zhao, C. Xiao, X. Lin, and W. Wang. Efficient graph similarity joins with edit distance constraints. In *ICDE*, pages 834–845, 2012.

[32] Z. Zheng, F. Li, M. Huang, and X. Zhu. Learning to link entities with knowledge base. In *NAACL*, pages 483–491, 2010.

[33] L. Zou, R. Huang, H. Wang, J. X. Yu, W. He, and D. Zhao. Natural language question answering over RDF: a graph data driven approach. In *SIGMOD Conference*, pages 313–324, 2014.

[34] L. Zou, J. Mo, L. Chen, M. T. Özsu, and D. Zhao. gstore: Answering sparql queries via subgraph matching. *PVLDB*, 4(8), 2011.

[35] Z. Zou, H. Gao, and J. Li. Discovering frequent subgraphs over uncertain graph databases under probabilistic semantics. In *KDD*, pages 633–642, 2010.

B. PROOF OF LEMMA 3

PROOF. (proof by induction)

Let $dif'(q, g^c)$ denote $\sum_{i=1}^{i=m} d(u_i, q) \ominus d(f(u_i), g^c)$. We just need to prove $dif'(q, g^c) \geq dif(q, g^c)$.

1) (Base Case.)

When $m = 1$, it is straightforward that $dif'(q, g^c) \geq dif(q, g^c)$.

When $m = 2$, assume the two vertex degree sets are $A = \{a_1, a_2\}$ $(a_1 \geq a_2)$, $B = \{b_1, b_2\}$ $(b_1 \geq b_2)$, we need to prove $dif(q, g^c) = (a_1 \ominus b_1) + (a_2 \ominus b_2) \leq dif'(q, g^c) = (a_1 \ominus b_2) + (a_2 \ominus b_1)$. There are four cases to be discussed as follows:

Case 1: When $a_1 \leq b_1$ and $a_2 \leq b_2$, $dif(q, g^c) = 0$, which is minimum.
Case 2: When $a_1 \leq b_1$ and $a_2 > b_2$, $dif(q, g^c) = a_2 - b_2$.

$$\begin{aligned} dif'(q, g^c) &= (a_1 \ominus b_2) + (a_2 \ominus b_1) \\ &= (a_1 \ominus b_2) \geq (a_2 \ominus b_2) = dif(q, g^c) \end{aligned}$$

Case 3: When $a_1 > b_1$ and $a_2 \leq b_2$, $dif(q, g^c) = a_1 - b_1$.

$$\begin{aligned} dif'(q, g^c) &= (a_1 \ominus b_2) + (a_2 \ominus b_1) \\ &= (a_1 \ominus b_2) = (a_1 - b_2) \\ &\geq (a_1 - b_1) = (a_1 \ominus b_1) = dif(q, g^c) \end{aligned}$$

Case 4: When $a_1 > b_1$ and $a_2 > b_2$, $dif(q, g^c) = (a_1 - b_1) + (a_2 - b_2)$.

$$\begin{aligned} dif'(q, g^c) &= (a_1 \ominus b_2) + (a_2 \ominus b_1) \\ &= a_1 - b_2 + a_2 \ominus b_1 \geq a_1 - b_2 + a_2 \ominus b_1 \\ &= dif(q, g^c) \end{aligned}$$

To summarize, we have proved that $dif'(q, g^c) \geq dif(q, g^c)$, where there are only two vertices in q and g^c, respectively.

2) (Hypothesis.) Provided that when $m \geq k$, $dif'_m(q, g^c) \geq dif_m(q, g^c)$.

(Induction.) Consider the case $m = (k+1)$. $dif_{k+1}(q, g^c) = dif_k(q, g^c) + a_{k+1} \ominus b_{k+1}$. Assume that $f(a_{k+1}) = b_i$ $(i < k+1)$ and $f^{-1}(b_{k+1}) = a_j$ $(j < k+1)$, thus, we have

$$dif'_{k+1}(q, g^c) = dif'_{k-1}(q, g^c) + a_{k+1} \ominus b_i + a_j \ominus b_{k+1}.$$

Let us consider $a_{k+1} \ominus b_i + a_j \ominus b_{k+1}$. According to the non-increasing order, it is straightforward to know $a_j > a_{k+1}$ and $b_i > b_{k+1}$. Hence, according to the proof about $m = 2$ in the basis, we know

$$a_{k+1} \ominus b_i + a_j \ominus b_{k+1} \geq a_j \ominus b_i + a_{k+1} \ominus b_{k+1}$$

Therefore,

$$\begin{aligned} dif'_{k+1}(q, g^c) &= dif'_{k-1}(q, g^c) + (a_{k+1} \ominus b_i) + (a_j \ominus b_{k+1}) \\ &\geq dif'_{k-1}(q, g^c) + (a_j \ominus b_i) + (a_{k+1} \ominus b_{k+1}) \\ &= dif'_k(q, g^c) + (a_{k+1} \ominus b_{k+1}) \end{aligned}$$

According to hypothesis, we know $dif'_k(q, g^c) \geq dif_k(q, g^c)$.

$$\begin{aligned} dif'_{k+1}(q, g^c) &\geq dif'_k(q, g^c) + (a_{k+1} \ominus b_{k+1}) \\ &\geq dif_k(q, g^c) + (a_{k+1} \ominus b_{k+1}) \\ &= dif_{k+1}(q, g^c) \end{aligned}$$

3) According to the above analysis, we can prove that $dif_{k+1}(q, g^c) \geq dif'_{k+1}(q, g^c)$ if $dif_k(q, g^c) \geq dif'_k(q, g^c)$. Since we have proved the basis, according to induction method, we know Lemma 3 holds. □

C. PROOF OF THEOREM 2

PROOF. Without loss of generality, let us assume that $|V(q)| = m < |V(g^c)| = n$.

$$\begin{aligned} & lb\_ged_{CSS}(q, g^c) - lb\_ged_{LM}(q, g^c) \\ &= |V(g^c)| + |E(g^c)| - \lambda_E(q, g^c) + \frac{dif(q, g^c)}{2} - \lambda_V(q, g^c) \\ &-(|V(g^c)| - \lambda_V(q, g^c) + \max\{|E(q)|, |E(g^c)|\} - \lambda_E(q, g^c)) \\ &= |E(g^c)| - \max\{|E(q)|, |E(g^c)|\} + \frac{dif(q, g^c)}{2} \end{aligned}$$

1) When $|E(g)| \geq |E(q)|$,

$$\begin{aligned} & lb\_ged_{CSS}(q, g^c) - lb\_ged_{LM}(q, g^c) \\ &= |E(g^c)| - \max\{|E(q)|, |E(g^c)|\} + \frac{dif(q, g^c)}{2} \\ &= |E(g^c)| - |E(g^c)| + \frac{dif(q, g^c)}{2} \\ &= \frac{dif(q, g^c)}{2} \geq 0. \end{aligned}$$

2) When $|E(g^c)| < |E(q)|$,

$$\begin{aligned} & lb\_ged_{CSS}(q, g^c) - lb\_ged_{LM}(q, g^c) \\ &= |E(g^c)| - |E(q)| + \frac{dif(q, g^c)}{2} \end{aligned}$$

Given two certain graphs q and g^c, it is straightforward to know $|E(q)| - |E(g^c)| = \frac{\sum_{u \in V(q)} d(u, q) - \sum_{v \in V(g^c)} d(v, g^c)}{2}$.

Since we know $|V(q)| = m < |V(g^c)| = n$, according to the definition of $dif(q, g^c)$ in Eq. 9, we have the following equation.

$$\begin{aligned} |E(q)| - |E(g^c)| &= \frac{\sum_{i=1}^{i=m} d(u_i, q) - \sum_{j=1}^{j=n} d(v_j, g^c)}{2} \\ &\leq \frac{\sum_{i=1}^{i=m} (d(u_i, q) - d(v_i, g^c))}{2} \\ &= \frac{dif(q, g^c)}{2} \end{aligned}$$

Hence, we know

$$\begin{aligned} & lb\_ged_{CSS}(q, g^c) - lb\_ged_{LM}(q, g^c) \\ &\geq |E(g^c)| - |E(q)| + \frac{dif(q, g^c)}{2} \\ &\geq |E(g^c)| - |E(q)| + (|E(q)| - |E(g^c)|) = 0 \end{aligned}$$

To summarize, $lb\_ged_{CSS}(q, g^c) \geq lb\_ged_{LM}(q, g^c)$ always holds, i.e., CSS-based is tighter than the label-multiset-based lower bound in [31]. □

D. ALGORITHM OF SIMJ PROCEDURE

D.1 SimJ Algorithm

Algorithm 1 SimJ_Procedure(D, U, τ, α)

Require: deterministic graphs D, uncertain graphs U, graph edit distance threshold τ, and similarity probability threshold α

Ensure: graph pairs $\{\langle q, g\rangle \in D \times U | SimP_\tau(q, g) \geq \alpha\}$

```
AS ← ∅
for ⟨q, g⟩ ∈ D × U do
  compute lb_ged_CSS(q, g) according to Theorem 3
  if lb_ged_CSS(q, g) ≤ τ then
    compute ub_SimP_τ(q, g) according to Theorem 4
    if ub_SimP_τ(q, g) ≥ α then
      SimP_τ(q, g) ← 0
      for possible world pw(g) ∈ PW(g) do
        compute lb_ged_CSS(q, pw(g)) by Theorem 2
        if lb_ged_CSS(q, pw(g)) ≤ τ then
          compute ged(q, pw(g))
          if ged(q, pw(g)) ≤ τ then
            SimP_τ(q, g) ← SimP_τ(q, g) + Pr(pw(g))
      if SimP_τ(q, g) ≥ α then
        put ⟨q, g⟩ into AS
return AS
```

D.2 Complexity Analysis

Complexity of computing CSS-based lower bound of GED for uncertain graphs (line 3 in Algorithm 1). Let us recall the lower bound $lb\_ged_{CSS}(q,g) = |V| + |E| - \lambda_E(q,g) + \frac{dif(q,g)}{2} - \lambda_V(q,g)$. Its dominating computation is caused by $\lambda_V(q,g)$, i.e., the size of the maximal matching in the vertex label bipartite graph. The maximal matching problem can be sovled by a classic Hungarian algorithm [10], with time complexity $O(|V|^3)$. Hence, the complexity of computing CSS-based lower of GED for uncertain graphs is $O(|V|^3)$, where $|V| = \max\{|V(g)|, |V(q)|\}$.

Complexity of computing upper bound of $SimP_\tau(q,g)$ for uncertain graphs (line 5 in Algorithm 1). Let us recall the upper bound $ub\_SimP_\tau(q,g) = \frac{E(Y)}{C(q,g)-\tau}$, where $E(Y) = \sum_{i=1}^{m} E(y_i)$ can be computed with the time complexity $O(|V| \cdot |l(v)|)$. The time complexity of computing $C(q,g)$ is $O(|V(q)| \cdot |V(g)|)$. Hence, the time complexity $O(min\{|V| \cdot |l(v)|, |V(q)| \cdot |V(g)|\})$.

Complexity of computing CSS-based lower bound of GED for certain graphs (line 9 in Algorithm 1). Let us recall the lower bound $lb_g ed_{CSS}(q,g^c) = |V(g^c)| + |E(g^c)| - \lambda_E(q,g^c) + \frac{dif(q,g^c)}{2} - \lambda_V(q,g^c)$, where $|V(g^c)|$ and $|E(g^c)|$ are constants. Since the computation complexity of $\lambda_V(q,g^c)$ and $\lambda_E(q,g^c)$ is $O(|V(q)| \cdot |V(g^c)| + |E(q)| \cdot |E(g^c)|)$ and the computation complexity of $\frac{dif(q,g^c)}{2}$ is $O(|V(q)|)$, the complexity of computing CSS-based lower of GED for certain graphs is $O(|E(q)| \cdot |E(g^c)|)$.

Complexity of verification (lines 8-15 in Algorithm 1). In the verification phase, we need to compute $SimP_\tau(q,g)$ by enumerating all possible worlds in the worst case. Moreover, it invokes the GED computation, which is a well-known NP-hard problem. Nevertheless, it is feasible to compute the graph edit distance since the semantic query graphs and SPARQL graphs are small in real applications.

Note that our proposed upper/lower bounds are efficient with the time complexity $O(max\{|E(q)| \cdot |E(g^c)|, |V|^3\})$ even if the verification procedure is NP-hard.

E. ALGORITHM OF GROUP-BASED OPTIMIZATION

Algorithm 2 SimJ_OPT(q, g, τ, α)

Require: uncertain graph q, deterministic graph g, graph edit distance threshold τ, and similarity probability threshold α
Ensure: $ub\_SimP_\tau(q,g)$

```
SimP_τ(q,g) ⟵ 0
divide g into k possible world groups PWG_1, ..., PWG_k
for i = 1 to k do
    compute lb_ged_CSS(q, PWG_i) according to Theorem 3
    if lb_ged_CSS(q, PWG_i) ≤ τ then
        compute ub_SimP_τ(q, PWG_i) according to Theorem 4
        t ⟵ ub_SimP_τ(q, PWG_i)
        ub_SimP_τ(q,g) ⟵ ub_SimP_τ(q,g) + t
return ub_SimP_τ(q,g)
```

F. EXPERIMENTAL RESULTS

F.1 Result Analysis

Effect of the number of relations k. We have analyzed the experimental results carefully, and find that the simple query patterns are easily recognized. Figure 17 presents the effect of the number of relations over the datasets of QALD-3 and WebQ, where the horizontal x-axis represents the number of relations (denoted by k), and vertical y-axis represents the proportion of correct patterns (i.e., the number of correct patterns with k relations divided by all correct patterns), denoted by ρ. It shows that the patterns with few relations are better recognized. The reason is that if a natural language question is complex, the generated sematic query graph may be incorrect probably.

Failure analysis. We also provide the failure analysis for the templates generated by our method. There are two key reasons for the errors. The first reason is that it fails to generate correct semantic query graphs for some natural language questions. For example, in the question "Who composed the music for Harold and Maude?", it fails in linking "Harold and Maude" to the corresponding entity "Harold_and_Maude". The second one is that some graph pairs have small graph edit distance, but they do not share the same query intension. We give the ratio of each reason in Figure 18.

What is the ruling party in <___>?	SELECT ?uri WHERE { <___> type <___>. <___> leaderParty ?uri. }
Give me all <___> directed by <___>	SELECT ?film WHERE { ?film type <___>. ?film director <___>. }
Which <___> has been developed by organizations founded in <___>?	SELECT ?product WHERE { ?company type Organization. ?company foundationPlace <___>. ?product developer ?company. ?product type <___>. }

Figure 16: Templates for the case study

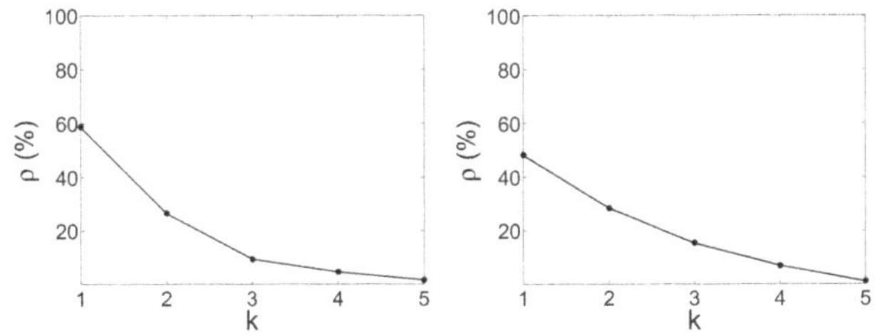

(a) Results on QALD-3 (b) Results on WebQ

Figure 17: Effect of k (the number of relations)

Reason	Incorrect Semantic Query Graph	Graph Edit Distance	Others
#(Ratio)	73%	21%	6%

Figure 18: Failure Analysis

F.2 Q/A Using Templates

Comparisons With Other Systems. In order to evaluate the quality of the templates, we use the questions of QALD-3 to test the effectiveness. We translate the questions into SPARQL queries utilizing these generated templates, and then search these SPARQL queries over DBpedia.

We utilize the evaluation measures that are also used in QALD task. The overall precision and recall are computed by taking the average mean of all single precision and recall values, as well as the overall F-measure[11].

[11]http://greententacle.techfak.uni-bielefeld.de/~cunger/qald/4/qald-4.pdf

$$Recall(n) = \frac{\text{number of correct system answers}}{\text{number of gold standard answers}}$$

$$Precision(n) = \frac{\text{number of correct system answers}}{\text{number of system answers}}$$

$$\text{F-Measure(n)} = \frac{2 \times Precision \times Recall}{Precision + Recall}$$

To confirm the effectiveness of our method, we compare it with gAnswer [33] and DEANNA [23]. As shown in Table 4, our template-based method is more effective, which indicates that the generated templates have high quality.

Table 4: Q/A results compared with other systems

Methods	Precision	Recall	F-1
Our method	0.65	0.65	0.65
gAnswer	0.41	0.41	0.41
DEANNA	0.21	0.21	0.21

Effect of matching proportion ϕ. If we cannot find a match between a template with the entire sentence of a new natural language question (NLQ for short), we choose the template that maximizes the matching proportion ϕ.

We can also generate SPARQL queries based on this partial match. To evaluate the effect of ϕ, we conduct experiments over real datasets by varying ϕ from 0.5 to 1. Table 5 shows that allowing partial template match improves both the recall and precision of RDF Q/A task. The main reason is by allowing partial match, we can answer more questions without affecting those can be answered correctly by setting $\phi = 1$ (i.e., take no account of the partial match).

Table 5: Effect of ϕ

ϕ	**0.5**	**0.6**	**0.7**	**0.8**	**0.9**	**1.0**
Precision	0.69	0.69	0.68	0.66	0.66	0.65
Recall	0.73	0.72	0.70	0.69	0.67	0.65
F-1	0.71	0.70	0.69	0.67	0.66	0.65

RBench: Application-Specific RDF Benchmarking

Shi Qiao
Case Western Reserve University
Cleveland, OH, 44106, USA
sxq18@case.edu

Z. Meral Özsoyoğlu
Case Western Reserve University
Cleveland, OH, 44106, USA
mxo2@case.edu

ABSTRACT
As more RDF data management systems and RDF data querying techniques emerge, RDF benchmarks providing a controllable and comparable testing environment for applications are needed. To address the needs of diverse applications, we propose an application-specific framework, called *RBench*, to generate RDF benchmarks. *RBench* takes an RDF dataset from any application as a template, and generates a set of synthetic datasets with similar characteristics including graph structure and literal labels, for the required "size scaling factor" and the "degree scaling factor". *RBench* analyzes several features from the given RDF dataset, and uses them to reconstruct the new benchmark graph. A flexible query load generation process is then proposed according to the design of *RBench*. Efficiency and usability of *RBench* are demonstrated via experimental results.

Categories and Subject Descriptors
H.2 [Systems]; K.6.2 [Management Of Computing And Information Systems]: Installation Management—*Benchmarks*

General Terms
RDF; Benchmark

Keywords
Application-Specific Benchmarking

1. INTRODUCTION
With the increasing popularity of RDF data, more and more RDF management systems and querying techniques are emerging [7,10, 12,20,31]. Performance evaluation of these systems and techniques are typically done by using synthetic RDF benchmark data [6,11, 18,24,35]. However, achieving the same levels of performance on real applications depends on how closely the synthetic RDF benchmark data mimic real datasets, and whether the existing RDF benchmarks provide a complete and expected testing environment as real data. Most existing RDF benchmarks adopt the traditional top-down approach to generate domain-specific benchmarks where predefined schema and domain knowledge are utilized. RDF data are defined with full flexibility where no schema is required, and different RDF datasets scale in different ways. Thus, as compared to domain-specific benchmark design, application-specific benchmarking [29] for RDF data is needed for diverse graph structure and literals of RDF datasets used in real-life applications.

SIGMOD'15, May 31–June 4, 2015, Melbourne, Victoria, Australia.

http://dx.doi.org/10.1145/2723372.2746479

1.1 Problem Definition
Similar to the definition of dataset scaling problem [29] (proposed as the central problem of application-specific benchmarking for relational databases), the application-specific benchmarking problem for RDF data is defined as follows.

> *Given an RDF data graph G, a size scaling factor s and a degree scaling factor d, generate a synthetic dataset $\tilde{G}$ which is similar to G, and has its number of edges (triples) and the average node degree changed by factors s and d, respectively.*

The size scaling factor s here is utilized to describe different benchmarking goals. Scaling up ($s > 1$) an empirical dataset can provide the scalability test environment for applications' software and hardware design which is essential for applications with sharp dataset size increases. Miniaturizing ($s < 1$) an empirical dataset allows efficient data communication, testing, and analysis. Synthetic copying ($s \approx 1$) of an empirical dataset can be used for anonymization to protect sensitive data. As compared with real datasets, controllable dataset size is an important advantage in performance evaluation using benchmark datasets.

The degree scaling factor d is introduced to simulate different types of data scaling applications. The fact that RDF datasets can change significantly over time even for primitive metrics, e.g., the node degree, is explained [14] as the *Densification Power Law* which states that the average degree of data graphs increases over time for real applications. Moreover, different applications may require completely different degree scaling factors. Another important reason to use the degree scaling factor in RDF benchmarking is that average degrees of graphs have a significant impact on query evaluation. For graphs with the same number of edges, queries can be much more complex to evaluate on dense graphs than sparse graphs.

A generated benchmark dataset is considered similar to the given dataset if their values for the dataset evaluation metrics and query evaluation times for different techniques are similar. For the dataset evaluation metrics, we use the *dataset coherence* [8], *relationship specialty* [22] and *literal diversity* [22]. Query evaluation time similarity is motivated by the expectation that the generated benchmarks are useful if they provide a controllable environment with comparable results so that performance of different query techniques on the given dataset can be estimated.

1.2 Our Contributions
Application-specific benchmarking has been proposed [29] for the database community to resolve the mismatch between a handful of domain-specific benchmarks and the multitude of data-centric applications. Compared with domain-specific design which requires predefined schema and domain knowledge, the application-specific design is more specifically suited to generate RDF benchmarks as no schema is needed, and most RDF datasets tend to include information from diverse domains. The main challenge of designing application-specific RDF benchmarks is to

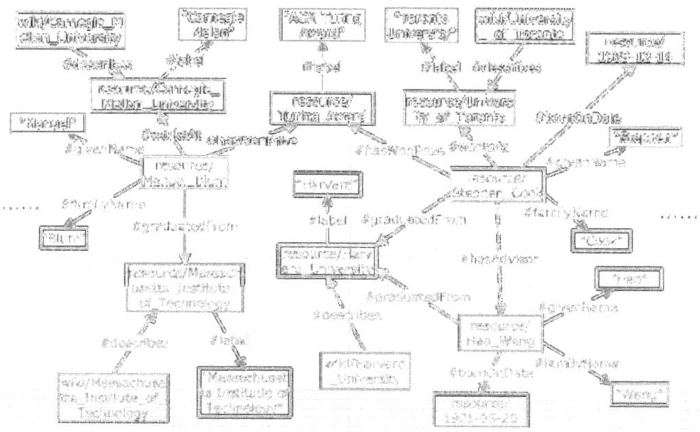

Figure 1. RDF graph example (*Yago*)

understand the characteristics of a given RDF dataset, and propose criteria and methods which can be utilized to generate synthetic data with similar characteristics.

Our main contributions are as follows:

1) To better understand and identify the limitations of existing RDF benchmarks, three evaluation metrics, namely, *dataset coherence, relationship specialty,* and *literal diversity,* are utilized to compare twelve RDF datasets (both real and synthetic). Benchmark evaluation results show that existing RDF benchmarks are limited in terms of the diversity of their graph structure and literal labels.

2) To resolve the limitations of existing RDF benchmarks, we propose an application-specific framework, called *RBench*, which takes any given RDF dataset as a template, analyses the characteristics of its graph structure and literal labels, and generates a similar synthetic dataset with the required size scaling factor s and the degree scaling factor d.

3) Based on the design of *RBench*, a query generation process is proposed to generate different types of queries systematically for any generated benchmark.

4) Three aspects of *RBench* are explored in experiments: time and memory complexity of benchmark generation, benchmark datasets evaluation, and query evaluation analysis. We empirically show that benchmark datasets generated by *RBench* can achieve different scaling factors to fulfil different benchmark generation tasks, consistent with real scaling datasets, and address the limitations of the previous application-specific benchmark generator [8].

The paper is organized as follows. Benchmark evaluation is performed in Section 2. Section 3 introduces *RBench* framework. In Section 4, we describe the random query workload generation. Evaluation experiments of *RBench* are presented in Section 5. Section 6 discusses the related work, and Section 7 concludes.

2. BENCHMARK EVALUATION

Evaluating existing RDF benchmarks with real datasets is an important step in designing a new benchmark generator. The evaluation results not only reveal the differences between real and synthetic data, but also provide hints on the directions to improve the existing RDF benchmarks. Three dataset evaluation metrics are utilized: *dataset coherence, relationship specialty* and *literal diversity*. *Dataset coherence* is first proposed in [8] as a measure of the structuredness of RDF datasets. *Relationship specialty* and *literal diversity* are introduced in [22] to provide a better way to differentiate benchmarks and real datasets.

We evaluate twelve RDF datasets (eight real RDF datasets and four benchmarks). We categorize the real datasets into three groups based on the types of applications: (1) Knowledge bases (DBpedia [5], YAGO [17,25,26,33] and WordNet [32]); (2) Information systems (Barton [30], LinkedMDB [16] and DBLP [15]); (3) Biology datasets (NCBI Taxonomy [19,21] and SGD: Saccharomyces Genome Database [21,23]). The benchmark datasets all use domain-specific design. BSBM [6] considers an e-commerce domain with types *Product, Offer, Vendor, Person* and *Review*. Relationships between products and vendors, and between users and product reviews are simulated. LUBM [11] and UOBM [35] consider the same University domain. SP2Bench [24] uses the publication domain, same as DBLP. All real datasets utilized in this paper are the newest versions available. All benchmark datasets are generated with approximately 20M (million) triples. We first list definitions utilized in the rest of the paper.

DEFINITION 2.1: An **RDF Graph** is a directed graph $G = \{V, E, l, f\}$ where V is a set of vertices representing either Subjects, Objects or both, in RDF triples. $E \subseteq V \times V$ is a set of directed edges representing predicates pointing from Subjects to Objects. l is a label set for subjects, objects and predicates. $f: V/E \rightarrow l$ denotes the mapping function between vertices/ edges to labels. Example RDF graph from Yago is shown in Figure 1.

DEFINITION 2.2: For RDF graph G,any node $n_i \in V$ associated with URI reference label is denoted as **Resource Node**[1]. All other nodes associated with literal labels are denoted as **Literal Nodes**.

DEFINITION 2.3: For an RDF graph G, any edge $e_i \in E$ between two resource nodes is denoted as **Relationship Edge**. All other edges (from resource nodes to literal nodes) are denoted as **Attribute Edges** (Literal nodes have no outgoing edges).

In Figure 1, resource nodes and relationship edges are in blue while literal nodes and attribute edges are in red. The reasons to distinguish relationship edges from attribute edges in an RDF dataset: (1) Subjects in triples are only resource nodes, and graph structures of attribute edges are simple (no cycles, no paths); (2) Relationship patterns among resources may change significantly as datasets evolve over time.

2.1 Dataset Coherence

Dataset coherence [8] measures how uniformly predicates are distributed among the same type/class (the terms type and class are used interchangeably in this paper) of resources in an RDF dataset. The type system utilized by the *coverage* and *coherence* metrics comes from the predicate "rdf:type" which defines instances (resources) of different RDF classes. The resources associated with multi-classes are analysed for each class separately in the *coverage* and *coherence* computation. To avoid potential bias, the weighted formula takes into consideration both the number of resources in each class, and the number of distinct predicates associated with the resources of each class. *Coverage* and *coherence* metrics are defined below.

DEFINITION 2.4: Given an RDF dataset and its type system T, ***coverage*** $Cov(t)$ for any type $t \in T$ is defined as

[1] Blank nodes associated with local identifiers are treated the same as resource nodes in this paper.

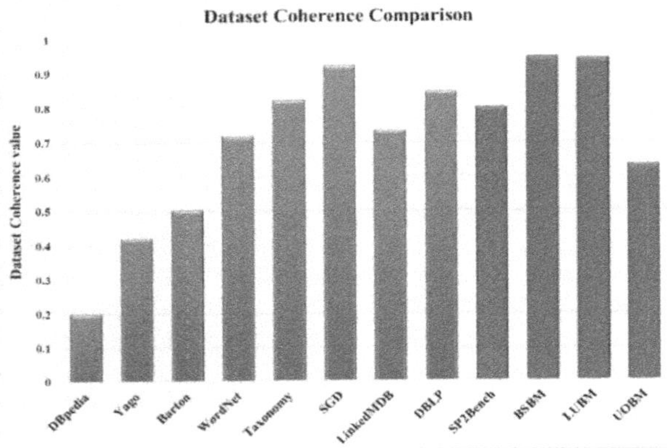

Figure 2. *Coherence* metric for all datasets

$$Cov(t) = \frac{\sum_{\forall p \in P(t)} c(\mathfrak{r}(t), p)}{|P(t)| \times |\mathfrak{r}(t)|}$$

where $\mathfrak{r}(t)$ is the set of resources of type t, $P(t)$ is the set of predicates associated with any resource in $\mathfrak{r}(t)$, $c(\mathfrak{r}(t), p)$ is the number of resources in $\mathfrak{r}(t)$ associated with predicate p, and $|P(t)|$, $|\mathfrak{r}(t)|$ are the sizes of these two sets.

DEFINITION 2.5: Given an RDF dataset $\mathcal{D}$ and its type system T, ***coherence*** $Coh(\mathcal{D})$ of the dataset $\mathcal{D}$ is then defined as

$$Coh(\mathcal{D}) = \sum_{\forall t \in T} \omega(t) \times Cov(t)$$

where $\omega(t) = \frac{|\mathfrak{r}(t)| + |P(t)|}{\sum_{\forall t' \in T}(|\mathfrak{r}(t')| + |P(t')|)}$.

Considering the example RDF graph in Figure 1, there are three types of resources: University, Person and Award. *Coherence* of the dataset is computed using the *weights* and *coverages* of all three types in the dataset. Here, we illustrate the computation of *weight* and *coverage* for type University. There are four resources and four distinct predicates for the University type. Each of these four resources has three distinct predicates. Thus, the *coverage* for University type is $\frac{3+3+3+3}{4 \times 4} = 0.75$. The weight of University type is computed as $\omega(\text{Univ}) = \frac{8}{8+10+3}$.

Coherence values of the twelve datasets are shown in Figure 2 where the first eight are real datasets (blue bar) and the remaining four are benchmark datasets (red bar). One can observe that the benchmark datasets are limited to a smaller range and higher *coherence* values as compared to those of real datasets. This means that domain-specific RDF benchmarks are associated with highly uniform graph patterns for resources of the same type. In other words, graph structure of domain-specific benchmarks are more "relational-like" because of a pre-defined schema. In comparison, some real datasets show extremely diverse graph patterns which include resources from all different domains and sources, e.g., *DBpedia*. Thus, existing RDF benchmarks differ from real datasets in this respect.

2.2 Relationship Specialty

The number of occurrences of the same predicate associated with each resource provides useful information on the graph structure of an RDF dataset, especially for relationship predicates. In a real dataset, it identifies the diverse relationship patterns for different resources, and makes some resources distinguishable from others. This kind of *relationship specialty* is common for real datasets in all different areas, (e.g., a movie star is liked by millions of fans in social networks; a common molecule is involved in thousands of reactions in biological pathways; a concept is linked by millions of concepts in Wiki; and a book is referenced by thousands of other publications in library information systems). Synthetic data are limited in capturing relationship *specialty* because either uniform relationship patterns are simulated for all resources, or a random relationship generation process is utilized. The motivation behind the *relationship specialty* metric is to capture this fundamental difference between real data and benchmark data.

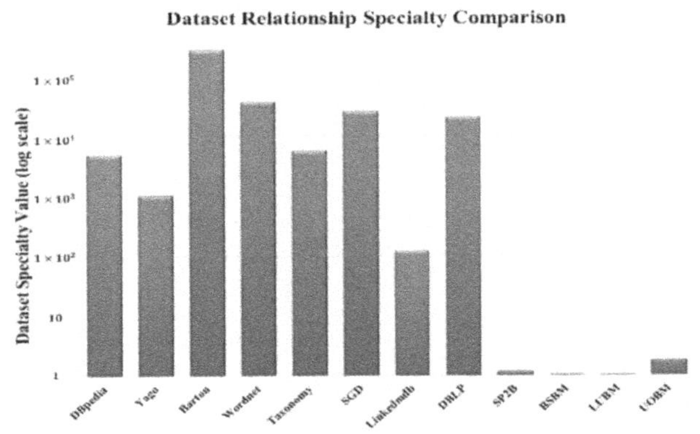

Figure 3. Relationship specialty for all datasets

The *specialty* value of a relationship predicate $\mathfrak{r}_i$ is defined [22] as the kurtosis value [13] of the distribution d_i which records the number of occurrences of $\mathfrak{r}_i$ associated with each resource. *Relationship specialty* of a dataset is defined in the form of a weighted sum of *specialty* values of all relationship predicates in the dataset where each relationship predicate contributes proportional to the number of triples associated with it:

$RS(\mathrm{D}) = \sum_{\mathfrak{r}_i \in R}\left(\frac{|T(\mathfrak{r}_i)|}{\sum_{\mathfrak{r}_j \in R}|T(\mathfrak{r}_j)|} \times \mathcal{K}_{\mathfrak{r}_i}\right)$, where $T(\mathfrak{r}_i)$ is the set of triples containing the relation predicate $\mathfrak{r}_i$, and $|T(\mathfrak{r}_i)|$ is the number of such triples, $\mathcal{K}_{\mathfrak{r}_i}$ is the *specialty* value of relationship $\mathfrak{r}_i$, and R is the set of all relationship predicates in dataset D.

The *relationship specialty* values for all twelve datasets are shown in Figure 3. As observed, the dataset *relationship specialty* of all benchmarks are below ten while the dataset *relationship specialty* of all real datasets ranges from 10^2 to 10^5 (indicating that the variance of the distribution is mostly related to infrequent extreme deviations). This is due to the fact that resources of the same type are treated similarly in benchmark data generation, while the roles of "importance" associated with resources are generally different in real datasets. For example, considering the number of friends associated with each student as an indication of popularity, the popularity of students in LUBM is similar while, in the real world, some students are much more popular than others. Unless the benchmark generator assigns different roles to resources for relationships which makes some resources distinguishable from others, *relationship specialty* will always identify benchmark data.

2.3 Literal Diversity

The diversity of literals is another factor that influences the quality of an RDF benchmark. This aspect is not well addressed by the existing RDF benchmarks. Only two simple literal generation processes are employed currently: (1) use a small set of predefined words plus digits (for LUBM, UOBM); (2) use a random selection from documents containing a large number of possible words (for BSBM, SP2B). It is clear that both methods may introduce bias to query evaluation as literals are most frequently queried by

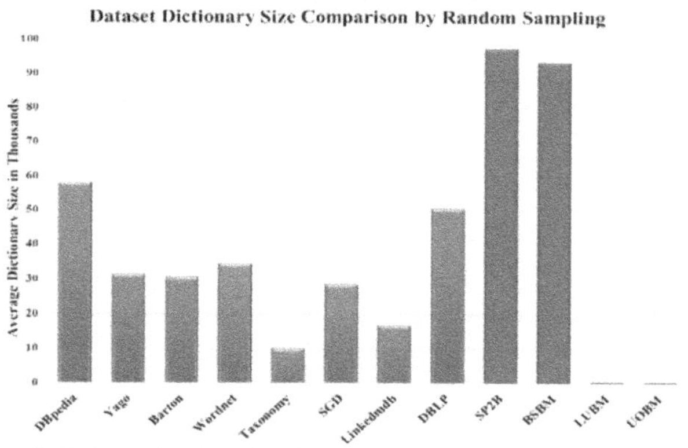

Figure 4. Dictionary sizes for all datasets with $\mathcal{M} = 100k$

keywords. The first method results in low keyword selectivity due to utilizing small number of fixed words as literals while the second method results in high keyword selectivity for relatively small benchmark dataset sizes due to the random selection.

Here, we use the dictionary size of literals from a randomly sampled set of attribute triples of size $\mathcal{M}$ to describe the *literal diversity* of a given dataset. Dictionary size, measured by the number of unique "words" $w_{\mathcal{M}}$ contained by the literals of an RDF dataset, provides important information about the diversity of literals. To provide efficient evaluation for datasets with millions of attribute triples, a random sampling of $\mathcal{M}$ attribute triples is utilized. As different attribute predicates may have significantly different ranges, e.g., "#hasGender" and "#hasName" predicates in a social network, the sample size $\mathcal{M}$ should be large enough to ensure that it covers all attribute predicates of an RDF dataset. In order to choose the random sample size $\mathcal{M}$, for the datasets in our experiments, we evaluated the dictionary sizes of multiple samples using different values of $\mathcal{M}$. For $\mathcal{M} = 100{,}000$, the coefficient of variation in dictionary sizes of different samples is less than 5% for all datasets shown in Figure 4, and hence, we used $\mathcal{M} = 100{,}000$ as the random sample size to compute the dictionary sizes. Clearly, LUBM and UOBM have extremely limited *literal diversity* which contain only less than 20 unique words in $100k$ literals. In comparison, SP2B and BSBM have much larger *literal diversity* due to random selection from a large set of candidate words. Compared with real datasets where a large number of frequently utilized literals are associated with multiple resources, most literals appear only in one attribute triple since the probability of generating the same set of random words in SP2B and BSBM is very low.

2.4 Insights from Benchmark Evaluation

Benchmark evaluation based on the metrics *coherence*, *relationship specialty* and *literal diversity* indicates that the existing RDF benchmarks are limited in their coverage of diverse structures and do not quite mimic the characteristics of real datasets. This motivates us to design an application-specific RDF benchmark generator which can generate benchmarks similar to the real ones. *Dataset coherence* is a direct evidence that the traditional top-down approach to generate domain-specific benchmarks is not a good option for RDF benchmarking. Using predefined schema to describe all resources of the same type is limited since most real applications use resources from multiple domains and multiple sources. This leads to diverse predicate patterns for resources of the same type (relatively smaller *dataset coherence*). *Relationship specialty* shows that uniform relationship patterns are utilized in current RDF benchmarks while a hidden "role" system exists in real

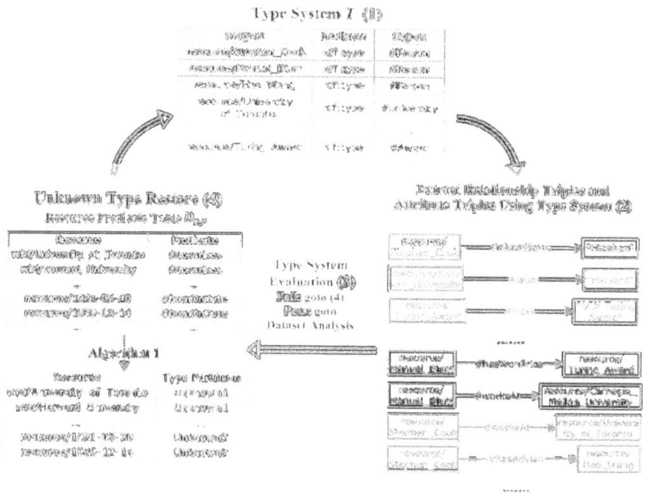

Figure 5. Dataset Preprocessing

datasets. This "role" system makes some resources distinguishable from others. *Relationship specialty* can also be viewed as a finer granularity in analyzing the degree distribution by considering different relationship predicates separately. The *literal diversity* highlights potential improvement for the existing RDF benchmarks.

3. *RBENCH*

Application-specific design is the key to overcome the limitations of existing domain-specific RDF benchmarks where predefined schemas are utilized. The challenge is to understand characteristics of a given RDF dataset, and define the criteria to generate a set of "similar" synthetic datasets. Next we propose a new framework, called *RBench*, which analyzes features of the graph structure and literal labels of a given RDF dataset, and uses these features to generate benchmark data with the desired scaling factors. *RBench* generates benchmarks in three steps: (1) preprocessing the given RDF dataset G; (2) generating a set of features characterizing the given dataset G in dataset analysis; (3) generating benchmark graph with the required scaling factors based on these features.

3.1 Dataset Preprocessing

Preprocessing a given RDF dataset G has four steps (Figure 5): (1) identifying the type system T associated with G by checking predicate "rdf:type"; (2) identifying relationship triples and attribute triples using type system T in G; (3) evaluating the type system T associated with G; and (4) restoring the type system for resources without type definition (if the evaluation of T fails).

The motivation for identifying different types of resources and edges/triples is to provide a finer granularity to better understand a given RDF dataset. As explained in section 2, attribute triples associated with each resource forms simple graph structure since literal nodes have no outgoing edges while the graph structure of relationship triples is much more complex. The labels of literals in attribute triples convey important semantics, and are frequently queried as keywords while the labels of resources are typically long strings with randomly generated IDs. Thus, the method to analyze relationship triples and attribute triples should take these differences into consideration. The type system associated with a given RDF dataset provides a more effective way to understand its data structure. Resources of the same type often share the same set of attribute predicates, and show similar relationship patterns. This can be observed in Figure 2 as most real RDF datasets (6 out of 8 in experiments) have *dataset coherence* values above 0.5. In other

Algorithm 1: RUT ($L_R, D_{R,P}, \tau$)

Input: L_R:list of Resources; $D_{R,P}$: resource, predicate table; τ: minimal required information gain

Output: T: type system for L_R

1 add all resource $r_i \in L_R$ to t_1 and add t_1 to T
2 *predPrtn*$(t_1, T, D_{R,P}) \rightarrow p_{t_1}, c_{t_1}$ and add (p_{t_1}, c_{t_1}) to P //P represents the partition plans
3 WHILE (1)
4 find $(p_{t_j}, c_{t_j}) \in P$ with max c_t //max information gain
5 IF $c_{t_j} \geq \tau$
6 partition t_j into t_j and t_{max+1} by checking whether resource $r_k \in t_j$ is associated with p_{t_j} //if true, $r_k \in t_j$; else $r_k \in t_{max+1}$
7 *predPrtn*$(t_j, T, D_{R,P}) \rightarrow p_{t_j}, c_{t_j}$
8 *predPrtn*$(t_{max+1}, T, D_{R,P}) \rightarrow p_{t_{max+1}}, c_{t_{max+1}}$
9 update t_j, t_{max+1} in T
10 update (p_{t_j}, c_{t_j}), $(p_{t_{max+1}}, c_{t_{max+1}})$ in P
11 ELSE BREAK
12 ENDIF
13 ENDWHILE
14 RETURN T

FUNCTION *predPrtn*$(t, T, D_{R,P})$
15 $p_t = null, c_t = 0$
16 FOR any predicate p_n associated with resources of t
17 partition t into t_+ and t_- by checking whether resource $r_d \in t$ is associated with p_n //if true, $r_d \in t_+$; else $r_d \in t_-$
18 update t as t_+, t_- in T as T'
19 $c_{t,p_n} = coh(T', D_{R,P})$ - $coh(T, D_{R,P})$
20 IF $c_{t,p_n} > c_t$
21 $p_t = p_n, c_t = c_{t,p_n}$
22 ENDIF
23 ENDFOR
24 RETURN p_t, c_t

words, the same set of predicates are associated with over half of resources of the same type. This is mainly due to the utilization of popular ontology systems. Many ontologies define standard sets of possible predicates for different types of resources which are adopted in the design of real RDF datasets. Note that some resources are associated with multiple type definitions. Similar to the strategy in [8], different possible type combinations are defined to distinguish resources with multiple types.

Although the type system associated with an RDF dataset provides useful information for dataset analysis, it is not required to be complete, and some resources are not associated with type definition. As *RBench* performs dataset analysis using the type system, it may become a potential limitation if a large number of resources are not fully utilized in the analysis process due to unknown types. For most of the datasets (both real and synthetic) utilized in section 2, the type systems associated with them are relatively complete, and over 90% of resources are well-defined with types. Resource analysis with defined types is sufficient for these datasets. But, type systems associated with some datasets are limited, e.g., Yago dataset (more than half of the resources do not have types). Thus, an evaluation of the type system is performed in order to validate the analysis results. For *RBench*, type system evaluation checks two aspects: 1) percentage of resources with type definition; 2) percentage of triples containing only resources with type definitions. If both percentages exceed the expected threshold (in this paper, 80%), the type system is claimed to be high quality, and passes the evaluation. Otherwise, the original type system fails the evaluation, and the process of restoring unknown types is utilized.

3.1.1 Restoring Unknown Types

The goal of restoring unknown types is to provide a complementary type system for datasets which have a large number of resources without type definition for better dataset analysis results. Simply using one new type "unknown" to label all resources without types provides too little information for dataset analysis. As we observed, most of these resources with unknown types result from incomplete type system. For example, missing types for resources integrate from other domains as in the case of the Yago dataset. This means some unknown types may be restored to provide a better type system for dataset analysis. Since URI labels of resources are not required to include semantic information, using these labels to identify the potential types of resources can't be achieved. However, resources of the same type tend to be described by a similar set of predicates, and some predicates can be utilized as features to distinguish different types of resources. This motivates us to recover unknown types by using predicates. As shown in Figure 5, step (4), the resource predicate table $D_{R,P}$ is constructed by using all triples associated with resources of the unknown type, which records all possible resource-predicate combinations in these triples. Then, the process to restore types is formulated as a decision tree problem. Internal nodes of the decision tree is partitioned into two branches by checking whether a predicate p is associated with the resource. Each leaf node represents a quality unknown type. Information gain is calculated by using the *coherence* metric. In other words, the partition based on predicate p is high quality if the *coherence* value of $D_{R,P}$ improves with the new types. As high *coherence* value often indicates more structured graph patterns associated with resources of the same type, using the *coherence* metric to compute information gain can facilitate better feature graph extraction for resources of unknown types. The process to generate the complementary type system is shown in **Algorithm 1**.

Algorithm 1 begins with labeling all resources without types as one new type t_1, and finds the predicate to partition t_1 to achieve the largest information gain by using function *predPrtn*$(t, T, D_{R,P})$ (steps 1-2). Function *predPrtn*$(t, T, D_{R,P})$ enumerates all possible partition plans for resources labeled as type t, and calculates the *coherence* increase for each partition plan. The partition plan with the highest *coherence* increase is returned. Then, Algorithm 1 finds the type t_j with the largest *coherence* increase c_{t_j} of all partition plans in P, and checks whether c_{t_j} meets the minimal required gain τ (steps 4-5). If c_{t_j} meets the minimal requirement, t_j is partitioned into two types t_j and t_{max+1} using the partition plan (p_{t_j}, c_{t_j}) and the partition plans for the new resulting types t_j and t_{max+1} are calculated (steps 6-10). If c_{t_j} is smaller than the minimal requirement, the algorithm terminates, and returns the resulting type system. The run time complexity of Algorithm 1 is $O(|L_R| \times |T| \times |p|)$ where $|L_R|$ represents the number of resources without types, $|T|$ is the number of types in the restored type system, and $|p|$ is the number of all distinct predicates associated with any resource in L_R. $|T|$ is bounded by $\frac{1}{\tau}$ since the *coherence* value is increased at least by τ for each loop (each new type), and the *coherence* value is at most 1. Thus, the run-time complexity of Algorithm 1 is $O(|L_R| \times |p|)$ if τ is set. The process of restoring unknown types runs offline at most once for each given dataset.

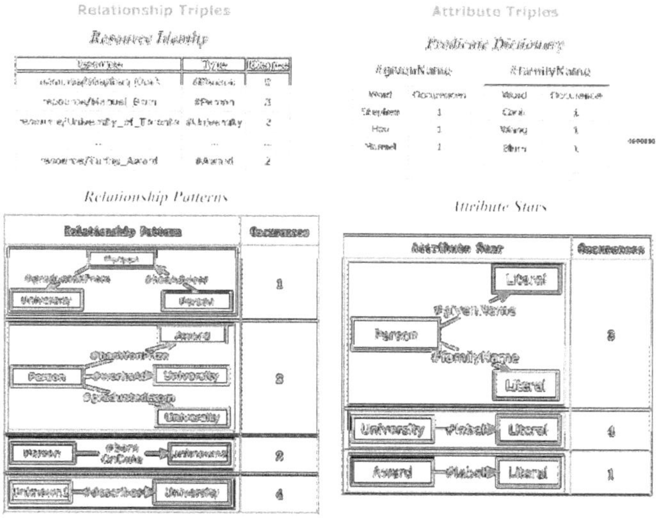

Figure 6. Dataset Analysis

3.2 Dataset Analysis

To provide a benchmark dataset "similar" to a given dataset G, we consider two aspects of similarity: similar characteristics for (i) literal labels, and (ii) the graph structure. As shown in Figure 6, four dataset features are defined to characterize the given dataset, namely, *resource identity* and *relationship patterns* for relationship triples; *predicate dictionary* and *attribute patterns/stars* for attribute triples.

3.2.1 Resource Identity

We define *resource identity* as the three-column table shown in Figure 6, containing the resource ID, resource type and the number of relationship edges associated with this resource (denoted as $\mathcal{R}$Degree in Figure 6). Though each resource can be uniquely identified by its URI label, most URI labels convey little semantics, and are not important in synthetic data generation. On the other hand, type of the resource is highly related with its predicates and the graph structure. $\mathcal{R}$Degree describes the importance associated with each resource in the relationship graph. It is also used as a threshold to assign the generated resources to *relationship patterns* in the benchmark graph generation.

3.2.2 Relationship Patterns

We introduce *relationship patterns* to characterize the structure of the given relationship graph (the subgraph of the given RDF graph which contains only relationship edges, e.g., the blue subgraph in Figure 1). By using these patterns as building blocks, a set of similar synthetic graphs with different required sizes can be generated. The relationship graph is analyzed via the resource types rather than the resource IDs to generate *relationship patterns.* For *RBench*, the *relationship patterns* are generated by decomposing the relationship graph into subgraphs. As shown in Figure 6, one *path pattern*, one *star pattern,* and two *edge patterns* are generated, and the occurrences of each pattern are recorded for the given relationship graph.

Choosing among different graph patterns generated by decomposing the relationship graph is a tradeoff between the flexibility to reconstruct the synthetic graphs and the ability to preserve structure similarity. Using only edge *patterns* is a flexible way to reconstruct benchmark graphs while preserving the least structure similarity (only the types of resources implicitly identified by predicates and the occurrences of different predicates are preserved). In comparison, using the entire relationship graph as one pattern, or recursively generating the largest spanning trees as patterns is good in preserving the highest structure similarity. However, with such approaches, only some specific size-scaling factors can be achieved when generating benchmark graphs (degree scaling factor $d \neq 1$ is infeasible).

As a response, *RBench* utilizes three types of *relationship patterns* (in preference order): *path patterns*, *star patterns* and *edge patterns*. The motivation is to achieve a flexible benchmark graph generation while frequently queried structures are preserved. To understand the frequently queried structures, the query workloads from different RDF benchmarks [6,11,18,24,35] are analyzed. Queries proposed in [6,11,24,35] are targeted at a specific domain. Most of these queries are path- or star-shaped, which contain less than 5 relationship triples. Queries proposed in [18] are clustered from over 30 million real user queries. These queries are more complex, but the number of relationship edges contained in most of them is still small (more than 80% of queries contain less than 5 relationship triples). Based on this observation, small path patterns and star patterns (with less than 5 relationship edges) are used for generating benchmark graphs to achieve a query performance similar to that of the given dataset. Using small patterns also provides flexible building blocks to achieve different scaling factors for benchmark graphs. *Path patterns* are generated before *star patterns* for two reasons: (1) *path patterns* represent transitive relationships among a set of resources, and play an important role in query evaluation; (2) no *path patterns* will be generated if *star patterns* are generated first (*path patterns* can be viewed as multiple two edge *star patterns*).

The decomposition process of the relationship graph for *RBench* can be achieved by scanning the relationship triples and maintaining lists of paths with the same-source nodes. For each relationship edge, the process tries to attach the edge to a decomposed path, and generates a new path by checking whether the object node in the edge is a source node for any decomposed path. After generating *path patterns* and *edge patterns*, the process tries to combine *edge patterns* with the same-source nodes to generate *star patterns*. Generating *star patterns* with large cardinality is avoided by using a preset threshold (set as 5 in experiments) to constrain the number of edges contained by each *star pattern*.

3.2.3 Predicate Dictionary

Predicate dictionaries characterize attribute predicate literals by recording words and occurrences in them as shown in Figure 6. Predicate dictionaries can be used to generate "similar" synthetic literals for attribute predicates where the word appearing more frequently has a higher probability to be selected to form new literals. This way, the percentage of synthetic literals containing a specific word is similar to the percentage of literals containing the word in the given dataset. This is motivated by the observation that the number of attribute triples containing a specific word (that frequently appears in literals) is almost proportional to the dataset size for real applications. Some attribute predicates are associated with literals which are not textual strings. For these attribute predicates, predicate dictionaries are not used.

3.2.4 Attribute Patterns/Stars

The graph structure of attribute triples can be characterized by *star patterns* as there are no outgoing edges for literal nodes (no paths, no circles). Similar to *relationship patterns*, these star patterns are abstracted into *attribute stars* by considering the node types, rather than node labels, as shown in Figure 6. Different resources of the same type may share the same *attribute star*, and occurrences of each *attribute star* in the given RDF dataset G are recorded. It is

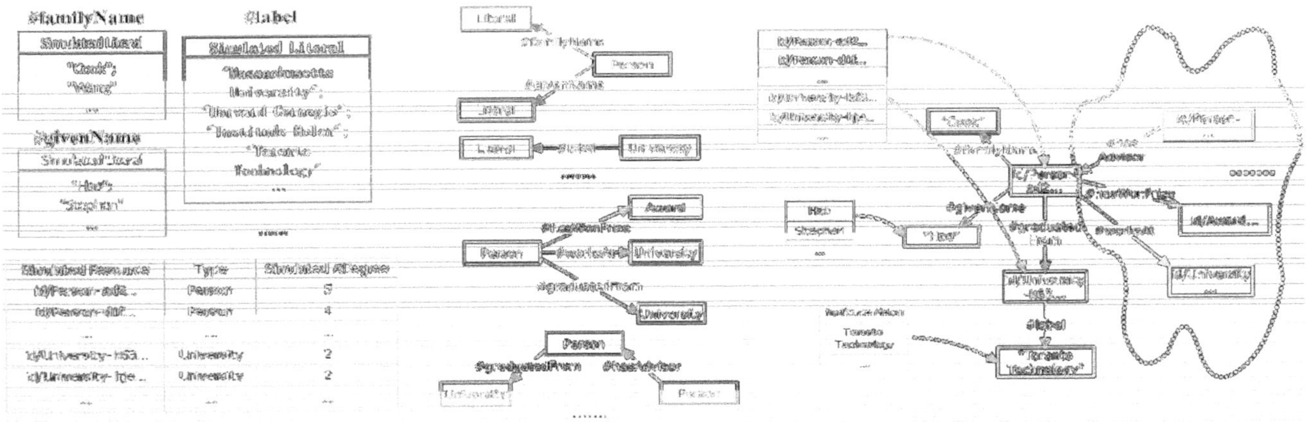

(a) Simulating Resources and Literals (b) Simulating Feature Graphs (c) Assigning Simulated Resources and Literals to Feature Graphs

Figure 7. Benchmark Graph Generation

also observed that the number of different *attribute stars* is significantly smaller than the number of resources, and most resources of the same type share the same set of attribute predicates.

3.3 Benchmark Graph Generation

Benchmark graph is generated in three steps: (1) generate resources and literals based on *resource identity* and *predicate dictionaries*; (2) generate feature graphs based on *attribute stars* and *relationship patterns*; (3) assign the generated resources and literals to the generated feature graphs. An example demonstrating the process of generating benchmark graphs is shown in Figure 7.

3.3.1 Resources and Literals

The generated resources are recorded in the same form as *resource identity*. As the labels of resources are URIs and have little semantics, labels of generated resources are in the form of types with random GUIDs (globally unique identifiers). Types are assigned to generated resources according to the type distribution (the percentage of resources belonging to each type) in *resource identity*. Also, the distribution of $\mathcal{R}$Degrees for resources of the same type in *resource identity* is utilized to assign $\mathcal{R}$Degrees to the generated resources by taking the degree scaling factor into consideration. The number of generated resources is $\frac{s}{d}$ times the number of resources in the given dataset where s the size scaling factor, and d is the degree scaling factor. To ensure the connectivity of the benchmark graph, triples with predicate "rdf:type" which describe the types of all generated resources are produced first in *RBench*.

Generating literals from *predicate dictionaries* is performed in a similar way as in SP2B [24] and BSBM [6]. In order to generate literals more efficiently, large numbers of candidate words for each attribute predicate are pre-generated as plain text files according to the occurrence distribution of these words in *predicate dictionaries*. Literals are generated by simply reading a sequence of words from these files. The length (the number of words) of the generated literals for each attribute predicate is set as the average length of literals in the given dataset. Using *predicate dictionaries* to generate literals is a good option for attribute predicates satisfying two properties: (1) the literals are textual strings; (2) the number of literal nodes is proportional to the dataset size. For other attribute predicates, the set of literals in the given dataset can be directly utilized in the benchmark.

3.3.2 Feature Graphs and Node Assignment

As shown in Figure 7, feature graphs are *attribute stars* and *relationship patterns*. The generated dataset changes the number of occurrences of *relationship patterns* in the given dataset by the size scaling factor s. For attribute triples, there are two alternatives: the number of occurrences of *attribute stars* in the generated dataset can be (1) the size scaling factor s times that in the given dataset; (2) or $\frac{s}{d}$ times that in the given dataset, where d is the degree scaling factor. With the first option, the number of triples in the resulting benchmark graph is exactly s times that in the given dataset. However, for real datasets that grow over time, the number of attribute triples associated with each resource may remain almost constant. Since the number of triples and the average degree in the generated benchmark are estimates, we consider both options (1) and (2).

Assignment of resources to generated *attribute stars* is based on the resource type of their root nodes. As shown in Figure 7, the generated resource with type "Person" can be assigned to any *attribute star* rooted at "Person". The literals assigned to generated *attribute stars* are extracted from pre-generated files based on attribute predicates. Assignment of resources to generated *relationship patterns* should not only match the type of the resource, but also consider the generated $\mathcal{R}$Degree. The rule of resource assignment to *relationship patterns* is that the sum of the degree of a resource in all assigned *relationship patterns* is not to exceed its generated $\mathcal{R}$Degree. Triples are generated simultaneously with node assignment for each edge in feature graphs. Node assignment process may generate duplicate triples when the same pair of resources is assigned to a specific predicate multiple times (either in one feature graph or multiple feature graphs). As the analysis of *attribute stars* and *relationship patterns* contains no duplicate triples, resources in these duplicate triples are swapped to generate distinct triples to ensure that the number of generated triples match the size requirement (empirically, the probability to generate duplicate triples is low as the number of distinct resource pairs is significantly larger than the number of generated triples for most RDF datasets).

4. QUERY WORKLOAD GENERATION

Query workloads defined for existing benchmarks [6,11,24,35] are strictly domain-specific, and limited in their coverage of diverse graph structures. Most queries are defined with SPARQL, a graph matching query language that uses graph patterns as basic query units. Attribute edges with specified labels provide the most effective way to locate the matching resources. The more attributes specified in the query, the less matching resources are found. In comparison, relationship edges in query patterns often lead to nested joins among resources, resulting in an increased number of

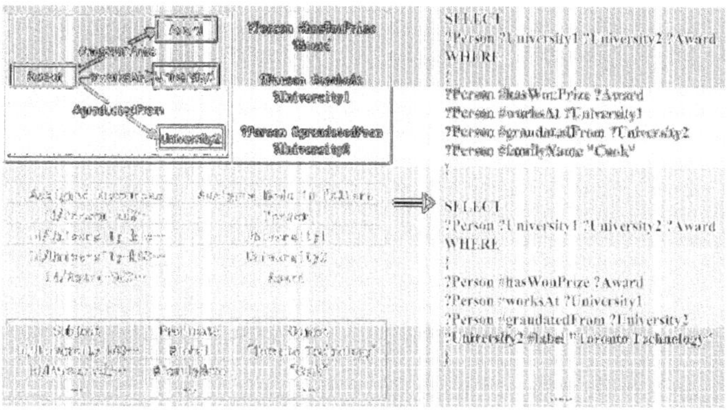

Figure 8. Query Generation Process

intermediate matching results. Thus, the types of queries utilized in *RBench* are defined based on the structures of relationship edges. Five types of queries are defined (based on the shapes of graph structures involving relationship edges similar to *relationship patterns*): node queries, edge queries, star queries, path queries, and subgraph queries (including tree queries and cyclic queries). Queries defined with similar structure types are also utilized in [1].

Query workload generation utilizes the results in dataset analysis to propose a systematic way to generate different types of queries. The first four types of queries are generated based on *attribute stars* and *relationship patterns*, and are generated in parallel with the benchmark generation. The top *k, where k* is an adjustable parameter, resource assignment combinations for each unique *relationship pattern* are recorded, and attribute triples associated with these recorded resources are retrieved. Similarly, for *attribute stars*, the top *k* resource and literal combinations assigned to each unique *attribute star* are recorded. Recorded *attribute stars* and *relationship patterns* with assigned resources and literals are utilized as the candidate queries. The process to generate *RBench* queries has the following four steps, which is illustrated in Figure 8 for a star query: (1) choose a *relationship pattern* according to the desired type, and formulate as triple patterns; (2) choose a recorded resource combination for this *relationship pattern,* and retrieve the attribute triples associated with the assigned resources; (3) formulate attribute triples as triple patterns by relabeling the resource node accordingly (e.g., "?Person #familyName 'Cook'"); (4) formulate *RBench* query to identify resource IDs by using a subset of these triple patterns in query generation. The main advantages of utilizing *attribute stars* and *relationship patterns* in generating query workload are: (a) all predicates of benchmark data are covered by candidate queries; (b) frequent *relationship patterns* among resources are covered by candidate queries; (c) it is easier to generate a set of identical queries for benchmarks with different scaling parameters by utilizing the candidate queries for the same set of *relationship patterns*. However, these queries may provide a biased coverage of the graph structure for the resulting benchmark graphs since the analysis of *relationship patterns* is based on the given graph. This bias can be reduced by using subgraph queries which are discussed next.

Subgraph queries are generated by first randomly selecting a subgraph from the benchmark graph, and then processing the subgraph to generate SPARQL queries by using the types of resources in formulating triple patterns. Subgraph selection begins by selecting a small component of the benchmark graph, and recursively adds one random edge adjacent to the already selected subgraph until the query template size requirement is reached (the selection takes the types of edges into consideration). For cyclic queries, Tarjan's strongly connected components algorithm [28] is utilized to identify cycles in the benchmark graph. The process to generate SPARQL queries from a subgraph is similar to generating other types of queries. Triple patterns are formulated by using resource types, and SPARQL queries are generated to identify resource IDs by using a subset of these triple patterns. Subgraph queries provide additional graph structure coverage for *RBench.*

RBench emphasizes benchmark data generation and query workload generation in the context of viewing and querying RDF data as graphs. This fits the trend in the database community, and the requirement of graph-based functionalities to query RDF data, such as querying for paths. Many new RDF management systems [2,9,36] rely on more sophisticated, structure-based indexes. Note that query workload generation utilized in *RBench* does not consider some complex functionalities of SPARQL, such as aggregation, and property paths. Most of these complex functionalities require pre-knowledge for the given datasets and users can generate SPARQL queries with complex functionalities by using subgraph queries. The design of *RBench* also takes RDF reasoning into consideration. *RBench* generation is based on the type system and predicates associated with the given dataset which preserve characteristics of the ontologies utilized in it. For relation patterns, *path patterns* are considered as the first priority before *star patterns* and *edge patterns* to preserve the transitive connections in the given dataset. However, reasoning queries are more related with a specific domain (a set of ontologies), and specifying reasoning queries often needs pre-knowledge of the dataset. Thus, the query workload generation for *RBench* focuses on generating graph templates directly from the given dataset. Comparing with benchmarks which focus on reasoning queries (LUBM [11] and UOBM [35]), the same set of queries can be executed on *RBench* benchmarks generated from them without any modification.

5. *RBENCH* EVALUATION

We evaluate *RBench* for three aspects: (i) time and memory complexity of RBench, (ii) benchmark evaluation, and (iii) query evaluation analysis. *RBench* framework is implemented with Visual C# 2010 and SQL Server 2008. All experiments were performed on a 2.93GHZ Intel(R) Xeon X5570 machine with 48GB ram running Windows Server 2008 R2.

5.1 Time and Memory Complexity Analysis

RBench generator is designed to preprocess and analyze each given RDF dataset once, and use the dataset analysis results to generate benchmarks with different parameters. The results of dataset preprocessing and dataset analysis are stored in SQL tables. Benchmarks are generated in six steps:

1. Parser Step: The given RDF dataset is scanned to generate three tables in SQL: relationship edge table, attribute edge table and resource type table.

2. Triple Extraction: The resource type table is loaded in memory to build dictionary look up for the types of each resource, and triples containing only resources defined with types are extracted by scanning the relationship edge table and attribute edge table. During this scan, resource identity table and predicate dictionary table are generated.

3. Type Restore: The current type system is evaluated. If the type system passes the evaluation, we continue to step 4. Otherwise, restoring unknown types is needed (by running Algorithm 1), and we go to step 2.

4. Pattern Decomposition: *Relationship patterns* and *attribute stars* are generated from the extracted relationship and attribute triples.

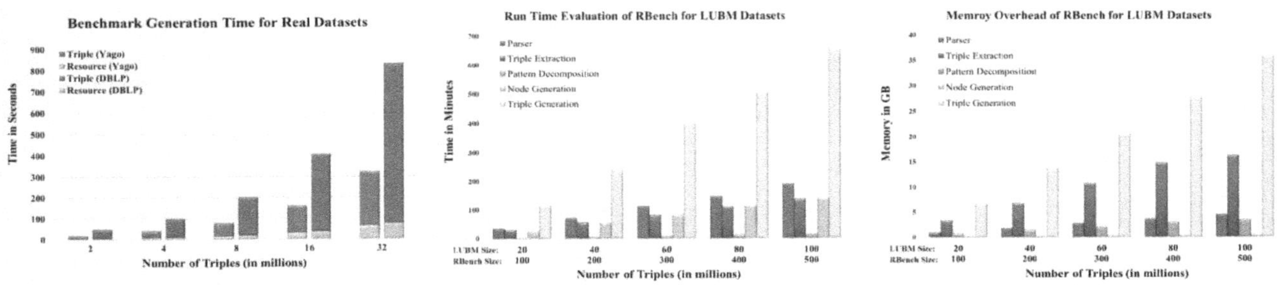

(a) (b) (c)

Figure 9. Time and Memory Complexity of RBench for Real and Benchmark Datasets

5. Resource Generation: The required number of resources are generated based on parameters s and d.

6. Triple Generation: Relationship triples are generated by assigning resources to *relationship patterns* and attribute triples are generated by assigning resources to *attribute stars*.

The most time-consuming part of *RBench* generator is writing the results into the database. By loading the resource type table into memory, the time complexity for steps 1, 2 and 4 are linear in the size of the given dataset. The time complexity of Algorithm 1 is $O(|L_R| \times |p|)$ as explained in Section 3.1.1. Compared with resource generation (step 5), resource assignment to *relationship patterns* (step 6) is more time consuming since the $\mathcal{R}$Degrees for all generated resources need to be maintained and updated. To provide efficient triple generation, the generated resources are loaded into memory to build the dictionary look-up. After step 4, only four tables are necessary to generate benchmarks: resource identity table, predicate dictionary table, relationship pattern table and attribute star table. Compared with the given RDF dataset, these four tables are much smaller (10-30% of disk space). The highest memory overhead of RBench is loading resource type table in step 2, and maintaining the generated resources with $\mathcal{R}$Degrees in step 6. Utilization of efficient resource type look-ips for triple extraction and triple generation processes is a must for generating benchmarks with millions of triples.

Time and space efficiency tests for *RBench* are performed by generating benchmarks from both real and synthetic datasets. For real datasets, we focus on evaluating the time complexity of generating benchmark graphs (step 5 and step 6). Figure 9 (a) shows benchmark graph generation time for *RBench* from DBLP dataset (~20 million triples) and Yago dataset (~ 20 million triples) for different sizes in number of million triples (here, d is 1 to ensure that the number of resources generated increases linearly with benchmark size). For synthetic datasets, we first generate LUBM datasets with different sizes (20 M to 100 M triples). *RBench* generator is then utilized to generate a benchmark dataset for each LUBM dataset by setting $s = 5$ and $d = 1$. The time for each step (except step 3 as LUBM has a complete type system) is shown in Figure 9 (b), and the peak of memory overhead for each step is also identified in Figure 9 (c). As observed, the dataset preprocessing and dataset analysis times are linear with the size of the given dataset, while the benchmark graph generation time is linear with the size of the generated benchmark. Note that, the type restoring process (step 3) is only required for Yago. **Algorithm 1** runs in less than 5 minutes on the Yago dataset with over 2 million resources without type definition. By observing the results, four unknown types are generated for Yago dataset as wiki resources, wiki category resources, wordnet resources and date resources. As Yago dataset brings knowledge from both Wikipedia and Wordnet, this result provides a better dataset analysis for Yago dataset. Triple generation (step 6) has the highest memory overhead since all generated resources with $\mathcal{R}$ Degrees are maintained in main memory.

5.2 Dataset Metrics & *RBench*

Benchmark evaluation aims to validate the claim that benchmark datasets generated by *RBench* have similar structure as the given RDF dataset. For this experiment, *RBench* is utilized to generate benchmarks from six datasets (both real and synthetic) utilized in Section 2. Three dataset metrics (*dataset coherence, relationship specialty* and *literal diversity*) are utilized to evaluate the generated *RBench* benchmarks. Results are shown in Figure 10 (*RBench* benchmarks are labeled as R-given dataset). For Figure 10 (a), (b) and (c), the degree scaling factor is set as 1 to generate *RBench* benchmarks (different size scaling factors are tested which give similar evaluation results for all datasets). As observed, the benchmark datasets generated by *RBench* yield similar evaluation results as the given dataset for all three metrics. Detailed analyses of these results are in following subsections.

5.2.1 Literal Diversity

The *literal diversity* of *RBench* datasets and the given datasets are identical by design, as shown in Figure 10 (a), due to utilizing *attribute stars* and *predicate dictionaries* features. *Attribute stars* provide information about the distribution of different attribute predicates and the attribute patterns associated with resources of each type. *Predicate dictionaries* capture the dictionary information for each attribute predicate, and are utilized to simulate the new literals. By utilizing *attribute stars* and *predicate dictionaries* in data generation, *RBench* benchmarks inherit the characteristics of attribute triples (both predicates and literals) from the given dataset. Different scaling factors have no impact on *literal diversity* evaluation.

5.2.2 Dataset Coherence

The *dataset coherence* measures how uniformly predicates are distributed among resources of each type. *RBench* provides an effective way to preserve the graph structures among types and predicates by utilizing *relationship patterns* and *attribute stars*. *Relationship patterns* and *attribute stars* are generated by considering the types of resources and the associated predicates in dataset analysis. Thus, predicates associated with resources of each type remain the same for *RBench* benchmarks and the given dataset. Feature graphs generated as star shapes provide identical structures between the center resource and its associated predicates. Since resources are all assigned as the centers for *attribute stars*, attribute predicates are distributed identically among resources of each type between benchmarks and the given dataset. The situation is different for relationship predicates: 1) *relationship patterns* are in

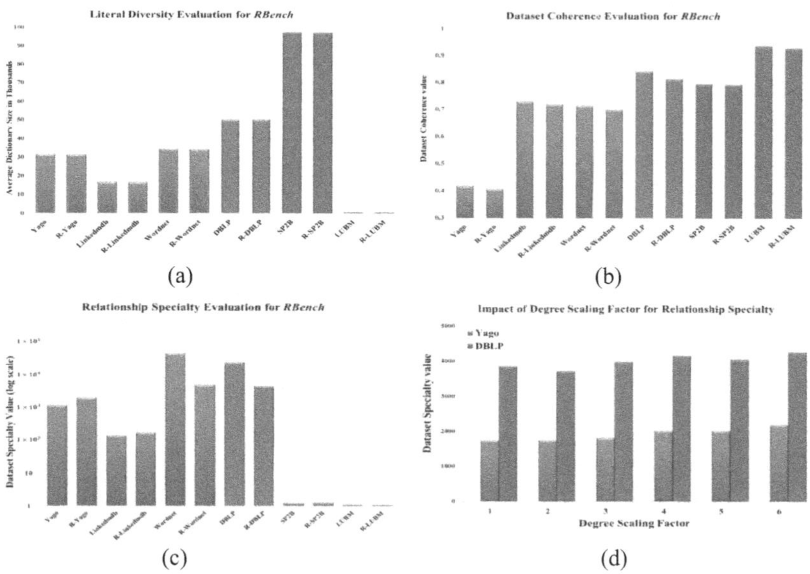

Figure 10. Benchmark Evaluation Results for *Literal Diversity* (a), *Dataset Coherence* (b) and *Relationship Specialty* (c, d)

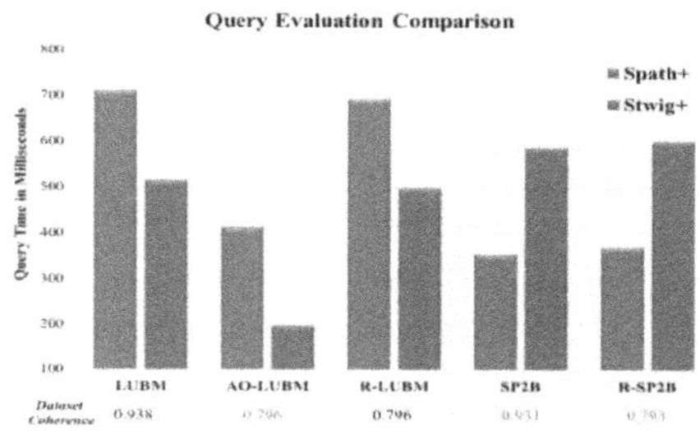

Figure 11. Query Evaluation for *AO Benchmark* and *RBench*

the shapes of paths, stars and edges; 2) resources are not always assigned to the centers of *patterns* with star shape. Since the generated resources are assigned to *relationship patterns* by considering types and $\mathcal{R}$ Degrees only, the distribution of relationship predicates among resources of each type may be slightly different from the given RDF dataset. As shown in Figure 10 (b), *dataset coherence* values of *RBench* benchmarks are slightly smaller than the given RDF datasets. As observed in the *coverage* metric computation, resource assignment to *relationship patterns* yields minor variance on the distribution of relationship predicates. For relationship predicates which are originally associated with most resources of a type in the given dataset, this variance leads to a small reduction in *coverage* values. As different degree scaling factors can be utilized to generate benchmark data, *RBench* benchmarks can achieve different *dataset coherence* values from the same given dataset.

A smaller than 1 degree scaling factor value results in (i) a much sparser graph, and (ii) the same predicates being associated with smaller numbers of resources, which lead to smaller *dataset coherence* values. *Dataset coherence* values increase if the degree scaling factor is increased to a value larger than 1.

5.2.3 Relationship Specialty

Star patterns (one type of *relationship patterns*) and the utilization of the generated $\mathcal{R}$Degrees in resource assignment are important to preserve *relationship specialty* of the given dataset. Most of the resources associated with the same relationship predicate significantly more frequently than others are decomposed as *star patterns*. These *star patterns* are assigned with new resources with large simulated $\mathcal{R}$Degrees. The utilization of $\mathcal{R}$Degrees provides a way to imply a hidden "role" system similar to real datasets. As observed in Figure 10 (c), *relationship specialty* values for *RBench* benchmarks and the given RDF datasets are not exactly the same; but the trend of *relationship specialty* for different datasets are illustrated in a consistent way between the given datasets and *RBench* benchmarks. Note that there is a significant difference between the *relationship specialty* values of synthetic datasets and real datasets, which is also preserved in the benchmarks generated by *RBench*.

Different degree scaling factors has little impact on relationship specialty since relationship specialty is measured by kurtosis, and degree scaling factors scale the distribution of relationship predicates for each resource uniformly. This is shown in Figure 10 (d) using *RBench* benchmarks generated from Yago and DBLP with different degree scaling factors.

5.3 Query Evaluation Analysis

Query evaluation analysis of *RBench* has two parts: 1) comparing *RBench* with the existing application-specific RDF benchmark generator [8]; 2) comparing *RBench* benchmarks with scaling datasets both from real applications and benchmarks.

5.3.1 Experimental Set Up

Query Techniques: Three query algorithms are utilized in the query evaluation analysis, namely, Spath [34], Stwig [27] and RDF3X [20]. Spath [34] is a graph template matching algorithm which takes paths as basic join units, and utilizes neighborhood signature-based pruning to improve query performance. Stwig [27] is a graph join algorithm which takes Stwig as basic join units, and utilizes the trinity memory (similar functionalities are implemented in single machine environment). RDF3X [20] is a SPARQL query algorithm which takes triples/edges as basic join units, and utilizes indexes over 6 permutations of the three dimensions (Subjects, Predicates and Objects) of RDF triples. Spath and Stwig are revised to support directed graphs with Visual C# 2010 (named as Spath+ and Stwig+ in experiments). The motivation to utilize these three query algorithms are: 1) to cover different basic join units (path pattern for Spath, star pattern for Stwig and edge pattern for RDF3X); and 2) to utilize diverse techniques to accelerate query processing (neighborhood index for Spath, trinity memory for Stwig, and dimension indexes for RDF3X).

Query Generation: Since the three query algorithms utilize different types of graph patterns as basic join units, subgraph queries are used to provide results without bias in query evaluation. Since Spath and Stwig do not utilize edge labels in query evaluation, the subgraph queries are formulated without specifying the predicates. Subgraph queries are generated as size 6 (6 triples/edges) with at most two attribute edges.

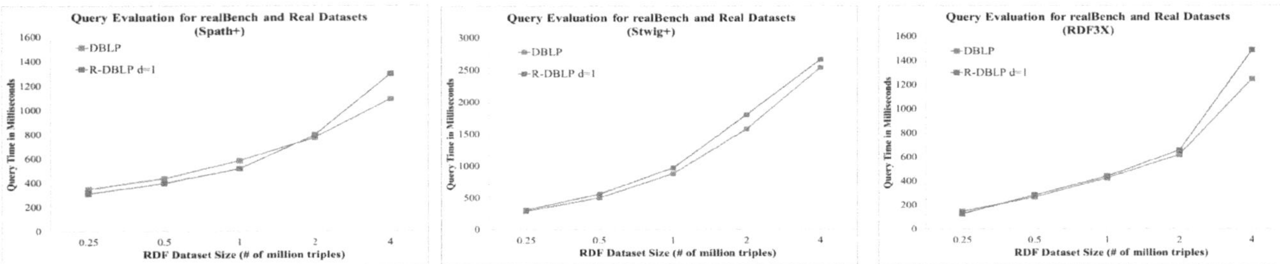

Figure 12. Query Performance Evaluation for *R*-DBLP and DBLP (Spath+, Stwig+ and RDF3X)

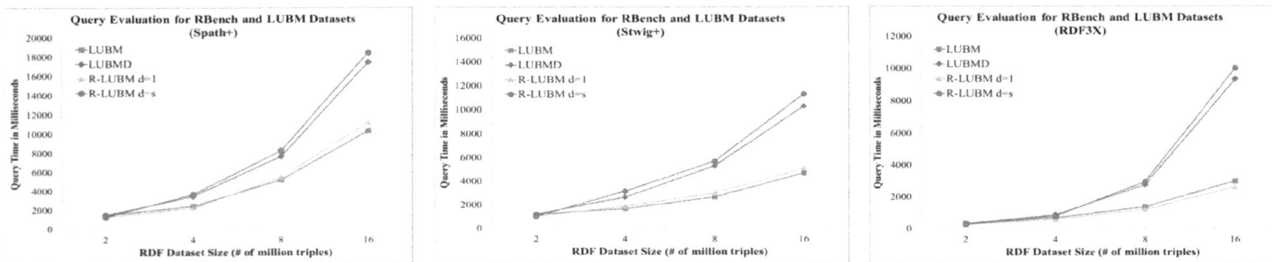

Figure 13. Query Performance Evaluation for *R*-LUBM, LUBM and LUBMD (Spath+, Stwig+ and RDF3X)

5.3.2 Application-Specific Benchmark Comparison

The application-specific benchmark generator [8] (referred as *AO benchmark)* is the only comparable benchmark generator for *RBench*. By using *AO benchmark* generator, a series of benchmarks with smaller sizes and smaller *coherence* values can be generated by selectively removing triples from the given dataset. *AO benchmark* focuses on providing benchmarks with varied "structuredness" from the given dataset and show that changing the characteristic (*coherence*) of the dataset changes query execution times. In comparison, *RBench* is designed to generate benchmarks preserving the characteristic of the given dataset. To show this difference, Stwig and Spath are chosen to evaluate subgraph queries for benchmarks generated by *AO Benchmark* and *RBench*. Five datasets are utilized: LUBM, AO-LUBM, R-LUBM, SP2B and R-SP2B. All five datasets utilized have similar sizes (about 1 million triples). LUBM is generated directly by using the LUBM generator. For AO-LUBM and R-LUBM, they are both generated from a larger LUBM dataset (with about 1.5 million triples). The *coherence* value of AO-LUBM is smaller than that of LUBM and is the same as the *coherence* of SP2B. Two sets of subgraph queries are generated for LUBM and SP2B (40 queries with 6 edges). The average query time of these 40 subgraph queries on different datasets are shown in Figure 11.

As observed, the query evaluation results of Spath and Stwig on SP2B are completely different compared with LUBM. By reducing the *coherence* of LUBM from 0.938 to 0.796, the queries are executed much faster on AO-LUBM than on LUBM. This reaffirms that changing the characteristics of the dataset (*coherence*) affects query evaluation times. In comparison, query evaluation shows similar results for *RBench*-generated datasets and the given datasets (both LUBM and SP2B), confirming that *RBench* generates benchmark datasets preserve the characteristics of the given datasets. Compared with *RBench*, the biggest drawback of the *AO benchmark* generator is that it can only provide benchmarks with sizes smaller than that of the given datasets.

5.3.3 Scaling Dataset Comparison

A major goal of the application-specific benchmarking is to provide a controllable testing environment for different applications. Different size scaling factor values are utilized to perform different tasks. For datasets approaching billion triples (e.g., *DBpedia* and *YAGO*), providing a smaller copy for efficient data communication and analysis is important. For application deployment, scalability testing which requires scaling up the existing dataset is critical to analyze potential workloads in the future. The purpose of scaling dataset comparison is to analyze whether the benchmarks with varied scaling factors generated by *RBench* provide a testing environment similar to the given datasets, i.e., whether the query performance evaluation of the same set of queries is consistent between the *RBench* benchmarks and the given datasets with varied sizes. For this purpose, two datasets are chosen: publication dataset (DBLP, real dataset) and university dataset (LUBM, benchmark dataset).

For DBLP, we use the yearly updated versions to generate five DBLP datasets with different sizes which contain publications of different time periods (M represents million): 0.25M triples (1980-84), 0.5M triples (1980-86), 1M triples (1980-90), 2M triples (1980-94) and 4M triples (1980-99). To generate the corresponding *RBench* benchmarks, the DBLP dataset containing publications from year 1980-90 (1 M triples) is utilized as the given dataset to analyze dataset features. Since the average node degree for different DBLP datasets remains almost the same over the years (slight increase), R-DBLP is generated by using the parameter d as 1 and s as 0.25, 0.5, 1, 2 and 4. Since *RBench* utilizes the DBLP dataset with 1M triples as the given dataset, different tasks of real application testing (*scaling up* and *miniaturization* of the given dataset) are addressed. The evaluated query workload is a set of 40 subgraph queries generated from the first version of the DBLP dataset (0.25M triples). Matching results of these queries on the first version of the DBLP dataset are duplicated on all R-LUBM datasets to ensure that the same set of queries can be executed. Query evaluation results (average run time for 40 queries) of algorithms Spath, Stwig and RDF3X are shown in Figure 12. As observed, all three algorithms show similar patterns between the DBLP dataset and the *RBench* benchmark for varied sizes. This confirms that *RBench* benchmarks provide a similar testing environment as those of the real scaling datasets.

LUBM dataset is used for both size scaling and degree scaling experiments. For size scaling, LUBM datasets are generated by changing the number of universities in LUBM generator. In this way, the size of LUBM dataset is increased by including more universities while its average node degree remains almost the same. To generate LUBM datasets for degree scaling (named as LUBMD), some preset parameters in the LUBM generator are multiplied by a scaling factor to allow more triples generated for each university, such as min/max number of publications for each faculty, min/max number of courses taken by a student. In this way, the LUBM dataset size is increased by including more triples in a university while the number of resources in a university changes very slightly. By using both scaling methods, 7 datasets are generated: LUBM2 (14 universities, 2M triples), LUBM4 (28 universities, 4M triples), LUBM8 (56 universities, 8M triples), LUBM16 (110 universities, 16M triples), LUBMD4 (14 universities, 4M triples), LUBMD8 (14 universities, 8M triples) and LUBMD16 (14 universities, 16M triples). R-LUBM is generated from LUBM2 by using two different settings of parameters, $d = 1$ and $d = s$ (s is set as 1, 2, 4 and 8). Setting d as 1 means that the dataset size increase is merely a result of newly added resources as the average degree for each resource remains the same. In the opposite direction, setting d as s indicates that the number of resources in a dataset remains the same; but the connections among resources are drastically increased. The results (average query run time for 40 subgraph queries) are shown in Figure 13. Compared with the LUBM dataset with similar average node degree, the running time of the same set of queries degrades much faster as the dataset size increases for all algorithms on LUBMD. As observed, R-LUBM with different parameters simulates both scaling situations successfully, and the query evaluation results on R-LUBM are consistent with those from LUBM and LUBMD datasets. Thus, *RBench* can provide a different testing environment to simulate different scaling datasets (both size and degree scaling) which are important for generating RDF benchmarks. Though the purpose here is not to compare the query performance of different algorithms, RDF3X tends to yield the best results for datasets with varied sizes. Indexing all permutations of the three dimensions of triples and the utilization of hash join and merge join are beneficial.

6. RELATED WORKS

Many RDF benchmarks have been developed recently. Considering the design, we categorize them as domain-specific [1,3,6,11,18, 24,35] and application-specific [8] benchmarks. LUBM [11], BSBM [6] and SP2B [24] are among the first RDF benchmarks which use strict pre-defined domain schema to generate synthetic data. Due to the small numbers of types and predicates utilized in these three benchmarks, the generated synthetic data has a limited variability; and inherent graph structures are repetitively generated. BSBM and SP2B both use SPARQL queries to test performances of different RDF management systems; and a variety of SPARQL features (such as FILTER, and OPTIONAL) are evaluated. The queries proposed by LUBM benchmark are plain SPARQL queries which focus on evaluating systems with different reasoning capabilities. UOBM [35] extends the ontology utilized in LUBM to include disjunctive axioms and negation, more relationships, and more properties for different types of resources. WatDiv [1] (Waterloo SPARQL Diversity Test Suite) is a great effort to allow customizable domain schema by using a dataset description language. WatDiv enables users to create their own test databases and/or to customize existing ones. The query template generator is also provided by WatDiv to generate queries with different graph structures. DBPSB benchmark [18] is the first domain-specific benchmark which uses non-artificial data and queries. The data are generated by duplicating or sampling triples directly from DBpedia. Queries utilized in DBPSB are analysed and clustered from 31.5M real user queries. The Linked Data Benchmark Council (LDBC) [3] works to bridge the best practices of the TPC (Transaction Processing Council) to the benchmark of RDF database industry. Two benchmarks, the Social Network Benchmark (SNB) and the Semantic Publishing Benchmark (SPB) are currently under development.

The *AO benchmark* proposed in [8] is the first effort of application-specific benchmarking for RDF data. Compared with *RBench*, the *AO benchmark* is designed to generate benchmarks with varied *structuredness* from the given dataset. By computing the impact of removing predicates for resources, the *AO benchmark* formulates an integer programming problem for selectively removing triples in the given dataset to achieve the desired smaller dataset *coherence* and smaller dataset sizes. *Coverage* and *coherence* metrics are introduced [8], as an intuitive way to combine primitive metrics into one single measure of *structuredness* of RDF datasets. A comprehensive study of the *structuredness* of RDF graphs is also presented in [4]. A framework is proposed [4] to discover a partitioning of the entities of an RDF graph into subsets which have high *structuredness* with respect to a specific function chosen by the user.

7. CONCLUSIONS

RBench provides application-specific benchmarking for RDF data. By utilizing the three dataset evaluation metrics (*dataset coherence, relationship specialty* and *literal diversity*), we show that existing domain-specific RDF benchmarks are limited in coverage for the diverse graph structures of real RDF datasets, and can not provide a comparable testing environment. As RDF data model is defined without a strict schema, the application-specific benchmarking is a better fit to generate RDF benchmarks. Motivated by this, we propose *RBench* which can be utilized to generate benchmarks from any given RDF dataset having similar characteristics of its graph structure and literal labels. The process to generate *RBench* benchmarks contains three steps: dataset preprocessing, dataset analysis and benchmark graph generation. Four features are utilized to analyze the characteristics of the given RDF dataset as *resource identity*, *relationship patterns*, *predicate dictionary* and *attribute stars*. Benchmark data are generated by simulating feature graphs based on *relationship patterns* and *attribute stars,* and then new resources and literals are assigned to feature graphs to reconstruct the benchmark graph. Consistent with the application-specific design, the query workload generation of *RBench* can generate different types of queries in parallel with the benchmark generation. Three aspects of *RBench* are evaluated through experiments: time and memory complexity of benchmark generation, benchmark dataset evaluation, and query evaluation analysis. By using real and synthetic datasets, we empirically show that *RBench* benchmarks can achieve different benchmark generation tasks with size and degree scaling, and provide the expected testing environment similar as the given scaling datasets.

There are several directions to extend the *RBench* framework. Providing benchmarks generated from multiple given datasets to simulate the results of the data integration of different applications; and addressing the attribute correlation and evaluating different choices of relationship patterns in different contexts for benchmark generation are among the future directions to explore.

8. ACKNOWLEDGEMENTS

Special thanks to Soumya Ray and Gültekin Özsoyoğlu for their suggestions and helpful comments for Algorithm 1, and for improving the presentation of this paper respectively. We also would like to thank anonymous reviewers for their valuable comments.

9. REFERENCES

[1] Aluç, G., Hartig, O., Özsu, M. T., & Daudjee, K. Diversified stress testing of RDF data management systems. In The Semantic Web–ISWC 2014, p. 197-212. 2014.

[2] Aluç, G., Ozsu, M. T., & Daudjee, K. Workload matters: Why RDF databases need a new design. Proceedings of the VLDB Endowment, 7(10), p. 837-840, 2014.

[3] Angles, R., Boncz, P. A., Larriba-Pey, J., Fundulaki, I., Neumann, T., Erling, O., Neubauer, P., Martínez-Bazan, N., Kotsev, V. & Toma, I. The linked data benchmark council: a graph and RDF industry benchmarking effort. ACM SIGMOD Record, 43(1), p. 27-31, 2014.

[4] Arenas, M., Diaz, G. I., Fokoue, A., Kementsietsidis, A., & Srinivas, K. A Principled Approach to Bridging the Gap between Graph Data and their Schemas. PVLDB 7(8): p. 601-612, 2014.

[5] Bizer, C., Lehmann, J., Kobilarov, G., Auer, S., Becker, C., Cyganiak, R., & Hellmann, S. DBpedia-A crystallization point for the Web of Data. Web Semantics: science, services and agents on the world wide web, 7(3), p. 154-165, 2009

[6] Bizer, C. & Schultz, A. The berlin SPARQL benchmark. Int. J. Semantic Web Inf. Syst., 5(2), p.1–24, 2009.

[7] Broekstra, J., Kampman, A., & Van Harmelen, F. Sesame: A generic architecture for storing and querying RDF and RDF schema. In The Semantic Web—ISWC, p. 54-68. Springer Berlin Heidelberg, 2002.

[8] Duan, S., Kementsietsidis, A., Srinivas, K., & Udrea, O. Apples and oranges: a comparison of RDF benchmarks and real RDF datasets. In Proceedings of the 2011 ACM SIGMOD International Conference on Management of data, p. 145-156. ACM, 2011 June.

[9] Erling, O. Virtuoso, a Hybrid RDBMS/Graph Column Store. IEEE Data Eng. Bull., 35(1), p. 3-8, 2012.

[10] Erling, O., & Mikhailov, I. RDF Support in the Virtuoso DBMS. In Networked Knowledge-Networked Media, p. 7-24. Springer Berlin Heidelberg, 2009.

[11] Guo, Y., Pan, Z., & Heflin, J. LUBM: A benchmark for OWL knowledge base systems. Web Semantics: Science, Services and Agents on the World Wide Web, 3(2), p.158-182, 2005.

[12] Harris, S. & Gibbins, N. 3store: Efficient bulk RDF storage. Proc. of PSSS, p.1-15, 2003.

[13] Jackson, S. L. Statistics plain and simple. Cengage Learning, 2013, ISBN: 1133312535.

[14] Leskovec, J., Kleinberg, J., & Faloutsos, C. Graphs over time: densification laws, shrinking diameters and possible explanations. In Proceedings of the eleventh ACM SIGKDD international conference on Knowledge discovery in data mining, p. 177-187. ACM, 2005 August.

[15] Ley, M. DBLP: some lessons learned. Proceedings of the VLDB Endowment, 2(2), p. 1493-1500, 2009.

[16] Linked Movie DataBase. http://www.linkedmdb.org/.

[17] Mahdisoltani, F., Biega, J., & Suchanek, F. M. YAGO3: A knowledge base from multilingual Wikipedias. In 7th Biennial Conference on Innovative Data Systems Research. CIDR 2015.

[18] Morsey, M., Lehmann, J., Auer, S., Ngomo. DBpedia SPARQL benchmark performance assessment with real queries on real data. In: Proc. 10th Int. Semantic Web Conference. p. 454–469, 2011.

[19] NCBI Taxonomy. http://www.ncbi.nlm.nih.gov/taxonomy/.

[20] Neumann, T., & Weikum, G. RDF-3X: a RISC-style engine for RDF. Proceedings of the VLDB Endowment, 1(1), p. 647-659, 2008.

[21] Nolin, M. A., Ansell, P., Belleau, F., Idehen, K., Rigault, P., Tourigny, N., Roe P., Hogan, J.M. & Dumontier, M. Bio2RDF network of linked data. In Semantic Web Challenge; International Semantic Web Conference (ISWC 2008), 2008.

[22] Qiao, S. & Ozsoyoglu, M. RDF Benchmarks vs Real RDF Datasets: How Different Are They Really. In BeRSys 2014.

[23] Saccharomyces Genome Database. http://www.yeastgenome.org/.

[24] Schmidt, M., Hornung, T., Lausen, G., & Pinkel, C. SP2Bench: a SPARQL performance benchmark. In Data Engineering, 2009. ICDE'09. IEEE 25th International Conference, p. 222-233, 2009, March.

[25] Suchanek, F. M., Kasneci, G., & Weikum, G. Yago: A large ontology from wikipedia and wordnet. Web Semantics: Science, Services and Agents on the World Wide Web, 6(3), p. 203-217, 2008.

[26] Suchanek, F. M., Kasneci, G., & Weikum, G. Yago: a core of semantic knowledge. In Proceedings of the 16th international conference on WWW, p. 697-706, ACM, 2007, May.

[27] Sun, Z., Wang, H., Wang, H., Shao, B., & Li, J. Efficient subgraph matching on billion node graphs. Proceedings of the VLDB Endowment, 5(9), p. 788-799, 2012.

[28] Tarjan, R. E. Depth-first search and linear graph algorithms. SIAM journal on computing, 1(2), p. 146-160, 1972.

[29] Tay, Y. C. Data generation for application-specific benchmarking. VLDB, Challenges and Visions, p.1471-1473, 2011.

[30] The MIT Barton Library dataset. http://simile.mit.edu/rdf-test-data/.

[31] Wilkinson, K., Sayers, C., Kuno, H. A., & Reynolds, D. Efficient RDF Storage and Retrieval in Jena2. In SWDB, Vol. 3, p. 131-150. 2003, September.

[32] WordNet: A lexical database for English (WordNet RDF/OWL Files). http://www.w3.org/2006/03/wn/wn20/.

[33] YAGO: Yet Another Great Ontology. http://www.mpi-inf.mpg.de/yago-naga/yago/.

[34] Zhao, P., & Han, J. On graph query optimization in large networks. Proceedings of the VLDB Endowment, 3(1-2), p. 340-351, 2010.

[35] Zhou, Y., Cuenca Grau, B., Horrocks, I., Wu, Z., & Banerjee, J. Making the most of your triple store: query answering in OWL 2 using an RL reasoner. In Proceedings of the 22nd international conference on World Wide Web, p. 1569-1580. 2013, May.

[36] Zou, L., Mo, J., Chen, L., Özsu, M. T., & Zhao, D. gStore: answering SPARQL queries via subgraph matching. Proceedings of the VLDB Endowment, 4(8), p. 482-493, 2011.

APPENDIX

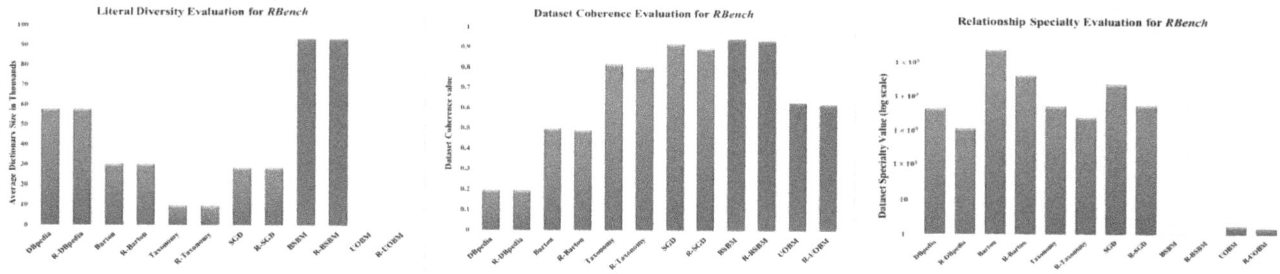

(a) (b) (c)

Figure 14. Benchmark Evaluation Results for *Literal Diversity* (a), *Dataset Coherence* (b) and *Relationship Specialty* (c)

ALEX: Automatic Link Exploration in Linked Data

Ahmed El-Roby*
University of Waterloo
aelroby@uwaterloo.ca

Ashraf Aboulnaga
Qatar Computing Research Institute
aaboulnaga@qf.org.qa

ABSTRACT

There has recently been an increase in the number of RDF knowledge bases published on the Internet. These rich RDF data sets can be useful in answering many queries, but much more interesting queries can be answered by integrating information from different data sets. This has given rise to research on automatically linking different RDF data sets representing different knowledge bases. This is challenging due to their scale and semantic heterogeneity. Various approaches have been proposed, but there is room for improving the quality of the generated links.

In this paper, we present **ALEX**, a system that aims at improving the quality of links between RDF data sets by using feedback provided by users on the answers to linked data queries. **ALEX** starts with a set of candidate links obtained using any automatic linking algorithm. **ALEX** utilizes user feedback to discover new links that did not exist in the set of candidate links while preserving link precision. **ALEX** discovers these new links by finding links that are similar to a link approved by the user through feedback on queries. **ALEX** uses a Monte-Carlo reinforcement learning method to learn how to explore in the space of possible links around a given link. Our experiments on real-world data sets show that **ALEX** is efficient and significantly improves the quality of links.

Categories and Subject Descriptors

H.2.5 [**Heterogeneous Databases**]

Keywords

Linked Data; RDF; Knoweldge Bases; Automatic Linking; Federated Query Processing; Reinforcement Learning

1. INTRODUCTION

In recent years, advances in the field of information extraction have helped in automating the construction and publishing of large RDF knowledge bases. Some of these knowledge bases are general-purpose [3, 9, 11], and others focus on specific domains such as movies[1], geographic information[2], music[3], and city data[4]. Publishing these RDF data sets on the web was encouraged by the Semantic Web principle of making data on the web readable and processable directly by machines [5]. However, publishing these data sets alone is not sufficient. The true power of linked data is realized only when the data sets are linked to each other so that their semantic properties can be fully exploited [8]. Linking data sets is crucial for answering queries that cannot be answered using one RDF data set alone. For example, consider the query "Find all New York Times articles about the NBA's MVP of 2013". Articles about people are available from the New York Times RDF knowledge base. However, we need to know who the "NBA's MVP of 2013" is, since this information cannot be found in the New York Times data set. Another data set like DBpedia could have the information that "LeBron James" is the "NBA's MVP of 2013". One can use the Web Ontology Language (OWL)[5] to define an *owl:sameAs* relation linking the two entities representing "LeBron James" from both data sets. This relation indicates that the two entities refer to the same individual, and enables the system to return all articles about "LeBron James" from the New York Times data set.

Some work has been done on aligning RDF schemas [4, 13] and automatically linking equivalent entities from different data sets [6, 12, 14]. That work aims to automatically introduce *owl:sameAs* links between two data sets. However, automatic linking approaches are best effort in nature, with no guarantees on output quality. They try to infer semantics automatically based on syntax, which is a difficult task in the absence of human guidance. As such, automatic linking of RDF knowledge bases can greatly benefit from user feedback on the quality of the generated links.

In this paper, we introduce **ALEX** (Automatic Link Exploration in Linked Data), a system that improves the quality of links between linked data RDF data sets by utilizing feedback that users provide on answers to their queries. **ALEX** allows users to issue queries over multiple RDF data sets that are linked using any automatic linking approach. These queries can be answered using one or more data sets. When the query answer is produced using links between multi-

*Work done while author was at the Qatar Computing Research Institute

SIGMOD'15, May 31–June 4, 2015, Melbourne, Victoria, Australia.

ACM 978-1-4503-2758-9/15/05 ...$15.00.
http://dx.doi.org/10.1145/2723372.2749428.

[1]http://www.linkedmdb.org/
[2]http://www.geonames.org/
[3]http://musicbrainz.org/
[4]http://www.data.gov/opendatasites
[5]http://www.w3.org/2001/sw/wiki/OWL

ple data sets, ALEX gives the user the opportunity to approve or reject the query answers. ALEX considers the approval/rejection of a query answer as an approval/rejection of the link(s) used to produce this answer, and it uses this feedback to improve the quality of links. ALEX uses a stochastic technique that generalizes the feedback provided by the user and is resilient to errors in that feedback. Errors in user feedback (approving a wrong answer or rejecting a correct answer) can arise due to errors in the data or errors made by the user.

ALEX starts with a set of automatically generated links that can be produced using any automatic linking algorithm (referred to as *candidate links*). ALEX removes incorrect links rejected by the user, but the main focus of ALEX is to find new links that are *similar* to the links approved by the user. The way ALEX finds similar links is as follows: An entity in an RDF data set is represented by a URI. Each entity has a set of attributes (RDF predicates), and values corresponding to these attributes (RDF objects). We represent a link between two entities from different data sets by a set of *features* made up of the attributes of the two entities. A feature is a pair of attributes where the first attribute comes from the first entity and the second comes from the second entity. Each feature has a value, which is the *similarity score* of the values of the two attributes. When a user approves a link by approving a query answer based on this link, ALEX chooses one feature and finds new candidate links for which the value of this feature (i.e., the similarity score) is within a (narrow) range around the value of the feature of the approved link.

An important question that ALEX needs to answer is: *Which feature to explore around for a given approved link?*. Exploring around a random feature is not effective since it incorrectly assumes that all features are of equal importance in determining whether the entities are equivalent. At the same time, ALEX has no prior knowledge of which features may be important, and the best feature to explore around can depend on the link being explored. For example, the title of the two entities may be a good feature to explore around for some link, while the date of birth may return better results for another link. Thus, ALEX needs a way to identify the feature to explore around for any approved link between any two entities.

In this paper, we propose that this problem can be solved using *Monte Carlo reinforcement learning* methods [22], where the system can *learn* which feature to explore around for different links. Using the terminology of reinforcement learning, ALEX aims at learning from interacting with the environment in order to learn the best action to take (feature to explore around) in order to maximize reward (positive user feedback). The feature is chosen by ALEX using a policy that is iteratively improved.

We also develop several optimizations that help ALEX to converge in fewer steps. These optimizations include reducing the search space of links, partitioning the data to exploit parallelism, using a blacklist to prevent known incorrect links from being proposed, and rolling back actions to undo actions that result in exploring many incorrect links.

Our experiments over real-world data sets show that ALEX can improve the quality of the initial set of candidate links, while not exposing the end-user to a large number of incorrect answers. Experiments also show that ALEX converges in a reasonable amount of time and is robust to changes in parameters values.

The contributions of this paper are as follows:

- To the best of our knowledge, we are the first to bridge the gap between automatic linking of data sets on one side and querying linked data on the other side by leveraging user feedback to discover new links between entities without prior knowledge of the data sets or how they were originally linked.
- We propose a reinforcement learning approach to find new links while preserving link precision.
- We develop optimizations to reduce execution time and converge in fewer steps.
- We prove that our approach is sound in terms of finding an optimal policy for links exploration.
- We demonstrate the validity of our approach by running experiments on large, real-world, multi-domain data sets.

The rest of the paper is organized as follows: Section 2 gives an overview of the related work. Section 3 gives some background on reinforcement learning and an overview of ALEX. We describe the details of ALEX in Section 4. In Section 5, we prove the soundness of ALEX. Section 6 shows our optimizations for faster convergence. In Section 7, we discuss our experiments. We conclude in Section 8.

2. RELATED WORK

Automatic Linking: Linked data has enabled seamless connections between open data sets [7]. The idea is to link entities from different data sets that are semantically equivalent to each other. There have been many works on semantic matching of entities, taking different approaches. The SILK framework [23] uses manually defined mapping rules that are applied on input data sets. New data sets require new mapping rules. OBJECTCOREF [14] uses training data to learn how to link entities. However, this requires having good training data that captures most aspects of the input data sets, which is difficult in practice. PARIS [21] is a powerful probabilistic holistic automatic linking algorithm that is fully automatic and does not require any prior information. It also produces better quality links than other approaches. Due to its generality and superior quality, we use PARIS in this paper as our automatic linking algorithm to produce the candidate links that are the starting point for ALEX. However, we emphasize that ALEX can work with any initial set of candidate links, regardless of how they were generated.

Incorporating User Feedback: User feedback has been used to improve schema matching in relational data. In [1], user feedback is used in an iterative exploratory process to guide the system towards the best data sources for the user, and the best mediated schema for these sources. In [15], user feedback is used to order candidate matches so that they can be confirmed by the user. The candidate matches are sorted based on their importance (i.e., they are involved in more queries or associated with more data). A user is asked to confirm or reject each match. In [16], the user is asked during the schema matching process about matches that the system is uncertain about in order to choose the correct match. In the Crowd ER system [24], users are also asked to confirm or reject entity matches. However, due to the large number of questions that can be asked, the system is more concerned with choosing questions that need to be answered first (questions that are more challenging to computers). In contrast to these approaches, ALEX does not ask the user to provide feedback on links but rather on answers to queries. The user wants to see the answers to the queries anyway, so providing feedback on query answers is easier for the user than providing feedback directly on links.

In [25], user feedback is obtained over the answers to a keyword search query. The feedback is represented as a constraint over the ordering of the returned answers, or as identification of good or bad answers. The feedback is then utilized to improve the ordering of answers to future queries. In contrast, ALEX does not expose the user to the ontology of the data sets or the details of the linked entities but rather directly improves the quality of links by utilizing user feedback on the answers to her queries.

In the context of linking open data, ZenCrowd [10] utilizes the crowd by forming micro-tasks using a probabilistic model for manual matching. Its goal is to link traditional web content to the Linked Open Data (LOD) cloud[6]. In this paper, we utilize user feedback to improve the quality of links *in* the LOD cloud to which ZenCrowd tries to link traditional web pages.

One goal of [2] that is related to our problem is to refine links in DBpedia by removing incorrect links to external web pages or resources. Users are shown a caption of the external source and determine if it matches the entity in DBpedia or not. In contrast to all the aforementioned approaches, the most distinct feature of ALEX is that it not only removes incorrect links from the set of candidate links, but also discovers new links that were not part of this set.

3. BACKGROUND AND OVERVIEW

3.1 Reinforcement Learning

In reinforcement learning [22], the learner and decision maker is called the *agent*. Everything else outside of the agent is considered to be the *environment*. A reinforcement learning system consists of four main components:

- *Policy*: The policy defines how a reinforcement learning agent interacts with the environment at a given state. It can be viewed as the mapping from an environment *state* to an *action* taken by the agent. The policy can be as simple as a lookup table, or it can involve extensive computations. It also can be either deterministic or stochastic. In ALEX, we use a stochastic policy. For example, consider a user providing positive feedback on the link (E_1, E_2), where E_1, and E_2 are entities. The policy π might state that when this link is encountered, explore around the feature $(E_1.label, E_2.name)$ with probability 0.8, and around the feature $(E_1.birth, E_2.birthDate)$ with probability 0.2. Formally, $\pi((E_1, E_2), (E_1.label, E_2.name)) = 0.8$ and $\pi((E_1, E_2), (E_1.birth, E_2.birthDate)) = 0.2$. When an action is chosen, say the one that has higher probability, then $\pi((E_1, E_2)) = (E_1.label, E_2.name)$. More details are presented in the following sections.
- *Reward Function*: The reward function defines the goal of the reinforcement learner. It can be viewed as a mapping from a state (or a state-action pair) to a *reward*. The goal of the agent is to maximize the total reward throughout its dynamic interactions with the environment. For example, assume a positive feedback over the link (E_1, E_2) resulted in the exploration of 5 links $\{link_1, \ldots, link_5\}$. Assume that positive feedback comes over $link_1$ and $link_5$, negative feedback comes on $link_3$, and no feedback is received over $link_2$ and $link_4$. In this case, the reward is $R(E_1, E_2) = 2 \times pReward - nReward$.
- *Value Function*: The value function defines what is good in the long run. A *value* of a state can be viewed as the total reward that can be collected from this state taking into account the states that are likely to follow and the rewards available from those states. The major difference between the reward function and the value functions is that the first indicates what is good in an immediate sense (next reward), whereas the second indicates the long-term value of a state (total rewards that can be collected in the future starting from the current state). The reward of a state may be low but its value can be high because other states that yield high rewards can be reached from this state.
- *Environment Model* (optional): This model simulates the behavior of the environment. For example, given a state and an action, the model can determine which state is next and the reward of the action. The model is used in planning because it enables the agent to determine which action to take without experiencing the state. However, there may be cases where a model is not available. In this case, the only way to determine the next state and reward given a state and action is by actually performing the action in the environment. In ALEX, the environment model is unknown because it is not possible to know in advance what feedback users will provide.

Reinforcement learning differs from other branches of machine learning in that the learning agent is not told what actions to take. The agent learns over time how to act by experiencing the return it gets from interacting with the dynamic environment. Reinforcement learning is more suitable than supervised learning [17] for interactive problems where it is impractical to obtain examples of the desired behaviors to use as training data that are correct and representative of most situations in the environment. The reinforcement learning agent learns how to act by trying different actions at different states and aiming to maximize the expected return at those states [22]. The challenge that faces the learning agent is finding a balance between the need to explore as many states as possible while exploiting the current knowledge to maximize the total reward. Also, reinforcement learning needs a way to evaluate the policy used to take actions in order to improve it. In ALEX, we use a Monte Carlo method to evaluate the policy through returns from interactions with the environment. This is a suitable approach in situations like ours where the model of the environment is not known.

3.2 Overview of ALEX

Before we present the details of ALEX, we present an end-to-end overview. ALEX can be integrated in a system that answers queries over multiple data sets of RDF linked data (e.g., data sets in the Linked Open Data cloud). In this paper, we use SPARQL[7] as the query language, although other query languages can be used. An application may send a SPARQL query that can only be answered using data from different data sets that are linked by *owl:sameAs* links. If a link is correct, answers returned based on this link should also be correct unless the data itself is erroneous (which is beyond the scope of this paper). The user evaluates the

[6]http://lod-cloud.net/

[7]http://www.w3.org/TR/sparql11-query/

returned answer and gives her feedback by marking the answer "correct" or "incorrect". If the feedback is positive, ALEX tries to find new *owl:sameAs* links that are similar to the approved link. If the feedback is negative, ALEX removes this link. ALEX works as follows:

- ALEX accepts the links between two data sets as input. These links are automatically generated by any automatic linking algorithm.
- Federated queries are issued over the linked data. A federated query is a query whose answer is not available in one data source, but can be answered using multiple data sources. The query is decomposed into subqueries for each involved data source. However, this fact is hidden from the user who issues the query as if all data is in one place. Answers are retrieved using a federated query processing system (e.g. FedX [19]). A user then gives her feedback on the returned answers. The feedback is as simple as approving or rejecting the returned answer. ALEX takes action immediately based on the feedback, since it assumes that this feedback is correct. However, ALEX has techniques to recover from incorrect feedback.
- ALEX represents each link as a state, starting from which it takes an action after receiving user feedback. The action, in the case of positive feedback, can be described as choosing a feature to explore around within some exploration distance. In the case of negative feedback, the wrong link is removed from the set of candidate links.
- The given feedback is translated into a reward in ALEX. This reward is positive in the case of an approved link (positive feedback), and negative in the case of a rejected one (negative feedback). The value of the reward can be the same for positive and negative feedback, or negative feedback can be penalized more.
- ALEX explores links in a space of feature sets. This space is populated in a pre-processing step, with a feature set for every pair of entities in the two data sets.
- Initially, ALEX chooses arbitrary actions whenever a state is encountered because there is no prior knowledge of what actions to take. Rewards are collected for each state-action pair encountered, and are aggregated to estimate the value of the state-action pair. This is called *policy evaluation.*
- Policy evaluation takes place until sufficient feedback is collected. We call this a feedback *episode.* At the end of an episode, *policy improvement* takes place. Policy improvement modifies the policy so that actions that maximize the reward are taken most of the time, while assigning a low but non-zero probability to other actions in order to ensure continuous exploration.
- These last two steps of policy evaluation and policy improvement are repeated until convergence. ALEX converges when the set of candidate links does not change after an iteration of policy evaluation - policy improvement or when a maximum number of iterations is reached. ALEX can also use a more relaxed convergence condition and stop if the change in the set of candidate links is less than 5%.

4. DISCOVERING NEW LINKS IN ALEX

Starting with the output of any automatic linking algorithm, ALEX's goal is to (1) discover new links that did not exist in the set of candidate links (which improves recall), and (2) preserve the correctness of links by quickly eliminating wrong links in the output (which improves precision).

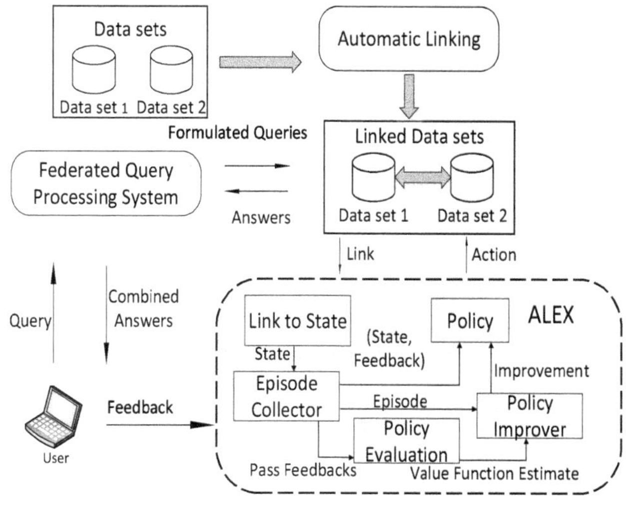

Figure 1: Architecture of a federated query system with ALEX.

Figure 1 shows the architecture of ALEX, in which a user issues a query over RDF data sets that are linked using some automatic linking algorithm. The query is answered by a federated query processing system that is able to answer queries that span multiple data sources (e.g., [18] or [19]). If a query answer is generated based on a link between two data sets, the user is given a chance to evaluate this answer and provide feedback about which answers are correct and which are not. This feedback is interpreted as feedback on the link that is used to generate the answer. That is, if the answer is correct then the link is correct, and if the answer is incorrect the link is incorrect. The feedback is sent to ALEX, which uses its current policy to take an action based on the current state. We emphasize that a user is not *required* to provide feedback on each query answer; if no feedback is provided on an answer, this answer will simply not trigger an action by ALEX. In ALEX, the state is represented by the feature set of the link used to answer the query, while the action is choosing one feature around which ALEX will explore to find new candidate links. The action results in adding these links to the set of candidate links.

An important aspect of reinforcement learning is improving the policy after using it for some time. In ALEX, this is achieved by grouping feedback on states into episodes, where each episode has a number of feedback items. The policy is evaluated while the episode of feedback is collected. Policy evaluation is defined as estimating the value of the states or state-action pairs encountered in an episode. Grouping feedback items into episodes makes the evaluation of the value of the states or state-action pairs more accurate. The larger the number of feedback items in an episode, the more accurate the estimation of the value. At the end of an episode, changes are made to improve the current policy to maximize the collected rewards, a process called policy improvement. The current policy defines the actions that ALEX takes within an episode, until the policy changes at the end of the episode through policy improvement. ALEX continues the iterations of policy evaluation and policy improvement until convergence.

4.1 States in ALEX

In a general reinforcement learning problem, the agent and the environment interact at every discrete time step, $t = 0, 1, 2, \ldots$. At each time step t, the agent perceives the state of the environment $s_t \in S$, where S is the set of all states in the environment. The agent then takes an action $a_t \in A(s_t)$, where $A(s_t)$ is the set of all actions available at the state s_t. As a result of the action taken, the agent receives a reward r_{t+1} and a new state s_{t+1} is reached. The agent's action is determined by the policy π_t where $\pi_t(s, a)$ is the probability that $a_t = a$ at $s_t = s$. In ALEX, the state is defined by the link that was approved or rejected by a user in a feedback item. The state is represented by the state feature set sf of many-to-many mappings between the attributes of the two entities that are linked by the link being considered. For example, consider the two entities E_1 and E_2 with n and m attributes, respectively, $E_1 = \{(p_{11}, o_{11}), (p_{12}, o_{12}), \ldots, (p_{1n}, o_{1n})\}$, and $E_2 = \{(p_{21}, o_{21}), (p_{22}, o_{22}), \ldots, (p_{2m}, o_{2m})\}$, where each attribute is the pair (predicate label, predicate value). An example entity is {(name, "LeBron James"), (birth date, 1984), (age, 29)}. We first construct a similarity matrix between the two entities using a similarity function that returns a score in the range $[0, 1]$. An element in the similarity matrix is $((p_{1x}, p_{2y}), score)$ where p_{1x} is a predicate from the first data set, p_{2y} is a predicate from the second data set, and $score$ is the similarity between the objects associated with these predicates, $score = sim(o_{1x}, o_{2y})$. Scores that are less than a specific threshold are discarded. ALEX uses a generic similarity function that depends on the type of the attributes to be compared (string, integer, float, date, etc.). The state feature set sf is then constructed by choosing the maximum value for each row in the similarity matrix if $n > m$ or each column if $m > n$. In this paper, we use the terms *state* and *link* interchangeably.

4.2 Actions in ALEX

Given a state s_t, ALEX takes an action a_t that is based on a policy π_t. The environment (the user in our case) then responds with a reward r_{t+1}. The ultimate goal of ALEX is to improve the policy π_t so that the maximum total reward is collected. The action of ALEX can be perceived as exploring an area surrounding the current state (the link between two entities) in a particular direction (one feature of the feature set). Given a state represented by a feature set sf of n features, the action a is also a feature set af of n features with a single non-zero feature that represents the offset by which ALEX should explore to discover new links. Formally, ALEX finds all the links that have similarity value between sf and $sf \pm af$. For example, consider the feature set $sf(E_1, E_2)$ ={((*label*, *name*), 0.8), ((*birth*, *year*), 0.6), ((*age*, *year*), 0.4)}. The first element of the feature set means that the predicate *label* from the first entity maps to the predicate *name* from the second entity, and the similarity between the predicate values is 0.8. A possible action can be represented by the action feature set $af(E_1, E_2)$ ={((*label*, *name*), 0.05), 0, 0}, which means that links that have a similarity score between attributes *label* and *name* in the range $[0.75, 0.85]$ should be added to the set of candidate links for future queries and possible feedback opportunities. The step size (0.05 here) is a parameter in ALEX.

ALEX can sometimes take an action that explores around a feature that has values that do not distinguish between entities. For example, it can decide to discover links around the feature (*rdf:type*, *rdf:type*) which has a categorical value *owl:thing*. Exploring around this feature and value is expected to return a large number of incorrect links because a large number of different entities share this attribute and value. ALEX can *learn* that this feature is not distinctive and avoid exploring around it in the future.

4.3 Rewards and Feedback

The goal of ALEX is to maximize the expected return, R_t, defined as the sum of all future rewards:

$$R_t = r_{t+1} + r_{t+2} + \ldots + r_T \tag{1}$$

where T is the final time step. In ALEX, the final time step is when a feedback episode ends. After that, the policy used during the episode is refined through policy improvement, and a new episode is started using the new policy.

In ALEX, the reward is the feedback given by the user. The feedback could be positive (approving a link) or negative (rejecting a link). The value of the reward can be equal in both cases, or we can severely penalize wrong links by giving them a negative value that is larger than the positive value of the approved link.

We also need to define the value of taking an action a at a state s under a policy π. The *action-value function* $Q^\pi(s, a)$ is defined by:

$$\begin{aligned} Q^\pi(s,a) &= E_\pi \{R_t | s_t = s, a_t = a\} \\ &= E_\pi \left\{ \sum_{k=t+1}^{T} r_k | s_t = s, a_t = a \right\} \end{aligned} \tag{2}$$

where E_π is the expected value given that ALEX follows policy π. A fundamental property of the value function is that it follows a recursive relationship between the current and future state-action values:

$$\begin{aligned} Q^\pi(s,a) &= E_\pi \left\{ \sum_{k=t+1}^{T} r_k | s_t = s, a_t = a \right\} \\ &= E_\pi \left\{ r_{t+1} + \sum_{k=t+2}^{T} r_k | s_t = s, a_t = a \right\} \\ &= \sum_{s'} P^a_{ss'} \left[R^a_{ss'} + E_\pi \left\{ \sum_{k=t+2}^{T} r_k | s_{t+1} = s', a_t = a \right\} \right] \end{aligned} \tag{3}$$

where $P^a_{ss'}$ is the probability that the next state is s' when action a is taken at state s at time step t: $P^a_{ss'} = Pr\{s_{t+1} = s' | s_t = s, a_t = a\}$, and $R^a_{ss'}$ is the expected value of the next reward when taking action a at state s to move to state s': $R^a_{ss'} = E\{r_{t+1} | s_t = s, a_t = a, s_{t+1} = s'\}$.

The relationship between the action-value of the current state and that of the next state can be obtained from Equation 3 as follows:

$$\begin{aligned} Q^\pi(s,a) &= \sum_{s'} P^a_{ss'} \left[R^a_{ss'} + \sum_{a'} \pi(s', a') \times \right. \\ &\qquad \left. E_\pi \left\{ \sum_{k=t+2}^{T} r_k | s_{t+1} = s', a_{t+1} = a' \right\} \right] \\ &= \sum_{s'} P^a_{ss'} \left[R^a_{ss'} + \sum_{a'} \pi(s', a') Q^\pi(s', a') \right] \end{aligned} \tag{4}$$

where $\pi(s', a')$ is the probability of choosing action a' at state s' according to policy π. In ALEX, when a positive feedback item is received over a link (state) s, and an action a is taken based on a policy π with probability $\pi(s, a)$, a number of new links (states) is discovered and added to the set of candidate links. When one of these states s' is later visited and feedback (positive or negative) is received over it, we know then the value of $R^a_{ss'}$. We assume that all states that are generated by an action a have equal probability of being visited. Thus, $P^a_{ss'} = \frac{1}{|s'|}$.

A policy π' is considered to dominate another policy π if and only if $Q^{\pi'}(s, a) \geq Q^{\pi}(s, a)$ for all $s \in S$. In this sense, π^* is considered to be an *optimal policy* if its value function dominates the value functions of all other policies. There may exist more than one optimal policy. An optimal policy implies an optimal action-value function:

$$Q^*(s, a) = max_\pi \; Q^{\pi}(s, a) \tag{5}$$

for all $s \in S$. Therefore, Equation 4 becomes:

$$Q^*(s, a) = \sum_{s'} P^a_{ss'} \left[R^a_{ss'} + max_{a'} Q^*(s', a')\right] \tag{6}$$

4.4 Iterative Improvement

After an episode of feedback is collected, ALEX improves the policy based on the value function evaluated during the episode. A new episode is then started and the policy evaluation - policy improvement iterations continue until ALEX converges. Convergence is defined by the candidate links not changing in an episode of feedback. In the following, we discuss how the policy is evaluated during an episode, and improved at the end of the episode.

4.4.1 Monte Carlo Policy Evaluation

The value function can only be evaluated through interactions between ALEX and the environment (the user and existing links). According to our definition of value, the value of a state or state-action pair can only be known if a user gives feedback on the current state and future states that follow. Since we need to evaluate the value function at the present time without waiting for future feedback, we need to estimate the value function according to the current state s, policy π, and action taken a. We use a Monte Carlo (MC) method for this estimation. Specifically, we use a Monte Carlo method to estimate the action-value of each state visited during each episode, while feedback is collected.

The existence of a state s in an episode is called a *visit*. We use a *first-visit* MC approach [22] for estimating the action-value function. In the first-visit MC approach, the average of returns following the first visit to s in which action a was taken is maintained. This means that if the state-action pair (s, a) is witnessed again during an episode, returns following that pair will not be considered. For example, if a state s_2 results from the state-action pair (s_1, a_1), and s_2 turns out to be a correct link, a positive reward is added to the return of state-action pair (s_1, a_1). Now, if from state s_2, action a_2 is taken and results in a wrong state s_3, a negative reward is added to (s_2, a_2) and (s_1, a_1). However, when state s_2 or s_3 is encountered again, no reward is added to the updated returns of the state-action pairs during the current episode. If a state, say s_2, is encountered in a future episode, that would be considered a new first visit. The first-visit MC approach converges asymptotically to $Q^{\pi}(s, a)$ [20].

The MC method requires π to be probabilistic. If π is deterministic rather than probabilistic at a state s, the same action a will always be taken. Thus, many relevant state-action pairs may never be visited. In such a case, there would be no need for learning how to choose among actions at any state. To compare the alternatives, we need to estimate the value of almost all actions from all witnessed states. ALEX ensures continual exploration to avoid this problem.

ALEX gives itself the option of choosing any action at any state. This means that at any state $s \in S$, and for all actions available in that state $a \in A(s)$, $\pi(s, a) > 0$. ALEX achieves this non-zero probability by using an ϵ-greedy policy so that it mostly chooses a greedy action that has the maximal estimated action value, but chooses a random action with low probability $\epsilon > 0$. In other words, with probability $1 - \epsilon + \frac{\epsilon}{|A(s)|}$ a greedy action is taken, and with probability $\epsilon - \frac{\epsilon}{|A(s)|}$, a non-greedy action is taken. This satisfies $\pi(s, a) \geq \frac{\epsilon}{|A(s)|} > 0$, which means that no action has zero probability of being selected by the current policy, thereby ensuring continuous exploration.

4.4.2 Policy Improvement

If the rewards, $R^a_{ss'}$, and the probabilities of moving to states given an action, $P^a_{ss'}$, are known in advance, Equation 6 has a unique solution since it is actually a system of N equations where N is the number of states in the environment. If the optimal value function is known, it is straightforward to determine an optimal policy: At any state s, choose the action that yields the maximum value of $Q^*(s, a)$ in Equation 6. In other words, a greedy policy with respect to the optimal evaluation function is the optimal policy. However, as explained earlier, the feedback on links and which states can be visited next are unknown in our problem. This means that the reward of the current action will not be known until the user gives feedback on the links discovered after the current action is taken. Also, the next state visited is not known in advance.

The previous section explained how a Monte Carlo method can be used to estimate Q^{π_k} for arbitrary probabilistic π_k, where k is the iteration number in the policy evaluation - policy improvement cycle. Policy improvement is done by making the policy greedy with respect to the current value function. That is, for any action-value function Q, the greedy policy is the one that, for all $s \in S$, chooses the action with the maximal Q value:

$$\pi(s) = argmax_a Q(s, a) \tag{7}$$

Equation 7 can be used as the basis for policy improvement as follows:

$$\begin{aligned} Q^{\pi_k}(s, \pi_{k+1}(s)) &= Q^{\pi_k}(s, argmax_a Q^{\pi_k}(s, a)) \\ &= max_a Q^{\pi_k}(s, a) \\ &\geq Q^{\pi_k}(s, \pi_k(s)) \end{aligned} \tag{8}$$

where, as explained above, π_{k+1} is the greedy policy with respect to Q^{π_k}. In Section 5, we prove π_{k+1} dominates π_k.

4.5 Interaction Between Policy Evaluation and Policy Improvement

The value function is repeatedly updated to approximate the actual value of the current state with respect to the current policy. Also, the policy is repeatedly improved with respect to the current value function. Iteratively, these two processes cause the policy to approach optimality, and the value function to approach its actual value.

As discussed before in Section 4.4.1, each evaluation step moves the value function Q^{π_k} towards its actual value. This

Algorithm 1: `ALEX` with ϵ-greedy policy

```
   input  : set of states S, set of actions A
   output: action-value function Q(s, a), Policy π(s)
1  // Initialize
2  for all s ∈ S do
3      for all a ∈ A(s) do
4          Q(s, a) = undefined;
5          π(s) = arbitrary action;
6          Returns(s, a) = empty list;
7      end
8  end
9  while set of candidate links different from last iteration
   do
10     // Policy Evaluation
11     while episode not complete do
12         receive feedback on a state s';
13         if first visit of s' then
14             append feedback value to all Returns(s, a)
               that led to s';
15         end
16         Q(s, a) = AVG(Returns(s, a));
17         if positive feedback then
18             a' = π(s');
19         else
20             remove link;
21         end
22     end
23     // Policy Improvement
24     for all states s in episode do
25         a* = argmax_a Q(s, a);
26         for all a ∈ A(s) do
27             if a = a* then
28                 π(s, a) = 1 − ε;
29             else
30                 π(s, a) = ε / |A(s)|;
31             end
32         end
33     end
34 end
```

value function converges to its actual value over many steps, at which point policy improvement can terminate. However, this process would require many feedback episodes for each policy improvement iteration. `ALEX` does not wait for complete policy evaluation before returning to policy improvement. In fact, only one episode of iterative policy evaluation is required between each two policy improvement steps.

Algorithm 1 shows how `ALEX` alternates between policy evaluation and policy improvement on an episode-by-episode basis. While collecting feedback in an episode, policy evaluation is done by estimating the action-value function $Q(s, a)$ (lines 11 to 22), the policy is then improved at all states visited in the episode by choosing the greedy action (line 25). It is not required for the policy to always be greedy. However, it is required to *move* towards a greedy policy. This will be proven to be sound in Section 5.

Algorithm 1 shows how policy improvement is done using an ϵ-greedy policy. When `ALEX` starts, it chooses arbitrary actions for new states visited for the first time or before the first policy improvement cycle (lines 2 to 8). Lines 24 to 33 show how policy improvement takes place after an episode by assigning the greedy action a probability of $1 - \epsilon$ while non-greedy actions are assigned a probability $\frac{\epsilon}{|A(s)|}$. This is to ensure continuous exploration while at the same time moving towards a greedy policy. During the next episode, when a state that exists in the policy is encountered, a greedy action is taken with high probability, while other actions are explored with low probability.

5. SOUNDNESS OF ALEX

In this section, we prove that: (1) Policy improvement always yields a better policy unless the policy is already optimal. (2) This property applies for the ϵ-greedy policy used in `ALEX`.

The value function we discussed thus far is the action-value function $Q^\pi(s, a)$, which defines the expected return at a state s when choosing an action a following some policy π. Another value function, which we need in our proof, defines the expected return, $V^\pi(s)$, for a state s under policy π:

$$V^\pi(s) = E_\pi\{R_t | s_t = s\} = E_\pi\left\{\sum_{k=t+1}^{T} r_k | s_t = s\right\} \tag{9}$$

This value function is called the *state-value function* for policy π. It defines the expected value given that `ALEX` follows policy π at state s. Similar to Equation 4, the value function of state s can be represented as a recursive relationship with the value function of the next state, s' (derivation in Appendix A):

$$V^\pi(s) = \sum_a \pi(s, a) \sum_{s'} P^a_{ss'}\left[R^a_{ss'} + V^\pi(s')\right] \tag{10}$$

Also, similar to Equation 6, the optimality equation for state value V^* is given by (derivation in Appendix A):

$$V^*(s) = max_{a \in A(s)} \sum_{s'} P^a_{ss'}\left[R^a_{ss'} + V^*(s')\right] \tag{11}$$

We now turn to proving that policy improvement always yields a better policy. Our proof will use the state-value function that we just defined. For ease of explanation, assume that the policy is deterministic. However, the concepts discussed here can be applied to probabilistic policies like the one used by `ALEX`.

The approach to proving that policy improvement always yields a better policy can be illustrated with an example: Assume that the policy currently being used is π, and that for some state s we want to change the policy to choose an action $\pi'(s) = a \neq \pi(s)$. The value of the state given that we follow policy π is given by $V^\pi(s)$. The question is whether it would be better or worse to change the policy so that it always chooses a at state s. The value of choosing a at s and then continuing for future states following the original policy π can be given by:

$$Q^\pi(s, a) = E_\pi\{r_{t+1} + V^\pi(s_{t+1}) | s_t = s, a_t = a\} = \sum_{s'} P^a_{ss'}\left[R^a_{ss'} + V^\pi(s')\right] \tag{12}$$

If it turns out that following policy π' only at state s (i.e., choosing action a), and then following policy π for future states gives greater state-value than the value of the state when following policy π, this situation can be represented by the following inequality:

$$Q^\pi(s, \pi'(s)) \geq V^\pi(s) \tag{13}$$

We want to show that if Equation 13 holds, then always following policy π' at state s yields a greater value than following policy π. That is, we want to prove that

$$V^{\pi'}(s) \geq V^{\pi}(s) \tag{14}$$

This can be proved by starting from Equation 13 and expanding $Q^{\pi}(s, \pi'(s))$ using Equation 12. The proof is presented in Appendix A.

So far, we have shown that we can evaluate how a change in the policy at a single state to a particular action affects the state-value of this state, given the policy and the evaluation function. Greedily choosing a policy that increases the action-value function at state s improves the overall policy. This reasoning can be extended to all states and all possible actions by selecting the action a that yields the highest $Q^{\pi}(s, a)$ at each state s. This is the greedy policy π' defined by:

$$\begin{aligned} \pi'(s) &= argmax_a Q^{\pi}(s, a) \\ &= argmax_a E\left\{r_{t+1} + V^{\pi}(s_{t+1}) | s_t = s, a_t = a\right\} \\ &= argmax_a \sum_{s'} P^a_{ss'}\left[R^a_{ss'} + V^{\pi}(s')\right] \end{aligned} \tag{15}$$

Thus far, we proved that a greedy policy π' is as good as, or better than, an arbitrary policy π. Now, if we assume that the greedy policy π' is as good as, but not better than, policy π (i.e.,$V^{\pi'} = V^{\pi}$), we get:

$$\begin{aligned} V^{\pi'}(s) &= max_a E\left\{r_{t+1} + V^{\pi'}(s_{t+1}) | s_t = s, a_t = a\right\} \\ &= max_a \sum_{s'} P^a_{ss'}\left[R^a_{ss'} + V^{\pi'}(s')\right] \end{aligned} \tag{16}$$

This equation is the same as the optimality Equation 11. Thus, $V^{\pi'}$ must be V^*, and π and π' must be the optimal policies. This means that policy improvement must give a better policy unless the policy is already optimal. This also proves Equation 8 because each π_{k+1} is uniformly better than π_k, or equal to it if both are optimal policies:

$$\begin{aligned} Q^{\pi_k}(s, \pi_{k+1}(s)) &\geq Q^{\pi_k}(s, \pi_k(s)) \\ &\geq V^{\pi_k}(s) \end{aligned} \tag{17}$$

To show that policy improvement applies for the ϵ-greedy probabilistic policy used by `ALEX`, let π' be the ϵ-greedy policy. We show in Appendix A that:

$$Q^{\pi}(s, \pi'(s)) \geq V^{\pi}(s) \tag{18}$$

Equation 18 shows that policy improvement is sound for the ϵ-greedy policy. Using a greedy policy guarantees improvement on every step except when an optimal policy is reached. This analysis is independent of how the action-value functions are determined at each iteration.

6. OPTIMIZATIONS TO ALEX

In this section, we describe some optimizations to improve execution time and reduce the number of iterations required for the convergence of `ALEX`.

6.1 Filtering to Reduce the Search Space

`ALEX` searches in the space of all possible links between entities in the two data sets. It is computationally expensive to: (1) Construct the space of feature sets for each pair of entities from both data sets. (2) Search for candidate links in this space. It is important to reduce the search space to eliminate unlikely links since the number of correct links is considerably small compared to the number of all possible links.

When computing a value for a feature (i.e., a similarity score between two objects associated with two predicates), we require the value to pass a certain threshold θ. Feature values less than θ are set to zero. Feature sets that do not have any positive values are dropped. In our experiments, we use $\theta = 0.3$.

6.2 Partitioning the Search Space

The search conducted by `ALEX` in the space of possible links can be parallelized by partitioning the space into independent partitions that do not require communication. In order to achieve this, we partition the larger data set and generate feature sets between each partition and all entities in the smaller data set. Assume the first data set Ds_1 is larger than the second data set Ds_2. We partition Ds_1 into $\{Ds_{11} \cup Ds_{12} \cup \cdots \cup Ds_{1n}\}$. Feature sets are generated for each pair $\{(Ds_{11}, Ds_2), (Ds_{12}, Ds_2), \cdots, (Ds_{1n}, Ds_2)\}$. Feedback can then be directed to all partitions so that `ALEX` can take actions and explore new links in the partition. The different partitions can be independently explored in parallel, either on different CPU cores of the same machine or on multiple machines in a distributed setting.

`ALEX` uses a simple partitioning technique that we call *equal-size partitioning*. Equal-size partitioning divides the larger data set into equal-sized partitions in a round-robin fashion. That is, the ith entity is in partition $i \bmod n$, where n is the number of partitions. Equal-size partitioning enables parallelism that significantly reduces execution time without sacrificing the quality of candidate links.

6.3 Optimizations for Fast Convergence

`ALEX`'s actions (exploring links that did not exist in the set of candidate links) lead to fast improvement in recall. However, `ALEX` can also generate incorrect links, which reduces precision. Negative feedback would eventually correct these errors by removing incorrect links. Based on negative feedback, `ALEX` learns that some action resulted in worse returns. During policy improvement, `ALEX` would change the policy so that this action is chosen only with small probability. However, relying only on policy improvement to remove incorrect links may result in slow convergence. In order to speed up convergence we develop two optimizations that improve precision without waiting for policy improvement: *blacklist* and *rollback*.

Blacklist: When negative feedback is received over a link, it is now known that the link is incorrect, so it is added to a list of incorrect links. The blacklist is used to prevent links that are known to be incorrect from being returned by `ALEX` when exploring links at any state in the future.

Rollback: The probabilistic nature of the ϵ-greedy policy used by `ALEX` allows it to choose incorrect actions at any state to learn how to make better choices when choosing future actions. Some actions may result in the discovery of a large number of incorrect links. When this happens, it is a wise choice to rollback and remove the links generated by such actions. `ALEX` traces feedback on links to know by which state-action pair these links were generated. When a sufficient number of negative feedback items is received over links generated by a specific state-action pair, a rollback process is initiated, and all links generated by this state-action pair are removed. However, links removed without being marked with negative feedback are not added to the blacklist since they may include some correct links. These links can be discovered later by another state-action pair with a better average return.

Data Set	Version	Field	Triples
DBpedia	3.5.1	Multi-domain	43.6M
OpenCyc	4.0	Multi-domain	1.6M
NYTimes	2010-01-13	Media	335K
Drugbank	2010-11-25	Life Sciences	767K
Lexvo	2013-02-09	Linguistics	715K
Semantic Web Dogfood	2014-05-29	Publications	337K
DBpedia (NBA)	3.5.1	Basketball Players	56K
OpenCyc (NBA)	4.0	Basketball Players	726

Table 1: Data sets used in the experiments.

The rollback optimization is particularly useful for handling incorrect feedback due to errors in the data or errors by the user. It may be possible to refine the feedback so that ALEX uses only high quality feedback obtained from a large number of users (e.g., using techniques from [16]). However, we should never expect feedback to be 100% correct, regardless of the measures taken to improve its quality. When incorrect feedback is received by ALEX, it will take an action that can be rolled-back if future feedback contradicts the incorrect feedback. A study of the effect of incorrect feedback is presented in Appendix C.

7. EXPERIMENTAL EVALUATION

7.1 Experimental Setup

Data sets: We use the real data sets shown in Table 1. DBpedia contains structured data extracted from Wikipedia, and OpenCyc[8] contains parts of the Cyc knowledge base of everyday knowledge. Both of these data sets cover multiple domains, and are in the center of the Linked Open Data cloud, with many links to other data sets. Each of our experiments aims to link one of these two data sets with one of the other data sets in Table 1, which are from different domains. NYTimes contains data about locations, people, and organizations. Lexvo[9] contains data about human languages. Semantic Web Dogfood contains data about conferences and workshops about the Semantic Web. Two subsets of the DBpedia and OpenCyc about NBA basketball players are extracted to evaluate ALEX in more domain-specific situations. In our experiments, we use the versions the of DBpedia, NYTimes, and Drugbank data sets from FedBench[10], a benchmark suite to test the efficiency of federated query processing systems, and we use OpenCyc and Lexvo from the Linked Open Data cloud.

Initial Set of Links: We use PARIS [21] as the automatic linking algorithm for generating the initial set of candidate links for ALEX. We chose PARIS because it was shown to outperform other techniques, and it is not domain specific. PARIS produces links where each link is associated with a score. In order to find better quality links from PARIS, we only consider links with score greater than 0.95. Lowering this threshold does not improve the recall value, but it lowers the precision.

[8]http://sw.opencyc.org/downloads/opencyc_owl_downloads/opencyc-latest.owl.gz

[9]http://www.lexvo.org/resources/lexvo_latest.rdf.gz

[10]http://fedbench.fluidops.net/

Ground Truth: The data sets that we use are part of the Linked Open Data cloud, which means that they are already linked. Some of the data sets are manually linked. Others are linked automatically and refined manually by human experts. We remove all existing links between the data sets and use them as our ground truth. In addition, we randomly inspect samples from the ground truth to remove any incorrect links. We then run PARIS over the pair of data sets to be linked to discover candidate links, which ALEX uses as initial candidate links. We manually inspect the initial candidate links generated by PARIS to find correct links that do not exist in the ground truth. If we find any such links, we add them to the ground truth.

Generating Feedback: We randomly choose a link out of the set of candidate links and compare it to the ground truth. If the link exists in the ground truth, a positive feedback item is returned to ALEX. If the link is incorrect (i.e., does not exist in the ground truth), a negative feedback item is returned.

Evaluation Metrics: We evaluate the efficiency of ALEX by comparing the candidate links it generates to the ground truth. We perform this comparison after each policy evaluation - policy improvement iteration, i.e., after each episode of feedback. We evaluate the quality of candidate links using precision $P = \frac{|C \cap G|}{|C|}$, recall $R = \frac{|C \cap G|}{|G|}$, and F-measure $F = \frac{2PR}{P+R}$, where C is the set of candidate links after each episode, and G is the ground truth.

We also measure the execution time that ALEX requires to converge. The execution time includes the exploration of new candidate links and improving the policy after each episode.

Default Settings: The step size in ALEX is the offset away from the feature score that ALEX searches around. For example, if a feature has a score of 0.8 and the step size is 0.05, ALEX will find links whose feature score is in the range [0.75, 0.85]. The default value of the step size is 0.05. The episode size is the number of feedback items collected before starting policy improvement. The default episode size is 1000. All our experiments use equal-size partitioning to partition the space of feature sets into 27 partitions.

Execution Environment: ALEX is implemented in Java. We ran our experiments on a shared server running Linux Ubuntu 12.04.3 with 64 AMD Opteron processors at 2.6 GHz and 256 GB of memory. Our memory usage for the largest data sets never exceeded 30 GB.

Section 7.2 evaluates the quality of the links discovered by ALEX, and Section 7.3 evaluates the efficiency of ALEX and the effect of the optimizations it employs.

7.2 Quality of Links

We envision ALEX being used in one of two settings: 1. Batch Mode: A service provider can give users the ability to query multiple, large linked RDF data sets. In this setting, the service provider collects feedback from many users over a large number of links between different parts of the data sets. ALEX applies the feedback in batches, using a large episode size, in order to ensure that there is sufficient feedback over different parts of the data sets. In this setting, we use the default episode size of 1000 (e.g., 1000 users providing 1 feedback item each). 2. Specific Domains: Individual users can develop applications that target more specific domains, either small data sets or subsets of large data sets. The user feedback is focused on a specific domain (e.g., a

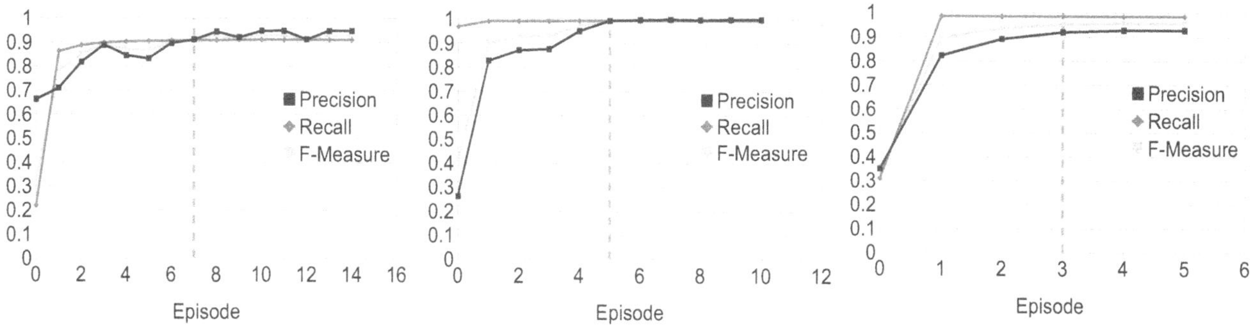

(a) DBpedia - NYTimes (b) DBpedia - Drugbank (c) DBpedia - Lexvo

Figure 2: Quality of links between DBpedia and NYTimes, Drugbank, and Lexvo.

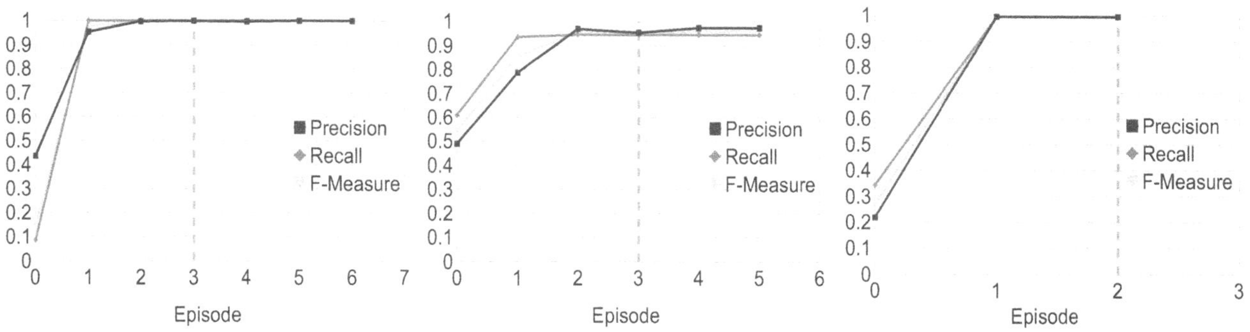

(a) OpenCyc - NYTimes (b) OpenCyc - Drugbank (c) OpenCyc - Lexvo

Figure 3: Quality of links between OpenCyc and NYTimes, Drugbank, and Lexvo.

small part of the DBpedia data set), and she expects to see quick improvement in link quality based on her feedback. In this setting, we use a small episode size of 10. We evaluate the first setting in Section 7.2.1 and the second setting in Section 7.2.2. In both settings, we use a strict rule for convergence. ALEX stops when there is no change at all in the set of candidate links between episodes. We also show the episode at which fewer than 5% of the links change compared to the previous episode. This can be used as a more relaxed convergence rule.

7.2.1 ALEX in Batch Mode

Figure 2 shows how ALEX performs in batch mode on the following pairs of data sets: DBpedia - NYTimes, DBpedia - Drugbank, and DBpedia - Lexvo. Figure 2(a) shows the quality of links between DBpedia and NYTimes after each episode (i.e., iteration of policy evaluation - policy improvement). The figure shows how the recall value is significantly improved after the first episode from a low value of around 0.2 (i.e., most ground truth links are not included) to almost 0.9. This means that a large number of links have been discovered and added to the set of candidate links after only one episode. In some iterations, the precision is hurt by adding some incorrect links to the set of candidate links. However, ALEX recovers fast and keeps improving both precision and recall until it converges. The vertical green line in this and subsequent figures shows the episode at which the number of changed links from the previous episode is less than 5%. This relaxed convergence happens after 7 episodes in this experiment, while full convergence (i.e., no change in links) happens after 14 episodes. A total of 7568 new links were discovered by ALEX. The total number of links in the ground truth is 10968.

While linking DBpedia and NYTimes demonstrates a case in which PARIS is able to generate a set of initial candidate links with relatively good precision but with bad recall, linking DBpedia and Drugbank demonstrates a case in which the initial candidate links have very good recall but bad precision. Figure 2(b) shows how ALEX performs in this case. The figure shows that the automatically generated links have a low starting precision value (less than 0.3), and high recall value (over 0.95). ALEX is able to significantly improve the precision value after three episodes. The recall value is also improved. ALEX converges after 10 episodes in this experiment (5 episodes with the relaxed condition), reaching an F-measure of 0.99. The total number of links in the ground truth for this pair of data sets is 1514. A total of 70 new links were discovered by ALEX. This is a small number since recall was already high. Most of the work done by ALEX is in removing incorrect links.

Figure 2(c) shows a different case, where both precision and recall have low values. The number of links in the ground truth is 4364. A total of 3011 new links were discovered by ALEX. The figure shows that ALEX significantly improves the recall after the first episode and no longer improves it after the second episode. However, it improves

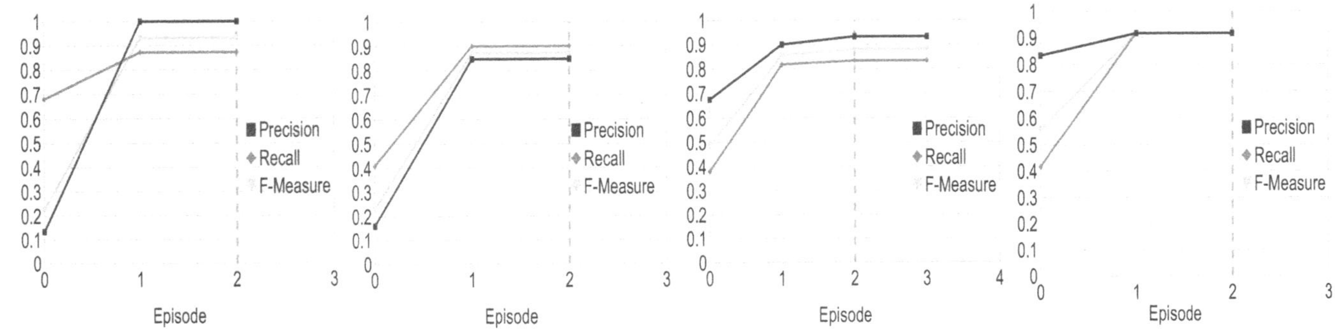

(a) DBpedia - Semantic Web Dogfood (b) OpenCyc - Semantic Web Dogfood (c) DBpedia (NBA) - NYTimes (d) OpenCyc (NBA) - NYTimes

Figure 4: Quality of links for specific domains: publications and NBA basketball players.

the precision for 3 more episodes until it converges after 5 episodes (3 episodes with the relaxed condition).

The results of similar experiments using OpenCyc instead of DBpedia are shown in Figure 3. ALEX performs as effectively in these experiments as it did in Figure 2. The number of ground truth links is 2965 for OpenCyc - NYTimes, 204 for OpenCyc - Drugbank, and 383 for OpenCyc - Lexvo.

7.2.2 *ALEX for Specific Domains*

In this section we investigate the performance of ALEX in the single-user, specific domain setting. We use a small episode size of 10 feedback items since users expect quick improvement in this setting. Figure 4(a) shows the performance of ALEX between DBpedia and the Semantic Web Dogfood data set which has information about conferences and workshops about the Semantic Web. The number of ground truth links between DBpedia and Semantic Web Dogfood is small (461), although the Semantic Web Dogfood data set has more triples than the NYTimes data set. The links mainly connect universities and technical companies from both datasets. A total of 84 new links were discovered by ALEX. Figure 4(a) shows that ALEX achieves very good quality of links and converges in 2 episodes (i.e., significant improvement after 10 feedback items, and full convergence after 20).

Figure 4(b) shows a similar experiment, replacing DBpedia with OpenCyc. In this case, there are 110 links in the ground truth, and ALEX discovers 51 new links.

In addition, we extract data about NBA basketball players from DBpedia and OpenCyc to demonstrate another domain-specific situation where an application is interested in finding all news about NBA basketball players (active or retired). Figures 4(c) and 4(d) show the results of this experiment. There are 93 ground truth links in Figure 4(c), and ALEX discovers 43 new links after one episode. The number of ground truth links in Figure 4(d) is 35, and ALEX discovers 19 new links.

7.3 Efficiency of ALEX

In this section, we investigate the efficiency (i.e., running time) of ALEX, and the effect of the different optimizations to speed up convergence, which were described in Section 6. For these experiments, we use the DBpedia and NYTimes data sets. These data sets are challenging for ALEX since they contain data from more heterogeneous domains than

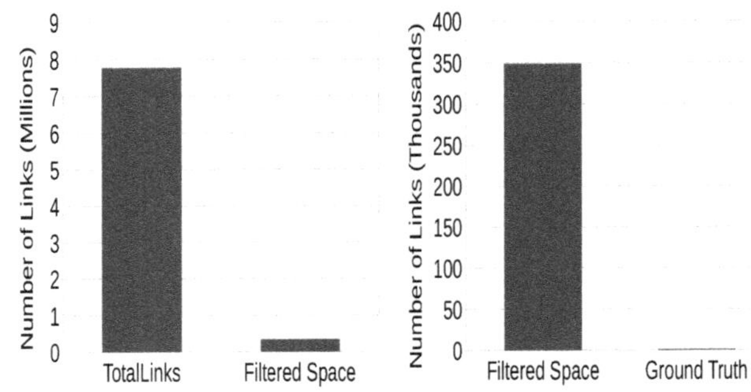

(a) Total links vs. filtered search space (b) Filtered search space vs. ground truth

Figure 5: Comparing number of links: total possible links vs. filtered search space vs. ground truth.

the rest of data sets. In addition, they are the data sets for which PARIS was able to discover only a small fraction of the links, as seen in Figure 2(a). This pair of data sets also has the largest number of links between a multi-domain data set and a data set from any other domain. Only the two multi-domain data sets have more links between them, and we use them to test efficiency in Appendix B.

Filtering to Reduce the Search Space: Figure 5(a) shows the total number of links that can be generated between the first partition of the DBpedia data set and the whole data set of NYTimes, compared to the number of links after filtering using a threshold $\theta = 0.3$. The figure shows that filtering reduces the search space by 95%.

Figure 5(b) shows the number of filtered links compared to number of the ground truth links that can be generated out of this partition. The figure shows that ground truth represents only 0.2% of the filtered links, demonstrating the efficiency of ALEX, which is able to discover correct links in such a large space.

Blacklist: Figure 6 shows a comparison between ALEX with and without the blacklist optimization. Figure 6(a) shows that using a blacklist gives a slight improvement in F-measure over not using it. However, Figure 6(b) shows that using a blacklist significantly decreases the fraction of negative feedback, which the user provides on incorrect links

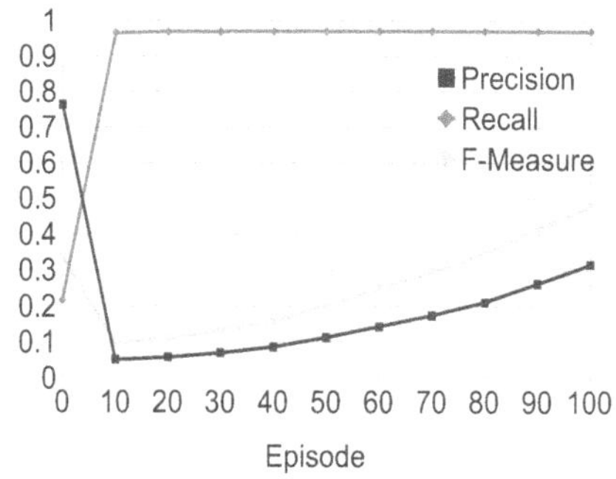

(a) Quality without rollback

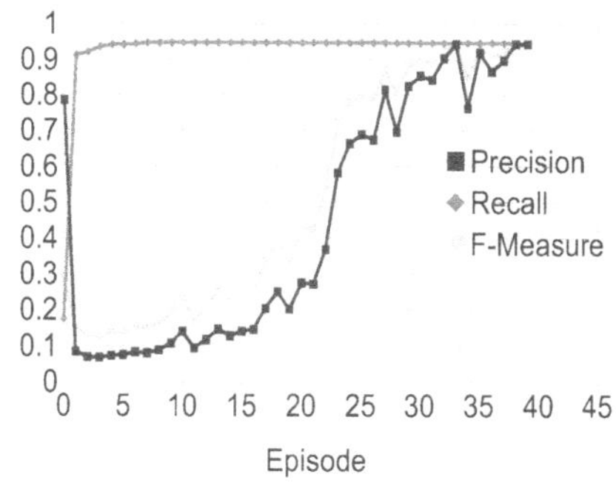

(b) A partition that converges

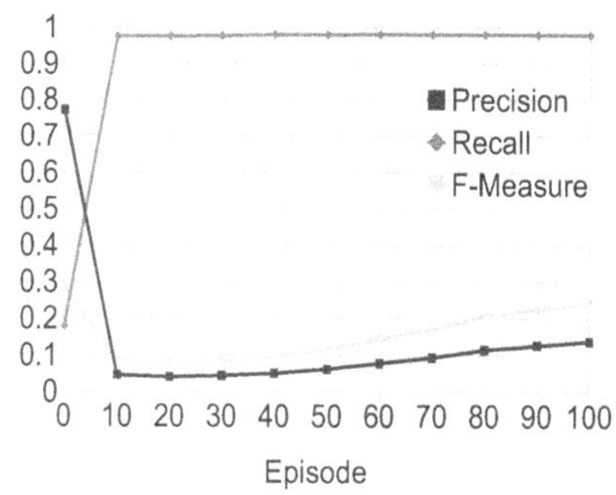

(c) A partition that does not converge

Figure 7: Effect of rollback: (a) quality without rollback, (b) a partition that converges, and (c) a partition that does not converge.

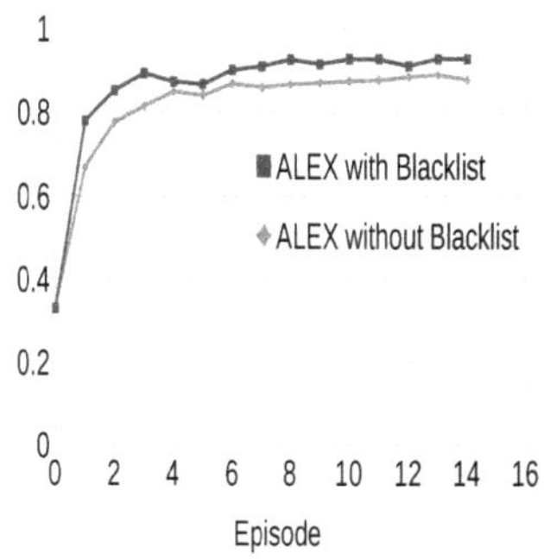

(a) F-measure

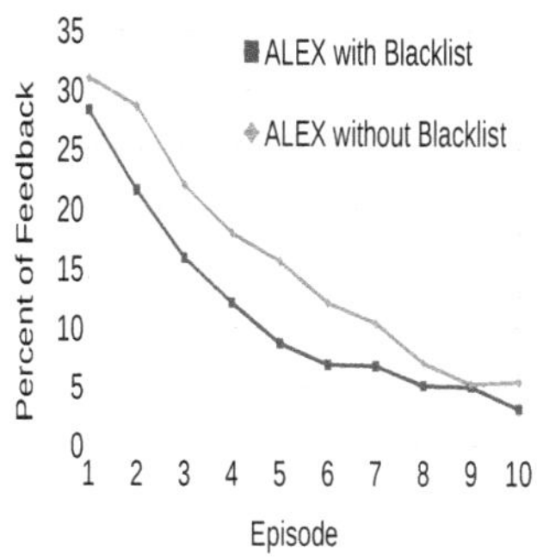

(b) Negative feedback

Figure 6: Effect of the blacklist: (a) F-measure, and (b) negative feedback.

between the data sets. Using a blacklist does not affect the execution time of ALEX. Intuitively, a black list is useful because when a user provides negative feedback on a link she should not need to provide this feedback again.

Rollback: ALEX learns by interacting with the environment. This means that it can sometimes make wrong decisions. These wrong decisions can result in exploring a large number of incorrect candidate links, significantly reducing the quality of the discovered links. If rollback is not used, ALEX can recover from wrong decisions only very slowly. Figure 7 shows the importance of the rollback optimization. Figure 7(a) shows the quality measures of ALEX without using the rollback optimization. This figure should be contrasted to Figure 2(a), which shows ALEX with rollback (the default). The figure shows that after the first episode, precision drops to a very low value. The figure also shows that it is hard to recover from the wrong decisions made during the first episode. After 100 episodes, which is the maximum number of iterations allowed by ALEX, precision is a little over 0.3. Figure 7(a) shows the overall quality of all partitions. If we examine partitions independently, we find that some partitions are able to recover from wrong decisions made by ALEX, while others are not. Figure 7(b) shows an example of a partition that is able to recover from the wrong decisions and converges in 40 episodes. The same partition converges in 7 episodes when rollback is applied. However, another partition, shown in Figure 7(c), cannot recover from wrong decisions.

Execution Time: In the experiment with DBpedia and NYTimes shown in Figure 2(a), ALEX finishes execution in 97 minutes, which is the execution time of the slowest partition. This is approximately 7 minutes per episode. The average execution time of all partitions is approximately 64 minutes. In the specific domain experiment shown in Figure 4(c), ALEX finishes in approximately 4 seconds. This is approximately 1.3 second per episode (10 feedback items). The faster convergence in the specific domain setting is because the data sets and the amount of feedback are smaller. Thus, in batch mode ALEX takes a few minutes per episode, while in interactive mode it takes a few seconds. We consider this to be acceptable efficiency.

Additional experiments are presented in the appendices. We study the efficiency of ALEX when linking the multi-domain data sets in Appendix B. We demonstrate that ALEX can recover from incorrect feedback in Appendix C. And we demonstrate that ALEX is not overly sensitive to parameter values in Appendix D.

8. CONCLUSION AND FUTURE WORK

In this paper, we presented ALEX, a system that utilizes user feedback on queries over linked data to remove incorrect links and discover new links that did not exist between the data sets. When a user provides positive feedback on a link, ALEX finds new links that are similar to this link. This exploration is conducted by taking one pair of attributes from the two data sets and exploring around the similarity value between these two attributes. ALEX uses a probabilistic policy to choose the attributes to explore around. This policy is learned and improved using a Monte Carlo reinforcement learning approach. Using this approach, ALEX learns how to find new links as the user continues giving feedback on query answers. ALEX uses several optimizations to speed up convergence. Our experiments with real world data sets show the effectiveness and efficiency of ALEX.

An important direction for future work is confirming the effectiveness of ALEX through user studies using real applications on the Linked Open Data cloud. In such studies, users are likely to generate some incorrect feedback, which should enable us to validate the robustness of ALEX beyond our current set of experiments.

9. REFERENCES

[1] A. Aboulnaga and K. El Gebaly. μbe: User guided source selection and schema mediation for internet scale data integration. In *IEEE Int. Conf. on Data Engineering (ICDE)*, 2007.

[2] M. Acosta, A. Zaveri, E. Simperl, D. Kontokostas, S. Auer, and J. Lehmann. Crowdsourcing linked data quality assessment. In *Proc. Int. Semantic Web Conf. (ISWC)*. 2013.

[3] S. Auer, C. Bizer, G. Kobilarov, J. Lehmann, R. Cyganiak, and Z. Ives. DBpedia: A nucleus for a web of open data. In *Proc. Int. Semantic Web Conf. (ISWC)*. 2007.

[4] D. Aumueller, H.-H. Do, S. Massmann, and E. Rahm. Schema and ontology matching with COMA++. In *Proc. ACM SIGMOD Int. Conf. on Management of Data*, 2005.

[5] T. Berners-Lee, J. Hendler, and O. Lassila. The semantic web. *Scientific American*, 2001.

[6] I. Bhattacharya and L. Getoor. Collective entity resolution in relational data. *ACM Trans. on Knowledge Discovery from Data (TKDD)*, 2007.

[7] C. Bizer, T. Heath, and T. Berners-Lee. Linked data-the story so far. *Int. Journal on Semantic Web and Information Systems*, 5(3), 2009.

[8] C. Bizer, T. Heath, K. Idehen, and T. Berners-Lee. Linked data on the web. In *Proc. Int. World Wide Web Conf. (WWW)*, 2008.

[9] K. Bollacker, C. Evans, P. Paritosh, T. Sturge, and J. Taylor. Freebase: a collaboratively created graph database for structuring human knowledge. In *Proc. ACM SIGMOD Int. Conf. on Management of Data*, 2008.

[10] G. Demartini, D. E. Difallah, and P. Cudré-Mauroux. ZenCrowd: leveraging probabilistic reasoning and crowdsourcing techniques for large-scale entity linking. In *Proc. Int. World Wide Web Conf. (WWW)*, 2012.

[11] O. Etzioni, M. Cafarella, D. Downey, S. Kok, A.-M. Popescu, T. Shaked, S. Soderland, D. S. Weld, and A. Yates. Web-scale information extraction in KnowItAll (preliminary results). In *Proc. Int. World Wide Web Conf. (WWW)*, 2004.

[12] A. Ferrara, D. Lorusso, and S. Montanelli. Automatic identity recognition in the semantic web. In *Proc. Int. Workshop on Identity and Reference on the Semantic Web (IRSW)*, 2008.

[13] J. Gracia, M. d'Aquin, and E. Mena. Large scale integration of senses for the semantic web. In *Proc. Int. World Wide Web Conf. (WWW)*, 2009.

[14] W. Hu, J. Chen, and Y. Qu. A self-training approach for resolving object coreference on the semantic web. In *Proc. Int. World Wide Web Conf. (WWW)*, 2011.

[15] S. R. Jeffery, M. J. Franklin, and A. Y. Halevy. Pay-as-you-go user feedback for dataspace systems. In *Proc. ACM SIGMOD Int. Conf. on Management of Data*, 2008.

[16] R. McCann, W. Shen, and A. Doan. Matching schemas in online communities: A web 2.0 approach. In *Proc. IEEE Int. Conf. on Data Engineering (ICDE)*, 2008.

[17] M. Mohri, A. Rostamizadeh, and A. Talwalkar. *Foundations of Machine Learning*. The MIT Press, 2012.

[18] B. Quilitz and U. Leser. Querying distributed RDF data sources with SPARQL. In *The Semantic Web: Research and Applications*. Springer, 2008.

[19] A. Schwarte, P. Haase, K. Hose, R. Schenkel, and M. Schmidt. FedX: Optimization techniques for federated query processing on linked data. In *Proc. Int. Semantic Web Conf. (ISWC)*. 2011.

[20] S. P. Singh and R. S. Sutton. Reinforcement learning with replacing eligibility traces. *Machine Learning*, 22(1-3), 1996.

[21] F. M. Suchanek, S. Abiteboul, and P. Senellart. PARIS: probabilistic alignment of relations, instances, and schema. *Proc. VLDB Endow. (PVLDB)*, 5(3), 2011.

[22] R. S. Sutton and A. G. Barto. *Introduction to Reinforcement Learning*. MIT Press, 1998.

[23] J. Volz, C. Bizer, M. Gaedke, and G. Kobilarov. Silk-A link discovery framework for the web of data. In *Proc. Workshop on Linked Data on the Web (LDOW)*, 2009.

[24] S. E. Whang, P. Lofgren, and H. Garcia-Molina. Question selection for crowd entity resolution. *Proc. VLDB Endow. (PVLDB)*, 6(6), 2013.

[25] Z. Yan, N. Zheng, Z. G. Ives, P. P. Talukdar, and C. Yu. Actively soliciting feedback for query answers in keyword search-based data integration. *Proc. VLDB Endow. (PVLDB)*, 6(3), 2013.

APPENDIX

A. DERIVATIONS AND PROOFS

A.1 State Value Function (Equation 10)

$$
\begin{aligned}
V^{\pi}(s) &= E_{\pi}\left\{\sum_{k=t+1}^{T} r_k | s_t = s\right\} \\
&= E_{\pi}\left\{r_{t+1} + \sum_{k=t+2}^{T} r_k | s_t = s\right\} \\
&= \sum_{a} \pi(s,a) \sum_{s'} P_{ss'}^{a}\left[R_{ss'}^{a} + E_{\pi}\left\{\sum_{k=t+2}^{T} r_k | s_{t+1} = s'\right\}\right] \\
&= \sum_{a} \pi(s,a) \sum_{s'} P_{ss'}^{a}\left[R_{ss'}^{a} + V^{\pi}(s')\right]
\end{aligned}
$$

A.2 Optimal Value Function (Equation 11)

$$
\begin{aligned}
V^{*}(s) &= max_a Q^{\pi^*}(s,a) \\
&= max_a E_{\pi^*}\left\{R_t | s_t = s, a_t = a\right\} \\
&= max_{a \in A(s)} E_{\pi^*}\left\{\sum_{k=t+1}^{T} r_k | s_t = s, a_t = a\right\} \\
&= max_{a \in A(s)} E_{\pi^*}\left\{r_{t+1} + \sum_{k=t+2}^{T} r_k | s_t = s, a_t = a\right\} \\
&= max_{a \in A(s)} E_{\pi^*}\left\{r_{t+1} + V^{*}(s_{t+1}) | s_t = s, a_t = a\right\} \\
&= max_{a \in A(s)} \sum_{s'} P_{ss'}^{a}\left[R_{ss'}^{a} + V^{*}(s')\right]
\end{aligned}
$$

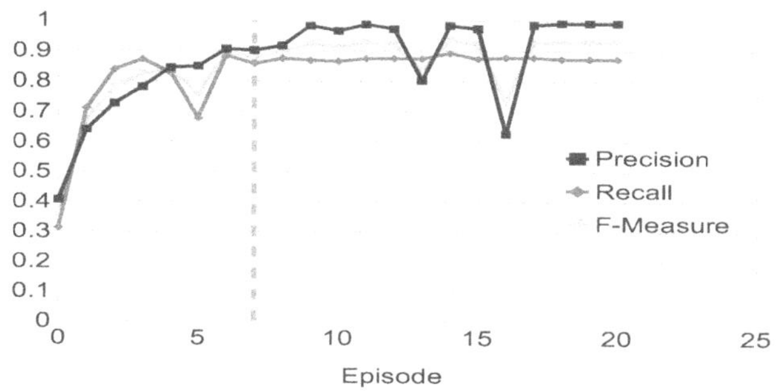

Figure 8: Quality of links between the two largest data sets: DBpedia and OpenCyc.

A.3 Policy Improvement Proof (Equation 14)

$$V^{\pi}(s) \leq Q^{\pi}(s, \pi'(s))$$
$$V^{\pi}(s) \leq E_{\pi'} \{r_{t+1} + V^{\pi}(s_{t+1}) | s_t = s\}$$
$$V^{\pi}(s) \leq E_{\pi'} \{r_{t+1} + Q^{\pi}(s_{t+1}, \pi'(s_{t+1})) | s_t = s\}$$
$$V^{\pi}(s) \leq E_{\pi'} \{r_{t+1} + E_{\pi'}\{r_{t+2} + V^{\pi}(s_{t+2})\} | s_t = s\}$$
$$V^{\pi}(s) \leq E_{\pi'} \{r_{t+1} + r_{t+2} + V^{\pi}(s_{t+2}) | s_t = s\}$$
$$V^{\pi}(s) \leq E_{\pi'} \{r_{t+1} + r_{t+2} + r_{t+3} + V^{\pi}(s_{t+3}) | s_t = s\}$$
$$V^{\pi}(s) \leq V^{\pi'}(s)$$

A.4 Proof of Improvement Using the ϵ-greedy Policy (Equation 18)

$$Q^{\pi}(s, \pi'(s)) = \sum_a \pi'(s, a) Q^{\pi}(s, a)$$
$$= \frac{\epsilon}{|A(s)|} \sum_a Q^{\pi}(s, a) + (1 - \epsilon) max_a Q^{\pi}(s, a)$$
$$\geq \frac{\epsilon}{|A(s)|} \sum_a Q^{\pi}(s, a) + (1 - \epsilon) \sum_a \frac{\pi(s, a) - \frac{\epsilon}{|A(s)|}}{1 - \epsilon} Q^{\pi}(s, a)$$

The transition from the equality to the inequality is because the sum of the second term is the weighted average with non-negative weights summing to one ($\sum_a \frac{\pi(s,a) - \frac{\epsilon}{|A(s)|}}{1-\epsilon}$), and therefore must be less than or equal to the largest number averaged ($max_a Q^{\pi}(s, a)$).

$$Q^{\pi}(s, \pi'(s)) \geq \frac{\epsilon}{|A(s)|} \sum_a Q^{\pi}(s, a) + \sum_a \pi(s, a) Q^{\pi}(s, a)$$
$$- \frac{\epsilon}{|A(s)|} \sum_a Q^{\pi}(s, a)$$
$$Q^{\pi}(s, \pi'(s)) \geq \sum_a \pi(s, a) Q^{\pi}(s, a)$$
$$Q^{\pi}(s, \pi'(s)) \geq V^{\pi}(s)$$

B. LINKING THE TWO MULTI-DOMAIN DATA SETS

We stress-test ALEX by using it to link the two multi-domain data sets in our experiments (DBpedia and OpenCyc), using the default episode size of 1000. Linking these two data sets is challenging because they are the largest in our experiments. Furthermore, they span multiple semantically diverse domains so they use a large number of labels for their predicates, and hence generate a large number of features. There are 41039 links between the two data sets in the ground truth, the largest in our experiments. Figure 8 shows that ALEX converges after 20 episodes with an F-measure greater than 0.9 (7 episodes with the relaxed condition). ALEX started with 12227 correct candidate links obtained from PARIS, and discovered 23476 additional correct links.

C. EFFECT OF INCORRECT FEEDBACK

In this paper, we assume that user feedback is always correct. However, in real-life scenarios, users may not agree on the correctness of query answers. Therefore, incorrect feedback items may be encountered. In order to evaluate ALEX in this context, we generate random incorrect feedback items such that 10% of the feedback items received by ALEX are incorrect. We evaluate ALEX with 10% incorrect feedback on the DBpedia - NYTimes data sets, using the default episode size of 1000. Figure 9 shows the precision, recall, and F-measure for ALEX with 10% incorrect feedback, and the corresponding values when all feedback is correct (from Figure 2(a)). The recall value in Figure 9(b) does not vary much, demonstrating that the reinforcement learning techniques used in ALEX to improve recall are robust to incorrect feedback. The precision values shown in Figure 9(a) are slightly worse when there is incorrect feedback, and this also affects the F-measure in Figure 9(c). ALEX improves precision by removing incorrect links from the set of candidate links, and these incorrect links can be removed only when negative feedback is received over them. When there is incorrect feedback, a constant stream of positive feedback is received over incorrect links, so these incorrect links stay in the set of candidate links. Nevertheless, the degradation in precision is relatively small, and ALEX is able to produce good results even in the presence of incorrect feedback.

D. SENSITIVITY OF ALEX

We use the DBpedia - NYTimes data sets to test the sensitivity of ALEX to the step size and episode size parameters.

Step Size: In this experiment, we use the default episode size of 1000, and we vary the step size. Changing the step size slightly affects how ALEX performs. Increasing the step size means that we expand the search area around the feature score chosen by the current policy at the current state. Decreasing the step size means that we narrow it. Figure 10 shows ALEX with step sizes 0.01, 0.05 (default), and 0.1. Figure 10(a) shows that the F-measure does not vary significantly with higher step size, getting slightly better. Figure 10(b) gives a deeper insight by showing the variance in recall, where the gap between different step sizes is more obvious. The figure shows how increasing the search area around feature score results in more correct links being discovered. Precision is not reported because it has a trend similar to that of Figure 2(a).

However, increasing the search area does not come for free. The total execution time is determined by the partition that finishes last. ALEX with a step size of 0.1 has much higher execution time than with a step size of 0.05 or 0.1. The last partition to finish for step size 0.1 takes over 210 minutes, whereas it takes 97 minutes for a step size of 0.05 and 89 minutes for a step size of 0.01.

Another drawback of increasing the step size is that ALEX will discover more incorrect links in the search area. This is

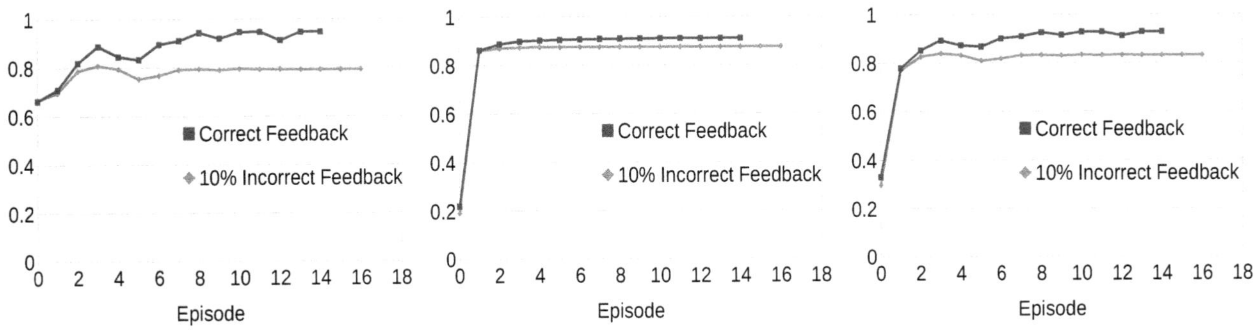

(a) Precision (b) Recall (c) F-measure

Figure 9: ALEX with correct feedback and with 10% incorrect feedback.

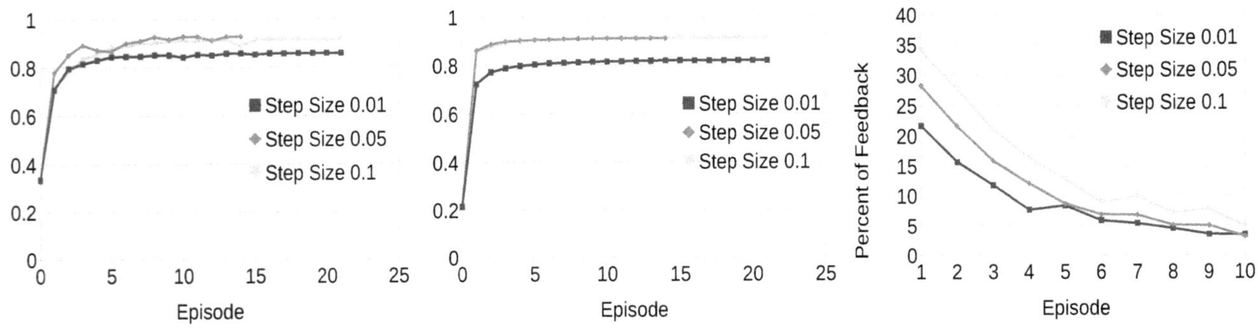

(a) F-measure (b) Recall (c) Negative feedback

Figure 10: ALEX with different step sizes: (a) F-measure, (b) recall, and (c) negative feedback.

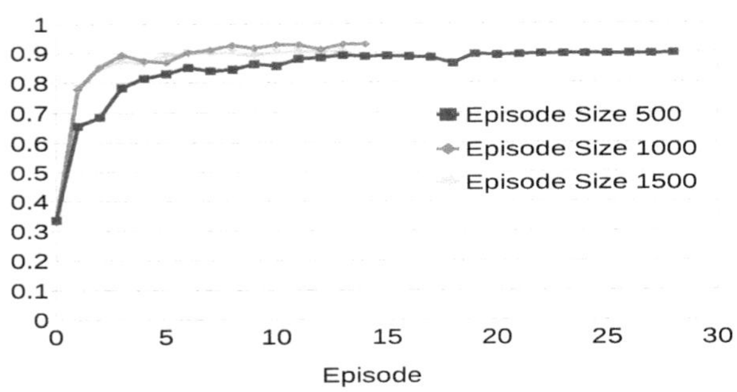

Figure 11: F-measure for ALEX with different episode sizes.

reflected directly in the number of negative feedback items received from the user. Figure 10(c) shows the percentage of feedback received in every episode that is negative. This negative feedback is caused by incorrect links. The figure shows this value for the first 10 episodes for different step sizes. The figure shows that during the first episode, ALEX with a step size of 0.1 receive almost 35% negative feedback of the 1000 feedback items in the episode, compared to less than 30% for a step size of 0.05 and a little over 20% for 0.01. For later episodes, ALEX improves its policy and learns to take better actions. This reduces the percentage of negative feedback. However, the trend that a bigger step size results in a larger percent of negative feedback continues.

Episode Size: Like changing the step size, changing the episode size slightly affects the quality of the discovered links. Figure 11 shows a comparison of ALEX using an episode size of 500, 1000 (default), and 1500. During each episode, policy evaluation uses the current policy to take action after every feedback item. At the end of an episode, the policy is improved for the next episode. Figure 11 shows the F-measure for the three episode sizes. The F-measures are very close to each other, with episode sizes 1000 and 1500 slightly outperforming episode size 500. A larger episode size results in ALEX taking fewer episodes to converge, since each episode has more feedback. ALEX converges in 26, 14, and 13 episodes for episode size 500, 1000, and 1500, respectively.

The experiments in this appendix show that ALEX is sensitive to changes in the values of its parameters. That is, the parameters have a noticeable effect on performance. However, the sensitivity is not so high as to make ALEX unstable and reliant on highly accurate parameter settings: the difference between the best case and the worst case performance is not too high, and reasonable choices of parameter values work well.

k-Shape: Efficient and Accurate Clustering of Time Series

John Paparrizos
Columbia University
jopa@cs.columbia.edu

Luis Gravano
Columbia University
gravano@cs.columbia.edu

ABSTRACT

The proliferation and ubiquity of temporal data across many disciplines has generated substantial interest in the analysis and mining of time series. Clustering is one of the most popular data mining methods, not only due to its exploratory power, but also as a preprocessing step or subroutine for other techniques. In this paper, we present k-Shape, a novel algorithm for time-series clustering. k-Shape relies on a scalable iterative refinement procedure, which creates homogeneous and well-separated clusters. As its distance measure, k-Shape uses a normalized version of the cross-correlation measure in order to consider the shapes of time series while comparing them. Based on the properties of that distance measure, we develop a method to compute cluster centroids, which are used in every iteration to update the assignment of time series to clusters. To demonstrate the robustness of k-Shape, we perform an extensive experimental evaluation of our approach against partitional, hierarchical, and spectral clustering methods, with combinations of the most competitive distance measures. k-Shape outperforms all scalable approaches in terms of accuracy. Furthermore, k-Shape also outperforms all non-scalable (and hence impractical) combinations, with one exception that achieves similar accuracy results. However, unlike k-Shape, this combination requires tuning of its distance measure and is two orders of magnitude slower than k-Shape. Overall, k-Shape emerges as a domain-independent, highly accurate, and highly efficient clustering approach for time series with broad applications.

1. INTRODUCTION

Temporal, or sequential, data mining deals with problems where data are naturally organized in sequences [34]. We refer to such data sequences as time-series sequences if they contain explicit information about timing (e.g., stock, audio, speech, and video) or if an ordering on values can be inferred (e.g., streams and handwriting). Large volumes of time-series sequences appear in almost every discipline, including astronomy, biology, meteorology, medicine, finance, robotics, engineering, and others [1, 6, 25, 27, 36, 52, 70, 76]. The ubiquity of time series has generated a substantial interest in querying [2, 19, 45, 46, 48, 62, 74, 79], indexing [9, 13, 41, 42, 44, 77], classification [37, 56, 68, 88], clustering [43, 54, 64, 87, 89], and modeling [4, 38, 86] of such data.

SIGMOD '15, May 31–June 4, 2015, Melbourne, Victoria, Australia.

http://dx.doi.org/10.1145/2723372.2737793.

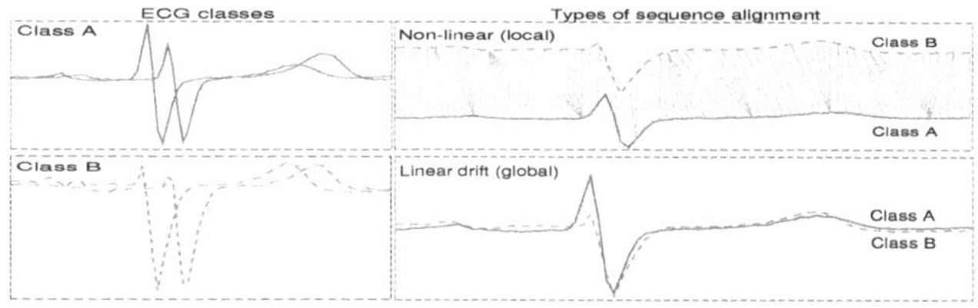

Figure 1: ECG sequence examples and types of alignments for the two classes of the ECGFiveDays dataset [1].

Among all techniques applied to time-series data, clustering is the most widely used as it does not rely on costly human supervision or time-consuming annotation of data. With clustering, we can identify and summarize interesting patterns and correlations in the underlying data [33]. In the last few decades, clustering of time-series sequences has received significant attention [5, 16, 25, 47, 60, 64, 66, 87, 89], not only as a powerful stand-alone exploratory method, but also as a preprocessing step or subroutine for other tasks.

Most time-series analysis techniques, including clustering, critically depend on the choice of distance measure. A key issue when comparing two time-series sequences is how to handle the variety of distortions, as we will discuss, that are characteristic of the sequences. To illustrate this point, consider the well-known ECGFiveDays dataset [1], with ECG sequences recorded for the same patient on two different days. While the sequences seem similar overall, they exhibit patterns that belong in one of the two distinct classes (see Figure 1): Class A is characterized by a sharp rise, a drop, and another gradual increase while Class B is characterized by a gradual increase, a drop, and another gradual increase. Ideally, a *shape-based* clustering method should generate a partition similar to the classes shown in Figure 1, where sequences exhibiting similar patterns are placed into the same cluster based on their *shape* similarity, regardless of differences in amplitude and phase. As the notion of shape cannot be precisely defined, dozens of distance measures have been proposed [11, 12, 14, 19, 20, 22, 55, 75, 78, 81] to offer invariances to multiple inherent distortions in the data. However, it has been shown that distance measures offering invariances to amplitude and phase perform exceptionally well [19, 81] and, hence, such distance measures are used for shape-based clustering [53, 59, 64, 87].

Due to these difficulties and the different needs for invariances from one domain to another, more attention has been given to the creation of new distance measures rather than to the creation of new clustering algorithms. It is generally believed that the choice of distance measure is more important than the clustering algorithm itself [7]. As a consequence, time-series clustering relies mostly on classic clustering methods, either by replacing the default distance measure with one that is more appropriate for time series, or by transforming time series into "flat" data so that existing clustering algorithms can be directly used [83]. However, the choice of clustering method can affect: (i) accuracy, as every method expresses homogeneity and separation of clusters differently; and (ii) efficiency, as the computational cost differs from one method to another. For example, spectral clustering [21] or certain variants of hierarchical clustering [40] are more appropriate to identify density-based clusters (i.e., areas of higher density than the remainder of the data) than partitional methods such as k-means [50] or k-medoids [40]. On the other hand, k-means is more efficient than hierarchical, spectral, or k-medoids methods.

Unfortunately, state-of-the-art approaches for shape-based clustering, which use partitional methods with distance measures that are scale- and shift-invariant, suffer from two main drawbacks: (i) these approaches cannot scale to large-volumes of data as they depend on computationally expensive methods or distance measures [53, 59, 64, 87]; (ii) these approaches have been developed for particular domains [87] or their effectiveness has only been shown for a limited number of datasets [53, 59]. Moreover, the most successful shape-based clustering methods handle phase invariance through a local, non-linear alignment of the sequence coordinates, even though a global alignment is often adequate. For example, for the ECG dataset in Figure 1, an efficient linear drift can reveal the underlying differences in patterns of sequences of two classes, whereas an expensive non-linear alignment might match every corresponding increase or drop of each sequence, making it difficult to distinguish the two classes (see Figure 1). Importantly, to the best of our knowledge, these approaches have never been extensively evaluated against each other, against other partitional methods, or against different approaches such as hierarchical or spectral methods. We present such an experimental evaluation in this paper, as discussed below.

In this paper, we propose k-Shape, a novel algorithm for shape-based time-series clustering that is efficient and domain independent. k-Shape is based on a scalable iterative refinement procedure similar to the one used by the k-means algorithm, but with significant differences. Specifically, k-Shape uses both a different distance measure and a different method for centroid computation from those of k-means. As argued above, k-Shape attempts to preserve the shapes of time-series sequences while comparing them. To do so, k-Shape requires a distance measure that is invariant to scaling and shifting. Unlike other clustering approaches [53, 64, 87], for k-Shape we adapt the cross-correlation statistical measure and we show: (i) how we can derive in a principled manner a time-series distance measure that is scale- and shift-invariant; and (ii) how this distance measure can be computed efficiently. Based on the properties of the normalized version of cross-correlation, we develop a novel method to compute cluster centroids, which are used in every iteration to update the assignment of time series to clusters.

To demonstrate the effectiveness of the distance measure and k-Shape, we have conducted an extensive experimental evaluation on 48 datasets and compared the state-of-the-art distance measures and clustering approaches for time series using rigorous statistical analysis. We took steps to ensure the reproducibility of our results, including making available our source code as well as using public datasets. Our results show that our distance measure is competitive, outperforming Euclidean distance (ED) [20], and achieving similar results as constrained Dynamic Time Warping (cDTW) [72], the best performing distance measure [19, 81], without requiring any tuning and performing one order of magnitude faster. For example, for the ECG dataset in Figure 1, our distance measure achieves a one-nearest-neighbor classification accuracy of 98.9%, significantly higher than cDTW's accuracy for the task, namely, 79.7%.

For clustering, we show that the k-means algorithm with ED, in contrast to what has been reported in the literature, is a robust approach and that inadequate modifications of the distance measure and the centroid computation can reduce its performance. Moreover, simple partitional methods outperform hierarchical and spectral methods with the most competitive distance measures, indicating that the choice of algorithm, which is sometimes believed to be less important than that of distance measure, is as critical as the choice of distance measure. Similarly, we show that k-Shape outperforms all scalable and non-scalable partitional, hierarchical, and spectral methods in terms of accuracy, with the only exception of one existing approach that achieves similar results, namely, k-medoids with cDTW. However, there are problems with this approach that can be avoided with k-Shape: (i) the requirement of k-medoids to compute the dissimilarity matrix makes it unable to scale and particularly slow, two orders of magnitude slower than k-Shape; (ii) its distance measure requires tuning, either through automated methods that rely on labeling of instances or through the help of a domain expert; this requirement is problematic for clustering, which is an unsupervised task. In contrast, k-Shape uses a simple, parameter-free distance measure. Overall, k-Shape is a highly accurate and scalable choice for time-series clustering that performs exceptionally well across different domains. k-Shape is particularly effective for applications involving similar but out-of-phase sequences, such as those of the ECG dataset in Figure 1, for which k-Shape reaches an 84% clustering accuracy, which is significantly higher than the 53% accuracy for k-medoids with cDTW.

In this paper, we start with an in-depth review of the state of the art for clustering time series, as well as with a precise definition of our problem of focus (Section 2). We then present our novel approach as follows:

- We show how a scale-, translate-, and shift-invariant distance measure can be derived in a principled manner from the cross-correlation measure and how this measure can be efficiently computed (Section 3.1).
- We present a novel method to compute a cluster centroid when that distance measure is used (Section 3.2).
- We develop k-Shape, a centroid-based algorithm for time-series clustering (Section 3.3).
- We evaluate our ideas by conducting an extensive experimental evaluation (Sections 4 and 5).

We conclude with a discussion of related work (Section 6) and the implications of our work (Section 7).

2. PRELIMINARIES

In this section, we review the relevant theoretical background (Section 2.1). We discuss distortions that are common in time series (Section 2.2) and the most popular distance measures for such data (Section 2.3). Then, we summarize existing approaches for clustering time-series data (Section 2.4) and for centroid computation (Section 2.5). Finally, we formally present our problem of focus (Section 2.6).

2.1 Theoretical Background

Hardness of clustering: Clustering is the general problem of partitioning n observations into k clusters, where a *cluster* is characterized with the notions of homogeneity — the similarity of observations within a cluster — and separation — the dissimilarity of observations from different clusters. Even though many clustering criteria to capture homogeneity and separation have been proposed [35], the minimum within-cluster sum of squared distances is most commonly used as it expresses both of them. Given a set of n observations $X = \{\vec{x}_1, \ldots, \vec{x}_n\}$, where $\vec{x}_i \in \mathbb{R}^m$, and the number of clusters $k < n$, the objective is to partition X into k pairwise-disjoint clusters $P = \{p_1, \ldots, p_k\}$, such that the within-cluster sum of squared distances is minimized:

$$P^* = \arg\min_P \sum_{j=1}^{k} \sum_{\vec{x}_i \in p_j} dist(\vec{x}_i, \vec{c}_j)^2 \tag{1}$$

where $\vec{c}_j$ is the centroid of partition $p_j \in P$. In Euclidean space this is an NP-hard optimization problem for $k \geq 2$ [3], even for number of dimensions $m = 2$ [51]. Because finding a global optimum is difficult, heuristics such as the k-means method [50] are often used to find a local optimum. Specifically, k-means randomly assigns the data points into k clusters and then uses an iterative procedure that performs two steps in every iteration: (i) in the assignment step, every data point is assigned to the cluster of its nearest centroid, which is determined with the use of a distance function; (ii) in the refinement step, the centroids of the clusters are updated to reflect the changes in cluster memberships. The algorithm converges either when there is no change in cluster memberships or when the maximum number of iterations is reached.

Steiner's sequence: In the refinement step, k-means computes new centroids to serve as representatives of the clusters. The centroid is defined as the data point that minimizes the sum of squared distances to all other data points and, hence, it depends on the distance measure used. Finding such a centroid is known as the Steiner's sequence problem [63]: given a partition $p_j \in P$, the corresponding centroid $\vec{c}_j$ needs to fulfill:

$$\vec{c}_j = \arg\min_{\vec{w}} \sum_{\vec{x}_i \in p_j} dist(\vec{w}, \vec{x}_i)^2, \quad \vec{w} \in \mathbb{R}^m \tag{2}$$

When ED is used, the centroid can be computed with the arithmetic mean property [18]. In many cases where alignment of observations is required, this problem is referred to as the multiple sequence alignment problem, which is known to be NP-complete [80]. In the context of time series, Dynamic Time Warping (DTW) (see Section 2.3) is the most widely used measure to compare time-series sequences with alignment, and many heuristics have been proposed to find the average sequence under DTW (see Section 2.5).

2.2 Time-Series Invariances

Based on the domain, sequences are often distorted in some way, and distance measures need to satisfy a number of invariances in order to compare sequences meaningfully. In this section, we review common time-series distortions and their invariances. For a more detailed review, see [7].

Scaling and translation invariances: In many cases, it is useful to recognize the similarity of sequences despite differences in amplitude (scaling) and offset (translation). In other words, transforming a sequence $\vec{x}$ as $\vec{x}' = a\vec{x} + b$, where a and b are constants, should not change $\vec{x}$'s similarity to other sequences. For example, these invariances might be useful to analyze seasonal variations in currency values on foreign exchange markets without being biased by inflation.

Shift invariance: When two sequences are similar but differ in phase (global alignment) or when there are regions of the sequences that are aligned and others are not (local alignment), we might still need to consider them similar. For example, heartbeats can be out of phase depending on when we start taking the measurements (global alignment) and handwritings of a phrase from different people will need alignment depending on the size of the letters and on the spaces between words (local alignment).

Uniform scaling invariance: Sequences that differ in length require either stretching of the shorter sequence or shrinking of the longer sequence so that we can compare them effectively. For example, this invariance is required for heartbeats with measurement periods of different duration.

Occlusion invariance: When subsequences are missing, we can still compare the sequences by ignoring the subsequences that do not match well. This invariance is useful in handwritings if there is a typo or a letter is missing.

Complexity invariance: When sequences have similar shape but different complexities, we might want to make them have low or high similarity based on the application. For example, audio signals that were recorded indoors and outdoors might be considered similar, despite the fact that outdoor signals will be more noisy than indoor signals.

For many tasks, some or all of the above invariances are required when we compare time-series sequences. To satisfy the appropriate invariances, we could preprocess the data to eliminate the corresponding distortions before clustering. For example, by z-normalizing [29] the data we can achieve the scaling and translation invariances. However, for invariances that cannot be trivially achieved with a preprocessing step, we can define sophisticated distance measures that offer distortion invariances. In the next section, we review the most common such distance measures.

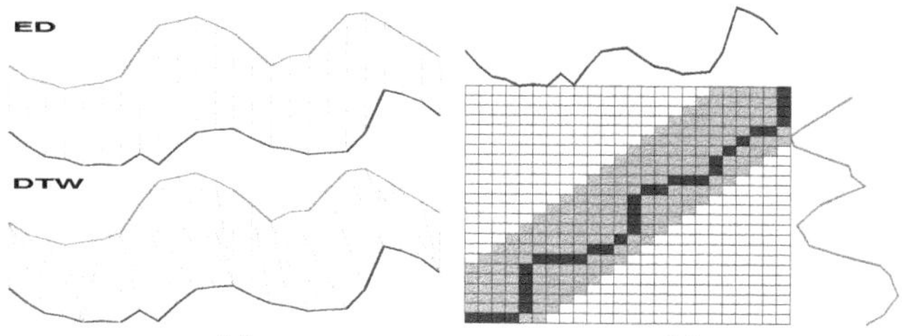

Figure 2: Similarity computation: (a) alignment under ED (top) and DTW (bottom), (b) Sakoe-Chiba band with a warping window of 5 cells (light cells in band) and the warping path computed under cDTW (dark cells in band).

2.3 Time-Series Distance Measures

The two state-of-the-art approaches for time-series comparison first z-normalize the sequences and then use a distance measure to determine their similarity, and possibly capture more invariances. The most widely used distance metric is the simple ED [20]. ED compares two time series $\vec{x} = (x_1, \ldots, x_m)$ and $\vec{y} = (y_1, \ldots, y_m)$ of length m as follows:

$$ED(\vec{x}, \vec{y}) = \sqrt{\sum_{i=1}^{m} (x_i - y_i)^2} \tag{3}$$

Another popular distance measure is DTW [72]. DTW can be seen as an extension of ED that offers a local (non-linear) alignment. To achieve that, an m-by-m matrix M is constructed, with the ED between any two points of $\vec{x}$ and $\vec{y}$. A *warping path* $W = \{w_1, w_2, \ldots, w_k\}$, with $k \geq m$, is a contiguous set of matrix elements that defines a mapping between $\vec{x}$ and $\vec{y}$ under several constraints [44]:

$$DTW(\vec{x}, \vec{y}) = \min \sqrt{\sum_{i=1}^{k} w_i} \quad (4)$$

This path can be computed on matrix M with dynamic programming for the evaluation of the following recurrence: $\gamma(i,j) = ED(i,j) + \min\{\gamma(i-1,j-1), \gamma(i-1,j), \gamma(i,j-1)\}$. It is common practice to constrain the warping path to visit only a subset of cells on matrix M. The shape of the subset matrix is called *band* and the width of the band is called *warping window*. The most frequently used band for constrained Dynamic Time Warping (cDTW) is the Sakoe-Chiba band [72]. Figure 2a shows the difference in alignments of two sequences offered by ED and DTW distance measures, whereas Figure 2b presents the computation of the warping path (dark cells) for cDTW constrained by the Sakoe-Chiba band with width 5 cells (light cells).

Recently, Wang et al. [81] extensively evaluated 9 distance measures and several variants thereof. They found that ED is the most efficient measure with a reasonably high accuracy, and that DTW and cDTW perform exceptionally well in comparison to other measures. cDTW is slightly better than DTW and significantly reduces the computation time. Several optimizations have been proposed to further speed up cDTW [65]. In the next section, we review clustering algorithms that can utilize these distance measures.

2.4 Time-Series Clustering Algorithms

Several methods have been proposed to cluster time series. All approaches generally modify existing algorithms, either by replacing the default distance measures with a version that is more suitable for comparing time series (raw-based methods), or by transforming the sequences into "flat" data so that they can be directly used in classic algorithms (feature- and model-based methods) [83]. Raw-based approaches can easily leverage the vast literature on distance measures (see Section 2.3), which has shown that invariances offered by certain measures, such as DTW, are general and, hence, suitable for almost every domain [19]. In contrast, feature- and model-based approaches are usually domain-dependent and applications on different domains require that we modify the features or models. Because of these drawbacks of feature- and model-based methods, in this paper we follow a raw-based approach.

The three most popular raw-based methods are agglomerative hierarchical, spectral, and partitional clustering [7]. For hierarchical clustering, the most widely used "linkage" criteria are the single, average, and complete linkage variants [40]. Spectral clustering [58] has recently started receiving attention [7] due to its success over other types of data [21]. Among partitional methods, k-means [50] and k-medoids [40] are the most representative examples. When partitional methods use distance measures that offer invariances to scaling, translation, and shifting, we consider them as shape-based approaches. From these methods, k-medoids is usually preferred [83]: unlike k-means, k-medoids computes the dissimilarity matrix of all data sequences and uses actual sequences as cluster centroids; in contrast, k-means requires the computation of artificial sequences as centroids, which hinders the easy adaptation of distance measures other than ED (see Section 2.1). However, from all these methods, only the k-means class of algorithms can scale linearly with the size of the datasets. Recently, k-means was modified to work with: (i) the DTW distance measure [64] and (ii) a distance measure that offers pairwise scaling and shifting of time-series sequences [87]. Both of these modifications rely on new approaches to compute cluster centroids that we will review next.

2.5 Time-Series Averaging Techniques

The computation of an average sequence or, in the context of clustering, a centroid, is a difficult task and it critically depends on the distance measure used to compare time series (see Section 2.1). We now review the state-of-the-art methods for the computation of an average sequence.

With Euclidean distance, the property of arithmetic mean is used to compute an average sequence (e.g., as is the case in the centroid computation of the k-means algorithm). However, as DTW is more appropriate for many time-series tasks [44, 65], several methods have been proposed to average time-series sequences under DTW. Nonlinear alignment and averaging filters (NLAAF) [32] uses a simple pairwise method where each coordinate of the average sequence is calculated as the center of the mapping produced by DTW. This method is applied sequentially to pairs of sequences until only one pair is left. Prioritized shape averaging (PSA) [59] uses a hierarchical method to average sequences. The coordinates of an average sequence are computed as the weighted center of the coordinates of two time-series sequences that were coupled by DTW. Initially, all sequences have weight one, and each average sequence produced in the nodes of the tree has a weight that corresponds to the number of sequences it averages. To avoid the high computation cost of previous approaches, Ranking Shape-based Template Matching Framework (RSTMF) [53] approximates an ordering of the time-series sequences by looking at the distances of sequences to all other cluster centroids, instead of computing the distances of all pairs of sequences.

Several drawbacks of these methods have led to the creation of a more robust technique called Dynamic Time Warping Barycenter Averaging (DBA) [64], which iteratively refines the coordinates of a sequence initially picked from the data. Each coordinate of the average sequence is updated with the use of barycenter[1] of one or more coordinates of the other sequences that were associated with the use of DTW. Among all these methods, DBA seems to be the most efficient and accurate averaging approach when DTW is used [64]. Another averaging technique that is based on matrix decomposition was proposed as part of K-Spectral Centroid Clustering (KSC) [87], to compute the centroid of a cluster when a distance measure for pairwise scaling and shifting is used. In our approach, which we will present in Section 3, we also rely on matrix decomposition to compute centroids.

2.6 Problem Definition

We address the problem of domain-independent, accurate, and scalable clustering of time series into k clusters, for a given value of the target number of clusters k.[2] Even though different domains might require different invariances to data distortions (see Section 2.2), we focus on distance measures that offer invariances to scaling and shifting, which are generally sufficient (see Section 2.3) [19]. Furthermore, to easily adopt such distance measures, we focus our analysis on raw-based clustering approaches, as we argued in Section 2.4. Next, we introduce k-Shape, our novel clustering algorithm.

[1] Barycenter is defined as $b(X_1, \ldots, X_a) = \frac{X_1 + \ldots + X_a}{a}$, where the sums in the numerator are vector additions.

[2] Although the exact estimation of k is difficult without a gold standard, we can do so by varying k and evaluating clustering quality with criteria that capture information intrinsic to the data alone [40].

3. K-SHAPE CLUSTERING ALGORITHM

Our objective is to develop a domain-independent, accurate, and scalable algorithm for time-series clustering, with a distance measure that is invariant to scaling and shifting. We propose k-Shape, a novel centroid-based clustering algorithm that can preserve the shapes of time-series sequences. Specifically, we first discuss our distance measure, which is based on the cross-correlation measure (Section 3.1). Based on this distance measure, we propose a method to compute centroids of time-series clusters (Section 3.2). Finally, we describe our k-Shape clustering algorithm, which relies on an iterative refinement procedure that scales linearly in the number of sequences and generates homogeneous and well-separated clusters (Section 3.3).

3.1 Time-Series Shape Similarity

As discussed earlier, capturing shape-based similarity requires distance measures that can handle distortions in amplitude and phase. Unfortunately, the best performing distance measures offering invariances to these distortions, such as DTW, are computationally expensive (see Section 2.3). To circumvent this efficiency limitation, we adopt a normalized version of the cross-correlation measure.

Cross-correlation is a measure of similarity for time-lagged signals that is widely used for signal and image processing. However, cross-correlation, a measure that compares one-to-one points between signals, has largely been ignored in experimental evaluations for the problem of time-series comparison. Instead, starting with the application of DTW decades ago [8], research on that problem has focused on elastic distance measures that compare one-to-many or one-to-none points [11, 12, 44, 55, 78]. In particular, recent comprehensive and independent experimental evaluations of state-of-the-art distance measures for time-series comparison — 9 measures and their variants in [19, 81] and 48 measures in [26] — did not consider cross-correlation. Different needs from one domain or application to another hinder the process of finding appropriate normalizations for the data and the cross-correlation measure. Moreover, inefficient implementations of cross-correlation can make it appear as slow as DTW. As a consequence of these drawbacks, cross-correlation has not been widely adopted as a time-series distance measure. In the rest of this section, we show how to address these drawbacks. Specifically, we will show how to choose normalizations that are domain-independent and efficient, and lead to a shape-based distance measure for comparing time series efficiently and effectively.

Cross-correlation measure: Cross-correlation is a statistical measure with which we can determine the similarity of two sequences $\vec{x} = (x_1, \ldots, x_m)$ and $\vec{y} = (y_1, \ldots, y_m)$, even if they are not properly aligned.[3] To achieve shift-invariance, cross-correlation keeps $\vec{y}$ static and slides $\vec{x}$ over $\vec{y}$ to compute their inner product for each *shift* s of $\vec{x}$. We denote a shift of a sequence as follows:

$$\vec{x}_{(s)} = \begin{cases} (\overbrace{0, \ldots, 0}^{|s|}, x_1, x_2, \ldots, x_{m-s}), & s \geq 0 \\ (x_{1-s}, \ldots, x_{m-1}, x_m, \underbrace{0, \ldots, 0}_{|s|}), & s < 0 \end{cases} \quad (5)$$

When all possible shifts $\vec{x}_{(s)}$ are considered, with $s \in [-m, m]$, we produce $CC_w(\vec{x}, \vec{y}) = (c_1, \ldots, c_w)$, the cross-correlation sequence with length $2m - 1$, defined as follows:

[3] For simplicity, we consider sequences of equal length even though cross-correlation can be computed on sequences of different length.

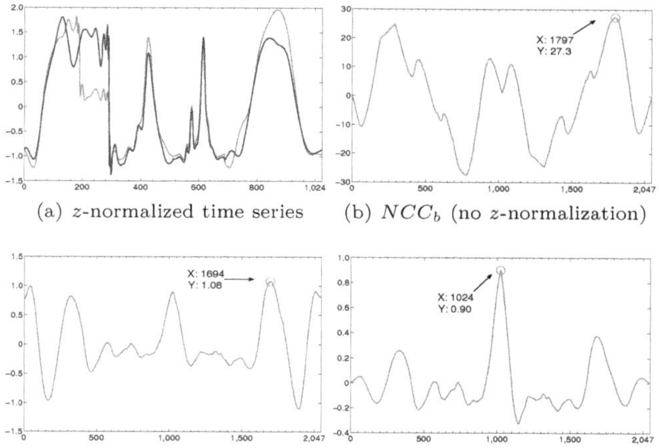

(a) z-normalized time series (b) NCC_b (no z-normalization)

(c) NCC_u with z-normalization (d) NCC_c with z-normalization

Figure 3: Time-series and cross-correlation normalizations.

$$CC_w(\vec{x}, \vec{y}) = R_{w-m}(\vec{x}, \vec{y}), \quad w \in \{1, 2, \ldots, 2m-1\} \quad (6)$$

where $R_{w-m}(\vec{x}, \vec{y})$ is computed, in turn, as:

$$R_k(\vec{x}, \vec{y}) = \begin{cases} \sum_{l=1}^{m-k} x_{l+k} \cdot y_l, & k \geq 0 \\ R_{-k}(\vec{y}, \vec{x}), & k < 0 \end{cases} \quad (7)$$

Our goal is to compute the position w at which $CC_w(\vec{x}, \vec{y})$ is maximized. Based on this value of w, the optimal shift of $\vec{x}$ with respect to $\vec{y}$ is then $\vec{x}_{(s)}$, where $s = w - m$.

Depending on the domain or the application, different normalizations for $CC_w(\vec{x}, \vec{y})$ might be required. The most common normalizations are the biased estimator, NCC_b, the unbiased estimator, NCC_u, and the coefficient normalization, NCC_c, which are defined as follows:

$$NCC_q(\vec{x}, \vec{y}) = \begin{cases} \frac{CC_w(\vec{x}, \vec{y})}{m}, & q = \text{"b"} \ (NCC_b) \\ \frac{CC_w(\vec{x}, \vec{y})}{m - |w|}, & q = \text{"u"} \ (NCC_u) \\ \frac{CC_w(\vec{x}, \vec{y})}{\sqrt{R_0(\vec{x}, \vec{x}) \cdot R_0(\vec{y}, \vec{y})}}, & q = \text{"c"} \ (NCC_c) \end{cases} \quad (8)$$

Beyond the cross-correlation normalizations, time series might also require normalization to remove inherent distortions. Figure 3 illustrates how the cross-correlation normalizations for two sequences $\vec{x}$ and $\vec{y}$ of length $m = 1024$ are affected by time-series normalizations. (Appendix A also elaborates on the classification accuracy of cross-correlation variants under other time-series normalizations.) Independently of the normalization applied to $CC_w(\vec{x}, \vec{y})$, the produced sequence will have length 2047. Initially, in Figure 3a, we remove differences in amplitude by z-normalizing $\vec{x}$ and $\vec{y}$ in order to show that they are aligned and, hence, no shifting is required. If $CC_w(\vec{x}, \vec{y})$ is maximized for $w \in [1025, 2047]$ (or $w \in [1, 1023]$), one of $\vec{x}$ or $\vec{y}$ should be shifted by $i - 1024$ to the right (or $1024 - i$ to the left). Otherwise, if $w = 1024$, $\vec{x}$ and $\vec{y}$ are properly aligned, which is what we expect in our example. Figure 3b shows that if we do not z-normalize $\vec{x}$ and $\vec{y}$, and we use the biased estimator, then NCC_b is maximized at $w = 1797$, which indicates a shifting of a sequence to the left $1797 - 1024 = 773$ times. If we z-normalize $\vec{x}$ and $\vec{y}$, and use the unbiased estimator, then NCC_u is maximized at $w = 1694$, which indicates a shifting of a sequence to the right $1694 - 1024 = 670$ times (Figure 3c). Finally, if we z-normalize $\vec{x}$ and $\vec{y}$, and use the coefficient normalization, then NCC_c is maximized at $w = 1024$, which indicates that no shifting is required (Figure 3d).

As illustrated by the example above, normalizations of the data and the cross-correlation measure can have a sig-

Algorithm 1: $[dist, y'] = SBD(x, y)$

```
Input: Two z-normalized sequences x and y
Output: Dissimilarity dist of x and y
        Aligned sequence y' of y towards x
length = 2^(nextpower2(2*length(x)-1))
CC = IFFT{FFT(x, length) * FFT(y, length)}     // Equation 12
NCC_c = CC / (||x|| ||y||)                     // Equation 8
[value, index] = max(NCC_c)
dist = 1 - value                               // Equation 9
shift = index - length(x)
if shift >= 0 then
    y' = [zeros(1, shift), y(1 : end - shift)] // Equation 5
else
    y' = [y(1 - shift : end), zeros(1, -shift)] // Equation 5
```

nificant impact on the cross-correlation sequence produced, which makes the creation of a distance measure a non-trivial task. Furthermore, as we have seen in Figure 3, cross-correlation sequences produced by pairwise comparisons of multiple time series will differ in amplitude based on the normalizations. Thus, a normalization that produces values within a specified range should be used in order to meaningfully compare such sequences.

Shape-based distance (SBD): To devise a shape-based distance measure, and based on the previous discussion, we use the coefficient normalization that gives values between -1 and 1, regardless of the data normalization. Coefficient normalization divides the cross-correlation sequence by the geometric mean of autocorrelations of the individual sequences. After normalization of the sequence, we detect the position w where $NCC_c(\vec{x},\vec{y})$ is maximized and we derive the following distance measure:

$$SBD(\vec{x},\vec{y}) = 1 - \max_{w}\left(\frac{CC_w(\vec{x},\vec{y})}{\sqrt{R_0(\vec{x},\vec{x})\cdot R_0(\vec{y},\vec{y})}}\right) \quad (9)$$

which takes values between 0 to 2, with 0 indicating perfect similarity for time-series sequences.

Up to now we have addressed shift invariance. For scaling invariance, we transform each sequence $\vec{x}$ into $\vec{x}' = \frac{\vec{x}-\mu}{\sigma}$, so that its mean μ is zero and its standard deviation σ is one.

Efficient computation of SBD: From Equation 6, the computation of $CC_w(\vec{x},\vec{y})$ for all values of w requires $\mathcal{O}(m^2)$ time, where m is the time-series length. The convolution theorem [39] states that the convolution of two time series can be computed as the Inverse Discrete Fourier Transform (IDFT) of the product of the individual Discrete Fourier Transforms (DFT) of the time series, where DFT is:

$$\mathcal{F}(x_k) = \sum_{r=0}^{|\vec{x}|-1} x_r e^{\frac{-2jrk\pi}{|\vec{x}|}}, \quad k = 0,\ldots,|\vec{x}|-1 \quad (10)$$

and IDFT is:

$$\mathcal{F}^{-1}(x_r) = \frac{1}{|\vec{x}|}\sum_{k=0}^{|\vec{x}|-1} \mathcal{F}(x_k) e^{\frac{2jrk\pi}{|\vec{x}|}}, \quad r = 0,\ldots,|\vec{x}|-1 \quad (11)$$

where $j = \sqrt{-1}$. Cross-correlation is then computed as the convolution of two time series if one sequence is first reversed in time, $\vec{x}^{(t)} = \vec{x}^{(-t)}$ [39], which equals taking the complex conjugate (represented by $*$) in the frequency domain. Thus, Equation 6 can be computed for every m as:

$$CC(\vec{x},\vec{y}) = \mathcal{F}^{-1}\{\mathcal{F}(\vec{x}) * \mathcal{F}(\vec{y})\} \quad (12)$$

However, DFT and IDFT still require $\mathcal{O}(m^2)$ time. By using a Fast Fourier Transform (FFT) algorithm [15], the time reduces to $\mathcal{O}(m\log(m))$. Data and cross-correlation normalizations can also be efficiently computed; thus the overall time complexity of SBD remains $\mathcal{O}(m\log(m))$. Moreover, recursive algorithms compute an FFT by dividing it into pieces of power-of-two size [24]. Therefore, to further improve the performance of the FFT computation, when $CC(\vec{x},\vec{y})$ is not an exact power of two we pad $\vec{x}$ and $\vec{y}$ with zeros to reach the next power-of-two length after $2m-1$. Algorithm 1 shows how this efficient and parameter-free measure is computed in a few lines of code using modern mathematical software.

In this section, we showed effective cross-correlation and data normalizations to derive a shape-based distance measure. Importantly, we also discussed how the cross-correlation distance measure can be efficiently computed. In our experimental evaluation (Sections 4 and 5), we will show that SBD is highly competitive, achieving similar results to cDTW and DTW while being orders of magnitude faster. We now turn to the critical problem of extracting a centroid for a cluster, to represent the cluster data consistently with the shape-based distance measure described above.

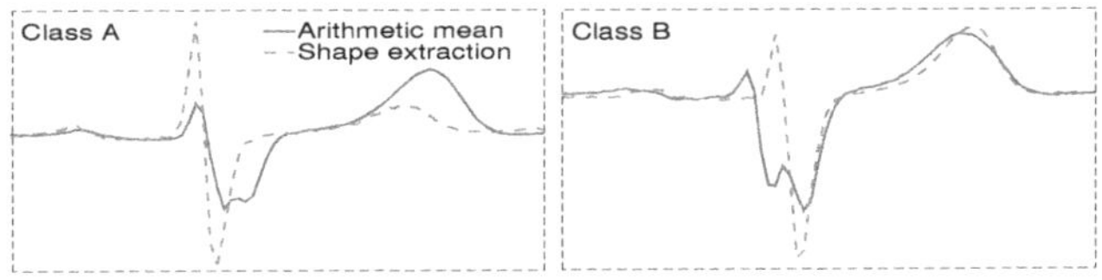

Figure 4: Examples of centroids for each class of the ECGFiveDays dataset, based on the arithmetic mean property (solid lines) and our shape extraction method (dashed lines).

3.2 Time-Series Shape Extraction

Many tasks in time-series analysis rely on methods that effectively summarize a set of time series by only one sequence. This summary sequence is often referred to as an *average sequence* or, in the context of clustering, as a *centroid*. The extraction of meaningful centroids is a challenging task that critically depends on the choice of distance measure (see Section 2.1). We now show how to determine such centroids for time-series clustering for the SBD distance measure, to capture shared characteristics of the underlying data.

The easiest way to extract an average sequence from a set of sequences is to compute each coordinate of the average sequence as the arithmetic mean of the corresponding coordinates of all sequences. This approach is used by k-means, the most popular clustering method. In Figure 4, the solid lines show such centroids for each class in the ECGFiveDays dataset of Figure 1: these centroids do not capture effectively the class characteristics (see Figures 1 and 4).

To avoid such problems, we cast the centroid computation as an optimization problem where the objective is to find the minimizer of the sum of squared distances to all other time series sequences (Equation 2). However, as cross-correlation intuitively captures the similarity — rather than the dissimilarity — of time series, we can express the computed sequence as the maximizer $\mu_k^\star$ of the squared similarities to all other time-series sequences. By rewriting Equation 2 as a maximization problem and from Equation 8, we obtain:

$$\begin{aligned}\vec{\mu_k}^\star &= \underset{\vec{\mu_k}}{\operatorname{argmax}} \sum_{\vec{x_i}\in P_k} NCC_c(\vec{x_i},\vec{\mu_k})^2 \\ &= \underset{\vec{\mu_k}}{\operatorname{argmax}} \sum_{\vec{x_i}\in P_k}\left(\frac{\max_w CC_w(\vec{x_i},\vec{\mu_k})}{\sqrt{R_0(\vec{x_i},\vec{x_i})\cdot R_0(\vec{\mu_k},\vec{\mu_k})}}\right)^2 \end{aligned} \quad (13)$$

Equation 13 requires the computation of an optimal shift for every $\vec{x_i} \in P_k$. As this approach is used in the context of it-

Algorithm 2: $C' = ShapeExtraction(X, C)$

```
Input: X is an n-by-m matrix with z-normalized time series.
       C is a 1-by-m vector with the reference sequence against
       which time series of X are aligned.
Output: C' is a 1-by-m vector with the centroid.
X' ← [ ]
for i ← 1 to n do
    [dist, x'] ← SBD(C, X(i))                    // Algorithm 1
    X' ← [X'; x']
S ← X'^T · X'                                    // S of Equation 15
Q ← I − (1/m) · O                                // Q of Equation 15
M ← Q^T · S · Q                                  // M of Equation 15
C' ← Eig(M, 1)                                   // Extract first eigenvector
```

erative clustering, we use the previously computed centroid as reference and align all sequences towards this reference sequence. This is a reasonable choice because the previous centroid will be very close to the new centroid. For this alignment, we use SBD, which identifies an optimal shift for every $\vec{x_i} \in P_k$. Subsequently, as sequences are already aligned towards a reference sequence before the centroid computation, we can also omit the denominator of Equation 13. Then, by combining Equations 6 and 7, we obtain:

$$\vec{\mu_k}^{\star} = \underset{\vec{\mu_k}}{\operatorname{argmax}} \sum_{\vec{x_i} \in P_k} \left(\sum_{l \in [1,m]} x_{il} \cdot \mu_{kl} \right)^2$$

For simplicity, we express this equation with vectors and assume that the $\vec{x_i}$ sequences have already been z-normalized to handle the differences in amplitude:

$$\begin{aligned} \vec{\mu_k}^{\star} &= \underset{\vec{\mu_k}}{\operatorname{argmax}} \sum_{\vec{x_i} \in P_k} (\vec{x_i}^T \cdot \vec{\mu_k})^2 \\ &= \underset{\vec{\mu_k}}{\operatorname{argmax}} \, \vec{\mu_k}^T \cdot \sum_{\vec{x_i} \in P_k} (\vec{x_i} \cdot \vec{x_i}^T) \cdot \vec{\mu_k} \end{aligned} \tag{14}$$

In the previous equation, only $\vec{\mu_k}$ is not z-normalized. To handle the centering (i.e., the subtraction of mean) of $\vec{\mu_k}$ we set $\vec{\mu_k} = \vec{\mu_k} \cdot Q$, where $Q = I - \frac{1}{m}O$, I is the identity matrix, and O is a matrix with all ones. Furthermore, to make $\vec{\mu_k}$ have unit norm, we divide Equation 14 by $\vec{\mu_k}^T \cdot \vec{\mu_k}$. Finally, by substituting S for $\sum_{\vec{x_i} \in P_k} (\vec{x_i} \cdot \vec{x_i}^T)$, we obtain:

$$\begin{aligned} \vec{\mu_k}^{\star} &= \underset{\vec{\mu_k}}{\operatorname{argmax}} \frac{\vec{\mu_k}^T \cdot Q^T \cdot S \cdot Q \cdot \vec{\mu_k}}{\vec{\mu_k}^T \cdot \vec{\mu_k}} \\ &= \underset{\vec{\mu_k}}{\operatorname{argmax}} \frac{\vec{\mu_k}^T \cdot M \cdot \vec{\mu_k}}{\vec{\mu_k}^T \cdot \vec{\mu_k}} \end{aligned} \tag{15}$$

where $M = Q^T \cdot S \cdot Q$. Through the above transformations, we have reduced the optimization of Equation 13 to the optimization of Equation 15, which is a well-known problem called maximization of the Rayleigh Quotient [30]. We can find the maximizer $\vec{\mu_k}^{\star}$ as the eigenvector that corresponds to the largest eigenvalue of the real symmetric matrix M.

Algorithm 2 shows how we can extract the most representative shape from the underlying data in a few lines of code. In Figure 4, the dashed lines show the centroids of each class in the ECGFiveDays dataset, extracted with Algorithm 2 and using randomly selected sequences as reference sequences. This method for shape extraction can more effectively capture the characteristics of each class (Figure 1) than by using the arithmetic mean property (solid lines in Figure 4). In the next section, we show how our shape extraction method is used in a time-series clustering algorithm.

Algorithm 3: $[IDX, C] = k\text{-}Shape(X, k)$

```
Input: X is an n-by-m matrix containing n time series of
       length m that are initially z-normalized.
       k is the number of clusters to produce.
Output: IDX is an n-by-1 vector containing the assignment of
        n time series to k clusters (initialized randomly).
        C is a k-by-m matrix containing k centroids of
        length m (initialized as vectors with all zeros).
1  iter ← 0
2  IDX' ← [ ]
3  while IDX != IDX' and iter < 100 do
4      IDX' ← IDX
       // Refinement step
5      for j ← 1 to k do
6          X' ← [ ]
7          for i ← 1 to n do
8              if IDX(i) = j then
9                  X' ← [X'; X(i)]
10         C(j) ← ShapeExtraction(X', C(j))       // Algorithm 2
       // Assignment step
11     for i ← 1 to n do
12         mindist ← ∞
13         for j ← 1 to k do
14             [dist, x'] ← SBD(C(j), X(i))       // Algorithm 1
15             if dist < mindist then
16                 mindist ← dist
17                 IDX(i) ← j
18     iter ← iter + 1
```

3.3 Shape-based Time-Series Clustering

We now present k-Shape, our novel algorithm for time-series clustering. k-Shape relies on the SBD distance measure of Section 3.1 and the shape extraction method of Section 3.2 to efficiently produce clusters of time series.

k-Shape Clustering Algorithm: k-Shape is a partitional clustering method that is based on an iterative refinement procedure similar to the one used in k-means. Through this iterative procedure, k-Shape minimizes the sum of squared distances (Equation 1) and manages to: (i) produce homogeneous and well-separated clusters, and (ii) scale linearly with the number of time series. Our algorithm compares sequences efficiently and computes centroids effectively under the scaling-, translation-, and shift invariances. k-Shape is a non-trivial instantiation of k-means and, in contrast to similar attempts in the literature [64, 87], its distance measure and centroid computation method make k-Shape the only scalable method that significantly outperforms k-means.

In every iteration, k-Shape performs two steps: (i) in the assignment step, the algorithm updates the cluster memberships by comparing each time series with all computed centroids and by assigning each time series to the cluster of the closest centroid; (ii) in the refinement step, the cluster centroids are updated to reflect the changes in cluster memberships in the previous step. The algorithm repeats these two steps until either no change in cluster membership occurs or the maximum number of iterations allowed is reached. In the assignment step, k-Shape relies on the distance measure of Section 3.1, whereas in the refinement step it relies on the centroid computation method of Section 3.2.

k-Shape (see Algorithm 3) expects as input the time series set X and the number of clusters k that we want to produce. Initially, we randomly assign the time series in X to clusters. Then, we compute each cluster centroid using Algorithm 2 (lines 5-10). Once the centroids are computed, we refine the memberships of the clusters by using the SBD distance measure (Algorithm 1) in lines 11-17. We repeat this procedure until the algorithm converges or reaches the maximum number of iterations (usually a small number, such as 100). The output of the algorithm is the assignment of sequences to clusters and the centroids for each cluster.

Complexity of k-Shape: As we claimed earlier, k-Shape scales linearly with the number of time series. To see why, we will analyze the computational complexity of Algorithm 3, where n is the number of time series, k is the number of clusters, and m is the length of the time series. In the assignment step, k-Shape computes the dissimilarity of n time series to k centroids by using SBD, which requires $\mathcal{O}(m \cdot \log(m))$ time. Thus, the time complexity of this step is $\mathcal{O}(n \cdot k \cdot m \cdot \log(m))$. In the refinement step, for every cluster, k-Shape computes matrix M, which requires $\mathcal{O}(m^2)$ time, and performs an eigenvalue decomposition on M, which requires $\mathcal{O}(m^3)$ time. Thus, the complexity of this step is $\mathcal{O}(\max\{n \cdot m^2, k \cdot m^3\})$. Overall, k-Shape requires $\mathcal{O}(\max\{n \cdot k \cdot m \cdot \log(m), n \cdot m^2, k \cdot m^3\})$ time per iteration. We see that this algorithm has a linear dependence in the number of time series, and the majority of the computation cost depends on the length of the time series. However, this length is usually much smaller than the number of time series (i.e., $m \ll n$) and, hence, the dependence on m is not a bottleneck. (Appendix B further examines the scalability of k-Shape.) In rare cases where m is very large (i.e., $m \gg n$), segmentation or dimensionality reduction approaches can be used to sufficiently reduce the length of the sequences [10, 49].

We now turn to the experimental evaluation of k-Shape against the state-of-the-art time-series clustering approaches.

4. EXPERIMENTAL SETTINGS

In this section, we describe the experimental settings for the evaluation of both SBD and our k-Shape algorithm.

Datasets: We use the largest public collection of class-labeled time-series datasets, namely, the UCR time-series collection [1]. It consists of 48 datasets,[4] both synthetic and real, which span several different domains. Each dataset contains from 56 to 9236 sequences. The sequences in each dataset have equal length, but from one dataset to another the sequence length varies from 24 to 1882. These datasets are annotated and every sequence can belong to only one class, which, in the context of clustering, should be interpreted as the cluster where the sequence belongs. Furthermore, the datasets are already z-normalized[5] and split into training and test sets. As we will see, we use this split of the datasets for the distance measure evaluation; we also use the training sets for tuning some of the baselines.

Platform: We ran our experiments on a cluster of 10 servers with identical configuration: Dual Intel Xeon X5550 (4-core with 2-way SMT) processor with clock speed at 2.67 GHz and 24 GB RAM. We utilized up to 16 processes continuously for a period of two months in order to perform all experiments included in this paper. Each server runs Ubuntu 12.04 (64-bit) and Matlab R2012b (64-bit).

Implementation: We implemented our approach and all state-of-the-art approaches that we compare against under the same framework, in Matlab, for a consistent evaluation in terms of both accuracy and efficiency. For repeatability purposes, we make all datasets and source code available.[6]

[4]Currently, 47 out of 48 datasets are listed in [1]. One dataset, namely, Insect, will become publicly available in the next release, according to the owners of the UCR repository [1].

[5]Several datasets as available in [1] are not z-normalized. (We have communicated about this issue with the site owners.) Therefore, our experiments start with a z-normalization step for all datasets.

[6]`http://www.cs.columbia.edu/~jopa/kshape.html`

Baselines: We evaluate both our distance measure, SBD, and our clustering approach, k-Shape. We compare SBD against the strongest state-of-the-art distance measures for time series (see Section 2.3 for a detailed discussion):

- **ED:** a simple, efficient — yet accurate — distance measure for time series [20]
- **DTW:** the best performing — but expensive — distance measure for time series [72]
- **cDTW:** the constrained version of DTW, with improved accuracy and efficiency [72]

We compare k-Shape against the three strongest types of scalable and non-scalable clustering methods, namely, partitional, hierarchical, and spectral methods (see Section 2.4 for a detailed discussion), combined with the most competitive distance measures. As scalable methods, we consider the classic k-means algorithm with ED (k-AVG+ED) [50] and the following variants of k-means:

- **k-AVG+Dist:** k-means with DTW and SBD as distance measures and the arithmetic mean of time series coordinates for centroid computation
- **k-DBA:** k-means with DTW as distance measure and the DBA method for centroid computation [64]
- **KSC:** k-means with a distance measure offering pairwise scaling and shifting of time series and computation of the spectral norm of a matrix (i.e., matrix decomposition) for centroid computation [87]

As non-scalable methods, among partitional methods we consider the Partitioning Around Medoids (PAM) implementation of the k-medoids algorithm [40]. Among hierarchical methods, we use agglomerative hierarchical clustering with single, average, and complete linkage criteria [40]. Finally, among spectral methods, we consider the popular normalized spectral clustering method [58]. These non-scalable approaches require a large number of distance calculations to compute the full dissimilarity matrix and, hence, they become unacceptably inefficient with high-cost distance measures. For this reason, we ignore DTW and focus instead on ED, cDTW, and SBD as distance measures. In Table 1 we summarize the combinations used in our evaluation. Overall, we compared k-Shape against 20 clustering approaches.

Parameter settings: Among the distance measures discussed above, only cDTW requires setting a parameter, to constrain its warping window. We consider two cases from the literature: (i) cDTW^{opt}: we compute the optimal window by performing a leave-one-out classification step over the training set of each dataset; (ii) cDTW^{w}: we use as window 5%, for cDTW^{5}, and 10%, for cDTW^{10}, of the length of the time series of each dataset; this second case is more realistic for an unsupervised setting such as clustering.[7] For the 1-NN classification computation, we also consider the state-of-the-art lower bounding approach LB$_{Keogh}$ [44], which prunes time series unlikely for a match when DTW and cDTW are used. We denote lower bounding with the LB subscript (e.g., cDTW$^{10}_{LB}$). For clustering, all the algorithms that we compare, except for hierarchical clustering, receive the target number of clusters k as input, which is equal to the number of classes for each dataset. For hierarchical clustering, we compute a threshold that cuts the produced dendrogram at the minimum height such that k clusters are formed. We set the maximum number of iterations for k-Shape, all variants of k-means, PAM, and spectral methods to 100. Finally, in every iteration of k-Shape, k-DBA, and KSC, we use the centroids of the previous run

[7]For non-scalable methods, we use cDTW^{5} for its efficiency, as noted in Table 1, even though cDTW^{10} and cDTW^{opt} perform similarly.

Name	Clustering Algorithm	Distance Measure
PAM+ED	Partitioning Around Medoids	ED
PAM+cDTW	Partitioning Around Medoids	$cDTW^5$
PAM+SBD	Partitioning Around Medoids	SBD
H-S+ED	Hierarchical with *single* linkage	ED
H-A+ED	Hierarchical with *average* linkage	ED
H-C+ED	Hierarchical with *complete* linkage	ED
H-S+cDTW	Hierarchical with *single* linkage	$cDTW^5$
H-A+cDTW	Hierarchical with *average* linkage	$cDTW^5$
H-C+cDTW	Hierarchical with *complete* linkage	$cDTW^5$
H-S+SBD	Hierarchical with *single* linkage	SBD
H-A+SBD	Hierarchical with *average* linkage	SBD
H-C+SBD	Hierarchical with *complete* linkage	SBD
S+ED	Normalized Spectral Clustering	ED
S+cDTW	Normalized Spectral Clustering	$cDTW^5$
S+SBD	Normalized Spectral Clustering	SBD

Table 1: Combinations of PAM, hierarchical, and spectral methods with ED, cDTW, and SBD for our evaluation.

as reference sequences to refine the centroids of the current run once.

Metrics: We compare all approaches on both runtime and accuracy. For runtime, we compute CPU time utilization and report time ratios for our comparisons. Following [19], we use the 1-NN classifier, which is a simple and parameter-free classifier, to evaluate distance measures. We report the classification accuracy (i.e., number of correctly classified instances over all instances) by performing 1-NN classification over the training and test sets of each dataset. Because the 1-NN classifier is deterministic, we make this computation once. Following [7], we use the Rand Index [67] to evaluate clustering accuracy over the fused training and test sets of each dataset. This metric is related to the classification accuracy and is defined as $R = \frac{TP+TN}{TP+TN+FP+FN}$, where TP is the number of time series pairs that belong to the same class and are assigned to the same cluster, TN is the number of time series pairs that belong to different classes and are assigned to different clusters, FP is the number of time series pairs that belong to different classes but are assigned to the same cluster, and FN is the number of time series pairs that belong to the same class but are assigned to different clusters. As hierarchical algorithms are deterministic, we report the Rand Index over one run. However, for partitional methods, we report the average Rand Index over 10 runs and for spectral methods the average Rand Index over 100 runs; in every run we use a different random initialization.

Statistical analysis: Following [7, 26], we analyze the results of every pairwise comparison of algorithms over multiple datasets using the Wilcoxon test [84] with a 99% confidence level. According to [17], the Wilcoxon test is less affected by outliers than is the t-test [69], as Wilcoxon does not consider absolute commensurability of differences. Moreover, using pairwise tests to reason about multiple algorithms is not fully satisfactory because sometimes the null hypotheses are rejected due to random chance. Therefore, we also use the Friedman test [23] followed by the post-hoc Nemenyi test [57] for comparison of multiple algorithms over multiple datasets, as suggested in [17]. The Friedman and Nemenyi tests require more evidence to detect statistical significance than the Wilcoxon test [26] (i.e., the larger the number of methods, the larger the number of datasets required) and, hence, as we already use all 48 datasets for the Wilcoxon test, we report statistical significant results with a 95% confidence level.

5. EXPERIMENTAL RESULTS

In this section, we discuss our experiments. First, we evaluate SBD against the state-of-the-art distance measures (Section 5.1). Then, we compare k-Shape against scalable (Section 5.2) and non-scalable (Section 5.3) clustering approaches. Finally, we highlight our findings (Section 5.4).

5.1 Evaluation of SBD

Comparison against ED: To understand if SBD (Section 3.1) is an effective measure for time-series comparison, we evaluate it against the state-of-the-art distance measures, using their 1-NN classification accuracies across 48 datasets (Section 4). Table 2 reports the performance of the state-of-the-art measures against the baseline ED. All distance measures, including SBD, outperform ED with statistical significance. For DTW, constraining its warping window significantly improves performance. In particular, $cDTW^{opt}$ performs at least as well as DTW in 36 datasets, $cDTW^5$ performs at least as well as DTW in 34 datasets, and $cDTW^{10}$ performs at least as well as DTW in 41 datasets. However, the statistical test suggests that there is no significant difference between $cDTW^{opt}$, $cDTW^5$, and $cDTW^{10}$. Figure 5a further illustrates the superiority of SBD over ED.

Comparison against DTW and cDTW: Figure 5b shows that the difference in accuracy between SBD and DTW is in most cases negligible: SBD performs at least as well as DTW in 30 datasets, but the statistical test reveals no evidence that either measure is better than the other. Considering the constrained versions of DTW, we observe that SBD performs similarly to or better than $cDTW^{opt}$, $cDTW^5$, and $cDTW^{10}$ in 22, 18, and 19 datasets, respectively. Interestingly, there is no significant difference between SBD and $cDTW^{10}$, but $cDTW^{opt}$ and $cDTW^5$ are significantly better than SBD. $cDTW^{opt}$, with its optimal tuning, identifies that across the 48 datasets the average warping window is 4.5%. This explains why $cDTW^5$ behaves similarly to $cDTW^{opt}$ and outperforms SBD, whereas the large majority of constrained $cDTW^w$ variants, including $cDTW^{10}$, do not outperform SBD. Importantly, the p-values for the Wilcoxon test between $cDTW^{opt}$ and SBD, and between $cDTW^5$ and SBD, are close to the confidence level, which indicates that deeper statistical analysis is required, as we discuss next.

Statistical analysis: To better understand the performance of SBD in comparison with $cDTW^{opt}$ and $cDTW^5$, we evaluate the significance of their differences in accuracy when considered all together. Figure 6 shows the average rank across datasets of each distance measure. $cDTW^{opt}$ is the top measure, with an average rank of 1.96, meaning that $cDTW^{opt}$ performed best in the majority of the datasets. The Friedman test rejects the null hypothesis that all measures behave similarly, and, hence, we proceed with a post-hoc Nemenyi test, to evaluate the significance of the differences in the ranks. The wiggly line in the figure connects all measures that do not perform statistically differently according to the Nemenyi test. We observe that the ranks of $cDTW^{opt}$, $cDTW^5$, and SBD do not present a significant difference, and ED, which is ranked last, is significantly worse than the others. In conclusion, SBD is a very competitive distance measure that significantly outperforms ED and achieves similar results to both constraint and unconstraint versions of DTW. Moreover, SBD is the most robust variant of the cross-correlation measure (see Appendix A).

Efficiency: We now show that SBD is not only competitive in terms of accuracy, but also highly efficient. We also

Distance Measure	>	=	<	Better	Average Accuracy	Runtime
DTW DTW_{LB}	29	2	17	✓	0.788	15573x 6040x
$cDTW^{opt}$ $cDTW^{opt}_{LB}$	31	15	2	✓	0.814	2873x 322x
$cDTW^{5}$ $cDTW^{5}_{LB}$	34	3	11	✓	0.809	1558x 122x
$cDTW^{10}$ $cDTW^{10}_{LB}$	33	1	14	✓	0.804	2940x 364x
SBD_{NoFFT} SBD_{NoPow2} SBD	30	12	6	✓	0.795	224x 8.7x 4.4x

Table 2: Comparison of distance measures. Columns ">", "=", and "<" denote the number of datasets over which a distance measure is better, equal, or worse, respectively, in comparison to ED. "Better" indicates that a distance measure outperforms ED with statistical significance. "Average accuracy" denotes the accuracy achieved in the 48 datasets whereas "Runtime" indicates the factor by which a distance measure is slower than ED.

demonstrate that implementation choices for SBD can significantly impact its speed. The last row of Table 2 shows the factors by which each SBD variation is slower than ED. The optimized version of SBD, denoted simply as SBD, is the fastest version, performing only 4.4x slower than ED. When we use SBD still with FFT but without the power-of-two-length optimization discussed in Section 3.1, the resulting measure, SBD_{NoPow2}, is 8.7x slower than ED. Furthermore, SBD_{NoFFT}, the version of SBD without FFT, is two orders of magnitude slower (224x) than ED and one order slower (51x) than SBD. Table 2 also shows that SBD is substantially faster than the DTW and cDTW variants. Specifically, SBD is three orders of magnitude (3533x) faster than DTW, two orders (652x) faster than $cDTW^{opt}$, two orders (353x) faster than $cDTW^5$, and two orders (667x) faster than $cDTW^{10}$. Even when we speed up the search of 1-NN classification computation, by pruning time series unlikely for a match using LB_{Keogh}, SBD is still significantly faster. In particular, SBD now becomes one order of magnitude faster (73x) than $cDTW^{opt}_{LB}$, one order faster (28x) than $cDTW^{5}_{LB}$, and one order faster (82.5x) than $cDTW^{10}_{LB}$, while remaining three orders faster (1370x) than DTW_{LB}.

5.2 k-Shape Against Other Scalable Methods

Comparison against k-AVG+ED: Having shown the robustness of SBD, we now compare our algorithm, k-Shape, against scalable state-of-the-art time-series clustering algorithms. Table 3 reports the performance of variants of k-means against k-AVG+ED, using their Rand Index on the 48 datasets (see Section 4). From all these variants of k-means, only k-Shape outperforms k-AVG+ED with statistical significance, and, in particular, k-Shape significantly outperforms every other method. In most cases, replacing ED in k-means with other distance measures not only does not improve accuracy significantly, but in certain cases results in substantially lower performance. For example, k-AVG+SBD achieves higher accuracy than k-AVG+ED in 67% of the datasets, but the differences in accuracy are not statistically significant. Interestingly, when DTW is combined with k-means, in k-AVG+DTW, the performance is significantly worse than with k-AVG+ED. Even in cases where both the distance measure and the centroid computation method of k-means are modified, the performance does

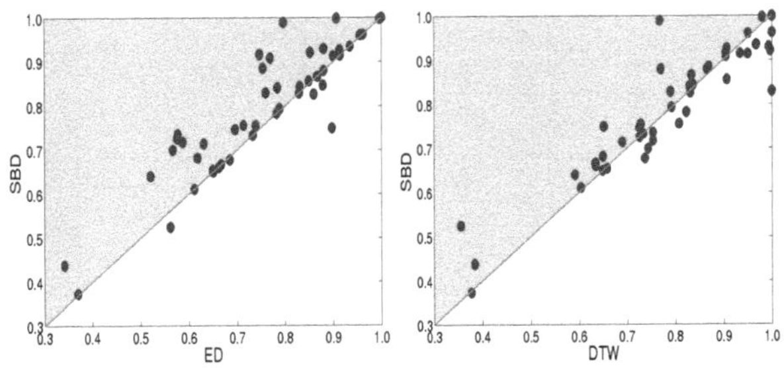

(a) SBD vs. ED (b) SBD vs. DTW

Figure 5: Comparison of SBD, ED, and DTW over 48 datasets. Circles above the diagonal indicate datasets over which SBD has better accuracy than the compared method.

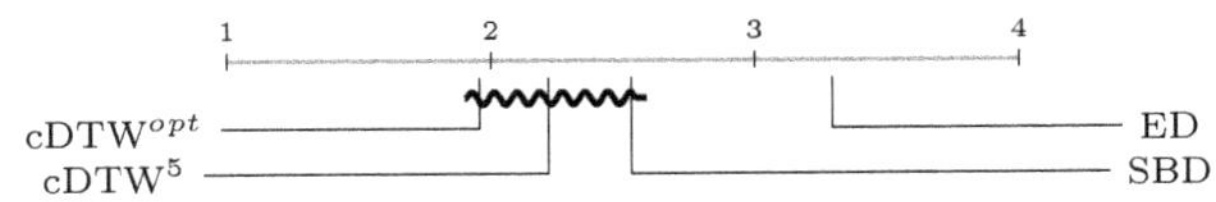

Figure 6: Ranking of distance measures based on the average of their ranks across datasets. The wiggly line connects all measures that do not perform statistically differently according to the Nemenyi test.

not improve significantly in comparison to k-AVG+ED. k-DBA outperforms k-AVG+DTW with statistical significance in 39 out of 48 datasets. Both of these approaches use DTW as distance measure, but k-DBA also modifies its centroid computation method. This modification significantly improves the performance of k-DBA over that of k-AVG+DTW, with an average improvement in Rand Index of 25.6%. Despite this improvement, k-DBA still does not perform better than k-AVG+ED in a statistical significant manner.[8] Another algorithm that modifies both the distance measure and the centroid computation method of k-means is KSC. Similarly to k-DBA, KSC does not outperform k-AVG+ED.

Comparison against k-DBA and KSC: Both k-DBA and KSC are similar to k-Shape in that they all modify both the centroid computation method and the distance measure of k-means. Therefore, to understand the impact of these modifications, we compare them against our k-Shape algorithm (see Figure 7). k-Shape is better in 30 datasets and worse in 18 datasets in comparison to KSC (Figure 7a), and is better in 35 datasets and worse in 13 datasets in comparison to k-DBA (Figure 7b). In both of these comparisons, the statistical test indicates the superiority of k-Shape.

Statistical analysis: In addition to the pairwise comparisons performed with the Wilcoxon test, we further evaluate the significance of the differences in algorithm performance when considered all together. Figure 8 shows the average rank across datasets of each k-means variant. k-Shape is the top technique, with an average rank of 1.89, meaning that k-Shape achieved better rank in the majority of the datasets. The Friedman test rejects the null hypothesis that all algorithms behave similarly, and, hence, we proceed with a post-hoc Nemenyi test, to evaluate the significance of the differences in the ranks. We observe that the ranks of KSC, k-DBA, and k-AVG+ED do not present a statistically significant difference, whereas k-Shape, which is ranked first, is significantly better than the others. To conclude, modi-

[8] Even when multiple refinements of k-DBA's centroids are performed per iteration, k-DBA still does not outperform k-AVG+ED. In particular, performing five refinements per iteration improves the Rand Index by 4% but runtime increases by 30%.

Algorithm	>	=	<	Better	Worse	Rand Index	Runtime
k-AVG+SBD	32	1	15	✗	✗	0.745	3.6x
k-AVG+DTW	10	0	38	✗	✓	0.584	3444x
KSC	22	0	26	✗	✗	0.636	448x
k-DBA	18	0	30	✗	✗	0.733	3892x
k-Shape+DTW	19	1	28	✗	✗	0.698	4175x
k-Shape	36	1	11	✓	✗	0.772	12.4x

Table 3: Comparison of k-means variants against k-AVG+ED. Columns ">", "=", and "<" denote the number of datasets over which an algorithm is better, equal, or worse, respectively, in comparison to k-AVG+ED. "Better" indicates that an algorithm outperforms k-AVG+ED with statistical significance whereas "Worse" indicates that k-AVG+ED outperforms an algorithm with statistical significance. "Rand Index" denotes the accuracy achieved in the 48 datasets whereas "Runtime" indicates the factor by which an algorithm is slower than k-AVG+ED.

fying k-means with inappropriate distance measures or centroid computation methods might lead to unexpected results. The same holds for k-Shape, where the use of DTW as its distance measure, in k-Shape+DTW, significantly drops its performance (i.e., k-Shape outperforms k-Shape+DTW with statistical significance in 36 out of 48 datasets).

Efficiency: k-Shape is the only algorithm that outperforms all k-means variants, including the simple, yet robust, k-AVG+ED. We now investigate whether k-Shape's superiority in terms of accuracy has an associated penalty in efficiency. Table 3 shows the factors by which each algorithm is slower than k-AVG+ED. Our approach, k-Shape, is one order of magnitude faster (36x) than KSC, two orders of magnitude faster (313x) than k-DBA, and 12.4x slower than k-AVG+ED.

5.3 k-Shape Against Non-Scalable Methods

Comparison against k-AVG+ED: Up to now, we have focused our evaluation on scalable clustering algorithms. In order to show the robustness of k-Shape in terms of accuracy beyond scalable approaches, we now ignore scalability and compare k-Shape against clustering methods that scale quadratically with the number of time series, namely, hierarchical, spectral, and k-medoids methods. Table 4 reports the performance of non-scalable methods against k-AVG+ED. Among all existing state-of-the-art methods that use ED or cDTW as distance measures, only partitional methods perform similarly to or better than k-AVG+ED. In particular, PAM+cDTW is the only method that outperforms k-AVG+ED with statistical significance. PAM+ED achieves better performance in 63% of the datasets in comparison to k-AVG+ED; however, this difference is not statistically significant. Moreover, PAM+cDTW performs better in 33 datasets, equal in 1 dataset, and worse in 14 datasets relative to PAM+ED. For this comparison, the statistical significance test indicates the superiority of PAM+cDTW.

All combinations of hierarchical clustering, with all different linkage criteria, perform poorly in comparison to k-AVG+ED. Interestingly, k-AVG+ED outperforms all of them with statistical significance. We observe that the major difference in performance among hierarchical methods is the linkage criterion and not the distance measure. This highlights the importance of the clustering method and not only of the distance measure for time-series clustering. Similarly to hierarchical methods, spectral methods also perform poorly against k-AVG+ED. S+cDTW performs better in more datasets than S+ED in comparison to k-AVG+ED:

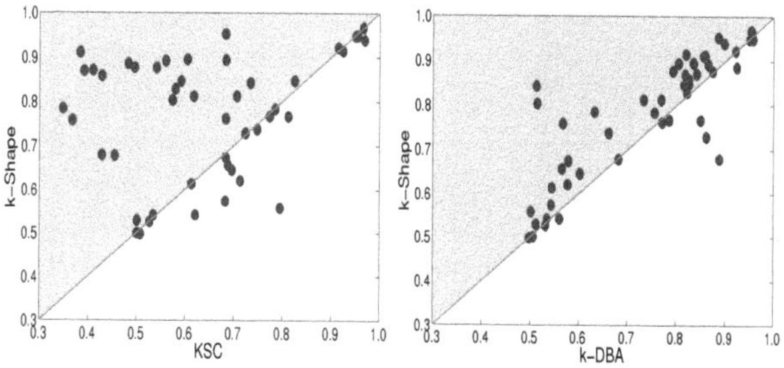

(a) k-Shape vs. KSC (b) k-Shape vs. k-DBA

Figure 7: Comparison of k-Shape, KSC, and k-DBA over 48 datasets. Circles above the diagonal indicate datasets over which k-Shape has better Rand Index.

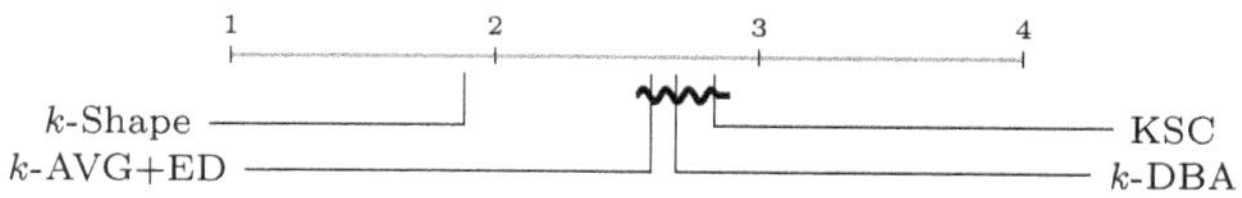

Figure 8: Ranking of k-means variants based on the average of their ranks across datasets. The wiggly line connects all techniques that do not perform statistically differently according to the Nemenyi test.

comparing S+cDTW with S+ED, S+cDTW achieves similar or better accuracy in 27 datasets, but this difference is not significant. Importantly, k-AVG+ED is significantly better than both S+ED and S+cDTW. Therefore, for hierarchical and spectral methods, these distance measures have a small impact on their performance.

k-Shape against PAM+cDTW: Among all methods that we evaluated, only PAM+cDTW outperforms k-AVG+ED with statistical significance. Therefore, we compare this approach with k-Shape. PAM+cDTW is better in 31, equal in 1, and worse in 16 datasets in comparison to k-Shape, but this difference is not significant. For completeness, we also evaluate SBD with hierarchical, spectral, and k-medoids methods. For hierarchical methods, H-C+SBD is better than H-A+SBD, and, in turn, H-A+SBD is better than H-S+SBD, all with statistical significance. For each linkage option, there is no significance in the accuracy between ED, SBD, and cDTW. S+SBD, in contrast to S+ED and S+cDTW, outperforms k-AVG+ED in 38 out of 48 datasets, with statistical significance. S+SBD is also significantly better than S+ED and S+cDTW, but S+SBD does not outperform k-Shape. Similarly, PAM+SBD performs equally to or better than k-AVG+ED in 36 out of 48 datasets. The statistical test suggests that PAM+SBD is significantly better than k-AVG+ED but not better than k-Shape.

Statistical analysis: We evaluate the significance of the differences in algorithm performance for all algorithms that significantly outperform k-AVG+ED. The Friedman test rejects the null hypothesis that all algorithms behave similarly, and, hence, as before, we proceed with a post-hoc Nemenyi test. Figure 9 shows that k-Shape, PAM+SBD, PAM+cDTW, and S+SBD do not present a significant difference in accuracy, whereas k-AVG+ED, which is ranked last, is significantly worse than the others.

From our extensive evaluation of existing scalable and non-scalable clustering approaches for time series that use ED, cDTW, or DTW as distance measures, PAM+cDTW is the only approach that achieves similar — but not better — results to k-Shape. In contrast to k-Shape, PAM+cDTW has two drawbacks that make it an unrealistic choice for time-series clustering: (i) its distance measure, cDTW, re-

Algorithm	>	=	<	Better	Worse	Rand Index
H-S+ED	3	1	44	✗	✓	0.328
H-S+cDTW	7	0	41	✗	✓	0.371
H-S+SBD	6	1	41	✗	✓	0.349
H-A+ED	3	1	44	✗	✓	0.599
H-A+cDTW	9	0	39	✗	✓	0.617
H-A+SBD	8	0	40	✗	✓	0.541
H-C+ED	8	0	40	✗	✓	0.690
H-C+cDTW	15	0	33	✗	✓	0.699
H-C+SBD	17	0	31	✗	✓	0.697
S+ED	7	1	40	✗	✓	0.602
S+cDTW	18	1	29	✗	✓	0.563
S+SBD	38	0	10	✓	✗	0.769
PAM+ED	30	1	17	✗	✗	0.762
PAM+cDTW	38	1	9	✓	✗	0.772
PAM+SBD	35	1	12	✓	✗	0.780

Table 4: Comparison of hierarchical, spectral, and k-medoids variants against k-AVG+ED. Columns ">", "=", and "<" denote the number of datasets over which an algorithm is better, equal, or worse, respectively, in comparison to k-AVG+ED. "Better" indicates that an algorithm outperforms k-AVG+ED with statistical significance whereas "Worse" indicates that k-AVG+ED outperforms an algorithm with statistical significance. "Rand Index" denotes the accuracy achieved in the 48 datasets.

quires tuning to improve its performance and reduce the computation cost; and (ii) the computation of the dissimilarity matrix that PAM+cDTW requires as input makes it unable to scale in both time and space. For example, the matrix computation alone is already two orders of magnitude slower than the computation required by k-Shape. Thus, k-Shape emerges as a domain-independent, highly accurate, and scalable approach for time-series clustering.

5.4 Summary of Results

In short, our experimental evaluation suggests that: (1) cross-correlation measures (e.g., SBD), which are not widely adopted as time-series distance measures, are as competitive as state-of-the-art measures, such as cDTW and DTW, but significantly faster; (2) the k-means algorithm with ED, in contrast to what has been reported in the literature, is a robust approach for time-series clustering, but inadequate modifications of its distance measure and centroid computation can reduce its performance; (3) the choice of clustering method, which was believed to be less important than that of distance measure, is as important as the choice of distance measure; and overall (4) k-Shape is a highly accurate and efficient method for time-series clustering.

6. RELATED WORK

This paper focused on efficient and domain-independent time-series clustering. Section 2 provided an in-depth discussion of the state of the art for time-series clustering, which we will not repeat for brevity. Specifically, Section 2.1 summarized the relevant theoretical background, Section 2.2 reviewed common distortions in time series, and Section 2.3 discussed the most popular state-of-the-art distance measures for time series. (We refer the reader to [19, 81] for a thorough review and evaluation of the alternative time-series distance measures.) Section 2.4 highlighted existing approaches for clustering time series. (We refer the reader to [83] for a more detailed view of these approaches.) Finally, Section 2.5 discussed the methods for centroid computation that are part of many time-series clustering algorithms.

As argued throughout the paper, we focus on shape-based clustering of time series. Beyond shape-based clustering

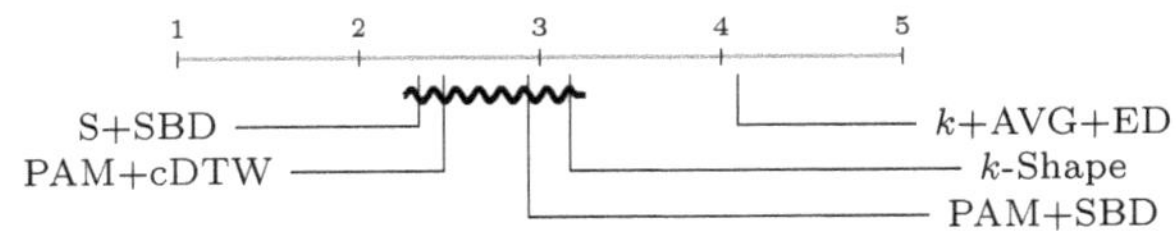

Figure 9: Ranking of methods that outperform k-AVG+ED based on the average of their ranks across datasets. The wiggly line connects all techniques that do not perform statistically differently according to the Nemenyi test.

algorithms, statistical-based approaches use measures that summarize characteristics [82], coefficients of models [38], or portions of time series (i.e., shapelets) [89] as descriptive features to cluster time series. Unfortunately, statistical-based approaches frequently require the non-trivial tuning of multiple parameters, which often leads to ad-hoc decisions, or their effectiveness has been established only for isolated domains and not in a domain-independent manner. Instead, shape-based approaches are general and leverage the vast literature on distance measures.

The best performing shape-based approaches from the literature are partitional methods combined with scale- and shift-invariant distance measures. Among partitional methods, k-medoids [40] is the most popular method as it enables the easy adoption of any shape-based distance measure [19, 81]. However, k-medoids requires the computation of the full dissimilarity matrix among all time series, which makes it particularly slow and unable to scale. Recent alternative approaches [32, 53, 59, 64, 87] have focused on k-means [50], which is scalable but requires the modification of the centroid computation method when the distance measure is altered, in order to support the same properties (e.g., scaling, translation, and shifting). Because DTW is the most prominent shape-based distance measure [19, 81], the majority of the k-means approaches have proposed new centroid computation methods to be used in conjunction with DTW [32, 53, 59, 64]. k-DBA has been shown to be the most robust of these approaches [64]. Another approach worth mentioning is KSC [87], which focuses on a different shape-based distance measure that offers simultaneously pairwise scaling and shifting of time series. Unfortunately, the effectiveness of such pairwise scaling and shifting, and, hence, KSC, has not been established beyond a limited number of datasets.

For completeness, we note that [28] used cross-correlation as distance measure and the arithmetic mean property for centroid computation for fuzzy clustering of fMRI data. (In Section 5 we showed that k-AVG+SBD is not competitive for our non-fuzzy setting.) Finally, cross-correlation was used to transform fMRI data into features for clustering [31], as well as for stream mining, pattern extraction, and time-series monitoring [61, 73, 85, 90].

7. CONCLUSIONS

We presented k-Shape, a partitional clustering algorithm that preserves the shapes of time series. k-Shape compares time series efficiently and computes centroids effectively under the scaling and shift invariances. Our extensive evaluation shows that k-Shape outperforms all state-of-the-art partitional, hierarchical, and spectral clustering approaches, with only one method achieving similar performance. Interestingly, this method is two orders of magnitude slower than k-Shape and its distance measure requires tuning, unlike that for k-Shape. Overall, k-Shape is a domain-independent, accurate, and scalable approach for time-series clustering.

Acknowledgments

We thank Or Biran, Eamonn Keogh, Kathy McKeown, Taesun Moon, and Kapil Thadani for invaluable discussions and feedback. We also thank Ken Ross for sharing computing resources for our experiments. This research was supported by the Intelligence Advanced Research Projects Activity (IARPA) via Department of Interior National Business Center (DoI/NBC) contract number D11PC20153. The U.S. Government is authorized to reproduce and distribute reprints for Governmental purposes notwithstanding any copyright annotation thereon. Disclaimer: The views and conclusions contained herein are those of the authors and should not be interpreted as necessarily representing the official policies or endorsements, either expressed or implied, of IARPA, DoI/NBC, or the U.S. Government. This material is also based upon work supported by a generous gift from Microsoft Research. John Paparrizos is an Alexander S. Onassis Public Benefit Foundation Scholar.

8. REFERENCES

[1] The UCR Time Series Classification/Clustering Homepage. `http://www.cs.ucr.edu/~eamonn/time_series_data`. Accessed: May 2014.

[2] R. Agrawal, C. Faloutsos, and A. N. Swami. Efficient similarity search in sequence databases. In *FODO*, pages 69–84, 1993.

[3] D. Aloise, A. Deshpande, P. Hansen, and P. Popat. NP-hardness of Euclidean sum-of-squares clustering. *Machine Learning*, 75(2):245–248, 2009.

[4] J. Alon, S. Sclaroff, G. Kollios, and V. Pavlovic. Discovering clusters in motion time-series data. In *CVPR*, pages 375–381, 2003.

[5] A. J. Bagnall and G. J. Janacek. Clustering time series from ARMA models with clipped data. In *KDD*, pages 49–58, 2004.

[6] Z. Bar-Joseph, G. Gerber, D. K. Gifford, T. S. Jaakkola, and I. Simon. A new approach to analyzing gene expression time series data. In *RECOMB*, pages 39–48, 2002.

[7] G. E. Batista, E. J. Keogh, O. M. Tataw, and V. M. de Souza. CID: An efficient complexity-invariant distance for time series. *Data Mining and Knowledge Discovery*, pages 1–36, 2013.

[8] D. J. Berndt and J. Clifford. Using dynamic time warping to find patterns in time series. In *AAAI Workshop on KDD*, pages 359–370, 1994.

[9] Y. Cai and R. Ng. Indexing spatio-temporal trajectories with Chebyshev polynomials. In *SIGMOD*, pages 599–610, 2004.

[10] F. Chan, A. Fu, and C. Yu. Haar wavelets for efficient similarity search of time-series: with and without time warping. *TKDE*, 15(3):686–705, 2003.

[11] L. Chen and R. Ng. On the marriage of Lp-norms and edit distance. In *VLDB*, pages 792–803, 2004.

[12] L. Chen, M. T. Özsu, and V. Oria. Robust and fast similarity search for moving object trajectories. In *SIGMOD*, pages 491–502, 2005.

[13] Q. Chen, L. Chen, X. Lian, Y. Liu, and J. X. Yu. Indexable PLA for efficient similarity search. In *VLDB*, pages 435–446, 2007.

[14] Y. Chen, M. A. Nascimento, B. C. Ooi, and A. K. Tung. Spade: On shape-based pattern detection in streaming time series. In *ICDE*, pages 786–795, 2007.

[15] J. W. Cooley and J. W. Tukey. An algorithm for the machine calculation of complex Fourier series. *Mathematics of Computation*, 19(90):297–301, 1965.

[16] G. Das, K.-I. Lin, H. Mannila, G. Renganathan, and P. Smyth. Rule discovery from time series. In *KDD*, pages 16–22, 1998.

[17] J. Demšar. Statistical comparisons of classifiers over multiple data sets. *The Journal of Machine Learning Research*, 7:1–30, 2006.

[18] E. Dimitriadou, A. Weingessel, and K. Hornik. A combination scheme for fuzzy clustering. *International Journal of Pattern Recognition and Artificial Intelligence*, 16(07):901–912, 2002.

[19] H. Ding, G. Trajcevski, P. Scheuermann, X. Wang, and E. Keogh. Querying and mining of time series data: Experimental comparison of representations and distance measures. *PVLDB*, 1(2):1542–1552, 2008.

[20] C. Faloutsos, M. Ranganathan, and Y. Manolopoulos. Fast subsequence matching in time-series databases. In *SIGMOD*, pages 419–429, 1994.

[21] M. Filippone, F. Camastra, F. Masulli, and S. Rovetta. A survey of kernel and spectral methods for clustering. *Pattern Recognition*, 41(1):176–190, 2008.

[22] E. Frentzos, K. Gratsias, and Y. Theodoridis. Index-based most similar trajectory search. In *ICDE*, pages 816–825, 2007.

[23] M. Friedman. The use of ranks to avoid the assumption of normality implicit in the analysis of variance. *Journal of the American Statistical Association*, 32:675–701, 1937.

[24] M. Frigo and S. G. Johnson. The design and implementation of FFTW3. *Proceedings of the IEEE*, 93(2):216–231, 2005.

[25] M. Gavrilov, D. Anguelov, P. Indyk, and R. Motwani. Mining the stock market: Which measure is best? In *KDD*, pages 487–496, 2000.

[26] R. Giusti and G. E. Batista. An empirical comparison of dissimilarity measures for time series classification. In *BRACIS*, pages 82–88, 2013.

[27] S. Goddard, S. K. Harms, S. E. Reichenbach, T. Tadesse, and W. J. Waltman. Geospatial decision support for drought risk management. *Communications of the ACM*, 46(1):35–37, 2003.

[28] X. Golay, S. Kollias, G. Stoll, D. Meier, A. Valavanis, and P. Boesiger. A new correlation-based fuzzy logic clustering algorithm for fMRI. *Magnetic Resonance in Medicine*, 40(2):249–260, 1998.

[29] D. Q. Goldin and P. C. Kanellakis. On similarity queries for time-series data: Constraint specification and implementation. In *CP*, pages 137–153, 1995.

[30] G. H. Golub and C. F. Van Loan. *Matrix computations*, volume 3. JHU Press, 2012.

[31] C. Goutte, P. Toft, E. Rostrup, F. Å. Nielsen, and L. K. Hansen. On clustering fMRI time series. *NeuroImage*, 9(3):298–310, 1999.

[32] L. Gupta, D. L. Molfese, R. Tammana, and P. G. Simos. Nonlinear alignment and averaging for estimating the evoked potential. *IEEE Transactions on Biomedical Engineering*, 43(4):348–356, 1996.

[33] M. Halkidi, Y. Batistakis, and M. Vazirgiannis. On clustering validation techniques. *Journal of Intelligent Information Systems*, 17(2-3):107–145, 2001.

[34] J. Han, M. Kamber, and J. Pei. *Data Mining: Concepts and Techniques.* Morgan Kaufmann Publishers Inc., 3rd edition, 2011.

[35] P. Hansen and B. Jaumard. Cluster analysis and mathematical programming. *Mathematical Programming*, 79(1-3):191–215, 1997.

[36] R. Honda, S. Wang, T. Kikuchi, and O. Konishi. Mining of moving objects from time-series images and its application to satellite weather imagery. *Journal of Intelligent Information Systems*, 19(1):79–93, 2002.

[37] B. Hu, Y. Chen, and E. Keogh. Time series classification under more realistic assumptions. In *SDM*, pages 578–586, 2013.

[38] K. Kalpakis, D. Gada, and V. Puttagunta. Distance measures for effective clustering of ARIMA time-series. In *ICDM*, pages 273–280, 2001.

[39] Y. Katznelson. *An introduction to harmonic analysis.* Cambridge University Press, 2004.

[40] L. Kaufman and P. J. Rousseeuw. *Finding groups in data: An introduction to cluster analysis*, volume 344. John Wiley & Sons, 2009.

[41] E. Keogh. A decade of progress in indexing and mining large time series databases. In *VLDB*, pages 1268–1268, 2006.

[42] E. Keogh, K. Chakrabarti, M. Pazzani, and S. Mehrotra. Locally adaptive dimensionality reduction for indexing large time series databases. In *SIGMOD*, pages 151–162, 2001.

[43] E. Keogh and J. Lin. Clustering of time-series subsequences is meaningless: Implications for previous and future research. *Knowledge and Information Systems*, 8(2):154–177, 2005.

[44] E. Keogh and C. A. Ratanamahatana. Exact indexing of dynamic time warping. *Knowledge and Information Systems*, 7(3):358–386, 2005.

[45] C. Kin-pong and F. Ada. Efficient time series matching by wavelets. In *ICDE*, pages 126–133, 1999.

[46] F. Korn, H. V. Jagadish, and C. Faloutsos. Efficiently supporting ad hoc queries in large datasets of time sequences. In *SIGMOD*, pages 289–300, 1997.

[47] C.-S. Li, P. S. Yu, and V. Castelli. MALM: A framework for mining sequence database at multiple abstraction levels. In *CIKM*, pages 267–272, 1998.

[48] X. Lian, L. Chen, J. X. Yu, G. Wang, and G. Yu. Similarity match over high speed time-series streams. In *ICDE*, pages 1086–1095, 2007.

[49] J. Lin, M. Vlachos, E. Keogh, and D. Gunopulos. Iterative incremental clustering of time series. In *EDBT*, pages 106–122, 2004.

[50] J. MacQueen. Some methods for classification and analysis of multivariate observations. In *BSMSP*, pages 281–297, 1967.

[51] M. Mahajan, P. Nimbhorkar, and K. Varadarajan. The planar k-means problem is NP-hard. In *WALCOM*, pages 274–285. 2009.

[52] R. N. Mantegna. Hierarchical structure in financial markets. *The European Physical Journal B-Condensed Matter and Complex Systems*, 11(1):193–197, 1999.

[53] W. Meesrikamolkul, V. Niennattrakul, and C. A. Ratanamahatana. Shape-based clustering for time series data. In *PAKDD*, pages 530–541. 2012.

[54] V. Megalooikonomou, Q. Wang, G. Li, and C. Faloutsos. A multiresolution symbolic representation of time series. In *ICDE*, pages 668–679, 2005.

[55] M. D. Morse and J. M. Patel. An efficient and accurate method for evaluating time series similarity. In *SIGMOD*, pages 569–580, 2007.

[56] A. Mueen, E. Keogh, and N. Young. Logical-shapelets: An expressive primitive for time series classification. In *KDD*, pages 1154–1162, 2011.

[57] P. Nemenyi. *Distribution-free Multiple Comparisons.* PhD thesis, Princeton University, 1963.

[58] A. Y. Ng, M. I. Jordan, and Y. Weiss. On spectral clustering: Analysis and an algorithm. In *NIPS*, pages 849–856, 2002.

[59] V. Niennattrakul and C. A. Ratanamahatana. Shape averaging under time warping. In *ECTI-CON*, pages 626–629, 2009.

[60] T. Oates. Identifying distinctive subsequences in multivariate time series by clustering. In *KDD*, pages 322–326, 1999.

[61] S. Papadimitriou, J. Sun, and P. S. Yu. Local correlation tracking in time series. In *ICDM*, pages 456–465, 2006.

[62] P. Papapetrou, V. Athitsos, M. Potamias, G. Kollios, and D. Gunopulos. Embedding-based subsequence matching in time-series databases. *TODS*, 36(3):17, 2011.

[63] F. Petitjean and P. Gançarski. Summarizing a set of time series by averaging: From Steiner sequence to compact multiple alignment. *Theoretical Computer Science*, 414(1):76–91, 2012.

[64] F. Petitjean, A. Ketterlin, and P. Gançarski. A global averaging method for dynamic time warping, with applications to clustering. *Pattern Recognition*, 44(3):678–693, 2011.

[65] T. Rakthanmanon, B. Campana, A. Mueen, G. Batista, B. Westover, Q. Zhu, J. Zakaria, and E. Keogh. Searching and mining trillions of time series subsequences under dynamic time warping. In *KDD*, pages 262–270, 2012.

[66] T. Rakthanmanon, E. J. Keogh, S. Lonardi, and S. Evans. Time series epenthesis: Clustering time series streams requires ignoring some data. In *ICDM*, pages 547–556, 2011.

[67] W. M. Rand. Objective criteria for the evaluation of clustering methods. *Journal of the American Statistical Association*, 66(336):846–850, 1971.

[68] C. A. Ratanamahatana and E. Keogh. Making time-series classification more accurate using learned constraints. In *SDM*, pages 11–22, 2004.

[69] J. Rice. *Mathematical statistics and data analysis.* Cengage Learning, 2006.

[70] E. J. Ruiz, V. Hristidis, C. Castillo, A. Gionis, and A. Jaimes. Correlating financial time series with micro-blogging activity. In *WSDM*, pages 513–522, 2012.

[71] N. Saito. *Local Feature Extraction and Its Applications Using a Library of Bases.* PhD thesis, Yale University, 1994.

[72] H. Sakoe and S. Chiba. Dynamic programming algorithm optimization for spoken word recognition. *IEEE Transactions on Acoustics, Speech and Signal Processing*, 26(1):43–49, 1978.

[73] Y. Sakurai, S. Papadimitriou, and C. Faloutsos. Braid: Stream mining through group lag correlations. In *SIGMOD*, pages 599–610, 2005.

[74] Y. Shou, N. Mamoulis, and D. Cheung. Fast and exact warping of time series using adaptive segmental approximations. *Machine Learning*, 58(2-3):231–267, 2005.

[75] A. Stefan, V. Athitsos, and G. Das. The move-split-merge metric for time series. *TKDE*, 25(6):1425–1438, 2013.

[76] K. Uehara and M. Shimada. Extraction of primitive motion and discovery of association rules from human motion data. In *Progress in Discovery Science*, pages 338–348. 2002.

[77] M. Vlachos, M. Hadjieleftheriou, D. Gunopulos, and E. Keogh. Indexing multidimensional time-series. *The VLDB Journal*, 15(1):1–20, 2006.

[78] M. Vlachos, G. Kollios, and D. Gunopulos. Discovering similar multidimensional trajectories. In *ICDE*, pages 673–684, 2002.

[79] H. Wang, Y. Cai, Y. Yang, S. Zhang, and N. Mamoulis. Durable queries over historical time series. *TKDE*, 26(3):595–607, 2014.

[80] L. Wang and T. Jiang. On the complexity of multiple sequence alignment. *Journal of Computational Biology*, 1(4):337–348, 1994.

[81] X. Wang, A. Mueen, H. Ding, G. Trajcevski, P. Scheuermann, and E. Keogh. Experimental comparison of representation methods and distance measures for time series data. *Data Mining and Knowledge Discovery*, 26(2):275–309, 2013.

[82] X. Wang, K. Smith, and R. Hyndman. Characteristic-based clustering for time series data. *Data Mining and Knowledge Discovery*, 13(3):335–364, 2006.

[83] T. Warren Liao. Clustering of time series data - a survey. *Pattern Recognition*, 38(11):1857–1874, 2005.

[84] F. Wilcoxon. Individual comparisons by ranking methods. *Biometrics Bulletin*, pages 80–83, 1945.

[85] D. Wu, Y. Ke, J. X. Yu, S. Y. Philip, and L. Chen. Detecting leaders from correlated time series. In *DASFAA*, pages 352–367, 2010.

[86] Y. Xiong and D.-Y. Yeung. Mixtures of ARMA models for model-based time series clustering. In *ICDM*, pages 717–720, 2002.

[87] J. Yang and J. Leskovec. Patterns of temporal variation in online media. In *WSDM*, pages 177–186, 2011.

[88] L. Ye and E. Keogh. Time series shapelets: A new primitive for data mining. In *KDD*, pages 947–956, 2009.

[89] J. Zakaria, A. Mueen, and E. Keogh. Clustering time series using unsupervised-shapelets. In *ICDM*, pages 785–794, 2012.

[90] Y. Zhu and D. Shasha. Statstream: Statistical monitoring of thousands of data streams in real time. In *VLDB*, pages 358–369, 2002.

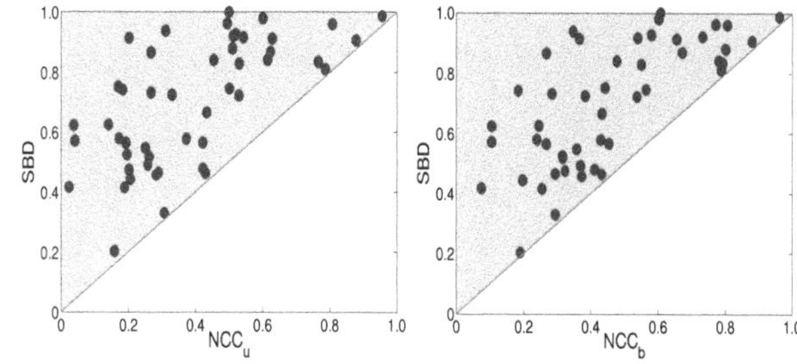

(a) SBD vs. NCC_u (b) SBD vs. NCC_b

Figure 10: Comparison of SBD, NCC_b, and NCC_u over 48 datasets under the *OptimalScaling* normalization. Circles above the diagonal indicate datasets over which SBD has better accuracy than the compared method.

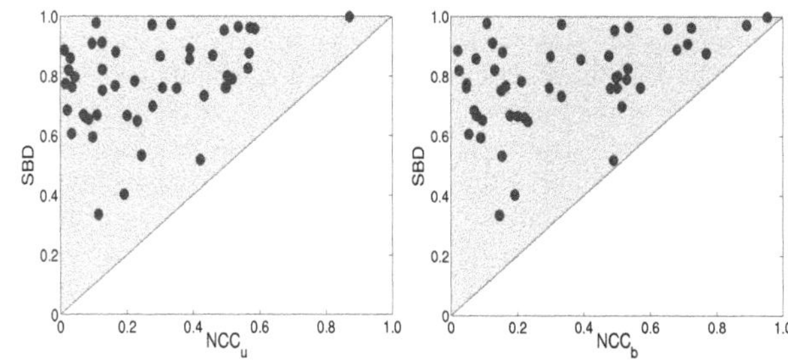

(a) SBD vs. NCC_u (b) SBD vs. NCC_b

Figure 11: Comparison of SBD, NCC_b, and NCC_u over 48 datasets under the *ValuesBetween0-1* normalization. Circles above the diagonal indicate datasets over which SBD has better accuracy than the compared method.

APPENDIX

A. CROSS-CORRELATION VARIANTS UNDER TIME-SERIES NORMALIZATIONS

As discussed in Section 3.1, the choice of normalizations for the data and the cross-correlation measure can significantly impact the cross-correlation sequence produced. To understand the sensitivity of cross-correlation variants to data normalizations we evaluate their performance using all 48 datasets from the UCR time-series collection [1]. This collection contains z-normalized datasets but the unnormalized versions are not available. Therefore, to experiment with unnormalized versions of these datasets and ensure that the initial sequences differ in amplitude, we first multiply each sequence with a random number chosen individually for that sequence. Then, we perform and study three common time-series normalizations: (1) *OptimalScaling*: to match two time series $\vec{x}$ and $\vec{y}$, we compute their optimal scaling coefficient $c = \frac{\vec{x} \cdot \vec{y}^T}{\vec{y} \cdot \vec{y}^T}$, which is used for every pairwise comparison (e.g., $SBD(\vec{x},\vec{y})$ is computed as $SBD(\vec{x}, c \cdot \vec{y})$); (2) *ValuesBetween0-1*: we normalize each sequence $\vec{x}$ such that its values fall between 0 and 1, by transforming it into $\vec{x}' = \frac{\vec{x} - min(\vec{x})}{max(\vec{x}) - min(\vec{x})}$; and (3) *z-normalization*: we normalize each sequence $\vec{x}$ such that its mean is 0 and its standard deviation is 1, by transforming it into $\vec{x}' = \frac{\vec{x} - mean(\vec{x})}{std(\vec{x})}$.

We evaluate the 1-NN classification accuracy of each cross-correlation variant, namely, SBD, NCC_u, and NCC_b, on each dataset for the three common time-series normalization scenarios. Figure 10 presents the results for the *OptimalScaling* normalization. In particular, SBD significantly outperforms both NCC_u (Figure 10a) and NCC_b (Figure 10b) in

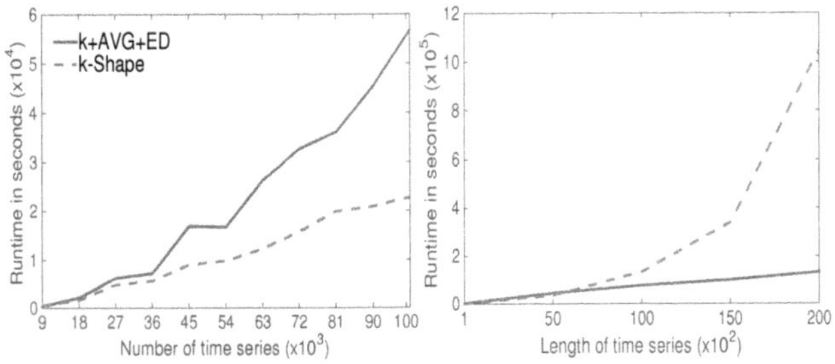

(a) Varying n for m=128 (b) Varying m for n=18K

Figure 12: Runtime of k-AVG+ED and k-Shape as a function of (a) the number of time series n and (b) the time series length m.

all 48 datasets, and, in turn, NCC_b outperforms NCC_u in 40 datasets, with statistical significance.

Similarly, for *ValuesBetween0-1* data normalization, SBD significantly outperforms NCC_u (Figure 11a) and NCC_b (Figure 11b) in all 48 datasets. NCC_b performs similarly to or better than NCC_u in 41 datasets and the Wilcoxon test suggests this difference in accuracy is statistically significant. Finally, for *z-normalization*, SBD and NCC_b achieve similar performance and both significantly outperform NCC_u.

Therefore, we can conclude that SBD is the most robust cross-correlation variant as it achieves better performance across multiple different time series normalizations. On average, SBD achieves accuracy values of 0.699, 0.779, and 0.795, for *OptimalScaling*, *ValuesBetween0-1*, and *z-normalization* normalizations, respectively.

B. SCALABILITY OF k-SHAPE

As discussed in Section 3.3, k-Shape requires $\mathcal{O}(\max\{n \cdot k \cdot m \cdot \log(m), n \cdot m^2, k \cdot m^3\})$ time per iteration to cluster n time series of length m into k clusters. The majority of the computational cost of our algorithm depends on the time-series length m, whereas its dependence on the number n of time series is linear. To better understand the scalability of k-Shape, we use the synthetic CBF dataset [71] because it enables experiments with varying values of both n and m without changing any of its general properties. Figure 12 reports the results of our scalability experiments where both n and m are up to one order of magnitude larger than the biggest dataset in the UCR archive [1]. We report the average CPU runtime of 5 runs. Specifically, in Figure 12a, we vary n while we set $m = 128$ as in the original CBF dataset: k-Shape, similarly to k+AVG+ED, scales linearly with the number of time series without any loss in accuracy for both methods. Importantly, k-Shape, remains significantly faster than k-AVG+ED with the increasing number of time series because k-Shape requires 45% fewer iterations to converge than k+AVG+ED does. Then, in Figure 12b, we vary m while we set $n = 18K$: k-Shape still outperforms k-AVG+ED for $m \ll n$ but k-Shape becomes slower, as expected, when the time-series length is large and approaches the total number of time series in the dataset. Similarly to the previous experiment, there is no loss in accuracy for either technique.

SMiLer: A Semi-Lazy Time Series Prediction System for Sensors

Jingbo Zhou
Interactive Digital Media Institute
National University of Singapore
jzhou@u.nus.edu

Anthony K. H. Tung
School of Computing
National University of Singapore
atung@comp.nus.edu.sg

ABSTRACT

It is useful to predict future values in time series data, for example when there are many sensors monitoring environments such as urban space. The Gaussian Process (GP) model is considered as a promising technique for this setting. However, the GP model requires too high a training cost to be tractable for large data. Though approximate methods have been proposed to improve GP's scalability, they usually can only capture global trends in the data and fail to preserve small-scale patterns, resulting in unsatisfactory performance.

We propose a new method to apply the GP for sensor time series prediction. Instead of (eagerly) training GPs on entire datasets, we custom-build query-dependent GPs on small fractions of the data for each prediction request.

Implementing this idea in practice at scale requires us to overcome two obstacles. On the one hand, a central challenge with such a semi-lazy learning model is the substantial model-building effort at kNN query time, which could lead to unacceptable latency. We propose a novel two-level inverted-like index to support kNN search using the DTW on the GPU, making such "just-in-time" query-dependent model construction feasible for real-time applications.

On the other hand, several parameters should be tuned for each time series individually since different sensors have different data generating processes in diverse environments. Manually configuring the parameters is usually not feasible due to the large number of sensors. To address this, we devise an adaptive auto-tuning mechanism to automatically determine and dynamically adjust the parameters for each time series with little human assistance.

Our method has the following strong points: (a) it can make prediction in real time without a training phase; (b) it can yield superior prediction accuracy; and (c) it can effectively estimate the analytical predictive uncertainty.

To illustrate our points, we present SMiLer, a semi-lazy time series prediction system for sensors. Extensive experiments on real-world datasets demonstrate its effectiveness and efficiency. In particular, by devising a two-level inverted-like index on the GPU with an enhanced lower bound of the DTW, SMiLer accelerates the efficiency of kNN search by one order of magnitude over its baselines. The prediction accuracy of SMiLer is better than the state-of-the-art competitors (up to 10 competitors) with better estimation of predictive uncertainty.

SIGMOD'15, May 31–June 4, 2015, Melbourne, Victoria, Australia.

http://dx.doi.org/10.1145/2723372.2749429.

Categories and Subject Descriptors: H.2.8 [Database management]: Database applications-Data mining

Keywords: Semi-lazy learning; Sensors; Time series; Predictive analysis; Gaussian Process; DTW; GPU

1. INTRODUCTION

With sensor data becoming prevalent, time series prediction of sensors is valuable in many applications including event prediction, air pollution forecasting, manufacturing condition monitoring and medical diagnoses. Since statistical regression methods are not powerful enough to handle large varieties of time series in realistic settings, machine learning methods have drawn much attention and are becoming popular for time series prediction.

Among the models, the Gaussian Process (GP) model have received significant interests for time series prediction [70, 34, 50, 16, 20, 35, 72, 23, 40]. This is due to its nonparametric nonlinear property and excellent modeling capability for a wide variety of behavior. In addition, the GP model can easily estimate analytical predictive uncertainty with conceptually simple closed-form expression.

A major limitation of the GP is its poor scalability that scales as $O(n^3)$ where n is the size of training data. To overcome this limitation, some approximation methods are usually adopted to find approximated representation of the whole dataset. The consequence is that the constructed GP models are more influenced by global distribution of the whole time series data, while local behavior and small-scale patterns are not captured. We refer this as the "*information loss*" problem. In addition, the GP models, as well as many other non-linear machine learning models, may also suffer from "*concept drift*" problem. In the case of sensors monitoring dynamic environments such as urban space, since the underlying model generating the data might gradually change, the constructed global GP models might be outdated by the time when sufficient historical data is collected to build the models. In this case, paying a high computational cost to construct a large, global model that fits the whole of the sensor time series may be wasteful.

EXAMPLE 1.1 (TRAFFIC SENSOR PREDICTION). *Time series prediction for traffic sensors can be very useful for many smart city applications such as abnormal event detection, traffic jam prediction and flow speed prediction [42]. While the standard GP model is not tractable for large data, the approximated GP models have relative low prediction accuracy, and also high training time cost. These observations are supported by our experiment evaluation for traffic sensors prediction (see Fig. 13(a) and Section 6.4.2).*

In this paper, we propose a new approach to employing the GP model in sensor time series prediction. Instead of attempting to eagerly train a global GP model on the entire dataset which may suffer from information loss and is not adaptive to concept drift, we propose to build a query-dependent GP model for each prediction request. In general, the methodology of our solution can be considered as a semi-lazy learning approach, which is a hybrid of the eager learning approach (e.g. GPs and SVMs) and the lazy learning approach (e.g. kNN regression). Its framework essentially follows the lazy learning paradigm until the last step, where sophisticated models, i.e. GPs in this paper, are applied on the kNN results of the submitted prediction request.

Fig. 2 shows an illustration of the semi-lazy learning GP prediction idea. We use the time series of a sensor in the last few time steps as the input request to retrieve a set of k-Nearest Neighbor (kNN) time series segments from historical data. The kNNs are then utilized to construct GPs for predicting the future value of the sensor.

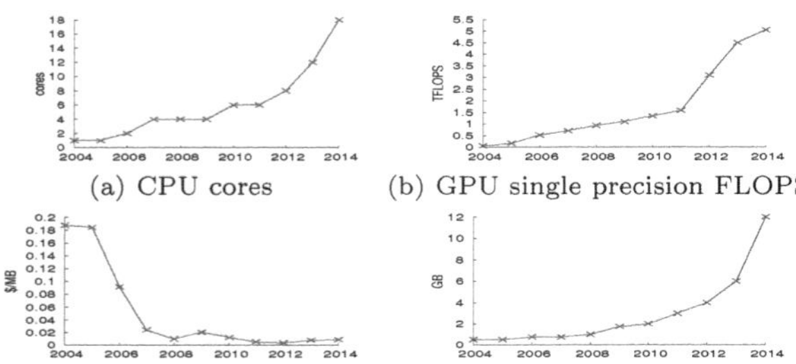

(a) CPU cores (b) GPU single precision FLOPS

(c) CPU memory price (d) GPU memory size

Figure 1: **Trends of computing performance over time.**[1]

Fig. 1 illustrates the growth in computing capability over recent years. We believe that such growths in modern hardware will increasingly make semi-lazy learning feasible: cheap and fast storage can support high speed similarity search (e.g. kNN) and powerful computing devices can support efficient online model construction (e.g. GP). The work in this paper is part of our "*Genie and Lamp*" project [1] which aims to provide a systematic investigation into the use of semi-lazy learning for predictive analytics.

Two main technical obstacles must be overcome to make the semi-lazy time series prediction scalable in practice. First, to build the query-dependent GP model, substantial model-building effort at kNN query time could lead to unacceptable latency. As will be explained in Section 4, we define a "*(Continuous) Suffix kNN Search*" problem which tries to identify small fractions of data for each prediction request. A property of the Suffix kNN Search is that each prediction request invokes a set of kNN queries sharing common suffix. To make such kNN search feasible in real-time applications, we develop an efficient search method using the popular Dynamic Time Warping (DTW) distance on the Graphic Processing Unit (GPU). Specifically, we design a novel two-level inverted-like index on the GPU and propose a new enhanced DTW lower bound to accelerate the search process.

[1]References of data source are presented in Appendix A.

Second, several parameters have to be configured. The underlying generating process of time series data may be diverse and continuously changing. As a result, we have to set different parameters for different sensors and even for the same sensor at different times. It is infeasible to manually set parameters for each sensor in a sensor network. To overcome this, we propose an adaptive auto-tuning mechanism to dynamically adjust the parameters for each sensor during continuous prediction without requiring user intervention.

Our method has several appealing advantages:

- It can make time series prediction of sensors in real time without a training phase in contrast to non-linear machine learning models like GPs and SVMs.
- It can yield superior prediction accuracy over several eager learning competitors. Since historical time series data is kept until prediction time in semi-lazy learning approach, a very rich set of models is preserved as part of the data. The query-dependent GP model caters to specifically making prediction for a submitted query without the need to build a generalized model that caters to the whole dataset.
- It can effectively estimate the analytical predictive uncertainty. Compared to traditional kNN regression, our method not only has higher prediction accuracy, but also can provide a closed-formed analytical expression to measure the prediction confidence.

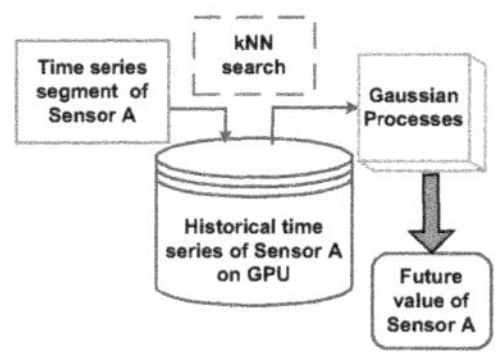

Figure 2: **An illustration for the semi-lazy (query-dependent) GP to time series prediction.**

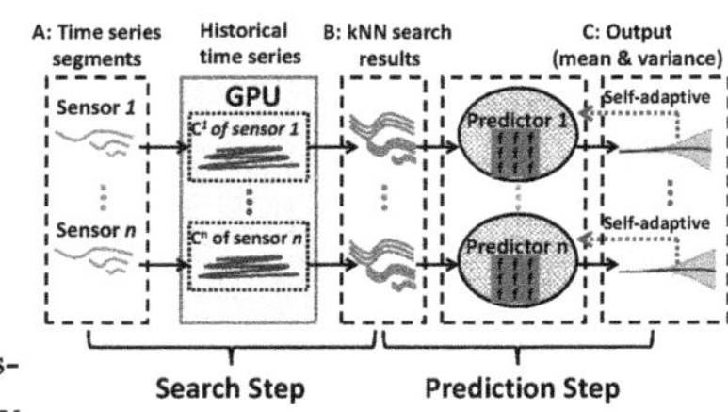

Figure 3: **Overview framework of SMiLer.**

To make our method feasible, we present **SMiLer**, *a SeMi-Lazy time series prediction system for sensors*. Fig. 3 shows an overall framework of SMiLer comprising of two main steps which overcome two mentioned obstacles respectively. More details about it will be clarified in Section 3.4. In summary, our key contributions are listed as follows.

- We propose a new method to enable the Gaussian Process model for time series prediction of sensors. It brings up a new insight for time series prediction from the semi-lazy learning perspective.
- We contrive a novel two-level inverted-like index on the GPU with an enhanced lower bound of the DTW, which can accelerate the proposed Suffix kNN Search problem to quickly identify small fractions of data for building query-dependent GP models.
- We devise an adaptive auto-tuning mechanism which can automatically learn and adjust the parameters of models over time for each sensor.
- We conduct extensive experiment study on several real-life datasets. SMiLer accelerates the efficiency of kNN search by one order of magnitude over its competitors. The prediction accuracy of SMiLer is better than several state-of-the-art competitors (up to 10 competitors

including GPs, SVMs, kNN and linear models with S-GD) with better estimation of predictive uncertainty.

The rest of this paper is organized as follows. Next, we discuss the related work in Section 2, followed by an overview of the framework of SMiLer in Section 3. Then we address the search problem in Section 4 and the model construction problem in Section 5. Finally, we evaluate our system in Section 6, and conclude the paper in Section 7.

2. RELATED WORK

In thi section, first, we review existing methods for time series prediction. Next, we give a discussion about GPs. Then, we investigate literatures about the semi-lazy approach. Finally, we briefly talk about kNN search under DTW distance.

2.1 Time series prediction methods

Existing time series prediction methods can be separated into two categories, i.e. statistical regression methods and machine learning methods. Statistical regression methods focus on finding parameterized functions, including linear models (e.g. ARIMA [15] and robust regression [59]) and nonlinear models (e.g. exponential smoothing [71, 38] and ((G)ARCH) models [31, 13]), which can predict the behavior of time series. Their major drawback is that they usually impose rigid assumptions on the time series data which may not be true in real-life applications.

Machine learning methods can be further grouped into two classes: the eager learning approach and the lazy learning approach. The eager learning approach usually has a pre-processing stage to train models for prediction such as Artificial Neural Networks (ANNs) [2, 68], Support Vector Machines (SVMs) [58, 46] and Gaussian Processes (GPs) [34, 50, 17, 72]. The common problem is that they usually require high computational cost. Although some approximate methods have been proposed, they are more influenced by the global distribution of the whole dataset, resulting in high potential of overfitting or underfitting [61]. Whereas, though some linear models with Stochastic Gradient Descent (SGD) can be efficiently trained, their prediction performance is not as good as the non-linear models in some applications.

The lazy learning approach typically is done by finding a set of k similar time series of the sensor and doing some simple computation (e.g. average) over these query results [44, 18, 11, 8]. These methods however cannot estimate the analytical predictive uncertainty directly. Bootstrap can partially remedy this drawback but requires high time cost. Furthermore, bootstrap cannot work well in high dimensional space when the time series segment is long. Besides, the accuracy of the semi-lazy learning approach still needs to be further improved.

2.2 GP for time series prediction

The Gaussian Process (GP) has received extensive attention for time series prediction [70, 34, 50, 16, 20, 35, 72, 23, 40]. GP has powerful and flexible model capability since it can be derived from both perspectives of neural networks and Bayesian nonparametric regression [49, 47]. The evaluation study in [55] further demonstrates that the GP can consistently outperform (or at least be comparable to) other modeling approaches like neural networks or local learning methods. In contrast to SVMs, GPs can innately predict analytical model uncertainty.

Unfortunately, the GP has a poor scalability (scaling as $O(n^3)$). Low-rank approximation is a popular method to improve its scalability [25, 56, 65, 43], but can only capture the global patterns of the data rather than the local behavior and patterns. There are also a few of papers about the localized models [33, 51, 48], which try to divide the data into different parts and build GP model for each part. Nevertheless, how to partition the data becomes a serious problem in high dimensional space. For this reason, the applications of this method are suitable for low dimensional spatial data analysis [33, 51, 48], but not for time series prediction.

We propose a new method to improve the scalability of GPs. The general idea is to build local GPs on the kNNs of prediction requests. This method can preserve the strength but not the weakness of the eager learning and the lazy learning approach. Using many local models to form an implicit global approximation, it can commit to a much richer hypothesis [73] but avoid an intractable training phase.

2.3 Semi-lazy prediction

To our best knowledge, SMiLer is the first work to exploit the semi-lazy learning approach to time series prediction. It is still desirable to discuss existing works about semi-lazy learning approach. There are indeed some works [74, 12] employing SVMs on kNN results for image classification. These methods are customized for image features (like tangle distance), and cannot be directly extended to support time series prediction. The authors in [67] propose a kNN based Kalman Filter GP regression. However, it still needs an offline processing to learn the hyperparameters, which makes it essentially still be an eager learning method.

Compared with the semi-lazy trajectory prediction[77, 76], SMiLer is a general framework for time series prediction, while the method in [77] is only applicable to object path prediction because its methodology is specially catered to the scenario where there are many moving objects in a dynamic environment. Furthermore, the method in [77] requires several parameters which have to be tuned manually; on the contrary SMiLer can minimize the user assistance by devising an adaptive auto-tuning mechanism. Additionally, except the semi-lazy GP idea, we also devote an extensive study to kNN search under the DTW distance leveraging the GPU and devise an adaptive mechanism for auto-tuning parameters, both of which are not touched by previous semi-lazy learning methods.

2.4 kNN search on Dynamic Time Warping

There have been many efforts to speed up kNN search under the DTW [41, 78, 30, 6, 54]. Various indexing methods in memory [6] and disk [37, 5, 36] are also studied in recent years. In [60], the authors compared the performance of GPUs and FPGAs with scanning method for DTW computation. We refer interested readers to [30]. As far as we know, our paper is the first study to design index on the G-PU to accelerate kNN search. We also propose an enhanced lower bound of the DTW suitable for GPU computation.

3. OVERVIEW

In this section, we give a formal description of our semi-lazy method for time series prediction, and discuss the challenges of our method. Table 1 lists the basic notations used throughout this paper.

Table 1: Table of Basic Notations.

C^i	time series of sensor i	c_t^i	value of C^i at t
$x_{j,d}^i$	d-length segment of C^i	$X_{k,d}^i$	data set $\{x_{j,d}^i\}_{j=1}^k$
$y_{j,h}^i$	h-step ahead value of $x_{j,d}^i$	Y_h^i	a vector of $y_{j,h}^i$
EKV	Ensemble kNN Vector	k	number of kNNs
ELV	Ensemble Length Vector	d	length of segment

3.1 Preliminaries

A time series C^i is a collection of observations made sequentially in time from a sensor i (or more generally, an unknown system), i.e., $C^i = \{c_0^i, c_1^i, .., c_j^i, ...\}$, where c_j^i is the value of C^i at timestamp j. We assume the sample rate of one sensor is always fixed[1], therefore, a time series is only a sequence of data points. $|C^i|$ denotes the length of C^i. A set of contiguous observations of C^i between two points c_t^i and c_{t+d}^i is called a *segment* and is denoted by $C_{t,d}^i$. We also call a segment with length d as a d-length segment.

At time t_0, the h-step ahead prediction is to predict the value of the sensor at time t_0+h. Taking a d-length segment $x_{0,d}^i = C_{t_0-d+1,d}^i = \{c_{t_0-d+1}^i, .., c_{t_0}^i\}$ as model input and denoting the h-step ahead value of $x_{0,d}^i$ by $y_{0,h}^i = c_{t_0+h}^i$, the h-step ahead prediction model is a mapping $f(\cdot)$ between $x_{0,d}^i$ and $y_{0,h}^i$, i.e. $y_{0,h}^i = f(x_{0,d}^i)$.

3.2 Semi-lazy time series prediction

In this section, we first present the general framework for semi-lazy time series prediction, and then introduce the adaptive auto-tuning mechanism.

3.2.1 Abstract semi-lazy time series predictor

Given a time series segment $x_{0,d}^i = \{c_{t_0-d+1}^i, .., c_{t_0}^i\}$ ending at time t_0, we can retrieve k nearest neighbor segments from time series C^i, i.e. $X_{k,d}^i = \{x_{j,d}^i\}_{j=1}^k = [x_{j,d}^i, ..., x_{k,d}^i]$ (where $x_{j,d}^i$ is a segment of C^i ending at time t_j, i.e. $x_{j,d}^i = \{c_{t_j-d+1}^i, .., c_{t_j}^i\}$). For each segment $x_{j,d}^i$, its h-step ahead value is $y_{j,h}^i = c_{t_j+h}^i$. We denote the h-step ahead values of every $x_{j,d}^i$ in $X_{k,d}^i$ by a vector $Y_h^i = [y_{1,h}^i, y_{2,h}^i, ..., y_{k,h}^i]^\top = [c_{t_1+h}^i, c_{t_2+h}^i, ..., c_{t_k+h}^i]^\top$. Now given $(X_{k,d}^i, Y_h^i)$, we formally define the semi-lazy time series predictor as below.

DEFINITION 3.1 (SEMI-LAZY TIME SERIES PREDICTOR). *Given a d-length time series segment $x_{0,d}^i = \{c_{t_0-d+1}^i, .., c_{t_0}^i\}$ of C^i ending at time t_0, the semi-lazy time series predictor is a model which can use the kNN data $(X_{k,d}^i, Y_h^i) = \{x_{j,d}^i, y_{j,h}^i\}_{j=1}^k$ and test input $x_{0,d}^i$ to obtain the posterior distribution of the h-step ahead observation $y_{0,h}^i$ (i.e. $c_{t_0+h}^i$):*

$$y_{0,h}^i = f(x_{0,d}^i, X_{k,d}^i, Y_h^i) \sim \mathcal{N}(u, \sigma^2) \quad (1)$$

where $f(\cdot)$ is an abstract predictor which can be instantiated with suitable probabilistic prediction model.

The semi-lazy time series predictor is built independently for each sensor, but multiple sensors can be processed in the same way. Hereafter, unless otherwise stated, we focus on the kNN search and prediction for one sensor.

The superscript "i" (e.g. $y_{0,h}^i$ and $x_{j,d}^i$) indicates that the variables are from sensor i. Hereafter, when we focus on one sensor, we omit the superscript i for convenience.

[1]This is not a real limitation since the user can easily re-interpolate data if the sample rate is changed.

3.2.2 Auto-tuning mechanism with ensemble method

We design an auto-tuning mechanism to eliminate the parameters of the semi-lazy prediction model as well as to improve the prediction accuracy. In Definition 3.1, for each predictor, there are two parameters: (1) k: the number of nearest neighbors and (2) d: the length of time series segment. For different sensors with different intrinsic properties, the semi-lazy predictors may desire different k and d. With the changing of the data generating process, the values of k and d also have to be adjusted.

We introduce an ensemble method to the semi-lazy model, which forms a matrix of abstract predictors $f_{i,j}$ for a sensor with different k and d. The final predictor is the mixture of all the $f_{i,j}$ predictors. Let us define an ensemble matrix λ:

$$\lambda = \begin{bmatrix} (k_0, d_0) & ... & (k_0, d_{n-1}) \\ ... & (k_i, d_j) & ... \\ (k_{m-1}, d_0) & ... & (k_{m-1}, d_{n-1}) \end{bmatrix} \quad (2)$$

where k_i is the number of nearest neighbors and d_j is the length of time series segment for predictor $f_{i,j}$. We group different k_i in the "*Ensemble kNN Vector*" denoted by $EKV = [k_0, ..., k_{m-1}]$, and group different d_j in the "*Ensemble Length Vector*" denoted by $ELV = [d_0, ..., d_{n-1}]$. In the ensemble matrix λ, each element $\lambda_{i,j}$ also indicates the weight of $f_{i,j}$ contributed to the final predictor. Hence, the ensemble prediction model for one sensor is formally defined as:

$$f_{em} = \frac{1}{\mathcal{C}_\lambda} \sum_{i=0}^{m-1} \sum_{j=0}^{n-1} \lambda_{i,j} f_{i,j} \quad (3)$$

where $\mathcal{C}_\lambda$ is the normalization constant by summing the weight of every element in λ, i.e. $\mathcal{C}_\lambda = \sum_{i=0}^{m-1} \sum_{j=0}^{n-1} \lambda_{i,j}$. Later we further propose an intelligent self-adaptive method to adjust λ during continuous prediction (see Section 5.1).

3.3 Challenges of semi-lazy prediction

Now we can summarize the challenges for semi-lazy time series prediction. First, we need to quickly identify the kNNs for each semi-lazy predictor. To overcome the unacceptable latency for kNN search, we resort to the help of the GPU to accelerate the search process in Section 4.

Specifically, we formalize the "*(Continuous) Suffix kNN Search*" problem in Section 4. With the ensemble method, we need to invoke a set of kNN queries for one sensor per prediction (see Eqn. (2)). We can see that, if $d_i < d_j$, x_{0,d_i} is just a suffix of x_{0,d_j} since both of them end at time t_0. Moreover, we usually need to continuously predict the future value of sensors. During the continuous prediction, some computation can also be reused. Based on the suffix property and the continuous prediction, we further propose a two-level inverted-like index on the GPU in Section 4.

Second, a proper model selection for the abstract predictor $f(\cdot)$ and an auto-tuning mechanism are required. We propose to use GPs as predictors and give a complete solution for the semi-lazy time series prediction in Section 5.2. We also fully depict the adaptive auto-tuning mechanism for dynamic adjusting the ensemble matrix λ in Section 5.1.

3.4 Framework of SMiLer

SMiLer is designed to make the semi-lazy time series prediction model feasible. Fig. 3 shows an overview framework of SMiLer to satisfy the above objectives.

In the first step, called Search Step, with the input of the last few time steps (Rectangle A in Fig. 3) of target sensors, we invoke the Continuous Suffix kNN Search with multiple k and d. The queries of one sensor are parallel processed on the data of itself by the the GPU. (see Section 4)

Next, in the Prediction Step, the kNN results (Rectangle B in Fig. 3) are input into the semi-lazy GP models to predict future value (with mean and variance) of each sensor (Rectangle C in Fig. 3). The adaptive auto-tuning mechanism is utilized to improve the prediction performance as well as to minimize users' assistance. (see Section 5)

4. DTW KNN SEARCH WITH THE GPU

We use DTW distance to find kNN segments on the GPU. There have been several similarity measures for time series, such as Euclidean distance [32], DTW [10], LCSS [66], ERP [21], EDR [22] and SpADe [24]. Euclidean distance is simple but sensitive to noise (e.g. shifting and scaling) problem which usually appears in time series. Among these measures, DTW is a simple but effective one which is robust to noise (e.g. shifting and scaling). Other distance measures can also handle time series similarity search, but they usually need a sophisticated index structure, which cannot be easily implemented on the GPU. Besides, there are some evidences showing that DTW is the best measures for time series data mining problems [30, 60, 54].

4.1 Problem formulation

The SMiLer Index is designed to identify a set of kNNs for the ensemble prediction model (refer to Section 3.2.2). The kNN search with different k in $EKV = [k_0, k_2, ..., k_{m-1}]$ (see Eqn. (2)) can be solved by invoking the NN search with maximum value k_n, and then selecting subsets of the result according to DTW distance order.

However, it is not trivial for kNN search with different query lengths but sharing common suffix. Suppose at time t_0 the set of the queries is $\{x_{0,d_0}, ..., x_{0,d_{n-1}}\}$ where $x_{0,d_i} = \{c_{t_0-d_i+1}, ..., c_{t_0}\}$. We can see that, if $d_i < d_j$, x_{0,d_i} is a suffix of x_{0,d_j} since both of them end at time t_0. An example of x_{0,d_0} and x_{0,d_1} is shown in Fig. 5. It is desirable to reduce the computation cost based on the suffix property.

Another opportunity arises from the continuous kNN search. Since the query input is gradually changing over time, we should also consider this property to improve efficiency.

Let us define some simplified notations. For a target sensor, "*Master Query*" denotes the longest query segment $MQ = x_{d_{n-1}} = \{q_0, ..., q_{d_{n-1}}\} = \{c_{t_0-d_{n-1}+1}, ..., c_{t_0}\}$. Since every x_{d_i} is a suffix of $x_{0,d_{n-1}}$, we also denote each query segment as "*Item Query*" $IQ_i = x_{0,d_i} = \{q_{d_n-d_i}, ..., q_{d_{n-1}}\} = \{c_{t_0-d_i+1}, ..., c_{t_0}\}$. Fig. 5(b) shows an example of MQ and its item queries IQ_0 and IQ_1. The "*Continuous Suffix kNN Search*" problem can be formally defined as:

DEFINITION 4.1 ((CONTINUOUS) SUFFIX kNN SEARCH). *Given a master query MQ of a sensor with $ELV = [d_0, ..., d_{n-1}]$, we can generate a set of item queries $\{IQ_0, ..., IQ_{n-1}\}$ where $|IQ_i| = d_i$ and IQ_i is a suffix of IQ_j if $d_i < d_j$. The Suffix kNN Search is to find kNN segments C_{t,d_i} for each item query IQ_i under DTW distance on time series C of the sensor. From time t to time $t+1$, we may continuously do Suffix kNN search with appending the latest observed point into MQ and delete the oldest point from MQ.*

In the following sections, we will exploit the SMiLer Index for the Continuous Suffix kNN Search on the GPU. Readers may refer to Appendix B.1 for a brief review about DTW. Recall that in this paper we only consider the DTW under Sakoe-Chiba band constraint with warping width ρ. We also provide a short introduction of the GPU in Appendix B.2.

4.2 Enhanced lower bound for DTW

We propose an enhanced lower bound for DTW, denoted by LB_{en}, which is derived from the existing lower bound LB_keogh [41] (refer to Appendix B.1).

Depending on which envelope is used, for convenience, we simply denote $LB_{EQ}(Q, C) = LB\_keogh(E(Q), C)$ and $LB_{EC}(Q, C) = LB\_keogh(E(C), Q)$. Examples of envelope, $LB_{EQ}(Q, C)$ and $LB_{EC}(Q, C)$ are shown in Fig. 5 (a)(b).

Based on LB_keogh, we propose an enhanced lower bound of DTW, denoted by LB_{en}, which are defined as:

$$LB_{en}(Q, C) = \max\{LB_{EQ}(Q, C), LB_{EC}(Q, C)\}$$

THEOREM 4.1. *$LB_{en}(Q, C)$ is a lower bound of $DTW(Q, C)$.*

PROOF. Since $LB_{EC}(Q, C) \leq DTW(Q, C)$ and $LB_{EQ}(Q, C) \leq DTW(Q, C)$, we have $LB_{en}(Q, C) \leq DTW(Q, C)$. □

4.3 SMiLer Index: a two-level inverted-like index

In this section, we present the SMiLer Index on the GPU memory as well as how to use this index to support the Continuous Suffix kNN search. The novel point of the SMiLer Index is that we can reuse the intermediate results to accelerate the computation of the DTW lower bound.

As shown in Fig. 4, indeed the SMiLer Index is a two-level inverted-like index which contains a "*window level index*" and a "*group level index*". This inverted index-like structure can enjoy the parallel capability of the GPU by using one block to process one posting list.

4.3.1 *Window level index of the SMiLer Index*

Following the DualMatch framework [45, 36], we divide the time series C into disjoint windows DW and divide the master query MQ into sliding windows SW where $\omega = |DW| = |SW|$. Examples of DW and SW are illustrated in Fig. 5(a)(b). Note that we divide sliding windows in time-reserved order (from right to left in Fig. 5(b)).

In the *window level index*, a keyword (index term) is a sliding window (of the master query) whose posting list stores lower bounds between the sliding window and disjoint windows of time series C. The window level inverted index can be constructed efficiently by the GPU. We use one block to treat one sliding window to parallel compute lower bounds (LB_{EQ} and LB_{EC}) between all SWs and DWs. Illustration of the window level index is shown in Fig. 4 and Fig. 5(c).

Remark 1: reuse based on the continuous query.

During continuous prediction, we can reuse the computed result on the window level index to avoid building the SMiLer Index from scratch. Suppose that at time $t_0 - 1$ there is a master query MQ'. Then at time t_0, the new master query MQ is constructed by adding one point to the head of MQ' and removing the last point of MQ'. Consequently, we only need to add a new sliding window to MQ and remove the last sliding window of MQ'.

Fig. 6 illustrates how to update the window level index during the continuous prediction. For a new master query at time t_0, we first clear the posting list of the last sliding window SW_n, and then place the posting list of the new sliding window SW' in the memory space of SW_n (see Fig.

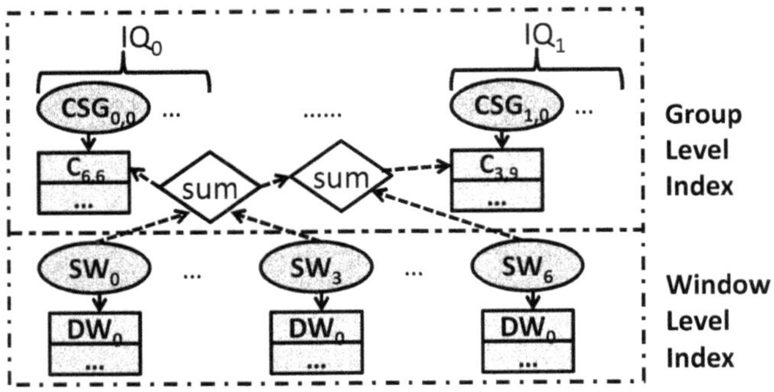

Figure 4: SMiLer Index: a two-level inverted-like index.

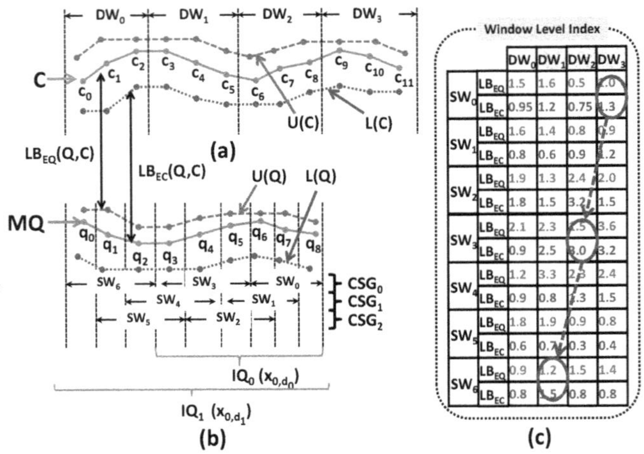

Figure 5: An illustration for SMiLer Index.

6(b)). The starting cursor (the red vertical arrow) of the window level index moves from SW_0 to SW'. Then at time $t_0 + 1$ (see Fig. 6 (c)), the new sliding window SW'' replaces the memory space of SW_{n-1} and the starting cursor moves to SW''. In addition, after adding a new point, the envelopes of previous ρ (i.e. warping width) sliding windows are changed. As a result, we need to re-calculate LB_{EQ} in the posting lists for these affected sliding windows. For example, if $\rho = 1$, LB_{EQ} of SW_0 is re-calculated in Fig. 6 (b), and LB_{EQ} of SW' is re-calculated in Fig. 6(c).

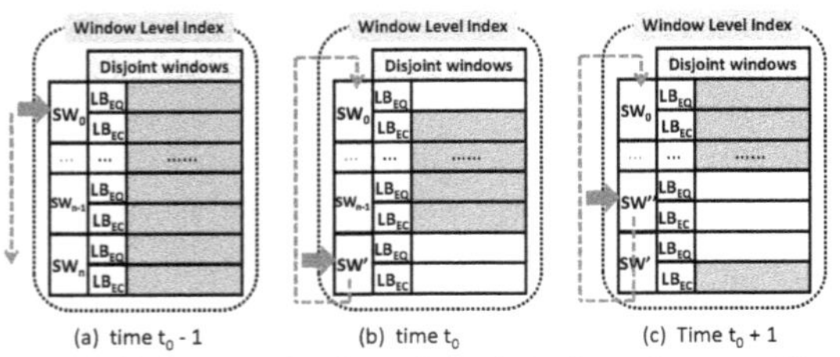

Figure 6: Reuse window level index for continuous prediction.

4.3.2 Group level index of the SMiLer Index

In the *group level index*, a keyword is a *Catenated Sliding Window Group (CSG)* (will be explained later) of item query IQ_i. The posting list of the CSG of IQ_i stores the lower bounds between IQ_i and a set of segments of C. The general idea for constructing group level index is that partial sum of posting lists in window level index are just the lower bounds between item queries and candidate segments. We first define the keyword in the group level index, i.e. the Catenated Sliding Window Group (CSG) which is inspired by the concept of "equivalence class" in [36].

DEFINITION 4.2 (CATENATED SLIDING WINDOW GROUP). *A Catenated Sliding Window Group (CSG) of query Q contains maximum number of sliding windows without overlap.*

$CSG_{i,b}$ denotes a CSG of item query IQ_i, where subscript i is identifier of IQ_i and subscript b is identifier of the first sliding window (from right to left) SW_b in the $CSG_{i,b}$. For a master query MQ without subscript, we denote it as CSG_b. Note that $CSG_{i,b}$ is always the prefix of CSG_b.

EXAMPLE 4.1. *In Fig. 5(b), master query MQ has three CSGs which are $CSG_0 = \{SW_0, SW_3, SW_6\}$, $CSG_1 = \{SW_1, SW_4\}$ and $CSG_2 = \{SW_2, SW_5\}$. The CSGs of IQ_0 are $CSG_{0,0} = \{SW_0, SW_3\}$, $CSG_{0,1} = \{SW_1\}$ and $CSG_{0,2} = \{SW_2\}$. $CSG_{0,b}$ of IQ_0 is always a prefix of CSG_b of MQ.*

Theorems of the CSG for index construction.

We introduce two important theorems for constructing the group level index. Before that, we first clarify the meaning of the alignment between a CSG and disjoint windows.

LEMMA 4.1. *Suppose that item query IQ_i has a $CSG_{i,b}$ whose sliding windows are aligned with a set of contiguous disjoint windows (from right to left) i.e. $\{DW_r, DW_{r-1}, ...\}$. Then this alignment indicates an alignment between IQ_i and a segment C_{t,d_i} where the value of subscript t of C_{t,d_i} is:*

$$t = (r - |CSG_{i,b}| + 1) * \omega - (d_i - b)\%\omega \tag{4}$$

where $|CSG_{i,b}|$ is the number of windows in $CSG_{i,b}$.

PROOF. See Appendix C.1. □

THEOREM 4.2. *For each pair of IQ_i and C_{t,d_i}, there is one and only one alignment between $CSG_{i,b}$ and corresponding disjoint windows.*

PROOF. See Appendix C.2. □

Then we can deduce the window enhanced lower bound LB_w, between IQ_i and C_{t,d_i} from the window level index.

THEOREM 4.3. *Given a $CSG_{i,b} = \{SW_b, SW_{b+w}, ...\}$ of IQ_i and a disjoint window DW_r, we can define the window enhanced lower bound LB_w between IQ_i and C_{t,d_i} as:*

$$LB_w(IQ_i, C_{t,d_i}) = \max \left\{ \begin{array}{l} \sum_{j=0}^{m-1} LB_{EQ}(SW_{b+j*\omega}, DW_{r-j}) \\ \sum_{j=0}^{m-1} LB_{EC}(SW_{b+j*\omega}, DW_{r-j}) \end{array} \right. \tag{5}$$

where $m = |CSG_{i,b}|$ and $t = (r - m + 1) * \omega - (d_i - b)\%\omega$. The following inequality always holds:

$$LB_w(IQ_i, C_{t,d_i}) \leq DTW(IQ_i, C_{t,d_i})$$

PROOF. See Appendix C.3. □

Group level index construction.

The construction of the group level index is based on the property of the Suffix kNN search and Theorem 4.3. Since IQ_i is always a suffix of IQ_j if $d_i < d_j$ for the Suffix kNN search, from Eqn. (5) we can see that the intermediate results of $LB_w(IQ_j, C_{t,d_i})$ just contain the lower bound between IQ_i and a candidate segment. We use this intuition to design the algorithm for building group level index.

For each item query IQ, we spin off a set of CSGs as the keywords to construct the group level index, where the posting lists of CSGs store the enhanced lower bounds between IQ and a set of time segments. Specifically, Theorem 4.2

tells us that we can get the lower bounds between IQ and every candidate time series segments in this way.

Eqn. (5) indicates that, by shift summing the posting lists of sliding windows within the same CSG of MQ, we can sequentially get all the lower bounds of IQ_i ($0 \le i \le n-1$) of MQ (see Example 4.2). In other words, based on the suffix property, by sequentially summing the posting lists of sliding windows within the same CSG of a master query, we can obtain the posting lists of the CSG for each item query.

This computation can also be efficiently parallel processed by the GPU. The idea is to use one block of the GPU to process one CSG and use each thread of the block to handle several disjoint windows (elements in posting lists). In Algorithm 1 (Appendix D), we show the pseudo code to compute the posting lists of CSGs on the GPU.

EXAMPLE 4.2. *We use a block of the GPU to scan posting lists sequentially in order of* $SW_0 \to SW_3 \to SW_6$ *(see Fig. 4). In the block, there is a thread (blue dashed arrow) visiting the elements of the posting lists in order of:* $(SW_0, DW_3) \to (SW_3, DW_2) \to (SW_6, DW_1)$ *(see Fig. 5(c)). To sum the first two elements, we get lower bound between* IQ_0 *and* $C_{6,6}$, $LB_{EC}(IQ_0, C_{6,6}) = LB_{EC}(SW_0, DW_3) + LB_{EC}(SW_3, DW_2)$ *(refer to Eqn. 5). With summing the third element, we have* $LB_{EC}(IQ_1, C_{3,9}) = LB_{EC}(IQ_0, C_{6,6}) + LB_{EC}(SW_6, DW_1)$, *which is an element of posting list of* $CSG_{1,0}$ *(see Fig. 4).*

Remark 2: reuse based on the Suffix kNN Search.

The reuse of the computed result on the group level index can be seen from two points. First, for a set of item queries sharing suffix, by sequentially summing the posting lists of sliding windows in suffix order, we can compute the lower bounds between all item queries and time series segments in one-pass scan (see Example 4.2), which can avoid scanning the GPU memory multiple times. Second, the elements in the posting lists of window level index are computed once but are reused multiple times for computing the lower bound of every item query.

4.3.3 kNNs: filtering, verification and selection

After building the SMiLer Index, we follow the filtering-verification framework to retrieve the kNN results. By scanning the posting lists of CSGs in the group level index, we can get the DTW lower bound between item query IQ_i and all candidates segments. We filter the segments whose lower bounds are larger than a threshold τ_i (*Filtering*), and then compute the real DTW distance between IQ_i and unfiltered segments C_{t,d_i} (*Verification*). Finally, we select the kNNs of each IQ_i from all unfiltered candidates (*Selection*).

Filtering. The method is to discard candidates whose lower bounds are larger than threshold τ_i during scanning the post lists in group level index. There are two methods to determine threshold τ_i for IQ_i. The first one is to select the segment with the k-th smallest lower bound, and then set τ_i as the DTW distance between the segment and IQ_i. The second method is to reuse the kNN results during continuous prediction. Suppose that at time $t_0 - 1$ there is a query item IQ'_i. Since the difference between IQ_i and IQ'_i should be slight, we can take the distance between the k-th NN segment of IQ'_i and IQ_i as threshold τ_i. In SMiLer, we use the first method to determine the τ_i in initial queries, and then use the second one for the following continuous queries.

Verification. In Algorithm 2 (Appendix E), we show the pseudo code to compute the DTW distance (with Sakoe-Chiba band) between item queries and un-filtered candidates. The novelty of Algorithm 2 lies in the use of a compressed warping matrix. The shared memory, which is much faster than the global memory, is quite small (up to 64KB). To store the warping matrix in the shared memory, we design a compressed warping matrix with size of $2\times(2*\rho+2)$ where ρ is the warping width. The essential idea is to temporarily store the matrix elements along the warp path, while the modulus operation (%) is employed to reuse the memory space. Please refer to Appendix E for more details.

Selection. We use a GPU k-selection algorithm to select kNNs with the smallest DTW distance from all unfiltered candidates. The main technique is distributive partitioning for k-selection on the GPU [3]. We adopt the existing work for GPU k selection [3] but with two incremental improvements: (1) we use one block to handle one k-selection for one query to support multiple k-selections; (2) we return all k smallest segments instead of only the k-th one.

4.4 Utility of the GPU

We summarize the utility of the GPU in the SMiLer Index from several perspectives. First of all, the SMiLer Index is essentially a two-level inverted-like index which can be parallel processed in as fine-grained manner as possible to fully utilize the GPU parallel computation capability. For example, we use one block to treat one sliding window to construct window level index; and we use one block to treat one CSG to construct group level index.

Second, based on properties of the *Continuous Suffix kNN Search*, the SMiLer Index can reuse intermediate results to improve efficiency (see Section 4.3.1, Remark 1: reuse based on the continuous query and Remark 2:reuse based on the Suffix kNN Search).

Third, the proposed enhanced lower bounds (LB_{en}) are innately applicable to GPU computation, which is not adopted by existing CPU based method like [45, 41, 36, 54]. Owing to the powerful parallel processing ability, we can obtain a tighter lower bound by computing both LB_{EC} and LB_{EQ} without increasing the response time.

Fourth, we try to ensure that processing in each thread block is as homogenous as possible. We use a two-phase scheme to filter and verify candidates instead of having them in one phase. The reason is that, due to the property of the SIMD architecture, the GPU hardware serializes different execution paths. If we mixed the filtering and verification, threads doing different processing need to wait for each other before continuing their processing which sacrifices efficiency.

Last, the SMiLer Index can easily scale up with multiple sensors, where we only need to create multiple SMiLer Indexes and invoke more blocks.

5. TIME SERIES PREDICTION VIA SEMI-LAZY LEARNING

Following by Section 3.2, we continue the discussion about our semi-lazy model. We first present the adaptive auto-tuning mechanism. Next, we introduce the instantiation of the *abstract predictor* with the Gaussian Process.

5.1 Adaptive auto-tuning mechanism with continuous prediction

The adaptive auto-tuning mechanism will dynamically adjust the ensemble matrix λ during continuous prediction

(Section 5.1.1). We also devise a sleep and recovery strategy (Section 5.1.2) to reduce the computational cost.

5.1.1 Auto-tuning with self-adaptive prediction

During the continuous prediction, we can self-adaptively learn to adjust the weight of each predictor in the ensemble matrix. The trick is that, after acquiring the true value of the sensor, we can evaluate each predictor by comparing the true value with the predicted one. Then we can increase the weight of predictors making good prediction.

Taking an abstract predictor $f_{i,j}$ as an example, we denote the true value of the sensor at time t as $y(t)$, and denote the predicted mean and variance as $u_{i,j}(t)$ and $\sigma^2_{i,j}(t)$. The likelihood function of $f_{i,j}$ after observing $y(t)$ is:

$$l_{i,j}(t) = l(y(t), u_{i,j}(t), \sigma^2_{i,j}(t)) \quad (6)$$

$$= \frac{1}{\sqrt{2\pi\sigma^2_{i,j}(t)}} exp(-\frac{(y(t) - u_{i,j}(t))^2}{2\sigma^2_{i,j}(t)}) \quad (7)$$

It is clear that the larger the likelihood $l_{i,j}(t)$ is, the better the predictor is. Then the weight of $f_{i,j}$ in the ensemble matrix at time t is adjusted as follows:

$$\bar{\lambda}_{i,j}(t) = \lambda_{i,j}(t-1) + \frac{l_{i,j}(t)}{\sum_i \sum_j l_{i,j}(t)} \quad (8)$$

After Eqn. (8), we need to further re-normalized $\bar{\lambda}_{i,j}(t)$ to get the final weight of the predictor $f_{i,j}$, i.e.:

$$\lambda_{i,j}(t) = \frac{\bar{\lambda}_{i,j}(t)}{\sum_i \sum_j \bar{\lambda}_{i,j}(t)} \quad (9)$$

In fact, combining Eqn. (8) and Eqn. (9), $\lambda_{i,j}(t)$ is an effectively exponential smoothing average of the posterior probability of the predictor $f_{i,j}$ over time.

5.1.2 Sleep and recovery

We further devise a strategy to control the sleep and recovery of every predictor. If $\lambda_{i,j}(t)$ is smaller than a threshold, we can temporarily make $f_{i,j}$ sleep to reduce the computational cost. The predictor would be recovered later.

The strategy is briefly presented here. In SMiLer, each predictor $f_{i,j}$ has a sleep counter $\varsigma_{i,j}$ specified how many steps it would sleep. If the weight $\lambda_{i,j}$ is smaller than threshold $\eta = \frac{1}{2*n*m}$ ($n*m$ is the number of elements of the ensemble matrix), we make predictor $f_{i,j}$ sleep, who will recover when the number of subsequent prediction steps exceeds $\varsigma_{i,j}$. If there are κ predictors recovered, the new weight of every recovered predictor is $\eta/(1-\kappa*\eta)$. After normalization, the weight of recovered predictors are equal to η.

Aiming to make the "weaker" predictor sleep longer, the sleep counter $\varsigma_{i,j}$ is also self-adaptive during the continuous prediction. $\varsigma_{i,j}$ is first initialized as 1, which means the predictor would only sleep for one step. If after recovery the predictor $f_{i,j}$ goes to sleep immediately in the next step, we will double the value of $\varsigma_{i,j}$. Otherwise, if the predictor successfully avoids the sleep trap, we would continuously halve the value of $\varsigma_{i,j}$ at very prediction step until $\varsigma_{i,j} = 1$.

5.2 Instantiation of the abstract predictor

5.2.1 A simple aggregation predictor

One simple predictor is a function to aggregate all the h-step ahead values of the kNN data. We define an Aggregation Regression (AR) function with pseudo-mean $\tilde{u}_0$ and pseudo-variance $\tilde{\sigma}^2_0$:

$$\hat{y}(t_0 + h) = f(x_{0,d}, X_{k,d}, Y_h) \quad (10)$$

$$= AR(x_{0,d}, X_{k,d}, Y_h) \sim \mathcal{N}(\tilde{u}_0, \tilde{\sigma}^2_0) \quad (11)$$

$$\tilde{u}_0 = \frac{\sum_{a=1}^k y_{a,h}}{k} \quad (12)$$

$$\tilde{\sigma}^2_0 = \frac{\sum_{a=1}^k (y_{a,h} - \tilde{u}_0)^2}{k} \quad (13)$$

AR predictor is simple and can be effectively computed, but its drawback is that the true value of $y(t_0 + h)$ may not follow the normal distribution defined by $\tilde{u}_0$ and $\tilde{\sigma}^2_0$.

5.2.2 Gaussian Process predictor

In this section, we introduce the Gaussian Process (GP) predictor, which has better prediction accuracy and good ability to estimate the predictive uncertainty. In Appendix B.3, we briefly recall some fundamentals of the GP.

For the GP predictor, given an input test segment $x_{0,d}$, the predictive distribution of $\hat{y}_{0,h}$ is obtained through conditioning on the kNN data $(X_{k,d}, Y_h)$ (recall Section 3.2.1). The predictive distribution is also a Gaussian distribution with mean u_0 and variance σ^2_0 as follows:

$$\hat{y}(t_0 + h) = f(x_{0,d}, X_{k,d}, Y_h) \quad (14)$$

$$= GP(x_{0,d}, X_{k,d}, Y_h) \sim \mathcal{N}(u_0, \sigma^2_0) \quad (15)$$

$$u_0 = c_0^\top C^{-1} Y_h \quad (16)$$

$$\sigma^2_0 = c(x_{0,d}, x_{0,d}) - c_0^\top C^{-1} c_0 \quad (17)$$

where C, c and c_0 are specified by the covariance function:

$$c(x_a, x_b) = \theta_0^2 exp\left(-\frac{1}{2}\frac{\|x_a - x_b\|^2}{\theta_1^2}\right) + \delta_{ab}\theta_2^2 \quad (18)$$

More details about Eqn. (16), Eqn. (17) and covariance function can be found in Appendix B.3. However, before making prediction, an important point is to determine the hyperparameters $\Theta = \{\theta_0, \theta_1, \theta_2\}$.

Online training for model optimization.

We use an online training method to determine the hyperparameters $\Theta = \{\theta_0, \theta_1, \theta_2\}$. For the eager learning approach, a heavy training process is employed to learn the optimal hyperparameters of GP in a pre-processing stage. In contrast, with the semi-lazy learning approach, we can afford the time to invoke an online training process to determine the hyperparameters because there are only a small number of training points (i.e. the kNN data $(X_{k,d}, Y_h)$). The advantage of this method is that the hyperparameters are specially trained for the test input $x_{0,d}$ (and its neighbors). In this way, we can avoid the underfitting or overfitting problems of the eager learning approach.

Now we explain how to train the GP predictor (to determine the hyperparameters) on the kNN dataset $(X_{k,d}, Y_h)$. For the GP, the predictive log probability when leaving out a training item $(x_{a,d}, y_a)$ is [56]:

$$logp(y_a|X_{k,d}, Y_{-a,h}, \Theta) = -\frac{1}{2}log\sigma^2_a - \frac{(y_a - u_a)^2}{2\sigma^2_a} - \frac{1}{2}log2\pi \quad (19)$$

where notation $Y_{-a,h}$ means all h-step ahead values in Y_h except y_a. The u_a and σ^2_a are computed according to Eqn. (16) and Eqn. (17) respectively. Thus, the leave-one-out

(LOO) log likelihood function on the whole kNN data is:

$$L(X_{k,d}, Y_h, \Theta) = \sum_{a=1}^{k} logp(y_a | X_{k,d}, Y_{-a,h}, \Theta) \quad (20)$$

The objective is to maximize the LOO log likelihood function (i.e. Eqn. (20)). To achieve this goal, we can compute its partial derivatives w.r.t. the hyperparameters and use the Conjugate Gradient (CG) optimization.

Since the expressions in Eqn. (16) and Eqn. (17) are almost identical for different points (only one column and one row removed in turn), the computation cost to optimize Eqn. (20) can be significantly reduced by the inversion of the partitioned matrix. An efficient approach to such training process can be found in [64].

Online training in continuous prediction.

In the continuous prediction, we can use an online optimization method to train the GP model. The intuition for the online training is that the hidden model generating the time series should change gradually. Consequently, the fixed steps pursuit training method is enough to find near-optimal value of the hyperparameters. Based on this point, in SMiLer, we only use the fixed five-step gradient descent to update the hyperparameters for the subsequential predictions. For a time series predictor GP, let $\theta_r(t)$ denote a hyperparameter at time t. We can use $\theta_r(t)$ as the inial seed value (instead of random seed values) to deduce the the parameter $\theta_r(t+1)$ by one step gradient descent. After the initial deducing, we further employ the CG optimization method (with fixed steps of descent) to obtain a near-optimal value of θ_r. By this method, the energy paid for the training process in previous steps is partially preserved.

6. EXPERIMENTS

6.1 Settings

Table 2: Default parameter for experiment.

Parameter	Description	value
ρ	warping width	8
ω	window length	16
ELV	Ensemble Length Vector	$\{32, 64, 96\}$
EKV	Ensemble kNN Vector	$\{8, 16, 32\}$

6.1.1 Environment and parameters

Experiments were conducted on a CPU-GPU platform. The GPU is a GeForce GTX TITAN with 6 GB memory. We implemented the GPU code using CUDA 6. The other program was implemented in C++ running on CentOS 6 with an Intel Core i7-3820 CPU server and 64 GB RAM.

Table 2 lists the default parameters in the experiment. For the DTW computation (SMiLer and its competitors), we set the warping width as $\rho = 8$. The window size ω is set as 16. Unless otherwise stated, in SMiLer we used a 3×3 ensemble matrix for prediction (see Section 3.2.2) where k and d are indicated in EKV and ELV respectively.

6.1.2 Datasets

We used three real-life time series datasets to evaluate our system. Two datasets are publicly available which can ensure the repeatability, and the remaining one is provided by our collaborators. We used z-normalization to normalize the time series of each sensor.

Table 3: Effect of the enhanced lower bound LB_{en}. The "time" (in seconds) is the total time for verifying un-filtered candidates of all sensors, and the "number" indicates the number of unfiltered candidates per query per sensor.

data	ROAD		MALL		NET	
	time	number	time	number	time	number
LB_{EQ}	2.30	12558	1.12	6632	0.11	753
LB_{EC}	1.55	9206	0.94	5707	0.11	725
LB_{en}	1.11	6739	0.63	3677	0.079	516

[**ROAD**] This dataset [27] consists of times series of 963 road traffic sensors of San Francisco bay area freeways in PEMS website [53]. Each sensor measured the occupancy rate of a road in the city for 15 months with 10-minute sample interval. In total, there are 61.0 million data points. The data set is available in the UCI Machine Learning Repository [7] and can be download freely [28].

[**MALL**] This dataset consists of time series of available car park lots in main shopping malls in Singapore. There are a total of 26 car parks with a record in every 10 minutes for 12 months. We duplicated every time series 40 times. In total, there are 1040 (26×40) sensor time series and 53.9 million data points (after duplication). The data is crawled from dataMall website [63] from Sept. 2013 to Sept. 2014.

[**NET**] This dataset is a time series of internet traffic data of a network backbone. It was collected for 3 months with 5-minute sample interval. We duplicated this time series 1024 times. In total, there are 1024 (1×1024) sensor time series and 20.4 million data points (after duplication). The data set can be download freely from DataMarket [29].

6.2 Search Step: Suffix kNN search on DTW

6.2.1 Competitors and experiment settings

We compared our DTW kNN search method of SMiLer, denoted as "*SMiLer-Idx*", with three kNN search competitors, namely FastGPUScan, GPUScan [60] and FastCPUScan. FastGPUScan first computes the DTW between the queries and all segments with the Sakeo-Chiba constraint, and then uses the GPU fast selection method to obtain the kNNs. GPUScan [60] is similar to FastGPUScan but without the Sakeo-Chiba constraint. FastCPUScan computes the DTW under the Sakeo-Chiba constraint with suitable pruning criteria studied in [41, 54]. For all datasets, we randomly selected a master query for each sensor to do the Suffix kNN search with 100 steps continuous query. The running time is the total time of all sensors per query step.

6.2.2 Evaluation with running time

Fig. 7 (y-axis is log-scaled) shows that SMiLer-Idx is one order of magnitude faster for the Suffix kNN Search compared with the best competitor FastGPUScan. SMiLer-Idx needs about 1 second to finish the search on all sensors, while FastGPUScan needs 10 seconds and FastCPUScan needs about 500 seconds. The time cost of SMiLer-Idx is quite stable with different numbers of nearest neighbors k.

Table 3 exhibits the utility of the lower bound LB_{en}. Both the number of unfiltered candidates and the time cost for verifying the candidates of LB_{en} are only about a half of the ones of LB_{EQ} and two-thirds of the ones of LB_{EC}.

Fig. 8 further demonstrates the effectiveness of the two-level inverted-like index of SMiLer. In Fig. 8, we use "*SMiLer-Dir*" to denote the method to compute the LB_{en} directly for

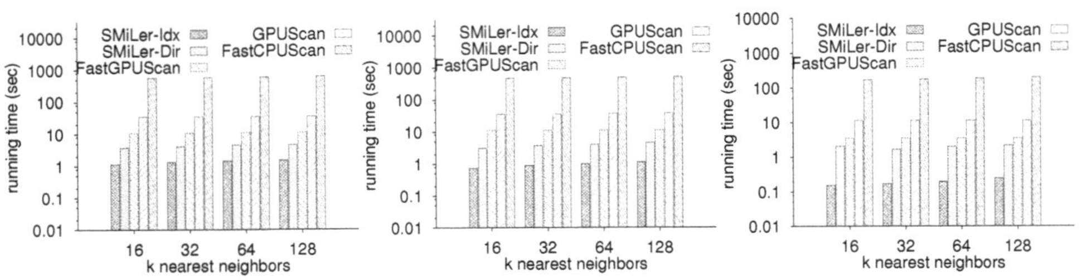

(a) ROAD (b) MALL (c) NET

Figure 7: Time cost (log-scaled) of the Suffix kNN Search on all sensors with varying k.

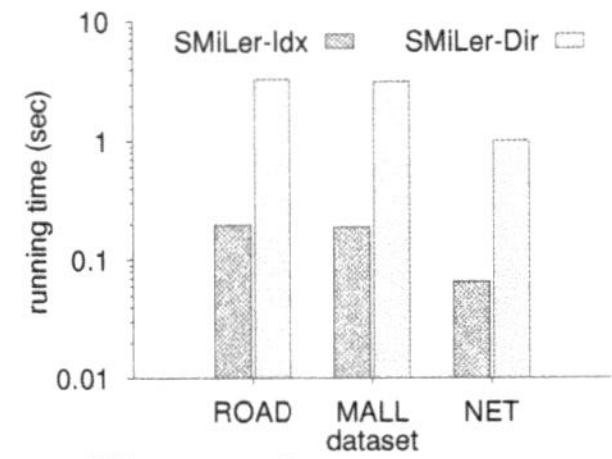

Figure 8: Time cost (log-scaled) for computing LB_{en} for all sensors.

each item query without building index at the window level (i.e. simply scanning the data to compute the lower bound). We can see that the SMiLer-Idx can significantly reduce the running time for computing LB_{en} by much more than one order of magnitude over SMiLer-Dir.

6.3 Prediction Step: effectiveness of SMiLer

6.3.1 *Competitors and experiment settings*

SMiLer-AR and **SMiLer-GP** denote our semi-lazy prediction models with different instantiated predictors. We category competitors into two groups: offline learning models and online learning models. The offline learning models, which are examples of eager learning, have a training phase; while the online learning models build the model on the fly with the incoming data. The offline learning models are:

- **PSGP**, i.e. Projected Sparse Gaussian Process, is an approximation to the Gaussian Process [56] by projecting all information onto a set of "active points" [25].We set the number of "active points" to 32, whose effect is also investigated in Section 6.4.2. We used an open-source project of PSGP [9].
- **VLGP**, i.e. Variational Learning Gaussian Process, is another state-of-the-art scalable Gaussian Process approximation model [65]. We set the number of inducing inputs as 32 whose effect is similar to the active points of PSGP. We use its implementation in [62].
- **NysSVR**, is a low-rank approximation of RBF kernel Support Vector Regression (SVR) model with Nyström method [69]. We set the reduced rank as 128.
- **SgdSVR**, is a linear SVR model with the Stochastic Gradient Descent (SGD) optimization method [75].
- **SgdRR**, is a robust regression [59] model with the SGD optimization method.

For NysSVR, SgdSVR and SgdRR, we used their implementation in Scikit-learn [52]. The grid search method by 10-fold cross validation is used to find their optimal parameters. We adopted the method in libSVM [19] to estimate the prediction confidence of SVR. The online learning models are:

- **LazyKNN**, is a lazy learning prediction method for time series prediction [4], where the predicted value is an average of the kNNs weighted by the inverse of DTW distance. We used the variance of the kNNs as the predicted variance.
- HoltWinters, which has two sub-methods: "**FullHW**" and "**SegHW**", is a popular statistical regression model for time series with periodical patterns [71, 38]. We used its implementation in "forecast" package of R [39]. We set the period as one day, and parameters were determined by minimizing the squared error. For "FullHW", we used all the available data to construct the model for each prediction, and for "SegHW", we used the last 10 days data to construct the model.
- **OnlineSVR** and **OnlineRR**, are similar with SgdSVR and SgdRR, but are trained in a one-pass online fashion [14]. We used the first one-third of the data to determine their parameters with grid search by 10-fold cross validation, and then used the following data to sequentially update the model with SGD.

Though some competitors are in R or Python, their core algorithms (except VLGP) are still implemented by C++ or Cython. Therefore, their running time is still comparable.

We evaluate the prediction performance by two measures: mean absolute error (MAE), which is an average of the absolute errors between the predicted value and the true value; and mean negative log predictive density (MNLPD), which is an average of negative log of the density of the true value under the predicted normal distribution. The MAE can evaluate the accuracy of the predicted result; while the MNLPD can assess the quality of the predictive uncertainty. For both measures, the smaller the value is, the better the method is.

For the ROAD dataset, we cut off a segment (i.e. leave-out testing) with 1000 points at the end of every time series. For MALL and NET datasets, since there is duplication, we randomly cut off a segment (leave-out testing) with 1000 points from every time series. Then we made 200-step continuous prediction along the segment. For PSGP, VLGP and NysSVR, we only tested on 50 randomly selected time series, since their training time costs for all sensors are too high to be acceptable (see Section 6.4.2 for more explanation).

Table 4: Running time comparison. The training time cost ("trn", in hours) is the total time for training the models for all sensors for one prediction step in the experiment. The prediction time ("prd", in milliseconds) is the average prediction time per sensor per query.

data	ROAD		MALL		NET	
	trn(h)	prd(ms)	trn(h)	prd(ms)	trn(h)	prd(ms)
SMiLer-GP	-	27.59	-	24.46	-	25.32
SMiLer-AR	-	1.48	-	0.95	-	0.25
FullHW	-	724.87	-	770.73	-	188.05
SegHW	-	58.52	-	64.23	-	83.32
LazyKNN	-	0.63	-	0.46	-	0.11
PSGP	1.8e3	0.037	1.6e3	0.031	126.3	0.024
VLGP	198.4	0.0068	274.3	0.011	57.5	0.0068
NysSVR	95.3	0.0085	86.2	0.0087	28.9	0.0088
SgdSVR	2.2	2.1e-4	2.3	2.2e-4	0.6	2.1e-4
SgdRR	13.5	2.7e-4	12.7	2.4e-4	4.0	2.5e-4
OnlineSVR	0.6	2.4e-4	0.5	2.2e-4	0.19	2.2e-4
OnlineRR	2.4	2.7e-4	2.3	2.5e-4	0.72	2.4e-4

6.3.2 *Evaluation with MAE and MNLPD*

Fig. 9 and Fig. 10 show the prediction performance of S-MiLer compared to offline learning and online learning mod-

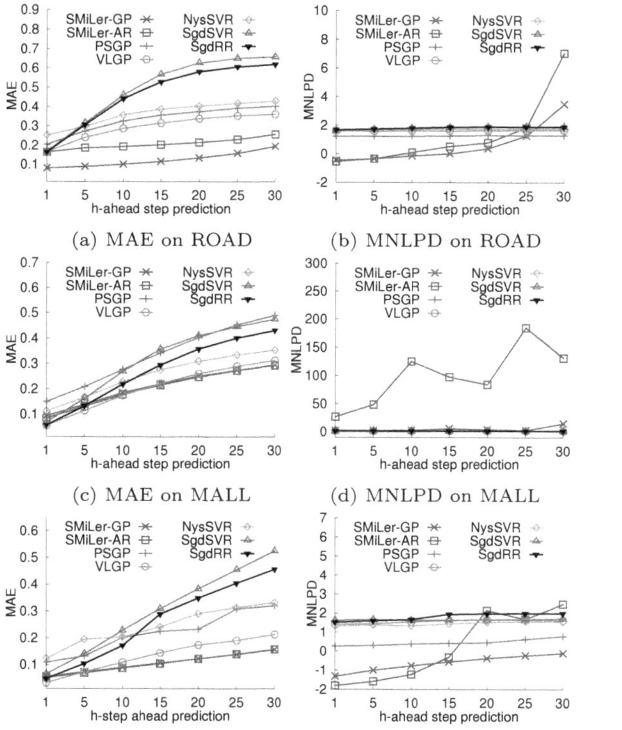

(a) MAE on ROAD (b) MNLPD on ROAD

(c) MAE on MALL (d) MNLPD on MALL

(e) MAE on NET (f) MNLPD on NET

Figure 9: MAE and MNLPD of offline learning models with varying h-step ahead prediction.

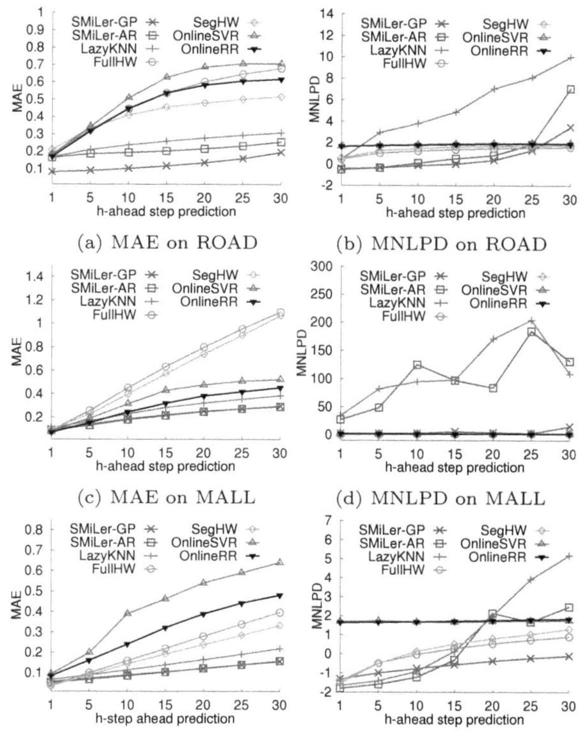

(a) MAE on ROAD (b) MNLPD on ROAD

(c) MAE on MALL (d) MNLPD on MALL

(e) MAE on NET (f) MNLPD on NET

Figure 10: MAE and MNLPD of online learning models with varying h-step ahead prediction.

els with varying look-ahead step h. From Fig. 9 (a)(c)(e) and Fig. 10 (a)(c)(e), we can see that SMiLer-GP always has a smaller MAE than all competitors. The reason is that, as a query-dependent GP model, SMiLer-GP caters to specifically making prediction for the submitted query without the need to cater for all parts of the data. Whereas the offline learning methods may result in over generalized global models, and the online learning methods may not have powerful enough modeling capability. An interesting point is that the MAE of SMiLer-AR is about 2 times larger than SMiLer-GP on the ROAD dataset (see Fig. 10(a)), while their MAE is almost identical on the MALL and NET datasets (see Fig. 10(c)(e)). It is because the ROAD dataset contains more dynamic traffic information while the MALL and NET datasets have some seasonal patterns. Therefore, SMiLer-GP, with strong GP predictors, has an innate advantage over SMiLer-AR on such complex data. Moreover, SMiLer-AP is worse than SMiLer-GP under MNLPD measure.

Fig. 9(b)(d)(f) and Fig. 10(b)(d)(f) demonstrate that SMiLer-GP is better than (or at least is comparable to) all competitors under MNLPD measure. In particular, SMiLer-GP is significantly better than SMiLer-AR and LazyKNN under the MNLPD measure. SMiLer-GP also has smaller MNLPD than the other competitors except after step 30.

6.3.3 *Effect of the adaptive auto-tuning mechanism*

Fig. 11 reveals the effect of the adaptive auto-tuning mechanism of SMiLer. SMiLerNE-GP and SMiLerNE-AR denote the experimental result of SMiLer without the ensemble method (i.e. only one predictor instead of a matrix of predictors). For SMiLerNE, we fixed the query segment length as $d = 64$ and the number of nearest neighbors as $k = 32$. SMiLerNW-GP and SMiLerNW-AR denote the SMiLer with the ensemble prediction but without the self-adaptive prediction. We can see that SMiLer-GP always has a better performance than SMiLerNW-GP and SMiLerNE-GP under both measures (MAE and MNLPD). But SMiLer-AR only holds similar conclusion on the MAE measure since it lacks ability to estimate predictive uncertainty.

6.4 Practicality of SMiLer

6.4.1 *Scalability of SMiLer*

Table 4 shows running time of SMiLer and its competitors. Except for FullHW and SegHW, SMiLer-GP requires a larger prediction time. However, we should note that SMiLer-GP does not have a training phase, but has the best prediction performance under both MAE and MNLPD. This shows a trade-off between the time and the accuracy.

Fig. 12 (a)(b) show the total time cost of SMiLer on all the sensors per prediction. The paybacks of the higher time cost of SMiLer-GP are more accurate prediction results (lower MAE) and better estimation of predictive uncertainty (lower MNLPD). If the predictive uncertainty is not a concern, the SMiLer-AR may still be a choice.

Note that, since the sample time interval is 5-10 minutes in the datasets, both SMiLer-AR and SMiLer-GP can perform prediction for all sensors in real time. Besides, the running time of SMiLer-GP can be further reduced by multithreading on multi-core architecture.

SMiLer scales well with the number of sensors in real-life applications. Fig. 12(c) shows the maximum number of sensors supported by one GPU. The space of SMiLer Index is $O(nM)$ where n is number of sensors and M is size of time series data per sensor. In our system, 6GB memory is large enough for all sensors (about 1000 sensors of ROAD data

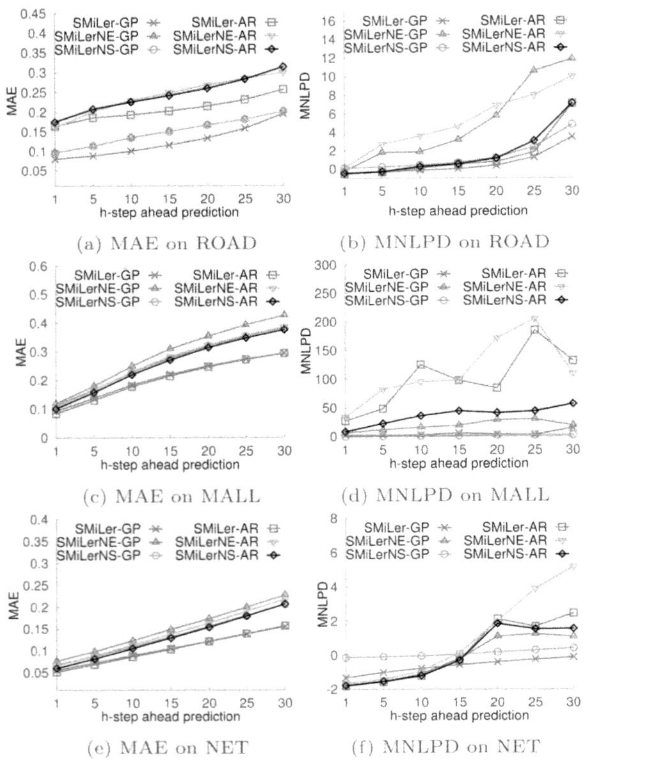

(a) MAE on ROAD (b) MNLPD on ROAD

(c) MAE on MALL (d) MNLPD on MALL

(e) MAE on NET (f) MNLPD on NET

Figure 11: Effect of the adaptive auto-tuning mechanism.

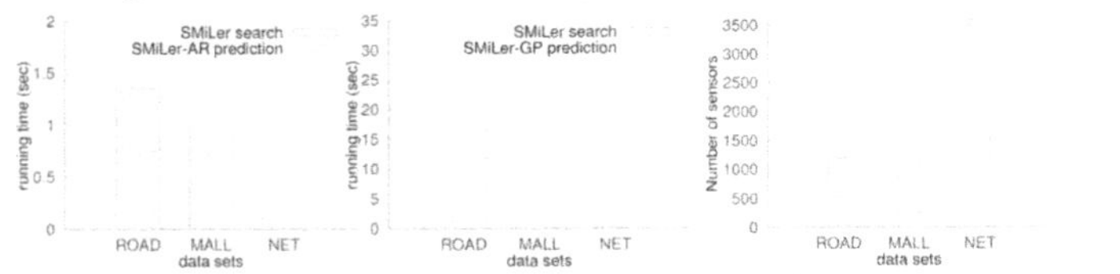

(a) SMiLer-AR (b) SMiLer-GP (c) capability of SMiLer

Figure 12: Scalability of SMiLer: (a) and (b) show total time cost of all sensors to make prediction, (c) shows maximum number of sensors per GPU on the data.

from a city) while each sensor has one year data. To support more sensors, there are two options. First, we can simply use multiple-GPU system. We also believe that the memory of the GPU will be continuous increasing while the number of sensors in a city is quite stable over years. Second, we can reduce M (the size of one sensor data). For example, if we take a sample of ten percent of ROAD dataset into the GPU, one GPU can support more than ten thousands of sensors. But its prediction performance may be degenerate. This is a trade-off between the space and the prediction performance.

6.4.2 Comparison of PSGP and SMiLer

We claim that SMiLer is more practical than its competitors. It seems that the low-rank approximation models, such as PSGP and VLGP, have a potential to achieve better prediction performance since their accuracy can be improved by increasing the "rank". We take PSGP as an example to reveal the impracticality of this solution.

Fig. 13 indicates why SMiLer-GP is more practical than PSGP. For each dataset, we randomly selected 50 sensors to make prediction using PSGP and averaged their training time and MAE. In Fig. 13, when we vary the number of active points, the left y-axis shows the MAE of PSGP and the right y-axis shows the average training time of PSGP for each sensor. The MAE of SMiLer-GP averaged on such 50 sensors is also illustrated with violet solid line. We can see that, after the number of active points is larger than a threshold (e.g. 32), the marginal improvement of MAE is small, but the increase of the time is exponential. For example, on the ROAD dataset, the total training time for its 963 sensors with 128 active points should be about 200 days (18000*963=17334000 seconds). However, SMiLer-GP still has lower MAE than PSGP on all the datasets even if we allow such an expensive training process for PSGP.

The experiment in this section and Fig. 13 (a) also experimentally demonstrates that SMiLer can overcome the critical challenges in the "*traffic sensor prediction*" problem introduced in Example 1.1 (see Section 1). Without having a training phase, SMiLer can still achieve much better prediction performance than the approximated low-rank GP model which requires high training time cost.

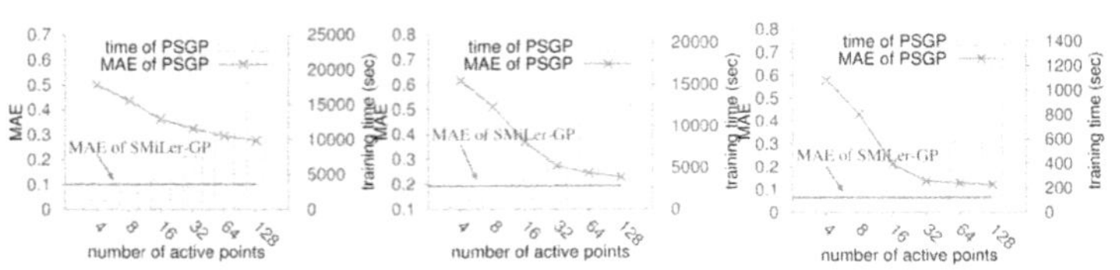

(a) ROAD (b) MALL (c) NET

Figure 13: Comparison of PSGP and SMiLer-GP: average training time per sensor of PSGP and their MAE.

7. CONCLUSIONS

We present SMiLer, a semi-lazy time series prediction system for sensors. The core idea is to employ the semi-lazy learning approach to enable GPs for time series prediction. Two challenging problems are solved, which are a suffix kNN search method under DTW and a semi-lazy GP prediction model. For the former problem, we depicted a GPU-based two-level inverted-like index for fast Suffix kNN search. For the latter one, we devised an adaptive auto-tuning mechanism integrating the ensemble and continuous prediction.

Extensive experiment study demonstrates that SMiLer performs the prediction with good accuracy, and can also scale well with carrying out prediction in real time.

8. ACKNOWLEDGMENTS

We would like to gratefully acknowledge Prof. H. V. Jagadish who provided insightful comments, inspiring advice and kind help on this paper. We would also like to give many thanks to Chang Fanxi Francis who generously shared MALL dataset to us for the experiment study. The work by Anthony K.H. Tung was partially supported by NUS FRC Grant R-252-000-370-112. This research was carried out at the NUS-ZJU Sensor-Enhanced social Media (SeSaMe) Centre. It is supported by the Singapore National Research Foundation under its International Research Centre @ Singapore Funding Initiative and administered by the Interactive Digital Media Programme Office.

9. REFERENCES

[1] Genie and lamp. http://www.comp.nus.edu.sg/~atung/gl/, 2014.

[2] R. Adhikari and R. Agrawal. A novel weighted ensemble technique for time series forecasting. In *PAKDD*, pages 38–49, 2012.

[3] T. Alabi, J. D. Blanchard, B. Gordon, and R. Steinbach. Fast k-selection algorithms for graphics processing units. *Journal of Experimental Algorithmics*, 17:4–2, 2012.

[4] N. S. Altman. An introduction to kernel and nearest-neighbor nonparametric regression. *The American Statistician*, 46(3):175–185, 1992.

[5] I. Assent, R. Krieger, F. Afschari, and T. Seidl. The ts-tree: efficient time series search and retrieval. In *EDBT*, pages 252–263, 2008.

[6] V. Athitsos, P. Papapetrou, M. Potamias, G. Kollios, and D. Gunopulos. Approximate embedding-based subsequence matching of time series. In *SIGMOD*, pages 365–378, 2008.

[7] K. Bache and M. Lichman. UCI machine learning repository. https://archive.ics.uci.edu/ml, 2013.

[8] T. Ban, R. Zhang, S. Pang, A. Sarrafzadeh, and D. Inoue. Referential knn regression for financial time series forecasting. In *ICONIP*, pages 601–608, 2013.

[9] R. Barillec, B. Ingram, D. Cornford, and L. Csató. Projected sequential gaussian processes: A c++ tool for interpolation of large datasets with heterogeneous noise. *Computers&Geosciences*, 37(3):295–309, 2011.

[10] D. Berndt and J. Clifford. Using dynamic time warping to find patterns in time series. In *AAAI94 workshop on knowledge discovery in databases*, pages 359–370, 1994.

[11] G. Biau, K. Bleakley, L. Györfi, and G. Ottucsák. Non-parametric sequential prediction of time series. *Journal of Nonparametric Statistics*, 22(3):297–317, 2010.

[12] E. Blanzieri and F. Melgani. Nearest neighbor classification of remote sensing images with the maximal margin principle. *IEEE Transactions on Geoscience and Remote Sensing*, 46(6):1804–1811, 2008.

[13] T. Bollerslev. Generalized autoregressive conditional heteroskedasticity. *Journal of econometrics*, 31(3):307–327, 1986.

[14] L. Bottou. On-line learning and stochastic approximations. In *On-line learning in neural networks*, pages 9–42. Cambridge University Press, 1999.

[15] G. E. Box, G. M. Jenkins, and G. C. Reinsel. *Time Series Analysis: Forecasting and Control.* Wiley, 4th edition, 2008.

[16] P. Boyle and M. Frean. Dependent gaussian processes. In *NIPS*, pages 217–224, 2004.

[17] S. Brahim-Belhouari and A. Bermak. Gaussian process for nonstationary time series prediction. *Computational Statistics & Data Analysis*, 47(4):705–712, 2004.

[18] D. Chakrabarti and C. Faloutsos. F4: large-scale automated forecasting using fractals. In *CIKM*, pages 2–9, 2002.

[19] C.-C. Chang and C.-J. Lin. Libsvm: a library for support vector machines. *ACM TIST*, 2(3):27, 2011.

[20] N. Chapados and Y. Bengio. Augmented functional time series representation and forecasting with gaussian processes. In *NIPS*, pages 457–464, 2007.

[21] L. Chen and R. Ng. On the marriage of lp-norms and edit distance. In *VLDB*, pages 792–803, 2004.

[22] L. Chen, M. T. Özsu, and V. Oria. Robust and fast similarity search for moving object trajectories. In *SIGMOD*, pages 491–502, 2005.

[23] T. Chen and J. Ren. Bagging for gaussian process regression. *Neurocomputing*, 72(7):1605–1610, 2009.

[24] Y. Chen, M. Nascimento, B. Ooi, and A. Tung. Spade: On shape-based pattern detection in streaming time series. In *ICDE*, pages 786–795, 2007.

[25] L. Csató and M. Opper. Sparse on-line gaussian processes. *Neural computation*, 14(3):641–668, 2002.

[26] C. Cuda. Programming guide. *NVIDIA Corporation*, 2014.

[27] M. Cuturi. Fast global alignment kernels. In *ICML*, pages 929–936, 2011.

[28] M. Cuturi. Pems-sf data set. https://archive.ics.uci.edu/ml/datasets/PEMS-SF, 2014.

[29] DataMarket. Internet traffic data. http://data.is/19Cbyed, 2014.

[30] H. Ding, G. Trajcevski, P. Scheuermann, X. Wang, and E. Keogh. Querying and mining of time series data: experimental comparison of representations and distance measures. *PVLDB*, 1(2):1542–1552, 2008.

[31] R. F. Engle. Autoregressive conditional heteroscedasticity with estimates of the variance of united kingdom inflation. *Econometrica*, pages 987–1007, 1982.

[32] C. Faloutsos and R. T. Snodgrass. Fast subsequence matching in time-series databases. In *SIGMOD*, pages 419–429, 1994.

[33] R. Furrer, M. G. Genton, and D. Nychka. Covariance tapering for interpolation of large spatial datasets. *Journal of Computational and Graphical Statistics*, 15(3), 2006.

[34] A. Girard, C. E. Rasmussen, J. Quinonero-Candela, and R. Murray-Smith. Gaussian process priors with uncertain inputs-application to multiple-step ahead time series forecasting. In *NIPS*, pages 545–552, 2002.

[35] T. Hachino and V. Kadirkamanathan. Time series forecasting using multiple gaussian process prior model. In *CIDM*, pages 604–609, 2007.

[36] W.-S. Han, J. Lee, Y.-S. Moon, S.-W. Hwang, and H. Yu. A new approach for processing ranked subsequence matching based on ranked union. In *SIGMOD*, pages 457–468, 2011.

[37] W.-S. Han, J. Lee, Y.-S. Moon, and H. Jiang. Ranked subsequence matching in time-series databases. In *VLDB*, pages 423–434, 2007.

[38] C. C. Holt. Forecasting seasonals and trends by exponentially weighted moving averages. *International Journal of Forecasting*, 20(1):5–10, 2004.

[39] R. J. Hyndman and Y. Khandakar. Automatic time series forecasting: The forecast package for r. *Journal of Statistical Software*, 27(i03), 2008.

[40] J.-T. Jeng, C.-C. Chuang, and C.-W. Tao. Hybrid svmr-gpr for modeling of chaotic time series systems with noise and outliers. *Neurocomputing*, 73(10):1686–1693, 2010.

[41] E. Keogh. Exact indexing of dynamic time warping. In *VLDB*, pages 406–417, 2002.

[42] Y. Liu, A. Choudhary, J. Zhou, and A. Khokhar. A scalable distributed stream mining system for highway traffic data. In *PKDD*, pages 309–321. 2006.

[43] K. H. Low, J. Yu, J. Chen, and P. Jaillet. Parallel gaussian process regression for big data: low-rank representation meets markov approximation. In *AAAI*, 2015.

[44] J. McNames. A nearest trajectory strategy for time series prediction. In *Proceedings of the International Workshop on Advanced Black-Box Techniques for Nonlinear Modeling*, pages 112–128, 1998.

[45] Y.-S. Moon, K.-Y. Whang, and W.-K. Loh. Duality-based subsequence matching in time-series databases. In *ICDE*, pages 263–272, 2001.

[46] K.-R. Müller, A. J. Smola, G. Rätsch, B. Schölkopf, J. Kohlmorgen, and V. Vapnik. Predicting time series with support vector machines. In *ICANN*, pages 999–1004, 1997.

[47] R. M. Neal. *Bayesian Learning for Neural Networks.* Springer-Verlag New York, Inc., Secaucus, NJ, USA, 1996.

[48] D. Nguyen-Tuong, M. Seeger, and J. Peters. Model learning with local gaussian process regression. *Advanced Robotics*, 23(15):2015–2034, 2009.

[49] A. O'Hagan and J. Kingman. Curve fitting and optimal design for prediction. *Journal of the Royal Statistical Society. Series B (Methodological)*, pages 1–42, 1978.

[50] C. J. Paciorek and M. J. Schervish. Nonstationary covariance functions for gaussian process regression. In *NIPS*, pages 273–280, 2003.

[51] C. Park, J. Z. Huang, and Y. Ding. Domain decomposition approach for fast gaussian process regression of large spatial data sets. *JMLR*, 12:1697–1728, 2011.

[52] F. Pedregosa, G. Varoquaux, A. Gramfort, V. Michel, B. Thirion, O. Grisel, M. Blondel, P. Prettenhofer, R. Weiss, V. Dubourg, et al. Scikit-learn: Machine learning in python. *JMLR*, 12:2825–2830, 2011.

[53] PeMS. Freeway performance measurement system. `http://pems.dot.ca.gov/`, 2014.

[54] T. Rakthanmanon, B. Campana, A. Mueen, G. Batista, B. Westover, Q. Zhu, J. Zakaria, and E. Keogh. Searching and mining trillions of time series subsequences under dynamic time warping. In *KDD*, pages 262–270, 2012.

[55] C. E. Rasmussen. *Evaluation of Gaussian Process and Other Methods for Non-linear Regression.* PhD thesis, University of Toronto, 1996.

[56] C. E. Rasmussen and C. K. Williams. *Gaussian processes for machine learning.* MIT Press, 2006.

[57] C. A. Ratanamahatana and E. Keogh. Three myths about dynamic time warping data mining. In *SDM*, pages 506–510, 2005.

[58] G. Ristanoski, W. Liu, and J. Bailey. Time series forecasting using distribution enhanced linear regression. In *PAKDD*, pages 484–495. 2013.

[59] P. J. Rousseeuw and A. M. Leroy. *Robust regression and outlier detection*, volume 589. John Wiley & Sons, 2005.

[60] D. Sart, A. Mueen, W. Najjar, E. Keogh, and V. Niennattrakul. Accelerating dynamic time warping subsequence search with gpus and fpgas. In *ICDM*, pages 1001–1006, 2010.

[61] N. Segata and E. Blanzieri. Fast and scalable local kernel machines. *JMLR*, 11:1883–1926, 2010.

[62] SheffieldML. Gpy gaussian process toolkit. `http://sheffieldml.github.io/GPy/`, 2014.

[63] L. T. A. Singapore. Carpark lots availability. `https://www.mytransport.sg/content/mytransport/home/dataMall.html`, 2014.

[64] S. Sundararajan and S. S. Keerthi. Predictive approaches for choosing hyperparameters in gaussian processes. *Neural Computation*, 13(5):1103–1118, 2001.

[65] M. K. Titsias. Variational learning of inducing variables in sparse gaussian processes. In *AISTATS*, pages 567–574, 2009.

[66] M. Vlachos, G. Kollios, and D. Gunopulos. Discovering similar multidimensional trajectories. In *ICDE*, pages 673–684, 2002.

[67] Y. Wang and B. Chaib-Draa. A knn based kalman filter gaussian process regression. In *IJCAI*, pages 1771–1777, 2013.

[68] P. J. Werbos. Generalization of backpropagation with application to a recurrent gas market model. *Neural Networks*, 1(4):339–356, 1988.

[69] C. Williams and M. Seeger. Using the nyström method to speed up kernel machines. In *NIPS*, pages 682–688, 2001.

[70] C. K. Williams and C. E. Rasmussen. Gaussian processes for regression. In *NIPS*, pages 514–520, 1996.

[71] P. R. Winters. Forecasting sales by exponentially weighted moving averages. *Management Science*, 6(3):324–342, 1960.

[72] W. Yan, H. Qiu, and Y. Xue. Gaussian process for long-term time-series forecasting. In *IJCNN*, pages 3420–3427, 2009.

[73] A. Zakai and Y. Ritov. Consistency and localizability. *JMLR*, 10:827–856, 2009.

[74] H. Zhang, A. C. Berg, M. Maire, and J. Malik. Svm-knn: Discriminative nearest neighbor classification for visual category recognition. In *CVPR*, pages 2126–2136, 2006.

[75] T. Zhang. Solving large scale linear prediction problems using stochastic gradient descent algorithms. In *ICML*, pages 116–123, 2004.

[76] J. Zhou, A. K. Tung, W. Wu, and W. S. Ng. R2-d2: a system to support probabilistic path prediction in dynamic environments via "semi-lazy" learning. *PVLDB*, 6(12):1366–1369, 2013.

[77] J. Zhou, A. K. Tung, W. Wu, and W. S. Ng. A "semi-lazy" approach to probabilistic path prediction in dynamic environments. In *KDD*, pages 748–756, 2013.

[78] Y. Zhu and D. Shasha. Warping indexes with envelope transforms for query by humming. In *SIGMOD*, pages 181–192, 2003.

APPENDIX

A. DATA SOURCE OF FIG. 1

The data of Fig. 1(a) is selected from `http://ark.intel.com/` according to the family of the Intel Xeon Processor E5 and 5000. Fig. 1(b) is depicted from data of Dr. Michael Galloy in `https://github.com/mgalloy/cpu-vs-gpu`. Fig. 1(c) is drawn according to a list maintained by Prof. John C. McCallum in `http://www.jcmit.com/memoryprice.htm` whose major source is `NewEgg.com`. The data of Fig. 1(d) is collected from `http://www.techpowerup.com/gpudb/` according to the family of the NVIDIA GeForce GPU.

B. CONCEPT AND BACKGROUND

B.1 Dynamic Time Wrapping

We give a short explanation of Dynamic Time Warping (DTW) here. For more details, please refer to [41]. Without losing the generality, we assume that all time series are of equal length (see [57]). We have two time series $Q = [q_1, q_2, ..., q_d]$ and $C = [c_1, c_2, .., c_d]$. The DTW computes the best possible alignment between Q and C with respect to the overall warping cost. In Fig. 14(a), a warping matrix γ is constructed where element (i, j) corresponds to the alignment between $q_i \in Q$ and $c_j \in C$. Indeed, computing DTW is to find a contiguous set of matrix elements, called warping path, which defines the optimal alignment between Q and C (see Fig. 14). Typically, the warping path is restricted to not more than ρ cells from the diagonal [41, 54, 5]. This constraint is called Sakoe-Chiba band where ρ is called the warping width. This band constraint not only reduces the computation cost of DTW, but also avoids the degenerated matchings (e.g. most of elements of a time series are matched to several elements of the other) [5]. In this paper, we only consider the DTW with Sakoe-Chiba band constraint. The definition of DTW with ρ warping path is:

$$\gamma(i,j) = dist(q_i, c_j) + \min \begin{cases} \gamma(i-1,j) \\ \gamma(i,j-1) \\ \gamma(i-1,j-1) \end{cases} \tag{21}$$

$$\gamma(0,0) = 0, \gamma(i,0) = \gamma(0,j) = \infty, \tag{22}$$

$$dist(q_i, c_j) = \infty \ if|i-j| > \rho \tag{23}$$

$$D(Q,C) = \gamma(d,d) \tag{24}$$

where $dist(\cdot)$ is the distance between observations.

Now we give an introduction about the popular lower bound of DTW – *LB_keogh* [41]. We first define the "envelope" of time series.

DEFINITION B.1 (TIME SERIES ENVELOPE). *Given a time series C and a warping width ρ, the envelope $\mathrm{E}(C)$ contains two sequences: upper envelope $\mathrm{U}(C)$ and lower envelope $\mathrm{L}(C)$, whose i-th elements are defined as:*

$$U_i^c = \max_{-\rho \le r \le \rho} (c_{i+r}), \quad L_i^c = \min_{-\rho \le r \le \rho} (c_{i+r}) \tag{25}$$

LB_keogh is the distance between E(C) and the query Q:

$$LB\_keogh(\mathrm{E}(C), Q) = \sum \begin{cases} dist(U_i^c, q_i) & q_i > U_i^c \\ dist(L_i^c, q_i) & q_i < L_i^c \\ 0 \ otherwise \end{cases} \quad (26)$$

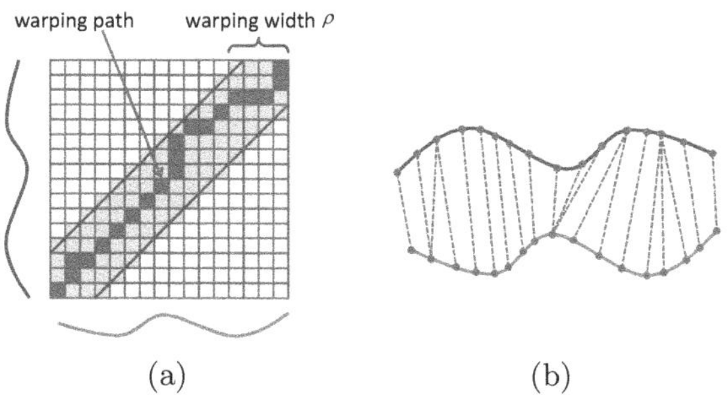

Figure 14: (a) An illustration for warping matrix with warping width and warping path; (b) Result alignment according to warping path.[1]

B.2 Graphics Processing Unit

The Graphics Processing Unit (GPU) is a computing device that provides a massively parallel execution environment for many threads. With all of the threads running on multiple processing cores, and executing the same program on separate data, the GPU shares many aspects of Single-Instruction-Multiple-Data (SIMD) architecture.

We implemented our algorithm on a NVIDIA GPU using the Compute Unified Device Architecture (CUDA) toolkit [26]. Each CUDA function is executed by an array of threads. A small batch (e.g. 256) of threads are organized as one block that possesses an associated pool of "shared memory" for the cooperation of the threads. Note that the shared memory is much faster than the global memory of the GPU.

B.3 Gaussian Process

We give a brief review of Gaussian Processes (GPs) here. Please refer to [56] for a comprehensive introduction. A Gaussian Process is a collection of random variables, any subset of which has a joint normal distribution. Suppose that a set of data pairs $(X, Y) = \{x_i, y_i\}_{i=1}^k$ are random variables, where x_i is a d-dimensional vector and y_i is the predicted value. We can assume that there is an underlying prediction function $f(\cdot)$ such that $\hat{y}_i = f(x_i)$ is based on the GP, which is fully specified by the mean function $m(x)$ and the covariance function $c(x_i, x_j)$. We usually further assume that the mean function is set to be zero, i.e.:

$$[y_1, y_2, ..., y_n]^\top \sim \mathcal{GP}(0, \Sigma) \quad (27)$$

where $\Sigma_{ij} = cov(y_i, y_j) = cov(f(x_i), f(x_j)) = c(x_i, x_j)$, which specifies the covariance between pairs of random variables. A widely-used covariance function is the squared exponential (SE) covariance function, i.e.,

$$\begin{aligned} cov(y_i, y_j) &= cov(f(x_i), f(x_j)) = c(x_i, x_j) \\ &= \theta_0^2 exp\left(-\frac{1}{2}\frac{\|x_i - x_j\|^2}{\theta_1^2}\right) + \delta_{ij}\theta_2^2 \end{aligned}$$

where δ_{ij} is a Kronecker delta. $\delta_{ij} = 1$ if and only if $i = j$ and $\delta_{ij} = 0$ otherwise. The vector $\Theta = \{\theta_0, \theta_1, \theta_2\}$ is a set of hyperparameters. In particular, θ_1 is called a *characteristic length-scale*, which determines how relevant an input is: if the length-scale has a very large value, the covariance becomes almost independent of that input, effectively removing it from the inference.

Now given data $(X, Y) = \{x_i, y_i\}_{i=1}^n$, and a test input vector x_0, we want to estimate the predictive distribution of the value y_0 corresponding to the input x_0. Given the Gaussian Process prior and Bayesian rules, the joint distribution of the observed values and the predicted value y_0 is given by

$$\begin{bmatrix} Y \\ y_0 \end{bmatrix} \sim \mathcal{GP}\left(0, \begin{bmatrix} C(X,X) & C(X,x_0) \\ C(x_0,X) & c(x_0,x_0) \end{bmatrix}\right) \quad (28)$$

where $C(X, x_0) = [c(x_1, x_0), ..., c(x_n, x_0)]^\top$ is the $n \times 1$ vector of variances between the test vector and training vectors (similar for the other entries $C(X, X), C(x_0, x_0)$ and $C(x_0, X)$). For simplicity, we use a compact notation as $C = C(X, X)$, $c_0 = C(X, x_0) = C^\top(x_0, X)$.

In the Gaussian Process model, for a test input x_0, the predictive distributive is simply obtained through conditioning on the training data. The joint distribution of the variables being Gaussian, the posterior distribution for the input test data $p(\hat{y}_0|x_0, X, Y)$ is also a Gaussian distribution, with the following mean and variance:

$$\hat{y}_0 = f(x_0, X, Y) \sim \mathcal{N}(u_0, \sigma_0^2) \quad (29)$$

$$u_0 = E(y_0) = c_0^\top C^{-1} Y \quad (30)$$

$$\sigma_0^2 = cov(y_0) = c(x_0, x_0) - c_0^\top C^{-1} c_0 \quad (31)$$

C. PROOF

C.1 Proof of Lemma 4.1

PROOF. We have two observations: (O1) For the item query IQ_i with $CSG_{i,b}$, the number of points in the right side of SW_b (exclusive) is b. Then, the number of points in the left side of SW_b adding the number of points of SW_b is $d_i - b$. According to the definition of CSG, in the left side of SW_b, only $(d_i - b)\%\omega$ points are not included in $CSG_{i,b}$.

(O2) If the rightmost aligned disjoint window is DW_r, then the leftmost aligned disjoint window is $DW_{r-|CSG_{i,b}|+1}$. The starting position (from left to right) of the point of $DW_{r-|CSG_{i,b}|+1}$ is $(r - |CSG_{i,b}| + 1) * \omega$.

Then, based on (O1) and (O2), in order to match IQ_i with a segment, we only need $(d_i - b)\%\omega$ number of points from the starting position of $DW_{r-|CSG_{i,b}|+1}$ to left forward. Therefore, the starting position of the aligned segment C_{t,d_i} is $t = (r - |CSG_{i,b}| + 1) * \omega - (d_i - b)\%w$. □

C.2 Proof of Theorem 4.2

PROOF. Suppose that the disjoint windows covered by segment C_{t,d_i} are $\{DW_r, DW_{r-1}, ..., DW_{r-m+1}\}$ where m is the number of the disjoint windows and r is the identifier of the rightmost disjoint window. We have $m = \lfloor\frac{(r+1)*\omega-t}{\omega}\rfloor$. We prove the corollary in two directions.

(I) There is one alignment. For the segment C_{t,d_i}, we can find a $CSG_{i,b}$ of IQ_i, where $b = t + d_i - (r+1) * w$ (b is the number of points in the right side of SW_b). The number of sliding windows in $CSG_{i,b}$ is $\lfloor\frac{d_i-b}{\omega}\rfloor$. By replacing b with $b = t + d_i - (r+1) * w$, it is computed that $m = \lfloor\frac{d_i-b}{\omega}\rfloor = \lfloor\frac{(r+1)*\omega-t}{\omega}\rfloor$. Therefore, $CSG_{i,b}$ can be aligned with the disjoint windows covered by C_{t,d_i}.

[1]The figure is reproduced and modified from [41].

(II) There is only one alignment. We prove it by contradiction. Suppose that for a segment C_{t,d_i} there are at least two CSGs, denoted by $CSG_{i,b'}$ and $CSG_{i,b''}$, which are aligned with the disjoint windows $\{DW_r, DW_{r-1}, ..., DW_{r-m+1}\}$. The number of points of C_{t,d_i} in the left side of DW_{r-m+1} is $b_l = (r-m+1)*\omega-t$ (b_l is the number of points from t to the starting point (exclusive) of the disjoint window DW_{r-m+1}). Then the total length of C_{t,d_i} is $d'_i = b_l + m*\omega + b'$ and $d''_i = b_l+m*\omega+b''$. Since $b' \neq b''$, it is obvious that $d'_i \neq d''_i$. But C_{t,d_i} have only one length, i.e. $d_i = d'_i = d''_i$. There is a contradiction. Therefore, there is only one alignment between the CSG and the disjoint windows.

Based on (I) and (II), we prove the claim. □

C.3 Proof of Theorem 4.3

PROOF. Suppose that the disjoint windows covered by segment C_{t,d_i} are $\{DW_r, DW_{r-1}, ..., DW_{r-m+1}\}$ where r is the identifier of the rightmost disjoint window and m is the number of disjoint windows such that $m = \lfloor\frac{(r+1)*\omega-t}{\omega}\rfloor$. Then, the number of points of C_{t,d_i} in the left side of DW_{r-m+1} is $b_l = (r-m+1)*\omega-t$ and the number of points of C_{t,d_i} in the right side of DW_r is $b_r = t+d_i-(r+1)*w$ (The calculation of b_l and b_r can be found in Appendix C.2).

For simplicity, let the distance between the point q_j and the envelop of c_i be $LB(E(c_i), q_j)$, i.e.

$$LB(E(c_i), q_j) = \begin{cases} dist(U_i^c, q_j) & q_j > U_i^c \\ dist(L_i^c, q_j) & q_j < L_i^c \\ 0 \ otherwise & \end{cases}$$

For the lower bound $LB_{EC}(IQ_i, C_{t,d_i})$, we have:

$$LB_{EC}(IQ_i, C_{t,d_i}) = \sum_{j=0}^{d_i-1} LB(E(c_{t+j}), q_j)$$

$$= \sum_{j=0}^{b_l-1} LB(E(c_{t+j}), q_j) + \sum_{j=d_i-b_r+1}^{d_i} LB(E(c_{t+j}), q_j)$$

$$+ \sum_{j=b_l}^{d_i-b_l-b_r} LB(E(c_{t+j}), q_j)$$

$$\geq \sum_{j=b_l}^{d_i-b_l-b_r} LB(E(c_{t+j}), q_j) = \sum_{a=0}^{m-1} LB_{EC}(SW_{b+a*\omega}, DW_{r-a})$$

In the same way, we can also get $LB_{EQ}(IQ_i, C_{t,d_i}) \geq \sum_{a=0}^{m-1} LB_{EQ}(SW_{b+a*\omega}, DW_{r-a})$. Combining these two inequalities, we have $LB_w(IQ_i, C_{t,d_i}) \leq LB_{en}(IQ_i, C_{t,d_i})$. According to Theorem 4.1, for the enhanced lower bound we also have $LB_{en}(IQ_i, C_{t,d_i}) \leq DTW(IQ_i, C_{t,d_i})$. Finally, we get $LB_w(IQ_i, C_{t,d_i}) \leq DTW(IQ_i, C_{t,d_i})$. □

D. ALGORITHM FOR COMPUTING LOWER BOUND IN GROUP LEVEL INDEX

Algorithm 1 shows the pseudo code for constructing the posting list of CSG in the group level index of the SMiLer Index. We use one thread to scan the elements of posting lists of sliding windows in the sliding window index to compute the lower bound of item queries. There are two key points. The first one is to do shift sum (recall Eqn. (5)) to compute the lower bound LB_{EQ} and LB_{EC} in Line 7 and Line 8 by sequentially accessing the window level index. The second one is to compute LB_w (recall Theorem 4.3) for each item query in Line 11. The computed LB_w is just the element of the posting list in the group level index.

Algorithm 1: Group level index construction: compute enhanced lower bound of the CSG.

// One block of the GPU takes one CSG
1 **for** *each* CSG_b *of master query* MQ **do**
2   **for** *each disjoint window* DW_r *of* C **do**
3     $j \leftarrow 0$ // count window number
4     $i \leftarrow 0$ // count item query number
5     $d \leftarrow b+\omega$ // ω is window length
      // n is number of item queries per MQ
6   **while** $i < n$ **do**
        // access window level index
7       $LB_q \leftarrow LB_{EQ}(SW_{b+j*\omega}, DW_{r-j})$
8       $LB_c \leftarrow LB_{EC}(SW_{b+j*\omega}, DW_{r-j})$
9   **if** $d+\omega > |IQ_i|$ *and* $d \leq |IQ_i|$ **then**
10        $t \leftarrow (r-j)*\omega-(d-b)\%\omega$
11        $LB_w(IQ_i, C_{t,d}) \leftarrow \max\{LB_q, LB_c\}$
12   Store $LB_w(IQ_i, C_{t,d})$ in posting list of $CSG_{i,b}$ of IQ_i
13        $i \leftarrow i+1$ // for next item query
14      $j \leftarrow j+1$, $d \leftarrow d+\omega$

E. ALGORITHM FOR COMPUTING DTW

Algorithm 2: Compute DTW distance

input : a query Q and a time series C ($|Q| = |C| = d$)
output: The DTW distance between Q and C
// This is pseudo-code for one thread.

1 $m = 2*\rho+2$;// ρ is warping width
2 $\gamma[m][2]$ // γ is allocated in shared memory
3 **for** $i \leftarrow 1$ *to* $m-1$ **do**
4   $\gamma(i, 0) = \infty$
5 $\gamma(0, 1) = \infty$
6 **for** $j \leftarrow 1$ *to* d **do**
7   $\gamma((j-\rho-1)\%m, j\%2) = \infty$
8   $\gamma((j+\rho)\%m, (j-1)\%2) = \infty$
9   **for** $i \leftarrow (j-\rho)$ *to* $(j+\rho)$ **do**
10    $\gamma(i\%m, j\%2) = dist(q_i, c_j) + \min \begin{cases} \gamma((i-1)\%m, j\%2) \\ \gamma(i\%m, (j-1)\%2) \\ \gamma((i-1)\%m, (j-1)\%2) \end{cases}$
11 **return** $\gamma(d\%m, d\%m)$// $|Q| = |C| = d$

In Algorithm 2, we show the pseudo code to compute the DTW distance (with Sakoe-Chiba band constraint) between a query Q and a time series C. It is worth noting that, in order to reduce the number of accesses to the global memory, the query Q should reside in the shared memory; and furthermore, the query Q must be placed in the inner loop of Algorithm 2 (i.e. Q should be placed in line 9 instead of line 6) [60].

SQLGraph: An Efficient Relational-Based Property Graph Store

Wen Sun†, Achille Fokoue‡, Kavitha Srinivas‡, Anastasios Kementsietsidis§, Gang Hu†, Guotong Xie†

†IBM Research - China
{sunwenbj, hugang, xieguot}@cn.ibm.com

‡IBM Watson Research Center
{achille, ksrinivs}@us.ibm.com

§Google Inc.
akement@google.com

ABSTRACT

We show that existing mature, relational optimizers can be exploited with a novel schema to give better performance for property graph storage and retrieval than popular noSQL graph stores. The schema combines relational storage for adjacency information with JSON storage for vertex and edge attributes. We demonstrate that this particular schema design has benefits compared to a purely relational or purely JSON solution. The query translation mechanism translates Gremlin queries with no side effects into SQL queries so that one can leverage relational query optimizers. We also conduct an empirical evaluation of our schema design and query translation mechanism with two existing popular property graph stores. We show that our system is 2-8 times better on query performance, and 10-30 times better in throughput on 4.3 billion edge graphs compared to existing stores.

Categories and Subject Descriptors

H.2 [**Database Management**]: Systems

General Terms

Property graphs; Gremlin

Keywords

Property graphs; Relational Storage; Gremlin

1. INTRODUCTION

There is increased interest in graph data management recently, fueled in part by the growth of RDF data on the web, as well as diverse applications of graphs in areas such as social network analytics, machine learning, and data mining. The dominant focus in the academic literature has been on RDF data management (e.g., [39, 18, 27, 24, 6, 25, 16]). Much of this work targets support of the graph data model over native stores or over distributed key-value stores. Few target relational systems because of concerns about the efficiency of storing sparse graph adjacency data in relational storage (e.g., Jena SDB [38], C-store [1]). Yet relational systems offer significant advantages over noSQL or native systems because they are fully ACID compliant, and they have industrial strength support for concurrency, locking, security and query optimization. For graph workloads that require these attributes, relational databases may be a very attractive mechanism for graph data management. In fact, in a recent paper, Bornea et al. [5] show that it is possible to shred RDF into relational storage in a very efficient manner with significant gains in performance compared to native graph stores.

Significant progress has been made as well on query optimization techniques for querying RDF graph data. The standard graph query language for RDF is called SPARQL, which is a declarative query language for specifying subgraphs of interest to the user. Many techniques have been proposed for optimizing SPARQL queries (e.g., [33, 34]), with some specifically targeting the problem of translating SPARQL to SQL (e.g., [7, 9, 13]). As a result, it has been possible to use relational databases for RDF data.

However, RDF is just one model for graph data management. Another model which is rapidly gaining popularity for graph storage and retrieval is the so-called property graph data model, which differs from RDF in two important ways: (a) it has an object model for representing graphs, (b) it has an accompanying query language called Gremlin which varies significantly from SPARQL.

The data model for property graphs is a directed labeled graph like RDF, but with attributes that can be associated with each vertex or edge (see Figure 2a for an example of a property graph). The attributes of a vertex such as *name* and *lang* are encapsulated in an object as key-value pairs. In RDF, they would be modeled as extra edges from the vertex to literals with the labels of *name* and *lang*, respectively. Similarly, the attributes of an edge are associated with an object, with attributes such as *weight* and its value represented as key-value pairs. One mechanism to model edge attributes in RDF is using reification, where four new edges are added to the graph to refer to the pre-existing edge. Thus, to model the edge between vertex *4* and *3*, there would be a new vertex *5* added to the graph. This vertex would have an edge labeled *subject* to *4*, an edge labeled *object* to *3*, and an edge label labeled *predicate* to *created*. The fourth edge would link *5*'s type to a *Statement*, to indicate that this vertex reflects metadata about another RDF statement (or edge). While this method of modeling edge attributes is very general, it is verbose and inefficient in terms of storage and retrieval. Other techniques in RDF

SIGMOD'15, May 31–June 4, 2015, Melbourne, Victoria, Australia.
ACM 978-1-4503-2758-9/15/05.
http://dx.doi.org/10.1145/2723372.2723732.

include adding a fourth element to each edge (such that each edge is now described with four elements), and this fourth element (*5* in our example) can now be used as a vertex in the graph, so that edge attributes such as *weight* can be added as edges from it. Property graphs provide a simplified version of this latter form of reification, by adding an object for every edge, and encapsulating edge attributes as key values. That is, the notion of one level of reification is built in to the notion of a property graph. How to deal with reification in RDF is however, not standard (see [14]), and hence, most of the literature directed at the study of RDF data management has ignored the issue of how to efficiently store RDF edge attributes.

Another important difference between property graphs and RDF is in the query language. While SPARQL, the query language for RDF, is declarative, Gremlin is a procedural graph traversal language, allowing the programmer to express queries as a set of steps or 'pipes'. For example, a typical query might start at all vertices filtered by some vertex attribute p, traverse outward from that vertex along edges with labels a, and so on. Each step produces an iterator over some elements (e.g., edges or vertices in the graph). In Gremlin, it is possible to have arbitrary code in some programming language such as Java or Groovy act as a pipe to produce side effects. This poses a significant challenge to query optimization, because much of the prior work on SPARQL cannot be re-applied for Gremlin.

Because the data model and query language for property graphs reflect an object-oriented view of graphs, they seem to be gaining popularity with Web programmers, as seen in the growing number of stores aimed at this model. Examples include Apache Titan[1], Neo4j[2], DEX [21], OrientDB[3], InfiniteGraph[4] to name a few. To our knowledge, all of them are built using either native support or other noSQL stores. For instance, Apache Titan supports BerkeleyDB (a key-value store), Cassandra, and HBase (distributed column stores). OrientDB is a document database like MongoDB, but doubles as a graph store. Neo4j and DEX support graphs natively. The question we ask in this paper, is whether one can provide efficient support for property graphs over relational stores. Specifically, we examine alternative schema designs to efficiently store property graphs in relational databases, while allowing the Web programmer access to a query language such as Gremlin. Note that because Gremlin is a procedural language, it may include side effects that make it impossible to translate into SQL. In this paper, we focus on Gremlin queries with no side-effects or complex Java code embedded in the query, to examine if such an approach is even feasible. We outline a generic mechanism to convert Gremlin queries into SQL and demonstrate that this approach does in fact produce efficient queries over relational storage.

There are two key ideas in Bornea et al. [5] that we examine in detail with respect to their applicability to property graphs: (a) the adjacency list of a vertex in a graph is accommodated on the same row as much as possible, (b) to deal with sparsity of graphs and uneven distribution of edge labels in the graph, each edge label is 'hashed' to a small set of columns and each column is overloaded to contain multiple edge labels. The hashes are optimized to minimize conflicts, by analysis of the dataset's characteristics. Bornea et al. [5] demonstrate the efficacy of these ideas to store the adjacency information in a graph, but the property graph model presents additional challenges in terms of storage of edge and vertex information. One option is to store edge or vertex information in another set of tables analogous to those described in [5]. Another option is to examine whether these additional attributes of a property graph model can be stored more efficiently in non-relational storage such as JSON storage since most commercial and open source database engines now support JSON. We examined both options to make informed decisions about the schema design for property graphs, and empirically evaluated their benefits. The outcome is a novel schema that combines relational with non-relational storage for property graphs, because as we show in a series of experiments, non-relational storage provides advantages over relational storage for lookup of edge and vertex attributes.

Our contributions in this paper are fourfold: (a) We propose a novel schema which exploits both relational and non-relational storage for property graphs, (b) We define a generic technique to efficiently translate a useful subset of Gremlin queries into SQL, (c) We modify two very different graph benchmarks (i.e., the DBpedia SPARQL benchmark and the LinkBench) to measure property graph performance because there are no accepted benchmarks yet for this query language[5]. Our benchmarks include graphs in the 300M-4.3 billion edge graphs. We are not aware of any comparison of property graph stores for graphs of this size. (d) We show that our ideas for property graph data management on relational databases yield performance that is 2-8X better than existing stores such as Titan, Neo4j and OrientDB on read only, single requester workloads. On concurrent workloads, that advantage grows to about 30X over existing stores.

2. RELATED WORK

Graph data management is a broad area and falls into three categories: (a) graph stores targeting the RDF data model, (b) graph stores targeting the property graph data model, (c) graph processing frameworks. The first two target subgraph queries over graph data, or selective graph traversal, whereas the third targets global graph manipulations where each step performs some complex logic at each vertex or edge. Our focus is on the graph data management in the first two cases in this paper.

Numerous schemes have been proposed for storage of graph data over relational and non-relational storage (see [31], [26] for surveys) in both centralized and distributed settings. These schemes include storage of edges in (a) vertical tables with extensive use of specialized indexes for performance [25], (b) predicate-oriented column stores to deal with sparsity [1], or to enable scale out [28], (c) different tables for each RDF type [38], (d) a relational hash table to store adjacency lists for each vertex [5]. To our knowledge, ours is the first work to explore combining relational with non-relational storage to address the problem of storing a graph along with metadata about each edge or vertex.

[1]http://thinkaurelius.github.io/titan/
[2]http://www.neo4j.org
[3]http://www.orientechnologies.com/orientdb/
[4]http://www.objectivity.com/infinitegraph

[5]Standardization efforts are underway, but the benchmarks are still in draft form as of today [2]

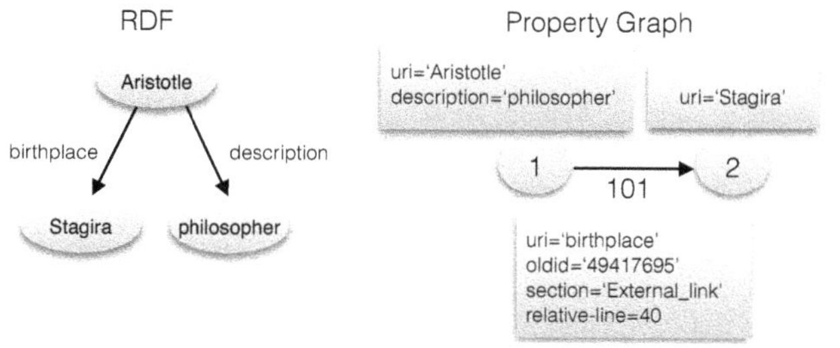

Figure 1: Conversion of RDF to Property graphs

As we stated earlier, compilation of declarative query languages such as SPARQL into SQL is a well-studied problem [7, 9, 13], both in terms of mapping SPARQL's semantics to SQL, and in terms of providing SPARQL views over legacy relational schemas [10, 29, 30]. There does not appear to be any work targeting the translation of Gremlin to SQL, perhaps due to the fact that it is a procedural language. Yet, for many graph applications, Gremlin is used to traverse graphs in a manner that can be expressed declaratively. In fact, one recent attempt contrasts performance on Gremlin with performance on other SPARQL-like declarative query languages on Neo4j [15].

There are numerous benchmarking efforts in the RDF space targeting query workloads for graphs. Examples include SP2Bench [32], LUBM [12], UOBM [19], BSBM [4] and DBpedia [22], but none of them can be easily modeled as property graphs because they do not have edge attributes, except for DBpedia. Other graph benchmarks such as HPC Scalable Graph Analysis Benchmark [11] and Graph500 [23] largely target graph processing frameworks, and once again have no edge attributes, or even edge labels. Ciglan et al. [8] proposed a general graph benchmark that evaluates the performance of 2-hop and 3-hop BFS kernals over a property graph, but the benchmark is not publicly accessible. PIG [20] is a benchmark for tuning or comparison of different property graph specific operations, but it targets a Blueprints API which performs atomic graph operations. A complex graph traversal can use these atomic graph operations in sequence, but the performance overhead is very serious in normal client-server workloads. An ongoing property graph benchmark project is the Linked Data Benchmark Council [2], where a Social Network Benchmark is under development targeting interactive graph workloads, but the current queries are still vendor-specific, and do not support Gremlin. LinkBench [3] is a benchmark for evaluating the performance of different databases on supporting social graph query workloads. It was initially designed for MySQL and HBase, and it generates synthetic datasets and queries based on traces of Facebook's production databases. Since none of the current benchmarks support Gremlin natively, we chose to adapt DBpedia and LinkBench as our target benchmarks for two different type of workloads. DBpedia's queries are more complex, but target a read only benchmark. LinkBench focuses on atomic graph operations like PIG, but has very good support for measuring concurrent read write workloads.

3. SCHEMA DESIGN

Bornea et al. [5] outlined a novel schema layout for storage of RDF data in relational databases, and demonstrated its efficacy against other native RDF systems. In this paper, we evaluate the generality of this design for the property graph data model. Recall that in property graphs, each vertex or edge can have multiple key-value pairs that serve as attributes on the vertex or edge. An important point to note is that access to these key-value pairs associated with an edge or vertex is usually through the vertex or edge identifier, unless specialized indexes have been created by a user on specific keys or values for the vertex or edge. In other words, access in property graph models tends to be like very much like a key-value lookup. To help make informed decisions on schema design for this specific model and its access patterns, we created a micro benchmark (a) to empirically examine whether adjacency information is best stored in a schema layout outlined for RDF as in [5] or whether a backend store supporting key-value lookups was more appropriate, and (b) to evaluate whether it is better to store vertex and edge attributes in key-value type stores or shredded within a relational model as in [5].

3.1 Micro Benchmark Design

For this micro-benchmark, we needed (a) fairly complex graph traversal queries to contrast differing approaches to storing adjacency and (b) simple vertex or edge attribute lookups to contrast different approaches for storing edge or vertex metadata. As stated earlier, there is a dearth of realistic graph datasets for property graphs. Some of the synthetic datasets that exist such as LinkBench are clearly not designed to study graph traversal performance, although they do provide a nice benchmark for edge attribute lookups. As a result, we turned to real graphs in the RDF space to adapt them for use as a micro-benchmark. This allows us to re-use the exact same graph for both studies, by just varying the queries.

To adapt the DBpedia 3.8 RDF data model into a property graph data model, we translated each triple in the RDF dataset into a property graph using the following rules: (a) any subject or object node in RDF became a vertex with a unique integer ID in the property graph, (b) object properties in RDF were specified as adjacency edges in the property graph, where the source and the target of the edge were vertex IDs, and the edge was identified by an integer ID, (c) datatype properties in RDF were specified as vertex attributes in the property graph, (d) provenance or context information, encoded in the DBpedia 3.8 dataset as n-quads were converted into edge attributes. Figure 1 shows the conversion of DBpedia from an RDF data model to property graphs. Note that URIs are abbreviated for succinctness. This conversion helped us study characteristics of query performance such as *k hop* traversal or vertex attribute lookup on the same real graph data, without having to revert to the creation of new synthetic datasets for each aspect of our study. We define the set of queries we used for each study on this same graph in the sections below.

3.2 Storing Adjacency

An interesting aspect of popular stores for storing property graphs is that they are based on noSQL key-value stores or document stores such as Berkeley DB, Cassandra, HBase or OrientDB. In storing sparse RDF graph data, earlier work has shown that [5] shredding vertex adjacency lists into a relational schema provides a significant advantage over other mechanisms such as property tables or vertical stores which

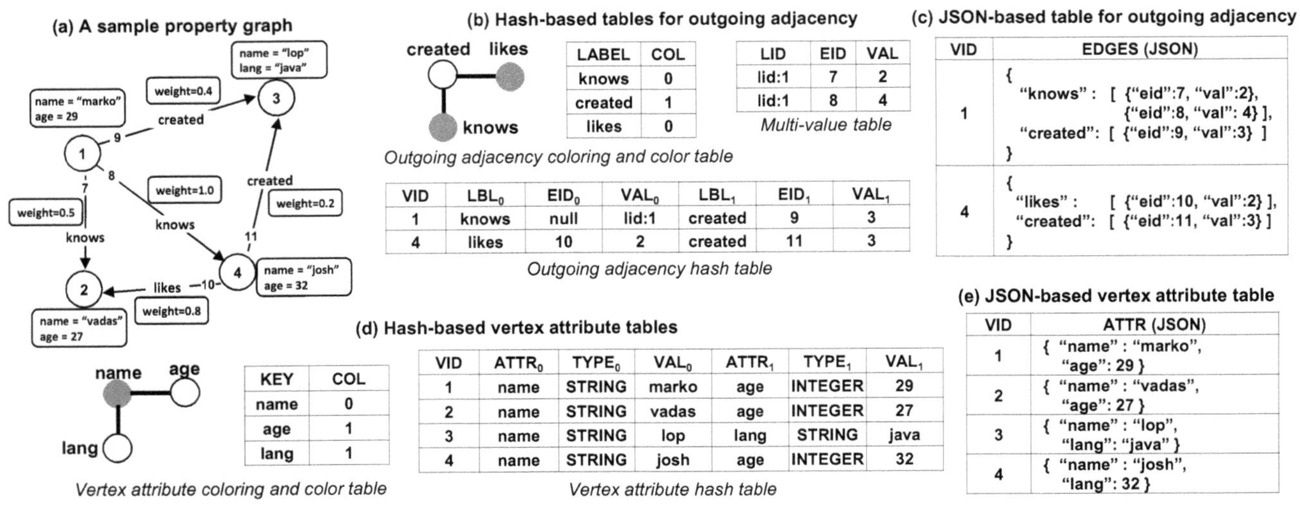

Figure 2: Hash-based and JSON-based schema for graph adjacency and attributes.

store all edge information in a single table. However, given the somewhat stylized access patterns in property graphs, it is unclear whether storing adjacency lists in non-relational key-value stores would provide more efficient storage. A relevant research question then is whether such stores provide more efficient access for property graphs.

Most modern relational databases such as DB2, Oracle or Postgresql have features to support both relational and non-relational storage within the same database engine, making it possible to perform an empirical comparison of the utility of relational versus non-relational storage structures for property graphs. Our first study was to compare relational versus non-relational methods for the storage of adjacency lists of a vertex.

For the relational schema, we re-used the approach specified in [5]; i.e., the adjacency list of an edge was stored in a relational table by hashing each edge label to a specific column pair, where one column in the pair stored the edge label, and the other column in the pair stored the value as shown in Figure 2b. In this schema, a given column is overloaded in terms of the number of different edge labels it can store to minimize the use of space. Figure 2 shows this column overloading, such that *likes* and *knows* edges are stored in the same column *0*, both having hashed to column *0*. RDF graphs can have thousands of edge labels, so overloading columns reduces sparsity in the relational table structure. However, this mechanism can also result in conflicts if one uses a hashing function that does not capitalize on the characteristics of the data. Bornea et al. [5] introduced a hashing function based on an analysis of the dataset characteristics. Specifically, the technique involves building a graph of edge label co-occurrences where two edge labels share an edge if they occur together in an adjacency list (e.g., *knows* and *created* in 2b). A graph coloring algorithm is then applied to this graph of edge label co-occurences, to ensure that two predicates that co-occur together in an adjacency list never get assigned to the same color. Because the color represents a specific column in the store, this hashing function minimizes conflicts by assigning predicates that co-occur together in a dataset to different columns. In the example, this means that *knows* and *created* would be assigned to different columns. With this type of hashing, Bornea et al. [5] showed that across multiple benchmarks, one can accomodate most adjacency lists on a single row, and moreover, this schema layout has significant advantages for query performance on many different RDF benchmarks[6].

We contrasted this relational schema to an approach where the entire adjacency list was stored as a JSON object. Our choice of JSON was driven by the fact that most modern relational engines support JSON stores in an efficient way, and this support co-exists with relational storage in the same database engine. A comparison can therefore be made between the two approaches in a more controlled setting. In a later section, we perform an experimental evaluation of our approach against other popular property graph stores, which rely on different key-value stores to rule out the possibility that any of the differences we see in are purely due to implementation specific differences within the engine for relational versus non relational data.

Our queries shown in Table 1 to study adjacency storage were focused around graph traversal, because these sorts of queries can highlight inefficiencies in adjacency storage. We created a set of queries on the DBpedia 3.8 property graph to vary (a) the number of hops that had to be traversed in the query, (b) the size of the starting set of vertices for the traversal, (c) the result size which reflects query selectivity as shown in Table 1. All the queries shown in Table 1 involved traversal over *isPartOf* relations between places, or *team* relationships between soccer players and their teams[7] In this and all other experiments, we always discarded the first run, so we could measure system performance with a warm cache. We ran each query 10 times, discarded the first run, and report the mean query time in our results.

The results shown in Figure 3 were unequivocal. Storing adjacency lists by shredding them in a relational table has significant advantages over storing them in a non-relational store such as JSON. Query times were significantly faster for the relational shredded approach (mean: 3.2 s, standard deviation: 2.2 s) compared to the non-relational JSON ap-

[6]Source code for ideas described in Bornea et al. is available at `https://github.com/Quetzal-RDF/quetzal`

[7]In the case of *team* relations, we traversed these relations ignoring the directionality of the edge.

Query	Query ID	Num. Hops	Input Size	Result Size
isPartOf	1	3	16000	257K
	2	6	16000	257K
	3	9	16000	257K
	4	5	100	4K
	5	5	1000	30K
	6	5	10000	196K
team	7	4	1	61K
	8	6	1	234K
	9	8	1	267K
	10	6	10	255K
	11	6	100	266K

Table 1: Adjacency queries

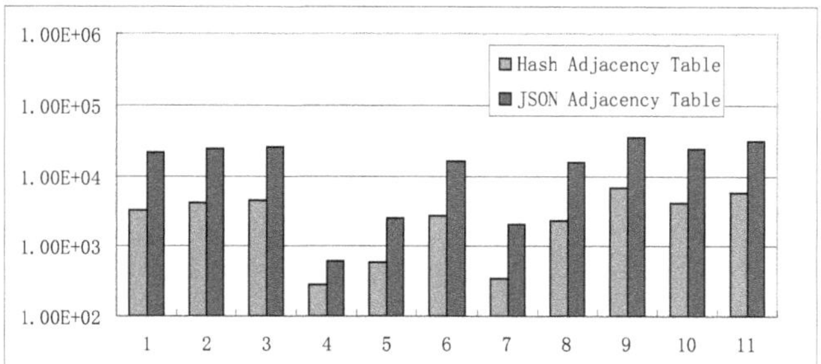

Figure 3: Results of the adjacency micro-benchmark.

proach (mean: 18.0 s, standard deviation: 11.9). These results suggest that there is value in re-using the relational shredded approach to store the adjacency information in a property graph model. Our next question was how to extend the shredded relational schema approach to store edge and vertex attributes in the property graph data model, which we address in the next section.

3.3 Storing Vertex and Edge Attributes

Query Type	ID	Attribute	Filter	Result Size
String	1	national	not null	239
	2	national	like %en	218
	3	genre	not null	28K
	4	genre	like %en	27K
	5	title	not null	231K
	6	title	like %en	222K
	7	label	not null	10M
	8	label	like %en	10M
Numeric	9	regionAffiliation	not null	223
	10	regionAffiliation	1958	3
	11	populationDensitySqMi	not null	28K
	12	populationDensitySqMi	100	32
	13	longm	not null	205K
	14	longm	1	3K
	15	wikiPageID	not null	11M
	16	wikiPageID	29899664	1

Table 2: Queries of the vertex attribute lookup micro-benchmark.

As we noted earlier, the key-value attributes on the vertices and edges is the only difference between property graphs and RDF graphs in structure. We started by examining whether we could extend the existing relational schema by adding two more tables for the storage of vertex and edge key value properties respectively. To store edge and key value attributes in these tables, we could use the same technique we

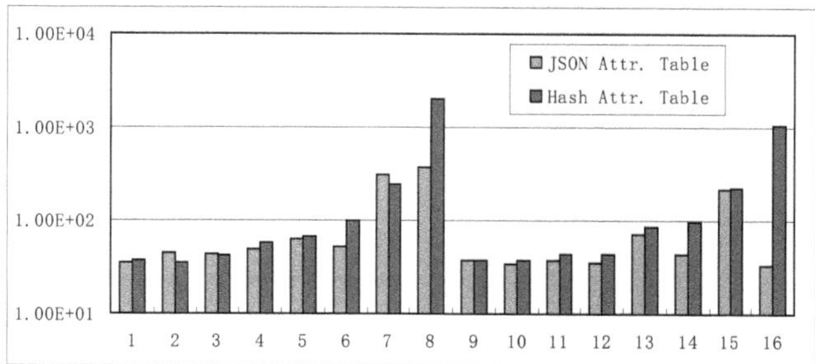

Figure 4: Results of the vertex attribute lookup micro-benchmark.

outlined in [5], by hashing attributes to columns in a standard relational table. However, note that access to these attributes tends to be very much like a simple key value lookup (because it does not involve joins). Shredding the key values into a relational table may be unnecessary. Hence, we compared the choice of a relational or non-relational approaches for storage of these attributes, just as we did in the prior sub-section. Once again, as shown in Figure 2 d, we shredded vertex or edge attributes using a coloring based hash function, and contrasted it with an approach that stored all the vertex or edge information in a single JSON column (see Figure 2 e).

	Vertex Attribute Hash Table	Outgoing Adjacency Hash Table	Incoming Adjacency Hash Table
No. of Hashed Labels	53K	13K	13K
Hashed Bucket Size	106	125	19
Spill Rows Percentage	3.2%	0	0.6%
Long String Table Rows	586K	0	0
Multi-Value Table Rows	49M	244M	243M

Table 3: Comparison of using hash tables for vertex attributes and adjacency.

To evaluate the efficacy of these different storage mechanisms, we used the same DBpedia benchmark but changed the queries so that they were lookups on a vertex's attributes[8]. In property graphs, a user would typically add specialized indexes for attributes that they wanted to lookup a vertex or an edge by. We therefore added indexes for queried keys and attributes both for the shredded relational table and when the vertex's attributes were stored in JSON. Table 2 shows the queries we constructed for this portion of our study. Across queries, we varied (a) whether the queried attribute values were strings or required casts to numeric, (b) whether the query was a simple lookup to check if the key of the attribute existed (the *not null* queries), or whether it required the value as well (these in addition could be equality comparisons such as the lookup to see if *longm* had the value 1, or string functions to evaluate if the query matched some substring), (c) whether the query was selective or not selective. The results are shown in Figure 4. Vertex attribute lookups on the JSON attribute table (mean: 92 ms, standard deviation: 108 ms) were better than the relational shredded table lookups (mean: 265 ms, standard deviation: 537 ms).

[8]We did not test lookup of an edge's attributes because the mechanism is the same.

VID+	SPILL	......	EID_j	LBL_j	VAL_j	......	EID_K	LBL_K	VAL_K
1	0		null	knows	101		9	created	3
4	0		10	like	2		11	created	3

(a) Outgoing Primary Adjacency (OPA)

VALID+	EID	VAL
101	7	2
101	8	4

(b) Outgoing Secondary Adjacency (OSA)

VID+	SPILL	......	EID_p	LBL_p	VAL_p	......	EID_q	LBL_q	VAL_q
2	0		7	knows	1		10	like	4
3	0		null	null	null		null	created	102
4	0		8	knows	1		null	null	null

(c) Incoming Primary Adjacency (IPA)

VALID+	EID	VAL
102	9	1
102	11	4

(d) Incoming Secondary Adjacency (ISA)

VID*	ATTR (JSON object)
1	{ "name"="marko", "age"=29 }
2	{ "name"="vadas", "age"=27 }
3	{ "name"="lop", "lang"="java" }
4	{ "name"="josh", "age"=32 }

(e) Vertex Attributes (VA)

EID*	INV	OUTV	LBL	ATTR (JSON object)
7	1	2	knows	{ "weight"=0.5 }
8	1	4	knows	{ "weight"=1.0 }
9	1	3	created	{ "weight"=0.4 }

(f) Edge Attributes (EA)

Figure 5: Schema of the proposed property graph store. "*" denotes the primary key, and "+" denotes the indexed column.

Another interesting aspect of using JSON in this dataset is shown in the characteristics of the shredded relational hash tables for vertex attributes for DBpedia, as shown in Table 3. Clearly, the relational hash table approach is efficient only to the degree that the entire adjacency list of a vertex is stored in a single row. For outgoing edges (and incoming edges) in DBpedia, if one considers just the adjacency data, this is mostly true with no spill rows in the outgoing adjacency hash table and 0.6% spills in the incoming adjacency hash table. The vertex attribute hash table however has more spills, and has a number of long strings in the attributes which cannot be put into a single row. Storing this data in a shredded relational table thus means more joins in looking up vertex attributes, either because rows have spilled due to conflicts, because long strings are involved, or because a vertex has multiple values for a given key. In JSON, we eliminate joins due to spills, long strings, or multi-valued attributes. Moreover, because the shredded relational table needs a uniform set of columns to store many different data types, it needs casts, which are eliminated in JSON. Thus, as long as these values do not participate in a join again, we see substantial gains in using JSON to store these attribute values. Note that JSON lookups for simple attribute lookups (the *not null*) queries were not different from the shredded relational table, suggesting that when joins are not involved, both storage systems do equally well.

3.4 The Proposed Schema

Given the results of the micro-benchmarks, we designed a novel schema that combined relational storage for adjacency information along with JSON storage for vertex and edge attributes. Figure 5 illustrates the proposed schema with the sample property graph in Figure 2a.

The primary tables for storing outgoing and incoming adjacency (OPA, and IPA) directly apply the coloring and hashing ideas in the RDF store [5] to store edge labels, their values and additionally an edge ID as a key for edge attributes, provided the edge has only a single value. An example in Figure 2 is the *like* edge between *4* and *2*. Ideally, all the outgoing (or incoming) edges of a vertex, will be stored in the same row, where the EID_i, LBL_i, and VAL_i columns are used to store the connected edge id, edge label, and outgoing (or incoming) vertex id respectively, assuming that the hashing function hashes the edge label to the ith column triad (in our example for *like* this would be the jth triad. If there are collisions of hashing, the SPILL column will be set for the vertex to indicate multiple rows are required to represent the outgoing adjacency information of the vertex. In addition, if the vertex has multiple outgoing edges with the same label, the outgoing edge ids and outgoing vertices are stored in the OSA (or correspondingly ISA) tables, as shown in the figure for the edge between *1* and its edges to *2* and *4*. Obviously, the effectiveness of this approach to storing adjacency is dependent on minimizing hashing conflicts. Bornea et al. [5] show that hashing based on dataset characteristics is relatively robust if its based on a reprentative small sample of the data. However, if updates change substantially the basic characteristics of the dataset on which the hashing functions were derived, reorganization is required for efficient performance.

The vertex attribute (VA) table as in Figure 5 (e) directly uses JSON column to store vertex attributes. The separate table avoids redundant storage of the attributes, in case vertices span multiple rows. The edge attribute (EA) table not only stores the edge attributes in JSON column, but also keeps a copy of the adjacency information of each edge. We incorporated this feature because it provides significant benefits on certain types of graph queries, as we discuss in the next section. Furthermore, as we discuss in the evaluation section, this redundancy does not actually result in greater storage costs on disk compared to existing systems, because most relational engines have very good compression schemes.

In addition, for VA and EA tables, the vertex and edge ids are used as the primary keys. For the other tables, we built indexes over the VID and VALID columns, to support efficient table joins by using the ids. We also added the equivalent of a combined index on INV and LBL, as well as OUTV and LBL (these are effectively the equivalent of SP and OP indexes in RDF triple stores). In addition, depending on the workloads of the property graph stores, more relational and JSON indexes can be built to accelerate specific query types or graph operations, which is similar to the functionality provided by most property graph stores.

3.5 Uses for Redundancy in the Schema

One weakness in the proposed schema for the storage of adjacency lists is that it always requires a join between the OSA and OPA (or correspondingly IPA and ISA) tables to find the immediate neighbors of a vertex. In cases where the result set is large in either table, this can be an expensive

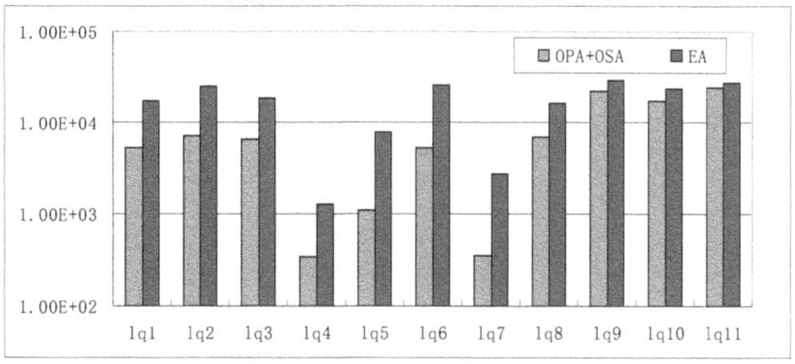

Figure 6: Results of the EA versus OPA-OSA path computation in ms.

operation compared to an index lookup in EA. We tested this hypothesis with another micro-benchmark on DBpedia. The query was to find all neighbors of a given vertex. We varied the selectivity of that query by choosing vertices with a small number of incoming edges, or a large number of incoming edges, as shown in Table 4. As shown in the table, a simple lookup of a vertex's neighbors can degrade if the query is not selective for the adjacency tables, compared to a lookup in EA.

The next question to ask is whether we need the adjacency tables at all? After all, the EA table contains adjacency information as well (it is basically a triple table) and can be used to compute paths. We therefore ran our long path queries using joins on the EA table alone, or using joins on OPA+OSA. The results shown in Figure 6 were once again unequivocal. On average, queries for paths were performed in 8.8 s when OPA+OSA were used to the answer the query compared to 17.8 s when EA was used. OPA+OSA was also somewhat less variable overall (a standard deviation of 8.2 s compared to 9.8 s for EA). The reason for this finding is due to the fact that shredding results in a much more compact table than a typical vertical representation. Thus, the cardinality of the tables involved in the joins is smaller, and it yields better results for path queries. We note that this complements [5]'s work which shows the advantages of shredding for so-called star queries, which are also very common in graph query workloads.

Query ID	ResultSize	EA	IPA+ISA
1	1	38	39
2	21	38	38
3	228	39	40
4	2282	39	40
5	21156	41	42
6	226720	58	77
7	2350906	74	440

Table 4: Comparison of getting vertex neighbors query performance in ms.

4. QUERY TRANSLATION

Gremlin, the de facto standard property graph query traversal language [37], is procedural, and this makes it difficult to compile it into a declarative query language like SQL. Nevertheless, Gremlin is frequently used to express graph traversal or graph update operations alone, and these can be mapped to declarative languages. In this paper, we focus on graph traversal queries and graph update operations with no side effects.

4.1 Gremlin Query Language in a Nutshell

A Gremlin query consists of a sequence of steps, called pipes. The evaluation of a pipe takes as input an iterator over some objects and yields a new iterator. Table 5 shows the different categories of Gremlin operations (or pipes).

Gremlin Operation Types	Description
Transform	Take an object and emit a transformation of it. Examples: both(), inE(), outV(), path()
Filter	Decide whether to allow an object to pass. Examples: has(), except(), simplePath()
Side Effect	Pass the object, but with some kind of side effect while passing it. Examples: aggregate(), groupBy(), as()
Branch	Decide which step to take. Examples: split/merge, ifThenElse, loop

Table 5: Operations supported by Gremlin query language.

The interested reader is referred to [36] for an exhaustive presentation of all Gremlin pipes. Here, we illustrate, on a simple example, the standard evaluation of a Gremlin query. The following Gremlin query counts the number of distinct vertices with an edge to or from at least one vertex that has 'w' as the value of its 'tag' attribute:

g.V.filter{it.tag=='w'}.both.dedup().count()

The first pipe of the query V returns an iterator it_1 over all the vertices in the graph g. The next pipe *filter{it.tag == 'w'}* takes as input the iterator it_1 over all vertices in the graph, and yields a new iterator it_2 that retains only vertices with 'w' as the value of their 'tag' attribute. The *both* pipe then takes as input the iterator it_2 and returns an iterator it_3 containing, for each vertex v in it_2, all vertices u such that the edge (v, u) or (u, v) is in the graph g (note that it_3 may contain duplicated values). The *dedup()* produces an iterator it_4 over unique values appearing in the iterator it_3. Finally, the last pipe *count()* returns a iterator with a single value corresponding to the number of elements in the previous iterator it_4.

4.2 Query Processing Framework

Since Gremlin operates over any graph database that supports the basic set of primitive CRUD (Create Read Update Delete) graph operations defined by the Blueprints APIs [35], a straightforward way to support Gremlin queries is to implement the Blueprints APIs over the proposed schema, as most of the existing property graph stores do. However, this approach results in a huge number of generated SQL queries for a single Gremlin query, and multiple trips between the client code and the graph database server, which leads to significant performance issues when they are not running in the same process on the same machine. For instance, for the example query in the previous section, for each vertex v returned by the pipe *filter{it.tag == 'w'}*, the Blueprints' method $getVertices(Direction.BOTH)$ will be invoked on v to get all its adjacent vertices in both directions, which will result in the evaluation, on the graph database server, of a SQL query retrieving all the vertices that have an edge to or from v.

Compared to random file system access or key-value lookups, SQL query engines are more optimized for set operations rather than for multiple key lookups. Hence, the basic idea of our query processing method is to convert a Gremlin query into a single SQL query. By doing so, we not only eliminate the chatty protocol between the client and the database server, but we also leverage multiple decades of query optimization research and development work that have gone into mature relational database management systems. In other words, by specifying the intent of the graph traversal in one shot as a declarative query, we can leverage the database engine's query optimizer to perform the query in an efficient manner.

The proposed query framework follows the following steps. The input Gremlin query is first parsed into an execution pipeline that is composed of a set of ordered Gremlin operations (i.e., pipes). The pipes are then sent to the query builder, where a set of pre-defined templates, which are of different types including SQL functions, user defined functions (UDFs), common table expression (CTE) fragments and stored procedures (SPs), are used to translate the pipes into SQL queries. Based on the order of the input pipes, the matched templates are composed together and optimized by the query optimizer. Finally, input Gremlin queries are converted into a single SQL query or stored procedure call to send to the relational engine for execution.

4.3 Gremlin Query Translation

In the standard implementation of Gremlin, the input or output of a pipe is an iterator over some elements. In our SQL based implementation, the input or output of a pipe is a table (a materialized table or a named Common Table Expression (CTE)) with a mandatory column named *val* that contains the input or output objects, and an optional column named *path* that represents the traversal path for each element in the *val* column (this path information is required by some pipes such as simplePath or path).

DEFINITION 1. *We define the translation of a gremlin pipe e, denoted* $[e]$, *as a function that maps the input table* t_{in} *of the pipe to a tuple of* (sp, spi, cte, t_{out}), *where*

- t_{out} *(also denoted* $[e].out$*) is the result table of the pipe.*
- *sp (also denoted* $[e].sp$*) is the list of stored procedure definitions used in the translation of e.*
- *spi (also denoted* $[e].spi$*) is the list of stored procedure invocations for a subset of stored procedures in sp.*
- *cte (also denoted* $[e].cte$*) is the list of pairs (cteName, cteDef) consisting of the name and the definition of Common Table Expressions (CTEs) used in the translation of e.*

If the translation is done through CTEs, then t_{out} is the name of one of the CTEs in *cte*; otherwise, it is the name of a temporary table created and populated by the invocation of the last element of *spi*.

Table 5 lists the Gremlin operations in different categories. Basically, for the different types of Gremlin operations (pipes), we designed different types of query templates to handle each Gremlin pipe based on operations that are standard in relational databases.

Transform Pipes. The transform pipes control the traversal between the the vertices in a graph. Based on results discussed in section 3.5 on how to best exploit the redundancy in the schema design section, for a transform from a set of vertices to their adjacent vertices, if the transform appears as the only graph traversal step in the query (i.e., for a simple look-up query), the most efficient translation, in general, uses the edge table (EA); otherwise, the translated CTE template joins with the hash adjacency tables. For example, the *out* pipe, which outputs the set of adjacent vertices of each input vertex, is translated by the following template parametrized by the input table t_{in} if the pipe is part of a multi-step traversal query:

```
[out](t_in)=(∅, ∅, cte, t1)
cte = {
(t0,SELECT t.val FROM t_in v,OPA p,
   TABLES(VALUES(p.val0), ... ,(p.valn))AS t(val)
   WHERE v.val=p.entry AND t.val is not null),
(t1,SELECT COALESCE(s.val, p.val)  AS  val
    FROM  t0 p LEFT OUTER JOIN OSA s on p.val=s.id)}
```

Otherwise, if the *out* pipe is the only graph traversal step in the query, the preferred translation uses the edge table (EA) as follows:

```
[out](t_in)=(∅, ∅, cte, t0)
cte = {(t0,SELECT p.outv AS val  FROM t_in v, EA p
   WHERE v.val=p.inv )}
```

A more complex transform pipe is the path pipe, which returns the traversal path of each input object (i.e., the path of each object through the pipeline up to this point). For illustration, let us consider the following labeled graph $g = (V = \{1, 2, 3, 4\}, E = \{(1, p, 2), (2, q, 3), (2, r, 4)\})$, the gremlin query $q_1 = g.V(1).out.out$ returns the vertices two hops aways from 1, namely 3 and 4. If we add the path pipe at the end of the previous query, the resulting query $q_2 = g.V(1).out.out.path$ evaluates to the actual traversal path of each result of query q_1 (i.e., a sequence of steps from 1 to a result of query q_1). The result of the evaluation of q_2 consists of the two sequences [1, 2, 3] and [1, 2, 4]. Thus, path pipe requires the system to record the paths of the traversal. Hence, if a path pipe p is present in a query, the additional *path* column has to be added to the CTE templates used to translate all pipes appearing before p to track the path of all output object. The translation of a pipe e that keeps track of the path of each object is denoted $[e]_p$. $[e]_p$ is similar to $[e]$ except that it assumes that the input table t_{in} has a column called *path* and it produces an output table t_{out} with a column named *path* for storing the updated path information. For example, when path information tracking is enabled, the *out* pipe is translated by the following template parametrized by the input table t_{in} (assuming the pipe is part of a multiple step traversal query):

```
[out]_p(t_in)=(∅, ∅, cte, t1)
cte = {
(t0,SELECT t.val AS val, (v.path || v.val) AS path
   FROM t_in v, OPA p,
   TABLES(VALUES(p.val0), ... ,(p.valn))AS t(val)
   WHERE v.val=p.entry AND t.val is not null),
(t1,SELECT COALESCE(s.val, p.val)  AS  val, p.path
    FROM  t0 p LEFT OUTER JOIN OSA s on p.val=s.id)}
```

Filter Pipes. The filter pipes typically filter out unrelated vertices or edges by attribute lookup. Hence, the corresponding CTE templates can simply apply equivalent SQL conditions on JSON attribute table lookup. For the filter conditions not supported by default SQL functions, such as the simplePath() pipe, we define UDFs to enable the filter condition translation.

Side Effect Pipes. Side effect pipes do not change the input graph elements, but generate additional information based on the input. In our current implementation, side effects are ignored, so side effect pipes act as identity functions (i.e., their output is identical to their input).

Branch Pipes. The branch pipes control the execution flow of other pipes. For split/merge pipes and ifElseThen()

pipes, we can simply use CTEs to represent all the possible branches, and use condition filters to get the desired branch.

For example, for a given input table t_{in} and an ifThenElse pipe $e = ifThenElse\{e_{test}\}\{e_{then}\}\{e_{else}\}$, we first translate the test expression e_{test} as a transform expression that yields a boolean value, and we also track provenance information in the path column. Let $test$ be the result of the translation: $test = [e_{test}]_p(t_{in})$. Using the output table of $test$ (i.e., $test.out$), we then define the CTE $thencte_{in}$ (resp. $elsecte_{in}$) corresponding to the input table for the evaluation of e_{then} (resp. e_{else}):

$thencte_{in}$=($then_{in}$,SELECT path[0] AS val FROM $\underline{test.out}$ WHERE val=true)
$elsecte_{in}$=($else_{in}$,SELECT path[0] AS val FROM $\underline{test.out}$ WHERE val=false)

The translation of the ifThenElse expresion e for the input table t_{in} can now be defined by collecting all the stored procedure definitions and invocations, and CTEs produced by the translations of 1) the test condition ($test = [e_{test}]_p(t_{in})$), 2) the then part ($then = [e_{then}](then_{in})$), and 3) the else part ($else = [e_{else}](else_{in})$):

$$
\begin{aligned}
&[e](t_{in}) = (sp, spi, cte, t_{out})\\
&\quad sp = test.sp \cup then.sp \cup else.sp\\
&\quad spi = test.spi \cup then.spi \cup else.spi\\
&\quad cte = test.cte \cup \{thencte_{in}, elsecte_{in}\}\\
&\qquad \cup\, then.cte \cup else.cte \cup \{(t_{out},\\
&\qquad \textbf{SELECT * FROM } then.out\\
&\qquad \textbf{UNION ALL SELECT * FROM } else.out)\}
\end{aligned}
$$

The result table t_{out} is simply defined as the union of results from the then part and else part.

For loop pipes, we evaluate the depth of the loop. For fixed-depth loops, we will directly expand the loop and translate it into CTEs. Otherwise, we translate the loop pipe into a recursive SQL or a stored procedure call, depending on the engine's efficiency in handling recursive SQL.

Figure 7 gives an example of using CTEs to translate our sample Gremlin query.

4.4 Limitations

Our focus in this paper is on graph traversal queries and graph update operations with no side effects. Specifically, side effect pipes are ignored (i.e. they are currently implemented as identity functions: their output is identical to their input). Likewise, pipes with complex Groovy/Java closures or expressions are also ignored because we currently do not perform a static analysis of closures and expressions to allow us to understand, for example, whether a Java method call in a closure or an expression has side effects (e.g., such an expression can appear as the stopping condition in a loop pipe or as the test condition in an IfThenElse pipe). As a result, we currently conservatively ignore pipes containing any expression other than simple arithmetic or comparison operators.

Modulo the limitations outlined in the previous paragraph, our translation process is fairly generic and produces CTEs as the result of the translation of most pipes (see Table 8 in the Appendix for the translation in detail). Stored procedures are only used as fallback option in the translation of recursive pipes when the depth of the loop cannot be statically determined.

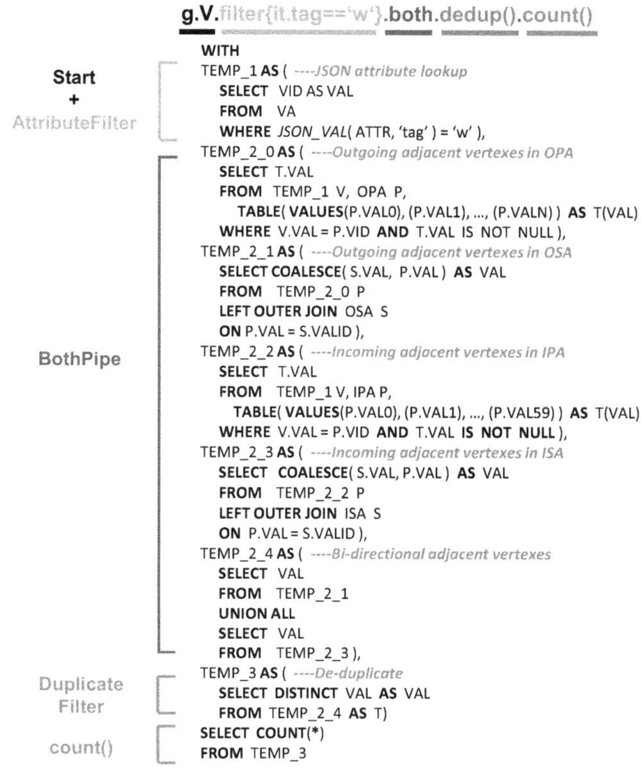

Figure 7: An example of Gremlin query translation.

4.5 Optimization

In this section, we describe optimizations applied to the query translation and evaluation steps as well as optimizations needed for efficient update operations.

4.5.1 *Query Translation and Evaluation Optimization*

A standard Gremlin query rewrite optimization technique in most property graph stores consists of replacing a sequence of the non selective pipe $g.V$ (retrieve all vertices in g) or $g.E$ (retrieve all edges in g) followed by a sequence of attribute based filter pipes (i.e., filter pipes that select only vertices or edges having specific edge labels, attribute names, or attribute name/value pairs) by a single GraphQuery pipe that combines the non selective pipe $g.V$ or $g.E$ with the potentially more selective filter pipes. A similar rewrite is done to replace a sequence of the potentially non selective pipe out, $outE$, in, or inE followed by a sequence of attribute based filter pipes by a single VertexQuery pipe. This VertexQuery rewrite is particularly efficient for the processing of supernodes (i.e., vertices with large number connections to other vertices). GraphQuery and VertexQuery rewrites allow for a more efficient retrieval of only relevant data by the underlying graph database (e.g., by leveraging indexes on particular attributes). We exploit such merging in our translation as shown in Figure 7, where the non selective first pipe $g.V$ is explicitly merged with the more selective filter $filter\{it.tag == \text{'}w\text{'}\}$ in the translation. To some extent, our translation of the whole Gremlin query into a single SQL generalizes the basic idea embodied in GraphQuery and VertexQuery pipes: providing more information about the query to the underlying graph database to enable a more efficient evaluation. However, as opposed to our approach that compiles the whole Gremlin query into a single SQL query, GraphQuery and VertexQuery do not go far enough: they are limited to efficient filtering of a single traversal step (in our example query, the rewrite optimization will yield g.queryGraph(filter{it.tag=='w'}, V).both.dedup().count()).

In the current implementation of our approach, we rely on the underlying relational database management system to provide the best evaluation strategy for the generated SQL query.

4.5.2 Graph Update Optimization

Basic graph update operations, including addition, update, and deletion of vertices and edges are implemented by a set of stored procedures. For our schema, this is especially important because graph data are stored into multiple tables, and some of these operations involve updates to multiple tables. Furthermore, some update operations, such as the deletion of a single supernode of the graph, can result in changes involving multiple rows in multiple tables, which can significantly degrade performance.

To address this issue, we optimized vertex deletions by setting the ID of the vertices and edges to be deleted to a negative value corresponding to its current ID. To delete a vertex with $ID = i$, we set its VID to $-i - 1$ in the vertex attribute and hash adjacency tables, so the relations of deleted rows are maintained across tables. Corresponding rows in the edge attribute tables are deleted. As a result of this update optimization, we add to each query the additional condition $VID \geq 0$ to ensure that vertices marked for deletion are never returned as answers to a query. An off-line cleanup process can perform the actual removal of the marked vertices, but this is not currently implemented in the system yet.

5. EVALUATION

Our goal in this section was to compare the performance of SQLGraph against two popular open source property graph systems, Titan and Neo4j. To keep systems comparable in terms of features, we focused on a comparison of property graph systems with full ACID support, targeting a single node in terms of scalability. Titan uses existing noSQL stores such as BerkeleyDB, Cassandra and HBase to support graph storage and retrieval, but the latter two backends focus on distributed storage, and do not provide ACID support. We therefore examined Titan with the BerkeleyDB configuration which targets single server, ACID compliant workloads[9]. Neo4j provides native storage for graphs, is fully ACID compliant, and is not based on any existing noSQL stores. We compared the efficacy of our schema and query translation for property graphs by comparing them with these two popular systems for property graphs. The fact that Titan and Neo4j are focused on rather different architectures was an important factor in our choice of these systems for the evaluation. In addition, we also tried to include the document-based graph store OrientDB in our comparisons, but encountered problems in data loading and concurrency support. We include a discussion of the performance of OrientDB where we could.

[9]Titan-BerkeleyDB is also known to have better performance than Titan with distributed store back-ends [17]

There are no explicit benchmarks targeted for Gremlin over property graphs yet. We therefore converted two different graph benchmarks into their property graph equivalents, as described below. We tried to vary the type of workload significantly in our choices for the two benchmarks. As in the micro benchmarks, our first choice was DBpedia, a benchmark which reflects structured knowledge from Wikipedia, as well as extractions from it. The structured knowledge is modeled as RDF, with additional metadata about where the knowledge was extracted from being represented as attributes of quads in RDF. Our second choice was LinkBench, a synthetic benchmark developed to simulate the social graph at Facebook [3].

To evaluate the performance of the different property graph stores on existing commodity single-node servers, we conducted our experiments on 4 identical virtual machines (one per system), each with 6-core 2.86GHz CPU, 24GB memory and 1TB storage running 64-bit Linux. All three property graph stores were running in server mode and responding to the requests from clients at localhost. We used a commercial relational engine to implement SQLGraph, and compared it to Neo4j 1.9.4 with its native http server as well as Titan 0.4.0 and OrientDB 1.7.8 with the Rexster http server 2.4.0. During testing, we assigned the same amount of memory (10G except in experiments that manipulated it explicitly) for the graph stores, and used their recommended configurations for best performance (if no recommended parameters found, we used the default ones). In addition, in our LinkBench testing, the largest dataset of billion-node graphs was beyond the storage capacity of the above servers. We conducted that experiment on a virtual machine instance equivalent to an Amazon EC2 hs1.8xlarge machine with 16-core CPU, 117GB memory, and 48TB storage to test it over the three graph stores. We report those experiments separately since they were conducted on different hardware.

5.1 DBPedia

For the DBPedia benchmark, we converted DBPedia 3.8 dataset to a property graph as described in Section 3.1. Two query sets were used to evaluate query performance of our graph store compared with Neo4j and Titan-BerkeleyDB. For the first query set, we converted the SPARQL query set used in [22] into Gremlin queries as described in Appendix B, and compared performance for the three graph stores[10]. The results are shown in Figure 8a, and these are separated from the results for the path queries in figure 8b. As shown in the figure 8a, Titan timed out on query 15 of the DBpedia SPARQL benchmark. We therefore provide two means for each system, one overall mean for the 20 benchmark queries (which for Titan excluded query 15), and an adjusted mean, excluding the times from query 15 for all three systems in figure 8d to allow a more fair comparison.

For the second query set, we used the 11 long-path queries described in Section 3.1 to examine graph traversal over the same dataset. This is a fairly common requirement in graph workloads, but it is not part of the current DBpedia SPARQL benchmark. The results are shown in Figure 8b. As can be seen from figure 8d, SQLGraph achieves the best performance for both path queries and benchmark

[10]All the queries in this benchmark and in LinkBench and their corresponding translations to Gremlin are available at `http://researcher.ibm.com/researcher/files/us-ksrinivs/supp-queries.pdf`

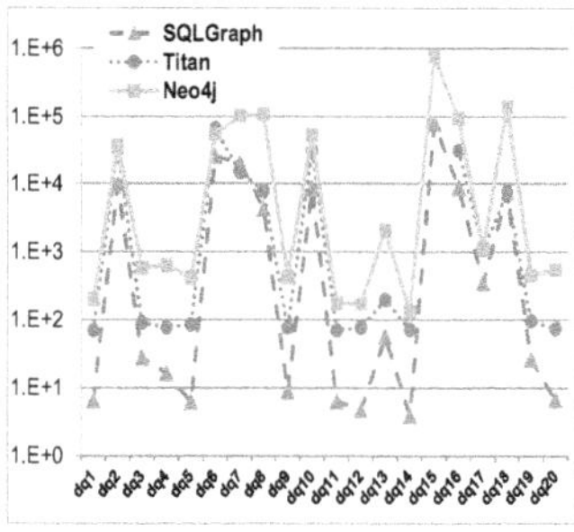

(a) Benchmark queries

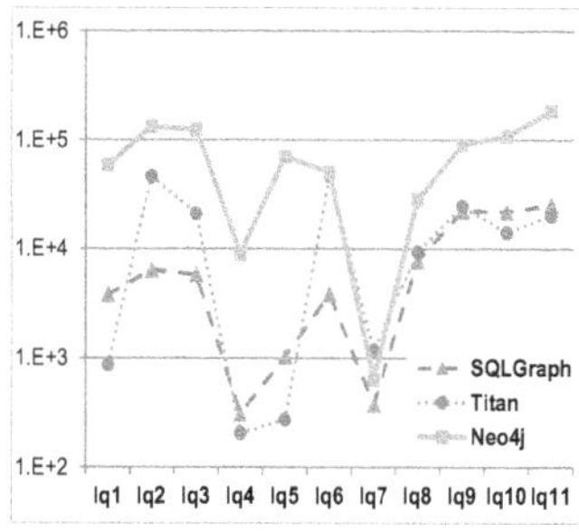

(b) Path queries

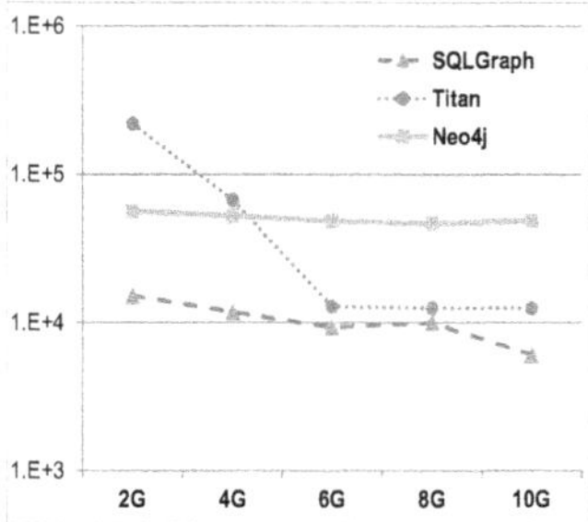

(c) Varying memory usage effects

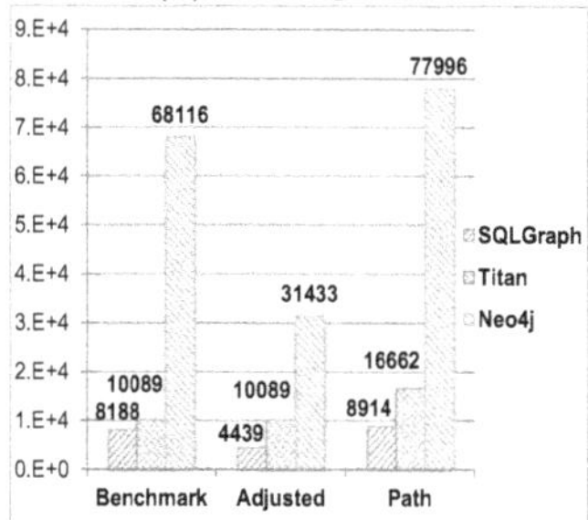

(d) DBpedia performance summary

Figure 8: DBpedia benchmark performance in ms.

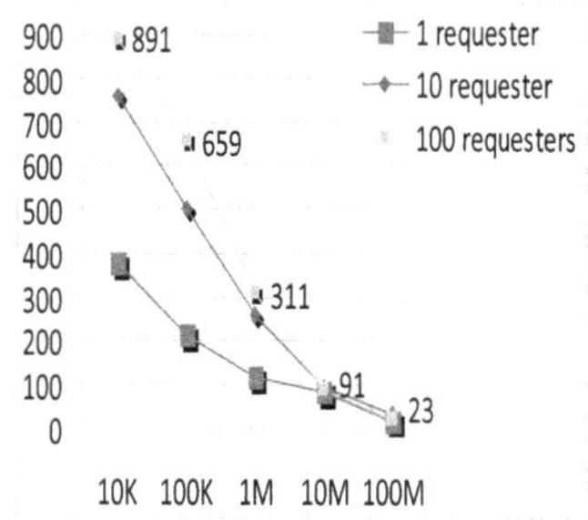

(a) SQLGraph

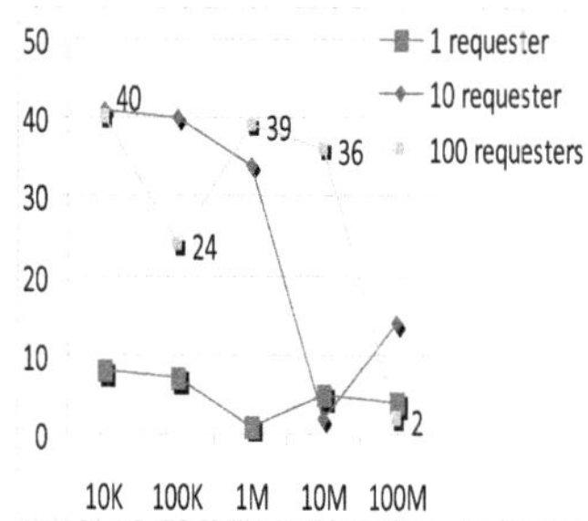

(b) Titan

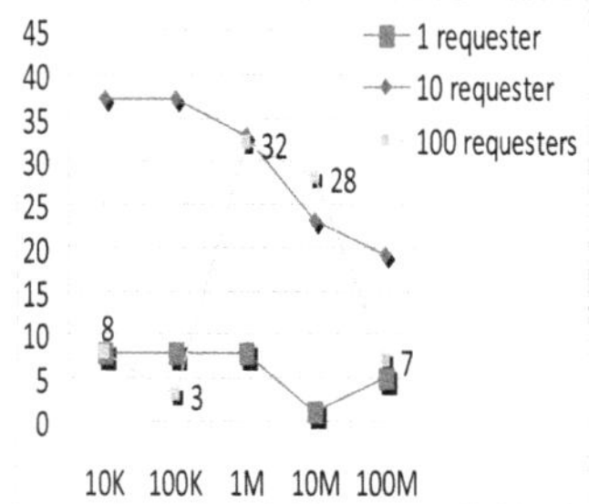

(c) Neo4j

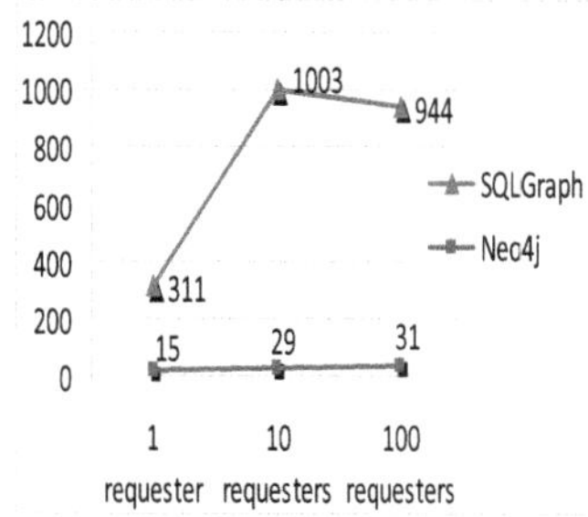

(d) 1 Billion node graph

Figure 9: LinkBench workload performance in op/sec.

queries. Specifically, SQLGraph is approximately 2X faster than Titan-BerkeleyDB, and about 8X faster than Neo4j. SQLGraph was also less variable in terms of its query performance; the standard deviation for SQLGraph for the benchmark queries excluding query 15 was 8.3 s, but Titan had a standard deviation of 17.5 s, and Neo4j had a standard deviation of 54.6 s. Path queries showed a similar trend, SQLGraph had a standard deviation of 9.4 s for path queries, Titan had 17.0 s, and Neo4j had 56.7 s.

In addition, we evaluated the performance of the different graph stores while varying the amount of memory available to the system. Our key objective here was to just ensure that the systems we were comparing against were not limited by available resources in the system. Figure 8c shows the comparison results for the 2,4,6,8, and 10 GB memory settings. In plotting the results, we computed the average times for each system across all queries in DBpedia (both the benchmark queries and the path queries), and we omitted query 15 from all systems so they could be compared. As shown in the figure, neither Titan nor Neo4j were showing any perceptible performance benefits when memory increased beyond 8G. We would like to note however, that Titan in particular has some rather aggressive caching strategies, compared to other systems. For instance, on the 10G memory usage case, Titan's mean (excluding query 15) for all the DBpedia queries was 380.1 s on the first run (cold cache), compared to 12.9 s on run 10. SQL graph's corresponding numbers for the first run was 24.1 s compared to 6.2 s on the tenth run, and Neo4j's average was 129.0 s on the first run compared to 55 s on the tenth.

One additional point to make is about the sizes of the database on disk. We pointed out earlier that our schema is redundant, in the sense that we store adjacency information in relational storage and store a copy of it in EA for edge specific queries. We also measured the sizes of the DBpedia dataset on disk for the 3 engines. DBpedia's size on disk for SQLGraph was 66GB, 98GB for Neo4j and 301GB for Titan. For OrientDB, we failed to load the DBPedia dataset after trying various configurations. The loading speed of OrientDB for such large graphs is extremely slow and it seems OrientDB cannot well support URIs as edge labels and property keys.

5.2 LinkBench

LinkBench [3] is a benchmark that simulates a typical social graph workload involving frequent graph updates. While its data model was not specified as a property graph, it can be directly transformed to a property graph by mapping "objects" into graph vertices with vertex attributes *type*, *version*, *update time*, and *data*, and mapping "associations" into graph edges with edge attributes *association type*, *visibility*, *timestamp*, and *data*.

To evaluate the performance of primitive graph CRUD operations, we adapted LinkBench to support the property graph CRUD operations in Gremlin language. The approximate distribution of CRUD operations reflects the distribution described in [3], as shown in Table 6.

We first generated 5 datasets with different scales, with the number of vertices ranging from 10 thousand to 100 million. Figure 9 shows the results of SQLGraph, Neo4j and Titan under different concurrency settings with LinkBench. In the figure, data values are only added for the 100 requesters case for clarity. As can be seen from the figure, SQLGraph's concurrency is much better than the other two graph stores, and it seems to be much less variable than the other two stores. For OrientDB, the throughput ranges from 2 to 9 op/sec for the 1-requester case, which is comparable to Neo4j and Titan. However, for the 10-requester and 100-requester settings, OrientDB reported concurrent update errors due to the lack of built-in locks. We also tested the scalability of these systems against a much larger graph dataset (1 billion nodes, 4.3 billion edges), but that evaluation could not be performed on the same VM configuration because of the scale of the graph. Furthermore, we could not test Titan on the 1 billion node graph because the queries timed out even on a superior VM, and we could not determine the reasons for its failure. We therefore show the results for the 1 billion node graph in a separate panel (d) of the figure. Still, compared with Neo4j, on the billion node graph, SQLGraph showed about 30 times better throughput.

Table 6 shows the distribution of LinkBench operations, and the average performance (as well as the maximum values) for each operation in seconds for the three systems. Note that we do not show the 100 requester case because we tried to find the point where each system was at its maximal performance. This was 10 requesters for all three systems on the 100 million node dataset. As can be seen from the table, SQLGraph is slower than the other two systems on the delete node, add link and update link operations on average, but its maximum time is still well within the maximum time of other systems. These operations constitute about 5% of the overall LinkBench workload. Thus, on write-heavy workloads, SQLGraph may have inferior update performance than Titan and Neo4j on average, because the update affects multiple underlying tables rather than a single operation. However when the dataset gets substantially bigger, one does not observe this behavior. Table 7 shows the same operations on the 1 billion node benchmark for the SQLGraph and Neo4j systems, now with 100 requesters since this was where Neo4j showed maximal performance. As can be seen in the table, SQLGraph now outperforms Neo4j on *all* operations on LinkBench.

Operation	Query Disbn	SQL-Graph	Titan	Neo4j
add node	2.6%	0.04(0.47)	0.30(3.34)	0.96(6.13)
update node	7.4%	0.12(1.75)	0.56(10.25)	1.12(6.87)
delete node	1.0%	2.24(5.81)	0.98(7.45)	0.73(4.06)
get node	12.9%	0.06(1.75)	0.51(9.18)	0.17(4.47)
add link	9.0%	1.68(4.83)	0.72(6.40)	1.02(6.30)
delete link	3.0%	0.12(1.54)	0.63(5.95)	0.28(4.50)
update link	8.0%	1.38(4.70)	0.72(9.29)	1.02(6.33)
count link	4.9%	0.03(0.53)	0.52(7.54)	0.22(5.31)
multiget link	0.5%	0.04(0.15)	0.44(1.27)	0.19(0.48)
get link list	50.7%	0.03(18.80)	0.58(369.30)	0.28(255.19)

Table 6: LinkBench operation distribution, and average performance in seconds for the 100M node graph, 10 requesters case. Maximum times are provided in parentheses.

As in the case of DBpedia, we measured the size of the largest 1B dataset for LinkBench, and found that SQLGraph took 850GB on disk, Neo4j took 1.1TB, and Titan took 1.7TB on disk. Similar to the DBPedia case, we failed to load largest LinkBench dataset to OrientDB. For the smaller datasets, OrientDB's footprint is between Neo4j and Titan.

6. FUTURE WORK AND CONCLUSIONS

We have shown that by leveraging both relational and non-relational storage in a relational database, along with very basic optimization techniques it is possible for relational systems to outperform graph stores built on key value stores or specialized data structures in the file system. More optimization opportunities exist, especially for Gremlin queries

Operation	SQLGraph	Neo4j
add node	0.002(0.160)	1.643(6.586)
update node	0.003(0.241)	2.429(490.562)
delete node	0.422(0.586)	4.527(2059.552)
get node	0.002(0.093)	1.453(7.259)
add link	0.405(0.723)	2.435(786.816)
delete link	0.003(0.152)	2.297(1273.229)
update link	0.307(0.704)	2.677(1132.209)
count link	0.002(0.266)	1.505(7.128)
multiget link	0.004(0.013)	2.387(1165.061)
get link list	0.002(1.297)	1.651(684.347)

Table 7: LinkBench operation distribution, and average performance in seconds for the 1B node graph, 100 requesters case. Maximum times are provided in parentheses.

without any side effects, if one builds a better compiler for the query language. This will be a focus for our future work.

7. REFERENCES

[1] D. J. Abadi, A. Marcus, S. R. Madden, and K. Hollenbach. Scalable semantic web data management using vertical partitioning. In *Proceedings of the 33rd international conference on very large data bases*, pages 411–422. VLDB Endowment, 2007.

[2] R. Angles, P. Boncz, J. Larriba-Pey, I. Fundulaki, T. Neumann, O. Erling, P. Neubauer, N. Martinez-Bazan, V. Kotsev, and I. Toma. The linked data benchmark council: A graph and RDF industry benchmarking effort. *SIGMOD Rec.*, 43(1):27–31, May 2014.

[3] T. G. Armstrong, V. Ponnekanti, D. Borthakur, and M. Callaghan. LinkBench: A database benchmark based on the Facebook social graph. In *Proceedings of the 2013 ACM SIGMOD International Conference on Management of Data*, pages 1185–1196, New York, NY, USA, 2013. ACM.

[4] C. Bizer and A. Schultz. The Berlin SPARQL benchmark. *International Journal On Semantic Web and Information Systems*, 2009.

[5] M. A. Bornea, J. Dolby, A. Kementsietsidis, K. Srinivas, P. Dantressangle, O. Udrea, and B. Bhattacharjee. Building an efficient RDF store over a relational database. In *Proceedings of the 2013 ACM SIGMOD International Conference on Management of Data*, pages 121–132. ACM, 2013.

[6] F. Bugiotti, F. Goasdoué, Z. Kaoudi, and I. Manolescu. RDF data management in the Amazon cloud. In *Proceedings of the 2012 Joint EDBT/ICDT Workshops*, EDBT-ICDT '12, pages 61–72, New York, NY, USA, 2012. ACM.

[7] A. Chebotko, S. Lu, and F. Fotouhi. Semantics preserving SPARQL-to-SQL translation. *Data and Knowledge Engineering*, 68(10):973 – 1000, 2009.

[8] M. Ciglan, A. Averbuch, and L. Hluchy. Benchmarking traversal operations over graph databases. In *28th International Conference on Data Engineering Workshops (ICDEW)*, pages 186–189. IEEE, 2012.

[9] R. Cyganiak. A relational algebra for SPARQL. *Digital Media Systems Laboratory HP Laboratories Bristol. HPL-2005-170*, page 35, 2005.

[10] F. Di Pinto, D. Lembo, M. Lenzerini, R. Mancini, A. Poggi, R. Rosati, M. Ruzzi, and D. F. Savo.

Optimizing query rewriting in ontology-based data access. In *Proceedings of the 16th International Conference on Extending Database Technology*, EDBT '13, pages 561–572, New York, NY, USA, 2013. ACM.

[11] D. Dominguez-Sal, P. Urbón-Bayes, A. Giménez-Vañó, S. Gómez-Villamor, N. Martínez-Bazán, and J.-L. Larriba-Pey. Survey of graph database performance on the HPC scalable graph analysis benchmark. In *Web-Age Information Management*, pages 37–48. Springer, 2010.

[12] Y. Guo, Z. Pan, and J. Heflin. LUBM: A benchmark for OWL knowledge base systems. *Journal of Web Semantics*, 3(2–3):158–182, 2005.

[13] S. Harris and N. Shadbolt. SPARQL query processing with conventional relational database systems. In *Web Information Systems Engineering–WISE 2005 Workshops*, pages 235–244. Springer, 2005.

[14] O. Hartig and B. Thompson. Foundations of an alternative approach to reification in RDF. *CoRR*, abs/1406.3399, 2014.

[15] F. Holzschuher and R. Peinl. Performance of graph query languages: Comparison of Cypher, Gremlin and native access in Neo4J. In *Proceedings of the Joint EDBT/ICDT 2013 Workshops*, pages 195–204, New York, NY, USA, 2013. ACM.

[16] J. Huang, D. J. Abadi, and K. Ren. Scalable SPARQL querying of large RDF graphs. *PVLDB*, 4(11):1123–1134, 2011.

[17] S. Jouili and V. Vansteenberghe. An empirical comparison of graph databases. In *SocialCom*, pages 708–715. IEEE, 2013.

[18] Z. Kaoudi and I. Manolescu. Cloud-based RDF data management. In *Proceedings of the 2014 ACM SIGMOD International Conference on Management of Data*, pages 725–729, New York, NY, USA, 2014. ACM.

[19] L. Ma, Y. Yang, Z. Qiu, G. Xie, Y. Pan, and S. Liu. Towards a complete OWL ontology benchmark. In *Proceedings of the 3rd European Conference on The Semantic Web*, ESWC'06, pages 125–139, Berlin, Heidelberg, 2006. Springer-Verlag.

[20] P. Macko, D. Margo, and M. Seltzer. Performance introspection of graph databases. In *Proceedings of the 6th International Systems and Storage Conference*, page 18. ACM, 2013.

[21] N. Martínez-Bazan, V. Muntés-Mulero, S. Gómez-Villamor, J. Nin, M.-A. Sánchez-Martínez, and J.-L. Larriba-Pey. DEX: High-performance exploration on large graphs for information retrieval. In *Proceedings of the Sixteenth ACM Conference on Conference on Information and Knowledge Management*, CIKM '07, pages 573–582, New York, NY, USA, 2007. ACM.

[22] M. Morsey, J. Lehmann, S. Auer, and A.-C. N. Ngomo. DBpedia SPARQL benchmark–performance assessment with real queries on real data. In *The Semantic Web–ISWC 2011*, pages 454–469. Springer, 2011.

[23] R. C. Murphy, K. B. Wheeler, B. W. Barrett, and J. A. Ang. Introducing the graph 500. *Cray Users Group (CUG)*, 2010.

[24] T. Neumann and G. Weikum. RDF-3X: A RISC-style engine for RDF. *Proc. VLDB Endow.*, 1(1):647–659, Aug. 2008.

[25] T. Neumann and G. Weikum. x-RDF-3X: Fast querying, high update rates, and consistency for RDF databases. *Proc. VLDB Endow.*, 3(1-2):256–263, Sept. 2010.

[26] K. Nitta and I. Savnik. Survey of RDF storage managers. In *DBKDA 2014, The Sixth International Conference on Advances in Databases, Knowledge, and Data Applications*, pages 148–153, 2014.

[27] N. Papailiou, I. Konstantinou, D. Tsoumakos, and N. Koziris. H2RDF: Adaptive query processing on RDF data in the cloud. In *Proceedings of the 21st International Conference Companion on World Wide Web*, WWW '12 Companion, pages 397–400, New York, NY, USA, 2012. ACM.

[28] N. Papailiou, D. Tsoumakos, I. Konstantinou, P. Karras, and N. Koziris. H2RDF+: an efficient data management system for big RDF graphs. In *Proceedings of the ACM SIGMOD International Conference on Management of Data, SIGMOD 2014, Snowbird, Utah, USA on June 22-27, 2014*. ACM, 2014.

[29] M. Rodríguez-Muro, R. Kontchakov, and M. Zakharyaschev. Ontology-based data access: Ontop of databases. In *International Semantic Web Conference, ISWC 2013*, pages 558–573. Springer, 2013.

[30] S. S. Sahoo, W. Halb, S. Hellmann, K. Idehen, S. Auer, J. Sequeda, and A. Ezzat. A survey of current approaches for mapping of relational databases to RDF. *W3C RDB2RDF XG Incubator Report*, 2009.

[31] S. Sakr and G. Al-Naymat. Relational processing of RDF queries: a survey. *ACM SIGMOD Record*, 38(4):23–28, 2010.

[32] M. Schmidt, T. Hornung, G. Lausen, and C. Pinkel. SP2Bench: a SPARQL performance benchmark. In *Data Engineering, 2009. ICDE'09. IEEE 25th International Conference on*, pages 222–233. IEEE, 2009.

[33] M. Schmidt, M. Meier, and G. Lausen. Foundations of SPARQL query optimization. In *Proceedings of the 13th International Conference on Database Theory*, ICDT '10, pages 4–33, New York, NY, USA, 2010. ACM.

[34] M. Stocker, A. Seaborne, A. Bernstein, C. Kiefer, and D. Reynolds. SPARQL basic graph pattern optimization using selectivity estimation. In *Proceedings of the 17th International Conference on World Wide Web*, WWW '08, pages 595–604, New York, NY, USA, 2008. ACM.

[35] Tinkerpop. Blueprints. Available: https://github.com/tinkerpop/blueprints/wiki, 2014.

[36] Tinkerpop. Gremlin pipes. Available: https://github.com/tinkerpop/pipes/wiki, 2014.

[37] Tinkerpop. Gremlin query language. Available: https://github.com/tinkerpop/gremlin/wiki, 2014.

[38] K. Wilkinson, C. Sayers, H. A. Kuno, and D. Reynolds. Efficient RDF Storage and Retrieval in Jena2. In *Semantic Web and Databases Workshop*, pages 131–150, 2003.

[39] P. Yuan, P. Liu, B. Wu, H. Jin, W. Zhang, and L. Liu. Triplebit: A fast and compact system for large scale RDF data. *Proc. VLDB Endow.*, 6(7):517–528, May 2013.

APPENDIX

A. GREMLIN TRANSLATION IN DETAIL

As described in section 4.3, Gremlin queries can be translated into SQL queries (CTEs) or stored procedure calls (SPs) based on a set of pre-defined templates. Table 8 gives a full list of Gremlin pipes that are currently supported by our query translator and the corresponding CTE templates. Here we only include the templates for the basic form of the pipes. Possible variations and combinations of the pipe translation have been discussed in section 4.

B. SPARQL TO GREMLIN QUERY CONVERSION

As described in section 5.1, our first DBPedia Gremlin query set was converted from the SPARQL queries used in [22]. Given the declarative nature of the SPARQL queries, we tried to implement each of the SPARQL query using graph traversals in Gremlin as efficient as possible. More specifically, we first identify the most selective URI as the Gremlin start pipe, and then use Gremlin transform pipes to implement the SPARQL triple patterns. Note that the traversal order of the transform pipes is also based on the selectivity of the different triple patterns. SPARQL filters are directly translated into Gremlin filter pipes, and SPARQL UNION operations are translated into Gremlin branch pipes if possible. In addition, the translated Gremlin queries will only return the size of the result set of the corresponding SPARQL queries, to minimize the result set composing and consumption differences of the different property graph stores.

Table 9 gives an example of SPARQL query to Gremlin query translation (dq2 in section 5.1). It can be seen that the URI *'http://dbpedia.org/ontology/Person'* is used in the start pipe to lookup the start vertex. Then the property filter pipe applies on the most selective literal *"Montreal Carabins"@en.* The out pipe and back pipe are used to traverse the graph. Two table pipes are used to store the results of the main branch and the optional branch. Ideally, the outer left join of the two tables generates the desired results of the original SPARQL query. However, due to the lack of built-in table operation support in Gremlin language, we directly return the sizes of the both tables in the translated Gremlin query.

Language	Query

SPARQL	PREFIX rdfs:
	<http://www.w3.org/2000/01/rdf-schema#>
	PREFIX dbpedia-owl: <http://dbpedia.org/ontology/>
	PREFIX foaf: <http://xmlns.com/foaf/0.1/>
	PREFIX dbpedia-prop: <http://dbpedia.org/property/>
	PREFIX rdf:
	<http://www.w3.org/1999/02/22-rdf-syntax-ns#>
	SELECT ?var4 ?var8 ?var10
	WHERE {
	?var5 dbpedia-owl:thumbnail ?var4 ;
	rdf:type dbpedia-owl:Person ;
	rdfs:label "Montreal Carabins"@en ;
	dbpedia-prop:pageurl ?var8 .
	OPTIONAL { ?var5 foaf:homepage ?var10 . }
	}

Gremlin	t1=new Table();
	t2=new Table();
	var5=[];
	g.V("_URI_", "http://dbpedia.org/ontology/Person").in('http://www.w3.org/1999/02/22-rdf-syntax-ns#type').has('http://www.w3.org/2000/01/rdf-schema#label','"Montreal Carabins"@en').aggregate(var5).as('var5').out('http://dbpedia.org/ontology/thumbnail').as('var4').back(1)
	.out('http://dbpedia.org/property/pageurl').as('var8')
	.table(t1).iterate();
	var5._().as('var5').out('http://xmlns.com/foaf/0.1/homepage').as('var10').table(t2).iterate();
	[t1.size(),t2.size()];

Table 9: An example of SPARQL to Gremlin query conversion.

Operation	CTE Template for Query Translation
out pipe	(t_0, SELECT t.val FROM $\underline{t_{in}}$ v,OPA p, TABLES(VALUES($p.val_0$), ... ,($p.val_n$))AS t(val) WHERE v.val=p.vid AND t.val is not null), (t_1,SELECT COALESCE(s.val, p.val) AS val FROM t_0 p LEFT OUTER JOIN OSA s on p.val=s.valid)
in pipe	(t_0, SELECT t.val FROM $\underline{t_{in}}$ v,IPA p, TABLES(VALUES($p.val_0$), ... ,($p.val_m$))AS t(val) WHERE v.val=p.vid AND t.val is not null), (t_1,SELECT COALESCE(s.val, p.val) AS val FROM t_0 p LEFT OUTER JOIN ISA s on p.val=s.valid)
both pipe	(t_0, SELECT t.val FROM $\underline{t_{in}}$ v,OPA p, TABLES(VALUES($p.val_0$), ... ,($p.val_n$))AS t(val) WHERE v.val=p.vid AND t.val is not null), (t_1, SELECT COALESCE(s.val, p.val) AS val FROM t_0 p LEFT OUTER JOIN OSA s on p.val=s.valid), (t_2, SELECT t.val FROM $\underline{t_{in}}$ v,IPA p, TABLES(VALUES($p.val_0$), ... ,($p.val_m$))AS t(val) WHERE v.val=p.vid AND t.val is not null), (t_3,SELECT COALESCE(s.val, p.val) AS val FROM t_2 p LEFT OUTER JOIN ISA s on p.val=s.valid), (t_4,SELECT * FROM t_1 UNION ALL SELECT * FROM t_3)
out vertex pipe	(t_0, SELECT p.outv AS val FROM $\underline{t_{in}}$ v, EA p WHERE v.val=p.eid)
in vertex pipe	(t_0, SELECT p.inv AS val FROM $\underline{t_{in}}$ v, EA p WHERE v.val=p.eid)
both vertex pipe	(t_0, SELECT t.val FROM $\underline{t_{in}}$ v, EA p, TABLES(VALUES($p.outv$), ($p.inv$)) AS t(val) WHERE v.val=p.eid)
out edges pipe	(t_0, SELECT p.eid AS val FROM $\underline{t_{in}}$ v, EA p WHERE v.val=p.outv)
in edges pipe	(t_0, SELECT p.eid AS val FROM $\underline{t_{in}}$ v, EA p WHERE v.val=p.inv)
both edges pipe	(t_0, SELECT p.eid AS val FROM $\underline{t_{in}}$ v, EA p WHERE v.val=p.outv OR v.val=p.inv)
range filter pipe	(t_0, SELECT * FROM $\underline{t_{in}}$ v LIMIT ? OFFSET ?)
duplicate filter pipe	(t_0, SELECT DISTINCT v.val FROM $\underline{t_{in}}$ v)
id filter pipe	(t_0, SELECT * FROM $\underline{t_{in}}$ v WHERE v.val == ?)
property filter pipe	(t_0, SELECT v.* FROM $\underline{t_{in}}$ v, VA p WHERE v.val=p.vid AND JSON_VAL(p.data, ?) == ?)
interval filter pipe	(t_0, SELECT v.* FROM $\underline{t_{in}}$ v, VA p WHERE v.val=p.vid AND JSON_VAL(p.data, ?) > ? AND JSON_VAL(p.data, ?) < ?)
label filter pipe	(t_0, SELECT v.* FROM $\underline{t_{in}}$ v, EA p WHERE v.val=p.eid AND p.lbl == ?)
except filter pipe	(t_0, SELECT * FROM $\underline{t_{in}}$ v WHERE v.val NOT IN (SELECT p.val FROM t_k p))
retain filter pipe	(t_0, SELECT * FROM $\underline{t_{in}}$ v WHERE v.val IN (SELECT p.val FROM t_k p))
cyclic path filter pipe	(t_0, SELECT * FROM $\underline{t_{in}}$ v WHERE isSimplePath(v.path) == 1)
back filter pipe	$meta.cte$ ∪ (t_0, SELECT * FROM $\underline{t_{in}}$ v WHERE v.val IN (SELECT p.path[0] FROM $meta.t_{out}$ p))
and filter pipe	$meta1.cte$ ∪ $meta2.cte$ ∪ (t_0, SELECT * FROM $\underline{t_{in}}$ v WHERE v.val IN (SELECT p.path[0] FROM $meta1.t_{out}$ p1 INTERSECT SELECT p.path[0] FROM $meta2.t_{out}$ p2))
or filter pipe	$meta1.cte$ ∪ $meta2.cte$ ∪ (t_0, SELECT * FROM $\underline{t_{in}}$ v WHERE v.val IN (SELECT p.path[0] FROM $meta1.t_{out}$ p1 UNION SELECT p.path[0] FROM $meta2.t_{out}$ p2))
if-then-else pipe	$test.cte$ ∪ $\{thencte_{in}, elsecte_{in}\}$ ∪ $then.cte$ ∪ $else.cte$ ∪ (t_{out}, SELECT * FROM then.out UNION ALL SELECT * FROM else.out)
split-merge pipe	$meta1.cte$ ∪ $meta2.cte$ ∪ (t_0, SELECT * FROM $meta1.t_{out}$ p1 UNION ALL SELECT * FROM $meta2.t_{out}$ p2)
loop pipe	expand to fixed-length ctes or call stored procedure
as pipe	∅, record the mapping between the as pipe and the (t_{out}) of the current translated ctes
aggregate pipe	∅, record the mapping between the aggregate pipe and the (t_{out}) of the current translated ctes
add vertex	∅, call stored procedure
add edge	∅, call stored procedure
delete vertex	∅, call stored procedure
delete edge	∅, call stored procedure

Table 8: Currently supported Gremlin pipes and the translation method. "?" denotes the parameters of the pipes.

Updating Graph Indices with a One-Pass Algorithm

Dayu Yuan [*‡], Prasenjit Mitra [†‡], Huiwen Yu [‡] and C. Lee Giles [‡]
[‡] The Pennsylvania State University [†] Qatar Computing Research Institute
dayyyuan@gmail.com, pmitra@qf.org.qa, huy117@psu.edu, giles@ist.psu.edu

ABSTRACT

Indices are commonly built into graph databases in order to support fast searches. Any given graph database and the distribution of queries will change over time. Therefore, the cost of processing queries using a static graph index increases because the index is built to optimize old snapshots of the database. There is growing research interest in determining how to update a graph index with the purpose of adapting to database and query changes. Updating features in a graph index is typically an NP-hard problem. In addition, because the features are chosen from a large number of frequent subgraphs, a multi-pass algorithm is not scalable to big datasets. In order to address this issue, we propose a time-efficient *one-pass algorithm* that is designed to update a graph index by scanning each frequent subgraph at most once. The algorithm replaces a feature with a new subgraph if the latter is "better" than the former one. We use the branch and bound technique to skip subgraphs that cannot outperform any of the features in the graph index. We further use a decomposed index and reduce the space complexity from $O(|G||Q|)$ to $O(|G| + |Q|)$, where G is database graphs and Q is a query workload. Through the empirical study, we show that the one-pass algorithm is 5–100 times faster than all previous algorithms for updating graph indices. In addition, the one-pass algorithm guarantees the return of a close to optimum solution. Our experiments show that when the one-pass algorithm is used to update an index, the query-processing speed is 1–2 times faster than that of other cutting-edge indices, i.e., the FGindex and the gIndex.

1. INTRODUCTION

Many chemical molecules, images, and CAD mechanical parts are modeled as graphs in scientific and commercial fields. [3, 22, 8]. The *subgraph search* and the *supergraph search* are two of the most popular query scenarios in graph databases. The subgraph search returns database graphs that contain the query as a subgraph [24], whereas the *supergraph search* returns database graphs with the query as a supergraph [3]. The subgraph isomorphism problem (SGI), which determines whether a database graph is a subgraph or a supergraph of a query, is an NP-complete problem [14]. It is time-consuming to compare a query with each database graph. In a considerable number of studies, researchers have tried to reduce the complexity of the problem by building *graph indices* to filter out false graphs so that the query is compared with only the remaining graphs [3, 4, 18, 24, 27]. A graph index is defined as a map from a feature f to the ids of the database graphs that contain f. A feature is a frequent subgraph in the database graphs.

[*]Current affiliation: Google

SIGMOD'15, May 31–June 4, 2015, Melbourne, Victoria, Australia.

http://dx.doi.org/10.1145/2723372.2746482.

EXAMPLE 1.1. *Figure 1(a) shows a database G_0 with 4 graphs $\{g', g'', g_1, g_2\}$ and an index I_0 built for G_0. I_0 has two features f_1 and f_2. Given a subgraph-search query q, f_1 filters out graphs $\{g'', g_2\}$. This is because f_1 is a subgraph of q and not a subgraph of either g'' or g_2. Thus, q cannot be a subgraph of either g'' or g_2. For the same reason, f_2 filters out graph $\{g', g_2\}$ for query q. After $\{g', g'', g_2\}$ are removed, it is sufficient to compare q and g_1 using one subgraph isomorphism test (SGI).*

In previous studies, graph indices are built by mining subgraph features from a snapshot of the graph database [3, 4, 18, 24, 27]. However database graphs and queries in real-life applications change over time. For example, almost 4000 graphs are added to the SCI finder database every day [28]. Since the graph database changes over time, features mined from the outdated database are not optimal for pruning false graphs from the new database.

EXAMPLE 1.2. *In Figure 1(b), the database removes two graphs $\{g', g''\}$ and adds two new graphs $\{g_3, g_4\}$. We refer to the new graph database as G_1. It is straightforward to remove g''s id from the graph index when g' is removed from the graph database. Also, when g_3 is added to the graph database, it is easy to find the features in g_3 and add g_3 as their supergraph in the graph index [25]. For the same query q, features f_1 and f_2 only prune g_2 from the new graph database. q must to be compared with three graphs $\{g_1, g_3, g_4\}$. This is because f_1 and f_2 are not optimized to prune graphs from G_1.*

When features are updated, the index becomes more attuned to the current database and query workload. Consequently, the performance of processing queries will improve. In most research to date [3, 4, 24, 27], the only solution proposed for updating features is that of re-mining the whole index afresh. To rebuild the index, such algorithms first mine all the frequent subgraphs and store them in memory, and then select k features from the frequent subgraphs by scanning each frequent subgraph multiple times [3, 4, 24, 26, 27]. This is both memory-consuming and time-consuming because the number of frequent subgraphs in real databases is usually very large [22]. In this paper, we propose a **one-pass** streaming algorithm to update features. The algorithm scans each frequent subgraph at most once. It mines a new subgraph h from the graph database by using a DFS coder [24] and replaces a feature f (a sub-

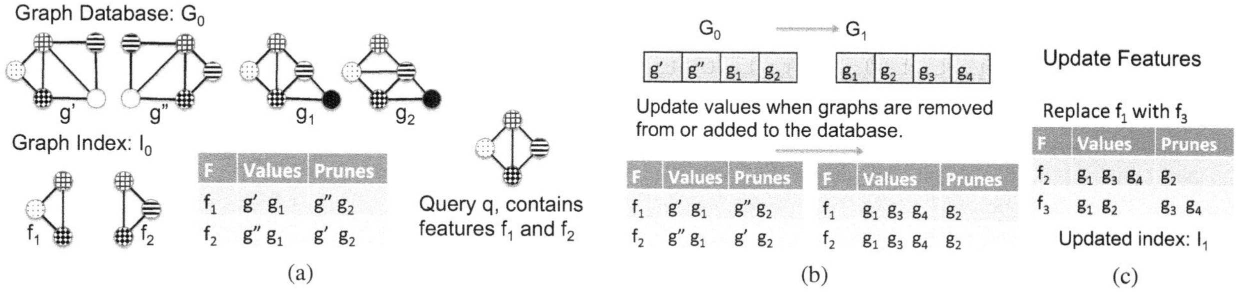

Figure 1: (a) Graph database and graph index (b) Changes of graph database (c) Update features

graph used for indexing) with h if h is "better" than f. The swap is determined by a swapping criterion.

EXAMPLE 1.3. *In Figure 1(c), the one-pass algorithm replaces feature f_1 with a new subgraph f_3. For query q, f_2 and f_3 filter out false graphs $\{g_2, g_3, g_4\}$. It is sufficient to compare q and g_1 using a SGI test. The number of SGI tests decreases from 3 (in Figure 1(b)) to 1.*

In comparison to previous feature-mining algorithms, the one-pass algorithm has the following advantages. *Firstly, it guarantees the return of a close to optimum solution.* We show in Section 3 that mining features to maximize the pruning power of a graph index can be modeled as a *maximum-coverage* problem for both subgraph and supergraph searches. The maximum-coverage problem is NP-hard. We prove that the one-pass algorithm has an approximation ratio of $1/4$ with a specially designed swapping criterion, which decides whether or not to replace an old feature with a new frequent subgraph. Most of the previous feature-mining algorithms are based on heuristics, and they do not have a theoretical approximation guarantee. Our experiment shows that the index updated with the one-pass algorithm outperforms two cutting-edge indices built afresh using heuristics-based algorithms, i.e., the gIndex and the FG-index (see Section 7). In addition, the one-pass algorithm *incrementally* updates the graph index. Each swap improves the performance of the graph index. Further, the graph index is always valid and can be used to process incoming queries during the index update.

Secondly, the one-pass algorithm is time-efficient. There is a traditional polynomial-time greedy algorithm for the maximum-coverage problem with an approximation ratio $1 - 1/e$ [3]. In updating the index, the greedy algorithm first mines all the frequent subgraphs and stores them in memory [3]. To find k features, the greedy algorithm must scan each frequent subgraph k times (see Section 3.3 for details). Hence, this approach is not time-efficient. *In one experiment, we used a dataset with* $40,000$ *graphs downloaded from www.emolecules.com. We found more than* 5×10^6 *frequent subgraphs by mining with a minimum support of* 0.01. *To select* $k = 10,000$ *features, the greedy algorithm scans the* 5×10^6 *subgraphs* $10,000$ *times, and takes more than* 10 *hours to finish the computation.* The one-pass algorithm is a streaming algorithm that scans each subgraph at most once. It takes much less memory and time than the greedy algorithm. In addition, we use the branch and bound technique to reduce the number of frequent subgraphs (see Section 5.1). We mine frequent subgraphs using a DFS coder [24], which extends a subgraph h' with an edge e and generates a subgraph $h = h' \circ e$. Before h is generated from the DFS coder, we estimate an upper bound of the pruning power of h. If the upper bound does not meet the swapping criterion of the one-pass algorithm, we can safely skip generating subgraph h, thereby reducing the number of frequent subgraphs.

We further optimize the running time of the one-pass algorithm with a new swapping criterion. Two swapping criteria have been studied theoretically for the maximum-coverage problem [1, 16]. However, neither of these criteria performs well on updating graph features. We found that one criterion [16], $swap_1$, is too loose in that it causes features to be frequently swapped in and out of the index. Hence, the algorithm is time-consuming. The second criterion [1], $swap_2$, is too strict, such that it fails to select enough frequent subgraphs with high pruning power because many subgraphs do not meet its very strict swapping criterion. We propose an adjustable swapping criterion to prevent the algorithm from becoming trapped in the local optimum. We also show that the adjustable swapping criterion has an approximation ratio $1/4$. The one-pass algorithm with the new swapping criterion runs as fast as that using $swap_2$. Further, the features mined by using the new swapping criterion have high pruning power on filtering out false graphs.

Finally, the one-pass algorithm is space-efficient. It does not need to pre-mine or store all the frequent subgraphs in memory. The default space required by the algorithm to compute the pruning power is $O(|G| \times |Q|)$, where G is the graph database and Q is a query set. This is not scalable for large datasets. We propose to use a decomposed index to record the pruning status for each $q_i \in Q$ and $g_j \in G$ separately and to compute the pruning status for (q_i, g_j) by a set minus operation (see Section 5.2). The decomposed index reduces the memory complexity to $O(k(|G| + |Q|))$ for updating an index of k features.

Organization: We summarize related work in Section 2. Then, we formally define the feature-update problem in Section 3. In Section 4, we introduce the one-pass algorithm designed to solve the feature-update problem. We introduce different techniques to reduce the running time and space complexity of the one-pass algorithm in Section 5. We evaluate the empirical performance of the one-pass algorithm in Section 7. Finally, we offer a conclusion in Section 8.

2. RELATED WORK

A graph $g = (V, E, L)$ is a triple that contains a set of vertices V, a set of edges E such that $E \subseteq V \times V$, and a set of labels L. Two graphs $g_1 = (V_1, E_1, L_1)$ and $g_2 = (V_2, E_2, L_2)$ are isomorphic if there is a bijection between V_1 and V_2 that preserves the labels and connectivity of the two graphs. A graph $h(V', E', L)$ is **subgraph isomorphic** to $g(V, E, L)$ if h is isomorphic to one of g's subgraphs. In this paper, we refer to h as a **subgraph** of g. Also, g is a **supergraph** of h, $g \supset h$. Index features are commonly mined from *frequent subgraphs* of a graph database:

DEFINITION 1 (FREQUENT SUBGRAPHS). *In graph database G, the* **supporting set** *of subgraph h, $G(h)$, comprises graphs that contain h as a subgraph. A subgraph h is* **frequent** *if and only if $|G(h)| > \sigma|G|$, where σ is a tunable parameter referred to as* **minimum support**.

2.1 Feature-Mining Algorithms

There are two types of algorithms for the index-feature mining problem: batch algorithms and direct-mining algorithms. **Batch algorithms** first mine and store all frequent subgraphs H and then select k features from H [3, 24, 4]. In order to prevent any interesting subgraphs from being missed, a batch algorithm usually sets a very small minimum support σ. It has been shown that in a chemical molecule dataset (the AIDS dataset), the growth of the number of frequent subgraphs has a power-law relationship with the decrease of the minimum support [26]. As discussed in many related works [22, 10, 11, 21], batch algorithms are both time-and memory-consuming, because they mine and store a large number of frequent subgraphs and their supporting sets.

Direct-mining algorithms have been proposed as a way to prevent mining and storing all the frequent subgraphs [22, 21, 13]. To search for an optimum feature, a direct-mining algorithm mines many frequent subgraphs (and their supporting sets), but does not store them in memory. This kind of algorithm only mines a small number of frequent subgraphs because of the use of pruning techniques like the branch and bound technique [21, 13] and the jump search [22]. Heuristic-based algorithms, such as the evolutionary computation algorithm GAIA [11], are also proposed to further reduce the search space for an optimum feature [26, 10, 15]. Mining one feature with direct-mining algorithms is much faster than using batch algorithms [22, 21, 13]. However, a direct-mining algorithm has to run k times to find k features [22, 26, 21]; therefore, frequent subgraphs and their supporting sets are computed multiple times. Hence, direct-mining algorithms are not scalable for large ks. In a recent version of CORK [21], Thoma et al. showed that mining k features with a direct-mining algorithm can take longer than doing the same with a batch algorithm [20].

2.2 Mining Features for Indexing

A comprehensive review shows that the feature-based graph index works best for graph searches in comparison to other indices, e.g., tree-like indices [9]. A feature-base graph index is built as follows: the algorithm first mines a set of features F from the dataset, and then builds an inverted index with $f \in F$ as a key and $G(f)$ as the value ($G(f)$ defined in Definition 1). For the subgraph search, the gIndex mines discriminative and frequent subgraphs for indexing [24]. A frequent subgraph h' is discriminative if and only if $|\bigcap_{h \subset h', h \in H} G(h)|/|G(h')| > \gamma$. The QuickSI mines discriminative and frequent subtrees for indexing [18]. The FG-index mines δ-TCFG subgraphs for indexing [4]. A frequent subgraph h' is δ-TCFG if and only if $\forall h \supset h'$ and $|G(h)|/|G(h')| < 1 - \delta$. The heuristic-based algorithms discussed above all select index features with the goal of reducing redundancies among the index features. Sun, Mitra, and Giles proposed a forward feature-mining algorithm with a rigorously defined objective function, MimR, which measures both the cumulative information gain and pairwise redundancies of index features [19]. However, the quality of the features mined with the forward feature-mining algorithm have no theoretical guarantee. For the supergraph search, Chen et al. mined index features by reducing the problem to a maximum-coverage (with cost) problem [3]. Zhang et al. proposed a heuristic-based algorithm to mine significant subgraphs for indexing [27]. A frequent subgraph h' is significant if and only if $|G(h')|/|\bigcup_{h \in H, h \supset h'} G(h)| \geq \sigma_{min}$. The algorithms discussed above are all batch algorithms. Yuan et al. proposed a direct-mining algorithm to update graph indices for the subgraph search [26].

Table 1 summarizes the feature-mining algorithm in previous works. The gIndex [24], FGindex [4] and cIndex [3] are all batch algorithms. Each of these algorithms mines and stores the whole set of frequent subgraphs H in memory (column 2), and each mines H only once (column 3). The gIndex [24] and the FGindex [4] select features based on heuristics; hence, they do not guarantee the return of a close to optimum solution (column 4). The greedy approximation algorithm used in the cIndex [3] has an approximation ratio $1 - 1/e$. CORK [21] and SubUpdate [26] are both direct-mining algorithms. Neither algorithm mines or stores the whole set of frequent subgraphs (column 2), but each mines frequent subgraphs k times to find k features (column 3). Both algorithms are constant factor approximation algorithms (column 4). GAIA [11] uses a randomized searching strategy to find the optimal solution, which simulates biological evolution. But it has no theoretical guarantee. The one-pass algorithm in this paper is a streaming algorithm, which only mines and scans each frequent subgraph at most once (column 3). Therefore, there is no need to either pre-mine or to store all the frequent subgraphs (column 2). Also, the one-pass algorithm has an approximation ratio of $1/4$ (column 4). In addition, only SubUpdate [26] and the one-pass algorithm update graph indices (column 5).

Table 1: Related Work on Feature Mining

Algorithm	Mine and store H	Mine times	Near optimal	Updatable
gIndex [24]	yes	**one**	no	no
FGindex [4]	yes	**one**	no	no
cIndex [3]	yes	**one**	**yes**	no
CORK [21]	**no**	multi	**yes**	no
GAIA [11]	**no**	**one**	no	no
SubUpdate [26]	**no**	multi	**yes**	**yes**
One-pass	**no**	**one**	**yes**	**yes**

2.3 Maximum Coverage

In this paper, we correlate the index-feature mining problem with the maximum-coverage problem.

DEFINITION 2 (MAXIMUM COVERAGE). *Given a ground set of elements $U = \{e_1, e_2, ...e_n\}$, a collection of sets $S = \{s_1, s_2, ... s_m\}$ on U, and a number k, find a sub-collection $S' \subseteq S$ such that $|\bigcup_{s_i \in S'} s_i|$ is maximized and $|S'| \leq k$.*

The maximum-coverage problem and a related problem, *set-cover*, are NP-hard problems [6]. A greedy algorithm is commonly used to solve both problems, whereby the greedy algorithm selects the set that maximizes the increase of item coverage in each iteration. The greedy algorithm has an approximation ratio $1 - 1/e$ for the maximum-coverage problem [12]. On a small dataset, the greedy algorithm runs fast especially with an auxiliary index. However, it is not scalable to large datasets. Cormode, Karloff, and Wirth proposed a disc-based greedy algorithm for the set-cover problem with an approximation ratio of $1 + p\ln(|U|)$ by first assigning sets to different buckets (p is a parameter controlling the size of the buckets) [7]. Chierichett, Kumar, and Tomkin proposed a map-reduce algorithm to solve the set-cover problem [5]. Although both algorithms address the scalability issue for the maximum-coverage problem, neither can be directly applied to updating index features. This is because each must mine the whole set of frequent subgraph features H, which is prohibitively space-consuming and time-consuming for the index update task.

The maximum-coverage problem has also been studied in a streaming scenario, in which each set is accessed only once. Saha and Getoor proposed a swap-based algorithm with an approximation ratio of $1/4$ [16]. k sets are first selected and stored in memory. For each set from the input, the algorithm determines whether to discard it or swap it with a selected set. Ausiello et al. introduced a similar swap-based algorithm with a different swap criterion [1]. The algorithm also has an approximation ratio of $1/4$ [1]. However, as we show in Section 4.2.1, neither swap criterion can be used to update graph indices: [16] is too loose, and [1] is too strict.

Table 2 lists the symbols and terms used in this paper.

Table 2: Symbols and Terms

g, G	database graphs
q, Q	query graphs
f, F	index features
h, H_σ	frequent subgraphs with min support σ
$G(h), Q(h)$	supporting set of frequent subgraph h

3. PROBLEM FORMULATION

In this section, we begin by introducing the framework of maintaining a graph database. Then, we formally define the feature-update problem, which is a key component of database maintenance. We further show that the traditional greedy algorithm is time-and memory-consuming and cannot be directly applied to updating graph indices. We focus on studying subgraph-search indices in this section. For the supergraph search problem, please refer to Appendix A.

3.1 Graph Database Framework

Graph databases use **filter + verify** algorithms to answer subgraph-search queries [3, 24, 4, 18, 27, 25]. The algorithm first **filters out** false graphs and then **verifies** each remaining graph with a subgraph isomorphism test. Verifying the remaining graphs is time-consuming because the subgraph isomorphism test is an NP-hard problem. Hence, it is essential to maximize the number of removed graphs to reduce the query-processing time. Many algorithms have been studied to mine features and build a graph index for fast query processing [3, 24, 4, 18, 27, 25] (lines 1 and 2 of Algorithm 1).

Algorithm 1 Graph Database Maintenance

Input: G
1: Mine index features F from G
2: Build a graph index I using F, (I is in shared memory)
   $I \leftarrow$ map(key $= f \in F$, value $= G(f)$ids)
3: **while** Receive a request R **do**
4:   **if** $R =$ process query q **then**
5:     Candidates $\leftarrow G\setminus$ false graphs
6:     **for all** g in Candidates **do**
7:       **if** SubgraphIsoTest(g, q) = True **then**
8:         Answer$\leftarrow$ Answer + g
9:       **end if**
10:     **end for**
11:     Send Answer
12:   **else if** $R =$ add (remove) a graph g to (from) G **then**
13:     **for all** $f \in F, f \subset g$ **do**
14:       $G \leftarrow G + g$ or $G \leftarrow G - g$
15:       Add (remove) g's id to (from) f's value in I.
16:     **end for**
17:   **end if**
18:   **if** F is outdated due to database or query changes **then**
19:     fork a new process to update features
20:     $(I, F) \leftarrow$ One-Pass Algorithm(G, Q, I, F), where Q is a query workload.
21:   **end if**
22: **end while**

The index is a map with a feature f as key, and the value of key f is the ids of database graphs that contain f as a subgraph. We put the index in shared memory so that it can be updated by a child process forked from the parent process. The index I listens to the next request R. If R is a query-processing request, the algorithm answers the query by first pruning false graphs and then verifying each remaining graph using a subgraph isomorphism test (lines 4 to 11). Otherwise, if R is to insert a new graph g into G, the algorithm first adds g to the graph database (line 14) and then appends g's id to each index feature $f \subset g$. A reverse operation can be performed to remove graph g from G. To handle the request of updating a graph $g \in G$ to g', the algorithm first delete g and then add g' to the graph database.

After changes of this graph database have taken places, features mined from the outdated database are not optimal for pruning false graphs from the new database. When the performance of the graph index has degraded significantly, the algorithm forks a process to update the index features using a one-pass algorithm (Algorithm 2). We introduce the one-pass algorithm in Section 4.

3.2 Updating Index Features

In this section, we introduce the notion of *pruning power* as a measure of the goodness of index features. Then, we formally define the feature update problem.

For the subgraph-search problem, an **inclusive logic** is proposed to filter out false graphs [4, 18, 24, 25]: given index features F, a graph g cannot be query q's supergraph (can be filtered out) if $\exists f \in F, f \subset q$, and $f \not\subset g$. In other words, for a query q, an index feature $f \subset q$ filters out $G \setminus G(f)$.

DEFINITION 3 (PRUNING POWER AND COVER). *We define the pruning power of a feature f as the cardinality of f's pruning cover, $C(f, G, Q)$,*

$$C(f, G, Q) = \{(q, g) | g \text{ is filtered out by feature } f \text{ for } q\} \quad (1)$$

For the subgraph search[1],

$$C(f, G, Q) = \{(g, q) | f \subset q \wedge f \not\subset g \text{ or } f \equiv q\}. \quad (2)$$

We further define the pruning cover of F as the union of the pruning cover of $f \in F, \forall f$. $C(F, G, Q) = \cup_{f \in F} C(f, G, Q)$.

When G and Q are clear from the context, we simplify $C(f, G, Q)$ to $C(f)$.

EXAMPLE 3.1. *Figure 2(b) shows the pruning cover of the features from the graph index in Figure 2(a). For example, feature f_1 filters out g_2 for queries q_1, q_2, and q_4. Also, for query q_1, graphs $\{g_2, g_3, g_4\}$ are filtered out by features in F. (Note that the third column in Figure 2(a) is not part of the graph index.)*

DEFINITION 4 (THE FEATURE UPDATE PROBLEM). *Given a graph database G, a set of queries Q, and a graph index I_0 with outdated features F_0, update F_0 to F with the goal of maximizing the pruning power of the index:*

$$F = argmax_F |C(F, G, Q)| \quad (3)$$

STATEMENT 1. *Feature Update $\equiv_p$ maximum-coverage.*

PROOF. According to the definition of pruning cover, each (q, g) pair is an element e and the pruning cover is a set of (q, g) pairs. It is easy to see that finding k features to maximize the pruning power of the index is equivalent to the maximum-coverage problem defined in Definition 2. □

[1] If a query $q \equiv f$, the index will directly return the answer $G(q) \equiv G(f)$. Hence, no verification is needed. We treat this as filtering out all graphs.

Graph Index

Key	G(f)	Q(f)
f_1	g_1, g_3, g_4	q_1, q_2, q_4
f_2	g_1, g_2	q_1, q_3
f_3	g_1, g_3	q_2
f_4	g_2, g_3	q_2, q_4
f_5	g_4	q_4

(a)

Q	q_1				q_2				q_3				q_4			
G	g_1	g_2	g_3	g_4	g_1	g_2	g_3	g_4	g_1	g_2	g_3	g_4	g_1	g_2	g_3	g_4
$C(f_1)$		1				1								1		
$C(f_2)$			1	1							1	1				
$C(f_3)$						1		1								
$C(f_4)$					1			1					1			1
$C(f_5)$													1	1	1	
$C(F_0)$		1	1	1	1	1		1			1	1	1	1	1	1

(b)

Figure 2: (a) Graph index and features supporting set on queries (b) Pruning cover

Discussion: A graph index usually stores k features in memory for indexing because it is not feasible to index all the frequent subgraphs for filtering given limited memory. When the index is updated, it is desirable to keep the same number of index features, $|F_0| = |F|$. Hence, a feature-update algorithm will remove an outdated feature for each newly added feature. We refer to each replacement of an outdated feature with a new feature as a *swap*. There are also cases in which extra features are needed for indexing due to the increase of available memory. To find k' features ($k' > k$), a swap-based algorithm can simply add $k' - k$ frequent subgraphs to F and then gradually update the k' features through numerous swaps.

3.2.1 Feature Update Vs. Feature Selection

The feature update problem has the same goal as the feature selection problem. The major difference between the two is that there is an existing index I_0 with feature F_0 for the feature update problem, whereas the feature selection problem lacks such an index.

Feature-selection algorithms can be used to "update" graph indices by simply ignoring F_0 and building a new index from scratch. However, this approach has two drawbacks. Firstly, most feature-selection algorithms are time-consuming. Instead of utilizing F_0, they select new features from scratch even if the majority of the features in F_0 are still good for indexing. Secondly, feature-selection algorithms do not improve the graph index incrementally. A graph index with a set of partially selected features may not perform as well as I_0 does. In other words, the new features are guaranteed to outperform F_0 only after the feature-selection algorithm completes. The feature-update algorithm (Section 4) we propose in this paper updates features by incrementally swapping a feature $f \in F_0$ with a new subgraph h if $|C(F_0 \setminus \{f\} \cup \{h\})| > |C(F_0)|$. Hence, the pruning power of the graph index increases monotonically. With each swap, the resulting index is guaranteed to outperform the version before the swap took place. Also, the feature-update algorithm runs much faster than the feature-selection algorithm because the former can update F_0 to a close-to-optimum solution after a few swaps, especially when the majority of features in F_0 are good for indexing.

In addition, a feature-update algorithm can build a graph index from scratch by simply picking k random frequent subgraphs as F_0 and gradually updating F_0. We also propose a **hybrid method**, which first mines features with a heuristic-based algorithm, e.g, the gIndex and the FG-index, and then runs the one-pass algorithm (Algorithm 2) to update the index features. Our experiment results show that the hybrid method is fast to run (Figure 11(b)) and the index constructed using the hybrid method has high pruning power (Figure 11(b)).

3.3 A Greedy Solution

The maximum-coverage problem has a greedy solution [3]. The greedy algorithm first mines all frequent subgraphs H_σ and stores H_σ in memory for random access. To select the tth feature (assume that $(t-1)$ features are selected), this algorithm first computes a *score* for each unselected subgraph $h \in H_\sigma$. The score of h is defined as the number of (q, g) pairs that are filtered out by h but not by the $(t-1)$ selected features. That is,

$$score(h) = |C(h) \setminus \cup_{i<t} C(f_i)|. \quad (4)$$

Then, the algorithm picks the frequent subgraph with the highest score. The algorithm computes the scores and picks the maximum-score frequent subgraph iteratively until k features are selected.

This greedy algorithm cannot be used to update real-life dataset, because it is both memory-consuming and time-consuming for the following reasons:

1. The greedy algorithm precomputes and stores all frequent subgraphs H_σ, which is both memory-consuming and time-consuming. The space for storing H_σ and their supporting sets is $O(|H_\sigma|(|G| + |Q|))$, and the time for mining H_σ is $O(|H_\sigma|(|G| + |Q|)T_{SGI})$ where T_{SGI} is the time of a subgraph isomorphism test.
2. The greedy algorithm computes a score for each unselected subgraph $h \in H_\sigma$ in order to select one maximum-score feature. The algorithm takes $O(k|H_\sigma|T_{score})$ time to compute scores for selecting k features, where T_{score} is the time to compute the score for one subgraph. An alternative approach is to update the scores (instead of recomputing them). However, this requires an auxiliary index, which further increases the memory required by the algorithm.
3. The greedy algorithm only selects features forwardly. A feature cannot be removed after being selected. Hence, the greedy algorithm cannot incrementally update index features.

4. THE ONE-PASS ALGORITHM

In this section, we introduce a one-pass algorithm to update features.

The algorithm uses a DFS coder to mine frequent subgraphs [22, 23]. The coder generates subgraphs in a stream according to the depth search order of an immaterialized pattern tree [22, 23].

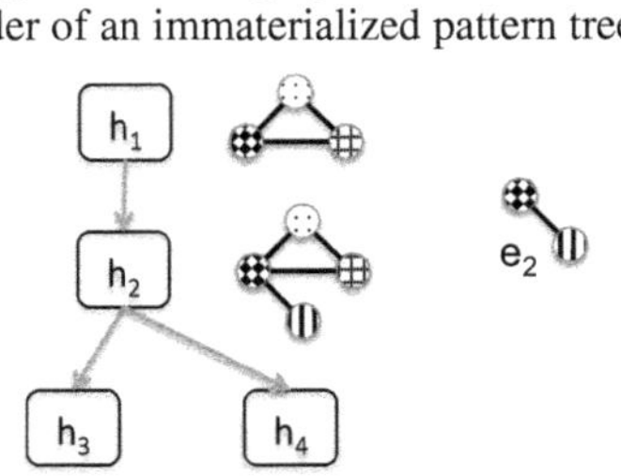

Figure 3: One branch of a pattern tree.

EXAMPLE 4.1. *Figure 3 shows a branch of the pattern tree. The DFS coder first generates a subgraph h_1, then extends h_1 with an edge e_2 to generate $h_2 = h_1 \circ e_2$. Then, the coder generates h_3 and h_4.*

A DFS coder supports the following two functions: (a) $next()$, which generates the next subgraph, and (b) $skip()$, which skips all the offspring of the current subgraph h in the pattern tree.

Algorithm 2 gives the one-pass algorithm in detail. Taking a set of features F_0 as input, the algorithm computes a *loss* score for each feature $f \in F_0$ and then inserts f into a minimum heap.

DEFINITION 5 (LOSS SCORE). *The loss score of a feature f, $L(f, F)$, is the decrease of the pruning power caused by removing f from F:*

$$L(f, F) = |C(f) \setminus C(F \setminus f)|. \tag{5}$$

Figure 4(a) shows the pruning cover of the index in Example 3.1. The loss scores $L(f, F_0)$ for $f \in F_0$ are shown in row 2 of Figure 4(b).

Q	q_1				q_2				q_3				q_4			
G	g_1	g_2	g_3	g_4	g_1	g_2	g_3	g_4	g_1	g_2	g_3	g_4	g_1	g_2	g_3	g_4
$C(F_0)$		1	1	1	1	1		1			1	1	1	1	1	1
$C(h_1)$						1	1							1	1	
$C(F_1)$		1	1	1	1	1	1	1			1	1	1	1	1	1
$C(h_2)$			1	1											1	1

(a)

Features F_0	f_1	f_2	f_3	f_4	f_5			
$L(f, F_0)$	1	4	0	2	1		$\lvert C(F_0)\rvert = 12$	$B(h_1, F_0)=1$
Features F_1	f_1	f_2	h_1	f_4	f_5			
$L(f, F_1)$	1	4	1	3	0		$\lvert C(F_1)\rvert = 13$	$B(h_2, F_0)=0$

(b)

Figure 4: Update features with the one-pass algorithm: (a) Pruning cover (b) Loss and benefit scores.

Algorithm 2 The One-Pass Algorithm

Input: G, Q, Index I_0 with features F_0
Output: Index I with updated features F

1: QUE $\leftarrow$ Min Heap
2: **for all** $f \in F_0$ **do**
3: Compute **loss**, $L(f, F_0)$ (Definition 5)
4: QUE.insert with score(f, $L(f, F_0)$)
5: **end for**
6: $F \leftarrow$ reference of features in QUE
7: Initialize a DFS coder D
8: **while** $h \leftarrow D$.next() **do**
9: Compute the supporting sets $Q(h)$ and $G(h)$
10: Compute **benefit** of h, $B(f) = |C(h) \setminus C(F_0)|$
11: $f^* \leftarrow$ QUE.pop()
12: **if** $B(h), L(f^*)$ meet the swapping criterion **then**
13: Replace f^* with h.
14: Update the loss score to $L(f, F), \forall f \in F$
15: Reorganize QUE according to the new loss score
16: **else if** The upper bound of $B(h', F)$ ($\forall h' \supset h$) does not meet the swapping criterion **then**
17: D.skip() (see Section5.1)
18: **end if**
19: **end while**

Then, the algorithm iteratively updates F_0. In each iteration, the algorithm generates a subgraph h using the above-mentioned DFS coder. Then, it computes h's supporting sets on both G and Q (line 9). Finding the supporting sets requires subgraph isomorphism tests. Therefore, the algorithm runs faster if it generates fewer subgraphs. Then, the algorithm computes a *benefit* score for h.

DEFINITION 6 (BENEFIT SCORE). *The benefit score of a subgraph h, $B(h, F)$, is the increase of the pruning power after adding h to index features F:*

$$B(h, F) = |C(h) \setminus C(F)|. \tag{6}$$

The benefit of h is compared with the minimum loss score of features F_0. The algorithm swaps h with the minimum-loss feature f^* if a swapping criterion is met (see Section 4.2 for details). After the swap, the feature set F changes. Hence, the algorithm updates the loss scores and reorganizes the minimum heap QUE. We also use the branch and bound technique to skip many of the frequent subgraphs (line 17) (see Section 5.1 for details). The algorithm runs iteratively until the DFS coder stops producing frequent subgraphs.

EXAMPLE 4.2. *The algorithm first mines a frequent subgraph h_1 with the pruning cover as shown in row 4 of Figure 4(a). h_1 has a benefit score of* 1, *and f_3 has a loss score of* 0. *The algorithm replaces f_3 with h_1 and updates the index features to $F_1 = \{h_1, f_1, f_2, f_4, f_5\}$. It also updates the loss scores $\forall f \in F_1$ (row 4 of Figure 4(b)). In the next iteration, the algorithm mines a frequent subgraph h_2 with* 0 *benefit score. As h_2 does not meet the swapping criterion, the algorithm skips h_2 and moves to the next iteration.*

Discussion: Compared with the batch algorithms [3, 4, 24] (see Section 2.1), this one-pass algorithm does not pre-mine or store all frequent subgraphs H_σ. In addition, with the branch and bound technique (Section 5.1), a much smaller number of frequent subgraphs $\mathcal{H}_\sigma$ is computed, $|\mathcal{H}_\sigma| \ll |H_\sigma|$. Compared with the direct-mining algorithms [13, 21, 22], this one-pass algorithm only mines and examines each frequent subgraph at most once, instead of k times to select k features.

4.1 Complexity Analysis

Because it only stores the k selected features and their supporting sets in memory, the one-pass algorithm has a space complexity of $O(k(|G| + |Q|))$. This is a large win in comparison with the $O(|H_\sigma|(|G| + |Q|))$ space complexity of the greedy algorithm (Section 3.3) because $k \ll |H_\sigma|$.

The one-pass algorithm has a time complexity of

$$O(|\mathcal{H}_\sigma|(|G|+|Q|)T_{SGI}+|\mathcal{H}_\sigma|T_{score}+N_{swap}k(T_{score}+log(k))), \tag{7}$$

where $|\mathcal{H}_\sigma|$ is the number of frequent subgraphs mined by the DFS coder and N_{swap} is the number of swaps (line 13). $O(|\mathcal{H}_\sigma|(|G| + |Q|)T_{SGI})$ is the time to compute the supporting sets (line 9). The time to compute the benefit score $B(h, F)$ is $O(|\mathcal{H}_\sigma|T_{score})$. Also, for each swap, the algorithm updates the loss scores for $f \in F$ and updates the minimum heap, which takes $O(k(T_{score}+log(k))$ time.

It is easy to observe from Equation 7 that the running time of the one-pass algorithm mainly depends on two factors: (1) the number of frequent subgraphs returned by the DFS coder, $|\mathcal{H}_\sigma|$, and (2) the number of swaps N_{swap}. In Section 4.2, we propose an adjustable swapping criterion to reduce N_{swap}. We also study the branch and bound technique to reduce $|\mathcal{H}_\sigma|$ in Section 5.

4.2 The Swapping Criterion

In this section, we propose a swapping criterion to reduce the number of swaps, N_{swap}, and thus reduce the running time of the algorithm.

4.2.1 Related Work and Discussion

Saha and Gettor proposed a swapping criterion for the maximum-coverage problem, which gives the one-pass algorithm an approximation ratio of $1/4$ [16].

DEFINITION 7 ($swap_1$). *Given features F, replace $f^* \in F$ with a subgraph h if $B(h, F) > 2L(f^*, F)$, where f^* is the feature with the minimum loss score in F.* [2]

Ausiello et al. [1] proposed another swapping criterion with an approximation ratio of $1/4$.

DEFINITION 8 ($swap_2$). *Replace f^* with h if $B(h, F) > L(f^*, F) + |C(F)|/k$, where $C(F)$ is the pruning cover of features F (see Definition 3).*

The pruning power of the features updated by $swap_2$ is much lower than that of the features updated by $swap_1$ (see Section 7). This is because $swap_2$ is too strict, as $|C(F)|/k \gg L(f^*, F)$. As a result, a lot of frequent subgraphs with high benefit scores fail to meet the criterion. Therefore, we have $|C(F_{swap_2})| \ll |C(F_{swap_1})|$.

The one-pass algorithm adopting $swap_1$ runs 2 to 10 times slower than that adopting $swap_2$. This is because $swap_1$ is too loose. The right side of $swap_1$, $L(f^*, F)$, can be very small and even zero in many iterations of Algorithm 2. Hence, many frequent subgraphs with a low benefit score are swapped in. In the latter iterations, these newly swapped-in frequent subgraphs are swapped out because of their low pruning power. Therefore, the algorithm is trapped in a local optimum: the frequent swapping-in and swapping-out of the features does not significantly improve the pruning power. Further, this swapping in and out prolongs the running time of the algorithm, as the algorithm must update $L(f, F), \forall f \in F$ (line 14 of Algorithm 2) after each swap of features.

4.2.2 Our solution

To balance the respective pros and cons of $swap_1$ and $swap_2$, we propose $swap_\alpha$, which can be seen as a linear combination of the two. With this swapping criterion, the one-pass algorithm has an approximation ratio of at least $1/4$ (see Appendix B for the proof).

DEFINITION 9 ($swap_\alpha$). *The one-pass algorithm replaces the feature f^* with a frequent subgraph h if*

$$B(h, F) > (1+\alpha)L(f^*, F) + (1-\alpha)|C(F)|/k$$

, where $\alpha \in [0, 1]$.

Discussion: The benefit of the term $(1-\alpha)|C(F)|/k$ is that it prevents the right side of $swap_\alpha$ from being too small. For example, even when $L(f^*, F) = 0$, a frequent subgraph h with a low benefit score will not be swapped in the index and then swapped out. In practice, $|C(F)|/k$ is two orders of magnitude (about 100 times) larger than $L(f^*, F)$. Hence, we need a normalizing factor to prevent $|C(F)|/k$ from totally dominating the swap criterion. Hence, we varied α from .95 to .995 and found that 0.99 worked the best in most of our experiments.

5. OPTIMIZING THE ALGORITHM

In addition to the number of swaps N_{swap}, the running time of the one-pass algorithm also depends on the number of frequent subgraphs mined by the DFS coder, as shown in Equation 7. In this section, first, we introduce a branch and bound technique (Section 5.1). Using this technique the one-pass algorithm can safely skip generating numerous frequent subgraphs without decreasing the solution quality. Second, to address the memory issues, we decomposed the index and used a fast algorithm to compute the benefit and loss scores, a procedure also described in this section.

[2] In [16], $L(f, F)$ is defined as $C(f) \setminus C(F \cup \{h\})$, where h is a frequent subgraph to be compared with f.

5.1 Branch and Bound

The one-pass algorithm mines frequent subgraphs with a DFS coder (line 8 of Algorithm 2), which generates subgraphs by depth-first traversing a feature tree, as shown in Figure 3. We observe that the benefit score of a frequent subgraph h, $B(h, F)$, is neither monotonically increasing nor decreasing. That is, it is undecidable which value of $B(h_1, F)$ and $B(h_2, F)$ is bigger given that $h_1 \subset h_2$. Therefore, the benefit score cannot be directly used to reduce the search space. An alternative method is to derive an upper bound, $Bupp(h, F)$ [13, 17, 21, 22]. $Bupp(h, F)$ is an upper bound of the benefit score of any subgraph h', where $h' \supset h$. That is, $Bupp(h, F) \geq B(h', F), \forall h' \supset h$. A branch starting from h can be skipped if $Bupp(h, F)$ does not meet the swapping criterion because no $h' \supset h$ will meet the swapping criterion either.

In the rest of this section, we derive a branch upper bound of $B(h, F)$ for the subgraph search. See Appendix A for how to derive the same for the supergraph search. In the case of an index update, we assume that $|G(q)|$ are stored in the query logs when the graph index processes queries.

Given $Q = \{q_1, q_2, ...q_n\}$, $C(F, G, \{q_i\})$ is F's pruning cover over G and $\{q_i\}$. As $C(F, G, \{q_i\})$ and $C(F, G, \{q_j\})$ $(i \neq j)$ are disjoint, it is easy to show that

$$|C(F, G, Q)| = \sum_{q_i \in Q} |C(F, G, \{q_i\})|. \quad (8)$$

By Definition 6,

$$B(h', F) = |C(h') \setminus C(F)| \quad (9)$$

$$= \sum_{q \in Q(h')} |C(h', G, \{q\}) \setminus C(F, G, \{q\})| \quad (10)$$

$$= \sum_{q \in Q(h')} |(G \setminus G(h')) \setminus C(F, G, \{q\})|. \quad (11)$$

For a query $q \in Q(h')$, $q \supset h'$, any database graph not containing h' cannot contain q as a subgraph either. That is, $(G \setminus G(h')) \subseteq (G \setminus G(q))$. Therefore,

$$B(h', F) \leq \sum_{q \in Q(h')} |(G \setminus G(q)) \setminus C(F, G, \{q\})| \quad (12)$$

$$= \sum_{q \in Q(h')} (|G \setminus G(q)| - |C(F, G, \{q\})|). \quad (13)$$

Equation 13 is because of the fact that $C(F, G, \{q\}) \subseteq (G \setminus G(q))$. Now we show that $C(F, G, \{q\}) \subseteq (G \setminus G(q))$. As introduced in Section 3.2, $C(F, G, \{q\}) = \cup_{f \subset q}(G \setminus G(f))$. Notice that for each feature, $f \subset q$, $(G \setminus G(f)) \subseteq (G \setminus G(q))$. Hence, $C(F, G, \{q\}) \subseteq (G \setminus G(q))$.

Based on Equation 13, we have a branch upper bound of the benefit score for the subgraph search:

$$Bupp(h, F) = \sum_{q \in Q(h)} (|G| - |G(q)| - |C(F, G, \{q\})|).$$

The upper bound is fast to compute as the one-pass algorithm already computes $|C(F, G, \{q\})|$ and $|G(q)|$.

5.2 Index Decomposition

To compute $B(h, F)$ and $L(f, F)$, the one-pass algorithm records whether each item pair (q, g) is in the pruning cover (Definition 3)

$C(F)$ and $C(F \setminus \{f\})$. As can be seen in Figure 2(b), the space complexity of keeping the coverage status is $O(|G||Q|)$, which is not scalable to large datasets. We propose a decomposed index that has a linear space $O(k|G| + k|Q|)$ to keep the covering status.

Space: k |G|

Key	Value
g_1	f_1 f_2 f_3
g_2	f_2 f_4
g_3	f_1 f_3 f_4
g_4	f_1 f_5

Space: k |Q|

Key	Value
q_1	f_1 f_2
q_2	f_1 f_3 f_4
q_3	f_2
q_4	f_1 f_4 f_5

Figure 5: Decomposed index

DEFINITION 10 (DECOMPOSED INDEX). *A decomposed index is a set of key-value pairs. A key is a query graph q or a database graph g. The value of key q is the features contained in q, which we refer to as $V(q)$.*

Figure 5 is a decomposed index built for Example 3.1 (Figure 2(b)). By using a decomposed index, we can use a set operation to find the features covering each (q, g) pair. For a subgraph search, a feature f covers (q, g) if $f \subset q \wedge f \not\subset g$ (see Section 3.2). Hence, features in $V(q)$ but not in $V(g)$, $V(q) \setminus V(g)$, cover (q, g).

EXAMPLE 5.1. *In Figure 2(b), (q_1, g_1) is not covered by any features in F. We get the same answer with the decomposed index, $V(q_1) \setminus V(g_1) = \{f_1, f_2\} \setminus \{f_1, f_2, f_3\} = \emptyset$. Similarly, (q_3, g_4) is covered by f_2 in Figure 2(b), and we have $V(q_3) \setminus V(g_4) = \{f_2\} \setminus \{f_1, f_5\} = \{f_2\}$ in the decomposed index. Also (q_2, g_2) is covered by f_1 and f_3 in Figure 2(b), and we have $V(q_2) \setminus V(g_2) = \{f_1, f_3, f_4\} \setminus \{f_2, f_4\} = \{f_1, f_3\}$.*

Complexity: The space required to store the decomposed index is $O(k(|Q| + |G|))$, where k is the number of features in the graph index. The time complexity to look up the covering status of each (q, g) pair is $O(k)$. Our empirical study shows that $|V(q)| \ll k$ and $|V(g)| \ll k$ for most queries and database graphs. Thus, the empirical running time is much lower than that of the theoretical worst case.

5.3 Fast Computing of Benefit and Loss

Recall that the benefit score of a frequent subgraph h is $B(h, F) = |C(h, G, Q) \setminus C(F, G, Q)|$. With a decomposed index (e.g., Figure 5), $B(h, F)$ can be computed by scanning each (q, g) pair in $C(h, G, Q)$ and looking up the index to determine whether (q, g) is covered by any feature in F. This is time-consuming for large datasets, as $|C(h, G, Q)| = O(|G||Q|)$.

We reduce the running time of computing $B(h, F)$ by first finding h's subgraph and supergraphs in F: $Sub(h, F)$, and $Sup(h, F)$. The computation of $Sub(h, F)$ and $Sup(h, F)$ is fast using a graph index such as Lindex [25]. With $Sub(h, F)$ and $Sup(h, F)$, we further define a subset of graphs and queries, $|G'| \ll |G|, |Q'| \ll |Q|$. Then, we argue that it is sufficient to compute $B(h, F)$ over G' and Q'. That is, instead of scanning each (q, g) pair in $C(h, G, Q)$, the algorithm iterates over (q, g) pairs in $C(h, G', Q')$, which takes $O(|G'||Q'|)$ time to run, where $O(|G'||Q'|) \ll O(|G||Q|)$.

DEFINITION 11 (G' AND Q'). *We define the partial graph set G' and Q' as follows:*

$$G'(h) = (G \setminus G(h)) \setminus \cup_{f \subset h} (G \setminus G(f)) \quad (14)$$

$$Q'(h) = Q(h) \setminus \cup_{f \supset h} Q(f). \quad (15)$$

We have the following equation:

$$C(h, G, Q) \setminus C(F) \equiv C(h, G', Q') \setminus C(F). \quad (16)$$

EXAMPLE 5.2. *Assume that the frequent subgraph h_1 in Example 4.2 is a subgraph of f_5 and a supergraph of f_1. $G(h_1) = \{g_1, g_4\}$, $Q(h_1) = \{q_2, q_4\}$. Based on this definition, $G'(h_1) = \{g_2, g_3\} \setminus \{g_2\} = \{g_3\}$, $Q'(h_1) = \{q_2, q_4\} \setminus \{q_4\} = \{q_2\}$. Based on Definition 3, $C(h_1, G, Q) = \{(g_2, q_2), (g_3, q_2), (g_2, q_4), (g_3, q_4)\}$ (row 4 of Figure 4(a)) and $C(h_1, G', Q') = \{g_3, q_2\}$. It is easy to see that $C(h_1, G, Q) \setminus C(F) \equiv C(h_1, G', Q') \setminus C(F)$. Hence, we can compute h_1's benefit score over G' and Q'. In this example, $|C(h_1, G', Q')| = 1$ and $|C(h_1, G, Q)| = 4$. Computing h_1's benefit over G' Q' saves three decomposed index look-ups.*

Now, we prove Equation 16 using the following two lemmas.

LEMMA 5.1. *A frequent subgraph h does not filter out any additional graphs for queries $\cup_{f \supset h} Q(f)$.*

PROOF. Each query $q \in \cup_{f \supset h} Q(f)$ uses features $\{f \in F | f \supset h\}$ for pruning. Because $f \supset h$, $G(h) \supset G(f)$, f filters out more false graphs than h does. Hence, h cannot filter out additional graphs for $q \in \cup_{f \supset h} Q(f)$. □

EXAMPLE 5.3. *For example, h in Example 5.2 has a supergraph feature f_5. $Q(f_5) = \{q_4\}$, and q_4 uses f_5 to filter out graphs $\{g_1, g_2, g_3\}$. The subgraph h_1, which filters out $\{g_2, g_3\}$, does not prune additional graphs for q_4.*

LEMMA 5.2. *h does not filters out additional graphs in $\cup_{f \subset h} (G \setminus G(f))$, as these graphs are filtered out by f.*

PROOF. For $\{f \in F | f \subset h\}$, any queries using h for pruning also use f for pruning. Graphs $G \setminus G(f)$ are filtered out by feature f; hence, graphs $\cup_{\{f \in F | f \subset h\}} (G \setminus G(f))$ are filtered out by features $\forall \{f \in F | f \subset h\}$. Thus, h does not filter out additional graphs in $\forall \{f \in F | f \subset h\}$. □

Based on Lemmas 5.1 and 5.2, items $\{(q_i, g_j) | \forall q_i \in \cup_{f \supset h} Q(f)$ or $g_j \in \cup_{f \subset h} (G \setminus G(f))\}$ are already in the pruning cover of F. Therefore, $C(h, G, Q) \setminus C(F) \equiv C(h, G', Q') \setminus C(F)$ (Equation 16). We thereby reduce the time to compute $B(h, F)$ from $O(|G||Q|)$ to $O(|G'||Q'|)$, $(|G'||Q'| \ll |G||Q|)$. The same technique can be used to compute $L(f, F)$ as well.

6. UPDATING A GRAPH INDEX WITH THE ONE-PASS ALGORITHM

In this section, we first discuss the gain and cost of running the one-pass algorithm to update the graph index. Then, we introduce ADWIN, which is a useful tool for monitoring graph stream changes. Using ADWIN, we can run the one-pass algorithm to update the features only after detecting significant changes in the graph database and queries.

6.1 Gain and Cost of the One-Pass Algorithm

Gain: The one-pass algorithm optimizes the pruning power of the index features. Hence, it reduces the query-processing time of the graph index. We define the gain of the one-pass algorithm as the decrease in the time taken to process queries Q using the updated index:

$$Gain = |Q||G|(r_{after} - r_{before})T_{SGI}, \quad (17)$$

where T_{SGI} is the average time for one subgraph isomorphism test and r is the pruning ratio of the index, $r = C(F)/(|Q||G|)$.

Because each swap of the one-pass algorithm increases the pruning power, the one-pass algorithm will never downgrade the performance of the index. That is, if we run the one-pass algorithm when there is no change in either the database or the query, the pruning power of the index increases if there is a feature swap during the index update. In one of our experiments, we run the one-pass algorithm to update the graph index over a stable graph database (Figure 11(b)) and observe an improvement in the index's pruning power after the update. In addition, the one-pass algorithm updates the index by gradually replacing features. The graph index can process queries in parallel to the one-pass algorithm (see Algorithm 1).

Cost: The running time of the one-pass algorithm inversely correlates to the "quality" of the index before the update. In one of our experiments, we compare four indices built using features mined by four different feature-mining algorithms. The query-processing times of these four indices differ. Then, we run the one-pass algorithm ($swap_\alpha$) to update indices. We observe strong correlations between the query-processing time of the index before the update and the time cost of the one-pass algorithm (see Figure 8(a)). That is, it is fast to run the one-pass algorithm to update a close-to-optimal index. In practice, we can ping the system periodically, e.g., late at night, and run the one-pass algorithm when the system is idle. If the pruning power of the current index is close to optimal, according to the above arguments, we will not introduce too much cost to the system by running an update. On the other hand, if the current index should be improved to adapt to the changes in the query stream or database graphs, it is good to start an update at an appropriate time. We use the monitoring tool ADWIN [2] to find the appropriate time.

6.2 Automatic Change Detection

In our experiments, we use ADWIN to monitor the query stream. It is straightforward to extend the usage to the database graphs. In this way, it is sufficient to use the one-pass algorithm when ADWIN detects changes in the graph database or the queries.

Bifet et al. showed that ADWIN is effective in detecting the changes of graph streams by estimating the frequencies of frequent subgraphs from the streams [2]. The ADWIN algorithm maintains a window with adaptive size that contains data with similar distributions. Whenever a change in the stream is detected, ADWIN shrinks the window by discarding all the data before the change and storing only the stream data that arrives after the change. Given a confidence δ, the probability that ADWIN will shrink the window size (detect a change) on a stable graph stream is at most δ. Meanwhile, the probability that ADWIN will fail to detect the change (false negative rate) is bounded by $(1 - \delta)$. For example, given a stream data X comprising two parts $\{X_1, X_2\}$, each part contains several queries. Assume that X_1 arrives earlier than X_2 in the graph stream and that they have different distributions with a mean of μ_1 and μ_2, respectively. The probability that ADWIN will not shrink the window size to remove X_1 is at most $(1 - \delta)$ if $\mu_1 - \mu_2 > 2\epsilon_{cut}, \epsilon_{cut} = \sqrt{\frac{1}{4}(\frac{1}{|X_1|} + \frac{1}{|X_2|}) \cdot ln\frac{4|X|}{\delta}}$.

Our empirical study shows that ADWIN is effective in detecting the changes of the query stream. After detecting a change in the query stream, we update the index using the one-pass algorithm. With the updated index, the overall query-processing time decreases by $1/3$, which is worth the cost of the index update using the one-pass algorithm (Figure 10(c)).

7. EXPERIMENT

In this section, we study the empirical performance of the one-pass algorithm.

Datasets: We study two datasets. The first one is the AIDS dataset, which contains $43,905$ chemical molecules [3, 24, 4]. The second one is the eMolecules dataset,[3] which contains more than $5.9M$ chemical molecules. For the subgraph search, we generate queries by first mining frequent subgraphs with very small minimum support, e.g., $\sigma = 0.008$, and then randomly sampling a subset as queries. For the supergraph search, we use the graphs in the AIDS and eMolecules datasets as queries and generate the graph database by mining frequent subgraphs.

Algorithms: We study the one-pass algorithm in comparison to the FG-index [4], the gIndex [24] and the greedy algorithm (see Section 3.3). We study three swapping criteria for the one-pass algorithm, namely, $swap_1$ [16], $swap_2$ [1], and $swap_\alpha$. As discussed in Section 4.2.2, we set $\alpha = 0.99$ by default. We use the branch and bound technique and the decomposed index (see Section 5) by default except when specified otherwise. To make the features mined or updated with different algorithms comparable, we use the same index structure, Lindex [25], to index the graph database. For the FG-index [4], we use Lindex+ to store the on-disk index features to answer queries that are frequent in the graph database, and we update the in-memory features of the FG-index with the one-pass algorithm.

7.1 Changes of the Graph Database

In this subsection, we study the performance of the one-pass algorithm on updating indices to accommodate changes in the graph database. First, we build three graph indices using the features mined from the AIDS dataset: (1) the FG-index, (2) the gIndex, and (3) the index with features mined using the greedy algorithm (Section 3.3), which we refer to as the **Greedy** index. To construct the FG-index and the gIndex, we set the default parameters as recommended in the original work [24, 4]. As a result, $7,462$ features are mined to build the gIndex and $5,694$ features are mined to build the FG-index. We mine $2,000$ features to build the Greedy index such that the three indices can have comparable performance on query processing. We test all indices on a test query set sampled from $H_{0.008}$. The greedy algorithm mines index features using a training set, which is also sampled from $H_{0.008}$. To ensure a fair evaluation, we use separate queries for training and testing.

To simulate the *changes of the graph database*, we replace 40% of the AIDS graphs with eMolecules graphs. As shown in Figure 6(a), the verification time increases significantly after the graph changes. This is because the features mined from the outdated database do not perform well on pruning false graphs in the new database. We use the counts of subgraph isomorphism tests (SGI) to measure the verification time.

To improve the pruning power of the graph index, we can either (1) mine features from the new graph database and build a new index from scratch or (2) update the index features with the proposed one-pass algorithm. Here, we use $swap_\alpha$ as the swapping criterion of the one-pass algorithm. Figure 6(b) compares the query-processing times of features mined or updated using these two approaches. By re-mining features and rebuilding indices, all indices can save more than half of the SGIs in the verification step. Also, it is promising that features updated by the one-pass algorithm perform as well as those mined from scratch on processing queries.

Figure 6(c) compares the time taken to mine features from scratch with the time taken to update features using the one-pass algorithm. We can see that the one-pass algorithm is much faster than mining features from scratch. For example, it takes 20 times longer to mine

[3] http://www.emolecules.com/

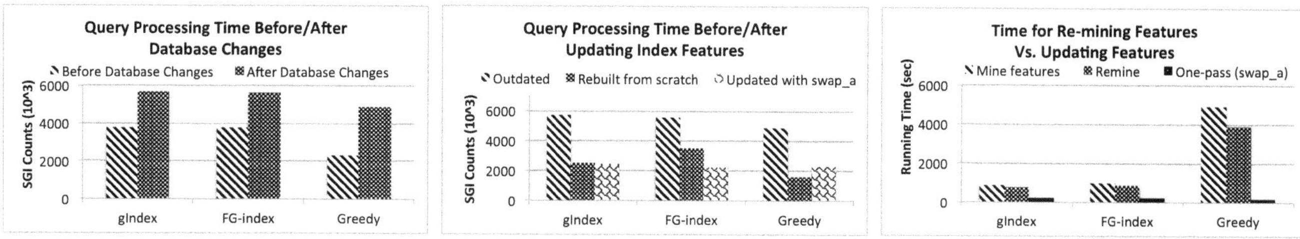

(a) (b) (c)

Figure 6: Changes of the graph database.

features using the greedy algorithm than to update the features with the one-pass algorithm ($swap_\alpha$). This further shows that it is time-consuming to update a graph index with the greedy algorithm, as discussed in Section 3.3.

Next, we study the performance of the one-pass algorithm with different swap criteria. Following the stated experiment settings, to accommodate to the changes of the graph database, we update the Greedy index using the one-pass algorithms $swap_1$, $swap_2$ and $swap_\alpha$. The Greedy index is the index built using the features mined by the greedy algorithm. Figure 7(a) compares the query-processing times of features mined using each of the three swapping criteria. As before, we use the SGI counts to measure the query-processing time. It can be seen that features updated using $swap_1$ and $swap_\alpha$ are similar in terms of query-processing time, which is about 50% of those features mined using $swap_2$. This supports the observation in Section 4.2.1 that $swap_2$ is too strict and as a result a lot of frequent subgraphs with high benefit scores fail to be swapped in as index features. Figure 7(b) compares the running time of the one-pass algorithm using these three swapping criteria. It is shown that $swap_\alpha$ and $swap_2$ are similar in terms of running time, which is $1/3$ of $swap_1$'s running time. This supports the observation in Section 4.2.1 whereby $swap_1$ is slow because it can get trapped in a local optimum.

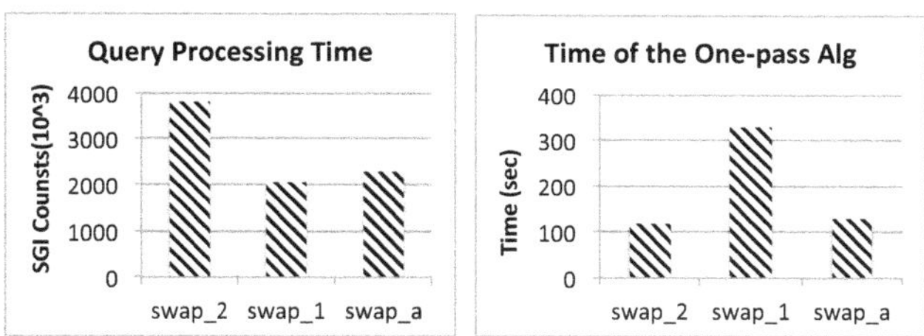

(a) (b)

Figure 7: Changes of the database: different swapping criteria.

We further study the running time of the one-pass algorithm on updating the outdated indices with different pruning powers. We compare four indices, the gIndex, the FG-index, $I(swap_\alpha)$ and the Greedy index. Index $I(swap_\alpha)$ is built by first randomly picking $2,000$ frequent subgraphs as features, and then gradually updating those features with the one-pass algorithm $swap_\alpha$. These four indices differ in terms of query-processing time: Greedy index $< I(swap_\alpha) <$ FG-index $<$ gIndex. Figure 8(a) shows strong correlations between the query-processing time of the index before the update and the time cost of running the one-pass algorithm. That is, the one-pass algorithm runs faster to update an index with high pruning power than to update an index with low pruning power.

7.2 Change of Queries

In this subsection, we study the performance of the one-pass algorithm on updating indices to accommodate changes of queries. As before, we build three graph indices using the features mined from the AIDS dataset: the FG-index, the gIndex, and the Greedy index. We first mine a query set Q_3 with a minimum support $\sigma = 0.003$. We build the Greedy index using the training queries sampled from Q_3. To ensure a fair evaluation, we use separate queries for training and testing. We refer to the Greedy index built with Q_3 as Greedy(train Q_3), and the Greedy index built with Q_8 as Greedy(train Q_8).

To simulate the change of queries, we use the above indices to process the queries mined with $\sigma = 0.008$, Q_8. As expected, the pruning power of the Greedy index decreases significantly. As we can see from Figure 8(b), the SGI counts of Greedy(train Q_3) total more than 3×10^6, whereas the SGI counts of Greedy(train Q_8) in Figure 6(a) total 2.3×10^6. Both Greedy indices are evaluated with the query set sampled from Q_8. Compared with Greedy(train Q_8), Greedy(train Q_3) has less pruning power because the latter is trained on Q_3, which is statistically different from the testing queries, which are sampled from Q_8.

As before, to improve the performance of the index, we can either rebuild an index from scratch or update the index features with the one-pass algorithm. Figure 8(b) compares the query-processing times of features mined or updated using the above two approaches. Unlike in the Section 7.1, we assume that the graph database is stable in this subsection and the queries change from Q_3 to Q_8. As the gIndex and the FG-index are query-independent, rebuilding the gIndex and the FG-index does not improve their pruning power. However, as shown in Figure 8(b), rebuilding the index improves the performance of the Greedy index on processing queries by more than 25%. Also, features updated by the one-pass algorithm perform as well as those mined from scratch on processing queries. In addition, after the one-pass algorithm updates the gIndex and the FG-index features, the query-processing time of both indices decreases significantly. This is because compared with the query-independent indices the one-pass algorithm updates index features in a way that is more attuned to the query workload.

Figure 8(c) compares the time taken to mine index features from scratch with the time taken to update index features. As before, updating index features with the one-pass algorithm is much faster than the process of mining features from scratch. Again, this shows the benefit of updating index features with the one-pass algorithm.

We also study the one-pass algorithm with different swap criteria: $swap_1$, $swap_2$, and $swap_\alpha$. We run the one-pass algorithm using these three swapping criteria to update the Greedy index, Greedy(train Q_3). Figure 9(a) compares the query-processing times of features mined using these three swapping criteria. We use the SGI counts to measure the query-processing time. As before, $swap_1$ and $swap_\alpha$ have similar pruning power, which is 25% better than the features mined using $swap_2$. Figure 9(b) compares the running times of the one-pass algorithm using the three swapping criteria. $swap_\alpha$ and $swap_2$ have similar running time. The running time of $swap_1$ is 8 times longer than that of $swap_\alpha$. This further shows the benefit of using $swap_\alpha$ as the swapping criterion for the one-pass algorithm.

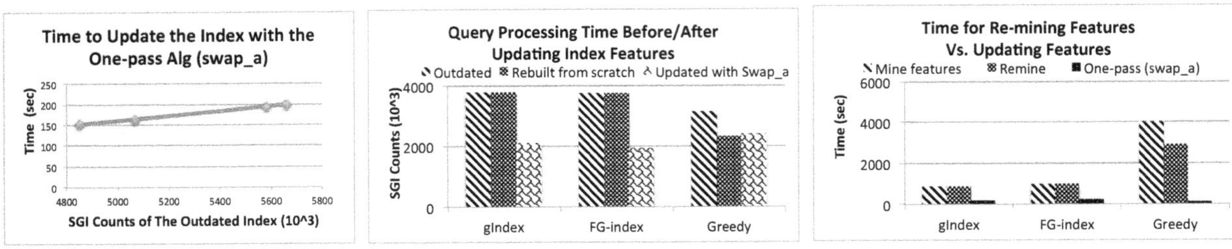

(a) (b) (c)

Figure 8: (a) Time cost of the one-pass algorithm to update different indices. (b,c) Changes of the queries.

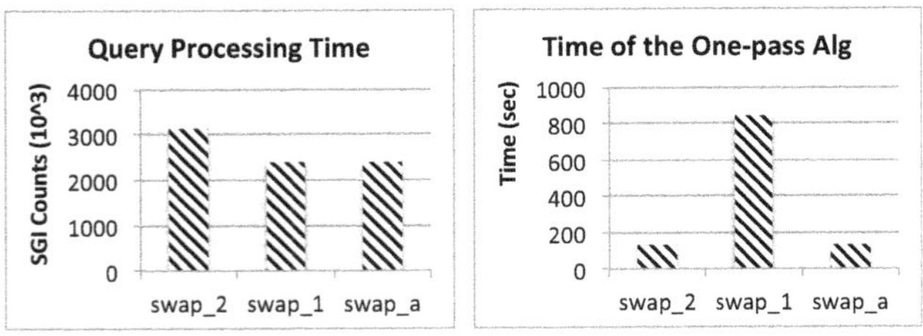

(a) (b)

Figure 9: Changes of queries: Different swapping criteria.

7.2.1 *Using Different Numbers of Features in the Index*

We further run the one-pass algorithm on indices that differ in terms of the number of features. We use the same experiment setting as in the query change-experiment. That is, we first mine features using the greedy algorithm on G and Q_3 and build Greedy(train Q_3). We mine $1,000$, $2,000$, $3,000$, $4,000$ and $5,000$ features and correspondingly build five Greedy indices. To accommodate the changes of the test queries from $H_{0.003}$ to $H_{0.008}$, we run the one-pass algorithm using $swap_\alpha$ as the swapping criterion to update the five Greedy indices.

Figure 10(a) shows the running time of the one-pass algorithm. We can see that the running time of the greedy algorithm is linear to the number of index features. However, the running time of the one-pass algorithm is stable. After further investigation, we observe that the running time of the one-pass algorithm largely depends on the number of swaps, N_{swap}, and the number of frequent subgraphs that are generated by the DFS coder in Algorithm 2, $|\mathcal{H}_\sigma|$. Although the five indices differ in terms of the number of features, the one-pass algorithm has similar N_{swap} and $|\mathcal{H}_\sigma|$ when we run the one-pass algorithm to update the give indices.

Figure 10(b) shows the query-processing time of the old indices, the updated indices, and the re-mined indices. As before, we use the SGI counts to measure the query-processing time. We can see that the pruning power of the updated indices is similar to that of the re-mined indices. In addition, the index with more features has higher pruning power (lower SGI counts) than the index with fewer features does .

7.3 Change Detection and Auto Update

In this subsection, we study the automatic update of indices. We monitor the change of queries with the ADWIN algorithm [2], so that the one-pass algorithm can be used automatically after detecting a change of the query distribution.

To simulate the change of queries, we generate a query stream containing $40,000$ queries. The first $10,000$ queries and the third $10,000$ queries are mined from the AIDS dataset with a minimum support $\sigma = 0.003$. The second $10,000$ and the fourth $10,000$ queries are mined with $\sigma = 0.01$. The Greedy index is initially constructed with training queries generated with $\sigma = 0.003$.

Figure 10(c) shows the query-processing performance of the index over this query stream. The graph index processes the queries in batches. Each batch has 100 queries. The average pruning power of each batch is computed and monitored by ADWIN. Once ADWIN detects give change points (marked with squares in Figure 10(c)), it calls the one-pass algorithm to update the index. After detecting a significant decrease in pruning power, we run the one-pass algorithm with the queries that come after the change point. As Figure 10(c) shows, after the update of the index using the one-pass algorithm, the query-processing algorithm that uses the updated index saves $1/3$ of the SGIs in the verification step. This further shows the advantage of the one-pass algorithm.

7.4 Improve the Existing Index

In the previous subsections, we studied the one-pass algorithm to accommodate to the changes of the graph database or queries. In this subsection, we use the one-pass algorithm to improve the index built by heuristic-based algorithms.

Figure 11(a) shows the mining time and the query-processing time of features mined by the gIndex, the FG-index and the greedy algorithm (Section 3.3). We sample both the training and the test queries from $H_{0.008}$. The gIndex and the FG-index are similar in terms of the features mining time and the SGI counts. The query-processing times of both the gIndex and the FG-index are longer than that of the Greedy index. However, the feature-mining time of the greedy algorithm is four times longer than the feature-mining times of both the gIndex and the FG-index.

We propose a **hybrid method**, which first mines features with the gIndex or the FG-index and then runs the one-pass algorithm (Algorithm 2) to update those index features. Figure 11(b) shows the query-processing time of the updated gIndex and the updated FG-index using the one-pass algorithm. Three swapping criteria, $swap_1$, $swap_2$, and $swap_\alpha$ are studied. We can see that the query-processing times of both gIndex and FG-index decrease significantly after their features are updated by the one-pass algorithm. For example, the one-pass algorithm reduces the SGI counts of the FG-index by half. Also, in Figure 11(b), the features of the gIndex (FG-index) that are updated using $swap_\alpha$ perform better than the features mined by the greedy algorithm on processing queries. (Note that the gIndex and the FG-index have more features than the Greedy index does.)

Figure 11(c) compares the running time of the feature mining algorithms and the one-pass algorithm. $swap_2$ and $swap_\alpha$ run the fastest, taking only $1/4$ of the time taken by the gIndex and by the FG-index. By taking only $1/5$ of the time of the greedy algorithm, the hybrid method can find features as good as those mined by the greedy algorithm in terms of pruning power.

Scalability: We randomly sample five datasets from the eMolecules dataset. We denote them by G_1 to G_5. G_1 to G_5, respectively, has 2^{16} to 2^{20} graphs. We mine features with $\sigma = 0.1$. Figure 12(a) shows that both the running time and the memory consumption of

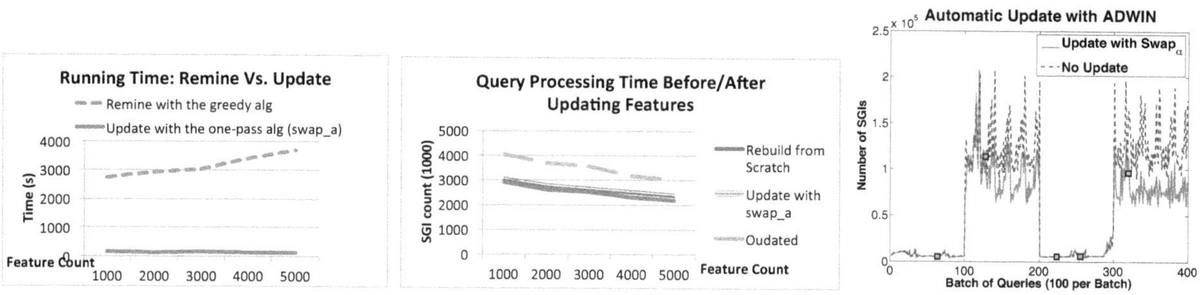

(a) (b) (c)

Figure 10: (a,b)Different number of features. (c) Automatic update of the Greedy index.

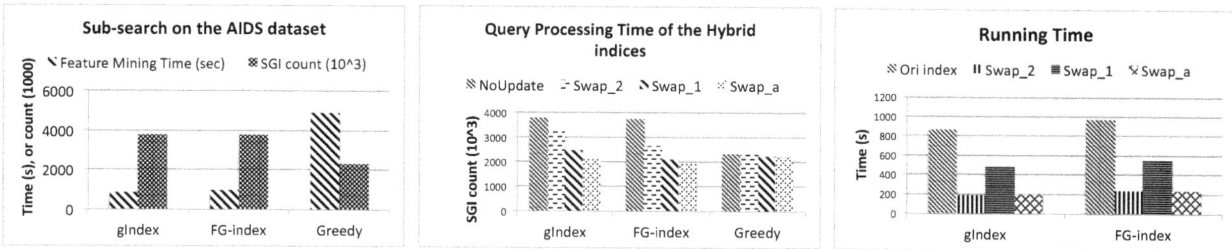

(a) (b) (c)

Figure 11: Optimize the gIndex and the FG-index with the one-pass algorithm.

the one-pass algorithm grow linearly to the data size (the figure is in log-log scale).

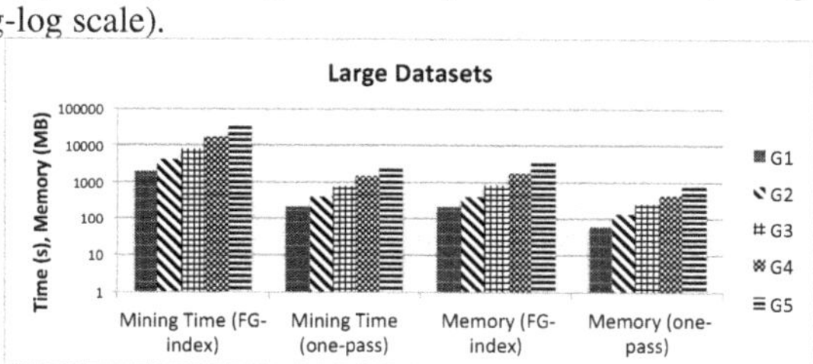

(a)

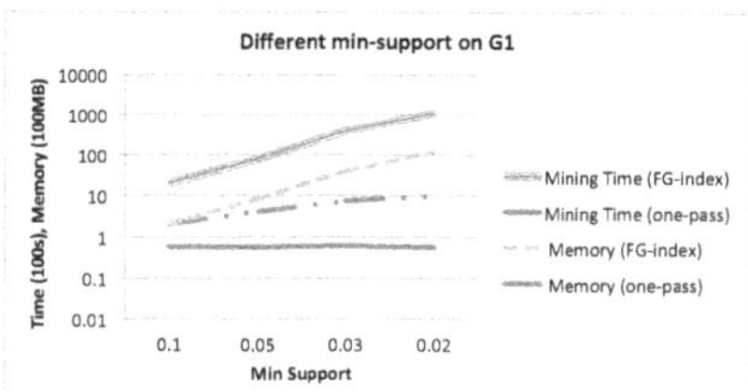

(b)

Figure 12: Scalability test.

We also mine index features with different minimum support values on G_1. As can be seen from Figure 12(b), the memory and the time used to mine FG-index features explode with respect to a decrease in the minimum support. This is because H_σ grows exponentially. On the other hand, the memory consumed by the one-pass algorithm does not change, and the running time of the one-pass algorithm is sub-linear to $|H_\sigma|$.

7.5 Supergraph Search

For the super graph search, we compare the performance of the one-pass algorithm with that of the greedy algorithm (cIndex [3]). We construct the original graph database by randomly sampling 10,000 frequent subgraphs mined from the AIDS dataset. We use the AIDS graph as queries. To simulate the update of the graph database, we randomly replace 50% of the graphs in the graph database with frequent subgraphs mined from the eMolecule dataset. As Figure 13(a) shows, 40% to 50% of the query-processing time can be saved by updating or rebuilding the graph index. In addition, the graph index updated with the one-pass algorithm has the same performance as the index built from scratch by the greedy algorithm. Also, the one-pass algorithm significantly outperforms the greedy algorithm on running time and memory consumption, as shown in Figure 13(b).

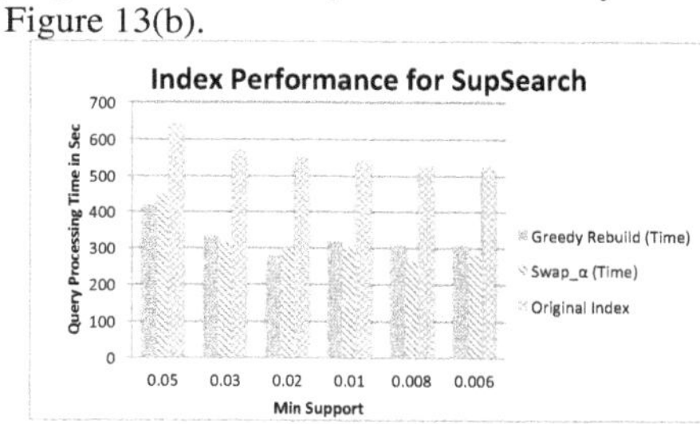

(a)

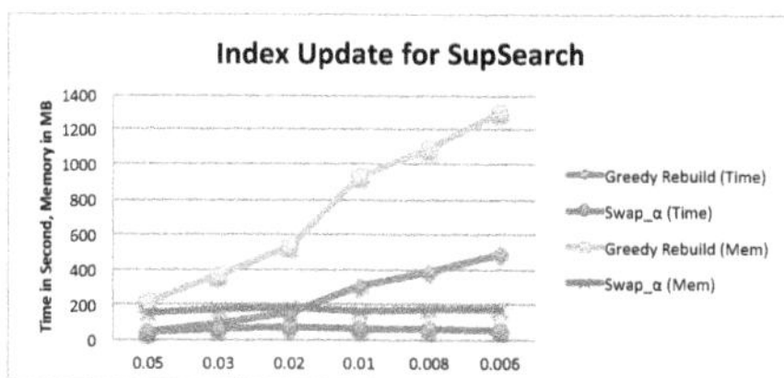

(b)

Figure 13: Database changes: supergraph search.

8. CONCLUSION

In this paper, we studied the feature-update problem for graph searches. We propose a one-pass algorithm, which scans each frequent subgraph at most once. An adjustable swap criterion is proposed to prevent the one-pass algorithm from osculating around a local optimum, thereby significantly reducing the running time of the algorithm. We also prove that when the new adjustable swap criterion is used, the algorithm has an approximation ratio of $1/4$. A branch and bound approach is further proposed to reduce the running time. In addition, we propose a decomposed index and reduce the memory consumption from quadratic to linear to the input size. Our empirical study shows that the one-pass algorithm is time and space efficient for both subgraph and supergraph searches.

9. REFERENCES

[1] G. Ausiello, N. Boria, A. Giannakos, G. Lucarelli, and V. T. Paschos. Online maximum k-coverage. In *FCT*, 2011.

[2] A. Bifet, G. Holmes, B. Pfahringer, and R. Gavaldà. Mining frequent closed graphs on evolving data streams. In *KDD*, pages 591–599, 2011.

[3] C. Chen, X. Yan, P. S. Yu, J. Han, D.-Q. Zhang, and X. Gu. Towards graph containment search and indexing. In *VLDB*, pages 926–937, 2007.

[4] J. Cheng, Y. Ke, W. Ng, and A. Lu. Fg-index: Towards verification-free query processing on graph databases. In *SIGMOD*, pages 857–872, 2007.

[5] F. Chierichetti, R. Kumar, and A. Tomkins. Max-cover in map-reduce. In *WWW*, pages 231–240, 2010.

[6] S. A. Cook. The complexity of theorem-proving procedures. In *STOC*, pages 151–158, 1971.

[7] G. Cormode, H. Karloff, and A. Wirth. Set cover algorithms for very large datasets. In *CIKM*, pages 479–488, 2010.

[8] M. El-Mehalawi and R. A. Miller. A database system of mechanical components based on geometric and topological similarity. *J. CAD*, 35(1):83–94, 2003.

[9] W.-S. Han, J. Lee, M.-D. Pham, and J. X. Yu. igraph: A framework for comparisons of disk-based graph indexing techniques. *Proc. VLDB Endow.*, 3:449–459, September 2010.

[10] N. Jin, C. Young, and W. Wang. Graph classification based on pattern co-occurrence. In *CIKM*, pages 573–582, 2009.

[11] N. Jin, C. Young, and W. Wang. Gaia: Graph classification using evolutionary computation. In *SIGMOD*, pages 879–890, 2010.

[12] D. S. Johnson. Approximation algorithms for combinatorial problems. In *STOC*, pages 38–49, 1973.

[13] T. Kudo, E. Maeda, and Y. Matsumoto. An application of boosting to graph classification. In *NIPS*, 2004.

[14] M. E. J. Newman. The structure and function of complex networks. *SIAM*, 45:167–256, 2003.

[15] S. Ranu and A. K. Singh. Graphsig: A scalable approach to mining significant subgraphs in large graph databases. In *ICDE*, pages 844–855, 2009.

[16] B. Saha and L. Getoor. On maximum coverage in the streaming model and application to multi-topic blog-watch. In *SDM*, April 2009.

[17] H. Saigo, N. Krämer, and K. Tsuda. Partial least squares regression for graph mining. In *SIGKDD*, pages 578–586, 2008.

[18] H. Shang, Y. Zhang, X. Lin, and J. X. Yu. Taming verification hardness: an efficient algorithm for testing subgraph isomorphism. *Proc. VLDB Endow.*, pages 364–375, 2008.

[19] B. Sun, P. Mitra, and C. L. Giles. Independent informative subgraph mining for graph information retrieval. In *CIKM*, pages 563–572, 2009.

[20] M. Thoma, H. Cheng, A. Gretton, J. Han, H.-P. Kriegel, A. Smola, L. Song, P. S. Yu, X. Yan, and K. M. Borgwardt. Discriminative frequent subgraph mining with optimality guarantees. *Statistical Analysis and Data Mining*, 3(5):302–318, 2010.

[21] M. Thoma, H. Cheng, A. Gretton, J. Han, H. peter Kriegel, A. J. Smola, L. Song, P. S. Yu, X. Yan, and K. M. Borgwardt. Near-optimal supervised feature selection among frequent subgraphs. In *SDM*, pages 1075–1086, 2009.

[22] X. Yan, H. Cheng, J. Han, and P. S. Yu. Mining significant graph patterns by leap search. In *SIGMOD*, pages 433–444, 2008.

[23] X. Yan and J. Han. gspan: Graph-based substructure pattern mining. In *ICDM*, page 721, 2002.

[24] X. Yan, P. S. Yu, and J. Han. Graph indexing: a frequent structure-based approach. In *SIGMOD*, pages 335–346, 2004.

[25] D. Yuan and P. Mitra. Lindex: a lattice-based index for graph databases. *The VLDB Journal*, 22(2):229–252, 2013.

[26] D. Yuan, P. Mitra, H. Yu, and C. Giles. Iterative graph feature mining for graph indexing. In *ICDE*, pages 198–209, April 2012.

[27] S. Zhang, J. Li, H. Gao, and Z. Zou. A novel approach for efficient supergraph query processing on graph databases. In *EDBT*, pages 204–215, 2009.

[28] L. Zou, L. Chen, J. X. Yu, and Y. Lu. A novel spectral coding in a large graph database. In *EDBT*, pages 181–192, 2008.

APPENDIX

A. SUPERGRAPH SEARCH

The supergraph search is a complementary search scenario to the subgraph search. Given a query graph q, a supergraph-search algorithm returns graphs that have q as a supergraph, $\{g \in G | g \subseteq q\}$. An **exclusive logic** is proposed for filtering [3]: A database graph g cannot be a subgraph of query q if g contains an index feature f that is not contained in q. Similar to Equation 2, we define the pruning cover as

$$C_{sup}(f, G, Q) = \{(g, q) | f \not\subset q \wedge f \subset g\}. \tag{18}$$

We define the benefit and loss scores as the same as that in Definitions 5 and 6. Hence,

$$\begin{aligned} B_{sup}(h', F) &= |C_{sup}(h, G, Q) \setminus C_{sup}(F, G, Q)| & (19)\\ &= \sum_{g \in G(h')} |(Q \setminus Q(h')) \setminus C_{sup}(F, \{g\}, Q)| \\ &\leq \sum_{g \in G(h')} |(Q \setminus Q(g)| - |C_{sup}(F, \{g\}, Q)| & (20)\\ &\leq \sum_{g \in G(h)} |(Q \setminus Q(g)| - |C_{sup}(F, \{g\}, Q)| \end{aligned}$$

Inequality 20 is because of $Q(h') \supseteq Q(g)$ and $C_{sup}(F, \{g\}, Q) \subseteq Q \setminus Q(g)$. Therefore, we have an upper bound as follows:

$$Bupp_{sup}(h, F) = \sum_{g \in G(h)} (|Q| - |Q(g)| - |C_{sup}(F, \{g\}, Q)|), \tag{21}$$

which is fast to compute.

B. APPROXIMATION RATIO

Let $O = \{o_1, o_2, ..., o_k\}$ be the optimum solution. W.l.o.g, we assume that the pruning covers of the optimum features are pairwise disjoint. Hence, $C(O, G, Q) = \sum_{i=1}^{k} |C(o_i)|$. Otherwise, resize $C(o_i)$ such that it contains only those elements not in $C(o_j)$, $\forall j < i$.

We refer to the initial set of features before the update as F_0, and we refer to the output of Algorithm 2 as F_{final}. We prove the approximation ratio with a charging schema similar to that in [16]. We charge the cost of the swap operations in the one-pass algorithm. When Algorithm 2 stops, we prove that the total cost charged is at most $4 \times |C(F_{final})|$ and the total cost also equals $|C(O)|$. Therefore, the approximation ratio is $\frac{|C(F_{final}|)}{|C(F^*)|} \geq 1/4$.

DEFINITION 12 (CHARGE SCHEMA). *Assume that in an iteration of the one-pass algorithm, the DFS coder mines a frequent subgraph $h = o_i$. We refer to the index features in this iteration as F_i. If the algorithm replaces a feature $f^* \in F_i$ with o_i, we charge each element $e \in C(o_i)$ by 1 (**element-charge**). Otherwise, if the algorithm does not select o_i, we (1) charge each element $e \in C(o_i) \cup C(F_i)$ by 1 (**element-charge**) and (2) charge each element in $C(F_i)$ by $\frac{B(o_i,F_i)}{|C(F_i)|}$ (**set-charge**).*

LEMMA B.1. *The total cost charged is $|C(O)|$.*

PROOF. (1) If the algorithm selects o_i, then the cost charged in that iteration is $|C(o_i)|$. (2) Otherwise, the charge is

$$|C(o_i) \cup C(F_i)| + |C(F_i)| \times \frac{B(o_i, F_i)}{|C(F_i)|} \quad (22)$$
$$= |C(o_i) \cup C(F_i)| + |C(o_i) \setminus C(F_i)| = |C(o_i)|.$$

Thus, the lemma is proved. □

LEMMA B.2. *The total cost charged is at most $4|C(F_{final})|$.*

PROOF. We prove the lemma by Claims B.1 and B.2 □

CLAIM B.1. *We prove that each element $e \in C(F_i)$ gets a set charge of at most $2/k$ for each o_i that is not selected by the one-pass algorithm.*

PROOF. As the algorithm does not select o_i,

$$B(o_i, F_i) \leq (1 - \alpha_i)|C(F_i)|/k + (1 + \alpha_i) \cdot L(f^*, F_i)$$
$$\leq (1 - \alpha_i)|C(F_i)|/k + (1 + \alpha_i) \cdot |L(f_t, F_i)|, \quad (23)$$

where f_t is an arbitrary feature in F_i.

Let us derive an upper bound for $k \cdot B(o_i, F_i)$. We first define a loss set, $\mathcal{L}(f, F) = C(f) \setminus C(F \setminus f)$. Thus, the loss score in Definition 5 is $L(f, F) = |\mathcal{L}(f, F)|$. It is easy to see that $\mathcal{L}(f_t, F_i) \bigcap \mathcal{L}(f_p, F_i) = \emptyset$ for $t \neq p$ and that $\cup_{f_t \in F_i} \mathcal{L}(f_t, F_i) \subseteq C(F_i)$. Thus, $\sum_{t=1}^{k} L(f_t, F_i) = | \cup_{f_t \in F_i} \mathcal{L}(f_t, F_i)| \leq |C(F_i)|$.

$$k \cdot B(o_i, F_i) \leq (1 - \alpha_i)|C(F_i)| + (1 + \alpha_i) \cdot \sum_{t=1}^{k} L(f_t, F_i)$$
$$\leq (1 - \alpha_i)|C(F_i)| + (1 + \alpha_i)|C(F_i)| = 2|C(F_i)|. \quad (24)$$

Therefore, the set charge for each element in F_i is $\frac{B(o_i,F_i)}{|C(F_i)|} \leq 2/k$. □

Hence, the total set charge is:

$$Setcharge = \sum_{1 \leq i \leq k} (|C(F_i)| \times 2/k) \quad (25)$$
$$\leq \sum_{1 \leq i \leq k} (|C(F_{final})| \times 2/k) = 2|C(F_{final})|.$$

CLAIM B.2. *The total element charge is at most $2|C(F_{final})|$.*

PROOF. The element cost is always charged on an element that is covered by F_i at the time of the charge. Each charged element will either be covered by F_{final} or uncovered due to the swap out of a feature. Hence,

$$elementcharge < |C(F_{final})| + \sum_{i \geq 0} |L(f_i, F_i)|, \quad (26)$$

where f_i^* is the 'i'th removed feature. We also define the 'i'th added frequent subgraph as h_i, and we define the features before the 'i'th update as F_i.

Next, we show that $\sum_{i \geq 0} |L(f_i, F_i)| \leq |C(F_{final})|$. By definition,

$$|C(F_{i+1})| - |C(F_i)| \quad (27)$$
$$= |C(h_i) \setminus C(F_i)| - |C(f_i) \setminus C(F_i \cup \{h_i\} \setminus \{f_i\})|$$
$$= B(h_i, F_i) - L(f_i, F_i \cup \{h_i\}) \geq B(h_i, F_i) - L(f_i, F_i)$$

Also, at each swap, the swap criterion is met:

$$B(h_i, F_i) > (1 - \alpha_i)|C(F_i)|/k + (1 + \alpha_i)L(f_i, F_i). \quad (28)$$

$$|C(F_i)|/k \geq L(f_i, F_i). \quad (29)$$

Based on Equations 28 and 29, we have $B(h_1, F_i) > 2L(f_i, F_i)$. By combining Equations 28 and 29 with Equation 27, we have

$$|C(F_{i+1})| - |C(F_i)| > L(f_i, F_i).$$

Therefore,

$$|C(F_{final})| > |C(F_{final})| - |C(F_0)| \quad (30)$$
$$= \sum_{i \geq 0} (|C(F_{i+1})| - |C(F_i)|) > \sum_{i \geq 0} L(f_i, F_i).$$

As the cost charged on the items that are uncovered due to swapping out features is less than $|C(F_{final}|$, and the cost charged on the items in the final cover is less than $|C(F_{final})|$, the total element charge $< 2|C(F_{final})|$. □

THEOREM 1. *Algorithm 2 with $swap_\alpha$ has an approximation ratio of $1/4$.*

PROOF. By Lemma B.1, the total cost charged is $|C(O)|$. From Lemma B.2, the total cost charged is at most $4|C(F_{final})|$ Hence, $|C(O)| \leq 4|C(F_{final})|$. The approximation ratio is $\frac{|C(F_{final})|}{C(O)} \geq 1/4$. □

Amazon Redshift and the Case for Simpler Data Warehouses

Anurag Gupta, Deepak Agarwal, Derek Tan, Jakub Kulesza, Rahul Pathak, Stefano Stefani, Vidhya Srinivasan

Amazon Web Services

Abstract

Amazon Redshift is a fast, fully managed, petabyte-scale data warehouse solution that makes it simple and cost-effective to efficiently analyze large volumes of data using existing business intelligence tools. Since launching in February 2013, it has been Amazon Web Service's (AWS) fastest growing service, with many thousands of customers and many petabytes of data under management.

Amazon Redshift's pace of adoption has been a surprise to many participants in the data warehousing community. While Amazon Redshift was priced disruptively at launch, available for as little as \$1000/TB/year, there are many open-source data warehousing technologies and many commercial data warehousing engines that provide free editions for development or under some usage limit. While Amazon Redshift provides a modern MPP, columnar, scale-out architecture, so too do many other data warehousing engines. And, while Amazon Redshift is available in the AWS cloud, one can build data warehouses using EC2 instances and the database engine of one's choice with either local or network-attached storage.

In this paper, we discuss an oft-overlooked differentiating characteristic of Amazon Redshift – simplicity. Our goal with Amazon Redshift was not to compete with other data warehousing engines, but to compete with non-consumption. We believe the vast majority of data is collected but not analyzed. We believe, while most database vendors target larger enterprises, there is little correlation in today's economy between data set size and company size. And, we believe the models used to procure and consume analytics technology need to support experimentation and evaluation. Amazon Redshift was designed to bring data warehousing to a mass market by making it easy to buy, easy to tune and easy to manage while also being fast and cost-effective.

1. Introduction

Many companies augment their transaction-processing database systems with data warehouses for reporting and analysis. Analysts estimate the data warehouse market segment at 1/3 of the overall relational database market segment (\$14B vs. \$45B for software licenses and support), with an 8-11% compound annual growth rate (CAGR)[1]. While this is a strong growth rate for a large, mature market, over the past ten years, analysts also estimate data storage at a typical enterprise growing at 30-40% CAGR. Over the past 12-18 months, new market research has begun to show an increase to 50-60%, with data doubling in size every 20 months.

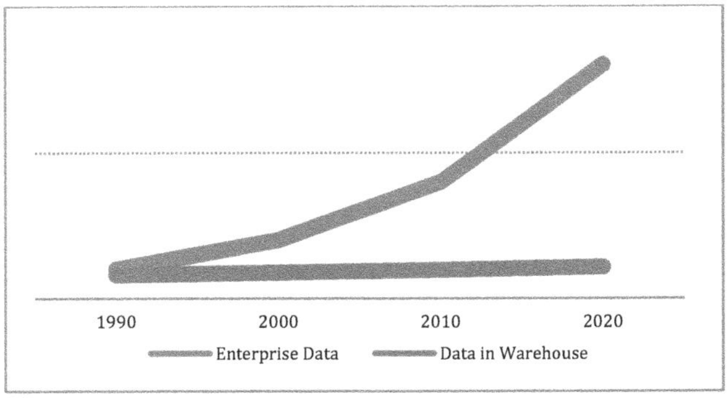

Figure 1: Data Analysis Gap in the Enterprise [10]

This implies most data in an enterprise is "dark data"[2]: data that is collected but not easily analyzed. We see this as unfortunate. If our customers didn't see this data as having value, they would not retain it. Many companies are trying to become increasingly data-driven. And yet, not only is most data already dark, the overall data landscape is only getting darker. Storing this data in NoSQL stores and/or Hadoop is one way to bridge the gap for certain use cases. However it doesn't address all scenarios.

In our discussions with customers, we found the "analysis gap" between data being collected and data available for analysis as due to four major causes.

1. Cost – Most commercial database solutions capable of analyzing data at scale require significant up-front expense. This is hard to justify for large datasets with unclear value.
2. Complexity – Database provisioning, maintenance, backup, and tuning are complex tasks requiring specialized skills. They require IT involvement and cannot easily be performed by line of business data scientists or analysts.
3. Performance – It is difficult to grow a data warehouse without negatively impacting query performance. Once built, IT teams sometimes discourage augmenting data or adding queries as a way of protecting current reporting SLAs.
4. Rigidity – Most databases work best on highly structured relational data. But a large and increasing percentage of data consists of machine-generated logs that mutate over time, audio and video, not readily accessible to relational analysis.

We see each of the above issues only increasing with data set size. To take one large-scale customer example, the Amazon Retail team collects about 5 billion web log records daily (2TB/day,

SIGMOD '15, May 31–June 4, 2015, Melbourne, Victoria, Australia
ACM 978-1-4503-2758-9/15/05.
http://dx.doi.org/10.1145/2723372.2742795

[1] Forecast data combined from IDC, Gartner, and 451 Research.
[2] http://www.gartner.com/it-glossary/dark-data

growing 67% YoY). It is very valuable to combine this data with transactional data stored in their relational and NoSQL systems. Using an existing scale-out commercial data warehouse, they were able to analyze 1 week of data per hour and maintain a cap of 15 months of log, using the largest configuration available. Using much larger Hadoop clusters, they were able to analyze up to 1 month of data per hour, though these clusters were very expensive to administer.

By augmenting their existing systems with a petabyte-scale Amazon Redshift cluster, the Amazon Enterprise Data Warehouse team was able to perform their daily load (5B rows) in 10 minutes, load a month of backfill data (150B rows) in 9.75 hours, take a backup in 30 minutes and restore it to a new cluster in 48 hours. Most interestingly, they were able to now run queries that joined 2 trillion rows of click traffic with 6 billion rows of product ids in less than 14 minutes, an operation that didn't complete in over a week on their existing systems.

Some of the above results emerge from Amazon Redshift's use of, by now, familiar data warehousing techniques, including columnar layout, per-column compression, co-locating compute and data, co-locating joins, compilation to machine code and scale-out MPP processing. While these techniques have not fully made their way into the largest data warehousing vendors, Amazon Redshift's approach is very close to that taken by other columnar MPP data warehousing engines.

Beyond these techniques used to scale out query processing and to reduce CPU, disk IOs, network traffic, Amazon Redshift had a number of additional design goals:

1. Minimize cost of experimentation – It is difficult to understand whether data is worth analyzing without performing at least a few experiments. Amazon Redshift provides a free trial allowing customers to evaluate the service for 60 days using up to 160GB of compressed SSD data at no charge. For subsequent experiments, they can spin up a cluster with no commitments for $0.25/hour/node. This is inclusive of hardware, software, maintenance and management.
2. Minimize time to first report – We measure the time it takes our customers to go from deciding to create a cluster to seeing the results of their first query. As seen in Figure 2, this can be as little as 15 minutes, even to provision a multi-PB cluster.
3. Minimize administration – Amazon Redshift tries to reduce the undifferentiated heavy lifting of creating and operating a data warehouse. We automate backup, restore, provisioning, patching, failure detection and repair. Advanced operations like encryption, cluster resizing and disaster recovery require only a few clicks to enable.
4. Minimize scaling concerns - Many data warehousing engines provide parallelization of loads and queries. We additionally try to parallelize administrative operations like cluster creation, patching, backup, restore and cluster resize. Pricing is also linear or sub-linear with data set growth.
5. Minimize tuning – We avoid knobs and apply techniques to make the ones we do provide "dusty" with disuse. For most users the default setting for these knobs as determined by the system would be sufficient. However, advanced users can choose to change it as needed. For example, we automatically pick compression types based on data sampling. We also avoid the use of indexing or projections, instead favoring multi-dimensional z-curves.

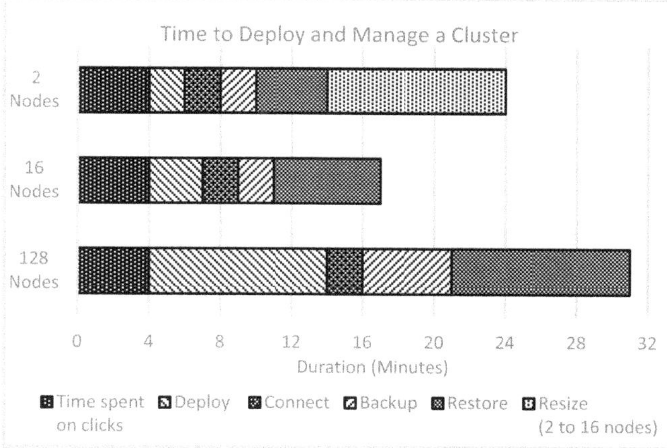

Figure 2: Common admin operation execution time by size

Amazon Redshift also obtains a number of advantages by operating as a managed service in the AWS cloud.

First and foremost, we are able to leverage the pricing and scale of Amazon EC2 for our instances, the durability and throughput of Amazon S3 for backup, and the security of Amazon VPC, to name just a few. This enables our customers to benefit from the innovation and price reductions delivered across a much larger team than ours alone.

Second, by making deployments and patching automatic and painless for our customers, we are able to deploy software at a high frequency. We have averaged the addition of one feature per week, over the past two years. Reducing the cost of deployment and the rapid feedback mechanisms available in running a service allows us to run a more agile OODA[3] loop compared to on-premise providers, ensuring we quickly provide the features our customers care most about.

Finally, since we manage a fleet of thousands of Amazon Redshift clusters, we benefit from automating capabilities that would not make economic sense for any individual on-premise DBA. An operation requiring one minute of per-node overhead is worth many days of investment for us to remove. Removing the root cause of a defect that causes an individual cluster to fail and restart once per thousand days is well worth our investment to reduce paging. As we scale, we have to continually improve the reliability, availability and automation across our fleet to manage operations, which makes failures increasingly uncommon for our customers.

In this paper, we discuss Amazon Redshift's system architecture, simplicity as a guiding principle, and lessons we've learned over the past two years operating the service.

2. System Architecture

The Amazon Redshift architecture consists of a **data plane**, the database engine providing data storage and SQL execution, a **control plane**, providing the workflows to monitor and manage the database, and other AWS services we depend on to support data plane and control plane execution. We summarize each below.

[3] http://en.wikipedia.org/wiki/OODA_loop

2.1 Data Plane

The Amazon Redshift engine is a SQL-compliant, massively-parallel, query processing and database management system designed to support analytics workload. We consider analytic workloads those that regularly ingest incremental sets of data that can be large in size and run queries that join, scan, filter and aggregate data that can comprise a significant fraction of the total stored data. The initial version of the engine was derived from a code base licensed from ParAccel. Data storage and compute is distributed across one or more nodes, which provides near-linear scalability for maintaining & querying datasets from 100s of gigabytes on up to petabyte scale. An Amazon Redshift cluster is comprised of a leader node and one or more compute nodes. We also support a single-node design where leader and compute work is shared on a single node.

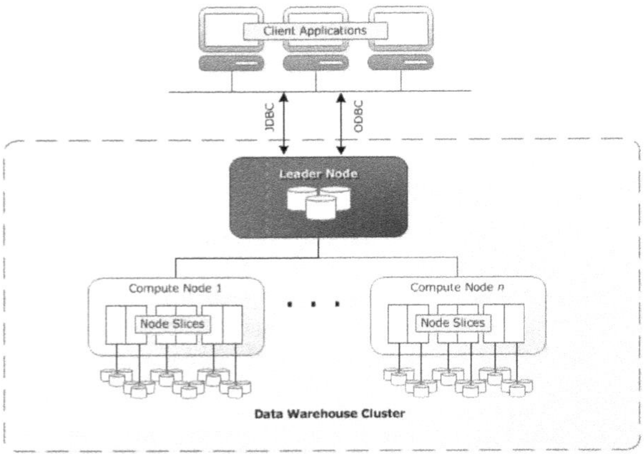

Figure 3: Amazon Redshift system architecture

The **leader node** accepts connections from client programs, parses requests, generates & compiles query plans for execution on the compute nodes, performs final aggregation of results when required, and coordinates serialization and state of transactions. The compute node(s) perform the heavy lifting inherent in both query processing and data manipulation against local data.

Data stored within each Amazon Redshift table is automatically distributed both across compute nodes, to enable scale out of large data sets, and within a compute node, to reduce contention across processing cores. A compute node is partitioned into slices; one slice for each core of the node's multi-core processor. Each slice is allocated a portion of the node's memory and disk space, where it processes a portion of the workload assigned to the node. The user can specify whether data is distributed in a round robin fashion, hashed according to a distribution key, or duplicated on all slices. Using distribution keys allows join processing on that key to be co-located on individual slices, reducing IO, CPU and network contention and avoiding the redistribution of intermediate results during query execution. Within each slice, data storage is column-oriented. Each column within each slice is encoded in a chain of one or more fixed size data blocks. The linkage between the columns of an individual row is derived by calculating the logical offset within each column chain. This linkage is stored as meta-data.

Data blocks are replicated both within the database instance and within Amazon Simple Storage Service (S3). Each data block is synchronously written to both its primary slice as well as to at least one secondary on a separate node. Cohorting is used to limit the number of slices impacted by an individual disk or node failure. Here, we attempt to balance the resource impact of re-replication against the increased probability of correlated failures as disk and node counts increase. Data blocks are also asynchronously and automatically backed up to Amazon S3, which is designed to provide 99.9999999% durability by storing multiple copies across multiple data centers. The primary, secondary and Amazon S3 copies of the data block are each available for read, making media failures transparent. Loss of durability requires multiple faults to occur in the time window from the first fault to re-replication or backup to Amazon S3. Customers can also choose to have their backups occur to Amazon S3 in a second region for further protection against disasters.

Query processing within Amazon Redshift begins with query plan generation and compilation to C++ and machine code at the leader node. The use of query compilation adds a fixed overhead per query that we feel is generally amortized by the tighter execution at compute nodes vs. the overhead of execution in a general-purpose set of executor functions. The executable and plan parameters are sent to each compute node participating in the query. At the compute nodes, the executable is run with the plan parameters and the intermediate results are sent back to the leader node for final aggregation. Each slice in the compute node may run multiple operations such as scanning, filtering, processing joins, etc., in parallel.

Data loading is a special case of query processing, using a modified version of the PostgreSQL COPY command. The Amazon Redshift version of COPY provides direct access to load data from Amazon S3, Amazon DynamoDB, Amazon EMR, or over an arbitrary SSH connection. COPY is parallelized across slices, with each slice reading data in parallel, distributing as needed, and sorting locally. By default, compression scheme and optimizer statistics are updated with load. While customers can override these, they represent some of the dustier knobs still remaining in the system. COPY also directly supports ingestion of JSON data as well as data that is encrypted and/or compressed.

2.2 Control Plane

In addition to the database engine software itself, each Amazon Redshift node has host manager software that helps with deploying new database engine bits, aggregating events and metrics, generating instance-level events, archiving and rotating logs, and monitoring the host, database and log files for errors. The host manager also has limited capability to perform actions, for example, restarting a database process on failure.

Most control plane actions are coordinated off-instance by a separate Amazon Redshift control plane fleet. These nodes are responsible for fleet-wide monitoring and alarming as well as initiating maintenance tasks based on telemetry from instance host managers or actions requested by end-customers through the console or API. Example tasks would include node replacements, cluster resize, backup, restore, provisioning, patching, etc.

2.3 Dependent AWS Services

In addition to the core Amazon Redshift software itself, we leverage multiple AWS services, most significantly Amazon Elastic Compute Cloud (EC2) for instances, Amazon S3 for backup, Amazon Simple Workflow (SWF) for control plane actions, Amazon CloudWatch for customer instance metrics, Amazon Simple Notification Service (SNS) for customer alarms, Amazon VPC for network isolation, Amazon Route53 for DNS lookup, AWS CloudTrail for audit logging, and AWS Key Management Service and AWS CloudHSM for key management.

We additionally leverage a number of internal AWS services for additional capabilities including deployment, short-term credentials, log harvesting, load balancing, metering, etc.

The use of these services has significantly accelerated Amazon Redshift development, both as we have avoided the need to build robust, fault-tolerant and secure components where available in other AWS services, as well as providing us with access to an ongoing innovation stream by our sister development teams. For example, Amazon EC2 has significantly enhanced intrusion detection, network QoS, packets per second, server health monitoring, and IO queue management over the past two years – all capabilities we have absorbed with no changes to our engine.

The overall Amazon Redshift system architecture can be seen as the integration of traditional parallel, distributed relational database architecture with service-oriented architecture for management. Our greatest differentiation occurs when we are able to leverage these together.

For example, many database providers provide backup integration to cold storage. However, they are rarely able to expect the availability of any specific provider. By operating in the AWS cloud, Amazon Redshift is able to rely upon the specific characteristics of Amazon S3 availability, durability and access APIs. This has allowed us to entirely automate backup, making it continuous, incremental and automatic, and removing the need for customer attention. More significantly, we are able to include Amazon S3 backups as part of our data availability and durability design, by doing block-level backups and "page-faulting" in blocks when unavailable on local storage. This also allowed us to implement a streaming restore capability, allowing the database to be opened for SQL operations after metadata and catalog restoration, but while blocks were still being brought down in background. Since the average working set for a data warehouse is a small fraction of the total data stored, this allows performant queries to be obtained in a small fraction of the time required for a full restore. A meaningful percentage of Amazon Redshift customers delete their clusters every Friday and restore from backup each Monday.

3. The Case for Simplicity

We believe the success of SQL-based databases came in large part from the significant simplifications they brought to application development through the use of declarative query processing and a coherent model of concurrent execution. The introduction of data warehousing and later columnar layouts extended this by simplifying schema design and reducing the expense of join processing. And while customers will always demand more powerful capabilities (e.g., consider the rise in popularity of the MapReduce paradigm), our approach to this customer pull is to balance it with the belief that additional power generally requires additional education and understanding. As one of our customers put it, 'I want a relationship with my data, not my database.'

3.1 Simplifying the Purchase Decision Process

'Time to first report' is a key metric for our team. We see the clock starting at the point a customer first looks at our website to evaluate our service and stopping when they are first able to issue a query and obtain a result from their database instance. We take a retail mindset to this, understanding one of our customers looking for data management technology on AWS is the same person looking for a laptop or CD on Amazon.com. Many of the same techniques in ecommerce applications apply. For example, one might look at click trails through web pages and evaluate where abandonment occurs.

These may not feel like software development concerns, but we have found that they impact product decisions. It helped us to have launched using the standard PostgreSQL ODBC/JDBC drivers, providing confidence that our customers existing tools ecosystem would largely work. Our linear pricing model (with discounts for commitment) has informed how we scale out to support larger databases. Reducing the up-front steps required to create and configure a database has reduced abandonment.

Looking at the specific process of cluster creation, our analogue to "package delivery", we've limited the information required to number and type of nodes, basic network configuration and administrative account information. We are working to reduce this further. At launch time, cluster creation times averaged 15 minutes, which we viewed as a significant benefit compared to on-premise database provisioning times. Some months later, we introduced support for preconfigured Amazon Redshift nodes available for faster creations and supporting standbys for node failure replacements. These reduced provisioning time to 3 minutes, and meaningfully reduced abandonment.

We have found reducing the cost of an error to be as important as improving delivery time. Our customers can more readily experiment if they can easily "return" or "exchange" their database. Customers creating their first database cluster will automatically get enough free hours for their first two months to continually run a database supporting 160GB of compressed SSD data. Beyond this level, the use of hourly pricing enables experimentation and trial of the service by reducing commitment. While pricing may seem orthogonal to product design, a service involves hardware capital expense and operations personnel and software design can meaningfully impact both.

For example, at any time, customers can resize their clusters up or down or to a different instance type, removing the need for up-front capacity and performance estimation. Underneath the covers, we provision a new cluster, put the original cluster in read-only mode, and run a parallel node-to-node copy from source cluster to target. The source cluster is available for reads until the operation completes, at which time, we move the SQL endpoint and decommission the source.

3.2 Simplifying Database Administration

Most Amazon Redshift customers do not have a designated DBA to administer their database. This reduces their costs and enables them to allocate resources towards higher value work with their data. Our service manages much of the undifferentiated heavy lifting involved in database administration, including provisioning, patching, monitoring, repair, backup and restore.

We believe database administration operations should be as declarative as queries, with the database determining parallelization and distribution. Amazon Redshift operations are data-parallel within the cluster, as well cluster-parallel for fleet-wide actions such as patching and monitoring. For example, the time required to backup an entire cluster is proportional to the data changed on a single node. System backups are taken automatically and are automatically aged out. User backups leverage the blocks already backed up in system backups and are kept until explicitly deleted. Disruptions to cloud infrastructure get wide publicity so some customers ask for disaster recovery by storing backups in a second region. In Amazon Redshift, that only requires setting a checkbox and specifying the region. Within the system, we will initiate backing up data blocks to both the local and the remote region. Disaster recovery backups have the same streaming restore capabilities as local backups, allowing customers to start issuing queries within minutes of starting a cluster in the remote region.

Encryption is similarly straightforward. Enabling encryption requires setting a checkbox in our console and, optionally, specifying a key provider such as a hardware security module (HSM). Under the covers, we generate block-specific encryption keys (to avoid injection attacks from one block to another), wrap these with cluster-specific keys (to avoid injection attacks from one cluster to another), and further wrap these with a master key, stored by us off-network or via the customer-specified HSM. All user data, including backups, is encrypted. Key rotation is straightforward as it only involves re-encrypting block keys or cluster keys, not the entire database. Repudiation is equally straightforward, as it only involves losing access to the customer's key or re-encrypting all remaining valid cluster keys with a new master. We also benefit from security features in the core AWS platform. For example, we use Amazon VPC to provide network isolation of the compute nodes providing cluster storage, isolating them from general-purpose access from the leader node, which is accessible from the customer's VPC.

Future work will remove the need for user-initiated table administration operations, making them closer to backup in operation. The database should be able to determine when data access performance is degrading and take action to correct itself when load is otherwise light.

3.3 *Simplifying Database Tuning*

Amazon Redshift has few tuning knobs in comparison to other database engines. We view this as a plus, removing burden from our customers in favor of putting responsibility on ourselves. The main things set by a customer are instance type and number of nodes for the database cluster, and sort and distribution model used for individual tables.

While customers can set other parameters, such as column compression type, we strive to make such knobs dusty with disuse, by simply setting them accurately ourselves. The database generally has as much or more information as available to the customer to set these well, including query patterns, data distribution and cost of compression.

We are striving to make other settings, such as sort column and distribution key equally dusty. One technique we are applying is to reduce the cost of a suboptimal decision. For example, a missing projection can result in a full table scan while an additional one can greatly impact load time. By comparison, a multidimensional index [JAO] using z-curves degrades more gracefully with excess participation and still provides utility if leading columns are not specified. Similarly, z-curves can reduce the span of nodes involved in a join, rather than making them entirely local or fully distributed.

Similarly, relaxation of how we map data and query computation to nodes and slices would allow a more elastic system, which could grow and shrink as load required.

4. Customer Use Cases

Below, we touch on some of the ways customers are using Amazon Redshift. What connects many of these and other cases is SQL. The ability to declaratively state one's intent and have it automatically converted into an optimized execution plan that is resilient to changes in access patterns and data distribution is a very significant benefit compared to other data-intensive computing techniques. This is only yet more important when computation needs to be distributed and parallelized across many nodes, and resources distributed across many concurrent queries. A common theme across these use cases for forward work is data movement and transformation, which today seems to lack the simplicity and power of in-database processing using declarative SQL. A standardized declarative model for data structure identification and transformation would be valuable.

Enterprise data warehousing: Many customers utilize Amazon Redshift for what we consider to be the traditional enterprise data warehousing use case. They populate data from a set of source relational databases, ingest at an hourly or nightly cadence, and access data through BI tools. These customers have appreciated the simplicity and transparency of the procurement process, the ability to evaluate the service at minimal cost, and the ability to use their existing ecosystem of BI and ETL tools. They are generally struggling with the maintenance overhead for their existing systems and see the value of managed systems that take care of undifferentiated heavy lifting.

When migrating from other systems, we find that our customers like their existing databases, but do not always have great relationships with their database vendors. They often come to us when faced with a decision point on their existing system, either being forced to upgrade hardware for a managed system, coming to the end of a term license and about to enter a protracted negotiation cycle, or reaching the scaling limit on one engine and being forced to migrate to a second from the same vendor with somewhat different SQL semantics and maintenance. These have guided us towards reducing "sharp edges" in our own service, by making scaling linear and straightforward, increasing compatibility with PostgreSQL and growing the tools ecosystem we support.

Semi-structured "Big Data" analysis: Many customers also use Amazon Redshift for the integrated analysis of log and transaction data. We see a number of customers migrating away from HIVE on Hadoop and obtain much better performance at a much lower cost. They are also able to make their systems directly available to business analysts in their organizations using SQL or BI tools, rather than burdening their engineers and data scientists with the responsibility to generate these reports. For these customers, simplicity is a key driver, as they generally are not staffed with DBAs to manage and maintain their systems. We see this use case as where the bulk of "dark data" resides, and see many opportunities to further simplify their lives. For example, we could support transient data warehouses on a source 'data lake' or automatically 'relationalizing' source semi-structured data into tables for efficient query execution.

Data Transformation: An increasing number of Amazon Redshift customers use the service as part of a data processing pipeline, taking large amounts of raw data, dropping it into the data warehouse to run large SQL jobs that generate output tables that they can then use in their online business. An example would be in ad-tech, where many billion ad impressions may be distilled into lookup tables that informs an ad exchange online service. We have also seen customers begin to directly integrate Amazon Redshift into their customer facing screens under analytic reports and graphs. We see these customers moving towards SQL for the benefits of being able to straightforwardly and declaratively indicate intent and have the underlying system perform the parallel query decomposition. We see a similar trend in the SQL on Hadoop community, with SQL being used to reduce the labor involved in writing Map Reduce jobs. Speed and expressibility are key attributes here, for example, guiding our work on approximate functions. In time, we would like to build distributed approximate equivalents for all non-linear exact operations within our engine.

"Small Data" - A large number of Amazon Redshift customers have never previously used a data warehouse, instead directly running their reports against their source transaction systems. Amazon Redshift's cost structure and removal of overhead administration has enabled these customers to create data warehouses and obtain the benefits of improved performance, OLTP system offload, and retention of history. These customers are used to a short time lag to source data changes, so automated change data capture and automatic schema creation and maintenance are important capabilities.

5. Lessons Learned

Amazon Redshift has grown rapidly since it became generally available in February 2013. While our guiding principles have served us well over the past two years, we now manage many thousands of database instances and below offer some lessons we have learned from operating databases at scale.

Design escalators, not elevators: Failures are common when operating large fleets with many service dependencies. A key lesson for us has been to design systems that degrade on failures rather than losing outright availability. These are a common design pattern when working with hardware failures, for example, replicating data blocks to mask issues with disks. They are less common when working with software or service dependencies, though still necessary when operating in a dynamic environment. Amazon overall (including AWS) had 50 million code deployments over the past 12 months. Inevitably, at this scale, a small number of regressions will occur and cause issues until reverted. It is helpful to make one's own service resilient to an underlying service outage. For example, we support the ability to preconfigure nodes in each data center, allowing us to continue to provision and replace nodes for a period of time if there is an Amazon EC2 provisioning interruption. One can locally increase replication to withstand an Amazon S3 or network interruption. We are adding similar mitigation strategies for other external dependencies that can fail independently from the database itself.

Continuous delivery should be to the customer: Many engineering organizations now use continuous build and automated test pipelines to a releasable staging environment. However, few actually push the release itself at a frequent pace. While customers would prefer small patches to large ones for the same reasons engineering organizations prefer to build and test continuously, patching is an onerous process. This often leads to special-case, one-off patches per customer that are limited in scope – while necessary, they make patching yet more fragile.

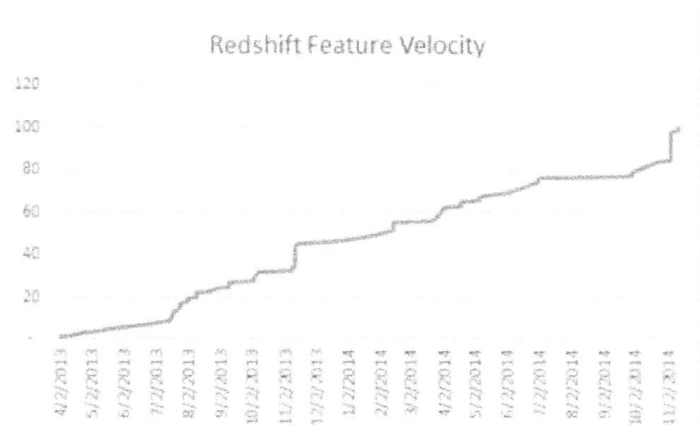

Figure 4: Cumulative features deployed over time

Amazon Redshift is set up to automatically patch customer clusters on a weekly basis in a 30-minute window specified by the customer. Patches are reversible and will automatically be reversed if we see an increase in errors or latency in our telemetry. At any point, a customer will only be on one of two patch versions, greatly improving our ability to reproduce and diagnose issues. We typically push new database engine software, including both features and bug fixes, every two weeks. We have found reducing this pace, for example to every four weeks, meaningfully increased the probability of a failed patch.

Use Pareto analysis to schedule work: In a rapidly growing service, operational load can easily overwhelm development capacity. We page ourselves on each database failure, understanding that, even if not a widespread concern, each issue is meaningful to the customer experiencing it. In Figure 5, Sev 2 refers to a severity 2 alarm that causes an engineer to get paged. This means operational load roughly correlates to business success. Within Amazon Redshift, we collect error logs across our fleet and monitor tickets to understand top ten causes of error, with the aim of extinguishing one of the top ten causes of error each week.

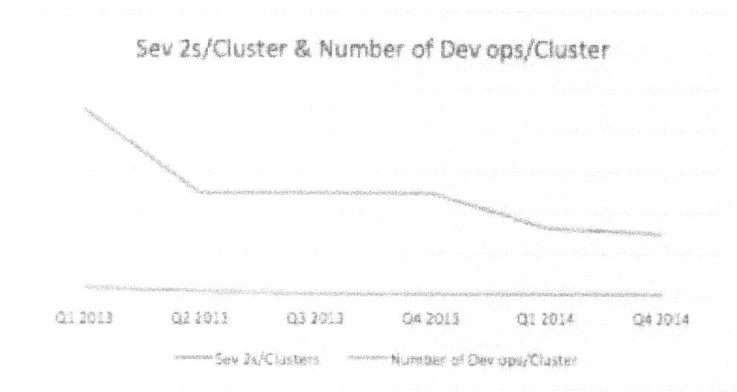

Figure 5: Tickets per cluster over time

Pareto analysis is equally useful in understanding customer functional requirements. However, it is more difficult to collect. We manage this by simply conducting over 1000 direct one-to-one conversations with customers each year. This provides a clear sample of customer needs and service gaps, providing us with actionable telemetry towards scheduling feature development. In future, we would like to add automated collection of usage statistics by feature, query plan shapes, etc. across our fleet.

6. Related Work

While Amazon Redshift, when launched, was the first widely available data warehouse-as-a-service, its core database technology (parser, optimizer, engine, storage organization, MPP architecture) was derived from technology licensed from ParAccel. ParAccel belongs to a group of column-oriented DBMS products that appeared from the middle through the end of the 2000s: Vertica, Ingres VectorWise, Infobright, Kickfire, and many others [1]. These systems had several similarities in their design philosophy and list of features, with many of them influenced by two pioneering modern column-store systems: C-Store [8] and MonetDB/X100 [3].

Redshift's compression techniques are similar to those used by Vertica, and their performance tradeoffs are well understood [2]. Redshift foregoes traditional indexes (or projections in C-Store/Vertica) and instead focuses on sequential scan speed through compiled code execution and column-block skipping based on value-ranges stored in memory. Infobright's Knowledge Grid and Netezza's Zone Maps also rely on block skipping which as a technique was first discussed in [5]. Code compilation techniques in query execution have received renewed attention in academia [6][9] and are also used in other systems such as Microsoft's Hekaton [4].

7. Conclusion

Amazon Redshift's price, performance, and simplicity extend the use cases for data warehousing beyond traditional enterprise data warehousing, into big data and software-as-service applications with embedded analytics. Unlike traditional data warehouse systems, which often require large upfront payments and months of vendor negotiations, hardware procurement and deployments, Amazon Redshift clusters can be provisioned in minutes, enabling customers to get started with no commitments and scale up to a petabyte scale cluster. Redshift also offers automated patching, provisioning, scaling, securing, backup, restore, and a comprehensive set of security features such as encryption at rest, in transit, HSM integration and audit logging.

By dramatically lowering the cost and effort associated with deploying data warehousing systems without compromising on features and performance, Amazon Redshift is not only changing how traditional enterprises think about data warehousing but also making data warehousing technology available to segments that had not previously considered it. This is evident in Redshift's customer base, which ranges from enterprises like NTT DOCOMO and Amazon.com with multi-petabyte systems, to high-scale startups like Pinterest and Flipboard with hundreds of terabytes, to small startups with hundreds of gigabytes in their data warehouses.

8. Acknowledgements

We first would like to acknowledge the contributions of each engineer on the Amazon Redshift team, who worked hard to deliver the first version, and continue to drive a fast pace of innovation while maintaining operational excellence of the service for our customers. We would also like to thank Raju Gulabani for his guidance through the launch of Amazon Redshift and its subsequent operation.

Amazon Redshift has lineage in the database engine work done by the ParAccel team, now at Actian, which in turn benefited from work from the PostgreSQL community. Their work was a very significant accelerant in the delivery of Amazon Redshift.

We also thank Christopher Olston and Sihem Amer-Yahia for shepherding this paper and all the reviewers for their valuable comments.

9. References

[1] Abadi D, Boncz P, Harizopoulos S, Idreos S, Madden S. The Design and Implementation of Modern Column-Oriented Database Systems. Foundations and Trends in Databases. 2013;5(3):197-280.

[2] Daniel J. Abadi, Samuel R. Madden, and Miguel Ferreira. Integrating compression and execution in column-oriented database systems. In Proceedings of the ACM SIGMOD Conference on Management of Data, pages 671–682, 2006.

[3] Peter Boncz, Marcin Zukowski, and Niels Nes. MonetDB/X100: Hyper- pipelining query execution. In Proceedings of the biennial Conference on Innovative Data Systems Research (CIDR), 2005.

[4] Cristian Diaconu, Craig Freedman, Erik Ismert, Per-Åke Larson, Pravin Mittal, Ryan Stonecipher, Nitin Verma, Mike Zwilling. Hekaton: SQL server's memory-optimized OLTP engine. SIGMOD Conference 2013: 1243-1254.

[5] Guido Moerkotte. Small Materialized Aggregates: A Light Weight Index Structure for Data Warehousing. VLDB '98 Proceedings of the 24rd International Conference on Very Large Data Bases. Pages 476-487.

[6] Thomas Neumann. Efficiently Compiling Efficient Query Plans for Modern Hardware. PVLDB 2011, Seattle, USA.

[7] J. A. Orenstein and T. H. Merrett. A class of data structures for associative searching. In *Proc. PODS*, pages 181–190, 1984.

[8] Michael Stonebraker, Daniel J. Abadi, Adam Batkin, Xuedong Chen, Mitch Cherniack, Miguel Ferreira, Edmond Lau, Amerson Lin, Samuel R. Madden, Elizabeth J. O'Neil, Patrick E. O'Neil, Alexan- der Rasin, Nga Tran, and Stan B. Zdonik. C-Store: A Column-Oriented DBMS. In Proceedings of the International Conference on Very Large Data Bases (VLDB), pages 553–564, 2005.

[9] J. Sompolski, M. Zukowski, and P. A. Boncz. Vectorization vs. compilation in query execution. In DaMoN, pages 33–40, 2011.

[10] Gartner : User Survey Analysis: Key Trends Shaping the Future of Data Center Infrastructure Through 2011
IDC: Worldwide Business Analytics Software 2012–2016 Forecast and 2011 Vendor Shares.

ShareInsights - An Unified Approach to Full-stack Data Processing

Mukund Deshpande
Persistent Systems Ltd.
'Bhageerath', Senapati Bapat Road,
Pune 411005, INDIA
mukund_deshpande@persistent.com

Dhruva Ray
Persistent Systems Ltd.
'Bhageerath', Senapati Bapat Road,
Pune 411005, INDIA
dhruva_ray@persistent.com

Sameer Dixit
Persistent Systems Ltd.
'Bhageerath', Senapati Bapat Road,
Pune 411005, INDIA
sameer_dixit@persistent.com

Avadhoot Agasti
Persistent Systems Ltd.
'Bhageerath', Senapati Bapat Road,
Pune 411005, INDIA
avadhoot_agasti@persistent.com

ABSTRACT

The field of data analysis seeks to extract value from data for either business or scientific benefit. This field has seen a renewed interest with the advent of big data technologies and a new organizational role called data scientist. Even with the new found focus, the task of analyzing large amounts of data is still challenging and time-consuming.

The essence of data analysis involves setting up data pipelines which consists of several operations that are chained together - starting from data collection, data quality checks, data integration, data analysis and data visualization (including the setting up of interaction paths in that visualization).

In our opinion, the challenges stem from from the technology diversity at each stage of the data pipeline as well as the lack of process around the analysis.

In this paper we present a platform that aims to significantly reduce the time it takes to build data pipelines. The platform attempts to achieve this in following ways.

1. Allow the user to describe the entire data pipeline with a single language and idioms - all the way from data ingestion to insight expression (via visualization and end-user interaction).

2. Provide a rich library of parts that allow users to quickly assemble a data analysis pipeline in the language.

3. Allow for a collaboration model that allows multiple users to work together on a data analysis pipeline as well as leverage and extend prior work with minimal effort.

We studied the efficacy of the platform for a data hackathon competition conducted in our organization. The hackathon provided us with a way to study the impact of the approach. Rich data pipelines which traditionally took weeks to build were constructed and deployed in hours. Consequently, we believe that the complexity of designing and running the data analysis pipeline can be significantly reduced; leading to a marked improvement in the productivity of data analysts/data scientists.

SIGMOD'15, May 31–June 4, 2015, Melbourne, Victoria, Australia.

ACM 978-1-4503-2758-9/15/05 ...$15.00.
http://dx.doi.org/10.1145/2723372.2742800.

Categories and Subject Descriptors

H.4 [**Information Systems Applications**]: Miscellaneous; D.3.2 [**Language Classifications**]: [Data-flow languages]

General Terms

Management, Design, Experimentation, Human Factors, Languages.

Keywords

Big data; Data analysis; Data visualization; Data pipeline

1. INTRODUCTION

The field of data analysis has seen dramatic changes in the last few years. These changes are seen primarily on the dimensions of data, evolving user needs and technology changes.

On the data side of the equation, the volume of data that needs to be analyzed has become extremely large. It is now routine to analyze terabytes of data and in some cases, petabytes as well. The nature of the data is also multi-structured with text, audio as well as visual data being analyzed side-by-side with structured tabular data. In line with an increased amount of public data being made available, the need for integrating it with private organization data has never been higher.

On the consumption side of the equation, users are making increasing demands on the data visualization component of data analysis. With the advent of multiple devices and form factors, data needs to be visualized and analyzed at multiple resolutions, possibly in environments with varying network connectivity. Also, the bar for aesthetics and ease of use for data visualization has gone up significantly. Users are demanding richer and more interesting widgets for displaying data and intuitive ways of interacting with them. Finally, with users being increasingly connected on networks (enterprise and social), the ability to share and collaborate with their peers for building and running the data pipeline is also becoming crucial.

On the technology side of the equation, the last few years have seen several technologies reaching mainstream - both big data technologies as well as advanced use of JavaScript for data visualization. Though big data technologies allow analyzing large data-sets, they have also brought an additional complexity of multiple technologies and different programming paradigms. Additionally, at every boundary, there remain integration challenges. Concomitantly, data crunching libraries in Python and R are seeing a revived interest and there appears to be a renewed interest in using these libraries in the data pipeline.

In our opinion, all of these challenges have made the task of doing data analysis increasingly difficult and time consuming.

The essence of data analysis involves setting up data pipelines which consists of several operations that are chained together - starting from data collection, data quality checks, data integration, data analysis and data visualization. (includes setting up interaction paths in that visualization)

Since, data pipelines operates on electronic media, the task of running and changing a data analysis pipeline is relatively easy; Consequently, in most cases, the data analysis pipeline is built and stabilized by incrementally building the pipeline. This iterative process mandates that it be very easy to change and edit an existing data pipeline. Sadly, that is not the state of the affairs[4].

In this paper, we present a platform which attempts to significantly ease the process of building complete data pipelines for businesses and data scientists. The platform and the supposed benefits were tested by running a data hackathon. Data pipelines and dashboards which took weeks to implement were completed in under six hours.

The paper is organized as follows. In section 2, we explain current approaches and the challenges faced in building data pipelines. In section 3, we illustrate key concepts of the unified representation provided on the ShareInsights platform by building complex data pipelines. Section 4 describes the key building blocks and features provided by the platform. Section 5 reports the findings of the hackathon used to verify the utility of the platform, Finally we conclude the paper with observations and future areas of work.

2. BUILDING A DATA ANALYSIS PIPELINE

In this section, we outline the current approaches to building data pipelines and the challenges faced by businesses and data scientists.

2.1 Current Approaches

2.1.1 *Data Warehouse stack*

This stack uses an extract-transform-load (ETL) mechanism to ingest, clean, transform and ultimately load processed data into the data warehouse[8]. Reporting tools query the warehouse to give reports to the end-user. The typical architecture is shown in figure 1.

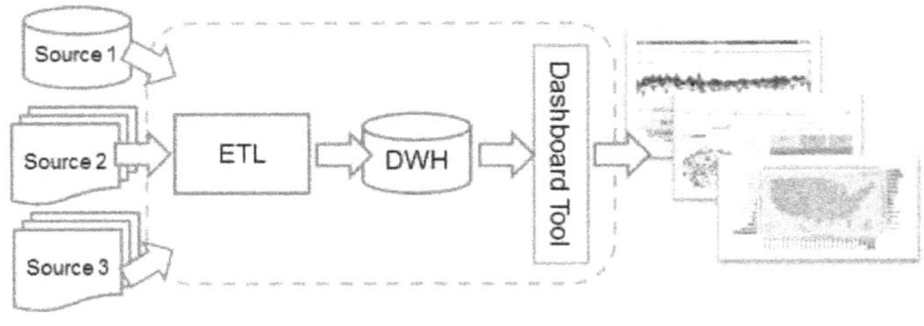

Figure 1: BI Architecture for data pipelines

This configuration is widely used and there is a relative maturity in the tooling and understanding of the data pipeline process. Almost all available tools provide a user interface for each step of the ETL process including reporting. Even so, building the pipeline requires investment in tool knowledge and relational data theory. Due to it's relational lineage, this stack was traditionally not adept at handling unstructured data.

2.1.2 *Big Data stack*

This stack leverages the Hadoop platform to do the traditional ETL processing described earlier. ETL is done with a map-reduce paradigm (as well as other programming styles) and uses a cluster of commodity hardware to scale[6]. Support for handling unstructured data is more natural on this platform.

With the advent of powerful client machines, fast JavaScript engines and rich widget libraries, JavaScript has become the de facto choice for creating interactive data visualizations.

The canonical architecture for this stack is shown in figure 2.

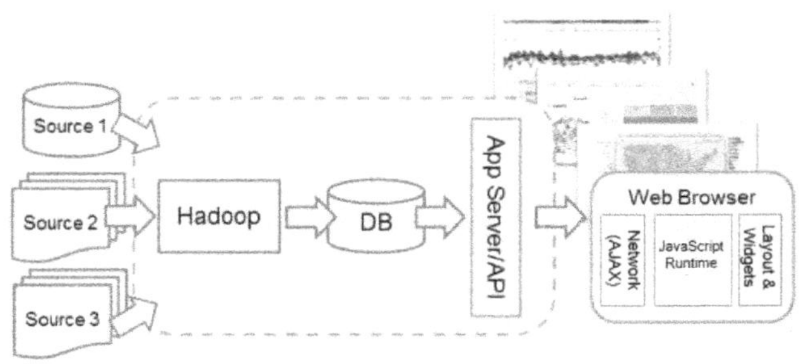

Figure 2: Big Data Architecture for data pipelines

2.2 Challenges

Both these approaches have serious challenges that limit the efficacy of developers building the data pipeline in organizations[14].

1. Multiple Technologies:
Data visualization technologies/tooling and data transformation technologies/tooling are inherently different. Apart from requiring different mind-sets, multiple technology stacks bring their attendant problems of data serialization, interface design and the like. This problem is more acute for the Big Data stack where engineers need to glue reporting to the transformed data.

2. Unavailability of Skills:
Given the diverse technology pieces present in the data pipeline, lack of skills is an acute problem that the industry faces. This translates to a lower team velocity to build data pipelines. The problem is made more acute as there is an explosion of technology options at each phase of the data pipeline.

3. Lack of Collaboration Model:
Although most technologies (whether it is ETL or reporting) provide lot of libraries to work with, the abstraction model is not necessarily enforced. It is quite common for the complexity to spread both in the library as well as the glue code that puts systems together. This problem is more acute for the Big Data stack - that uses JavaScript based interactive visualization - where the user needs to resort to significant custom programming. This hampers collaboration and it is very hard to leverage prior work. More importantly, since there is no systemic enforcement of abstractions, existing code needs to be understood before re-use. This leads to significant overheads.

3. SHAREINSIGHTS PLATFORM

The platform's unique contribution is to present an unified representation across the data stack so that common idioms can be used for the **entire** data pipeline. Since data pipeline architects are dealing with one logical model for the whole pipeline, we believe that it would translate into a faster turnaround.

In the subsequent sections, we explain the key abstractions and techniques provided by the platform using examples.

Use Case : Analysis of Apache Open Source Projects.

The Apache activity analysis dashboard analyzes open source projects on http://www.apache.org. It computes a project activity index to allow for relative comparison of project activity in the same (and/or complementary) technology category . This dashboard is shown in figure 3.

The raw data for this dashboard comes from bug tickets, project commit history, stack overflow traffic and project collaborators information. We allow dashboard users to tweak the weightage given to each of the four parameters - check-ins, bug issues, contributors and releases (the four sliders at the top of the dashboard) to determine the overall project activity (and thereby relevance) in the project cloud. Once the weight factors have been decided, users can change the date range of their analysis using the provided date slider. Finally, clicking on a project bubble will reveal statistics about the selected project.(figure 13).

In the following sections, we demonstrate the key abstractions of our system using this example.

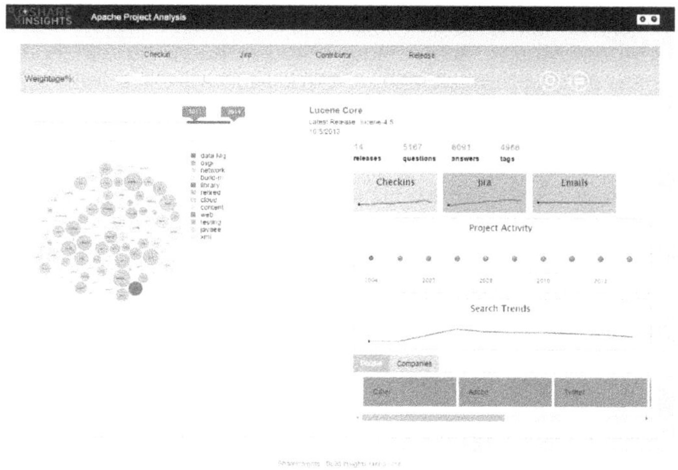

Figure 3: Apache Open Source Project Analysis

3.1 Flow File

All data pipelines are expressed in a flow file. Each flow file has a name and contains the data pipelines associated with it. Each flow file has a Data (D) configuration section, a Widget (W) configuration section, a Task (T) configuration section, a Flow (F) configuration section - to process data objects through tasks (T) - and a Layout (L) configuration section to position widgets (W) in the dashboard.

These sections are elaborated below.

3.2 Data Section

This section contains the data objects (sources and sinks) used by the data pipeline. Every dashboard needs data objects to work off from. The data section allows the dashboard to configure these data objects. Data object configuration involves specifying the protocol and protocol parameters used to fetch the data as well as parameters to understand the payload.

The platform provides popular protocol connectors - such as File (local, remote), HTTP/S, FTP, JDBC, ad-hoc queries over JDBC - and recognizes popular data payload formats such as CSV, AVRO, XML and JSON documents.

A sample data object configuration described in figure 4 indicates that the data source is a CSV file. (present in the data directory of the dashboard)

```
D.stack_summary :
    separator : ','
    source : 'stackoverflow.csv'
    format : 'csv'
```

Figure 4: Data source configuration

Additionally, users need to explicitly call out the schema of the payload as shown in figure 5.

```
stack_summary:
  [project ,question ,answer ,tags]
```

Figure 5: Data source schema

These column names may be used to configure tasks which transform data sources into other forms. In this example, the data object columns are questions, answers and tags related to the projects being analyzed by this data pipeline. Even though, this example shows data read from a local file, the data object can be configured to directly talk to the provider APIs. This is shown in figure 6. The => notation maps JSON paths in the payload to column names.

```
D:
   stack_questions : [
      question => title ,
      tags => tags ,
   ]
D. stack_questions:
   source : https://api.stackexchange.com/
   2.2/questions?order=desc&
   sort=activity&site=stackoverflow

   protocol : http
   format : json
   request_type : get
   http_headers :
     X-Access-Key : XXX
```

Figure 6: Configure data source with provider APIs

3.3 Task Section

The task section contains all the task configurations used by the data pipeline.

Tasks operate on data objects and are consumed in data flows (shown in section 3.4). The platform comes pre-loaded with a set of useful transformations. The input data to a task is determined contextually; the preceding data object or task (tasks also output temporary data objects). Tasks are generally configured by specifying column names to operate on.

For example a filter task would use a column name in a filter expression as shown in figure 7. Note that the task configuration assumes that it will be used in a context where the data source has a **rating** column.

```
classification :
    type : filterby
    filter_expression :rating < 3
```

Figure 7: Filter task

Tasks can be reused in multiple flows as long as the preceding data source has the column the task consumes.

Task transformations can add columns (e.g. join operation) or reduce columns (e.g. group operation) or preserve columns (e.g. filter operation) to the transformed data source.

3.4 Flow Section

The flow section contains a collection of flows. Each flow allows data-sets to be transformed into other forms. We leverage the Unix pipe notation to express data transformation semantics.

A sample flow is shown in the F section of figure 8. The flow transforms **svn_jira_summary** to **checkin_jira_emails data sink** with a groupby task (using a composite key).

```
D:
...
  svn_jira_summary:[project ,year ,noOfBugs
    noOfCheckins ,noOfEmailsTotal ...]

  checkin_jira_emails:[project ,year ,
     total_checkins ,total_jira ,
     total_emails ]
F:
...
D. checkin_jira_emails :
  D. svn_jira_summary | T. get_svnjira_count
T:
...
get_svnjira_count :
    type : groupby
    groupby : [project ,year]
    aggregates :
        - operator : sum
          apply_on : noOfCheckins
          out_field : total_checkins
        - operator : sum
          apply_on : noOfBugs
          out_field : total_jira
        - operator : sum
          apply_on : noOfEmailsTotal
          out_field : total_emails
```

Figure 8: A data transformation flow

We constrain each flow to start with (optionally) multiple data sources (i.e fan-in) and end with (optionally) multiple data outputs (fan-out). The input data objects are transformed to output data objects via transform (or task) operators configured in the task section. Data sinks are automatically configured by the system. (As outlined in section 3.2). Note that data-sink is purely a concept for clarity of explanation. The system internally makes no differentiation between a data source and a data sink.

3.4.1 Sharing processed data objects

Data objects (sources or sinks) can be shared in the following ways.

Enable Remote Access.
To make the data object available to the dashboard (over a network connection), specify **endpoint** to true as shown in figure 9. Data objects which hold aggregated or summarized data for visualization purposes would set this property to true.

Enable Group Access.
To make the data object available to other dashboards, specify a name by which this data object will be referenced by other dashboards. In figure 10, **checkin_jira_emails** is published as a named data source - **project_chatter**. Other dashboards can use this data object by name without having to configure it in their own dashboards. (The platform

```
D.checkin_jira_emails:
    endpoint : true
       OR
#+ is an alias for endpoint :true
+D.checkin_jira_emails:
    D.svn_jira_summary|T.get_svnjira_count
```

Figure 9: A data sink configured as an endpoint

searches for this data object - in the shared objects list - when referenced in another dashboard)

This concept allows for creation of dashboards with the sole intention of building flows to transform raw data sources into a shared set of data entities on the platform.

```
D.checkin_jira_emails:
        publish : project_chatter
        endpoint : true
```

Figure 10: A published data sink

Data sources and sinks can be configured with both publish and endpoint values. If none of these keywords are used, it is assumed to be a throw-away data source/sink.

3.4.2 *Linear flow specification*

Data sinks can also be input to other flows as demonstrated in figure 11.

```
D.temp_release_count : D.releases
                 | T.calculate_total_release

D.rel_qa_tags : (
          D.temp_release_count,
          D.stack_summary
) | T.combine_stack_summary
```

Figure 11: A flow using intermediate data object

Note that the user can only specify simple (as in linear) flows. Since data sinks can become data sources for other flows, it is possible to build up arbitrarily complicated transformation paths.

On submission, the platform internally builds a directed acyclic graph (DAG) from the collection of flows specified by the user.

3.5 Widget Section

The widget section contains a collection of widget configurations. Widgets show transformed (endpoint) data and needs to be minimally configured with a data source and the type of widget (Line, Pie, Bubble etc). The platform comes pre-loaded with a set of commonly used widgets. Every widget has a set of attributes which associate (or bind) with data source columns. These attributes are called data attributes or widget columns[9]. The remaining attributes of a widget are visual attributes. Visual attributes are available in various categories such as legend, axis, dimension configurations and the like.

```
D:
...

project_data:[project,year,total_wt...]

W:
...

project_technology_bubble :
  # Data Attributes
  type : BubbleChart
  source : D.project_data | T.get_date
         | T.aggregate_project_bubbles
  text : project
  size : total_wt
  legend_text : technology
  # Visual Attributes
  default_selection : True
  default_selection_key : text
  default_selection_value : 'pig'
  ...
  legend :
    show_legends : true
    ...
```

Figure 12: Widget configuration

Figure 12 shows how the project bubble widget is configured using project_data (endpoint data) as a source. The widget columns are **text** and **size** and are bound to the **project** and **total_wt** columns of the data schema respectively.

Note that multiple widgets can be configured with the same data source.

Most of the widgets used by the Apache dashboard are provided by the platform. The widget which lets the user decide the relative weight of each parameter to compute project activity index is a custom widget - written using the platform extension APIs.(Section 4.2)

3.5.1 *Widget to Widget Interaction*

Dashboards allow users to interact with widgets to explore data patterns. Common examples include filter and drill-down operations. For example, a pie wedge selection may be used to filter rows in a data grid. In general, the visual information-seeking mantra: "overview first, zoom and filter, then details on demand" [13] has never been more relevant.

In the Apache dashboard, selection of a project in the bubble widget reflects the project statistics at the right as shown in figure 13.

Figure 14 demonstrates how this interaction is represented as a flow in the widget source.

Notice that the interaction specification is represented as a data transformation flow - identical in all respects to flows in the Flow (F) section. These transformations also use tasks defined in the task (T) section. Popular widget flow tasks provided by the platform are group, filter and map.

The task **filter_projects** configuration is shown in figure 15. This task filters by the **project** column of the data source with values retrieved from widget **project category bubble**'s **text** widget column property. Note that we

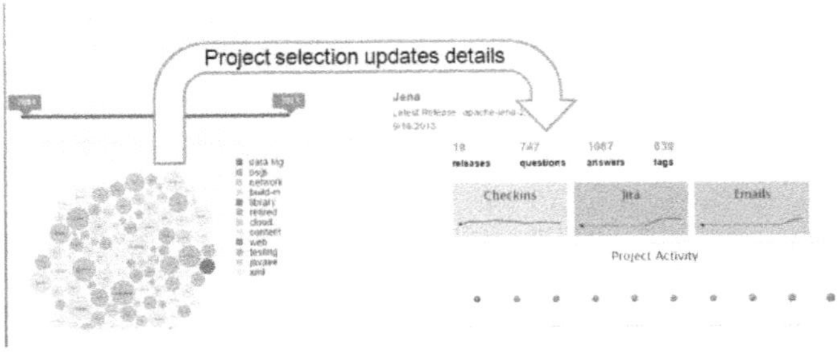

Figure 13: Project selection updates project details

W:

```
...

project_name :
   # Data Attributes
   type : HTML
   tag : section
   source : D.project_latest_release
                  | T.filter_projects
```

Figure 14: Widget interaction modeling

treat widgets as data objects and widget columns as data columns(attributes).

Note the **absence** of event handlers and traditional imperative programming constructs to handle widget - widget interaction.

T:

```
...

filter_projects :
  type : filterby
  filterby : [project]

  #widget data source
  filter_source :W.project_category_bubble

  #widget column
  filter_val : [text]
```

Figure 15: A filter task configured for use in interaction flows

3.6 Layout Section

The layout section arranges the widgets on the dashboard screen. The platform models any dashboard as a grid of widgets. Every cell in the grid holds a reference to a widget name or can itself be a layout. Every row in the grid is broken into twelve columns (arbitrary) of equal width. Each cell specifies how many columns it will span. A sample layout is specified in figure 16.

To explain the key concepts, we have only used few configuration items from the complete Apache project analysis

```
L:
  description : Apache Project Analysis
  rows :
   #Row 1 has a cell spans 12 columns
   - [span12 : W.apache_custom_widget]

   #Row 2 has two cells
   #Cell 1 spans 4 cols
   #Cell 2 spans 8 cols
   - [span4 :W.year_slider_layout ,
      span8 :W.right_project_info_layout]

  ...

   - [span5 :W.project_category_bubble ,
      span7 :W.right_sliders_layout]
```

Figure 16: Apache dashboard layout

dashboard. The complete listing of this dashboard can be availed on request from any of the authors.

The flow file grammar (simplified) is presented in appendix B for reference.

3.7 Data Sharing

Use Case : Tweet Analysis .

In this section, we demonstrate data sharing by creating two data pipelines. The first data pipeline transforms source tweet data into shared data objects. The second data pipeline consumes these shared data objects to create an interactive dashboard. We also illustrate the ability to handle unstructured data and the notion of custom tasks. The dashboard we want to build is shown in figure 17.

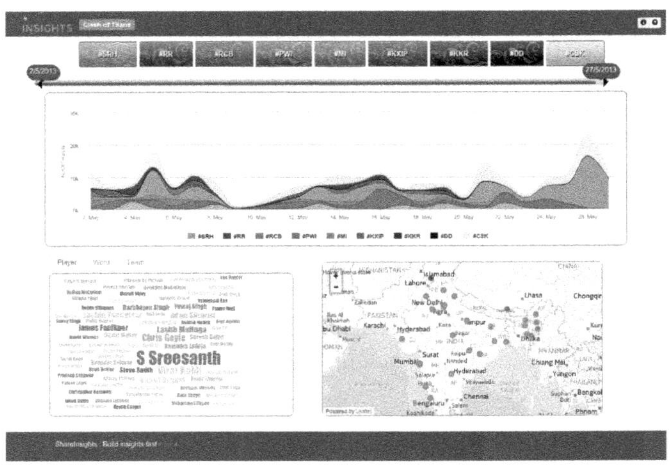

Figure 17: Tweet analysis for IPL

The raw data for this dashboard comes from the tweets collected during the Indian Premier League (IPL) competition. The dashboard allows users to select teams and a date range. The remaining widgets are filtered for the selected team and date range. The streamgraph [3] depicts the relative team tweet volumes, the word clouds show popular words(players, team names) and the map shows the favorite team for major cities in India. (The diameter of the marker is proportional to total tweets for that team and location)

3.7.1 Data-Processing Mode

The platform allows dashboards to be created in a data-processing mode only. In this mode, the flow file has only a data section (D), flow section (F) and a task section (T). The (transformed) aggregated data from the flows are made 'available' (as defined in section 3.4.1) for consumption in other dashboards. We demonstrate using one representative flow. The data section is shown in figure 18.

```
D:
ipltweets : [
    postedTime => created_at ,
    body => text ,
    location => user.location
]
players_tweets : [
    date ,
    player ,#normalized name of player
    count #count of tweets for a player
]
```

Figure 18: IPL Data Section

In this case, source data are tweets retrieved from Gnip provided APIs [7]. Each tweet is a document with hierarchical data items. Users need to map paths in this document (in a similar fashion to XPath or JSONPath queries) to column names. In figure 18, **user.location** path is mapped to a schema attribute - **location**. The flow in figure 19 takes raw tweets (from **ipltweets**) and transforms it to a schema represented by **players_tweets**.

```
F:
...
D.players_tweets : D.ipltweets |
        T.players_pipeline |
        T.players_count
D.players_tweets :
  endpoint : true
  publish : players_tweets
```

Figure 19: Transform raw tweet data

The first step transforms (in parallel) the date to a standard format and extracts player names from the tweet by looking at an user provided dictionary (which maps the multitude of player names - abbreviations, nick names etc - to a standardized player name). This is shown (and explained with comments) in figure 20 and figure 21.

```
players_pipeline :
    parallel:[
        T.norm_ipldate ,T.extract_players
    ]
```

Figure 20: Transform 1 : Normalize date and extract player in parallel

```
norm_ipldate :
  type : map
  operator : date
  transform:postedTime #attribute to map
  input_format:'E MMM dd HH:mm:ss Z yyyy'
  output_format : yyyy-MM-dd
  output : date # output column
extract_players :
  type : map
  operator : extract
  transform : body #attribute to transform
  dict : players.txt #standard names map
  output : player #output column
```

Figure 21: Transform 1 : Normalize date and extract player tasks

The first step of the transformation thus produces the schema shown in figure 22.

```
players_tweets : [
  postedTime, body, location # ipltweets
  date,   #normalized date
  player   #normalized player name
]
```

Figure 22: Intermediate schema

The second step of the transformation takes the intermediate schema and groups by date and player to give the count of tweets for the composite key (date + player). This is shown in figure 23. This produces data in the scheme described in figure 18.

```
players_count :
  type : groupby
  groupby : [date, player]
```

Figure 23: Transform 2 : Group by date and player

Some of the important transformation tasks are provided by the platform. Users however can extend the capability of the platform by providing their own transformation tasks. User defined tasks are treated on par with system provided tasks and are represented in the flow file in an identical fashion. The complete listing for this dashboard is available in appendix A.1.

3.7.2 Data-consumption Mode

The shared data object (**player_tweets**) is now available to other consumers (dashboards) on the platform. The consumption dashboard typically has a layout section (L), widget section (W) and a task section (T) for modeling widget interaction. When widgets use the shared data object as their source, the platform automatically searches the shared data objects on the platform for matches. Breaking up the data processing and data consumption activities results in benefits which are outlined in greater detail in section 4.5.3. The complete listing for this dashboard is available in appendix A.2.

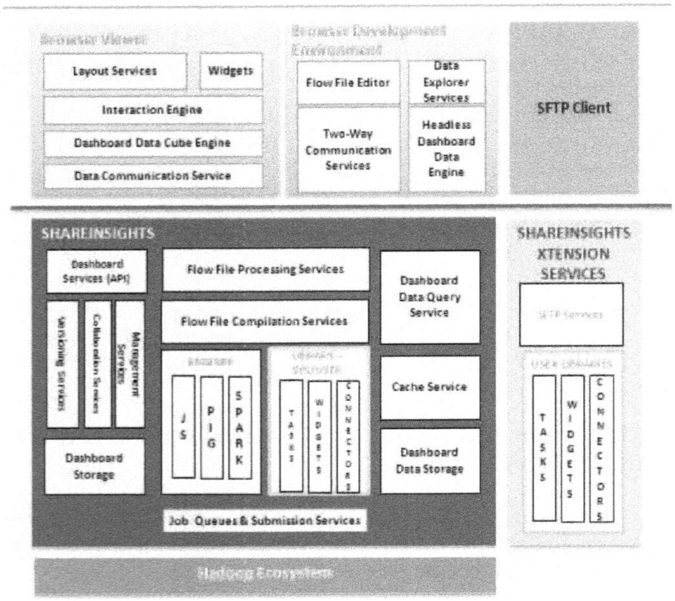

Figure 24: ShareInsights Platform Blocks

4. THE SHAREINSIGHTS PLATFORM

In this section, we provide details on the building blocks of the ShareInsights platform (See figure 24).

4.1 Flow File Compilation Services

The flow file compilation module is the heart of the platform. The compilation module builds an abstract syntax tree (AST) from the flows specified in the flow and widget section. The AST eventually gets converted into either a Pig[12]/Spark[15] job - for data processing - and a data cube (in JavaScript) - for ad-hoc widget interaction (group, filter etc). This is shown diagrammatically in figure 25.

The AST provides opportunities to optimize the complete flow. For example, tasks can be re-arranged to minimize data transfers to the browser.

Additionally, the generated output needs to be cognizant of the operating environment settings (constraints) such as screen resolution and client computing resources.

Screen Resolution : At one end of the spectrum, mobile devices have limited screen space - further limiting interaction methods - and at the other end, power analysts have large monitors that affords richer visualization and interaction methods.

Client Computing Resources : It is not guaranteed that the user will have a powerful device for accessing the visualization. Additionally, JavaScript support may be varied across devices and in the worst case even turned off.

These constraints influence what analysis can be displayed meaningfully and the platform needs to choose the appropriate representation and execution engine.

4.2 ShareInsights Extension Services

The ShareInsights platform comes with a library of data connectors, data formats, tasks and widgets. Through the platform extension services, users can bring their own extensions to the platform. The section lists the possible ways to extend the platform.

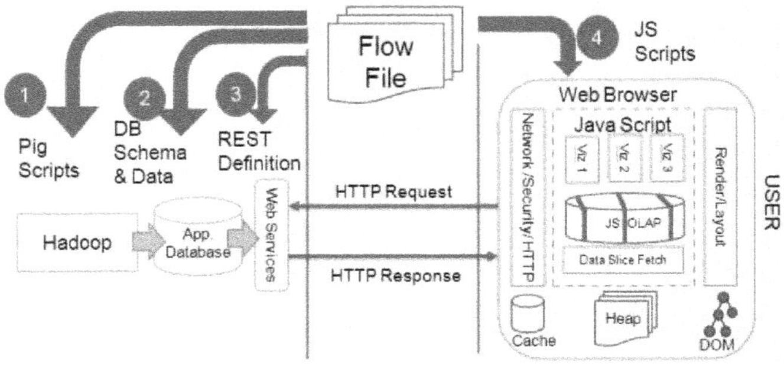

Figure 25: Flow file compilation

Connectors : The Connectors API allows to connect data sources via new protocols to the platform.

Data formats : The Data formats API allows for recognizing and processing new data formats.

Tasks : The Tasks API allows for introducing new kinds of tasks on the platform. Tasks can be broadly categorized as

1. Transforming a column value into another value. These kinds of tasks are called operators and work off a given data point.

2. Transforming a bag of values into a point value. These kinds of tasks are called user defined aggregates.

3. Transforming a data object via the underlying engine (e.g. Spark) APIs. For example, the platform **group** operator generates calls to the engine group operator.

4. Transforming a data object via a native map reduce job. This is very useful as many organizations have existing map reduce jobs and they can be part of the platform through this route.

Since, we support multiple execution contexts, each task (potentially) has an implementation for each run-time environment - Hadoop and JavaScript (browser) run-times. To encourage adoption and lower barriers of entry, tasks can be written in either Java, JavaScript, Python or R and can use existing libraries on those environments. For example Python natural language processing libraries can be wrapped with our APIs and used in the flow file.

Widgets : The Widgets API allows new widgets to be introduced to the platform. Commercial and open source widgets can easily be made part of the platform by implementing this interface.

Styling : The dashboard look and feel can be changed or enhanced using Cascading Style Sheets (CSS). Stylesheet authors can use widget names specified in the flow file as style targets in the CSS file.

4.3 ShareInsights Development Services

ShareInsights uses regular desktop software for contributors to be productive and requires no additional installs. Data pipeline analysts interact with ShareInsights via the development interface or the extension services interface. These interfaces are described in the subsequent sections.

4.3.1 Development interface

ShareInsights uses the browser exclusively for data-pipeline development. All ShareInsights dashboard operations (create, edit, run, save etc) as well as data operations can be accessed via intuitive REST APIs.

For example, to create a dashboard from scratch, users need to navigate to the following URL : https://<server-base-path>/dashboards/<dashboard-name>/create.

Running this command would take the user to a web editor to edit the dashboard as shown in figure 26. The key components of the editor are also highlighted in the same figure. The data explorer will be covered in section 4.4.

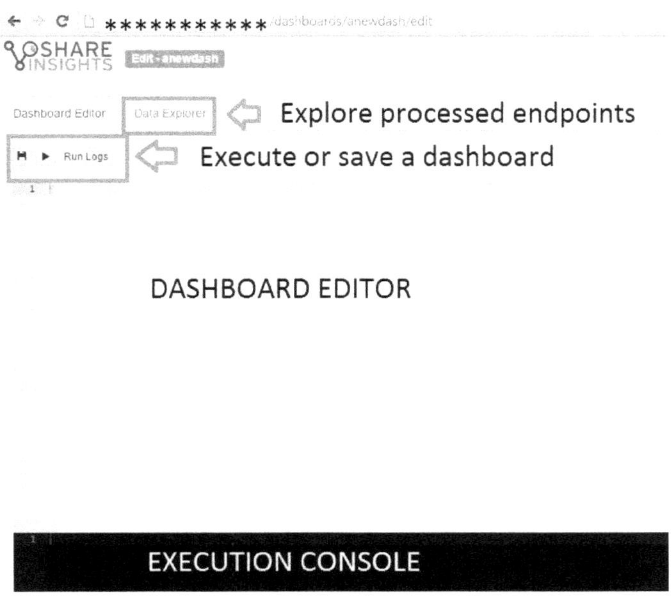

Figure 26: Dashboard Editor

4.3.2 Extension Services interface

The ShareInsights platform provides a secure file transfer protocol (SFTP) interface to upload the various types of extensions - widgets, connectors, tasks and stylesheets. The interface is file based and each dashboard has appropriately named folders for task, widgets etc. Additionally, users can upload dashboard data to a 'data' folder. All data files in this folder can be referred in the data object configuration (using relative paths from this data folder).

4.4 ShareInsights Data API

The generated interactive dashboard code from the flow file follows a Single Page Architecture style [10].

Dashboard data is retrieved via a REST API provided by the platform(for endpoint data - see section 3.4.1). This is described in the following sections.

Dashboard endpoint data.

To see all endpoint data associated with a dashboard, the following URL (/<dashboard-name>/ds) can be accessed via the browser or curl - as shown in figure 27.

Once the endpoint data names are known, they can be used to further browse data and perform ad-hoc queries as demonstrated in the following sections.

Figure 27: Endpoint data for dashboard

Browsing dashboard endpoint data.

Data browsing can be achieved either from the raw REST APIs as shown in figure 28 or from the platform provided data explorer.

Figure 28: Query endpoint data

The data explorer effectively runs the dashboard in a headless mode and displays the data in a tabular format. The data explorer for the Apache dashboard is shown in figure 29.

Figure 29: Data Explorer (UI for endpoint data)

Ad-hoc queries on dashboard endpoint data.

The platform also exposes a simplified query language for ad-hoc queries. In figure 30, the count of items in each category is returned by querying the data endpoint - **projects**. (/ds/<dataset-name>/groupby/<column>/ <aggregate-function>/<column>)

Figure 30: Ad-hoc query on endpoint data

4.5 Collaboration Services

ShareInsights encourages collaboration in the data analysis ecosystem via the following mechanisms.

4.5.1 Branch and Merge Model

The ShareInsights platform leverages the collaboration model found in distributed version control systems (DVCS), like Git. Since the entire data pipeline is represented as a single text file, it makes it very amenable to manage via a source control system. CRUD operations on flow files map to source commits. A DVCS encourages collaboration via branching and repeated merging. This model is mature and is the preferred way to manage code assets [2]. ShareInsights leverages this model for flow files.

Additionally, since the flow file has clearly demarcated sections, the anxieties with merging and repeated branching should be significantly lower.

4.5.2 Configuration Driven Development

The flow file has been designed to let users configure tasks, data, widgets and even flows. Configuration is the activity of setting property values.(as seen from earlier examples)

The only **active** elements in the flow file then are the flows in the flow(F) section and widget sources (for widget to widget interaction). Here too, we have restricted the representation to linear flows. There are no control structures other than the notion of chaining via pipes. Consequently, it is easier to pick up paths which matter when users modify existing flows (users 'fork' existing dashboards to modify). We believe that this will reduce barriers to experimentation.

4.5.3 Flow file Groups

The canonical form of the flow file is to have all sections. However, this is optional. The system allows for creation of flow files which have only the data, flow and task sections. Processed data objects can be shared - either by publishing and/or making it a visualization endpoint - for consumption by other dashboards. The set of dashboards which share data objects and the set of dashboards which consumes them form a natural flow file group.

This technique has the following benefits

1. It addresses the problem of allowing other users to benefit and leverage prior work.(an important aspect of collaboration). It is a common experience that data cleaning takes a significant percentage of the total time [5]. The platform ecosystem encourages that this effort is not repeated across data pipelines.

2. It allows for teams to be deployed in their area of strength. To glean insights effectively, it is a common practice to divide and conquer; each dashboard attempts to answer specific questions or guide users towards a certain dimension of the problem space. Consequently, there could be multiple non-intersecting dashboards in the problem space - each consuming only a subset of data flows. The team which designs dashboards have possibly a different mindset from the team which focuses on publishing processed data for the problem space. This technique then allows each subteam to focus on their strengths and work fairly independently.

3. It allows for efficient processing of raw data sources. In this configuration, long running data flows are executed only by the dashboard which shares the data objects.

4. As a corollary to the above point, teams building interactive dashboards on processed data can get extremely quick feedback to changes in the flow file.(as long running data pipelines will not be executed when the flow file is saved) This is vital to encourage rapid changes during dashboard design.

5. RACE2INSIGHTS

To test the value provided by the unified representation, we organized an internal competition called Race2Insights where untrained users were challenged to create interactive dashboards within six hours.

5.1 Competition setup

This section describes the format and the setup of the competition.

Data-sets:
: We identified seven interesting data-sets that contained both public and enterprise data. Each data-set had multiple files that contained both transaction as well as reference data about business entities. Teams were randomly allocated a data-set and were encouraged to augment with other interesting data-sets.

Teams and Team Composition:
: Fifty two teams participated in the competition. Each team had five members. Participants were encouraged to form teams with known colleagues. Teams had varying skill level ranging from zero to little programming background at one end of the spectrum to significant skills in data processing at the other end.

Training:
: Participants were exposed to the platform five days prior to the competition. Training videos and handson lab sessions were conducted for participants to familiarize them with the nuances of flow file creation. A day before the competition, participants were assigned the data-set (chosen by a lottery system) and only schema details were shared. Teams were encouraged to paper-prototype and design the data pipelines. Access to systems were switched off.

Competition day:
: On the day of the competition, the actual data-sets were published and teams were given six hours to build interactive dashboards to demonstrate business insights for their problem space.

Judging:
Two rounds of panel-style judging were performed. Teams had to present their dashboard to an internal and an external committee. Teams had to present the flow file to the internal committee for review as well as highlight any extensions they may have written or additional data-sets used. The external committee purely evaluated the dashboard in terms of business value for that domain.

5.2 Learnings

The section describes some of the findings from the hackathon.

5.2.1 Dashboards from competition data

The data generated during the competition as well as the practice sessions - application logs, flow file growth, error messages, execution logs - were used to build dashboards (using the platform) to illustrate usage of the platform during the competition hours.

The dashboard shown in figure 31 highlights the popular operators and widgets.

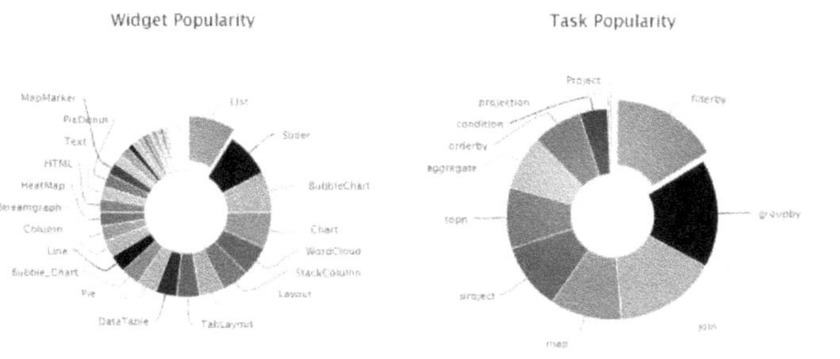

Figure 31: Platform usage

Another interesting plot shows the correlation between practice and success. Practice runs versus competition runs (a run = a dashboard execution) for the various teams are shown in figure 35. The finalists are teams{5,9,12,18,33,35,41}. The winning teams are teams{12, 18, 33}.

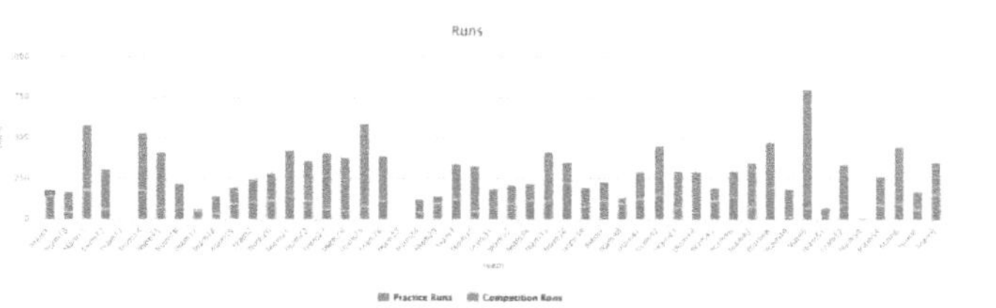

Figure 32: Does practice matter?

5.2.2 Observations

1. Teams produced extremely rich dashboards in six hours. Prior to building this platform, equivalent dashboards took four to six weeks to develop. A few dashboards are shown in figure 33 and 34.

2. Some of the winning teams wrote custom tasks to process the data. For example, one team wrote a task to predict resolution dates of service tickets based on keywords present in the ticket. The custom task looks no different from a platform provided task and was used by other team members as a black box.

   The extension points provided by the platform are crucial as it is not possible to anticipate all possibilities. The ability to not differentiate between a platform task and a user defined one is also critical for a consistent conceptual model.

Figure 33: Service Desk Ticket Analysis

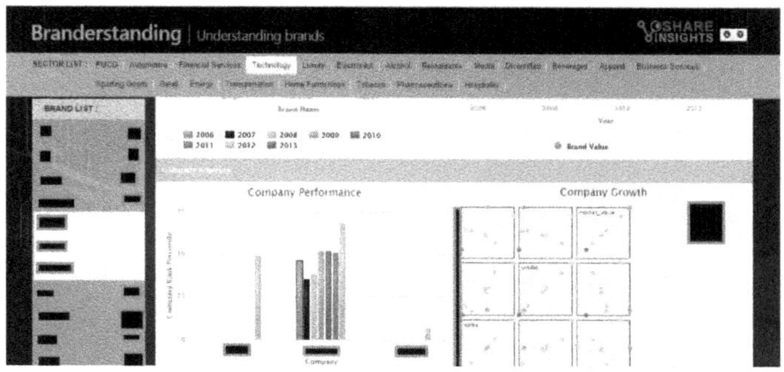

Figure 34: 'Branderstanding'

3. Teams 'forked' off existing (help or sample) dashboards to get started. Figure 35 shows the flow file size for each team at the start of the competition.

4. Data cleaning is non trivial task. Teams prepared synthetic data for practice runs. During the actual competition, the real data provided forced teams to define more elaborate pipelines to cleanse the data.

5. More training was required to grasp widget to widget interaction specification.

6. Browser based development and deployment - a zero install footprint - helped the competition logistics during the actual competition hours as well as during training sessions by allowing teams to participate remotely.

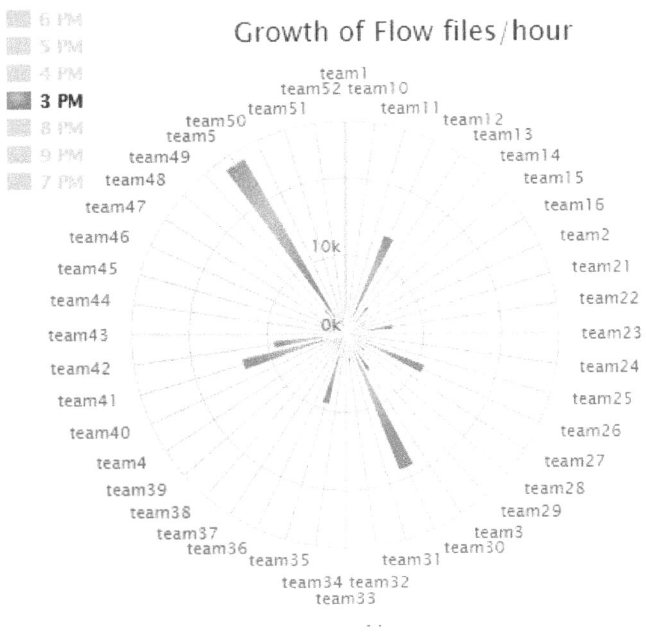

Figure 35: Fork to go (Size in bytes)

7. Error reporting (during dashboard execution) leaked the abstraction. The most popular debugging strategy was to go to a stable version and then incrementally add till the error resurfaced.

6. FUTURE DIRECTIONS

This section outlines some of the key enhancements to the platform.

Future platform versions will focus on exploiting the AST generated from the flow file to do execution optimization. For example one can conceive of rearranging user flows to minimize data transfers to the client. The uniform interface for widget and flow tasks will facilitate this feature.

Also, since the flow file is an abstraction layer, more work needs to be done to enable users to pin-point errors quickly. (Without leaking the underlying engine errors or debug logs). Also, tools to identify performance bottlenecks need to be provided.

We want to auto-construct meta-dashboards which provide statistics and analysis of all the data columns used in the data pipeline. Since, data cleaning is a non-trivial activity[5], we believe this feature would be of immense help for huge data sizes.

Since data is published on the platform, it potentially allows for discovery of data-sets to enrich an existing data pipeline. This is an important feature [11] [1].

7. CONCLUSION

Having an unified representation to model all stages of the data pipeline from data ingestion to interactive visualization design has significant benefits in terms of reduced time to build. Configuration driven development reduces the complexities associated with control structures and cleanly segregated sections allow for reuse and easy modification. The abstraction hides technology differences at every layer of the data stack and empowers the data analyst/data scientist to focus on building value for end-users. The notion of allowing transformed data to be a shared entity allows for re-use (by other data pipelines) of the non trivial effort which goes behind curating and cleansing data.

8. ACKNOWLEDGMENTS

We thank the following individuals for their involvement with the ShareInsights platform. Reshma Godse, Kalyani Zomte and Leena Rajendran for their involvement as the lead engineers of the platform, Vinayak Datar and Kartik Vyas for their customer facing roles and Nilesh Joshi for systems infrastructure support.

9. REFERENCES

[1] C. Bizer, P. Boncz, M. L. Brodie, and O. Erling. The meaningful use of big data: Four perspectives – four challenges. *SIGMOD Rec.*, 40(4):56–60, Jan. 2012.

[2] C. Brindescu, M. Codoban, S. Shmarkatiuk, and D. Dig. How do centralized and distributed version control systems impact software changes? In *Proceedings of the 36th International Conference on Software Engineering*, ICSE 2014, pages 322–333, New York, NY, USA, 2014. ACM.

[3] L. Byron and M. Wattenberg. Stacked graphs ; geometry & aesthetics. *IEEE Transactions on Visualization and Computer Graphics*, 14(6):1245–1252, Nov. 2008.

[4] S. Chaudhuri. What next?: A half-dozen data management research goals for big data and the cloud. In *Proceedings of the 31st Symposium on Principles of Database Systems*, PODS '12, pages 1–4, New York, NY, USA, 2012. ACM.

[5] T. Dasu and T. Johnson. *Exploratory Data Mining and Data Cleaning*. John Wiley & Sons, Inc., New York, NY, USA, 1 edition, 2003.

[6] J. Dean and S. Ghemawat. Mapreduce: Simplified data processing on large clusters. *Commun. ACM*, 51(1):107–113, Jan. 2008.

[7] Gnip.com. Twitter data - gnip : https://gnip.com/sources/twitter/, 2015.

[8] R. Kimball and M. Ross. *The Data Warehouse Toolkit: The Complete Guide to Dimensional Modeling*. John Wiley & Sons, Inc., New York, NY, USA, 2nd edition, 2002.

[9] R. Krishnamurthy and M. M. Zloof. RBE: rendering by example. In *Proceedings of the Eleventh International Conference on Data Engineering, March 6-10, 1995, Taipei, Taiwan*, pages 288–297, 1995.

[10] M. Mikowski and J. Powell. *Single Page Web Applications: JavaScript End-to-end*. Manning Publications Co., Greenwich, CT, USA, 1st edition, 2013.

[11] K. Morton, M. Balazinska, D. Grossman, and J. D. Mackinlay. Support the data enthusiast: Challenges for next-generation data-analysis systems. *PVLDB*, 7(6):453–456, 2014.

[12] C. Olston, B. Reed, U. Srivastava, R. Kumar, and A. Tomkins. Pig latin: A not-so-foreign language for data processing. In *Proceedings of the 2008 ACM SIGMOD International Conference on Management of*

Data, SIGMOD '08, pages 1099–1110, New York, NY, USA, 2008. ACM.

[13] B. Shneiderman. The eyes have it: A task by data type taxonomy for information visualizations. In *Proceedings of the 1996 IEEE Symposium on Visual Languages*, VL '96, pages 336–, Washington, DC, USA, 1996. IEEE Computer Society.

[14] M. Winslett. Databases in virtual organizations: A collective interview and call for researchers. *SIGMOD Rec.*, 34(1):86–89, Mar. 2005.

[15] M. Zaharia, M. Chowdhury, M. J. Franklin, S. Shenker, and I. Stoica. Spark: Cluster computing with working sets. In *Proceedings of the 2Nd USENIX Conference on Hot Topics in Cloud Computing*, HotCloud'10, pages 10–10, Berkeley, CA, USA, 2010. USENIX Association.

APPENDIX

A. IPL FLOW GROUP

A.1 Data Processing Dashboard

```
D:
    ipltweets : [
       postedTime => created_at ,
       body => text ,
       displayName => user.location
    ]
    players_tweets : [
       date , player , count
    ]
    teams_tweets : [
       date , team , count
    ]
    dim_teams : [
       team_number , team ,
       team_fullName , sort_order ,
       color , noOfTweets
    ]
    team_players : [
       player , team_fullName ,
       team , player_id , noOfTweets
    ]
    latlong : [
       state , point_one , point_two ,
       point_three
    ]
    player_tweets : [player ,
       team , date , player_id ,
       team_fullName , noOfTweets
    ]
    team_tweets : [
        sort_order , date , color ,
        team , team_fullName , noOfTweets
    ]
    tm_rgn_raw_cnt : [
        date , team , state , count
    ]
    tm_rgn_tm_dtls : [
        sort_order , noOfTweets , color ,
        state , team , date , team_fullName
    ]
    team_region_tweets : [
       point_one , point_two ,
       point_three , state ,
       team_fullName , team ,
       color , sort_order ,
       date , noOfTweets
    ]
    tagcloud_tweets_raw : [
       date , word , count
    ]
    tagcloud_tweets : [
       date , word , count
    ]
#
F:
    D.players_tweets : D.ipltweets |
        T.players_pipeline |
        T.players_count

    D.player_tweets : (
        D.players_tweets ,
        D.team_players
    ) | T.join_player_team

    D.teams_tweets : D.ipltweets |
        T.teams_pipeline |
        T.teams_count

    D.team_tweets : (
        D.teams_tweets ,
        D.dim_teams
    ) | T.join_dim_teams

    D.tm_rgn_raw_cnt : D.ipltweets |
        T.teams_pipeline_region |
        T.teams_regions_count

    D.tm_rgn_tm_dtls : (
        D.tm_rgn_raw_cnt ,
        D.dim_teams
    ) | T.join_dim_teams_two

    D.team_region_tweets : (
        D.tm_rgn_tm_dtls ,
        D.latlong
    ) | T.join_latlong

    D.tagcloud_tweets_raw :
        D.ipltweets |
        T.word_date_extraction |
        T.words_count

    D.tagcloud_tweets :
        D.tagcloud_tweets_raw |
        T.topwords

#
T:
  players_pipeline :
    parallel : [
        T.norm_ipldate ,
        T.extract_players
    ]
```

```
teams_pipeline :
  parallel : [
      T.norm_ipldate,
      T.extract_teams
  ]
teams_pipeline_region :
  parallel : [
      T.norm_ipldate,
      T.extract_location,
      T.extract_teams
  ]
word_date_extraction :
  parallel : [
       T.norm_ipldate,
       T.extract_words
  ]
norm_ipldate :
  type : map
  operator : date
  transform : postedTime
  input_format:'E MMM dd HH:mm:ss Z yyyy'
  output_format : yyyy-MM-dd
  output : date
extract_players :
  type : map
  operator : extract
  transform : body
  dict : players.txt
  output : player
extract_teams :
  type : map
  operator : extract
  transform : body
  dict : teams.csv
  output : team
extract_location :
  type : map
  operator : extract_location
  transform : displayName
  match : city
  country : IND
  output : state
extract_words :
  type : map
  operator : extract_words
  transform : body
  output : word

join_player_team :
  type : join
  left : players_tweets by player
  right : team_players by player
  join_condition : left outer
  project :
    players_tweets_date : date
    players_tweets_player : player
    players_tweets_state : state
    players_tweets_count : noOfTweets
    team_players_team : team
    team_players_team_fullName:
                         team_fullName
    team_players_player_id :
                         player_id
```

```
join_dim_teams :
  type : join
  left : teams_tweets by team
  right : dim_teams by team_fullName
  join_condition : left outer
  project :
    teams_tweets_date : date
    teams_tweets_team : team_fullName
    teams_tweets_count : noOfTweets
    dim_teams_team : team
    dim_teams_sort_order : sort_order
    dim_teams_color : color

join_dim_teams_two :
  type : join
  left:tm_rgn_raw_cnt by team
  right : dim_teams by team_fullName
  join_condition : left outer
  project :
    tm_rgn_raw_cnt_date : date
    tm_rgn_raw_cnt_team : team_fullName
    tm_rgn_raw_cnt_state : state
    tm_rgn_raw_cnt_count : noOfTweets
    dim_teams_Team : team
    dim_teams_sort_order : sort_order
    dim_teams_color : color

join_latlong :
 type : join
 left : tm_rgn_tm_dtls by state
 right : latlong by state
 join_condition : left outer
 project :
  tm_rgn_tm_dtls_team_fullName :
                           team_fullName
  tm_rgn_tm_dtls_state: state
  tm_rgn_tm_dtls_date: date
  tm_rgn_tm_dtls_noOfTweets: noOfTweets
  tm_rgn_tm_dtls_team: team
  tm_rgn_tm_dtls_sort_order: sort_order
  tm_rgn_tm_dtls_color: color
  latlong_point_one : point_one
  latlong_point_two : point_two
  latlong_point_three : point_three

players_count :
    type : groupby
    groupby : [date, player]
teams_count :
    type : groupby
    groupby : [date, team]
teams_regions_count :
    type : groupby
    groupby : [date, team, state]
words_count :
    type : groupby
    groupby : [date, word]
topwords :
    type : topn
    groupby : [date]
    orderby_column : [count DESC]
    limit : 20
```

A.2 Data consumption Dashboard

For brevity of the source listing, it is assumed that all the data objects used by widgets in this listing have been published (with identical names) and end-pointed in listing A.1.

```
# ————————————————————————————————————
L:
 description : Clash of Titans
 rows :
   - [span12 : W.teams ]
   - [span11 :  W.iplduration ]
   - [span11 : W.relativeteamtweets ]
   - [span6  : W.word_team_player_tweets ,
      span5  : W.regiontweets ]

# ————————————————————————————————————
W:

iplduration :
   type : Slider
   source : ['2013-05-02','2013-05-27']
   static : true
   range : true
   slidertype : date

relativeteamtweets:
   type : Streamgraph
   source : D.team_tweets |
         T.filter_by_date |
         T.filter_by_team
   #widget columns
   x : date
   y : noOfTweets
   color : color
   serie : team
   xAxis:
       type: 'datetime'
   yAxis:
       allowDecimals: false
       min: 0
       max: 25000

teams :
   type : List
   source : D.dim_teams
   #widget columns
   text : team
   #Visual attributes
   image_position : right

playertweets:
   type : WordCloud
   source : D.player_tweets |
           T.filter_by_date |
           T.filter_by_team |
           T.aggregate_by_player
   #widget columns
   text : player
   size : noOfTweets
   #visual attributes
   show_tooltip : true
   tooltip_text : [player ,noOfTweets]

teamtweets:
   type : WordCloud
   source : D.team_tweets |
             T.filter_by_date |
             T.aggregate_by_team
   #widget columns
   text : team
   size : noOfTweets
   #visual attributes
   show_tooltip : true
   tooltip_text : [team, noOfTweets ]

wordtweets:
   type : WordCloud
   source : D.tagcloud_tweets |
             T.filter_by_date |
               T.aggregate_by_word
   #widget columns
   text : word
   size : count
   #visual attributes
   show_tooltip : true
   tooltip_text : [word, count ]

regiontweets :
   type : MapMarker
   source : D.team_region_tweets |
          T.filter_by_date |
          T.filter_by_team |
          T.aggregate_by_team_region
   country : IND
   markers :
     - marker1 :
         type : circle_marker
         #widget columns
         latlong_value : point_one
         markersize : noOfTweets
         fill_color : color
         tooltip_text : [
           state ,
           team ,
           noOfTweets
         ]

#sub layouts

teamtweetstab:
   type : Layout
   rows :
     - [span11 : W.teamtweets]

playertweetstab:
   type : Layout
   rows :
     - [span11 : W.playertweets]

wordtweetstab:
   type : Layout
   rows :
     - [span11 : W.wordtweets]
```

```
word_team_player_tweets :
   type : TabLayout
   tabs :
      -    name : 'Player'
           body : W.playertweetstab
      -    name : 'Word'
           body : W.wordtweetstab
      -    name : 'Team'
           body : W.teamtweetstab

# ------------------------------------------

T:


aggregate_by_player :
   type : groupby
   groupby : [player]
   aggregates :
      - operator : sum
        apply_on : noOfTweets
        out_field : noOfTweets


aggregate_by_team :
   type : groupby
   groupby : [team]
   aggregates :
      - operator : sum
        apply_on : noOfTweets
        out_field : noOfTweets

aggregate_by_word :
   type : groupby
   groupby : [word]
   aggregates :
      - operator : sum
        apply_on : count
        out_field : count
        orderby_aggregates : true


filter_by_date :
   type : filterby
   filterby : [date]
   filter_source : W.iplduration


filter_by_team :
   type : filterby
   filterby : [team]
   filter_source : W.teams
   filter_val : [text]


aggregate_by_team_region :
   type : groupby
   groupby : [team,point_one,state,color]
   aggregates :
      - operator : sum
        apply_on : noOfTweets
        out_field : noOfTweets
```

B. FLOW FILE GRAMMAR

```
/* -------- Parser rules ---------- */
flowFile :
   dataSection? flowSection?
   taskSection?
   dataDetailsSection? EOF ;

/* ---------- data section -------- */
dataSection : 'D' ':' dataItem+ ;
dataItem : dataItemName ':' '[' hdrs ']';
dataItemName : IDENTIFIER ;
hdrs : hdrField (',' hdrField)* ;
hdrField : IDENTIFIER ;

/* ---------- flow section -------- */
flowSection : 'F' ':' flow+ ;
flow:'D.' outputData ':' multiDataStart*
     'D.' inputDataInFlow
     (',' 'D.' inputDataInFlow)*
     multiDataEnd
     ( '|' 'T.' taskInDataFlow )+;
multiDataStart : ROUND_BRACKET_OPEN ;
multiDataEnd : ROUND_BRACKET_CLOSE ;
outputData : IDENTIFIER ;
inputDataInFlow : IDENTIFIER ;
taskInDataFlow : IDENTIFIER ;

/* ---------- task section -------- */
taskSection : 'T' ':' task+ ;
task
  :
  taskName ':'
  'type' ':' taskType
  (paramName ':'
     '['*
     '('* paramValue (',' paramValue)* ')'*
     ']'* )+
  ;
taskName : IDENTIFIER ;
taskType : IDENTIFIER ;
paramName : IDENTIFIER ;
paramValue : IDENTIFIER;

/* ---- data details section ---- */
dataDetailsSection : dataItemInDetail+ ;
dataItemInDetail :
   'D.' dataItemNameInDetail ':' prop+ ;
prop :
     (dd_paramName ':' dd_paramValue )+;
dataItemNameInDetail : IDENTIFIER ;
dd_paramName : IDENTIFIER ;
dd_paramValue : IDENTIFIER;

/* -------- Lexer rules ---------- */
ROUND_BRACKET_OPEN : '(' ;
ROUND_BRACKET_CLOSE : ')' ;
IDENTIFIER : [a-zA-Z_]+[a-zA-Z0-9_]* ;
WS : [ \t\r\n\u000C]+ -> skip ;
LINE_COMMENT : '#' ~[\r\n]* -> skip ;
```

An Incremental Anytime Algorithm for Multi-Objective Query Optimization*

Immanuel Trummer and Christoph Koch
{firstname}.{lastname}@epfl.ch
École Polytechnique Fédérale de Lausanne

ABSTRACT

Query plans offer diverse tradeoffs between conflicting cost metrics such as execution time, energy consumption, or execution fees in a multi-objective scenario. It is convenient for users to choose the desired cost tradeoff in an interactive process, dynamically adding constraints and finally selecting the best plan based on a continuously refined visualization of optimal cost tradeoffs. Multi-objective query optimization (MOQO) algorithms must possess specific properties to support such an interactive process: First, they must be anytime algorithms, generating multiple result plan sets of increasing quality with low latency between consecutive results. Second, they must be incremental, meaning that they avoid regenerating query plans when being invoked several times for the same query but with slightly different user constraints. We present an incremental anytime algorithm for MOQO, analyze its complexity and show that it offers an attractive tradeoff between result update frequency, single invocation time complexity, and amortized time over multiple invocations. Those properties make it suitable to be used within an interactive query optimization process. We evaluate the algorithm in comparison with prior work on TPC-H queries; our implementation is based on the Postgres database management system.

Categories and Subject Descriptors

H.2.4 [**Database Management**]: Systems

Keywords

Query optimization; multi-objective; incremental; anytime

1. INTRODUCTION

Classical query optimization considers only one cost metric for query plans and aims at finding a plan with minimal cost [12]. This model is insufficient for scenarios where multiple cost metrics are of interest. Multi-Objective Query Optimization (MOQO) judges query plans based on multiple cost metrics such as monetary fees of execution (e.g., in cloud computing) and energy consumption in addition to execution time [11, 14, 15]. Plans are associated with cost vectors instead of cost values and the goal is to find a plan with an optimal tradeoff between conflicting cost metrics. The optimal tradeoff is user-specific since different users might have different priorities. Prior work in MOQO assumes that users select the optimal cost tradeoff indirectly by specifying weights and constraints prior to query optimization. User studies have however shown that users have generally troubles to accurately express their preferences indirectly in a multi-objective scenario without having prior knowledge of the available tradeoffs [17]. It is more natural for users to select the preferred tradeoff out of a set of alternatives and this procedure tends to lead users to better choices. We apply those results from general multi-objective optimization to MOQO and postulate that MOQO should be an interactive process (at least for queries with non-negligible execution time) in which users select the query plan with optimal cost tradeoff out of a set of alternatives. The following examples illustrate two out of many possible application scenarios.

EXAMPLE 1. *In cloud computing, there is a tradeoff between execution time and fees as buying more resources can speed up execution. Users performing SQL processing in the cloud can benefit from a visualization of available cost tradeoffs before they select a query plan for execution.*

EXAMPLE 2. *In approximate query processing, there is a tradeoff between execution time and result precision since sampling can be used to reduce execution time. Visualizing available tradeoffs helps users to hand-tune the execution of queries that process large data sets or are executed frequently.*

It is not necessary to make users aware of all alternative query plans for their query. It is sufficient if users have an overview of the *Pareto-Optimal* plans; a plan is Pareto-optimal if no alternative plan has better cost according to all cost metrics at the same time (this definition is slightly simplified). For two or three cost metrics, the Pareto-optimal plan cost tradeoffs can be visualized as a curve or as a surface in three-dimensional space. For higher number of cost metrics, users could successively visualize the Pareto surface for different combinations of cost metrics or look at aggregates (minima and maxima) for the different cost metrics. Having an overview of the available cost tradeoffs, users can directly select the query plan which fits best to their priorities.

An ideal interactive MOQO optimizer presents an overview of all Pareto-optimal cost tradeoffs quickly after receiving

*This work was supported by ERC grant 279804.

SIGMOD'15, May 31–June 4, 2015, Melbourne, Victoria, Australia.

http://dx.doi.org/10.1145/2723372.2746484.

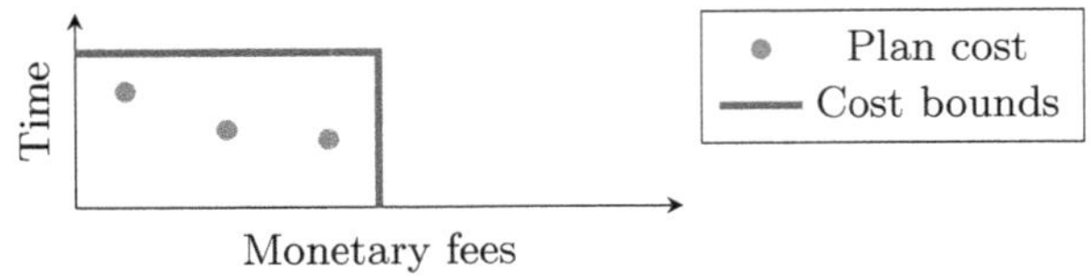

(a) The optimizer quickly visualizes a first approximation of Pareto-optimal query plan costs

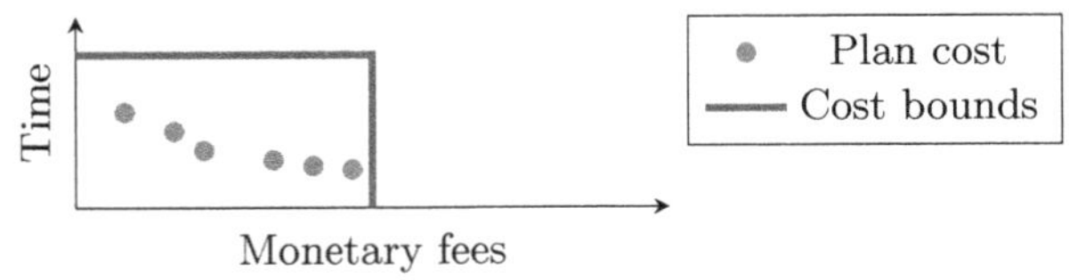

(b) The approximation is continuously refined without user interaction

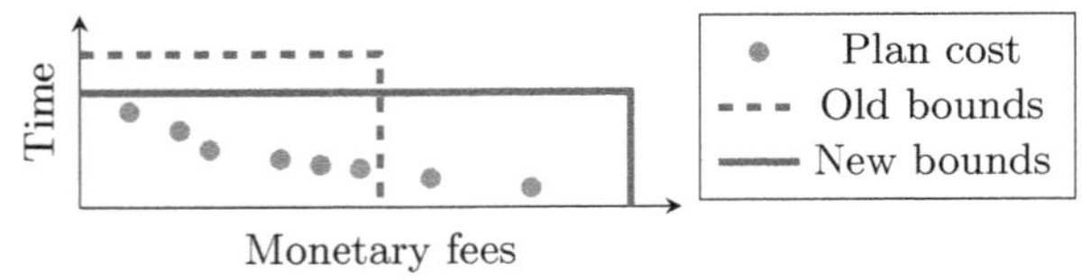

(c) The user can always adapt the optimization focus by dragging bounds into a new position

Figure 1: Example interaction between user and interactive anytime optimizer: the user selects a query plan by finally clicking on the desired cost tradeoff.

the user query as input. The problem is that the number of Pareto plans might be extremely large already for medium-sized queries and prior work has shown that calculating all Pareto-optimal plans is often not realistic within a reasonable time frame [14]. This leads to approximation algorithms for MOQO that quickly find a representative set of query plans whose cost vectors approximate the Pareto-optimal cost tradeoffs with a given target precision [11, 14]. There is a tradeoff between optimization time and target precision; choosing a finer target precision increases optimization time. Approximate MOQO can take several tens of seconds for TPC-H queries when choosing a rather fine-grained target precision which is inconvenient for an interactive interface. It is impossible to know which precision the user requires to make his decision. It is also unclear how much time optimization will take for a given query and target precision since this depends on the size of the result plan set which is the output of optimization. The most natural approach is therefore an interface that iteratively refines the approximation of the Pareto cost tradeoffs, while allowing continuous user interaction; users may for instance interact with the MOQO optimizer by selecting a query plan for execution (thereby ending optimization) or by setting cost bounds for different cost metrics (which can be exploited to speed up optimization as bounds restrict the search space). Figure 1 illustrates the interaction between user and optimizer: query plans are evaluated according to the two cost metrics (execution) time and monetary fees in the example, and plan costs are represented as points in a two-dimensional space.

Existing approximation algorithms for MOQO [14] are however ill-suited to be used within such an interface for several reasons. First, they require to specify a target precision in advance and return results only once a full result

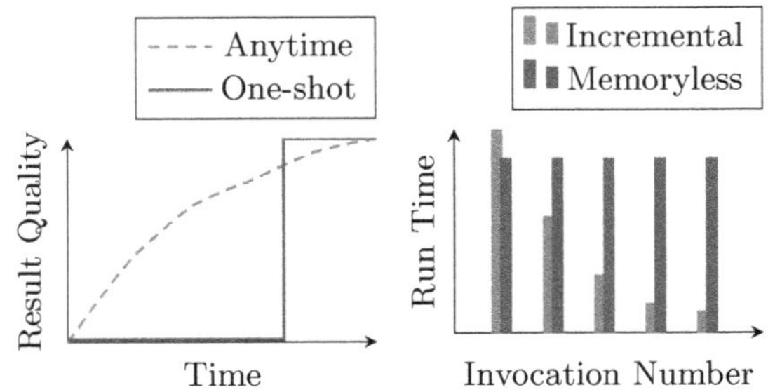

(a) Anytime versus one-shot algorithms

(b) Incremental versus memoryless algorithms

Figure 2: Incremental anytime algorithms

plan set is generated that is guaranteed to approximate the Pareto plan set with the target precision. An interactive scenario rather requires algorithms that return several result plan sets of increasing approximation precision with high frequency (low waiting time between consecutive result sets). Algorithms that continuously improve result quality instead of returning only one result at the end of execution are generally called *anytime algorithms* in contrast to *one-shot algorithms*. Figure 2(a) illustrates the difference. A second shortcoming of existing MOQO algorithms is that they are *non-incremental*: they cannot systematically exploit results of prior invocations to speed up optimization for very similar input problems. Users might for instance adapt the cost bounds several times when optimizing a single query which changes part of the input for the optimization algorithm (the bounds change while the query remains the same). Starting optimization from scratch every time that this happens is inefficient since the same query plans might get regenerated several times. An interactive scenario rather requires an *incremental* algorithm that maintains state across several invocations for the same query to minimize redundant computation. Figure 2(b) illustrates the difference between incremental and memoryless algorithms.

The original scientific contribution of this paper is an *incremental anytime algorithm for MOQO*. This algorithm has the anytime property since it generates a rough approximation of the Pareto plan set quickly that is refined in multiple steps, having low latency between consecutive refinements. The algorithm is incremental since it maintains state across consecutive invocations for the same query with different cost bounds, thereby avoiding to regenerate the same plans. Hence our algorithm is suitable for interactive MOQO.

We summarize the contributions of this paper:

1. We present an incremental anytime algorithm for interactive MOQO; it continuously refines the approximation of the Pareto-optimal cost tradeoffs and avoids regenerating plans over multiple invocations.

2. We analyze the space complexity of that algorithm, the time complexity of a single invocation, and the amortized complexity of several invocations.

3. We experimentally evaluate an implementation of that algorithm within the Postgres database management system comparing with non-incremental non-anytime MOQO algorithms, using TPC-H queries as test cases.

The remainder of this paper is organized as follows. Section 2 discusses related work. Section 3 introduces the formal model that is used throughout the remainder of the paper. Section 4 discusses the incremental anytime algorithm for interactive MOQO in detail. Section 5 proves correctness of the algorithm, analyzes its space complexity, the time complexity of a single invocation, and the amortized time of several invocations. Section 6 contains experimental results for TPC-H queries; the presented algorithm was implemented on top of the Postgres optimizer.

2. RELATED WORK

We discuss prior work solving similar problems as we do (MOQO) and prior work using similar algorithmic techniques as we do (work on anytime algorithms, incremental algorithms, and approximation algorithms). Classical query optimization [12] judges query plans based on only one cost metric. Single-objective query optimization algorithms are not applicable to MOQO in the general case; a detailed explanation can be found in prior work [7, 14]. MOQO algorithms were proposed in the context of the Mariposa system [13] where query plans are evaluated based on the two cost metrics execution time and execution fees: Papadimitriou and Yannakakis propose a fully polynomial-time approximation scheme for MOQO [11]. Their algorithm combines polynomial run time with formal approximation guarantees but does not optimize join order (only the mapping from query plan nodes to processing sites is optimized for a fixed join order) and is therefore not applicable to the query optimization problem addressed in this paper. It has been shown that even single-objective query optimization cannot be approximated in polynomial time if join order is optimized [5]; those results apply to MOQO as well since MOQO is a generalization of single-objective query optimization. Ganguly et al. [7] described an algorithm for MOQO based on dynamic programming; this algorithm produces the full set of Pareto-optimal cost tradeoffs but its execution time can be excessive in practice [14]. In prior work [14], we proposed several approximation schemes for MOQO. We assumed that users specify a preference function in the form of weights and cost bounds prior to optimization; the optimizer searches for a plan maximizing that preference function. Specifying a preference function in advance is however often difficult for users [17]; this is why we assume now that users select their preferred query plan in an interactive process. Our prior algorithms are unsuitable to be used within an interactive process since they are not incremental, meaning that consecutive invocations for the same query result in large amounts of redundant work, and since they are not anytime algorithms, meaning that they do not improve result precision in regular intervals. We discuss and justify the design constraints that an interactive interface imposes on the optimization algorithm in more detail in Section 4. During formal analysis (see Section 5) and experimental evaluation (see Section 6), we use algorithms as baseline that are very similar to the ones proposed in our prior work. Other MOQO algorithms are tailored towards specific combinations of cost metrics [18, 1]; while such special-purpose algorithms achieve good performance, they break when taking into account additional cost metrics [14]. The algorithm proposed in this paper is applicable for a broad range of plan cost metrics such as execution time, energy consumption, monetary fees, result precision and others; we cover the same metrics as the generic approximation schemes that were discussed before [14].

Anytime algorithms are algorithms whose result quality improves gradually as computation time progresses [19]; they are often applied to computationally intensive problems in situations where computation might be interrupted. MOQO is computationally intensive and user input may interrupt the current optimization at any time in our interactive scenario. Anytime algorithms have been proposed for *query processing* [16, 8] while we use them for *query optimization*. Chaudhuri motivated the development of anytime algorithms for classical query optimization [6]. We argue that anytime algorithms are even more beneficial for MOQO due to the higher computational cost and due to the additional challenge of user interaction. Incremental algorithms avoid redundant work when solving similar problem instances in consecutive invocations (e.g., when calculating shortest paths for several graphs with similar structure [2]). In our case we solve many consecutive optimization problems for the same query but with different bounds and different approximation precision. Bizarro et al. proposed an incremental algorithm for parametric query optimization [4]; plan cost depends on unknown parameters in their scenario and the optimizer might have to optimize the same query for many different combinations of parameter values. Storing result plans together with the corresponding input parameters allows to bypass future optimizer invocations for similar parameter values. Parametric query optimization is related to MOQO since both extend the problem model of classical query optimization; parametric query optimization associates plans however with cost functions while MOQO associates plans with cost vectors. MOQO algorithms are in general not applicable for parametric query optimization and vice versa, a detailed discussion of the differences can be found in prior work [15]. Existing algorithms for multi-objective parametric query optimization [15] are neither incremental nor anytime algorithms. The algorithm presented in this paper is an approximation scheme [9]: it differs from an exhaustive algorithm since it does not guarantee to return the optimal result. It offers however formal worst-case guarantees on how far the quality of the produced result is from the optimum; this distinguishes our algorithm from pure heuristics. Approximation schemes for MOQO have been proposed before [14] but they are neither anytime algorithms nor incremental. Our algorithm is iterative which connects it to other iterative query optimization algorithms [10, 14]. The algorithm proposed by Kossmann and Stocker [10] is however only applicable to single-objective query optimization while our prior iterative algorithm [14] is non-incremental, meaning that results generated in prior iterations are not reused, and the goal was to minimize total query optimization time rather than the time between consecutive results.

3. MODEL

We model a *Query* as a set Q of tables that need to be joined. We use this simple query model to describe our algorithm in Section 4 but we outline in Section 4.3 how the algorithm can be extended to support a richer query model. A *Query Plan* either scans a single table or is composed out of two *Sub-Plans* such that the result of those sub-plans is finally joined. We denote by $p = p_1 \bowtie p_2$ the plan p that uses p_1 and p_2 as sub-plans and joins their results.

Query plans are associated with scalar cost values in classical query optimization [12]. As we consider multiple cost metrics in MOQO, each plan is associated with a *Cost Vector* instead of a cost value. We denote by $\mathbf{c}(p) \in \mathbb{R}^l_+$ the cost vector associated with plan p. Each component of that vector represents the cost value according to one of the l metrics. Note that cost values are always non-negative. We use boldface for vectors (e.g., $\mathbf{c}$) to distinguish them from scalar values. The algorithm presented in Section 4 supports the same class of cost metrics as prior generic approximation schemes [14]; this set includes for instance execution time, monetary execution fees, result precision, energy consumption, or various measures of resource consumption concerning system resources such as buffer space, number of cores, or IO bandwidth. The class of supported cost metrics is characterized more thoroughly during formal analysis in Section 5. The focus of this paper is on optimization and not on costing; we do not provide our own cost formulas but assume that cost models from prior work are used to estimate the cost of query plans.

Considering one cost metric, a query plan p_1 is at least as good as another query plan p_2 if the cost of p_1 is lower than or equivalent to the cost of p_2. With multiple cost metrics, a plan p_1 is at least as good as p_2 if its cost is lower than or equivalent to the cost of p_2 according to each cost metric; if this is the case then we say that p_1 *Dominates* p_2 and denote it by $\mathbf{c}(p_1) \preceq \mathbf{c}(p_2)$. If p_1 dominates p_2 and p_1 has lower cost than p_2 according to at least one metric then we say that p_1 *Strictly Dominates* p_2 and denote it by $\mathbf{c}(p_1) \prec \mathbf{c}(p_2)$. Consider the set P of all possible plans for a fixed query: we call each plan $p^* \in P$ *Pareto-Optimal* if there is no alternative plan $p \in P$ such that $\mathbf{c}(p) \prec \mathbf{c}(p^*)$. We call the set $P^* \subseteq P$ a *Pareto Plan Set* if for each possible plan $p \in P$ there is a plan $p^* \in P^*$ with $\mathbf{c}(p^*) \preceq \mathbf{c}(p)$. Note that several subsets of P can be Pareto plan sets.

Full Pareto plan sets can be excessively large; this motivates to approximate the real Pareto set. Let $\alpha > 1$ be the *Precision Factor*. Then each subset P^*_α of P is an α-*Approximate Pareto Plan Set* if for each possible plan $p \in P$ there is a plan $p^* \in P^*_\alpha$ such that $\mathbf{c}(p^*) \preceq \alpha\mathbf{c}(p)$. Each Pareto plan set is an approximate Pareto plan set with factor $\alpha = 1$. By multiplying the cost vector of plan p by a factor greater than 1, we make its cost appear higher than it actually is; this reduces the requirements compared to the definition of the Pareto plan set. The higher α is chosen, the lower the approximation precision and the smaller the corresponding approximate Pareto plan set can be. We derive size bounds in Section 5.

Often, users care only about query plans whose cost is upper-bounded for certain cost metrics. Users might for instance have a deadline which implies an upper bound on execution time, or a monetary budget limiting execution cost. We model *Cost Bounds* by a cost vector $\mathbf{b}$ with the semantics that users are only interested in plans p with $\mathbf{c}(p) \preceq \mathbf{b}$. If $\mathbf{c}(p) \preceq \mathbf{b}$ for some plan p then we also say that it *Respects* the cost bounds while it otherwise *Exceeds* the bounds. If a user specifies cost bounds $\mathbf{b}$ then he is interested in an approximation of a subset of the Pareto plan set: an α-*Approximate* $\mathbf{b}$-*Bounded Pareto Plan Set* is a subset P^* of the set P of possible plans such that for each plan $p \in P$ with $\alpha\mathbf{c}(p) \preceq \mathbf{b}$ there is a plan $p^* \in P^*$ such that $\mathbf{c}(p^*) \preceq \alpha\mathbf{c}(p)$. The input to the *Approximate Bounded MOQO Problem* is a query Q, an approximation factor α, and cost bounds $\mathbf{b}$. The result is a α-approximate $\mathbf{b}$-bounded Pareto plan set for query Q. During *Interactive MOQO*, many approximate bounded MOQO problems may have to be solved, reflecting gradually refined approximation precision and bounds that may change due to user input.

We finally discuss the parameters used in our formal analysis: n is the number of query tables, m the cardinality of the biggest table in the data base. Parameter l is the number of cost metrics. We treat n as variable while we treat m and l as constants during complexity analysis. Those assumptions are consistent with prior work on MOQO approximation algorithms [14].

4. DESCRIPTION OF ALGORITHM

We describe the Incremental Anytime MOQO Algorithm, short IAMA, for interactive MOQO in this section. Existing MOQO algorithms [14] assume that users specify a preference function prior to optimization; the goal of optimization is to find a plan that optimizes this preference function. IAMA differs since users select the optimal query plan for their query in an interactive process. IAMA consists of two main parts: the *main control loop* and the *incremental optimizer*. The main control loop handles the interaction with the user and decides which part of the plan search space to explore next. It uses the incremental optimizer as a subfunction to generate fresh query plans. The incremental optimizer generates query plans for the given query; it allows to focus plan generation by specifying an area of interest within the plan cost space and to choose the resolution with which Pareto-optimal cost tradeoffs are approximated. Choosing a higher resolution yields more accurate results while choosing a lower resolution reduces optimization time. The main control loop uses the optimizer to increase approximation precision step by step for a given area in the cost space which leads to the anytime behavior of IAMA.

The incremental optimizer was designed with two performance constraints in mind. First, it must be *incremental*, meaning that it avoids regenerating the same query plans in consecutive invocations; this is important as the optimizer is invoked many times for a given query while only the resolution and the area of interest in the cost space change. Second, the time of any single optimizer invocation must be *proportional* to the resolution and to the size of the chosen cost space area. Both optimizer properties are crucial to enable an interactive process: If the optimizer was not incremental then each invocation would start from scratch and generating a fine-grained approximation could easily take several tens of seconds. Receiving user input during such a long time is likely which only leaves the choice between blocking the interface until optimization is finished (leading to poor user experience) or interrupting optimization without being able to reuse any results (making it unlikely that high resolutions are ever reached). If invocation time was not guaranteed to be at most proportional to the input parameters then the interface might not be able to generate a first approximation of optimal cost tradeoffs quickly.

The proposed optimizer algorithm satisfies both performance constraints. It uses a variant of the classical dynamic programming approach to query optimization [12] and generates optimal plans for joining table sets out of optimal plans for joining subsets. A single-objective optimizer would store one cost-optimal plan per table set[1] while the IAMA optimizer might have to store many alternative query plans that all realize Pareto-optimal cost tradeoffs. The IAMA optimizer becomes incremental by maintaining two plan sets across invocations: the *result plan set* and the *candidate plan set*. Both sets may contain completed query plans, joining all tables in the current query, as well as partial query plans, joining only a subset of tables. Result plans have already been verified to be crucial in order to approximate a specific cost space area with a specific resolution. Candidate plans have only been determined to be potentially useful for a given cost space area and resolution. A future optimizer invocation will decide whether they are relevant indeed.

Both plan sets are indexed by plan cost and by resolution level. Using a data structure supporting multi-dimensional range queries allows to efficiently retrieve plans whose cost is within a certain range and which are registered for a certain range of resolution levels. Indexing plans by their cost vectors enables the optimizer to focus on certain cost space areas. Indexing candidate plans by resolution allows to avoid checking relevance of the same candidate for the same resolution twice. We will formally prove in Section 5 that the proposed algorithm indeed verifies relevance only once per resolution and candidate plan. Indexing result plans by resolution is required to guarantee that optimization time is always proportional to the chosen resolution. When inserting new partial candidate plans during an optimizer invocation, they should for instance only be combined with result plans that are registered for the current resolution level or lower. We illustrate how our algorithm works by means of a highly simplified example before providing details.

EXAMPLE 3. *We consider the two cost metrics execution time and monetary fees (e.g., in a cloud scenario) and optimize the simple query $R \bowtie S$. The user selects very tight cost bounds on execution fees. The initial goal of the optimizer is to quickly produce a coarse-grained approximation of the optimal cost tradeoffs for the query. Therefore, optimization starts with the lowest possible resolution level 0.*

The optimizer starts by considering alternatives scan plans for the two single relations R and S. If the optimizer encounters a scan plan whose cost exceed the user bounds then this plan is stored as candidate for later optimizer invocations as it might become useful once the user changes the bounds. If the optimizer encounters several plans for the same table whose cost are roughly comparable then only one of them is stored as result plan while the others are stored as candidates; the other plans might become useful once the resolution is refined. In a second step, the optimizer combines result scan plans to form join plans answering the entire query. The optimizer separates result plans from candidate plans in the same fashion as before and shows the cost of the result plans to the user.

Without user intervention, the resolution is increased to 1. Now the optimizer reconsiders some of the scan plans for R and S that were stored as candidates. The optimizer does not reconsider candidate plans whose cost exceed the bounds since the user did not change them. The optimizer reconsiders candidate plans whose cost was roughly comparable to the cost of a result plan. Two plans whose costs were considered equivalent at resolution level 0 might not be equivalent anymore at resolution level 1; such plans are inserted as result plans. Then the optimizer uses the freshly inserted result scan plans to combine fresh plans for the entire query.

Assume the user relaxes the tight bound on monetary fees. Now the resolution is reset to 0 in order to quickly generate a rough approximation of available cost tradeoffs for the new bounds. The optimizer only reconsiders candidate scan plans whose costs exceeded the previous bounds but no candidates whose cost was considered equivalent to one of the result plans at resolution 0 or 1. Freshly inserted result plans are used to combine fresh plans for the entire query; the user view is updated.

Section 4.1 describes the main control loop and Section 4.2 discusses the pseudo-code of the incremental optimizer. Section 4.3 proposes finally several extensions.

4.1 Main Control Loop

Algorithm 1 is the main function of IAMA. Its input is a query and its output is the query plan that the user selects for execution in an interactive process. Algorithm 1 contains the main control loop from lines 12 to 25; each iteration of the main loop generates new query plans by invoking the OPTIMIZE procedure (its implementation is discussed in the next subsection), visualizes their cost using the VISUALIZE procedure (we do not provide pseudo-code for this procedure), and selects the focus for the next optimizer invocation, taking into account user input, if any.

The optimization focus is described by the two local variables $\mathbf{b}$ and r. Variable $\mathbf{b}$ is a vector of upper cost bounds restricting the area of interest in the cost space. Variable $\mathbf{b}$ is used as parameter for the optimizer invocation and the optimizer focuses on generating plans that respect the cost bounds (i.e., plans whose cost vector is dominated by $\mathbf{b}$). The cost bounds are initialized to default values (this can also be the value ∞, indicating that no bounds are set by default) and can be adapted by the user in each iteration of the main control loop. Adapting the bounds gives users the opportunity to focus plan search on the relevant part of the cost space, thereby speeding up optimization. Variable r represents the resolution with which the Pareto-optimal cost tradeoffs are approximated. At a low resolution, the optimizer does not distinguish query plans with similar cost vectors and generates a relatively small set of representative query plans. At a high resolution, the optimizer generates more query plans and the approximation of the set of Pareto-optimal cost tradeoffs is therefore more fine-grained. Assuming a two-dimensional visualization of cost vectors, a high resolution translates into pixels representing alternative cost tradeoffs being closer together while a low resolution means that those pixels are far apart from each other (see Figure 1 from Section 1 for an example: the resolution increases from Figure 1(a) to Figure 1(b)). This motivates the use of the term *resolution*. We assume that a predetermined number of resolution levels is used; the value domain of variable r is the set of resolution levels $\{0, \ldots, r_M\}$. Variable r is initialized with the lowest possible resolution and is increased by one in each iteration of the main control loop if no user input is received. If the user changes the cost bounds then the resolution is set to zero again. Gradually increasing resolution allows to keep each optimizer invocation short (note that this reasoning is only valid since the

[1]Single-objective optimizers might still store several cost-optimal plans for a table set if they produce different tuple orderings that might speed up following operations; we neglect tuple orderings here to simplify the explanations.

```
1: // Generate Pareto plan set of increasing resolution
2: // for query Q until user selects query plan
3: function IncAnyMOQO(Q)
4:     // Initialize bounds and resolution
5:     b ← default bounds
6:     r ← 0
7:     // Fill in scan plans for single tables
8:     for q ∈ Q, p ∈ScanPlans(q) do
9:         Prune(Res^q, Cand^q, b, r, p)
10:    end for
11:    // Main control loop
12:    repeat
13:        // Generate more plans
14:        Optimize(Q, Res, Cand, b, r)
15:        // Visualize cost of known plans
16:        Visualize(Res^Q[0..b, 0..r])
17:        // Update bounds or refine resolution
18:        if User changed bounds then
19:            b ← user-specified bounds
20:            r ← 0
21:        else
22:            // Refine resolution until r_M is reached
23:            r ← min(r_M, r + 1)
24:        end if
25:    until User selects plan p
26:    // Return result plan
27:    return p
28: end function
```

Algorithm 1: Main function for interactive query optimization: processes user input, visualizes plan cost, and invokes incremental optimization procedure.

optimizer is incremental). Under the reasonable assumption that the time for one iteration of the main loop is mainly determined by optimization time, the short optimization times lead to high iteration frequencies. This guarantees that the plan cost visualization is updated frequently and that the interface remains responsive. Resetting the resolution after a bounds change makes sure that first results become visible quickly after the user adapts the cost space area of interest.

Variable *Res* stores the set of result plans and variable *Cand* the set of candidate plans. Both sets contain partial plans that join subsets of Q in addition to completed plans that join all tables in Q; we use the superscript notation to refer to subsets of plans that join specific table sets (e.g., Res^q for $q \subseteq Q$ denotes the subset of result plans that join table set q). Plans in both sets are also indexed by their cost vectors and by the resolution at which they were inserted (result set) or at which they should be considered for insertion (candidate set). We refer to subsets of plans that are associated with a specific resolution range and cost range using square brackets: $Res^q[\mathbf{0}..\mathbf{b}, 0..r]$ selects for instance all result plans that join table set q, were inserted at a resolution between 0 and r (both limits inclusive), and whose cost is dominated by $\mathbf{b}$. The analogous notation applies for candidate plans. Those plan selections correspond to range queries in the space that is spanned by all of the plan cost metrics and by the resolution level as additional dimension. A classic survey on data structures supporting range queries was compiled by Bentley and Friedman [3]. Different data structures offer different tradeoffs between insertion and retrieval time. We will later prove and exploit the fact that the number of plan insertions is bounded for a fixed query while the number of retrieval operations is not (see Section 5.4). Prioritizing fast retrieval over fast insertion times and selecting a corresponding data structure seems therefore advantageous.

```
// Generate plans for query Q, insert them into result
// set Res if they are relevant for current resolution r
// and bounds b or insert them into candidate set Cand
// if they might become relevant later.
procedure Optimize(Q, Res, Cand, b, r)
    // Check candidate plans
    for q ⊆ Q do
        for p_C ∈ Cand^q[0..b, 0..r] do
            Cand^q ← Cand^q \ {p_C}
            Prune(Res^q, Cand^q, b, r, p_C)
        end for
    end for
    // Generate plans using fresh candidates
    for k ← 2 to |Q| do
        for q ⊆ Q : |q| = k do
            for q_1 ⊂ Q : q_1 ≠ ∅; q_2 ← Q \ q_1 do
                for p_F ∈Fresh(Res^{q_1}, Res^{q_2}, b, r) do
                    Prune(Res^q, Cand^q, b, r, p_F)
                end for
            end for
        end for
    end for
end procedure
```

Algorithm 2: Incremental optimization algorithm for multi-objective query optimization.

Both sets, result plans and candidate plans, are initially empty in each invocation of Algorithm 1. They are initialized before the main control loop starts, by inserting plans for scanning single query tables using procedure Prune. The pruning procedure decides whether to insert plans into the result or candidate set and its implementation will be discussed in the next subsection. New plans can get generated and inserted into *Res* and *Cand* in each invocation of the Optimize procedure. Note that we assume call-by-reference parameter passing such that the optimizer subfunction can alter the state of *Res* and *Cand*. Procedure Visualize visualizes only cost tradeoffs of completed query plans which respect the current cost bounds and are appropriate for the current resolution; the input set to procedure Visualize is therefore the subset of completed query plans described by $Res^Q[\mathbf{0}..\mathbf{b}, 0..r]$.

4.2 Incremental Optimizer

Algorithm 2 is the incremental optimizer procedure that is invoked in each iteration of the main loop (lines 12 to 25 in Algorithm 1). It obtains as input the current query Q, the set of result and candidate plans (which it may alter), as well as cost bounds $\mathbf{b}$ and resolution r. After the optimizer invocation, the result set is guaranteed to contain a $\mathbf{b}$-bounded approximation of the Pareto plan set for query Q with resolution r. This may or may not require the optimizer to insert new plans into the result set. As the optimizer is incremental, it will only insert new plans in addition to the ones already contained in *Res* if this is required to satisfy the previously mentioned guarantee. The optimizer may also insert plans into the candidate plan set *Cand*, discard plans from the candidate set, or re-index candidate plans for a different resolution. The purpose of the candidate set is to avoid redundant work over different optimizer invocations: a non-incremental MOQO algorithm [14] discards query plans that are not useful for the current invocation. IAMA keeps them as candidate plans instead and does not need to regenerate them in later invocations. Re-indexing and discarding candidate plans also minimizes redundant work: if it has been verified during the current optimizer invocation that a certain candidate plan is irrelevant for a given resolution then it is not necessary to recheck that candidate plan for the same resolution again in future invocations. Re-indexing that candidate plan for a higher resolution makes sure that the knowledge gained in the current invocation (about the irrelevance of that candidate) is not lost. If candidate plans are irrelevant even for the highest resolution then they can be safely discarded.

Algorithm 2 consists of two phases. In the first phase (lines 6 to 12), the optimizer *reconsiders candidate plans that were generated in previous invocations*. It iterates over all table subsets of Q in arbitrary order and retrieves for each set all candidate plans that are indexed for the current resolution and the current cost bounds. All considered plans are deleted from the candidate set and pruned; the pruning procedure might insert them again as candidates but for a higher resolution than the current one. The pruning procedure (whose pseudo-code is discussed later) might also insert them into the result plan set. The second phase of Algorithm 2 (lines 13 to 22) generates new plans by combining plans in the result sets. During that phase, the optimizer iterates over table sets of increasing cardinality; for each table set, it considers all possible splits into two non-empty subsets. For each split of a set q into two subsets q_1 and q_2, the optimizer considers combining a plan joining the tables in q_1 with one joining the tables in q_2 to obtain a plan joining all tables in q. In contrast to classical query optimization algorithms [12], the incremental optimizer does not combine all plans in the result plan sets but only considers fresh combinations of sub-plans that were not generated in prior optimizer invocations. Function FRESH (whose pseudo-code is discussed next) returns only such plans.

Algorithm 3 shows pseudo-code for the pruning procedure PRUNE and for function FRESH generating fresh query plans. Procedure PRUNE inserts a new query plan into the result set if its cost vector cannot be approximated by any alternative result plan at the current resolution. We use the expression $\text{INSERT}(S, p)$ for some set S and a plan p as shortcut for $S \leftarrow S \cup \{p\}$. Resolution levels r translate into an approximation factor α_r by which the cost vector of the new plan is multiplied before it is compared with the cost vectors of the alternative plans (line 7). The approximation factors α_r are chosen such that $\alpha_r > 1$ and $\alpha_r > \alpha_{r+1}$ for all resolution levels r; we demonstrate the effects of different choices for the number of resolution levels and approximation factors in Section 6. Scaling the cost vector of the new plan by a factor greater than one makes it more likely that the scaled vector is dominated by the cost vector of one of the alternative result plans, meaning that the new plan is not inserted into the result set; the new plan can only be inserted if its cost is for each cost metric lower than the cost of any other result plan by factor α_r at least. The higher the factor α_r, the less likely it is that the new plan is inserted. This means that the result plan set tends to grow with shrinking approxima-

1: // Insert plan p for query q into result set Res if p is
2: // relevant for current resolution r and bounds $\mathbf{b}$.
3: // Insert p into candidate set $Cand$ if p could
4: // become relevant later.
5: **procedure** PRUNE($Res^q, Cand^q, \mathbf{b}, r, p$)
6: // Compare p with alternative plans and bounds
7: **if** $\exists p_A \in Res^q[\mathbf{0}..\mathbf{b}, 0..r] : \mathbf{c}(p_A) \preceq \alpha_r \cdot \mathbf{c}(p)$ **then**
8: // p_A approximates p for resolution r
9: // $\rightarrow$ keep p as candidate for higher resolutions
10: **if** $r < r_M$ **then**
11: INSERT($Cand^q[\mathbf{c}(p), r+1], p$)
12: **end if**
13: **else if** $\mathbf{c}(p) \npreceq \mathbf{b}$ **then**
14: // Cost of p exceeds the bounds
15: // $\rightarrow$ keep p as candidate for different bounds
16: INSERT($Cand^q[\mathbf{c}(p), r], p$)
17: **else**
18: // p is immediately relevant
19: // $\rightarrow$ add p to result plan set
20: INSERT($Res^q[\mathbf{c}(p), r], p$)
21: **end if**
22: **end procedure**
23: // Given two sets of sub-plans Res^{q_1} and Res^{q_2}, filter
24: // to relevant plans for resolution r and bounds $\mathbf{b}$ and
25: // generate all fresh combinations of sub-plans.
26: **function** FRESH($Res^{q_1}, Res^{q_2}, \mathbf{b}, r$)
27: // Filter to relevant sub-plans
28: $P_1 \leftarrow Res^{q_1}[\mathbf{0}..\mathbf{b}, 0..r]$
29: $P_2 \leftarrow Res^{q_2}[\mathbf{0}..\mathbf{b}, 0..r]$
30: // Generate relevant sub-plan pairs
31: $pairs \leftarrow \Delta P_1 \times (P_2 \setminus \Delta P_2)$
32: $pairs \leftarrow pairs \cup ((P_1 \setminus \Delta P_1) \times \Delta P_2)$
33: $pairs \leftarrow pairs \cup (\Delta P_1 \times \Delta P_2)$
34: // Generate fresh plans
35: $fresh \leftarrow \emptyset$
36: **for** $\langle p_1, p_2 \rangle \in pairs$:ISFRESH(p_1, p_2) **do**
37: $fresh \leftarrow fresh \cup \{p_1 \bowtie p_2\}$
38: **end for**
39: **return** $fresh$
40: **end function**

Algorithm 3: Sub-functions of the optimization procedure.

tion factor and growing resolution; as the time complexity grows in the size of the result set, the complexity grows with increasing resolution as well. We calculate precise bounds in Section 5. We also show in Section 5 that an invocation of the optimizer function with resolution r yields an α_r^n-approximate Pareto plan set, where $n = |Q|$ designates the number of tables in the query. The underlying reason is intuitively that each pruning operation may in the worst case introduce an approximation error that accumulates over different pruning operations; the number of pruning operations for a single query plan is proportional to n. Knowing the relationship between α_r and the result precision allows to choose the factors α_r such that a desired target precision is still reached for the maximal expected number of tables; alternatively, the choice of α_r can be adapted to the current query. If the scaled cost vector of the new plan is dominated at the current resolution, it is inserted as candidate plan for higher resolutions or discarded if the maximal resolution has been reached. If the cost vector of the new plan exceeds the current bounds, it may become useful again once the bounds change; in that case the new plan is therefore inserted as candidate for the current resolution again.

As discussed before, our goal is to make the time complexity of one optimizer invocation proportional to the current resolution and cost bounds, independently from how many candidate and result plans have accumulated from prior invocations. This goal leads to two subtle design decisions concerning the pruning function that are nevertheless crucial in order to obtain the complexity properties we were aiming for: First, the new plan is only compared to alternative plans that have been inserted at the current resolution level or at a lower one. The disadvantage is that we might insert the new plan even if plans that are preferable over the new plan were already inserted at a higher resolution; the advantage is however that the number of plan comparisons is proportional to the size of the result plan set at the current resolution. The second decision is that we do not discard result plans that are dominated by the new plan in case that the new plan is inserted into the result set. This differs from prior MOQO approximation schemes which always keep the result plan sets as small as possible [14]. The reason that we do not discard result plans is that they might have been used already as sub-plans to combine other query plans in prior invocations of the optimizer; this might have happened at the current resolution or at a higher one. Discarding a result plan would require to discard at the same time all plans that use it as sub-plan to keep the result plan sets for different table sets consistent (we also assume that plans are represented by pointers to their sub-plans as discussed in Section 5.2); the number of plans to discard is not necessarily proportional to the size of the result plan set at the current resolution. We renounce discarding result plans to keep the time complexity of the current optimizer invocation proportional to the current resolution.

Function FRESH uses result plans for two table subsets q_1 and q_2 to combine new plans that are *fresh*, i.e., they have not been generated in prior optimizer invocations. The expression ΔS designates for some plan set S a subset of plans that potentially were not yet combined with all other plans indexed for the current resolution and cost range. During invocation series in which the bounds are tightened while resolution is refined, we can include all plans that were inserted in the current invocation in ΔS (in such cases we are sure that all previously inserted plans respecting the current bounds were already combined with each other) and set $\Delta S = S$ otherwise. We can use auxiliary data structures that index plans based on the invocation at which they were inserted in combination with the index on cost and resolution; this allows to evaluate the expressions ΔS and $(S \setminus \Delta S)$ efficiently. For each cross product between plan sets, we check first if one of the two operand sets is empty before evaluating the entire expression. Predicate ISFRESH evaluates to true for plans that were not yet combined in prior invocations; we can use a hash table to perform this check efficiently. Fresh plans are returned and will be pruned.

4.3 Extensions

The algorithm presented in the last subsections is simplified and does not possess several features that are standard in query optimization. The code can easily be extended to incorporate the features discussed next and the implementation used for our experiments in Section 6 supports them as well. First, the presented code only optimizes join order but not the choice of join operators. Supporting different join operators just requires to add an inner loop iterating over all applicable join operators and creating corresponding plans in function FRESH (see Algorithm 3). Second, alternative operators might produce the same set of result tuples while some of them generate them in an order that can be exploited by future operations. This is why dynamic-programming based query optimizers distinguish plans generating different *interesting tuple orders* [12] during pruning; the cost-based plan comparison is restricted to plans generating similar tuple orders and it is straight-forward to generalize this principle to the multi-objective case. Third, the presented code is based on a simple query model, representing queries as sets of tables that need to be joined. Predicates and projections can be handled by applying them as early as possible in the join tree and the required code extensions are standard [12]. The seminal paper by Selinger [12] describes how complex SQL statements containing nested queries can be decomposed into simple select-project-join query blocks that can be optimized by our algorithm.

5. FORMAL ANALYSIS

We analyze the algorithm presented in Section 4: More precisely, we analyze the optimizer sub-function that is represented in Algorithm 2. Section 5.1 proves formal worst-case guarantees on how closely the result plan sets, produced by the optimizer, approximate the real Pareto plan set. Section 5.2 analyzes space complexity and Section 5.3 analyzes the time complexity of a single optimizer invocation. In Section 5.4, we analyze the amortized time complexity of several consecutive optimizer invocations for the same query.

5.1 Result Precision

The following analysis is based on the *Principle of Near-Optimality* [14] (PONO) for MOQO which states that replacing optimal sub-plans within a complete query plan by near-optimal sub-plans still yields a near-optimal complete plan for a broad class of cost metrics. The class of cost metrics to which the PONO applies is characterized by the *Aggregation Function*, i.e. by the recursive function that calculates the cost of a plan according to that metric out of the cost of the two sub-plans: the PONO applies to all cost metrics whose aggregation function can be represented using a combination of the operators sum, maximum, minimum, and multiplication by a constant. This applies for instance to metrics such as energy consumption or execution time[2]. The PONO has also been shown to apply for several other metrics whose aggregation formulas do not fit into the latter scheme, such as failure resilience or result precision. A formal definition of the PONO follows.

DEFINITION 1 (PONO). *Let p be a query plan with sub-plans p_1 and p_2 and pick an arbitrary $\alpha \geq 1$. Derive p^* from p by replacing p_1 by p_1^* and p_2 by p_2^*. Then $\mathbf{c}(p_1^*) \preceq \alpha\mathbf{c}(p_1)$ and $\mathbf{c}(p_2^*) \preceq \alpha\mathbf{c}(p_2)$ together imply $\mathbf{c}(p^*) \preceq \alpha\mathbf{c}(p)$.*

The following theorems are based on the PONO. We also assume *Monotone Cost Aggregation*, meaning that the cost of a plan must be higher or equal to the cost of its sub-plans according to each cost metric.

[2]The energy consumption of a plan is the sum of the energy consumption of the sub-plans. The plan execution time is the maximum of the execution times of the sub-plans for parallel execution, and the sum for sequential execution.

THEOREM 1. *After invoking* OPTIMIZE *with bounds* $\mathbf{b}$ *and resolution* r *for query* Q, $Res^q[\mathbf{0}..\mathbf{b}, 0..r]$ *contains an* α_r*-approximate* $\mathbf{b}$*-bounded Pareto plan set for each table* $q \in Q$.

PROOF. For each table q, all applicable scan plans are generated and pruned before the main loop starts. Let p be an arbitrary scan plan for an arbitrary table q. Once procedure OPTIMIZE is invoked later for resolution r and bounds $\mathbf{b}$, there are two possibilities for p: either p was inserted into the result plan set in prior invocations or it is not in the result plan set at the start of the current invocation. If p was not inserted before then we must make sure that it is either inserted in the current invocation or not required to form an α_r-approximate $\mathbf{b}$-bounded Pareto plan set.

If p was not inserted before then it must be included in $Cand^q[\mathbf{0}..\mathbf{b}, 0..r]$ unless it exceeds the bounds $\mathbf{b}$ or can be approximated by an alternative plan. In both cases, p is not required for an α_r-approximate $\mathbf{b}$-bounded Pareto plan set. If p is however in $Cand^q[\mathbf{0}..\mathbf{b}, 0..r]$ at the start of the current invocation then procedure OPTIMIZE will retrieve and prune p; plan p will be inserted if it is required for an α_r-approximate $\mathbf{b}$-bounded Pareto plan set. □

THEOREM 2. *After invoking* OPTIMIZE *with bounds* $\mathbf{b}$ *and resolution* r *for query* Q, $Res^q[\mathbf{0}..\mathbf{b}, 0..r]$ *contains an* α_r^k*-approximate* $\mathbf{b}$*-bounded Pareto plan set for each table subset* $q \subseteq Q$ *with cardinality* $k = |q|$.

PROOF. The proof is an induction over the number of tables k. Theorem 1 proves the induction start for $k = 1$. Assume that the inductional assumption has been proven for all $k < K$. Let $q \subseteq Q$ be a set of K tables and p an arbitrary plan that joins those tables with $\alpha_r^K \mathbf{c}(p) \preceq \mathbf{b}$. Plan p must have two sub-plans p_1 and p_2 that each join at most $K - 1$ tables. Let q_1 and q_2 be the set of tables joined by p_1 and p_2 respectively. We assume monotone cost aggregation which implies $\alpha_r^K \mathbf{c}(p_1) \preceq \mathbf{b}$ and $\alpha_r^K \mathbf{c}(p_2) \preceq \mathbf{b}$. The inductional assumption applies to p_1 and p_2 such that $Res^{q_1}[\mathbf{0}..\mathbf{b}, 0..r]$ will contain a plan p_1^* with $\mathbf{c}(p_1^*) \preceq \alpha_r^{K-1}\mathbf{c}(p_1)$ and $Res^{q_2}[\mathbf{0}..\mathbf{b}, 0..r]$ will contain a plan p_2^* with $\mathbf{c}(p_2^*) \preceq \alpha_r^{K-1}\mathbf{c}(p_2)$ after the optimizer invocation. Plans p_1^* and p_2^* can be combined into a plan p^* that joins the same tables as p and has similar cost according to the PONO: $\mathbf{c}(p^*) \preceq \alpha_r^{K-1}\mathbf{c}(p)$. Plan p^* is generated either in the current optimizer invocation with resolution r and bounds $\mathbf{b}$ or in one of the prior invocations. If p^* is generated in the current invocation then it is inserted unless an alternative plan p^{**} with $\mathbf{c}(p^{**}) \preceq \alpha_r \mathbf{c}(p^*) \preceq \alpha_r^K \mathbf{c}(p)$ is already in the result set. In that case the theorem holds. If p^* was generated in prior invocations then it was either inserted into the result set, or it was already pruned at resolution r and its cost too similar to one of the result plans, or it will be pruned in the current iteration. In all cases the theorem holds. □

Knowing the relationship between the precision factors α_r and the approximation quality of the result plan sets allows to choose the factor α_{r_M} for the maximal resolution in function of the desired target precision.

5.2 Space Consumption

The optimizer (meaning procedure OPTIMIZE, see Algorithm 2) is called once per iteration of the main loop. We analyze the accumulated space consumption of several optimizer invocations for the same query. We denote the resolution used in the i-th invocation by r_i and the cost bounds used in the i-th invocation by $\mathbf{b}_i$. Resolution $r = \min_i r_i$ designates the minimal resolution used over all invocations and vector $\mathbf{b}$ dominates all used cost bounds: $\forall i : \mathbf{b}_i \preceq \mathbf{b}$. Result and candidate plan sets are the variables with dominant space consumption in IAMA. We upper-bound the number of plans stored in those sets after all optimizer invocations to obtain the accumulated space complexity.

LEMMA 1. *Let* q *be a set containing* k *tables. Then* Res^q *contains* $O(k^l \log^l_{\alpha_r}(m))$ *result plans.*

PROOF. The cost of a query plan joining k tables is asymptotically bounded by $O(m^{2k})$ for a broad range of cost metrics [14]. Given an approximation factor $\alpha_r > 1$, the number of cost values in the interval $[1, m^{2k}]$ such that there are no two cost values c_1 and c_2 with $c_1 \leq \alpha_r c_2$ and $c_2 \leq \alpha_r c_1$ is bounded by $O(k \log_{\alpha_r}(m))$. Generalizing to l dimensions, the number of cost vectors taken from $[1, m^{2k}]^l$ such that there are no two vectors $\mathbf{c}_1$ and $\mathbf{c}_2$ with $\mathbf{c}_1 \preceq \alpha_r \mathbf{c}_2$ and $\mathbf{c}_2 \preceq \alpha_r \mathbf{c}_1$ is bounded by $O(k^l \log^l_{\alpha_r}(m))$. The pruning function of IAMA only inserts query plans into the result set if their cost vectors cannot be approximated by any other plan in the result set, using approximation factor α_r for the comparison. Therefore, the result set for q can never contain two plans whose cost vectors can mutually approximate each other. So the bound on the number of cost vectors translates into a bound on the number of plans. □

The preceding lemma exploits an upper bound on the plan cost derived from the number of joined tables. The cost bounds additionally restrict the maximal number of result plans since plans are only inserted into the result set if they respect the current bounds. We denote by $rpt(k, \mathbf{b}, r)$ the asymptotic upper bound on the number of result plans joining a set of k tables when using bounds $\mathbf{b}$ and resolution r. The next lemma derives a bound on the number of candidate plans from the bound on the number of result plans.

LEMMA 2. $Cand^q$ *contains* $O(2^k rpt^2(k, \mathbf{b}, r))$ *candidate plans for a table set* q *with* k *tables.*

PROOF. Each candidate plan for q is constructed by combining two result plans that join subsets of q. There are $O(2^k)$ possibilities of splitting a set with k tables into two subsets. Assume that q is split into two subsets q_1 and q_2. The cardinalities of Res^{q_1} and Res^{q_2} are both bounded by $rpt(k, \mathbf{b}, r)$ since rpt grows monotonically in k and $|q_1|, |q_2| < k$. The number of possible splits times the number of subplan combinations bounds the number of candidates. □

We refer to the asymptotic upper bound on the number of candidate plans per table set by $cpt(k, \mathbf{b}, r)$ in the following. The total space complexity of IAMA is obtained by summing the number of result and candidate plans over all table sets.

THEOREM 3. *The accumulated space consumption of several optimizer invocations for an* n*-table query is in* $O(3^n rpt^2(n, \mathbf{b}, r))$.

PROOF. Each plan can be represented in $O(1)$ space: scan plans are represented by the ID of the table being scanned; other plans can be represented by the IDs of the two subplans generating the operands for the final join. Plan cost vectors have constant space consumption since l is treated as a constant (see Section 3). We assume $O(l) = O(1)$ indexing space overhead per plan which is true for many data structures supporting range queries, including the cell data structure [3]. The number of candidate plans dominates the number of result plans. Summing over all table sets we obtain a space complexity of $O(\sum_{k=1}^{n}\binom{n}{k}cpt(k,\mathbf{b},r))$. Using the definition of *cpt*, considering that $cpt(k,\mathbf{b},r) \leq cpt(n,\mathbf{b},r)$ for $k \leq n$, and exploiting $\sum_{k=0}^{n}\binom{n}{k}2^k = 3^n$ yields the final complexity. □

5.3 Time of Single Optimizer Invocation

We analyze the time complexity of a single optimizer invocation for a query with n tables, for bounds $\mathbf{b}$, and for resolution r. The following analysis is valid independently from which invocations of OPTIMIZE precede the analyzed invocation. We simplify and assume that retrieving F plans by a range query takes $O(F)$ time. We can for instance use a data structure similar to the cell data structure, described by Bentley and Friedmann [3]: we partition the resolution and plan cost space into cells[3], associate a list of plans with every cell, and make those lists accessible via direct lookup. Assuming suitable cell sizes and plan cost distributions such that the number of empty cells as well as the number of plans in partially included cells is negligible for most range queries, retrieval is in $O(F)$ time and single plan insertion in $O(1)$.

LEMMA 3. *Invoking* PRUNE *for a plan joining k tables is in $O(rpt(k,\mathbf{b},r))$ time.*

PROOF. The pruning procedure retrieves all result plans joining the same tables as the new plan if they respect the bounds $\mathbf{b}$ and are indexed for resolution r or smaller. The number of plans is in $O(rpt(k,\mathbf{b},r))$ and so is the retrieval time. The cost vector of the new plan is compared against the cost vectors of all retrieved plans. One comparison requires to compare l cost values but l is a constant (see Section 3). Adding the new plan takes constant time. □

LEMMA 4. *Invoking* FRESH *for two table sets with maximally k tables is in $O(rpt^2(k,\mathbf{b},r))$ time.*

PROOF. Function FRESH iterates over pairs of result plans. The plans from those sets are combined pair-wise forming $O(rpt^2(k,\mathbf{b},r))$ pairs. Constructing a new plan and calculating its cost from the cached cost of the sub-plans using recursive cost formulas is in $O(1)$. □

We use the previous results to calculate the time complexity of the OPTIMIZE procedure.

THEOREM 4. *Invoking* OPTIMIZE *for a query with n tables is in $O(3^n rpt^3(n,\mathbf{b},r))$ time.*

PROOF. The first part of the OPTIMIZE procedure checks which candidate plans have become relevant. For one table set with k tables, this requires to retrieve and prune all candidate plans that respect bounds $\mathbf{b}$ and are marked as potentially relevant for resolution r or smaller which takes $O(cpt(k,\mathbf{b},r)rpt(k,\mathbf{b},r)) = O(2^k rpt^3(k,\mathbf{b},r))$ time. The second part of the OPTIMIZE procedure generates fresh plans using the newly inserted result plans and prunes the generated new plans. For one table set with k tables, this requires again $O(2^k rpt^3(k,\mathbf{b},r))$ time, using the complexity results for pruning and plan generation. Summing over all table sets yields a time complexity of $O(\sum_{k=1}^{n}\binom{n}{k}2^k rpt^3(k,\mathbf{b},r))$ which is in $O(3^n rpt^3(n,\mathbf{b},r))$. □

[3]We can use logarithmic partitioning for the cost space which should lead to a more uniform distribution of plans over cells since the area in the cost space that a result plan approximately dominates is defined by multiplying its cost vector by a constant factor.

The time complexity of one optimizer invocation only depends on the parameters (resolution and cost bounds) of the current invocation but not on parameters used for previous invocations. This means that plans stored from previous iterations do not cause any time overhead.

5.4 Amortized Optimization Time over Several Optimizer Invocations

We analyzed the time complexity of a single optimizer invocation in the preceding subsection. Now we analyze the amortized time complexity of a large series of invocations for the same query. After each invocation, the optimizer keeps plans that could be relevant for future invocations, thereby avoiding redundant computation. The amortized time complexity of a series of invocation is therefore lower than the time complexity of a single invocation. Resolution r and bounds $\mathbf{b}$ vary between invocations while query Q is fixed. We assume an invocation series where the Δ operator in function FRESH filters plans to the ones that were inserted in the current invocation (e.g., if the user keeps tightening the bounds and the resolution is refined). The next lemmata bound the amount of redundant computation.

LEMMA 5. *Each possible plan is generated at most once.*

PROOF. Scan plans are only generated before the main loop of Algorithm 1 is entered; this code is executed only once per query. Other plans are only generated in function FRESH and we explicitly make sure to generate plans only for fresh sub-plan combinations using predicate ISFRESH. □

LEMMA 6. *Each sub-plan pair is generated at most once.*

PROOF. Each possible plan is inserted at most once into the result plan set since it is generated at most once (according to the previous lemma) and since each plan is removed from the candidate set once it is inserted into the result set. Assume that optimizer invocations are numbered and denote for two arbitrary plans p_1 and p_2 by i_1 and i_2 the invocations at which they become result plans. Then the corresponding plan pair can only be considered at invocation $\max(i_1, i_2)$: it cannot be considered before since at least one of the plans is not in the result set at this point and it cannot be considered afterwards since none of the two plans was freshly inserted at that time. □

Candidate plans are considered for insertion (into the result set) in the first phase of the OPTIMIZE procedure. Each possible plan is only considered a limited number of times according to the following lemma.

LEMMA 7. *Each generated plan is retrieved at most r_M+1 times from the candidate plan set.*

PROOF. Each retrieved candidate plan is deleted from the candidates and pruned. During pruning, the plan can be inserted as candidate again (and considered in future invocations). All considered plans respect the current bounds.

Therefore, no plan can be re-inserted as candidate because it exceeds the bounds. It can only be re-inserted as candidate if it is approximately dominated by another plan. But then the plan becomes candidate only for a higher resolution than the current one. As there are only $r_M + 1$ resolution levels, the plan can be re-considered only so many times. □

The preceding two lemmata bound the total amount of work that is necessary per query plan over several optimizer invocations. The following theorem analyzes amortized complexity of a large series of optimizer invocations.

THEOREM 5. *Procedure* OPTIMIZE *has amortized time complexity $O(3^n)$ for a large number of invocations.*

PROOF. We split time T^i_{opt} for the i-th optimizer invocation into a time component T^i_{dep} that depends on the number of retrieved and generated plans and another time component T^i_{idp} which does not, such that $T^i_{opt} = T^i_{dep} + T^i_{idp}$.

We express T^i_{dep} in the following. Newly generated or retrieved plans must be pruned and we assume that pruning time dominates plan generation, retrieval, and insertion time. Let s_i be the number of plans and plan pairs that were generated or retrieved as candidates in the i-th invocation. The pruning time for a query with n tables must be in $O(rpt(n, \infty, r_M))$, using Lemma 3 and the fact that pruning time becomes maximal for the highest resolution and without bounds. Hence we obtain $T^i_{dep} \in O(s_i \cdot rpt(n, \infty, r_M))$.

Even if no plans are retrieved or generated, there is still time overhead for verifying whether candidate plans have to be pruned or fresh plans can be generated. This requires us to iterate over all table sets (searching for candidates) and to iterate over each split of each table set (searching for fresh plans). Using a similar reasoning as in the previous proofs, we obtain $T^i_{idp} \in O(3^n)$.

The time $T = \sum_{i=1}^{x} T^i_{opt}$ denotes the time of x consecutive optimizer invocations for the same query. We certainly have $T \in O((rpt(n, \infty, r_M) \cdot \sum_{i=1}^{x} s_i) + x \cdot 3^n)$. However, as the total number of generated plans for a fixed query is bounded (see Section 5.2), as each plan and plan pair is generated only once (Lemmata 5 and 6), and as each plan is retrieved at most $r_M + 1$ times (Lemma 7), we can bound $\sum_{i=1}^{x} s_i$ independently from the number of invocations x. This means that for a sufficiently large number of invocations, the time component that is independent of the number of retrieved and generated plans must become dominant. □

As IAMA avoids redundant work, its averaged time complexity over many iterations equals the time complexity of single-objective query optimization with bushy plans.

6. EXPERIMENTAL EVALUATION

Section 6.1 describes and justifies the experimental setup and Section 6.2 discusses the experimental results.

6.1 Experimental Setup

We evaluate an incremental anytime algorithm for MOQO, its simplified pseudo-code was presented in Section 4, in comparison with two baselines: the *memoryless algorithm* is equivalent to the iterative MOQO algorithm proposed in a prior publication [14] except that we use a different precision refinement policy, the *one-shot algorithm* corresponds to the non-iterative MOQO algorithm presented in the same publication [14]. The memoryless algorithm produces the same sequence of result plan sets as the incremental anytime algorithm; it is however non-incremental and produces each plan set from scratch. The one-shot algorithm produces the result plan set with highest resolution directly, avoiding any intermediate steps; it therefore lacks the anytime property and takes a long time to produce the first result. We compare the algorithms according to average and maximal time of a single optimizer invocation within a series of invocations for the same query. It is crucial to minimize the time for single optimizer invocations in an interactive scenario: if single optimizer invocations take too long then it is unlikely that they won't be interrupted by user interaction. We do not evaluate space consumption: all three evaluated algorithms finally produce a result plan set with the same resolution so the total space consumption does not differ significantly between them. We evaluate all algorithms in a scenario without user interaction to make the comparison as fair as possible; the cost bounds are initially fixed to ∞.

Our implementation is based on an extended version of the Postgres 9.2 database system: this version features an optimizer that considers multiple plan cost metrics and was already used in prior work to evaluate MOQO algorithms [14]. We reuse the cost models of the three plan cost metrics execution time, consumed system resources (namely the number of reserved cores), and result precision. We chose a scenario with three plan cost metrics on purpose since this is the maximal number of metrics that allows to visualize Pareto-optimal cost tradeoffs to the user (in the form of a surface in 3D); it is of course still possible to provide users with aggregate information about available cost tradeoffs for higher numbers of metrics. Our implementation only covers the parts of the optimization algorithms that are required for this benchmark. We evaluate the algorithms on TPC-H queries containing at least one join. The performance of the algorithms is strongly correlated with the number of joined tables. In the following figures, we report average numbers over all queries with the same number of tables to make those correlations visible. Also, the Postgres optimizer may split up optimization of one TPC-H query into multiple optimizations of sub-queries with different numbers of tables. In those cases, we measured optimization times for different sub-queries separately. The relative performance of the evaluated algorithms also depends on the number of resolution levels. We experimented with different numbers of resolution levels (i.e., we used different values for r_M) and applied the formula $\alpha_r = \alpha_T + \alpha_S(r_M - r)/r_M$ to calculate the precision factors used during pruning; we use different values for the target precision α_T and for the precision step α_S. All experiments were executed on a MacBook air with 4 GB RAM and an Intel Core i5 processor with 1.4 GHz.

6.2 Experimental Results

Figure 3 shows average times per optimizer invocation for a moderate target precision of $\alpha_T = 1.01$ and $\alpha_S = 0.05$. Choosing $\alpha_T = 1.01$ means that the final result plan set is an $1.01^8 \approx 1.08$-approximate Pareto plan set, based on the formal analysis from Section 5.1 and on the fact that TPC-H queries have at most eight tables. Hence the costs of the result query plans are formally guaranteed to be not higher than optimal by more than about 8 percent. These are rather weak guarantees and, correspondingly, optimization takes never more than ten seconds, even for the two baselines. Such optimization times are not unusual for

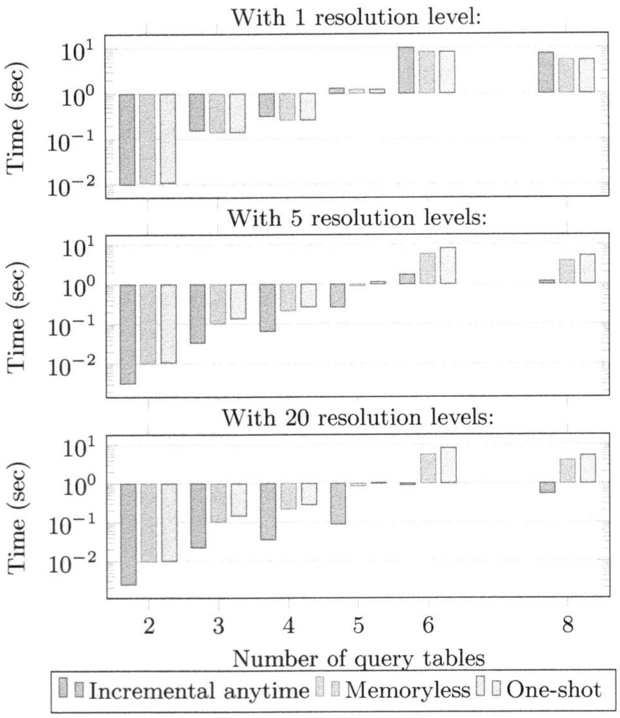

Figure 3: Average time per optimizer invocation for TPC-H sub-queries and target precision $\alpha_T = 1.01$

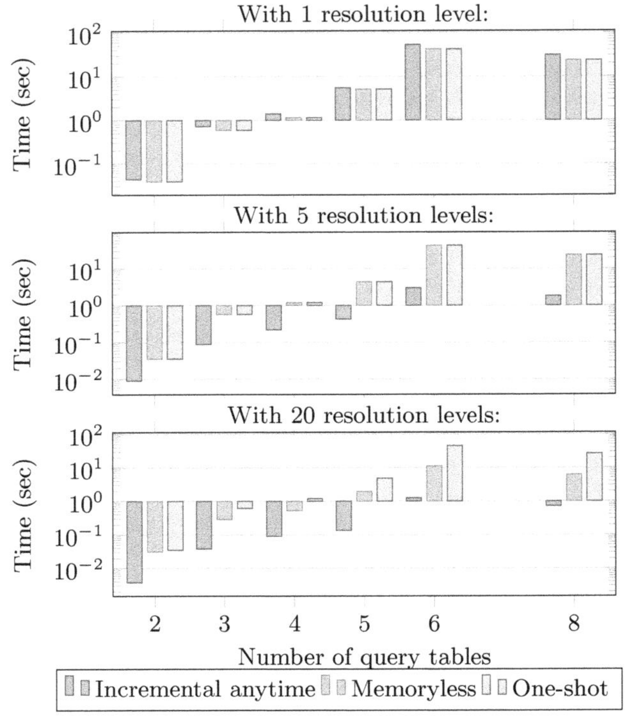

Figure 4: Average time per optimizer invocation for TPC-H sub-queries and target precision $\alpha_T = 1.005$

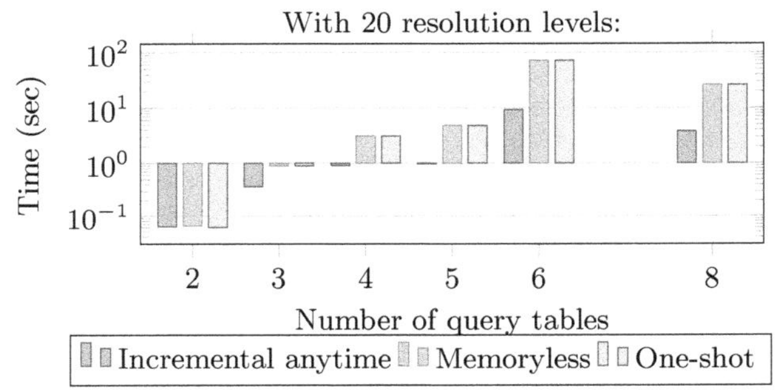

Figure 5: Maximal time per optimizer invocation for TPC-H sub-queries and target precision $\alpha_T = 1.005$

MOQO [14]. The plan search space size increases in the number of query tables and so do optimization times[4]. Note that no TPC-H sub-query joins seven tables which is the reason for the missing bar at that position. When considering only one resolution level, the incremental anytime algorithm (IAMA) cannot show its strengths and is slower than the two baselines by at most 37%. This overhead is due to plan indexing and the extended pruning function. The situation changes once we increase the number of resolution levels: already with five resolution levels, IAMA is up to four times faster than the one-shot algorithm and up to three times faster than the memoryless algorithm. With 20 resolution levels, IAMA is up to one order of magnitude faster than both baselines. Only IAMA is able to exploit different resolution levels by splitting up optimization into several incremental optimization steps. The behavior of the one-shot algorithm does not depend on the number of resolution levels; the memoryless algorithm generates the same sequence of result plan sets as IAMA but is not incremental and has to start optimization from scratch in each invocation.

Figure 4 shows analogous results for target precision $\alpha_T = 1.005$ (and $\alpha_S = 0.5$); using that target precision during pruning, all evaluated algorithms guarantee to generate 1.04-approximate Pareto plan sets so the precision is higher than before. This results in optimization times of between 41 and 53 seconds for all three algorithms with one resolution level. This makes incremental computation even more necessary than in the last example. IAMA is up to 14 times faster than the memoryless algorithm and beats the one-shot algorithm by up to factor 37. This means that the relative advantage that IAMA gives over non-incremental algorithms increases, the more difficult the optimization task is (e.g., higher target precision or higher number of tables). Figure 5 finally shows not the average but the maximal time for one optimizer invocation: IAMA is up to eight times faster than both baselines and we believe that this ratio could be extended by a more optimized sequence of precision factors. The two baselines are in practice equivalent when considering maximum time: for the memoryless algorithm, the invocation with maximal execution time is usually the last one in which it has to accomplish the same work as the one-shot algorithm.

[4]There is a slight decrease from six to eight tables since the only TPC-H query joining eight tables refers to many small tables for which less sampling strategies are considered.

7. CONCLUSION

User preferences are difficult to formalize so MOQO should be an interactive process. We presented an incremental anytime algorithm that is well suited for interactive MOQO.

8. REFERENCES

[1] S. Agarwal, A. Iyer, and A. Panda. Blink and it's done: interactive queries on very large data. In *VLDB*, volume 5, pages 1902–1905, 2012.

[2] G. Ausiello and G. Italiano. Incremental paths algorithms for minimal length paths. *Journal of Algorithms*, 12(4):12–21, 1991.

[3] J. L. Bentley and J. H. Friedman. Data structures for range searching. *ACM Computing Surveys*, 11(4):397–409, 1979.

[4] P. Bizarro, N. Bruno, and D. DeWitt. Progressive parametric query optimization. *KDE*, 21(4):582–594, 2009.

[5] S. Chatterji and S. Evani. On the complexity of approximate query optimization. In *PODS*, pages 282–292, 2002.

[6] S. Chaudhuri. Query optimizers: time to rethink the contract? *SIGMOD*, pages 961–968, 2009.

[7] S. Ganguly, W. Hasan, and R. Krishnamurthy. Query optimization for parallel execution. In *SIGMOD*, pages 9–18, 1992.

[8] J. M. Hellerstein, P. J. Haas, and H. J. Wang. Online aggregation. In *SIGMOD*, pages 171–182, 1997.

[9] P. Klein and N. Young. Approximation algorithms for NP-hard optimization problems. In *Algorithms and Theory of Computation Handbook*. 2010.

[10] D. Kossmann and K. Stocker. Iterative dynamic programming: a new class of query optimization algorithms. *ACM TODS*, 25(1):43–82, 2000.

[11] C. Papadimitriou and M. Yannakakis. Multiobjective query optimization. In *PODS*, pages 52–59, 2001.

[12] P. G. Selinger, M. M. Astrahan, D. D. Chamberlin, R. A. Lorie, and T. G. Price. Access path selection in a relational database management system. In *SIGMOD*, pages 23–34, 1979.

[13] M. Stonebraker, P. Aoki, R. Devine, W. Litwin, and M. Olson. Mariposa: a new architecture for distributed data. In *ICDE*, pages 54–65, 1994.

[14] I. Trummer and C. Koch. Approximation schemes for many-objective query optimization. In *SIGMOD*, pages 1299–1310, 2014.

[15] I. Trummer and C. Koch. Multi-objective parametric query optimization. *VLDB*, 8(3):221–232, 2015.

[16] S. V. Vrbsky and Jane W.-S. Liu. APPROXIMATE-a query processor that produces monotonically improving approximate answers. *KDE*, 5(6):1056–1068, 1993.

[17] R. Willis, CEWillis, C., & Perlack. Multiple objective decision making: generating techniques or goal programming. *Journal of the Northeastern Agr. Econ. Council*, 9(1):0–5, 1980.

[18] Z. Xu, Y. C. Tu, and X. Wang. PET: Reducing Database Energy Cost via Query Optimization. *VLDB*, 5(12):1954–1957, 2012.

[19] S. Zilberstein. Using anytime algorithms in intelligent systems. *AI Magazine*, 17(3):73–83, 1996.

Output-sensitive Evaluation of Prioritized Skyline Queries

Niccolò Meneghetti
Dept. of Computer Science and Engineering
University at Buffalo
Buffalo, NY 14260-2000
niccolom@buffalo.edu

Denis Mindolin
Bloomberg L.P.
731 Lexington Avenue
New York, NY 10022
dmindolin1@bloomberg.net

Paolo Ciaccia
DISI
University of Bologna
Mura Anteo Zamboni, 7
40126 Bologna Italy
paolo.ciaccia@unibo.it

Jan Chomicki
Dept. of Computer Science and Engineering
University at Buffalo
Buffalo, NY 14260-2000
chomicki@buffalo.edu

ABSTRACT

Skylines assume that all attributes are equally important, as each dimension can always be traded off for another. Prioritized skylines (*p-skylines*) take into account *non-compensatory* preferences, where some dimensions are deemed more important than others, and trade-offs are constrained by the relative importance of the attributes involved.

In this paper we show that querying using non-compensatory preferences is computationally efficient. We focus on preferences that are representable with *p-expressions*, and develop an efficient in-memory divide-and-conquer algorithm for answering p-skyline queries. Our algorithm is *output-sensitive*; this is very desirable in the context of preference queries, since the output is expected to be, on average, only a small fraction of the input. We prove that our method is well behaved in both the worst- and the average-case scenarios. Additionally, we develop a general framework for benchmarking p-skyline algorithms, showing how to sample prioritized preference relations uniformly, and how to highlight the effect of data correlation on performance. We conclude our study with extensive experimental results.

Categories and Subject Descriptors

H.2.3 [**Database Management**]: Languages—*Query languages*; H.2.4 [**Database Management**]: Systems—*Query processing*

General Terms

Algorithms, Experimentation, Performance

SIGMOD'15, May 31–June 4, 2015, Melbourne, Victoria, Australia.

http://dx.doi.org/10.1145/2723372.2723736.

Keywords

preference, preference query, skyline, p-skyline, Pareto accumulation, Prioritized accumulation

1. INTRODUCTION

Output-sensitive algorithms are quite popular in computational geometry. Starting from the classical results on convex hulls by Kirkpatrick and Seidel [26] and Chan [9], output-sensitive solutions have been explored in several problem domains. Let's denote the input- and the output-size by n and v, respectively. An output-sensitive algorithm is designed to be efficient when v is a small fraction of n. More specifically, its asymptotic complexity should depend explicitly on v, and gracefully degrade to the level of the best known output-*insensitive* algorithms when $v \in \Omega(n)$. Preference queries [11, 12, 22] provide an interesting domain for output-sensitive algorithms. Starting from a large set of tuples, the goal is to extract those that maximize a given binary preference relation. Preference queries are not aimed at retrieving tuples that perfectly match user's interests, but rather at filtering out those that clearly do not. Hence, if preferences are modeled properly, the user should expect to see only a fairly limited number of results.

The most basic preferences a user can express are those that depend on a single attribute: for example, a user may state that she prefers cheap cars over expensive ones, or that she is more comfortable driving with the manual transmission rather than with the automatic one. Single-attribute preferences are easy to elicit and we will assume they are known a priori.

Several ways exist to combine simple, one-dimensional preferences into composite, multi-dimensional ones. A popular approach is to look for tuples that are *Pareto*-optimal. A tuple is Pareto-optimal when no other tuple Pareto-dominates it, being better in one dimension and no worse in all the other dimensions. Within the database community, the set of tuples satisfying Pareto-optimality is called a *skyline* [7, 13]. It is important to notice that skylines always allow to trade off one dimension for another: even if a tuple is dominated in several dimensions, it can still be part of the skyline as long as it guarantees an arbitrarily small advantage on some other dimensions. In other words, one dimension can always compensate for another. It has been proved that skylines contain all the tuples maximizing any arbitrary scoring function[1]. Hence, if we assume that users make their decisions according to some hidden utility function, under reasonable assumptions we are guaranteed that their preferred tuple will belong to the skyline. The first output-sensitive algorithm for skyline queries is due to Kirkpatrick and Seidel [25].

Prioritized-skylines [22, 29] take a rather different approach: single-dimensional preferences are composed according to a specific priority order, that is dictated by the user. For example: let's assume a customer is looking for a cheap, low-mileage vehicle, and she would prefer to have a manual transmission *as long as there is no extra charge for it.* Such customer exhibits preferences over three dimensions (price, mileage and transmission), but the preference on price is deemed more important than the one on transmission type. In other words, the user is not willing to negotiate on price if the only reward is to obtain a better transmission. Notice that we have no reason to assume that the preference on mileage is either more or less important than any of the other two. Prioritized skylines are a special-case of *non-compensatory decision making*, a phenomenon that has been extensively studied in economics and psychology [31, 16, 17]. A non-compensatory preference arises whenever a user refuses to negotiate a trade-off between attributes (for example: a higher price for a better transmission), deeming one dimension infinitely more important than the other. P-skylines allow to model this kind of preferences naturally. Semantically, they generalize skylines: when the user considers all the attributes to be equally important, the p-skyline contains only Pareto-optimal tuples. A p-skyline query always returns a subset of the skyline; in practice, it usually returns just a small portion of it.

The main contribution of this paper is to develop a novel output-sensitive algorithm for p-skyline queries. We show the problem is $\mathcal{O}\left(n \log^{d-2} v\right)$ in $d \geq 4$ dimensions, and $\mathcal{O}\left(n \log v\right)$ in two and three dimensions. Hence, our work generalizes the results in [25] to the context of p-skylines. Our solution differs significantly from [25], as we show how to exploit the semantics of prioritized preferences for devising an effective divide-and-conquer strategy. Additionally, we prove the algorithm is $\mathcal{O}(n)$ in the average case.

We conclude our work presenting extensive experimental results on real-life and synthetic data. Apart from the nice asymptotic properties, our algorithm proves to be practical for processing realistically sized data sets. For our evaluations we use data sets with up to one million records and up to 20 attributes. To the best of our knowledge our benchmarks are in line with most of the studies of skyline queries in the literature.

2. NOTATION AND RELATED WORK

In this document we adopt the following typographic conventions: sets of tuples (or operators returning set of tuples) are written as capital letters (like D, B, W or $M(D)$), sets of attributes are written in calligraphic font (like $\mathcal{A}$, $\mathcal{C}$ or $\mathcal{E}$), actual attributes are written in boldface font (for example: $\mathbf{A}_1, \mathbf{A}_2, \ldots$).

[1]Assuming the function is defined on all dimensions.

$\mathcal{A}$	a relation schema
D	a relation instance
$\mathbf{A}_1, \mathbf{A}_2, \ldots$	attributes
$t_1, t_2, \ldots$	tuples
π	a p-expression
$\succ_\pi$	the strict partial order induced by π
$M_{\text{sky}}(D)$	the skyline of D
$M_\pi(D)$	the p-skyline of D, w.r.t. π
n	the size of the input (# of tuples)
v	the size of the output (# of tuples)
d	the number of relevant attributes
$W \not\succeq_\pi B$	no tuple in W is better than (or indistinguishable from) any tuple in B
Γ_π, Γ_π^r	the p-graph of π and its trans. reduction
$\mathcal{V}ar(\pi)$	the attributes appearing in π
$\mathcal{S}ucc_\pi(\mathbf{A}_i)$	immediate successors of $\mathbf{A}_i$ in Γ_π^r
$\mathcal{D}esc_\pi(\mathbf{A}_i)$	descendants of $\mathbf{A}_i$ in Γ_π^r
$\mathcal{P}re_\pi(\mathbf{A}_i)$	immediate predecessors of $\mathbf{A}_i$ in Γ_π^r
$\mathcal{A}nc_\pi(\mathbf{A}_i)$	ancestors of $\mathbf{A}_i$ in Γ_π^r
$\mathcal{R}oots_\pi$	attributes having no ancestors in Γ_π^r
$\mathcal{B}etter_\pi(t', t)$	attributes where t' is preferred to t
$\mathcal{T}op_\pi(t', t)$	topmost attributes in Γ_π^r where t and t' disagree
$d_{\mathbf{A}_i}$	the depth of $\mathbf{A}_i$, the length of the longest path in Γ_π^r from any root to $\mathbf{A}_i$
$C_d(v, n)$	worst-case complexity of skyline queries
$F_d(b, w)$	w.c. complexity of screening queries
$C_d^*(v, n)$	w.c. complexity of p-skyline queries
$F_d^*(b, w)$	w.c. complexity of p-screening queries

For the convenience of the reader the above table summarizes the most common notations used throughout the paper. All notational conventions are formally introduced and explained in more details in the following sections.

2.1 Modeling Preferences

Several frameworks have been proposed for modeling preferences in databases, many of which are surveyed in [34]. In this paper we follow the *qualitative* approach [11, 22, 12], as we assume user's wishes are modeled as strict partial orders. We denote by $\mathcal{A} = \{\mathbf{A}_1, \mathbf{A}_2, \ldots\}$ a finite set of attributes defining a relation schema, and by U the set of all possible tuples over such schema. Without lack of generality, we assume attributes can be either discrete or range over the set of rational numbers. A *preference* is a strict partial order $\succ$ over U, a subset of $U \times U$ being transitive and irreflexive. The assertion $t' \succ t$ (t' *dominates* t) means the user prefers t' over t, i.e. she's always willing to trade the tuple t for the tuple t' if she is given the chance. Given a relation instance $D \subseteq U$ and a preference $\succ$, a *preference query* retrieves all the maximal elements of the partially ordered set $(D, \succ)$. Following the notation of [25], we denote by $M_\succ(D)$ the set of all these maximal tuples:

$$M_\succ(D) = \{t \in D \mid \nexists\, t' \in D \text{ s.t. } t' \succ t\}$$

Every preference $\succ$ induces an indifference relation ($\sim$): $t' \sim t$ holds whenever $t' \not\succ t$ and $t \not\succ t'$. A preference $\succ$ is a *weak order* when $\sim$ is transitive. A weak order extension of $\succ$ is simply an arbitrary weak order containing $\succ$. Two tuples t' and t are *indistinguishable* with respect to $\succ$ when they agree on all attributes that are relevant for deciding $\succ$. In such case we write $t' \approx t$. We denote by $t' \succeq t$ the fact that t' is either better than or indistinguishable from t. If D and D' are two relation instances, we write $D' \not\succeq D$ when there is no pair of tuples (t', t) in $D' \times D$ such that $t' \succeq t$.

Declaring a preference by enumerating its elements is impractical in all but the most trivial domains. Kießling [22] suggested to define preferences in a constructive fashion, by iteratively composing single-attribute preferences into more complex ones. From his work we borrow two composition operators, namely the *Pareto accumulation* ($\otimes$) and the *Prioritized accumulation* (&). Denote $\succ_1$ and $\succ_2$ two strict partial orders; their Pareto accumulation $\succ_{1\otimes 2}$ is defined as follows

$$\forall\, t', t \quad t' \succ_{1\otimes 2} t \iff \begin{array}{l}(t' \succ_1 t \,\wedge\, t' \succeq_2 t) \,\vee \\ (t' \succ_2 t \,\wedge\, t' \succeq_1 t)\end{array}$$

In other words, $t' \succ_{1\otimes 2} t$ holds when t' is better according to one of the preferences $\succ_1$ and $\succ_2$, and better or indistinguishable from t according to the other. Hence, the two preferences are equally important. The prioritized composition of $\succ_1$ and $\succ_2$ is defined as follows

$$\forall\, t', t \quad t' \succ_{1\&2} t \iff t' \succ_1 t \,\vee\, (t' \approx_1 t \,\wedge\, t' \succ_2 t)$$

Clearly $\succ_{1\&2}$ gives more weight to the first preference, as $\succ_2$ is taken into consideration only when two tuples are indistinguishable w.r.t. $\succ_1$. Both operators are associative and the Pareto accumulation is commutative [22]. Several standard query languages have been extended to support preference constructors like the Pareto- and the Prioritized accumulation, including SQL [24], XPATH [23], and SPARQL [33]. To the best of our knowledge we are the first to develop an output-sensitive algorithm supporting both of these constructors.

A *p-expression* [29] is a formula denoting multiple applications of the above operators. P-expressions respect the following grammar:

$$\begin{array}{rcl} pExpr & \rightarrow & paretoAcc \mid prioritizedAcc \mid attribute \\ paretoAcc & \rightarrow & pExpr \otimes pExpr \\ prioritizedAcc & \rightarrow & pExpr \;\&\; pExpr \\ attribute & \rightarrow & \mathbf{A}_1 | \mathbf{A}_2 | \ldots \end{array}$$

where all non-terminal symbols are lower-case and each terminal symbol is either a composition operator ($\otimes$ or &) or a single-attribute preference, with the restriction that no attribute should appear more than once. A single-attribute preference (also denoted by $\succ_{\mathbf{A}_i}$) is simply an arbitrary total order defined over the attribute's domain. Without lack of generality, we will assume users rank values in natural order (i.e. they prefer small values to larger ones), unless stated differently. With a little abuse of notation, we will use single-attribute preferences for ranking either tuples or values, depending on the context.

EXAMPLE 1. *Assume that a dealer is offering the following cars*

id	**P** *(price)*	**M** *(mileage)*	**T** *(transmission)*
t_1	\$ 11,500	50,000 miles	*automatic*
t_2	\$ 11,500	60,000 miles	*manual*
t_3	\$ 12,000	50,000 miles	*manual*
t_4	\$ 12,000	60,000 miles	*automatic*

and that we are looking for a cheap vehicle, with low mileage, possibly with manual shift. Notice that while the first car is Pareto-optimal for price and mileage, if we want a manual transmission we need to give up either on getting the best price or the best mileage. Depending on our priorities, we can model our preferences in different ways. All the following are well-formed and meaningful p-expressions:

1. $\mathbf{P}$
2. $(\mathbf{P} \otimes \mathbf{M}) \;\&\; \mathbf{T}$
3. $(\mathbf{P} \;\&\; \mathbf{T}) \otimes \mathbf{M}$
4. $\mathbf{M} \;\&\; \mathbf{T} \;\&\; \mathbf{P}$

Expression (1) states that we care only about price. If that is the case, we should buy either t_1 or t_2. Expression (2) states that we are looking for cars that are Pareto-optimal w.r.t. price and mileage, and that we take into consideration transmission only to decide between cars that are indistinguishable in terms of price and mileage. In this case t_1 is the best option. Expression (3) is more subtle: we are looking for cheap cars, with low mileage and manual transmission, but we are not willing to pay an extra price for the manual transmission. In this case we should buy either t_1 or t_2, since t_1 dominates t_3 and t_4. Finally, expression (4) denotes a lexicographic order: amongst the cars with the lowest mileage, we are looking for one with manual transmission, and price is the least of our concerns. In this case we should buy t_3.

Given a p-expression π we denote by $\succ_\pi$ the preference relation defined by it. Notice that $\succ_\pi$ is guaranteed to be a strict partial order [22]. We denote by $\mathcal{V}ar(\pi)$ the set of attributes that appear inside π, i.e. those that are relevant for deciding $\succ_\pi$. Notice that $t' \approx_\pi t$ holds iff t' and t agree on every attribute in $\mathcal{V}ar(\pi)$; in the following we will simply say that t and t' are indistinguishable w.r.t. attributes in $\mathcal{V}ar(\pi)$.

Definition 1. Given a relation instance $D \subseteq U$ and a p-expression π, a *p-skyline query* returns the set $M_\pi(D)$ of the maximal elements of the poset $(D, \succ_\pi)$.

The computational complexity of p-skyline queries depends strongly on the size of the input, the size of the output, and the number of attributes that are relevant to decide $\succ_\pi$. Hence, our analysis will take in consideration mainly three parameters: n, the number of tuples in the input, v the number of tuples that belong to the p-skyline, and d, the cardinality of $\mathcal{V}ar(\pi)$.

Every p-expression π implicitly induces a priority order over the attributes in $\mathcal{V}ar(\pi)$. Mindolin and Chomicki [29] modeled these orders using p-graphs, and showed how they relate to the semantics of p-skyline preferences. We will follow a similar route designing our divide-and-conquer strategy for p-skyline queries. Hence, we need to introduce some of the notation used in [29].

Definition 2. A p-graph Γ_π is a directed acyclic graph having one vertex for each attribute in $\mathcal{V}ar(\pi)$. The set $E(\Gamma_\pi)$ of all edges connecting its vertices is defined recursively as follows:

- if π is a single-attribute preference, then $E(\Gamma_\pi) \equiv \emptyset$
- if $\pi = \pi_1 \otimes \pi_2$ then $E(\Gamma_\pi) \equiv E(\Gamma_{\pi_1}) \cup E(\Gamma_{\pi_2})$
- if $\pi = \pi_1 \;\&\; \pi_2$ then $E(\Gamma_\pi) \equiv E(\Gamma_{\pi_1}) \cup E(\Gamma_{\pi_2}) \cup (\mathcal{V}ar(\pi_1) \times \mathcal{V}ar(\pi_2))$

Intuitively, a p-graph Γ_π contains an edge from $\mathbf{A}_i$ to $\mathbf{A}_j$ iff the preference on $\mathbf{A}_i$ is more important than the one on $\mathbf{A}_j$. Notice that p-graphs are transitive by construction and, since p-expressions do not allow repeated attributes, they are guaranteed to be acyclic. In order to simplify the notation in the following sections we will not use p-graphs directly, but we will refer mostly to their transitive reductions[2] Γ^r_π (see Figure 1). In relation to Γ^r_π we define the following sets of attributes:

$\mathcal{S}\text{ucc}_\pi(\mathbf{A}_i)$	immediate successors of $\mathbf{A}_i$
$\mathcal{D}\text{esc}_\pi(\mathbf{A}_i)$	descendants of $\mathbf{A}_i$
$\mathcal{P}\text{re}_\pi(\mathbf{A}_i)$	immediate predecessors of $\mathbf{A}_i$
$\mathcal{A}\text{nc}_\pi(\mathbf{A}_i)$	ancestors of $\mathbf{A}_i$
$\mathcal{R}\text{oots}_\pi$	nodes having no ancestors

We will denote by $d_{\mathbf{A_i}}$ the depth of $\mathbf{A}_i$, i.e. the length of the longest path in Γ^r_π from any root to $\mathbf{A}_i$ (roots have depth 0).

EXAMPLE 2. *A customer is looking for a low-mileage* ($\mathbf{M}$) *car; amongst barely used models, she is looking for a car that is available near her location* ($\mathbf{D}$) *for a good price* ($\mathbf{P}$)*, possibly still under warranty* ($\mathbf{W}$)*. In order to obtain a comprehensive warranty she is willing to pay more, but not to drive to a distant dealership, since regular maintenance would require her to go there every three months. All else being equal, she prefers cars equipped with heated seats* ($\mathbf{H}$) *and manual transmission* ($\mathbf{T}$)*. Her preferences can be formulated using the following p-expression:*

$$\mathbf{M} \ \& \ ((\mathbf{D}\&\mathbf{W}) \otimes \mathbf{P}) \ \& \ (\mathbf{T} \otimes \mathbf{H})$$

Figure 1(a) shows the corresponding p-graph and Figure 1(b) its transitive reduction. Notice the p-graph is not a weak order, thus the attributes cannot be simply ranked.

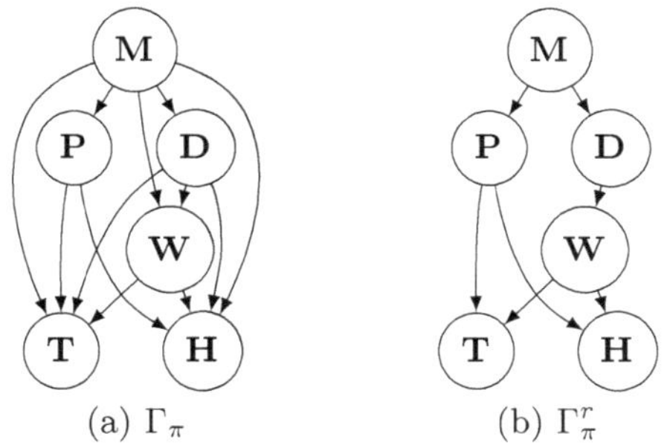

Figure 1: (a) the p-graph of the expression $\mathbf{M}$ & $((\mathbf{D}\&\mathbf{W}) \otimes \mathbf{P})$ & $(\mathbf{T} \otimes \mathbf{H})$ and (b) its transitive reduction.

The following result from [29] highlights the relation between p-graphs and the semantics of p-skylines:

PROPOSITION 1. *[29] Denote by t and t′ two distinct tuples, by $\mathcal{B}etter_\pi(t', t)$ the set of attributes where t′ is preferred to t, and by $\mathcal{T}op_\pi(t', t)$ the topmost elements in Γ^r_π where t and t′ disagree. The following assertions are equivalent:*

1. $t' \succ_\pi t$
2. $\mathcal{B}etter_\pi(t', t) \supseteq \mathcal{T}op_\pi(t', t)$
3. $\mathcal{D}esc_\pi(\mathcal{B}etter_\pi(t', t)) \supseteq \mathcal{B}etter_\pi(t, t')$

In other words, $t' \succ_\pi t$ holds iff the two tuples are distinguishable and every node in the p-graph for which t is preferred has an ancestor for which t' is preferred. We will take advantage of this result in Sections 4 and 6.

[2]Since every p-graph is a finite strict partial order, the transitive reduction Γ^r_π is guaranteed to exist and to be unique: it consists of all edges that form the only available path between their endpoints.

2.2 Skyline queries

A *skyline query* can be seen as a special case of p-skyline query: the Pareto-optimality criterion over an arbitrary set of attributes $\{\mathbf{A}_i, \mathbf{A}_j, \mathbf{A}_k, \ldots\}$ can be formulated as follows

$$\mathbf{A}_i \otimes \mathbf{A}_j \otimes \mathbf{A}_k \otimes \ldots$$

From now on we will denote by *sky* the above expression, and by $M_{\text{sky}}(D)$ the result of a skyline query. Clearly, the meaning of this notation will depend on the content of $\mathcal{V}ar(\text{sky})$.

PROPOSITION 2. *[29] Let π and π' be two p-expressions such that $\mathcal{V}ar(\pi) = \mathcal{V}ar(\pi')$. The following containment properties hold*

$$\succ_\pi \subset \succ_{\pi'} \Leftrightarrow E(\Gamma_\pi) \subset E(\Gamma_{\pi'}) \quad (1)$$

$$\succ_\pi = \succ_{\pi'} \Leftrightarrow E(\Gamma_\pi) = E(\Gamma_{\pi'}) \quad (2)$$

From Proposition 2 we can directly infer that $M_\pi(D) \subseteq M_{\text{sky}}(D)$ as long as $\mathcal{V}ar(\pi) = \mathcal{V}ar(sky)$.

Skyline queries have been very popular in the database community. Over several years a plethora of algorithms have been proposed, including BNL [7], SFS [14], LESS [20], SALSA [2], BBS [30], and many others. For the purpose of this paper we briefly review BNL, together with its extensions. BNL (block-nested-loop) allocates a fixed-size memory buffer able to store up to k tuples, the *window*, and repeatedly performs a linear scan of the input; during each iteration i each tuple t is compared with all the elements currently in the window. If t is dominated by any of those, it is immediately discarded, otherwise all the elements of the window being dominated by t are discarded and t is added to the window. If there is not enough space, t is written to a temporary file T_i. At the end of each iteration i all the tuples that entered the window when T_i was empty are removed and added to the final result; the others, if any, are left in the window to be used during the successive iteration $(i+1)$, that will scan the tuples stored in T_i. The process is repeated until no tuples are left in the temporary file.

SFS (sort-filter-skyline) improves BNL with a pre-sorting step; at the very beginning the input is sorted according to a special ranking function, ensuring that no tuple dominates another that precedes it. The resulting algorithm is pipelineable and generally faster than BNL. LESS (Linear Elimination Sort for Skyline [20]) and SALSA (Sort and Limit Skyline algorithm [2]) improve this procedure by applying an elimination filter and an early-stop condition.

Skylines have been studied for several decades in computational geometry, as an instance of the *maximal vector problem* [28, 6, 25]. The first divide and conquer algorithm is due to Kung, Luccio and Preparata [28] and is similar to the one used in this paper: the general idea is to split the data set in two halves, say B and W, so that no tuple in W is indistinguishable from or dominates any tuple in B ($W \not\succeq_{\text{sky}} B$); then, the skyline of both halves is computed recursively, obtaining $M_{\text{sky}}(B)$ and $M_{\text{sky}}(W)$. The last step is to remove from $M_{\text{sky}}(W)$ all tuples dominated by some element in $M_{\text{sky}}(B)$. This operation is called *screening*. Let W' be the set of tuples from $M_{\text{sky}}(W)$ that survive the screening, the algorithm returns the set $M_{\text{sky}}(B) \cup W'$, containing each and every skyline point. The base case for the recursion is when B and W are small enough to make the computation of the skyline trivial.

In [3] Bentley et al. developed a similar, alternative algorithm, and in [4] proposed a method that is provably fast in the average-case. Kirkpatrick and Seidel [25] were the first to propose an output-sensitive procedure. More recently, [32] developed a divide-and-conquer algorithm that is efficient in external memory, while several results have been obtained using the word-RAM model [18, 10, 1]. Following [25] we denote by $C_d(v, n)$ the worst-case complexity of skyline queries, and by $F_d(b, w)$ the worst-case complexity of screening, assuming $b = |B|$ and $w = |W|$. The following complexity results were obtained in [25, 27, 28]. In this paper we will prove similar results in the context of p-skylines.

PROPOSITION 3. *[25] The following upper-bounds hold on the complexity of the maximal vector problem:*

1. $C_d(v,n) \leq \mathcal{O}(n)$ *for* $d = 1$
2. $C_d(v,n) \leq \mathcal{O}(n \log v)$ *for* $d = 2, 3$
3. $C_d(v,n) \leq \mathcal{O}\left(n \log^{d-2} v\right)$ *for* $d \geq 4$
4. $C_d(v,n) \leq \mathcal{O}(n)$ *when* $v = 1$

PROPOSITION 4. *[25, 27, 28] The following upper-bounds on the complexity of the screening problem hold:*

1. $F_d(b,w) \leq \mathcal{O}(b + w)$ *for* $d = 1$
2. $F_d(b,w) \leq \mathcal{O}((b + w) \log b)$ *for* $d = 2, 3$
3. $F_d(b,w) \leq \mathcal{O}\left((b + w) \log^{d-2} b\right)$ *for* $d \geq 4$
4. $F_d(b,w) \leq \mathcal{O}(w)$ *when* $b = 1$

3. OUTPUT-SENSITIVE P-SKYLINE

In this section we present our output-sensitive algorithm for p-skyline queries. We first introduce a simple divide and conquer algorithm, named Dc, showing the problem is $\mathcal{O}\left(n \cdot \log^{d-2} n\right)$. Later we extend it, making it output-sensitive and ensuring an asymptotic worst-case complexity of $\mathcal{O}\left(n \cdot \log^{d-2} v\right)$. Before discussing our algorithms in detail, we need to generalize the concept of screening to the context of p-skylines:

Definition 3. Given a p-expression π and two relation instances B and W, such that $W \not\succeq_\pi B$, *p-screening* is the problem of detecting all tuples in W that are not dominated by any tuple in B, according to $\succ_\pi$.

Extending the notation of [27], we denote by $\left[{B \atop W}\right]_\pi$ the problem of p-screening B and W, and by $F^*_d(b, w)$ its worst-case complexity[3]. In Section 4 we will show $F^*_d(b, w)$ is $\mathcal{O}\left((b + w) \cdot (\log b)^{d-2}\right)$. For the moment we take this result as given. We denote by $C^*_d(v, n)$ the worst-case complexity of p-skylines, where n and v are the input- and the output-size.

The complete code of Dc is given in the Figure on the right. Similarly to the divide and conquer algorithm by [28], the strategy of Dc is to split the input data set into two chunks, B and W, so that no tuple in W dominates or is indistinguishable from any tuple in B ($W \not\succeq_\pi B$). The algorithm then computes recursively the p-skyline of B, $M_\pi(B)$, and performs the p-screening of W against $M_\pi(B)$, i.e. it prunes all tuples in W that are dominated by some element of $M_\pi(B)$. Eventually, it recursively computes the p-skyline of the tuples that survived the p-screening, and returns it, together with $M_\pi(B)$, the p-skyline of B.

[3]As in Section 2: $d = |\mathcal{V}ar(\pi)|$, $b = |B|$ and $w = |W|$.

Algorithm Dc (divide & conquer)

Input: a p-expression π, a relation instance D_0
Output: the p-skyline $M_\pi(D_0)$

1: **procedure** DC(π, D_0)
2:     **return** DCREC(π, D_0, $\mathcal{R}oots_\pi$, $\emptyset$)

3: **procedure** DCREC(π, D, $\mathcal{C}$, $\mathcal{E}$)
4:     **if** $\mathcal{C} = \emptyset$ or $|D| \leq 1$ **then return** D
5:     select an attribute **A** from the candidates set $\mathcal{C}$
6:     **if** all tuples in D assign the same value to **A then**
7:         $\mathcal{E}' \leftarrow \mathcal{E} \cup \{\mathbf{A}\}$
8:         $\mathcal{C}' \leftarrow \mathcal{C} \setminus \{\mathbf{A}\}$
9:         $\mathcal{C}'' \leftarrow \mathcal{C}' \cup \{\mathbf{V} \in \mathcal{S}ucc_\pi(\mathbf{A}) : \mathcal{P}re_\pi(\mathbf{V}) \subseteq \mathcal{E}'\}$
10:         **return** DCREC(π, D, $\mathcal{C}''$, $\mathcal{E}'$)
11:     **else**
12:         $(B, W, m^*) \leftarrow$ SPLITBYATTRIBUTE(D, **A**)
13:         $B' \leftarrow$ DCREC(π, B, $\mathcal{C}$, $\mathcal{E}$)
14:         $W' \leftarrow$ PSCREEN(π, B', W, $\mathcal{C} \setminus \{\mathbf{A}\}$, $\mathcal{E}$)
15:         $W'' \leftarrow$ DCREC(π, W', $\mathcal{C}$, $\mathcal{E}$)
16:         **return** $B' \cup W''$

17: **procedure** SPLITBYATTRIBUTE(D, **A**)
18:     Select m^* as the median w.r.t. $\succ_\mathbf{A}$ in D
19:     Compute the set $B = \{t \in D \mid t \succ_\mathbf{A} m^*\}$
20:     Compute the set $W = \{t \in D \mid m^* \succeq_\mathbf{A} t\}$
21:     **return** (B, W, m^*)

In order to understand how Dc works, it is important to understand how the input data set is split into B and W: the goal is to ensure that no tuple in B is dominated by (or indistinguishable from) any tuple in W. The general idea is to select an attribute from $\mathcal{V}ar(\pi)$, say **A**, and compute the median tuple m^* w.r.t. $\succ_\mathbf{A}$, over the entire data set; then we can put in B all tuples that assign to **A** a better value than the one assigned by m^*, and put in W all the other tuples. If we want to be sure that $W \not\succeq_\pi B$ holds, we need to make sure that the preference on attribute **A** is not overridden by some other, higher-priority attribute. Hence, we need to choose **A** so that all tuples in both B and W agree w.r.t. all the attributes in $\mathcal{A}nc_\pi(\mathbf{A})$. In order to choose **A** wisely, Dc keeps track of two sets of attributes, namely $\mathcal{E}$ and $\mathcal{C}$, ensuring the following invariants hold:

I1 : If an attribute belongs to $\mathcal{E}$ then no pair of tuples in D can disagree on the value assigned to it. In other words: all tuples in D are indistinguishable w.r.t. all attributes in $\mathcal{E}$.

I2 : An attribute in $\mathcal{A} \setminus \mathcal{E}$ belongs to $\mathcal{C}$ if and only if all its ancestors belong to $\mathcal{E}$.

Clearly, attribute **A** is always chosen from $\mathcal{C}$. Let's see how Dc works in more detail: at the beginning $\mathcal{E}$ is empty and $\mathcal{C}$ contains all the root nodes of Γ^r_π; at every iteration the algorithm selects some attribute **A** from $\mathcal{C}$ and finds the median tuple m^* in D w.r.t. $\succ_\mathbf{A}$. If all tuples in D assign to **A** the same value, the algorithm updates $\mathcal{C}$ and $\mathcal{E}$ accordingly and recurs (lines 7-10). Otherwise (lines 12-16) m^* is used to split D into B and W: B contains all the tuples preferred to m^*, W those that are indistinguishable from or dominated by m^*, according to $\succ_\mathbf{A}$. Clearly $W \not\succeq_\mathbf{A} B$ holds by construction, and $W \not\succeq_\pi B$ is a direct consequence of invariants I1 and I2. Hence, the algorithm can compute $M_\pi(B)$ recursively (line 13), perform the p-screening $\left[{M_\pi(B) \atop W}\right]_\pi$ (line

14), and compute the p-skyline of the remaining tuples (line 15). The procedure PSCREEN at line 14 will be discussed in Section 4.

EXAMPLE 3. *Let's see how* DC *would determine the p-skyline for the data set of Example 1, with respect to the p-expression* $\pi = (\mathbf{P} \mathbin{\&} \mathbf{T}) \otimes \mathbf{M}$. *The p-graph of* π *contains three nodes and only one edge, from* **P** *to* **T**. *The following diagram shows the invocation trace of the procedure* DCREC. *Each box represents an invocation, its input, output and a short explanation of the actions performed. For the lack of space we omit the invocations that process only one tuple.*

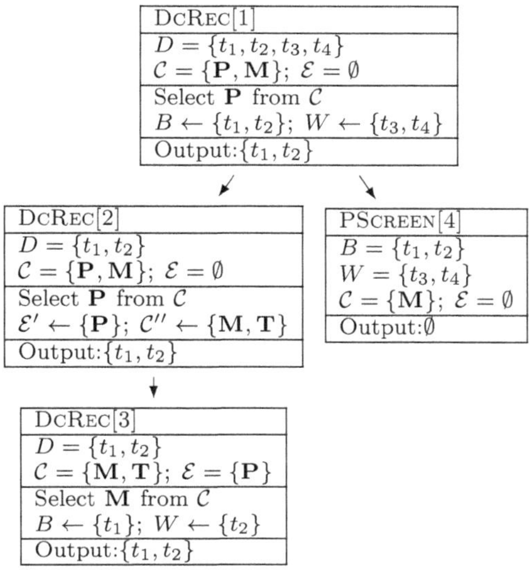

During the first invocation, the original set of cars is split into two halves, with respect to price. *The algorithm then recurs on the first half,* $\{t_1, t_2\}$, *in order to compute its p-skyline. The second invocation performs no work, except updating* $\mathcal{C}$ *and* $\mathcal{E}$: *attribute* **P** *is moved from* $\mathcal{C}$ *to* $\mathcal{E}$, *and attribute* **T** *enters* $\mathcal{C}$. *The third invocation computes the p-skyline of* $\{t_1, t_2\}$, *splitting w.r.t.* mileage *(no tuple is pruned). Back to the first invocation of* DCREC, *the procedure* PSCREEN *is used for removing from* $\{t_3, t_4\}$ *all tuples dominated by some element in* $\{t_1, t_2\}$. *Both* t_3 *and* t_4 *are pruned. Since no tuple survived the screening, the algorithm directly returns* $\{t_1, t_2\}$ *without making an additional recursive call.*

The complexity analysis for DC is straightforward. If we denote by $T(n)$ its running time and we assume $|B| \simeq |W|$ at every iteration, the following upper bound holds for some fixed constant k_0

$$T(n) \leq k_0 n + 2 \cdot T\left(\frac{n}{2}\right) + F^*_{d-1}\left(\frac{n}{2}, \frac{n}{2}\right)$$

where the linear term $k_0 n$ models the time spent by the SPLITBYATTRIBUTE procedure; notice the p-screening operation at line 14 doesn't need to take attribute **A** into consideration, hence only $d-1$ attributes need to be taken into account. Since we assumed $F^*_d(b, w)$ is $\mathcal{O}\left((b+w) \cdot (\log b)^{d-2}\right)$, we can apply the master theorem [5, 15] and conclude that

$$T(n) \leq \mathcal{O}\left(n \cdot \log^{d-2} n\right)$$

We show now how to make DC output-sensitive. Before moving to the algorithm, we introduce some basic complexity results for $C^*_d(v, n)$ when $v = 1$ and for $F^*_d(b, w)$ when $b = 1$.

LEMMA 1. *Given a relation instance* $D \subseteq U$ *and a p-expression* π, *locating a single, arbitrary element of* $M_\pi(D)$ *takes linear time.*

PROOF. We can use an arbitrary weak order extension of $\succ_\pi$ and locate a maximal element $p^* \in D$ in linear time. It is easy to see p^* must belong to $M_\pi(D)$. From now on, we will denote this procedure as PSKYLINESP(π, D). □

As a corollary to Lemma 1 we can state that $C^*_d(1, n) \leq \mathcal{O}(n)$. A similar result holds for p-screening:

LEMMA 2. $F^*_d(1, w) \leq \mathcal{O}(w)$ *for any positive d and w.*

PROOF. If B contains only one element, then we can easily perform p-screening in linear time: we only need one dominance test for each element of W. From now on, we will refer to this procedure as PSCREENSP(π, B, W). □

Algorithm Osdc (output-sensitive divide & conquer)

Input: a p-expression π, a relation instance D_0
Output: the p-skyline $M_\pi(D_0)$

```
1: procedure OSDC(π, D0)
2:     return OSDCREC(π, D0, Roots_π, ∅)

3: procedure OSDCREC(π, D, C, E)
4:     if C = ∅ or |D| ≤ 1 then return D
5:     select an attribute A from the candidates set C
6:     if all tuples in D assign the same value to A then
7:         E' ← E ∪ {A}
8:         C' ← C \ {A}
9:         C'' ← C' ∪ {V ∈ Succ_π(A) : Pre_π(V) ⊆ E'}
10:        return OSDCREC(π, D, C'', E')
11:    else
12:        (B, W, m*) ← SPLITBYATTRIBUTE(D, A)
13:        p*  ← PSKYLINESP(π, B)
14:        B'  ← PSCREENSP(π, {p*}, B \ {p*})
15:        W'  ← PSCREENSP(π, {p*}, W)
16:        B'' ← OSDCREC(π, B', C, E)
17:        W'' ← PSCREEN(π, B'', W', C \ {A}, E)
18:        W''' ← OSDCREC(π, W'', C, E)
19:        return {p*} ∪ B'' ∪ W'''
```

Now that we have defined the two procedures PSCREENSP and PSKYLINESP, we can introduce our output-sensitive algorithm, OSDC (see the Figure above). The divide and conquer strategy is similar to the one in DC, except for the look-ahead procedure at lines 13-15: at each recursion the algorithm spends linear time to extract a single p-skyline point p^* and prune from both B and W all tuples dominated by it. As a consequence, if at some point in the execution either B or W contains only a single p-skyline point, then either B' or W' will be empty, and the corresponding recursive call (line 16 or 18) will terminate immediately (line 4). We use Algorithm OSDC for proving the following theorem:

THEOREM 1. $C^*_d(v, n)$ *is* $\mathcal{O}\left(n \cdot \log^{d-2} v\right)$.

PROOF. If we run OSDC, the following upper bound holds on $C^*_d(v, n)$, for some fixed constant k_0

$$C^*_d(v, n) \leq k_0 n + C^*_d\left(v', \frac{n}{2}\right) + C^*_d\left(v'', \frac{n}{2}\right) + F^*_{d-1}\left(v', \frac{n}{2}\right)$$

where $v' + v'' + 1 = v$. The linear term $k_0 n$ models the time spent at lines 12-15, the second and the third terms the recursive calls at lines 16 and 18, while the last term is the p-screening operation at line 17. In order to keep track of the partitioning of v into smaller chunks during the recursion, we need to introduce some additional notational conventions. Let's denote by $v_{\ell,j}$ the size of the $j{-}th$ portion of v obtained at depth ℓ into the recursion. We can organize the different $v_{\ell,j}$ variables into a binary tree, as in Figure 2. Clearly, only

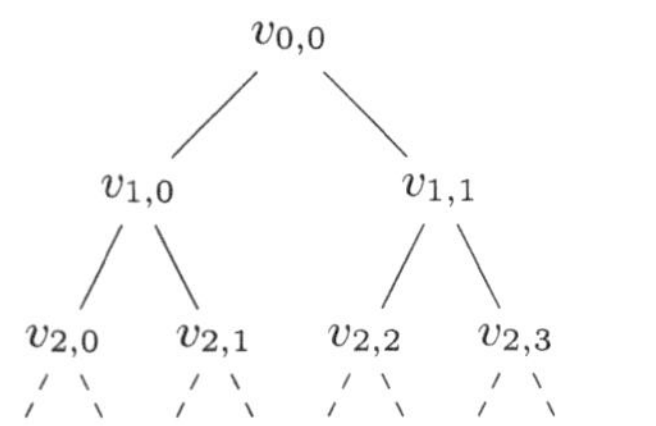

Figure 2

a finite subtree rooted in $v_{0,0}$ will cover the variables having a strictly positive value. The root $v_{0,0}$ is equal to v and, for all ℓ and j, $v_{\ell,j}$ is either $1 + v_{\ell+1,2j} + v_{\ell+1,2j+1}$ or zero. Notice there are exactly v assignments to (ℓ, j) such that $v_{\ell,j} > 0$, and the recursion proceeds up to a level $\ell_{\max}$ such that $v_{\ell_{max}+1,j} = 0$ for all j. Using this notation:

$$C^*_d(v,n) \le \sum_{\ell=0}^{\ell_{\max}} \sum_{\{j: v_{\ell,j}>0\}} k_0 \frac{n}{2^\ell} + F^*_{d-1}\left(v_{\ell+1,2j}, \frac{n}{2^{\ell+1}}\right)$$

We don't know $\ell_{\max}$ a priori; depending on the input it could be anywhere between $\log v$ and $\min(v, \log n)$. On the other hand, we do know the above sum has exactly v terms, and that their cost increases when the value of ℓ decreases. Therefore, in the worst-case scenario only the first $\log v$ levels of recursion are used, i.e. $\ell_{\max} = \log v$.

$$C^*_d(v,n) \le \sum_{\ell=0}^{\log v} \left[k_0 n + 2^\ell \cdot F^*_{d-1}\left(v_{\ell+1,2j}, \frac{n}{2^{\ell+1}}\right)\right]$$

Assuming $F^*_d(b,w)$ is $\mathcal{O}\left((b+w) \cdot (\log b)^{d-2}\right)$, there is a constant k_1 such that

$$C^*_d(v,n) \le k_0 n \log v + k_1 n \cdot \sum_{\ell=0}^{\log v - 1} \left(\log\left(v_{\ell+1,2j}\right)\right)^{d-3}$$

Since in the worst-case scenario only the first $\log v$ levels of recursion are used, we have that $v_{\ell,j} \le v/2^\ell \le n/2^\ell$, hence

$$C^*_d(v,n) \le k_0 n \log v + k_1 n \cdot \sum_{\ell=0}^{\log v - 1} \left(\log(v) - (\ell+1)\right)^{d-3}$$

If we set $h = \log(v) - (\ell + 1)$, we obtain

$$C^*_d(v,n) \le k_0 n \log v + k_1 n \cdot \sum_{h=0}^{\log v - 1} h^{d-3}$$

We can conclude that $C^*_d(v,n) \le \mathcal{O}\left(n \cdot (\log v)^{d-2}\right)$ □

4. COMPLEXITY OF P-SCREENING

We can now analyze the complexity of p-screening. We start from the simple case $d \le 3$. When $d = 1$ the problem coincides with regular screening, and it is linear. When $d = 2$ or $d = 3$ the following lemmas apply

LEMMA 3. *$F^*_2(b,w) \le \mathcal{O}((b+w)\log b)$ for any $b > 1$ and $w > 0$.*

PROOF. A p-expression with only two attributes can be either a lexicographical order or a regular skyline. In the first case p-screening takes $\mathcal{O}(b+w)$ time, in the second it takes $\mathcal{O}((b+w)\log b)$ time, as per Proposition 4. □

LEMMA 4. *$F^*_3(b,w) \le \mathcal{O}((b+w)\log b)$ for any $b > 1$ and $w > 0$.*

PROOF. A p-expression π over three attributes can come in five possible forms:

Case 1 When $\pi = \mathbf{A}_1 \otimes \mathbf{A}_2 \otimes \mathbf{A}_3$ p-screening consists of a regular screening in three dimensions: its complexity is $\mathcal{O}((b+w) \cdot \log b)$, as per Proposition 4.

Case 2 When $\pi = \mathbf{A}_1 \,\&\, \mathbf{A}_2 \,\&\, \mathbf{A}_3$, p-screening can be done in $\mathcal{O}(b+w)$ time, since π represents a lexicographical order. In $\mathcal{O}(b)$ time we can find a maximal element p^* in B, in additional $\mathcal{O}(w)$ time we can check for each $t \in W$ whether $p^* \succ_\pi t$ holds.

Case 3 When $\pi = \mathbf{A}_1 \,\&\, (\mathbf{A}_2 \otimes \mathbf{A}_3)$ we can proceed as follows: let a^*_1 be the best value for attribute $\mathbf{A}_1$ amongst all tuples in B, let W_b, W_e and W_w contain all the tuples in W assigning to $\mathbf{A}_1$ a value respectively better, equal and worse than a^*_1; we have that

$$\begin{bmatrix} B \\ W \end{bmatrix}_\pi = W_b \cup \begin{bmatrix} M_{\mathbf{A}_1}(B) \\ W_e \end{bmatrix}_{\mathbf{A}_2 \otimes \mathbf{A}_3}$$

Since $M_{\mathbf{A}_1}(B)$, W_b, W_e and W_w can be computed in linear time, the overall complexity is dominated by the two-dimensional screening, that takes $\mathcal{O}((b+w)\log b)$, as per Proposition 4.

Case 4 When $\pi = (\mathbf{A}_1 \otimes \mathbf{A}_2) \,\&\, \mathbf{A}_3$ we can proceed as follows: first we compute the set

$$W' = \begin{bmatrix} B \\ W \end{bmatrix}_{\mathbf{A}_1 \otimes \mathbf{A}_2}$$

in $\mathcal{O}((b+w)\log b)$ time, then we sort B by the lexicographic order $\succ_{\mathbf{A}_1 \& \mathbf{A}_2 \& \mathbf{A}_3}$; given an assignment to $\mathbf{A}_1$ and $\mathbf{A}_2$ finding the best value for $\mathbf{A}_3$ in B takes only $\mathcal{O}(\log b)$, therefore pruning all the remaining dominated points from W' takes $\mathcal{O}(w \log b)$.

Case 5 When $\pi = (\mathbf{A}_1 \,\&\, \mathbf{A}_2) \otimes \mathbf{A}_3$ we can proceed as follows: let k be the number of distinct values for $\mathbf{A}_1$ in B, we can partition both B and W into k subsets, such that $B_k \not\preceq_{\mathbf{A}_1} B_{k-1} \not\preceq_{\mathbf{A}_1} \dots \not\preceq_{\mathbf{A}_1} B_1$ and[4] $B_{i+1} \not\preceq_{\mathbf{A}_1} W_i \not\preceq_{\mathbf{A}_1} B_{i-1}$, for each i in $\{1, \dots, k\}$; then, for each i and j in $\{1, \dots, k\}$ such that $i \le j$ we perform the screening of W_j against B_i. When $i = j$ the screening is 2-dimensional, and takes $\mathcal{O}(|B_i \cup W_j| \log |B_i|)$ time; when $i < j$ the screening is 1-dimensional and takes $\mathcal{O}(|B_i \cup W_j|)$ time. All the 1-dimensional screenings take $\mathcal{O}(b+w)$ overall, while the 2-dimensional ones take $\mathcal{O}((b+w)\log b)$.

□

[4]Here we assume $B_0 = B_{k+1} = \emptyset$

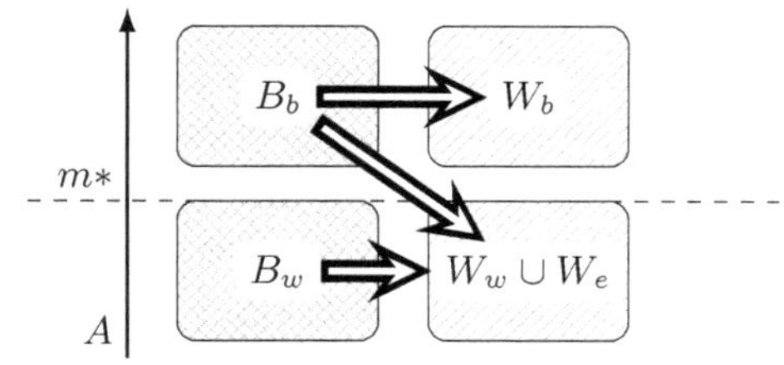

Figure 3: Dividing p-screening into simpler subproblems. Each box represents a set of tuples, each arrow a p-screening operation.

Algorithm PSCREEN (see the Figure on the right) shows how to perform p-screening in $\mathcal{O}\left((b+w)\log^{d-2} b\right)$ when $d \geq 3$. The algorithm is inspired by the one proposed by Kung, Luccio and Preparata [28]: in order to perform the p-screening $\left[{B \atop W}\right]_\pi$, we split B in two halves, namely B_b and B_w, ensuring that no tuple in B_w dominates or is indistinguishable from any tuple in B_b ($B_w \not\succeq_\pi B_b$). We can obtain B_b and B_w with the same strategy we used in DC: we select an attribute $\mathbf{A}$, making sure that all tuples in *both* B *and* W agree w.r.t all the attributes in $\mathcal{A}nc_\pi(\mathbf{A})$. Then we find the median tuple m^* w.r.t. $\succ_\mathbf{A}$ and split B accordingly. Clearly $B_w \not\succeq_\pi B_b$ holds, as all tuples in B_b are better than all tuples in B_w w.r.t. $\succ_\mathbf{A}$, while the preference on $\mathbf{A}$ is not overridden by other higher-priority attributes. Then we proceed splitting W into three chunks: the set W_b of tuples being preferred to m^* (according to $\succ_\mathbf{A}$), those being indistinguishable from m^* (W_e) and those being dominated (W_w). Since we chose $\mathbf{A}$ so that all tuples in *both* B and W agree w.r.t. all attributes in $\mathcal{A}nc_\pi(\mathbf{A})$, we are guaranteed that no tuple in B_w can dominate (or be indistinguishable from) any tuple in W_b[5]. Hence, the problem of p-screening B and W is reduced to following three smaller sub-problems, as depicted in Figure 3:

$$\text{(i)} \begin{bmatrix} B_b \\ W_b \end{bmatrix}_\pi \quad \text{(ii)} \begin{bmatrix} B_b \\ W_w \cup W_e \end{bmatrix}_\pi \quad \text{(iii)} \begin{bmatrix} B_w \\ W_w \cup W_e \end{bmatrix}_\pi$$

We can solve these three sub-problems by recursion. The recursion will stop when we run out of attributes ($d \leq 3$) or tuples ($|B| \leq 1$). Notice that for sub-problem (ii) we do not need to take attribute $\mathbf{A}$ into consideration, hence, for that recursion branch, we reduced the dimensionality by one unit. In order to choose attribute $\mathbf{A}$ properly, PSCREEN adopts the same strategy of DC: it keeps track of two sets of attributes, $\mathcal{C}$ and $\mathcal{E}$, ensuring the following invariants:

I1 : If an attribute belongs to $\mathcal{E}$ then no pair of tuples in $B \cup W$ can disagree on the value assigned to it. That is, all tuples in $B \cup W$ are indistinguishable with respect to all attributes in $\mathcal{E}$.

I2 : An attribute in $\mathcal{A} \setminus \mathcal{E}$ belongs to $\mathcal{C}$ if and only if all its ancestors belong to $\mathcal{E}$.

We can now analyze the pseudo-code of PSCREEN in more detail. Lines 19-24 define the core logic of the recursion, lines 4-17 handle the base-cases, while lines 25-29 contain auxiliary methods. The algorithm takes as input two sets of tuples, B and W, such that $W \not\succeq_\pi B$. At each iteration the algorithm selects an attribute $\mathbf{A}$ from $\mathcal{C}$ (line 9), and tests whether the tuples in B are distinguishable w.r.t. $\mathbf{A}$. If they are, the block at lines 19-24 is executed, otherwise the one at lines 11-17.

Algorithm PScreen

Input:
a p-expression π
two relation instances, B and W, s.t. $W \not\succeq_\pi B$
Output: the set W' of all tuples in W that are not dominated by any tuple in B

1: **procedure** PSCREEN(π, B, W)
2: **return** PSCREENREC($\pi, B, W, \mathcal{R}oots_\pi, \emptyset$)

3: **procedure** PSCREENREC(π, B, W, $\mathcal{C}$, $\mathcal{E}$)
4: **if** $\mathcal{C}$ is empty **then return** $\emptyset$
5: **else if** $|B| = 1$ **then**
6: **return** PSCREENSP(π, B, W)
7: **else if** $|\mathcal{C} \cup \mathcal{D}esc_\pi(\mathcal{C})| \leq 3$ **then**
8: apply Lemma 4 and **return**
9: select an attribute $\mathbf{A}$ from the candidates set $\mathcal{C}$
10: **if** all tuples in B assign the value a to $\mathbf{A}$ **then**
11: $(W_b, W_e, W_w) \leftarrow$ SPLITBYVALUE($W, \mathbf{A}, a$)
12: $\mathcal{C}' \leftarrow \mathcal{C} \setminus \{\mathbf{A}\}$
13: $W'_w \leftarrow$ PSCREENREC($\pi, B, W_w, \mathcal{C}', \mathcal{E}$)
14: $\mathcal{E}' \leftarrow \mathcal{E} \cup \{\mathbf{A}\}$
15: $\mathcal{C}'' \leftarrow \mathcal{C}' \cup \{\mathbf{V} \in \mathcal{S}ucc_\pi(\mathbf{A}) : \mathcal{P}re_\pi(\mathbf{V}) \subseteq \mathcal{E}'\}$
16: $W'_e \leftarrow$ PSCREENREC($\pi, B, W_e, \mathcal{C}'', \mathcal{E}'$)
17: **return** $W'_w \cup W'_e \cup W_b$
18: **else**
19: $(B_b, B_w, m^*) \leftarrow$ SPLITBYATTRIBUTE($B, \mathbf{A}$)
20: $(W_b, W_e, W_w) \leftarrow$ SPLITBYVALUE($W, \mathbf{A}, m^*$)
21: $W'_b \leftarrow$ PSCREENREC($\pi, B_b, W_b, \mathcal{C}, \mathcal{E}$)
22: $W'_w \leftarrow$ PSCREENREC($\pi, B_w, W_w \cup W_e, \mathcal{C}, \mathcal{E}$)
23: $W''_w \leftarrow$ PSCREENREC($\pi, B_b, W'_w, \mathcal{C} \setminus \{\mathbf{A}\}, \mathcal{E}$)
24: **return** $W'_b \cup W''_w$

25: **procedure** SPLITBYVALUE(D, $\mathbf{A}$, m^*)
26: Compute the set $D_b = \{t \in D \mid t[\mathbf{A}] \succ_\mathbf{A} m^*\}$
27: Compute the set $D_e = \{t \in D \mid t[\mathbf{A}] \approx_\mathbf{A} m^*\}$
28: Compute the set $D_w = \{t \in D \mid m^* \succ_\mathbf{A} t[\mathbf{A}]\}$
29: **return** (D_b, D_e, D_w)

Let's analyze the first case. At line 19 B is split into B_b and B_w, at line 20 W is split into W_b, W_e and W_w. At lines 21, 22 and 23 the algorithm recurs three times, in order to solve the three sub-problems discussed above. We can now analyze the base-cases: when $\mathcal{C}$ is left empty (line 4), all tuples in W are dominated by all tuples in B, so the algorithm returns the empty set; when B contains only one element, the algorithm applies the procedure from Lemma 2 (lines 5-6); when only three attributes are left to be processed, the algorithm applies Lemma 4. When it is not possible to split B, since all its tuples agree on some value a for $\mathbf{A}$, the algorithm splits W into three sets (W_b, W_e and W_w) containing tuples that are respectively better, indistinguishable from and worse than a, w.r.t. $\succ_\mathbf{A}$. Then it proceeds to solve $\left[{B \atop W_w}\right]_\pi$ and $\left[{B \atop W_e}\right]_\pi$. Notice $\mathcal{C}$ and $\mathcal{E}$ are updated at lines 12, 14 and 15 in order to satisfy the invariants I1 and I2.

THEOREM 2. *$F^*_d(b+w) \leq \mathcal{O}\left((b+w)\log^{d-2} b\right)$ for any $d > 3$, b and w.*

PROOF. We show that the above upper bound holds if we apply Algorithm PSCREEN to perform p-screening. The proof is by induction on d, and will use the simplifying assumptions that (i) $b = 2^m$ for some positive m and (ii) the splitting operation at line 19 divides B into two almost equally sized halves. Since we proved the base case $d = 3$ in

[5]Notice that for every pair of tuples (t', t) in $B_w \times W_b$ attribute $\mathbf{A}$ belongs to both $\mathcal{T}op_\pi(t', t)$ and $\mathcal{B}etter_\pi(t, t')$. From Proposition 1 we can conclude that $B_w \not\succeq_\pi W_b$ holds.

Lemma 4, the rest of the proof has a similar structure to the one proposed in [27, 28]. During each recursion Algorithm PSCREEN splits the set W in two parts; using a notation similar to the one presented in Figure 2, from now on we will denote by $w_{\ell,j}$ the size of the j-th portion of W obtained at depth ℓ in the recursion. Clearly $w_{0,0} = |W|$, and for each ℓ in $\{0, 1, \ldots, \log b - 1\}$ the sum $\sum_{j=1}^{2^\ell} w_{\ell,j}$ is equal to $|W|$. It is easy to see the following upper bound holds on F_d^*, for some fixed constant k_0

$$\begin{aligned} F_d^*(b, w_{0,0}) &\leq k_0(b + w_{0,0}) + F_{d-1}^*(b, w_{0,0}) \qquad (3) \\ &+ F_d^*\left(\frac{b}{2}, w_{1,0}\right) + F_d^*\left(\frac{b}{2}, w_{1,1}\right) \end{aligned}$$

the linear term $k_0(b+w_{0,0})$ models the time spent for finding the median m^* and split B and W accordingly (lines 19 and 20), and the other three terms model the recursive calls at lines 21,22, and 23. Inequality 3 holds during each recursion, therefore

$$\begin{aligned} F_d^*\left(\frac{b}{2^\ell}, w_{\ell,j}\right) &\leq k_0\left(\frac{b}{2^\ell} + w_{\ell,j}\right) + F_{d-1}^*\left(\frac{b}{2^\ell}, w_{\ell,j}\right) \qquad (4) \\ &+ F_d^*\left(\frac{b}{2^{\ell+1}}, w_{\ell+1,2j}\right) \\ &+ F_d^*\left(\frac{b}{2^{\ell+1}}, w_{\ell+1,2j+1}\right) \end{aligned}$$

We can apply (4) to the last two terms of (3) and repeat the operation until we obtain the following

$$\begin{aligned} F_d^*(b, w) &\leq \sum_{\hat{\ell}=0}^{\log b-1} \sum_{k=1}^{2^{\hat{\ell}}} k_0\left(\frac{b}{2^{\hat{\ell}}} + w_{\hat{\ell},k}\right) \\ &+ \sum_{\hat{\ell}=0}^{\log b-1} \sum_{k=1}^{2^{\hat{\ell}}} F_{d-1}^*\left(\frac{b}{2^{\hat{\ell}}}, w_{\hat{\ell},k}\right) \\ &+ \sum_{k=0}^{2^{\log b-1}} F_d^*(1, w_{\log b-1,k}) \end{aligned}$$

By inductive hypothesis, we can assume

$$F_{d-1}^*(b, w) \leq \mathcal{O}\left((b + w)(\log b)^{d-3}\right)$$

Also, from Lemma 2 we know $F_d^*(1, w)$ is $\mathcal{O}(w)$. Therefore, there exist constants k_0, k_1 and k_2 such that, for every b and w, the following holds

$$\begin{aligned} F_d^*(b, w) &\leq k_0 \cdot (b + w)\log b \\ &+ k_1 \cdot \sum_{\hat{\ell}=0}^{\log b-1} \sum_{j=1}^{2^{\hat{\ell}}} \left(\frac{b}{2^\ell} + w_{\hat{\ell},j}\right) \cdot \left(\log \frac{b}{2^\ell}\right)^{d-3} \\ &+ k_2 \cdot w \end{aligned}$$

Solving the sum over j, we get

$$\begin{aligned} F_d^*(b, w) &\leq k_0 \cdot (b + w)\log b \\ &+ k_1 \cdot (b + w) \cdot \sum_{\hat{\ell}=0}^{\log b-1} \left(\log b - \hat{\ell}\right)^{d-3} + k_2 \cdot w \end{aligned}$$

If we set $h = \log b - \hat{\ell}$, we obtain

$$\begin{aligned} F_d^*(b, w) &\leq k_0 \cdot (b + w)\log b \\ &+ k_1 \cdot (b + w) \cdot \sum_{h=1}^{\log b} h^{d-3} + k_2 \cdot w \end{aligned}$$

Since $\sum_{h=1}^{\log b} h^{d-3}$ is $\mathcal{O}\left((\log b)^{d-2}\right)$, it follows that

$$F_d^*(b, w) \leq \mathcal{O}\left((b + w) \cdot (\log b)^{d-2}\right)$$

This concludes our proof. □

5. AVERAGE-CASE ANALYSIS

The average-case performance for regular skyline algorithms has been studied extensively in several papers [20, 4, 6]. The most usual assumption is that the data is distributed so that each attribute is independent from the others (*statistical independence*) and the probability of two tuples agreeing on the same value for the same attribute is negligible (*sparseness*). These two assumptions are usually called, collectively, *component independence* (or CI, as in [6]). Under the CI assumption LESS has been shown to be $\mathcal{O}(n)$ in the average-case, while SFS resulted to be $\mathcal{O}(n \log n)$ [20]. In this section we show how to modify OSDC, in order to ensure a linear average-case complexity. We start by making two key observations:

Observation 1 Over all the preference relations that can be expressed using p-expressions, the skyline relation $\succ_{\text{sky}}$ represents a worst-case scenario for an output-sensitive algorithm like OSDC. This follows directly from the containment property (Proposition 2): it is easy to see that for every $\succ_\pi$ we have that $M_\pi(D) \subseteq M_{\text{sky}}(D)$ holds as long as $\mathcal{V}ar(\pi) = \mathcal{V}ar(sky)$.

Observation 2 Buchta [8] proved that, under the CI assumption, the expected size of $M_{\text{sky}}(D)$ is $H_{d-1,n}$, the $(d-1)$-th order harmonic of n. Godfrey [19] observed that, if we drop the assumption of sparseness, the size of $M_{\text{sky}}(D)$ is likely to *decrease*.

Hence, computing regular skylines over data sets respecting the CI assumption is a corner-case scenario for an output-sensitive p-skyline algorithm, in the sense that introducing priorities between attributes or dropping the sparseness assumption would only improve the algorithm's performance. In order to show that our procedure is well-behaved in the average-case, we will prove it is well-behaved under the assumptions discussed above. More specifically, we will show how to make a simple modification to OSDC and ensure an average performance of $\mathcal{O}(n)$ for skyline queries under the CI assumption. The general idea is to follow a two-stage approach, similar to the one proposed in [4]:

1. During the first phase a linear scan prunes all the points dominated by a virtual tuple t^*, that is chosen so that the probability that no point dominates it is less than $1/n$, and the average number of points not dominated by it is $o(n)$. Such t^* can be chosen using the strategy presented in [4].
2. With probability $(n-1)/n$ the virtual tuple t^* is dominated by a real tuple in D, and so the algorithm can compute the final answer by running OSDC only on the $o(n)$ points that survived the initial linear scan.

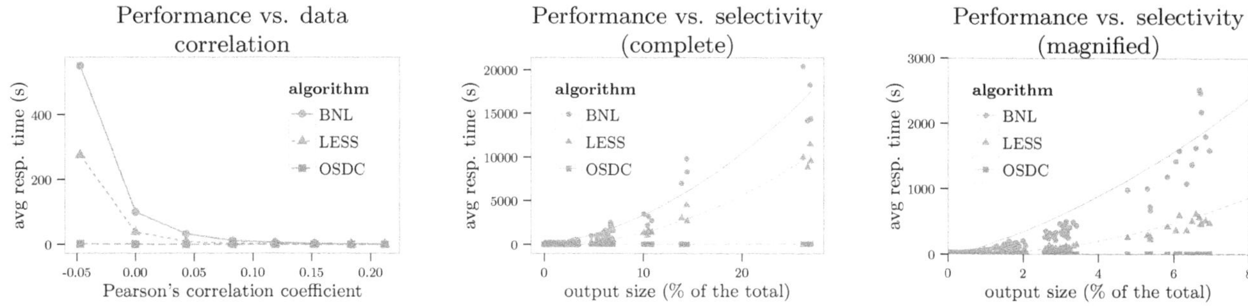

Figure 4: The effect of data correlation and query selectivity on performance (synthetic data sets)

3. With probability $1/n$ the final answer needs to be computed by running OSDC over the whole data set D.

It is easy to see that the amortized, average cost of this procedure is $\mathcal{O}(n)$, while the worst-case complexity is still $\mathcal{O}(n \log^{d-2} v)$.

6. P-SKYLINES IN EXTERNAL MEMORY

In the past scan-based skyline algorithms like BNL, SFS, SALSA or LESS have generated a considerable interest in the database community. While all these algorithms exhibit a sub-optimal worst-case performance of $\mathcal{O}(n^2)$, they are known to be well-behaved in the average-case scenario, and, for larger values of d, to be even more practical than divide-and-conquer algorithms like [6] (we refer the reader to [20] for an exhaustive discussion of the topic). Additionally, scan-based algorithms are easy to embed into existing database systems, as they are easily pipelinable, and support execution in external memory (where they still exhibit a sub-optimal, quadratic worst-case performance, as discussed in [32]). In this section we show how to adapt two scan-based skyline algorithms, SFS and LESS, in order to support p-skyline queries. Our goal is twofold: on one hand we want to show that OSDC is faster than the scan-based solutions, a part for its nice asymptotic properties (this will be done in the Section 7); on the other hand we want to develop a p-skyline algorithm that supports execution in external memory.

Both SFS and LESS sort the input dataset so that no tuple can dominate another preceding it; to achieve a similar result with prioritized preferences, we propose to presort the input w.r.t. the following weak order extension of $\succ_\pi$

$$\succ_\pi^{\text{ext}} = \succ_{\text{sum}_0} \;\&\; \succ_{\text{sum}_1} \;\&\; \ldots \;\&\; \succ_{\text{sum}_{d-1}} \qquad (5)$$

Each $\succ_{\text{sum}_i}$ is defined as follows:

$$t' \succ_{\text{sum}_i} t \iff \sum_{\mathbf{A} \in \mathcal{V}ar(\pi):d_{\mathbf{A}}=i} t'[\mathbf{A}] < \sum_{\mathbf{A} \in \mathcal{V}ar(\pi):d_{\mathbf{A}}=i} t[\mathbf{A}]$$

That is, $t' \succ_{\text{sum}_i} t$ holds when the sum over all attributes at depth i computed for t' is lower than the same sum computed for t. After the sorting step, if $t' \succ_\pi^{\text{ext}} t$ holds tuple t' is going to be processed before tuple t.

THEOREM 3. *The relation $\succ_\pi^{ext}$ defined above is a weak order extension of $\succ_\pi$.*

PROOF. First we want to show that for each pair of tuples (t', t) in U^2, $t' \succ_\pi^{\text{ext}} t$ implies $t \not\succ_\pi t'$. We can denote by i^* the smallest index i such that $(t' \succ_{\text{sum}_{i^*}} t)$. Since the sum over all attributes at depth i^* is smaller for t' rather than for t, there must be at least one attribute $\mathbf{A}$ at depth i^* favoring t' over t. It is easy to see that such $\mathbf{A}$ belongs to $\mathcal{T}op_\pi(t', t)$; from Proposition 1, point 2, we can conclude that $t \not\succ_\pi t'$. We are left to prove that $\succ_\pi^{\text{ext}}$ is a weak order: this follows directly from (5), noting that each $\succ_{\text{sum}_i}$ is a weak order, and the prioritized composition of weak orders is a weak order itself. □

7. EXPERIMENTAL RESULTS

To the best of our knowledge there is no published work on measuring p-skyline queries performance. The problem is difficult, since the response time depends on many factors, including the topology of the p-graph and data properties like size, correlation and likelihood of duplicated values.

In the following sections we try to address this issue by proposing a novel p-skyline testing framework. First we show how to sample random p-expressions from a uniform distribution, and how to generate meaningful synthetic data sets. Later we present our experimental results from both real and synthetic data sets.

7.1 Sampling random p-expressions

P-expressions can encode a wide variety of preferences: they can represent lexicographic orders, classical skylines, or any combination of the two. In order to keep evaluations fair and unbiased we should not polarize benchmarks on specific preferences. Instead, our goal is to randomly sample p-expressions from a uniform distribution, ensuring all preferences are equally represented.

Given the number of attributes d, sampling a random p-expression means building a random p-graph over d vertices, ensuring that all legal p-graphs have the same probability of being generated. We present a result from [29] to characterize the set of p-graphs we want to sample from.

THEOREM 4. *[29] Given a set of d attributes $\mathcal{A}$, a graph Γ over $\mathcal{A}$ is a p-graph if and only if:*

1. *Γ is transitive and irreflexive.*
2. *Γ respects the* envelope *property:*
   $\forall \mathbf{A}_1, \mathbf{A}_2, \mathbf{A}_3, \mathbf{A}_4$ all different in $\mathcal{A}$, $(\mathbf{A}_1, \mathbf{A}_2) \in \Gamma \wedge (\mathbf{A}_3, \mathbf{A}_4) \in \Gamma \wedge (\mathbf{A}_3, \mathbf{A}_2) \in \Gamma \Rightarrow (\mathbf{A}_3, \mathbf{A}_1) \in \Gamma \vee (\mathbf{A}_1, \mathbf{A}_4) \in \Gamma \vee (\mathbf{A}_4, \mathbf{A}_2) \in \Gamma$.

Iterating over all graphs that respect the above constraints is practical only for small values of d. For larger values we

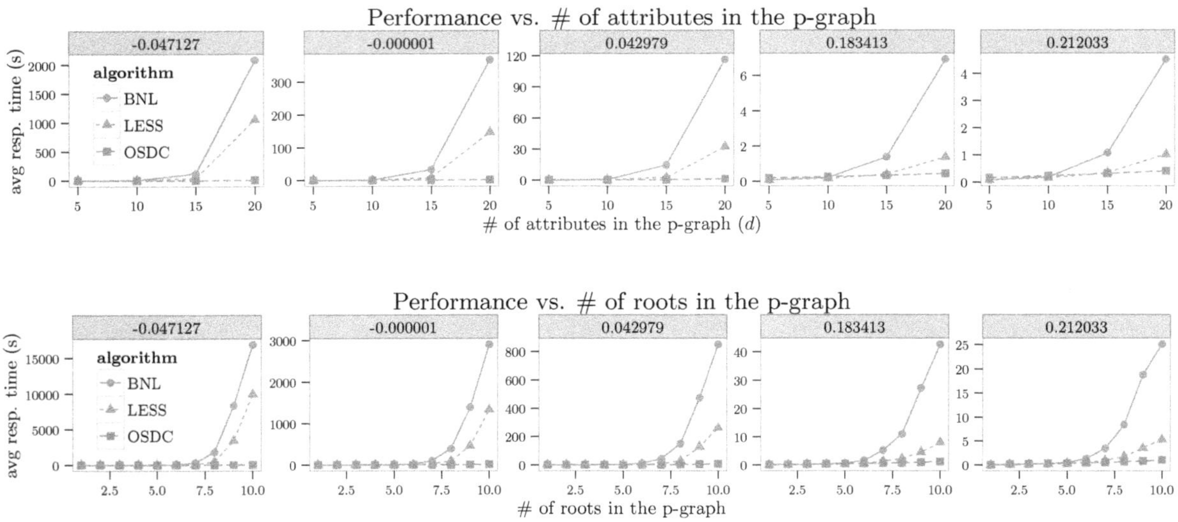

Figure 5: The effect of the p-graph's topology on performance (synthetic data sets)

use the following strategy: we convert the constraints into a boolean satisfaction problem and sample from its solutions near-uniformly using SampleSAT [35]. SampleSAT performs a random walk over the possible solutions of a SAT problem, alternating greedy WalkSAT moves with simulated annealing steps. The ratio of the frequencies of the two kinds of steps, denoted by f, determines the trade-off between the uniformity of the sampling and the time spent to obtain it. For our tests on synthetic data we used $f = 0.5$ for generating 200 p-expressions, with d ranging from 5 to 20 attributes.

7.2 Synthetic data sets

Several papers, starting from [7], showed how data correlation affects the performance of skyline queries. We wanted to test whether similar considerations apply to p-skylines. Notice the role of correlation in this context is subtle: depending whether two variables have the same priority or not, a correlation between them may have different effects. For this reason we decided to generate synthetic data sets where each pair of dimensions exhibits approximatively the same linear correlation. Let's denote by $\vec{1}$ a d-dimensional all-ones vector $(1, 1, \ldots, 1)$, and by M a $d \times d$ matrix whose rows form an orthonormal basis for $\mathbb{R}^d$, the first one being parallel with $\vec{1}$. Notice that M represents a rotation centered on the origin. Let M_D be a $d \times d$ diagonal matrix, having $(\alpha, 1, \ldots, 1)$ as its main diagonal. We propose to test p-skyline algorithms over a multivariate Gaussian distribution $\mathcal{N}_\alpha$, centered on the origin, with covariance matrix $\Sigma_\alpha = M \times M_D \times M^{-1}$. According to this distribution each pair of distinct dimensions exhibits the same correlation, determined by the parameter α. It is important to notice that $\mathcal{N}_\alpha$, amongst all the distributions where all pairs of variables have the same correlation, is the one with *maximum entropy*, given the parameter α.

For our tests we sampled several data sets, varying the value of α; each set contains one million tuples over $d = 20$ attributes. Since p-skylines make sense only when some tuples agree on some attributes, we rounded the data off to four decimal digits of precision, in order to ensure the presence of duplicated values. As a result, the uncorrelated data sets (those with $\alpha = 1$) have approximatively $7,000$ distinct values in each column. We compared the performance of OSDC against BNL and LESS. To keep the comparison fair we implemented an in-memory version of BNL, setting the size of the window to be large enough to store the whole input. This way, the algorithm could answer each query with a single iteration. We adapted LESS using the strategy discussed in Section 6. We ran it using several different thresholds on the size of the elimination filter, ranging between 50 and $10,000$ tuples. For each experiment we report only the fastest response times. In order to avoid any overhead, we precomputed the ranking $\succ_\pi^{\text{ext}}$. All the algorithms were implemented using Java, and tested on an Intel Core i7-2600 (3.4 GHz) machine equipped with 8 GB of RAM. We ran all the experiments using the Java Runtime Environment version 1.7.0, limiting the maximum heap size to 4 GB.

On the average we observed OSDC to be significantly faster than LESS and BNL. Here we analyze these results in relation with data correlation, and we study how the topology of p-expressions affects the performance of each algorithm. Figure 4 (left) focuses on the effect of data correlation. We average the response time over all queries, and plot it against the observed Pearson's correlation coefficient[6]. The Figure shows that LESS and BNL compete with OSDC in presence of positive data correlation, but their performance decreases quickly on anti-correlated data. OSDC, on the other hand, remains mostly unaffected by data correlation.

In Figure 5 we investigate the relation between performance and the topology of p-graphs. We group queries according to the number of attributes (top) and roots (bottom) in their p-graphs, and we aggregate response times w.r.t. data correlation. For lack of space we report only five levels of correlation, the most significant ones. Independently from data correlation, OSDC exhibits a distinct performance advantage on queries with more than 10 attributes,

[6]The correlation coefficient was measured after rounding the data sets.

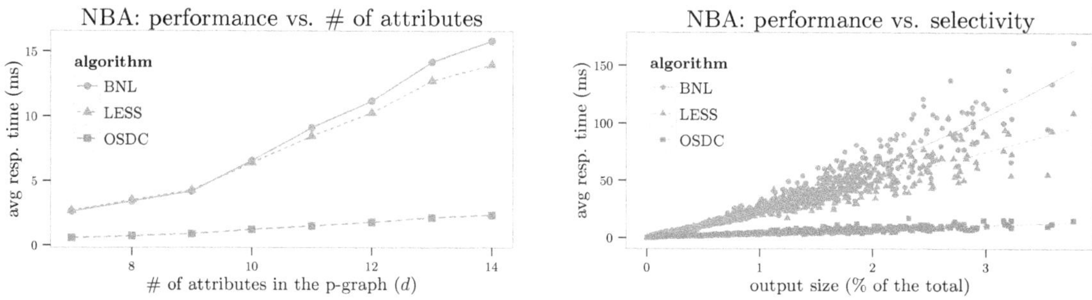

Figure 6: NBA data set (21,959 tuples over 14 attributes)

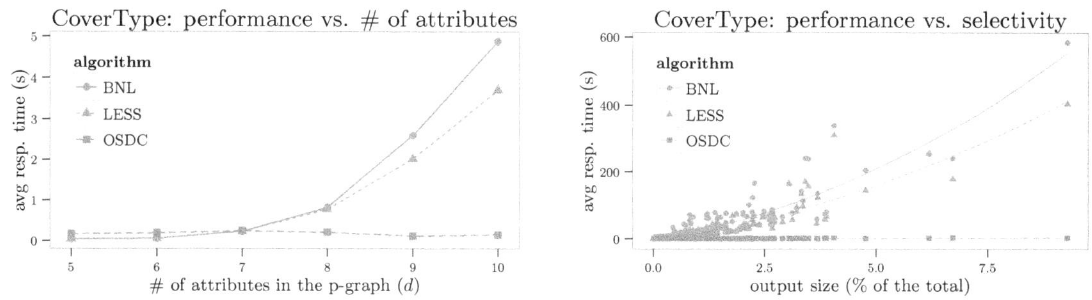

Figure 7: CoverType data set (581,012 tuples over 10 attributes).

especially if there are more than five roots; LESS shows a similar advantage in presence of positive data correlation, while BNL results are competitive mostly on queries with less than five roots. During our experiments we observed that both p-graph topology and data correlation have a direct influence on the size of the output: highly-prioritized p-expressions (those with few roots) are likely to produce smaller p-skylines; similarly, positively correlated data is likely to produce smaller result-sets. Therefore, we summarize our results by plotting the average response time against the size of the output (Figure 4, on the right). As expected, OSDC and LESS show a clear advantage for large result-sets while BNL remains competitive only for queries returning few tuples. The lines on the graph represent second-order polynomial regressions.

7.3 Real data sets

We tested our algorithms over the following real, publicly available data sets:

NBA NBA[7] is a very popular data set for evaluating skyline algorithms. We used the following regular season statistics: *gp*, *minutes*, *pts*, *reb*, *asts*, *stl*, *blk*, *turnover*, *pf*, *fga*, *fta*, *tpa*, *weight*, *height*. After dropping null values, the data set contains 21,959 tuples. We generated 8,000 random p-expressions with d ranging from 7 to 14. For this data set we used the assumption that larger values are preferred.

CoverType Forest Covertype[8] contains a collection of cartographic observations performed by the US Forest Service and the US Geological Survey. We extracted a data set of 581,012 tuples over 10 attributes. We generated 6,000 random p-expressions with d ranging from 5 to 10. For this data set we used the assumption that smaller values are preferred.

[7] www.databasebasketball.com

[8] archive.ics.uci.edu/ml/datasets/Covertype

Our results are presented in Figures 6 and 7. In the graphs on the left response times are aggregated by the number d of attributes in each p-expression. In the plots on the right response times are put in relation with the size of the output. On both data sets our findings confirmed our average-case analysis and the results we obtained from synthetic data: OSDC outperforms LESS and BNL, especially when the output-size is over 1% of the input-size.

8. CONCLUSIONS AND FUTURE WORK

In this paper we generalized the results of [25] to the context of p-skylines. We proved that p-skylines can be computed in $\mathcal{O}\left(n \log^{d-2} v\right)$ in the worst-case scenario, and in $\mathcal{O}\left(n\right)$ in the average-case. Additionally, we proposed a novel framework for benchmarking p-skyline queries, showing how to sample p-expressions uniformly, with the purpose of running unbiased tests. We designed our divide-and-conquer strategy assuming the input data always fits in the main memory; it would be interesting to verify whether we can drop this assumption, and develop an output-sensitive algorithm that runs efficiently in external memory, taking inspiration from [32, 21]. Another interesting aspect to investigate concerns the estimation of the expected size of the output. Can we exploit the semantics of p-skylines for predicting the expected output-size of a query? This would be helpful for choosing the most convenient algorithm for answering it, on a case-by-case basis. We leave the answers to all these questions open for future work.

9. REFERENCES

[1] P. Afshani. Fast computation of output-sensitive maxima in a word RAM. In C. Chekuri, editor, *SODA*, pages 1414–1423. SIAM, 2014.

[2] I. Bartolini, P. Ciaccia, and M. Patella. Efficient sort-based skyline evaluation. *ACM Trans. Database Syst.*, 33(4):31:1–31:49, Dec. 2008.

[3] J. L. Bentley. Multidimensional divide-and-conquer. *Commun. ACM*, 23(4):214–229, 1980.

[4] J. L. Bentley, K. L. Clarkson, and D. B. Levine. Fast linear expected-time algorithms for computing maxima and convex hulls. In D. S. Johnson, editor, *SODA*, pages 179–187. SIAM, 1990.

[5] J. L. Bentley, D. Haken, and J. B. Saxe. A general method for solving divide-and-conquer recurrences. *SIGACT News*, 12(3):36–44, Sept. 1980.

[6] J. L. Bentley, H. T. Kung, M. Schkolnick, and C. D. Thompson. On the average number of maxima in a set of vectors and applications. *J. ACM*, 25(4):536–543, 1978.

[7] S. Börzsönyi, D. Kossmann, and K. Stocker. The skyline operator. In *Proceedings of the 17th International Conference on Data Engineering*, pages 421–430, 2001.

[8] C. Buchta. On the average number of maxima in a set of vectors. *Inf. Process. Lett.*, 33(2):63–65, 1989.

[9] T. M. Chan. Optimal output-sensitive convex hull algorithms in two and three dimensions. *Discrete & Computational Geometry*, 16(4):361–368, 1996.

[10] T. M. Chan, K. G. Larsen, and M. Pătraşcu. Orthogonal range searching on the RAM, revisited. In *Proceedings of the Twenty-seventh Annual Symposium on Computational Geometry*, SoCG '11, pages 1–10, New York, NY, USA, 2011. ACM.

[11] J. Chomicki. Querying with intrinsic preferences. In C. S. Jensen, K. G. Jeffery, J. Pokorný, S. Saltenis, E. Bertino, K. Böhm, and M. Jarke, editors, *EDBT*, volume 2287 of *Lecture Notes in Computer Science*, pages 34–51. Springer, 2002.

[12] J. Chomicki. Preference formulas in relational queries. *ACM Trans. Database Syst.*, 28(4):427–466, Dec. 2003.

[13] J. Chomicki, P. Ciaccia, and N. Meneghetti. Skyline queries, front and back. *SIGMOD Record*, 42(3):6–18, 2013.

[14] J. Chomicki, P. Godfrey, J. Gryz, and D. Liang. Skyline with presorting. In *ICDE*, pages 717–719, 2003.

[15] T. H. Cormen, C. E. Leiserson, R. L. Rivest, and C. Stein. *Introduction to Algorithms (3. ed.)*. MIT Press, 2009.

[16] S. A. Drakopoulos. Hierarchical choice in economics. *Journal of Economic Surveys*, 8(2):133–153, 1994.

[17] P. C. Fishburn. Axioms for lexicographic preferences. *The Review of Economic Studies*, pages 415–419, 1975.

[18] H. N. Gabow, J. L. Bentley, and R. E. Tarjan. Scaling and related techniques for geometry problems. In R. A. DeMillo, editor, *STOC*, pages 135–143. ACM, 1984.

[19] P. Godfrey. Skyline cardinality for relational processing. In D. Seipel and J. M. T. Torres, editors, *FoIKS*, volume 2942 of *Lecture Notes in Computer Science*, pages 78–97. Springer, 2004.

[20] P. Godfrey, R. Shipley, and J. Gryz. Maximal vector computation in large data sets. In K. Böhm, C. S. Jensen, L. M. Haas, M. L. Kersten, P.-Å. Larson, and B. C. Ooi, editors, *VLDB*, pages 229–240. ACM, 2005.

[21] X. Hu, C. Sheng, Y. Tao, Y. Yang, and S. Zhou. Output-sensitive skyline algorithms in external memory. In S. Khanna, editor, *SODA*, pages 887–900. SIAM, 2013.

[22] W. Kießling. Foundations of preferences in database systems. In *VLDB*, pages 311–322. Morgan Kaufmann, 2002.

[23] W. Kießling, B. Hafenrichter, S. Fischer, and S. Holland. Preference XPATH: A query language for e-commerce. In H. U. Buhl, A. Huther, and B. Reitwiesner, editors, *Wirtschaftsinformatik*, page 32. Physica Verlag / Springer, 2001.

[24] W. Kießling and G. Köstler. Preference SQL - design, implementation, experiences. In *VLDB*, pages 990–1001. Morgan Kaufmann, 2002.

[25] D. G. Kirkpatrick and R. Seidel. Output-size sensitive algorithms for finding maximal vectors. In *Symposium on Computational Geometry*, pages 89–96, 1985.

[26] D. G. Kirkpatrick and R. Seidel. The ultimate planar convex hull algorithm? *SIAM J. Comput.*, 15(1):287–299, 1986.

[27] H. T. Kung. On the computational complexity of finding the maxima of a set of vectors. In *SWAT (FOCS)*, pages 117–121, 1974.

[28] H. T. Kung, F. Luccio, and F. P. Preparata. On finding the maxima of a set of vectors. *J. ACM*, 22(4):469–476, 1975.

[29] D. Mindolin and J. Chomicki. Preference elicitation in prioritized skyline queries. In *VLDB J.*, pages 157–182, 2011.

[30] D. Papadias, Y. Tao, G. Fu, and B. Seeger. Progressive skyline computation in database systems. *ACM Trans. Database Syst.*, 30(1):41–82, 2005.

[31] A. Scott. Identifying and analysing dominant preferences in discrete choice experiments: an application in health care. *Journal of Economic Psychology*, 23(3):383–398, 2002.

[32] C. Sheng and Y. Tao. Worst-case i/o-efficient skyline algorithms. *ACM Transactions on Database Systems (TODS)*, 37(4):26, 2012.

[33] W. Siberski, J. Z. Pan, and U. Thaden. Querying the semantic web with preferences. In I. F. Cruz, S. Decker, D. Allemang, C. Preist, D. Schwabe, P. Mika, M. Uschold, and L. Aroyo, editors, *International Semantic Web Conference*, volume 4273 of *Lecture Notes in Computer Science*, pages 612–624. Springer, 2006.

[34] K. Stefanidis, G. Koutrika, and E. Pitoura. A survey on representation, composition and application of preferences in database systems. *ACM Trans. Database Syst.*, 36(3):19:1–19:45, Aug. 2011.

[35] W. Wei, J. Erenrich, and B. Selman. Towards efficient sampling: Exploiting random walk strategies. In D. L. McGuinness and G. Ferguson, editors, *AAAI*, pages 670–676. AAAI Press / The MIT Press, 2004.

Learning Generalized Linear Models Over Normalized Data

Arun Kumar Jeffrey Naughton Jignesh M. Patel
Department of Computer Sciences,
University of Wisconsin-Madison
{arun, naughton, jignesh}@cs.wisc.edu

ABSTRACT

Enterprise data analytics is a booming area in the data management industry. Many companies are racing to develop toolkits that closely integrate statistical and machine learning techniques with data management systems. Almost all such toolkits assume that the input to a learning algorithm is a single table. However, most relational datasets are not stored as single tables due to normalization. Thus, analysts often perform key-foreign key joins before learning on the join output. This strategy of learning *after* joins introduces redundancy avoided by normalization, which could lead to poorer end-to-end performance and maintenance overheads due to data duplication. In this work, we take a step towards enabling and optimizing learning *over* joins for a common class of machine learning techniques called generalized linear models that are solved using gradient descent algorithms in an RDBMS setting. We present alternative approaches to learn over a join that are easy to implement over existing RDBMSs. We introduce a new approach named *factorized learning* that pushes ML computations through joins and avoids redundancy in both I/O and computations. We study the tradeoff space for all our approaches both analytically and empirically. Our results show that factorized learning is often substantially faster than the alternatives, but is not always the fastest, necessitating a cost-based approach. We also discuss extensions of all our approaches to multi-table joins as well as to Hive.

Categories and Subject Descriptors

H.2 [**Information Systems**]: Database Management

Keywords

Analytics; feature engineering; joins; machine learning

1. INTRODUCTION

There is an escalating arms race to bring sophisticated statistical and machine learning (ML) techniques to enterprise applications [3, 5]. A number of projects in both industry and academia aim to integrate ML capabilities with data processing in RDBMSs, Hadoop, and other systems [2, 4, 9, 15, 18, 21, 22, 33, 34]. Almost all such implementations of ML algorithms require that the input dataset be a single table. However, most relational datasets are not as stored single tables due to normalization [27]. Thus, analysts often perform key-foreign key joins of the base tables and *materialize* a single temporary table that is used as the input to the ML algorithm, i.e., they learn *after* joins.

Example: Consider an insurance company analyst modeling customer churn (will a customer leave the company or not) – a standard classification task. She builds a logistic regression model using the large table that stores customer details: `Customers(CustomerID, Churn, Age, Income, ..., EmployerID)`. Note that one of the features, `EmployerID`, is the ID of the customer's employer. It is a foreign key that refers to a separate table that stores details about companies and other organizations: `Employers(EmployerID, Revenue, NumEmployees, ...)`. She joins the two tables on the `EmployerID` as part of her "feature engineering" because she thinks the features of the employer might be helpful in predicting how likely a customer is to churn. For example, she might have a hunch that customers employed by large corporations are less likely to churn. She writes the output of the join as a single temporary table and feeds it to an ML toolkit that implements logistic regression.

Similar examples arise in a number of other application domains, e.g., detecting malicious users by joining data about user accounts with account activities, predicting census mail response rates by joining data about census districts with individual households, recommending products by joining data about past ratings with users and products, etc.

Learning after joins imposes an artificial barrier between the ML-based analysis and the base relations, resulting in several practical issues. First, the table obtained after the join can be much larger than the base tables themselves because the join introduces redundancy that was originally removed by database normalization [8, 27]. This results in unnecessary overheads for storage and performance as well as waste of time performing extra computations on data with redundancy. Second, as the base tables evolve, maintaining the materialized output of the join could become an overhead. Finally, analysts often perform exploratory analysis of different subsets of features and data [20, 33]. Materializing temporary tables after joins for learning on each subset could slow the analyst and inhibit exploration [7]. Learning *over* joins, i.e., pushing ML computations through joins to the base tables, mitigates such drawbacks.

SIGMOD'15, May 31 – June 04, 2015, Melbourne, VIC, Australia.

http://dx.doi.org/10.1145/2723372.2723713.

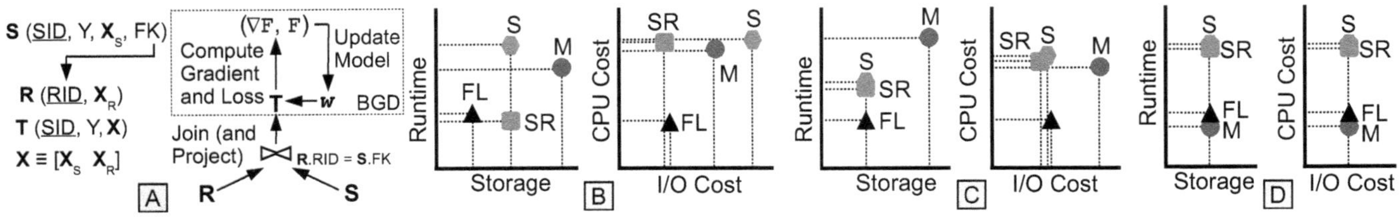

Figure 1: Learning over a join: (A) Schema and logical workflow. Feature vectors from S (e.g., Customers) and R (e.g., Employers) are concatenated and used for BGD. The loss (F) and gradient (∇F) for BGD can be computed together during a pass over the data. Approaches compared: Materialize (M), Stream (S), Stream-Reuse (SR), and Factorized Learning (FL). High-level qualitative comparison of storage-runtime tradeoffs and CPU-I/O cost tradeoffs for runtimes of the four approaches (S is assumed to be larger than R, and the plots are not to scale) (B) When the hash table on R does not fit in buffer memory, S, SR, and M require extra storage space for temporary tables or partitions. But, SR could be faster than FL due to lower I/O costs. (C) When the hash table on R fits in buffer memory, but S does not, SR becomes similar to S and neither need extra storage space, but both could be slower than FL. (D) When all data fit comfortably in buffer memory, none of the approaches need extra storage space, and M could be faster than FL.

From a technical perspective, the issues that arise from the redundancy present in a denormalized relation (used for learning after joins) are well known in the context of traditional relational data management [27]. But the implications of this type of redundancy in the context of ML algorithms are much less well understood. Thus, an important challenge to be addressed is if it is possible to devise approaches that learn over joins and avoid introducing such redundancy without sacrificing either the model quality, learning efficiency, or scalability compared to the currently standard approach of learning after joins.

As a first step, in this paper, we show that, for a large generic class of ML techniques called Generalized Linear Models (GLMs), it is possible to learn over joins and avoid redundancy without sacrificing quality and scalability, while actually improving performance. Furthermore, all our approaches to learn GLMs over joins are simple and easy to implement using existing RDBMS abstractions, which makes them more easily deployable than approaches that require deep changes to the code of an RDBMS. We focus on GLMs because they include many popular classification and regression techniques [17, 24]. We use standard gradient methods to learn GLMs: Batch Gradient Descent (BGD), Conjugate Gradient (CGD), and (L)BFGS [26]. For clarity of exposition, we use only BGD, but our results are also applicable to these other gradient methods. BGD is a numerical optimization algorithm that minimizes an objective function by performing multiple passes (*iterations*) over the data.

Figure 1(A) gives a high-level overview of our problem. We call the approach of materializing **T** before BGD as *Materialize*. We focus on the hybrid hash algorithm for the join operation [31]. We assume that **R** is smaller in size than **S** and estimate the I/O and CPU costs of all our approaches in a manner similar to [31]. We propose three alternative approaches to run BGD over a join in a single-node RDBMS setting – *Stream*, *Stream-Reuse* and *Factorized Learning*. Each approach avoids some forms of redundancy. *Stream* avoids writing **T** and could save on I/O. *Stream-Reuse* also exploits the fact that BGD is iterative and avoids repartitioning of the base relations after the first iteration. But, neither approach avoids redundancy in the computations for BGD. Thus, we design the *Factorized Learning* (in short, *Factorize*) approach that avoids computational redundancy as well. *Factorize* achieves this by interleaving the computations and I/O of the join operation and BGD. None of our approaches compromise on model quality. Furthermore, they are all easy to implement in an RDBMS using the abstraction of user-defined aggregate functions (UDAFs), which provides scalability and ease of deployment [13, 16].

The performance picture, however, is more complex. Figures 1(B-D) give a high-level qualitative overview of the tradeoff space for all our approaches in terms of the storage space needed and the runtimes (split into I/O and CPU costs). Both our analytical and experimental results show that *Factorize* is often the fastest approach, but which approach is the fastest depends on a combination of factors such as buffer memory, input table dimensions, and number of iterations. Thus, a cost model such as ours is required to select the fastest approach for a given instance of our problem. Furthermore, we identify that *Factorize* might face a scalability bottleneck since it maintains an aggregation state whose size is linear in the number of tuples in **R**. We propose three extensions to mitigate this bottleneck and find that none of them dominate the others in terms of runtime, which again necessitates our cost model.

We extend all our approaches to multi-table joins, specifically, the case in which **S** has multiple foreign keys. Such a scenario arises in applications such as recommendation systems in which a table of ratings refers to both the user and product tables [28]. We show that optimally extending *Factorize* to multi-table joins involves solving a problem that is NP-Hard. We propose a simple, but effective, greedy heuristic to tackle this problem. Finally, we extend all our approaches to the shared-nothing parallel setting and implement them on Hive. We find near-linear speedups and scaleups for all our approaches.

In summary, our work makes the following contributions:

- To the best of our knowledge, this is the first paper to study the problem of learning over joins of large relations without materializing the join output. Focusing on GLMs solved using BGD, we explain the tradeoff space in terms of I/O and CPU costs and propose alternative approaches to learn over joins.
- We propose the *Factorize* approach that pushes BGD computations through a join, while being amenable to a simple implementation in existing RDBMSs.

ML Technique	F_e (a, b) (For Loss)	G (a, b) (For Gradient)
Logistic Regression (**LR**)	$\log(1 + e^{-ab})$	$\frac{-a}{1 + e^{ab}}$
Least-Squares Regression (**LSR**), Lasso, and Ridge	$(a - b)^2$	$2(b - a)$
Linear Support Vector Machine (**LSVM**)	$\max\{0, 1 - ab\}$	$-a\delta_{ab<1}$

Table 1: GLMs and their functions.

- We compare the performance of all our approaches both analytically and empirically using implementations on PostgreSQL. Our results show that *Factorize* is often, but not always, the fastest approach. A combination of factors such as the buffer memory, the dimensions of the input tables, and the number of BGD iterations determines which approach is the fastest. We also validate the accuracy of our analytical models.
- We extend all our approaches to multi-table joins. We also demonstrate how to parallelize them using implementations on Hive.

Outline. In Section 2, we present a brief background on GLMs and BGD and some preliminaries for our problem. In Section 3, we explain our cost model and simple approaches to learn over joins. In Section 4, we present the new approach of *Factorized Learning* and its extensions. In Section 5, we discuss our experimental setup and results. We discuss related work in Section 6 and conclude in Section 7.

2. BACKGROUND AND PRELIMINARIES

We provide a brief introduction to GLMs and BGD. For a deeper description, we refer the reader to [17, 24, 26].

Generalized Linear Models (GLMs). Consider a dataset of n examples, each of which includes a d-dimensional numeric *feature vector*, $\mathbf{x}_i$, and a numeric *target*, y_i ($i = 1$ to n). For regression, $y_i \in \mathbb{R}$, while for (binary) classification, $y_i \in \{-1, 1\}$. Loosely, GLMs assume that the data points can be separated into its target classes (for classification), or approximated (for regression), by a hyperplane. The idea is to compute such a hyperplane $\mathbf{w} \in \mathbb{R}^d$ by defining an optimization problem using the given dataset. We are given a *linearly-separable* objective function that computes the *loss* of a given model $\mathbf{w} \in \mathbb{R}^d$ on the data: $F(\mathbf{w}) = \sum_{i=1}^{n} F_e(y_i, \mathbf{w}^T\mathbf{x}_i)$. The goal of an ML algorithm is to minimize the loss function, i.e., find a vector $\mathbf{w}^* \in \mathbb{R}^d$, s.t., $\mathbf{w}^* = \arg\min_{\mathbf{w}} F(\mathbf{w})$. Table 1 lists examples of some popular GLM techniques and their respective loss functions. The loss functions of GLMs are *convex* (bowl-shaped), which means any local minimum is a global minimum, and standard gradient descent algorithms can be used to solve them.[1]

Batch Gradient Descent (BGD). BGD is a simple algorithm to solve GLMs using iterative numerical optimization. BGD initializes the model $\mathbf{w}$ to some $\mathbf{w}_0$, computes the gradient $\nabla F(\mathbf{w})$ on the given dataset, and updates the model as $\mathbf{w} \leftarrow \mathbf{w} - \alpha\nabla F(\mathbf{w})$, where $\alpha > 0$ is the stepsize parameter. The method is outlined in Algorithm 1. Like F, the gradient is also linearly separable: $\nabla F(\mathbf{w}) = \sum_{i=1}^{n} G(y_i, \mathbf{w}^T\mathbf{x}_i)\mathbf{x}_i$. Since the gradient is the direction of steepest ascent of F,

[1]Typically, a convex penalty term called a *regularizer* is added to the loss to constrain $\|\mathbf{w}\|$ [17].

Algorithm 1 Batch Gradient Descent (BGD)

Inputs: $\{\mathbf{x}_i, y_i\}_{i=1}^{n}$ (Data), $\mathbf{w}_0$ (Initial model)

1: $k \leftarrow 0$, $r_{prev} \leftarrow$ null, $r_{curr} \leftarrow$ null, $\mathbf{g}_k \leftarrow$ null
2: **while** (Stop (k, r_{prev}, r_{curr}, $\mathbf{g}_k$) = False) **do**
3: $\quad r_{prev} \leftarrow r_{curr}$
4: $\quad (\mathbf{g}_k, r_{curr}) \leftarrow (\nabla F_{k+1}, F_{k+1})$ ▷ 1 pass over data
5: $\quad \mathbf{w}_{k+1} \leftarrow \mathbf{w}_k - \alpha_k \mathbf{g}_k$ ▷ Pick α_k by line search
6: $\quad k \leftarrow k + 1$
7: **end while**

BGD is also known as the method of steepest descent [26]. Table 1 also lists the gradient functions of the GLMs. We shall use F and $F(\mathbf{w})$ interchangeably.

BGD updates the model repeatedly, i.e., over many *iterations* (or *epochs*), each of which requires (at least) one pass over the data. The loss value typically drops over iterations. The algorithm is typically stopped after a pre-defined number of iterations, or when it *converges* (e.g., the drop in the loss value across iterations, or the norm of the gradient, falls below a given threshold). The stepsize parameter (α) is typically tuned using a line search method that potentially computes the loss many times (similar to step 4) [26].

On large data, it is likely that computing F and ∇F dominates the runtime of BGD [12, 13]. Fortunately, both F and ∇F can be computed scalably in a manner similar to distributive aggregates like `SUM` in SQL. Thus, it is easy to implement BGD using the abstraction of a user-defined aggregate function (UDAF) that is available in almost all RDBMSs [13, 16]. However, unlike `SUM`, BGD performs a "multi-column" or vector aggregation since all feature values of an example are needed to compute its contribution to the gradient. For simplicity of exposition, we assume that feature vectors are instead stored as arrays in a single column.

Joins Before Learning. From our conversations with analysts at companies across various domains – insurance, consulting, Web search, security, and e-commerce – we have learned that analysts often perform joins to replace foreign key references with actual feature values as part of their feature engineering effort.[2] In this work, we focus chiefly on a two-table join. We term the main table with the entities to learn on as the *entity table* (denoted **S**). We term the other table as the *attribute table* (denoted **R**). A column in **S** is a foreign key that refers to **R**.

Problem Statement. Suppose there are n_S examples (tuples) in **S**, and n_R tuples in **R**. Assume that the feature vectors are split across **S** and **R**, with $d_S - 1$ features in $\mathbf{X}_S$ and $d_R = d - d_S + 1$ in $\mathbf{X}_R$. Thus, the "width" of **S** is $2 + d_S$, including the ID, foreign key, and target. The width of **R** is $1 + d_R$, including the ID. Typically, we have $n_S \gg n_R$, similar to how fact tables have more tuples than dimension tables in OLAP [16, 27]. We now state our problem formally (illustrated in Figure 1(A)).

Given two relations **S** *($\underline{SID}$, Y, $\boldsymbol{X}_S$, FK) and* **R** *($\underline{RID}$, $\boldsymbol{X}_R$) with a key-foreign key relationship (***S***.FK refers to* **R***.RID), where $\boldsymbol{X}_S$ and $\boldsymbol{X}_R$ are feature vectors and Y is the target, learn a GLM using BGD over the result of the projected*

[2]An alternative is to simply ignore the foreign key, or treat it as a large, sparse categorical feature. Such feature engineering judgements are largely analyst-specific [7, 20, 33]. Our work simply aims to make feature engineering easier.

Symbol	Meaning
R	Attribute table
S	Entity table
T	Join result table
n_R	Number of rows in **R**
n_S	Number of rows in **S**
d_R	Number of features in **R**
d_S	Number of features in **S** (includes Y)
p	Page size in bytes (1MB used)
m	Allocated buffer memory (pages)
f	Hash table fudge factor (1.4 used)
|R|	Number of **R** pages ($\lceil \frac{8n_R(1+d_R)}{p} \rceil$)
|S|	Number of **S** pages ($\lceil \frac{8n_S(2+d_S)}{p} \rceil$)
|T|	Number of **T** pages ($\lceil \frac{8n_S(1+d_S+d_R)}{p} \rceil$)
Iters	Number of iterations of BGD (≥ 1)

Table 2: Notation for objects and parameters used in the cost models. I/O costs are counted in number of pages. Dividing by the disk throughput yields the estimated runtimes. NB: As a simplifying assumption, we use an 8B representation for all values: IDs, target, and features (categorical features are assumed be have been converted to numeric ones [17]).

equi-join $\mathbf{T}(\underline{SID}, Y, [\boldsymbol{X_S}\ \boldsymbol{X_R}]) \leftarrow \pi(\mathbf{R} \bowtie_{RID=FK} \mathbf{S})$ *such that the feature vector of a tuple in* **T** *is the concatenation of the feature vectors from the joining tuples of* **S** *and* **R**.

3. LEARNING OVER JOINS

We now discuss alternative approaches to run BGD over a table that is logically the output of a key-foreign key join.

3.1 Assumptions and Cost Model

For the rest of the paper, we focus only on the data-intensive computation in step 4 of Algorithm 1 – computing $(\nabla F, F)$. The data-agnostic computations of updating $\mathbf{w}$ are identical across all approaches proposed here, and typically take only a few seconds.[3] Tables 2 and 3 summarize our notation for the objects and parameters.

We focus on the classical hybrid hash join algorithm (considering other join algorithms is part of future work), which requires $(m-1) > \sqrt{\lceil f|\mathbf{R}| \rceil}$ [31]. We also focus primarily on the case $n_S > n_R$ and $|\mathbf{S}| \geq |\mathbf{R}|$. We discuss the cases $n_S \leq n_R$ or $|\mathbf{S}| < |\mathbf{R}|$ in the appendix.

3.2 BGD After a Join: Materialize (M)

Materialize (M) is the current popular approach for handling ML over normalized datasets. Essentially, we write a new table and use it for BGD.

1. Apply hybrid hash join to obtain and write **T**.
2. Read **T** to compute $(\nabla F, F)$ for each iteration.

Following the style of the discussion of the hybrid hash join algorithm in [31], we now introduce some notation. The number of partitions of $\mathbf{R}$ is $B = \left\lceil \frac{\lceil f|\mathbf{R}| \rceil - (m-2)}{(m-2)-1} \right\rceil$. Partition

[3]CGD and (L)BFGS differ from BGD only in these data-agnostic computations, which are easily implemented in, say, Python, or R [12]. If a line search is used to tune α, we need to compute only F, but largely the same tradeoffs apply.

Symbol	Meaning	Default Value (CPU Cycles)
hash	Hash a key	100
comp	Compare two keys	10
copy	Copy a double	1
add	Add two doubles	10
mult	Multiply two doubles	10
funcG	Compute *G(a, b)*	150
funcF	Compute $F_e(a, b)$	200

Table 3: Notation for the CPU cost model. The approximate default values for CPU cycles for each unit of the cost model were estimated empirically on the machine on which the experiments were run. Dividing by the CPU clock frequency yields the estimated runtimes. For G and F_e, we assume LR. LSR and LSVM are slightly faster.

sizes are $|\mathbf{R}_0| = \left\lfloor \frac{(m-2)-B}{f} \right\rfloor$, and $|\mathbf{R}_i| = \left\lceil \frac{|\mathbf{R}|-|\mathbf{R}_0|}{B} \right\rceil (1 \leq i \leq B)$, with the ratio $q = \frac{|\mathbf{R}_0|}{|\mathbf{R}|}$, where $\mathbf{R}_0$ is the first partition and $\mathbf{R}_i$ are the other partitions as per the hybrid hash join algorithm [31]. We provide the detailed I/O and CPU costs of Materialize here. The costs of the other approaches in this section can be derived from these, but due to space constraints, we present them in the appendix.

I/O Cost. If $(m-1) \leq \lceil f|\mathbf{R}| \rceil$, we partition the tables:

```
  (|R|+|S|)                 //First read
+ 2.(|R|+|S|).(1-q)         //Write, read temp partitions
+ |T|                       //Write output
+ |T|                       //Read for first iteration
+ (Iters-1).|T|             //Remaining iterations
- min{|T|,[(m-2)-f|R_i|]} //Cache T for iter 1
- min{|T|,(m-1)}.(Iters-1)  //MRU for rest
```

If $(m-1) > \lceil f|\mathbf{R}| \rceil$, we need not partition the tables:

```
  (|R|+|S|)
+ (Iters+1).|T|
- min{|T|,[(m-2)-f|R|]}
- min{|T|,(m-1)}.(Iters-1)
```

CPU Cost

```
  (nR+nS).hash               //Partition R and S
+ nR.(1+dR).copy             //Construct hash on R
+ nR.(1+dR).(1-q).copy       //R output partitions
+ nS.(2+dS).(1-q).copy       //S output partitions
+ (nR+nS).(1-q).hash         //Hash on R and S partitions
+ nS.comp.f                  //Probe for all of S
+ nS.(1+dS+dR).copy          //T output partitions
+ Iters.[                    //Compute gradient and loss
    nS.d.(mult+add)          //w.xi for all i
  + nS.(funcG+funcF)         //Apply G and F_e
  + nS.d.(mult+add)          //Scale and add
  + nS.add                   //Add for total loss
  ]
```

3.3 BGD Over a Join: Stream (S)

This approach performs the join *lazily* for each iteration.

1. Apply hybrid hash join to obtain **T**, but instead of writing **T**, compute $(\nabla F, F)$ on the fly.
2. Repeat step 1 for each iteration.

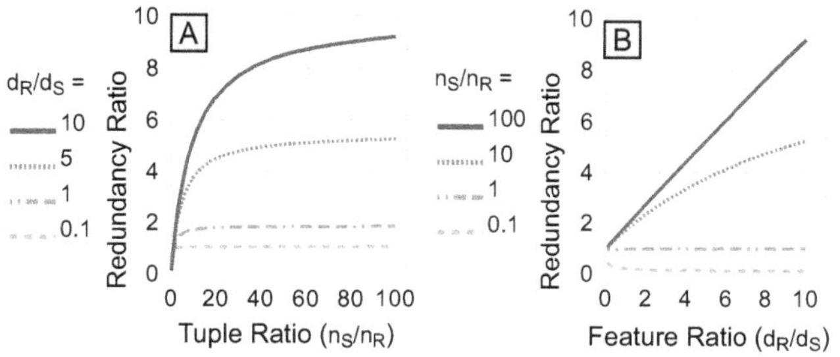

Figure 2: Redundancy ratio against the two dimension ratios (for $d_S = 20$). (A) Fix $\frac{d_R}{d_S}$ and vary $\frac{n_S}{n_R}$. (B) Fix $\frac{n_S}{n_R}$ and vary $\frac{d_R}{d_S}$.

The I/O cost of Stream is simply the cost of the hybrid hash join multiplied by the number of iterations. Its CPU cost is a combination of the join and BGD.

Discussion of Tradeoffs. The I/O and storage tradeoffs between Materialize and Stream (Figure 1(B)) arise because it is likely that many tuples of **S** join with a single tuple of **R** (e.g., many customers might have the same employer). Thus, $|\mathbf{T}|$ is usually larger than $|\mathbf{S}|+|\mathbf{R}|$. Obviously, the gap depends upon the dataset sizes. More precisely, we define the *redundancy ratio (r)* as the ratio of the size of **T** to that of **S** and **R**:

$$r = \frac{n_S(1+d_S+d_R)}{n_S(2+d_S)+n_R(1+d_R)} = \frac{\frac{n_S}{n_R}(1+\frac{d_R}{d_S}+\frac{1}{d_S})}{\frac{n_S}{n_R}(1+\frac{2}{d_S})+\frac{d_R}{d_S}+\frac{1}{d_S}}$$

This ratio is useful because it gives us an idea of the factor of speedups that are potentially possible by learning over joins. Since it depends on the dimensions of the inputs, we plot the redundancy ratio for different values of the *tuple ratio* ($\frac{n_S}{n_R}$) and (inverse) *feature ratio* ($\frac{d_R}{d_S}$), while fixing d_S. Figure 2 presents the plots. Typically, both dimension ratios are > 1, which mostly yields $r > 1$. But when the tuple ratio is < 1, $r < 1$ (see Figure 2(A)). This is because the join here becomes selective (when $n_S < n_R$). However, when the tuple ratio > 1, we see that r increases with the tuple ratio. It converges to $\frac{1+\frac{d_R}{d_S}+\frac{1}{d_S}}{1+\frac{2}{d_S}} \approx 1+\frac{d_R}{d_S}$. Similarly, as shown in Figure 2(B), the redundancy ratio increases with the feature ratio, and converges to the tuple ratio $\frac{n_S}{n_R}$.

3.4 An Improvement: Stream-Reuse (SR)

We now present a simple modification to Stream – the Stream-Reuse approach – that can significantly improve performance.

1. Apply hybrid hash join to obtain **T**, but instead of writing **T**, run the first iteration of BGD on the fly.
2. Maintain the temporary partitions of **S** and **R** on disk.
3. For the remaining iterations, reuse the partitions of **S** and and **R** for the hybrid hash join, similar to step 1.

The I/O cost of Stream-Reuse gets rid of the rewriting (and rereading) of partitions at every iteration, but the CPU cost is reduced only slightly. Stream-Reuse makes the join "iteration-aware" – we need to divide the implementation of the hybrid hash join in to two steps so as to reuse the partitions across iterations. An easier way to implement (without changing the RDBMS code) is to manually handle pre-partitioning at the logical query layer after consulting the optimizer about the number of partitions. Although the latter is a minor approximation to SR, the difference in performance (estimated using our analytical cost models) is mostly negligible.

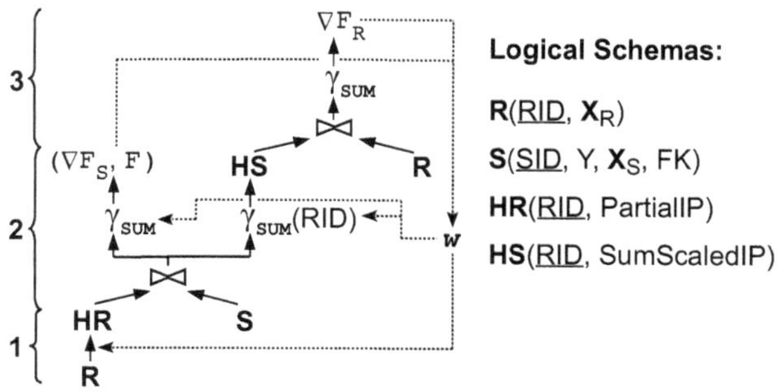

Figure 3: Logical workflow of factorized learning, consisting of three steps as numbered. HR and HS are logical intermediate relations. PartialIP refers to the partial inner products from R. SumScaledIP refers to the grouped sums of the scalar output of $G()$ applied to the full inner products on the concatenated feature vectors. Here, γ_{SUM} denotes a `SUM` aggregation and $\gamma_{SUM}(RID)$ denotes a `SUM` aggregation with a `GROUP BY` on RID.

4. FACTORIZED LEARNING

We now present a new technique that interleaves the I/O and CPU processing of the join and BGD. The basic idea is to avoid the redundancy introduced by the join by dividing the computations of both F and ∇F and "pushing them through the join". We call our technique *factorized learning* (Factorize, or FL for short), borrowing the terminology from "factorized" databases [8]. An overview of the logical computations in FL is presented in Figure 3.

The key insight in FL is as follows: given a feature vector $\mathbf{x} \in \mathbf{T}$, we have $\mathbf{w}^T\mathbf{x} = \mathbf{w}_S^T\mathbf{x}_S + \mathbf{w}_R^T\mathbf{x}_R$. Since the join duplicates $\mathbf{x}_R$ from **R** when constructing **T**, the main goal of FL is to avoid redundant inner product computations as well as I/O over those feature vectors from **R**. FL achieves this goal with the following three steps (numbered in Figure 3).

1. Compute and save the partial inner products $\mathbf{w}_R^T\mathbf{x}_R$ for each tuple in **R** in a new table **HR** under the PartialIP column (part 1 in Figure 3).
2. Recall that the computation of F and ∇F are clubbed together, and that $\nabla F \equiv [\nabla F_S \; \nabla F_R]$. This step computes F and ∇F_S together. Essentially, we join **HR** and **S** on RID and complete the computation of the full inner products on the fly, and follow that up by applying both $F_e()$ and $G()$ on each example. By aggregating both these quantities as it performs the join, FL completes the computation of $F = \sum F_e(y, \mathbf{w}^T\mathbf{x})$ and $\nabla F_S = \sum G(y, \mathbf{w}^T\mathbf{x})\mathbf{x}_S$. Simultaneously, FL also performs a `GROUP BY` on RID and sums up $G(y, \mathbf{w}^T\mathbf{x})$, which is saved in a new table **HS** under the SumScaledIP column (part 2 in Figure 3).
3. Compute $\nabla F_R = \sum G(y, \mathbf{w}^T\mathbf{x})\mathbf{x}_R$ by joining **HS** with **R** on RID and scaling the partial feature vectors $\mathbf{x}_R$ with SumScaledIP (part 3 in Figure 3).

Example: Consider logistic regression (LR). In step 2, as the full inner product $\mathbf{w}^T\mathbf{x}$ is computed by joining **HR** and

$\mathbf{S}$, FL computes $log(1 + exp(-y\mathbf{w}^T\mathbf{x}))$ and adds it into F. Immediately, FL also computes $\frac{-y}{1+exp(y\mathbf{w}^T\mathbf{x})} = g$ (say), and adds it into SumScaledIP for that RID. It also computes $g\mathbf{x}_S$ and adds it into ∇F_S.

Overall, FL computes $(\nabla F, F)$ without any redundancy in the computations. FL reduces the CPU cost of floating point operations for computing inner products from $O(n_S(d_S + d_R))$ to $O(n_S d_S + n_R d_R)$. The reduction roughly equals the redundancy ratio (Section 3.3). Once $(\nabla F, F)$ is computed, $\mathbf{w}$ is updated and the whole process is repeated for the next iteration of BGD. Note that to compute only F, step 3 of FL can be skipped. FL gives the same results as Materialize and Stream. We provide the proof in the appendix.

PROPOSITION 4.1. *The output $(\nabla F, F)$ of FL is identical to the output $(\nabla F, F)$ of both Materialize and Stream.*[4]

While it is straightforward to translate the logical plan shown in Figure 3 into SQL queries, we implement it using a slightly different scheme. Our goal is to take advantage of some physical properties of this problem that will help us improve performance by avoiding some table management overheads imposed by the RDBMS. Basically, since **HR** and **HS** are both small 2-column tables keyed by RID, we maintain them together in a simple in-memory associative array **H** with the bucket for each RID being a pair of double precision numbers (for PartialIP and SumScaledIP). Thus, we perform random reads and writes on **H**, and replace both the joins (from parts 2 and 3 in Figure 3) with simple aggregation queries with *user-defined aggregation functions* (UDAFs) that perform simple scans over the base tables. Overall, our implementation of FL works as follows, with each step corresponding to its respective part in Figure 3:

1. Read **R**, hash on RID and construct **H** in memory with partial inner products ($\mathbf{w}_R^T\mathbf{x}_R$) saved in PartialIP. It can be expressed as the following SQL query: `SELECT UDAF1(R.RID,R.xR,wR) FROM R`.
2. Read **S**, probe into **H** using the condition $FK = RID$, complete the inner products by adding PartialIP from **H** with partial inner products on each tuple ($\mathbf{w}_S^T\mathbf{x}_S$), update F in the aggregation state by adding into it (essentially, a `SUM`), update ∇F_S in the aggregation state by adding into it (a `SUM` over vectors), and add the value of $G(\mathbf{w}^T\mathbf{x})$ into SumScaledIP (essentially, a `SUM` with a `GROUP BY` on RID). As a query: `SELECT UDAF2(S.FK,S.y,S.xS,wS) FROM S`.
3. Read **R**, probe into **H** on RID, compute partial gradients on each example and update ∇F_R in memory (essentially, a `SUM` over vectors). As a query: `SELECT UDAF3(R.RID,R.xR) FROM R`.
4. Repeat steps 1-3 for each remaining iteration.

I/O Cost

```
Iters.[
   (|R|+|S|+|R|)            //Read for each iter
  - min{|R|,(m-1)-|H|} ]    //Cache R for second pass
- (Iters - 1).[
   min{|R|,(m-1)-|H|}       //Cache R for next iter
  + min{|S|,max{0,(m-1)-|H|-|R|}} ] //Cache S too
```

[4]The proof assumes exact arithmetic. Finite-precision arithmetic may introduce minor errors. We leave a numerical analysis of FL to future work.

CPU Cost

```
Iters.[
    nR.hash                  //Hash R for stats
  + nR.dR.(mult+add)         //Partial w.xi for col 1
  + nR.copy                  //Update column 1 of H
  + nS.(hash+comp.f)         //Probe for all of S
  + nS.(dS-1).(mult+add) //Partial w.xi for col 2
  + nS.(add+funcG+funcF) //Full w.xi and functions
  + nS.(dS-1).(mult+add) //Partial scale and add
  + nS.add                   //Add for total loss
  + (nS-nR).add              //Compute column 2 of H
  + nR.copy                  //Update column 2 of H
  + nR.(hash+comp.f)         //Probe for all of R
  + nR.dR.(mult+add)         //Partial scale and add
]
```

The above costs present an interesting insight into FL. While it avoids computational redundancy in computing $(\nabla F, F)$, FL performs extra computations to manage **H**. Thus, FL introduces a non-obvious computational tradeoff. Similarly, FL requires an extra scan of **R** per iteration, which introduces a non-obvious I/O tradeoff. As we will show later in Section 5, these tradeoffs determine which approach will be fastest on a given instance of the problem.

As an implementation detail, we found that, while it is easy to manage **H** as an associative array, the caching of **R** for the second pass is not straightforward to implement. This is because the pages of **R** might be evicted when **S** is read, unless we manually keep them in memory. We found that the performance benefit due to this is usually under 10% and thus, we ignore it. But if an RDBMS offers an easy way to "pin" pages of a table to buffer memory, we can use it in FL.

Finally, we note that FL requires **H** to be maintained in buffer memory, which requires $m - 1 > |\mathbf{H}|$. But note that $|\mathbf{H}| = \left\lceil \frac{f.n_R.(1+2).8}{p} \right\rceil$, which is only $O(n_R)$. Thus, in many cases, **H** will probably easily fit in buffer memory. Nevertheless, to handle cases when **H** does not fit in buffer memory, we present a few extensions to FL.

4.1 Scaling FL along n_R

We explore three extensions to FL to mitigate its scalability bottleneck: FLSQL, FLSQL+, and FL-Partition (FLP).

4.1.1 FLSQL

FLSQL applies the traditional approach of optimizing SQL aggregates (e.g., `SUM`) over joins using logical query rewriting [10,32]. Instead of maintaining **H** in memory, it directly converts the logical plan of Figure 3 into SQL queries by managing **HR** and **HS** as separate tables:

1. Read **R**, and write **HR** with partial inner products.
2. Join **HR** and **S** and aggregate (`SUM`) the result to compute (∇F_S,F).
3. Join **HR** and **S** and write **HS** after a `GROUP BY` on RID. **HS** contains sums of scaled inner products.
4. Join **HS** and **R** and aggregate (`SUM`) the result to compute ∇F_R.
5. Repeat steps 1-4 for each remaining iteration.

Note that both **HR** and **HS** are of size $O(n_R)$. Also, note that we have to read **S** twice – once for computing an aggregate and the other for creating a new table.

4.1.2 FLSQL+

FLSQL+ uses the observation that since $n_S \gg n_R$ typically (and perhaps $d_S < d_R$), it might be faster to write a wider table in step 2 of FLSQL instead of reading **S** twice:

1. Read **R**, and write **HR** with partial inner products.
2. Join **HR** and **S** and write **HS+** after a `GROUP BY` on RID. **HS+** contains both sums of scaled inner products and partial gradient vectors.
3. Join **HS+** and **R** and aggregate (`SUM`) the result to compute F and ∇F.
4. Repeat steps 1-3 for each iteration..

Note that **HR** is of size $O(n_R)$ but **HS+** is of size $O(n_R d_S)$, since it includes the partial gradients too. Thus, whether this is faster or not depends on the dataset dimensions.

4.1.3 FL-Partition (FLP)

The basic idea behind FLP is simple – pre-partition **R** and **S** so that the smaller associative arrays can fit in memory:

1. Partition **R** and **S** on RID (resp. foreign key) into $\{\mathbf{R}_i\}$ and $\{\mathbf{S}_i\}$ so that each $\mathbf{H}_i$ corresponding to $\mathbf{R}_i$ fits in memory.
2. For each pair $\mathbf{R}_i$ and $\mathbf{S}_i$, apply FL to obtain partial $(\nabla F, F)_i$. Add the results from all partitions to obtain full $(\nabla F, F)$.
3. Repeat steps 1-2 for each remaining iteration, reusing the partitions of **R** and **S**, similar to Stream-Reuse.

Note that we could even partition **S** and **R** into more than necessary partitions to ensure that $\mathbf{R}_i$ is cached for the second pass, thus improving the performance slightly. All the above extensions preserve the correctness guarantee of FL. We provide the proof in the appendix.

PROPOSITION 4.2. *The output $(\nabla F, F)$ of FLP, FLSQL, and FLSQL+ are all identical to the output $(\nabla F, F)$ of FL.*

4.2 Extensions

We explain how we can extend our approaches to multi-table joins. We then briefly discuss how we can extend our approaches to a shared-nothing parallel setting.

4.2.1 Multi-table Joins

Multi-table key-foreign key joins do arise in some applications of ML. For example, in a movie recommendation system such as Netflix, ratings of movies by users (e.g., 1-5 stars) are typically stored in a table that has foreign key references to two tables – one with user details, and another with movie details. Thus, there is one entity table and many attribute tables (considering other schema scenarios is part of future work). Extending Materialize and Stream (and Stream-Reuse) to multi-table joins is trivial, since data processing systems such as RDBMSs and Hive already support and optimize multi-table joins [1, 29].

Extending FL is also straightforward, provided we have enough memory to store the associative arrays of all attribute relations simultaneously for step 2. But we face a technical challenge when the memory is insufficient. One solution is to adapt the FLP strategy, but partitioning all input relations might be an overkill. Instead, it is possible to improve performance by formulating a standard discrete optimization problem to determine the subset of input relations to partition so that the overall runtime is minimized.

Formally, we are given k attribute tables $\mathbf{R}_i(\underline{RID_i}, \mathbf{X}_i)$, $i = 1$ to k, and the entity table $\mathbf{S}(\underline{SID}, Y, \mathbf{X}_S, FK_1, \ldots, FK_k)$, with k foreign keys. Our approach reads each $\mathbf{R}_i$ and converts it to its associative array $\mathbf{HR}_i$ (step 1 of FL), and then applies a simplified GRACE hash join [31] recursively on the right-deep join tree with **S** as the outer table.[5] We have $m < \sum_{i=1}^{k} |\mathbf{HR}_i|$, and thus, we need to partition **S** and some (or all) of $\{\mathbf{HR}_i\}$. Let s_i (a positive integer) be the number of partitions of $\mathbf{HR}_i$ (so, **S** has $\Pi_{i=1}^{k} s_i$ partitions). We now make three observations. First, minimizing the total cost of partitioning is equivalent to maximizing the total savings from not partitioning. Second, the cost of partitioning $\mathbf{R}_i$, viz., $2|\mathbf{R}_i|$, is independent of s_i, provided the page size p is large enough to perform mostly sequential writes (note that $s_i \le |\mathbf{R}_i|$). Thus, it only matters if $s_i = 1$ or not. Define a binary variable x_i as $x_i = 1$, if $s_i = 1$, and $x_i = 0$, if $s_i > 1$. Finally, we allocate at least one page of memory for each $\mathbf{R}_i$ to process each partition of **S** (this needs $m > k$, which is typically not an issue). We now formally state the problem (FL-MULTJOIN) as follows:

$$\max \sum_{i=1}^{k} x_i |\mathbf{R}_i|, \ s.t. \ \sum_{i=1}^{k} x_i(|\mathbf{HR}_i| - 1) \le m - 1 - k$$

Basically, we count the I/Os saved for those $\mathbf{R}_i$ that do not need to be partitioned since $\mathbf{HR}_i$ fits entirely in memory. We prove the following result:

THEOREM 4.1. *FL-MULTJOIN is* NP*-Hard in l, where $l = |\{i | m - k \ge |\mathbf{HR}_i| > 1\}| \le k$.*

Essentially, this result means that FL-MULTJOIN is trivial if either none of $\mathbf{HR}_i$ fit in memory individually or all fit simultaneously, but is harder if a few (not all) can fit simultaneously. Our proof provides a reduction from the classical 0/1 knapsack problem [14]. Due to space constraints, we present the proof in the appendix. We adopt a standard $O(klog(k))$ time greedy heuristic for the knapsack problem to solve FL-MULTJOIN approximately [11]. Essentially, we sort the list of attribute tables on $\frac{|\mathbf{R}_i|}{(|\mathbf{HR}_i| - 1)}$, and pick the associative arrays to fit in memory in decreasing order of that ratio until we run out of memory. We leave more sophisticated heuristics to future work.

4.2.2 Shared-nothing Parallelism

It is trivial to parallelize Materialize and Stream (and Stream-Reuse) since most parallel data processing systems such as parallel RDBMSs and Hive already provide parallel joins. The only requirement is that the aggregations needed for BGD need to be *algebraic* [16]. But since both F and ∇F are just sums across tuples, they are indeed algebraic. Hence, by implementing them using the parallel user-defined aggregate function abstraction provided by Hive [1] (and most parallel RDBMSs), we can directly leverage existing parallelism infrastructure [13].

FL needs a bit more attention. All three of its steps can also be implemented using parallel UDAFs, But merging independent copies of **H** requires reinserting the individual entries, rather than just summing them up. Also, since **H** is $O(n_R)$ in size, we might exceed available memory when multiple aggregation states are merged. While this issue might

[5]Hybrid hash requires a more complex analysis and we leave it for future work. But note that GRACE and hybrid hash have similar performance in low memory settings [31].

be resolved in Hadoop automatically by spilling to disk, a faster alternative might be to employ the FLP strategy – by using the degree of parallelism and available memory on each node, we pre-partition the inputs and process each partition in parallel separately. Of course, another alternative is to employ FLSQL or FLSQL+, and leave it to Hive to manage the intermediate tables that correspond to **H** in FL. While these strategies might be slightly slower than FLP, they are much easier to implement. We leave a detailed comparison of alternatives that take communication costs into consideration to future work.

5. EXPERIMENTS

We present empirical and analytical results comparing the performance all our approaches to learn over joins against Materialize. Our goal in this section is three-fold: (1) Get a high-level picture of the tradeoff space using our analytical cost models. (2) Drill down deeper into the relative performance of various approaches using our implementations and also validate the accuracy of our cost models. (3) Evaluate the efficiency and effectiveness of each of our extensions.

Data. Unfortunately, publicly-available large real (labeled) datasets for ML tasks are rare [6]. And to the best of our knowledge, there is no publicly-available large real database with the key-foreign key relationship we study. Nevertheless, since this paper focuses on performance at scale, synthetic datasets are a reasonable option, and we use this approach. The ranges of dimensions for our datasets are modeled on the real datasets that we found in practice. Our synthesizer samples examples based on a random class boundary (for binary classification with LR) and adds some random noise. The codes for our synthesizer and all our implementations are available for download from our project webpage.[6]

5.1 High-level Performance Picture

We compare the end-to-end performance of all approaches in a single-node RDBMS setting. Using our analytical cost models, we vary the buffer memory and plot the I/O, CPU, and total runtimes of all approaches to get a high-level picture of the tradeoff space. Figure 4 presents the results.

The plots show interesting high-level differences in the behavior of all the approaches. To help explain their behavior, we classify memory into three major regions: the hash table on **R** does not fit in memory (we call this the *relative-small-memory*, or RSM region), the hash table on **R** does fit in memory but **S** does not (*relative-medium-memory*, or RMM), and when all tables comfortably fit in memory (*relative-large-memory*, or RLM). These three regions roughly correspond to the three parts of the curve for S in Figure 4. Factorize (FL) seems the fastest in all three regions for this particular set of parameter values. At RSM, Stream (S) is slower than Materialize (M) due to repeated repartitioning. Stream-Reuse (SR), which avoids repartitioning, is faster, and is comparable to FL. But at RMM, we see a crossover and S is faster than M since M needs to read a larger table. Since no partitioning is needed, SR is comparable to S, while FL is slightly faster. At RLM, we see another crossover and M becomes slightly faster than S (and SR) again, while FL is even faster. This is because the CPU costs dominate at RLM, and M has lower CPU costs than S (and SR). The I/O-CPU breakdown shows that the

[6] http://pages.cs.wisc.edu/~arun/orion

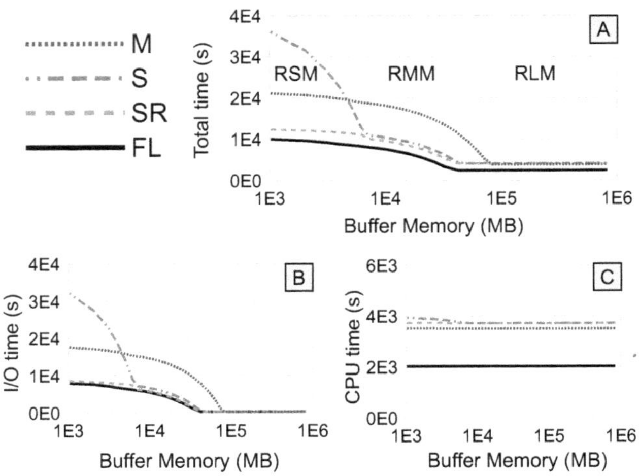

Figure 4: Analytical cost model-based plots for varying the buffer memory (m). (A) Total time, (B) I/O time (with $100MB/s$ I/O rate), and (C) CPU time (with $2.5GHz$ clock). The values fixed are $n_S = 10^8$ (in short, $1E8$), $n_R = 1E7$, $d_S = 40$, $d_R = 60$, and $Iters$ = 20. Note that the x axes are in logscale.

Memory Region	Parameter Varied		
	n_S for n_S / n_R	d_R for d_R / d_S	Iters
RSM	n_R = 5E7, d_S = 40 d_R = 60, Iters = 20	n_S = 5E8, n_R = 5E7 d_S = 40, Iters = 20	n_S = 5E8, n_R = 5E7 d_S = 40, d_R = 60
RMM	n_R = 1E7, d_S = 40 d_R = 60, Iters = 20	n_S = 1E8, n_R = 1E7 d_S = 40, Iters = 20	n_S = 1E8, n_R = 1E7 d_S = 40, d_R = 60
RLM	n_R = 5E6, d_S = 6 d_R = 9, Iters = 20	n_S = 5E7, n_R = 5E6 d_S = 6, Iters = 20	n_S = 5E7, n_R = 5E6 d_S = 6, d_R = 9

Table 4: Parameters used for the single-node setting results in Figure 5. NB: $xEy \equiv x \times 10^y$.

overall trends mirror the I/O costs at RSM and RMM but mirrors the CPU costs at RLM. Figure 4(C) shows that FL has a lower CPU cost by a factor that roughly equals the redundancy ratio (≈ 2.1). But as expected, the difference is slightly lower since FL performs extra computations to manage an associative array.

5.2 Performance Drill Down

Staying with the single-node RDBMS setting, we now drill down deeper into each memory region and study the effect of the major dataset and algorithm parameters using our implementations. For each memory region, we vary each of three major parameters – tuple ratio ($\frac{n_S}{n_R}$), feature ratio ($\frac{d_R}{d_S}$), and number of BGD iterations ($Iters$) – one at a time, while fixing all the others. We use a decaying stepsize (α) rather than a line search for simplicity of exposition. Thus, $Iters$ is also the actual number of passes over the dataset [13, 26]. Finally, we assess whether our cost models are able to accurately predict the observed performance trends and discuss some practical implications.

Experimental Setup: All four approaches were prototyped on top of PostgreSQL (9.2.1) using UDAFs written in C and control code written in Python. The experiments were run

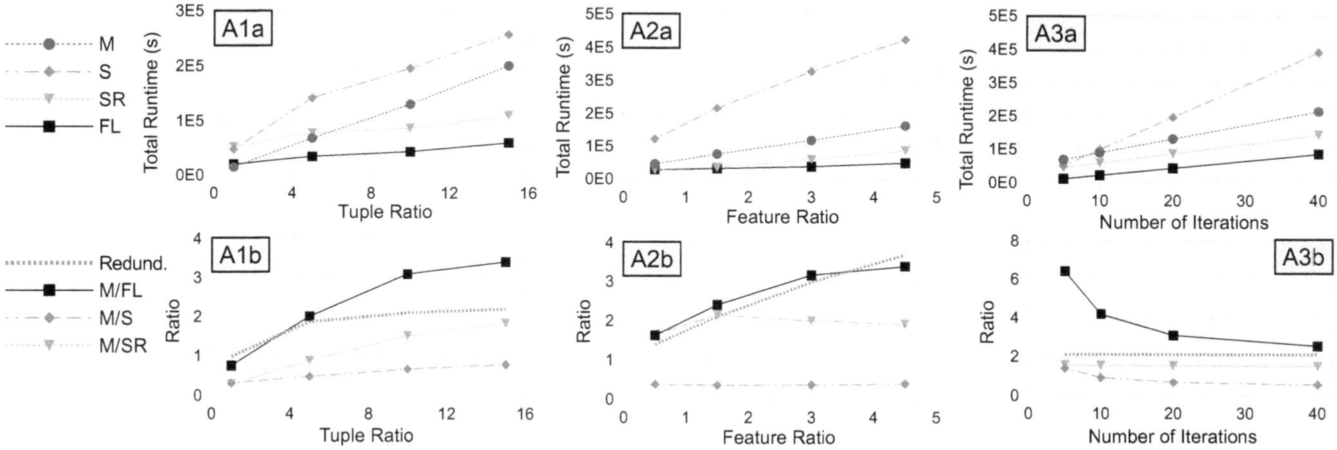

(A) RSM: Total runtimes and relative performance (speedup) against M and redundancy ratios.

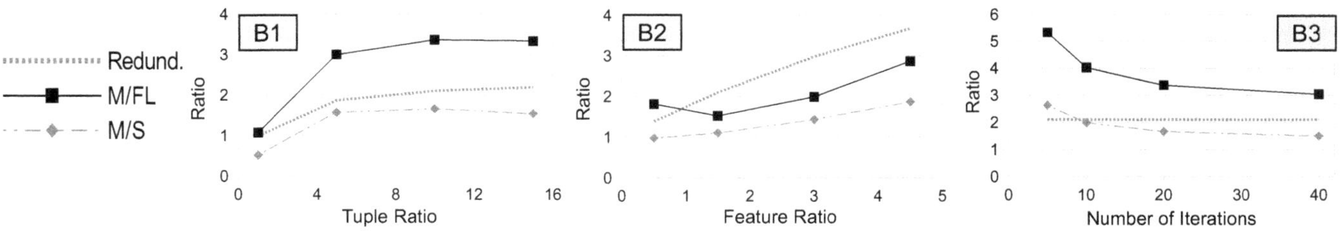

(B) RMM: Relative performance (speedup) against M and redundancy ratios.

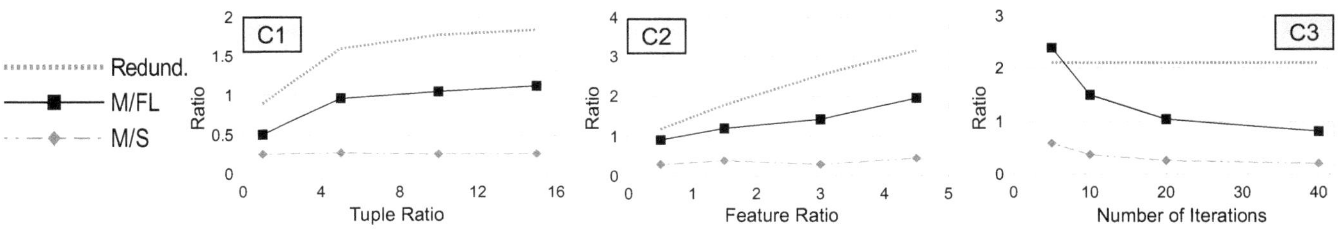

(C) RLM: Relative performance (speedup) against M and redundancy ratios.

Figure 5: Implementation-based performance against each of (1) tuple ratio ($\frac{n_S}{n_R}$), (2) feature ratio ($\frac{d_R}{d_S}$), and (3) number of iterations ($Iters$) – separated column-wise – for the (A) RSM, (B) RMM, and (C) RLM memory region – separated row-wise. SR is skipped for RMM and RLM since its runtime is very similar to S. The other parameters are fixed as per Table 4.

on machines with Intel Xeon X5650 2.67GHz CPUs, 24GB RAM, 1TB disk, and Linux 2.6.18-194.3.1.el5. The dataset sizes are chosen to fit each memory region's criteria.

Results: The implementation-based runtimes and speedup (and redundancy) ratios for RSM are plotted in Figure 5(A). The corresponding parameter values chosen (for those parameters that are not varied) are presented in Table 4. We present the corresponding speedup ratios for RMM in Figure 5(B) and for RLM in Figure 5(C). Due to space constraints, we skip the runtime plots for RMM and RLM here but present them in the appendix.

- **RSM:** The plots in Figure 5(A) shows that S is the slowest in most cases, followed by the state-of-the-art approach, M. SR is significantly faster than M, while FL is the fastest. This trend is seen across a wide range of values for all 3 parameters – tuple ratio, feature ratio, and number of iterations. All the approaches seem to scale almost linearly with each parameter. Figure 5(A1a) shows a small region where SR is slower than M. This arises because the cost of partitioning both **R** and **S** is slightly more than the cost of materializing **T** at low tuple ratios. In many cases, the performance of SR is comparable to FL, even though the latter performs an extra read of **R** to compute ∇F. The speedup plots show that the speedup of FL over M is mostly higher than the redundancy ratio (r) – this is because the cost of materializing **T** is ignored by r. Figure 5(A3b) confirms this reason as it shows the speedup dropping with iterations since the cost of materialization gets amortized. In contrast, the speedups of SR over M are mostly lower than r.
- **RMM:** The plots in Figure 5(B) show that S could become faster than M (as predicted by Figure 4). SR (skipped here for brevity) is roughly as fast as S, since

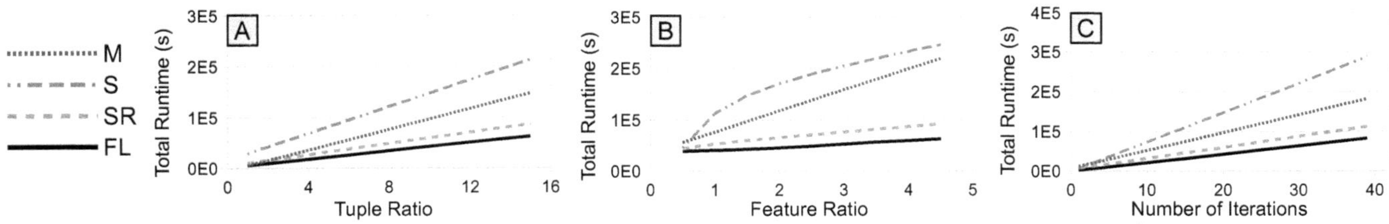

Figure 6: Analytical cost model-based plots of performance against each of (A) $\frac{n_S}{n_R}$, (B) $\frac{d_R}{d_S}$, and (C) $Iters$ for the RSM region. The other parameters are fixed as per Table 4.

no partitioning occurs. FL is the fastest in most cases, but interestingly, Figure 5(B2) shows that the speedup of FL over M is lower than the redundancy ratio for larger feature ratios. This is because $|\mathbf{R}|$ increases and FL reads it twice, which means its relative runtime increases faster than the redundancy ratio.

- **RLM:** The plots in Figure 5(C) show that M is faster than S again. Interestingly, the speedup of FL over M is smaller than r in most cases. In fact, Figures 5(C1,C2) show that M is faster than FL at low dimension ratios (but slower at higher ratios). Figure 5(C3) shows that the amortization of materialization cost could pay off for large values of $Iters$. The lower speedup of FL occurs because all the data fit in memory and the runtime depends mainly on the CPU costs. Thus, the relative cost of managing $\mathbf{H}$ in FL for each iteration (note that M needs to write $\mathbf{T}$ only once) against the cost of BGD's computations for each iteration determines the relative performance. This is also why S (and SR) are much slower than M. Since the CPU cost of BGD increases with the dimension ratios, FL, which reduces the computations for BGD, is faster than M at higher values of both ratios.

Cost Model Accuracy. Our main goal for our analytical models was to understand the fine-grained behavior of each approach and to enable us to quickly explore the relative performance trends of them all for different parameter settings. Thus, we now verify if our models predicted the trends correctly. Figure 6 presents the performance results predicted by our cost models for the RSM region. A comparison of the respective plots of Figure 5(A) with Figure 6 shows that the runtime trends of each approach are largely predicted correctly, irrespective of what parameter is varied. As predicted by our models, crossovers occur between M and S at low $Iters$, between M and SR at low tuple ratios, and between M and FL at low tuple ratios. We found similar trends for RMM and RLM as well but due to space constraints, we present their plots in the appendix.

Since no single approach dominates all others, we also verify if our cost model can predict the fastest approach correctly. We found that, overall, it correctly predicts the fastest approach in 95% of the cases shown in Figure 5. The accuracy of the predicted runtimes, however, varies across approaches and memory regions. For example, the standard R^2 score for FL on RMM is 0.77, while that for SR on RSM is 0.27. Similarly the median percentage error for FL on RSM is 14%, while that for S on RLM is 73%. Due to space constraints, we present more details in the appendix. We think it is interesting future work to improve the absolute accuracy of our cost model, say, by making our models more fine-grained, and by performing a more careful calibration.

Discussion. We briefly discuss a few practical aspects of our proposed approaches.

Application in a System: Recent systems such as Columbus [20, 33] and MLBase [21] provide a high-level language that includes both relational and ML operations. Such systems optimize the execution of logical ML computations by choosing among alternative physical plans using cost models. While we leave it to future work, we think it is possible to apply our ideas for learning over joins by integrating our cost models with their optimizers. An alternative way is to create hybrid approaches, say, like the hybrid of SR and FL that we present in the appendix. The disadvantage is that it is more complex to implement. It is also not clear if it is possible to create a "super-hybrid" that combines FL with both SR and M. We leave a detailed study of hybrid approaches to future work.

Convergence: The number of iterations ($Iters$) parameter might be unknown a priori if we use a convergence criterion for BGD such as the relative decrease in loss. To the best of our knowledge, there is no proven technique to predict the number of iterations for a given quality criterion for any gradient method. While Figures 5(A3b,B3,C3) show that FL is faster irrespective of $Iters$, crossovers might occur for other parameter values. In cases where crossovers are possible, we think a "dynamic" optimizer that tracks the costs of many approaches might be able switch to a faster approach after a particular iteration.

Summary. Our results with both implementations and cost models show that Factorize can be significantly faster than the state-of-the-art Materialize, but is not always the fastest. Stream is often, but not always, faster than Materialize, while Stream-Reuse is faster than Stream and sometimes comparable to Factorize. A combination of the buffer memory, dataset dimensions, and the number of BGD iterations affects which approach is the fastest. Our cost models largely predict the trends correctly and achieve high accuracy in predicting the fastest approach. Thus, they could be used by an optimizer to handle learning over joins.

5.3 Evaluation of Extensions

We now focus on evaluating the efficiency and effectiveness of each of our extensions – scaling FL to large values of n_R, multi-table joins for FL, and shared-nothing parallelism.

5.3.1 Scaling FL along n_R

Using our analytical cost models, we now compare the performance of our three extensions to FL when $\mathbf{H}$ cannot fit in memory. Note that $|\mathbf{H}| \approx 34n_R$ bytes, which implies that for $m = 24$GB, FL can scale up to $n_R \approx 750E6$. Attribute tables seldom have so many tuples (unlike entity tables).

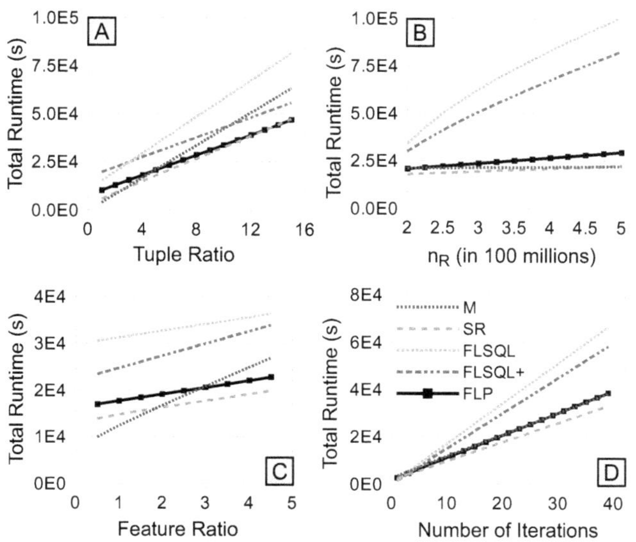

Figure 7: Analytical plots for when m is insufficient for FL. We assume m = 4GB, and plot the runtime against each of n_S, d_R, $Iters$, and n_R, while fixing the others. Wherever they are fixed, we set $(n_S, n_R, d_S, d_R, Iters) = (1E9, 2E8, 2, 6, 20)$.

Set	I/O Cost	M	FL		
			PA	GH	OP
1	Partitioning	1,384	171	31	28
	Iters = 10	4,745	2,098	1,959	1,955
2	Partitioning	3,039	338	164	145
	Iters = 10	10,239	3,941	3,766	3,748

Table 5: I/O costs (in 1000s of 1 MB pages) for multi-table joins. Set 1 has $k = 5$, i.e., 5 attribute tables, while Set 2 has $k = 10$. We set $n_S = 2E8$, $d_S = 10$, while n_i and d_i $(i > 0)$ range from $1E7$ to $6E7$ and 35 to 120 respectively. We set $m = 4$GB.

Hence, we use a smaller value of $m = 4$GB. We also vary n_R for this comparison. Figure 7 presents the results.

The first observation is that FLSQL is the slowest in most cases, while FLSQL+ is slightly faster. But, as suspected, there is a crossover between these two at low tuple ratios. More suprisingly, FLP and SR have similar performance across a wide range of all parameters (within this low memory setting), with SR being slightly faster at high feature ratios, while M becomes faster at low feature ratios.

5.3.2 Multi-table Joins for FL

We compare three alternative approaches to solve FL-MULTJOIN using our analytical cost model – Partition-All (PA), a baseline heuristic that partitions all $\mathbf{R}_i$ in $O(k)$ time, Optimal (OP), which solves the problem exactly in $O(2^k)$ time, and the $O(klog(k))$ time greedy heuristic (GH). We perform this experiment for two different sets of inputs: one with $k = 5$ and the other with $k = 10$, with a range of different sizes for all the tables. We report the I/O costs for the plan output by each approach. Table 5 presents the results.

For Set 1 ($k = 5$), PA has a partitioning cost that is nearly 6 times that of OP. But GH is only about 12% higher than OP, and both GH and OP partition only one of the five attribute tables. As expected, PA closes the gap on total cost as we start running iterations for BGD. At $Iters = 10$, PA has only 7% higher cost than OP, whereas M is 140% higher. A similar trend is seen for Set 2, with the major difference being that the contribution of the partitioning cost to the total cost becomes higher for both GH and OP, since they partition six out of the ten attribute tables.

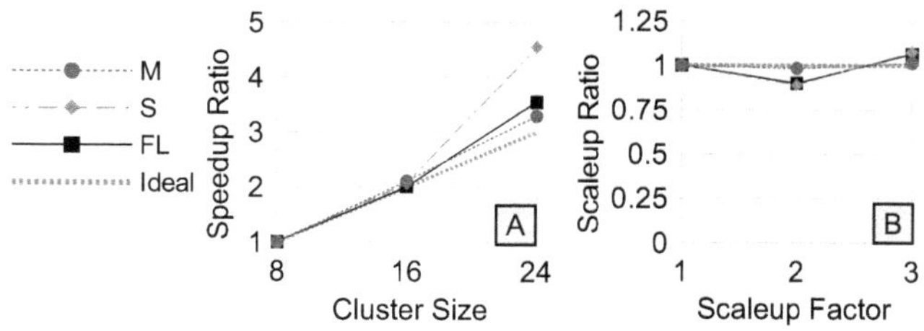

Figure 8: Parallelism with Hive. (A) Speedup against cluster size (number of worker nodes) for $(n_S, n_R, d_S, d_R, Iters) = (15E8, 5E6, 40, 120, 20)$. Each approach is compared to itself, e.g., FL on 24 nodes is 3.5x faster than FL on 8 nodes. The runtimes on 24 nodes were 7.4h for S, 9.5h for FL, and 23.5h for M. (B) Scaleup as both the cluster and dataset size are scaled. The inputs are the same as for (A) for 8 nodes, while n_S is scaled. Thus, the size of T varies from 0.6TB to 1.8TB.

5.3.3 Shared-nothing Parallelism

We compare our Hive implementations of M, S, and FL.[7] Our goal is to verify if similar runtime tradeoffs as for the RDBMS setting apply here, and also measure the speedups and scaleups. The setup is a 25-node Hadoop cluster, where each node has two 2.1GHz Intel Xeon processors, 88GB RAM, 2.4TB disk space, and runs Windows Server 2012. The datasets synthesized are written to HDFS with a replication factor of three.[8] Figure 8 presents the results.

Figure 8(A) shows that all three approaches achieve near-linear speedups. The speedups of S and FL are slightly super-linear primarily because more of the data fits in the aggregate memory of a larger cluster, which makes an iterative algorithm such as BGD faster. Interestingly, S is comparable to FL on 8 nodes (S takes 33.5h, and FL, 33.8h), and is faster than FL on 24 nodes (7.4h for S, and 9.5h for FL). Using the Hive query plans and logs, we found that FL spends more time (16%) on Hive startup overheads than S (7%) since it needs more MapReduce jobs. Nevertheless, both S and FL are significantly faster than M, which takes 76.7h on 8 nodes and 23.5h on 24 nodes. We also verified that FL could be faster than S on different inputs. For example, for $(n_S, n_R, d_S, d_R) = (1E9, 100, 20, 2000)$ on 8 nodes, FL is 4.2x faster than S. Thus, while the exact crossover points are different, the runtime tradeoffs are similar to the RDBMS setting in that FL dominates M and S as the redundancy ratio increases. Of course, the runtimes could be better on a different system, and a more complex cost model that includes communication and startup costs might be able to

[7] Due to engineering issues in how we can use Hive's APIs, we use FLSQL+ instead of FLP for FL in some cases.

[8] Although the aggregate RAM was slightly more than the raw data size, not all of the data fit in memory. This is due to implementation overheads in Hive and Hadoop that resulted in Hive using an aggregate of 1.2TB for a replicated hash table created by its broadcast hash join implementation.

predict the trends. We consider this as an interesting avenue for future work. Figure 8(B) shows that all approaches achieve near-linear scaleups. Overall, we see that similar runtime tradeoffs as for the RDBMS setting apply, and that our approaches achieve near-linear speedups and scaleups.

6. RELATED WORK

We now discuss how our problem and our approaches are related to prior work in the literature.

Factorized computation: The abstraction of factorized databases was proposed recently to improve the efficiency of RDBMSs [8]. The basic idea is to succintly represent relations with join dependencies using algebraically equivalent forms that store less data physically. By exploiting the distributivity of Cartesian product over a union of sets, they enable faster computation of relational operations over such databases. However, as they admit, their techniques apply only to in-memory datasets. Our work can be seen as a special case that only has key-foreign key joins. We extend the general idea of factorized computation to ML algorithms over joins. Furthermore, our work considers datasets that may not fit in memory. We explore the whole tradeoff space and propose new approaches that were either not considered for, or are inapplicable to, relational operations. For example, the iterative nature of BGD for learning GLMs enables us to design the Stream-Reuse approach. Recent work [28] has also shown that combining features from multiple tables can improve ML model quality, and that factorizing computations can improve efficiency. They focus on a specific ML algorithm named factorization machine that is used for a recommendation systems application. Using a simple abstraction called "block-structured dataset" that encodes the redundancy information in the data, they reduce computations. However, as they admit, their techniques apply only to in-memory datasets. We observe that designing block-structured datasets essentially requires joins of the base tables – a problem not recognized in [28]. Hence, we take a first-principles approach towards the problem of learning over joins. By harnessing prior work from the database literature, and avoiding explicit encoding of redundancy information, we handle datasets that may not fit in memory. We devise multiple approaches that apply to a large class of ML models (GLMs) and also extend them to a parallel setting. Finally, our empirical results show that factorizing computation for ML may not always be the fastest approach, necessitating a cost model such as ours.

Query optimization: As noted in [8], factorized computations generalize prior work on optimizing SQL aggregates over joins [10, 32]. While BGD over joins is similar at a high level to executing a `SUM` over joins, there are major differences that necessitate new techniques. First, BGD aggregates feature vectors, not single features. Thus, BGD requires more complex statistics and rearrangement of computations as achieved by factorized learning. Second, BGD is iterative, resulting in novel interplays with the join algorithm, e.g., the Stream-Reuse approach. Finally, there exist non-commutative algorithms such as Stochastic Gradient Descent (SGD) that might require new and more complex tradeoffs. While we leave SGD for future work, this paper provides a framework for designing and evalutating solutions for that problem. Learning over joins is also similar in spirit to multi-query optimization (MQO) in which the system optimizes the execution of a bunch of queries that are presented together [30]. Our work deals with join queries that have sequential dependencies due to the iterative nature of BGD, not a bunch of queries presented together.

Analytics systems: There are many commercial and open-source toolkits that provide scalable ML and data mining algorithms [2, 18]. However, they all focus on implementations of individual algorithms, not on pushing ML algorithms through joins. There is increasing research and industrial interest in building systems that achieve closer integration of ML with data processing. These include systems that combine linear algebra-based languages with data management platforms [4, 15, 34], systems for Bayesian inference [9], systems for graph-based ML [23], and systems that combine dataflow-based languages for ML with data management platforms [21, 22, 33]. None of these systems address the problem of learning over joins, but we think our work is easily applicable to the last group of systems. We hope our work contributes to more research in this direction. Analytics systems that provide incremental maintenance over evolving data for some ML models have been studied before [19, 25]. However, neither of those papers address learning over joins. It is interesting future work to study the interplay between these two problems.

7. CONCLUSION AND FUTURE WORK

Key-foreign key joins are often required prior to applying ML on real-world datasets. The state-of-the-art approach of materializing the join output before learning introduces redundancy avoided by normalization, which could result in poor end-to-end performance in addition to storage and maintenance overheads. In this work, we study the problem of learning over a join in order to avoid such redundancy. Focusing on generalized linear models solved using batch gradient descent, we propose several alternative approaches to learn over a join that are also easy to implement over existing RDMBSs. We introduce a new approach named factorized learning that pushes the ML computations through a join and avoids redundancy in both I/O and computations. Using analytical cost models and real implementations on PostgreSQL, we show that factorized learning is often substantially faster than the alternatives, but is not always the fastest, necessitating a cost-based approach. We also extend all our approaches to multi-table joins as well as a shared nothing parallel setting such as Hive.

With increasing research and industrial interest in closely integrating advanced analytics with data processing, we think our work lays a foundation for more research on integrating ML with relational operations in the context of feature engineering. As for future work, we are working on extending factorized learning to other popular algorithms to solve GLMs such as stochastic gradient descent and coordinate descent methods. Another area is pushing other popular ML techniques such as non-linear SVMs, decision trees, neural networks, and clustering algorithms through joins. Since the data access behavior of these techniques might differ from that of GLMs with BGD, it is not clear if it is straightforward to extend our ideas to these techniques. We also intend to formally analyze the effects of the redundancy introduced by database dependencies on ML algorithms. Finally, we intend to expand the scope of the problem to consider aggregate queries as well as the task of feature selection.

8. REFERENCES

[1] Apache Hive. hive.apache.org.
[2] Apache Mahout. mahout.apache.org.
[3] IBM Report. www-01.ibm.com/software/data/bigdata/.
[4] Oracle R Enterprise.
[5] SAS Report on Analytics. sas.com/reg/wp/corp/23876.
[6] A. Agarwal et al. A Reliable Effective Terascale Linear Learning System. *JMLR*, 15:1111–1133, 2014.
[7] M. Anderson et al. Brainwash: A Data System for Feature Engineering. In *CIDR*, 2013.
[8] N. Bakibayev et al. Aggregation and Ordering in Factorised Databases. In *VLDB*, 2013.
[9] Z. Cai et al. Simulation of Database-valued Markov Chains Using SimSQL. In *SIGMOD*, 2013.
[10] S. Chaudhuri and K. Shim. Including Group-By in Query Optimization. In *VLDB*, 1994.
[11] G. B. Dantzig. Discrete-Variable Extremum Problems. *Operations Research*, 5(2):pp. 266–277, 1957.
[12] S. Das et al. Ricardo: Integrating R and Hadoop. In *SIGMOD*, 2010.
[13] X. Feng, A. Kumar, B. Recht, and C. Ré. Towards a Unified Architecture for in-RDBMS Analytics. In *SIGMOD*, 2012.
[14] M. R. Garey and D. S. Johnson. *Computers and Intractability: A Guide to the Theory of NP-Completeness.* W. H. Freeman & Co., 1979.
[15] A. Ghoting et al. SystemML: Declarative Machine Learning on MapReduce. In *ICDE*, 2011.
[16] J. Gray et al. Data Cube: A Relational Aggregation Operator Generalizing Group-By, Cross-Tab, and Sub-Totals. *Data Min. Knowl. Discov.*, 1(1):29–53, Jan. 1997.
[17] T. Hastie et al. *The Elements of Statistical Learning: Data mining, Inference, and Prediction.* Springer-Verlag, 2001.
[18] J. Hellerstein et al. The MADlib Analytics Library or MAD Skills, the SQL. In *VLDB*, 2012.
[19] M. L. Koc and C. Ré. Incrementally Maintaining Classification using an RDBMS. In *VLDB*, 2011.
[20] P. Konda, A. Kumar, C. Ré, and V. Sashikanth. Feature Selection in Enterprise Analytics: A Demonstration using an R-based Data Analytics System. In *VLDB*, 2013.
[21] T. Kraska et al. MLbase: A Distributed Machine-learning System. In *CIDR*, 2013.
[22] A. Kumar et al. Hazy: Making it Easier to Build and Maintain Big-data Analytics. *CACM*, 56(3):40–49, March 2013.
[23] Y. Low et al. GraphLab: A New Framework For Parallel Machine Learning. In *UAI*, 2010.
[24] T. M. Mitchell. *Machine Learning.* McGraw Hill, 1997.
[25] M. Nikolic et al. LINVIEW: Incremental View Maintenance for Complex Analytical Queries. In *SIGMOD*, 2014.
[26] J. Nocedal and S. J. Wright. *Numerical Optimization.* Springer, 2006.
[27] R. Ramakrishnan and J. Gehrke. *Database Management Systems.* McGraw-Hill, Inc., New York, NY, USA, 2003.
[28] S. Rendle. Scaling Factorization Machines to Relational Data. In *VLDB*, 2013.
[29] P. G. Selinger et al. Access Path Selection in a Relational Database Management System. In *SIGMOD*, 1979.
[30] T. K. Sellis. Multiple-Query Optimization. *ACM TODS*, 13(1):23–52, Mar. 1988.
[31] L. D. Shapiro. Join Processing in Database Systems with Large Main Memories. *ACM TODS*, 11(3):239–264, Aug. 1986.
[32] W. P. Yan and P.-Å. Larson. Eager Aggregation and Lazy Aggregation. In *VLDB*, 1995.
[33] C. Zhang, A. Kumar, and C. Ré. Materialization Optimizations for Feature Selection Workloads. In *SIGMOD*, 2014.
[34] Y. Zhang, W. Zhang, and J. Yang. I/O-Efficient Statistical Computing with RIOT. In *ICDE*, 2010.

Acknowledgments

We thank David DeWitt, Stephen J. Wright, Robert McCann, Jiexing Li, Bruhathi Sundarmurthy, Wentao Wu, and the members of the Microsoft Jim Gray Systems Lab for their feedback on this paper. This work is supported by a research grant from the Microsoft Jim Gray Systems Lab. All views expressed in this work are that of the authors and do not necessarily reflect any views of Microsoft.

APPENDIX

A. COSTS OF STREAM

I/O Cost. If $(m-1) \leq \lceil f|\mathbf{R}|\rceil$:

```
Iters * [
  (|R| + |S|)              //First read
+ (|R| + |S|).(1 - q)      //Write temp partitions
+ (|R| + |S|).(1 - q)      //Read temp partitions
]
```

If $(m-1) > \lceil f|\mathbf{R}|\rceil$:

```
Iters * [
  (|R| + |S|)
- min{|R|+|S|,(m-1) - f|R|]}.(Iters - 1)
]
```

CPU Cost

```
Iters.[
    (nR+nS).hash              //Partition R and S
  + nR.(1+dR).copy            //Construct hash on R
  + nR.(1+dR).(1-q).copy      //R output partitions
  + nS.(2+dS).(1-q).copy      //S output partitions
  + nR.(1-q).hash             //Hash rest of R
  + nS.(1-q).hash             //Hash rest of S
  + nS.comp.f                 //Probe for all of S
  + nS.d.(mult+add)           //Compute w.xi
  + nS.(funcG+funcF)          //Apply functions
  + nS.d.(mult+add)           //scale and add
  + nS.add                    //Add for total loss
]
```

B. COSTS OF STREAM-REUSE

I/O Cost. If $(m-1) \leq \lceil f|\mathbf{R}|\rceil$:

```
  (|R| + |S|)              //First read
+ (|R| + |S|).(1 - q)      //Write temp partitions
+ (|R| + |S|).(1 - q)      //Read of iter 1
+ (Iters - 1).(|R| + |S|)  //Remaining iterations
- (Iters - 1).min{|R|+|S|,[(m-2) - f|R0|]} //Cache
```

If $(m-1) > \lceil f|\mathbf{R}|\rceil$:

```
  (|R| + |S|)
+ (Iters - 1).|S|
- (Iters - 1).min{|S|,[(m-1) - f|R|]}
```

CPU Cost

```
  (nR+nS).hash            //Partition R and S
+ nR.(1+dR).copy          //Construct hash on R
+ nR.(1+dR).(1-q).copy    //R output partitions
+ nS.(2+dS).(1-q).copy    //S output partitions
+ nR.(1-q).hash           //Hash rest of R
+ nS.(1-q).hash           //Hash rest of S
+ nS.comp.f               //Probe for all of S
+ (Iters-1).[
    nR.hash               //Construct hash on R
  + nR.(1+dR).copy        //Construct hash on R
  + nS.(hash + comp.f)    //Probe for all of S
]
+ Iters.[                   //Compute gradient
    nS.d.(mult+add)         //Compute w.xi
  + nS.(funcG+funcF)        //Apply functoins
  + nS.d.(mult+add)         //Scale and add
  + nS.add                  //Add for total loss
]
```

C. PROOF OF PROPOSITION 4.1

Given $\mathbf{S} = \{(sid, fk, y, \mathbf{x}_S)_i\}_{i=1}^{n_S}$, and $\mathbf{R} = \{(rid, \mathbf{x}_R)_i\}_{i=1}^{n_R}$, with $n_S > n_R$, the output of the join-project query $\mathbf{T} \leftarrow \pi(\mathbf{R} \bowtie_{\mathbf{R}.rid=\mathbf{S}.fk} \mathbf{S})$ is $\mathbf{T} = \{(sid, y, \mathbf{x})_i\}_{i=1}^{n_S}$. Note that sid is the primary key of $\mathbf{S}$ and $\mathbf{T}$, while rid is the primary key of $\mathbf{R}$, and fk is a foreign key in $\mathbf{S}$ that points to sid of $\mathbf{R}$. Denote the joining tuples $s \in \mathbf{S}$ and $r \in \mathbf{R}$ that produce a given $t \in \mathbf{T}$ as $S(t)$ and $R(t)$ respectively. Also given is $\mathbf{w} \in \mathbb{R}^d$, which is split as $\mathbf{w} = [\mathbf{w}_S\ \mathbf{w}_R]$, where $|\mathbf{w}_R| = d_R$.

Materialize and Stream both operate on $\mathbf{T}$ (the only difference is *when* the tuples of $\mathbf{T}$ are produced). Thus, they output identical values of $\nabla F = \sum_{t\in\mathbf{T}} G(t.y, \mathbf{w}^T t.\mathbf{x})t.\mathbf{x}$ and $F = \sum_{t\in\mathbf{T}} F_e(t.y, \mathbf{w}^T t.\mathbf{x})$. Denote their output $(\nabla F^*, F^*)$, with $\nabla F^* = [\nabla F_S^*\ \nabla F_R^*]$, in a manner similar to $\mathbf{w}$.

We first prove that the output F of FL equals F^*. As per the logical workflow of FL (see Figure 3), we have $\mathbf{HR} = \{(rid, pip)_i\}_{i=1}^{n_R}$, s.t. $\forall h \in \mathbf{HR}, \exists r \in \mathbf{R}\ s.t.\ h.rid = r.rid \wedge h.pip = \mathbf{w}_R^T r.\mathbf{x}_R$. Also, we have $\mathbf{U} \leftarrow \pi(\mathbf{HR} \bowtie_{\mathbf{HR}.rid=\mathbf{S}.fk} \mathbf{S})$ expressed as $\mathbf{U} = \{(sid, rid, y, \mathbf{x}_S, pip)_i\}_{i=1}^{n_S}$. FL aggregates $\mathbf{U}$ to compute $F = \sum_{u\in\mathbf{U}} F_e(u.y, (\mathbf{w}_S^T u.\mathbf{x}_S + u.pip))$. But $u.pip = HR(u).pip = \mathbf{w}_R^T R(HR(u)).\mathbf{x}_R$ and $\mathbf{w}_S^T u.\mathbf{x}_S = \mathbf{w}_S^T S(u).\mathbf{x}_S$. Due to their join expressions, we also have that $\forall u \in \mathbf{U}$, there is exactly one $t \in \mathbf{T}\ s.t.\ u.sid = t.sid$, which implies $F_e(u.y, (\mathbf{w}_S^T u.\mathbf{x}_S + u.pip)) = F_e(t.y, \mathbf{w}^T t.\mathbf{x})$. That along with the relationship $\mathbf{w}^T t.\mathbf{x} = \mathbf{w}_S^T S(t).\mathbf{x}_S + \mathbf{w}_R^T R(t).\mathbf{x}_R$ implies $F = F^*$.

Next, we prove that the output ∇F_S of FL equals ∇F_S^*. As $\mathbf{S}$ is scanned, FL scales and aggregates the feature vectors to get $\nabla F_S = \sum_{u\in\mathbf{U}} G(u.y, (\mathbf{w}_S^T u.\mathbf{x}_S + u.pip))\mathbf{x}_S$. Applying the same argument as for F, we have that $\forall u \in \mathbf{U}$, there is exactly one $t \in \mathbf{T}\ s.t.\ u.sid = t.sid$, which implies $G(u.y, (\mathbf{w}_S^T u.\mathbf{x}_S + u.pip)) = G(t.y, \mathbf{w}^T t.\mathbf{x})$, Thus, we have $\nabla F_S = \nabla F_S^*$.

Finally, we prove that the output ∇F_R of FL equals ∇F_R^*. We have the logical relation $\mathbf{HS} \leftarrow \gamma_{SUM(rid)}(\pi(\mathbf{U}))$ as $\mathbf{HS} = \{(rid, fip)_i\}_{i=1}^{n_R}$, obtained by completing the inner products, applying G, and grouping by rid. We have $\forall h \in \mathbf{HS}, h.fip = \sum_{u\in\mathbf{U}:u.rid=h.rid} G(u.y, (\mathbf{w}_S^T u.\mathbf{x}_S + u.pip))$. We then have another relation $\mathbf{V} \leftarrow \pi(\mathbf{HS} \bowtie_{\mathbf{HS}.rid=\mathbf{R}.rid} \mathbf{R})$ as $\mathbf{V} = \{(rid, fip, \mathbf{x}_R)_i\}_{i=1}^{n_R}$. Now, FL simply aggregates $\mathbf{V}$ to compute $\nabla F_R = \sum_{v\in\mathbf{V}} (v.fip)v.\mathbf{x}_R$. Due to their join expressions, we also have that $\forall v \in \mathbf{V}$, there is exactly one $r \in \mathbf{R}\ s.t.\ v.rid = r.rid$. Since rid imposes a partition on $\mathbf{T}$, we define the partition corresponding to v as $\mathbf{T}_v = \{t \in T | t.rid = v.rid\}$. Thus, $v.fip = \sum_{t\in\mathbf{T}_v} G(t.y, \mathbf{w}^T t.\mathbf{x})$, which coupled with the distributivity of product over a sum, implies $\nabla F_R = \nabla F_R^*$. □

D. PROOF OF PROPOSITION 4.2

The proof for FLSQL is identical to FL, since FLSQL simply materializes some intermediate relations, while the proofs for FLSQL+ and FLP are along the same lines. For FLP, we also use the fact that addition is associative over $\mathbb{R}$ and $\mathbb{R}^d$, and both F and ∇F are just sums of terms. □

E. PROOF OF THEOREM 4.1

We restate the FL-MULTJOIN problem and the theorem.

Problem. Given m, k, $\{|\mathbf{R}_i|\}_{i=1}^k$, $\{|\mathbf{HR}_i|\}_{i=1}^k$ as inputs and k binary variables $\{x_i\}$ to optimize over:

$$\max \sum_{i=1}^{k} x_i |\mathbf{R}_i|,\ s.t.\ \sum_{i=1}^{k} x_i(|\mathbf{HR}_i| - 1) \leq m - 1 - k$$

Theorem. FL-MULTJOIN is NP-Hard in l, where $l = |\{i | m - k \geq |\mathbf{HR}_i| > 1\}| \leq k$.

Proof. We prove by a reduction from the 0/1 knapsack problem, which is proven to be NP-Hard. The 0/1 knapsack problem is stated as follows. Given a weight W and n items with respective weights $\{w_i\}$ and values $\{v_i\}$ as inputs and n binary variables $\{z_i\}$ to optimize over, compute $\max \sum_{i=1}^n z_i v_i,\ s.t.\ \sum_{i=1}^n z_i w_i \leq W$. While not necessary, W, $\{w_i\}$, and $\{v_i\}$ are all generally taken to be positive integers. The reduction is obvious now. Set $k = n$, $m = W + k + 1$, $|\mathbf{R}_i| = v_i$ and $|\mathbf{HR}_i| = 1 + w_i, \forall i = 1\ to\ k$. Also, $w_i > W \implies z_i = 0$, while $w_i = 0 \implies z_i = 1$. Thus, the actual size of the knapsack problem is $|\{i | W \geq w_i > 0\}|$, which after reduction becomes $|\{i | m - k \geq |\mathbf{HR}_i| > 1\}| = l$. Thus, FL-MULTJOIN is NP-Hard in l. □

F. ADDITIONAL RUNTIME PLOTS

The implementation-based runtime results for RMM and RLM are presented in Figure 9. The analytical cost model-based plots for the same are in Figure 12. Note that the parameters for both these figures are fixed as per Table 4.

G. CASE $|\mathbf{S}| < |\mathbf{R}|$ OR TUPLE RATIO ≤ 1

In this case, an RDBMS optimizer would probably simply choose to build the hash table on $\mathbf{S}$ instead of $\mathbf{R}$. It is straightforward to extend the models of M, S, and, SR to this case. FL, however, is more interesting. Prima facie, it appears that we can switch the access of the tables – construct $\mathbf{H}$ using $\mathbf{S}$, and join that with $\mathbf{R}$, etc. This way, we need only one scan of $\mathbf{R}$ and two of $\mathbf{S}$. The two twists to the FL approach described earlier are: (1) The associative array must store the SID, RID, Y, and PartialIP. (2) We need to doubly index the array since the first join is on RID with $\mathbf{R}$, while the second is on SID with $\mathbf{S}$. Of course, we could use a different data structure as well. Nevertheless, our plots suggest something subtly different.

First, as long as $n_S > n_R$, even if $|\mathbf{S}| < |\mathbf{R}|$, it might still be beneficial to construct $\mathbf{H}$ using $\mathbf{R}$ first as before. This is because the other approaches still perform redundant computations, and FL might still be faster. Figure 10 presents the runtimes for such a setting for varying values of buffer memory as well as the other parameters. The figures confirm our observations above. Of course, it is possible that the above modified version of FL might be faster than the original verion in some cases.

Second, when $n_S \leq n_R$ (irrespective of the sizes of $\mathbf{R}$ and $\mathbf{S}$), there is probably little redundancy in the computations, which means that Materialize is probably the fastest approach. This is because FL performs unnecessary computations on $\mathbf{R}$, viz., with tuples that do not have a joining tuple in $\mathbf{S}$. The above modified version of FL might also be slower than Materialize since the latter obtains a new dataset that probably has almost no redundancy. Figure 11 presents the runtimes for such a setting for varying values of buffer memory as well as the other parameters. The figures confirm our observations above. Of course, in the above, we have implicitly assumed that at most 1 tuple in $\mathbf{S}$ joins with a tuple in $\mathbf{R}$. If we have multiple tuples in $\mathbf{S}$ joining with $\mathbf{R}$, Materialize might still have computational redundancy. In such cases, a more complex hybrid of Materialize and FL might be faster, and we leave the design of such a hybrid approach to future work.

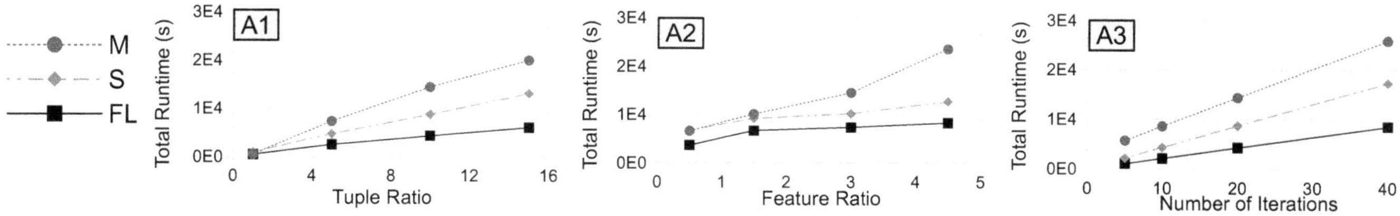

(A) RMM: Total runtimes.

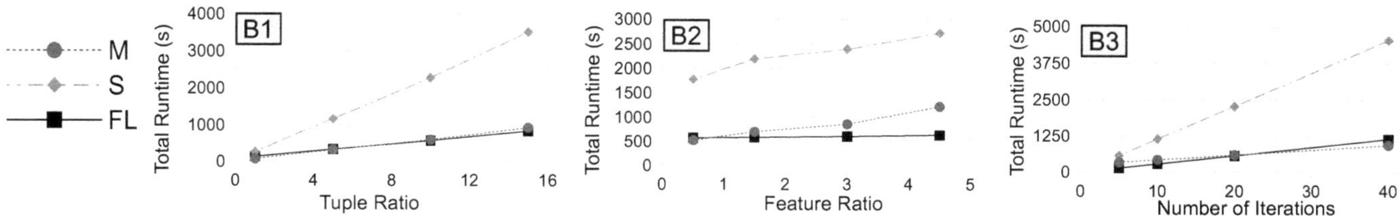

(B) RLM: Total runtimes.

Figure 9: Implementation-based performance against each of (1) tuple ratio ($\frac{n_S}{n_R}$), (2) feature ratio ($\frac{d_R}{d_S}$), and (3) number of iterations (*Iters*) – separated column-wise – for (A) RMM, and (B) RLM – separated row-wise. SR is skipped since its runtime is very similar to S. The other parameters are fixed as per Table 4.

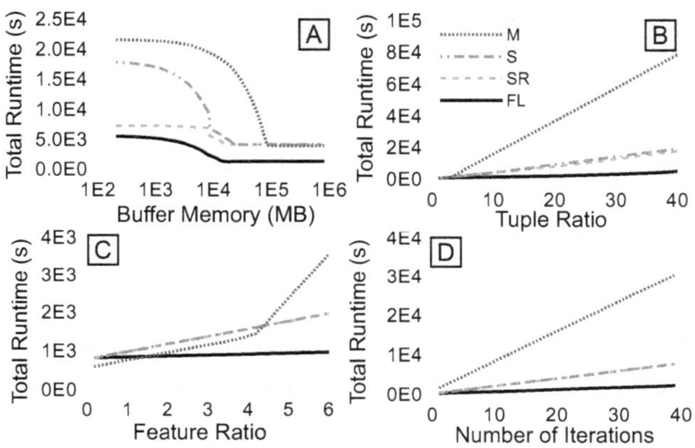

Figure 10: Analytical plots for the case when $|\mathbf{S}| < |\mathbf{R}|$ but $n_S > n_R$. We plot the runtime against each of m, n_S, d_R, $Iters$, and n_R, while fixing the others. Wherever they are fixed, we set $(m, n_S, n_R, d_S, d_R, Iters) = (24GB, 1E8, 1E7, 6, 100, 20)$.

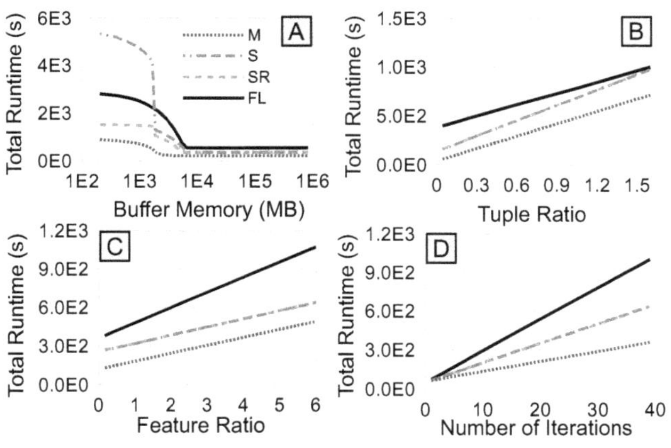

Figure 11: Analytical plots for the case when $n_S \leq n_R$ (mostly). We plot the runtime against each of m, n_S, d_R, $Iters$, and n_R, while fixing the others. Wherever they are fixed, we set $(m, n_S, n_R, d_S, d_R, Iters) = (24GB, 2E7, 5E7, 6, 9, 20)$.

H. MORE COMPLEX APPROACHES

These approaches are more complex to implement since they might require changes to the join implementations.

H.1 Stream-Reuse-Rock (SRR)

1. Similar to Stream-Reuse.
2. Only twist is that for alternate iterations, we flip the order of processing the splits from $0 \to B$ to $B \to 0$ and back so as to enable the hash table in cache to be reused across iterations ("rocking the hash-cache").

I/O Cost. If $(m-1) \leq \lceil f|\mathbf{R}| \rceil$:

```
I/O Cost of Stream-Reuse
+ (Iters - 1).min{|R|+|S|,[(m-2) - f|R_0|]}    //Cache
- ⌊Iters/2⌋.[|R_i| + min{|R|+|S|,(m-2)-f|R_i|}]    //H(R_B)
- ⌊(Iters-1)/2⌋.[|R_0| + min{|R|+|S|,(m-2)-f|R_0|}] //H(R_0)
```

If $(m-1) > \lceil f|\mathbf{R}| \rceil$:

```
I/O Cost of Stream-Reuse
```

SRR also makes the join implementation "iteration-aware".

CPU Cost

```
CPU Cost of Stream-Reuse
- ⌊Iters/2⌋.[                 //Cache HASH(R_B)
  nR.((1-q)/B).[hash + (1+dR).copy]
]
- ⌊(Iters-1)/2⌋.[             //Cache HASH(R_0)
  nR.q.[hash + (1+dR).copy]
]
```

H.2 Hybrid of Stream-Reuse-Rock and Factorize (SFH)

1. Let $\mathbf{R}'$ be an augmentation of $\mathbf{R}$ with two columns padded to store statistics. So, $|\mathbf{R}'| = \left\lceil \frac{8n_R \cdot (1+d_R+2)}{p} \right\rceil$.
2. Let $B = \left\lceil \frac{f|\mathbf{R}'|-(m-1)}{(m-1)-1} \right\rceil$. Let $|\mathbf{R}'_0| = \left\lfloor \frac{(m-2)-B}{f} \right\rfloor$, $|\mathbf{R}'_i| = \left\lceil \frac{|\mathbf{R}'|-|\mathbf{R}'_0|}{B} \right\rceil (1 \leq i \leq B)$, and $q = \frac{|\mathbf{R}'_0|}{|\mathbf{R}'|}$.
3. Similar to hybrid hash join on $\mathbf{R}'$ and $\mathbf{S}$.

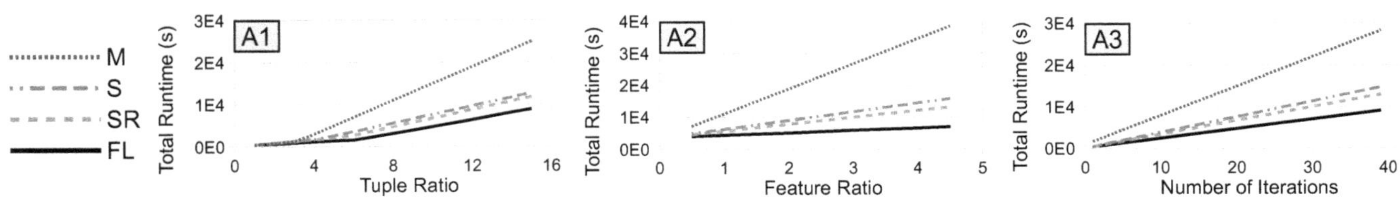

(A) RMM: Total runtimes.

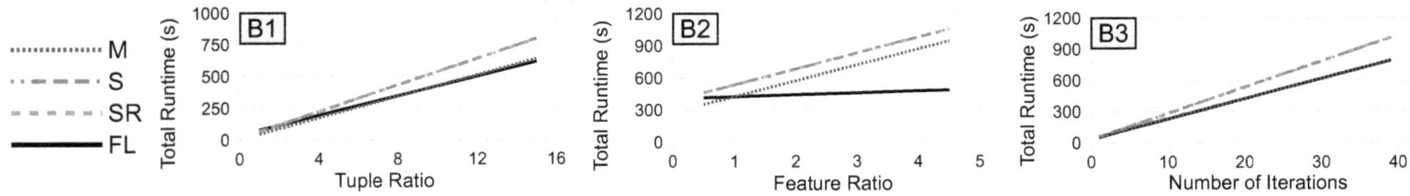

(B) RLM: Total runtimes.

Figure 12: Analytical plots of runtime against each of (1) $\frac{n_S}{n_R}$, (2) $\frac{d_R}{d_S}$, and (3) $Iters$, for both the (A) RMM, and (B) RLM memory regions. The other parameters are fixed as per Table 4.

4. Only twist is that PartialIP from $\mathbf{R}'_i$ is computed when the $\mathbf{H}$ is constructed on $\mathbf{R}_i$, while SumScaledIP is computed when $\mathbf{S}_i$ is read.
5. Repeat for remaining iterations, reusing the same partitions and rocking the hash-cache as in SRR.

We omit the I/O and CPU costs of SFH here since they are easily derviable from the other approaches.

I. COST MODEL ACCURACY DETAILS

Table 6 presents the discrete prediction accuracy, i.e., how often our cost model predicted the fastest approach correctly for each experiment and memory region corresponding to the results of Figure 5. This quantity matters because a typical cost-based optimizer uses a cost model only to predict the fastest approach. Table 7 presents the standard R^2 score for predicting the absolute runtimes. We split them by approach and memory region because the models are different for each. Similarly, Table 8 presents the mean and median percentage error in the predictions.

Experiment	RSM	RMM	RLM	
Tuple Ratio	75%	75%	100%	83%
Feature Ratio	100%	100%	100%	100%
Iterations	100%	100%	100%	100%
	92%	92%	100%	**95%**

Table 6: Discrete prediction accuracy of cost model.

Approach	RSM	RMM	RLM
Materialize	0.65	0.23	0.65
Stream	0.55	0.88	-1.2
Stream-Reuse	0.27	–	–
Factorize	0.77	0.77	0.67

Table 7: Standard R^2 scores for predicting runtimes.

J. COMPARING GRADIENT METHODS

While our focus in this paper has been on performance at scale for learning over joins, we briefly mention an interesting finding regarding the behavior of different gradient methods on a dataset with the redundancy that we study. This particular experiment is agnostic to the approach we use to learn over the join. Figure 13 plots the loss for three popular gradient methods for LR – BGD, CGD, and LBFGS – against the number of iterations and the number of passes. As expected, BGD takes more iterations to reach a similar loss as CGD. However, the behavior of LBFGS (with five gradients saved to approximate the Hessian) is more perplexing. Typically, LBFGS is known to converge faster than CGD in terms of number of iterations [6,26] but we observe otherwise on this dataset. We also observe that LBFGS performs many extra passes to tune the stepsize, making it slower than even BGD in this case. However, it is possible that a different stepsize tuning strategy might make LBFGS faster. While we leave a formal explanation to future work, we found that the Hessians obtained had high condition numbers, which we speculate might make LBFGS less appealing [26].

Approach	RSM	RMM	RLM
Materialize	33% / 30%	33% / 23%	31% / 29%
Stream	33% / 30%	20% / 16%	73% / 75%
Stream-Reuse	42% / 37%	–	–
Factorize	22% / 14%	26% / 19%	25% / 26%

Table 8: Mean / median percentage error for predicting runtimes.

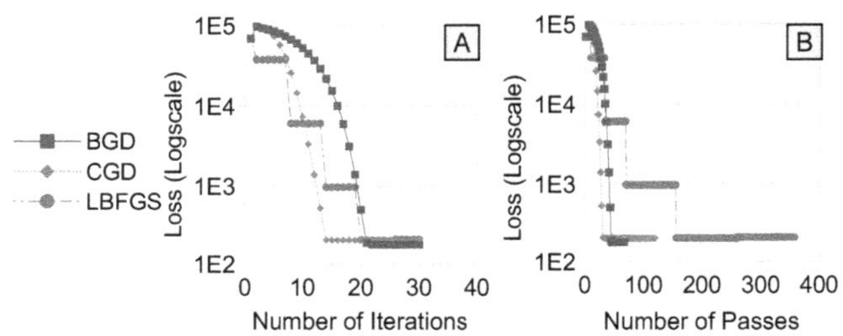

Figure 13: Comparing gradient methods: Batch Gradient Descent (BGD), Conjugate Gradient (CGD), and Limited Memory BFGS (LBFGS) with 5 gradients saved. The parameters are $n_S = 1E5$, $n_R = 1E4$, $d_S = 40$, and $d_R = 60$. (A) Loss after each iteration. (B) Loss after each pass over the data (extra passes needed for line search to tune α).

Utilizing IDs to Accelerate Incremental View Maintenance*

Yannis Katsis
UC San Diego
ikatsis@cs.ucsd.edu

Kian Win Ong
UC San Diego
kianwin@cs.ucsd.edu

Yannis Papakonstantinou
UC San Diego
yannis@cs.ucsd.edu

Kevin Keliang Zhao
UC San Diego
kezhao@cs.ucsd.edu

ABSTRACT

Prior Incremental View Maintenance (IVM) algorithms specify the view tuples that need to be modified by computing diff sets, which we call *tuple-based diffs* since a diff set contains one diff tuple for each to-be-modified view tuple. *idIVM* assumes the base tables have keys and performs IVM by computing *ID-based diff* sets that compactly identify the to-be-modified tuples through their IDs.

This work makes the following contributions: (a) An ID-based IVM system for a large subset of SQL that includes the algebraic operators selection, join, grouping and aggregation, generalized projection involving functions, antisemijoin (and therefore negation/difference) and union. The system is based on a modular approach, allowing one to extend the supported language simply by adding one algebraic operator at-a-time, along with equations describing how ID-based changes are propagated through the operator. (b) An efficient algorithm that creates an IVM plan for a given view in four passes that are polynomial in the size of the view expression. (c) A formal analysis comparing the ID-based IVM algorithm to prior IVM approaches and analytically showing when one outperforms the other. (d) An experimental comparison of the ID-based IVM algorithm to prior IVM algorithms showing the superiority of the former in common use cases.

Categories and Subject Descriptors

H.2 [**Database Management**]: Systems

Keywords

materialized views; incremental view maintenance

1. INTRODUCTION

Materialized views are widely used to speed up query evaluation by storing the results of commonly asked queries. Being materialized, these views have to be brought up to date when the underlying data change. This is typically done through *Incremental View Maintenance (IVM)*. Abstracting out the details of different IVM approaches, a typical IVM algorithm takes as input three diff tables $\mathcal{D}_R^+$, $\mathcal{D}_R^-$ and $\mathcal{D}_R^u$ per base relation R, containing the tuples that were inserted, deleted and updated in R and computes the corresponding diff tables $\mathcal{D}_V^+$, $\mathcal{D}_V^-$ and $\mathcal{D}_V^u$ for the view V, containing the changes that have to be performed on V to bring it up to date.

*Supported by NSF III-1018961 and NSF III-1219263, PI'd by Prof. Papakonstantinou, who has commercial interest in this research. Also supported by NSF III-1117527.

SIGMOD'15, May 31–June 4, 2015, Melbourne, Victoria, Australia.

ACM 978-1-4503-2758-9/15/05 ...$15.00.
http://dx.doi.org/10.1145/2723372.2750546.

```
devices(did, category)
parts(pid, price)
devices_parts(did, pid)
```

(a) Database schema

```
CREATE VIEW V AS
SELECT did, pid, price
FROM parts NATURAL JOIN
  devices_parts NATURAL JOIN
  devices
WHERE category = "phone"
```

(b) View definition

Figure 1: Database schema and view for running example

In prior IVM work, each diff table $\mathcal{D}_V^+$, $\mathcal{D}_V^-$ and $\mathcal{D}_V^u$ contains one diff tuple for each view tuple that has to be inserted, deleted and updated, respectively. This is why we refer to such diffs as *tuple-based diffs* (in short *t-diffs*). In this work we show that if the base tables contain keys, one can represent the view modifications in a much more compact way through a novel type of diffs, called *ID-based diffs* (in short *i-diffs*), which identify the to-be-modified view tuples through their IDs. In contrast to t-diff tuples, a single i-diff tuple can represent modifications to *multiple* view tuples. This difference is crucial, as i-diffs are more efficient to compute than t-diffs, requiring in general fewer base table accesses as we will explain next. This leads to more efficient ID-based IVM algorithms, under common assumptions. The following example demonstrates the difference between t-diffs and i-diffs. To differentiate between the two types of diffs, in the rest of the paper we will be using the standard symbol Δ to refer to the newly introduced i-diffs and the symbol $\mathcal{D}$ to refer to traditional t-diffs.

EXAMPLE 1.1. *Consider the database of an electronic device manufacturer, storing a list of devices and their parts. Figure 1a shows the respective database schema, consisting of the relations* ***devices***, ***parts*** *and* ***devices_parts***. *The key attributes of each relation are shown underlined. Also consider the view* ***V*** *of Figure 1b returning the list of parts for devices of type 'phone'.*

Figure 2 shows an example of tuple-based and ID-based incremental maintenance of ***V***. *The initial database and view instance are shown on the left and t-diffs and i-diffs for a sample change in relation* ***parts*** *on the right in Figures 2a and 2b, respectively. Consider the action of updating the price of part "P1" from $10 to $11. This modification is represented through identical t-diff and i-diff tuples, as seen in the t-diff table $\mathcal{D}^u_{parts}$ and i-diff table Δ^u_{parts}, respectively. However, this is no longer true when we look at the diffs that represent the resulting updates that have to happen to the view. Note that the change of the "P1" price in* ***parts*** *has to be propagated as updates of all "P1" tuples in the view (which in this case are the first two tuples). While the t-diff table $\mathcal{D}^u_V$ describes these changes by two diff tuples, each describing an entire view tu-*

Initial Database Instance DB

devices	
did	**category**
D1	phone
D2	phone
D3	tablet

devices_parts	
did	**pid**
D1	P1
D2	P1
D1	P2

parts	
pid	**price**
P1	10
P2	20

Initial View Instance V(DB)

V		
did	**pid**	**price**
D1	P1	10
D2	P1	10
D1	P2	20

Initial Instances

D^u_{parts}		
pid	**price_ old**	**price_ new**
P1	10	11

Q_D: SELECT did, pid, price_old, price_new FROM D^u_{parts} INNER JOIN devices_parts INNER JOIN devices

D^u_V			
did	**pid**	**price_ old**	**price_ new**
D1	P1	10	11
D2	P1	10	11

(a) Tuple-based diffs

Δ^u_{parts}		
pid	**price_ old**	**price_ new**
P1	10	11

Q_Δ: SELECT * FROM Δ^u_{parts}

Δ^u_V		
pid	**price_ old**	**price_ new**
P1	10	11

(b) ID-based diffs

Figure 2: Example of tuple-based and ID-based IVM

ple that has to be updated, the i-diff table Δ^u_V describes the same modifications through a single diff tuple (which intuitively instructs updating all "P1" tuples in the view).

Obviously ID-based diffs are more compact than their tuple-based counterparts. More importantly though i-diffs are in general more efficient to compute than t-diffs. Intuitively, the performance gains come from the fact that in contrast to t-diffs, i-diffs do not need to recreate the entire view tuples to be modified and thus can avoid some base table accesses. We use this observation to design an ID-based IVM algorithm, which is shown both analytically and experimentally to perform in most cases fewer base-table and view accesses than prior tuple-based approaches.

EXAMPLE 1.2. *Queries $Q_{\mathcal{D}}$ and Q_Δ show how the diffs for the view can be computed from the base tables and the diff for base relation* ***parts****. While computing the t-diff requires joining $\mathcal{D}^u_{parts}$ with the base tables* ***devices_parts*** *and* ***devices*** *(see $Q_{\mathcal{D}}$) to find all devices containing part "P1", producing the i-diffs simply amounts to finding the modified parts (and not the devices in which they are contained) and can therefore be accomplished by accessing only Δ^u_{parts} and avoiding all joins with the base relations (see Q_Δ).*

Note that the fewer base table accesses of i-diff computations are not, just by themselves, an absolute proof of superior performance of the i-diffs, as maintaining the view should also count the cost of applying the i-diffs to the view. While both the ID-based and tuple-based approaches will have to join the resulting view diffs with the view, the ID-based approach has the drawback of potentially trying to join more diff tuples by creating *dummy* i-diff tuples, i.e., i-diff tuples describing changes for tuples that do not even exist in the view. For example, assume that **parts** included a tuple (P3, 20) and Δ^u_{parts} included a change of P3's price. Then Δ^u_V would include a dummy P3 tuple, i.e., the system would pay the price of attempting to update the P3's in V, albeit there would be no P3 in V. We call this effect *overestimation*. Nevertheless, our theoretical and experimental analysis show that under common circumstances the i-diff approach is indeed superior. Furthermore, we show that the advantage of ID-based IVM grows as the queries become more complex.

Contributions. This paper makes the following contributions:

(a) An ID-based IVM system, called *idIVM*, applicable when the base relations have primary keys. The *idIVM* is based on a modular, algebraic approach, allowing one to extend the supported view definition language simply by adding one relational algebra operator at-a-time and providing *i-diff propagation equations* describing how ID-based changes are propagated through it.

(b) A set of i-diff propagation equations for a large subset of SQL (denoted by Q_{SPJADU}) that includes the algebraic operators select, project, join, grouping and aggregation with associative functions, generalized projection involving functions, antisemijoin[1] and union. Although the framework can be easily extended to more expressive view definition languages as described above, our analytical and experimental results focus on Q_{SPJADU}, as it is expressive enough to cover a large number of practical use cases.

(c) An efficient 4-pass algorithm that creates an IVM plan for a given algebraically-expressed view and a given set of modification types in four passes that are polynomial in the size of the view expression: The first pass computes the IDs of intermediate results. The second pass instantiates the operator IVM equations to the specifics of the view's operators. The third pass composes individual equations into the queries of the IVM plan. Finally, the fourth pass applies minimization and other optimizations particular to the IVM problem. Unlike general purpose minimization the considered minimization is polynomial.

(d) An algorithm that given a view expression decides what types of i-diffs should be mined from the modification log or captured from triggers. The problem is non-trivial since, as we will see, the number of types of i-diffs that are applicable, given a base schema and a view schema, is exponential in the size of the schemas. The presented algorithm uses the view definition to decide the much smaller number of sufficient and efficient i-diffs.

(e) A formal analysis proving that for Q_{SPJADU} views in many use cases the ID-based IVM with the i-diff propagation equations described in the paper is more efficient than tuple-based IVMs. The analysis is based on a fine-grained cost model counting data accesses and includes a discussion under the specific conditions under which tuple-based IVMs can perform better.

(f) An experimental evaluation of the proposed IVM system for Q_{SPJADU} views indicating that in most cases it significantly outperforms traditional tuple-based approaches. The experimental results show speedups of 2 to more than 50 over tuple-based IVMs.

Note that ID-based IVM optimization is orthogonal and can be combined with many of the other IVM issues studied in the literature [12, 8], such as materialized view selection [3, 25, 19], self maintenance [5, 11] and compilation into code [2]. We briefly describe these prior IVM works and their synergies in Section 8.

Outline. The paper is structured as follows: Section 2 defines ID-based diffs (i-diffs). Section 3 presents the architecture of *idIVM*. It consists of two main parts: The first transforms base table mod-

[1]Therefore capturing queries with negation. The difference operator is a special case of antisemijoin.

ifications to i-diffs and the second, given a set of i-diffs, creates a DML script for maintaining the view. For ease of exposition, we present them in the reverse order, i.e. Section 4 describes the algorithm for the DML script generation and Section 5 describes the transformation of changes to i-diffs. Sections 6 and 7 compare analytically and experimentally the efficiency of the generated script to those produced by tuple-based IVM approaches. Finally, Sections 8 and 9 discuss related work and conclude the paper, respectively.

2. ID-BASED DIFFS

For the following discussion we consider a relational database DB whose base tables contain keys and a relational view $V(\bar{I}, \bar{A})$ over DB, containing a set of key attributes (which we will refer to as IDs) $\bar{I}$ and a set of non-key attributes $\bar{A}$.

EXAMPLE 2.1. *The view V of our running example contains IDs $\bar{I}$ = {did, pid} and non-ID attributes $\bar{A}$ = {price}. In the following we will be using the initial instance of V of Figure 2.*

View definition language. Although, as we will see, the framework can be easily extended to more expressive view definition languages, unless otherwise stated, we consider views from the language Q_{SPJADU}, which contains all SQL queries that can be formulated using the algebraic operators Selection, Projection (involving functions), Join (with arbitrary join conditions), Aggregation with associative functions sum, avg and count, Antisemijoin (and thus Difference), and Union[2].

General Structure of an i-diff. Let $V(\bar{I}, \bar{A})$ be a view with IDs $\bar{I}$ and non-ID attributes $\bar{A}$. An *ID-based diff* (in short *i-diff*) of type $t \in \{+, -, u\}$ for relation V is in its most general form a relation $\Delta_V^t(\bar{I}', \bar{A}'_{pre}, \bar{A}''_{post})$ satisfying the following properties:

- It contains a subset $\bar{I}'$ of the view's IDs $\bar{I}$. These are used to identify the tuples to be modified.
- It may contain two sets $\bar{A}'_{pre}$ and $\bar{A}''_{post}$ of attributes, such that $\bar{A}', \bar{A}''$ are sets of non-ID attributes of V. An attribute A_{pre} and A_{post} intuitively stores the pre-state value (i.e., initial value before the change) and respectively post-state value (i.e., new value after the change) of attribute A of V.

Depending on their type, i-diffs may not contain both pre-state and post-state attributes. In particular, insert i-diffs (i.e, of type $t = +$), do not contain pre-state attributes, since they represent insertions of tuples that did not exist before. Similarly, delete i-diffs (i.e., of type $t = -$) do not contain post-state attributes. Only update diffs (i.e., of type $t = u$) may contain both old and new attribute values. We next describe the semantics for each i-diff type:

Update i-diff. An update i-diff instance Δ_V^u for view $V(\bar{I}, \bar{A})$ is a relation instance with schema $\Delta_V^u(\bar{I}', \bar{A}'_{pre}, \bar{A}''_{post})$, where $\bar{I}'$ is a subset of the IDs $\bar{I}$ of V and $\bar{A}'$, $\bar{A}''$ are potentially different subsets of the non-ID attributes $\bar{A}$ of V (with $\bar{A}'$ being potentially the empty set).

Intuitively, each tuple $(\bar{i}', \bar{a}'_{pre}, \bar{a}''_{post})$ in Δ_V^u specifies that all tuples in V with values $\bar{i}'$ for their $\bar{I}'$ attributes should have the values of their $\bar{A}''$ attributes updated to $\bar{a}''_{post}$. Formally, applying Δ_V^u on an instance I_V of V is equivalent to applying the following DML statement on I_V:

APPLY Δ_V^u: UPDATE V
SET $\bar{A}'' = \bar{A}''_{post}$
FROM Δ_V^u
WHERE $V.\bar{I}' = \Delta_V^u.\bar{I}'$ [3]

In the rest of the paper, the instance I_V will be implied from the context and therefore for simplification we will simply refer to a diff as being applied on the view V.

Note, that although not affecting its semantics, an update i-diff may also contain pre-state values of some non-ID attributes of V. As we will see later, this additional information is leveraged by the IVM algorithm to reduce the number of accesses to the database.

EXAMPLE 2.2. *Applying the following update i-diff*

Δ_V^u	pid	price_{pre}	price_{post}
	P1	10	11

leads to the update of the price of both tuples in V with pid = "P1" from 10 to 11.

Remark. In the following we consider only i-diffs where $\bar{I}'$ forms a primary key of the i-diff. The reason is that if $\bar{I}'$ is not a key, then update i-diffs are not well-defined and insert i-diff applications may lead to primary key violations.

Insert i-diff. An insert i-diff instance Δ_V^+ for a view $V(\bar{I}, \bar{A})$ is a relation instance with schema $\Delta_V^+(\bar{I}, \bar{A}_{post})$, or in other words a relation containing the post-state values for all attributes of the view and no pre-state values.

Intuitively, an insert i-diff instance Δ_V^+ contains a set of tuples that should be inserted into V. Formally, applying Δ_V^+ has the same effect as applying the following DML statement on V:

APPLY Δ_V^+: INSERT INTO V
SELECT $\bar{I}$, $\bar{A}_{post}$ AS $\bar{A}$ FROM Δ_V^+
WHERE ROW($\bar{I}$, $\bar{A}_{post}$) NOT IN
(SELECT $\bar{I}$, $\bar{A}$ FROM V)

EXAMPLE 2.3. *Applying the following insert i-diff*

Δ_V^+	did	pid	price_{post}
	D3	P2	20
	D4	P3	30

inserts tuples <D3, P2, 20> and <D4, P3, 30> in V.

Remark. The WHERE clause in the above DML statement ensures that an attempt is made to insert a tuple into V only if it is does not already exist in V in the exact same form. This allows multiple insert i-diffs to try to insert the same tuple.

Delete i-diff. A delete i-diff instance Δ_V^- for a relation $V(\bar{I}, \bar{A})$ is a relation instance with schema $\Delta_V^-(\bar{I}', \bar{A}'_{pre})$, where $\bar{I}'$ is a subset of the IDs $\bar{I}$ of V and $\bar{A}'$ is a potentially empty subset of the non-IDs $\bar{A}$ of V.

Intuitively, Δ_V^- specifies the tuples that should be deleted from V based on the values of the $\bar{I}'$ attributes. Formally, applying Δ_V^- has the same effect as applying the following DML statement on V:

APPLY Δ_V^-: DELETE FROM V
WHERE ROW($\bar{I}'$) IN (SELECT $\bar{I}'$ FROM Δ_V^-)

Note that, similarly to update i-diffs, a delete i-diff may also specify the pre-state values of the deleted tuples, which are used to create more efficient IVM solutions.

[2]To maintain the IDs for the bag union, we employ a special union all operator, outputting a special attribute **b**, denoting which child branch (b = 0/1 for left and right, resp.) a tuple came from.

[3]Note that for conciseness the UPDATE statement is written using PostgreSQL's special UPDATE FROM syntax. However, it could be equivalently written using standard SQL syntax.

EXAMPLE 2.4. *Applying the following delete i-diff*

Δ_V^-	pid	price$_{pre}$
	P1	10

leads to the deletion of both tuples with pid = "P1" from V.

Effective i-diff instances. Given a set of i-diff instances $\bar{\Delta}$ for a relation V, applying them on V leads in general to different results depending on the order of application. However, in this work we only look at sets of i-diffs where any order of applying them on V yields the same result. To this end, we define the notion of *effective* i-diff instances. Given the pre-state V^{pre} and post-state V^{post} of a relation V, an i-diff instance Δ_V^t is said to be *effective* w.r.t. V^{pre} and V^{post} if for each value of a tuple of V it reflects its final value. Formally, it is effective iff it satisfies the following properties:

- If Δ_V^t is an insert i-diff: Every tuple inserted by the i-diff exists in the post-state (i.e., $\Delta_V^+ \subseteq V^{post}$).
- If Δ_V^t is a delete i-diff over schema $\Delta_V^-(\bar{I}', \bar{A}'_{pre})$: Every tuple deleted by the i-diff does *not* exist in the post-state relational instance (i.e., $\pi_{\bar{I}'}\Delta_V^- \cap \pi_{\bar{I}'}V^{post} = \emptyset$).
- If Δ_V^t is an update i-diff over schema $\Delta_V^u(\bar{I}', \bar{A}'_{pre}, \bar{A}''_{post})$: Every tuple updated by Δ_V^u that exists in the post-state instance, has all updated attributes $\bar{A}''_{post}$ set to the corresponding values in that instance (i.e., $\pi_{\bar{I}',\bar{A}''_{post}}\Delta_V^u \ltimes_{\bar{I}'} V^{post} \subseteq \pi_{\bar{I}',\bar{A}''}V^{post}$).

It can be shown that a set of effective i-diffs lead to the same result regardless of the order in which they are applied. In the following the i-diff instances we consider are assumed to be effective. We will discuss in Sections 4 and 5 how *idIVM* makes sure that it always operates on effective i-diff instances.

i-diff schemas. It should be obvious that a single modification could be represented through i-diffs of different schemas. In particular, one can include pre-state or post-state values for different sets of attributes. More importantly, different base table i-diffs may lead to IVM solutions of different efficiencies. For instance, an update of a t tuple of relation $R(\bar{I}, A_1, A_2)$ on attribute A_1 can be represented by either an i-diff that contains only the post-state of A_1, or both the post-state of A_1 and A_2 (even though the value of A_2 did not change). However, the first i-diff will in general lead to a more efficient solution, since for the second i-diff the IVM algorithm will have to account also for the change of A_2, although this is not needed. This generates a novel challenge of selecting which base tables i-diff schemas to create, as explained next.

IDs and functional dependencies. As discussed earlier, the set $\bar{I}$ of ID attributes of a view V forms a key of that view. Moreover, any i-diff Δ_V for the view V identifies the tuples of V to be updated, deleted or inserted through a subset of that key. However, this cannot be an *arbitrary* subset of the key. The key $\bar{I}$ of a view is split into components $(\bar{I}_1, \bar{I}_2, \dots \bar{I}_n)$, such that for each component of the key there is a functional dependency $\bar{I}_i \rightarrow \bar{A}_i$ from this component $\bar{I}_i$ to a subset $\bar{A}_i$ of non-key attributes of the view. The i-diff can identify the tuples of the view to be modified through a subset of these key components.

EXAMPLE 2.5. *For instance, in our running example, V has ID/key $\bar{I}$ = {did, pid}, which can be decomposed into two components $\bar{I}_1$ = did and $\bar{I}_2$ = pid, since there is the functional dependency pid → price (in a more general view V′ containing also attributes of the* **devices** *relation there would also be a functional dependency from did to those attributes). Thus the tuples of V can be identified by an i-diff either through did or through pid (as is the case in our example).*

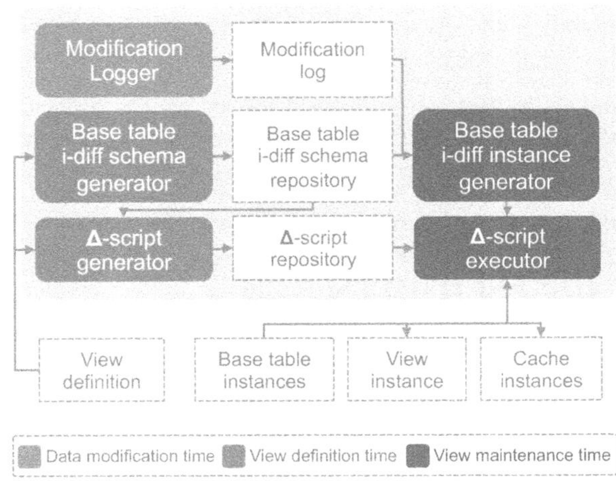

Figure 3: *idIVM* architecture

3. SYSTEM ARCHITECTURE

Figure 3 depicts the architecture of *idIVM*; an ID-based IVM system based on i-diffs and built on top of a relational DBMS. The modules of the system are shown as rounded boxes, while the system's data structures are depicted as white rectangles. *idIVM* can be setup to maintain the view either eagerly (i.e., whenever the base data change, known as *eager IVM* [6, 7, 10]) or lazily at some later point in time (known as *deferred* IVM [9, 15, 17]). In either case, the modification logging module of the *idIVM* remains the same. Furthermore, the only part of the architecture that is substantially different in the two approaches is the i-diff propagation rules and cache maintenance rules (see Figure 4). This paper describes the deferred IVM rules. *idIVM* contains modules executed at three different times (shown through color-coding in Figure 3): (a) when the views are defined (orange), (b) whenever the data in the underlying database change (green), and (c) whenever the views are maintained (blue). We present next briefly each of these stages:

View definition time. The most interesting and novel computations happen when a view is added to the system. At that point *idIVM* precomputes in the form of DML scripts how to translate i-diffs on the base tables to view updates. This computation happens through the synergy of two components: First, it employs a *base table i-diff schema generator* to decide which i-diff schemas to generate for the base tables. As we have discussed in Section 2, this is a non-trivial problem, as the same update could be modelled through i-diffs of different schemas. Once the base table i-diff schemas have been decided, *idIVM* invokes the Δ*-script generator* creating a DML script that accesses the generated i-diffs, the base tables and the potential caches (which as we will see can be used to speedup the IVM) to maintain the view. The resulting Δ-script is stored in a repository to be used at view maintenance time.

Data modification & view maintenance time. Given this offline computation, the system's online component is simple: When the base data are modified, a *modification logger* logs these changes for later use. When the time comes to maintain the view, the *base table i-diff instance generator* consults the modification log and converts it to instances of the base table i-diff schemas precomputed at view definition time. A Δ*-script executor* then retrieves the Δ-script corresponding to the view from the Δ-script repository and executes it to propagate the changes represented by the base table i-diff instances to the view instance.

We next describe the Δ-script generation, leaving the discussion of how to convert base table modifications to i-diffs for Section 5.

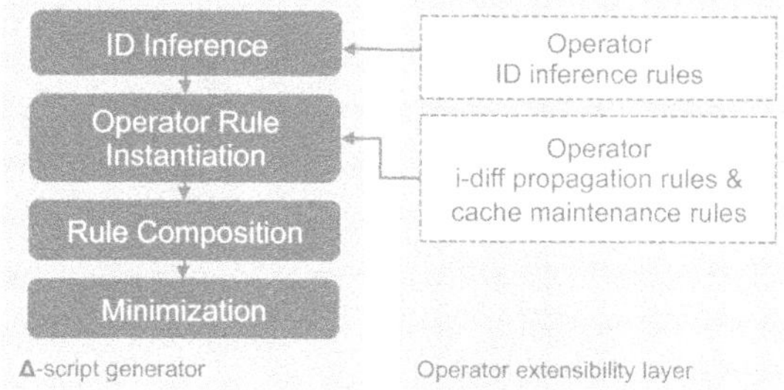

Figure 4: Δ-script generator architecture

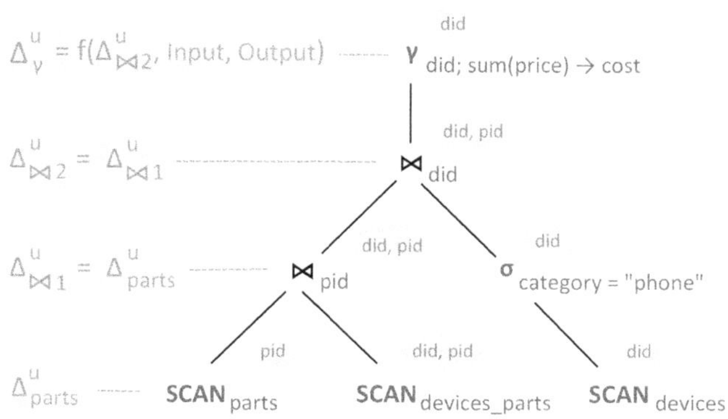

(a) Algebraic plan (annotated by the Δ-script generator)

```
CREATE VIEW V' AS
SELECT did, sum(price) AS cost
FROM parts NATURAL JOIN
     devices_parts NATURAL JOIN
     devices
WHERE category = "phone"
GROUP BY did
```

(b) View definition

Figure 5: View definition and plan for extended running example

4. Δ-SCRIPT GENERATION ALGORITHM

Given a view definition and a set of base table i-diff schemas, the Δ-script generation algorithm creates a DML script that includes (a) queries over the base table i-diffs, the base tables and the auxiliary caches (which as we will see are used by *idIVM* to speed up the IVM) that compute the corresponding view i-diffs and (b) UPDATE / INSERT / DELETE statements of the form described in Section 2 that apply these i-diffs on the view.

The Δ-script generator is based on the algebraic IVM approach [21, 10, 22]: Each relational operator type (e.g., selection, projection, join, etc.) is annotated with a set of *rules*, describing how to transform an (effective) i-diff over its input schema to an (effective) i-diff over its output schema. Given this information, the Δ-script for a view V can be composed from the individual rules for each operator that appears in an algebraic plan of V. Intuitively, the algorithm is computing how to maintain the entire view by first computing how to maintain all intermediate subviews in the algebraic plan. This approach enables a modular implementation in which the supported view definition language can be easily extended by adding rules for additional relational algebra operators. In this work we present the rules for all operators included in Q_{SPJADU} (i.e., selection, join, generalized projection involving functions, grouping with aggregation, antisemijoin, and union). Similarly to prior algebraic IVM approaches, we assume that the algebraic plan of the view on which the algorithm operates is given as input.

Operator	Output ID attributes
$SCAN(R)$	$key(R)$
$\sigma_\phi(R)$	$ID(R)$
$\pi_{\bar{D}}(R)$	$ID(R)$
$R \times S$	$ID(R) \cup ID(S)$
$R \bowtie_\phi S$	$ID(R) \cup ID(S)$
$R \bar{\ltimes}_\phi S$	$ID(R)$
bag union $R \cup S$	$ID(R) \cup ID(S) \cup \{b\}$
group by $\gamma_{\bar{G}, f(\bar{M})\ldots}(R)$	$\bar{G}$

Table 1: Operator ID inference rules

EXAMPLE 4.1. *To showcase the algorithm, we extend the view of our running example to also perform an aggregation, returning the total cost of the parts for each device. Figures 5b and 5a show the view definition V' and a corresponding algebraic plan, respectively. The shaded components are annotations inserted by the algorithm, which we explain below.*

idIVM performs the 4 efficient passes of Figure 4.

Pass 1: Inferring ID information for intermediate views. Since i-diffs determine the view tuples that have to be modified through their IDs, the view and all intermediate subviews should contain as part of their output schema a set of ID attributes that form a key of the corresponding view. *idIVM* determines the ID attributes that should be contained in the output schema of each subview through the use of *ID inference rules*. An ID inference rule is supplied for each operator type supported by the system and describes how the IDs of the view rooted at an operator p can be computed from the IDs of the subviews rooted at p's children. Table 1 shows the ID inference rules for operators in Q_{SPJADU}.[4] *idIVM* uses these rules to perform a postorder traversal of the plan checking at each operator whether the IDs inferred by these rules exist in the operator's output schema. If this is not the case, *idIVM* automatically extends the plan to include the required ID attributes.

EXAMPLE 4.2. *Figure 5a shows the set of IDs for each operator in a shaded oval on the top right side of the operator.*

Note that extending the view with additional ID attributes simply increases the width of the view instance (i.e., the number of columns) but does not affect its cardinality (i.e., the number of tuples). In particular, if V_{orig} is an original view with attributes $\bar{A}$ and V_{ID} is the view inferred by the ID-inference algorithm, then for all instances of the base tables the original view can be computed from the original view simply by projecting out the additional attributes introduced by the ID-inference algorithm (i.e., $V_{orig} = \pi_{\bar{A}} V_{ID}$). Given that the number of additional ID attributes is usually small compared to the number of attributes already in the view, we do not expect the extension of the view schema with ID attributes to significantly affect the query evaluation performance. Importantly, the above observations hold not only for operators in Q_{SPJADU} but *for any* SQL operator (for the reader wondering how this can be the case for the duplicate elimination operator δ, given that in general $\delta(\pi_{A,B}(R))$ is different from $\delta(\pi_{ID,A,B}(R))$, consider an implementation where the duplicate elimination operator δ above is replaced by the group by operator $\gamma_{A,B}$).

Pass 2: Instantiating rules for each intermediate operator. To construct the Δ-script for the view, the algorithm employs operator rules that describe how each operator can propagate i-diffs over its input to i-diffs over its output.

Operator rules. An operator describes how to transform an i-diff Δ^t_{input} over one of its input schemas to an i-diff Δ^t_{output} over its

[4] Union refers to the *union all* operator described in Section 2.

output schema through a set of queries known as *i-diff propagation rules*. These queries can access (a) the operator's input i-diff Δ^t_{input} and (b) the data corresponding to the subview rooted at the operator or at one of its child operators. The latter is the way in which *idIVM* allows operator rules to access data from the base tables. Since an operator does not have knowledge of the exact place in the query plan where it appears to ask for a query result over the base tables, it can access the base table data only indirectly by asking for the subview rooted at one of its children through the use of the $Input_{i=l,r}$ (standing for left and right input, resp. for binary operators) or for the subview rooted at itself using the $Output$ keyword, respectively. The input subviews can be requested either in their pre-state form (i.e., using the instances of the base tables before the diffs were applied to them) or in the post-state (i.e., using the final instances of the base tables after the diffs were applied to them). An i-diff propagation rule can specify which of the two versions of the input it needs through the subscripts pre and $post$. The output is always provided in pre-state.

EXAMPLE 4.3. *For instance, a general grouping and aggregate operator* $V = \gamma_{\bar{G},f(\bar{X})\rightarrow c}(Input)$ *contains among others the i-diff propagation rule:* $\Delta^u_V = \gamma_{\bar{G},f(\bar{X})\rightarrow c}(Input_{post} \ltimes_{\bar{G}} \Delta^+_{Input})$, *which semijoins the post-state of the subview rooted at the operator's child with an input insert i-diff to find all tuples that belong to groups affected by the insertions and use them to recompute the value of the aggregate function for these groups. The* $Input_{post}$ *keyword is the way in which the operator asks for the (post-state of) some base data (in this case the base data defined by the subview rooted at the operator's child, which for the aggregate operator of Figure 5a is the subview* ***parts*** $\bowtie_{pid}$ ***devices_parts*** $\bowtie_{did}$ $\sigma_{category=\text{"phone"}}$ ***devices****).*

There are two different classes of operators in *idIVM*: The first consists of operators which can produce an output effective i-diff by looking at one input i-diff at a time. These operators are called *non-blocking* operators, in contrast to *blocking* operators which need to inspect the entire set of input i-diffs before creating an effective output i-diff. The operator type affects how the operator's i-diff propagation rules are expressed. For non-blocking operators, each rule is expressed over a single input i-diff, while for blocking operators, a rule is expressed over all input i-diffs.

EXAMPLE 4.4. *The general aggregate operator* γ *of Example 4.3 is a non-blocking operator, since it can decide how to propagate an input insert i-diff without looking at other input i-diffs (e.g., delete or update i-diffs). The reason is that for each insert i-diff tuple it recomputes the entire affected group from the base data thus reflecting indirectly also the changes incurred by other input i-diffs. On the other hand, imagine a more efficient aggregate operator designed specifically for the SUM aggregate function. This operator avoids recomputing entire groups by combining all input i-diffs to figure out the amount by which the aggregate value of each group has changed. While it avoids some base table accesses, it requires knowledge of all input i-diffs and is thus a blocking operator.*

Tables 4-13 show the i-diff propagation rules for the operators considered in this work, including join, union, generalized projection involving functions, antisemijoin and aggregation. Rules for aggregation are provided in four different versions (see Tables 7, 9, 11, and 12); one for general aggregation functions and others for specialized functions, such as SUM, COUNT and AVG.

Some operator rules may also benefit from special caches to speed up IVM. For instance, an aggregate AVG operator in the presence of a COUNT and SUM cache can incrementally maintain its output without accessing the base tables. To accomodate such cases, *idIVM* allows operators to declare special *operator caches*

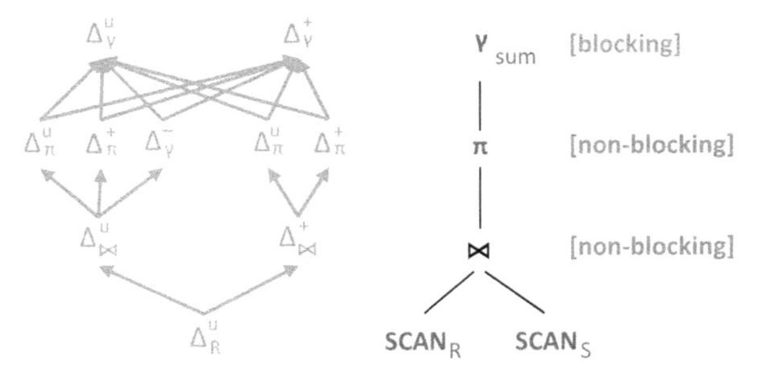

Figure 6: Rule DAG structure

and associated *cache maintenance rules*, describing how to compute the i-diffs that maintain the caches. The i-diff propagation rules can then be expressed also over the operator cache schemas and the operator cache i-diffs. Table 12 shows the cache maintenance rules and i-diff propagation rules for the AVG operator.

Rule instantiation. In its second pass, the Δ-script generator algorithm employs the predefined operator rules to compute how each base table i-diff is propagated from operator to operator in the view plan. This is done as follows: For each base table i-diff schema Δ^t_R, the algorithm starts from the scan operator of the corresponding base table R and in a bottom-up fashion instantiates the rules for all operators in the path from the scan operator to the root of the plan.[5] The rule instantiation simply consists in selecting from all rules for the particular operator the ones that apply in the particular case (based on the input i-diff schema and other conditions) and replacing the abstract schema used in the rules with the concrete schema of the particular operator instance (e.g., for an operator $V = \pi_x(R)$ the general projection i-diff propagation rule $\Delta^+_V = \pi_{\bar{a},f(\bar{X})\rightarrow c}\Delta^+_R$ becomes $\Delta^+_V = \pi_x\Delta^+_R$).

EXAMPLE 4.5. *Consider an update i-diff schema* $\Delta^u_{parts}(pid, price_{pre}, price_{post})$ *modeling updates on the price attribute of table* ***parts*** *of our running example. Figure 5a shows on the left the corresponding instantiated rules generated by the algorithm. The exact rule for the aggregate operator is omitted due to lack of space. However, it is important to note that it is a rule that mentions the input i-diff and the input and the output of the operator, respectively.*

Note that for a single input i-diff an operator may create multiple output i-diffs. For instance, an update i-diff going through a selection operator may lead to insert, update and delete i-diffs, depending on whether a tuple satisfied the condition before and after the change. Whenever the rules of an operator create multiple output i-diffs, the above computation continues conceptually in parallel for each generated i-diff schema. This leads to a directed *rule DAG*, whose nodes are instantiated rules and whose edges point from a rule to all rules that were created using its output schema. Figure 6 shows such a structure. Note how blocking rules convert the structure that would otherwise be a tree into a DAG.

Pass 3: Composing operator-level instantiated rules into a Δ-script. Each rule in the DAG is a query expressed over the output schema of its parent rules (note that the DAG in Figure 6 is shown inverted with its root shown at the bottom). Thus each i-diff for the view (which corresponds to a leaf) can be computed by composing the instantiated rules of its ancestors. The exact order in which these compositions are performed does not matter, since all considered i-diffs are effective. This is guaranteed by the fact that (a) the base table diff instance generator creates effective diffs (as we will discuss in Section 5) and (b) i-diff propagation rules transform effective input i-diffs to effective output i-diffs.

[5]If the base table R appears with multiple aliases, this process is repeated for every scan operator of R.

$$\Delta^u_{Cache} = \Delta^u_{parts};$$
$$\text{APPLY } \Delta^u_{Cache};$$
$$\Delta^u_{V'} = \pi_{did, cost \to cost_{pre}, cost + cost_\Delta \to cost_{post}}(V' \bowtie \gamma_{did, sum(price_\Delta) \to cost_\Delta}(\pi_{did, pid, (price_{post} - price_{in}) \to price_\Delta}(\Delta^u_{Cache} \bowtie \pi_{price \to price_{in}} Cache)));$$
$$\text{APPLY } \Delta^u_{V'};$$

Figure 7: Δ-script for running example

To make the generated plan more efficient, *idIVM* employs also additional caching, other than the caching used internally by operators. In particular, for aggregate operators, whose rules typically ask for the base data corresponding to their input/output (through the $Input_i$ and $Output$ keywords, resp.), *idIVM* attempts[6] to create an *intermediate* cache in which it materializes this result. This cache is treated as any other view and maintained during the IVM process. In particular, *idIVM* first composes all rules that create the i-diffs for the cache and then using them as input, composes the rest of the rules up to the next cache until it reaches the view.

EXAMPLE 4.6. *For instance, as we have seen in Figure 5a, the instantiated rule for the aggregation mentions both the input and the output of the operator. Thus,* idIVM *tries to generate two intermediate caches; one before the aggregate and another after the aggregate. Since however the output of the aggregate coincides with the view (which is already materialized),* idIVM *creates only the first cache and utilizes the already existing view as the second.*

The result of this composition is a Δ-script, containing queries that compute i-diffs for an intermediate cache/view and APPLY operators that use the DML statements corresponding to each i-diffs type (shown in Section 2) to apply these i-diffs to the cache/view.

EXAMPLE 4.7. *In our running example* idIVM *employs an intermediate cache below the aggregate operator. Thus, it composes the rules up to that point, updates the cache and then uses it as input to compose the rules up to the view, which is subsequently updated. This leads to the Δ-script of Figure 7.*

Pass 4: Optimizing the generated Δ-script. As a last step, *idIVM* optimizes the Δ-script by performing semantic optimization, which minimizes each individual query included in the plan. In contrast to general minimization, this minimization takes into account the special semantics of i-diff tables. As described in Section 2, given a base table $R(\bar{I}, \bar{A})$ in its post-state and i-diffs $\Delta^+_R(\bar{I}, \bar{A}_{post})$, $\Delta^-_R(\bar{I}, \bar{A}'_{pre})$, and $\Delta^u_R(\bar{I}, \bar{A}'_{pre}, \bar{A}''_{post})$ over this table, the following constraints hold: (a) $C_1 : \Delta^+_R \subseteq R$, (b) $C_2 : \pi_{\bar{I}} \Delta^-_R \cap \pi_{\bar{I}} R = \emptyset$, and (c) $C_3 : \pi_{\bar{I}, \bar{A}''_{post}} \Delta^u_R \ltimes_{\bar{I}} R \subseteq \pi_{\bar{I}, \bar{A}''} R$. *idIVM* minimizes w.r.t. constraints C_1 - C_3 by employing on top of the standard relational rewrite rules also the rewrite rules presented in Figure 8. Semantic minimization is crucial in eliminating inefficiencies introduced by composing individual operator rules, improving in some cases performance by more than 50%.

Designing operator i-diff propagation rules. The efficiency of the Δ-script obviously depends on the provided i-diff propagation rule definitions. Reasoning about the efficiency of individual rules is hard, as rules affect each other (e.g., a rule avoiding base table accesses may not bring in some information that could be used by rules later in the plan, thus leading to higher access cost later).

[6]Intermediate caches are not generated when they are expected to contain multi-valued dependencies (for instance due to a many-to-many join), since in that case reading the result from the cache would incur more tuple accesses than simply recomputing it on the fly from the base tables. *idIVM* exploits foreign key constraints to infer the absence of multi-valued dependencies.

For semijoin

$\Delta^+_R \ltimes_{R.\bar{I}} \sigma_{\phi(\bar{X})} R \to \sigma_{\phi(\bar{X}_{post})} \Delta^+_R$
$R \ltimes_{R.\bar{I}} \sigma_{\phi(\bar{Y})} \Delta^+_R \to \pi_{\bar{I}, \bar{A}_{post} \to \bar{A}} \sigma_{\phi(\bar{Y})} \Delta^+_R$
$\Delta^u_R \ltimes_{R.\bar{I}} \sigma_{\phi(\bar{X})} R \to \sigma_{\phi(\bar{X}_{post})} \Delta^u_R$, if $\bar{X} \subseteq \bar{A}''$
$R \ltimes_{R.\bar{I}} \sigma_{\phi(\bar{Y})} \Delta^u_R \to \pi_{\bar{I}, \bar{A}''_{post} \to \bar{A}} \sigma_{\phi(\bar{Y})} \Delta^u_R$, if $\bar{A}'' = \bar{A}$
$\Delta^-_R \ltimes_{R.\bar{I}} \sigma_{\phi(\bar{X})} R \to \emptyset$
$R \ltimes_{R.\bar{I}} \sigma_{\phi(\bar{X})} \Delta^-_R \to \emptyset$

For antisemijoin

$\Delta^+_R \bar{\ltimes}_{R.\bar{I}} \sigma_{\phi(\bar{X})} R \to \sigma_{\neg\phi(\bar{X}_{post})} \Delta^+_R$
$\Delta^u_R \bar{\ltimes}_{R.\bar{I}} \sigma_{\phi(\bar{X})} R \to \sigma_{\neg\phi(\bar{X}_{post})} \Delta^u_R$, if $\bar{X} \subseteq \bar{A}''$
$\Delta^-_R \bar{\ltimes}_{R.\bar{I}} \sigma_{\phi(\bar{X})} R \to \Delta^-_R$
$R \bar{\ltimes}_{R.\bar{I}} \sigma_{\phi(\bar{X})} \Delta^-_R \to R$

For join

$\Delta^+_R \bowtie_{R.\bar{I}} R \to \Delta^+_R$
$\Delta^u_R \bowtie_{R.\bar{I}} R \to \Delta^u_R$
$\Delta^-_R \bowtie_{R.\bar{I}} R \to \emptyset$
* *up to renaming*

Figure 8: Rewrite rules for semantic optimization

However, in this work we show that we do not have to get into this reasoning process. Simply creating rules that individually avoid accessing the base tables when possible leads to efficient Δ-scripts, as shown by our analytical and experimental results. To avoid data accesses, the rules are even allowed to *overestimate*, i.e. skip some filtering that would require base table accesses and propagate to their output i-diffs dummy tuples that do not affect the view.

EXAMPLE 4.8. *For instance, the selection operator allows a delete input i-diff to pass through the operator unmodified. However, this means that the output i-diff will also instruct the deletion of tuples that do not satisfy the selection conditions and thus do not exist in the view. Although this is an overestimated i-diff, it does not affect the correctness of the generated Δ-script, since the latter will simply try to delete some tuples from the view that do not exist. On the other hand, this rule locally minimizes the base table accesses, as it avoids accessing the base tables to filter out the tuples that do not satisfy the selection condition.*

5. FROM MODIFICATIONS TO I-DIFFS

We saw above how given a set of base table i-diffs, *idIVM* maintains the view. In this section we explain how these base table i-diffs are generated from base table modifications. This is a non-trivial problem, since as explained in Section 2, a single modification can be represented through i-diffs of different schemas, each leading potentially to Δ-scripts of different efficiencies.

idIVM solves the i-diff generation problem through the synergy of three components shown in Figure 3: (a) a modification logger recording the base table modifications at data modification time, (b) a base table i-diff *schema* generator deciding at view definition time which base table i-diff schemas to generate, and (c) a base table i-diff *instance* generator, translating at view maintenance time the modifications recorded in the log to instances of the pre-computed i-diff schemas. Logging changes to the base tables can be easily performed through known techniques, such as DBMS log inspections, timestamp queries or triggers (currently used by *idIVM*). Therefore we focus next on the other two components.

Generating i-diff schemas. Given a view definition V, *idIVM* generates suitable base-table i-diff schemas for all base tables mentioned in V. Insertions and deletions are straightforward cases: Consider a base table $R(\bar{I}, \bar{A})$ with key attributes $\bar{I}$ and non-key attributes $\bar{A}$. For each such table, the i-diff schema generator creates a single insert i-diff schema $\Delta^+_R(\bar{I}, \bar{A}_{post})$ (containing all attributes of R) and a single delete i-diff schema $\Delta^-_R(\bar{I}, \bar{A}_{pre})$ (containing all non-ID attributes of R in pre-state form). This is based on the observation that pre-state values can lead only to a more efficient Δ-script as they may reduce overestimation and the respective view index lookups. For instance, as shown in Table 6 with blue, a selection operator can exploit pre-state attributes to filter out the tuples of an incoming delete i-diff that do not satisfy the condition.

The same does not hold though for post-state attributes included in update i-diffs. Including more post-state attributes in an update i-diff schema leads to a generally less efficient Δ-script, as it has to account also for changes in these attributes. Creating one update i-diff schema for each subset of attributes of each base table is obviously not an option, due to the exponentiality involved.

In *idIVM* we solve this problem by observing that the base table attributes can be divided into sets of attributes whose updates lead to the same Δ-script and can thus be grouped together in a single i-diff schema. For each operator *op* in the algebraic view plan, let C_{op}, be the set of (non-key) base table attributes involved in any condition (e.g., selection, join etc)[7]. We refer to C_{op} as the *set of conditional attributes for op.* The set of (non-key) base table attribute not included in any C_{op} for any operator *op* in the view's plan is referred to as the *set of non-conditional attributes* NC. Non-conditional attributes may still affect the view (since they could be included in the view's output), but intuitively they do not affect the generated Δ-script (up to projections). Updates on each set of conditional attributes C_{op} on the other hand may lead to a different Δ-script, since the updated values may affect whether the i-diffs make it past *op*'s condition. Therefore for each base table $R(\bar{I}, \bar{A})$, the i-diff schema generation algorithm creates (a) for each set C_{op} an update i-diff $\Delta^u_R(\bar{I}, \bar{A}_{pre}, \bar{A}'_{post})$, s.t. $\bar{A}' = \bar{A} \cap C_{op}$ and (b) an additional update i-diff $\Delta^u_R(\bar{I}, \bar{A}_{pre}, \bar{A}''_{post})$, containing the non-conditional attributes of R (i.e., $\bar{A}'' = \bar{A} \cap NC$).

Populating i-diff instances. Every time *idIVM* is invoked to maintain the view, the i-diff instance generator simply populates the i-diff tables created at view definition time. This is done by extracting the changes since the last view maintenance from the modification log and adding them as diff-tuples to all i-diff tables that contain at least one of the modified attributes (in the case of updates) and to the single insert and delete i-diff tables (in the case of inserts and deletes, respectively). Note, that when extracting the modifications from the log, the algorithm combines multiple modifications to the same tuple to a single modification, so as to generate *effective* diffs. As discussed in Sections 2 and 4, this is crucial for the algorithm's correctness.

6. PERFORMANCE ANALYSIS

We next analytically compute the speedup ratio of ID-based over tuple-based IVM (i.e., the ratio $\frac{\text{tuple-based cost}}{\text{ID-based cost}}$). A speedup ratio greater than 1 signifies that the ID-based approach has a lower cost than the tuple-based approach and thus is more efficient than the latter, while a speedup ratio lower than 1 signifies the opposite.

To compute the speedup we first compute the individual cost of each IVM approach. The cost of the ID-based/tuple-based approach is measured in the combined number of tuple accesses and index lookups incurred by the $\Delta/\mathcal{D}$-script, generated by the corresponding approach. For the purposes of this analysis, we assume that both approaches have access to view indices on the view IDs and additionally the tuple-based IVM has access to appropriate base table indices (which are not required by the ID-based approach). We also try to be as general as possible regarding the query plan that the DBMS might choose to execute a particular $\Delta/\mathcal{D}$-script. However, since DBMSs employ complex optimizations that cannot be comprehensively accounted for in an analytical model, the computed cost and the associated speedups reported in this Section should only be used as rough estimates of the actual cost of performing IVM that illustrate the difference in performance between the two approaches. For an experimental comparison of the two IVM approaches, please refer to Section 7.

We next present the speedup for two representative cases: (a) SPJ views, which by default do not involve intermediate caches and (b) Aggregate views involving grouping and associative functions, which (by default) are supported by caches. For a detailed analysis explaining how this speedup was computed, please refer to Appendix A.

6.1 SPJ Views

Consider the SPJ view V_{spj}:

$$\texttt{SELECT } \bar{S} \texttt{ FROM } R, R_1, \ldots, R_n \texttt{ WHERE } c$$

whose FROM clause involves a single alias of a table R, (b) a t-diff $\mathcal{D}_R$ on R and (c) a corresponding i-diff Δ_R. [8]

Parameters affecting speedup. The speedup of the ID-based approach over the tuple-based approach can be expressed in terms of two parameters: the *i-diff compression factor* p and the *tuple-based computation cost per base table diff tuple* a. The i-diff compression factor $p = |\mathcal{D}_{V_{\text{spj}}}|/|\Delta_{V_{\text{spj}}}|$ is the ratio of the size of the tuple-based diff to the size of the ID-based diff for the view. p may be less than 1 (when i-diffs summarize the modifications to the view in a more compact way than t-diffs, as shown in Figure 2) but may also be greater than 1 (when i-diffs are overestimating and trying to modify tuples that do not exist in V_{spj}). The second parameter is the number of accesses a that the tuple-based approach has to perform on average to compute the t-diff tuples for the view that result from a given t-diff tuple for the base table. This cost will typically vary, depending on the plan chosen by the DBMS to evaluate the tuple-based $\mathcal{D}$-script.

Speedup ratio. The speedup ratio of the ID-based approach over the tuple-based approach is given by the following formula:

(a) if $\Delta_R/\mathcal{D}_R$ is an update i-diff/t-diff on attributes of R that are not involved in selection or join conditions in V_{spj}, then

$$\text{A: Speedup ratio} = \tfrac{a+2p}{1+p}$$

(b) else (i.e., if $\Delta_R/\mathcal{D}_R$ is any other update i-diff/t-diff or it is an insert or delete i-diff/t-diff)

$$\text{B: Speedup ratio} \geq min\left(\tfrac{a+2p}{1+p}, 1\right)$$

Discussion. Let us first explain why update diffs on attributes of R that are non-conditional may lead to a different speedup ratio than other types of diffs. Since the updates do not affect how a tuple behaves w.r.t. selections or joins, they are guaranteed to lead to updates (i.e., neither inserts, nor deletes) on the view. When this is the case (case (a) above), the ID-based IVM algorithm can simply propagate the base table i-diffs to the view without accessing the base tables, leading to a speedup ratio of $\frac{a+2p}{1+p}$. This speedup is in most practical cases greater than 1 (meaning that the ID-based is more efficient than the tuple-based approach). For the tuple-based approach to perform better, it should be the case that $a < 1 - p$, which can be satisfied only in the corner case when the following conditions simultaneously hold: (a) the tuple-based approach incurs $a < 1$ tuple accesses for each tuple in $\mathcal{D}^u_R$ on average (which can only happen if many tuples of $\mathcal{D}^u_R$ share the same join attribute values and thus the joined tuples can be retrieved once and reused for all of them) and (b) the ID-based approach is severely overestimating (i.e., $p \ll 1$). We have experimentally verified that by following this pattern it is possible to create contrived scenarios in which the tuple-based IVM outperforms the ID-based approach.

[7]Base table key attributes do not need to be considered for updates as they are immutable.

[8]Recall that we use the symbols Δ and $\mathcal{D}$ to represent i-diffs and t-diffs, respectively.

However, in all other cases, the ID-based approach performs better (with a difference that raises proportionally to p).

When the base table diffs are insert or delete diffs or they are updates on attributes involved in conditions (case (b) above), then they will lead in general to updates, inserts and/or deletes on the view. If they lead to updates and deletes only, then the resulting speedup is the same as in the first case (i.e., $\frac{a+2p}{1+p}$) and thus the ID-based approach is expected to perform better in most cases. However, if they lead to inserts, then the two approaches will perform identically and hence exhibit a speedup of 1. Finally, if the base table diffs lead to a combination of updates, deletes and inserts, then the speedup will be a linear combination of the above two speedups and thus will be greater than the smaller of the two (hence the use of inequality and the min function in the above formula).

Thus for SPJ queries the ID-based IVM will always (up to the corner case described above) perform at least as good as the tuple-based IVM and in most cases better then the latter. The two approaches will only perform identically if the IVM workload is heavy on modifications that lead to insertions to the view.

6.2 Aggregate Views

Consider the aggregate view V_{agg}:

SELECT $\bar{G}, f(\bar{X})$ AS g FROM $R, R_1, \ldots, R_n$
WHERE c GROUP BY $\bar{G}$

whose FROM clause involves a single alias of R, and f is an associative aggregation function such as sum (b) a t-diff $\mathcal{D}_R$ on R and (c) a corresponding i-diff Δ_R.

To ease exposition, we isolate the aggregation operator of the query, expressing it through the plan $V_{\text{agg}} = \gamma_{\bar{G}, f(\bar{X}) \to g} V_{\text{spj}}$, where V_{spj} is the plan for the SPJ query presented in Section 6.1. We study the interesting case, where the ID-based IVM has identified that an intermediate cache storing the input of the aggregate operator, which is the result of the SPJ query, is beneficial (since without cache both approaches would perform identically). The tuple-based approach does not use a cache, since it cannot benefit from it.

Both approaches operate in two two stages: They first compute the diff to maintain the SPJ subview V_{spj} and then use it to maintain the final aggregate view V_{agg}. The second step is the same in both cases. Thus the difference in performance comes from computing the diff for the V_{spj}, which in the case of the ID-based approach is also used to maintain the cache. Let a and p be defined as above for the subview V_{spj} (i.e., let $p = |\mathcal{D}_{V_{\text{spj}}}|/|\Delta_{V_{\text{spj}}}|$ and let a be the average cost incurred by the tuple-based diff to compute for each base table diff tuple the corresponding diff tuples for the view V_{spj}).

Speedup ratio. The speedup ratio of the ID-based approach over the tuple-based approach is given by the following formula:

(a) if Δ_R/$\mathcal{D}_R$ is an update i-diff/t-diff on non-conditional attributes of R, then

$$\text{Speedup ratio} = \frac{a+x}{1+p+x}$$

(b) else

$$\text{Speedup ratio} \geq min\left(\frac{a+x}{1+p+x}, \frac{a+x}{a+k+x}\right)$$

where x is a cost related to grouping that is shared by both approaches and thus can be safely ignored for the purposes of our discussion and k is a parameter concerning insert diffs that we will explain later.

Discussion. Similarly to SPJ views, we differentiate between cases where the base table diffs lead to update or delete diffs on the view V_{spj} and cases where they lead to insert diffs on V_{spj}.

In the first case the speedup ratio is $s_1 = \frac{a+x}{1+p+x}$. This speedup is always going to be at least 1, meaning that the tuple-based approach can never perform better than the ID-based approach. This happens because the cost a incurred by the tuple-based approach for each diff tuple in $\mathcal{D}_R$ is at least $1 + p$, since for each such tuple it will have to incur at least one index access (to find the tuple of the other relations it joins with) and p tuple accesses (to read the tuples it joins with to create the corresponding p tuples in the view). Note that these are lower bounds that apply when the view V_{spj} contains only one join. If it contains more joins, the speedup ratio and thus the performance benefit of ID-based IVM will be even higher.

On the other hand when base table diffs lead to insert diffs on the view V_{spj}, the ID-based approach will be performing the same plan with the tuple-based approach but will also be inserting tuples into the cache. Thus if k is the number of tuples created in V_{spj} on average as a result of a single diff in $\mathcal{D}_R$, then the speedup will be $s_2 = \frac{a+x}{a+k+x}$. This speedup is less than 1 (meaning that the tuple-based approach will be performing better), but now the loss is bounded, as it is always 1 per tuple inserted into V_{spj}.

Similarly to SPJ views, when the base table diffs are updates on non-conditional attributes (case (a) above), the generated diffs on the view V_{spj} are guaranteed to be update or delete diffs and thus the speedup ratio will be equal to s_1. In any other case (case (b)), the generated view diffs will in general be combinations of update, delete, and insert diffs and thus the speedup will be a linear combination of s_1 and s_2 (and thus bounded by the smaller of them).

To summarize, for all base table diffs that do not lead to inserts in the cache, the ID-based approach is guaranteed to perform not worse (and the more complex the query the better) than the tuple-based approach. It only performs worse in workloads heavy on modifications that lead to insertions to the view, because it has to maintain a cache, so that the update and delete diffs can benefit from it. However, even this loss is bounded and we expect it to not be significant in practice. Moreover, this loss will be balanced out by the speedup on diffs that lead to deletes and updates in the view, which benefit from the cache.

Relation	Tuples
User	1M
FriendList	100M
Microblog (i.e. tweets)	20M
Retweets	4M (#tweets × 10% × 2 retweets per tweet)
Mentions	8M (#tweets × 20% × 2 mentions per tweet)
Rel_Event_Microblog	16M (#tweets × 40% × 2 events per tweet)

(a) BSMA relation sizes

Query	Description
Q7	Mentioned users within a time range
Q10	Users who are retweeted within a time range
Q11	Pair of retweeting users, grouped by retweeting times
Q15	Users talking about events within a time range
Q18	Pairwise count of mentions
Q*1	Aggregate of friends of friends within the same city
Q*2	Aggregate of retweeters for every user
Q*3	Aggregate of users who tweet about topics

(b) BSMA queries and additional Queries

Figure 9: Configuration of social analytics experiments

7. EXPERIMENTAL EVALUATION

To compare the performance of ID-based and tuple-based IVM, we ran two sets of experiments. In our first set of experiments we studied the performance of both approaches on a diverse workload of views, by applying them on views commonly used in social networks. In our second set of experiments we studied the effect of varying different parameters on both the view and the data (such as selectivity, fanout, number of joins and base-table diff size).

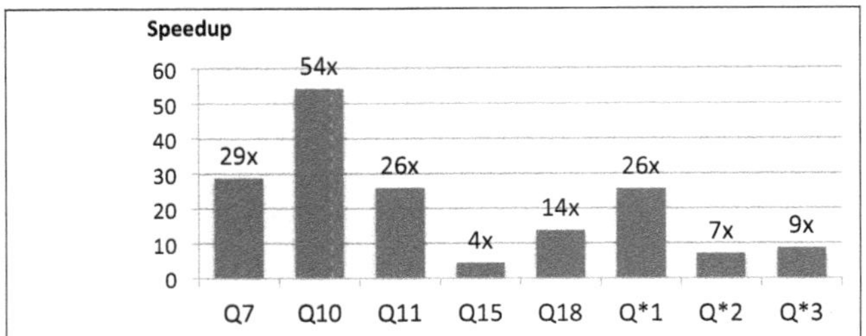

	Q7	Q10	Q11	Q15	Q18	Q*1	Q*2	Q*3
ID IVM (sec)	0.07	0.07	0.09	0.73	0.16	14.24	0.64	0.43
Tuple IVM (sec)	2.04	3.98	2.26	3.23	2.15	364.50	4.56	3.75

Figure 10: Speedup & IVM time for extended set of BSMA queries

In all cases we used *idIVM* to generate the Δ-script and $\mathcal{D}$-script (the latter was produced using our implementation of *idIVM* with tuple-based diff propagation rules instead of the standard ID-based propagation rules). We then measured the times to run each script in PostgreSQL. All experiments were run using Ubuntu LTS 12.04, OpenJDK JRE 7 and PostgreSQL 9.1, on top of an Amazon Web Services (AWS) m1.large dedicated instance configured with 1,200 input/output operations per sec (IOPS) for 16KB blocks. The configured IOPS provide predictable throughput for random block accesses. Each experiment was run with cold PostgreSQL page buffers and Linux disk buffers, which is the common case when large number of views need to be maintained.

7.1 IVM in social analytics

To study the relative performance of ID-based and tuple-based IVM on a diverse set of real queries, we applied both IVM approaches to a workload of analytics views over social media. Maintaining analytics over social media is a primary use case for IVM techniques because: (a) large base tables are produced by social media such as Twitter and Facebook, (b) rapid, frequent updates occur on the base tables, and (c) analytic views that monitor metrics and trends need to be updated continuously.

To generate the workload, we utilized the Benchmark for Social Media Analytics (BSMA) [26]. Figure 9a shows the size of the relations generated, while Figure 9b provides a summary of the workload, which comprises:

- 100 update diffs on the **User** table for attributes $tweetsnum$ (i.e number of tweets) and $favornum$ (i.e. number of favorites)
- Views corresponding to queries Q7, Q10, Q11, Q15 and Q18 from BSMA, which exhibit join chains and aggregates, hence resulting in high cost for view re-computation. These queries are also minimally extended to: (a) extend the `SELECT` clause with attributes $tweetsnum$ and $favornum$ (b) remove the `ORDER BY` and `LIMIT` and the ID parameter in the WHERE clause in order to create larger views where the benefit of the IVM becomes apparent.
- An additional 3 aggregate views over the BSMA schema, labeled as Q*1, Q*2 and Q*3. Whereas queries Q7, Q10, Q11, Q15 and Q18 include aggregation, this aggregation is not affected by the updated attributes. Since, as we have discussed in Section 6 the ID-based and tuple-based approaches behave differently in the presence of aggregates affected by the updates, we designed views Q*1, Q*2 and Q*3 to include such aggregates.

Figure 10 shows the speedup ratio of the ID-based over the tuple-based approach for each of the views. The speedup varies widely between the 8 different views and its value does not seem to be determined by whether a view contains an aggregate affected by an update or not. From the reported views, it is interesting to look at the extreme cases with either very high or low speedup. Queries Q10 and Q*1 create a huge benefit for the ID-based IVM due to the fact that the tuple-based IVM has to incur a large number of data accesses, which can be avoided by the ID-based IVM. Interestingly, this need for data accesses is created in different ways by each of the two queries. In Q10 it is created by a long join chain (Q10 joins 4 relations), while in Q*1 it is created by a combination of a long join chain with a high selectivity that appears at the end of the join chain (so that the tuple-based has to perform a lot of data accesses before it can decide that a tuple will be dropped). Finally, Q15 displays a relatively low speedup because the resulting view and the number of tuples that need to be updated in the view is very large. This makes the view update time component (which is shared by both the ID-based and the tuple-based approaches) dominate the IVM cost, thus leading to a relatively small speedup. However, it should be noted that even in this case the ID-based approach outperforms the tuple-based approach by a factor of 4.

Relation	Tuples	Size
parts	5M	170MB
devices	5M	170MB
devices_parts	50M	3GB

(a) Relation sizes

Parameter	Defaults
d: Diff size	200
s: Selectivity	20%
f: Fanout	10
j: Joins	2

(b) Parameters

$$\Delta^u_{parts} = \mathcal{D}^u_{parts}(\underline{pid}, price_{pre}, price_{post})$$

(c) Base-table Diff

Figure 11: Configuration of varying parameter experiments

7.2 Effect of data & query parameters

To study in a more controlled fashion how the structure of the view and the data affects the ID-based and tuple-based IVM, we next ran a second set of experiments, in which we picked a single view and measured the performance of both ID-based and tuple-based IVM on maintaining the view, while varying different parameters of both the view definition and the underlying data. For ease of exposition we employed the view used in our running example and shown in Figure 5a.

Experimental setup. Figure 11 shows the properties of the dataset and the view used in the experiments. Figure 11a shows the sizes of the relations, Figure 11c presents the employed base-table diff (which captures updates on the prices of parts) and Figure 11b lists the parameters that we varied in the experiments and their default values. We varied four parameters: (a) The size d of the base-table diff (i.e., the number of price updates that happened), (b) the number of joins performed by the view (as we will explain later we extended the view that by default performs two joins with additional joins), (c) The selectivity s of the selection condition *category="phone"* (i.e., the percentage of **devices** tuples that satisfy the condition), and (d) the fanout f from **parts** to **devices_parts**, i.e. the number of parts for each device. (Note that the fanout from association table **devices_parts** to entity table **devices** is always 1.) For each experiment varying a parameter, we used for all other parameters their default values shown in Figure 11b.

Figure 12 shows the view maintenance times for ID-based IVM versus tuple-based IVM and the resulting speedup of ID-based over tuple-based IVM. The cost of each approach is broken down to its components. Column A represents ID-based IVM, with the top stack (diagonally striped) corresponding to cache update time (recall that the input of an aggregate is materialized as an intermediate cache), and the bottom stack (solid colored) corresponding to view update time. No stack is shown for the cache/view diff computation time as both are negligible. Column B represents tuple-based IVM, with the top stack (horizontally striped) corresponding to view diff computation time, and the bottom stack (solid colored) correspond-

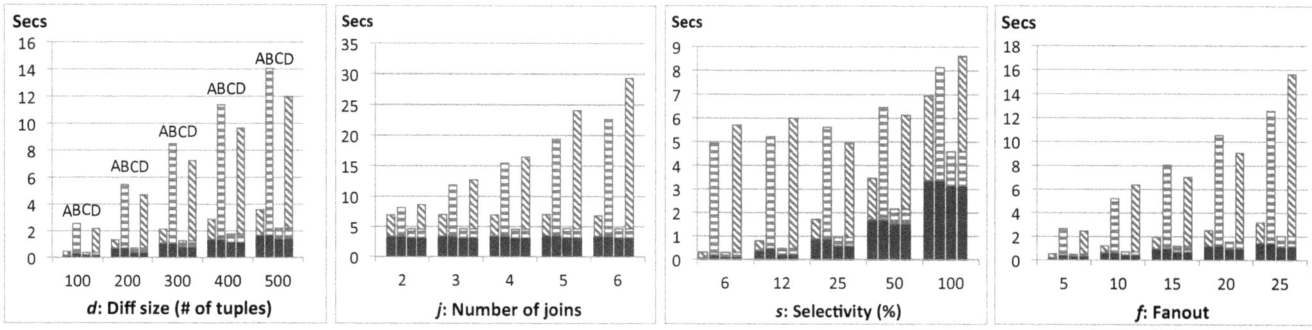

d	100	200	300	400	500
Speedup	5.5	4.1	3.9	4.0	3.9

(a) Varying Diff Size

j	2	3	4	5	6
Speedup	1.2	1.7	2.2	2.8	3.3

(b) Varying Number of Joins

s	6	12	25	50	100
Speedup	15.9	6.6	3.3	1.9	1.2

(c) Varying Selectivity

f	5	10	15	20	25
Speedup	5.0	4.3	4.1	4.1	3.9

(d) Varying Fanout

A ID-based IVM | B Tuple-based IVM | C SDBT-fixed | D SDBT-streams | Cache Update | View Diff Computation | View Update

Figure 12: View maintenance time of ID-based IVM vs tuple-based IVM and two DBToaster-inspired systems for varying parameters

ing to view update time. No stack is shown for cache update time, since as we have explained the tuple-based approach does not use a cache as it cannot benefit from it. Columns C and D correspond to simulations of DBToaster [2], which we discuss in Section 7.3. We next explain the effect of varying each of the parameters.

Varying the base-table diff size. Figure 12a illustrates the effects of varying the diff size d linearly from 100 to 500 tuples[9]. As shown on the figure, the speedup stays within 4-5. The experiment also shows a slight downward trend on the speedup. This is because as d increases, the chance also increases for reading a block of the **devices** table (out of its 20k blocks) from PostgreSQL's page buffers. In the running example, this buffering benefits tuple-based IVM, but not ID-based IVM.

Varying the number of joins. Figure 12b illustrates the effect of joins on the speedup. For this experiment we consider more complex views by augmenting the original view definition with j additional joins as follows: (i) **devices_parts** is joined with tables $R_1 \dots R_j$, such that each join is 1-to-1 on (pid, did). This simulates joins across vertically-decomposed tables, which is common practice in data warehousing. (ii) The selection $\sigma_{\text{category=“phone”}}$ is disabled in order to focus on the effects of each additional join. Figure 12b shows that the total running time of ID-based IVM is unaffected by linearly varying j between 2 (i.e., the original view with no additional joins) to 6 (the view with four additional joins). On the other hand, the total running time of the tuple-based IVM increases with each additional join, making the speedup of ID-based IVM arbitrarily high, as the complexity of the query increases. This happens due to the fact that tuple-based IVM has to perform all joins in order to compute the entire view tuples that have to be modified, in contrast to the ID-based IVM that can simply propagate the base-table diff to the view and avoid performing any joins.

Varying the selectivity of the selection condition. Figure 12c shows how the speedup is affected by the selectivity s (i.e., the number of **devices** tuples that satisfy the condition). We vary s on a log scale from 6% to 100%. Allowing more tuples to pass through the selection adversely affects the performance of ID-based IVM. The reason is that more tuples of the **devices** table join with the other tables and thus the size of the intermediate cache employed by the ID-based approach increases. This in turn leads to a higher cost of updating the cache. It should be noted however that even at 100% selectivity, ID-based IVM is faster than tuple-based IVM, albeit at a lower speedup of 1.2. Thus, ID-based IVM is at least on par with tuple-based IVM, and performs better in the common case where the selection filters a subset of the base table tuples.

Varying the fanout. Finally, Figure 12d illustrates the effects of varying the fanout f of the join (**parts, devices_parts**) linearly between 5 to 25. For all values of the fanout, the ID-based IVM performs better than the tuple-based IVM by a factor of 4-5 times.

We highlight that the ID-based approach consistently outperforms the tuple-based approach. This is the case even though the experimental conditions were designed to explicitly benefit the tuple-based IVM. In particular, (a) we assumed the existence of appropriate base table indices to speedup tuple-based joins (without counting the associated index maintenance cost) and (b) we did not use a cache for the tuple-based IVM, to avoid the cache maintenance cost, since tuple-based maintenance of associative aggregate functions does not benefit from caches. When these optimizations are inadmissible, ID-based IVM will exhibit an even higher speedup.

7.3 Comparison to the state of the art

Finally, we compared *idIVM* to DBToaster [2]; the current state of the art IVM system, which, while being essentially a tuple-based system, has been shown to significantly outperform prior IVM approaches. DBToaster's performance is the result of five major optimizations: (a) performing IVM one diff tuple at a time (which leads to reducing $\mathcal{D}$-script joins with a diff table into selections), (b) compiling the $\mathcal{D}$-script into code, instead of SQL statements, (c) utilizing an in-memory implementation, (d) aggressively pushing aggregations down, and (e) materializing a large number of intermediate views (i.e., caches) that are used to maintain the original view and each other. On the other hand, *idIVM* benefits most from using (a) ID-based diffs and (b) update diffs (in contrast to DBToaster, where updates are simulated through inserts and deletes).

These differences make the two systems not directly comparable. Since *idIVM* could in principle also benefit from DBToaster's optimizations a-d, we next focus on comparing *idIVM* to the intermediate view materialization strategy used by DBToaster. To this end, we designed a DBToaster-inspired implementation (denoted as Simulated DBToaster or SDBT) that runs on top of a DBMS and uses the same intermediate views as the original DBToaster implementation (up to aggregation push-down). We then executed SDBT on all scenarios considered in Section 12. Since, in contrast to *idIVM*, DBToaster creates different intermediate views depending on the types of allowed base-table diffs, we ran two different versions of SDBT: one assuming that only diffs to the **parts** table are

[9]Similar trends can be observed for diff sizes up to 15,000 tuples. This is the point where it is beneficial to recompute the view rather than apply IVM, as discussed in prior work [13].

possible (referred to as SDBT-fixed) and one assuming that all base tables may change (referred to as SDBT-streams). Columns C and D in Figure 12 show the times of SDBT-fixed and SDBT-streams, respectively. We observe that *idIVM* in all cases significantly outperforms SDBT-streams, while it is in most cases slightly slower then SDBT-fixed. It should be noted however that we allowed both SDBT-fixed and SDBT-streams to employ update t-diffs. Had they simulated updates through inserts and deletes, as is the case in DBToaster, their performance would have been worse.

Note that SDBT captures only one of the optimizations used in DBToaster. Furthermore, SDBT (alike *idIVM* and tuple-based IVM) operates on large data, residing in secondary storage and managed via a database (PostgreSQL in this case). Due to the mix of optimizations involved and its main memory orientation, DBToaster behaves differently from SDBT. Experiments we conducted with DBToaster showed for instance that the compilation to code and in-memory implementation lead to 50-300 times faster execution than the PostgreSQL-based SDBT-fixed. On the other hand, the in-memory execution severely limits DBToaster's scalability (allowing it to scale only up to 2% of the data size used in our experiments when diffs are allowed on all base tables). Moreover, the lack of set-processing makes DBToaster's performance deteriorate much faster than SDBT with increasing diff sizes (e.g, DBToaster's speedup over SDBT-fixed drops from 300x for a diff size of 100 tuples to 50x when the diff size becomes 500).

8. RELATED WORK

IVM is a long studied problem with a lot of influential works [6, 5, 7, 21, 13]. *idIVM* falls under the category of IVM works that employ the *algebraic* [21, 10, 22, 18] approach. Due to the vast amount of related work in IVM, we focus next on approaches that are particularly related to the main aspects of our work, which are: (a) exploiting primary key information together with the associated (b) overestimation and (c) caching. Note that we cover all works in these areas, even if they do not follow the algebraic approach. For comprehensive surveys on IVM, the reader is referred to [12, 8].

Exploiting primary key constraints. The idea of exploiting primary key constraints to speed up IVM was first presented in [11, 23]. However, in contrast to our work, [11, 23] study only self-maintenance (potentially together with some auxiliary views) and not general view maintenance where some data from the base relations may be required to maintain the view. Furthermore, they are limited to maintenance of SPJ (including outer-join) views and their algorithms are not easily extensible to more general classes of queries as they operate by looking holistically at the view definition, in contrast to our modular algebraic approach. The first work that exploited primary keys in an extensible algebraic setting and introduced the notion of partial diffs, is [16]. However, the partial diffs of [16] always contain the entire primary key of the view. Thus, they are not true ID-based diffs, but instead (relaxed) tuple-based diffs, that may lack some of the (non-key) attributes of the view but will still incur the same number of accesses as tuple-based approaches. Finally, primary key information has also been used to optimize the rules for maintaining the output of particular operators (e.g., outer-join in [18]) within a tuple-based approach. However, these approaches do not look at exploiting the keys to avoid tuple-based diffs altogether, as done in this work.

Overestimation. Our definition of overestimation is similar to *safe overestimation* described in [4] and *ineffective updates* in [16]. While overestimation in these works appears only because of selection conditions, *idIVM* exploits also overestimation that arises because of joins, which do not appear in the former, since they are both (relaxed) tuple-based approaches.

Caching. Several works looked at the problem of materializing additional results to speed up IVM. These can be classified into two broad categories. The first category includes approaches where the cached results are operator-specific. Examples of such works include the IVM of aggregation under the assumption that previous aggregation results are available [22, 20] and of top-k results by caching additional view tuples that are beyond the top k in order to reduce the frequency of accessing the base tables [27]. These caches correspond to our notion of operator caches and can thus be incorporated in our framework as part of an operator definition. The second category contains approaches where the cached results are not tied to a particular operator, but are additional views that are then exploited holistically during the IVM of the original view [24, 19, 23, 2]. In contrast to our work that uses only caches that correspond to subplans of the original plan, these works benefit by employing caches that may not be subplans of a single plan. This aggressive materialization allows more efficient IVM, though at the cost of maintaining an increased number of intermediate views. A prime example of such approaches is DBToaster [2], which is discussed extensively in Section 7.3. However, by not being ID-based such approaches always access at least one materialized view, in contrast to our approach, which in some cases can avoid accessing base tables or cached views altogether. Finally, a related area to caching in IVM is view selection, consisting of works that decide which views to materialize to speed up query evaluation [1, 14]. Such approaches can be used in the context of *idIVM* to decide which intermediate caches to materialize.

9. CONCLUSIONS AND FUTURE WORK

We have shown how to exploit IDs towards an IVM algorithm that is more efficient than existing tuple-based approaches under common assumptions. An extension of this work involves minimizing base table accesses for insert i-diffs. Although in this work insert i-diffs incur the same base table accesses as tuple-based approches, more elaborate rules for i-diff's avoid base table accesses by instead utilizing data that potentially already exist in the view. However, in contrast to the current ID-based approach where one can know statically based on the i-diff schema whether base table accesses will be needed, the extended (for insert i-diff) version of the algorithm has to find out dynamically at run-time whether accesses are needed, depending on the i-diff instance.

10. ACKNOWLEDGEMENTS

We thank the anonymous reviewers and Gaurav Saxena, Alok Singh, and Romain Vernoux for their detailed comments on prior versions of this paper. We also thank Christoph Koch, Mohammad Dashti, and Oliver Kennedy for extensive private communications on DBToaster.

11. REFERENCES

[1] S. Agrawal, S. Chaudhuri, and V. R. Narasayya. Automated selection of materialized views and indexes in sql databases. In *VLDB*, 2000.

[2] Y. Ahmad, O. Kennedy, C. Koch, and M. Nikolic. Dbtoaster: Higher-order delta processing for dynamic, frequently fresh views. *PVLDB*, 5(10):968–979, 2012.

[3] E. Baralis, S. Paraboschi, and E. Teniente. Materialized views selection in a multidimensional database. In *VLDB*, 1997.

[4] A. Behrend and T. Jörg. Optimized incremental etl jobs for maintaining data warehouses. In *IDEAS*, pages 216–224, 2010.

[5] J. A. Blakeley, N. Coburn, and P.-Å. Larson. Updating derived relations: Detecting irrelevant and autonomously computable updates. *ACM Trans. Database Syst.*, 14(3):369–400, 1989.

[6] J. A. Blakeley, P.-Å. Larson, and F. W. Tompa. Efficiently updating materialized views. In *SIGMOD Conference*, pages 61–71, 1986.

[7] S. Ceri and J. Widom. Deriving production rules for incremental view maintenance. In *VLDB*, 1991.

[8] R. Chirkova and J. Yang. Materialized views. *Foundations and Trends in Databases*, 4(4):295–405, 2012.

[9] L. S. Colby, T. Griffin, L. Libkin, I. S. Mumick, and H. Trickey. Algorithms for deferred view maintenance. In *SIGMOD*, 1996.
[10] T. Griffin and L. Libkin. Incremental maintenance of views with duplicates. In *SIGMOD*, pages 328–339, 1995.
[11] A. Gupta, H. V. Jagadish, and I. S. Mumick. Data integration using self-maintainable views. In *EDBT*, pages 140–144, 1996.
[12] A. Gupta and I. S. Mumick. Maintenance of materialized views: Problems, techniques, and applications. *IEEE Data Eng. Bull.*, 1995.
[13] A. Gupta, I. S. Mumick, and V. S. Subrahmanian. Maintaining views incrementally. In *SIGMOD*, pages 157–166. ACM Press, 1993.
[14] H. Gupta and I. S. Mumick. Selection of views to materialize in a data warehouse. *IEEE Trans. Knowl. Data Eng.*, 17(1):24–43, 2005.
[15] H. He, J. Xie, J. Yang, and H. Yu. Asymmetric batch incremental view maintenance. In *ICDE*, pages 106–117, 2005.
[16] T. Jörg and S. Deßloch. View maintenance using partial deltas. In *Datenbanksysteme für Business, Technologie und Web*, 2011.
[17] H. A. Kuno and G. Graefe. Deferred maintenance of indexes and of materialized views. In *DNIS*, pages 312–323, 2011.
[18] P.-Å. Larson and J. Zhou. Efficient maintenance of materialized outer-join views. In *ICDE*, pages 56–65, 2007.
[19] H. Mistry, P. Roy, S. Sudarshan, and K. Ramamritham. Materialized view selection and maintenance using multi-query optimization. In *SIGMOD Conference*, pages 307–318, 2001.
[20] T. Palpanas, R. Sidle, R. Cochrane, and H. Pirahesh. Incremental maintenance for non-distributive aggregate functions. In *VLDB*, pages 802–813, 2002.
[21] X. Qian and G. Wiederhold. Incremental recomputation of active relational expressions. *IEEE TKDE*, 3(3):337–341, 1991.
[22] D. Quass. Maintenance expressions for views with aggregation. In *VIEWS*, pages 110–118, 1996.
[23] D. Quass, A. Gupta, I. S. Mumick, and J. Widom. Making views self-maintainable for data warehousing. In *4th International Conference on Parallel and Distributed Information Systems*, 1996.
[24] K. A. Ross, D. Srivastava, and S. Sudarshan. Materialized view maintenance and integrity constraint checking: Trading space for time. In *SIGMOD*, pages 447–458, 1996.
[25] A. Shukla, P. Deshpande, and J. F. Naughton. Materialized view selection for multidimensional datasets. In *VLDB*, 1998.
[26] F. Xia, Y. Li, C. Yu, H. Ma, and W. Qian. BSMA: A benchmark for analytical queries over social media data. *PVLDB*, 7(13), 2014.
[27] K. Yi, H. Yu, J. Yang, G. Xia, and Y. Chen. Efficient maintenance of materialized top-k views. In *ICDE*, pages 189–200, 2003.

APPENDIX

A. DETAILED PERFORMANCE ANALYSIS

We next describe the detailed performance analysis of the ID-based and tuple-based approaches that led to the equations of Section 6. The analysis covers two representative cases: (a) SPJ views, which by default do not involve intermediate caches and (b) Aggregate views involving grouping and associative functions, which (by default) are supported by caches. In the following we assume that both approaches have access to view indices on the view IDs and additionally the tuple-based IVM has access to appropriate base table indices (which are not required by the ID-based approach).

A.1 SPJ Views

Consider (a) the SPJ view V_{spj}:

$$\texttt{SELECT } \bar{S} \texttt{ FROM } R, R_1, \ldots, R_n \texttt{ WHERE } c$$

whose FROM clause involves a single alias of a table R, (b) a t-diff $\mathcal{D}_R$ on R and (c) a corresponding i-diff Δ_R on R. We distinguish between two cases, depending on the type of the diff $\mathcal{D}_R/\Delta_R$.

A.1.1 Update diffs on non-conditional attributes

We first study base table update diffs on attributes of R that do not participate in any join or selection condition in V_{spj}. Consider such an update t-diff/i-diff on attributes $\bar{A}''$ of R:

$$\mathcal{D}_R^u = \Delta_R^u(\bar{I}, \bar{A}'_{pre}, \bar{A}''_{post})$$

where $\bar{I}$ is the key of R.

Since we are interested in the IVM of an update on R, we decompose the condition c into 3 subconditions $c_R, c_{rest}, c_{R-rest}$ in conjunctive normal form, s.t. every one of their conjuncts involves only attributes of R, only attributes of $R_1, \ldots, R_n$ and both attributes of R and $R_1, \ldots, R_n$, respectively. It is easy to see that V_{spj} can be computed through the algebraic expression $\pi_S(\sigma_{c_R} R \bowtie_{c_{R-rest}} E)$, where $E = \sigma_{c_{rest}}(R_1 \times \ldots \times R_n)$.

In general, the i-diff Δ_R^u (resp. t-diff $\mathcal{D}_R^u$) will lead to $\Delta_{V_{\text{spj}}}^u$, $\Delta_{V_{\text{spj}}}^+$ and $\Delta_{V_{\text{spj}}}^-$ in the ID-based approach (resp. $\mathcal{D}_{V_{\text{spj}}}^u$, $\mathcal{D}_{V_{\text{spj}}}^+$ and $\mathcal{D}_{V_{\text{spj}}}^-$ in the tuple-based approach). However, since the updated attributes $\bar{A}''$ of R do not participate in the join condition c_{R-rest} or the selection condition c_R, the update diff on R will only lead to an update diff on V_{spj}. Furthermore, since the selection σ_{c_R} simply filters out tuples of $\mathcal{D}_R^u$, it has the same effect as using a smaller initial diff, and is therefore ignored in the rest of the analysis.

$\mathcal{D}/\Delta$-script. The scripts returned by the IVM algorithms are:

ID-based approach	Tuple-based approach
$\Delta_{V_{\text{spj}}}^u = \mathcal{D}_R^u$	$\mathcal{D}_{V_{\text{spj}}}^u = \pi_{\bar{S}} \mathcal{D}_R^u \bowtie_{c_{R-rest}} E$
APPLY $\Delta_{V_{\text{spj}}}^u$	APPLY $\mathcal{D}_{V_{\text{spj}}}^u$

The ID-based approach simply propagates the base table diff by exploiting the fact that no tuples need to be inserted or deleted from the view, since the modified attributes $\bar{A}''$ do not participate in the join condition.

Cost analysis. Both the ID-based IVM cost and the tuple-based IVM cost are the sum of the *diff computation cost* of $\Delta_{V_{\text{spj}}}^u$ (respectively $\mathcal{D}_{V_{\text{spj}}}^u$) and the *view modification cost*, which is the cost of applying the modifications dictated by $\Delta_{V_{\text{spj}}}^u$ (respectively $\mathcal{D}_{V_{\text{spj}}}^u$) on the materialized view. We measure both costs in terms of block accesses to indices and tuples. Employing common assumptions on the index structures[10], the cost of retrieving (using an index) the m tuples whose $\bar{X}$ attributes have given $\bar{x}$ values can be approximated by $1 + m$ (i.e., 1 index lookup and m tuple accesses). We next analyze each of the cost components.

Diff computation cost. Since the ID-based approach simply propagates Δ_R^u to the view as is, its diff computation cost is zero. On the other hand, the cost of the tuple-based IVM varies widely depending on the computation of $\mathcal{D}_{V_{\text{spj}}}^u = \pi_{\bar{S}} \mathcal{D}_R^u \bowtie_{c_{R-rest}} E$.

We consider the common case where the join condition c_{R-rest} is a conjunction of equalities of the form $R.J = R_i.J_i$. Furthermore, we assume that the database is optimized for tuple-based IVM, having all necessary indices for the efficient computation of $\mathcal{D}_{V_{\text{spj}}}^u = \mathcal{D}_R^u \bowtie_{c_{R-rest}} E$. Since the diff-table $\mathcal{D}_R^u$ is considered in the IVM literature to be smaller than the base tables, the DBMS will typically execute the above query through a *diff-driven loop* plan: For each tuple t of $\mathcal{D}_R^u$ it executes the subplan $\sigma_{c'_{R-rest}} E$, where c'_{R-rest} is an instantiation of the c_{R-rest} condition where the attributes of R have been replaced with their values in t. Let us name a the average number of accesses performed for each tuple of $\mathcal{D}_R^u$, i.e., the average number of accesses in each execution of $\sigma_{c'_{R-rest}} E$. Then the diff computation cost of the tuple-based approach is $|\mathcal{D}_R^u| a$. The DBMS may also choose to evaluate the

[10] We assume that indices satisfy the following conditions:
1. An index is either a hash index, or a B-tree with leaf nodes in secondary storage and non-leaf nodes in memory.
2. The retrieved tuples, if any, are not clustered together.
3. Caching of index leaves and/or tuples has minimal effects on the overall cost, as the cache is significantly smaller than the database.

Costs	ID-based	Tuple-based	
		Diff-driven loop plan	Other plan
Diff computation	0	$\lvert\mathcal{D}_R^u\rvert a$	E
View index lookups	$\lvert\mathcal{D}_R^u\rvert$	$\lvert\mathcal{D}_R^u\rvert p$	$\lvert\mathcal{D}_R^u\rvert p$
View tuple accesses		$\lvert\mathcal{D}_R^u\rvert p$	

Table 2: Costs of ID-based and tuple-based IVM on V_{spj}

query with a plan other than a diff-driven loop, but this is expected to happen only when the diff tables are very large, when the use of an IVM approach becomes questionable.

View modification cost. To apply $\Delta^u_{V_{\mathrm{spj}}}$ (resp. $\mathcal{D}^u_{V_{\mathrm{spj}}}$) to the view, the DBMS will typically utilize the view index to locate the view tuples that need to be modified. In either of the approaches there will be as many view index lookups as tuples in the view diff (i.e., $|\Delta^u_{V_{\mathrm{spj}}}| = |\mathcal{D}^u_R|$ lookups for the ID-based and $|\mathcal{D}^u_{V_{\mathrm{spj}}}|$ lookups for the tuple-based approach, respectively). Once the to-be-modified view tuples have been identified (which are in both cases equal to $|\mathcal{D}^u_{V_{\mathrm{spj}}}|$), both approaches will incur $|\mathcal{D}^u_{V_{\mathrm{spj}}}|$ view tuple accesses to update them. Table 2 shows the view index lookups and view tuple accesses for each approach utilizing the i-diff compression factor $p = |\mathcal{D}^u_{V_{\mathrm{spj}}}|/|\Delta^u_{V_{\mathrm{spj}}}|$.[11]

Discussion. Table 2 summarizes the costs for the tuple-based and ID-based approach. Combining them leads to the following speedup ratio of the ID-based over the tuple-based approach (assuming a diff-driven loop plan for the tuple-based approach):

$$\text{Speedup ratio for } V_{\mathrm{spj}} = \frac{|\mathcal{D}^u_R|(a+p+p)}{|\mathcal{D}^u_R|(1+p)} = \frac{a+2p}{1+p} \quad (1)$$

The relative performance difference between the two approaches varies depending on the value of the compression factor p. When $p \geq 1$, the ID-based approach is guaranteed to be more efficient with its absolute gain (i.e., the difference of accesses from the tuple-based approach) raising proportionally to p. When $0 < p < 1$, the ID-based approach is also more efficient in the typical case when the tuple-based approach has to do at least one access for each tuple in $\mathcal{D}^u_R$ (which means that $a > 1$). For the tuple-based approach to perform better it should be the case that $a < 1 - p$, which can be satisfied only if the following conditions simultaneously hold: (a) the tuple-based approach incurs $a < 1$ tuple accesses for each tuple in $\mathcal{D}^u_R$ on average (which can only happen if many tuples of $\mathcal{D}^u_R$ share the same join attribute values and thus the joined tuples can be retrieved once and reused for all of them) and (b) the ID-based approach is severely overestimating (i.e., $p \ll 1$).

A.1.2 Other diffs

Consider now insert and delete i-diffs/t-diffs on the base relation R, as well as update i-diffs/t-diffs on attributes of R that are involved in some join or selection condition in V_{spj}. Such base table diffs will lead in general to a combination of $\Delta^u_{V_{\mathrm{spj}}}$, $\Delta^+_{V_{\mathrm{spj}}}$ and $\Delta^-_{V_{\mathrm{spj}}}$ in the ID-based approach (resp. $\mathcal{D}^u_{V_{\mathrm{spj}}}$, $\mathcal{D}^+_{V_{\mathrm{spj}}}$ and $\mathcal{D}^-_{V_{\mathrm{spj}}}$ in the tuple-based approach). For the cases in which a base table diff is translated into an update or delete i-diff/t-diff on the view, the ID-based and tuple-based algorithms will behave as described in Section A.1.1 and thus the speedup ratio will be $\frac{a+2p}{1+p}$. On the other hand, in the case when a base table diff is translated into an insert i-diff/t-diff on the view, the ID-based and tuple-based algorithm will produce identical scripts, leading to a speedup of 1 (i.e., the ID-based algorithm will degenerate to the tuple-based algorithm but will not behave worse than the latter).

[11]In the unlikely case, where the DBMS chooses to identify the to-be-modified tuples by performing a full scan of the view instead of using the index, the view modification cost becomes the same for both approaches. In this case, the difference between the two approaches reduces to the difference between their computation costs.

A.2 Aggregate Views

Consider (a) the aggregate view V_{agg}:

```
SELECT Ḡ, f(X̄) AS g FROM R, R1, ..., Rn
WHERE c GROUP BY Ḡ
```

whose FROM clause involves a single alias of a table R, and f is an associative aggregation function such as sum, (b) a t-diff $\mathcal{D}_R$ on R and (c) a corresponding i-diff Δ_R on R.

To ease exposition, we isolate the aggregation operator of the query, expressing it through the plan $V_{\mathrm{agg}} = \gamma_{\bar{G}, f(\bar{X}) \to g} V_{\mathrm{spj}}$, where V_{spj} is the algebraic plan for the SPJ query presented in Section A.1.

We consider the case where the ID-based algorithm has determined that it is beneficial to create an intermediate cache storing the result of the SPJ subview V_{spj}, since otherwise both approaches will be performing identically. The tuple-based does not employ a cache, as it cannot benefit from it.

Similarly to the case of SPJ views, we distinguish between two cases depending on the type of the base table diff $\mathcal{D}_R/\Delta_R$.

A.2.1 Update diffs on non-conditional attributes

Consider an update t-diff/i-diff on attributes $\bar{A}''$ of R that are not involved in any condition in V_{agg}:

$$\mathcal{D}^u_R = \Delta^u_R(\bar{I}, \bar{A}'_{pre}, \bar{A}''_{post})$$

where $\bar{I}$ is the key of R.

Cache diff computation / modification cost. The ID-based approach maintains an intermediate cache, which is equivalent to V_{spj}. The cache incurs *cache diff computation* cost and *cache modification cost*, which are also equivalent to the diff computation and view modification cost of V_{spj}. There is no intermediate cache for the tuple-based approach.

View diff computation cost. We consider the case where f is *incrementally computable*. That is, there is an incremental function $f_{\mathcal{D}}$ that inputs $\mathcal{D}^u_{V_{\mathrm{spj}}}(\bar{S}, \bar{X}_{pre}, \bar{X}_{post})$ where $\bar{S}$ is the key of V_{spj}, and outputs $\mathcal{D}^u_{V_{\mathrm{agg}}}(\bar{G}, g_{pre}, g_{post})$. For example, when f is the sum function, $f_{\mathcal{D}}$ is also f, since sum is an associative aggregation function. Given $f_{\mathcal{D}}$, the tuple-based approach computes $\mathcal{D}^u_{V_{\mathrm{agg}}} = \gamma_{\bar{G}, f_{\mathcal{D}}(\bar{X}) \to g} \mathcal{D}^u_{V_{\mathrm{spj}}}$.

Given that $|\mathcal{D}^u_R|$ is much smaller than base tables, the number of groups in $\mathcal{D}^u_{V_{\mathrm{agg}}}$ will be smaller than the number of groups in V_{agg}. The efficient implementation for γ is thus hash aggregation with in-memory buckets, which can be pipelined. Due to pipelining, no additional block accesses are incurred for γ. Thus, the tuple-based approach has the same diff computation cost for V_{spj} and V_{agg}.

As an optimization, the ID-based approach uses the UPDATE RETURNING statement to update the cache and return the result of the update in a single step. Thus, $\Delta^u_{V_{\mathrm{spj}}}$ is obtained without additional accesses over cache modification costs. Similar to the tuple-based approach, $\Delta^u_{V_{\mathrm{agg}}} = \gamma_{\bar{G}, f_{\Delta}(\bar{X}) \to g} \Delta^u_{V_{\mathrm{spj}}}$, and the γ uses pipelined hash aggregation. Thus, the ID-based approach also has the same diff computation cost for V_{spj} and V_{agg}.

View modification cost. To apply $\Delta^u_{V_{\mathrm{agg}}}$ (resp. $\mathcal{D}^u_{V_{\mathrm{agg}}}$) to the view, both approaches will incur an index lookup and a tuple access per tuple in the i-diff (resp. t-diff). We denote the grouping compression factor $g = |\mathcal{D}^u_{V_{\mathrm{agg}}}|/|\mathcal{D}^u_{V_{\mathrm{spj}}}|$ in Table 3. **Discussion.** For V_{agg}, Table 3 summarizes the costs for both ID-based and tuple-based approaches. Combing them leads to the following speedup ratio of the ID-based over the tuple-based approach (assuming a diff-driven loop plan for the tuple-based approach):

$$\text{Speedup ratio for } V_{\mathrm{agg}} = \frac{a+2pg}{1+p+2pg} \quad (2)$$

Costs	ID-based	Tuple-based	
		Diff-driven loop plan	Other plan
Cache diff computation	0	–	
Cache index lookups	$\lvert\mathcal{D}^u_R\rvert$	–	
Cache tuple accesses	$\lvert\mathcal{D}^u_R\rvert p$	–	
View diff computation	0	$\lvert\mathcal{D}^u_R\rvert a$	E
View index lookups	$\lvert\mathcal{D}^u_R\rvert pg$		
View tuple accesses	$\lvert\mathcal{D}^u_R\rvert pg$		

Table 3: Costs of ID-based and tuple-based IVM on V_{agg}

For the tuple-based approach to perform better on V_{agg}, it should be the case that $\frac{a+2pg}{1+p+2pg} < 1$, which implies that $a < 1 + p$. However, we will show that this is never possible. The average cost a spent by the tuple-based IVM for each diff tuple in $\mathcal{D}^u_R$ will always be at least $1+p$, as for each such tuple t the algorithm would have to perform (a) at least one index access to check whether t joins with some of the other relations in the FROM clause and (b) at least p tuple accesses to retrieve the tuples it joins with from the other relations to create p diff tuples in $\mathcal{D}^u_{V_{\text{spj}}}$. Note that these are the lower bounds for a that happen when the query contains just a single join $R \bowtie R_1$. For longer join chains the tuple-based IVM will have to perform additional index and tuple accesses, yielding even worse performance compared to the ID-based approach.

Note that the above analysis exploits the absence of multivalued dependencies in V_{spj} (which is a necessary condition for *idIVM* to create a cache). If there was a multivalued dependency, multiple tuples in $\mathcal{D}^u_R$ could share the same computation (and thus it would not be the case that each of them would incur at least $1 + p$ accesses).

A.2.2 Other diffs

Similarly to the SPJ views, an insert and delete base table diff or an update diff on an attribute of R involved in a condition, might lead to insert, update and delete diffs on V_{spj}. For the cases that lead to deletes and updates on V_{spj} the cost will be the same as the one outlined in Section A.2.1.

On the other hand when base table diffs lead to insert diffs on the view V_{spj}, the ID-based approach will be performing the same plan with the tuple-based approach but will also be inserting tuples into the cache. Let k be the number of tuples created in V_{spj} on average as a result of a single diff in $\mathcal{D}_R$. Then the cost of the tuple-based and ID-based approach is $|\mathcal{D}_R|(a+2pg)$ and $|\mathcal{D}_R|(k+a+2pg)$, respectively. Thus the speedup ratio is $\frac{a+2pg}{a+k+2pg}$. This speedup is less than 1 (meaning that the tuple-based approach will be performing better). However, this loss is bounded, as it is always 1 per tuple inserted into V_{spj}.

B. I-DIFF PROPAGATION RULES

For $\Delta^+_{Input_l}(\bar{I}, \bar{A}''_{post})$
$\Delta^+_V = \Delta^+_{Input_l} \times Input^{post}_r$
For $\Delta^+_{Input_r}(\bar{I}, \bar{A}''_{post})$
$\Delta^+_V = Input^{post}_l \times \Delta^+_{Input_r}$
For $\Delta^-_{Input_l}(\bar{I}, \bar{A}'_{pre})$ ($\Delta^-_{Input_r}$ is symmetric)
$\Delta^-_V = \Delta^-_{Input_l}$
For $\Delta^u_{Input_l}(\bar{I}, \bar{A}'_{pre}, \bar{A}''_{post})$ ($\Delta^u_{intpu_r}$ is symmetric)
$\Delta^u_V = \Delta^u_{Input_l}$

Table 4: Rules for $\times$

For $\Delta^+_{Input_l}(\bar{I}, \bar{A}_{post})$ (For $\Delta^+_{Input_r}$ replace 0 by 1)
$\Delta^+_V = \pi_{*,b\to 0}\Delta^+_{Input_l}$
For $\Delta^-_{Input_l}(\bar{I}, \bar{A}'_{pre})$ (For $\Delta^-_{Input_r}$ replace 0 by 1)
$\Delta^-_V = \pi_{*,b\to 0}\Delta^-_{Input_l}$
For $\Delta^u_{Input_l}(\bar{I}, \bar{A}'_{pre}, \bar{A}''_{post})$ (For $\Delta^u_{Input_r}$ replace 0 by 1)
$\Delta^-_V = \pi_{*,b\to 0}\Delta^u_{Input_l}$

Table 5: Rules for $\cup$

For $\Delta^+_{Input}(\bar{I}, \bar{A}_{post})$
$\Delta^+_V = \sigma_{\phi(\bar{X})}\Delta^+_{Input}$
For $\Delta^-_{Input}(\bar{I}, \bar{A}'_{pre})$
$\Delta^-_V = \sigma_{\phi(\bar{X}_{pre})}\Delta^-_{Input}$
For $\Delta^u_{Input}(\bar{I}, \bar{A}'_{pre}, \bar{A}''_{post})$

if $\bar{X} \subseteq \bar{I} \cup \bar{A}''_{post}$ then
$\quad \Delta^u_V = \sigma_{\phi(\bar{X}_{pre})}\sigma_{\phi(\bar{X})}\Delta^u_{Input}$
else
$\quad \Delta^u_V = \Delta^-_{Input}$

if $\bar{X} \cap \bar{A}''_{post} = \emptyset$ then
$\quad \Delta^+_V =$ not triggered
else if $\bar{X} \subseteq \bar{I} \cup \bar{A}''_{post}$ then
$\quad \Delta^+_V = Input^{post} \ltimes_{\bar{I}} \sigma_{\neg\phi(\bar{X}_{pre})}\sigma_{\phi(\bar{X})}\Delta^u_{Input}$
else
$\quad \Delta^+_V = \sigma_{\neg\phi(\bar{X}_{pre})}\sigma_{\phi(\bar{X})}(Input^{post} \ltimes \Delta^u_{Input})$

if $\bar{X} \cap \bar{A}''_{post} = \emptyset$ then
$\quad \Delta^-_V =$ not triggered
else if $\bar{X} \subseteq \bar{I} \cup \bar{A}''_{post}$ then
$\quad \Delta^-_V = \pi_{\bar{I},\bar{A}'_{pre}}\sigma_{\phi(\bar{X}_{pre})}\sigma_{\neg\phi(\bar{X})}\Delta^u_{Input}$
else
$\quad \Delta^-_V = \pi_{\bar{I},\bar{A}'_{pre}}\sigma_{\phi(\bar{X}_{pre})}\sigma_{\neg\phi(\bar{X})}Input^{post} \ltimes \Delta^u_{Input}$

Blue portion applies when pre-state attributes present.

Table 6: Rules for $\sigma_{\phi(\bar{X})}$

For $\Delta^-_{Input}(\bar{I}, \bar{A}'_{pre})$ where $\bar{I} \subseteq \bar{G}$
$\Delta^-_V = \Delta^-_{Input}$
For any $\Delta^t_{Input}(\bar{I}, \bar{A}')$ and f, we can recompute groups

if $\bar{G} \subseteq (\bar{I} \cup \bar{A}')$ then
$\quad \Delta^u_V = \gamma_{\bar{G},f(\bar{X})\to c}(\Delta^t_{Input} \rtimes_{\bar{G}} Input^{post})$
else
$\quad \Delta^u_V = \gamma_{\bar{G},f(\bar{X})\to c}(\Delta^t_{Input} \rtimes_{\bar{I}} Input^{post} \rtimes_{\bar{G}} Input^{post})$

(Do not handle group creation/deletion)

Table 7: Rules for $\gamma_{\bar{G},f(\bar{X})\to c}$

For $\Delta^+_{Input}(\bar{I}, \bar{A}_{post})$
$\Delta^+_V = \pi_{\bar{D},f(\bar{X})\to c,\bar{I}}\Delta^+_{Input}$
For $\Delta^-_{Input}(\bar{I}, \bar{A}'_{pre})$

if $\bar{X} \subseteq \bar{I} \cup \bar{A}'_{pre}$ then
$\quad \Delta^-_V = \pi_{(\bar{D}\cap(\bar{I}\cup\bar{A}'_{pre}))\cup f(\bar{X}_{pre})\to c_{pre},\bar{I}}\Delta^-_{Input}$
else
$\quad \Delta^-_V = \pi_{\bar{D}\cap(\bar{I}\cup\bar{A}'_{pre}),\bar{I}}\Delta^-_{Input}$

For $\Delta^u_{Input}(\bar{I}, \bar{A}'_{pre}, \bar{A}''_{post})$

if $(\bar{I} \cup \bar{A}''_{post}) \cap \bar{X} = \emptyset$ then
$\quad \Delta^u_V = \sigma_{isupd}\pi_{\bar{D}',\bar{I}}\Delta^u_{Input}$
else if $\bar{X} \subseteq \bar{I} \cup \bar{A}''_{post}$ then
$\quad \Delta^u_V = \sigma_{isupd}\pi_{\bar{D}',f(\bar{X})\to c_{post},f(\bar{X}_{pre})\to c_{pre},\bar{I}}\Delta^u_{Input}$
else
$\quad \Delta^u_V = \sigma_{isupd}\pi_{\bar{D}',f(\bar{X})\to c_{post},f(\bar{X}_{pre})\to c_{pre},\bar{I}}$
$\qquad (Input^{post} \ltimes_{\bar{I}} \Delta^u_{Input})$
where σ_{isupd} selects tuples corresponding to actual updates (i.e., where $c_{pre} \neq c_{post}$ or $a_{pre} \neq a_{post}$ for some attribute a), $\bar{D}' = (\bar{D} \cap (\bar{I} \cup \bar{A}''_{post})) \cup (\bar{D}_{pre} \cap \bar{A}'_{pre})$, and $\bar{D}_{pre}$ is the pre-state counterpart of $\bar{D}$.

Blue portion applies when pre-state attributes present.

Table 8: Rules for $\pi_{\bar{D},f(\bar{X})\to c}$

For $\Delta^u_{Input}(\bar{I}, \bar{A}'_{pre}, \bar{A}''_{post})$, and $\bar{G} \cap \bar{A}''_{post} = \emptyset$
$\Delta^i_1 = \pi_{\bar{I}, x_{post}-x_{in}\to x_\Delta}(\Delta^u_{Input} \bowtie \pi_{x\to x_{in}} Input^{pre})$
For $\Delta^-_{Input}(\bar{I}, \bar{A}'_{pre})$
$\Delta^j_2 = \pi_{\bar{I}, 0-x_{in}\to x_\Delta}(\Delta^-_{Input} \bowtie \pi_{x\to x_{in}} Input^{pre})$
For $\Delta^+_{Input}(\bar{I}, \bar{A}''_{post})$
$\Delta^k_3 = \pi_{\bar{I}, x\to x_\Delta}(\Delta^+_{Input} \bar{\ltimes} Input^{pre})$
For converting Δ to output update i-diffs
Happens after all $\Delta^i_1, \Delta^j_2, \Delta^k_3$ are computed. $\Delta^u_V = \pi_{\bar{G}, c\to c_{pre}, c+c_\Delta\to c_{post}}(Output \bowtie$ $\gamma_{\bar{G}, sum(x_\Delta)\to c_\Delta}(\Delta^i_1 \cup \Delta^j_2 \cup \Delta^k_3))$

(Do not handle group creation/deletion)

Table 9: Rules for $\gamma_{\bar{G}, sum(\bar{X})\to c}$

For $\Delta^+_{Input_l}(\bar{I}, \bar{A}_{post})$
$\Delta^+_V = \Delta^+_{Input_l} \bowtie_{\phi(\bar{X})} Input^{post}_r$
For $\Delta^+_{Input_r}(\bar{I}, \bar{A}_{post})$
$\Delta^+_V = Input^{post}_l \bowtie_{\phi(\bar{X})} \Delta^+_{Input_r}$
For $\Delta^-_{Input_l}(\bar{I}, \bar{A}'_{pre})$ ($\Delta^-_{Input_r}$ is symmetric)
$\Delta^-_V = \sigma_{\phi(\bar{X}_{pre})}\Delta^-_{Input_l}$
For $\Delta^u_{Input_l}(\bar{I}, \bar{A}'_{pre}, \bar{A}''_{post})$ ($\Delta^u_{Input_r}$ is symmetric)

if $\bar{X} \subseteq \bar{I} \cup \bar{A}''_{post}$ then
$\quad\Delta^u_V = \sigma_{\phi(\bar{X}_{pre})}\sigma_{\phi(\bar{X})}\Delta^u_{Input_l}$
else
$\quad\Delta^u_V = \Delta^u_{Input_l}$

if $\bar{I} \cap \bar{A}''_{post} = \emptyset$ then
$\quad\Delta^+_V =$ not triggered
else if $\bar{X} \subseteq \bar{I} \cup \bar{A}''_{post}$ then
$\quad\Delta^+_V = (Input^{post}_l \ltimes_{\bar{I}} \sigma_{\neg\phi(\bar{X}_{pre})}\sigma_{\phi(\bar{X}_{post})}\Delta^u_{Input_l})$
$\qquad\bowtie_{\phi(\bar{X})} Input^{post}_r$
else
$\quad\Delta^+_V = \pi_{Input_l, Input_r}\sigma_{\neg\phi(\bar{X}_{pre})}\sigma_{\phi(\bar{X}_{post})}$
$\qquad(Input^{post}_l \bowtie \Delta^u_{Input_l} \bowtie_{\phi(\bar{X})} Input^{post}_r)$

if $\bar{I} \cap \bar{A}''_{post} = \emptyset$ then
$\quad\Delta^-_V =$ not triggered
else if $\bar{X} \subseteq \bar{I} \cup \bar{A}''_{post}$ then
$\quad\Delta^-_V = \pi_{\bar{I}, \bar{A}'_{pre}}\sigma_{\phi(\bar{X}_{pre})}\sigma_{\neg\phi(\bar{X}_{post})}\Delta^u_{Input_l}$
else
$\quad\Delta^-_V = \pi_{\bar{I}, \bar{A}'_{pre}}\sigma_{\phi(\bar{X}_{pre})}\sigma_{\neg\phi(\bar{X}_{post})}Input^{post}_l$
$\qquad\bowtie \Delta^u_{Input_l} \bowtie_{\phi(\bar{X})} Input^{post}_r$

Blue portion applies when pre-state attributes present.

Table 10: Rules for $\bowtie_{\phi(\bar{X})}$

For $\Delta^u_R(\bar{I}, \bar{A}'_{pre}, \bar{A}''_{post})$, and $\bar{G} \cap \bar{A}''_{post} = \emptyset$
$\Delta^i_1 = \emptyset$
For $\Delta^-_R(\bar{I}, \bar{A}'_{pre})$
$\Delta^j_2 = \pi_{\bar{I}, -1\to x_\Delta}(\Delta^-_R \bowtie \pi_{x\to x_{in}} Input)$
For $\Delta^+_R(\bar{I}, \bar{A}''_{post})$
$\Delta^k_3 = \pi_{\bar{I}, 1\to x_\Delta}(\Delta^+_R \bar{\ltimes} Input)$
For converting Δ to output update i-diffs
Happens after all $\Delta^i_1, \Delta^j_2, \Delta^k_3$ are computed. $\Delta^u_V = \pi_{\bar{G}, c\to c_{pre}, c+c_\Delta\to c_{post}}(Output \bowtie$ $\gamma_{\bar{G}, sum(x_\Delta)\to c_\Delta}(\Delta^i_1 \cup \Delta^j_2 \cup \Delta^k_3))$

(Do not handle group creation/deletion)

Table 11: Rules for $\gamma_{\bar{G}, count(\bar{X})\to c}$

Operator cache schemas: $Cache_{sum}(\bar{G}, c_{sum}), Cache_{count}(\bar{G}, c_{count})$
Cache maintenance rules: For $\Delta^u_{Cache_{sum}}$: Use rules of $\gamma_{\bar{G}, sum(\bar{X})\to c}$ (Table 9) For $\Delta^u_{Cache_{count}}$: Use rules of $\gamma_{\bar{G}, count(\bar{X})\to c}$ (Table 11)
i-diff propagation rules: $\Delta^u_V = \pi_{\bar{G}, c^{sum}_{pre}/c^{count}_{pre}\to c_{pre}, c^{sum}_{post}/c^{count}_{post}\to c_{post}}($ $\quad\Delta^u_{Cache_{count}} \bowtie_{\bar{G}} \Delta^u_{Cache_{sum}})$

Table 12: Rules for $\gamma_{\bar{G}, avg(\bar{X})\to c}$

For $\Delta^+_{Input_l}(\bar{I}, \bar{A}''_{post})$
$\Delta^+_V = \Delta^+_{Input_l} \bar{\ltimes}_\phi Input^{post}_r$
For $\Delta^-_{Input_l}(\bar{I}, \bar{A}'_{pre})$
$\Delta^-_V = \Delta^-_{Input_l}$
For $\Delta^u_{Input_l}(\bar{I}, \bar{A}'_{pre}, \bar{A}''_{post})$
$\Delta^u_V = \Delta^u_{Input_l}$

if $\bar{X} \cap \bar{A}''_{post} = \emptyset$ then
$\quad\Delta^+_V =$ not triggered
if $\bar{X} \subseteq \bar{I} \cup \bar{A}''_{post}$ then
$\quad\Delta^+_V = Input^{post}_l \ltimes_{\bar{I}_{Input_l}} (\Delta^u_{Input_l} \bar{\ltimes}_{\phi(\bar{X}_{post}, \bar{Y})} Input^{post}_r)$
else
$\quad\Delta^+_V = (Input^{post}_l \ltimes_{\bar{I}_{Input_l}} \Delta^u_{Input_l})\bar{\ltimes}_{\phi(\bar{X}_{post}, \bar{Y})} Input^{post}_r$

if $\bar{X} \cap \bar{A}''_{post} = \emptyset$ then
$\quad\Delta^-_V =$ not triggered
if $\bar{X} \subseteq \bar{I} \cup \bar{A}''_{post}$ then
$\quad\Delta^-_V = \pi_{\bar{I}}(\Delta^u_{Input_l} \ltimes_{\phi(\bar{X}_{post}, \bar{Y})} Input^{post}_r)$
else
$\quad\Delta^-_V = \pi_{\bar{I}}((Input^{post}_l \ltimes_{\bar{I}_{Input_l}} \Delta^u_{Input_l})$
$\qquad\ltimes_{\phi(\bar{X}_{post}, \bar{Y})} Input^{post}_r)$

For $\Delta^+_{Input_r}(\bar{I}, \bar{A}''_{post})$
$\Delta^-_V = \pi_{\bar{I}}(Input^{post}_l \ltimes_{\phi(\bar{X}_{post}, \bar{Y})} \Delta^+_{Input_r})$
For $\Delta^-_{Input_r}(\bar{I}, \bar{A}'_{pre})$

if $\bar{Y} \subseteq \bar{I} \cup \bar{A}'_{pre}$ then
$\quad\Delta^+_V = (Input^{post}_l \ltimes_{\phi(\bar{X}_{pre}, \bar{Y})} \Delta^-_{Input_r})$
$\qquad\bar{\ltimes}_{\phi(\bar{X}_{post}, \bar{Y})} Input^{post}_r$
else
$\quad\Delta^+_V = (Input^{post}_l \ltimes_{\phi(\bar{X}_{pre}, \bar{Y})} (Input^{pre}_r \ltimes \Delta^-_{Input_r}))$
$\qquad\bar{\ltimes}_{\phi(\bar{X}_{post}, \bar{Y})} Input^{post}_r$

For $\Delta^u_{Input_r}(\bar{I}, \bar{A}'_{pre}, \bar{A}''_{post})$
Treat input update as combination of insert and delete

if $\bar{Y} \cap \bar{A}''_{post} = \emptyset$ then
$\quad\Delta^-_V =$ not triggered
else
$\quad\Delta^-_V = \pi_{\bar{I}}(Input^{post}_l \ltimes_{\phi(\bar{X}_{post}, \bar{Y})} (Input^{post}_r \ltimes \Delta^u_{Input_r}))$

if $\bar{Y} \cap \bar{A}''_{post} = \emptyset$ then
$\quad\Delta^+_V =$ not triggered
else if $\bar{Y} \subseteq \bar{I} \cup \bar{A}'_{pre}$ then
$\quad\Delta^+_V = (Input^{post}_l \ltimes_{\phi(\bar{X}_{pre}, \bar{Y})} \Delta^-_{Input_r})$
$\qquad\bar{\ltimes}_{\phi(\bar{X}_{post}, \bar{Y})} Input^{post}_r$
else
$\quad\Delta^+_V = (Input^{post}_l \ltimes_{\phi(\bar{X}_{pre}, \bar{Y})} (Input^{pre}_r \ltimes \Delta^-_{Input_r}))$
$\qquad\bar{\ltimes}_{\phi(\bar{X}_{post}, \bar{Y})} Input^{post}_r$

Table 13: Rules for $\bar{\ltimes}_{\phi(Input_l.\bar{X}, Input_r.\bar{Y})}$

S4: Top-k Spreadsheet-Style Search for Query Discovery

Fotis Psallidas[1] * Bolin Ding[2] Kaushik Chakrabarti[2] Surajit Chaudhuri[2]
[1]Columbia University, New York, NY
[2]Microsoft Research, Redmond, WA
fotis@cs.columbia.edu, {bolind, kaushik, surajitc}@microsoft.com

ABSTRACT

An enterprise information worker is often aware of a few example tuples that should be present in the output of the query. Query discovery systems have been developed to discover project-join queries that contain the given example tuples in their output. However, they require the output to exactly contain all the example tuples and do not perform any ranking. To address this limitation, we study the problem of efficiently discovering top-k project join queries which approximately contain the given example tuples in their output. We extend our algorithms to incrementally produce results as soon as the user finishes typing/modifying a cell. Our experiments on real-life and synthetic datasets show that our proposed solution is significantly more efficient compared with applying state-of-the-art algorithms.

Categories and Subject Descriptors

H.2.4 [**Database Management**]: Systems—*query processing, textual databases*

Keywords

SQL query discovery; example spreadsheet; relevance ranking

1. INTRODUCTION

Modern data warehouses usually have large and complex data schemas. A decision-support query on such a data warehouse typically touches a small portion of the schema. However, to express such a query, the enterprise information worker needs to comprehend the entire schema and locate the schema elements of interest. This is extremely burdensome for most users.

Query discovery has recently been proposed as a solution to this problem [18, 22]. An enterprise information worker is often aware of *a few example tuples* that should be present in the output of a query. These example tuples together form an *example spreadsheet*, one per each row. Previous systems discover *project-join queries* (*PJ queries*) that contain the given example tuples, or the example spreadsheet, in their output [18, 22]. This liberates users from understanding the entire schema. We illustrate this below.

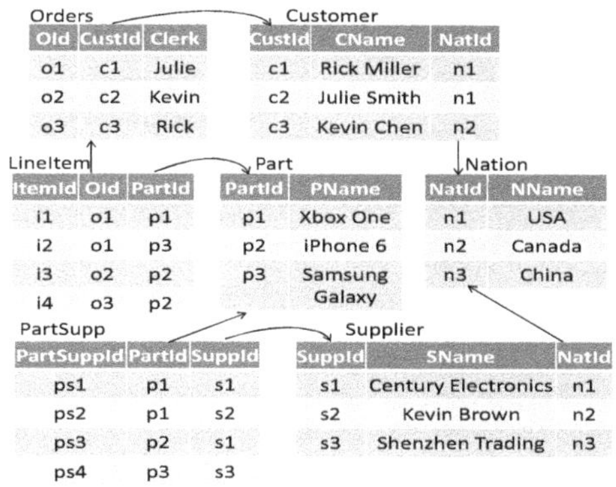

Figure 1: A sample database

EXAMPLE 1. *Consider a database instance of a TPC-H subschema in Figure 1. The database contains information about customers, the countries they live in, the orders they placed, the parts purchased in each order, the suppliers of those parts, and the countries the suppliers are based in. The arrows point in the direction of foreign-key to primary-key relationships between pairs of relations.*

*Suppose the user wants to discover the PJ query that outputs all customers and, for each customer, outputs her name, the name of the country she lives in, and the names of the parts she ordered. The PJ query and its output is shown in Figure 2(b)-(i). She is aware of an example spreadsheet of three example tuples that should be present in the query result: a customer named 'Rick' (does not know his full name) who lives in 'USA' and ordered an 'Xbox', a customer named 'Julie' (not sure where she lives) who ordered an 'iPhone' and a customer named 'Kevin' who lives in 'Canada' (not sure what he ordered). She can provide this information by typing these example tuples into an example spreadsheet (in forms of, e.g., Microsoft Excel and Google Sheets) as shown in Figure 2(a). Note that some cells in the example spreadsheet can be empty. The system returns the desired PJ query in Figure 2(b)-(i) as it contains all the example tuples in its output relation. The example tuples and corresponding tuples in the output are shaded with the same color. The system maps the columns of the example spreadsheet to the projected columns in the query for users to better understand the PJ query discovered; the latter are labeled by the name of the corresponding column in the example spreadsheet (*A*,* B *and* C*).*

One main limitation of these previous systems is that they require the output relations of PJ queries to *exactly* contain all the example tuples and do not perform any ranking. As a result, they cannot i) tolerate errors that the user might make while providing the example tuples and ii) perform IR-style relevance ranking.

*Work done while visiting Microsoft Research

SIGMOD'15, May 31–June 4, 2015, Melbourne, Victoria, Australia.

http://dx.doi.org/10.1145/2723372.2749452.

	A	B	C
1	Rick	USA	Xbox
2	Julie		iPhone
3	Kevin	Canada	

(a)

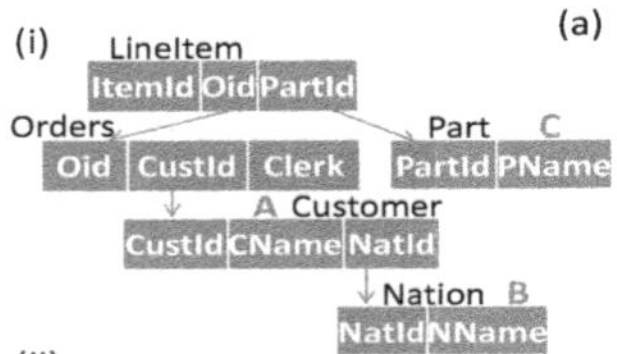

Customer. CName	Nation. Nname	Part. Pname
Rick Miller	**USA**	**Xbox** One
Rick Miller	USA	Samsung..
Julie Smith	USA	**iPhone** 6
Kevin Chen	**Canada**	iPhone 6

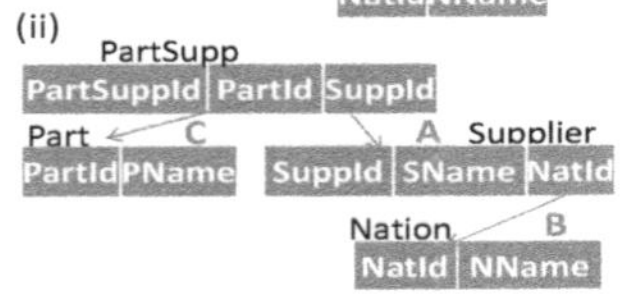

Supplier. SName	Nation. Nname	Part. Pname
Century...	**USA**	**Xbox** One
Century...	USA	**iPhone** 6
Kevin Brown	**Canada**	Xbox One
Shenzhen...	China	Samsung..

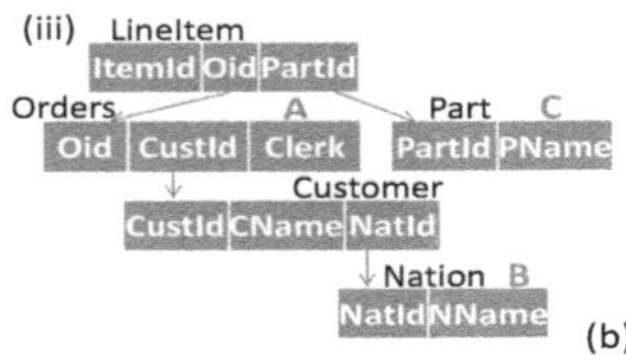

Orders. Clerk	Nation. Nname	Part. Pname
Julie	**USA**	**Xbox** One
Julie	USA	Samsung..
Kevin	USA	iPhone 6
Rick	Canada	iPhone 6

(b)

Figure 2: (a) Example spreadsheet (b) PJ queries and their outputs

• *Tolerating errors*: Suppose the user wants to discover the query that outputs all orders and, for each order, outputs the name of clerk who processed the order, the country of the customer who placed the order, and the parts in the order. She provides an example tuple: a clerk named 'Rick' processed an order from a customer in 'USA', and the order consisted of the part 'Xbox'. However, it is not 'Rick' but another clerk 'Julie' who processed that order. The desired PJ query and its output is shown in Figure 2(b)-(iii). We say that she has made a *relationship error* with respect to that PJ query as, although 'Rick' is a correct domain value (he is indeed a clerk), the provided relationship of 'Rick' with 'USA' and 'Xbox' is wrong.

The user can also make *domain errors*. Suppose the user wants to discover the query that outputs all suppliers and, for each supplier, outputs its name, the country it is based in and the parts it supplies. She then provides such an example tuple: a supplier named 'Rick' based in 'USA' who supplies the part 'Xbox'. The desired PJ query and its output is shown in Figure 2(b)-(ii). There is a domain error with respect to the PJ query as there is no supplier named 'Rick'.

• *Performing relevance ranking*: Suppose there is a supplier with name 'Welton USA' who supplies Xbox One. Consider the first example tuple in Figure 2(a). In addition to the the PJ query shown in Figure 2(b)-(i), some other PJ queries may also contain that example tuple in their outputs (e.g., a customer 'Rick Miller' who ordered 'Xbox One' which is supplied by 'Welton USA'). The former is more relevant, as country name 'USA' is a better match to 'USA' in the example tuple than supplier name 'Welton USA'.

To address the above issues, in this paper, we propose to *discover not only the PJ queries which exactly contain the given example tuples, or the example spreadsheet, in its output but also those that partially contain them.* We compute a relevance score for each PJ query that quantifies how well its output contain the example tuples and return *PJ queries with the top-k highest scores.*

Technical challenges. In a large real-world database, there are numerous ways of projecting and connecting tables and rows through foreign keys. So there could be millions of PJ queries that partially contain the user-specified example tuples in their output relations.

The first technical challenge is to develop a scoring model that allows us to tolerate relationship/domain errors and quantifies how well the user-given example spreadsheet is contained in the output of PJ queries, in order to perform a relevance ranking of them.

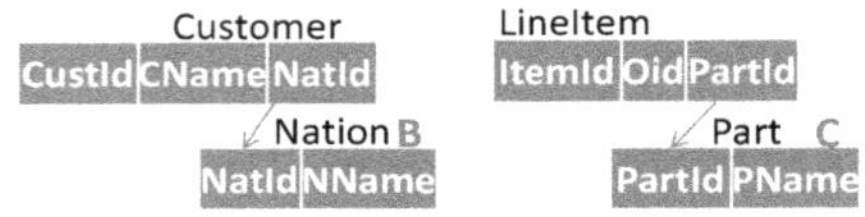

Figure 3: Common sub-expressions (sub-PJ queries) in Figure 2(b)

The second and the main technical challenge is to compute the top-k PJ queries *efficiently*. One important application of our system is to provide *online* data-search and discovery services in data processing tools, e.g., in Excel Online [3] and Google Sheets [1]. While a user may spend a significant amount of time in specifying the query, i.e., the example spreadsheet in our system, it has been shown that, in the context of online search, query latency is critical to user satisfaction. Increases in latency directly lead to lower utilization and higher rates of query abandonment [7, 16].

Overview of our solution and key insights. In this paper, we adapt a *candidate-enumeration and evaluation* framework, which is also used in keyword search systems for relational databases [5, 12, 15]. In the first step, called *PJ query enumeration*, we enumerate all candidate PJ queries that are potential answers for a user-specified *example spreadsheet*. The only requirement for these candidate PJ queries, called *minimality*, is that no table or projection column can be dropped without "losing" in relevance score. In the second step, called *PJ query evaluation*, we execute candidate PJ queries, and compare their output relations with the example spreadsheet to calculate their scores. A naive solution is to execute all the candidates and output the top-k with the highest scores.

It is important to note that the first step is very efficient, as it is pursued on the schema-level and no join is required. So it constitutes a negligible fraction of the overall query processing time. The second step, evaluating scores of PJ queries, is expensive (as it requires joins). As our scoring model quantifies how well the user-given example spreadsheet is contained in the output of join and projection, we need to at least examine rows in the join output, which may partially contain an example tuple. So this challenge translates to that of *evaluating as few PJ queries as possible.* The naive solution, evaluating all the candidates, is hence infeasible (we will compare it with the approaches we propose in Section 6).

Although calculating the exact relevance scores is expensive, we derive their upper bounds in a much more efficient way (without executing any join). Inspired by the work on multi-step kNN search [20], we evaluate PJ queries in decreasing order of their upper bound scores, and terminate with the top-k as soon as the max upper-bound score of un-evaluated queries is no higher than the current top-k score. This approach is referred to as BASELINE.

Our main insight to improve BASELINE is that there are many common sub-expressions, called *sub-PJ queries*, that are *shared* among the PJ queries. For example, the PJ queries (i) and (iii) in 2(b) share the two sub-PJ queries shown in Figure 3. If we can compute the output relations of these sub-PJ queries once, and cache (or memorize) them in memory, we can re-use them multiple times later when we evaluate queries containing these two sub-PJ queries. This reduces the overall evaluation cost significantly.

A novel component, called *caching-evaluation scheduler*, in our system determines, for the set of candidate PJ queries, i) the order following which these PJ queries will be evaluated; ii) output relations of which sub-PJ queries to be cached; and iii) when to put the output relations into the cache and when to remove them, as we have only a budgeted amount of memory. There are two aspects in the objective of this component: one is to evaluate *as few PJ queries as possible* to discover the top-k; and the other one is to utilize the cached output relations as much as possible to reduce the overall *evaluation cost.* We will formalize the task of this component and refer to it as *caching-evaluation scheduling problem.*

Contributions and organization. We have built a *spreadsheet-style search system* (called S4) to tackle the challenges based on the above insights. Our contributions are summarized as follows:

- We introduce a novel scoring model for a PJ query w.r.t. an example spreadsheet. It allows us to tolerate both types of errors and perform IR-style relevance ranking of PJ queries (Section 2).
- We introduce our system based on a candidate-enumeration and evaluation framework, and we enable a flexible caching-evaluation component in the system architecture (Section 3).
- To tackle the technical challenges of our task, we first introduce some basic operators in our system and propose BASELINE strategy. It aims to evaluate as few PJ queries as possible (Sections 4).
- We then introduce our cache-aware optimization techniques to improve BASELINE. We propose the *caching-evaluation scheduling problem* with the objective of minimizing the overall evaluation cost. We prove it is NP-complete. Several novel heuristics are proposed to solve this problem, and the resulting strategy is called FASTTOPK. We can prove that FASTTOPK has performance guarantee in the worst-case in two aspects: i) it does not evaluate too many PJ queries in addition to the necessary ones; and ii) the gap between the evaluation cost introduced by FASTTOPK strategy and the optimal evaluation cost is bounded in the worst case. We also introduce how to extend our system and strategies to handle incremental updates on the example spreadsheet (Section 5).
- We perform experimental study on real-life and synthetic datasets to evaluate the efficiency of our approaches, together with a user study to evaluate the effectiveness of our scoring model (Section 6).

2. SYSTEM TASK AND SCORING MODEL

We first present our data model, and formally define our system task of *discovering top-k project-join queries for a given example spreadsheet*. Then, we present the model to compute the relevance score of a project-join query w.r.t. an example spreadsheet.

2.1 Data Model

We consider a database $\mathcal{D}$ with m relations $R_1, R_2, \cdots, R_m$. For a relation R, let $R[i]$ denote its ith column, and $\text{col}(R) = \{R[i]\}_{i=1,\ldots|\text{col}(R)|}$ denote the set of columns of R. For a tuple r in R, denote $r \in R$ and let $r[i]$ be its *cell* value on the column $R[i]$.

Let $\mathcal{G}(\mathcal{V}, \mathcal{E})$ denote the *directed schema graph* of $\mathcal{D}$ where the vertices in $\mathcal{V}$ represent the relations in $\mathcal{D}$, and the edges in $\mathcal{E}$ represent foreign key references between two relations: there is an edge from R_j to R_k in $\mathcal{E}$ iff the primary key defined on R_k is referenced by a foreign key defined in R_j. There can be multiple edges from R_j to R_k and we label each edge with the corresponding foreign key's attribute name. For simplicity, we omit edge labels in our examples and description if they are clear from the context.

In a relation R_i, we refer to a column as *text column* if its values are strings. Figure 1 shows an example database with a total of seven relations. There five text columns: Customer.CustName, Nation.NatName, Orders.Clerk, Part.PartName, and Supplier.SuppName. In the rest of this paper, we focus on only text columns and primary or foreign key columns of the relations.

2.2 Discovering Top-k PJ Queries by Example Spreadsheet

Example spreadsheet. An example spreadsheet is a multi-column table and serves as an interactive interface for PJ query discovery. Each cell of this spreadsheet is typed by the user, and could either be empty or contain some text. Figure 2(a) gives an example.

DEFINITION 1. (Example spreadsheet) *An example spreadsheet T is a table with multiple rows $\{t\}$ and columns* $\text{col}(T)$. *Each row $t \in T$ is called an example tuple, where each cell is either a string (i.e., one or more terms) or empty. Let $t[i]$ denote its cell value on the column $i \in \text{col}(S)$, and let $t[i] = \emptyset$ if $t[i]$ is empty. Each row t contains at least one term and so does each column $T[i]$.*

Project-Join (PJ) queries. We aim to discover queries in directed-tree shapes with projections and foreign key joins that generate a table from $\mathcal{D}$ to expand the user-given example spreadsheet T.

DEFINITION 2. (Project-Join Queries) *A* project-join query $Q = (\mathcal{J}, \mathcal{C}, \phi)$ *for T is specified by:*

- *a* join tree $\mathcal{J} \subseteq \mathcal{G}$, *i.e., a directed subtree of the schema graph $\mathcal{G}(\mathcal{V}, \mathcal{E})$ of the database $\mathcal{D}$ representing all the relations (vertices of $\mathcal{J}$) and joins (edges of $\mathcal{J}$) involved in the query – let* $\text{col}(\mathcal{J})$ *be the set of all columns of relations in $\mathcal{J}$,*
- *a set of* projection columns $\mathcal{C} \subseteq \text{col}(\mathcal{J})$ *from the relations in $\mathcal{J}$, which the join result is projected onto, and*
- *a* column mapping $\phi : \text{col}(T) \rightarrow \mathcal{C}$ *from columns of the example spreadsheet T to the projection columns in $\mathcal{C}$ – it is a surjective function, i.e., $\forall c \in \mathcal{C} : \exists i \in \text{col}(T)$ s.t. $\phi(i) = c$.*

It is important to ensure that there is no redundant table or projection column in the discovered PJ queries. Intuitively, a table or a projection column is redundant if, after it is dropped from the PJ query, the output relation matches the example spreadsheet equally well or even better. We formally define them as *minimal PJ queries* and only consider them as the candidates to be discovered.

DEFINITION 3. (Minimal Project-Join Queries) *A PJ query $Q = (\mathcal{J}, \mathcal{C}, \phi)$ w.r.t. an example spreadsheet T is* minimal *iff*

i) for any degree-1 vertex (relation) R in $\mathcal{J}$, there is a column $i \in \text{col}(T)$ s.t. $\phi(i) \in \text{col}(R)$, i.e., every degree-1 relation R has a column of the example spreadsheet mapped to it; and

ii) for every column i of T which is mapped to column $R[j]$ of a relation R in $\mathcal{J}$ through ϕ (i.e., $\phi(i) = R[j]$), there exists at least one term in column $T[i]$ appearing in column $R[j]$.

In the rest of this paper, when we refer to *PJ queries*, we refer to minimal project-join queries. For the example database in Figure 1, three PJ queries and their output relations are shown in Figure 2(b).

Let $\mathcal{A}(Q)$ be the output relation when Q is executed on database $\mathcal{D}$: joins in $\mathcal{J}$ are executed first, and then the results are projected on columns $\mathcal{C}$. Columns of the example spreadsheet T are mapped to columns $\mathcal{C}$ of the output relation $\mathcal{A}(Q)$ according to ϕ.

Property i) in Definition 3 is similar to the *minimality* of *candidate networks* in keyword search literatures like [5, 12, 15]. In our case, degree-1 relations not satisfying i) can be excluded from $\mathcal{J}$ s.t. we have no less distinct tuples in the output relation $\mathcal{A}(Q)$, because they have no column in the projection and the join tree is still valid after the removal of them.

Property ii) says that a column i in the example spreadsheet T should not be mapped to a column $R[j]$ in the projection $\mathcal{C}$ if none of the terms in the column $T[i]$ appears in $R[j]$ (and the corresponding column in $\mathcal{A}(Q)$). Intuitively, if the two columns $T[i]$ and $R[j]$ have no overlap in their vocabularies, they are likely from two different domains so it is meaningless to map $T[i]$ to $R[j]$. In fact, we can drop the column i from T to get a smaller example spreadsheet T', and drop the column $R[j]$ from the projection $\mathcal{C}$ and the mapping ϕ, denoting as $\mathcal{C}' = \mathcal{C} - \{R[j]\}$ and ϕ'; in our scoring model, we can prove that the relevance score of $Q' = (\mathcal{J}, \mathcal{C}', \phi')$ w.r.t. T' is no less than the score of $Q = (\mathcal{J}, \mathcal{C}, \phi)$ w.r.t. T.

Based on our scoring model introduced next in Section 2.3, we will show that we do not "lose" in score by looking only at the minimal PJ queries (Proposition 1). A bit more formally, for any non-minimal PJ query $Q = (\mathcal{J}, \mathcal{C}, \phi)$, we can find a minimal PJ query $Q' = (\mathcal{J}', \mathcal{C}', \phi')$ with $\mathcal{J}'$ as a subtree of $\mathcal{J}$ and/or ϕ' as a sub-mapping of ϕ such that the score of Q' is no less than the score of Q. For example, consider the example spreadsheet in Figure 2(a) *without* column C, Figure 2(b)-(i) is no longer a minimal PJ query, as the degree-1 relation Part violates property i) and removing it will not reduce the score. Another example is, in Figure 2, it does not make sense to map column A in the example spreadsheet to column Nation.NName – any PJ query with this mapping violates property ii), and we can remove this pair of columns from the example spreadsheet/PJ query without reducing the score.

End-to-end system task. For a user-given example spreadsheet T, the goal of our system is *to find minimal PJ queries with the top-k highest scores w.r.t. T*. The incremental version of our task is: suppose we have found the top-k PJ queries for a user-given example spreadsheet T, after one or more cells in T are updated by the user, how to find the updated top-k PJ queries efficiently.

2.3 Scoring Model for PJ Queries

The score of a PJ query Q w.r.t. an example spreadsheet T quantifies how well the Q's output $\mathcal{A}(Q)$ contains rows in T. We first present the scoring model and then show how it allows us to tolerate relationship and domain errors for performing relevance ranking.

An IR system computes a score of a document w.r.t. a keyword query, which quantifies how well the former contains the terms in the latter. A straightforward way to compute the score of Q w.r.t. T is to treat T as a "*query*" (by concatenating all text in T) and $\mathcal{A}(Q)$ as a "*document*" (again, by concatenating) and apply a traditional IR relevance scoring model [23]. We do not adopt this model as we need to quantify how well $\mathcal{A}(Q)$ contains each example tuple with their columns aligned according to the mapping ϕ; it is difficult to do so in this model as it removes the row/column boundaries.

Containment score w.r.t. single example tuple. We first define a score $\mathsf{score}(t \mid \mathcal{A}(Q))$ to quantify how well $\mathcal{A}(Q)$ contains *a single example tuple* $t \in T$. Let $\mathsf{score}(t \mid r)$ denote the similarity between an example tuple $t \in T$ and a row $r \in \mathcal{A}(Q)$ in the PJ query output (referred to as *row-row similarity*). By definition of containment, $\mathsf{score}(t \mid \mathcal{A}(Q))$ should be high as long as there is one row $r \in \mathcal{A}(Q)$ in the PJ query's output relation with a high row-row similarity $\mathsf{score}(t \mid r)$ with t; so we refer to the *most similar tuple* for t to define the containment score:

$$\mathsf{score}(t \mid Q) = \max_{r \in \mathcal{A}(Q)} \mathsf{score}(t \mid r). \quad (1)$$

Row-row similarity. One way to get row-row similarity $\mathsf{score}(t \mid r)$ between an example tuple $t \in T$ and a row $r \in \mathcal{A}(Q)$ in the PJ query output is to treat t as a "query" (by concatenating the terms in all cells in t) and r as a "document" (again, by concatenating). Again, this model is not suitable as we need to respect the mapping ϕ while computing the row-row similarity. We need to compare a cell $t[i]$ with the cell $r[\phi(i)]$ it is mapped to. Let $\mathsf{score}_{\text{cell}}(t[i] \mid r[j])$ denote the cell similarity between an example tuple cell $t[i]$ and a cell $r[j]$ in an output row. We compute the row-row similarity by summing up the cell similarities for all columns.

$$\mathsf{score}(t \mid r) = \sum_{i \in \text{col}(T)} \mathsf{score}_{\text{cell}}(t[i] \mid r[\phi(i)]). \quad (2)$$

We use a simple cell similarity $\mathsf{score}_{\text{cell}}(t[i] \mid r[j])$ as: how many terms in $t[i]$ appear in $r[j]$ if $t[i]$ is non-empty and 0 otherwise. We discuss how to adapt a more complicated IR-style cell similarity to perform relevance ranking in Appendix A.2.

Row containment score w.r.t. entire example spreadsheet. We are now ready to define the *row-wise containment score* to quantify how well $\mathcal{A}(Q)$ contains *all* the example tuples in T, denoted as $\mathsf{score}_{\text{row}}(T \mid Q)$. The more individual tuples in the example spreadsheet $\mathcal{A}(Q)$ contains, the higher should be the final score. So, a natural way is to sum up containment scores for all the example tuples in the example spreadsheet:

$$\mathsf{score}_{\text{row}}(T \mid Q) = \sum_{t \in T} \mathsf{score}(t \mid Q) = \sum_{t \in T} \max_{r \in \mathcal{A}(Q)} \mathsf{score}(t \mid r). \quad (3)$$

EXAMPLE 2. *We compute the score $\mathsf{score}_{\text{row}}(T \mid Q)$ of PJ query Q in Figure 2(b)-(iii) w.r.t. the example spreadsheet T in Figure 2(a). Recall that cell similarity $\mathsf{score}_{cell}(t[i] \mid r[j])$ is how many terms in $t[i]$ appear in $r[j]$ if non-empty, and 0 otherwise. For each row in T, the most similar row in $\mathcal{A}(Q)$ is shaded with the same color (yellow, pink and green for the three rows). The single tuple containment scores are 2, 1, and 1 respectively. So, $\mathsf{score}_{\text{row}}(T \mid Q) = 4$. Similarly, the score between the same example spreadsheet and PJ query in Figure 2(b)-(ii) is $2 + 1 + 2 = 5$.*

Tolerating errors. Naturally, the scoring function should have the following property: *higher the number of errors in the example spreadsheet with respect to the output of a PJ query Q, lower the score of Q*. The above score $\mathsf{score}_{\text{row}}$ satisfies this property. For example, the example spreadsheet in Figure 2(a) has 2 errors in the output of PJ query in Figure 2(b)-(ii) (Rick and Julie in column A do not appear in column Supplier.SName for the first two example tuples), while it has 3 errors in the output of PJ query (iii) (one term missed for each example tuple). From Example 2, we see that (ii) has a higher score $\mathsf{score}_{\text{row}}$ than (iii). However, it *penalizes relationship and domain errors equally*. Relationship errors are more common, so we want to penalize them less than domain errors. We next introduce column containment score for that purpose.

Column containment score. We define column containment score that penalizes *only domain errors*. Subsequently, we will put it together with the row containment score $\mathsf{score}_{\text{row}}$ to penalize the two classes of errors differently. A cell in column $i \in \text{col}(T)$ in an example spreadsheet T has a domain error in a PJ query Q iff it has one term not occurring in the mapped column $\phi(i)$ of the join tree $\mathcal{J}$ of Q. The column-wise containment score that quantifies how well the cells in each column $i \in \text{col}(T)$ are contained in the mapped column $\phi(i)$ will penalize only domain errors.

For each cell in the example spreadsheet T, we first find the *most similar cell* in the mapped column $\phi(i)$ of the join tree $\mathcal{J}$ of Q. We sum up the similarities between cells paired in this way to obtain the *column-wise containment score*:

$$\mathsf{score}_{\text{col}}(T \mid Q) = \sum_{i \in \text{col}(T)} \sum_{t \in T} \max_{r \in \mathcal{J}[\phi(i)]} \mathsf{score}_{\text{cell}}(t[i] \mid r[\phi(i)]), \quad (4)$$

where let $\mathcal{J}[\phi(i)]$ be the relation $T[i]$ is mapped to in database $\mathcal{D}$.

EXAMPLE 3. *We compute the column-wise containment score $\mathsf{score}_{\text{col}}$ of the PJ query Q in Figure 2(b)-(ii) w.r.t. the example spreadsheet T in Figure 2(a). Column* A *in T is mapped to column* Supplier.SuppName *(in the database in Figure 1) through ϕ. Only one (*Rick*) out of the three terms in T.*A *appears in* Supplier.SuppName. *For each of the other two columns in T, both terms can be found in the corresponding column in the database. So $\mathsf{score}_{\text{col}}(T \mid Q) = 5$. Similarly, the column-wise containment score of the PJ query Q in Figure 2(b)-(iii) is $3+2+2 = 7$. In contrast to Example 2, now (iii) has a higher score than (ii) because (iii) has no domain errors while (ii) has 2 domain errors.*

Putting it together. We obtain the final *relevance score* $\mathsf{score}(T \mid Q)$ of a PJ query Q w.r.t. an example spreadsheet T by taking a lin-

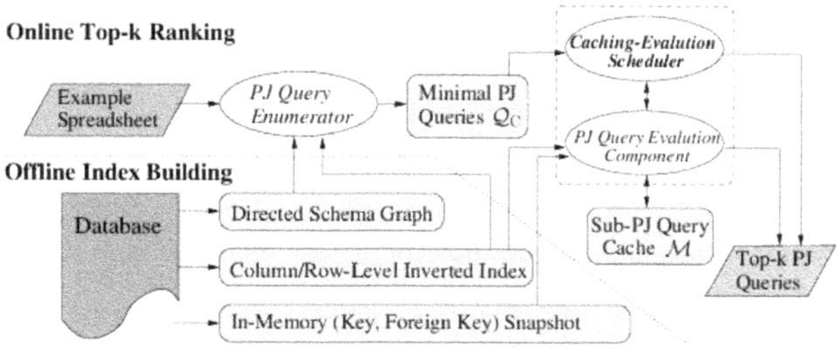

Figure 4: S4 System Architecture

ear combination of row-wise and column-wise containment scores. We introduce a parameter $0 \le \alpha \le 1$ to control the relative penalty of the two classes of errors. Similar to prior work, we also penalize PJ queries with larger join trees as the relationship among the mapped columns in $\mathcal{J}$ is looser. We penalize it with a factor of $1 + \ln(1 + \ln |\mathcal{J}|)$, where $|\mathcal{J}|$ is the number of relations in $\mathcal{J}$.

$$\mathsf{score}(T \mid Q) = \frac{\alpha \cdot \mathsf{score}_{\mathrm{row}}(T \mid Q) + (1 - \alpha) \cdot \mathsf{score}_{\mathrm{col}}(T \mid Q)}{1 + \ln(1 + \ln |\mathcal{J}|)}. \tag{5}$$

Minimality and scores. In Proposition 1 below, we show why we are interested in finding only minimal PJ queries (Definition 3).

PROPOSITION 1. *Consider a user-given example spreadsheet T and a PJ query $Q = (\mathcal{J}, \mathcal{C}, \phi)$ in a database $\mathcal{D}$. If property i) in Definition 3 is not satisfied, let R be a degree-1 relation in $\mathcal{J}$ with no column in T mapped to it. Define a smaller $\mathcal{J}' = \mathcal{J} - R$ and $Q' = (\mathcal{J}', \mathcal{C}, \phi)$. We have* $\mathsf{score}(T \mid Q) \le \mathsf{score}(T \mid Q')$.

If property ii) is violated, let i be a column in T s.t. no term in $T[i]$ appears in the database column $R[j]$ it is mapped to. We can remove the column i from T to get a smaller example spreadsheet T', and remove the column $R[j]$ from the projection $\mathcal{C}$ and the mapping ϕ: let $\mathcal{C}' = \mathcal{C} - \{R[j]\}$ and ϕ' be the range-restriction of ϕ by $\mathcal{C}'$, i.e., $\phi'(i) = \phi(i)$ iff $\phi(i) \in \mathcal{C}'$ and undefined otherwise. Let $Q'' = (\mathcal{J}, \mathcal{C}', \phi')$. We have $\mathsf{score}(T \mid Q) = \mathsf{score}(T' \mid Q'')$.

3. SYSTEM ARCHITECTURE

The S4 system architecture is depicted in Figure 4, with two major components: *offline index building* and *online top-k ranking*.

3.1 Offline Index Building

First, we have the *directed schema graph* $\mathcal{G}(\mathcal{V}, \mathcal{E})$ in memory, which keeps schema-level information about the database $\mathcal{D}$, including names of relations/columns (in $\mathcal{V}$), and foreign keys (in $\mathcal{E}$).

Secondly, for the purpose of PJ query enumeration and evaluation (computing their scores), we build two types of in-memory indexes that are extensions to *inverted indexes* in traditional IR.

• *Column-level inverted index.* Given a term w, index inv(w) returns all the database columns where w appears in at least one row.

• *Row-level inverted index.* For a term w and a column $R[i]$ in relation R, inv(w, $R[i]$) returns all rows in R, where w appears in column i, and its term frequency in each cell.

Finally, the PJ queries need to be executed and scored without accessing the database in disk. Attivio Active Intelligence Engine uses a similar index to perform "query-time join" [24]. We call it:

• *In memory (key, foreign key) snapshot of the database.* We have the primary-key column and foreign-key columns of each row in each relation of the database materialized in memory.

3.2 Online Top-k Ranking

We adopt a *PJ-query enumeration-ranking* framework for online top-k ranking. Our system processes a user-specified example spreadsheet in two steps as follows to output the top-k PJ queries.

PJ query enumeration. The set of minimal PJ queries, denoted as $\mathcal{Q}_C$, for the example spreadsheet could all be candidate answers for the top-k. The component, *PJ Query Enumerator*, generates this set of PJ queries. We adapt the *CN generation* algorithm described in [13] for this component. Since the generation of $\mathcal{Q}_C$ (without computing their scores) can be done by accessing only the schema graph and column-level inverted index, it is quite efficient. Moreover, we compute an *upper bound* of its score for each PJ query in $\mathcal{Q}_C$. This upper bound can be also computed efficiently without executing any join. More details about the generation of $\mathcal{Q}_C$ and upper-bound score computation will be given in Section 4.1.

PJ query ranking. Taking PJ queries in $\mathcal{Q}_C$ as the input, the main contribution of this paper is about how to identify those with the top-k highest scores from $\mathcal{Q}_C$. To this end, *PJ Query Evaluation Component* evaluates *some queries* in $\mathcal{Q}_C$ to get their scores. By *evaluating a PJ query*, we mean executing the query to compute its score w.r.t. the example spreadsheet. Because our scoring model quantifies how well the example spreadsheet is contained in the output of join and projection of a PJ query, to get the row containment score, we need to at least examine rows which either completely or partially contain the example tuples in the output. This process requires to execute joins and thus is the bottleneck in online top-k ranking. Details about the evaluation of PJ queries will be given in Section 4.1 (basic version) and Section 5.1 (cache-aware version).

Caching-Evaluation Scheduler finds a strategy that specifies: i) which queries to be evaluated to get the top-k, ii) the order of evaluations, and iii) how to use the in-memory *Sub-PJ Query Cache* to speedup the evaluations. We focus on this scheduler in the rest part. We present a baseline strategy in Section 4 without utilizing the cache and a more efficient cache-aware strategy in Section 5.

4. BASELINE EVALUATION STRATEGY

In Section 4.1, we first introduce the basic operators in our evaluation strategy: how to enumerate all candidate PJ queries $\mathcal{Q}_C$ for an example spreadsheet and compute their upper-bound scores and exact scores. We also analyze their costs. For interactive speed, it is affordable to enumerate $\mathcal{Q}_C$ first and compute the upper-bound scores but it would be too expensive to compute the exact scores for all queries in $\mathcal{Q}_C$. To design more efficient approaches, in Section 4.2, we study what is the minimal set of queries we have to evaluate to get the top-k given those upper bounds. We end this section with a worst-case optimal baseline strategy in Section 4.3.

4.1 Basic Operators in Evaluation Strategy

Before introducing our evaluation strategies, we give more details about the basic operators in our system and analyze their costs.

4.1.1 *Enumerating Minimal PJ Queries $\mathcal{Q}_C$*

For a user-specified example spreadsheet T, we utilize the directed schema graph $\mathcal{G}(\mathcal{V}, \mathcal{E})$ and column-level inverted index to generate $\mathcal{Q}_C$. For each column $T[i]$ in T, we first find all the columns $\mathcal{C}_i$ in $\mathcal{D}$ which contain at least one term in $T[i]$, called *candidate projection columns*. $\mathcal{C}_i$ is essentially the union of inv(w)'s for all terms w's in $T[i]$, i.e., $\mathcal{C}_i = \bigcup_{\mathsf{w} \in T[i]} \mathsf{inv}(\mathsf{w})$.

Consider the example table in Figure 2. The candidate projection columns for column A are: Customer.CustName, Orders.Clerk (containing all the 3 terms in A) and Supplier.SuppName (containing only the first term, Rick). For column B, there is only one, Nation.NatName (containing both terms in B). And for column C, Part.PartName (contains both terms) is the only one.

Given candidate projection columns $\mathcal{C}_i$'s generated in the above process, to enumerate $\mathcal{Q}_C$, we can pick one column from each $\mathcal{C}_i$ to form $\mathcal{C}$ and mapping ϕ, and generate directed Steiner trees to get

$\mathcal{J}$ that connect to relations in $\mathcal{C}$, using the *CN generation* algorithm described in [13]. It is important to note that all PJ queries violating i) and ii) in Definition 3 are pruned during the enumeration.

4.1.2 *Computing Upper Bounds of Relevance Scores*

It can be shown that the score of a PJ query Q w.r.t. T, $\mathsf{score}(T \mid Q)$, can be upper bounded by its column-wise score $\mathsf{score}_{\mathrm{col}}$ for any value parameter α. This simple but effective upper bound can be computed in a light-weight way, without executing any join in Q. We will use this upper bound frequently in the rest of this paper.

PROPOSITION 2. (Upper Bound of Score) *For any* $0 \leq \alpha \leq 1$,

$$\mathsf{score}(T \mid Q) \leq \frac{\mathsf{score}_{\mathrm{col}}(T \mid Q)}{1+\ln(1+\ln|\mathcal{J}|)} \triangleq \overline{\mathsf{score}}(T \mid Q). \quad (6)$$

It suffices to show that $\mathsf{score}_{\mathrm{row}}(T \mid Q) \leq \mathsf{score}_{\mathrm{col}}(T \mid Q)$ to prove Proposition 2. The intuition is that, in $\mathsf{score}_{\mathrm{row}}(T \mid Q)$, each row in T is matched to the most similar row in the output relation $\mathcal{A}(Q)$, while in $\mathsf{score}_{\mathrm{col}}(T \mid Q)$, each cell in T is matched to the most similar cell in the corresponding column of $\mathcal{A}(Q)$. The latter has a weaker constraint in matching so it produces a higher score.

Computing $\overline{\mathsf{score}}$ and column containment score $\mathsf{score}_{\mathrm{col}}$. To compute the upper bound $\overline{\mathsf{score}}$, it suffices to compute the column containment score $\mathsf{score}_{\mathrm{col}}$ in Equation (4). To compute $\mathsf{score}_{\mathrm{col}}$, for each term w appearing in column i of T, suppose column i is mapped to column j of a relation R, we need to scan $\mathsf{inv}(\mathsf{w}, R[j])$ once to compute the cell similarity $\mathsf{score}(t[i] \mid r[j])$ for each cell $t[i]$ in T and each cell $r[j]$ in R. Then $\mathsf{score}_{\mathrm{col}}$ can be computed directly as in (4). Refer to Algorithm 1 for more details.

```
Initialize cell similarities score_cell to be 0 for all entries.
For each column i of T: it is mapped to R[j] of relation R
   For each tuple t ∈ T and each term w in t[i]
      Retrive row-level inverted index inv(w, R[j]);
      For each row r ∈ inv(w, R[j]): score_cell(t[i] | r[j])++.
Compute score_col(T | Q) from score_cell as in (4).
Compute score‾(T | Q) as in (6).
```

Algorithm 1: Computing $\mathsf{score}_{\mathrm{col}}(T \mid Q)$ and $\overline{\mathsf{score}}(T \mid Q)$

PROPOSITION 3. *Consider an example spreadsheet T and a PJ query* $Q = (\mathcal{J}, \mathcal{C}, \phi)$ *in a database. For each column i in T and each term* w *in the column* $T[i]$*, suppose i is mapped to a column* $R[j]$ *in a relation R of* $\mathcal{J}$*, let* $l_{\mathsf{w}} = |\mathsf{inv}(\mathsf{w}, R[j])|$ *be the number of rows in R that contain* w *in the column* $R[j]$*, i.e., the size of row-level inverted index* $\mathsf{inv}(\mathsf{w}, R[j])$ *for term* w *in column* $R[j]$*. Algorithm 1 computes* $\overline{\mathsf{score}}$ *and* $\mathsf{score}_{\mathrm{col}}$ *in* $O(\sum_{\mathsf{w} \in T} l_{\mathsf{w}})$ *time.*

4.1.3 *Evaluating PJ Queries for Relevance Scores*

We now introduce how to *evaluate* PJ queries, i.e., *to compute the exact relevance score* $\mathsf{score}(T \mid Q)$. According to (5), the only missing part is the row containment score $\mathsf{score}_{\mathrm{row}}(T \mid Q)$.

Computing score and row containment score $\mathsf{score}_{\mathrm{row}}$. As in (3), for each example tuple t in T, we need to find the most similar row in the output relation $\mathcal{A}(Q)$. Indeed, we can first execute the PJ query Q, for example, sending it as a SQL query to the database (as in [22]), and then examine each row in the output relation $\mathcal{A}(Q)$. To utilize our in-memory indexes and compute the scores more efficiently, we design an execution plan for Q using hash joins. More details are in Appendix B.1. Follwoing is its complexity.

PROPOSITION 4. *Consider an example spreadsheet T and a PJ query* $Q = (\mathcal{J}, \mathcal{C}, \phi)$ *in a database. For each term* w *in T, let* l_{w} *be defined as in Proposition 3. For each relation R in* $\mathcal{J}$*, let* $|R|$ *be the number of rows and* $d_{\mathcal{J}}(R)$ *be the degree of R in* $\mathcal{J}$*. We can compute* $\mathsf{score}(T \mid Q)$ *in* $O(\sum_{R \in \mathcal{J}} |R| \cdot d_{\mathcal{J}}(R) + \sum_{\mathsf{w} \in T} l_{\mathsf{w}})$ *time.*

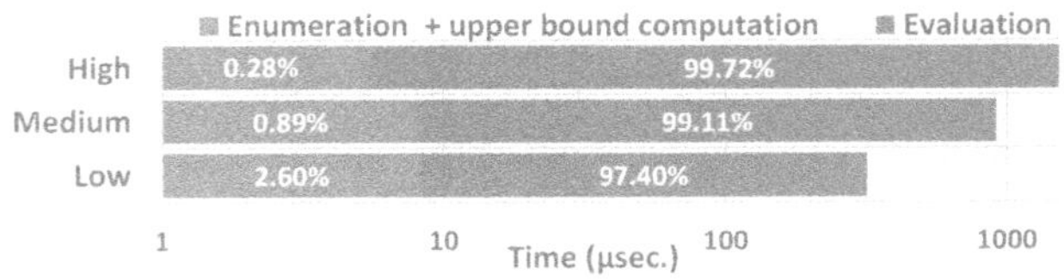

Figure 5: Average running time of "query enumeration + upper bound computation" v.s. "query evaluation" per PJ query

4.1.4 *Cost Analysis*

It is quite common to enumerate candidate database queries in previous keyword search literature [5, 13, 12, 15]. Similarly in our case, we only access the schema graph and column-level inverted index to enumerate $\mathcal{Q}_{\mathrm{C}}$ (no need to execute any actual join).

Now, comparing the complexity of computing upper bounds of scores (Proposition 3) with computing exact scores (Proposition 4), we find that the additional cost, $O(\sum_{R \in \mathcal{J}} |R| \cdot d_{\mathcal{J}}(R))$, to compute the exact score is truly the bottleneck. In the worst case, this cost is proportional to the total number of rows in all relations involved in a PJ query. On the other hand, the cost, $O(\sum_{\mathsf{w} \in T} l_{\mathsf{w}})$, to compute the upper bound is only proportional to the number of rows that contain keyword terms in projection columns of the PJ query.

Figure 5 compares i) the time for query enumeration plus upper bound computation (orange bars), with ii) the time to compute exact scores via query evaluation (blue bars), on average per query. We generate 50 example spreadsheets for CSUPP dataset and divide them into three buckets (H, M, L) based on the frequency of terms in the dataset (from highly frequent to lowly). Please refer to Section 6.1 for more details about the setting. All PJ queries are generated for those example spreadsheet, and for each, we compute both the upper-bound score and the exact score. The experimental result also shows that query enumeration plus upper bound computation requires a negligible fraction of the overall processing time. So, in the rest part, we assume that *$\mathcal{Q}_{\mathrm{C}}$ can be enumerated first for each given example spreadsheet* and $\overline{\mathsf{score}}$ *is associated with each query in $\mathcal{Q}_{\mathrm{C}}$ generated in the query enumeration step.*

4.2 Minimal Evaluation Set

From both theoretical and experimental analysis in the last subsection, we find that the bottleneck in our PJ-query enumeration-ranking framework is to *evaluate candidate PJ queries in* $\mathcal{Q}_{\mathrm{C}}$, i.e., to *execute PJ queries and compute their exact scores*; and on the other hand, we can enumerate all PJ queries in $\mathcal{Q}_{\mathrm{C}}$ and compute the upper bounds of scores for all of them quite efficiently. Now the major challenge translates to that of *evaluating as few PJ queries in $\mathcal{Q}_{\mathrm{C}}$ as possible to get the top-k with highest scores*, given that *an upper bound of score is associated with each one in $\mathcal{Q}_{\mathrm{C}}$*.

In the rest of this paper, we will write $\overline{\mathsf{score}}(T \mid Q)$ as $\overline{\mathsf{score}}(Q)$ and $\mathsf{score}(T \mid Q)$ as $\mathsf{score}(Q)$ if T is clear from the context.

Given the set of queries in $\mathcal{Q}_{\mathrm{C}}$ and their upper-bound scores, we now analyze what is the minimal (sub)set $\mathcal{Q}_{\min} \subseteq \mathcal{Q}_{\mathrm{C}}$ of queries we have to evaluate to get the top-k with the highest scores in $\mathcal{Q}_{\mathrm{C}}$. Let $\mathcal{Q}_{\mathrm{C}} = \{Q_1, Q_2, \ldots, Q_N\}$, where Q_i's are ordered by their upper-bound scores $\overline{\mathsf{score}}(Q_1) \geq \ldots \geq \overline{\mathsf{score}}(Q_N)$. Intuitively, if we evaluate queries in $\mathcal{Q}_{\mathrm{C}}$ in this order, we can *terminate* if

$$\mathrm{top}_k\{\mathsf{score}(Q_1), \ldots, \mathsf{score}(Q_i)\} > \overline{\mathsf{score}}(Q_{i+1}), \quad (7)$$

where $\mathrm{top}_k\{\ldots\}$ is the k-th largest number in the set, we can assert that the top-k queries are among $\{Q_1, \ldots, Q_i\}$. Let i^* be the minimal index i that satisfies the *termination condition* in (7), let

$$\mathcal{Q}_{\min} = \{Q_1, Q_2, \ldots, Q_{i^*}\} \subseteq \mathcal{Q}_{\mathrm{C}}. \quad (8)$$

We can show that, informally, if based on only the upper-bound information $\overline{\text{score}}$, $\mathcal{Q}_{\min}$, called *minimal evaluation set*, is the minimal subset of queries in $\mathcal{Q}_C$ we have to evaluate to get the top-k.

PROPOSITION 5. (Optimality of $\mathcal{Q}_{\min}$) *Given a set of PJ queries $\mathcal{Q}_C$ and upper bounds $\overline{\text{score}}$ of their scores. Any multi-step ranking algorithm to find queries with the top-k scores in $\mathcal{Q}_C$ has to evaluate all queries in the set $\mathcal{Q}_{\min}$ (in* (8)*) to compute their scores.*

The formalization of the class of *multi-step ranking algorithms* and the proof of this proposition are given in Appendix C.

4.3 Worst-Case Optimal Baseline Strategy

Based on the upper bounds of scores and the optimality of $\mathcal{Q}_{\min}$ introduced in the above two subsections, we have a simple but "worst-case optimal" strategy BASELINE described in Algorithm 2.

The idea is to evaluate queries $Q_1, Q_2, \ldots$ in $\mathcal{Q}_C$ one by one (to get the exact scores) in the descending order of upper-bound scores. Recall that upper-bound scores (line 1) can be computed efficiently and are associated with all queries in $\mathcal{Q}_C$, as discussed in Sections 4.1.2 and 4.1.4. For each Q_i, we use the operator introduced in Section 4.1.3 to compute its true score (line 4). If after we finish evaluating Q_i, (7) is satisfied, then we can terminate and output the current top-k among the evaluated PJ queries.

Input: queries in $\mathcal{Q}_C$ and upper bounds of their scores
Output: top-k PJ queries in $\mathcal{Q}_C$ with the highest scores

1: Sort queries in $\mathcal{Q}_C$: $\overline{\text{score}}(Q_1) \geq \ldots \geq \overline{\text{score}}(Q_N)$.
2: Initialize $\mathcal{Q}_{\text{topk}} \leftarrow \emptyset$.
3: For $i = 1$ to N do
4: Evaluate Q_i to compute score(Q_i).
5: Let $\mathcal{Q}_{\text{topk}} \leftarrow \mathcal{Q}_{\text{topk}} \cup \{Q_i\}$; if $|\mathcal{Q}_{\text{topk}}| > k$, keep only queries in $\mathcal{Q}_{\text{topk}}$ with the top-k highest scores.
6: If termination condition (7) is satisfied, exit the loop.
7: Output $\mathcal{Q}_{\text{topk}}$.

Algorithm 2: Baseline Evaluation Strategy: BASELINE

It is not hard to show that BASELINE evaluates only queries in $\mathcal{Q}_{\min}$ and thus is worst-case optimal for finding top-k.

THEOREM 1. (Correctness and Optimality) BASELINE *correctly finds the PJ queries with the top-k highest scores among $\mathcal{Q}_C$, and evaluates only queries in the minimal evaluation set $\mathcal{Q}_{\min}$.*

Disadvantages of the baseline. BASELINE strategy in Algorithm 2 is worst-case optimal in terms of the number of PJ queries it evaluates. But the evaluation cost (or, response time) can be potentially improved significantly. BASELINE has several disadvantages. First, this baseline algorithm does not utilize frequent common subexpressions in $\mathcal{Q}_C$. Indeed, we can cache the output relations of some subexpressions so that they can be re-used for more than one PJ query $\mathcal{Q}_C$. Secondly, as we do not have infinite memory, to maximize the benefit we get from caching, we need to make the decisions of which subexpressions to be cached and when, for a batch of PJ queries. BASELINE examines queries in $\mathcal{Q}_C$ one-by-one, so such decisions cannot be made wisely. The strategy we introduce in Section 5 improves BASELINE from the above two angles.

5. OPTIMIZING CACHING-EVALUATION

We introduce our cache-aware optimization techniques in this section to overcome the disadvantages of BASELINE. The goal is still to find PJ queries with the top-k scores in $\mathcal{Q}_C$ w.r.t. the user-given example spreadsheet T. We will first discuss how to evaluate a PJ query. i.e., compute its score, when output relations of some sub-parts of it are cached, together with a cost model which quantify the cost of such cache-aware evaluation, in Section 5.1. We then formulate the *cache-evaluation scheduling problem*, i.e., an abstract version of the task to be solved by caching-evaluation scheduler in Section 5.2. Core technical challenges we resolve here are: to determine the order of PJ queries in $\mathcal{Q}_C$ to be evaluated, which sub-PJ queries to be cached, and for how long, with the goal of minimizing the evaluation cost, or maximizing the benefit we get from caching. We show that it is NP-hard. Section 5.3 introduces a near-optimal solution to this problem. We will discuss how to extend our approach for incremental computation in Section 5.4.

5.1 Cache-Aware Evaluation of PJ Queries

Recall that the evaluation of $\text{score}_{\text{col}}$ is light-weight without exectuing any join of relations as discussed in Section 4.1.2. So here, we focus on computing $\text{score}_{\text{row}}$ of a PJ query Q w.r.t. T.

Caching sub-PJ queries in evaluation. Let's formally define a *sub-PJ query* of Q, and discuss how to evaluate PJ query Q if the output relations of some sub-PJ queries of Q have been cached.

DEFINITION 4. (Sub-PJ Query) $Q' = (\mathcal{J}', \mathcal{C}', \phi_{\mathcal{C}'})$ *is said to be a sub-PJ query of a PJ query $Q = (\mathcal{J}, \mathcal{C}, \phi)$, iff $\mathcal{J}'$ is a subtree of $\mathcal{J}$; $\mathcal{C}' \subseteq \mathcal{C}$ is a subset of columns from relations in $\mathcal{J}'$ which the columns in T are mapped to; and $\phi_{\mathcal{C}'}$ is a range-restriction of ϕ by $\mathcal{C}'$, i.e., $\phi_{\mathcal{C}'}(i) = \phi(i)$ iff $\phi(i) \in \mathcal{C}'$ and is undefined iff $\phi(i) \in \mathcal{C} - \mathcal{C}'$. We denote $Q' \preceq Q$ if Q' is a sub-PJ query of Q.*

Two types of subtrees are considered here: i) $\mathcal{J}'$ is a subtree of $\mathcal{J}$ rooted at some internal node, containing all leaves below; and ii) a type-i) subtree plus the parent of its root.

Figure 3 shows two sub-PJ queries Q_1' (left) and Q_2' (right) of the PJ query Q in Figure 2(b)-(i).

We have a *sub-PJ query cache* $\mathcal{M}$ in our system, which temporarily stores the output relations of some sub-PJ queries in a budgeted amount of memory. The execution plans of PJ-queries can be easily extended to take advantage of the cached output relations of sub-PJ queries: for a PJ query Q and a set of cached sub-PJ queries in $\mathcal{M}$, instead of starting from the leaves of Q, we start from the output relations of maximal sub-PJ queries of Q in $\mathcal{M}$ and follow the execution plan of Q afterward. Q' is said to be a *maximal sub-PJ query of Q in $\mathcal{M}$*, iff $Q' \preceq Q$ and there is no Q'' whose output relation is cached in $\mathcal{M}$ such that $Q' \prec Q'' \preceq Q$. Intuitively, we want to utilize the output relations cached in $\mathcal{M}$ as much as possible. More details are given in Appendix B.2.

Cost model of evaluation. We do not have unlimited memory to cache every single sub-PJ query. So our scheduling-evaluation scheduler needs to determine which sub-PJ queries to be cached and for how long, so as to maximize the benefit we obtain from caching, or equivalently, to minimize the total evaluation cost. To this end, a cost model needs to be introduced.

We define $\text{cost}(Q)$ to be the cost of evaluating a (sub-)PJ query Q, without utilizing the cache, and $\text{cost}(Q, \mathcal{M})$ be the cost of evaluating Q when a set of sub-PJ queries $\mathcal{M}$ have their output relations in the cache. We abuse the notation $\mathcal{M}$ a bit – we use it to denote both the set of sub-PJ queries as well as their cached output relations. Details about the cost model can be found in (12)-(13) in Appendix B.3, which is calibrated to the execution plans we use.

5.2 Caching-Evaluation Scheduling Problem

We are given a set of PJ queries $\mathcal{Q}_C = \{Q_1, Q_2, \ldots, Q_N\}$, ordered by their upper-bound scores $\overline{\text{score}}(Q_1) \geq \overline{\text{score}}(Q_2) \geq \ldots \geq \overline{\text{score}}(Q_N)$. Let $\mathcal{T}(Q_i)$ be the set of all *sub-PJ queries* of Q_i and $\mathcal{T}(\mathcal{Q}) = \bigcup_{Q_i \in \mathcal{Q}} \mathcal{T}(Q_i)$ for a set of PJ queries $\mathcal{Q} \subseteq \mathcal{Q}_C$.

We first introduce a general framework of our caching-evaluation strategies to find the top-k answers from $\mathcal{Q}_C$, and then define the *caching-evaluation scheduling problem* to find the best strategy.

Operators. To utilize output relations of sub-PJ queries shared by multiple PJ-queries in $\mathcal{Q}_C$, we maintain a cache $\mathcal{M}$ of size at most B. Three types of operators are allowed:

a) Evaluate($Q, \mathcal{M}$): to evaluate a PJ query or a sub-PJ query Q using output relations cached in $\mathcal{M}$, and get its relevance score $\mathsf{score}(T \mid Q)$ (for $Q \in \mathcal{Q}_C$) and output relation $\mathcal{A}(Q)$.

b) Add($Q, \mathcal{M}$): to store the output relation $\mathcal{A}(Q)$ in $\mathcal{M}$.

c) Delete($Q, \mathcal{M}$): to delete $\mathcal{A}(Q)$ from $\mathcal{M}$.

The size of $\mathcal{M}$, denoted as $|\mathcal{M}|$, is the amount of memory we need to keep the output relations of (sub-)PJ queries in $\mathcal{M}$. We want to ensure that, at any time, $|\mathcal{M}|$ could be at most B.

Caching-evaluation schedule and termination condition. Initially, the cache $\mathcal{M}$ is empty, and for every PJ query $Q_i \in \mathcal{Q}_C$ we only know its upper-bound score. We want to apply the above three types of operators in some order on PJ queries in $\mathcal{Q}_C$ and their sub-PJ queries. The goal is that, at some point, the set of evaluated queries, denoted as $\mathcal{Q}_E$, satisfies: $\mathcal{Q}_E \supseteq \mathcal{Q}_{\min}$, i.e., the top-$k$ have been found. Note that $\mathcal{Q}_{\min}$ is not known in advance.

Objective. Each type-a operator Evaluate($Q, \mathcal{M}$) (Q is either a PJ query from $\mathcal{Q}_C$ or a sub-PJ query) has a cost, cost($Q, \mathcal{M}$), as defined in (13) in Appendix B.3. The goal is to minimize the total evaluation cost of type-a operators. Each type-b/c operator also has a cost but it is negligible compared to type-a's cost.

Problem statement (CACHE-EVAL SCHEDULER) *Given a set of PJ queries $\mathcal{Q}_C = \{Q_1, Q_2, \ldots, Q_N\}$, with their upper-bound scores $\overline{\mathsf{score}}(Q_1) \geq \overline{\mathsf{score}}(Q_2) \geq \ldots \geq \overline{\mathsf{score}}(Q_N)$, w.r.t. an example spreadsheet T, a sequence of operators in type-a,b,c are chosen to be executed and the objective is to:*

$$\text{minimize} \sum_{\text{Op. Evaluate}(Q,\mathcal{M})\text{'s executed}} \mathrm{cost}(Q, \mathcal{M})$$

$$\text{s.t. } \mathcal{M} \text{ has size at most } B \text{ at any time, and eventually } \mathcal{Q}_E \supseteq \mathcal{Q}_{\min}.$$

THEOREM 2. (Hardness) *Even when the set $\mathcal{Q}_{\min}$ is known, the* CACHE-EVAL SCHEDULER *problem is NP-complete, with $|\mathcal{Q}_C| + |\mathcal{T}(\mathcal{Q}_C)|$ as the input size, where $|\mathcal{T}(\mathcal{Q}_C)|$ is the total number of sub-PJ queries of queries in $\mathcal{Q}_C$.*

5.3 A Near-Optimal Strategy

We will introduce a near-optimal strategy, FASTTOPK, for the CACHE-EVAL SCHEDULER problem. It is based on two heuristics: *guessing the minimal evaluation set* and *caching critical sub-PJ queries*. We will also analyze the theoretical guarantee on performance it provides, in terms of the evaluation cost.

5.3.1 Guessing The Minimal Evaluation Set

The first challenge is that the minimal evaluation set $\mathcal{Q}_{\min}$ is unknown to us. Our strategy BASELINE (Algorithm 2) examines only queries in $\mathcal{Q}_{\min}$ because it evaluates queries one by one, but $\mathcal{Q}_{\min}$ is known only after it terminates. Ideally, if we know $\mathcal{Q}_{\min}$ in advance, we can find *frequent* sub-PJ queries in $\mathcal{Q}_{\min}$ (the ones contained by many PJ queries), and cache their output relations so that they can be re-used multiple times in the evaluation. Indeed, we can consider all queries in $\mathcal{Q}_C$ in one batch, but since $\mathcal{Q}_{\min}$ is usually a small subset of $\mathcal{Q}_C$, sub-PJ queries that are frequent in $\mathcal{Q}_C$ may not be frequent in $\mathcal{Q}_{\min}$ or even do not exist in $\mathcal{Q}_{\min}$ – so our decision of which sub-PJ queries to be cached based on their frequencies in $\mathcal{Q}_C$ is likely to be sub-optimal.

We note that $\mathcal{Q}_{\min}$ is a "prefix" of $\mathcal{Q}_C$, and can be uniquely specified by the index i^* as in (7)-(8). So our heuristic to resolve this challenge is to create a few batches $\mathcal{B}_0, \mathcal{B}_1, \mathcal{B}_2, \ldots$ of queries in the order of $Q_1, Q_2, \ldots, Q_i, \ldots$ to approximate $\mathcal{Q}_{\min}$. We will optimize the cache-evaluation schedule for queries in each batch. After we finish evaluating each batch of queries in $\mathcal{B}_j$, we check the termination condition (7), and eventually we stop at $\mathcal{B}_{j^*}$ after evaluating queries in $\mathcal{Q}_E = \mathcal{B}_0 \cup \mathcal{B}_1 \cup \ldots \cup \mathcal{B}_{j^*} \supseteq \mathcal{Q}_{\min}$. On one hand, we want to create as few batches as possible, i.e., j^* is small, so common sub-PJ queries across different queries can be found in one batch and we can cache and re-use their output relations; and on the other hand, we do not want to evaluate too many additional queries that are not in $\mathcal{Q}_{\min}$, i.e., $\mathcal{Q}_E - \mathcal{Q}_{\min}$ is small.

The following batch-forming strategy balances the two concerns. The first batch of queries to be evaluated is $\mathcal{B}_0 = \{Q_1, \ldots, Q_k\}$, as Q_i's are ordered by the upper-bound scores and B_0 has the least number of queries we have to evaluate to get the top-k. After finishing evaluating this batch, if the termination condition in (7) is not satisfied, we will consider the next batch with a slightly larger number of queries: $\mathcal{B}_1 = \{Q_{k+1}, \ldots, Q_{k(1+\epsilon)}\}$. Again, if the termination condition is satisfied, we can stop and output the top-k; and otherwise, we consider the next batch. In general, the jth batch is $\mathcal{B}_j = \{Q_{k(1+\epsilon)^{j-1}+1}, \ldots, Q_{k(1+\epsilon)^j}\}$, for some constant $\epsilon > 0$.

This high-level procedure is outlined in Algorithm 3. Recall the discussion in Section 4.1, upper-bound scores can be computed efficiently and are associated with all queries in $\mathcal{Q}_C$ (line 1). The loop (lines 4-9) forms batches one-by-one as described above. The value of i in line 7 of every loop is the index of the last PJ query evaluated up to now, so line 9 can check the termination condition in (7) to see whether the top-k have been found.

Input: queries in $\mathcal{Q}_C$ and upper bounds of their scores
Output: top-k PJ queries in $\mathcal{Q}_C$ with the highest scores

1: Sort queries in $\mathcal{Q}_C$: $\overline{\mathsf{score}}(Q_1) \geq \ldots \geq \overline{\mathsf{score}}(Q_N)$.
2: Initialize $\mathcal{Q}_{\text{topk}} \leftarrow \emptyset$.
3: Let the first batch be $\mathcal{B}_0 \leftarrow \{Q_1, \ldots, Q_k\}$, $i \leftarrow k$, and $j \leftarrow 0$.
4: Do
5: BatchEval($\mathcal{B}_j$) to get $\mathsf{score}(Q)$'s for all $Q \in \mathcal{B}_j$.
6: Let $\mathcal{Q}_{\text{topk}} \leftarrow \mathcal{Q}_{\text{topk}} \cup \mathcal{B}_j$;
keep only queries in $\mathcal{Q}_{\text{topk}}$ with the top-k highest scores.
7: Let $i \leftarrow k(1+\epsilon)^j$ and then $j \leftarrow j+1$.
8: Form next batch: $\mathcal{B}_j = \{Q_{i+1}, Q_{i+2}, \ldots, Q_{k(1+\epsilon)^j}\}$.
9: While ($\text{top}_k\{\mathsf{score}(Q_1), \ldots, \mathsf{score}(Q_i)\} \leq \overline{\mathsf{score}}(Q_{i+1})$)
10: Output $\mathcal{Q}_{\text{topk}}$.

Algorithm 3: Near-Optimal Strategy: FASTTOPK

Suppose the algorithm terminates with $i = i_{\text{end}}$. In Section 5.3.3, we will utilize the fact that $i^* \leq i_{\text{end}} \leq i^*(1+\epsilon)$, where $i^* = |\mathcal{Q}_{\min}|$ is the least number of PJ queries any strategy has to evaluate, to give a performance guarantee of our strategy. Intuitively, based on this fact, we have that the size of $\mathcal{Q}_E$, the set of queries evaluated by FASTTOPK (Algorithm 3), is at most $(1+\epsilon)|\mathcal{Q}_{\min}|$. So FASTTOPK does not examine too many additional queries that are not in $\mathcal{Q}_{\min}$. To bound the total evaluation cost, we can also show that there are at most $O(\log_{1+\epsilon}(|\mathcal{Q}_{\min}|/k))$ batches.

The only missing building block in FASTTOPK (Algorithm 3) is now the subroutine BatchEval($\mathcal{B}_j$) in line 5.

5.3.2 Caching Critical Sub-PJ Queries

Let's focus on the subroutine BatchEval($\mathcal{B}_j$). We want to evaluate a batch $\mathcal{B}_j$ of queries using operators in type-a/b/c, so that the total cost is minimized. The basic idea of our approach for this subroutine is to partition queries in a batch $\mathcal{B}_j$ into groups, such that each group of PJ queries share at least one heavy-cost sub-PJ query, called *critical sub-PJ query*. The output relation of this sub-PJ query is cached in $\mathcal{M}$ if its size is no more than the budget B. We will later show that this seemingly simple heuristic has strong theoretical/practical performance guarantee.

Critical sub-PJ query. Let $\mathcal{T}(Q_i)$ be the set of all sub-PJ queries of Q_i, and $\mathcal{T}(\mathcal{B}_j) = \bigcup_{Q_i \in \mathcal{B}_j} \mathcal{T}(Q_i)$. A sub-PJ query $Q^* \in \mathcal{T}(Q_i)$ is said to be *critical* to Q_i in $\mathcal{B}_j$, if i) Q^* is shared by more than one query: there exists $Q_{i'} \in \mathcal{B}_j$ s.t. $i' \neq i$ and $Q^* \in \mathcal{T}(Q_{i'}) \cap \mathcal{T}(Q_i)$; and ii) Q^* has the highest cost, $\text{cost}(Q^*)$, among those in $\mathcal{T}(Q_i)$ satisfying condition i).

It is intuitive that the output relation of a critical sub-PJ query is worth caching in $\mathcal{M}$, because it can benefit the evaluation of at least one PJ query in $\mathcal{B}_j$, as condition i); and it has the highest cost among all such sub-PJ queries of a PJ query, as condition ii), so that we can benefit the most from caching it. We describe this heuristic for BatchEval($\mathcal{B}_j$) more formally in Algorithm 4.

Input: queries in a batch $\mathcal{B}_j$ and cache budget B
Task: get score(Q) by evaluating every $Q \in \mathcal{B}_j$

1: Sort the M sub-PJ queries in $\mathcal{T}(\mathcal{B}_j)$ as:
   $\text{cost}(Q'_1) \geq \text{cost}(Q'_1) \geq \ldots \geq \text{cost}(Q'_M)$.
2: While $\mathcal{B}_j$ is not empty
3: Clear $\mathcal{M}$ using type-c operators Delete.
4: Pick $Q^* = \text{argmax}_{Q' \in \mathcal{T}(\mathcal{B}_j)} \{\text{cost}(Q') \mid |\mathcal{A}(Q')| \leq B \wedge \exists i_1 \neq i_2 : Q' \in \mathcal{T}(Q_{i_1}) \cap \mathcal{T}(Q_{i_2})\}$.
5: If no such Q^* can be found, evaluate all the remaining queries in $\mathcal{B}_j$ and terminate.
6: Let $\text{Critical}^{-1}(Q^*) \leftarrow \{Q_i \in \mathcal{B}_j \mid Q^* \in \mathcal{T}(Q_i)\}$.
7: Execute Evaluate($Q^*, \mathcal{M}$) and Add($Q^*, \mathcal{M}$). (evaluate Q^* and store its output relation in $\mathcal{M}$)
8: For each $Q_i \in \text{Critical}^{-1}(Q^*)$ do
9: Evaluate Q_i using $\mathcal{M}$: call Evaluate($Q_i, \mathcal{M}$).
10: Let $\mathcal{B}_j \leftarrow \mathcal{B}_j - \text{Critical}^{-1}(Q^*)$.

Algorithm 4: BatchEval($\mathcal{B}_j$): strategy for evaluating a batch of queries for their scores while minimizing the cost

In line 1, all sub-PJ queries of $Q = (\mathcal{J}, \mathcal{C}, \phi) \in \mathcal{B}_j$ can be enumerated efficiently by retrieving the rooted subtree at each node in $\mathcal{J}$. As discussed in Appendix B.3, the cost of each sub-PJ query Q'_i can be computed efficiently from (12) by summing up the sizes of relations in Q'_i and row-level inverted indexes for columns in the projection of Q'_i. For each iteration (lines 2-10), the critical sub-PJ query Q^* in $\mathcal{B}_j$ with the highest cost and output relation of size no more than B is picked (line 4). Since we are focusing on foreign-key joins, we will use the number of rows in the root relation of Q' multiplying the number of columns in the output relation as the size of the output relation, $|\mathcal{A}(Q')|$. The set of queries in $\mathcal{B}_j$ containing Q^* as a sub-PJ query is put into a set $\text{Critical}^{-1}(Q^*)$ is (line 6). We first evaluate and cache the output relation of Q^* in $\mathcal{M}$ (lines 7). Then all queries having Q^* as its sub-PJ query are evaluated to get their scores using $\mathcal{M}$ (lines 8-9), and removed form $\mathcal{B}_j$ (line 10). After that, the cache $\mathcal{M}$ is cleared up (line 3).

EXAMPLE 4. *Consider a batch of three PJ queries, $\mathcal{B}_j = \{Q_1, Q_2, Q_3\}$, where Q_1-Q_3 are depicted in Figure 2(b)-(i), (ii), (iii), respectively. Two sub-PJ queries Q'_1 and Q'_2 of them are shown in Figure 3 (left and right, respectively). Both are contained in two queries Q_1 and Q_3, so could potentially be critical sub-PJ queries to Q_1 and Q_3. If Q'_2 has the largest cost $\text{cost}(Q'_2)$ among all such sub-PJ queries, then Q'_2 is a critical to both Q_1 and Q_3, and line 4 will pick $Q^* = Q'_2$. We have $\text{Critical}^{-1}(Q^*) = \{Q_1, Q_3\} \subseteq \mathcal{B}_j$ in line 6. Our strategy* FASTTOPK *would cache $\mathcal{A}(Q'_2)$ in $\mathcal{M}$ first (line 7), and then use it to evaluate Q_1 and Q_3 (lines 8-9). After that, only Q_2 is left in $\mathcal{B}_j$ and will be evaluated as in line 5.*

Although this subroutine is applied for each batch independently in Algorithm 3 to find the top-k in $\mathcal{Q}_C$, we will later show that it has an overall performance guarantee, using the fact that the total number of batches is small (the last value of j in Algorithm 3).

THEOREM 3. (Putting Together and Correctness) FASTTOPK *strategy (Algorithm 3 with subroutine* BatchEval *as Algorithm 4), correctly finds the queries in $\mathcal{Q}_C$ with the top-k highest scores.*

5.3.3 Performance Analysis

We will start with the time complexity of our strategy FASTTOPK, and then analyze its approximation ratio.

Time complexity. The online response time of our system is determined by i) time spent on generating PJ queries in $\mathcal{Q}_C$ and their upper bounds, ii) spent on evaluating PJ queries, and iii) spent optimizing the scheduling of caching and evaluations (FASTTOPK strategy). i) is negligible compared to ii) (analyzed in Section 4.1.4). ii) is modeled as the objective in our CACHE-EVAL SCHEDULER problem and the goal of FASTTOPK is to reduce it as much as possible. The purpose of the following theorem is to show that, excluding the time spent on executing operators in type-a/b/c, the time spent by FASTTOPK on iii) is negligible compared to ii).

THEOREM 4. (Time Complexity) *Given a set of PJ queries in $\mathcal{Q}_C$ and their sub-PJ queries $\mathcal{T}(\mathcal{Q}_C)$ with costs and upper-bound scores associated, the time complexity of* FASTTOPK *is $O(N + M_{\text{all}}(s_{\max} + \log M_{\text{all}}))$ (excluding the running time of operators in type-a/b/c chosen by* FASTTOPK *to be run), where $N = |\mathcal{Q}_C|$ is the number of PJ queries in $\mathcal{Q}_C$, $M_{\text{all}} = \sum_{Q_i \in \mathcal{Q}_C} |\mathcal{T}(Q_i)|$ here is the total number of sub-PJ queries of queries in $\mathcal{Q}_C$, and $s_{\max}$ is the max size of a join tree $\mathcal{J}$ of a PJ query in $\mathcal{Q}_C$. Because of the definition of a sub-PJ query, we have $M_{\text{all}} = \Theta(s_{\max} \cdot N)$.*

Performance ratio. FASTTOPK strategy (Algorithms 3-4) provide a feasible solution (a scheduling of operators in type a/b/c) to the CACHE-EVAL SCHEDULER problem. We now compare the cost of this strategy with the cost of the optimal solution (which is hard to be found as shown in Theorem 2).

For a set of PJ queries $\mathcal{Q} = \{Q_i\}$, let $\text{cost}_{\text{TOT}}(\mathcal{Q})$ be the total cost of evaluating queries in $\mathcal{Q}$ one by one without caching:

$$\text{cost}_{\text{TOT}}(\mathcal{Q}) = \sum_{Q_i \in \mathcal{Q}} \text{cost}(Q_i).$$

Let $\text{cost}_{\text{OPT}}(\mathcal{Q})$ be the cost of evaluating all queries in $\mathcal{Q}$ using the optimal strategy in the CACHE-EVAL SCHEDULER problem.

Let $\text{cost}_{\text{SOL}}(\mathcal{Q})$ be the cost of evaluating all queries in $\mathcal{Q}$ using our FASTTOPK strategy in Algorithms 3-4.

THEOREM 5. (Performance Ratio) *Given PJ queries in $\mathcal{Q}_C$ with upper-bound scores associated, the strategy* FASTTOPK *in Algorithms 3-4 evaluates a set of PJ queries $\mathcal{Q}_E$ s.t.*

$$|\mathcal{Q}_{\min}| \leq |\mathcal{Q}_E| \leq (1+\epsilon)|\mathcal{Q}_{\min}|, \tag{9}$$

and the benefit from caching

$$\begin{aligned} &\text{cost}_{\text{TOT}}(\mathcal{Q}_E) - \text{cost}_{\text{SOL}}(\mathcal{Q}_E) \qquad (10) \\ \geq &\frac{1}{2c^2}\left(\text{cost}_{\text{TOT}}(\mathcal{Q}_E) - \log_{1+\epsilon}\left(\frac{|\mathcal{Q}_{\min}|}{k}\right) \cdot \text{cost}_{\text{OPT}}(\mathcal{Q}_E)\right) \end{aligned}$$

where c is the number of columns in T.

Informally, the above theorem gives guarantees for our FASTTOPK strategy from two aspects: i) it does not evaluate too many additional PJ queries in additional to the necessary ones in $\mathcal{Q}_{\min}$, as in (9); and ii) $\text{cost}_{\text{TOT}}(\mathcal{Q}_{\text{E}}) - \text{cost}_{\text{SOL}}(\mathcal{Q}_{\text{E}})$ is the benefit we obtained from caching, and is lower bounded by the gap between the total cost and the cost of the optimal strategy (RHS of (10)).

5.3.4 *Heuristics for Further Improvement*

Our strategy can be further improved. Although not improving the performance ratio in Theorem 5, the following two heuristics are effective to improve its performance in practice.

The first heuristic is as follows. Consider each iteration of lines 3-10 in Algorithm 4, only one output relation (the one of Q^*) is cached in $\mathcal{M}$. Indeed, if there is still room in $\mathcal{M}$, it will always be beneficial to cache more sub-PJ queries to speed up the evaluation of queries in $\text{Critical}^{-1}(Q^*)$. So our heuristic here is to order queries in $\text{Critical}^{-1}(Q^*)$ in such a way that "similar" queries (sharing common sub-PJ queries) are consecutive. While we evaluate these queries one-by-one in this order, the standard LRU replacement algorithm is applied to insert and replace output relations of sub-PJ queries in $\mathcal{M}$ – but note that we never replace the output relation of Q^* until finishing evaluating all queries in $\text{Critical}^{-1}(Q^*)$. Such an order can be formed as follows. Starting with any query in $\text{Critical}^{-1}(Q^*)$, in each step, we pick the query, which shares the most sub-PJ queries with the last one but is not in the order yet, to be the next one in this order. Repeat until all queries are placed in the order.

The second heuristic is an extension to our termination condition in (7). We call it the *skipping condition*. During the execution of FASTTOPK, we maintain the current kth highest score for all the queries that have been evaluated. In line 9 of Algorithm 4, before we evaluate Q_i, we first check whether its upper-bound score is higher than the current top-k score – if not, we can safely skip the evaluation of Q_i. This heuristic is particularly powerful and necessary for the last batch of queries in Algorithm 3, as this batch is usually large and contains queries not in $\mathcal{Q}_{\min}$.

5.4 Incremental Computation

Our strategy can be easily extended for incremental computation. The incremental version of our end-to-end system task is: suppose we have found the top-k PJ queries for a user-given example spreadsheet T, after one or more cells in T are updated – the updated example spreadsheet is denoted as T' – how to find the top-k PJ queries for T' by re-using the evaluation results for T.

If the user adds/deletes a column in T, we re-start and generate a completely new caching-evaluation schedule using FASTTOPK (Algorithms 3-4), because in this case, the set of PJ queries, $\mathcal{Q}_{\text{C}}'$, to be evaluated for T' are different from $\mathcal{Q}_{\text{C}}$ for T.

We focus on speeding up the case when the set of columns in T are unchanged, but some rows are updated (with one or more cells). In this case, $\mathcal{Q}_{\text{C}}'$ may have large overlap with $\mathcal{Q}_{\text{C}}$ and thus evaluation results for $\mathcal{Q}_{\text{C}}$ can be re-used. The basic ideas are to derive a tighter upper bound of $\mathsf{score}(T' \mid Q)$ based on the unchanged part of T and to schedule the incremental part of evaluation for $\mathcal{Q}_{\text{C}}'$ carefully. Refer to Appendix A.1 for more details.

6. EXPERIMENTAL EVALUATION

We present an experimental study of the techniques proposed in this paper. We evaluate and compare three algorithms.

- NAIVE: evaluates all the enumerated PJ queries in $\mathcal{Q}_{\text{C}}$;
- BASELINE (Algorithm 2): as described in Section 4.3;
- FASTTOPK (Algorithms 3-4): as described in Section 5.

We compare the performance of the three algorithms, and evaluate their sensitivity with respect to various parameters (Section 6.2). We also conduct a user study to evaluate the effectiveness of our scoring model (Section 6.3). Additional experiments about incremental computation are deferred to the appendix.

6.1 Settings of Experiments

We have implemented all the algorithms using C++/CLI (Common Language Infrastructure) on a Windows 8.1 machine with an Intel i7-4770 CPU at 3.4GHz with 16GB RAM.

Datasets. We use two datasets to evaluate the system performance: CSUPP and AdventureWorks. Our primary dataset, CSUPP, is a real-life database containing information related to customer service and IT support from a Fortune 500 Company. It has a size of 95GB. AdventureWorks, ADVW for short, is a synthetic database with information related to sales, purchasing, product management and contact management with size 300MB [2]. Although ADVW has a small size, we use it for its realistic and complex schema (93 primary key-foreign key edges compared with 63 in CSUPP), and also scale up its dimension/fact tables by creating new rows.

	# Relations	# Columns	# Text Columns	# Edges
CSUPP	105	1721	821	63
ADVW	71	650	104	93

For the user study, we use the real database IMDB [4] with information about movies, because our judges are more familiar with the movie domain compared with CSUPP or ADVW.

Index building. To build the inverted indexes, we tokenize each cell in each text column in the database. We discard tokens containing non-alphanumeric characters and those with more than 15 characters. For each token, we construct a list consisting of column identifiers (which uniquely identifies a column across all columns in the database) of all columns containing it. This forms the *column-level inverted index*. For each token in each column, we construct a list consisting of the row identifiers (which identifies the row within the relation) of all cells containing it in the column. This forms *the row-level inverted index*. We also build an *in-memory (key, foreign key) snapshot* as discussed in Section 3.1. We store all indexes in memory. Table 1 shows the index sizes. For both databases, the total index size is about **7%** of the database size.

	Inv. index (MiB)	(key,fk) snap. (MiB)	Tokens
CSUPP	4759.7	1237.4	6434684
ADVW	6.86	12.57	125083

Table 1: Index sizes

Example spreadsheet (ES) generation. We manually choose 10 semantically meaningful join queries with 6 or more text columns. We execute them and project the results on all the text columns involved. We generate an ES with m rows and n columns by (i) randomly choosing one of the semantically meaningful join queries and (ii) randomly choosing m rows and n columns from its output. We keep only the first token of the cell and all cells of the ES are non-empty. We use $m = 3$ and $n = 3$ in all our experiments.

To simulate real-life inputs, we introduce relationship errors in the ESs (default is 2 errors). To introduce a relationship error, we randomly select a cell of an ES generated above and replace it with the value of another cell in the same column in the join query's output. As before, we keep only the first token of the chosen cell.

We generate 50 ESs for CSUPP and 450 ESs for ADVW. We divide the 50 ESs for CSUPP into 3 buckets, namely *low*, *medium*, and *high*, based on the sizes of row-level inverted indexes of terms in the ESs (from lowly frequent to highly frequent). There are 25, 15, and 10 ESs in the three buckets, respectively. This is to test how our approaches are sensitive about the frequency of terms.

Description	Symbol	Ranges and default values
Param. in scoring model	α	$0.5, 0.6, 0.7, 0.8, 0.9, 1.0$
k in top-k	k	$5, 10, 20, 50, 100$
Batch increase factor	ϵ	$0.2, 0.4, 0.6, 0.8, 1.0, 2.0$
Cache size (MiB)	B	$100, 200, 500, 1000, 2000$
# relationship errors	e	$0, 1, 2, \ldots, (m-1) * n$

Table 2: Parameters we vary in our experiments along with their description, value ranges, and default values (underlined)

6.2 System Performance

We compare the algorithms by: (i) execution time and (ii) number of PJ query-row evaluations (times PJ queries are evaluated on rows in the ES). (ii) indicates the benefit of *using upper bounds* $\overline{\mathsf{score}}$ *of scores for early termination.* (i) indicates the combined benefit of *caching shared sub-PJ queries* and *early termination.*

In our experiments, we vary the 5 parameters in Table 2. Unless otherwise specified, we use the underlined default values. We use CSUPP as the dataset in Exp-I to IV, and ADVW in Exp-IIV.

Exp-I: Comparing FASTTOPK with NAIVE and BASELINE. Figure 6 shows the average execution times (in log scale) of the three algorithms for each of the three ES buckets (low, medium and high). The execution time here is partitioned into query "enumeration + upper bound computation" and "evaluation" (evaluating PJ queries to compute their scores). Figure 6 shows that the "enumeration + upper bound computation" part takes a tiny fraction of the overall execution time for all the three approaches.

We used default values of the 5 parameters shown in Table 2 for this experiment. FASTTOPK outperforms NAIVE *by factors of 11, 10 and 5* for the low, medium and high buckets respectively. NAIVE often takes several minutes to return answers, and it can be found from Figure 6 that the crucial bottleneck is query evaluation to compute scores. Such inefficiency motivates the problem addressed in this paper for interactive query discovery.

The improvement of execution time in BASELINE and FASTTOPK is the combined benefit gained from using the upper bounds $\overline{\mathsf{score}}$ for early termination and caching shared sub-PJ queries.

Without using the upper bounds, NAIVE has to go through and evaluate all the PJ queries enumerated in $\mathcal{Q}_C$; but with the help of the upper bounds, BASELINE and FASTTOPK can terminate as soon as the condition in (7) is satisfied. Figure 7 plots the numbers of queries evaluated by the three approaches. The significantly smaller numbers of queries evaluated by BASELINE and FASTTOPK explain their faster execution time compared with NAIVE.

In Figure 6, FASTTOPK outperforms BASELINE *by factors of 5, 3 and 1.5* for the low, medium and high buckets respectively. This shows the benefit gained from solving the problem of *caching-evaluation scheduling* by our FASTTOPK strategy.

Exp-II: Vary cache size. Figure 8 shows execution time of the two algorithms for the low/high ES buckets. FASTTOPK outperforms the BASELINE for all cache sizes. Higher the cache size, more the sharing, larger the gap. With a cache size of B = 2GiB, FASTTOPK outperforms BASELINE *by a factor of 6X for the low-cost ESs* and *by 3.7X for medium-cost ESs.* The gap is smaller for high-cost ESs; FASTTOPK outperforms BASELINE *by a factor of 2.3X* for B = 2GiB. It is because the results of many of those common sub-PJ queries are too large to fit in the cache. We need a larger cache to obtain the full benefit of sharing for high-cost ESs and get speedups. The trend for the medium ES bucket is similar.

Exp-III: Vary parameter α. Figure 9(a) shows the execution times of the two algorithms with different values of α. Since $(1-\alpha)$ is the weight on the column containment score $\mathsf{score}_{\mathrm{col}}$ and the upper bound score is proportional to $\mathsf{score}_{\mathrm{col}}$, smaller values of α imply tighter upper bound scores and thus faster early termination.

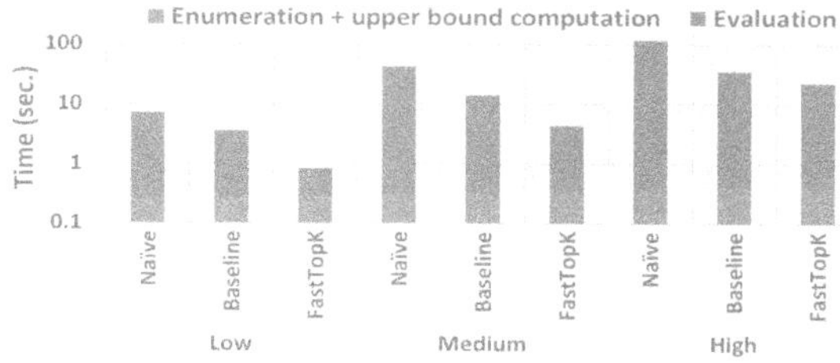

Figure 6: Comparison of FASTTOPK with NAIVE and BASELINE

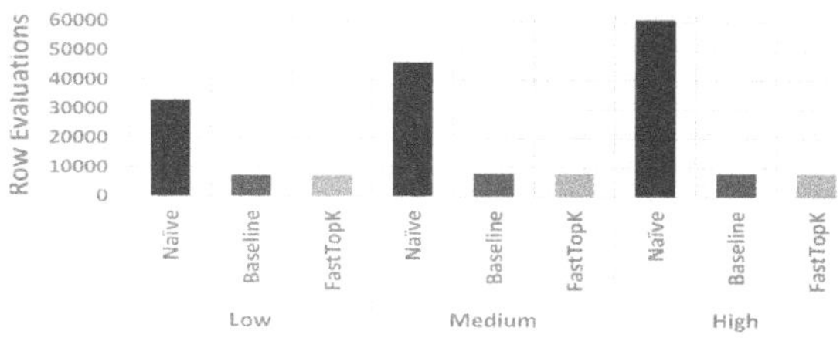

Figure 7: Amount of queries evaluated by NAIVE (without using upper bound $\overline{\mathsf{score}}$), BASELINE (using $\overline{\mathsf{score}}$), and FASTTOPK (using $\overline{\mathsf{score}}$)

Hence, the number of PJ query-row evaluations and the execution time of both algorithms increase in α. FASTTOPK outperforms the BASELINE *by a factor of 3.5X* for all values of α. While they evaluate almost the same number of PJ queries, FASTTOPK performs better due to caching shared outputs of common sub-PJ queries.

Exp-IV: Vary k. With increase in k, both approaches evaluate more PJ queries before they terminate, and thus need more execution time. They perform almost the same number of PJ Query-row evaluations. But, due to shared evaluation, FASTTOPK outperforms BASELINE *by a factor of 3-4X* for k's as in Figure 9(b).

Exp-V: Vary number of relationship errors. We generate different sets of ESs with different numbers of relationship errors (varying from 0 to 5). Higher the number of errors, lower the final scores of the top-k PJ queries. A lower kth highest score delays the satisfaction of the termination condition. So the number of PJ query-row evaluations increase significantly with the number of errors. Overall, FASTTOPK outperforms BASELINE *by a factor of 2-6X.*

Exp-IV: Vary ϵ. We find that FASTTOPK is robust to ϵ. There is negligible change in execution time as we vary ϵ from 0.2 to 2.0, so we omit the plot in the paper. One would expect the performance to suffer when ϵ is high (say, 2.0) since FASTTOPK would evaluate many PJ queries outside the minimum evaluation set. However, due to both cache-evaluation scheduling and the skipping condition, it does not incur much more cost of evaluating such PJ queries.

Exp-IIV: Scale up dimension tables and fact tables. In this experiment, we start with the original ADVW database and scale it up to create databases with different statistical properties.

First, we scale up the dimension tables by creating new rows containing the same values as existing rows (but different row identifiers). We do not modify the fact tables, i.e., the new rows are not referenced by any fact rows. Figure 10(a) shows that the average execution time (over 450 ESs) of FASTTOPK increases slowly as we increase the scale factor (# new rows created for each existing row) from 1 to 2000. This is due to increase in cost of retrieving rows from the row-level inverted index. There is no increase in join cost (hash lookups) as the fact table is unchanged.

Next, we scale up the fact tables by creating new fact rows that reference the same dimension table rows as existing fact rows. We do not modify the dimension tables. This is to test the case that relations with a huge number of tuples and relatively few unique values in certain columns. Figure 10(b) shows the average execution time of FASTTOPK as we increase the scale factor (# new fact rows created for each existing fact row) from 1 to 50. The execution time

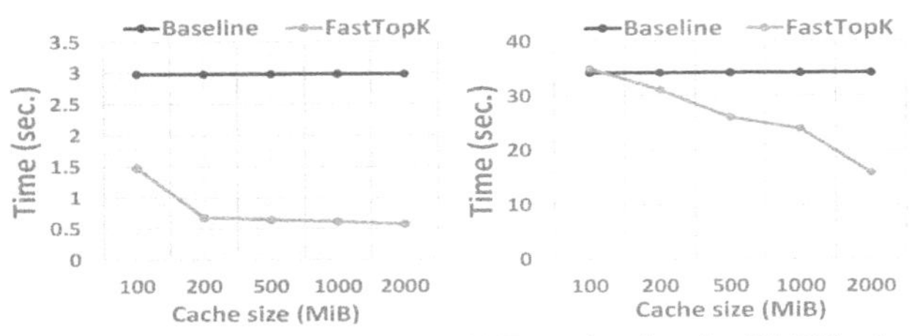

(a) Execution time for "low" bucket (b) Execution time for "high" bucket

Figure 8: Varying cache size B for ESs in "low"/"high" bucket

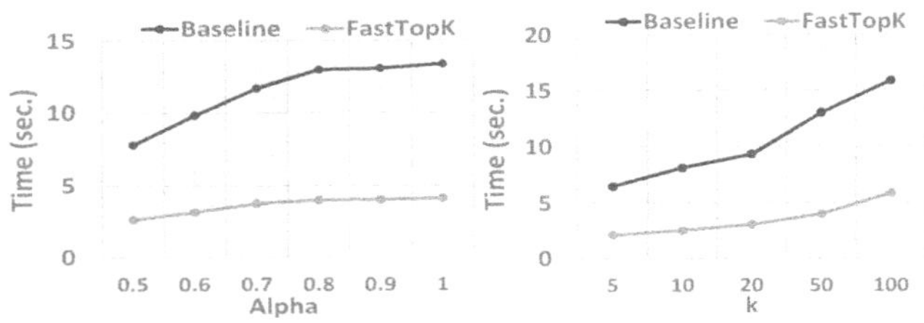

(a) Varying score weight α (b) Varying k

Figure 9: Varying α and k for ESs in "medium" bucket

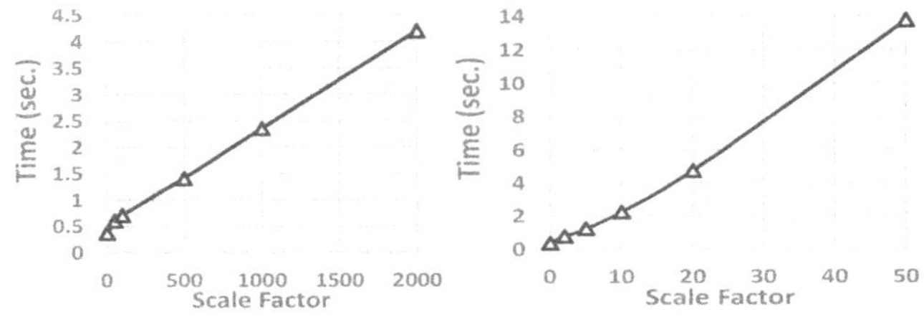

(a) Scaling up dimension tables (b) Scaling up fact tables

Figure 10: Varying scale factor in ADVW.

increases at a much faster rate (superlinear) compared with the first case. This is due to increase in join cost (hash lookups), although the inverted index retrieval cost does not change. This also shows that the join cost dominates the overall cost of query processing.

Finally, if we scale up the dimension tables and the fact tables simultaneously, we have a combined effect of both on the performance. For the space limit, we do not include those results here.

6.3 User Study

We have conducted a user study in IMDB to evaluate the effectiveness of our scoring model. We use the IMDB database for this study as our judges are more familiar with the movie domain compared with CSUPP or ADVW. For the fairness of evaluation, we generate ESs from a source different from IMDB. We use HTML tables extracted from the web [8]. We select HTML tables about movies by creating a list of movies and checking for overlap of the subject column of the table with that list. We generate 52 ESs from randomly selected rows and columns of randomly selected movie HTML tables. For each ES, we compute the top-10 PJ queries and present it to the three judges via a web-based user interface.

We have all the human judges get familiar with and agree on the organization of the IMDB database, and give them access to each original HTML table, so that they can mark each PJ query as relevant or non-relevant to an ES. Different subsets of ESs are assigned to different judges. On average, judges marked 2.3 results as relevant per ES. The overall mean reciprocal rank (MRR)[1] is 0.79; it shows that the relevant result(s) typically appear at the top.

To study the effectiveness for varying characteristics of the ES, we divide the 52 ESs into 3 buckets high (highly frequent terms), medium, and low, based on posting list sizes of the terms in the ESs. The MRRs for the high, medium and low buckets are 0.87, 0.78 and 0.71, respectively. The MRR is quite stable across all the buckets; the MRR values are slightly lower for the low and medium buckets due to presence of a few ESs containing foreign language movies (which are not well-covered by IMDB) in these buckets.

7. RELATED WORK

Our work is most related to query discovery using example tuples [25, 18, 27, 22]. These works can be divided into two categories: those that discover queries whose output is exactly the user-provided table [25, 27] and those that discover queries whose output contains the user-provided example tuples [18, 22]. None of the above works allow approximate containment and top-k ranking based on the degree of containment. This gives rise to unique challenges (exploiting common subexpressions while terminating early) which does not arise in these previous works.

Our work is also related to the vast body of work on keyword search in databases [5, 12, 6, 15, 14]. Some of these works perform top-k ranking and early termination [12, 15]; some of them return answers incrementally [14]. However, the input and output is quite different: they take keyword search queries as input and return interconnected tuple structures (i.e., tuples connected via foreign key references) that contain some or all the keywords. Since the ranking objects are different, our problem requires a new scoring model, and thus new upper bounds of scores and early termination algorithms need to be invented. Specifically, none of those approaches exploit common subexpressions while still terminating early.

Top-k ranking and early termination techniques have been an area of intense research [20, 10]. These techniques compute a lightweight upper bound score for each object, and evaluate them (i.e., compute the exact score) in the descending order of upper bound scores to terminate early. They do not consider sharing computation among the evaluation of different objects.

While sharing some similarity with the line of works on multiple-query optimization (e.g., [19, 21] for traditional databases, and, recently, [9, 26] in MapReduce environment), our problem needs to be tackled with significantly different techniques. There are two major differences. First, multiple-query optimization problem is to evaluate all queries/jobs in a given set, while our problem is to find the top-k – one aspect of our objective is to evaluate as few queries as possible. Secondly, multi-query optimization techniques consider optimize only for cost and have no budget constraints. As we have only a budgeted amount of memory and the number of possible PJ queries is large, our system needs to determine when to insert output relations into the cache and when remove/replace them with new ones wisely. While our PJ queries have a more restrictive form (i.e., with only foreign-key join tree and projection), our caching scheme is much more flexible – this leads to a different technical problem (caching-evaluation scheduling).

8. CONCLUSION AND FUTURE WORK

In this paper, we proposed and studied the problem of discovering top-k project join queries which approximately contain a user-given set of example tuples in their outputs. The main technical challenge is to share results of common subexpressions among the PJ queries and still terminate early. We formalize the problem as the caching-evaluation scheduling problem, show its hardness, and develop a near-optimal solution. Our experiments demonstrate that our solution is both efficient and effective in finding the top-k.

Our ranker captures some classes of errors; extending it to other types of errors (e.g., spelling errors and fuzzy matching) and evaluating its quality on real enterprise users are open challenges.

[1] Defined as $\frac{1}{\text{number of inputs}} \sum_{\text{each input}} \frac{1}{\text{rank of the first right answer}}$

9. REFERENCES

[1] https://docs.google.com/spreadsheets/.

[2] https://msftdbprodsamples.codeplex.com/releases.

[3] https://www.office.com/start/default.aspx.

[4] http://www.imdb.com/interfaces.

[5] S. Agrawal, S. Chaudhuri, and G. Das. Dbxplorer: A system for keyword-based search over relational databases. In *ICDE*, 2002.

[6] G. Bhalotia, A. Hulgeri, C. Nakhe, S. Chakrabarti, and S. Sudarshan. Keyword searching and browsing in databases using banks. In *ICDE*, 2002.

[7] J. Brutlag. Speed matters for google web search (2009): http://services.google.com/fh/files/blogs/google_delayexp.pdf.

[8] M. J. Cafarella, A. Y. Halevy, Y. Zhang, D. Z. Wang, and E. Wu. Uncovering the relational web. In *WebDB*, 2008.

[9] I. Elghandour and A. Aboulnaga. Restore: Reusing results of mapreduce jobs. *PVLDB*, 5(6):586–597, 2012.

[10] R. Fagin, A. Lotem, and N. Naor. Optimal Aggregation Algorithms for Middleware. *J. Comput. Syst. Sci.*, 66(4), 2002.

[11] M. R. Garey, D. S. Johnson, and L. J. Stockmeyer. Some simplified np-complete problems. In *STOC*, 1974.

[12] V. Hristidis, L. Gravano, and Y. Papakonstantinou. Efficient ir-style keyword search over relational databases. In *VLDB*, 2003.

[13] V. Hristidis and Y. Papakonstantinou. Discover: keyword search in relational databases. In *VLDB*, 2002.

[14] G. Li, S. Ji, C. Li, and J. Feng. Efficient type-ahead search on relational data: A tastier approach. In *SIGMOD*, 2009.

[15] Y. Luo, X. Lin, W. Wang, and X. Zhou. Spark: top-k keyword query in relational databases. In *SIGMOD*, 2007.

[16] M. Mayer. http://glinden.blogspot.com/2006/11/marissa-mayer-at-web-20.html.

[17] E. Millar, D. Shen, J. Liu, and C. K. Nicholas. Performance and scalability of a large-scale n-gram based information retrieval system. *J. Digit. Inf.*, 1(5), 2000.

[18] L. Qian, M. J. Cafarella, and H. V. Jagadish. Sample-driven schema mapping. In *SIGMOD*, 2012.

[19] P. Roy, S. Seshadri, S. Sudarshan, and S. Bhobe. Efficient and extensible algorithms for multi query optimization. In *SIGMOD*, 2000.

[20] T. Seidl and H. Kriegel. Optimal multi-step k-nearest neighbor search. In *SIGMOD*, 1998.

[21] T. K. Sellis. Multiple-query optimization. *ACM Trans. Database Syst.*, 13(1):23–52, 1988.

[22] Y. Shen, K. Chakrabarti, S. Chaudhuri, B. Ding, and L. Novik. Discovering queries based on example tuples. In *SIGMOD*, 2014.

[23] A. Singhal. Modern information retrieval: A brief overview. *IEEE Data Eng. Bull.*, 24(4):35–43, 2001.

[24] T. Smith, W. Johnson, R. Tamm-Daniels, and S. Probstein. Querying joined data within a search engine index. *US Patent No. 8073840*, 2011.

[25] Q. T. Tran, C.-Y. Chan, and S. Parthasarathy. Query by output. In *SIGMOD*, 2009.

[26] G. Wang and C. Chan. Multi-query optimization in mapreduce framework. *PVLDB*, 7(3):145–156, 2013.

[27] M. Zhang, H. Elmeleegy, C. M. Procopiuc, and D. Srivastava. Reverse engineering complex join queries. In *SIGMOD*, 2013.

APPENDIX

A. EXTENSION AND DISCUSSION

A.1 Incremental Computation

Let $T' = T^{\text{old}} \cup T^{\text{new}}$, where T^{old} is the set of unchanged rows that are identical to the ones in T, and T^{new} is the set of new rows or updated rows in T'. Recall that $\mathcal{Q}_{\text{E}} \subseteq \mathcal{Q}_{\text{C}}$ is the set of PJ queries that have been evaluated for T. For the new set of queries, $\mathcal{Q}_{\text{C}}'$, generated by the PJ query enumerator for T', can be partitioned into $\mathcal{Q}_{\text{C}}' = \mathcal{Q}_{\text{C}}^{\text{old}} \cup \mathcal{Q}_{\text{C}}^{\text{new}}$, where $\mathcal{Q}_{\text{C}}^{\text{old}} = \mathcal{Q}_{\text{C}}' \cap \mathcal{Q}_{\text{E}}$ and $\mathcal{Q}_{\text{C}}^{\text{new}} = \mathcal{Q}_{\text{C}}' - \mathcal{Q}_{\text{E}}$. For each query in $\mathcal{Q}_{\text{C}}^{\text{old}}$, since it has been evaluated for T, we keep and re-use its score w.r.t. rows in T^{old}; and for each query in $\mathcal{Q}_{\text{C}}^{\text{new}}$, since it is new or unevaluated before, we need to (re-)evaluate it for every row in T'. We will discuss how to utilize the "partial scores" of queries in $\mathcal{Q}_{\text{C}}^{\text{old}}$ to get better upper bounds of scores, and how to take the incremental changes into consideration when scheduling caching-evaluation.

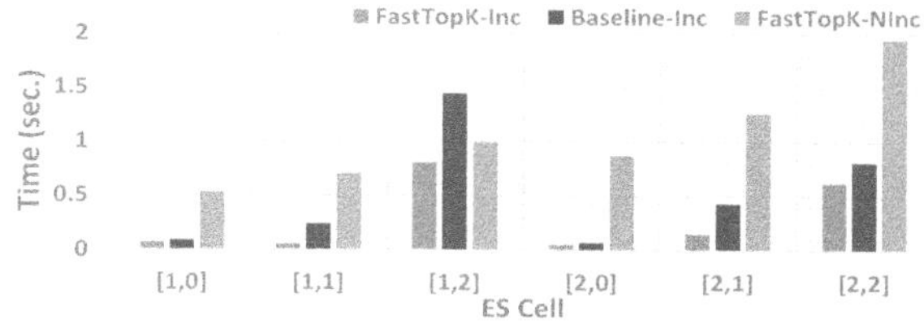

Figure 11: Execution time for incremental input [row, column]

Improved upper-bound scores for $\mathcal{Q}_{\text{C}}^{\text{old}}$. For a query $Q \in \mathcal{Q}_{\text{C}}^{\text{old}}$, a better upper bound of its score can be computed as a combination of its old score w.r.t. rows in T^{old} and column-wise score w.r.t. the rest part of T'. For any $0 \leq \alpha \leq 1$, we have

$$\mathsf{score}(T' \mid Q) \leq \mathsf{score}(T^{\text{old}} \mid Q) + \frac{\mathsf{score}_{\text{col}}(T^{\text{new}} \mid Q)}{1 + \ln(1 + \ln |\mathcal{J}|)} \quad (11)$$
$$\leq \overline{\mathsf{score}}(T' \mid Q) \quad \text{(the one defined in Proposition 2).}$$

Note that $\mathsf{score}(T^{\text{old}} \mid Q)$ in (11) is known, as Q has been evaluated for rows in T^{old}. $\mathsf{score}_{\text{col}}$ can be computed as in Section 4.1.2. Compared to $\overline{\mathsf{score}}$, RHS of (11) is a better upper bound of score, and thus implies a smaller minimal evaluation set $\mathcal{Q}'_{\min}$ for T'. So our strategies terminate more quickly using this upper bound.

Incremental caching-evaluation scheduling. We only need to modify our cost model so that the incremental updates can be automatically considered in our strategy FASTTOPK (Algorithms 3-4). In our current cost model (12)-(13) in B.3, we need to evaluate each query $Q = (\mathcal{J}, \mathcal{C}, \phi)$ for every row in T. The new cost model to handle updates will take into consideration the number of rows in T' we need to evaluate Q on. i) For a (sub-)PJ query $Q \in \mathcal{T}(\mathcal{Q}_{\text{C}}^{\text{old}}) - \mathcal{T}(\mathcal{Q}_{\text{C}}^{\text{new}})$, we only need to evaluate it for rows in T^{new}, so we define $\text{cost}'(Q) = |T^{\text{new}}| \cdot \text{cost}(Q)$ and $\text{cost}'(Q, \mathcal{M}) = |T^{\text{new}}| \cdot \text{cost}(Q, \mathcal{M})$; ii) for a (sub-)PJ query $Q \in \mathcal{T}(\mathcal{Q}_{\text{C}}^{\text{new}}) - \mathcal{T}(\mathcal{Q}_{\text{C}}^{\text{old}})$, we need to evaluate it for all rows in T', so we define $\text{cost}'(Q) = |T'| \cdot \text{cost}(Q)$ and $\text{cost}'(Q, \mathcal{M}) = |T'| \cdot \text{cost}(Q, \mathcal{M})$; and iii) for a (sub-)PJ query $Q \in \mathcal{T}(\mathcal{Q}_{\text{C}}^{\text{old}}) \cap \mathcal{T}(\mathcal{Q}_{\text{C}}^{\text{new}})$, we create two copies of it – the one belonging to queries in $\mathcal{Q}_{\text{C}}^{\text{old}}$ is associated with cost as i) and the one belong to queries in $\mathcal{Q}_{\text{C}}^{\text{new}}$ is associated with cost as ii). Such a weighted cost model is applied in FASTTOPK to get updated top-k PJ queries.

Experimental Results

We generate complete 3×3 example spreadsheets in CSUPP as described in Section 6.1. We simulate incremental input by starting with the completely filled-out first row and then adding one cell at a time from the complete example spreadsheet (i.e., 6 cell additions). Our simulator adds cells row-by-row, from left to right. We average our results over the 50 example spreadsheets.

We evaluate three approaches for incremental input:

(i) FASTTOPK-NINC: always treating an example spreadsheet as a new one and applying FASTTOPK on it;

(ii) FASTTOPK-INC: described in Section 5.4 and above; and

(iii) BASELINE-INC: extending BASELINE using the same ideas as FASTTOPK-INC without caching-evaluation scheduling

Refer to Section 6.1 for the settings of experiments. Figure 11 shows the execution times of the three algorithms for the 6 cell additions via row-wise typing. FASTTOPK-INC significantly outperforms both BASELINE-INC and FASTTOPK-NINC. FASTTOPK-

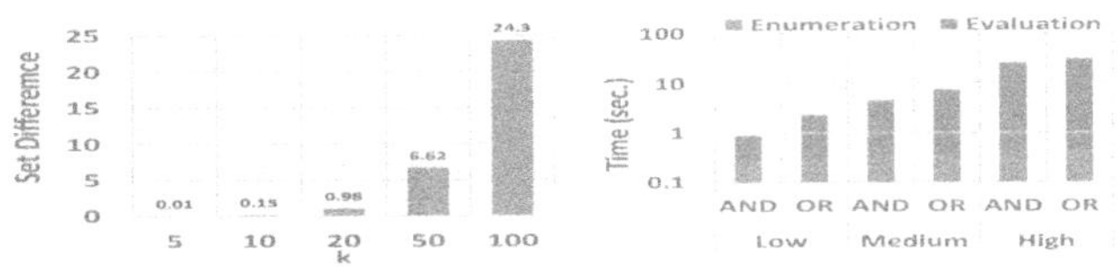

(a) Difference in result sets (b) Execution time

Figure 12: AND-column mapping v.s. OR-column mapping

NINC performs poorly since it does not use previously computed scores for the unchanged example tuples. This is especially true for the first few cells in a new row (e.g., [2,0], [2,1]). In these cases, the incremental approaches evaluate the PJ queries only for the changed example tuple (only a few terms) while FASTTOPK-NINC evaluates them for both changed and unchanged example tuples. BASELINE-INC suffers as it does not share results of sub-PJ queries as in the non-incremental case.

A.2 Generalizing Cell Similarity

We can extend cell similarity to perform IR-style relevance ranking as in [23]. For example, we can define cell similarity to be higher if there is an exact match between an example tuple cell and output row cell (as opposed to the latter only containing some terms of the former). And we can incorporate terms weights (based on inverse document frequency and document length) in cell similarity.

We can also extend cell similarity to handle spelling errors, synonyms, and fuzzy matching. For example, to handle fuzzy matching, we can built the inverted indexes (both column-level and row-level) on n-grams as terms instead of words [17]. When processing an example spreadsheet, we split each cell into n-grams (instead of words) and retrieve the inverted indexes corresponding to those n-grams. For spelling errors, we can simply replace a term in the example spreadsheet with a list of similar terms (within certain edit distance), look up them in our inverted indexes, and take the union of posting lists. Synonyms can be handled similarly.

A.3 AND v.s. OR Semantics

Our definition of PJ queries (Definition 2) requires that every column in the example spreadsheet is mapped to some column in the database. We can relax this constraint by allowing that only a subset of the example spreadsheet columns is mapped to the set of database columns, i.e., simply ignoring some example spreadsheet columns. Consider a PJ query $Q = (\mathcal{J}, \mathcal{C}, \phi)$, this relaxation changes our mapping from "$\phi : \text{col}(T) \to \mathcal{C}$" to "$\phi : \text{col}(T) \to \mathcal{C} \cup \{\perp\}$". When a column i in the example spreadsheet T is mapped to $\perp$, this column does not correspond to any column in the output relation of Q. We call our old column mapping, *AND-column mapping*, and the new relaxed one, *OR-column mapping*.

Our approaches can be extended to handle OR-column mapping easily. A simple extension is as follows. For a user-given example spreadsheet T with c columns, our system can create 2^c example spreadsheets $T_0, T_1, \ldots, T_{2^c-1}$, each of which consists of a subset of columns of T. We then process them using our FASTTOPK strategy one by one. The 2^c top-k resulting lists are aggregated to generate the overall top-k. Since c is small in practice, the cost of this approach is affordable. A more direct way is to enumerate all PJ queries under this OR semantics. To this end, we can apply the *Candidate Network Generator* in [12] to generate an extended set of candidate PJ queries in $\mathcal{Q}_C{}^+$, each of which has a subset of example spreadsheet columns mapped to its projection. Then both of our strategies BASELINE and FASTTOPK still work on $\mathcal{Q}_C{}^+$.

Experimental Results

Refer to Section 6.1 for the settings of experiments. We use CSUPP dataset and corresponding example spreadsheets to compare FASTTOPK with AND-column mapping (the one described in the main body of this paper) with the extended version of FASTTOPK with OR-column mapping (the simple extension described above).

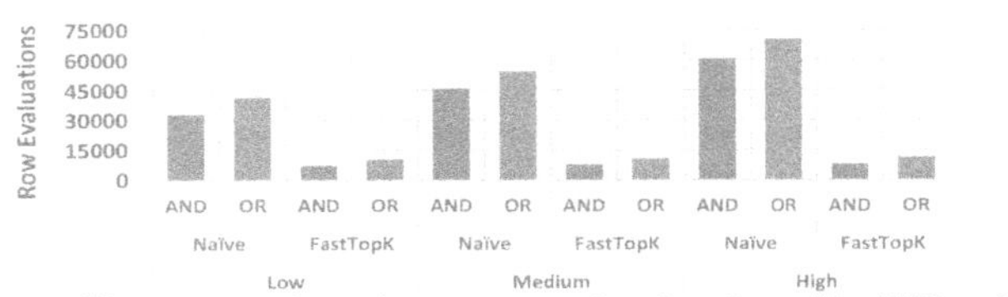

Figure 13: Amount of queries enumerated and evaluated in AND and OR semantics by NAIVE (not using $\overline{\text{score}}$) and FASTTOPK (using $\overline{\text{score}}$)

Figure 12(a) shows the average set difference between the result sets with AND and OR-column mapping for the 50 example spreadsheets for various values of k. For smaller values of k, there is almost no difference between the two result sets. For example, the top 10 results are identical for 49 out of the 50 ESs. It means that, even when we allow OR-column mapping in PJ queries, the top ones are likely to have all the columns in example spreadsheets mapped to their projections (AND semantics).

Figure 12(b) shows the average execution times of the two approaches. Note that "enumeration" here means "query enumeration + upper-bound score computation". The OR-semantics implementation is only a bit slower than the AND-semantics one since the execution time for the T_i created from the biggest subset of columns in T (i.e., the entire example spreadsheet) dominates the execution time. This shows that our system can be easily adapted to support OR-semantics whenever necessary, e.g., when the system returns an empty result for some user-specified example spreadsheet.

Figure 13 plots the number of PJ queries enumerated and evaluated in AND and OR semantics. NAIVE evaluates all the PJ queries enumerated in both semantics. We can find that, in the AND semantics, less PJ queries are enumerated than in OR because of stronger constraints in the column mapping ϕ. Using upper bounds $\overline{\text{score}}$, the number of PJ queries actually evaluated by FASTTOPK is much less than the total number of queries enumerated.

B. COMPUTING EXACT SCORES

B.1 Execution Plan for PJ Queries

We need to execute the PJ query Q and, for each tuple t in the example spreadsheet, examine every row in the output relation $\mathcal{A}(Q)$ to compute the terms $\max_{r \in \mathcal{A}(Q)} \text{score}(t \mid r)$ in (3). We utilize the *(key, foreign key)-snapshot* of the database (discussed in Section 3.1), and select a pre-optimized plan to execute Q in memory. Our execution plan for Q borrows ideas from hash joins:

Stage I *(scanning row-level inverted indexes to score cells)*: For each term w in each cell $t[i] \in T$, suppose column i is mapped to column j in a relation R in the database $\mathcal{D}$ through ϕ, we retrieve the row-level inverted index $\text{inv}(\text{w}, R[j])$ to compute cell similarities $\text{score}_{\text{cell}}(t[i] \mid r[j])$ (as lines 1-5 of Algorithm 1) for rows $r \in R$. $\text{score}_{\text{cell}}$ is then associated to primary keys of rows in R.

Stage II *(bottom-up hash joins)*: Starting from the leaf relations in $\mathcal{J}$, the primary key of each row, associated with cell similarities, is inserted into a hash table if cell similarity is non-zero in at least one cell – after that, a leaf relation is called *evaluated*.

Recursively, **Stage II-A *(scan/hash lookup)*:** for each relation above, if all of its children relations have been *evaluated*, we can start to *scan* its rows in the in-memory (key, foreign key)-snapshot of this relation, and for each row, *look up* all foreign keys (in different columns) in the corresponding hash tables popped up from the children relations to conduct the foreign-key joins. **Stage II-B *(building hash table)*:** Then, the primary key of each row in the

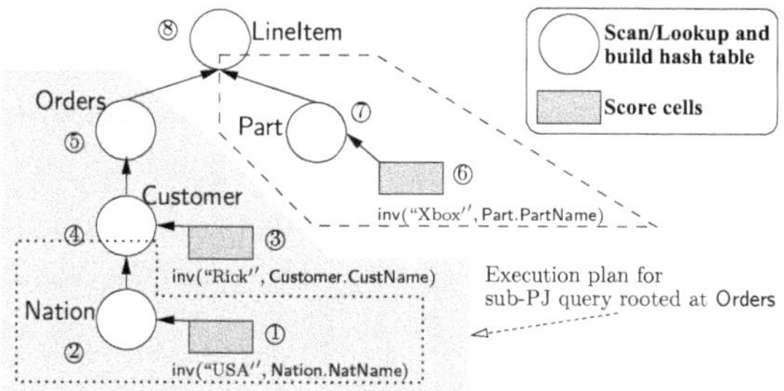

Figure 14: Execution plan for the PJ query in Figure 2(b)-(i) and its sub-PJ queries (operators executed in the order of 1, 3, 6, 2, 4, 5, 7, 8)

join output with nonzero cell similarities (in at least one cell) is put into a hash table. After that this relation is called *evaluated.*

Stage III *(computing scores)*: After the root relation is evaluated, we get the output relation $\mathcal{A}(Q)$, with cell similarities associated in each row of $\mathcal{A}(Q)$, and then we can compute the row containment score as in (1)-(3). Note at at each relation, we only need to keep primary/foreign key columns and columns in the projection $\mathcal{C}$. □

The above evaluation plan can be executed either for Q with one row of T, or with all rows of T together.

Figure 14 shows the execution plan for the PJ query in Figure 2(b)-(i) on the first row of the example table in Figure 2(a). A rectangle node represents the operation to retrieve row-level inverted indexes and compute cell similarities in Stage-I. A circle node represents the operations (scanning, hash lookups, and building hash table) we perform on a relation (labeled beside) in Stage-II, after all of its children are evaluated. For example, on the Orders node, we lookup foreign key Orders.CustId of each row in the hash table built by the node Custmer, and then build a hash table with Orders.OId (key in the hash table) and cell similarities on column Customer.CustName and column Nation.NatName. On the root node LineItem, we need to look up two foreign keys PartId and OId in the hash tables popped up by its two children Part and Orders, respectively. Operations are performed in the order of ①, ③, ⑥, ②, ④, ⑤, ⑦, ⑧ to compute the final score.

B.2 Speedup Execution using Cache

The execution plans of PJ-queries can be easily extended to take advantage the cached sub-PJ queries: for a PJ query Q and a set of cached sub-PJ queries in $\mathcal{M}$, instead of starting from the leaves of Q, we start from the output relations of maximal sub-PJ queries of Q in $\mathcal{M}$ and follow the execution plan of Q afterwards.

For example, Figure 3 shows two sub-PJ queries Q'_1 (left) and Q'_2 (right) of the PJ query Q in Figure 2(b)-(i). Intuitively, the execution plan of a sub-PJ query $Q' \preceq Q$ is a subtree of the execution plan of Q. For example, the dotted polygon and the dashed polygon in Figure 14 are the execution plans of Q'_1 and Q'_2, respectively.

In the execution plan of Q in Figure 14, if both Q'_1 and Q'_2 are materialized in $\mathcal{M}$, we can start from their output relations in $\mathcal{M}$ and execute only the operations ③, ④, ⑤, and ⑧ (only the join with Part is needed in ⑧). If a even larger one Q'_3 (rooted at Orders), whose plan is the shaded polygon in Figure 14, is cached, we can start from the output relations of Q'_1 and Q'_3 (Q'_2 is no more a maximal one) and execute only the operation ⑧.

B.3 Cost Model for Computing Exact Scores

For the PJ-query $Q = (\mathcal{J}, \mathcal{C}, \phi)$ w.r.t. T, there are three major operators involved in our execution plan in B.1: i) retrieving row-level inverted index; ii) scanning a relation while doing hash lookups; and iii) building a hash table. The running time of each of these operators is constant. So a natural and light-weight cost model of the execution plan for Q is to count the number of operations ii) and iii) executed on tuples in the relations of $\mathcal{J}$ and the number of tuples retrieved from inverted indexes. For a (sub-)PJ query Q, define the cost of evaluating Q as:

$$\text{cost}(Q) = \sum_{R \in \mathcal{V}(\mathcal{J})} |R| \cdot d_{\mathcal{J}}(R) + \sum_{i \in \text{col}(T)} \sum_{\text{w} \in T[i]} |\text{inv}(\text{w}, \mathcal{J}[\phi(i)])|. \quad (12)$$

The first component on the RHS of (12) quantifies the total number of hash lookups/inserts: $d_{\mathcal{J}}(R)$ is the degree of relation R in $\mathcal{J}$, as for each tuple in R, the number of hash lookups is equal to the number of children of R in $\mathcal{J}$, and for every relation except the root relation in R, we need to build a hash table by inserting tuples in this relation. The second component quantifies the number of tuples we need to retrieve from row-level inverted indexes: here let $\mathcal{J}[\phi(i)]$ be the column which i is mapped to in a relation of $\mathcal{J}$.

More generally, we have a set of sub-PJ queries cached in $\mathcal{M}$. The cost of the execution plan for Q when we reuse output relations of sub-PJ queries in $\mathcal{M}$ is defined to be:

$$\text{cost}(Q, \mathcal{M}) = \text{cost}(Q) - \sum_{\substack{\text{maximal } Q' \in \mathcal{M} \\ Q' \preceq Q}} \text{cost}(Q'), \quad (13)$$

as the output relations of maximal sub-PJ queries Q' of Q in $\mathcal{M}$ can be directly retrieved from $\mathcal{M}$ and reused.

Both $\text{cost}(Q)$ and $\text{cost}(Q, \mathcal{M})$ can be computed efficiently. In (12)-(13), $|R|$, the number of tuples in R, and $|\text{inv}(\text{w}, \mathcal{J}[\phi(i)])|$, the length of a row-level inverted index, can be gotten in constant time. So the total time is $O(\mathcal{V}(\mathcal{J}) + \#\text{ terms in } T)$.

C. PROOFS

Proof of Proposition 1. For the first part (property i)), since no column in T is mapped to R, by excluding R from Q, the column containment score is unchanged, i.e., $\text{score}_{\text{col}}(T \mid Q) = \text{score}_{\text{col}}(T \mid Q')$. So it suffices to prove $\text{score}_{\text{row}}(T \mid Q) \leq \text{score}_{\text{row}}(T \mid Q')$. Consdier the output relations $\mathcal{A}(Q)$ and $\mathcal{A}(Q')$, for any $t \in \mathcal{A}(Q)$, we have $t \in \mathcal{A}(Q')$, because Q' has less key-foreign key constraints in joins. So from (1), we have, for each $t \in T$, $\text{score}(t \mid Q) \leq \text{score}(t \mid Q')$. Then the conclusion follows from (3)

For the second part (property ii)), $\text{score}_{\text{col}}(T \mid Q) = \text{score}_{\text{col}}(T' \mid Q'')$ is also obvious as no term in the removed column $T[i]$ appears in the removed $R[j]$. It suffices to prove $\text{score}_{\text{row}}(T \mid Q) = \text{score}_{\text{row}}(T' \mid Q'')$. Comparing Q with Q'', their join trees are the same and the projection in Q'' is a subset of the projection in Q. So the output relation $\mathcal{A}(Q'')$ is essentially the projection of $\mathcal{A}(Q)$ on $\mathcal{C}'$. And since the column $R[j]$ excluded in Q'' contains no term in the spreadsheet column $T[i]$, the above claim follows. □

Proof of Proposition 2. From (5), it suffices to show $\text{score}_{\text{row}}(T \mid Q) \leq \text{score}_{\text{col}}(T \mid Q)$. Putting (2) into (3), and comparing it with (4), we can derive this relationship. □

Proof of Proposition 3. For each term w in a column i of T, if $T[i]$ is mapped to $R[j]$, we need to scan the row-level inverted index $\text{inv}(\text{w}, R[j])$ – the term in (4), $\text{score}_{\text{cell}}(t[i] \mid r[\phi(i)])$, is obtained by aggregating the results for different terms. The total cost is dominated by $O(\sum_{\text{w} \in T} l_{\text{w}})$, i.e., lengths of inverted indexes. □

Proof of Proposition 4. Again, the row-level inverted indexes need to be scanned to compute the terms $\text{score}_{\text{cell}}(t[i] \mid r[\phi(i)])$ in (2). To compute the terms $\max_{r \in \mathcal{A}(Q)} \text{score}(t \mid r)$ in (3), we need to scan the output relation $\mathcal{A}(Q)$ at least once. The complexity of generating $\mathcal{A}(Q)$ using the hash-join execution plan introduced in Appendix B.1 is $O(\sum_{R \in \mathcal{J}} |R| \cdot d_{\mathcal{J}}(R))$. □

Proof of Proposition 5. Let's first define the class of algorithms, called *multi-step ranking* algorithms. A multi-step ranking algorithm takes i) a set of PJ queries $\mathcal{Q}_{\text{C}}$, and ii) upper bounds $\overline{\text{score}}$

of their scores, as input. In each step, it picks one or more PJ queries in $\mathcal{Q}_{\mathrm{C}}$ with unknown scores and *evaluates* them, i.e., computes $\mathsf{score}(Q)$; based on the known scores, it continues to pick the next one or more PJ queries to evaluate, until the *top-k* of known scores is larger than the *max* of upper-bound scores of queries with unknown scores. The following proof follows from [20].

Recall $\mathcal{Q}_{\min} = \{Q_1, Q_2, \ldots, Q_{i^*}\} \subseteq \mathcal{Q}_{\mathrm{C}}$, and i^* is the minimal i s.t. $\mathrm{top}_k\{\mathsf{score}(Q_1), \ldots, \mathsf{score}(Q_i)\} > \overline{\mathsf{score}}(Q_{i+1}) \geq \overline{\mathsf{score}}(Q_{i+2}) \geq \ldots \geq \overline{\mathsf{score}}(Q_N)$. We prove this proposition via contradiction. Consider any multi-step ranking algorithm that evalutes a set of PJ queries $\mathcal{Q}'$ and claims that all queries with the top-k scores in $\mathcal{Q}_{\mathrm{C}}$ have been found in $\mathcal{Q}'$. Pick any $Q_p \in \mathcal{Q}_{\min} - \mathcal{Q}'$. Let Q_q be the PJ query in $\mathcal{Q}'$ with the kth highest score, i.e., $\mathsf{score}(Q_q) = \mathrm{top}_k\{\mathsf{score}(Q) \mid Q \in \mathcal{Q}'\}$.

i) If $\overline{\mathsf{score}}(Q_p) \geq \mathsf{score}(Q_q)$: Since the algorithm has not evaluated Q_p, the adversary can set $\mathsf{score}(Q_p) = \overline{\mathsf{score}}(Q_p)$. Then $\mathsf{score}(Q_p) \geq \mathsf{score}(Q_q) = \mathrm{top}_k\{\mathsf{score}(Q) \mid Q \in \mathcal{Q}'\}$, so Q_p is missed from the top-k and the output of the algorithm is incorrect.

ii) If $\overline{\mathsf{score}}(Q_p) < \mathsf{score}(Q_q)$: Consider the set of top-k PJ queries in $\mathcal{Q}'$, $\mathcal{Q}'_{\mathrm{topk}} = \{Q \mid \mathsf{score}(Q) \geq \mathsf{score}(Q_q)\} \cap \mathcal{Q}'$. We have $\mathcal{Q}'_{\mathrm{topk}} \subseteq \{Q_1, Q_2, \ldots, Q_{p-1}\}$, because for any $Q \in \mathcal{Q}'_{\mathrm{topk}}$, we have $\overline{\mathsf{score}}(Q) > \overline{\mathsf{score}}(Q_p)$. Then it follows that $\mathrm{top}_k\{\mathsf{score}(Q_1), \ldots, \mathsf{score}(Q_{p-1})\} > \overline{\mathsf{score}}(Q_p)$. Note that $p \leq i^*$, and thus it contradicts with the minimality of i^*.

Both i) and ii) lead to contradiction, so we have $\mathcal{Q}_{\min} \subseteq \mathcal{Q}'$. □

Proof of Theorem 1. To prove the correctness, we only need to show that if (7) is satisfied, the top-k are among $Q_1, Q_2, \ldots, Q_i$. This is true, because, from the way how Q_i's are ordered in (7) and BASELINE, for any $j > i$, we have $\mathsf{score}(Q_j) \leq \overline{\mathsf{score}}(Q_{i+1})$.

The second part, it evaluates only queries in $\mathcal{Q}_{\min}$, is trivial. □

Proof of Theorem 2. Given a sequence of type-a,b,c operators, to check whether it is a feasible solution, we only need to check when it eventually evaluates all PJ queries in $\mathcal{Q}_{\min}$ and, at any time, the cache size it uses is no more than B. So when $\mathcal{Q}_{\min}$ is known, the problem is in NP. We use a reduction from the HAMILTONIAN PATH problem to show CACHE-EVAL SCHEDULER is NP-hard.

Consider a HAMILTONIAN PATH instance: given a undirected graph $G(V, E)$, whether there exist an ordering of all vertices v_1, $v_2, \ldots, v_n \in V$ ($|V| = n$) s.t. $(v_i, v_{i+1}) \in E$ for $i = 1, \ldots, n-1$. This problem is NP-complete even in a restricted class of graphs, where every vertex has degree equal to three [11]. Now let's construct an instance of our CACHE-EVAL SCHEDULER problem. For each vertex $v \in V$, create a PJ query Q_v in $\mathcal{Q}_{\min}$. For each edge $e = (v, u)$, create a sub-PJ query Q_e^{sub} and let Q_e^{sub} be a sub-PJ query of both Q_v and Q_u. So for each created PJ query Q_v, we have the set of all sub-PJ queries of Q_v to be $\mathcal{T}(Q_v) = \{Q_e^{\mathrm{sub}} \mid e \text{ is incident on } v\}$. Finally, let $|\mathcal{A}(Q_e^{\mathrm{sub}})| = B$ for every $e \in E$, i.e., at any time, we can only keep the output relation of one sub-PJ query in our cache; and let $\mathrm{cost}(Q_e^{\mathrm{sub}}) = C_1$ be equal for every e and $\mathrm{cost}(Q_v) = C_2$ be equal for every $v \in V$. To prove the NP-hardness, it suffices to show such a claim: there is a Hamiltonian path in G if and only if there exists a sequence of operators to evaluate $\mathcal{Q}_{\min}$ with cost no more than $n \cdot C_2 - (n-1) \cdot C_1$.

To prove the claim, we need to transform a path into a sequence of operators and vice versa. A subpath $v_{i-1}v_iv_{i+1}$ in the Hamiltonian path corresponds to: when evaluting $Q_{v_{i-1}}$, we put $Q^{\mathrm{sub}}_{(v_{i-1},v_i)}$ in cache and reuse it to evaluate Q_{v_i}; and after that, we clear the cache and put $Q^{\mathrm{sub}}_{(v_i,v_{i+1})}$ in cache. Details are omitted here. □

Proof of Theorem 3. The correctness follows directly from Theorem 1. The set of PJ queries FASTTOPK evaluate is always a superset of those evaluated by BASELINE (i.e., all queries in $\mathcal{Q}_{\min}$ have been evaluated when FASTTOPK terminates). □

Proof of Theorem 4. The second part, $M_{\mathrm{all}} = \Theta(s_{\max} \cdot N)$, is directly from our definition of sub-PJ queries.

For the overall time complexity, we focus on Algorithm 4 first. For each sub-PJ query Q', we need $O(s_{\max})$ time to get $\mathrm{cost}(Q')$ and $|\mathcal{A}(Q')|$, which are used in lines 1 and 4. So we need a total of $O(M \cdot s_{\max})$ time for all sub-PJ queries. Sorting all sub-PJ queries in line 1 needs $O(M \cdot \log M)$ time. The remaining question is how to get Q^* and $\mathrm{Critical}^{-1}(Q^*)$ efficiently (lines 4, 6, and 8). Note that $\mathcal{B}_j$ is the set of unevaluated PJ queries. For each sub-PJ query Q', we keep a hash set $HS(Q')$ of *unevaluated* PJ queries it belongs to. For each PJ query Q, we also keep a list $LT(Q)$ of sub-PJ queries it contains. So after a PJ-queriy Q is evaluated, each $HS(Q')$ can be updated in constant time if Q' is a sub-PJ query of Q. To get Q^* in all iterations, we only need to scan all sub-PJ quries $Q'_1, \ldots, Q'_M$ in order and check whether $|HS(Q')| > 1$ for each. $\mathrm{Critical}^{-1}(Q^*)$ can be directed retrived from $HS(Q^*)$. So the time complexity of Algorithm 4 is $O(M(s_{\max} + \log M))$.

In Algorithm 3, the additional time besides invoking Algorithm 4 is at most $O(N \cdot (\log N + \log k))$ (soring plus keeping the top-k).

So from $x \log x + y \log y \leq (x + y)\log(x + y)$, we have the overall time complexity is $O(N + M_{\mathrm{all}}(s_{\max} + \log M_{\mathrm{all}}))$. □

Proof of Theorem 5. The first part (9) is directly from the definition of $\mathcal{Q}_{\min}$ and the way we construct batches in Algorithm 3.

To prove the main result (10), we first prove, for each batch $\mathcal{B}$

$$\mathrm{cost}_{\mathrm{TOT}}(\mathcal{B}) - \mathrm{cost}_{\mathrm{SOL}}(\mathcal{B}) \geq \frac{1}{2c^2}\left(\mathrm{cost}_{\mathrm{TOT}}(\mathcal{B}) - \mathrm{cost}_{\mathrm{OPT}}(\mathcal{B})\right). \tag{14}$$

That is, the cost saved by FASTTOPK is no less than $1/2c^2$ of the optimal save. Summing up (14) for all batches $\mathcal{B} = \mathcal{B}_0, \mathcal{B}_1, \ldots$, since they are disjoint and $\cup \mathcal{B}_j = \mathcal{Q}_{\mathrm{E}}$, we have

$$\begin{aligned} &\mathrm{cost}_{\mathrm{TOT}}(\mathcal{Q}_{\mathrm{E}}) - \Sigma_{\mathcal{B}_j}\mathrm{cost}_{\mathrm{SOL}}(\mathcal{B}_j) \\ \geq &\frac{1}{2c^2}\left(\mathrm{cost}_{\mathrm{TOT}}(\mathcal{Q}_{\mathrm{E}}) - \Sigma_{\mathcal{B}_j}\mathrm{cost}_{\mathrm{OPT}}(\mathcal{B}_j)\right). \end{aligned} \tag{15}$$

FASTTOPK works batch-by-batch, so we have i) $\sum_{\mathcal{B}_j} \mathrm{cost}_{\mathrm{SOL}}(\mathcal{B}_j) = \mathrm{cost}_{\mathrm{SOL}}(\mathcal{Q}_{\mathrm{E}})$. Since $\mathcal{B}_j \subseteq \mathcal{Q}_{\mathrm{E}}$, we have ii) $\mathrm{cost}_{\mathrm{OPT}}(\mathcal{B}_j) \leq \mathrm{cost}_{\mathrm{OPT}}(\mathcal{Q}_{\mathrm{E}})$. And it is obvious that iii) the total number of batches processed by Algorithm 3 is at most $\log_{1+\epsilon}(|\mathcal{Q}_{\min}|/k)$. Our performance ratio (10) follows from (15) and i)-iii).

The only missing part is the proof for (14). Let the batch of PJ queries $\mathcal{B} = \{Q_1, \ldots, Q_n\}$. Suppose in the optimal solution,

$$\mathrm{cost}_{\mathrm{TOT}}(\mathcal{B}) - \mathrm{cost}_{\mathrm{OPT}}(\mathcal{B}) \leq \sum_{Q_i \in \mathcal{B}} \mathrm{cost}(Q_i) - \mathrm{cost}(Q_i, \mathcal{M}_i^*), \tag{16}$$

where $\mathcal{M}_i^*$ is the status of cache before Q_i is evaluated. From (13),

$$\mathrm{cost}(Q_i) - \mathrm{cost}(Q_i, \mathcal{M}_i^*) = \sum_{\substack{\text{maximal } Q' \in \mathcal{M}_i^* \\ Q' \preceq Q_i}} \mathrm{cost}(Q'). \tag{17}$$

On the other hand, in Algorithm 4, when Q_i is to be evaluated, we have cache $\mathcal{M}_i = \{Q^*\}$ (lines 8-9), where Q^* is the most costly sub-PJ query among those in $\{\text{maximal } Q' \in \mathcal{M}_i^* \mid Q' \preceq Q_i\}$ based on its selection (line 4). There are at most c maximal sub-PJ queries for Q_i (as there are at most c leaves in the join tree), so

$$\mathrm{cost}(Q_i) - \mathrm{cost}(Q_i, \mathcal{M}_i) \geq \frac{1}{c}\left(\mathrm{cost}(Q_i) - \mathrm{cost}(Q_i, \mathcal{M}_i^*)\right). \tag{18}$$

Among all PJ queries in $\mathcal{B}$, in the worst case, a fraction $\frac{1}{2c}$ of them can benefit as much as (18) from the cache. So putting (18) back to (16), we can obtain (14). The proof can be completed. □

Proactive Annotation Management in Relational Databases*

Karim Ibrahim, Xiao Du, and Mohamed Y. Eltabakh
Computer Science Department, Worcester Polytechnic Institute
Worcester, MA, US
kaibrahim@cs.wpi.edu, xiaodu@cs.wpi.edu, meltabakh@cs.wpi.edu

ABSTRACT

Annotation management and data curation has been extensively studied in the context of relational databases. However, existing annotation management techniques share a common limitation, which is that they are all *passive* engines, i.e., they only manage the annotations obtained from external sources such as DB admins, domain experts, and curation tools. They neither learn from the available annotations nor exploit the annotations-to-data correlations to further enhance the quality of the annotated database. Delegating such crucial and complex tasks to end-users—especially under large-scale databases and annotation sets—is clearly the wrong choice. In this paper, we propose the *Nebula* system, *an advanced and proactive annotation management engine in relational databases*. Nebula complements the state-of-art techniques in annotation management by learning from the available annotations, analyzing their content and semantics, and understanding their correlations with the data. And then, Nebula proactively discovers and recommends potentially missing annotation-to-data attachments. We propose context-aware ranking and prioritization of the discovered attachments that take into account the relationships among the data tuples and their annotations. We also propose approximation techniques and expert-enabled verification mechanisms that adaptively maintain high-accuracy predictions while minimizing the experts' involvement. Nebula is realized on top of an existing annotation management engine, and experimentally evaluated to illustrate the effectiveness of the proposed techniques, and to demonstrate the potential gain in enhancing the quality of annotated databases.

Categories and Subject Descriptors

H.2 [**Database Management**]: Systems—*Relational Databases*

Keywords

Proactive Annotation Management; Keyword Search; Annotated Database.

1. INTRODUCTION

Data curation and annotation is becoming an integral component to modern relational database systems. This is due to several factors including: (1) Many emerging applications that use database systems, especially scientific applications [6, 10, 21, 28], rely on data curation for capturing various types of metadata information, e.g., attaching related articles to the data, highlighting erroneous or conflicting values, and capturing the data's lineage. (2) Annotations do not follow the rigid schema of relational databases, instead a single annotation can be attached to individual table cells, rows, columns, or arbitrary sets and combinations of them. And thus, annotation management gives end-users and higher-level applications the flexibility to annotate their data in a seamless way. And (3) The increasing scale of the generated annotations as well as their richness in semantics have triggered the need for querying the annotations in more systematic and efficient ways, and for incorporating them into the data processing cycle.

For the aforementioned reasons, annotation management has been extensively studied in the context of relational databases, e.g., [9, 13, 16, 18, 20]. These techniques address several aspects ranging from efficient storage and indexing [18, 20], abstract querying and propagation [9, 16, 20], summarization and summary-aware annotation propagation [22, 32], view-related annotations [13, 25], and semantic annotations [11, 12, 14, 16, 19]. However, the growing scale of the managed datasets and their annotations, and the increasing rate at which both the data and the annotations are dynamically changing, pose new challenges to annotation management that have not been addressed before. One of these challenges—which is the key focus of this paper—is that in many cases the database may become *"under annotated"*. That is, a given annotation may not be attached to all data tuples to which the annotation applies. The following scenarios highlight various reasons that cause a database to be under annotated.

Motivation Scenario 1 – Embedded References to DB Objects: *Common uses of annotations include attaching documents or articles to specific data tuples, and linking free-text comments to data values. For example, referring to Figure 1, a biological scientist "Bob" investigating a set of genes may attach a related scientific article to one of his genes-under-investigation* `JW0013`*. Whereas, another scientist "Alice" may attach a comment to one of her genes-of-interest* `JW0019`*. Interestingly, each of these annotations apply to (and are related to) other tuples in the database beyond those to which they are manually attached. For example, the article also references gene names* `yaaB` *and* `yaaI`*, and refers to protein* `G-Actin`*. Similarly, Alice's comment references genes* `JW0014` *and* `grpC`*. Unfortunately, there are many reasons that may hinder Bob and Alice from creating these missing attachments, e.g., Bob and Alice may not know that the other objects actually exist in the database—A scientists usually focuses on a small subset of the data—, Bob may not have time to read the entire article, extract all its references to other objects, and then search the database to add the links, and Alice may not be willing to put any effort in attaching her comment to gene* `JW0014` *since that gene is not of interest to her. As a result, the database becomes under annotated.*

*This project is partially supported by NSF-CRI 1305258 grant.

SIGMOD'15, May 31–June 4, 2015, Melbourne, Victoria, Australia.

http://dx.doi.org/10.1145/2723372.2749435.

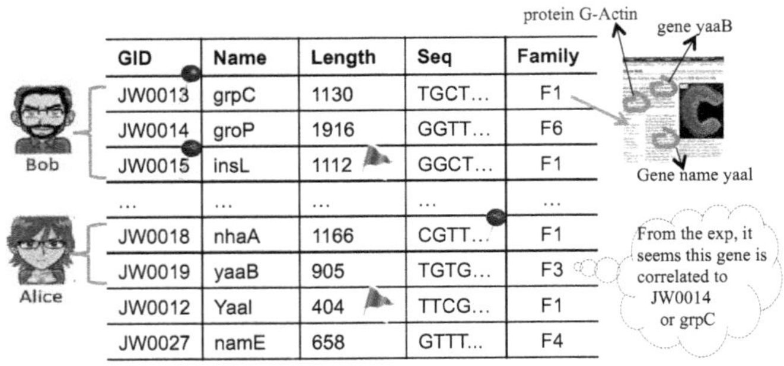

Figure 1: Example of Under-Annotated DB.

Motivation Scenario 2– Implicit Correlations Between Annotations and Data: *In real-world applications, correlations between the annotations and the data may exist. For example, continuing with our demonstration in Figure 1, some genes in the database may get annotated with "Rounded Flag" and "Triangle Flag" annotations as indicated in the figure. By analyzing the correlations between the annotations and the data, we may discover that most genes having value* `F1` *in the* `Family` *column have an attached "Rounded Flag" annotation. Such correlation suggests that gene* `JW0012` *is probably missing this annotations. Correlations may even exist among the annotations themselves. Unfortunately, manually defining correlation patterns between the annotations and the data, e.g., by DB admins, may not be feasible. This is because these correlations may not be known in advance, hard to capture and express, dynamically changing over time, or even not 100% conformed. As a result, links and associations between the annotations and the data can be easily missed without detection.*

These real-world scenarios are common in many applications, and they yield the database under annotated. As a result, crucial and valuable information can be lost, and the benefits from annotation management may decrease over time. Nevertheless, the state-or-art techniques in annotation management, e.g., [9, 15, 20, 32], are all *passive* systems that only manage the available annotations. The underlying assumption in these techniques is that the completeness in annotating the data is a task that is performed outside the annotation management engine, i.e., delegated to end-users and higher-level applications. Clearly, this assumption is error prone, impractical in some cases, and does not scale as motivated by the above scenarios. Instead, we need an advanced and *proactive* annotation management engine that is capable of learning from the available annotations, analyzing their associations and correlations with the data, and discovering and recommending potentially new attachments between the annotations and the data.

In this paper, we propose the *"Nebula"* system, *a proactive annotation management engine in relational databases.* We will focus only on addressing the challenges of the 1st motivation scenario, i.e., the discovery and management of embedded references. Nebula extends the annotation management engine with advanced capabilities for analyzing and extracting semantics from annotations, identifying potential references and relationships to other database objects, and proactively providing recommendations for establishing these missing attachments. The key challenges to be addressed include:

(1) Identifying and extracting potential keywords from an annotation that possibly reference other objects in the database. This is a challenging task not only because the annotation itself can be a large document or free-text value, but also because the database objects are dynamically changing, too many to easily enumerate, and can be referenced in different ways.

(2) Searching the database for objects matching the identified keywords. DBMSs are optimized for structured query search, e.g., SQL queries. However, searching based on keywords requires advanced techniques and always involves uncertainty in the answer—not to mention that the generated keywords themselves inherit a degree of uncertainty since they are automatically generated.

(3) Ranking and prioritizing the predicted attachments. It is not a straightforward task especially because the ranking should not depend only on the confidence generated from the database search, but it should also capture the relationships between the data tuples and whether or not they have other annotations in common. Therefore, such annotation-related context need to modeled and integrated within the system.

(4) Verifying the predicted attachments. Depending solely on either of the system-generated confidence estimations or the domain experts to verify the attachments may not be a practical solution. We need a hybrid verification approach that offers high confidence in the attachments while minimizing the involvement of domain experts and DB admins.

The overall processing stages and key contributions of Nebula are presented in Appendix A- Figure 16. These contributions are summarized as follows:

- Introducing the new problem of *proactive annotation management.* We propose formal definition and modeling for the concept of *"annotated database"* and the problem of *"discovery and management of embedded references"*. We also propose quantification criteria for *"under-annotated databases"*. (Section 3)
- Developing techniques for extracting the potential keywords (embedded references) from the annotations and translating them to keyword queries to identify the corresponding database objects. Instead of re-inventing the wheel, we leverage the existing work in the area of *keyword search over RDBMSs* with substantial extensions and optimizations to solve the problem at hand. (Sections 4, 5)
- Proposing several refinement and optimization techniques that include: (1) Adjusting the predictions' ranking based on the annotations' context and the relationships among the data tuples, (2) Sharing the search execution among multiple concurrent queries, and (3) Developing approximate searching techniques that search only a very small—but highly promising—subset of the data records instead of searching the entire database. (Section 6)
- Developing assessment criteria and adaptive verification techniques for verifying the predicted attachments. The techniques learn from training datasets and previously verified annotations to balance between achieving a high prediction accuracy and minimizing the involvement of domain experts. (Section 7)
- Implementing the Nebula prototype engine on top of an existing annotation management system [18]. As such, Nebula builds on existing annotation-related functionalities, e.g., seamless storage, organization, and propagation of annotations, and adds the proposed proactive capabilities. The experimental evaluation using real-world workloads demonstrates the effectiveness of the proposed techniques in predicting the missing attachments, e.g., some of the proposed optimizations achieve up to 15x speedup without sacrificing the accuracy. (Section 8)

2. RELATED WORK

Data curation and annotation is an emerging research topic due to the increasing virtue and merit of the collected metadata in modern applications. In the context of relational databases, various techniques have been proposed to address different aspects of annotation management. The techniques in [18, 20] focus on providing efficient storage organization, indexing and compact representation for the annotations. Some techniques, e.g., [9, 16, 20], focus on extending the query algebra and operators to seamlessly propagate the annotations at query time. While other techniques focus on supporting special types of annotations, e.g., provenance annotations [11, 12, 16], hierarchical annotations [15, 23], belief annotations [19], and summary-based annotations [31, 32].

Despite the contributions offered by the above techniques, a common limitation to all of them is that they are all *passive* systems that manage only the available annotations. Detecting whether or not a database is under-annotated and discovering the missing attachments is beyond the scope of these techniques. The techniques proposed in [18, 25] offer mechanisms for automating the attachment of annotations to data tuples by enabling the curator (annotator) to specify *predicates* over the database as part of an annotation's definition. As such, newly added data tuples satisfying these predicates will have the corresponding annotation automatically attached to them. However, these techniques cannot be applied to the problem at hand since they deal only with structured predicates in the form of SQL queries (over the DB schema) without taking the annotations' content into account.

In some domains, e.g., scientific applications, publically available databases may go under a curation process [1, 2, 3, 29]. In this process domain experts manually curate the data, ensure correct and high-quality annotations are attached to the data, and potentially add or remove further attachments between the annotations and the data. Certainly, this curation process is very time consuming, error prone and does not scale well, and more importantly consumes valuable cycles from domain experts and scientists. The proposed Nebula system is not intended to entirely eliminate the curation process. Instead, it is a complementary system by which a significant effort in discovering missing attachments and relationships between the data and the annotations can be automated. And hence, freeing domain experts to do what they know best, which is scientific experimentation.

Another related area of research is the *keyword search in relational database*. It is related to the proposed work because the embedded references are ultimately a set of keywords scattered within the annotations. Existing keyword search techniques, e.g., [5, 7, 27, 30], have made it feasible to execute unstructured queries (a.k.a. keyword queries) over structured databases. Some techniques require a pre-processing phase over the data and building appropriate indexes before answering queries [5, 27, 30]. Other techniques rely on metadata information, e.g., schema information, data types, domain constraints, in generating candidate SQL queries that may answer the keyword query [7]. Nebula will leverage such extensive work and existing techniques without re-inventing the wheel. However, as we will discuss in Section 4, a naive approach that relies solely on keyword search techniques would not be a practical solution and will not lead to the desired results. Therefore, Nebula uses such techniques as one component—which can be black box—within a bigger processing framework.

3. PROBLEM STATEMENT

In this section, we formally define an annotated database, and formulate the problem of proactive annotation management (*Stage 0* in Figure 16).

Definition 3.1 (Annotated Database). *An annotated database $\mathcal{D}$ is modeled as a weighted bipartite graph $\mathcal{D} = \{\mathcal{A}, \mathcal{T}, \mathcal{E}\}$, where set $\mathcal{A}$ consists of nodes representing the available annotations, set $\mathcal{T}$ consists of nodes representing the data tuples in the database, and the edges $\mathcal{E}$ represent the associations and attachments between the annotations and the data tuples in a many-to-many relationship.*

Figure 2 illustrates an example of an annotated database $\mathcal{D}$. Each edge $e(\mathtt{a} \in \mathcal{A}, \mathtt{t} \in \mathcal{T}) \in \mathcal{E}$ is assigned a weight $e.w \in [0,\ 1]$ representing the confidence in this edge. $\mathcal{E}$ consists of two types of edges: (1) Solid-line edges (called *True Attachments*), and these are the attachments manually established by external sources, e.g., end-users, DB admins, and curators. These edges are assumed to be correct and 100% accurate, i.e., have $e.w$ = 1, as illustrated in Figure 2. And (2) Dotted-line edges (called *Predicted Attachments*), and these are the edges that Nebula proactively predicts to be missing attachments, and assigns an estimated confidence value ($e.w < 1$) to each of them. When a *Predicted Attachment* edge e is verified and accepted by the system (Section 7), e changes its type to a *True Attachment* edge with $e.w$ = 1.

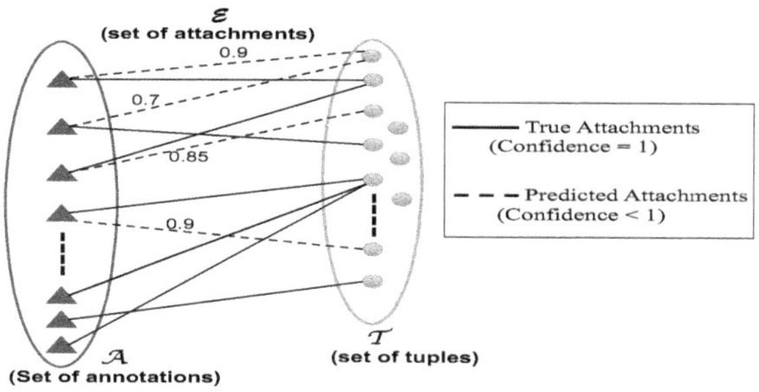

Figure 2: Modeling of an Annotated Database $\mathcal{D}$.

In an ideal world represented by an ideal database $\mathcal{D}_{ideal} = \{\mathcal{A}, \mathcal{T}, \mathcal{E}_{ideal}\}$, each annotation $\mathtt{a} \in \mathcal{A}$ is attached to all (and only those) data tuples in $\mathcal{T}$ to which a is related. And hence, $\mathcal{E}_{ideal}$ contains neither false-negative (denoted by F_N) nor false-positive (denoted by F_P) edges, i.e., $\mathcal{D}_{ideal}.F_N = \mathcal{D}_{ideal}.F_P = 0$. In our context, an annotation is said to be related to a data tuple according to the following definitions.

Definition 3.2 (Embedded Reference). *An embedded reference to a tuple t within an annotation* a *is defined as a set of keywords* $\{k_1,\ k_2,\ ...,\ k_m\}$ *not necessarily consecutive within* a*'s text that collectively refer to and identify t.*

Definition 3.3 (Annotation-to-Data Relationship). *An annotation* a *is said to be related to data tuple t if* a *is manually attached to t, or* a *contains an embedded reference to t.*

For example, Alice's comment in Figure 1 contains two embedded references, which are `"gene...JW0014"` and `"gene...grpC"`. And thus, Alice's comment is related to the `JW0019` gene tuple (since it is manually attached to it), and to the `JW0013` and `JW0014` gene tuples (since it contains an embedded reference to each of them).

Unlike the ideal database $\mathcal{D}_{ideal}$, a real-world database $\mathcal{D}$ may diverge from $\mathcal{D}_{ideal}$. The following two evaluation metrics will measure the quality of $\mathcal{D}$ w.r.t $\mathcal{D}_{ideal}$ using the set-difference semantics between the two sets $\mathcal{E}_{ideal}$ and $\mathcal{E}$ as follows:

$$\mathcal{D}.F_N = |\mathcal{E}_{ideal} - \mathcal{E}|\ /\ |\mathcal{E}_{ideal}|, \quad \in [0,\ 1] \tag{1}$$

$$\mathcal{D}.F_P = |\mathcal{E} - \mathcal{E}_{ideal}|\ /\ |\mathcal{E}|, \quad \in [0,\ 1] \tag{2}$$

where $\mathcal{D}.F_N$ captures the ratio of the false-negative edges in $\mathcal{E}$, i.e., the edges in $\mathcal{E}_{ideal}$ that are missing in $\mathcal{E}$. Whereas, $\mathcal{D}.F_P$ captures the ratio of the false-positive edges in $\mathcal{E}$, i.e., the edges in $\mathcal{E}$ that are not present in $\mathcal{E}_{ideal}$. Based on Equations 1 & 2, an annotated database $\mathcal{D}$ without any predicted edges, i.e., without dotted-line edges, is guaranteed to have $\mathcal{D}.F_P$ = 0, but $\mathcal{D}.F_N$ might be large. Our goal is thus, to minimize $\mathcal{D}.F_N$ by discovering the missing attachments, while keeping $\mathcal{D}.F_P$ as small as possible.

Definition 3.4 (Discovery of Embedded References). *Given an annotation* $\mathtt{a} \in \mathcal{A}$, *which is manually attached to data tuples* $\{t_1, t_2, ..., t_k\} \subset \mathcal{T}$, *our goal is to discover all other data tuples* $\{t'_1, t'_2, ..., t'_m\} \subset \mathcal{T}$ *(if any) to which* a *is related, i.e.,* $\exists\ e(\mathtt{a}, \mathtt{t}'_\mathtt{i}) \in \mathcal{E}_{\mathtt{ideal}}\ \&\ \mathtt{e}(\mathtt{a}, \mathtt{t}'_\mathtt{i}) \notin \mathcal{E},\ \forall\ 1 \leq \mathtt{i} \leq \mathtt{m}.$ [1]

[1]We assume that *spam-like* annotations, e.g., an annotation that references all (or most) data tuples, do not exist. Detecting and handling this type of annotations is beyond the scope of this paper [26].

Definition 3.5 (Annotation's Focal). *The focal of a given annotation* $a \in \mathcal{A}$ *is denoted as* $Foc(a)$*, and defined as* $Foc(a) = \{t_1, t_2, ..., t_k\} \subset \mathcal{T}$*, where* $t_1, t_2, ..., t_k$ *are the data tuples to which* a *is manually attached.*

For example, referring to Bob's annotation in Figure 1, the article's focal is the JW0013 gene tuple. Moreover, according to Definition 3.4, Bob's article may have three potential missing attachments to the JW0019 and JW0012 gene tuples, as well as a missing attachment to the G-Actin protein tuple (if they exist in the database). As will be presented later, the annotation's focal—as part of the annotation's context—will play a key role in the discovery process w.r.t searching and ranking .

4. NAIVE BASELINE APPROACH

A naive approach to solve the problem at hand is to directly apply any of the existing keyword search techniques to discover the data tuples related to a given annotation a. The naive approach involves the following two main steps: (1) Passing annotation a as input to a keyword search technique, i.e., the annotation's content becomes a sequence of keywords to the search technique, and (2) The search technique would search the entire database to identify the data tuples satisfying the input keywords. Without loss of generality, Nebula uses the keyword search technique proposed in [7] as it has shown superiority over other techniques, and it incorporates metadata repositories—which are already part of Nebula's system—into its computations.

As a brief overview, the algorithm in [7] starts by assigning weights to each of the input keywords capturing whether a keyword has a potential mapping to a schema item, e.g., a table name or column name, or a database value. It is possible to have several of these potential mappings for each keyword. From these mappings, the algorithm constructs what are called *configurations*, where each configuration captures one possible semantics of the keyword query. And then, each configuration maps to one or more SQL queries over the database. Each query has an assigned confidence weight that captures the algorithm's estimated confidence of matching this query with the intended semantics. Finally, the produced data tuples from the SQL queries represent the answer to the keyword query, each tuple inherits the confidence of its query.

Limitations of Naive Approach: Clearly, the naive approach has severe limitations and drawbacks that affect not only the performance, but also the accuracy in producing the expected results. These limitations include:

• *Vague and Imprecise Input*: Keyword search techniques expect as input a short sequence of related keywords—usually less than 5 keywords. In contrast, in our case, an input annotation can be a general comment or big article (Refer to Bob's and Alice's annotations in Figure 1). As a result, the keyword search technique will encounter significant degradation in accuracy due to the imprecise input, produce very noisy results that most likely will be worthless, and will take substantial time in processing many input keywords. Therefore, the challenge is to pre-process the input annotation, identify potential keywords that are more likely to be embedded references, and then form meaningful and concise keyword query(s) that existing techniques can handle efficiently.

• *Absence of Annotation-Related Context:* Keyword search techniques are oblivious to the annotation-related context. For example, in keyword search, an input query is not attached to any data tuples. And hence, the query has no starting or focal point that may affect the produced answerset. In contrast, each annotation has a focal, which may affect the desired answerset, e.g., affecting the selection of the candidate attachments as well as their ranking and confidence weights. For example, since Alice's comment is attached to one of the genes, this increases the chance that the highlighted keyword "JW0014" from the comment is also referring to another gene— especially if such pair of genes has other annotations in common. Therefore, the challenge is to incorporate and integrate the annotation-related context into the search process to the extent that searching the entire database can be avoided.

• *Lack of Optimizations and Verifications*: Our problem involves several optimization opportunities and design issues that are beyond the scope of the standard keyword search techniques. For example, existing techniques are designed to answer one query at a time. In contrast, in our problem, a single annotation may generate multiple keyword queries at once. Therefore, handling these multiple queries as a group opens new opportunities not only for optimizing their execution, but also for correlating and ranking their results. Moreover, the predicted attachments between the annotations and the data need to be verified through some mechanisms—depending on the application's sensitivity, the verification may either be fully-automated or require experts' involvement.

ConceptRefs **Table (Part of** ***NebulaMeta*****)**

DB concepts that may be referenced within annotations

Concept	TableName	Referenced BY
Gene	Gene	Gene.ID | Gene.Name
Gene Family	Gene	Gene.Family
Protein	Protein	PID | (PName & PType)
...	....	....

The expected ways to reference the concept inside annotations

Figure 3: Example of Nebula's Auxiliary Information.

5. FROM ANNOTATIONS TO KEYWORD QUERIES

In this section, we present techniques for pre-processing a given annotation, identifying the potential embedded references, and forming keyword search queries from those references (*Stage 1* in Figure 16). To construct meaningful keyword queries, Nebula relies on a variety of auxiliary information sources, e.g, domain knowledge, lexical and semantic database repositories, syntactic patterns and descriptions in the data, etc. The goal is to assign weights to the different words in the annotation capturing the probability that a word would be part of an embedded reference vs. being a regular English word. And then, based on these probabilities, we generate potential keyword queries.

5.1 Nebula's Auxiliary Information

Nebula integrates a variety of sources into its metadata repository, called *"NebulaMeta"*, which includes: (1) Publically available lexical and semantic knowledge databases, e.g., WordNet [4], which maintain synonyms and hyponyms of the English words. (2) Domain and expert knowledge capturing the synonyms and equivalent names of the database tables and columns—especially that the table and column names may have abbreviations without obvious semantics, e.g., a column name "GID" will have an equivalent name like "Gene ID" that is more semantically clear. (3) Domain information for the different columns in the database as well as any available ontologies and vocabularies, e.g., the values within a Gene.Function column may follow a specific ontology. In this case, these ontologies will be stored—along with their links to the database columns—in NebulaMeta. And then, during the search phase, estimating whether or not a given keyword w references a database column, e.g., Gene.Function, will depend on whether or not w is present in the corresponding ontology. (4) Syntactic description and patterns of the column values, e.g., the values in the Gene.ID column in Figure 1 conform with the regular expression of $JW[0...9]^4$, whereas the values in the Gene.Name column usually consist of four letters following the regular expression of $[a...z]^3[A...Z]$. These patterns can be even extracted using automated techniques, e.g., [8]. (5) Samples drawn randomly from specific database columns (See the *ConceptRefs* ta-

QueryGeneration()

Input:
- *a* = Input Annotation
- *NebulaMeta* = Nebula's Auxiliary Information sources
- Cutoff threshold ε

Output:
- Set of keyword search queries Q = {q1, q2, …, qn}

Step 1. Generation of *Concept-Map*
```
For (each word w in a) Loop
    For (each table or column name c in ConceptRef) Loop
        // Estimate the probability that w maps to c
        Compute p(w,c) based on NebulaMeta
    End Loop
    If ( p(w,c) < ε for all c) Then
        replace w in the Concept-Map with '-'
    End If
End Loop
```

Step 2. Generation of *Value-Map*
```
For (each word w in a) Loop
    For (each column c in ConceptRef) Loop
        // Estimate the probability that w maps to domain(c)
        Compute d(w,c) based on NebulaMeta
    End Loop
    If ( d(w,c) < ε for all c) Then
        replace w in the Value-Map with '-'
    End If
End Loop
```

Step 3. Overlaying maps & Context-Based Adjustment
```
Context-Map ← Overlay Concept-Map and Value-Map.
Context-Map ← ContextBasedAdjustment(Context-Map).
```

Step 4. Generating the keyword search queries
```
Q ← ContextMap-To-Queries(Context-Map).
```

(a) Pseudocode generating keyword queries from annotation a

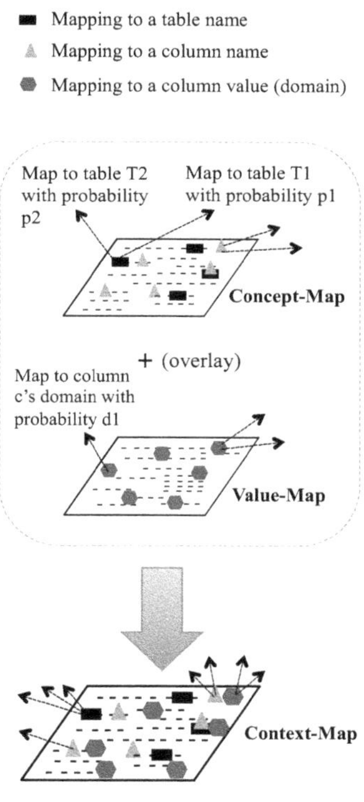

(b) Signature Maps

Matching	Pattern	Reward
Type-1	{ ■, ▲, ⬢ } (related to the same concept)	+ β_1%
Type-2	{ ■, ⬢ } (related to the same concept)	+ β_2% (< β_1)
Type-3	{ ▲, ⬢ } (related to the same concept)	+ β_3% (< β_2)

(c) Context-Based Matching Types

ContextMap-To-Queries()

Input: - Context-Map
- α = Influence range size // Number of words on both sides

Output: Set Q = {q1, q2, …, qn} // Set of keyword queries

```
1.  For (each word w in Context-Map) Loop
2.      w.bestMapping ← the highest-weight mapping of w
3.      w. bestMatch ← Search within w.range for the best matching
4.      If (w.bestMatch exists) Then
5.          Generate new query q = the keywords of w.bestMatch
6.          Set q.weight = Σ (v.weight) ∀v in w.bestMatch keywords
7.          Q ← add query q
8.      Else If (w.range is empty and w is hexagon shape) Then
9.          w' ← The closest rectangle or triangle keyword before w
10.         If (w' has a mapping matching with w.bestMaping) Then
11.             Form a new query q and add it to Q as in Lines 5-7.
12.         End If
13.     End If
14. End Loop
15. Eliminate duplicates within Q by keeping the highest-weight
    q in each group.
16. Normalize the weights within Q by dividing by the largest weight.
```

(d) From Context-Map to Keyword Queries

Figure 4: Extracting Keyword Search Queries From Annotation a.

ble below) if they have no attached ontology or syntactic patterns. And (6) Domain and expert knowledge capturing the key concepts in the database, and the most probable ways, i.e., columns' combinations, for referring to these concepts within the annotations.

As an example, the *ConceptRefs* system table in Figure 3 is part of *NebulaMeta*. It stores the key concepts in a biological database and the most probable ways for referencing them inside the annotations. For example, among the key concepts are *Gene*, *Protein*, and *Gene Family* (1st column). Concepts do not have to belong to separate database tables, e.g., the genes and gene families are stored in the same *Gene* table (2nd column). The 3rd column captures the most probable ways by which a concept may be referenced within an annotation, e.g., a gene is most probably referenced by either its GID or Name columns, while a protein is more likely to be referenced using either its PID column, or the combination of PName and PType columns. In the context of this paper, we assume that populating the *ConceptRefs* table is performed by the domain experts [2].

5.2 Signature Maps and Queries Generation

5.2.1 *Generation of Signature Maps*

We outline the key steps in the query-generation algorithm (called *QueryGeneration()*) in Figure 4(a). The algorithm's inputs include: (1) an input annotation a (which is newly inserted into the database), (2) the *NebulaMeta* auxiliary information, and (3) a cutoff threshold ϵ. The algorithm starts by generating two types of maps, called *signature maps*, which emphasize and highlight the important keywords within annotation a.

Step1 in the algorithm generates the *Concept-Map*. This map highlights the words that are more likely to reference a table name or a column name included in the *ConceptRefs* auxiliary table. The algorithm loops over each word *w* in the annotation (outer loop), and each table name and column name *c* included in *ConceptRefs* (inner loop), and estimates a matching weight between them, i.e., $p(w,c)$. To compute $p(w,c)$, we consider whether or not: (1) w is exactly matching c, (2) w is matching equivalent names of c (defined by domain experts), or (3) w is matching synonyms of c. The first two matching types give higher weight than the third type, otherwise the weight is zero. If *w* does not have a good matching with any of the concepts, i.e., $p(w,c) < \epsilon, \forall c$, where ϵ is an input threshold, then *w* is ignored and replaced with '$-$' in the *Concept-Map* as depicted in Figure 4(b). For the ease of illustration and further discussion, we use a *rectangle*, and *triangle* shapes to indicate potential mappings from the word to either of a table name, or a column name, respectively. Notice that each of the emphasized words may have multiple potential mappings.

The second generated map is called *Value-Map* (Step 2 in the *QueryGeneration()* algorithm). This map highlights the keywords that are more likely to reference a value within the database—more specifically a value in any of the columns included in the *ConceptRefs* auxiliary table. The algorithm loops over each word *w* in the annotation (outer loop), and each of the target columns *c*, and computes a weight indicating the probability that *w* belongs to the domain of *c*, i.e., $d(w,c)$. To compute $d(w,c)$, we consider whether or not: (1) w has the same data type as c, (2) w belongs to c's ontology (if any), (3) w follows c's regular expression pattern (if any), and (4) w has good matching with c's drawn sample (if c has no associated ontology or regular expression pattern). The more positive matching of these factors, the higher the weight. Similar to Step 1, if $d(w,c) < \epsilon, \forall c$, then *w* is ignored and replaced with '$-$' in the *Value-Map* as depicted in Figure 4(b). Each emphasized word in

[2]In extreme cases, a module can be developed for learning from the available annotations the key concepts in the database that they frequently reference, and by which column(s). However, this is beyond the scope of this paper.

Value-Map—highlighted as a *hexagon* shape—may have multiple potential mappings to different column domains, each with different $d(w, c)$ probability.

In Step 3, the algorithm overlays the two maps on top of each other such that the emphasized words will be put into the others' context. The generated map is referred to as the *Context-Map* as illustrated in Figure 4(b). The next step is to adjust the assigned weights—either $p(w, c)$ or $d(w, c)$—depending on the surrounding context and how well the mappings will match with the neighbors' mappings. Therefore, *QueryGeneration()* will call Function *ContextBasedAdjustment()* to adjust the probabilities as will be described in the next section.

5.2.2 Context-Based Weight Adjustment

Before describing how the weights are adjusted based on the surrounding context, we will first introduce the matching types used in the adjustment process. We identify three types of matching based on the context, which are summarized in Figure 4(c). *Type-1* matching (the strongest match) means that we are able to form a matching that consists of a table name, column name, and a value within that column. This is indicated in Figure 4(c) by having a set of three shapes {rectangle, triangle, hexagon}. For example, if words *{"gene", "Id", "JW0018"}* are within one context, then they form a *Type-1* matching. As a result, the probabilities of mapping the 1st word to the gene table, the 2nd word to the ID column within that table, and the 3rd word to a value within this column should all be rewarded and increased. The *Type-2* matching is a weaker match but still common. It means that a matching can be formed consisting of a table name and a database value (without a column name), e.g., a comment may include "gene yaaB". Again the mappings that result in such a match will be rewarded, but with a smaller benefit compared to *Type-1* matching. Finally, the Type-3 matching in which the formed matching consists of the column name and a value (without a table name). This is the weakest match and its rewarding is smaller compared to the other types.

Based on these context-based matching types, the *ContextBasedAdjustment()* Function works as follows (A pseduocode of the function is presented in Appendix A- Figure 17). The function loops over each word *w* in *Context-Map* and creates an influence range around *w*, called *w.range.* The influence range *w.range* is α words to the left and to the right of *w*, where α is an input parameter to the function. This range represents the surrounding context of *w* within which the matching patterns are most likely to be found. Therefore, for each potential mapping of *w*, referred to as *w.mapping*, the function will search within *w.range* if any of Type-1 matchings can be formed. If any, then for each match, the weight of *w.mapping* will be increased by β_1 precent. Otherwise, the search continues to the lower-ranked matches, i.e., Type-2 followed by Type-3 matches. The best match of these types will increment the weight of *w.mapping* by β_2, or β_3 percent, respectively, where $\beta_3 < \beta_2 < \beta_1$ as indicated in Figure 4(c).

5.2.3 Generation of Keyword Search Queries

The last step of the *QueryGeneration()* algorithm is to form potential keyword queries from the *Context-Map* (Step 4). The algorithm is outlined in Figure 4(d). The algorithm will first loop over each keyword *w*, and only *w*'s highest-weight mapping will be considered, say *w.bestMapping* (Line 2). Based on this mapping, the algorithm will form the best possible matching within *w*'s influence rage (*w.range*), i.e., forming Type-1 match, and if not then forming Type-2 match, and if not then forming Type-3 match (Line 3). This best match (if any) will form a keyword search query $q = \{k_1, k_2, k_3\}$ (for Type-1 matching), or $q = \{k_1, k_2\}$ (for Type-2 or Type-3 matching). We then set the weight of *q* to be the sum of weights assigned to its keywords' selected mappings, and then add it to the output set *Q* (Lines 5-7).

```
IdentifyRelatedTuples()
Input: Q = { q1, q2, ..., qn}  // Set of keyword queries,
       D ← the annotated database
Output: T = {t1, t2, ..., tx}  // Set of candidate tuples
Step 1: Executing the keyword queries
1.  For (each query q in Q) Loop
2.      q.answer = KeywordSearch(q, D)   //each tuple t has t.conf [0, 1]
3.      For (each tuple t in q.answer) Loop
4.          t.conf = t.conf x q.weight    //incorporate the query's weight
5.      End Loop
6.      T ← add q.answer to T
7.  End Loop
Step 2: Group tuples and reward the frequent ones
9.  Group tuples in T based on tuples content
10. For (each group g of tuple t) Loop
11.     t.conf = Σ ti.conf, forall ti in g
Step 3: Normalize the weights
12. maxC = maximum confidence in T
13. For (each t in T) Loop
14.     t.conf /= maxC
15. End Loop
```

Figure 5: Identifying DB tuples Related to annotation a.

We consider one important special case while generating the keyword queries, in which the concept keyword (a rectangle or triangle shape), may appear earlier in the text and it may not repeat with each of the following values (a hexagon shape) belonging to this concept. This case is common in human writing as studied in [17, 24]. For example, in Alice's comment the keyword "`gene`" is not repeated before the keywords "`JW0014`" or "`grpC`" since the context is already around genes. To address this special case (Lines 8-12), the algorithm checks if a hexagon-shape keyword *w* has an empty influence range *w.range*. If that is the case, then the algorithm searches backward (starting from *w*'s position) until it finds the closest concept, i.e., a rectangle- or triangle-shape keyword, say *w'*. If *w.bestMapping* and a mapping from *w'* can form a Type-2 or Type-3 match, then a keyword query $q = \{w', w\}$ will be formed. Otherwise, *w* will be ignored. The last steps of the *ConceptMap-To-Queries()* Function (Lines 15-16) are to eliminate any duplicates within *Q* by keeping only the highest-weight *q* from each group, and then normalize the weights of the remaining queries to be between [0, 1].

6. EXECUTION, REFINEMENT, AND OPTIMIZED PROCESSING

The next step after generating the set of keyword queries *Q* is to execute them (*Stage 2* in Figure 16). In the following, we will present the basic version of the execution algorithm, and then propose several refinement and optimization strategies to enhance its performance and accuracy. Due to space limitations, we will omit one of the proposed optimizations, which concerns the *shared query execution* among the keyword queries in *Q*. In summary, the underlying keyword search technique in [7] will generate for each query $q \in Q$ one or more candidate SQL query(s), each captures a potential semantic of *q* (Refer to Section 4). Therefore, Nebula exploits possible sharing opportunities among the SQL queries instead of executing them in isolation.

6.1 Basic Execution Algorithm

The *IdentifyRelatedTuples()* algorithm in Figure 5 outlines the key execution steps. In Step 1, each keyword query $q \in Q$ is submitted to the search technique in [7] for execution—As indicated before, any other technique can be used (Line 2). Each tuple *t* in the answerset will be assigned a confidence value *t.conf* that is computed by internal criteria specific to the underlying search technique. Nevertheless, Nebula adjusts this confidence according to the query's weight $q.weight$ by multiplying them together (Lines 3-6). And then, the answerset is added to the final output T. In the next step (Step 2), the algorithm rewards the tuples that appear in the answerset of more than one query. The intuition is that if a tuple t satisfies multiple queries generated from the same annotation, then this increases the probability that t is actually related to the annotation. Therefore, the algorithm groups the tuples, and sums the confidences within each group (Lines 9-11). Finally, in Step 3, the confidences are normalized relative to the largest confidence value (Step 3). By the end of this step, T will contain the final output set of the candidate data tuples that are likely to be referenced by annotation $\mathtt{a}$. Each tuple t carries a confidence $t.conf \in [0, 1]$ reflecting Nebula's confidence of this attachment.

It is important to highlight that while searching for the relevant tuples given a keyword query, the underlying search algorithm internally leverages the FK-PK relationships among the database tables to produce meaningful related tuples (Line 2). That is why Nebula does not re-examine or adjust the weights based on these relationships. Moreover, Nebula does not explicitly take the structural similarity among the data tuples into account because, by default, all tuples inside a single table will have the same structure. And thus, this property cannot effectively discriminate between tuples in the database. Instead, we incorporate another, more effective, property based on the annotations' focal as described in the next section.

6.2 Focal-Based Confidence Adjustment

An annotation's focal (Def. 3.5) can be leveraged in different ways to enhance Nebula's accuracy in discovering the embedded referenced. We will first introduce a new data structure, called *"Annotations Connectivity Graph"* (a.k.a ACG). ACG is illustrated in Figure 6, where each annotated tuple in the database is represented by a node in the graph. An edge $e(t_i, t_j)$ connects two tuples t_i and t_j iff there are common annotations between the two tuples. Each edge has a weight $e.weight$ (indicated by α_i in Figure 6) representing the ratio between the common annotations to the total number of annotations attached to both t_i and t_j tuples. The ACG structure is incrementally built offline by Nebula as more annotations are attached to the data tuples.

The intuition behind using ACG to adjust the confidence of the candidate data tuples is as follows. Assume annotation $\mathtt{a}$ has two tuples in its focal, i.e., $Foc(\mathtt{a}) = \{\mathtt{t}_1, \mathtt{t}_4\}$ as illustrated in Figure 6. After analyzing $\mathtt{a}$ and extracting the potential embedded references, the data tuples produced from the *IdentifyRelatedTuples()* Function are $T = \{t_3, t_5, t_7, t_x\}$, where t_x is not even present in ACG. Certainly, the fact that t_3 is connected to both t_1 and t_4, i.e., already share other annotations with them, increases Nebula's confidence that $\mathtt{a}$ might also be referencing t_3—especially if α_1 and α_2 are closer to 1. The same applies to t_5 but with slightly less confidence degree since t_5 shares some annotations with only one focal tuple, i.e., t_4. Whereas, for t_7 and t_x, the ACG structure does not suggest an increase in their confidence.

To reflect the ACG structure on the candidate tuples' confidence, we extend Step 2 in *IdentifyRelatedTuples()* Function (Refer to Figure 5) by adding the following lines of code after the grouping step, i.e., after the loop in Lines 10-11.

```
For (each t ∈ T) Loop
    For (each e(t, f) ∈ ACG, ∀ f ∈ Foc(a)) Loop
        t.conf += e.weight x t.conf
    End For
End For
```

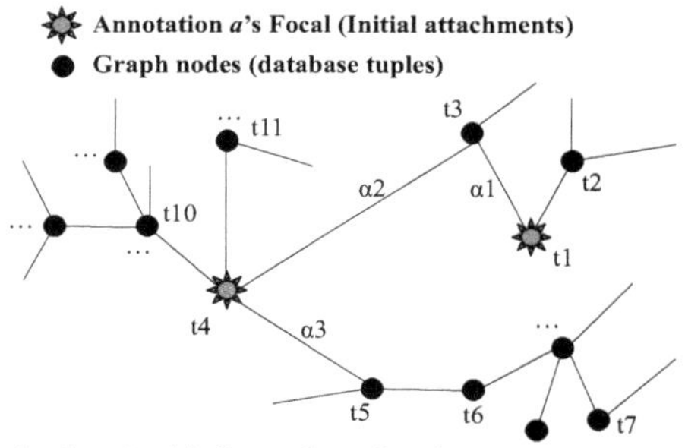

Each edge $e(t_i, t_j)$ indicates that t_i & t_j share common annotations. The e.weight (α) is the ratio between the common annotations to the total annotations attached to t_i & t_j.

Figure 6: Annotations Connectivity Graph (ACG).

That is, for each direct edge each $e(t, f)$ between tuple t and one of the annotation's focal f, t's confidence will be increased according to the e's weight. The higher the weight and the larger the number of direct edges to focal tuples, the higher the reward that tuple t receives. The adjustment model can be easily extended to take into account the shortest path—in terms of the number of hops—between t and each focal tuple instead of only the direct edges. In this case, tuple t_7, for example, will get some reward based on its 4-hop distance from t_4, e.g., by multiplying the weights of the in-between edges. However, Nebula currently incorporates only the direct edges to adjust the weights since the latter extension is semantically weaker and may cause model overfitting.

6.3 Approximate Searching with Focal-Based Spreading

The key intuition here is that as the ACG structure gets mature over time, i.e., models more and more annotations, the graph gets relatively stable and not many new edges are added. In this case, there is a good chance that the embedded references in a given annotation will be referring to direct (or close) neighbors of the annotation's focal. And thus, instead of searching the entire database—which is a very expensive operation—, we can focus the search only on the neighbors of the annotation's focal. Towards this goal, we first introduce the notion of ACG stability as follows.

Definition 6.1 (ACG Stability). *The ACG structure is said to be stable iff for the most recent batch of annotations of size B with total number of attachments to database tuples M ($M \geq B$), the number of newly added edges to ACG is N, where $N/M < \mu$.*

where the batch size B, and the stability threshold $\mu < 1$ are configuration parameters. The ACG's stability property—which is a Boolean value— changes from one batch to another. For ease of computations, the system considers non-overlapping batches (not sliding batches). That is, when the current batch collects B annotations, the ACG's stability property will be re-computed based on that batch. And then, the counters are reset for the next batch. When the ACG structure is marked as stable, then Nebula follows the intuition described above, and searches only neighbors of the annotation's focal.

We investigated several variants of implementing this intuition inside Nebula. One variant, called *Fixed-Scope*, is to search a fixed *K-hop* neighbors of the annotation's focal. This is performed by extending Step 1 in Figure 5 and replacing Lines 1- 2 by the following lines:

```
- miniDB = Form a materialized view of the K-hop
      neighbors of tuple f in ACG, ∀f ∈ Foc(a)
- For (each query q ∈ Q) Loop
    - q.answer = KeywordSearch(q, miniDB)
    ...
```

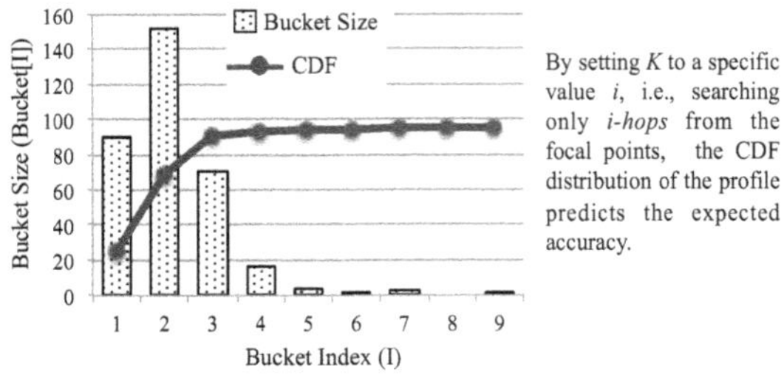

Figure 7: Metadata Profile for Dynamic Selection of K.

That is, the system will perform the keyword search operation over a mini database *miniDB* consisting of only the *K-hop* neighbors of the annotation's focal, where K is a parameter that specifies the radius around the focal tuples. For example, referring to Figure 6, the 1-hop neighbors of annotation a consists of $\{t_2, t_3, t_5, t_{10}, t_{11}\}$. Each tuple in *miniDB* will follow the schema of its own table, and thus creating a materialized mini version of the original database.

A key question in the focal-based spreading search is: *How to specify the value of K?* Blindly setting K to a large value may cause unnecessarily processing overhead, while setting it to a small value may cause the accuracy to be unacceptably low. To help guiding this decision, Nebula creates and maintains a profile on how the ACG structure changes over time. The profile is a simple histogram structure consisting of an array of integers, called *Bucket*, and is built as follows. Assume an annotation a with focal tuples $Foc(\mathtt{a})$, for which Nebula predicts a set of True Attachment tuples $T = \{t_1, t_2, ..., t_x\}$. This means that a will be attached to each of these tuples, and hence an edge will be added to ACG between each t_i and each of the focal tuples $Foc(\mathtt{a})$ (unless the edge already exists). Before adding these edges, Nebula will perform the following step.

```
For (each t ∈ T) Loop
   - S = shortest path from t to any of Foc(a)
        assuming un-weighted ACG.
   - //Update the profile
   - profile.Bucket[S.length] += 1;
End For
```

While computing S, we assume un-weighted ACG since we care about the smallest number of hops from t to reach any of the annotation's focal. And then, we update the profile by incrementing the bucket corresponding to $S.length$, i.e., Bucket[S.length] is incremented by 1. The intuition is that, if we were to discover t by searching only the neighbors of the annotation's focal, then K would need to be at least equal to $S.length$ (or larger), otherwise t would have been missed. By accumulating more points in the profile over time, the distribution of points across the different buckets would give us a good guidance on where to set K (See Figure 7). For example, according to the example profile illustrated in Figure 7, by setting by setting $K = 2$, or $K = 3$, we expect to discover 71%, or 93% of the candidates, respectively. The reason is that based on the history, 71%, and 93% of the candidates produced from the entire database search were 2-hop, and 3-hop away from at least one of the focal tuples, respectively. The profile can be then used either by the DB admins to manually select K, or by the system to automatically select K given a desired accuracy.

7. VERIFICATION AND ASSESSMENT

So far, we presented various techniques and optimizations for discovering and predicting the missing attachments of a given annotation a to a set of data tuples $T = \{t_1, t_2, ..., t_x\}$. In this section, we address how these predicted attachments are verified and how the different techniques are assessed (*Stage 3* in Figure 16).

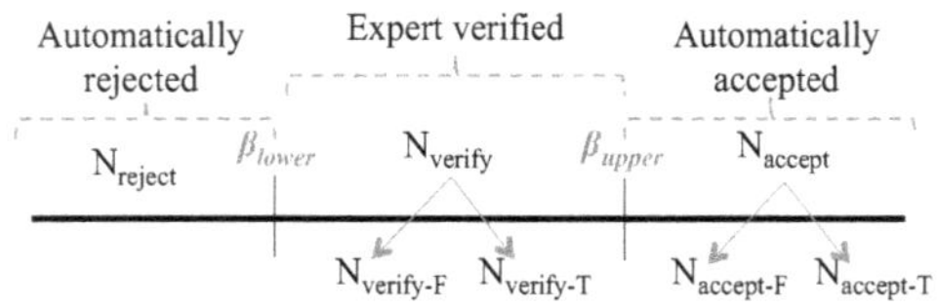

Figure 8: Verification Bounds and Assessment Variables.

Definition 7.1 (Verification Task). *A verification task v is defined as v = (v_{id}, a, t, confidence, evidence), where v_{id} is a unique system-generated identifier, a is an annotation, t is a database tuple to which Nebula predicted a missing attachment, confidence is the estimated confidence of the attachment, and evidence is the set of evidences supporting Nebula's prediction. The result of v is a Boolean decision of either accepting the attachment (becomes a True Attachment), or rejecting and discarding the attachment.*

In the current implementation, *v.evidence* contains all the keyword queries q generated from a for which t is part of the answer. The objective from reporting *v.evidence* is to help the DB admins in the verification process. Since manual verification of all verification tasks—which can be many—is not a practical solution, Nebula relies on two thresholds β_{lower} and β_{upper} as highlighted in Figure 8, where a verification task v having *v.confidence* $< \beta_{lower}$ will be automatically rejected (discard from the system). Whereas, if *v.confidence* $> \beta_{upper}$, then v will be automatically accepted (becomes a True Attachment with 100% confidence). In contrast, if $\beta_{lower} \leq$ *v.confidence* $\leq \beta_{upper}$, then v would require expert involvement for verification. In this case, v is called a *"pending verification task"*, and stored in a system table for further processing. This table can be queried by database admins (or authorized users) to report the pending tasks and verify them. To verify a task, the following extended SQL command is introduced:

```
[Verify | Reject] Attachement <v_id>;
```

The new command is needed because if the attachment is verified and accepted, then a sequence of actions will be performed by the system transparently from end-users. These actions include: (1) Attaching annotation a to tuple t (it becomes a True Attachment), (2) Updating the ACG structure to reflect the new attachment (Refer to Figure 6), and (3) Updating the metadata profile that guides the focal-based spreading technique (Refer to Figure 7). Notice that the same actions will be performed for each automatically accepted task whose *v.confidence* $> \beta_{upper}$.

Assessment: The verification decisions will be assessed according to four criteria. We assume that the number of attachments between a and the data tuples in the ideal world D_{ideal} is denoted by N_{ideal}. The predictions of the system can be categorized into five categories according to the β_{lower} and β_{upper} bounds as depicted in Figure 8. The number of automatically rejected predictions is denoted by N_{reject}. The number of manually-verified predictions is denoted by N_{verify}, which is further divided into $N_{verify-T}$ (if the verification is positive), or $N_{verify-F}$ (if the verification is negative), such that $N_{verify} = N_{verify-T} + N_{verify-F}$. Finally, the number of automatically accepted predictions is denoted by N_{accept}, which is further divided into $N_{accept-T}$ (if the prediction is correct), or $N_{accept-F}$ (if the prediction is wrong), such that $N_{accept} = N_{accept-T} + N_{accept-F}$. Based on these variables, the assessment criteria is defined as follows.

Definition 7.2 (Assessment Criteria). *For a given annotation* a, *the prediction of* a*'s missing attachments is assessed based on four criteria: (1) The false-negative ratio F_N, (2) The false-positive ratio F_P, (3) The manual effort involved in the verification process M_F, and (4) The manual hit ratio (conversion ratio) M_H. The criteria factors are defined as:*

```
BoundsSetting()
Input:
    - Training dataset D_Training, Tolerance threshold Ψ (e.g., 0.1)
Output: Setting values for β_lower and β_upper

Step 1: Distort the training dataset and generate D_incomplete
1. For (each annotation a) Loop
2.      - Remove all of a's attachments to the data tuples
3.        which are referenced within a, except one.
4. End Loop

Step 2: Compute the assessment criteria
5. For (each annotation a in D_incomplete) Loop
6.      - Let Nebula predicts the missing attachments
7.      For (each possible setting of β_lower and β_upper ) Loop
8.           - Compute F_N, F_P, M_F, and M_H (w.r.t D_Training)
9.      End For
10. End For

Step 3: Select the best β_lower & β_upper
11. For (each possible setting of β_lower and β_upper ) Loop
12.     - Compute average over all annotations: G_FN, G_FP, G_MF, G_MH
13. End For
14. Select the settings of β_lower and β_upper that minimizes G_MF
15.       while keeping G_FN < Ψ and G_FP < Ψ.
```

Figure 9: Adaptively Adjusting β_{lower} & β_{upper} Bounds.

$$F_N = \frac{N_{ideal} - (N_{verify-T} + N_{accept-T} + N_{focal})}{N_{ideal}}$$

$$F_P = \frac{N_{accept-F}}{(N_{verify-T} + N_{accept} + N_{focal})}$$

$$M_F = N_{verify}$$

$$M_H = N_{verify-T} \; / \; N_{verify}$$

The F_N and F_P factors capture the accuracy and completeness of the prediction, whereas M_F and M_H capture the required effort by domain experts in the verification process. Notice that the only source producing false positives, i.e., $F_P > 0$, is the automatically accepted predictions that are actually wrong $N_{accept-F}$.

Adaptively Adjusting the β_{lower} and β_{upper} Bounds: The specification of the two bounds β_{lower} and β_{upper} is clearly an important factor since they affect the accuracy of the accepted/rejected predictions as well as the balance between automating the verification decision vs. involving the domain experts in the process. For example, if $\beta_{upper} = 1$, then no predictions will be automatically accepted and they must be manually verified. In contrast, if $\beta_{lower} = \beta_{upper}$, then all the predictions will be decided automatically without any expert involvement. The optimal scenario is to minimize F_N and F_P with zero involvement from domain experts, i.e., $M_F = 0$. This is due to the potential long delays in human actions, the inability to scale to many verification tasks, and more importantly their valuable time that should not be consumed in the verification process. However, entirely eliminating the experts from the process may not be feasible due to the uncertainty involved in deciding whether or not an annotation is related to a data tuple. Therefore, β_{lower} and β_{upper} should be adjusted to generate acceptable F_N and F_P while minimizing M_F.

To help adjusting β_{lower} and β_{upper} to proper values, we periodically deploy the algorithm presented in Figure 9. Nebula uses a training dataset $D_{Training}$ in which each annotation a is attached to all (and only those) tuples related to a. $D_{Training}$ is built by selecting a subset of the annotations from the underlying database, e.g., selecting few 100s of the available annotations, and then manually verifying their attachments and adding any missing ones. And then, the algorithm distorts the dataset by considering each annotation a and removing all its attachments to the data tuples except one. The resulted distorted dataset is called $D_{incomplete}$ (Step 1 in Figure 9). The system will then try to discover the missing attachments (Line 6), and then assess such prediction for different settings of β_{lower} and β_{upper} (Lines 7-9). Notice that all the variables defined in Figure 8 can be automatically computed (including $N_{verify-F}$ and $N_{verify-T}$) since $D_{Training}$ dataset is available. For example, $N_{verify-F}$ will correspond to the verification tasks located between β_{lower} and β_{upper} that do not have a matching in $D_{Training}$. In Step 3, we average the assessment measures over all the annotations for each setting for β_{lower} and β_{upper}, and then take the best setting that minimizes the expert involvement (M_F) while keeping F_N and F_P within an acceptable range.

Further enhancements can be applied to the *BoundsSetting()* algorithm—which are omitted from Figure 9 for simplicity. These enhancements include: (1) In Step 1, we may consider different degrees of dataset distortion, e.g., we may remove all attachments of a given annotation except 2 or 3 links, which creates less-distorted versions of the dataset. And (2) In Step 3, Lines 7-9, instead of blindly exploring different values of β_{lower} and β_{upper}, we can use M_H factor to guide the adjustment of the bounds. For example, if M_H is high (closer to 1), then this means that most manually-verified predictions are accepted. In this case, the algorithm may lower β_{upper} (moving it to the left) to allow accepting more predictions automatically without passing them for verification.

It is worth mentioning that in practice Nebula does not require the D_{ideal} dataset to be present—which is the typical cases in real-world applications. In this case, the assessment criteria can be computed periodically by the domain experts as follows: (1) Given a set of m newly added annotations, the domain experts will examine them and identify the True attachments, i.e., N_{ideal}, (2) Nebula will provide its predictions for each annotation in m divided into the three categories depicted in Figure 8, i.e., *Reject*, *Verify*, and *Accept*, and (3) The domain experts will compute the assessment criteria factors for each annotation, and can even compute additional statistics, e.g., min, max, and average, across the m annotations.

8. EXPERIMENTS

Nebula is implemented on top of an existing annotation management system [18], which offers end-to-end annotation management functionalities, e.g., mechanisms for adding annotations, transparent storage and indexing, and automated propagation of annotations along with the queries' answers at query time. The experiments are conducted using an AMD Opteron Quadputer compute server with two 16-core AMD CPUs, 128GB memory, and 2 TBs SATA hard drive. Figure 10 summarizes the key experimental parameters, which are described in the following section.

8.1 Experimental Setup and Workloads

Curated Biological Datasets: We use a subset of the UniProt real-world annotated biological database [3]. UniProt offers a comprehensive repository for protein and functional information for various species. We extracted three main tables including *Protein*, *Gene*, and *Publication*. The tables are connected through the following relationships: The *Protein* table has a many-to-one relationship with *Gene*, and many-to-many relationships with *Publication*. The *Gene* table has also a many-to-many relationship with *Publication*. The dataset consists of approximately 750,000 protein records ($\approx$ 4.7GBs), 1.3 x 10^6 gene records ($\approx$ 8GBs), and 12 x 10^6 publication records ($\approx$ 4.5GBs). Thus, the total size of the dataset is approximately 18GBs.

We divide the dataset to form three experimental subsets with different sizes, which are: (1) *Small-Size Dataset* (D_{small}) in which we select 10% of the proteins, genes, and their related publications ($\approx$ 2GBs), (2) *Mid-Size Dataset* (D_{mid}) in which we select 50% of the proteins, genes, and their related publications ($\approx$ 9GBs), and (3) *Large-Size Dataset* (D_{large}) in which we use the entire extracted records ($\approx$ 18GBs). The *NebulaMeta* repository

Symbol	Description
D_{small}, D_{mid}, D_{large}	The databases with different sizes of 2.5GB, 10GB, and 20GB, respectively.
$L_{i\text{-}j}$	A set of publications (annotations) with number of links between *i* and *j*. Takes values: $L_{1\text{-}3}$, $L_{4\text{-}6}$, $L_{7\text{-}10}$
L^m	A set of 15 annotations, each of a max size *m* bytes, where *m* in {50, 100, 500, 1000}. L^m contains 5 annotations from each of $L_{1\text{-}3}$, $L_{4\text{-}6}$, $L_{7\text{-}10}$.
ε	The cutoff threshold for signature-map generation. Takes values 0.4, 0.6, or 0.8.
Δ	Distortion degree. Takes values 1, 2, or 3. $\Delta = x$ means dropping all links of an annotation except x links.
K	# of hops in focal-based spreading search

Figure 10: Summary of Workload Parameters.

is manually populated by adding the two concepts of "Gene" and "Protein" to the *ConceptRefs* table, and identifying their `ID`, and `Name` columns to be the referencing columns. We also specified regular expression patterns over the values in `Gene.ID` and `Gene.Name` columns.

Annotation Workload: We use the publication records in the dataset to represent the annotations over the gene and protein records. To create the workload for each of the three datasets, i.e., $D = \{D_{small}, D_{mid}, or D_{large}\}$, the following procedure is followed (A visual representation of the datasets and the workload mixture is presented in Appendix A- Figure 18):

(1) The annotated dataset D is assumed to be an ideal and complete dataset, i.e., when verifying Nebula's recommendations, D will be treated as the reference D_{ideal} dataset.

(2) A workload over D is created by selecting a mixture of annotations, which will act as the new annotations to be inserted into the database. The workload consists of four distinct sets, denoted as $L^{50}, L^{100}, L^{500}, L^{1000}$, where each L^m consists of a total of 15 annotations, each of a max size of m bytes.

(3) The 15 annotations within each L^m are selected such that they are divided equally across three distinct subsets (5 from each subset), which are denoted as L_{1-3}, L_{4-6}, and L_{7-10}. Set L_{i-j} contains annotations having a number between i and j (inclusive) of embedded references to the `Gene` and/or `Protein` tables (See Figure 18). For example, "$L^{100}.L_{4-6}$" is a set in the workload that contains 5 annotations, each of a max size of 100 bytes, and each contains between 4 to 6 embedded references to the gene and/or protein records. This step involves a manual effort to identify the publications that have the desired number of embedded references under each group [3]. The workload is designed in such way to ensure the inclusion of annotations with various sizes as well as diverse number of embedded references.

(4) The ACG structure for dataset D is built from the FK-PK relationships between the publication records and the gene and protein records, i.e., two tuples—from any of the `Protein` and `Gene` tables—having common a publication will have an edge between them in ACG. The only exception is that the annotations used in the workload, i.e., part of the L^m sets, do not participate in building the ACG. This is because they will be treated as new annotations. The ACG is built at once and not in an incremental fashion.

As summarized in Figure 10, the other important parameters include the cutoff threshold ϵ, which is used in generating the signature maps, the distortion degree Δ, where an annotation **a** with $\Delta = x$ means that all of **a**'s links to the gene and protein records will be dropped except x links, and parameter K, which represents the number of considered hops in the focal-based spreading search.

[3] Set "$L^{50}.L_{7-10}$" was always empty since not as many embedded references can fit within a 50-char annotation. Therefore, we substituted the missing annotations by additional ones added to L_{1-3} and L_{4-6} subsets.

8.2 Performance Evaluation

Generation of Keyword Queries: In Figure 11, we focus on studying the performance of generating the keyword queries from a given annotation. These experiments are independent of the database size since they focus only on analyzing the annotation's content. Therefore, we use the workload created from the largest dataset D_{large}. Each experiment is repeated 15 times, one for each annotation in L^m, and the average values are presented in the figures. In the *Naive* approach, the entire annotation is assumed to be a single query, and thus we assume the needed time to generate the query in this case is zero. In Nebula , the generation goes through three phases, which are: (1) The generation of the *Concept* and *Value* signature maps, (2) The overlaying and context-based weight adjustment, and (3) The generation of the keyword queries. The execution time taken by each of these phases is illustrated in Figure 11(a). We study the performance under various cutoff threshold (ϵ) and annotation sets (L^m), which are presented on the x-axis. As illustrated in Figure 11(a), the first phase (map generation) takes around 2/3 of the execution time, and then the other two phases consume around 1/3 of the time. As the cutoff threshold gets larger, less number of keywords qualify to be added to the signature maps, and thus less work is needed to align them and generate candidate keyword queries.

In Figure 11(b), we present the number of generated keyword queries from the previous experiment under the different L^m and ϵ values. The cutoff threshold $\epsilon = 0.4$ is clearly very low and causes the number of generated queries to be relatively high—Recall that each annotation has less than 10 embedded references, and thus in the ideal case, we should expect around 10 keyword queries. This large number of generated queries is due to the fact that many keywords from the annotation will pass the 0.4 threshold. In contrast, for $\epsilon = 0.6$ & 0.8 the thresholds are tighter and less number of queries are generated. Although this is a good sign, this figure does not capture whether or not the queries represent the actual embedded references within the annotation. Therefore, we manually investigate the generated SQL queries and check whether a query refers to something other than an embedded reference (False Positive), or some embedded references are not captured by any query (False Negatives). We report the results in Figure 11(c).

The presented numbers in Figure 11(c) indicate that for $\epsilon = 0.4$ no embedded references were missed, i.e., the false negative percent is zero. However, very large percentage of the generated queries search keywords that are not embedded references, e.g., 91% of the generated queries in the case of L^{1000} are false positives. The 0.6 cutoff is superior over the 0.4 value since the 0.6 threshold also has zero false negatives but significantly less false positives (as well as less number of total queries as illustrated in Figure 11(b)). The tightest threshold 0.8 misses few embedded references, yet its false positive results are very low compared to the other values, e.g., it has zero false positives under L^{50}. Even under larger annotation sizes, e.g., L^{1000}, where the false positive percentage reaches 54% for $\epsilon = 0.8$, the effect is not as severe as in the cases of $\epsilon = 0.4$ *or* 0.6 because: (1) The number of queries for the 0.8 threshold is relatively very small (Refer to Figure 11(b)), and (2) As the number of false-positive queries becomes smaller, less noise propagates to the subsequent phases, i.e., the tuple-level weight adjustment (Section 6.1), and the focal-based confidence adjustment (Section 6.2). And thus, these phases become more effective and produce better-quality results.

In general, there is no golden value for ϵ that works the best in all cases. However, as our experiments show, and has been also reported in literature in related keyword search problems [7], values between 0.5 and 0.8 usually yield good results. In the rest of the experiments, we will exclude the 0.4 threshold from the comparison as it has no advantage over the 0.6 threshold.

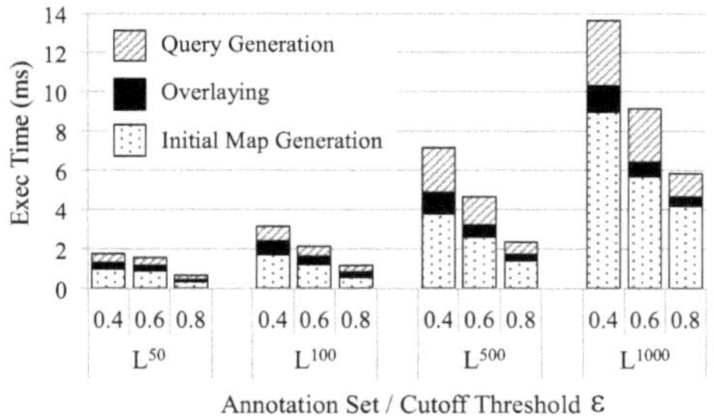

(a) Overhead of Query Generation Phases

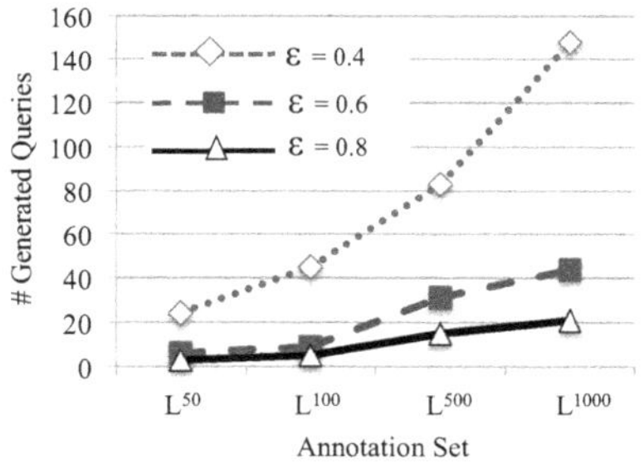

(b) Number of Generated Keyword Queries

Annotation Set	False Negative %			False Positive %		
	Cutoff Threshold ε			Cutoff Threshold ε		
	0.4	0.6	0.8	0.4	0.6	0.8
L^{50}	0	0	33.3	83	50	0
L^{100}	0	0	0	84	66	40
L^{500}	0	0	12	90	72	53
L^{1000}	0	0	10	91.5	77	54

(c) Query-Level False Positives and Negatives

Figure 11: Performance of Keyword Query Generation Phases.

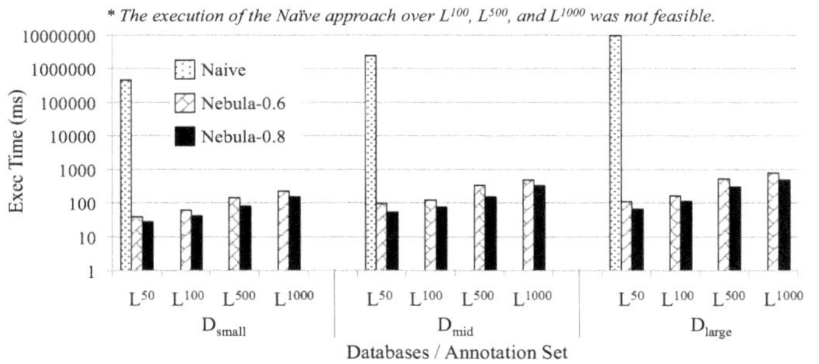

(a) Execution Time Overhead

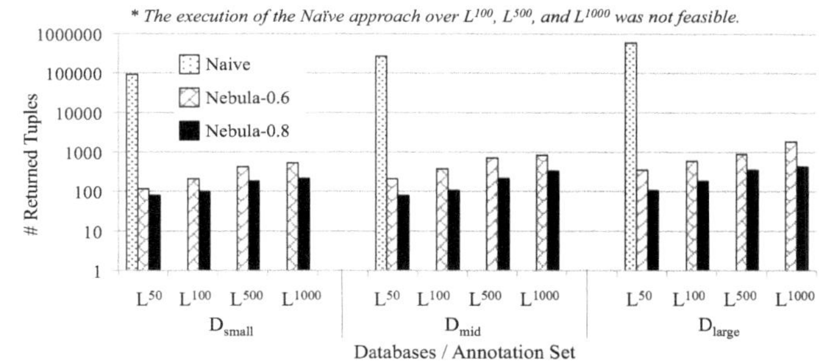

(b) Number of Returned Tuples

Figure 12: Performance of Candidate Tuple Generation.

Execution of Keyword Queries: After generating the keyword queries, we study their execution performance in Figure 12. The x-axis presents the different database sizes as well as the various annotation sets L^m under each database. The comparison includes the *Naive* approach in which the keyword query includes the entire content of the annotation. In Figure 12(a), we measure the total execution time, i.e., the time of one query in the case of the *Naive* approach, and the sum of the execution times from the n queries generated from Nebula. As indicated in the figure, the *Naive* approach is five orders-of-magnitudes slower than the other two cases; *Nebula*-0.6 (using $\epsilon = 0.6$), and *Nebula*-0.8 (using $\epsilon = 0.8$). Moreover, under larger annotation sets, e.g., L^{100} or larger, it was not even feasible to execute the *Naive* approach.

The performance between *Nebula*-0.6 and *Nebula*-0.8 is relatively comparable. The differences in execution time are mainly due to the number of queries being executed as well as the number of produced tuples, which is depicted in Figure 12(b). The number of produced tuples from the queries again confirm that the *Naive* approach is useless as it returns 100s of thousands of tuples under the smallest annotation set L^{50}. This is due to the keyword query itself being very imprecise, and hence the underlying search technique returns a significant portion of the database. It is important to highlight that for *Nebula*-0.6 and *Nebula*-0.8 the number of returned tuples does not grow in the same ratio as the database size grows. This is because many of the queries are on columns with unique values, and thus the increase in the database size does not necessarily reflect on the number of returned tuples.

Referring back to Figure 12(a), the reported execution time of Nebula's techniques represent the sum of times from executing each keyword query in isolation, i.e., no multi-query sharing. This is the default mode, especially if the underlying keyword search technique is used as black box. Nevertheless, as we highlighted in Section 6, if we enable shared execution among the SQL queries generated from the keyword search technique, then significant savings can be achieved. For completeness, we report in Figure 13 the performance gain from such query sharing. We repeat the same experiment as in Figure 12(a) while comparing *Nebula*-0.6 and *Nebula*-0.8 with their sharing-enabled variants. The results indicate around 40% to 50% speedup in execution time while producing the same number of output tuples.

Finally, the performance of executing the keyword queries using the approximate focal-based spreading technique is presented in Figure 14. In this experiment, we set the database to the largest one D_{large}, the cutoff threshold to $\epsilon = 0.6$ (as it has zero false negatives), and the annotation set to L^{100} (an average-size set). Moreover, there is no sharing while executing the queries. This experiment is sensitive to the number of initial attachments between an annotation and the database records (the focal points). Therefore, we vary the distortion degree Δ over the x-axis, which controls the number of focal points that an annotation will have, and measure the performance under various values of K, i.e., the number of hops around each focal point. The results in Figure 14(a) illustrate that the execution time is around 15x faster than the basic search without sharing. Moreover, when compared with multi-query sharing, it is around 8x faster. This is mostly due to searching a small—but highly-promising—subset of the database.

Clearly, as the two key parameters Δ and K increase, the number of the searched tuples will increase, which will reflect on increasing both the execution time (Figure 14(a)), and the number of produced tuples (Figure 14(b)). By comparing Figures 12(b) and 14(b), we observe that the number of produced tuples is significantly less in the latter case. Therefore, the advantages of the focal-based spreading search are not limited only to speeding up the execution time, but also to reducing the verification overhead, which will be studied next. We repeated the experiments in Figure 14 using different dataset sizes and cutoff ϵ thresholds, and the insights from the results are almost the same, i.e., significant gain in execution time and an order-of-magnitude reduction in the candidate tuples.

Verification and Assessment: Since the ideal database D_{ideal} is known in our experiments, i.e., for a given annotation $\mathbf{a}$ we know all of its attachments to the database tuples, then the assessment criteria introduced in Definition 7.2 can be easily computed. Even the *expert-verified* factors $N_{verify-F}$ and $N_{verify-T}$ can be automatically computed, i.e., $N_{verify-T}$ represents all the candidate

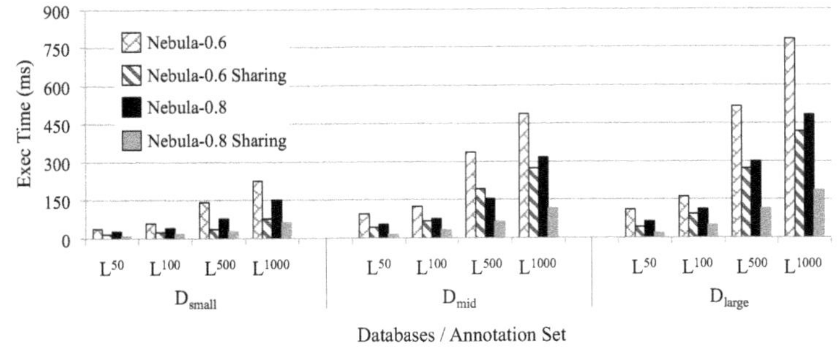

Figure 13: Shared Query Execution.

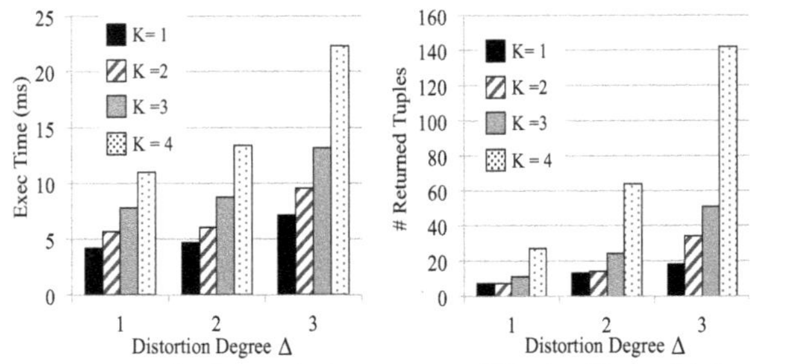

(a) Execution Time Overhead **(b) Number of Returned Tuples**

Figure 14: Focal-Spreading Approximate Search.

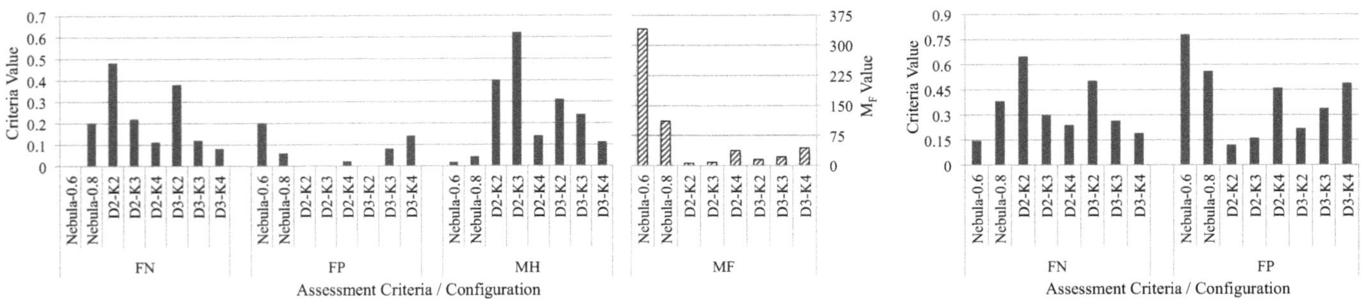

(a) Assessment Criteria With Auto-Configured β_{lower} & β_{upper} (β_{lower} = 0.32 & β_{upper} = 0.86)

(b) Assessment Criteria without Expert Involvement ($\beta_{lower} = \beta_{upper}$ = 0.5)

Figure 15: Evaluation of the Verification and Assessment Criteria.

tuples that lie between β_{lower} and β_{upper} and their links to a exist in D_{ideal}, while $N_{verify-F}$ represents those tuples that lie between β_{lower} and β_{upper} and their links to a do not exist in D_{ideal}. This is under the assumption that experts do not make errors. The evaluation is repeated 15 times, once for each annotation in L^{100}, and the average values are presented in the figures.

In Figure 15, we fix the annotation set to L^{100}, and the database to the largest one D_{large}. We then evaluate each of the four assessment criterion under eight different configurations (the x-axis), which include the basic algorithm without approximation under two cutoff thresholds *Nebula*-0.6 and *Nebula*-0.8, and six configurations for the focal-based approximate searching with various Δ and K parameters. In Figure 15(a), the verification bounds β_{lower} and β_{upper} are automatically adjusted using the algorithm presented in Section 7. The $D_{Training}$ dataset is built by randomly selecting 500 annotations from the database, and manually verifying their attachments. The algorithm has set the bounds to $\beta_{lower} = 0.32$ and $\beta_{upper} = 0.86$. The results show that there is no single configuration that dominates the others in all criteria factors. Nevertheless, in general, *Nebula*-0.8 is performing better than *Nebula*-0.6, especially when considering the manual effort needed from the experts' side (the M_F factor). Yet, *Nebula*-0.8 introduces around 20% false negatives. The second observation is that the focal-based approximate techniques are performing very well, especially under $K = 3$ or $K = 4$.

In the above experiment, we exclude the evaluation of the Naive approach w.r.t. the assessment criteria since it does not scale to annotation sizes beyond L^{50} (Refer to Figure 12). However, to confirm the infeasibility of this approach, we computed the assessment factors $\{F_N, F_P, M_F, M_H\}$ for the L^{50} case in which 587,040 tuples have been returned (Figure 12(b)), and the results are $\{0, 0.93, 318427, 1.6e-5\}$, respectively. This means that for a single annotation, the domain experts will need to verify 318,427 annotations from which only 5 will be accepted. These numbers provide a clear evidence that *Nebula* enables a new functionality in annotated databases that is not possible otherwise.

In Figure 15(b), we evaluate an extreme case in which we manually set the verification bounds $\beta_{lower} = \beta_{upper} = 0.5$. In this case, there will be no expert involvement in the verification process. The results show that the F_P values get significantly higher, and hence the techniques create many wrong associations between the annotation and the data tuples. Moreover, the F_N values also get higher by a noticeable percentage. We repeated the same experiment by setting β_{lower} and β_{upper} to the same value (but different from 0.5), and in all cases the F_N and F_P were relatively very high compared to the results in Figure 15(a). Our conclusion is that it may not be feasible to entirely exclude the experts from the verification process while achieving good results. However, the results in Figure 15(a) are promising and show that with a reasonable involvement, we can achieve acceptable results.

9. CONCLUSION

In this paper, we presented the un-addressed problem of *proactive annotation management in relational databases*. We focused on one sub-problem, which is the discovery and management of embedded references within the annotations. To address this problem, we proposed the *Nebula* engine that complements the state-of-art in annotation management with proactive capabilities. The key contributions introduced by Nebula are: (1) Proposing techniques for analyzing the annotations' content and discovering the embedded references, (2) Extending the state-of-art in RDBMS-based keyword search techniques to efficiently search and find the data tuples corresponding to the embedded references, (3) Proposing various annotation-aware optimizations including focal-based weight adjustment, approximate searching with focal-based spreading, and multi-query shared execution, and (4) Developing an expert-enabled verification mechanisms that adaptively minimize the experts' involvements while maintaining high-accuracy predictions. The experimental evaluation illustrates the significant gain in enhancing the quality of annotated databases, the effectiveness of the proposed optimization techniques, and the reduction in the time- and resource-consuming process of manual curation.

10. REFERENCES

[1] EcoliHouse: A Publicly Queryable Warehouse of E. coli K12 Databases. http://www.porteco.org/.

[2] PubChem- Database of Chemical Molecules. https://pubchem.ncbi.nlm.nih.gov.

[3] The Universal Protein Resource Databases (UniProt) . http://www.ebi.ac.uk/uniprot/.

[4] WordNet: Lexical Database. . *http://wordnet.princeton.edu/*.

[5] DBXplorer: A System for Keyword-Based Search over Relational Databases. In *ICDE*, pages 5–16, 2002.

[6] P. Alper, K. Belhajjame, C. Goble, and P. Karagoz. Small Is Beautiful: Summarizing Scientific Workflows Using Semantic Annotations. In *IEEE BigData Congress*, pages 318–325, 2013.

[7] S. Bergamaschi, E. Domnori, F. Guerra, R. Trillo Lado, and Y. Velegrakis. Keyword Search over Relational Databases: A Metadata Approach. In *SIGMOD*, pages 565–576, 2011.

[8] S. Bergamaschi, C. Sartori, F. Guerra, and M. Orsini. Extracting Relevant Attribute Values for Improved Search. *IEEE Internet Computing*, 11(5):26–35, 2007.

[9] D. Bhagwat, L. Chiticariu, and W. Tan. An annotation management system for relational databases. In *VLDB*, pages 900–911, 2004.

[10] S. Bowers and B. LudŁscher. A Calculus for Propagating Semantic Annotations through Scientific Workflow Queries. In *In Query Languages and Query Processing (QLQP)*, 2006.

[11] S. Bowers, T. Mcphillips, S. Riddle, M. K. Anand, and B. Ludascher. Kepler/pPOD: Scientific Workflow and Provenance Support for Assembling the Tree of Life. In *Provenance and Annotation Workshop (IPWA)*, pages 70–77, 2008.

[12] P. Buneman, J. Cheney, W.-C. Tan, and S. Vansummeren. Curated databases. In *Proceedings of the 27th ACM symposium on Principles of database systems (PODS)*, pages 1–12, 2008.

[13] P. Buneman and et. al. On propagation of deletions and annotations through views. In *PODS*, pages 150–158, 2002.

[14] P. Buneman, S. Khanna, and W. Tan. Why and where: A characterization of data provenance. *Lec. Notes in Comp. Sci.*, 1973:316–333, 2001.

[15] P. Buneman, E. V. Kostylev, and S. Vansummeren. Annotations are relative. In *Proceedings of the 16th International Conference on Database Theory*, ICDT '13, pages 177–188, 2013.

[16] L. Chiticariu, W.-C. Tan, and G. Vijayvargiya. DBNotes: a post-it system for relational databases based on provenance. In *SIGMOD*, pages 942–944, 2005.

[17] R. Cole, J. Mariani, and H. Uszkoreit, editors. *Survey of the State-of-the-Art in Human Language Technology*. Cambridge University Press and Giardini, 1997.

[18] M. Y. Eltabakh, W. G. Aref, A. K. Elmagarmid, M. Ouzzani, and Y. N. Silva. Supporting annotations on relations. In *EDBT*, pages 379–390, 2009.

[19] W. Gatterbauer, M. Balazinska, N. Khoussainova, and D. Suciu. Believe it or not: adding belief annotations to databases. *Proc. VLDB Endow.*, 2(1):1–12, 2009.

[20] F. Geerts, A. Kementsietsidis, and D. Milano. Mondrian: Annotating and querying databases through colors and blocks. In *ICDE*, pages 82–93, 2006.

[21] J. Gray, D. T. Liu, M. Nieto-Santisteban, A. Szalay, D. J. DeWitt, and G. Heber. Scientific data management in the coming decade. *SIGMOD Record*, 34(4):34–41, 2005.

[22] K. Ibrahim, D. Xiao, and M. Y. Eltabakh. Elevating Annotation Summaries To First-Class Citizens In InsightNotes. In *EDBT Conference*, 2015.

[23] E. V. Kostylev and P. Buneman. Combining dependent annotations for relational algebra. In *Proceedings of the 15th International Conference on Database Theory (ICDT)*, pages 196–207, 2012.

[24] R. Kumar and A. Tomkins. A Characterization of Online Browsing Behavior. In *Proceedings of the International Conference on World Wide Web*, pages 561–570, 2010.

[25] Q. Li, A. Labrinidis, and P. K. Chrysanthis. ViP: A User-Centric View-Based Annotation Framework for Scientific Data. In *SSDBM*, pages 295–312, 2008.

[26] X. Li, M. Zhang, Y. Liu, S. Ma, Y. Jin, and L. Ru. Search Engine Click Spam Detection Based on Bipartite Graph Propagation. In *Proceedings of the 7th ACM International Conference on Web Search and Data Mining*, pages 93–102, 2014.

[27] Y. Luo, X. Lin, W. Wang, and X. Zhou. Spark: Top-k Keyword Query in Relational Databases. In *SIGMOD*, pages 115–126, 2007.

[28] G. Palma and et. al. Measuring Relatedness Between Scientific Entities in Annotation Datasets. In *International Conference on Bioinformatics, Computational Biology and Biomedical Informatics*, pages 367:367–367:376, 2013.

[29] N. P. Savchuk, K. V. Balakin, and S. E. Tkachenko. Exploring the chemogenomic knowledge space with annotated chemical libraries. *Current Opinion in Chemical Biology*, 8(4):412, 2004.

[30] S. Tata and G. M. Lohman. SQAK: Doing More with Keywords. In *SIGMOD*, pages 889–902, 2008.

[31] D. Xiao, A. Bashllari, and T. M. M. Y. Eltabakh. Even Metadata is Getting Big: Annotation Summarization using InsightNotes. In *SIGMOD Conference*, 2015.

[32] D. Xiao and M. Y. Eltabakh. InsightNotes: summary-based annotation management in relational databases. In *SIGMOD Conference*, pages 661–672, 2014.

APPENDIX

A. SUPPORTING FIGURES

In this section, we include several supporting and illustrative figures. Figure 16 presents the main processing stages of the Nebula system along with the key contributions in each stage, which are: *Stage 0:* The modeling of an annotated database, the insertion of new annotations, and identifying the focal points (Section 3), *Stage 1:* The analysis of the annotation's content, constructing signature maps, and the generation of keyword-search queries (Section 5), *Stage 2:* The execution of the queries either over the entire database, or over a small subset surrounding the focal points (Section 6), and *Stage 3:* The verification of the generated candidate attachments and assessing the results' quality (Section 7). Figure 17 presents a detailed pseudocode for the *ContextBasedAdjustment()* Function, which is introduced in Section 5.2.2, and called from the *QueryGeneration()* Function (Figure 4(a)). The function adjusts the weights assigned to each candidate keyword in the annotation based on the keyword's surrounding context. Finally, Figure 18 presents a visual representation of the experimental datasets and the annotation workload based on which Nebula is evaluated (Section 8).

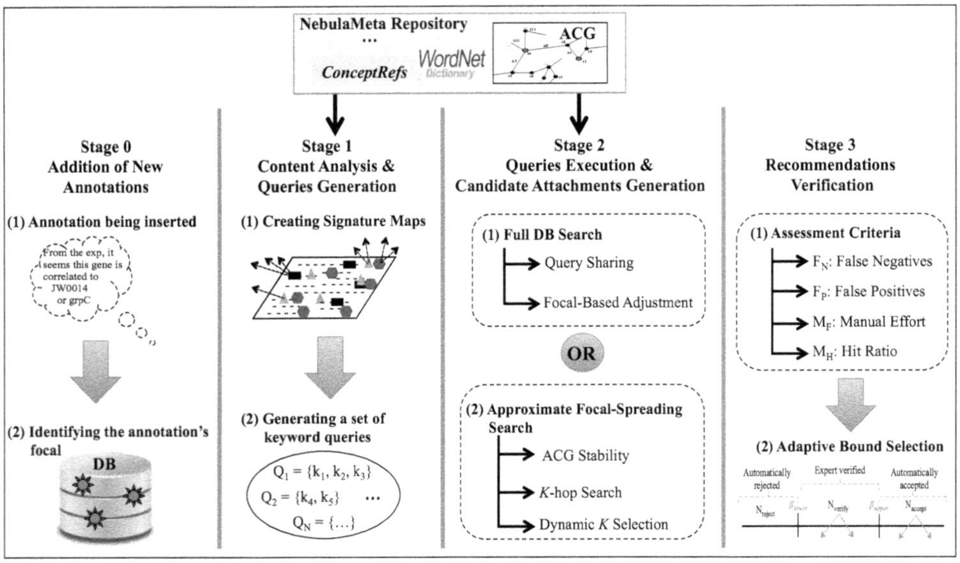

Nebula's Main Processing Stages. Nebula has three main processing stages triggered by the insertion of a new annotation (Stage 0), which are:

Stage 1: In which the annotation's content is analyzed, the metadata information (NebualMeta) is consulted, and signature maps are generated. The signature maps highlight the keyword combinations that potentially represent embedded references. Those combinations will create a pool of *keyword-search* queries.

Stage 2: In which the queries are executed to produce candidate attachments between the new annotation and other tuples in the DB. Nebual has two execution modes: (1) Full DB Search, and (2) Approximate Focal-Spreading Search. In both modes, NebulaMeta plays a key role in adjusting the confidence degree, and/or limiting the search space. The results are candidate attachments called "*verification tasks*".

Stage 3: In which the verification tasks are either automatically accepted, automatically rejected, or manually verified by experts (depending on their confidence scores). Nebula deploys adaptive algorithms to set the bounds between these three decisions. The goal is to achieve a high-quality prediction while maintaining experts' involvement to a minimal acceptable degree.

Figure 16: The Main Processing Stages of Nebula.

```
ContextBasedAdjustment()
Input:  - Context-Map
        - α = Influence range size                    // Number of words on both sides
Output: Updated Context-Map
1.  For (each word w in Context-Map) Loop
2.      w.range = Form an influence range around w of size α (both sides)
3.      For (each potential mapping w.mapping of w) Loop
4.          If (w.mapping can form with other mappings in w.range a Type-1 match) Then
5.              Increment w.mapping weight by β1% for each match
6.          Else If (w.mapping can form with other mappings in w.range a Type-2 match) Then
7.              Increment w.mapping weight by β2% for each match
8.          Else If (w.mapping can form with other mappings in w.range a Type-3 match) Then
9.              Increment w.mapping weight by β3% for each match
10.         End If
11.     End Loop
12. End Loop
```

ContextBasedAdjustment() Function (Section 5.2.2). The function loops over each word *w* in *Context-Map* and creates an influence range around *w* called "*w.range*" (Line 2). The influence range *w.range* is α words to the left and to the right of *w*. This range represents the surrounding context of *w* within which the matching patterns are most likely to be found.

For each potential mapping of *w*, referred to as *w.mapping*, the function will search within *w.range* for any of *Type-1* matching. If any can be formed, then for each match, the weight of *w.mapping* will be increased by β_1% (Lines 4-5). Otherwise, the search continues to the lower-ranked matches, i.e., *Type-2* and *Type-3* matches, as illustrated in Lines 6-10. Any match of these types will increment the weight of *w.mapping* by β_2%, or β_3%, respectively.

Figure 17: Pseudocode of the *ContextBasedAdjustment()* Function.

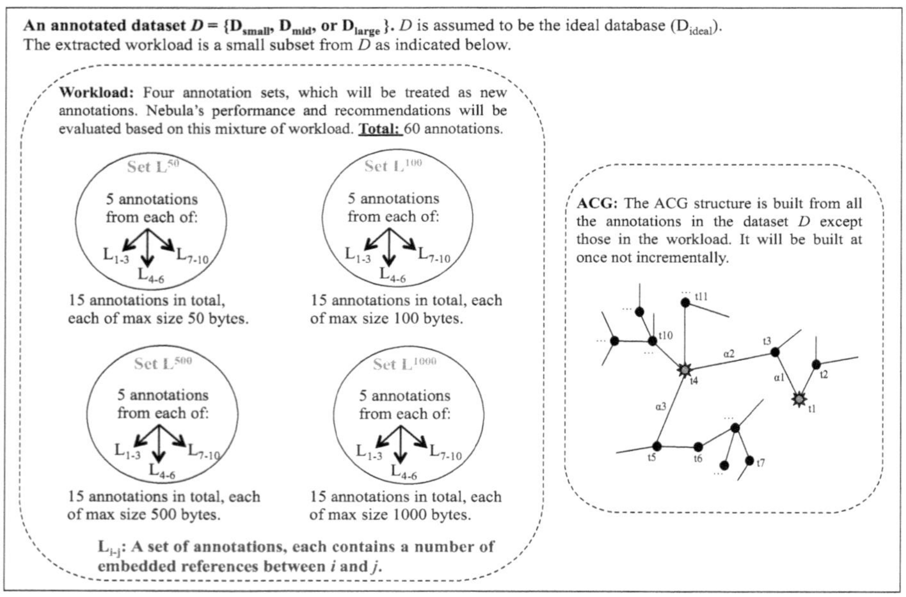

Experimental Datasets and Workload (Section 8.1). Nebula is evaluated under three datasets D_{small}, D_{mid}, D_{large}. From each dataset, a workload is extracted as illustrated in the figure. The total number of annotations within a workload is 60 divided into 4 disjoint groups: L^{50}, L^{100}, L^{500}, and L^{1000}. The annotations in each group are further selected from 3 disjoint subsets: L_{1-3}, L_{4-6}, and L_{7-10}.

The ACG structure is built from all of the annotations in the dataset (D_{small}, D_{mid}, or D_{large}) excluding the annotations selected within the workload.

Figure 18: Visual Representation of the Experimental Datasets and the Extracted Annotation Workload.

Weighted Coverage based Reviewer Assignment

Ngai Meng Kou *1 Leong Hou U *2 Nikos Mamoulis #3 Zhiguo Gong *4
*Department of Computer and Information Science, University of Macau, Macau SAR
#Department of Computer Science, University of Hong Kong, Hong Kong SAR
1yb27406@umac.mo 2ryanlhu@umac.mo 3nikos@cs.hku.hk 4fstzgg@umac.mo

ABSTRACT

Peer reviewing is a standard process for assessing the quality of submissions at academic conferences and journals. A very important task in this process is the assignment of reviewers to papers. However, achieving an appropriate assignment is not easy, because all reviewers should have similar load and the subjects of the assigned papers should be consistent with the reviewers' expertise. In this paper, we propose a generalized framework for fair reviewer assignment. We first extract the domain knowledge from the reviewers' published papers and model this knowledge as a set of topics. Then, we perform a *group assignment* of reviewers to papers, which is a generalization of the classic Reviewer Assignment Problem (RAP), considering the relevance of the papers to topics as weights. We study a special case of the problem, where reviewers are to be found for just one paper (Journal Assignment Problem) and propose an exact algorithm which is fast in practice, as opposed to brute-force solutions. For the general case of having to assign multiple papers, which is too hard to be solved exactly, we propose a greedy algorithm that achieves a 1/2-approximation ratio compared to the exact solution. This is a great improvement compared to the 1/3-approximation solution proposed in previous work for the simpler coverage-based reviewer assignment problem, where there are no weights on topics. We theoretically prove the approximation bound of our solution and experimentally show that it is superior to the current state-of-the-art.

Keywords

Paper Reviewer Assignment; Group Coverage; Stage Deepening Greedy

1. INTRODUCTION

Peer reviewing is a widely accepted process for assessing submitted papers to academic venues. One of the most challenging tasks in this process is to perform the assignment of reviewers to papers in a way that would maximize the quality of reviews. This problem is known as the *Reviewer Assignment Problem* (RAP) [4, 6, 7, 10, 14, 15, 18, 19, 21, 23, 29]. In order to improve the quality of the assignment, existing conference management systems (e.g., Conference Management Toolkit[1] and EasyChair[2]) ask reviewers to bid on their preferred papers; the assignment is then conducted based on the bids, as a classic matching problem [20]. Still, there are well-known drawbacks of this approach. For example, reviewers could be too lazy to go through the complete list of paper titles and abstracts. Alternatively, the reviewer assignment can be performed *automatically*, based on similarity models between the papers and the reviewers.

SIGMOD'15, May 31–June 4, 2015, Melbourne, Victoria, Australia.
Copyright © 2015 ACM 978-1-4503-2758-9/15/05 ...$15.00.
http://dx.doi.org/10.1145/2723372.2723727.

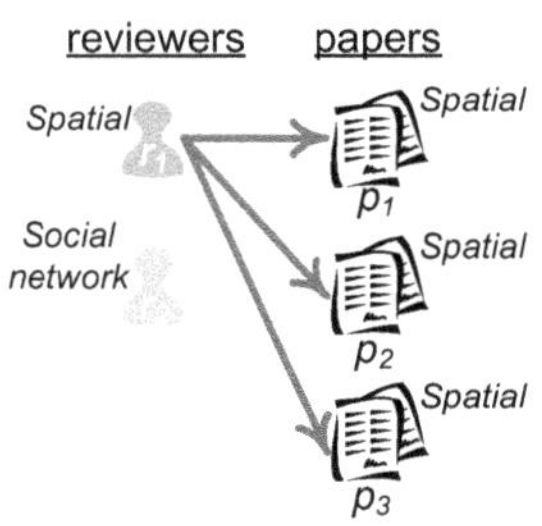

(a) Retrieval-based

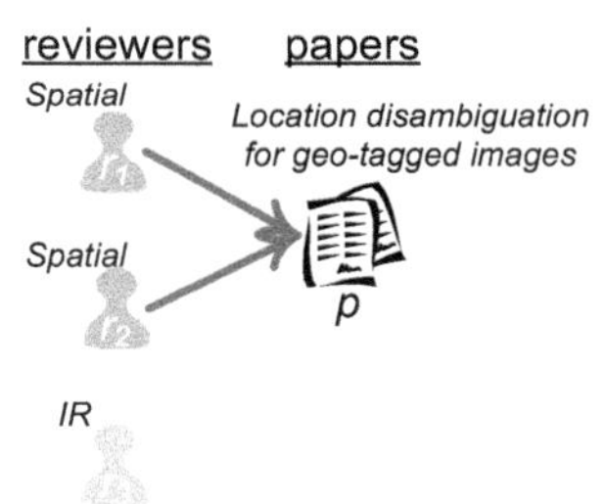

(b) Assignment-based

Figure 1: Drawbacks of previous RAP definitions

1.1 Previous Work

RAP was first regarded as a retrieval problem by Dumais and Nielsen [10]. The retrieval-based RAPs [4, 10, 19, 23] attempt to retrieve qualified reviewers for each paper based on their similarity to the paper, where similarity is measured using topic discovery models [10, 18, 21, 23], Bayesian probabilistic matrix factorization and linear regression [6], interval fuzzy ontologies [29], root mean square error of bids [7], or vector space models [4]. This category of approaches produce imbalanced assignments, where some reviewers may receive too many papers to review. An example is given in Figure 1(a), where reviewer r_1, whose research interest is mainly in spatial databases, receives 3 related papers to review but another reviewer (r_2) receives no paper by this assignment. Another line of work [6, 7, 14, 18, 21, 27, 29] regard RAP as an assignment problem subject to a maximum workload per reviewer and the number of required reviews per paper. These assignment-based RAPs aim at

[1]`http://cmt.research.microsoft.com/cmt/`
[2]`http://www.easychair.org/`

finding the best assignment (i.e., an assignment objective is optimized) subject to the aforementioned constraints. The quality of each assignment pair is individually considered; however, it may turn out that an interdisciplinary paper is reviewed by a group of reviewers with too narrow expertise. For instance, assuming that each paper is supposed to be assigned to 2 reviewers in Figure 1(b), the review quality of p may improve if one of the reviewers (e.g., r_1 or r_2) is replaced by r_3.

The drawback of assigning reviewers independently was first stated in [15], where papers and reviewers are modeled as term vectors and the expertise of a reviewer group on a term is the sum of term values of the reviewers in the group. The assignment objective is to minimize the difference between the papers and their assigned groups for each term in their vectors. A hill-climbing algorithm is proposed in [15] to find a local optimal value for this problem, without a quality guarantee; in addition, [15] does not consider how to automatically construct reviewer groups. Recently, Long et al. [22] formulated and solved RAP as a Set-coverage Group-based Reviewer Assignment Problem (SGRAP). The intuition is that the quality of the reviews on a paper should be measured based on the entire group of reviewers assigned to it. In other words, a paper is well-reviewed only if the assigned reviewers have the expertise to cover every single topic of the paper. Long et al. [22] transform the expertise of reviewers and the content of papers into sets of topics and assess the quality of assigning a group of reviewers $\{r_i, \cdots, r_j\}$ to paper p by the *set coverage ratio*, i.e., $|\mathbb{T}_{r_i} \cup \cdots \cup \mathbb{T}_{r_j} \cap \mathbb{T}_p|/|\mathbb{T}_p|$, where $\mathbb{T}_{r_i}$ is the set of topics in the expertise of r_i and $\mathbb{T}_p$ is the set of p's topics. This assessment well considers every topic of a paper in the assignment process. However, all topics of a paper are assumed to have identical importance, which is not always true in the real world. For instance, a paper could be related to many topics, but only one of them is the main subject of the paper.

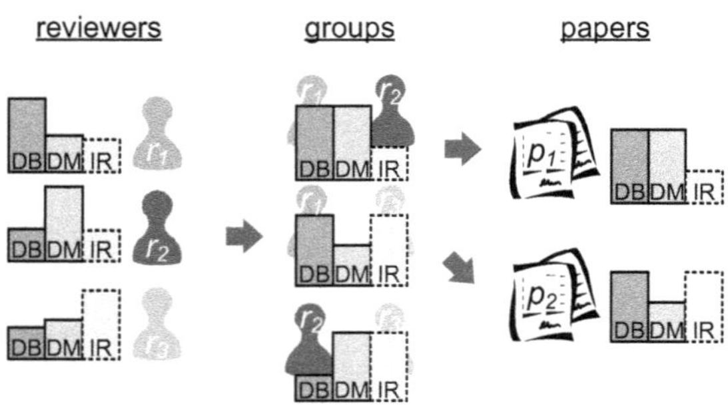

Figure 2: Weighted-coverage GRAP

1.2 Contributions

In this work, we revise the quality measure for a group of reviewers assigned to a paper from *set coverage* to *weighted coverage*. We model the expertise of reviewers and the content of papers as T-dimensional *topic vectors* (instead of topic sets). The quality of an assignment pair is estimated by considering the T-dimensional vectors of reviewers and the paper. In Figure 2, for example, the best group to review paper p_1 is $\{r_1, r_2\}$ because the topic vectors of these two reviewers, when taken together, best match the topic vector of p_1 (i.e., high relevance to DB and DM, lower relevance to IR). Our *weighted coverage* (to be defined in detail in Section 2) well addresses the topic equilibrium problem mentioned above, where the topics are no longer viewed as equally important. Based on the above, we define and solve RAP as a Weighted-coverage Group-based Reviewer Assignment Problem (WGRAP). Our contributions are as follows.

Introduction and generality of WGRAP. We introduce WGRAP as an appropriate definition of RAP that considers (i) the load balancing of reviewers to papers and (ii) the coverage of the topics of the assigned papers by the reviewers' expertise, proportionally to the importance of the paper topics. We show that all previous RAP definitions (retrieval-based RAP, assignment-based RAP, SGRAP) are special cases of WGRAP.

Journal Reviewer Assignment (JRA). As a case of WGRAP, we first study the problem of assigning a single journal paper p to a set of δ_p reviewers, chosen from a pool R of candidates. We propose an exact Branch-and-Bound Algorithm (BBA), which finds the best reviewer group based on a well-designed execution order. BBA finds the result much faster compared to a brute force method that examines all reviewer combinations, an integer linear programming approach, and a commercial constraint programming solver.

An approximation algorithm for WGRAP. The general WGRAP, where multiple papers are to be assigned to multiple reviewers, is an NP-hard problem; it is a generalization of SGRAP, the hardness of which was shown in Long et al. [22]. Since finding the exact solution for WGRAP is too expensive, we propose a polynomial-time approximation algorithm. Compared to the greedy algorithm of [22], which has 1/3 approximation ratio, our algorithm improves the approximation ratio significantly (to at least 1/2) and it is applicable to both WGRAP and SGRAP. The main idea of our approach is to divide the assignment into stages, such that exactly one reviewer is assigned to each paper at each stage (solved in PTIME as a linear assignment problem). More importantly, our approximation guarantee holds for any submodular objective function (we investigate the applicability of alternative objective functions in Appendix B).

Stochastic refinement of a WGRAP solution. We propose a stochastic process for refining the assignment computed by our approximation algorithm. In a nutshell, our approach first builds a probability model that captures the suitability of reviewers to be assigned to papers. Then, it iteratively attempts to swap assignment pairs, following the probability model, until the process converges to a solution that cannot be further improved.

Experimental evaluation. We conduct an experimental evaluation using real data from DBLP. Our results show our approximation algorithm paired with the stochastic refinement postprocessing finds an assignment of much better quality compared to previous work, within reasonable time.

The rest of this paper is organized as follows. Section 2 provides the necessary definitions, formulates WGRAP, and analyzes its relationship to previous RAP definitions. Section 3 includes our solution to JRA. In Section 4, we study the general case of WGRAP, by reviewing the greedy algorithm of [22], proposing our solution, analyzing its approximation ratio, and presenting our stochastic refinement process. Our experiments are presented in Section 5. Finally, Section 6 concludes with a discussion about future work.

2. PRELIMINARIES AND DEFINITIONS

In this section, we first define fundamental concepts, including topics, reviewer groups, and weighted coverage. Subsequently, we give the formal definition of our WGRAP and discuss how we can specialize WGRAP into three RAP definitions studied before.

2.1 Topic Coverage and Assignment Quality

As introduced in Section 1, we assume that there are T research topics (i.e., subjects) and that the expertise of reviewers and the content of papers are modeled as T-dimensional topic vectors, denoted as $\vec{r_i} = (\vec{r_i}[1], \cdots, \vec{r_i}[T])$ (for reviewer r_i) and $\vec{p_j} = (\vec{p_j}[1], \cdots, \vec{p_j}[T])$ (for paper p_j), respectively. For instance, $\vec{r_i}[1]$ refers to the relevance (i.e., expertise) of reviewer r_i to the first topic, while $\vec{p_j}[1]$ is the relevance of paper p_j to the first topic. For simplicity, we sometimes refer to $\vec{r_i}[t]$ (resp. $\vec{p_j}[t]$) as the *weight* of reviewer r_i (resp. paper p_j) on topic t. Given the publications record of r_i and the abstract of p_j, $\vec{r_i}$ and $\vec{p_j}$ can be extracted by topic modeling, e.g., Latent Dirichlet Allocation (LDA) [5]. Even though topic extraction is not the main focus of our work, it remains an important component of our framework. Thus, we will discuss its details in Section 2.4.

The topic vector of a reviewer $\vec{r}$ can be viewed as the confidence of the reviewer over different topics. Intuitively, if topic t of a paper p is well covered by an assigned reviewer r (i.e., $\vec{r}[t] \geq \vec{p}[t]$), then it is safe to assume that r is fully confident to review p on topic t. Specifically, we can measure how well a reviewer r *covers* topic t by $\min\{\vec{r}[t], \vec{p}[t]\}$. This quantity, also encapsulates the relative importance (i.e., *weight*) of t's coverage compared to other topics. For example, if a topic t' is more relevant to paper p than t is (i.e., $\vec{p}[t'] > \vec{p}[t]$), then the coverage of reviewer r on t' should be more important than the coverage of r on t. Thereby, the quality of assigning r to review p can be calculated by the *weighted coverage* of the two vectors as follows.

DEFINITION 1 (WEIGHTED COVERAGE SCORE $c(\vec{r}, \vec{p})$). *The quality of assigning $\vec{r}$ to review $\vec{p}$ is the summation of the coverage weights over different topics.*

$$c(\vec{r}, \vec{p}) = \frac{\sum_{t=1}^{T} \min\{\vec{r}[t], \vec{p}[t]\}}{\sum_{t=1}^{T} \vec{p}[t]} \qquad (1)$$

The denominator $\sum_{t=1}^{T} \vec{p}[t]$ normalizes $c(\vec{r}, \vec{p})$ to take values from 0 to 1.[3] As an example, Figure 3(a) shows the quality of assigning r to review p, calculated based on the coverage weights over three topics. Besides Definition 1, we study alternative scoring functions for the quality of a reviewer-paper assignment in Appendix B.

We now discuss how we measure the quality of assigning a *group of reviewers* $g = \{r_i, \cdots, r_j\}$ to a specific paper p.

[3] The normalization is not necessary if we already have $\sum_{t=1}^{T} \vec{p}[t] = 1$ for each paper p, i.e., the relevance of each paper to the topics is already a normalized vector. Besides, we can also assume that the reviewer vectors are normalized, i.e., $\sum_{t=1}^{T} \vec{r}[t] = 1$ for each reviewer r. Otherwise, we might allow one reviewer r_1 to dominate another reviewer r_2 with respect to expertise (i.e., r_1's expertise in each topic is greater than the corresponding expertise of r_2), which means that r_1 could be considered more qualified than r_2 in general. Regardless the situation, we keep the denominator in Eq. 1 to make the definition of weighted coverage general.

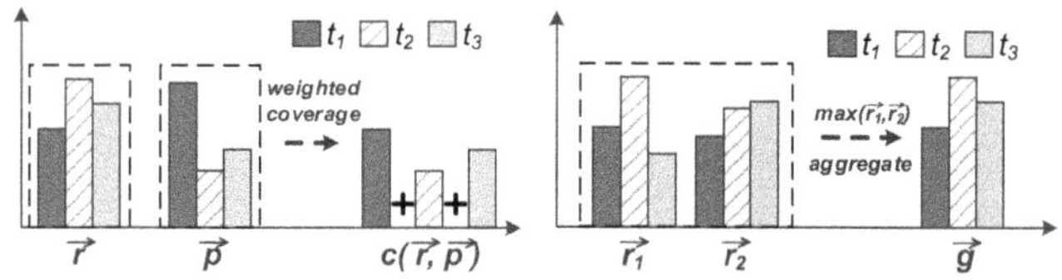

(a) Weighted coverage (b) Group topic vector

Figure 3: Weighted coverage and group topic vector

Given the topic vectors of the group (i.e., $\{\vec{r_i}, \cdots, \vec{r_j}\}$), the expertise of the reviewer group $\vec{g}$ is a vector which stores for every topic t the *maximum expertise of any reviewer in the group* in t. The rationale is that the reviewer who is the most expert in t will have the highest confidence in reviewing the aspects of the paper related to t and her opinion will most probably dominate the opinions on these aspects from other reviewers in the group. Formally,

DEFINITION 2 (EXPERTISE OF A REVIEWER GROUP). *Given* $g = \{r_i, \cdots, r_j\}$, $\vec{g} = (\max_{r \in g} \vec{r}[1], \cdots, \max_{r \in g} \vec{r}[T])$.

As an example, Figure 3(b) shows a reviewer group $g = \{r_1, r_2\}$. The expertise of g is $\vec{g} = (\vec{r_1}[1], \vec{r_1}[2], \vec{r_2}[3])$. The quality of assigning group g to review a paper p can now also be conveniently calculated using Equation 1; i.e., as $c(\vec{g}, \vec{p})$, after computing $\vec{g}$.

2.2 Weighted-coverage Group-based Reviewer Assignment Problem (WGRAP)

Without loss of generality, we assume that there are P papers (i.e., $\mathbb{P} = \{p_1, \cdots, p_P\}$) and R reviewers (i.e., $\mathbb{R} = \{r_1, \cdots, r_R\}$), where each paper should be reviewed by δ_p reviewers (group size constraint) and each reviewer should be given at most δ_r papers (reviewer workload). In addition, we assume that there are enough reviewers for the given papers, i.e., $R \cdot \delta_r \geq P \cdot \delta_p$.

The goal of our *Weighted-coverage Group-based Reviewer Assignment Problem* (WGRAP) is to find the best assignment $\mathbb{A} \subseteq \mathbb{P} \times \mathbb{R}$ such that the *objective* (i.e., the summation of the weighted coverage scores per topic) is maximized subject to the workload constraints. For the ease of discussion, we use $\mathbb{A}[x]$ to denote the assignment pair(s) of x. For instance, if $\mathbb{A} = \{(r_1, p_1), (r_2, p_1)\}$, then $\mathbb{A}[r_1] = \{(r_1, p_1)\}$ and $\mathbb{A}[p_1] = \mathbb{A}$. WGRAP is formally defined as follows:

DEFINITION 3 (WGRAP). *Given a set of papers $\mathbb{P}$ and a set of reviewers $\mathbb{R}$, WGRAP finds an assignment $\mathbb{A} \subseteq \mathbb{P} \times \mathbb{R}$, such that*

$$\begin{aligned}
&\max && \sum_{p \in \mathbb{P}} c(\vec{g}, \vec{p}) && \\
&\textit{where} && g = \{r \mid (r,p) \in \mathbb{A}[p]\} && \\
&\textit{s.t.} && |\mathbb{A}[r]| \leq \delta_r && \forall r \in \mathbb{R} \\
& && \textit{(reviewer workload)} && \\
& && |\mathbb{A}[p]| = \delta_p && \forall p \in \mathbb{P} \\
& && \textit{(group size constraint)} &&
\end{aligned}$$

In WGRAP, the assignment quality of each paper is calculated by the weighted-coverage of the assigned reviewers (cf. Definition 1); i.e., we want the assigned group of reviewers per paper to cover as much as possible every single topic of the paper. The quality of an assignment $\mathbb{A}$ is measured by the objective function of Definition 3, i.e., $\sum_{p\in\mathbb{P}} c(\vec{g}, \vec{p})$, where $g = \{r|(r,p) \in \mathbb{A}[p]\}$. We sometimes refer to this quality measure as the *coverage score* of assignment $\mathbb{A}$, simply denoted by $c(\mathbb{A})$. Table 1 summarizes the frequently used notations in this paper.

Symbol	Description	Symbol	Description
p	paper	r	reviewer
g	reviewer group	$\mathbb{T}$	set of topics
$\mathbb{P}$	set of papers	$\mathbb{R}$	set of reviewers
$\mathbb{A}$	assignment	$\mathbb{O}$	optimal assignment
δ_p	group size constraint	δ_r	reviewer workload

Table 1: Notations

2.3 Relationship to other RAPs

In this section, we briefly introduce three popular types of RAPs and discuss their relationship to our WGRAP.

Retrieval-based RAP (RRAP). This type of RAP is first proposed by Dumais and Nielsen [10]. Their model firstly suggests the top-δ_r most relevant papers to each reviewer and then each reviewer picks $\delta_r/2$ papers (out of δ_r) to review. As discussed in Section 1, RRAP may end up in imbalanced assignments, where some paper may be assigned to no reviewers. This is due to the lack of the group size constraint (i.e., the number of reviewers of a paper, δ_p) in RRAP. The formal definition of RRAP is shown as follows.

DEFINITION 4 (RRAP). *Given $\mathbb{P}$ and $\mathbb{R}$, RRAP finds an assignment $\mathbb{A} \subseteq \mathbb{P} \times \mathbb{R}$ such that*

$$\max \quad \sum_{p\in\mathbb{P}} \sum_{r\in\mathbb{A}[p]} c(\vec{r}, \vec{p})$$
$$s.t. \quad |\mathbb{A}[r]| = \delta_r \qquad \forall r \in \mathbb{R}$$

WGRAP can be reduced to RRAP by two steps, (1) removing the group size constraint and (2) revising the objective function, i.e., making $\sum_{r\in\mathbb{A}[p]} c(\vec{r}, \vec{p})$ equal to $c(\vec{g}, \vec{p})$. For the second step, we can simply extend the topic vectors from T dimensions to $R \cdot T$ dimensions such that: (i) the original topic vectors of papers are repeated R times, (ii) for the i-th reviewer, the i-th T dimensions include its original topic vector and the others are 0. This reduction can be done in polynomial time.

Assignment-based RAP (ARAP). The second type of RAP addresses the workload problem: every paper is reviewed by a certain amount of reviewers [18]. The formal definition of ARAP is as follows.

DEFINITION 5 (ARAP). *Given $\mathbb{P}$ and $\mathbb{R}$, ARAP finds an assignment $\mathbb{A} \subseteq \mathbb{P} \times \mathbb{R}$ such that*

$$\max \quad \sum_{p\in\mathbb{P}} \sum_{r\in\mathbb{A}[p]} c(\vec{r}, \vec{p})$$
$$s.t. \quad |\mathbb{A}[r]| \le \delta_r \qquad \forall r \in \mathbb{R}$$
$$|\mathbb{A}[p]| = \delta_p \qquad \forall p \in \mathbb{P}$$

Since ARAP already considers reviewer size constraint, WGRAP can be reduced to ARAP by simply revising the objective function (similarly to the reduction to RRAP).

Set-coverage GRAP (SGRAP). We omit the formal definition of SGRAP [22], since it is identical to our WGRAP except for how the coverage function $c(\vec{g}, \vec{p})$ is defined for a group of reviewers assigned to a paper. WGRAP can easily be reduced to SGRAP if we transform each topic set $\mathbb{T}$ into a binary T-dimensional topic vector. The i-th value of a topic vector (e.g., $\vec{p}[i]$) is set to 1 if the i-th topic exists in the topic set (e.g., $\mathbb{T}_p$). Otherwise, it is set to 0. This conversion makes the coverage functions of SGRAP and WGRAP become identical, i.e.,

$$c(\mathbb{T}_g, \mathbb{T}_p) = \frac{|\mathbb{T}_g \cap \mathbb{T}_p|}{|\mathbb{T}_p|} = \frac{\sum_{t=1}^{T} \min\{\vec{g}[t], \vec{p}[t]\}}{\sum_{t=1}^{T} \vec{p}[t]} = c(\vec{g}, \vec{p})$$

where $\vec{g}[t], \vec{p}[t] \in \{0,1\}$. Thus, SGRAP is a special case of WGRAP (where all scores are integral); this means that our solutions for WGRAP can be applied to SGRAP as well.

Summary. To the best of our knowledge, WGRAP is the first RAP formulation that assesses the reviewer assignment quality by a group-based objective function under weighted coverage of topics. Our evaluation approach well addresses certain drawbacks of previous approaches, including the load balancing problem (using the *group size constraint*), the diversity of reviewer groups (using a *group-based objective function*), and the topic equilibrium problem (using *weighted-coverage*).

	RRAP	ARAP	SGRAP	WGRAP
Constraint				
Group size	X	√	√	√
Objective				
Group-based	X	X	√	√
Obj. function	Weight	Weight	Set	Weight

Table 2: Comparison of different RAPs

2.4 Topic Vector Extraction

We now briefly introduce how we can extract the topic vectors (i.e., $\vec{p}$ and $\vec{r}$) from the corresponding papers and reviewers. A naïve method is to collect the vectors manually; e.g., collecting paper topics from keywords specified by the authors or asking the reviewers to declare their expertise by some check boxes. However, such information is not always available. As an example, in a journal review process, the expertise of potential reviewers is typically not declared by them in advance, or the pool of potential reviewers is dynamic. A more reasonable approach would be to extract the topic vectors of potential reviewers automatically from their publication records.

In this work, we first use the Author-Topic Model (ATM) of [25] to extract the topic set $\mathbb{T}$ and the topic vector of reviewers $\{\vec{r_1}, \cdots, \vec{r_R}\}$ based on their publication records. The topic vector of papers $\{\vec{p_1}, \cdots, \vec{p_P}\}$ is estimated by Expectation-Maximization (EM) [30] based on $\mathbb{T}$. For completeness, we show the details of our adapted ATM in Appendix A.

3. JOURNAL REVIEWER ASSIGNMENT

In this section, we study a special case of WGRAP, where only a single paper has to be reviewed (i.e., $\mathbb{P} = \{p\}$). This case finds practical application in the scenario of *Journal Reviewer Assignment* (JRA), where the editor is looking for δ_p qualified reviewers for a single submission. Thus, we can ignore the reviewer workload δ_r, since each assigned reviewer assesses the given paper just once. Formally, Definition 3 is reduced to JRA as follows:

DEFINITION 6 (JRA). *Given a journal paper p and a set of reviewers $\mathbb{R}$, the journal reviewer assignment finds an assignment $\mathbb{A} \subseteq \{p\} \times \mathbb{R}$ such that*

$$\begin{array}{ll} \max & c(\vec{g}, \vec{p}) \\ where & g = \{r|(r,p) \in \mathbb{A}[p]\} \\ s.t. & |\mathbb{A}[p]| = \delta_p \end{array}$$

The best reviewer group is one of the δ_p-combinations out of R reviewers and there are $C^R_{\delta_p}$ such combinations. The following lemma proves the NP-hardness of JRA.

LEMMA 1. *JRA is an NP-hard problem.*

PROOF. We will show that another NP-hard problem, i.e., the *maximum coverage problem* [11], can be reduced to an instance of JRA in polynomial time. Given a collection of sets $\mathbb{S} = \{s_1, s_2, ...\}$, where each set s_i is a subset of a domain set $\mathbb{D} = \{e_1, \cdots, e_n\}$, and a number k, the maximum coverage problem finds a subset $\mathbb{S}' \subseteq \mathbb{S}$ of sets such that $|\mathbb{S}'| = k$ and the number of covered elements from $\mathbb{D}$, i.e., $|\cup_{s_i \in \mathbb{S}'} s_i|$, is maximized. A special case of JRA is that the target paper p is only relevant to n topics and each topic has the same importance, i.e., $\vec{p}[t] \in \{0, 1/n\}$ and $\sum_{1 \le t \le T} \vec{p}[t] = 1$. We transform each subset $s_i \in \mathbb{S}$ to a T-dimensional vector $\vec{s_i}$, where $\vec{s_i}[e] = 1/n$ if element e is in s_i, otherwise $\vec{s_i}[e] = 0$. We also set $k = \delta_p$ (i.e., the group size constraint). All these transformations take $O(|\mathbb{S}|n)$ time. The problem now becomes to find a subset $\mathbb{S}' \subseteq \mathbb{S}$ of k collections such that $c(\vec{g}, \vec{p})$, where $g = \{s_i | s_i \in \mathbb{S}'\}$ is maximized. This problem is equivalent to the maximum coverage problem as every newly covered (missing) topic of $\mathbb{S}'$ increases (decreases) by exactly $1/n$ of the total coverage score. □

Even though JRA is NP-hard (it considers $C^R_{\delta_p}$ reviewer combinations), we can still solve it within acceptable time if R and δ_p are not very large. For example, in practice $\delta_p = 3$ and R is in the order of a few hundreds. To the best of our knowledge, Brute Force Search (BFS) (i.e., enumerating every possible reviewer group) and Integer Linear Programming (ILP) [24] can be used to compute JRA exactly. However, these two solutions do not scale well. BFS is very sensitive to R and δ_p, because it examines every possible reviewer group and ILP suffers from floating-point precision issues, when there are too many constrained functions and variables (these are proportional to R and δ_p). We develop a novel algorithm, Branch-and-Bound Algorithm (BBA), which finds the best reviewer group based on a well-designed execution order. A promising result is that BBA finds the exact solution almost in real time in practical cases. For example, BBA finds the best set of 5 reviewers out of 200 candidates within 2.2 seconds on a commodity machine while BFS and ILP take 5.1 hours and 45.6 minutes, respectively, to solve the same problem.

BBA operates on the search space of JRA (cf. Figure 4), that can be viewed as a tree structure. Each *non-root* node represents a reviewer r_i and it has up to $R - 1$ children nodes (i.e., all reviewers except r_i). The depth of the tree is determined by the group size constraint δ_p; the nodes along a path from the root to a leaf indicate one possible reviewer group. For instance, path *root* $\rightarrow r_1 \rightarrow r_3$ indicates reviewer group $\{r_1, r_3\}$.

To search for the best reviewer group, we apply the classic backtracking paradigm which partitions the search process

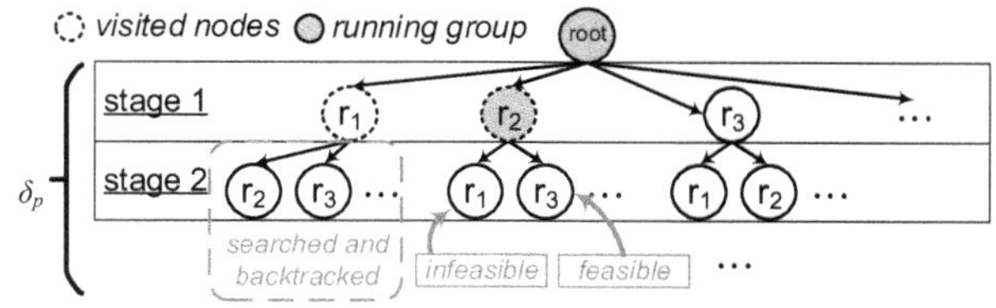

Figure 4: Search space of JRA

into δ_p stages. When the search moves from stage s to stage $s+1$, a *feasible* reviewer (see Definition 7) is inserted into the running reviewer group g. The feasibility condition ensures that every group combination is only examined at most once in the entire search process. When search reaches the last stage (i.e., stage δ_p), the coverage score of g is calculated and the best-so-far result is updated, if applicable. Search backtracks to the previous stage if there are no more feasible reviewers at the current stage.

DEFINITION 7 (FEASIBILITY OF REVIEWER). *Given a running group g and the visited information, a reviewer r is feasible only if r is not yet visited along the execution path (i.e., along the first stage to the running stage).*

In Figure 4, when examining the branches under r_2 (at stage 1), r_1 (at stage 2) is infeasible since r_1 has been visited at stage 1 already. In other words, every possible reviewer group containing r_1 has been considered as soon as r_1 has been selected at stage 1, therefore r_1 should be omitted from the subsequent processes. As another example, r_3 is still feasible since the visited information of the branches under r_1 has been reset when it backtracks to stage 1.

	t_1	t_2	t_3
$\vec{p}$	0.35	0.45	0.2
$\vec{r_1}$	0.15	0.75	0.1
$\vec{r_2}$	0.75	0.15	0.1
$\vec{r_3}$	0.1	0.35	0.55

(a) Topic vectors

SL_1	SL_2	SL_3
0.75(r_2)	0.75(r_1)	0.55(r_3)
0.15(r_1)	0.35(r_3)	0.1(r_1)
0.1(r_3)	0.15(r_2)	0.1(r_2)

(b) T-sorted lists, SL_i

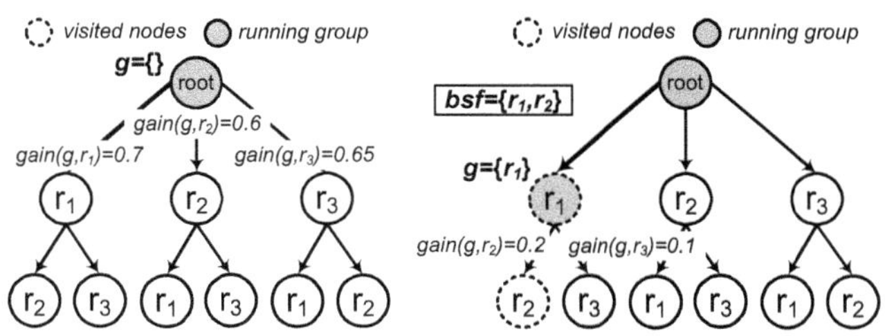

(c) Picking r_1 at stage 1 (d) Early termination at stage 2

Figure 5: Searching for the best reviewer group

To efficiently locate the best reviewer group, we need to prioritize the traversal order (*branching*) and terminate search branches that cannot lead to a better solution as early as possible (*bounding*). Given the reviewer vectors $\{\vec{r_1}, \cdots, \vec{r_R}\}$, we prepare T sorted lists where the t-th sorted list SL_t keeps the t-th values of the reviewer vectors in an descending order. An example of three reviewers and their corresponding sorted lists is shown in Figure 5(a) and 5(b), respectively.

In the following, we show how to prioritize and bound the search process by accessing the T sorted lists back-and-forth. At each stage s, we construct a set of T running cursors, $\Pi^s = \{\pi_1^s, \cdots, \pi_T^s\}$ and every cursor always points at a feasible reviewer. Initially, every cursor (e.g., π_i^1) points at the beginning of the corresponding sorted list (e.g., SL_i).

Branching. Intuitively, a reviewer r is a good candidate for the running group g if adding r into g has large *marginal gain*, which is defined as follows:

DEFINITION 8 (MARGINAL GAIN, $gain(g, r, p)$). *Given a running reviewer group g and a reviewer candidate r, the marginal gain of adding r into g is calculated by*

$$gain(g, r, p) = c(\overrightarrow{g \cup \{r\}}, \vec{p}) - c(\vec{g}, \vec{p}) \tag{2}$$

We use the running cursors to locate the best yet feasible reviewer to be considered in the branching process. More specifically, we add r into g only if r has the maximum marginal gain among the reviewers pointed by the cursors at current stage s. After having added r into g, we move *forward* every affected cursor (i.e., pointing to r) to the next *feasible reviewer* and continue to the next stage. The initial positions of the next stage cursors Π^{s+1} are cloned from Π^s since every reviewer group is necessarily examined once (cf. the feasibility condition in Definition 7). In our running example, r_1 is the first picked reviewer since its marginal gain (i.e., $gain(g, r_1, p) = c(\vec{r_1}, \vec{p}) = 0.7$) is the maximum among all three cursors (see Figure 5(c)). r_1 is marked as visited at stage 1 and we move forward the affected cursor (i.e., π_2^1) to the next feasible reviewer (i.e., $0.35(r_3)$).

Bounding. We use the running cursors to estimate the upper bound of the running group g as follows:

$$UB(g, \Pi^s) = c(\vec{ub}, \vec{p}) \tag{3}$$

where $\vec{ub}[i] = \max(\vec{g}[t_i], \pi_i^s), \forall_{1 \le i \le T}$. Equation 3 is the upper bound of g since the cursors always move forward so that every cursor always point to the best yet feasible reviewer. If the upper bound of g is no longer promising (i.e., smaller than the score of the best reviewer group found so far), then we backtrack to the previous stage and reset the visited information at the current stage.

In our running example (cf. Figure 5(d)), assume that we already have examined a reviewer group $bsf = \{r_1, r_2\}$ (e.g., $c(\vec{bsf}, \vec{p}) = 0.9$) and bsf is our best result so far. The running cursors at stage 2 point to $0.1(r_3), 0.35(r_3)$, and $0.55(r_3)$, respectively. Before examining another feasible reviewer (e.g., r_3) at stage 2, we estimate the upper bound of g by Equation 3 where $\vec{ub} = \{0.15, 0.75, 0.55\}$ and $UB(g, \Pi^2) = 0.8$. Since the upper bound of the running group $g(=\{r_1\})$ is not better than the best-so-far result, we backtrack to stage 1 and reset the visited information at stage 2 (e.g., changing the dashed line of r_2 back to solid line at stage 2).

Algorithm 1 shows a pseudocode of BBA for clarity. Search is terminated when there is no feasible cursor at stage 1 (cf. Line 5 of Algorithm 1). BBA fully exploits the sorted lists to boost the brand-and-bound process by maintaining the running cursors properly. Even though BBA does not improve the worst-case computational cost of JRA, its branching prioritization (by the marginal gain estimation) and its early termination (by the upper bound estimation) significantly reduce the computational cost in practice. The space overhead of BBA is mainly due to the sorted lists that consume $O(R \cdot T)$ space (i.e., negligible space for modern commodity machines). Note that BBA can easily be adapted to return the top-k reviewer sets (i.e., by replacing bsf by a heap structure that keeps the k best-so-far reviewer groups).

Algorithm 1 Branch-and-Bound Algorithm (BBA)

Input: paper p, reviewer set $\mathbb{R}$, reviewer group size δ_p
Output: result bsf
Algorithm $bba(p, \mathbb{R}, \delta_p)$
1: construct T sorted lists
2: initialize the running cursor set for 1st stage, Π^1
3: set running group $g \leftarrow \emptyset$ and *best-so-far* group $bsf \leftarrow \emptyset$
4: set running stage $s \leftarrow 1$
5: **while** $\exists_{\pi_i^1 \in \Pi^1} \pi_i^1 \neq nil$ **do**
6: $\quad r \leftarrow \text{argmax}_{r \in \{\pi_1^s, \cdots, \pi_T^s\}} gain(g, r, p)$ ▷ by Eq. 2
7: $\quad$ estimate $UB(g, \Pi^s)$ ▷ by Eq. 3
8: $\quad$ **if** $r = \emptyset$ or $UB(g, \Pi^s) \le c(\vec{bsf}, \vec{p})$ **then** ▷ bounding
9: $\quad\quad$ reset visited information at stage s
10: $\quad\quad$ backtrack to previous stage (i.e., $s \leftarrow s - 1$)
11: $\quad\quad$ **goto** line 5
12: $\quad g \leftarrow g \cup \{r\}$ and mark r as visited at stage s ▷ branching
13: $\quad$ **if** $|g| = \delta_p$ **then** ▷ a complete assignment is found
14: $\quad\quad$ **if** $c(\vec{g}, \vec{p}) > c(\vec{bsf}, \vec{p})$ **then** $bsf \leftarrow g$
15: $\quad\quad g \leftarrow g \backslash \{r\}$ ▷ backtracking
16: $\quad$ **else**
17: $\quad\quad$ **for** $\pi_i^s \in \{\pi_1^s, \cdots, \pi_T^s\}$ **do**
18: $\quad\quad\quad$ move π_i^s *forward* when π_i^s is infeasible
19: $\quad\quad$ set $\Pi^{s+1} \leftarrow \Pi^s$
20: $\quad\quad$ move to next stage (i.e., $s \leftarrow s + 1$)
21: **return** bsf

4. CONFERENCE REVIEWER ASSIGNMENT

In this section, we study the general WGRAP (Definition 3), which applies in a scenario of *Conference Reviewer Assignment* (CRA), where P received papers must be assigned to R program committee members. The objective is to find an assignment $\mathbb{A} \subseteq \mathbb{P} \times \mathbb{R}$ such that the assignment maximizes the topic coverage scores subject to the reviewer group and workload constraints. Compared to JRA, the number of papers increases from 1 to P, therefore the search space increases from $C_{\delta_p}^R$ to $(C_{\delta_p}^R)^P$. Such an increase makes finding the exact solution infeasible even for small problems (e.g., when $R = 100$ and $P = 100$). Thus we develop a polynomial-time approximation algorithm for CRA.

4.1 Greedy Algorithm

We first investigate the application of the approximation algorithm [22], which was proposed for SGRAP, to WGRAP. This greedy algorithm finds a solution for SGRAP with $1/3$ approximation ratio. The assignment $\mathbb{A}$ is constructed incrementally; at each iteration, the algorithm picks the feasible pair of reviewer and paper $(r, p)_{best}$ which has the largest marginal gain when added to the current $\mathbb{A}$ among all feasible pairs. The iterative process terminates only when all papers are fully assigned, i.e., $\mathbb{A}[p] = \delta_p, \forall p \in \mathbb{P}$. Formally:

$$\begin{aligned} (r, p)_{best} &= \underset{(r,p) \in \mathbb{F}}{\text{argmax}}\ gain(\mathbb{A}[p], r, p), \\ \text{where } \mathbb{F} &= \{(r, p) \in \mathbb{R} \times \mathbb{P} \mid (r, p) \notin \mathbb{A} \wedge \\ & \quad |\mathbb{A}[r]| < \delta_r \wedge |\mathbb{A}[p]| < \delta_p\} \end{aligned} \tag{4}$$

$\mathbb{F}$ indicates the set of feasible reviewer-paper pairs and $\mathbb{A}[p]$ (used in the $gain(\cdot)$ function) represents the running group of reviewers for p (i.e., reviewers already assigned to p).

The greedy algorithm needs $P \cdot \delta_p$ iterations[4] and each iteration takes $O(P \cdot R)$ time to locate a pair (i.e., evaluating the $gain$ score). We can easily reduce the cost of this step to logarithmic time if we keep the feasible pairs into a heap that organizes them in descending order of their marginal gains. This can be done because the gain function is monotonically decreasing with the size of $\mathbb{A}$. Thus, the time complexity of Greedy is $O(P\delta_p \log(PR))$.

The greedy algorithm is shown to provide an assignment with 1/3 approximation ratio for SGRAP [22]. Since SGRAP is a special case of WGRAP (cf. Section 2.3), the greedy algorithm finds at worst an 1/3-approximation solution for WGRAP.[5] The greedy algorithm simply splits the assignment process into $P \cdot \delta_p$ iterations and disregards how the selections between iterations are correlated. In the next section, we introduce a more sophisticated method that performs only δ_p iterations and significantly increases the approximation ratio up to $1 - 1/e$.

4.2 Stage Deepening Greedy Algorithm

Our intuition is to reduce the number of iterations and assign multiple pairs at each iteration. This way, we can improve the quality of the resulting assignment because we have higher flexibility in which pairs are added to $\mathbb{A}$ at each iteration. One way to apply our idea is to find the best reviewer group (i.e., δ_p reviewers) for any paper at each stage (i.e., iteration), which reduces the number of iterations to P (from $P \cdot \delta_p$). However, finding the best reviewer group for a specific paper (i.e., the JRA problem) is already NP-hard, therefore such a solution would not be a polynomial-time solution. Thus, our goal is to partition the stages such that (i) each stage requires polynomial time and (ii) the approximation ratio is guaranteed. We first discuss how we perform the assignment in δ_p stages and then analyze the approximation ratio of our method in Section 4.3.

To satisfy condition (i), we construct a sub-problem which assigns exactly one reviewer to every paper at each stage; in this way, at each stage we solve a PTIME linear assignment problem. To fulfil condition (ii), we confine the reviewer workload at each stage, i.e., every reviewer is assigned at most $\lceil \delta_r/\delta_p \rceil$ papers at each stage. The necessity of this confinement will be discussed in Section 4.3; the practical benefit is that every reviewer enters into the tail stages of the assignment process, as shown in the following example. Consider a WGRAP with 3 reviewers and 3 papers with topic vectors as in the tables below. Let $\delta_p = 2$ and $\delta_r = 2$. If we greedily assign r_1 to 2 papers (i.e., $c(\overrightarrow{r_1}, \overrightarrow{p_2}) = 0.6$ and $c(\overrightarrow{r_1}, \overrightarrow{p_3}) = 0.6$) at the first stage, then no reviewer (other than r_1) can cover t_3 at the second stage. On the other hand, the overall assignment score will be improved if we reserve one workload of r_1 for the second stage.

	t_1	t_2	t_3
$\overrightarrow{r_1}$	0.1	0.5	0.4
$\overrightarrow{r_2}$	1	0	0
$\overrightarrow{r_3}$	0	1	0

	t_1	t_2	t_3
$\overrightarrow{p_1}$	0.6	0	0.4
$\overrightarrow{p_2}$	0.5	0.5	0
$\overrightarrow{p_3}$	0.5	0.5	0

[4]if there are not enough reviewers, it needs $R \cdot \delta_r$ iterations.

[5]The proof in [22] is also applicable to WGRAP, as a greedy algorithm for the problem of maximizing a submodular function (i.e., $c(\cdot)$) over a 2-system (i.e., feasible set of assignments) achieves a 1/3-factor approximation [12].

Definition 9 (Stage-WGRAP). *Given the running stage s and previous stage results $\mathbb{A}_1, \cdots, \mathbb{A}_{s-1}$, Stage-WGRAP finds an assignment $\mathbb{A}_s$ such that*

$$\begin{array}{lll} \max & \sum_{p \in \mathbb{P}} c(\overrightarrow{g}, \overrightarrow{p}) & \\ \textit{where} & g = \{r | (r,p) \in \mathbb{A}_1[p] \cup \cdots \cup \mathbb{A}_s[p]\} & \\ s.t. & |\mathbb{A}_s[r]| \leq \lceil \delta_r/\delta_p \rceil & \forall r \in \mathbb{R} \\ & \textit{(reviewer workload)} & \\ & |\mathbb{A}_s[p]| = 1 & \forall p \in \mathbb{P} \\ & \textit{(group size constraint)} & \end{array}$$

We denote the discussed sub-problem as Stage-WGRAP and define it in Definition 9. When $s = 1$, this sub-problem is clearly a linear assignment problem (cf. Definition 5), since each group includes only a single reviewer at the first stage.

Lemma 2. *Stage-WGRAP can be computed incrementally from stage 1 to s in polynomial time.*

Proof. So far we know that $\mathbb{A}_1$ can be computed in polynomial time. Given $\mathbb{A}_1$, the objective function at stage 2 can be rewritten as:

$$\begin{aligned} \sum_{p \in \mathbb{P}} c(\overrightarrow{g}, \overrightarrow{p}) &= \sum_{p \in \mathbb{P}} c(\overrightarrow{\mathbb{A}_1[p] \cup \mathbb{A}_2[p]}, \overrightarrow{p}) \\ &= \sum_{p \in \mathbb{P}} c(\overrightarrow{\mathbb{A}_1[p]}, \overrightarrow{p}) + \sum_{p \in \mathbb{P}} gain(\mathbb{A}_1[p], \mathbb{A}_2[p], p) \end{aligned}$$

As $c(\overrightarrow{\mathbb{A}_1[p]}, \overrightarrow{p})$ is fixed at stage 1 already, our objective is to find $\mathbb{A}_2$ such that the marginal gain $\sum_{p \in \mathbb{P}} gain(\mathbb{A}_1[p], \mathbb{A}_2[p], p)$ of the assignment is maximized. This is obviously another linear assignment problem. By simple induction, we can compute Stage-WGRAP incrementally from stage 1 to s in polynomial time, i.e.,

$$\begin{aligned} \sum_{p \in \mathbb{P}} c(\overrightarrow{g}, \overrightarrow{p}) &= \sum_{p \in \mathbb{P}} c(\overrightarrow{\mathbb{A}_1[p] \cup \cdots \cup \mathbb{A}_s[p]}, \overrightarrow{p}) \\ &= \sum_{p \in \mathbb{P}} c(\overrightarrow{\mathbb{A}_1[p] \cup \cdots \cup \mathbb{A}_{s-1}[p]}, \overrightarrow{p}) \\ &\quad + \sum_{p \in \mathbb{P}} gain(\mathbb{A}_1[p] \cup \cdots \cup \mathbb{A}_{s-1}[p], \mathbb{A}_s[p], p) \end{aligned} \tag{5}$$

□

Figure 6 illustrates WGRAP and Stage-WGRAP. Algorithm 2 is a pseudocode for our Stage Deepening Greedy Algorithm (SDGA). At each stage, we can apply a classic linear assignment algorithm (e.g., Hungarian algorithm [20], Minimum-cost flow assignment [3]) to compute the assignment in polynomial time. For instance, the Hungarian algorithm takes $O((\max\{P, R\})^3)$ to compute a linear assignment; therefore, the time complexity of SDGA using the Hungarian algorithm is $O(\delta_p(\max\{P, R\})^3)$ and the space requirement is $O((\max\{P, R\})^2)$. Both time and space complexities are acceptable (for commodity machines) as P and R are in the order of a few hundreds (or thousands) in academic conferences.

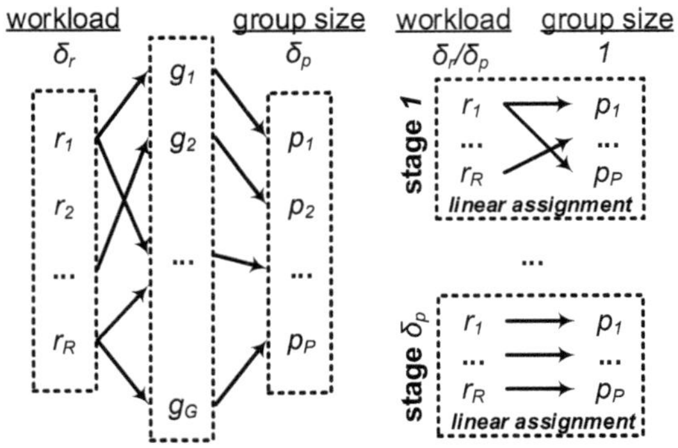

(a) WGRAP (b) Stage-WGRAP

Figure 6: WGRAP and Stage-WGRAP

Algorithm 2 Stage Deepening Greedy Algorithm

Input: paper set $\mathbb{P}$, reviewer set $\mathbb{R}$, workload constraint δ_r, group size constraint δ_p
Output: assignment $\mathbb{A}$
Algorithm $SDGA(\mathbb{P}, \mathbb{R}, \delta_r, \delta_p)$
1: **for** $s \leftarrow 1$ to δ_p **do**
2: $\mathbb{A}_s \leftarrow$ *Stage-WGRAP*$(\{\mathbb{A}_1, \cdots, \mathbb{A}_{s-1}\}, \mathbb{P}, \mathbb{R})$ ▷ by Eq. 5
3: **return** $\mathbb{A}_1 \cup \cdots \cup \mathbb{A}_{\delta_p}$

4.3 Approximation Ratio of SDGA

In this section, we show that SDGA provides a solution of WGRAP with an approximation ratio $(1-1/e)$ (when δ_r is divisible by δ_p) and $1/2$ (otherwise).

4.3.1 Integral cases: δ_r/δ_p is an integer

Optimal assignment, $\mathbb{O}$. We first introduce some notations that are used throughout this section. For any WGRAP, we denote by $\mathbb{O}$ its optimal assignment. In the following, we show how we can split $\mathbb{O}$ into δ_p isolated sets, $\{\mathbb{O}_1, \cdots, \mathbb{O}_{\delta_p}\}$, such that $\mathbb{O} = \mathbb{O}_1 \cup \cdots \cup \mathbb{O}_{\delta_p}$, $\mathbb{O}_i \cap \mathbb{O}_j = \emptyset, \forall 1 \le i < j \le \delta_p$, and for every stage s,

$$|\mathbb{O}_s[r]| \le \lceil \delta_r/\delta_p \rceil, \forall r \in \mathbb{R}, \text{ and } |\mathbb{O}_s[p]| = 1, \forall p \in \mathbb{P} \quad (6)$$

This partitioning can be done in $O(|\mathbb{O}|^2)$ time in a nested loops fashion. First, we arbitrarily divide the reviewer-paper pairs in $\mathbb{O}$ into disjoint sets $\mathbb{O}_1, \cdots, \mathbb{O}_{\delta_p}$. Then, the outer loop scans every assignment pair from $\mathbb{O}_1, \cdots, \mathbb{O}_{\delta_p}$; if the current pair (e.g., in $\mathbb{O}_s$) violates the constraints of Equation 6, an inner loop is run to the partitions (e.g., $\mathbb{O}_{s+1}, \cdots, \mathbb{O}_{\delta_p}, \mathbb{O}_1, \cdots, \mathbb{O}_{s-1}$) to swap the pair with one that is valid.

Stage marginal gain and assignment gap. For the ease of our discussion, we use $c(\mathbb{O})$ to denote the *coverage score* (i.e., quality) of an assignment $\mathbb{O}$, i.e., $c(\mathbb{O}) = \sum_{p \in \mathbb{P}} c(\vec{g}, \vec{p})$ where $g = \{r | (r,p) \in \mathbb{O}[p]\}$ and we use $\mathbb{O}_{1\cdots s}$ to denote the union set of $\mathbb{O}_1 \cup \cdots \cup \mathbb{O}_s$.

We define the stage marginal gain of the SDGA assignment at the running stage s as

$$\Delta(\mathbb{A}, s) = c(\mathbb{A}_{1\cdots s}) - c(\mathbb{A}_{1\cdots s-1}) \quad (7)$$

and the *assignment gap* (i.e., the difference) between the optimal score and the running SDGA score (from stage 1 to $s-1$) as

$$gap(\mathbb{O}, \mathbb{A}, s) = c(\mathbb{O}) - c(\mathbb{A}_{1\cdots s-1}) \quad (8)$$

To show the approximation ratio, we first show that the marginal gain of SDGA at stage s is always larger than the $1/\delta_p$-assignment gap. This is a commonly used step in showing the approximation ratio of maximum coverage problems [11].

LEMMA 3. $\Delta(\mathbb{A}, s) \ge gap(\mathbb{O}, \mathbb{A}, s)/\delta_p$

PROOF. As the coverage score is always positive, we begin with the fact that the coverage score becomes higher when we have a larger assignment, i.e.,

$$\begin{aligned} c(\mathbb{O}) \le & c(\mathbb{A}_{1\cdots s-1} \cup \mathbb{O}) \\ gap(\mathbb{O}, \mathbb{A}, s) \le & c(\mathbb{A}_{1\cdots s-1} \cup \mathbb{O}_{1\cdots\delta_p}) - c(\mathbb{A}_{1\cdots s-1}) \\ = & c(\mathbb{A}_{1\cdots s-1} \cup \mathbb{O}_1) - c(\mathbb{A}_{1\cdots s-1}) + \\ & c(\mathbb{A}_{1\cdots s-1} \cup \mathbb{O}_{1\cdots 2}) - c(\mathbb{A}_{1\cdots s-1} \cup \mathbb{O}_1) + \\ & \cdots + \\ & c(\mathbb{A}_{1\cdots s-1} \cup \mathbb{O}_{1\cdots\delta_p}) - c(\mathbb{A}_{1\cdots s-1} \cup \mathbb{O}_{1\cdots\delta_p-1}) \end{aligned}$$

where each term $c(\mathbb{A}_{1\cdots s-1} \cup \mathbb{O}_{1\cdots i}) - c(\mathbb{A}_{1\cdots s-1} \cup \mathbb{O}_{1\cdots i-1})$ indicates the marginal gain of adding $\mathbb{O}_i$ into the set $\mathbb{A}_{1\cdots s-1} \cup \mathbb{O}_{1\cdots i-1}$. Accordingly, there must exist an $\mathbb{O}_i$ such that the marginal gain is larger than $gap(\mathbb{O}, \mathbb{A}, s)/\delta_p$, i.e.,

$$c(\mathbb{A}_{1\cdots s-1} \cup \mathbb{O}_{1\cdots i}) - c(\mathbb{A}_{1\cdots s-1} \cup \mathbb{O}_{1\cdots i-1}) \ge gap(\mathbb{O}, \mathbb{A}, s)/\delta_p$$

Since $c(\cdot)$ is a submodular function[6], $c(\mathbb{A}_{1\cdots s-1} \cup \mathbb{O}_i) - c(\mathbb{A}_{1\cdots s-1}) \ge c(\mathbb{A}_{1\cdots s-1} \cup \mathbb{O}_{1\cdots i}) - c(\mathbb{A}_{1\cdots s-1} \cup \mathbb{O}_{1\cdots i-1})$. Thus,

$$c(\mathbb{A}_{1\cdots s-1} \cup \mathbb{O}_i) - c(\mathbb{A}_{1\cdots s-1}) \ge gap(\mathbb{O}, \mathbb{A}, s)/\delta_p$$

What remains is to show that $c(\mathbb{A}_{1\cdots s-1} \cup \mathbb{A}_s) \ge c(\mathbb{A}_{1\cdots s-1} \cup \mathbb{O}_i)$. This inequality is true since (i) we always find the optimal assignment at each stage independently and (ii) the stages are equally partitioned (i.e., workload=δ_r/δ_p) so that $\mathbb{A}_s$ and $\mathbb{O}_i$ always share the same sets of reviewers and papers. □

THEOREM 1. *SDGA is a $(1-1/e)$-approximation algorithm for WGRAP if δ_r is divisible by δ_p.*

PROOF.

$$\begin{aligned} & c(\mathbb{O}) - c(\mathbb{A}_{1\cdots\delta_p}) \\ = & c(\mathbb{O}) - c(\mathbb{A}_{1\cdots\delta_p-1}) - \Delta(\mathbb{A}, \delta_p) && \text{(by Eq. 7)} \\ = & gap(\mathbb{O}, \mathbb{A}, \delta_p) - \Delta(\mathbb{A}, \delta_p) && \text{(by Eq. 8)} \\ \le & gap(\mathbb{O}, \mathbb{A}, \delta_p)(1 - 1/\delta_p) && \text{(by Lemma 3)} \\ \le & gap(\mathbb{O}, \mathbb{A}, \delta_p - 1)(1 - 1/\delta_p)^2 && \text{(Eq.7, 8 and Lemma 3)} \\ \le & \cdots \\ \le & (1 - 1/\delta_p)^{\delta_p} c(\mathbb{O}) && \text{(after } \delta_p \text{ iterations)} \\ \le & (1/e) c(\mathbb{O}) \\ \therefore\ & c(\mathbb{A}_{1\cdots\delta_p}) \ge (1 - 1/e) c(\mathbb{O}) \end{aligned}$$

□

4.3.2 General cases: δ_r/δ_p is a real number

$\mathbb{O}$ cannot be split into equal sets $\{\mathbb{O}_1, \cdots, \mathbb{O}_{\delta_p}\}$ if δ_r is not divisible by δ_p. As SDGA computes the approximate assignment stage by stage, for the first $\delta_p - 1$ stages, the claim of Lemma 3 is satisfied. Thereby, we can derive the

[6]For the sake of readability, this is shown in Appendix B.

following inequality from the proof of Theorem 1, by simply ignoring the contribution at the last stage:

$$c(\mathbb{O}) - c(\mathbb{A}_{1\cdots\delta_p}) \leq (1 - 1/\delta_p)^{\delta_p - 1} c(\mathbb{O})$$

Thus, the approximation ratio is at least $1 - (1 - 1/\delta_p)^{\delta_p - 1}$. We conclude the approximation ratio of SDGA in Theorem 2.

THEOREM 2. *SDGA is a 1/2-approximation algorithm for WGRAP.*

PROOF. Trivial. $1 - (1 - 1/\delta_p)^{\delta_p - 1}$ is monotonically increasing to δ_p. When $\delta_p \in \mathcal{I}$ and $\delta_p \geq 2$, the smallest value of this function is 1/2. □

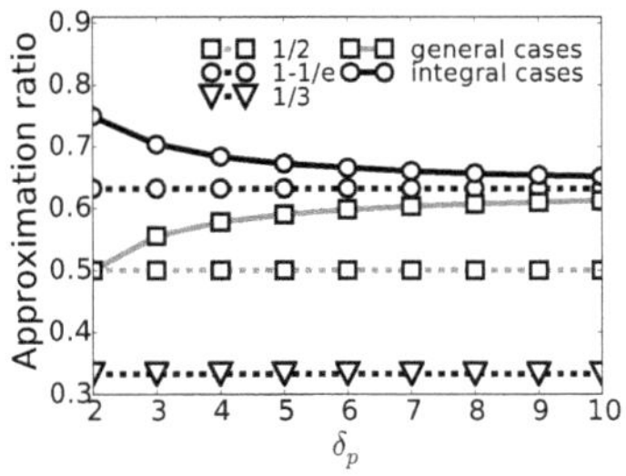

Figure 7: The effect of δ_p

As the approximation ratio of both integral (i.e., $1 - (1 - 1/\delta_p)^{\delta_p}$) and general cases (i.e., $1 - (1 - 1/\delta_p)^{\delta_p - 1}$) is sensitive to δ_p, we plot the ratio according to the value of δ_p in Figure 7 for clarity. In general cases, the approximation ratio increases to 5/9 for $\delta_p = 3$ (e.g., a typical setting in major database conferences) and to 0.5904 for $\delta_p = 5$ (e.g., a setting used in some IR conferences).

Supporting Conflicts of Interest (COIs). Our approximation algorithm can also seamlessly support COIs with the same approximation guarantee. The reason is that for any pair (r, p), which is a COI, the pair must not appear any stage of $\mathbb{O}_i$ and $\mathbb{A}_i$. Thus, $\mathbb{O}_i$ and $\mathbb{A}_i$ still share the same workload of reviewers and papers.

4.4 Stochastic Refinement

The approximate result $\mathbb{A}$ of SDGA can be further improved by postprocessing. *Local search* [17] is a widely used postprocessing technique for approximation algorithms. In our context, local search attempts to swap two or multiple assignment pairs such that the assignment quality (i.e., coverage score) gets improved. The search terminates when the improvement becomes not obvious (i.e., convergence) or the search time exceeds a pre-defined threshold.

However, a simple application of local search is not expected to be effective for WGRAP since the search space is huge, i.e., $O((C^R_{\delta_p})^P)$, even for small data instances. In such a huge space, local search is not likely to find a good result by only considering local information, e.g., greedily swapping two pairs (or a short chain of pairs) to improve the coverage score. In this section, we propose an effective refinement method, which swaps pairs based on a stochastic process.

Assume that the probability $\mathcal{P}(r|p)$ of the assignment pair (r, p) to be in the optimal assignment $\mathbb{O}$ can be estimated

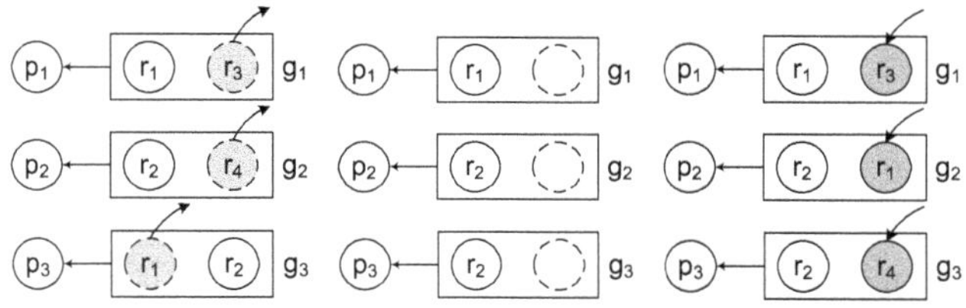

(a) $\mathcal{P}$-based removal (b) Available slots (c) stage-WGRAP

Figure 8: An illustration of stochastic refinement

(how to estimate this will be discussed shortly). Our idea is to try the replacement of some pairs from $\mathbb{A}$ according to this probability. More specifically, we attempt to remove pairs (r, p) by a stochastic process (i.e., (r, p) has high chance to be removed when $\mathcal{P}(r|p)$ is low) and then add back pairs for papers with less reviewers than δ_p. In order to make this process systematic, we only remove one reviewer from each paper; this way, the result can be completed by a linear assignment (i.e., similarly to the process at the last stage of SDGA). The basic idea of the stochastic refinement is illustrated in Figure 8. In our approach, we iteratively apply stochastic refinement on the result of SDGA, until the process converges: if the assignment result does not improve in the last ω refinement rounds, then we assume that further refinement is not likely to improve the quality, therefore we terminate the process.

What remains is to estimate the probability $\mathcal{P}(r|p)$ of reviewer r correctly being assigned to paper p. A simple approach would be to consider the probabilities of all reviewers identical, i.e., $\mathcal{P}(r|p) = 1/R$. This uniformity assumption simply disregards the expertise of a reviewer to a paper. Thus, we consider a more data oriented approach which estimates the probability based on the coverage score of reviewers for each paper. The estimation can be done in $O(PR)$.

Assume that for each paper p, we have the coverage score of all reviewers (Definition 1). A reviewer r is more likely assigned to a paper p in $\mathbb{O}$ if $c(\vec{r}, \vec{p})$ is high. However, if r has high coverage score for many papers, then we should lower r's probability to be assigned to each of those papers.[7] Accordingly, we define the probability of reviewer r to be correctly assigned to paper p as follows:

$$\mathcal{P}(r|p) \propto c(\vec{r}, \vec{p}) / \sum_{p' \in \mathbb{P}} c(\vec{r}, \vec{p}'), \tag{9}$$

where the numerator indicates how good (r, p) is and the denominator penalizes reviewers that have high coverage scores in many papers.

Equation 9 models the probability used by our stochastic refinement process to remove assignment pairs from $\mathbb{A}$. After running several refinement iterations, the effect of the probabilities degrades dramatically since the process may get stuck in a local maximum. Thereby, we slightly modify Equation 9 to reflect this by an exponential decay function as follows:

$$\mathcal{P}(r|p) \propto \max\{1/R, e^{-\lambda I} \cdot c(\vec{r}, \vec{p}) / \sum_{p' \in \mathbb{P}} c(\vec{r}, \vec{p}')\} \tag{10}$$

[7]This shares the same intuition as the TF-IDF model in IR.

where I indicates the number of refinement iterations run so far. We use $1/R$ as a constant so that every reviewer has a chance to be involved into the refinement process. We summarize our stochastic refinement process in Algorithm 3.

Algorithm 3 Stochastic Refinement Algorithm

Input: assignment $\mathbb{A}$ (from SDGA), papers $\mathbb{P}$, reviewers $\mathbb{R}$, workload δ_r, group size δ_p
Output: refined assignment $\mathbb{A}$
Algorithm $SRA(\mathbb{A}, \mathbb{P}, \mathbb{R}, \delta_p, \delta_r)$
for all $p \in \mathbb{P}$ **do**
  for all $r \in \mathbb{R}$ **do** computes $c(\vec{r}, \vec{p})$
while $c(\mathbb{A})$ does not converge **do**
  for all $(r, p) \in \mathbb{A}$ **do**
    computes $\mathcal{P}(r|p)$ by Eq. 10
  for all $p \in \mathbb{P}$ **do**
    removes a reviewer r from $\mathbb{A}[p]$ based on $1 - \mathcal{P}(r|p)$
  $\mathbb{A}_s \leftarrow$ *Stage-WGRAP*$(\mathbb{A}, \mathbb{P}, \mathbb{R})$
  $\mathbb{A} \leftarrow \mathbb{A} \bigcup \mathbb{A}_s$
return $\mathbb{A}$

5. EXPERIMENTS

	Data Mining	Databases	Theory
Venues	SIGKDD'08,'09 ICDM'08,'09 SDM'08,'09 CIKM'08,'09	SIGMOD'08,'09 VLDB'08,'09 ICDE'08,'09 PODS'08,'09	STOC'08,'09 FOCS'08,'09 SODA'08,'09
#Papers	545, 648	617, 513	281, 226
Reviewers	SIGKDD'08,'09	SIGMOD'08,'09	STOC'08,'09
#Reviewers	203, 145	105, 90	228, 222

Table 3: Data used in the evaluation

To evaluate our methods, we conducted experiments using academic publications in three research areas (Data Mining, Databases and Theory) over two years (2008 and 2009). We obtained the data from [26], since in this dataset the paper abstracts are available.[8] As set of reviewers, we take the program committee list from one venue of the corresponding area (e.g., the PC of SIGMOD 2008 is used to simulate the reviewers of the Databases area for year 2008). To extract the topic vectors of reviewers (cf. Section 2.4 and Appendix A), we collect the abstracts of their publication records from 2000 to 2009. We set the number of topics T to 30 (treated as a constant in this work). As we do not have records about the submitted papers at a conference, we simulate an artificial conference by taking the publications from 3 to 4 similar venues of the same year as the submitted papers (e.g., the submissions for Databases in 2008 are all considered to be all published papers in 2008 in SIGMOD, VLDB, ICDE, and PODS). The number of submitted papers and the set of reviewers for each area and year are summarized in Table 3.

All methods were implemented in C++, complied using VC2010, and the experiments were performed on a machine equipped with Intel Core 4-Cores (8-Threads) i7-2600 3.4GHz and 3.17GB main memory. The machine was running Windows 7 Enterprise 32bit.

[8]Abstracts are used in the process of extracting the topic vectors. See Section 2.4 and Appendix A for details.

5.1 Journal Reviewer Assignment

We first evaluate the efficiency of our Branch-and-Bound Algorithm (BBA) for JRA. We compare BBA with two competitors, Brute Force Search (BFS) and Integer Linear Programming (ILP). We use *lp_solve* [2] to solve ILP which is a C++ library based on the revised simplex method. In this section, we only evaluate the effect of δ_p (i.e., reviewer group size) and R (i.e., number of reviewer candidates) since the search space is only sensitive to the depth (i.e., δ_p) and the fan-out (i.e., R) of the tree. By default, the pool of candidate reviewers $\mathbb{R}$ includes all authors who published at least 3 papers in any of the three areas in 2005-2009 (a total of 1002 authors). In each experiment, we vary a single parameter, while setting the others to specific values. To evaluate the effect of R, we randomly select R reviewers candidates from the default pool $\mathbb{R}$. We report the average response time of all methods on 20 papers (i.e., p is randomly selected from the three areas).

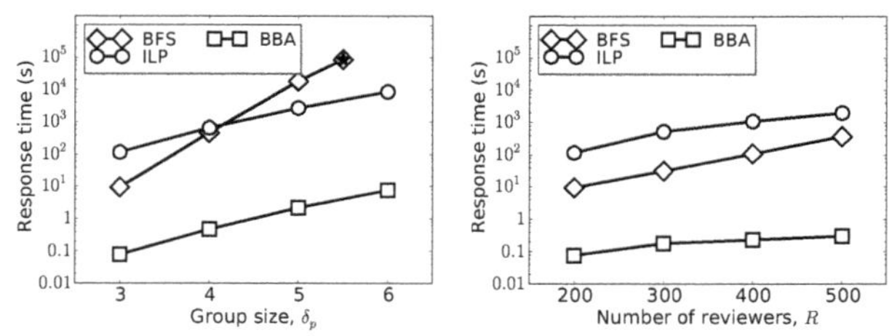

(a) Effect of δ_p ($R = 200$) (b) Effect of R ($\delta_p = 3$)

Figure 9: Scalability evaluation of JRA

Figure 9(a) shows the response time of the methods as a function of group size δ_p, after setting R to 200. ILP and BBA are less sensitive to δ_p due to the effectiveness of the branching techniques (i.e., executing promising branches first). BFS cannot finish within 24 hours and ILP takes 2.4 hours to compute the result when $\delta_p = 6$, while BBA only takes 7.7 seconds to locate the optimal reviewer group. BBA is at least two orders of magnitude faster than ILP and BF.

Figure 9(b) shows the response time of the methods as a function of reviewer size R, after setting δ_p to 3. All methods are less sensitive to R than δ_p. Again, our method (BBA) is less sensitive to R than the other two methods due to the effect of branching and bounding. When $R = 500$, BBA is 1,252 and 6,661 times faster than BFS and ILP, respectively. For R=1,000 (not shown in Figure 9(b)), BBA is just 2.1 times slower (0.64 s) than BBA for $R = 500$ (0.3 s) while BFS and ILP are 33.9 and 3.4 times slower than their respective runs for $R = 500$. For completeness, we put two additional scalability experiments (i.e., changing the default value of R to 300 and of δ_p to 4) in Appendix C.

As JRA can be viewed as a general constraint programming problem [9], we also attempted to solve JRA by a commercial CP solver, IBM ILOG CPLEX Optimizer 12.6 (CPLEX) [8]. For a small problem instance (with $R = 30$ and $\delta_p = 3$), CPLEX takes 14.35 s to find the optimal assignment and uses 90 ms to return the first feasible assignment group. Our method (BBA) takes only 4 ms to return the optimal assignment. To our understanding, typical constraint programming techniques are not favorable to the group assignment problem due to the lack of a tight upper bound (cf. Equation 3).

5.2 Conference Reviewer Assignment

In the next set of experiments, we simulate the assignment process of two conferences (in the Databases and Data Mining areas of 2008)[9], for which the statistics (e.g., R and P) can be found in Table 3. We compare our proposed techniques, SDGA, and SDGA with stochastic refinement (denoted by SDGA-SRA), to other competitors, including Stable Matching (SM) [13] (i.e., a widely accepted approach in resource allocation problems), ILP (i.e., the objective is not a group coverage function), Greedy [22], and Best Reviewer Group Greedy (BRGG) (i.e., at each iteration, we find the best pair of group and paper (g, p) instead of best reviewer and paper (r, p), a method discussed in the beginning of Section 4.2). Regarding SM and ILP, they do not consider the quality of each assignment group at its entirety so that an interdisciplinary paper may be reviewed by a group of reviewers with too narrow expertise. Still, we include them in the experiments, for the sake of completeness. For SDGA-SRA, we set the convergence threshold $\omega = 10$. We also set the reviewer workload δ_r to the minimum possible value (i.e., $\delta_r = \lceil P \cdot \delta_p / R \rceil$). This setting is commonly used in the real world as the program chair would like to minimize the workload of each reviewer and make the assignment as balanced as possible. Moreover, this setting makes the problem more challenging as every reviewer must be involved in the assignment process.

	SM	ILP	BRGG	Greedy	SDGA	SDGA-SRA
DB ($\delta = 3$)	0.1	7.6	11.6	0.1	5.9	46.3
DB ($\delta = 5$)	0.1	8.7	15.5	0.2	9.5	48.8
DM ($\delta = 3$)	0.1	16.0	30.2	0.3	5.5	44.3
DM ($\delta = 5$)	0.1	17.3	21.4	0.3	9.1	47.7

Table 4: Response time (s) of approximate methods

Even though the response time is not the main focus when evaluating approximation algorithms, it remains a significant performance factor in practice. We report the response time of all tested methods in Table 4. As expected, SDGA and SDGA-SRA are more costly than Greedy, due to the fact that these methods examine a larger part of the search space. Still, the response time, e.g., 5.9 s (SDGA) and 46.3 s (SDGA-SRA), is reasonable as the assignment is only computed once for a conference.

Optimality ratio. A reasonable approach to evaluate the quality of each assignment $\mathbb{A}$ is to compute its *approximation ratio* $c(\mathbb{A})/c(\mathbb{O})$ to the optimal assignment $\mathbb{O}$. However, computing $\mathbb{O}$ may take very long time even for small instances, due to the hardness of the problem. Instead, we compute the *optimality ratio* $c(\mathbb{A})/c(\mathbb{A}_\mathbb{I})$ of $\mathbb{A}$ to an *ideal assignment* $\mathbb{A}_\mathbb{I}$. To compute $\mathbb{A}_\mathbb{I}$, for each paper, we greedily assign to each paper the best set of δ_p reviewers, disregarding their workloads. $\mathbb{A}_\mathbb{I}$ may violate the constraint that each reviewer is assigned to at most δ_r, therefore, in general, $c(\mathbb{A}_\mathbb{I}) > c(\mathbb{O})$. Hence, $c(\mathbb{A})/c(\mathbb{A}_\mathbb{I})$ is a lower bound of $c(\mathbb{A})/c(\mathbb{O})$.

Figure 10 shows the optimality ratio of the methods as a function of reviewer group size δ_p. Although SDGA outperforms the simple methods SM, ILP and BRGG by a visible margin, SDGA performs similarly to Greedy. This is not

[9] As the results for different areas are similar, we moved the simulation for Data Mining/Database areas of 2009 and Theory area for 2008/2009 to Appendix C.

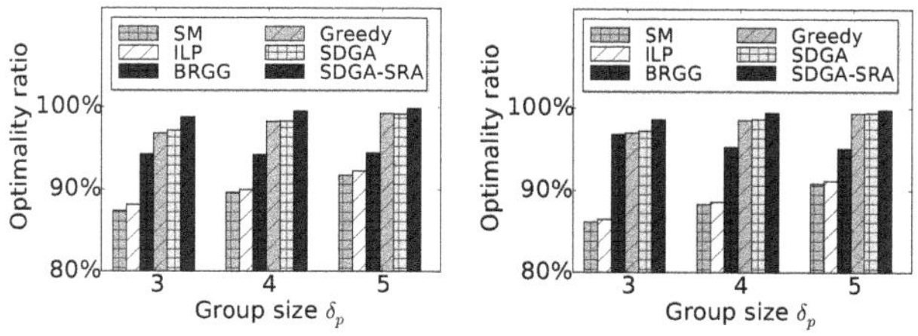

(a) Databases (b) Data Mining

Figure 10: Optimality ratio

surprising, as Greedy is shown to provide good results in many NP-hard problems in practice. Still, in the majority of our tests (one exception can be found in Databases when $\delta_p = 5$), the optimality ratio of SDGA is better than that of Greedy due to the stage deepening technique. Given its stronger approximation guarantee and the better practical performance, we recommend SDGA as the best approach for WGRAP. In addition, after applying our stochastic refinement (SDGA-SRA), the optimality ratio becomes very close to 1, consistently outperforming the ratio of Greedy (from 0.39% for $\delta_p = 5$ on Data Mining to 1.91% for $\delta_p = 3$ on Databases). A substantial amount of papers get better coverage scores; for example, 389 (out of 617) papers, for $\delta_p = 3$ on Databases.

Superiority ratio. Next we investigate the assignment quality of each paper by a *superiority ratio* metric. Given two approximate result $\mathbb{A}_X$ and $\mathbb{A}_Y$, the ratio of X over Y is calculated as

$$ratio(X, Y) = \mid \{p \in \mathbb{P} | c(\overrightarrow{\mathbb{A}_X[p]}, \overrightarrow{p}) \geq c(\overrightarrow{\mathbb{A}_Y[p]}, \overrightarrow{p})\} \mid / \ P,$$

where the numerator indicates the number of papers, which get better or equal coverage score in $\mathbb{A}_X$ than $\mathbb{A}_Y$. The superiority ratio is an important quality factor, as it shows how many papers will get an assignment of better quality by the approximate solutions.

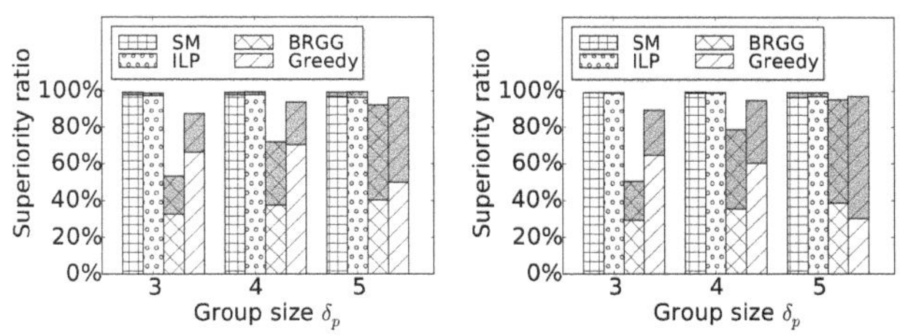

(a) Databases (b) Data Mining

Figure 11: Superiority ratio of SDGA-SRA

Figure 11 demonstrates the superiority ratio of SDGA-SRA over the three competitors, as a function of the reviewer group size δ_p. SDGA is omitted since SDGA-SRA is derived from SDGA. Each bar indicates the superiority ratio of SDGA-SRA over a competitor; the dark grey portion indicates the ratio of tie cases. For instance, almost every paper gets by SDGA-SRA a better or equal quality to SM and ILP, and at least 89.4% of the papers gets better or equal quality to Greedy. This result reveals that the stage execution paradigm of SDGA and the stochastic process (SRA) help in finding a better reviewer group for each paper. SDGA-SRA is not better than BRGG since a portion of papers gets very good reviewer groups at the early stages of BRGG. However, this strategy harms the latter stage assignments, leading to a low coverage ratio (cf. Figure 10).

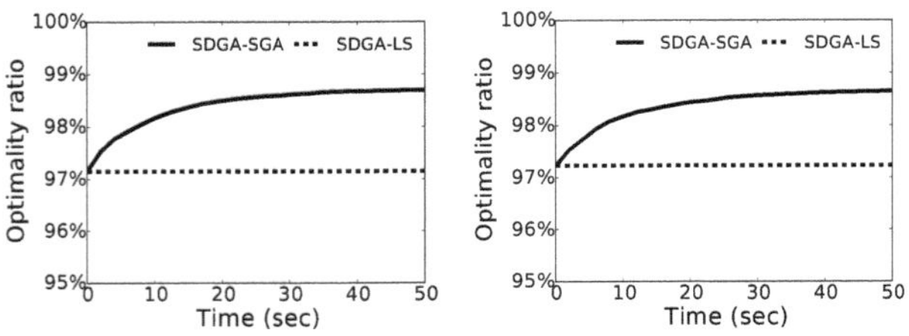

(a) Databases (b) Data Mining

Figure 12: Optimality ratio to stochastic refinement executions

Effectiveness of stochastic refinement. Next, we demonstrate the effect of our stochastic refinement process. We compare it with a standard, *Local Search* (LS) refinement approach. Our stochastic refinement can improve the optimality ratio by 1.4% and 1.2% in databases and data mining, respectively, after 20 seconds; while local search does not improve the overall quality since it gets stuck in a local maximum.

Summary. Our fully optimized approximate solution, SDGA-SRA, outperforms other methods by a wide margin considering different performance factors. More importantly, SDGA-SRA finds a solution with at least $1 - 1/e$ approximation ratio (for integral cases) and 1/2 ratio (for general cases), which is the best ratio achieved to the best of our knowledge. More comparisons, discussions, and case studies can be found in Appendix C. All paper assignment results are available via our project homepage (`http://degroup.cis.umac.mo/reviewerassignment/`).

6. CONCLUSION

In this paper, we formulated the automatic reviewer assignment to papers as a Weighted-coverage Group-based Reviewer Assignment Problem (WGRAP). Our formulation does not have the drawbacks of previous work. First, it balances the review load. Second, it uses a quality metric based on the coverage of the paper topics by the reviewers' expertise, giving weight to the topics according to their relevance to the papers. We studied the special case of Journal Reviewer Assignment and proposed an efficient algorithm that finds an exact solution for it. For the general WGRAP, we proposed a polynomial-time approximation algorithm, which improves the approximation ratio of previous work from 1/3 to 1/2. Finally, we proposed a stochastic refinement process that further improves the quality of the solution found by our algorithm. Our experimental results show that our algorithm paired with the stochastic refinement postprocessing achieves much better results compared to previous approaches and also runs within reasonable time. In the future, we plan to study alternative RAP formulations, e.g., where the quality of the assignment depends on both reviewer relevance to the paper topics and reviewer preferences based on available bids.

7. ACKNOWLEDGMENTS

This project was supported by grants MYRG188-FST11-GZG, MYRG109(Y1-L3)-FST12-ULH and MYRG2014-00106-FST from University of Macau RC, grant FDCT/106/2012/A3 from Macau FDCT, and grant HKU 715413E from Hong Kong RGC. We thank Y. Benjo for using his open source ATM project [1], the authors of [26] for the DBLP Citation network dataset, and the anonymous reviewers for their insightful comments.

8. REFERENCES

[1] `https://github.com/ybenjo/LDA`. Accessed: 2013-09-01.

[2] lp_solve 5.5. `http://lpsolve.sourceforge.net/5.5/`. Accessed: 2014-11-11.

[3] R. K. Ahuja, T. L. Magnanti, and J. B. Orlin. *Network flows: theory, algorithms and applications*. Prentice Hall, 1993.

[4] H. K. Biswas and M. Hasan. Using publications and domain knowledge to build research profiles: An application in automatic reviewer assignment. In *ICICT*, 2007.

[5] D. M. Blei, A. Y. Ng, and M. I. Jordan. Latent dirichlet allocation. *Journal of Machine Learning Research*, 3:993–1022, 2003.

[6] L. Charlin, R. S. Zemel, and C. Boutilier. A framework for optimizing paper matching. In *UAI*, 2011.

[7] D. Conry, Y. Koren, and N. Ramakrishnan. Recommender systems for the conference paper assignment problem. In *RecSys*, 2009.

[8] I. Corp. Ibm cplex cp optimizer 12.6. `http://www-01.ibm.com/software/commerce/optimization/cplex-cp-optimizer/index.html`. Accessed: 2014-12-29.

[9] R. Dechter. *Constraint processing*. Morgan Kaufmann, 2003.

[10] S. T. Dumais and J. Nielsen. Automating the assignment of submitted manuscripts to reviewers. In *SIGIR*, 1992.

[11] U. Feige. A threshold of ln n for approximating set cover. *J. ACM*, 45(4):634–652, July 1998.

[12] M. Fisher, G. Nemhauser, and L. Wolsey. An analysis of approximations for maximizing submodular set functions—ii. In *Polyhedral Combinatorics*, volume 8 of *Mathematical Programming Studies*, pages 73–87. 1978.

[13] D. Gale and L. S. Shapley. College admissions and the stability of marriage. *The American Mathematical Monthly*, 120(5):386–391, 2013.

[14] D. Hartvigsen, J. C. Wei, and R. Czuchlewski. The conference paper-reviewer assignment problem. *Decision Sciences*, 30(3):865–876, 1999.

[15] S. Hettich and M. J. Pazzani. Mining for proposal reviewers: lessons learned at the national science foundation. In *KDD*, 2006.

[16] T. Hofmann. Probabilistic latent semantic indexing. In *SIGIR*, 1999.

[17] D. S. Johnson, C. H. Papadimitriou, and M. Yannakakis. How easy is local search? (extended abstract). In *FOCS*, 1985.

[18] M. Karimzadehgan and C. Zhai. Constrained multi-aspect expertise matching for committee review assignment. In *CIKM*, 2009.

[19] M. Karimzadehgan, C. Zhai, and G. G. Belford. Multi-aspect expertise matching for review assignment. In *CIKM*, 2008.

[20] H. W. Kuhn. Variants of the hungarian method for assignment problems. *Naval Research Logistics Quarterly*, 3(4):253–258, 1956.

[21] X. Li and T. Watanabe. Automatic paper-to-reviewer assignment, based on the matching degree of the reviewers. In *KES*, 2013.

[22] C. Long, R. C.-W. Wong, Y. Peng, and L. Ye. On good and fair paper-reviewer assignment. In *ICDM*, 2013.

[23] D. M. Mimno and A. McCallum. Expertise modeling for matching papers with reviewers. In *KDD*, 2007.

[24] G. L. Nemhauser and L. A. Wolsey. *Integer and combinatorial optimization*, volume 18. Wiley New York, 1988.

[25] M. Rosen-Zvi, T. Griffiths, M. Steyvers, and P. Smyth. The author-topic model for authors and documents. In *UAI*, 2004.

[26] J. Tang, J. Zhang, L. Yao, J. Li, L. Zhang, and Z. Su. Arnetminer: extraction and mining of academic social networks. In *KDD*, 2008.

[27] F. Wang, S. Zhou, and N. Shi. Group-to-group reviewer assignment problem. *Computers & OR*, 40(5):1351–1362, 2013.

[28] X. Wang and A. McCallum. Topics over time: a non-markov continuous-time model of topical trends. In *KDD*, 2006.

[29] N. Xue, J.-X. Hao, S. Jia, and Q. Wang. An interval fuzzy ontology based peer review assignment method. In *ICEBE*, 2012.

[30] C. Zhai, A. Velivelli, and B. Yu. A cross-collection mixture model for comparative text mining. In *KDD*, 2004.

APPENDIX

A. TOPIC DISCOVERY

Topic modeling is a widely accepted method in Text Mining [5, 16, 25, 28, 30]. The objective is to extract a set of relevant and representative topics from a set of articles. Recent work [18, 19, 23] on the reviewer assignment problem adopt topic modeling for the extraction of topic vectors for reviewers and papers. As the topics can also be defined manually, the quality of topic extraction is orthogonal and independent to the development and necessity of WGRAP and any new findings on topic extraction are readily applicable and beneficial to WGRAP.

In this work, we apply the Author-Topic Model (ATM) [25] to extract the topic vectors of reviewers based on their publication records. Figure 13 illustrates the adapted ATM for our problem, where each variable is represented by a node (solid nodes for observed variables and hollow nodes for unknown variables to be estimated) and their dependencies are indicated by the arrows. The number of times each variable is replicated is indicated by the right-bottom number of each box. In our figure, there are R reviewers and the total number of their publications is D (i.e., $\{d_1, \cdots, d_D\}$). ATM assumes that every word of a document can be generated independently using the following iterative procedures.

1. Generate $\overrightarrow{r_i} \sim Dir(\alpha)$, $i \in \{1, \ldots, R\}$, where $Dir(\alpha)$ is the Dirichlet distribution for parameter α.
2. Generate $\overrightarrow{t_i} \sim Dir(\beta)$, $i \in \{1, \ldots, T\}$.
3. Generate each word w in a publication d as follows.
   (a) Generate a reviewer r_i based on $p(r|d)$, where $p(r|d)$ is a uniform distribution over reviewers who are the authors of d.
   (b) Generate a topic t_j based on $p(t|\overrightarrow{r_i})$
   (c) Generate a word w_k based on $p(w|\overrightarrow{t_j})$

Our goal is to estimate the topic vector of reviewers $\{\overrightarrow{r_1}, \cdots, \overrightarrow{r_R}\}$ and the topic set $\{\overrightarrow{t_1}, \cdots, \overrightarrow{t_T}\}$ such that the generated documents are as similar as possible to the observed variables D (i.e., the generative probability is maximized). The estimation can be done by Gibbs Sampling, as suggested in [25].

Given the topic set, we can easily derive the topic vector $\overrightarrow{p}$ of each submitted paper by Expectation Maximization (EM) [30] as follows.

$$\overrightarrow{p} = \underset{\overrightarrow{p}}{\operatorname{argmax}} \prod_{i=1}^{W_p} \sum_{j=1}^{T} p(w_i|t_j)\overrightarrow{p}[t_j], \tag{11}$$

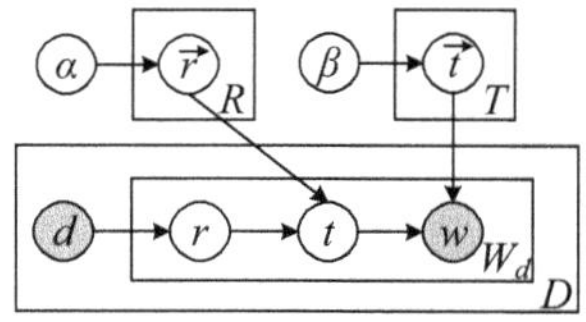

Figure 13: Author-Topic Model

where $\mathbb{W}_p$ indicates the set of words in p and $p(w_i|t_j)$ is estimated by ATM.

B. SUBMODULARITY AND ALTERNATIVE SCORING FUNCTIONS

According to the proofs of Lemma 3 and Theorem 1, the approximation ratio of SDGA still holds even when the objective function $c(\mathbb{A}) = \sum_{p \in \mathbb{P}} c(\overrightarrow{g}, \overrightarrow{p})$ (where $g = \{r|(r,p) \in \mathbb{A}[p]\}$) is replaced by alternative submodular functions. In this section, we first prove the submodularity of $c(\mathbb{A})$ subject to two conditions of the scoring function $c(\overrightarrow{r}, \overrightarrow{p})$. We then study 3 additional scoring functions and discuss their effect to WGRAP.

Proof of submodularity. $c(\mathbb{A})$ is submodular while (C.1) $c(\overrightarrow{r}, \overrightarrow{p})$ is a summation of topic scores, i.e. the contribution of different topics is independently counted, and (C.2) $c(\overrightarrow{r}, \overrightarrow{p})$ is monotonically increasing function w.r.t. $\overrightarrow{r}$, i.e., the assignment quality does not decrease when the expertise of a reviewer r (or a reviewer group g) increases. Obviously, our default scoring function (cf. Definition 1) fulfills these two conditions. A formal proof follows.

LEMMA 4. *The objective function $c(\mathbb{A})$ is submodular if (C.1) $c(\overrightarrow{r}, \overrightarrow{p})$ is a summation of topic scores and (C.2) $c(\overrightarrow{r}, \overrightarrow{p})$ is a monotonically increasing function w.r.t. $\overrightarrow{r}$.*

PROOF. $c(\mathbb{A})$ is submodular iff, $\forall (r,p), (r',p') \in \mathbb{R} \times \mathbb{P}$,

$$c(\mathbb{A} \cup \{(r,p)\}) - c(\mathbb{A}) \geq$$
$$c(\mathbb{A} \cup \{(r',p')\} \cup \{(r,p)\}) - c(\mathbb{A} \cup \{(r',p')\})$$

If $p \neq p'$, the marginal gains of (r,p) and (r',p') are independent. In other words, the gain of assigning (r,p) is not affected by whether we have assigned (r',p'), i.e.:

$$c(\mathbb{A} \cup \{(r,p)\}) - c(\mathbb{A}) =$$
$$c(\mathbb{A} \cup \{(r',p')\} \cup \{(r,p)\}) - c(\mathbb{A} \cup \{(r',p')\})$$

If $p = p'$, assignment pairs (r,p) and (r',p') refer to the same paper. In this case, r and r' belong to the same reviewer group g. According to the first condition (C.1), each topic t independently contributes to $c(\overrightarrow{r}, \overrightarrow{p})$. For the ease of our discussion, we use $f(\overrightarrow{r}[t], \overrightarrow{p}[t])$ to denote the contribution at topic t.

When $\overrightarrow{r}[t] \geq \overrightarrow{r}'[t]$,

$$\begin{aligned}
&f(\overrightarrow{g \cup \{r\}}[t], \overrightarrow{p}[t]) - f(\overrightarrow{g}[t], \overrightarrow{p}[t]) && \text{by Def. 2}\\
=&f(\overrightarrow{g \cup \{r, r'\}}[t], \overrightarrow{p}[t]) - f(\overrightarrow{g}[t], \overrightarrow{p}[t]) && \text{by C.2}\\
\geq&f(\overrightarrow{g \cup \{r, r'\}}[t], \overrightarrow{p}[t]) - f(\overrightarrow{g \cup \{r'\}}[t], \overrightarrow{p}[t]) && (12)
\end{aligned}$$

When $\overrightarrow{r}[t] < \overrightarrow{r}'[t]$,

$$f(\overrightarrow{g \cup \{r, r'\}}[t], \overrightarrow{p}[t]) - f(\overrightarrow{g \cup \{r'\}}[t], \overrightarrow{p}[t]) \quad \text{by Def. 2}$$
$$= f(\overrightarrow{g \cup \{r, r'\}}[t], \overrightarrow{p}[t]) - f(\overrightarrow{g \cup \{r, r'\}}[t], \overrightarrow{p}[t]) = 0 \quad (13)$$

Thereby,

$$f(\overrightarrow{g \cup \{r\}}[t], \overrightarrow{p}[t]) - f(\overrightarrow{g}[t], \overrightarrow{p}[t]) \quad \text{by C.2 and Eq. 13}$$
$$\geq f(\overrightarrow{g \cup \{r, r'\}}[t], \overrightarrow{p}[t]) - f(\overrightarrow{g \cup \{r'\}}[t], \overrightarrow{p}[t]) \quad (14)$$

Thus, we now prove the marginal gain of assigning (r, p) may decrease if we have assigned (r', p') first, i.e.:

$$c(\mathbb{A} \cup \{(r,p)\}) - c(\mathbb{A}) \quad \because g \text{ reviews } p$$
$$= \sum_{t=1}^{\mathbb{T}} f(\overrightarrow{g \cup \{r\}}[t], \overrightarrow{p}[t]) - f(\overrightarrow{g}[t], \overrightarrow{p}[t])$$

by Eq. 12 and 14

$$\geq \sum_{t=1}^{\mathbb{T}} f(\overrightarrow{g \cup \{r, r'\}}[t], \overrightarrow{p}[t]) - f(\overrightarrow{g \cup \{r'\}}[t], \overrightarrow{p}[t])$$
$$= c(\mathbb{A} \cup \{(r', p')\} \cup \{(r,p)\}) - c(\mathbb{A} \cup \{(r', p')\})$$

□

Alternative scoring functions. We study three alternative scoring functions, namely the reviewer coverage score, the paper coverage score, and the dot-product score. The reviewer (paper) coverage score employs a winner-takes-all strategy where the reviewer (paper) contributes to topic t if and only if $r[t] \geq p[t]$ (i.e., r is qualified to review p at topic t). The score computed by this strategy is based on only the reviewer expertise (paper contents). The dot-product score is widely used in many vector based similarity computations. All of these three functions are submodular, i.e., the satisfy the conditions of Lemma 4.

Table 6 is a toy example with two reviewers and one paper, demonstrating the effect of these scoring functions. The reviewer coverage score c_R prefers a reviewer with strong expertise on some specific topic(s) of the paper so that r_1 is preferred to r_2 due to r_1's expertise at these topic(s). The paper coverage score c_P focuses on whether a topic in the paper can be completely understood by the reviewer. Actually, we recommend to use the reviewer (paper) coverage score only when we are very confident about the reviewers' expertise information (paper topic distribution). The dot-product score c_D offers a fair evaluation based on both paper contents and reviewer expertise. However, it may overestimate the importance of some topic, e.g., topic t_1 of r_1 is 0.9, which likely returns a large score, although the paper's relevance to t_1 is 0.6 only. In this example, our default scoring function (i.e., weighted coverage c), is the only method that prefers r_2 to r_1. This result is more intuitive as r_2 is more similar to p than r_1 is. It should be noted that the main focus of this work is not to evaluate the appropriateness of the scoring functions. Instead, we provide flexibility in the choice of the objective function, as long as it is a submodular function, in which case our theoretical results (Theorem 1) hold.

name	symbol	function (numerator only)
weighted coverage (default)	c	$\sum_{t=1}^{T} \min\{\overrightarrow{r}[t], \overrightarrow{p}[t]\}$
reviewer coverage	c_R	$\sum_{t=1}^{T} \begin{cases} \overrightarrow{r}[t] & \text{if } \overrightarrow{r}[t] \geq \overrightarrow{p}[t] \\ 0 & \text{otherwise} \end{cases}$
paper coverage	c_P	$\sum_{t=1}^{T} \begin{cases} \overrightarrow{p}[t] & \text{if } \overrightarrow{r}[t] \geq \overrightarrow{p}[t] \\ 0 & \text{otherwise} \end{cases}$
dot-product	c_D	$\sum_{t=1}^{T} \overrightarrow{r}[t] \cdot \overrightarrow{p}[t]$

Table 5: Alternative scoring functions

	t_1	t_2
$\overrightarrow{p}$	0.6	0.4
$\overrightarrow{r_1}$	0.9	0.1
$\overrightarrow{r_2}$	0.5	0.5

	$\overrightarrow{r_1}$	$\overrightarrow{r_2}$
$c_R(\overrightarrow{r}, \overrightarrow{p})$	0.9	0.5
$c_P(\overrightarrow{r}, \overrightarrow{p})$	0.6	0.4
$c_D(\overrightarrow{r}, \overrightarrow{p})$	0.58	0.5
$c(\overrightarrow{r}, \overrightarrow{p})$	0.7	0.9

Table 6: An example using the 4 scoring functions

C. ADDITIONAL EXPERIMENTS

Additional scalability evaluation of JRA. Figures 14(a) and 14(b) show the response time of the methods as a function of group size δ_p and number of reviewers R, respectively. The overall trend is similar to the result in Section 5.1. When $\delta = 6$, BF cannot finish in 48 hours and ILP takes 18.9 hours to compute the result while BBA only takes 53.8 seconds. Figure 15 evaluates the effect of k (i.e., top-k reviewer groups) under the default setting. BBA returns the best 1,000 reviewer groups within 2 seconds.

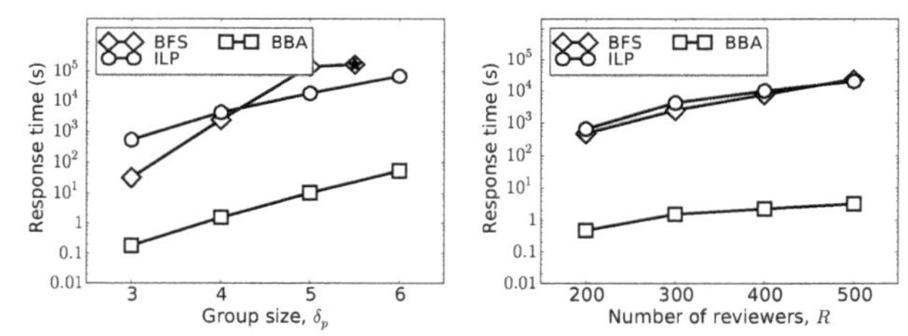

(a) Effect of δ_p ($R = 300$) (b) Effect of R ($\delta_p = 4$)

Figure 14: Additional scalability evaluation of JRA

Lowest coverage score. The lowest coverage score, $\min_{p \in \mathbb{P}} c(\overrightarrow{g}, \overrightarrow{p})$, models the quality of the worst assignment in a CRA approximate result. As Table 7 shows, SDGA-SRA significantly outperforms the other methods with respect to this metric, especially for low δ_p values. This is because the stage assignment of SDGA achieves a result closer to the optimal, when there are only few stages.

Effect of the convergence threshold ω in SRA. The convergence threshold ω is a parameter used to terminate the stochastic refinement process. For larger ω values, the execution time increases and we also expect the assignment quality to increase. Figure 16 demonstrates the effect of ω for $\delta_p = 3$, where the line indicates the response time and the bar represents the optimality ratio. Although the optimality ratio increases with ω, the response time decreases at a higher rate. We select $\omega = 10$ as our default setting

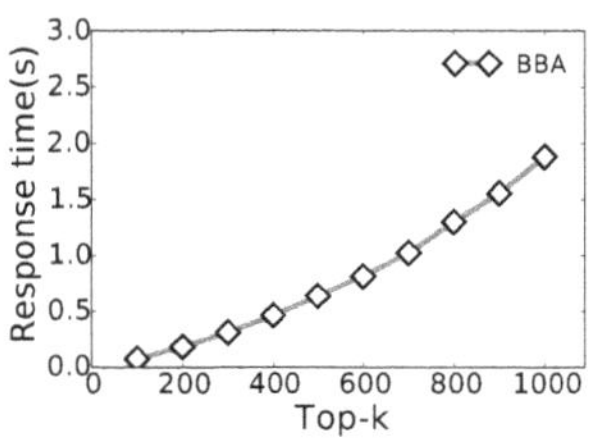

Figure 15: The effect of k on BBA

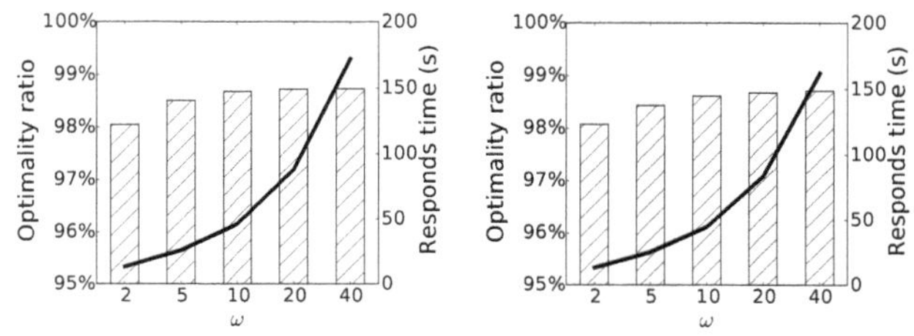

(a) Database (b) Data Mining

Figure 16: The effect of ω ($\delta_p = 3$)

	δ_p	SM	ILP	BRGG	Greedy	SDGA-SRA
DB08	3	0.03	0.42	0.16	0.56	0.59
	4	0.42	0.44	0.16	0.59	0.59
	5	0.53	0.46	0.16	0.59	0.59
DM08	3	0.45	0.45	0.40	0.77	0.75
	4	0.28	0.57	0.36	0.77	0.75
	5	0.44	0.58	0.36	0.77	0.76
T08	3	0.20	0.49	0.25	0.69	0.76
	4	0.59	0.49	0.48	0.79	0.79
	5	0.47	0.59	0.45	0.79	0.79
DB09	3	0.51	0.56	0.32	0.71	0.77
	4	0.33	0.56	0.26	0.78	0.78
	5	0.53	0.61	0.33	0.78	0.78
DM09	3	0.42	0.59	0.41	0.81	0.84
	4	0.36	0.62	0.30	0.86	0.86
	5	0.67	0.63	0.34	0.86	0.86
T09	3	0.16	0.50	0.13	0.66	0.70
	4	0.10	0.56	0.05	0.70	0.70
	5	0.23	0.63	0.19	0.70	0.70

Table 7: Lowest coverage score in $\mathbb{A}$

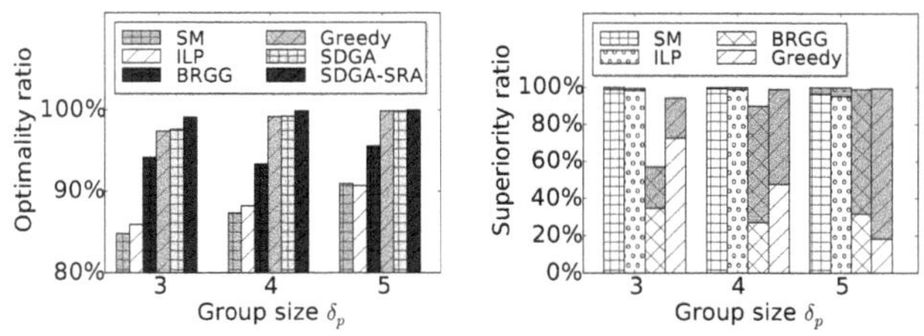

(a) Optimality ratio (b) Superiority ratio

Figure 17: CRA experiments in Theory (2008)

in this work as it offers good tradeoff between effectiveness and efficiency.

Additional quality evaluation of CRA. Figures 17 and 18 show the optimality ratio and the superiority ratio for the Theory area of 2008 and all three datasets for 2009. The overall trends have no difference to the results observed for the areas of Databases and Data Mining in 2008.

Case study (1). We take a closer look at the set of reviewers assigned to paper "Kun Liu, Evimaria Terzi: *Towards identity anonymization on graphs.* SIGMOD 2008: 93-106", in our Databases 2008 experiment. The result of different approaches are shown in Figure 19, where a bar indicates the coverage score for a specific topic and we only report the 5 most related topics in terms of their probability distribution (i.e., the probability of the remaining topics is low). For clarity, we show the related topics and their keywords in Table 8. Due to lack of space, we omit the result of SM (it performs similarly to ILP). As shown in Table 8 and Figure 19, the extracted topics (i.e., topic bars) accurately capture the contents of the paper (in fact, they also match the paper keywords provided by the authors, i.e., `Anonymity`, `Degree Sequence`, and `Dynamic Programming`).

We now analyze the expertise of the selected reviewers. Chris Clifton is an expert on data privacy, particularly with respect to analysis of private data, so he has relatively high weight on topic t_2 compared to the other topics. As another example, Philip Yu is an active scholar who has published at least 856 papers (according to DBLP) and works on diverse research topics. The majority of his research is related to data mining, therefore he has relatively high weight on topic t_5. We add a note that the expertise of Philip Yu only reveals that he offers strong support to review topic t_5 but this does not mean that he is not qualified for t_2 (since we treat the qualification of every committee member identically by normalization).

Regarding the assignment result, SDGA-SRA (i.e., our proposed implementation of WGRAP) returns the best assignment according to the coverage of the paper's topics. Note that SDGA-SRA is the only method which can find an expert (i.e., Philip Yu) to support topic t_5. Accordingly, the paper is expected to be reviewed in a more diverse way.

topic	keywords
t_1	algorithms, techniques, based, large, propose, efficient,...
t_2	privacy, access, control, security, sensitive, secure,...
t_3	stream, algorithm, approximation, online, string, traffic,...
t_4	graph, xml, similarity, matching, approximate, variety,...
t_5	clustering, stream, high, mining, classification, graph,...

Table 8: Topics and keywords (for Case study 1)

Case study (2). Table 9 and Figure 20 analyze the assignment of another paper "Mirit Shalem, Ziv Bar-Yossef: *The Space Complexity of Processing XML Twig Queries Over Indexed Documents.* ICDE 2008: 824-832", having keywords `XML`, `computational complexity`, `indexing`, `query processing`. The coverage scores of all assignment results are relatively high compared to Case study (1). Again, SDGA-SRA is the only method that includes Christoph Koch, who has strong background in XML query processing, in the group of reviewers.

Note that our assignment results are computed solely based on the paper abstracts. The assignment quality is expected to be further improved if the topic extraction process uses the article's main text and the expertise on topics is self-tuned by the reviewers.

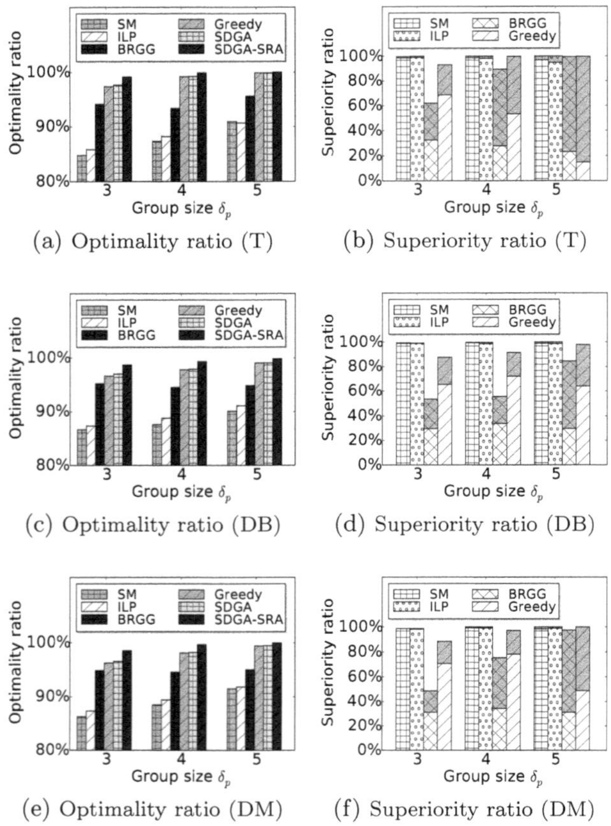

(a) Optimality ratio (T) (b) Superiority ratio (T)

(c) Optimality ratio (DB) (d) Superiority ratio (DB)

(e) Optimality ratio (DM) (f) Superiority ratio (DM)

Figure 18: CRA experiments in 2009 datasets

topic	keywords
t_1	algorithms, techniques, based, large, propose, efficient,...
t_2	query, processing, model, relational, optimization,...
t_3	xml, xquery, xpath, query, evaluation, tree, structure,...
t_4	graph, xml, similarity, matching, approximate, variety,...
t_5	stream, system, operators, plan, maintenance, processing,...

Table 9: Topics and keywords (for Case study 2)

Quality evaluation of scoring functions. Figures 21(a), 21(b), and 21(c) show the optimality ratio of 3 alternative objective functions (cf. Table 5) on Databases area in 2008. The overall trends have no difference to those observed when using our default objective function (cf. Definition 1). Besides evaluating alternative scoring functions, we attempt to scale the expertise of the reviewers using their h-indices. Specifically, we scale the vector of each reviewer by a number in the range [1,2] as follows:

$$\vec{r} = (1 + \frac{h_r - h_{min}}{h_{max} - h_{min}})\vec{r} \quad (15)$$

where h_r denotes the h-index of reviewer r, while h_{max} and h_{min} denote the minimum and maximum h-indices of all reviewers, respectively. Similar to other experiments, SDGA-SRA performs well after the scaling (cf. Figure 21(d)).

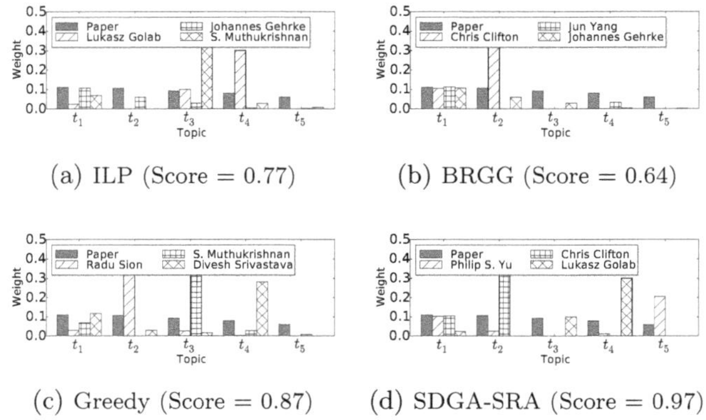

(a) ILP (Score = 0.77) (b) BRGG (Score = 0.64)

(c) Greedy (Score = 0.87) (d) SDGA-SRA (Score = 0.97)

Figure 19: Case study 1

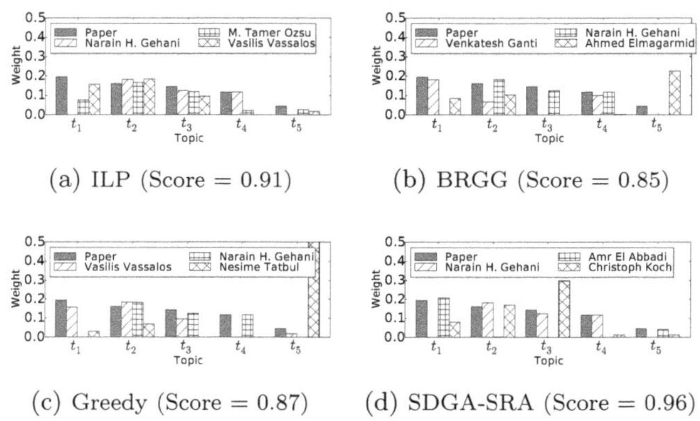

(a) ILP (Score = 0.91) (b) BRGG (Score = 0.85)

(c) Greedy (Score = 0.87) (d) SDGA-SRA (Score = 0.96)

Figure 20: Case study 2

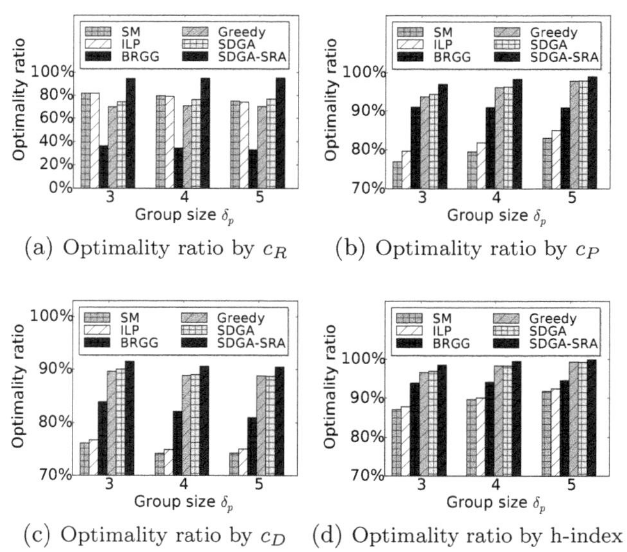

(a) Optimality ratio by c_R (b) Optimality ratio by c_P

(c) Optimality ratio by c_D (d) Optimality ratio by h-index

Figure 21: The effect of alternative scoring functions

Distributed Online Tracking

Mingwang Tang[1], Feifei Li[1], Yufei Tao[2]
[1]University of Utah [2]Chinese University of Hong Kong
{tang, lifeifei}@cs.utah.edu taoyf@cse.cuhk.edu.hk

In online tracking, an observer S receives a sequence of values, one per time instance, from a data source that is described by a function f. A tracker T wants to continuously maintain an approximation that is within an error threshold of the value $f(t)$ at any time instance t, with small communication overhead. This problem was recently formalized and studied in [32, 34], and a principled approach with optimal competitive ratio was proposed. This work extends the study of online tracking to a distributed setting, where a tracker T wants to track a function f that is computed from a set of functions $\{f_1, \ldots, f_m\}$ from m distributed observers and respective data sources. This formulation finds numerous important and natural applications, e.g., sensor networks, distributed systems, measurement networks, and pub-sub systems. We formalize this problem and present effective online algorithms for various topologies of a distributed system/network for different aggregate functions. Experiments on large real data sets demonstrate the excellent performance of our methods in practice.

Categories and Subject Descriptors

H.2.m [**Information Systems**]: Database Management – *Miscellaneous*

Keywords

Distributed online tracking, online tracking, tracking

1. INTRODUCTION

The increasing popularity of smart mobile devices and the fast growth in the deployment of large measurement networks generate massive distributed data continuously. For example, such data include, but are not limited to, values collected from smart phones and tablets [3], measurements from large sensor-based measurement networks [12, 22, 31], application data from location based services (LBS) [28], and network data from a large infrastructure network.

Tracking a user function over such distributed data *continuously* in an online fashion is a fundamental challenge. This is a useful task in many applications. A concrete example is the MesoWest project [18]. It collects many aspects of weather data from distributed measurement stations. Users and scientists in MesoWest would like to continuously track the aggregate values (e.g., maximum or minimum) of atmospheric readings, e.g. temperature, from a number of stations in vicinity. Another example is the SAMOS project (Shipboard Automated Meteorological Oceanography System) [27], which collects marine meteorological and near-surface oceanographic observations from distributed research vessels and voluntary ships at sea.

Similar examples can be easily found in location based services and other distributed systems. This problem is also useful in the so called publish/subscribe systems [4, 13], where a subscriber (tracker) may register a function (also known as a query) with a publisher (observer). Data continuously arrive at the publisher. The publisher needs to keep the subscriber informed about the value of her function f, when f is continuously applied over the *current data value*. When a subscriber's function of interest depends on data values from multiple publishers, it becomes a distributed tracking problem.

It is always desirable, sometimes even critical, to reduce the amount of communication in distributed systems and applications, for a number of reasons [1, 5–7, 12, 22, 23, 25, 31]. Many devices rely on on-board battery and incur high power consumption when they communicate, e.g., in sensors and smart phones. Hence, reducing the number of messages they need to send helps extend their battery time. Another reason is to save the network bandwidth. From the user's point of view, less communication often leads to economic gains, e.g., most smart phones have a monthly budget for their data plan, or for nodes in remote areas in a large measurement network, communication via satellites come with a high price tag. From the network infrastructure's point of view (e.g., ISP such as Comcast), too much communications from any application could significantly congest their network and slow down the performance of the network (keep in mind that there could be many user applications running at the same time that share the available network bandwidth).

To achieve exact *continuous online tracking* of arbitrary functions, the solution is to ask all stations to always send readings back to a central coordinator (the tracker), from which various functions can be easily computed and then tracked. This baseline approach, unfortunately, generates excessive communications: every new reading from any station must be forwarded to the tracker to ensure the correctness of the output values of the function being tracked.

SIGMOD'15, May 31–June 4, 2015, Melbourne, Victoria, Australia.

http://dx.doi.org/10.1145/2723372.2737790.

But the good news is, in many application scenarios, exact tracking is often unnecessary. Users are willing to trade-off accuracy with savings in communication. In some applications, approximation is often necessary not just for reducing communication, but also for policy constraints, e.g, due to privacy concerns in location based services [2] and law requirements.

To formalize this accuracy and communication trade-offs, we refer to a distributed site that continuously receives data from a data source as an *observer*, and the centralized site that wants to track a function (or multiple functions) computed over data from multiple, distributed data sources as the *tracker*. Without loss of generality, we assume that the tracker is tracking only one function, which if f. Clearly, f's output is a function of time, and denoted as $f(t)$ for a time instance t. More precisely, it is a function of multiple data values at time instance t, one from each observer. Based on the above discussion, producing the exact values of $f(t)$ continuously for all time instances is expensive. Thus, the tracker's goal is to maintain an approximation $g(t)$, which is his best knowledge of $f(t)$ at any time instance t using small amount of communication (accumulated so far). Focusing on functions that produce a one-dimensional output, we require that $g(t) \in [f(t)-\Delta, f(t)+\Delta]$ for any $t \in [0, t_{\text{now}}]$, for some user-defined error threshold Δ.

Under this set up, when $\Delta = 0$, $g(t)$ always equals $f(t)$ and the baseline exact solution is needed, which is communication-expensive. On the other hand, in the extreme case when $\Delta = +\infty$, $g(t)$ can be a random value, and effectively there will be no communication needed at all. These two extremes illustrate the possible accuracy-communication trade-off enabled by this framework.

Key challenge. It is important to note that our problem is a *continuous online* problem that requires a good approximation for *every time instance*. This is different from many distributed tracking problems in the literature that use the popular *distributed streaming model*, where the goal is to produce an approximation of certain functions/properties computed over the *union of data stream elements seen so far* for all observers, from the beginning of the time till now. It is also different from many existing work on monitoring a function over distributed streams, where the tracker only needs to decide if $f(t)$'s value has exceeded a given (constant) threshold or not at any time instance t.

When there is only one observer, our problem degenerates to a centralized, two-party setting (observer and tracker). This problem has only been recently studied in [32, 34]. where they have studied both one-dimensional and multi-dimensional online tracking in this centralized setting. They have given an online algorithm with $O(\log \Delta)$ competitive-ratio, and shown that this is optimal. In other words, any online algorithm for solving this problem must use at least a factor of $O(\log \Delta)$ more communication than the offline optimal algorithm. Note that, however, this problem is different from the classic problem of two-party computation [30] in communication complexity. For the latter problem, two parties Alice and Bob have a value x and y respectively, and the goal is to compute some function $f(x, y)$ by communicating the minimum number of bits between them. Note that in online tracking, only Alice (the observer) sees the input, Bob (the tracker) just wants to keep track of it. Furthermore, in communication complexity both inputs x and y are given in advance, and the goal is to study the worst-case communication; while in online tracking, the inputs arrive in an online fashion and it is easy to see that the worst-case (total) communication bound for online tracking is meaningless, since the function f could change drastically at each time step. For same reasons, our problem, distributed online tracking, is also different from distributed multi-party computation.

Our contributions. In this paper, we extend the online tracking problem that was only recently studied in [32,34] to the distributed setting with common aggregation functions (e.g., MAX), and investigate principled methods with formal theoretical guarantees on their performance (in terms of communication) when possible. We design novel methods that achieve good communication costs in practice, and formally show that they have good approximation ratios.

Our contributions are summarized below.

- We formalize the distributed online tracking problem in Section 2 and review the optimal online tracking method from [32, 34] in the centralized setting.
- We examine a special extension of the centralized setting with one observer but many relaying nodes, known as the *chain case*. We study the chain model in Section 3 and design a method with $O(\log \Delta)$ competitive ratio. We also show that our method has achieved the optimal *competitive-ratio* in this setting.
- We investigate the "broom" model in Section 4 by leveraging our results from the chain model, where there are m distributed observers at the leaf-level and a single chain connecting them to the tracker. We design novel method for MAX function and show that our method has very good approximation ratio among the class of online algorithms for the broom model.
- We extend our results to the general tree model in Section 5, which is an extension of the broom model. We again show that our method has good approximation ratio among the class of online algorithms for the general-tree model.
- We discuss other functions and topologies in Section 6.
- We conduct an extensive experiments to evaluate the effectiveness of our methods in practice in Section 7. We used several real data sets and the results have confirmed that our methods are indeed superior compared to other alternatives and baseline methods.

Furthermore, we review the related work in Section 8, and conclude the paper in Section 9. Unless otherwise specified, proofs are provided in Appendix A.

2. PROBLEM FORMULATION AND BACKGROUND

Formally, there are m observers $\{s_1, \ldots, s_m\}$ at m distributed sites, and a tracker T. These m observers are connected to T using a network topology. We consider two common topologies in this work, the *broom* topology and the *general-tree* topology as shown in Figure 1. Observers always locate at the leaves, and the tracker always locates at the root of the tree. Both topologies are constructed based on a *chain topology* as shown in Figure 2(a), and the centralized setting studied in [32, 34] is a special case of the chain topology as shown in Figure 2(b). A relay node does

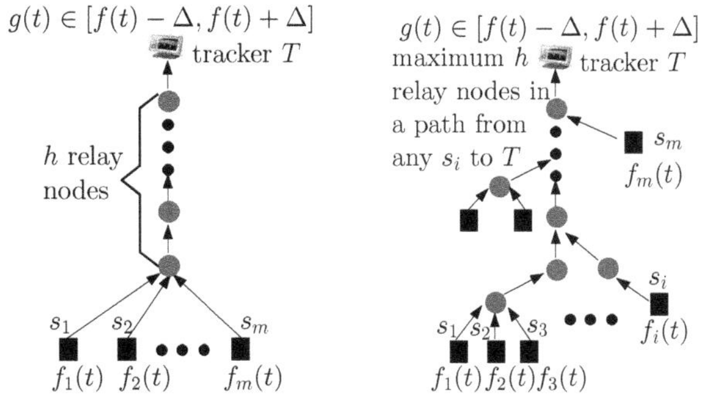

(a) broom model. (b) general-tree.

Figure 1: Track $f(t) = f(f_1(t), f_2(t), \cdots, f_m(t))$.

not directly observe a function (or equivalently data values) that contributes to the computation of f, but it can receive messages from its child (or preceding) node(s), and send messages to its parent (or succeeding) node.

It is important to note that our general-tree topology has *already covered the case* in which an intermediate replay node u may be an observer at the same time, who also observes values (modeled by a function) that contributes to the computation of function f. This is because we can always conceptually add an observer node s directly below (and connected to) such an intermediate node u. Let s report the data values that is observed by u, we can then only view u as a relay node (while making no changes to all other connections to u that already exist). More details on this issue will be presented in Section 6.

That said, in practice, a relay node can model a router, a switch, a sensor node, a computer or computation node in a complex system (e.g., Internet, peer-to-peer network), a measurement station in a monitoring network, etc.

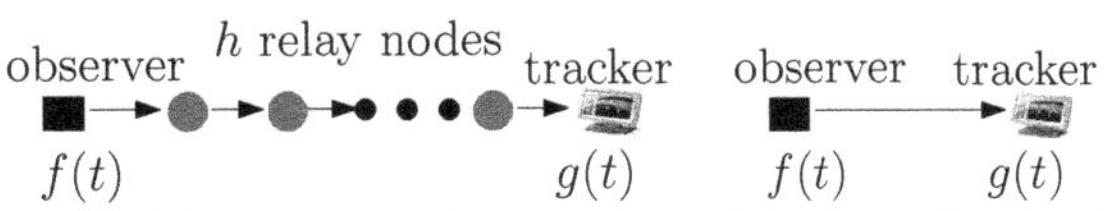

(a) chain topology. (b) centralized setting [32,34].

Figure 2: Special cases: $g(t) \in [f(t) - \Delta, f(t) + \Delta]$.

Each observer's data value changes (arbitrarily) over time, and can be described by a function. We dub the function at the ith observer f_i, and its value at time instance t $f_i(t)$. The tracker's objective is to continuously track a function f that is computed based on the values of functions from all observers at time instance t, i.e., it's goal is to track $f(t) = f(f_1(t), f_2(t), \ldots, f_m(t))$ continuously over all time instances. Since tracking $f(t)$ exactly is expensive, an approximation $g(t)$ is allowed at the tracker T, subject to the constraint that $g(t) \in [f(t) - \Delta, f(t) + \Delta]$ for any time instance $t \in [0, t_{\text{now}}]$. $\Delta \in \mathbb{Z}^+$ is a user-defined error threshold, that defines the maximum allowed error in approximating $f(t)$ with $g(t)$.

The goal is to find an online algorithm that satisfies this constraint while minimizing the communication cost.

Note that depending on the dimensionality for the outputs of $f(t)$, as well as $f_1(t), f_2(t), \ldots$, and $f_m(t)$, we need to track either a one-dimensional value or a multi-dimensional value that changes over time. This work focuses on the one-dimensional case. In other words, we assume that $f(t)$, and $f_1(t), \ldots, f_m(t)$ are all in a one-dimensional space.

2.1 Performance metric of an online algorithm

There are different ways to formally analyze the performance of an online algorithm.

For an online problem P (e.g., caching), let $\mathcal{I}$ be the set of all possible valid input instances, and $\mathcal{A}$ be the set of all valid online algorithms for solving the problem P. Suppose the optimal *offline* algorithm for P is $\mathsf{offline}$. Given an input instance $I \in \mathcal{I}$, and an algorithm $A \in \mathcal{A}$ (or $\mathsf{offline}$), we denote the cost of running algorithm A on I as $\mathsf{cost}(A, I)$. In our setting, the cost is the total number of messages sent in a topology.

A widely used metric is the concept of *competitive ratio*. Formally, for an algorithm $A \in \mathcal{A}$, the competitive ratio of A [24], denoted as $\mathsf{cratio}(A)$, is defined as:

$$\mathsf{cratio}(A) = \max_{I \in \mathcal{I}} \frac{\mathsf{cost}(A, I)}{\mathsf{cost}(\mathsf{offline}, I)}.$$

Another popular metric is to analyze the performance of an algorithm A compared to other algorithms in a class of online algorithms. Formally, we can define the *ratio* of A on an input instance I as follows:

$$\mathsf{ratio}(A, I) = \frac{\mathsf{cost}(A, I)}{\mathsf{cost}(A_I^*, I)},$$

where A_I^* is the online algorithm from the class $\mathcal{A}$ that has the lowest cost on input I, i.e., $A_I^* = \text{argmin}_{A' \in \mathcal{A}} \mathsf{cost}(A', I)$.

Lastly, we can quantify an algorithm A's performance by considering its worst case *ratio*, i.e.,

$$\mathsf{ratio}(A) = \max_{I \in \mathcal{I}} \mathsf{ratio}(A, I).$$

Note that the definitions of $\mathsf{ratio}(A, I)$ and $\mathsf{ratio}(A)$ are inspired by the classic work that has motivated and defined the concept of "instance optimality" [14]. In fact, if $\mathsf{ratio}(A)$ is a constant, then indeed A is an *instance optimal online algorithm*.

Clearly, we always have, for any online problem P and its online algorithm A, $\mathsf{cratio}(A) \leq \mathsf{ratio}(A)$.

2.2 State-of-the-art method

Prior work has studied the online tracking problem in the *centralized, two party setting* [32, 34], as shown in Figure 2(b). They studied both one-dimensional tracking and multi-dimensional tracking, defined by the dimensionality of the output value for the function $f(t)$ at the observer. Since we focus on the one dimension case, here we only review the one-dimension tracking method from [32,34]. Finding a good online algorithm for this seemingly very simple set up turns out to be a very challenging problem.

Consider the simple case where the function takes integer values at each time step, i.e., $f : \mathbb{Z} \to \mathbb{Z}$, and the tracker requires an absolute error of at most Δ. The natural solution is to let the observer first communicate $f(t_0)$ to the tracker at the initial time instance t_0; then every time $f(t)$ has changed by more than Δ since the last communication, the observer updates the tracker with the current value of $f(t)$. However, this natural solution has an unbounded competitive ratio compared with the offline optimal method. Consider the case where $f(t)$ starts at $f(0) = 0$ and then oscillates between 0 and 2Δ. The above algorithm will communicate for an infinite number of times while the offline optimal solution only needs to send one message: $g(0) = \Delta$.

This example demonstrates the hardness of the online tracking problem. For functions in the form of $f : \mathbb{Z} \to \mathbb{Z}$, Yi and Zhang proposed the method in Algorithm 1, and showed the following results.

Algorithm 1: OptTrack (Δ) (from [32, 34])

```
let S = [f(t_now) − Δ, f(t_now) + Δ] ∩ Z
while S ≠ ∅ do
    let g(t_now) be the median of S;
    send g(t_now) to tracker T; set t_last = t_now;
    wait until |f(t) − g(t_last)| > Δ;
    S ← S ∩ [f(t) − Δ, f(t) + Δ]
```

Theorem 1 *(from [32, 34]) To track a function $f : \mathbb{Z} \to \mathbb{Z}$ within error Δ, any online algorithm has to send $\Omega(\log \Delta \cdot \mathsf{OPT})$ messages in the worst case, where OPT is the number of messages needed by the optimal offline algorithm. And,* OptTrack *is an $O(\log \Delta)$-competitive online algorithm to track any function $f : \mathbb{Z} \to \mathbb{Z}$ within Δ. Furthermore, if f takes values from the domain of reals (or any dense set), the competitive ratio of any online algorithm is unbounded.*

Theorem 1 establishes the optimality of the OptTrack method, since it shows that any online algorithms for centralized online tracking (between two nodes) has a competitive ratio that is at least $\log \Delta$, and OptTrack's competitive ratio $O(\log \Delta)$ has met this lower bound.

Note that the negative results on real domains and other dense domains do not rule out the application of OptTrack in practice on those cases. In practice, most functions (or data values for a sequence of inputs) have a fixed precision, e.g., any real number in a 64-bit machine can be described by an integer from an integer domain with size 2^{64}.

To the best of our knowledge, and as pointed out in [32, 34], no prior work has studied the distributed online tracking problem as we have formalized earlier in this section.

3. THE CHAIN CASE

We first examine a special case that bridges centralized and distributed online tracking. Considering the tree topology in Figure 1, it is easy to observe that each observer is connected to the tracker via a single path with a number of relay nodes (if multiple paths exist, we simply consider the shortest path). Hence, online tracking in the chain topology as shown in Figure 2(a) is a basic building block for the general distributed online tracking problem. We refer to this problem as the *chain online tracking.*

The centralized online tracking as reviewed in Section 2.2 and shown in Figure 2(b) is a special case of chain online tracking, with 0 relay node.

Baseline methods. For a chain topology with h relay nodes, a tempting solution is to distribute the error threshold Δ equally to all relay nodes and apply $(h+1)$ independent instances of the OptTrack algorithm. Suppose we have h relay nodes $\{n_1, \ldots, n_h\}$, an observer s, and a tracker T. Let $n_0 = s$ and $n_{h+1} = T$, for every pair of nodes $\{n_{i-1}, n_i\}$ for $i \in [1, h+1]$, we can view n_i as a tracker and its preceding node n_{i-1} as an observer, and require that n_i tracks n_{i-1}'s function within an error threshold of $\frac{\Delta}{h+1}$.

Let $y_i(t)$ be the function at n_i for $i \in [1, h+1]$, then $y_i(t)$ is the output of running OptTrack with an error threshold $\frac{\Delta}{h+1}$, where n_{i-1} is the observer, $y_{i-1}(t)$ is the function to be tracked, and n_i is the tracker. Since $n_0 = s$ and $y_0(t) = f(t)$, we have two facts:

(1) $y_1(t) \in [f(t) - \frac{\Delta}{h+1}, f(t) + \frac{\Delta}{h+1}]$ for any time instance t.

(2) $y_i(t) \in [y_{i-1}(t) - \frac{\Delta}{h+1}, y_{i-1}(t) + \frac{\Delta}{h+1}]$ for any $i \in [2, h+1]$ and any time instance t.

Since the tracker T is simply node n_{h+1}, thus, $g(t) = y_{h+1}(t)$. Using the facts above, it is easy to verify that $g(t)$ will be always within $f(t) \pm \Delta$ as required. We denote this method as ChainTrackA (chain-track-average).

We can generalize ChainTrackA to derive other similar methods. Instead of distributing the error threshold uniformly along the chain, one can distribute a random error threshold Δ_i to node n_i for $i = 1, \ldots, h+1$, subject to the constraint that $\sum_{i=1}^{h+1} \Delta_i = \Delta$. We denote this method as ChainTrackR (chain-track-random). Using a similar argument, ChainTrackR also ensures that $g(t)$ at T is always within $f(t) \pm \Delta$.

Unfortunately, these seemingly natural solutions do not perform well, even though they are intuitive extensions of the optimal online tracking method between two nodes to multiple nodes.

Given any valid algorithm A for chain online tracking, let $y_i(t)$ be the best knowledge of $f(t)$ at node n_i at any time instance t, for $i = 1, \ldots, h+1$. The first observation on a chain topology is given by the following lemma.

Lemma 1 *For an algorithm A (either online or offline) that solves the chain online tracking problem, we must have $y_i(t) \in [f(t) - \Delta, f(t) + \Delta]$ for any $i \in [1, h+1]$ in order to reduce communication while ensuring correctness. This holds for any $t \in [0, t_{now}]$.*

Lemma 1 formalizes a very intuitive observation on a chain topology. This result helps us arrive at the following.

Lemma 2 *Both* ChainTrackA *and* ChainTrackR*'s competitive ratios are $+\infty$ for the chain online tracking problem.*

Proof. We prove the case for ChainTrackA. The proof for ChainTrackR is similar and omitted for brevity.

Consider a function f at the observer s (which is node n_0) whose values always change no more than Δ around a constant a. In other words, $f(t) \in [a - \Delta, a + \Delta]$ for any time instance t.

By the construction of ChainTrackA, we must have:

(1) $y_i(t) \in [f(t) - \frac{i}{h+1}\Delta, f(t) + \frac{i}{h+1}\Delta]$ for any $i \in [1, h]$;

(2) $g(t) = y_{h+1}(t) \in [f(t) - \Delta, f(t) + \Delta]$.

Consider an adversary Alice that tries to explore the worst case for ChainTrackA. Suppose that t_0 is the initial time instance. Alice first sets $f(t_0) = a - \Delta$. It takes $h+1$ messages to let n_{h+1} learn a valid value for $g(t_0)$ at time t_0. By the facts above, it must be $y_i(t_0) \in [a - \Delta - \frac{i}{h+1}\Delta, a - \Delta + \frac{i}{h+1}\Delta]$ for any $i \in [1, h]$.

Alice then sets $f(t_1) = a + \Delta$. Now $y_i(t_0)$ is more than Δ away from $f(t_1)$ for any $i \in [1, h]$. By Lemma 1, such $y_i(t_0)$'s are not allowed, hence, any node n_i cannot simply set $y_i(t_1) = y_i(t_0)$. Instead, every node n_i needs to receive an update message to produce a valid tracking value $y_i(t_1)$. This leads to h messages. Again, based on the design of ChainTrackA, $y_i(t_1) \in [a + \Delta - \frac{i}{h+1}\Delta, a + \Delta + \frac{i}{h+1}\Delta]$.

Alice sets $f(t_2) = a - \Delta$, by a similar argument, this will again trigger h messages. She repeatedly alternates the subsequent values for f between $a + \Delta$ and $a - \Delta$. ChainTrackA pays at least h messages for any $t \in [t_0, t_{now}]$, which leads to $O(ht_{now})$ messages in total. However, the offline optimal algorithm on this problem instance only needs to set $g(t_0) = y_{h+1}(t_0) = a$ at t_0, which takes $h+1$ messages, and keeps all subsequent $g(t_i)$ same as $g(t_0)$.

Hence, cratio(ChainTrackA) $= ht_{now}/(h+1) = t_{now} = +\infty$. $\square$

Optimal chain online tracking. Recall that the centralized, two-party online tracking (simply known as online tracking) is a special case of chain online tracking with no relay nodes, i.e., $h = 0$. The OptTrack method in Algorithm 1 achieves an $O(\log \Delta)$-competitive ratio for the online tracking problem. Furthermore, it is also shown that $O(\log \Delta)$ is the lower bound for the competitive ratio of any online algorithms for online tracking [32,34]. Yet, when generalizing it to chain online tracking with either ChainTrackA or ChainTrackR, the competitive ratio suddenly becomes unbounded. The huge gap motivates us to explore other alternatives, which leads to the optimal chain online tracking method, ChainTrackO (chain-tracking-optimal).

This algorithm is shown in Algorithm 2, and its construction is surprisingly simple: allocate all error threshold to the very first relay node!

Algorithm 2: ChainTrackO (Δ, h)

Let the tracking output at a node n_i be $y_i(t)$.
Run OptTrack (Δ) between observer s and the first relay node n_1, by running n_1 as a tracker.
for *any node n_i where $i \in [1, h]$* **do**
  Whenever $y_i(t)$ has changed, send $y_i(t)$ to node n_{i+1} and set $y_{i+1}(t) = y_i(t)$.

Basically, ChainTrackO ensures that $y_1(t)$ is always within $f(t) \pm \Delta$ using the OptTrack method. For any other relay node n_i for $i \in [2, h+1]$, it maintains $y_i(t) = y_{i-1}(t)$ at all time instances t. The tracker T maintains $g(t) = y_{h+1}(t)$ (recall node n_{h+1} is the tracker node). In other words, $g(t) = y_{h+1}(t) = y_h(t) = \cdots = y_2(t) = y_1(t)$ for any t.

Lemma 3 *ChainTrackO's competitive ratio is $O(\log \Delta)$ for chain online tracking with h relay nodes.*

Proof. While running algorithm OptTrack between the observer s and node n_1, we define a round as a time period $[t_s, t_e]$, such that $S = [f(t_s) - \Delta, f(t_s) + \Delta]$ at t_s and $S = \emptyset$ at t_e from line 1 and line 2 in Algorithm 1. By the proof of Theorem 1 in [32,34], we know that OptTrack will communicate $O(\log \Delta)$ messages in a round. Thus, by the construction of Algorithm 2, ChainTrackO has to communicate $O(h \log \Delta)$ messages in this round.

For a round $[t_s, t_e]$, consider any time instance $t \in [t_s, t_e]$. Lemma 1 means that $y_i(t) \in [f(t) - \Delta, f(t) + \Delta]$ for any $i \in [1, h+1]$ in the offline optimal algorithm. Suppose node n_i receives no message in this round, then it must be the case that:

$$y_i(x) \in \cap_{t=t_s}^{x} [f(t) - \Delta, f(t) + \Delta] \text{ for any } x \in [t_s, t_e]. \quad (1)$$

Consider the set $S(x)$ at node n_1 at time x, where $S(x)$ is the set S at time x in Algorithm 1. By the construction of Algorithm 1, $S(x) = \cap_t [f(t) - \Delta, f(t) + \Delta]$ for a subset of time instances t from $[t_s, x]$ (only when $|f(t) - g(t)| > \Delta, S \leftarrow S \cap [f(t) - \Delta, f(t) + \Delta]$). Clearly, we must have:

$$\cap_{t=t_s}^{x} [f(t) - \Delta, f(t) + \Delta] \subseteq S(x) \text{ for any } x \in [t_s, t_e]. \quad (2)$$

By the end of this round, $S(t_e)$ becomes $\emptyset$ by the definition of a round, which means that $\cap_{t=t_s}^{x} [f(t) - \Delta, f(t) + \Delta]$ has become $\emptyset$ at some time $x \leq t_e$ by (2). But this means that (1) cannot be true. Hence, our assumption that node n_i receives no message in this round must be wrong. This argument obviously applies to any node n_i for $i \in [1, h+1]$, which implies that an offline optimal algorithm must have sent at least $h+1$ messages in this round.

Thus, cratio(ChainTrackO) $= ((h+1)\log \Delta)/(h+1) = \log \Delta$. $\square$

ChainTrackO is optimal among the class of online algorithms that solve the chain online tracking problem, in terms of its competitive ratio. Specifically, $O(\log \Delta)$ is the lower bound for the competitive ratio of any online algorithms for chain online tracking. Let C-OPT(h) be the number of messages sent by the offline optimal algorithm for a chain online tracking problem with h relay nodes.

Lemma 4 *Any online algorithms for chain online tracking of h relay nodes must send $\Omega(\log \Delta \cdot \text{C-OPT}(h))$ messages.*

4. THE BROOM CASE

A base case for distributed online tracking is the "broom" topology as shown in Figure 1(a). A broom topology is an extension of the chain topology where there are m observers (instead of only one) connected to the first relay node. Similarly as before, we denote the ith relay node as n_i, and n_1 is the first relay node that connects directly to m observers. In fact, a broom topology reduces to a chain topology when $m = 1$.

Since there are m functions, one from each observer, an important distinction is that the function to be tracked is computed based on these m functions. Specifically, the goal is to track $f(t)$ where $f(t) = f(f_1(t), \ldots, f_m(t))$ for some function f at T subject to an error threshold Δ. Clearly, the design of online tracking algorithms in this case will have to depend on the function f. We *focus on the max aggregate function* in this work, and discuss other aggregate functions in Section 6. Hence, in subsequent discussions, $f(t) = \max(f_1(t), \ldots, f_m(t))$ and $g(t)$ must be in the range $[f(t) - \Delta, f(t) + \Delta]$ at T, for any time instance t.

A baseline. A baseline method is to ask T to track each function $f_i(t)$ within $f_i(t) \pm \Delta$ for $i \in [1, m]$ using a function $g_i(t)$. The tracker computes $g(t) = \max(g_1(t), \ldots, g_m(t))$ for any time instance t. For the ith function, this can be done by using the ChainTrackO method for a chain online tracking instance, where the chain is the path from observer s_i to tracker T. Given that $g_i(t) \in [f_i(t) - \Delta, f_i(t) + \Delta]$ for all $i \in [1, m]$, it is trivial to show that $g(t) \in [f(t) - \Delta, f(t) + \Delta]$. We denote this approach as the m-Chain method.

Improvement. Recall that ChainTrackO allocates all error threshold to the first relay node n_1 in its chain; all other relay nodes simply forward every update arrived at n_1 (from observer s) to T. Hence, in the m-Chain method, it is n_1 that actually tracks $g_1(t), \ldots, g_m(t)$ and n_1 simply passes every update received for $g_i(t)$ through the chain to T. This clearly generates excessive communication. In light of this, we consider a class A_{broom} of online algorithms for broom online tracking as follows:

1. Every node u in a broom topology keeps a value $y_u(t)$ which represents the knowledge of u about $f(t)$ in the subtree rooted at u at time t. For a leaf node u (an observer), $y_u(t)$ is simply its function value $f_u(t)$.

2. Each leaf node u's function is tracked by its parent v within error Δ using $g_u(t)$, i.e., $|g_u(t) - f_u(t)| \leq \Delta$ for every time instance t. Note that $g_u(t)$ does not need to be $f_u(t)$. Specifically, a leaf u sends a new value $g_u(t)$ to its parent v *only when* $|g_u(last) - f_u(t)| > \Delta$, where $g_u(last)$ is the previous update u sent to v.

Note that in *both broom and tree models*, we *do not* analyze the competitive ratio (cratio) of their online algorithms. The reason is that in a broom or a tree topology, since the offline optimal algorithm offline can see the entire input instance in advance, offline can "communicate" between leaf nodes for free. These are observers that are distributed in the online case. As a result of this, there always exists an input instance where the performance gap between an online algorithm and offline is infinitely large.

Hence, in the following discussion, we will analyze the performance of an online algorithm using the concept of ratio as defined in Section 2.1 with respect to the class A_{broom}.

In a broom topology, we use $y_i(t)$ to denote $y_u(t)$ for a node u that is the ith relay node n_i.

Lemma 5 *Any algorithm $A \in A_{broom}$ must track functions $f_1(t), \ldots, f_m(t)$ with an error threshold that is exactly Δ at the first relay node n_1 in order to minimize* ratio(A).

Lemma 5 implies that $y_u(t)$ at every relay node u must be tracked by its parent node exactly, since all error thresholds have to be allocated to the first relay node n_1.

That said, whenever $y_i(t)$ changes, the message will be popped up along the chain to the tracker T. Formally,

Lemma 6 *Whenever $y_i(t) \neq y_i(t-1)$ at node n_i for any $i \in [1, h]$, any $A \in A_{broom}$ must send an update from n_i to n_{i+1}, and this update message must be $y_i(t)$.*

PROOF. This lemma is an immediate result of the above discussion. □

Lemmas 5 and 6 do *not* imply that A_{broom} does not have many choices, because there are still many possible tracking strategies between n_1 and the m leaf nodes (observers). But these two lemmas do help us reach the following theorem.

Theorem 2 *For any algorithm A in A_{broom}, there exists an input instance I and another algorithm $A' \in A_{broom}$, such that* cost(A, I) *is at least h times worse than* cost(A', I)*, i.e., for any $A \in A_{broom}$,* ratio$(A) = \Omega(h)$.

Theorem 2 implies that there does not exist an "overall optimal" algorithm A in A_{broom} that always achieves the smallest cost on all input instances from $\mathcal{I}$. Such an algorithm A would imply ratio$(A) = 1$, which contradicts the above.

Next, we present an online algorithm whose performance is close to the lower bound established by Theorem 2.

The BroomTrack method. We design the BroomTrack algorithm in Algorithm 3. Similarly as before, n_{h+1} refers to the tracker T and $g(t) = y_{h+1}(t)$.

Algorithm 3: BroomTrack (Δ, m, h)

run m instances of OptTrack (Δ), one instance per pair (s_i, n_1). note that s_i is the observer at the ith leaf node and n_1, the first relay node, behaves as a tracker in OptTrack, for $i \in [1, m]$;
let $g_j(t)$ be the tracking result at n_1 at time t for $f_j(t)$;
for *any time instance t* **do**
  if *no update in any* OptTrack *instances at n_1* **then** set $y_1(t) = y_1(t-1)$;
  else
    set $y_1(t) = \max(g_1(t), g_2(t), \ldots, g_m(t))$;
  for $i = 1, \ldots, h$ **do**
    if $t = 0$ *or* $y_i(t) \neq y_i(t-1)$ **then**
      send $y_i(t)$ to n_{i+1} and set $y_{i+1}(t) = y_i(t)$;
    else set $y_i(t) = y_i(t-1)$;

The idea of Algorithm 3 is inspired by the same principle we explored in the design of ChainTrackO for chain online tracking, which is to ask the first relay node to do all the tracking, and the remaining relay nodes simply "relay" the updates sent out by n_1. Specifically, n_1 tracks each function f_i from observer s_i *with error threshold* Δ, and monitors the maximum value among these tracking results; n_1 takes this value as $y_1(t)$, his tracking result for $f(t)$. Other than the first time instance $t = 0$, only a change in this value, when $y_1(t) \neq y_1(t-1)$, will cause a communication through the entire chain, to send $y_1(t)$ to the tracker T and set $g(t) = y_1(t)$. Otherwise, every node in the chain, including the tracker, simply sets $y_u(t) = y_u(t-1)$ without incurring any communication in the chain (from n_1 to T).

The correctness of BroomTrack is obvious: $|g_i(t) - f_i(t)| \leq \Delta$ for any i and t. And, at the tracker T, for any time instance t, $g(t) = y_1(t)$ and $y_1(t) = \max(g_1(t), \ldots, g_m(t))$ immediately lead to $|g(t) - f(t)| \leq \Delta$, for $f(t) = \max(f_1(t), \ldots, f_m(t))$.

Theorem 3 *With respect to online algorithms in A_{broom},* ratio(BroomTrack) $< h \log \Delta$.

PROOF. Given an input instance $I \in \mathcal{I}$, we denote M_i as the number of messages between s_i and n_1 for tracking function f_i up to t_{now} by algorithm BroomTrack. Thus, n_1 will receive $\sum_{i=1}^{m} M_i$ messages from $s_1, \ldots, s_m$. In the worst case, all of them get propagated up from n_1 to the root. So cost(BroomTrack, I) $\leq h \sum_{i=1}^{m} M_i$.

On the other hand, for any algorithm A ($A \neq$ BroomTrack) in A_{broom}, it takes at least $\frac{M_i}{\log \Delta}$ messages between s_i and n_1 to track $f_i(t)$ on the input I by Theorem 1. Further, A needs to propagate at least one message through the chain at the first time instance. Thus, cost$(A, I) \geq h + \frac{\sum_{i=1}^{m} M_i}{\log \Delta}$. Hence, for any $I \in \mathcal{I}$, the following holds:

$$\text{ratio}(\text{BroomTrack}, I) \leq \frac{h \sum_{i=1}^{m} M_i}{h + \frac{\sum_{i=1}^{m} M_i}{\log \Delta}} < h \log \Delta.$$

Hence, ratio(BroomTrack) $< h \log \Delta$. □

Similarly, we can show that m-Chain's ratio is $O(h \log \Delta)$ with respect to online algorithms in A_{broom}.

Corollary 1 ratio(m-Chain) $= O(h \log \Delta)$.

5. THE GENERAL TREE CASE

In a general tree topology, every leaf node is still an observer, but it is no longer necessary for all leaf nodes to appear in the same level in the tree. Furthermore, they do not need to share a single chain to the tracker T. We still assume that there are m observers and the tracker T locates at the root. Similarly as before, every non-leaf node (except the root node) is considered a relay node. Using a simililar definition as that for the class A_{broom} in the broom model, we can define A_{tree} as the class of online algorithms for the tree online tracking problem.

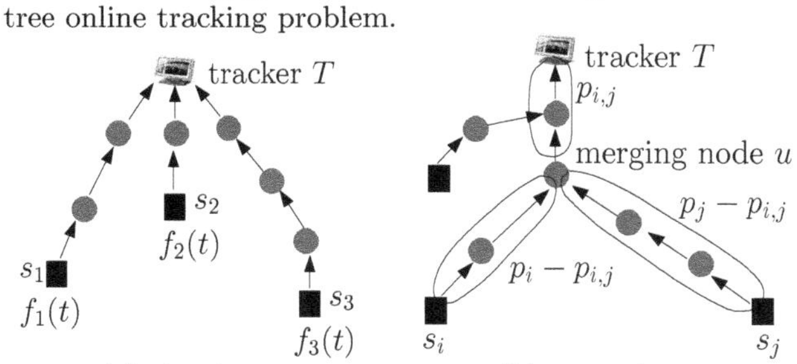

(a) simple tree. (b) general tree.

Figure 3: Tree online tracking.

A trivial case is shown in Figure 3(a). Any leaf node (an observer) is connected through a path to the tracker at the root, and no two paths share a common node except the root node. Every such path is a chain, hence, we can run the m-CHAIN method in this case. It is easy to show that m-CHAIN method is *an instance optimal* online method for this simple case, with respect to the class A_{tree}. In other words, its ratio is $O(1)$ with respect to A_{tree}.

So in the general case, an observer at a leaf node is still connected to the tracker through a single path. But a path may join another path at a non-root node u. We call such node u a "merging node". Let p_i be the ith path connecting observer s_i to T. A path p_i may join another path p_j at a merging node u, as illustrated in Figure 3(b). The common part of p_i and p_j is a chain from u to T, and is denoted as $p_{i,j}$ for any such i, j. Note that a path p_i may join with multiple, different paths at either one or more merging node(s), as shown in Figure 3(b). We use $(p - p')$ to denote the *subpath in a path* p that is *not a part of* another path p'.

When two paths p_i and p_j shares a merging node u, they form a *generalized broom model* in the sense that u connects to s_i and s_j through two separate chains, $(p_i - p_{i,j})$ and $(p_j - p_{i,j})$ respectively, and u itself connects to T through a single chain (that is $p_{i,j}$). When both s_i and s_j are directly connected under the merging node u, paths p_i and p_j become exactly a broom model (with two observers).

Given this observation, inspired by Theorem 2, we first have the following negative result.

Corollary 2 *There is no instance optimal algorithm for* A_{tree}.

Also inspired by the above observation, we can extend the idea behind BROOMTRACK to derive the TREETRACK method for tree online tracking. It basically runs a similar version of BROOMTRACK on all generalized broom models found in a tree topology. This algorithm is shown in Algorithm 4 and its correctness is established by Lemma 7.

Lemma 7 *Consider a node u. suppose $y_1, \ldots, y_\ell$ are the most recent updates of its ℓ child nodes. let z be the most recent update sent from u to its parent node. Define $y = \max\{y_1, \ldots, y_\ell\}$. If $y \neq z$, then u must send an update to its parent node, and this update message must be y.*

Algorithm 4: TREETRACK (Δ, a general tree R)

---

for *any non-leaf node u in R with an observer s_i as a leaf node directly connected under u* **do**
  run an instances of OPTTRACK (Δ) between u and s_i, where u is the tracker and s_i is the observer;
for *any non-leaf node u in R at any time instance* **do**
  let $y_1, \ldots, y_\ell$ be the most recent updates of its ℓ child nodes;
  let z be the most recent update of u to its parent;
  set $y = \max\{y_1, \ldots, y_\ell\}$;
  if $y \neq z$ **then**
    send y as an update to u's parent node in R
$g(t)$ at tracker T is the maximum value among the most recent updates T has received from all its child nodes.

Lastly, if we denote h_{max} as the max length (the number of relay nodes in a path) of any path in a general tree, we can show the following results for TREETRACK.

Corollary 3 ratio(TREETRACK) $= O(h_{max} \log \Delta)$ *with respect to* A_{tree}.

6. OTHER FUNCTIONS AND TOPOLOGIES

6.1 Other functions for f

It is trivial to see that all of our results hold for min as well. That said, for any *distributive aggregates* on any topology, our methods can be extended to work for these aggregates. A *distributive aggregate* can be computed in a divide-and-conquer strategy, i.e., $f(f_1(t), \ldots, f_m(t)) = f(f(f_{a_1}(t), \ldots, f_{a_i}(t)), f(f_{a_{i+1}}(t), \ldots, f_{a_m}(t)))$, where $\{(a_1, \ldots, a_i), (a_{i+1}, \ldots, a_m)\}$ represents a (random) permutation and partition of $\{1, \ldots, m\}$. Other than max and min, another examples is sum. In online tracking, since we assume that the number of observers is a constant, hence, tracking average is equivalent to tracking sum (because the count is a constant).

So consider sum as an example, we can extend m-CHAIN to both broom and tree models, by allocating Δ/m error for each chain. BROOMTRACK and TREETRACK can be extended as well, by: (1) allocating error thresholds *only* to a chain connecting to a merging node; (2) and making sure that the sum of error thresholds from *all chains to all merging nodes* equals Δ. The rest of the algorithm is designed in a similar fashion as that in BROOMTRACK and TREETRACK, respectively. It is easy to see that, no matter there are how many merging nodes, there are exactly m such chains. So a simple scheme is to simply allocate the error threshold Δ equally to any chain connecting to a merging node. Of course, the ratio of these algorithms needs to be analyzed with respect to the class of online algorithms for sum, which will be different from that in the max case. Such analyses are beyond the scope of this paper, and will be studied in the full version of this work.

More interestingly, our methods can be extended to work with *holistic aggregate* (aggregates that cannot be computed distributively) in certain case, such as *any quantiles* in a *broom* topology. Specifically, we can modify both m-CHAIN and BROOMTRACK for max to derive similar m-CHAIN and

BROOMTRACK methods for distributed online tracking with any quantile function in a broom topology. Suppose $f(t) = \phi(f_1(t), \ldots, f_m(t))$, where $\phi(S)$ represents an ϕ-quantile from a set S of one dimension values for any $\phi \in (0, 1)$. When $\phi = 0.5$, we get the median function.

The only change needed for m-CHAIN is to change f = max to $f = \phi$-quantile at the tracker, when applying f over $g_1(t), \ldots, g_m(t)$.

For BROOMTRACK, the only change we need to make is in line 6 in Algorithm 3, by replacing max with ϕ-quantile, i.e., $y_1(t) = \phi(g_1(t), \ldots, g_m(t))$. The following lemma ensures the correctness of these adaptions.

Lemma 8 *Let* $y_1(t) = \phi(g_1(t), \ldots, g_m(t))$ *and* $f(t) = \phi(f_1(t), \ldots, f_m(t))$. *If* $|g_i(t) - f_i(t)| \leq \Delta$ *for all* $i \in [1, m]$, *then it must be* $|y_1(t) - f(t)| \leq \Delta$.

The proof is provided in Appendix A. Furthermore, using similar arguments, we can show a similar lower bound and upper bound, as that for the max case, on the ratio of these algorithms with respect to the class of online algorithms for tracking a quantile function in the broom model.

For the general-tree model, the m-CHAIN method still works for tracking any quantile function (since the tracker T tracks $f_1(t), \ldots, f_m(t)$ within error Δ with $g_1(t), \ldots, g_m(t)$). However, the TREETRACK method no longer works. The fundamental reason is that one cannot combine quantiles from two subtrees to obtain the quantile value of the union of the two subtrees. A similar argument holds against combining the tracking results from two subtrees in the case of quantile online tracking.

6.2 Other topologies

As we already mentioned in Section 2, the general tree topology can be used to cover the cases when a relay node also serves as an observer at the same time. The idea is illustrated in Figure 4(a). A conceptual observer s' can be added as a leaf-level child node to such a relay node u. Our algorithms and results are carried over to this case. The only difference is that there is no need to run OPTTRACK between s' and u. Instead, u gets $g'(t) = f'(t)$ for free, where $f'(t)$ is the function at s' (the function at u when he acts as an observer). This is useful when intermediate nodes in a network or a distributed system also observe data values of interest to the computation of f being tracked.

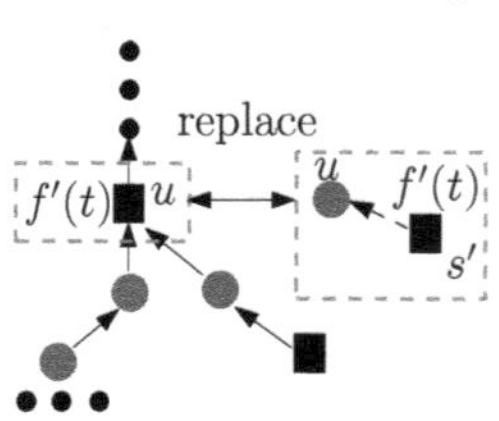

(a) observer at relay node.

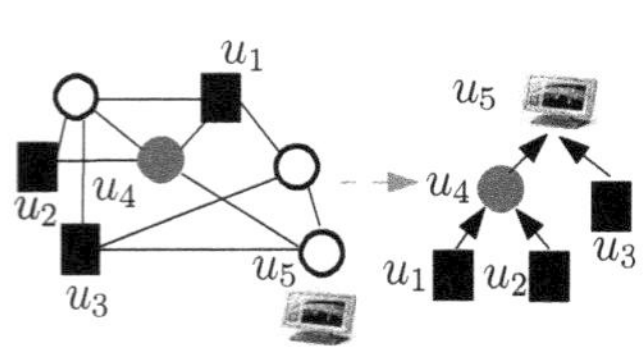

(b) graph topology.

Figure 4: Other topologies.

Lastly, our results from the general tree topology also extend to a graph. On a graph topology G, a distributed online tracking instance has a tracker T at a node from the graph, and m observers on m other nodes on the graph. We can find the shortest path from an observer s_i to T on the graph G, for each $i \in [1, m]$, where the length of a path is determined by the number of graph nodes it contains. Then, a general tree topology can be constructed (conceptually) from these m shortest paths by merging any common graph node from these paths into a single parent node with proper child nodes. T is the root node, and each observer is a leaf node. An example is shown in Figure 4(b).

6.3 Asynchronous updates

So far in our discussion, we assumed that observers receive *synchronous updates* at all time instances, i.e., each observer receives an update on the value of its function at each time instance. In some applications, this may not be the case and observers may receive *asynchronous updates*, in which not only the data arrival rates for different observers may be different, but also the data arrival rate for a single observer may also change over time. Asynchronous updates seem to present new challenges, nevertheless, all our methods can handle asynchronous updates gracefully, in the same way as they do for synchronous updates.

Consider any time instance t for an observer s and its function f, and assume that there are x values, $\{v_1, \ldots, v_x\}$ arriving at s at t. Recall that in our solution framework, u and s simply runs the centralized tracking algorithm OPTTRACK with error parameter Δ [32,34] (say we consider max as an example).

If we treat these values arriving at t as x updates in x time instances $t.1, \ldots, t.x$, and simply continue to run our tracking method between s and u, then u always has an approximation g that is within $f \pm \Delta$ *continuously*. This holds for any observer even if they have different arrival rates. The key observation is that when u receives an update from one observer s_i, but not from another observer s_j, either because s_j didn't receive an update for its function or it did receive an update but OPTTRACK didn't trigger an update message to u, u still holds a valid approximation for each observer's function, guaranteed by the independent centralized tracking (OPTTRACK) instance between u and any observer attached to u!

7. EXPERIMENT

All algorithms were implemented in C++. We tested various distributed topologies, and executed all experiments in a Linux machine with an Intel Core I7-2600 3.4GHz CPU and 8GB memory. Every single communication between *two directly connected nodes* u and v contributes one message.

Data sets. We used two real data sets. The first data set is a temperature data set (TEMP) from the MesoWest project [18], a national environmental measurement network. It contains temperature measurements from Jan 1997 to Oct 2011 from 26,383 distinct stations across the United States. We randomly select a subset of stations as the observers and treat readings from a station as the values of the function for that observer.

The second data set is wind direction measurements (WD) from the SAMOS project [27], a weather observation network based on research vessels and voluntary ships at sea. Raw readings from the research vessel Wecoma were obtained which consist of approximately 11.8 million records observed during a 9 month interval in 2010. Wecoma reports a measurement as frequent as 1 second, but may report no readings for a number of seconds between two measurements. We partition these records by a week interval, which leads to 36 chunks. Then we randomly select a subset of data chunks and treat the readings from each chunk as the values of an observer's function.

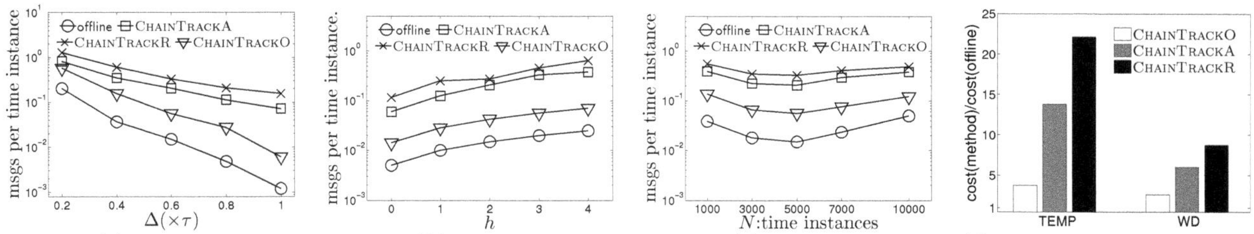

(a) vary Δ. (b) vary h. (c) vary N. (d) cost(method)/cost(offline)

Figure 5: Performance of chain tracking methods on TEMP.

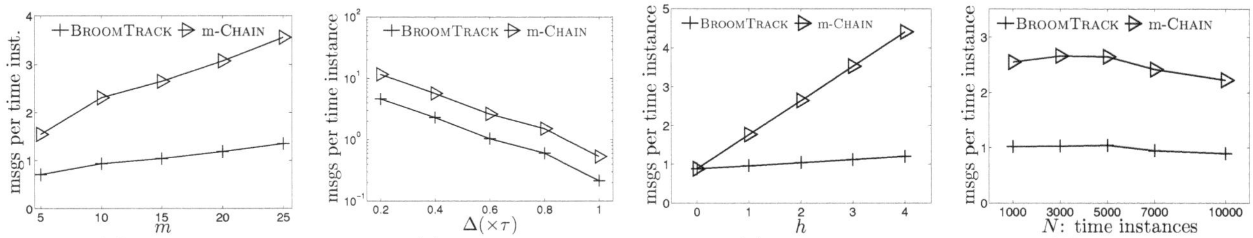

(a) vary m (b) vary Δ. (c) vary h. (d) vary N.

Figure 6: Performance of broom tracking methods on TEMP.

In all data sets, values at each observer are sorted by their timestamps (from MesoWest or SAMOS). By default, at each time instance, we feed each observer one reading as its observed function value at that time instance, which leads to synchronous updates across observers, i.e., each observer receives a single update at each time instance. These two data sets provide quite different distributions: we plot the function values of the function from an observer using a small sample (1000 time instances) in Figure 7.

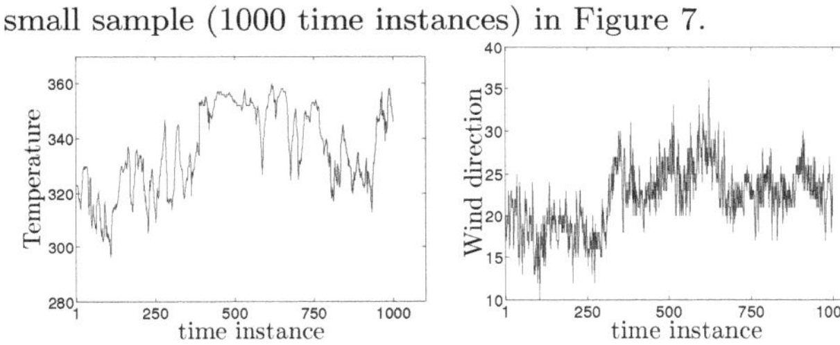

(a) TEMP (b) WD

Figure 7: $f_1(t)$ for TEMP and WD, for $t \in [1, 1000]$.

Setup. We use TEMP as the default data set. The default values of key parameters are: the number of time instances $N = 5000$; the number of relay nodes in a chain or a broom topology by default is $h = 2$. The default aggregate function f is max. For any function f_i, we compute its standard deviation (std) with respect to $t \in [1, N]$. We set $\tau = \text{avg}(\text{std}(f_1), \ldots, \text{std}(f_m))$ for $f = \max$. We then set the default Δ value to 0.6τ. For the broom model, we set the default number of observers $m = 15$, i.e., number of leaf nodes connecting to the first relay node.

Note that leaf nodes can sit on different levels in a general tree topology. To produce a tree topology, each child node of an internal node with fanout F becomes a leaf node with probability p. We stop expanding nodes when they reach the tree level that equals the tree height H. We set $F = 3$, $p = 0.5$ and $H = 4$ as default values when generating a general tree topology.

For each experiment, we *vary the values for one parameter while setting the other parameters at their default values.* We report the *average total number of messages per time instance* in a topology for different methods. This is denoted as "msgs per time instance" in our experimental results.

7.1 Chain model

Figure 5(a) shows the communication cost when we vary Δ from 0.2τ to τ. Clearly, the communication cost reduces for all methods as Δ increases, since larger Δ values make a tracking algorithm less sensitive to the change of function values. ChainTrackO outperforms both ChainTrackA and ChainTrackR for all Δ values by an order of magnitude. Compared with the cost of the offline optimal method, denoted as offline, ChainTrackO performs well consistently. Averaging over the whole tracking period, offline needs 0.015 message per time instance and ChainTrackO takes only 0.056 message per time instance when $\Delta = 0.6\tau$.

Figure 5(b) shows the communication cost as h increases from 0 to 4. Note that when $h = 0$ the chain model becomes the centralized setting (one observer connects to the tracker directly). Not surprisingly, all methods need more messages on average as the chain contains more relay nodes while h increases. Among the three online algorithms, ChainTrackO gives the best performance for all h values. Meanwhile, we verified that its competitive ratio is indeed independent of h, by calculating the ratio between the number of messages sent by ChainTrackO and offline.

We then vary the number of time instances N from 1000 to 10,000 in Figure 5(c). We observe that the communication cost of all methods first decreases and then increases around $N = 5000$. This is explained by the dynamic nature of functions values over time, due to the real data sets we have used in our experiments.

Figure 5(d) shows the ratio between the cost of a method and the cost of offline, on both TEMP and WD data sets. Clearly, on both data sets, ChainTrackO has significantly outperformed both ChainTrackA and ChainTrackR. The cost of ChainTrackO is very close to the cost of offline.

7.2 Broom model

Figure 6(a) shows the communication cost as we vary m the number of observers in a broom topology from 5 to 25. We see that BroomTrack outperforms m-Chain for all m values and the gap enlarges for larger m values. In particular, when $m = 15$ m-Chain takes on average 2.64 mes-

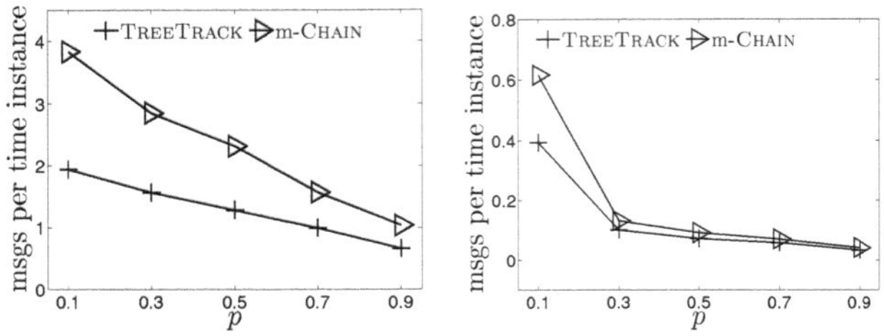

(a) TEMP (b) WD

Figure 8: General tree: vary p.

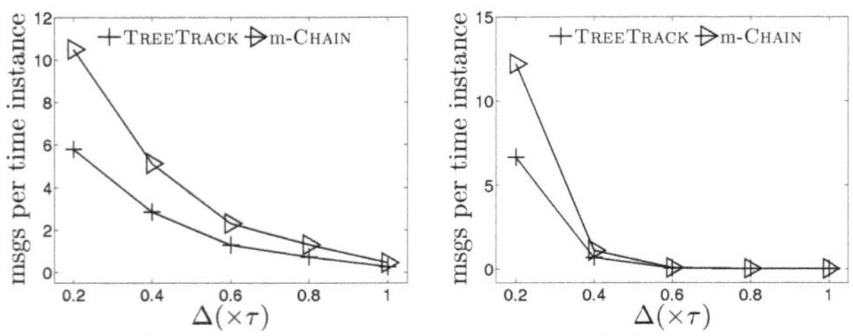

(a) TEMP (b) WD

Figure 9: General tree: vary Δ.

sages per time instance while BROOMTRACK takes only 1.04 messages per time instance, in a broom topology with 15 observers and 2 relay nodes. Note that if we were to track function values exactly, this means that we will need 45 messages per time instance! In the following, we use $m = 15$ as the default value in a broom topology.

Figure 6(b) shows the communication cost when we change Δ from 0.2τ to τ. For all Δ values, BROOMTRACK has outperformed m-CHAIN by more than 3 times consistently. Again, for similar reasons, a larger Δ value always leads to less communication.

We change h, the number of relay nodes in a broom topology, from 0 to 4 in Figure 6(c). When $h = 0$, there is no relay node and all observers are directly connected to the tracker itself. Therefore, BROOMTRACK and m-CHAIN give the same communication cost when $h = 0$. We see that m-CHAIN suffers from the increase of h much more significantly compared to BROOMTRACK, and BROOMTRACK scales very well against more relay nodes. In particular, its number of messages per time instance only increases slightly from 0.88 to 1.20 when h goes from 0 to 4. Again, if we were to track all functions exactly, when the broom has 4 relay nodes and 15 observers, we will need 75 messages per time instance!

We vary N from 1000 to 10,000 in Figure 6(d). It shows that the average number of messages per time instance is quite stable and only decreases slightly when N goes beyond 5000 for both BROOMTRACK and m-CHAIN methods. This is caused by the change in the distribution of function values with respect to the time dimension.

7.3 General tree topology

We first vary p, when generating a tree topology, from 0.1 to 0.9 in Figure 8. The corresponding number of observers in the trees that were generated ranges from 27 to 7. Note that larger p values tend to produce less number of observers, since more nodes become leaf nodes (observers) early and they stop generating subtrees even though the height of the tree has not been reached yet in the tree generation process. Not surprisingly, the communication cost of both method reduces as p increases on both data sets. Averaging over the whole tracking period, when $p = 0.5$ TREETRACK takes 1.28 messages per time instance while m-CHAIN takes 2.21 messages per time instance on TEMP data set. This particular tree has 15 leaf nodes (observers) and 22 nodes in total. In the same tree topology, if we were to track function values exactly, we will need 41 messages per time instance! On WD data set, both methods need even less number of messages per time instance as shown in Figure 8(b). We set $p = 0.5$ as the default value in general-tree topologies.

Figure 9 shows the communication cost when we vary Δ from 0.2τ to τ. Again, TREETRACK outperforms m-CHAIN for all Δ values on both TEMP and WD data sets. In particular, these results show that TREETRACK is very effective in tracking changes of function values in a tree. For example, Figure 9(b) shows that TREETRACK takes on average 0.07 message per time instance when $\Delta = 0.6\tau$ on WD data set.

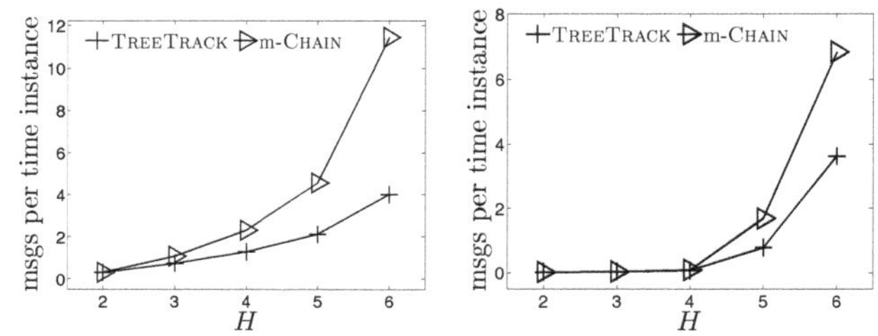

(a) TEMP (b) WD

Figure 10: General tree: vary H.

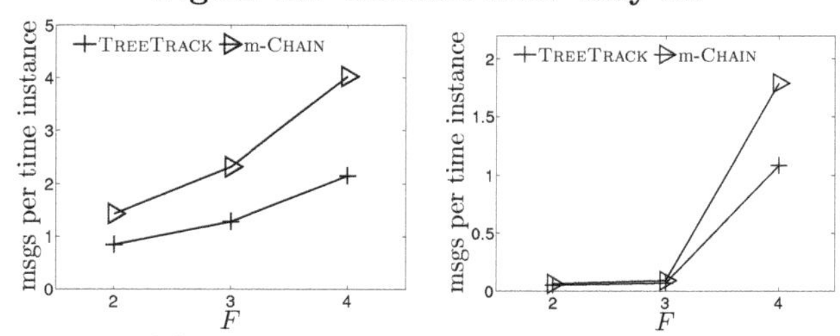

(a) TEMP (b) WD

Figure 11: General tree: vary F.

Next, we grow the size of a tree by increasing H, the height of a tree, from 2 to 6 in Figure 10. Note that the number of nodes in a general tree increases exponentially in terms of H. Therefore, both methods show an increase in communication cost as H increases on both data sets. Nevertheless, we still see a significant performance improvement of TREETRACK over m-CHAIN as H increases on both WD and TEMP data sets. Also note that even though the communication cost increases as a tree grows higher, TREETRACK is still very effective. For example, when $H = 6$, we have a general tree of 91 nodes and 61 of them are leaf nodes (observers). Tracking these functions exactly would require more than 300 messages per time instance. But in this case, TREETRACK has sent on average only 3.6 messages and 4 messages on WD and TEMP data sets respectively.

We vary the fan-out F from 2 to 4 in Figure 11. Not surprisingly, both m-CHAIN and TREETRACK show an increasing communication cost as F increases on both data sets since larger F values lead to more nodes in a tree. But the cost of TREETRACK increases much slowly. And in all cases, TREETRACK performs much better than m-CHAIN, and is still orders of magnitude more effective if we compare its cost against the cost of tracking all functions exactly.

7.4 Other functions

Next, we investigate our online algorithms for tracking sum and median aggregate functions respectively. We evaluate their performance using the default parameter values on both data sets, over both broom and tree models. Note that under the default setting, if we were to tracking function values exactly, we will need 45 messages per time instance in the broom instance and 41 messages per time instance in the tree instance.

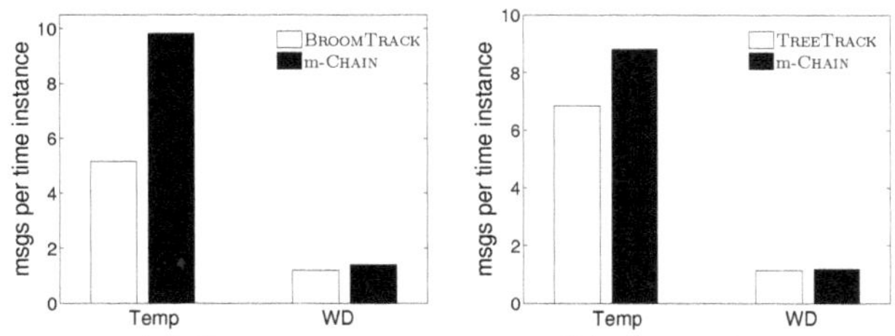

(a) Broom (b) General tree

Figure 12: Track sum on broom and general tree.

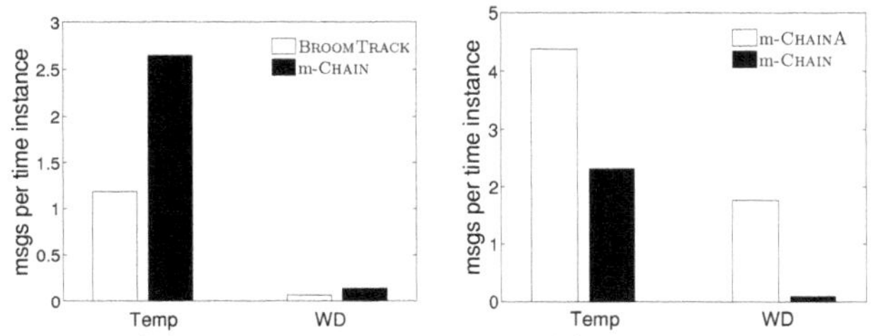

(a) Broom (b) General tree

Figure 13: Track median on broom and general tree.

We first explore the performance of our methods for tracking sum function in Figure 12, for both broom and tree models. In this case, we define $\tau = \text{std}(f(t))$ for $t \in [1, N]$, where we calculate the values of $f(t)$ offline based on functions $f_1(t), \ldots, f_m(t)$, i.e., $f(t) = \sum_{i=1}^{m} f_i(t)$. Our improved methods (BROOMTRACK and TREETRACK) still outperforms m-CHAIN in communication cost on both data sets.

Figure 13 compares the performance of different methods for tracking median function on both broom and tree models. Figure 13(a) shows that BROOMTRACK outperforms m-CHAIN in communication cost on both data sets. We evaluate the performance of m-CHAIN and m-CHAINA in Figure 13(b) for general-tree topology since TREETRACK does not work in this case. Here, m-CHAINA is a m-chain tracking method that calls CHAINTRACKA for each chain. It confirms our analysis that allocating tracking error to the first relay node indeed is better than allocating error threshold over different relay nodes in a chain, and m-CHAIN performs much better than m-CHAINA on both data sets.

7.5 Asynchronous updates

By default, we experimented with synchronous updates at all observers, i.e., each observer receives an update per time unit. As discussed in Section 6.3, our methods handle asynchronous updates as well. Next, we show experiments to track the max over observers with different data arrival rates using the WD dataset. We use $m = 15$ observers and default values for other parameters.

In particular, in this experiment, we take *one minute* as a time instance for the SAMOS data set [27]. Each ship in SAMOS collects measurement as frequent as 1 second, but it is also possible that a ship didn't report any measurements for a number of seconds. This leads to different arrival rates for different observers when they measure updates in minute interval. Figure 14(a) shows the data arrival rate over time for an observer over the first 3,500 minutes. Clearly, its data arrival rate fluctuates over time.

Figure 14(b) shows the communication cost over time of BROOMTRACK and m-CHAIN under dynamic data arrival rates at 15 observers. We also show msgs per minute for the exact tracking method ($m = 15$ and $h = 2$), which is denoted by the blue line in Figure 14(b). Clearly, both BROOMTRACK and m-CHAIN outperform exact tracking, and BROOMTRACK performs the best over all time instances.

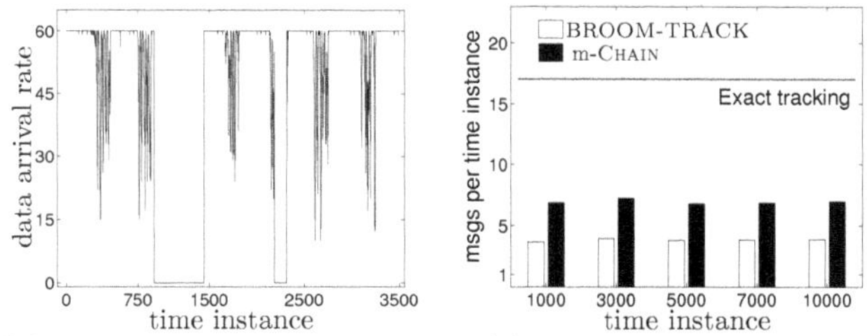

(a) Arrival rate at an observer (b) Communication cost

Figure 14: Broom: max, asynchronous updates.

8. RELATED WORK

Online tracking is a problem that has only been recently studied in [32,34], which we have reviewed in details in Section 2. Only the centralized setting was studied in [32,34].

In the popular *distributed streaming model*, the goal is to produce an approximation of certain functions/properties computed over the *union of data stream elements seen so far* for all observers, from the beginning of the time till now, for example, [5–7,19,33]). There are studies in distributed streaming model on a time-based sliding window of size W [10,11,17,23,26]. Their objective is to compute an aggregate of interest over the union of all elements (from a single or multiple streams) between 0 and t_{now} or a sliding window of size W (with respect to t_{now}) [5–7,19,33].

When a time-based sliding window is used, e.g., [10,11,17], by setting the window size $W = 1$, their problems resemble some similarity to our problem. However, there are two important distinctions. Firstly, prior works for computing aggregates over distributed streams using time-based sliding window focus on computing *aggregates defined over item frequencies* (in fact, this is the case for most streaming algorithms), while our problem is to track an aggregate over *item values*. Secondly, for aggregation over time-based sliding window [10,11,17] and streaming algorithms in general, the approximation error is typically quantified by an error parameter $\varepsilon \in (0, 1)$ over the *total frequency* of all item counts in the current window, while an error parameter $\Delta \in \mathbb{Z}^+$ is used in our problem to bound the error in the *output value* of an aggregation over current *item values* from all sites.

In distributed settings with multiple observers, to the best of our knowledge and as pointed out by the prior studies that have proposed the state-of-the-art centralized method [32, 34], a comprehensive study of the distributed online tracking problem with theoretical guarantees is still an open problem. Cormode et al. studied a special instance of this problem, but focused on only *monotone functions* [8,9]. When f is the top-k function, a heuristic method has been proposed in [1] which provides no theoretical analysis. In contrast, our work focuses on common aggregation functions and principled methods with theoretical guarantees on their communication costs.

Several existing studies explored the problem of threshold monitoring over distributed data [20, 21, 29], where the goal is to monitor continuously if $f(t)$ (a function value computed over the data values of all observers at time instance t) is above a user-defined threshold or not. Note that, in threshold monitoring the tracker only needs to verify if the function value has exceeded a threshold or not, instead of keeping an approximation that is always within $f(t) \pm \Delta$. The geometric-based methods have been further explored to provide better solutions to the threshold monitoring problem [16], and the function approximation problem in the distributed streaming model [15] (which as analyzed above is different from the online tracking problem).

9. CONCLUSION

This paper studies the problem of distributed online tracking. We first extend the recent results for online tracking in the centralized, two party model to the chain model, by introducing relay nodes between observer and tracker. We then investigate both the broom model and the tree model, as well as other different tracking functions. Extensive experiments on real data sets demonstrate that our methods perform much better than baseline methods. Many interesting directions are open for future work, including but not limited to formally analyzing the ratios of our methods when extending them to different aggregates, investigating online tracking with an error threshold that may change over time.

10. ACKNOWLEDGMENT

Mingwang Tang and Feifei Li were supported in part by NSF grants 1251019 and 1200792. Feifei Li was also supported in part by NSFC grant 61428204. The research of Yufei Tao was supported by grants GRF 4168/13 and GRF 142072/14 from HKRGC.

11. REFERENCES

[1] B. Babcock and C. Olston. Distributed top-k monitoring. In *SIGMOD*, pages 28–39, 2003.

[2] A. R. Beresford and F. Stajano. Location privacy in pervasive computing. *IEEE Pervasive Computing*, 2(1):46–55, 2003.

[3] B. Chandramouli, S. Nath, and W. Zhou. Supporting distributed feed-following apps over edge devices. *PVLDB*, 6(13):1570–1581, 2013.

[4] B. Chandramouli, J. Phillips, and J. Yang. Value-based notification conditions in large-scale publish/subscribe systems. In *VLDB*, pages 878–889, 2007.

[5] G. Cormode and M. N. Garofalakis. Sketching streams through the net: Distributed approximate query tracking. In *VLDB*, pages 13–24, 2005.

[6] G. Cormode and M. N. Garofalakis. Streaming in a connected world: querying and tracking distributed data streams. In *EDBT*, 2008.

[7] G. Cormode, M. N. Garofalakis, S. Muthukrishnan, and R. Rastogi. Holistic aggregates in a networked world: Distributed tracking of approximate quantiles. In *SIGMOD Conference*, pages 25–36, 2005.

[8] G. Cormode, S. Muthukrishnan, and K. Yi. Algorithms for distributed functional monitoring. In *SODA*, pages 1076–1085, 2008.

[9] G. Cormode, S. Muthukrishnan, and K. Yi. Algorithms for distributed functional monitoring. *ACM Transactions on Algorithms*, 7(2):21, 2011.

[10] G. Cormode and K. Yi. Tracking distributed aggregates over time-based sliding windows. In *PODC*, pages 213–214, 2011.

[11] G. Cormode and K. Yi. Tracking distributed aggregates over time-based sliding windows. In *SSDBM*, pages 416–430, 2012.

[12] A. Deshpande, C. Guestrin, S. Madden, J. M. Hellerstein, and W. Hong. Model-driven data acquisition in sensor networks. In *VLDB*, pages 588–599, 2004.

[13] Y. Diao, S. Rizvi, and M. J. Franklin. Towards an internet-scale xml dissemination service. In *VLDB*, pages 612–623, 2004.

[14] R. Fagin, A. Lotem, and M. Naor. Optimal aggregation algorithms for middleware. *J. Comput. Syst. Sci.*, 66(4):614–656, 2003.

[15] M. N. Garofalakis, D. Keren, and V. Samoladas. Sketch-based geometric monitoring of distributed stream queries. *PVLDB*, 6(10):937–948, 2013.

[16] N. Giatrakos, A. Deligiannakis, M. N. Garofalakis, I. Sharfman, and A. Schuster. Prediction-based geometric monitoring over distributed data streams. In *SIGMOD*, pages 265–276, 2012.

[17] L.-K. L. Ho-Leung Chan, Tak-Wah Lam and H.-F. Ting. Continuous monitoring of distributed data streams over a time-based sliding window. *Algorithmica*, 62(3-4):1088–1111, 2012.

[18] J. Horel, M. Splitt, L. Dunn, J. Pechmann, B. White, C. Ciliberti, S. Lazarus, J. Slemmer, D. Zaff, and J. Burks. Mesowest: cooperative mesonets in the western united states. *Bull. Amer. Meteor. Soc.*, 83(2):211–226, 2002. http://www.mesowest.org.

[19] Z. Huang, K. Yi, and Q. Zhang. Randomized algorithms for tracking distributed count, frequencies, and ranks. In *PODS*, pages 295–306, 2012.

[20] S. R. Kashyap, J. Ramamirtham, R. Rastogi, and P. Shukla. Efficient constraint monitoring using adaptive thresholds. In *ICDE*, pages 526–535, 2008.

[21] R. Keralapura, G. Cormode, and J. Ramamirtham. Communication-efficient distributed monitoring of thresholded counts. In *SIGMOD*, pages 289–300, 2006.

[22] S. Madden, M. J. Franklin, J. M. Hellerstein, and W. Hong. Tinydb: an acquisitional query processing system for sensor networks. *ACM Trans. Database Syst.*, 30(1):122–173, 2005.

[23] A. Manjhi, V. Shkapenyuk, K. Dhamdhere, and C. Olston. Finding (recently) frequent items in distributed data streams. In *ICDE*, pages 767–778, 2005.

[24] R. Motwani and P. Raghavan. *Randomized Algorithms*. Cambridge University Press, 1995.

[25] C. Olston, B. T. Loo, and J. Widom. Adaptive precision setting for cached approximate values. In *SIGMOD Conference*, pages 355–366, 2001.

[26] O. Papapetrou, M. N. Garofalakis, and A. Deligiannakis. Sketch-based querying of distributed sliding-window data streams. *PVLDB*, 5(10):992–1003, 2012.

[27] SAMOS. Shipboard Automated Meteorological and Oceanographic System. http://samos.coaps.fsu.edu.

[28] J. H. Schiller and A. Voisard, editors. *Location-Based Services*. Morgan Kaufmann, 2004.

[29] I. Sharfman, A. Schuster, and D. Keren. A geometric approach to monitoring threshold functions over distributed data streams. In *SIGMOD*, pages 301–312, 2006.

[30] A. C.-C. Yao. Some complexity questions related to distributive computing (preliminary report). In *STOC*, pages 209–213, 1979.

[31] Y. Yao and J. Gehrke. Query processing in sensor networks. In *CIDR*, 2003.

[32] K. Yi and Q. Zhang. Multi-dimensional online tracking. In *SODA*, pages 1098–1107, 2009.

[33] K. Yi and Q. Zhang. Optimal tracking of distributed heavy hitters and quantiles. In *PODS*, pages 167–174, 2009.

[34] K. Yi and Q. Zhang. Multidimensional online tracking. *ACM Transactions on Algorithms*, 8(2):12, 2012.

APPENDIX

A. PROOFS

Lemma 1 *For an algorithm A (either online or offline) that solves the chain online tracking problem, we must have $y_i(t) \in [f(t) - \Delta, f(t) + \Delta]$ for any $i \in [1, h+1]$ in order to reduce communication while ensuring correctness. This holds for any $t \in [0, t_{now}]$.*

PROOF. We prove a general fact that holds for any relay node and the tracker. Consider any node n_i for $i \in [1, h]$, and its successor n_{i+1}. We prove that the error (defined as $|y_{i+1}(t) - f(t)|$) at n_{i+1} cannot be lower than that at n_i for any time instance t. This is true because no matter what n_i tells n_{i+1}, n_i can also tell that to itself. In other words, n_i has at least the same amount of information that n_{i+1} does in order to reduce the tracking error.

That said, since we must have $|y_{h+1}(t) - f(t)| \leq \Delta$ at any time instance t at the tracker node n_{h+1}, combined with the fact above, it implies that $|y_i(t) - f(t)| \leq \Delta$ for any t and $i \in [1, h]$. □

Lemma 4 *Any online algorithms for chain online tracking of h relay nodes must send $\Omega(\log \Delta \cdot \textsf{C-OPT}(h))$ messages.*

PROOF. Suppose A is an online algorithm for chain online tracking with h relay nodes. The approximations of $f(t)$ at different nodes are $y_1(t), y_2(t), \ldots, y_h(t), y_{h+1}(t)$ respectively (note that n_{h+1} is the tracker T, and $g(t) = y_{h+1}(t)$).

Consider an adversary Alice, who maintains an integer set R such that any $y \in R$ at time instance t is a valid representative for the value of $f(t)$, for $t \in [t_s, t_e]$. Note that a round is defined as a period $[t_s, t_e]$, such that $R = [f(t_s) - \Delta, f(t_s) + \Delta]$ at t_s and $R = \emptyset$ at t_e. Let d_i be the number of integers in R after the i-th update sent out by algorithm A from the observer. Initially, $R = [f(t_s) - \Delta, f(t_s) + \Delta]$ and $d_0 = 2\Delta + 1$.

In each round $[t_s, t_e]$, we will show that there exists a sequence of $f(t)$ values such that A has to send $\Omega(\log \Delta \cdot \textsf{C-OPT}(h))$ messages, but the optimal offline method has to send only $\textsf{C-OPT}(h)$ messages.

Consider a time instance $t \in [t_s, t_e]$ after the i-th update sent by algorithm A. Let x be the median of R. Without loss of generality, suppose more than $\frac{h+1}{2}$ values among $\{y_1(t), y_2(t), \ldots, y_{h+1}(t)\}$ are in the range $[\min(R), x]$, let $Y_{\leq}(t)$ be the set of such values and $z = \max(Y_{\leq}(t))$.

Alice sets $f(t+1) = z + \Delta + 1$. It is easy to verify that $f(t+1) - y_i(t) > \Delta$ for any $y_i(t) \in Y_{\leq}(t)$. Hence, any node n_i, such that $y_i(t) \in Y_{\leq}(t)$, must receive an update at $(t+1)$ to ensure that $y_i(t+1) \in [f(t+1) - \Delta, f(t+1) + \Delta]$ by Lemma 1. This means that A has to send at least $\frac{h+1}{2}$ messages (the size of $Y_{\leq}(t)$) from t to $t+1$.

After the $(i+1)$-th update sent out by A from the observer, R has to be updated as $R \leftarrow R \cap [f(t+1) - \Delta, f(t+1) + \Delta]$, i.e., $R = [z + 1, x + (d_i - 1)/2]$ and its size reduces by at most half at each iteration when A sends out an update from the observer. It's easy to see that $d_{i+1} \geq (d_i - 1)/2$. Using the same argument, we will get a similar result if more than $\frac{h+1}{2}$ values of $\{y_1(t), \ldots, y_{h+1}(t)\}$ are in the range $[x, \max(R)]$. In that case, we set $f(t+1) = z - \Delta - 1$ where $z = \min(Y_{\geq}(t))$.

That said, it takes at least $\Omega(\log \Delta)$ iterations for R to be a constant, since R's initial size is $O(\Delta)$ and its size reduces by at most half in each iteration. When R becomes empty, Alice starts a new round. By then, an offline optimal algorithm must have to send at least one update from the observer to the tracker (as $g(t)$ must hold a value from R to represent $f(t)$ for $t \in [t_s, t_e]$), which takes at least $O(h)$ messages. Hence, in any such round $[t_s, t_e]$, when $R = \emptyset$ at t_e, $\textsf{C-OPT}(h) = O(h)$, but A has to send at least $\Omega(\frac{h+1}{2} \log \Delta)$ messages, which completes the proof. □

Lemma 5 *Any algorithm $A \in A_{broom}$ must track functions $f_1(t), \ldots, f_m(t)$ with an error threshold that is exactly Δ at the first relay node n_1 in order to minimize $\textsf{ratio}(A)$.*

PROOF. Assume that the claim does not hold. This means there exists an algorithm $A \in A_{broom}$ that allows node n_1 to track at least one function $f_i(t)$ using an error threshold δ that is less than Δ. Without loss of generality, consider $i = 1$. In this case, we can show that $\textsf{ratio}(A) = +\infty$ by constructing an input instance I as follows.

In this instance I, $f_j(t) = -2\Delta$ for $j = 2, \ldots, m$ and any time instance t; $f_1(t) = (-1)^{t \bmod 2}\Delta$. In other words, $f_1(t)$ alternates between $-\Delta$ and Δ and all other functions are set to a constant -2Δ. In this case, clearly, $f(t) = \max(f_1(t), \ldots, f_m(t)) = f_1(t)$ for all time instances t. But since the error threshold allocated to n_1 for f_1 is $\delta < \Delta$, A needs to send $+\infty$ number of messages when t goes $+\infty$, no matter how it designs its online tracking algorithm between n_1 and s_1.

But the optimal online algorithm *for this particular instance* only needs to send $(m + h + 1)$ number of messages in the first time instance. This algorithm A_I^* sets $g_1(t_1) = f_1(t_1) + \Delta$, and $g_i(t_1) = f_i(t_1)$ for all $i > 1$ at the first time instance t_1. It then asks each observer s_i to only send an update to n_1 if and only if at a time instance t, $f_i(t)$ has changed more than Δ from its last communicated value to n_1. At any time instance, n_1 sends $y_1(t) = \max(g_1(t), \ldots, g_m(t))$ to T, through the chain defined by $n_2, \ldots, n_h$, if $y_1(t)$ is different from the last communicated value from n_1 to T. It is easy to verify that this algorithm belongs to A_{broom} and it works correctly on all possible instances. On the above input instance, at the first time instance t_1, it will send $g_1(t_1) = 0$, and $g_2(t_1) = \cdots = g_m(t_m) = -2\Delta$ to n_1 from observers $s_1, \ldots, s_m$ (n_1 also forwards only $y_1(t) = 0$ to T). But it will incur no more communication in all subsequent time instances. Hence, its communication cost is $(m + h + 1)$.

Thus, on this input instance I, $\textsf{ratio}(A, I)/\textsf{ratio}(A_I^*, I) = +\infty$. As a result, $\textsf{ratio}(A) = +\infty$.

Note that the optimal algorithm for a particular input instance may perform badly on other input instances. The definition of $\textsf{ratio}$ is to quantify the difference in the worst case between the performance of an online algorithm A against the best possible performance for a valid input instance. □

Theorem 2 *For any algorithm A in A_{broom}, there exists an input instance I and another algorithm $A' \in A_{broom}$, such that $\textsf{cost}(A, I)$ is at least h times worse than $\textsf{cost}(A', I)$, i.e., for any $A \in A_{broom}$, $\textsf{ratio}(A) = \Omega(h)$.*

PROOF. For simplicity and without loss of generality, it suffices to prove the theorem for $m = 2$, i.e., a broom topology that has only 2 observers at the leaf level. We denote the two observers as s_1 and s_2 respectively. For an algorithm $A \in A_{broom}$, we will play as an adversary to construct two bad input instances I_1 and I_2 with respect to A.

Initially, we set $f_1(t_1) = \Delta$. Suppose in algorithm A s_1 sends a value x_1 to n_1. Note that x_1 must be an integer in $[0, 2\Delta]$. When $x_1 > 0$ we'll construct input instance I_1; otherwise we'll construct instance I_2 for $x_1 = 0$.

Time instance	$f_1(t)$	$g_1(t)$	$f_2(t)$	$g_2(t)$	$y_1(t)$
Initialization					
t_1	Δ	x_1	$x_1 + \frac{3}{2}\Delta$	x_2	x_2
t_2	$x_1 + \Delta$	x_1	$\ll 0$	$\ll 0$	x_1
Round					
t_{2i+1}	$x_1 + \Delta$	x_1	$x_1 + \frac{3}{2}\Delta$	x_2	x_2
t_{2i+2}	$x_1 + \Delta$	x_1	$\ll 0$	$\ll 0$	x_1

Table 1: Input instance I_1 and behavior of A.

Table 1 shows the construction of I_1 and the behavior of A on I_1. At time t_1, we set $f_2(t_1) = x_1 + \frac{3}{2}\Delta$ and s_2 sends a value x_2 to n_1. Clearly, x_2 is strictly larger than x_1 since $x_2 \geq x_1 + \frac{\Delta}{2}$. Hence, at node n_1, $g_1(t_1) = x_1$ and $g_2(t_1) = x_2$. We have $y_1(t_1) = \max(g_1(t_1), g_2(t_1)) = x_2$ and it will be propagated all the way up to the tracker at the root node by Lemma 6.

At time t_2, we update $f_1(t_2) = x_1 + \Delta$ and $f_2(t_2)$ to a value that is $\ll 0$. Note that s_1 sends no message to n_1 since $|x_1 - f_1(t_2)| \leq \Delta$; meanwhile, s_2 needs to send an update message that is $\ll 0$ to n_1 because $|g_2(t_1) - f_2(t_2)| > \Delta$ and $f_2(t_2) \ll 0$. Now, $y_1(t_2)$ will be set back to x_1 which will be propagated up to the tracker T.

The rest of I_1 is constructed in rounds. Right before each round, we always ensure that $y_1(t) = x_1$ and $g_2(last) \ll 0$. Each round i contains two time instances t_{2i+1} and t_{2i+2}. In a round i, we keep f_1's value at $x_1 + \Delta$ and alternate the values of f_2 between $x_1 + \frac{3}{2}\Delta$ and some value that is $\ll 0$. Specifically, at time t_{2i+1}, s_2 will send a value x_2 to n_1 and $g_2(t_{2i+1})$ will be set to x_2. But s_1 will not send any message and $g_1(t_{2i+1})$ will still be x_1. Because $|x_2 - (x_1 + \frac{3}{2}\Delta)| \leq \Delta$, clearly, $x_2 > x_1$. Hence, $y_1(t_{2i+1}) = x_2$, and by Lemma 6, $y_1(t_{2i+1}) = x_2$ will be propagated up to the tracker. At the following time t_{2i+2}, s_2 sends another update message to n_1 that sets $g_2(t_{2i+2})$ to be $\ll 0$, and s_1 again sends no update message and $g_1(t_{2i+2})$ is still x_1. Hence, $y_1(t_{2i+2})$ goes back to x_1. Again, this update on $y_1(t)$ will be propagated up to the tracker according to Lemma 6.

In summary, for every time instance in a round, A will incur h messages. Hence, $\mathsf{cost}(A, I_1)$ equals $O(ht_{now})$.

Next, we show the existence of another algorithm A' in A_{broom} which only sends $O(h + t_{now})$ messages on the same input I_1.

Time instance	$f_1(t)$	$g_1(t)$	$f_2(t)$	$g_2(t)$	$y_1(t)$
Initialization					
t_1	Δ	0	$x_1 + \frac{3}{2}\Delta$	$x_1 + \Delta$	$x_1 + \Delta$
t_2	$x_1 + \Delta$	$x_1 + \Delta$	$\ll 0$	$\ll 0$	$x_1 + \Delta$
Round					
t_{2i+1}	$x_1 + \Delta$	$x_1 + \Delta$	$x_1 + \frac{3}{2}\Delta$	$x_1 + \Delta$	$x_1 + \Delta$
t_{2i+2}	$x_1 + \Delta$	$x_1 + \Delta$	$\ll 0$	$\ll 0$	$x_1 + \Delta$

Table 2: A' on input instance I_1.

At time t_1, A' sends $g_1(t_1) = 0$ from s_1 and $g_2(t_1) = x_1 + \Delta$ from s_2 to n_1, for $f_1(t_1) = \Delta$ and $f_2(t_1) = x_1 + \frac{3}{2}\Delta$ respectively. Hence, $y_1(t_1) = x_1 + \Delta$ and it will be propagated up to the tracker at the root.

At time t_2, $f_1(t_2) = x_1 + \Delta$. This forces s_1 to send a new update message to n_1 because $|f_1(t_2) - g_1(t_1)| = |x_1 + \Delta - 0| > \Delta$ (note that while constructing I_1, we assumed that $x_1 > 0$). At this time, A' sends $g_1(t_2) = x_1 + \Delta$ for tracking $f_1(t_2) = x_1 + \Delta$. On s_2, $f_2(t_2) \ll 0$ which also forces an update message $g_2(t_2) \ll 0$ to be sent to n_1. But $y_1(t_2) = \max(g_1(t_2), g_2(t_2))$, which still equals $y_1(t_1) = x_1 + \Delta$! Thus, $y_1(t_2) = x_1 + \Delta$ does not need to sent up to the tracker along the chain.

In subsequent rounds, A' is able to maintain $y_1 = x_1 + \Delta$ with respect to I_1 in each round as shown in Table 2. That said, it only takes two messages for updating $g_2(t)$ at n_1 in each round. Therefore, $\text{cost}(A', I_1) = h + 4 + 2 \times r$ for r rounds, which is $O(h + t_{now})$ since each round has two time instances. This means that $\mathsf{cost}(A', I_1) = O(h + t_{now})$.

Similarly, we can construct a bad input instance I_2 for algorithm A when $x_1 = 0$ as shown by Table 3. And for this input instance, there exists another algorithm A'' in A_{broom} that only takes $(h + 3 + 2 \times r) = O(h + t_{now})$ messages on input I_2 as shown by Table 4.

Time instance	$f_1(t)$	$g_{s_1}(t)$	$f_2(t)$	$g_{s_2}(t)$	$y_1(t)$
Initialization					
t_1	Δ	0	$\Delta + 1$	x_2	x_2
t_2	Δ		$\ll 0$	$\ll 0$	0
Round					
t_{2i+1}	Δ		$\Delta + 1$	x_2	x_2
t_{2i+2}	Δ		$\ll 0$	$\ll 0$	0

Table 3: A on input instance I_2.

Time instance	$f_1(t)$	$g_{s_1}(t)$	$f_2(t)$	$g_{s_2}(t)$	$y_1(t)$
Initialization					
t_1	Δ	1	$\Delta + 1$	1	1
t_2	Δ		$\ll 0$	$\ll 0$	1
Round					
t_{2i+1}	Δ		$\Delta + 1$	1	1
t_{2i+2}	Δ		$\ll 0$	$\ll 0$	1

Table 4: A'' on input instance I_2.

That said, for any algorithm $A \in A_{broom}$, there always exists an input instance I and an algorithm $A' \in A_{broom}$, such that $\mathsf{cost}(A, I) = O(ht_{now})$ and $\mathsf{cost}(A', I) = O(h + t_{now})$. In other words, $\mathsf{ratio}(A) = \Omega(h)$. □

Corollary 2 *There is no instance optimal algorithm for A_{tree}.*

PROOF. Since we have excluded the trivial case in the tree model, a tree topology must have at least two paths p_i and p_j that shares a merging node u. The paths p_i and p_j form a generalized broom model as discussed above. Suppose path $p_{i,j}$ consists of h relay nodes.

By Theorem 2, for any algorithm $A \in A_{tree}$, there always exists an input instance I and another algorithm $A' \in A_{tree}$, such that the cost of A on I on path $p_{i,j}$ is at least h times worse than the cost of A' on I on path $p_{i,j}$. The cost of A on I on path $(p_i - p_{i,j})$ and path $(p_j - p_{i,j})$ is at best the same as the cost of A' on I on these two paths. □

Lemma 7 *Consider a node u. suppose $y_1, \ldots, y_\ell$ are the most recent updates of its ℓ child nodes. let z be the most recent update sent from u to its parent node. Define $y = \max\{y_1, \ldots, y_\ell\}$. If $y \neq z$, then u must send an update to its parent node, and this update message must be y.*

PROOF. Without loss of generality, assume that $y = y_i$. The jth child node of u is referred to as the node j, and its function is denoted as f_j.

We prove the theorem by induction. First, consider the base case when u only has leaf nodes as its child nodes (i.e., u only has observers as its child nodes). We first show that u must send an update to its parent.

case 1: $y > z$: For node i, set f_i to $y+\Delta$. For node $j \neq i$, if $y_j \geq y - 2\Delta$, then set f_j to $y - \Delta$.

case 2: $y < z$: For node i, set f_i to $y-\Delta$. For node $j \neq i$, if $y_j \geq y - 2\Delta$, then set f_j to $y - \Delta$.

With some technicality, we can show that in both cases: (1) $y \in [f(t)-\Delta, f(t)+\Delta]$ where $f(t) = \max(f_1(t), \ldots, f_\ell(t))$; and (2) $z \notin [f(t) - \Delta, f(t) + \Delta]$. Hence, node u must send an update to its parent. Now suppose that node u sends an update y', but $y' \neq y$.

case 1: $y > y'$: For node i, set f_i to $y+\Delta$. For node $j \neq i$, if $y_j \geq y - 2\Delta$, then set f_j to $y - \Delta$.

case 2: $y < y'$: For node i, set f_i to $y-\Delta$. For node $j \neq i$, if $y_j \geq y - 2\Delta$, then set f_j to $y - \Delta$.

It is easy to show that y' is not in $[f_i(t) - \Delta, f_i(t) + \Delta]$, but by construction $f(t) = f_i(t)$. So the update cannot be such an y'.

Now consider the case where u is a node such that the statement holds for all its descendants. We will show that the statement also holds for u. First, we show that u must send an update.

The fact that the statement holds for all the descendants of u implies that each y_j must be the most recent update of some leaf node in the jth subtree of u (rooted at u's jth child node). Let v be the leaf node corresponding to y_i.

case 1: $y > z$. For v, set f_v to $y + \Delta$. For any leaf node $w \neq v$, if $y_w \geq y - 2\Delta$, then set f_w to $y - \Delta$.

case 2: $y < z$. For v, set f_v to $y - \Delta$. For any leaf node $w \neq v$, if $y_w \geq y - 2\Delta$, then set f_w to $y - \Delta$.

Using a similar argument as that in the base case, we can show that u must send an update to its parent. Now suppose that node u sends an update y', but $y' \neq y$.

case 1: $y > y'$. For v, set f_v to $y + \Delta$. For any leaf node $w \neq v$, if $y_w \geq y - 2\Delta$, then set f_w to $y - \Delta$.

case 2: $y < y'$. For v, set f_v to $y - \Delta$. For any leaf node $w \neq v$, if $y_w \geq y - 2\Delta$, then set f_w to $y - \Delta$.

Again by a similar argument as that in the base case, we can show that such an y' cannot be the update message. □

Corollary 3 *$\mathsf{ratio}(\text{TreeTrack}) = O(h_{max} \log \Delta)$ with respect to A_{tree}.*

Proof. Given an input instance I and any algorithm $A \in A_{tree}$, suppose the number of messages between a leaf node (an observer) s_i and its parent node as M_i. It's easy to see that $\mathsf{cost}(\text{TreeTrack}, I) \leq h_{max} \sum_{i=1}^{m} M_i$. Meanwhile, any algorithm A' in A_{tree} satisfies $\mathsf{cost}(A', I) \geq h_{max} + \frac{\sum_{i=1}^{m} M_i}{\log \Delta}$ as a direct application of Theorem 1. Thus,

$$\mathsf{ratio}(\text{TreeTrack}, I) \leq \frac{h_{max} \sum_{i=1}^{m} M_i}{h_{max} + \sum_{i=1}^{m} M_i / \log \Delta} < h_{max} \log \Delta.$$

Therefore, $\mathsf{ratio}(\text{TreeTrack}) = O(h_{max} \log \Delta)$. □

Lemma 8 *Let $y_1(t) = \phi(g_1(t), \ldots, g_m(t))$ and $f(t) = \phi(f_1(t), \ldots, f_m(t))$. If $|g_i(t) - f_i(t)| \leq \Delta$ for all $i \in [1, m]$, then it must be $|y_1(t) - f(t)| \leq \Delta$.*

Proof. We prove this with contradiction, and we illustrate the proof using median ($\phi = 0.5$). Other quantile functions can be similarly proved. To ease the discussion for quantiles, we assume no duplicates. Cases with duplicates can be easily handled with a proper tie-breaker. Let's say $f(t) = f_i(t)$ for some i.

Suppose this is not true, then it must be $|y_1(t) - f_i(t)| > \Delta$. Without loss of generality, let's say $y_1(t) - f_i(t) > \Delta$. This means that $y_1(t) > g_i(t)$, since $|g_i(t) - f_i(t)| \leq \Delta$.

There are two cases. First, consider m is an odd number. Since $f_i(t)$ is the median of $f_1(t), \ldots, f_m(t)$, there must be $\frac{m-1}{2}$ functions $f_{\ell_1}, \ldots, f_{\ell_{(m-1)/2}}$ in $f_1(t), \ldots, f_m(t)$, such that $f_{\ell_i}(t) < f_i(t)$.

Consider $f_{\ell_i}(t)$ for any $i \in [1, (m-1)/2]$, the facts that $|g_{\ell_i}(t) - f_{\ell_i}(t)| \leq \Delta$, $f_{\ell_i}(t) < f_i(t)$ and $y_1(t) - f_i(t) > \Delta$ imply that $g_{\ell_i}(t) < y_1(t)$.

But now there are $(m+1)/2$ functions ($g_{\ell_1}, \ldots, g_{\ell_{(m-1)/2}}$, and $g_i(t)$), from $g_1(t), \ldots, g_m(t)$, that are less than $y_1(t)$, which contracts that $y_1(t)$ is the median of $g_1(t), \ldots, g_m(t)$.

The other case when m is an even number can be argued in the same fashion, as long as median is properly defined (as either the $(m-1)/2$th value or the $(m+1)/2$th value in the sorted sequence). □

Knowledge Curation and Knowledge Fusion: Challenges, Models, and Applications

Xin Luna Dong
Google Inc.
Mountain View, CA
lunadong@google.com

Divesh Srivastava
AT&T Labs-Research
Bedminster, NJ
divesh@research.att.com

ABSTRACT

Large-scale knowledge repositories are becoming increasingly important as a foundation for enabling a wide variety of complex applications. In turn, building high-quality knowledge repositories critically depends on the technologies of knowledge curation and knowledge fusion, which share many similar goals with data integration, while facing even more challenges in extracting knowledge from both structured and unstructured data, across a large variety of domains, and in multiple languages.

Our tutorial highlights the similarities and differences between knowledge management and data integration, and has two goals. First, we introduce the Database community to the techniques proposed for the problems of entity linkage and relation extraction by the Knowledge Management, Natural Language Processing, and Machine Learning communities. Second, we give a detailed survey of the work done by these communities in knowledge fusion, which is critical to discover and clean errors present in sources and the many mistakes made in the process of knowledge extraction from sources. Our tutorial is example driven and hopes to build bridges between the Database community and other disciplines to advance research in this important area.

1. INTRODUCTION

Large-scale knowledge repositories have immense value for both humans and computers, and have been shown to be effective in facilitating web search and other complex tasks. Over the years we have seen many techniques proposed for (semi-) automatically building progressively larger repositories of knowledge, from Freebase [4] and YAGO [23, 16], to NELL [6], DeepDive [21], and Knowledge Vault [9] (see Table 1 for a comparison). Major companies including Google, Microsoft, Facebook, and Walmart have also launched their own efforts to organize knowledge [8].

Knowledge curation shares many similar goals with *data integration*: to integrate data of large diversity in representations of entities and of relations, to provide a unified interface to access and query the data, and to leverage the collective wisdom from a multitude of data sources. In turn, it faces many challenges that the data integration community has been facing for decades: identifying different mentions of the same real-world entity, matching different ways of representing the same attribute of an entity or the same relation between entities, discovering erroneous and out-of-date data, and so on. Web-scale knowledge discovery faces even more challenges, as the desire is to extract knowledge from both structured data and unstructured data on the web, across multiple domains and across many languages.

The goal of this tutorial is two-fold. First, we aim to introduce to the Database community the techniques proposed by other communities such as Knowledge Management, Natural Language Processing, and Machine Learning, in resolving the heterogeneity inherent in web-scale data, towards building a single coherent repository of the knowledge in the world. We describe critical techniques in this process, focusing on entity linkage and relation extraction. We point out the similarities and differences of the techniques with the data extraction, schema alignment, and entity resolution techniques that have been well studied in the Database community.

Second, we give a detailed survey of *knowledge fusion*, an important tool to discover and clean both errors present in data sources, and the many mistakes that can be made in the process of knowledge extraction from sources. Comparing with *data fusion*, which aims at resolving conflicts from sources [3, 12], knowledge fusion considers an additional dimension of errors–the errors made by knowledge extractors. We present how existing data fusion techniques can be adapted to solve the knowledge fusion problem; in addition, we present the knowledge fusion techniques from the Machine Learning community based on AdaBoost learning [9], random walk inference [18], and deep learning [7].

Comparing with previous tutorials that have covered data fusion [12, 13], this tutorial has only a very small portion introducing data fusion techniques, mainly for the purpose of comparison to highlight the new challenges faced by knowledge fusion. Comparing with previous tutorials on knowledge management [2, 24], this tutorial focuses more on the post-processing step of knowledge fusion, and on drawing parallels between the research that has been done by the Database community on data integration, data cleaning, and data management, and the research outside our community on knowledge extraction and curation. We hope our tutorial can build bridges across these communities and inspire more

SIGMOD'15, May 31–June 4, 2015, Melbourne, Victoria, Australia.
ACM Copyright 2015 ACM 978-1-4503-2758-9/15/05$15.00
http://dx.doi.org/10.1145/2723372.2731083.

Name	# Entity types	# Entity instances	# Relation types	# Confident facts (relation instances)
Knowledge Vault (KV)	1100	45M	4469	271M
DeepDive [21]	4	2.7M	34	7M[a]
NELL [6]	271	5.19M	306	0.435M[b]
PROSPERA [20]	11	N/A	14	0.1M
YAGO2 [16]	350,000	9.8M	100	4M[c]
Freebase [4]	1,500	40M	35,000	637M[d]
Knowledge Graph (KG)	1,500	570M	35,000	18,000M[e]

Table 1: Comparison of knowledge bases [9]. KV, DeepDive, NELL, and PROSPERA rely solely on extraction, Freebase and KG rely on human curation and structured sources, and YAGO2 uses both strategies. Confident facts means with a probability of being true at or above 0.9.

[a]Ce Zhang (U Wisconsin), private communication.
[b]Bryan Kiesel (CMU), private communication.
[c]Core facts, `http://www.mpi-inf.mpg.de/yago-naga/yago/downloads.html`
[d]This is the number of non-redundant base triples, excluding reverse predicates and "lazy" triples derived from flattening CVTs (complex value types).
[e]`http://insidesearch.blogspot.com/2012/12/get-smarter-answers-from-knowledge_4.html`

inter-disciplinary research to leverage our expertise on data management for improving knowledge management.

2. TARGET AUDIENCE

The target audience for this tutorial is anyone with an interest in understanding knowledge management. The assumed level of mathematical sophistication is that of the typical conference attendees. Apart from a basic understanding of database technology, there is no prerequisite for this tutorial.

3. TUTORIAL OUTLINE

Knowledge curation and fusion are broad topics. Our tutorial is example driven and organized as follows.

3.1 Motivation

Our tutorial starts with a variety of examples of existing knowledge bases built by the academia and by industry (see Table 1). We motivate the importance of knowledge management by a few real-world examples such as web search.

3.2 Knowledge Extraction

We then briefly introduce the key techniques in knowledge extraction, namely, entity linkage and relation extraction.

Entity linkage is analogous to entity resolution (or record linkage) for structured data (surveyed in [15]). Whereas entity resolution focuses on structured records that refer to the real world, entity linkage considers entity mentions in text and semi-structured data (*e.g.*, DOM trees). There have been over 100 papers on this topic [17]; we focus on the techniques presented in the seminal paper [22].

Relation extraction is analogous to data extraction and schema alignment in data integration. We briefly review techniques for extracting relations from free text, DOM trees, web tables, and web annotations. In particular, we focus on two techniques: *distance supervision* based on existing schemas and training data [19], and *open IE* without requiring any human input [1, 14].

We end this session with a brief analysis of the knowledge extracted by 16 extractors from the web in the Knowledge Vault project [9].

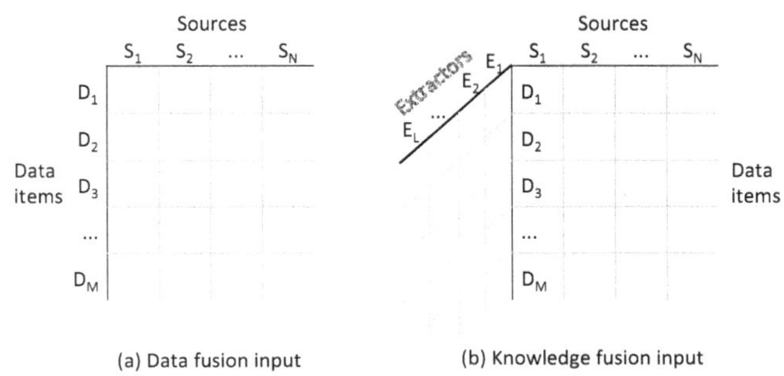

Figure 1: Input for data fusion is two-dimensional whereas input for knowledge fusion is three-dimensional [10].

3.3 Knowledge Fusion Models

The background of knowledge extraction serves as a good motivation for knowledge fusion, where we need to address both erroneous data present in web sources and mistakes in knowledge extraction. In characterizing knowledge fusion, we highlight the key difference from data fusion depicted in Figure 1; that is, data fusion assumes we know exactly the data provided by each source so the input is two-dimensional, whereas knowledge fusion reasons about the data extracted from the sources by multiple extractors so the input is three-dimensional.

We then present three types of knowledge fusion techniques. The first type takes signals such as the number of extractors that extract a triple and the extraction confidence, and learns a binary classifier for the correctness of an extracted triple. We present the techniques and the training data that are used in such supervised learning [9].

The second type learns graph-based priors to verify extracted knowledge. As an example, knowing that X and Y are both the parents of Z would increase the confidence that X and Y have a spouse relationship. This problem can be considered as link prediction–predicting edges from existing edges in a graph. We present two techniques: path ranking algorithm (PRA) [18] and neural network model (MLP) [7].

The third type extends data fusion techniques, which leverage agreements between sources and give higher trust to high-quality sources. We show how basic data fusion techniques have been extended to take care of the mistakes made during knowledge extraction [10].

For each type of techniques, we briefly show experimental results on Knowledge Vault data for validation.

3.4 Knowledge Fusion Applications

We then briefly discuss potential applications for knowledge fusion. In particular, we highlight two applications. The first one generates a new signal for evaluating the quality of web sources: *knowledge-based trust* [11]. We discuss the techniques that are critical to generate such measures and our observations on how it complements existing measures such as *PageRank* [5]. The second one, called *Data X-Ray*, is a diagnosis framework that analyzes the common features among the identified wrong knowledge triples to provide insights on possible underlying systematic errors made in the process of knowledge curation [25].

3.5 Open Problems

We end our tutorial with a discussion of open problems in knowledge curation and knowledge fusion. It includes improving entity linkage on DOM-tree data by exploring the structure of the data, combining corpus-based matching and distance supervision for better relation extraction, advancing knowledge fusion for openIE, and so on. In particular, we issue a call to arms–*no valuable data left behind*, where we hope to significantly enrich knowledge bases by exploiting the large volume of "tail" data, including data about less popular entities, in less popular verticals, about non-current (historical) facts, from smaller sources, in languages other than English, and so on. How to effectively combine the techniques designed for structured data and those oriented towards unstructured data is the key for enabling greater success in this area.

4. CONCLUSIONS

This tutorial surveys the state-of-the-art techniques for knowledge curation and knowledge fusion. Our tutorial explores the similarities and differences between the techniques proposed for data integration and for knowledge management, aiming to build bridges between the research in the Database community and in other disciplines to develop more comprehensive techniques in this active research area.

5. BIOGRAPHIES

Xin Luna Dong is a Senior Research Scientist at Google Inc. She is one of the major contributors for the Knowledge Vault project and has led the Solomon data fusion project. She is a co-chair for WAIM'15 and has served as an area chair for Sigmod'15, ICDE'13, and CIKM'11.

Divesh Srivastava is the head of the Database Research Department at AT&T Labs-Research. He is an ACM fellow, on the board of trustees of the VLDB Endowment, the managing editor of PVLDB, and an associate editor of the ACM Transactions on Database Systems. He has served as PC co-chair of many conferences, including VLDB'07.

6. REFERENCES

[1] M. Banko, M. J. Cafarella, S. Soderland, M. Broadhead, and O. Etzioni. Open information extraction from the web. In *IJCAI*, 2007.

[2] D. Barbosa, H. Wang, and C. Yu. Shallow information extraction for the knowledge web. In *ICDE*, 2013.

[3] J. Bleiholder and F. Naumann. Data fusion. *ACM Computing Surveys*, 41(1):1–41, 2008.

[4] K. Bollacker, C. Evans, P. Paritosh, T. Sturge, and J. Taylor. Freebase: a collaboratively created graph database for structuring human knowledge. In *SIGMOD*, pages 1247–1250, 2008.

[5] S. Brin and L. Page. The anatomy of a large-scale hypertextual Web search engine. *Computer Networks and ISDN Systems*, 30(1–7):107–117, 1998.

[6] A. Carlson, J. Betteridge, B. Kisiel, B. Settles, E. H. Jr., and T. Mitchell. Toward an architecture for never-ending language learning. In *AAAI*, 2010.

[7] J. Dean. Large scale deep learning. In *CIKM*, 2014.

[8] O. Deshpande, D. S. Lamba, M. Tourn, S. Das, S. Subramaniam, A. Rajaraman, V. Harinarayan, and A. Doan. Building, maintaining, and using knowledge bases: A report from the trenches. In *Sigmod*, 2013.

[9] X. L. Dong, E. Gabrilovich, G. Heitz, W. Horn, N. Lao, K. Murphy, T. Strohmann, S. Sun, and W. Zhang. Knowledge vault: A web-scale approach to probabilistic knowledge fusion. In *SIGKDD*, 2014.

[10] X. L. Dong, E. Gabrilovich, G. Heitz, W. Horn, K. Murphy, S. Sun, and W. Zhang. From data fusion to knowledge fusion. *PVLDB*, 2014.

[11] X. L. Dong, E. Gabrilovich, K. Murphy, V. Dang, W. Horn, C. Lugaresi, S. Sun, and W. Zhang. Knowledge-based trust: Estimating the trustworthiness of web sources. http://arxiv.org/abs/1502.03519, 2015.

[12] X. L. Dong and F. Naumann. Data fusion–resolving data conflicts for integration. *PVLDB*, 2009.

[13] X. L. Dong and D. Srivastava. Big data integration. *PVLDB*, 2013.

[14] O. Etzioni, A. Fader, J. Christensen, S. Soderland, and Mausam. Open information extraction: the second generation. In *IJCAI*, 2011.

[15] L. Getoor and A. Machanavajjhala. Entity resolution: Theory, practice, & open challenges. *PVLDB*, 5(12):2018–2019, 2012.

[16] J. Hoffart, F. M. Suchanek, K. Berberich, and G. Weikum. YAGO2: A Spatially and Temporally Enhanced Knowledge Base from Wikipedia. *Artificial Intelligence*, 2012.

[17] H. Ji. Entity linking and wikification reading list. http://nlp.cs.rpi.edu/kbp/2014/elreading.html, 2014.

[18] N. Lao, T. Mitchell, and W. Cohen. Random walk inference and learning in a large scale knowledge base. In *EMNLP*, 2011.

[19] M. Mintz, S. Bills, R. Snow, and D. Jurafksy. Distant supervision for relation extraction without labeled data. In *Prof. Conf. Recent Advances in NLP*, 2009.

[20] N. Nakashole, M. Theobald, and G. Weikum. Scalable knowledge harvesting with high precision and high recall. In *WSDM*, pages 227–236, 2011.

[21] F. Niu, C. Zhang, and C. Re. Elementary: Large-scale Knowledge-base Construction via Machine Learning and Statistical Inference. *Intl. J. on Semantic Web and Information Systems*, 2012.

[22] L. Ratinov, D. Roth, D. Downey, and M. Anderson. Local and global algorithms for disambiguation to wikipedia. In *NAACL*, 2011.

[23] F. M. Suchanek, G. Kasneci, and G. Weikum. YAGO - A Core of Semantic Knowledge. In *WWW*, 2007.

[24] F. M. Suchanek and G. Weikum. Knowledge bases in the age of big data analytics. In *VLDB*, 2014.

[25] X. Wang, X. L. Dong, and A. Meliou. Data X-Ray: A diagnostic tool for data errors. In *Sigmod*, 2015.

Smooth Task Migration in Apache Storm

Mansheng Yang
National University of Singapore
mansheng@u.nus.edu

Richard T.B. Ma
National University of Singapore
tbma@comp.nus.edu.sg

ABSTRACT

Task migration happens when distributed data processing systems scale in real-time. To handle the task migration process more gracefully, we propose three task migration methods: (i) worker level migration, (ii) executor level migration, and (iii) executor level migration with reliable messaging. We implement our migration methods on Apache Storm. Our experiments show that, compared with Storm's original migration implementation, our methods significantly reduce the performance degradation and the number of task failures during each migration.

1. INTRODUCTION

Modern distributed data processing systems support real-time elastic scaling, i.e., the ability to dynamically add or remove computing nodes and redistribute tasks. To scale an application, the system computes a new task configuration, reallocates computing resources, and performs *migration* to redistribute the tasks. A simple and common migration method is to stop the running application and start it afresh with the new configuration. This approach is easy to implement and free of synchronization concerns but the application is completely interrupted during the restart. The state-of-the-art strategy adopted by prior work [2, 3, 4] is to identify the tasks to move and pause the tasks that communicate with them until the migration is completed. However, in most cases, this approach results in pausing many components in the system and thus no jobs can be completed during the migration.

We tackle the problem of smooth task migration in such systems, i.e., migration with minimal performance degradation to the system, and specifically focus on Apache Storm [1]. Storm runs an application on a number of *workers*, which are OS processes on a cluster of nodes. Every worker runs a number of *executors*, each of which resides in an independent OS thread and performs the actual computation. When scaling an application, the system redistributes the executors among a new set of workers. Figure 1 gives an example of scaling in Storm. Migration in Storm does not handle task states as they reside at the application layer and are not visible to the system layer. Currently, Storm uses the simple method described above to perform migration: it shuts down all workers of the application and then starts new ones with the new configuration. During the shutdown, it waits for the workers to complete tasks that are in progress. This simple scheme has a few performance drawbacks. (i) The migration process takes about 20 seconds. (ii) No jobs are completed when the workers are restarting. (iii) Many tasks fail during migration due to messaging failures. Although Storm has built-in reliability support to retry these tasks, this still raises serious performance concerns.

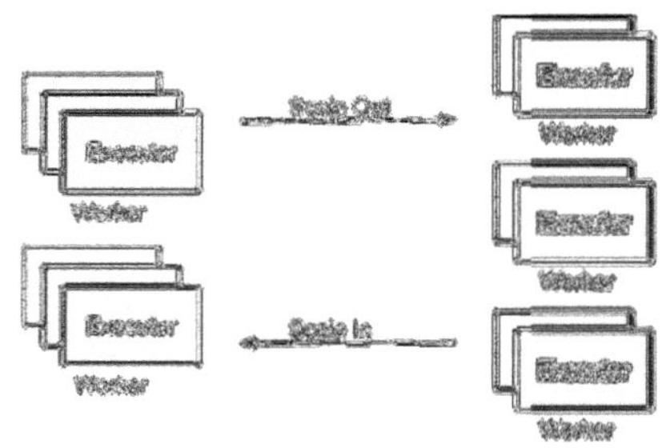

Figure 1: Scaling a Storm Application

We present three migration methods to solve these performance issues: (i) worker level (WL) migration, (ii) executor level (EL) migration, (iii) executor level migration with reliable messaging (ELR). Base on our experimental results, we provide detailed discussions on the performance gains of these methods.

2. TECHNICAL OVERVIEW

2.1 Worker Level Migration

One major performance issue caused in the original implementation is the restart of workers: both safely shutting down and starting the workers take significant amount of time. Worker level migration avoids this overhead by reusing the existing workers. Instead of killing all the workers, we keep the workers alive, only kill the executors, and start them on the workers that they are newly assigned to. When scaling up the system, we only start the newly added workers; when scaling down the system, we only shut down the removed workers.

2.2 Executor Level Migration

Worker level migration removes the overhead of worker restart, but as all the executors need to be restarted, this still dis-

SIGMOD'15, May 31 - June 04, 2015, Melbourne, VIC, Australia
ACM 978-1-4503-2758-9/15/05.
http://dx.doi.org/10.1145/2723372.2764941

rupts the running application in the migration. By managing migration at the executor level, we can run the application without disruption during the migration: (i) As before, workers are kept alive and added or removed only when necessary. (ii) If an executor does not need to move to a different worker after a migration, we keep it running without interruption; otherwise, we kill the executor and restart it on the corresponding worker. (iii) We implement a migration-friendly task scheduler to minimize the number of moving executors in migration. The implementation in Storm requires great care of the running executors.

2.3 Reliable Messaging

The above methods improve migration performance by reducing the migration time. However, messaging failures in the migration also result in job failures and thus negative performance impact. To address this issue, we also improved the messaging system in Storm on top of executor level migration as follows. (i) We capture all failed messages at various places in the system, which are usually caused by inconsistent states among workers when the workers are updating their states in a migration. Using a message retry mechanism we implemented, these messages are then retried later at a scheduled time. (ii) We save messages from executors that are being shut down, and send them to the correct workers using the same message retry mechanism.

3. MAJOR RESULTS

We evaluated the performance of the proposed methods for both a scaling-out and a scaling-in scenarios, using Storm's migration method as the baseline. Using a frequent pattern mining application and synthetic datasets, we performed experiments to measure the time taken to complete 500 jobs and the number of failed jobs for each method. We ran the experiments multiple times and collected the mean values. In the scaling-out setting, we increased the number of workers from 4 to 6. The workers were all saturated before the scaling, so after the migration the task completion rate increased. In the scaling-in setting, we reduced the number of workers from 4 to 2. The task completion rate remained the same after the migration as the workers were not saturated before the scaling. The difference in the assumption of worker saturation condition is due to the fact that typically, the system is scaled out when more resources are needed and scaled in when there are some unutilized resources.

Figure 2 depicts the results. During the first 5 seconds, the task completion rate is low for all methods because the system was still warming up. The migration started at around the 20th second. The proposed methods quickly responded to the migration and adjusted the configuration, while Storm's method spent some time trying to finish the jobs in progress and slowly shutting down the workers. This is why Storm's method performed better than two of the proposed methods for a short period of time just after the migration started. At the 40th second, when Storm's method finished the migration, the proposed methods all have stabilized at normal working state for more than 15 seconds. Compared with Storm's method, the three proposed methods reduce the finishing time of a single migration period by about 8, 12 and 15 seconds, respectively. When comparing the number of failed jobs with Storm baseline, we observe: (i) the worker level migration reduces the number by about one third, (ii) the executor level migration by about

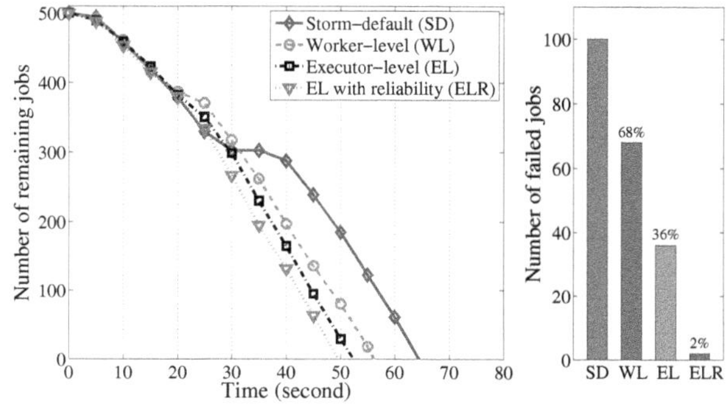

(a) Scaling out

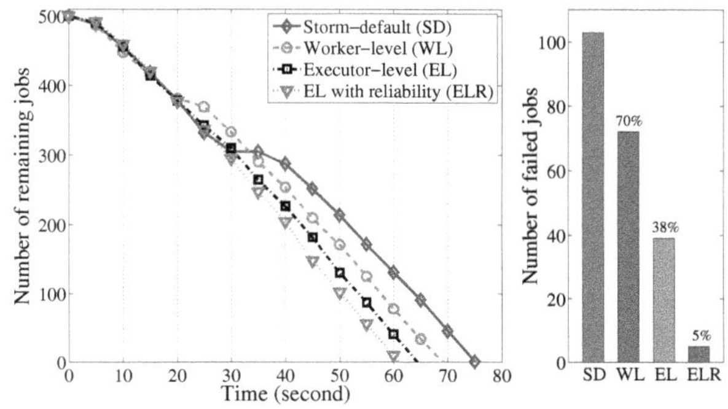

(b) Scaling in

Figure 2: Performance of Migration Methods

two thirds, (iii) and the executor level migration with reliable messaging reduces that to less than 5%. These results demonstrate that our proposed methods greatly improve Storm's method, and the executor level migration with reliable messaging achieves the most significant improvement. In real world situations where the system is frequently scaled to react to changing workload, the performance gains can be accumulated and have a bigger impact.

For future work, we plan to extend the system and our methods to support efficient migration of task states.

4. ACKNOWLEDGMENTS

The author would like to thank Tom Z. J. Fu and Jianbing Ding from Advanced Digital Sciences Center Illinois at Singapore for their help in the project.

5. REFERENCES

[1] Apache storm. `http://storm.apache.org`.

[2] R. Castro Fernandez, M. Migliavacca, E. Kalyvianaki, and P. Pietzuch. Integrating scale out and fault tolerance in stream processing using operator state management. In *SIGMOD 2013*, pages 725–736. ACM, 2013.

[3] T. Heinze, Z. Jerzak, G. Hackenbroich, and C. Fetzer. Latency-aware elastic scaling for distributed data stream processing systems. In *DEBS 2014*, pages 13–22. ACM, 2014.

[4] S. Schneider, H. Andrade, B. Gedik, A. Biem, and K.-L. Wu. Elastic scaling of data parallel operators in stream processing. In *IPDPS 2009*, pages 1–12, May 2009.

JAFAR: Near-Data Processing for Databases

Oreoluwa Babarinsa
Harvard University
obabarinsa@seas.harvard.edu

Stratos Idreos
Harvard University
stratos@seas.harvard.edu

ABSTRACT

As main-memory sizes have grown, data systems have been able to process entire large-scale data-sets in memory. However, because memory speeds have been not been keeping pace with CPU speeds, the cost of moving data into CPU caches has begun to dominate certain operations within in-memory data systems. Recent advances in hardware architectures point to near memory computation capabilities becoming possible soon. This allows us to rethink how database systems process queries and how they split computation across the various computational units. In this paper, we present JAFAR, a near data processing accelerator for pushing selects down to memory. Through a detailed simulation of JAFAR hardware we show it has the potential to provide up to 900% improvement for select operations in modern column-stores.

1. INTRODUCTION

The Development of In-memory Data Systems. Rapidly diminishing costs of main memory per gigabyte have led to the development of in-memory data systems, significantly increasing throughput and performance compared to disk-based systems. However, while disk accesses are no longer the performance bottleneck for in-memory data systems, the cost of moving data from main memory across the memory buses and into CPU caches is still significant [2]. Big data applications like data analytics tend to be more memory bound than CPU-bound. This trend, called "memory wall" [11], will only become worse as CPU performance improvement continues to surpass memory performance improvement.

Furthermore, while there have been fruitful efforts in tuning database operators to be cache-aware and efficient in multi-core settings [3], ultimately, data still must be moved from main memory to the CPUs, incurring a significant cost. There is extensive literature on optimizing the memory behavior of DBMS workloads, such as improving cache hit rates with multi-core optimized joins [3]. Past work, however, does not directly try to reduce movement of relevant data from memory to the CPUs.

Near Data Processing. Reducing data movement can be achieved by moving the computation closer to the data itself by having specialized hardware that performs computation close to the data. This is known as *near-data processing* (NDP). In the hardware architecture community, NDP has been proposed in various forms in the past [7, 10]. However, NDP hardware did not see widespread adoption, when it was originally proposed due to strong past gains in CPU performance. However, due to diminishing returns from technology scaling, there has been a recent resurgence in NDP research [2]. Historically, proposals for NDP systems have emphasized design for general purpose computation [5, 6, 8].

Our Contribution. In this paper, we study NDP for columnar data systems [1]. We present JAFAR, short for "Just a Filtering Accelerator on Relations". JAFAR is a hardware accelerator embedded in a DRAM module that implements the select operator of a modern column-store. According to our experiments, JAFAR is capable of achieving up to 9× speedup on the selection operator.

2. JAFAR

JAFAR allows for processing database filtering operations directly in memory. When a select operator is pushed to JAFAR by the database system, JAFAR starts filtering data directly in memory. The key idea is that JAFAR requests data from memory as normal but it filters data without pushing data further up in the memory hierarchy. To achieve that JAFAR receives input directly from the IO buffer of the DRAM module, as shown in Figure 1a. JAFAR targets integer input data, covering a spectrum of use cases. Modern data systems typically store columns of data employing dictionary compression, allowing a variety of data types to be represented by integers or fixed-width data.

The internals of JAFAR are depicted in Figure 1b. For each 64 bit word that it receives, an integer comparison is performed against the value of the element corresponding to the query predicate. For range filters, two arithmetic logic units (ALUs) operate in parallel. JAFAR tracks the offset of the current row in the page. If the result of the filter is true, then the offset is converted into a bitmask and written into an output buffer, which is a bitset indicating which rows pass the filter. The output buffer thus holds n bits to represent the state of n filter operations. Every n cycles, the output buffer is filled, the bitset is written back to main memory at a pre-programmed location. The CPU controls JAFAR via memory-mapped accelerator control registers and is notified on completion by polling a shared memory location.

We design and simulate JAFAR using an accelerator modeling tool called Aladdin [9] and the surrounding system with the gem5 simulator [4]. Aladdin is a power and performance modeling tool that converts a C-style representation of the workload being accelerated into a data dependence graph, which represents the structure and execution of the accelerator datapath itself.

SIGMOD '15 May 31 - June 04, 2015, Melbourne, VIC, Australia
ACM 978-1-4503-2758-9/15/05
http://dx.doi.org/10.1145/2723372.2764942.

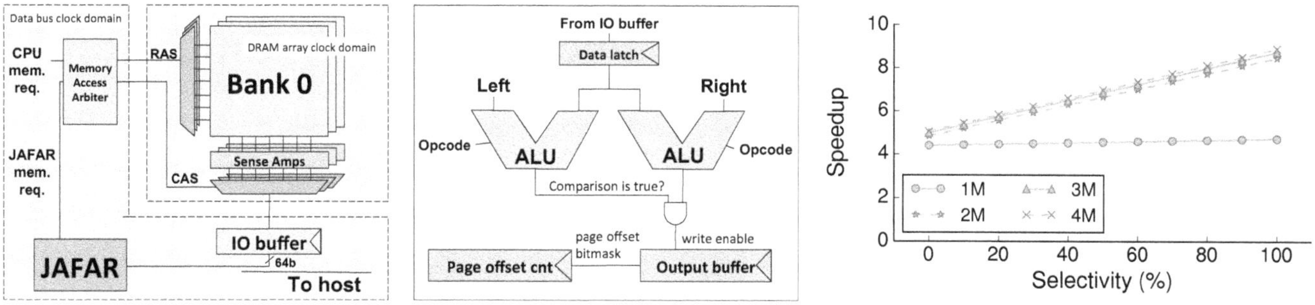

(a) DDR3 DRAM module (b) JAFAR architecture (c) Speedup increases with selectivity

Figure 1: JAFAR design and evaluation

3. EXPERIMENTAL ANALYSIS

Experimental Setup. Using the gem5 simulator we simulate a machine with a single 1 GHZ CPU with 64KB L1, 128KB L2 cache, and 2GB of DRAM. We experiment using a synthetic dataset consisting of integers between 0 and 10^6, randomly generated from a uniform distribution. We evaluate JAFAR using scans and selections of varying selectivity over different data sizes. Figure 1c shows on the y-axis the speedup achieved when running a scan followed by a selection using JAFAR when compared with a CPU-only execution. On the x-axis we vary the selectivity from 10% to 100%. The four different lines correspond to different data sizes. We calculate speed-up by comparing the run-time of a query on our simulated machine with and without JAFAR handling scans.

Impact of Dataset Size. We first discuss the impact of dataset size on JAFAR (the different lines in Figure 1c). JAFAR speedup is small for small datasets (< 1M rows), but increases to a maximum of 9× for large datasets. This is because on large datasets, most of the program execution is spent in the accelerated selection operation. For smaller datasets, the amount of time in the accelerated part of the code is reduced, thus leading to a smaller speedup. In this experiment, there is no memory contention when JAFAR is running because the CPU is spin-waiting until JAFAR finishes.

Impact of Selectivity. In addition to the data size, selectivity plays an important role in the achieved speed-up due to JAFAR, especially for data sizes larger than 1M (note the top three lines in in Figure 1c). We observe that JAFAR performance increases with query selectivity. This behavior is attributed to a key difference between how JAFAR operates compared to a traditional CPU-based execution. CPU executes additional code on a record when a row passes the filter. On the other hand, JAFAR always writes the contents of the output buffer back to main memory each time the buffer is full, without delaying the filtering operation. Hence, JAFAR has constant execution time regardless of the query selectivity. Combining that with the increasing number of commands the CPU needs to execute for increasing selectivity, results to the observed linear increase in speedup for higher selectivity.

Contention. JAFAR provides considerable speedup on filtering operations, increasing both with data size and query selectivity. However, so far we did not consider memory contention effects, which are important because JAFAR was designed as a drop-in NDP accelerator which can can only operate while the memory controller is idle. To quantify this effect, we measure the idle periods when using a modern data system. We use several filter-heavy TPC-H queries running on MonetDB on a NUMA machine with 4 sockets, each equipped with an Intel Xeon E7-4820 v2 Ivy processor running at 2.0GHz with 16MB of L3 cache. We find that the memory controller idle periods range between 200 and 800 memory bus clock cycles, with an average of 500 cycles. Thus, on average, JAFAR can process $500/4 = 125$ 32-byte data blocks, or a total of 4KB of data, per idle period. Due to space restrictions we do include this analysis here. More details can be found in a subsequent publication [12].

4. SUMMARY & FUTURE WORK

We present JAFAR, an NDP hardware accelerator embedded into DRAM that provides up to 9× speedup on filtering operations in modern column-stores. A more complete version of this study is now available [12], where we analyze the performance gains when running analytical queries and quantify memory contention.

Our future research plans include the design of further operators, as well as studying NDP opportunities for row-stores and hybrid systems. Another important topic is to identify what are the minimum changes required at the host system and software stack as well as study possible optimizations based on data types.

Acknowledgments. The authors would like to thank Sam Xi and Manos Athanassoulis, member of Harvard DASlab, for their help during this project.

5. REFERENCES

[1] D. J. Abadi, P. Boncz, S. Harizopoulos, S. Idreos, and S. Madden. The Design and Implementation of Modern Column-Oriented Database Systems. *Foundations and Trends in Databases*, 5(3):197–280, 2013.

[2] R. Balasubramonian, J. Chang, T. Manning, J. H. Moreno, R. Murphy, R. Nair, and S. Swanson. Near-Data Processing: Insights from a MICRO-46 Workshop. *IEEE Micro*, 34(4):36–42, 2014.

[3] C. Balkesen, J. Teubner, G. Alonso, and M. T. Ozsu. Main-memory hash joins on multi-core CPUs: Tuning to the underlying hardware. In *Proceedings of the IEEE International Conf. on Data Engineering (ICDE)*, pages 362–373, 2013.

[4] N. L. Binkert et al. The gem5 simulator. *SIGARCH Computer Architecture News*, 39(2):1–7, 2011.

[5] M. Gokhale, W. Holmes, and K. Iobst. Processing in Memory: The Terasys Massively Parallel PIM Array. *IEEE Computer*, 28(4):23–31, 1995.

[6] M. Hall et al. Mapping Irregular Applications to DIVA, a PIM-based Data-intensive Architecture. In *Proceedings of the ACM/IEEE Conf. on Supercomputing*, 1999.

[7] W. H. Kautz. Cellular Logic-in-Memory Arrays. *IEEE Transactions on Computers*, 18(8):719–727, 1969.

[8] D. Patterson, T. Anderson, N. Cardwell, R. Fromm, K. Keeton, C. Kozyrakis, R. Thomas, and K. Yelick. A Case for Intelligent RAM. *IEEE Micro*, 17(2):34–44, 1997.

[9] Y. S. Shao, B. Reagen, G.-Y. Wei, and D. Brooks. Aladdin: A Pre-RTL, Power-performance Accelerator Simulator Enabling Large Design Space Exploration of Customized Architectures. In *Proc. of the Annual International Symposium on Computer Architecture (ISCA)*, pages 97–108, 2014.

[10] H. S. Stone. A Logic-in-Memory Computer. *IEEE Transactions on Computers*, 19(1):73–78, 1970.

[11] W. A. Wulf and S. A. McKee. Hitting the Memory Wall: Implications of the Obvious. *ACM SIGARCH Computer Architecture News*, 23(1):20–24, 1995.

[12] S. Xi, O. Babarinsa, M. Athanassoulis, and S. Idreos. Beyond the Wall: Near-Data Processing for Databases. In *Proceedings of the International Workshop on Data Management on New Hardware (DAMON)*, 2015.

Job Scheduling with Minimizing Data Communication Costs

[Extended Abstract]

Trevor Clinkenbeard*
David R. Cheriton School of Computer Science
Faculty of Mathematics, University of Waterloo
tclinken@uwaterloo.ca

Anisoara Nica
SAP SE
Waterloo, Ontario, Canada
Anisoara.Nica@sap.com

ABSTRACT

The research presented in this paper analyzes different algorithms for scheduling a set of potentially interdependent jobs in order to minimize the total runtime, or makespan, when data communication costs are considered. On distributed file systems, such as the HDFS, files are spread across a cluster of machines. Once a request, such as a query, having as input the data in these files is translated into a set of jobs, these jobs must be scheduled across machines in the cluster. Jobs consume input files stored in the distributed file system or in cluster nodes, and produce output which is potentially consumed by future jobs. If a job needs a particular file as input, the job must either be executed on the same machine, or it must incur a time penalty to copy the file, increasing latency for the job. At the same time, independent jobs are ideally scheduled at the same time on different machines, in order to take advantage of parallelism. Both minimizing communication costs and maximizing parallelism serve to minimize the total runtime of a set of jobs. Furthermore, the problem gets more complex when certain jobs must wait for previous jobs to provide input, as is frequently the case when a set of jobs represents the steps of a query on a distributed database.

Keywords

Distributed databases; Job scheduling

1. INTRODUCTION

Previous research has studied specific cases of minimizing data communication costs. Golab et al. [2] used the theory of graph partitioning to find a near-optimal algorithm to place files in a distributed file system in order to minimize data communication cost given an a known workload. In contrast, the goal of this paper is not merely to minimize data communication cost, but to consider the cost of data communication in order to minimize the total runtime of a set of dynamic jobs. We also assume that input files may already reside in some cluster nodes, and our solutions attempt to schedule new jobs considering the current state of distributed filesystem.

Apache Spark is a popular distributed processing paradigm which implements the efficient Sparrow scheduler [4]. The Sparrow scheduler is designed to efficiently schedule jobs with processing times on the order of 100ms. Thus, Sparrow relies on randomness and unsophisticated heuristics, in order to schedule jobs in real time with very low latency. In contrast, here we aim to design a dynamic scheduler for a set of heterogeneous, including both large and small, jobs. Our algorithms take significantly longer to schedule jobs, but produce more optimal scheduling, a trade-off which favors scheduling jobs with relatively long processing times.

The inputs to our problem are a set $\mathcal{M}$ of machines, a set $\mathcal{J}$ of atomic jobs, and a set $\mathcal{D}$ of data files. Each job $j_i \in \mathcal{J}$ has an estimated processing time r_i, a set of input files $I_i \subset \mathcal{D}$, and an output file $o_i \in \mathcal{D}$. Each file $d_i \in \mathcal{D}$ has a (possibly estimated) size t_i. Some jobs in $\mathcal{J}$ are already scheduled on a machine in $\mathcal{M}$. Let the set of unscheduled jobs be $u\mathcal{J}$ (e.g., the set of jobs of currently unscheduled requests). Our goal is to output a function $m : u\mathcal{J} \to \mathcal{M}$, mapping each unscheduled job to a machine on which it is to be executed. In the case where jobs are interdependent, i.e. $o_i \in I_k$ for some jobs $j_i, j_k \in \mathcal{J}$, we must also produce an order in which to process jobs on each machine. The goal of the output is to minimize total runtime.

The first step in developing our scheduling algorithms was to interpret the set of jobs, files, and dependencies as a directed acyclical graph. Vertices represent files and jobs, while dependencies are represented by arcs. All jobs depend on their input files, and all output files depend on the jobs which produce them. A job's processing time, r_i, provides the weight of the arc to the job's output file. The file sizes, t_i, along with the average network communication speed, give potential weights for the rest of the arcs (these weights are only assigned if the input file is not already stored on the same machine as the job is executed on).

Based on this general outline for a graph, the first algorithm implemented was a greedy algorithm based on the well-known critical path method [3]. Using the arc weights assigned, repeatedly select the job with the longest weighted chain of dependents (i.e. the job at the head of the critical path). Greedily schedule this job on a machine which minimizes the current makespan and ideally balances the load

*The student author and the adviser Dr. Anisoara Nica worked on this project during Fall 2014 co-op term at SAP Waterloo, Canada.

SIGMOD '15, May 31–June 4, 2015, Melbourne, Victoria, Australia.
ACM 978-1-4503-2758-9/15/05.
http://dx.doi.org/10.1145/2723372.2764943.

between different machines. Repeat this process until all jobs are scheduled.

This algorithm is much more efficient than arbitrary or random scheduling algorithms in all our experiments. However, it is very greedy, and does not fully consider the structure of the directed acyclical graph. Other algorithms explored used linear programming, implemented using SAP SciPlex software.

In the linear programming algorithms, variables are used to represent the projected finish time of each machine. The obvious objective is to minimize the maximum of these machine finish times, the makespan. This works optimally for scheduling just one set of jobs. However, if we wish to schedule more jobs in the future, it is also important to balance the load across machines. For example, consider a multinode cluster in which a large number of jobs are already scheduled to run on machine m. Now assume we wish to schedule a new, smaller, set of independent jobs. If the only objective is to minimize makespan, these jobs can be scheduled anywhere on the cluster except on machine m, since the makespan depends only on m's finish time. However, we would prefer to balance these jobs effectively across the other machines which cannot be achieved if only makespan is minimized. Thus, we experimented with different objective functions, such as minimizing a weighted sum of the makespan and some other linear functions based on the load balance. Unfortunately, we are restricted to using linear functions. The greedy algorithm has no such restrictions, so it can use a more effective load balancing objective function.

The first linear programming algorithm implemented ignored the possibility of inter-job dependencies. In this case, the ordering of jobs on a particular machine is irrelevant. By using boolean variables x_{ik} representing job i being scheduled on machine k, and introducing the appropriate constraints, it is possible to find a completely optimal solution.

Introducing inter-job dependencies complicates the problem significantly. It is no longer feasible to find a completely optimal solution. Instead, we split the graph of jobs into "layers." We repeatedly select a set S of unscheduled jobs which don't depend on any other unscheduled jobs. These jobs can be scheduled in a nearly optimal way using linear programming, once constraints are added to ensure that a new job cannot start on a particular machine until that machine is finished executing the jobs already scheduled there.

While breaking the jobs into "layers" greatly simplifies the problem, and the above algorithm performs well in most cases, inter-job dependencies introduce an important technicality. A machine may be starved as its next scheduled job waits for data from another machine. However, in the meantime, the machine can load other data necessary for its waiting jobs. This is difficult to represent using linear programming, because we had previously been adding all load times to the runtime of a job. With this consideration in mind, though, a job could potentially load an input file from another machine, without causing any additional delay to later jobs scheduled on the machine. By adding additional constraints to find the order of jobs on a machine, this problem can be avoided with a more expensive but slightly more optimal linear programming solution.

2. RESULTS AND DISCUSSIONS

To test the algorithms, nine machines were used. 75 files of size 100MB were generated and placed on the HDFS initially.

Table 1: Average Total Runtimes (in seconds): (1) first n_1 jobs are randomly scheduled; (2) n_2 jobs are scheduled with one of the scheduling algorithms *Random*, *Greedy*, and *Linear Programming* given the state of the cluster having n_1 jobs already scheduled.

n_1	n_2	*Random*	*Greedy*	*Linear Programming*
0	20	362.6	162.0	167.5
0	40	415.1	270.3	275.6
20	20	421.2	254.8	327.2

A set of random jobs and dependencies were randomly generated, using random graph generation techniques inspired by Cordeiro et al. [1]. Jobs are created with a randomly assigned constant processing time, uniformly distributed between 30 and 60 seconds. Each job produces a 100MB output file. On average, a given job consumes a given file with probability 0.1, but jobs are ordered to prevent any cyclical dependencies.

Table 1 contains preliminary testing results, giving the average total runtime in seconds. The first n_1 jobs are randomly scheduled, then an additional n_2 jobs are scheduled, considering the state of the cluster with the already scheduled n_1 jobs. In general, the linear programming algorithm and the greedy algorithm perform similarly for smaller sets of jobs. Both algorithms are much better than a random scheduling. The greedy algorithm is better for load balancing, though, as seen in the case where half of the jobs are already scheduled arbitrarily. These scheduled jobs are likely to be scheduled unevenly across machines, so the greedy algorithm is favored due to its load balancing capabilities.

In the future, we plan to run more extensive tests on larger sets of jobs. The linear programming algorithms are promising, in that they can be less greedy than the other algorithm tested. However, utilizing linear programming to effectively balance jobs across many machines is still an open problem. Lastly, certain real life complications were ignored in this study. In practice, machines have memory constraints, and they can get rid of unused files to free up space. Furthermore, we have made the assumption that each job has constant processing time, regardless of the machine it is run on. In reality, some machines are faster than others, so it is not always this simple. These issues further complicate the scheduling problem, and can be the subject of further research.

3. REFERENCES

[1] D. Cordeiro, G. Mounie, S. Perarnau, D. Trystram, J.-M. Vincent, and F. Wagner. Random graph generation for scheduling simulations. In *SIMUTools*, Torremolinos, Malaga, Spain, March 2010.

[2] L. Golab, M. Hadjieleftheriou, H. Karloff, and B. Saha. Distributed data placement to minimize communication costs via graph partitioning. In *SSDBM*, Aalborg, Denmark, June 2014.

[3] J. Kelley and M. Walker. Critical-path planning and scheduling. In *Proceedings of the Eastern Joint Computer Conference*, 1959.

[4] K. Ousterhout, P. Wendell, M. Zaharia, and I. Stoica. Sparrow: Scalable scheduling for sub-second parallel jobs. Technical Report UCB/EECS-2013-29, U.C. Berkeley, April 2013.

One Loop Does Not Fit All

Styliani Pantela
Harvard University
stylianipantela@college.harvard.edu

Stratos Idreos
Harvard University
stratos@seas.harvard.edu

ABSTRACT

Just-In-Time (JIT) compilation increasingly becomes a key technology for modern database systems. It allows the creation of code on-the-fly to perfectly match an active query. In the past, it has been argued that a query should be compiled to a single loop that performs all query actions, for example, all selects over all relevant columns. On the other hand, vectorization – a common feature in modern data systems – allows for better results by evaluating the query predicates sequentially in different tight for-loops.

In this paper, we study JIT compilation for modern in-memory column-stores in detail and we show that, contrary to the common belief that vectorization outweighs the benefits of having one loop, there are cases in which creating a single loop is actually the optimal solution. In fact, deciding between multiple or a single loop is not a static decision; instead, it depends on (per column) query selectivity. We perform our experiments on a modern column-store prototype that supports vectorization and we show that, depending on selectivity, a different code layout is optimal. When a select operator is implemented with a no-branch design, for low selectivity creating multiple loops performs better than a single loop. A single tight loop performs better otherwise.

1. INTRODUCTION

Just-In-Time Code Generation. JIT code generation for query execution is a method employed by database management systems in order to avoid the interpretation overhead that comes with declarative languages like SQL [6]. Upon receiving the query, the engine makes decisions on optimization and compiles SQL into a low level representation that will then be linked, loaded and executed. This method avoids pitfalls that could be incurred by the separation of operators, a key insight exploited in HyPer [3]. HyPer uses JIT code generation for an in-memory column store system by avoiding intermediate materialization of results until a pipeline breaker appears. The generated code breaks operator boundaries combining together as many operators as possible in a single loop. It keeps intermediate results in registers and generates code in LLVM IR and suggests that *one loop fits all.*

SIGMOD'15, May 31–June 4, 2015, Melbourne, Victoria, Australia.
ACM 978-1-4503-2758-9/15/05.
http://dx.doi.org/10.1145/2723372.2764944.

Furthermore, Sompolski et al. [5] extensively study the ideas of JIT compilation and vectorized query processing in column stores and prove that it is beneficial to introduce JIT query compilation to a vectorized system and that there are still benefits of vectorization to a tuple-at-a-time compiled system. The premise of JIT code generation in a compact loop is that it avoids the creation of intermediate results [5]. Sompolski et al. argue that if we reduce the generation of intermediate results by using a select_fetch operator instead of using a fetch followed by a separate select, the approach of using one loop is worse that simply evaluating one predicate after another sequentially, in a vectorized way.

Contributions. In this paper we experiment with modern in-memory column store systems and look closely at the case of conjunctive selects. We show that in a multi-threaded setting, it is beneficial to switch to the one loop technique most of the time. However, in cases of low selectivity and branchless execution it is beneficial to opt for having multiple loops.

2. ONE LOOP DOES NOT FIT ALL

In this section we present our experimental analysis and we demonstrate that a single JIT solution is not optimal across all workload scenarios.

Experimental Setup. We use an in-memory column store prototype. Every column is assumed to fit in main memory and the tuples are 8 bytes long for a total of one billion tuples per column. We evaluate our system on a 4-way Intel Xeon E7-4820 configuration with 64 hardware threads and 1 TB of main memory and use GCC 4.7.2 (Debian 4.7.2-5).

Test Queries. We focus our experiments on conjunctive select queries of the form of Query 1. Such queries stress the decision between a single and multiple loops, as they include several predicates.

Query 1 Select Query

```
SELECT R.d FROM R
WHERE R.a < v1 AND R.b < v2
AND R.c < v3 AND R.d < v4
```

Execution Strategies. The first strategy of execution breaks the evaluation of the query into four tight loops; one for each predicate. In this case vectorized execution can be exploited. Each loop operates on a vector of tuples that fits into the L1 cache and performs the select over the respec-

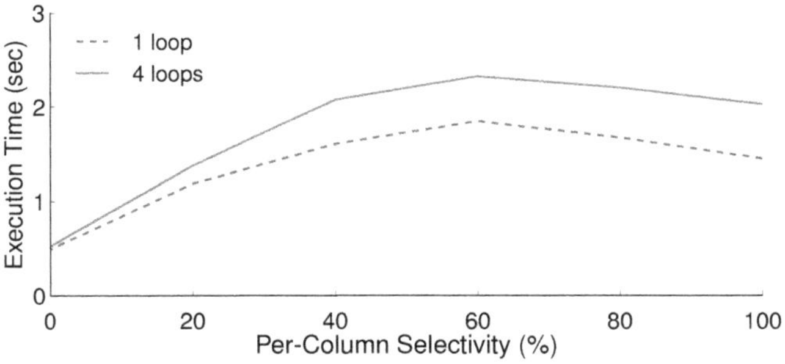

Figure 1: With branches

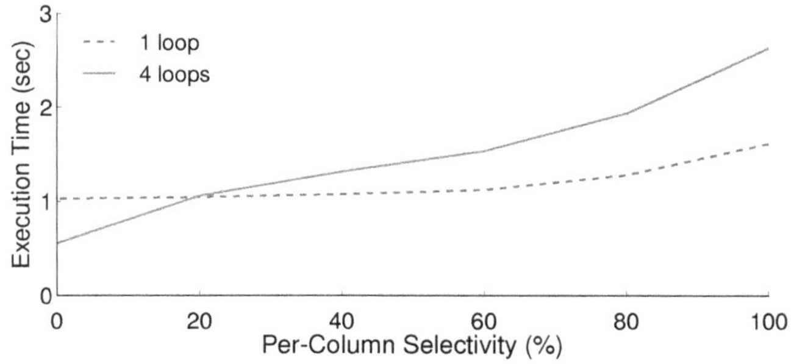

Figure 2: Branchless

tive column using column store operations [1]. After the first select, we can minimize intermediate results by using a fetch_select operator to perform a column projection and selection in one step, following prior art [2] (Algorithm 1).

Algorithm 1 *4 Loops Strategy* for Query 1

```
inter = select(R.a, v1)
inter = select_fetch(R.b, v2, inter)
inter = select_fetch(R.c, v3, inter)
dest  = select_fetch(R.d, v4, inter)
```

The second execution strategy uses one tight loop for the evaluation of all of predicates (Algorithm 2).

Algorithm 2 *1 Loop Strategy* for Query 1

```
dest = select(R.a, v1, R.b, v2,
              R.c, v3, R.d, v4)
```

Optimizations. Multi-threaded execution helps to improve performance; we fully utilize the eight available cores by using eight threads. Following prior work [4] we evaluate the two execution strategies with two different implementations: with and without branching. The order of evaluation of the predicates is inconsequential because the data is randomly generated using a uniform distribution, and the per-column selectivity is the same across all predicates. Finally, we use loop unrolling to optimize the branchless version of vectorized processing.

Results. Figure 1 shows the performance of the two execution strategies for different column selectivity in an implementation that uses branching. The performance is affected by branch mispredictions as selectivity varies. The *1 Loop Strategy* (Algorithm 1) outperforms the *4 Loops Strategy* (Algorithm 2) for any selectivity and the gap is increased in high selectivity. Furthermore, Figure 2 compares the two execution strategies in a branchless context. The *1 Loop Strategy* is outperforming the *4 Loops Strategy* for higher selectivity but is slower for lower selectivity.

Although it is argued that vectorization comes with a lot of benefits [5], the functional overhead we pay along with the cost of materializing intermediate results is significant in both the branchless and the with cases. The intuition behind our observation is that in the *1 Loop Strategy*, all columns of the predicates will be scanned fully regardless of the selectivity. However, for low selectivity, most of the tuples across the columns are not going to qualify. This results in reading data that is not going to be used. On the other hand, using separate loops for each predicate results in scanning fewer cache lines when the first filter selects very few tuples.

Comparing Figure 1 and 2 we observe that optimizing for performance requires the branched execution (especially for low selectivity), where we should always opt for the *1 Loop Strategy*. On the other hand, the branchless version yields more predictable performance. For low selectivity the *4 Loops Strategy* outperforms the *1 Loop Strategy*, and vice versa for high selectivity.

Finally, we observe that the difference between the two execution strategies in Figure 1 and Figure 2 is increasing and appears to be dominated by the extra cost of the creation of intermediate results for the vectorized execution.

3. SUMMARY & FUTURE WORK

We study code generation for in-memory column store systems, covering the case of conjunctive selects. We show that there is no single solution that works optimally across all workloads; selectivity is the crucial factor. Our conclusion is that a robust system using branchless execution should choose to alternate between the two methods based on predicted selectivity.

Future steps include a more detailed breakdown of hardware metrics like CPU cycles and branch mispredictions for varying selectivity in order to further support our findings on which strategy performs better. Another open question is whether employing SIMD instructions when comparing the two strategies will yield different results. In order to establish a general heuristic, we plan to extend our analysis by evaluating disjunctive queries, and varying data distribution and correlations across columns.

Acknowledgments. This project is supported by the National Science Foundation under Grant No. IIS-1452595. The authors would like to thank Lukas Maas and Manos Athanassoulis, members of Harvard DASlab, for their help.

4. REFERENCES

[1] D. Abadi, P. Boncz, S. Harizopoulos, S. Idreos, and S. Madden. The design and implementation of modern column-oriented database systems. *Foundations and Trends in Databases*, 5:197–280, 2013.

[2] S. Idreos, M. L. Kersten, and S. Manegold. Database Cracking. In *Proceedings of the International Conference on Innovative Data Systems Research (CIDR)*, pages 68–78, 2007.

[3] T. Neumann. Efficiently Compiling Efficient Query Plans for Modern Hardware. *Proceedings of the VLDB Endowment*, 4(9):539–550, 2011.

[4] K. A. Ross. Selection Conditions in Main Memory. *ACM Transactions on Database Systems*, 29(1):132–161, 2004.

[5] J. Sompolski, M. Zukowski, and P. Boncz. Vectorization vs. Compilation in Query Execution. In *Proceedings of the International Workshop on Data Management on New Hardware (DAMON)*, pages 33–40, 2011.

[6] S. D. Viglas. Just-in-time Compilation for SQL Query Processing. *Proceedings of the VLDB Endowment*, 6(11):1190–1191, 2013.

DunceCap: Compiling Worst-Case Optimal Query Plans

[Extended Abstract]

Adam Perelman*
Stanford University
adamperelman@cs.stanford.edu

Christopher Ré†
Stanford University
chrismre@cs.stanford.edu

ABSTRACT

Modern data analytics workloads frequently involve complex join queries where the pairwise-join-based algorithms used by most RDBMS engines are suboptimal. In this study, we explore two algorithms that are asymptotically faster than pairwise algorithms for a large class of queries. The first is Yannakakis' classical algorithm for acyclic queries. The second is a more recent algorithm which works for any query and which is optimal with respect to the worst-case size of the output. We introduce a query compiler, DunceCap, which uses these two algorithms and variations on them to produce optimal query plans, and find that these plans can outperform standard RDBMS algorithms as well as simple worst-case optimal algorithms by an order of magnitude on a variety of queries.

1. INTRODUCTION

Traditional RDBMS join algorithms are based on pairwise joins. Modern OLAP and graph processing workloads, however, typically involve complex queries, often with many large tables and sometimes with cycles in the query graph, where traditional pairwise algorithms are suboptimal and more efficient techniques are needed[1].

Theoreticians have developed several algorithms that are asymptotically superior to any pairwise plan for a variety of queries. In this section, we introduce two such algorithms. The first is Yannakakis' classical algorithm for acyclic queries[5]. The second is a worst-case optimal algorithm recently introduced by Ngo, Porat, Ré, and Rudra (henceforth NPRR) which can be used for any query, whether cyclic or acyclic[3].

*This author is grateful to Susan Tu for many collaborations on this project, to Chris Aberger and Andres Nötzli for implementation advice, and to Rohan Puttagunta and Manas Joglekar for valuable insights into join theory.

†We gratefully acknowledge support from a National Science Foundation CAREER Award under No. IIS-1353606.

SIGMOD'15, May 31–June 4, 2015, Melbourne, Victoria, Australia.
ACM 978-1-4503-2758-9/15/05.
http://dx.doi.org/10.1145/2723372.2764945.

1.1 Yannakakis' Algorithm

For a given join query $Q = R_1 \bowtie \cdots \bowtie R_n$, we define its hypergraph representation as $\mathcal{F} = (V, E)$, where V is the set of attributes in the query $V = \bigcup R_i$, and E is the set of relations $E = \{R_i\}$. We define a query as acyclic if and only if its hypergraph representation is acyclic. If a query Q is acyclic, then there exists a *full reducer* for Q, which is a sequence of pairwise semi-joins such that after execution of this semi-join plan, all relations $R_i \in Q$ are both pairwise consistent and globally consistent. That is, none of the relations have *dangling tuples*: tuples that do not correspond to any tuple in the query result. Based on this insight, Yannakakis' algorithm works as follows: first, we run a full reducer. Then, we compute the output via a sequence of pairwise joins. At each step, every tuple in the intermediate result corresponds to at least one tuple in the final output, so the run-time of this algorithm is linear in the size of the input and the output[5].

However, this algorithm only works for acyclic queries. For cyclic queries, we can extend Yannakakis as follows: first, we compute the minimum-width tree decomposition for the query; this is a standard technique to modify algorithms for acyclic graphs so that they can run on cyclic graphs. Within each bag of the hypertree decomposition, we use a traditional pairwise plan to compute the join of the relations in the bag. Once all the within-bag joins are complete, we are left with a tree of relations, which we join via Yannakakis' classical algorithm.

1.2 Worst-Case Optimal Join Algorithm

More recently, NPRR introduced a new algorithm that is guaranteed to run in time proportional to the worst-case size of the output, regardless of whether the query is cyclic or acyclic. Rather than using relational algebra operations as its building blocks, the NPRR algorithm reduces any join query to a sequence of set-theoretic operations, in particular set intersections and set unions[3].

2. QUERY COMPILER

Our query compiler, DunceCap, takes as input a list of relations over which to perform a natural join. It then compiles the query into a C++ query plan which executes either Yannakakis, NPRR, or a HybridJoin algorithm.

Our HybridJoin algorithm is very similar to Yannakakis' algorithm. However, after computing the minimum-width hypertree decomposition for a query, HybridJoin uses NPRR instead of a pairwise plan to compute the join of the relations

Query	Relational Algebra Expression
Triangle (K_3)	$R(A,B) \bowtie S(B,C) \bowtie T(A,C)$
4-clique (K_4)	$R(A,B) \bowtie S(B,C) \bowtie T(C,D)$ $\bowtie U(A,D) \bowtie V(A,C) \bowtie W(B,D)$
Lollipop ($L_{3,1}$)	$R(A,B) \bowtie S(B,C) \bowtie T(C,A)$ $\bowtie U(A,D)$
Lollipop ($L_{4,1}$)	$R(A,B) \bowtie S(B,C) \bowtie T(C,D) \bowtie U(D,A)$ $\bowtie V(A,C) \bowtie W(B,D) \bowtie X(A,E)$

Table 1: Common graph-pattern queries.

Dataset	Algorithm	Query			
		K_3	K_4	$L_{3,1}$	$L_{4,1}$
Facebook	Yannakakis	0.159	10.6	0.65	148.6
	NPRR	0.086	2.51	18.2	54.7
	HybridJoin	0.086	2.51	0.354	12.7
	LogicBlox	0.52	4.13	11.4	241.5
Arxiv GR-GC	Yannakakis	0.032	0.259	0.075	1.34
	NPRR	0.027	0.120	0.087	0.715
	HybridJoin	0.027	0.120	0.054	0.363
	LogicBlox	0.49	0.55	0.73	2.14

Table 2: Runtime (in seconds) of each count query. LogicBlox, a commercial system that implements a worst-case optimal algorithm, uses 48 cores; all other algorithms are single-threaded.

within each bag. Once the within-bag joins are complete, we compute the output via Yannakakis' algorithm.

3. EXPERIMENTS

We ran the common graph-pattern queries described in Table 1 on two real-world graph datasets from the Stanford Network Analysis Project (SNAP): the Arxiv GR-GC dataset (5242 nodes, 14496 edges) and the Facebook dataset (4039 nodes, 88234 edges)[2].

3.1 Algorithm Comparison

Running times are listed in Table 2. For all queries except $L_{3,1}$, the NPRR algorithm is faster than the Yannakakis algorithm, implying that the cost of pairwise within-bag joins in the Yannakakis algorithm outweighs the lack of a full reducer in the NPRR algorithm. For the $L_{3,1}$ query, the opposite is true. However, for all queries, the HybridJoin algorithm achieves the best running time, implying that it effectively combines Yannakakis and NPRR.

We compare our running times with LogicBlox, the only commercial system which implements a worst-case optimal join algorithm[4]. The comparison is not perfect: LogicBlox is implemented in Java instead of C++, and incurs overhead for fault tolerance, task distribution, and so on. On the other hand, while the LogicBlox implementation uses all 48 cores on our machine, DunceCap use a single thread. By profiling our algorithms on different queries, we estimate that for long-running queries, differences in overhead account for a factor of about 2 in our runtime improvement over LogicBlox, and algorithmic differences account for a factor of about 10, although these vary depending on the query.

3.2 Attribute Ordering and NPRR

The order in which NPRR performs the set intersections for each attribute in a query depends on the *global attribute ordering* chosen by the algorithm. The theoretical worst-case optimal bound on the algorithm holds regardless of the attribute ordering. However, our results show that in practice, the choice of ordering can change runtime by over an order of magnitude. Whereas Table 2 assumes runtimes given the optimal attribute ordering, Table 3 shows the runtime for NPRR given two example attribute orderings (the orderings use the attribute names defined in Table 1).

Query	Attribute Order	Dataset	
		Facebook	Arxiv GR-GC
$L_{3,1}$	A,B,C,D	1.817	0.087
	D,A,B,C	25.64	0.495
$L_{4,1}$	A,B,C,D,E	54.68	0.715
	E,A,B,C,D	1358.0	6.729

Table 3: Runtime (in seconds) of NPRR on lollipop queries given each global attribute ordering.

In our experiments, the best attribute ordering for a query corresponds to its minimum-width hypertree decomposition. In particular, given the best attribute ordering for a lollipop query, NPRR begins by computing intersections for attributes that would have been placed in the same bag by a minimum-width hypertree decomposition. It does not consider the remaining attribute from the other bag until the very end of the algorithm. By staying within a single bag of the decomposition for as long as possible, this strategy keeps intermediate results relatively small. In contrast, the worst attribute orderings cause NPRR to begin with attributes that are from different bags of the decomposition, leading to larger intermediate results. Thus, the hypertree decomposition of a query is helpful for determining the optimal attribute ordering.

4. CONCLUSION AND FUTURE WORK

In this study, we compared the performance of Yannakakis' algorithm, a worst-case optimal algorithm, and a hybrid algorithm, finding that the hybrid algorithm effectively combines the best runtime characteristics of both Yannakakis and NPRR. This algorithmic refinement causes our query plans to outperform a commercial system that implements a worst-case optimal algorithm by an order of magnitude.

We see several promising directions for future work. First, we hope to incorporate work on fast set-intersections via SIMD algorithms into our query engine[1]. Second, a better understanding of these join algorithms requires an exploration of how each can be parallelized. Third, recent research has begun to explore "beyond worst-case" algorithms, which are instance-optimal rather than schema-optimal. There is potential for significant advances to be made by exploring the tradeoffs between our algorithms and these beyond-worst case algorithms.

5. REFERENCES

[1] C. R. Aberger, A. Nötzli, K. Olukotun, and C. Ré. EmptyHeaded: Boolean Algebra Based Graph Processing, Mar. 2015.

[2] J. Leskovec and A. Krevl. Snap datasets: Stanford large network dataset collection, June 2014.

[3] H. Q. Ngo, E. Porat, C. Ré, and A. Rudra. Worst-case optimal join algorithms: [extended abstract]. In *PODS '12*, pages 37–48, New York, NY, USA, 2012. ACM.

[4] T. L. Veldhuizen. Leapfrog triejoin: a worst-case optimal join algorithm. *CoRR*, abs/1210.0481, 2012.

[5] M. Yannakakis. Algorithms for acyclic database schemes. VLDB '81, pages 82–94. VLDB Endowment, 1981.

DunceCap: Query Plans Using Generalized Hypertree Decompositions

[Extended Abstract]

Susan Tu *
Stanford University
sctu@stanford.edu

Christopher Ré †
Stanford University
chrismre@stanford.edu

ABSTRACT

Joins are central to data processing. However, traditional query plans for joins, which are based on choosing the order of pairwise joins, are provably suboptimal. They often perform poorly on cyclic graph queries, which have become increasingly important to modern data analytics. Other join algorithms exist: Yannakakis', for example, operates on acyclic queries in runtime proportional to the input size plus the output size [7]. More recently, Ngo et al. published a join algorithm that is optimal on worst-case inputs [5]. My contribution is to explore query planning using these join algorithms. In our approach, every query plan can be viewed as a generalized hypertree decomposition (GHD). We score each GHD using the minimal fractional hypertree width, which Ngo et al. show allows us to bound its worst-case runtime. We benchmark our plans using datasets from the Stanford Large Network Dataset Collection [4] and find that our performance compares favorably against that of LogicBlox, a commercial system that implements a worst-case optimal join algorithm.

1. PRELIMINARIES

We begin by describing Yannakakis' and a worst-case optimal join algorithm.

1.1 Yannakakis

Yannakakis' algorithm consists of constructing the tree T_{GYO} implicit in performing the Graham-Yu-Ozsoyoglu (GYO) reduction. For every leaf v in T_{GYO} with relation R, compute $R := R \ltimes S$ where S is the relation in the leaf's parent. Now recursively fully reduce T_{GYO} without v. Then compute $S := S \ltimes R$. Finally, join each leaf in the tree with its parent. Since the semijoins "filter out" input tuples that will not appear in the final result, they prevent wasted work in the final join phase.

1.2 Worst-Case Optimal Join Algorithms

We implemented the worst-case optimal join algorithm described in Ngo, Rudra, and Ré's survey [5]., which we reproduce below as Algorithm 1. To see a situation in which this algorithm is optimal, consider the triangle query $R_1(A,B) \bowtie R_2(B,C) \bowtie R_3(C,A)$. As a concrete example (taken from [6]), consider having all three relations contain $(1,2)$, $(1,3)$, $(1,4)$, $(2,1)$, $(3,1)$, $(4,1)$. The maximum number of tuples that could result from a triangle query is $O(M^{3/2})$. Algorithm 1 is $O(M^{3/2})$; any pairwise join is $\Omega(M^2)$.

Algorithm 1 Worst-case optimal join algorithm

```
Input: Query Q, hypergraph H = (V, E)
def WorstCaseOptimalJoin(⋈_{F∈E} R_F)
    Q = ∅
    If |V| = 1 then
        return ∩_{F∈E} R_F
    Let I = {v}, J = V \ I for some v ∈ V.
    A = WorstCaseOptimalJoin(⋈_{F∈E|I∩F≠∅} π_I(R_F))
    For every a ∈ A:
        partialQ{a} = WorstCaseOptimalJoin(
            ⋈_{F∈E|J∩F≠∅} π_J(R_F ⋉ {a}))
        Q = Q ∪ {a} × partialQ{a}
    return Q
```

2. APPROACH

DunceCap (DC), our query compiler, uses a hybrid algorithm to perform joins. Algorithm 1 is guaranteed to be optimal only for *worst-case* data but can be used for any query, whereas Yannakakis can only be used on acyclic queries. We might ask, given a cyclic query, how can we separate the query into subqueries such that the results of the subqueries can be joined using Yannakakis? (The subqueries would be computed using Algorithm 1.) The subquery that takes the most time in such a partition of work would contribute the dominant term in the worst case analysis, and if we parallelize the computation of the subqueries, the largest subquery will be the bottleneck computation. We therefore seek to minimize the size of the largest subquery output.

*Thanks to Adam Perelman, with whom I worked to implement the two join algorithms and who implemented the count query. Thanks to Chris Aberger and Andres Nötzli for implementation advice, and to Rohan Puttagunta and Manas Joglekar for theory help.

†This project is supported by the National Science Foundation CAREER Award (No. IIS-1353606).

SIGMOD'15, May 31–June 4, 2015, Melbourne, Victoria, Australia.
ACM 978-1-4503-2758-9/15/05.
http://dx.doi.org/10.1145/2723372.2764946.

2.1 Generalized Hypertree Decomposition

A theory problem that maps well to this problem of allocating subqueries to Algorithm 1 is finding a minimal width generalized hypertree decomposition (GHD). A GHD of a join query $\bowtie_{i\in\{1,...,d\}} R_i$ is a tree T where each node contains at least one relation, each relation appears in at least one node (we also refer to these nodes as *bags*), and if a bag v and a bag u both contain an attribute A, all bags on the path between v and u contain A. Where $\alpha(v)$ denotes the number of attributes in node v and V is the set of all nodes in the GHD, the generalized hypertree width is $max_{v\in V}(\alpha(v)-1)$. While finding a minimal width GHD is NP-hard [3], our inputs are so small (our inputs are relations and their attributes, not tuples) that we can use Algorithm 2 to enumerate a GHD of every possible width.

Algorithm 2 Algorithm for enumerating GHDs

```
def enumerateGHDs(ℰ, attributes)
For every n in 1 to |ℰ|:
  For every possible subset S of size n in ℰ:
    For any R ∈ ℰ \ S:
      If R.attributes ∩ attributes ⊈ S.attributes
        return []
    Find connected components in ℰ \ S,
    ignoring attributes in S
    For every connected component C_i:
      subtrees{C_i} = enumerateGHDs(
        C_i, S.attributes)
    subtrees = {{c_1, c_2, ...} | each c_i ∈ subtrees{C_i}}
    result = []
    For each s in subtrees:
      result.append(S with s as children)
    return result
```

2.1.1 Fractional Hypertree Width

The Atserias, Grohe, and Marx bound tells us that the output size is upper bounded by $\prod_{F\in\mathcal{E}} |R_F|^{x_F}$, under the constraints $\forall v \in \mathcal{V}, \sum_{F:v\in F} x_F \geq 1$ and $x_F \geq 0$ [2]. We would therefore like to minimize $\prod_{F\in\mathcal{E}} |R_F|^{x_F}$, subject to those constraints. If we assume that $|R_F| = N$ for all $F \in \mathcal{E}$ (which is true for graph queries), we can take the log of our objective and divide by $log(N)$. Then our linear program is: minimize $\sum_{F\in\mathcal{E}} x_F$, subject to $\forall v \in \mathcal{V}, \sum_{F:v\in F} x_F \geq 1$ and $x_F \geq 0$. Its solution is known as the fractional hypertree width (FHW). We can score all the GHDs according to the FHW instead of the generalized hypertree width.

2.2 Attribute Ordering

Because we represent our tables using tries, it is advantageous, for the joins in Yannakakis, to have the join attributes at or near the first level of the trie. We therefore compute a global attribute ordering by performing a pre-order traversal of our plan's GHD. If attribute A comes before B in the global attribute ordering, in the tries we index A before B, and we perform intersections on A before B in Algorithm 1.

3. RESULTS

We benchmarked our query plans on the Arxiv GR-QC collaboration network (5242 nodes, 14496 edges) and Facebook friend lists (4039 nodes, 88234 edges) [4]. (Each edge is represented as a tuple in our input tables.) Execution times are presented in Tables 1 and 2. Our numbers compare favorably with LogicBlox's despite their use of all 48 cores. We currently use 1 thread but are faster on all queries except for the 4-clique query on Facebook.

Query	DC 1 bag	DC min FHW	LogicBlox	Count
Triangle	0.051	0.051	0.56	290E3
(3,1)-Lollipop	0.133	0.069	0.92	~10E6
(4,1)-Lollipop	5.576	0.817	6.06	~342E6
4-Clique	0.538	0.538	1.37	~8E6

Table 1: Time (s) to run queries that count the occurrences of various graph structures on the Arxiv dataset. Note that for triangle and 4-clique, the 1-bag plan is the minimal FHW plan. Datasets are not pruned, so each triangle is counted 6x, etc. Benchmarks were run on a machine with 48 cores on 4 Intel Xeon E5-4657L v2 CPUs and 1 TB of RAM.

Query	DC 1 bag	DC min FHW	LogicBlox	Count
Triangle	0.281	0.281	0.88	~10E6
(3,1)-Lollipop	3.427	0.529	21.47	~1.4E9
(4,1)-Lollipop	416.753	48.408	1084.83	~121E9
4-Clique	29.437	29.437	26.23	~720E6

Table 2: Time (s) to run queries on the Facebook dataset. Queries and experimental setup are the same as in Table 1.

Note that there can be quite a drastic difference in execution times between the minimal FHW and any other arbitrary plan: For example, the query plan for the (4,1)-lollipop count query that puts a single edge from the 4-clique part of the structure into a bag and the rest in another bag takes over 14 seconds to run on the Arxiv dataset. The optimal plan, which places the 4-clique in a bag and the remaining edge in a bag (FHW=2), takes 817 ms. We also benchmarked all the 1 or 2-bag plans we generate for the (3,1)-Lollipop count query. The 2 plans with FHW=1.5 take 69 and 69 ms, the plans with FHW=2 take 137 to 10866 ms, and the plans with FHW=3 take 641 and 11967 ms. These times show that plans with lower FHW are indeed faster.

4. FUTURE WORK

EmptyHeaded is an graph pattern engine that uses SIMD parallelism to implement fast set intersections [1], which we plan to leverage in the base case of Algorithm 1. We plan to more thoroughly test our system on different queries (including non-graph queries where the relations have more attributes) and datasets.

5. REFERENCES

[1] C. R. Aberger, A. Nötzli, K. Olukotun, and C. Ré. EmptyHeaded: Boolean Algebra Based Graph Processing. *ArXiv e-prints*, Mar. 2015.

[2] A. Atserias, M. Grohe, and D. Marx. Size bounds and query plans for relational joins, 2008.

[3] G. Gottlob, Z. Miklós, and T. Schwentick. Generalized hypertree decompositions: Np-hardness and tractable variants. *J. ACM*, 56(6):30:1–30:32, Sept. 2009.

[4] J. Leskovec and A. Krevl. SNAP Datasets: Stanford large network dataset collection, June 2014.

[5] H. Q. Ngo, E. Porat, C. Ré, and A. Rudra. Worst-case optimal join algorithms. PODS '12, pages 37–48, New York, NY, USA, 2012. ACM.

[6] H. Q. Ngo, C. Re, and A. Rudra. Skew strikes back: New developments in the theory of join algorithms. *CoRR*, abs/1310.3314, 2013.

[7] M. Yannakakis. Algorithms for acyclic database schemes. VLDB '81, pages 82–94. VLDB Endowment, 1981.

Author Index

www.ingramcontent.com/pod-product-compliance
Ingram Content Group UK Ltd.
Pitfield, Milton Keynes, MK11 3LW, UK
UKHW051419290926
15471UKWH00009B/1679

9 781450 338646